McDougal Littell

life

— The —

Americans

Reconstruction through the 20th Century

ANNOTATED TEACHER'S EDITION

liberty

pursuit *of* happiness

Authors

from left to right: Gerald A. Danzer, Professor of History and Director of the M.A. Program for Teachers of History at the University of Illinois at Chicago; J. Jorge Klor de Alva, Class of 1940 Professor of Comparative Ethnic Studies and Anthropology at the University of California at Berkeley; Nancy Woloch, history teacher at Barnard College; Louis E. Wilson, Associate Professor and Chair of the Afro-American and African Studies Department at Smith College.

Acknowledgments
Page 644: Excerpt from the song "Little Boxes," words and music by Malvina Reynolds. Copyright © 1962 by Schroder Music Company (ASCAP), renewed 1990. Used by permission of Schroder Music Company. All rights reserved.

ISBN 0-395-89081-0
Printed in the United States of America.
4 5 6 7 8 9–DWO–02 01 00 99

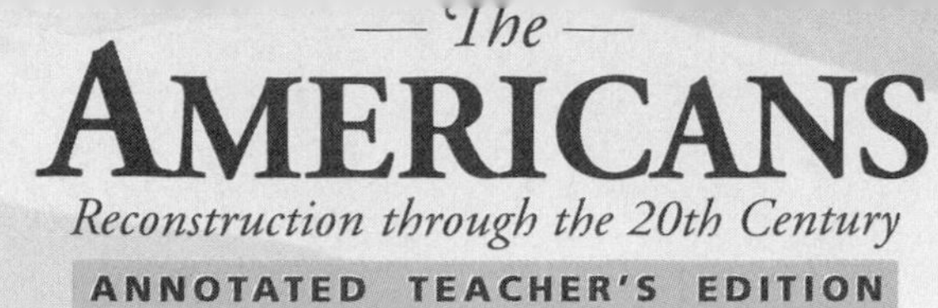

Table of Contents

Program Overview

The Americans: Reconstruction through the 20th Century is a highly integrated program that provides teachers with a practical and motivational approach to teaching modern U.S. history and to helping students think critically and reflectively. (For more information on each element, see pages T6–T21.)

ANNOTATED TEACHER'S EDITION

This comprehensive book provides all the material you need to organize and focus instruction.

PUPIL EDITION

The story of modern America—its diverse people, its varied landscape, its sturdy democracy, and its great events—is told through the voices of Americans from all walks of life. As students read the narrative, they will place historical events in context and will consider the events' meaning for the future.

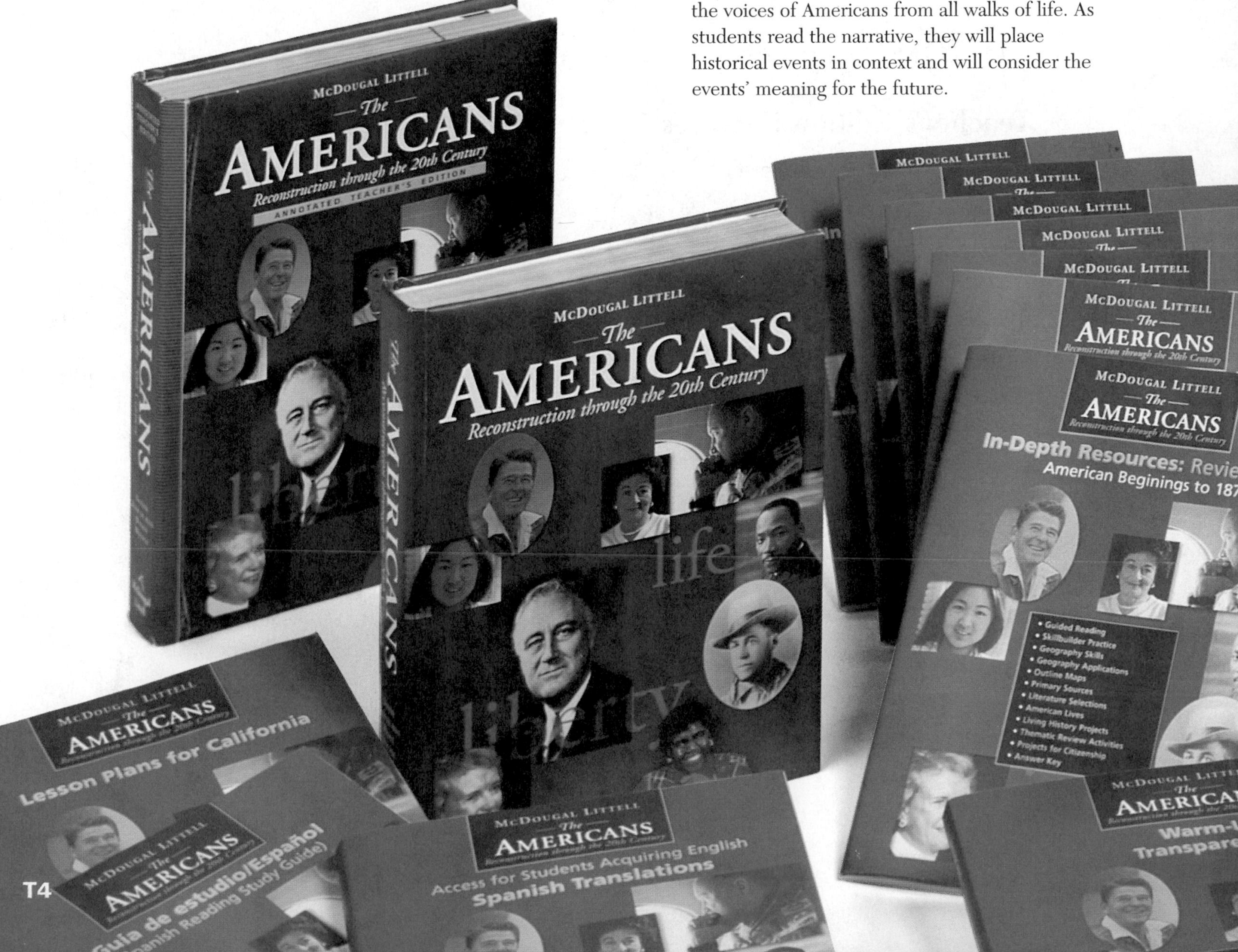

TECHNOLOGY RESOURCES

Documentary videos integrated with the text, five separate CD-ROM options, audiotapes, a videodisc portfolio, and extensive Internet resources provide a full range of technology enrichment options.

TEACHER'S RESOURCE MATERIALS

Extensive teacher's resource materials include everything teachers need in one easy-to-use package: in-depth resources organized by unit, a comprehensive guide to block scheduling, a complete assessment package, and more.

Making History Human

Stories, as every teacher knows, can capture students' imaginations, hold their attention, and teach important concepts all at once. When students experience the events of modern American history through the eyes of individuals, those events take on new meaning. Students therefore begin to make personal connections to the past.

The Americans: Reconstruction through the 20th Century focuses on the human face of modern history. When students dig into the events and see the people clearly, modern history for them will be more real, more accessible, and more exciting.

PERSONAL VOICES
Woven into the text are quotations from people who were involved in historical events. All Personal Voices are primary sources—authentic documents resonating with the passions and sharp personal observations of people who lived through the historical periods discussed.

A PERSONAL VOICE
Here we are, tremendously exhilarated, and there's a sea of dead. . . . [The platoon leader] was much moved. . . . He said, "Joe, lets make a resolution with these Russians here and also the ones on the bank: this would be an important day in the lives of the two countries." . . . It was a solemn moment. There were tears in the eyes of most of us. . . . We embraced. We swore never to forget.

JOSEPH POLOWSKY, quoted in *The Good War*

ONE AMERICAN'S STORY
Every major section of a chapter begins with the true story of an American who was touched by events discussed in the section. The American may have been a key decision-maker or simply an ordinary person caught up in the pivotal events of modern U.S. history. Several subjects of One American's Story features are also the subjects of *American Stories* videos that extend and enrich the text.

***AMERICAN STORIES* VIDEOS**
Fifteen videos integrate the lives of individuals with historical events described in the text. These short documentary films introduce individuals who lived and struggled through some of the most vivid times in modern American history.

JUMP AT THE SUN: Zora Neale Hurston and the Harlem Renaissance

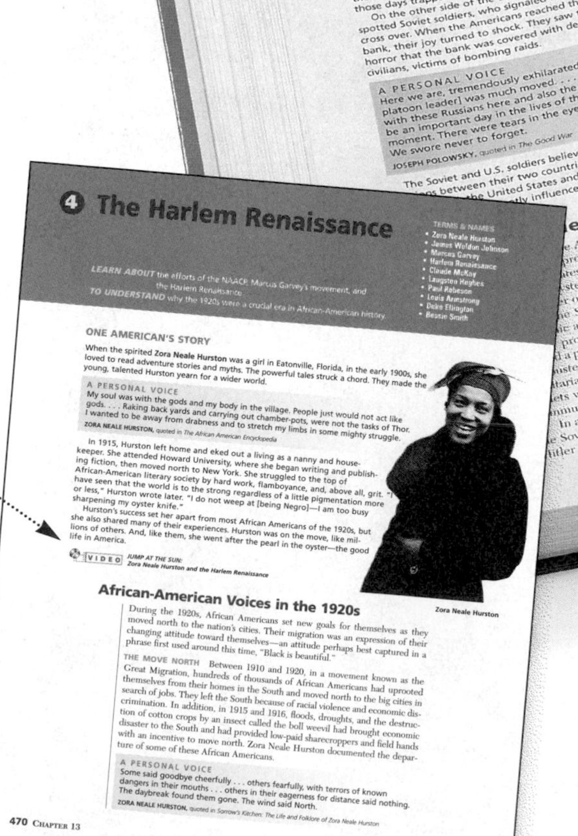

4 The Harlem Renaissance

TERMS & NAMES
- Zora Neale Hurston
- James Weldon Johnson
- Marcus Garvey
- Harlem Renaissance
- Claude McKay
- Langston Hughes
- Paul Robeson
- Louis Armstrong
- Duke Ellington
- Bessie Smith

LEARN ABOUT the efforts of the NAACP, Marcus Garvey's movement, and the Harlem Renaissance
TO UNDERSTAND why the 1920s were a crucial era in African-American history.

ONE AMERICAN'S STORY

When the spirited **Zora Neale Hurston** was a girl in Eatonville, Florida, in the early 1900s, she loved to read adventure stories and myths. The powerful tales struck a chord. They made the young, talented Hurston yearn for a wider world.

A PERSONAL VOICE
My soul was with the gods and my body in the village. People just would not act like gods. . . . Raking back yards and carrying out chamber-pots, were not the tasks of Thor. I wanted to be away from drabness and to stretch my limbs in some mighty struggle.
ZORA NEALE HURSTON, quoted in *The African American Encyclopedia*

In 1915, Hurston left home and eked out a living as a nanny and housekeeper. She attended Howard University, where she began writing and publishing fiction, then moved north to New York. She struggled to the top of African-American literary society by hard work, flamboyance, and, above all, grit. "I have seen that the world is to the strong regardless of a little pigmentation more or less," Hurston wrote later. "I do not weep at [being Negro]—I am too busy sharpening my oyster knife."

Hurston's success set her apart from most African Americans of the 1920s, but she also shared many of their experiences. Hurston was on the move, like millions of others. And, like them, she went after the pearl in the oyster—the good life in America.

VIDEO *JUMP AT THE SUN: Zora Neale Hurston and the Harlem Renaissance*

Zora Neale Hurston

African-American Voices in the 1920s

During the 1920s, African Americans set new goals for themselves as they moved north to the nation's cities. Their migration was an expression of their changing attitude toward themselves—an attitude perhaps best captured in a phrase first used around this time, "Black is beautiful."

THE MOVE NORTH Between 1910 and 1920, in a movement known as the Great Migration, hundreds of thousands of African Americans had uprooted themselves from their homes in the South and moved north to the big cities in search of jobs. They left the South because of racial violence and economic discrimination. In addition, in 1915 and 1916, floods, droughts, and the destruction of cotton crops by an insect called the boll weevil had brought economic disaster to the South and had provided low-paid sharecroppers and field hands with an incentive to move north. Zora Neale Hurston documented the departure of some of these African Americans.

A PERSONAL VOICE
Some said goodbye cheerfully . . . others fearfully, with terrors of known dangers in their mouths . . . others in their eagerness for distance said nothing. The daybreak found them gone. The wind said North.
ZORA NEALE HURSTON, quoted in *Sorrow's Kitchen: The Life and Folklore of Zora Neale Hurston*

470 CHAPTER 13

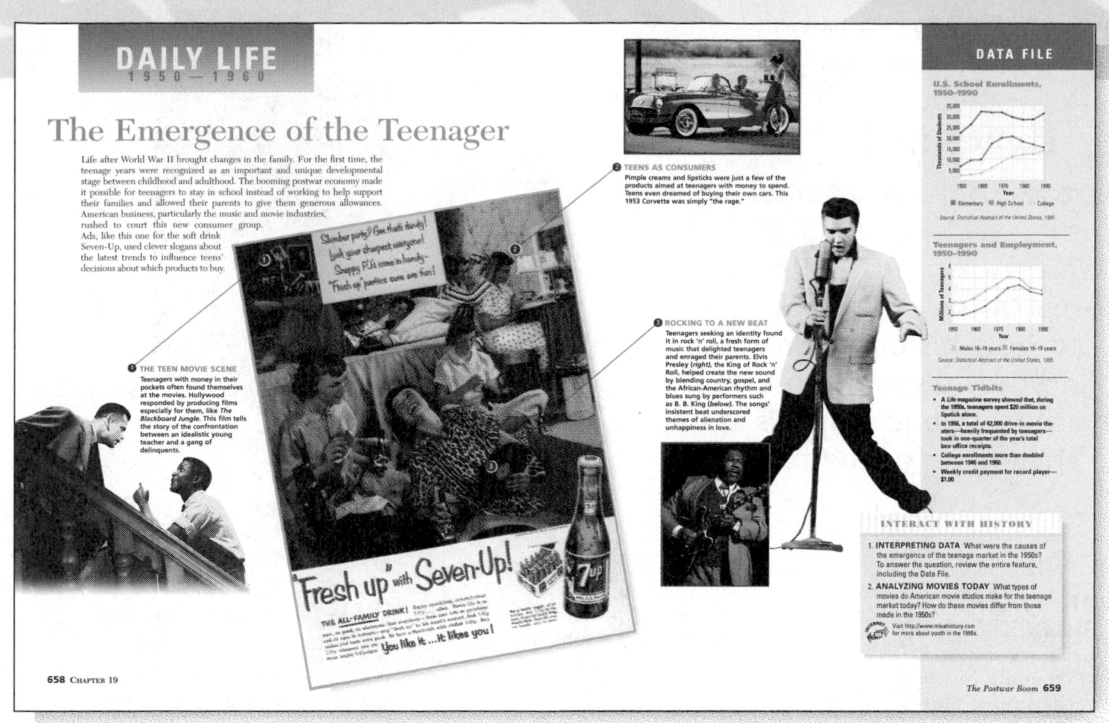

DAILY LIFE 1950–1960

The Emergence of the Teenager

Life after World War II brought changes in the family. For the first time, the teenage years were recognized as an important and unique developmental stage between childhood and adulthood. The booming postwar economy made it possible for teenagers to stay in school instead of working to help support their families and allowed their parents to give them generous allowances. American business, particularly the music and movie industries, rushed to court this new consumer group. Ads, like this one for the soft drink Seven-Up, used clever slogans about the latest trends to influence teens' decisions about which products to buy.

1 THE TEEN MOVIE SCENE
Teenagers with money in their pockets often found themselves at the movies. Hollywood responded by producing films especially for them, like *The Blackboard Jungle*. This film tells the story of the confrontation between an idealistic young teacher and a gang of delinquents.

2 TEENS AS CONSUMERS
Pimple creams and lipsticks were just a few of the products aimed at teenagers with money to spend. Teens even dreamed of buying their own cars. This 1953 Corvette was simply "the rage."

3 ROCKING TO A NEW BEAT
Teenagers seeking an identity found it in rock 'n' roll, a fresh form of music that delighted teenagers and enraged their parents. Elvis Presley (*right*), the King of Rock 'n' Roll, helped create the new sound by blending country, gospel, and the African-American rhythm and blues sung by performers such as B. B. King (*below*). The songs' insistent beat underscored themes of alienation and unhappiness in love.

DATA FILE

U.S. School Enrollments, 1950–1990

Teenagers and Employment, 1950–1990

Source: Statistical Abstract of the United States, 1995

Teenage Tidbits

- A *Life* magazine survey showed that, during the 1950s, teenagers spent $20 million on lipstick alone.
- In 1956, a total of 42,000 drive-in movie theaters—heavily frequented by teenagers—took in one-quarter of the year's total box-office receipts.
- College enrollments more than doubled between 1946 and 1960.
- Weekly credit payment for record player—$1.00

INTERACT WITH HISTORY

1. INTERPRETING DATA What were the causes of the emergence of the teenage market in the 1950s? To answer the question, review the entire feature, including the Data File.
2. ANALYZING MOVIES TODAY What types of movies do American movie studios make for the teenage market today? How do these movies differ from those made in the 1950s?

Visit http://www.mlushistory.com for more about youth in the 1950s.

658 Chapter 19

The Postwar Boom 659

DAILY LIFE

What has American life been like through the 20th century? What is it like now? How have the lives of young people changed? The Daily Life features show how people worked and played, while providing some thought-provoking facts about their lives.

KEY PLAYERS

HARRY S. TRUMAN 1884–1972

Young Harry S. Truman, the son of a Missouri livestock trader and his wife, did not seem destined for greatness. When he graduated from high school in 1901, he drifted from job to job—drugstore clerk, newspaper mailroom clerk, timekeeper, bank clerk, bookkeeper, farmer, World War I soldier. After the war, he invested in a men's clothing store; but the business failed, and he spent the next 15 years paying off business debts.

Discouraged by his business failure, Truman sought a career in politics. As a politician, his blunt and outspoken style won loyal friends and bitter enemies. As president, his decisiveness and willingness to accept responsibility for his decisions ("The Buck Stops Here" read a sign on his desk) earned him respect that has grown in the decades following his presidency.

JOSEPH STALIN 1879–1953

As a young revolutionary, Iosif Vissarionovich Dzhugashvili took the name Stalin, which means "man of steel."

His father was a failed shoemaker and an alcoholic. His mother helped support the family as a washerwoman. Following her wishes, Stalin entered a seminary, but he was eventually expelled for revolutionary activism.

Stalin is credited with turning the Soviet Union into a world power, but at a terrible cost to its citizens. He ruled with terror and brutality and saw "enemies" everywhere, even among friends and supporters. He subdued the population with the use of secret police and labor camps, and he is believed to have been responsible for the murder of millions of people in the Soviet Union.

KEY PLAYERS

Great men and women in positions of power or influence have often played key roles in modern American history. They are featured in short biographies that allow students to see them as individuals in both triumph and adversity.

Making History Relevant

Educators know that history comes alive when students are actively involved in their own learning. In *The Americans: Reconstruction through the 20th Century*, students make connections between the past and the present. They think about how historical events have influenced their lives. And they discover that history binds us together in the present and helps us understand how to meet the challenges of the future.

ON THE WORLD STAGE
While focusing on the modern history of the United States, the text never loses sight of the rest of the world. These short features help students relate events in the United States to international events.

ON THE WORLD STAGE

WAR ON THE EASTERN FRONT

The Russian army surprised the Germans by mobilizing rapidly in the early months of the war. Russian troops advanced quickly into German territory. The Germans turned the Russians back, however, at the Battle of Tannenberg in August 1914.

Throughout 1915, the Russians suffered successive defeats and continued to fall back into their own territory. By the end of 1915 they had suffered about 2.5 million casualties. Beyond the casualties, the war also caused massive bread shortages within Russia.

Demanding bread and peace, revolutionaries ousted the czar in March 1917 and established a provisional government led by Alexander Kerensky, who refused to pull Russia out of the war. In November, the Bolsheviks, led by Vladimir Lenin and Leon Trotsky, overthrew the Kerensky government. They then set up a Communist state and sought peace with the Central Powers.

HISTORICAL SPOTLIGHT
Shining a spotlight on special persons or events can make history come alive for students as they gain information that extends and enriches the main text.

HISTORICAL SPOTLIGHT

PAUL ROBESON

Paul Robeson was an all-American football player and Phi Beta Kappa member at Rutgers University. After earning a law degree in 1923, he entered on a distinguished international career as a singer and actor. (He is shown here playing Othello.) He was a vocal civil rights activist and a supporter of left-wing union activities, and he was sympathetic to the Soviet culture and political philosophy.

In 1950, when he refused to sign an affidavit indicating whether he had ever been a member of the Communist Party, the State Department revoked his passport for seven years. During that time, he was unable to perform abroad and was blacklisted at home. His income fell from $150,000 to $3,000 a year.

LIVING HISTORY
Every chapter begins with a project that actively involves students in their own learning as they explore an aspect of the period that interests them. At the end of the chapter, they finish the project and add it to their American history portfolios.

PLANNING A FIFTIES PARTY

Plan a 1950s party for your classmates and friends. To recreate the time as authentically as possible, use the information in the chapter and additional research or interviews to learn the following about fifties teenagers:

- how they dressed
- what they did for entertainment
- what music they listened to
- what they liked to eat

PORTFOLIO PROJECT Create an invitation that tells guests what to wear and what they can expect to hear, see, taste, and do at the party. Keep a copy of the invitation in a folder. At the end of the chapter, you will write a radio advertisement for your party and add it to your American history portfolio.

TRACING THEMES
Paying attention to themes in the history classroom can help students understand that the forces guiding their lives also governed the lives of previous generations. By looking at broad themes over time, students can begin to make connections between the past and the present.

ISSUES FOR THE 21ST CENTURY
Eight articles examine key social, economic, and political issues for today and tomorrow. The issues covered are foreign policy, immigration, crime and public safety, education, health care, women and the glass ceiling, poverty, and entitlements.

THEMATIC REVIEW
This section appears at the end of Review Unit 1: Beginnings to 1877. It connects the key events of early U.S. history to each of the ten themes in *The Americans: Reconstruction through the 20th Century*. This review helps students see the continuity between early history and modern history.

NOW & THEN

SPIES
Spying is still an active business in both the United States and Russia. In February 1994, Aldrich Ames was arrested for spying. Ames was a "mole" within the CIA who turned over to the Russians the names of all the important U.S. spies at work in Russia, causing ten CIA agents to be executed and others to be imprisoned. Ames was convicted and sentenced to life in prison.

NOW & THEN
When students see connections between the past and the present, modern American history becomes more real, more accessible, and more exciting to them. These features connect events discussed in the text with situations and events of today.

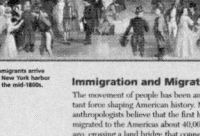

Making History Thought Provoking

Developing an ability to think critically and reflectively is an important goal of social studies instruction, because with this ability, students become citizens who can make informed and responsible decisions. *The Americans: Reconstruction through the 20th Century* incorporates a variety of materials that help students develop the thinking skills that are crucial to successful learning.

DIFFICULT DECISIONS IN HISTORY
The history of the United States is filled with difficult decisions—decisions that have often had long-term and far-reaching effects. Reflecting on these decisions and their results is an effective way for students to study the process of decision making and to examine their own thinking patterns.

Difficult Decisions IN HISTORY

TO PROHIBIT ALCOHOL OR NOT?

The question of whether to outlaw alcohol divided Americans. Many reformers and religious groups thought drinking was sinful, unhealthy, and devastating to families. They believed that the government should protect the public's health and morals by making alcohol illegal.

Other Americans, including liberals, conservatives, intellectuals, and immigrant groups, did not believe alcohol consumption to be sinful or dangerous in moderation. They believed that consuming alcohol was a personal, not a government, decision and resisted any group's trying to tell them how to live.

1. Examine the pros and cons of each position. Which do you agree with? What other factors, if any, do you think would influence your position?
2. If you had been a legislator asked to vote for the Eighteenth Amendment, what would you have said? Explain.
3. What issues might the experiment of prohibition relate to today? Should the government attempt to prohibit immoral behavior?

Visit http://www.mlushistory.com for more about prohibition and its repeal.

POINT/COUNTERPOINT
In this feature, students encounter opposing viewpoints on historical controversies. The viewpoints are expressed in the words of primary sources, such as editorials; in the words of people involved in the controversies; and in the words of historians. Being open-minded enough to explore several sides of crucial issues is important training for thoughtful decision making.

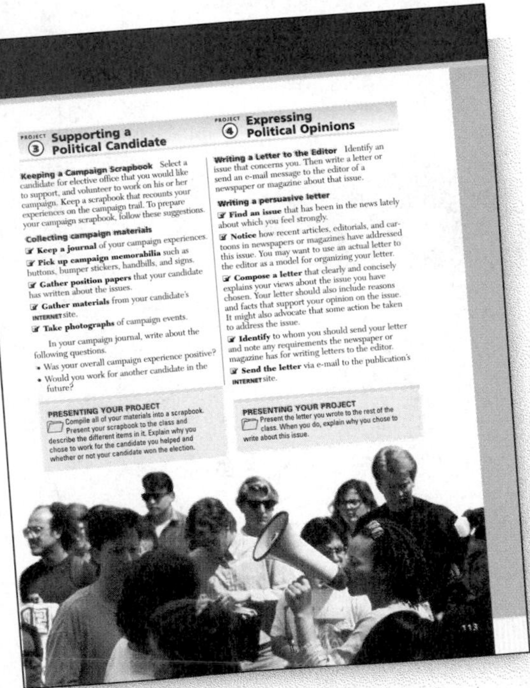

PROJECT 3 Supporting a Political Candidate

Keeping a Campaign Scrapbook Select a candidate for elective office that you would like to support, and volunteer to work on his or her campaign. Keep a scrapbook that recounts your experiences on the campaign trail. To prepare your campaign scrapbook, follow these suggestions.

Collecting campaign materials
- **Keep a journal** of your campaign experiences.
- **Pick up campaign memorabilia** such as buttons, bumper stickers, handbills, and signs.
- **Gather position papers** that your candidate has written about the issues.
- **Gather materials** from your candidate's INTERNET site.
- **Take photographs** of campaign events.

In your campaign journal, write about the following questions.
- Was your overall campaign experience positive?
- Would you work for another candidate in the future?

PRESENTING YOUR PROJECT
Compile all of your materials into a scrapbook. Present your scrapbook to the class and describe the different items in it. Explain why you chose to work for the candidate you helped and whether or not your candidate won the election.

PROJECT 4 Expressing Political Opinions

Writing a Letter to the Editor Identify an issue that concerns you. Then write a letter or send an e-mail message to the editor of a newspaper or magazine about that issue.

Writing a persuasive letter
- **Find an issue** that has been in the news lately about which you feel strongly.
- **Notice** how recent articles, editorials, and cartoons in newspapers or magazines have addressed this issue. You may want to use an actual letter to the editor as a model for organizing your letter.
- **Compose a letter** that clearly and concisely explains your views about the issue you have chosen. Your letter should also include reasons and facts that support your opinion on the issue. It might also advocate that some action be taken to address the issue.
- **Identify** to whom you should send your letter and note any requirements the newspaper or magazine has for writing letters to the editor.
- **Send the letter** via e-mail to the publication's INTERNET site.

PRESENTING YOUR PROJECT
Present the letter you wrote to the rest of the class. When you do, explain why you chose to write about this issue.

113

PROJECTS FOR CITIZENSHIP
Students learn and apply the skills of responsible and informed citizenship through eight projects, which are part of the chapter entitled "The Living Constitution." Additional Projects for Citizenship are included in Chapter Assessments throughout the textbook.

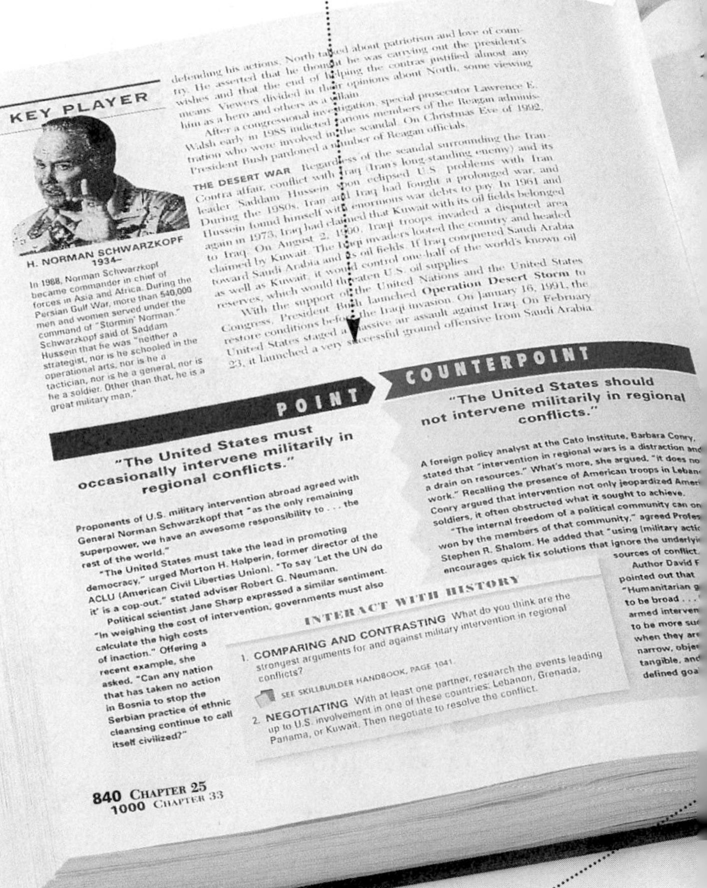

defending his actions. North talked about patriotism and love of country. He asserted that he thought he was carrying out the president's wishes and that the end of helping the contras justified almost any means. Viewers divided in their opinions about North, some viewing him as a hero and others as a villain.

After a congressional investigation, special prosecutor Lawrence E. Walsh early in 1988 indicted various members of the Reagan administration who were involved in the scandal. On Christmas Eve of 1992, President Bush pardoned a number of Reagan officials.

THE DESERT WAR Regardless of the scandal surrounding the Iran-Contra affair, conflict with Iraq (Iran's long-standing enemy) and its leader Saddam Hussein soon eclipsed U.S. problems with Iran. During the 1980s, Iran and Iraq had fought a prolonged war, and Hussein found himself with enormous war debts to pay. In 1961 and again in 1973, Iraq had claimed that Kuwait with its oil fields belonged to Iraq. On August 2, 1990, Iraqi troops invaded a disputed area claimed by Kuwait. The Iraqi invaders looted the country and headed toward Saudi Arabia and its oil fields. If Iraq conquered Saudi Arabia as well as Kuwait, it would control one-half of the world's known oil reserves, which would threaten U.S. oil supplies.

With the support of the United Nations and the United States Congress, President Bush launched **Operation Desert Storm** to restore conditions before the Iraqi invasion. On January 16, 1991, the United States staged a massive air assault against Iraq. On February 23, it launched a very successful ground offensive from Saudi Arabia.

KEY PLAYER

H. NORMAN SCHWARZKOPF
1934–

In 1988, Norman Schwarzkopf became commander in chief of forces in Asia and Africa. During the Persian Gulf War, more than 540,000 men and women served under the command of "Stormin' Norman." Schwarzkopf said of Saddam Hussein that he was "neither a strategist, nor is he schooled in the operational arts, nor is he a tactician, nor is he a general, nor is he a soldier. Other than that, he is a great military man."

POINT

"The United States must occasionally intervene militarily in regional conflicts."

Proponents of U.S. military intervention abroad agreed with General Norman Schwarzkopf that "as the only remaining superpower, we have an awesome responsibility to . . . the rest of the world."

"The United States must take the lead in promoting democracy," urged Morton H. Halperin, former director of the ACLU (American Civil Liberties Union). "To say 'Let the UN do it' is a cop-out," stated adviser Robert G. Neumann.

Political scientist Jane Sharp expressed a similar sentiment. "In weighing the cost of intervention, governments must also calculate the high costs of inaction." Offering a recent example, she asked, "Can any nation that has taken no action in Bosnia to stop the Serbian practice of ethnic cleansing continue to call itself civilized?"

COUNTERPOINT

"The United States should not intervene militarily in regional conflicts."

A foreign policy analyst at the Cato Institute, Barbara Conry, stated that "intervention in regional wars is a distraction and a drain on resources." What's more, she argued, "it does no work." Recalling the presence of American troops in Leban Conry argued that intervention not only jeopardized Amer soldiers, it often obstructed what it sought to achieve.

"The internal freedom of a political community can on won by the members of that community," agreed Profes Stephen R. Shalom. He added that "using [military actio encourages quick fix solutions that ignore the underlyi sources of conflict.

Author David F pointed out that "Humanitarian g to be broad . . . armed interven to be more su when they are narrow, objec tangible, and defined goa

INTERACT WITH HISTORY

1. **COMPARING AND CONTRASTING** What do you think are the strongest arguments for and against military intervention in regional conflicts?

SEE SKILLBUILDER HANDBOOK, PAGE 1041.

2. **NEGOTIATING** With at least one partner, research the events leading up to U.S. involvement in one of these countries: Lebanon, Grenada, Panama, or Kuwait. Then negotiate to resolve the conflict.

840 CHAPTER 25
1000 CHAPTER 33

ASSESSMENTS
Section and chapter assessments explicitly draw on various critical-thinking strategies to help students focus on concept formation—on the crucial process of practicing to become proficient thinkers.

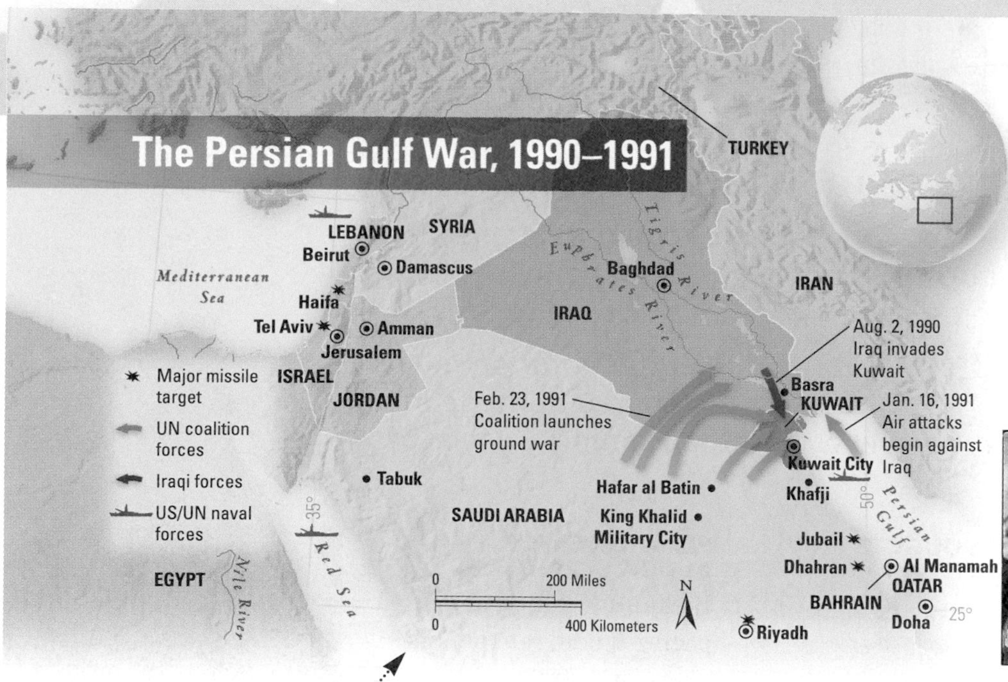

The Persian Gulf War, 1990–1991

TURKEY
LEBANON
SYRIA
Beirut
Damascus
Mediterranean Sea
Haifa
Tel Aviv
Amman
Jerusalem
ISRAEL
JORDAN
Baghdad
IRAQ
IRAN
Euphrates River
Tigris River
Aug. 2, 1990 Iraq invades Kuwait
Basra
KUWAIT
Jan. 16, 1991 Air attacks begin against Iraq
Feb. 23, 1991 Coalition launches ground war
Kuwait City
Khafji
Persian Gulf
Tabuk
Hafar al Batin
SAUDI ARABIA
King Khalid Military City
Jubail
Dhahran
Al Manamah
QATAR
BAHRAIN
Doha
Riyadh
EGYPT
Nile River
Red Sea
35°
50°
25°
0 200 Miles
0 400 Kilometers
N

✱ Major missile target
UN coalition forces
Iraqi forces
US/UN naval forces

GEOGRAPHY SKILLBUILDER
REGION *What did the UN coalition probably hope to achieve by moving forces into southern Iraq?* **MOVEMENT** *How did the movements of coalition ground forces show that the intention of the coalition in the Gulf War was primarily defensive, not offensive?*

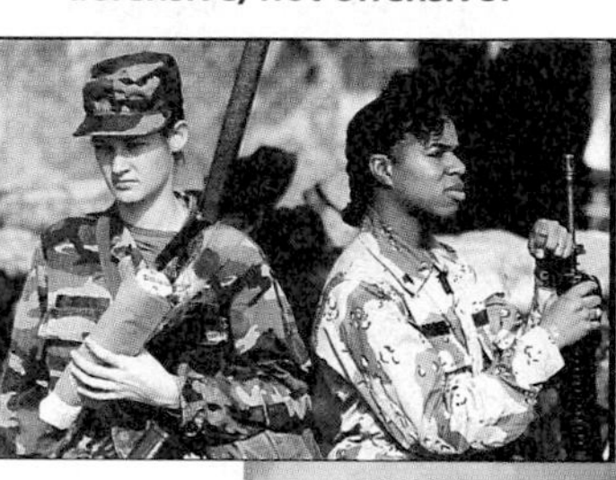

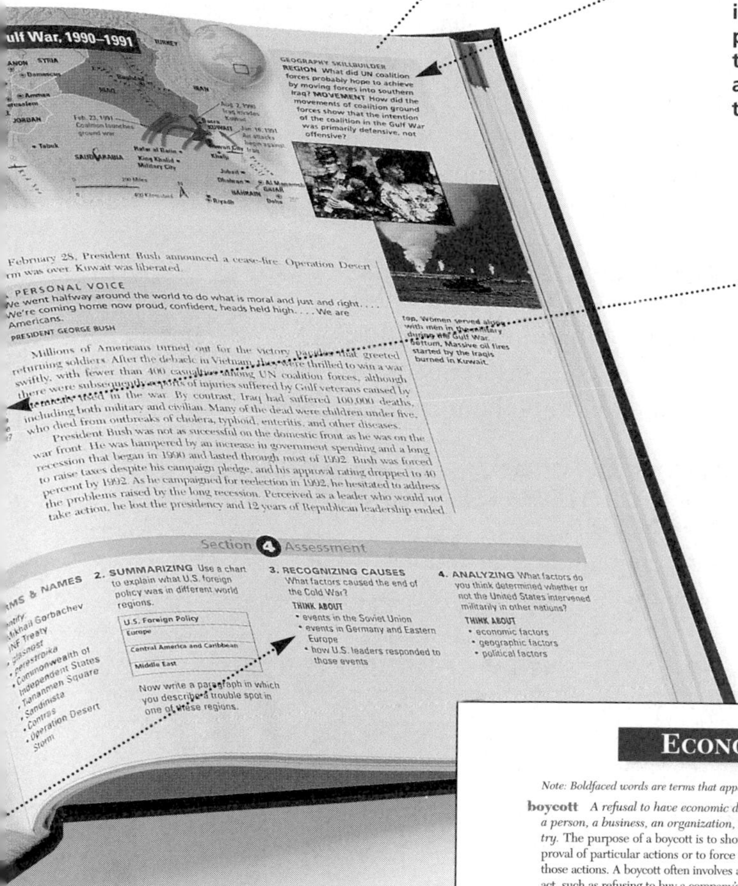

VISUALS
State-of-the-art maps and graphs appear throughout the text. Layers of visual information, accompanied by thought provoking questions, encourage students to explore relationships, make predictions, and compare outcomes as they interpret these powerful visuals.

THINK THROUGH HISTORY
These questions in the margins of the text help students think critically about historical events. By using these questions, teachers can encourage and reward thinking in their classrooms.

THINK THROUGH HISTORY
C. *Clarifying*
What issues led to conflict in the Middle East?

DENMARK'S RESISTANCE

In 1942, the Nazis began pressuring occupied Denmark to enforce the Nuremberg Laws against its Jews. The Danes resisted fiercely. Denmark's aged king, Christian X, is reported to have said,

> "The Jews are part of the Danish nation. We have no Jewish problem. . . . If the Jews are forced to wear the yellow star, I and my whole family shall wear it as a badge of honor."

Not only the royal family but thousands of Danes from all walks of life did just that.

ANOTHER PERSPECTIVE
These short features expose students to different perspectives on historical events. By looking at events from a perspective other than the one given in the main text, students can develop their skills of analysis and reflection.

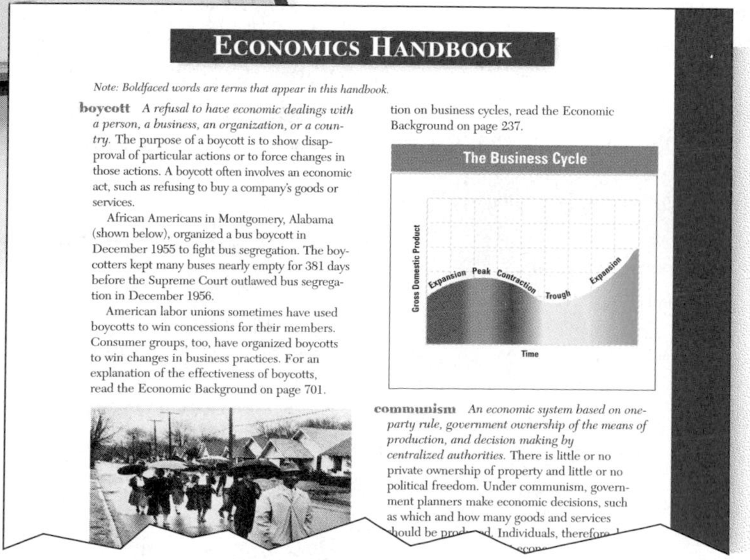

ECONOMICS HANDBOOK
This special section at the back of the textbook explains 29 key economics terms in depth. At appropriate places throughout the textbook, students are referred to the handbook.

ECONOMICS HANDBOOK

Note: Boldfaced words are terms that appear in this handbook.

boycott *A refusal to have economic dealings with a person, a business, an organization, or a country.* The purpose of a boycott is to show disapproval of particular actions or to force changes in those actions. A boycott often involves an economic act, such as refusing to buy a company's goods or services.

African Americans in Montgomery, Alabama (shown below), organized a bus boycott in December 1955 to fight bus segregation. The boycotters kept many buses nearly empty for 381 days before the Supreme Court outlawed bus segregation in December 1956.

American labor unions sometimes have used boycotts to win concessions from their members. Consumer groups, too, have organized boycotts to win changes in business practices. For an explanation of the effectiveness of boycotts, read the Economic Background on page 701.

tion on business cycles, read the Economic Background on page 237.

The Business Cycle

Gross Domestic Product
Expansion
Peak
Contraction
Trough
Expansion
Time

communism *An economic system based on one-party rule, government ownership of the means of production, and decision making by centralized authorities.* There is little or no private ownership of property and little or no political freedom. Under communism, government planners make economic decisions, such as which and how many goods and services should be produced. Individuals, therefore ...

Teacher's Resource Materials

From block scheduling to teaching students acquiring English, teachers are structuring their history lessons to make them work in today's diverse classrooms.

The Americans: Reconstruction through the 20th Century provides a full range of options to help you teach our shared heritage in ways that meet the common, and even the uncommon, needs of your students.

IN-DEPTH RESOURCES

One book for each unit, organized by chapter, includes the following complete set of options for reinforcement, practice, enrichment, and extension:

- **Guided Reading** worksheets develop essential reading skills.
- **Skillbuilder Practice** worksheets supplement the Skillbuilder Handbook in the pupil edition.
- **Geography Skills** worksheets teach map-reading skills.
- **Geography Application** worksheets provide practice in geography skills.
- **Primary Source** materials feature political cartoons, facsimile pages, historical documents, diary entries, letters, and much more.
- **Literature Selection** pages let your students experience history through relevant works of literature.
- **American Lives** pages provide additional short biographies to augment those in each chapter.
- **Living History Project** worksheets help students organize and complete their Living History projects.
- **Standards for Evaluation** charts provide rubrics for assessing students' Living History projects.

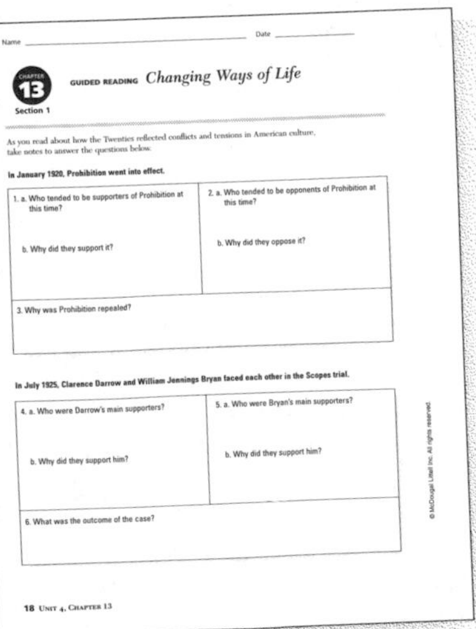
Name ______ Date ______

Chapter 13 Section 1 GUIDED READING *Changing Ways of Life*

As you read about how the Twenties reflected conflicts and tensions in American culture, take notes to answer the questions below.

In January 1920, Prohibition went into effect.

1. a. Who tended to be supporters of Prohibition at this time?
   b. Why did they support it?
2. a. Who tended to be opponents of Prohibition at this time?
   b. Why did they oppose it?
3. Why was Prohibition repealed?

In July 1925, Clarence Darrow and William Jennings Bryan faced each other in the Scopes trial.

4. a. Who were Darrow's main supporters?
   b. Why did they support him?
5. a. Who were Bryan's main supporters?
   b. Why did they support him?
6. What was the outcome of the case?

18 Unit 4, Chapter 13

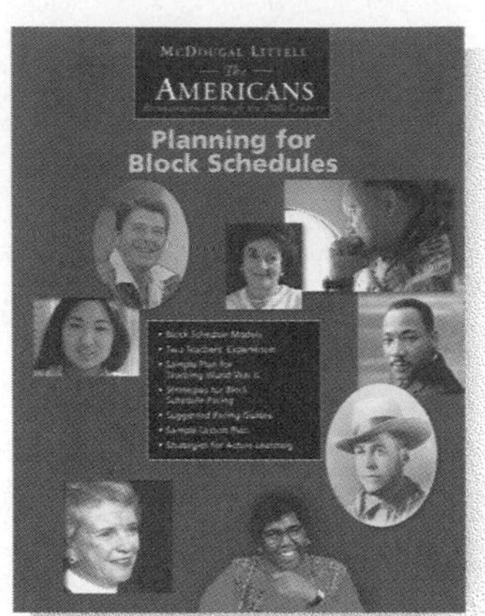

PLANNING FOR BLOCK SCHEDULES

Includes teaching models, a pacing guide, sample lesson plans, and strategies for active learning.

LESSON PLANS

Thorough two-page lesson plans for all sections of the textbook. Included are suggestions for block schedules, students acquiring English, less proficient readers, and technology.

TELESCOPING THE TIMES: CHAPTER SUMMARIES

Helps you address differences in reading speed, the need for condensed instruction in block scheduling, reinforcement, and reteaching.

TRANSLATIONS OF CHAPTER SUMMARIES: CAMBODIAN, CANTONESE, HMONG, AND VIETNAMESE

Four booklets containing translations of the chapter summaries in *Telescoping the Times.*

ACCESS FOR STUDENTS ACQUIRING ENGLISH: SPANISH TRANSLATIONS

Provides strategies for teaching ESL students in addition to Spanish translations of Chapter Summaries, Guided Reading, Skillbuilder Practice, Geography Application, and Outline Maps.

READING STUDY GUIDE

Provides access to American history content and reading support for less proficient readers and students acquiring English.

SPANISH READING STUDY GUIDE

Provides access in Spanish to American history content and reading support for Spanish-speaking students.

WRITING FOR SOCIAL STUDIES

Support for writing history research papers, historical narratives, essays, interviews, oral histories, book reviews, and short reports.

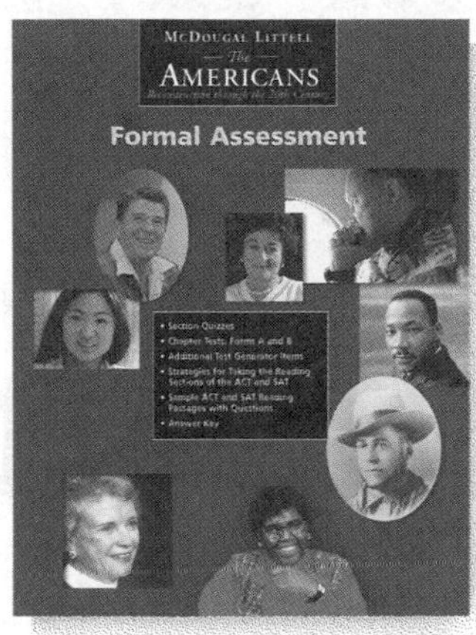

FORMAL ASSESSMENT

Section Quizzes
Chapter Tests, Forms A and B
Additional Test Questions
ACT/SAT Test Practice

ALTERNATIVE ASSESSMENT

Provides explanations and forms for a variety of assessment options, including cooperative learning, group discussion, role-playing, oral presentation, peer assessment, self-assessment, and portfolio assessment.

TEST GENERATOR

Includes all questions in the Section Quizzes and Chapter Tests, forms A and B—plus ten new test items for each chapter, leveled for basic and advanced students.

HISTORY FROM VISUALS: TRANSPARENCY PACKS

Enliven lessons with four volumes of transparencies:

HUMANITIES

Political cartoons, fine art, photographs, and other artworks.

CRITICAL THINKING

Charts, graphs, and infographics, plus a cause-and-effect chart for each chapter.

GEOGRAPHY

Thirty-four new maps, plus a map of U.S. growth with overlays.

WARM-UPS

Visual support for the 5-Minute Warm-Up activities that begin the lesson plans for all sections in the Teacher's Edition.

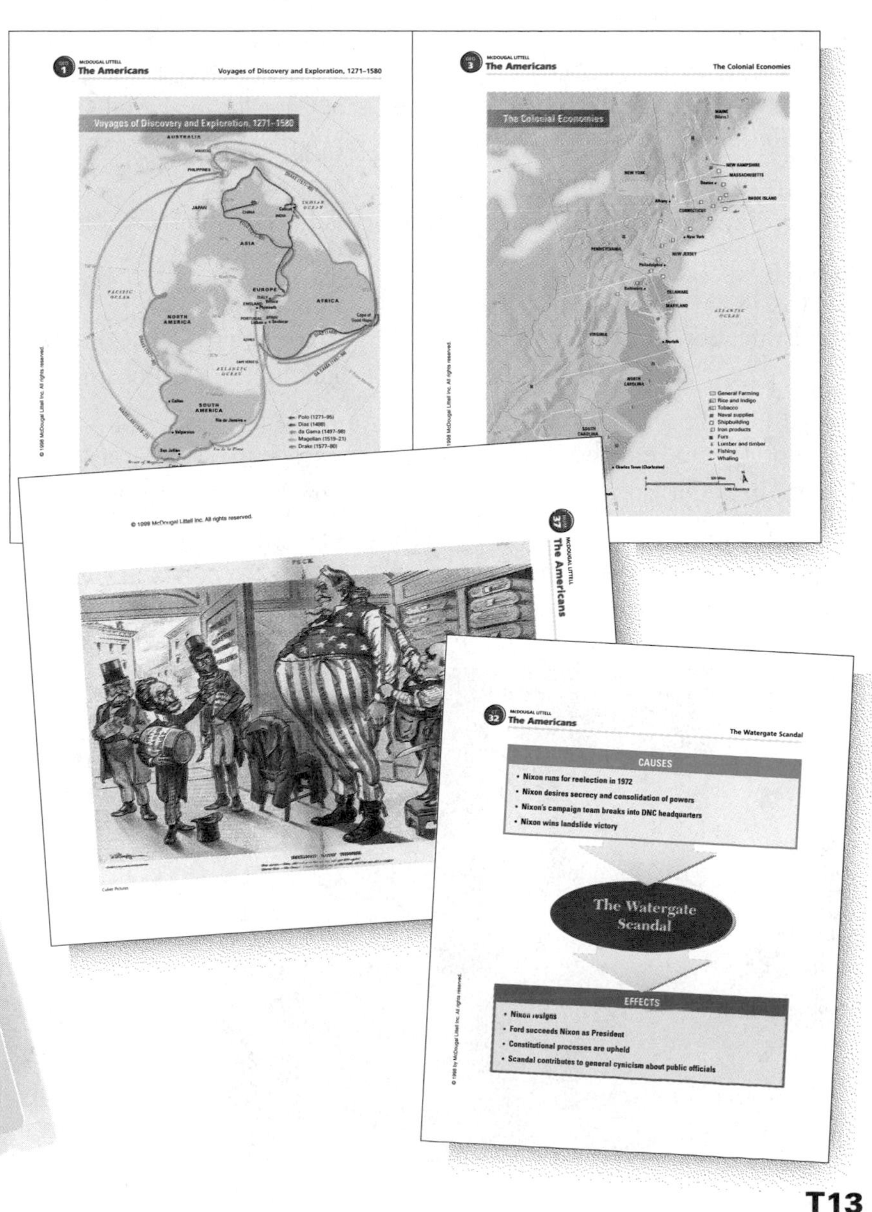

American Stories Video Series

American Stories is a powerful new video series integrated with the text of *The Americans: Reconstruction through the 20th century.* Fifteen fascinating documentaries, each 8–10 minutes long, help you to introduce various sections of the text.

In addition, an invaluable Teacher's Resource Book helps you to fully exploit the power of the videos with everything from teaching tips to lesson-extending information and activities.

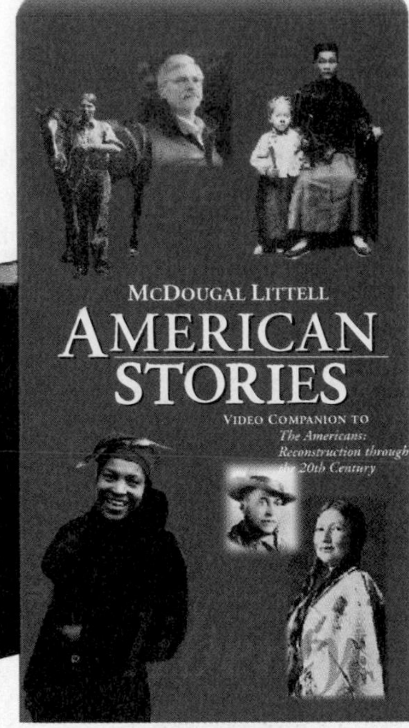

In English and Spanish

VIDEOCASSETTES

Volume 1: Videos 1–3
Volume 2: Videos 4–6
Volume 3: Videos 7–9
Volume 4: Videos 10–12
Volume 5: Videos 13–15

Video 1
WAR OUTSIDE MY WINDOW
Mary Chesnut's Diary of the Civil War

Video 2
TEACHER OF A FREED PEOPLE
Robert Fitzgerald and Reconstruction

Video 3
A WALK IN TWO WORLDS
The Education of Zitkala-Ša, a Sioux

Video 4
GUSHER!
Pattillo Higgins and the Great Texas Oil Boom

Video 5
FROM CHINA TO CHINATOWN
Fong See's American Dream

Video 6
A CHILD ON STRIKE: The Testimony of Camella Teoli, Mill Girl

Video 7
ACE OF ACES
Eddie Rickenbacker and the First World War

Video 8
JUMP AT THE SUN: Zora Neale Hurston and the Harlem Renaissance

Video 9
BROKE BUT NOT BROKEN: Ann Marie Low Remembers the Dust Bowl

Video 10
A SONG FOR HIS PEOPLE: Pedro J. González and the Fight for Mexican-American Rights

Video 11
ESCAPING THE FINAL SOLUTION: Kurt Klein and Gerda Weissmann Klein Remember the Holocaust

Video 12
THE COLD WAR COMES HOME: Hollywood Blacklists the Kahn Family

Video 13
JUSTICE IN MONTGOMERY: Jo Ann Gibson Robinson and the Bus Boycott

Video 14
MATTERS OF CONSCIENCE: Stephan Gubar and the Vietnam War

Video 15
POISONED PLAYGROUND: Lois Gibbs and the Crisis at Love Canal

VIDEODISCS

Disc 1: Videos 1–5
Disc 2: Videos 6–10
Disc 3: Videos 11–15

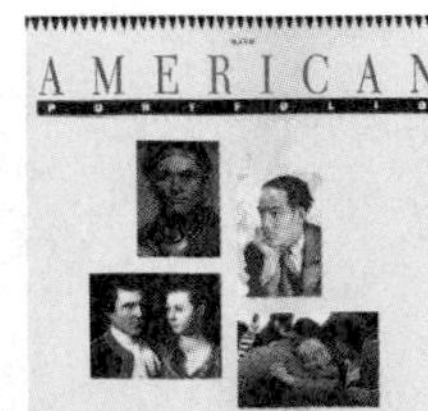

AMERICAN PORTFOLIO: A VIDEODISC FOR U.S. HISTORY

Enhance any lesson with more than 1,500 still images, more than 70 maps (many of them animated), and approximately 25 minutes of historical film footage.

CD-ROM Resources

Electronic Library of Primary Sources

Support, enrich, and extend each chapter of the text with a compendium of carefully selected primary sources. Discover a wealth of documents that have shaped modern American history, along with personal accounts drawn from letters, diaries, and oral histories.

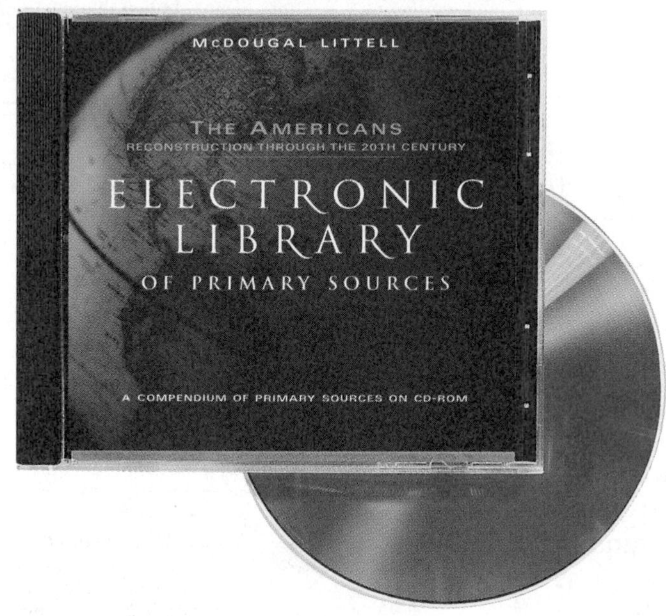

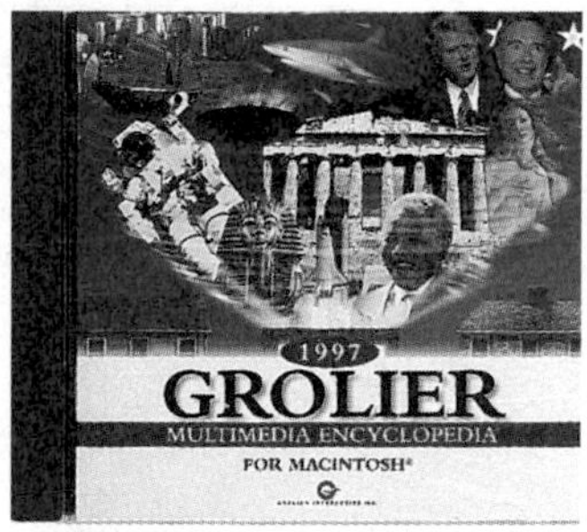

GROLIER MULTIMEDIA ENCYCLOPEDIA

This multimedia encyclopedia includes over 50,000 entries and 1,200 maps. Articles, historical time lines, and hyperlinks to World Wide Web sites are easily accessed, offering students multiple avenues to research topics of interest.

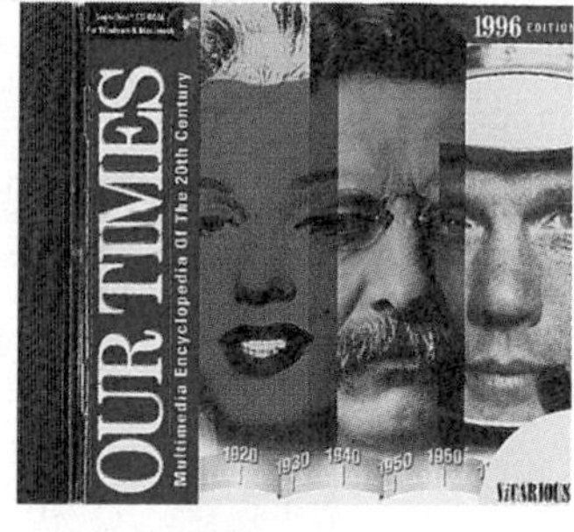

OUR TIMES MULTIMEDIA ENCYCLOPEDIA OF THE 20TH CENTURY

Students can find out what was happening, and who was who, in a multimedia exploration of the 20th century. Compelling video and audio tours, narrated by James Earl Jones, summarize key cultural, scientific, and political events. More information is available as students browse 52,000 articles and 2,500 charts, maps, and graphs. The content of *Our Times* is hyperlinked to *The Columbia Encyclopedia,* Fifth Edition.

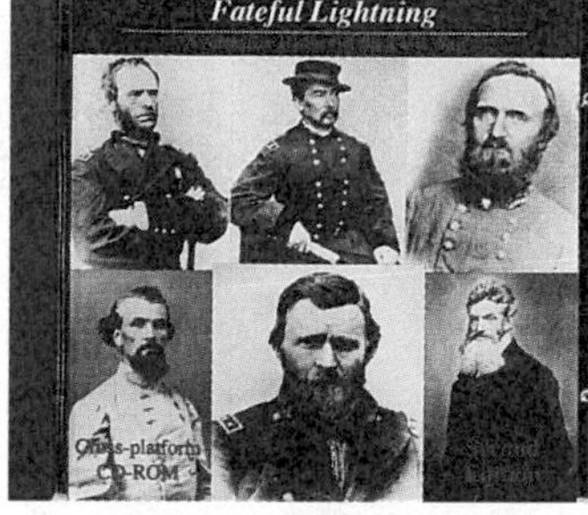

FATEFUL LIGHTNING: A NARRATIVE HISTORY OF THE CIVIL WAR

A comprehensive narrative is enhanced with animated maps that detail campaigns and battles of the Civil War. In addition, reenactment video, contemporary photographs of Civil War battle sites, and music of the era help bring the sights and sounds of the Civil War to life. This CD-ROM provides valuable enrichment for a review of early American history.

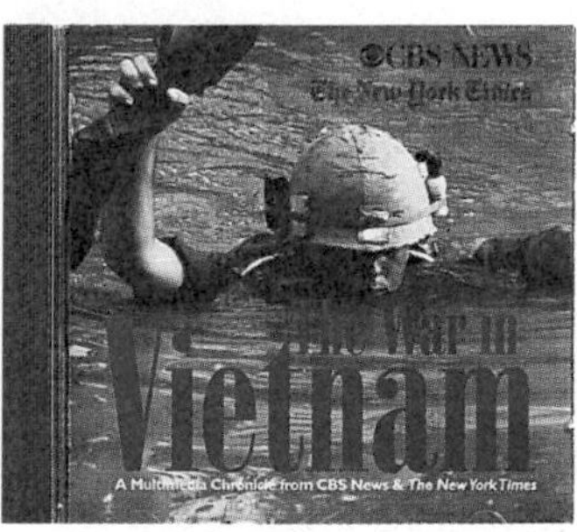

THE WAR IN VIETNAM

Over 1,000 articles from the *New York Times* and 40 minutes of video from CBS News are cross-indexed and arranged along time lines to provide students an opportunity to see, hear, and read about the Vietnam War as it was actually reported. Additional enhancements include interactive maps and special databases, such as a searchable list of names on the Vietnam Veterans Memorial in Washington, D.C.

TEACHER'S EDITION FEATURES

Chapter Planning Guide

As you write your lessons to meet the needs of today's classroom, you can depend on outstanding support in the Teacher's Edition of *The Americans: Reconstruction through the 20th Century.*

Support begins with the convenient two-page planning guide found at the beginning of every chapter. From key ideas to technology connections, the guide features invaluable information and options to help you devise an effective course of instruction.

PLANNING GUIDE

CHAPTER 22

The Vietnam War Years

	Key Ideas	COPYMASTERS	ASSESSMENT
SECTION 1 Moving Toward Conflict *pp. 724–728*	*America slowly involves itself in the war in Vietnam as it seeks to halt the spread of communism.*	***In-Depth Resources: Unit 6*** • Guided Reading, p. 35 ***Lesson Plans,*** pp. 177–178	PE ***Section 1 Assessment,*** p. 728 TE ***Self-Assessment,*** p. 728 ***Formal Assessment*** • Section Quiz, p. 270 ***Alternative Assessment Book*** • Standards for Evaluating a Cooperative Activity
SECTION 2 U.S. Involvement and Escalation *pp. 729–734*	*The United States sends troops to fight in Vietnam, but the war quickly turns into a stalemate.*	***In-Depth Resources: Unit 6*** • Guided Reading, p. 36 • Skillbuilder Practice: Distinguishing Fact from Opinion, p. 40 • Primary Source: Letter from a Soldier in Vietnam, p. 45 • American Lives: Robert McNamara, p. 52 ***Lesson Plans,*** pp. 179–180	PE ***Section 2 Assessment,*** p. 734 TE ***Self-Assessment,*** p. 734 ***Formal Assessment*** • Section Quiz, p. 271 ***Alternative Assessment Book*** • Standards for Evaluating a Cooperative Activity
SECTION 3 A Nation Divided *pp. 735–740*	*An antiwar movement emerges in the United States, pitting those who oppose the government's war policy against those who support it.*	***In-Depth Resources: Unit 6*** • Guided Reading, p. 37 • Primary Sources: Protest Buttons, p. 46; The New Left, p. 47 ***Lesson Plans,*** pp. 181–182	PE ***Section 3 Assessment,*** p. 740 TE ***Self-Assessment,*** p. 740 ***Formal Assessment*** • Section Quiz, p. 272 ***Alternative Assessment Book*** • Standards for Evaluating a Cooperative Activity
SECTION 4 1968: A Tumultuous Year *pp. 741–746*	*A shocking enemy attack in Vietnam, two assassinations, and a chaotic political convention help make 1968 the most explosive year of the decade.*	***In-Depth Resources: Unit 6*** • Guided Reading, p. 38 • Geography Application: The Ho Chi Minh Trail, p. 41 • Primary Source: Lyndon B. Johnson on Vietnam and Reelection, p. 48 • American Lives: John Lewis, p. 53 ***Lesson Plans,*** pp. 183–184	PE ***Section 4 Assessment,*** p. 746 TE ***Self-Assessment,*** p. 746 ***Formal Assessment*** • Section Quiz, p. 273 ***Alternative Assessment Book*** • Standards for Evaluating a Cooperative Activity
SECTION 5 The End of the War and Its Legacy *pp. 747–753*	*The nation's longest war ends after nearly ten years and leaves a lasting impact on U.S. policy and American society.*	***In-Depth Resources: Unit 6*** • Guided Reading, p. 39 • Outline Map: The Vietnam War, p. 43 • Literature: from *In Country* by Bobbie Ann Mason, p. 49 ***Lesson Plans,*** pp. 185–186	PE ***Section 5 Assessment,*** p. 753 TE ***Self-Assessment,*** p. 753 ***Formal Assessment*** • Section Quiz, p. 274 ***Alternative Assessment Book*** • Standards for Evaluating a Cooperative Activity
CHAPTER RESOURCES	**Chapter Overview** *The United States enters a war in Vietnam, which results in the deaths of tens of thousands of American soldiers, the division of society into bitterly opposed camps, and a lasting impact on U.S. foreign policy.*	***In-Depth Resources: Unit 6*** • Living History Project: Worksheet, p. 54; Standards, p. 55 ***Telescoping the Times*** • Chapter Summary, pp. 43–44 ***Planning for Block Schedules***	PE ***Chapter Assessment,*** pp. 756–757 PE ***Alternative Assessment,*** p. 757 ***Formal Assessment*** • Chapter Test, forms A and B, pp. 275–280 ***Test Generator*** ***Alternative Assessment Book*** See explanation and forms for different kinds of alternative assessments including portfolio assessment.

KEY
PE Pupil's Edition
TE Teacher's Edition
http://www.mlushistory.com

721A

KEY IDEAS

A chronological, section-by-section summary of the key ideas in the chapter. The column of key ideas builds to a unifying theme for the whole chapter.

COPYMASTERS

For each section there is a bulleted listing of valuable ancillary support available.

ASSESSMENT

Locates pages on which assessment, self-assessment, evaluation guidelines, quizzes, and tests are available for the section or chapter.

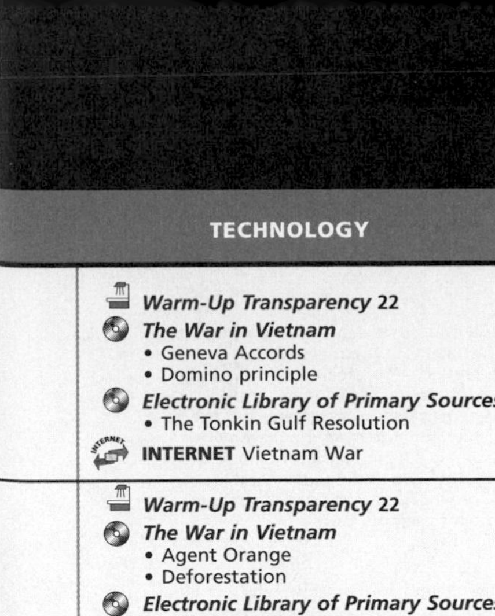

TECHNOLOGY

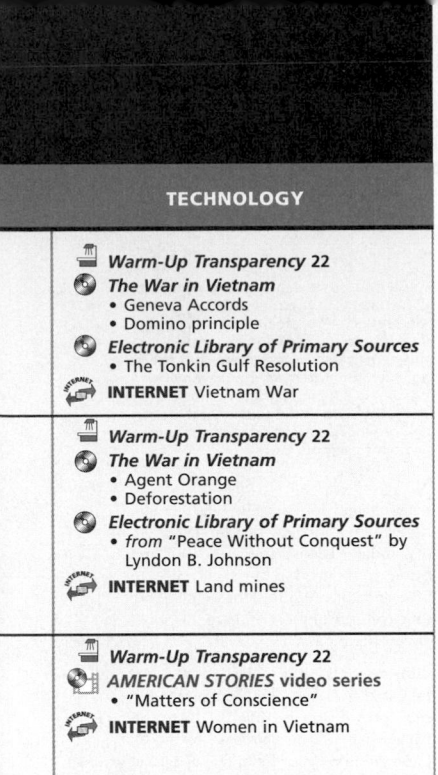

- *Warm-Up Transparency 22*
- *The War in Vietnam*
  - Geneva Accords
  - Domino principle
- *Electronic Library of Primary Sources*
  - The Tonkin Gulf Resolution
- **INTERNET** Vietnam War

- *Warm-Up Transparency 22*
- *The War in Vietnam*
  - Agent Orange
  - Deforestation
- *Electronic Library of Primary Sources*
  - *from* "Peace Without Conquest" by Lyndon B. Johnson
- **INTERNET** Land mines

- *Warm-Up Transparency 22*
- *AMERICAN STORIES* video series
  - "Matters of Conscience"
- **INTERNET** Women in Vietnam

- *Warm-Up Transparency 22*
- *Critical Thinking Transparencies*
  - CT64, Impact of Tet Offensive
- *The War in Vietnam*
  - Tet Offensive
- *Electronic Library of Primary Sources*
  - from *The Strategy of Confrontation*
- **INTERNET** Tet offensive

- *Warm-Up Transparency 22*
- *Humanities Transparencies*
  - H28, Fall of Saigon
  - H45, The Blind Leading the Blind
- *Geography Transparencies*
  - G30, Vietnam War: 1964–1975
- *Critical Thinking Transparencies*
  - CT30, The War in Vietnam
- *The War in Vietnam*
  - from the Pentagon Papers
  - Supreme Court decision
  - the boat people
- *Electronic Library of Primary Sources*
  - Kent State
- **INTERNET** Interact with History p. 755 (PE)

- *American Portfolio: A Videodisc for U.S. History,* user's guide, pp.244–245, 251–253, 255
- *Chapter Summary Audiotapes*
  - Unit 6, Chapter 22
- **INTERNET http://www. mlushistory.com**

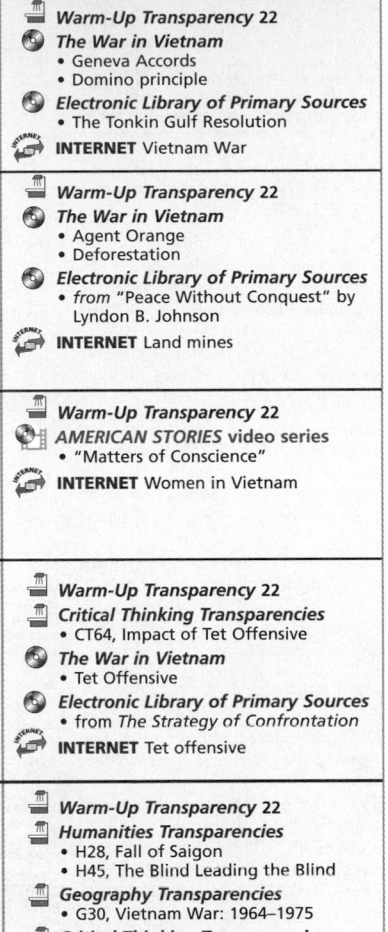

Block Scheduling (90 MINUTES)

Day 1

Section 1, pp. 724–728

Section Assessment, p. 728

COOPERATIVE ACTIVITY
- Researching Buddhism, p. 726 (TE)

Day 2

Section 2, pp. 729–734

Section Assessment, p. 734

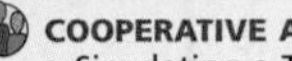

COOPERATIVE ACTIVITY
- Simulating a TV Interview, p. 733 (TE)

Day 3

Section 3, pp. 735–740

AMERICAN STORIES video series "Matters of Conscience"

Section 4, pp. 741–746

Section Assessments, pp. 740, 746

COOPERATIVE ACTIVITIES
- Composing "Hawk" or "Dove" Song Lyrics, p. 739 (TE)
- Creating a 1968 Yearbook, p. 745 (TE)

Day 4

Section 5, pp. 747–753

American Literature: Literature of the Vietnam War, pp. 754–755

Chapter Assessment, pp. 756–757

COOPERATIVE ACTIVITY
- Writing Editorials, p. 749 (TE)

YEARLY PACING *Chapter 22 Total:* 4 days *Yearly Total:* 85 days

See *Planning for Block Schedules* for special activities and pacing strategies.

Customizing for Special Populations

Students Acquiring English

Access for Students Acquiring English: Spanish Translations
- Guided Reading for Sections 1–5, pp. 241–245
- Chapter Summary, pp. 239–240
- Skillbuilder Practice: Distinguishing Fact from Opinion, p. 246
- Geography Application: The Ho Chi Minh Trail, p. 247
- Outline Map: The Vietnam War, p. 249

Spanish Reading Study Guide, pp. 223–234

Translations of Chapter Summaries, Hmong, Cantonese, Vietnamese, and Cambodian

Chapter Summary Audiotapes in Spanish Unit 6, Chapter 22

AMERICAN STORIES video series
- "Matters of Conscience" (Spanish track)

INTERNET The Diverse Classroom

Gifted and Talented Students

In-Depth Resources: Unit 6
- Primary Sources: Letter from a Soldier in Vietnam, p. 45; Protest Buttons, p. 46; The New Left, p. 47; Lyndon B. Johnson on Vietnam and Reelection, p. 48
- American Lives: Robert McNamara, p. 52; John Lewis, p. 53

Less Proficient Readers

In-Depth Resources: Unit 6
- Guided Reading for Sections 1–5, pp. 35–39
- Skillbuilder: Distinguishing Fact from Opinion, p. 40
- Geography Application: The Ho Chi Minh Trail, p. 41
- Outline Map: The Vietnam War, p. 43

Reading Study Guide
- pp. 223–234

Telescoping the Times
- Chapter Summary, pp. 43–44

Chapter Summary Audiotapes, Unit 6, Chapter 22

Connections to Literature READINGS FOR STUDENTS

In-Depth Resources: Unit 6
- from *In Country* by Bobbie Ann Mason, p. 49

McDougal Littell *The Language of Literature* American Literature
- Estela Portillo Trambley, "Village," p. 937
- George Olsen, from *Dear America: Letters Home from Vietnam,* p. 945
- Yusef Komunyakaa, "Camouflaging the Chimera," p.949
- Wendy Wilder Larsen and Tran Thi Nga, "Deciding," p. 952
- Tim O'Brien, "Ambush," p. 956
- Lanford Wilson, *Wandering,* p. 972
- Denise Levertov, "At the Justice Department, November 15, 1969," p. 979

McDougal Littell *Literature Connections*

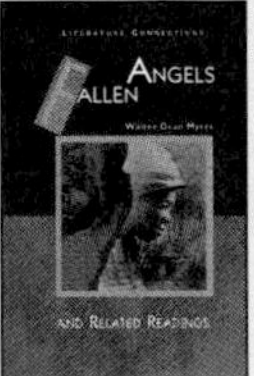

- Walter Dean Myers *Fallen Angels (with related readings) This novel presents the experiences of a small group of men who come of age in the Vietnam War. Richie Perry enlists in the army mainly to escape his problems at home and finds himself in the middle of a war that is more traumatic and confusing than the life he fled.*

Teacher's Edition **721B**

BLOCK SCHEDULING

A pacing guide for block scheduling.

CUSTOMIZING FOR SPECIAL POPULATIONS

Suggested resources for teaching students acquiring English, gifted and talented students, and less proficient readers. From the Reading Study Guide and chapter summaries in Spanish to additional primary-source material, these suggestions offer practical help for basic classroom needs.

LITERATURE CONNECTIONS

Literature Connections from McDougal Littell are stand-alone books with related readings that offer in-depth literary supplements. A SourceBook provides student support materials for each selection.

TECHNOLOGY

Lists connections to technology resources available for each section, from CD-ROMs to Internet resources.

ENRICHMENT READING

Lists additional suggested literature options.

THE LANGUAGE OF LITERATURE

Connections to McDougal Littell's American literature text, *The Language of Literature,* can help in planning American studies courses.

TEACHER'S EDITION FEATURES

Lesson Support

The Teacher's Edition for *The Americans: Reconstruction through the 20th Century* supports instruction with everything from fascinating tidbits to practical graphic organizers. Side columns focus on core instruction, with optional ideas and teaching strategies being featured at the bottom of the pages.

GRAPHIC ORGANIZERS

Convey key information in a clear and convincing way to help students grasp concepts.

REFERENCES TO RESOURCE MATERIALS

Identify where to find additional support for teaching the section.

5-MINUTE WARM-UP

Recognizing Facts and Details

To explore the conditions of child labor, have students look at the photo on page 499 and answer these questions.

1. What was the age group of these factory workers? How were they dressed?
2. What details do you notice about the factory and the machinery?

WARM-UP TRANSPARENCY 9

OBJECTIVE ③ **INSTRUCT**

Building the Great Society

▶ ***Starting with the Student*** Have students use a chart like the one below to organize what they learn about the Great Society programs. Students should list each program and describe its purpose.

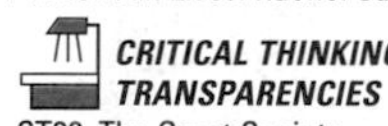

▶ ***Discussing Key Ideas***

- Johnson presents his legislative program, which he calls the Great Society.
- Great Society programs bring about change in education, Social Security, housing, and immigration.
- The Great Society also seeks to protect the environment and consumers.

IN-DEPTH RESOURCES: UNIT 6
Primary Source: from *Unsafe at Any Speed,* p. 10
American Lives: Rachel Carson, p. 15

CRITICAL THINKING TRANSPARENCIES
CT28, The Great Society

NOW & THEN
Medicare on the Line

Critical Thinking: Evaluating Ask students whether they think cutbacks should be made in Medicare. Is Medicare an entitlement? Should other federal programs be cut to help balance the budget? Or is Medicare in its present state too expensive to maintain?

Building the Great Society

In May of 1964, Johnson had summed up his grand vision for America in a phrase: the **Great Society.** In a speech at the University of Michigan, the president declared that "the Great Society demands an end to poverty and racial injustice." But, he told the enthusiastic crowd, that was "just the beginning." Johnson envisioned a legislative program that would create not only a higher living standard and equal opportunity but also promote a richer quality of life.

NOW & THEN

MEDICARE ON THE LINE

When President Johnson signed the Medicare bill in 1965, only half of the nation's elderly had health insurance. Today, thanks largely to Medicare, most do. However, most experts agree that the country cannot afford to sustain Medicare in its present form for much longer, especially if the nation hopes to balance the federal budget.

Three trends are fueling these concerns: (1) people are living longer, (2) health care continues to become more advanced and more expensive, and (3) the large baby boomer generation is moving toward retirement age. Medicare costs are increasing 10 percent a year. In 1994, federal spending on Medicare was about $160 billion; in 2002, without changes in the program, it could top $345 billion.

Both Democrats and Republicans in Washington agree that cuts have to be made, but experience has shown that the issue is a political hot potato. Many people consider Medicare an "entitlement" that they expect to receive when they retire. Although most Americans want a balanced budget, a 1996 survey revealed that only 16 percent favored large cutbacks in Medicare to achieve it.

A PERSONAL VOICE

The Great Society is a place where every child can find knowledge to enrich his mind and to enlarge his talents. It is a place where leisure is a welcome chance to build and reflect, not a feared cause of boredom and restlessness. It is a place where the city of man serves not only the needs of the body and the demands of commerce but the desire for beauty and the hunger for community. It is a place where man can renew contact with nature. It is a place which honors creation for its own sake and for what it adds to the understanding of the race. It is a place where men are more concerned with the quality of their goals than the quantity of their goods.

LYNDON JOHNSON, "The Great Society," May 22, 1964

LBJ set lofty goals for his nation and for himself. Like his idol FDR, he wanted to change America. He also knew that he had to act quickly to capitalize on his new mandate. During the years 1965 and 1966, the Johnson administration introduced a flurry of bills to Congress. By the time Johnson left the White House in 1969, Congress had passed 206 of his measures. For most of them, the president personally led the battle to get them passed.

LANDMARK LEGISLATION Johnson considered education "the key which can unlock the door to the Great Society." The Elementary and Secondary Education Act of 1965 provided more than $1 billion in federal aid to help public and parochial schools purchase textbooks and new library materials. This was the first major federal aid package for education in the nation's history.

LBJ and Congress brought about the first major change in Social Security since its adoption in 1935 by establishing Medicare and Medicaid. **Medicare** provides hospital insurance and low-cost medical insurance for almost every American age 65 or older. **Medicaid** extended health insurance to welfare recipients.

D. Answer Both provide government-sponsored health insurance.

THINK THROUGH HISTORY
D. Comparing *How are Medicare and Medicaid similar?*

Congress also appropriated money to build some 240,000 units of low-rent public housing and help low- and moderate-income families pay for better private housing. It established a new federal department, the Department of Housing and Urban Development (HUD). As secretary of the new department, Johnson appointed Robert Weaver, the first African-American cabinet member in American history.

The Great Society also brought profound changes to the nation's immigration laws. The Immigration Act of 1924 and the National Origins Act of 1929 had established immigration quotas that discriminated strongly against people from outside Western Europe. The **Immigration Act of 1965** replaced the national origins system with an annual quota of 170,000 immigrants from the Eastern Hemisphere and 120,000 from the Western Hemisphere. Within this overall quota, no more than 20,000 persons from any one nation could enter the United States each year. Close relatives of American residents were exempt from the quotas. This act opened the door for many non-European immigrants to settle in the United States.

E. Answer It replaced the national origins system, which discriminated against people from outside Western Europe.

THINK THROUGH HISTORY
E. THEME Immigration and Migration *How did the Immigration Act of 1965 change the nation's immigration system?*

TEACHING OPTIONS

Exploring Themes

Immigration and Migration Discuss the Immigration Act of 1965. Ask students how the legislation affected immigration to the United States. *Possible Response: It allowed the influx of people from Asia, Latin America, and other non-European regions.* In what ways was the act consistent with the ideals and goals of the Great Society? *Possible Response: It offered the opportunity of a better life to people in need.* How does the act's provisions continue to affect the United States today? *Possible Response: People allowed into the country under the act have greatly influenced mainstream American culture and lifestyle.*

Making Connections Across the Curriculum

Government Discuss the creation of the Department of Housing and Urban Development. Ask students why the new federal department was created. *To address the problems of the nation's cities.* Why was the department considered necessary by the mid-1960s? *Possible Response: Explosive urban growth in the 1950s had resulted in many urban problems, including overcrowding and inadequate housing.* Then ask students to discuss any recently formed federal departments or programs, such as the war on drugs, created to address current problems.

MAKING CONNECTIONS (THEMATIC AND CROSSCURRICULAR)

Provide insightful observations and meaningful examples showing how a particular topic relates to key themes and other areas of study.

5-MINUTE WARM-UPS

Provide starter activities that prepare students to read and understand every section in the textbook.

Great Society Programs, 1964–1967

Category	Year	Program	Year	Program
Poverty	1964	**Tax Reduction Act** cut corporate and individual taxes to stimulate growth.	1965	**Medical Care Act** established Medicare and Medicaid programs.
	1964	**Economic Opportunity Act** created Job Corps, VISTA, Project Head Start, and other programs to fight "war on poverty."	1965	**Appalachian Regional Development Act** targeted aid for highways, health centers, and resource development in that economically depressed area.
Cities	1965	**Omnibus Housing Act** provided money for low-income housing.	1966	**Demonstration Cities and Metropolitan Area Redevelopment Act** funded slum rebuilding, mass transit, and other improvements for selected "model cities."
	1965	**Department of Housing and Urban Development** was formed to administer federal housing programs.		
Education	1965	**Elementary and Secondary Education Act** directed money to schools for textbooks, library materials, and special education.	1965	**National Foundation on the Arts and the Humanities** was created to financially assist painters, musicians, actors, and others in arts.
	1965	**Higher Education Act** funded scholarships and low-interest loans for college students.	1967	**Corporation for Public Broadcasting** was formed to fund educational TV and radio broadcasting.
Discrimination	1964	**Civil Rights Act** outlawed discrimination in public accommodations, housing, and jobs; increased federal power to prosecute civil rights abuses.	1965	**Voting Rights Act** ended the practice of requiring voters to pass literacy tests and permitted the federal government to monitor voter registration.
	1964	**Twenty-fourth Amendment** abolished the poll tax in federal elections.	1965	**Immigration Act** ended national-origins quotas established in 1924.
Environment	1965	**Wilderness Preservation Act** set aside over 9 million acres for national forest lands.	1965	**Clean Air Act Amendment** directed the federal government to establish emission standards for new motor vehicles.
	1965	**Water Quality Act** required states to clean up their rivers.	1967	**Air Quality Act** set federal air pollution guidelines and extended federal enforcement power.
Consumer Advocacy	1966	**Truth in Packaging Act** set standards for labeling consumer products.	1966	**Highway Safety Act** required states to set up highway safety programs.
	1966	**National Traffic and Motor Vehicle Safety Act** set federal safety standards for the auto and tire industries.	1966	**Department of Transportation** was created to deal with national air, rail, and highway transportation.

Skillbuilder Answer The programs were wide-ranging, which reflected an expanding role for the federal government in addressing certain areas of American society.

The Great Society addressed more than economic and social ills—it also embraced, among other things, protecting the environment and consumers. In 1962, *Silent Spring*, a book by Rachel Carson, had called attention to a hidden danger: the effects of pesticides on the environment. Carson's book and the following public outcry resulted in the Water Quality Act of 1965, which required states to clean up rivers. "Today we begin to be masters of our environment," declared Johnson as he signed the bill into law. He also ordered the federal government to search out the worst chemical polluters. "There is no excuse . . . for chemical companies and oil refineries using our major rivers as pipelines for toxic wastes." Such words and actions helped trigger the environmental movement in the United States. (See Chapter 24.)

Hand in hand with environmental protection arose a new concern for consumer protection. Consumer advocates convinced Congress to pass major safety laws, including a truth-in-packaging law that set standards for labeling consumer goods. Ralph Nader, a young lawyer, wrote a book, *Unsafe at Any Speed*, that sharply criticized the U.S. automobile industry for ignoring safety

SKILLBUILDER
INTERPRETING CHARTS
What did the Great Society programs indicate about the federal government's changing role?

Ralph Nader

Issues for the 21st Century

Curing the Health Care System

Connect medical programs in the 1960s to health care issues today by having students read pages 892–893. Then have them answer these questions.

1. Why did President Johnson want to establish Medicare and Medicaid? *To provide health care for the elderly and for the poor.*
2. Why are these medical programs in danger now? *Rising costs; running out of money; increasing numbers of seniors.*

HISTORY FROM VISUALS

Great Society Programs, 1964–1967

Reading the Chart Point out that the chart organizes the Great Society programs in distinct categories. Then ask students in which year the greatest number of programs were passed. *1965.* How is this fact connected to the results of the 1964 election? *Johnson hurried through a flurry of bills soon after the election to take advantage of his mandate.*

Extension Ask students what the scope of the Great Society programs suggests about the Johnson administration. *Possible Responses: The administration was ambitious, compassionate, liberal.* Why did the number of programs drop off after 1967? *Possible Response: Because Johnson began to focus his energies on the Vietnam War.*

Block Schedule TEACHING OPTION **Time Needed: 30 Minutes**

Cooperative Activity: Outlining Provisions for a Great Society Program

Task: Groups of four to five students will select a category and outline provisions for a Great Society-inspired program that addresses a problem today.

Purpose: To get a sense of the scope and purpose of the Great Society programs.

Activity: Students should get together in groups and discuss some of the major problems that face society today. Encourage students to use the categories and bills listed in the chart on page 687 to spark ideas. Students should then agree on a problem they would like to address and write an outline describing the problem and a proposed solution. The outline should detail the roles of the individuals and groups involved in the solution.

Building a Portfolio: Students who add their outlines to their portfolios should attach a note explaining the extent to which the government should involve itself in the issue.

ALTERNATIVE ASSESSMENT BOOK
Standards for Evaluating a Cooperative Activity

Standards for Evaluation
Outlines should . . .
- address an important problem in society
- describe the roles of the people involved in effecting a solution
- be consistent with the vision of the Great Society programs

HISTORY FROM VISUALS

Provides a variety of notes, learning strategies, and extension activities to help students make the most of charts, graphs, political cartoons, and key historical photographs.

ANSWERS

Answers to Think Through History and Skillbuilder questions are conveniently placed on the page in the Teacher's Edition.

COOPERATIVE ACTIVITIES

Suggest some great ways for students to work together and enhance their interest in and understanding of history.

ISSUES FOR THE 21ST CENTURY

Highlights appropriate points to connect historical events with the eight contemporary issues covered in Issues for the 21st Century in the pupil text.

Issues for the 21st Century

The Debate over Immigration

Connect immigration in the late 1800s with immigration today by having students read pages 880–883. Then have them answer these questions.

1. What factor contributed to the rise of nativism in the 1800s? *Suspicion of growing numbers of immigrants.*
2. What has been the trend in the admission of immigrants to the United States since 1940? *Steady increase.*
3. Compare the arguments against immigration to the United States today with the arguments used in the 1800s. *They are similar.*

Block Schedules

"Some of my favorite active-learning strategies, such as role-playing and simulations, work even better with the block."

Debra Brown, teacher, Houston, Texas

"While I was not an ardent fan of block scheduling during the planning stage, I quickly became a convert after working under a block schedule for a few months."

Marsee Perkins, teacher, Orlando, Florida

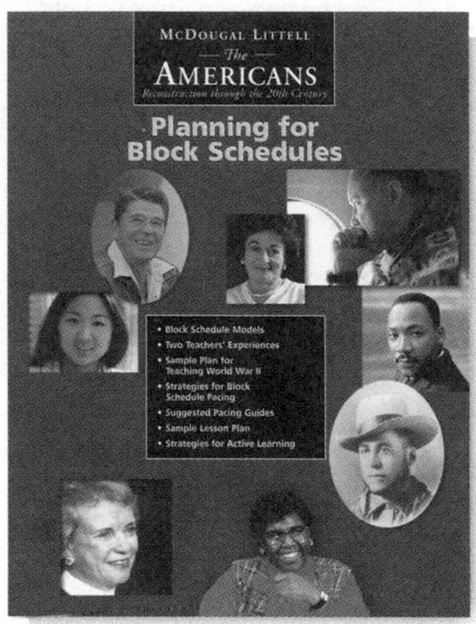

What is block scheduling, this new way of organizing the school day? What benefits does it offer teachers and students? For Debra Brown and Marsee Perkins, the block schedule has some clear advantages. You can find out about various types of block schedules and get the advice of these two experienced teachers by examining *Planning for Block Schedules,* found in the teacher resource materials for *The Americans: Reconstruction through the 20th Century.*

In contrast to the traditional school day of six to eight single class periods, block schedules have fewer classes, each lasting anywhere from 85 to 100 minutes. The longer classes provide teachers with convenient periods of teaching time and students with fewer subjects on which to concentrate. Block schedules can take a variety of forms: *Planning for Block Schedules* shows several of the most common of these.

Sample Alternate-Day (A/B) Schedule

Period	Length in Minutes	Monday	Tuesday	Wednesday	Thursday	Friday	Monday
BLOCK ONE	112	Class A	Class D	Class A	Class D	Class A	Class D
passing	8						
BLOCK TWO	112	Class B	Class E	Class B	Class E	Class B	Class E
passing							
lunch							
passing							

Sample Semester Plan (4/4) Schedule

Period	Length in Minutes	First Semester	Second Semester
BLOCK ONE	90	Class A	Class E
passing	8		
BLOCK TWO	90	Class B	Class F
passing	8		
lunch	50		

…ING STRATEGIES FOR ACTIVE LEARNING

…llaborative and Cooperative Learning

…ents working in pairs or small groups take responsibility for their own learn- …in a way that students in more passive roles sometimes do not. Whether you …ose to set up a formal cooperative learning classroom or to use occasional col- …orative teams, varying the grouping in your classroom can help to break up …e longer block schedule periods and add flexibility to your menu of activities.

…FOR THE BLOCK SCHEDULE CLASSROOM

…sson Plan　Class

…hase	Time	Activity	Materials
…nation	10 mins	**Warm Up:** Students work in small groups to list themes they consider most important from their reading about the 1920s. Each group writes a single sentence stating what in their opinion were the consequences of the Scopes Trial.	*The Americans,* Chapter 21, Sections 1 and 2, and "Youth in the Roaring Twenties"
	20 mins	**Lecture:** Students take notes on changes and conflicts occurring during the 1920s, including the clash between religious fundamentalism and science.	
Application	45 mins	**Simulation:** Students re-create Clarence Darrow's cross-examination of William Jennings Bryan, taking the following roles: Darrow, Bryan, Stewart, newspaper reporters, and spectators on both sides.	*In-Depth Resources: Unit 6,* Primary Source from The Scopes Trial *In-Depth Resources: Unit 6,* Literature Selection, Section 1, from *Inherit the Wind*
Syntheseis	15 mins	**Discussion:** Students discuss the issues raised in the Scopes trial and how they relate to other issues of the times (social changes, the role of women, Prohibition and so on).	
Homework		**Reflection:** Students write a paragraph summarizing the outcome and significance of the Scopes trial, telling whether their thoughts have changed since their groups discussed the question at the opening of class.	
		Reading: *The Americans,* Chapter …	*In-Depth Resources:* …

Block schedules offer teachers opportunities for using a variety of active-learning strategies. *Planning for Block Schedules* provides explanations of and suggestions for implementing a variety of collaborative and cooperative activities that work well in block-schedule classrooms.

As you plan your own classes, you will find helpful sample lesson plans and blank forms in *Planning for Block Schedules.*

Internet Resources

McDougal Littell's American history Web site—mlushistory.com—offers you an opportunity to become part of a nationwide community of teachers and students using *The Americans: Reconstruction through the 20th Century.* With a user-friendly format, our American history curriculum center helps you meet the challenges of teaching in today's diverse classroom by providing access to a wide range of resources related to the chapters of the textbook.

Chapter Links Our editors have gathered some of the best links on the Internet to help you extend each lesson, expand your research, and boost your own creativity.

Today in History Browse the archive of significant events in American history. Compiled by the Library of Congress, this site contains links to photos and prints, primary source documents, motion pictures, maps, and sound recordings.

Professional Development Calendar Consult this on-line calendar for the latest information on upcoming events and conferences related to social studies education.

Discussion Groups Exchange ideas, brainstorm, or network with your colleagues. Join the History Discussion Group to post or answer history or program-related questions. Check out the Idea Exchange Discussion Group for more general teaching strategies and topics.

Monthly Special Feature Author profiles, Web-site guests, and other special events are all a part of this monthly feature.

Teacher Links Library Need more information on anything from Reconstruction to the Clinton presidency? Explore hundreds of annotated links to sites dealing with specific topics discussed in *The Americans: Reconstruction through the 20th Century*.

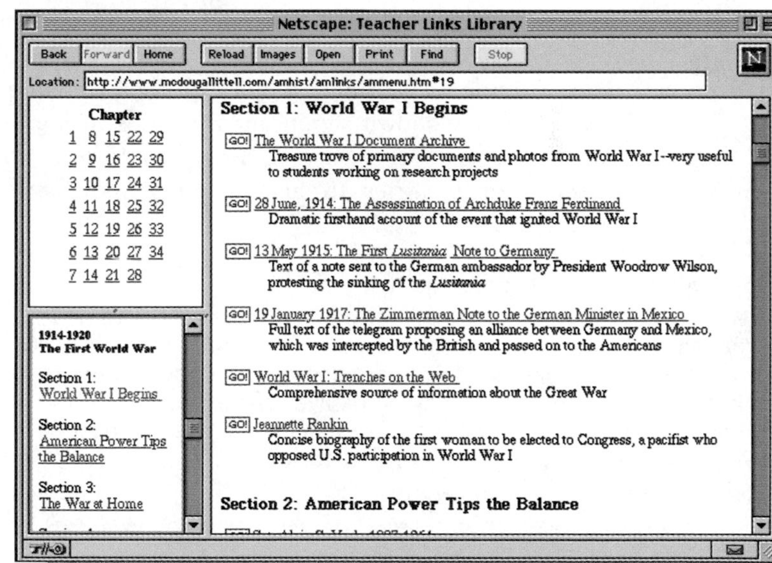

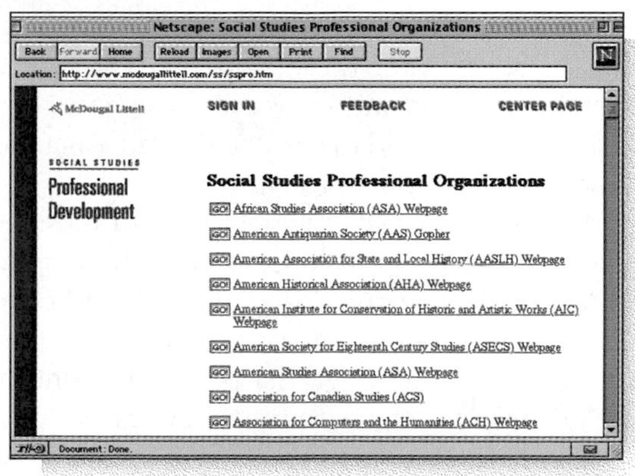

Reading and Learning History from Textbooks

DONNA M. OGLE
Professor, Reading and Language
National-Louis University

Active, engaged readers make the best learners. Researchers have found that successful readers connect text information with what they already know. These readers build associations among ideas, create visual images of what they are reading, and continually refine their interpretations as they gather more information.

Encouraging active, engaged reading is difficult for teachers when they find that many students have learned to ignore their textbooks. This is often due to texts that are too difficult conceptually and are too dense in information. It is possible, however, for teachers and students to find texts that meet their needs.

SUPPORTING READERS

Often we see students who don't have a foundation of information and experience on which to build. If there are not strong connections, experiences, or foundations, then the amount of support and elaboration provided by the text and teacher are critical. That support and elaboration can be provided in a variety of ways.

Personal Connections For some students, personal stories and human connections can bring a subject such as history alive. Taking a personal point of view and thinking as if they were living the experiences can deepen students' learning. Studies on these techniques have generally shown significant increases in learning. *The Americans: Reconstruction through the 20th Century* uses personal stories throughout to support student learning.

A PERSONAL VOICE
Here we are, tremendously exhilarated, and there's a sea of dead. . . . [The platoon leader] was much moved. . . . He said, "Joe, lets make a resolution with these Russians here and also the ones on the bank: this would be an important day in the lives of the two countries." . . . It was a solemn moment. There were tears in the eyes of most of us. . . . We embraced. We swore never to forget.

JOSEPH POLOWSKY, quoted in *The Good War*

Visual Information Visual information is a resource that many readers rely on heavily when reading unfamiliar material. When text content is unfamiliar, the visual materials accompanying the text can provide strong support for the creation of meaning, especially in expository material. Pictures create a visual context and make abstractions of time and space more real; photos and artifacts create a grounding for new ideas; maps and other spatial features, such as charts, help readers associate and compare ideas. The more opportunity there is to learn through the visual sense, the more avenues for thinking are stimulated and supported.

Learning Styles We know that readers have different styles of constructing meaning—some rely heavily on verbal input and discussion, some need visual supports, and others may learn best by taking notes and making drawings or graphic organizers as they study. Students may become engaged in learning when they challenge ideas, make comparisons, and trace causes and effects. The richer the thinking you encourage, the more likely students are to learn. Posing problems, comparing and contrasting ideas, and presenting different points of view on issues stimulates deeper engagement and leads to more learning than does a simple exposition of factual information. The Point/Counterpoint feature does just that.

POINT	COUNTERPOINT
"The United States must occasionally intervene militarily in regional conflicts."	"The United States should not intervene militarily in regional conflicts."

Students Acquiring English Second-language learners, in particular, need to have information and ideas presented to them in multiple ways. Since many of these students are unfamiliar with the concepts and events of American history, being able to "see" history helps them make it real to themselves. Attending to illustrations of all kinds is essential for these students. The more ways the same information and ideas are presented, the more likely they are to be able to construct an adequate understanding of what they are studying.

In addition, the greater variety of materials second-language learners can read on the same topic, the more deeply they will understand the language and concepts. Seeing the same concepts presented by different authors in different types of writing (first-person accounts, newspapers, official documents) and from different points of view helps these students build a better understanding of new ideas and terminology. Then, having opportunities to discuss ideas and share interpretations can solidify their growing understanding.

EVOLVING FORMS OF READING

Today's students need to be able to read in ways earlier generations did not.

Nonlinear Materials Today, students must

- gather ideas from multiple sources: resource books, magazines, computerized databases, CD-ROMs, the Internet
- know how to evaluate these sources and make decisions about their content
- find their way through nonlinear materials, such as by deciding which area of a computer screen contains the information they want
- make decisions about what level of knowledge and elaboration they need

Graphic Layouts Today's readers must deal with information presented in a variety of formats, such as

- multiple columns of text with many pictures, graphs, and maps
- single-column texts with with large marginal areas used for problems, illustrations, highlighted information, and thought-provoking ideas
- combinations of layouts

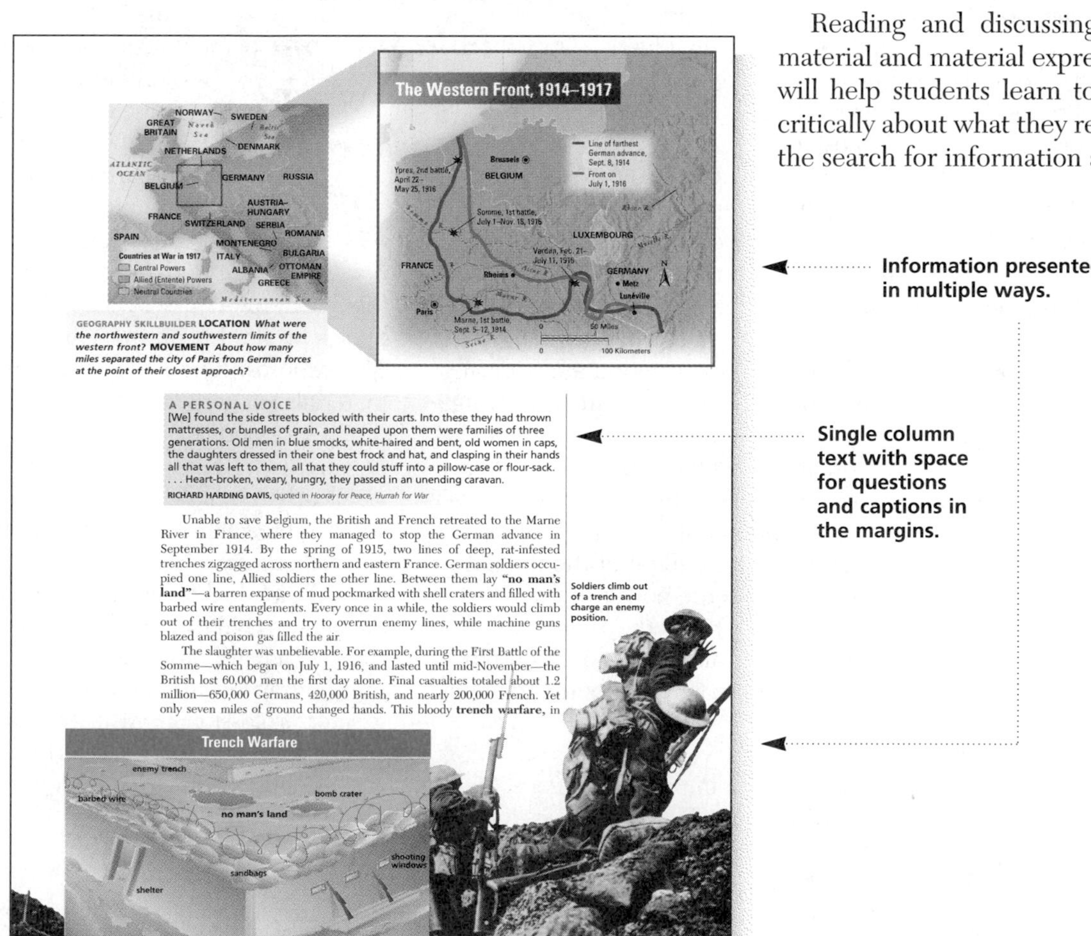

GEOGRAPHY SKILLBUILDER **LOCATION** *What were the northwestern and southwestern limits of the western front?* **MOVEMENT** *About how many miles separated the city of Paris from German forces at the point of their closest approach?*

A PERSONAL VOICE

[We] found the side streets blocked with their carts. Into these they had thrown mattresses, or bundles of grain, and heaped upon them were families of three generations. Old men in blue smocks, white-haired and bent, old women in caps, the daughters dressed in their one best frock and hat, and clasping in their hands all that was left to them, all that they could stuff into a pillow-case or flour-sack. . . . Heart-broken, weary, hungry, they passed in an unending caravan.

RICHARD HARDING DAVIS, quoted in *Hooray for Peace, Hurrah for War*

Unable to save Belgium, the British and French retreated to the Marne River in France, where they managed to stop the German advance in September 1914. By the spring of 1915, two lines of deep, rat-infested trenches zigzagged across northern and eastern France. German soldiers occupied one line, Allied soldiers the other line. Between them lay **"no man's land"**—a barren expanse of mud pockmarked with shell craters and filled with barbed wire entanglements. Every once in a while, the soldiers would climb out of their trenches and try to overrun enemy lines, while machine guns blazed and poison gas filled the air

The slaughter was unbelievable. For example, during the First Battle of the Somme—which began on July 1, 1916, and lasted until mid-November—the British lost 60,000 men the first day alone. Final casualties totaled about 1.2 million—650,000 Germans, 420,000 British, and nearly 200,000 French. Yet only seven miles of ground changed hands. This bloody **trench warfare,** in

Soldiers climb out of a trench and charge an enemy position.

Information presented in multiple ways.

Single column text with space for questions and captions in the margins.

THE TEACHER'S ROLE

Are our students prepared with strategies for reading and learning in the 21st century? Are they able to shift easily from one form of text presentation to another? Do they know how to construct meaning from multiple sources?

Strategies for Teachers You can help your students become active, engaged, and confident readers. Here are some strategies you might try:

- Observe your students and ask them how they read.
- Do a "think aloud" as students begin to read a text. Ask them to tell you where they look on the page; when they look at the charts, maps, and pictures; and when they read the headings and titles.
- Introduce the text layout and features, and discuss students' options for reading.
- Show students that all the material on a page does not have to be read in order.
- Have students experiment with reading the graphics first before reading the text on a page.
- Demonstrate how headings and subheadings can help readers find specific information.
- Use graphic organizers and reading guides to help students gain confidence.

Reading and discussing different types of written material and material expressing different points of view will help students learn to look deeply into and think critically about what they read. Help them learn to enjoy the search for information and ideas!

Teaching United States History Thematically

Mary E. Connor

In the following article, Mary E. Connor, a U.S. history teacher at Westridge School in Pasadena, California, explains several advantages of thematic teaching and gives strategies for teaching themes successfully.

How can today's educators convey the essentials of American history in a way that is engaging and memorable? One possible answer is a course organized around themes rather than chronological periods. The primary benefit of teaching the subject thematically is that it affords a better grasp of the principal developments in U.S. history by treating issues in depth.

A common problem in many high school U.S. history courses is the neglect of teaching about the recent past. It is not uncommon to hear of classes that never get to the events of more recent decades. The signal beauty of the thematic approach lies in the fact that students can hold informed discussions about current issues by mid-October. For example, as part of the first theme I teach—The American Character and the American Belief System—a discussion of welfare reform can take place within a framework of knowledge about basic (and opposing) American values of self-reliance and social egalitarianism.

A thematic approach allows students to become involved with narratives and articles about one topic. Consider how a teacher might cover the traditional material in exploring the theme America in the World. The teacher outlines the history of imperialism, both world wars, and the Cold War. Students study World War II and Vietnam in depth. For World War II, students might read Studs Terkel's *The Good War* or *War Without Mercy* by John Dower. For Vietnam, differing interpretations of the Vietnam experience can be found in the movie *Coming Home* and in the book *A Rumor of War* by Philip Caputo. The cumulative effect of looking at the scope of American foreign affairs over a six-week period seizes the imagination.

In developing a theme, students could be given options for assignments. For example, for the theme Immigration and Migration, a student might research the immigrants of the 19th century or interview a recent immigrant to America. One class that took my course interviewed immigrants from thirty countries on five continents. These interviews revealed that virtually no one felt discriminated against because of race or ethnicity, all believed they had achieved the American dream, all preferred living in this country to anywhere else despite its problems, and the most difficult adjustment was learning the English language. This analysis of the immigrant experience took on added meaning as students discussed California Proposition 187.

"The signal beauty of the thematic approach lies in the fact that students can hold informed discussions about current issues by mid-October."

In following a thematic approach, students journey from the past to the present ten times—validating the venerable principle of repetition. There are frequent opportunities for discussing contemporary issues within a historical framework. For example, after studying the theme Women in America, students discuss the challenges faced by women today and the current status of the women's movement.

Still another benefit of the thematic approach lies in the power of the narrative. Sometimes the vitality of historical accounts can be lost using the traditional approach, but thematic units have their own inner dynamic and can help students develop broader perspectives on important issues in American history. This includes such topics as African-American history from slavery to the Million Man March and the progress of efforts toward creating a peaceful world.

Moving through successive themes rather than chronological periods allows for greater creativity. The curriculum no longer determines how one does history, and each theme permits varied and absorbing activities. Students can investigate their own family background to better understand how their own histories are part of a larger history. Ellis Island, the Great Depression, and the D-Day invasion all may acquire a new luster if one's own or a friend's grandparent was there. This is especially poignant when the persons in question were on different sides.

Another important element in my thematic course is that of choice in student research. During the summer before taking the class, students receive a list of books organized by the themes in the course. Students read two books, preferably on the same theme. This exposes them to superb source materials and provides them with in-depth knowledge before the school year begins.

Clearly, it will be easier for the seasoned teacher to move to a fully thematic course. However, one can move toward the ideal by expanding on themes encountered in the textbook. Teaching thematically requires more preparation, but the rewards are high: for the teacher, greater professional satisfaction; for students, greater interest, performance, and retention. And your students are likely to thank you.

This essay is adapted from an article that appeared in the April/May 1997 issue of *Social Education*.

Teaching Themes and Current Events in *The Americans: Reconstruction through the 20th Century*

For teachers and districts who wish to organize their modern U.S. history courses thematically, *The Americans: Reconstruction through the 20th Century* serves as a valuable resource. The lists below show how to organize the text around ten themes for a fully thematic course. In addition, the lists show how each theme may be linked to current issues and events by using the Epilogue: Issues for the 21st Century (pages 876–901 in the pupil text).

Ten Themes in *The Americans: Reconstruction through the 20th Century*

1. **America in the World**
2. **The American Dream**
3. **Science and Technology**
4. **Economic Opportunity**
5. **Immigration and Migration**
6. **Women in America**
7. **Civil Rights**
8. **Constitutional Concerns**
9. **Cultural Diversity**
10. **Democracy in America**

America in the World

America Claims an Empire, pp. 362–389
The First World War, pp. 392–421
Revolution Abroad and Reaction at Home, pp. 430–433
A Return to "Normalcy," pp. 436–438
World War Looms, pp. 540–567
The War for Europe and North Africa, The War in the Pacific, pp. 578–583
The Origins of the Cold War, The Cold War Heats Up, pp. 606–618
Two Nations Live on the Edge, pp. 625–629
Kennedy and the Cold War, pp. 670–676
The Vietnam War Years, pp. 724–755
Nixon's Foreign Policy Triumphs, pp. 791–792
A Human Rights Foreign Policy, Triumph and Crisis in the Middle East, pp. 804–807
American Foreign Policy After the Cold War, pp. 836–841
Clinton's Foreign Policy, p. 849
The New Global Economy, pp. 853–857
TODAY: Foreign Policy After the Cold War, pp. 878–879

The American Dream

Settling on the Great Plains, pp. 230–234
Tracing Themes: What Is the American Dream?, The Problems of Urbanization, pp. 280–287
Dawn of Mass Culture, pp. 314–321
New Ways to Play, pp. 322–323
Changing Ways of Life, pp. 452–457
Daily Life: Youth in the Roaring Twenties, Education and Popular Culture, pp. 462–469
American Literature: Literature in the Jazz Age, pp. 476–477
Hardship and Suffering During the Depression, pp. 490–494
Society and Culture, The Impact of the New Deal, pp. 523–533
Science Fiction Reflects Cold War Realities, pp. 630–631
The American Dream in the Fifties, Geography Spotlight: The Road to Suburbia, Popular Culture, Daily Life: The Emergence of the Teenager, pp. 643–659
The New Frontier, pp. 677–682
A Nation Divided, pp. 735–755
Culture and Counterculture, Daily Life: Signs of the Sixties, pp. 773–779
Daily Life: Television Reflects American Life, pp. 798–799
Environmental Activism, pp. 808–813
American Society in a Conservative Age, pp. 827–833
The Suburban Nation, pp. 866–868
America and a New Millennium, pp. 870–871
TODAY: Tough Choices About Entitlements, pp. 900–901

Science and Technology

The Expansion of Industry, pp. 246–249
Science and Urban Life, pp. 298–302
Science and Religion Clash, pp. 456–457
The Atomic Bomb Ends the War, pp. 589–592
Tracing Themes: Science and Technology, pp. 594–595
Race to the Moon, p. 680
Technology and Modern Life, pp. 860–865
TODAY: Exploring Education Today, pp. 888–891

Economic Opportunity

Settlers Push Westward, pp. 215–216
The Growth of the Cattle Industry, Settling on the Great Plains, pp. 222–234
The Expansion of Industry, pp. 246–249
The Age of the Railroads, Big Business Emerges, Workers of the Nation Unite, pp. 252–269
China and the Open Door Policy, The Impact of U.S. Territorial Gains, pp. 378–381
A Time of Labor Unrest, pp. 433–435
The Business of America, Economic Opportunity: Consumer Spending, pp. 441–447
The Great Depression Begins, 480–499
A New Deal Fights the Depression, The Second New Deal Takes Hold, pp. 504–516
Economic Controls, pp. 575–577
Opportunity and Adjustment, pp. 596–598
Readjustment and Recovery, Economic Challenges, pp. 636–639
The Other America, pp. 660–663
The Promise of Progress, pp. 678–680
The Great Society, pp. 683–691
Geography Spotlight: Migrant Workers pp. 766–767
Nixon Confronts a Stagnant Economy, p. 790
Carter's Domestic Agenda, pp. 802–804
Conservative Policies Under Reagan and Bush, pp. 822–824, 825
The Urban Crisis, pp. 829–830
The Clinton Record, pp. 847–849
Welfare and Health Reform, p. 851
Balancing the Budget, p. 852
The New Global Economy, pp. 853–857
The Graying of America, p. 868
TODAY: Breaking the Cycle of Poverty, pp. 896–899

(continued on next page)

Immigration and Migration

Settlers Push Westward, pp. 215–216
The New Immigrants, pp. 274–279
Tracing Themes: Immigration and Migration, pp. 422–423
Limiting Immigration, pp. 438–439
Latinos and Native Americans Seek Equality, Geography Spotlight: Migrant Workers pp. 760–767
Geography Spotlight: Sunbelt, Rustbelt, Ecotopia, pp. 834–835
Immigration in the 1990s, pp. 869–870
TODAY: The Debate over Immigration, pp. 880–883

Women in America

One American's Story, p. 230
Women's Work, p. 233
Women in Public Life, pp. 337–340
Woman Suffrage, pp. 356–358
Women in the War, pp. 415–416
The Twenties Woman, pp. 458–461
New Opportunities for Women, pp. 517–518
Women in the Military, p. 571
Women Fight for Equality, pp. 768–772
The Equal Rights Struggle, pp. 830–831
American Literature: Women Writers Reflect American Diversity, pp. 858–859
TODAY: Women and the Glass Ceiling, pp. 894–895

Civil Rights

Segregation and Discrimination, pp. 309–313
The Limits of Progressivism, pp. 358–359
Mexican-American Fortunes, Native American Gains, p. 520
Minorities in the Armed Services, pp. 571–572
Discrimination and Reaction, pp. 598–601
Truman Supports Civil Rights, pp. 639–640
Walking the Middle of the Road, p. 642
The Other America, pp. 660–663
Civil Rights, pp. 694–719
Nixon's Southern Strategy, pp. 788–790
Carter and Civil Rights, p. 804
The Fight for Rights Continues, pp. 831–833
TODAY: Exploring Education Today, pp. 888–891

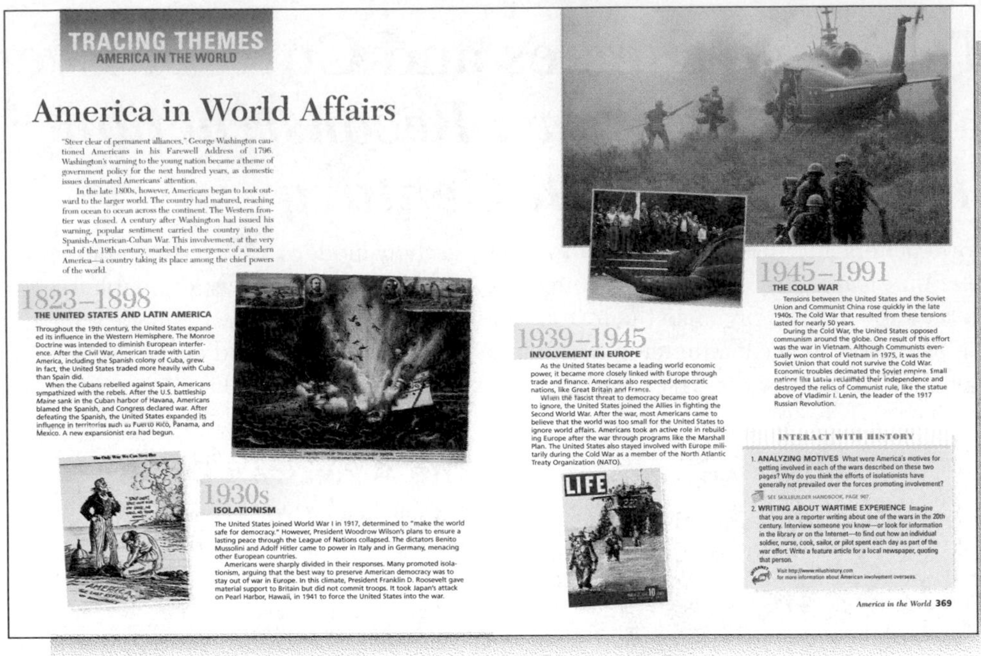

Constitutional Concerns

Attacks on Civil Liberties, pp. 412–414
Revolution Abroad and Reaction at Home, pp. 420–433
Scandal Hits Harding's Administration, pp. 439–440
Science and Religion Clash, pp. 456–457
Internment of Japanese Americans, p. 675
The Cold War at Home, pp. 619–624
Taking on Segregation, pp. 696–703
Nixon's Southern Strategy, pp. 788–790
Watergate: Nixon's Downfall, pp. 793–797
Judicial Power Shifts to the Right, p. 824
The Fight for Rights Continues, pp. 831–833
TODAY: Crime and Public Safety, pp. 884–887

Cultural Diversity

Native American Cultures in Crisis, pp. 214–220
Social Changes During the War, pp. 414–415
The Harlem Renaissance, pp. 472–474
Mexican-American Fortunes, Native American Gains, p. 520
The Other America, pp. 660–663
Latinos and Native Americans Seek Equality, Geography Spotlight: Migrant Workers pp. 760–767
The Fight for Rights Continues, pp. 831–833
American Literature: Women Writers Reflect American Diversity, pp. 858–859
Immigration in the 1990s, pp. 869–870
Tracing Themes: Cultural Diversity: Sharing Cultures, pp. 872–873
TODAY: The Debate over Immigration, pp. 880–883

Democracy in America

Farmers and the Populist Movement, pp. 235–239
The Emergence of the Political Machine, pp. 288–290
Politics in the Gilded Age, pp. 291–293
The Origins of Progressivism, pp. 330–336
Teddy Roosevelt's Square Deal, Progressivism Under Taft, Wilson's New Freedom, pp. 341–359
A New Deal Coalition, pp. 520–522
Republicans Take the Middle Road, p. 641
The Great Society, pp. 683–691
Latinos and Native Americans Seek Equality, Geography Spotlight: Migrant Workers pp. 760–767
Expanding Democracy, pp. 786–792
A Conservative Movement Emerges, pp. 818–821
Clinton Wins the Presidency, pp. 846–847
The Republican Congress, pp. 850–851
The Election of 1996, pp. 851–852
Campaign Finance Reform, p. 852
TODAY: Tough Choices About Entitlements, pp. 900–901

Pacing Guide

The following pacing guide shows how the chapters in *The Americans: Reconstruction through the 20th Century* can be adapted to fit your specific course needs.

The guide includes pacing suggestions for reviewing early American history. The review periods for each course are as follows.

In-Depth Coverage	Content to Review	Time for Review	In-Depth Coverage Begins with
Civil War to the Present	Review Chapters 1–3	10 days	Review Chapter 4
1877 to the Present	Review Unit 1 and Thematic Review	15 days	Unit 2
20th Century	Units 1 and 2	20 days	Unit 3
1920s to the Present	Units 1–3	30 days	Unit 4

This pacing guide is based on 170 days of instruction during the school year. For **block schedules**, based on 85 days of instruction, see *Planning for Block Schedules* in the teacher's resource materials.

	Civil War to Present	1877 to Present	20th Century	1920s to Present
Review Unit 1 American Beginnings to 1877				
Review Chapter 1 Beginnings to 1763: Exploration and the Colonial Era	(days)	(days)	(days)	(days)
1. The Americas, West Africa, and Europe	1	1	.5	.5
2. Spanish North America	.5	.5	.5	.5
3. Early British Colonies	1	1	.5	.5
4. The Colonies Come of Age	.5	.5	.5	.5
Review Chapter 2 1763–1800 Revolution and the Early Republic				
1. Colonial Resistance and Rebellion	.5	.5	.5	.5
★ The Declaration of Independence	.5	.5	.5	.5
2. The War for Independence	.5	.5	.5	.5
3. Confederation and the Constitution	.5	.5	.5	.5
4. Launching the New Nation	.5	.5	.5	.5
The Living Constitution	1	1	1	1
Review Chapter 3 1800–1850 The Growth of a Young Nation				
1. The Jeffersonian Era	1	1	.5	.5
2. The Age of Jackson	.5	.5	.5	.5
3. Manifest Destiny	1	1	1	.5
4. The Market Revolution	.5	1	.5	.5
5. Reforming American Society	.5	1	.5	.5

For **block schedules**, see *Planning for Block Schedules* in the teacher's resource materials.

	Civil War to Present	1877 to Present	20th Century	1920s to Present
Review Chapter 4 1850–1877 The Union in Peril				
1. The Divisive Politics of Slavery	2	1	.5	.5
2. The Civil War Begins	2	1	.5	.5
3. The North Takes Charge	2	1	.5	.5
4. Reconstruction and Its Effects	2	1	1	.5
Thematic Review of Unit 1 Beginnings Through Reconstruction	**1**	**1**	**1**	**1**
Total Days for Unit	**19**	**16**	**12**	**11**
Unit 2 1877–1917 Bridge to the 20th Century				
Chapter 5 1877–1900 Changes on the Western Frontier				
1. Native American Cultures in Crisis	2	2	.5	.5
2. The Growth of the Cattle Industry	2	2	.5	.5
3. Settling on the Great Plains	1	1	.5	.5
4. Farmers and the Populist Movement	2	2	.5	.5
Chapter 6 1877–1900 A New Industrial Age				
1. The Expansion of Industry	2	2	.5	.5
2. The Age of the Railroads	1	2	.5	.5
3. Big Business Emerges	1	2	.5	.5
4. Workers of the Nation Unite	2	2	.5	.5
Chapter 7 1877–1914 Immigrants and Urbanization				
1. The New Immigrants	2	2	.5	.5
2. The Problems of Urbanization	2	2	.5	.5
3. The Emergence of the Political Machine	2	2	.5	.5
4. Politics in the Gilded Age	2	2	.5	.5
Chapter 8 1877–1917 Life at the Turn of the Century				
1. Science and Urban Life	2	2	.5	.5
2. Education and Culture	1	1	.5	.5
3. Segregation and Discrimination	2	2	.5	.5
4. Dawn of Mass Culture	3	3	.5	.5
Total Days for Unit	**29**	**31**	**8**	**8**

For **block schedules**, see *Planning for Block Schedules* in the teacher's resource materials.

	Civil War to Present	1877 to Present	20th Century	1920s to Present
Unit 3 1890–1920 Modern America Emerges				
Chapter 9 1890–1920 The Progressive Era				
1. The Origins of Progressivism	1	1	2	1
2. Women in Public Life	2	2	2	.5
3. Teddy Roosevelt's Square Deal	2	3	3	1
4. Progressivism Under Taft	1	1	2	.5
5. Wilson's New Freedom	1	1	2	1
Chapter 10 1890–1920 America Claims an Empire				
1. Imperialism and America	2	2	2	1
2. The Spanish–American–Cuban War	1	1	2	.5
3. Acquiring New Lands	2	2	2	.5
4. America as a World Power	2	2	3	1
Chapter 11 1914–1920 The First World War				
1. World War I Begins	2	2	2	1
2. American Power Tips the Balance	2	2	2	1
3. The War at Home	1	1	3	1
4. Wilson Fights for Peace	2	2	2	1
Total Days for Unit	**21**	**22**	**29**	**11**
Unit 4 1920–1940 The Twenties and the Great Depression				
Chapter 12 1920–1929 Politics of the Roaring Twenties				
1. Americans Struggle with Postwar Issues	2	2	3	3
2. "Normalcy" and Isolationism	2	2	2	2
3. The Business of America	2	2	2	3
Chapter 13 1920–1929 The Roaring Life of the 1920s				
1. Changing Ways of Life	2	2	3	3
2. The Twenties Woman	2	2	2	3
3. Education and Popular Culture	1	1	2	2
4. The Harlem Renaissance	3	3	3	3
Chapter 14 1929–1933 The Great Depression Begins				
1. The Nation's Sick Economy	2	2	2	2
2. Hardship and Suffering During the Depression	2	2	3	3
3. Hoover Struggles with the Depression	1	1	2	2

For **block schedules**, see *Planning for Block Schedules* in the teacher's resource materials.

	Civil War to Present	1877 to Present	20th Century	1920s to Present
Chapter 15 1933–1940 The New Deal				
1. A New Deal Fights the Depression	2	2	2	2
2. The Second New Deal Takes Hold	1	1	2	2
3. The New Deal Affects Many Groups	2	2	2	2
4. Society and Culture	1	1	3	3
5. The Impact of the New Deal	2	2	2	2
Total Days for Unit	**27**	**27**	**35**	**37**
Unit 5 1931–1960 World War II and Its Aftermath				
Chapter 16 1931–1941 World War Looms				
1. Dictators Threaten World Peace	1	1	2	2
2. War in Europe	2	2	2	3
3. The Holocaust	2	2	3	3
4. America Moves Toward War	2	2	2	2
Chapter 17 1941–1945 The United States in World War II				
1. Mobilization on the Home Front	1	1	1	2
2. The War for Europe and North Africa	2	2	2	3
3. The War in the Pacific	2	2	3	3
4. The Impact of the War	3	3	3	3
Chapter 18 1945–1960 Cold War Conflicts				
1. Origins of the Cold War	1	1	1	2
2. The Cold War Heats Up	1	1	2	3
3. The Cold War at Home	2	2	3	3
4. Two Nations Live on the Edge	2	2	2	2
Chapter 19 1946–1960 The Postwar Boom				
1. Postwar America	1	1	1	2
2. The American Dream in the Fifties	2	2	3	3
3. Popular Culture	3	3	3	3
4. The Other America	2	2	2	2
Total Days for Unit	**29**	**30**	**35**	**41**

For **block schedules**, see *Planning for Block Schedules* in the teacher's resource materials.

	Civil War to Present	1877 to Present	20th Century	1920s to Present
Unit 6 1954–1975 Living with Great Turmoil				
Chapter 20 1960–1968 The New Frontier and the Great Society				
1. Kennedy and the Cold War	2	2	2	3
2. The New Frontier	1	1	2	2
3. The Great Society	2	2	2	3
Chapter 21 1954–1970 Civil Rights				
1. Taking on Segregation	2	2	2	2
2. The Triumphs of a Crusade	2	2	2	3
3. Challenges and Changes in the Movement	1	1	3	3
Chapter 22 1954–1975 The Vietnam War Years				
1. Moving Toward Conflict	1	1	2	2
2. U.S. Involvement and Escalation	1	1	1	2
3. A Nation Divided	2	2	3	3
4. 1968: A Tumultuous Year	1	1	1	2
5. The End of the War and Its Legacy	2	2	2	2
Chapter 23 1960–1975 An Era of Social Change				
1. Latinos and Native Americans Seek Equality	2	2	2	2
2. Women Fight for Equality	2	2	2	2
3. Culture and Counterculture	2	2	3	3
Total Days for Unit	**23**	**23**	**29**	**34**
Unit 7 1968–1997 Passage to a New Century				
Chapter 24 1968–1980 An Age of Limits				
1. The Nixon Administration	2	2	2	2
2. Watergate: Nixon's Downfall	2	2	2	3
3. The Ford and Carter Years	1	1	1	2
4. Environmental Activism	2	2	2	3

For block schedules, see *Planning for Block Schedules* in the teacher's resource materials.

Chapter 25 1980–1992 The Conservative Tide	Civil War to Present	1877 to Present	20th Century	1920s to Present
1. A Conservative Movement Emerges	2	2	2	2
2. Conservative Policies Under Reagan and Bush	2	1	2	1
3. American Society in a Conservative Age	2	2	2	3
4. Foreign Policy After the Cold War	2	2	2	3
Chapter 26 1992–1997 The United States in Today's World				
1. The Clinton Presidency	1	1	1	1
2. The New Global Economy	2	2	2	2
3. Technology and Modern Life	1	1	1	1
4. The Changing Face of America	1	1	1	1
Total Days for Unit	**20**	**20**	**20**	**24**
Epilogue: Issues for the 21st Century	2	2	2	2
Total for Year	**170**	**170**	**170**	**170**

McDougal Littell

life

— *The* —

Americans

Reconstruction through the 20th Century

liberty

pursuit *of* happiness

"The Genius of America lies in its capacity to forge a single nation from peoples of remarkably diverse racial, religious, and ethnic origins. . . . The American identity will never be fixed and final: it will always be in the making."

Arthur M. Schlesinger

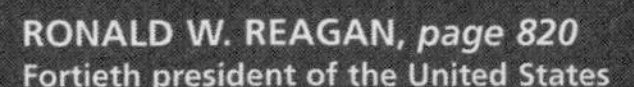

RONALD W. REAGAN, *page 820*
Fortieth president of the United States

NORMAN SCHWARZKOPF, *page 840*
U.S. general during the Persian Gulf War

GERDA WEISSMANN KLEIN, *page 554*
Holocaust survivor

MAYA LIN, *page 752*
Designer of the Vietnam Veterans Memorial

DR. MARTIN LUTHER KING, JR.
page 702
Civil rights leader

SANDRA DAY O'CONNOR, *page 824*
U.S. Supreme Court justice

FRANKLIN D. ROOSEVELT, *page 505*
Thirty-second president of the United States

PEDRO J. GONZÁLEZ, *page 517*
Musician, radio personality, and civil rights activist

BARBARA JORDAN, *page 793*
United States representative from Texas

Authors

Gerald A. Danzer, Ph.D.

Gerald A. Danzer is Professor of History and Director of the M.A. Program for Teachers of History at the University of Illinois at Chicago. He served from 1992 to 1994 as Chair of the Council for Effective Teaching and Learning at UIC and was Director of the Chicago Neighborhood History Project. Dr. Danzer's area of specialization is historical geography, in which he has written *Discovering the Past Through Maps and Views* and numerous other publications. Before entering university teaching, Dr. Danzer taught high school history in the Chicago area. Dr. Danzer received his Ph.D. in history from Northwestern University.

J. Jorge Klor de Alva, J.D. and Ph.D.

J. Jorge Klor de Alva is Class of 1940 Professor of Comparative Ethnic Studies and Anthropology at the University of California at Berkeley and former Professor of Anthropology at Princeton University. Dr. Klor de Alva's interests include interethnic relations, historical ethnography, and educational reform. His publications include *The Aztec Image of Self and Society* and *Interethnic Images: Discourse and Practice in the New World, 1492–1992*, as well as more than ten other books and more than seventy scholarly articles. Dr. Klor de Alva earned his J.D. from the University of California at Berkeley and his Ph.D. in history/anthropology from the University of California at Santa Cruz.

Louis E. Wilson, Ph.D.

Louis E. Wilson is Associate Professor and Chair of the Afro-American and African Studies Department at Smith College. Previously Dr. Wilson was on the faculty at the University of Colorado, Boulder, and was a senior Fulbright Scholar at the University of Ghana, Legon. Dr. Wilson is the author of *The Krobo People of Ghana to 1892: A Political, Social, and Economic History* and *Genealogical and Militia Data on Blacks, Indians, and Mustees from Military American Revolutionary War Records*. Dr. Wilson is currently writing a book entitled *Forgotten Patriots: African Americans and Native Americans in the American Revolution from Rhode Island*. In 1991, Dr. Wilson received The Blackwell Fellowship and Prize as Outstanding Black New England Scholar. Dr. Wilson received his Ph.D. in history from the University of California at Los Angeles.

Nancy Woloch, Ph.D.

Nancy Woloch teaches history at Barnard College, where she has been on the faculty since 1988. Dr. Woloch's scholarly interest has been the history of women in the United States, and in this area she has published *Women and the American Experience* and *Early American Women: A Documentary History, 1600–1900*. She is also the author of *Muller v. Oregon* and the co-author of *The American Century*. Dr. Woloch was the recipient of a National Endowment for the Humanities Fellowship for Younger Humanists. She received her Ph.D. in history and American studies from Indiana University.

Acknowledgments begin on page 1013.

ISBN 0-395-89080-2

Printed in the United States of America.
1 2 3 4 5 6 7 8 9–DWO–02 01 00 99 98 97

BEN NIGHTHORSE CAMPBELL, *page 763*
U.S. senator from Colorado

ELIZABETH DOLE, *page 831*
U.S. secretary of transportation

QUEEN LILIUOKALANI, *page 364*
Queen of Hawaii

BEV SCOTT, *page 617*
U.S. soldier and Korean War veteran

JOHN F. KENNEDY, *page 670*
Thirty-fifth president of the United States

— *The* —
AMERICANS

Reconstruction through the 20th Century

Gerald A. Danzer

J. Jorge Klor de Alva

Louis E. Wilson

Nancy Woloch

McDougal Littell
A HOUGHTON MIFFLIN COMPANY
Evanston, Illinois • Boston • Dallas

Consultants and Reviewers

Constitution Consultant

Melvin Dubnick
Professor of Political Science
Rutgers University, Trenton
Trenton, New Jersey

Contributing Writer

Miriam Greenblatt
Educational Writer and Consultant
Highland Park, Illinois

Multicultural Advisory Board

The multicultural advisers reviewed the manuscript for appropriateness of historical content.

Pat A. Browne
Director of the Indianapolis Public Schools Office of African Centered Multicultural Education
Indianapolis Public Schools
Indianapolis, Indiana

Ogle B. Duff
Associate Professor of English
University of Pittsburgh
Pittsburgh, Pennsylvania

Mary Ellen Maddox
Black Education Commission Director
Los Angeles Unified School District
Los Angeles, California

Jon Reyhner
Associate Professor and Coordinator of the Bilingual Multicultural Education Program
Northern Arizona University
Flagstaff, Arizona

Curtis L. Walker
Executive Officer, Office of Equity and Compliance
Pittsburgh Public Schools
Pittsburgh, Pennsylvania

Ruben Zepeda
Compliance Advisor, Language Acquisition and Curriculum Development
Los Angeles, California

Content Consultants

The content consultants reviewed the manuscript for historical depth and accuracy and for clarity of presentation.

Catherine Clinton
Fellow of the W. E. B. Du Bois Institute
Harvard University
Cambridge, Massachusetts

Theodore Karaminski
Professor of History
Loyola University
Chicago, Illinois

Joseph Kett
Professor of History
University of Virginia
Charlottesville, Virginia

Jack Rakove
Professor of History
Stanford University
Stanford, California

Harvard Sitkoff
Professor of History
University of New Hampshire
Durham, New Hampshire

Teacher Review Panels

The following educators provided ongoing review during the development of prototypes, the table of contents, and key components of the program.

Florida Teacher Panel

David Debs
Mandarin High School
Jacksonville, Florida

Ronald Eckstein
Hudson High School
Hudson, Florida

Sharman Feliciani
Land O'Lakes High School
Land O'Lakes, Florida

Flossie Gautier
Bay High School
Panama City, Florida

Glenn Hallick
Vanguard High School
Ocala, Florida

Mary Kenney
Astronaut High School
Titusville, Florida

Lou Morrison
Lake Weir High School
Ocala, Florida

Brenda Sims Palmer
Lehigh High School
Lehigh Acres, Florida

Marsee Perkins
Maynard Evans High School
Orlando, Florida

Kent Rettig
Pensacola High School
Pensacola, Florida

Jim Sutton
Edgewater High School
Orlando, Florida

Illinois Teacher Panel

Rosemary Albright
Conant High School
Hoffman Estates, Illinois

Jeff Anhut
Wheaton Warrenville South High School
Wheaton, Illinois

James Crider
Downers Grove South High School
Downers Grove, Illinois

John Devine
Elgin High School
Elgin, Illinois

George Dyche
West Aurora High School
Aurora, Illinois

Diane Ring
St. Charles High School
St. Charles, Illinois

Jim Rosenberg
Crystal Lake South High School
Crystal Lake, Illinois

Pam Zimmerman
Stevenson High School
Lincolnshire, Illinois

Texas Teacher Panel

Patricia Brison
Bellaire High School
Bellaire, Texas

Debra Brown
Eisenhower High School
Houston, Texas

Gwen Cash
Clear Creek High School
League City, Texas

Kyle Howard
Cooper High School
Lubbock, Texas

Melody Kenney
Turner High School
Carrollton, Texas

James Lee
Lamar High School
Arlington, Texas

Janie Maldonado
Lanier High School
Austin, Texas

LeAnna Morse
Memorial High School
McAllen, Texas

Gloria Remijio
Del Valle High School
El Paso, Texas

Alice White
Bryan Adams High School
Dallas, Texas

Manuscript Reviewers

The following educators reviewed the prototype chapter and the manuscript of the entire book.

Arman Afshani
North Tonawanda High School
North Tonawanda, New York

Debra Brown
Eisenhower High School
Houston, Texas

Dianne Bumgarner
Ashbrook High School
Mt. Holly, North Carolina

Sherry Burgin
Garland High School
Garland, Texas

Maurice Bush
South Point High School
Crouse, North Carolina

Bruce Campbell
Bemidji High School
Bemidji, Minnesota

Al Celaya
Robert E. Lee High School
Tyler, Texas

Mary E. Connor
Westridge School
Pasadena, California

James Crider
Downers Grove South High School
Downers Grove, Illinois

Eric DeMeulanaere
Burton Academic High School
San Francisco, California

Gail Dent
Lincoln High School
San Francisco, California

Dr. Simone Dorman
Burton Academic High School
San Francisco, California

Kenward Goode
Robert E. Lee High School
Tyler, Texas

Gary Gregus
Shakopee High School
Shakopee, Minnesota

Patti Harrlod
Edmond Memorial High School
Edmond, Oklahoma

Terry Holt
South Rowan High School
China Grove, North Carolina

Al Juengling
Lane Technical High School
Chicago, Illinois

James Lee
Lamar High School
Arlington, Texas

Judith Mahnke
Wallenberg High School
San Francisco, California

Gary Marksbury
Lakewood High School
Lakewood, California

Internet Resources

McDougal Littell's American history Web site—mlushistory.com—offers you an opportunity to become part of a nationwide community of teachers and students using *The Americans: Reconstruction through the 20th Century.* With a user-friendly format, our American history curriculum center helps you meet the challenges of teaching in today's diverse classroom by providing access to a wide range of resources related to the chapters of the textbook.

Chapter Links Our editors have gathered some of the best links on the Internet to help you extend each lesson, expand your research, and boost your own creativity.

Today in History Browse the archive of significant events in American history. Compiled by the Library of Congress, this site contains links to photos and prints, primary source documents, motion pictures, maps, and sound recordings.

Professional Development Calendar Consult this on-line calendar for the latest information on upcoming events and conferences related to social studies education.

Discussion Groups Exchange ideas, brainstorm, or network with your colleagues. Join the History Discussion Group to post or answer history or program-related questions. Check out the Idea Exchange Discussion Group for more general teaching strategies and topics.

Monthly Special Feature Author profiles, Web-site guests, and other special events are all a part of this monthly feature.

Teacher Links Library Need more information on anything from Reconstruction to the Clinton presidency? Explore hundreds of annotated links to sites dealing with specific topics discussed in *The Americans: Reconstruction through the 20th Century.*

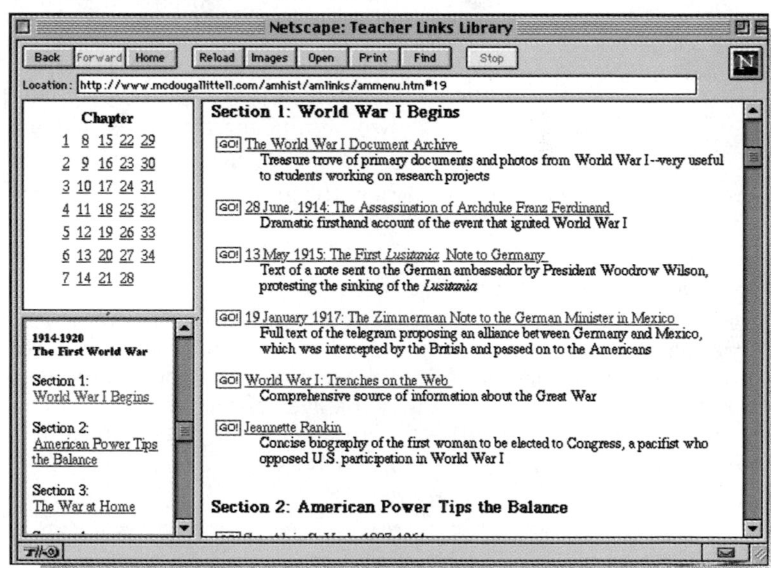

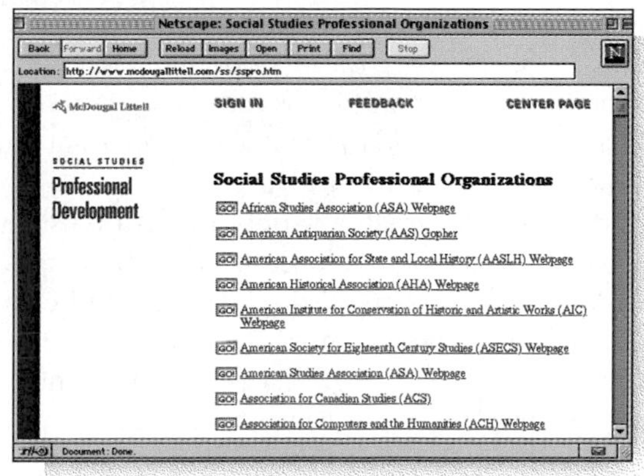

To learn more about our products, contact your local sales representative or purchase materials online at http://www.mcdougallittell.com

http://www.mcdougallittell.com

Reading and Learning History from Textbooks

DONNA M. OGLE
Professor, Reading and Language
National-Louis University

Active, engaged readers make the best learners. Researchers have found that successful readers connect text information with what they already know. These readers build associations among ideas, create visual images of what they are reading, and continually refine their interpretations as they gather more information.

Encouraging active, engaged reading is difficult for teachers when they find that many students have learned to ignore their textbooks. This is often due to texts that are too difficult conceptually and are too dense in information. It is possible, however, for teachers and students to find texts that meet their needs.

SUPPORTING READERS

Often we see students who don't have a foundation of information and experience on which to build. If there are not strong connections, experiences, or foundations, then the amount of support and elaboration provided by the text and teacher are critical. That support and elaboration can be provided in a variety of ways.

Personal Connections For some students, personal stories and human connections can bring a subject such as history alive. Taking a personal point of view and thinking as if they were living the experiences can deepen students' learning. Studies on these techniques have generally shown significant increases in learning. *The Americans: Reconstruction through the 20th Century* uses personal stories throughout to support student learning.

A PERSONAL VOICE

Here we are, tremendously exhilarated, and there's a sea of dead. . . . [The platoon leader] was much moved. . . . He said, "Joe, lets make a resolution with these Russians here and also the ones on the bank: this would be an important day in the lives of the two countries." . . . It was a solemn moment. There were tears in the eyes of most of us. . . . We embraced. We swore never to forget.

JOSEPH POLOWSKY, quoted in *The Good War*

Visual Information Visual information is a resource that many readers rely on heavily when reading unfamiliar material. When text content is unfamiliar, the visual materials accompanying the text can provide strong support for the creation of meaning, especially in expository material. Pictures create a visual context and make abstractions of time and space more real; photos and artifacts create a grounding for new ideas; maps and other spatial features, such as charts, help readers associate and compare ideas. The more opportunity there is to learn through the visual sense, the more avenues for thinking are stimulated and supported.

Learning Styles We know that readers have different styles of constructing meaning—some rely heavily on verbal input and discussion, some need visual supports, and others may learn best by taking notes and making drawings or graphic organizers as they study. Students may become engaged in learning when they challenge ideas, make comparisons, and trace causes and effects. The richer the thinking you encourage, the more likely students are to learn. Posing problems, comparing and contrasting ideas, and presenting different points of view on issues stimulates deeper engagement and leads to more learning than does a simple exposition of factual information. The Point/Counterpoint feature does just that.

POINT	COUNTERPOINT
"The United States must occasionally intervene militarily in regional conflicts."	"The United States should not intervene militarily in regional conflicts."

Students Acquiring English Second-language learners, in particular, need to have information and ideas presented to them in multiple ways. Since many of these students are unfamiliar with the concepts and events of American history, being able to "see" history helps them make it real to themselves. Attending to illustrations of all kinds is essential for these students. The more ways the same information and ideas are presented, the more likely they are to be able to construct an adequate understanding of what they are studying.

In addition, the greater variety of materials second-language learners can read on the same topic, the more deeply they will understand the language and concepts. Seeing the same concepts presented by different authors in different types of writing (first-person accounts, newspapers, official documents) and from different points of view helps these students build a better understanding of new ideas and terminology. Then, having opportunities to discuss ideas and share interpretations can solidify their growing understanding.

Terry McRae
Robert E. Lee High School
Tyler, Texas

Peyton Mullins
Robert E. Lee High School
Tyler, Texas

Brenda Sims Palmer
Lehigh High School
Lehigh Acres, Florida

David Pasternak
Edison Technical High School
Rochester, New York

Dean Pedersen
North Fayette High School
West Union, Iowa

Kent Rettig
Pensacola High School
Pensacola, Florida

Diane Ring
St. Charles High School
St. Charles, Illinois

Susan Roe
C. E. Jordan High School
Durham, North Carolina

Tom Sewell
Inglemoor High School
Bothell, Washington

Marcie Smith
Hurst-Euless-Bedford Independent School District
Bedford, Texas

Mary Smith
Secondary Social Studies Coordinator
Cypress-Fairbanks Independent School District
Houston, Texas

Clara Spence
Millikan High School
Long Beach, California

Wayne Sylvester
Pentucket High School
Westbury, Massachusetts

Bill Von Vihl
Conifer High School
Conifer, Colorado

Pattie Willbanks
Robert E. Lee High School
Tyler, Texas

Nancy Williams
Jersey Village High School
Houston, Texas

Student Board

The following students reviewed prototype materials for the book.

John Afordakos
Chantilly High School
Fairfax County, Virginia

Marisha Cook
Rockford East High School
Rockford, Illinois

Matthew Cornejo
New Bedford High School
New Bedford, Massachusetts

Kevin Dodd
Lanier High School
Austin, Texas

Melissa Dugan
Mount Lebanon High School
Mount Lebanon, Pennsylvania

Denise Ford
Douglas Byrd Sr. High School
Cumberland County, North Carolina

Rebecca Freeman
Foshay Learning Center
Los Angeles, California

Tonya Gieseking
Broad Ripple High School
Indianapolis, Indiana

Yolande Godfrey
Ocean Township High School
Ocean Township, New Jersey

Norma Jaquez
Odessa High School
Ector County, Texas

Mary McCarthy
Penfield High School
Penfield, New York

Dan McKinley
Bulkeley High School
Hartford, Connecticut

Ms. Kris Miller
Midland High School
Cabell County, West Virginia

Brandi Nicholas
Meadowdale High School
Dayton, Ohio

Michael Pancherz
Clark Lake High School
Houston, Texas

Elizabeth Porter
Burnsville High School
Burnsville, Minnesota

Edwin Reyes
Miami Palmetto High School
Dade County

Misty Sisk
Jackson High School
Jacksonville, Florida

Christopher Sizemore
Community High School
Ann Arbor, Michigan

Jennifer Vasquez
Gilbert High School
Gilbert, Arizona

Everett Wheeler-Bell
East High School
Denver, Colorado

LuKisha Williams
Mackenzie High School
Detroit, Michigan

Review Unit 1
To 1877

American Beginnings to 1877

EVOLVING FORMS OF READING

Today's students need to be able to read in ways earlier generations did not.

Nonlinear Materials Today, students must

- gather ideas from multiple sources: resource books, magazines, computerized databases, CD-ROMs, the Internet
- know how to evaluate these sources and make decisions about their content
- find their way through nonlinear materials, such as by deciding which area of a computer screen contains the information they want
- make decisions about what level of knowledge and elaboration they need

Graphic Layouts Today's readers must deal with information presented in a variety of formats, such as

- multiple columns of text with many pictures, graphs, and maps
- single-column texts with with large marginal areas used for problems, illustrations, highlighted information, and thought-provoking ideas
- combinations of layouts

The Western Front, 1914–1917

GEOGRAPHY SKILLBUILDER **LOCATION** *What were the northwestern and southwestern limits of the western front?* **MOVEMENT** *About how many miles separated the city of Paris from German forces at the point of their closest approach?*

A PERSONAL VOICE

[We] found the side streets blocked with their carts. Into these they had thrown mattresses, or bundles of grain, and heaped upon them were families of three generations. Old men in blue smocks, white-haired and bent, old women in caps, the daughters dressed in their one best frock and hat, and clasping in their hands all that was left to them, all that they could stuff into a pillow-case or flour-sack. . . . Heart-broken, weary, hungry, they passed in an unending caravan.

RICHARD HARDING DAVIS, quoted in *Hooray for Peace, Hurrah for War*

Unable to save Belgium, the British and French retreated to the Marne River in France, where they managed to stop the German advance in September 1914. By the spring of 1915, two lines of deep, rat-infested trenches zigzagged across northern and eastern France. German soldiers occupied one line, Allied soldiers the other line. Between them lay **"no man's land"**—a barren expanse of mud pockmarked with shell craters and filled with barbed wire entanglements. Every once in a while, the soldiers would climb out of their trenches and try to overrun enemy lines, while machine guns blazed and poison gas filled the air.

The slaughter was unbelievable. For example, during the First Battle of the Somme—which began on July 1, 1916, and lasted until mid-November—the British lost 60,000 men the first day alone. Final casualties totaled about 1.2 million—650,000 Germans, 420,000 British, and nearly 200,000 French. Yet only seven miles of ground changed hands. This bloody **trench warfare,** in

Soldiers climb out of a trench and charge an enemy position.

Trench Warfare

Information presented in multiple ways.

Single column text with space for questions and captions in the margins.

THE TEACHER'S ROLE

Are our students prepared with strategies for reading and learning in the 21st century? Are they able to shift easily from one form of text presentation to another? Do they know how to construct meaning from multiple sources?

Strategies for Teachers You can help your students become active, engaged, and confident readers. Here are some strategies you might try:

- Observe your students and ask them how they read.
- Do a "think aloud" as students begin to read a text. Ask them to tell you where they look on the page; when they look at the charts, maps, and pictures; and when they read the headings and titles.
- Introduce the text layout and features, and discuss students' options for reading.
- Show students that all the material on a page does not have to be read in order.
- Have students experiment with reading the graphics first before reading the text on a page.
- Demonstrate how headings and subheadings can help readers find specific information.
- Use graphic organizers and reading guides to help students gain confidence.

Reading and discussing different types of written material and material expressing different points of view will help students learn to look deeply into and think critically about what they read. Help them learn to enjoy the search for information and ideas!

Teaching United States History Thematically

Mary E. Connor

In the following article, Mary E. Connor, a U.S. history teacher at Westridge School in Pasadena, California, explains several advantages of thematic teaching and gives strategies for teaching themes successfully.

How can today's educators convey the essentials of American history in a way that is engaging and memorable? One possible answer is a course organized around themes rather than chronological periods. The primary benefit of teaching the subject thematically is that it affords a better grasp of the principal developments in U.S. history by treating issues in depth.

A common problem in many high school U.S. history courses is the neglect of teaching about the recent past. It is not uncommon to hear of classes that never get to the events of more recent decades. The signal beauty of the thematic approach lies in the fact that students can hold informed discussions about current issues by mid-October. For example, as part of the first theme I teach—The American Character and the American Belief System—a discussion of welfare reform can take place within a framework of knowledge about basic (and opposing) American values of self-reliance and social egalitarianism.

A thematic approach allows students to become involved with narratives and articles about one topic. Consider how a teacher might cover the traditional material in exploring the theme America in the World. The teacher outlines the history of imperialism, both world wars, and the Cold War. Students study World War II and Vietnam in depth. For World War II, students might read Studs Terkel's *The Good War* or *War Without Mercy* by John Dower. For Vietnam, differing interpretations of the Vietnam experience can be found in the movie *Coming Home* and in the book *A Rumor of War* by Philip Caputo. The cumulative effect of looking at the scope of American foreign affairs over a six-week period seizes the imagination.

In developing a theme, students could be given options for assignments. For example, for the theme Immigration and Migration, a student might research the immigrants of the 19th century or interview a recent immigrant to America. One class that took my course interviewed immigrants from thirty countries on five continents. These interviews revealed that virtually no one felt discriminated against because of race or ethnicity, all believed they had achieved the American dream, all preferred living in this country to anywhere else despite its problems, and the most difficult adjustment was learning the English language. This analysis of the immigrant experience took on added meaning as students discussed California Proposition 187.

"The signal beauty of the thematic approach lies in the fact that students can hold informed discussions about current issues by mid-October."

In following a thematic approach, students journey from the past to the present ten times—validating the venerable principle of repetition. There are frequent opportunities for discussing contemporary issues within a historical framework. For example, after studying the theme Women in America, students discuss the challenges faced by women today and the current status of the women's movement.

Still another benefit of the thematic approach lies in the power of the narrative. Sometimes the vitality of historical accounts can be lost using the traditional approach, but thematic units have their own inner dynamic and can help students develop broader perspectives on important issues in American history. This includes such topics as African-American history from slavery to the Million Man March and the progress of efforts toward creating a peaceful world.

Moving through successive themes rather than chronological periods allows for greater creativity. The curriculum no longer determines how one does history, and each theme permits varied and absorbing activities. Students can investigate their own family background to better understand how their own histories are part of a larger history. Ellis Island, the Great Depression, and the D-Day invasion all may acquire a new luster if one's own or a friend's grandparent was there. This is especially poignant when the persons in question were on different sides.

Another important element in my thematic course is that of choice in student research. During the summer before taking the class, students receive a list of books organized by the themes in the course. Students read two books, preferably on the same theme. This exposes them to superb source materials and provides them with in-depth knowledge before the school year begins.

Clearly, it will be easier for the seasoned teacher to move to a fully thematic course. However, one can move toward the ideal by expanding on themes encountered in the textbook. Teaching thematically requires more preparation, but the rewards are high: for the teacher, greater professional satisfaction; for students, greater interest, performance, and retention. And your students are likely to thank you.

This essay is adapted from an article that appeared in the April/May 1997 issue of *Social Education*.

Teaching Themes and Current Events in *The Americans: Reconstruction through the 20th Century*

For teachers and districts who wish to organize their modern U.S. history courses thematically, *The Americans: Reconstruction through the 20th Century* serves as a valuable resource. The lists below show how to organize the text around ten themes for a fully thematic course. In addition, the lists show how each theme may be linked to current issues and events by using the Epilogue: Issues for the 21st Century (pages 876–901 in the pupil text).

Ten Themes in *The Americans: Reconstruction through the 20th Century*

1. **America in the World**
2. **The American Dream**
3. **Science and Technology**
4. **Economic Opportunity**
5. **Immigration and Migration**
6. **Women in America**
7. **Civil Rights**
8. **Constitutional Concerns**
9. **Cultural Diversity**
10. **Democracy in America**

America in the World

The American Dream

Science and Technology

Economic Opportunity

(continued on next page)

Immigration and Migration

Settlers Push Westward, pp. 215–216
The New Immigrants, pp. 274–279
Tracing Themes: Immigration and Migration, pp. 422–423
Limiting Immigration, pp. 438–439
Latinos and Native Americans Seek Equality, Geography Spotlight: Migrant Workers pp. 760–767
Geography Spotlight: Sunbelt, Rustbelt, Ecotopia, pp. 834–835
Immigration in the 1990s, pp. 869–870
TODAY: The Debate over Immigration, pp. 880–883

Women in America

One American's Story, p. 230
Women's Work, p. 233
Women in Public Life, pp. 337–340
Woman Suffrage, pp. 356–358
Women in the War, pp. 415–416
The Twenties Woman, pp. 458–461
New Opportunities for Women, pp. 517–518
Women in the Military, p. 571
Women Fight for Equality, pp. 768–772
The Equal Rights Struggle, pp. 830–831
American Literature: Women Writers Reflect American Diversity, pp. 858–859
TODAY: Women and the Glass Ceiling, pp. 894–895

Civil Rights

Segregation and Discrimination, pp. 309–313
The Limits of Progressivism, pp. 358–359
Mexican-American Fortunes, Native American Gains, p. 520
Minorities in the Armed Services, pp. 571–572
Discrimination and Reaction, pp. 598–601
Truman Supports Civil Rights, pp. 639–640
Walking the Middle of the Road, p. 642
The Other America, pp. 660–663
Civil Rights, pp. 694–719
Nixon's Southern Strategy, pp. 788–790
Carter and Civil Rights, p. 804
The Fight for Rights Continues, pp. 831–833
TODAY: Exploring Education Today, pp. 888–891

TRACING THEMES
AMERICA IN THE WORLD

America in World Affairs

"Steer clear of permanent alliances," George Washington cautioned Americans in his Farewell Address of 1796. Washington's warning to the young nation became a theme of government policy for the next hundred years, as domestic issues dominated Americans' attention.

In the late 1800s, however, Americans began to look outward to the larger world. The country had matured, reaching from ocean to ocean across the continent. The Western frontier was closed. A century after Washington had issued his warning, popular sentiment carried the country into the Spanish-American-Cuban War. This involvement, at the very end of the 19th century, marked the emergence of a modern America—a country taking its place among the chief powers of the world.

1823–1898
THE UNITED STATES AND LATIN AMERICA

Throughout the 19th century, the United States expanded its influence in the Western Hemisphere. The Monroe Doctrine was intended to diminish European interference. After the Civil War, American trade with Latin America, including the Spanish colony of Cuba, grew. In fact, the United States traded more heavily with Cuba than Spain did.

When the Cubans rebelled against Spain, Americans sympathized with the rebels. After the U.S. battleship *Maine* sank in the Cuban harbor of Havana, Americans blamed the Spanish, and Congress declared war. After defeating the Spanish, the United States expanded its influence in territories such as Puerto Rico, Panama, and Mexico. A new expansionist era had begun.

1930s
ISOLATIONISM

The United States joined World War I in 1917, determined to "make the world safe for democracy." However, President Woodrow Wilson's plans to ensure a lasting peace through the League of Nations collapsed. The dictators Benito Mussolini and Adolf Hitler came to power in Italy and in Germany, menacing other European countries.

Americans were sharply divided in their responses. Many promoted isolationism, arguing that the best way to preserve American democracy was to stay out of war in Europe. In this climate, President Franklin D. Roosevelt gave material support to Britain but did not commit troops. It took Japan's attack on Pearl Harbor, Hawaii, in 1941 to force the United States into the war.

1939–1945
INVOLVEMENT IN EUROPE

As the United States became a leading world economic power, it became more closely linked with Europe through trade and finance. Americans also respected democratic nations, like Great Britain and France.

When the fascist threat to democracy became too great to ignore, the United States joined the Allies in fighting the Second World War. After the war, most Americans came to believe that the world was too small for the United States to ignore world affairs. Americans took an active role in rebuilding Europe after the war through programs like the Marshall Plan. The United States also stayed involved with Europe militarily during the Cold War as a member of the North Atlantic Treaty Organization (NATO).

1945–1991
THE COLD WAR

Tensions between the United States and the Soviet Union and Communist China rose quickly in the late 1940s. The Cold War that resulted from these tensions lasted for nearly 50 years.

During the Cold War, the United States opposed communism around the globe. One result of this effort was the war in Vietnam. Although Communists eventually won control of Vietnam in 1975, it was the Soviet Union that could not survive the Cold War. Economic troubles decimated the Soviet empire. Small nations like Latvia reclaimed their independence and destroyed the relics of Communist rule, like the statue above of Vladimir I. Lenin, the leader of the 1917 Russian Revolution.

INTERACT WITH HISTORY

1. **ANALYZING MOTIVES** What were America's motives for getting involved in each of the wars described on these two pages? Why do you think the efforts of isolationists have generally not prevailed over the forces promoting involvement?
   SEE SKILLBUILDER HANDBOOK, PAGE 907.
2. **WRITING ABOUT WARTIME EXPERIENCE** Imagine that you are a reporter writing about one of the wars in the 20th century. Interview someone you know—or look for information in the library or on the Internet—to find out how an individual soldier, nurse, cook, sailor, or pilot spent each day as part of the war effort. Write a feature article for a local newspaper, quoting that person.

Visit http://www.mlushistory.com for more information about American involvement overseas.

America in the World 369

Constitutional Concerns

Attacks on Civil Liberties, pp. 412–414
Revolution Abroad and Reaction at Home, pp. 420–433
Scandal Hits Harding's Administration, pp. 439–440
Science and Religion Clash, pp. 456–457
Internment of Japanese Americans, p. 675
The Cold War at Home, pp. 619–624
Taking on Segregation, pp. 696–703
Nixon's Southern Strategy, pp. 788–790
Watergate: Nixon's Downfall, pp. 793–797
Judicial Power Shifts to the Right, p. 824
The Fight for Rights Continues, pp. 831–833
TODAY: Crime and Public Safety, pp. 884–887

Cultural Diversity

Native American Cultures in Crisis, pp. 214–220
Social Changes During the War, pp. 414–415
The Harlem Renaissance, pp. 472–474
Mexican-American Fortunes, Native American Gains, p. 520
The Other America, pp. 660–663
Latinos and Native Americans Seek Equality, Geography Spotlight: Migrant Workers pp. 760–767
The Fight for Rights Continues, pp. 831–833
American Literature: Women Writers Reflect American Diversity, pp. 858–859
Immigration in the 1990s, pp. 869–870
Tracing Themes: Cultural Diversity: Sharing Cultures, pp. 872–873
TODAY: The Debate over Immigration, pp. 880–883

Democracy in America

Farmers and the Populist Movement, pp. 235–239
The Emergence of the Political Machine, pp. 288–290
Politics in the Gilded Age, pp. 291–293
The Origins of Progressivism, pp. 330–336
Teddy Roosevelt's Square Deal, Progressivism Under Taft, Wilson's New Freedom, pp. 341–359
A New Deal Coalition, pp. 520–522
Republicans Take the Middle Road, p. 641
The Great Society, pp. 683–691
Latinos and Native Americans Seek Equality, Geography Spotlight: Migrant Workers pp. 760–767
Expanding Democracy, pp. 786–792
A Conservative Movement Emerges, pp. 818–821
Clinton Wins the Presidency, pp. 846–847
The Republican Congress, pp. 850–851
The Election of 1996, pp. 851–852
Campaign Finance Reform, p. 852
TODAY: Tough Choices About Entitlements, pp. 900–901

Review Unit 1
To 1877

Unit 2
1877–1917

Bridge to the 20th Century

Modern America Emerges

Unit 3
1890–1920

Unit 4
1920–1940

The Twenties and the Great Depression

World War II and Its Aftermath

Unit 5
1931–1960

Unit 6
1954–1975

Living with Great Turmoil

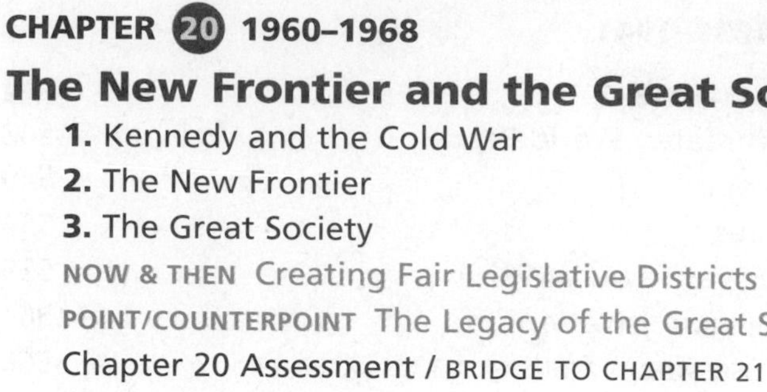

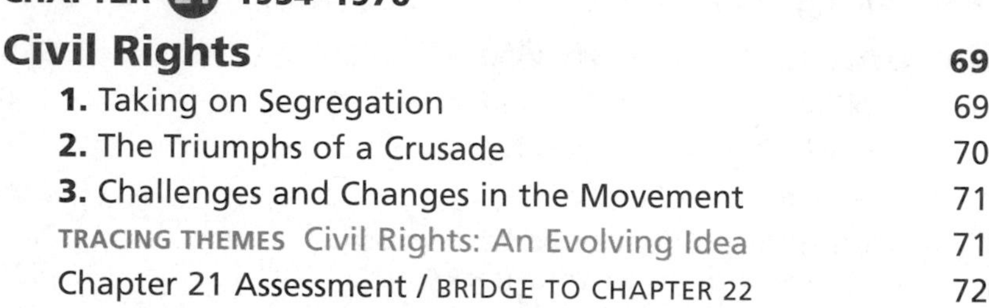

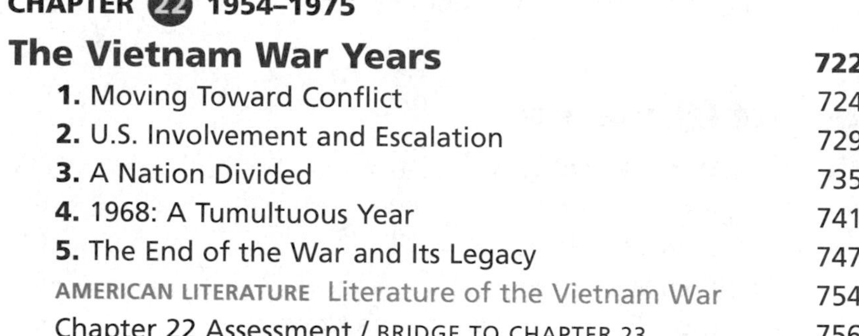

Passage to a New Century

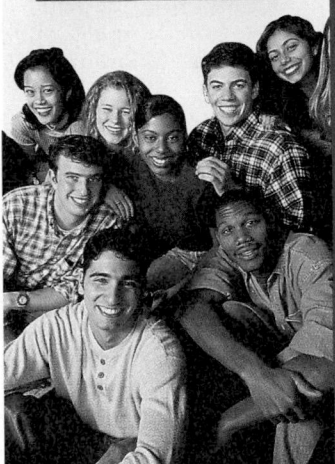

Unit 7
1968–1997

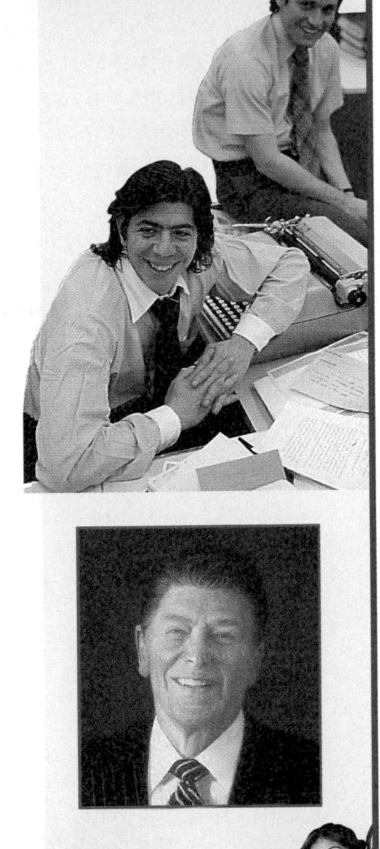

Skillbuilder Handbook

The Skillbuilder Handbook is at the back of the book on pages 903–932. Refer to it when you need help in answering Think Through History questions, doing the activities entitled Interact with History, or answering questions in Section Assessments and Chapter Assessments. The handbook will also help you answer questions about maps, charts, and graphs.

Section 1: Understanding Historical Readings

1.9 Making Inferences

Making inferences from a piece of historical writing means drawing conclusions based on facts, examples, and the author's use of language. For example, if you are reading about the Spanish-American-Cuban War, the writer may not come right out and explain why the United States fought that war. Therefore, you must make inferences about the reasons. To make inferences, use clues in the text and your own personal experience, historical knowledge, and common sense.

UNDERSTANDING THE SKILL

Strategy: Finding clues in the text The following passage is from a speech by President Ronald Reagan. In it, he describes the economic program that he presented to Congress in 1981. From Reagan's language and choice of facts, what can you infer about his opinions with regard to the economy? The chart below lists some inferences that can be drawn from the first paragraph.

On the Program for Economic Recovery

All of us are aware of the punishing inflation which has for the first time in 60 years held to double-digit figures for 2 years in a row. Interest rates have reached absurd levels of more than 20 percent and over 15 percent for those who would borrow to buy a home. All across this land one can see newly built homes standing vacant, unsold because of mortgage interest rates. Almost 8 million Americans are out of work. . . .

I am proposing a comprehensive four-point program . . . aimed at reducing the growth in government spending and taxing, reforming and eliminating regulations which are unnecessary and unproductive or counterproductive, and encouraging a consistent monetary policy aimed at maintaining the value of the currency.

Now, I know that exaggerated and inaccurate stories about these cuts have disturbed many people. . . . Some of you have heard from constituents, I know, afraid that social security checks, for example, were going to be taken away from them. . . . Those who, through no fault of their own, must depend on the rest of us—the poverty stricken, the disabled, the elderly, all those with true need—can rest assured that the social safety net of programs they depend on are exempt from any cuts.

From the facts in the text and historical knowledge, you can infer that Reagan is placing responsibility for the poor economy on the Democrats.

From Reagan's language, you can infer that he blames the poor economy on government spending and taxing.

From Reagan's language, you can infer that he is aware of criticism, although he finds it "exaggerated" and "inaccurate."

Strategy: Making a chart

Clues in the Text: Facts, Examples, Language	Personal Experience, Historical Knowledge, Common Sense	Inference
• Inflation in double digits • Interest rates over 20% • 8 million unemployed • Inflation is "punishing" • Interest rates "absurd"	• Reagan defeated Democratic incumbent Jimmy Carter in the 1980 election.	Reagan blames the Democrats for the current economic problems.

Make your own inferences. Record clues in the text, as well as what you know about the topic on the basis of your own experience, knowledge, and common sense.

APPLYING THE SKILL

Make your own chart Turn to Chapter 10, Section 3, and read the passage headed "The Impact of U.S. Territorial Gains." Create a chart like the one above, making inferences based on clues in the text and on your own personal experience, historical knowledge, and common sense.

912 Skillbuilder Handbook

Section 3: Print, Visual, and Technological Sources

3.6 Using the Internet

The **Internet** is a network of computers associated with universities, libraries, news organizations, government agencies, businesses, and private individuals worldwide. Every page of information on the Internet has its own address, or **URL.**

With a computer connected to the Internet, you can reach pages provided by many organizations and services. You can find the call number of a library book, read an article in a periodical, view photographs, or receive moving pictures and sound.

The international collection of sites, known as the **World Wide Web** is a good source of up-to-the minute information about current events as well as in-depth research on historical subjects. This textbook contains many suggestions for navigating the Internet through the World Wide Web. You can begin by entering the address (URL) for McDougal Littell's site, which is

http://www.mlushistory.com

UNDERSTANDING THE SKILL

Strategy: Finding clues on the screen The computer screen below shows the Web page of the Library of Congress in Washington, D.C.

Go directly to a Web page. If you know the address of a particular Web page, type the address in the strip at the top of the screen and press RETURN. After a few seconds, that Web page will appear on your screen.

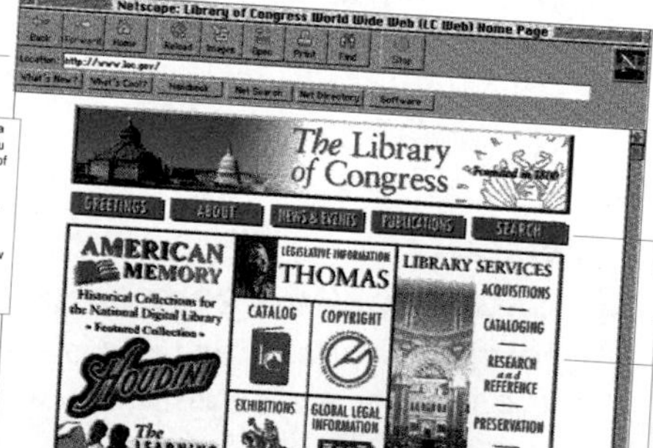

Learn about the page. Click on one of the topics across the top of the page to learn more about the Library of Congress and how to use its Web site.

Explore the features of the page. Click on any one of the images or topics to find out more about a specific subject. For example, you can search the library's catalog by clicking on the image of a book or on the word *catalog* above it.

APPLYING THE SKILL

Do your own Internet research Turn to Chapter 21, Section 2, "The Triumphs of a Crusade." Read the section, making a list of topics you would like to research. If you have a computer with Internet access, go to the McDougal Littell site (http://www.mlushistory.com), where you will learn more about how to conduct a search.

930 Skillbuilder Handbook

VIDEO *American Stories is a powerful video series integrated with the text of The Americans. Fifteen fascinating documentaries, each eight to ten minutes long, help introduce various sections of the text.*

PATTILLO HIGGINS

ZITKALA-ŠA

ZORA NEALE HURSTON

TONY KAHN

LOIS GIBBS

1861–1902

1. **WAR OUTSIDE MY WINDOW** Mary Chesnut's Diary of the Civil War—Chapter 4
2. **TEACHER OF A FREED PEOPLE** Robert Fitzgerald and Reconstruction—Chapter 4
3. **A WALK IN TWO WORLDS** The Education of Zitkala-Ša, a Sioux—Chapter 5

1901–1912

4. **GUSHER!** Pattillo Higgins and the Great Texas Oil Boom—Chapter 6
5. **FROM CHINA TO CHINATOWN** Fong See's American Dream—Chapter 7
6. **A CHILD ON STRIKE** The Testimony of Camella Teoli, Mill Girl—Chapter 9

1914–1937

7. **ACE OF ACES** Eddie Rickenbacker and the First World War—Chapter 11
8. **JUMP AT THE SUN** Zora Neale Hurston and the Harlem Renaissance—Chapter 13
9. **BROKE BUT NOT BROKEN** Ann Marie Low Remembers the Dust Bowl—Chapter 14

1924–1962

10. **A SONG FOR HIS PEOPLE** Pedro J. González and the Fight for Mexican-American Rights—Chapter 15
11. **ESCAPING THE FINAL SOLUTION** Kurt Klein and Gerda Weissmann Klein Remember the Holocaust—Chapter 16
12. **THE COLD WAR COMES HOME** Hollywood Blacklists the Kahn Family—Chapter 18

1949–present

13. **JUSTICE IN MONTGOMERY** Jo Ann Gibson Robinson and the Bus Boycott—Chapter 21
14. **MATTERS OF CONSCIENCE** Stephan Gubar and the Vietnam War—Chapter 22
15. **POISONED PLAYGROUND** Lois Gibbs and the Crisis at Love Canal—Chapter 24

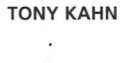

TRACING THEMES

DAILY LIFE

GEOGRAPHY SPOTLIGHT

AMERICAN LITERATURE

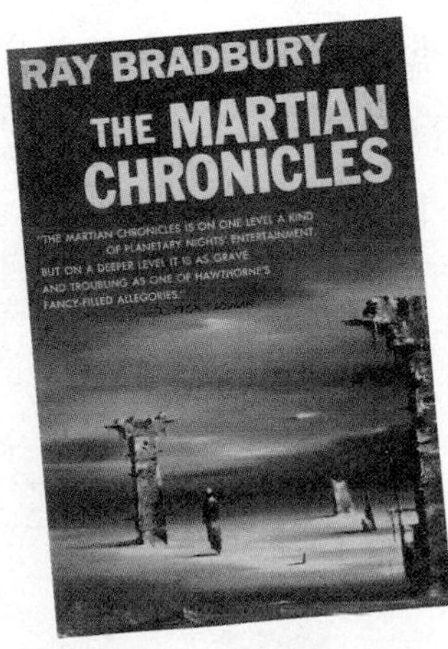

* indicates topics with Internet links

NOW & THEN

KEY PLAYERS

* indicates topics with Internet links

Special Features

ECONOMIC BACKGROUND

POINT COUNTERPOINT

ON THE WORLD STAGE

Difficult Decisions IN HISTORY

* indicates topics with Internet links

HISTORICAL SPOTLIGHT

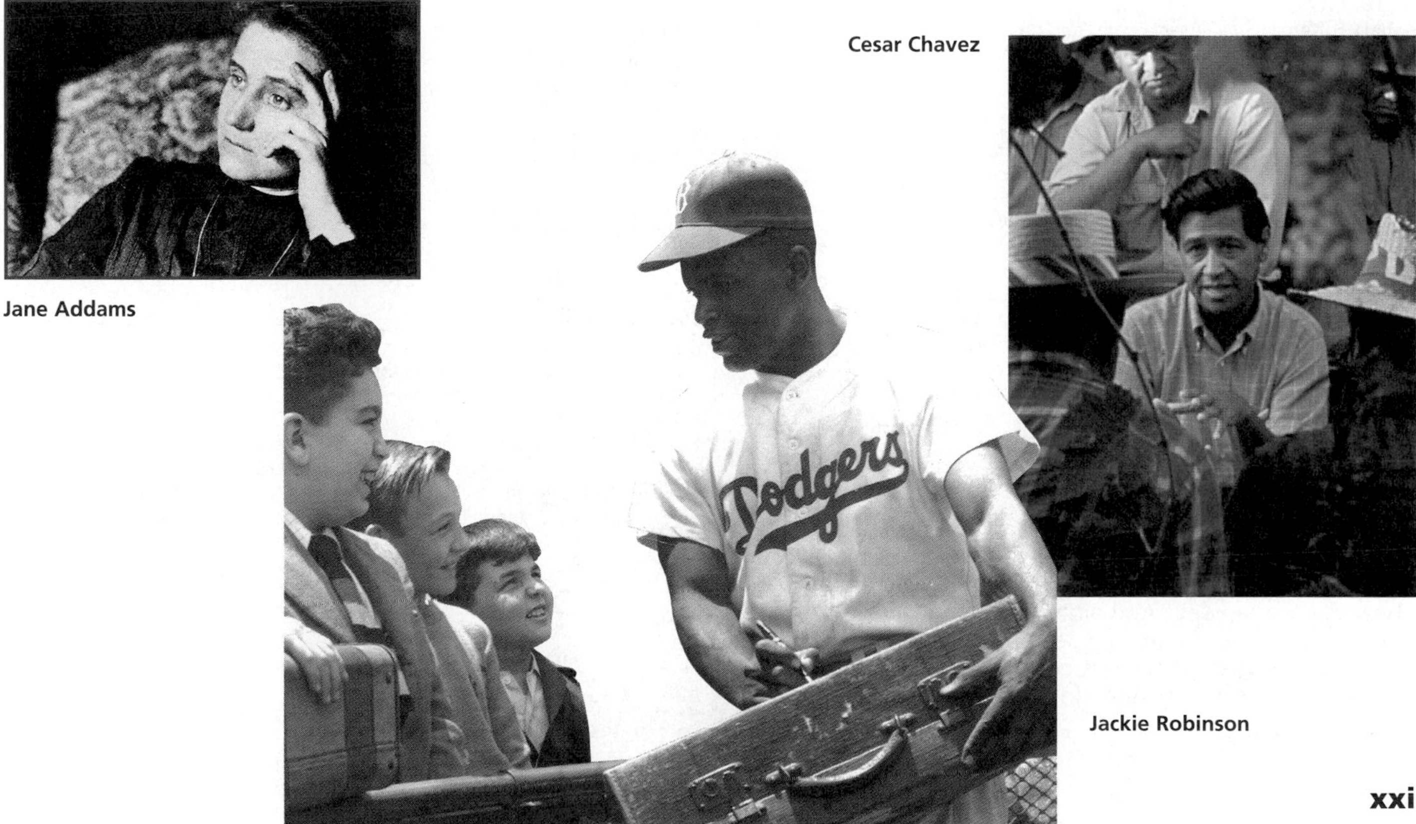

Jane Addams

Cesar Chavez

Jackie Robinson

Primary Sources and Personal Voices

A PERSONAL VOICE
Look at me! Look at my arm! I have ploughed, and planted, and gathered into barns, and no man could head me. And ain't I a woman? I could work as much and eat as much as a man—when I could get it—and bear the lash as well! And ain't I a woman? I have borne thirteen children, and seen most all sold off to slavery, and when I cried out with a mother's grief, none but Jesus heard! And ain't I a woman?
SOJOURNER TRUTH, quoted in *Narrative of Sojourner Truth*

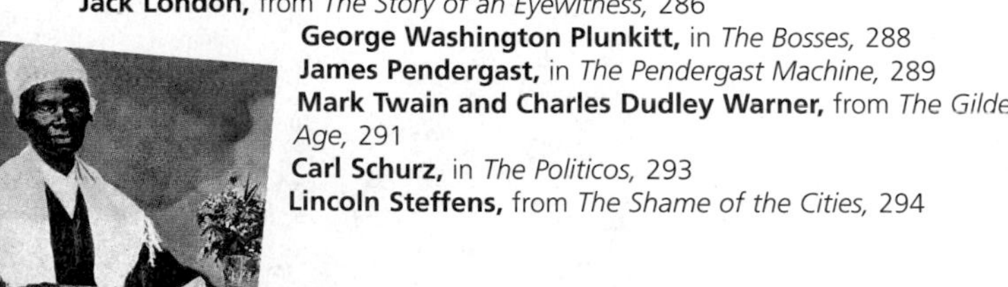

A PERSONAL VOICE
"Government of the people, by the people, for the people, shall not perish from the earth."
ABRAHAM LINCOLN, the Gettysburg Address

Chapter 8

E. F. Farrington, in *The Great Bridge,* 298
Frederick Law Olmsted, in *Frederick Law Olmsted's New York,* 300
William Torrey Harris, in *Public Schools and Moral Education,* 303
Anonymous, in *The One Best System,* 304
Ida B. Wells, in *Crusade for Justice,* 309
Booker T. Washington, from Atlanta Exposition Address, 1895, 311
Bruce Blen, in *Amusing the Million,* 314
Albert Bigelow Paine, in *Coney Island,* 315
Edwin Milton Royle, in *Victorian America,* 317
Henry Steele Commager, in *The American Mind,* 324

Chapter 9

Camella Teoli, at congressional hearings, March 1912, 330
Eugene Debs, in *Debs: His Life, Writings and Speeches,* 332
Susette La Flesche, in *Bright Eyes,* 337
Sophia Smith, in *Alma Mater,* 339
Upton Sinclair, from *The Jungle,* 341
W. E. B. Du Bois, from *The Souls of Black Folk,* 347
Ida M. Tarbell, from *The History of the Standard Oil Company,* 348
Lincoln Steffens, from *The Shame of the Cities,* 349
Upton Sinclair, from *The Jungle,* 349
Gifford Pinchot, from *The Fight for Conservation,* 350
Woodrow Wilson, in *The New Freedom,* 353
Carrie Chapman Catt, from a letter to Maud Wood Park, August 30, 1916, 354
William Monroe Trotter, from address to President Wilson, November 12, 1914, 359
John Muir, from "The American Forests," *Our National Parks,* 360

A PERSONAL VOICE
"Let us, while this war lasts, forget our special grievances and close our ranks shoulder to shoulder."
W. E. B. DU BOIS, *The Souls of Black Folk*

Chapter 10

Queen Liliuokalani, in *Those Kings and Queens of Old Hawaii,* 364
Albert J. Beveridge, in *Beveridge and the Progressive Era,* 365
James Creelman, in *New York World,* May 17, 1896, 370
Luis Muñoz Rivera, in *The Puerto Ricans,* 375
Andrew Carnegie, in *Distant Possessions,* 377
Mark Twain, in *To the Person Sitting in Darkness,* 381
Joseph Bucklin Bishop, in *The Impossible Dream,* 382
Woodrow Wilson, from statement on Latin America, March 11, 1913, 386
Walter Hines Page, from "The War with Spain and After," *Atlantic Monthly,* June 1898, 390

Chapter 11

Jeannette Rankin, in *Jeannette Rankin: First Lady in Congress,* 394
Richard Harding Davis, in *Hooray for Peace, Hurrah for War,* 397
Woodrow Wilson, in *American Voices,* 401
Captain Eddie Rickenbacker, in *Rickenbacker,* 402
Arthur Taber, in *Hooray for Peace, Hurrah for War,* 404
Florence Bullard, in *Over There,* 407
Eddie Rickenbacker, in *Hooray for Peace, Hurrah for War,* 408
Justice Oliver Wendell Holmes, Jr., from dissenting opinion in *Abrams* v. *United States,* 409
Harriot Stanton Blatch, in *We, the American Women,* 411
Woodrow Wilson, in *Cobb of "The World,"* 412
W. E. B. Du Bois, from "Close Ranks," 414
Richard Wright, in *12 Million Black Voices,* 415
Edith Bolling Galt Wilson, in *Hooray for Peace, Hurrah for War,* 417
General John J. Pershing, in *Over Here and Over There,* 421
Mary Simkhovitch, from *Neighborhood: My Story of Greenwich House,* 424

Chapter 12

Irving Fajans, in *The Jewish Americans,* 430
Bartolomeo Vanzetti, in *The National Experience,* 432
Woodrow Wilson, in *Labor in Crisis,* 434
Ernesto Galarza, in *The Hispanic Americans,* 436
Warren G. Harding, in *The Rise of Warren Gamaliel Harding,* 436
Madison Grant, in *United States History: Ideas in Conflict,* 438
Warren G. Harding, in *Only Yesterday,* 439
A Ford salesman, in *Flappers, Bootleggers, and "Typhoid Mary,"* 441
Sinclair Lewis, from *Babbitt,* 443
Listerine advertisement, 444
Business owner, in *In the Time of Silent Cal,* 445
William Ashdown, in *The Twenties: Fords, Flappers, and Fanatics,* 448

Chapter 13

Billy Sunday, in *How Dry We Were: Prohibition Revisited,* 452
Walter L. George, from *Hail Columbia!,* 453
Herbert Asbury, from *Gem of the Prairies,* 455
Clarence Darrow and William Jennings Bryan, in *Bryan and Darrow at Dayton,* 457
G. Stanley Hall, from "Flapper Americana Novissima," *Atlantic Monthly,* June 1922, 458
G. Stanley Hall, from "Flapper Americana Novissima," *Atlantic Monthly,* June 1922, 459
Helen Wright, in *Wage-Earning Women,* 461
Graham McNamee, in *Time* magazine, October 3, 1927, 464
F. Scott Fitzgerald, in *The Lawless Decade,* 467
Sinclair Lewis, from *Babbitt,* 468
Zora Neale Hurston, in *The African American Encyclopedia,* 470
Zora Neale Hurston, in *Sorrow's Kitchen: The Life and Folklore of Zora Neale Hurston,* 470
Marcus Garvey, from a speech at Liberty Hall, New York City, 1922, 471
James Weldon Johnson, from "Harlem: The Culture Capital," 472
Langston Hughes, from *The Big Sea,* 474
Louis Armstrong, in *The Negro Almanac,* 474
Alain Locke, in *Afro-American Writing: An Anthology of Prose and Poetry,* 475
F. Scott Fitzgerald, from *The Great Gatsby,* 476
Edna St. Vincent Millay, "First Fig," 477
Langston Hughes, "Dream Variations," 477
F. Scott Fitzgerald, from "Echoes of the Jazz Age," 478

Chapter 14

Gordon Parks, from *A Choice of Weapons,* 482
Frederick Lewis Allen, in *Only Yesterday,* 486
Ann Marie Low, from *Dust Bowl Diary,* 490
A visitor to a shantytown outside Oklahoma City, in *Hard Times,* 491
Herman Shumlin, in *Hard Times,* 491
Thomas Wolfe, from *You Can't Go Home Again,* 493
Meridel Le Seuer, in *America in the Twenties,* 493
Oscar Ameringer, in *The American Spirit,* 495
A. Everette McIntyre, in *Hard Times,* 499
Oscar Ameringer, from *Testimony Before a Subcommittee of the Committee on Labor, House of Representatives,* 500

A PERSONAL VOICE
"Last weekend was the worst dust storm we ever had."
ANN MARIE LOW, *Dust Bowl Diary*

Primary Sources and Personal Voices

A PERSONAL VOICE

Never shall I forget that night, the first night in the camp, which has turned my life into one long night. . . . Never shall I forget the little faces of the children, whose bodies I saw turned into wreaths of smoke beneath a silent blue sky. Never shall I forget those flames which consumed my faith forever. Never shall I forget that nocturnal silence which deprived me, for all eternity, of the desire to live. Never shall I forget those moments which murdered my God and my soul and turned my dreams to dust. Never shall I forget these things, even if I am condemned to live as long as God Himself. Never.

ELIE WIESEL, *Night*

A PERSONAL VOICE

"Seeing how badly they treated Mexicans back in the days of my youth, I could have started a rebellion. But now [1984] there could be a cultural understanding so that . . . we might understand each other."

PEDRO J. GONZÁLEZ, quoted in *Los Angeles Times,* December 9, 1984

A PERSONAL VOICE
"Today . . . [m]y faith in the Constitution is whole."

BARBARA JORDAN, quoted in *Notable Black American Women*

A PERSONAL VOICE
"It is not just those of us who have reached the top who are fighting this daily battle."

GERALDINE FERRARO, quoted in *Vital Speeches of the Day*

Historical and Political Maps

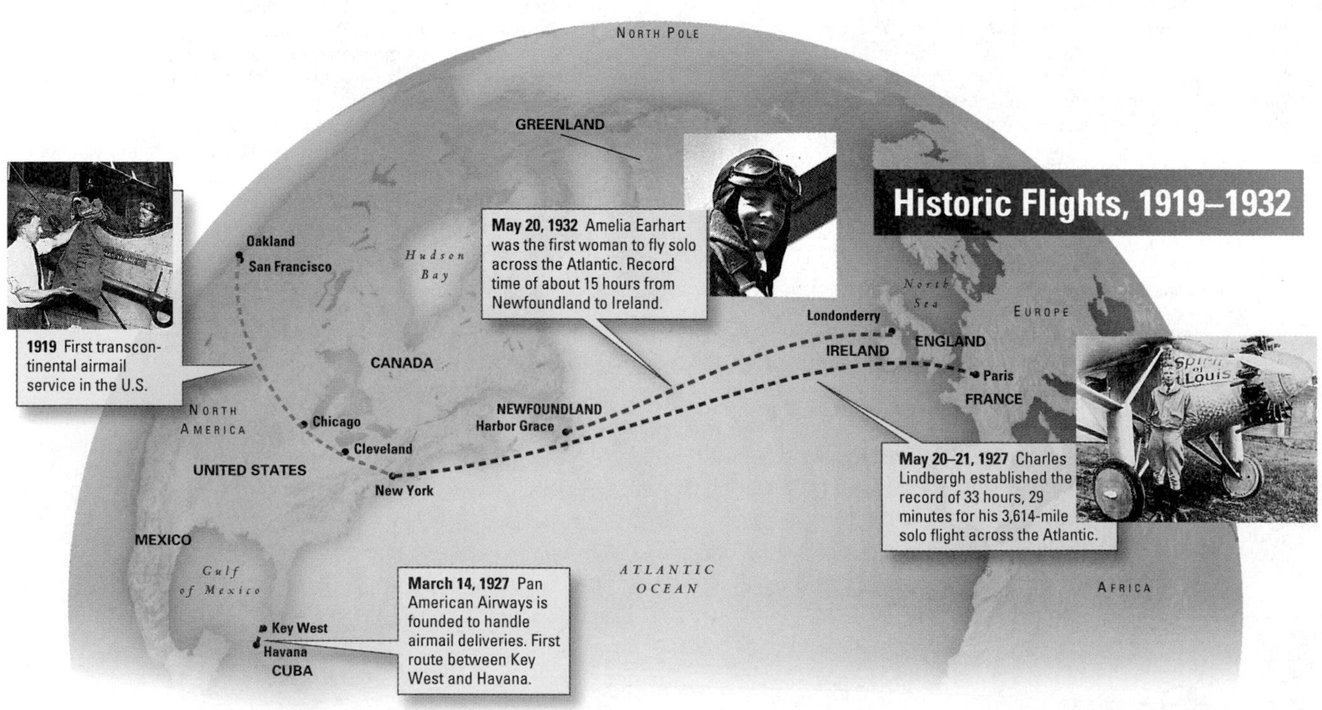

Historic Flights, 1919–1932
North Pole
GREENLAND
Hudson Bay
North Sea
Europe
Oakland
San Francisco
CANADA
North America
UNITED STATES
Chicago
Cleveland
New York
NEWFOUNDLAND
Harbor Grace
Londonderry
IRELAND
ENGLAND
Paris
FRANCE
MEXICO
Gulf of Mexico
Key West
Havana
CUBA
ATLANTIC OCEAN
Africa
1919 First transcontinental airmail service in the U.S.
May 20, 1932 Amelia Earhart was the first woman to fly solo across the Atlantic. Record time of about 15 hours from Newfoundland to Ireland.
May 20–21, 1927 Charles Lindbergh established the record of 33 hours, 29 minutes for his 3,614-mile solo flight across the Atlantic.
March 14, 1927 Pan American Airways is founded to handle airmail deliveries. First route between Key West and Havana.

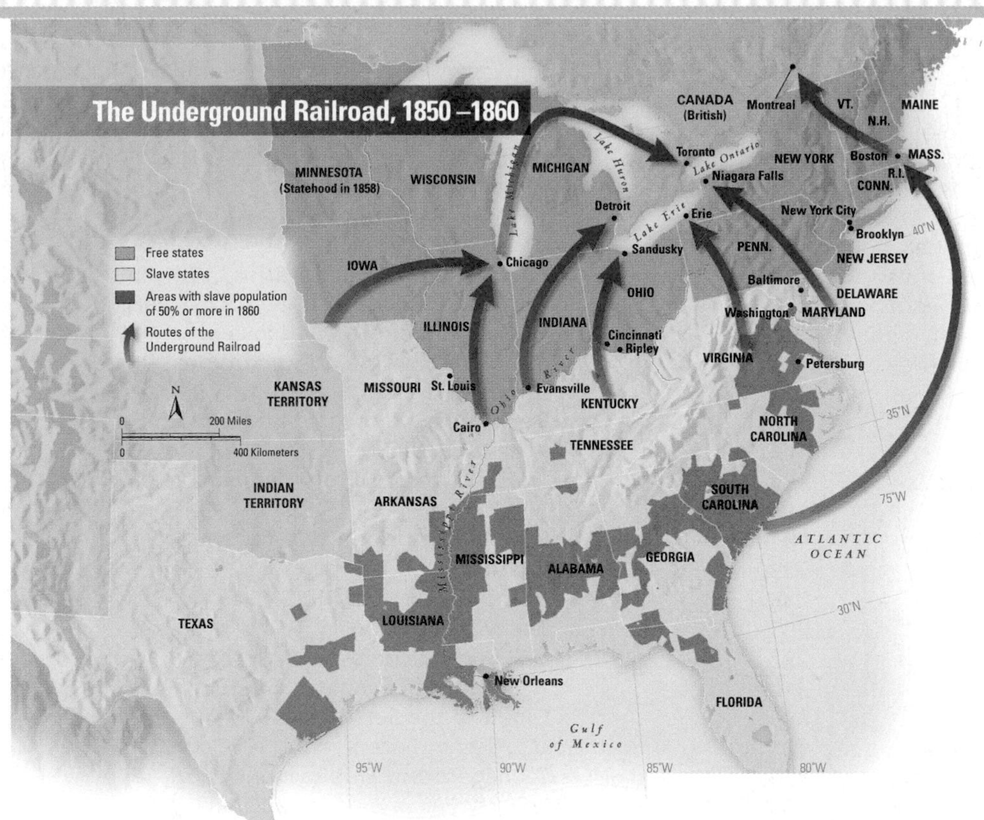

The Underground Railroad, 1850 –1860
Free states
Slave states
Areas with slave population of 50% or more in 1860
Routes of the Underground Railroad
200 Miles
400 Kilometers
CANADA (British)
Montreal
VT.
N.H.
MAINE
Toronto
Lake Ontario
Niagara Falls
NEW YORK
Boston
MASS.
R.I.
CONN.
MINNESOTA (Statehood in 1858)
WISCONSIN
MICHIGAN
Lake Michigan
Lake Huron
Detroit
Lake Erie
Erie
New York City
Brooklyn
IOWA
Chicago
Sandusky
PENN.
NEW JERSEY
OHIO
Baltimore
DELAWARE
Washington
MARYLAND
ILLINOIS
INDIANA
Cincinnati
Ripley
VIRGINIA
Petersburg
KANSAS TERRITORY
MISSOURI
St. Louis
Ohio River
Evansville
KENTUCKY
Cairo
NORTH CAROLINA
TENNESSEE
INDIAN TERRITORY
ARKANSAS
Mississippi River
SOUTH CAROLINA
ATLANTIC OCEAN
MISSISSIPPI
ALABAMA
GEORGIA
TEXAS
LOUISIANA
New Orleans
FLORIDA
Gulf of Mexico
40°N
35°N
30°N
75°W
95°W
90°W
85°W
80°W

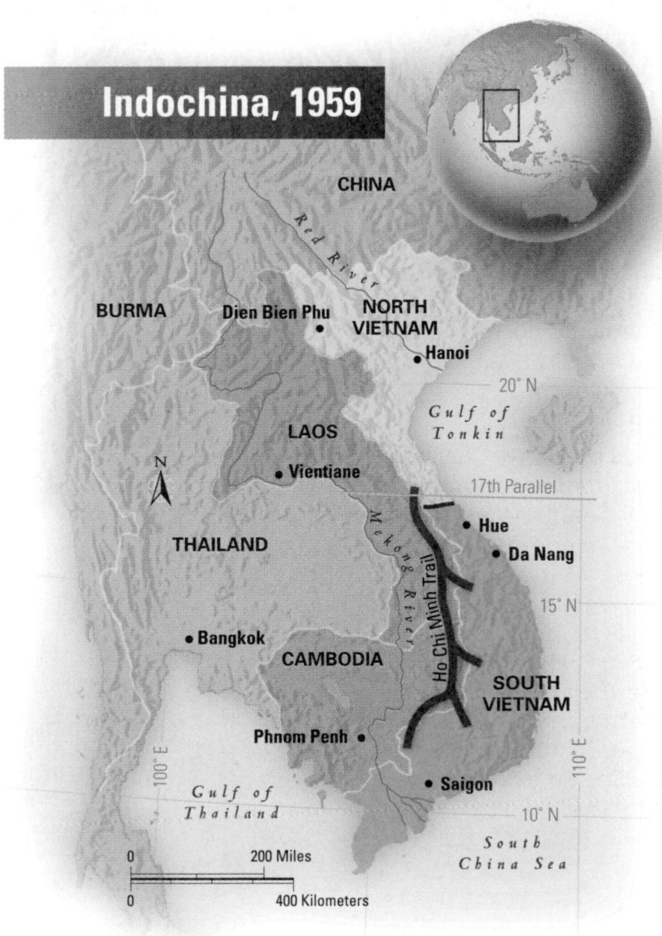

Indochina, 1959
CHINA
Red River
BURMA
Dien Bien Phu
NORTH VIETNAM
Hanoi
20° N
Gulf of Tonkin
LAOS
Vientiane
17th Parallel
Hue
Da Nang
THAILAND
Mekong River
Ho Chi Minh Trail
15° N
Bangkok
CAMBODIA
SOUTH VIETNAM
Phnom Penh
100° E
110° E
Saigon
Gulf of Thailand
10° N
200 Miles
400 Kilometers
South China Sea

Charts, Graphs, Infographics, Tables, and Time Lines

Charts

Graphs

U.S. Wheat Production and Wheat Prices

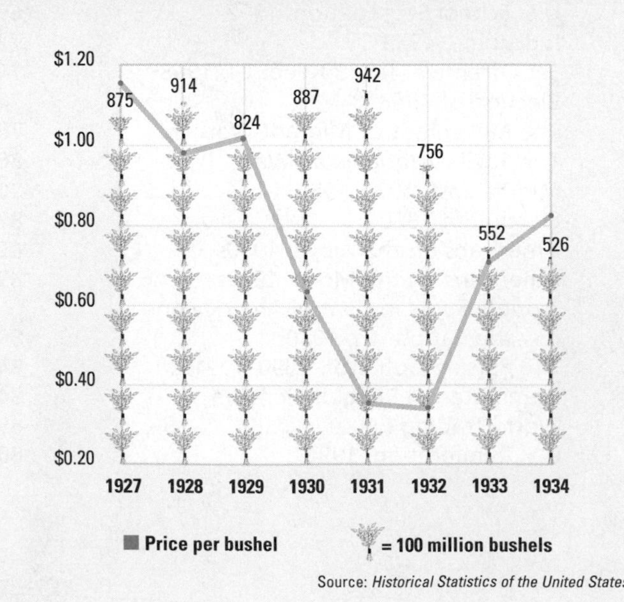

Source: *Historical Statistics of the United States.*

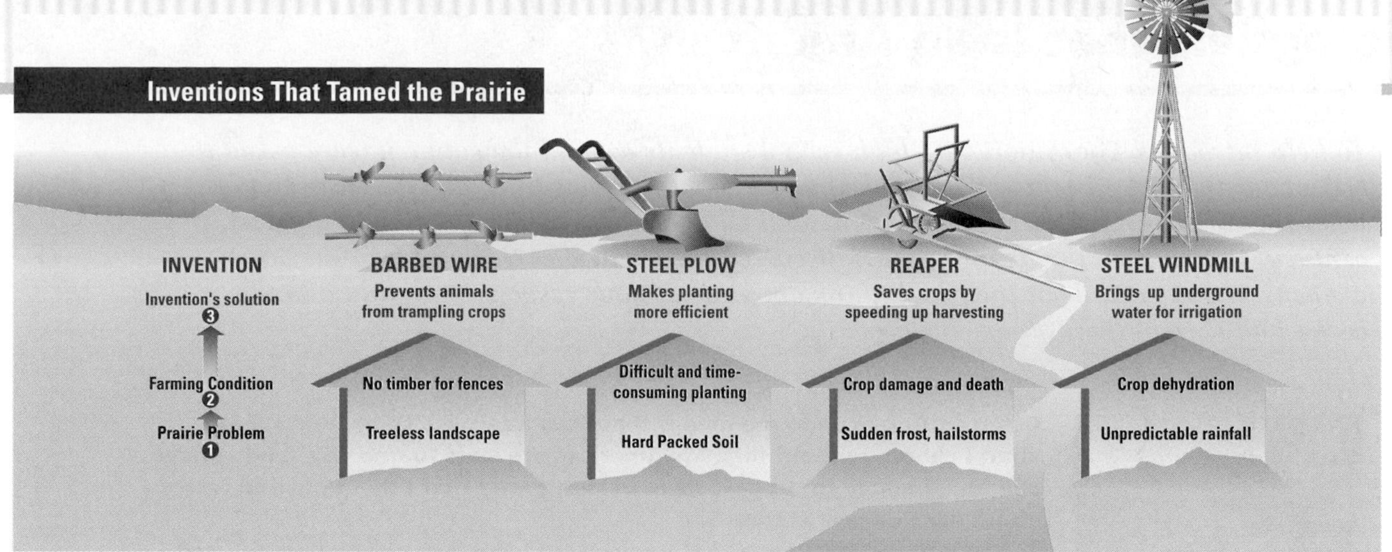

Infographics

Other Applications of World War II Technology

TECHNOLOGY	MILITARY USE	PEACETIME USE
Semi-conductors	Navigation	Transistors, radios, electronics
Computers	Code breaking	Software programs, video games
Freeze-dried food	Soldiers' rations	TV dinners, space-shuttle rations
Synthetic materials	Parachutes, weapons parts, tires	Telephones, automobile fenders, pacemakers
Infrared technology	Night tracking	TV remote controls, police surveillance, medical treatment
Radar	Tracking and surveillance	Weather tracking, air traffic control, archaeological digs, microwave ovens

Tables

Time Lines

Prologue: What Is an American?

To help introduce The Americans, *high school students around the country were asked to talk about the United States. They talked about what it means to be an American today, what the American dream means to them, and what changes await America in the 21st century. In addition, the young women discussed the challenges they see for American women. As you read what they said, think about what your responses would be to the issues and themes these students raise.*

KNEMARA SON, CALIFORNIA

Being an American to me means that I can freely do, think, and speak what I choose without fear. My American dream is to one day, when I have children, be able to support them in such a way that I don't have to worry about my financial status.

The greatest challenge that America is facing is that of being able to completely dissolve the chains of racism. We can best face this challenge by taking it head on, by accepting each and every individual for who they are.

NELLY DELEON, NEW JERSEY

Being an American means to me opportunity. My parents immigrated from Guatemala more than 14 years ago to give us a chance to become successful. My American dream is to graduate from a top college and become a leader.

I believe America's greatest challenge is racism. One way to face this challenge is for television to stop showing stereotyped characters.

ADAM BROWN, TEXAS

One part of being an American involves two closely related words, *freedom* and *choice*. We have the freedom to do many tasks and the choice to decide which tasks to do. We have the freedom to choose what to make of ourselves—whether we will be successful.

Our greatest challenge is to keep the basic principles our nation was built upon. Our democracy is like a house. Without a foundation, the house will crumble and topple. We must add or renovate, not demolish and destroy.

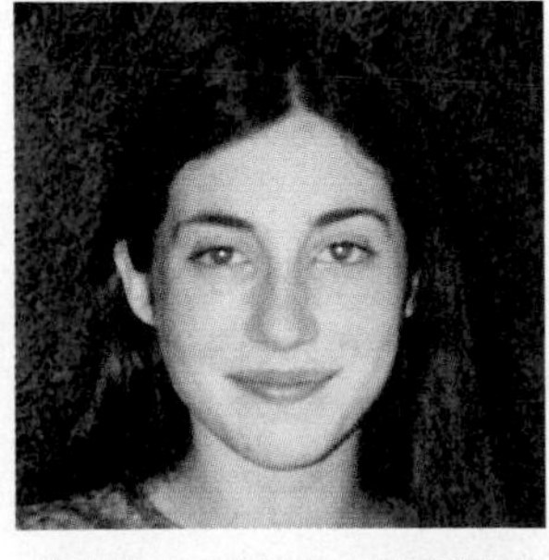

MICHELLE TAYLOR, CALIFORNIA

Being an American is the freedom to speak our minds, the right to be treated equally, and the ability to participate in our government's decisions.

I hope that one day, America's violence and poverty will be extinguished. America's greatest challenge is poverty, which increases violence and crime in our neighborhoods. We can best face this challenge by providing more jobs and increasing people's awareness of the importance of education.

ROBERT YICK, CALIFORNIA

Being an American means that you uphold the values of the Constitution. My American dream is to become a soldier and to spend my life supporting and defending the Constitution.

In the future, I hope that Americans can pull together and focus their energy on solving many of the world's ills as well as the country's. The 21st century will bring an era of constant change. We must prepare for that change by learning about our mistakes in the past so we do not repeat them.

AMY GRASS, COLORADO

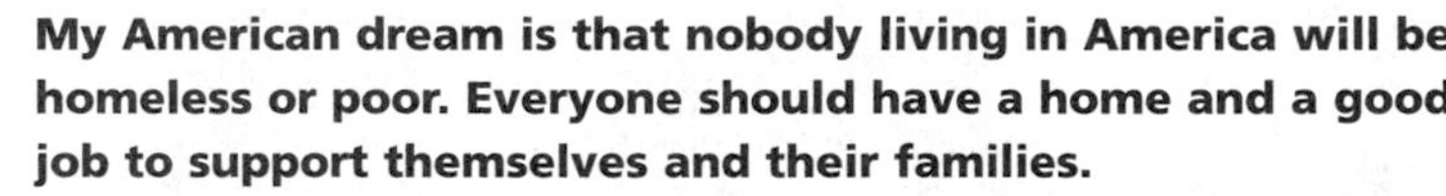

My American dream is that nobody living in America will be homeless or poor. Everyone should have a home and a good job to support themselves and their families.

The most important challenge facing women in the 21st century is equal opportunity. Although women's position in society has greatly improved, it is still not perfect. I think women will have great opportunities making discoveries with technology and working beside others as equals.

EDUARDO HERRERA, TEXAS

The American dream that I visualize for myself is what almost any human being would want. I want a fulfilling job, a comfortable home, but most importantly, I want to be able to raise my family in a safe environment.

I am proud to be an American because of the freedom and opportunities I have enjoyed. My parents moved to this country from Mexico in order to enable my brothers and sisters and me to receive a quality education. I am proud of the fact that America has given me an appreciation of freedom, liberty, and democracy that I will be able to pass on to others.

IJEOMA OSUAGWU, TEXAS

To me, being an American means obtaining success through honest hard work and perseverance in a society that encourages anybody who offers their best. My American dream is to pursue a profession in law and to be an asset to the community at large. Through education, careful planning, wise choices, and hard work, I know I am more than capable of accomplishing my goal.

As a female, I believe the social transition to working has been an important challenge for women. The biggest challenge for American women in the future will be balancing home life with work life.

Tracing Themes in United States History

The students whose responses you just read touched on several themes, including the promise of technology, the rights enjoyed by Americans, and the roles of women in the 21st century. As you study U.S. history, you will encounter these and other themes again and again. The Americans *focuses on ten themes, described on these pages. What do you think are the important issues raised by each theme?*

The American Dream

You live in a nation founded on dreams of freedom, opportunity, and progress. The most enduring of these visions is the American dream—the belief held by most Americans that if they work hard and play by the rules, then they and their children will be better off. But just what does "better off" mean? More money in the bank? A cleaner environment? That is something you and your generation will have to decide. (See **Tracing Themes** on page 280.)

NOW THEN **What American dreams do you observe people today pursuing?**

America in the World

From the earliest colonial times, the United States has been influenced by the events, people, and forms of government in other nations—and America has influenced world affairs. Today, relationships between the United States and other countries are more critical than ever, as modern communications and transportation have drawn the world closer together. As America continues to participate in world affairs, questions of trade, diplomacy, and regional conflict will grow in importance. (See **Tracing Themes** on page 368.)

NOW THEN **What do you think America's role should be in the world of the 21st century?**

Economic Opportunity

America has always been a land of economic opportunity. Blessed with fertile land and abundant resources, this has been a country where anyone who has worked hard has had a chance to prosper. Indeed, American history is full of heartening "rags-to-riches" success stories. Just as inspiring are the heroic struggles of women and minorities who fought to improve their economic prospects. As your generation enters the work force, you and your friends will have the opportunity to write your own success stories. (See **Tracing Themes** on page 446.)

NOW THEN **What do you think are the most exciting economic opportunities for Americans today?**

Science and Technology

Americans have always had a deep respect for the power of science and technology to improve life. In the past two centuries, new inventions, new technologies, and scientific breakthroughs have transformed the United States—and continue to appear at a dizzying pace. Which ones will change your life? You can be sure that some will, and in ways that no one can yet predict. (See **Tracing Themes** on page 594.)

NOW THEN **How do you think science and technology will change American life in the 21st century?**

Women in America

Half of all Americans are women. But only recently have their contributions and concerns found their way into history books. American women have helped shape the social and political history of every era. In their private roles as wives and mothers, they have strengthened families and raised America's children. In their more public roles as workers, reformers, and crusaders for equal rights, they have attacked the nation's worst social ills and challenged barriers to women's full participation in American life. (See **Tracing Themes** on page 66.)

NOW THEN **What do you think is the most important goal for American women today?**

Cultural Diversity

E Pluribus Unum—Out of Many, One. Pick up a dollar bill and you'll find this Latin motto on the Great Seal of the United States. From first settlement, this has been a land of many peoples, cultures, and faiths. This mixing of ethnic, racial, and religious groups has produced a rich and uniquely American culture. It has also led to competition and conflict. Today, the United States is more diverse than ever. The nation's motto still remains *E Pluribus Unum.* (See **Tracing Themes** on page 872.)

NOW THEN How do you think America today is enriched by its diversity?

Immigration and Migration

Restlessness seems to be part of the national character of Americans. This country was first settled by and has remained a magnet for immigrants. One out of every eleven people living in the United States today was born in another country. Moreover, every year one out of every six Americans moves to a new address. (See **Tracing Themes** on page 422.)

NOW THEN Why do you think people continue to have the dream of immigrating to the United States?

Constitutional Concerns

The United States Constitution consists of the basic principles on which the government of the United States was established in 1789. Since then, these principles have been tested and argued about endlessly. Some 10,000 amendments have been proposed to the Constitution in efforts to improve it. Remarkably, only 27 have been adopted. Constitutional amendments continue to be proposed, so stay tuned. The work of constitution making is far from over! (See **Tracing Themes** on page 174.)

NOW THEN If you could add one amendment to the Constitution, what would it be? Why?

Democracy in America

When Americans first began their experiment with democracy, only white men with property could vote or hold office. Over the past two centuries, women, African Americans, and other groups have fought for and won the right to vote and participate in government. Today the challenge is getting people to exercise the right to vote. In 1996, only 49 percent of eligible voters cast ballots in the presidential election. (See **Tracing Themes** on page 108.)

NOW THEN What do you think can be done to bring more Americans into the democratic process?

Civil Rights

The American system of government is based on a simple but revolutionary idea: Every citizen has certain rights and liberties. Among them are the right to participate in government and to exercise such liberties as freedom of speech and worship. Deciding who should have what rights, how these rights should be exercised, and how to protect a person's civil rights is anything but easy. Defining and protecting our civil rights is not likely to get any easier. (See **Tracing Themes** on page 718.)

NOW THEN What issue of civil rights do you think is most critical in the United States today?

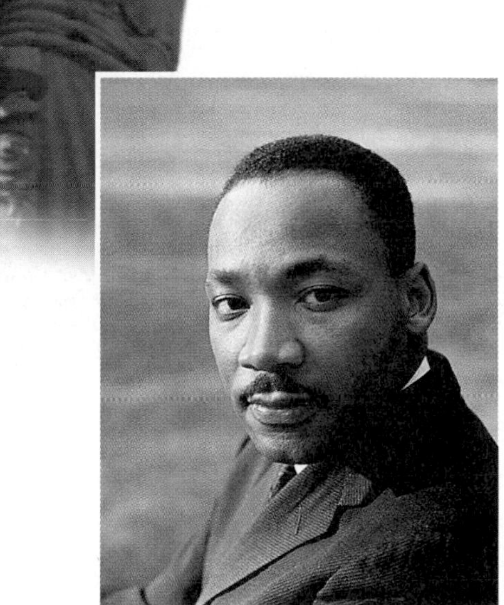

History shapes people, and people shape history. Just as surely, the land—where it lies and what it looks like—shapes the people, and the people in turn shape the land. This shaping process is the subject matter of geography. Paying attention to the following themes of geography can help you recognize when geographic forces are at work in the story of the United States.

These themes can also help you understand how you and people you know have been affected by your geographic surroundings.

Location

Location is fundamental. Geographers speak of absolute location—the latitude and longitude of an area—and of relative location—where an area is in relation to another area.

In absolute terms, the city of San Francisco lies at 37°45' north latitude and 122°25' west longitude. This information allows you to pinpoint San Francisco on a map. In relative terms, San Francisco lies at the western edge of the huge landmass of North America and looks out across the vast Pacific Ocean. This information helps explain San Francisco's history as an area where people and ideas have come together.

NOW THEN **Locate your city or town on both a political and a physical map. How has location influenced the history of your city or town?**

Place

Place, in geography, refers to what an area looks like, in both physical and human terms. The physical setting of an area—its landforms, soil, climate, and resources—are aspects of place. So are the numbers and cultures of the people who inhabit an area.

San Francisco's site at the tip of a hilly peninsula provides a natural harbor that has made the city an important international port. It is connected to the American River—where gold was discovered in 1848—by other rivers, which made it a boom town in the mid-1800s. Its position along a major fault line has subjected it to periodic earthquakes, the most disastrous in 1906.

During its history, San Francisco has attracted people from within North America as well as from Europe, Asia, and various Pacific islands, making it one of the most diverse cities in the United States.

NOW THEN **What is unique about the place where you live and the people who live there? What past events contributed to its uniqueness?**

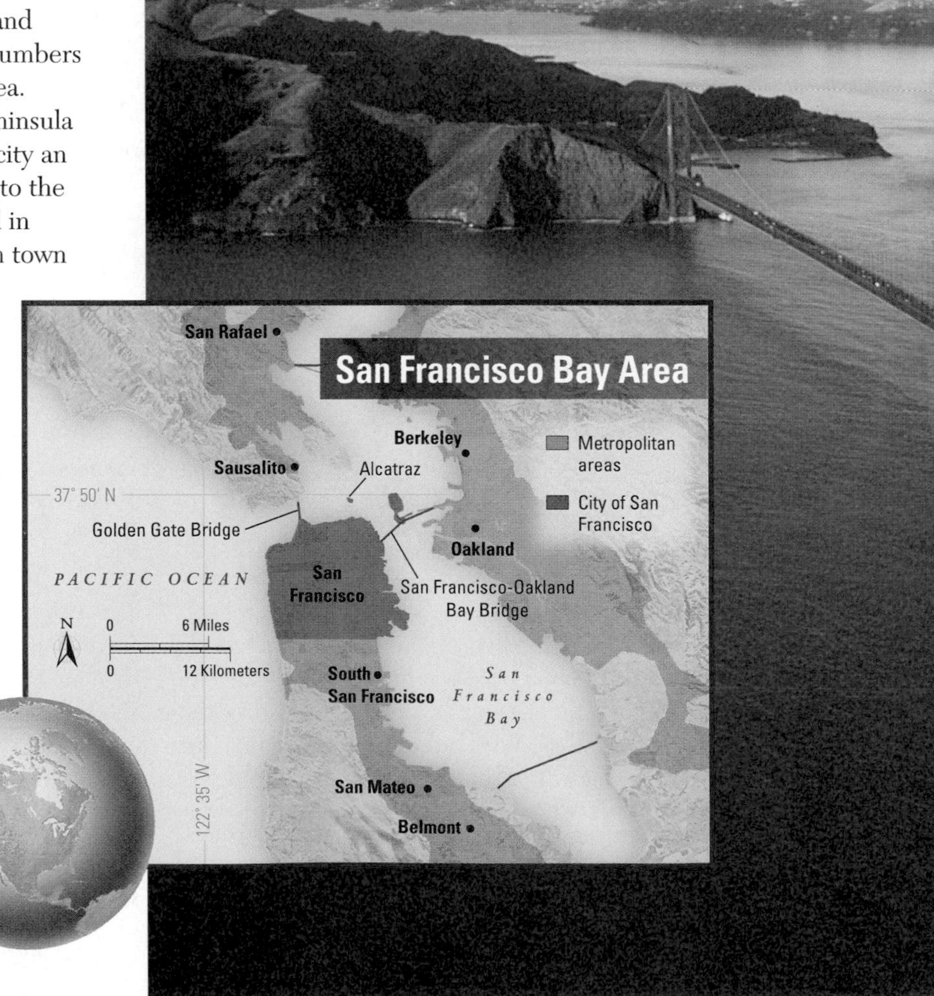

Region

Geographers use the idea of region as a way of summarizing the characteristics that different places have in common. Regions can be small or large, and a place can belong to more than one region.

As a part of the Pacific Coast region of the United States, San Francisco shares with cities like Seattle, Washington, and Portland, Oregon, a mild, rainy climate and an economic interest in international shipping. As a part of California, San Francisco shares concerns about the economic and environmental health of the state as a whole.

NOW THEN **To what region or regions does your area belong? How have the characteristics and concerns of your region changed over the last generation?**

Movement

One place or region can influence another even when the distance between them is great. Geographers seek evidence of this influence in the movement of people, raw materials, manufactured goods, and even ideas. Over time, patterns of movement can provide clues to an area's past or hints about its future.

San Francisco has been the site of many important movements of people and cultures. It has been a port of entry for immigrants, many of them Asian. It also lies along the path that Spanish missionaries trod in their quest to convert California's native peoples. The movements of these and other groups into San Francisco have helped to make the area what it is today.

NOW THEN **When and by what groups was your area settled? What trends in movement can you see today that may shape the future of your area?**

Human-Environment Interaction

Wherever people live, especially in large numbers, they affect the environment in the way they modify—and add to—their natural surroundings. They build shelters to defend against extremes of climate. They clear trees to create farmland. They turn the earth inside out to extract its resources.

People in the San Francisco Bay area have built bridges in order to move more easily from one point to another. And, over time, people have modified the bay itself, reducing its area by about one-third as they filled in tidelands for development.

NOW THEN **How have people in your area modified their surroundings? What consequences might these modifications have for your area in the future?**

REVIEW UNIT 1

American Beginnings to 1877

"The true foundation of republican government is the equal right of every citizen."
THOMAS JEFFERSON

Discussing the Quotation

Jefferson says that equality is universal. But as many Americans have known, that was not true in 1787: "When the Constitution . . . was completed, . . . I was not included in that 'We the People.' . . . But through . . . amendment, interpretation, and court decision, I finally have been included." Barbara Jordan, African-American member of Congress

FOR DISCUSSION:

- What does Jefferson mean by "equal rights"?
- Why does Jordan say she was "not included" in the Constitution?
- How did the Constitution itself make it possible for equal rights to become available to more people?

Discussing the Art

Stearns makes Washington the main figure in four ways. His natural height (over six feet) is enhanced by placing him on a dais. His presence alone seems to balance the majority of the figures on the left side of the painting. Finally, the papers he holds are presumably the Constitution itself.

FOR DISCUSSION:

- Why was Washington a good subject for patriotic painting at a time of rising sectional tensions?
- How does the image show the inequality that Jordan describes in her quotation?

4 The people

Some delegates are talking, but most are intent on listening to Washington. Though he is off to one side, he is clearly the focal point of the painting.

5 Abraham Baldwin

Abraham Baldwin of Georgia helped draft the Great Compromise of the Constitution. The compromise created two houses of Congress to settle the dispute between small states and large states over state representation in the national legislature.

6 George Washington

Washington played a vital role at the convention, more in his presence alone than in his actions as presiding officer. Many delegates were concerned about the power of the new federal government. Confidence in Washington's judgment and the assumption that he would be the first president helped ease much of this concern.

REVIEW CHAPTER 1

PLANNING GUIDE

Exploration and the Colonial Era

	Key Ideas	COPYMASTERS	ASSESSMENT
SECTION 1 **The Americas, West Africa, and Europe** *pp. 4–13*	*Long before the founding of the United States, the ancestors of its early inhabitants live in diverse societies in North America, Africa, and Europe.*	***In-Depth Resources: Unit 1*** • Guided Reading, p. 9 • Skillbuilder Practice: Interpreting Maps, p. 13 • Primary Source: *from* The Iroquois Constitution, p. 20 ***Lesson Plans,*** pp. 1–2	PE ***Section 1 Assessment,*** p. 13 TE ***Self-Assessment,*** p. 13 ***Formal Assessment*** • Section Quiz, p. 5 ***Alternative Assessment Book*** • Standards for Evaluating a Cooperative Activity
SECTION 2 **Spanish North America** *pp. 14–21*	*Following Columbus's voyage in 1492, Europeans explore North, Central, and South America, and Spanish conquistadores claim an empire for Spain.*	***In-Depth Resources: Unit 1*** • Guided Reading, p. 10 • Skillbuilder Practice, p. 14 • Outline Map, p. 18 • Primary Source: from *The Journal of Christopher Columbus*, p. 21 • Literature: from *The Memoirs of Christopher Columbus* by Stephen Marlowe, p. 25 ***Lesson Plans,*** pp. 3–4	PE ***Section 2 Assessment,*** p. 21 TE ***Self-Assessment,*** p. 21 ***Formal Assessment*** • Section Quiz, p. 6 ***Alternative Assessment Book*** • Standards for Evaluating a Cooperative Activity
SECTION 3 **Early British Colonies** *pp. 22–32*	*English settlers overcome hardship to found colonies in North America where they can survive economically and express their religious and moral ideals.*	***In-Depth Resources: Unit 1*** • Guided Reading, p. 11 • Primary Source: from *Travels and Works of Captain John Smith*, p. 23 • American Lives: John Winthrop, p. 28 ***Lesson Plans,*** pp. 5–6	PE ***Section 3 Assessment,*** p. 32 TE ***Self-Assessment,*** p. 32 ***Formal Assessment*** • Section Quiz, p. 7 ***Alternative Assessment Book*** • Standards for Evaluating a Cooperative Activity
SECTION 4 **The Colonies Come of Age** *pp. 33–41*	*A thriving agricultural economy in the South and a commercial economy in the North help England and its colonies prosper, although colonists begin to question British authority. Britain defeats France for dominance in the New World.*	***In-Depth Resources: Unit 1*** • Guided Reading, p. 12 • Skillbuider Practice: Visual Sources, p. 15 • Geography Application: The Triangular Trade, p. 16 • Primary Source: from *The Autobiography* by Benjamin Franklin, p. 24 • American Lives: Olaudah Equiano, p. 29 ***Lesson Plans,*** pp. 7–8	PE ***Section 4 Assessment,*** p. 41 TE ***Self-Assessment,*** p. 41 ***Formal Assessment*** • Section Quiz, p. 8 ***Alternative Assessment Book*** • Standards for Evaluating a Cooperative Activity
CHAPTER RESOURCES	**Chapter Overview** *Native Americans develop complex societies. Starting in 1492, Europeans and then Africans bring their cultures to the New World. British colonies thrive, and Britain dominates North America after defeating France at war.*	***In-Depth Resources: Unit 1*** • Living History Project: Worksheet, p. 30; Standards, p. 31 ***Telescoping the Times*** • Chapter Summary, pp. 1–2 ***Planning for Block Schedules***	PE ***Chapter Assessment,*** pp. 44–45 PE ***Alternative Assessment,*** p. 45 ***Formal Assessment*** • Chapter Test, forms A and B, pp. 9–14 ***Test Generator*** ***Alternative Assessment Book*** See explanation and forms for different kinds of alternative assessments including portfolio assessment.

KEY
PE Pupil's Edition
TE Teacher's Edition
http://www.mlushistory.com

TECHNOLOGY

Warm-Up Transparency 1
Humanities Transparencies
- H2, Ritual Cache Figures

Critical Thinking Transparencies
- CT35, Inventions, 1190–1500

Grolier Multimedia Encyclopedia
Electronic Library of Primary Sources
- "Portuguese-African Slave Trade"

INTERNET Pueblo and West Africa

Warm-Up Transparency 1
Humanities Transparencies
- H1, Map of North America
- H3, Indians Giving Cortés a Necklace

Geography Transparencies
- G1, Discovery and Exploration

Critical Thinking Transparencies
- CT1, Exploration of the Americas

Electronic Library of Primary Sources
- *from* "A Letter" by Columbus
- from *La Relación*

INTERNET Christopher Columbus

Warm-Up Transparency 1
Geography Transparencies
- G2, The European Colonies, 1650
- G35, Original Thirteen Colonies

Critical Thinking Transparencies
- CT2, Puritan Migration
- CT36, American Colonies

Grolier Multimedia Encyclopedia
Electronic Library of Primary Sources
- "The First Supply" by John Smith
- from *The Book of General Laws*

INTERNET Massachusetts Bay Colony and the Quakers

Warm-Up Transparency 1
Humanities Transparencies
- H4, Women Working in an Onion Field

Geography Transparencies
- G3, Colonial Economies

Critical Thinking Transparencies
- CT37, Africans in the Colonies
- CT3, French and Indian War

Grolier Multimedia Encyclopedia
Electronic Library of Primary Sources
- from *Olaudah Equiano*
- "Relations with the Indians"
- from "How Our Cities Looked"

INTERNET Colonies and slave trade

American Portfolio: A Videodisc for U.S. History, user's guide, pp. 1–10, 12–28, 32
Chapter Summary Audiotapes
- Unit 1, Chapter 1

INTERNET http://www.mlushistory.com

Block Scheduling (90 MINUTES)

Day 1
Section 1, pp. 4–13
Section 2, pp. 14–21
Section Assessments, pp. 13, 21

COOPERATIVE ACTIVITIES
- Mapping Native American Cultures, p. 6 (TE)
- Planning an Itinerary, p. 9 (TE)
- Designing Storyboards, p. 15 (TE)
- Mapping Corn Production, p. 17 (TE)
- Writing About Popé's Rebellion, p. 20 (TE)

Day 2
Section 3, pp. 22–32
Section 4, pp. 33–41
Geography Spotlight: Jamestown Settlement, pp. 24–25
Daily Life: Colonial Courtship, pp. 42–43
Section Assessments, pp. 32, 41
Chapter Assessment, pp. 44–45

COOPERATIVE ACTIVITIES
- Investigating Puritan Life, p. 26
- Mapping Colonial Economic Activities, p. 31 (TE)
- Annotated Maps, p. 39 (TE)

YEARLY PACING *Chapter 1 Total:* 2 days *Yearly Total:* 85 days

See *Planning for Block Schedules* for special activities and pacing strategies.

Customizing for Special Populations

Students Acquiring English
Access for Students Acquiring English: Spanish Translations
- Guided Reading for Sections 1–4, pp. 13–16
- Chapter Summary, pp. 11–12
- Skillbuilder Practice: Interpreting Maps, p. 17; Developing Historical Perspectives, p. 18; Visual Sources, p. 19
- Geography Application: The Triangular Trade, p. 20
- Outline Map: Spain Explores North America, p. 22

Spanish Reading Study Guide, pp. 5–14
Translations of Chapter Summaries, Hmong, Cantonese, Vietnamese, and Cambodian

Chapter Summary Audiotapes in Spanish Unit 1, Chapter 1

INTERNET The Diverse Classroom

Gifted and Talented Students
In-Depth Resources: Unit 1
- Primary Sources: *from* The Iroquois Constitution, p. 20; from *The Journal of Christopher Columbus,* p. 21; from *Travels and Works of Captain John Smith,* p. 23; from *The Autobiography* by Benjamin Franklin, p. 24
- American Lives: John Winthrop, p. 28; Olaudah Equiano, p. 29

Less Proficient Readers
In-Depth Resources: Unit 1
- Guided Reading for Sections 1–4, pp. 9–12
- Skillbuilder Practice: Interpreting Maps, p. 13; Developing Historical Perspective, p. 14; Visual Sources, p. 15
- Geography Application: The Triangular Trade, p. 16
- Outline Map: Spain Explores North America, p. 18

Reading Study Guide
- pp. 5–14

Telescoping the Times
- Chapter Summary, pp. 1–2

Chapter Summary Audiotapes, Unit 1, Chapter 1

Connections to Literature READINGS FOR STUDENTS

In-Depth Resources: Unit 1
- **from *The Memoirs of Christopher Columbus: A Novel* by Stephen Marlowe,** p. 25

Enrichment Reading
- **Michael Dorris**
  The Crown of Columbus.
  New York: HarperCollins, 1991.
  In this novel an anthropologist finds a lost diary of Columbus and embarks on a quest for the truth about the great explorer.
- **Jessamyn West**
  Massacre at Fall Creek.
  New York: Harcourt, 1975.
  In the early 1800s, five men are charged with murdering several Native Americans. This novel follows their trials.

McDougal Littell *The Language of Literature* American Literature
- **William Bradford, from *Of Plymouth Plantation,*** p. 88
- **Alicia Crane Williams, *Women and Children First: The Mayflower Pilgrims,*** p. 96
- **Salem Court, The Examination of Sarah Good,** p. 154

McDougal Littell *Literature Connections*

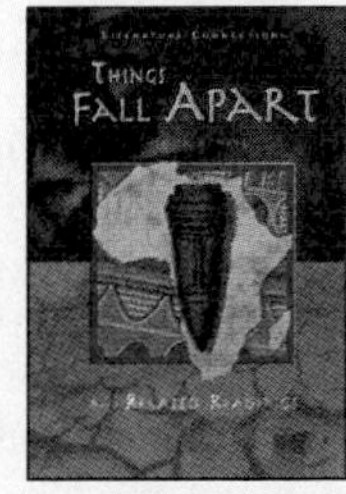

- **Chinua Achebe, *Things Fall Apart*** *(with related readings) Contact with outside forces brings deep changes to a traditional community.*

REVIEW
CHAPTER
1

OVERVIEW

Exploration and the Colonial Era

▶ *Accessing Prior Knowledge*

Ask students what reasons they or their families would have to move to another state or community.

Discuss the effects such a move would have on them.

▶ *Predicting Outcomes*

Have students study the art and time line on pages 2–3 and tell what peoples lived in the Americas by 1763. Then ask students what they think might happen as a result of these people coming together.

REVIEW CHAPTER 1

Exploration and the Colonial Era

SECTION 1

The Americas, West Africa, and Europe

Long before the founding of the United States, the ancestors of its early inhabitants live in diverse societies in North America, Africa, and Europe.

SECTION 2

Spanish North America

Following Columbus's voyage in 1492, Europeans explore North, Central, and South America, and Spanish conquistadores claim an empire for Spain.

SECTION 3

Early British Colonies

English settlers overcome hardship to found colonies in North America where they can survive economically and express their religious and moral ideals.

SECTION 4

The Colonies Come of Age

A thriving agricultural economy in the South and a commercial economy in the North help England and its colonies prosper, although colonists begin to question British authority. Britain defeats France for dominance in the New World.

"Here individuals of all nations are melted into a new race . . . whose labors and posterity will one day cause great change in the world."

Michel Guillaume Jean de Crèvecoeur

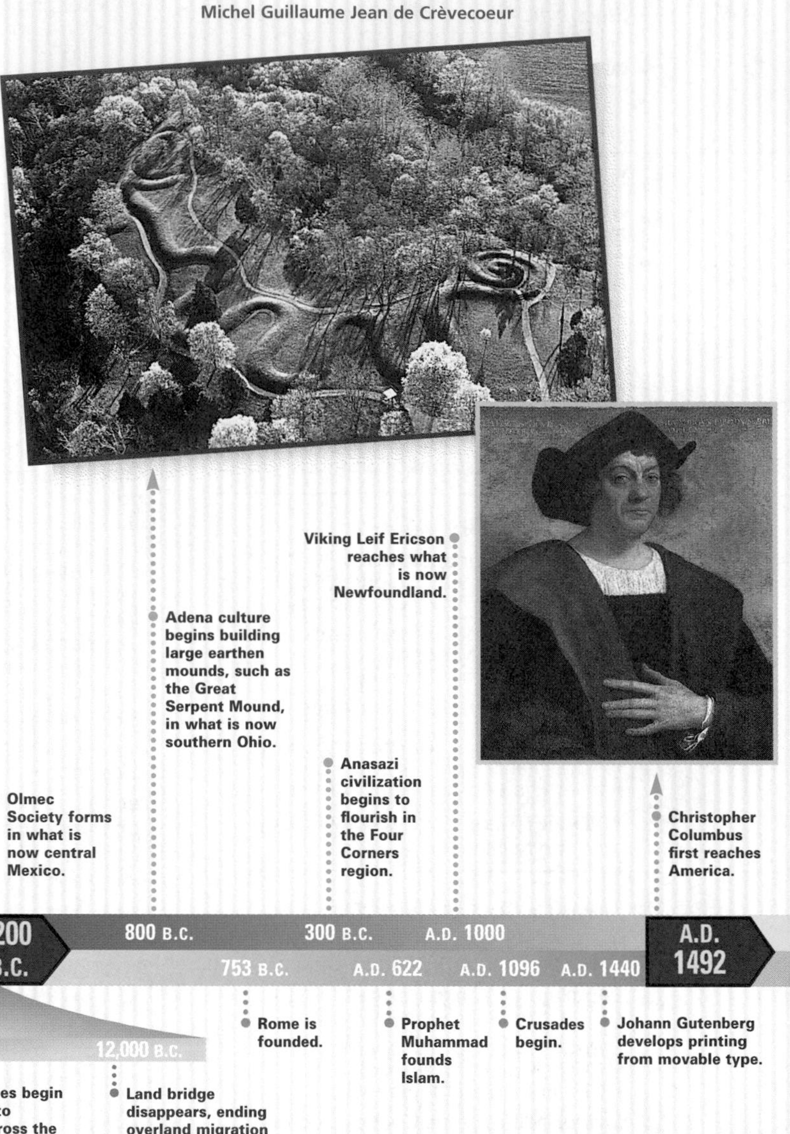

THE AMERICAS
THE WORLD
38,000 B.C.
Asian peoples begin to migrate to America across the Beringia land bridge.
12,000 B.C.
Land bridge disappears, ending overland migration from Asia.
1200 B.C.
Olmec Society forms in what is now central Mexico.
800 B.C.
Adena culture begins building large earthen mounds, such as the Great Serpent Mound, in what is now southern Ohio.
753 B.C.
Rome is founded.
300 B.C.
Anasazi civilization begins to flourish in the Four Corners region.
A.D. 622
Prophet Muhammad founds Islam.
A.D. 1000
Viking Leif Ericson reaches what is now Newfoundland.
A.D. 1096
Crusades begin.
A.D. 1440
Johann Gutenberg develops printing from movable type.
A.D. 1492
Christopher Columbus first reaches America.

THEMES IN CHAPTER 1

Immigration and Migration	*Science and Technology*	*Cultural Diversity*	*Democracy in America*
Everyone in the United States has ancestors who originally came from somewhere else. All eras in U.S. history have been shaped by the movement of peoples across America in search of opportunity.	New war technology gave European monarchs the tools to forge powerful nations. New maritime technology propelled these nations to sea. Later, the Enlightenment spread from Europe to the Americas, bringing with it a belief in reason and science that prompted many inventions and discoveries.	European exploration led to the meeting of many diverse cultures in America. Drawn to North America from many countries, for many reasons, settlers carved out diverse colonies. An influx of European immigrants and African slaves made the thirteen colonies a cultural mosaic.	English settlers who traveled to the Americas carried their political traditions and ideals with them. Dissenters such as Roger Williams and Anne Hutchinson, and visionaries such as William Penn introduced freedoms unknown in Europe, such as religious tolerance and expanded suffrage.
See Teacher's Edition notes, pp. 5, 16, 23, 27.	See Teacher's Edition notes, pp. 12, 37.	See Teacher's Edition notes, pp. 8, 29, 36.	See Teacher's Edition note, p. 28.

LIVING HISTORY

WRITING A COLONIZATION TALE

Many stories have been written about people who start new colonies—in outer space, on imaginary islands, and on unexplored continents. Write your own first-person story of a colony, set in the present day or in the past. It can be in the form of a short story, a ballad, or a comic book.

As you tell the tale, be sure to explain the reasons you left your home, who went with you, what provisions you took, how you traveled, where you settled, and the problems you faced on the journey and once you arrived. Create a map or a diagram of your settlement showing important features of the landscape and of the colony.

PORTFOLIO PROJECT Save your tale in a folder for your American history portfolio. You will revise and share your work at the end of the chapter.

- 1494 — Treaty of Tordesillas defines Portuguese and Spanish claims in the Western Hemisphere.
- 1500 — Iroquois League is formed.
- 1521 — Hernán Cortés conquers the Aztec Empire.
- 1588 — England defeats the Spanish Armada.
- 1591 — Songhai empire falls to Moroccan invaders.
- 1607 — English settlers establish Jamestown.
- 1630 — Puritans found the Massachusetts Bay Colony.
- 1649 — Charles I is beheaded; Puritan leader Oliver Cromwell assumes power in England.
- 1651 — English Parliament passes the first Navigation Act.
- 1660 — English monarchy is restored.
- 1675 — King Philip's War begins.
- 1687 — Issac Newton publishes theories of motion and gravitation.
- 1707 — Act of Union unites England and Wales with Scotland to form Great Britain.
- 1732 — Benjamin Franklin publishes *Poor Richard's Almanack.*
- 1754 — French and Indian War begins.
- 1756 — Olaudah Equiano arrives as a slave in the West Indies.
- 1763 — Treaty of Paris ends the French and Indian War.
- 1763 — Treaty of Paris recognizes British control over much of India.

ALTERNATIVE ASSESSMENT

LIVING HISTORY

WRITING A COLONIZATION TALE

Discuss ways to go about writing the tale:

- Brainstorm possible topics for colonization tales. Ask students to mention stories they think would be good models.
- Discuss possible approaches for developing the tales. Would a short story work, or would a comic book be better?
- Discuss the importance of using descriptive details to create a vivid picture of their colony.
- Discuss the importance of telling a story that includes a beginning, a middle, and an end.

Project Planning Guide

Step 1	Students choose the topic for their colonization tale.
Step 2	Students brainstorm details.
Step 3	Students write a draft of their tale.
Step 4	Students revise and edit their tale and prepare a final copy.

IN-DEPTH RESOURCES: UNIT 1
See worksheet and standards for evaluation, pp. 30, 31.

RECOMMENDED RESOURCES

Books for the Teacher

Davidson, Basil. *The Lost Cities of Africa.* Boston: Little, 1987.

Hofstadter, Richard. *America at 1750.* New York: Vintage, 1973.

Jennings, Francis. *The Founders of America.* New York: Norton, 1993.

Miller, John. *Life in Colonial America.* New York: Dell, 1966.

Weber, David J. *The Spanish Frontier in North America.* New Haven: Yale, 1992.

Books for the Student

Bennett, Jr., Lerone. *Before the Mayflower: A History of Black America.* New York: Penguin, 1984.

Fuentes, Carlos. *The Buried Mirror.* Boston: Houghton, 1992. Spain's influence in the New World.

Scott, John Anthony. *The British Colonies in North America, 1607–1750.* New York: Fact on File, 1992.

Foner, Eric, ed. *Nat Turner.* Englewood Cliffs, NJ: Prentice-Hall, 1971.

Videos

Great Explorers. National Geographic, 1978. Filmstrip. Columbus, Magellan, Drake, Cook.

Life in a California Mission. AIMS Media, 800-367-2467. Mission daily life.

Colonial Economy. CRM Films, 800-421-0833. Analyzes colonial economy.

Los colonos ingleses. Films for the Humanities & Sciences, 800-257-3767. English colonies—narrated in Spanish.

Benjamin Franklin: Citizen-Sage of a New Age. American Lifestyle Series. Laserdisc. AIMS Media, 1980.

Software

Columbus: Day by Day. CD-ROM. Educational Software Institute, 800-955-5570.

The Native Americans. CD-ROM. Philips Media Software, 800-883-3767.

Section 1 Overview

OBJECTIVES

1. To describe the ancient cultures in the Americas.
2. To identify the diverse Native American groups in North America.
3. To describe West African societies of the 1400s.
4. To understand European societies of the 1400s and the forces that led them to undertake exploration.

SKILLBUILDERS

- Understanding geography: region, p. 7
- Interpreting charts, p. 13

CRITICAL THINKING

- Theme: Immigration and Migration, p. 4
- Recognizing effects, pp. 5, 11
- Finding main ideas, p. 5
- Contrasting, p. 6
- Making predictions, p. 7
- Forming generalizations, p. 9
- Making inferences, pp. 10, 13
- Analyzing motives, p. 13
- Summarizing, p. 13
- Analyzing, p. 13

FOCUS & MOTIVATE

5-MINUTE WARM-UP

Making Inferences
To gain insight into the diverse cultures in the Americas, have students look at the images on pages 5–7 and answer these questions.

1. What do the pictures show?
2. Based on these images, how would you describe the civilizations that lived in the Americas at that time?

WARM-UP TRANSPARENCY 1

▶ ***Starting with the Student***
Have students read One American's Story on page 4 to learn how one woman helped preserve the knowledge and customs of her Native American culture. Ask students to describe traditions, memories, or family stories they would like to preserve for future generations.

1 The Americas, West Africa, and Europe

LEARN ABOUT ancient American, Native American, West African, and European societies
TO UNDERSTAND the diverse cultures that came to make up American society.

TERMS & NAMES
- Aztec
- Anasazi
- Pueblo
- Iroquois
- Songhai
- Benin
- Kongo
- Islam
- Reformation
- joint-stock company

ONE AMERICAN'S STORY

As a storyteller and medicine woman for the Kashaya Pomo, a Native American tribe, Essie Parrish kept alive a time when her people flourished along the Sonoma coast of northern California. One day in 1958, she invited Robert Oswalt, an anthropologist at the University of California, to join her on a journey back to the 1540s.

A PERSONAL VOICE

In the old days, before the white people came up here, there was a boat sailing on the ocean from the south. Because before that . . . [the Kashaya Pomo] had never seen a boat, they said, "Our world must be coming to an end. Couldn't we do something? This big bird floating on the ocean is from somewhere, probably from up high. . . ." [T]hey promised Our Father [a feast,] saying that destruction was upon them.

When they had done so, they watched [the ship] sail way up north and disappear. . . . They were saying that nothing had happened to them—the big bird person had sailed northward without doing anything—because of the promise of a feast. . . . Consequently they held a feast and a big dance.

ESSIE PARRISH, quoted in *Kashaya Texts*

By the 1950s, the Kashaya Pomo population was declining and Parrish feared that stories like this one might be lost. Parrish, Oswalt, and other researchers worked to produce a broad picture of the Native American world before it was changed forever by the arrival of Europeans and West Africans.

In this chapter, you will learn about three complex societies that met in North America in the late 1400s: the European, the West African, and the Native American. However, it is with the ancient peoples of the Americas that the story truly begins. Through the work of archaeologists, Americans today are able to see what it might have been like to live among those very first immigrants to the Americas.

Essie Parrish

Ancient Cultures in the Americas

Hunters roaming over 10,000 years ago in what is now southern Arizona used this large spear point to kill a woolly mammoth.

No one knows for sure when the first humans arrived in the Americas, but it may have been as long as 40,000 years ago. At that time, the glaciers of the last Ice Age had locked up huge amounts of the earth's water, lowering sea levels and creating a land bridge between Asia and Alaska across what is now the Bering Strait. Ancient people walked across the frozen strip called Beringia into North America, possibly following the animals they hunted for food. Some may have come down the Pacific coast in boats, which they made from the bones and hides of animals.

HUNTING AND GATHERING From the discovery of flaked spearheads and charred bones at ancient sites, archaeologists have inferred that the earliest Americans lived as big-game hunters. The woolly mammoth was their most challenging and rewarding prey. Weighing over a ton, the mammoth provided food, skins for clothing, and bones for making shelter and tools.

Around 12,000 to 10,000 years ago, temperatures warmed, glaciers melted, and sea levels once again rose. As the Ice Age ended, the land bridge disappeared under the Bering Sea, bringing to an end land travel between the Asian

THINK THROUGH HISTORY
A. THEME ***Immigration and Migration*** *The United States has been called a nation of immigrants. In what ways does its earliest human history support that description?*

A. Answer The very first Americans came from Asia across the Beringia land bridge. All Americans, including those called Native Americans, had their origins on other continents.

SECTION 1 RESOURCES

PRINT RESOURCES

IN-DEPTH RESOURCES: UNIT 1
Guided Reading, p. 9
Skillbuilder Practice: Interpreting Maps, p. 13
Primary Source: *from* The Iroquois Constitution, p. 20

READING STUDY GUIDE, p. 5

ACCESS FOR STUDENTS ACQUIRING ENGLISH
Guided Reading (Spanish), p. 13
Skillbuilder Practice: Interpreting Maps (Spanish), p. 17

SPANISH READING STUDY GUIDE, p. 5

FORMAL ASSESSMENT
Section Quiz, p. 5

ALTERNATIVE ASSESSMENT BOOK
See forms for supporting and scoring alternative activities.

TECHNOLOGY RESOURCES

HUMANITIES TRANSPARENCIES
H2, Ritual Cache Figures

CRITICAL THINKING TRANSPARENCIES
CT35, Inventions, 1190–1500

CD-ROM Electronic Library of Primary Sources
Grolier Multimedia Encyclopedia

VIDEO *American Portfolio: A Videodisc for U.S. History* user's guide, pp. 1–10, 12

INTERNET http://www.mlushistory.com

and North American continents. As the climate grew warmer, the large animals no longer thrived. People gradually switched to hunting smaller game and gathering nuts, wild rice, chokecherries, gooseberries, and currants. They invented snares—and later, bows and arrows—to hunt game such as deer and jackrabbits. They wove nets to fish the streams and lakes.

AGRICULTURE DEVELOPS While many ancient groups settled in North America, others continued south into what is now Mexico and South America. Between 10,000 and 5,000 years ago, an agricultural revolution quietly took place in what is now central Mexico. There, people began to raise plants as food. Some archaeologists believe that maize, or corn, was one of the first plants to be domesticated, that is, cultivated for human use. Gourds, pumpkins, peppers, and beans followed. Eventually, agricultural techniques spread throughout the Americas.

THINK THROUGH HISTORY
B. *Recognizing Effects* *What were the effects of agriculture on the hunting and gathering people of the Americas?*

B. Answer Made it possible for people to stay in one place, accumulate and store food, and build larger, more stable societies and complex cultures.

MAYA, AZTEC, AND INCA SOCIETIES FLOURISH The rise of agriculture made it possible for people to remain in one place and to accumulate and store surplus food. As their surplus increased, people had the time to develop skills and to advance complex ideas about the world. From this agricultural base, around 3,000 years ago, the Native Americans began to form larger communities and build flourishing civilizations.

Archaeologists believe that as early as 1200 B.C., in what is now southern Mexico, the Olmec people created a thriving civilization. Other civilizations appeared in the wake of the Olmec's mysterious collapse, around 400 B.C. These societies included the Maya, who built a dynamic culture in Guatemala and the Yucatán Peninsula between A.D. 250 and 900, and the **Aztecs,** who settled the Valley of Mexico in the 1200s. In South America, the most prominent empire builders were the Inca, who rose around A.D. 1400 to create a glittering empire that stretched nearly 2,500 miles along the mountainous western coast of South America.

COMPLEX SOCIETIES ARISE IN NORTH AMERICA In time, several North American groups, including the Hohokam and the **Anasazi,** introduced into the arid deserts of the Southwest such domesticated crops as corn, beans, and squash. Between 300 B.C. and A.D. 1400, each group had elaborated its own culture. The Hohokam settled in the valleys of the Salt and Gila rivers in what is now central Arizona, while the Anasazi took to the mesa tops, cliff sides, and canyon bottoms of the Four Corners region—the area where the present-day states of Utah, Colorado, Arizona, and New Mexico converge.

C. Answer They built complex societies that domesticated crops, built monumental structures, carried out trade, and worked with copper and stone.

THINK THROUGH HISTORY
C. *Finding Main Ideas* *What were some of the achievements of the first Americans?*

To the east of the Mississippi River, another series of complex societies developed—the Adena, the Hopewell, and the Mississippian. Originating around 800 B.C. and continuing one after the other into the 1500s, these societies excelled at trade and at building massive earthen structures, called mounds. Some Adena and Hopewell structures consisted of huge burial mounds filled with finely crafted copper ornaments and stone pipes. Other mounds bore likenesses of animals that can be seen clearly only from the air. The Mississippians, the last and most widespread of the Mound Builder societies, constructed gigantic pyramidal mounds.

These early peoples were the ancestors of the many and diverse Native American groups that inhabited North America on the eve of its encounter with the European world.

HISTORICAL SPOTLIGHT

THE "OTHER" PYRAMIDS

The stone pyramids of Egypt, which were used as elaborate tombs for Egyptian kings more than 4,000 years ago, are some of today's most recognizable structures. However, they were not the only pyramids to tower over the ancient world.

On the American side of the Atlantic, the Maya built giant flat-topped pyramids with stairs leading to rooftop temples, where Mayan priests performed religious ceremonies.

Farther north, at Cahokia in what is now Illinois, the Mississippian peoples constructed more than 100 massive earthen mounds, which served as tombs, temples, and foundations for elaborate homes. The largest of these mounds is Monk's Mound, which is 100 feet high and covers about 16 acres at its base—3 acres more than the largest pyramid in Egypt.

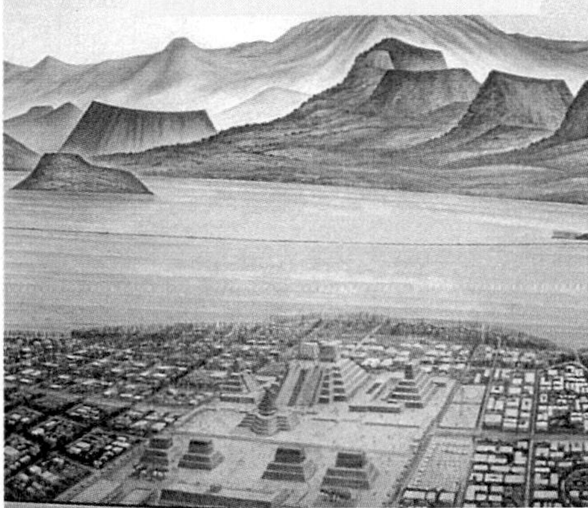

The Aztec capital, Tenochtitlán, featured a central pyramid and was surrounded by the waters of Lake Texcaco, which protected it like a moat.

OBJECTIVE
① INSTRUCT

Ancient Cultures in the Americas

▶ *Starting with the Student*
As students read about the different cultures in the Americas, have them create a chart listing each group and its characteristics.

Culture	Descriptions

▶ *Discussing Key Ideas*
- The first peoples may have come to the Americas 40,000 years ago.
- The cultural achievements in the Americas rival those of ancient cultures elsewhere in the world.

IN-DEPTH RESOURCES: UNIT 1
Guided Reading, p. 9

ACCESS FOR STUDENTS ACQUIRING ENGLISH
Guided Reading (Spanish), p. 13

HISTORICAL SPOTLIGHT
The "Other" Pyramids

Critical Thinking: Making Comparisons Refer students to the picture of pyramids built by the Aztecs on page 5. Based on information in the text, what reasons might explain the similarity between Aztec pyramids and those of other cultures in the Americas? *Possible Response: Trade might have brought the groups in contact with each other, promoting an exchange of ideas.*

TEACHING OPTIONS

Exploring Themes

Immigration and Migration Discuss with students the meaning of the words *immigration* and *migration.* *(Immigration is the act of moving to a region of which one is not a native. Migration is the act of moving from one area or region to another.)* Discuss the "push-pull" factors that have always compelled people to immigrate and migrate. *These factors include the need for food, the need for adventure, the wish to escape from or be united with family members, and the need for economic and employment opportunities. While many immigrants sought religious and political freedom, others suffered the complete loss of freedom through enslavement.*

Teaching Less Proficient Readers

Clarifying Ideas As they read Section 1, pages 4–13, have less proficient readers apply the five steps of the SQ3R study method:

1. ***Survey*** Skim paragraphs and topic headings and look over the map and the time lines.
2. ***Question*** Jot down any questions about the early peoples of the Americas, West Africa, and Europe.
3. ***Read*** Read pages 4–13, looking for answers to the questions.
4. ***Recite*** Discuss and record the answers found.
5. ***Review*** Review the information, checking for answers to any questions that remain.

OBJECTIVE

② INSTRUCT

Native American Societies of the 1400s

▶ ***Discussing Key Ideas***

- Native Americans adapt to and live in diverse physical settings.
- Trade links Native American peoples and promotes the sharing of ideas and cultures.
- Native Americans base their identity on a strong attachment to the land, which can be neither traded nor sold.

IN-DEPTH RESOURCES: UNIT 1
Primary Source: *from* The Iroquois Constitution, p. 20

NOW & THEN

Who Owns the Past?

Critical Thinking: Analyzing an Issue Call on students to state the central issue in the debate over preserving Native American artifacts and skeletal remains. What are the two main points of view on this issue? Ask students to suggest arguments in support of each point of view. Compare these arguments to identify the main areas of agreement and disagreement. What, if any, compromises can students suggest?

Native American Societies of the 1400s

The varied regions of the North American continent provided for many different styles of life. The native groups that populated the continent's coasts, deserts, and forests 500 years ago were as diverse as their surroundings.

CALIFORNIA AND THE NORTHWEST COAST The inhabitants of California adapted their lives to the region's varied physical settings. The Kashaya Pomo lived in marshlands along the central coast, hunting waterfowl with slingshots and nets. To the north of them, the Yurok and Hupa searched the forests for acorns and set up fish traps in mountain streams.

The waterways and forests of the Northwest Coast sustained large communities year-round. On a coastline that stretched from what is now southern Alaska to Oregon, groups such as the Kwakiutl, Nootka, and Haida collected shellfish from the beaches and hunted the ocean for whales, sea otters, and seals. Men, women, and children together harvested thousands of pounds of salmon as the fish swam upstream to spawn, or lay their eggs.

The Kwakiutl celebrated their abundance by carving and painting magnificent totems, or symbols of the ancestral spirits that guided each family. As a display of status, leading Kwakiutl families organized potlatches, elaborate ceremonies in which they gave away large quantities of their possessions. The family might spend up to 12 years preparing for such an event. The Kwakiutl believed that accounts balanced out over time, since the host of one potlatch would be a guest at many future ones.

WHO OWNS THE PAST?

The silent bones of the distant past have stirred a present-day controversy. In November of 1990, Congress passed the Native American Graves Protection and Repatriation Act to regulate the excavation of Native American burial sites. A provision of the act requires the return of skeletal remains and other artifacts to Native Americans who can prove they are culturally connected with the material.

This provision has sparked a debate. Some archaeologists claim that tribal remains should be dug up and made part of the nation's heritage. Native American groups contend the artifacts belong to their heritage and should stay either buried or with them. Other archaeologists have sided with Native Americans, saying that ancestral remains belong with their descendants and not in a museum.

THE SOUTHWEST In the dry Southwest, the **Pueblo** and Pima tribes, descendants of the Hohokam and Anasazi, lived in a harsher environment than the people of either California or the Northwest Coast. By 1300, the Pueblo and the related Hopi tribes had moved away from the cliff houses of their Anasazi ancestors. The Pueblo built new settlements near waterways such as the Rio Grande. The Hopi continued to live near the cliffs, collecting rainwater in rock cisterns to use for irrigation and cooking. Throughout the region, people lived in multistory houses made of adobe, coaxing corn, beans, melons, and squash from the sun-parched but fertile soil. In the manner of their ancestors, they built underground kivas, or ceremonial chambers, where the Pueblo men held religious ceremonies and councils.

EASTERN WOODLANDS Beneath the forest canopy of the Northeast, members of the **Iroquois** nation hunted game, such as wild turkeys, deer, and bear. Nuts, berries, and tree fruit ripened in the summer and fall. Fish filled the region's many lakes and rivers.

The tribes that lived in the Eastern woodlands built villages in forest clearings and blended agriculture with hunting and gathering. They traveled by foot over trails or by canoe over inland waterways. Most groups developed woodworking tools, such as stone axes, to craft everything from snowshoes to canoes. In the Northeast, where winters could be long and harsh, people relied heavily on wild animals for clothing and food. In the warmer Southeast, groups lived mainly off the land, growing such crops as corn, squash, and beans.

D. Answer Groups that lived along the coasts were able to rely on the ocean for their food; those in the Southwest relied mostly on crops; groups in the Eastern woodlands could hunt, fish, and gather food.

THINK THROUGH HISTORY
D. *Contrasting* *What ways did food production differ among the Native American societies?*

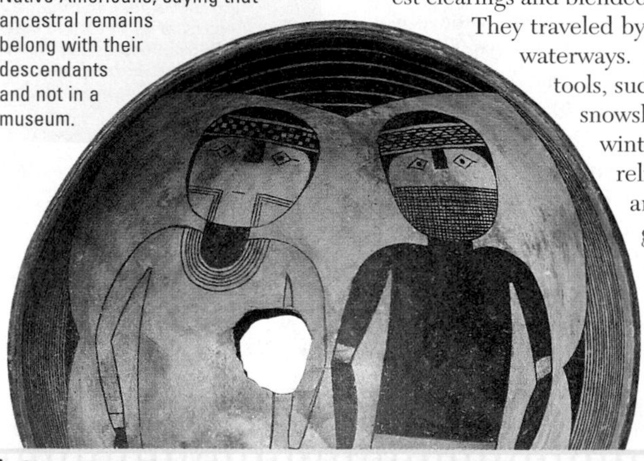

The Mogollon [mō´gə-yōn´] people of New Mexico placed bowls such as these in graves to accompany the dead. These offerings were ritually "killed" at burial to release their spirits, which accounts for the large hole in the center of this bowl.

Block Schedule TEACHING OPTION **Time Needed: 40 Minutes**

Cooperative Activity: Mapping Native American Cultures

Task: Groups of students will research the four Native American culture regions and create displays for each region.

Purpose: To help students understand how Native Americans created societies to fit the environments in which they lived.

Activity: Divide the class into four groups and assign one of the regions to each group. Have students research the cultural areas and write reports and develop visual displays for them. Make sure that groups research the geographical environments of the regions and tell how the different environments produced different kinds of cultural groups. Also have students include pictures of native arts and artifacts, myths, poems, or other materials.

Building a Portfolio: Students should write a note indicating their contribution to the report before adding it to their portfolio.

ALTERNATIVE ASSESSMENT BOOK
Standards for Evaluating a Cooperative Activity

Standards for Evaluation
Reports should . . .

- clearly describe the environments
- show how the environments and the cultures are related
- include specific examples, such as pictures or poems

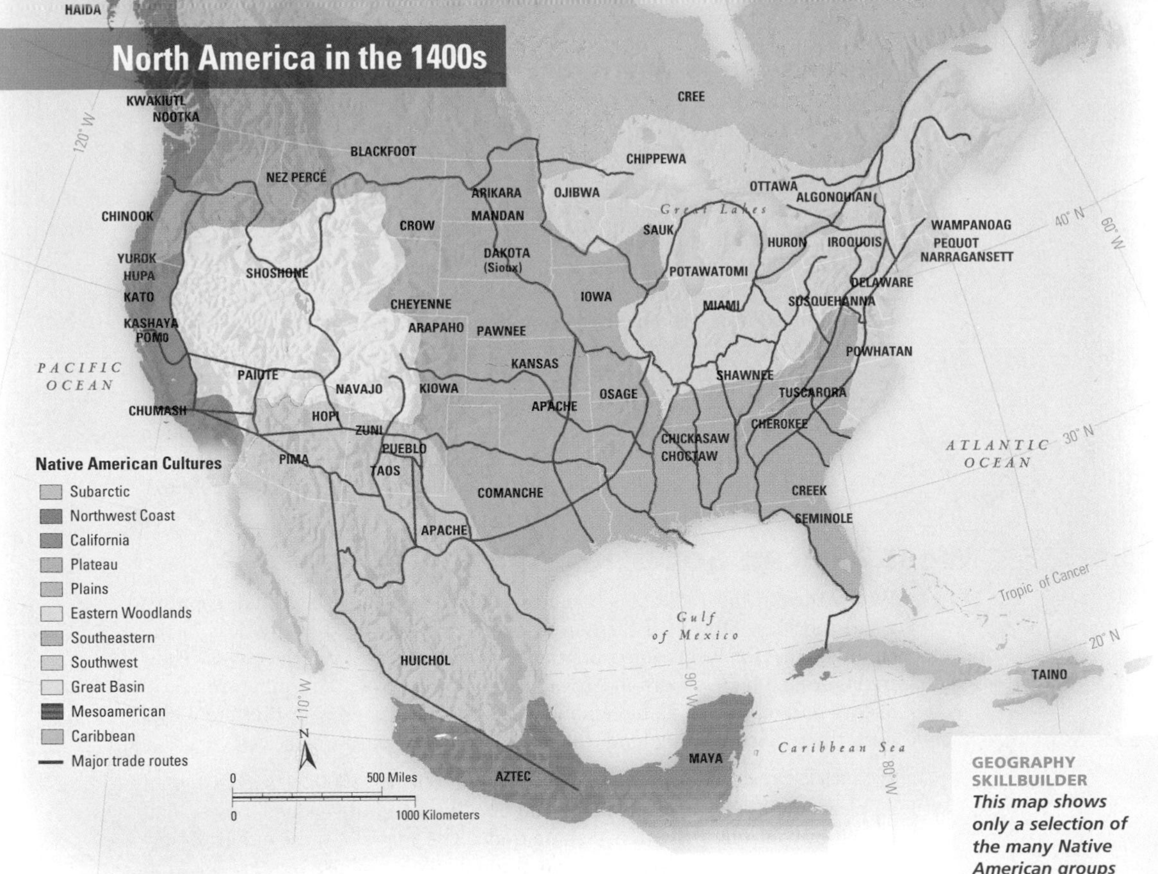

GEOGRAPHY SKILLBUILDER
This map shows only a selection of the many Native American groups and trade routes that existed in the 1400s. **REGION** *What groups lived in the Eastern woodlands cultural region?*

Skillbuilder Answer
Wampanoag, Pequot, Narragansett, Delaware, Powhatan, Susquehanna, Iroquois, Algonquian, Ottawa, Huron, Shawnee, Miami, Potawatomi, Sauk, Ojibwa, Chippewa

TRADING NETWORKS Many of the Native American cultures had in common certain patterns of trade, views of the land, religious beliefs, and social values. The tribes became known for specific products or skills. For instance, the Nootka of the Northwest Coast mastered whaling, the Ojibwa of the upper Great Lakes collected wild rice, and the Taos of the Southwest made pottery. These items, and many more, were traded both locally and over long distances. Trading centers flourished at points where two cultures came together. Traders received and passed along items from far-off places they had never even seen. So extensive was the network of forest trails and river roads that an English sailor named David Ingram claimed in 1568 to have walked along Native American trade routes all the way from Mexico to the Atlantic Coast.

E. Answer Students may say they will give away the land or refuse to deal in land, either one eventually resulting in clashes.

THINK THROUGH HISTORY
E. Making Predictions *Given the Native American view of the land, what response do you expect Native Americans will have when Europeans arrive and attempt to buy and sell land?*

VIEWS OF THE LAND Native Americans traded many things, but land was not one of them. They looked upon the land as the source of life, not as a commodity to be sold or bartered. "We cannot sell the lives of men and animals," said one Blackfoot chief in the 1800s, "therefore we cannot sell this land."

Native Americans altered the land as little as possible. A shaman, or priestess, of the Wintu of California expressed this age-old respect for the land as she spoke to the anthropologist Dorothy Lee.

A PERSONAL VOICE

When we dig roots we make little holes. When we build houses, we make little holes. . . . We shake down acorns and pinenuts. We don't chop down the trees. We use only dead wood [for fires]. But the White people plow up the ground, pull down the trees. . . . The tree says, "Don't. I am sore. Don't hurt me."

WINTU WOMAN, quoted in *Freedom and Culture*

A Kwakiutl artisan created this painted wooden animal mask to be worn in a religious ceremony.

HISTORY FROM VISUALS
North America in the 1400s

Reading the Map Explain to students that this map is a special-purpose map. A special-purpose map shows information about a topic, such as rainfall, temperatures, or population distribution. Ask: What is the special topic of this map? *Native American trade routes.*

Extension Tell students that historical fiction is designed to give an imaginative look into the past. It is part fact and part fiction. Assign students to write a two-page work of historical fiction in which they describe the travels of a Native American trader along one of the routes shown on the map.

MORE ABOUT . . .
The Power of Dreams

Native Americans throughout the Americas believed that spirits spoke to them in dreams and visions. One widespread vision preserved in the oral histories of Native Americans across the continents involved the coming of light-skinned strangers. A few, such as the Aztecs, believed the strangers were gods. Many others saw them as destroyers. Recalled one Wintu woman at the turn of the century, "My grandpa, before white people came, had a dream. . . . My grandpa say: 'White Rabbit'—he mean white people—'gonta devour our grass, our seed, our living. We won't have nothing.'"

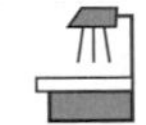

HUMANITIES TRANSPARENCIES
H2, Ritual Cache Figures

TEACHING OPTION

Skillbuilder Mini-Lesson: Interpreting Maps

Explaining the Skill Three useful tools for understanding maps are the legend, the compass rose, and the scale. The legend shows at a glance what each color or symbol represents. For example, on the map above, yellow indicates the Great Basin cultural region. The compass rose shows the map's orientation by pointing to the north, and the scale indicates how much actual distance is represented on the map. By measuring between two locations on the map and then comparing the measurement to the scale, readers can determine the actual distance between the two places. See Skillbuilder Handbook, pages 926–927.

Applying the Skill: North America in the 1400s

Ask students to point out the legend, compass rose, and scale on this map. Then ask the following questions:

1. What cultural region is southernmost on this map? *Mesoamerican*
2. What trade routes clearly went over water? *Great Lakes and from Florida to Cuba*
3. About how far, in miles, were the Blackfoot people from the Tuscarora? *About 1,700 miles*

IN-DEPTH RESOURCES: UNIT 1
Skillbuilder Practice: Interpreting Maps, p. 13

OBJECTIVE

③ **INSTRUCT**

West African Societies of the 1400s

▶ ***Discussing Key Ideas***

- The central governments of three West African kingdoms oversee empires based on trade and tribute.
- Most West Africans live in villages, where life centers on the extended family.
- Trade brings goods, ideas, and a major religion—Islam—to West Africa.
- Trade with Portugal opens new markets for African goods but also begins traffic in slaves.

MORE ABOUT . . .

West African Storytelling

In West Africa, the task of preserving a people's history was the role of the griots—a class of professional storytellers. Traditionally assigned to important families or rulers, griots spent years learning all the important facts about a people and memorizing them. In addition, they served as advisors, masters of ceremony, and official spokespersons.

The first enslaved Africans to arrive in the Americas carried this tradition of storytelling with them and used it as a way to keep alive their connections with the ancestral homeland.

RELIGIOUS BELIEFS AND SOCIAL ORGANIZATION Nearly all Native Americans thought of the natural world as filled with spiritual presences. Past generations remained alive for them as guides in the present. All objects—both living and nonliving—possessed voices that might be heard if one listened closely. Some cultures had one Supreme Being, variously called "Great Spirit," "Great Mystery," and "the Creative Power."

The basic unit of organization among all Native American groups was the family, defined broadly by most groups to include aunts, uncles, cousins, and other relatives. Some tribes organized the families into clans, or groups of families descended from a common ancestor. The groups broke into smaller bands for more efficient hunting but reassembled to celebrate important occasions.

In the late 1400s, on the eve of the first encounter with Europeans, the rhythms of Native American family life were well-established. All phases of a person's life—birth, marriage, and death—were guided by traditions that often went back hundreds or thousands of years. On the other side of the Atlantic, in West Africa, customs equally as old guided another diverse group of people.

West African Societies of the 1400s

West Africa in the 1400s was home to a variety of long-established, sophisticated societies. Most of the enslaved people brought to the Americas in the centuries that followed came from this region, especially from the coasts. Their traditions and beliefs, born in Africa, played a major role in forming American history and culture. Notable among West African societies in the late 1400s were three powerful kingdoms, the Songhai, Benin, and Kongo.

THE KINGDOM OF SONGHAI From about 600 to 1600, a succession of empires—first Ghana, then Mali, and finally **Songhai**—gained power and wealth by controlling the trans-Sahara trade. The rulers of these empires grew rich by taxing the goods that passed through their realms. In 1067 an Arab geographer in Spain, named Al Bakri, described the duties (import and export taxes) levied in Ghana.

A PERSONAL VOICE

For every donkey loaded with salt that enters the country, the king takes a duty of one golden dinar [about one-eighth ounce of gold], and two dinars from every one that leaves. From a load of copper the duty due to the king is five mithquals [also about one-eighth ounce of gold], and from a load of merchandise ten mithquals. . . . The [gold] nuggets found in all the mines . . . are reserved for the king, only gold dust being left for the people.

AL BAKRI, quoted in *Africa in the Days of Exploration*

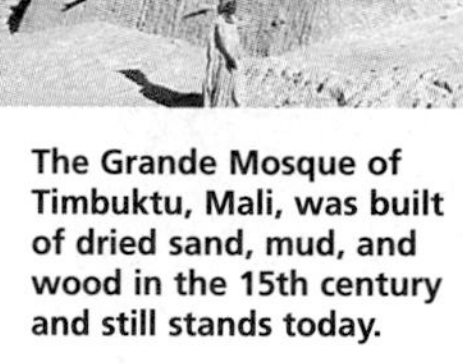

The Grande Mosque of Timbuktu, Mali, was built of dried sand, mud, and wood in the 15th century and still stands today.

With such wealth, the rulers who controlled the north-south trade routes could gather large armies and conquer new territory. They could also build cities, administer laws, and support the arts and education.

KINGDOMS OF BENIN AND KONGO At its height in the 1500s, Songhai's reach extended across much of West Africa. However, it did not control the forest kingdoms along the southern coast. Peoples such as the Akan, Ibo, Ewe, Edo, and Yoruba thrived there in the 1400s and 1500s. A brisk trade with Songhai and North Africa, and later with Portugal, helped the forest kingdoms grow. In the 1400s, one of these kingdoms, **Benin,** dominated a large region around the Niger Delta. Leading the expansion was a powerful oba, or ruler, named Ewuare, who developed Benin City.

TEACHING OPTIONS

Teaching Gifted and Talented Students

A Virtual Field Trip Request that students familiar with the Internet go to http://www.mlushistory.com. After accessing the web site, users should click on Social Studies and then follow the path to *The Americans* to explore the resources provided for Chapter 1. Ask students to choose one of the topic areas for further study. Among the possibilities might be the Iroquois, the spread of Islam, the Reformation, the Renaissance, the Christopher Columbus controversy, Plymouth, the Quaker religion, or Benjamin Franklin.

http://www.mlushistory.com

Exploring Themes

Cultural Diversity Discuss with students similarities and differences between the three representative West African kingdoms. What geographic factors helped to account for the different ways of life in Songhai and the forest kingdoms? Why, for example, did Islam fail to reach into Benin or Kongo? How did trade cause these diverse peoples to interact with each other? To build on this discussion, assign the cooperative activity suggested on page 9.

Within this great walled city, the oba headed a highly organized system of government; he appointed chiefs who governed the kingdom's districts. He controlled all trade in the kingdom, managed the development of industries such as goldsmithing and brass-smithing, and exchanged ambassadors with Portugal.

A thousand miles south, in western Central Africa, the powerful kingdom of **Kongo** arose on the lower Congo River. In the late 1400s, Kongo consisted of a series of small kingdoms organized under a single leader called the Manikongo, who lived in what is today Angola. The Manikongo, who could be either a man or a woman, held the smaller kingdoms together by a system of royal marriages, taxes, and, sometimes, war and tribute. By the 1470s, the Manikongo oversaw an empire estimated at over 4 million people.

An unknown Yoruba artist in the kingdom of Ife produced this bronze head of a king in the 1100s. The highly developed bronze artistry of Ife was handed down to the kingdom of Benin, which arose later in the same area.

The people of the Kongo, or Bakongo, mined, smelted, and worked iron ore into well-wrought tools and weapons. They turned the weaving of palm leaf threads into a fine art, producing a fabric like velvet. The Portuguese sailors who first reached Kongo in 1483 were struck by similarities between the Kongo and their own world. Its system of government—a collection of provinces centralized under one strong king—resembled that of most European nations at the time.

WEST AFRICAN CULTURE Within kingdoms or states, most people lived in small villages, where life revolved around family, the community, and tradition. Bonds of kinship—that is, ties among people of the same line of descent—formed the basis of most aspects of life. Some societies were matrilineal—that is, people traced their lineage through their mother's family.

Within a family, age determined rank. The oldest living descendant of the group's common ancestor exercised control over family members and also represented them in councils of the larger groups to which the family belonged. These larger groups shared a common language, a common past, and often, a common territory. One leader or chief might speak for the group as a whole, but this person rarely spoke without consulting a council of elders.

Political leaders from chiefs to kings claimed authority on the basis of religion. Religious rituals were central to the everyday activities of farmers, hunters, and fishers. Like Native Americans, West African people saw spiritual forces in both living and nonliving objects. They also gave great significance to the voices of departed ancestors who were thought to speak to the elders in dreams. Although West Africans might consult, through prayer and ritual, with a variety of ancestral spirits and lesser gods, most believed in a single Creator, and so had little trouble seeing why Christians and Muslims—followers of Islam—believed in a supreme God. However, the traditional cultures could not understand why Christian and Muslim conquerors insisted that West Africans give up worshipping spirits. Out of this difference grew many cultural conflicts.

Throughout West Africa, people supported themselves by farming, herding, hunting, fishing, and also by mining and trading. Almost all groups believed in collective ownership of land. Individuals farmed the land, but land returned to the family or village when not in use.

F. Answer Songhai, Benin, and Kongo all had strong centralized governments and powerful rulers; the ordinary people lived in rural villages, where their lives centered on the family and tradition.

THINK THROUGH HISTORY
F. *Forming Generalizations* *What did the kingdoms of West Africa have in common?*

TRADING PATTERNS WITH THE WIDER WORLD By the 1400s, West Africa had long been connected to the wider world through trade. The Songhai city of Timbuktu was the hub of a well-established trading network that connected nearly all of West Africa to the ports of North Africa, and through these ports to markets in Europe and Asia. Along trade routes across the Sahara, desert caravans carried goods from Mediterranean cities and salt from Saharan mines to exchange for gold, ivory, kola nuts, and dyed cotton cloth from the forest kingdoms to the south.

HISTORICAL SPOTLIGHT

ISLAM

The prophet Muhammad (about A.D. 570–632) worked as a merchant in Mecca, a trading city on the Arabian peninsula. When he was about 40, he believed the angel Gabriel appeared to him and told him to preach a new religion to the Arabs. This religion became known as Islam, which in Arabic means "surrender [to Allah]." (*Allah* is the Arabic word for God.) The followers of Islam are called Muslims, "those who submit to God's will."

The words that Muhammad received from God were recorded by his followers in the Qur'an, the holy book of Islam. The Qur'an teaches that "there is no God but Allah, and Muhammad is His Prophet." (Islam, like Judaism and Christianity, is monotheistic, or based on belief in one god.) The Qur'an also sets forth certain duties for righteous Muslims, including a series of daily prayers, the giving of charity, and a pilgrimage to the holy city of Mecca.

MORE ABOUT . . .
Mali

In 1324, Mansa Musa, the Muslim leader of Mali, took a pilgrimage to Mecca that left Europeans awestruck. Statistics from witnesses in Cairo, Egypt, dazzled listeners: the king's caravan consisted of 600,000 people, including 500 slaves—each armed with a six-pound gold staff—and 80 camels—each loaded with bags of gold dust weighing up to 100 pounds apiece.

The event literally put Mali on the maps of Europe. In 1377 a Spanish mapmaker drew a wall at the northern edge of the Sahara Desert. On the other side sat the Mali king luring Arab traders across the sands with a huge gold nugget.

ELECTRONIC LIBRARY OF PRIMARY SOURCES
On the Beginnings of the Portuguese-African Slave Trade by Gomes Eanes de Zurara

HISTORICAL SPOTLIGHT
Islam

Critical Thinking: Making Comparisons Ask students to begin a chart comparing three of the world's monotheistic religions: Christianity, Islam, and Buddhism. Suggest that they use the following headings to organize their research: Name of Supreme Being, Holy Book, Distinguishing Duties or Beliefs, Key Prophets or Founders, Approximate Age.

GROLIER MULTIMEDIA ENCYCLOPEDIA Islamic Art and Architecture

Block Schedule TEACHING OPTION **Time Needed: 40 Minutes**

Cooperative Activity: Planning an Itinerary

Task: Students will plan an itinerary for a merchant traveling from Tripoli to Timbuktu in about the year 1500.

Purpose: To help students understand the economic exchanges that fueled the growth of West African empires.

Activity: Assign groups of students to plan a North African trading expedition to Timbuktu. Students should determine a route, trade items carried to Timbuktu, trade items sought in Timbuktu, number of camels, estimated travel time, etc. (Helpful tip: Arabian camels can carry up to 100 pounds in weight. They travel about 4 miles per hour and can cover up to 47 miles a day.)

Building a Portfolio: Students who add the itineraries to their portfolios should attach notes pointing out aspects of the material they think are especially strong.

ALTERNATIVE ASSESSMENT BOOK
Standards for Evaluating a Cooperative Activity

Standards for Evaluation
Itineraries should . . .

- reflect routes and distances shown on a map
- include specific exchanges, such as those made at the Saharan salt mines
- use concrete details and lists of trade items

NOW & THEN
Kente Cloth

Critical Thinking: Analyzing a Quote Read aloud this quote by one African-American youth: "A lot of us are getting back to our culture, such as dressing in African materials. This gives us self-esteem and identity." Ask students to summarize the connection between African fabrics and African-American pride. Then assign the feature. Explore why kente cloth is especially valued by African Americans.

OBJECTIVE
④ INSTRUCT

European Societies of the 1400s

▶ ***Starting with the Student***

- To discuss the value of exploration, determine by a show of hands whether students would support an increase in taxes to pay for a costly U.S. mission into deep space.
- Have students share reasons they would support or oppose the exploration.

▶ ***Discussing Key Ideas***

- Europeans live in a hierarchical world that includes nobility, clergy, artisans, merchants, and peasants.
- The Roman Catholic Church is a major influence on the culture of western Europe.
- Monarchs consolidate their power and forge national identities.
- The Portuguese take the lead in using state-of-the-art navigation techniques to sail to Asia.

NOW & THEN

KENTE CLOTH

Today people of African descent all over the world value the multicolored fabric known as kente cloth as a symbol of Africa. For African Americans who choose to wear kente cloth or display it in their homes, the fabric serves as a tangible link to West African cultures from which their ancestors came.

Artisans of the Asante (Ashanti) people of modern Ghana have woven kente cloth for centuries. Working at looms, they produce long strips of cloth of complex designs and varying colors. These strips are then sewn together into a brilliant fabric that sparkles with reds, greens, blues, golds, and whatever other hues the weavers chose as dyes.

Along with goods, traders from North Africa also brought across the Sahara the Islamic faith, which gained increasing influence over savanna cultures. **Islam,** founded in Arabia in 622 by the prophet Muhammad, spread quickly across the Middle East and North Africa. By the 1200s, Islam had become the court religion of the large savanna empire of Mali, and it was later embraced by the rulers of Songhai. Despite its official status, however, Islam did not influence the daily lives and worship practices of many West Africans until after the 1400s.

THE PORTUGUESE Mariners from Portugal made trading contacts along the West African coast starting in the 1440s. In the 1480s, they claimed two uninhabited islands off the African coast where they established large sugar plantations. To work these plantations, which required much human labor, the Portuguese began importing enslaved people from the West African mainland.

These early contacts with Portuguese traders had two significant consequences for West Africa and the Americas. First, direct trade between the Portuguese and the coastal people of West Africa bypassed the routes across the Sahara and pulled the coastal region closer to Europe. Second, the Portuguese began the European trade in enslaved West Africans.

The success of these plantations created a model that eventually would be duplicated on a much vaster scale in the Americas. While slavery had been known in African societies, Africans were not born into slavery nor were they destined to remain slaves their entire lives. Conditions became different for Africans in the Americas. There a new kind of slavery emerged that continued from one generation to the next and was based on skin color.

European Societies of the 1400s

In the late 1400s, most Europeans, like most Native Americans and most Africans, lived in small villages, bound to the land and to rhythms of life that had been in place for centuries. For the majority of Europeans, change came slowly.

THE SOCIAL HIERARCHY European societies were hierarchical—arranged by order of rank or class. Monarchs and nobles, the landowning elite, held most of the wealth and power at the top of the hierarchy. The clergy were also high-ranking. Most people at the bottom of the social order were agricultural laborers, or peasants. A system of loyalties and responsibilities bound the various groups together. The nobility offered their peasants land and protection. In return, the peasants supplied nobles with livestock or crops—and with service in time of war.

Within the social structure, few individuals moved beyond the positions into which they were born. One group that did achieve mobility was the growing number of artisans and merchants, the people who crafted and sold goods for money. Although this group was relatively small in the 1400s, the profit they earned from sales would eventually make them a valuable source of tax revenue to monarchs seeking to finance costly overseas exploration and expansion.

G. Answer Power and wealth were concentrated in the hands of the nobles, monarchs, and church, with few opportunities for advancement offered peasants who needed to work hard simply to subsist.

THINK THROUGH HISTORY
G. Making Inferences *Why do you think few Europeans moved out of their original positions in the social hierarchy?*

CHRISTIANITY SHAPES THE EUROPEAN OUTLOOK The Roman Catholic Church was the dominant institution in western Europe. The leader of the church—the pope—and his bishops held great political as well as spiritual authority. It was the role of parish priests to convey the church's interpretation

TEACHING OPTIONS

Teaching Less Proficient Readers

Cause-and-Effect Chart Make sure students understand the meaning of cause and effect. (See the Skillbuilder Lesson on page 908.) Then use a graphic organizer like the one below to help students identify the causes and effects of the Crusades.

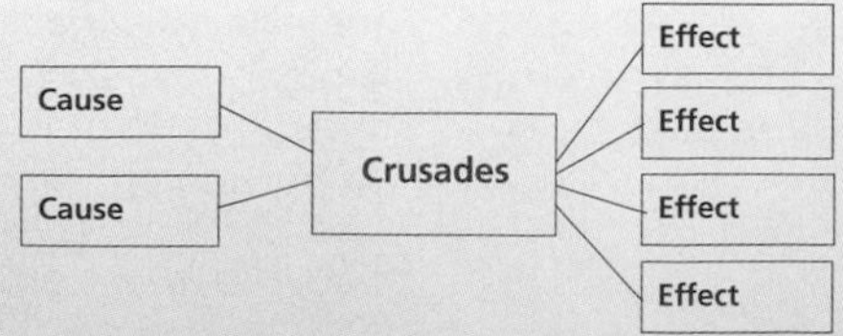

Teaching Gifted and Talented Students

Researching the Crusades Have interested students research the Crusades and compose reports and displays to present to the rest of the class. Several recent books that you might suggest are *The Oxford Illustrated History of the Crusades,* 1995, published by Oxford University Press; *Dungeon, Fire, and Sword: The Knights Templar in the Crusades* by John J. Robinson, 1991, published by M. Evans & Co.; *Holy War: The Crusades and Their Impact on Today's World* by Karen Armstrong, 1991, published by Doubleday. Suggest that students work together to decide who will focus on which topic, such as Christianity and Islam, knighthood, or trade, during this period.

of God's word to the people. Their message encouraged people to endure the hardships of life on earth with the promise of eternal life in heaven, or salvation.

Hand-in-hand with the belief in salvation was the call to convert people of other faiths to Christianity. The Bible encouraged Christians to "Go into all the world and preach the word to all creation." The emergence of Islam in the 600s posed a challenge. Within 100 years after the birth of Islam, Muslim armies had taken control of a region stretching from the Indus River to Morocco, and by 732, Muslims had conquered most of the Iberian Peninsula.

Christian armies from all over western Europe responded to the church's call to force the Muslims out of the Holy Land around Jerusalem. From 1096 to 1270, Europeans launched a series of military expeditions, or Crusades, to the Middle East under the banner of the Christian cross.

In the end, these bloody Crusades failed to "rescue" the Holy Land, but they had two consequences that would help push European society toward exploration and expansion. First, the Crusades sparked an increase in trade, as Europeans brought home with them a new taste for products from Asia. Second, the Crusades weakened the power of European nobles, many of whom lost their lives or fortunes in the wars. Monarchs eventually took advantage of the nobles' weakened ranks to consolidate their own power.

The failure of these campaigns reduced the prestige of the pope and contributed to a decline in the authority of the church. Many were eager for reforms. In the early 1500s, the desire for change led to a movement called the **Reformation,** which divided Christianity in western Europe into Catholicism and Protestantism. This split deepened the rivalries among European nations during the period of North American colonization 100 years later and sent some Protestants and some Catholics across the Atlantic to seek religious freedom.

THINK THROUGH HISTORY
H. Recognizing Effects *How did religious events in Europe help spur exploration and settlement of new lands?*

H. Answer The Crusades stimulated trade and increased the power of monarchs, who sponsored exploration; the Reformation created dissenting groups of Christians, some of whom sought religious freedom in North America.

Peasants tend to their fields outside the walls of a lavish castle near Paris, France. This illustration comes from *Les très riches heures,* a prayer book made for a French nobleman.

COMMERCE EXPANDS AND NATIONS ARISE The Crusades opened up Asian trade routes, supplying Europeans with luxuries from the east, especially spices such as cinnamon, cloves, nutmeg, and pepper. In those days European farmers slaughtered most of their pigs and cattle in late autumn and, in the absence of refrigeration, preserved the meat by packing it between layers of salt. Spices helped disguise the bad taste of the meat.

Two modern business institutions emerged in Italy at this time: international banking houses and corporations. International banks could transfer money and credit among business operations in different cities. Corporations emerged as **joint-stock companies,** in which numerous investors pooled their wealth. These companies financed many of the colonial expeditions to the Americas.

During the 1400s, Europe's population grew rapidly, stimulating prosperity and contributing to the expansion of commerce and the growth of towns. Population pressures would eventually lead some people to leave Europe for the new colonies in the Americas.

By the late 1400s, four major nations were taking shape in Europe: Portugal, Spain, France, and England. Ambitious kings and queens extended their reach by collecting new taxes, raising professional armies, and forming

HISTORY FROM VISUALS
The European Social Order

Viewing the Painting Ask students to notice that the image from Très riches heures can be studied as a primary source because it was created during the Middle Ages. It contains information about dress, dwellings, work, crops, and seasons. Have students summarize what they can learn from the image.

Extension This painting depicts the month of June. Have students find copies of the paintings depicting the other months in the prayer book and analyze those for information they contain. Then have them create a contemporary version of the book, showing activities from 12 months of the year.

MORE ABOUT . . .
Early Exploration

By the time Portuguese ships sailed down the west coast of Africa, the Chinese had already sailed well beyond their shores. By 1414, the Chinese explorer Zheng He had led a fleet of ships—the largest of which was 440 feet long—throughout the Indian Ocean. He and his crew reached ports in Indochina, Indonesia, and southeast India, and they would eventually reach the east coast of Africa. The Chinese are thought to have invented the first magnetic compass.

Block Schedule TEACHING OPTION **Time Needed: 30 Minutes**

Cooperative Activity: Advertising a Joint-Stock Company

Task: Students will create an advertisement luring investors to buy shares in a joint-stock company.

Purpose: To show how joint-stock companies spurred trade and colonization by reducing financial risks.

Activity: Assign students to design advertisements for investors in the Dutch East Indies Company—a joint-stock company set up to establish trading posts along the coast of Africa and on islands off India. The goal is to wrest part of the trade in spices and tea away from Italian merchants and from the Portuguese who have already carved footholds in the area.

Building a Portfolio: Suggest that students add a letter to their portfolio that begins, "This advertisement demonstrates knowledge of. . . ."

ALTERNATIVE ASSESSMENT BOOK
Standards for Evaluating a Cooperative Activity

Standards for Evaluation
Advertisements should . . .

- make clear the financial incentives offered by a joint-stock company
- state how investments will be used
- demonstrate a knowledge of persuasive techniques

KEY PLAYER
"King" Isabella

Critical Thinking: Summarizing Ask students to write an obituary summarizing Queen Isabella's accomplishments. Encourage them to analyze the role she played in the colonization of America. As a variation, students might present the obituary in the form of a poem entitled "A Woman's Place."

GROLIER MULTIMEDIA ENCYCLOPEDIA Queen Isabella I

MORE ABOUT . . .
Prince Henry the Navigator

Prince Henry may have been nicknamed the Navigator, but he rarely went exploring himself; instead, he planned and financed explorations. His own biggest adventure came at age 19, when he and his two brothers, hoping to prove themselves worthy of knighthood, led an armada and captured Ceuta, a Muslim stronghold on the African coast opposite Gibraltar.

Prince Henry required that his mariners keep accurate and detailed logs. They were expected to record all new geographical information on charts. Once they returned to port, their information was combined with data Henry collected from other travelers, including Marco Polo. Gradually the science of mapmaking benefited from the accumulated details of many voyages of discovery.

CRITICAL THINKING TRANSPARENCIES
CT35, Inventions, 1190–1500

KEY PLAYER

"KING" ISABELLA
1451–1504

Queen Isabella, who played a central role in European exploration by sponsoring Christopher Columbus's voyages to the Americas, made her mark on the Old World as well. As co-ruler of Spain, Isabella actively participated in her country's religious and military affairs.

In championing Spain's Catholicism, the queen often fought openly with the pope to make sure that her candidates were appointed to positions in the Spanish church. In addition, Isabella had tasted battle far more than most rulers, either male or female. The queen rode among her troops in full armor, personally commanding them in Ferdinand's absence. Whenever Isabella appeared on a horse, her troops shouted, "Castile, Castile, for our King Isabella!"

stronger central governments. Among their new allies were the merchants, who willingly paid taxes in exchange for the protection and expansion of trade.

Beginning in the 1300s, monarchs invested some of their tax revenues in new weapons—such as longbows and cannons—which they used to limit the power of the independent nobles. These new weapons, along with the hand-held firearms that were developed in the 1400s, also gave them military advantages over the Africans and Native Americans whom they later encountered.

These monarchs had powerful motives to finance the search for new lands and trading routes: they needed money to maintain their standing armies and large bureaucracies. By the mid-1400s, Europe's gold and silver mines were running low. So the monarchs of Portugal, Spain, France, and England began looking overseas for wealth.

THE RENAISSANCE SPIRIT TAKES HOLD "Thank God it has been permitted to us to be born in this new age, so full of hope and promise," exclaimed Matteo Palmieri, a scholar in 15th-century Italy. Palmieri's enthusiasm captured the spirit of the Renaissance, a term meaning "rebirth." Started in Italy, a region stimulated by commercial contact with Asia and Africa, the Renaissance soon spread to the rest of Europe. European scholars rediscovered the texts of ancient philosophers, mathematicians, geographers, and scientists. They also investigated Islamic scholarly works which had been carried home from the Crusades.

Renaissance painters, sculptors, writers, and architects created works of lasting influence, sometimes based on classical models. This was the time of Italian artists Leonardo da Vinci, Michelangelo, and Raphael. Although their themes were still often religious in nature, Renaissance artists tended to portray their subjects more realistically than earlier artists, using new techniques such as perspective. Leonardo, exploring to find out how things worked, kept notebooks in which he made detailed drawings of human anatomy and of his inventions, including a flying machine. This energetic spirit of inquiry infected the early explorers and adventurers who, like Christopher Columbus, came from the Renaissance culture. The Renaissance encouraged people to think of themselves as individuals, to have confidence in what they might achieve, and to look forward to the fame their achievements might bring.

The spread of the Renaissance was advanced by Johann Gutenberg's introduction of printing from movable type in the 1450s. This development made books easier and cheaper to produce, allowing larger numbers of people to own and read them. The first book to be mass-produced was Gutenberg's edition of the Bible. Other works soon followed, among them the travel stories of Marco Polo.

EUROPE ENTERS A NEW AGE OF EXPANSION The European interest in overseas expansion probably began in the 1200s with the journey of Marco Polo to China. With the printing of Polo's vivid—and sometimes exaggerated—account in 1477, the East came alive in European minds. Polo had traveled to Asia by overland routes, undertaking a long and dangerous journey. The expense and peril of such routes led Europeans to seek alternatives. In the 1400s, Europeans used the work of Ptolemy, a second-century scholar, and of Arab and Jewish scholars to revive the art of cartography, or mapmaking. Although imperfect, the new maps inspired Europeans to start exploring for water routes to Asia.

TEACHING OPTIONS

Exploring Themes

Science and Technology Point out that technological advances often bring about great social changes, both positive and negative. Then have students, individually or in groups, find technological advances mentioned in this section—the use of firearms, the invention of printing from movable type, the use of new navigational instruments, and the design of the caravel. Have students make a chart in which they assess the changes that each of these inventions brought to Europe. As a final question, ask: How did these inventions help push Europe into an age of expansion?

Making Connections Across Time

From Printing Press to Computer Explore how the printing press created a "knowledge revolution" in the 1400s and 1500s. Do students think the computer has created a comparable knowledge explosion today? Challenge students familiar with the Internet to go to http://www.mlushistory.com to explore some of today's access to information. Students should click on Social Studies and then find *The Americans,* Chapter 1. As students explore the many resources related to our understanding of history in the Americas, ask what they most enjoy about the experience. What concerns them?

http://www.mlushistory.com

The Caravel

The caravel, the ship used by most early Portuguese and Spanish explorers, had many advantages over earlier vessels. It was lighter, swifter, and more maneuverable than other ships.

1 The triangular lateen sails, an innovation borrowed from Muslim sailors, allowed the caravel to sail efficiently against the wind. Rigged with lateens, the ship could tack (sail on a zigzag course) more directly into the wind than could a square-rigged ship.

2 The sternpost rudder made the caravel highly maneuverable.

3 The shallow draft made the ship ideal for exploration close to shore.

4 The large hold was capable of carrying the considerable cargo needed for long voyages.

SKILLBUILDER
INTERPRETING CHARTS
How did the lateen sail differ from earlier sails? How was this a major advantage?

Skillbuilder Answer **Sails:** The lateen sail was triangular instead of square. **Advantage:** *Possible Answer:* It gave the caravel the advantage of sailing in almost any direction, as opposed to having wind direction determine where the ship could go.

SAILING TECHNOLOGY IMPROVES European ship captains in the 1400s experimented with the compass and the astrolabe, navigating tools that helped sailors plot direction at sea. They also took advantage of innovations in sailing ships that allowed them to sail against the wind.

One leader in developing and employing these innovations was Prince Henry the Navigator of Portugal, who established a school to train mariners and sponsored early voyages. According to a contemporary chronicler, Gomes Eanes de Zurara, his driving motivation was the need to know.

> A PERSONAL VOICE
> The noble spirit of this Prince . . . was ever urging him both to begin and to carry out very great deeds. . . . He had also a wish to know the land that lay beyond the isles of Canary and that Cape called Bojador. . . . It seemed to him that if he or some other lord did not endeavor to gain that knowledge, no mariners or merchants would ever dare to attempt it.
>
> GOMES EANES DE ZURARA, *The Chronicle of the Discovery and Conquest of Guinea*

"The best ships that sailed the seas . . ."

ALVISE DA CADAMOSTO, OF THE CARAVEL

I. Answer To increase their knowledge of the world and to boost trading profits by finding a water route to Asia.

THINK THROUGH HISTORY
I. Analyzing Motives *What were Portugal's motives in exploring the African coast?*

For almost 40 years, Prince Henry sent his captains sailing south along the west coast of Africa. Exploration continued after the prince's death, with Bartolomeu Dias rounding the southern tip of Africa in 1488 and Vasco da Gama reaching India ten years later. By sailing around Africa to eastern Asia via the Indian Ocean, Portuguese traders were able to cut their costs and increase their profits.

As cartographers redrew their maps to show this eastern route to Asia, an Italian sea captain named Christopher Columbus believed there was an even shorter route—one that headed west across the Atlantic.

Section 1 Assessment

1. TERMS & NAMES
Identify:
- Aztec
- Anasazi
- Pueblo
- Iroquois
- Songhai
- Benin
- Kongo
- Islam
- Reformation
- joint-stock company

2. SUMMARIZING Recreate the tree diagram below on your paper. Fill it in with an example of how a Native American society adapted to the environment of each region shown.

Environmental Adaptation
- Northwest Coast example:
- California example:
- Southwest example:
- Eastern Woodlands example:

3. ANALYZING What factors do you think contributed to the thriving trade system that flourished in West Africa? Use evidence from the text to support your response.

THINK ABOUT
- geographic location and features
- the kinds of goods exchanged
- the societies that emerged in West Africa

4. MAKING INFERENCES Why do you think other European nations lagged behind Portugal in the race for overseas exploration? Support your reasons with details from the text.

THINK ABOUT
- the geography of Portugal
- the power of monarchs in the 1400s
- the economic and political situation of European nations during this time

ANSWERS

1. TERMS & NAMES
- Aztec, p. 5
- Anasazi, p. 5
- Pueblo, p. 6
- Iroquois, p. 6
- Songhai, p. 8
- Benin, p. 8
- Kongo, p. 9
- Islam, p. 10
- Reformation, p. 11
- joint-stock company, p. 11

2. SUMMARIZING
Possible Responses: **Northwest Coast:** The Kwakiutl adapted to coast and ocean—collected shellfish; hunted whales, otters, and seals. **California:** The Kayasha Pomo adapted to marshlands—snared waterfowl. **Southwest:** The Pueblo adapted to arid climate—lived in adobe houses; grew corn, beans, melons, and squash. **Eastern Woodlands:** The Iroquois adapted to woodlands—hunted wild game.

3. ANALYZING
Possible Responses: The Songhai city of Timbuktu was located just south of the Sahara where it funneled goods coming across the desert from Europe and North Africa; the Niger River was a natural pathway for trade between Songhai and Benin; Benin, on the coast, was well situated to develop trade with Portugal; Europeans wanted African goods, such as gold, ivory, kola nuts, and cotton; Portuguese wanted African slaves for their offshore plantations; the sophisticated societies of West Africa were well organized and governed.

4. MAKING INFERENCES
Possible Responses: Portugal was along the Atlantic Ocean. Other European nations did not yet have adequate funds, trained mariners, innovative sailing ships, or a leader such as Prince Henry.

HISTORY FROM VISUALS
The Caravel

Reading the Diagram Be sure students know the meaning of words such as *lateen, sternpost, rudder, draft,* and *hold* as they read the diagram.

Extension Have students write a short essay or poem explaining how the caravel proved the old adage "Bigger is not always better."

ASSESS & RETEACH

Section 1 Assessment
Have students work together to answer the questions. Tell them to note the locations of the answers in the text.

Self-Assessment
Have students complete these two sentences:

I thought the history of our nation began with _____.

Now I think that it should begin with _____ because _____.

Section Quiz
FORMAL ASSESSMENT
Section Quiz, p. 5

Reteach
Use the images of the Aztec capital (p. 5), the Native American trade routes (p. 7), the mosque (p. 8), the peasants (p. 11), and the caravel (p. 13) to review the main ideas of the section.

CLOSE

Commercial expansion led to competition among nations and made monarchs more willing to finance overseas ventures. Christopher Columbus took advantage of these rivalries to win support for a voyage that changed the course of world history.

Section 2 Overview

1. To describe Spanish exploration of the Americas and its effects on Native Americans, Africans, and Europeans.
2. To describe the pattern of conquest that the Spanish used to subdue Native American peoples.
3. To summarize the goals of Spanish explorers and settlers who pushed into what is now the United States and to understand why Native Americans resisted.

SKILLBUILDERS

- Understanding geography: movement, place, p. 15
- Understanding geography: human-environment interaction, p. 17

CRITICAL THINKING

- Summarizing, pp. 15, 21
- Analyzing causes, p. 16
- Forming opinions, p. 18
- Contrasting, p. 19
- Theme: Cultural Diversity, p. 21
- Making inferences, p. 21
- Analyzing effects, p. 21
- Finding main ideas, p. 21

FOCUS & MOTIVATE

5-MINUTE WARM-UP

Interpreting Maps
To learn about exploration in the Americas, have students study the map on page 15 and answer these questions.

1. What countries were involved in the exploration of the Americas between 1492 and 1682?
2. What part of the Americas was explored by the French?

WARM-UP TRANSPARENCY 1

▶ ***Starting with the Student***
Ask students to imagine how it would feel to venture into the unknown, where there are no accounts from someone who has gone before, no maps, and no assurance of ever coming back.

2 Spanish North America

LEARN ABOUT Columbus's transatlantic voyages and the Spanish conquests of Central and North America
TO UNDERSTAND how these encounters permanently affected the lives of Africans, Europeans, and Native Americans.

TERMS & NAMES
- **Christopher Columbus**
- **Taino**
- **Treaty of Tordesillas**
- **Columbian Exchange**
- **conquistador**
- **Hernán Cortés**
- **New Spain**
- **mestizo**
- ***encomienda***
- **New Mexico**

ONE EUROPEAN'S STORY

In January 1492, the Genoese mariner **Christopher Columbus** stood before the Spanish court with what was at the time a wild dream: he would find a route to Asia by sailing west across the Atlantic Ocean. While Queen Isabella was intrigued by the plan, her advisers were less enthusiastic, because of the great distances involved, and she turned him away.

Influential people in the Spanish court spoke on his behalf, however, and their arguments finally won the Crown's support. On August 3, 1492, Columbus embarked on a journey destined to change the course of world history. A seeker of fame and fortune, he began his journal by restating the deal he had struck with Spain.

Christopher Columbus

A PERSONAL VOICE
Based on the information that I had given Your Highnesses about the land of India and about a Prince who is called the Great Khan [of China] . . . Your Highnesses decided to send me . . . to the regions of India, to see . . . the peoples and the lands, and to learn of . . . the measures which could be taken for their conversion to our Holy Faith. . . . I was to go by way of the west, whence until today we do not know with certainty that anyone has gone.
CHRISTOPHER COLUMBUS, *The Log of Christopher Columbus*

Columbus did not really reach Asia. He stepped onto an island he thought was off the coast of Asia but was actually in the Caribbean Sea. Instead of finding the Great Khan, he set in motion a process that brought together the American, European, and African worlds.

Columbus Crosses the Atlantic

Columbus's small fleet of ships, the *Niña*, the *Pinta*, and the *Santa María*, sailed out of a Spanish port in the predawn hours of August 3, 1492. At about 2 A.M. on October 12, 1492, a lookout aboard the *Pinta* caught sight of white sand dunes sparkling in the moonlight. "Tierra! Tierra!" he shouted. "Land! Land!"

At dawn Columbus went ashore where he encountered a group of people who would become known as the **Taino,** from their word for "noble ones." He planted Spanish banners and renamed their island San Salvador ("Holy Savior"), claiming it for Spain. When he did not find gold on San Salvador, he left to look elsewhere. Columbus spent 96 days exploring four coral islands in the Bahamas and the coastlines of two larger Caribbean islands, known today as Cuba and Hispaniola. Along the way, he claimed lands and bestowed names. "It was my wish to bypass no island without taking possession," wrote the captain. Nor did he wish to neglect his promise to spread Christianity. "In every place I have entered, islands and lands, I have always planted a cross," he noted on November 16.

Convinced that he had landed on islands off Asia, known to Europeans as the Indies, Columbus called the people he met *los indios.* Thus the name *Indian* came to be mistakenly applied to all the diverse peoples of the Americas.

SECTION 2 RESOURCES

PRINT RESOURCES

IN-DEPTH RESOURCES: UNIT 1
Guided Reading, p. 10
Skillbuilder Practice: Developing Historical Perspective, p. 14
Outline Map: Spain Explores North America, p. 18
Primary Source: from *The Journal of Christopher Columbus,* p. 21
Literature: from *The Memoirs of Christopher Columbus,* p. 25

READING STUDY GUIDE, p. 6

ACCESS FOR STUDENTS ACQUIRING ENGLISH
Guided Reading (Spanish), p. 14
Skillbuilder Practice (Spanish), p. 18
Outline Map: Spain Explores North America (Spanish), p. 22

SPANISH READING STUDY GUIDE, p. 6

FORMAL ASSESSMENT Section Quiz, p. 6

ALTERNATIVE ASSESSMENT BOOK
See forms for supporting and scoring alternative activities.

TECHNOLOGY RESOURCES

HUMANITIES TRANSPARENCIES
H1, Map of North America
H3, Indians Giving Cortés a Necklace

GEOGRAPHY TRANSPARENCIES
G1, Voyages of Discovery and Exploration

CRITICAL THINKING TRANSPARENCIES
CT1, Exploration of the Americas

CD-ROM Electronic Library of Primary Sources

VIDEO *American Portfolio: A Videodisc for U.S. History* user's guide, pp. 12–16

INTERNET http://www.mlushistory.com

THINK THROUGH HISTORY
A. *Summarizing* *What were the main activities that Columbus undertook after arriving in the Americas?*

A. Answer He claimed lands for Spain, renamed them, searched for gold, and attempted to spread Christianity among the Taino.

The Spanish monarchs were thrilled with Columbus's discoveries and funded three more voyages. Departing again for the Americas in September 1493, Columbus was no longer an explorer but an empire builder. He commanded a fleet of 17 ships and several hundred soldiers armed with cannons, crossbows, and swords. He also oversaw 5 priests and more than 1,000 colonists ready to settle the land.

THE IMPACT ON NATIVE AMERICANS By the time Columbus set sail for his return to Hispaniola in 1493, Europeans had already developed a pattern for colonization in the Old World, that is, the establishment of settlements under the control of a parent country. In these settlements, they had glimpsed the profitability of the plantation system, realized the economic benefits of using native peoples for forced labor, and learned to use European weapons to dominate native or local peoples. These tactics would be used in the Americas.

The natives of the Caribbean, however, did not succumb to Columbus and the Spaniards without fighting. After several rebellions, the Taino who inhabited Hispaniola were forced to submit to Columbus, but they revolted again in 1495. The Spanish response was swift and strong. A later settler, the missionary Bartolomé de Las Casas criticized the Spaniards' brutal response to the natives.

Skillbuilder Answer
Movement: Four.
Place: Maine.

GEOGRAPHY SKILLBUILDER
MOVEMENT ***How many voyages to the Americas did Columbus make?*** **PLACE** ***According to this map, which later U.S. state did Europeans reach first, California or Maine?***

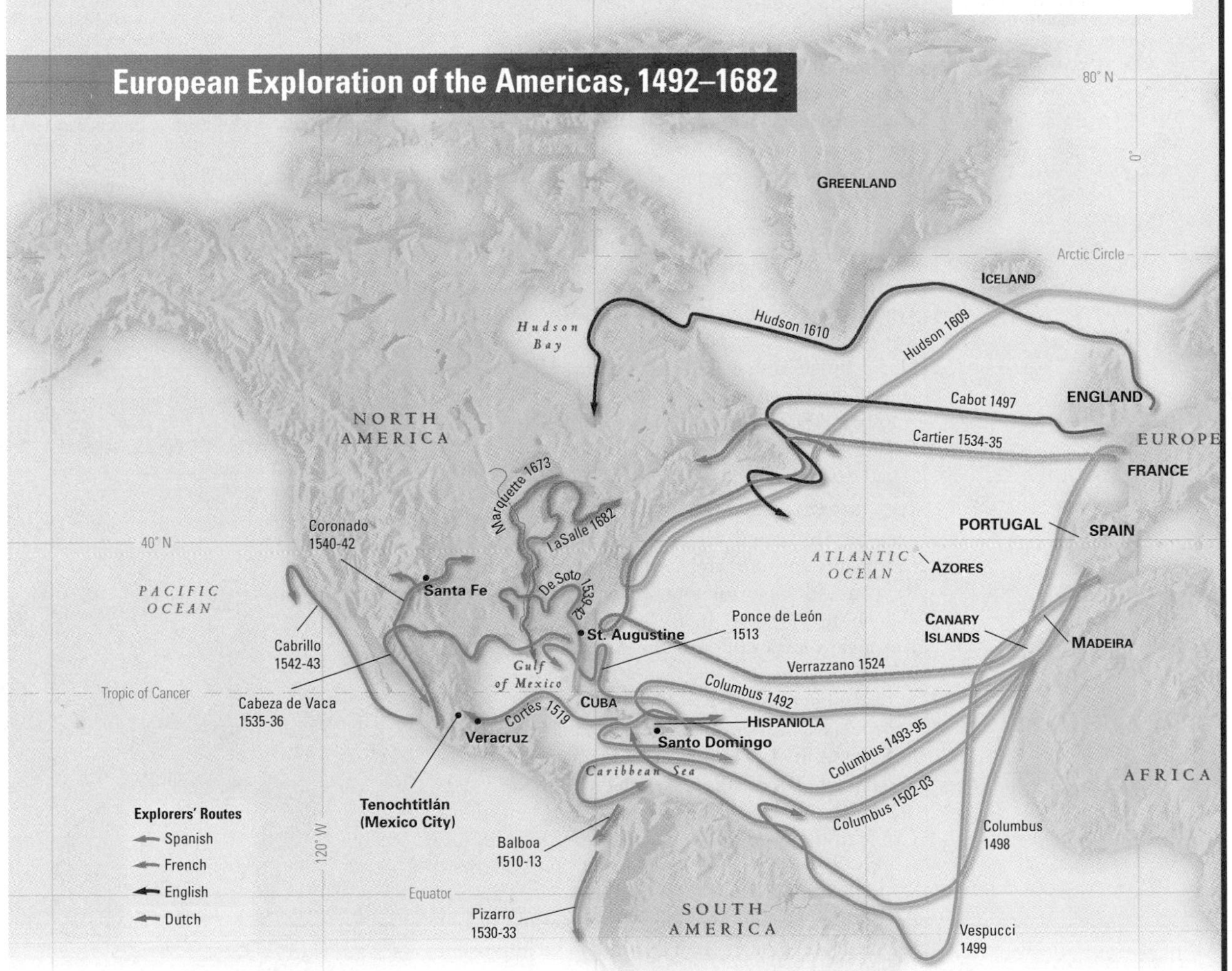

OBJECTIVE
① **INSTRUCT**

Columbus Crosses the Atlantic

▶ ***Discussing Key Ideas***

- Two worlds collide when Columbus and the Taino meet.
- Europeans begin coming to the Americas.
- European diseases decimate Native American populations.
- The Columbian Exchange brings about a massive exchange of plants and animals.

IN-DEPTH RESOURCES: UNIT 1
Guided Reading, p. 5
Primary Source: from *The Journal of Christopher Columbus,* p. 21

ACCESS FOR STUDENTS ACQUIRING ENGLISH
Guided Reading (Spanish), p. 14

HISTORY FROM VISUALS

European Exploration of the Americas, 1492–1682

Reading the Map Explain that the arrows show more than the routes followed by each explorer. They also connect European nations with the lands they later sought to claim. Which explorer laid the basis for Spanish claims to California? *Cabrillo.* Which explorer laid the basis for French claims to Canada? *Cartier.*

Extension Divide the class into small groups and have each group research and write a brief biography of an explorer whose travels are shown on the map.

IN-DEPTH RESOURCES: UNIT 1
Outline Map: Spain Explores North America, p. 18

Block Schedule TEACHING OPTION **Time Needed: 30 Minutes**

Cooperative Activity: Designing Storyboards

Task: Students will create storyboards showing Spanish colonization of Hispaniola from the Native American perspective.

Purpose: To illustrate the effects of the arrival of the Spaniards on such peoples as the Taino.

Activity: Have groups of students create storyboards that present a visual history of the Spanish conquest of the Taino. Suggest that students use the art in this section as a model.

A helpful tip might be to tell students to think of storyboards as frames in a filmstrip or a comic book.

Building a Portfolio: Before adding the storyboards to portfolios, students might script a story line, or a broad statement of the theme.

ALTERNATIVE ASSESSMENT BOOK
Standards for Evaluating a Cooperative Activity

Standards for Evaluation
Storyboards should . . .

- depict key events from the arrival of Columbus on Hispaniola to the coming of the first enslaved Africans
- show an understanding of the effects of colonization upon the Taino

MORE ABOUT . . .
Christopher Columbus

Even death did not stop Columbus's journeys across the Atlantic. After he died in 1506, his remains rested for several decades in Valladolid, Spain. But it was decided that his body should rest on the other side of the Atlantic.

With great ceremony, he was laid to rest in Santo Domingo, the capital of Hispaniola. When Spain ceded the island to France, officials moved his remains to Cuba. When the United States seized Cuba from Spain, the remains—or alleged remains—were returned to Spain.

IN-DEPTH RESOURCES: UNIT 1
Literature: from *The Memoirs of Christopher Columbus: A Novel,* p. 25

ELECTRONIC LIBRARY OF PRIMARY SOURCES
from A Letter to the Treasurer of Spain by Christopher Columbus

MORE ABOUT . . .
Native American Resistance

Cuban history records an account of a Native American from Hispaniola named Hatuey who fiercely resisted the Spanish. Captured while seeking to organize Native Americans in Cuba, Hatuey faced death at the stake.

A friar promised him paradise if he converted to Christianity. Hatuey asked if there were any Spaniards in paradise. The friar replied that only the good ones were. Hatuey gave the following response:

"The best are good for nothing, and I will not go where there is a chance of meeting one of them."

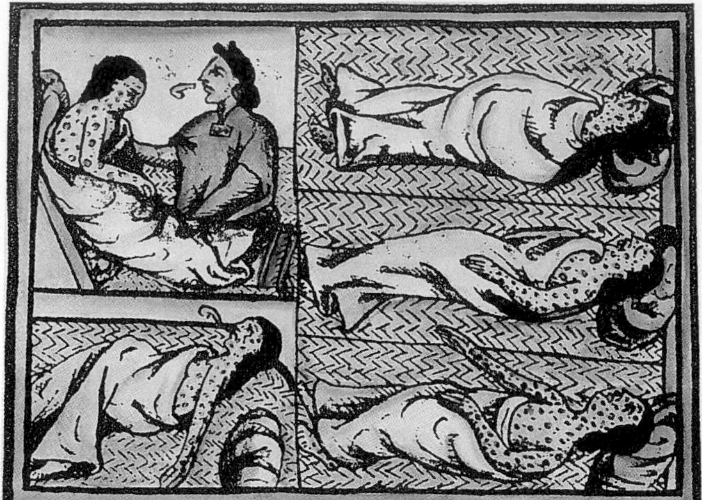

In Mexico, a medicine man ministers to an Aztec with smallpox, a deadly disease brought to the Americas by Europeans.

A PERSONAL VOICE

This tactic, begun here . . . , spread throughout these Indies and will end when there is no more land nor people to subjugate and destroy in this part of the world.

BARTOLOMÉ DE LAS CASAS, quoted in *Columbus: The Great Adventure*

The arrival of the Europeans devastated Native Americans by another means, disease. Because the Taino had not developed any natural immunity to measles, mumps, chickenpox, smallpox, typhus, and other diseases Europeans unknowingly brought with them, they died by the thousands once they were exposed. According to one estimate, nearly one-third of Hispaniola's 300,000 inhabitants died during Columbus's time there. By 1508, fewer than 60,000 were alive on the island, and 60 years later, only two villages remained.

B. Answer The resistance of the Native Americans made them difficult to control as laborers; many of them died from diseases brought by Europeans; the Portuguese were already trafficking in African slaves.

THINK THROUGH HISTORY
B. Analyzing Causes *What factors led to the use of enslaved Africans in the early Spanish colonies?*

THE IMPACT ON AFRICANS With the decline of the native work force, due mainly to disease, the European settlers of the Americas turned to Africa for slaves. As more natives died, the price of enslaved Africans rose, and more Europeans joined the African slave trade to get in on the profits. By 1515, the first shipment of sugar produced in the Americas by African slaves arrived in Spain. Just 23 years after Columbus first set foot in the Americas, African slavery was on its way to becoming an essential part of the European–American economic system.

The Atlantic slave trade devastated many African societies, particularly in West Africa. Starting in the 1500s, African cultures lost many of their young and more able members. One estimate is that 250,000 enslaved Africans were landed in the Americas during the 1500s alone. Another 200,000 arrived between 1601 and 1621. Before the Atlantic slave trade ended in the 1800s, it had drained Africa of at least 12 million people.

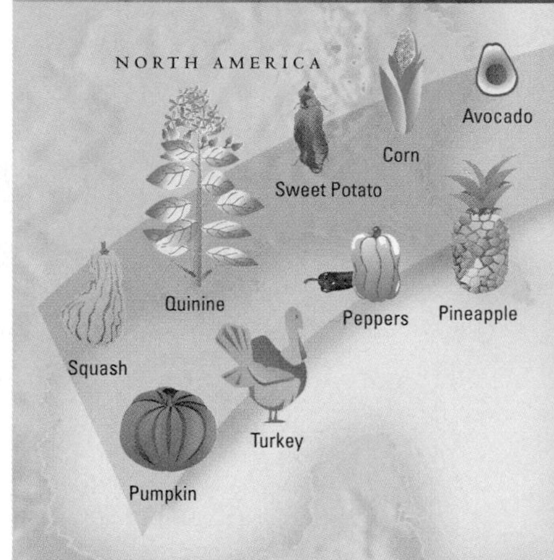

THE IMPACT ON EUROPEANS Columbus's voyages had profound effects on Europeans as well. Merchants and monarchs saw a chance to increase their wealth and influence. Some people saw a chance to improve their lives in a new world. Europeans began to cross the Atlantic by the thousands in what would become one of the biggest voluntary migrations in world history.

Overseas expansion inflamed national rivalries in Europe. In 1494, Spain and Portugal signed the **Treaty of Tordesillas,** in which they agreed to divide the Western Hemisphere between them. Lands to the west of an imaginary north-south line in the Atlantic, including most of the Americas, could be explored and colonized by Spain. Lands to the east of the line, including Brazil, would belong to Portugal. The agreement proved to be impossible

TEACHING OPTION

Exploring Themes

Immigration and Migration With the arrival of the first enslaved Africans in the Americas, the stage was set for the variety of peoples—Native American, European, and African—that would create the diverse nations of this hemisphere. Even today, with thousands of immigrants flooding into the United States from Asia and Latin America, the makeup of the U.S. population still reflects the deep impact of contact. Share with students this data from the 1990 census.

Ancestry Groups of Americans

Group	Millions
1. German	58
2. Irish	39
3. English	33
4. African	24
5. Italian	15
6. Mexican	12
7. French	10
8. Polish	9
9. Native American	9
10. Dutch	6

to enforce, and it meant nothing to the English, Dutch, or French, all of whom began colonizing the Americas during the late 1500s and early 1600s.

THE COLUMBIAN EXCHANGE The voyages of Columbus and those after him led to the discovery of plants and animals in the Americas that were new to Europeans and Africans. Ships took items such as corn, potatoes, and tobacco from the Americas to Europe and to Africa. In return, they brought livestock, grains, fruit, and coffee back. This global transfer of living things, called the **Columbian Exchange,** began with Columbus's first voyage and continues today.

The Spanish Claim a New Empire

In the wake of Columbus's voyages, Spanish explorers called **conquistadores** (conquerors) sailed across the Atlantic to claim new colonies for Spain. Lured by the prospect of lands filled with gold and silver, they pushed first into the Caribbean islands and along the coast of Central and South America. Then they swept through Mexico and south to the tip of South America. With the help of superior weapons, native allies, and the spread of disease, the conquistadores destroyed native communities as they went.

CORTÉS SUBDUES THE AZTECS Soon after landing in Mexico, the conquistador **Hernán Cortés** learned of a vast and wealthy empire in the region's interior. With a force of 600 men, 17 horses, numerous dogs, and 10 cannons, he trudged inland. The Aztecs, members of the diverse Nahua peoples of central Mexico, dominated the region. Cortés convinced those Nahua who had long resented the spread of Aztec power to join his ranks. After marching for 200 miles through difficult mountain passes, Cortés and his legions finally spotted the magnificent Aztec capital of Tenochtitlán. With 140,000 residents, the city was one of the largest urban centers in the world.

The Aztec emperor, Montezuma, convinced at first that Cortés was an armor-clad god, agreed to give the Spanish explorer a share of the empire's gold. Not satisfied with the existing gold, Cortés eventually forced the Aztecs to

Skillbuilder Answer
Possible Answer: It has given the people of each hemisphere new foods and sources of nutrition.

GEOGRAPHY SKILLBUILDER
HUMAN-ENVIRONMENT INTERACTION
How do you think the Columbian Exchange has enriched each hemisphere?

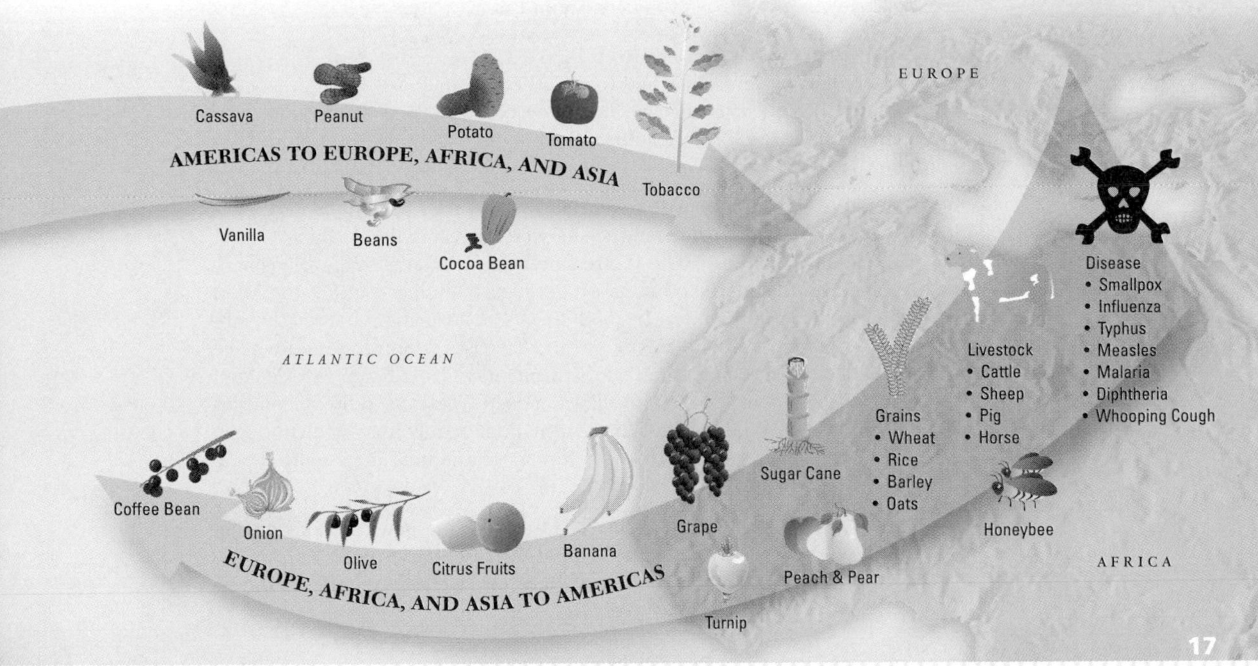

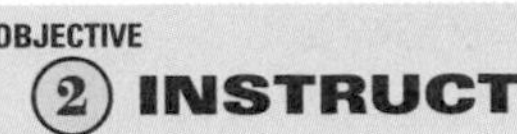
OBJECTIVE
② INSTRUCT

The Spanish Claim a New Empire

▶ ***Discussing Key Ideas***
- Cortés subdues the Aztecs aided by Spanish firearms, diseases, and native allies.
- Wealth from the Americas turns Spain into the most powerful nation in Europe.
- Dreams of new conquests and competition from other European nations leads Spain northward.
- Finding little gold in the northern borderlands, the Spaniards focus instead on the conversion of the Native Americans.

HISTORY FROM VISUALS
The Columbian Exchange

Reading the Map Point out the number of continents involved in the exchange. *Four.* Ask students why this back-and-forth flow of goods has been called an "ecological revolution."

Extension Have students expand the map and add other items involved in the exchange. A source of information is *The Seeds of Change,* a book sponsored by the Smithsonian Institution on the 500th anniversary of Columbus's arrival in the Americas.

Block Schedule TEACHING OPTION **Time Needed: 30 Minutes**

Cooperative Activity: Mapping Corn Production

Task: Students will research global corn production and show the results on a map.

Purpose: To show the impact of the Columbian Exchange.

Activity: Assign students to research corn production by nation, with each group focusing on a different nation. Tell them this information can be found in almanacs such as *The Information Please Almanac* or *The World Almanac.* Have them record their findings on an outline map of the world. Recommend that they develop a key to show categories of production. (Helpful tip: Amounts are recorded in thousands of metric tons and range from less than 100 to over 200,000.) Students should also think of an appropriate title for their map, such as "Corn: The Native American Gift to the World."

ALTERNATIVE ASSESSMENT BOOK
Standards for Evaluating a Cooperative Activity

KEY PLAYER

Hernán Cortés

Critical Thinking: Drawing Conclusions Ask students to list some of the personal qualities that made Cortés a successful explorer. Can they think of modern-day explorers who might need such qualities? *Possible answers might include his uncommon bravery and his determination. Astronauts today need those qualities.*

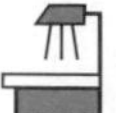

GEOGRAPHY TRANSPARENCIES

G1, Voyages of Discovery and Exploration

HUMANITIES TRANSPARENCIES

H1, Map of North America

H3, Indians Giving Cortés a Necklace

CRITICAL THINKING TRANSPARENCIES

CT1, Exploration of the Americas

ELECTRONIC LIBRARY OF PRIMARY SOURCES from *La Relación* by Álvar Núñez Cabeza de Vaca

MORE ABOUT . . .

The Last Aztec Emperor

Facing Cortés on the final days of the Aztec empire was an 18-year-old ruler named Cuauhtemoc, the nephew of Montezuma. Although disease had laid waste to the Aztecs, Cuauhtemoc led one final assault against the Spaniards, who ultimately captured and hanged him. Cuauhtemoc's courage has made him a hero to modern Mexicans. It is his statue, rather than a statue of Cortés, that today stands at the center of one of the busiest intersections in Mexico City.

KEY PLAYER

HERNÁN CORTÉS
1485–1547

Cortés made himself the enemy of thousands of Native Americans, but the daring conquistador did not have many friends among Spaniards either. Spanish authorities on Cuba, where Cortés owned land, accused the conquistador of murdering his wife, Catalina Juárez. "There were ugly accusations, but none proved," wrote Juárez's biographer.

In addition, the Cuban governor, Diego Velázquez, who resented Cortés's arrogance, relieved him of the command of a gold-seeking expedition to the mainland. Cortés left Cuba anyway. As he fought his way through Mexico, Cortés had to battle not only the Native Americans, but also the Spanish forces that Velázquez sent to arrest him.

mine more gold and silver. In the spring of 1520, the Aztecs rebelled against the intruders. The Aztecs are believed to have stoned their ruler to death, as a traitor, before driving out Cortés's forces.

While they had successfully repelled the Spanish invaders, the natives found they could do little to stop the spread of European diseases. When Cortés launched a counterattack in 1521, the Aztec force had been greatly reduced by smallpox and measles. After several months of fighting, the invaders sacked and burned Tenochtitlán, and the Aztec surrendered. Cortés laid plans for the colony of **New Spain,** whose capital he called Mexico City. Within three years, Spanish churches and homes rose from the foundations of old native temples and palaces.

THINK THROUGH HISTORY
C. *Forming Opinions* *Among the factors that allowed the Spanish to subdue the Aztecs, which do you think was most important, and why?*

C. Answer Students may say superior weapons because they overwhelmed the enemy immediately; disease because it undermined the enemy in the long run; or native allies because they offered inside knowledge of the enemy.

THE SPANISH PATTERN OF CONQUEST In building their American empire, the Spaniards lived among the native people and sought to impose their own culture upon them. The settlers, mostly men, tended to intermarry with native women. This practice eventually created a large **mestizo**—or mixed Spanish and Native American—population. Nonetheless, the Spanish also oppressed the people among whom they lived. In their effort to exploit the land for its resources, they forced native workers to labor under a system known as ***encomienda.*** Natives farmed, ranched, or mined for Spanish landlords, who received the rights to their labor from Spanish authorities. The holders of *encomiendas* promised the Spanish rulers to act fairly and to respect the workers. Instead, many of them abused their charges and sometimes even worked the laborers to death in dangerous mines.

Priests demanded an end to the harsh *encomienda* system. In 1511, Fray Antonio de Montesinos delivered a fiery sermon in which he attacked the use of the native population for slave labor.

A PERSONAL VOICE

Tell me, by what right or justice do you hold these Indians in such a cruel and horrible servitude? . . . Why do you keep them so oppressed and exhausted, without giving them enough to eat or curing them of the sicknesses they incur from the excessive labor you give them? . . . Are you not bound to love them as you love yourselves? Don't you understand this? Don't you feel this?

FRAY ANTONIO DE MONTESINOS, quoted in *Reflections, Writing for Columbus*

"As we approached, splendid chiefs came to meet us. . . ."

BERNAL DÍAZ DEL CASTILLO, CONQUISTADOR WITH CORTÉS

As more and more natives died from disease, the labor system grew even more brutal, for the Spanish overseers expected the same production from fewer laborers. In 1542, the Spanish monarchy abolished the system, and to meet their labor needs, the Spaniards began to use enslaved Africans.

SPAIN ENJOYS A GOLDEN AGE Gold and silver from the conquered lands flowed across the Atlantic, enriching Spain, which became the wealthiest, most powerful nation in Europe in the 1500s. Between 1522 and 1528, various lieutenants of Cortés conquered other native peoples, including many of the Maya in Yucatán and Central America. In 1532, Francisco Pizarro plundered the fabulously wealthy Inca empire on the western coast of South America. The Spanish built a far-reaching empire, which included New Spain (Mexico and part of what is now Guatemala), as well as lands in Central and South America and the Caribbean. While other European nations barely imagined American colonies of their own, the Spanish built immense cathedrals and a university in Mexico City.

THE CONQUISTADORES PUSH NORTH Dreaming of new conquests—and fearing that other European nations might invade their empire from the north—Spain undertook a series of expeditions into what is now the southern

TEACHING OPTIONS

Teaching Less Proficient Readers

Taking Notes Distribute three-by-five-inch index cards to students. Have them turn each subhead under "The Spanish Claim a New Empire" into a question; for example, How did Cortés subdue the Aztecs? Instruct students to write each question on the front of one of the index cards. Tell students to answer the question by taking notes on the back of each card as they read. Repeat this process with the rest of the section. Students can exchange their "flash cards" to quiz each other or to review for the section quiz.

Making Connections Across the Curriculum

Writing Students' English teachers might use the dramatic events about the arrival of the Spaniards at Tenochtitlán for a writing assignment, such as a monologue or a soliloquy that one of the following people might have delivered: Doña Marina, Cortés, or Montezuma. As students prepare to write their assignments, suggest that they think about what was happening, about the thoughts and feelings that the person might be experiencing, and about how these would color their perceptions of the events.

United States. Finding little gold or silver there, Spain nonetheless established a string of outposts to protect its American empire and to spread its culture and religion to the Native Americans.

In 1513, Juan Ponce de León, a Spanish soldier who had conquered Puerto Rico five years earlier, set out to investigate the land he named *La Florida.* For almost five decades, the Spanish sought gold in the region, battling the local residents, contending with disease, and facing starvation. Finally, in 1562, Spain abandoned further exploration of Florida.

This decision was reversed when France showed an active interest in the region. Spanish warrior Pedro Menéndez de Avilés drove out the French, and in 1565 he established the outpost of St. Augustine on the Florida coast. The fort suffered attacks by various European nations trying to wedge their way into the Caribbean in quest of their own colonies. However, the Spanish settlement survived to become the oldest European-founded city in the United States.

Spain Explores the Southwest and West

The first Spanish expeditions into what is now the southwestern United States began in the decade following Pizarro's triumph over the Incas in South America. In 1540, Francisco Vásquez de Coronado led the most ambitious venture, as he traveled throughout much of what is now Texas, Oklahoma, Arizona, New Mexico, and Kansas in search of another wealthy empire to conquer. After wandering for two years, the only precious metal he carried home was his own battered gold-plated armor.

In the winter of 1609–1610, Pedro de Peralta, governor of Spain's northern holdings, called **New Mexico,** led settlers to a tributary of the upper Rio Grande. Together they built a capital called Santa Fe, or "Holy Faith." In the next two decades, a string of Christian missions arose among the Pueblos in the area. A 1,500-mile trail known as el Camino Real, or "the Royal Road," was used to carry goods back and forth between Santa Fe and Mexico City.

Spain, however, had little interest in the trade goods that trickled in from the borderlands—cattle hides, piñon nuts, and the wool-and-cotton blankets woven by Pueblo artisans. Instead, the Spanish rulers saw the scattered missions, forts, and small ranches that dotted the lands of New Mexico as tools for advancing the Catholic religion. They also viewed them as buffers against advances by other European countries into New Spain.

THINK THROUGH HISTORY
D. Contrasting *How did Spain's colony in New Mexico differ from its colonies in New Spain?*
D. Answer New Spain was rich in gold and silver; New Mexico had fewer riches, and the emphasis there was on spreading the Catholic religion and protecting the colonies to the south.

While the conquistadores came to the Americas in search of wealth, the Spanish priests who accompanied them came in search of converts. Spain instructed its priests to teach Native Americans "the trades and skills with which they might live richly." Franciscan friars, priests dedicated to the teachings of St. Francis of Assisi, took up this task. To win new converts, the brown-robed priests learned the native languages and offered spiritual as well as political protection to the newly baptized.

This depiction of the Virgin Mary and the infant Jesus from the early 1900s reflects the intermingling of Spanish and Native American cultures in New Mexico.

THE SPANISH OPEN MISSIONS IN TEXAS In 1519 Alonso Álvarez de Piñeda of Spain had mapped the coast of what is today Texas. Soon afterward, in 1528, the first Europeans had begun to settle in the interior. Over the next two hundred years, using the San Antonio area as their administrative center, the Spanish sent more than 30 expeditions inland to explore and to settle. The land was already sparsely inhabited by Native Americans, including members of the large and diverse Apache group, whom Spanish missionaries sought to convert to Christianity. The first two Spanish missions in Texas were founded near what is now El Paso in 1682.

Beginning in 1718, a number of missions opened along the San Antonio River. Several of these had moved from East Texas locations where they had

OBJECTIVE
③ **INSTRUCT**

Spain Explores the Southwest and West

▶ ***Discussing Key Ideas***

- Spanish priests in New Mexico advance the Catholic religion and try to transform the Native American cultures.
- Spanish missions and presidios serve as buffers against settlement by other European countries.
- The Spanish open missions in Texas and California, where Native Americans provide labor for agriculture and assorted industries.
- Brutal suppression of native religious practices leads the Pueblo in New Mexico to rebel.

MORE ABOUT . . .
St. Augustine

St. Augustine owes its existence, in large part, to pirates. The trouble started with a Spanish cargo of treasure. Intercepted by a French corsair, or pirate ship, the cargo landed in the court of French king Francis I. This opened a new trade—pirating from the Spanish.

After pirates repeatedly set fire to St. Augustine, the Spanish ordered construction of a fort called Castillo de San Marcos. Built in 1672 from huge blocks of coquina, a rock made from fused seashells, the fort served as an active Spanish outpost well into the 1700s. Today it stands as one of the oldest major national landmarks in the United States.

TEACHING OPTION

Skillbuilder Mini-Lesson: Developing Historical Perspective

Explaining the Skill Historical perspective is a way of looking at a time in history based on the conditions that existed then instead of judging by what we think now. For example, some students might initially think Native Americans were weak to succumb to the Spanish invaders so quickly. However, knowing about medicine can help students realize that the Europeans had developed immunities to the diseases they brought whereas Native Americans had no such immunities.

Applying the Skill: Developing Historical Perspective Discuss the battle picture on page 3 and ask:

What details are surprising? *The Spanish seem very powerful compared to the Aztecs. It looks as if Native Americans are fighting along with the Spaniards.*

How does this picture affect your understanding of the Spanish conquest of Mexico? *Some students may say they now realize the Spanish had Native American allies. Others might be surprised at the conquistadores' apparent strength.*

IN-DEPTH RESOURCES: UNIT 1
Skillbuilder Practice: Developing Historical Perspective, p. 14

HISTORY FROM VISUALS

Spanish Missions

Viewing the Photographs Ask students to describe the architecture of the Spanish missions shown in the pictures. *Distinctive elements include arches, bell towers, adobe construction, stucco finishes, and the symbolism of the cross.* Why do students think the missions took such a long time to construct? *Students may say the missions were extensive settlements consisting of many buildings, some of them, like the churches, requiring elaborate planning and materials.*

Extension Have students create a map of the 21 California missions showing dates and descriptions of each mission. Have them research the Native American groups associated with one of the missions and tell how mission life affected them.

MORE ABOUT . . .

Everyday Life in New Mexico

While the Spanish sought to impose their culture on the Native Americans, some of the native ways were adopted by the Spanish. In the early 1600s many settlers along the frontier exchanged their Spanish fabrics for *gamuza*—the softly tanned deer or antelope hide called chamois in English and worn by the Native Americans, including fringed leather jackets and buckskin boots.

Spanish Missions

An outstanding example of Spanish architecture in North America, the church of Mission San José in San Antonio was built between 1768 and 1782, although the mission itself was founded in 1720. Among the mission's restored buildings is the first flour mill in Texas, built about 1790.

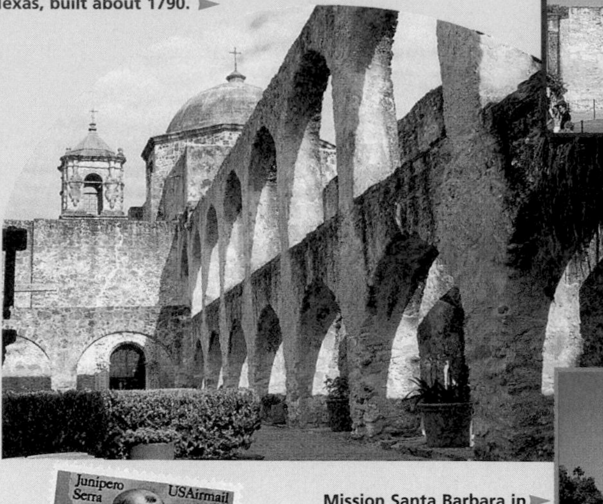

Mission San Diego de Alcalá, founded in 1769, was the first of the 21 missions in California.

The Alamo served as the chapel of Mission San Antonio de Valero, founded in 1718. Today it draws many visitors in downtown San Antonio.

Fray Junípero Serra came to Mexico from Majorca, Spain, as a missionary priest in 1749 and later traveled the length of California founding missions.

Mission Santa Barbara in California was founded in 1786. Native Americans provided the labor to build this stone church, still in use, and to raise the crops to feed the missionaries and themselves.

failed due to malaria, drought, the resistance of Native Americans, and competition from the French. Founded in 1720, Mission San José y San Miguel de Aguayo in San Antonio was by many accounts the most beautiful and successful Texas mission. Its compound included buildings for living, worshipping, storing grain, spinning and weaving cotton and wool, carpentry, iron working, and tailoring. Its church could hold 2,000 worshippers and featured a famous rose window considered a masterpiece.

A STRING OF MISSIONS SPANS CALIFORNIA Before the arrival of the Europeans, many Native American groups inhabited what is now California. They thrived on the region's rich resources, having developed ways of coping with periodic droughts and food shortages. They traded surplus foods with their neighbors and practiced their own religions. In 1542 Spanish navigator Juan Rodriguez Cabrillo, exploring the west coast of North America, gave one of its natural harbors the Spanish name San Diego. In 1769, the Spanish missionary Father Junípero Serra founded the first California mission at San Diego.

By 1823, the Franciscans had founded a string of 21 missions, each one day's walk (about 30 miles) from the next. The missionaries—sent by the Spanish government in part to prevent the further land claims by the British and Russians—were usually accompanied by military escorts. Many of the missions were protected by forts, called *presidios,* built nearby. A *presidio* and a mission founded in 1776 in San Francisco preceded the development of that city in the 1830s. The aims of the missionaries in California, as in Texas, were to convert the Native Americans to Christianity, to educate them in European ways and skills, and to secure the area for Spanish settlement.

The impact of the Spanish missions on Native American cultures has been a subject of much historical controversy. Recent historians assert that the mission

Block Schedule TEACHING OPTION **Time Needed: 40 Minutes**

Cooperative Activity: Writing About Popé's Rebellion

Task: Students will create a short story.

Purpose: To understand causes and effects of Popé's Rebellion.

Activity: Have groups of students recount the story of Popé's Rebellion. Each group will write only one part of the story based on the following four parts.

1. Arrival of the Spanish: *Popé could hardly believe his eyes! Rumbling toward his village was a strange group of people.*
2. Forced Conversion of the Pueblo: *"You must give up your religion," said the Spanish.*
3. Planning the Rebellion: *"We must plan carefully to defeat the terrible Spaniards."*
4. The Rebellion and Its Outcome: *Popé burned with hatred as the battle began.*

Building a Portfolio Students might title their stories and add them to their portfolios.

ALTERNATIVE ASSESSMENT BOOK
Standards for Evaluating a Cooperative Activity

Standards for Evaluation
Stories should . . .

- show clear understanding of the rebellion
- focus on their particular part of the story
- use language that helps re-create the situation

system negatively affected many Native American communities in several ways. The Spanish required Native Americans who converted to Christianity to live inside the missions, separating them from their families and cultures. Native Americans who tried to leave were punished. The Spanish also forced Native Americans to provide labor for farming and construction, give up their self-government, and adopt European dress, diet, and living arrangements.

THINK THROUGH HISTORY
E. THEME ***Cultural Diversity*** *What lasting effects do you think Spanish exploration and settlement have had on the cultural diversity of the United States?*

The missions helped the Spanish gain control over the region. After Mexico won its independence from Spain in 1821, however, the Spanish could no longer support the missions financially and began to secularize them, or convert them to nonreligious ownership and government. Native Americans were expected to receive one-half of the mission lands, but this plan was not carried out. Native American groups, like the Diegueño, Luiseño, and Cahuilla had been severely weakened, and others like the Gabrielino disappeared altogether.

E. Answer Students may say that European diseases decimated native populations and eliminated some groups; that some Native Americans were educated in European ways but lost some of their own skills; and that the influence of Spanish culture can still be seen from Florida and Texas through the Southwest and into California, for instance in architecture.

RESISTANCE TO THE SPANISH Though they mounted several armed attacks on the missions, Native Americans were not successful in resisting the missionaries in California. Tension also marked the relationship between the priests and their converts in New Mexico. As they sought to transform Native American cultures, Spanish priests and soldiers destroyed objects held sacred by local communities and suppressed many ceremonial dances and rituals. During the 1670s, priests and soldiers around Santa Fe began forcing Native Americans to help support the missions by paying a tribute—such as a bushel of maize or a deer hide—and forcing Native Americans to work for them. Those who refused to pay tribute or who practiced their native religion were beaten.

F. Answer The Native Americans were well organized; the Spanish priests had alienated a large number over a large area during the previous decades.

THINK THROUGH HISTORY
F. *Making Inferences* *What can you infer from the fact that 17,000 Native Americans from all over New Mexico took part in the uprising led by Popé?*

The Spanish priests punished the Pueblo religious leader Popé for his worship practices, which they interpreted as witchcraft. In 1680, the angered leader led an uprising of some 17,000 warriors from villages all over New Mexico. The triumphant fighters destroyed Catholic churches, executed priests, and drove the Spaniards back into New Spain. For the next 14 years—until the Spanish regained control of the area—the southwestern part of the future United States once again belonged to the Native Americans.

The rulers of Spain, however, had even greater concerns for their colonies. In 1588, England had defeated the Spanish Armada—a naval fleet assembled to invade England—ending Spain's dominance on the Atlantic Ocean. England also began forging colonies of its own along the eastern shore of North America. While the Spanish heritage still lives in the peoples and cultures of the Southwest and Southeast, the English—who migrated to their colonies in much larger numbers—eventually dominated North America.

Section 2 Assessment

1. TERMS & NAMES
Identify:
- Christopher Columbus
- Taino
- Treaty of Tordesillas
- Columbian Exchange
- conquistador
- Hernán Cortés
- New Spain
- mestizo
- *encomienda*
- New Mexico

2. SUMMARIZING Create a time line of the major events and significant dates of Columbus's voyages and the Spanish exploration of the New World. Use the dates already plotted on the time line below as a guide.

1492 | 1493 | 1494 | 1508 | 1513 | 1520–21 | 1532

3. ANALYZING EFFECTS What do you think were the most important long-term consequences of Columbus's encounters in the Americas?

THINK ABOUT
- conquering and claiming land
- forced labor of Native Americans and Africans
- the impact on Africa, Europe, and the Americas

4. FINDING MAIN IDEAS State three main ideas about Spanish exploration and settlement north of Mexico and the Spaniards' interaction with Native Americans there.

THINK ABOUT
- the explorations of Ponce de León and Coronado
- the establishment of St. Augustine and Santa Fe
- the activities of Spanish missionaries
- Native American acts of resistance

ANSWERS

1. TERMS & NAMES
- Christopher Columbus, p. 14
- Taino, p. 14
- Treaty of Tordesillas, p. 16
- Columbian Exchange, p. 17
- conquistador, p. 17
- Hernán Cortés, p. 17
- New Spain, p. 18
- mestizo, p. 18
- *encomienda*, p. 18
- New Mexico, p. 19

2. SUMMARIZING
Possible Responses: **1492:** Columbus's first voyage to the Americas. **1493:** Columbus's return trip. **1494:** The Treaty of Tordesillas. **1508:** Fewer than 60,000 of the original 300,000 native inhabitants remained alive on Hispaniola. **1513:** Ponce de León explored La Florida. **1520–21:** Aztecs rebelled, and Cortés retook Tenochtitlán. **1532:** Pizarro conquered the Incas.

3. ANALYZING EFFECTS
Possible Responses: The pattern of violating human rights in the process of conquering new lands; the African slave trade; the emergence of various nations in North and South America; the permanent alteration of global environments and societies as a result of the Columbian Exchange; the multicultural character of the United States.

4. FINDING MAIN IDEAS
Possible Responses: Early Spanish explorers failed to find gold or silver north of Mexico, so settlement was limited to missions and defensive outposts; missionaries provided Native Americans with material goods, but suppressed their culture; some Native Americans converted to Christianity, but others resisted violently.

MORE ABOUT . . .
The Spanish Armada

After a series of English raids on his treasure ships, King Philip II of Spain assembled a fleet of warships, or armada, to invade England. In the summer of 1588, this group of about 130 ships—carrying nearly 19,000 soldiers—sailed into the English channel. England, however, was prepared.

English warships outmaneuvered the Spanish vessels and bombarded the Armada with their heavier long-range cannons. Powerful storms also destroyed much of the fleet. The defeat of the Spanish Armada opened the way for the rest of Europe to venture into the Americas.

ASSESS & RETEACH

Section 2 Assessment
Suggest that students jot down important points that they want to include in each answer before beginning to write.

Self-Assessment
Have students explore their own understanding of the conflicts between cultures by listing the Spanish expectations and Native American responses.

Section Quiz
FORMAL ASSESSMENT
Section Quiz, p. 6

Reteach
Use the map on pages 16–17 (the Columbian Exchange) to review the main ideas of the section.

CLOSE

Little more than 60 years after the arrival of Cortés in Mexico, Spain had carved out a huge empire in the Americas. One of the biggest challenges to Spain would come from England, a nation with a large population of restless and landless people.

Section 3 Overview

1. To describe the English settlement at Jamestown.
2. To identify the motives that led Puritans to New England and the colonies they founded.
3. To explain the pattern of life at New Netherland and Pennsylvania.
4. To understand the economic relationship between England and its North American colonies.

SKILLBUILDERS

- Understanding geography: place, p. 28
- Understanding geography: region, p. 29
- Interpreting charts, p. 32

CRITICAL THINKING

- Making inferences, pp. 23, 29, 32
- Summarizing, pp. 23, 32
- Evaluating decisions, p. 25
- Creating a model, p. 25
- Analyzing motives, p. 26
- Analyzing issues, p. 27
- Making predictions, p. 28
- Contrasting, p. 30
- Theme: Democracy in America, p. 30
- Clarifying, p. 31
- Forming opinions, p. 32

FOCUS & MOTIVATE

5-MINUTE WARM-UP

Predicting Outcomes
To learn about the conflicts between the colonists and Native Americans in New England, ask students to read A Personal Voice on page 28 and answer these questions.

1. What is Miantonomo's basic concern?
2. What do you think might happen between the English colonists and the Native Americans given these conditions?

WARM-UP TRANSPARENCY 1

▶ ***Starting with the Student***
- If students were to create an ideal community, what features would it have?
- In this ideal community, how would students handle dissenters?

3 Early British Colonies

TERMS & NAMES
- John Smith
- Jamestown
- indentured servant
- Puritan
- John Winthrop
- King Philip's War
- William Penn
- Quaker
- mercantilism
- Navigation Acts

LEARN ABOUT the founding of Jamestown, the New England colonies, and the middle colonies, and their continuing relations with England
TO UNDERSTAND the diversity of the colonies and their evolving difficulties with the mother country.

ONE AMERICAN'S STORY

John Smith craved adventure. Smith's father had urged him to be a merchant, but the restless Englishman wanted to be a soldier. In 1600, at age 20, Smith helped Hungary fight a war against the Turks. For his heroic battle efforts, the Hungarians knighted him. Four years later, he offered his services as a colonist to the Virginia Company, a group of merchants charged with starting an English colony in North America. He later recalled his vision of the opportunities that awaited those who settled the Americas.

A PERSONAL VOICE
What man who is poor or who has only his merit to advance his fortunes can desire more contentment than to walk over and plant the land he has obtained by risking his life? . . . Here nature and liberty . . . give us freely that which we lack or have to pay dearly for in England. . . . What pleasure can be greater than to grow tired from . . . planting vines, fruits, or vegetables? . . .

JOHN SMITH, *The General History of Virginia*

Smith would need all of his abilities to steer the new colony, **Jamestown,** through what turned out to be a disastrous beginning. Despite disease, starvation, battles with Native Americans, and conflicts among its own members, the colony survived to become England's first permanent settlement in North America.

John Smith

An English Settlement at Jamestown

In April of 1607, nearly four months after the Virginia Company's three ships had left England, they reached the North American shore. Sailing part way up a broad river leading into Chesapeake Bay, the colonists selected a small, defensible peninsula as a location for Jamestown, which they named for their king.

A DISASTROUS START John Smith sensed trouble from the beginning. Because the investors in the colony demanded a quick return on their investment, the colonists seemed more interested in searching for riches than in farming. Disease from infected river water struck them first, followed soon by hunger. After several months, one settler described the terrifying predicament: "Thus we lived for the space of five months in this miserable distress, . . . our men night and day groaning in every corner of the fort, most pitiful to hear."

Smith used his diplomatic and military skills to hold the colony together. He forced the colonists to farm, and he received food and support from the nearby Powhatan peoples. Then Smith was injured and returned to England. Over the next several years, the colony struggled, as disorganized colonists were threatened by Powhatan who had become angry. By the winter of 1609, conditions in Jamestown had deteriorated to the point of famine. The colony was saved, however, by the arrival of new colonists and by the development of a highly profitable crop, tobacco.

This poster reflects an attempt to attract settlers to the early Virginia colony.

SECTION 3 RESOURCES

PRINT RESOURCES

IN-DEPTH RESOURCES: UNIT 1
Guided Reading, p. 11
Primary Source: from *Travels and Works of Captain John Smith,* p. 23
American Lives: John Winthrop, p. 28

READING STUDY GUIDE, p. 9

ACCESS FOR STUDENTS ACQUIRING ENGLISH
Guided Reading (Spanish), p. 15

SPANISH READING STUDY GUIDE, p. 9

FORMAL ASSESSMENT
Section Quiz, p. 7

ALTERNATIVE ASSESSMENT BOOK
See forms for supporting and scoring alternative activities.

TECHNOLOGY RESOURCES

GEOGRAPHY TRANSPARENCIES
G2, The European Colonies, 1650
G35, Original Thirteen Colonies

CRITICAL THINKING TRANSPARENCIES
CT2, Puritan Migration
CT36, American Colonies

CD-ROM Electronic Library of Primary Sources
Grolier Multimedia Encyclopedia
VIDEO *American Portfolio: A Videodisc for U.S. History* user's guide, pp. 17–26

INTERNET http://www.mlushistory.com

TOBACCO REQUIRES A SUPPLY OF LABOR By the late 1620s, colonists exported more than 1.5 million pounds of tobacco to England each year. The crop was so valuable that it could even be used as currency, that is, to exchange for goods and services. In order to grow tobacco, the Virginia Company needed field laborers. In 1618, they introduced the headright system, under which each new arrival received land. Immigration to the colony jumped.

Most of those who arrived in Virginia, however, came as **indentured servants.** In exchange for passage to North America, and food and shelter upon arrival, an indentured servant agreed to a limited term of servitude—usually four to seven years. Indentured servants were usually from the lower classes of English society and therefore had little to lose by leaving for a new world.

THINK THROUGH HISTORY
A. *Making Inferences* *Tobacco in the early colonies has been referred to as "brown gold." Why do you think this is so?*

A. Answer Because it could be used, like money, to exchange for other things; because its cultivation helped save the colonies economically.

The first Africans arrived in Virginia aboard a Dutch merchant ship in 1619. After a few years, most of them received land and freedom. It would be several decades before the English colonists in North America began the systematic use of enslaved Africans as laborers.

COLONISTS CLASH WITH NATIVE AMERICANS The colonists' desire for more land—to accommodate their growing population and the demand for more crop space—led to warfare with the original inhabitants of Virginia. Unlike the Spanish, the English followed a pattern of driving away the people they defeated. Their conquest over the native peoples was total and complete, which is one reason a large mestizo population never developed in the United States.

The leaders of Jamestown demanded tributes of corn and labor from the local native people. Soldiers pressed these demands by setting Powhatan villages on fire and taking hostages, especially children. One of the captives, Chief Powhatan's daughter, Pocahontas, married colonist John Rolfe in 1614. This led to a half-hearted truce. However, the peace would not last, as colonists continued to move farther into Native American territory and seize more land to grow tobacco. In 1622, in a well-planned attack, Powhatan raiding parties struck at colonial villages up and down the James River, and killed more than 340 colonists. England sent more troops and settlers to strengthen the colony and to conquer the Powhatan. By 1644, nearly 10,000 English men and women lived in Virginia, while the Powhatan population continued to fall.

ECONOMIC DIFFERENCES SPLIT VIRGINIA The English colonists who migrated to North America in increasing numbers battled not only Native Americans but sometimes each other. By the 1670s, one-quarter of the free white men in Virginia were former indentured servants who had little money to buy land, could not vote, and enjoyed almost no rights in colonial society. These poor colonists lived mainly on the western outskirts of Virginia, where they constantly fought with Native Americans for land.

Virginia's governor, William Berkeley, refused to back the western settlers in their struggles with the Native Americans, and the colonists, under the leadership of a young planter named Nathaniel Bacon, rebelled in 1676. Bacon marched on Jamestown in September of 1676 to confront colonial leaders with a number of grievances, including the frontier's lack of representation in Virginia's colonial legislature, the House of Burgesses. Although Bacon's Rebellion ultimately failed, it exposed the restlessness of the colony's former indentured servants. Virginia's "rabble," as many planters called the frontier settlers, resented being taxed and governed without their consent—a complaint that both wealthy and poor colonists would voice against Great Britain 100 years later in 1776.

B. Answer The colonial system offered them few rights and little protection from Native Americans.

THINK THROUGH HISTORY
B. *Summarizing* *Why were the frontier settlers discontented with the colonial system?*

HISTORICAL SPOTLIGHT

THE MYSTERY OF ROANOKE

England's first attempt to plant a colony in North America ended under a shroud of mystery. In 1585, an English navigator named Sir Walter Raleigh (pictured above with his son) led a small group of colonists to Roanoke Island on what are now called the Outer Banks of North Carolina. The first colonists soon abandoned the settlement and returned to England.

In 1587, Raleigh sent a second group of colonists, led by John White, to reestablish the Roanoke settlement. White sailed back to England for more supplies but did not return until 1590.

Upon his arrival, White discovered that the colonists had vanished. All that remained at the village were some rusted debris and the word "CROATOAN" (the name of a nearby island) carved into a post. Historians believe that the lost colonists may have starved to death or either joined with or been attacked by local Native American tribes.

OBJECTIVE
① INSTRUCT

An English Settlement at Jamestown

▶ ***Discussing Key Ideas***

- English investors found Jamestown.
- The colony struggles because of poor preparation and a desire for a quick return on investments.
- Production of tobacco saves the colony.
- A shortage of labor leads Virginia to turn to indentured servants and, later, enslaved Africans.

IN-DEPTH RESOURCES: UNIT 1
Guided Reading, p. 11
Primary Source: from *Travels and Works of Captain John Smith*, p. 23

ACCESS FOR STUDENTS ACQUIRING ENGLISH
Guided Reading, (Spanish), p. 15

HISTORICAL SPOTLIGHT

The Mystery of Roanoke

Critical Thinking: Making Inferences Have students find Roanoke on a map of North America. Then tell them that White had planned to set up his settlement on the Chesapeake Bay, perhaps along the mouth of the James River, but that the ship captain refused to go farther than Roanoke. Have students speculate on reasons for the captain's decision. *He considered the dangers of shallows, narrow channels, and reefs.*

ELECTRONIC LIBRARY OF PRIMARY SOURCES
What Happened Till the First Supply, by John Smith

TEACHING OPTIONS

Making Global Connections

The West Indies and the Chesapeake For a time the Spanish held a monopoly on tobacco, cultivating the sweet-tasting variety native to the West Indies and selling it at a high price in Europe. When Virginians began to cultivate tobacco on the low-lying alluvial plains around the Chesapeake Bay, they sold their more plentiful crops at lower prices than the Spaniards did. As a result, the Spanish turned their West Indian tobacco plantations into sugar plantations—producing a product that would eventually lure New England merchants to the Caribbean.

Exploring Themes

Immigration and Migration Indentured servitude still exists in parts of the developing world. In India and Pakistan, for example, poverty-stricken parents will bond their children to shops where they receive food and clothes in exchange for their labor. Adults sometimes bond themselves, too, so that they can pay off old debts or gain the use of land. Ask interested students to investigate efforts to end this practice by such groups as Free the Children, a Canadian organization founded by teenager Craig Kielburger.

Geography Spotlight

OBJECTIVES

1. To show how geography played a role in determining locations of settlements.
2. To identify the criteria settlers tried to meet in establishing Jamestown.

FOCUS & MOTIVATE

▶ ***Starting with the Student***
Tell students to imagine that they are part of a group of people moving to another part of the world.

- What specific criteria would you set for choosing a new locale?
- How might these change if the area to which you were moving was a wilderness with few inhabitants?

ELECTRONIC LIBRARY OF PRIMARY SOURCES
What Happened Till the First Supply by John Smith

MORE ABOUT . . .
Malaria

Malaria is caused by a parasite that lives in *Anopheles* mosquitoes and is transmitted to a human host by the mosquito's bite. The mosquito's role in spreading the disease was scientifically proved only in the late 19th century by a French physician, Charles Louis Alphonse Laveran. Laveran's work on tropical diseases won him the 1907 Nobel Prize for medicine.

GEOGRAPHY SPOTLIGHT

The Jamestown Settlement

Every time people choose a new place to settle, they consider two aspects of its geographic location: the site and the situation. Site refers to the physical characteristics of a particular spot: the landforms, the quality of the soil, and the type of vegetation. Situation, on the other hand, concerns the relationship between the site and its surrounding area. How close is it to the sea? to other settlements? to resources? to avenues of transportation like roads or harbors?

The first settlers of Jamestown were mainly concerned about defense. The English feared attack from two groups: (1) the rival power Spain, whose powerful navy could attack by sea, and (2) Native Americans, who could attack by land. The colonists also needed an area that would support their settlement with fresh water and fertile soil.

As the leaders of the Jamestown expedition explored the Chesapeake Bay and its rivers, they argued about where to erect a fort and plant their settlement. No one place seemed to meet all the criteria. The place they chose was well situated for defense. The land was flat and nearly surrounded by water. In other ways, however, the site was disastrous. Much of the land was marshy, and there were swarms of mosquitoes. At that time no one knew that some mosquitoes carried deadly malaria.

SETTLEMENT CRITERIA When the Virginia Company sent the Jamestown expedition, it gave specific instructions regarding the settlement's location. The four major criteria are shown in these maps. Three of the four criteria concern defense. The settlements were actually attacked twice by Native Americans—in 1622 and 1644—but a much feared invasion by the Spanish never occurred.

The fourth criterion—that the site be healthful and fertile—involved its suitability for living. While fertile, the island proved to be unhealthful.

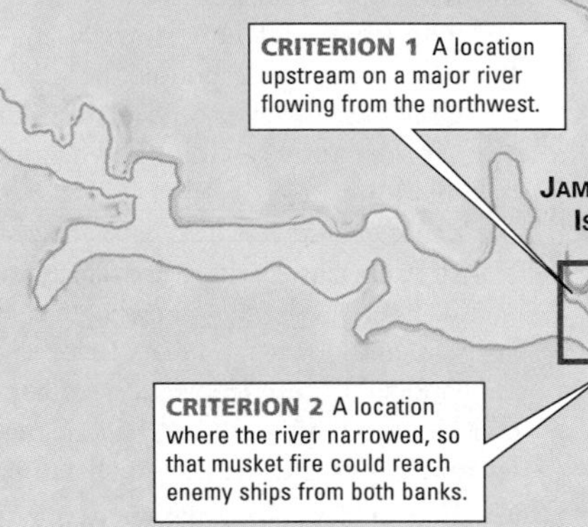
CRITERION 1 A location upstream on a major river flowing from the northwest.
JAMESTOWN ISLAND
James River
CRITERION 2 A location where the river narrowed, so that musket fire could reach enemy ships from both banks.

Pottery jug found on the site of James Fort.

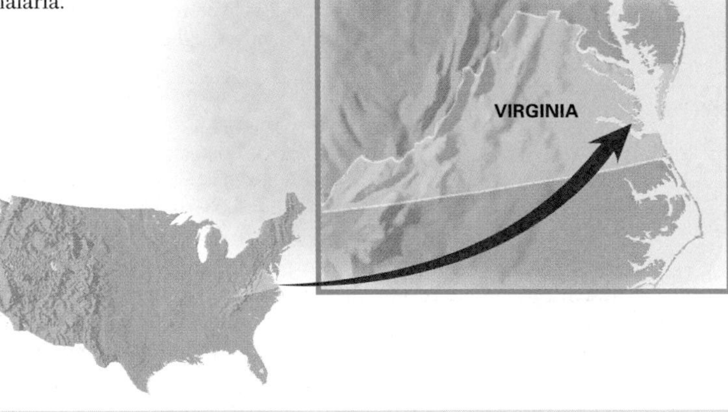
VIRGINIA

RECOMMENDED RESOURCES

Books

Bridenbaugh, Carl. *Jamestown, 1544–1699.* New York: Oxford UP, 1980. A brief, respected history.

Deetz, James. *In Small Things Forgotten.* Garden City, NY: Anchor, 1996. Objects from everyday colonial life.

Noël Hume, Ivor. *Martin's Hundred.* New York: Dell, 1982. Lost James River colony.

Smith, John. *Captain John Smith's History of Virginia.* Indianapolis: Bobbs-Merrill, 1979. Selections from Smith's work, first published in 1624.

Videos

Cavaliers and Craftsmen: Colonial Williamsburg & Jamestown. Atlas Video, 1986. Reenacts everyday life, with background period music.

Colonial America: The Beginnings. CRM Films. Focuses on the settling of America and early colonial life.

Search for a Century. Colonial Williamsburg Foundation, 1980. Documents the dig for the early Virginia colony lost in 1618 at Martin's Hundred.

Where America Began. Finley-Holiday Film Corp., 1988. Tours the restorations at Jamestown, Williamsburg, and Yorktown, Virginia.

Software

ColonyQuest. Decision Development Corp., distributed by ESI. A simulation placing students in Jamestown in about 1610, where as settlement leaders they must establish a tobacco plantation, hire workers, and face many other challenges.

SITE AND SITUATION The map below shows the situation of Jamestown on the James River, and the map to the right gives a detailed view of the site the colonists selected—a marshy island in the James River.

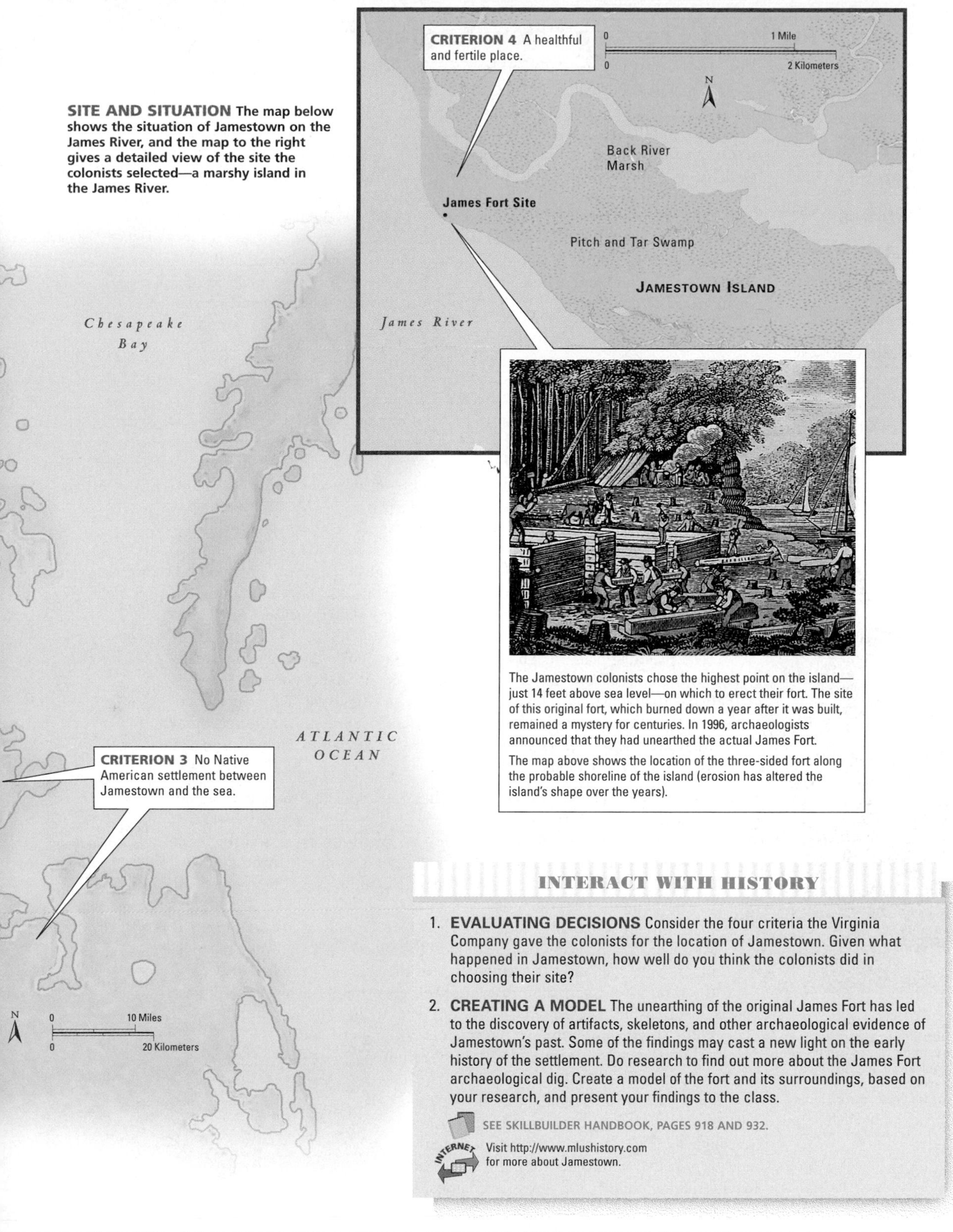

The Jamestown colonists chose the highest point on the island—just 14 feet above sea level—on which to erect their fort. The site of this original fort, which burned down a year after it was built, remained a mystery for centuries. In 1996, archaeologists announced that they had unearthed the actual James Fort.

The map above shows the location of the three-sided fort along the probable shoreline of the island (erosion has altered the island's shape over the years).

INTERACT WITH HISTORY

1. **EVALUATING DECISIONS** Consider the four criteria the Virginia Company gave the colonists for the location of Jamestown. Given what happened in Jamestown, how well do you think the colonists did in choosing their site?

2. **CREATING A MODEL** The unearthing of the original James Fort has led to the discovery of artifacts, skeletons, and other archaeological evidence of Jamestown's past. Some of the findings may cast a new light on the early history of the settlement. Do research to find out more about the James Fort archaeological dig. Create a model of the fort and its surroundings, based on your research, and present your findings to the class.

SEE SKILLBUILDER HANDBOOK, PAGES 918 AND 932.

INTERNET Visit http://www.mlushistory.com for more about Jamestown.

INSTRUCT

▶***Discussing Key Ideas***

- Defense was a key concern in choosing the site of the Jamestown colony.
- Because of their concern for defense and ignorance about malaria-carrying mosquitoes, the settlers chose a marshy area that proved unhealthful.

HISTORY FROM VISUALS

Reading the Images

Study the maps and the four points specifying an ideal location.

- To what "sea" does point 3 refer? *Atlantic Ocean*
- Why do you think the criteria stressed a river location near the sea? *Possible Responses: Easier to find and supply; easier to escape; good for trade; water was chief means of transport.*

MORE ABOUT . . .

The James Fort Discovery

"We are at ground zero, the genesis of America," observed William Kelso, leader of the team that unearthed the James Fort artifacts in 1996. The man whose skeleton they found, and who may have bled to death from the musket ball embedded in his leg, may have been George Kendall, possibly put to death as a suspected spy for Spain.

INTERACT WITH HISTORY

1. Evaluating Decisions

Possible Responses *In meeting three of the four criteria, the colonists did well, considering the unknown nature of the terrain. Because they failed to choose a healthful site, the colonists did poorly, since the high death rate almost nullified the positive effects of the other criteria. The colonists were still vulnerable to attack as well as disease. The colonists were still placed in a precarious position because the Virginia Company cared mainly about profits and neglected the colonists' welfare.*

2. Creating a Model

Standards for Evaluation

Information should . . .

- be presented as a physical model or a computer graphic display
- include details obtained through up-to-date sources such as periodicals, the Internet, and/or the Jamestown restoration itself or another appropriate organization
- focus on any new details that the findings provide about the suitability of the Jamestown site and the early history of the settlement

OBJECTIVE

② INSTRUCT

Puritans Create a "New England"

▶ ***Discussing Key Ideas***

- Puritan settlers come to America to practice their religion freely.
- They seek to build a model society.
- The Puritans are intolerant of other religious beliefs.
- Dissenters form the colony of Rhode Island.
- Conflicts over land and religion trigger wars with Native Americans.

MORE ABOUT . . .

John Winthrop

John Winthrop studied at Trinity College in the University of Cambridge. While there, he became a Puritan. He grew increasingly troubled by the problems faced by Puritans in England. Winthrop tasted the wrath of royalists when his beliefs cost him a lucrative job as an attorney in the royal courts.

IN-DEPTH RESOURCES: UNIT 1
American Lives: John Winthrop, p. 28

ELECTRONIC LIBRARY OF PRIMARY SOURCES
from *The Book of the General Laws by the Inhabitants of New-Plimouth*

CRITICAL THINKING TRANSPARENCIES
CT2, Puritan Migration

Puritans Create a "New England"

"The Holy Spirit illumines the heart of every true believer."

ANNE HUTCHINSON

King Henry VIII (1491–1547) had brought the Reformation to England in the 1530s when he broke with Roman Catholicism to form the Church of England. Although the new church was free of Catholic control, one religious group, the **Puritans,** felt that the church had kept too much of the Catholic ritual and tradition. They wanted to purify the church by eliminating all traces of Catholicism. Some Puritans felt they should remain in the Church of England and reform it from within. Others, called Separatists, did not think that was possible. The Separatists met in secret because James I was determined to punish those who did not follow the Anglican form of worship.

One congregation of Separatists, known today as the Pilgrims, fled from England to Holland and eventually migrated to America. There, in 1620, this small group of families founded the Plymouth Plantation, the second permanent English colony in North America. Their Mayflower Compact, named for the ship on which they sailed to North America, became an important landmark in the development of American democracy.

THE MASSACHUSETTS BAY COLONY Other Puritans who were not Separatists turned their thoughts toward New England in the 1620s. They felt the burden of increasing religious persecution, political repression, and dismal economic conditions. **John Winthrop,** a lawyer who would be the first governor of the Massachusetts Bay Colony, and some of his well-connected friends obtained a royal charter for a joint-stock enterprise, the Massachusetts Bay Company. The migration that this company began in 1630 was greater in size and more thorough in planning than any previous expedition to North America. During that year, 17 ships carried about 1,000 English men, women, and children—Puritans and non-Puritans—to the Massachusetts Bay Colony. Aboard these vessels were ample provisions and the many skilled artisans needed to establish good English farms and villages.

THINK THROUGH HISTORY
C. ***Analyzing Motives*** *Why did the Puritans leave England?*

C. Answer Religious persecution, political repression, and poor economic conditions.

The planning paid off. The colony's success quickly encouraged a steady flow of colonists from across the Atlantic—about 20,000 people between 1630 and 1640—in a movement called the Great Migration. The port town of Boston soon became the colony's thriving capital. Settlers established other towns nearby and eventually incorporated the Plymouth Colony into the Massachusetts Bay Colony.

This statue of Anne Hutchinson stands in Boston, Massachusetts. Ironically, she was banished from Massachusetts for leading religious discussions.

THE PURITANS The Puritans believed they had a special covenant, or agreement, with God. To fulfill their part, they were to create a moral society that would serve as a beacon for others to follow. Winthrop expressed the sense of mission that bound the Puritans together, in a sermon delivered aboard the flagship *Arbella:* "We [in New England] shall be as a City upon a Hill; the eyes of all people are on us."

Although Puritans made no effort to create a democracy, the Massachusetts Bay Company extended the right to vote not only to stockholders but to all adult male members of the Puritan church—40 percent of the colony's men. As their system of self-government evolved, so did the close relationship between the government and the Puritan church. The Puritan view dominated Massachusetts society: taxes supported the Puritan church, and laws required church attendance.

Puritans cherished their Bibles, passing them down as family treasures from one generation to the next. This Bible belonged to Governor William Bradford of the Plymouth Colony.

Unlike settlers in Virginia, Puritans generally crossed the Atlantic as families rather than as single men or women. Within the family, authority rested with the father. Husbands and wives shared child-rearing responsibilities, but wives were expected to defer to their husbands in

Block Schedule TEACHING OPTION **Time Needed: 40 Minutes**

Cooperative Activity: Investigating Puritan Life

Task: Students will investigate the Puritans in colonial Massachusetts and create a visual display of their research.

Purpose: To understand the customs and traditions, family life, and community life of the Puritans in Massachusetts.

Activity: Divide the class into small groups to research and create displays of various aspects of Puritan life. Have students begin their research before they go to the library by identifying topics and dividing them among the groups. Topics might include food, clothing, religious practices, social customs, laws and traditions, work and income, education, and entertainment. Then students can research their topics, collecting facts, figures, and images that help depict and explain life in a Puritan community. Ask them to create visual displays that include drawings, sketches, maps, charts, color photocopies, and diagrams, as well as written descriptions of their findings and present them to the class.

ALTERNATIVE ASSESSMENT BOOK
Standards for Evaluating a Cooperative Activity

all other matters of importance. Puritan laws criminalized such sins as drunkenness, swearing, theft, and idleness.

DISSENT IN THE PURITAN COMMUNITY The Puritans came to America to follow their own form of worship, and they were intolerant of people who had other religious beliefs. Puritan leaders felt particularly threatened by two dissenters, Roger Williams and Anne Hutchinson, whose beliefs challenged the social order upon which the colony was founded.

Roger Williams, an extreme Separatist, expressed two controversial views. First, he declared that the English settlers had no rightful claim to the land unless they purchased it from Native Americans. Second, he declared that government officials had no business punishing settlers for their religious beliefs. He felt every person should be free to worship according to his or her conscience.

To the Puritan leaders of Massachusetts, the first idea was absurd, and the second was heresy—it violated the religious beliefs of the Puritans. The outraged General Court ordered Williams to be arrested and returned to England. Before this order was carried out, Williams fled Massachusetts. In January 1636, he headed south to Narragansett Bay. There he negotiated with the local Narragansett tribe for land to set up a new colony, which he called Providence. In Providence, later the capital of Rhode Island, Williams guaranteed separation of church and state and religious freedom.

Another dissenter, Anne Hutchinson, posed an even greater threat to strict Puritans in part because, as a woman, she was expected to defer to authority. In Bible readings at her home, Hutchinson taught that "the Holy Spirit illumines [enlightens] the heart of every true believer." In other words, worshippers did not need the church or its ministers to interpret the Bible for them. Although she had many supporters, Hutchinson was put on trial for violating the laws of the family, church, and state. Punished with banishment, Hutchinson, with her family and a band of followers, moved to Rhode Island in 1638. After her trial, the Massachusetts colony increased restrictions on women's activities.

THINK THROUGH HISTORY
D. *Analyzing Issues* *In what principles did the government of Providence differ from that of Massachusetts Bay?*

D. Answer Separation of church and state and religious tolerance.

NATIVE AMERICANS RESIST COLONIAL EXPANSION While Williams and his followers were settling Rhode Island, thousands of other white settlers fanned out to western Massachusetts and to new colonies in New Hampshire and Connecticut. From the beginning, Native Americans had helped the colonists, providing them with land, giving them agricultural advice, and engaging them in trade—trade that helped many Puritan merchants prosper.

However, as Native Americans saw their own people killed by European diseases and their lands taken over by settlers, they feared an end to their way of life. Disputes between the Puritans and Native Americans arose over land and religion. For every acre a colonial farmer needed to support life, a Native American needed 20 acres for hunting, fishing, and agriculture. To Native Americans, no one owned the land—it was there for everyone to use. Europeans, however, viewed the natives' agreement to share the land with them as an outright sale.

Similar misunderstandings existed over religion. At first, Puritans tried to convert Native Americans. Over time, as hostility between the two groups increased, the New England colonists set out to remove or destroy native societies. For their part, Native Americans developed a similarly hard view toward the white invaders.

KEY PLAYER

METACOM (?–1676)

As a youth, Metacom watched his father, Massasoit, befriend the Puritans and offer them land, advice, and protection from other tribes. As a sign of friendship, the Puritans gave Massasoit's sons English names. Metacom received the name Philip, after Philip of Macedon, the father of Alexander the Great.

However, English names did not make English subjects. In 1662, after the death of his father and older brother, 24-year-old Metacom became chief of the Wampanoag. Whereas his father had kept peace with the English, Metacom found it increasingly difficult to live on their terms, as he saw white settlers take more and more land and subject his people to much humiliation.

Metacom bided his time for 13 years while he secretly forged an alliance among Northeastern tribes. The breaking point came in 1675, when Puritan authorities executed three Wampanoag for the murder of a tribal informer. In retaliation, Metacom and his allies attacked colonial villages, and King Philip's War began.

KEY PLAYER
Metacom

Critical Thinking: Evaluating Decisions
Ask students to evaluate Metacom's decisions in his relations with the English settlers, first biding his time, and then after 13 years forging a secret alliance that eventually led to war. *Some students will suggest that he was justified, having been pushed to the breaking point; others will suggest that he should have made earlier attempts to reach a compromise with the English.*

MORE ABOUT . . .
Puritan Women
Puritan emphasis on reading the Bible encouraged a higher rate of literacy among Puritan women in New England than among women in England or elsewhere in the colonies. As late as the 1750s, only one out of three women in England could sign her name. In the colonies as a whole in the 17th century, fewer than half of all women could read and even fewer could write. Most Puritan women, however, learned to read and write at home. They were expected, though, to keep their writings private.

TEACHING OPTIONS

Exploring Themes

Immigration and Migration When the Puritans moved into New England, they introduced new ideas of land use that conflicted with those held by Native Americans. They cut down trees and farmed tracts of land which were owned by individual families. When New Englanders defeated the Native Americans who lived in the region, they also set in motion forces that would reshape the region's landscape. The densely forested woodlands would soon be sacrificed for well-defined villages and towns.

Making Connections Across Time

Pequot Land Rights In 1973, Elizabeth George Plouffe, the last Pequot occupying a tiny reservation, died. When Connecticut moved to convert the land into a park, Plouffe's grandson, Richard "Skip" Hayward, honored a promise to "hold onto the land." After a series of court suits, Hayward and the Pequot who joined him won a $900,000 settlement. The Pequot invested the money in a giant casino complex and used the profits to revitalize their culture. Since the 1970s, the number of Pequot has grown from about 50 to more than 250.

HISTORY FROM VISUALS

New England Colonies to 1675

Reading the Map Explain to students that the New England colonies grew into a distinct region. Refer them to the map and ask: What colonies made up this region? How would students describe the geographic location of these colonies?

Extension Based on the map, what hypotheses can students form about the way New Englanders might have earned their living? Have students evaluate their hypotheses by examining the map on page 32.

OBJECTIVE ③ **INSTRUCT**

Settlement of the Middle Colonies

▶ ***Discussing Key Ideas***

- The Dutch establish New Netherland to expand their fur trade.
- New Netherland opens its door to a wide variety of people.
- William Penn founds Pennsylvania on Quaker principles of tolerance.
- His respect of Native American land rights promotes peace.

GEOGRAPHY TRANSPARENCIES
G2, European Colonies, 1650

The first major conflict arose in Connecticut in 1637, when the Pequot nation decided to take a stand against the colonists. The colonists formed an alliance with the Narragansett, old enemies of the Pequot. The end came in May 1637, when about 90 English colonists and hundreds of their Native American allies surrounded a Pequot fort on the Mystic River. After setting the fort on fire, the colonists shot Pequot men, women, and children as they tried to escape or surrender.

That day, both the Pequot and the Narragansett witnessed warfare more brutal than any they had ever known. The massacre led a Narragansett leader named Miantonomo to warn other tribes, including the Montauk of Long Island, about the English.

New England Colonies to 1675

Skillbuilder Answer
Place: Plymouth, Massachusetts.
Place: Boston's proximity to the sea and good harbor made it easily accessible for ships carrying supplies and settlers.

GEOGRAPHY SKILLBUILDER
PLACE What was the earliest major European settlement in the New England colonies?
PLACE What characteristics did Boston have that made it a good place for a settlement?

A PERSONAL VOICE

You know our fathers had plenty of deer and skins, our plains were full of deer, as also our woods, and of turkeys, and our coves full of fish and fowl. But these English have gotten our land, they with scythes cut down the grass, and with axes fell the trees; their cows and horses eat the grass, and their hogs spoil our clam banks, and we shall all be starved. . . .

For so are we all Indians as the English are, and say brother one to another, so must we be one as they are, otherwise we shall be all gone shortly.

MIANTONOMO, quoted in *Changes in the Land*

KING PHILIP'S WAR Great tension continued for nearly 40 years. The colonial population had swelled to more than 50,000. Deprived of their land and livelihood, many Native Americans had to work for the English to earn a living. They also had to obey Puritan laws, such as the prohibition of hunting or fishing on Sunday, the Sabbath day. The Wampanoag chief Metacom, whom the English called King Philip, organized his tribe and several others into an alliance to wipe out the invaders.

The eruption of **King Philip's War** in the spring of 1675 startled the Puritans with its intensity. Native Americans attacked and burned outlying settlements throughout New England. Within months they were striking the outskirts of Boston. The alarmed and angered colonists responded by killing as many Native Americans as they could, even some from friendly tribes. For over a year, the two sides waged a war of mutual brutality and destruction. Finally, food shortages, disease, and heavy casualties wore down the Native Americans' resistance, and they gradually surrendered or fled.

Dutch settlers in New Netherland trade with Native Americans.

THINK THROUGH HISTORY
E. *Making Predictions* *What long-term effects would you predict followed King Philip's War?*

E. Answer
Students might suggest lasting bitterness between Native Americans and Europeans and the colonialists' continual encroachment on Native American lands.

Settlement of the Middle Colonies

While English Puritans were establishing colonies in New England, the Dutch were founding one to the south. As early as 1609, Henry Hudson—an Englishman employed by the Dutch—had sailed up the river that now bears his name. The Dutch soon established a fur trade with the Iroquois and built trading posts on the Hudson River at Fort Orange (now Albany) and on Manhattan Island, at the mouth of the river.

TEACHING OPTIONS

Exploring Themes

Democracy in America Although most Puritans believed in the concept of government by consent, they did not uphold the idea of religious freedom. Majority rule in Massachusetts Bay had little room for individual dissenters, such as Roger Williams and Anne Hutchinson. Protection of the rights of religious minorities was established in Rhode Island, where Williams formulated the principles of separation of church and state and religious tolerance.

Making Connections Across Cultures

The Jews of Rhode Island In the spring of 1658, 15 Spanish and Portuguese Jewish families arrived in Newport, Rhode Island. They were attracted by a statement by Roger Williams that declared, *I affirm, that [in keeping with] liberty of conscience . . . , that none of the Papists [Catholics], Protestants, Jews and Turks [Muslims] be forced to . . . worship [in a certain way].* By 1759, the Jewish community had grown wealthy enough to break ground for the Touro Synagogue, the oldest synagogue in the United States and a national historic site.

THE DUTCH FOUND NEW NETHERLAND In 1621, the Dutch government granted the newly formed Dutch West India Company permission to colonize New Netherland and expand the thriving fur trade. New Amsterdam (now New York City), founded in 1625, became the capital of the colony. By the 1630s, the Dutch had built a number of enormous estates along both sides of the Hudson River. In 1655, they extended their claims by taking over New Sweden, a tiny colony of Swedish and Finnish settlers that had established a rival fur trade along the Delaware River.

To encourage settlers to come and stay, the colony opened its doors to a variety of people. Gradually, more Dutch as well as Germans, French, Scandinavians, and other Europeans settled the area. The colony also included many Africans, free as well as enslaved. By the 1660s, in fact, one-fifth of New Netherland's population was of African ancestry. The Dutch reputation for religious tolerance also drew people of many faiths, including Protestants, Catholics, Muslims, and Jews.

THINK THROUGH HISTORY
F. *Making Inferences* *What were the important characteristics of New Netherland society?*

F. Answer Ethnic diversity, religious tolerance, and generally good relations with Native Americans.

These settlers generally enjoyed friendlier relations with the Native Americans than did the English colonists in New England and Virginia. The Dutch were less interested in conquering the Native Americans than in trading with them for furs.

In 1644, the English took over the colony without a fight. The duke of York, the new proprietor, or owner, of the colony, renamed it New York. The duke later gave a portion of this land to two of his friends, naming this territory New Jersey for the British island of Jersey.

THE QUAKERS SETTLE PENNSYLVANIA The acquisition of New Netherland was one step in England's quest to extend its American empire after 1660, when the English monarchy was restored after a period of civil war and Puritan rule. The new king, Charles II, owed a debt to the father of a young man named **William Penn.** As payment, Charles gave the younger Penn a large property that the king insisted be called Pennsylvania, or "Penn's Woods," after the father. Following this, in 1682, Penn acquired more land from the duke of York, the three counties that became Delaware.

William Penn belonged to the Society of Friends, or **Quakers,** a Protestant sect whose religious and social beliefs were radical for the time. They held services without formal ministers, allowing any person to speak as the spirit moved him or her. They dressed plainly, refused to defer to persons of rank, opposed war, and refused to serve in the military. For their radical views, they were scorned and harassed by Anglicans and Puritans alike.

Penn wanted to establish a good and fair society in keeping with Quaker ideals of equality, cooperation, and religious toleration. Penn guaranteed every adult male settler 50 acres of land and the right to vote. His plan for government called for a representative assembly and freedom of religion. As a lasting symbol of his Quaker beliefs, Penn also helped plan a capital he called the "City of Brotherly Love," or Philadelphia.

As a Quaker, Penn believed that people approached in friendship would respond in friendship. So even before setting foot in North America, Penn, aware that the Delaware—the tribe that inhabited the settlement area—had already been ravaged by European diseases and war, arranged to have a letter read to them.

ON THE WORLD STAGE

THE ENGLISH CIVIL WAR AND RESTORATION

From 1642 to 1649, England was torn apart by a great civil war between loyalists to the king and those who were loyal to Parliament, many of whom were Puritans. The armies of Parliament were victorious, and Charles I was executed in 1649. For a decade, England became a commonwealth, or republic, headed first by Oliver Cromwell, a Puritan, and then by his son Richard.

However, the English grew weary of the rather grim and sober Puritan rule, and in 1660 the monarchy was restored under Charles II. Following the Restoration, new colonies took shape, including New York and Pennsylvania. In 1663, Charles awarded a group of key supporters the land between Virginia and Spanish Florida, which became North and South Carolina. The addition of these colonies, as well as Maryland, which had been chartered in 1632, and Georgia, later chartered in 1732, brought the number of England's colonies to 13.

Skillbuilder Answer The Delaware River.

GEOGRAPHY SKILLBUILDER
REGION ***What major river formed part of the border separating New Netherland from the English middle colonies?***

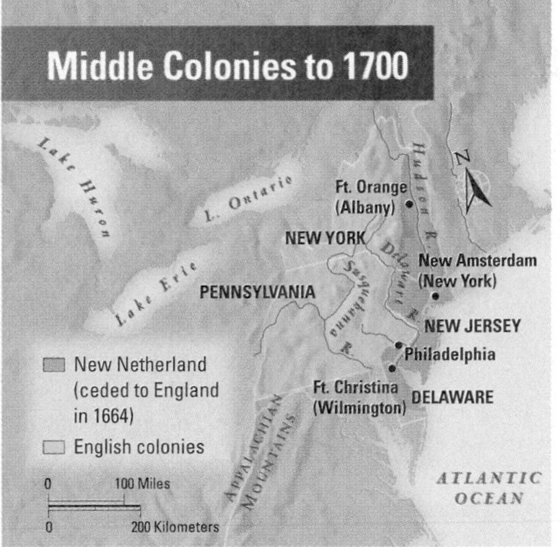

ON THE WORLD STAGE
The English Civil War and Restoration

Critical Thinking: Finding Main Ideas Read this explanation of the English Civil War by a Puritan.

"The question in dispute between the King's party and us was whether the King should govern as a god by will . . . ; or whether the people should be governed by laws made by themselves and live under a Government derived from their own consent."

Ask, What was the main issue in the war? *How the people should be governed.*

MORE ABOUT . . .
Philadelphia

William Penn worked with the surveyor Thomas Holme to systematically plan the layout of Philadelphia. It consisted of a 22-by-8 block grid. Penn set aside the central block for the "capital square" and four other blocks for public use. From 1683 to 1799, Philadelphia served as the capital of Pennsylvania.

GROLIER MULTIMEDIA ENCYCLOPEDIA
George Fox, Founder of the Society of Friends

HISTORY FROM VISUALS
Middle Colonies to 1700

Reading the Map
Have students examine the map key. Ask, How does this key help you to understand why the English called New Netherland "the Dutch wedge"? *It comes between the British colonies.*

TEACHING OPTIONS

Exploring Themes

Cultural Diversity To attract settlers, the Dutch of New Netherland opened their colony to people of all backgrounds, including free Africans. William Penn followed the Dutch example in Pennsylvania. From these actions resulted colonies of extraordinary diversity and vitality.

Making Connections Across Cultures

Dutch Words The cultural exchanges that occurred among the peoples of colonial America can be illustrated by the number of Dutch words that have slipped into English usage. According to New York's New Netherland Project, a sampling includes: *cookie, snack, skating, duffel, knapsack, stove, dollar, caboodle, hodgepodge, pinkie, yacht, cruiser,* and more. Ask students to find other words from other cultures that have become part of American English.

MORE ABOUT . . .

The Delaware

Europeans renamed the Lenape of Pennsylvania the Delaware because they lived along the Delaware River and its tributaries. In reality, the Delaware formed part of a large group of peoples that extended into the colony of New Netherland.

The westward push of settlers forced the Delaware across the Appalachians and eventually across the Mississippi River.

By 1990, the Delaware numbered about 9,300, with most living on reservations or in towns in Oklahoma and in Ontario, Canada.

England and Its Colonies Prosper

▶ ***Discussing Key Ideas***

- Under the economic system of mercantilism, England benefits from trading with its colonies.
- The colonies often benefit from mercantilism as well.
- The Navigation Acts control trade to and from the colonies.
- The colonies typically have a governor, an advisory council, and an elected assembly.
- A spirit of self-determination grows among the colonists.

A PERSONAL VOICE

Now I would have you well observe, that I am very sensible of the unkindness and injustice that has been too much exercised towards you by the people of these parts of the world, who have sought . . . to make great advantages by you, . . . sometimes to the shedding of blood. . . . But I am not such a man. . . . I have great love and regard toward you, and I desire to win and gain your love and friendship by a kind, just, and peaceable life. . . .

WILLIAM PENN, quoted in *A New World*

Like Roger Williams before him, Penn believed that the land belonged to the Delaware and other Native Americans, and he saw to it that they were paid for it. To be sure that his colonists treated the native people fairly, he regulated trade with them and provided for a court made up of both colonists and Native Americans to settle any differences. The Native Americans respected Penn.

As a proprietor, Penn needed to attract settlers—farmers, builders, and traders—to create a profitable colony. After opening the colony to Quakers, he vigorously recruited immigrants from around western Europe using glowing advertisements. In time, settlers came in great numbers, including thousands of Germans who brought with them craft skills and farming techniques that helped the colony to thrive.

This 19th-century painting portrays the signing of a peace treaty in 1682 between William Penn and the Delaware Indians—an event some historians believe never took place. A Quaker silver collar (*top*) is offered to local Native Americans as a token of peace.

Penn himself spent only about four years in Pennsylvania. Meanwhile, his idealistic vision had faded but did not disappear. The Quakers became a minority in a colony thickly populated by people from all over western Europe. Slavery was introduced, and, in fact, many prominent Quakers in Pennsylvania owned slaves. However, the principles of equality, cooperation, and religious tolerance on which he had founded his vision would eventually become fundamental values of the new American nation.

G. Answer Penn sought the respect and friendship of the Native Americans and paid them for their land; the Puritans sought to push the Native Americans off the land once attempts to convert them had failed.

THINK THROUGH HISTORY
G. *Contrasting* *How did Penn's actions toward the Native Americans differ from those of the Puritans?*

H. Answer English settlers brought with them the belief in self-government. Dissenters such as Roger Williams and Anne Hutchinson and idealists like William Penn introduced freedoms such as religious tolerance and expanded suffrage.

THINK THROUGH HISTORY
H. THEME *Democracy in America* *What were some of the sources of democratic ideals in the early colonies?*

England and Its Colonies Prosper

The new British colonies existed primarily for the benefit of England. The colonies exported to England a rich variety of raw materials, such as lumber and furs, and in return they imported the manufactured goods that England produced. This economic relationship benefited both England and its colonies, and their economies flourished.

MERCANTILISM AND THE NAVIGATION ACTS Beginning in the 16th century, the nations of Europe competed for wealth and power through a new economic system called mercantilism, in which colonies played a critical role. According to the theory of **mercantilism,** a nation could increase its wealth and power in two ways: by obtaining as much gold and silver as possible, and by establishing a favorable balance of trade, in which it sold more goods than it bought. A nation's ultimate goal was to become self-sufficient so that it did not have to depend on other countries for goods.

The key to this process was the establishment of colonies. By 1732, there were 13 English colonies, from Massachusetts in the North producing timber and ships, to Georgia in the South growing indigo and rice. Colonies provided products, especially raw materials, that

The silver Spanish piece of eight *(left)* and the gold British guinea *(right)* were coins used by colonial merchants.

TEACHING OPTIONS

Making Connections Across the Curriculum

Economics Clarify that the balance of trade is the result of money made and spent on imports and exports. Encourage students to discuss arguments that still persist about whether trade should be regulated by government or not. *Benefits of free trade include lower consumer prices, higher-wage export jobs, and overseas economic stability that may help curb wars, terrorism, etc. Drawbacks include job losses in some industries, possible loss of manufacturing base, and loss of revenue to foreign creditors.*

Making Connections Across Cultures

Appalachian Roots Note that the political-religious factionalism in the British Isles at this time helped prompt immigration to America. The Scots-Irish of Appalachia descend largely from Scottish Protestants who for a time settled in Ireland before moving on to the New World. With them they brought their cultural traditions—which is why the Virginia reel looks and sounds so much like an Irish reel, and why so many English-Scottish border ballads ("Barbara Allan," for example) have their counterparts in Appalachian folk songs.

could not be found in the home country. For example, England, with its scarcity of forests, could now import lumber from New England rather than from Scandinavia. In addition to playing the role of supplier, the colonies under mercantilism also provided a market for the home country to sell the goods it produced.

Beginning in 1651, England's Parliament, the country's legislative body, moved to tighten control of colonial trade by passing a series of measures known as the **Navigation Acts.** These acts ordered the following:

1. No country could trade with the colonies unless the goods were shipped in either colonial or English ships.
2. All vessels had to be manned by crews that were at least three-quarters English or colonial.
3. The colonies could export certain products, including tobacco and sugar—and later rice, molasses, and furs—only to England.
4. Almost all goods traded between the colonies and Europe first had to be unloaded at an English port.

The system created by the Navigation Acts obviously benefited England. It proved to be good for most colonists as well. By restricting trade to English or colonial ships, the acts spurred a boom in the colonial shipbuilding industry and helped support the development of numerous other colonial industries.

THINK THROUGH HISTORY
I. *Clarifying* *Under mercantilism, what was the relationship between a home country and its colonies?*

I. Answer The colonies existed primarily to benefit the parent country by supplying it with materials and buying its goods.

Trade between England and the colonies benefited many colonial merchants. This painting depicts the wealthy New England trader Moses Marcy.

COLONIAL GOVERNMENTS Whatever their form of charter, most colonies were similar in the structure of their governments. In nearly every colony, a governor appointed by the Crown served as the highest authority. The governor presided over an advisory council, usually appointed by the governor, and a local assembly elected by landowning white males. The governor had the authority to appoint and dismiss judges and oversee colonial trade.

In addition to raising money through taxes, the colonial assembly initiated and passed laws. The governor could veto any law but did so at a risk—because the colonial assembly, not the Crown, paid the governor's salary. Using this power of the purse liberally, the colonists influenced the governor in a variety of ways, from the approval of laws to the appointment of judges.

GROWING SPIRIT OF SELF-DETERMINATION The colonies were developing a taste for self-government that would ultimately create the conditions for rebellion. Nehemiah Grew, a British mercantilist, voiced one of the few early concerns when he warned his fellow countrymen about the colonies' growing self-determination in 1707.

A PERSONAL VOICE

The time may come . . . when the colonies may become populous and with the increase of arts and sciences strong and politic, forgetting their relation to the mother countries, will then confederate and consider nothing further than the means to support their ambition of standing on their own legs.

NEHEMIAH GREW, quoted in *The Colonial Period of American History*

The 13 colonies that became the original United States were founded over a period of 125 years. The first permanent English settlement, at Jamestown, Virginia (1607), was founded as an investment by the Virginia Company and became viable once tobacco had become established. The last colony, Georgia (1732), came into being partly to protect the other Southern colonies against Spanish expansion from Florida. Together the colonies represented a wide variety of people, skills, motives, industries, resources, and agricultural products.

HISTORY FROM VISUALS

New England Trader

Reading the Art Ask students what words they would use to describe the man in the painting. *Possible Responses: Wealthy, comfortable, satisfied, leisurely.*

Extension Ask what the scene implies about colonial expansion or mercantilism. *Highly beneficial; brought prosperity.*

MORE ABOUT . . .

Great Britain

During the period covered by this section, England completed the process of unifying its island. This process started when England joined with Wales in 1536. However, nearly 200 more battle-filled years passed before the English unified the island by incorporating Scotland to the north. Since around 1100, the Scots, descendants of a Celtic tribe that had migrated from Ireland, had continually resisted English attempts at control.

Weary of constant warfare, the two nations signed the Act of Union in 1707, which joined them under the United Kingdom of Great Britain. The Scots dissolved their parliament and sent members to the British Parliament. Tensions continued throughout the century, however, as the Scots revolted on several occasions. Today the United Kingdom of Great Britain and Northern Ireland includes England, Scotland, Wales, and Northern Ireland.

Block Schedule TEACHING OPTION **Time Needed: 40 Minutes**

Cooperative Activity: Mapping Colonial Economic Activities

Task: Students will create a pictorial map showing the economic activities of the 13 English colonies.

Purpose: To illustrate the economic diversity of the colonies.

Activity: Request volunteers to draw a wall-size outline map of the 13 colonies. Tell them to show only the political boundaries on the map. (They might use an opaque projector to copy the map on page 32 onto poster paper.) Then assign groups of students one or more of the colonies, and have them think of various symbols to show the ways in which people earned a living in these colonies at this time. For extra credit, have students devise symbols that illustrate the main economic activities in French and Spanish possessions.

Note: If you have any students with a strong interest in cartography, refer them to *Pictorial Maps,* by Nigel Holmes (NY: Watson-Guptill Publications, 1991) as a reference.

ALTERNATIVE ASSESSMENT BOOK
Standards for Evaluating a Cooperative Learning Activity

HISTORY FROM VISUALS

The Thirteen Colonies to the Mid-1700s

Reading the Map

Tell students that this map provides many different types of information. Have them identify some of these categories: *physical topography east of the Mississippi, political boundaries of the colonies, economic activities of the colonies, European holdings east of the Mississippi River, etc.*

GEOGRAPHY TRANSPARENCIES
G35, Original Thirteen Colonies

ASSESS & RETEACH

Section 3 Assessment

Have students edit each other's answers, indicating whether or not answers match directions such as "summarizing" and "forming opinions."

Self-Assessment

Have students create their own questionnaire about this section and then answer the questions. Students can then review the section in pairs to find information they still need to answer all the questions.

Section Quiz

FORMAL ASSESSMENT
Section Quiz, p. 7

Reteach

Use the Guided Reading worksheet for Section 3 to help review the main ideas of this section.

IN-DEPTH RESOURCES
Guided Reading, p. 11

CLOSE

While tough trade and industrial policies encouraged colonial dissatisfaction, it was England's policy of salutary neglect that had the greatest impact and moving the colonies toward independence.

The Thirteen Colonies to the Mid-1700s

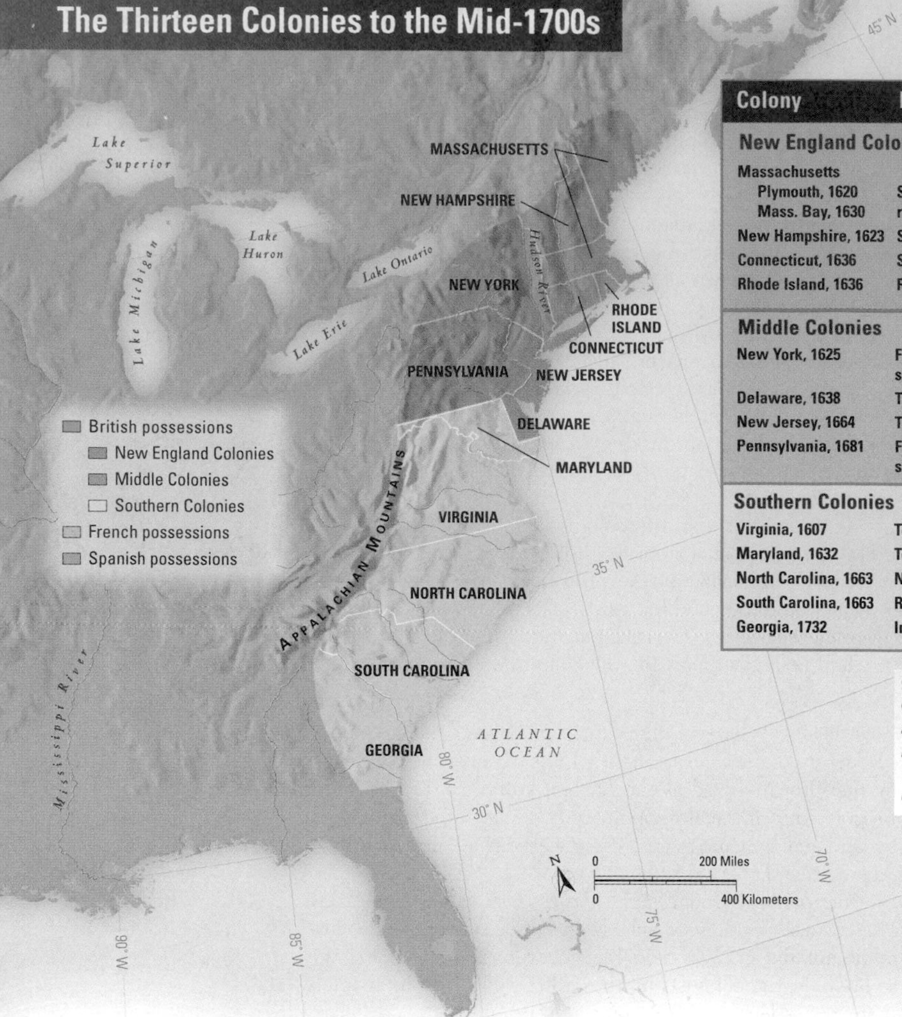

Colony	Economic Activities
New England Colonies	
Massachusetts	
Plymouth, 1620 Mass. Bay, 1630	Shipbuilding, shipping, fishing, lumber, rum, meat products
New Hampshire, 1623	Ship masts, lumber, fishing, trade
Connecticut, 1636	Shipping, livestock, foodstuffs
Rhode Island, 1636	Rum, iron foundries, shipbuilding, snuff, livestock
Middle Colonies	
New York, 1625	Furs, wheat, glass, shoes, livestock, shipping, shipbuilding, rum, beer, snuff
Delaware, 1638	Trade, foodstuffs
New Jersey, 1664	Trade, foodstuffs, copper
Pennsylvania, 1681	Flour, foodstuffs, paper, iron, wheat, flax, shipbuilding
Southern Colonies	
Virginia, 1607	Tobacco, wheat, cattle, iron
Maryland, 1632	Tobacco, wheat, snuff
North Carolina, 1663	Naval supplies, tobacco, furs
South Carolina, 1663	Rice, indigo, silk
Georgia, 1732	Indigo, rice, naval supplies, lumber

SKILLBUILDER **INTERPRETING CHARTS** *How did the New England and middle colonies' economies differ in general from the South's economy? What may have accounted for this difference?*

Aside from a desire for more economic and political breathing room, however, the colonies had little in common that would unite them against Britain. In particular, the Northern and Southern colonies were developing distinct societies, based on sharply contrasting economic systems.

Section 3 Assessment

1. TERMS & NAMES

Identify:
- John Smith
- Jamestown
- indentured servant
- Puritan
- John Winthrop
- King Philip's War
- William Penn
- Quaker
- mercantilism
- Navigation Acts

2. SUMMARIZING Identify the effects of each of the causes listed in the chart below.

Cause	Effect
Persecution of Puritans in England	
Puritan belief in hard work	
Roger Williams's dissenting beliefs	
Rapid colonial expansion in New England	
Defeat of King Philip	

3. FORMING OPINIONS In your judgment, what were the benefits and drawbacks of using indentured servants for labor in Virginia? Support your judgment with references to the text.

THINK ABOUT
- the labor demands of growing tobacco
- the characteristics and cost of indentured servants
- the causes and consequences of Bacon's Rebellion

4. MAKING INFERENCES In 1707 the British mercantilist Nehemiah Grew forecast that the colonies, "forgetting their relation to the mother countries, will then confederate and consider nothing further than the means to support their ambition of standing on their own legs." Explain why the British did not want this to happen.

THINK ABOUT
- the goals of mercantilism
- what might happen to Great Britain's economy if Grew's prediction came true

ANSWERS

1. TERMS & NAMES

John Smith, p. 22
Jamestown, p. 22
indentured servant, p. 23
Puritan, p. 26
John Winthrop, p. 26
King Philip's War, p. 28
William Penn, p. 29
Quaker, p. 29
mercantilism, p. 30
Navigation Acts, p. 31

2. SUMMARIZING

Possible Responses: Cause: Persecution—Effect: Puritan migration to New England. Cause: Belief in hard work—Effect: Rapid growth and success of Massachusetts Bay. Cause: Dissent—Effect: Founding of new colony based on his principles. Cause: Rapid colonial expansion—Effect: Conflict with Native Americans, including wars. Cause: Defeat—Effect: End of Native American power in southeastern New England.

3. FORMING OPINIONS

Possible Responses: Benefits: indentured servants were available, willing, and economical labor. Drawbacks: terms of service relatively short; since they earned little or no money during service, former servants were unable to buy land, remained poor, and had few rights.

4. MAKING INFERENCES

Possible Responses: Under mercantilism, Great Britain prized the economic value of the American colonies. The colonists' economic and political independence might weaken the British economy.

4 The Colonies Come of Age

TERMS & NAMES
- triangular trade
- middle passage
- Enlightenment
- Benjamin Franklin
- Great Awakening
- Jonathan Edwards
- French and Indian War
- William Pitt
- Pontiac
- Proclamation of 1763

LEARN ABOUT the economic, intellectual, and religious life of the colonies in the 1700s and the British victory over France
TO UNDERSTAND the economies of the North and South, the development of slavery, and the consolidation of British territory in North America.

ONE AMERICAN'S STORY

In 1773, Philip Vickers Fithian left his home in Princeton, New Jersey, for the unfamiliar world of Virginia. Fithian, a theology student, had agreed to tutor the children of Robert Carter III and his wife at their Virginia manor house. The magnificent brick mansion, which anchored their 13,500-acre plantation, sat on a hill overlooking the Potomac and Nomini rivers. Surrounding the house were more than 30 smaller houses, most of them living quarters for servants and slaves.

Fithian kept a journal of his one-year stay there, in which he recalled an evening walk along the property.

A PERSONAL VOICE

We stroll'd down the Pasture quite to the River, admiring the Pleasantness of the evening, & the delightsome Prospect of the River, Hills, Huts on the Summits, low Bottoms, Trees of various Kinds, and Sizes, Cattle & Sheep feeding some near us, & others at a great distance on the green sides of the Hills.

PHILIP VICKERS FITHIAN, *Journal & Letters of Philip Vickers Fithian*

The Shirley plantation house in Virginia is representative of many old Southern mansions. Built in 1723, it was the birthplace of the mother of Civil War general Robert E. Lee.

Plantations like the Carters' played a dominant role in the South's economy, which came to rely heavily on agriculture. The development of this plantation economy led to a largely rural society, in which African slaves played an important role.

A Plantation Economy Arises in the South

While there were cities in the South, on the whole the region developed as a self-sufficient, rural society. Plantations sprang up along the rivers, making it possible for planters to ship their goods directly to the Northern colonies and Europe without the need for public dock facilities. Farmers also had no need for city warehouses, since they stored their goods on the plantation. Finally, because plantation owners produced much of what they needed on their property, they did not often need shops, bakeries, and markets.

THINK THROUGH HISTORY
A. Clarifying *Why didn't the planters in the South (Virginia) need many cities?*
A. Answer They raised their own food, stored their own crops, and shipped their own goods directly from docks on the property.

Plantations specialized in raising a single crop grown primarily for sale rather than for the farmer's own use. In Maryland, Virginia, and North Carolina, planters grew tobacco. Planters in South Carolina and Georgia harvested rice and later indigo (for blue dye) as cash crops.

LIFE IN A DIVERSE SOUTHERN SOCIETY While small farmers made up the majority of the Southern population, prosperous plantation owners controlled much of the South's economy, as well as its political and social institutions. By the mid-1700s, life was good for many other Southern colonists as well. Because of a large growth in the entire colonies' export trade, colonial standards of living rose dramatically from 1700 to 1770. Thousands of German immigrants settled throughout Maryland, Virginia, and as far south as South Carolina. A wave of Scots and Scots-Irish also came to the South, mainly along the fertile hills of western North Carolina.

Section 4 Overview

OBJECTIVES
1. To characterize the plantation economy in the South.
2. To recognize the varied economy in the North.
3. To summarize the impact of Enlightenment thinking on people in the colonies.
4. To summarize the influence of the Great Awakening.
5. To understand the French and Indian War.

SKILLBUILDERS
- Interpreting graphs, p. 36
- Understanding geography: region, p. 41

CRITICAL THINKING
- Clarifying, p. 33
- Making inferences, pp. 35, 40
- Synthesizing, p. 35
- Finding main ideas, p. 36
- Recognizing effects, pp. 37, 38
- Contrasting, p. 39
- Summarizing, p. 41
- Analyzing issues, p. 41
- Making decisions, p. 41

FOCUS & MOTIVATE

5-MINUTE WARM-UP

Drawing Conclusions
Have students study the definitions and visuals on page 34.

1. What was the purpose of the triangular trade?
2. How did the European traders feel toward the enslaved Africans?

WARM-UP TRANSPARENCY 1

▶ ***Starting with the Student***
Is it possible to be wealthy without relying on the work of poorer people? Explain.

OBJECTIVE
1 INSTRUCT

A Plantation Economy Arises in the South

▶ ***Discussing Key Ideas***
- The Southern economy is dominated by large, self-sufficient plantations.

(continued on next page)

SECTION 4 RESOURCES

PRINT RESOURCES
IN-DEPTH RESOURCES: UNIT 1
Guided Reading, p. 12
Skillbuilder Practice: Visual Sources, p. 15
Geography Application: The Triangular Trade, p. 16
Primary Source: from *The Autobiography,* p. 24
American Lives: Olaudah Equiano, p. 29

READING STUDY GUIDE, p. 11

ACCESS FOR STUDENTS ACQUIRING ENGLISH
Guided Reading (Spanish), p. 16
Skillbuilder Practice: Visual Sources (Spanish), p. 19
Geography Application: The Triangular Trade (Spanish), p. 20

SPANISH READING STUDY GUIDE, p.11

FORMAL ASSESSMENT Section Quiz, p. 8

ALTERNATIVE ASSESSMENT BOOK
See forms for supporting and scoring alternative activities.

TECHNOLOGY RESOURCES
HUMANITIES TRANSPARENCIES
H4, Women Working in an Onion Field

GEOGRAPHY TRANSPARENCIES
G3, Colonial Economies

CRITICAL THINKING TRANSPARENCIES
CT37, Africans in the Colonies; CT3, French and Indian War

CD-ROM Electronic Library of Primary Sources
Grolier Multimedia Encyclopedia

VIDEO *American Portfolio: A Videodisc for U.S. History* user's guide, pp. 23–25, 27–28, 32

INTERNET http://www.mlushistory.com

(continued from page 33)

- Slaves come to America by the "middle passage," aboard slave ships where 20 percent of them died.
- Slaves from a variety of African cultures maintain their traditions.
- Sometimes they resist their plight, as in the Stono Rebellion of 1739.

IN-DEPTH RESOURCES: UNIT 1
Guided Reading, p. 12
Geography Application: the Triangular Trade, p. 16

ACCESS FOR STUDENTS ACQUIRING ENGLISH
Guided Reading (Spanish), p. 16

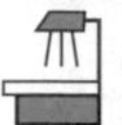

CRITICAL THINKING TRANSPARENCIES
CT37, Africans in the Colonies

HISTORY FROM VISUALS
Slave Ship

Reading the Art Ask students what words they would use to describe the scene depicted. *Possible Responses: Crowded, unsanitary, dark, communal.* Ask students what the diagram of the slave ship suggests about the slave traders' attitude toward their passengers.

Extension Have students discuss the degree of accuracy in the scene, based on the information in the text. *Some students may feel that the scene presents a somewhat idealized view by showing two slaves conversing, another relaxing in the foreground, and so on.*

As in the North, women in Southern society shared second-class citizenship. They could not vote, preach, or own property. Occupying an even lower rung on Southern society's ladder were indentured servants. Those who lived through their harsh years of labor—and many did not—saw their lives improve only slightly as they struggled to survive on the western outskirts of the Southern colonies. Their numbers declined toward the end of the century.

SLAVERY BECOMES ENTRENCHED As the indentured-servant population fell, the English colonists turned to enslaved Africans as an alternative. Slaves cost more than indentured servants, but they worked for a lifetime rather than for a period of bondage. By 1690, about 13,000 slaves were working in the Southern colonies. By 1750, the number of slaves in the South had increased to more than 200,000.

During the 17th century, Africans had become part of a transatlantic trading network described as the **triangular trade.** (See *trade* on page 940 in the Economics Handbook.) The term *triangular* referred to a process in which merchants carried rum and other goods from New England to Africa; exchanged their merchandise for slaves, whom they transported to the West Indies and sold for sugar and molasses; then shipped these goods to New England to be distilled into rum.

> ***"Every man was allowed a space six feet long by sixteen inches wide."***
>
> FROM *BLACK CARGOES*

THE MIDDLE PASSAGE The voyage that brought Africans to the West Indies and later to North America was known as the **middle passage,** after the middle leg of the transatlantic trade triangle. Extreme cruelty characterized this journey. In the ports of West Africa, European traders branded Africans for identification and packed them into the dark holds of large ships. On board a slave ship, Africans were beaten into submission and often fell victim to diseases that spread rapidly. Some committed suicide. Nearly 20 percent of the Africans aboard each slave ship perished during the brutal trip to the New World. One enslaved African, Olaudah Equiano, recalled the inhumane conditions on his trip from West Africa to the West Indies at age 11 in 1756.

A British naval officer painted the above scene of the deck of the slave ship *Albanez* in 1846. It portrays conditions that were found on many slave ships. The diagram at the right shows how slave traders often crammed as many slaves as possible on their ships.

TEACHING OPTION

Skillbuilder Mini-Lesson: Interpreting Visual Sources

Explaining the Skill Visual sources such as the images of slave ships on page 34 can reveal much about the times in which they were created. The artist's choice of details, the mood created with color and light, and the purpose of the piece, either known or guessed, all give the observer information.

Applying the Skill: Interpreting Visual Sources Have students examine the images of slave ships on this page and note who created them. Then ask these questions:

1. What conditions would you expect on board the ship in the diagram? *Cramped; hot; painful.*
2. What mood does the painting convey? *Blue suggests a calm, cool environment. Sunlight gives a sense of well being.*
3. What seem to be the artists' attitudes toward their subjects? *Students may say that neither artist views Africans as worthy of respect. The artist of the diagram views the captives simply as cargo. The painter seems to think, or wants others to think, that conditions on board were humane.*

IN-DEPTH RESOURCES: UNIT 1
Skillbuilder Practice: Visual Sources, p. 15

THINK THROUGH HISTORY
B. *Making Inferences* *If 20 percent of the enslaved Africans died on the journey to America, why did the merchants treat them so badly?*

B. Answer Possibly it was less expensive to replace the slaves than to keep them alive and healthy; possibly, because of racism, the merchants did not view the slaves as fully human and therefore deserving of humane treatment.

A PERSONAL VOICE

The closeness of the place and the heat of the climate, added to the number in the ship, which was so crowded that each had scarcely room to turn himself, almost suffocated us. This produced copious perspirations, so that the air soon became unfit for respiration from a variety of loathsome smells, and brought on a sickness among the slaves, of which many died.

OLAUDAH EQUIANO, *The Interesting Narrative of the Life of Olaudah Equiano*

Olaudah Equiano

AFRICANS COPE IN THEIR NEW WORLD Africans who survived the ocean voyage entered an extremely difficult life of bondage in North America. Probably 80 to 90 percent worked in the fields. The other 10 to 20 percent worked as domestic slaves or as artisans. Domestic slaves worked in the houses of their owners, cooking, cleaning, and helping to raise the owners' children. Artisans developed skills as carpenters, blacksmiths, and bricklayers and were sometimes loaned out to the owner's neighbors.

In the midst of the horrors of slavery, Africans developed a way of life based strongly on their cultural heritage. They kept alive their musical, dance, and storytelling traditions. They wove baskets and molded pottery as they had done in Africa. When a slave owner sold a parent to another plantation, other slaves stepped in to raise the children left behind.

Slaves resisted their position of subservience. Throughout the colonies, planters reported slaves' faking illness, breaking tools, and staging work slowdowns. A number of slaves tried to run away, even though escape attempts were severely punished.

Some slaves pushed their resistance to open revolt. One uprising, the Stono Rebellion, began on a September Sunday in 1739. That morning, about 20 slaves gathered at the Stono River just south of Charles Town. Wielding guns and other weapons, they killed several planter families and marched south, beating drums and inviting other slaves to join them in their plan to flee to Spanish-held Florida. Many slaves died in the fighting that followed. Those captured were executed. Despite the rebellion's failure, it sent a chill through many Southern colonists and led to the tightening of harsh slave laws already in place.

C. Answer Slaves preserved as much of their cultural heritage as possible, while they resisted the tyranny of their owners in numerous ways.

THINK THROUGH HISTORY
C. *Synthesizing* *How did enslaved Africans maintain their sense of self-worth?*

Industry Grows in the North

The development of thriving commercial cities and diverse economic activities gradually made the North radically different from the South. Grinding wheat, harvesting fish, and sawing lumber became thriving industries. By the 1770s, the colonists had built one-third of all British ships and were producing more iron than England did. Many colonists prospered. In particular, the number of merchants grew. By the mid-1700s, merchants were one of the most powerful groups in the North.

COLONIAL CITIES AND TRADE The expansion in trade caused port cities to grow. Charles Town was the only major port in the South. In contrast, the North boasted Boston, New York, and Philadelphia—which eventually became the second largest port in the British empire, after London. Toward the end of the 1700s, Yankee traders were sailing around Cape Horn at the tip of South America to trade with the Spanish missionaries as far away as California. There they exchanged manufactured goods for hides, tallow, wine, olive oil, and grain raised with the help of the Native American labor on the missions.

The Northern colonies attracted a variety of immigrants. During the 18th century, about 585,000 Europeans migrated to America. Before 1700, most immigrants came as indentured servants from England, but by 1755 more than a third of European immigrants were coming from other countries. The Germans and the Scots-Irish were the largest non-English European immigrant

MORE ABOUT . . .
Olaudah Equiano

Also known as Gustavus Vassa, Equiano was enslaved and sold in the West Indies in about 1762. Eventually freed, he became an active abolitionist in England and helped lead the way for the establishment of Freetown, Sierra Leone, as an African sanctuary for freed slaves. In 1789 Equiano published *The Interesting Narrative of the Life of Olaudah Equiano, or Gustavus Vassa, the African.* The book was a best seller, which Equiano later followed with his *Miscellaneous Verses.*

ELECTRONIC LIBRARY OF PRIMARY SOURCES
from *The Interesting Narrative of the Life of Olaudah Equiano*

IN-DEPTH RESOURCES: UNIT 1
American Lives: Olaudah Equiano, p. 29

OBJECTIVE
② INSTRUCT

Industry Grows in the North

▶ ***Discussing Key Ideas***

- The Northern colonies have a diversified economy that is thriving by the mid-18th century.
- Large port cities develop as Native Americans are pushed further inland.
- Immigrants from many countries help make Northern society diverse.
- While slavery exists in the North, it does not play as important a role as it does in the South.
- Social and economic tensions contribute to the Salem witchcraft trials.

TEACHING OPTIONS

Teaching Gifted and Talented Students

Comparing and Contrasting Ask students to research the lives of wealthy landowners in Britain and compare and contrast them with the lives of plantation owners in the Southern colonies. Students' final reports might take the form of a fictional correspondence between a planter and an English aristocrat or a short piece of historical fiction in which the son or daughter of a wealthy Southern planter goes to England to be educated. Encourage students to speculate on how the English aristocracy would treat their American counterparts.

Making Connections Across the Curriculum

Biology Explain that specific populations may develop immunities to diseases to which they are often exposed. Such immunity can occur when those who contract severe cases of the disease die and those with total or partial resistance survive and pass on their resistance genetically. Native Americans, for example, died in great numbers because they had no resistance to the diseases brought over by Europeans. Black Africans' ability to fight off malaria is a genetically transmitted trait that also makes them prone to the often fatal disease of sickle-cell anemia. Students might research and report on other genetically transmitted diseases and immunities.

MORE ABOUT . . .
Slavery in the North

Because the North had fewer slaves and its economy was less dependent on them, laws governing slaveholding did not evolve to the degree that they did in the South. Thus, while slavery in the North could be as brutal as in the South, it was less widespread. In those areas in the North where male slaves could hire themselves out for wages, it was not unknown for a slave to earn enough cash to purchase his own and his family's freedom.

HISTORY FROM VISUALS
Colonial Diversity—1700 and 1755

Reading the Graph Ask who was the second-largest colonial ethnic group both in 1700 and in 1755. *Africans.*

Extension Ask from what part of Europe the immigrants to the 13 colonies appear to have come. *Northern; western.*

ELECTRONIC LIBRARY OF PRIMARY SOURCES

from How Our Cities Looked by Lord Adam Gordon

A Letter Regarding Relations with the Indians by Samuel Sewall

GROLIER MULTIMEDIA ENCYCLOPEDIA

Salem Witch Trials

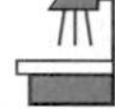

HUMANITIES TRANSPARENCIES

H4, Women Working in an Onion Field

GEOGRAPHY TRANSPARENCIES

G3, Colonial Economies

Philadelphia in 1720 was a bustling colonial port.

groups. Germans began arriving in Pennsylvania in the 1680s. Most were fleeing economic devastation. The Scots-Irish—descendants of Scottish Protestants who had colonized northern Ireland in the 1500s and early 1600s—came a bit later. Other ethnic groups included the Dutch in New York, Scandinavians in Delaware, and Jews in such cities as Newport and Philadelphia.

Native Americans had largely disappeared from the cities of the North. The Swedish naturalist Peter Kalm, visiting New York and Pennsylvania in 1748, described his impressions of the vanished native population.

Colonial Diversity

1700

African	11%
Dutch	4%
Scottish	3%
Other European	2%
English/Welsh	80%

1755

African	20%
German	7%
Scots-Irish	7%
Irish	5%
Scottish	4%
Dutch	3%
Other European	2%
English/Welsh	52%

Source: *The Enduring Vision*

SKILLBUILDER
INTERPRETING GRAPHS ***What new ethnic groups had settled in the American colonies by 1755?***

Skillbuilder Answer
Germans, Scots-Irish, and Irish.

A PERSONAL VOICE

The country, especially all along the coasts, in the English colonies, is inhabited by Europeans, who in some places are already so numerous that few parts of Europe are more populous. The Indians have sold the country to the Europeans, and have retired farther up; in most parts you may travel 20 Swedish miles, or about 120 English miles, from the seashore before you reach the first habitations of the Indians. And it is very possible for a person to have been at Philadelphia and other towns on the seashore for half a year together without so much as seeing an Indian.

PETER KALM, *Travels into North America*

FARMING IN THE NORTH The farms in New England and the Middle colonies, unlike plantations, typically produced several cash crops rather than a single one like rice or tobacco. Because raising wheat and corn did not require as much labor as tobacco and rice, Northerners had less incentive to turn to slavery. However, slavery did exist in New England and was extensive throughout the middle colonies, as were racial prejudices against blacks—free or enslaved. While still considered property, most slaves in New England did enjoy greater legal protections than slaves elsewhere in the colonies.

THINK THROUGH HISTORY
D. *Finding Main Ideas* *In what ways was the Northern economy diverse?*

D. Answer
Northern farms produced a variety of foodstuffs; the North had many cities, with a wide variety of industries and occupations such as lumbering, shipbuilding, and iron making.

THE ROLE OF WOMEN AND THE TRIALS IN SALEM In 1692, hysteria spread through the town of Salem in the Massachusetts Bay Colony as hundreds were accused of practicing witchcraft. In all, 19 women and men were tried, convicted, and hanged as witches, one was pressed to death for refusing to answer the charges, and many more were jailed.

The temporary witchcraft hysteria expressed underlying social tensions. The accusers typically lived in the poorer half of town and brought charges against those who lived in the more prosperous area. Furthermore, many of the accused were women who might be considered too independent by Puritan standards: they had conducted business outside the home, did not attend church, or intended to live on their own. As in the South, women in the North had extensive work responsibilities but few legal or social rights.

TEACHING OPTIONS

Exploring Themes

Cultural Diversity Stress that the influx of European immigrants, especially in the North, and of African slaves, especially in the South, brought cultural diversity to the colonies. Clarify that European immigrants were not confined to the North; for example, many of the Scots-Irish, instead of settling in western Pennsylvania, headed further south into Appalachia; and quite a few Scots fleeing the Jacobite rebellions settled in North Carolina. Point out that some French and Spanish immigrants also came to North America around this time but usually settled in French and Spanish colonies elsewhere on the continent.

Making Connections Across Time

Urban Light and Blight Have students compare and contrast the benefits and drawbacks of city life in colonial times with those of urban life today. They might list the colonial benefits and drawbacks mentioned or implied here—bustling commerce, cultural diversity, fuel shortages, problems with the water supply, poor sanitation, and so on—and then consider whether these same qualities manifest themselves in cities today. What generalizations, if any, do students feel they can make about urban life?

The Enlightenment

During the 1700s, the Enlightenment, which was an intellectual movement that began in Europe, and the Great Awakening, a colonial religious movement, led to changes in thinking throughout the 13 colonies.

EUROPEAN IDEAS INSPIRE THE COLONISTS During the Renaissance in Europe, scientists had begun looking beyond religious beliefs and traditional assumptions for answers about how the world worked. Careful observation and logic led to the discovery of some of the natural laws and principles governing the world and human behavior. The work of Nicolaus Copernicus, Galileo Galilei, and Sir Isaac Newton established that the earth revolved around the sun and not vice versa. This observation, which removed the earth from the "center" of the universe, was at first fiercely resisted. The early scientists also concluded that the world is governed by fixed mathematical laws. These ideas about nature led to a movement called the **Enlightenment** in which philosophers stressed reason and the scientific method.

Enlightenment ideas traveled from Europe to the colonies. One colonist, **Benjamin Franklin,** eagerly took to the notion of obtaining truth through experimentation and reason. For example, his most famous experiment—flying a kite in a thunderstorm—demonstrated that lightning is a form of electrical power. Franklin's experiments resulted in several practical inventions, including lightning rods, bifocal eyeglasses, and a stove that heated rooms more efficiently than did earlier models. Colonial ministers, physicians, astronomers, botanists, and inventors took most readily to the techniques of applied science emerging from the European Enlightenment. Many practical scientists belonged to the American Philosophical Society, formed in 1744, in which Benjamin Franklin was a central figure.

The British minister George Whitefield was a major force behind the Great Awakening. In his seven journeys to the American colonies between 1739 and 1769, Whitefield preached dramatic sermons that brought many listeners to tears.

Enlightenment ideas spread quickly through the colonies by means of books and pamphlets. Literacy was particularly high in New England because the Puritans had long supported public education partly to make it possible for everyone to read the Bible. However, Enlightenment views were disturbing to some people. The Enlightenment suggested that people could use science and logic—rather than the pronouncements of church authorities—to arrive at truths. As English poet John Donne had written, "[The] new philosophy calls all in doubt."

The Enlightenment also had a profound effect on political thought in the colonies. Colonial statesmen such as Thomas Jefferson, influenced by Enlightenment philosophers, reasoned that individuals have natural rights that governments must respect. Enlightenment principles eventually would lead many colonists to question the authority of the British monarchy.

E. Answer Colonists reasoned that individuals have natural rights, which the government must respect; colonists began questioning the authority of the British monarch.

THINK THROUGH HISTORY
E. *Recognizing Effects* *What effects did the Enlightenment have on political thought in the colonies?*

The Great Awakening

By the early 1700s, the Puritans had lost some of their influence. Under the new Massachusetts charter of 1691, Puritans were required to practice religious tolerance and could no longer limit voting privileges to members of their own church. Furthermore, as Puritan merchants had prospered, they had developed a taste for fine houses, stylish clothes, and good food and wine. Their interest in maintaining the strict Puritan code had declined: material comfort was accompanied in the early 1700s by a drop in church membership. A series of revivals,

OBJECTIVE
③ **INSTRUCT**

The Enlightenment

▶ ***Discussing Key Ideas***

- An intellectual movement called the Enlightenment develops in Europe.
- Colonists absorb the Enlightenment values emphasizing reason and the scientific method.
- Enlightenment ideas influence political thinking as well.

MORE ABOUT . . .
The Enlightenment

A major idea from the Enlightenment was that a social contract existed between a government and those it governed. This meant that those who were governed gave their consent to be governed in return for certain benefits. They also had the right to change a government that did not meet its side of the contract. This idea was made widespread by English philosopher John Locke, whose work was read by Virginia's Thomas Jefferson, a noted Enlightenment thinker and chief author of the Declaration of Independence.

OBJECTIVE
④ **INSTRUCT**

The Great Awakening

▶ ***Discussing Key Ideas***

- A religious revival movement called the Great Awakening spreads through the colonies.

(continued on next page)

TEACHING OPTIONS

Exploring Themes

Science and Technology Stress that the Enlightenment that spread from Europe to the Americas brought with it an optimistic belief in science and reason that prompted a general spirit of inquiry and invention as well as an openness to new ideas. Point out that electricity was still a new and mysterious idea when Franklin conducted his famed experiments, which duplicated and expanded the work being done in France and England at the time. Franklin himself coined or popularized several of the terms used in the study of electricity—*conductor, battery, positive,* and *negative,* for example.

Teaching Less Proficient Readers

Clarifying Ideas In reading pages 37–41, less proficient readers may find it helpful to apply the five steps of the SQ3R study method, as follows:

1. **Survey** the pages by skimming paragraphs for headings and topic sentences and by looking over the art.
2. **Question** the information by jotting down any questions.
3. **Read** the pages, looking for answers to these questions.
4. **Recite** or record any answers they find.
5. **Review** the information, answering any remaining questions.

(continued from page 37)

- The Great Awakening stirs people to rededicate themselves to God.
- An effect of both the religious revival and the Enlightenment is an emphasis on individualism and the questioning of authority.

KEY PLAYERS

Franklin and Edwards

Critical Thinking: Compare and Contrast

Have students compare and contrast Franklin's and Edwards's ideas, particularly the two men's views of the individual and of destiny. A Venn diagram may be helpful in making this comparison.

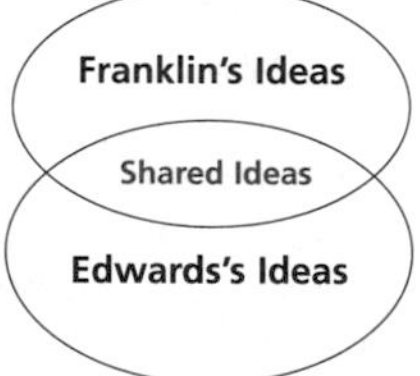

IN-DEPTH RESOURCES: UNIT 1

Primary Source: from *The Autobiography* by Benjamin Franklin, p. 24

MORE ABOUT . . .

George Whitefield

Whitefield's tremendous success as a preacher can be attributed in part to his acting ability. In his sermons he would first play the role of God and then switch to the role of the devil. "What a spell he casts over an audience," said Jonathan Edwards's wife, "by proclaiming the simplest of truths of the Bible. I have seen upwards of a thousand people hang on his words with breathless silence, broken only by an occasional half-suppressed sob."

KEY PLAYERS

BENJAMIN FRANKLIN
1706–1790

A true student of the Enlightenment, Benjamin Franklin devised an orderly method to develop moral perfection in himself. In his autobiography, he records how he decided on a list of virtues he thought he should have. Then, every night, he reviewed whether his behavior lived up to those standards and recorded his faults in a notebook.

Originally, he concentrated on only 12 virtues until a Quaker friend told him he was too proud. Franklin promptly added a 13th virtue to the list—the virtue of humility, which he never quite achieved.

Franklin took great pleasure in seeing his character improve. He wrote: "I was surpris'd to find myself so much fuller of faults than I had imagined; but I had the satisfaction of seeing them diminish."

JONATHAN EDWARDS
1703–1758

Unlike Benjamin Franklin, Jonathan Edwards did not believe that humans had the power to perfect themselves. Descended from a long line of Puritan ministers, he believed that "however you may have reformed your life in many things," all were sinners who were destined for hell unless they had a "great change of heart."

Edwards was a brilliant thinker who entered Yale College when he was only 13. His preaching was one of the driving forces of the Great Awakening. Ironically, when the religious revival died down, Edwards's own congregation rejected him for being too strict about doctrine. Edwards moved to Stockbridge, Massachusetts, in 1751, where he lived his remaining years as missionary to a Native American settlement.

aimed at restoring the intensity and dedication of the early Puritan church, moved through the colonies. They came to be known collectively as the **Great Awakening.**

SPREAD OF RELIGIOUS REVIVALS

Among those clergy who sought to revive the fervor of the original Puritan vision was **Jonathan Edwards,** of Northampton, Massachusetts. One of the most learned theologians of his time, Edwards preached that it was not enough for people simply to come to church. In order to be saved, they must feel their sinfulness and feel God's love for them. In his most famous sermon, delivered in 1741, Edwards vividly described God's mercy toward sinners.

A PERSONAL VOICE

The God that holds you over the pit of Hell, much as one holds a spider, or some loathsome insect over the fire, abhors [hates] you, and is dreadfully provoked: his wrath towards you burns like fire; he looks upon you as worthy of nothing else but to be cast into the fire . . . and yet it is nothing but his hand that holds you from falling into the fire every moment.

JONATHAN EDWARDS, "Sinners in the Hands of an Angry God"

Preachers traveled from village to village, attracting thousands to outdoor revival meetings, giving impassioned sermons, and stirring people to rededicate themselves to God. By reaching out to individuals, the revivals tended to democratize the religious experience.

The Great Awakening lasted throughout the 1740s and 1750s. The revivals brought many colonists, as well as Native Americans and African Americans, into organized Christian churches for the first time. As the movement gained momentum, it also challenged the authority of established churches. Some colonists abandoned their old Puritan or Anglican congregations. At the same time, independent denominations, such as the Baptists and Methodists, gained new members. The Great Awakening also led to an increased interest in higher education, as several Protestant denominations founded colleges such as Princeton, Brown, Columbia, and Dartmouth to train ministers for their rapidly growing churches.

While the Great Awakening emphasized emotionalism and the Enlightenment emphasized logic, the two movements had similar consequences. Both caused people to question traditional authority. Moreover, both stressed the importance of the individual—the Enlightenment by emphasizing human reason, and the Great Awakening by de-emphasizing the role of church authority. Because these movements helped lead the colonists to question Britain's authority over their lives, they were important in creating the intellectual and social atmosphere that eventually led to the American Revolution.

"Resolve to perform what you ought; perform without fail what you resolve."

BENJAMIN FRANKLIN

F. Answer It made Christianity more diverse ethnically and racially, and it strengthened new denominations and weakened older ones.

THINK THROUGH HISTORY
***F. Recognizing Effects** What effects did the Great Awakening have on organized religion in the colonies?*

TEACHING OPTIONS

Making Connections Across the Cultures

French Americans Note that beginning in the 16th century small groups of Huguenots, or French Protestants, came to the New World to escape religious persecution. After the English acquired Acadia (Nova Scotia and nearby areas, including New Brunswick and part of Quebec and Maine), many French settlers fled or were deported from the region. Those who resettled in the French territory of Louisiana became known as Cajuns, a corruption of *Acadians,* while French settlers who came directly to Louisiana were called Creoles. When the U.S. purchased Louisiana in 1803, these French Americans too became part of the American mosaic.

Making Connections Across the Curriculum

Literature Note that both Franklin's autobiography and Edwards's sermon are American literary landmarks. The autobiography is viewed as a pioneering expression of the recurring American theme of self-reliance; the sermon is noted for its powerful, poetic style.

Have students identify and evaluate the central metaphor in the passage from Edwards's sermon cited in A Personal Voice on page 38. Central metaphor: *God holding a person over Hell compared to a person holding a spider or another "loathsome insect" over the fire. Evaluations will vary.*

The French and Indian War

As the French empire in North America expanded, it collided with the growing British empire. By the 1750s, France and Great Britain had already fought three indecisive wars in the previous half-century. Each war had begun in Europe but spread to their colonies around the world, including those in North America. In 1754, after six relatively peaceful years, the French–British conflict reignited.

French explorer Jacques Cartier

RIVALS FOR AN EMPIRE From the start the French colony in North America, called New France, differed from the British colonies. France had begun its North American empire in 1534, when Jacques Cartier had explored the St. Lawrence River. In 1608, Samuel de Champlain had founded the town of Quebec, the first permanent French settlement in North America.

After establishing Quebec, the French penetrated the heart of the North American continent. French priest Jacques Marquette and the trader Louis Jolliet explored the Great Lakes and the upper Mississippi River. Robert Cavelier, Sieur de La Salle, explored the lower Mississippi in 1682 and claimed the entire river valley for France, naming it Louisiana in honor of the king, Louis XIV.

By 1760 the European population of New France had grown to only about 80,000—compared with more than a million in the British colonies. Typical French colonists were young, single men who engaged in the fur trade and Catholic priests who sought to convert Native Americans. They did not settle in the English pattern, to build towns or raise families. The French were not so much interested in occupying the territories they claimed as in exploiting them economically. However, they usually enjoyed better relations with Native Americans, in part because they needed the local people as partners in the fur trade. In fact, several military alliances developed out of the French–Native American trade relations.

THINK THROUGH HISTORY
G. *Contrasting* *How was the French empire in North America unlike the British empire?*

G. Answer France focused on developing the fur trade rather than on creating permanent settlements; enjoyed better relations with Native Americans; sent missionaries to convert Native Americans to Catholicism.

EARLY FRENCH VICTORIES One major area of contention between France and Great Britain was the rich Ohio River valley just west of Pennsylvania and Virginia. In 1754, the French built Fort Duquesne at the place where the Allegheny and Monongahela rivers join to form the Ohio, where Pittsburgh now stands. The Virginia government had already granted 200,000 acres of land in the Ohio country to a group of wealthy planters, so the Virginia governor sent militiamen to order the French to leave.

The small band, led by an ambitious 22-year-old colonel named George Washington, established an outpost about 60 miles from Fort Duquesne, called Fort Necessity. In the battle that followed, the French inflicted such heavy losses on the outnumbered Virginians that Washington was forced to surrender. This was the opening of the **French and Indian War,** the fourth war between Great Britain and France for control of North America.

A year after his defeat, Washington again headed into battle, this time as an aide to the British general Edward Braddock. Braddock's first task was to relaunch an attack on Fort Duquesne. As Braddock and nearly 1,500 soldiers neared the fort, French soldiers and their Native American allies ambushed them. The British soldiers—accustomed to enemies who marched in straight rows rather than ones who fought from behind trees—turned and fled. The cowardice of the British army surprised Washington, who showed great courage himself.

As Washington tried to rally the troops, two horses were shot from under him and four bullets pierced his coat—yet he escaped unharmed. Nine days after the battle, he wrote to his mother, "The English soldiers . . . were struck with such a panic that they behaved with more cowardice than it is possible to

OBJECTIVE
⑤ **INSTRUCT**

The French and Indian War

▶ ***Discussing Key Ideas***

- France's colonial claims in Canada and America are based on the efforts of several explorers.
- Rivalries smolder between the French and English colonies.
- Britain and France fight the French and Indian War for control of America.
- Britain gains control of Canada and most of Northern America east of the Mississippi.

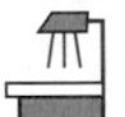

CRITICAL THINKING TRANSPARENCIES
CT3, French and Indian War

MORE ABOUT . . .
The Fur Trade

Fashionable top hats made from beaver skins were extremely popular in Europe beginning in the late 16th century. Because of this demand for beaver, the fur trade proved enormously successful for all involved until the fur supply began to decrease and silk hats replaced beaver hats as the fashion in Europe.

Block Schedule TEACHING OPTION **Time Needed: 30 Minutes**

Cooperative Activity: Annotated Maps

Task: Groups of students will work together to create annotated maps of the battles and territorial gains of the French and Indian War.

Purpose: To understand the sequence of events and the geographical results of a war.

Activity: Students should include brief descriptions of events as well as boundaries and labels. These should include critical information about battles, such as number of people involved, dates, and results. To illustrate the changing nature of the situation, students might create two or three maps, or perhaps a single map with overlays or a set of computer graphics.

Building a Portfolio: Students might include the final products (or printouts of the final products) in their portfolios.

ALTERNATIVE ASSESSMENT BOOK
Standards for Evaluating a Cooperative Activity

Standards for Evaluation
Maps should . . .

- include appropriate geographical features
- provide descriptions of battles with dates
- use colors or patterns to clarify territorial changes
- correctly place all information

MORE ABOUT . . .
William Pitt

William Pitt (1708–1778) was the statesman often credited with securing, through victory in the French and Indian War, Britain's leading position as a colonial power. Pitt insisted on huge government expenditures as well as young, new generals to fortify his army. His first battle, an attack on Fort Ticonderoga, was a disaster, but after that, Pitt's brilliant military strategy assured victory for the British.

MORE ABOUT . . .
The Iroquois

The Iroquois League, a confederacy of Iroquoian-speaking tribes in what is now upstate New York, unified between 1570 and 1600. Later, the confederacy came into conflict with the French, who were allies of the Hurons and Algonquins—both rivals of the Iroquois in the fur trade. Few French settled in this part of New York, partly because of frequent Iroquois attacks.

MORE ABOUT . . .
Pontiac

Pontiac became tribal chief of the Ottawa in 1755, and in 1762 he organized the alliance of the Great Lakes tribes that fought in Pontiac's War. A shrewd military strategist, Pontiac arranged surprise attacks on several British forts and is especially admired for his capture of Detroit. In 1769, three years after concluding a peace treaty with the British, Pontiac was killed by a member of the Peoria tribe, an incident that sparked a bitter intertribal war.

In the French and Indian War, the colonists and the British fought side by side for nine years. In this scene, the British general Edward Braddock meets defeat and death on his march to Fort Duquesne in July of 1755.

conceive." Of his own troops, he reported, "The Virginia troops showed a good deal of bravery, and were near all killed; for I believe out of three companies that were there, there are scarce 30 men left alive." Many other colonists in addition to Washington began to question the ability of the British army, which suffered defeat after defeat during 1755 and 1756.

BRITAIN DEFEATS AN OLD ENEMY Angered by French victories, Britain's King George II selected new leaders to run his government in 1757. One of these was **William Pitt,** an energetic, self-confident politician. Under Pitt, the reinvigorated British and colonial troops finally began winning battles. These successes prompted the powerful Iroquois to agree to support them, giving Britain some Native American allies to balance those of France.

In September 1759, the war took a dramatic and decisive turn on the Plains of Abraham just outside of Quebec. Under cover of night, British troops led by General James Wolfe approached Quebec by scaling the high cliffs that protected the city. Catching the French by surprise, they fought and won a short but deadly battle. The British triumph at Quebec gave them victory in the war.

The war officially ended in 1763 with the signing of the Treaty of Paris. Great Britain claimed Canada and virtually all of North America east of the Mississippi River. Britain also took Florida from Spain, which had allied itself with France. The treaty permitted Spain to keep possession of its lands west of the Mississippi and the city of New Orleans, which it had gained from France in 1762. France retained control of only a few small islands near Newfoundland and in the West Indies. The French, having lost so much territory in the war, harbored resentment against the English. This led the French later to respond positively when Benjamin Franklin requested their assistance in the colonies' rebellion against Great Britain. Thus, the British eventually paid an unexpected price for the acquisition of Canada.

VICTORY BRINGS NEW PROBLEMS Others who lost ground in the war were the Native Americans, who found the victorious British harder to bargain with than the French had been. Native Americans resented the growing number of British settlers crossing the Appalachian Mountains and feared the settlers would soon drive away the game they depended on for survival. In the spring of 1763, the Ottawa leader **Pontiac** recognized that the French loss was a loss for Native Americans.

THINK THROUGH HISTORY
H. *Making Inferences* *How did Great Britain's victory over France affect Native Americans?*

H. Answer It deprived Native Americans of their French ally, at the same time worsening Native American conflict with colonists over lands to the west of existing British colonies. The British were harder to deal with than the French.

A PERSONAL VOICE

When I go to see the English commander and say to him that some of our comrades are dead, instead of bewailing their death, as our French brothers do, he laughs at me and at you. If I ask for anything for our sick, he refuses with the reply that he has no use for us. For all this you can well see that they are seeking our ruin. Therefore, my brothers, we must all swear their destruction and wait no longer.

PONTIAC, quoted in *Red and White*

Led by Pontiac, Native Americans captured eight British forts in the Ohio Valley and laid siege to two others. In response, British officers deliberately

TEACHING OPTIONS

Teaching Gifted and Talented Students

Tracing Changing Developments Interested students might work with a partner to research and report on the complexity of French-British relations in Canada from about 1700. Final reports might take the form of two annotated fictional family trees, one for a family of French background and another for a family of British background, in which family members across the centuries make remarks about the current British-French situation. Encourage volunteers to give oral readings of their final efforts.

Making Connections Across Time

Biological Warfare Elicit that the incident with the smallpox-infested blankets is a simple example of biological warfare, which attempts to devastate an enemy by spreading disease or another biological danger. Encourage students to discuss modern examples of both biological and chemical warfare or terrorism and the efforts being made to dissuade them. You might mention that the incident with the smallpox-infested blankets has never been proven to all scholars' satisfaction.

European Claims in North America, 1754–1763

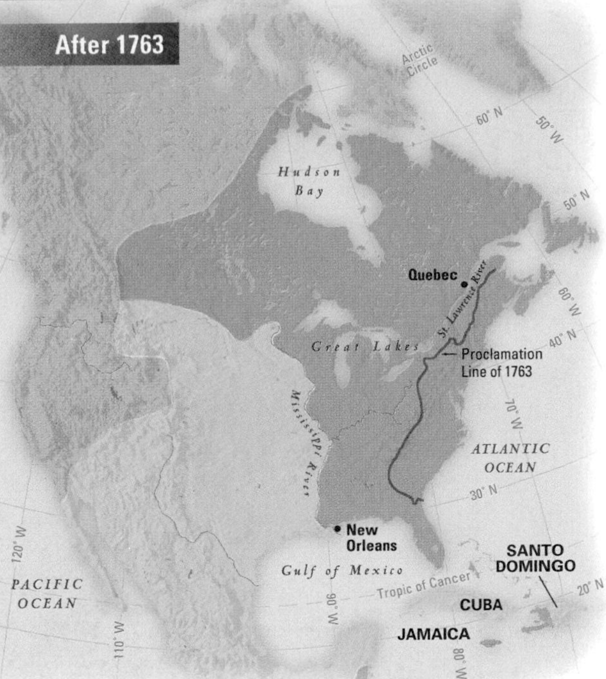

GEOGRAPHY SKILLBUILDER
REGION ***What happened to France's possessions between 1754 and 1763?***

Skillbuilder Answer
They were divided between Britain and Spain—Canada and most of France's possessions east of the Mississippi went to Britain, and New Orleans and the possessions west of the Mississippi to Spain.

presented blankets contaminated with smallpox to two Delaware chiefs during peace negotiations, and the virus spread rapidly among the Native Americans. Weakened by disease and tired of fighting, most Native American groups negotiated treaties with the British by the end of 1765.

To avoid further costly conflicts with Native Americans, the British government prohibited colonists from settling west of the Appalachian Mountains. The **Proclamation of 1763** established a Proclamation Line along the Appalachians, which the colonists were not supposed to cross. The ban angered colonists, who were eager to expand westward from the increasingly crowded Atlantic seaboard. The British could not enforce the Proclamation of 1763 any more effectively than they could enforce the Navigation Acts, and colonists continued to stream onto Native American lands.

Section 4 Assessment

1. TERMS & NAMES
Identify:
- triangular trade
- middle passage
- Enlightenment
- Benjamin Franklin
- Great Awakening
- Jonathan Edwards
- French and Indian War
- William Pitt
- Pontiac
- Proclamation of 1763

2. SUMMARIZING Recreate the tree diagram below on your paper and fill it in with historical examples that illustrate the main idea in the top box.

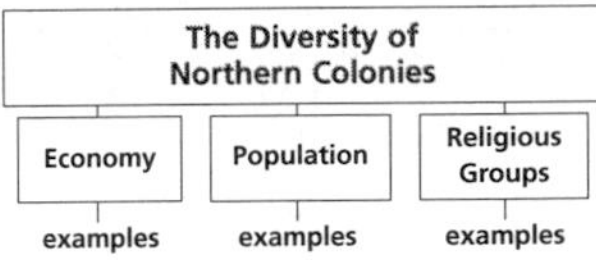

Name the advantages and the disadvantages that this kind of society might have.

3. ANALYZING ISSUES In what ways was slavery a brutal system? Consider the whole of the slave experience, and support your statement with examples from the text.

THINK ABOUT
- the way in which slaves were taken from Africa
- the conditions under which slaves worked
- the lives slaves led
- the attitudes toward African slaves

4. MAKING DECISIONS If you had been a Native American living in the Northeast during the French and Indian War, would you have formed a military alliance with France or with Great Britain? Support your choice with reasons.

THINK ABOUT
- Native Americans' past relations with France and Britain
- what Native Americans might have gained or lost as a result of a victory by either nation

ANSWERS

1. TERMS AND NAMES

triangular trade, p. 34
middle passage, p. 34
Enlightenment, p. 37
Benjamin Franklin, p. 37
Great Awakening, p. 38
Jonathan Edwards, p. 38
French and Indian War, p. 39
William Pitt, p. 40
Pontiac, p. 40
Proclamation of 1763, p. 41

2. SUMMARIZING

Possible Responses:
Economy—several cash crops; fisheries, mills, manufacturing.
Population—English, Germans, Scots-Irish, and other immigrant groups; African slaves.
Religious Groups—Anglicans, Roman Catholics, Quakers, Methodists, other Protestant denominations, Jews.

3. ANALYZING ISSUES

Possible Responses: Free people were enslaved on the basis of race alone and were treated as merchandise; neither slaves nor their children could free themselves from the system; slaves were transported and lived under inhumane conditions; work was long and grueling; families were often torn apart; slaves' lives were completely controlled.

4. MAKING DECISIONS

Possible Responses: France: Past relations were friendly; economic cooperation in the fur trade and military alliances; French rarely seized land for agricultural settlements. Britain: Native Americans impressed because the British were winning battles; by aligning with the winner, Native Americans might avoid Britain's retaliation for their support of France.

HISTORY FROM VISUALS
European Claims in North America, 1754–1763

Reading the Map Ask whether the British acquired all of present-day Canada in 1763. *No.*

Extension Have students use a map or an atlas to identify the present-day U.S. states that Britain acquired as a result of the French and Indian War.

ASSESS & RETEACH

Section 4 Assessment

Have a student volunteer direct the class in a group review of the questions and responses.

Self-Assessment

Have students write their own questions, exchange them with a partner, and answer their partner's questions. Partners can then review the section together to find information for any incorrect answers.

Section Quiz

FORMAL ASSESSMENT
Section Quiz, p. 8

Reteach

Use the Personal Voices, marginal quotes, and Key Players to help review the main ideas of this section.

CLOSE

The Northern and Southern British colonies came of age in different ways, but the colonists shared the influences of the Enlightenment and the Great Awakening. Though victory in the French and Indian War benefited Britain, it also contributed to deteriorating relations between the mother country and the colonies.

Daily Life

OBJECTIVES

1. To compare and contrast the courtship customs of different colonial groups.
2. To summarize marriage statistics among different colonial groups.

FOCUS & MOTIVATE

▶ ***Starting with the Student*** Have students imagine that they are reporting current-day American social customs to foreign readers.

- What would you say about the age at which typical Americans begin dating? About the age at which they marry?
- What specific courtship or dating customs would you mention?

MORE ABOUT . . .
The Puritans

In contrast to Church of England teachings, the Puritans felt marriage should be a civil contract, claiming that nowhere in the Bible was it tied to the ministry. Performed by Governor Bradford, the first Pilgrim marriage was between recent widow Susanna Fuller White and widower Edward Winslow, who went on to become the colony's governor and in that capacity performed marriages himself.

DAILY LIFE
1630–1763

Colonial Courtship

The concept of teenage dating was nonexistent in colonial times. Young people were considered either children or adults, and as important as marriage was in the colonies, sweethearts were older than you might suspect. The practices of courtship and marriage varied among the different communities, as you will see in the examples below.

FRONTIER OR BACKCOUNTRY PEOPLE Andrew Jackson, depicted with his wife in the painting above, "stole" his wife (she was willing) from her first husband. Jackson was following a custom of the backcountry people, who lived along the western edge of the colonies. These colonists, mostly Scots-Irish, based their marriages on the old custom of "abduction"—stealing the bride, often with her consent. Even regular marriages began with the groom and his friends coming to "steal" the bride. Much drinking and dancing accompanied these wild and hilarious weddings.

PURITANS For Puritans, marriage was a civil contract, not a religious or sacred union. Although adults strictly supervised a couple's courting, parents allowed two unusual practices. One was the use of a courting stick, a long tube through which the couple could whisper to each other while the family was in another room. The other was the practice of "bundling": a young man spent the night in the same bed as his sweetheart, with a large bundling board (shown below) between them.

Before marrying, the couple had to allow Puritan leaders to voice any objections to the marriage at the meeting house. If there were no objections, the couple would marry in a very simple civil ceremony and share a quiet dinner.

RECOMMENDED RESOURCES

Books

Emrich, Duncan. *The Folklore of Weddings and Marriage.* New York: American Heritage, 1970. An illustrated study of marriage and the marriage ceremony.

Lemay, J. A. Leo. *Robert Bolling Woos Anne Miller.* Charlottesville: UP of Virginia, 1990. Love and courtship in colonial Virginia in 1760.

Longfellow, Henry W. "The Courtship of Miles Standish" in *Evangeline and Selected Tales and Poems.* New York: New American Library, 1964. A Romantic-era narrative poem about a famous colonial-era courtship.

Rothman, Ellen K. *Hands and Hearts.* New York: Basic, 1984. A history of courtship in America.

Videos

Colonial America, 1500–1600. Master Vision, 1982. Colonial customs and traditions.

The Colonial Way of Life. CRM Films. Diverse American colonists create a unified culture.

The Marriage of Pocahontas. Dir. Emma De'ath. Ambrose Video, 1995. A look at a famous marriage and its historical effects.

THE SOUTH Many African slaves married in a "jumping the broomstick" ceremony, in which the bride and groom jumped over a broomstick to seal their union. Although there is disagreement among scholars, some suggest that the painting above depicts a slave wedding on a South Carolina plantation in the late 1700s.

QUAKERS A Quaker couple intent on marrying needed the consent not only of their parents but also of the whole Quaker community. Quakers who wanted to marry had to go through a 16-step courtship phase before they could wed. Quaker women, however, were known to reject men at the last minute.

VIRGINIA In Virginia, marriage was a sacred union that often involved a union of properties. Parents were heavily involved in the negotiations. In this illustration from a dance manual *(left)*, a young upper-class couple work to improve their social graces by practicing an elaborate dance step.

DATA FILE

Average Age at Marriage in Colonial Times

GROUP	MALES	FEMALES
Puritans	26	23
Virginians	26	19
Quakers		
in Delaware	31	29
in Penn. & N.J.	26	22
Philadelphians	26	23
Frontier People	21	19
Modern Americans	25	24

Who Married in Colonial Times?

PURITANS:

- 98% of males and 94% of females married
- Grooms a few years older than brides
- Only one bachelor in original Puritan community; spinsters called "thornbacks"
- Discouraged marriages between first cousins

VIRGINIANS:

- 25% of males never married; most females married
- Grooms nearly 10 years older than brides
- Allowed first-cousin marriages

QUAKERS:

- 16% of women single at age 50
- Forbade first-cousin marriages

FRONTIER PEOPLE:

- Almost all women and most men married
- Ages of bride and groom about the same
- Married at youngest age

Who Could Divorce in Colonial Times?

Puritans: Yes
Virginians: No
Quakers: No

Source: David Hackett Fischer, *Albion's Seed*

INTERACT WITH HISTORY

1. **COMPARING** What was a common characteristic of courtship among Puritans, Quakers, and Virginians?
2. **CREATING A GRAPH** Create a bar graph using the figures shown in the data file table. What patterns do you notice in the data? What reasons would you suggest for the fact that men and women are now closer in age when they marry than they were in colonial times?

SEE SKILLBUILDER HANDBOOK, PAGES 909 AND 931.

Visit http://www.mlushistory.com for more about colonial daily life.

INSTRUCT

▶ *Starting with the Student*

- Have students share details about marriage customs in their families or ethnic groups.
- Ask which details about colonial courtship and marriage students found most surprising, and why.

▶ *Discussing Key Ideas*

- Colonial courtship customs varied among groups.
- Most people married when they were over 20.

HISTORY FROM VISUALS

Reading the Images Have students study the art and accompanying text, including the data file on page 43.

- Jot down adjectives to describe the different scenes depicted. *Possible Responses: Frontier: romantic, celebratory; South: informal, communal; Quaker: simple, idyllic; Virginia: formal, elegant.*
- Why do you think so many waited until they were past 20 to marry even though life was shorter then? *Possible Responses: Financial reasons; needed to prepare wedding clothes.*
- Why do you think almost all females in Virginia married, while only 75 percent of males did so? *Possible Responses: More males than females; Virginia Co. encouraged single males to emigrate.*

INTERACT WITH HISTORY

1. Comparing

Possible Responses *The family and/or community had a say in whether or not couples could wed; courting couples were allowed to spend some time together; most people were past 20 when they married; most courtships led to marriage.*

2. Creating a Graph

Standards for Evaluation
Graphs should . . .

- accurately represent the data in the table
- clearly show relationships among the data
- lead students to recognize patterns in the data, such as the fact that grooms are older than their brides in all cases, frontier couples married considerably earlier than others, and so on
- lead students to reasonable conclusions or hypotheses about why brides and grooms are closer in age today

REVIEW CHAPTER 1
ASSESSMENT ANSWERS

REVIEWING THE CHAPTER

TERMS & NAMES

1. Anasazi, p. 5
2. joint-stock company, p. 11
3. Christopher Columbus, p. 14
4. Columbian Exchange, p. 17
5. Jamestown, p. 22
6. indentured servant, p. 23
7. Puritan, p. 26
8. mercantilism, p. 30
9. middle passage, p. 34
10. Enlightenment, p. 37

MAIN IDEAS

Answers will vary.

11. Perhaps 40,000 years ago, the earliest Americans walked across a land bridge from Asia, possibly following animals. Others may have traveled down the Pacific coast in boats.
12. Trading networks; view of the land; the extended family.
13. Mediterranean goods and Saharan salt exchanged for gold, ivory, kola nuts, cotton cloth, and slaves; Islamic faith.
14. Bartholomeu Dias, Africa, 1488; Vasco da Gama, India, 1498.
15. Plantation colonies; forced labor; European weapons and coercive tactics.
16. Frontier settlers were angry at powerful planters for refusing to back them in conflicts with Native Americans.
17. Both argued for greater individual religious freedom. Williams escaped before being arrested, while Hutchinson was tried and banished.
18. Wealth; favorable balance of power; economic self-sufficiency. Great Britain founded colonies and controlled their trade.
19. Violent: revolts. Nonviolent: faking illness, working slowly, escape.
20. Franklin's experiments and inventions, Jefferson's view of individuals' natural rights, and the colonists' questioning of authority.

Review Chapter  Assessment

REVIEWING THE CHAPTER

TERMS & NAMES Explain the historical significance of each term, place, or person listed below.

1. Anasazi	**6. indentured servant**
2. joint-stock company	**7. Puritan**
3. Christopher Columbus	**8. mercantilism**
4. Columbian Exchange	**9. middle passage**
5. Jamestown	**10. Enlightenment**

MAIN IDEAS

SECTION 1 *(pages 4–13)*

The Americas, West Africa, and Europe

11. Describe the theories that explain when and how the first people came to the Americas.
12. Name three broad cultural patterns that the diverse Native American societies shared.
13. What exchanges of goods and ideas occurred as a result of trade routes across the Sahara?

SECTION 2 *(pages 14–21)*

Spanish North America

14. What were the most significant Portuguese explorations?
15. What methods of colonization did Spain use in the Americas?

SECTION 3 *(pages 22–32)*

Early British Colonies

16. What were the causes of Bacon's Rebellion?
17. How were the experiences of Roger Williams and Anne Hutchinson similar and different?

SECTION 4 *(pages 33–41)*

The Colonies Come of Age

18. What were a nation's goals under mercantilism and how did Great Britain strive to achieve these goals?
19. Describe examples of both violent and nonviolent resistance to slavery in the South.
20. How were the philosophical ideas of the Enlightenment expressed in the American colonies?

THINKING CRITICALLY

1. **COLONISTS AND NATIVE AMERICANS** Using a chart like the one below, summarize the way settlers and Native Americans interacted in the four listed regions.

Region	Interaction
New Mexico	→
Virginia	→
New England	→
Pennsylvania	→

2. **FORMING GENERALIZATIONS** How would you describe the civilizations that existed in North and South America prior to the arrival of the Europeans?
3. **GEOGRAPHY OF THE COLONIES** Look carefully at the map on page 41. What was the purpose of the Proclamation of 1763? Why might the British government have chosen the Appalachian mountain range as the location for the Proclamation Line?
4. **TRACING THEMES** **SCIENCE AND TECHNOLOGY** What technological innovations helped Europeans explore overseas? What technologies helped them overcome the native peoples they encountered?
5. **ANALYZING PRIMARY SOURCES** During the 1700s, there was an influx of European immigrants to the northern colonies. Read the following excerpt from Gottlieb Mittelberger's memoir *Journey to Pennsylvania in the Year 1750,* in which he reflects on his painful experiences as a German immigrant.

> Work and labor in this new and wild land are very hard and manifold. . . . Besides, there is . . . an arduous journey lasting half a year, during which he has to suffer, more than with the hardest work. . . . [If he has no money,] he must work his debt off as a slave and poor serf. Therefore, let everyone stay in his own country and support himself and his family honestly. Besides, I say that those who suffer themselves to be persuaded and enticed away by the man-thieves are very foolish if they believe that roasted pigeons will fly into their mouths in America or Pennsylvania without their working for them.
>
> **GOTTLIEB MITTELBERGER,** *Journey to Pennsylvania in the Year 1750*

How does Mittelberger characterize the ordeal of newcomers to America? If you were thinking of immigrating to America in the 1700s, would Mittelberger's warning about the hardships influence your decision? Why or why not?

THINKING CRITICALLY

1. COLONISTS AND NATIVE AMERICANS

Possible Responses: New Mexico: Settlers tried to impose Catholic faith and Spanish culture on Native Americans but met strong resistance.
Virginia: Settlers conquered Native Americans and seized their land.
New England: Some settlers tried to convert Native Americans to Christianity, but many wanted to remove or destroy native societies; Native Americans helped early colonists but later mounted organized resistance.
Pennsylvania: Quakers respected Native American rights and negotiated treaties for land.

2. FORMING GENERALIZATIONS

Possible Responses: The civilizations were varied and sophisticated. Aztec, Maya, and Inca empires in Central and South America ruled large territories with many inhabitants in highly sophisticated societies. Some early societies in North America excelled at trade and built massive earthen mounds. Later Native American groups developed extensive trade networks, kinship systems, religions, and agricultural techniques.

ALTERNATIVE ASSESSMENT

1. ROLE-PLAYING A TRIAL
How did lawyers defend their clients against some of the colonies' very strict laws?

Using legal documents from colonial days, find out the legal punishments for infractions of certain laws in specific colonies, such as boys running away in Massachusetts.

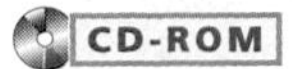
Use the CD-ROM *Electronic Library of Primary Sources* and other reference materials to research a specific law and punishment in 17th-century America.

- **Cooperative Learning** With a group of students, plan to act out a trial. Each student should play a different part, including judge, defendant, prosecuting attorney, defending lawyer, and witnesses. Each person should know the law.
- Act out the trial in front of the rest of the class, who will act as the colonial jury. Let the jury decide the verdict and the punishment. Then, discuss the outcome.

2. MAKING DECISIONS
Imagine you are living in Europe in the 1750s and considering coming to the American colonies. Use the following list to help you think through the decisions you would need to make in order to form a plan.

- What major choices would you need to make about coming to the colonies?
- What information would you want to gather in order to make your choices?
- What options would each choice present to you?
- What would be the consequences of each of the options?
- What actions would you take to implement your final decisions?

3. PORTFOLIO PROJECT

Use the Living History activity to expand your portfolio.

LIVING HISTORY

REVISING YOUR COLONIZATION TALE

You have written your own colonization tale. Now think about how you might revise it.

- Consider the experiences of actual colonists and the people they found already living where they settled. What details from these histories could you adapt for your story?
- Ask a friend to read the tale and comment on its content and organization. Make changes as appropriate.

After you have revised your tale, add a title page and a cover page. Then share your story with the class or add it to other students' stories to create a classroom anthology of colonization tales. Add your work to your American history portfolio.

Bridge to Chapter 2

Review Chapter 1

THE AMERICAS, WEST AFRICA, AND EUROPE The first humans came to North America across a land bridge from Asia as early as 38,000 B.C. Prior to the 1400s, North America was home to diverse Native American groups who were the descendants of these first Americans. At the same time, West Africa was home to village communities and to wealthy kingdoms with ties to Europe through trade. In the late 1400s, political, social, economic, cultural, and technological changes spurred Europeans to explore the African coast and to cross the Atlantic.

SPANISH NORTH AMERICA Within a century of Columbus's first voyage to the Americas, Spain had created a colonial empire that made the country wealthy. Spanish missionaries attempted to convert Native Americans and built missions throughout Texas, California, and the Southwest. Settlers intermarried with natives to create a mestizo population.

EARLY BRITISH COLONIES Overcoming hardships, the English created their first lasting colony at Jamestown. Better planning led to the development of successful colonies to the north, including Massachusetts Bay Colony. The colony of Providence was founded by dissenters from Puritan New England. New Netherland and Pennsylvania were founded on idealistic grounds and enjoyed religious and ethnic diversity and good relations with Native Americans.

THE COLONIES COME OF AGE Both the agricultural South and the commercial North played important roles as part of Great Britain's mercantile empire. Influenced by the Enlightenment and the Great Awakening, colonists began to question the authority of the colonial power. Great Britain expanded its North American holdings by acquiring former French and Spanish territories after defeating the French in war.

Preview Chapter 2

Following the French and Indian War, Great Britain tried to limit settlement west of the Appalachian mountains to avoid increased hostilities with Native Americans. Great Britain's policies to raise more revenue and tighten its control over the American colonies provoked colonial resistance, which eventually escalated into the American Revolution. You will learn about these significant developments in the next chapter.

ALTERNATIVE ASSESSMENT

1. ROLE-PLAYING A TRIAL
Standards for Evaluation
An effective trial should meet the following criteria:

- Demonstrates knowledge of the law and crime that is being prosecuted.
- Follows proper courtroom procedure.
- Presents thoughtful, logical arguments.
- Shows an understanding of the colonial period and its laws and customs.

2. MAKING DECISIONS
Possible Responses:

- Decisions: Which colony to come to, how to travel, when to come, whom to bring, what to bring.
- Information: About colonies: Climate, work opportunities, social and religious atmosphere, quality of life. About travel: cost, length of trip, difficulties on the way. About people and supplies: How will the trip affect family members? How are the living and traveling conditions in America? What is needed once you get there?
- Options: You have 13 colonies to choose from, each with distinctive characteristics. You probably have fewer choices about when to travel, and may be limited by cost and availability.
- Consequences: Most important will be the opportunities for you to make a living, so you must consider your own skills and circumstances as well as what you know about the colonies. The negative consequences of bringing along family members who are not prepared could be severe.
- Actions: You would need to make plans to travel to a port, book passage on a ship, sell your possessions and bring along money and supplies, and possibly contact colonists or returned visitors for current information.

3. PORTFOLIO
LIVING HISTORY
Standards for Evaluation
A tale should meet the following criteria:

- Focuses on an interesting aspect of the past or the present.
- Includes a variety of detail that enriches the story.
- Has a plot that shows what it's like to be a colonist.
- Gives a clear sense of time and place.
- Is thoughtfully organized with a beginning, middle, and end.

THINKING CRITICALLY

3. GEOGRAPHY OF THE COLONIES
Possible Responses: The purpose of the line was to prevent colonists from going farther west into Native American lands; the Appalachian range presented a clear line of demarcation and provided a natural barrier to migration west.

4. TRACING THEMES SCIENCE AND TECHNOLOGY
Possible Responses: Mapmaking; printing with movable type; improved sailing technology such as the caravel with its lateen sails; navigation instruments such as the compass and astrolabe. Weapons such as longbows, cannons, and hand-held firearms.

5. ANALYZING PRIMARY SOURCES
Possible Responses: Mittelberger describes the physical discomforts of the transatlantic journey, the arduous labor of the indentured servant, and his disillusionment about life in America. Some students might heed Mittelberger's warning, saying that the adjustments they would face would be too overwhelming. Others might disregard his warning, citing their ability to overcome the hardships and their belief that the effort would be worthwhile in preparing a better life for future generations.

REVIEW CHAPTER 2

PLANNING GUIDE

Revolution and the Early Republic

	Key Ideas	COPYMASTERS	ASSESSMENT
SECTION 1 Colonial Resistance and Rebellion *pp. 48–55*	*Ideas about freedom and self-determination spur the colonies to unite in their resistance to Britain and declare independence.*	***In-Depth Resources: Unit 1*** • Guided Reading, p. 32 • Primary Source: The Boston Tea Party, p. 41 ***Lesson Plans,*** pp. 9–10	PE ***Section 1 Assessment,*** p. 55 TE ***Self-Assessment,*** p. 55 ***Formal Assessment*** • Section Quiz, p. 17 ***Alternative Assessment Book*** • Standards for Evaluating a Cooperative Activity
SECTION 2 The War for Independence *pp. 59–65*	*With the help of European allies, the colonists defeat the mighty British army and establish a new nation.*	***In-Depth Resources: Unit 1*** • Guided Reading, p. 33 • Skillbuilder Practice: Analyzing Causes; Recognizing Effects, p. 36 • Geography Application: The Siege of Yorktown, p. 39 • Primary Sources: Political Cartoon, p. 43; *from* Valley Forge Diary, p. 44 • American Lives: Salomon, p. 49 ***Lesson Plans,*** pp. 11–12	PE ***Section 2 Assessment,*** p. 65 TE ***Self-Assessment,*** p. 65 ***Formal Assessment*** • Section Quiz, p. 18 ***Alternative Assessment Book*** • Standards for Evaluating a Cooperative Activity
SECTION 3 Confederation and the Constitution *pp. 68–75*	*The delegates to the 1787 Philadelphia convention create a new Constitution to replace the Articles of Confederation. After the Bill of Rights is added, the Constitution is finally ratified.*	***In-Depth Resources: Unit 1*** • Guided Reading, p. 34 • Skillbuilder Practice: Analyzing Issues, p. 37 • Primary Source: *from* The U.S. Constitution, First Draft, p. 45 • Literature: from *Legacy* by James A. Michener, p. 46 • American Lives: Patrick Henry, p. 50 ***Lesson Plans,*** pp. 13–14	PE ***Section 3 Assessment,*** p. 75 TE ***Self-Assessment,*** p. 75 ***Formal Assessment*** • Section Quiz, p. 19 ***Alternative Assessment Book*** • Standards for Evaluating a Cooperative Activity
SECTION 4 Launching the New Nation *pp. 78–83*	*George Washington shapes the young nation, which faces conflict with European powers outside its borders and with Native Americans within its borders.*	***In-Depth Resources: Unit 1*** • Guided Reading, p. 35 • Skillbuilder Practice: Contrasting, p. 38 ***Lesson Plans,*** pp. 15–16	PE ***Section 4 Assessment,*** p. 83 TE ***Self-Assessment,*** p. 83 ***Formal Assessment*** • Section Quiz, p. 20 ***Alternative Assessment Book*** • Standards for Evaluating a Cooperative Activity
The Living Constitution *pp. 86–107*	*The full text of the Constitution including explanatory notes and critical thinking questions.*	***In-Depth Resources: Unit 1*** • Guided Reading, pp. 53, 54, 55, 56 • Skillbuilder Practice, p. 57 • Geography Application, p. 58 • American Lives, pp. 60, 61 • Projects for Citizenship, pp. 64–71 ***Lesson Plans,*** pp. 17–24	***Formal Assessment*** • Section Quizzes, pp. 29, 30, 31, 32 ***Alternative Assessment Book*** • Standards for Evaluating a Cooperative Activity
CHAPTER RESOURCES	**Chapter Overview** *Colonists declare their independence and win a war to gain the right to govern themselves. Leaders meet to write the Constitution. George Washington guides the new nation, but conflict between the two major political parties increases. The country also faces conflict with European nations.*	***In-Depth Resources: Unit 1*** • Living History Project: Worksheet, p. 51; Standards, p. 52 • Constitution Living History Project: Worksheet, p. 62; Standards, p. 63 ***Telescoping the Times*** • Chapter Summary, pp. 3–4 ***Planning for Block Schedules***	PE ***Chapter Assessment,*** pp. 84–85 PE ***Alternative Assessment,*** p. 85 PE ***Constitution Assessment,*** pp. 110–111 PE ***Alternative Assessment,*** p. 111 ***Formal Assessment*** • Chapter Test, forms A and B, pp. 21–26 • Constitution Test, forms A and B, pp. 33–38

KEY
PE Pupil's Edition
TE Teacher's Edition
http://www.mlushistory.com

TECHNOLOGY

Warm-Up Transparency 2

Humanities Transparencies
- H5, *Battle of Bunker Hill*
- H31, Political Cartoon

Electronic Library of Primary Sources
- *from* "Resolutions"
- *from* "An Account" by Paul Revere
- from *Common Sense* by Thomas Paine

INTERNET Colonial resistance

Warm-Up Transparency 2

Humanities Transparencies
- H6, Signing the Treaty of Paris, 1783
- H32, Mrs. General Washington

Geography Transparencies
- G4, North America, 1783

Critical Thinking Transparencies
- CT4, The War for Independence

Grolier Multimedia Encyclopedia

INTERNET Declaration of Independence

Warm-Up Transparency 2

Geography Transparencies
- G5, Land Ceded by States: 1782–1802

Critical Thinking Transparencies
- CT5, The Constitutional Convention

Electronic Library of Primary Sources
- *from* "Notes on Slavery"
- *from* "Constitution" by Franklin
- "On the Federal Government"
- from *Federalist 51* by Publius

INTERNET Valley Forge

Warm-Up Transparency 2

Humanities Transparencies
- H7, The Republican Court

Grolier Multimedia Encyclopedia

Electronic Library of Primary Sources
- "Regarding the Whiskey Rebellion"

INTERNET George Washington

Warm-Up Transparency for the Constitution

INTERNET The Constitution

American Portfolio: A Videodisc for U.S. History, user's guide, pp. 28–38, 40–43, 45

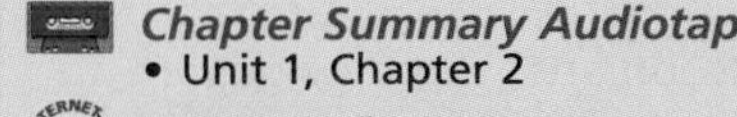

Chapter Summary Audiotapes
- Unit 1, Chapter 2

INTERNET http://www. mlushistory.com

Block Scheduling (90 MINUTES)

Day 1

Section 1, pp. 48–55

Section 2, pp. 59–65

Tracing Themes: Women in America, pp. 66–67

Section Assessments, pp. 55, 65

COOPERATIVE ACTIVITIES
- Letters from Committees of Correspondence, p. 50 (TE)
- Creating a Political Pamphlet, p. 53 (TE)
- Paraphrasing the Declaration, p. 57
- Reporting on the Revolution, p. 60

Day 2

Section 3, pp. 68–75

Section 4, pp. 78–83

Geography Spotlight: The Land Ordinance of 1785, pp. 76–77

Section Assessments, pp. 75, 83

Chapter Assessment, pp. 84–85

COOPERATIVE ACTIVITIES
- Letters to the Editor, p. 69 (TE)
- Creating a Media Ad, p. 72 (TE)
- Writing a Treaty, p. 82 (TE)

Day 3

The Living Constitution, pp. 86–107

Tracing Themes: Democracy in America, pp. 108–109

Assessment, pp. 110–111

COOPERATIVE ACTIVITIES
- Proposing Laws, p. 90 (TE)
- Proposing and Ratifying Amendments, p. 98 (TE)
- Preparing Voting Requirements, p. 106 (TE)
- Reviewing the Constitution, p. 107 (TE)

YEARLY PACING *Chapter 2 Total:* 3 days *Yearly Total:* 85 days

See *Planning for Block Schedules* for special activities and pacing strategies.

Customizing for Special Populations

Students Acquiring English

Access for Students Acquiring English: Spanish Translations
- Guided Reading for Sections 1–4, pp. 26–29
- Guided Reading for Constitution, pp. 35–38
- Chapter Summary, pp. 24–25
- Skillbuilder Practice: Analyzing Causes; Recognizing Effects, p. 30; Analyzing Issues, p. 31; Contrasting, p. 32; Clarifying, p. 39
- Geography Application: The Siege of Yorktown, p. 33; The Electoral College, p. 40
- Projects for Citizenship, pp. 42–49

Spanish Reading Study Guide, pp. 15–24

Translations of Chapter Summaries, Hmong, Cantonese, Vietnamese, and Cambodian

Chapter Summary Audiotapes in Spanish Unit 1, Chapter 2

INTERNET The Diverse Classroom

Gifted and Talented Students

In-Depth Resources: Unit 1
- Primary Sources: The Boston Tea Party, p. 41; Political Cartoon, p. 43; *from* Valley Forge Diary, p. 44; *from* The U.S. Constitution, First Draft, p. 45
- American Lives: Haym Salomon, p. 49; Patrick Henry, p. 50; James Madison, p. 60; Thurgood Marshall, p. 61
- Projects for Citizenship, pp. 64–71

Less Proficient Readers

In-Depth Resources: Unit 1
- Guided Reading for Sections 1–4, pp. 32–35
- Skillbuilder: Analyzing Causes; Recognizing Effects, p. 36; Analyzing Issues, p. 37; Contrasting, p. 38
- Geography Application: The Siege of Yorktown, p. 39

Reading Study Guide
- pp. 15–24

Telescoping the Times
- Chapter Summary, pp. 3–4

Chapter Summary Audiotapes, Unit 1, Chapter 2

Connections to Literature READINGS FOR STUDENTS

In-Depth Resources: Unit 1
- **from *Legacy* by James A. Michener,** p. 46

Enrichment Reading
- **Kenneth Roberts**
  Oliver Wiswell.
  New York: Doubleday, 1940. *This historically accurate story of the American Revolution is told from the viewpoint of a Tory.*
- **Washington Irving**
  Rip Van Wikle and the Legend of Sleepy Hollow.
  Tarrytown, NY: Sleepy Hollow Press, 1980. *These much loved ghost stories are set in colonial America.*

McDougal Littell *The Language of Literature*
American Literature
- **Patrick Henry,**
  "Speech in the Virginia Convention," p. 206
- **Phillis Wheatley,**
  "Letter to the Rev. Samson Occom," p. 216
- **Abigail Adams,**
  "Letter to John Adams," p. 216
- **Benjamin Franklin,**
  ***from* Poor Richard's Almanack,** p. 226
- **Red Jacket,**
  Lecture to a Missionary, p. 229

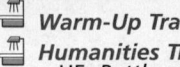

REVIEW CHAPTER 2
OVERVIEW

Revolution and the Early Republic

▶ ***Accessing Prior Knowledge***

Ask students to describe a sports event or contest in which a seemingly weaker person defeated a stronger one. Students should give reasons for why they think that happened.

▶ ***Predicting Outcomes***

Discuss with students Patrick Henry's quotation on this page. Ask them what makes the quotation so powerful. Then ask them what predictions they can make about the Revolution based on the quotation.

MORE ABOUT . . .
Patrick Henry

A lawyer noted for fine oratory, Patrick Henry was elected to the Virginia House of Burgesses in 1764, served as a delegate to the First Continental Congress, and was Virginia's governor during the Revolution. A member of his state's convention to ratify the Constitution, he is widely credited with getting the Bill of Rights included.

REVIEW CHAPTER 2

Revolution and the Early Republic

SECTION 1
Colonial Resistance and Rebellion
Ideas about freedom and self-determination spur the colonies to unite in their resistance to Britain and declare independence.

SECTION 2
The War for Independence
With the help of European allies, the colonists defeat the mighty British army and establish a new nation.

SECTION 3
Confederation and the Constitution
The delegates to the 1787 Philadelphia convention create a new Constitution to replace the Articles of Confederation. After the Bill of Rights is added, the Constitution is finally ratified.

SECTION 4
Launching the New Nation
George Washington shapes the young nation, which faces conflict with European powers outside its borders and with Native Americans within its borders.

"Give me liberty or give me death."
Patrick Henry

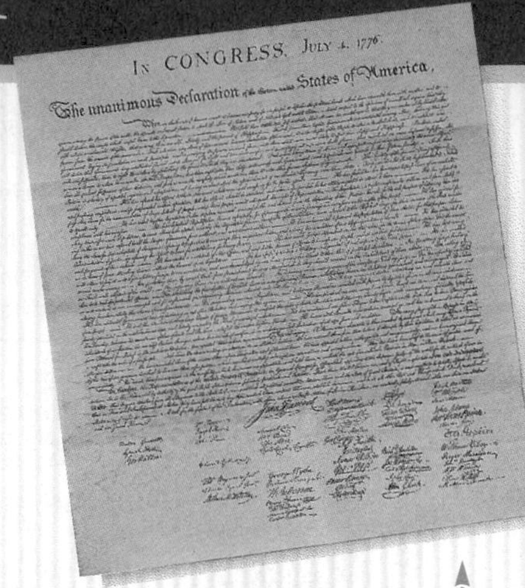
In CONGRESS, July 4, 1776.
The unanimous Declaration of the ... States of America,

THE UNITED STATES — 1763

- 1765 British Parliament passes the Stamp Act.
- 1773 Colonists stage the Boston Tea Party.
- 1774 Parliament passes the Intolerable Acts.
- 1774 First Continental Congress convenes.
- 1775 Second Continental Congress convenes.
- 1776 Colonists declare independence.
- 1781 The British surrender at Yorktown.

THE WORLD

- 1765 British Captain James Cook reaches Australia.
- 1774 Reign of Louis XVI begins in France.
- 1776 Adam Smith's *Wealth of Nations* is published.
- 1785 British preacher Edmund Cartwright invents first power loom.

THEMES IN CHAPTER 2

Economic Opportunity

Britain's economic policies toward the colonies were a major cause of the Revolution. The new nation's economy was largely based on agricultural products, which the government used to develop a profitable trade with Europe.

See Teacher's Edition notes, pp. 49 and 79.

Women in America

During the Revolution, women managed farms and businesses while the men were off fighting. They also performed tasks such as making supplies for the troops. Those women who traveled with their soldier husbands usually remained in the army camps.

See Teacher's Edition note, p. 62.

Constitutional Concerns

One of the greatest problems faced by the new confederation was unequal representation of citizens within states, which led to rebellion against unfair taxation. Eventually, a bill of rights created a government in which the needs of the nation were balanced with the rights of the individual.

See Teacher's Edition notes, pp. 70 and 74.

Immigration and Migration

Soon after the new government was launched, the United States began extending its borders. Many courageous people were willing to brave hardships and dangers to pioneer the country's westward expansion.

See Teacher's Edition note, p. 81.

LIVING HISTORY

CREATING A CONSTITUTION

Imagine that you are a delegate to a constitutional convention. Work with a small group of classmates to create a constitution for your class or school. Be sure your constitution answers such questions as the following:

- How will laws be passed?
- How will laws be enforced?
- How can laws be changed?

PORTFOLIO PROJECT As you work out compromises for your new government, save your notes in a folder. You will present your constitution and add it to your American history portfolio.

1786 — Daniel Shays leads a rebellion against higher taxes.

1787 — First of the *Federalist Papers* is published by Hamilton, Jay, and Madison.

1788 — The Constitution, which James Madison helped write at the Pennsylvania State House (*above*), is ratified.

1789 — George Washington is inaugurated as first president.

1792 — George Washington is elected president.

1794 — Whiskey Rebellion breaks out.

1796 — John Adams is elected president.

1800

1787 — Sierra Leone in Africa is made a haven for freed American slaves.

Turkey declares war on Russia.

1789 — The French Revolution starts.

1793 — French king Louis XVI is executed.

ALTERNATIVE ASSESSMENT

LIVING HISTORY

CREATING A CONSTITUTION

Encourage students to imagine that they are creating a new school from the ground up. They will decide how it will be organized and run. Students should begin by determining the primary goals of their school and how those goals can best be met. Students should address the following issues:

- Who will run the school?
- Who will decide what will be taught?
- How will students be evaluated?
- What ground rules for student and staff behavior will there be?
- How will the guilt or innocence of someone accused of breaking rules be determined?

Students should add to this list as they plan a new school.

IN-DEPTH RESOURCES: UNIT 1
See worksheet and standards for evaluation, pp. 51, 52.

RECOMMENDED RESOURCES

Books for the Teacher

Draper, Theodore. *A Struggle for Power.* New York: Times, 1996. Thorough study of the British and the colonists.

Madison, James. *Notes of Debates in the Federal Convention of 1787.* New York: Norton, 1987.

Morris, Richard B. *Witnesses at the Creation.* New York: Holt, 1985.

Sugden, John. *Tecumseh's Last Stand.* Norman: U of Oklahoma P, 1985. Readable story.

Books for the Student

Bailyn, Bernard. *Faces of Revolution.* New York: Vintage, 1992. Profiles of a wide variety of subjects.

Hibbert, Christopher. *Redcoats and Rebels: The American Revolution Through British Eyes.* New York: Norton, 1990.

Rutland, Robert. *James Madison and the Search for Nationhood.* Washington, DC: Library of Congress, 1981. Illustrated sketch of Madison's life and work; full of letters.

Videos

The American Revolution. History Channel home video. Six-tape documentary.

Bill of Rights in Action. Encyclopaedia Britannica, 800-554-9862. Connection of Bill of Rights to current issues.

The Building of the Capitol. Republic Pictures Home Video, 800-826-2295. Creating Washington, D.C.

Naca una nación. Films for the Humanities & Sciences, 800-257-3767. The Revolution in Spanish.

The Problems of Confederation. RMI Media, 800-745-5480.

Software

U.S. History: Government, Part 1. CD-ROM Educational Software Institute, 800-955-5570.

Section 1 Overview

OBJECTIVES

1. To explain the effects of the French and Indian War.
2. To summarize colonial resistance to British taxation.
3. To trace the mounting tension in Massachusetts.
4. To examine efforts made to avoid war between the colonies and the British.
5. To summarize the historical background of the Declaration of Independence.

SKILLBUILDER

- Interpreting charts, p. 49

CRITICAL THINKING

- Analyzing causes, p. 49
- Summarizing, p. 49
- Theme: Economic Opportunity, p. 50
- Forming opinions, p. 52
- Making inferences, pp. 54, 55
- Finding main ideas, pp. 54, 55
- Synthesizing, p. 55
- Making predictions, p. 55

FOCUS & MOTIVATE

5-MINUTE WARM-UP

Perceiving Cause and Effect

To explore the conflict between the colonists and the British, have students study the chart on page 49 and answer these questions.

1. What caused tensions between Great Britain and the colonists?
2. How did British actions affect the colonists?

WARM-UP TRANSPARENCY 2

▶ ***Starting with the Student***
Ask students how small quarrels between people mushroom into larger fights.

OBJECTIVE 1 **INSTRUCT**

The Colonies and Britain Grow Apart

▶ ***Discussing Key Ideas***

- To help pay for the huge war debt, George Grenville

(continued on next page)

1 Colonial Resistance and Rebellion

TERMS & NAMES
- Sugar Act
- Stamp Act
- Samuel Adams
- Boston Massacre
- Boston Tea Party
- King George III
- John Locke
- *Common Sense*
- Thomas Jefferson
- Declaration of Independence

LEARN ABOUT the growing conflict between Great Britain and the American colonies ***TO UNDERSTAND*** the American Revolution and how it began.

ONE AMERICAN'S STORY

Crispus Attucks, a sailor of African and Native American ancestry, was leading an angry group of laborers from Dock Square in Boston to the customshouse the night of March 5, 1770. British soldiers, stationed in the tension-filled city to keep the peace, had clashed with colonists that afternoon. By evening another enraged crowd gathered and marched to the customshouse on snowy King Street. At first, the crowd heckled the British sentry on guard, calling him a lobster-back to mock his red uniform. Then more soldiers arrived, and the mob began hurling stones and snowballs at them. At that moment, Crispus Attucks and his followers arrived.

Crispus Attucks

A PERSONAL VOICE

This Attucks . . . appears to have undertaken to be the hero of the night; and to lead this army with banners . . . up to King street with their clubs . . . this man with his party cried, do not be afraid of them. . . . He had hardiness enough to fall in upon them, and with one hand took hold of a bayonet, and with the other knocked the man down.

JOHN ADAMS, quoted in *The Black Presence in the Era of the American Revolution*

Attucks's action ignited the troops. Ignoring orders not to shoot civilians, one soldier and then several others fired on the crowd. Five people were killed; three were wounded. Crispus Attucks was, according to a newspaper account, the first to die.

Relations between Britain and the colonists had been strained since the Proclamation of 1763, but now the tensions had boiled over. No one knew it that clear, cold night, but Crispus Attucks would become one of the first colonists to die in an all-out war for freedom.

The Colonies and Britain Grow Apart

> ***"They that give up essential liberty to obtain a little temporary safety deserve neither liberty nor safety."***
>
> BENJAMIN FRANKLIN

Because the Proclamation of 1763 sought to halt expansion by the colonists west of the Appalachian Mountains, it convinced the colonists that the British government did not care about their needs. A second result of the French and Indian War—Britain's financial crisis—brought about new laws that reinforced the colonists' opinion.

PROBLEMS RESULTING FROM THE WAR After the war, the British government stationed 10,000 troops in its newly acquired territories to keep the Native Americans and former French subjects under control. Although the British government saw this army as protection for the colonies, the colonists viewed the troops as a standing army that might turn against them if they exercised too much liberty.

To maintain the troops in North America, Britain had borrowed so much money during the war that it nearly doubled its national debt. Hoping to lower the debt, King George III, who had succeeded his grandfather in 1760, chose a financial expert, George Grenville, to serve as prime minister in 1763.

The new prime minister noticed that the American customs service, which collected duties, or taxes on imports, was losing money. Grenville concluded that the colonists were smuggling goods into the country without paying duties. To stop the practice, in 1764 he prompted Parliament to enact a law known as the **Sugar Act.**

SECTION 1 RESOURCES

PRINT RESOURCES

IN-DEPTH RESOURCES: UNIT 1
Guided Reading, p. 32
Primary Source: The Boston Tea Party, p. 41

READING STUDY GUIDE, p. 15

ACCESS FOR STUDENTS ACQUIRING ENGLISH
Guided Reading (Spanish), p. 26

SPANISH READING STUDY GUIDE, p. 15

FORMAL ASSESSMENT
Section Quiz, p. 17

ALTERNATIVE ASSESSMENT BOOK
See forms for supporting and scoring alternative activities.

TECHNOLOGY RESOURCES

HUMANITIES TRANSPARENCIES
H5, *Battle of Bunker Hill* by Howard Pyle
H31, Political Cartoon on the Battle of Bunker Hill by Matthew Darly

CD-ROM Electronic Library of Primary Sources

VIDEO *American Portfolio: A Videodisc for U.S. History* user's guide, pp. 28–34

INTERNET http://www.mlushistory.com

The Sugar Act did three things. It halved the duty on foreign-made molasses (in the hopes that colonists would pay a lower tax rather than risk arrest by smuggling). It placed duties on certain imports that had not been taxed before. Most important, it strengthened the enforcement of the law by allowing prosecutors to try smuggling cases in a vice-admiralty court rather than a colonial court. There, each case would be decided by a single judge rather than by a jury of sympathetic colonists.

Colonial merchants complained that the Sugar Act would reduce their profits, and many charged that the British government violated their rights. Merchants and traders claimed that Parliament had no right to tax the colonists because the colonists had elected no representatives to the body. The new regulations, however, had little effect on colonists besides merchants and traders.

THINK THROUGH HISTORY
A. Analyzing Causes *What were the economic causes of tension between the colonists and Britain?*

A. Answer The colonists believed that the Sugar Act would reduce their profits and that these taxes violated their rights because they were not represented in Parliament.

Tension Between Britain and the Colonies

CAUSE	EFFECT
British station troops along the colonies' western borders to control Native Americans.	Colonists view the troops as a threat to their own activities and desire for liberty.
Britain establishes proclamation line to contain colonial expansion westward.	Proclamation line angers colonists, who ignore the boundary and continue moving westward.
British Parliament imposes greater taxes on the colonists to help pay the massive war debt.	Many colonial merchants protest the increased duties as taxation without representation.

SKILLBUILDER
INTERPRETING CHARTS
What three actions of the British offended the colonists?

Skillbuilder Answer
British troops in North America, Proclamation line, taxation without representation.

TWO VIEWS COLLIDE By the end of 1764, the colonies and Great Britain were disagreeing more and more about how the colonies should be taxed and governed. After the war, colonists fumed as Britain installed a standing army on their frontier and passed measures that violated long-standing rights of British citizens. While most colonists still considered themselves loyal subjects of the king, they grew increasingly dissatisfied with the way Parliament governed them. These feelings of dissatisfaction soon would swell into outright rebellion.

The Colonies Organize to Resist Britain

To finance its debts, Parliament continued to turn hungry eyes on the colonies' resources. British leaders saw nothing tyrannical in their plans for additional colonial rules and taxes. Their actions, however, set the stage for conflict.

THE STAMP ACT The seeds of increased tension were sown in March 1765 when Parliament, persuaded by Prime Minister Grenville, passed the **Stamp Act.** It was the first tax that affected colonists directly because it was levied on goods and services. Previous taxes, such as those levied by the Sugar Act, had been indirect, involving duties on imports.

The Stamp Act required that stamps be placed on many kinds of items, including wills, newspapers, and playing cards. In May of 1765, the colonists united to defy the law. Boston shopkeepers, artisans, and laborers organized a secret resistance group called the Sons of Liberty. By the end of the summer, members of the group protested throughout the colonies.

The colonial assemblies also made a strong collective protest. In October 1765, delegates from nine colonies gathered for a Stamp Act Congress in New York City. There they issued a Declaration of Rights and Grievances, which stated that Parliament lacked the power to impose taxes on the colonies because the colonists were not represented in Parliament. Colonial merchants added their weight to the resistance. In October 1765, merchants in New York, Boston, and Philadelphia agreed to a boycott of British goods until the Stamp Act was repealed. The widespread boycott worked, and in March 1766 Parliament repealed the law.

B. Answer Colonists protested, adopted resolutions denouncing the Stamp Act, and boycotted British goods.

THINK THROUGH HISTORY
B. Summarizing *How did the colonists respond to the Stamp Act?*

The colonists' view of the stamp tax is clear in the skull and crossbones emblem that warns of the effects of the Stamp Act.

THE TOWNSHEND ACTS Within a year after Parliament repealed the Stamp Act, however, Parliament passed the Townshend Acts, proposed by Charles Townshend, a newly appointed minister. These were duties levied on imports as they came into the colonies from Britain. The acts also imposed a three-penny tax on tea, the most popular drink in the colonies.

(continued from page 48)

imposes more tariffs on the colonists.
- Some colonists believe that the new regulations violate their rights as British citizens.

IN-DEPTH RESOURCES UNIT 1
Guided Reading, p. 32

ACCESS FOR STUDENTS ACQUIRING ENGLISH
Guided Reading (Spanish), p. 26

HISTORY FROM VISUALS
Tension Between Britain and the Colonies

Reading the Chart Point out that on the chart the causes are all actions and the effects are usually feelings.

Extension Have students list additional actions and effects as they read through this chapter.

OBJECTIVE
② INSTRUCT

The Colonies Organize to Resist Britain

Discussing Key Ideas
- The Stamp Act of 1765 provokes such widespread protest that Parliament repeals it.
- Not long afterward, Britain imposes the Townshend Acts which also meet with widespread resistance.

ELECTRONIC LIBRARY OF PRIMARY SOURCES
from "Resolutions for American Duties," Members of the British Parliament

TEACHING OPTIONS

Exploring Themes

Economic Opportunity Underscore the strong role economic factors played in causing the Revolution. Remind students that Britain not only imposed new taxes but also followed policies that squelched the colonies' economic development and their expansion into the newly acquired territories. Stress that the taxes especially outraged colonists because they had no representation in the taxing body, the British Parliament. Be sure students understand the difference between a direct tax—similar to a sales tax today—and an indirect tax, or duty paid by a shipper or importer that is passed along to consumers via a price increase.

Teaching Less Proficient Readers

Guided Reading Suggest that students focus their reading by turning each heading and subheading into a question and then reading the material below it to find the answer. For example, the main section heading on page 49 could be turned into this question:

How did the colonies organize to resist Britain?

The subheadings in this section could be turned into these questions: What was the Stamp Act? What were the Townshend Acts?

MORE ABOUT . . .
John Hancock

A close associate of Samuel Adams, John Hancock also represented Massachusetts at the Continental Congress. Hancock was its president when members signed the Declaration of Independence; that is why his signature came first and was the largest.

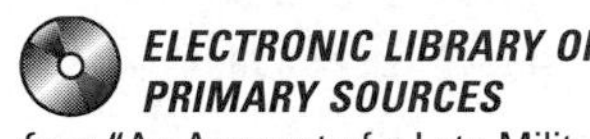

Tension Mounts in Massachusetts

▶ ***Discussing Key Ideas***

- Colonial resistance and British countermeasures lead to the Boston Massacre of 1770 and the Boston Tea Party of 1773.
- George III gets Parliament to punish Boston by passing laws that colonists call the Intolerable Acts.
- In 1774, the First Continental Congress meets in Philadelphia to draw up a declaration of colonial rights.

ELECTRONIC LIBRARY OF PRIMARY SOURCES
from "An Account of a Late Military Massacre" by Paul Revere

Enraged, colonists protested that they were being taxed without representation in Parliament. Boston's **Samuel Adams,** one of the founders of the Sons of Liberty, called for another boycott of British goods. Also, American women of every rank in society boycotted British-made cloth and British tea.

Conflict intensified in June 1768. British agents in Boston seized the *Liberty,* a ship belonging to local merchant John Hancock, and accused him of smuggling. The seizure triggered riots against customs agents. In response, the British stationed 4,000 troops in Boston—one soldier for every four citizens. This show of force led the colonists one step closer to revolution.

THINK THROUGH HISTORY
C. THEME ***Economic Opportunity*** *What economic factors contributed to the colonists' dissatisfaction and eventually to the American Revolution?*

C. Answer Britain squelched the colonies' economic development and expansion into new territories, and imposed taxes without the consent of the colonists.

Tension Mounts in Massachusetts

The presence of British soldiers in Boston's streets charged the air with hostility. The city soon erupted in bloody clashes between British soldiers and colonists and later in a daring tea protest, all of which pushed the colonists and Britain closer to war.

VIOLENCE ERUPTS IN BOSTON On March 5, 1770, a mob gathered in front of the Boston customshouse and taunted the British soldiers standing guard there. When Crispus Attucks and other dockhands appeared on the scene, an armed clash erupted, leaving Attucks and four others dead in the snow. Instantly, Samuel Adams and other agitators labeled this confrontation the **Boston Massacre,** thus presenting it as a British attack on defenseless citizens. Propaganda about the "massacre," including an engraving of the incident by the colonist Paul Revere (shown below), inflamed Massachusetts colonists as nothing had before.

Despite strong feelings on both sides, the political atmosphere relaxed somewhat during the next three years. Lord Frederick North, the new prime minister, realized that the Townshend Acts cost more to enforce than they would ever bring in. Therefore, North convinced Parliament to repeal the Townshend Acts, except for the tax on tea.

Tensions rose again in 1772 after a group of Rhode Island colonists attacked a British customs schooner that patrolled the coast for smugglers. In response, King George named a special commission to seek out the suspects and bring them to England for trial.

The plan to haul Americans to England for trial ignited widespread alarm. The assemblies of Massachusetts and Virginia set up committees of correspondence to communicate with other colonies about this and other threats to American liberties. By

Paul Revere's engraving of the Boston Massacre appeared in the *Boston Gazette* and was sold as a poster.

British Actions and Colonial Reactions, 1765 –1775

	British Action	Colonial Reaction
1765 STAMP ACT	Britain passes the Stamp Act, a tax law requiring colonists to purchase special stamped paper for printed items.	Colonists harass stamp distributors, boycott British goods, and prepare a Declaration of Rights and Grievances.
1767 TOWNSHEND ACTS	Britain taxes certain colonial imports and stations troops at major colonial ports to protect customs officers.	Colonists protest "taxation without representation" and organize a new boycott of imported goods.
1770 BOSTON MASSACRE	British troops stationed in Boston are taunted by an angry mob. The troops fire into the crowd, killing five men.	Colonial agitators label the conflict a massacre and publish a dramatic engraving depicting the violence.

Block Schedule TEACHING OPTION **Time Needed: 20 Minutes**

Cooperative Activity: Letters from Committees of Correspondence

Task: Groups of students will pretend to be committees of correspondence, writing letters committee members might have written in 1774.

Purpose: To understand the colonists' reactions to British actions.

Activity: Each group should pretend to live in different colonies and should address its letter to different groups in colonial society.

Students might supplement historical details from their texts with information that they research in library books or other references.

Building a Portfolio: Remind students to choose their strongest work for their portfolio. If they feel that this assignment qualifies, they should place a copy of it in their portfolio.

ALTERNATIVE ASSESSMENT BOOK
Standards for Evaluating a Cooperative Activity

Standards for Evaluation
Letters should . . .

- report on events occurring around 1774 in the writer's area
- include the writer's feelings
- indicate the rebellious political climate and possibly suggest a course of action

1774, such committees formed a buzzing communication network linking leaders in nearly all the colonies.

THE BOSTON TEA PARTY Early in 1773, Lord North faced a new problem. The British East India Company, which held an official monopoly on tea imports, had been hit hard by the colonial boycotts. With its warehouses bulging with 17 million pounds of tea, the company was nearing bankruptcy. To save it, North devised the Tea Act, which granted the company the right to sell tea to the colonies free of the taxes that colonial tea sellers had to pay. This action cut colonial merchants out of the tea trade, because the East India Company could sell its tea directly to consumers for less. North hoped the American colonists would simply buy the cheaper tea; instead, they protested violently.

On the moonlit evening of December 16, 1773, a large group of Boston rebels disguised themselves as Native Americans and proceeded to take action against three British tea ships anchored in the harbor. In this incident, later known as the **Boston Tea Party,** the "Indians" dumped 15,000 pounds of the East India Company's tea into the waters of Boston Harbor.

THE INTOLERABLE ACTS **King George III** was infuriated by this organized destruction of British property, and he pressed Parliament to act. In 1774, Parliament responded by passing a series of measures that colonists called the Intolerable Acts. One law shut down Boston Harbor because the colonists had refused to pay for the damaged tea. Another, the Quartering Act, authorized British commanders to house soldiers in vacant private homes and other buildings. In addition to these measures, General Thomas Gage, commander in chief of British forces in North America, was appointed the new governor of Massachusetts. To keep the peace, he placed Boston under martial law, or rule imposed by military forces.

King George hoped to isolate Massachusetts by singling it out for special punishment, but his actions only strengthened the colonies' unity. The committees of correspondence quickly moved into action and assembled the First Continental Congress. In September 1774, 56 delegates met in Philadelphia and drew up a declaration of colonial rights. They defended the colonies' right to run their own affairs. They supported the protests in Massachusetts and stated that if the British used force against the colonies, the colonies should fight back. They also agreed to reconvene in May 1775 if their demands weren't met.

This bottle contains tea that colonists threw into Boston Harbor during the Boston Tea Party.

NOW & THEN

TAXES

Anger among taxpayers is not a thing of the past. On June 4, 1996, Wisconsin voters threw Republican state senator George Petak out of office. The reason? Petak had promised voters he wouldn't vote to raise sales taxes to fund a new stadium for the Milwaukee Brewers baseball team, but at the last minute he changed his mind and voted for the tax. Voters were so angry they forced a recall election and voted Petak out of office.

A View of the Town of Concord, **painted by an unknown artist, shows British troops drilling on the village green.**

1773 TEA ACT		1774 INTOLERABLE ACTS		1775 LEXINGTON AND CONCORD	
British Action	**Colonial Reaction**	**British Action**	**Colonial Reaction**	**British Action**	**Colonial Reaction**
Britain gives the East India Company special concessions in the colonial tea business and shuts out colonial tea merchants.	Colonists in Boston rebel, dumping 15,000 pounds of East India Company tea into Boston Harbor.	King George tightens control over Massachusetts by closing Boston Harbor and quartering troops.	Colonial leaders form the First Continental Congress meet and draw up a declaration of colonial rights.	General Gage orders troops to march to Concord, Massachusetts, and seize colonial weapons.	Minutemen intercept the British and engage in battle—first at Lexington, and then at Concord.

NOW & THEN
Taxes

Critical Thinking: Comparing Ask students how the Wisconsin voters' political status was different from that of colonial Americans. *The voters were able to vote their senator out of office; the colonists had no vote on taxation.*

IN-DEPTH RESOURCES: UNIT 1
Primary Source: The Boston Tea Party, p. 41

MORE ABOUT . . .
The Intolerable Acts

The term "Intolerable Acts," like "the Boston Massacre," was a colonial term, not a British one. In addition to the retaliatory measures against Boston, the acts included the Quebec Act, which attempted to appease residents in the territory Britain had recently acquired from France. This was done by awarding to Quebec's jurisdiction all the land and fur trade between the Ohio and Mississippi rivers. The 13 colonies were outraged not only by the loss of revenue this represented but also by the prospect of encroaching Roman Catholicism, then still widely condemned both in England and in Protestant America.

TEACHING OPTIONS

Making Connections Across Time

Advances in Communications Point out that communications were slow in colonial times; in fact, the extremely slow communications between Britain and the American colonies contributed both to mutual misunderstandings and to Britain's inability to conduct the war effectively.

Ask how "committees of correspondence" might communicate today. *Possibilities include radio or TV broadcasts for mass communication; newspapers or newsletters, which can now be distributed far more rapidly; ham radio; telephone; Fax machine; e-mail; and the Internet.*

Teaching Less Proficient Readers

Organizing Information To help students understand the chain of events that led to the start of the Revolution, put the following diagram on the chalkboard. Help them fill in the events.

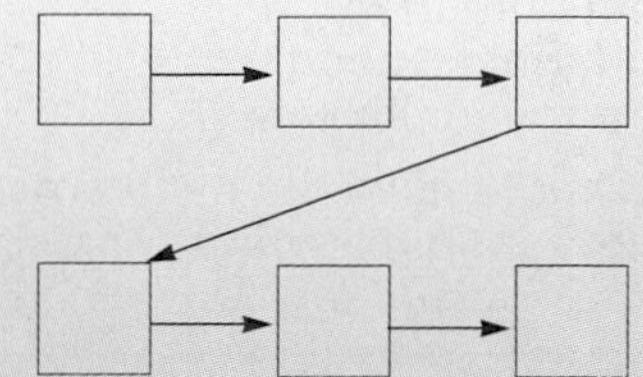

OBJECTIVE

④ **INSTRUCT**

The Road to Revolution

▶ ***Discussing Key Ideas***

- Warned that approaching British troops will attempt to seize their stockpiled weapons, civilian soldiers—minutemen—make their stand on April 19, 1775, in Concord.
- The shots fired prove to be the opening shots of the American Revolution.
- As delegates to the Second Continental Congress, held in Philadelphia, argue over independence, events overtake them.
- In June 1775, British troops outside Boston engage the colonial militia in the Battle of Bunker Hill.
- The Continental Congress offers peace with the Olive Branch Petition, which George III rejects.

HUMANITIES TRANSPARENCIES:

H5, *Battle of Bunker Hill*

H31, Political Cartoon on Bunker Hill

The Road to Revolution

After the First Continental Congress met, colonists in many eastern New England towns stepped up military preparations. Minutemen, or civilian soldiers, quietly stockpiled firearms and gunpowder. General Gage soon learned about these activities. In the spring of 1775, he ordered troops to march from Boston to nearby Concord, Massachusetts, and to seize illegal weapons.

FIGHTING AT LEXINGTON AND CONCORD Colonists in Boston watched the British troop movements. On the night of April 18, 1775, Paul Revere, William Dawes, and Samuel Prescott rode out to spread word that 700 British troops were headed for Concord. The king's troops reached Lexington, Massachusetts, near Concord, on April 19. As they neared the town, they saw 70 minutemen on the village green. The British commander ordered the minutemen to leave, and the colonists began to move out without laying down their muskets. Then someone fired, and the British soldiers shot into the departing militia. Eight minutemen were killed and nine more were wounded, but only one British soldier was injured.

The British marched on to Concord, where they found an empty arsenal. After a brief skirmish with minutemen, the British soldiers lined up to march back to Boston, but the march quickly became a slaughter. Between 3,000 and 4,000 minutemen had assembled by now, and they fired on the marching troops from behind stone walls and trees. British soldiers fell by the dozen. Only the arrival of reinforcements from Boston saved them from complete disaster.

Bloodied and humiliated, the remaining British soldiers made their way back to Boston that night. By now the colonists had become enemies of Britain and held Boston and the British troops there under siege.

In May of 1775, colonial leaders convened a second Continental Congress in Philadelphia to debate their next move. Beyond their meeting hall, however, events continued moving quickly, as minutemen and British soldiers clashed in a bloody battle outside Boston and an increasingly furious King George readied his country for war.

"I am determined to defend my rights and maintain my freedom or sell my life in the attempt."

NATHANAEL GREENE, QUAKER AND PACIFIST

D. Answer Possible responses: Yes, they failed to notice how angry and unified the colonies were becoming, and how years of resentment were sure to end in revolt. No, the British believed that taxing the colonies was justified because the colonies existed to benefit the British empire, and they expected continued loyalty from the colonists.

THINK THROUGH HISTORY
D. *Forming Opinions* *Do you think the British underestimated the colonists in 1770–1775?*

THE SECOND CONTINENTAL CONGRESS The loyalties that divided colonists sparked endless debates at the Second Continental Congress. Some delegates called for independence, while others argued for reconciliation with Great Britain. John Adams of Massachusetts suggested that each colony set up its own government and that the Congress declare the colonies independent. Furthermore, he argued, the Congress should consider the militiamen besieging Boston as the Continental Army and therefore name a general to lead them. Moderate John Dickinson of Pennsylvania strongly disagreed with Adams's call for revolt. In private, he confronted Adams.

A PERSONAL VOICE

> What is the reason, Mr. Adams, that you New England men oppose our measures of reconciliation? . . . If you don't concur with us in our pacific system, . . . we will carry on the opposition by ourselves in our own way.
>
> **JOHN DICKINSON,** quoted in *Patriots: The Men Who Started the American Revolution*

The debates raged on into June. The Congress agreed to recognize the colonial militia as the Continental Army and appointed as its commander a 43-year-old veteran of the French and Indian War, George Washington. Acting like an independent government, the Congress also authorized the printing of paper money to pay the troops and organized a committee to deal with foreign nations. These actions came just in time.

THE BATTLE OF BUNKER HILL Cooped up in Boston, British General Thomas Gage decided to strike at militiamen on Breed's Hill, north of the city and near

TEACHING OPTIONS

Making Connections Across the Curriculum

Literature Upon the completion of a monument to the Battle of Concord, Ralph Waldo Emerson wrote:

By the rude bridge that arched the flood,
  Their flag to April's breeze unfurled,
Here once the embattled farmers stood,
  And fired the shot heard round the world.

Ask in what sense the first shot fired by the minutemen at Concord was "the shot heard round the world." *Possible Response: It was the shot that marked the beginning of the American Revolution.*

Teaching Gifted and Talented Students

Create a Political Cartoon Ask students to work independently or with a partner to create a political cartoon based on an event described in the subsection "The Road to Revolution." For example, students might make a cartoon depicting the attack on the British at Concord, or the meeting of delegates at the Second Continental Congress. Point out to students that cartoons should exaggerate events, use recognizable symbols that are relevant to the event, appeal to a particular audience, and be witty.

Bunker Hill. On June 17, 1775, Gage sent out 2,400 redcoats, British soldiers so named for the scarlet jackets they wore. The British, sweating in wool uniforms and heavy packs, began marching up Breed's Hill in their customary broad lines. The colonists held their fire until the last minute and then began to mow down the advancing redcoats. The surviving British troops made a second attack and then a third. The third assault succeeded, but only because the militiamen ran low on ammunition.

By the time the smoke cleared, the colonists had lost 311 men, while the British had suffered over 1,000 casualties. The misnamed Battle of Bunker Hill would prove to be the deadliest battle of the war.

By July the Second Continental Congress was readying the colonies for war, though still hoping for peace. On July 8 the Congress sent the king the so-called Olive Branch Petition, urging a return to "the former harmony" between Britain and the colonies. King George rejected the petition. He also issued a proclamation stating that the colonies were in rebellion and urging Parliament to order a naval blockade of the American coast.

This painting shows "Bunker's Hill" before the battle, as shells from Boston set nearby Charlestown ablaze. At the battle, the British demonstrated a maneuver they used throughout the war. They massed together, were visible for miles, and failed to take advantage of ground cover.

The Patriots Declare Independence

Although most colonists found fault with the British army and British officeholders, they had feelings of loyalty to the king and were uncertain about the idea of independence. However, in the months following the Olive Branch Petition, colonial public opinion began to shift.

THE IDEAS BEHIND THE REVOLUTION This shift in public opinion occurred because of a set of powerful ideas that spread throughout the colonies in the 1760s and 1770s. These ideas grew out of the European intellectual movement known as the Enlightenment. Enlightenment thinkers stressed reason and logic, and they believed that humans could progress and develop a better society.

One of the key Enlightenment thinkers was English philosopher **John Locke.** Locke maintained that people have natural rights to life, liberty, and property. Furthermore, he contended, people willingly come together in a

MORE ABOUT . . .
John Dickinson

Called the "penman of the Revolution," John Dickinson won fame for his newspaper series *Letters from a Farmer in Pennsylvania,* which presented his powerful arguments against the Townshend Acts. As a Pennsylvania delegate to the Continental Congress, he refused to sign the Declaration of Independence, still hoping for reconciliation with Britain. He nevertheless fought valiantly in the Patriot militia and later represented Delaware at the Constitutional Convention.

OBJECTIVE
5 INSTRUCT

The Patriots Declare Independence

Starting with the Student
Ask students whether they have ever had to make a direct statement of what they believed were their rights in a particular situation. Then ask them how they went about doing this and what the response was.

Discussing Key Ideas
- Thomas Paine's *Common Sense* makes a persuasive case for independence.
- Thomas Jefferson's Declaration of Independence, adopted by the Continental Congress on July 4, 1776, expresses the argument in more philosophical terms.

Block Schedule TEACHING OPTION **Time Needed: 20 Minutes**

Cooperative Activity: Creating a Political Pamphlet

Task: Small groups of students will create political pamphlets that support or oppose independence.

Purpose: To understand the colonists' feelings about the war.

Activity: Each group should work together to produce a folded pamphlet designed to persuade colonists to support or oppose independence. Tell students to imagine that the pamphlet will be printed and circulated soon after a particular episode or event—the Battle of Bunker Hill, for example, or the signing of the Declaration of Independence.

Building a Portfolio: Students who choose to place a pamphlet in their portfolio should attach a note to it pointing out their contributions.

ALTERNATIVE ASSESSMENT BOOK
Standards for Evaluating a Cooperative Activity

Standards for Evaluation
Pamphlets should . . .
- express a point of view for or against independence
- use persuasive language
- end with some kind of call to action
- include an eye-catching front page

MORE ABOUT . . .
Thomas Paine

Thomas Paine came to Philadelphia in 1774 on the advice of Ben Franklin, whom Paine had met in London. Two years later, Paine published *Common Sense,* donating most of his profits to the Revolutionary cause. He later returned to England, where his defense of the French Revolution, *The Rights of Man,* prompted an indictment for treason. Fleeing to France, he was caught up in the Reign of Terror and imprisoned there. While in prison, he published *The Age of Reason,* an attack on organized religion that won him many enemies.

ELECTRONIC LIBRARY OF PRIMARY SOURCES:
from *Common Sense* by Thomas Paine

COMMON SENSE;
ADDRESSED TO THE
INHABITANTS
OF
AMERICA,
On the following interesting
SUBJECTS.
I. Of the Origin and Design of Government in general, with concise Remarks on the English Constitution.
II. Of Monarchy and Hereditary Succession.
III. Thoughts on the present State of American Affairs.
IV. Of the present Ability of America, with some miscellaneous Reflections.
Man knows no Master save creating Heaven,
Or those whom choice and common good ordain.
THOMSON.
PHILADELPHIA;
Printed, and Sold, by R. BELL, in Third-Street.
MDCCLXXVI.

Thomas Paine helped to overcome many colonists' doubts about separating from Britain with his pamphlet *Common Sense.*

social contract—an agreement in which the people consent to choose and obey a government so long as it safeguards their natural rights. If the government violates that social contract by taking away or interfering with those rights, people have the right to resist and even overthrow the government.

In addition to the philosophy of natural rights, colonial leaders who favored independence were influenced by traditions of liberty in past civilizations, particularly in the Greek city-state of Athens and in Rome. Both civilizations had traditions of individual liberty, and both developed forms of representative government.

Other influences on colonial leaders who favored independence were religious traditions that supported the cause of liberty. One minister of the time, Jonathan Mayhew, wrote that he had learned from the holy scriptures that wise, brave, and virtuous men were always friends of liberty. Some ministers even spoke from their pulpits in favor of liberty.

E. Answer Americans seeking independence found support for their views in Locke's assertion that people have a right to resist or overthrow an unfair government.

THINK THROUGH HISTORY
E. Making Inferences *Why might the ideals of the Enlightenment appeal to the colonists?*

THOMAS PAINE'S *COMMON SENSE* Such lofty ideas were important in creating the atmosphere for revolution. Just as important, though, were the ideas of Thomas Paine. In a 47-page widely read pamphlet titled ***Common Sense,*** Paine attacked King George and the monarchy. Paine, a recent immigrant, argued that responsibility for British tyranny lay with "the royal brute of Britain." Paine explained that his own revolt against the king had begun with Lexington and Concord.

Thomas Paine

A PERSONAL VOICE

> No man was a warmer wisher for a reconciliation than myself, before the fatal nineteenth of April, 1775, but the moment the event of that day was made known, I rejected the hardened, sullen-tempered Pharaoh of England forever . . . the wretch, that with the pretended title of FATHER OF HIS PEOPLE can unfeelingly hear of their slaughter, and composedly sleep with their blood upon his soul.
>
> **THOMAS PAINE,** *Common Sense*

Paine declared that the time had come for colonists to proclaim an independent republic. He argued that independence, which was the American "destiny," would allow America to trade freely with other nations for guns and ammunition and win foreign aid from British enemies. Finally, Paine stated, independence would give American colonists the chance to create a better society—one free from tyranny, with equal social and economic opportunities for all.

Common Sense was widely read (some 500,000 copies were sold) and widely applauded. In April 1776, George Washington wrote, "I find *Common Sense* is working a powerful change in the minds of many men."

F. Answer Paine believed that independence would allow America to trade freely with other nations for guns and ammunition, thereby winning foreign aid from British enemies. He also believed that independence would give all American colonists equal social and economic opportunities.

THINK THROUGH HISTORY
F. Finding Main Ideas *What ideas did Thomas Paine use to justify independence from Britain?*

These documents are laws that were issued by the Second Continental Congress, which served as the government of the United States during the Revolutionary War.

TEACHING OPTIONS

Making Connections Across the Curriculum

Literature In addition to *Common Sense,* Paine is famous for his series of pamphlets *The Crisis.* The first of these appeared in December 1776, when the dispirited American troops had just retreated across New Jersey. Paine's patriotic message, beginning "These are the times that try men's souls," proved so stirring that General Washington ordered the pamphlet read to all his troops. Paine continued the series until 1783; he also served as aide-de-camp to General Nathanael Greene.

Encourage students to discuss patriotic songs, speeches, or other literature that they find especially inspiring.

Making Connections Across TIme

Independence Day Note that Independence Day was first celebrated in Philadelphia on July 4, 1777, the one-year anniversary of the adoption of the Declaration of Independence. Flag Day, June 14, commemorates the Continental Congress's 1777 adoption of the Stars and Stripes as the U.S. flag; it is a legal holiday only in Pennsylvania.

Ask students if they feel that present-day celebrations of these holidays show sufficient appreciation of the events they commemorate. Should Flag Day be a legal holiday in all 50 states? Have students explain their answers.

DECLARING INDEPENDENCE In May 1776, events pushed the wavering Continental Congress toward a decision. North Carolina had declared itself independent, and a majority of Virginians told their delegates that they favored independence. At last, the Congress urged each colony to form its own government. On June 7, Virginia delegate Richard Henry Lee moved that "these United Colonies are, and of a right ought to be, free and independent States."

While talks on this fateful motion were under way, the Congress appointed a committee to prepare a formal declaration explaining the reasons for the colonies' actions. Virginia lawyer **Thomas Jefferson**, known for his broad knowledge and skillfully crafted prose, was chosen to express the committee's points.

Jefferson's masterful **Declaration of Independence** drew on Locke's philosophy of natural rights. Jefferson referred to these rights as unalienable rights—ones that can never be taken away. He described these rights as "Life, Liberty and the pursuit of Happiness." In keeping with Locke's idea of a social contract, Jefferson then declared that governments derive their powers from the consent of the governed—that is, from the people. This consent gave the people the right "to alter or to abolish" any government that threatened their unalienable rights and to install a government that would uphold these principles. On the basis of this reasoning, the American colonies declared their independence from Britain. The Declaration listed the numerous ways in which the British king had taken away the "unalienable rights" of the Americans.

The Declaration states flatly that "all men are created equal." When this phrase was written, it expressed the common belief that free citizens were political equals. It was not meant to embrace women, Native Americans, and African-American slaves—a large number of Americans. However, Jefferson's words presented ideals that would later help these groups challenge traditional attitudes.

G. Answer When a government fails to protect people's unalienable rights, these people have a right to rebel and form a government that will protect their rights.

THINK THROUGH HISTORY
G. *Finding Main Ideas* *What reasons did Jefferson give to justify revolt by the colonies?*

In his first draft, Jefferson included an eloquent attack on the cruelty and injustice of the slave trade. However, South Carolina and Georgia, the two colonies most dependent on slavery, objected. In order to gain the votes of those two states, Jefferson dropped the offending passage.

On July 2, 1776, the delegates voted unanimously that the American colonies were free, and on July 4, 1776, they adopted the Declaration of Independence. While delegates created a formal copy of the Declaration, the document was read to a crowd in front of the Philadelphia State House—now called Independence Hall. A rush of pride and anxiety ran through the supporters of independence when they heard the closing vow: "We mutually pledge to each other our Lives, our Fortunes, and our Sacred Honor."

ASSESS & RETEACH

Section 1 Assessment
Students might work in pairs to respond to the questions.

Self-Assessment
To assess what they have learned, students might write their own questions, exchange them with a partner, and try to answer their partner's questions.

Section Quiz
FORMAL ASSESSMENT
Section Quiz, p. 17

Reteach
Use the Guided Reading Worksheet for Section 1 to help in reviewing the main ideas of this section.

IN-DEPTH RESOURCES: UNIT 1
Guided Reading, p. 32

CLOSE

Swept up in escalating violence and spurred by inspiring political rhetoric, the colonies declared their independence and began a revolution that divided colonial loyalties.

Section  Assessment

1. TERMS & NAMES
Identify:
- Sugar Act
- Stamp Act
- Samuel Adams
- Boston Massacre
- Boston Tea Party
- King George III
- John Locke
- *Common Sense*
- Thomas Jefferson
- Declaration of Independence

2. SYNTHESIZING Create a cluster diagram like the one shown and fill it with events that demonstrate the conflict between Great Britain and the American colonies.

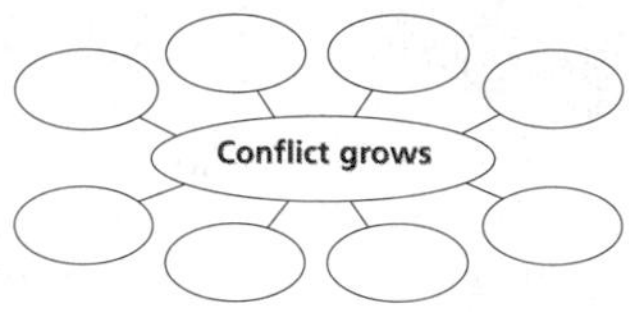

Choose one event to further explain in a paragraph.

3. MAKING PREDICTIONS Imagine that King George had accepted the Olive Branch Petition and tried a diplomatic resolution with the Congress. Do you think colonists would still have pressed for independence?

THINK ABOUT
- the attitudes of the king and Parliament toward the colonies
- the impact of fighting at Lexington, Concord, and Breed's Hill
- the writings of Thomas Paine

4. MAKING INFERENCES Why do you think that when Jefferson borrowed Locke's ideas, he changed the rights of men from "life, liberty, and property" to "life, liberty, and the pursuit of happiness"?

THINK ABOUT
- Jefferson's reputation as a lawyer and scholar
- the politically charged climate of rebellion and loyalty
- the socioeconomic groups living in America

ANSWERS

1. TERMS AND NAMES
Sugar Act, p. 48
Stamp Act, p. 49
Samuel Adams, p. 50
Boston Massacre, p. 50
Boston Tea Party, p. 51
King George III, p. 51
John Locke, p. 53
Common Sense, p. 54
Thomas Jefferson, p. 55
Declaration of Independence, p. 55

2. SYNTHESIZING
Possible Responses: forming Sons of Liberty; protesting Stamp Act; seizure of the *Liberty;* Boston Massacre; Boston Tea Party; closing Boston Harbor; Quartering Act; placing Boston under martial law; stockpiling arms; stationing British troops at Concord; Battle of Lexington; colonists' retaliation at Concord.

3. MAKING PREDICTIONS
Possible Responses: Students answering yes might cite British efforts to keep the colonists subservient; colonists' memories of recent battles; Thomas Paine's persuasive arguments for independence. Students answering no might say that most Americans were loyal to the king and did not want independence.

4. MAKING INFERENCES
Possible Responses: He felt that "pursuit of happiness" had universal appeal and that no one could argue against it; as a lawyer, he knew the emotional power of words; perhaps he felt that the wording might sway those who opposed independence; he knew that many Americans didn't own property, and he wanted to include them.

The Declaration of Independence

The text printed here shows the spelling and punctuation of the handwritten original. Selected words and phrases are explained below, to help students understand some of the 18th-century language and to help clarify meaning.

unalienable Rights rights that cannot be taken away

light and transient causes unimportant reasons

shewn shown

usurpations *unjust seizures of power*

Despotism *rule by a tyrant with absolute power*

let facts be submitted to a candid world The colonists can no longer suffer the abuses of their government and thus must change it. What follows is a list of charges against King George III.

He *King George III*

inestimable priceless

Th Jefferson

John Adams

Phil. Livingston

Benj. Franklin

Roger Sherman

In Congress, July 4, 1776.

A Declaration by the Representatives of the United States of America, in General Congress assembled.

When in the Course of human events, it becomes necessary for one people to dissolve the political bands which have connected them with another, and to assume among the powers of the earth, the separate and equal station to which the Laws of Nature and of Nature's God entitle them, a decent respect to the opinions of mankind requires that they should declare the causes which impel them to the separation.

We hold these truths to be self-evident, that all men are created equal, that they are endowed by their Creator with certain unalienable Rights, that among these are Life, Liberty and the pursuit of Happiness; that, to secure these rights, Governments are instituted among Men, deriving their just powers from the consent of the governed; that whenever any Form of Government becomes destructive of these ends, it is the Right of the People to alter or to abolish it, and to institute new Government, laying its foundation on such principles and organizing its powers in such form, as to them shall seem most likely to effect their Safety and Happiness. Prudence, indeed, will dictate that Governments long established should not be changed for light and transient causes; and accordingly all experience hath shewn that mankind are more disposed to suffer, while evils are sufferable, than to right themselves by abolishing the forms to which they are accustomed. But when a long train of abuses and usurpations, pursuing invariably the same Object, evinces a design to reduce them under absolute Despotism, it is their right, it is their duty, to throw off such Government, and to provide new Guards for their future security.

Such has been the patient sufferance of these Colonies; and such is now the necessity which constrains them to alter their former Systems of Government. The history of the present King of Great Britain is a history of repeated injuries and usurpations, all having in direct object the establishment of an absolute Tyranny over these States. To prove this, let facts be submitted to a candid world.

He has refused his Assent to Laws, the most wholesome and necessary for the public good.

He has forbidden his Governors to pass Laws of immediate and pressing importance, unless suspended in their operation till his assent should be obtained; and, when so suspended, he has utterly neglected to attend to them.

He has refused to pass other Laws for the accommodation of large districts of people, unless those people would relinquish the right of Representation in the Legislature, a right inestimable to them, and formidable to tyrants only.

He has called together legislative bodies at places unusual, uncomfortable, and distant from the depository of their public Records, for the sole purpose of fatiguing them into compliance with his measures.

He has dissolved Representative Houses repeatedly, for opposing with manly firmness his invasions on the rights of the people.

He has refused for a long time, after such dissolutions, to cause others to be elected; whereby the Legislative powers, incapable of Annihilation, have returned to the people at large for their exercise; the State remaining in the mean time exposed to all the dangers of invasions from without, and convulsions within.

He has endeavoured to prevent the population of these States; for that purpose obstructing the Laws for Naturalization of Foreigners; refusing to pass others to encourage

RECOMMENDED RESOURCES

Books for the Teacher

Fleming, Thomas. *1776: Year of Illusions.* New York: Norton, 1975. Provides context of events surrounding the Declaration.

Wills, Garry. *Inventing America.* New York: Doubleday, 1980. The Declaration in American thought.

Books for the Student

Ferriss, Robert, ed. *Signers of the Declaration.* Washington, D.C.: National Park Service, 1973. Biography of each signer.

Lengyel, Cornel. *Four Days in July.* New York: Doubleday, 1958. Focus on the July 1–4 debates in Congress.

Videos

The Adams Chronicles, 1976. Films Inc., 800-323-4222. Early Declaration debate.

Andrew Jackson/Thomas Jefferson. Great American Lives Series. Videodisc. Educational Software Institute, 800-955-5570.

The Declaration of Independence by the Colonies. Encyclopaedia Britannica, 800-554-9862.

1776. Dir. Peter H. Hunt, 1972. Home video. (G) Broadway musical about debate over Declaration takes some liberties but is mostly accurate and entertaining.

Software

The American Revolution. CD-ROM. Educational Software Institute, 800-955-5570.

The Pennsylvania Gazette, Folio III 1766–1783: The American Revolution. CD-ROM. Accessible Archives, 697 Sugartown Road, Malvern, PA 19355.

their migration hither, and raising the conditions of new Appropriations of Lands.

He has obstructed the Administration of Justice, by refusing his Assent to Laws for establishing Judiciary powers.

He has made Judges dependent on his Will alone, for the tenure of their offices, and the amount and payment of their salaries.

He has erected a multitude of New Offices, and sent hither swarms of Officers to harass our people and eat out their substance.

He has kept among us, in times of peace, Standing Armies, without the Consent of our legislatures.

He has affected to render the Military independent of and superior to the Civil power.

He has combined with others to subject us to a jurisdiction foreign to our constitution and unacknowledged by our laws; giving his Assent to their Acts of pretended Legislation:

For quartering large bodies of armed troops among us;

For protecting them, by a mock Trial, from punishment for any Murders which they should commit on the Inhabitants of these States;

For cutting off our Trade with all parts of the world;

For imposing Taxes on us without our Consent;

For depriving us, in many cases, of the benefits of Trial by Jury;

For transporting us beyond Seas to be tried for pretended offenses;

For abolishing the free System of English Laws in a neighboring Province, establishing therein an Arbitrary government, and enlarging its Boundaries so as to render it at once an example and fit instrument for introducing the same absolute rule into these Colonies;

For taking away our Charters, abolishing our most valuable laws, and altering fundamentally the Forms of our Governments;

For suspending our own Legislatures, and declaring themselves invested with power to legislate for us in all cases whatsoever.

He has abdicated Government here, by declaring us out of his Protection and waging War against us.

He has plundered our seas, ravaged our Coasts, burnt our towns, and destroyed the lives of our people.

He is at this time transporting large Armies of foreign Mercenaries to compleat the works of death, desolation, and tyranny, already begun with circumstances of Cruelty & perfidy scarcely paralleled in the most barbarous ages, and totally unworthy the Head of a civilized nation.

He has constrained our fellow Citizens, taken Captive on the high Seas, to bear Arms against their Country, to become the executioners of their friends and Brethren, or to fall themselves by their Hands.

He has excited domestic insurrections amongst us, and has endeavoured to bring on the inhabitants of our frontiers the merciless Indian Savages, whose known rule of warfare is an undistinguished destruction of all ages, sexes and conditions.

ANOTHER PERSPECTIVE

DECLARATION REACTIONS

The Declaration did not speak to certain conditions of inequality within the colonies themselves. Husbands dominated their wives, for example, and slaves lived under complete control of their owners. Speaking on behalf of women, Abigail Adams had this to say to her husband John, who served in the Continental Congress:

> "Remember the Ladies, and be more generous and favourable to them than your ancestors. Do not put such unlimited power into the hands of the Husbands. Remember all Men would be tyrants if they could. If particular care . . . is not paid to the Ladies, we are determined to foment a Rebellion."
>
> **ABIGAIL SMITH ADAMS**, Letter to John Adams, March 31, 1776

Citing the Declaration, some enslaved African Americans petitioned for freedom. Eight Boston slaves signed this petition:

> "[Following] the . . . example of the good People of these States, your Petitioners . . . can not but express their astonishment that it has never been considered that . . . they may be restored to the enjoyment of that freedom which is the natural right of all Men."
>
> Petition of "a great number of Negroes who are detained in a State of Slavery" to the Massachusetts General Court, January 13, 1777

eat out their substance drain the resources of the colonies by forcing them to support more government officials

quartering furnishing with housing

foreign Mercenaries professional soldiers hired to serve in a foreign army

domestic insurrections rebellions at home

Block Schedule TEACHING OPTION **Time Needed: 30 Minutes**

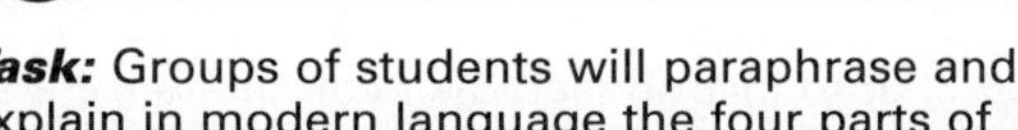

Cooperative Activity: Paraphrasing the Declaration

Task: Groups of students will paraphrase and explain in modern language the four parts of the Declaration.

Purpose: To closely read one of the greatest documents in U.S. history.

Activity: Assign each group one of the four sections of the Declaration: (1) Preamble, (2) Declaration of Rights, (3) List of Grievances, (4) Statement of Independence. (Several groups should work on selected portions of the List of Grievances.) Students will rewrite the section in modern English, using words everyone in the group understands and agrees to use. Each group should also include information on the background and the meaning of the passage(s).

Building a Portfolio: Students who feel their work is especially good may wish to add the paraphrases to their portfolios.

ALTERNATIVE ASSESSMENT BOOK
Standards for Evaluating a Cooperative Activity

Standards for Evaluation
Paraphrases of the Declaration should . . .

- be expressed in clear, coherent language
- show evidence of research into word meanings
- include background explanations of ideas

Petitioned for Redress *asked the king to correct the abuses*

unwarrantable jurisdiction *unjustified control*

magnanimity *generosity and unselfishness*

conjured *brought to mind*

consanguinity *relationship by blood or by a common ancestor*

rectitude righteousness; moral uprightness

This engraving shows Thomas Jefferson's design for the Great Seal of the United States.

In every stage of these Oppressions We have Petitioned for Redress in the most humble terms; Our repeated Petitions have been answered only by repeated injury. A Prince, whose character is thus marked by every act which may define a Tyrant, is unfit to be the ruler of a free people.

Nor have We been wanting in attentions to our British brethren. We have warned them from time to time of attempts by their legislature to extend an unwarrantable jurisdiction over us. We have reminded them of the circumstances of our emigration and settlement here. We have appealed to their native justice and magnanimity, and we have conjured them by the ties of our common kindred, to disavow these usurpations, which would inevitably interrupt our connections and correspondence. They too have been deaf to the voice of justice and of consanguinity. We must, therefore, acquiesce in the necessity, which denounces our Separation, and hold them, as we hold the rest of mankind, Enemies in War, in Peace Friends.

We, therefore, the Representatives of the United States of America, in General Congress, Assembled, appealing to the Supreme Judge of the world for the rectitude of our intentions, do, in the name, and by the Authority of the good People of these Colonies solemnly publish and declare, That these United Colonies are, and of Right ought to be, Free and Independent States; that they are Absolved from all Allegiance to the British Crown, and that all political connection between them and the State of Great Britain is, and ought to be, totally dissolved; and that as Free and Independent States, they have full Power to levy War, conclude Peace, contract Alliances, establish Commerce, and do all other Acts and Things which Independent States may of right do.

And for the support of this Declaration, with a firm reliance on the protection of divine Providence, we mutually pledge to each other our Lives, our Fortunes, and our sacred Honor.

[Signed by]

John Hancock [President of the Continental Congress]

[GEORGIA]
Button Gwinnett
Lyman Hall
George Walton

[RHODE ISLAND]
Stephen Hopkins
William Ellery

[CONNECTICUT]
Roger Sherman
Samuel Huntington
William Williams
Oliver Wolcott

[NORTH CAROLINA]
William Hooper
Joseph Hewes
John Penn

[SOUTH CAROLINA]
Edward Rutledge
Thomas Heyward, Jr.
Thomas Lynch, Jr.
Arthur Middleton

[MARYLAND]
Samuel Chase
William Paca
Thomas Stone
Charles Carroll

[VIRGINIA]
George Wythe
Richard Henry Lee
Thomas Jefferson
Benjamin Harrison
Thomas Nelson, Jr.
Francis Lightfoot Lee
Carter Braxton

[PENNSYLVANIA]
Robert Morris
Benjamin Rush
Benjamin Franklin
John Morton
George Clymer
James Smith
George Taylor
James Wilson
George Ross

[DELAWARE]
Caesar Rodney
George Read
Thomas McKean

[NEW YORK]
William Floyd
Philip Livingston
Francis Lewis
Lewis Morris

[NEW JERSEY]
Richard Stockton
John Witherspoon
Francis Hopkinson
John Hart
Abraham Clark

[NEW HAMPSHIRE]
Josiah Bartlett
William Whipple
Matthew Thornton

[MASSACHUSETTS]
Samuel Adams
John Adams
Robert Treat Paine
Elbridge Gerry

HYPOTHESIZING

Ask students to imagine this nation without the Declaration of Independence. Think about

- the Declaration as a call to arms
- the influence of the Declaration on the Constitution
- the impact of the Declaration on the colonists

TEACHING OPTION

Making Connections Across Cultures

Slavery In his rough draft of the Declaration, Thomas Jefferson included a strongly worded attack on the institution of slavery. The passage was dropped to gain the votes of South Carolina and Georgia—both slave-owning states.

Jefferson wrote: "He [King George] has waged cruel war against human nature itself, violating it's most sacred rights of life and liberty in the persons of a distant people who never offended him, captivating and carrying them into slavery in another hemisphere, or to incur miserable death in their transportation thither. This piratical warfare, the opprobrium of infidels powers, is the warfare of the Christian king of Great Britain." Jefferson also characterizes the slave trade as "execrable commerce" and an "assemblage of horrors."

Have students discuss the possible impact on U.S. history this passage might have had if it had been included in the Declaration.

2 The War for Independence

TERMS & NAMES
- Loyalists
- Patriots
- Saratoga
- Valley Forge
- inflation
- Marquis de Lafayette
- Charles Cornwallis
- Yorktown
- Treaty of Paris
- egalitarianism

LEARN ABOUT campaigns of the Revolutionary War and the colonists' maneuvers to reverse British advances
TO UNDERSTAND how the Americans won the war.

ONE AMERICAN'S STORY

Benjamin Franklin, the famous American writer, scientist, statesman, and diplomat, represented the colonies in London throughout the growing feud with Britain. As resistance in the colonies turned to bloodshed, however, Franklin fled London in 1775 and sailed home to Philadelphia.

But one thing nagged him: his son William sided with the Crown. William Franklin, the royal governor of New Jersey, had an English wife, was stubbornly loyal to King George, and opposed the rebellious atmosphere in the colonies. William regularly wrote letters to the British authorities in which he reported on the conflict in the colonies. In a letter written on August 2, 1775, to Lord Dartmouth, William stated his position and that of others who resisted revolutionary views.

A PERSONAL VOICE
There is indeed a dread in the minds of many here that some of the leaders of the people are aiming to establish a republic. Rather than submit . . . we have thousands who will risk the loss of their lives in defense of the old Constitution. [They] are ready to declare themselves whenever they see a chance of its being of any avail.
WILLIAM FRANKLIN, quoted in *A Little Revenge: Benjamin Franklin and His Son*

William Franklin

Because of William's stand on colonial issues, communication between him and his father virtually ceased. The break between Benjamin Franklin and his son mirrored the chasm that now divided the colonies from Britain. The notion of fighting Britain frightened and horrified some colonists even as it inspired others. But, in the end, a set of ideas spurred the colonists to declare independence from their home country.

Americans Choose Sides

Americans now faced a difficult, bitter choice: revolution or loyalty to the Crown. All over the colonies this issue divided communities, friends, and even families.

LOYALISTS AND PATRIOTS The exact number of **Loyalists**—those who opposed independence and remained loyal to the Crown—is unknown. Many with Loyalist sympathies changed sides as the war progressed.

Some Loyalists felt a tie to the king because they had served as judges or governors. Most Loyalists, however, were people of modest means. They included some people who lived far from the cities and knew little of the events that turned other colonists into revolutionaries. Other people remained loyal because they thought that the British were going to win and they wanted to avoid punishment as rebels. Still others thought that the Crown would protect their rights more effectively than the new colonial governments would.

Patriots—the supporters of independence—drew their numbers from people who saw economic opportunity in an independent America. The patriot cause included farmers, artisans, merchants, landowners, and elected officials. Patriots made up nearly half the population. Many Americans remained neutral.

A. Answer Loyalists maintained respect for the king and preferred British rule; Patriots agreed with Paine and wanted to be free of tyrannical rules imposed by Britain.

THINK THROUGH HISTORY
A. *Forming Generalizations* *How did the thinking of Loyalists differ from that of Patriots?*

Section 2 Overview

OBJECTIVES
1. To contrast the attitudes of Loyalists and Patriots.
2. To trace the war through the battle of Saratoga.
3. To examine civilian life during the Revolution.
4. To trace the war in the South through the siege of Yorktown.
5. To recognize the symbolic value of the Revolution.

SKILLBUILDERS
- Interpreting charts, p. 60
- Understanding geography: location, place, p. 60
- Understanding geography: place, movement, p. 63

CRITICAL THINKING
- Forming generalizations, p. 59
- Recognizing effects, pp. 61, 65
- Identifying problems, p. 62
- Theme: Women in America, p. 62
- Making predictions, p. 65
- Analyzing issues, p. 65
- Summarizing, p. 65
- Analyzing causes, p. 65

FOCUS & MOTIVATE

5-MINUTE WARM-UP

Describing Character
To better understand the importance of George Washington, have students read Key Player on page 61 and answer these questions.
1. Why was Washington a national hero?
2. List the qualities that you think describe George Washington's character.

WARM-UP TRANSPARENCY 2

▶ ***Starting with the Student***
Ask students what the American Revolution means to them.

OBJECTIVE
1 INSTRUCT

Americans Choose Sides

▶ ***Discussing Key Ideas***
- Americans become either Loyalists or Patriots.

(continued on next page)

SECTION 2 RESOURCES

PRINT RESOURCES

IN-DEPTH RESOURCES: UNIT 1
Guided Reading, p. 33
Skillbuilder Practice: Analyzing Causes; Recognizing Effects, p. 36
Geography Application: The Siege of Yorktown, p. 39
Primary Sources: Cartoon, p. 43; *from* Valley Forge Diary, p. 44
American Lives: Haym Salomon, p. 49

READING STUDY GUIDE, p. 17

ACCESS FOR STUDENTS ACQUIRING ENGLISH
Guided Reading (Spanish), p. 27
Skillbuilder Practice (Spanish), p. 30
Geography Application: The Siege of Yorktown (Spanish), p. 33

SPANISH READING STUDY GUIDE, p. 17

FORMAL ASSESSMENT
Section Quiz, p. 18

ALTERNATIVE ASSESSMENT BOOK
See forms for supporting and scoring alternative activities.

TECHNOLOGY RESOURCES

HUMANITIES TRANSPARENCIES
H6, Signing of the Treaty of Paris, 1783
H32, Mrs. General Washington

GEOGRAPHY TRANSPARENCIES
G4, North America: 1783

CRITICAL THINKING TRANSPARENCIES
CT4, The War for Independence

CD-ROM *Grolier Multimedia Encyclopedia*

VIDEO *American Portfolio: A Videodisc for U.S. History* user's guide, pp. 34–38, 43

INTERNET http://www.mlushistory.com

(continued from page 59)

- Within ethnic and religious groups, and even within families, loyalties are often divided.

IN-DEPTH RESOURCES: UNIT 1
Guided Reading, p. 33
Primary Source: Political Cartoon, p. 43

ACCESS FOR STUDENTS ACQUIRING ENGLISH
Guided Reading (Spanish), p. 27

HISTORY FROM VISUALS
Military Strengths and Weaknesses

Reading the Chart Ask students what they would add to the British weaknesses. *Possible Response: Use of mercenaries, who had no real stake in the outcome.*

OBJECTIVE
② **INSTRUCT**

The War Moves to the Middle States

▶ ***Discussing Key Ideas***
- The American victory at Saratoga is a turning point in the Revolution.
- The Continental Army spends a brutal winter in Valley Forge, Pennsylvania.

HISTORY FROM VISUALS
Revolutionary War, 1775–1778

Reading the Map Have students follow the American campaign on the map.

Extension Have students name the site at which Burgoyne's troops scored a victory on the way to Saratoga. *Fort Ticonderoga.*

TAKING SIDES The conflict presented dilemmas for other groups as well. The Quakers generally supported the Patriots but did not fight, because they did not believe in war. Many African Americans fought on the side of the Patriots, but others joined the Loyalists because the British promised freedom to slaves who would fight for the Crown. Most Native Americans supported the British because they viewed colonial settlers as a bigger threat to their lands.

Now the colonies were plunged into two wars: a war for independence and a civil war in which Americans found themselves on opposing sides. The price of choosing sides could be high. In declaring their independence, the Patriots had invited war with the mightiest empire on earth.

Military Strengths and Weaknesses

UNITED STATES	GREAT BRITAIN
Strengths:	**Strengths:**
• Familiarity of home ground	• Strong, well-trained army and navy
• Leadership of George Washington and other officers	• Strong central government with available funds
• Inspiring cause—independence	• Support of colonial Loyalists and Native Americans
Weaknesses:	**Weaknesses:**
• Most soldiers untrained and undisciplined	• Large distance separating Britain from battlefields
• Shortage of food and ammunition	• Troops unfamiliar with terrain
• Inferior navy	• Weak military leaders
• No central government to enforce wartime policies	

SKILLBUILDER
INTERPRETING CHARTS *What do you think was the key strength for the colonists? The key weakness for Britain?*

Skillbuilder Answer **Colonists:** *Possible Responses:* familiarity of home ground, strong leadership, and the inspiring cause of independence. **British:** *Possible Responses:* unfamiliarity with the terrain, weak military leadership, and the large distance between Britain and the battlefield.

The War Moves to the Middle States

The colonists suffered an initial loss to the British in the battle for New York, which along with the other middle states served as the Revolutionary War's early battleground. "These are the times that try men's souls," Thomas Paine lamented after the Continental Army's early defeats.

EARLY VICTORIES AND DEFEATS The British retreated from Boston in March 1776, moving the theater of war to the middle states. As part of a plan to stop the rebellion by isolating New England, the British decided to seize New York City. Two brothers, General William Howe and Admiral Richard Howe, sailed into New York Harbor in the summer of 1776 with a force of about 32,000 soldiers, including thousands of German mercenaries, or hired soldiers. The Americans called these troops Hessians, because many of them came from the German region of Hesse.

Washington rallied 23,000 men to New York's defense. But he was vastly outnumbered, and most of his troops were untrained recruits with poor equipment. The battle for New York ended in late August with heavy losses and an

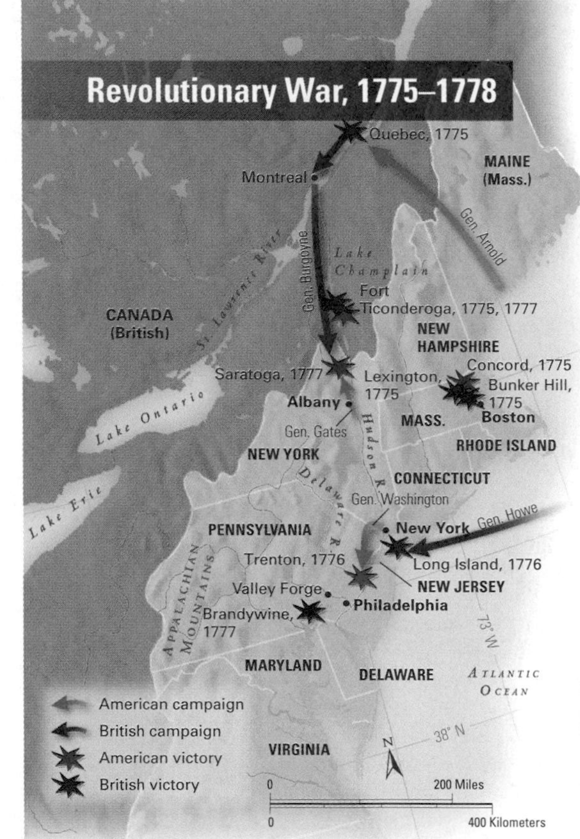

GEOGRAPHY SKILLBUILDER
LOCATION *From which cities did General Burgoyne march his troops to Saratoga?*
PLACE *What characteristics did many of the battle sites have in common? Why do you think this was so?*

Skillbuilder Answer **Location:** Quebec, Montreal. **Place:** Sites— They were near either Atlantic Ocean or a riv Reason—Rivers and oceans, which provide troops with transporta were strategically important to both sides

Block Schedule TEACHING OPTION **Time Needed: 30 Minutes**

Cooperative Activity: Reporting on the Revolution

Task: Groups of students will create front pages of newspaper issues reporting on different Revolutionary battles.

Purpose: To understand the military, psychological, and historical effects of different Revolutionary battles.

Activity: Each group should decide how often its paper comes out (daily, weekly) and who the audience is (Loyalists, Patriots, or both, or perhaps people overseas). Students should choose one battle and, if necessary, do further research to cover it completely. The front page might include straight news, interviews, background pieces, and human-interest features (about soldiers or civilians affected by war, for example). Different students might serve as researchers, writers, editors, and layout designers.

Building a Portfolio: Remind students to choose their strongest work for their portfolio.

ALTERNATIVE ASSESSMENT BOOK
Standards for Evaluating a Cooperative Activity

Standards for Evaluation
Front pages should . . .
- include headlines and the newspaper's name
- present facts accurately, telling who, what, where, when, how, and why
- contain several types of articles—straight news, interviews, and so on
- be geared to a particular audience

American retreat. By late fall, the British had pushed Washington's army across the Delaware River into Pennsylvania.

Washington desperately wanted some sort of victory to inspire his men. He resolved to risk everything on one bold stroke set for Christmas night, 1776. In the face of a fierce storm, he led 2,400 men across the ice-choked Delaware River in small rowboats. By 8 o'clock the next morning, the men had marched nine miles through sleet and snow to the objective—Trenton, New Jersey, held by a garrison of Hessians. In a surprise attack, the Americans defeated the British. This victory was followed by another victory against British troops at Princeton, New Jersey.

THINK THROUGH HISTORY
B. *Recognizing Effects* *Why were the victories at Trenton and Princeton so important to the Continental Army?*
B. Answer These victories restored the soldiers' confidence after numerous losses.

In the spring of 1777, General Howe had a plan to seize the American capital at Philadelphia. His troops left New York by sea, sailed up the Chesapeake Bay, and landed near the capital in late August. Washington's troops tried to block the redcoats at nearby Brandywine Creek. The Americans lost the battle, and the pleasure-loving General Howe settled in to enjoy the hospitality of Philadelphia's grateful Loyalists. Later, a strike against the British in nearby Germantown also resulted in an American defeat.

SARATOGA AND VALLEY FORGE In the meantime, one of Howe's fellow British generals was marching straight into the jaws of disaster. In a complex scheme, General John Burgoyne planned to lead an army down a route of lakes from Canada to Albany, where he would meet Howe's troops as they arrived from New York City. The two generals would then join forces to isolate New England from the rest of the colonies.

However, Burgoyne first had to travel through forested wilderness, which bogged down his army. At the same time, militiamen and soldiers from the Continental Army gathered from all over New York and New England. Every time the two sides clashed, Burgoyne lost several hundred men. Even worse, Burgoyne didn't realize that Howe was preoccupied with occupying Philadelphia and wasn't coming to meet him.

American troops finally surrounded Burgoyne at **Saratoga,** where he surrendered his battered army to General Horatio Gates on October 17, 1777. The surrender at Saratoga dramatically changed Britain's war strategy. From that time on, the British generally kept their men along the coast, close to the big guns and supply bases of the British fleet.

Saratoga was important psychologically as well as militarily. Americans now had proof that they could defeat the British regulars. At the same time, British confidence took a heavy blow.

The full impact of Saratoga was felt when the news reached Paris and London. Although the French had secretly sent weapons and ammunition to the Patriots since early 1776, the Saratoga victory bolstered French trust in the American army so much that France agreed to support the Revolution openly. The French signed an alliance, a treaty of cooperation, with the Americans in February 1778, agreeing not to make peace with Britain unless Britain recognized American independence.

While this hopeful turn of events took place in Paris, Washington and his Continental Army fought to stay alive at winter camp in **Valley Forge,** Pennsylvania. Unfortunately, the Continental Congress had little money for supplies for the troops. Throughout the winter, 10,000 soldiers braved harsh conditions, with tattered clothes and little food. More than 2,000 soldiers died, yet the survivors didn't desert. Their endurance and suffering filled Washington's letters to the Congress and his friends.

KEY PLAYER

GEORGE WASHINGTON
1732–1799

During the Revolutionary War, Commander in Chief George Washington became a national hero. An imposing man, Washington stood six feet two inches tall. He was broadshouldered, calm, and dignified, and he was an expert horseman. But it was Washington's character that won hearts and, ultimately, the war.

Time and again, Washington roused dispirited men into a fighting force. At Princeton, he galloped on his white horse into the line of fire, shouting and encouraging his men. At Valley Forge, he bore the same cold and privation as every suffering soldier. Time and again, Washington's tactics saved his smaller, weaker force to fight another day. By the end of the war, the entire nation idolized General Washington, and adoring soldiers crowded near him just to touch his boots when he rode by.

MORE ABOUT . . .
The Opposing Armies

The Continental Army was officially formed by the Continental Congress in June 1775 from the standing militias that all colonies except Pennsylvania possessed. The Congress also voted to raise ten new companies of riflemen and put George Washington in charge of the entire army. The British hired German mercenaries, most of them Hessians (from Hesse-Kassel in what is now central Germany), to supplement their forces.

KEY PLAYER
George Washington

Critical Thinking: Analyzing Effects Ask students how the British at Trenton might have felt about Washington. *Possible Response: They might have considered him sneaky and perhaps dishonorable to attack the day after Christmas.*

GROLIER MULTIMEDIA ENCYCLOPEDIA
George Washington

IN-DEPTH RESOURCES: UNIT 1
Primary Source: *from* Valley Forge Diary, p. 44

TEACHING OPTIONS

Teaching Less Proficient Readers

Learning Visually Visual learners may find it easier to absorb information about Revolutionary battles if they map the details out themselves. Encourage students to expand on the maps in this and the next section of their text, creating a single map with all the important battle sites. You may want to give students copies of Geography Transparency 4 to help them create their own maps. Each visual learner might work with a more verbal partner who supplies appropriate details from the text and/or from additional research about the Revolution.

GEOGRAPHY TRANSPARENCIES
G4, North America, 1783

Making Connections Across Time

Revolutionary Battlefields The site of the Battle of Saratoga is now a historical park tourists can drive through, stopping at various exhibits along the way. In fact, most of the other battlesites mentioned here and elsewhere in the chapter have commemorative monuments, parks, or museums that people can visit today. Have students choose different Revolutionary sites to describe to classmates in oral reports or special exhibits. Students might include personal accounts or photos as well as information from tourist brochures, travel books, Internet sites, local historical societies, and/or organizations such as the Sons of the Revolution.

ECONOMIC BACKGROUND

"Not Worth a Continental"

Critical Thinking: Making Inferences

Ask students what effect the inflated currency may have had on Patriot morale, and why. *Negative effect: The bad economic situation could have angered people and sapped their support of the Patriot cause; Positive effect: The Patriots may have had an incentive to win quickly—to end the economic hardship.*

IN-DEPTH RESOURCES: UNIT 1
American Lives: Haym Salomon, p. 49

OBJECTIVE

③ INSTRUCT

Life During the Revolution

▶ ***Starting with the Student***
Ask students these questions:

- How does financial hardship affect people's behavior and attitudes?
- How might the effects of financial hardship be different during a time of war than during peacetime?

▶ ***Discussing Key Ideas***

- Inflation and shortages spell economic hardship for colonists; eventually, financiers organize the government's finances.
- Women contribute to the war effort by helping to arm, clothe, and feed the army, and even by fighting.

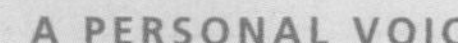

ECONOMIC BACKGROUND

"NOT WORTH A CONTINENTAL"

When Congress began printing the paper money called Continentals, it had no gold or silver to back up the currency; it simply promised that the money would be good when the war was won. But Americans had their doubts about a victory—and about the worth of the Continentals. Furthermore, everyday goods were in short supply due to the British blockade and the heavy demands for staples by the army.

Consequently, prices for goods rose. Congress responded to the rising prices by printing more money but quickly learned that having too much money in circulation lowers its value. The value of Continental currency dropped so much that people began to use the phrase "not worth a Continental" to refer to anything worthless. (See *inflation* on page 936 in the Economics Handbook.)

A PERSONAL VOICE

It may be said that no history . . . can furnish an instance of an Army's suffering uncommon hardships as ours have done. . . . To see men without Clothes to cover their nakedness, without Blankets to lay on, without Shoes, . . . and submitting to it without a murmur, is a mark of patience and obedience which in my opinion can scarcely be paralleled.

GEORGE WASHINGTON, quoted in *Ordeal at Valley Forge*

It would take months for French aid to arrive. In the meantime, the British controlled New York and parts of New England and wintered comfortably in Philadelphia while the meager army of Patriots struggled to survive.

Life During the Revolution

The Revolutionary War touched the life of every American, not just the men on the battlefield and the leaders struggling to pilot America through the storm. The war upset the economy and forced people into new ways of living and thinking.

FINANCING THE WAR One huge problem that the Continental Congress faced was paying the troops. When the Congress ran out of hard currency—silver and gold—it borrowed money by selling bonds to American investors and foreign governments, especially France. It also printed paper money called (like the Revolutionary soldiers) Continentals. As Congress printed more and more money, its value plunged, causing rising prices, or **inflation.** The Congress also struggled against great odds to equip the beleaguered army.

THINK THROUGH HISTORY
C. *Identifying Problems* *What economic problems did the Americans face in financing the war?*

C. Answer
Colonists faced inflation—the rise in the price of goods.

In 1781, the Congress appointed a rich Philadelphia merchant named Robert Morris as superintendent of finance. His associate was Haym Salomon, a Jewish political refugee from Poland. Morris and Salomon begged and borrowed on their personal credit. They raised funds from Philadelphia's Quakers and Jews. In time, they organized the government's finances and set up a supply system for the army. On September 8, 1781, a Continental major wrote in his diary, "This day will be famous in the Annals of History for being the first on which the Troops of the United States received one Month's Pay in Specie [coin]."

Molly Pitcher was the heroine of the Battle of Monmouth in New Jersey, which was fought in 1778. For her heroism, Washington made her a sergeant.

CIVILIANS AT WAR The demands of war also affected civilians. When men marched off to fight, many wives stepped into their husbands' shoes, managing farms and businesses as well as households and families.

Hundreds of women followed their husbands to the battlefield, where they washed and cooked for the troops. A few women risked their lives in combat. Mary Ludwig Hays (known as Molly Pitcher) took her husband's place at a cannon when he was wounded at the Battle of Monmouth.

These women sparked a slight shift in attitudes. Traditional society viewed women as subordinate to their husbands, but during the war, women tasted new freedoms and felt a growing sense of self-confidence. While the Revolution did not win major freedoms for women, it did shape a new ideal for them: to rear the next generation to be Patriots.

D. Answer
Women managed farms and businesses as well as households and families. Some women washed and cooked for troops in the battlefields. A few women risked their lives in combat.

THINK THROUGH HISTORY
D. THEME *Women in America* *What important roles did women play in the American Revolution?*

TEACHING OPTIONS

Making Connections Across Cultures

Jews in Early America Most of the first Jews in America were Sephardic (Southern European) Jews whose ancestors had fled to Holland from Spain and Portugal to escape the Inquisition. They settled first in New Amsterdam (later New York) and then in other colonies. Traditionally merchants, not farmers (in medieval times, farming was often forbidden to Europe's Jews), they remained mostly in port cities. Haym Salomon, a Polish Jew, was a later arrival, coming to New York in 1772. Arrested by the British for spying, he escaped to Philadelphia, where he aided the Patriot cause.

Exploring Themes

Women in America Women played an important role in the Revolution managing farms and businesses while the men were off fighting. Women also supported the Patriot cause by making ammunition, clothing, and other supplies for the troops and by helping to feed and house soldiers in their area. Those women who traveled with their soldier husbands usually remained in the army camps, doing cooking, washing, and sewing; attending to wounds and illnesses when necessary; and occasionally taking up arms themselves.

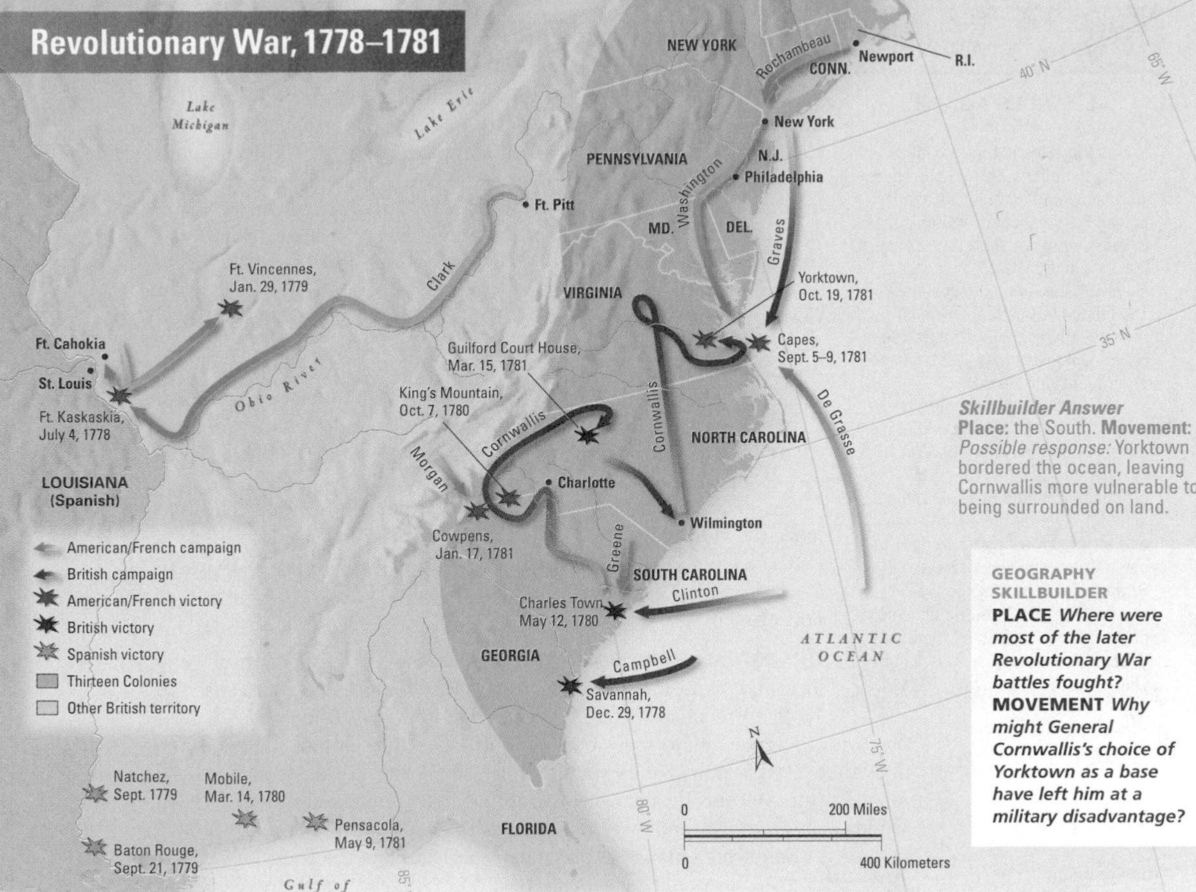

Skillbuilder Answer
Place: the South. **Movement:** *Possible response:* Yorktown bordered the ocean, leaving Cornwallis more vulnerable to being surrounded on land.

GEOGRAPHY SKILLBUILDER

PLACE *Where were most of the later Revolutionary War battles fought?*
MOVEMENT *Why might General Cornwallis's choice of Yorktown as a base have left him at a military disadvantage?*

During the Revolutionary War, fighting also took place on the western frontier. The American general George Rogers Clark captured Ft. Kaskaskia and Ft. Vincennes from the British. The Spanish, who entered the war on the American side in 1779, captured several British outposts on the Gulf Coast.

The war opened some doors for African Americans. Thousands of slaves escaped to freedom in the chaos of war. Some fled to the cities, where they passed as free people, or to the frontier, where they sometimes joined Native American tribes. About 5,000 African Americans served in the Continental Army, where their courage, loyalty, and talent impressed white Americans. Native Americans, however, remained on the fringes of the Revolution, preferring to remain independent and true to their own cultures.

Winning the War

In February 1778, in the midst of the frozen winter at Valley Forge, American troops began an amazing transformation. Friedrich von Steuben, a Prussian captain and talented drillmaster, volunteered his services to Washington at Valley Forge and went to work "to make regular soldiers out of country bumpkins." Other foreign military men, such as the **Marquis de Lafayette,** also arrived to offer their help. A brave, idealistic 20-year-old French aristocrat, Lafayette joined Washington's staff and bore the misery of Valley Forge, lobbied for French reinforcements in France in 1779, and led a command in Virginia in the last years of the war. With the help of such European military leaders, the raw Continental Army became an effective fighting force.

HISTORY FROM VISUALS

Revolutionary War, 1778–1781

Reading the Map After students have read the section on the Yorktown surrender, ask them what the blue arrow in the Atlantic Ocean represents on the map. *The French naval force blocking the entrance to Chesapeake Bay.*

Extension Ask students what conclusions they might draw, based on the map, about the Spanish strategy. *Possible Response: Spain took advantage of the British forces' being occupied elsewhere to make inroads along the Gulf of Mexico.*

Winning the War

▶ ***Discussing Key Ideas***

- European idealists such as Lafayette contribute to the American cause.
- The Southern campaign pits American forces led by Nathanael Greene against British forces under Cornwallis.
- French and American forces unite for a month-long siege at Yorktown, where Cornwallis surrenders on October 17,1781.
- The Treaty of Paris of 1783 grants American independence and sets the new nation's boundaries.

TEACHING OPTION

Skillbuilder Mini-Lesson: Analyzing Causes, Recognizing Effects

Explaining the Skill History often involves more than a simple string of causes and effects, with one following after another. For example, a cause can have more than one effect, and an effect can become the cause of something else.

Applying the Skill Have students read On the World Stage on page 64 and then chart the causes and effects of French intervention in the Revolutionary War. Students' charts might look like this:

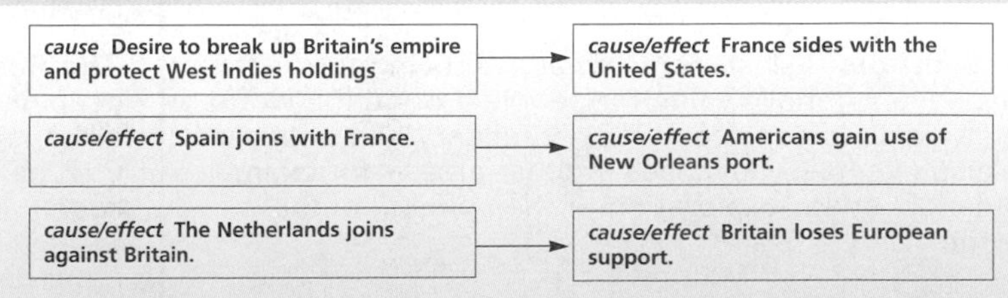

cause Desire to break up Britain's empire and protect West Indies holdings → *cause/effect* France sides with the United States.

cause/effect Spain joins with France. → *cause/effect* Americans gain use of New Orleans port.

cause/effect The Netherlands joins against Britain. → *cause/effect* Britain loses European support.

IN-DEPTH RESOURCES: UNIT 1
Skillbuilder Practice: Analyzing Causes, Recognizing Effects, p. 36

ON THE WORLD STAGE

Alliances Against Britain

Critical Thinking: Drawing Conclusions Ask students whether the French alliance with the Americans should have come as a surprise to the British. *Possible Response: No, Anglo-French rivalry in both the New World and the Old World was strong throughout the 18th century; since France and England had already been at war several times in the past hundred years, French involvement was to be expected.*

IN-DEPTH RESOURCES: UNIT 1
Geography Application: The Siege of Yorktown, p. 39

HUMANITIES TRANSPARENCIES
H6, Signing of the Treaty of Paris, 1783
H32, "Mrs. General Washington Bestowing Thirteen Stripes on Britannia"

ON THE WORLD STAGE

ALLIANCES AGAINST BRITAIN

During the 18th century, the major European nations were intense rivals who competed for colonies and power. France, hoping to break up Britain's empire and protect French holdings in the West Indies, allied itself with the American colonies. The French feared that if Britain regained the colonies, it might seize French colonies in the West Indies in order to pay for the war.

The French alliance with the Americans was decisive in that it transformed the American War for Independence into a full-scale European conflict. In 1779, Spain joined the war as an ally of France and allowed the American navy to use the Spanish port of New Orleans as a base for the war at sea. In 1780, the Netherlands also declared war on Britain. By then Britain faced an international fight with no allies of its own.

THE BRITISH MOVE SOUTH After their devastating defeat at Saratoga, the British began to shift their operations to the South. At the end of 1778, a British expedition easily took Savannah, Georgia. In their greatest victory of the war, the British under Generals Henry Clinton and **Charles Cornwallis** captured Charles Town, South Carolina, in May 1780 and marched 5,500 American soldiers off as prisoners of war. Clinton then left for New York, leaving Cornwallis to command the British forces in the South and to conquer South and North Carolina. For most of 1780, Cornwallis succeeded.

In January 1781 American soldiers defeated the British at Cowpens, South Carolina. The British expected the outnumbered Americans to flee; but the Continental Army fought back, forcing the redcoats to surrender.

Angered by the defeat at Cowpens, Cornwallis attacked American troops under General Nathanael Greene two months later at Guilford Court House, North Carolina. Cornwallis won the battle, but the victory cost him nearly a fourth of his troops.

After the exhausting battle in the Carolinas, Cornwallis chose to move the fight to Virginia. He led his army of 7,200 onto the peninsula between the James and York rivers and camped at **Yorktown.** Cornwallis planned to fortify Yorktown, take Virginia, and then move north to join Clinton's forces.

THE BRITISH SURRENDER AT YORKTOWN A combination of good luck and well-timed decisions now favored the American cause. In 1780, a French army of 6,000 landed in Newport, Rhode Island, after the British left the city to focus on the South. The French had stationed one fleet there and were operating another in the West Indies. At this crucial moment, the Marquis de Lafayette suggested that the American and French armies join forces with the two French fleets to attack Cornwallis at Yorktown. Following Lafayette's plan, the Americans and the French closed in on Cornwallis. A French naval force defeated a British fleet and then blocked the entrance to the Chesapeake Bay, thereby obstructing British sea routes to the bay. Meanwhile, 17,000 French and American troops surrounded the British on the Yorktown peninsula and bombarded them day and night.

The Continental Congress officially adopted a flag with 13 stripes and 13 stars in 1777.

The siege of Yorktown lasted about a month. On October 17, 1781, with his troops outnumbered by more than two to one, Cornwallis finally surrendered. On October 19, a triumphant Washington, the French generals, and their troops assembled to accept the British surrender.

Peace talks began in Paris in 1782. Representatives of four nations—the United States, Great Britain, France, and Spain—joined the negotiations. Many observers expected the savvy European diplomats to outwit the Americans at the bargaining table. But an able team of negotiators—John Adams, Benjamin Franklin, and John Jay of New York—demanded that Britain recognize American independence before any other negotiations began. Once Britain agreed to full independence, the talks officially opened.

In September 1783, the delegates signed the **Treaty of Paris,** which confirmed U.S. independence and set the boundaries of the new nation. The United States now stretched from the Atlantic Ocean to the Mississippi River and from Canada to the Florida border.

Some provisions of the treaty promised future trouble. The British made no attempt to protect the land interests of their Native American allies, and the

TEACHING OPTIONS

Making Connections Across Time

Events as Symbols Ask students what events in more recent times have symbolic value for people around the world. Encourage students to consider not only military and political events but also events or advances in other areas—for example, a landmark in space exploration or the opening of the Olympic games.

Making Connections Across Cultures

The Revolution and the Iroquois The Revolution brought deep division to the centuries-old Iroquois League, which had allied itself with Britain in the past. The Mohawks, Senecas, Cayugas, and Onondagas remained generally pro-British, with some of their tribal leaders even journeying to London to meet with King George. The Oneidas and Tuscaroras, on the other hand, had become largely pro-American. After the war, many Iroquois who had sided with the British gave up their lands in what became western New York and, like other Loyalists, fled to Canada.

THINK THROUGH HISTORY
E. *Making Predictions* *What problems do you think might be caused by the unresolved issues of the Treaty of Paris?*

treaty did not specify when the British would evacuate their American forts. On the other side, the Americans agreed that British creditors could collect debts owed them by Americans and promised to allow Loyalists to sue in state courts for recovery of their losses. The state governments, however, later failed to honor this agreement.

The War Becomes a Symbol of Liberty

E. Answer Students should be able to predict that the problems will include conflict with British over their forts and conflict with Native Americans over land.

Revolutionary ideals set a new course for American society. During the war, class distinctions between rich and poor had begun to blur as the wealthy wore homespun clothing and as military leaders showed respect for all of their men. Changes like these stimulated the rise of **egalitarianism**—a belief in the equality of all people. This belief fostered a new attitude: the idea that ability, effort, and virtue, not wealth or family, defined one's worth.

The egalitarianism of the 1780s, however, applied only to white males. Most African Americans were still enslaved, and even those who were free usually faced discrimination and poverty. Still, the idea of human equality as asserted in the Declaration of Independence had great significance for African Americans, since it spurred the growth of opposition to slavery.

The postwar egalitarianism also did not bring any new political rights to women. A few states made it possible for women to divorce, but common law still dictated that married women's property belonged to their husbands. Women had shown, though, that they were capable of serving their nation. In so doing, they created a foundation for future changes in their status both in the family and in society.

F. Answer The war fostered the idea that ability, effort, and virtue—not family or wealth—defined one's worth. This egalitarianism, however, applied only to white men.

THINK THROUGH HISTORY
F. *Analyzing Issues* *Why did the belief in equality rise after the American Revolution? What were the exceptions to this egalitarianism?*

For Native Americans, the Revolution brought uncertainty. During both the French and Indian War and the Revolution, many Native American communities had been either destroyed or displaced, and the Native American population east of the Mississippi had declined by about 50 percent. Postwar developments further threatened Native American interests, as settlers seeking economic opportunity began to move onto tribal lands left unprotected by the Treaty of Paris.

In the closing days of the Revolution, the Continental Congress had chosen a quotation from the works of the Roman poet Virgil as a motto for the reverse side of the Great Seal of the United States. The motto, Novus Ordo Seclorum, means "a new order of the ages." Establishing a government and resolving internal problems in that new order would be a tremendous challenge for citizens of the newborn United States.

Difficult Decisions IN HISTORY

WHAT SHOULD A LOYALIST DO?

After the war, Loyalists who stayed in America were viewed as traitors. The many who had lost their land during the war, or would later have their land taken by state governments, were forced to start over from scratch.

Loyalists who chose to leave faced other problems. Many set out for Canada, only to find the climate harsh. Former slaves who went to Canada found the white Loyalists hostile; most of them eventually resettled in Sierra Leone, West Africa. Loyalists who went to England encountered such a high cost of living that they soon were in debt.

1. If you had been a Loyalist living in America at the end of the war, where would you have chosen to live? Why?
2. What should the new American government have done with the Loyalists? Explain and support your opinion.

Section 2 Assessment

1. TERMS & NAMES
Identify:
- Loyalists
- Patriots
- Saratoga
- Valley Forge
- inflation
- Marquis de Lafayette
- Charles Cornwallis
- Yorktown
- Treaty of Paris
- egalitarianism

2. SUMMARIZING Choose five significant battles, events, or developments described in this section. For each, write a newspaper headline that summarizes its significance. Then choose one of the headlines and write the first paragraph of an article to go with it.

3. ANALYZING CAUSES Do you think the colonists could have won their independence without aid from foreigners? Explain.

THINK ABOUT
- the military needs of the Americans and the strengths of the French
- the outcomes at Cowpens and Guilford Court House
- the Americans' belief in their fight for independence

4. RECOGNIZING EFFECTS What were the effects of the Revolutionary War on the American colonists?

THINK ABOUT
- political effects
- economic effects
- social effects

ANSWERS

1. TERMS AND NAMES

Loyalists, p. 59
Patriots, p. 59
Saratoga, p. 61
Valley Forge, p. 61
inflation, p. 62
Marquis de Lafayette, p. 63
Charles Cornwallis, p. 64
Yorktown, p. 64
Treaty of Paris, p. 64
egalitarianism, p. 65

2. SUMMARIZING

Possible Responses: Von Steuben, Lafayette Lead Europeans in Aiding Rebels; Colonists Conquer Brits at Yorktown; Successful Treaty Negotiations Include Seeds of Trouble; Leaders of Revolution Claim Slavery Violates Human Equality; Native Americans Uncertain About Future with New Nation.

3. ANALYZING CAUSES

Possible Responses: **No** The colonists needed the French fleet to block sea routes in order to win the battle at Yorktown; the American troops needed Von Steuben's training. **Yes** The determination of the American Patriots would have carried them to victory; American troops were weakening the British and winning in the Carolinas; once isolated at Yorktown, the British might still have been defeated.

4. RECOGNIZING EFFECTS

Possible Responses: Politically, the colonists gained a great deal of stature, as they became leaders of a large, independent country. Economically, the war forced many colonists to confront inflation. Socially, the war sparked a growing sense of egalitarianism.

OBJECTIVE
(5) INSTRUCT

The War Becomes a Symbol of Liberty

▶ ***Discussing Key Ideas***
- For many people, the Revolution becomes a symbol of liberty.
- Postwar egalitarianism emphasizes ability, effort, and virtue over wealth or breeding in defining a man's worth.

DIFFICULT DECISIONS IN HISTORY
What Should a Loyalist Do?
Critical Thinking: Evaluating Conduct a survey, after students have answered the questions, to find out where they think most Loyalists would have chosen to live.

ASSESS & RETEACH

Section 2 Assessment
Students might work in pairs to respond to the questions.

Self-Assessment
To assess what they have learned, students might write their own questions, exchange them with a partner, and try to answer their partner's questions.

Section Quiz
FORMAL ASSESSMENT
Section Quiz, p. 18

Reteach
Use the Think Through History questions to help in reviewing this section.

CRITICAL THINKING TRANSPARENCIES
CT4, War for Independence

CLOSE

With the aid of France and other nations, the American Patriots managed to defeat one of the world's most powerful nations in a war that became a symbol of liberty for centuries to come.

Tracing Themes

OBJECTIVES

1. To explain women's contributions to the American Revolution.
2. To summarize the struggle for political power by American women over the centuries.

FOCUS & MOTIVATE

▶ ***Starting with the Student*** Have students consider their own definitions of the term "women's rights." Ask them,

- Which aspects of the definition relate to political power?
- In their opinion, what is the state of women's rights in America today?

MORE ABOUT . . .

Women in Political Power

In addition to holding more elected offices than ever before, American women in the late 20th century have broken the "glass ceiling" in appointed political offices. In the 1980s, President Reagan appointed the first woman to the Supreme Court, Sandra Day O'Connor. A decade later, President Clinton appointed Janet Reno to be the first woman attorney general of the United States. On Clinton's reelection in 1996, he appointed the first woman, Madeleine K. Albright (who had been serving as UN ambassador), to the top Cabinet position of secretary of state. (See "Women and the Glass Ceiling" on pages 894–895.)

TRACING THEMES
WOMEN IN AMERICA

Women and Political Power

Throughout the history of the United States, women have played whatever roles they felt were necessary to build and to better this country. Women also have worked and fought to expand their own political power, a power that throughout much of American history has been denied them.

1770s
PROTEST AGAINST BRITAIN

In the tense years leading up to the American Revolution, women found ways to participate in the protest movement against the British. Colonial women boycotted tea and British-made clothing. In the painting to the right, depicting Sarah Morris Mifflin and her husband Thomas, Sarah Mifflin spins her own thread rather than use British thread.

1848
SENECA FALLS

As America grew, women became acutely aware of their unequal status in society, particularly their lack of suffrage, or the right to vote. In 1848, two women—Elizabeth Cady Stanton, shown at the right, and Lucretia Mott—launched the first woman suffrage movement in the United States at the Seneca Falls Convention in Seneca Falls, N.Y. During the convention, the participants crafted the Declaration of Sentiments, in which they demanded greater rights for women, including the right to vote.

A WOMAN'S DECLARATION

ELIZABETH CAD
the cruel and unju
the office of her f
child, to find a way
to the abolitionist
ly into the curre
foundation for th
for woman's right
inspiring leader. T
executed the first
Falls, New York, J
truly the history o

Elizabeth Cady Stanton.

1920
THE RIGHT TO VOTE

More than a half-century after organizing for the right to vote, women finally won their struggle. In 1920, the United States adopted the Nineteenth Amendment, which granted women the right to vote. Pictured to the right is one of the many suffrage demonstrations of the early 1900s that helped garner public support for the amendment.

RECOMMENDED RESOURCES

Books

Gurko, Miriam. *The Ladies of Seneca Falls.* New York: Schocken, 1976. America's woman suffrage movement.

Hoffert, Sylvia D. *When Hens Crow.* Bloomington: Indiana UP, 1995. Women's rights in pre-Civil War America.

Schneir, Miriam, ed. *Feminism: The Essential Historical Writings.* New York: Random, 1972. Includes the Seneca Falls declaration, Sojourner Truth's speeches, Virginia Woolf's writings, and much more.

Videos

One Woman, One Vote. PBS Video, 1995. TV documentary about the woman suffrage movement.

Sojourner Truth: Ain't I a Woman? Coronet/MTI, 1989. Focuses on Truth's famous speech.

Women in American Life. National Women's History Project, 1988. From the Civil War to the late 1970s.

Software

Women in America. CD-ROM. Woodbridge, CT: Research Publications, 1994.

TimeLiner 4.0. Tom Snyder Productions. Software for making time lines, available with a *Women in History Data Disk* containing 17 sample time lines that cover prominent women as well as the women's movement.

1972-1982

THE EQUAL RIGHTS AMENDMENT MOVEMENT

During the mid-1900s, as more women entered the work force, many women recognized the continuing inequalities in their status, including lack of equal pay for equal work. Some women hoped that the passage of the Equal Rights Amendment would give them the same social and economic rights as men. Although millions supported the amendment, many men and women feared that the measure would prompt unwanted change. The ERA ultimately failed to be ratified.

ERA YES

VOTES FOR US WHEN WE ARE WOMEN

1996

WOMEN IN CONGRESS

In spite of the failure of the ERA, many women have achieved strong positions for themselves—politically as well as socially and economically. Pictured above are several of the 58 women members of the 104th U.S. Congress.

INTERACT WITH HISTORY

1. **SYNTHESIZING** How did women's political status change from 1770 to 1996?

SEE SKILLBUILDER HANDBOOK, PAGE 921.

2. **RESEARCHING AND REPORTING** Think of a woman who has played an important role in your community, either in the past or in the present. What kinds of things did this woman do? What kind of support did she receive in the community? What kinds of problems did she run into?

INSTRUCT

▶ ***Starting with the Student***
Ask students which women in political life they most admire, and why.

▶ ***Discussing Key Ideas***
- Throughout much of American history, women, despite their contributions to such causes as the American Revolution, are denied real political power.
- Winning the right to vote in 1920, women have gradually achieved political power at the polls and as elected officials.

HISTORY FROM VISUALS

Reading the Images
Have students study the pictures on these pages.

- Ask students why they think there are so many flags in the photo of the suffrage demonstration. *Possible Responses: To win sympathy for woman suffrage by appealing to patriotism; to show the justice of the women's cause by reminding people of American values.*

INTERACT WITH HISTORY

1. Synthesizing

Possible Responses: *Women in the 1770s supported the protests against the British by working to boycott British products. In the 1840s, women began the long process of demanding the right to vote, which was finally granted in 1920. In the 1970s and 1980s, more women were in the workforce than ever before, and many supported an Equal Rights Amendment to the Constitution, which ultimately failed to be ratified. By 1996, many women were serving in Congress.*

2. Researching and Reporting

Standards for Evaluation
Reports should . . .

- stress the achievements of a community leader, past or present
- clearly express the significance of the woman's role in the community
- examine community support that she received and problems that she encountered, if any
- support general statements with factual details

Section 3 Overview

OBJECTIVES

1. To describe the political and economic problems faced by the Confederation.
2. To summarize the key conflicts at the Constitutional Convention and explain how they were resolved through compromise.
3. To describe the form of government established by the Constitution.
4. To explain how and why the Bill of Rights was added to the Constitution.
5. To recognize that the structure of the Constitution helps to make it a document capable of meeting changing needs.

SKILLBUILDERS

- Interpreting charts, pp. 69, 71

CRITICAL THINKING

- Comparing, p. 69
- Making inferences, p. 70
- Evaluating decisions, p. 70
- Finding main ideas, p. 73
- Theme: Constitutional Concerns, p. 74
- Forming generalizations, p. 75
- Following chronological order, p. 75
- Evaluating, p. 75
- Forming opinions, p. 75

FOCUS & MOTIVATE

5-Minute Warm-Up

Recognizing Facts and Details

To find out about the issues involved in establishing a national government, have students read A Personal Voice on page 72 and answer these questions.

1. What did Madison consider to be essential to the preservation of liberty?
2. How did Madison believe that different powers of government should be handled?

WARM-UP TRANSPARENCY 2

▶ ***Starting with the Student***

Ask students to think about disputes they have had that were successfully resolved by compromise.

3 Confederation and the Constitution

LEARN ABOUT conflicting interpretations of the role of national government
TO UNDERSTAND how the Constitution became the law of the land.

TERMS & NAMES
- **republic**
- **Articles of Confederation**
- **Northwest Ordinance of 1787**
- **Shays's Rebellion**
- **James Madison**
- **checks and balances**
- **ratification**
- **Federalist**
- **Antifederalist**
- **bill of rights**

ONE AMERICAN'S STORY

John Jay enjoyed relating an incident that took place at King's College in New York City in 1764, a few weeks before the end of his senior year. Jay was present when some of his classmates got out of hand and broke a dining table in the college hall. The president of King's College questioned the students, but each denied knowing who was responsible. Jay also denied breaking the table, but when the president asked if he knew who was guilty, Jay replied, "I do not choose to tell you, sir."

Infuriated, the president had the students appear before a faculty committee. Jay came prepared with a copy of the college rules. He defended himself by pointing out that the rules did not require one student to inform on another. The faculty disagreed with Jay's interpretation of the rules and suspended him.

Years later, Jay's commitment to principle and to the spirit of unity would serve him well when he argued for ratification of the newly written Constitution. He warned of how other nations would view the United States if it did not unify itself.

A PERSONAL VOICE

What a poor pitiful figure will America make in their eyes! How liable would she become not only to their contempt, but to their outrage; and how soon would dear-bought experience proclaim that when a people or family so divide, it never fails to be against themselves.

JOHN JAY, *Federalist,* Number 4

Whether Jay was defending himself or his country's Constitution, he relied on strong principles and a commitment to unity. His arguments played a key role in ratifying the Constitution.

John Jay

Experimenting With Confederation

In adopting the Declaration of Independence, Americans had set out to build a stable republic, a government of the people. However, the task of creating a new government posed a great challenge. Fighting the Revolutionary War gave the states a common goal, but they remained reluctant to unite under a strong central government.

BASIS FOR A REPUBLIC Americans believed in republicanism—the idea that governments should be based on the consent of the people. However, they also believed that a democracy—government directly by the people—placed power in the hands of the uneducated masses. Therefore, they favored a **republic**—a government in which citizens rule through their elected representatives—which placed power in the hands of capable leaders.

THE CONFEDERATION IS FORMED The Second Continental Congress set up a new plan of government called the **Articles of Confederation.** The plan established a new form of government called a confederation, or alliance, among the 13 states.

SECTION 3 RESOURCES

PRINT RESOURCES

IN-DEPTH RESOURCES: UNIT 1
Guided Reading, p. 34
Skillbuilder Practice: Analyzing Issues, p. 37
Primary Source: *from* The U.S. Constitution, First Draft, p. 45
Literature: from *Legacy* by James A. Michener, p. 46
American Lives: Patrick Henry, p. 50

READING STUDY GUIDE, p. 19

ACCESS FOR STUDENTS ACQUIRING ENGLISH
Guided Reading (Spanish), p. 28
Skillbuilder Practice: Analyzing Issues (Spanish), p. 31

SPANISH READING STUDY GUIDE, p. 19

FORMAL ASSESSMENT
Section Quiz, p. 19

ALTERNATIVE ASSESSMENT BOOK
See forms for supporting and scoring alternative activities.

TECHNOLOGY RESOURCES

GEOGRAPHY TRANSPARENCIES
G5, Land Ceded by States: 1782–1802

CRITICAL THINKING TRANSPARENCIES
CT5, The Constitutional Convention

CD-ROM Electronic Library of Primary Sources

VIDEO *American Portfolio: A Videodisc for U.S. History* user's guide, pp. 40, 41, 45

INTERNET http://www.mlushistory.com

The Articles set up a Congress in which each state would have one vote regardless of population. Power was divided between the states and the national government. The national government had the power to declare war, make peace, and sign treaties. It could borrow money, set standards for coins and for weights and measures, and establish a postal service. After approval by all 13 states, the Articles of Confederation went into effect in March 1781.

One of the first issues the Confederation faced had to do with the lands west of the Appalachians, where many people settled after the Revolutionary War. To help govern these lands, Congress passed the Land Ordinance of 1785, which established a plan for surveying the land, as is shown in the Geography Spotlight on pages 76–77. In the **Northwest Ordinance of 1787,** Congress provided a procedure for dividing the land into no fewer than three and no more than five territories. The ordinance also set requirements for the admission of new states, which, however, overlooked Native American land claims.

THINK THROUGH HISTORY
A. Comparing *What was the difference between the Land Ordinance of 1785 and the Northwest Ordinance of 1787?*

A. Answer The Land Ordinance of 1785 established a plan for surveying the land, whereas the Northwest Ordinance of 1787 provided for dividing the land into three to five territories and established the requirements for the admission of new states.

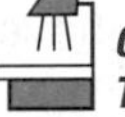

John Baptist de Coigne, a Kaskaskia chief, was among a group of Indians from the Northwest Territory who met with leaders of the U.S. government in 1793. He expressed the Native American view of the westward expansion of white settlers during the previous ten years:

> Order your people to be just. They are always trying to get our lands. They come on our lands, they hunt on them; kill our game and kill us. Keep them on one side of the line, and us on the other. Listen, my father, to what we say, and protect the nations of the Wabash and the Mississippi in their lands.

THE CONFEDERATION ENCOUNTERS PROBLEMS The Land Ordinance of 1785 and the Northwest Ordinance of 1787 became the Confederation's greatest achievements. In dealing with more immediate issues, the Confederation encountered overwhelming problems.

The most serious problem was that each state functioned independently by pursuing its own interests rather than those of the nation as a whole. In addition, the Confederation didn't recognize the differences in population among the states. Furthermore, the Articles could not be amended without the consent of all the states. Therefore, changes in government were difficult to achieve.

The lack of support by states for national concerns weakened the ability of Congress to deal with foreign-relations problems. First, since the United States could not repay its debts to British merchants, Britain refused to evacuate its military forts on the Great Lakes. In addition, in 1784 Spain closed the Mississippi River to American navigation. This deprived Western farmers of a means of shipping their crops to Eastern markets through New Orleans.

The most serious economic problem was the huge debt that the Congress had amassed during the Revolutionary War. To pay for these debts, the states raised taxes. The high taxes caused problems for individuals, especially farmers, who found themselves unable to pay both the taxes and the mortgages on their land. As a result, many farmers lost their land to the banks.

Skillbuilder Answer All states *Possible response:* Without the ability to collect taxes or to regulate interstate or foreign trade and with no executive branch or national court system, the government was weak.

SKILLBUILDER
INTERPRETING CHARTS
How many states' votes were needed to approve changes in the Articles of Confederation? Why did the listed weaknesses lead to an ineffective government?

Drafting the Constitution

The farmers' situation illustrated the inability of the Confederation government to handle the nation's problems. Protests by Massachusetts farmers pointed to the need for a stronger national government. This need would be addressed by the Constitutional Convention.

NATIONALISTS STRENGTHEN THE GOVERNMENT By 1786 many farmers in western Massachusetts had reached the breaking point and protested the increased taxes. They petitioned their state assembly for relief from the taxes—but their pleas fell on deaf ears.

The farmers' discontent boiled over into mob action in January of 1787 when Daniel Shays, a fellow farmer, led a motley army of 1,200 farmers. The group attempted to force the courts to close to

Weaknesses of the Articles of Confederation
• Congress could not enact and collect taxes.
• Each state had only one vote in Congress, regardless of population.
• Nine out of 13 states needed to agree to pass any law.
• Articles could be amended only if all states approved.
• There was no executive branch to enforce laws of Congress.
• There was no national court system to settle legal disputes.
• There were 13 separate states that lacked national unity.

OBJECTIVE
① INSTRUCT

Experimenting with Confederation

▶Discussing Key Ideas
- Equal representation among the states leads to crisis in national unity.
- War debt and national disunity create chaos in foreign relations.

IN-DEPTH RESOURCES: UNIT 1
Guided Reading, p. 34

ACCESS FOR STUDENTS ACQUIRING ENGLISH
Guided Reading (Spanish), p. 28

GEOGRAPHY TRANSPARENCIES
G5, Land Ceded by States: 1782–1802

ANOTHER PERSPECTIVE
John Baptist de Coigne
Role-Playing Ask students to write a response to the Kaskaskia chief's requests from the viewpoint of a government leader in 1793.

HISTORY FROM VISUALS
Weaknesses of the Articles of Confederation
Reading the Chart Have students identify at least one consequence of each weakness listed in the chart.

OBJECTIVE

Drafting the Constitution

▶Discussing Key Ideas
- Delegates at the convention seek to increase the

(continued on next page)

Block Schedule TEACHING OPTION **Time Needed: 20 Minutes**

Cooperative Activity: Letters to the Editor

Task: Students will write letters to the editor, expressing the viewpoint of a citizen regarding problems of the Confederation.

Purpose: To understand how weaknesses of the Confederation affected citizens.

Activity: Assign groups of three to five students to investigate problems the Confederation encountered. Then have group members assume the roles of a farmer, a merchant, or another citizen and write a letter to the editor of a newspaper stating how these problems affect them.

Building a Portfolio: If students feel their letter qualifies as an example of their best work, they should place it in their portfolio.

ALTERNATIVE ASSESSMENT BOOK
Standards for Evaluating a Cooperative Activity

Standards for Evaluation
Letters should . . .
- state the problem from the citizen's viewpoint and relate it to a weakness of government
- suggest a way to solve the problem
- use appropriate style for a letter to the editor

(continued from page 69)

strength of the national government while preserving states' rights.
- Delegates puzzle over balancing the interests of a variety of societal groups.

MORE ABOUT . . .
Daniel Shays

Although the farmers' revolt of 1787 bears his name, Daniel Shays was only one of several leaders of the rebellion. Shays held political office at Pelham, Massachusetts, and he became sympathetic to the farmers' plight. When the state militia scattered the rebels at Springfield, Shays escaped to Vermont. The government placed a death penalty on his head but later pardoned him.

KEY PLAYER
James Madison

Critical Thinking: Analyzing Character
Ask students what limitations Madison had to overcome. *Possible Response: Madison was sickly, with a weak speaking voice.*

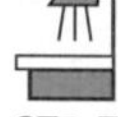
CRITICAL THINKING TRANSPARENCIES
CT5, The Constitutional Convention

OBJECTIVE

③ **INSTRUCT**

Creating a New Government

▶ ***Discussing Key Ideas***
- Delegates at the Constitutional Convention distribute power between the states and the national government.

(continued on next page)

Shays's Rebellion not only resulted in the death of four rebels but also greatly disturbed some of the nation's leaders.

prevent the courts from taking away their farms. Shays's army then marched toward the arsenal at Springfield, Massachusetts. State officials hurriedly called out the militia to head off the army of farmers, killing four of the rebels and scattering the rest.

Shays's Rebellion, as the farmers' protest came to be called, caused panic and dismay throughout the nation. It was clearly time to talk about a stronger national government. Since the states had placed such severe limits on the government to prevent abuse of power, the government was unable to solve many of the nation's problems.

News of the rebellion spread throughout the states. The incident convinced 12 states to send delegates to a convention called by Congress in Philadelphia in May of 1787.

THINK THROUGH HISTORY
B. *Making Inferences* *Why do you think news of Shays's Rebellion made states decide to participate in the Philadelphia convention?*

B. Answer They may have feared other uprisings. Shays's Rebellion showed the weakness of the national government in dealing with economic problems.

CONFLICT LEADS TO COMPROMISE Most of the delegates recognized the need to strengthen the central government. Within the first five days of the meeting, they gave up the idea of fixing the Articles of Confederation and decided to form a whole new government.

One big issue the delegates faced was giving fair representation to both large and small states. **James Madison** proposed the Virginia Plan, which called for a bicameral, or two-house, legislature, with membership based on each state's population. Delegates from the small states vigorously objected to the Virginia Plan because it gave more power to states with large populations. Small states supported William Paterson's New Jersey Plan, which proposed a single-house congress in which each state had an equal vote.

Proponents of the plans became deadlocked, and the debate dragged on through the hot and humid summer days. Finally, Roger Sherman suggested the Great Compromise, which offered a two-house Congress to satisfy both small and big states. Each state would have equal representation in the Senate, or upper house. The size of the population of each state would determine its representation in the House of Representatives, or lower house. Voters of each state would choose members of the House. The state legislatures would choose members of the Senate.

The Great Compromise settled one major issue but led to conflict over another. Southern delegates, whose states had large numbers of slaves, wanted slaves included in the population count that determined the number of representatives in the House. Northern delegates, whose states had few slaves, argued against counting slaves as part of the population. Not counting them would give the northern states more representatives than the southern states in the House of Representatives. The Three-Fifths Compromise called for three-fifths of a state's slaves to be counted as population.

KEY PLAYERS

JAMES MADISON
1751–1836

The oldest of 12 children, James Madison grew up in Virginia. He was a sickly child who suffered all his life from physical ailments. Because of a weak speaking voice, he decided not to become a minister and thus entered politics.

Madison's Virginia Plan resulted from extensive research that he had done on political systems before the meeting. He asked Edmund Randolph, a fellow delegate from Virginia, to present the plan because his own voice was too weak to be heard throughout the assembly.

Besides providing brilliant political leadership, Madison kept a record of the debates that took place at the convention. Because of his plan and his leadership, Madison is known as the Father of the Constitution.

THINK THROUGH HISTORY
C. *Evaluating Decisions* *Do you think the delegates made a wise choice in deciding to replace the Articles of Confederation rather than revise them? Why or why not?*

C. Answer Some students might say the government under the Articles had too many problems to be fixed by revisions. Other students might say by creating a new government the delegates violated what they were authorized to do.

Creating a New Government

After the delegates reached agreement on the difficult questions of slavery and representation, they dealt with other issues somewhat more easily. They divided power between the states and the national government, and they separated the national government's power into three branches. Thus, they created an entirely new government.

DIVISION OF POWERS The new system of government was a form of federalism that divided power between the national government and the state governments. The powers granted to the national government by the Constitution are known as delegated powers, or enumerated powers. These

TEACHING OPTIONS

Exploring Themes

Constitutional Concerns Discuss the forms of protest Massachusetts farmers used in seeking relief from their economic problems. Ask students,

- How was Shays's Rebellion like the American Revolution? *Possible Response: Students may point out that the farmers' actions reflected the values stated in the Declaration of Independence.*
- Why did the farmers' revolt cause fear and disapproval among Americans? *Possible Response: It emphasized the weakness of government.*

Teaching Gifted and Talented Students

Analyzing a Primary Source Document Tell students to log on to the McDougal Littell web page and explore the Internet resources for Chapter 2 of *The Americans.* They will find a treasure trove of resources about the Constitutional Convention. After exploring, they should choose one resource to examine in depth, and write a description and review of the material to share with the class.

 http://www.mlushistory.com

include such powers as control of foreign affairs and regulating trade between the states. Powers not specifically granted to the national government but kept by the states are called reserved powers. These include powers such as providing for and supervising education. Some powers, such as the right to tax and establish courts, were shared by both the national and the state governments.

SEPARATION OF POWERS The delegates also limited the authority of the national government. First, they created three branches of government: a legislative branch to make laws, an executive branch to carry out laws, and a judicial branch to hear cases. Then the delegates established a system of **checks and balances** to prevent any one branch from dominating the other two. Look at the chart on page 97 to see how the checks and balances system works.

The procedure the delegates established for electing the president reflected their fear of placing too much power in the hands of the people. Instead of choosing the president directly, each state would choose a number of electors equal to the number of senators and representatives the state had in Congress. This group of electors chosen by the states, known as the electoral college, would then cast ballots for the presidential candidates.

Key Conflicts in the Constitutional Convention

CENTRAL GOVERNMENT vs. STRONG STATES	
• Authority derives from the people. • In a new plan of government, the central government should be stronger than the states.	• Authority comes from the states. • Under a modified Articles of Confederation, the states should remain stronger than the central government.
LARGE STATES vs. SMALL STATES	
• Congress should be composed of two houses. • Number of delegates to both houses of Congress should be assigned according to population.	• Congress of one house should be preserved. • Each state should have one vote.
NORTH vs. SOUTH	
• Slaves should not be counted when deciding the number of congressional delegates. • Slaves should be counted when levying taxes.	• Slaves should be counted when determining congressional representation. • Slaves should not be counted when levying taxes.

SKILLBUILDER
INTERPRETING CHARTS
Why do you think the Southern states wanted slaves counted for determining the number of representatives in the House of Representatives?

Skillbuilder Answer
Possible answer: Including slaves would increase the South's official population and its proportional number of representatives.

CHANGING THE CONSTITUTION After four months of debate and compromise, the delegates succeeded in creating a Constitution that was an enduring document. In other words, by making the Constitution flexible, the delegates enabled it to pass the test of time. They provided a means of changing the Constitution through the amendment process. See the chart on page 98.

Ratifying the Constitution

George Washington adjourned the convention on September 17, 1787. The convention's work was over, but the new government could not become a reality until the voters agreed. So the Constitution of the United States of America was sent to the Congress, which submitted it to the states for approval.

FEDERALISTS AND ANTIFEDERALISTS The framers set up a procedure for **ratification**—official approval by the people of the United States—that called for each state to hold a special convention. The voters would elect the delegates to the convention, who would then vote to accept or reject the Constitution. Ratification required approval by at least nine states.

Supporters of the Constitution called themselves **Federalists,** a name referring to a balance of power between the states and the national government. Their opponents became known as **Antifederalists** because they opposed having such a strong central government and thus were against the Constitution.

Both sides waged a war of words in the public debate over ratification. The *Federalist Papers,* a series of 85 essays defending the Constitution, appeared in New York newspapers between October 1787 and April 1788. They were written by three influential men who supported ratification: Alexander Hamilton, James Madison, and John Jay, who together adopted the pen name "Publius."

(continued from page 70)

- The three branches of government are created, along with corresponding checks and balances of power.

IN-DEPTH RESOURCES: UNIT 1
Primary Source: *from* The U.S. Constitution, First Draft, p. 45

HISTORY FROM VISUALS
Key Conflicts in the Constitutional Convention

Reading the Chart Have pairs of students read aloud the contrasting sides of each conflict.

Extension Explain how the Great Compromise and the Three-Fifths Compromise resolved conflicts.

ELECTRONIC LIBRARY OF PRIMARY SOURCES
from "Notes on Slavery at the Federal Convention, 1787" by James Madison

OBJECTIVE
④ **INSTRUCT**

Ratifying the Constitution

Discussing Key Ideas
- Antifederalists demand a bill of rights so that citizens are protected from the potential tyranny of a strong national government.
- In 1788, the new Constitution is ratified by the minimum number of states; three years later, the Bill of Rights is ratified.

ELECTRONIC LIBRARY OF PRIMARY SOURCES
"On the Constitution" by Benjamin Franklin
from "On the Federal Government" by Tench Coxe

TEACHING OPTION

Skillbuilder Mini-Lesson: Analyzing Issues

Explaining the Skill Analyzing an issue involves finding and describing different parts of the issue. To analyze the issue of drug abuse, students might identify what the central problems are, who is involved, and what solutions might be possible.

Applying the Skill: The Division of Powers Have students read the paragraphs on the division of powers and answer the following questions to begin analyzing the issue of who should have power and how it should be divided.

1. What is the central problem related to this issue? *How to strengthen the power of the national government while preserving the rights of the states.*
2. What solution was found to this issue? *Give the central government powers dealing with other countries and between states. Give states power over local concerns and activities within the state.*
3. How successful does the solution seem? *Many students will say that it is successful because the country still operates under the original system.*

IN-DEPTH RESOURCES: UNIT 1
Skillbuilder Practice: Analyzing Issues, p. 37

MORE ABOUT . . .
The Federalist Papers

The authorship of the *Federalist Papers* remained secret until 1804, when it was revealed by Alexander Hamilton. Hamilton was facing the duel that would cost him his life. He wrote a brief note crediting the authors of the *Federalist Papers,* but was somewhat inaccurate in stating which essays each author had written. Historians attribute 51 of the essays to Hamilton, 29 to Madison, and the remaining five to Jay.

IN-DEPTH RESOURCES: UNIT 1
American Lives: Patrick Henry, p. 50

ELECTRONIC LIBRARY OF PRIMARY SOURCES from *Federalist 51,* by Publius

NOW & THEN
South Africa Creates a Bill of Rights

▶ ***Starting with the Student***

- What do students know about the system of apartheid?
- Why might a country with a history of institutionalized racism need an extremely detailed bill of rights?

▶ ***Discussing Key Ideas***

- Before 1994, the South African government operates on the principle of apartheid, or "apartness."
- In 1996, South African lawmakers ratify a constitution guaranteeing equal rights to blacks and whites.
- A very detailed and comprehensive bill of rights is created to counteract any lingering effects of institutionalized racism.

The *Federalist Papers* provided an analysis and a defense of the Constitution that remain important today. *Letters from the Federal Farmer,* written by Richard Henry Lee, was the most widely read Antifederalist publication. Lee listed the rights the Antifederalists believed should be protected, such as freedom of the press and of religion, guarantees against unreasonable searches of people and their homes, and the right to a trial by jury.

One of the most important numbers of the *Federalist Papers* is Number 51, by James Madison. In the following excerpt from that essay, Madison explains why the drafters of the Constitution separated the power of government into three branches and separated the legislative branch into two houses.

A PERSONAL VOICE

In order to lay a due foundation for that separate and distinct exercise of the different powers of government, which to a certain extent, is admitted on all hands to be essential to the preservation of liberty, it is evident that each department should have a will of its own; and consequently should be so constituted, that the members of each should have as little agency as possible in the appointment of the members of the others. . . .

In republican government the legislative authority, necessarily, predominates. The remedy for this inconveniency is, to divide the legislature into different branches; and to render them by different modes of election, and different principles of action, as little connected with each other, as the nature of their common functions, and their common dependence on the society, will admit. . . .

JAMES MADISON, *Federalist,* Number 51, 1788

"You are not to inquire how your trade may be increased, nor how you are to become a great and powerful people, but how your liberties can be secured."

PATRICK HENRY

ON THE ROAD TO RATIFICATION All state constitutions guaranteed individual rights, and seven of them included a **bill of rights**—a formal summary of citizens' rights and freedoms. However, the proposed U.S. Constitution contained no guarantee that the government would protect the rights of the people or of the states. Even some supporters of the Constitution viewed its lack of a bill of rights as a serious drawback to ratification.

The Antifederalists' demand for a bill of rights stemmed from their fear of a strong central government. The states, with their guarantees of individual liberties, served as protectors of the people. Antifederalists argued that since the Constitution weakened the states, the people needed a national bill of rights to protect them. They wanted written guarantees that the people would have freedom of speech, of the press, and of religion. They demanded assurance of the right to trial by jury and the right to bear arms.

NOW & THEN

South Africa Creates a Bill of Rights

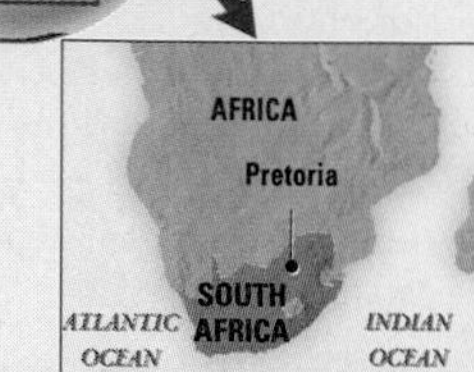

On May 8, 1996 South African lawmakers leaped to their feet and danced in the aisles of South Africa Parliament. They had just passed a landmark constitution guaranteeing equal rights for blacks and whites in the new South Africa. Included in this constitution is a bill of rights modeled in part on the United States Bill of Rights, though with significant differences.

The South African bill of rights, like the Bill of Rights in the United States Constitution, grew out of a history o

South Africa's President Nelson Mandela, *center,* with two of his deputy presidents, celebrates the approval of the new constitution by the constitutional assembly in Parliament at Cape Town, South Africa, on May 8, 1996. The deputy on the left is Thabo Mbeki, and the deputy on the right is F. W. de Klerk, a former president of South Africa.

Block Schedule — TEACHING OPTION — Time Needed: 40 Minutes

Cooperative Activity: Creating a Media Ad

Task: Groups of students will prepare a script for a media ad presenting Federalist or Antifederalist views.

Purpose: To examine arguments over ratification of the Constitution.

Activity: Students should consider how Federalists or Antifederalists might use television or radio to promote ideas, and then choose a particular medium and message. Groups should prepare a script for a 30-second ad promoting a particular viewpoint. Students should include ideas for accompanying sound and/or pictures.

Building a Portfolio: Students should identify their contributions to the script on the copy they place in their portfolios.

ALTERNATIVE ASSESSMENT BOOK
Standards for Evaluating a Cooperative Activity

Standards for Evaluation
Media ads should . . .

- accurately depict the viewpoint of Federalists or Antifederalists
- state reasons supporting the viewpoint
- include persuasive language
- be appropriate for the chosen medium

THINK THROUGH HISTORY
D. Finding Main Ideas *Why did the Antifederalists insist that the Constitution must have a bill of rights?*

Federalists insisted that the Constitution granted only limited powers to the national government so that it could not violate the rights of the states or of the people. They also pointed out that the Constitution gave the people the power to protect their rights through the election of trustworthy leaders. In the end, though, the Federalists yielded to people's overwhelming desire and promised to add a bill of rights if the states would ratify the Constitution.

Delaware led the country in ratifying the Constitution, by unanimous vote, in December 1787. In June 1788, New Hampshire fulfilled the requirement for ratification by becoming the ninth state to approve the Constitution.

D. Answer The Antifederalists argued that because the Constitution granted significant powers to the national government, the Constitution must have explicit safeguards to prevent the government from abusing those powers.

oppression and tyranny. For most of the twentieth century, South Africa's white minority government denied basic rights to blacks and other people of color. This system of racial discrimination, known as apartheid, finally came crashing down in 1994 with the election of a coalition government under Nelson Mandela. Soon after, the new government began the long process of creating a new constitution and bill of rights.

From the start, South African lawmakers made the writing of the constitution a public event. They invited ideas and opinions, which led to a vigorous public debate. In contrast, the United States Constitution was written in private by a small group of men.

In addition, the South African bill of rights is a much broader and more detailed document than the U.S. Bill of Rights. For example, two pages are devoted to the rights of arrested, detained, and accused persons. One page is devoted to the rights of children. The document forbids discrimination of all kinds and protects the rights of minorities. It also guarantees every citizen the right to freedom of travel within the country, which was often denied blacks under apartheid. In addition, the bill of rights guarantees a range of social and economic rights—including the right to adequate housing, food, water, education, and health care—which were often denied blacks under apartheid. Nevertheless, the cost of providing these basics will make it difficult for the government to deliver on these promises.

Nelson Mandela, the first black president of South Africa, greets a crowd celebrating the new constitution. Mandela, who had been imprisoned in1962 for fighting for rights for black South Africans, was released from prison in 1990. He became South Africa's president after receiving 62 percent of the vote in the 1994 election.

INTERACT WITH HISTORY

1. **COMPARING AND CONTRASTING** What makes South Africa's bill of rights similar to the U.S. Bill of Rights? How is it different?
2. **RESEARCHING SOUTH AFRICA** Using library resources, find out more about the South African constitution and bill of rights. Also research conditions in South Africa that led to the writing of a new constitution. With a partner, prepare a short oral report on your findings and present it to the class.

SEE SKILLBUILDER HANDBOOK, PAGES 909 AND 924.

Visit http://www.mlushistory.com for more about South Africa.

MORE ABOUT . . .
Nelson Mandela

Nelson Mandela was born in Umtata, a village in the Transkei territory of South Africa where his father was a tribal chief. In 1944, working as a lawyer, Mandela joined the African National Congress, or ANC. This group was opposed to the policy of apartheid. Mandela gained national fame in the 1950s for leading protests against the government. In 1962, Mandela was arrested and convicted of sabotage and conspiracy and sentenced to life imprisonment. Many South African groups refused to negotiate with the government until Mandela was released. Finally, after almost 30 years in prison, Mandela was released in 1990. Just four years later, Mandela became South Africa's first black president.

MORE ABOUT . . .
The South African Constitution

The following is an excerpt from the Preamble: *We, the people of South Africa, / Recognise the injustices of our past; / Honour those who suffered for justice and freedom in our land; / Respect those who have worked to build and develop our country; and / Believe that South Africa belongs to all who live in it, united in our diversity. . . .*

INTERACT WITH HISTORY

1. Comparing and Contrasting

Possible Responses: *The two bills of rights are similar in that they were both inspired by the experiences of an oppressive and tyrannical regime. The two bills are different in that the South African government made the writing of the constitution a national event, inviting opinions and vigorous public debate. The United States Constitution was written in private by a small group of men. Also, the South African bill of rights is more detailed and comprehensive than the U.S. Bill of Rights.*

2. Researching South Africa

Review with students how to find and use resources other than encyclopedias. You may want to review how to use periodical indexes, the card catalog or electronic filing system used by your library, particular search engines on the Internet, and Internet newsgroups. You may also want to give students a few pointers for public speaking. For example: speak slowly, clearly, and loud enough for the whole class to hear you; do not read your report to the class, outline your talk on note cards so that you can speak naturally; if eye contact with the audience is too difficult, look at the tops of people's heads.

MORE ABOUT . . .
The Bill of Rights

In 1941, President Franklin D. Roosevelt proclaimed December 15 as Bill of Rights Day. This day of national observance commemorates the date on which the Bill of Rights became part of the Constitution in 1791.

OBJECTIVE

(5) INSTRUCT

Continuing Relevance of the Constitution

▶ ***Discussing Key Ideas***

- The Constitution is a "living" document, capable of meeting the changing needs of the nation's citizens.
- The "elastic clause" allows Congress to make laws necessary to carry out the expressed powers detailed in the Constitution.
- The Constitution provides the basic framework of government but leaves the details to the people running the government.
- The Constitution can be changed when necessary through amendments.

Nevertheless, Virginia and New York had not voted, and the new government needed these very large and influential states. James Madison, Edmund Randolph, and George Washington campaigned for ratification in Virginia. Madison's logical arguments and Washington's influence brought Federalist victory there. Virginia ratified the Constitution in June 1788. John Jay and Alexander Hamilton campaigned effectively in New York, which ratified the Constitution in July 1788. Although Rhode Island did not accept the Constitution until 1790, the new government became a reality in 1789.

ADOPTION OF A BILL OF RIGHTS James Madison carried out the pledge to add guarantees of rights by writing a list of amendments for Congress to consider. In September 1789, Congress submitted 12 amendments to the state legislatures for ratification. By December 1791, the required three fourths of the states had ratified 10 of the amendments, which became known as the Bill of Rights.

A parade in New York in 1788 celebrates the new Constitution and features the "Ship of State" float. It has Alexander Hamilton's name on it to emphasize the key role he played in launching the new government.

The first eight amendments spell out the personal liberties the states had requested. The First Amendment guarantees citizens' rights to freedom of religion, speech, the press, and political activity. The Second and Third Amendments protect citizens from the threat of standing armies. According to these amendments, the government cannot deny citizens the right to bear arms as members of a militia of citizen-soldiers, nor can the government house troops in private homes in peacetime. The Fourth Amendment prevents the search of citizens' homes without proper warrants. The Fifth through Eighth Amendments guarantee fair treatment for individuals accused of crimes. The Ninth Amendment makes it clear that people's rights are not restricted to just those specifically mentioned in the Constitution. Finally, the Tenth Amendment clarifies that the people and the states have all the powers that the Constitution does not specifically give to the national government or deny to the states.

The protection of rights and freedoms did not apply to all Americans at the time the Bill of Rights was adopted. Native Americans and slaves were excluded. Women were not mentioned in the Constitution. A growing number of free blacks did not receive adequate protection from the Constitution. Although many states permitted free blacks to vote, the Bill of Rights offered them no protection against whites' discrimination and hostility. The expansion of democracy came from later amendments. The flexibility of the U.S. Constitution has made it a model for governments around the world.

E. Answer Possible response: It showed that the Constitution could be changed to meet the fundamental rights and protection of the people.

THINK THROUGH HISTORY
E. THEME *Constitutional Concerns* *How did the adoption of the Bill of Rights show the flexibility of the Constitution?*

Continuing Relevance of the Constitution

The United States Constitution is the oldest written national constitution still in existence. It is a "living" document, capable of meeting the changing needs of Americans. One reason for this capability lies in Article I, Section 8, of the Constitution, which gives Congress the power "to make all laws which shall be necessary and proper for carrying into execution" the powers that the Constitution enumerates. This clause is referred to as the "elastic

TEACHING OPTIONS

Exploring Themes

Constitutional Concerns Identify groups of Americans who were excluded from protection under the Bill of Rights in 1791. Discuss why those groups were excluded. What rights were denied them? Emphasize that governments reflect the ideas and values of the time. The civil rights movement and the women's movement brought about the inclusion and equal protection under law of excluded groups. By organizing, petitioning the government, and raising public awareness, excluded groups gained access to those rights previously withheld from them.

Making Connections Across the Cultures

Native Americans One of the world's oldest democracies is that of the Iroquois Confederacy. It has been suggested that Benjamin Franklin, once a colonial Indian commissioner, had been inspired by the Iroquois when he wrote the Articles of Confederation in 1777. Find out more about how the Iroquois Confederacy was structured and run. Write a one- to two-page paper comparing and contrasting the Iroquois Confederacy with the United States Government of 1788. Use reference works such as *500 Nations: An Illustrated History of North American Indians* by Alvin M. Josephy, Jr.

clause" because it stretches the power of the government. The framers of the Constitution included these implied powers to expand the authority of the government to meet unforeseen circumstances. Deciding which laws are "necessary and proper" has often evoked controversy. However, many recent pieces of legislation are based on the implied powers of the Constitution.

Jay Friedland of Surf Watch and Bruce Taylor of the National Law Center for Children and Families debate the merits of the Communications Decency Act of 1996.

Another factor that has made the Constitution endure for so many years is that the document lays out the basic provisions of government, such as the powers of each branch. However, it has not detailed what these powers involve. For example, Article III provides for a Supreme Court and other courts but it does not provide details about establishing these courts. The Constitution leaves those details to the people who run the government. The Constitution also uses very broad language, allowing the document to be interpreted to fit the problems at hand. A more specific document would have to be altered frequently in order to meet changing situations.

The Constitution, however, can be formally changed when necessary through amendments. The Constitution provides ways for amendments to be proposed and ways for amendments to be ratified. However, the writers made the amendment process difficult in order to avoid changes that were not thoroughly thought out. Through the ratification process, the writers of the Constitution have also ensured that any amendment has the overwhelming support of the people.

In more than 200 years, only 27 amendments have been added to the Constitution. These amendments have helped the government meet the challenges of a changing world, while still preserving the rights of the American people.

F. Answer The Constitution has remained relevant because (a) it was written in terms broad enough to allow for interpretation and application to specific situations, and (b) it has the capability of being changed, if necessary, to reflect today's issues.

THINK THROUGH HISTORY
F. Forming Generalizations
Explain why the Constitution has remained relevant today.

NOW & THEN

CONSTITUTIONAL ISSUES IN THE 1990s

The framers of the Constitution created a "living" document that could meet the changing needs of the nation. One of the major changes in the United States in the 1990s has been the growth of new communications networks such as the Internet. Concern about the easy access to material on the Internet led to the passage of the Communications Decency Act of 1996. The legislation sought to protect children from obscene materials on the Internet. In 1997, however, the Supreme Court overturned the act on the grounds that it threatened free-speech rights.

Another issue facing the country in the 1990s has been the increased use of handguns in committing crimes. In 1993, to stem this increase, Congress passed the Brady gun-control bill, which required background checks of prospective gun buyers. The checks were to be made by local law enforcement officers. In 1997 the Supreme Court ruled in favor of states' rights, stating that Congress can't force local law enforcement officials to enforce a federal program.

Section 3 Assessment

1. TERMS & NAMES
Identify:
- republic
- Articles of Confederation
- Northwest Ordinance of 1787
- Shays's Rebellion
- James Madison
- checks and balances
- ratification
- Federalist
- Antifederalist
- bill of rights

2. FOLLOWING CHRONOLOGICAL ORDER Create a time line like the one below, showing at least five important events of the first ten years of the new nation.

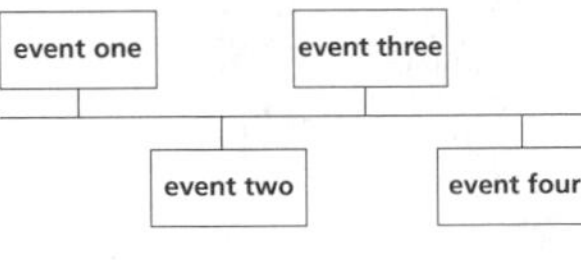

What was the most important event, and why do you think it the most important?

3. EVALUATING Do you think the Federalists or the Antifederalists had the more valid arguments? Support your opinion with examples from the text.

THINK ABOUT
- whom each group represented
- Americans' experience with the Articles of Confederation
- Americans' experience with Great Britain

4. FORMING OPINIONS Several states ratified the Constitution only after being assured that a bill of rights would be added to it. In your opinion, what is the most important value of the Bill of Rights?

THINK ABOUT
- the powers of the national government and of the states
- why people demanded a bill of rights
- the rights that the Bill of Rights guarantees

ANSWERS

1. TERMS AND NAMES
republic, p. 68
Articles of Confederation, p. 68
Northwest Ordinance of 1787, p. 69
Shays's Rebellion, p. 70
James Madison, p. 70
checks and balances, p. 71
ratification, p. 71
Federalist, p. 71
Antifederalist, p. 71
bill of rights, p. 72

2. FOLLOWING CHRONOLOGICAL ORDER
Possible Responses:
1776 Declaration of Independence
1777 Congress adopts the Articles of Confederation
1779 12 states, all but Maryland, accept new government
1781 Maryland approves the Articles of Confederation and they go into effect
1785 The Land Ordinance of 1785
1787 The Northwest Ordinance of 1787

3. EVALUATING
Possible Responses:
Arguments for Federalists include the strength of a government with central authority and the protections coming from the division of power and the system of checks and balances. Antifederalists may say that centralized authority could lead to abuses of power and that the country was too large to be managed by one government.

4. FORMING OPINIONS
Possible Responses:
Students may say guaranteeing individual freedoms and protecting people against the government.

NOW & THEN
Constitutional Issues in the 1990s
Critical Thinking: Evaluating Decisions Ask students if they agree with the Supreme Court's decisions regarding the Communications Decency Act of 1996 and the Brady gun-control bill. Encourage students to provide reasons for their opinion.

ASSESS & RETEACH

Section 3 Assessment
Divide students into groups and assign one of the assessment questions to each group. After groups have answered the questions, form new groups consisting of one member from each of the original groups. Have students share the answers to the questions.

Self-Assessment
Have each student review the answers derived from the group-sharing sessions.

Section Quiz
FORMAL ASSESSMENT
Section Quiz, p. 19

Reteach
Have students work in groups to outline the section. Instruct them to use the boldfaced headings as main ideas. Then have them fill in the supporting details from the text.

CLOSE

Debates over ratification of the Constitution centered on the lack of protection for individual rights. By pledging to add a bill of rights, Federalists succeeded in gaining ratification. The same Constitution remains in effect today.

Geography Spotlight

OBJECTIVES

1. To describe how the Land Ordinance of 1785 promoted settlement of the Old Northwest.
2. To explain how the Land Ordinance of 1785 and the Northwest Ordinance of 1787 established patterns for all future expansion.

FOCUS & MOTIVATE

▶ ***Starting with the Student*** Have students imagine that they are state planners in charge of developing a large rural or suburban parcel of land.

- What goals would they have in developing the land?
- What services would they provide or practices would they encourage to ensure that those settling on the land become productive citizens?

MORE ABOUT . . .
The Northwest Ordinance
The Northwest Ordinance was a landmark law in the history of the republic. In an unusual move, the ordinance stipulated that the territories of the Old Northwest would not be colonies of the states but would instead be able to join the union on an equal footing with older states. Left out of the equation, of course, were the Native Americans who already inhabited the area and were already in conflict with incoming settlers.

GEOGRAPHY SPOTLIGHT

The Land Ordinance of 1785

When states ceded, or gave up, their western lands to the United States, the new nation became "land rich" even though it was "money poor." Government leaders searched for a way to use the land to fund such services as public education.

The fastest and easiest way to raise money would be to sell huge parcels of thousands of acres at a time. However, then only rich people would be able to purchase land. The Land Ordinance of 1785 came down on the side of small landowners by making the parcels affordable.

The Land Ordinance established a plan for dividing the land. The government would first survey the land, dividing it into townships of 36 square miles, as shown on the map below. Then each township would be divided into 36 sections of 1 square mile, or about 640 acres each. An individual or a family could purchase a section and divide it into farms or smaller units. A typical farm of the period was equal to one-quarter section, or 160 acres. The minimum price per acre was one dollar.

The map on the next page was probably drawn by Rufus Putnam. It shows how a township, now in Meigs County, Ohio, was divided in 1787 into parcels of full square-mile sections and smaller, more affordable plots. The names of the original buyers are written on the full sections.

Government leaders hoped the buyers would occupy their lands, develop farms, and establish democratic communities. In this way American settlements would spread across the western territories in an orderly way. Government surveyors repeated the process thousands of times as Americans transformed the continent with their frontier geometry.

In 1787, the Congress further provided for the orderly development of the Northwest Territory by passing the Northwest Ordinance. The ordinance established how states would be created out of the territory.

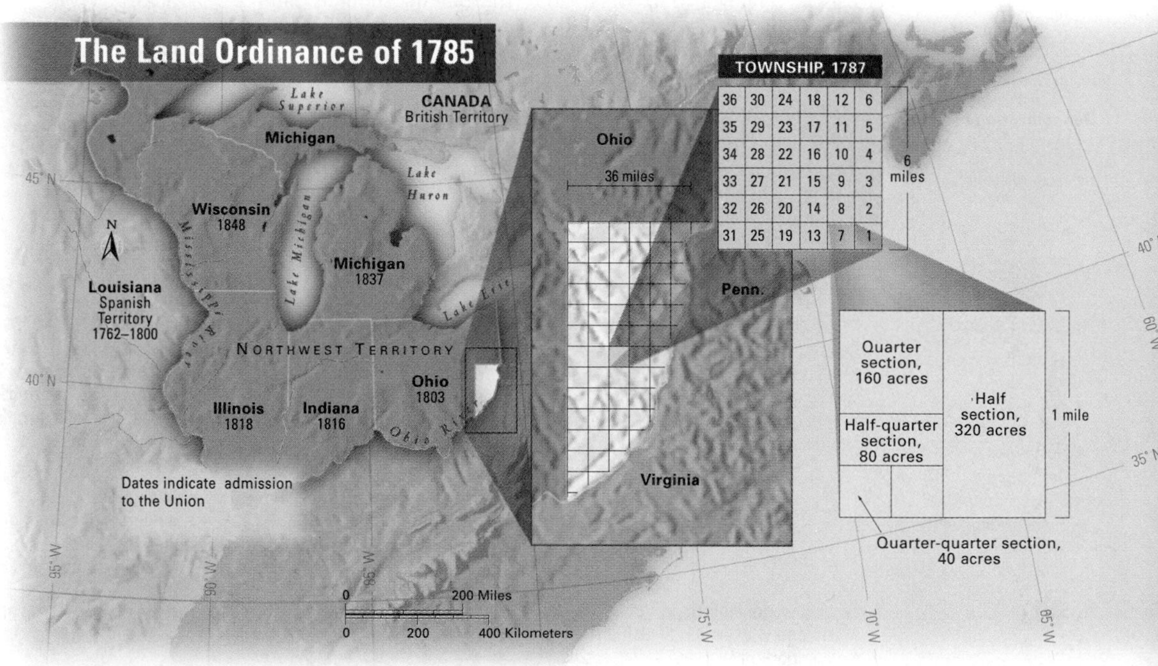

RECOMMENDED RESOURCES

Books

Eckert, Allan W. *Gateway to Empire.* Boston: Little, 1983. A history of the Old Northwest.

Hunter, Lloyd A. *Pathways to the Old Northwest.* Indianapolis: Indiana Historical Society, 1988. A study of the Northwest Ordinance.

Onuf, Peter S. *Statehood and Union: A History of the Northwest Ordinance.* Bloomington: Indiana UP, 1987.

Williams, Frederick D., ed. *The Northwest Ordinance.* East Lansing: Michigan State UP, 1989. A collection of essays.

Videos

Settling the Old Northwest. Encyclopaedia Britannica. A dynamic account of the conflicts between Native Americans and early settlers.

U.S. Expansion: The Northwest Territory. Coronet/MTI, 1989. A history of the Old Northwest from Native American days to the growth of Chicago in the late 19th century.

Westward Movement I: Settlers of the Old Northwest Territory. Encyclopaedia Britannica. A study of settlement in the post-Revolutionary era.

A TOWNSHIP

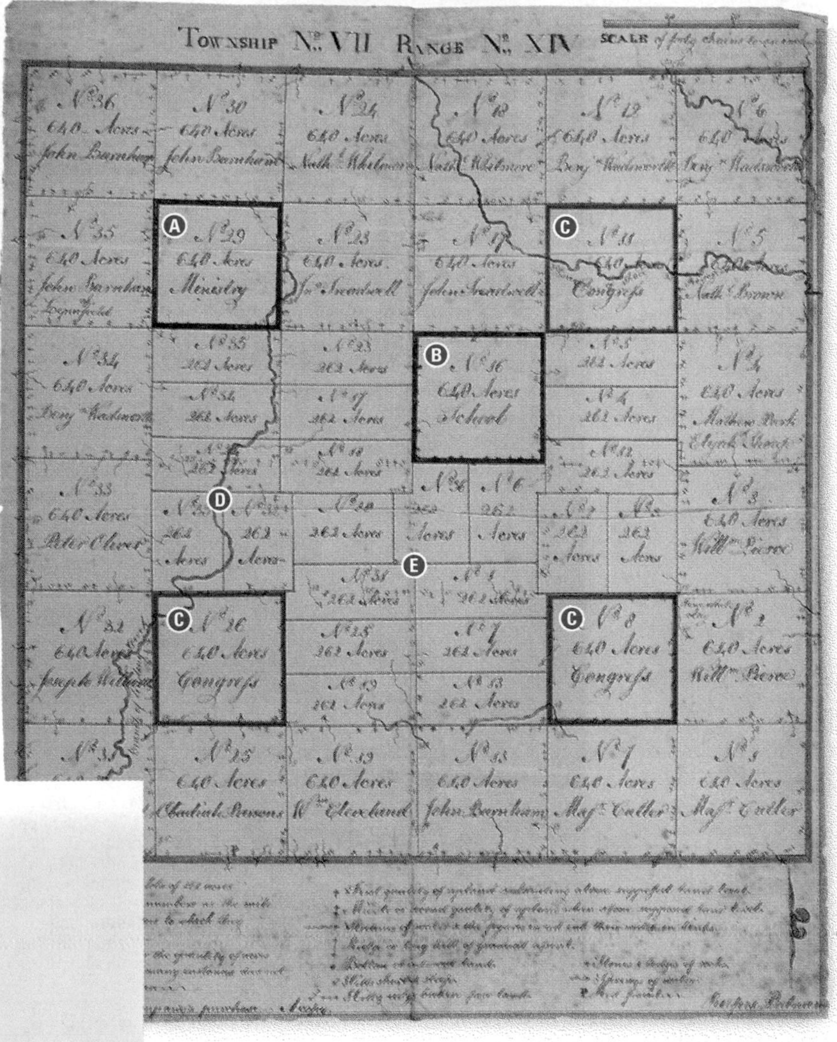

A RELIGION To encourage the growth of religion within the township, the surveyors set aside a full section of land. Most of the land within the section was sold to provide funds for a church and a minister's salary. This practice was dropped after a few years because of concern about the separation of church and state.

B EDUCATION The ordinance encouraged public education by setting aside section 16 of every township for school buildings. Local people used the money raised by the sale of land within this section to build a school and hire a teacher. This section was centrally located so that students could reach it without traveling too far.

C REVENUE Congress reserved two or three sections of each township for sale at a later date. Congress planned to sell the sections then at a tidy profit. The government soon abandoned this practice because of criticism that it should not be involved in land speculation.

D WATER Rivers and streams were very important to early settlers, who used them for transportation. Of most interest, however, was a meandering stream, which indicated flat bottomland that was highly prized for its fertility.

E SMALL PARCELS The interior of the township was divided into smaller parcels for sale to individuals.

INTERACT WITH HISTORY

1. **SYNTHESIZING** How did the Land Ordinance of 1785 provide for the orderly development of the Northwest Territory? How did it make land affordable?

   SEE SKILLBUILDER HANDBOOK, PAGE 921.

2. **CHOOSING A TOWNSHIP SECTION** Use the information in this feature to answer the questions.
   - If you were living in 1787 and wanted to purchase a full section of land in the township shown on this page, which one would you select? Would you want to be near water? Would you want to be near the center of the township? Would it be important to you to be close to a school? Explain your choice.
   - List advantages that your section seems to offer.

INSTRUCT

▶ *Starting with the Student*
- Have students find out more about land settlement in their own area. Into what sort of lots or tracts was the land originally divided?

▶ *Discussing Key Ideas*
- The Land Ordinance of 1785 encourages small landowners to settle in the Northwest Territories.
- The Northwest Ordinance of 1787 establishes the process by which the territories would enter the union as states.
- The two ordinances set a pattern for the nation's future westward expansion.

HISTORY FROM VISUALS

Reading the Images Have students study and compare the different maps and insets.
- In what sense was the area in question the "Northwest"? *It was the northwesternmost land possessed by the new nation at this time.*
- What bodies of water essentially defined the boundaries of the Old Northwest? *The Great Lakes, the Ohio River, and the Mississippi River.*

INTERACT WITH HISTORY

1. Synthesizing

Possible Response: *It surveyed the land and established a plan for parceling it out. Instead of dividing the land into huge parcels that only the rich could afford, it allowed families or individuals to purchase smaller parcels and to subdivide them further if necessary.*

2. Choosing a Township Section

Possible Responses: *Among the advantages students may consider important are fertile soil; reasonably flat, passable terrain; distance from Native Americans; and proximity to a church, to a school, to one or more streams, to friends or loved ones also settling in the area, and/or to the more built-up "civilization" in Pennsylvania and Virginia in the east. Students should choose a parcel that has the maximum number of the advantages that they consider important.*

Section 4 Overview

OBJECTIVES

1 To explain how the United States confronted the difficult task of forming a new government.

2 To describe how political differences between Alexander Hamilton and Thomas Jefferson evolved into a two-party system.

3 To summarize developing foreign policy with France, Great Britain, and Spain.

4 To explain how the United States dealt with Native Americans and with British interests west of the Appalachians.

5 To identify some of the deep divisions between Federalists and Republicans.

SKILLBUILDERS

- Interpreting charts, pp. 80, 83

CRITICAL THINKING

- Drawing conclusions, p. 78
- Contrasting, pp. 79, 80
- Recognizing effects, p. 81
- Theme: Immigration and Migration, p. 81
- Finding main ideas, p. 83
- Making predictions, p. 83
- Summarizing, p. 83
- Evaluating leadership, p. 83
- Forming opinions, p. 83

FOCUS & MOTIVATE

5-MINUTE WARM-UP

Drawing Conclusions

To gain insight into the problems facing the new leaders of the United States, have students read the quotation in the side margin on page 78 and answer these questions.

1. What situation is Madison referring to in the quotation?
2. How will launching a new government be more difficult as a result of this situation?

WARM-UP TRANSPARENCY 2

▶ ***Starting with the Student***

- How do students handle disputes with their friends? How do they handle disputes with strangers?

(continued on next page)

4 Launching the New Nation

TERMS & NAMES
- Judiciary Act of 1789
- Alexander Hamilton
- cabinet
- Democratic-Republican
- two-party system
- protective tariff
- John Jay
- XYZ Affair
- Alien and Sedition Acts
- nullification

LEARN ABOUT the first steps taken by the Washington administration
TO UNDERSTAND how key decisions set precedents for the nation's future.

ONE AMERICAN'S STORY

George Washington had no desire to be president after the Constitutional Convention. His dream was to settle down to a quiet life at his Virginia estate, Mount Vernon. The American people had other ideas, though. They wanted a strong national leader of great authority as their first president. As the hero of the Revolution, Washington was the unanimous choice in the first presidential ballot. When the news reached him on April 14, 1789, Washington reluctantly accepted the call to duty. Two days later he set out for New York City to take the oath of office.

A PERSONAL VOICE

About ten o clock I bade adieu [farewell] to Mount Vernon, to private life, and to domestic felicity [happiness]; and with a mind oppressed with more anxious and painful sensations than I have words to express, set out for New York . . . with the best dispositions [intentions] to render service to my country in obedience to its call, but with less hope of answering its expectations.

GEORGE WASHINGTON, *The Diaries of George Washington*

George Washington

When Washington took office as the first president of the United States under the Constitution, he and Congress faced a daunting task to create an entirely new government. The momentous decisions that these early leaders made have resounded through American history.

Washington Heads the New Government

"*We are in a wilderness without a single footstep to guide us.*"

JAMES MADISON

Although the Constitution provided a strong foundation, it was not a detailed blueprint for governing. To create a working government, Washington and Congress had to make many practical decisions.

JUDICIARY ACT OF 1789 One of the first tasks Washington and Congress tackled was the creation of a judicial system. The Constitution had authorized Congress to set up a federal court system, headed by a Supreme Court, but it failed to spell out the details.

The **Judiciary Act of 1789** spelled out some of the details. The legislation provided for a Supreme Court and federal circuit and district courts. The Judiciary Act allowed state court decisions to be appealed to a federal court when constitutional issues were raised. It also guaranteed that federal laws would remain "the supreme law of the land."

A. Answer If states could pass laws that contradicted federal law, the authority of the federal government might be undermined and therefore jeopardize the stability of the Union.

THINK THROUGH HISTORY
A. *Drawing Conclusions* *Why did federal law have to be "the supreme law of the land" in the new nation?*

WASHINGTON SHAPES THE EXECUTIVE BRANCH At the same time that Congress shaped the judiciary, Washington faced the task of building an executive branch. To help the president govern, Congress created three executive departments: the Department of State, to deal with foreign affairs; the Department of War, to handle military matters; and the Department of the Treasury, to manage finances.

To head these departments, Washington chose capable leaders—Thomas Jefferson as secretary of state, **Alexander Hamilton** as secretary of the treasury,

SECTION 4 RESOURCES

PRINT RESOURCES

IN-DEPTH RESOURCES: UNIT 1
Guided Reading, p. 35
Skillbuilder Practice: Contrasting, p. 38

READING STUDY GUIDE, p. 21

ACCESS FOR STUDENTS ACQUIRING ENGLISH
Guided Reading (Spanish), p. 29
Skillbuilder Practice: Contrasting (Spanish), p. 32

SPANISH READING STUDY GUIDE, p. 21

FORMAL ASSESSMENT
Section Quiz, p. 20

ALTERNATIVE ASSESSMENT BOOK
See forms for supporting and scoring alternative activities.

TECHNOLOGY RESOURCES

HUMANITIES TRANSPARENCIES
H7, The Republican Court

CD-ROM *Grolier Multimedia Encyclopedia*
Electronic Library of Primary Sources

VIDEO *American Portfolio: A Videodisc for U.S. History* user's guide, pp. 41, 42

INTERNET http://www.mlushistory.com

Henry Knox as secretary of war. He also appointed Edmund Randolph as attorney general, the chief lawyer of the federal government. These department heads soon became the president's chief advisers, or **cabinet.**

HAMILTON AND JEFFERSON: TWO CONFLICTING VISIONS Washington appointed Hamilton and Jefferson to executive posts not only because they were brilliant thinkers but also because they had very different political ideas. By having both men in his cabinet, Washington ensured a range of opinion in his administration. No two men embodied the political differences in the nation more than Hamilton and Jefferson.

Hamilton believed in a strong central government led by a prosperous, educated elite of upper-class citizens. Jefferson distrusted a strong central government and the rich. He favored strong state and local governments rooted in popular participation. Hamilton believed that commerce and industry were the keys to a strong nation; Jefferson favored a society of farmer-citizens.

THINK THROUGH HISTORY
B. *Contrasting* *How did Jefferson's and Hamilton's views of government differ?*

B. Answer Jefferson emphasized the rights of states and average citizens. Hamilton emphasized the rights of the national government and ruling elite.

The differences between Hamilton and Jefferson caused bitter disagreements. The differences were particularly evident when dealing with the nation's financial problems.

KEY PLAYERS

ALEXANDER HAMILTON
1755–1804

Born into poverty in the British West Indies, Alexander Hamilton was orphaned at age 11 and went to work as a shipping clerk. He later made his way to New York, where he attended King's College (now Columbia University). He joined the army during the Revolution and became an aide to General Washington. Intensely ambitious, Hamilton quickly moved up in society. Although in his humble origins Hamilton was the opposite of Jefferson, he had little faith in the common citizen and sided with the interests of upper-class Americans. Hamilton said of Jefferson's beloved common people: "Your people, sir, your people is a great beast!"

THOMAS JEFFERSON
1743–1826

The writer of the Declaration of Independence, Thomas Jefferson began his political career at age 26, when he was elected to Virginia's colonial legislature. In 1779 he was elected governor of Virginia, and in 1785 he was appointed minister to France. He served as secretary of state from 1790 to 1793. A Southern planter, Jefferson was also an accomplished scholar, the architect of Monticello (his Virginia house), an inventor (of, among other things, a machine that made copies of letters), and the founder of the University of Virginia in 1819. Despite his elite background and his ownership of slaves, he was a strong ally of the small farmer and average citizen.

HAMILTON'S ECONOMIC PLAN As secretary of the treasury, Hamilton's job was to put the nation's economy on a firm footing. To do this, he proposed a plan to manage the country's debts and a plan to establish a national banking system.

The public debt of the United States in 1790 (most of it incurred during the Revolution) was many millions of dollars. Hamilton proposed to pay off the foreign debt. He also proposed that the federal government assume the debts of the states, a suggestion that made many people in the South furious because some Southern states had already paid off most of their debts. Although this would increase the federal debt, Hamilton reasoned that assuming state debts would give creditors—the people who originally loaned the money—an incentive to support the new federal government. If the government failed, these creditors would never get their money back.

This line of reasoning also motivated Hamilton's proposal for a national bank that would be funded by both the federal government and wealthy private investors. This bank would issue paper money and handle tax receipts and other government funds.

Hamilton's proposals aroused a storm of controversy. Opponents of a national bank, such as James Madison, argued that since the Constitution made no provision for a national bank, Congress had no right to authorize it. This

(continued from page 78)

- How do they think the U.S. government should handle disputes with other countries today?

OBJECTIVE
① INSTRUCT

Washington Heads the New Government

▶***Discussing Key Ideas***

- Washington chooses trusted leaders to advise him on foreign affairs, military matters, and finances.
- Hamilton and Jefferson disagree on the role of government and on economic issues.
- Hamilton proposes creating a national bank.
- In order to gain favor from Southerners for his ideas, Hamilton suggests that the capital be moved to the District of Columbia.

IN-DEPTH RESOURCES: UNIT 1
Guided Reading, p. 35

ACCESS FOR STUDENTS ACQUIRING ENGLISH
Guided Reading (Spanish), p. 29

KEY PLAYERS
Jefferson and Hamilton
Critical Thinking: Compare and Contrast
Ask students to create a chart comparing the lives of Jefferson and Hamilton. *Possible Headings: Family, Early Life, Beliefs, Political Career.*

GROLIER MULTIMEDIA ENCYCLOPEDIA
Thomas Jefferson, Alexander Hamilton

TEACHING OPTIONS

Exploring Themes

Economic Opportunity Discuss how the U.S. economy has changed over the past 200 years. Early on, the U.S. economy relied on agriculture, a system favored by Jefferson. After the Industrial Revolution in the 1800s, the economy relied more on manufacturing, a system favored by Hamilton.

Ask students how Jefferson and Hamilton might view the state of the economy today. *Possible Responses: Jefferson would be saddened by the decline of family-owned farms and of working-class wages. Hamilton would approve of the growth of industry but be shocked at the huge national debt.*

Teaching Less Proficient Readers

Activating Prior Knowledge Before students begin reading pages 78 and 79, initiate a brief discussion about debts and banks. Ask the following questions:

- What institution can people turn to when they don't have enough money to pay for something?
- How do banks make a profit?
- What happens when people have trouble paying off their debts to a bank?

Have students keep the answers to these questions in mind as they read about Hamilton's economic plans.

HISTORY FROM VISUALS

Contrasting Views of the Federal Government

Reading the Chart
Encourage students to explain what is meant by a "loose" and a "strict" interpretation of the Constitution.

Extension Ask students to identify modern issues that divide Americans due to the differences between "loose" and "strict" interpretations of the Constitution. *Possible Response: The controversies over gun control and the right to bear arms.*

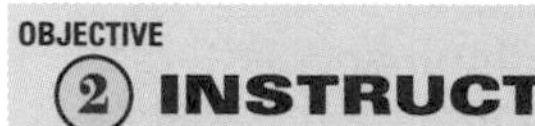

OBJECTIVE ② **INSTRUCT**

The First Political Parties

▶ ***Starting with the Student***
Have students make a list of the advantages and disadvantages of a two-party political system. Students might organize their list in a chart like this:

Two-Party System	
Advantages	Disadvantages
1.	1.
2.	2.
3.	3.

▶ ***Discussing Key Ideas***
- The two-party system is established.
- The Whiskey Rebellion consolidates federal power in domestic affairs.

HUMANITIES TRANSPARENCIES
H7, The Republican Court

ELECTRONIC LIBRARY OF PRIMARY SOURCES *from* "Proclamation Regarding the Whiskey Rebellion" by George Washington

Contrasting Views of the Federal Government

HAMILTON	JEFFERSON
• Concentrating power in federal government	• Sharing power with state and local governments
• Fear of mob rule	• Fear of absolute power or ruler
• Republic of a wise elite	• Limited national government
• Loose interpretation of the Constitution	• Democracy of virtuous farmers and tradespeople
• National bank constitutional (loose interpretation)	• Strict interpretation of the Constitution
• Economy based on shipping and manufacturing	• National bank unconstitutional (strict interpretation)
• Payment of national and state debts (favoring creditors)	• Economy based on farming
• Supporters: merchants, manufacturers, landowners, investors, lawyers, clergy	• Payment of only the national debt (favoring debtors)
	• Supporters: the "plain people" (farmers, tradespeople)

SKILLBUILDER **INTERPRETING CHARTS** ***Whose view of the federal government was a wealthy person more likely to favor? Why? How do you think Jefferson differed from Hamilton in his view of people and human nature?***

Skillbuilder Answer
Wealthy: Hamilton's. Because Hamilton's view favored a national bank, shipping and manufacturing, and payment of debts. **Human nature:** *Possible answers:* Jefferson had greater faith in people's ability to govern themselves. His view reflected a more positive view of human nature.

argument began the debate between those, like Hamilton, who favored a loose interpretation of the Constitution and those, like Madison, who favored a strict interpretation—a vital debate that has continued throughout U.S. history.

In the end Hamilton, Jefferson, and Madison struck a deal. Southerners accepted Hamilton's plan for the Bank of the United States in exchange for moving the nation's capital from New York City to a new city in the South, on the banks of the Potomac River. The new capital was Washington, D.C.

The First Political Parties

President Washington tried to remain above the arguments between Hamilton and Jefferson and to encourage them to work together despite their basic differences. These differences were so great, however, that the two men continued to clash over government policy; their conflict divided the cabinet and fueled the growing division in national politics.

FEDERALISTS AND DEMOCRATIC-REPUBLICANS The split in Washington's cabinet helped give rise to the country's first political parties. The two parties formed around one of the key issues in American history: the power and size of the federal government in relation to state and local governments. Those who shared Hamilton's vision of a strong central government (mostly Northerners) called themselves Federalists. Those who supported Jefferson's vision of strong state governments (mostly Southerners) called themselves **Democratic-Republicans.**

The very existence of political parties worried many leaders, including Washington, who saw parties as a danger to national unity. Despite criticism, however, the two parties continued to develop. The **two-party system**—initially Federalists and Democratic-Republicans—was well established by the time Washington left office.

THE WHISKEY REBELLION: FEDERAL AND REGIONAL INTERESTS During Washington's second term, an incident occurred that reflected the tension between federal and regional interests. Previously, Congress had passed a **protective tariff,** an import tax on goods produced in Europe. This tax brought in a great deal of revenue, but Secretary Hamilton wanted more. So he pushed through an excise tax—a tax on a product's manufacture, sale, or distribution—to be levied on the manufacture of whiskey.

THINK THROUGH HISTORY
C. *Contrasting* *How did the Federalists and the Democratic-Republicans differ?*

C. Answer
Federalists believed in a strong central government, while Democratic-Republicans believed in a limited central government.

TEACHING OPTION

Skillbuilder Mini-Lesson: Contrasting

Explaining the Skill Finding the differences between ideas, institutions, behaviors, or events helps students understand historical events more clearly. Often, one concept is easier to grasp if its features can be contrasted with similar features of something else. For example, understanding the rules of rugby might be made easier by contrasting them with the rules of soccer or football.

Applying the Skill: Think Through History Question To answer the Think Through History question on this page, students will first need to identify the issue about which the Federalists and Democratic-Republicans disagreed (the role of the central government). Encourage students to study the chart on page 80 and discuss how those points reflect the differences in the two points of view. *Possible Answers: Federalists lacked faith in the common people and thought the country would be better served by well-educated people experienced in government. Democratic-Republicans had more respect for common people and instead feared that leaders with economic power might become too powerful and abuse the rights of common folk.*

IN-DEPTH RESOURCES: UNIT 1
Skillbuilder Practice: Contrasting, p. 38

Most whiskey producers were small frontier farmers, who were furious. In 1794, farmers in western Pennsylvania refused to pay the tax and attacked the tax collectors and the soldiers sent to guard them. Hamilton looked upon the Whiskey Rebellion as an opportunity for the federal government to show that it could enforce the law along the western frontier. Accordingly, some 15,000 militiamen were called up to end the conflict.

The Whiskey Rebellion was a milestone in the consolidation of federal power in domestic affairs. At the same time, the new government faced critical problems and challenges in foreign affairs.

Foreign Affairs Trouble the Nation

In 1789 a revolution had come to France, which ended the French monarchy and brought hope for a government based on the will of the people. By 1793, France was engaged in war with Great Britain as well as in conflicts with other European countries.

REACTIONS TO FRENCH CONFLICTS Most Americans initially supported the French Revolution. The alliance between France and the United States, created by the Treaty of 1778, served as a bond between the two nations. Because of their alliance with the United States, the French expected American help.

The American reaction, however, tended to split along party lines. Democratic-Republicans wanted to honor the 1778 treaty and support France. Federalists wanted to back the British. President Washington took a middle position. On April 22, 1793, he issued a declaration of neutrality, a statement that the United States would support neither side in the conflict.

French revolutionaries storm the Bastille in Paris, France, on July 14, 1789.

D. Answer Travel and trade were difficult on the frontier, and the Mississippi offered the easiest means of transport for frontier farmers and merchants.

THINK THROUGH HISTORY
D. *Recognizing Effects* *Why did the United States want access to the Mississippi River?*

TREATY WITH SPAIN In 1795 Thomas Pinckney negotiated the Pinckney Treaty with Spain, which settled disagreements between these two countries. According to the treaty, Spain gave up all claims to land east of the Mississippi and recognized the 31st parallel as the northern boundary of Florida. Spain also agreed to open the Mississippi River to American traffic and allow American traders to use the port of New Orleans. This treaty was important because it paved the way for U.S. expansion west of the Appalachians.

Native Americans Resist White Settlers

Pioneers had been moving west of the Appalachians since before the Revolution. After the war, pioneers in even greater numbers migrated west in pursuit of fertile and abundant land. They assumed that the 1783 Treaty of Paris gave them free rein to settle the area. However, the British still maintained forts in direct violation of the treaty. In addition to the British presence, the settlers met fierce resistance from the original inhabitants.

THINK THROUGH HISTORY
E. THEME ***Immigration and Migration*** *Why did settlers move westward in greater numbers after the Revolution?*

E. Answer They moved westward in search of rich and abundant farmland and greater opportunities.

FIGHTS IN THE NORTHWEST Native Americans in the Northwest Territory never accepted the provisions of the Treaty of Paris. They continued to claim their tribal lands and demanded direct negotiations with the United States. When white settlers moved into their territory, the Native Americans often attacked them.

OBJECTIVE
③ INSTRUCT

Foreign Affairs Trouble the Nation

▶ ***Discussing Key Ideas***
- The American people are divided over whether or not to support the French Revolution.
- The United States secures the rights from Spain to claim land west of the Appalachians.

OBJECTIVE
④ INSTRUCT

Native Americans Resist White Settlers

▶ ***Starting with the Student***
Have students create a cause-and-effect chart like the one below to show the effects stemming from Native Americans' rejection of the Treaty of Paris.

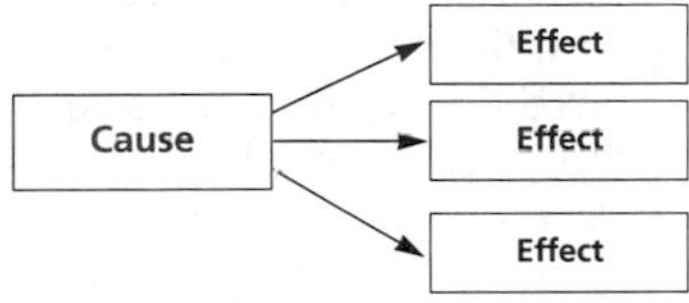

▶ ***Discussing Key Ideas***
- Through battle, the United States obtains lands in Ohio from Native Americans.
- Britain signs the Jay Treaty, which gives the United States control of western territories.

TEACHING OPTIONS

Exploring Themes

Immigration and Migration Discuss the reasons for the westward migration. Explain that many settlers sought rich farmland and greater opportunities in the West. They were willing to endure hardships and fight Native Americans to achieve their goals.

Ask students where Americans tend to migrate today, and why they move to these places. *Possible Responses: The West, the Southwest, the Southeast; the weather and economy in these places appeal to many people.*

Making Connections Across the Cultures

The Native American Perspective Remind students that the Native Americans had been the sole inhabitants of the West for hundreds of years. The westward expansion eventually destroyed their way of life. Recently, Native American groups have worked to regain ancestral works of art and skeletal remains from museums and collectors. (For more information, see Now & Then, "Who Owns the Past," in Chapter 1, p. 6.)

Ask students why Native Americans might be doing this. *Possible Response: Native Americans want their culture and traditions to be respected.*

MORE ABOUT . . .

The Battle of Fallen Timbers

Although well-trained, General Wayne's troops were greatly outnumbered. Nearly 2,000 Shawnee, Ottawa, and Chippewa planned to attack Wayne's men. But Wayne had devised a plan of his own. He sent an advance party to draw the Native American warriors out of hiding. The warriors chased the American soldiers, who led them to Wayne's troops. Forced out in the open to fight a conventional battle, the Native Americans were surrounded on all sides. The battle was over within 40 minutes.

OBJECTIVE

(5) **INSTRUCT**

Adams Provokes Criticism

▶ ***Starting with the Student***

- As citizens, do students have the right to criticize the government?
- Do they think there should be any limits to what they can say?

▶ ***Discussing Key Ideas***

- Tensions mount between the United States and France, but Adams avoids war.
- The Alien and Sedition Acts divide Federalists and Republicans.

The Miami war chief Little Turtle negotiates with General Anthony Wayne.

To gain control over the area that would become Ohio, the federal government sent an army led by General Josiah Harmar. In 1790, Harmar's troops clashed with a confederacy of Native American groups led by a Miami chieftain named Little Turtle. The Native Americans won that battle. The following year, the Miami Confederacy inflicted an even worse defeat on a federal army led by General Arthur St. Clair.

BATTLE OF FALLEN TIMBERS Finally, in 1792, President Washington appointed General Anthony Wayne to lead troops against the Native Americans. Known as "Mad Anthony" for his reckless courage, Wayne spent a year drilling his men.

On August 20, 1794, Wayne defeated the Miami Confederacy at the Battle of Fallen Timbers, near present-day Toledo, Ohio. The following year, the Miami Confederacy signed the Treaty of Greenville, agreeing to give up most of the land in Ohio in exchange for an annual payment of $10,000. This settlement continued a pattern in which Native Americans gave up their land to settlers and the government for much less than it was worth.

> ***"We have beaten the enemy twice under different commanders."***
>
> LITTLE TURTLE

JAY'S TREATY At the time of the Battle of Fallen Timbers, **John Jay** was in London to negotiate a treaty with Britain. One of the disputed issues was which nation would control territories west of the Appalachian Mountains. When news of Wayne's victory at Fallen Timbers arrived, the British agreed to evacuate their posts in the Northwest Territory because they did not wish to fight both the United States and Napoleon's France, with whom they were in conflict, at the same time.

Although Jay's Treaty, signed on November 19, 1794, was a diplomatic victory, the treaty provoked outrage at home. For one thing, it allowed the British to continue their fur trade on the American side of the U.S.-Canadian border. This angered Western settlers. Also, the treaty did not resolve a dispute over neutral American trade in the Caribbean. Americans believed that their ships had the right to free passage there. The British, however, had seized a number of these ships, confiscating their crews and cargo. Despite serious opposition, the treaty managed to pass the Senate.

Adams Provokes Criticism

Portrait of a young John Adams by Joseph Badger

The bitter political fight over Jay's Treaty, along with the growing division between the Federalists and Democratic-Republicans, convinced Washington not to seek a third term. In the election of 1796, Americans faced a new situation: a contest between opposing parties. The Federalists nominated Vice-President John Adams for president and Thomas Pinckney for vice-president. The Democratic-Republicans chose Thomas Jefferson, with Aaron Burr as his running mate.

In the election, Adams received 71 electoral votes, while Jefferson received 68. Because the Constitution stated that the runner-up should become vice-president, the country found itself with a Federalist president and a Democratic-Republican vice-president. What had seemed sensible when the Constitution was written had become a problem because of the unexpected rise of political parties.

ADAMS TRIES TO AVOID WAR Soon after taking office, President Adams faced his first crisis: a looming war with France. The French government, which regarded Jay's Treaty as a violation of the French-American alliance, began to seize American ships bound for Britain. To negotiate a solution, Adams sent a three-man team to Paris to meet with the French foreign minister, Talleyrand.

Block Schedule TEACHING OPTION **Time Needed: 30 Minutes**

Cooperative Activity: Writing a Treaty

Task: Student groups will draft a treaty that deals fairly with the Native Americans.

Purpose: To help students understand that the Native Americans were frequently cheated in their dealings with the U.S. government.

Activity: Divide groups of eight to ten students into two teams. Have one team represent the interests of the United States. Have the other team represent the interests of the Native American people. Students should draw up a treaty that makes fair concessions to both sides. For example, the United States might allow the Native Americans to continue using the land, and the Native Americans might agree to leave the settlers in peace.

Building a Portfolio: Students adding the treaty to their portfolios should include a note pointing out their own contribution to the treaty.

ALTERNATIVE ASSESSMENT BOOK
Standards for Evaluating a Cooperative Activity

Standards for Evaluation
Treaties should . . .

- use neutral language to address the positions of both parties equally
- include specific provisions for the use of the land
- include provisions for enforcing the treaty

Instead, the French sent three low-level officials, whom Adams called X, Y, and Z. The French officials demanded a $250,000 bribe as payment for seeing Talleyrand. News of this insult, which became known as the **XYZ Affair,** provoked a wave of anti-French feeling at home.

The Federalists called for a full-scale war against France, but Adams refused to take that step. Through diplomacy, the two countries eventually smoothed over their differences. Adams damaged his standing among the Federalists, but he kept the United States out of war.

THE ALIEN AND SEDITION ACTS Although Democratic-Republicans cheered Adams for avoiding war with France, they criticized him on other issues. Tensions between Federalists and Democratic-Republicans increased. Adams regarded Democratic-Republican ideas as dangerous to the welfare of the nation. He and other Federalists accused the Democratic-Republicans, and many immigrants who supported them, of favoring foreign powers.

To counter what they saw as a growing threat to the government, the Federalists in 1798 pushed through Congress four measures that became known as the **Alien and Sedition Acts.** Three of these measures, the Alien Acts, raised the residence requirement for American citizenship. The fourth measure, the Sedition Act, set fines and jail terms for anyone expressing opinions considered damaging to the government. Outraged Democratic-Republicans called the laws a violation of the free speech that was guaranteed by the First Amendment.

F. Answer They basically denied citizens the right to criticize their government or elected officials. This violated freedom of speech under the First Amendment.

THINK THROUGH HISTORY
F. Finding Main Ideas *How did the Alien and Sedition Acts threaten political freedoms?*

Skillbuilder Answer
Constitutionality: The states (probably through their legislatures).
Principles: *Possible answer:* A far weaker federal government would have developed—with more powerful states than we have today.

SKILLBUILDER
INTERPRETING CHARTS
According to the Virginia and Kentucky Resolutions, who had the right to determine the constitutionality of federal laws? If the country had accepted the principles of these resolutions, how would the balance of power between federal and state governments have changed?

Federal and State Conflicts

Alien and Sedition Acts	Virginia and Kentucky Resolutions
• The president was authorized to deport or imprison any alien considered "dangerous to the peace and safety of the United States."	• Virginia and Kentucky claimed the right to declare null and void the Alien and Sedition Acts because they violated the Bill of Rights.
• Fines and a prison sentence could be imposed on anyone trying to hinder the operation of the government or making "false, scandalous, and malicious statements" against the government.	• Virginia and Kentucky claimed the right to declare null and void federal laws going beyond powers granted by the Constitution to the central government.

VIRGINIA AND KENTUCKY RESOLUTIONS Protests against the Alien and Sedition Acts included the Virginia and Kentucky Resolutions, which were adopted by the Virginia and Kentucky legislatures to challenge the Acts. The Kentucky Resolutions in particular asserted the principle of **nullification—**that states had the right to nullify, or consider void, any act of Congress that they deemed unconstitutional. Virginia and Kentucky viewed the Alien and Sedition Acts as unconstitutional because they violated the First Amendment.

The resolutions showed that the balance of power between the states and the federal government remained controversial. In fact, the election of 1800 would center on this critical debate.

THINK THROUGH HISTORY
G. Making Predictions *What issues that arose during the Adams administration might continue to trouble the nation in the next administration?*

G. Answer Issues of centralized versus decentralized power, as well as foreign relations, will continue to trouble the nation.

Section 4 Assessment

1. **TERMS & NAMES**
   Identify:
   - Judiciary Act of 1789
   - Alexander Hamilton
   - cabinet
   - Democratic-Republican
   - two-party system
   - protective tariff
   - John Jay
   - XYZ Affair
   - Alien and Sedition Acts
   - nullification

2. **SUMMARIZING** In a chart, list the leaders, beliefs, and goals of the country's first political parties.

Federalists	Democratic-Republicans

   If you had lived in that time, which party would you have favored? Why?

3. **EVALUATING LEADERSHIP** How would you judge the leadership qualities of President Washington in his decision to put two such opposed thinkers as Hamilton and Jefferson in his cabinet?
   THINK ABOUT
   - both men's merits
   - their philosophies
   - the conflicts that developed

4. **FORMING OPINIONS** Do you agree with the Democratic-Republicans that the Alien and Sedition Acts were a violation of the First Amendment? Were they necessary? Support your opinion.
   THINK ABOUT
   - the intent of the First Amendment
   - what was happening in Europe
   - what was happening in the United States

ANSWERS

1. TERMS AND NAMES
Judiciary Act of 1789, p. 78
Alexander Hamilton, p. 78
cabinet, p. 79
Democratic-Republican, p. 80
two-party system, p. 80
protective tariff, p. 80
John Jay, p. 82
XYZ Affair, p. 83
Alien and Sedition Acts, p. 83
nullification, p. 83

2. SUMMARIZING
Federalists: Hamilton; led by educated, upper class; favored commerce, strong government, loose interpretation of the Constitution, and national bank.
Democratic-Republicans: Jefferson; supported common people; favored agriculture, weak central government, strict interpretation of the Constitution; opposed national bank.

3. EVALUATING LEADERSHIP
Many students will think Washington was a strong leader who listened to both sides of an issue and was secure enough not to be threatened by surrounding himself with brilliant people who would give him the very best advice. Others may think he should have chosen cabinet members whose views did not conflict so sharply.

4. FORMING OPINIONS
Those who agree with the Federalists will say that the country needed to control the vocal members of the Democratic-Republican Party from seeming to threaten the stability of the young government. Those who agree with the Democratic-Republicans will see these measures as a violation of freedom of speech.

HISTORY FROM VISUALS
Federal and State Conflicts

Reading the Chart Point out that the Alien and Sedition Acts (left column) came from the federal government. The states of Virginia and Kentucky (right column) reacted to those new laws.

Extension Ask students to speculate about the further effects of the resolutions made by Virginia and Kentucky. *Possible Response: In the future, other states might be encouraged to question the power and authority of the federal government.*

GROLIER MULTIMEDIA ENCYCLOPEDIA
Second Amendment

ASSESS & RETEACH

Section 4 Assessment
Encourage students to work in small groups to answer the questions.

Self-Assessment
To explore their understanding of Section 4, have students create a web identifying three or four issues that divided Federalists and Democratic-Republicans. Then have them mark those issues which seem relevant today.

Section Quiz
FORMAL ASSESSMENT
Section Quiz, p. 20

Reteach
Ask students to create a time line to map events discussed in Section 4.

CLOSE

The new government overcame obstacles in shaping its domestic affairs. It also struggled to establish relations with other countries. However, many people disagreed with the government's decisions. Foreign policy has continued to divide the nation throughout its history.

REVIEW CHAPTER 2
ASSESSMENT ANSWERS

REVIEWING THE CHAPTER

TERMS & NAMES
1. Stamp Act, p. 49
2. *Common Sense,* p. 54
3. Thomas Jefferson, p. 55
4. Valley Forge, p. 61
5. Articles of Confederation, p. 68
6. Shays's Rebellion, p. 70
7. James Madison, p. 70
8. bill of rights, p. 72
9. Alexander Hamilton, p. 78
10. nullification, p. 83

MAIN IDEAS

11. Eight colonists were killed at Lexington, dozens of British soldiers died in the fighting at Concord and on the march back to Boston.
12. He meant that free white males were political equals, not that all Americans had equal opportunity.
13. Civilians lent money to the government, made ammunition and clothing, and took over the civilian roles of those who became soldiers.
14. It had to form a government, handle problems resulting from provisions in the peace treaty, and live up to its ideals.
15. A huge debt from the Revolutionary War, no power to tax, no control over interstate or foreign trade, and no power to deal with foreign relations.
16. Big and little states compromised; the Three-Fifths Compromise settled the issue of counting slaves.
17. For: It created a strong central government but reserved powers for the states and created a system of checks and balances for the central government. Against: Strong central government might increase taxes; citizens' rights/freedoms were not protected enough.
18. Creating a judicial system, building an executive branch, developing a cabinet.
19. It consolidated federal power in domestic affairs.
20. It continued a pattern in which Native Americans gave up their land and received much less for their land than it was worth from settlers and the government.

Review Chapter  Assessment

REVIEWING THE CHAPTER

TERMS & NAMES For each term below, write a sentence explaining its connection to the American Revolution or the early years of the Republic. For each person below, explain his role in the Revolution or in launching the new nation.

1. **Stamp Act**
2. ***Common Sense***
3. **Thomas Jefferson**
4. **Valley Forge**
5. **Articles of Confederation**
6. **Shays's Rebellion**
7. **James Madison**
8. **bill of rights**
9. **Alexander Hamilton**
10. **nullification**

MAIN IDEAS

SECTION 1 *(pages 48–55)*

Colonial Resistance and Rebellion

11. What were the results of fighting at Lexington and Concord?
12. What did Jefferson mean, and not mean, by the phrase "all men are created equal"?

SECTION 2 *(pages 59–65)*

The War for Independence

13. Explain how civilians supported the war effort in the colonies.
14. Describe three significant challenges facing the United States when the American Revolution ended.

SECTION 3 *(pages 68–75)*

Confederation and the Constitution

15. In what ways was the confederation too weak to handle the nation's problems?
16. In what ways did compromise play a critical role in the drafting of the Constitution?
17. What were the arguments for and against ratifying the Constitution?

SECTION 4 *(pages 78–83)*

Launching the New Nation

18. What were the first steps taken by the Washington administration in building a new government?
19. Why was the Whiskey Rebellion a significant event in the early days of the new government?
20. How did the expanding nation deal with the Native Americans?

THINKING CRITICALLY

1. **TRACING THEMES** **WOMEN IN AMERICA** If you were a woman civilian at the beginning of the American Revolution, what problem caused by the war do you think would affect you the most?
2. **DEMOCRATIC VALUES** Paraphrase the first two sentences of the Declaration of Independence, simplifying and modernizing the language.
3. **GEOGRAPHY OF THE REVOLUTIONARY WAR** Look at the maps on pages 60 and 63. How did the region in which the war was fought change from 1775 to 1781?
4. **EVALUATING COMPROMISES** Which compromise during the Constitutional Convention was more important in your view, the Great Compromise or the Three-Fifths Compromise? Explain your choice.
5. **FEDERALISTS AND DEMOCRATIC-REPUBLICANS** Create a chart listing some of the more important differences in beliefs and goals between Federalists and Democratic-Republicans. Whose ideas do you think made more sense? Explain your choice.

Federalists	Democratic-Republicans

6. **ANALYZING PRIMARY SOURCES** Read the following observation by Madison about Benjamin Franklin and the chair in which George Washington sat during the Constitutional Convention.

> Whilst the last members were signing it, Doctr. Franklin looking towards the President's chair, at the back of which a rising sun happened to be painted, observed to a few members near him, that painters had found it difficult to distinguish in their art a rising from a setting sun. I have, said he, often and often in the course of the session . . . looked at that [sun] behind the President without being able to tell whether it was rising or setting: But now at length I have the happiness to know that it is a rising, and not a setting sun.
>
> **JAMES MADISON,** *The Records of the Federal Convention of 1787*

THINKING CRITICALLY

1. TRACING THEMES WOMEN IN AMERICA
Possible Responses: The problem of trying to keep a large family fed, safe, and healthy with so little food and so few other provisions; the excessive workload created by having to make so many items, to manage houses and workplaces or farms, and to send supplies to troops.

2. DEMOCRATIC VALUES
Possible Responses: When the people of a colony must break away from a ruling country and become a separate country, which is natural and right for them to do, they must give their reasons for doing so out of respect. We believe that all men are created equal and that they have rights that cannot be taken away. These rights are to life, to freedom, and to live as they wish. Government, which gets its power from the people, exists to protect the people.

3. GEOGRAPHY OF THE REVOLUTIONARY WAR
Possible Responses: Early battles were focused in the North; the conflict spread to include the South and the territory to the west.

ALTERNATIVE ASSESSMENT

1. **CREATING A POLITICAL PAMPHLET**
   In the years leading up to the American Revolution, how did political rhetoric influence and inspire the colonists?
   Write a political pamphlet that takes a stand on a controversial issue from the 1760s or 1770s.
   - Use library resources to research the sources of conflict between England and the colonists from 1760 to 1775.
   - Choose a political issue or act that sparked protest from the colonists, and write a political pamphlet that either defends Parliament and the king or urges colonial resistance. Use Thomas Paine's *Common Sense* as a mode.
   - Clearly state your points and persuade your readers with reasons and examples.
   - Revise and edit your writing and turn it into pamphlet form, adding visuals if you wish.
   - Share your pamphlet with classmates.

2. **DEBATING ISSUES**

   How did the delegates to the Constitutional Convention in Philadelphia achieve compromise in drafting the U.S. Constitution?
   Use the CD-ROM *Electronic Library of Primary Sources* and other resources to investigate an issue debated in the Constitutional Convention.
   - Choose an issue of disagreement. Read the section of the Constitution that contains the final compromise as well as documents that show the various sides of the issue before a compromise was reached.
   - **Cooperative Learning** Work in pairs. Each partner should draft a three-minute speech defending one side of the issue.
   - Present your debate to the class, giving a short rebuttal after the other point of view has been given. Have the class evaluate the two sides of the argument before reminding your classmates how the issue was resolved.

   Add your debate speech to your American history portfolio.

3. **PORTFOLIO PROJECT**
   Use the living history activity to expand your portfolio.

LIVING HISTORY

REVISING YOUR CONSTITUTION

You and your group have drafted a new constitution for your class or school. With the other members of your group, revise your constitution, asking yourself the following questions:

- Do we need to add, delete, or change anything?
- Is a bill of rights needed?

Then present your constitution to your class. Compare your constitution with those presented by other groups, noting its strengths and weaknesses. Finally, put a copy of your constitution and your evaluation in your American history portfolio.

Bridge to the Constitution and Chapter 3

Review Chapter 2

REVOLUTION BEGINS Beginning in 1765, Parliament attempted to collect more tax revenue from the colonies. Colonists responded with waves of protest. They angrily complained about taxation without representation. The battles at Concord and Lexington in April 1775, and at Bunker Hill along with the writings of Thomas Paine, spurred increasing support for independence. On July 4, 1776, the Second Continental Congress adopted the Declaration of Independence, formally breaking the ties between the colonies and Great Britain.

WAR AND VICTORY After the Americans' victory at Saratoga, France agreed to use its military power to openly support the revolution. The decisive battle of the war occurred at Yorktown, where American and French forces combined to conquer the British on October 17, 1781. The peace treaty of 1783 recognized the independence of the United States.

CREATING A NEW GOVERNMENT After much disagreement, the states adopted the Articles of Confederation in 1781. However, the problems the new government faced prompted states to send delegates to the Constitutional Convention, which planned to revise the Articles of Confederation. However, the Convention decided to create an entirely new Constitution. Ratification of the Constitution required that at least nine of the thirteen states approve it.

THE NEW GOVERNMENT George Washington proved to be a wise leader of the new nation. President Washington managed to keep the nation out of war by taking a position of neutrality. Adams's presidency brought the passage of the Alien and Sedition Acts. The nation continued to expand its borders.

Preview the Constitution and Chapter 3

The Constitution overcame many problems the nation had had under the Articles of Confederation. You will learn more about the Constitution next. Then in Chapter 3 you will learn how the country continued to grow and how the spirit of democracy set the stage for the reform era of the early 1800s.

ALTERNATIVE ASSESSMENT

1. CREATING A POLITICAL PAMPHLET
Standards for Evaluation
An effective political pamphlet will meet the following criteria.
- Focuses on one political act or issue from the 1760s or 1770s that caused conflict between the colonists and England.
- Takes a clear stand on one side or the other.
- States arguments clearly and persuades effectively.
- Is presented in a clear and attractive manner.

2. DEBATING ISSUES
Standards for Evaluation
A position speech should meet the following criteria.
- Clearly and concisely states a position.
- Rebuttal is logical and effective and addresses specific points in the opposing argument.
- Displays thorough knowledge of the subject.

3. PORTFOLIO PROJECT
LIVING HISTORY
Standards for Evaluation
A constitution should meet the following criteria.
- Creates a clear and well-ordered structure for the school.
- Specifies rules for students and staff to follow.
- Supports the goals of government envisioned by students.
- Contains clear explanations of rules and procedures.

IN-DEPTH RESOURCES: UNIT 1
See the form for scoring this activity on page 52.

THINKING CRITICALLY

4. EVALUATING COMPROMISES
Possible Responses: Students who choose the Great Compromise might mention that it was absolutely essential to reach a compromise between the large states and the small states, or an effective new government could not be created. Students who choose the Three-Fifths Compromise might point out how critical it was to reach an agreement on the issue of slaves, or a government consisting of the Southern states and the Northern states could never be formed.

5. FEDERALISTS AND DEMOCRATIC-REPUBLICANS
Possible Responses: Federalists: believed in strong central government, economy based on shipping and manufacturing, republic ruled by a wise elite. Democratic-Republicans: believed in limited central government and strong state governments, an agrarian economy, and a democratic system based on broader popular participation.

6. ANALYZING PRIMARY SOURCES
Possible Responses: Students might say Franklin is referring to the new nation. They will probably say that after a long summer of debating the issues, the delegates must have felt relieved that they had come up with a plan that they thought most could live with.

OVERVIEW

The Living Constitution

▶ *Accessing Prior Knowledge*

Have students complete the following statement:

The best thing about living in a democracy is _____.

Call on students to read their responses. Tell them that they will learn how the Constitution helps to promote democracy in the United States.

▶ *Predicting Outcomes*

Have students read the opening quotation on this page. Ask students what comparisons President Wilson draws. Ask them what they think the comparisons might suggest about the purpose of the Constitution.

FOCUS & MOTIVATE

5-MINUTE WARM-UP

Recognizing Facts and Details

To gain insight into the structure of the Constitution, ask students to answer these questions.

1. What are the five purposes of the Constitution, as stated in the Preamble?
2. How many articles and amendments does the Constitution have?

WARM-UP TRANSPARENCY FOR CONSTITUTION

The Living Constitution

Table of Contents for the Constitution of the United States

"The Constitution was not made to fit us like a straightjacket. In its elasticity lies its chief greatness."

President Woodrow Wilson

The official purpose of the delegates who met in Philadelphia in 1787 was to change the Articles of Confederation. They soon made a fateful decision, however, to ignore the Articles and to write an entirely new constitution.

Purposes of the Constitution

The delegates who met in Philadelphia in 1787—the "framers"—had five purposes to fulfill in their effort to create an effective constitution.

1. Establish Legitimacy

First, the framers had to establish the new government's legitimacy—its right to rule. Every government must do so.

For the framers of the Constitution, legitimacy had to be based on a compact or contract among those who are to be ruled. This is why the Constitution starts with the words "We the people of the United States . . . do ordain and establish this Constitution."

2. Create Appropriate Structures

The framers' second purpose was to create appropriate structures for the new government. The framers were committed to the principles of representative democracy. They also believed that any new government must include an important role for state governments and ensure that the states retained some legitimacy to rule within their borders.

To achieve their goals, the framers created the Congress, the presidency, and the judiciary to share the powers of the national government. They also created a system of division of powers between the national government and the state governments.

THEMES IN THE LIVING CONSTITUTION

The American Dream

The Constitution incorporates the vision 18th-century Americans had for their new nation and provides the flexibility to adapt to a changing society. It remains as vital today as it was 200 years ago.

See Teacher's Edition note, p. 89.

Immigration and Migration

The United States is often called a nation of immigrants. Through naturalization, hundreds of thousands of immigrants become U.S. citizens each year. The Constitution gives Congress the power to establish a uniform rule of naturalization.

See Teacher's Edition note, p. 92.

Civil Rights

The Fourteenth Amendment guarantees equal protection of the law for all citizens. Subsequent civil rights legislation provides for equal opportunity as well. The broadening of equality through affirmative action policies has sometimes led to conflict.

See Teacher's Edition note, p. 103.

Women in America

Ratification of the Nineteenth Amendment was the culmination of years of struggle by women's movements in the United States. Beginning in 1878, a woman suffrage amendment was introduced annually in Congress for 40 years.

See Teacher's Edition note, p. 105.

3. Describe and Distribute Power

Having created such an elaborate set of structures, the framers had as their third purpose the description and distribution of governmental powers among those structures. The powers of the national government, which are those of Congress, are listed in Article 1, Section 8, of the Constitution. Many of the executive powers belonging to the president are listed in Article 2, Sections 2 and 3. The courts are given judicial powers in Article 3. The words of Article 4 imply that the states retain authority over many public matters.

4. Limit Government Powers

The fourth purpose of the framers was to limit the powers of the structures they created. Limits on the national government's powers are found in Article 1, Section 9. Some of the limits on the powers of state governments are found in Article 1, Section 10. There the framers enumerate things that are delegated to the national government and so cannot be done by the states.

5. Allow for Change

The framers' fifth purpose was to include some means for changing the Constitution. Here they faced a dilemma: they wanted to make certain that the government endured by changing with the times, but they did not want to expose the basic rules of government to so many changes that the system would be unstable. So in Article 5 they created a difficult but not impossible means for amending the Constitution.

How well did the framers fulfill their five purposes? The Constitution has been an effective framework for governing the United States for more than 200 years. As you read this government "contract," ask yourself how each provision reflects the framers' success in fulfilling their five major purposes.

LIVING HISTORY

RESEARCHING A CONSTITUTIONAL QUESTION

As you study the Constitution, think about a constitutional question that interests you. Here are some possible questions:

- How much, if at all, can the federal government or a state government restrict the sale of firearms?
- Under what conditions does the president have the power to order American troops into battle without congressional approval?
- Under what conditions may a police officer conduct a search of the inside of an automobile?

Once you have chosen a constitutional question, research that question in articles and books on the Constitution. Also check the indexes of well-known newspapers, such as the *New York Times,* for articles that are relevant.

PORTFOLIO PROJECT Save your research in a folder for your American history portfolio. After studying the Constitution, you will write an opinion essay on the constitutional question you chose.

The Constitution, which appears on pages 88–107, is printed on a purple background, while the explanatory notes next to each article, section, or clause are printed on white. Each article is divided into sections, and the sections are subdivided into clauses. Headings have been added, and the spelling and punctuation modernized for easier reading. Portions of the Constitution no longer in use have been crossed out. The Constitutional Insight questions and answers will help you understand significant issues related to the Constitution.

ALTERNATIVE ASSESSMENT

LIVING HISTORY

RESEARCHING A CONSTITUTIONAL QUESTION

Discuss ways of conducting the research.

- To help guide the research and investigate the constitutional issue in depth, write questions using the words *who, what, where, when, why,* and *how.*
- Explore a variety of sources. Refer to the *Readers' Guide to Periodical Literature* and the *Social Science Index.* Also, check the Internet.
- Examine Supreme Court cases pertaining to a constitutional issue. For example, *United States* v. *Miller,* 1939, relates to the sale of firearms; *Horton* v. *California,* 1990, to police searches without a warrant.
- Review your sources and look for information that answers your research questions.
- Take notes, using one or more of the following techniques: quoting the source directly, paraphrasing, and summarizing.

IN-DEPTH RESOURCES: UNIT 1
See worksheet and standards for evaluation, pp. 62, 63.

RECOMMENDED RESOURCES

Books for the Teacher

Garraty, John, ed. *Quarrels That Have Shaped the Constitution.* New York: Harper, 1988. Landmark cases.

Lyons, Owen, and others. *Exiled in the Land of the Free.* Santa Fe, N.M.: Clear Light, 1992. Argues that Native American political organization influenced the Constitution.

St. John, Jeffrey. *Forge of Union, Anvil of Liberty.* Ottawa, Ill.: Jameson, 1992. Story of Bill of Rights and first election.

Books for the Student

Ketcham, Ralph, ed. *The Anti-Federalist Papers and the Constitutional Convention Debates.* New York: Mentor, 1986. Leading tracts against the Constitution.

Morris, Richard B. *Witnesses at the Creation.* New York: Holt, 1985. Lives of Madison, Hamilton, and Jay.

Videos

The Congress. Direct Cinema, 800-525-0000. History of the institution.

The Constitution in the Information Age. Sweet Pea Communications, 800-235-4922. Relevance of Constitution today.

Skokie: Rights or Wrong? New Day Films, 22 Riverview Drive, Wayne, NJ 07470. Debate over a free speech issue today.

Software

How a Bill Becomes a Law. Diskette. Word Associates, 3226 Robincrest Drive, Northbrook, IL 60062.

U.S. Constitution Tutor. Diskette. Educational Software Institute, 800-955-5570.

U.S. History: Government, Part 1. CD-ROM. Educational Software Institute, 800-955-5570.

Preamble Article 1

OBJECTIVES

1. To explain the purpose for establishing the Constitution.
2. To identify powers of the legislature.

SKILLBUILDERS

- Interpreting charts, p. 90
- Interpreting political cartoons, p. 91

FOCUS & MOTIVATE

▶ ***Starting with the Student***
- What do students prize most about living in a democracy?

OBJECTIVE

1 INSTRUCT

PREAMBLE

▶ ***Discussing Key Ideas***
- The Constitution reflects the most treasured goals of the American people.

OBJECTIVE

2 INSTRUCT

ARTICLE 1. THE LEGISLATURE

▶ ***Discussing Key Ideas***
- The legislature is directly responsible to the people.
- Qualifications and terms of office differ for senators and representatives.
- The enumerated powers are the powers of Congress.
- The Constitution limits the power of Congress.

IN-DEPTH RESOURCES: UNIT 1
Guided Reading, p. 53
American Lives: James Madison, p. 60

ACCESS FOR STUDENTS ACQUIRING ENGLISH
Guided Reading (Spanish), p. 35

THINK THROUGH THE CONSTITUTION
Possible Responses:

A. Yes—Citizens vote directly for congressional representatives and write them letters voicing views and concerns. No—The effectiveness of the president's leadership and decision-making most affects citizens.

B. Yes—keeps representatives more accountable to their constituents. No—limits representatives' time to carry out their agendas.

PREAMBLE

Constitutional Insight **Preamble** *Why does the Preamble say "We the people of the United States . . . ordain and establish" the new government?* The Articles of Confederation was an agreement among the states. But the framers of the Constitution wanted to be sure its legitimacy came from the American people, not from the states, which might decide to withdraw their support at any time. This is a basic principle of the Constitution.

ARTICLE 1

Constitutional Insight **Section 1** *Why does the first article of the Constitution focus on Congress rather than on the presidency or the courts?* The framers were intent on stressing the central role of the legislative branch in the new government, because it is the branch that represents the people most directly and is most responsive to them. This is why Section 8 of this article lists the major powers of the national government as legislative powers.

A. THINK THROUGH THE CONSTITUTION ***Do you think Congress is still the branch of the federal government that is most directly responsible to the people? Why or why not?***

Constitutional Insight **Section 2.1** *Why are members of the House of Representatives elected every two years?* The House of Representatives was designed to be a truly representative body, with members who reflect the concerns and sentiments of their constituents as closely as possible. The framers achieved this timely representation by establishing two years as a reasonable term for members of the House to serve.

B. THINK THROUGH THE CONSTITUTION ***Do you think electing members of the House of Representatives every two years is a good idea? Why or why not?***

The original manuscript of the Constitution is now kept in the National Archives in Washington, D.C.

The Constitution

Preamble. *Purpose of the Constitution*

We the people of the United States, in order to form a more perfect Union, establish justice, insure domestic tranquility, provide for the common defense, promote the general welfare, and secure the blessings of liberty to ourselves and our posterity, do ordain and establish this Constitution for the United States of America.

Article 1. *The Legislature*

SECTION 1. CONGRESS All legislative powers herein granted shall be vested in a Congress of the United States, which shall consist of a Senate and House of Representatives.

SECTION 2. THE HOUSE OF REPRESENTATIVES

1. Elections The House of Representatives shall be composed of members chosen every second year by the people of the several states, and the electors in each state shall have the qualifications requisite for electors of the most numerous branch of the state legislature.

2. Qualifications No person shall be a Representative who shall not have attained to the age of twenty-five years, and been seven years a citizen of the United States, and who shall not, when elected, be an inhabitant of that state in which he shall be chosen.

3. Number of Representatives Representatives ~~and direct taxes~~ shall be apportioned among the several states which may be included within this Union, according to their respective numbers, ~~which shall be determined by adding to the whole number of free persons, including those bound to service for a term of years, and excluding Indians not taxed, three fifths of all other persons.~~ The actual enumeration shall be made within three years after the first meeting of the Congress of the United States, and within every subsequent term of ten years, in such manner as they shall by law direct. The number of Representatives shall not exceed one for every thirty thousand, but each state shall have at least one Representative; ~~and until such enumeration shall be made, the state of New Hampshire shall be entitled to choose three, Massachusetts eight, Rhode Island and Providence Plantations one, Connecticut five, New York six, New Jersey four, Pennsylvania eight, Delaware one, Maryland six, Virginia ten, North Carolina five, South Carolina five, and Georgia three.~~

Requirements for Holding Federal Office

POSITION	MINIMUM AGE	RESIDENCY	CITIZENSHIP
Representative	25	state in which elected	7 years
Senator	30	state in which elected	9 years
President	35	14 years in the United States	natural-born
Supreme Court Justice	none	none	none

CONSTITUTION RESOURCES

PRINT RESOURCES

IN-DEPTH RESOURCES: UNIT 1
Guided Reading, pp. 53, 54, 55, 56
Skillbuilder Practice: Clarifying, p. 57
Geography Application: The Electoral College, p. 58
American Lives: James Madison, p. 60; Thurgood Marshall, p. 61

READING STUDY GUIDE, pp. 25, 27, 29, 31

ACCESS FOR STUDENTS ACQUIRING ENGLISH
Guided Reading (Spanish), pp. 35, 36, 37, 38
Skillbuilder Practice: Clarifying (Spanish), p. 39
Geography Application: The Electoral College (Spanish), p. 40

SPANISH READING STUDY GUIDE, pp. 25, 27, 29, 31

FORMAL ASSESSMENT
Section Quiz, pp. 29, 30, 31, 32

ALTERNATIVE ASSESSMENT BOOK
See forms for supporting and scoring alternative activities.

TECHNOLOGY RESOURCES

INTERNET http://www.mlushistory.com

4. Vacancies When vacancies happen in the representation from any state, the executive authority thereof shall issue writs of election to fill such vacancies.

5. Officers and Impeachment The House of Representatives shall choose their Speaker and other officers; and shall have the sole power of impeachment.

SECTION 3. THE SENATE

1. Numbers The Senate of the United States shall be composed of two Senators from each state, chosen ~~by the legislature thereof,~~ for six years; and each Senator shall have one vote.

2. Classifying Terms ~~Immediately after they shall be assembled in consequence of the first election, they shall be divided as equally as may be into three classes. The seats of the Senators of the first class shall be vacated at the expiration of the second year, of the second class at the expiration of the fourth year, and of the third class at the expiration of the sixth year, so that one third may be chosen every second year; and if vacancies happen by resignation, or otherwise, during the recess of the legislature of any state, the executive thereof may make temporary appointments until the next meeting of the legislature, which shall then fill such vacancies.~~

3. Qualifications No person shall be a Senator who shall not have attained to the age of thirty years, and been nine years a citizen of the United States, and who shall not, when elected, be an inhabitant of that state for which he shall be chosen.

4. Role of Vice-President The Vice-President of the United States shall be President of the Senate, but shall have no vote, unless they be equally divided.

5. Officers The Senate shall choose their other officers, and also a President pro tempore, in the absence of the Vice-President, or when he shall exercise the office of President of the United States.

6. Impeachment Trials The Senate shall have the sole power to try all impeachments. When sitting for that purpose, they shall be on oath or affirmation. When the President of the United States is tried, the Chief Justice shall preside: and no person shall be convicted without the concurrence of two thirds of the members present.

7. Punishment for Impeachment Judgment in cases of impeachment shall not extend further than to removal from office, and disqualification to hold and enjoy any office of honor, trust or profit under the United States; but the party convicted shall nevertheless be liable and subject to indictment, trial, judgment and punishment, according to law.

SECTION 4. CONGRESSIONAL ELECTIONS

1. Regulations The times, places and manner of holding elections for Senators and Representatives shall be prescribed in each state by the legislature thereof; but the Congress may at any time by law make or alter such regulations, ~~except as to the places of choosing Senators.~~

2. Sessions The Congress shall assemble at least once in every year, ~~and such meeting shall be on the first Monday in December, unless they shall by law appoint a different day.~~

Constitutional Insight **Section 3.1** *Why are members of the Senate elected every six years?* The framers feared the possibility of instability in the government. So they decided that senators should have six-year terms and be elected by the state legislatures rather than directly by the people. The Seventeenth Amendment, as you will see later, changed part of this. The framers also staggered the terms of the senators so that only one-third of them are replaced at any one time. This stabilizes the Senate still further.

C. THINK THROUGH THE CONSTITUTION ***Do you think it is important today for the Senate to have more stability than the House of Representatives? If so, why?***

Constitutional Insight **Sections 3.6 and 3.7** *Have high-level public officials ever been impeached?* Impeachment is a formal accusation of criminal behavior or serious misbehavior that the House of Representatives can bring against a public official (such as the president, a member of the president's cabinet, or a judge). Once accused by the House, the official must stand trial before the Senate, which can find him or her guilty or not guilty. Only one president, Andrew Johnson, was ever impeached, but the Senate failed to find him guilty by one vote.

D. THINK THROUGH THE CONSTITUTION ***Do you think a president should be impeached if he or she is connected to a crime? Should a president be put on trial for a crime while he or she is still in office? Explain.***

HISTORY FROM VISUALS

Requirements for Holding Federal Office

Reading the Chart Have students refer to the column heads as they compare qualifications for holding office in the three branches of government.

Extension Create a concept web to show the qualifications a person should have for the job of Supreme Court justice.

MORE ABOUT . . .

Senators and Vice-Presidents

The Senate is apparently a fertile breeding ground for future vice-presidents. Since World War II, eight vice-presidents formerly served as senators. They are Harry Truman, Alben Barkley, Richard Nixon, Lyndon Johnson, Hubert Humphrey, Walter Mondale, Dan Quayle, and Al Gore.

THINK THROUGH THE CONSTITUTION

Possible Responses:

C. Yes—Membership of the House can change drastically with biennial elections. No—Both representatives and senators should be elected frequently so they remain sensitive to constituents' current needs.

D. Yes—Presidents should be impeached for criminal involvement, because they should comply with higher ethical standards than average citizens. Presidents should stand trial during office, because they are not above the law. No—Impeaching a president is too disruptive and mars the country's international reputation. Presidents' criminal trials should occur after their terms of office to maintain national stability.

TEACHING OPTIONS

Exploring Themes

The American Dream In 1963, Dr. Martin Luther King, Jr.'s "I Have a Dream" speech echoed the vision of America reflected in the Preamble: "When the architects of our republic wrote the magnificent words of the Constitution and the Declaration of Independence, they were signing a promissory note to which every American was to fall heir. This note was a promise that all men would be guaranteed the unalienable rights of life, liberty, and the pursuit of happiness." As students read the Preamble, ask them if all Americans today enjoy the "blessings of liberty."

Making Global Connections

South Africa's Constitution In 1996, South Africa joined the ranks of the world's democracies by adopting a permanent constitution to protect the rights of all its citizens. The country's first democratically elected lawmakers voted in favor of the 150-page document that ends white minority rule. The South African Constitution includes a bill of rights and spells out the organization of its legislature, which mirrors the U.S. Congress. South Africa's Parliament consists of the National Assembly, similar to the House of Representatives, and the National Council of Provinces, similar to the Senate.

HISTORY FROM VISUALS

How a Bill in Congress Becomes a Law

Reading the Chart Read each step in the sequence, noting that many steps have more than one possible outcome.

Extension Point out that a standing committee is a permanent group in each house of Congress that studies bills. A conference committee is a temporary group made up of senators and representatives to produce a compromise bill that both houses will approve. Students might investigate and report on standing committees in each house of Congress.

MORE ABOUT . . .

Congressional Record

The *Congressional Record,* begun in 1873, is published daily while Congress is in session. It prints everything spoken in Congress except secret matters, such as those involving national security. Members of Congress receive a copy of the *Record* for the previous day's session. They may make changes in their speeches before the speeches appear in the *Record.*

THINK THROUGH THE CONSTITUTION

Possible Response:

E. The chairman shapes procedures that can determine the outcome of proposed legislation.

How a Bill in Congress Becomes a Law

1 A bill is introduced in the House or the Senate and referred to a standing committee for consideration.

2 A bill may be reported out of committee with or without changes—or it may be shelved.

3 Either house of Congress debates the bill and may make revisions. If passed, the bill is sent to the other house.

4 If the House and the Senate pass different versions of a bill, both versions go to a conference committee to work out the differences.

5 The conference committee submits a single version of the bill to the House and the Senate.

6 If both houses accept the compromise version, the bill is sent to the president to be signed.

7 If the president signs the bill, it becomes law.

8 If the president vetoes the bill, the House and the Senate may override the veto by a vote of two thirds of the members present in each house, and then the bill becomes law.

SKILLBUILDER **INTERPRETING CHARTS** *How is the constitutional principle of checks and balances reflected in the process of a bill's becoming a law?*

Skillbuilder Answer *Possible Answer: Both* the House and Senate must pass a common version of a bill, which the president may accept or reject (veto). If the president rejects it, it still will become a law with a two-thirds vote in each house. So, the House and Senate can check each other *and* the president, while the president can check the Congress.

Constitutional Insight **Section 5.2** *What kinds of rules does Congress make for itself?* The Constitution gives each house control over most of its rules of procedure and membership. Rules are important, for they help shape the kinds of laws and policies that pass each body. Senate rules allow a filibuster, whereby a senator holds the floor as long as he or she likes in order to block consideration of a bill he or she dislikes. In recent years, a "cloture" rule has been used to end debate if 60 or more members vote to do so.

In contrast, the House of Representatives has rules to limit debate. A rules committee has the primary task of determining how long a bill on the floor of the House may be discussed, and whether any amendments can be offered to the bill. In recent years, the power of the Rules Committee has been limited, but being able to shape the rules remains a powerful tool of members of Congress.

E. THINK THROUGH THE CONSTITUTION ***Why do you think the position of chairman of the Rules Committee is a powerful one?***

SECTION 5. RULES AND PROCEDURES

1. Quorum Each house shall be the judge of the elections, returns and qualifications of its own members, and a majority of each shall constitute a quorum to do business; but a smaller number may adjourn from day to day, and may be authorized to compel the attendance of absent members, in such manner, and under such penalties, as each house may provide.

2. Rules and Conduct Each house may determine the rules of its proceedings, punish its members for disorderly behavior, and, with the concurrence of two thirds, expel a member.

3. Congressional Records Each house shall keep a journal of its proceedings, and from time to time publish the same, excepting such parts as may in their judgment require secrecy; and the yeas and nays of the members of either house on any question shall, at the desire of one fifth of those present, be entered on the journal.

4. Adjournment Neither house, during the session of Congress, shall, without the consent of the other, adjourn for more than three days, nor to any other place than that in which the two houses shall be sitting.

Block Schedule TEACHING OPTION **Time Needed: 30 Minutes**

Cooperative Activity: Proposing Laws

Task: Groups of students will brainstorm a list of issues and propose a law.

Purpose: To understand the complexities and opposing interests involved in making laws.

Activity: Divide students into small groups. Assign groups a special interest to represent or have them choose one of their own. Group members will propose a law and write at least three arguments to support it. Each group should present its law and supporting arguments to the class.

Building a Portfolio: Students who wish to add the proposals to their portfolios should highlight their own contributions.

ALTERNATIVE ASSESSMENT BOOK
Standards for Evaluating a Cooperative Activity

Standards for Evaluation
Proposals should . . .

- clearly state the proposed law
- reflect the interests of the group they represent
- include at least three logical arguments to support the law

SECTION 6. PAYMENT AND PRIVILEGES

1. Salary The Senators and Representatives shall receive a compensation for their services, to be ascertained by law, and paid out of the treasury of the United States. They shall in all cases, except treason, felony and breach of the peace, be privileged from arrest during their attendance at the session of their respective houses, and in going to and returning from the same; and for any speech or debate in either house, they shall not be questioned in any other place.

2. Restrictions No Senator or Representative shall, during the time for which he was elected, be appointed to any civil office under the authority of the United States, which shall have been created, or the emoluments whereof shall have been increased, during such time; and no person holding any office under the United States shall be a member of either house during his continuance in office.

SECTION 7. HOW A BILL BECOMES A LAW

1. Tax Bills All bills for raising revenue shall originate in the House of Representatives; but the Senate may propose or concur with amendments as on other bills.

2. Lawmaking Process Every bill which shall have passed the House of Representatives and the Senate shall, before it become a law, be presented to the President of the United States; if he approves he shall sign it, but if not he shall return it with his objections to that house in which it shall have originated, who shall enter the objections at large on their journal, and proceed to reconsider it. If after such reconsideration two thirds of that house shall agree to pass the bill, it shall be sent, together with the objections, to the other house, by which it shall likewise be reconsidered, and if approved by two thirds of that house, it shall become a law. But in all such cases the votes of both houses shall be determined by yeas and nays, and the names of the persons voting for and against the bill shall be entered on the journal of each house respectively. If any bill shall not be returned by the President within ten days (Sundays excepted) after it shall have been presented to him, the same shall be a law, in like manner as if he had signed it, unless the Congress by their adjournment prevent its return, in which case it shall not be a law.

3. Role of the President Every order, resolution, or vote to which the concurrence of the Senate and House of Representatives may be necessary (except on a question of adjournment) shall be presented to the President of the United States; and before the same shall take effect, shall be approved by him, or being disapproved by him, shall be repassed by two thirds of the Senate and House of Representatives, according to the rules and limitations prescribed in the case of a bill.

"It's awful the way they're trying to influence Congress. Why don't they serve cocktails and make campaign contributions like we do?"

SKILLBUILDER **INTERPRETING POLITICAL CARTOONS**
What point do you think the cartoonist is making about influencing Congress?

Skillbuilder Answer The cartoonist is suggesting that Congress can be influenced in various ways.

Constitutional Insight **Section 7.2** *How often do presidents use the veto, and how often is that action overridden?* The use of the veto, which is the refusal to approve a bill, depends on many factors, especially the political conditions of the time. Some presidents—for example, John Adams and Thomas Jefferson—never used the veto power of the presidency. Others used it hundreds of times. Usually, Congress is unable to produce the votes (those of two-thirds of the members present in each house) needed to override presidential vetoes. The following chart gives selected numbers of presidential vetoes.

F. THINK THROUGH THE CONSTITUTION *Do you think it should be easier for Congress to override a president's veto? Why or why not?*

Presidential Vetoes

PRESIDENT	VETOES	VETOES OVERRIDDEN
Andrew Johnson 1865–1869	29	15
Franklin D. Roosevelt 1933–1945	635	9
George Bush 1989–1993	46	1

HISTORY FROM VISUALS

Political Cartoon

Reading the Cartoon Ask students to identify who the person speaking in the cartoon represents. *"Bigshot" interests—business lobbyists.* Whose interests do the people carrying the signs represent? *Working people, the poor.*

Extension Have students revise the cartoon, adding a caption that the people carrying the picket signs might say.

HISTORY FROM VISUALS

Presidential Vetoes

Reading the Chart Explain that the numbers under the headings "Vetoes" and "Vetoes Overridden" reflect a power struggle between the president and Congress.

Extension Calculate the percentage of vetoes overridden for each of the presidents listed. *Johnson—52%; Roosevelt—1%; Bush—2%.* Have students add to the chart by researching the veto records of other U.S. presidents. Suggest they include a fourth column, with the heading "Percentage of Vetoes Overridden."

THINK THROUGH THE CONSTITUTION

Possible Responses:

F. Yes—to curb presidential power; No—to curb congressional power over president's decisions on legislation.

TEACHING OPTION

Making Connections Across the Curriculum

U.S. Government The word *filibuster* stems from the Dutch word for pirate. Instead of plundering the seas by force, filibusterers on the Senate floor steal time by their endless jabber. Their goal—to stall or kill a legislative measure—is often realized. During the last 100 years or so, filibusters have halted the passage of roughly 200 measures.

In an effort to tongue-tie filibusterers, senators adopted the cloture rule, a procedure for ending debate, in 1917 and amended the rule in 1979 and 1986. Ask students to speculate why many senators are reluctant to advocate cloture motions. *Many senators heed the tradition of open debate and want to preserve the tactic of filibustering—an effective political weapon they too might want to employ in the future.*

Republican Senator Strom Thurmond of South Carolina holds the filibustering record—24 hours, 18 minutes. Despite the long-winded display he staged on the Senate floor, Thurmond failed to avert the passage of the Civil Rights Act of 1957.

MORE ABOUT . . .
The Images on Money

The faces on various denominations of paper money compose a gallery of famous political leaders in American history. On the back are notable symbols, scenes, or architecture.

Amount	Front	Back
$1	George Washington	Great Seal
$2	Thomas Jefferson	Signing of the Declaration of Independence
$5	Abraham Lincoln	Lincoln Memorial
$10	Alexander Hamilton	U.S. Treasury
$20	Andrew Jackson	White House
$50	Ulysses S. Grant	U.S. Capitol
$100	Benjamin Franklin	Independence Hall

THINK THROUGH THE CONSTITUTION
Possible Response:

G. The clause provides the necessary flexibility for the federal government, which has expanded over time, to carry out its functions by implied powers.

Constitutional Insight **Section 8** *Just how powerful is the national government?* In the Constitution, the powers of the national government are the powers given to Congress in Section 8 of Article 1. The first 17 clauses of Section 8, which are specific, are often called the national government's enumerated powers. They confer on Congress a host of powers dealing with issues ranging from taxation and the national debt to calling out the armed forces of the various states to governing the nation's capital district (Washington, D.C.).

The 18th and final clause is different. It gives Congress the power to do what is "necessary and proper" to carry out the previous list of powers. Thus, the enumerated powers of Congress "to lay and collect taxes," "to borrow money," "to regulate commerce," and "to coin money" imply the power to create a bank in order to execute these enumerated powers. Early in the country's history, this "elastic clause," as it has been called, was used by Congress to establish the controversial Bank of the United States in 1791 and the Second Bank of the United States in 1816.

G. THINK THROUGH THE CONSTITUTION ***Why do you think the elastic clause is still important today?***

Section 8.6 **Because of frequent counterfeiting of the U.S. $100 bill, especially in Asia, a new design was created in 1996. It includes an enlarged portrait of Benjamin Franklin, a security thread running beneath the longer serial number, a microprinted word on the 1 in the number 100, color-shifting ink, and a watermark to the right of Franklin's portrait. These all make the bill more difficult to counterfeit than it previously was.**

SECTION 8. POWERS GRANTED TO CONGRESS

1. Taxation The Congress shall have power to lay and collect taxes, duties, imposts and excises, to pay the debts and provide for the common defense and general welfare of the United States; but all duties, imposts and excises shall be uniform throughout the United States;

2. Credit To borrow money on the credit of the United States;

3. Commerce To regulate commerce with foreign nations, and among the several states, and with the Indian tribes;

4. Naturalization, Bankruptcy To establish a uniform rule of naturalization, and uniform laws on the subject of bankruptcies throughout the United States;

5. Money To coin money, regulate the value thereof, and of foreign coin, and fix the standard of weights and measures;

6. Counterfeiting To provide for the punishment of counterfeiting the securities and current coin of the United States;

7. Post Office To establish post offices and post roads;

8. Patents, Copyrights To promote the progress of science and useful arts, by securing for limited times to authors and inventors the exclusive right to their respective writings and discoveries;

9. Federal Courts To constitute tribunals inferior to the Supreme Court;

10. International Law To define and punish piracies and felonies committed on the high seas, and offenses against the law of nations;

11. War To declare war, ~~grant letters of marque and reprisal~~, and make rules concerning captures on land and water;

12. Army To raise and support armies, but no appropriation of money to that use shall be for a longer term than two years;

13. Navy To provide and maintain a navy;

14. Regulation of Armed Forces To make rules for the government and regulation of the land and naval forces;

15. Militia To provide for calling forth the militia to execute the laws of the Union, suppress insurrections and repel invasions;

16. Regulations for Militia To provide for organizing, arming, and disciplining the militia, and for governing such part of them as may be employed in the service of the United States, reserving to the states respectively the appointment of the officers, and the authority of training the militia according to the discipline prescribed by Congress;

17. District of Columbia To exercise exclusive legislation in all cases whatsoever, over such district (not exceeding ten miles square) as may, by cession of particular states, and the acceptance of Congress, become the seat of the government of the United States, and to exercise like authority over all places purchased by the consent of the legislature of the state in which the same shall be, for the erection of forts, magazines, arsenals, dockyards, and other needful buildings;—and

18. Elastic Clause To make all laws which shall be necessary and proper for carrying into execution the foregoing powers, and all other powers vested by this Constitution in the government of the United States, or in any department or officer thereof.

TEACHING OPTIONS

Exploring Themes

Immigration and Migration Legal immigrants may become naturalized citizens of the United States by following a procedure established by Congress. Applicants must be at least 18 years old and must have resided permanently in the United States for a minimum of the previous five years. They must prove that they are of good moral character and that they are loyal to American principles of government. Applicants must pass an examination that tests their knowledge of U.S. history and government. A final hearing takes place in a court, where the applicant takes a loyalty oath in front of a judge.

Making Connections Across the Curriculum

Literature In Mark Twain's novel *A Connecticut Yankee in King Arthur's Court,* an inventive 19th-century mechanic discovers he has journeyed in time to 6th-century Camelot. Twain's ingenuity was not limited to creating colorful characters. He too dabbled as an inventor and, through a power granted to Congress in Section 8.8, was issued patents for the following contrivances:

- 1871—suspenders
- 1873—"Mark Twain's Self-Pasting Scrapbook"
- 1885—an educational game designed to enhance players' memory of key dates in history

SECTION 9. POWERS DENIED CONGRESS

1. Slave Trade ~~The migration or importation of such persons as any of the states now existing shall think proper to admit, shall not be prohibited by the Congress prior to the year one thousand eight hundred and eight, but a tax or duty may be imposed on such importation, not exceeding ten dollars for each person.~~

2. Habeas Corpus The privilege of the writ of habeas corpus shall not be suspended, unless when in cases of rebellion or invasion the public safety may require it.

3. Illegal Punishment No bill of attainder or ex post facto law shall be passed.

4. Direct Taxes No capitation, ~~or other direct,~~ tax shall be laid, unless in proportion to the census or enumeration herein before directed to be taken.

5. Export Taxes No tax or duty shall be laid on articles exported from any state.

6. No Favorites No preference shall be given by any regulation of commerce or revenue to the ports of one state over those of another: nor shall vessels bound to, or from, one state be obliged to enter, clear, or pay duties in another.

7. Public Money No money shall be drawn from the treasury, but in consequence of appropriations made by law; and a regular statement and account of the receipts and expenditures of all public money shall be published from time to time.

8. Titles of Nobility No title of nobility shall be granted by the United States: and no person holding any office of profit or trust under them shall, without the consent of the Congress, accept of any present, emolument, office, or title, of any kind whatever, from any king, prince, or foreign state.

SECTION 10. POWERS DENIED THE STATES

1. Restrictions No state shall enter into any treaty, alliance, or confederation; grant letters of marque and reprisal; coin money; emit bills of credit; make anything but gold and silver coin a tender in payment of debts; pass any bill of attainder, ex post facto law, or law impairing the obligation of contracts, or grant any title of nobility.

2. Import and Export Taxes No state shall, without the consent of the Congress, lay any imposts or duties on imports or exports, except what may be absolutely necessary for executing its inspection laws; and the net produce of all duties and imposts, laid by any state on imports or exports, shall be for the use of the treasury of the United States; and all such laws shall be subject to the revision and control of the Congress.

3. Peacetime and War Restraints No state shall, without the consent of Congress, lay any duty of tonnage, keep troops or ships of war in time of peace, enter into any agreement or compact with another state, or with a foreign power, or engage in war, unless actually invaded, or in such imminent danger as will not admit of delay.

NOW & THEN

MODERN-DAY PIRATES (SECTION 8.10)

Few pirates sail the high seas nowadays—they are more likely to be surfing the Internet. Software piracy, or the illegal duplication and sale of software, cost the American software industry an estimated $500 million in 1995. Most of this loss was due to pirated software products that were illegally duplicated in China. As a result of software piracy, legitimate software producers lose markets in China and in much of the Third World, where the pirated goods are sold. For example, it is estimated that 99 percent of all software sold in Indonesia is pirated.

In 1995, Congress threatened the Chinese government with $2 billion in punitive tariffs if it didn't crack down on piracy. China threatened to retaliate with its own set of equally harsh trade sanctions. However, the two countries narrowly averted a trade war just hours before tariffs would have been imposed, when the Chinese government agreed to shut down 15 factories producing pirated CD-ROMs and software.

Constitutional Insight **Section 9** *Why didn't the framers include a bill of rights in the original Constitution?* Actually, they did. Article 1, Section 9, defines limits on the powers of Congress, just as the first ten amendments (which we call the Bill of Rights) do. While some of the provisions focus on such issues as slavery and taxation, there are three explicit prohibitions dealing with citizens' rights:

- **Writ of habeas corpus.** Section 9, Clause 2, says that, except in time of rebellion or invasion, Congress cannot suspend people's right to a writ of habeas corpus. This means that people cannot be held in prison or jail without being formally charged with a crime.
- **Bill of attainder.** Section 9, Clause 3, prohibits the passage of any law that convicts or punishes a person directly and without the benefit of a trial. Any legislative action that would punish someone without recourse to a court of law is called a bill of attainder.
- **Ex post facto law.** The same clause prohibits ex post facto laws. Such a law would make illegal an act that was legal when it was performed.

The fact that these particular rights were protected by the original document issued by the framers reflects both the framers' experiences during the Revolution and their fear of excessive government power.

H. THINK THROUGH THE CONSTITUTION ***Why are American citizens today so intent on having protections against government violations of their rights?***

NOW & THEN
Modern-Day Pirates

Critical Thinking: Drawing Conclusions Ask, Which clauses of Article I, Section 8, grant Congress the power to deal with software piracy? *3, 8, 10.* Why do you think China agreed to the demands of Congress? *Possible Responses: To avert a trade war; to avoid a tense economic relationship.*

MORE ABOUT . . .
Habeas Corpus

During the Civil War, President Lincoln suspended the writ of habeas corpus to suppress disloyalty and dissent. Consequently, over 13,000 suspected Confederate sympathizers in the Union were arrested without trial, although most were soon released. Initially, Jefferson Davis, president of the Confederacy, condemned Lincoln for dragging "upright men and innocent women . . . to distant dungeons." By 1862, Davis had made an about-face on this issue; that year he too suspended habeas corpus.

FORMAL ASSESSMENT
Quiz: Preamble and Article 1, p. 29

THINK THROUGH THE CONSTITUTION
Possible Response:
H. Today's Americans still prize personal freedom and fear government's potential to abuse power.

TEACHING OPTION

Making Global Connections

Titles of Nobility Though the U.S. Constitution bars public officials from assuming titles of nobility, this has not been the practice in many other countries around the world. Here are some examples.

Royal Title	Status	Country of Origin
Czar/Czarina	ruler	Russia (until 1917)
Emir	prince or chieftain	Middle East
Pharaoh	ruler	ancient Egypt
Rajah	prince	India
Shah	ruler	Iran (until 1979)
Sultan	ruler	Muslim states

OBJECTIVE

① To explain the powers and duties of the president.

FOCUS & MOTIVATE

▶ ***Starting with the Student***

- What traits do students think a president needs to lead the country? Why?

OBJECTIVE ① **INSTRUCT**

ARTICLE 2. THE EXECUTIVE

▶ ***Discussing Key Ideas***

- The Constitution empowers the president to carry out the nation's laws.

IN-DEPTH RESOURCES: UNIT 1
Guided Reading, p. 54

ACCESS FOR STUDENTS ACQUIRING ENGLISH
Guided Reading (Spanish), p. 36

MORE ABOUT . . .
The Electoral College

In 1824, Andrew Jackson received the largest number of popular votes but did not have an electoral majority. The House of Representatives chose John Quincy Adams to be president.

IN-DEPTH RESOURCES: UNIT 1
Geography Application: The Electoral College, p. 58.

THINK THROUGH THE CONSTITUTION
Possible Responses:

I. To make sure laws are faithfully executed.

J. To ensure smooth and orderly transfer of leadership.

ARTICLE 2

Constitutional Insight **Section 1.1** *What exactly is "executive power"?* We know the president has it, but nowhere is it explicitly defined. It is most often defined as the power to carry out the laws of the land, but of course no one person can handle such a chore alone. A more appropriate definition is found in Section 3 of this article, which empowers the president to "take care that the laws be faithfully executed." In this sense, the president isn't merely an administrator, but the chief administrator.

I. THINK THROUGH THE CONSTITUTION ***Why is it important to have an executive who is the chief administrator?***

Constitutional Insight **Section 1.6** *What happens when the vice-president succeeds a dead or incapacitated president?* Section 1.6 provides that the vice-president shall assume the duties of the presidential office. But until the Twenty-fifth Amendment was added to the Constitution in 1967, there was no explicit statement in the document that the vice-president is to become president. That tradition owes its origin to John Tyler, the tenth president of the United States, who in 1841 succeeded William Henry Harrison—the first president to die in office. Tyler decided to take the oath of office and assume the title of president of the United States. Congress voted to go along with his decision, and the practice was repeated after Lincoln was assassinated. It would take another century for the written provisions of the Constitution to catch up with the practice.

J. THINK THROUGH THE CONSTITUTION ***Why is it important to know the order of succession if a president dies in office?***

Article 2. *The Executive*

SECTION 1. THE PRESIDENCY

1. Terms of Office The executive power shall be vested in a President of the United States of America. He shall hold his office during the term of four years and, together with the Vice-President, chosen for the same term, be elected as follows:

2. Electoral College Each state shall appoint, in such manner as the legislature thereof may direct, a number of electors, equal to the whole number of Senators and Representatives to which the state may be entitled in the Congress; but no Senator or Representative, or person holding an office of trust or profit under the United States, shall be appointed an elector.

3. Former Method of Electing President ~~The electors shall meet in their respective states, and vote by ballot for two persons, of whom one at least shall not be an inhabitant of the same state with themselves. And they shall make a list of all the persons voted for, and of the number of votes for each; which list they shall sign and certify, and transmit sealed to the seat of the government of the United States, directed to the President of the Senate. The President of the Senate shall, in the presence of the Senate and House of Representatives, open all the certificates, and the votes shall then be counted. The person having the greatest number of votes shall be the President, if such number be a majority of the whole number of electors appointed; and if there be more than one who have such majority, and have an equal number of votes, then the House of Representatives shall immediately choose by ballot one of them for President; and if no person have a majority, then from the five highest on the list the said house shall in like manner choose the President. But in choosing the President, the votes shall be taken by states, the representation from each state having one vote; a quorum for this purpose shall consist of a member or members from two thirds of the states, and a majority of all the states shall be necessary to a choice. In every case, after the choice of the President, the person having the greatest number of votes of the electors shall be the Vice-President. But if there should remain two or more who have equal votes, the Senate shall choose from them by ballot the Vice-President.~~

4. Election Day The Congress may determine the time of choosing the electors, and the day on which they shall give their votes; which day shall be the same throughout the United States.

5. Qualifications No person except a natural-born citizen, ~~or a citizen of the United States at the time of the adoption of this Constitution~~, shall be eligible to the office of President; neither shall any person be eligible to that office who shall not have attained to the age of thirty-five years, and been fourteen years a resident within the United States.

6. Succession In case of the removal of the President from office, or of his death, resignation, or inability to discharge the powers and duties of the said office, the same shall devolve on the Vice-President, and the Congress may by law provide for the case of removal, death,

TEACHING OPTION

Making Connections Across the Curriculum

U.S. Government The Presidential Succession Act, passed in 1886 and amended as necessary, determines who would assume the duties of president if the president and vice-president should die or become disabled. The order of succession for the next ten leaders follows.

1. Speaker of the House of Representatives
2. President pro tempore of the Senate
3. Secretary of state
4. Secretary of the treasury
5. Secretary of defense
6. Attorney general
7. Secretary of the interior
8. Secretary of agriculture
9. Secretary of commerce
10. Secretary of labor

Ask, What if the person designated to succeed does not meet the qualifications for president stated in the Constitution? *The presidency would pass to the next eligible member who fulfills those qualifications.*

resignation, or inability, both of the President and Vice-President, declaring what officer shall then act as President, and such officer shall act accordingly, until the disability be removed, or a President shall be elected.

7. Salary The President shall, at stated times, receive for his services a compensation, which shall neither be increased nor diminished during the period for which he shall have been elected, and he shall not receive within that period any other emolument from the United States, or any of them.

8. Oath of Office Before he enter on the execution of his office, he shall take the following oath or affirmation:—"I do solemnly swear (or affirm) that I will faithfully execute the office of President of the United States, and will to the best of my ability, preserve, protect and defend the Constitution of the United States."

SECTION 2. POWERS OF THE PRESIDENT

1. Military Powers The President shall be commander in chief of the army and navy of the United States, and of the militia of the several states, when called into the actual service of the United States; he may require the opinion, in writing, of the principal officer in each of the executive departments, upon any subject relating to the duties of their respective offices, and he shall have power to grant reprieves and pardons for offenses against the United States, except in cases of impeachment.

2. Treaties, Appointments He shall have power, by and with the advice and consent of the Senate, to make treaties, provided two thirds of the Senators present concur; and he shall nominate, and by and with the advice and consent of the Senate, shall appoint ambassadors, other public ministers and consuls, judges of the Supreme Court, and all other officers of the United States, whose appointments are not herein otherwise provided for, and which shall be established by law; but the Congress may by law vest the appointment of such inferior officers, as they think proper, in the President alone, in the courts of law, or in the heads of departments.

3. Vacancies The President shall have power to fill up all vacancies that may happen during the recess of the Senate, by granting commissions which shall expire at the end of their next session.

SECTION 3. PRESIDENTIAL DUTIES He shall from time to time give to the Congress information of the state of the Union, and recommend to their consideration such measures as he shall judge necessary and expedient; he may, on extraordinary occasions, convene both houses, or either of them, and in case of disagreement between them, with respect to the time of adjournment, he may adjourn them to such time as he shall think proper; he shall receive ambassadors and other public ministers; he shall take care that the laws be faithfully executed, and shall commission all the officers of the United States.

Constitutional Insight **Section 2.1** *Just how much authority does the president have as "commander in chief" of the armed forces?* While Congress has the power to declare war and to support and maintain an army and navy, only the president has the power to give orders to American military forces. There have been several instances in U.S. history when presidents have used that authority in spite of congressional wishes.

The president involved the armed forces of the United States in the Korean War from 1950 to 1953 without a congressional declaration of war. Likewise, American presidents involved hundreds of thousands of American troops in the Vietnam War.

K. THINK THROUGH THE CONSTITUTION ***Why is it important that the commander in chief of the armed forces of the United States be the president (a civilian) rather than a military general?***

NOW & THEN

THE WAR POWERS RESOLUTION (SECTION 2.1)

How much power the president has to make war has long been a subject of debate. In 1964, President Lyndon B. Johnson persuaded the Senate to pass the Gulf of Tonkin Resolution, which virtually gave Johnson a free hand in conducting the Vietnam War.

Reacting to criticism of the Vietnam War, Congress in 1973 enacted the War Powers Resolution, making the president more accountable to Congress for any military actions he or she might take. Every president since Richard Nixon has called the resolution unconstitutional. Nevertheless, within 48 hours of sending troops into an international crisis, every president has sent a report to Congress that included the information required by the War Powers Resolution.

In the Persian Gulf War of 1990–1991, President George Bush sent American troops into Kuwait without congressional action. Subsequently, Congress passed a joint resolution authorizing the use of American military forces in the Persian Gulf War.

In 1993, President Bill Clinton sent additional American forces into Somalia, where our country already had troops. He notified Congress of this action within the required 48 hours. As of 1996 the constitutionality of the War Powers Resolution had not been challenged or determined.

Constitutional Insight **Section 3** *Is it necessary for the president to deliver a State of the Union address before a joint session of Congress at the start of each legislative year?* The Constitution requires only that the president report to Congress on the state of the Union from time to time, and nowhere does it call for an annual address. That tradition started in 1913 with President Woodrow Wilson, who wanted to influence Congress to take action without delay on some legislation that he thought was important. Unlike most presidents since John Adams, President Wilson delivered his State of the Union addresses in person.

L. THINK THROUGH THE CONSTITUTION ***How does the president use the State of the Union address today?***

NOW & THEN
The War Powers Resolution

Critical Thinking: Drawing Conclusions How does the War Powers Resolution balance the power of the executive and legislative branches of government? Students might create a chart with the following headings to illustrate their answer.

Executive Power	Legislative Power

MORE ABOUT . . .
Executive Title

The proper form of address for the chief executive is "Mr. President" (or "Madam President"). George Washington chose this title, in spite of suggestions that he should assume a more noble one. For example, John Adams thought Washington should be called "His Highness, the President of the United States of America, and Protector of their Liberties."

THINK THROUGH THE CONSTITUTION
Possible Responses:

K. To make military decisions from a broader perspective; to safeguard the nation from becoming a military dictatorship.

L. To inform Congress of key domestic and foreign policies that the administration will address; to recommend legislative measures.

TEACHING OPTIONS

Making Connections Across the Curriculum

Music "Hail to the Chief who in triumph advances!" This line from Sir Walter Scott's narrative poem *The Lady of the Lake* became the inspiration for James Sanderson's song "Hail to the Chief." It made its debut as music paying homage to the nation's chief executive in 1821 at James Monroe's second-term inauguration ceremony. This song had become a tribute to the president by 1845, when James Polk assumed office. Today bands typically play the instrumental arrangement of "Hail to the Chief." You may wish to have students listen to the song on the following sound recording: United States Marine Band, *The President's Own,* Washington S. Marine Corps, 1983.

Teaching Less Proficient Readers

Organizing Information To help students keep track of the president's powers, put this organizational tree on the chalkboard and help them fill in the missing examples.

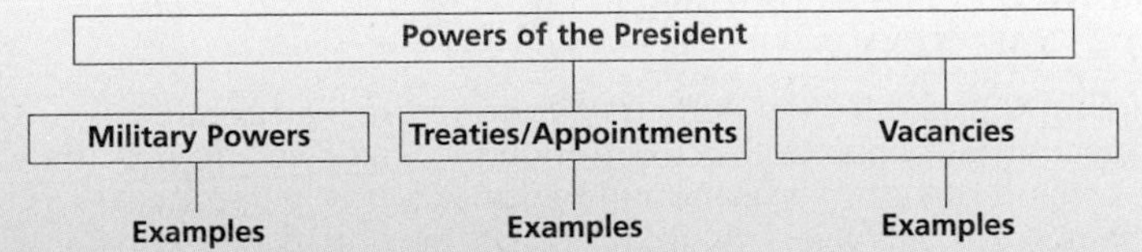

Article 3

OBJECTIVE

① To explain how judicial review expands the power of the judiciary.

FOCUS & MOTIVATE

▶ ***Starting with the Student***

- Have students think about courtroom scenes they have seen on television or at the movies. How would they describe the roles the judges played?

OBJECTIVE

① INSTRUCT

ARTICLE 3. THE JUDICIARY

▶ ***Discussing Key Ideas***

- The Constitution gives judicial power to the Supreme Court.
- Through judicial review, courts determine the constitutionality of laws or government actions.

FORMAL ASSESSMENT
Quiz: Articles 2 and 3, p. 30

HISTORY FROM VISUALS

The Checks and Balances of the Federal System

Reading the Chart Suggest to students that they read the chart by pairing branches to see how they check each other.

THINK THROUGH THE CONSTITUTION
Possible Response:
M. To ensure that laws and government actions do not violate the Constitution.

Although Andrew Johnson (the only president to be impeached) was impeached by an overwhelming vote of the House of Representatives in 1868, at his trial before the Senate he was found not guilty by just one vote.

ARTICLE 3

Constitutional Insight **Section 2.1** *What is judicial review? Is it the same as judicial power?* Actually, they are not the same. Judicial power is the authority to hear cases involving disputes over the law or the behavior of people. Judicial review, in contrast, is a court's passing judgment on the constitutionality of a law or government action that is being disputed. Interestingly, nowhere does the Constitution mention judicial review. There are places where it is implied (for example, in Section 2 of Article 6), but the only explicit description of the responsibility of the courts is the reference to judicial power in Section 1 of Article 3.

M. THINK THROUGH THE CONSTITUTION *Why is judicial review, although not mentioned in the Constitution, an important activity of the Supreme Court?*

The Supreme Court of the United States in 1996. In the front row *(left to right)* are Associate Justices Antonin Scalia and John Paul Stevens, Chief Justice William H. Rehnquist, and Associate Justices Sandra Day O'Connor and Anthony Kennedy. In the back row are Associate Justices Ruth Bader Ginsburg, David Souter, Clarence Thomas, and Stephen Breyer.

SECTION 4. IMPEACHMENT The President, Vice-President and all civil officers of the United States shall be removed from office on impeachment for, and conviction of, treason, bribery, or other high crimes and misdemeanors.

Article 3. *The Judiciary*

SECTION 1. FEDERAL COURTS AND JUDGES The judicial power of the United States shall be vested in one Supreme Court, and in such inferior courts as the Congress may from time to time ordain and establish. The judges, both of the Supreme and inferior courts, shall hold their offices during good behavior, and shall, at stated times, receive for their services a compensation, which shall not be diminished during their continuance in office.

SECTION 2. THE COURTS' AUTHORITY

1. General Authority The judicial power shall extend to all cases, in law and equity, arising under this Constitution, the laws of the United States, and treaties made, or which shall be made, under their authority;—to all cases affecting ambassadors, other public ministers and consuls;—to all cases of admiralty and maritime jurisdiction;—to controversies to which the United States shall be a party;—to controversies between two or more states;~~—between a state and citizens of another state~~;—between citizens of different states;—between citizens of the same state claiming lands under grants of different states, and between a state, or the citizens thereof, and foreign states, ~~citizens or subjects.~~

2. Supreme Court In all cases affecting ambassadors, other public ministers and consuls, and those in which a state shall be party, the Supreme Court shall have original jurisdiction. In all the other cases before mentioned, the Supreme Court shall have appellate jurisdiction, both as to law and fact, with such exceptions, and under such regulations, as the Congress shall make.

3. Trial by Jury The trial of all crimes, except in cases of impeachment, shall be by jury; and such trial shall be held in the state where the said crimes shall have been committed; but when not committed within any state, the trial shall be at such place or places as the Congress may by law have directed.

SECTION 3. TREASON

1. Definition Treason against the United States shall consist only in levying war against them, or in adhering to their enemies, giving them aid and comfort. No person shall be convicted of treason unless on the testimony of two witnesses to the same overt act, or on confession in open court.

2. Punishment The Congress shall have power to declare the punishment of treason, but no attainder of treason shall work corruption of blood, or forfeiture except during the life of the person attainted.

TEACHING OPTIONS

Teaching Gifted and Talented Students

Read aloud the following front-page headline from the *New York Times* of August 9, 1974:

NIXON RESIGNS
URGES A TIME OF 'HEALING';
FORD WILL TAKE OFFICE TODAY

Explain that the House Judiciary Committee's articles of impeachment against President Richard Nixon for high crimes and misdemeanors spurred his resignation. Have students research Nixon's alleged violations of the Constitution and report their findings to the class.

Making Global Connections

Judicial Review In Switzerland the power of judicial review rests with the people, rather than the courts. The Swiss are frequently at the polling booths, casting their ballots in nationwide referenda—a practice dating back to 1848. Their votes are the final word on the constitutionality of laws. What if a citizen disapproves of the parliament's passage of a law? One individual can pressure all Swiss residents to vote on it by convincing 50,000 people to sign a petition. Ask students if they consider Switzerland's procedure for judicial review better than the process of judicial review conducted by the courts in the United States.

The Checks and Balances of the Federal System

EXECUTIVE BRANCH

Checks on the Judicial Branch
- Appoints federal judges
- Can pardon or reprieve people convicted of federal crimes

Checks on the Legislative Branch
- Can veto bills of Congress
- Can call special sessions of Congress
- Can influence public opinion
- Can propose legislation

LEGISLATIVE BRANCH

Checks on the Executive Branch
- Congress can override a presidential veto
- Congress approves funding for presidential programs
- Congress can impeach and remove the president or other high officials
- Senate approves or rejects treaties
- Senate confirms or rejects federal appointments

Checks on the Judicial Branch
- Congress establishes lower federal courts
- Senate confirms or rejects appointments of judges
- Congress can impeach and remove federal judges

JUDICIAL BRANCH

Checks on the Executive Branch
- Appointed for life, federal judges are free from presidential control
- Can declare presidential actions unconstitutional

Checks on the Legislative Branch
- Can decide the meaning of laws
- Can declare acts of Congress unconstitutional

Article 4. *Relations Among States*

SECTION 1. STATE ACTS AND RECORDS Full faith and credit shall be given in each state to the public acts, records, and judicial proceedings of every other state. And the Congress may by general laws prescribe the manner in which such acts, records, and proceedings shall be proved, and the effect thereof.

SECTION 2. RIGHTS OF CITIZENS

1. Citizenship The citizens of each state shall be entitled to all privileges and immunities of citizens in the several states.

2. Extradition A person charged in any state with treason, felony, or other crime, who shall flee from justice, and be found in another state, shall on demand of the executive authority of the state from which he fled, be delivered up, to be removed to the state having jurisdiction of the crime.

3. Fugitive Slaves ~~No person held to service or labor in one state, under the laws thereof, escaping into another, shall, in consequence of any law or regulation therein, be discharged from such service or labor, but shall be delivered up on claim of the party to whom such service or labor may be due.~~

SECTION 3. NEW STATES

1. Admission New states may be admitted by the Congress into this Union; but no new state shall be formed or erected within the jurisdiction of any other state; nor any state be formed by the junction of two or more states, or parts of states, without the consent of the legislatures of the states concerned as well as of the Congress.

2. Congressional Authority The Congress shall have power to dispose of and make all needful rules and regulations respecting the territory or other property belonging to the United States; and nothing in this Constitution shall be so construed as to prejudice any claims of the United States, or of any particular state.

SECTION 4. GUARANTEES TO THE STATES The United States shall guarantee to every state in this Union a republican form of government, and shall protect each of them against invasion; and on application of the legislature, or of the executive (when the legislature cannot be convened), against domestic violence.

ARTICLE 4

Constitutional Insight **Section 2.1** *Why do college students attending public universities outside their state of residence have to pay higher tuition fees?* The Supreme Court has interpreted the "privileges and immunities" clause to allow higher tuition fees (and fees for hunting permits, etc.) for nonresidents when a state can give a "substantial reason" for the difference. Since state colleges and universities receive some financial support from the states' taxpayers, the difference is regarded as justified in most states. If a student establishes residency in the state, he or she can pay in-state tuition after one year.

N. THINK THROUGH THE CONSTITUTION ***Do you think it is fair that a nonresident must pay higher tuition fees at a state college than a resident of the state? Explain.***

Constitutional Insight **Section 3.1** *Should there be a West Virginia?* The Constitution states that "no new state shall be formed or erected within the jurisdiction of any other state" without the permission of the legislature of the state involved and of the Congress. Vermont, Kentucky, Tennessee, and Maine were created from territory taken from existing states, with the approval of the sitting legislatures. West Virginia, however, is a different story. During the Civil War, the residents of the westernmost counties of Virginia were angry with their state's decision to secede from the Union. They petitioned Congress to have their counties declared a distinct state. Congress agreed, and so the state of West Virginia was created. After the Civil War, the legislature of Virginia gave its formal approval, perhaps because it was in no position to dispute the matter.

O. THINK THROUGH THE CONSTITUTION ***Suppose a section of Texas should decide to become a new state today. Could it do this? Why or why not?***

Article 4

OBJECTIVE

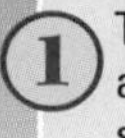
To describe how the states are interdependent and subject to the federal government.

FOCUS & MOTIVATE

▶ ***Starting with the Student***
- Ask, What would happen if criminals could escape punishment by fleeing to another state?

OBJECTIVE

① INSTRUCT

ARTICLE 4. RELATIONS AMONG STATES

▶ ***Discussing Key Ideas***
- States must respect one another's laws, records, and court rulings.
- U.S. citizens have equal rights in all states.
- Congress has authority over the states.

IN-DEPTH RESOURCES: UNIT 1
Guided Reading, p. 55

ACCESS FOR STUDENTS ACQUIRING ENGLISH
Guided Reading (Spanish), p. 37

THINK THROUGH THE CONSTITUTION
Possible Responses:

N. Yes—Higher tuition fees for nonresidents are fair because state tax dollars, which residents have to pay, help support state colleges. No—Based on Section 2.1, all U.S. citizens should be entitled to attend any state college nationwide without penalty of higher tuition fees.

O. Yes, if Congress and the legislature of Texas gave their approval.

TEACHING OPTION

Making Connections Across the Curriculum

Geography Floods, drought, hurricanes, earthquakes, tornadoes—all of these natural disasters can be classified as examples of "domestic violence." As ordained in Article 4, Section 4, the federal government guarantees that it will protect the states in the event of such disasters. The Federal Civil Defense Act of 1950 permits the president to declare a national disaster following these kinds of emergencies and to pave the way for supplying federal funds and aid to victims.

Have students research the natural disasters that are most likely to occur in their region of the country. For example, students who live along the San Andreas Fault in California might investigate earthquakes, while students who live in the Plains states might explore tornadoes. Encourage students to create visual aids, such as maps, diagrams, or cause-and-effect charts, to illustrate their findings.

Articles 5 and 6

OBJECTIVES

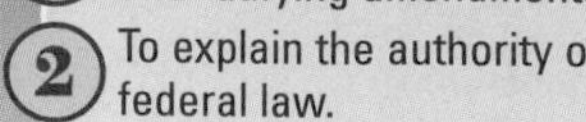

1. To cite ways of proposing and ratifying amendments.
2. To explain the authority of federal law.

SKILLBUILDER

- Interpreting charts, p. 98

FOCUS & MOTIVATE

▶ ***Starting with the Student***

- Do students think rules at home and school should be flexible? Why or why not?
- Baseball teams must bow to umpires' rulings. How does this situation compare to states' compliance with federal laws?

OBJECTIVE

① INSTRUCT

ARTICLE 5. AMENDING THE CONSTITUTION

▶ ***Discussing Key Ideas***

- The Constitution establishes guidelines for proposing and ratifying amendments.

OBJECTIVE

② INSTRUCT

ARTICLE 6. SUPREMACY OF THE NATIONAL GOVERNMENT

▶ ***Discussing Key Ideas***

- States yield to national law.

THINK THROUGH THE CONSTITUTION
Possible Response:
P. National disunity might result if U.S. citizens were subject to conflicting laws.

Amending the Constitution

PROPOSAL STAGE

- Two-thirds vote of members present in both houses of Congress (33 amendments proposed)

or

- National convention convened by Congress at request of two-thirds of state legislatures (no amendments proposed)

RATIFICATION STAGE

- Three-fourths of state legislatures (25 amendments ratified)

or

- Conventions in three-fourths of the states (one amendment, the 21st, ratified)

SKILLBUILDER **INTERPRETING CHARTS** ***Why does it take more votes to ratify an amendment than to propose one?***

Skillbuilder Answer The Framers of the Constitution wanted to make it more difficult to ratify amendments than to propose them, so that ideas could be considered but not too easily accepted.

Article 5. *Amending the Constitution*

The Congress, whenever two thirds of both houses shall deem it necessary, shall propose amendments to this Constitution, or, on the application of the legislatures of two thirds of the several states, shall call a convention for proposing amendments, which, in either case, shall be valid to all intents and purposes, as part of this Constitution, when ratified by the legislatures of three fourths of the several states, or by conventions in three fourths thereof, as the one or the other mode of ratification may be proposed by the Congress; provided ~~that no amendment which may be made prior to the year one thousand eight hundred and eight shall in any manner affect the first and fourth clauses in the ninth section of the first article; and that~~ no state, without its consent, shall be deprived of its equal suffrage in the Senate.

Article 6. *Supremacy of the National Government*

SECTION 1. VALID DEBTS All debts contracted and engagements entered into, before the adoption of this Constitution, shall be as valid against the United States under this Constitution, as under the Confederation.

SECTION 2. SUPREME LAW This Constitution, and the laws of the United States which shall be made in pursuance thereof; and all treaties made, or which shall be made, under the authority of the United States, shall be the supreme law of the land; and the judges in every state shall be bound thereby, anything in the constitution or laws of any state to the contrary notwithstanding.

SECTION 3. LOYALTY TO CONSTITUTION The Senators and Representatives before mentioned, and the members of the several state legislatures, and all executive and judicial officers, both of the United States and of the several states, shall be bound by oath or affirmation to support this Constitution; but no religious test shall ever be required as a qualification to any office or public trust under the United States.

ARTICLE 6

Constitutional Insight **Section 2** *Just how "supreme" is the "law of the land"?* The Constitution and all federal laws and treaties are the highest law of the land. All state constitutions and laws and all local laws rank below national law and cannot be enforced if they contradict national law. For example, if the United States enters into a treaty protecting migratory Canadian geese, the states must change their laws to fit the provisions of that agreement. That was the decision of the Supreme Court in the case of *Missouri* v. *Holland* (1920). The state of Missouri argued that the national government could not interfere with its power to regulate hunting within its borders, but the Supreme Court concluded that the treaty was a valid exercise of national power and therefore took priority over state and local laws. The states had to adjust their rules and regulations accordingly.

P. THINK THROUGH THE CONSTITUTION ***What would happen if the national law were not supreme?***

Block Schedule TEACHING OPTION **Time Needed: 40 Minutes**

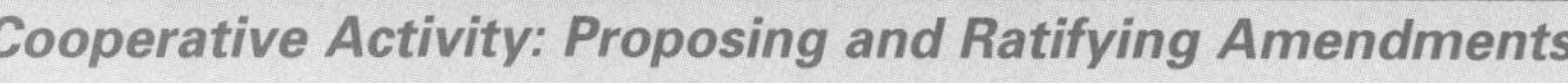

Cooperative Activity: Proposing and Ratifying Amendments

Task: Student groups will attempt to propose an amendment by two-thirds majority of the group and ratify the amendment by three-fourths majority of the class.

Purpose: To gain understanding of the amendment process.

Activity: Divide students into groups of six. Each group will propose an amendment by a two-thirds majority of its members. Each group will then present its amendment to the class for ratification. A three-fourths majority vote is required. Conclude with a class discussion of the following questions:

- Which was more difficult to achieve–a two-thirds majority to propose the amendment or a three-fourths majority to ratify it?
- Do you think the procedure for amending the Constitution provides enough flexibility for the document to change with the times? Why or why not?

ALTERNATIVE ASSESSMENT BOOK
Standards for Evaluating a Cooperative Activity

Article 7. *Ratification*

The ratification of the conventions of nine states shall be sufficient for the establishment of this Constitution between the states so ratifying the same.

Done in convention by the unanimous consent of the states present, the seventeenth day of September in the year of our Lord one thousand seven hundred and eighty-seven and of the independence of the United States of America the twelfth. In witness whereof we have hereunto subscribed our names.

George Washington*—President and deputy from Virginia*

NEW HAMPSHIRE: *John Langdon, Nicholas Gilman*

MASSACHUSETTS: *Nathaniel Gorham, Rufus King*

CONNECTICUT: *William Samuel Johnson, Roger Sherman*

NEW YORK: *Alexander Hamilton*

NEW JERSEY: *William Livingston, David Brearley, William Paterson, Jonathan Dayton*

PENNSYLVANIA: *Benjamin Franklin, Thomas Mifflin, Robert Morris, George Clymer, Thomas FitzSimons, Jared Ingersoll, James Wilson, Gouverneur Morris*

DELAWARE: *George Read, Gunning Bedford, Jr., John Dickinson, Richard Bassett, Jacob Broom*

MARYLAND: *James McHenry, Dan of St. Thomas Jenifer, Daniel Carroll*

VIRGINIA: *John Blair, James Madison, Jr.*

NORTH CAROLINA: *William Blount, Richard Dobbs Spaight, Hugh Williamson*

SOUTH CAROLINA: *John Rutledge, Charles Cotesworth Pinckney, Charles Pinckney, Pierce Butler*

GEORGIA: *William Few, Abraham Baldwin*

ARTICLE 7

Constitutional Insight *Why was ratification by only 9 states sufficient to put the Constitution into effect?* In taking such a momentous step as replacing one constitution (the Articles of Confederation) with another, the framers might have been expected to require the agreement of all 13 states. But the framers were political realists. They knew that they would have a difficult time winning approval of the proposed constitution from all 13 states. But they also knew that they had a good chance of getting 9 or 10 of the states "on board" and that the rest would follow. Their strategy worked, but just barely. Although they had the approval of 8 states by June 1788, 2 of the most important states—Virginia and New York—had not yet decided to ratify. Without the approval of these influential states, the new government would have had a difficult time surviving. Finally, by the end of July, both had given their blessing to the new constitution, but not without intense debate. And then there was the last holdout—Rhode Island. Not only had Rhode Island refused to send delegates to the Constitutional Convention in 1787, but it turned down ratification several times before finally giving its approval under a cloud of economic and even military threats from neighboring states. Rhode Island entered the Union reluctantly on May 29, 1790.

Q. THINK THROUGH THE CONSTITUTION ***Do you think all 50 states would ratify the Constitution today? Why or why not?***

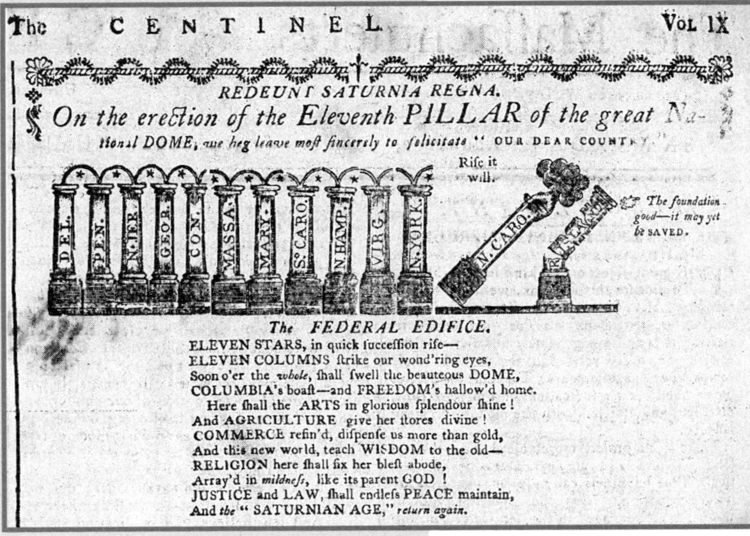

This cartoon celebrated the ratification of the Constitution by New York, the 11th state to ratify it. This left only North Carolina and Rhode Island to complete all 13 pillars of the federal structure.

Article 7

OBJECTIVE

1 To explain how the Constitution was ratified.

FOCUS & MOTIVATE

▶ ***Starting with the Student***

- Ask students belonging to school clubs if all members approve of their clubs' rules.

OBJECTIVE

1 INSTRUCT

ARTICLE 7. RATIFICATION

▶ ***Discussing Key Ideas***

- Ratification requires approval by nine states.

HISTORY FROM VISUALS

Political Cartoon

Reading the Cartoon Ask students to describe the pillars representing North Carolina and Rhode Island. *North Carolina's pillar is toppling, and Rhode Island's is cracking.*

Extension Point out that the 13 pillars are arranged in the order (from left to right) that these states ratified the Constitution.

FORMAL ASSESSMENT
Quiz: Articles 4–7, p. 31

THINK THROUGH THE CONSTITUTION

Possible Responses:

Q. Yes—All states would recognize the Constitution's value and flexibility. No—Unresolved differences over states' sovereignty and rights might emerge.

TEACHING OPTION

Making Connections Across Time

Durability and Flexibility of the Constitution Have students compare the following views of the Constitution. What does each of the quotes say about the document's durability and flexibility?

- "A Constitution is framed for ages to come, and is designed to approach immortality as nearly as human institutions can approach it. . . . The people made the Constitution, and the people can unmake it. It is the creature of their own will, and lives only by their will."
  John Marshall, *Cohens* v. *Virginia,* 1821
- "When the Constitution was first framed, I predicted that it would last fifty years. I was mistaken. . . . But I was mistaken only in point of time. The crash will come, but not so quick as I thought."
  Aaron Burr, 1835
- "Amendments to the Constitution ought to not be too frequently made; . . . [if] continually tinkered with it would lose all its prestige and dignity, and the old instrument would be lost sight of altogether in a short time."
  President Andrew Johnson, 1866

Bill of Rights

OBJECTIVE

1 To identify basic freedoms guaranteed by the first ten amendments.

FOCUS & MOTIVATE

▶ ***Starting with the Student***

- Ask students to name their rights as U.S. citizens. Then have them create a chart comparing the rights they cited with the Bill of Rights.

OBJECTIVE

1 INSTRUCT

BILL OF RIGHTS

▶ ***Discussing Key Ideas***

- The Bill of Rights protects individuals by limiting the power of the national government.

IN-DEPTH RESOURCES: UNIT 1
Guided Reading, p. 56

ACCESS FOR STUDENTS ACQUIRING ENGLISH
Guided Reading (Spanish), p. 38

THINK THROUGH THE CONSTITUTION
Possible Responses:

A. Sometimes one person's freedom of speech infringes on another's personal freedom.

B. Most oppose invasion of privacy and want protection against police brutality.

C. The verdict of the first trial would have no enduring validity.

BILL OF RIGHTS

Constitutional Insight **AMENDMENT 1** *Do Americans have an absolute right to free speech?* The right to free speech is not without limits. In the case of *Schenck* v. *the United States* (1919), Justice Oliver Wendell Holmes wrote that this right does "not protect a man in falsely shouting fire in a theatre and causing panic." Thus, there are some forms of speech that are unprotected by the First Amendment. This allows Congress to make laws regarding certain types of expression.

A. THINK THROUGH THE CONSTITUTION ***Why is there controversy over freedom of speech today?***

Constitutional Insight **AMENDMENT 4** *Can the police search your car without a court-issued search warrant when they stop you for speeding?* The answer, according to Supreme Court decisions, depends on whether they have good reasons—called "probable cause"—for doing so. If a state trooper notices bloody clothing on the back seat of a vehicle she stops for a traffic violation, there might be probable cause for her to insist on searching the vehicle. There is probably not sufficient reason for a search if the trooper is merely suspicious of the driver because of the way he is acting. In such cases, the trooper may make a casual request, such as "Do you mind if I look inside your vehicle?" If the answer is no, then according to the Court, the driver has waived his or her constitutional right against unreasonable searches.

B. THINK THROUGH THE CONSTITUTION ***Why do you think the right against unreasonable searches and seizures is highly important to most people?***

Constitutional Insight **AMENDMENT 5** *Can you be tried twice for the same offense?* The prohibition against "double jeopardy" protects you from having the same charge twice brought against you for the same offense, but you can be retried on different charges related to that offense.

C. THINK THROUGH THE CONSTITUTION ***What do you think could happen if a person could be tried twice for the same offense?***

Bill of Rights: Amendments 1–10

Passed by Congress September 25, 1789. Ratified December 15, 1791.

AMENDMENT 1. RELIGIOUS AND POLITICAL FREEDOM (1791) Congress shall make no law respecting an establishment of religion, or prohibiting the free exercise thereof; or abridging the freedom of speech, or of the press; or the right of the people peaceably to assemble, and to petition the government for a redress of grievances.

AMENDMENT 2. RIGHT TO BEAR ARMS (1791) A well-regulated militia being necessary to the security of a free state, the right of the people to keep and bear arms shall not be infringed.

AMENDMENT 3. QUARTERING TROOPS (1791) No soldier shall, in time of peace, be quartered in any house without the consent of the owner, nor in time of war, but in a manner to be prescribed by law.

AMENDMENT 4. SEARCH AND SEIZURE (1791) The right of the people to be secure in their persons, houses, papers, and effects, against unreasonable searches and seizures, shall not be violated, and no warrants shall issue, but upon probable cause, supported by oath or affirmation, and particularly describing the place to be searched, and the persons or things to be seized.

AMENDMENT 5. RIGHTS OF ACCUSED PERSONS (1791) No person shall be held to answer for a capital or otherwise infamous crime, unless on a presentment or indictment of a grand jury, except in cases arising in the land or naval forces, or in the militia, when in actual service in time of war or public danger; nor shall any person be subject for the same offense to be twice put in jeopardy of life or limb; nor shall be compelled in any criminal case to be a witness against himself, nor be deprived of life, liberty, or property, without due process of law; nor shall private property be taken for public use, without just compensation.

TEACHING OPTION

Skillbuilder Mini-Lesson: Clarifying

Explaining the Skill Clarifying, or confirming one's understanding of what someone else has said, is a basic skill in communicating and in studying any subject. Clarifying readings from primary sources such as the Constitution should first involve defining unfamiliar words and working through complicated sentence structures to restate the ideas in simpler language.

Applying the Skill **Understanding the Constitution** Ask students to read the first amendment on this page, then answer the following questions:

1. What does *respecting* mean? *about, in relation to*
2. What word does *thereof* refer to? *religion*
3. What does *abridging* mean? *to curtail or diminish*
4. What is a redress of grievances? *righting a wrong*
5. What rights are covered in this amendment? *Freedom of religion; freedom of speech and the press; and freedom to hold meetings and to ask the government to solve problems or make up for wrongdoings.*

IN-DEPTH RESOURCES: UNIT 1
Skillbuilder Practice: Clarifying, p. 57

AMENDMENT 6. RIGHT TO A SPEEDY, PUBLIC TRIAL (1791) In all criminal prosecutions, the accused shall enjoy the right to a speedy and public trial, by an impartial jury of the state and district wherein the crime shall have been committed, which district shall have been previously ascertained by law, and to be informed of the nature and cause of the accusation; to be confronted with the witnesses against him; to have compulsory process for obtaining witnesses in his favor, and to have the assistance of counsel for his defense.

AMENDMENT 7. TRIAL BY JURY IN CIVIL CASES (1791) In suits at common law, where the value in controversy shall exceed twenty dollars, the right of trial by jury shall be preserved, and no fact tried by a jury shall be otherwise reexamined in any court of the United States, than according to the rules of the common law.

AMENDMENT 8. LIMITS OF FINES AND PUNISHMENTS (1791) Excessive bail shall not be required, nor excessive fines imposed, nor cruel and unusual punishments inflicted.

These people are holding a candlelight vigil to protest capital punishment (the death penalty) as cruel and unusual, an issue the Supreme Court has addressed in relation to the Eighth Amendment.

AMENDMENT 9. RIGHTS OF PEOPLE (1791) The enumeration in the Constitution, of certain rights, shall not be construed to deny or disparage others retained by the people.

AMENDMENT 10. POWERS OF STATES AND PEOPLE (1791) The powers not delegated to the United States by the Constitution, nor prohibited by it to the states, are reserved to the states respectively, or to the people.

Constitutional Insight **AMENDMENT 6** *What are the Miranda rights?* The term comes from the Supreme Court's decision in *Miranda* v. *Arizona* (1966), in which the justices established basic rules that the police must follow when questioning a suspect. If suspected, you must be told that you have a right to remain silent and that anything you say "can and will" be used against you. You also need to be informed that you have a right to an attorney and that the attorney may be present during questioning.

D. THINK THROUGH THE CONSTITUTION *How do the Miranda rights protect you?*

Constitutional Insight **AMENDMENT 8** *Is the death penalty "cruel and unusual punishment"?* This question was tackled by the Supreme Court in *Furman* v. *Georgia* (1972), a case in which a majority of the justices declared capital punishment unconstitutional. At least two of the justices in the majority felt that the death penalty was inherently cruel and unusual and thus in violation of the Eighth Amendment. Three other members of the Court felt that the death penalty was unconstitutional because it was not applied consistently with regard to race, gender, and other factors. In the case of *Gregg* v. *Georgia* (1976), however, the Court declared that punishment by death does not inherently violate the Eighth Amendment. Today a majority of states, and the federal government, sanction some forms of capital punishment in their legal codes.

E. THINK THROUGH THE CONSTITUTION *Do you think the death penalty is cruel and unusual punishment? Explain your position.*

Constitutional Insight **AMENDMENT 9** *Do you have a right to privacy?* Until 1965, no such right had ever been explicitly stated by the courts. That year, in the case of *Griswold* v. *Connecticut*, the Court said there is an implied right of American citizens to make certain personal choices without interference from the government; this case concerned the right to use birth control. Years later, in *Roe* v. *Wade* (1973), the same logic was used to declare unconstitutional a Texas law restricting a woman's right to an abortion in the first stages of pregnancy. Since that decision, both the right to privacy and abortion rights have become the focus of major political controversies.

F. THINK THROUGH THE CONSTITUTION *How do you define the right to privacy?*

MORE ABOUT . . .
Amendment 6

The Sixth Amendment guarantees trial by an impartial jury from the place where the crime was committed. Today, pretrial media coverage may make it difficult for potential jurors to avoid forming opinions before hearing the evidence. In such cases, the court may grant a change of venue, which allows the case to be tried in a different location.

THINK THROUGH THE CONSTITUTION
Possible Responses:

D. They protect citizens from being tricked, led, or forced into divulging information that might be used to convict them of a crime.

E. Yes—too extreme a measure to deter crime; conflicts with many people's moral and ethical beliefs. No—justifiable punishment for murder conviction; less cruel than life imprisonment.

F. The guarantee that government will not intrude in people's personal lives and dictate their decisions.

TEACHING OPTION

Making Global Connections

The United Nations Stance on Human Rights In 1948, the United Nations General Assembly adopted the Universal Declaration of Human Rights. This document sets forth the basic privileges and freedoms of every person in the world. The preamble states in part that "recognition of the inherent dignity and of the equal and inalienable rights of all members of the human family is the foundation of freedom, justice and peace in the world."

In 1989, the United Nations adopted the Convention on the Rights of the Child, consisting of 41 articles of rights based on this premise: "[T]he child, by reason of his physical and mental immaturity, needs special safeguards and care. . . . [I]n all countries of the world, there are children living in exceptionally difficult situations." Children's rights proclaimed in the articles include education, health and medical care, and liberty.

Have students examine the Universal Declaration of Human Rights and the articles in the Convention on the Rights of the Child and compare them with the U.S. Bill of Rights.

Amendments 11–27

OBJECTIVE

① To summarize Constitutional Amendments 11–27.

FOCUS & MOTIVATE

▶ ***Starting with the Student***

- Ask students to think about how parents change the standards for their children's behavior as time passes.
- Why do parents drop some old rules and create new ones?

OBJECTIVE

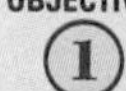 **INSTRUCT**

AMENDMENTS 11–27

▶ ***Discussing Key Ideas***

- Amendments 11–27 reflect ways the Constitution has developed to meet the changing needs of society and historical trends.
- Amendments 15, 19, and 26 give voting rights to specific groups.

THINK THROUGH THE CONSTITUTION

Possible Responses:

A. Reflected the growing role of political parties in nominating presidential and vice-presidential candidates; ensured that the president and vice-president belong to the same party.

Constitutional Insight **AMENDMENT 12** *How did the election of 1800 lead to the Twelfth Amendment?* The election ended in a tie vote between the Republican running mates, Thomas Jefferson and Aaron Burr, and it therefore had to be decided by the House of Representatives. Finally, Alexander Hamilton decided that his political enemy Jefferson would make a better president than Burr, and the election was decided in Jefferson's favor on the House's 36th ballot. Almost immediately Hamilton and others designed an amendment that established that the presidential electors would vote for both a presidential and a vice-presidential candidate. This amendment prevents a repeat of the problem in the 1800 election.

A. THINK THROUGH THE CONSTITUTION ***Why is the Twelfth Amendment important?***

Amendments 11–27

AMENDMENT 11. LAWSUITS AGAINST STATES (1798) Passed by Congress March 4, 1794. Ratified February 7, 1795. Proclaimed 1798.

Note: Article 3, Section 2, of the Constitution was modified by the Eleventh Amendment.

The judicial power of the United States shall not be construed to extend to any suit in law or equity, commenced or prosecuted against one of the United States by citizens of another state, or by citizens or subjects of any foreign state.

AMENDMENT 12. ELECTION OF EXECUTIVES (1804) Passed by Congress December 9, 1803. Ratified June 15, 1804.

Note: A portion of Article 2, Section 1, of the Constitution was superseded by the Twelfth Amendment.

The electors shall meet in their respective states and vote by ballot for President and Vice-President, one of whom, at least, shall not be an inhabitant of the same state with themselves; they shall name in their ballots the person voted for as President, and in distinct ballots the person voted for as Vice-President, and they shall make distinct lists of all persons voted for as President, and of all persons voted for as Vice-President, and of the number of votes for each, which lists they shall sign and certify, and transmit sealed to the seat of the government of the United States, directed to the President of the Senate;—the President of the Senate shall, in the presence of the Senate and House of Representatives, open all the certificates and the votes shall then be counted;—the person having the greatest number of votes for President shall be the President, if such number be a majority of the whole number of electors appointed; and if no person have such majority, then from the persons having the highest numbers not exceeding three on the list of those voted for as President, the House of Representatives shall choose immediately, by ballot, the President. But in choosing the President, the votes shall be taken by states, the representation from each state having one vote; a quorum for this purpose shall consist of a member or members from two thirds of the states, and a majority of all the states shall be necessary to a choice. And if the House of Representatives shall not choose a President whenever the right of choice shall devolve upon them, ~~before the fourth day of March next following~~, then the Vice-President shall act as President, as in the case of the death or other constitutional disability of the President. The person having the greatest number of votes as Vice-President shall be the Vice-President, if such number be a majority of the whole number of electors appointed, and if no person have a majority, then from the two highest numbers on the list, the Senate shall choose the Vice-President; a quorum for the purpose shall consist of two thirds of the whole number of Senators, and a majority of the whole number shall be necessary to a choice. But no person constitutionally ineligible to the office of President shall be eligible to that of Vice-President of the United States.

AMENDMENT 13. SLAVERY ABOLISHED (1865) Passed by Congress January 31, 1865. Ratified December 6, 1865.

Note: A portion of Article 4, Section 2, of the Constitution was superseded by the Thirteenth Amendment.

TEACHING OPTION

Teaching Less Proficient Readers

Summarizing Main Ideas Pair less proficient readers with more proficient readers to summarize the key points of Amendments 11–27. Have student pairs follow these steps.

1. **Skim** pages 102–107 together, noting the boldfaced titles of the amendments and sections.
2. **Closely read** each amendment, one at a time, along with any accompanying Constitutional Insight.
3. **Rewrite** the title of each amendment as a main-idea sentence that highlights the most important concept.

To help students get started, you may wish to write some examples on the chalkboard as models:

Amendment 12: Presidential electors will cast votes for president and vice-president on separate ballots.

Amendment 13: Slavery must end in the United States and its territories.

Amendment 14: All native-born and naturalized Americans are granted citizenship and will enjoy the privileges of equal protection under the law.

Section 1 Neither slavery nor involuntary servitude, except as a punishment for crime whereof the party shall have been duly convicted, shall exist within the United States, or any place subject to their jurisdiction.

Section 2 Congress shall have power to enforce this article by appropriate legislation.

AMENDMENT 14. CIVIL RIGHTS (1868) Passed by Congress June 13, 1866. Ratified July 9, 1868.

Note: Article 1, Section 2, of the Constitution was modified by Section 2 of the Fourteenth Amendment.

Section 1 All persons born or naturalized in the United States, and subject to the jurisdiction thereof, are citizens of the United States and of the state wherein they reside. No state shall make or enforce any law which shall abridge the privileges or immunities of citizens of the United States; nor shall any state deprive any person of life, liberty, or property, without due process of law; nor deny to any person within its jurisdiction the equal protection of the laws.

Section 2 Representatives shall be apportioned among the several states according to their respective numbers, counting the whole number of persons in each state, ~~excluding Indians not taxed~~. But when the right to vote at any election for the choice of electors for President and Vice-President of the United States, Representatives in Congress, the executive and judicial officers of a state, or the members of the legislature thereof, is denied to any of the ~~male~~ inhabitants of such state, ~~being twenty-one years of age,~~ and citizens of the United States, or in any way abridged, except for participation in rebellion, or other crime, the basis of representation therein shall be reduced in the proportion which the number of such ~~male~~ citizens shall bear to the whole number of ~~male~~ citizens ~~twenty-one years of age~~ in such state.

Section 3 No person shall be a Senator or Representative in Congress, or elector of President and Vice-President, or hold any office, civil or military, under the United States, or under any state, who, having previously taken an oath, as a member of Congress, or as an officer of the United States, or as a member of any state legislature, or as an executive or judicial officer of any state, to support the Constitution of the United States, shall have engaged in insurrection or rebellion against the same, or given aid or comfort to the enemies thereof. But Congress may, by a vote of two thirds of each house, remove such disability.

Section 4 The validity of the public debt of the United States, authorized by law, including debts incurred for payment of pensions and bounties for services in suppressing insurrection or rebellion, shall not be questioned. But neither the United States nor any state shall assume or pay any debt or obligation incurred in aid of insurrection or rebellion against the United States, or any claim for the loss or emancipation of any slave; but all such debts, obligations and claims shall be held illegal and void.

Section 5 The Congress shall have power to enforce, by appropriate legislation, the provisions of this article.

Constitutional Insight **AMENDMENT 14, Section 1** *Which personal status takes priority—that of U.S. citizen or that of state citizen?* The Fourteenth Amendment firmly notes that Americans are citizens of both the nation and the states but that no state can "abridge the privileges or immunities" of U.S. citizens, deprive them "of life, liberty, or property, without due process of law," or deny them "equal protection of the laws."

What does it mean to have "equal protection of the laws"? The laws of the national government and those of the states apply in the same way to all citizens. The Supreme Court has declared that not only does the due-process clause of the Fifth Amendment apply to the states as well as to the national government, but other parts of the Bill of Rights, such as that protecting freedom of speech, also apply. The civil rights movement received a boost from the Supreme Court's decision in *Brown* v. *Board of Education of Topeka, Kansas* (1954), which declared that the legal segregation of schools and, by implication, other public services and facilities was unconstitutional. The Court reasoned that "separate facilities are inherently unequal."

B. THINK THROUGH THE CONSTITUTION *Do you agree or disagree with the Supreme Court's decision that separate facilities are unequal? Explain your position.*

The lawyers who successfully challenged segregation in the *Brown* v. *Board of Education* case in 1954 included *(left to right)* George E. C. Hayes, Thurgood Marshall, and James M. Nabrit.

MORE ABOUT . . .

Thurgood Marshall (1908–1993)

Reacting to the *Brown* v. *Board of Education* ruling, Thurgood Marshall (pictured on this page) declared, "I was so happy, I was numb." The outcome of the case—Marshall's most stunning victory up to that time—heralded his brilliant legal career to come. In 1967, he became the first African American to serve as a Supreme Court justice. He dedicated his life to championing civil rights and battling racial injustice.

IN-DEPTH RESOURCES: UNIT 1
American Lives: Thurgood Marshall, p. 61.

THINK THROUGH THE CONSTITUTION
Possible Responses:
B. Agree—if separate facilities vary widely in quality and are vehicles for fostering discrimination. Disagree—if separate facilities are uniform in quality.

TEACHING OPTIONS

Making Connections Across Cultures

Korematsu* v. *United States After the Japanese attack on Pearl Harbor in 1941, the U.S. government moved 120,000 Japanese Americans to internment camps. Two-thirds of these people were native-born U.S. citizens. Because of their Japanese heritage, the government claimed they were a security risk. In *Korematsu* v. *United States* (1944), the Supreme Court upheld internment as a justifiable wartime measure. In 1988, however, Congress made a public apology and paid $20,000 to each person who had been sent to a government camp. Ask students which parts of the Constitution apply to this case. *Possible Responses: Article 1, Section 9; Amendments 5, 14.*

Exploring Themes

Civil Rights In the 1960s, the government began promoting affirmative action to help many African Americans, women, and other minorities gain education and jobs. Affirmative-action programs involve making special efforts to hire or enroll groups that have suffered from discrimination in the past. In the late 1970s, though, some people began to criticize these programs as "reverse discrimination" that set hiring or enrollment quotas depriving whites of opportunities. The fate of affirmative action is yet to be decided. Ask students how affirmative action might have made up for past violations of civil rights.

MORE ABOUT . . .
Income Tax

A pay-as-you-go tax plan began in 1913. It provided for employers to withhold tax from employees' paychecks and send the money directly to the Internal Revenue Service. On April 15 of each year, taxpayers file a tax return stating how much taxable income they received the previous year. If the amount withheld is less than they are required to pay according to a tax rate schedule, they must pay additional taxes. If it is more than they are required to pay, they receive a refund.

THINK THROUGH THE CONSTITUTION
Possible Responses:

C. Reasons include unawareness of candidates and issues; voter apathy.

D. Yes— provides revenue to support federal government and its programs. No—provides federal government with the incentive to overspend at the taxpayers' expense; can be imposed unfairly.

E. The senators are more directly responsible to voters.

F. Yes—to help ensure that citizens adhere to the same high standards of ethical behavior. No—to avoid possible invasion of privacy.

Constitutional Insight **AMENDMENT 15** *Can you be denied the right to vote?* The Fifteenth Amendment prohibits the United States or any state from keeping citizens from voting because of race or color or because they were once slaves. However, a person convicted of a crime can be denied the right to vote, as can someone found to be mentally incompetent.

C. THINK THROUGH THE CONSTITUTION ***Why do you think so many people do not exercise the right to vote?***

Constitutional Insight **AMENDMENT 16** *How has the ability of Congress to impose taxes been amended?* The Sixteenth Amendment permits a federal income tax and in so doing changes Article 1, Section 2, Clause 3, and Section 9, Clause 4, by stating that Congress has the power to levy an income tax, which is a direct tax, on people without apportioning such a tax among the states according to their populations.

D. THINK THROUGH THE CONSTITUTION ***Do you think Congress should have the power to impose an income tax on the people of the nation? Explain your answer.***

Constitutional Insight **AMENDMENT 17** *How has the way senators are elected been changed?* The Seventeenth Amendment changes Article 1, Section 3, Clause 2, by stating that senators shall be elected by the people of each state rather than by the state legislatures.

E. THINK THROUGH THE CONSTITUTION ***Why is the direct election of senators by the people of each state important?***

Constitutional Insight **AMENDMENT 18** *Besides its being the only amendment to have been repealed, what is distinctive about the Prohibition amendment?* So far, it is the only amendment that has dealt directly with a public policy issue. The failure of Prohibition is often cited by opponents of proposed constitutional amendments that seek to change people's behavior.

F. THINK THROUGH THE CONSTITUTION ***Do you think Congress should try to legislate morality? Why or why not?***

Federal agents prepare to smash containers of illegal whiskey.

AMENDMENT 15. RIGHT TO VOTE (1870) Passed by Congress February 26, 1869. Ratified February 3, 1870.

Section 1 The right of citizens of the United States to vote shall not be denied or abridged by the United States or by any state on account of race, color, or previous condition of servitude.

Section 2 The Congress shall have power to enforce this article by appropriate legislation.

AMENDMENT 16. INCOME TAX (1913) Passed by Congress July 12, 1909. Ratified February 3, 1913.

Note: Article 1, Section 9, of the Constitution was modified by the Sixteenth Amendment.

The Congress shall have power to lay and collect taxes on incomes, from whatever source derived, without apportionment among the several states, and without regard to any census or enumeration.

AMENDMENT 17. DIRECT ELECTION OF SENATORS (1913) Passed by Congress May 13, 1912. Ratified April 8, 1913.

Note: Article 1, Section 3, of the Constitution was modified by the Seventeenth Amendment.

Clause 1 The Senate of the United States shall be composed of two Senators from each state, elected by the people thereof, for six years; and each Senator shall have one vote. The electors in each state shall have the qualifications requisite for electors of the most numerous branch of the state legislatures.

Clause 2 When vacancies happen in the representation of any state in the Senate, the executive authority of such state shall issue writs of election to fill such vacancies: Provided, that the legislature of any state may empower the executive thereof to make temporary appointments until the people fill the vacancies by election as the legislature may direct.

Clause 3 This amendment shall not be so construed as to affect the election or term of any Senator chosen before it becomes valid as part of the Constitution.

AMENDMENT 18. PROHIBITION (1919) Passed by Congress December 18, 1917. Ratified January 16, 1919. Repealed by Amendment 21.

Section 1 ~~After one year from the ratification of this article the manufacture, sale, or transportation of intoxicating liquors within, the importation thereof into, or the exportation thereof from the United States and all territory subject to the jurisdiction thereof for beverage purposes is hereby prohibited.~~

Section 2 ~~The Congress and the several states shall have concurrent power to enforce this article by appropriate legislation.~~

Section 3 ~~This article shall be inoperative unless it shall have been ratified as an amendment to the Constitution by the legislatures of the several states, as provided in the Constitution, within seven years from the date of the submission hereof to the states by the Congress.~~

TEACHING OPTION

Making Connections Across the Curriculum

Film In 1927, moviegoers flocked to see *Underworld,* featuring Chicago mobsters who reaped huge profits as bootleggers—providers of illegal liquor. This film set the stage for a series of gangster films to follow. They portrayed the lawlessness and rise of organized crime stemming from the rampant violation of the Eighteenth Amendment. In real life, hoodlums like Al Capone controlled large-scale bootlegging operations. On the silver screen, characters modeled after Al Capone and his thugs masterminded crime waves and struggled to outsmart federal agents. Among the most popular films were *Little Caesar* (1930), *The Public Enemy* (1931), and *Scarface* (1932).

Though actual bootleggers became extinct with the repeal of Prohibition in 1933, fictional bootleggers still played leading roles in gangster films until the end of the decade. The movie *The Roaring Twenties,* released in 1939, was one of the last films to glamorize the era of speakeasies and "bathtub gin."

AMENDMENT 19. WOMAN SUFFRAGE (1920) Passed by Congress June 4, 1919. Ratified August 18, 1920.

Clause 1 The right of citizens of the United States to vote shall not be denied or abridged by the United States or by any state on account of sex.

Clause 2 Congress shall have power to enforce this article by appropriate legislation.

AMENDMENT 20. "LAME DUCK" SESSIONS (1933) Passed by Congress March 2, 1932. Ratified January 23, 1933.

Note: Article 1, Section 4, of the Constitution was modified by Section 2 of this amendment. In addition, a portion of the Twelfth Amendment was superseded by Section 3.

Section 1 The terms of the President and Vice-President shall end at noon on the 20th day of January, and the terms of Senators and Representatives at noon on the 3rd day of January, of the years in which such terms would have ended if this article had not been ratified; and the terms of their successors shall then begin.

Section 2 The Congress shall assemble at least once in every year, and such meeting shall begin at noon on the 3rd day of January, unless they shall by law appoint a different day.

Section 3 If, at the time fixed for the beginning of the term of the President, the President elect shall have died, the Vice-President elect shall become President. If a President shall not have been chosen before the time fixed for the beginning of his term, or if the President elect shall have failed to qualify, then the Vice-President elect shall act as President until a President shall have qualified; and the Congress may by law provide for the case wherein neither a President elect nor a Vice-President elect shall have qualified, declaring who shall then act as President, or the manner in which one who is to act shall be selected, and such person shall act accordingly until a President or Vice-President shall have qualified.

Section 4 The Congress may by law provide for the case of the death of any of the persons from whom the House of Representatives may choose a President whenever the right of choice shall have devolved upon them, and for the case of the death of any of the persons from whom the Senate may choose a Vice-President whenever the right of choice shall have devolved upon them.

Section 5 Sections 1 and 2 shall take effect on the 15th day of October following the ratification of this article.

Section 6 This article shall be inoperative unless it shall have been ratified as an amendment to the Constitution by the legislatures of three fourths of the several states within seven years from the date of its submission.

AMENDMENT 21. REPEAL OF PROHIBITION (1933) Passed by Congress February 20, 1933. Ratified December 5, 1933.

Section 1 The eighteenth article of amendment to the Constitution of the United States is hereby repealed.

Section 2 The transportation or importation into any state, territory, or possession of the United States for delivery or use therein of intoxicating liquors, in violation of the laws thereof, is hereby prohibited.

Constitutional Insight **AMENDMENT 19** *When did women first get the right to vote in the United States?* Women had the right to vote in the state of New Jersey between 1776 and 1807. In the late 19th century, some states and territories began to extend full or limited suffrage to women. Then, in 1920, the Nineteenth Amendment prohibited the United States or any state from denying women the right to vote.

G. THINK THROUGH THE CONSTITUTION *How does the right of women to vote affect politics today?*

Constitutional Insight **AMENDMENT 20** *Why is the Twentieth Amendment usually called the lame duck amendment?* A lame duck is a person who continues to hold office after his or her replacement has been elected. Such a person is called a lame duck because he or she no longer has any strong political influence. The Twentieth Amendment reduces the time between the election of a new president and vice-president in November and their assumption of the offices, which it sets at January 20 instead of March 4. It also reduces the time new members of Congress must wait to take their seats from 13 months to about 2 months. They are now seated on January 3 following the November election. As a result, the lame duck period is now quite short.

H. THINK THROUGH THE CONSTITUTION *Why may the framers have specified a longer lame duck period?*

On January 20, 1937, President Roosevelt took the oath of office for his second term. This was the first time the inauguration took place on January 20, thanks to the Twentieth Amendment.

Constitutional Insight **AMENDMENT 21** *What is unique about the Twenty-first Amendment?* Besides being the only one that explicitly repeals another amendment, it was the first, and is so far the only, one to have been ratified by the state convention method outlined in Article 5. Congress, probably fearing that state legislatures would not deal swiftly with the issue of repeal, chose to have each state call a special convention to consider the amendment. The strategy worked well, for the elected delegates to the conventions represented public opinion on the issue and ratified the amendment without delay.

I. THINK THROUGH THE CONSTITUTION *Why is it necessary to pass another amendment to revoke or remove an existing amendment?*

MORE ABOUT . . .
Woman Suffrage

Although American women had campaigned for the right to vote since the mid-1800s, they were not the first to receive that right. New Zealand granted woman suffrage in 1893, and Australian women could vote in national elections in 1902.

THINK THROUGH THE CONSTITUTION
Possible Responses:

G. Political effects include higher voter turnout, more women candidates and office holders, and greater focus on women's issues.

H. In the late 1700s representatives spent a much longer time traveling from their home states to the nation's capital.

I. To ensure an orderly legal procedure.

TEACHING OPTION

Connecting to Themes

Women in America By 1920 women had full voting rights in 15 states. Twelve other states granted them the right to vote in presidential elections. The Nineteenth Amendment had strong support in the House of Representatives in 1918. One representative left his wife's deathbed, at her request, to vote for the amendment. Another representative was brought in on a stretcher. The amendment passed the House but was defeated in the Senate until 1919.

Carrie Lane Chapman Catt became president of the National American Woman Suffrage Association in 1900. After the Nineteenth Amendment went into effect in 1920, Catt shifted the organization's focus to voter education and formed the League of Women Voters. This organization sponsored the presidential debates in 1976, 1980, and 1984.

NOW & THEN

Congressional Term Limits

Critical Thinking: Forming Opinions The issue of restricting the term of office for senators and representatives still sparks debate. Those who serve for several terms often bring with them a wealth of legislative experience and contribute to the stability of Congress. Do you think forcing experienced leaders to leave Congress because of term limits would disrupt this stability? Why or why not?

THINK THROUGH THE CONSTITUTION

Possible Responses:

J. Agree—curbs presidential powers; limits one-party control of White House; avoids possibility of dictatorial rule. Disagree—extended terms desirable during crises such as war; disrupts agenda of an effective president.

K. Yes—Washington, D.C., residents would have essentially the same privileges as the citizens of the nation's 50 states. No—The capital's size and population are not comparable to those of the other 50 states.

L. Since poll taxes can no longer be used to keep African Americans from voting, more African-American candidates have won elections.

Constitutional Insight **AMENDMENT 22** *Why are presidents subject to a two-term limit?* The Twenty-second Amendment legislates the tradition of a two-term limit started by George Washington and broken by Franklin Roosevelt (elected to four terms).

J. THINK THROUGH THE CONSTITUTION ***Do you agree or disagree that a president of the United States should serve no more than two terms? Explain your answer.***

NOW & THEN

CONGRESSIONAL TERM LIMITS (AMENDMENT 22)

In the early 1990s there was a national movement to establish congressional term limits. However, in 1995, the Supreme Court struck down all state laws limiting congressional terms, stating that they were unconstitutional because they did not deal with age, residency, or citizenship.

As a result of the Supreme Court decision, Congress would need to pass a constitutional amendment to establish congressional term limits. In 1947 Congress did pass an amendment—the 22nd—to limit a president to two terms.

Constitutional Insight **AMENDMENT 23** *Why were residents of the District of Columbia without a vote in presidential elections?* First, the district was merely an idea at the time the Constitution was written. Second, no one expected the district to include many residents. Third, the framers designed the electoral college on a state framework. By 1960, however, the fact that nearly 750,000 Americans living in the nation's capital could not vote in presidential elections was an embarrassment. The Twenty-third Amendment gives Washington, D.C., residents the right to vote in presidential elections by assigning them electoral votes.

K. THINK THROUGH THE CONSTITUTION ***Do you think the District of Columbia should be made a separate state?***

Constitutional Insight **AMENDMENT 24** *Why was the poll tax an issue important enough to require an amendment?* The poll tax was used in some places to prevent African-American voters—at least the many who were too poor to pay the tax—from participating in elections. As the civil rights movement gained momentum, the abuse of the poll tax became a major issue, but the national government found it difficult to change the situation because the constitutional provisions in Article 1, Section 4, leave the qualifications of voters in the hands of the states. The Twenty-fourth Amendment changed this by prohibiting the United States or any state from including payment of any tax as a requirement for voting.

L. THINK THROUGH THE CONSTITUTION ***What impact do you think the Twenty-fourth Amendment has had on elections?***

Section 3 This article shall be inoperative unless it shall have been ratified as an amendment to the Constitution by conventions in the several states, as provided in the Constitution, within seven years from the date of the submission hereof to the states by the Congress.

AMENDMENT 22. LIMIT ON PRESIDENTIAL TERMS (1951)
Passed by Congress March 21, 1947. Ratified February 27, 1951.

Section 1 No person shall be elected to the office of the President more than twice, and no person who has held the office of President, or acted as President, for more than two years of a term to which some other person was elected President shall be elected to the office of the President more than once. ~~But this article shall not apply to any person holding the office of President when this article was proposed by the Congress, and shall not prevent any person who may be holding the office of President, or acting as President, during the term within which this article becomes operative from holding the office of President or acting as President during the remainder of such term.~~

Section 2 This article shall be inoperative unless it shall have been ratified as an amendment to the Constitution by the legislatures of three fourths of the several states within seven years from the date of its submission to the states by the Congress.

AMENDMENT 23. VOTING IN DISTRICT OF COLUMBIA (1961)
Passed by Congress June 17, 1960. Ratified March 29, 1961.

Section 1 The district constituting the seat of government of the United States shall appoint in such manner as Congress may direct:

A number of electors of President and Vice-President equal to the whole number of Senators and Representatives in Congress to which the district would be entitled if it were a state, but in no event more than the least populous state; they shall be in addition to those appointed by the states, but they shall be considered, for the purposes of the election of President and Vice-President, to be electors appointed by a state; and they shall meet in the district and perform such duties as provided by the twelfth article of amendment.

Section 2 The Congress shall have power to enforce this article by appropriate legislation.

AMENDMENT 24. ABOLITION OF POLL TAXES (1964) Passed by Congress August 27, 1962. Ratified January 23, 1964.

Section 1 The right of citizens of the United States to vote in any primary or other election for President or Vice-President, for electors for President or Vice-President, or for Senator or Representative in Congress, shall not be denied or abridged by the United States or any state by reason of failure to pay any poll tax or other tax.

Section 2 The Congress shall have power to enforce this article by appropriate legislation.

AMENDMENT 25. PRESIDENTIAL DISABILITY, SUCCESSION (1967)
Passed by Congress July 6, 1965. Ratified February 10, 1967.

Note: Article 2, Section 1, of the Constitution was affected by the Twenty-fifth Amendment.

Section 1. In case of the removal of the President from office or of his death or resignation, the Vice-President shall become President.

Block Schedule TEACHING OPTION **Time Needed: 30 Minutes**

Cooperative Activity: Preparing Voting Requirements

Task: Student groups will discuss voting requirements they would like to see enacted for the next election.

Purpose: To gain insight into the decision-making process for establishing voting rights.

Activity: Divide students into groups of six. Each group will address the following questions:

- Should the age of eligibility for voting be amended in any way?
- Who do you think should be eligible to vote? Whose voting rights should be denied?
- Do you think that voting rights should be limited to people who are able to read and write?
- Should an elementary school diploma be a voting requirement? What about a high school diploma?
- Should military or community service be a requirement?

Groups should discuss their voting requirements with the class.

ALTERNATIVE ASSESSMENT BOOK
Standards for Evaluating a Cooperative Activity

Section 2 Whenever there is a vacancy in the office of the Vice-President, the President shall nominate a Vice-President who shall take office upon confirmation by a majority vote of both houses of Congress.

Section 3 Whenever the President transmits to the President pro tempore of the Senate and the Speaker of the House of Representatives his written declaration that he is unable to discharge the powers and duties of his office, and until he transmits to them a written declaration to the contrary, such powers and duties shall be discharged by the Vice-President as Acting President.

Section 4 Whenever the Vice-President and a majority of either the principal officers of the executive departments or of such other body as Congress may by law provide, transmit to the President pro tempore of the Senate and the Speaker of the House of Representatives their written declaration that the President is unable to discharge the powers and duties of his office, the Vice-President shall immediately assume the powers and duties of the office as Acting President.

Thereafter, when the President transmits to the President pro tempore of the Senate and the Speaker of the House of Representatives his written declaration that no inability exists, he shall resume the powers and duties of his office unless the Vice-President and a majority of either the principal officers of the executive department[s] or of such other body as Congress may by law provide, transmit within four days to the President pro tempore of the Senate and the Speaker of the House of Representatives their written declaration that the President is unable to discharge the powers and duties of his office. Thereupon Congress shall decide the issue, assembling within forty-eight hours for that purpose if not in session. If the Congress, within twenty-one days after receipt of the latter written declaration, or, if Congress is not in session, within twenty-one days after Congress is required to assemble, determines by two thirds vote of both houses that the President is unable to discharge the powers and duties of his office, the Vice-President shall continue to discharge the same as Acting President; otherwise, the President shall resume the powers and duties of his office.

AMENDMENT 26. 18-YEAR-OLD VOTE (1971) Passed by Congress March 23, 1971. Ratified July 1, 1971.

Note: Amendment 14, Section 2, of the Constitution was modified by Section 1 of the Twenty-sixth Amendment.

Section 1 The right of citizens of the United States, who are eighteen years of age or older, to vote shall not be denied or abridged by the United States or by any state on account of age.

Section 2 The Congress shall have power to enforce this article by appropriate legislation.

AMENDMENT 27. CONGRESSIONAL PAY (1992) Passed by Congress September 25, 1789. Ratified May 7, 1992.

No law, varying the compensation for the services of the Senators and Representatives, shall take effect, until an election of Representatives shall have intervened.

President Richard M. Nixon *(above)* signs the Twenty-sixth Amendment to the Constitution, adopted in 1971. A teenager *(right)* exercises her right to vote.

Constitutional Insight **AMENDMENT 26** *Why was the Twenty-sixth Amendment passed?* Granting 18-year-olds the right to vote became an issue in the 1960s, during the Vietnam War, when people questioned the justice of requiring 18-year-old men to submit to the military draft but refusing them the right to vote. In 1970, Congress passed a voting rights act giving 18-year-olds the right to vote in elections. When the constitutionality of this act was challenged, the Supreme Court decided that states had to honor the 18-year-old vote for congressional and presidential elections but could retain higher age requirements for state and local elections. To avoid confusion at the polls, the Twenty-sixth Amendment was passed by both houses of Congress in March 1971 and ratified by July 1, 1971. It guarantees 18-year-olds the right to vote in national and state elections.

M. THINK THROUGH THE CONSTITUTION ***Do you think 18-year-olds should have the right to vote? Why or why not?***

Constitutional Insight **AMENDMENT 27** *How long did it take to ratify this amendment?* Although the Twenty-seventh Amendment was one of the 12 amendments proposed in 1789 as part of the Bill of Rights, it was not ratified until 1992. This amendment, which deals with congressional compensation, allows the members of Congress to vote for an increase in their pay but prohibits the increase from taking effect until after an election.

N. THINK THROUGH THE CONSTITUTION ***Do you think members of Congress should be able to vote themselves a pay increase? Explain your answer.***

MORE ABOUT . . .
Amendment 25

In 1973 Vice-President Spiro Agnew resigned from office. Under the provisions of the Twenty-fifth Amendment, Congress approved President Nixon's appointment of Gerald Ford to fill the vacancy. When Nixon resigned a year later, Ford became president. President Ford then named Nelson Rockefeller as vice-president. Congress approved Rockefeller's appointment. That was the only time in history when neither the president nor the vice-president had been elected to office.

FORMAL ASSESSMENT
Quiz: The Amendments, p. 32

THINK THROUGH THE CONSTITUTION
Possible Responses:

M. Yes—capable of learning about candidates and issues; mature enough to make informed decisions; old enough for military service. No—capable of following military orders but not mature enough to make sound, independent decisions.

N. Yes—If members abused this privilege, they could be voted out of office. No—As public servants, they should not be granted this privilege.

Block Schedule TEACHING OPTION **Time Needed: 30 Minutes**

Cooperative Activity: Reviewing the Constitution

Task: To review the Constitution.

Purpose: To gain a deeper understanding of the Constitution.

Activity: Assign groups of four students two articles or sections of the document to summarize and explain in contemporary language. You may vary the number of articles or sections assigned depending on their length, as well as the size of your class. All groups will present their summaries and, in effect, teach one another the whole document.

Suggest that students create bulleted lists of key points as a study aid. Here is an example:

Article 2. The Executive

Section 2. Powers of the President

- Acts as commander in chief of the armed forces
- Makes treaties (with the consent of Congress)
- Appoints ambassadors
- Appoints Supreme Court justices

ALTERNATIVE ASSESSMENT BOOK
Standards for Evaluating a Cooperative Activity

Tracing Themes

OBJECTIVES

1. To summarize the expansion of voting rights in America.
2. To identify constitutional amendments passed to expand voting rights and the year in which each was ratified.

FOCUS & MOTIVATE

▶ ***Starting with the Student*** Lead students in a discussion of the significance of voting.

- Why do students think so many people, especially between the ages of 18 and 21, fail to vote?
- How might people's attitudes toward voting change if the privilege were suddenly denied?

MORE ABOUT . . .

The Voting Rights Act of 1965

A landmark of the civil rights movement, the Voting Rights Act of 1965 had several important provisions. One did away with devices like literacy tests used in many Southern states to prevent African Americans from voting. Another gave the United States attorney general authority to enroll voters in areas where groups such as African Americans were clearly not voting in reasonable numbers.

TRACING THEMES
DEMOCRACY IN AMERICA

Voting Rights

When the American colonists declared their independence from Great Britain in 1776, the state constitutions that were drafted established not only the governing bodies of the states but also the voting rights of the people. These voting rights were maintained by the central government under the Articles of Confederation.

When the delegates met in Philadelphia in 1787, they decided to create a new government instead of revising the Articles of Confederation. In Article 1, Section 2, and Article 2, Section 1, of the Constitution, they left it to the state legislatures to determine who was qualified to vote for representatives in Congress and for presidential electors.

1789
MALE PROPERTY OWNERS

In the early years of the United States, property qualifications for male voters, which had long existed, were relaxed in some states (Pennsylvania, Delaware, North Carolina, Georgia, and Vermont) to include all male taxpayers. Most state constitutions also required that a voting male be at least 21 years of age.

Those who qualified to vote were generally white, although some states allowed free African Americans to vote (New Jersey did until 1807, as did New York until 1821, Rhode Island until 1822, and Pennsylvania until 1837). Slaves could not vote in any state. Women could not vote, except in New Jersey, until 1807. Native Americans could vote in no states.

The picture at right is from a 1789 painting of Daniel Boardman, a white male property owner. What about the portrait suggests that he was a qualified voter?

1870
AFRICAN-AMERICAN MALES

The Fifteenth Amendment to the Constitution attempted to guarantee African-American males the right to vote by stating that the right of U.S. citizens "to vote shall not be denied or abridged [curtailed] by the United States or by any state on account of race, color, or previous condition of servitude." The picture above shows African-American males voting in a state election in 1867. African-American males, however, were often kept from voting through the use of poll taxes, which were finally abolished by the Twenty-fourth Amendment in 1964, and literacy tests, which were suspended by the Voting Rights Act of 1965.

RECOMMENDED RESOURCES

Books

Bott, Alexander J. *Handbook of United States Election Laws and Practices.* Westport, CT: Greenwood, 1991. An in-depth look at the right to vote.

Cultice, Wendell W. *Youth's Battle for the Ballot.* Westport, CT: Greenwood, 1992. Historical changes in America's voting age.

Frost, Elizabeth, and Kathryn Cullen-Dupont. *Women's Suffrage in America.* New York: Facts on File, 1992. Primary sources in the struggle for woman suffrage.

Lusane, Clarence. *No Easy Victories.* Danbury, CT: Franklin, 1996. The African-American struggle for the vote.

Videos

Electing the President. Encyclopaedia Britannica. The electoral process from Washington's day to recent times.

One Woman, One Vote. PBS Video, 1995. TV documentary about the woman suffrage movement.

United States Elections: How We Vote. Encyclopaedia Britannica. A walk through the election process.

Software

Social Reform Movements. Clearvue, dist. ESI. American reform movements linked to an encyclopedia and dictionary.

U.S. Constitution Tutor. Word Associates, dist. ESI. Tutorial and tests on the Constitution.

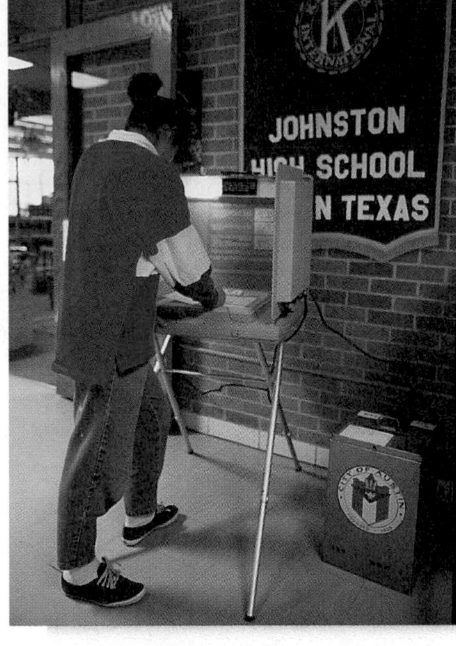

1971
EIGHTEEN-YEAR-OLD VOTE

The Twenty-sixth Amendment, ratified in 1971, granted the right to vote to citizens of the United States "eighteen years of age or older." Voting rights for young people had become an issue in the 1960s, during the Vietnam War. Many people questioned drafting 18-year-olds to fight but refusing them the right to vote. The picture at left shows a young person exercising her new right to vote.

1920
WOMAN SUFFRAGE

In 1920, the Nineteenth Amendment, granting voting rights to women, was finally ratified. Women's fight to gain voting and other rights had been going on ever since colonial times. Abigail Adams, in a letter in 1776, reminded her husband that in writing a new code of laws he and his colleagues should "remember the ladies." Elizabeth Cady Stanton, Susan B. Anthony, and many other women, such as those shown marching in a woman suffrage parade in 1919, worked tirelessly for women's voting rights.

Four years after ratification of the Nineteenth Amendment, in 1924, citizenship—including the right to vote—was extended to Native Americans.

INTERACT WITH HISTORY

1. **DRAWING CONCLUSIONS** What does the information on these pages demonstrate about voting rights in the United States? How did the Constitution help bring about the changes?

SEE SKILLBUILDER HANDBOOK, PAGE 920.

2. **INTERPRETING DATA** Research voter turnout statistics from the 1800s and compare them to contemporary statistics.

Visit http://www.mlushistory.com for more about voting news.

INSTRUCT

▶ *Starting with the Student*
- Have students research and report on the motor-voter law passed in the early 1990s.
- Ask students to find out more about voting and voting restrictions in their state. How far in advance need a person register in order to vote in the next election? Can a person register by mail? What must a person do if he or she moves within the state? What rules govern voting in party primaries?

▶ *Discussing Key Ideas*
- American voting rights gradually expand over the years.
- The Fifteenth, Nineteenth, and Twenty-sixth Amendments to the Constitution expand the vote to African-American males, women, and Americans between 18 and 21, respectively.

HISTORY FROM VISUALS
Reading the Images

Have students examine the art on these pages.

- What words do you think of when you examine each picture?
- Why do you think the women marching for suffrage held that particular sign? *Possible Responses: To appeal to men's love for or loyalty to their mothers; to stress a valuable role of women in society.*

INTERACT WITH HISTORY

1. Drawing Conclusions

Possible Answers: *Voting rights in the United States gradually expanded over time. Various groups (women, African Americans, 18-year-olds) often had to struggle to achieve the right to vote.*

The initial clause concerning who could vote was expanded by constitutional amendments.

2. Interpreting Data

Strategies for researching voter turnout statistics can include:
- Check the library for histories of presidential elections. These books often include extensive discussions of voter turnout.
- Infotrak, a computer database of thousands of magazines, permits a key word search and will supply many references under "voter turnout."
- The *Congressional Quarterly* weekly reports are a good source of current information.
- The *Readers' Guide to Periodical Literature* is a basic source for magazine articles.

THE LIVING CONSTITUTION
ASSESSMENT ANSWERS

REVIEWING THE CONSTITUTION

MAIN IDEAS
Answers will vary.

1. House members are elected from congressional districts and Senate members from each state. The legislature makes laws.
2. The number of representatives is based on population, while each state has two senators only.
3. Any four powers: to tax, borrow money, regulate commerce, coin money, establish post offices, create federal courts, declare war, raise armed forces, make laws.
4. Congress: to suspend *habeas corpus,* illegally punish people, levy direct taxes, levy export taxes on goods from any state, show preference among states, take money illegally from the treasury, confer titles of nobility.

   States: all powers listed in Article 1, Section 10, for example, to enter treaties on their own, coin money, illegally imprison people, lay import/export taxes, engage in war on their own.
5. To carry out the laws made by Congress.
6. The Electoral College, by vote of the states' electors.
7. If convicted upon impeachment.
8. The president nominates them; the Senate approves.
9. Those appealed from lower courts; not to hear a case means the lower court ruling stands with no further appeal.
10. It exemplifies cooperation among the states.
11. Three-fourths of the states, or 38 states.
12. To protect citizens' rights and to get the Constitution ratified.
13. No, there are limits; you cannot yell, "Fire!" in a crowded theater and incite a riot.
14. They were worried by Eisenhower's illness and Kennedy's assassination.
15. The Twenty-seventh Amendment; prevents Congress's use of taxpayers' money for members' own gain.

The Living Constitution Assessment

REVIEWING THE CONSTITUTION

MAIN IDEAS

Article 1. The Legislature

1. Why does the legislative branch of the government represent the people most directly? What is the principal job of this branch?
2. Why are there more members of the House of Representatives than of the Senate?
3. Name four powers Congress has.
4. What powers are denied to Congress? to the states?

Article 2. The Executive

5. What is the main function of the executive branch?
6. Who officially elects the president of the United States? Explain.
7. How can the president lose his or her job before election time?

Article 3. The Judiciary

8. How are Supreme Court justices appointed?
9. What kinds of cases go before the Supreme Court? Why is the Court's decision whether to hear a case important?

Article 4. Relations Among States

10. Extradition is the sending of a fugitive back to the state in which he or she is accused of committing a crime. How is this an example of relations among states?

Article 5. Amending the Constitution

11. How many states must ratify an amendment for it to become part of the Constitution? Why do you think it takes that many?

The Amendments

12. Why was the Bill of Rights added to the Constitution almost immediately after the Constitution was ratified?
13. Does the First Amendment allow complete freedom of speech—the right to say anything you want at any time, anywhere? Explain your answer.
14. Why do you think an amendment was added to spell out exactly how presidential succession should be handled?
15. What is the newest amendment? What protection does that amendment give to the American people?

THINKING CRITICALLY

1. **FEDERAL POWER** How does the Constitution reflect the fear of too strong a central government?
2. **CONSTITUTIONAL POWERS** The powers of the federal government are separated among the three branches. Create a chart that shows how the Constitution's framers used checks and balances to ensure that no one branch of the government could become much stronger than the others.

Executive	Legislative	Judicial

3. **PASSAGE OF BILLS** Because of the process by which bills become laws, what problems may occur when the president and a majority of members of Congress are from different political parties?
4. **RIGHT OF APPEAL** Many people today object to the fact that convicted criminals "clog up the courts" with their many appeals to have new trials. What gives criminals the right to appeal? Do you think their appeals should be limited? Explain your opinion.
5. **AMENDMENTS** Why did the framers make it so difficult to amend the Constitution? Do you agree or disagree with their philosophy? Explain.
6. **SPEEDY TRIAL** The Bill of Rights guarantees a defendant a speedy, public trial. What may have motivated the framers to include this right? Do you think it is being observed today? Explain.
7. **TRACING THEMES DEMOCRACY IN AMERICA** The 15th, 19th, and 26th amendments give voting rights to specific groups. Why was it necessary for Congress to spell out these groups' rights in amendments?
8. **ELASTICITY OF THE CONSTITUTION** Reread the quotation from President Wilson on page 86. Do you agree or disagree? Provide information to support your position.

THINKING CRITICALLY

1. FEDERAL POWER
Possible Responses: Students might point out that the Constitution divides powers among three branches; provides checks by each branch on the others; states in the Preamble that the people are the source of power.

2. CONSTITUTIONAL POWERS
Executive: may veto legislation; appoints Supreme Court justices and other federal judges; may grant reprieves and pardons; may call special sessions of Congress.
Legislative: makes the laws; may override presidential vetoes; may impeach and try the president, cabinet officers, and federal judges; controls money; establishes lower courts; the Senate approves treaties and presidential appointments.
Judicial: decides the meaning of laws; may declare acts of Congress or executive acts unconstitutional; free from presidential control because justices are appointed for life.

3. PASSAGE OF BILLS
President may veto bills; Congress may override veto; a stalemate could occur.

4. RIGHT OF APPEAL
Article 3, Section 2, gives the right to appeal. ***Possible Responses:*** Some students might say appeals should be limited to keep from overloading the courts. Others might say that appeals should be every person's right.

5. AMENDMENTS
They didn't want the swaying opinions of the times to prompt changes in the law of the land without a great deal of thought. ***Possible Responses:*** Making it difficult to amend the Constitution makes sure that it doesn't get changed too often. But some may say that the process is so difficult that some good changes never get made.

9. **ANALYZING PRIMARY SOURCES** Read the following excerpt from the *Federalist Papers,* a series of essays written to urge ratification of the Constitution. After you read it, answer the questions that follow.

> Ambition must be made to counteract ambition. The interest of the man must be connected with the constitutional rights of the place. It may be a reflection on human nature that such devices should be necessary to control the abuses of government. But what is government itself but the greatest of all reflections on human nature? If men were angels, no government would be necessary. . . . In framing a government which is to be administered by men over men, the great difficulty lies in this: You must first enable the government to control the governed; and in the next place, oblige it to control itself. A dependence on the people is, no doubt, the primary control on the government; but experience has taught mankind the necessity of auxiliary precautions.
>
> **JAMES MADISON,** *Federalist,* Number 51

a. Based on this passage, how do you think Madison judged human nature? Do you agree with his view? Explain your answer.

b. How does the Constitution enable the government to control the governed? How does the Constitution provide for the government to control itself?

10. **INTERPRETING POLITICAL CARTOONS** What do you think the cartoonist is suggesting about FDR's third term?

ALTERNATIVE ASSESSMENT

1. **RESEARCHING SUPREME COURT CONTROVERSIES**
The Supreme Court has often been a source of controversy. Become an expert on one controversy surrounding the Court—either a controversy related to a ruling or one related to members of the Court itself.

Present a complete explanation of the controversy to your classmates, showing both sides and the results.

Use the CD-ROM *Our Times,* focusing on a part such as "The Right to Remain Silent," "Death Sentence for Jim Crow," "Scottsboro Boys," "Anita Hill Hearings," or "The Battle for Baby M." Or use newspaper and magazine articles to research your controversy.

- List the facts on each side of the controversy. Clarify the controversy as objectively as you can. Summarize the results. Finally, add your own opinion and reasons for it.
- Present your explanation to the class. Make sure to present the facts first, then your opinion.

2. **RESEARCHING THE COSTS OF ELECTIONS**
How much money was spent in the last presidential election by each candidate? How much was spent by the current senators and representatives from your state? Use magazines, newspapers, or the Internet to help you find this information. Some candidates may have home pages on the Internet. Look them up if you can. How are candidates using the Internet? Present your discoveries to the class.

3. **DEBATING AN AMENDMENT**
Cooperative Learning Think about controversial issues of today, such as gun control, the death penalty, and the rights of the accused. Choose a pertinent amendment to support, eliminate, or change in light of these issues. With three likeminded classmates, form a team to debate your position against a group who disagrees. Research and plan your arguments carefully. Then hold a debate in front of your class. Allow the class to choose the winner.

4. **PORTFOLIO PROJECT**
Use the Living History activity to expand your portfolio.

LIVING HISTORY

WRITING ABOUT A CONSTITUTIONAL QUESTION
Write an essay on the constitutional issue that you have researched. State your opinion about the issue and then support that opinion with reasons based on your research. Edit and polish your essay and then have a classmate read it and suggest improvements. Finally, read your essay aloud or post it on a bulletin board for others to read. Afterward, put it in your American history portfolio.

ALTERNATIVE ASSESSMENT

1. RESEARCHING SUPREME COURT CONTROVERSIES
Standards for Evaluation
An explanation should meet the following criteria.

- Maintains an objective tone while stating the facts of the controversy.
- Shows evidence of thorough research from a variety of sources.
- Presents a clear and concise summary of the controversy.
- States an opinion on the controversy and supports the opinion with appropriate facts and examples.

2. RESEARCHING THE COSTS OF ELECTIONS
Standards for Evaluation
Students who do well on this assignment will . . .

- Find specific information about campaign costs.
- Break the information into separate sections for the presidential candidates, and the senators and the representatives from the students' own state.
- Indicate how some candidates are using the Internet.

3. DEBATING AN AMENDMENT
Standards for Evaluation
A debate should meet the following criteria.

- Presents clear arguments to support a position on one amendment.
- Supports each argument with specific examples.
- Acknowledges and answers opposing arguments.

4. PORTFOLIO PROJECT
LIVING HISTORY
Standards for Evaluation
A good essay will meet the following criteria.

- Explains and summarizes a specific constitutional issue.
- Clearly states an opinion about the issue.
- Supports the opinion with quotations and other specific research.
- Is expressed in language that is clear and correct.

IN-DEPTH RESOURCES: UNIT 1
See the form for scoring this activity on page 63.

THINKING CRITICALLY

6. SPEEDY TRIAL
To protect citizens from illegal imprisonment. ***Possible Responses:*** Observed today in principle but the process of honoring a defendant's rights does slow down legal procedures. All the legal protections of the rights of an accused today may make it impossible for a person to have a speedy trial.

7. TRACING THEMES DEMOCRACY IN AMERICA
Original voters were white, male property owners. Each group enfranchised since then fought for its rights.

8. ELASTICITY OF THE CONSTITUTION
Possible Responses: Many students will agree, citing the Supreme Court's ability to interpret and Congress's ability to amend the document. Those who disagree might say that it's too hard to change the Constitution.

9. ANALYZING PRIMARY SOURCES
a. Madison feels that humans are imperfect, will take advantage when possible, and need to be controlled. ***Possible Responses:*** Some students might agree that human beings are imperfect and need to be controlled, especially those who hold governing positions. Other students might suggest that human beings are imperfect and governing officials must have authority to maintain law and order.
b. The Constitution gives the federal government power over the states and citizens to make and enforce laws; it provides for the government to control itself through the system of checks and balances among the branches.

10. INTERPRETING POLITICAL CARTOONS
That Roosevelt wants a third term.

OBJECTIVES
PROJECT 1

1. To learn about candidates currently campaigning for office.
2. To evaluate the accuracy and completeness of campaign information.
3. To use a range of sources to write an endorsement.

PROJECT 2

1. To learn reasons for seeking U.S. citizenship.
2. To explore the process of gaining U.S. citizenship from both the immigrants' and the government's point of view.

Projects for Citizenship

Applying the Constitution

The United States Constitution is admired the world over. But a healthy democracy depends on the full participation of its citizens—including you. Here are eight projects that will help you learn the rewards and challenges of responsible citizenship.

Visit http://www.mlushistory.com for more information that will help you with these Citizenship Projects.

PROJECT 1 Becoming an Educated Voter

Endorsing a Candidate Choose a campaign for elective office and learn about the issues and the candidates in the campaign. After doing your research, write an endorsement, or a statement in favor, of one of the candidates.

Learning about the candidates

☑ **Examine news media.** During campaigns, some media offer endorsements that explain why particular candidates are worthy of support.

☑ **Get information from political parties.** They provide information on the candidates, but their perspective is biased toward their own candidates. The major parties have INTERNET sites.

☑ **Contact interest groups,** such as the Sierra Club and the National Association of Manufacturers. They provide information on candidates' positions on the issues and support candidates who share their beliefs.

☑ **Contact independent organizations,** such as the League of Women Voters and Project Vote Smart. They publish nonpartisan voters' guides.

As you use each source, think about the following questions.

- What does the author of this source stand to gain from supporting a particular candidate?
- Is the information in the source complete and accurate?

PRESENTING YOUR PROJECT

After you have written your endorsement, you might send it to a media outlet, such as a newspaper or a television station, or post it on the INTERNET. Or you might send it to your local or school newspaper for possible publication.

PROJECT 2 Learning the Process of Becoming a Citizen

Writing a News Report Write a news report about how people become naturalized U.S. citizens. Find out about the reasons immigrants want to become American citizens and the process they must follow. Learn what obstacles they face and who helps them in earning U.S. citizenship. Take the following steps in preparing your report.

Learning about the process

☑ **Interview** one or more people who have become U.S. citizens. Ask them to describe the citizenship process and their reasons for, and feelings about, becoming citizens.

☑ **Contact people** who work on immigration and citizenship issues, such as the Immigration and Naturalization Service (INS), an immigration attorney, or an immigrants' rights group. Ask them to describe the requirements that people must meet to become U.S. citizens.

☑ **Write or call** your local, state, and congressional representatives. Find out what unique circumstances, if any, immigrants to your community or state face. Learn about what measures are taken at the local or state level to help new immigrants adjust to American life.

☑ **Find information** in the library or on the INTERNET about the process of becoming a citizen.

PRESENTING YOUR PROJECT

Write a newspaper report or record your findings on audio or video tape as a broadcast news report. Report the information provided by your sources and identify your sources of information so that readers can verify the accuracy of your story. Then present your news report to the class in a clear and orderly manner, like a professional journalist.

A student expresses her opinions on political issues as she addresses an audience.

PROJECT 1
Becoming an Educated Voter

Tips for Teaching

- If students have access to the Internet, they may be able to complete this project in three to five days. Without access, a time line of two weeks is more reasonable.
- If a local campaign is under way, you might invite the candidates to address the class, to send representatives, or to send information.
- Help students sort out fallacies in political advertising, such as either-or thinking, false analogies, and begging the question.

Standards for Evaluation
The endorsement should meet the following criteria.

- Includes the candidate's stand on several major issues.
- Incorporates endorsements from news media and interest groups as well as information from the candidate's party and nonpartisan voting groups.
- Is clearly written and well supported.
- Is sent to an appropriate media outlet.

IN-DEPTH RESOURCES: UNIT 1
See additional suggestions for completing this project on page 64.

PROJECT 2
Learning the Process of Becoming a Citizen

Tips for Teaching

- Urge students to begin by setting up the interview.
- Ask students to read an overview of the topic in an easily accessible reference source, such as an almanac. This will provide them with the framework of immigration law.
- Provide addresses or phone numbers for local representatives.
- Emphasize that a news report begins with a strong lead and saves less interesting or dramatic details for later.

Standards for Evaluation
The news report should meet the following criteria.

- Includes the reasons people become citizens.
- Details the process of becoming a citizen.
- Reflects a variety of sources, including people who have experienced the process, people who work on immigration and naturalization issues, and government representatives.
- Is clearly and accurately written or recorded in the form of a news report.

IN-DEPTH RESOURCES: UNIT 1
See additional suggestions for completing this project on page 65.

Projects for Citizenship

OBJECTIVES
PROJECT 3

1. To learn about candidates in a current campaign for office.
2. To learn about political campaigning through volunteer work.

PROJECT 4

1. To express an opinion on an issue by writing a letter to the editor.
2. To explore an issue fully by reading about it and then developing and supporting an argument about it.

PROJECT 3 Supporting a Political Candidate

Keeping a Campaign Scrapbook Select a candidate for elective office that you would like to support, and volunteer to work on his or her campaign. Keep a scrapbook that recounts your experiences on the campaign trail. To prepare your campaign scrapbook, follow these suggestions.

Collecting campaign materials

- ☑ **Keep a journal** of your campaign experiences.
- ☑ **Pick up campaign memorabilia** such as buttons, bumper stickers, handbills, and signs.
- ☑ **Gather position papers** that your candidate has written about the issues.
- ☑ **Gather materials** from your candidate's INTERNET site.
- ☑ **Take photographs** of campaign events.

In your campaign journal, write about the following questions.

- Was your overall campaign experience positive?
- Would you work for another candidate in the future?

PRESENTING YOUR PROJECT
Compile all of your materials into a scrapbook. Present your scrapbook to the class and describe the different items in it. Explain why you chose to work for the candidate you helped and whether or not your candidate won the election.

PROJECT 4 Expressing Political Opinions

Writing a Letter to the Editor Identify an issue that concerns you. Then write a letter or send an e-mail message to the editor of a newspaper or magazine about that issue.

Writing a persuasive letter

- ☑ **Find an issue** that has been in the news lately about which you feel strongly.
- ☑ **Notice** how recent articles, editorials, and cartoons in newspapers or magazines have addressed this issue. You may want to use an actual letter to the editor as a model for organizing your letter.
- ☑ **Compose a letter** that clearly and concisely explains your views about the issue you have chosen. Your letter should also include reasons and facts that support your opinion on the issue. It might also advocate that some action be taken to address the issue.
- ☑ **Identify** to whom you should send your letter and note any requirements the newspaper or magazine has for writing letters to the editor.
- ☑ **Send the letter** via e-mail to the publication's INTERNET site.

PRESENTING YOUR PROJECT
Present the letter you wrote to the rest of the class. When you do, explain why you chose to write about this issue.

113

PROJECT 3
Supporting a Political Candidate

Tips for Teaching

- This project may span more than a month and may be best conducted in spring or early fall. You may wish to set interim due dates for the journal in progress and some of the materials.
- Encourage students to use their journals to make personal reflections on campaigning, the candidate, and their role.
- Ask students to provide labels or captions for all materials they include in their scrapbook.

Standards for Evaluation
The campaign scrapbook should meet the following criteria.

- Includes a variety of campaign materials including position papers and photographs of campaign events.
- Incorporates personal reflection by means of selected journal entries.
- Reflects reasons why the student chose to support the candidate.
- Supports the student's choice of the candidate and includes the campaign outcome.

IN-DEPTH RESOURCES: UNIT 1
See additional suggestions for completing this project on page 66.

PROJECT 4
Expressing Political Opinions

Tips for Teaching

- Explain that students may choose an international, national, state, or local issue.
- Urge students to identify the most convincing arguments in the letters they gather and to analyze why the arguments are effective.
- Point out places in newspapers and magazines that give information on requirements for letters and where they should be sent.
- Emphasize that persuasive letters maintain an even, reasoned tone.

Standards for Evaluation
The letter to the editor should meet the following criteria.

- Focuses on a single issue.
- Explains the writer's point of view and includes reasons and facts to support it.
- Reflects knowledge of opposing viewpoints and others' approach to the issue.
- Is clearly and concisely written and reflects the standards for submission set by the intended place of publication.

IN-DEPTH RESOURCES: UNIT 1
See additional suggestions for completing this project on page 67.

Projects for Citizenship

OBJECTIVES
PROJECT 5

1. To learn the roles and procedures for conducting a business meeting.
2. To learn the process for creating and passing a resolution.
3. To develop skills required to take group action.

PROJECT 6

1. To learn to develop a proposition.
2. To explore an issue fully by preparing and anticipating arguments.
3. To stage an actual debate.

PROJECT 5 Organizing a Meeting

Passing a Resolution Work with other members of your class to hold a meeting to create and pass a resolution on an important issue in your school or community. Use the following guidelines to help you run a smooth and effective meeting.

Running a successful meeting

☑ **Call the meeting** to order when there is a quorum, or a minimum number of members in attendance to conduct business.

☑ **Select** two class members—one to act as the chair to preside over the meeting and one to act as the secretary to record minutes and the final resolution.

☑ **The chair should open** the meeting and take motions, or proposals for action, from the floor. The motions will introduce resolutions for your group to discuss and eventually vote on.

☑ **The chair should preside** as the motions are discussed, ensuring full and fair discussion for all members who want to express their views.

☑ **The chair should call for a vote** on the motion after the discussion is completed. Voting may be by secret ballot, by a show of hands, or by voice vote. The secretary counts the votes, and the chair announces whether the motion has been carried or defeated.

☑ **The chair declares** the meeting adjourned, or closed, when all business has been completed.

☑ **The secretary records** the minutes, including any resolutions that were passed.

PROJECT 6 Debating an Issue

Staging a Debate Work with other class members to stage a debate. First, develop a proposition, such as "Resolved: Universities have the moral obligation to prohibit the use of hate speech." Make sure that the proposition has clear affirmative and negative sides. Then select teams of two or three students to argue the proposition. Other members of the class may help the teams develop their cases.

Preparing for a debate

☑ **The teams must prepare** a case, or set of arguments. Each team identifies the issues and evidence that support its side of the proposition. Each team also must consider the other side of the proposition, because it needs to attack, or rebut, the opposing team's arguments.

☑ **Appoint** a moderator and a timekeeper to run the debate.

☑ **Begin the debate** by having the moderator state the proposition. One side must argue in the affirmative, or in support of the proposition. The other must argue in the negative, or against the proposition.

☑ **Present your case** in two parts. First, team members put forward their arguments in constructive speeches. Then they attack the opposing team's arguments in rebuttal speeches. Affirmative and negative speakers alternate, and their speeches are limited to a set period of time (traditionally ten minutes for constructive speeches and five minutes for rebuttal speeches).

PRESENTING YOUR PROJECT
Have the secretary present your resolution to the rest of the class. He or she should also use the minutes of the meeting to respond to any questions about how the final resolution was created.

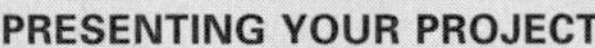

PRESENTING YOUR PROJECT
Stage the debate for your classmates or for other members of your school or community. Have a panel of students or community leaders serve as judges to choose a winner.

The young man at the podium emphasizes a point as these students stage a classroom debate.

PROJECT 5
Organizing a Meeting
Tips for Teaching

- Explain that organizations ranging from trustees of the local library to boards of corporations conduct business by creating resolutions, discussing their probable impact and the alternatives to them, and voting on them.
- Explain what a quorum is, and encourage groups to define a quorum before conducting their meeting.
- Introduce parliamentary rules of order, including types of motions and how they are moved, seconded, and passed.
- Invite students to discuss reasons why parliamentary procedure is followed at group meetings.

Standards for Evaluation
The presentation of the resolution should meet the following criteria.

- Includes minutes that show the meeting was run according to parliamentary procedure, conducted by a chair, and recorded by a secretary.
- Shows, both through the minutes and through responses to questions, how the resolution was created and passed.

IN-DEPTH RESOURCES: UNIT 1
See additional suggestions for completing this project on page 68.

PROJECT 6
Debating an Issue
Tips for Teaching

- You may want to have several small groups research and write propositions; then have the large group vote on which proposition they want to debate.
- It may work best to assign students to argue the pro and con positions.
- Review the propositions carefully to be sure they will engender meaty, productive debates.
- You may wish to model the moderator's role.
- If possible, show students a videotape of a presidential or other debate, pointing out the moderator, the time limits, and the rebuttals.

Standards for Evaluation
The debate should meet the following criteria.

- Focuses on a proposition with a clear affirmative and negative side.
- Presents a well-developed and supported case for each side of the argument.
- Includes effective rebuttals.
- Is conducted by a moderator and is timed.

IN-DEPTH RESOURCES: UNIT 1
See additional suggestions for completing this project on page 69.

Projects for Citizenship

OBJECTIVES
PROJECT 7

1. To learn methods by which to influence legislation or public policy.
2. To practice documenting an argument for a specific course of action.
3. To practice gathering and presenting group support for an issue.

PROJECT 8

1. To learn more about organizations that serve the community.
2. To experience community volunteer work.

PROJECT 7 Understanding How to Lobby

Planning a Lobbying Campaign Form a committee with other students in the class to organize a lobbying campaign—a campaign to influence legislation or public policy. Create a plan for the lobbying campaign that includes materials to be presented to government officials. In creating your plan, keep the following points in mind.

Creating a lobbying plan

☑ **Establish a clear goal.** Decide what you want to achieve with your lobbying efforts. Make sure all members of the group understand and agree with the established goal.

☑ **Identify the appropriate people to lobby**—the people who can best help you to achieve your goal. Establish the best lobbying procedure to follow—in other words, whether it would be preferable to lobby legislators or appointed officials. For example, if your group is planning to lobby to have a bill passed, you would lobby the legislators who will vote on the bill. However, if your group wants to lobby for a local improvement—such as cleaning up an abandoned factory site—you should lobby the local officials who make those decisions.

☑ **Gather statistics** and other information that support your case. Explore a variety of resources, including the library, the INTERNET, and interviews with appropriate state or local officials. Use the information you gather to develop a brief written report that can be given to the officials you intend to lobby.

☑ **Organize public opinion** in favor of your case. Gather signatures on petitions or conduct a letter-writing campaign to encourage people who support your goal to contact government officials. You can also create fliers calling attention to your cause.

☑ **Present your case** to government officials firmly but politely. Practice your presentation several times before you actually appear before them.

PRESENTING YOUR PROJECT

Share your lobbying plan with the rest of the class in the form of a written proposal that includes materials, such as petition forms, that you will use in your lobbying effort. If you implement your lobbying plan, describe to the class what response you received from the officials you lobbied.

PROJECT 8 Volunteering in Your Community

Making an Oral Report
Identify a local community organization that you might want to help. Find out what kinds of volunteer activities the organization has, such as answering phones in the office, serving food to the homeless, or cleaning vacant lots. Then volunteer to participate in one of those activities. Prepare an oral report to present to the rest of the class about your experiences as a volunteer. Keep the following points in mind as you choose which organization to help.

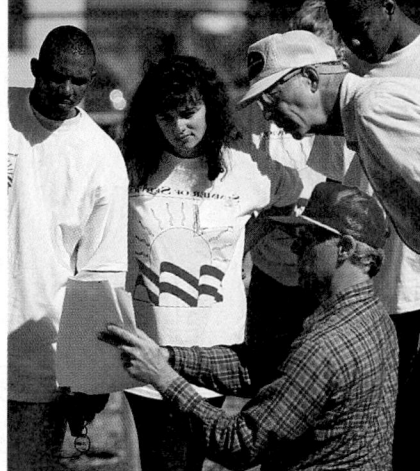

A group of young volunteers in the Summer of Service project discusses plans with carpenters.

Suggestions for volunteering

☑ **Think about** the kind of public service projects that might interest you. You might talk to your parents, a teacher, friends, a local church, or a local political organization to learn what kinds of volunteer services are needed in your community.

☑ **Call local community organizations** to find out what kinds of volunteer opportunities they offer and decide whether you would like to volunteer for those projects.

☑ **Identify the cause** you want to support and a community organization that addresses that cause.

☑ **Identify the type of work** you want to do and work with that organization.

PRESENTING YOUR PROJECT

Deliver an oral report to your class about your experiences as a volunteer. Explain why you chose the specific volunteer activity that you did. Describe the activity you performed. Then tell them what effect your volunteering had as well as whether you felt the experience was a good one.

PROJECT 7
Understanding How to Lobby

Tips for Teaching

- Provide two weeks or more for this project. Encourage students to work through it step by step, in the order it is presented.
- Explain how lobbies work in Washington and the role they have historically played in the passage of major legislation.
- Discuss the power of organized lobby efforts in contrast to individual efforts to affect legislation.

Standards for Evaluation
The lobbying plan should meet the following criteria:

- Reflects a clear goal.
- Is aimed at the appropriate audience.
- Organizes public support through such means as petitioning, advertising, or letter writing.
- Includes a clearly written proposal, backed up by statistics and evidence of public support.

IN-DEPTH RESOURCES: UNIT 1
See additional suggestions for completing this project on page 70.

PROJECT 8
Volunteering in Your Community

Tips for Teaching

- This long-term activity may extend over several months.
- You might require students to contact a certain minimum number of organizations, or you might require different groups to contact different types of organizations. Encourage students to explore many options before committing to a job.
- Remind students that when they volunteer for an organization, their behavior must reflect the goals and standards for conduct of the organization they serve. Invite pairs to role-play situations in which volunteers are required to put the organization's goals or rules of conduct ahead of their own.

Standards for Evaluation

The oral report describing the volunteer experience should meet the following criteria.

- Identifies the community organization's purpose.
- Gives reasons why the student volunteered.
- Describes the volunteer work.
- Discusses ways in which the experience benefited the volunteer, the organization, and the community.

IN-DEPTH RESOURCES: UNIT 1
See additional suggestions for completing this project on page 71.

REVIEW CHAPTER 3

PLANNING GUIDE

The Growth of a Young Nation

	Key Ideas	COPYMASTERS	ASSESSMENT
SECTION 1 The Jeffersonian Era *pp. 118–123*	*Thomas Jefferson leads the growing country into the 19th century as it confirms its status as a free and independent nation.*	***In-Depth Resources: Unit 1*** • Guided Reading, p. 72 • Skillbuilder Practice: Making Inferences, p. 77; Synthesizing, p. 78 • American Lives: Tecumseh, p. 93 ***Lesson Plans,*** pp. 25–26	PE ***Section 1 Assessment,*** p. 123 TE ***Self-Assessment,*** p. 123 ***Formal Assessment*** • Section Quiz, p. 41 ***Alternative Assessment Book*** • Standards for Evaluating a Cooperative Activity
SECTION 2 The Age of Jackson *pp. 124–132*	*Sectionalism causes tensions, but a strong national spirit—represented by Andrew Jackson—holds the nation together.*	***In-Depth Resources: Unit 1*** • Guided Reading, p. 73 • Outline Map: Indian Removal Act of 1830, p. 83 • Primary Source: from *The Webster-Hayne Debates,* p. 85 • American Lives: Henry Clay, p. 94 ***Lesson Plans,*** pp. 27–28	PE ***Section 2 Assessment,*** p. 132 TE ***Self-Assessment,*** p. 132 ***Formal Assessment*** • Section Quiz, p. 42 ***Alternative Assessment Book*** • Standards for Evaluating a Cooperative Activity
SECTION 3 Manifest Destiny *pp. 133–141*	*Americans continue to move westward toward the Pacific Ocean, and the United States claims new territories—sometimes as the result of war.*	***In-Depth Resources: Unit 1*** • Guided Reading, p. 74 • Skillbuilder Practice: Analyzing Assumptions, p. 79 • Geography Application: Mexico Cedes Land, p. 81 • Primary Source: *from* James K. Polk's Speech, p. 87 • Literature: from *Roughing It* by Mark Twain, p. 90 ***Lesson Plans,*** pp. 29–30	PE ***Section 3 Assessment,*** p. 141 TE ***Self-Assessment,*** p. 141 ***Formal Assessment*** • Section Quiz, p. 43 ***Alternative Assessment Book*** • Standards for Evaluating a Cooperative Activity
SECTION 4 The Market Revolution *pp. 144–149*	*The Industrial Revolution comes to America, creating new opportunities for some and new problems for others.*	***In-Depth Resources: Unit 1*** • Guided Reading, p. 75 ***Lesson Plans,*** pp. 31–32	PE ***Section 4 Assessment,*** p. 149 TE ***Self-Assessment,*** p. 149 ***Formal Assessment*** • Section Quiz, p. 44 ***Alternative Assessment Book*** • Standards for Evaluating a Cooperative Activity
SECTION 5 Reforming American Society *pp. 152–157*	*As the country's economy and political systems change, a new spiritual awakening and a series of social reform movements sweep the nation.*	***In-Depth Resources: Unit 1*** • Guided Reading, p. 76 • Skillbuilder Practice: Identifying Problems, p. 80 • Primary Sources: Propaganda Images, p. 88; *from* The Seneca Falls "Declaration of Sentiments," p. 89 ***Lesson Plans,*** pp. 33–34	PE ***Section 5 Assessment,*** p. 157 TE ***Self-Assessment,*** p. 157 ***Formal Assessment*** • Section Quiz, p. 45 ***Alternative Assessment Book*** • Standards for Evaluating a Cooperative Activity
CHAPTER RESOURCES	**Chapter Overview** *In the first half of the 1800s, the United States grows—adding land and people. The economy grows throughout the nation, but the different regions develop varied ways of life and attitudes.*	***In-Depth Resources: Unit 1*** • Living History Project: Worksheet, p. 95; Standards, p. 96 ***Telescoping the Times*** • Chapter Summary, pp. 5–6 ***Planning for Block Schedules***	PE ***Chapter Assessment,*** pp. 160–161 PE ***Alternative Assessment,*** p. 161 ***Formal Assessment*** • Chapter Test, forms A and B, pp. 46–51 ***Test Generator*** ***Alternative Assessment Book*** See explanation and forms for different kinds of alternative assessments including portfolio assessment.

KEY
PE Pupil's Edition
TE Teacher's Edition
http://www.mlushistory.com

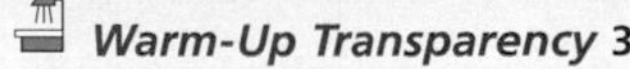

TECHNOLOGY

Warm-Up Transparency 3

Critical Thinking Transparencies
- CT6, The War of 1812

Electronic Library of Primary Sources

INTERNET Louisiana Purchase and War of 1812

Warm-Up Transparency 3

Humanities Transparencies
- H33, Jackson destroying the Bank

Critical Thinking Transparencies
- CT7, Industrial Revolution
- CT41, Cotton and Slave Population

Electronic Library of Primary Sources

INTERNET Trail of Tears and Jackson

Warm-Up Transparency 3

Humanities Transparencies
- H9, General Winfield Scott

Critical Thinking Transparencies
- CT9, Westward Movement
- CT43, Growth of U.S.: 1790–1850

Grolier Multimedia Encyclopedia
- Stephen F. Austin, Texas Revolution

Electronic Library of Primary Sources

INTERNET American expansion West

Warm-Up Transparency 3

Geography Transparencies
- G9, American Cities, 1820, 1860

Grolier Multimedia Encyclopedia
- Samuel Morse
- Charles Goodyear

Electronic Library of Primary Sources

INTERNET 19th-century workers and inventors

Warm-Up Transparency 3

Humanities Transparencies
- H8, "Religion Camp Meeting"

Geography Transparencies
- G8, Distribution of Slaves

Critical Thinking Transparencies
- CT42, Increasing School Enrollment

Grolier Multimedia Encyclopedia
- Lucretia Mott

Electronic Library of Primary Sources

INTERNET 19th-century reformers

American Portfolio: A Videodisc for U.S. History, user's guide, pp. 45–51, 53–61, 63–67, 69–73, 75–86

Chapter Summary Audiotapes
- Unit 1, Chapter 3

INTERNET http://www.mlushistory.com

Block Scheduling (90 MINUTES)

Day 1

Section 1, pp. 118–123

Section 2, pp. 124–132

Section Assessments, pp. 123, 132

COOPERATIVE ACTIVITIES
- Taking Part in an Expedition, p. 120 (TE)
- Sectionalism and Nationalism, p. 127 (TE)
- Discussing States' Rights, p. 130 (TE)

Day 2

Section 3, pp. 133–141

Section 4, pp. 144–149

Geography Spotlight: Mapping the Oregon Trail, pp. 142–143

Daily Life: Working at Mid-Century, pp. 150–151

Section Assessments, pp. 141, 149

COOPERATIVE ACTIVITIES
- Interviewing Settlers, p. 135 (TE)
- Creating a Newspaper, p. 140 (TE)
- Writing a List of Demands, p. 148 (TE)

Day 3

Section 5, pp. 152–157

American Literature: Abolitionist Literature, pp. 158–159

Section Assessment, p. 157

Chapter Assessment, pp. 160–161

COOPERATIVE ACTIVITY
- Daily Lives in Contrast, p. 155 (TE)

YEARLY PACING ***Chapter 3 Total:*** 3 days ***Yearly Total:*** 85 days

See *Planning for Block Schedules* for special activities and pacing strategies.

Customizing for Special Populations

Students Acquiring English

Access for Students Acquiring English: Spanish Translations
- Guided Reading for Sections 1–5, pp. 52–56
- Chapter Summary, pp. 50–51
- Skillbuilder Practice: Making Inferences, p. 57; Synthesizing, p. 58; Analyzing Assumptions, p. 59; Identifying Problems, p. 60
- Geography Application: Mexico Cedes Land to the United States, p. 61
- Outline Map: Indian Removal Act of 1830, p. 63

Spanish Reading Study Guide, pp. 35–46

Translations of Chapter Summaries, Hmong, Cantonese, Vietnamese, and Cambodian

Chapter Summary Audiotapes in Spanish Unit 1, Chapter 3

INTERNET The Diverse Classroom

Gifted and Talented Students

In-Depth Resources: Unit 1
- Primary Sources: from *The Webster-Hayne Debates,* p. 85; *from* James K. Polk's Speech on War with Mexico, p. 87; Propaganda Images, p. 88; *from* The Seneca Falls "Declaration of Sentiments," p. 89
- American Lives: Tecumseh, p. 93; Henry Clay, p. 94

Less Proficient Readers

In-Depth Resources: Unit 1
- Guided Reading for Sections 1–5, pp. 72–76
- Skillbuilder Practice: Making Inferences, p. 77; Synthesizing, p. 78; Analyzing Assumptions, p. 79; Identifying Problems, p. 80
- Geography Application: Mexico Cedes Land to the United States, p. 81
- Outline Map: Indian Removal Act of 1830, p. 83

Reading Study Guide
- pp. 35–46

Telescoping the Times
- Chapter Summary, pp. 5–6

Chapter Summary Audiotapes, Unit 1, Chapter 3

Connections to Literature READINGS FOR STUDENTS

In-Depth Resources: Unit 1
- **from *Roughing It* by Mark Twain,** p. 90

Enrichment Reading
- **Barbara Kingsolver**
  Pigs in Heaven.
  New York: Harper & Rowe, 1994.
  In this modern novel, a Native American child is the center of a complex situation involving family and heritage.
- **James Michener**
  Texas.
  New York: Ballantine, 1987.
  Spanning four and a half centuries, this saga of Texas begins in the early 1500s. Paths of the characters and their descendants cross and recross as the narrative develops.

McDougal Littell *The Language of Literature*
American Literature
- **Henry Wadsworth Longfellow, "A Psalm of Life" p. 272**
- **Ralph Waldo Emerson, *from* "Self-Reliance" p. 291**
- **Margaret Fuller, *from* "Memoirs" p. 294**

McDougal Littell *Literature Connections*

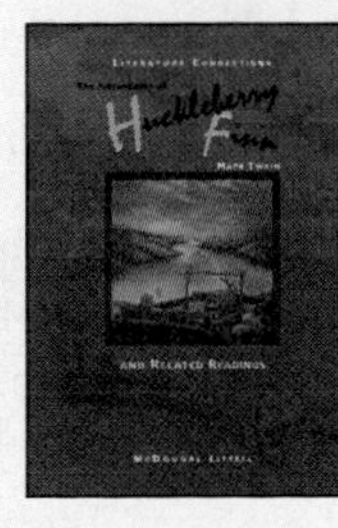

Mark Twain,
The Adventures of Huckleberry Finn
(with related readings)
Through a remarkable river journey with two unforgettable characters, Twain captures the essence of mid-19th century America.

OVERVIEW

The Growth of a Young Nation

▶ *Accessing Prior Knowledge*

Ask students whether or not Americans should have been optimistic about the prospects for their nation in the early 19th century. Students should explain what kinds of things a nation needs in order to prosper.

▶ *Predicting Outcomes*

Ask the students to read the quotation by Ignatius Donnelly. What does it suggest to them could happen to the United States in the early 19th century?

MORE ABOUT . . .
Ignatius Donnelly

Ignatius Donnelly (1831–1901) was a reformer and politician who helped form the Populist Party. The Populist Party advocated reforms to help common people, especially laborers and farmers, many of whom migrated west. Born in Philadelphia, Donnelly took his own advice about moving west and in 1857 settled in Minnesota.

REVIEW CHAPTER 3

The Growth of a Young Nation

SECTION 1
The Jeffersonian Era
Thomas Jefferson leads the growing country into the 19th century as it confirms its status as a free and independent nation.

SECTION 2
The Age of Jackson
Sectionalism causes tensions, but a strong national spirit—represented by Andrew Jackson—holds the nation together.

SECTION 3
Manifest Destiny
Americans continue to move westward toward the Pacific Ocean, and the United States claims new territories—sometimes as the result of war.

SECTION 4
The Market Revolution
The Industrial Revolution comes to America, creating new opportunities for some and new problems for others.

SECTION 5
Reforming American Society
As the country's economy and political systems change, a new spiritual awakening and a series of social reform movements sweep the nation.

"Why should we weep to sail in search of fortune? Cheer for the West, the new and happy land."
Ignatius Donnelly

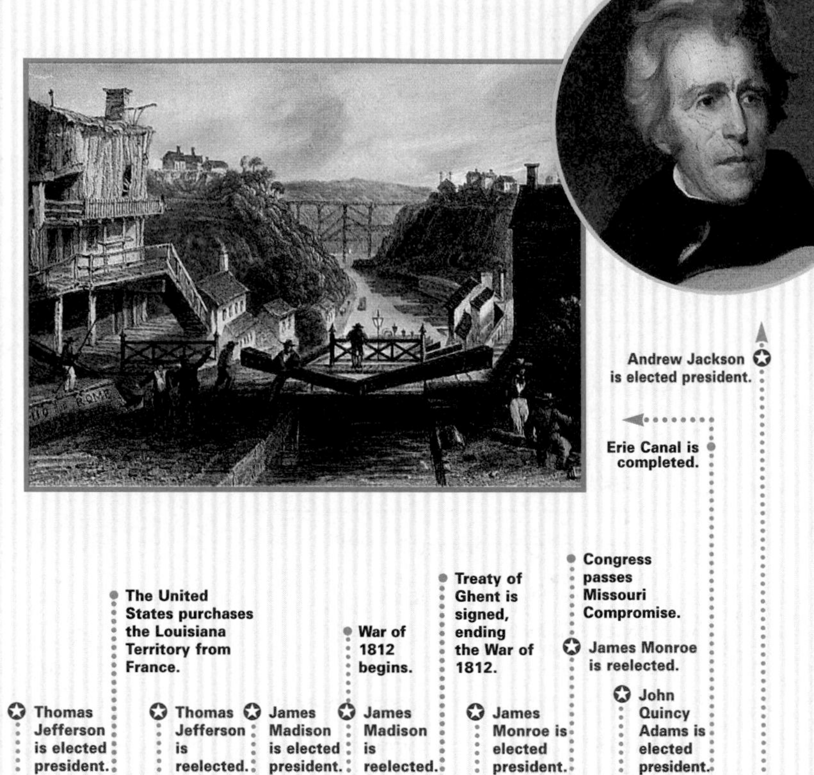

Thomas Jefferson is elected president.
The United States purchases the Louisiana Territory from France.
Thomas Jefferson is reelected.
James Madison is elected president.
War of 1812 begins.
James Madison is reelected.
Treaty of Ghent is signed, ending the War of 1812.
James Monroe is elected president.
Congress passes Missouri Compromise.
James Monroe is reelected.
John Quincy Adams is elected president.
Erie Canal is completed.
Andrew Jackson is elected president.

THE UNITED STATES: 1800, 1803, 1804, 1808, 1812, 1814, 1816, 1820, 1824, 1825, 1828

THE WORLD: 1804, 1810, 1815, 1821

- 1804: Haiti declares independence from France.
- 1810: Mexican War of Independence begins.
- 1815: Napoleon is defeated at Waterloo.
- 1821: Mexico wins its independence from Spain.

THEMES IN CHAPTER 3

America in the World	*Democracy in America*	*Immigration and Migration*	*Science and Technology*
The nation establishes a foreign policy with two main goals—supporting the independence of new nations in the Western Hemisphere and defending the commercial interests of the United States. See Teacher's Edition note, p. 121.	Although increasing numbers of Americans gained the right to vote in this era, Native Americans, African Americans, and women continued to face discrimination. See Teacher's Edition notes, pp. 129, 154.	Americans heed the call of the Mexican government and migrate to Texas in search of economic opportunity. Eventually these migrants would rebel against Mexico and join the United States. See Teacher's Edition note, p. 136.	By the 1830s, new manufacturing techniques had revolutionized industry and transformed society in New England. However, not everyone benefited from these changes. See Teacher's Edition note, p. 146.

LIVING HISTORY

CREATING A POLITICAL ADVERTISEMENT

As you will read, Andrew Jackson was the first presidential candidate to really develop a political "image" as a campaign strategy. He was followed by Martin Van Buren and William Henry Harrison. This image-making is a large part of politics today—as you can see by watching political advertisements on television and noticing how the candidates are portrayed.

- Study pictures and words that help create a candidate's image.
- Then pick a current political candidate and create your own political advertisement, in the form of a poster, for that candidate.
- Aim for a particular look or impression you want the public to get—positive or negative.
- Choose pictures and words that help convey that image.

PORTFOLIO PROJECT Keep your poster in a folder for your American history portfolio. At the end of the chapter, you will compare your poster with others' posters.

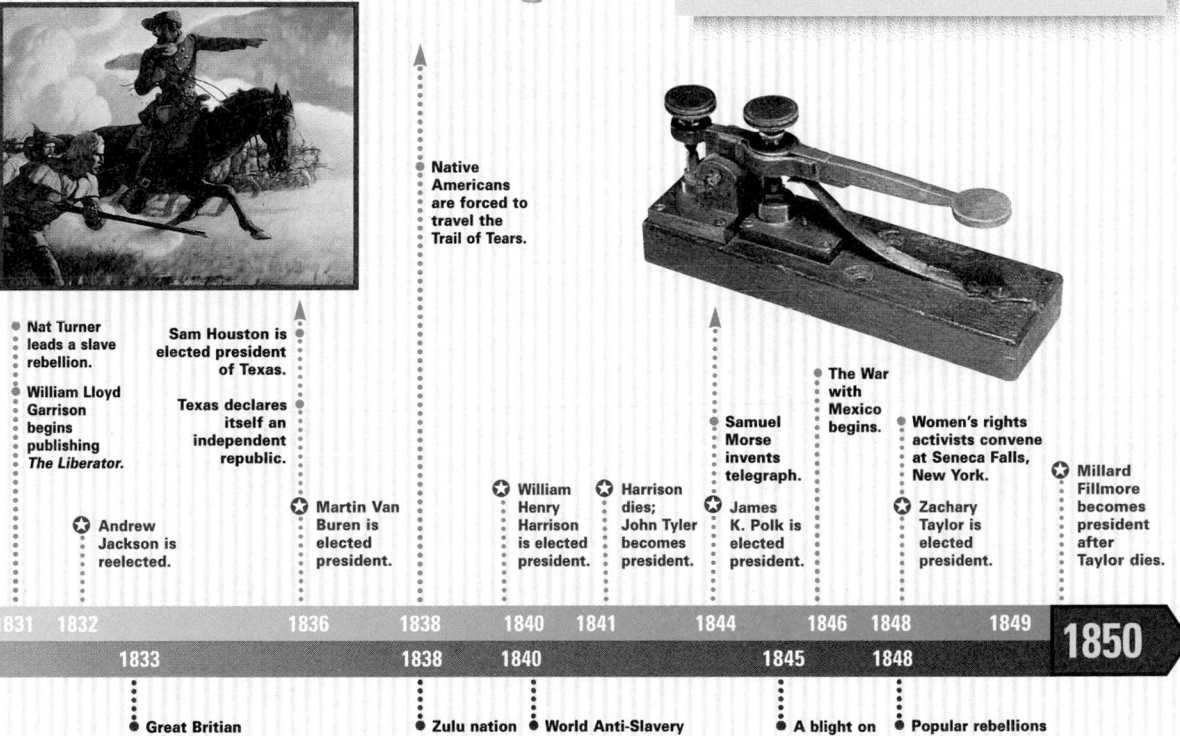

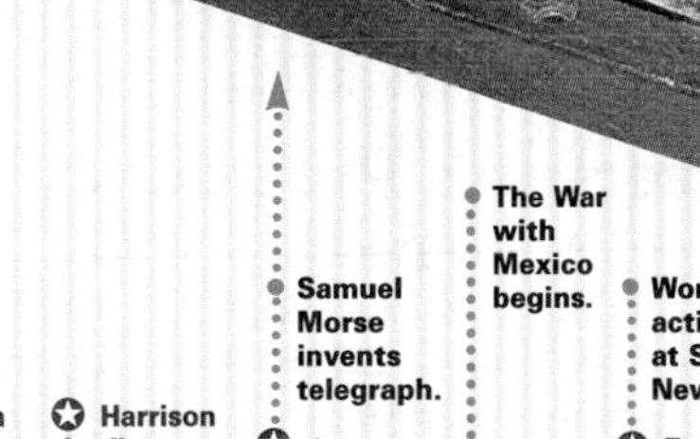

- 1831: Nat Turner leads a slave rebellion. William Lloyd Garrison begins publishing *The Liberator*.
- 1832: Andrew Jackson is reelected.
- 1833: Great Britian abolishes slavery in the empire.
- 1836: Sam Houston is elected president of Texas. Texas declares itself an independent republic. Martin Van Buren is elected president.
- 1838: Native Americans are forced to travel the Trail of Tears.
- 1838: Zulu nation in Africa clashes with Boer settlers.
- 1840: William Henry Harrison is elected president.
- 1840: World Anti-Slavery Convention is held in London.
- 1841: Harrison dies; John Tyler becomes president.
- 1844: Samuel Morse invents telegraph. James K. Polk is elected president.
- 1845: A blight on potatoes causes famine in Ireland.
- 1846: The War with Mexico begins.
- 1848: Women's rights activists convene at Seneca Falls, New York. Zachary Taylor is elected president.
- 1848: Popular rebellions erupt across Europe and force reform.
- 1849: Millard Fillmore becomes president after Taylor dies.
- 1850

LIVING HISTORY

CREATING A POLITICAL ADVERTISEMENT

Discuss ways of planning the political campaign poster, suggesting the following steps to students.

- Choose a politician widely photographed in the media.
- Research the politician's strengths and weaknesses.
- Decide whether you want to create an ad for or against the politician.
- Determine which qualities of the politician you will stress.
- Find photos that reflect those qualities.
- Create a pithy slogan that sums up your message.

To help students organize their information, suggest that they make a web diagram like the one below.

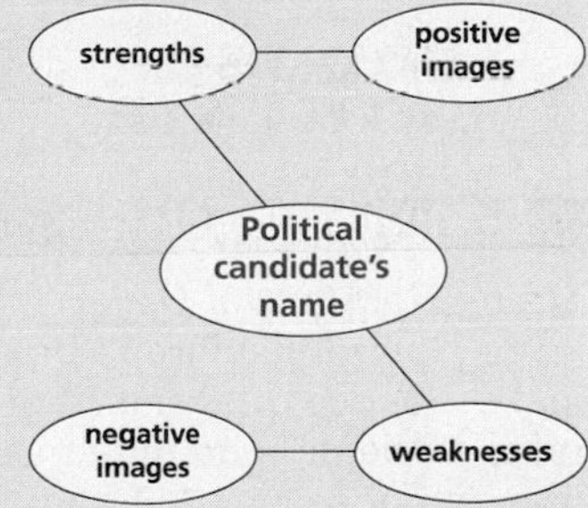

IN-DEPTH RESOURCES: UNIT 1
See worksheet and standards for evaluation, pp. 95, 96.

RECOMMENDED RESOURCES

Books for the Teacher

Cunningham, Noble, Jr. *In Pursuit of Reason: The Life of Thomas Jefferson.* Baton Rouge: Louisiana State UP, 1987.

Walters, Ronald G. *American Reformers 1815–1860.* New York: Hill, 1978.

White, Richard. *It's Your Misfortune and None of My Own.* Norman: Oklahoma UP, 1991. A history of the American expansion in the West.

Books for the Student

Douglass, Frederick. *A Narrative of the Life of Frederick Douglass.* New York: Macmillan, 1962.

Griffith, Elisabeth. *In Her Own Right.* New York: Oxford UP, 1992. Life of Elizabeth Cady Stanton.

Hickey, Donald R. *The War of 1812: A Forgotten Conflict.* Urbana: U of Illinois P, 1989.

Videos

Canals and Steamboats. Agency for Instructional Technology, 800-457-4509.

A History of Slavery in America. Schlessinger Video Productions, 1994, 800-843-3620.

Adelante Mujeres 1992. Women Make Movies, 212-925-0606. Story of Mexican-American women.

The Alamo. A&E Home Video, 1966.

Software

The Industrial Revolution in America. CD-ROM. Educational Software Institute, 800-955-5570.

Social Reform Movements. CD-ROM. Educational Software Institute, 800-955-5570.

The Santa Fe Trail. Diskette. Educational Activities, 800-645-3739.

Section 1 Overview

OBJECTIVES

1. To identify some of the significant changes brought about during Thomas Jefferson's presidency.
2. To explain the causes and consequences of the War of 1812.
3. To summarize the ways nationalism shaped American foreign policy, including the Monroe Doctrine.

SKILLBUILDERS

- Understanding geography: movement, p. 120
- Understanding geography: place, region, p. 123

CRITICAL THINKING

- Making inferences, p. 119
- Clarifying, p. 119
- Finding main ideas, p. 121
- Summarizing, pp. 122, 123
- Theme: America in the World, p. 122
- Forming opinions, p. 123
- Recognizing effects, p. 123

FOCUS & MOTIVATE

5-MINUTE WARM-UP

Using Sequential Order
To recognize the chronological sequence of events, have students read the time line on pages 116–117 and answer these questions.

1. Which event happened first—the Louisiana Purchase or Thomas Jefferson's reelection as president?
2. Who was president when the War of 1812 began?

WARM-UP TRANSPARENCY 3

▶ ***Starting with the Student***
- Ask students what issues, personalities, and events have dominated the era in which they live.
- What name or title might summarize this era?

1 The Jeffersonian Era

TERMS & NAMES
- Jeffersonian republicanism
- *Marbury* v. *Madison*
- John Marshall
- judicial review
- Louisiana Purchase
- impressment
- war hawks
- Tecumseh
- James Monroe
- Monroe Doctrine

LEARN ABOUT the important issues during the presidencies of Thomas Jefferson, James Madison, and James Monroe
TO UNDERSTAND the development of the United States during the first quarter of the 19th century.

ONE AMERICAN'S STORY

Patrick Gass witnessed many remarkable events in the young nation. Born in 1771, before the American Revolution, he died nearly a century later, on April 2, 1870. During his lifetime, the nation grew rapidly into an economic power, greatly increased its population, and expanded its reach across the continent to the Pacific Ocean. Gass played an important role in that expansion as part of the most famous frontier exploration: the Lewis and Clark expedition. Setting out in 1804, this expedition traveled overland from St. Louis, Missouri, to the Pacific. Along the way, Gass kept a journal in which he took notes on the people and places he saw and the dramatic events he witnessed. Gass described one of those events in his journal entry for May 14, 1805.

Patrick Gass

A PERSONAL VOICE
This forenoon we passed a large creek on the North side and a small river on the South. About 4 in the afternoon we passed another small river on the South side near the mouth of which some of the men discovered a large brown bear, and six of them went out to kill it. They fired at it; but having only wounded it, it made battle and was near seizing some of them, but they all fortunately escaped, and at length succeeded in dispatching it. These bears are very bold and ferocious; and very large and powerful. The natives say they have killed a number of their brave men.

PATRICK GASS, *A Journal of the Voyages and Travels of a Corps of Discovery*

Lewis and Clark helped lay the foundations for expansion by charting the Western regions of the continent for the new government. Their era ushered in great changes for the United States. Pioneers and settlers followed the lead of Lewis and Clark and expanded American influence to the West, and new inventions ignited dynamic economic change. Meanwhile, Americans continued to shape the government in their growing nation.

Jefferson's Presidency

In the late 1790s, Thomas Jefferson and his followers were highly critical of President Adams. They felt Adams and the Federalists were grabbing too much power for the national government and were endangering the liberties won during the revolution. As the election of 1800 approached, Jefferson led his party, the Democratic-Republicans (known as Republicans), against Adams.

THE ELECTION OF 1800 The presidential campaign of 1800 was a hard-fought struggle between Adams and Jefferson. Each party hurled wild charges at the other. Republicans called Adams a tool of the rich who wanted to turn the executive branch into a British-style monarchy. Federalists cried that Jefferson was a dangerous supporter of revolutionary France and an atheist.

In the balloting, Jefferson defeated Adams by eight electoral votes. However, since Jefferson's running mate, Aaron Burr, received the same number of votes as Jefferson in the Electoral College, the House of Representatives had to choose the winner. For six days the House voted—35 ballots in all. Finally, Alexander Hamilton intervened. Although he opposed Jefferson's philosophy of

SECTION 1 RESOURCES

PRINT RESOURCES

IN-DEPTH RESOURCES: UNIT 1
Guided Reading, p. 72
Skillbuilder Practice: Making Inferences, p. 77; Synthesizing, p. 78
American Lives: Tecumseh, p. 93

READING STUDY GUIDE, p. 35

ACCESS FOR STUDENTS ACQUIRING ENGLISH
Guided Reading (Spanish), p. 52
Skillbuilder Practice: Making Inferences (Spanish), p. 57; Synthesizing (Spanish), p. 58

SPANISH READING STUDY GUIDE, p. 35

FORMAL ASSESSMENT
Section Quiz, p. 41

ALTERNATIVE ASSESSMENT BOOK
See forms for supporting and scoring alternative activities.

TECHNOLOGY RESOURCES

CRITICAL THINKING TRANSPARENCIES
CT6, The War of 1812

CD-ROM Electronic Library of Primary Sources

VIDEO *American Portfolio: A Videodisc for U.S. History* user's guide, pp. 45–51

INTERNET http://www.mlushistory.com

government, he feared Burr even more. Hamilton persuaded enough Federalists to cast blank votes to give Jefferson a majority of two votes. Burr then became vice-president.

The deadlock revealed a flaw in the electoral process established by the Constitution. As a result, Congress passed the Twelfth Amendment, which called for electors to cast separate ballots for president and vice-president. This system is still in effect today.

Despite the bitter feelings provoked in the campaign, Jefferson's inauguration took place without incident and proved that the American republic could handle political change. In his inaugural address, Jefferson extended the hand of peace to his opponents. "Every difference of opinion is not a difference of principle," he said. "We are all Republicans; we are all Federalists."

SIMPLIFYING THE GOVERNMENT Jefferson's theory of government, often called **Jeffersonian republicanism,** held that the people should control the government and that a simple government best suited the needs of the people. In accord with his belief in decentralized power, Jefferson tried to shrink the government and cut costs wherever possible. He reduced the size of the army, halted a planned expansion of the navy, and lowered expenses for government social functions. He also rolled back Hamilton's economic program by eliminating all internal taxes and reducing the influence of the Bank of the United States.

THINK THROUGH HISTORY **A. *Making Inferences*** *How did Jefferson's actions reflect his philosophy?*

A. Answer He acted to restore Republican ideals in place of Federalist policies; he simplified the government.

As president, Jefferson also tried to reduce the role of the Federalists in government. Under Washington and Adams, Federalists filled most government positions. Jefferson replaced some Federalist officials with Republican ones so that by 1803, the government bureaucracy was more evenly balanced between Republicans and Federalists.

JOHN MARSHALL AND THE SUPREME COURT Federalists continued to exert great influence in the judicial branch, however. Just before leaving office, President Adams had tried to influence future judicial decisions by filling federal judgeships with Federalists. Adams's effort to pack the courts angered Jefferson and the Republicans. Since the documents authorizing some of the appointments were signed but not delivered by the time Adams left office, Jefferson argued that these appointments were invalid.

This argument led to one of the most important Supreme Court decisions of all time in ***Marbury* v. *Madison*** (1803). William Marbury, a Federalist, was one of Adams's late judicial appointments, but he never received his official papers. When he demanded that Secretary of State James Madison deliver the papers, Madison refused. In a famous ruling, the Federalist chief justice **John Marshall** declared that part of Congress's Judiciary Act of 1789, which would have forced Madison to hand over the papers, was unconstitutional.

B. Answer It is the principle that the Supreme Court has the right to review acts of Congress to see if they are constitutional. The Supreme Court checks the power of Congress.

THINK THROUGH HISTORY **B. *Clarifying*** *What is judicial review, and why is it important?*

John Marshall, Chief Justice of the United States **(about 1832), by William James Hubard.**

This decision was in part a victory for the Republicans, since the Federalist Marbury never received his commission. However, the decision strengthened the Supreme Court by establishing the principle of **judicial review**—the ability of the Supreme Court to declare an act of Congress unconstitutional. This principle became a cornerstone of American law and government.

THE LOUISIANA PURCHASE Federalists were not alone in expanding the power of the federal government. Jefferson himself contributed to the nation's growth with the **Louisiana Purchase.** As Americans continued their westward migration across the Appalachians, Jefferson unexpectedly had an opportunity to

HISTORICAL SPOTLIGHT

PROSSER'S REBELLION

Gabriel Prosser, an African-American slave in Virginia, demanded the rights promised all Americans under a republic. Denied any political voice, Prosser felt he had no other option than to fight for those rights; thus, he attempted to lead an armed rebellion.

On August 30, 1800, he assembled a thousand slaves from nearby plantations for a planned attack on Richmond (the state capital), with the intention of making Virginia a state for African Americans. The attack was thwarted by a violent storm and by the Virginia militia, and Prosser was captured and hanged, but other slave revolts would soon follow.

OBJECTIVE

① INSTRUCT

Jefferson's Presidency

▶ Discussing Key Ideas

- Jefferson's inauguration marks the first transfer of power from one party to another.
- Jefferson decentralizes the federal government.
- U.S. Supreme Court Chief Justice John Marshall establishes the principle of judicial review.
- France sells the Louisiana Territory to the United States.
- Jefferson sends an expedition led by Lewis and Clark to explore the new territory.

IN-DEPTH RESOURCES: UNIT 1
Guided Reading, p. 72
ACCESS FOR STUDENTS ACQUIRING ENGLISH
Guided Reading (Spanish), p. 52

HISTORICAL SPOTLIGHT

Prosser's Rebellion

Critical Thinking: Making Inferences Ask students why Prosser felt he had to rebel to fight for his rights. *Possible Response: Since Prosser was a slave, all of his political rights were limited, and he probably felt an armed rebellion would be the only way to win freedom for himself and fellow slaves.*

TEACHING OPTION

Skillbuilder Mini-Lesson: Making Inferences

Explaining the Skill Making inferences from a piece of historical writing means drawing conclusions based on facts, examples, and the author's use of language instead of from explicit statements. For example, a writer may not explicitly say how Thomas Jefferson's political philosophy relates to his policies as president, but you can still make inferences about how Jefferson's philosophy shaped his policies.

Applying the Skill: Jefferson's Response to Marshall Have students review the concept of Jeffersonian republicanism and Chief Justice John Marshall's decision in *Marbury* v. *Madison* on this page.

1. What is the central tenet of Jeffersonian republicanism? *A simple government is best.*
2. What was the main effect of the Supreme Court decision in *Marbury? It gave more power to the Supreme Court.*
3. Infer from the preceding points what Thomas Jefferson thought about Marshall's opinion in *Marbury. Jefferson opposed it because it gave more power to the judicial branch of the federal government (despite the fact Jefferson's side won the case).*

IN-DEPTH RESOURCES: UNIT 1
Skillbuilder Practice: Making Inferences, p. 77

HISTORY FROM VISUALS

The Lewis and Clark Expedition, 1804–1806

Reading the Map Point out that the descriptive labels are numbered from 1 to 8 and should be read in a counter-clockwise direction. The arrows point to the locations where the events took place. You might display a physical map of the region to give students an idea of the terrain the exploration party covered.

Extension Ask students to write a journal entry based on one of the labels shown on the map.

ELECTRONIC LIBRARY OF PRIMARY SOURCES

from A Letter to Meriwether Lewis by Thomas Jefferson

from A List of Requirements by Meriwether Lewis

MORE ABOUT . . .

Sacajawea

Ask students to consider what knowledge Sacajawea would have had about the area of the country being explored that could have helped the expedition.

Possible Response: Her knowledge of food sources, local topography, and dominant weather patterns in addition to her knowledge of Native American groups and languages.

Skillbuilder Answer **Total miles** About 2500 miles. **Miles per day** Approximately 5 miles per day.

GEOGRAPHY SKILLBUILDER:
MOVEMENT *About how many miles did the expedition travel on its route to the Pacific Ocean?*
MOVEMENT *On average, how many miles per day did they travel from Ft. Clatsop to the place where the party split up on July 3, 1806?*

expand American territory. In 1800, Napoleon Bonaparte of France persuaded Spain to return to France the Louisiana Territory, which Spain had received from France in 1762. Jefferson decided to see whether he could buy New Orleans, an important port city in Louisiana, from the French.

By 1803, however, Napoleon abandoned his hopes for an empire in America and suddenly offered to sell the entire Louisiana Territory to the United States. With no time to consult their government, American representative James Monroe and ambassador Robert Livingston went ahead and closed the deal for $15 million. Jefferson, though, was not certain that the purchase was constitutional. He doubted whether the Constitution gave the government the power to acquire new territory. At the same time, he realized that the vast new lands could form the "empire of liberty" that was his vision for the nation. After a delay, he submitted the treaty finalizing the purchase, and the Senate

The Lewis and Clark Expedition, 1804–1806

Sacajewea, a young woman and member of the Shoshone nation, served as interpreter and guide for the expedition.

1 May 14, 1804 Depart camp near St. Louis about 4 P.M. Heavy rain.
2 August 20, 1804 Sergeant Floyd dies, only fatality of expedition, and is buried.
3 November 3, 1804 Hard wind from northwest. Begin to set up winter camp. December 17, 1804 Coldest weather yet—45 degrees below zero. Sentinels have to be changed every half hour.
4 April 7, 1805 Party of 32, including Clark's black servant York, French-Canadian trader Charbonneau, his wife Sacajawea, and their son, depart at 5 P.M. to continue journey. High northwest wind but otherwise fair weather.
5 April 25–26, 1805 High winds and cold enough for water to freeze on oars. Lewis searches by land for Yellowstone River. Rejoins Clark at junction of Missouri and Yellowstone.
6 December 8, 1805–March 23, 1806. Winter camp at Ft. Clatsop. Lack of provisions forces departure. Wind high.
7 July 3, 1806 Party breaks up. Lewis takes direct route to falls of Missouri. Clark takes route to Jefferson and Yellowstone rivers. August 11, 1806 Mistaken for elk, Lewis accidentally shot in thigh by member of party. In pain, he rejoins Clark's party next day.
8 September 23, 1806 Reach St. Louis at 12 noon, Lewis's shortcut having saved 579 miles. Total mileage: 7,689.
Fort Clatsop
Traveler's Rest
Three Forks
Fort Mandan
CANADA (British)
LOUISIANA PURCHASE (1803)
St. Louis
NEW SPAIN
New Orleans
0 500 Miles
0 1,000 Kilometers
N
Journey west, 1804–1805
Journey home, 1806
Lewis's route
Clark's route
Fort

Lewis & Clark's compass

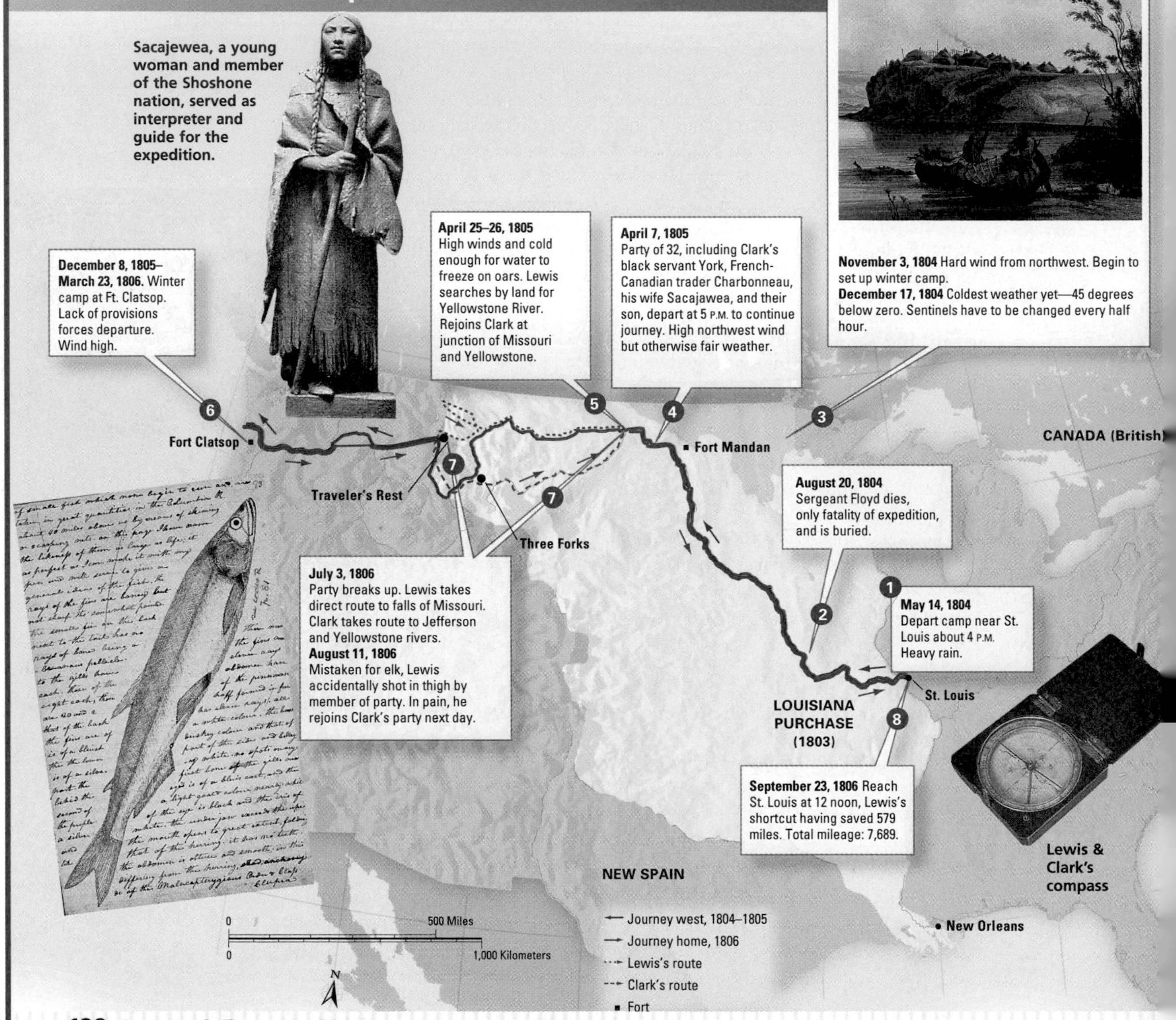

Block Schedule TEACHING OPTION **Time Needed: 50 Minutes**

Cooperative Activity: Taking Part in an Expedition

Task: Have groups of four to five students explore an area with which they are unfamiliar—a park, neighborhood, zoo, public recreation area—and write a report on what they find there.

Purpose: To help students understand what is involved in organizing and carrying out an exploratory expedition.

Activity: Students should prepare for their expedition by making a list of the equipment they will need. During the expedition, students should take notes on the area's terrain and climate and the people they encounter there. They should also make judgments about the area. Do they recommend that others visit it? Why or why not?

Building a Portfolio: If students consider that this report represents some of their best work, they may want to place the report in their portfolio.

Standards for Evaluation
Reports should . . .

- provide a detailed account of the area's geography, climate, and population
- include students' assessment of the area as a good or bad place to visit

ALTERNATIVE ASSESSMENT BOOK
Standards for Evaluating a Cooperative Activity

ratified it. The Louisiana Purchase more than doubled the size of the United States. Jefferson, who wanted to simplify and decentralize the government, had instead expanded the power of the government.

THE LEWIS AND CLARK EXPEDITION Jefferson was eager to have the new territory explored. In 1803, he appointed Meriwether Lewis to lead an expedition from St. Louis to the Pacific coast. Lewis chose William Clark to be second in command. Jefferson instructed Lewis and Clark to carry out scientific studies along the way and to document the native cultures they found.

The Lewis and Clark expedition took two years and four months—and was a great success. It brought back valuable information about the West and showed that transcontinental travel was possible. It also pointed the way for settlement of the West and strengthened American claims to the Oregon Territory on the northwest coast. The Louisiana Purchase and the Lewis and Clark expedition contributed to the success of Jefferson's first term in office, but trouble with Britain loomed on the horizon.

Madison and the War of 1812

Jefferson's popularity soared after the Louisiana Purchase, and he won reelection in 1804. During his second term, though, renewed fighting between Britain and France threatened American shipping. Although Jefferson made several attempts to end these threats, ultimately his successors had to deal with the problem. In 1812 Republican James Madison, who was elected president in 1808 over a Federalist named Charles C. Pinckney, led the nation into the War of 1812 against Great Britain to provide security for American commerce.

"The Great Spirit gave this great land to his red children."

TECUMSEH

THE CAUSES OF THE WAR Although France and Britain both threatened U.S. ships between 1805 and 1812, Americans focused their anger on the British. One reason was the policy of **impressment,** the British practice of seizing Americans at sea and "impressing," or drafting, them into the British navy.

Jefferson convinced Congress to declare an embargo, a ban on exporting products to other countries. He believed the embargo would hurt Britain and the other European powers and force them to honor American neutrality. Unfortunately, the embargo stifled American business, and Congress lifted the embargo in 1809.

Anger against Britain did not vanish, however. A group of young congressmen from the South and the West, known as the **war hawks,** continued to demand war. The leaders of this group were Representatives John C. Calhoun of South Carolina and Henry Clay of Kentucky, who was also the Speaker of the House of Representatives.

C. Answer They were angry that the British were supplying arms to Native Americans in the Indiana Territory.

THINK THROUGH HISTORY
C. Finding Main Ideas *For what reason did the war hawks demand war against England?*

The presence of Native Americans in the Indiana Territory upset the war hawks who wanted to expand white settlement. A confederacy of Native Americans, led by the Shawnee chief **Tecumseh,** organized to defend their homeland in the Indiana Territory against white settlers. In 1811, while Tecumseh was absent, his brother attacked American troops but was defeated. When the war hawks discovered that the Native American confederacy was using arms from British Canada, they again called for war against Britain.

THE COURSE OF THE WAR By the spring of 1812, President Madison had decided to go to war against Britain, and Congress approved the war declaration in early June.

Republican funding cuts had left the American military ill prepared for war, but the British were too preoccupied with Napoleon in Europe to pay much attention to the Americans. U.S. attempts to invade Canada in 1812 failed, but

OBJECTIVE
② INSTRUCT

Madison and the War of 1812

▶Starting with the Student
Have students create a chart like the one below, listing the positive and negative results of the war.

War of 1812: Results	
Positive	Negative

▶Discussing Key Ideas
- The United States declares war against Britain, but the U.S. military is ill prepared.
- After both sides suffer losses, the United States and Great Britain sign a peace treaty.

CRITICAL THINKING TRANSPARENCIES
CT6, The War of 1812

IN-DEPTH RESOURCES: UNIT 1
American Lives: Tecumseh, p. 93

MORE ABOUT . . .
Tecumseh
Tecumseh was a remarkable Native American leader. Beginning in the 1790s and continuing until his death in 1813, he led a movement for Indian unity. White settlers' invasion of Shawnee lands and their destruction of Shawnee crops fueled Tecumseh's hatred of whites. Nevertheless, he would not tolerate the torture of whites by his people.

TEACHING OPTIONS

Making Connections Across Cultures

African Americans in Jackson's Army General Andrew Jackson issued a call to the "Free Colored Inhabitants" of Louisiana in an attempt to recruit troops to resist British forces. His urgent call read: "To every noble-hearted, generous freeman of color, volunteering to serve during the present contest with Great Britain . . . will be paid the same bounty in money and lands, now received by the white soldiers. . . ." He went further and said, "You will not, by being associated with white men in the same corps, be exposed to improper comparisons or unjust sarcasm." A number of freemen did respond to his appeal.

Exploring Themes

America in the World The War of 1812 was caused by American desires to protect their national honor and economic interest against the British. The Monroe Doctrine, established a decade later, was designed to protect U.S. interests by preventing European economic and political control over the Western Hemisphere. Although most European leaders thought little about American threats, the British Navy gave the doctrine teeth. The British wanted to keep other European powers from colonizing the Western Hemisphere and used their navy to stop them.

MORE ABOUT . . .
Andrew Jackson

When he was only 13, Jackson fought in the Revolutionary War and was captured by the British. A British officer slashed Jackson with his sword when the boy refused to clean his boots. As a general during the War of 1812, Jackson proved his toughness once again. On the way to New Orleans in 1813, he received orders to disband his army, but he disobeyed them. After fighting in New Orleans, Jackson led his men back to Tennessee through 500 miles of wilderness. "He's tough," one soldier said of Jackson. "Tough as hickory," replied another. Thus, Jackson earned his nickname, "Old Hickory."

OBJECTIVE

③ **INSTRUCT**

Nationalism Shapes Foreign Policy

▶ ***Discussing Key Ideas***

- The United States works out agreements with Great Britain and Spain that help ensure its security and expand its borders.
- The Monroe Doctrine supports the independent nations of the Western Hemisphere against European interference.

ELECTRONIC LIBRARY OF PRIMARY SOURCES
from First Inaugural Address by James Monroe

Tecumseh was killed at the Battle of the Thames in 1813, leading to the end of his confederacy. An American fleet under Commodore Oliver Hazard Perry defeated a British fleet on Lake Erie, but by the end of 1813, the superior strength of the British navy kept most American ships bottled up in port.

The most stunning British victory came in August of 1814, when they brushed aside American troops and sacked Washington, D.C. Madison and other federal officials fled the city as the British burned the Capitol, the Presidential Mansion, and other public buildings. The most impressive American victory occurred at the Battle of New Orleans. On January 8, 1815, General Andrew Jackson of Tennessee gathered troops to protect the city. The British commander ordered his 8,000 troops to attack. The 5,400 Americans lay lodged behind walls of cotton bales. Hundreds of British troops died while just a handful of Americans lost their lives.

THINK THROUGH HISTORY
D. *Summarizing* *What successes and failures did Americans have during the War of 1812?*

D. Answer **Successes:** Defeated Tecumseh's confederacy; defeated a British fleet on Lake Erie; won Battle of New Orleans. **Failures:** Failed to invade Canada; navy bottled up; Washington, D.C. sacked.

THE CONSEQUENCES OF THE WAR Ironically, British and American diplomats had already signed a peace agreement before the Battle of New Orleans, but news of the pact had not reached Jackson in time. The Treaty of Ghent, signed on Christmas Eve, 1814, declared an armistice, or end to the fighting. The war had three important consequences. First, it led to the end of the Federalist party, whose members generally opposed the war. Second, it encouraged the growth of American industries to replace products no longer available from Britain because of the war. Third, it confirmed the status of the United States as a free and independent nation.

Nationalism Shapes Foreign Policy

Within a few years, the United States and Great Britain were able to reach agreement on many of the issues left open at Ghent. During the first term of President **James Monroe,** elected in 1816, Secretary of State John Quincy Adams established a foreign policy based on nationalism—a belief that national interests should be placed ahead of regional concerns, such as slavery in the South or tariffs in the Northeast.

TERRITORY AND BOUNDARIES High on Adams's list of national interests was the security of the nation and the expansion of its territory. To further these interests, Adams worked out the Rush-Bagot Treaty (1817) with Great Britain to reduce the Great Lakes fleets of both countries to only a few military vessels. Adams also arranged the Convention of 1818, which fixed the northern U.S. border at the 49th parallel west to the Rocky Mountains. Finally, he reached a compromise with Britain to jointly occupy the Oregon Territory, the territory west of the Rockies, for ten years. Then, Adams convinced Don Luis de Onís, the Spanish minister to the United States, to transfer Florida to the United States. This deal was confirmed in the Adams-Onís Treaty (1819).

THINK THROUGH HISTORY
E. THEME *America in the World* *What were some of the issues on which Britain and the U.S. reached agreement after the Treaty of Ghent?*

E. Answer Trade; number of warships on the Great Lakes; northern boundary of the United States; joint occupation of the Oregon Territory.

THE MONROE DOCTRINE Meanwhile, many Americans wanted to reduce European power in North America. Accordingly, in his 1823 message to Congress, President Monroe warned all European powers not to interfere with affairs in the Western Hemisphere and promised that the United States would not interfere in European affairs.

A PERSONAL VOICE

Our policy in regard to Europe . . . is not to interfere in the internal affairs of any of its powers. . . . But in regard to those continents [of the Western Hemisphere], circumstances are eminently and conspicuously different. It is impossible that the allied [European] powers should extend their political system to any portion of either continent without endangering our peace and happiness.

PRESIDENT JAMES MONROE, *Annual Message to Congress,* December 2, 1823

TEACHING OPTION

Skillbuilder Mini-Lesson: Synthesizing

Explaining the Skill Synthesizing involves combining information from a number of sources to come up with a new, more complete understanding of a subject. Students might first think about ideas or facts they have just learned and then put those new ideas in the context of information they already have. Last, they should work to develop new understandings or ideas about the information.

Applying the Skill: Nationalism To understand how to synthesize information, students might begin by identifying the national interests covered in this section. These national interests include:

1. The causes of the War of 1812.
2. The desire of the United States to annex new territories such as Louisiana, Florida, and Oregon.
3. National security.

The next step is to examine American foreign policies, such as the Monroe Doctrine, in the context of these interests.

IN-DEPTH RESOURCES: UNIT 1
Skillbuilder Practice: Synthesizing, p. 78

Boundary Settlements of the United States, 1803–1819

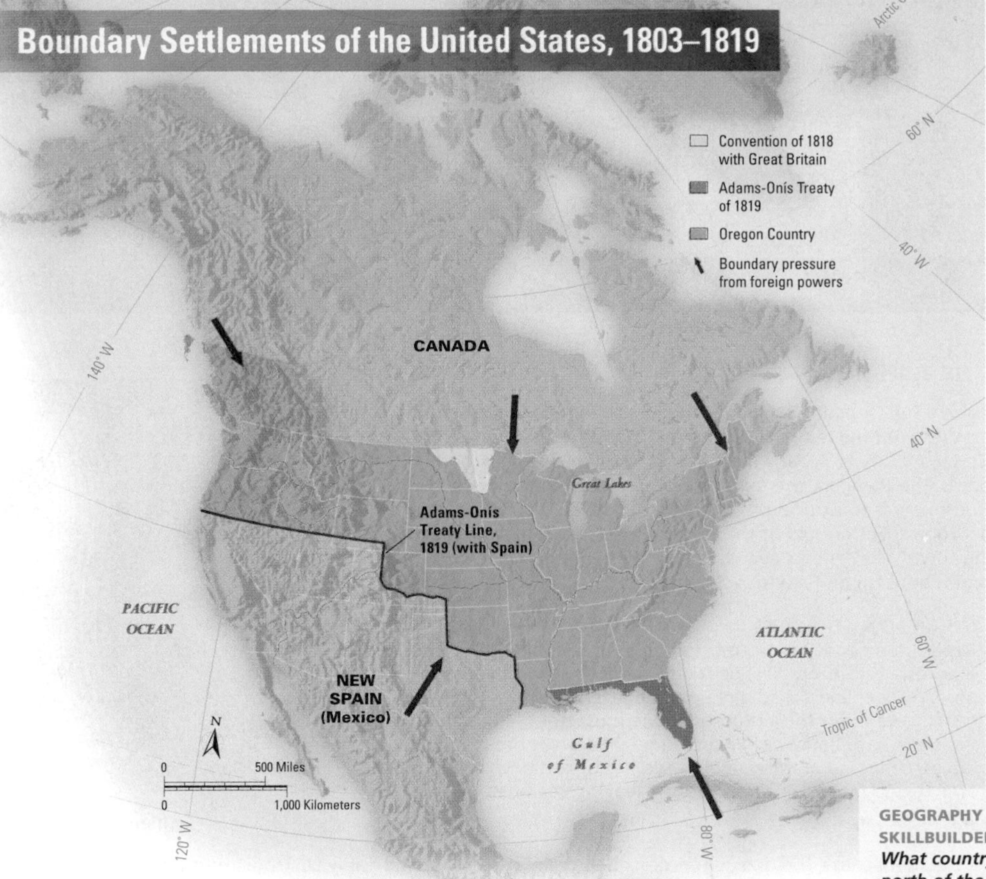

GEOGRAPHY SKILLBUILDER PLACE *What country lies north of the territory Great Britain ceded to the U.S. in the Convention of 1818?* **REGION** *What body of water lies due south of the eastern lands gained by the U.S. in the Adams-Onís Treaty?*

Skillbuilder Answer
Place: Canada.
Region: Gulf of Mexico.

These principles became known as the **Monroe Doctrine.** Because the United States lacked the armed forces to support the doctrine, European nations ignored Monroe's speech. However, the Monroe Doctrine became an important basis for future American policy.

The Monroe Doctrine provided an example of how the United States was becoming a stable nation, confidently charting its future. But sectional differences challenged national unity, requiring strong patriotic sentiments and leaders like Andrew Jackson to hold the nation together.

Section  Assessment

1. TERMS & NAMES
Identify:
- Jeffersonian republicanism
- *Marbury* v. *Madison*
- John Marshall
- judicial review
- Louisiana Purchase
- impressment
- war hawks
- Tecumseh
- James Monroe
- Monroe Doctrine

2. SUMMARIZING In the web below, show the consequences of the War of 1812.

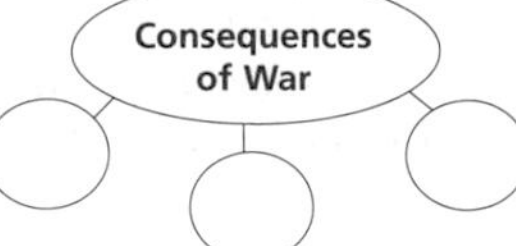

3. FORMING OPINIONS How successful was Thomas Jefferson as president in achieving his goal of simplifying the government?

THINK ABOUT
- the Louisiana Purchase
- military spending
- Jefferson's attitude toward the national bank

4. RECOGNIZING EFFECTS Why was *Marbury* v. *Madison* such an important case, both in the early days of the country and for the nation's future?

THINK ABOUT
- what was being argued
- Chief Justice Marshall's decision
- the effects on the future

HISTORY FROM VISUALS
Boundary Settlements of the United States, 1803–1819

Reading the Map Have students note that the arrow pointing toward Florida represents boundary pressure from Spain and Portugal, and that the arrow pointing toward Alaska represents the boundary pressure from Russia.

Extension Ask students to list some of the reasons the United States wanted to expand its boundaries to the West. *Possible Responses: To increase its resources; to facilitate trade with Asia; to increase its power.*

ASSESS & RETEACH

Section 1 Assessment
Have students work with a partner to answer the questions.

Self-Assessment
To explore their understanding of Section 1, ask students to make a two-column chart. In the first column, they should jot down what they knew previously about the events covered in the section. In the second column, they should list what they have learned.

Section Quiz
FORMAL ASSESSMENT
Section Quiz, p. 41

Reteach
Use the section quiz to help review the main ideas of the section.

CLOSE

The Monroe Doctrine signaled the growing confidence of the United States on the world stage. Democratic institutions would soon begin to expand, giving more Americans the opportunity to participate in their government.

ANSWERS

1. TERMS & NAMES
Jeffersonian republicanism, p. 119
Marbury v. *Madison*, p. 119
John Marshall, p. 119
judicial review, p. 119
Louisiana Purchase, p. 119
impressment, p. 121
war hawks, p. 121
Tecumseh, p. 121
James Monroe, p. 122
Monroe Doctrine, p. 123

2. SUMMARIZING
Answers should include these three points. First, the War of 1812 led to the end of the Federalist Party. Second, it encouraged the growth of American industries. Third, it confirmed the status of the United States as a free and independent nation.

3. FORMING OPINIONS
Jefferson's record is mixed. He succeeded in decreasing some activities of the federal government, such as reducing the size of the military and reducing the influence of the Bank of the United States. Nevertheless, he expanded federal power when he felt it was necessary, as in the case of the Louisiana Purchase.

4. RECOGNIZING EFFECTS
The case was significant because it affirmed the principle of judicial review—that the Supreme Court could declare a law unconstitutional (in this case, the Judiciary Act of 1789) and thus be an effective check on the legislative branch. From this point on, judicial review has played an important role in American government.

Section 2 Overview

OBJECTIVES

1. To describe regional economic differences in the early United States.
2. To summarize early tensions between nationalism and sectional interests.
3. To explain Andrew Jackson's rise to the presidency.
4. To describe the reasons for the removal of Native Americans from the Southeast.
5. To explain the major political issues of Jackson's presidency.
6. To identify the presidents that followed Jackson and the issues they faced.

SKILLBUILDERS

- Interpreting graphics, p. 125
- Understanding geography: region, 127
- Understanding geography: place, movement, p. 129

CRITICAL THINKING

- Analyzing causes, p. 124
- Comparing, p. 125
- Finding main ideas, p. 126
- Summarizing, pp. 127, 132
- Making inferences, pp. 128, 132
- Making decisions, p. 129
- Making predictions, pp. 131, 132
- Analyzing motives, p. 131
- Recognizing effects, p. 132

FOCUS & MOTIVATE

5-Minute Warm-Up

Analyzing Information
To understand some of the problems of nationalism and sectionalism, have students look at the map on page 127 and answer the following questions.

1. Which region contained most of the slave states?
2. Find the area where your state would be on the map. Was slavery allowed there under the Missouri Compromise?

WARM-UP TRANSPARENCY 3

2 The Age of Jackson

LEARN ABOUT major issues facing Andrew Jackson and other American politicians between 1820 and 1844
TO UNDERSTAND the importance of nationalism and sectionalism in the era dominated by Andrew Jackson.

TERMS & NAMES
- Henry Clay
- American System
- John C. Calhoun
- Missouri Compromise
- Andrew Jackson
- Jacksonian democracy
- John Quincy Adams
- Trail of Tears
- Daniel Webster
- Martin Van Buren
- John Tyler

ONE AMERICAN'S STORY

Robert Fulton built a boat propelled by a steam engine. In 1807 his *Clermont* made the 150-mile trip up the Hudson River from New York City to Albany in 32 hours. Another one of Fulton's boats, the *Paragon,* the third steamboat to operate on the Hudson, was so luxurious that it had a paneled dining room and bedrooms. Fulton said of the *Paragon* that it was a "whole floating town" that "beats everything on the globe." Fulton posted regulations on his luxurious steamboats.

Robert Fulton

A PERSONAL VOICE

As the steamboat has been fitted up in an elegant style, order is necessary to keep it so; gentlemen will therefore please to observe cleanliness, and a reasonable attention not to injure the furniture; for this purpose no one must sit on a table under the penalty of half a dollar each time, and every breakage of tables, chairs, sofas, or windows, tearing of curtains, or injury of any kind must be paid for before leaving the boat.

ROBERT FULTON, quoted in *Steamboats Come True: American Inventors in Action*

Steamboats like the one Fulton described did more than comfortably transport passengers. They also carried freight and played an important role in uniting the nation economically. Although tensions continued to arise between the different sections of the nation, a growing national spirit kept the country together. This spirit was perhaps best personified by Andrew Jackson—a self-made man from the growing West who was both confident and dynamic.

Regional Economies Create Differences

In the early decades of the 19th century, the economies of the various regions of the United States developed differently. The Northeast began to industrialize while the South and West continued to be more agricultural.

EARLY INDUSTRY IN THE UNITED STATES The Industrial Revolution began in Great Britain in the 18th century when inventors devised new ways to generate power from running water and coal. Inventors then developed power-driven machinery and ways to use this machinery to produce goods quickly. These techniques were gradually transferred to America.

The industry that began to emerge in the Northeast took manufacturing out of American households and artisans' workshops and put it in factories. The rise of factories lowered the costs of producing many goods and, as a result, increased markets and profits. These changes in manufacturing started an Industrial Revolution—a massive change in social and economic organization resulting in large-scale industrial production.

Industrial investment was greatest in New England, whose economy depended on shipping and foreign trade. Agriculture there was not highly profitable, so New Englanders were more ready than other Americans to embrace new forms of manufacturing—and prime among these were mechanized textile mills.

A. Answer Its economy depended on shipping and trade, and agriculture wasn't very profitable.

THINK THROUGH HISTORY
A. Analyzing Causes *Why was industrial investment greatest in New England?*

SECTION 2 RESOURCES

PRINT RESOURCES

IN-DEPTH RESOURCES: UNIT 1
Guided Reading, p. 73
Outline Map: Indian Removal Act, p. 83
Primary Source: from *The Webster-Hayne Debates,* p. 85
American Lives: Henry Clay, p. 94

READING STUDY GUIDE, p. 37

ACCESS FOR STUDENTS ACQUIRING ENGLISH
Guided Reading (Spanish), p. 53

SPANISH READING STUDY GUIDE, p. 37

FORMAL ASSESSMENT
Section Quiz, p. 42

ALTERNATIVE ASSESSMENT BOOK
See forms for supporting and scoring alternative activities.

TECHNOLOGY RESOURCES

HUMANITIES TRANSPARENCIES
H33, President Andrew Jackson destroying the Bank of the United States: Lithograph cartoon, 1828

CRITICAL THINKING TRANSPARENCIES
CT7, Industrial Revolution
CT41, Cotton Production and Slave Population

CD-ROM Electronic Library of Primary Sources

VIDEO *American Portfolio: A Videodisc for U.S. History* user's guide, pp. 53–61, 63–67

INTERNET http://www.mlushistory.com

In 1793, a British immigrant named Samuel Slater had established in Pawtucket, Rhode Island, the first successful mechanized textile factory in America. Others imitated his operation. However, Slater's factory and those modeled after it still only produced one part of finished cloth: thread. Later entrepreneurs would expand American textile production by mechanizing all the stages in the manufacture of cloth. (See *free enterprise* on page 935 in the Economics Handbook.)

Samuel Slater memorized the plans for a cotton mill while he was still in Britain. He then came to America and built a mill from memory.

TWO AGRICULTURAL SYSTEMS DEVELOP Farmers moving to the Northwest Territory often set up small farms to grow virtually all they needed and rarely sold their produce to distant markets.

Soon, however, farmers discovered that they could specialize in one or two crops or types of livestock (such as corn and cattle), sell what they produced to urban markets, and then purchase with cash whatever else they needed from stores. Increasingly, these were items made in Northern factories. As a result, a market economy began to develop in which agriculture and manufacturing each supported the growth of the other.

B. Answer Small farms developed in the North, while large plantations developed in the South.

THINK THROUGH HISTORY
B. *Comparing* *How were the agricultural systems of the North and South different?*

Eli Whitney's invention of a cotton gin (short for "cotton engine") in 1793 helped set the South on a different course from the North. Whitney's gin made it possible for Southern farmers to grow cotton more profitably. Armed with cotton gins, nonslaveholding farmers began growing cotton. Wealthier planters followed, and they employed an enormous slave labor force to grow it.

SLAVERY SPREADS The emergence of a Cotton Kingdom in the South contributed to the expansion of slavery. Plantation owners took their slaves with them as they traveled westward into Alabama, Mississippi, and Louisiana. Between 1790 and 1820, the enslaved population increased from 697,681 to 1,538,022. In the North, things were different. By 1804, states north of Delaware had abolished slavery or enacted laws for gradual emancipation. Slavery declined in the North, but some slaves remained there for decades.

Skillbuilder Answer A machine could remove the seeds more quickly and less expensively than could a person.

SKILLBUILDER
INTERPRETING GRAPHICS *Why was using the cotton gin more efficient than removing seeds by hand?*

The Cotton Gin

BEFORE COTTON GIN — 1 worker cleans 1 lb. of cotton a day

AFTER COTTON GIN — 1 worker cleans 50 lbs. of cotton a day

1. Raw cotton is placed in the gin.
2. A hand crank turns a series of rollers.
3. A roller with tight rows of wire teeth removes seeds from the cotton fiber.
4. The teeth pass through a slotted metal grate, pushing the cotton fiber through but not the seeds, which are too large to pass.
5. The cotton seeds fall into a hopper.
6. A second roller, with brushes, removes the cleaned cotton from the roller.
7. A "clearer compartment" catches the cleaned cotton.

OBJECTIVE
① **INSTRUCT**

Regional Economies Create Differences

▶***Starting with the Student***
- Ask students which leaders today show the greatest potential for unifying the American people.
- What characteristics make these leaders effective?

▶***Discussing Key Ideas***
- The Industrial Revolution changes manufacturing practices in the Northeast and brings about social and economic changes.
- The invention of the cotton gin makes possible large-scale, profitable cotton growing in the South.
- The slave population in the South increases to provide labor needed for cotton.

IN-DEPTH RESOURCES: UNIT 1
Guided Reading, p. 73

ACCESS FOR STUDENTS ACQUIRING ENGLISH
Guided Reading (Spanish), p. 53

HISTORY FROM VISUALS
The Cotton Gin

Reading the Chart Have students calculate how many pounds of cotton per day ten workers could clean before and after the invention of the cotton gin. *Before—10 pounds; after—500 pounds*

Extension Ask students how the cotton gin made life both easier and more difficult for workers.

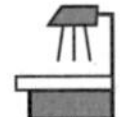

CRITICAL THINKING TRANSPARENCIES
CT7, Industrial Revolution
CT41, Cotton Production and Slave Population

TEACHING OPTION

Making Connections Across the Curriculum

Math Between 1790 and 1820 the population of enslaved African Americans in the United States increased from 697,681 to 1,538,022. How many more slaves were in the United States in 1820 than in 1790? *1,538,022 minus 697,681 equals 840,341.* What percentage increase in the number of slaves occurred between 1790 and 1820? *840,341 divided by 697,681 equals 120%.*

Between 1790 and 1820 the resident population of the United States increased from 3,929,214 to 9,638,483. How many more people lived in the United States in 1820 than in 1790? *9,638,483 minus 3,929,214 equals 5,709,269* What percentage increase in total population did the United States experience over this period? *5,709,269 divided by 3,929,214 equals 145%.* Which grew faster in this period—total population or slave population? *Total population (both in absolute terms and in relative terms).*

OBJECTIVE

② **INSTRUCT**

Balancing Nationalism and Sectionalism

▶ ***Discussing Key Ideas***

- The American System seeks to unite the nation's economic interests.
- Roads and canals are constructed to promote the exchange of goods between regions.
- The Missouri Compromise defuses a crisis over slavery.

NOW & THEN

Freight Transportation

Ask students to research the fate of the Erie Canal, formerly one of the most important transportation routes in the United States. What is the canal used for today? *Possible Responses: Today the main function of the canal is recreational, with boating, camping, and hiking areas. There are also historical sites and museums along the canal.*

MORE ABOUT . . .

Henry Clay

Clay was known as the "Great Compromiser" because he settled so many disputes. He ran unsuccessfully for president five times—perhaps because he remained true to his principles. Clay once said, "I had rather be right than be President." Clay was a faithful defender of the Union; his tombstone includes this quotation from one of his speeches: "I know no North—no South—no East—no West."

IN-DEPTH RESOURCES: UNIT 1
American Lives: Henry Clay, p. 94

Balancing Nationalism and Sectionalism

These economic differences often created political tensions between the different sections of the nation. Throughout the first half of the 19th century, however, American leaders managed to keep the nation together.

CLAY'S AMERICAN SYSTEM As the North, South, and West developed different economies, President Madison developed a plan to unify the nation. In 1815 he presented his plan to Congress. It included three major points: 1. establishing a protective tariff; 2. rechartering the national bank; and, 3. sponsoring the development of transportation systems and other internal improvements.

House Speaker **Henry Clay** promoted the plan as the "American System." As Clay explained it, the **American System** would unite the nation's economic interests. The industrial North would manufacture goods that farmers in the South and West would buy. Meanwhile, the agricultural South and West would raise most of the grain, meat, and cotton needed in the North. A national currency and an improved transportation network would facilitate this exchange of goods. With each part of the country sustaining the other, Americans would finally be economically independent of Britain and other European nations.

NOW & THEN

FREIGHT TRANSPORTATION

Freight in the United States is today carried by many means of transportation, as the following graph shows.

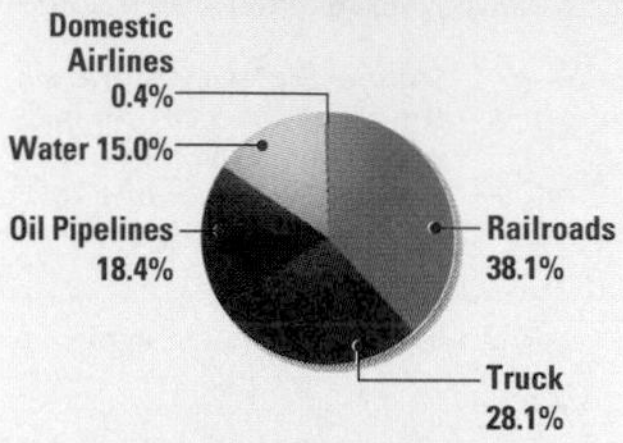

In the 1820s and 1830s, canals were the main means of freight transportation. After 1850, the railroads took the lead in freight transportation. The construction of the interstate highway system, beginning in the 1950s, produced 41,000 miles of highways and made trucks an important means of freight transportation.

Source: *Statistical Abstract of the United States, 1995. The United States Waterways and Ports: A Chronology*, Vol. 1, 1541–1871.

THINK THROUGH HISTORY

C. Finding Main Ideas *What was the intention of the American System?*

C. Answer The American System was supposed to unite the nation's economic interests by having the North produce manufactured goods that farmers in the South and West would buy, while the South and West would raise the grain, livestock, and cotton needed in the North.

TARIFFS AND THE NATIONAL BANK Madison and Clay supported tariffs on imports to protect U.S. industry from British competition. British-manufactured goods were often cheaper than American products. Placing a tariff on imports increased the cost of foreign goods and thereby eliminated their price advantage.

Most Northeasterners welcomed protective tariffs. However, people in the South and West, whose livelihoods did not depend on manufacturing, were not as eager to tax European imports. They resented government intervention that made goods more expensive. Nevertheless, Clay, who was from the West (Kentucky), and **John C. Calhoun,** a Southerner (South Carolina), convinced congressmen from their regions to approve the Tariff of 1816. (See *tariff* on page 939 in the Economics Handbook.)

Also in 1816, Congress voted to charter the Second Bank of the United States (BUS) for a 20-year period. At the time, regional banks issued their own currency, and often banks and businesses in a region honored only the currency issued there. This regional system made it difficult for people in one part of the country to do business with those in another. The BUS would make available a currency guaranteed to be accepted nationwide.

INTERNAL IMPROVEMENTS Improved transportation systems were also necessary for economic growth. However, building roads and canals was expensive, and funding was a major issue. Although the federal government experimented with building highways—constructing the National Road in 1811—the states funded the improvements to their own transportation systems.

One of the most impressive projects was the Erie Canal. This 363-mile canal was begun in 1817, and by 1825 it linked the Hudson River to Lake Erie—or, in effect, the Atlantic Ocean to the Great Lakes. Other states became eager to build their own canals when they saw the financial benefits that New York state reaped from the Erie Canal. Just 12 years after it had opened, canal tolls had completely paid for its construction. Partly because of the canal, New York City became the dominant port in the country. In their rush to make similar profits, other states built more than 3,000 miles of canals by 1837.

TEACHING OPTIONS

Making Connections Across the Curriculum

Economics The Tariff of 1816 helped to stabilize the U.S. economy by encouraging citizens to purchase domestic rather than imported goods. Discuss the advantages and disadvantages of placing a tariff on particular imported products or placing a tariff on all imports from a particular country. *Possible Responses: Products—domestic products become more attractive to consumers, but decreased competition reduces the need to strive for quality. Countries—money is raised from tariffs, but the taxed country will have less money to buy exported U.S. goods.*

Teaching Less Proficient Readers

Have students make a two-column chart to help clarify the regional attitudes toward the Tariff of 1816 and slavery in the territories. Put the chart below on the chalkboard and have students fill in the missing information.

Regional Attitudes	
Tariff of 1816	Slavery in the Territories
Northeasterners liked the tariff because it helped them sell their products	
Southerners . . .	

GEOGRAPHY SKILLBUILDER
REGION *What two slave states bordered the free state of Illinois?*
REGION *In what two territories was slavery permitted?*

Skillbuilder Answer
Region: Missouri and Kentucky.
Region: Arkansas Territory and Florida Territory.

THE MISSOURI COMPROMISE In spite of these efforts to unify the national economy, sectional conflicts remained part of American politics. In 1819 settlers in Missouri requested admission to the Union. Northerners and Southerners disagreed, however, on whether Missouri should be admitted as a free state or a slave state.

Southerners accused Northerners of trying to end slavery. Northerners accused Southerners of plotting to extend the institution into new territories. Tempers flared to the point that people on both sides raised the possibility of civil war and the end of the Union.

Behind the leadership of Henry Clay, however, Congress managed to avert disaster with a series of agreements known as the **Missouri Compromise.** In this deal, Maine was admitted as a free state and Missouri as a slave state. The rest of the Louisiana Territory was split into two parts. The dividing line was set at 36°30′ north latitude. South of the line, slavery was legal. North of the line—except in Missouri—slavery was banned. When President Monroe signed the Missouri Compromise in 1820, the problem of slavery in federal territories seemed to be settled.

D. Answer Maine was admitted as a free state and Missouri as a slave state. The rest of the Louisiana Territory was split into two parts at 36° 30′ north latitude. South of the line, slavery was legal. North of the line—except for Missouri—slavery was banned.

THINK THROUGH HISTORY
D. Summarizing *What agreements composed the Missouri Compromise?*

ANOTHER PERSPECTIVE

SLAVERY AND THE UNION

Former president Thomas Jefferson feared for the Union's future after the Missouri Compromise. His words would prove prophetic:

"This momentous question, like a firebell in the night, awakened and filled me with terror. I considered it at once as the knell of the Union. It is hushed, indeed, for the moment. But this is a reprieve only, not a final sentence."

THOMAS JEFFERSON, letter to John Holmes, April 22, 1820

Jackson's Path to the Presidency

Despite these sectional tensions, the story of America in the early 19th century was one of expansion—expanding economies, expanding territory, and expanding democracy. **Andrew Jackson** symbolized this growth and tension. Although he was a slaveowner, Jackson valued the Union more than states' rights. Although he was a wealthy planter, he was the hero of common people. Indeed, his faith in the common person as the source of American strength was the center of his political philosophy, which is often called **Jacksonian democracy.** Also, like the young nation, he was dynamic and confident.

THE ELECTION OF 1824 **John Quincy Adams,** who had succeeded James Monroe as President, was not effective as the nation's chief executive. Trouble for Adams began with his election in 1824. Jackson and Adams were the two main candidates. Jackson actually won more popular votes than any other candidate, but he lacked the majority of electoral votes required to take office. The House of Representatives had to decide the outcome. Because of his power in the House, Henry Clay could swing the election either way. Clay disliked

HISTORY FROM VISUALS
The Missouri Compromise, 1820–1821

Reading the Map Ask students how the Missouri Compromise promoted sectionalism. *Possible Response: It revealed how the issue of slavery divided the country into the North and the South.*

ANOTHER PERSPECTIVE
Slavery and the Union

Critical Thinking: Analyzing Ask students why Jefferson's words were prophetic. *Possible Response: The slavery issue would lead to the Civil War.*

Extension Ask students to rephrase Jefferson's quote in their own words. Have them explain the metaphors in the word pairs *knell* and *hushed,* and *reprieve* and *sentence.*

OBJECTIVE
③ INSTRUCT

Jackson's Path to the Presidency

▶***Discussing Key Ideas***
- Jackson creates problems for Adams's presidency.
- The easing of property requirements for voting greatly enlarges the electorate.
- Jackson appeals to the common citizen.
- Expanded suffrage helps Jackson win the 1828 election.
- Jackson's spoils system rewards loyal supporters.

Block Schedule TEACHING OPTION **Time Needed: 40 Minutes**

Cooperative Activity: Sectionalism and Nationalism

Task: Have students play the roles of congress members from various regions as they address the issues confronting the nation during President Monroe's first term.

Purpose: To understand the tensions between nationalist sentiment and sectional interest in the late 1810s.

Activity: Have each student pretend that he or she is a representative or senator from a different state. Students should think about the regional interests of their states and work with others to draft legislation on a tariff, a national bank, internal improvements, and the expansion of slavery to the western territories. They should then pass legislation on these issues that satisfies the concerns of each region.

Building a Portfolio: Students should keep a copy of the legislation they passed for their history portfolio.

ALTERNATIVE ASSESSMENT BOOK
Standards for Evaluating a Cooperative Activity

Standards for Evaluation
Legislation should. . .
- address all the major issues of the era
- demonstrate the strong national sentiments of the era
- satisfy the concerns of the different regions of the country

DIFFICULT DECISIONS IN HISTORY

Voting Restrictions

Critical Thinking: Analyzing Tell students that many Americans in the Age of Jackson believed the United States should be governed by a small aristocratic group of educated and public-spirited landowners. Ask students where these ideas might have originated. *Possible Response: Many people probably adopted this idea from their mother country, Great Britain, or from another country ruled by a monarchy or divided by a class system.*

HISTORY FROM VISUALS

Painting

Reading the Painting Discuss the details in the painting such as the dress of the people and the behavior of the animals. Ask students: Did Cruikshank think the visitors to the White House were orderly or not? *Some of the people are not dressed in suits. One of the horses is bucking. A man is clinging to the back of a carriage. This is probably a disorderly gathering.*

Extension Based on the images in the painting and the title of the painting, ask students what Cruikshank thought about the expansion of voting rights in the 1820s. *Cruikshank probably thought the expansion was bad because the rabble didn't know how to vote any better than it knew how to behave at the White House.*

Difficult Decisions IN HISTORY

VOTING RESTRICTIONS

In 1821, New York legislator Nathan Sanford argued that the old requirements that restricted voting rights to property holders should change. At the time, only those white males who owned property could vote. Those who agreed with this restriction argued that the vested interest of property owners in the stability of the government made them more responsible. Those who disagreed with property restrictions argued that those who did not own property were also affected by the laws and so should be able to vote.

Sanford believed that all taxpayers should have the right to vote, and not just those paying property taxes. He proposed that every white male citizen who had lived within the state for six months should be entitled to vote.

1. Examine the issues Sanford raised about who should vote. What other issues would you have brought up in the debate?
2. If you had been a New York legislator taking part in this debate in 1821, would you have revised voting restrictions or not? Explain your reasons.

Jackson personally and feared his lack of political experience. Adams, on the other hand, supported Clay's American System. As a result, Adams was elected president by a majority of the states represented in the House.

Jacksonians, or followers of Jackson, accused Adams of stealing the presidency. Then, because Adams appointed Clay secretary of state, the Jacksonians claimed Adams had struck a corrupt bargain. The split between Clay and Jackson tore apart the Democratic-Republican party. While Clay and his faction were called the National Republican Party, the Jacksonians became known as the Democratic Party.

EXPANDING DEMOCRACY CHANGES POLITICS During Adams's presidency, most states had eased voting requirements, thereby enlarging the voting population. In the election of 1824, approximately 350,000 white males voted for the presidency. In 1828, over three times that number voted, and their votes helped Andrew Jackson win the presidency. The expansion of voting rights meant that a candidate for president had to be able to speak to the concerns and hopes of common people.

During the 1828 campaign, Jackson characterized Adams as a part of the upper class and portrayed himself as a man of humble origins—even though he had become a wealthy plantation owner. Jackson won the election by a landslide. He was so popular that record numbers of people came to Washington to see "Old Hickory" inaugurated. Mrs. Samuel Harrison Smith described the scene.

A PERSONAL VOICE

The President, after having been literally nearly pressed to death and almost suffocated and torn to pieces by the people in their eagerness to shake hands with Old Hickory [Jackson], had retreated through the back way, or south front, and had escaped to his lodgings at Gadsby's. Cut glass and china to the amount of several thousand dollars had been broken in the struggle to get the refreshments. . . . Ladies fainted, men were seen with bloody noses, and such a scene of confusion took place as is impossible to describe; those who got in could not get out by the door again but had to scramble out of windows.

MRS. SAMUEL HARRISON SMITH, letter dated March 1829

THE SPOILS SYSTEM Jackson announced that in order to give common people a chance to participate in government, his appointees to federal jobs would serve a maximum of four-year terms. Unless there was a regular turnover of personnel, he declared, officeholders would become inefficient and corrupt.

Robert Cruikshank created this satirical print entitled *The President's Levee, or All Creation Going to the White House* in 1829.

This policy of "rotation in office" enabled Jackson to give away huge numbers of jobs to friends and political allies. He fired many federal employees, most of them holdovers from the Adams administration, and gave their jobs to loyal Jacksonians. Jackson's administration practiced the spoils system in filling government jobs. This system got its name from the saying, "To the victor belong the spoils of the enemy." In the spoils system, new administrations fire former appointees and replace them with their own supporters.

THINK THROUGH HISTORY
E. *Making Inferences* *How might the spoils system help a president consolidate power?*

E. Answer The spoils system could help a president consolidate power by removing political opponents from office and replacing them with loyal friends.

TEACHING OPTIONS

Making Connections Across the Curriculum

U.S. Government Today, almost all adults over the age of 18 can vote in national and local elections, with the exception of a few groups of people, including those convicted of serious crimes. Discuss with students whether denying some convicted criminals the right to vote is constitutional. *Possible Responses: Some students may say that once the crime is committed, the criminal forfeits all rights of citizenship; others may feel that after serving their prison terms the criminals should regain the right to vote.*

Making Connections Across Time

Electoral College The electoral college method of electing the president has always been controversial. Have students research another close presidential race in which the effectiveness of the Electoral College has been questioned, such as Kennedy vs. Nixon or Harrison vs. Cleveland. In a brief one- to two-page paper, students could explain the results of the election and why people used those results to find fault with the Electoral College.

The Removal of Native Americans

One of the most important aspects of Jackson's presidency was his policy toward Native Americans. Some Americans hoped to assimilate Native Americans, or bring them into mainstream American culture. In fact, some Southeastern tribes did begin to adopt the culture of their white neighbors. The Cherokee, for example, created a government with a legislature and constitution modeled after those of the United States. However, these "civilized tribes" still occupied large areas of valuable land—and white farmers and miners wanted that land.

THINK THROUGH HISTORY
F. Making Decisions *Imagine you are a congressman from Georgia. Would you have voted for the Indian Removal Act?*

F. Answer Some students might answer no because they think removal was wrong. Others might say yes if they wanted to get reelected.

THE INDIAN REMOVAL ACT In 1830 Congress passed the Indian Removal Act. Under this law, the federal government provided funds to negotiate treaties that would force the Native Americans to move west. About 90 treaties were signed. For Jackson, the removal policy was "not only liberal, but generous," because it would enable Native Americans to maintain their way of life.

In 1830, Jackson pressured several tribes to move west of the Mississippi River. However, the Cherokee Nation fought these efforts in the courts. In 1832, the Supreme Court ruled in *Worcester* v. *Georgia* that the Cherokee Nation was a distinct political community. As such, the state of Georgia could not regulate the Cherokee Nation by law or invade Cherokee lands. However, Jackson refused to abide by the Supreme Court decision, saying, "John Marshall has made his decision; now let him enforce it."

THE TRAIL OF TEARS Other Cherokee efforts to prevent removal failed, and in 1838, President Martin Van Buren (Jackson's successor) ordered the removal of the nearly 20,000 Cherokee that still remained in the East. U.S. troops under the command of General Winfield Scott rounded up the Cherokee and drove them into camps to await the journey. A Baptist missionary described the scene.

Skillbuilder Answer
Place: Indian Territory. **Movement:** Many sickened and died on the journey, and others completed the journey to find inferior land—these events probably demoralized many Native Americans.

GEOGRAPHY SKILLBUILDER
PLACE ***Where were most of the tribes moved?*** **MOVEMENT** ***What do you think were the effects of this removal on Native Americans?***

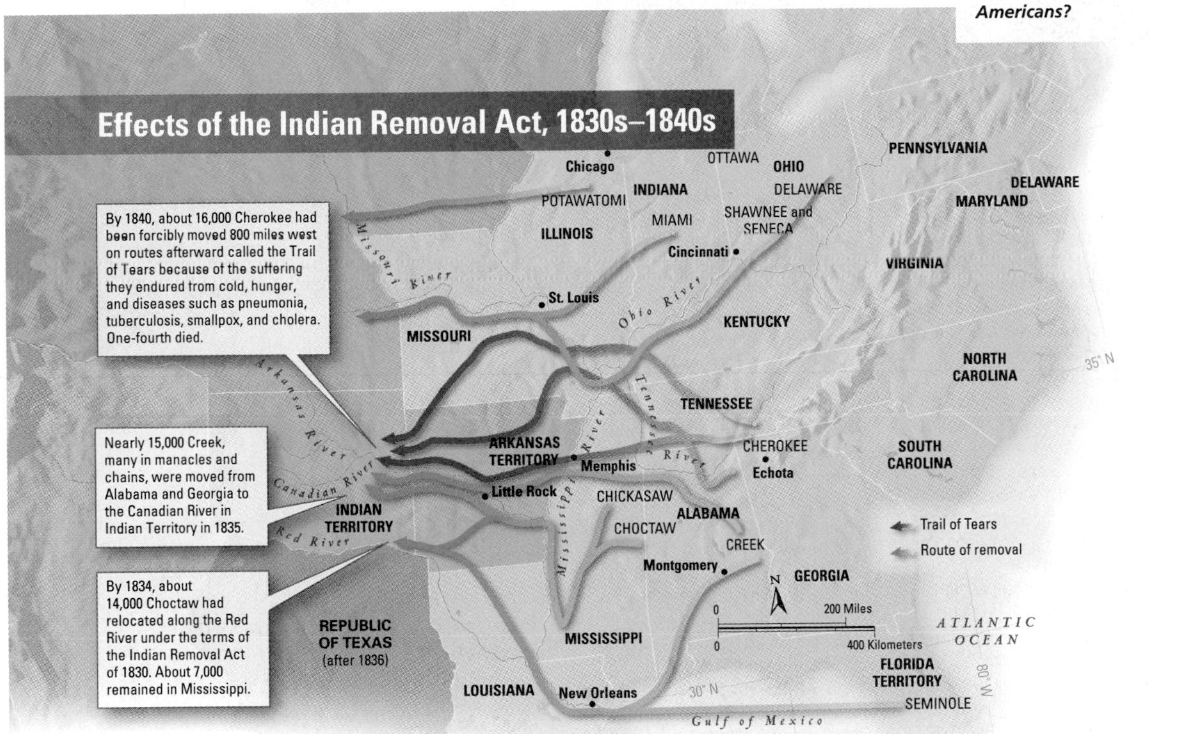

Effects of the Indian Removal Act, 1830s–1840s

By 1840, about 16,000 Cherokee had been forcibly moved 800 miles west on routes afterward called the Trail of Tears because of the suffering they endured from cold, hunger, and diseases such as pneumonia, tuberculosis, smallpox, and cholera. One-fourth died.

Nearly 15,000 Creek, many in manacles and chains, were moved from Alabama and Georgia to the Canadian River in Indian Territory in 1835.

By 1834, about 14,000 Choctaw had relocated along the Red River under the terms of the Indian Removal Act of 1830. About 7,000 remained in Mississippi.

Trail of Tears
Route of removal

OBJECTIVE
4 INSTRUCT

The Removal of Native Americans

Discussing Key Ideas
- Congress passes the Indian Removal Act of 1830, which forces Native Americans to move west.
- Many Cherokee die during the long, forced journey known as the Trail of Tears.

ELECTRONIC LIBRARY OF PRIMARY SOURCES
from A Message to Congress on Indian Policy by Andrew Jackson

HISTORY FROM VISUALS
Effects of the Indian Removal Act, 1830s–1840s

Reading the Map Ask students to study the routes taken by the Chickasaw and Choctaw out of Mississippi and by the Delaware, Shawnee, and Seneca out of Ohio. Why might these routes have been so circuitous? *Possible Response: The trails followed the courses of major rivers.*

Extension Remind students that much of the Cherokee's journey was made on foot. Then ask why so many Cherokee died during the forced removal. *Possible Response: Over 25 percent of the Cherokee along the Trail of Tears died of exhaustion and disease.*

IN-DEPTH RESOURCES: UNIT 1
Outline Map: The Indian Removal Act of 1830, p. 83

TEACHING OPTIONS

Exploring Themes

Democracy in America Discuss how the Cherokee fought for just treatment after Congress passed the Indian Removal Act of 1830. Ask students what the Cherokee's actions reveal about them. *Possible Responses: They were not violent; they were law-abiding.*

What do Jackson's actions following the Supreme Court's decision reveal about the government? *Possible Response: The executive branch did not always enforce the Supreme Court's decisions.*

Making Connections Across the Curriculum

Literature Tell students about *The Last of the Mohicans* by James Fenimore Cooper, published in 1826. This popular book was one in a series about Natty Bumppo and his noble Native American friends who live a happy life in the wilderness. The settlers who move into Bumppo's paradise, however, spoil the wilderness by trying to civilize it.

Invite students to read *The Last of the Mohicans* and to compare the treatment of Bumppo's friends with the government's treatment of the Native Americans in the 1820s.

OBJECTIVE

5 INSTRUCT

Tariffs, States' Rights, and the National Bank

▶ ***Discussing Key Ideas***

- Southern opposition to tariff laws leads to a crisis over nullification in 1832, but Henry Clay forges a compromise on the issue.
- President Jackson succeeds in killing the Second Bank of the United States.

KEY PLAYERS

Calhoun and Jackson

Critical Thinking: Analyzing Ask students to explain why the two men disagreed with each other over the nullification issue. *Possible Responses: As a Southerner, Calhoun probably supported nullification and states' rights as ways to protect slavery, which he believed was necessary to the Southern economy. Jackson saw himself as the leader of the whole nation and viewed nullification as a personal attack as well as an attack on national unity.*

IN-DEPTH RESOURCES: UNIT 1
Primary Source: *from* The Hayne-Webster Debates, p. 85

ELECTRONIC LIBRARY OF PRIMARY SOURCES
from Address to the People of the United States by John C. Calhoun

A PERSONAL VOICE

The Cherokees are nearly all prisoners. They had been dragged from their houses and encamped at the forts and military places, all over the nation. In Georgia especially, multitudes were allowed no time to take anything with them except the clothes they had on. Well-furnished houses were left as prey to plunderers, who, like hungry wolves, follow in the train of the captors. These wretches rifle the houses, and strip the helpless, unoffending owners of all they have on earth. Females who have been habituated to comforts and comparative affluence are driven on foot before the bayonets of brutal men.

EVAN JONES, *Baptist Missionary Magazine,* June 16, 1838

Beginning in October of 1838, the Cherokee were sent off in groups of about 1,000 each on the 800-mile journey, mostly on foot. As winter came, more and more Cherokee died. The Cherokee buried more than a quarter of their people along the **Trail of Tears,** the routes Cherokee followed from Georgia to the Indian Territory. When they reached their final destination, they ended up on land often inferior to that which they had been forced to leave.

KEY PLAYERS

JOHN C. CALHOUN
1782–1850

John Caldwell Calhoun entered national politics in 1811 with his election to the House of Representatives, where he was labeled a war hawk for his support of the War of 1812. Then, in 1817, President Monroe asked him to become his secretary of war. In that capacity, he improved the army's organization.

In 1824, this brilliant, ambitious, and handsome man with dark, flashing eyes won by a landslide the office of vice-president—a position he held under John Quincy Adams. In 1828, he won the vice-presidency again, this time as the running mate of Adams's opponent, Andrew Jackson.

A hard and humorless man, Calhoun took a tough position on slavery, arguing that it was not only necessary but even good: "There never has yet existed a wealthy and civilized society in which one portion of the community did not . . . live on the labor of the other."

ANDREW JACKSON
1767–1845

Andrew Jackson thought of himself as a man of the people. He had been born in poverty in the Carolina backcountry, the son of Scots-Irish immigrants. He was the first president since George Washington without a college education.

At the time of his election at the age of 61, however, Jackson was hardly one of the common people. He had built a highly successful career in Tennessee in law, politics, land speculation, cotton planting, and soldiering. His home, the Hermitage, was a mansion, not a log cabin. Anyone who owned more than a hundred slaves, as Jackson did, was a very wealthy man.

Because he had a suspicious nature, he disliked men whose power came from privilege. Lurking beneath the surface of his iron will was a deep streak of anger. When crossed, he lashed out, and he found it hard to forgive. He was also the only president to have killed a man in a duel.

Tariffs, States' Rights, and the National Bank

Two other important issues tested Jackson's leadership and the limits of federal power. One involved tariffs and states' rights. The other concerned the national bank.

THE NULLIFICATION CRISIS In 1824 and again in 1828, Congress increased the Tariff of 1816. Jackson's vice-president, John C. Calhoun of South Carolina, called the 1828 tariff a Tariff of Abominations. The South's economy depended on cotton exports. Yet the high tariff on manufactured goods reduced British exports to the United States, and because of this, Britain bought less cotton. With the decline of British goods, the South was now forced to buy the more expensive Northern manufactured goods. From the South's point of view, the North was getting rich at the expense of the South.

To try to free South Carolinians from the tariff, Calhoun developed a theory of nullification. Calhoun's theory held that the U.S. Constitution was based on a compact among the sovereign states. If the Constitution had been established by 13 sovereign states, he reasoned, then they must

Block Schedule TEACHING OPTION **Time Needed: 30 Minutes**

Cooperative Activity: Discussing States' Rights

Task: Have groups of four students write and perform a discussion between Jackson, Calhoun, and Clay over the crisis in South Carolina.

Purpose: To help students clarify the positions taken during the crisis.

Activity: Each student in a group will have a specific role. Three students will play the parts of Jackson, Calhoun, and Clay. One student will direct the enactment. All students in a group will work together to write the dialogue. After the dialogues have been completed, perform them in class.

Building a Portfolio: Students who want to include the dialogue scripts in their portfolios should attach a note describing their role in the group and explaining why they are proud of their work.

ALTERNATIVE ASSESSMENT BOOK
Standards for Evaluating a Cooperative Activity

Standards for Evaluation
Dialogues should. . .

- reveal each man's position during the crisis
- be clear, concise, and well-organized
- convey a sense of the emotions produced by the crisis

THINK THROUGH HISTORY
G. *Making Predictions* *What do you think might be the consequences of Calhoun's nullification theory for federal–state relations?*

G. Answer Some might argue that nullification would weaken federal authority and lead to disunion. Others might say that it would merely return proper authority to the states.

still be sovereign, and each had the right to determine whether acts of Congress were constitutional. If a state found an act to be unconstitutional, the state could declare the offending law nullified, or inoperative, within its borders. If the states did not have this right, Calhoun argued, then a majority in the federal government might trample on the rights of a minority. (See Tracing Themes on pages 174–175.)

The Senate debated the tariff question (and the underlying states' rights issue) with Senator **Daniel Webster** of Massachusetts opposing nullification and South Carolina Senator Robert Hayne airing Calhoun's views.

Two years later, in 1832, the issue of states' rights was put to a test when Congress passed another tariff law that South Carolina legislators found unacceptable. South Carolinians declared the tariffs of 1828 and 1832 "null, void, and no law." Then they threatened to secede, or withdraw from the Union, if customs officials tried to collect duties.

Jackson was furious. He took South Carolina's action as a challenge to him personally as well as to the nation as a whole. He believed that South Carolina's action in declaring a federal law null and void flouted the will of the people as expressed in the U.S. Constitution. Jackson urged Congress to pass the Force Bill to allow the federal government to use the military against South Carolina if state authorities resisted paying proper duties.

A bloody confrontation seemed likely until Henry Clay forged a compromise in 1833. Clay proposed a tariff bill that would gradually lower duties over a ten-year period. The compromise also included passage of the Force Bill. The tension between states' rights and federal authority subsided—temporarily.

THINK THROUGH HISTORY
H. *Analyzing Motives* *What were some of Jackson's reasons for opposing the Second Bank of the United States?*

H. Answer He thought the national bank was a tool of the upper classes and a threat to democracy.

JACKSON'S BANK WAR Although Jackson defended federal power in the nullification crisis, he tried to decrease federal power when it came to the Second Bank of the United States (BUS). Jackson believed that the national bank was an agent of the wealthy, whose members cared nothing for the common people. Jackson and his allies made certain that the public saw the BUS as a privileged institution that served to "make the rich richer and the potent more powerful."

In 1832 Jackson won reelection despite the efforts of Clay and Webster to make a campaign issue out of Jackson's opposition to the bank. After his reelection in 1832, he tried to kill the BUS by withdrawing all government deposits from the bank's branches and placing them in certain state banks called "pet banks" because of their loyalty to the Democratic Party.

In an attempt to save the BUS, bank president Nicholas Biddle had the bank call in—or demand repayment of—loans, and he refused to make new loans. This practice did little but force many merchants and manufacturers into bankruptcy. Pressure from financial leaders finally forced Biddle to adopt a more generous loan policy. Finally, in 1836, when its charter expired, the BUS became just another bank.

Jackson won the bank war, but his tactics and policies angered many people. Believing that Jackson had acted more like a king than a president, his foes dubbed him "King Andrew the First." Then, in 1834, the discontented—including National Republicans like Henry Clay and Daniel Webster—channeled their frustrations into action. They formed a new political party, called the Whig Party, named after a party in Britain that had tried to limit royal power.

In this cartoon, Andrew Jackson (portrayed as a king) tramples on the Constitution.

HISTORY FROM VISUALS
Political Cartoon

Reading the Cartoon Discuss the irony of the line at the top of the cartoon: "Born to command." Then ask students: Why might Jackson consider himself to be more powerful than the Constitution? *Possible Response: His veto power.*

Extension Ask students why portraying Jackson as a king was a powerful way to grab the public's attention. *Possible Response: After the Revolutionary War, Americans were suspicious of kings and monarchies.*

MORE ABOUT . . .
The Bank of the United States (BUS)

Jackson distrusted banks, any bank. In fact, he once told Nicholas Biddle, "I do not dislike your Bank any more than all banks." However, Jackson felt he could wield power over the national bank. When he vetoed the BUS, Jackson gave political, social, and economic reasons for his disapproval. Above all, he claimed that he vetoed the bank in the name of the people.

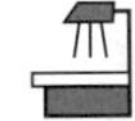
HUMANITIES TRANSPARENCIES
H33, President Andrew Jackson destroying the Bank of the United States: Lithograph cartoon, 1828

TEACHING OPTION

Teaching Gifted and Talented Students

Create a Political Cartoon Invite students to work independently or with a group to create a political cartoon based on an event or a person described in Section 2. For example, students might make a cartoon depicting Jackson's distrust of the national bank, or one illustrating some aspect of Hayne and Webster's debate. Suggest that students keep the following points in mind as they draw their cartoons.

- A political cartoon should exaggerate events or a person's actions.
- The cartoon should contain recognizable symbols relevant to the event or person depicted.
- The cartoon should be designed to appeal to a particular audience.
- The cartoon should be witty.

OBJECTIVE

⑥ INSTRUCT

Successors Deal with Jackson's Legacy

▶ ***Discussing Key Ideas***

- President Van Buren confronts the Panic of 1837.
- Whig Party candidate William Henry Harrison wins the 1840 presidential election.
- After Harrison dies, John Tyler becomes president and opposes Whig economic programs.

ON THE WORLD STAGE

The International Panic of 1837

Critical Thinking: Cause and Effect Ask students to create a cause-and-effect chart that lists some of the causes and effects of the panic. *Possible Responses: Causes —Troubled European economies, British and U.S. loans recalled; Effects —falling prices, unemployment, poverty.*

ASSESS & RETEACH

Section 2 Assessment

Pair less proficient students with those who are more proficient to answer the questions.

Self-Assessment

Have students write two questions they would like to ask Andrew Jackson. Students should then answer those questions as they believe he would have done.

Section Quiz

FORMAL ASSESSMENT
Section Quiz, p. 42

Reteach

Use the maps to help review the section's main ideas.

CLOSE

While democratic institutions expanded to include more Americans during the Age of Jackson, the nation also expanded westward.

Successors Deal with Jackson's Legacy

When Jackson announced that he would not run for a third term in 1836, the Democrats chose Vice-President **Martin Van Buren** as their candidate. The newly formed Whig Party ran three regional candidates against him. With Jackson's support, however, Van Buren easily won the election.

ON THE WORLD STAGE

THE INTERNATIONAL PANIC OF 1837

Although the financial crisis that came to be known as the Panic of 1837 was in part caused by Jackson's policies toward the Bank of the United States, these were not the only causes. The U.S. economy was affected by the economies of other nations.

During the 1830s, for example, British investment in the United States boomed as British banks made huge loans to U.S. banks. Then, when hard times came to European nations, these nations recalled their loans to Britain, forcing the British banks to recall their loans to American banks.

However, since U.S. banks had already lent the money, they, in turn, had to ask their customers to repay their loans. This forced many people to sell their goods, which caused the prices of goods to plummet.

MARTIN VAN BUREN Along with the presidency, however, Van Buren inherited the consequences of Jackson's bank war. Many of the pet banks that accepted federal deposits were wildcat banks that printed bank notes wildly in excess of the gold and silver they had on deposit. Such wildcat banks were doomed to fail when people tried to redeem their currency for gold or silver.

By May 1837, many banks stopped accepting paper currency. In the Panic of 1837, bank closings and the collapse of the credit system cost many people their savings, bankrupted hundreds of businesses, and put more than a third of the population out of work. Van Buren tried to help by reducing federal spending, but that caused already declining prices to drop further.

THINK THROUGH HISTORY
I. *Recognizing Effects* *How did Jackson's actions hurt the nation's economy?*

I. Answer Jackson had funds deposited in pet banks—many of which turned out to be wildcat banks.

HARRISON AND TYLER In 1840 Van Buren ran for reelection against Whig Party candidate William Henry Harrison—but this time the Whigs had two advantages. One was that voters blamed Van Buren for the weak economy. Second, the Whigs used Jackson's campaign strategy—they portrayed Harrison, the old war hero, as a man of the people and Van Buren as an aristocrat.

Harrison won and immediately tried to enact the Whig program to revitalize the economy, which was still in a severe depression. Then, a month after his inauguration, he died. **John Tyler,** Harrison's vice-president, became president. Tyler, a strong-minded Virginian and former Democrat, opposed many parts of the Whig program. He halted hopes for significant Whig reforms.

A LEGACY OF TWO PARTIES Just as in the 1790s, when people had divided politically into Democratic-Republicans and Federalists, people in the 1830s divided into two distinct parties—Democrats and Whigs. These parties dominated national politics until the 1850s. Meanwhile, the style of politics had changed drastically since the 1790s. Political speeches became a form of mass entertainment, involving far more Americans in the political process. Also, the West was playing an increasing role in national politics. That trend would only continue as more Americans moved to places like Texas and California.

Section 2 Assessment

1. TERMS & NAMES

Identify:

- Henry Clay
- American System
- John C. Calhoun
- Missouri Compromise
- Andrew Jackson
- Jacksonian democracy
- John Quincy Adams
- Trail of Tears
- Daniel Webster
- Martin Van Buren
- John Tyler

2. SUMMARIZING In a chart, write newspaper headlines that tell the significance of each date.

Dates	Headlines
1820	
1828	
1832	
1832	
1838	

3. MAKING INFERENCES In what ways do you think the Missouri Compromise and the nullification crisis of 1832 might be considered important milestones in American history before the Civil War? Use evidence from the text to support your response.

THINK ABOUT
- the expansion of slavery into the West
- Calhoun's nullification theory
- Thomas Jefferson's ideas about slavery and the Union

4. MAKING PREDICTIONS How do you think Jackson might have countered the Whig Party's accusation that he was acting like a king? Support your answer with evidence from the text.

THINK ABOUT
- his policies and political appeal
- the image of himself that Jackson projected to his supporters

ANSWERS

1. TERMS & NAMES

Henry Clay, p. 126
American System, p. 126
John C. Calhoun, p. 126
Missouri Compromise, p. 127
Andrew Jackson, p. 127
Jacksonian democracy, p. 127
John Quincy Adams, p. 127
Trail of Tears, p. 130
Daniel Webster, p. 131
Martin Van Buren, p. 132
John Tyler, p. 132

2. SUMMARIZING

Possible Responses:
1820—Congress Passes Compromise on Missouri Issue
1828—Jackson Wins Presidency
1832—South Carolina Nullifies Federal Tariff—Secession May Follow; Jackson Vows to Kill Bank
1838—Cherokee Follow Trail of Tears to Indian Territory

3. MAKING INFERENCES

Possible Responses: The Missouri Compromise and the nullification crisis were milestones in the struggle between nationalism and sectionalism. Jefferson recognized that the issue of slavery posed a grave threat to national unity, just as the nullification crisis threatened to destroy the Union.

4. MAKING PREDICTIONS

Possible Responses: Jackson believed he served the best interests of the common people, unlike the Whigs, who he said were agents of the aristocracy. Jackson might also contend that he used, not abused, the power of his office to preserve the democratic principles of the Constitution.

3 Manifest Destiny

LEARN ABOUT the experiences of Americans in the West during the first half of the 19th century
TO UNDERSTAND the causes and consequences of American expansion.

TERMS & NAMES
- manifest destiny
- Santa Fe Trail
- Oregon Trail
- Stephen F. Austin
- Texas Revolution
- the Alamo
- Sam Houston
- James K. Polk
- Bear Flag Republic
- Treaty of Guadalupe Hidalgo

ONE AMERICAN'S STORY

In 1821, Stephen F. Austin led the first of several groups of American settlers to a fertile area along the Brazos River. Drawn by the promise of inexpensive land and economic opportunity, Austin established a colony of American settlers in Tejas, or Texas, then the northernmost province of the Mexican state of Coahuila. However, Austin's plans didn't work out as well as he had hoped; 12 years later, he found himself in a Mexican prison and his new homeland in an uproar. After his release, Austin spoke about the impending crisis between Texas and Mexico.

A PERSONAL VOICE

Texas needs peace, and a local government; its inhabitants are farmers, and they need a calm and quiet life. . . . [But] my efforts to serve Texas involved me in the labyrinth of Mexican politics. I was arrested, and have suffered a long persecution and imprisonment. . . . I fully hoped to have found Texas at peace and in tranquillity, but regret to find it in commotion; all disorganized, all in anarchy, and threatened with immediate hostilities. . . . Can this state of things exist without precipitating the country into a war? I think it cannot.

STEPHEN F. AUSTIN, quoted in *Lone Star: A History of Texas and Texans*

Stephen F. Austin

Austin's prediction was correct. War did erupt in Texas—twice. First, Texans rebelled against the Mexican government. Then, the United States went to war against Mexico over the boundaries of Texas. These conflicts were the climax of decades of competition over the western half of North America—a competition that involved the United States, Mexico, Native Americans, and various European nations. The end result of the competition would be U.S. control over a huge swath of the continent, from the Atlantic to the Pacific.

Settling the Frontier

As various presidents established policies in the early 19th century that expanded U.S. territory, American settlers pushed into the Northwest Territory. These settlers cleared forests, transformed lush prairies into farms, and turned waterfronts into bustling cities and centers of commerce.

AMERICANS PURSUE MANIFEST DESTINY For a quarter century after the War of 1812, only a few Americans explored the West. Then, in the 1840s, expansion fever gripped the country. Americans began to believe that their movement westward was predestined by God. John L. O'Sullivan, editor of *The United States Magazine and Democratic Review,* described the annexation of Texas in 1845 as "the fulfillment of our **manifest destiny** to overspread the continent allotted by Providence for the free development of our yearly multiplying millions." Americans immediately seized on the phrase "manifest destiny" to express their belief that the United States was ordained to expand to the Pacific Ocean and into Mexican and Native American territory. They also believed that this destiny was manifest, or obvious and inevitable.

A. Answer The term refers to the belief that U.S. expansion into the West was inevitable and a good thing.

THINK THROUGH HISTORY
A. Clarifying *Explain the concept of manifest destiny.*

Section 3 Overview

OBJECTIVES

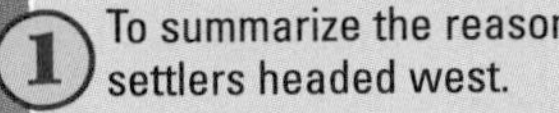
1. To summarize the reasons settlers headed west.

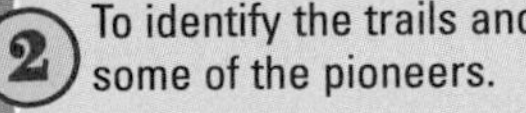
2. To identify the trails and some of the pioneers.

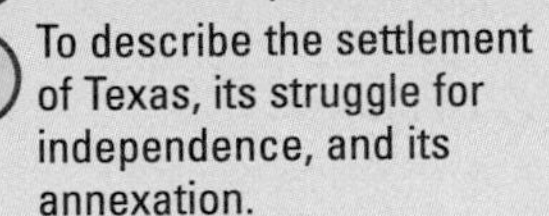
3. To describe the settlement of Texas, its struggle for independence, and its annexation.

4. To explain the causes and consequences of the War with Mexico.

SKILLBUILDERS
- Understanding geography: region, movement, p. 135
- Understanding geography: place, region, p. 137
- Understanding geography: location, region, p. 139

CRITICAL THINKING
- Clarifying, p. 133
- Recognizing effects, pp. 134, 141
- Theme: Immigration and Migration, p. 135
- Analyzing motives, p. 136
- Contrasting, p. 138
- Making inferences, p. 139
- Finding main ideas, p. 140
- Making predictions, p. 141
- Forming opinions, p. 141

FOCUS & MOTIVATE

5-MINUTE WARM-UP

Drawing Conclusions
Have students read page 133 and answer these questions.

1. Why did Americans believe in manifest destiny?
2. Does Austin's quote confirm or contradict manifest destiny?

WARM-UP TRANSPARENCY 3

▶ ***Starting with the Student***
Ask students if they would have moved west.

OBJECTIVE

1 INSTRUCT

Settling the Frontier

▶ ***Discussing Key Ideas***
- The concept of manifest destiny expresses American attitudes toward expansion.

(continued on next page)

SECTION 3 RESOURCES

PRINT RESOURCES

IN-DEPTH RESOURCES: UNIT 1
Guided Reading, p. 74
Skillbuilder Practice: Analyzing Assumptions, p. 79
Geography Application: Mexico Cedes Land, p. 81
Primary Source: *from* James K. Polk's Speech, p. 87
Literature: from *Roughing It* by Mark Twain, p. 90

READING STUDY GUIDE, p. 39

ACCESS FOR STUDENTS ACQUIRING ENGLISH
Guided Reading (Spanish), p. 54
Skillbuilder Practice: Analyzing Assumptions (Spanish), p. 59
Geography Application (Spanish), p. 61

SPANISH READING STUDY GUIDE, p. 39

FORMAL ASSESSMENT Section Quiz, p. 43

ALTERNATIVE ASSESSMENT BOOK
See forms for supporting and scoring alternative activities.

TECHNOLOGY RESOURCES

HUMANITIES TRANSPARENCIES
H9, General Winfield Scott

CRITICAL THINKING TRANSPARENCIES
CT9, Westward Movement
CT43, Growth of U.S. Population and Area: 1790–1850

CD-ROM *Grolier Multimedia Encyclopedia*
Electronic Library of Primary Sources

VIDEO *American Portfolio: A Videodisc for U.S. History* user's guide, pp. 79–86

INTERNET http://www.mlushistory.com

(continued from page 133)

- Many settlers move west in search of economic opportunity.
- Tension continues between Native Americans and settlers.

IN-DEPTH RESOURCES: UNIT 1
Guided Reading, p. 74

ACCESS FOR STUDENTS ACQUIRING ENGLISH
Guided Reading (Spanish), p. 54

GROLIER MULTIMEDIA ENCYCLOPEDIA
Stephen F. Austin, Texas Revolution

HISTORICAL SPOTLIGHT
Jim Beckwourth
Critical Thinking: Evaluating Before they read about Jim Beckwourth, ask students to list the qualities of a successful pioneer. *Possible Responses: Courage, independence, strength, adaptability, resourcefulness.* Then ask them to read about Beckwourth and tell whether he possessed these characteristics.

OBJECTIVE
② INSTRUCT

Trails West

▶ ***Discussing Key Ideas***

- American traders travel the Santa Fe Trail to New Mexico.
- Missionaries and pioneers seeking land endure months of hardship on the Oregon Trail.
- The Mormons go west to flee from persecution.
- The United States obtains from Britain all rights to the Oregon Territory.

HISTORICAL SPOTLIGHT

JIM BECKWOURTH 1798–1867?

James Pierson Beckwourth was the toughest kind of pioneer, a mountain man. The son of a white man and an African-American woman, he ventured westward with a fur-trading expedition in 1823 and found the place that would become his home for nearly the next quarter century—the Rocky Mountains. He greatly impressed the Crow, who gave him the name "Bloody Arm" because of his skill as a fighter.

Beckwourth served from 1837 until 1850 as an Army scout and trading-post operator. In 1850, he discovered a passage in the Sierra Nevada range that led to California's Sacramento Valley and decided to settle down near the pass and become a rancher. "In the spring of 1852 I established myself in Beckwourth Valley, and finally found myself transformed into a hotel-keeper and chief of a trading-post."

ECONOMIC CAUSES OF MIGRATION Most Americans had practical reasons for moving west. The abundance of land was the greatest attraction. Whether for farming or speculation, land ownership was an important step toward prosperity. As the number of western settlers climbed, merchants and manufacturers followed, seeking new markets for their goods.

Many Americans endured the rigors of the westward trek because of personal economic problems in the East. The Panic of 1837, for example, had disastrous consequences and convinced many Americans that they would be better off attempting a fresh start in the West.

SETTLERS AND NATIVE AMERICANS As American settlers moved west, they continued to have contact with Native American communities. Many Native Americans tried to keep their cultural traditions, but some tried to assimilate into mainstream American culture. A few fought to keep whites out of Native American lands.

The U.S. government responded to the settlers' fears of attack by calling a conference near what is now Laramie, Wyoming. The result was the 1851 Treaty of Fort Laramie, which provided various Native American groups with control of the central plains, a 400-mile-wide slice of flat land east of the Rocky Mountains that stretched roughly from the Arkansas River north to Canada. The Native Americans promised not to attack settlers and agreed to allow the construction of government forts and roads. In exchange, the government pledged to honor the agreed-upon boundaries and to make annual payments to the tribes.

Still the settlers flowed westward, trampling Native American hunting lands, while the U.S. government repeatedly violated its side of the treaty.

THINK THROUGH HISTORY
B. *Recognizing Effects* *What were the effects of the U.S. government policies toward Native Americans at this time?*

B. Answer The U.S. government at first agreed to boundaries that protected Native American territories, but did not fulfill these agreements and moved Native Americans to different lands.

Trails West

The settlers who made the trek used a series of old Native American trails and new routes to go West.

THE SANTA FE TRAIL One of the busiest routes was the **Santa Fe Trail,** which led 780 miles from Independence, Missouri, to Santa Fe, New Mexico. On the Santa Fe Trail each spring between 1821 and 1848, American traders loaded their covered wagons with goods and set off toward Santa Fe. For about the first 150 miles, traders traveled individually. After that, fearing attacks by Native Americans, traders banded into organized groups of up to 100 wagons.

Cooperation, though, came to an abrupt end when Santa Fe came into view. Traders raced off on their own as each tried to be the first to enter the Mexican province of New Mexico. After a few days of trading, they loaded their wagons with goods, restocked their animals, and headed back to Missouri.

"Eastward I go only by force, but westward I go free."

HENRY DAVID THOREAU

THE OREGON TRAIL The **Oregon Trail** was blazed in 1836 by two Methodist missionaries named Marcus and Narcissa Whitman. By driving their wagon as far as Fort Boise (near present-day Boise, Idaho), they proved that wagons could travel on the Oregon Trail, which started in Independence, Missouri, and ended in Portland, Oregon.

Following the Whitmans' lead, some Oregon pioneers bought wooden-wheeled wagons called prairie schooners, covered with sailcloth and pulled by oxen. Most of the pioneers walked, however, pushing handcarts loaded with a few precious possessions, food, and other supplies. The trip took months, even if all went well.

TEACHING OPTION

Skillbuilder Mini-Lesson: Analyzing Assumptions

Explaining the Skill In using historical sources, historians look for assumptions, or beliefs that are taken for granted, behind what writers say. Sometimes assumptions are stated directly; at other times they are implied. For example, the statement "You wouldn't understand; you're only ten" implies that no ten-year-old is capable of understanding the subject in question. Some assumptions can be proved with actual evidence; others are unfounded.

Applying the Skill: Manifest Destiny Have students analyze the underlying assumptions in the quotation from John O'Sullivan on page 133. Then ask,

1. What underlying beliefs are reflected in the statement? *Providence, or God, is on the side of white Americans; the main value of land is in supporting people; white Americans are superior to others; some things are inevitable.*
2. What, if any, examples of stereotyping do you see? *He refers to white Americans as a special group favored by Providence. By contrast and implication, those Native Americans who already occupy the land are not worthy.*

IN-DEPTH RESOURCES: UNIT 1
Skillbuilder Practice: Analyzing Assumptions, p. 79

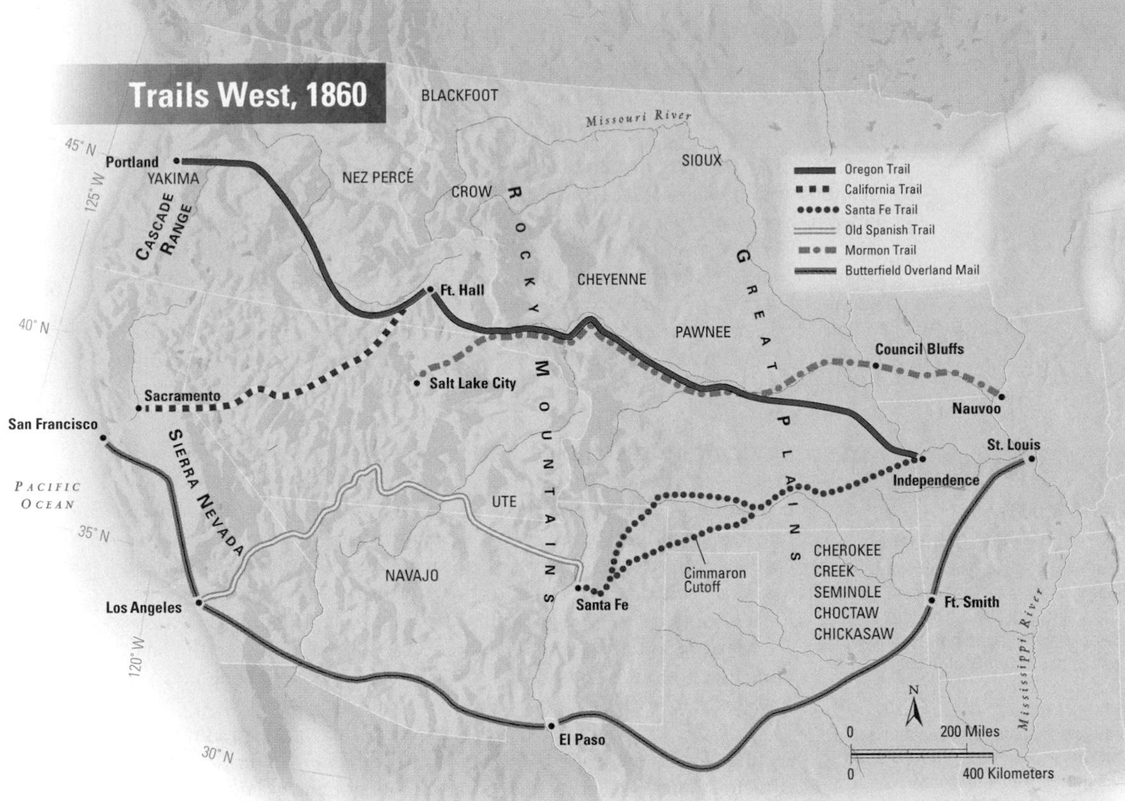

GEOGRAPHY SKILLBUILDER

REGION *Approximately how long was the trail from St. Louis to El Paso?*

MOVEMENT *At a wagon train speed of 15 miles a day, about how long would that trip take?*

Skillbuilder Answer
Region: About 1,100 miles.
Movement: Roughly 74 days.

THE MORMON MIGRATION One group migrated westward along the Oregon Trail to escape persecution. These people were the Mormons, a religious community that would play a major role in the development of the West. Founded by Joseph Smith in upstate New York in 1827, the Mormon community moved to Ohio and then Illinois to escape persecution. After an anti-Mormon mob murdered Smith, a new leader named Brigham Young urged the Mormons to move farther west. Thousands of believers walked to Nebraska, across Wyoming to the Rockies, and then southwest. In 1847, the Mormons stopped at the edge of the desert near the Great Salt Lake. Realizing that the land's isolation would protect the Mormons from attack, Young boldly declared, "This is the place."

THINK THROUGH HISTORY
C. THEME ***Immigration and Migration*** *Why did the Mormons move farther West in their search for a home?*

C. Answer The Mormons were fleeing religious persecution.

Soon they had coaxed settlements and farms from the bleak landscape by irrigating their fields. Salt Lake City blossomed out of the land the Mormons called Deseret.

SETTING BOUNDARIES In the early 1840s, Great Britain still claimed areas near the Canadian border in parts of what are now Maine and Minnesota. The Webster-Ashburton Treaty of 1842 settled these territorial disputes in the East and the Midwest, but the two nations merely continued the "joint occupation" of the Oregon Territory that the two countries had first established in 1818. In 1846 the two countries agreed to extend the mainland boundary along the 49th parallel westward from the Rocky Mountains to Puget Sound, establishing the current boundary between the United States and Canada. Unfortunately, establishing the boundary in the Southwest with Mexico would not be so peaceful.

HISTORY FROM VISUALS
Trails West, 1860

Reading the Map Point out the topographic features on the map. Ask students to discuss what effect the terrain along the trails would have had on the settlers' progress. *Possible Response: Most of the trails took the settlers over rugged mountain ranges and across rivers. Crossing such terrain probably slowed travel time considerably.*

Extension Ask students to determine the length of the longest trail. *The Butterfield Overland Mail route is longest at approximately 1,800 miles.*

MORE ABOUT . . .
The Westward Settlers

After Lodisa Frizzell began her journey westward, she wrote in her diary: "Who is there that does not recollect their first night when started on a long journey, the well-known voices of our friends still ring in our ears." Many of the women who traveled west described missing their friends. Men, on the other hand, seemed less preoccupied with losing old friends. As one man wrote in his diary about his wife, "She thought much of home—friends—prospects —& present condition. I tried to have her get above these things."

 ***ELECTRONIC LIBRARY OF PRIMARY SOURCES***
from *The Discovery of the Oregon Trail* by Robert Stuart

Block Schedule TEACHING OPTION **Time Needed: 30 Minutes**

Cooperative Activity: Interviewing Settlers

Task: One student will interview four or five others who role-play settlers on the westward trails.

Purpose: To explore life on the westward trails in depth.

Activity: Each group decides who will be the interviewer and who will role-play the settlers. The interviewer should pose as a reporter of the time who wants to convey the true flavor of life on the trails to a newspaper audience. The interviewer should prepare a list of questions, asking settlers why they are heading west, what they have experienced on the trail, and what they hope for the future. Have students tape their interviews. Play each audiotape in class.

Building a Portfolio: Students who add their audiotape to their portfolio should include a note detailing their role in the interviews.

ALTERNATIVE ASSESSMENT BOOK
Standards for Evaluating a Cooperative Activity

Standards for Evaluation
Audiotapes should . . .

- detail specific experiences on the trails
- contain information explaining why settlers decided to go West
- convey the hopes and fears of the settlers

OBJECTIVE

③ INSTRUCT

Texan Independence

▶ ***Discussing Key Ideas***

- Three centuries of Spanish rule in Mexico end when Mexicans win their independence in 1821.
- Mexican leaders encourage Americans to settle in Texas.
- Tension rises between Texans and Mexicans, resulting in the Texas Revolution.

NOW & THEN

Tex-Mex Culture

Critical Thinking: Generalizing Discuss the cultural interactions between Mexicans and Texans today. Ask students to form a generalization explaining what typically happens when any two cultural groups live close to each other. *Possible response: They adopt aspects of each other's culture.*

Have student pairs create a concept web like the one below as they brainstorm elements that define a culture.

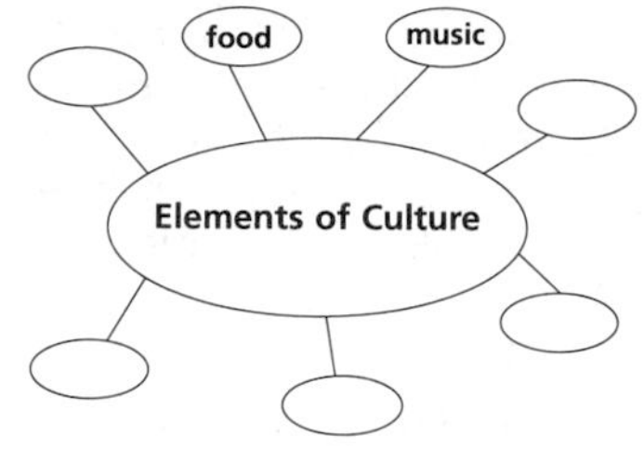

Texan Independence

After 300 years of Spanish rule, only a few thousand Mexican settlers had migrated to what is now Texas. After 1820, that changed as Texas became an important region in Mexico and then an independent nation.

LATINO AND NATIVE AMERICAN POPULATIONS The mission system that Spain used to organize frontier areas in Mexico declined after Mexico had won independence from Spain in 1821. After freeing the missions from Spanish control, the Mexican government offered the surrounding lands to government officials and ranchers. While some Native Americans were forced to remain as unpaid laborers, many others fled the missions, returning to their nomadic ways. When Mexicans captured Native Americans for forced labor, groups of hostile Comanche and Apache retaliated by sweeping through Texas, terrorizing Mexican settlements and stealing livestock that supported many of the American and Mexican settlers, or Tejanos.

NOW & THEN

TEX-MEX CULTURE

Ever since Mexico first invited Anglo settlers to Texas in the 1820s, the Anglo and Mexican cultures of Texas have shaped one another, especially in terms of music, food, and language.

For example, *Tejano* music reflects roots in Mexican mariachi as well as American country and western music and is now a $100 million industry. As for food, salsa now outsells ketchup in the United States, and you can hear ads for *"un* Quarter Pounder *con queso"* (a Quarter Pounder with cheese) on Spanish-language radio.

As Enrique Madrid, who lives in the border area between Texas and Mexico, says, "We have two very powerful cultures coming to terms with each other every day on the banks of [the Rio Grande] and creating a new culture."

MEXICAN INDEPENDENCE AND TEXAN LAND GRANTS The new Mexican government tried to improve its economy by easing trade restrictions. This policy made trade between Mexico's northern provinces and the United States more attractive than trade between northern Mexico and the rest of Mexico. Gradually, the ties loosened between central Mexico and the northern Mexican provinces. Furthermore, horse thieves and Native Americans continued to menace Mexican settlements in New Mexico and Texas. To make the land more secure and stable, the Mexican government encouraged Americans to settle in Texas.

THINK THROUGH HISTORY
D. *Analyzing Motives* *What did Mexico hope to gain from American settlement in Texas?*

D. Answer Mexico hoped to protect against raids by Native Americans and horse thieves.

In 1821, 1823, and 1824, Mexico offered enormous land grants to agents, who were called *empresarios.* The *empresarios,* in turn, attracted American settlers, who eagerly bought cheap land in return for a pledge to obey Mexican laws. Many Americans rushed at the chance, and the population of Anglo, or English-speaking, settlers from the United States soon surpassed the population of Tejanos who lived in Texas.

The most successful *empresario,* **Stephen F. Austin,** established a colony in Texas between the Brazos and Colorado rivers. By 1825, Austin had issued 297 land grants to the group that later became known as Texas's Old Three Hundred. Each family received 177 inexpensive acres of farmland, 4,428 acres for stock grazing, as well as a 10-year exemption from paying taxes.

Land had a low price, but life proved difficult at the outset, especially for women. A Kentucky blacksmith named Noah Smithwick later recalled life in Texas.

A PERSONAL VOICE

Men talked hopefully of the future; children reveled in the novelty of the present; but the women—ah, there was where the situation bore the heaviest. . . . There was no house to keep in order; the meager fare was so simple as to require little time for its preparation. There was no poultry, no dairy, no garden, no books . . . no schools, no churches—nothing to break the dull monotony of their lives, save an occasional wrangle among the children and dogs.

NOAH SMITHWICK, quoted in *Texas: An Album of History*

THE TEXAS REVOLUTION As Texas's Anglo population grew, differences intensified between Anglos and the Mexican government over cultural issues, including slavery. The overwhelmingly Protestant Anglo settlers spoke English instead of Spanish. Furthermore, many of the settlers were Southerners, who

TEACHING OPTIONS

Teaching Less Proficient Readers

To help students understand the impact of Mexican independence, have them create a cause-and-effect chart like the one below and fill in the missing information.

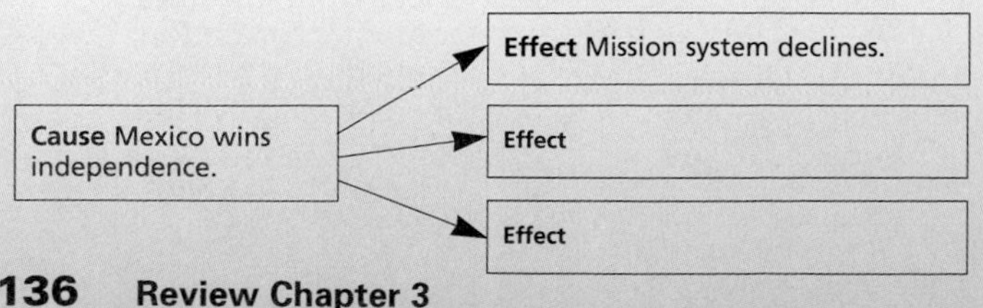

Exploring Themes

Immigration and Migration Discuss the migration of Americans to Texas. Ask students why the settlers wanted to move to Texas. *Possible Response: They were attracted by the abundant, low-priced land.* Ask them how they think the settlers' eagerness to settle in Texas reflected the idea of manifest destiny. *Possible Response: The settlers may have felt that Texas was destined to become a part of the United States.*

had brought slaves with them to Texas. Mexico, which had abolished slavery in 1829, insisted in vain that the Texans free their slaves.

In 1830, Mexico sealed its borders against any further immigration from the United States and slapped a heavy tax on the importation of American goods. Despite immigration restrictions, the Anglo population of Texas doubled between 1830 and 1834. In 1834, Austin won a repeal of Mexico's 1830 prohibition of immigration. By 1835, more than 1,000 Americans were streaming into Texas each month.

Meanwhile, Mexican politics had become increasingly unstable. Austin had traveled to Mexico City late in 1833 to present petitions for greater self-government for Texas to Mexican president Antonio López de Santa Anna. While Austin was there, Santa Anna had Austin imprisoned for inciting revolution. After Santa Anna suspended local powers in Texas and other Mexican states, several rebellions erupted, including what would be known as the **Texas Revolution.**

Austin had unsuccessfully argued with Santa Anna for self-government for Texas. When he returned to Texas in 1835, he was convinced that war was its "only recourse." Determined to force Texas to obey Mexican law, Santa Anna marched toward San Antonio at the head of a 4,000-man army. At the same time, Austin and his followers issued a call for Texans to arm themselves.

"REMEMBER THE ALAMO!" In San Antonio the commander of the Anglo troops, Lieutenant Colonel William Travis, moved his men into **the Alamo,** a mission and fort. Travis believed that maintaining control of the Alamo would prevent Santa Anna's movement farther north.

From February 23 until March 6, 1836, Santa Anna and his men attacked the rebels holed up in the Alamo. In a February 24 letter, Lt. Colonel Travis addressed "the People of Texas and all Americans in the World." He wrote, "Our flag still waves proudly from the walls—*I shall never surrender or retreat.*" The 12-day siege finally ended when Mexican troops scaled the Alamo's walls. All 187 U.S. defenders and hundreds of

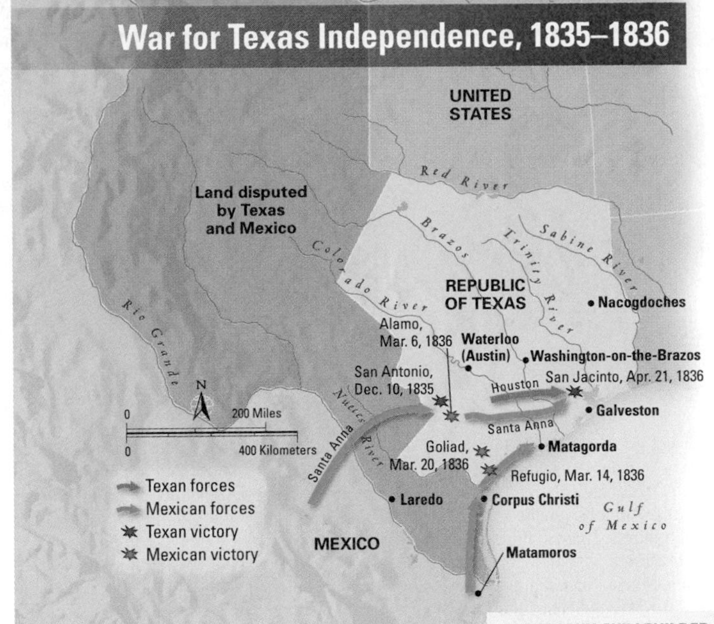

GEOGRAPHY SKILLBUILDER
PLACE *What geographical feature marked the northern border of the Republic of Texas?*
REGION *As of 1836, what does the map show as a major disagreement still remaining between Texas and Mexico?*

Skillbuilder Answer
Place: The Red River.
Region: *Possible Answer:* Both the Republic of Texas and Mexico claimed a large stretch of territory west of the Republic of Texas.

Henry Arthur McArdle conveys the brutality of the fighting in *Dawn at the Alamo,* painted between 1876 and 1883.

HISTORY FROM VISUALS

War for Texas Independence, 1835–1836

Reading the Map Point out that the blue stars on the map represent Texan victories, and the green stars Mexican victories. Have students make a two-column chart showing the Texans' win-loss record, based on information in the map. *Responses: Texan wins—San Antonio and San Jacinto; Texan losses—Alamo, Goliad, and Refugio.*

MORE ABOUT . . .

Davy Crockett at the Alamo

A Mexican soldier who fought at the Alamo witnessed Crockett's valor during the siege. This soldier wrote:

"Of the many soldiers who took deliberate aim at him and fired, not one ever hit him. On the contrary, he never missed a shot. He killed at least eight of our men, besides wounding several others. This being observed by a lieutenant who had come in over the wall, he sprang at him and dealt him a deadly blow with his sword, just over the right eye, which felled him to the ground, and in an instant he was pierced by not less than 20 bayonets."

ELECTRONIC LIBRARY OF PRIMARY SOURCES
Alamo Massacre by Andrea Castañón Villanueva

TEACHING OPTIONS

Making Connections Across Time

Immigration Restrictions Today Point out that in the early 1830s, Mexico wanted to police its borders to keep American immigrants out of Texas. Tell students that today American officials patrol the borders to keep illegal Mexican immigrants out of the United States. Ask students to compare the reasons the Americans migrated to Mexico with the reasons compelling Mexicans to enter the United States today. *Possible Response: Many of the Americans sought economic opportunity in Texas, while many of the Mexicans today seek greater economic opportunities in the United States.*

Making Connections Across Cultures

Shifting National Identity When Stephen F. Austin entered Texas in 1821, he said, "I bid an everlasting farewell to my native country, determined to fulfill rigidly all the duties and obligations of a Mexican citizen." Austin sincerely tried to "Mexicanize" himself. He learned Spanish and signed his name as "Don Estévan F. Austin." However, he became disillusioned with the Mexican government after his imprisonment in Mexico. Weak and pale and plagued by a nagging cough, Austin reluctantly called for war.

KEY PLAYERS
Santa Anna and Sam Houston

Critical Thinking: Compare and Contrast Have students create a chart comparing Santa Anna's and Houston's character traits. *Possible Responses: Santa Anna—ambitious, power-hungry, arrogant; Houston—adventurous, versatile, intelligent.*

The War with Mexico

▶ ***Starting with the Student***
Have students make a time line like the one below to chronicle U.S. military victories during the war with Mexico.

▶ ***Discussing Key Ideas***

- Polk blockades the Rio Grande after Mexico rejects his offer to buy territory.
- The War with Mexico sparks controversy between the North and South over slavery.
- Claiming that Mexico struck the first blow, the United States declares war against Mexico.
- U.S. forces quickly gain control of New Mexico and California.
- The United States successfully invades Mexico.

IN-DEPTH RESOURCES: UNIT 1
Primary Source: *from* James Polk's Speech on War with Mexico, p. 87

KEY PLAYERS

SANTA ANNA
1795–1876

Antonio López de Santa Anna reportedly once said, "If I were God, I would wish to be more." Santa Anna began his career fighting for Spain in the war over Mexican independence. Later, he switched sides to fight for Mexico.

Declaring himself the "Napoleon of the West," Santa Anna took control of the government shortly after Mexico won independence in 1821. He spent the next 35 years alternately serving as president, leading troops into battle, and living in exile. Santa Anna served as president of Mexico 11 times. Repeatedly ousted from office, he was viewed as unprincipled, extravagant, and inept at governing.

SAM HOUSTON
1793–1863

Sam Houston ran away from home in Tennessee at about 15 and lived for three years with the Cherokee. He later fought in the U.S. Army, studied law, was elected to Congress, and became governor of Tennessee.

In his memoirs Houston told of listening in vain for the signal guns indicating that the Alamo still stood. "I listened with an acuteness of sense which no man can understand whose hearing has not been sharpened by the teachings of the dwellers of the forest."

The Republic of Texas chose Houston to be its first president. When Texas became a state, he was elected to the U.S. Senate.

Mexicans died—estimates suggest as many as 1,500. Only a few women and children were spared.

On March 2, 1836, as the battle for the Alamo raged, Texans declared their independence from Mexico. On March 16, they ratified a constitution based on that of the United States. David G. Burnet became president of Texas's temporary government, and Lorenzo de Zavala, a Mexican-American foe of Santa Anna, became vice-president.

TEXAS WINS ITS INDEPENDENCE Later in March, Santa Anna's troops executed 445 rebels at Goliad. The Alamo and Goliad battles whipped the Texan rebels into a fury. Six weeks after the defeat at the Alamo, the rebels' commander in chief, **Sam Houston,** and 900 men surprised a group of Mexicans near the San Jacinto River. With shouts of "Remember the Alamo!" the Texans killed 630 of Santa Anna's soldiers in 15 minutes and captured Santa Anna, who allegedly attempted to escape by dressing in a private's uniform. The victorious Texans set Santa Anna free only after he signed the Treaty of Velasco, which granted independence to Texas.

The Mexican government later refused to acknowledge the forced treaty and still hoped to regain Texas. However, France and Great Britain both recognized Texas's new status. In July 1836, Sam Houston was elected president of the Republic of Texas.

TEXAS JOINS THE UNION Most Texans hoped that the United States would annex their republic, but U.S. opinion divided along sectional lines. Southerners sought to extend slavery, which already had been established in Texas. Northerners feared that the annexation of more slave territory would tip the uneasy balance in the Senate in favor of slave states—and prompt war with Mexico.

The 1844 U.S. presidential campaign focused on westward expansion. The winner, **James K. Polk,** a slaveholder, firmly favored the annexation of Texas "at the earliest practicable period." On December 29, 1845, Texas entered the Union.

THINK THROUGH HISTORY
E. *Contrasting* *Explain the differences between the Northern and Southern positions on the annexation of Texas.*

E. Answer The North did not want to admit a slave state, which would tip the balance of power between free and slave states. The South wished to annex Texas and extend slavery, which already existed in Texas.

The War with Mexico

Furious over the U. S. annexation of Texas, the Mexican government recalled its ambassador from Washington. Events moved quickly toward war.

POLK URGES WAR President Polk believed that war with Mexico would bring not only Texas into the Union, but also New Mexico and California. The president supported Texan claims in disputes with Mexico over the Texas–Mexico

TEACHING OPTIONS

Making Connections Across the Curriculum

Government Discuss Polk's message to Congress, which convinced members to vote in favor of declaring war against Mexico. Point out that Polk needed to sway the Congress because, according to the Constitution, only Congress can declare war. Ask students why the Constitution did not give this authority to the president. *Possible Response: Because the framers believed it would give the president too much power.* Then ask how some presidents have sidestepped this constitutional provision. *Possible Response: By waging undeclared wars.*

Making Connections Across Time

The Gulf of Tonkin Incident Explain that in 1964, President Lyndon Johnson announced that North Vietnamese torpedo boats had attacked two U.S. destroyers in the Gulf of Tonkin, off the North Vietnamese coast. Despite much confusion surrounding the details, the incident prompted Johnson to launch bombing raids on North Vietnam and to ask Congress to take "all necessary means to repel any armed attack against the forces of the United States and to prevent further aggression." Have students compare Johnson's maneuver with Polk's effort to instigate war. *Possible Response: Both claimed the enemy was the aggressor.*

border. While Texas insisted that its southern border extended to the Rio Grande, Mexico maintained that Texas's border stopped at the Nueces River, 100 miles northeast of the Rio Grande.

In November 1845, Polk sent John Slidell to Mexico to offer $25 million to purchase California and New Mexico and to gain Mexican approval of the Rio Grande as the Texas border. When Slidell arrived in Mexico City, the Mexican leader, General José Herrera, refused to receive him. Hoping for Mexican aggression that would unify Americans behind a war, Polk ordered General Zachary Taylor to march to the Rio Grande and blockade the river. Mexico viewed this action as a violation of its territorial rights. Many Americans shared Polk's goals for expansion, but the public was divided over resorting to military action.

At first, Southern Whigs denounced the Democratic president's attitude toward war. However, many Southerners saw Texas as an opportunity to extend slavery and increase Southern power in Congress. Furthermore, the Wilmot Proviso, a proposed amendment to a military appropriations bill of 1846, prohibited slavery in lands that might be gained from Mexico. This attack on slavery solidified Southern support for war.

Many Northerners opposed war. Opponents of slavery saw the war as a plot to expand slavery and ensure Southern domination of the Union. In a resolution adopted by the Massachusetts legislature, Charles Sumner proclaimed that "the lives of Mexicans are sacrificed in this cause; and a domestic question, which should be reserved for bloodless debate in our own country, is transferred to fields of battle in a foreign land."

F. Answer Northerners opposed war, seeing it as a way to extend slavery. Many Southerners favored war for the same reason.

THINK THROUGH HISTORY
F. Making Inferences *How did the issue of slavery affect the debate over the war with Mexico?*

Skillbuilder Answer
Location: San Antonio, Corpus Christi. **Region:** Mexico.

GEOGRAPHY SKILLBUILDER
LOCATION ***From which locations in Texas did U.S. forces come to Buena Vista?***
REGION ***In which country were most of the battles fought?***

The War with Mexico, 1846–1848

Acquired by U.S. in Texas annexation of 1845
Acquired by U.S. in Treaty of Guadalupe Hidalgo, 1848
Acquired by U.S. in Gadsden Purchase, 1853
Battle site
U.S. forces
Mexican forces

The United States, 1830

The United States, 1853

MORE ABOUT . . .
Zachary Taylor

Taylor's victories during the war with Mexico made him a popular hero in the United States. Recruiting posters declared, "Here's to Old Zach! Glorious Times! Roast Beef, Ice Cream, and Three Months' Advance!" Taylor's exploits even inspired dances, such as the "Rough and Ready Polka" and the "General Taylor Quick Step."

HISTORY FROM VISUALS
The War with Mexico, 1846–1848

Reading the Map Ask students to compare the two maps of the United States and Mexico dated 1830 and 1853. Then ask them what proportion of the Mexican territory shown on the map was lost to the United States as a result of the war. *About one-half.*

Extension Ask students how they think this loss of territory affected Mexico and how the gain of territory affected the United States. *Possible Responses: Mexico lost valuable farmland and other natural resources; the United States gained immeasurable wealth and more room to expand.*

HUMANITIES TRANSPARENCIES
H9, *General Winfield Scott*

TEACHING OPTIONS

Making Connections Across Cultures

Mexico's Battle Point out that Mexico won its independence from Spain in 1821. In the mid–1830s, the country fought over Texas. In 1846, Mexico was drawn into full-scale war with the United States. Mexico's inexperience in lawmaking and self-government led to reliance on corrupt military leaders such as Santa Anna. Still, pride in their heritage and traditions induced Mexicans to fight valiantly in the war and to refer to American soldiers as the "barbarians of the North."

Making Global Connections

Civil Disobedience In 1846, American writer Henry David Thoreau refused to pay a poll tax that would help support the Mexican War. He was jailed overnight for his action. This protest prompted him to write the essay "Civil Disobedience," which describes resistance to government laws that conflict with an individual's moral code. In India, under the leadership of Mohandas K. Gandhi (1869–1948), civil disobedience campaigns led to Britain's granting of independence to India in 1947. Echoing Thoreau's belief, Gandhi wrote, "Complete civil disobedience is rebellion without the element of violence in it. [A civil resister] . . . becomes an outlaw claiming to disregard every unmoral State law."

ANOTHER PERSPECTIVE
Los Niños Héroes
Critical Thinking: Analyzing Ask students to list some words that describe the boy heroes. *Possible Responses: Proud, brave, valiant, patriotic.* Ask what the young heroes might represent to Mexicans. *Possible Response: A proud Mexican spirit that does not bow to the United States.*

NOW & THEN
Blue Jeans: The Hot Commodity
Critical Thinking: Evaluating Ask students how Levi Strauss's decision to make pants for the miners reflected the entrepreneurial spirit. *Possible Responses: Using his own capital, Strauss took a chance on creating a new industry; he saw a possible demand and manufactured the goods to meet it.*

IN-DEPTH RESOURCES: UNIT 1
Geography Application: Mexico Cedes Land to the United States, p. 81

ELECTRONIC LIBRARY OF PRIMARY SOURCES
from Treaty of Guadalupe Hidalgo

CRITICAL THINKING TRANSPARENCIES
CT9, Westward Movement
CT43, Growth of U.S. Population and Area: 1790–1850

LOS NIÑOS HÉROES

Though most Americans know little about the war with Mexico, Mexicans view the war as a crucial event in their history.

On September 14, 1847, General Winfield Scott captured Mexico City after the hard-fought Battle of Chapultepec, the site of the Mexican military academy. There, six young cadets leaped from Chapultepec Castle, to commit suicide rather than surrender to the U.S. Army. A monument that honors *Los Niños Héroes* (the boy heroes) inspires pilgrimages every September 13 to commemorate the battle.

THE WAR BEGINS With General Taylor stationed at the Rio Grande in 1846, John C. Frémont led an American military exploration party into California, another violation of Mexico's territorial rights. The Mexican government had had enough.

Mexican troops crossed the Rio Grande. In a skirmish near Matamoros, Mexican soldiers killed 11 U.S. soldiers. Polk immediately sent a war message to Congress, declaring that by shedding "American blood upon American soil," Mexico had started the war. Over the objections of many Northerners and Whigs, Congress voted for war.

In 1846 Polk ordered Colonel Stephen Kearny to march from Fort Leavenworth, Kansas, to Santa Fe, New Mexico. They were met there by a New Mexican contingent that included upper-class Mexicans who wanted to join the United States. New Mexico fell to the United States without a shot.

THE BEAR FLAG REPUBLIC In California, a group of American settlers led by Frémont, seized the town of Sonoma in June 1846. Hoisting a flag that featured a grizzly bear, the rebels proudly declared their independence from Mexico and proclaimed the nation of the **Bear Flag Republic.** Kearny arrived from New Mexico and joined forces with Frémont and an American naval expedition. The Mexican troops quickly gave way, leaving U.S. forces in control of California.

For American troops in Mexico, one military victory followed another. In September 1846, Taylor attacked and captured Monterrey, but allowed the Mexican garrison to escape. General Winfield Scott's forces took advantage of Santa Anna's disrupted strategy and captured Veracruz in March. Then Scott's army set off for Mexico City, which they captured on September 14, 1847. Covering 260 miles, Scott's army had lost not a single battle.

NOW & THEN

BLUE JEANS: THE HOT COMMODITY

Though gold miners in 1848 counted on striking it rich, some of the largest fortunes went to those who clothed the miners. Levi Strauss, founder of Levi Strauss and Company, the San Francisco blue jeans manufacturer, originally intended to sell canvas tents to the California miners. However, he soon found that the canvas could be made into sturdy pants with rivets on the seams and pockets for the miners' tools.

What began as an article of clothing designed to meet a simple need is today woven into the fabric of American culture and the global economy. Having cashed in on the California gold rush, Levi Strauss and Company is now panning for blue jeans "gold" in India, where the market for blue jeans is estimated at $130 million. Blue jeans, the universal souvenir, are carried in countless suitcases to countries all over the world.

AMERICA CLAIMS THE SPOILS OF WAR For Mexico, the war marked an ugly milestone in its relations with the United States. It lost 50,000 men and nearly half its land. America's victory came at the cost of about 13,000 men. Of these, nearly 2,000 died in battle or from wounds and more than 11,000 perished from diseases, such as yellow fever. However, the magnitude of the land gained by the United States enlarged the nation by about one-third.

On February 2, 1848, the United States and Mexico signed the **Treaty of Guadalupe Hidalgo.** Mexico agreed to the Rio Grande border for Texas and ceded the New Mexico and California territories to the United States. The United States agreed to pay $15 million for the Mexican cession, which included present-day California, Nevada, New Mexico, Utah, most of Arizona, and parts of Colorado and Wyoming.

In 1853, President Franklin Pierce authorized James Gadsden to pay Mexico an additional $10 million for another piece of territory south of the Gila River. Along with the settlement of the Oregon boundary and the Treaty of Guadalupe Hidalgo, the Gadsden Purchase established the current borders of the lower 48 states.

THINK THROUGH HISTORY
G. *Finding Main Ideas* *Explain the importance of the Treaty of Guadalupe Hidalgo and the Gadsden Purchase.*

G. Answer
Together with the settlement of the Oregon question, the Treaty of Guadalupe Hidalgo and the Gadsden Purchase settled the boundaries of the mainland United States.

THE CALIFORNIA GOLD RUSH The United States quickly benefited from its new territories as gold was discovered at Sutter's Mill in the California Sierra Nevadas. Soon after the news reached San Francisco, the whole town hustled to the Sacramento Valley to pan for gold. On June 6, 1848, Monterey's mayor, Walter Colton, sent a scout to report on what was happening. When the scout returned on June 14, the mayor described the scene that had taken place in the middle of the town's main street.

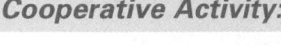

Block Schedule TEACHING OPTION **Time Needed: 20 Minutes**

Cooperative Activity: Creating a Newspaper About the Gold Rush

Task: Groups of four or five students will put together a newspaper about the discovery of gold in California.

Purpose: To explore the causes and effects of the California gold rush.

Activity: Group members should divide the tasks. Some students might write background articles on the discovery; others might do features on the miners. Students should also include editorials and advertisements relevant to the period (for example, ads for Levi Strauss's blue jeans). Pictures, photos, and other graphics should illustrate the articles and ads.

Building a Portfolio: Students who wish to add their newspaper to their portfolio should include a note summarizing their contributions to the project.

ALTERNATIVE ASSESSMENT BOOK
Standards for Evaluating a Cooperative Activity

Standards for Evaluation
Newspapers should . . .
- include stories that answer the journalist's five W's—who, what, where, when, why
- convey the excitement of gold fever
- include graphics that illustrate the stories and ads

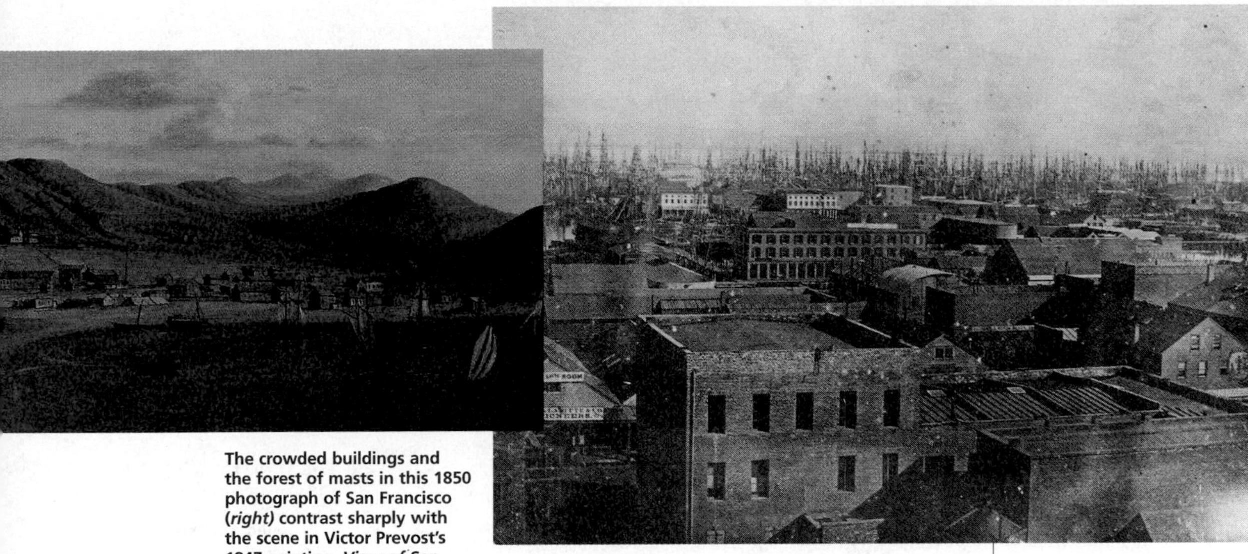

The crowded buildings and the forest of masts in this 1850 photograph of San Francisco (*right*) contrast sharply with the scene in Victor Prevost's 1847 painting, ***View of San Francisco (above).***

A PERSONAL VOICE

The blacksmith dropped his hammer, the carpenter his plane, the mason his trowel, the farmer his sickle, the baker his loaf, and the tapster [bartender] his bottle. All were off for the mines. . . . I have only a community of women left, and a gang of prisoners, with here and there a soldier who will give his captain the slip at first chance. I don't blame the fellow a whit; seven dollars a month, while others [prospectors] are making two or three hundred a day!

WALTER COLTON, quoted in *California: A Bicentennial History*

H. Answer It might become a large and important state very quickly.

THINK THROUGH HISTORY
H. *Making Predictions* *What do you think will be the consequences of the California Gold Rush?*

As gold fever traveled eastward, overland migration to California skyrocketed from 400 in 1848 to 44,000 in 1850. The rest of the world soon caught the fever. Among the so-called forty-niners, the prospectors who flocked to California in 1849 in the California gold rush, were people from Asia, South America, and Europe.

The discovery of gold revolutionized California's economy. Because of its location as a supply center, San Francisco became "a pandemonium of a city." The city's population exploded from 1,000 in 1848 to 35,000 in 1850. Ferrying people and supplies, ships clogged San Francisco's harbor with a forest of masts. These ships linked Californian markets to the expanding markets of the rest of the United States.

Section 3 Assessment

1. TERMS & NAMES
Identify:
- manifest destiny
- Santa Fe Trail
- Oregon Trail
- Stephen F. Austin
- Texas Revolution
- the Alamo
- Sam Houston
- James K. Polk
- Bear Flag Republic
- Treaty of Guadalupe Hidalgo

2. RECOGNIZING EFFECTS Draw a chart showing how the boundaries of the U.S. mainland were formed from 1845–1853.

Year	Boundary Change
1845	Texas annexed

3. RECOGNIZING EFFECTS What were the benefits and drawbacks of Americans' belief in manifest destiny? Use specific references to the section to support your response.

THINK ABOUT
- the various reasons for the move westward
- the settlers' point of view
- the impact on Native Americans
- the impact on the nation as a whole

4. FORMING OPINIONS Would you have supported the war with Mexico? Why or why not? Explain your answer, including details from the chapter.

THINK ABOUT
- the positions of Northerners and Southerners on the war
- the different viewpoints of the United States and Mexico

ANSWERS

1. TERMS & NAMES
manifest destiny, p. 133
Santa Fe Trail, p. 134
Oregon Trail, p. 134
Stephen F. Austin, p. 136
Texas Revolution, p. 137
the Alamo, p. 137
Sam Houston, p. 138
James K. Polk, p. 138
Bear Flag Republic, p. 140
Treaty of Guadalupe Hidalgo, p. 140

2. RECOGNIZING EFFECTS
1845—Texas joins the Union; 1846—Britain and United States set northwest boundary at 49th parallel; 1848—Treaty of Guadalupe Hidalgo includes Mexican cession; 1853—Gadsden Purchase.

3. RECOGNIZING EFFECTS
Possible Responses: Students may state that manifest destiny provided a strong push for westward expansion across the continent. Students should also recognize that the disregard for and poor treatment of Native Americans by other Americans constituted a drawback of the belief in manifest destiny.

4. FORMING OPINIONS
Possible Responses: Students should recognize that their position on the war would have been determined in part by their position on slavery (proslavery forces supported the war and antislavery forces opposed it). They may also point out that, from the Mexican perspective, the war was an unjust attempt by the United States to obtain a huge portion of land from a weaker country.

HISTORY FROM VISUALS
Pictures of San Francisco

Reading the Pictures Ask students to compare and contrast the two pictures. What differences do they see in the pictures? *Possible Responses: There are more ships and buildings in the photograph than in the painting. Also the photo is taken from the ground while the painting gives a view from the water, emphasizing the surrounding hills.*

Extension Ask students what life might have been like in such a rapidly changing community. *Possible Responses: It would be chaotic. New people would constantly arrive and the buildings and streets in the area would change often.*

ASSESS & RETEACH

Section 3 Assessment
Have students work individually to answer the questions; then have them share with the class their responses to item 4.

Self-Assessment
Have students illustrate what they have learned about the war with Mexico by listing in a two-column chart the key causes and effects of the war.

Section Quiz
FORMAL ASSESSMENT
Section Quiz, p. 43

Reteach
Review the maps on page 139 to reinforce students' understanding of the war with Mexico and its impact on U.S. territory.

CLOSE

The United States continued to expand its settlements and strengthened its control over territories in the West. At the same time, the nation's economy underwent a market revolution that changed the way people worked and lived.

Geography Spotlight

OBJECTIVES

1. To explain Preuss's map of the Oregon Trail.
2. To describe the hardships that settlers faced in traversing the trail.

FOCUS & MOTIVATE

▶ ***Starting with the Student***
Ask students to imagine traveling to a place they never visited before. Ask the following:

- Why would a map be useful?
- What troubles would a person encounter in creating the first accurate map of the area?

MORE ABOUT . . .
The Oregon Trail

About 2,000 miles long, the Oregon Trail was the longest-used overland route to the West. Fur traders and missionaries used the trail years before Frémont's mapping expedition. In 1843, a year after Frémont's first expedition, the missionaries Marcus and Narcissa Whitman led 1,000 settlers along the trail. All told, about 12,000 pioneers traversed the trail to Oregon, their wagon wheels cutting so deep that the tracks are still visible today along some parts of the trail. After railroads made wagon trains obsolete, the trail was used to drive cattle and sheep east to market.

GEOGRAPHY SPOTLIGHT

Mapping the Oregon Trail

In 1841, Congress appropriated $30,000 for a survey of the Oregon Trail and named John C. Frémont to head the expeditions. Frémont earned his nickname "the Pathfinder" by leading three expeditions—which included artists, scientists, and cartographers, among them the German-born cartographer Charles Preuss—to explore the American West between 1842 and 1848. When Frémont submitted the report of his first expedition, Congress immediately ordered the printing of 10,000 copies, which were widely distributed.

The "Topographical Map of the Road from Missouri to Oregon," drawn by Preuss, appeared in seven sheets. Though settlers first used this route in 1836, it was not until 1846 that Preuss published his map to guide them. The trickle of settlers westward would soon become a flood. Maps like the Preuss map, a portion of which is shown here, became essential to the economic development of the West.

THE OREGON TRAIL The long, narrow map at right is called a "strip" map, a map that shows a thin strip of the earth's surface—in this case, the last stretch of the trail before reaching Fort Wallah-Wallah.

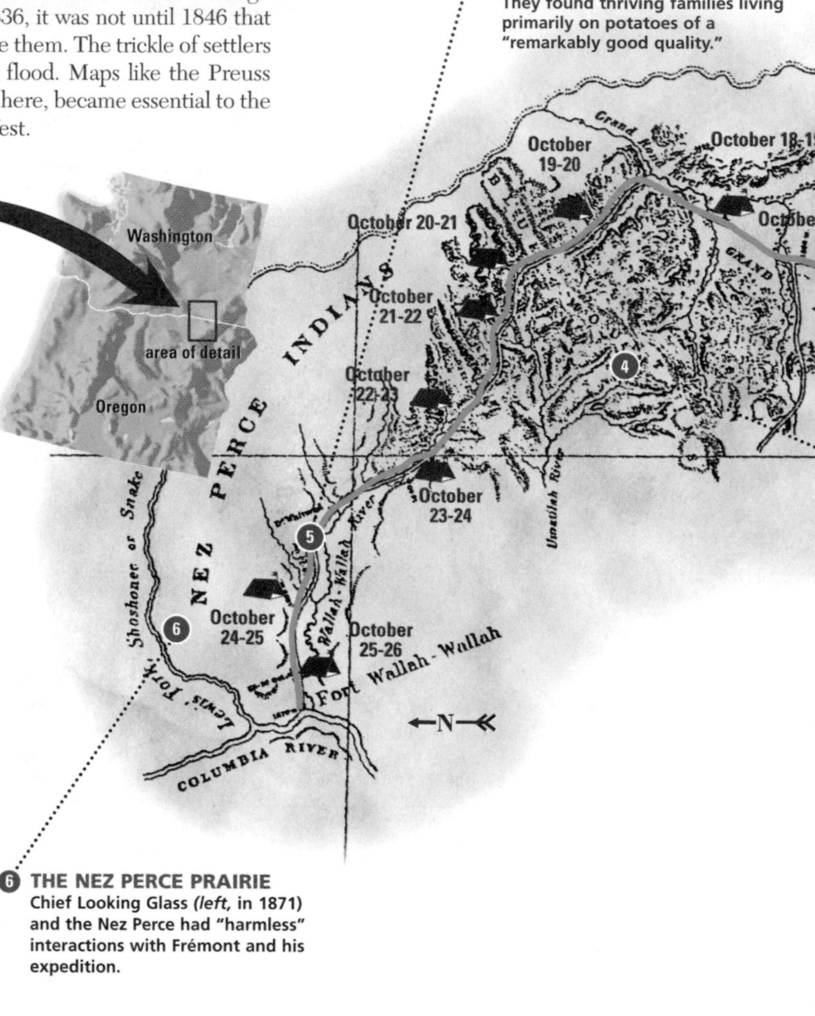

5 THE WHITMAN MISSION The explorers came upon the Whitmans' missionary station. They found thriving families living primarily on potatoes of a "remarkably good quality."

6 THE NEZ PERCE PRAIRIE Chief Looking Glass (*left*, in 1871) and the Nez Perce had "harmless" interactions with Frémont and his expedition.

RECOMMENDED RESOURCES

Books

Egan, Ferol. *Frémont, Explorer for a Restless Nation.* Garden City, NY: Doubleday, 1977. A biography of Frémont.

Ghent, William James. *The Road to Oregon.* London: Longmans, 1929. A noted chronicle of the Oregon Trail.

Guthrie, A. B. *The Way West.* Boston: Houghton, 1949. A Pulitzer Prize–winning novel about the Oregon Trail.

Parkman, Francis. *The Oregon Trail.* New York: Viking, 1989. Reprint of the famous 1849 chronicle of Parkman's 1,700-mile journey from Missouri to Wyoming and back.

Videos

As the Wind Rocks the Cradle. APL Educational Video, 1991. A pioneer woman describes her experiences on the trail west.

The Real West. Filmic Archives. The Oregon Trail and the people of the American West, narrated by Gary Cooper.

Settling the Oregon Territory. Encyclopaedia Britannica. How a belief in manifest destiny brought settlers to Oregon.

The West. PBS Video, 1996. Ken Burns's nine-part look at the American West includes Episode 2, "Empire upon the Trails."

Software

Oregon Trail I and II. MECC, 1993. Award-winning simulation of a covered-wagon journey from Missouri to Oregon.

Wagon Train 1848. MECC. Puts users in the shoes of pioneers traveling the Oregon Trail.

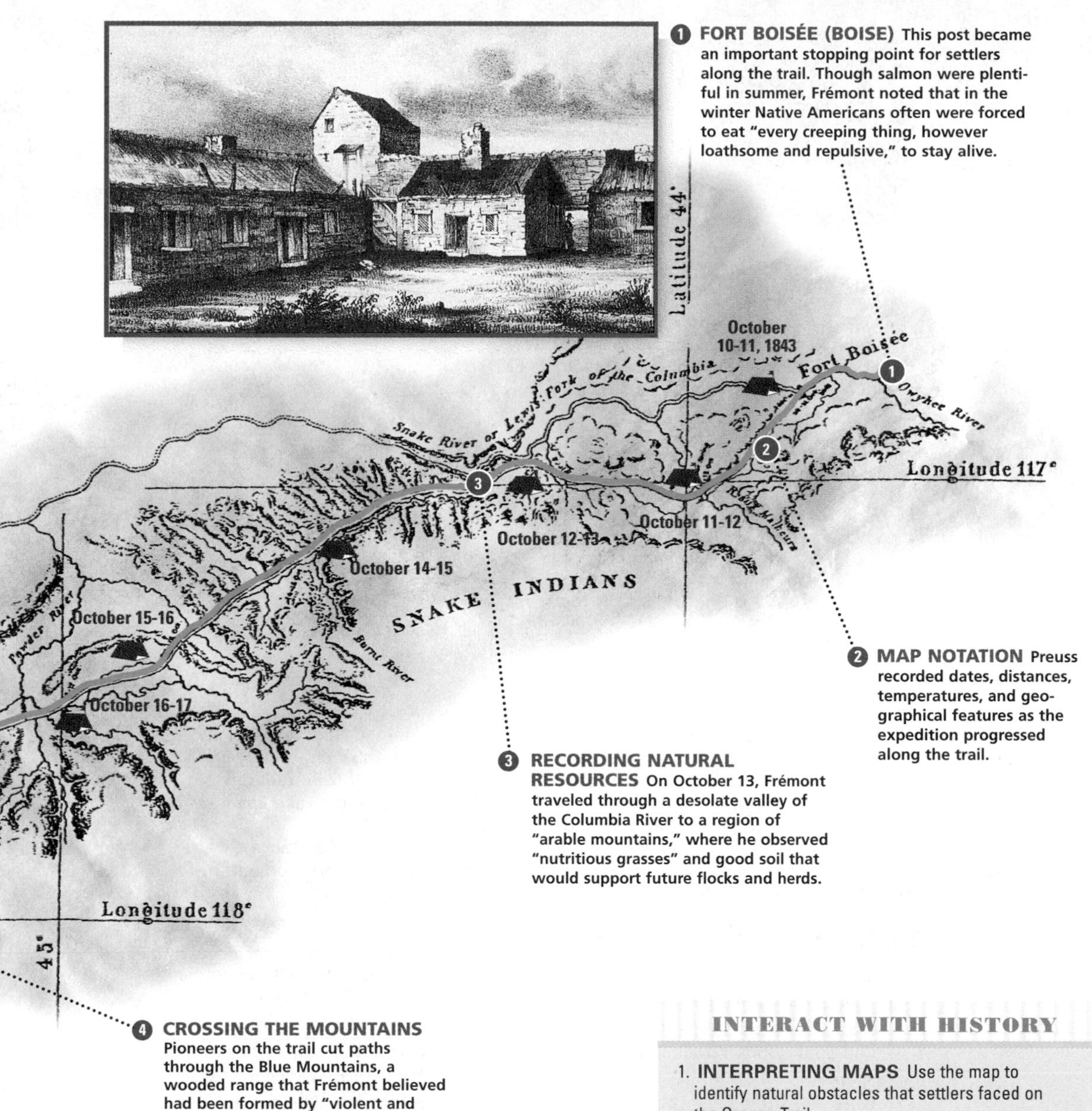

1 FORT BOISÉE (BOISE) This post became an important stopping point for settlers along the trail. Though salmon were plentiful in summer, Frémont noted that in the winter Native Americans often were forced to eat "every creeping thing, however loathsome and repulsive," to stay alive.

2 MAP NOTATION Preuss recorded dates, distances, temperatures, and geographical features as the expedition progressed along the trail.

3 RECORDING NATURAL RESOURCES On October 13, Frémont traveled through a desolate valley of the Columbia River to a region of "arable mountains," where he observed "nutritious grasses" and good soil that would support future flocks and herds.

4 CROSSING THE MOUNTAINS Pioneers on the trail cut paths through the Blue Mountains, a wooded range that Frémont believed had been formed by "violent and extensive igneous [volcanic] action."

INTERACT WITH HISTORY

1. **INTERPRETING MAPS** Use the map to identify natural obstacles that settlers faced on the Oregon Trail.
2. **CREATING A MAP** Do research to find out more about early mapping efforts for other western trails. Then choose one of the trails and sketch an enlarged map of one section. Label features such as rivers and mountains, and provide notes highlighting areas of particular interest

SEE SKILLBUILDER HANDBOOK, PAGES 926 AND 932.

INTERNET Visit http://www.mlushistory.com for more about the Oregon Trail.

INSTRUCT

Starting with the Student

- Have students compare the strip map with a road map of the area today. Ask them what names indicate present-day geographical sites on the strip map. *Names include Fort Boise (Boise, Idaho); Snake River; Columbia River; and Fort Wallah-Wallah, (Wallah-Wallah, Washington)*
- Have students imagine they were updating the mapping of the Oregon Trail for a contemporary story. Ask them what features and landmarks they would have the mapmakers add.

Discussing Key Ideas

- The Oregon Trail was mapped in 1842 during an expedition led by John C. Frémont and paid for by Congress.
- Settlers traveling the trail encountered many obstacles.

HISTORY FROM VISUALS

Reading the Images Have students examine the strip map and its labels. Then ask them these questions:

- Which way is north on the strip map? How do you know? *Left is north; the latitude lines are vertical instead of horizontal, and the line for 45 degrees is left of the line for 44 degrees.*
- How many days did it take the Frémont expedition to get from Fort Boise to Fort Wallah-Wallah? *14 days (from October 11 to October 25).*

INTERACT WITH HISTORY

1. Interpreting Maps

Possible Responses: *The settlers faced food shortages, especially in winter; desolate terrain; mountains; forests; and Native Americans who were not as friendly as Chief Looking Glass.*

You may want to mention that one of the worst problems confronting settlers traveling the trail was cholera, an often fatal illness that was contracted by drinking from contaminated watering holes along the trail.

2. Creating a Map

Standards for Evaluation
Maps should . . .

- be drawn roughly to scale
- accurately reflect one portion of a western trail
- include accurate geographic labels
- include notes highlighting areas of particular interest

Section 4 Overview

OBJECTIVES

1. To describe the rise of new markets, entrepreneurs, and inventions and their effect on the American economy in the early 19th century.
2. To explain the ways that workplaces changed during the market revolution.
3. To summarize the efforts of workers to improve their economic security.

CRITICAL THINKING

- Theme: Economic Opportunity, p. 145
- Recognizing effects, p. 146
- Making inferences, pp. 147, 149
- Forming generalizations, p. 148
- Evaluating decisions, p. 148
- Summarizing, p. 149
- Analyzing issues, p. 149
- Making predictions, p. 149

FOCUS & MOTIVATE

5-MINUTE WARM-UP

Using Context Clues for Technical Terms

To understand the economic changes in the United States in the 19th century, have students read the first three paragraphs of The Market Revolution on pages 144–145 and answer these questions.

1. What is the meaning of the term *market revolution?*
2. Which of the following would most likely be a means of production—a radio, a computer, or an automobile? Explain.

WARM-UP TRANSPARENCY 3

▶ ***Starting with the Student***

- Ask students what inventions and technologies have made their lives more enjoyable.
- Have them discuss how these technologies might have affected the economy.

4 The Market Revolution

LEARN ABOUT the inventions and economic developments in early 19th-century America
TO UNDERSTAND the development of a market economy in the United States.

TERMS & NAMES

- **the market revolution**
- **free enterprise**
- **entrepreneurs**
- **Samuel F. B. Morse**
- **Lowell textile mills**
- **strike**
- **immigration**
- **Great Potato Famine**
- **National Trades' Union**
- ***Commonwealth* v. *Hunt***

ONE AMERICAN'S STORY

At sunrise on July 4, 1817, a cannon blast from the United States arsenal in Rome, New York, announced the groundbreaking for the Erie Canal. With visiting dignitaries and local residents in attendance, Samuel Young opened the ceremony.

A PERSONAL VOICE

We have assembled here to commence the excavation of the Erie Canal. This work when accomplished will connect our western inland seas with the Atlantic Ocean. . . . By this great highway, unborn millions will easily transport their surplus productions to the shores of the Atlantic, procure their supplies, and hold a useful and profitable intercourse with all the maritime nations of the earth. . . . Let us proceed then to the work, animated by the prospect of its speedy accomplishment, and cheered with the anticipated benedictions of a grateful posterity.

SAMUEL YOUNG, quoted in *Erie Water West*

An Erie Canal lock in Lockport, New York, shown here in an 1838 engraving, was one of 83 locks that helped link the Great Lakes with the Northeast.

When the canal was completed, it stretched 363 miles from Albany, New York, to Lake Erie. On November 4, 1825, a fleet of boats traveled to the gala opening celebration in New York City and fulfilled Young's predictions. The lead boat, the Seneca Chief, carried whitefish from Lake Erie and flour and butter from Michigan, Ohio, and Buffalo, New York, to the people of New York City. At the celebration, New York's governor, DeWitt Clinton, poured a keg of water from Lake Erie into the Atlantic Ocean as the crowd cheered the "Wedding of the Waters."

As Young implied, the freight of the *Seneca Chief* symbolized the economic importance of the canal. The canal ushered in a new era, in which technology and improved transportation sent new products to markets across the United States.

The Market Revolution

Changes like those brought by the Erie Canal contributed to vast economic changes in the United States. The changes that occurred in the first half of the 19th century are known as **the market revolution,** in which people bought and sold goods rather than making them for themselves. Workers began to spend their money on goods produced by other workers. Farmers began to shift from self-sufficiency (raising a wide variety of food for their own families) to specialization (raising one or two crops that they could sell at home or abroad).

U.S. MARKETS EXPAND Over a few decades, goods and services multiplied while incomes rose. In fact, in the decade of the 1840s, the national economy grew more than it had in the first 40 years of the century. The quickening pace of U.S. economic growth coincided with the growth of **free enterprise,** the economic system in which private businesses and individuals control the means of production—such as factories, machines, and land—and use them to earn profits. (See *free enterprise* on page 935 in the Economics Handbook.)

These businessmen, called **entrepreneurs** from a French word that means "to undertake," invested their own money in new industries. In doing

SECTION 4 RESOURCES

PRINT RESOURCES

IN-DEPTH RESOURCES: UNIT 1
Guided Reading, p. 75

READING STUDY GUIDE, p. 41

ACCESS FOR STUDENTS ACQUIRING ENGLISH
Guided Reading (Spanish), p. 55

SPANISH READING STUDY GUIDE, p. 41

FORMAL ASSESSMENT
Section Quiz, p. 44

ALTERNATIVE ASSESSMENT BOOK
See forms for supporting and scoring alternative activities.

TECHNOLOGY RESOURCES

GEOGRAPHY TRANSPARENCIES
G9, American Cities, 1820, 1860

CD-ROM *Grolier Multimedia Encyclopedia*
Electronic Library of Primary Sources

VIDEO *American Portfolio: A Videodisc for U.S. History*
user's guide, pp. 53–55, 60–61

INTERNET http://www.mlushistory.com

this, entrepreneurs risked losing their investment if a venture failed, but they also stood to earn huge profits if they succeeded. Alexander Mackay, a Scottish journalist who lived in Canada and traveled in the United States, applauded the entrepreneurs' competitive spirit.

A PERSONAL VOICE

America is a country in which fortunes have yet to be made. . . . All cannot be made wealthy, but all have a chance of securing a prize. This stimulates to the race, and hence the eagerness of the competition.

ALEXANDER MACKAY, quoted in *The Western World*

INVENTIONS AND IMPROVEMENTS Inventor-entrepreneurs began to develop goods to make life more comfortable for more people. While some inventions simply made life more enjoyable, others fueled the economic revolution and transformed manufacturing, transportation, and communication.

New communication links began to put people into instant contact with one another. **Samuel F. B. Morse,** a New England artist, developed the telegraph in 1837. In 1844, Morse tapped out in code the words "What hath God wrought?" The message sped from Washington, D.C., over a metal wire. In less than a second, Morse's words had reached Baltimore, Maryland, prompting an immediate reply. Businessmen used the new communication device to transmit orders and relay up-to-date information on prices and sales. The new railroads employed the telegraph to keep trains moving regularly and to warn engineers of safety hazards. By 1853, 23,000 miles of telegraph wire crossed the country.

As the telegraph improved the movement of information, better transportation systems improved the movement of people and goods. Farmers and manufacturers alike sought more direct ways to ship their goods to market. In 1807, Pennsylvanian Robert Fulton had ushered in the steamboat era when his boat, the *Clermont,* made the 150-mile trip up the Hudson River from New York City to Albany in 32 hours—very fast for the era. Ships traveled upstream as well as downstream because they were powered by steam engines. By 1830, 200 steamboats traveled the nation's western rivers that flowed into the Mississippi River and slashed freight rates as well as voyage times.

Water transport was particularly important in moving raw materials such as lead and copper and heavy machinery. Where waterways didn't exist, Americans made them. By 1816, America had dug a mere 100 miles of canals. A quarter of a century later, the country boasted more than 3,300 miles of canals.

The heyday of the canals lasted only until the 1860s, though, due to the rapid emergence of railroads. Although shipping by rail cost significantly more in the 1840s than did shipping by canal, railroads offered the important advantage of speed. In addition, trains could operate in the winter, and they brought goods to people who did not live near waterways. By the 1840s, steam engines pulled freight at ten miles an hour—more than four times faster than canal boats traveled. By 1850, almost 10,000 miles of track had been laid.

NEW MARKETS LINK REGIONS By the 1840s, improved transportation and communication made America's regions interdependent. Steamboats went up as well as down the Mississippi, linking North to South. The Erie Canal, railroads, and telegraph wires now linked the East and the West. The growing links between America's regions contributed to the development of regional specialties.

A. Answer New methods of communication and transportation made the operation of business more efficient and profitable.

THINK THROUGH HISTORY
A. THEME ***Economic Opportunity*** *How did new communication methods and modes of transportation help the U.S. economy grow?*

HISTORICAL SPOTLIGHT

SAMUEL F. B. MORSE 1791–1872

While Samuel Morse was a student at Yale University, he learned about the new science of electricity and constructed batteries in a chemistry class. More interested in art than science, however, Morse embarked on a career in painting. Realizing that he could not support himself as an artist, Morse continued his scientific work.

By the end of 1837, Morse and an associate named Leonard Gale had built an electromagnetic telegraph. Morse's first model could send messages 10 miles on a wire that wound continuously around his workroom.

Congress granted Morse $30,000 in 1843 to build a test line between Baltimore and Washington, D.C. The successful transmission of his coded message won the inventor international fame.

OBJECTIVE **1 INSTRUCT**

The Market Revolution

Discussing Key Ideas

- The market revolution spurs economic growth.
- Inventions and innovations boost America's industrial output.
- Using factory-made, mechanized equipment, farmers help meet the nation's increased demand for food.
- New inventions lead to improvements in transportation and communication.

IN-DEPTH RESOURCES: UNIT 1
Guided Reading, p. 75

ACCESS FOR STUDENTS ACQUIRING ENGLISH
Guided Reading (Spanish), p. 55

HISTORICAL SPOTLIGHT
Samuel F. B. Morse

Critical Thinking: Making Inferences Ask students to speculate on the impact the telegraph had on the press's reporting of the news. *Possible Response: The telegraph could have been used to transmit news as soon as it happened to any newspaper connected to a telegraphic system.* Ask them what machines today have replaced the telegraph. *Possible Responses: Telephones, computers, communications satellites.* Ask students to find the Morse code in an encyclopedia and to create a brief message using the code. Then have students form pairs and translate their partner's message.

GROLIER MULTIMEDIA ENCYCLOPEDIA
Samuel Morse; Charles Goodyear

TEACHING OPTIONS

Making Connections Across Time

Transporting Freight Today Tell students that trains are still used more than any other means of transportation to convey freight in the United States. Trucks carry the second largest amount. Ships are also used, because they provide the least expensive means of sending freight. Air transport is used only infrequently because of the high costs involved. Ask students to do some research and to create a chart to compare the advantages and disadvantages of these forms of freight transportation today.

Making Connections Across the Curriculum

Literature Nineteenth-century American writers Walt Whitman, Emily Dickinson, and Henry David Thoreau all found railroads and locomotives fascinating. Ask students to read the following literary examples:

- "To a Locomotive in Winter" by Walt Whitman (poem)
- "I Like to See It Lap for Miles" by Emily Dickinson (poem)
- "Sounds" from *Walden* by Henry David Thoreau (prose)

Invite students to compare and contrast each writer's portrayal of the locomotive.

ON THE WORLD STAGE

Britain's Cotton Imports

Critical Thinking: Interpreting

Ask students to explain the significance of the statement, "Cotton is King."

Possible Responses: Cotton reigns as the most significant source of income in the South's economy; cotton dominates life in the South; cotton's influence extends to Great Britain, where cotton directly or indirectly provides jobs.

NOW & THEN

From Telegraph to Internet

▶ ***Starting with the Student***

Have students think about futuristic inventions for communicating that have been featured in science fiction movies or stories. Ask the following:

- What are these devices and how do they work?
- If these devices actually existed, how would they revolutionize people's lives?

▶ ***Discussing Key Ideas***

- The telegraph, the telephone, and the Internet all represent important breakthroughs in communication.
- Advances in computer technology pave the way for more sophisticated electronic communication systems.
- The Internet provides instant global communication.

ON THE WORLD STAGE

BRITAIN'S COTTON IMPORTS

By 1836, the American South, the world's leading producer of cotton, was also the leading supplier of cotton to Great Britain. In all, Great Britain imported three-quarters of its cotton from the South. Cotton directly or indirectly provided work for one in five people in Britain, then the world's leading industrial power.

For its part, Britain relied so heavily on Southern cotton that cotton growers incorrectly assumed that the British would actively support the South during the Civil War. "No power on earth dares to make war upon[cotton]," a South Carolina senator boldly declared in 1858, "Cotton is king." (See *trade* on page 940 in the Economics Handbook.)

Heavy investment in canals and railroads transformed the Northeast into the center of American commerce. Following the opening of the Erie Canal in 1825, New York City became the central link between American agriculture and European markets. In fact, more cotton was exported through New York than through any other American city.

The most striking development of the era, however, was the rise in manufacturing. Although most Americans still lived in rural areas and only 14 percent of workers had manufacturing jobs, these workers produced more and better goods at lower prices than had ever been produced before. Many of these goods became affordable for ordinary Americans, and improvements in transportation allowed people to purchase items from distant places. Some products, like farm equipment, helped make people more productive, too.

THINK THROUGH HISTORY
B. Recognizing Effects *How did the transportation revolution connect U.S. regions to one another and to the rest of the world?*

B. Answer
Canals, railroads, and improved roads reduced the price of shipping goods from one region to another, and moved products from the country's interior to international ports like New York City.

As the Northeast began to industrialize, many people moved to farm the fertile soil of the Midwest. First, however, they had to work very hard to make the land arable, or fit to cultivate. Many wooded areas had to be cleared before fields could be planted. The invention of the steel plow by John Deere and the reaper by Cyrus McCormick helped farmers shift from subsistence farming to growing cash crops, such as wheat and corn. The same trains and canals that brought them plows and reapers from distant factories would then carry their crops to markets in the East and in Europe.

Meanwhile, most of the South remained agricultural and relied on such crops as cotton, tobacco, and rice. Southerners who had seen the North's "filthy, overcrowded, licentious factories" looked with disfavor on industrialization. Even if wealthy Southerners wanted to build factories, they usually lacked the capital to do so because they had invested so much in land and slaves.

NOW & THEN

From Telegraph to Internet

What do the telegraph and the Internet have in common? They are both tools for instant communication. While the telegraph relied on a network of wires that spanned the country, the Internet—an international network of smaller computer networks—allows any computer user to communicate instantly with any other computer user in the world.

1837

Samuel Morse invents the telegraph, the first instant electronic communicator. Morse taps on a key to send bursts of electricity down a wire to the receiver, where an operator "translates" the coded bursts into understandable language—within seconds after they are sent.

1876

Alexander Graham Bell invents the telephone, which relies on a steady stream of electricity, rather than electrical bursts, to transmit sounds. Advances in the telephone have made it possible today to pick up a phone and talk to someone halfway around the world or even in space!

1953

Improvements in electronic communication lead to the development of one of the first computers, at the University of Pennsylvania. The government soon begins using computers for scientific and intelligence work. However, during the Cold War, fear of nuclear war leads to the search for a communication system safe from bombing and not dependent on a central authority.

TEACHING OPTION

Exploring Themes

Science and Technology Discuss the economic and social changes brought about by the new technology used in the factories. Ask students whether they think the new manufacturing techniques ultimately improved the quality of people's lives in the mid-19th century or created more problems. Then ask them to compare these positive and negative effects with those resulting from the new technologies—computers, fax machines, robotics—in today's society.

Possible Response: *The new technology in the mid-19th century created many new jobs for unskilled workers, but the work was tedious and the conditions in the factories were unhealthy. The new technology in the late-20th century eliminated many jobs for unskilled workers but made life easier for many people.*

Changing Workplaces

The new market economy in the United States did not only affect what people bought and sold; it also changed the ways Americans worked. Moving production from the home to the factory split families, created new communities, and transformed relationships between employers and employees.

Mid-19th-century "mill girls" often worked 12-hour days, six days a week—but for many, it was their first chance to earn money. These Massachusetts mill workers are holding shuttles, which were used during weaving.

THE LOWELL TEXTILE MILLS Francis Cabot Lowell, Nathan Appleton, and Patrick Tracy Jackson built a weaving factory in Waltham, Massachusetts, and outfitted it with power machinery. Mechanizing the process and housing the tools in the same place slashed the production time, as well as the cost, of textile manufacture. By 1822 Appleton and Jackson had profited so much from their factory that they decided to build a larger operation in Lowell, Massachusetts, a town named for their deceased partner, Francis Lowell. By the late 1820s, the **Lowell textile mills** had become booming enterprises. Thousands of people—mostly young women who came to Lowell because their families' farms were declining—went there to work.

THINK THROUGH HISTORY
C. *Making Inferences* *What do you think were the advantages of factory production?*

C. Answer It made production less expensive and more efficient.

In the early 19th century, skilled artisans worked in shops attached to their own homes. The most experienced, called masters, might be assisted by journeymen (skilled workers employed by masters) and by apprentices (young workers learning their craft). The rapid spread of factory production revolutionized industry in the next two decades. New machines allowed unskilled workers to perform tasks that once had taken the effort of trained artisans. To do this work, though, the unskilled workers needed to work in the factory.

1964

Scientists come up with the idea of a decentralized computer network that sends messages in small packets from one computer station to another. The Pentagon develops several supercomputer centers that can transfer data from individual computers to other computers on high-speed transmission lines. However, this first and very successful network is soon overworked and outdated. As more universities and individuals join the network, they refine the system and form the complex of networks called the Internet.

1997

Today, on the Internet, through e-mail (electronic mail) or on-line conversation, any two people can have instant dialogue. The Internet is growing incredibly fast, partly because of the relatively reasonable cost of belonging to a network and using its services. The Internet has become the modern tool for instant global communication not only of words, but images, too. And it is just as amazing now as the telegraph was in its time.

INTERACT WITH HISTORY

1. **CONTRASTING** Based on what you have read, what advantages does the Internet have over the telegraph?
2. **USING THE INTERNET** Access the Internet and try to find information about the origin and use of this modern-day communication phenomenon.

SEE SKILLBUILDER HANDBOOK, PAGES 909 AND 930.

Visit http://www.mlushistory.com for more about using the Internet.

OBJECTIVE
② **INSTRUCT**

Changing Workplaces

▶ ***Starting With the Student***
Have students create a chart like the one below to compare the life of a farm girl with that of a factory worker. Students should compare such factors as hours worked, conditions, wages, lodging, and tasks performed.

Factors	Farm Girl	Factory Worker
Hours		
Conditions		
Wages		
Lodging		
Tasks		

▶ ***Discussing Key Ideas***
- Mechanization allows many industries to carry out the manufacturing process in factories.
- Unskilled workers leave their farms to labor in the factories.
- Mill owners seek young female employees because they can control the girls' behavior and pay them less than men.
- Factory work involves long hours, unhealthy conditions, and hard work.

INTERACT WITH HISTORY

1. Contrasting

Possible Responses: *Advantages of the Internet include the efficiency of transmission; more direct communication, either by e-mail or on-line conversations; messages not coded; greater potential to broaden its application; more affordable for people to purchase.*

2. Using the Internet

Have students use the following steps to explore the Internet:

1. Go to http://www.mlushistory.com.
2. Choose Links for *The Americans.*
3. Choose *The Americans,* Chapter 9.

To help guide students in their research, encourage them to generate a list of questions about the history and use of the Internet.

MORE ABOUT . . .
Factory Life

By the late 1820s, conditions in the boarding houses where the factory workers lived had begun to worsen. Six or eight women shared a crowded room, often squeezing three in one bed. After working 13 or more hours a day, the women were often fed only bread and gravy for supper. In 1828, mill women in Dover, New Hampshire, went on strike—the first organized by mill women on their own. The community was shocked as several hundred young women paraded down the street, carrying banners and setting off gunpowder. Like other early strikes, however, this one was soon over, and the leaders were dismissed and blacklisted.

ELECTRONIC LIBRARY OF PRIMARY SOURCES
from Pleasures of Factory Life by Sarah Bagley

OBJECTIVE

(3) **INSTRUCT**

Workers Seek Better Conditions

▶***Discussing Key Ideas***

- Workers in the 1830s and 1840s organize dozens of strikes.
- Some Irish immigrants are willing to work for low wages, while others join unions and organize strikes.
- The National Trades' Union wins the right to strike by appealing to the Massachusetts Supreme Court.

WORK IN THE LOWELL MILLS The Lowell mills provide a good example of new work regulations that workers faced in the factories. In Lowell, a work force consisting almost entirely of unmarried farm girls worked under the control of female supervisors. At their boarding houses, the "mill girls" lived under strict curfews. The supervisors monitored the girls' behavior and church attendance.

Mill owners sought female employees because women provided an abundant source of labor, and owners could pay lower wages to women than men. To the girls in the mills, though, textile work offered better pay than their only alternatives: teaching, sewing, and domestic work. In an 1846 letter to her father in New Hampshire, 16-year-old Mary Paul expressed her satisfaction with her situation at Lowell.

A PERSONAL VOICE

I have a very good boarding place, have enough to eat. . . . The girls are all kind and obliging. . . . I think that the factory is the best place for me and if any girl wants employment, I advise them to come to Lowell.

MARY PAUL, quoted in *Women and the American Experience*

WORK CONDITIONS WORSEN Before long, however, work conditions deteriorated. The workday at Lowell was more than 12 hours long. These hours probably didn't seem unduly long to farm girls, but heat, darkness, and poor ventilation in the factories contributed to discomfort and illness. Overseers nailed windows shut to seal in the humidity to prevent the threads from breaking, so that in the summer the weaving rooms felt like ovens. In the winter, pungent smoke from whale-oil lamps blended with the cotton dust to make breathing difficult.

Conditions worsened in the 1830s. Managers forced workers to increase their pace. Between 1836 and 1850, Lowell owners tripled the number of spindles and looms but hired only 50 percent more workers to operate them. In the mid-1840s one mill manager said, "I regard my workpeople just as I regard my machinery. So long as they can do my work for what I choose to pay them, I keep them, getting out of them all I can."

"I regard my workpeople just as I regard my machinery."

TEXTILE MILL MANAGER, 1840s

D. Answer Many endured long hours, low pay, and hard, dangerous work.

THINK THROUGH HISTORY
D. *Forming Generalizations* *What problems did workers in different occupations have in common?*

Workers Seek Better Conditions

When confronted with deteriorating work conditions, workers began to organize to maintain control over the work places. Strikes began to break out when workers protested poor working conditions and low wages.

WORKERS STRIKE In 1834, when the Lowell mills announced a 15 percent wage cut, 800 mill girls organized a **strike,** a work stoppage to force an employer to respond to demands. The Lowell strikers of 1834 issued a proclamation declaring that they would not return to work "unless our wages are continued to us as they have been." For its part, the company threatened to recruit local women to fill the strikers' jobs. Criticized by the Lowell press and clergy, most of the strikers agreed to return to work at reduced wages. The mill owners fired the strike leaders. In 1836, Lowell mill workers struck again, but as in 1834, the company won, and most of the strikers returned to their jobs.

Skilled artisans also sought better wages and working conditions. These artisans, who had originally organized to preserve their own interests, began to ally themselves with unskilled workers. When Philadelphia coal workers struck for a 10-hour day in 1835, carpenters, shoemakers, and other artisans joined them in what became the first general strike in the United States. Although only 1 or 2 percent of workers in the United States were organized, the 1830s and 1840s saw dozens of strikes—many for higher wages, but some for shorter hours. Employers won most of these strikes because they could easily replace unskilled workers with strike breakers. Many of these strikebreakers were immigrants who

THINK THROUGH HISTORY
E. *Evaluating Decisions* *Based on the results, do you think the decision to strike at Lowell was a good one?*

E. Answer Students may say the decision was a good one because it made the workers' grievances known. Others may say it was not a good decision because it did not bring about change.

Block Schedule TEACHING OPTION **Time Needed: 20 Minutes**

Cooperative Activity: Writing a List of Demands

Task: Groups of four to five students will write a list of demands for improving work and living conditions at a Lowell mill.

Purpose: To help students understand the conditions the mill workers endured.

Activity: Students will meet with their groups and discuss the conditions in the mills. They should draft a list of demands to be presented to the mill owners. Remind students to write their list from the viewpoint of 1830s mill women. The tone of the writing should be respectful, and the demands should be reasonable. Ask the groups to read their lists to the class.

Building a Portfolio: Students who add their list of demands to their portfolio should include a note explaining what they liked most about this activity.

ALTERNATIVE ASSESSMENT BOOK
Standards for Evaluating a Cooperative Activity

Standards for Evaluation
Demands should . . .

- refer to specific conditions in the mills
- present specific, reasonable ideas to improve these conditions
- maintain the respectful tone of New England women in the 1830s

had just escaped even worse poverty in Europe. (See *strike* on page 938 in the Economics Handbook.)

IMMIGRATION INCREASES European **immigration** rose dramatically in the United States between 1830 and 1860. In the decade 1845–1854 alone, nearly 3 million immigrants were added to a population that had numbered only about 20 million. Most of them came from northern and western Europe.

Irish immigrants congregated in the large cities of the East, where they performed whatever work they could find. Nearly a million Irish immigrants had settled in America between 1815 and 1844. Between 1845 and 1854, Irish immigration soared after a blight on potatoes caused the **Great Potato Famine.** The famine killed as many as 1 million of the Irish people and drove about 1.3 million more to America.

Irish immigrants faced prejudice, both because they were Roman Catholic and because they were poor. Frightened by allegations of a Catholic conspiracy to take over the country, Protestant mobs in big cities rampaged through Irish neighborhoods. Native-born artisans, whose wages had fallen because of competition from unskilled laborers and factory production, considered Irish immigrants the most unfair competition of all. Their willingness to work for low wages under terrible conditions made the Irish easy prey for employers who sought to break strikes with cheap labor. Other Irish immigrants, however, soon began to view unions as an opportunity to advance their prospects.

The swelling numbers of immigrants arriving at New York Harbor in the mid-19th century made scenes like this one, painted by Samuel Waugh in 1847, common.

NATIONAL TRADES' UNION During the 1830s, the trade unions in different towns began to join together to expand their power. Journeymen's organizations from several industries united in 1834 to form the **National Trades' Union,** which represented a variety of trades. The national trade union movement faced fierce opposition from bankers and owners. In addition, workers' efforts to organize were at first hampered by court decisions declaring strikes illegal.

In 1842, however, the Massachusetts Supreme Court supported the workers' right to strike in the case of ***Commonwealth* v. *Hunt.*** Chief Justice Lemuel Shaw declared that Boston's journeymen bootmakers could act "in such a manner as best to subserve their own interests."

Protests in the workplace came in response to changes in the new industrial system in the United States, but this was not the only area of American life that experienced unrest in the mid-19th century. Indeed, a series of religious and social reform movements went hand in hand with these economic changes.

F. Answer The movement was important because it tried to unite workers from a variety of occupations into one labor organization.

THINK THROUGH HISTORY
F. Making Inferences *Why was the national trade union movement important?*

Section 4 Assessment

1. TERMS & NAMES
Identify:
- the market revolution
- free enterprise
- entrepreneurs
- Samuel F. B. Morse
- Lowell textile mills
- strike
- immigration
- Great Potato Famine
- National Trades' Union
- *Commonwealth* v. *Hunt*

2. SUMMARIZING Create a time line like the one below, on which you label and date the important developments in manufacturing during the early 19th century.

1800 1810 1820 1830 1840 1850

Write a paragraph explaining which development was most important and why.

3. ANALYZING ISSUES Do you think the positive effects of mechanizing the manufacturing process outweighed the negative effects? Why or why not?

THINK ABOUT
- changes in job opportunities for artisans, women, and unskilled male laborers
- changes in employer-employee relationships
- working conditions in factories
- the cost of manufactured goods

4. MAKING PREDICTIONS In the first half of the 19th century, transportation and communication linked the country more than ever before. How will these advances affect ordinary Americans?

THINK ABOUT
- the new kinds of transportation
- changes in communications
- American westward migration

ANSWERS

1. TERMS & NAMES
the market revolution, p. 144
free enterprise, p. 144
entrepreneurs, p. 144
Samuel F. B. Morse, p. 145
Lowell textile mills, p. 147
strike, p. 148
immigration, p.149
Great Potato Famine, p.149
National Trades' Union, p. 149
Commonwealth v. *Hunt,* p. 149

2. SUMMARIZING
Possible Answers: 1807—The steamboat *Clermont* travels from New York City to Albany; 1822—Lowell and his associates decide to open a larger textile mill; 1825—Erie Canal opens; 1834—First strike at the Lowell mill; National Trades' Union formed; 1835—Strike in Philadelphia; 1842—*Commonwealth* v. *Hunt;* 1844—Morse sends first telegraph message.

3. ANALYZING ISSUES
Possible Responses: Some students may refer to the reduced cost of manufactured items and to expanding opportunities for women and unskilled male laborers. Other students may mention the breaking up of families and communities when people left home to work in factories.

4. MAKING PREDICTIONS
Possible Answers: Most students may indicate that new means of communication and transportation would help Americans in increasingly distant regions of the continent stay in close contact and maintain economic links.

MORE ABOUT . . .
Irish Immigration
More than half of the Irish immigrants who fled to the United States were women, many of whom became maids or textile workers. By the 1840s, in fact, Irish women were replacing native-born American women in the Lowell mills. Irish men who could secure skilled jobs also competed with native-born white workers. As a result, according to one immigrant, there was "no love for [the Irish worker]—no protection of life—[he] can be shot down, run through, kicked, cuffed, spat upon. . . ."

GEOGRAPHY TRANSPARENCIES
G9, American Cities, 1820, 1860

ASSESS & RETEACH

Section 4 Assessment
Have students work on the questions individually, then compare their answers with those of a partner.

Self-Assessment
Have students write up to three questions about content they may not completely understand. Students should then try to answer those questions by skimming the section.

Section Quiz
FORMAL ASSESSMENT
Section Quiz, p. 44

Reteach
Review the main ideas of the section using the Guided Reading Worksheet for Section 4.

IN-DEPTH RESOURCES: UNIT 1
Guided Reading, p. 75

CLOSE
The market revolution marked the beginnings of America's rise as an industrial power. It contributed to the creation of wealth for some Americans but also caused economic inequality.

Daily Life

OBJECTIVES

1. To describe working conditions in mid-19th-century America.
2. To compare and contrast the lot of mill workers, field slaves, and farmers of the day.

FOCUS & MOTIVATE

▶ ***Starting with the Student***
Ask students who have part-time jobs to describe the working conditions at their workplace.

- How do working conditions today compare to conditions during the mid-19th century?
- What changes in their working conditions would they propose to their bosses?

MORE ABOUT . . .
The Industrial Revolution
When the small arms industry at the end of the 18th century pioneered the use of standard parts needed for mass production, that in turn expanded textile, metal, tool, and other industries. By 1860, manufacturing accounted for over a third of all U.S. production. Workers in industrialized nations enjoyed higher living standards than ever before, especially when they began to fight for shorter hours, higher wages, and better factory conditions.

DAILY LIFE
1820–1850

Working at Mid-Century

In the years before the Civil War, most workers labored from dawn to dusk, six days a week, without benefits. Although many Northerners criticized the South for exploiting slave labor, Southerners criticized the industrial wage system, mostly in the North, for exploiting free workers. Both North and South used children—cheap labor—for full workdays. While 10-year-old slave children worked in the fields like adults, one Northern mill employed 100 children aged 4–10. Look for similarities and differences in the lives of the workers discussed here, and consider how work life has changed from then to now.

Courtesy George Eastman House

MILL WORKERS Approximately 80 percent of textile-mill workers were young women between the ages of 15 and 30. The girls' day began with a bell for a quick breakfast in the boarding house, followed by a march to the factory, where they tended the spinning machines all day. They put up with heavy dust, the roar of machines, and hot air into which water was sprayed to prevent threads from breaking, with windows nailed shut to keep in the humidity.

When competitive pressure was on the owners, the girls had to speed up their work and endure lower wages. Children made $1 a week; older girls, $3; men, $6.

LENGTH OF DAY: 12 hours
TYPE OF LABOR: operating machines
PAYMENT: $1 to $6 a week

TIME TABLE OF THE LOWELL MILLS,
Arranged to make the working time throughout the year average 11 hours per day.
TO TAKE EFFECT SEPTEMBER 21st., 1853.
The Standard time being that of the meridian of Lowell, as shown by the Regulator Clock of AMOS SANBORN, Post Office Corner, Central Street.

From March 20th to September 19th, inclusive.
COMMENCE WORK, at 6.30 A. M. LEAVE OFF WORK, at 6.30 P. M., except on Saturday Evenings.
BREAKFAST at 6 A. M. DINNER, at 12 M. Commence Work, after dinner, 12.45 P. M.

From September 20th to March 19th, inclusive.
COMMENCE WORK at 7.00 A. M. LEAVE OFF WORK, at 7.00 P. M., except on Saturday Evenings.
BREAKFAST at 6.30 A. M. DINNER, at 12.30 P.M. Commence Work, after dinner, 1.15 P. M.

BELLS.

From March 20th to September 19th, inclusive.

Morning Bells.	*Dinner Bells.*	*Evening Bells.*
First bell,.............4.30 A. M.	Ring out,...............12.00 M.	Ring out,.............6.30 P. M.
Second, 5.30 A. M.; Third, 6.20.	Ring in,.............12.35 P. M.	Except on Saturday Evenings.

From September 20th to March 19th, inclusive.

Morning Bells.	*Dinner Bells.*	*Evening Bells.*
First bell,.............5.00 A. M.	Ring out,.............12.30 P. M.	Ring out at.............7.00 P. M.
Second, 6.00 A. M.; Third, 6.50.	Ring in,.............1.05 P. M.	Except on Saturday Evenings.

SATURDAY EVENING BELLS.
During APRIL, MAY, JUNE, JULY, and AUGUST, Ring Out, at 6.00 P. M.
The remaining Saturday Evenings in the year, ring out as follows:

SEPTEMBER.	NOVEMBER.	JANUARY.
First Saturday, ring out 6.00 P. M.	Third Saturday ring out 4.00 P. M.	Third Saturday, ring out 4.25 P. M.
Second " " 5.45 "	Fourth " " 3.55 "	Fourth " " 4.35 "
Third " " 5.30 "		
Fourth " " 5.20 "		
OCTOBER.	DECEMBER.	FEBRUARY.
First Saturday, ring out 5.05 P. M.	First Saturday, ring out 3.50 P. M.	First Saturday, ring out 4.45 P. M.
Second " " 4.55 "	Second " " 3.55 "	Second " " 4.55 "
Third " " 4.45 "	Third " " 3.55 "	Third " " 5.00 "

RECOMMENDED RESOURCES

Books

Danhof, Clarence H. *Change in Agriculture.* Cambridge: Harvard UP, 1969. American agricultural innovations from 1820 to 1870.

Davis, Rebecca Harding. *Life in the Iron Mills.* Old Westbury, NY: Feminist, 1972. An *Uncle Tom's Cabin* for factory workers, first published in 1861.

Laurie, Bruce. *Artisans into Workers.* New York: Hill, 1989. The history of labor in 19th-century America.

Mellon, James, ed. *Bullwhip Days.* New York: Weidenfeld, 1988. African Americans recall slavery.

Robinson, Harriet H. *Loom and Spindle.* Kailua, HI: Press Pacifica, 1976. Autobiography of a textile worker.

Zimiles, Martha. *Early American Mills.* New York: Potter, 1973. Early factories in New England.

Videos

Black People in the Slave South, 1850. Encyclopaedia Britannica.

The Industrial Revolution: Beginnings in the United States. Encyclopaedia Britannica.

The Plantation South. Encyclopaedia Britannica. The Southern plantation system.

Software

The Industrial Revolution in America. Queue. The rise of industry before and after the Civil War.

Haymaking (1864), Winslow Homer

FARMERS Because farmers' livelihoods depended on the weather, soil conditions, and the market prices of crops, their earnings were unpredictable—but generally very low.

Fathers and sons spent their days clearing land, plowing and planting, and hoeing the fields. Mothers and daughters raised vegetable gardens for family consumption, helped harvest crops, cared for livestock, made clothing, and cared for the family.

LENGTH OF DAY: dawn until after dark
TYPE OF LABOR: planting, tending crops, caring for livestock
PAYMENT: dependent on crop prices

FIELD SLAVES The field slave's day during harvest began with a bell an hour before dawn, a quick breakfast, and then a march to the fields. Men, women, and children spent the entire day picking cotton, bundling it, and coming back after dark carrying bales of cotton to the gin house. They then made their own suppers and ate quickly before falling asleep on wooden planks.

None of the other antebellum workers had such harsh and often brutal discipline imposed on them as slaves did. For most, the master's whip was the constant threat for lagging in their work.

LENGTH OF DAY: predawn until after dark
TYPE OF LABOR: picking and bundling cotton
PAYMENT: substandard food and shelter

DATA FILE

Annual Cost of Maintaining a Field Slave

A typical Southern plantation owner in 1848–1860 would spend the following to take care of a field slave for one year.

Taxes $0.80
Medical Care $1.75
Food/Clothing $8.50
Supervision $10.00
TOTAL $21.05

Source: *Slavery and the Southern Economy*, Harold D. Woodman, editor

Workers in the Mid-19th Century

Average monthly earnings from 1830 to 1850 for a few common occupations:

JOB	YEAR	MONTHLY EARNINGS
Artisan	1830	$ 45
Laborer	1830	$ 26
Teacher, male	1840	$ 15
Teacher, female	1840	$ 7
Northern farm hand	1850	$ 13
Southern farm hand	1850	$ 9

Source: *Historical Statistics of the United States*

Workers in the 1990s

Average monthly salary for each profession.

JOB	MONTHLY SALARY
Teacher—elementary	$ 2,758
Teacher—high school	$ 2,900
Construction worker	$ 2,399
Service worker	$ 1,518

Source: *Employment and Statistics, June 1996, U.S. Department of Labor; Statistical Abstract of the United States, 1994*

INTERACT WITH HISTORY

1. **INTERPRETING DATA** What attitudes about women and children do you see reflected in work and pay patterns during the mid-19th century?
2. **CREATING A GRAPH** Use the data in the charts above to create a graph that shows wage levels for workers in the mid-19th century. Clearly label jobs, wages, and years on your graph.

SEE SKILLBUILDER HANDBOOK, PAGE 931.

Visit http://www.mlushistory.com for more about child labor.

INSTRUCT

▶ *Starting with the Student*

- Ask students to imagine that they lived in mid-19th-century America. What job would they have chosen and why?
- Have students comment on any surprising information in the data file. You might point out that while a teacher's salary was low, the job often came with free living quarters adjoining the schoolhouse.

▶ *Discussing Key Ideas*

- Mid-19th-century labor conditions are very harsh.
- Women usually receive lower wages than men.
- Child labor and slave labor are exploited.

HISTORY FROM VISUALS

Reading the Images

Study the pictures and the graphics in the data file.

- Of the three types of work shown, which earned the most and provided the best conditions? *Mill worker.*
- Why do you think women were paid less than men? *Possible Responses: Women were supposedly not supporting families; to leave more for men who were supporting families; sexist prejudice; women may have been more timid about demanding raises; in jobs requiring physical strength, women may have been less productive; women generally had less education.*

INTERACT WITH HISTORY

1. Interpreting Data

Possible Responses: *Work patterns reflected a sexist attitude toward women and a low opinion of both women and children. Attitudes included a willingness to exploit them and a willingness to treat lower-class women and children badly even while coddling upper-class women and children.*

2. Creating a Graph

Standards for Evaluation

Graphs should . . .

- make appropriate use of the data provided in the data file
- accurately show differences in wages for different occupations and for different years
- be clearly labeled

Section 5 Overview

OBJECTIVES

1. To explain how the spiritual awakening of the early 19th century inspired the reform movements of the era.
2. To describe the institution of slavery and the rising movement to abolish it.
3. To discuss the central role that women played in 19th-century reform movements.

SKILLBUILDER

- Interpreting graphs, p. 155

CRITICAL THINKING

- Contrasting, p. 153
- Recognizing effects, pp. 153, 155
- Making predictions, pp. 154, 157
- Finding main ideas, p. 155
- Theme: Women in America, p. 156
- Summarizing, p. 157
- Forming opinions, p. 157
- Making inferences, p. 157

FOCUS & MOTIVATE

5-MINUTE WARM-UP

Analyzing Graphs
To examine slavery in antebellum America, have students look at the graph on page 155 and answer these questions.

1. How much more likely was a slave to live on a farm with fewer than 10 slaves than on a plantation with more than 100?
2. Was a slave owner more likely to own fewer than 10 slaves or more than 100?

WARM-UP TRANSPARENCY 3

▶ ***Starting with the Student***
What elements of society today do students think should change? Why?

OBJECTIVE
① INSTRUCT

A Spiritual Awakening Inspires Reform

▶ ***Discussing Key Ideas***

- The Second Great Awakening inspires

(continued on next page)

5 Reforming American Society

LEARN ABOUT the problems that many reformers saw in American society in the mid-19th century and their efforts to solve them
TO UNDERSTAND the impact of reform movements such as abolition and women's rights in American history.

TERMS & NAMES
- **Second Great Awakening**
- **Unitarians**
- **Ralph Waldo Emerson**
- **transcendentalism**
- **William Lloyd Garrison**
- **Frederick Douglass**
- **Nat Turner**
- **Elizabeth Cady Stanton**
- **Seneca Falls convention**
- **Sojourner Truth**

ONE AMERICAN'S STORY

James Forten's great-grandfather had been brought from Africa to the American colonies in chains, but James was born free. In 1781, the 15-year-old James went to sea to fight for American independence. Captured by the British and offered passage to England, the patriotic youth refused, saying, "I am here a prisoner for the liberties of my country; I never, NEVER, shall prove a traitor to her interests."

By the 1830s Forten had become a wealthy sailmaker. A leader of Philadelphia's free black community, Forten took an active role in a variety of political causes. When some people argued that free blacks should return to Africa, Forten disagreed and responded with sarcasm.

A PERSONAL VOICE

> Here I have dwelt until I am nearly sixty years of age, and have brought up and educated a family. . . . Yet some ingenious gentlemen have recently discovered that I am still an African; that a continent three thousand miles, and more, from the place where I was born, is my native country. And I am advised to go home. . . . Perhaps if I should only be set on the shore of that distant land, I should recognize all I might see there, and run at once to the old hut where my forefathers lived a hundred years ago.
>
> **JAMES FORTEN,** quoted in *Forging Freedom: The Formation of Philadelphia's Black Community 1720–1840*

James Forten

Forten's unwavering belief that he was an American not only led him to oppose colonization—the effort to resettle free blacks in Africa—but also pushed him fervently to oppose slavery. Forten was joined in his opposition to slavery by a growing number of Americans in the 19th century. Abolition, the movement to abolish slavery, became the most important of a series of reform movements in America.

A Spiritual Awakening Inspires Reform

Many of these movements had their roots in a spiritual awakening that swept the nation after 1790. People affected by these movements began to emphasize individual responsibility for seeking salvation and insisted that people could improve themselves and society. These religious attitudes were closely linked to the ideas of Jacksonian democracy that stressed the importance and power of the common person.

THE SECOND GREAT AWAKENING The **Second Great Awakening** was a widespread movement to awaken religious sentiments. Preachers like Charles Grandison Finney offered passionate sermons to inspire emotional, spiritual responses from their audiences. The primary forum for their message was the revival meeting, where participants attempted to revive religious faith through impassioned preaching. Some preachers could draw audiences of 25,000 or more at outdoor revival meetings.

Revival meetings might last for days as participants studied the Bible, reflected on their lives, and heard emotional sermons. Revivalism had a strong impact on the American public. According to one estimate, in 1800 just one in 15 Americans belonged to a church, but by 1850 one in 6 was a member. Yet revivalism was not to everyone's liking.

SECTION 5 RESOURCES

PRINT RESOURCES

IN-DEPTH RESOURCES: UNIT 1
Guided Reading, p. 76
Skillbuilder Practice: Identifying Problems, p. 80
Primary Sources: Propaganda Images, p. 88; *from* The Seneca Falls "Declaration of Sentiments," p. 89

READING STUDY GUIDE, p. 43

ACCESS FOR STUDENTS ACQUIRING ENGLISH
Guided Reading (Spanish), p. 56
Skillbuilder Practice: Identifying Problems (Spanish), p. 60

SPANISH READING STUDY GUIDE, p. 43

FORMAL ASSESSMENT Section Quiz, p. 45

ALTERNATIVE ASSESSMENT BOOK
See forms for supporting and scoring alternative activities.

TECHNOLOGY RESOURCES

HUMANITIES TRANSPARENCIES
H8, "Religion Camp Meeting" by J. Maze Burbank

GEOGRAPHY TRANSPARENCIES
G8, Distribution of Slaves, 1790 and 1860

CRITICAL THINKING TRANSPARENCIES
CT42, Increasing School Enrollment: 1840–1860

CD-ROM *Grolier Multimedia Encyclopedia*
Electronic Library of Primary Sources

VIDEO *American Portfolio: A Videodisc for U.S. History* user's guide, pp. 69–73, 75–78

INTERNET http://www.mlushistory.com

UNITARIANS AND TRANSCENDENTALISTS Another growing religious group was the **Unitarians,** who shared with revivalism a faith in the individual. But instead of appealing to emotions, Unitarians emphasized reason as the path to perfection. In New England, the Unitarians attracted a wealthy and educated following. In place of the conversions produced by the revivals, the Unitarians believed that spiritual awakening was a gradual process. Unitarians, like revivalists, held the conviction that individual and social reform were both possible and important.

THINK THROUGH HISTORY
A. *Contrasting* *How did the Unitarians' approach to religious conversion differ from that of the revivalists?*

A. Answer The Unitarians believed conversion was a gradual process, while revivalists expected an emotional conversion.

Some reform-minded individuals who sought an alternative to traditional religion admired the ideas of a New England minister, writer, and philosopher, **Ralph Waldo Emerson**. After the death of his young wife in 1831, Emerson fell into a religious crisis. Grief-stricken, Emerson traveled to England, where he met artists who advocated romanticism, an artistic style that encouraged people to develop unique and emotional forms of expression. From these romantic ideals, Emerson developed a philosophy called **transcendentalism,** which emphasized that truth could be found in nature, intuition, and imagination. Exalting the dignity of the individual, many transcendentalists fought for humanitarian reforms such as the abolition of slavery.

NOW & THEN

MODERN REVIVALISM

Evangelical Christianity reemerged in several different religious organizations in the late 20th century. One example is the Christian Coalition, a religiously based citizen-action organization with more than 1.7 million members. Many members of such groups hold religious beliefs that are similar to the revivalists' of the 1800s.

As with the Second Great Awakening, members of these religious organizations often are active in political movements that spring from personal religious beliefs. Indeed, some of the organizations use television much like Finney used the revival meeting to encourage believers to act on their faith.

THE AFRICAN-AMERICAN CHURCH The urge to reform was growing among African Americans, too. As revivals spread through the South, many slaveholders feared that enslaved African Americans might use the message of individual salvation to attack slavery. Slaves in the rural South—though they were segregated in pews of their own—worshipped in the same churches, heard the same sermons, and sang the same hymns as did the slave owners. Enslaved African Americans, however, interpreted the Christian message as a promise of freedom.

In the East, many free African Americans worshipped in separate black churches, like Richard Allen's Bethel African Church in Philadelphia. While enslaved, Allen had experienced a religious conversion. He went on to purchase his freedom and establish the Bethel African Church, which by 1816 would become the African Methodist Episcopal Church. Membership in the African Methodist Episcopal Church grew rapidly, in part because it offered more than simply a place to worship. The church became a political, cultural, and social center for African Americans, providing schools and other services that whites denied free blacks.

B. Answer Among African Americans such as Richard Allen, religion reinforced their desire for freedom. Meanwhile, whites like William Lloyd Garrison came to the abolition movement from work in other reform movements.

This early-19th-century tray depicts the African-American preacher Lemuel Haynes preaching to the parishioners in a Vermont Congregational church.

Slavery and Abolition

By the 1820s, more than 100 antislavery societies were advocating that African Americans be resettled in Africa. In 1817, the American Colonization Society had been founded to encourage black emigration. Whites began to join African Americans in criticizing slavery. The most radical white abolitionist was a young editor named **William Lloyd Garrison.**

THINK THROUGH HISTORY
B. *Recognizing Effects* *How did religious reform contribute to the abolition movement?*

Active in religious reform movements in Massachusetts, Garrison began a publishing career in 1828 as the editor of an antislavery paper. Three years later he established his own paper, *The Liberator,* to deliver an uncompromising message: immediate emancipation—the freeing of slaves—with no payment to slaveholders. Every issue of *The Liberator* forcefully stated his position.

(continued from page 152)

spiritual reform through emotional meetings where revivalists urge individual salvation.

- The Unitarians and Transcendentalists also have faith in the individual but emphasize reason rather than emotion.
- The African-American church gives its members a place to worship, a sense of community, and the support to oppose slavery.

IN-DEPTH RESOURCES: UNIT 1
Guided Reading, p. 76

ACCESS FOR STUDENTS ACQUIRING ENGLISH
Guided Reading (Spanish), p. 56

HUMANITIES TRANSPARENCIES
H8, "Religion Camp Meeting" by J. Maze Burbank

NOW & THEN
Modern Revivalism
Critical Thinking: Compare and Contrast Ask students to discuss the growth of the Christian Coalition. Then ask students: In what ways are the members of the Coalition and the revivalists of the 19th century similar?
Possible Response: Members of both movements had deep faith and used their power to effect social change.

OBJECTIVE
② INSTRUCT

Slavery and Abolition

▶***Discussing Key Ideas***
- White abolitionist William Lloyd Garrison alienates many whites with his radical views.

(continued on next page)

TEACHING OPTIONS

Making Connections Across the Curriculum

Literature Ralph Waldo Emerson stood at the center of one of the most vibrant literary communities of American history. His friends included fellow transcendentalist Henry David Thoreau, essayist Margaret Fuller, and the famous novelists Nathaniel Hawthorne and Herman Melville. These people produced much of the first great body of American literature.

Making Connections Across Time

The African-American Church Today Tell students that in the early 1960s, Martin Luther King, Jr., and other African-American ministers initiated a nonviolent struggle against discrimination that led to the civil rights movement. In 1995, another religious leader, Nation of Islam minister Louis Farrakhan, united African-American men on his Million Man March.

What does the power and authority of these leaders suggest?
Possible Response: Black churches continue to have great influence with many African Americans.

(continued from page 153)

- Escaped slave Frederick Douglass becomes an eloquent voice in the antislavery movement.
- Life under slavery is hard, but enslaved people struggle to control their lives.
- Nat Turner leads a slave rebellion, but the uprising fails and Turner is hanged.
- After the Turner rebellion, slaveholders tighten restrictions on slaves and more staunchly oppose abolition.

MORE ABOUT . . .

Frederick Douglass

Douglass worked for racial equality throughout his life. In the early 1840s, for example, Douglass protested segregated seating on trains by sitting in cars reserved for whites. Once, when he refused to leave the car, a group of white men tried to force him out of his seat. When Douglass resisted, the men pulled the railroad seat out of the floor of the car—with Douglass hanging on to the seat.

ELECTRONIC LIBRARY OF PRIMARY SOURCES

from A Lecture on the Anti-Slavery Movement by Frederick Douglass
from Declaration of Sentiments by the American Anti-Slavery Society
The Question of Negro Slavery by William J. Grayson
from *Incidents in the Life of a Slave Girl* by Harriet A. Jacobs

A PERSONAL VOICE

I am aware that many object to the severity of my language, but is there not cause for severity? I will be as harsh as truth, and as uncompromising as justice. On this subject [immediate emancipation], I do not wish to think or speak or write with moderation. . . . I am in earnest—I will not equivocate—I will not excuse—I will not retreat a single inch—AND I WILL BE HEARD.

WILLIAM LLOYD GARRISON, *The Liberator*

Before Garrison's call for the immediate emancipation of slaves, support for that position had been limited. In the 1830s, however, that position gained support. Garrison founded the New England Anti-Slavery Society in 1832 and then helped found the national American Anti-Slavery Society the following year. Many whites who opposed abolition, however, hated Garrison. In 1835 a Boston mob dragged him through town at the end of a rope. Nevertheless, Garrison enjoyed widespread black support; three out of four early subscribers to *The Liberator* were African Americans.

FREDERICK DOUGLASS One of those eager readers was **Frederick Douglass.** Born into slavery in 1817, Douglass had been taught to read and write by the wife of one of his owners. Her husband ordered her to stop teaching Douglass, however, because reading "would forever unfit him to be a slave." When Douglass realized that knowledge could be his "pathway from slavery to freedom," he studied harder.

"I consider it settled that the black and white people of America ought to share common destiny."

FREDERICK DOUGLASS, 1851

By 1838, Douglass held a skilled job as a ship caulker in Baltimore. He plied his trade well and earned the highest wages in the yard, but Douglass's slave owner took his pay each week. After a disagreement with his owner, Douglass decided to escape. Borrowing the identity of a free black sailor and carrying official papers, Douglass stepped onto a train. When he reached New York, he tasted freedom for the first time.

Garrison heard him speak and was so impressed that he sponsored Douglass to speak for the American Anti-Slavery Society. Hoping that abolition could be achieved without violence, Douglass broke with Garrison in 1847 and began his own antislavery newspaper. He named it *The North Star,* after the star that guided runaway slaves to freedom. For every escapee like Douglass, however, thousands more continued to be enslaved.

THINK THROUGH HISTORY
C. *Making Predictions* *What impact do you think Douglass will have on the abolition movement?*

C. Answer He might inspire other African Americans to fight slavery. He might convince whites to abandon their belief in white supremacy and encourage them to become abolitionists.

LIFE UNDER SLAVERY The institution of slavery had evolved since the 18th century. In those days, most slaves were male, had recently arrived from the Caribbean or Africa, and spoke one of several languages other than English. By 1830, however, the numbers of male and female slaves had become more equal. The majority had been born in America and spoke English. However, two things remained constant in the lives of slaves—hard work and a lack of freedom.

Most enslaved African Americans lived and worked on large plantations and worked long, hard days in the fields. Some slaves on plantations worked in the slave owner's house as servants. Although work in the house was less physically demanding than work in the fields, servants endured closer scrutiny by the slave owner. Many slave owners owned only a few slaves. Often they worked in the fields alongside their slaves.

While wealthy planters lived in luxurious houses, enslaved persons lived in small,

TEACHING OPTIONS

Exploring Themes

Democracy in America Discuss the different ways both white and black abolitionists fought against slavery. Note that some abolitionists favored force, while others used nonviolent methods.

Ask students which method was probably more effective. *Possible Responses: Violent methods might have been more effective in bringing antislavery views to the public's attention; nonviolent methods might have been more likely to win people's sympathy and support.*

Teaching Gifted and Talented Students

***Writing an Article for* The Liberator** Ask students to use the library or other resources to find excerpts from *The Liberator.* Then have them write an article for the paper. The article should:

- address an injustice in the world today
- call for some action to be taken
- maintain the tone and style of Garrison's antislavery paper

Encourage students to compile their articles in an "anti-injustice" paper that the rest of the class can read.

Southern Plantations

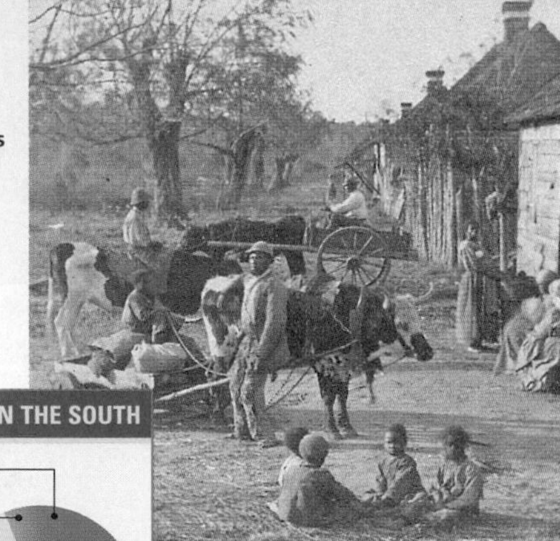

Southern plantations varied widely in prosperity, as these photographs show.

AFRICAN AMERICANS IN THE SOUTH

Slaves in groups of 10–99	61%
Free African Americans	6%
Slaves in groups of 100 or more	8%
Slaves in groups of 1–9	25%

Sources: 1860 figures from *Eighth Census of the United States*; Lewis C. Gray, *History of Agriculture in the Southern United States*

SKILLBUILDER
INTERPRETING GRAPHS
According to the pie graph, what was the smallest group of African Americans living in the South in 1860? Who do you think owned the smaller groups of slaves (groups of 1 to 9)?

Skillbuilder Answers
Smallest Group: Free African Americans. **Groups of 1 to 9:** *Possible answer:* Owners of small farms; families living in the towns and cities of the South.

cramped quarters that offered little protection from extreme weather and had few furnishings. Most poor whites, and many small slave owners, had housing that was little better than that of slaves. Even so, whites had greater opportunities than slaves, who were denied education and civil rights.

THINK THROUGH HISTORY
D. *Finding Main Ideas* *Despite the differences in their living situations, what common problems did enslaved African Americans face?*

D. Answer Whether they worked in the fields or in the planter's house, or if they worked on large plantations or in cities, enslaved African Americans faced hard work and a lack of freedom.

Some enslaved people developed specialized skills and were in demand in Southern cities. Slave owners often "hired out" their slaves to factory owners. In return, the slave owners collected the pay of their slaves without having to supervise their activities. As a result, urban slaves spent more time beyond the watch of their slave owners.

TURNER'S REBELLION Still, whether in cities or on farms, slaves never lost sight of their goal of freedom. For some, it was time to take action. **Nat Turner,** a slave in Virginia, organized a rebellion.

While in the woods, he experienced a vision that he interpreted as a call to "lead and organize his fellow slaves in a struggle for freedom." In August 1831, a partial eclipse of the sun convinced Turner that the time was ripe. Gathering more than 50 followers as he moved from plantation to plantation, Turner's band attacked four plantations and killed about 70 whites. By the fifth attack, an alarm alerted whites who captured and executed 16 members of Turner's band. Though Turner himself hid out for several weeks, eventually he was captured, tried, and hanged.

E. Answer The rebellion frightened many slave owners. Some tried to abolish slavery, but most argued for tighter restrictions on slaves to prevent further rebellions.

THINK THROUGH HISTORY
E. *Recognizing Effects* *How did Turner's rebellion affect slaveholders' attitudes about slavery?*

SLAVE OWNERS OPPOSE ABOLITION The Turner rebellion frightened and outraged slaveholders. In some states, people argued that the only way to prevent slave revolts was through emancipation. Others, however, chose to tighten restrictions on all African Americans to prevent them from plotting insurrections.

Some proslavery advocates began to argue that slavery was a beneficial institution. They used the Bible to defend slavery and cited passages that counseled servants to obey their masters. Some, even Christian ministers, argued that slavery benefited blacks by fostering Christian civilization among them.

Nevertheless, opposition to the existence of slavery refused to disappear. Much of the strength of the abolition movement came from the efforts of women—many of whom contributed to other reform movements, including a women's rights movement.

HISTORY FROM VISUALS
African Americans in the South

Reading the Graph Discuss with students that free African Americans were not owned as slaves. They are represented on the graph so that their numbers can be compared with the number of slaves in the South.

Extension Ask students why so few Southern blacks were free. *Possible Response: Most couldn't afford to buy their freedom; others left the South where they risked being enslaved.*

GEOGRAPHY TRANSPARENCIES
G8, Distribution of Slaves, 1790 and 1860

MORE ABOUT . . .
Free African Americans

Not all blacks in the United States were slaves. On the eve of the Civil War, there were about 250,000 free blacks in the United States. There were several ways that slaves won their freedom. Some ran away like Frederick Douglass. Some managed to earn some money and then purchase their freedom. Others were freed by owners who had moral qualms about slavery. Although many free blacks still faced discrimination and possible enslavement, some became wealthy. Some of these people purchased slaves of their own—usually relatives whom they intended to make free.

IN-DEPTH RESOURCES: UNIT 1
Primary Source: Propaganda Images, p. 88

Block Schedule TEACHING OPTION **Time Needed: 20 Minutes**

Cooperative Activity: Daily Lives in Contrast

Task: Groups of students will research the daily lives of plantation owners and slaves in the 1830s and present a "A Day in the Life of . . ." report.

Purpose: To help students understand the underlying attitudes and needs of these two important groups.

Activity: Assign some groups to focus on plantation owners and some groups to focus on slaves. Using library resources and the Internet, students will search for information and visuals to make their presentations effective. Some groups may wish to create posters that divide a day into various segments; others may use photographs of restored plantations and of artifacts from the period to enhance their "A Day in the Life of . . ." presentations.

ALTERNATIVE ASSESSMENT BOOK
Standards for Evaluating a Cooperative Activity

OBJECTIVE

3 INSTRUCT

Women and Reform

▶ ***Discussing Key Ideas***

- Although women are encouraged to stay at home, some women join the reform movements of the era—including abolition and education reform.
- Most men oppose women's participation in the abolition movement, but this only pushes them to fight for women's rights.

 ***GROLIER MULTIMEDIA ENCYCLOPEDIA***
Lucretia Mott

ELECTRONIC LIBRARY OF PRIMARY SOURCES
Disappointment Is the Lot of Women

 ***CRITICAL THINKING TRANSPARENCIES***
CT42, Increasing School Enrollment: 1840–1860

Issues for the 21st Century

Women and the Glass Ceiling

Connect women's status in the 19th century with women's status today by having students read pages 894–895 and answer these questions.

1. What gains have women made since the early 19th century in their struggle for equality? *Possible Response: Job opportunities and political rights for women have expanded.*
2. How did the women reformers of the 19th century help create these changes? *Possible Response: They fought for suffrage and better education for women.*

Women and Reform

In the early 19th century, women faced limited options. Prevailing customs encouraged women to restrict their activities after marriage to the home and family. Housework and child care were considered the only proper activities for married women, and they were denied full participation in the larger community.

KEY PLAYER

ELIZABETH CADY STANTON
1815–1902

Stanton was an ardent abolitionist, and she timed her marriage in 1840 so that she and her new husband could travel together to London for the World's Anti-Slavery Convention.

She also believed that women deserved the same rights as men and even persuaded the minister to omit the word "obey" from her vow in the marriage ceremony because she felt no need to "obey one with whom I supposed I was entering into an equal relation."

At the antislavery convention, Stanton and the other women delegates were barred from participation in the convention and were forced to sit and listen from a curtained gallery. There she met Lucretia Mott. Stanton and Mott vowed "to hold a convention as soon as we returned home, and form a society to advocate the rights of women." Eight years later, the Seneca Falls convention fulfilled that vow.

WOMEN MOBILIZE FOR REFORM Despite such limits, women actively participated in all the important reform movements of the 19th century. Like many middle-class men, middle-class white women had been inspired by the optimistic message of the Second Great Awakening to improve society. From abolition to education, women worked for reform despite the cold reception they got from many men. Eventually women reformers sought equal rights for themselves.

Perhaps the most important reform effort that women participated in was abolition. Women abolitionists raised money, distributed literature, and collected signatures for antislavery petitions to Congress. Sarah and Angelina Grimké, the daughters of a South Carolina slaveholder, spoke eloquently for abolition. In 1836 Angelina Grimké published *An Appeal to the Christian Women of the South,* in which she called upon women to "overthrow this horrible system of oppression and cruelty."

In addition to abolition, women played key roles in the temperance movement, the effort to prohibit the drinking of alcohol. Women like Mary C. Vaughan encouraged other women to support temperance reform. "We are learning," she said, "that our part in the drama of life is something beside inactive suffering and passive endurance."

EDUCATION FOR WOMEN Until the 1820s, American girls had few formal educational opportunities beyond elementary school. As Sarah Grimké complained, a woman who knew "chemistry enough to keep the pot boiling, and geography enough to know the location of the different rooms in her house" was considered learned enough.

To remedy this situation, Emma Willard opened one of the nation's first academically oriented schools for girls in Troy, New York, in 1821. In addition to classes in domestic sciences, the Troy Female Seminary offered classes in math, history, geography, languages, art, music, writing, and literature. In 1837 Mary Lyon founded another important institution of higher learning for women, Mount Holyoke Female Seminary (later known as Mount Holyoke College) in South Hadley, Massachusetts.

Black women had enjoyed even fewer educational opportunities than their white counterparts. In 1831 Prudence Crandall, a white Quaker, opened a school for girls in Canterbury, Connecticut. Two years later she admitted an African-American girl named Sarah Harris. The townspeople protested against desegregated education, so Crandall decided to have only African-American students. This aroused even more opposition, and in 1834 Crandall closed the school and left town.

F. Answer Some new schools like the Troy Female Seminary opened with expanded curriculums, but these gains did not extend to African-American women.

THINK THROUGH HISTORY
F. THEME ***Women in America*** *What gains did women make in education in the 1820s and 1830s? Did these gains extend to African-American women?*

WOMEN'S RIGHTS MOVEMENT EMERGES The reform movements of the mid-19th century fed the growth of the women's movement by providing women with increased opportunities to act outside the home. **Elizabeth Cady Stanton** and Lucretia Mott had been ardent abolitionists. Male abolitionists discriminated against them at the World's Anti-Slavery Convention in 1840, so the pair resolved to hold a women's rights convention. In 1848, more than 300

TEACHING OPTION

Skillbuilder Mini-Lesson: Identifying Problems

Explaining the Skill Identifying problems in history means finding and describing the difficulties faced by a group of people at a certain time. Being able to point to and explain a problem can lead to a thorough understanding of a situation. In reading history, students will find that some problems may be stated directly, while others might be implied by the ways people act. For example, gang violence in a community probably indicates that problems exist in other areas of community life, such as economic opportunities, housing conditions, and family structure.

Applying the Skill: Women and Reform Help students identify some of the problems women worked to reform in the early 1800s. *Slavery; lack of education and equality for women.*

Next ask whether the problems were stated directly in the text or were implied by people's actions. *Most are stated directly. Some people's treatment of women reformers suggests that traditional views of women's roles were restrictive.*

IN-DEPTH RESOURCES: UNIT 1
Skillbuilder Practice: Identifying Problems, p. 80

women convened in Seneca Falls, New York. Before the convention started, Stanton and Mott composed an agenda and a detailed statement of grievances.

The participants at the **Seneca Falls convention** approved all parts of the declaration unanimously—including several resolutions to encourage women to participate in all public issues on an equal basis with men—except one. The one exception, which still passed by a narrow majority, was the resolution calling for women to have the right to vote. The right of suffrage remained a controversial aim. Opponents of woman suffrage believed women should not vote because they were too dependent—on husbands and fathers for economic and legal protection—to exercise the right freely.

In spite of all the activity among middle-class white women, African-American women found it difficult to gain recognition of their problems. Sojourner Truth did not let that stop her. Born into slavery and given the name Isabella Baumfree, she took the name **Sojourner Truth** when she decided to sojourn (travel) arguing for abolition. At a women's rights convention in 1851, Truth refuted the arguments that because she was a woman she was weak, or because she was black, she was not feminine. The person who chaired the convention recorded remarks long attributed to Truth.

With her dignified bearing and powerful voice, Sojourner Truth made audiences snap to attention. Truth fought for women's rights, abolition, prison reform, and temperance.

A PERSONAL VOICE

Look at me! Look at my arm! I have ploughed, and planted, and gathered into barns, and no man could head me. And ain't I a woman? I could work as much and eat as much as a man—when I could get it—and bear the lash as well! And ain't I a woman? I have borne thirteen children, and seen most all sold off to slavery, and when I cried out with my mother's grief, none but Jesus heard me! And ain't I a woman?

SOJOURNER TRUTH, quoted in *Narrative of Sojourner Truth*

G. Answer It will intensify feelings for and against slavery and help lead to the Civil War.

THINK THROUGH HISTORY
G. *Making Predictions* *What effect will the abolition movement have on attitudes toward slavery?*

As Truth showed, hard work was a fact of life for most women. But she also pointed to the problem of slavery that continued to vex the nation. As abolitionists intensified their attacks, proslavery advocates strengthened their defenses. Before long the issue of slavery threatened to destroy the Union.

Section 5 Assessment

1. TERMS & NAMES

Identify:
- Second Great Awakening
- Unitarians
- Ralph Waldo Emerson
- transcendentalism
- William Lloyd Garrison
- Frederick Douglass
- Nat Turner
- Elizabeth Cady Stanton
- Seneca Falls convention
- Sojourner Truth

2. SUMMARIZING In a diagram similar to the one shown, fill in historical events, ideas, or people that relate to the main idea.

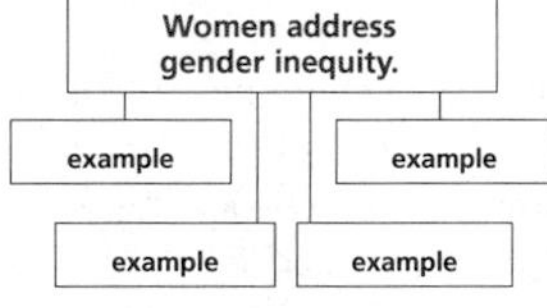

Write a paragraph about the most effective method of dealing with inequity.

3. FORMING OPINIONS Which do you think was a more effective strategy—violence or nonviolence—for achieving the abolitionists' goal of eliminating slavery? Why?

THINK ABOUT
- Garrison's attitude
- Frederick Douglass's views
- Southerners' reactions to Nat Turner's rebellion

4. MAKING INFERENCES Consider the philosophical and religious ideas expressed during the Second Great Awakening. How did they influence the activities of 19th-century reformers?

THINK ABOUT
- concepts of individualism and Jacksonian democracy
- the views of Finney, Allen, and Emerson
- the activities of Garrison, Douglass, Stanton, and Truth

ANSWERS

1. TERMS & NAMES

Second Great Awakening, p. 152
Unitarians, p. 153
Ralph Waldo Emerson, p. 153
transcendentalism, p.153
William Lloyd Garrison, p. 153
Frederick Douglass, p. 154
Nat Turner, p. 155
Elizabeth Cady Stanton, p. 156
Seneca Falls convention, p. 157
Sojourner Truth, p. 157

2. SUMMARIZING

Students' examples might be drawn from the following: Stanton, Mott, Troy Female Seminary, Seneca Falls convention, Sojourner Truth.

3. FORMING OPINIONS

Possible Responses: Some students may indicate that violence was a more effective strategy because it forced the nation to pay more attention to the issue of slavery. Others, however, may point out that antislavery violence brought equally strong reactions from slaveholders, who responded with violence of their own.

4. MAKING INFERENCES

Possible Responses: Most students may note that the reformers shared a strong belief in the power of the individual to improve himself or herself as well as the rest of society. Also the efforts of many reformers aimed at creating greater freedom and equality.

KEY PLAYER
Elizabeth Cady Stanton

Critical Thinking: Contrasting Ask students to contrast Stanton with the 19th-century image of the ideal woman. How did her activities differ from those of more traditional women?
Possible Responses: Stanton was strong willed rather than passive. She voiced her opinions and took part in the world outside her own home.

IN-DEPTH RESOURCES, UNIT 1
Primary Source: *from* The Seneca Falls "Declaration of Sentiments," p. 89

ASSESS & RETEACH

Section 5 Assessment

Have pairs of students work on the questions and share their answers with another pair of students.

Self-Assessment

To document what students have learned, have them make a list of the insights they have gained into the changing status of women in the mid-1800s.

Section Quiz

FORMAL ASSESSMENT
Section Quiz, p. 45

Reteach

Have students skim the section, noting the major reformers and their causes. Ask them to create a list to help them keep track of this information.

CLOSE

By the mid-1800s, women reformers active in the antislavery movement began to be concerned about their own rights. They fought for many other reforms, too. Between 1830 and 1860, more and more people began to oppose slavery, which led the nation to the Civil War.

AMERICAN LITERATURE

Abolitionist Literature

Words were a powerful weapon in the struggle to end slavery. Autobiographical accounts of former slaves—including Solomon Northup and Frederick Douglass—shocked their audiences and underscored the sad reality conveyed in the religious folk songs, or spirituals, that slaves sang as they worked in the fields.

The voices of hundreds of black abolitionists found support in Harriet Beecher Stowe's antislavery novel, *Uncle Tom's Cabin.* The book, a huge bestseller, had such a profound effect on Northerners' attitudes toward slavery that when Abraham Lincoln met Stowe during the Civil War, he said, "So this is the little lady who made the big war."

UNCLE TOM'S CABIN

Harriet Beecher Stowe's powerful antislavery novel portrays the brutality that the enslaved Uncle Tom and his family endures at the hands of cruel slaveowners. In this passage, the slave Eliza, having learned that her baby will be sold to another master, attempts to escape the slave trader Haley by crossing the icy Ohio River from Kentucky to Ohio. Sam and Andy are fellow slaves.

Eliza was standing by the window, looking out in another direction, when Sam's quick eye caught a glimpse of her. Haley and Andy were two yards behind. At this crisis, Sam contrived to have his hat blown off. . . .

A thousand lives seemed to be concentrated in that one moment to Eliza. Her room opened by a side door to the river. She caught her child, and sprang down the steps towards it. The trader caught a full glimpse of her, just as she was disappearing down the bank; and throwing himself from his horse, calling loudly on Sam and Andy, he was after her like a hound after a deer. In that dizzy moment her feet to her scarce seemed to touch the ground, and a moment brought her to the water's edge. Right on behind they came; and, nerved with strength such as God gives only to the desperate, with one wild cry and flying leap, she vaulted sheer over the turbid current by the shore, on to the raft of ice beyond. It was a desperate leap—impossible to anything but madness and despair; and Haley, Sam, and Andy, instinctively cried out, and lifted up their hands, as she did it.

The huge green fragment of ice on which she alighted pitched and creaked as her weight came on it, but she stayed there not a moment. With wild cries and desperate energy she leaped to another and still another cake;—stumbling—leaping—slipping—springing upwards again! Her shoes are gone—her stockings cut from her feet—while blood marked every step; but she saw nothing, felt nothing, till dimly, as in a dream, she saw the Ohio side, and a man helping her up the bank.

Harriet Beecher Stowe, *Uncle Tom's Cabin* (1852)

American Literature

OBJECTIVES

1. To learn how abolitionist messages were conveyed through literature.
2. To compare the effectiveness of different forms of abolitionist literature.

FOCUS & MOTIVATE

▶ ***Starting with the Student***
Ask students what books they have read and films they have seen about the American slave experience.

- What general impressions did these books and films give of slavery?
- How do you think these books differ in theme and content from books and other writings produced during the slavery era?

INSTRUCT

▶ ***Discussing Key Ideas***

- Abolitionists use many different literary forms to attack slavery.
- *Uncle Tom's Cabin* by Harriet Beecher Stowe uses the form of a novel to discuss the moral issues surrounding slavery.
- The spiritual "Follow the Drinking Gourd" uses metaphors to guide runaway slaves along the Underground Railroad.
- Frederick Douglass writes a moving personal account of the evils of slavery.

RECOMMENDED RESOURCES

Books

Brown, William Wells. *The Narrative of William W. Brown, a Fugitive Slave.* Boston: Anti-Slavery Office, 1847. A narrative of the author's experiences as a slave in St. Louis and elsewhere.

Douglass, Frederick. *My Bondage and My Freedom.* Urbana: U of Illinois P, 1987. The 1855 autobiography.

Garrison, William Lloyd. *William Lloyd Garrison and the Fight Against Slavery.* Boston: St. Martin's, 1995. Selections from *The Liberator.*

Stowe, Harriet Beecher. *Uncle Tom's Cabin.* New York: Norton, 1994. An authoritative text with background and criticism.

Henson, Josiah. *Father Henson's Story of His Own Life.* New York: Corinth, 1962. Autobiography of a slave who lived from 1789 to 1883.

Sound Recordings

African American Spirituals. Washington, D.C.: Smithsonian/Folkways, 1994. CD that includes "There Is a Balm in Gilead."

Anderson, Marian. *He's Got the Whole World in His Hands.* New York, NY: RCA Victor, 1994. A compact disc of spirituals.

Douglass, Frederick. *Narrative of the Life of Frederick Douglass.* Prince Frederick, Md: Recorded Books, 1991. An unabridged book on tape.

Video

Spirituals in Concert. New York: CAMI Video, 1991. Includes performances by Kathleen Battle and Jessye Norman.

No. 10 from the Harriet Tubman series (1939–1940), Jacob Lawrence, Casein tempera on gessoed hardboard, 17 7/8" x 12", Hampton University Museum, Hampton, VA.

FOLLOW THE DRINKING GOURD

This spiritual is believed to contain coded messages from escaped slaves and their sympathizers that hint at the road north to freedom. The "drinking gourd" may be another term for the Big Dipper constellation. The "great big river" probably refers to the Mississippi River. "Peg foot" may allude to a white ex-sailor nicknamed Pegleg Joe, a "conductor" on the Underground Railroad.

When the sun comes back and the first quail calls,
Follow the drinking gourd.
For the old man is a-waiting for to carry you to freedom
If you follow the drinking gourd.

The river bank will make a very good road,
The dead trees show you the way.
Left foot, peg foot traveling on,
Follow the drinking gourd.

Where the little river meets the great big river,
Follow the drinking gourd.
The old man is a-waiting for to carry you to freedom
If you follow the drinking gourd.

[Refrain] Follow the drinking gourd,
Follow the drinking gourd,
For the old man is a-waiting for to carry you to freedom
If you follow the drinking gourd.

TRADITIONAL, "Follow the Drinking Gourd"

NARRATIVE OF THE LIFE OF FREDERICK DOUGLASS

Frederick Douglass was born into slavery but escaped to the North at the age of 21. The first of his autobiographies, *Narrative of the Life of Frederick Douglass, an American Slave* was published in 1845, seven years after he made his way to freedom. Douglass's writing revealed the conditions of slavery and helped to destroy common stereotypes of African Americans. Here he recalls how his owner's new wife attempted to teach him to read.

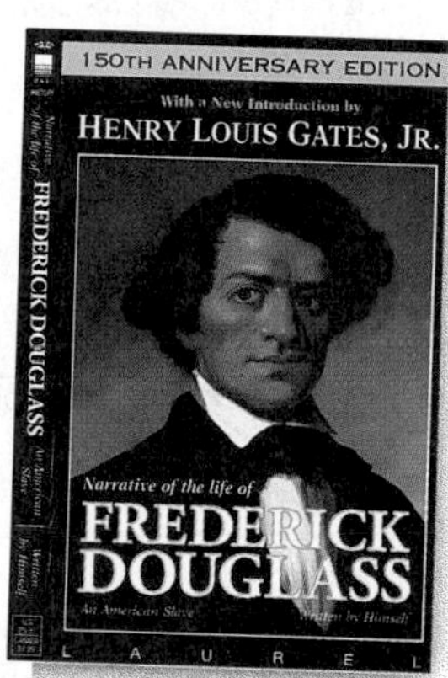

Very soon after I went to live with Mr. and Mrs. Auld, she very kindly commenced to teach me the A, B, C. After I had learned this, she assisted me in learning to spell words of three or four letters. Just at this point of my progress, Mr. Auld found out what was going on, and at once forbade Mrs. Auld to instruct me further, telling her, among other things, that it was unlawful, as well as unsafe, to teach a slave to read. . . . "Now," said he, "if you teach [Douglass] how to read, there would be no keeping him. It would forever unfit him to be a slave. He would at once become unmanageable, and of no value to his master. . . ." These words sank deep into my heart, stirred up sentiments within that lay slumbering, and called into existence an entirely new train of thought . . . . From that moment, I understood the pathway from slavery to freedom. . . . I set out with high hope, and a fixed purpose, at whatever cost of trouble, to learn how to read.

FREDERICK DOUGLASS, *Narrative of the Life of Frederick Douglass, an American Slave* (1845)

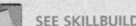

INTERACT WITH HISTORY

1. **COMPARING** Which of the three selections do you find most effective in conveying an abolitionist message, and why?

SEE SKILLBUILDER HANDBOOK, PAGE 909.

2. **RESEARCHING SPIRITUALS** Use books and musical recordings to prepare an oral report about African-American spirituals before the Civil War.

Visit http://www.mlushistory.com for more about pre-Civil War literature.

HISTORY FROM VISUALS

▶ *Reading the Image*

Ask students what the painting by Jacob Lawrence shows. Students should be able to identify the flight over mountainous terrain under a starry sky. Forked branches and a serpent-like figure suggest imminent danger. A central figure—perhaps Harriet Tubman—is dragging chains but reaching forward into the unknown.

MORE ABOUT . . .

The Writings of Frederick Douglass

Frederick Douglass built his reputation for eloquence as a speaker, not as a writer. When some people said that so brilliant a speaker could never have been a slave, Douglass decided to write his autobiography. In it, as well as in speeches and other writings, he tried to create a heroic image of himself. He did this for two reasons: to inspire other African Americans to believe that their skin color need not prevent them from achieving the American dream and to convince whites to give blacks a fair chance in life.

INTERACT WITH HISTORY

1. Comparing

Possible answers: *Students who choose* Uncle Tom's Cabin *might say that Stowe created sympathetic fictional characters whose sufferings could emotionally affect her readers. Students who choose Douglass's autobiography might cite how compelling his eloquent firsthand account is, as well as the fact that readers might have been influenced by the literary triumph of an African-American man who had overcome the obstacles of enslavement. Students who choose "Follow the Drinking Gourd" may say its effectiveness lies in the compelling quality of the lyrics, the soulful tune, or the mysterious double meanings.*

2. Researching Spirituals

Standards for Evaluation

Oral reports should . . .

- provide accurate information from both books and recordings
- describe the origins of African-American spirituals
- demonstrate the ways in which spirituals included abolitionist themes

REVIEW CHAPTER 3
ASSESSMENT ANSWERS

REVIEWING THE CHAPTER

TERMS & NAMES

1. Jeffersonian republicanism, p. 119
2. Monroe Doctrine, p. 123
3. Missouri Compromise, p. 127
4. Jacksonian democracy, p. 127
5. manifest destiny, p. 133
6. Stephen F. Austin, p. 136
7. market revolution, p. 144
8. Lowell textile mills, p. 147
9. Frederick Douglass, p. 154
10. Elizabeth Cady Stanton, p. 156

MAIN IDEAS

11. It doubled the size of the nation; Jefferson expanded the power of the presidency.
12. An end to the War of 1812.
13. Easing of voting requirements increased the number of voters; over three times as many white males voted in 1828 as in 1824, and they helped elect Andrew Jackson.
14. He regarded it as insensitive to the needs of common people and believed its financial strength and power threatened American democracy.
15. Many Americans were eager to control the Western lands, and they believed it was a destiny ordained by God.
16. A Mexican army killed 187 defenders of the Alamo, while 1,500 Mexicans also died. Fury over the massacre spurred the Texans to win their independence.
17. Transportation systems strengthened Northern industry and commerce. The steel plow and the reaper improved Midwest agriculture. Steam engines allowed the South to ship agricultural products north.
18. Workers went on strike and organized unions when their working conditions deteriorated and their wages fell. They organized to try to regain control over their workplaces.
19. Belief in the individual's ability to improve himself or herself and society, and in a democratic God who would offer salvation to all. Ideas like these could be found in the Second Great Awakening.
20. To gain support for women's rights and declare women's equality with men.

Review Chapter 3 Assessment

REVIEWING THE CHAPTER

TERMS & NAMES For each item below, write a sentence explaining its historical significance during the first half of the 19th century. For each person below, explain his or her role in the events of this period.

1. **Jeffersonian republicanism**
2. **Monroe Doctrine**
3. **Missouri Compromise**
4. **Jacksonian democracy**
5. **manifest destiny**
6. **Stephen F. Austin**
7. **market revolution**
8. **Lowell textile mills**
9. **Frederick Douglass**
10. **Elizabeth Cady Stanton**

MAIN IDEAS

SECTION 1 *(pages 118–123)*

The Jeffersonian Era

11. How did the Louisiana Purchase affect the United States?
12. What did the Treaty of Ghent accomplish?

SECTION 2 *(pages 124–132)*

The Age of Jackson

13. What changes occurred in the voting population and in voting patterns between the presidential elections of 1824 and 1828?
14. Why did Jackson oppose the Bank of the United States?

SECTION 3 *(pages 133–141)*

Manifest Destiny

15. Why was the concept of manifest destiny such an appealing one to Americans in the 1840s?
16. Describe the battle of the Alamo and explain why it is an important symbol in U.S. history.

SECTION 4 *(pages 144–149)*

The Market Revolution

17. How did the inventions and innovations of the mid-19th century encourage various regions to specialize in certain industries?
18. Why did workers go on strike and begin to form trade unions?

SECTION 5 *(pages 152–157)*

Reforming American Society

19. What new religious ideas set the stage for the reform movements of the mid-19th century?
20. What was the purpose of the Seneca Falls convention?

THINKING CRITICALLY

1. **AMERICAN GOALS** What were America's goals and ideals during this period of expansion and economic change? Draw a chart in which you list goals from the period, how they were achieved, and in what ways their effects were positive or negative.

Goal	How Achieved	Positive/Negative Effects

2. **NATIONAL CHARACTER** Westward expansion helped shape the personal identity of Americans in the early 19th century. What values and traits characterized many Western settlers of this era? Think about Jim Beckwourth's life (profiled in the Historical Spotlight in Section 3) and the rise of the common person during the Age of Jackson.
3. **DEFINING AMERICAN ATTITUDES** Reread the quotation by Ignatius Donnelly on page 116. How do you think his sentiments reflect American attitudes of the time?
4. **GEOGRAPHY OF THE OREGON TRAIL** Review the map on pages 142–143. In what ways would this map have been helpful to settlers following the Oregon Trail to a new home? Explain your answers.
5. **TRACING THEMES ECONOMIC OPPORTUNITY** Based on the descriptions of workers' lives in the mid-19th century, what similarities and differences can you see among workers in different industries? Support your answer with references to the text.
6. **ANALYZING PRIMARY SOURCES** Read the following excerpt from Ralph Waldo Emerson's essay, "Man, the Reformer," published in 1841. Then answer the questions below.

> What is a man born for but to be a Reformer, a Re-maker of what man has made; a renouncer of lies; a restorer of truth and good. . . . The power, which is at once spring and regulator in all efforts of reform, is faith in Man, the conviction that there is infinite worthiness in him which will appear at the call of worth, and that all particular reforms are the removing of some impediment. . . . I see at once how paltry is all this generation of unbelievers, and what a house of cards their institutions are, and I see what one brave man, what one great thought might effect.
>
> **RALPH WALDO EMERSON,** "Man, the Reformer"

How does Emerson characterize reformers' beliefs and goals? Do you think he presents an accurate profile? Support your opinion with historical examples of reformers.

THINKING CRITICALLY

1. AMERICAN GOALS
Possible Answers: Goals: finding new markets; increasing personal economic opportunities; expanding the borders of the country. How achieved: by increasing westward expansion and trade; by inventing new machines; by going to war to acquire new land. Positive effects: expanded U.S. political and economic power across the continent; made the United States more technologically advanced. Negative effects: displaced Native Americans; expanded slavery; lost lives in warfare.

2. NATIONAL CHARACTER
Possible Responses: Belief in social equality, social mobility, and individual freedom; greater confidence in the democratic process and expanded voting rights; the admission of new states to the Union; optimism; resourcefulness and versatility; rugged individualism.

3. DEFINING AMERICAN ATTITUDES
Possible Responses: Students may point out that the quotation expresses the optimism of manifest destiny. Although the westward journey may have been hard and people may have left behind homes and loved ones, there was great wealth to be had in the new territories of the West.

ALTERNATIVE ASSESSMENT

1. MAPPING THE EFFECTS OF EXPANSION

During the 1830s and 1840s, the U.S. government expanded its control over territories in the West. What effect did changing borders have on different population groups?

Cooperative Learning Working with a small group, draw two maps of the United States and its territories, one showing the 1830 boundary, the other showing the 1850 boundary.

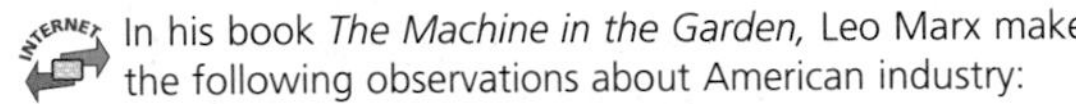

Use the CD-ROM *Electronic Library of Primary Sources* and other resources to identify the following on each map:

1. the location of Native American tribes
2. the U.S.-Mexican border
3. the routes of the major trails that settlers followed

- Prepare an oral presentation in which you compare these maps, analyzing the differences. Give political, economic, and historical reasons why the maps show differences.

2. RESEARCHING EARLY INDUSTRIALIZATION

INTERNET In his book *The Machine in the Garden,* Leo Marx makes the following observations about American industry:

By 1829 . . . a profitable factory system was firmly established in New England; new roads and canals and cities were transforming the landscape; on rivers and in ocean harbors the steamboat was proving the superiority of mechanized transport. . . . And it was the miraculous machinery of the age, beyond all else, which made it obvious that things were getting better all the time.

- Research a technological innovation from the early 19th century and its impact on the nation. For Internet research, visit http://www.mlushistory.com.
- Write an essay presenting your findings. Add your essay to your American history portfolio.

3. PORTFOLIO PROJECT

Use the Living History activity to expand your portfolio.

LIVING HISTORY

PRESENTING YOUR POLITICAL ADVERTISEMENT

You have created a poster with others that portrays a certain image of your political candidate.

- Share your poster with others and compare and contrast the images that various class members created for their candidates.
- Choose the most negative, the most positive, and the most effective from the poster's images.
- Discuss what makes an effective political ad and what kind of image would be considered positive today.
- Finally, add your poster to your American history portfolio.

Bridge to Chapter 4

Review Chapter 3

AMERICA'S CHANGING GOVERNMENT During the early part of the 19th century, the United States government evolved with the changing times. With the election of Thomas Jefferson in 1800, the new nation demonstrated its commitment to democracy by ensuring a peaceful transfer of power to a new government. During the first few decades, the roles of different branches of the government shifted when compelling reasons arose—as when Jefferson expanded the power of the presidency to buy Louisiana from France.

WESTWARD EXPANSION Many Americans believed in manifest destiny, the idea that America would inevitably expand to the Pacific Ocean. Settlers headed west in search of greater opportunity. As they did, they connected the western territories to American culture, politics, and markets. This caused a great deal of tension in Texas, where Anglo Texans led a successful rebellion against Mexico. When Texas joined the United States, war erupted between the United States and Mexico, resulting in American control of all the land between Texas and California.

THE MARKET REVOLUTION As the nation expanded westward, its economy also grew. New inventions in transportation helped create a market revolution in which the distant regions of the nation developed diverse economies and traded goods with one another.

REFORM IN AMERICA Along with these political, economic, and geographic changes came social changes. The Second Great Awakening and other spiritual movements led to a series of movements aimed at reforming American society. From temperance to women's rights to abolition, American reformers attempted to improve their society.

Preview Chapter 4

These reform efforts would have momentous consequences for the nation. As abolitionists persistently raised the question of slavery within the Union, regional tensions arose. You will read in Chapter 4 how these tensions led to the Civil War.

ALTERNATIVE ASSESSMENT

1. MAPPING THE EFFECTS OF EXPANSION

Standards for Evaluation

A map should meet the following criteria.

- Displays historically accurate representations of U.S. territory as of 1830 and 1850.
- Reflects careful research, with information drawn from a variety of sources.
- Contains clear, complete map keys, including color codes and symbols for locations and routes highlighted on the maps.

2. RESEARCHING EARLY INDUSTRIALIZATION

Standards for Evaluation

An essay should meet the following criteria.

- Focuses on a particular invention and describes its innovative characteristics in detail.
- Provides concrete examples of how that invention affected society.
- Displays thorough research—at least two sources should be from the Internet.
- Makes logical connections in a clear and concise manner.

3. PORTFOLIO PROJECT

LIVING HISTORY

Standards for Evaluation

A poster should meet the following criteria.

- Presents a clear and coherent message.
- Utilizes images to communicate information about the politician.
- Includes a brief, catchy slogan that promotes or discredits the candidate.
- Shows consistency.

IN-DEPTH RESOURCES: UNIT 1

See the form for scoring this activity on page 96.

THINKING CRITICALLY

4. GEOGRAPHY OF THE OREGON TRAIL

Possible Responses: Most students should indicate that the map contains valuable information about the terrain and shows the location of bodies of water and forts.

5. TRACING THEMES ECONOMIC OPPORTUNITY

Possible Responses: Similarities: long hours and low wages; Differences: slaves had harsh lives, farmers faced uncertain weather conditions, and factory workers confronted hazardous work conditions.

6. ANALYZING PRIMARY SOURCES

Possible Responses: Emerson suggests that all reform is positive and good because it is brought about by humans, in whom he has a deep faith. He sees reformers as working for the "truth and good" in society. Students might refer to the positive changes brought about during the mid-19th-century reform era, and to the contributions made by specific reformers. Students who do not share Emerson's attitude toward reform might suggest that reform is a lengthy, not always successful, process, and that some reformers were motivated by their own selfish interests rather than by the public good. They may also suggest that one person alone cannot accomplish much.

REVIEW CHAPTER 4

PLANNING GUIDE

The Union in Peril

	Key Ideas	COPYMASTERS	ASSESSMENT
SECTION 1 The Divisive Politics of Slavery *pp. 164–173*	*The issue of slavery leads to increased tension and violence between the North and the South and finally brings the nation to the brink of war.*	***In-Depth Resources: Unit 1*** • Guided Reading, p. 97 • Skillbuilder Practice: Analyzing Causes, p. 101 • Geography Application: Slave Populations in the United States, p. 104 • Primary Source: *from* The Lincoln-Douglas Debates, p. 108 • American Lives: Harriet Tubman, p. 116 ***Lesson Plans,*** pp. 35–36	PE ***Section 1 Assessment,*** p. 173 TE ***Self-Assessment,*** p. 173 ***Formal Assessment*** • Section Quiz, p. 54 ***Alternative Assessment Book*** • Standards for Evaluating a Cooperative Activity
SECTION 2 The Civil War Begins *pp. 176–183*	*The Civil War becomes a more prolonged, deadly conflict than anyone had predicted and has a significant impact on civilians, soldiers, and African Americans.*	***In-Depth Resources: Unit 1*** • Guided Reading, p. 98 • Skillbuilder Practice, p. 102 • Outline Map, p. 106 • Primary Source: Emancipation Proclamation, p. 110 ***Lesson Plans,*** pp. 37–38	PE ***Section 2 Assessment,*** p. 183 TE ***Self-Assessment,*** p. 183 ***Formal Assessment*** • Section Quiz, p. 55 ***Alternative Assessment Book*** • Standards for Evaluating a Cooperative Activity
SECTION 3 The North Takes Charge *pp. 184–191*	*The South surrenders to the North. However, the war has an enduring effect on the nation and on American lives.*	***In-Depth Resources: Unit 1*** • Guided Reading, p. 99 • Primary Source: On the Burning of Columbia, South Carolina, p. 111 ***Lesson Plans,*** p. 39–40	PE ***Section 3 Assessment,*** p. 191 TE ***Self-Assessment,*** p. 191 ***Formal Assessment*** • Section Quiz, p. 56 ***Alternative Assessment Book*** • Standards for Evaluating a Cooperative Activity
SECTION 4 Reconstruction and Its Effects and Thematic Review *pp. 192–201, 204–209*	*Reconstruction results in many political, social, and economic changes in the South before coming to an end in 1877.*	***In-Depth Resources: Unit 1*** • Guided Reading, p. 100 • Skillbuilder Practice: Evaluating Decisions, p. 103 • Primary Source: *from* An Inquiry on the Condition of the South, p. 112 • American Lives: Thaddeus Stevens, p. 117 • Literature: from *Jubilee* by Margaret Walker, p. 113 • Thematic Review Activities, p. 120 ***Lesson Plans,*** p. 41–42, 43–44	PE ***Section 4 Assessment,*** p. 201 TE ***Self-Assessment,*** pp. 201, 209 ***Formal Assessment*** • Section Quiz, p. 57 • Thematic Review Essay Questions, p. 66 ***Alternative Assessment Book*** • Standards for Evaluating a Cooperative Activity
CHAPTER RESOURCES	**Chapter Overview** *Slavery divides the nation. North and South enter a long and destructive civil war that ends slavery. African Americans briefly enjoy full civil rights, but new laws discriminate against them.*	***In-Depth Resources: Unit 1*** • Chapter 4 Living History Project: Worksheet, p. 118; Standards, p. 119 • Thematic Review Living History Project: Worksheet, p. 121; Standards, p. 122 ***Telescoping the Times*** • Chapter Summary, pp. 7–8 ***Planning for Block Schedules***	PE ***Chapter Assessment,*** pp. 202–203 PE ***Alternative Assessment,*** p. 203 ***Formal Assessment*** • Chapter Test, forms A and B, pp. 58–63 ***Test Generator*** ***Alternative Assessment Book*** See explanation and forms for different kinds of alternative assessments including portfolio assessment.

KEY
- PE Pupil's Edition
- TE Teacher's Edition
- http://www.mlushistory.com

TECHNOLOGY

- *Warm-Up Transparency* 4
- *Humanities Transparencies*
  - H10, No. 10 Harriet Tubman series
- *Geography Transparencies*
  - G10, Presidential Elections: 1856, 1860
- *Critical Thinking Transparencies*
  - CT10, Compromise of 1850
  - CT44, Population Growth: 1820–1860
- *Grolier Multimedia Encyclopedia*
- *Electronic Library of Primary Sources*
- **INTERNET** Underground Railroad

- *Warm-Up Transparency* 4
- *Geography Transparencies*
  - G11, Union and Confederacy: 1861
  - G37, Slavery and the Civil War
- *Electronic Library of Primary Sources*
- **INTERNET** Civil War

- *Warm-Up Transparency* 4
- *Humanities Transparencies*
  - H11, *Abraham Lincoln*
- *Critical Thinking Transparencies*
  - CT11, Civil War
  - CT45, North vs. South
- *Grolier Multimedia Encyclopedia*
- *Electronic Library of Primary Sources*
- *AMERICAN STORIES* video series "War Outside My Window"
- **INTERNET** Gettysburg

- *Warm-Up Transparencies* 4 and TR
- *Humanities Transparencies*
  - H12, *The Fifteenth Amendment*
  - H34, A. Johnson, Tailor
- *Geography Transparencies*
  - G12, The Barrow Plantation
- *Critical Thinking Transparencies*
  - CT12, Reconstruction
  - CT46, Agricultural Production
- *Grolier Multimedia Encyclopedia*
- *Electronic Library of Primary Sources*
- *AMERICAN STORIES* video series "Teacher of a Freed People"
- **INTERNET** Reconstruction

- *American Portfolio: A Videodisc for U.S. History,* user's guide, pp. 87–93, 96–109, 111–113, 115–120
- *Chapter Summary Audiotapes*
  - Unit 1, Chapter 4
- **INTERNET http://www. mlushistory.com**

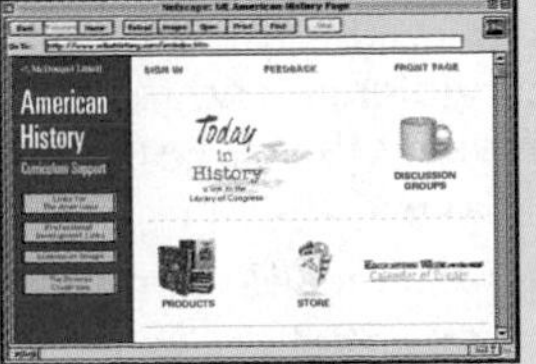

Block Scheduling (90 MINUTES)

Day 1

Section 1, pp. 164–173
Section 2, pp. 176–183
Tracing Themes: Constitutional Concerns, pp. 174–175
Section Assessments, pp. 173, 183

COOPERATIVE ACTIVITIES
- Experiencing the Underground Railroad, p. 166 (TE)
- Writing a Newspaper Account, p. 171 (TE)
- Researching the Battle of Bull Run, p. 177 (TE)

Day 2

Section 3, pp. 184–191
Section 4, pp. 192–201
Section Assessments, pp. 191, 201
Chapter Assessment, pp. 202–203

COOPERATIVE ACTIVITIES
- News Account of a City Under Siege, p. 186 (TE)
- Debating President Johnson's Impeachment, p. 194 (TE)

Day 3

Thematic Review of Unit 1, pp. 204–209

COOPERATIVE ACTIVITIES
- Exhibiting Immigrant Experiences, p. 205 (TE)
- Writing About the American Dream, p. 209 (TE)

YEARLY PACING ***Chapter 4 Total:*** 3 days ***Yearly Total:*** 85 days

See *Planning for Block Schedules* for special activities and pacing strategies.

Customizing for Special Populations

Students Acquiring English

Access for Students Acquiring English: Spanish Translations
- Guided Reading for Sections 1–4, pp. 67–70
- Chapter Summary, pp. 65–66
- Skillbuilder Practice: Analyzing Causes, p. 71; Following Chronological Order, p. 72; Evaluating Decisions, p. 73
- Geography Application: Slave Populations in the United States, p. 74
- Outline Map: The States Choose Sides, p. 76
- Activities, p. 78

Spanish Reading Study Guide, pp. 47–56

Translations of Chapter Summaries, Hmong, Cantonese, Vietnamese, and Cambodian

Chapter Summary Audiotapes in Spanish Unit 1, Chapter 4

AMERICAN STORIES video series
- "War Outside My Window"
- "Teacher of a Freed People" (Spanish track)

INTERNET The Diverse Classroom

Gifted and Talented Students

In-Depth Resources: Unit 1
- Primary Sources: *from* The Lincoln-Douglas Debates, p. 108; The Emancipation Proclamation, p. 110; On the Burning of Columbia, South Carolina, p. 111; *from* An Inquiry on the Condition of the South, p. 112
- American Lives: Harriet Tubman, p. 116; Thaddeus Stevens, p. 117

Less Proficient Readers

In-Depth Resources: Unit 1
- Guided Reading for Sections 1–4, pp. 97–100
- Skillbuilder: Analyzing Causes, p. 101; Following Chronological Order, p. 102; Evaluating Decisions, p. 103
- Geography Application: Slave Populations in the United States, p. 104
- Outline Map: The States Choose Sides, p. 106

Reading Study Guide
- pp. 47–56

Telescoping the Times
- Chapter Summary, pp. 7–8

Chapter Summary Audiotapes, Unit 1, Chapter 4

Connections to Literature READINGS FOR STUDENTS

In-Depth Resources: Unit 1
- **from *Jubilee* by Margaret Walker,** p. 113

Enrichment Reading
- **Stephen Crane**
  The Red Badge of Courage.
  New York: Pocket Books, 1994
  This classic novel of the Civil War tells of a young soldier's battle experiences.
- **Gore Vidal**
  Lincoln.
  New York: Ballantine, 1985
  This novel reveals the political and personal struggles of President Lincoln as he guides the nation through the Civil War while confronting his own personal and family tragedies.

McDougal Littell *The Language of Literature* American Literature
- **Frederick Douglass, from *Narrative of the Life of Frederick Douglass, an American Slave,*** p. 446
- **Frances Ellen Watkins Harper, "Free Labor,"** p. 458
- **Ambrose Bierce, "An Occurrence at Owl Creek Bridge,"** p. 464

McDougal Littell *Literature Connections*

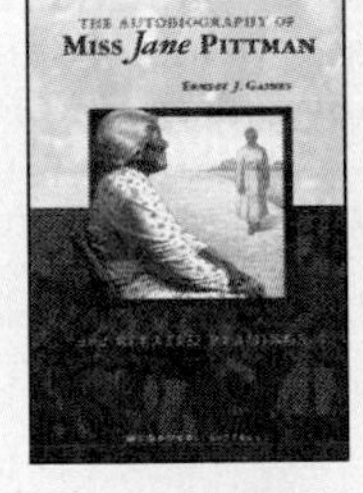

- **Ernest Gaines, *The Autobiography of Miss Jane Pittman***
  (with related readings) In this novel a black woman who has lived 110 years tells her memorable story both as a slave and as a witness to the civil rights movement of the 1960s.

OVERVIEW

The Union in Peril

▶ *Accessing Prior Knowledge*

Ask students what they know about the Civil War. What books have they read and what television programs and movies have they seen about the war? Who were some of the war's key players? What impressions have students formed about the Union and the Confederacy?

▶ *Predicting Outcomes*

Have students look at the image of carpetbaggers on the time line. Then ask them what the image implies about some of the people who took part in Reconstruction. What does it suggest about what might happen during this period?

REVIEW CHAPTER 4

The Union in Peril

SECTION 1

The Divisive Politics of Slavery

The issue of slavery leads to increased tension and violence between the North and the South and finally brings the nation to the brink of war.

SECTION 2

The Civil War Begins

The Civil War becomes a more prolonged, deadly conflict than anyone had predicted and has a significant impact on civilians, soldiers, and African Americans.

SECTION 3

The North Takes Charge

The South surrenders to the North. However, the war has an enduring effect on the nation and on American lives.

WAR OUTSIDE MY WINDOW

SECTION 4

Reconstruction and Its Effects

Reconstruction results in many political, social, and economic changes in the South before coming to an end in 1877.

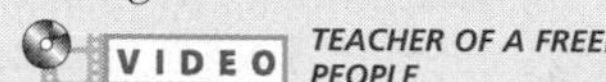

"Can we as a nation continue together permanently—forever—half slave and half free?"

Abraham Lincoln, 1855

Harriet Tubman is a conductor on the Underground Railroad.

The confederacy forms and elects Jefferson Davis president. The Confederates take Fort Sumter.

THE UNITED STATES

- **1850** Compromise of 1850 is passed. California enters the Union.
- **1852** Harriet Beecher Stowe publishes *Uncle Tom's Cabin*. Franklin Pierce is elected president.
- **1856** James Buchanan is elected president.
- **1857** *Dred Scott* decision is announced.
- **1860** Abraham Lincoln is elected president.
- **1861** The confederacy forms and elects Jefferson Davis president. The Confederates take Fort Sumter.
- **1863** Lincoln issues the Emancipation Proclamation.

THE WORLD

- **1852** South African Republic is established.
- **1857** Mexico institutes a new constitution.
- **1862** Otto von Bismarck is named minister-president of Prussia.

THEMES IN CHAPTER 4

Women in America

Although the era of the 1840s and 1850s saw a few women, including Harriet Tubman and Harriet Beecher Stowe, attain prominence, many women led harsh lives, struggling to eke out an existence for themselves and their families.

See Teacher's Edition note, p. 167.

Constitutional Concerns

By 1860, the issue of slavery had so divided the nation that South Carolina challenged the Constitution and seceded from the Union. Ten other states followed South Carolina's example. During the Civil War, President Lincoln used his constitutional war powers to end slavery by issuing the Emancipation Proclamation. After the war, fundamental rights, such as the right to vote or to own land, came under scrutiny.

See Teacher's Edition notes, pp. 172, 179, 198.

Civil Rights

The Fourteenth Amendment laid the groundwork for future civil rights legislation. However, the Ku Klux Klan used violence and terror to take away the civil rights of African Americans.

See Teacher's Edition notes, pp. 193, 199.

LIVING HISTORY

RESEARCHING A BIOGRAPHY

Research the life of someone who lived through the Civil War or the Reconstruction period. This person could be an African American, a woman, a Confederate soldier, a Union soldier, a scalawag, a carpetbagger, a planter, or a businessperson. To get ideas, look through books on the Civil War or Reconstruction. Include details of

- the person's early life
- the person's experiences during the war or Reconstruction
- the effects of those experiences on his or her later life

Add photos, quotations from diaries, or anecdotes to make your biography more interesting.

PORTFOLIO PROJECT Save your materials in a folder. At the end of the chapter, you will write a biography of the person for your American history portfolio.

TILDEN. HAYES.
OF THE TWO EVILS
CHOOSE THE LEAST.

1864 — Abraham Lincoln is reelected.

1865 — Lee surrenders at Appomattox. Lincoln is assassinated. Andrew Johnson becomes president.

1867 — Carpetbaggers take part in Reconstruction.

1867 — Emperor Maximilian is executed in Mexico.

1868 — President Johnson is impeached. Fourteenth Amendment is ratified. Ulysses S. Grant is elected president.

1870 — Fifteenth Amendment is ratified.

1870 — Unification of Italy is completed.

1872 — Ulysses S. Grant is reelected.

1873 — Financial panic results in depression.

1876 — Hayes-Tilden presidential election results in deadlock.

1876 — Japan forces Korea to open ports to trade.

1877 — Federal troops withdraw from the South, ending Reconstruction. Rutherford B. Hayes becomes president.

ALTERNATIVE ASSESSMENT

LIVING HISTORY

RESEARCHING A BIOGRAPHY

Discuss ways of doing research for the biography.

- Who would students like to know more about—someone of their age, sex, and cultural background, or someone very different? Have them look for a subject who lived through the Civil War or Reconstruction.
- Is sufficient information about their subject available? Have students select someone who is well-known and about whom adequate data exist.
- Ask students to collect quotes and anecdotes that show how their subject reacted to events and what other people thought about the person.

Project Planning Guide

Step 1	Students choose the person they will write about.
Step 2	Students do preliminary research.
Step 3	Students collect information, quotes, anecdotes, and pictures about their subject.
Step 4	Students organize their information in a folder before writing the biography.

IN-DEPTH RESOURCES: UNIT 1
See worksheet and standards for evaluation, pp. 118, 119.

RECOMMENDED RESOURCES

Books for the Teacher

Foote, Shelby. *The Civil War.* 3 vols. New York: Random House, 1958-1974. Highly readable history of the war.

Franklin, John Hope. *Reconstruction After the Civil War,* 2nd ed. Chicago: U of Chicago P, 1994. By a distinguished African-American historian.

Stampp, Kenneth. *America in 1857.* New York: Oxford UP, 1990. Sectional conflict as Buchanan takes office.

Books for the Student

Botkin, B.A., ed. *Lay My Burden Down.* New York: Dell, 1973. Remembrances of slavery collected by Federal Writers' Project.

Foner, Eric. *A Short History of Reconstruction.* New York: Oxford UP, 1991. Brief but thorough and readable overview.

Smith, George Winston, and Charles Judah, eds. *Life in the North During the Civil War.* Albuquerque: U of New Mexico P, 1966. Letters, speeches, diaries, and newspaper articles detailing the home front.

Videos

The Civil War. Prod. Ken Burns. PBS, 1989. A compelling documentary in six parts.

Reconstructing the South. Dir. Paul Bosner. PBS Video, 1987. RMI Media, 800-745-5480.

Roots of Resistance. PBS Home Video, 1989. 800-424-7963. Story of Underground Railroad.

A Woman Called Moses. Dir. Paul Wendkos. Xenon Home Video, 1978. Life of Tubman.

Software

African American History: Slavery to Civil Rights. CD-ROM. Queue, 1995. Educational Software Institute, 800-955-5570.

The Civil War. CD-ROM. Compton's New Media, 1992.

A House Divided: The Lincoln–Douglas Debates. CD-ROM. Grafica Multimedia, 1995.

Section 1 Overview

OBJECTIVES

1. To explain how the debate over slavery in the territories caused deep division between the North and the South.
2. To describe the increasing tension between proslavery and antislavery factions over the treatment of fugitive slaves and the spread of slavery to the territories.
3. To identify the political parties that emerged largely as a result of the rift over the issue of slavery.
4. To list the events that heightened tension between the sections and led to Southern secession.

SKILLBUILDERS

- Interpreting charts, p. 165
- Understanding geography: location, p. 167
- Understanding geography: place, region, p. 168

CRITICAL THINKING

- Analyzing causes, p. 165
- Finding main ideas, pp. 166, 169
- Analyzing issues, p. 168
- Analyzing motives, p. 170
- Theme: Constitutional Concerns, p. 170
- Comparing, p. 171
- Recognizing effects, p. 173
- Making predictions, p. 173
- Summarizing, p. 173
- Evaluating, p. 173

FOCUS & MOTIVATE

5-MINUTE WARM-UP

Making Inferences
To understand the hostility between the North and the South, have students look at the political cartoon on page 169 and answer these questions.

1. What does the caption suggest about the artist's attitude toward the South and Southern chivalry?
2. What can you infer about the men in the background? Whose side is each one on? How can you tell?

WARM-UP TRANSPARENCY 4

1 The Divisive Politics of Slavery

TERMS & NAMES
- secession
- Millard Fillmore
- Underground Railroad
- Harriet Tubman
- Harriet Beecher Stowe
- Franklin Pierce
- James Buchanan
- Dred Scott
- Abraham Lincoln
- Jefferson Davis

LEARN ABOUT the political crises and hostilities resulting from the growing tension between North and South over slavery
TO UNDERSTAND how the controversy over slavery led to the South's secession.

ONE AMERICAN'S STORY

Senator John C. Calhoun was a sick man, so sick that he had missed four months of debate over whether California should enter the Union as a free state. On March 4, 1850, wrapped in flannels, he tottered onto the Senate floor. Explaining that he was too ill to deliver a speech that he had prepared, Calhoun asked Senator James M. Mason of Virginia to deliver it for him.

A PERSONAL VOICE
I have, Senators, believed from the first that the agitation of the subject of slavery would, if not prevented by some timely and effective measure, end in disunion. . . . The agitation has been permitted to proceed . . . until it has reached a period when it can no longer be disguised or denied that the Union is in danger. You have thus had forced upon you the greatest and the gravest question that can ever come under your consideration: How can the Union be preserved?
JOHN C. CALHOUN, quoted in *The Compromise of 1850,* edited by Edwin C. Rozwenc

Senator Calhoun called on the North to give the South "justice, simple justice." He demanded that slavery be allowed throughout the territories won in the war with Mexico. If it was not, he declared, the South would secede, or withdraw, from the Union.

Senator William H. Seward of New York opposed slavery, saying that "there is a higher law than the Constitution." Seward believed that freedom came from God. The North would not rest, he implied, until slavery had been abolished everywhere.

Once again, the issue of slavery had brought about a political crisis, deepening the gulf between the North and the South.

John C. Calhoun

Slavery in the Territories

The rift between regions had begun to increase in 1846. On August 8 of that year, David Wilmot, a Democratic congressman from Pennsylvania, added an amendment to a military appropriations bill that proposed that "neither slavery nor involuntary servitude shall ever exist" in any territory the United States might acquire as a result of the war with Mexico. In practical terms, the Wilmot Proviso meant that California, as well as the territories of Utah and New Mexico, would be closed to slavery forever.

THE WILMOT PROVISO Northerners gradually came to support the Wilmot Proviso. They feared that adding slave territory would give slave states more members in Congress and deny economic opportunity to free workers. Southerners, on the other hand, opposed the proviso, which some believed raised complex constitutional issues. Slaves were property, they claimed, and property was protected by the Constitution. Many Southerners also feared that laws like the Wilmot Proviso would swing the balance of power permanently toward the North. The Senate repeatedly rejected the proviso. Nonetheless, Congressman Alexander H. Stephens of Georgia issued a dire prediction.

SECTION 1 RESOURCES

PRINT RESOURCES

IN-DEPTH RESOURCES: UNIT 1
Guided Reading, p. 97
Skillbuilder Practice: Analyzing Causes, p. 101
Geography Application: Slave Populations, p. 104
Primary Source: *from* The Lincoln-Douglas Debates, p. 108
American Lives: Harriet Tubman, p. 116

READING STUDY GUIDE, p. 47

ACCESS FOR STUDENTS ACQUIRING ENGLISH
Guided Reading (Spanish), p. 67
Skillbuilder Practice: Analyzing Causes (Spanish), p. 71
Geography Application: Slave Populations (Spanish), p. 74

SPANISH READING STUDY GUIDE, p. 47

FORMAL ASSESSMENT Section Quiz, p. 54

ALTERNATIVE ASSESSMENT BOOK
See forms for supporting and scoring alternative activities.

TECHNOLOGY RESOURCES

HUMANITIES TRANSPARENCIES
H10, No. 10 Harriet Tubman series by Jacob Lawrence

GEOGRAPHY TRANSPARENCIES
G10, Presidential Elections: 1856, 1860

CRITICAL THINKING TRANSPARENCIES
CT10, Compromise of 1850; CT44, Population Growth

CD-ROM *Grolier Multimedia Encyclopedia*
Electronic Library of Primary Sources

VIDEO *American Portfolio: A Videodisc for U.S. History* user's guide, pp. 87–93, 107–108

INTERNET http://www.mlushistory.com

A PERSONAL VOICE

The North is going to stick the Wilmot amendment to every appropriation and then all the South will vote against any measure thus clogged. Finally a tremendous struggle will take place and perhaps [President] Polk in starting one war may find half a dozen on his hands. I tell you, the prospect ahead is dark, cloudy, thick, and gloomy.

ALEXANDER H. STEPHENS, quoted in *The Coming of the Civil War*

STATEHOOD FOR CALIFORNIA The next flare-up of the political fire came from California. As a result of the gold rush, California had grown so quickly in population that it skipped the territorial phase of becoming a state. From September to November 1849, the Californians held a constitutional convention, during which they adopted a state constitution, elected a governor and a legislature, and applied for admission to the Union.

A. Answer Although California's voters opposed slavery, most of the state lay south of the Missouri Compromise line. Many Southerners had hoped that the Missouri Compromise would apply to new territories.

THINK THROUGH HISTORY
A. Analyzing Causes *Why did California's application for statehood cause an uproar?*

California's new constitution forbade slavery, a fact that alarmed and angered many Southerners. They had assumed that because most of California lay south of the Missouri Compromise line of 36°30', the state would be open to slavery. They wanted the compromise struck in 1820 to apply to territories west of the Louisiana Purchase, thus ensuring that California would become a slave state.

President Zachary Taylor, although himself a slaveholder, supported California's admission as a free state because he believed that its climate and terrain were not suited to slavery. More important, he felt that the South could counter abolitionism most effectively by letting the individual territories, rather than Congress, decide whether to allow slavery. However, Taylor soon found that feelings in the South were more passionate than he had expected. Southerners saw the move to block slavery in the territories as an attack on the Southern way of life—and began to question whether the South should remain in the Union.

THE COMPROMISE OF 1850 The 31st Congress opened in December 1849 in an atmosphere of distrust and bitterness. The question of statehood for California topped the agenda. Of equal concern was the border dispute in which the slave state of Texas claimed the eastern half of the New Mexico Territory, where the issue of slavery had not yet been settled. As passions mounted, threats of Southern **secession**, the formal withdrawal of a state from the Union, became more frequent.

Once again, Henry Clay worked to shape a compromise that both the North and the South could accept. After obtaining Webster's support, Clay

Skillbuilder Answers
States' rights: Calhoun believed maintaining states' rights was more important than the preservation of the Union; Webster believed saving the Union was more important than states' rights.
Provisions: The compromise had provisions to satisfy each side. For the North, it admitted California as a free state. For the South, it set up a stricter fugitive slave law.

SKILLBUILDER
INTERPRETING CHARTS ***How did Calhoun and Webster disagree over states' rights? How did the compromise try to satisfy both sides?***

The Compromise of 1850

CALHOUN'S GOAL	TERMS OF THE COMPROMISE	WEBSTER'S GOAL
Calhoun believed strongly in states' rights over federal power and held the interests of the slaveholding South as his highest priority. He had long believed that "the agitation of the subject of slavery would . . . end in disunion." He blamed the sectional crisis on Northern abolitionists and argued that the South had "no concession or surrender to make" on the issue of slavery.	• California admitted as a free state • Utah and New Mexico territories decide about slavery • Texas-Mexico boundary dispute resolved, and Texas paid $10 million by federal government • The trading of enslaved persons is banned—but slavery is not—in the District of Columbia • Stricter fugitive slave law	Webster had argued with Northern Whigs that slavery should not be extended into the territories. Upon hearing Calhoun's threat of secession, he took to the Senate floor and endorsed Clay's compromise "for the preservation of the Union . . . a great, popular, constitutional government, guarded by legislation, by law, by judicature, and developed by the whole affections of the people."

Starting with the Student
- How can differences among students affect the climate of a school?
- What kinds of differences could lead to problems of unity within a country?

OBJECTIVE
① INSTRUCT

Slavery in the Territories

Discussing Key Ideas
- The Wilmot Proviso forbids slavery in California, Utah, and New Mexico.
- California applies for admission to the Union as a free state.
- The Compromise of 1850 seeks to appease both the North and the South.

IN-DEPTH RESOURCES: UNIT 1
Guided Reading, p. 97
Geography Applications: Slave Populations in the United States, p. 104

ACCESS FOR STUDENTS ACQUIRING ENGLISH
Guided Reading (Spanish), p. 67

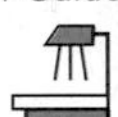
CRITICAL THINKING TRANSPARENCIES
CT44, Population Growth: 1820–1860

HISTORY FROM VISUALS
The Compromise of 1850

Reading the Chart Ask students to look at the goals of both Calhoun and Webster on the chart. Then ask them to list the key terms of the compromise. Using both the text and the chart, put an *S* (South) or an *N* (North) next to each term to show which side benefited from it.

CRITICAL THINKING TRANSPARENCIES
CT10, Compromise of 1850

TEACHING OPTION

Skillbuilder Mini-Lesson: Analyzing Causes

Explaining the Skill In history, causes are typically connected to geographical, economic, or social forces, or to political or governmental actions. Causes might also be related to the feelings or ambitions of a group or an individual. For example, economic considerations and desire for a better life were behind the movement of many settlers to the West.

***Applying the Skill:* Think Through History Question** To answer the Think Through History question on this page, students will need to identify the events, actions, and emotions that led to the uproar over California's application for statehood. Ask students these questions:

1. What laws or government actions caused the confusion over California's application? *Missouri Compromise*
2. Why did this law pose a problem? *It stated that territory south of the 36°30' line would be open to slavery.*
3. What emotions were involved? *Sectional loyalties were inflamed. Both antislavery and proslavery states wanted California to side with them.*

IN-DEPTH RESOURCES: UNIT 1
Skillbuilder Practice: Analyzing Causes, p. 101

MORE ABOUT . . .
Stephen A. Douglas

Stephen Douglas's political cleverness, oratorical skill, and personal drive earned him the nickname the Little Giant—a reference to the fact that he stood only 5'4" tall.

GROLIER MULTIMEDIA ENCYCLOPEDIA
Stephen Douglas

OBJECTIVE
(2) INSTRUCT

Protest, Resistance, and Violence

▶ ***Discussing Key Ideas***

- Conductors such as Harriet Tubman help slaves escape on the Underground Railroad.
- *Uncle Tom's Cabin* ignites fierce reaction in both the North and the South.
- Violence erupts in Kansas and in the Senate over slavery.

MORE ABOUT . . .
The Underground Railroad

Among the slaves who escaped by means of the Underground Railroad were William and Ellen Craft. Ellen, who was very light skinned, played the part of a sickly white man, with William as her slave. Since she did not know how to read or write, she put her right arm in a sling. The couple escaped to England, where they became literate.

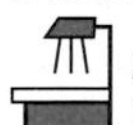
HUMANITIES TRANSPARENCIES
H10, No. 10 Harriet Tubman series by Jacob Lawrence

"There's two things I got a right to and these are Death and Liberty. One or the other I mean to have."

HARRIET TUBMAN

Harriet Tubman was called "Moses" by those she helped escape on the Underground Railroad. In her later years, Tubman opened a home for elderly African Americans.

presented to the Senate a series of resolutions later called the Compromise of 1850, which he hoped would settle "all questions in controversy between the free and slave states, growing out of the subject of Slavery."

Clay's compromise, summarized in the chart shown on page 165, contained provisions to appease Northerners as well as Southerners. To please the North, the compromise provided that California be admitted to the Union as a free state. To please the South, the compromise proposed a new and more effective fugitive slave law. Both sections were happy with a provision that allowed residents of the New Mexico and Utah territories popular sovereignty, the right to vote for or against slavery.

On February 5 Clay defended his resolutions and begged both the North and the South to consider them thoughtfully. The alternative was disunion—and, in Clay's opinion, quite possibly war. Within a month, Calhoun presented the Southern case for slavery in the territories. He was followed three days later by Daniel Webster, who appealed for national unity.

Despite the efforts of Clay and Webster, the Senate rejected the proposed compromise in July. Tired, ill, and discouraged, Clay withdrew from the fight and left Washington. In the final months, Senator Stephen A. Douglas of Illinois picked up the pro-compromise reins. To avoid another defeat, Douglas unbundled the package of resolutions and reintroduced them one at a time, hoping to obtain a majority vote for each measure individually. The unexpected death of President Taylor aided Douglas's efforts. Taylor's successor, **Millard Fillmore,** quickly made it clear that he supported the compromise.

At last, in September, after eight months of effort, the Compromise of 1850 became law. For the moment, the crisis over slavery in the territories had passed. However, relief was short-lived. The next crisis loomed on the horizon—enforcement of the new fugitive slave law.

Protest, Resistance, and Violence

The harsh terms of the Fugitive Slave Act surprised many people. Under the law, alleged fugitives were not entitled to a trial by jury. In addition, anyone convicted of helping a fugitive was liable for a fine of $1,000 and imprisonment for up to six months.

Infuriated by the Fugitive Slave Act, some Northerners resisted it by organizing vigilance committees to send endangered African Americans to safety in Canada. Others resorted to violence to rescue fugitive slaves. Still others worked to help slaves escape from slavery.

FUGITIVE SLAVES AND THE UNDERGROUND RAILROAD Attempting to escape from slavery was a dangerous process. It meant traveling on foot at night without any sense of distance or direction, except for the North Star and other natural signs. It meant avoiding patrols of armed men on horseback and struggling through forests and across rivers. Often it meant going without food for days at a time. Once fugitives reached the North, many chose to remain there. Others journeyed to Canada to be completely out of reach of their owners.

As time went on, free African Americans and white abolitionists developed a secret network of people who would hide fugitive slaves at great risk to themselves. The system of escape routes they used became known as the **Underground Railroad.** "Conductors" on the routes hid fugitives in secret tunnels and false cupboards, provided them with food and clothing, and escorted or directed them to the next "station."

One of the most famous conductors was **Harriet Tubman,** born a slave in Maryland in 1820 or 1821. As a young girl, she suffered a

B. Answer "Conductors" would hide fugitive slaves and help them work their way North from one "station" to the next.

THINK THROUGH HISTORY
B. Finding Main Ideas *How did the Underground Railroad operate?*

Block Schedule TEACHING OPTION **Time Needed: 30 Minutes**

Cooperative Activity: Experiencing the Underground Railroad

Task: Groups of students will prepare oral reports describing specific people and events that were part of the Underground Railroad.

Purpose: To examine in depth the motivations of individuals who participated in the Underground Railroad.

Activity: Have students work in small groups to research the Underground Railroad in depth. Tell them to examine both historical and fictional accounts to explore the powerful feelings of escaped slaves and of the people who took risks to help them. For example, they might examine books by Alex Haley and Virginia Hamilton or look for the autobiography of John Parker, a conductor on the Underground Railroad. Tell students to focus their reports on stories of individuals. These persons might be guides such as Harriet Tubman, homeowners who offered shelter, drivers who provided transportation to the next "station," or the escaped persons themselves.

ALTERNATIVE ASSESSMENT BOOK
Standards for Evaluating a Cooperative Activity

severe head injury when a plantation overseer hit her with a lead weight. The blow damaged her brain, causing her to lose consciousness several times a day. To compensate for her disability, Tubman increased her strength until she became strong enough to perform tasks that most men could not do. In 1849, after Tubman's owner died, she decided to make a break for freedom and succeeded in reaching Philadelphia.

Shortly after passage of the Fugitive Slave Act, Tubman resolved to become a conductor on the Underground Railroad. In all, she made 19 trips back to the South and is said to have helped 300 slaves—including her own parents—flee to freedom. Southern authorities put a price of $40,000 on her head, but neither Tubman nor the slaves she helped were ever captured. Later, she became an ardent speaker for abolition.

CAUTION!!
COLORED PEOPLE
OF BOSTON, ONE & ALL,
You are hereby respectfully CAUTIONED and advised, to avoid conversing with the
Watchmen and Police Officers of Boston,
For since the recent ORDER OF THE MAYOR & ALDERMEN, they are empowered to act as
KIDNAPPERS
AND
Slave Catchers,
Keep a Sharp Look Out for KIDNAPPERS, and have TOP EYE open.
APRIL 24, 1851.

About 30,000 fugitive slaves had arrived in the North by 1850. Abolitionists used posters and handbills—such as this one, made in Boston in 1851—to warn fugitives about slave catchers.

UNCLE TOM'S CABIN Meanwhile, another abolitionist voice spoke out in a book that brought slavery into the homes of a great many Americans. In 1852, **Harriet Beecher Stowe** published *Uncle Tom's Cabin,* which stressed that slavery was not just a political contest, but also a great moral struggle. (See the American Literature feature on pages 158–159.) The book stirred strong reactions from Northerners and Southerners alike. Northern abolitionists increased their protests against the Fugitive Slave Act, while Southerners criticized the book as an attack on the South. The furor over *Uncle Tom's Cabin* had barely begun to settle when the issue of slavery in the territories surfaced once again.

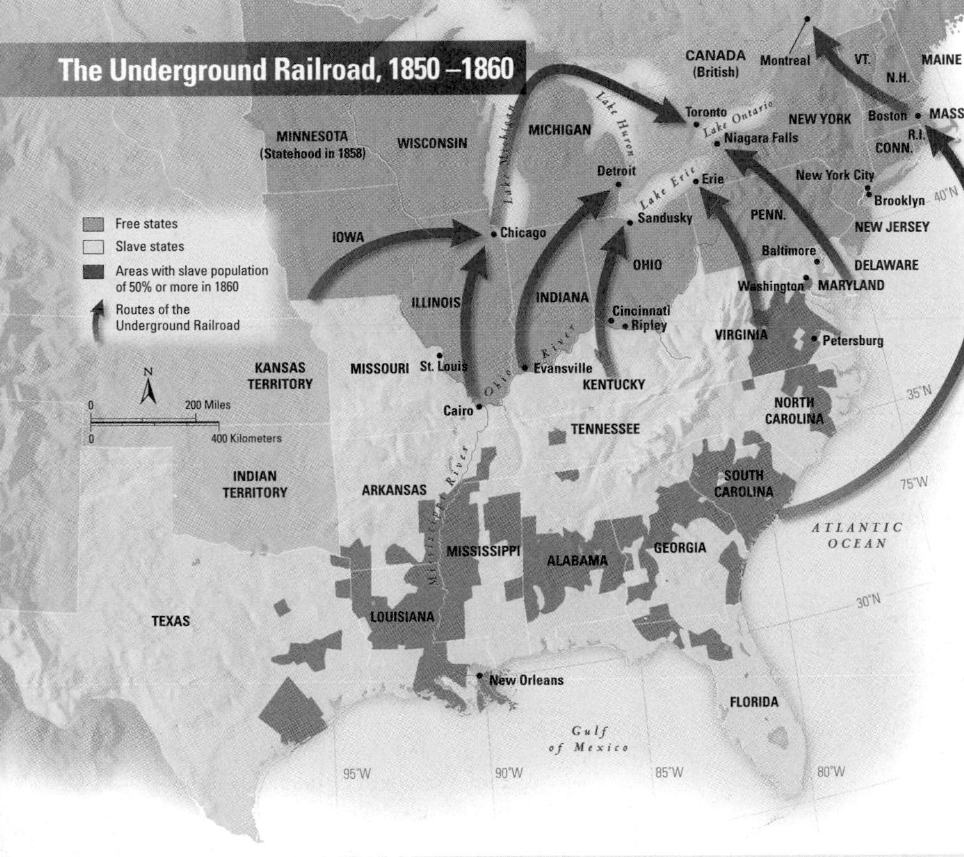

GEOGRAPHY SKILLBUILDER
LOCATION *Name three cities that were destinations on the Underground Railroad.*
LOCATION *Why do you think these cities were destinations?*

Skillbuilder Answers
Location: *Possible Answers:* Chicago, Detroit, Montreal, Erie (Penn.), Sandusky (Ohio).
Location: These cities were all far away from the South. Also, their size allowed fugitives more opportunities for hiding.

MORE ABOUT . . .
Uncle Tom's Cabin

At least a dozen Southern writers wrote novels that tried to prove that *Uncle Tom's Cabin* was a pack of lies. The most successful was *Aunt Eva's Cabin.* Its illustrations included the windows of Aunt Eva's cabin hung with lace curtains, presumably as evidence that her life as a slave was comfortable and happy, perhaps even better than that of free workers.

ELECTRONIC LIBRARY OF PRIMARY SOURCES
from "The Story of Eliza Harris" by Levi Coffin

HISTORY FROM VISUALS
The Underground Railroad, 1850–1860

Reading the Map Point out that the arrows show the movement of people from the South to the North. Ask students to notice the multiple routes and their lengths and to imagine the numbers of people required to make the operation work.

Extension Ask students to discuss the importance of the waterways in the slaves' journeys north. *The use of rivers, canals, and lakes was a way of avoiding capture; the ports served as entryways to the North and Canada.*

IN-DEPTH RESOURCES: UNIT 1
American Lives: Harriet Tubman, p. 116

ELECTRONIC LIBRARY OF PRIMARY SOURCES
"On Slavery" by Harriet Tubman
from The Fugitive Slave Act

TEACHING OPTIONS

Exploring Themes

Women in America A large proportion of the women who migrated to the urban North were poor and needed to provide income to care for themselves and their families. Some worked as servants; others worked in paper-box factories or as tobacco packers. Many of them worked in the sewing trades, as milliners, seamstresses, and vest makers. During the 1850s, under the "sweating system," entire families worked 12 to 16 hours a day for as little as a dollar for all. The introduction of Elias Howe's sewing machine (1846) enabled one woman to do the work of six, drastically reducing the demand for a woman's labor.

Making Connections Across the Curriculum

***Literature:* Uncle Tom's Cabin** Although Harriet Beecher Stowe was an enormously gifted woman, her father stated that he would have given a hundred dollars if she had been born a male instead. Stowe had already published much of her writing before the huge success of *Uncle Tom's Cabin.* Her work included sketches, columns, books, and sermonettes. She stated that she wrote for the money and insisted that she would not simply live her life as a "domestic slave." Suggest that interested students do a dramatic reading and presentation of *Uncle Tom's Cabin.*

HISTORY FROM VISUALS
Free and Slave States and Territories, 1820–1854

Reading the Map Point out that the three maps should be studied both individually and as a group. Have students note the changing political balance over the years and ask them to note the reasons for the changes.

Extension What major changes took place in the West between 1820 and 1850? *California became a free state, the Southwest territories were opened to slavery, the Northwest territories were closed to slavery.*

MORE ABOUT . . .
Border Ruffians

Violence was nothing new for the "border ruffians." Fifteen years before the struggle over Kansas, these ruffians had persecuted and burned the Mormons out of Missouri. When Senator David Atchison wrote to Jefferson Davis about his plans for Kansas, he said: "We will be compelled to shoot, burn & hang, but the thing will soon be over. We intend to 'Mormonize' the Abolitionists."

MORE ABOUT . . .
John Brown

Most people who knew the abolitionist John Brown believed him to be mentally unbalanced—it was generally said that insanity ran in his family. An unsuccessful businessman, Brown tried a variety of ventures from farming to land speculation, but he failed every time. Brown began to hate slavery when he saw a white man beating a young slave with a shovel.

GEOGRAPHY SKILLBUILDER
PLACE *How did the number of slave states change between 1820 and 1854?* **PLACE** *How did the status of California change, as shown on the maps?* **REGION** *How did the Kansas-Nebraska Act affect the amount of land that was open to slavery?*

TENSION IN KANSAS AND NEBRASKA The Compromise of 1850 had provided for popular sovereignty in New Mexico and Utah. To Senator Stephen Douglas, popular sovereignty seemed like an excellent way to decide whether slavery would be allowed in the Nebraska Territory. The only difficulty was that, unlike New Mexico and Utah, this territory, which was within the Louisiana Purchase area, lay north of the Missouri Compromise line of 36°30' and therefore was legally closed to slavery.

As a result, Douglas introduced a bill in Congress on January 23, 1854, that would divide the area into two territories: Nebraska in the north and Kansas in the south. If passed, the bill would repeal the Missouri Compromise and establish popular sovereignty for both territories. Congressional debate was bitter. Some Northern congressmen saw the bill as part of a plot to turn the territories into slave states. Southerners strongly defended the proposed legislation, with nearly 90 percent of Southern congressmen voting for it. After months of struggle, the Kansas-Nebraska Act became law in 1854.

Free and Slave States and Territories, 1820–1854

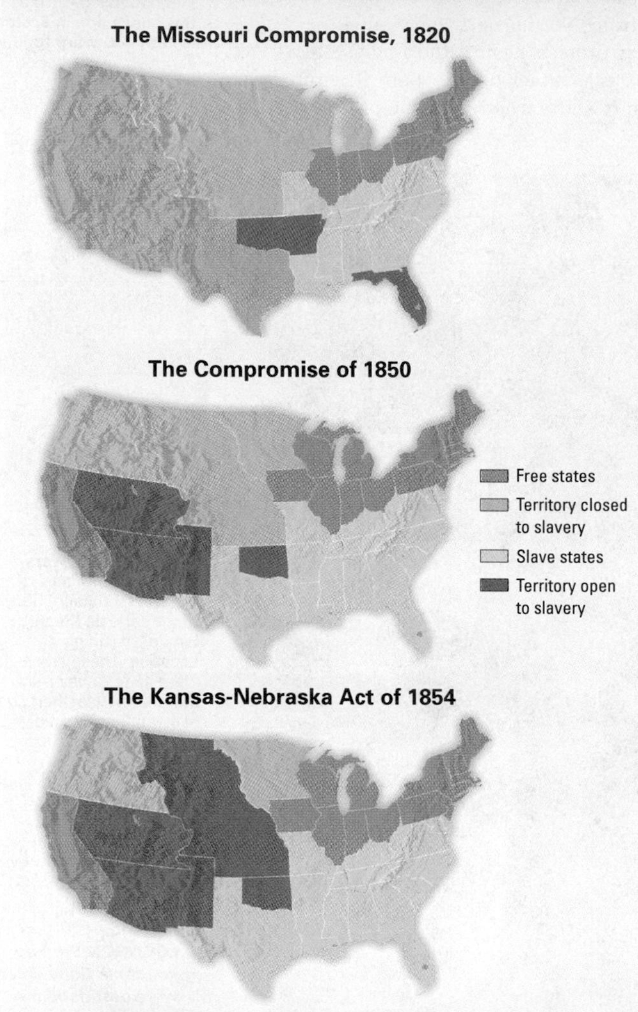

"BLEEDING KANSAS" The race for Kansas was on. By March 1855 Kansas had enough settlers to hold an election for a territorial legislature. However, thousands of "border ruffians" from the slave state of Missouri crossed into Kansas, voted illegally, and won a fraudulent majority for the proslavery candidates. Furious over these events, abolitionists organized a rival government in Topeka in the late summer of 1855.

It wasn't long before violence surfaced in the struggle for Kansas. A posse of 800 armed men looted and burned the antislavery town of Lawrence, Kansas. Seeking revenge, the antislavery fanatic John Brown murdered five men in the proslavery settlement of Pottawatomie Creek. The massacre triggered dozens of incidents throughout Kansas, earning the territory the name "Bleeding Kansas."

VIOLENCE IN THE SENATE Violence was not restricted to Kansas. In May, Senator Charles Sumner of Massachusetts delivered an impassioned speech in the Senate, entitled "The Crime Against Kansas." For two days he verbally attacked the South, slavery, and Senator Andrew P. Butler of South Carolina for his proslavery beliefs.

Skillbuilder Answers
Place: Slave states increased by three.
Place: *Possible Answer:* In 1820 that region was a territory open to slavery; as a result of the Compromise of 1850, it entered the Union as a free state. **Region:** *Possible Answer:* The Act increased the land that was open to slavery.

THINK THROUGH HISTORY
C. *Analyzing Issues* *Explain why popular sovereignty was so controversial.*

C. Answer It was controversial because it meant a repeal of the Missouri Compromise and because it opened any new territory or state to slavery.

TEACHING OPTION

Making Connections Across Cultures

Riots The violent outbreaks in Kansas can be characterized as riots. Since the beginning of history, riots have occurred throughout the world. Social scientists generally classify riots into two groups: instrumental riots and expressive riots.

Instrumental riots happen when groups use violence to protest specific issues. Sometimes the violence is an attempt to change policies or to improve specific conditions. The situation in Kansas involved a wild mix of protests over the actions of the proslavery and antislavery groups, inflamed passions over the issue of slavery, and instances of misunderstanding and misinformation.

Expressive riots occur when people in a minority group use violence to protest their conditions, such as poor housing, few job opportunities, inferior schools, and police brutality.

Ask students to consider the kinds of violence they read about or witness today. They should think about their own neighborhoods as well as places around the world such as the Middle East, Bosnia, and South Africa. What parallels can they draw with the eruptions in Kansas in the 1850s? What do they think are the long-term effects of violence?

The caption of this 1856 cartoon gives the Northern view of Preston Brooks's beating of Charles Sumner.

Soon thereafter, Butler's nephew, Congressman Preston S. Brooks, walked into the Senate chamber and struck Sumner on the head five or six times with a cane until the cane broke. Sumner suffered brain damage and did not return to his Senate seat for more than three years.

Southerners applauded Brooks and showered him with new canes. Northerners condemned the incident as yet another example of Southern brutality and antagonism toward free speech. Northerners and Southerners, it appeared, had met an impasse.

The widening gulf between the North and the South had far-reaching implications for party politics as well. As the two sections grew further apart, the old national parties ruptured and new political parties emerged, including a party for antislavery Northerners.

The Birth of the Republican Party

By the end of 1856, the nation's political landscape had a very different appearance than it had exhibited in 1848. The Whig Party had split over the issue of slavery and had lost support in both the North and the South. The Democratic Party, which had survived numerous crises in its history, was still alive, though scarred. The new Republican Party moved within striking distance of the presidency.

D. Answer The slavery issue had scarred the Democratic Party, but it divided and eventually led to the demise of the Whig Party.

THINK THROUGH HISTORY
D. *Finding Main Ideas* *What impact did the slavery issue have on the Democratic and Whig parties?*

SLAVERY DIVIDES WHIGS In 1852 the rift in the Whig Party widened when the Whigs nominated a pro-Northern candidate for president. The Whig vote in the South fell dramatically, which helped produce a victory for the Democratic candidate, **Franklin Pierce.** In 1854 the Kansas-Nebraska Act completed the demise of the Whigs. Unable to agree on a national platform, the Southern faction splintered as its members looked for a proslavery, pro-Union party to join, while Whigs in the North sought a political alternative of their own.

One alternative that appeared was the Know-Nothing Party, so-called because members were instructed to answer questions about their activities by saying, "I know nothing." The Know-Nothings expressed a belief in nativism, the favoring of native-born people over immigrants.

HISTORICAL SPOTLIGHT

HOUSTON'S FINAL BATTLE

Slavery had widespread support in Texas, but some people, including Sam Houston, did not want the issue to destroy the Union. In 1859, Houston ran for governor on an independent ticket, pledging allegiance to the Union. Touring Texas in a buggy, sometimes appearing without a shirt on hot days, the old war hero's popularity helped tip the election in his favor.

In 1860, however, as politicians battled over presidential nominations, the public controversy over slavery reached fever pitch in Texas. Fires were set in several northern Texas towns and charged, rightly or wrongly, to abolitionists.

After Lincoln's election in November, Texas Unionists argued against secession but daily lost ground. In March 1861, Texas joined the Confederate States of America. When called upon to take the oath of allegiance to the Confederacy, Governor Sam Houston refused. He was removed from office shortly thereafter.

HISTORY FROM VISUALS

Southern Chivalry

Reading a Political Cartoon Ask students to identify the two most important characters in this cartoon. What side did each character represent? Ask for opinions on the meaning of the caption.

Extension Have students review the main events of this section and then create a cartoon based on one of the most important personalities or events.

HISTORICAL SPOTLIGHT

Houston's Final Battle

Critical Thinking: Making Predictions Ask students why Houston refused to take the oath of allegiance to the Confederacy. What might he have gained by joining the Confederates? What might he have lost?

OBJECTIVE
③ INSTRUCT

The Birth of the Republican Party

▶***Starting with the Student*** Ask students what advantages or disadvantages would result if we had three or more parties in a presidential race.

▶***Discussing Key Ideas***
- Slavery divides and eventually destroys the Whig Party; anti-immigrant sentiment generates the Know-Nothing Party.
- The Republican Party attracts a wide spectrum of voters but is united by opposition to slavery.

TEACHING OPTION

Teaching Less Proficient Readers

Organizing Data This section deals with a large amount of data—names and dates—which sometimes discourages the less proficient reader. Pair less proficient readers with more proficient ones. Have pairs make a chart listing the names of each party, including important dates arranged chronologically, as well as the important political positions each party took. This chart should cover pages 169 to 170. Use the model at right as a graphic organizer. When complete, it should enable the less proficient reader to use the data in understanding the material. Students can use the chart later to review the section.

Political Parties Arising in the United States, 1844–1856

Name	Date	Political positions
Liberty	1844	Opposed slavery
Know-Nothing		
Republican		
Free Soil		

OBJECTIVE
④ INSTRUCT

Slavery and Secession

▶*Discussing Key Ideas*

- The Supreme Court's pro-slavery decision in the Dred Scott case further inflames the North.
- The Lincoln–Douglas debates over slavery in the territories propel Lincoln into the public eye.
- Lincoln is elected president in 1860, but his victory prompts some Southern states to secede.
- The secessionist states form the Confederacy and elect Jefferson Davis as their president.

ELECTRONIC LIBRARY OF PRIMARY SOURCES
from the Inaugural Address of Jefferson Davis, 1861

MORE ABOUT . . .
Dred Scott

Dred Scott's owner was a New Yorker named John F. A. Sanford (the Supreme Court misspelled his name, listing the case as *Scott* v. *Sandford).* He had purchased Scott to further his goal of having a slave case tried before the Supreme Court. When the case was over, Sanford freed Scott; his wife, Harriet; and their two daughters. Scott worked as a porter, but he died of tuberculosis two years before the Civil War began.

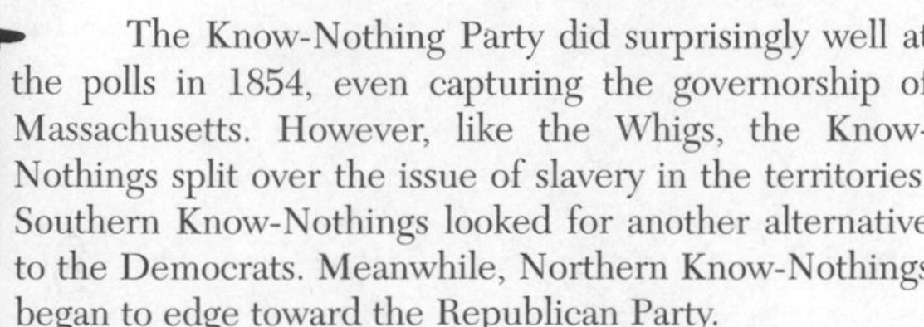

The Know-Nothing Party did surprisingly well at the polls in 1854, even capturing the governorship of Massachusetts. However, like the Whigs, the Know-Nothings split over the issue of slavery in the territories. Southern Know-Nothings looked for another alternative to the Democrats. Meanwhile, Northern Know-Nothings began to edge toward the Republican Party.

ANTISLAVERY PARTIES FORM Two forerunners of the Republican Party had emerged during the 1840s: the abolitionist Liberty Party in 1844 and the Free-Soil Party in 1848. Both parties opposed slavery. However, what Free-Soilers primarily objected to was the extension of slavery into the territories. They believed that the spread of slavery would force white workers to compete with slaves for jobs and would directly threaten the free labor system.

THINK THROUGH HISTORY
E. *Analyzing Motives* *Why did most Free-Soilers object to the extension of slavery into the territories?*

E. Answer Most Free-Soilers believed that the spread of slavery into the territories threatened the free labor system.

"Free Trade, Free Labor, Free Speech, and Free Men"

FREE-SOILERS' CAMPAIGN SLOGAN, 1844

To prevent this spread, the new Republican Party was formally organized in 1854. The party was united in opposing the Kansas-Nebraska Act and in keeping slavery out of the territories. Otherwise, though, it embraced a wide range of opinions. As the party grew, it took in Free-Soilers, antislavery Whigs and Democrats, and nativists, mostly from the North. The conservative faction hoped to resurrect the Missouri Compromise. At the opposite extreme were some radical abolitionists. Support from such diverse groups helped strengthen the Republican Party.

The presidential election of 1856 proved that the Republicans were a political force in the North. Republican candidate John C. Frémont came in a strong second against Democratic nominee **James Buchanan** by winning 11 of the 16 free states. The hard-fought election showed that the Democrats could win the presidency with a national candidate who could compete in the North without alienating Southerners. The election also signaled the decline of the Know-Nothing Party. However, the dissension that characterized party politics in the 1850s was only a pale preview of the turmoil that would divide the nation before the end of the decade.

Dred Scott's lawsuit dragged on for years and set off even more controversy over slavery.

Slavery and Secession

For the strongest of leaders, the passions inspired by the issue of slavery were difficult to control. For President Buchanan, an indecisive man and a poor politician, slavery-related controversies plagued his administration. The first one arose just two days after he took office on March 4, 1857.

THE DRED SCOTT DECISION **Dred Scott** was a slave whose owner took him from the slave state of Missouri to free territory in Illinois and Wisconsin and back to Missouri. Scott appealed to the Supreme Court for his freedom on the grounds that living in a free state—Illinois—and a free territory—Wisconsin—had made him a free man.

The Supreme Court ruled against Dred Scott on March 6, 1857. According to the ruling, Scott lacked any legal standing to sue in federal court because he was not, and never could be, a citizen. Moreover, the Court ruled that being in free territory did not make a slave free. The Fifth Amendment protected property, including slaves. For territories to exclude slavery would be to deprive slaveholders of their property. Southern slaveholders celebrated the decision. They believed that the ruling not only permitted the extension of slavery but guaranteed it.

F. Answer The Court defined slaves as property, which is protected by the Constitution. The Missouri Compromise was rendered unconstitutional because it banned slavery south of the 36°30′ north latitude line.

THINK THROUGH HISTORY
F. THEME *Constitutional Concerns* *How did the Supreme Court use the Constitution to uphold slavery in the* Dred Scott *decision? How did that decision render the Missouri Compromise unconstitutional?*

TEACHING OPTIONS

Teaching Gifted and Talented Students

Writing Poems In 1933, Stephen Vincent Benét and his wife, Rosemary Benét, published *A Book of Americans,* a collection of poems about American heroes, as well as weaker characters in American political history. One of the latter is James Buchanan. In their poem about Buchanan, the Benéts satirize the flaws of this unpopular president, including how "He twiddled his four years through, / And left the mess for somebody else / As weak men always do." Have interested students read the Benéts' poems, and then write a poem of their own, using the Benéts' work as a model.

Making Connections Across Time

Supreme Court Judges Justices of the Supreme Court are appointed by the president with the consent of the Senate and serve for life. Presidents try to appoint judges who they believe will conform to the ideals of the president's party, although many judges go on to serve well beyond the term of the president who appointed them.

The Dred Scott case was only the second one in American history in which the Supreme Court reversed a legislative act. In this case, a majority of the Supreme Court justices were Southerners. Ask students if they think a majority of Northerners on the court would have resulted in a different outcome.

G. Answer Both were against slavery; however, Lincoln thought the federal government should keep slavery out of the territories, while Douglas thought the states should decide.

THINK THROUGH HISTORY
G. *Comparing* *Explain the similarities and differences between Lincoln's position on slavery and that of Douglas.*

The slaveholders' interpretation was tested in 1857 when the proslavery government in Kansas developed a constitution and applied for admission to the Union. Free-Soilers, who greatly outnumbered proslavery settlers in Kansas, voted against the constitution in a referendum. However, President Buchanan endorsed the constitution. His endorsement angered fellow Democrat Stephen A. Douglas, who did not care "whether [slavery] is voted down or voted up." What he cared about was popular sovereignty. Douglas persuaded Congress to authorize another referendum on the constitution and, in 1858, voters rejected the constitution once again.

LINCOLN–DOUGLAS DEBATE That summer witnessed the start of one of Illinois's greatest political contests: the 1858 race for the U.S. Senate between Democratic incumbent Douglas and Republican challenger **Abraham Lincoln.** To many outsiders it must have seemed like an uneven match. Douglas was a two-term senator with an outstanding record and a large campaign chest, while Lincoln was a self-educated man who had been elected to one term in Congress in 1846.

To counteract the "Little Giant's" well-known name and extensive financial resources, Lincoln challenged Douglas to a series of debates on the issue of slavery in the territories. Douglas accepted the challenge, and the stage was set for some of the most celebrated debates in U.S. history.

The Lincoln-Douglas debates created quite a spectacle, partly due to the 6'4" Lincoln's one-foot height advantage over Douglas.

At the debates, Lincoln made a physically striking contrast to his opponent, over whom he towered. While Douglas was stocky and energetic, Lincoln was thin and gangling. While Douglas dressed smartly, Lincoln's clothes were plain and rumpled. The pair also had very different speaking styles. Douglas exuded self-confidence, using his fists to pound home his points. Lincoln, on the other hand, used plain language to deliver his comments.

The two men's positions were simple and consistent. Neither wanted slavery in the territories, but they disagreed on how to keep it out. Douglas believed deeply in popular sovereignty. Lincoln, on the other hand, believed that slavery was immoral. However, he did not expect individuals to give up slavery, unless Congress passed free-soil legislation.

In their second debate, Lincoln asked his opponent a crucial question: Could the settlers of a territory vote to exclude slavery before the territory became a state? Everyone knew that the *Dred Scott* decision said no—that territories could not exclude slavery. Popular sovereignty, Lincoln implied, was thus an empty phrase.

Douglas replied that, if the people of a territory were Free-Soilers, then all they had to do was elect representatives who would not provide legal enforcement of slave property laws in that territory. In other words, people could get around the *Dred Scott* decision.

Douglas won the Senate seat, but his response had widened the split in the

MORE ABOUT . . .
The Lincoln–Douglas Debates

At the time of the Lincoln–Douglas debates, newspapers seldom reported political events objectively because the papers depended on political organizations for their survival. Affiliating with a political party guaranteed a newspaper a certain number of subscribers, as well as legal and political advertising. In exchange, the paper was expected to print the party line. Partisan reporting appeared not only on the editorial pages, but on the news pages as well. As a result, people reading the "text" of the Lincoln–Douglas debates were not reading exact transcriptions of what the two men said.

Granted, newspapers reporting the debates utilized the new technique of verbatim reporting by trained stenographers. But after the stenographers sent in their notes, partisan editors took over. They eliminated ungrammatical sentences, divided run-on sentences, and remedied other problems, but only for whichever candidate their paper supported. Thus, the best way for a Chicagoan in 1858 to learn what Lincoln actually said was to read the pro-Democratic *Times,* while Douglas's actual words were most accurately presented in the *Republican Press* and *Tribune* (known today as the *Chicago Tribune*).

IN-DEPTH RESOURCES: UNIT 1
Primary Source: *from* The Lincoln–Douglas Debates, p. 108

Block Schedule TEACHING OPTION **Time Needed: 20 Minutes**

Cooperative Activity: Writing a Newspaper Account

Task: Pairs of students will write newspaper accounts of one of the Lincoln–Douglas debates, emphasizing the personal characteristics of each candidate.

Purpose: To help students understand the personal characteristics that often influence voters.

Activity: Describe the setting, the personal characteristics of each debater, the main point of disagreement between the two candidates, the reactions of the public. For help with their research, students with access to computers may want to check *A House Divided: The Lincoln–Douglas Debates.* CD-ROM. Grafica Multimedia, 1995.

Building a Portfolio: Students adding articles to their portfolios should attach a note pointing out their own contribution to the article.

ALTERNATIVE ASSESSMENT BOOK
Standards for Evaluating a Cooperative Activity

Standards for Evaluation
Articles should . . .

- list at least one political view of each candidate
- include examples of personal characteristics
- give examples of public reaction
- include a description of the locale of the debate

ECONOMIC BACKGROUND

The Panic of 1857

Have students create a cause and effect chart, showing the steps that led from the initial employee's embezzlement of company funds in 1857 to the business failures in 1859.

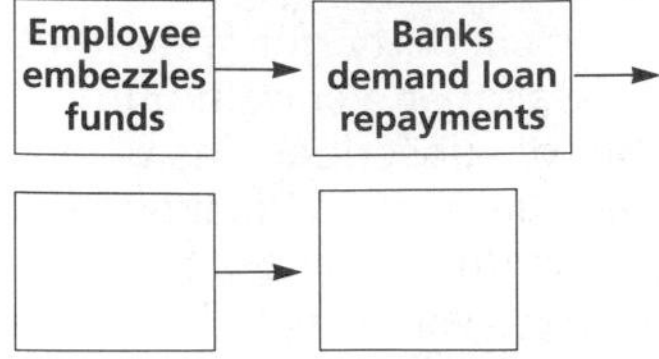

MORE ABOUT . . .

John Brown's Execution

Among those standing at attention as John Brown mounted the gallows steps were three men who were to play a major role in the drama of the Civil War. One was a Richmond actor named John Wilkes Booth, who assassinated President Lincoln in 1865. Another was Thomas J. Jackson, later known as "Stonewall" Jackson for his stand on the battlefield of Bull Run. The third was Edmund Ruffin, who is credited with firing the first shot at Fort Sumter, South Carolina.

HISTORY FROM VISUALS

Election of 1860

Reading the Map Have students note that the numbers on the map indicate the number of electoral votes for each state.

Extension Discuss how the election might have had different results if the Democratic Party had not split.

GEOGRAPHY TRANSPARENCIES

G10, Presidential Elections: 1856, 1860

ECONOMIC BACKGROUND

THE PANIC OF 1857

The Buchanan administration became widely unpopular not only because of the president's handling of the slavery issue but also because of the economic depression during his tenure.

The Panic of 1857 began on August 24 when the New York City branch of an Ohio insurance company went bankrupt because an employee had embezzled its funds. As news spread by telegraph, depositors rushed to recover their money. To pay them, the banks demanded immediate repayment of loans from businesses. Unable to both repay and finance daily operations, many crippled businesses closed down, and hundreds of thousands of men and women lost their jobs.

In the last four months of the year, nearly 5,000 businesses collapsed, and another 8,000 had failed by 1859. (See *depression* on page 934 in the Economics Handbook.)

Democratic Party. As for Lincoln, his attacks on the "vast moral evil" of slavery drew national attention, and some Republicans began thinking of him as an excellent candidate for the presidency in 1860.

HARPERS FERRY While politicians debated the slavery issue, John Brown was plotting a slave rebellion. On the night of October 16, 1859, he led a band of 18 men, black and white, into Harpers Ferry, Virginia (now West Virginia). His aim was to seize the federal arsenal there, distribute the captured arms to slaves in the area, and start a general slave uprising.

No such uprising occurred, though. Instead, troops killed ten of Brown's men and captured their leader. Brown was turned over to Virginia where he was found guilty of treason and condemned to death.

Public reaction to Brown's execution was immediate and intense in both sections of the country. In the North, bells tolled, guns fired salutes, and huge crowds gathered to hear fiery speakers denounce the South. The response was equally extreme in the South, where mobs assaulted whites who were suspected of holding antislavery views.

LINCOLN IS ELECTED PRESIDENT Despite the tide of hostility that now flowed between North and South, the Republican Party eagerly awaited its presidential convention in May 1860. When the convention began, almost everyone believed that the party's candidate would be Senator William H. Seward.

However, the delegates ultimately rejected Seward and his talk of an "irrepressible conflict" between the North and the South and nominated Lincoln, who seemed to them to be more moderate in his views. Although Lincoln pledged to halt the further spread of slavery, he also tried to reassure Southerners that a Republican administration would not "interfere with their slaves or with them about their slaves." Nonetheless, in Southern eyes, Lincoln was a "black Republican," whose election would be "the greatest evil that has ever befallen this country."

Election of 1860

ELECTORAL AND POPULAR VOTES

Party	Candidate	Electoral votes	Popular vote
Republican	Abraham Lincoln	180	1,865,593
Southern Democratic	J. C. Breckinridge	72	848,356
Constitutional Union	John Bell	39	592,906
Northern Democratic	Stephen Douglas	12	1,382,713

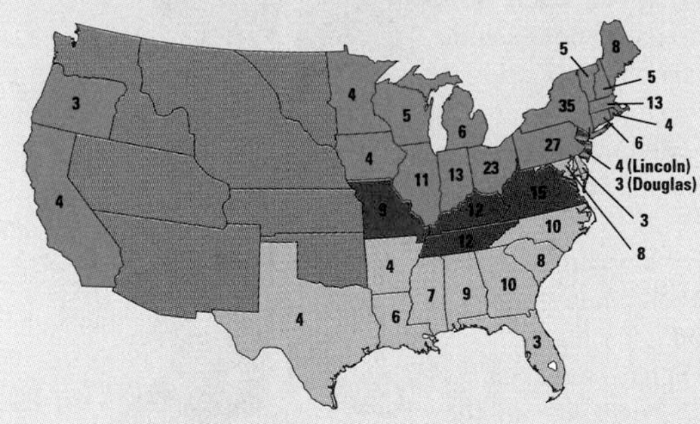

As the campaign developed, three major candidates besides Lincoln vied for office. The Democratic Party finally split over slavery. Northern Democrats rallied behind Douglas and his doctrine of popular sovereignty. Southern Democrats, who supported the Dred Scott decision, lined up behind Vice-President John C. Breckinridge of Kentucky. Former Know-Nothings and Whigs from the South organized the Constitutional Union Party and nominated John Bell of Tennessee as their candidate.

Lincoln emerged as the winner with less than half the popular vote and with no electoral votes from the South. He did not even appear on the ballot in most of the slave states because of Southern hostility toward him. The outlook for the Union was grim.

SOUTHERN SECESSION Lincoln's victory convinced Southerners—who had viewed the struggle over slavery partly as a conflict between the states' right of self-determination

TEACHING OPTIONS

Making Connections Across the Curriculum

Music Tell students that at Jefferson Davis's inauguration, cheering crowds sang "Dixie." The song later became the unofficial anthem of the Confederacy. Play "Dixie" for the class and ask why they think the song had such an important role in the history of the Civil War. *Both the original lyrics and the tune reminded Southerners of the good life that existed before the war.*

Exploring Themes

Constitutional Concerns With the secession of South Carolina from the Union, the Constitution faced one of its greatest challenges yet: Did a state have the right to secede from the Union? And when Mississippi, Alabama, Florida, Georgia, Louisiana, and Texas followed, forming the Confederacy, drafting their own constitution, and electing their own president, what was the Union then to do? After the initial confusion, strong feelings began to surface, and still more states seceded, agreeing with the rest of the Confederacy that their rights as states had been totally disregarded by the North.

and federal government control—that they had lost their political voice in the national government. Some Southern states decided to act. South Carolina led the way, seceding from the Union on December 20, 1860. When the news reached Northern-born William Tecumseh Sherman, superintendent of the Louisiana State Seminary of Learning and Military Academy (now Louisiana State University), he poured out his fears for the South.

THINK THROUGH HISTORY
H. *Recognizing Effects* *How did Lincoln's election affect the South?*

H. Answer
Lincoln's election convinced the South that Northerners intended to end slavery everywhere and that it was time to secede.

A PERSONAL VOICE

> This country will be drenched in blood. . . . [T]he people of the North . . . are not going to let the country be destroyed without a mighty effort to save it. . . . Besides, where are your men and appliances of war to contend against them? . . . You are rushing into war with one of the most powerful, ingeniously mechanical and determined people on earth—right at your doors. . . . Only in spirit and determination are you prepared for war. In all else you are totally unprepared.
>
> **WILLIAM TECUMSEH SHERMAN,** quoted in *None Died in Vain*

Yet even Sherman underestimated the depth and intensity of the South's commitment to its cause. Most white Southerners feared that an end to their entire way of life was at hand and saw secession as the only way to preserve it. Mississippi followed South Carolina's lead, as did Florida, Alabama, Georgia, Louisiana, and Texas.

In February 1861, delegates from the secessionist states met in Montgomery, Alabama, where they formed the Confederate States of America, or Confederacy. They also drew up a constitution that closely resembled that of the United States, but with a few notable differences. The most important difference was that it "protected and recognized" slavery in new territories.

The Confederates then unanimously elected former senator **Jefferson Davis** of Mississippi as president. Davis had made his position on the crisis clear, noting that to present a show of strength to the North, the South should "offer no doubtful or divided front."

The North had heard threats of secession before. When it finally happened, no one was shocked. But one key question remained in everyone's mind: Would the North allow the South to leave the Union without a fight?

HISTORICAL SPOTLIGHT

SECESSION AND THE BORDER STATES

Four slave states—Maryland, Kentucky, Missouri, and Delaware—were undecided about secession. Lincoln believed that these states would be essential to the success of the Union if war broke out. They had large populations, numerous factories, and access to the Ohio River, which would be needed to move troops and supplies. Moreover, Maryland nearly surrounded Washington, D.C., the seat of government.

Lincoln faced a choice: free the slaves and make abolitionists happy, or ignore slavery for the moment to keep from alienating the border states. He chose the latter, but that did not prevent violent conflicts between secessionists and Unionists in Maryland, Kentucky, and Missouri. With the intervention of the militia, and some political maneuvering in those states' legislatures, Lincoln kept the four border states in the Union.

Section 1 Assessment

1. TERMS & NAMES
Identify:
- secession
- Millard Fillmore
- Underground Railroad
- Harriet Tubman
- Harriet Beecher Stowe
- Franklin Pierce
- James Buchanan
- Dred Scott
- Abraham Lincoln
- Jefferson Davis

2. SUMMARIZING Create a time line highlighting the events that heightened the conflict between the North and the South and led to secession. Use a form similar to the one below.

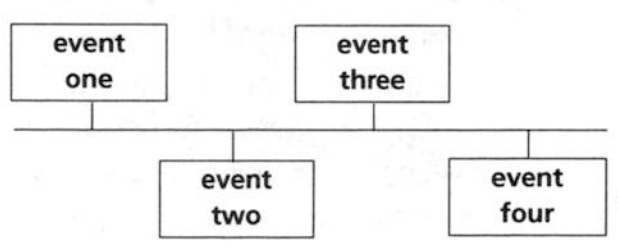

Select one event and explain in a paragraph how it was representative of the North-South conflict.

3. MAKING PREDICTIONS Review issues and events in this section that reflect the growing conflict between the North and the South. Do you think there are any points at which a different action or leader might have resolved the conflict?

THINK ABOUT
- issues raised by the Wilmot Proviso, the Compromise of 1850, the Fugitive Slave Act, and the Kansas-Nebraska Act
- the new political parties
- the Supreme Court's ruling in the *Dred Scott* decision
- the election of Abraham Lincoln for president in 1860

4. EVALUATING John Brown, Harriet Tubman, Harriet Beecher Stowe, and Stephen Douglas all opposed slavery. Explain whether you consider any of these people to be heroes.

THINK ABOUT
- each person's beliefs and actions
- the results of their actions
- the impact of their actions on Americans in the 1850s

ANSWERS

1. TERMS AND NAMES
secession, p. 165
Millard Fillmore, p. 166
Underground Railroad, p. 166
Harriet Tubman, p. 166
Harriet Beecher Stowe, p. 167
Franklin Pierce, p. 169
James Buchanan, p. 170
Dred Scott, p. 170
Abraham Lincoln, p. 171
Jefferson Davis, p. 173

2. SUMMARIZING
1846 Wilmot Proviso prohibits slavery in territories won in the war with Mexico.
1850 Congress passes Fugitive Slave Act.
1852 Harriet Beecher Stowe publishes *Uncle Tom's Cabin.*
1854 Congress passes the Kansas-Nebraska Act.
1857 Supreme Court rules against Dred Scott.
1860 Republican Abraham Lincoln is elected president.

3. MAKING PREDICTIONS
Possible Response: Some students may suggest that a president stronger than Buchanan or congressional leaders less opinionated than Calhoun might have been able to bring the North and the South to compromise earlier. Others may think that no one could have headed off the conflict, because of the complete division over slavery.

4. EVALUATING
Possible Response: Student responses should reflect understanding of the strengths and weaknesses of each individual and an awareness of their contributions to the abolition movement.

HISTORICAL SPOTLIGHT
Secession and the Border States
Critical Thinking: Evaluating Ask students to explore the following questions:
- What does Lincoln's decision to ignore slavery and retain the border states say about his character?
- What adjectives could best describe Lincoln's abilities as a leader?

ASSESS & RETEACH

Section 1 Assessment
Assign pairs of students to help each other answer the questions.

Self- Assessment
Have students mark those questions on the Section 1 Assessment that they could not answer. Ask them to work with a partner to locate the portions of the text that best answer each question.

Section Quiz
FORMAL ASSESSMENT
Section Quiz, p. 54

Reteach
Use the Guided Reading Worksheet for Section 1 to help review the main ideas of the section.

IN-DEPTH RESOURCES: UNIT 1
Guided Reading, p. 97

CLOSE

Proponents on both sides of the slavery issue tried to find a compromise that would prevent a complete dissolution of the Union. However, tensions continued to increase and led to new political alliances and violence. Lincoln's election in 1860 marked the final break between the North and the South.

Tracing Themes

OBJECTIVES

1. To explain the significance of the states' rights issue.
2. To summarize the historic conflicts between state and federal power.

FOCUS & MOTIVATE

▶ ***Starting with the Student***
Ask students to imagine a job with two bosses who give conflicting orders.

- What might have caused the conflict, and what would the results be?
- What would you do if you were faced with such a situation?

MORE ABOUT . . .
States' Rights

Clarify that the Supreme Court's 1996 decision took the side of the states against the U.S. Justice Department, which, to effect a recent expansion of the Voting Rights Act, had set up the minority districts to try to counter previous gerrymandering that had kept most African-American candidates from winning congressional seats in those states.

TRACING THEMES
CONSTITUTIONAL CONCERNS

States' Rights

The power struggle between states and the federal government has caused controversy since the country's beginning. At its worst, the conflict resulted in the Civil War. Even in the 1990s, state and federal governments have squared off on several issues.

- In 1996, the Supreme Court ruled that congressional districts in Texas and North Carolina that had been redrawn to increase minority representation were unconstitutional.
- In 1994, Florida sued the federal government to reimburse the state $1.5 billion for providing social services, such as education and health care, to illegal immigrants. A federal judge dismissed the case.

Constitutional conflicts between states' rights and federal jurisdiction are pictured here. As you read, see how each issue was resolved.

1787
CONSTITUTIONAL CONVENTION

ISSUE: The Constitution tried to resolve the original debate over states' rights versus federal authority.

At the Constitutional Convention in Philadelphia, delegates wanted to create a federal government that was stronger than the one created by the Articles of Confederation. But delegates disagreed about whether the federal government should have more power than the states. They also disagreed about whether large states should have more power than small states in the national legislature. The convention compromised—the Constitution reserves certain powers for the states, delegates other powers to the federal government, divides some powers between state and federal governments, and tries to balance the differing needs of the states through two houses of Congress.

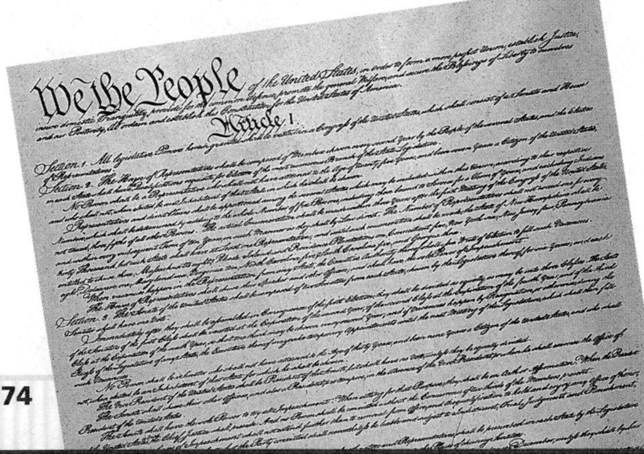

We the People

Article 1

1832
NULLIFICATION

ISSUE: The state of South Carolina moved to nullify, or declare void, a tariff set by Congress.

In the cartoon above, President Andrew Jackson, *right,* is playing a game called bragg. One of his opponents, Vice-President John C. Calhoun, is hiding two cards, "Nullification" and "Anti-Tariff," behind him. Jackson is doing poorly in this game, but he eventually won the real nullification dispute. When Congress passed high tariffs on imports in 1832, politicians from South Carolina, led by Calhoun, tried to nullify the tariff law, or declare it void. Jackson threatened to enforce the law with federal troops. Congress reduced the tariff to avoid a confrontation, and Calhoun resigned the vice-presidency.

RECOMMENDED RESOURCES

Books

Ellis, Richard E. *The Union at Risk.* New York: Oxford UP, 1987. An exploration of Jacksonian democracy, states' rights, and the nullification crisis.

Mason, Alpheus Thomas, ed. *The States' Rights Debate,* rev. ed. New York: Oxford UP, 1972. A collection of views on antifederalism and the Constitution.

Wilkinson, J. Harvie. *From Brown to Bakke.* New York: Oxford UP, 1979. An account of 20th-century Supreme Court decisions regarding school integration.

Videos

The Civil War: Union at Risk. Encyclopaedia Britannica, 1989. A look at constitutional issues and the war.

Federalism. MTI Film & Video, 1986. Focuses on federal vs. state and local government powers. Part of *The Constitution: That Delicate Balance,* an award-winning documentary series.

Hamilton and Jefferson on Democracy. Encyclopaedia Britannica, 1982. Part of the *Bill of Rights in Action* series.

Software

U.S. Government: The First 200 Years. Clearvue, dist. ESI. Various political issues.

1957

LITTLE ROCK CENTRAL HIGH SCHOOL

ISSUE: Some Southern governors refused to obey federal desegregation mandates for schools.

In 1957, President Eisenhower mobilized federal troops in Little Rock, Arkansas, to enforce the Supreme Court's 1954 ruling in the case of *Brown* v. *Board of Education of Topeka.* This ruling made segregation in public schools illegal. The Arkansas National Guard escorted nine African-American students into Little Rock Central High School against the wishes of Governor Orval Faubus, who had tried to prevent the students from entering the school. After this incident, Faubus closed the high schools in Little Rock in 1958 and 1959, thereby avoiding desegregation.

1860

SOUTH CAROLINA'S SECESSION

ISSUE: The conflict over a state's right to secede, or withdraw, from the Union led to the Civil War.

In December 1860, Southern secessionists cheered "secession" enthusiastically in front of the Mills House *(above),* a hotel in Charleston, South Carolina. South Carolina seceded after the election of Abraham Lincoln, whom the South perceived as anti-states' rights and antislavery. Lincoln took the position that states did not have the right to secede from the Union. In 1861, he ordered that provisions be sent to the federal troops stationed at Fort Sumter in Charleston harbor. South Carolinians fired on the fort—and the Civil War was under way. The Union's victory in the war ended the most serious challenge to federal authority: states did not have the right to secede from the Union.

INTERACT WITH HISTORY

1. **CREATING A CHART** For each incident pictured, create a chart that tells who was on each side of the issue, summarizes each position, and explains how the issue was resolved.
2. **USING PRIMARY AND SECONDARY SOURCES** Research one of the controversies in the bulleted list in the opening paragraph or another states' rights controversy of the 1990s. Decide which side you support. Write a paragraph explaining your position on the issue.

 SEE SKILLBUILDER HANDBOOK, PAGES 924 AND 931.

INSTRUCT

▶ *Starting with the Student*

- Have students voice their general opinion of federal vs. state and local government powers. What roles do they feel each should play in governance?
- Ask students to think of issues that involve a dispute between their local government and the state or the federal government.

▶ *Discussing Key Ideas*

- The conflict between state and federal governments has existed since the nation was created.
- At its worst, it resulted in the Civil War.
- Today it continues to play a role in several controversies.

HISTORY FROM VISUALS

Reading the Images

Have students study the illustrations of the four issues discussed on these pages and answer the following questions.

- What would you say is the emotion or attitude of the people (or their words) in each scene? *Possible Responses: 1787—formality, calm deliberation; 1832—confrontation, craftiness; 1860—jubilation; 1957—fear, grim determination.*
- What emotions does each scene prompt in you?

INTERACT WITH HISTORY

1. Creating a Chart

Standards for Evaluation
Charts should . . .

- state the group on each side of the issue and indicate leading figures in each group, if relevant
- summarize each side's position
- indicate how the issue was resolved
- supplement factual details provided on these pages with additional research, if necessary

2. Using Primary and Secondary Sources

To help get students started, you might ask them to react to one of these questions:

- To what degree should the U.S. government be allowed to redraw congressional districts in states that have historically tried to curtail black representation?
- Should state laws or ballot initiatives prescribing term limits for the U.S. Congress be constitutional?
- Should the federal government be able to pass unfunded mandates on state and local governments?

Section 2 Overview

OBJECTIVES

1. To explain military strategies and describe initial battles of the Civil War.
2. To discuss Lincoln's motives for issuing the Emancipation Proclamation.
3. To identify the social and economic changes brought about by the war.

SKILLBUILDER

- Understanding geography: region, place, p. 177

CRITICAL THINKING

- Forming generalizations, pp. 176, 181, 183
- Evaluating decisions, p. 178
- Making inferences, pp. 179, 180
- Analyzing causes, p. 183
- Theme: Women in America, p. 183
- Summarizing, p. 183
- Recognizing effects, p. 183

FOCUS & MOTIVATE

5-MINUTE WARM-UP

Describing Character

To compare Abraham Lincoln and Jefferson Davis, have students read the Key Players on page 179 and answer these questions.

1. Write five adjectives that describe Lincoln and five that describe Davis.
2. Which man was better suited to be a president? Why?

WARM-UP TRANSPARENCY 4

▶ Starting with the Student

Have students think of crises in which someone had to make a tough decision.

OBJECTIVE

① **INSTRUCT**

Union and Confederate Forces Clash

▶ Discussing Key Ideas

- The Union and the Confederacy adopt military strategies suited to their objectives and resources.

(continued on next page)

2 The Civil War Begins

LEARN ABOUT the early military actions, political issues, and experiences of soldiers and civilians during the Civil War

TO UNDERSTAND the social, political, and economic changes brought about by the deadly conflict.

TERMS & NAMES

- Fort Sumter
- Bull Run
- Stonewall Jackson
- Ulysses S. Grant
- Robert E. Lee
- Antietam
- Emancipation Proclamation
- conscription
- income tax
- Clara Barton

ONE AMERICAN'S STORY

On April 18, 1861, the federal supply ship *Baltic* dropped anchor off the coast of New Jersey. Aboard was Major Robert Anderson, a 35-year army veteran on his way from Charleston, South Carolina, to New York City. That day, Anderson wrote a report to the secretary of war in which he described his most recent command.

A PERSONAL VOICE

Having defended Fort Sumter for thirty-four hours, until the quarters were entirely burned, the main gates destroyed by fire, . . . the magazine surrounded by flames, . . . four barrels and three cartridges of powder only being available, and no provisions but pork remaining, I accepted terms of evacuation . . . and marched out of the fort . . . with colors flying and drums beating . . . and saluting my flag with fifty guns.

ROBERT ANDERSON, quoted in *Fifty Basic Civil War Documents*

Major Robert Anderson observes the firing at Fort Sumter.

As soon as the Confederacy was formed, Confederate soldiers began taking over federal installations in their states—especially forts. By the time of Lincoln's inauguration on March 4, only four Southern forts remained in Union hands. The most important was **Fort Sumter,** on an island in Charleston harbor.

The day after his inauguration, Lincoln received word that the Confederacy was demanding that the Union surrender Fort Sumter or face an attack. Lincoln decided to neither abandon Fort Sumter nor reinforce it. He would merely send in "food for hungry men." Lincoln left it to Jefferson Davis to initiate hostilities. At 4:30 A.M. on April 12, Confederate batteries began thundering away to the cheers of Charleston's citizens. The deadly struggle between North and South was under way.

Union and Confederate Forces Clash

News of Fort Sumter's fall united the North. When Lincoln called for volunteers, the response throughout the Northern states was overwhelming. However, Lincoln's call for troops provoked a very different reaction in the states of the upper South. In April and May, Virginia, Arkansas, North Carolina, and Tennessee seceded, bringing the number of Confederate states to eleven. The western counties of Virginia opposed slavery, so they seceded from Virginia and were admitted into the Union as West Virginia in 1863. The four remaining slave states—Maryland, Delaware, Kentucky, and Missouri—remained in the Union.

A. Answer The North had more resources such as manpower, factories, and railroad lines. The South had cotton profits, good generals, and the motivation of defending its homeland.

THINK THROUGH HISTORY

A. Forming Generalizations *What were the strengths of the North and the South?*

STRENGTHS AND STRATEGIES The Union and the Confederacy were unevenly matched. The Union enjoyed enormous advantages in resources over the South—more manpower, more factories, greater food production, and a more extensive railroad system. The Confederacy's advantages included "King Cotton," first-rate generals, and highly motivated soldiers.

Both sides adopted military strategies suited to their objectives and

SECTION 2 RESOURCES

PRINT RESOURCES

IN-DEPTH RESOURCES: UNIT 1
Guided Reading, p. 98
Skillbuilder Practice: Following Chronological Order, p. 102
Outline Map: The States Choose Sides, p. 106
Primary Source: The Emancipation Proclamation, p. 110

READING STUDY GUIDE, p. 49

ACCESS FOR STUDENTS ACQUIRING ENGLISH
Guided Reading (Spanish), p. 68
Skillbuilder Practice: Following Chronological Order (Spanish), p. 72
Outline Map: The States Choose Sides (Spanish), p. 76

SPANISH READING STUDY GUIDE, p. 49

FORMAL ASSESSMENT
Section Quiz, p. 55

ALTERNATIVE ASSESSMENT BOOK
See forms for supporting and scoring alternative activities.

TECHNOLOGY RESOURCES

GEOGRAPHY TRANSPARENCIES
G11, Union and Confederacy: 1861
G37, Slavery and the Civil War

CD-ROM Electronic Library of Primary Sources *Fateful Lightning*

VIDEO *American Portfolio: A Videodisc for U.S. History* user's guide, pp. 96–101, 106–109, 111, 115

INTERNET http://www.mlushistory.com

resources. The Union, which had to conquer the South to win, devised a three-part plan: (1) the Union navy would blockade Southern ports, so they could neither export cotton nor import much-needed manufactured goods, (2) Union riverboats and armies would move down the Mississippi River and split the Confederacy in two, and (3) Union armies would capture the Confederate capital at Richmond, Virginia. The Confederacy's strategy was mostly defensive, although Southern leaders encouraged their generals to attack the North if the opportunity arose.

BULL RUN The first bloodshed occurred about three months after Fort Sumter fell near the little creek of **Bull Run,** just 25 miles from Washington, D.C.

The battle was a seesaw affair. In the morning the Union army gained the upper hand, but the Confederates held firm, inspired by General Thomas J. Jackson. "There is Jackson standing like a stone wall!" another general shouted, originating the nickname **Stonewall Jackson.** In the afternoon Confederate reinforcements helped win the first victory for the South.

Fortunately for the Union, the Confederates were too exhausted to follow up their victory with an attack on Washington. Still, Confederate morale soared. Many Confederate soldiers, confident that the war was over, left the army and went home.

HISTORICAL SPOTLIGHT

PICNIC AT BULL RUN

Before the First Battle of Bull Run, the inexperienced soldiers expected the war to "be a picnic." The civilian population was similarly naive about the realities of battle. Carrying baskets of food and iced champagne, they rode out to observe the first encounter of the war. Photographer Mathew Brady, who would travel with the Union army throughout the war, joined the onlookers.

However, the battle did not turn out to be the enjoyable entertainment viewers expected. When the Confederates forced the Union troops to retreat, their progress was held up by the carriages of the panicking civilians. In the hasty retreat of the defeated Union forces, most of Brady's photographic equipment was smashed.

UNION ARMIES IN THE WEST Lincoln responded to the defeat at Bull Run by dramatically stepping up enlistments. He also appointed General George McClellan to lead the Union forces encamped near Washington. While McClellan drilled his men, the Union forces in the west began the fight for control of the Mississippi River.

In February 1862 a Union army invaded western Tennessee. At its head was General **Ulysses S. Grant,** a brave and decisive military commander. In just 11 days, Grant's forces captured two Confederate forts, Fort Henry on the Tennessee River and Fort Donelson on the Cumberland River.

Skillbuilder Answers **Region:** The West. **Place:** Kentucky, Pennsylvania, and Maryland.

GEOGRAPHY SKILLBUILDER

REGION *In which region of the country did Northern forces have the most success?*
PLACE *In which states did Confederate troops attempt invasions of the North?*

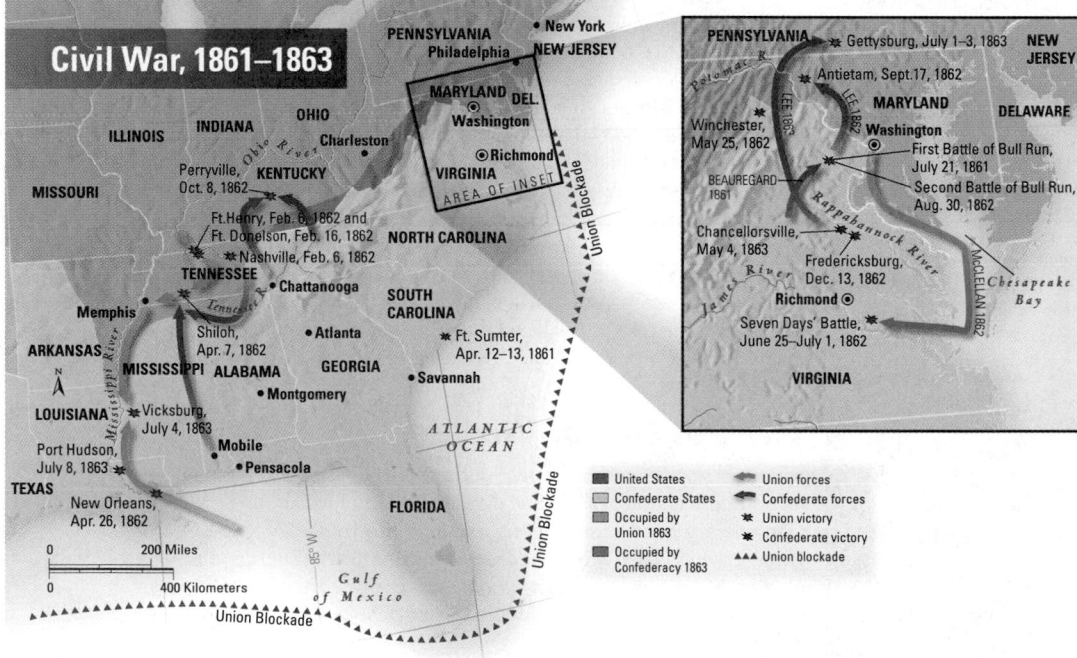

Civil War, 1861–1863

United States
Confederate States
Occupied by Union 1863
Occupied by Confederacy 1863
Union forces
Confederate forces
Union victory
Confederate victory
Union blockade

(continued from page 176)

- The South wins the first battle of the war.
- Both sides fight to save their capitals.

IN-DEPTH RESOURCES: UNIT 1
Guided Reading, p. 98
Outline Map: The States Choose Sides, p. 106

ACCESS FOR STUDENTS ACQUIRING ENGLISH
Guided Reading (Spanish), p. 68

HISTORICAL SPOTLIGHT
Picnic at Bull Run

Critical Thinking: Analyzing What factors do you think contributed to both soldiers' and civilians' false perceptions about the war? *Possible Responses: Naiveté about the horrors of warfare; underestimation of the enemy's resolve.*

HISTORY FROM VISUALS
Civil War, 1861–1863

Reading the Map Explain how the two maps depict the North's three-pronged strategy: Illustrating the goal to blockade Southern ports, the string of tiny blue triangles wraps around the Confederacy's southern and eastern coastline. The blue arrows winding along the Mississippi River show the North's success in dividing the Confederacy. The blue arrow pointing near Richmond reveals how the North is maneuvering to capture the Confederate capital.

GEOGRAPHY TRANSPARENCIES
G11, Union and Confederacy, 1861
G37, Slavery and the Civil War

FATEFUL LIGHTNING
Civil War Maps

Block Schedule TEACHING OPTION **Time Needed: 30 Minutes**

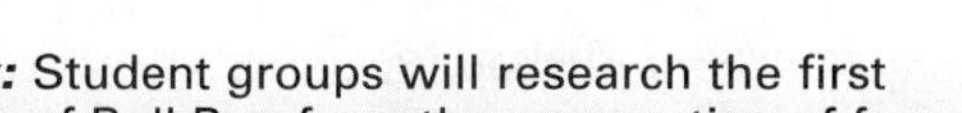
Cooperative Activity: Researching the Battle of Bull Run

Task: Student groups will research the first Battle of Bull Run from the perspective of four different people and then role-play the parts.

Purpose: To explore an event from multiple points of view.

Activity: Assign teams of four, and have each member choose one of the following roles—a Northern soldier, a Southern soldier, a civilian spectator, and a newspaper reporter. Students should then examine books about the Battle of Bull Run and relevant primary sources. Have students write descriptions based on their research and read them aloud. Classmates should guess whose point of view is represented in each description.

Building a Portfolio: Students adding their descriptions to their portfolios should attach a note pointing out their own contributions.

ALTERNATIVE ASSESSMENT BOOK
Standards for Evaluating a Cooperative Activity

Standards for Evaluation
Descriptions should . . .

- present vivid details about the location of the battle and the people
- include battle movements
- give sufficient information to reveal the narrator of each piece

MORE ABOUT . . .

Robert E. Lee

Lee had opposed secession. However, after Fort Sumter fell, he declined an offer to head the Union army and cast his lot with his beloved state of Virginia. After the Civil War was over, Lee tried to convince Southerners to accept the outcome. "Make your sons Americans," he urged. Although he pledged renewed allegiance to the Union, Lee was not pardoned. Congress did not restore Lee's full citizenship until 1975.

ELECTRONIC LIBRARY OF PRIMARY SOURCES

Letters to His Family by Robert E. Lee

HISTORICAL SPOTLIGHT

Boys in War

Critical Thinking: Analyzing Ask students why some people glorify war. At what age should men be drafted during wartime?

OBJECTIVE

(2) INSTRUCT

The Politics of War

▶ ***Discussing Key Ideas***

- Economic factors push Britain to neutrality.
- Lincoln issues the Emancipation Proclamation, which is met with mixed reactions from all sides.
- Lincoln and Davis take strong measures to suppress dissent.
- The Union and the Confederacy pass unpopular draft laws.

Admiral David Farragut, shown here in a photograph by Mathew Brady, won a strategic victory for the Union in taking the port city of New Orleans.

Two months later, Grant narrowly escaped disaster near Shiloh, a small church in Tennessee close to the Mississippi border. After Grant failed to have his troops dig trenches or set out adequate guards and patrols, thousands of Confederate soldiers carried out a surprise attack on the Union forces. Grant averted disaster by reorganizing his troops and driving the Confederate forces away the next day. However, Shiloh demonstrated what a bloody slaughter the war was becoming. Nearly one-fourth of the 100,000 men who fought there were killed, wounded, or captured.

As Grant pushed toward the Mississippi River, David G. Farragut, commanding a Union fleet of about 40 ships, seized New Orleans, the Confederacy's largest city and busiest port. By June, Farragut had taken control of much of the lower Mississippi.

Between Grant and Farragut, the Union had nearly achieved its goal of cutting the Confederacy in two. Only Port Hudson, Louisiana, and Vicksburg, Mississippi, still stood in the way.

THE WAR FOR THE CAPITALS As the campaign in the west progressed and the Union navy tightened its blockade of Southern ports, the North's plan to capture the Confederate capital at Richmond faltered. One of the problems was General McClellan. Although an excellent administrator and popular with his troops, McClellan was incredibly cautious. After he spent five full months training an army of 150,000 men, even the patient Lincoln commented that he would like to "borrow McClellan's army if the general himself was not going to use it."

McClellan finally got under way in the spring of 1862. He led his army toward Richmond, where it met a Confederate army commanded by **Robert E. Lee.** Lee was very different from McClellan—modest rather than vain, and willing to go beyond military textbooks in his tactics. Determined to save the Confederate capital, Lee drove McClellan away from Richmond.

Now it was Lee's turn to move against Washington. In September his troops crossed the Potomac into the Union state of Maryland. At this point McClellan had an incredible stroke of luck. A Union corporal found a copy of Lee's orders wrapped around some cigars! The plan revealed that Lee's and Stonewall Jackson's armies were separated for the moment.

For once McClellan acted aggressively and ordered his men forward after Lee. The two armies fought on September 17 near a creek called the **Antietam.** The clash proved to be the bloodiest single-day battle in American history, with casualties totaling more than 26,000. Instead of pursuing the battered Confederate army into Virginia and possibly ending the war, however, McClellan did nothing.

In November, Lincoln fired McClellan, the general whom the President characterized as having "the slows." This solved one problem. However, the president still faced the problems of smoothing over diplomatic conflicts with Britain and answering the demands of abolitionists.

B. Answer Most students may say the decision was a good one, because McClellan failed to act decisively when he had a chance to win the war.

THINK THROUGH HISTORY

B. Evaluating Decisions *Do you think Lincoln's decision to fire McClellan was a good one? Why or why not?*

HISTORICAL SPOTLIGHT

BOYS IN WAR

Both the Union and Confederate armies had soldiers who were under 18 years of age. Examination of some Confederate recruiting lists for 1861–1862 reveals that approximately 5 percent were 17 or younger—with some as young as 13. The percentage of boys in the Union army was lower, perhaps 1.5 percent. These figures, however, do not count the great number of boys who ran away to follow each army without officially enlisting.

Some boy soldiers performed heroically. In fact, Union soldier Arthur MacArthur (father of World War II hero Douglas MacArthur) became a colonel when he was only 18. Others experienced the hazards rather than the glories of war. For example, Charlie Jackson of Memphis, Tennessee, was killed at Shiloh at the end of his first and only day of fighting.

The Politics of War

After secession occurred, many Southerners believed that dependence on Southern cotton would force Great Britain to formally recognize the Confederacy as an independent nation. Unfortunately for the South, Britain accumulated a huge cotton inventory just before the outbreak of war. Moreover, Northern wheat and corn replaced cotton as an essential import. Britain decided that neutrality was the best policy—at least for a while.

TEACHING OPTION

Skillbuilder Mini-Lesson: Following Chronological Order

Explaining the Skill Understanding the relationships between events—causes and effects, problems and solutions—depends on knowing how the events relate in time. Even the childhood taunt, "Well, you did it first!" shows how important chronological thinking is in our lives. Using dates provided in the text and clue words about time, students can place events they read about in correct chronological order.

Applying the Skill Help students put the events described on this page in chronological order by asking them to identify dates and clue words about time: *Two months later, After Grant, the next day, As Grant pushed, By June, As the campaign, spring of 1862, At this point, on September 17, In November.*

Ask students what the word *as* shows at the beginning of the second paragraph. *Several things were going on at the same time.*

IN-DEPTH RESOURCES: UNIT 1

Skillbuilder Practice: Following Chronological Order, p. 102

BRITAIN REMAINS NEUTRAL In the fall of 1861, an incident occurred to test that neutrality. Two Confederate diplomats traveling to Britain aboard a British merchantmen were stopped and arrested by the captain of an American warship. The British threatened war against the Union and dispatched 8,000 troops to Canada. Aware of the need to fight just "one war at a time," Lincoln decided to free the two prisoners, publicly claiming that the captain had acted without orders.

THINK THROUGH HISTORY
C. *Making Inferences* *Why did the Union and Confederacy care about British neutrality?*

C. Answer Students should recall that Great Britain had a strong navy and great industrial power. Neither the North nor South wanted the British to actively support the other side.

PROCLAIMING EMANCIPATION As the South struggled in vain to gain foreign recognition, abolitionist feeling grew in the North. Although Lincoln disliked slavery, he did not believe that the federal government had the power to abolish it where it already existed. Lincoln stated, "My paramount object in this struggle is to save the Union, and is not either to save or destroy Slavery."

As the war progressed, however, Lincoln did find a way to use his constitutional war powers to end slavery. The Confederacy used the labor of slaves to build fortifications and grow food. Lincoln's powers as commander in chief allowed him to order his troops to seize enemy resources. Therefore, he decided that, just as he could order the Union army to take Confederate supplies, he could also authorize the army to emancipate slaves. Emancipation was not just a moral issue; it became a weapon of war.

On January 1, 1863, Lincoln issued his **Emancipation Proclamation.** The following portion captured national attention.

KEY PLAYERS

ABRAHAM LINCOLN
1809–1865

People question why Lincoln believed so passionately in the Union. A possible answer lies in his life story. He was born into poverty, the son of illiterate parents. Lincoln once said that in his boyhood there was "absolutely nothing to excite ambition for education," yet he hungered for knowledge.

He educated himself and, after working as rail splitter, flatboatman, storekeeper, and surveyor, he taught himself to be a lawyer. This led to careers in law and politics—and eventually to the White House. In Europe at that time, people were more or less fixed in the station into which they had been born. In the United States—founded on the belief that all men were created equal—Lincoln was free to achieve whatever he could. Small wonder that he fought to preserve the democracy he described as "the last best hope of earth."

JEFFERSON DAVIS
1808–1889

Davis, who was named after Thomas Jefferson, was born in Kentucky but grew up in Mississippi. After graduating from West Point, he alternated army service with life as a planter. He served in the U.S. Senate from 1847 to 1851 and again from 1857 to 1861, resigning when Mississippi seceded.

His election as president of the Confederacy dismayed him. As his wife Varina wrote, "I thought his genius was military, but as a party manager he would not succeed. He did not know the arts of the politician and would not practice them if understood, and he did know those of war." Varina was right. Davis fought frequently with other Confederate leaders and was blamed for the refusal of many Southern states to put the Confederacy's welfare above their own.

FROM THE EMANCIPATION PROCLAMATION

I do order and declare that all persons held as slaves within these said designated States and parts of States are, and henceforward shall be free; and that the Executive Government of the United States, including the military and naval authorities thereof, will recognize and maintain the freedom of said persons.

And I hereby enjoin upon the people so declared to be free, to abstain from all violence, unless in necessary self-defense, and I recommend to them, that in all cases, when allowed, they labor faithfully for reasonable wages.

And I further declare and make known that such persons of suitable condition will be received into the armed service of the United States to garrison forts, positions, stations, and other places, and to man vessels of all sorts in said service.

And, upon this, sincerely believed to be an act of justice, warranted by the Constitution, upon military necessity, I invoke the considerate judgment of mankind and the gracious favor of Almighty God.

ABRAHAM LINCOLN, *The Emancipation Proclamation,* January 1, 1863

KEY PLAYERS
Lincoln and Davis

Critical Thinking: Compare and Contrast
Have students create a chart like the one below to show the similarities and differences between Lincoln and Davis.

	Lincoln	Davis
Early Life		
Education		
Career		

MORE ABOUT . . .
Reactions to the Proclamation

In 1963, Martin Luther King, Jr., expressed his admiration for the Emancipation Proclamation in his speech, "I Have a Dream," delivered on the steps of the Lincoln Memorial. "Five score years ago, a great American, in whose symbolic shadow we stand, signed the Emancipation Proclamation. This momentous decree came as a great beacon light of hope to millions of Negro slaves who have been seared in the flames of withering injustice. It came as a joyous daybreak to end the long night of captivity."

IN-DEPTH RESOURCES: UNIT 1
Primary Source: The Emancipation Proclamation, p. 110

TEACHING OPTION

Exploring Themes

Constitutional Concerns Though the slavery issue was one of the root causes of the Civil War, most Northerners and Southerners were unwilling to admit it. Lincoln held that the federal government had no power over slavery in the slave states and insisted that his main goal was preservation of the Union. Gradually, however, the more radical members of Congress began to pass laws intended to free the slaves. Lincoln did not think such laws were constitutional and refused to enforce them. By the end of 1862, Lincoln recognized the need to take action. He used his war powers as commander in chief to authorize the Union army to free the slaves just as he authorized Union soldiers to seize Confederate supplies. The culmination of these measures was the Emancipation Proclamation of January 1, 1863.

ANOTHER PERSPECTIVE

The Cherokee and the War

Critical Thinking: Analyzing Causes Have students create a diagram like the one below and fill it in with the causes that shaped the Cherokee's shifting loyalties during the Civil War.

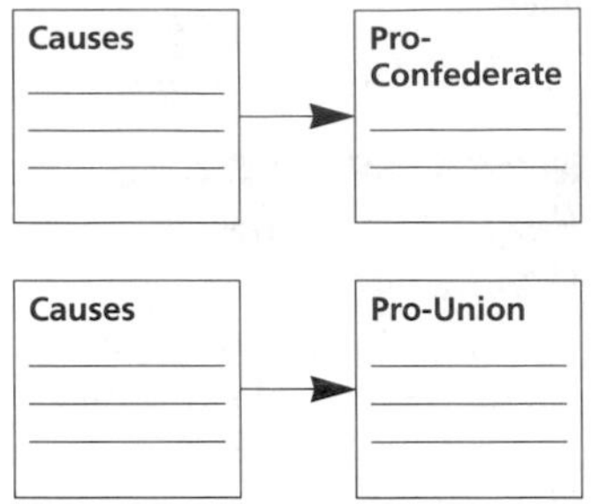

MORE ABOUT . . .

The New York Draft Riots

In a letter to the editor, published in the *New York Times* on July 15, 1863, a rioter justified why the draft resisters resorted to violence: "You will, no doubt, be hard on us rioters tomorrow morning, but the 300-dollar law [the Enrollment Act] has made us nobodies, vagabonds and cast-outs of society, for whom nobody cares when we must go to war and be shot down. We are the poor rabble, and the rich rabble is our enemy by this law. Therefore we give our enemy battle here."

THE CHEROKEE AND THE WAR

Another nation divided by the Civil War was the Cherokee Nation, located in the Indian Territory that eventually became part of Oklahoma. Both the North and the South wanted the Cherokee on their side because Indian Territory was an excellent grain- and livestock-producing area. For their part, the Cherokee felt drawn to both sides—to the Union because federal treaties guaranteed Cherokee political and property rights, and to the Confederacy because many Cherokee owned slaves.

After an attempt at neutrality, the Cherokee signed a treaty with the South in October 1861. However, the alliance did not last. Efforts by the pro-Confederate leader Stand Watie to govern the Cherokee Nation failed, and federal troops invaded Indian Territory. Many Cherokee deserted from the Confederate army and went into hiding or fled to Kansas, where they joined the Union army. In February 1863 the Cherokee Nation revoked the Confederate treaty.

The proclamation did not free any slaves immediately because it applied only to areas behind Confederate lines, outside Union control. Nevertheless, for many, the proclamation gave the war a high moral purpose by turning the struggle into a fight to free the slaves.

However, the Emancipation Proclamation did not please everyone in the North. The Democrats claimed that it would only further antagonize the South. Many Union soldiers accepted it grudgingly, saying they would support emancipation if that was what it took to reunify the nation.

Confederates reacted to the proclamation with fury. They became more determined than ever to fight to preserve their way of life. After the Emancipation Proclamation, compromise was no longer possible. From January 1863 on, it was a war to the death.

THINK THROUGH HISTORY
D. ***Making Inferences*** *In what way was the Emancipation Proclamation a part of Lincoln's military strategy?*
D. Answer It allowed free blacks to enlist in the Union army and added moral inspiration to the cause of the North.

BOTH SIDES FACE POLITICAL PROBLEMS Neither side in the Civil War was completely unified. The North harbored thousands of Confederate sympathizers, while the South had thousands of Union sympathizers.

Lincoln dealt forcefully with disloyalty and dissent. For example, when a Baltimore crowd attacked a Union regiment on its way to Washington a week after Fort Sumter, Lincoln sent federal troops to Maryland. In that state—and eventually in others—he also suspended the writ of habeas corpus, which prevents the government from holding citizens without formally charging them with crimes. Lincoln even seized telegraph offices to make sure no one used the wires for subversion. Although Jefferson Davis at first denounced Lincoln's actions, he, too, suspended habeas corpus in 1862.

Lincoln's action in dramatically expanding presidential powers to meet the crises of wartime set a precedent in U.S. history. Since then, some presidents have cited war or "national security" as a reason to expand the powers of the executive branch of government.

CONSCRIPTION Although both armies originally relied on volunteers, heavy casualties and widespread desertions led to **conscription,** a draft that would force certain members of the population to serve in the army. The Confederacy passed a draft law in 1862, and the Union followed suit in 1863. Many people objected to the laws because they allowed exemption from the draft for the rich.

Northern resentment over the draft led to several riots. The worst one occurred in New York City and was instigated by Irish immigrants. After four days of rioting in July 1863, more than 100 persons lay dead.

Violence erupted in New York City in July 1863 as thousands of rioters resisted the draft.

TEACHING OPTIONS

Making Connections Across Cultures

Immigrants in the Union Army About 500,000 Union soldiers were immigrants. Many did not speak English, which made it difficult for them to follow orders from native-born officers. The largest contingent were the Germans, who numbered about 200,000. Although most were scattered in various units, some fought in separate regiments such as the Steuben Volunteers and the German Rifles. The second-largest foreign-born contingent were the Irish, who numbered nearly 150,000. Other groups, such as Canadians, French, Italians, and Scandinavians, also joined the ranks of Union soldiers.

Teaching Less Proficient Readers

Making Comparisons Pair less proficient readers with more proficient ones to analyze Lincoln's and Davis's policies for handling dissent. Have the student pairs follow these steps:

1. Read page 180 of the text together.
2. Discuss civilians' opposition to war in both the North and the South.
3. Create a Venn diagram like the one shown here.

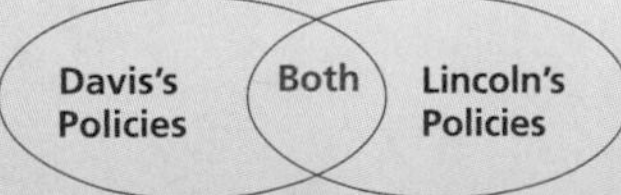

Life During Wartime

Draft riots were not the only significant development away from the battlefield. Sweeping changes occurred in the wartime economies of both sides as well as in the roles played by African Americans and women.

AFRICAN AMERICANS FIGHT FOR FREEDOM When the Civil War started, it was a white man's war. Neither the Union nor the Confederacy accepted African Americans as soldiers. Then in 1862, Congress passed a law allowing African Americans to serve in the military. It was only after the Emancipation Proclamation, however, that large-scale enlistment occurred.

African Americans, like those of Battery A of the 2nd United States Colored Artillery (shown here at gun drill), made up 10 percent of Union forces.

Although African Americans made up only 1 percent of the North's population, by war's end about 180,000 African Americans had fought for the Union—nearly 10 percent of the Northern army. African-American soldiers took part in about 500 battles, and 23 won the Medal of Honor.

In spite of their dedication, African-American soldiers in the Union army suffered discrimination. They served in separate regiments commanded by white officers and earned lower pay until the last year of the war. They also suffered a higher mortality rate than did white soldiers because many African Americans were assigned to labor duty in garrisons ridden with deadly disease. Then, too, the Confederacy did not treat captured African-American soldiers as prisoners of war. Those who were not executed on the spot were returned to slavery.

Most Southerners opposed the idea of African-American soldiers. Georgia general Howell Cobb claimed that "if slaves will make good soldiers our whole theory of slavery is wrong." Nevertheless, the South did arm some slaves in the spring of 1865 as the war drew to a close.

As Union forces pushed deeper into Confederate territory, thousands of slaves fled from their owners and sought freedom behind the lines of the Union army. Others waited on the plantations for the Northern troops to liberate their areas.

Some of the slaves that stayed on the plantations began to resist their owners. Fearful of a general slave uprising, Southerners tightened slave patrols and spread rumors about how Union soldiers abused runaways. No general uprising occurred, but slave resistance gradually weakened the plantation system. By 1864 even many Confederates realized that slavery was doomed.

THINK THROUGH HISTORY
E. *Forming Generalizations* *How did African Americans contribute to the struggle to end slavery?*

E. Answer By fighting for the North, by running away from slavery, and by resisting plantation owners.

THE WAR AFFECTS REGIONAL ECONOMIES The decline of the plantation system was not the only economic effect that the Civil War caused. In general, the war expanded the North's economy and shattered the South's.

The Confederacy soon faced a food shortage due to the drain of manpower into the army, the Union occupation of food-growing areas, and the loss of slaves to work in the fields. Meat became a once-a-week luxury at best, and even such staples as rice and corn were in short supply. Food prices skyrocketed, and the inflation rate rose 9,000 percent.

The situation grew so desperate that in 1863 hundreds of women and children—and some men—stormed bakeries and rioted for bread. In April, Mrs. Roger A. Pryor talked to an 18-year-old member of a mob in Richmond.

GLORY FOR THE 54TH MASSACHUSETTS

In July 1863, the African-American 54th Massachusetts Infantry, including a son of the famous abolitionist Frederick Douglass, led an assault on Fort Wagner, near Charleston harbor. The attack failed and more than 40 percent of the soldiers were killed. Among the survivors were Douglass's son and Sergeant William Carney, the first African American to win a Congressional Medal of Honor. Among the dead was the white commander, Colonel Robert G. Shaw.

As the New York *Tribune* pointed out, "If this Massachusetts 54th had faltered when its trial came, 200,000 troops for whom it was a pioneer would have never been put into the field. . . . It did not falter." Shaw's father declared that his son lay "with his brave, devoted followers who fell dead over him and around him. . . . What a bodyguard he has!"

OBJECTIVE
③ INSTRUCT

Life During Wartime

▶***Starting with the Student*** Have students imagine that the original prices of most consumer goods have increased by 90 times because of skyrocketing inflation. Then ask them the following questions.

- How much would a pair of gym shoes cost?
- How much would a pizza cost?

▶***Discussing Key Ideas***

- By 1862 African Americans are accepted as Union soldiers but still face discrimination.
- Overall, the Northern wartime economy expands while the South's falters.
- Soldiers withstand deplorable conditions and inhumane treatment.
- The work of Clara Barton and other nurses helps lower soldiers' death rates.

HISTORICAL SPOTLIGHT
Glory for the 54th Massachusetts

Critical Thinking: Making Characterizations Ask students to list adjectives that characterize the conduct of the African-American 54th Massachusetts Infantry. *Possible Responses: Courageous, loyal, gallant, fearless, daring, resolute.*

TEACHING OPTIONS

Making Connections Across the Curriculum

Economic Opportunity Though the Civil War caused the South's economy to topple, it invigorated some sectors of the North's economy, especially those tied to the war. For example, clothing and weapon manufacturers found the war to be a profitable venture—a source of huge profits from government contracts. Ask students why the demand for similar items in the Confederacy didn't stimulate the South's economy. *The South didn't have the industries and resources to satisfy the demand.*

Making Global Connections

Bread Riots During the French Revolution The angry mob of Southern women rioting for bread in 1863 is reminiscent of a scene from the French Revolution. The soaring price of bread left many poor mothers in Paris unable to feed their children. In October 1789, thousands of these women, brandishing pitchforks and sticks, marched to the palace of Versailles. They demanded that the French royal family—King Louis XVI, Marie Antoinette, and their son—accompany them to Paris. On the mob's return trip to Paris, some women shouted to onlookers that they had seized "the baker, the baker's wife, and the baker's boy."

MORE ABOUT . . .
The South's Economic Woes

The leaders of the Confederacy soon realized that they could not afford a long war. Treasury Secretary Christopher Memminger, chosen to tackle the impending financial crisis, had limited experience. When he took office, not one sheet of bank-note paper was available for printing money. When this shortage was remedied, so much money was printed that inflation was inevitable. Memminger became the overseer of an economy financing a war on credit with nothing but paper to back it.

MORE ABOUT . . .
Soldiers' Pastimes

Today, special officers are assigned full time to provide recreation for soldiers between battles. During the Civil War, though, soldiers were responsible for amusing themselves. The most common diversion was reading, especially in the Union army, which had a high percentage of fairly literate soldiers and an abundance of newspapers. Soldiers passed the papers around until they disintegrated. Although some men read literary works such as Shakespeare's plays, the majority enjoyed thrillers and lurid dime novels.

ELECTRONIC LIBRARY OF PRIMARY SOURCES

from *Letters to Eliza from a Union Soldier* by George Fowle

from *Diary of a Confederate Soldier* by John S. Jackman

A PERSONAL VOICE

As she raised her hand to remove her sunbonnet, her loose calico sleeve slipped up, and revealed a mere skeleton of an arm. She perceived my expression as I looked at it, and hastily pulled down her sleeve with a short laugh. "This is all that's left of me!" she said. "It seems real funny, don't it? . . . We are going to the bakeries and each of us will take a loaf of bread. That is little enough for the government to give us after it has taken all our men."

MRS. ROGER A. PRYOR, quoted in *Battle Cry of Freedom*

Overall, the war's effect on the economy of the North was much more positive. The army's need for supplies supported woolen mills, steel foundries, and many other industries. The economic boom had a dark side, though. Wages did not keep up with prices, and many people's standard of living declined. When white male workers went out on strike, employers hired free blacks, immigrants, and women to replace them for lower wages.

As the Northern economy grew, Congress decided to help pay for the war by tapping its citizens' wealth and collecting the nation's first **income tax,** a tax that takes a specified percentage of an individual's earned income. This tax ended in 1872. In 1894, when Congress passed another income tax law, the Supreme Court declared it unconstitutional. (See *taxation* on page 939 in the Economics Handbook.)

SOLDIERS SUFFER ON BOTH SIDES Both Union and Confederate soldiers had marched off to war thinking it would prove to be a glorious affair. They were soon disillusioned, not just by heavy battlefield casualties but also by such unhealthy conditions as filthy surroundings, a limited diet, and inadequate medical care. In the 1860s, the technology of killing had far outrun the technology of medical care.

Except when fighting or marching, most soldiers lived amid heaps of rubbish, spoiled food scraps, and open pits containing human excrement. In addition, soldiers had little regard for personal cleanliness. As a result, body lice, dysentery, and diarrhea were common.

Army food rations were far from appealing. Union troops subsisted on beans, bacon, pickled beef, and hardtack—square biscuits that were supposedly

Wounded Union troops recuperate after battle near makeshift field hospitals.

TEACHING OPTIONS

Making Connections Across the Curriculum

Art In October 1861, *Harper's Weekly* magazine sent American painter Winslow Homer (1836–1910) to the front lines of the Civil War. In a letter to his father, Homer wrote that his assignment as a "special artist" was to "go with the skirmishes in the next battle." During the next two years, he contributed several illustrations depicting various images of the war—combat scenes and everyday experiences. For example, the oil painting *Home, Sweet Home* shows two Union infantrymen standing near a campfire. A tin plate on the ground holds a square biscuit called hardtack.

Making Connections Across Time

Army Food Rations American soldiers during the Civil War, like their 20th-century counterparts, subsisted on food rations. World War II soldiers' "K Rations" included biscuits, canned meat, instant coffee, chewing gum, and sugar tablets. American soldiers who served in the Persian Gulf War ate "Meals Ready to Eat," or MRE's. Prepared meals, such as corned beef hash, were sealed in plastic pouches and had a shelf life of three years. The brand name of a popular dog food was a common slang expression used to describe MRE's.

hard enough to stop a bullet. Confederate troops fared equally poorly. Their most common food was "cush," a stew of small cubes of beef and crumbled cornbread mixed with bacon grease.

F. Answer Poor sanitation, malnutrition, and exposure caused disease and starvation.

THINK THROUGH HISTORY
F. *Analyzing Causes* *Why did so many prisoners of war die?*

If conditions in the army camps were bad, those in war prisons were atrocious. The Confederate camps were overcrowded and unsanitary. The South's lack of food and tent canvas also contributed to the appalling conditions. Prison camps in the North were only slightly better. Northern prisons provided more space and adequate amounts of food. However, thousands of Confederates, unaccustomed to cold winters and housed in quarters with little or no heat, contracted pneumonia and died. Historians estimate that 15 percent of Union prisoners in Southern prisons died, while 12 percent of Confederate prisoners died in Northern prisons.

Union nurses, such as Clara Barton, *below*, and Louisa May Alcott, themselves faced the hazards of disease in field hospitals.

WOMEN WORK TO IMPROVE CONDITIONS Soon after Fort Sumter fell, a group of Northern women and doctors convinced the federal government to set up the United States Sanitary Commission. The "Sanitary" proved a great success. It sent out agents to teach soldiers such things as how to avoid polluting their water supply. It developed hospital trains and hospital ships to transport wounded men from the battlefield.

Women volunteers held "sanitary fairs" to raise money for medicines and bandages, and some 3,000 women served as Union army nurses. At the age of 60, Dorothea Dix became the nation's first superintendent of women nurses. To discourage women from looking for romance, Dix insisted applicants be at least 30 and "very plain-looking." Impressed by the work of women nurses he observed, the surgeon general required that at least one-third of Union hospital nurses be women.

One dedicated Union nurse was **Clara Barton.** Barton cared for the sick and wounded, often at the front lines of battle. As a result of the Sanitary Commission's work and the tireless efforts of people like Clara Barton, the death rate among Union wounded, although terrible by 20th-century standards, showed considerable improvement over previous wars.

G. Answer Women in both the North and the South cared for the sick and wounded. Their efforts helped lower the death rate on the battlefield.

THINK THROUGH HISTORY
G. THEME *Women in America* *How did women help improve conditions on the battlefield?*

The Confederacy did not have a sanitary commission, but thousands of Southern women volunteered for nursing duty. Sally Tompkins, for example, performed so heroically in her hospital duties that she eventually was commissioned as a captain. Belle Boyd acted as both a nurse and a Confederate spy.

The nation as a whole benefited because women devoted so much time and energy to nursing. A series of battles in the Mississippi Valley and in the East soon sent casualties flooding into Northern and Southern hospitals alike.

NOW & THEN

BATTLEFIELD MEDICINE

In the Vietnam War (1954–1973) about one in every 400 wounded Americans died. In the Civil War, about one out of six died.

Medical knowledge was extremely limited in the mid-19th century. Doctors knew nothing about bacteria and how they infect the body, so they never sterilized their instruments. Antibiotics were unknown, so the only way to stop gangrene was by amputation. Anesthetics such as chloroform and ether were often in short supply.

Although both the Union and the Confederacy had a special ambulance corps to evacuate the wounded to field hospitals, many wounded died before the horse-drawn carts could get them there.

Section 2 Assessment

1. **TERMS & NAMES**
Identify:
- Fort Sumter
- Bull Run
- Stonewall Jackson
- Ulysses S. Grant
- Robert E. Lee
- Antietam
- Emancipation Proclamation
- conscription
- income tax
- Clara Barton

2. **SUMMARIZING** Create a diagram like the one shown in which you list the military actions, political issues, and social and economic changes of the first two years of the Civil War.

Civil War

	Military Actions	Political Issues	Social & Economic Changes
1.			
2.			

3. **RECOGNIZING EFFECTS** What effects did the Civil War have on women and African Americans?
THINK ABOUT
- the impact of the Emancipation Proclamation
- the efforts of women to battle disease
- discriminatory practices that persisted for both groups

4. **FORMING GENERALIZATIONS** How did the South's economy affect Confederate soldiers and civilians?
THINK ABOUT
- industrial production in the South as compared with that in the North
- decreased demand for cotton in Britain
- food shortages in the South
- the high rate of inflation in the Confederacy

ANSWERS

1. TERMS & NAMES
Fort Sumter, p. 176
Bull Run, p. 177
Stonewall Jackson, p. 177
Ulysses S. Grant, p. 177
Robert E. Lee, p. 178
Antietam, p. 178
Emancipation Proclamation, p. 179
conscription, p. 180
income tax, p. 182
Clara Barton, p. 183

2. SUMMARIZING
Military Actions: Bull Run, Shiloh, Antietam; **Political Issues:** Emancipation Proclamation, dealing with dissent, conscription; **Social and Economic Changes:** African Americans join Union Army, food shortage in South, battlefield medicine.

3. RECOGNIZING EFFECTS
Possible Responses: The roles of both groups were expanded. The Emancipation Proclamation allowed African Americans to fight for the Union. Many new jobs opened to women: nurses were in demand on both sides; Northern women replaced white males who went on strike.

4. FORMING GENERALIZATIONS
Possible Responses: Confederate soldiers and civilians both suffered. Industries in the South could not provide enough supplies for soldiers, and Britain, no longer dependent on Southern cotton, did not support the Confederacy. Civilians faced severe food shortages and high inflation rates.

NOW AND THEN
Battlefield Medicine
Have students make a concept web showing current technological advances that help save the lives of wounded soldiers.

Possible Responses: X-rays, antibiotics, new prostheses, better anesthetics, sterilized equipment.

ASSESS & RETEACH

Section 2 Assessment
Have students work individually to answer the questions. Then have them share their ideas for item 4 with the class.

Self-Assessment
Have students make a time line of key events from the fall of 1861 to the summer of 1863.

Section Quiz
FORMAL ASSESSMENT
Section Quiz, p. 55

Reteach
Use the graphic organizers students created for item 2 of the Section Assessment to review the changes brought about by the first two years of the war.

CLOSE

High death tolls on the battlefields shattered the illusion that the war would end swiftly. The first two years of the Civil War created political, social, and economic changes as people struggled with personal loss and the impending end of slavery.

Section 3 Overview

1. To show how the Union victories at Gettysburg and Vicksburg helped turn the tide for the North.
2. To trace the final events of the war, leading to the surrender at Appomattox.
3. To summarize the key economic, political, technological, and social effects of the Civil War.
4. To explain how the Civil War dramatically changed the lives of individuals.

SKILLBUILDERS

- Understanding geography: movement, location, p. 185
- Understanding geography: movement, p. 188
- Interpreting graphs, p. 189

CRITICAL THINKING

- Recognizing effects, pp. 185, 190
- Making predictions, pp. 186, 191
- Finding main ideas, p. 186
- Analyzing motives, p. 188
- Making inferences, p. 189
- Summarizing, p. 191
- Analyzing issues, p. 191

FOCUS & MOTIVATE

5-Minute Warm-Up

Interpreting Graphs
To understand the human loss suffered during the Civil War, have students study the bar graph on page 189 and answer these questions.

1. How many Union soldiers died during the war? How many Confederate soldiers died? What is the combined number of Union and Confederate losses?
2. How does the number of Civil War deaths compare with the number of deaths in other U.S. wars?

WARM-UP TRANSPARENCY 4

▶ ***Starting with the Student***
Watch the video "War Outside My Window" to find out Mary Chesnut's first-hand impressions of the Civil War.

- Using the *Teacher's Resource Book* as a guide,

(continued on next page)

❸ The North Takes Charge

TERMS & NAMES
- Gettysburg
- Vicksburg
- Gettysburg Address
- William Tecumseh Sherman
- Appomattox
- Thirteenth Amendment
- John Wilkes Booth

LEARN ABOUT the battles and events of the final two years of the war and the war's consequences
TO UNDERSTAND the political, economic, and social impact of the Civil War on the nation.

ONE AMERICAN'S STORY

Mary Chesnut was the daughter of a South Carolina governor and the wife of a U.S. senator who resigned his office to serve in the Confederate government. During the war, she recorded her observations and thoughts in a diary. Because of her prominent social position, she witnessed many key events of the time, including the formation of the Confederate government and the attack on Fort Sumter. Chesnut's diary describes not only these important events but also the details of daily life in the South—marriages and flirtations, hospital work, and dinner parties. In 1864, Chesnut went to hear Benjamin H. Palmer, a minister and professor, speak about the war. His pessimistic words filled her with foreboding about the future of the Confederacy.

A PERSONAL VOICE
September 21st . . . I did not know before how utterly hopeless was our situation. This man is so eloquent. It was hard to listen and not give way. Despair was his word—and martyrdom. He offered us nothing more in this world than the martyr's crown. . . . He spoke of these times of our agony. And then came the cry: "Help us, oh God. Vain is the help of man." And so we came away—shaken to the depths.
MARY CHESNUT, quoted in *Mary Chesnut's Civil War*

Mary Boykin Chesnut, whose portrait was painted in 1856 by Samuel Osgood, kept a detailed account of life during the Civil War.

By September 1864, the Northern armies had won several decisive battles. In spite of these victories, many Confederates refused to believe that the South would be defeated. Mary Chesnut must have had some idea of the threat posed to her way of life, however. In 1863 she wrote that the South, "the only world we cared for," had been "literally kicked to pieces."

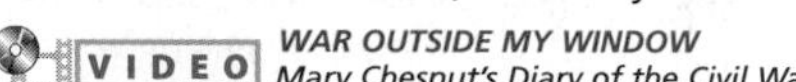
VIDEO *WAR OUTSIDE MY WINDOW*
Mary Chesnut's Diary of the Civil War

The Tide Turns

The year 1863 actually had begun well for the South. In December 1862, Lee's army had inflicted a bloody defeat on the Army of the Potomac at Fredericksburg, Virginia. Then, in May, the South defeated the North again at Chancellorsville, Virginia. The North's only consolation after Chancellorsville came as the result of an accident. As General Stonewall Jackson returned from a patrol on May 2, Confederate guards accidentally shot him in the left arm. A surgeon amputated his arm the following day. When Lee heard the news, he exclaimed, "He has lost his left arm but I have lost my right." For Lee, the true loss was still to come; Jackson caught pneumonia and died on May 10.

Despite Jackson's tragic death, Lee decided to press his military advantage and invade the North. He needed supplies and he thought that a major Confederate victory on Northern soil might tip the balance of power in the Union to the pro-Southern politicians. Accordingly, he crossed the Potomac into Maryland and then pushed on into Pennsylvania.

SECTION 3 RESOURCES

PRINT RESOURCES

IN-DEPTH RESOURCES: UNIT 1
Guided Reading, p. 99
Primary Source: On the Burning of Columbia, South Carolina, p. 111

READING STUDY GUIDE, p. 51

ACCESS FOR STUDENTS ACQUIRING ENGLISH
Guided Reading (Spanish), p. 69

SPANISH READING STUDY GUIDE, p. 51

FORMAL ASSESSMENT
Section Quiz, p. 56

ALTERNATIVE ASSESSMENT BOOK
See forms for supporting and scoring alternative activities.

TECHNOLOGY RESOURCES

HUMANITIES TRANSPARENCIES
H11, *Abraham Lincoln riding into Richmond, Virginia*

CRITICAL THINKING TRANSPARENCIES
CT11, Civil War
CT45, North vs. South

CD-ROM *Grolier Multimedia Encyclopedia*
Electronic Library of Primary Sources

VIDEO *American Stories* video series
American Portfolio: A Videodisc for U.S. History user's guide, pp. 102–107, 111–113, 115

INTERNET http://www.mlushistory.com

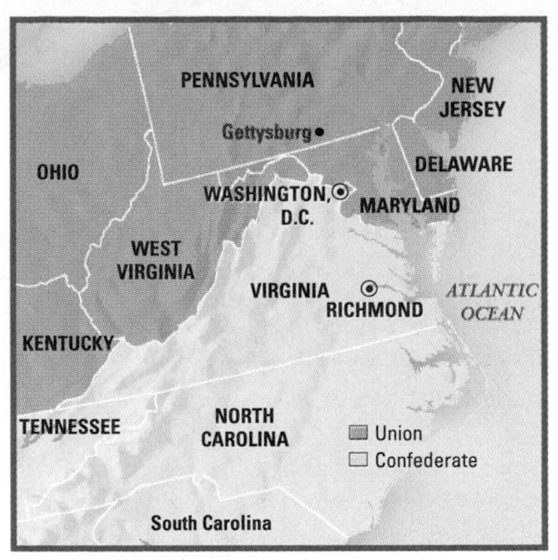

GEOGRAPHY SKILLBUILDER
MOVEMENT *Which side clearly took the offensive in the Battle of Gettysburg?*
LOCATION *Based on the information in the larger map, indicate what factor may have made it easier for reinforcements to enter the Gettysburg area.*

Skillbuilder Answers **Movement:** The Confederates took the offensive. **Location:** *Possible Answer:* Roads from many directions converge in the Gettysburg area.

THE BATTLE OF GETTYSBURG Near the sleepy town of Gettysburg, Pennsylvania, the most decisive battle of the war was fought. The Battle of **Gettysburg** began on July 1 when Confederate soldiers led by A. P. Hill encountered a couple of brigades of Union cavalry under the command of John Buford, an experienced officer from Illinois.

Buford ordered his men to take defensive positions on the hills and ridges surrounding the town. When Hill's troops marched toward the town from the west, Buford's men were waiting. The shooting attracted more troops, and both sides called for reinforcements. By the end of the first day of fighting, 90,000 Union troops under the command of General George Meade had taken the field against 75,000 Confederates, led by General Lee.

By the second day of battle, the Confederates had driven the Union troops from Gettysburg and had taken control of the town. However, the Northerners still held positions on Cemetery Ridge, the high ground south of Gettysburg. The Confederates repeatedly attacked the Union lines. Although the Union troops were forced to concede some territory, their lines withheld the withering Confederate onslaught.

On July 3, Lee ordered an artillery barrage on the center of the Union lines on Cemetery Ridge. Believing they had silenced the Union guns, the Confederates then charged the lines. Suddenly, Northern artillery renewed its barrage, and the infantry fired on the rebels as well. Devastated, the Confederates staggered back to their lines. After the battle, Lee gave up any hopes of invading the North and led his army back to Virginia.

The three-day battle produced staggering losses: 23,000 Union men and 28,000 Confederates were killed or wounded. Despite the devastation, Northerners were enthusiastic about breaking "the charm of Robert Lee's invincibility." Lee would continue to lead his men brilliantly in the next two years of the war, but neither he nor the Confederacy would ever recover from the loss at Gettysburg—or the surrender of Vicksburg, which occurred the very next day.

A. Answer It cost a huge number of casualties and demoralized the Confederates.

THINK THROUGH HISTORY
A. *Recognizing Effects* *Why was the Battle of Gettysburg a disaster for the South?*

(continued from page 184)

hold a class discussion about Chesnut's vivid portrayal of the Civil War era.

***AMERICAN STORIES* video series**
"War Outside My Window"
Videocassette: Volume 1

Videodisc: Disc 1, Side A, Chapter 2

OBJECTIVE
① INSTRUCT

The Tide Turns

Discussing Key Ideas

- With huge losses on both sides, Union troops defeat the Confederates at the battle of Gettysburg.
- Grant's victory at Vicksburg cuts the Confederacy in two.
- Lincoln's Gettysburg Address clarifies the North's reasons for fighting the war.

IN-DEPTH RESOURCES: UNIT 1
Guided Reading, p. 99

ACCESS FOR STUDENTS ACQUIRING ENGLISH
Guided Reading (Spanish), p. 69

HISTORY FROM VISUALS

Battle of Gettysburg, July 1863

Reading the Map Review the color coding on the map key representing Union and Confederate positions for each day of the battle. Have students reread the portions of the text corresponding to the military maneuvers that occurred on July 1–3 to help them visualize how these map symbols illustrate the daily progression of the battle.

TEACHING OPTION

Teaching Less Proficient Readers

Tracking Sequence To help less proficient readers trace the sequence of military actions during the Battle of Gettysburg, put the following set of three flow charts on the board. Then have students fill in the boxes with key events arranged in chronological order.

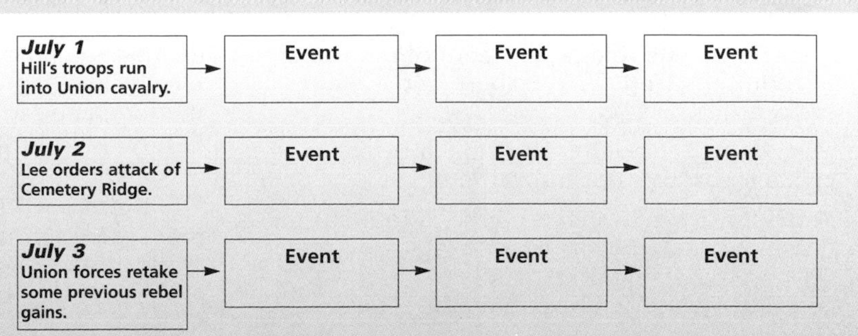

MORE ABOUT . . .
The Siege of Vicksburg

A few of the hillside caves where civilians hid during the siege were surprisingly homelike. Some of those living in the dugout rooms contained rugs, beds, and chairs. However, most of those living in makeshift caves in Vicksburg suffered extreme discomfort. One woman remarked, "It was living like plant roots."

ANOTHER PERSPECTIVE
On Lincoln's Speech

Critical Thinking: Evaluating Have students identify the qualities of Lincoln's speech that Edward Everett most admired. Ask them if Everett would have agreed with this quotation from Shakespeare's play *Hamlet:* "Brevity is the soul of wit."

OBJECTIVE
② **INSTRUCT**

The Confederacy Wears Down

▶ ***Discussing Key Ideas***

- The South's morale deteriorates.
- Grant appoints Sherman commander of the Military Division of the Mississippi.
- Grant's attack on Lee's forces in Virginia results in heavy casualties.
- Sherman's march through the South causes widespread destruction.
- The fall of Atlanta contributes to Lincoln's re-election in 1864.
- Lee's surrender to Grant at Appomattox in 1865 marks the end of the Civil War.

GRANT WINS AT VICKSBURG While the Army of the Potomac was destroying Confederate hopes in Gettysburg, Union general Ulysses S. Grant fought to gain control of the Mississippi River. **Vicksburg** was one of the two remaining Confederate strongholds on the river. Grant's efforts were unsuccessful—until the spring of 1863.

ANOTHER PERSPECTIVE

ON LINCOLN'S SPEECH

At the time of the Gettysburg Address, many dismissed it as a poor speech. Lincoln himself was displeased with his performance. "That speech won't scour," he said afterward. "It's a flat failure."

A writer for the London *Times* also criticized the speech. "The ceremony was rendered ludicrous by . . . the sallies of that poor President Lincoln."

However, Edward Everett, the other speaker, recognized the speech's greatness. Writing to Lincoln, he said, "I should be glad if I could flatter myself that I came as near to the central idea of the occasion, in two hours, as you did in two minutes."

Grant began by weakening the Confederate defenses that protected Vicksburg. Then he and his troops rushed to the Mississippi city, hoping to take it while the rebels were reeling from their losses. Grant ordered two frontal assaults on Vicksburg, neither of which succeeded. So, in the last week of May 1863, Grant settled in for a siege. He set up a steady barrage of artillery for several hours a day, forcing the city's residents into caves that they dug out of the yellow clay hillsides.

After food supplies ran so low that people were reduced to eating dogs and mules, the Confederate commander of Vicksburg asked Grant for terms of surrender. The city fell on July 4. Five days later Port Hudson, Louisiana, the last Confederate holdout on the Mississippi, also fell—and the Confederacy was cut in two.

THINK THROUGH HISTORY
B. *Making Predictions* *What impact do you think the defeats of Gettysburg and Vicksburg will have on the South?*

B. Answer Most students will say that the defeats will cripple the South.

THE GETTYSBURG ADDRESS In November 1863, a ceremony was held to dedicate a cemetery in Gettysburg. The authorities invited Edward Everett, a noted orator, to deliver the main speech at the dedication. When Lincoln accepted a belated invitation to attend, the authorities invited him to add "a few appropriate remarks."

After Everett gave a flowery two-hour oration, Lincoln spoke for a little more than two minutes. According to some contemporary historians, Lincoln's **Gettysburg Address** "remade America." Before Lincoln's speech, people said, "The United States are." Afterwards, they said, "The United States is." In other words, the speech helped the country to realize that it was not just a collection of individual states; it was a single nation.

"Government of the people, by the people, for the people, shall not perish from the earth."
ABRAHAM LINCOLN

THE GETTYSBURG ADDRESS

Fourscore and seven years ago our fathers brought forth on this continent a new nation, conceived in Liberty and dedicated to the proposition that all men are created equal.

Now we are engaged in a great civil war, testing whether that nation, or any nation so conceived and so dedicated, can long endure. We are met on a great battlefield of that war. We have come to dedicate a portion of that field, as a final resting-place for those who here gave their lives that that nation might live. It is altogether fitting and proper that we should do this.

But, in a larger sense, we can not dedicate—we can not consecrate—we can not hallow—this ground. The brave men, living and dead, who struggled here, have consecrated it, far above our poor power to add or detract. The world will little note, nor long remember, what we say here, but it can never forget what they did here. It is for us the living, rather, to be dedicated here to the unfinished work which they who fought here have thus far so nobly advanced. It is rather for us to be here dedicated to the great task remaining before us—that from these honored dead we take increased devotion to that cause for which they gave the last full measure of devotion—that we here highly resolve that these dead shall not have died in vain—that this nation, under God, shall have a new birth of freedom—and that government of the people, by the people, for the people, shall not perish from the earth.

ABRAHAM LINCOLN, *The Gettysburg Address, November 19, 1863*

C. Answer That it was one nation rather than just a collection of states, that it was worth dying for, and that it should not be destroyed.

THINK THROUGH HISTORY
C. *Finding Main Ideas* *What ideas about the United States did Lincoln express in the Gettysburg Address?*

The Confederacy Wears Down

The twin defeats at Gettysburg and Vicksburg cost the South much of its limited manpower. The Confederacy was already low on food, shoes, uniforms,

Block Schedule TEACHING OPTION **Time Needed: 30 Minutes**

Cooperative Activity: News Accounts of a City Under Siege

Task: Students role-play a team of reporters covering the siege of Vicksburg and write news articles.

Purpose: To heighten students' awareness of civilians' ordeals during wartime.

Activity: Have groups of three to four students research the siege of Vicksburg's impact on civilians. Assuming the identity of a war correspondent, each group member should choose an angle of the siege to cover. Examples include the extreme psychological stress, the food shortages, and the people's plummeting morale. Group members should review one another's drafts and suggest revisions.

Building a Portfolio: Students who think their news accounts represent their strongest work should place them in their portfolios.

ALTERNATIVE ASSESSMENT BOOK
Standards for Evaluating a Cooperative Activity

Standards for Evaluation
News accounts should . . .

- show evidence of research beyond the text
- include vivid details, anecdotes, and factual information
- create a sense of immediacy

guns, and ammunition. No longer able to attack, it could hope only to hang on long enough to destroy Northern morale and work toward an armistice. That plan proved increasingly unlikely, however, in part because Southern newspapers, state legislatures, and individuals began to call openly for peace, and in part because Lincoln finally found not just one but two generals who would fight.

MORALE IN THE CONFEDERACY As the war progressed, morale on the Confederacy's home front deteriorated. Farmers resented the tax that took part of their crops. Some soldiers deserted after receiving pleading letters from home about the lack of food and the shortage of labor to work the farms. In every Southern state except South Carolina, there were soldiers who decided to fight for the Union army. Peace movements sprang up in some states.

In the meantime, members of the Confederate Congress squabbled among themselves. Some even resorted to physical attacks, using everything from fists and inkstands to revolvers and Bowie knives. In South Carolina, the governor was upset when troops from his state were placed under the command of officers from another state. Such discord made it impossible for Jefferson Davis to govern effectively.

GRANT AND SHERMAN WAGE TOTAL WAR In March 1864, President Lincoln appointed Ulysses S. Grant commander of all Union armies. Grant in turn appointed **William Tecumseh Sherman** as commander of the military division of the Mississippi. These two appointments would change the course of the war.

Old friends and comrades in arms, both men believed in total war. They shared the conviction that it was essential to fight not only the South's armies and government but its civilian population as well. They reasoned that the strength of the people's will kept the war going. If the Union destroyed that will to fight, the Confederacy would collapse.

Grant's overall strategy was to grind up Lee's army in Virginia while Sherman raided Georgia. Even if his casualties ran twice as high as those of Lee—and they did—the North could afford it. The South could not.

During the period from May to June 1864, Grant lost 65,000 men—which the North could replace—to Lee's 35,000 men—which the South could not replace. Democrats and Northern newspapers called Grant a butcher. However, Grant kept going because he had promised Lincoln, "Whatever happens, there will be no turning back."

KEY PLAYERS

ULYSSES S. GRANT
1822–1885

U. S. Grant took a long time to discover himself—just about as long as it took the rest of the world to figure out who he was. Born Hiram Ulysses Grant, he allowed a clerk at West Point to record his name incorrectly as Ulysses Simpson Grant. Thereafter, he went by the name U.S. Grant.

Grant once said of himself, "A military life held no charms for me." Yet, a military man was what he was destined to be. He fought in the war with Mexico—even though he termed it "wicked"—because he believed his duty was to serve his country. His next post was in the West, where Grant grew so lonely for his family that he resigned.

When the Civil War broke out, the Illinois governor made Grant a colonel of volunteers because the federal government didn't want him! However, once Grant began fighting in Tennessee, Lincoln was quick to recognize his special strength. When newspapers demanded Grant's dismissal after Shiloh, Lincoln replied firmly, "I can't spare this man. He *fights.*"

ROBERT E. LEE
1807–1870

Lee was an aristocrat, related to some of Virginia's leading families. In fact, his father, Light-Horse Harry Lee, had been one of George Washington's best generals, and his wife was the great-granddaughter of Martha Washington. His sense of family honor may have contributed to his allegiance to his state. As a man who believed slavery was evil (but owned several slaves nonetheless), Lee fought for the Confederacy only because of his loyalty to his beloved Virginia. "I did only what my duty demanded. I could have taken no other course without dishonor," he said.

As a general, Robert E. Lee was tactically brilliant, but he seldom challenged Confederate civilian leaders about their failure to provide his army with adequate food, clothing, or weapons. On the other hand, his soldiers almost worshiped him because he never abused them and always insisted on sharing their hardships. His men called him Uncle Robert, just as the Union troops called Grant Uncle Sam.

KEY PLAYERS
Grant and Lee

Critical Thinking: Compare and Contrast
Have students create a two-column chart comparing Grant and Lee. *Possible Headings: Background, Military Career, Leadership Style, Character Traits.*

MORE ABOUT . . .
Sherman on War

Before burning Atlanta, Sherman ordered its citizens evacuated. The mayor of Atlanta wrote a letter of protest, to which Sherman replied that war is inherently cruel and cannot be changed into something humane. "The only way the people of Atlanta can hope once more to live in peace and quiet at home, is to stop the war, which can only be done by admitting that it began in error and is perpetuated in pride. We don't want . . . your lands, or any thing you have, but we do want and will have a just obedience to the laws of the United States."

IN-DEPTH RESOURCES: UNIT 1
Primary Source: On the Burning of Columbia, South Carolina, p. 111

ELECTRONIC LIBRARY OF PRIMARY SOURCES
from A Letter to General Hood by General Sherman
from A Letter to General Sherman by General Hood

TEACHING OPTIONS

Making Connections Across Time

Military Tactics Civil War historian Bruce Catton offered these observations on total war: "In the Civil War it was all or nothing. . . . Once a little blood had been shed, there was no halfway point at which the two sides could get together and compromise. . . . If you are fighting a total war, the enemy's army is not your own target. What you are really shooting for is the ability to carry on the fight. This means you will hit wherever you can with any weapon that comes into your hand." The Civil War set the stage for the way the two world wars in the twentieth century would be waged: Both military and civilian populations participated.

Making Connections Across the Curriculum

Journalism The telegraph, invented in 1844, had its greatest effect on news reporting during the Civil War. Journalists covering battle sites, such as Fredericksburg, Spotsylvania, and Petersburg, relayed their accounts by telegraph. Because technical difficulties sometimes occurred while transmitting their stories, journalists tried to report the outcome of the battle first and then describe the events more concisely. This approach to newswriting was the forerunner of the form called the *inverted pyramid,* in which the lead sentence summarizes the most important point of the story.

HISTORY FROM VISUALS

Civil War, 1863–1865

Reading the Map Emphasize the close distance between Washington, D.C., and Richmond, Virginia, as shown on the inset. Also point out the parallel movements of Union and Confederate forces in the vicinity of the capitals during the final two years of the Civil War.

Extension Ask students to describe the path of Sherman's march. *Response: Southeast through Georgia to the Atlantic coast.*

MORE ABOUT . . .

The 1864 Election Campaign

Mudslinging in presidential campaigns is nothing new. In 1864, McClellan's partisans hurled such epithets at Lincoln as "filthy storyteller, despot, liar, robber, swindler, buffoon, and Ignoramus Abe." Even more vicious was the accusation that the President had laughed and joked during a visit to Antietam shortly after the bloody battle there. A close Lincoln supporter urged him to issue a denial. Lincoln, however, told his supporter to "let the thing alone" and added: "If I have not established character enough to give the lie to this charge, I can only say that I am mistaken in my own estimate of myself. In politics, every man must skin his own skunk. These fellows are welcome to the hide of this one. Its body has already given forth its unsavory odor."

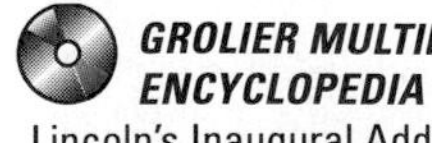

GROLIER MULTIMEDIA ENCYCLOPEDIA

Lincoln's Inaugural Addresses

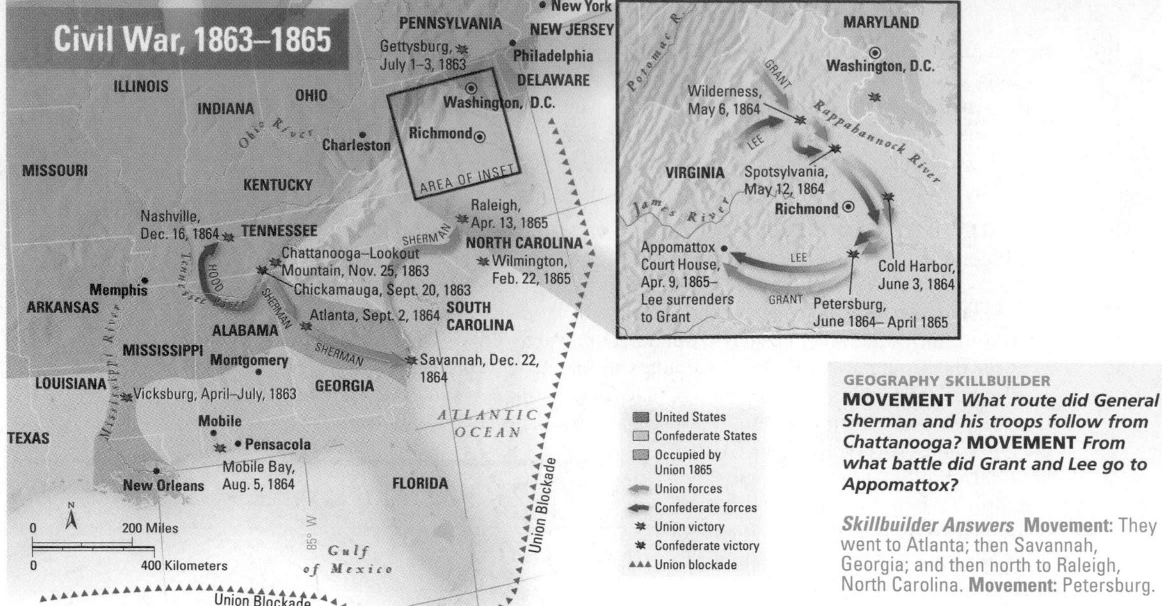

GEOGRAPHY SKILLBUILDER

MOVEMENT *What route did General Sherman and his troops follow from Chattanooga?* **MOVEMENT** *From what battle did Grant and Lee go to Appomattox?*

Skillbuilder Answers **Movement:** They went to Atlanta; then Savannah, Georgia; and then north to Raleigh, North Carolina. **Movement:** Petersburg.

"Atlanta is ours."

WILLIAM TECUMSEH SHERMAN

SHERMAN'S MARCH In the meantime, Sherman marched southeast through Georgia to the sea, creating a wide path of destruction. He was determined to make Southerners "so sick of war that generations would pass away before they would again appeal to it." By mid-November he had burned most of Atlanta.

After reaching the ocean, Sherman's forces—followed by 25,000 former slaves—turned north to help Grant "wipe out Lee." On its northward march, the army inflicted even more destruction in South Carolina than it had in Georgia. As an Ohio private explained, "Here is where treason began and, by God, here is where it shall end!" In contrast, when Sherman's troops entered North Carolina, which had been the last state to secede, they stopped destroying private homes and instead began handing out food and other supplies to people they encountered.

THINK THROUGH HISTORY

D. *Analyzing Motives* *What were Sherman's objectives in marching his troops from Atlanta to Savannah?*

D. Answer Sherman wanted to show Southerners the destructive nature of war and thus destroy the will of Confederate civilians to continue the war.

THE ELECTION OF 1864 Despite the war, politics in the Union went on as usual. As the 1864 presidential election approached, Lincoln faced heavy opposition from the Democrats and from a faction within his own party. Many Democrats, dismayed at the war's length and its high casualty rates, joined pro-Southerners to nominate George McClellan on a platform of an immediate armistice. Still resentful over having been fired by Lincoln, McClellan was delighted to run. Lincoln's other opponents, the Radical Republicans, formed a third political party and nominated John C. Frémont as their candidate.

Lincoln was pessimistic about his chances. "I am going to be beaten," he said in August, "and unless some great change takes place, badly beaten." However, some great change did take place. News of General Sherman's victories buoyed the North. By the end of September, Frémont had withdrawn from the presidential race. With the help of absentee ballots cast by Union soldiers, Lincoln won a second term with 55 percent of the popular vote.

THE SURRENDER AT APPOMATTOX By late March 1865, it was clear that the end of the Confederacy was near. Grant was approaching Richmond from the west, while Sherman was approaching from the south. On April 2—in response to news that Lee and his troops had been overcome by Grant's forces at Petersburg—President Davis and his government abandoned their capital, setting it afire to keep the Northerners from taking it. Union troops entered

TEACHING OPTION

Teaching Gifted and Talented Students

Researching the Election of 1864 Ask students to investigate the election of 1864. Students should identify the candidates, the political parties they represented, the events that influenced the election, and the final outcome. The research should include the final figures of the popular and electoral vote:

- Abraham Lincoln—212 electoral votes; 2,206,938 popular votes.
- George McClellan—21 electoral votes; 1,803,787 popular votes.

Encourage students to use charts and graphs to report their findings. For example, they may wish to create bar graphs showing the number of electoral and popular votes each candidate received and circle graphs to show the percentages of electoral and popular votes.

Richmond the following day. Despite their efforts to extinguish the flames, fire destroyed some 900 buildings and damaged hundreds more.

THINK THROUGH HISTORY
E. *Making Inferences* *Why do you think Lincoln didn't want to punish the Confederacy?*

On April 9, 1865, at a private home in a Virginia village called **Appomattox** Court House, Lee and Grant met to arrange a Confederate surrender. At Lincoln's request, the terms were generous. Grant paroled Lee's soldiers and sent them home with their possessions and three days worth of rations. Officers were permitted to keep their side arms. Within a month all remaining Confederate resistance collapsed. After four long years, the Civil War was over.

Though both Union and Confederate soldiers were lucky to escape the war with their lives, thousands—like this young amputee—faced an uncertain future.

The War Changes the Nation

E. Answer He wanted to bring the South back into the Union as smoothly as possible.

In 1869 Professor George Ticknor of Harvard commented that since the Civil War, "It does not seem to me as if I were living in the country in which I was born." The Civil War caused tremendous political, economic, technological, and social change in the United States. It also exacted a high price in terms of human life.

The human costs of the Civil War were staggering. Approximately 360,000 Union soldiers and 260,000 Confederates died, nearly as many as in all other American wars combined. One soldier was killed or wounded for every four slaves who became free. In addition, military service occupied the lives of some 3,000,000 men—nearly 10 percent of the nation's population of 31,000,000—for four long years. It disrupted their education, their careers, and their families.

POLITICAL CHANGES The United States underwent great political change because of the Civil War. Before the war, Southern states had used the threat of secession when federal policies angered them. After the war, no state ever threatened secession again. The states' rights issue did not go away; it simply led in directions other than secession. Late-20th-century arguments about states' rights focus on such issues as whether the state or national government should determine how to use local resources.

The Civil War also greatly increased the federal government's power. During the war, the federal government passed laws, including income tax and conscription laws, that gave it much more control over individual citizens. As a result, U.S. citizens could no longer assume that the national government in Washington was too far away to bother with them.

Skillbuilder Answers
Losses: The total losses for the Civil War nearly equaled the total for all other wars. **Inflation:** *Possible Answer:* The shortages of food and other supplies were more severe in the South, so most products cost more than in the North.

ECONOMIC CHANGES The Civil War dramatically widened the economic gap between North and South. During the war, the economy of the Northern states boomed. By war's end, the North had produced more coal, iron, merchant ships, and other products than the entire country had in 1860. The Southern economy, on the other hand, was devastated. The war not only marked the end of slavery as a labor system but also wrecked most of the region's industry, wiped out 40 percent of the livestock, destroyed much of the South's farm machinery and railroads, and left thousands of acres of uncultivated farmland in weeds. The economic gulf between the regions would not diminish until the 20th century.

The Costs of the Civil War

CASUALTIES

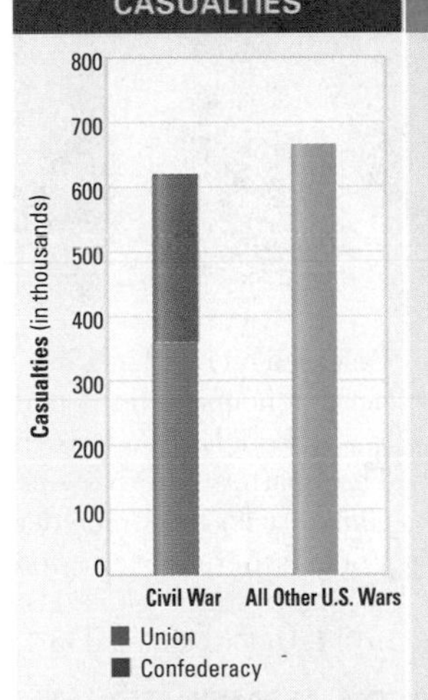

Sources: *The World Book Encyclopedia; Historical Statistics of the United States: Colonial times to 1970; The United States Civil War Center*

ECONOMIC COSTS

- Federal loans and taxes to finance the war totaled $2.6 billion.
- Taxes brought in another $667 million.
- Federal debt on June 30, 1865 rose to $2.7 billion.
- Confederate debt ran over $700 million.
- Union inflation reached 182% in 1864 and 179% in 1865.
- Confederate inflation rose to 9,000% by the end of the war.

SKILLBUILDER **INTERPRETING GRAPHS** *Based on the bar graph, how did the combined Union and Confederate losses compare with those of other wars? Why was inflation worse in the Confederacy than in the Union?*

MORE ABOUT . . .
Lee's Farewell

On April 10, 1865, General Robert. E. Lee addressed the Army of Northern Virginia. These were his parting words: "With an increasing admiration of your constancy and devotion to your country, and a grateful remembrance of your kind and generous consideration of myself, I bid you an affectionate farewell."

HUMANITIES TRANSPARENCIES
H11, *Abraham Lincoln riding into Richmond, Virginia*

OBJECTIVE
③ INSTRUCT

The War Changes the Nation

▶ ***Discussing Key Ideas***
- The Civil War greatly increases the federal government's authority.
- The economic rift between the North and the South widens.
- New technologies transform warfare.

HISTORY FROM VISUALS
The Costs of the Civil War

Reading the Graph In this case, "costs" involve both money and lives.

CRITICAL THINKING TRANSPARENCIES
CT45, North vs. South

TEACHING OPTIONS

Making Connections Across the Curriculum

Business Some great business tycoons of the post–Civil War era launched their careers during the war. Entrepreneurial skills, new available technology, and the capital gained from wartime profits helped the following men become industrial giants.

- Philip Armour—a meat packer who later introduced refrigeration and canned meats to the American public.
- John D. Rockefeller—an oil mogul who began refining oil in 1862 and by 1870 had monopolized the oil industry.
- Andrew Carnegie—a rags-to-riches businessman who later became the captain of the steel industry.

Making Connections Across the Curriculum

Economics The enormous casualties of the Civil War created long-term economic hardship for many American women—especially wives of soldiers either killed or wounded in battle and unmarried women. To survive financially, most of these women found themselves scraping by on meager incomes. Sewing, their chief marketable skill, commanded very low wages. Even those with professional job skills faced a difficult transition. Teacher, writer, and editor Eliza Frances Andrew was forced to earn a living in the 1870s "though wholly unprepared either by nature or training for a life of self-dependence."

OBJECTIVE

④ INSTRUCT

The War Changes Lives

▶ ***Starting with the Student***

- Ask students what they know about the kinds of problems war veterans face when they return to civilian life.
- Have them discuss why this transition is often so difficult.

▶ ***Discussing Key Ideas***

- The Thirteenth Amendment abolishes slavery.
- Civil War veterans adapt to civilian life.
- Lincoln is assassinated in 1865.

MORE ABOUT . . .
Booth's Alleged Co-Conspirators

Mary Surratt, a widow, ran a boarding house in Washington, D.C., where John Wilkes Booth sometimes met with a small group of followers. After Booth assassinated Lincoln, Surratt was accused of acting as an accomplice in the crime. The prosecution suppressed Booth's diary, which cast doubt on Surratt's guilt, and evidently she did not take part in planning the assassination. Nevertheless, she was convicted and hanged on July 7, 1865. Dr. Samuel Mudd, who set Booth's broken leg after he fled from Ford's Theater, was sentenced to life imprisonment, as were two other men. Edward Spangler, a stagehand at Ford's Theater charged with having held Booth's horse during the assassination, received a prison term of six years.

A REVOLUTION IN WARFARE The Civil War was one of the first modern wars. The two deadliest technological improvements were the rifle and the minié ball, a soft lead bullet that was more destructive than earlier bullets. Two other modern weapons used were hand grenades and land mines.

Another technological improvement was the ironclad ship, which could splinter wooden ships, withstand cannon fire, and resist burning. On March 9, 1862, every navy in the world became obsolete after the North's ironclad *Monitor* traded broadsides with the South's ironclad *Merrimack*. Although the battle ended in a draw, it signaled the end of wooden warships.

THINK THROUGH HISTORY
F. *Recognizing Effects* *How did technology affect the Civil War?*

F. Answer Deadlier weapons caused greater destruction. Ironclad ships made wooden ones obsolete.

The War Changes Lives

The war not only revolutionized weaponry but also changed individual lives. Perhaps the biggest change came for African Americans.

THE THIRTEENTH AMENDMENT The Emancipation Proclamation freed only those slaves who lived in the rebelling states. The government had to decide what to do about the border states, where slavery still existed. The president believed that the only solution was a constitutional amendment abolishing slavery.

Former slaves, like the four-generation family shown here, celebrated the passage of the Thirteenth Amendment, which abolished slavery.

After some political maneuvering, the **Thirteenth Amendment** was ratified at the end of 1865. The U.S. Constitution now stated, "Neither slavery nor involuntary servitude, except as a punishment for crime whereof the party shall have been duly convicted, shall exist within the United States."

LEADERS RETURN TO CIVILIAN LIFE After the war ended, military leaders in both the North and the South had to find new directions for their lives.

William Tecumseh Sherman remained in the army and spent most of his time fighting Native Americans in the West. When Republicans tried to convince him to run for the presidency in 1884, he replied, "If nominated I will not run; if elected I will not serve." He died in 1891.

Jefferson Davis was captured in Georgia a month after fleeing Richmond and imprisoned. Released on bond in 1867, he spent the rest of his life writing his memoirs. He never renounced his belief in the Confederate cause and died in 1889.

Robert E. Lee lost Arlington, the plantation that his wife had inherited. The quartermaster general of the Union had turned Lee's front lawn into a cemetery for the Union dead so that no one would ever live in the house again. Congress refused to restore Lee's citizenship even though he swore renewed allegiance to the United States. Still, Lee never spoke bitterly of Northerners or the Union. He died in 1870.

THE ASSASSINATION OF LINCOLN Whatever plans Lincoln had to reunify the nation after the war, he never got to implement them. On April 14, 1865, five days after Lee surrendered to Grant at Appomattox, Lincoln and his wife went to Ford's Theatre in Washington to see a British comedy, *Our American Cousin*. As the play drew to its close, a man crept up behind Lincoln and shot the president in the back of his head.

The assassin, **John Wilkes Booth**—a 26-year-old actor and Southern sympathizer—then leaped down from the presidential box to the stage. In doing so,

TEACHING OPTIONS

Making Connections Across Time

Assassinations Lincoln was the first of four presidents to fall prey to an assassin's bullet. In 1881, a mentally disturbed office seeker shot President James Garfield while entering a railroad station in Washington, D.C. In 1901, an anarchist at the Pan-American Exposition in Buffalo, New York, shot President William McKinley soon after his reelection. In 1963, a sniper killed John Kennedy, who was riding in a motorcade in Dallas, Texas. Andrew Jackson, Franklin Roosevelt, Harry Truman, Gerald Ford, and Ronald Reagan were all targets of failed assassination attempts.

Making Connections Across the Curriculum

Literature Walt Whitman describes Lincoln's funeral train in the poem "When Lilacs Last in the Dooryard Bloom'd":

Coffin that passes through lanes and streets,
Through day and night with the great cloud darkening
 the land,
With the pomp of the inloop'd flags with the cities
 draped in black,
With the show of the States themselves as of crape-veil'd
 women standing,
With processions long and winding and the flambeaus
 of the night,
With the countless torches lit, with the silent sea of faces.

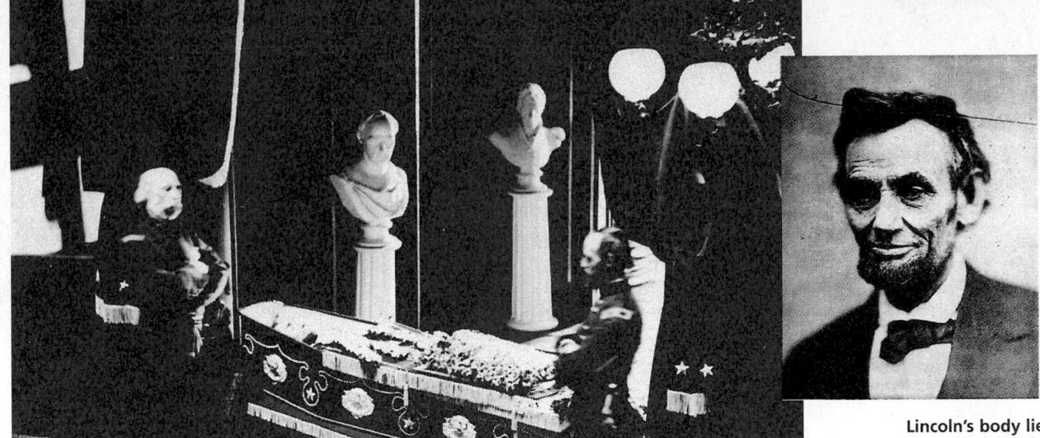

Lincoln's body lies in state *(above left).* The last known photograph of the president was taken by Alexander Gardner on April 10, 1865—four days before Lincoln was assassinated *(above right).*

he caught his spur on one of the flags draped across the front of the box. Booth landed hard on his left leg and broke it.

Despite his broken leg, Booth managed to escape. Twelve days later, however, Union cavalry trapped him in a Virginia tobacco shed, shot him, and then dragged him out. Booth is said to have died whispering, "Tell my mother I died for my country. I did what I thought was best."

Lincoln, who never regained consciousness, died on April 15. It was the first time a president of the United States had been assassinated. Secretary of the Navy Gideon Welles recorded people's reactions in his diary.

A PERSONAL VOICE

It was a dark and gloomy morning, and rain set in. . . . On the Avenue in front of the White House were several hundred colored people, mostly women and children, weeping and wailing their loss. This crowd did not appear to diminish through the whole of that cold, wet day; they seemed not to know what was to be their fate since their great benefactor was dead, and their hopeless grief affected me more than almost anything else, though strong and brave men wept when I met them.

GIDEON WELLES, quoted in *Voices from the Civil War*

G. Answer Some students may say that Southerners rejoiced at the news. Others may think that Southerners were upset by Lincoln's death, because he had dealt fairly with the Confederates.

THINK THROUGH HISTORY
G. Making Predictions *How do you think Southerners reacted to the news of Lincoln's assassination?*

The funeral train that carried Lincoln's body from Washington to his hometown of Springfield, Illinois, took 14 days for its journey. Approximately 7 million Americans, or almost one-third of the entire Union population, turned out to publicly mourn their martyred leader.

The Civil War had ended. Slavery and secession were no more. Now the country faced two different problems: how to restore the Southern states to the Union and how to integrate approximately 4 million newly freed African Americans into national life.

Section  3 Assessment

1. TERMS & NAMES

Identify:
- Gettysburg
- Vicksburg
- Gettysburg Address
- William Tecumseh Sherman
- Appomattox
- Thirteenth Amendment
- John Wilkes Booth

2. SUMMARIZING Copy the multiple-effects chart below on your paper and fill it in with consequences of the Civil War.

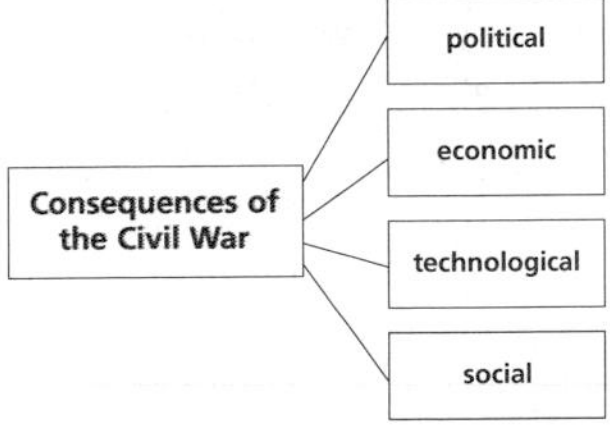

3. ANALYZING ISSUES Grant and Sherman presented a logical rationale for using the strategy of total war. Do you think the end—defeating the Confederacy—justified the means—causing harm to civilians? Explain.

THINK ABOUT
- their reasons for targeting the civilian population
- Sherman's quoted remarks about Georgia on page 188
- Sherman's march through Georgia and South Carolina

4. MAKING PREDICTIONS What do you think the government will do to help the South rebuild after the Civil War?

THINK ABOUT
- the economic devastation of the South
- the human costs of the war
- the numbers of newly freed slaves

ANSWERS

1. TERMS & NAMES

Gettysburg, p. 185
Vicksburg, p. 186
Gettysburg Address, p. 186
William Tecumseh Sherman, p. 187
Appomattox, p. 189
Thirteenth Amendment, p. 190
John Wilkes Booth, p. 190

2. SUMMARIZING

Possible Response: **Political**—Freed enslaved people; ended secession threat. **Economic**—Stimulated economic growth of the North and contributed to economic decline of the South. **Technological**—Introduced rifle, minié ball, and ironclad ship. **Social**—Disrupted families because of the staggering loss of lives.

3. ANALYZING ISSUES

Possible Responses: Students who think that the end does justify the means might say that winning the war and abolishing slavery is worth the cost of civilian lives. Students who think that the end does not justify the means might claim that killing defenseless citizens in any war is immoral.

4. MAKING PREDICTIONS

Possible Responses: Special funding or a farm act to help the South rebuild its farms and acquire new equipment; a livestock program to help farmers replace animals; training programs for unskilled newly freed slaves; programs for severely injured veterans; a special tax on Northern businesses to benefit the rebuilding of Southern businesses.

MORE ABOUT . . .
Lincoln's Last Working Day

On his last day in the White House, Lincoln spent several hours working at his desk. One of his acts was pardoning a Union soldier sentenced to death for deserting his company. He also met with Nancy Bushrod, a former slave whose husband was a Union soldier. Lincoln assured her that she would receive her husband's pay.

ASSESS & RETEACH

Section 3 Assessment

Have student pairs give feedback on each other's responses and then revise their final answers.

Self-Assessment

Have students get together in small groups to discuss and evaluate the charts they created for item 2.

Section Quiz

FORMAL ASSESSMENT
Section Quiz, p. 56

Reteach

Use Critical Thinking Transparency 11 on the causes and effects of the Civil War to review the war and its legacy.

CRITICAL THINKING TRANSPARENCIES
CT11, Civil War

CLOSE

The Union victory in the Civil War settled the disputes over states' rights and slavery. The war exacted a terrible toll in human life and had long-term economic, political, and social consequences. After the war, the nation turned to the problems of restoring the South and helping the freed African Americans lead new lives.

Section 4 Overview

OBJECTIVES

1. To explain the differing ideas Lincoln, Johnson, and Congress had about Reconstruction.
2. To summarize economic conditions in the postwar South.
3. To describe the obstacles African Americans faced.
4. To identify reasons for the collapse of congressional Reconstruction.

SKILLBUILDERS

- Interpreting charts, pp. 194, 198
- Interpreting political cartoons, p. 195

CRITICAL THINKING

- Contrasting, p. 193
- Recognizing effects, p. 194
- Making inferences, pp. 194, 198
- Identifying problems, p. 195
- Forming generalizations, pp. 197, 201
- Analyzing issues, p. 200
- Theme: Civil Rights, p. 201
- Making predictions, p. 201
- Summarizing, p. 201
- Forming opinions, p. 201

FOCUS & MOTIVATE

5-MINUTE WARM-UP

Recognizing Facts and Details

To explore the educational opportunities for former slaves, have students read One American's Story on page 192 and answer these questions.

1. What did Fitzgerald use to teach reading?
2. How many students did Fitzgerald have in his school? How many showed exceptional promise in composition?

WARM-UP TRANSPARENCY 4

▶ ***Starting with the Student*** Watch the video "Teacher of a Freed People: Robert Fitzgerald and Reconstruction" to find out how Reconstruction affected one African American.

4 Reconstruction and Its Effects

LEARN ABOUT the political, social, and economic changes that took place between 1865 and 1877 as a result of Reconstruction policies
TO UNDERSTAND why Reconstruction and the efforts to rebuild Southern society after the Civil War ultimately collapsed.

TERMS & NAMES
- **Andrew Johnson**
- **Reconstruction**
- **Fourteenth Amendment**
- **Fifteenth Amendment**
- **scalawag**
- **carpetbagger**
- **sharecropping**
- **tenant farming**
- **Ku Klux Klan**
- **Rutherford B. Hayes**

ONE AMERICAN'S STORY

Robert G. Fitzgerald was born a free African American in Delaware in 1840. During the Civil War, he served in both the U.S. Army and the U.S. Navy. In 1866, the Freedmen's Bureau sent Fitzgerald to teach in a small Virginia town. The bureau had been established in 1865 by Congress to provide former slaves with food, educational opportunities, legal aid, and other assistance. Fitzgerald's students were former slaves of all ages who were eager to learn reading, writing, spelling, arithmetic, and geography. Since textbooks were scarce, Fitzgerald often had to teach from the *Farmer's Almanac* and the Bible. A year after his arrival, Fitzgerald looked back on what he had accomplished.

Robert Fitzgerald

A PERSONAL VOICE

I came to Virginia one year ago on the 22nd of this month. Erected a school, organized and named the Freedman's Chapel School. Now (June 29th) have about 60 who have been for several months engaged in the study of arithmetic, writing, etc. etc. This morning sent in my report accompanied with compositions from about 12 of my advanced writers instructed from the Alphabet up to their [present] condition, their progress has been surprisingly rapid.

ROBERT G. FITZGERALD, quoted in *Proud Shoes*

Fitzgerald spent 14 months in Virginia and then went to North Carolina, where he lived until his death in 1919. He was one of many who labored diligently against the ignorance and poverty that slavery had forced upon most African Americans. The need to help former slaves, however, was just one of many issues the nation confronted during Reconstruction. In addition, the government, led by **Andrew Johnson,** who succeeded Abraham Lincoln as president, had to determine how to bring the defeated Confederate states back into the Union.

TEACHER OF A FREED PEOPLE
Robert Fitzgerald and Reconstruction

The Politics of Reconstruction

Reconstruction, the time period following the Civil War, lasted from 1865 to 1877. This was the period during which the United States began to rebuild after the Civil War. The term also refers to the process the federal government used to readmit the defeated Confederate states to the Union. Complicating the process was the fact that Abraham Lincoln, Andrew Johnson, and the members of Congress all had different ideas about how Reconstruction should be handled.

LINCOLN'S PLAN FOR RECONSTRUCTION Lincoln made it clear that he favored a lenient Reconstruction policy. In December 1863, Lincoln announced his Proclamation of Amnesty and Reconstruction, also known as the Ten-Percent Plan. Under this plan, the government would pardon all Confederates—except high-ranking officials and those accused of crimes

SECTION 4 RESOURCES

PRINT RESOURCES

IN-DEPTH RESOURCES: UNIT 1
Guided Reading, p. 100
Skillbuilder Practice: Evaluating Decisions, p. 103
Primary Source: *from* An Inquiry, p. 112
Literature: from *Jubilee* by Margaret Walker, p. 113
American Lives: Thaddeus Stevens, p. 117

READING STUDY GUIDE, p. 53

ACCESS FOR STUDENTS ACQUIRING ENGLISH
Guided Reading, p. 70; Skillbuilder Practice, p. 73

SPANISH READING STUDY GUIDE, p. 53

FORMAL ASSESSMENT Section Quiz, p. 57

ALTERNATIVE ASSESSMENT BOOK
See forms for supporting and scoring alternative activities.

TECHNOLOGY RESOURCES

HUMANITIES TRANSPARENCIES
H12, *The Fifteenth Amendment;* H34, A. Johnson, Tailor

GEOGRAPHY TRANSPARENCIES
G12, The Barrow Plantation, 1860, 1881

CRITICAL THINKING TRANSPARENCIES
CT12, Reconstruction; CT46, Agricultural Production

CD-ROM *Grolier Multimedia Encyclopedia*
Electronic Library of Primary Sources

VIDEO *American Stories* video series
American Portfolio: A Videodisc for U.S. History user's guide, pp. 116–120

INTERNET http://www.mlushistory.com

against prisoners of war—who would swear allegiance to the Union. As soon as ten percent of those who had voted in 1860 took this oath of allegiance, a Confederate state could form a new state government and send representatives and senators to Congress.

Under Lincoln's terms, four states—Arkansas, Louisiana, Tennessee, and Virginia—moved toward readmission to the Union. However, Lincoln's Reconstruction plan angered a minority of Republicans in Congress, known as Radical Republicans. The Radicals, led by Senator Charles Sumner of Massachusetts and Representative Thaddeus Stevens of Pennsylvania, wanted to destroy the political power of former slaveholders. Most of all, they wanted African Americans to be given full citizenship and the right to vote.

In July 1864, the Radicals passed the Wade-Davis Bill, which declared that for a state government to be formed, a majority—not just ten percent—of those eligible to vote in 1860 would have to take a solemn oath to support the Constitution.

Lincoln vetoed the bill after Congress adjourned. The Radicals called the veto an outrage and asserted that Congress had supreme authority. Thus, the stage was set for a presidential-congressional confrontation on the issue of Reconstruction.

JOHNSON'S PLAN FOR RECONSTRUCTION Lincoln was assassinated before he could implement his Reconstruction plan. In May 1865, his successor, Andrew Johnson, announced his own plan. To the dismay of the Radicals, Johnson's plan differed little from Lincoln's. The major difference was that Johnson tried to break the planters' power by excluding high-ranking Confederates and wealthy Southern landowners from taking the oath needed for voting privileges.

Most white Southerners, on the other hand, were relieved by Johnson's policies. In addition, even though Johnson had promised to punish traitors, he pardoned more than 13,000 former Confederates because he believed that "white men alone must manage the South."

The seven remaining ex-Confederate states quickly agreed to Johnson's terms. In the following months, these states set up new state governments and elected representatives to Congress. In December 1865, the newly elected Southern legislators arrived in Washington to take their seats. Many of them had held high-ranking positions in the Confederate government and army. Johnson pardoned them all, which infuriated the Radicals.

In response, Congress refused to admit the new Southern legislators. At the same time, moderate Republicans pushed for new laws to remedy weaknesses they saw in Johnson's plan. In February 1866, Congress voted to continue and enlarge the Freedmen's Bureau. A month later, Congress passed the Civil Rights Act of 1866, which gave African Americans citizenship and forbade states from passing discriminatory laws—black codes—that severely restricted African Americans' lives.

Johnson shocked everyone when he vetoed both the Freedmen's Bureau Act and the Civil Rights Act. Congress, Johnson contended, had gone far beyond "anything contemplated by the authors of the Constitution."

CONGRESSIONAL RECONSTRUCTION Angered by Johnson's actions, radical and moderate Republican factions decided to work together to shift the control of the Reconstruction process from the executive branch to the legislature. In mid-1866, they overrode the president's vetoes of the Civil Rights and Freedmen's Bureau acts. In addition, Congress drafted the **Fourteenth Amendment,** which prevented states from denying rights and privileges to any

A. Answer Both presidents favored a lenient approach to Southerners, while the Radicals wanted to punish the South severely and wanted to grant African Americans civil rights, including the vote.

THINK THROUGH HISTORY
A. Contrasting *How did the views of Presidents Lincoln and Johnson on Reconstruction differ from the views of the Radical Republicans?*

KEY PLAYER

THADDEUS STEVENS
1792–1868

The Radical Republican leader Thaddeus Stevens had a commanding physical presence—piercing eyes, a thin-lipped mouth, and a tall, thin body. In spite of a deformed foot, he was an expert horseman and swimmer. He was also famous for his quick wit and sarcasm. One colleague called him "a rude jouster in political and personal warfare."

Before being elected to Congress, he had practiced law in Pennsylvania, where he defended runaway slaves. Stevens hated slavery and in time came to hate white Southerners as well. He declared, "I look upon every man who would permit slavery . . . as a traitor to liberty and disloyal to God."

After Stevens died, at his own request he was buried in an integrated cemetery, because he wanted to show in death "the principles which I advocated throughout a long life: equality of man before his Creator."

***AMERICAN STORIES* video series**
"Teacher of a Freed People"
Videocassette: Volume 1
Videodisc: Disc 1, Side A, Chapter 3

OBJECTIVE
① INSTRUCT

The Politics of Reconstruction

▶Discussing Key Ideas
- Presidents Johnson and Lincoln hold similar views on Reconstruction.
- Radical and moderate Republicans unite in their opposition to Johnson.
- Radicals' dislike of Johnson leads them to impeach him.
- The Fifteenth Amendment guarantees African Americans the right to vote.

IN-DEPTH RESOURCES: UNIT 1
Guided Reading, p. 100

ACCESS FOR STUDENTS ACQUIRING ENGLISH
Guided Reading (Spanish), p. 70

HUMANITIES TRANSPARENCIES
H12, *The Fifteenth Amendment*

KEY PLAYER
Thaddeus Stevens
Critical Thinking: Evaluating Decisions
Discuss Stevens's reasons for being buried in an integrated cemetery. How effective do students think this gesture was in underscoring his beliefs?

IN-DEPTH RESOURCES: UNIT 1
American Lives: Thaddeus Stevens, p. 117

TEACHING OPTIONS

Teaching Gifted and Talented Students

Analyzing the Fourteenth Amendment Ask gifted and talented students to analyze the effectiveness of the Fourteenth Amendment. Have them think about the following questions: What was the outcome of the ratification of the Fourteenth Amendment? What possible changes in the amendment might have made it more effective? Why was a separate piece of legislation, the Civil Rights Act of 1866, required? Students may wish to do some additional research on the questions before drafting a short written response.

Exploring Themes

Civil Rights Discuss with students the recent history of civil rights. Point out that despite constitutional guarantees such as the Fourteenth Amendment, new civil-rights legislation has been required repeatedly. Yet the Fourteenth Amendment remains the anchor of the new legislation. The 1954 ruling outlawing school segregation, for example, was based on the Fourteenth Amendment. Ask students if they are satisfied that all born or naturalized citizens today receive equal protection under the law. Ask them to give reasons for their answers.

HISTORY FROM VISUALS

Major Reconstruction Legislation

Reading the Chart Ask students which legislation dealt with the civil rights of former slaves. *The Civil Rights Acts of 1866 and 1875 and the Enforcement Act of 1870.*

Extension Have students write two or three sentences explaining why, in their opinion, the Enforcement Act of 1870 was necessary.

ELECTRONIC LIBRARY OF PRIMARY SOURCES

from the Black Codes of Mississippi of 1865

from Civil Rights Act of 1866

MORE ABOUT . . .

The Impeachment of President Johnson

The House of Representatives has the sole power to impeach federal officials, who are then tried in the Senate. On February 24, 1868, the House impeached President Johnson, primarily on charges that he violated the Tenure of Office Act. Johnson's lawyers disputed these charges by pointing out that President Lincoln, not Johnson, had appointed Secretary Stanton, so the act did not apply.

Following Lincoln's assassination and Johnson's assumption of the presidency, the office of vice-president was left vacant. If the Senate had convicted Johnson, he would have been succeeded by the president pro tempore of the Senate—Benjamin Wade, the Radical Republican coauthor of the Wade-Davis Bill.

HUMANITIES TRANSPARENCIES

H34, A. Johnson, Tailor

Major Reconstruction Legislation

LEGISLATION	PROVISIONS
Freedmen's Bureau Acts (1865–66)	Offered assistance, such as medical aid and education, to freed slaves and war refugees
Civil Rights Act of 1866	Granted citizenship and equal protection under the law to African Americans
Reconstruction Act of 1867	Abolished governments formed in the former Confederate states Divided those states into five military districts Set up requirements for readmission into the Union
Enforcement Act of 1870	Protected the voting rights of African Americans and gave the federal government power to enforce the Fifteenth Amendment
Civil Rights Act of 1875	Outlawed racial segregation in public services Assured the right of African Americans to serve as jurors

Readmissions

STATE	DATE
Alabama	1868
Arkansas	1868
Florida	1868
Georgia	1870
Louisiana	1868
Mississippi	1870
North Carolina	1868
South Carolina	1868
Tennessee	1866
Texas	1870
Virginia	1870

SKILLBUILDER

INTERPRETING CHARTS
What was the primary focus of the major Reconstruction legislation?

Skillbuilder Answer
Reestablishing the union and providing for the needs and rights of the freed slaves.

U.S. citizen, now defined as "all persons born or naturalized in the United States." The amendment did not give African Americans the vote, but it declared that the congressional representation of each state would be reduced in proportion to the number of male citizens denied the vote.

However, President Johnson believed that it was wrong to force states to accept an amendment that their legislators had no part in drafting. Therefore, he advised the Southern states to reject the amendment. All but Tennessee did reject it, and the amendment was not ratified until 1868.

In the 1866 elections, moderate and radical Republicans gained control of Congress, ensuring them the numbers they needed to override presidential vetoes. They joined together to pass the Reconstruction Act of 1867, which did not recognize state governments formed under the Lincoln and Johnson plans—except for that of Tennessee, which had ratified the Fourteenth Amendment. The act divided the other ten former Confederate states into five military districts. The states were required to grant African-American men the vote and ratify the Fourteenth Amendment in order to reenter the Union.

Johnson vetoed the Reconstruction legislation. Congress promptly overrode the veto.

THINK THROUGH HISTORY
B. *Recognizing Effects* *How did the election of 1866 affect Republicans' ability to carry out their Reconstruction plan?*

B. Answer The election gave them a majority large enough to pass laws and to override vetoes.

"I say, as to the leaders, punishment. I say leniency, conciliation, and amnesty to the thousands whom they have misled and deceived."

ANDREW JOHNSON

JOHNSON IMPEACHED Because the Radicals thought Johnson was blocking Reconstruction, they looked for grounds on which to impeach him. They found grounds when Johnson removed Secretary of War Edwin Stanton from office in 1868. Johnson's removal of the cabinet member violated the Tenure of Office Act, which stated that a president could not remove cabinet officers during the term of the president who had appointed them without the Senate's approval. The House brought 11 charges of impeachment against Johnson, 9 of which were based on his violation of the Tenure of Office Act.

Johnson's trial before the Senate began in March 1868 and lasted 11 weeks. Until the final moment, no one could predict the outcome. When the last senator declared "not guilty," the vote was 35 to 19, one short of the two-thirds majority needed to convict the president.

U.S. GRANT ELECTED In the 1868 presidential election, the Civil War hero Ulysses S. Grant won by a margin of only 310,000 votes. About 500,000 Southern African Americans had voted, most of them for Grant. The importance of the African-American vote to the Republican Party was obvious.

After the election, the Radicals introduced the **Fifteenth Amendment,** which states that no one can be kept from voting because of "race, color, or previous condition of servitude." The Fifteenth Amendment, which was ratified by the states in 1870, was an important victory for the Radicals.

C. Answer Republicans needed the African-American vote to have a voice in the South.

THINK THROUGH HISTORY
C. *Making Inferences* *Why was the African-American vote so important to the Republicans?*

Block Schedule TEACHING OPTION **Time Needed: 40 Minutes**

Cooperative Activity: Debating President Johnson's Impeachment

Task: Student groups will debate the impeachment of President Johnson.

Purpose: To understand the issues that led to the impeachment of the president by the House and to the Senate's decision not to convict him.

Activity: Groups of three to four students will choose lots to determine which position they will uphold—for or against the president's conviction. They will then debate the issue in front of the rest of the class, who will act as the Senate and will vote on the impeachment on the basis of the arguments presented by the two sides.

ALTERNATIVE ASSESSMENT BOOK
Standards for Evaluating a Cooperative Activity

Standards for Evaluation
Presentations should . . .

- show evidence of sound research using multiple sources
- exhibit good oral presentation skills
- use specific details in an effort to persuade the audience

Reconstructing Society

Under the congressional Reconstruction program, state constitutional conventions met and Southern voters elected new, Republican-dominated governments. By 1870, all of the former Confederate states had completed the process. However, even after all the states were back in the Union, the Republicans did not end the process of Reconstruction because they wanted to make economic changes in the South.

CONDITIONS IN THE POSTWAR SOUTH The economic effects of the war on the South were devastating. Southern planters returned home to find that the value of their property had plummeted. Those who had invested in Confederate bonds had little hope of recovering their investments. Throughout the South, many small farms were ruined.

Many Southern families, like this one, lost their homes and most of their possessions because of economic problems after the Civil War.

The region's population was also devastated. More than one-fifth of the adult white men of the Confederacy died in the war. Tens of thousands of Southern African-American men also died, either fighting for the Union or working in Confederate labor camps.

The Republican governments began public works programs to repair the physical damage and to provide social services. However, economic problems made the tasks of rebuilding the South difficult. To raise money, most Southern state governments increased taxes. The deepening financial crisis drained existing resources and slowed the region's recovery.

THINK THROUGH HISTORY
D. *Identifying Problems* *What were the main postwar problems that Reconstruction governments in the South had to solve?*

D. Answer Repairing physical damage, meeting social needs, and raising money.

POLITICS IN THE POSTWAR SOUTH Another difficulty facing the new Republican governments was that the three groups that constituted the Republican Party in the South—scalawags, carpetbaggers, and African Americans—often had conflicting goals.

Although the terms *scalawags* and *carpetbaggers* were negative labels imposed by the Republicans' Democratic foes, historians still use the terms when referring to the two groups.

Scalawags were white Southerners who joined the Republican Party. The majority were small farmers who wanted to improve their economic position and did not want the former wealthy planters to regain power. **Carpetbaggers** were Northerners who moved to the South after the war. This negative name came from the belief that they arrived with so few belongings that they carried everything in small traveling bags made of carpeting.

The third and largest group of Southern Republicans—African Americans—gained voting rights as a result of the Fifteenth Amendment. During Reconstruction, African-American men registered to vote for the first time; eight out of ten of them supported the Republican Party. Although many former slaves could neither read nor write and were politically inexperienced, they were eager to exercise their voting rights.

Skillbuilder Answer That they are greedy Northerners who intend to plunder the South.

SKILLBUILDER
INTERPRETING POLITICAL CARTOONS
This cartoon from a Southern Democratic newspaper depicts Carl Schurz, a liberal Republican who advocated legal equality for African Americans. What does the portrayal suggest about carpetbaggers?

A PERSONAL VOICE

We are not prepared for this suffrage. But we can learn. Give a man tools and let him commence to use them and in time he will learn a trade. So it is with voting. We may not understand it at the start, but in time we shall learn to do our duty.

WILLIAM BEVERLY NASH, quoted in *The Trouble They Seen: Black People Tell the Story of Reconstruction*

OBJECTIVE ② **INSTRUCT**

Reconstructing Society

▶ ***Discussing Key Ideas***

- A devastated economy and a drastically reduced population make rebuilding the South difficult.
- Southern Republicans—scalawags, carpetbaggers, and African Americans—have very different aims.
- Former slaves test new freedoms, form churches and schools, and take an active role in politics.

ELECTRONIC LIBRARY OF PRIMARY SOURCES
from An Interview with a Former Slave by Annie Ruth Davis

HISTORY FROM VISUALS
Political Cartoon

Reading the Cartoon Have students identify specific details used by the cartoonist to convey his view that the carpetbagger is greedy. *Possible Responses: The large sack full of goods that he carries; the clenching of his fists; the tight grip he has on his bag; his pinched facial expression.*

Extension Horace Greeley described carpetbaggers as having "both arms around the Negroes and their hands in their rear pockets, seeing if they can't pick a dollar out of them." Have students draw a cartoon expressing this or another point of view on carpetbaggers.

TEACHING OPTION

Skillbuilder Mini-Lesson: Evaluating Decisions

Explaining the Skill Historians look at decisions made in the past and evaluate them based, in part, on the short- and long-term consequences of those decisions. For example, students might at first be glad they accepted an after-school job because of the extra spending money it provides. However, that decision may not seem as good after their school performance slips from having less time to study.

***Applying the Skill:* Evaluating the Decision to Impeach Johnson** Have students review the description of Johnson's impeachment on page 194.

1. What were the short-term effects of this decision? *Johnson was made to look guilty and powerless in relation to Congress.*
2. What were the long-term effects? *The long trial and near conviction diminished Johnson's authority and ensured that he would not be re-elected.*
3. Was the decision to impeach Johnson a good one?

IN-DEPTH RESOURCES: UNIT 1
Skillbuilder Practice: Evaluating Decisions, p. 103

MORE ABOUT . . .
African-American Colleges

The nation's first colleges for African Americans opened during Reconstruction. Fisk University in Nashville, Tennessee, was established as a liberal arts college in 1866. Howard University, named for Gen. Oliver O. Howard, head of the Freedmen's Bureau, opened in 1867 in Washington, D.C. It offered courses in law, medicine, education, and pharmacy. Hampton Institute in Hampton, Virginia, emphasized industrial arts. It was founded in 1868. Between 1878 and 1912 it received federal aid for educating Native Americans as well.

MORE ABOUT . . .
African-American Churches

Before the Civil War, African Americans were accepted only as associate members in some urban Protestant churches. Even if church membership was predominantly black, church property could be owned only by white trustees. After the war, however, most African Americans withdrew from biracial churches and formed their own congregations. In South Carolina, for example, African-American membership in biracial churches dropped from 42,000 at the beginning of the Civil War to only about 600 in the 1870s.

The differences among the goals of scalawags, carpetbaggers, and African Americans led to a lack of unity in the Republican Party. In particular, few scalawags shared the Republican commitment to civil rights and suffrage for African Americans. In addition, some Republican governors began to appoint white Democrats to office in an attempt to persuade more white voters to vote Republican. This policy made blacks feel that they had been betrayed.

The new status of African Americans required fundamental changes in the attitudes of most Southern whites. However, many white Southerners refused to accept blacks' new status and resisted the idea of equal rights.

FORMER SLAVES IMPROVE THEIR LIVES At first, many former slaves were cautious about testing the limits of their freedom. As the reality of freedom slowly sank in, however, freed African Americans faced many decisions. What were they to do? They had no land, no jobs, no tools, no money, and few skills besides those of farming. How would they feed and clothe themselves? How and where would they live?

One of the first decisions that former slaves faced was whether to remain where they were. During slavery, white planters had forbidden them to travel without a pass and had enforced that rule by patrolling the roads. During Reconstruction, thousands of African Americans took advantage of their new freedom to move to Southern towns and cities where they could find jobs. Between 1865 and 1870, the African-American population of the ten largest Southern cities doubled.

Many former slaves also sought an education. With the assistance of the Freedmen's Bureau, African-American churches, Northern charitable organizations, and state governments, African Americans organized their own schools, colleges, and universities. Initially, most teachers in black schools were Northern whites, about half of whom were women. However, educated African Americans like Robert G. Fitzgerald also became teachers, and by 1869, black teachers outnumbered whites in these schools.

This quilt, made in the 1880s by an African-American woman named Harriet Powers, illustrates how former slaves found ways to proclaim their beliefs—in this case, biblical stories—both publicly and artistically.

After the war African Americans also founded their own churches. Because churches were the principal institution that African Americans fully controlled, African-American ministers emerged as influential community leaders. They often played an important role in the broader political life of the country as well.

BLACKS IN RECONSTRUCTION After the war, African Americans took an active role in the political process. Not only did they vote, but, for the first time, they held office in local, state, and federal government.

Nevertheless, even though there were more black voters than white voters in the South, African-American

NOW & THEN
From Sharecropper to Shareholder

In the several generations since emancipati[on] many African-American families have made [a] long, difficult journey from sharecropper t[o] business owner. For many, education was t[he] key. Higher education, like other opportun[ities] has been slower to come to blacks than to whites. Some African Americans have gott[en] ahead by opening businesses, such as groce[ry] stores, which don't require them to have a college degree. Higher education is usually needed for further advancement, however.

1875
Sharecropping was one of the few choices open to former slaves, as well as to poor whites, following the Civil War. As sharecroppers, people could farm land on the plantation for themselves, but they had to turn over much of the profit to the landowner. This system gave them little chance of getting ahead.

TEACHING OPTIONS

Making Connections Across Time

African-American Ministers as Community Leaders Discuss with students the continued importance of the church in the African-American community. One example you might mention is the large number of church leaders who have assumed community and political leadership. Ask for names of African-American ministers who have played important roles in modern times. *Possible Response: Students may suggest Martin Luther King, Jr., or Jesse Jackson. Some students may mention Malcolm X, who served a similar role in the Black Muslim community.*

Making Connections Across the Curriculum

U.S. Government Tell students that African-American voters turned out in large numbers when they first received the right to vote. Ask students if they know the percent of registered voters who voted during recent community, state, or national elections. Interested students might volunteer to research the latest records available to them. If possible, have them look for voting records broken down by ethnic groups.

E. Answer They sought an education, organized their own schools, founded their own churches, and took an active role in the political process.

THINK THROUGH HISTORY
E. *Forming Generalizations* *How did Southern African Americans respond to their new status?*

officeholders remained in the minority. Out of 125 Southerners elected to the U.S. Congress during congressional Reconstruction, only 16 were African Americans. Among these was Hiram Revels, the first African-American senator.

African-American state legislators worked to pass laws against segregation. In 1871, for example, Texas passed a law prohibiting railroads from making distinctions between groups of passengers, and several other states followed suit. However, many antisegregation laws were not enforced.

African Americans themselves were often more interested in black community than in total integration. By establishing separate African-American institutions, they were able to promote African-American leadership and escape the interference of the whites who had dominated their lives.

1997

His grandfather was a sharecropper; his father, a mail clerk. Now Vernon Jordan is an influential corporate director, an attorney, and an adviser to President Clinton. He realized the value of education in achieving his own goals and served as director of the Voter Education Project and as executive director of the United Negro College Fund to help other African Americans achieve their goals. Jordan currently serves as a director of the Ford Foundation and of 11 of America's largest corporations.

1990

In the 1990s, the number of African-American–owned businesses is increasing nearly twice as fast as the number of majority-owned businesses, and not simply because blacks are a growing portion of the population. Education has played a major role.

Recent Trends for African Americans

AFRICAN-AMERICAN EDUCATION | NEW BLACK-OWNED BUSINESSES

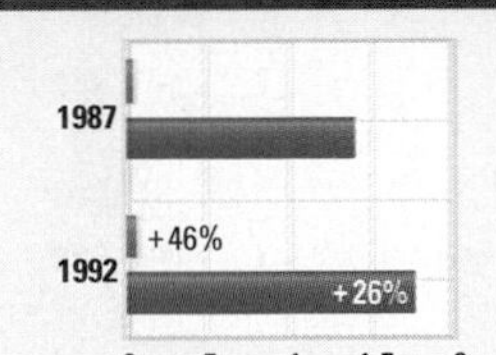

Source: *The U.S. Census Bureau*

INTERACT WITH HISTORY

1. **INTERPRETING GRAPHS** How does the number of new African-American-owned businesses compare with the number of new businesses overall for the period shown? What conclusions can you draw from this information and from success stories like Vernon Jordan's?

SEE SKILLBUILDER HANDBOOK, PAGE 929.

2. **INTERVIEWING AND REPORTING** Interview someone you know who has started a small business. Ask the person what he or she needed in order to get started. Ask about experience, education, money, and business partners. Present a short report to the class. Together create a class chart summarizing what you have learned about the effects of various factors on success in business.

MORE ABOUT . . .
Hiram Revels

Hiram Revels was born of free parents in Fayetteville, North Carolina. Because he could not obtain an education in the South, he attended Knox College in Illinois. Revels settled in Mississippi in 1865. In 1870, he became the first African American elected to the U.S. Senate. Ironically, he held the seat that had once belonged to Jefferson Davis.

NOW & THEN
From Sharecropper to Shareholder

▶ ***Starting with the Student*** Ask students to give their reactions to Vernon Jordan's life story.

- Ask them to speculate about the personality traits that make such success possible.
- What family values and dynamics do students think help children develop their fullest potential within the social constraints they face?

▶ ***Discussing Key Ideas***

- The number of African-American-owned businesses is increasing at nearly twice the rate of majority-owned businesses.
- The percentage of African Americans receiving a high school education has increased significantly, but the percentage receiving college degrees has increased only marginally.

INTERACT WITH HISTORY

1. Interpreting Graphs

Possible Responses: *The number of new African-American businesses is increasing at almost twice the rate of all new businesses. The actual number of new African-American businesses—around 200,000—is only a fraction of the almost 2 million total new businesses.*

Students may say that the increasing number of African-American businesses reflects increasing opportunities for African Americans to get an education and to accumulate the resources to open their own businesses.

2. Interviewing and Reporting

You may wish to make the following suggestions to students:

- Begin by telephoning the businessperson to set up an appointment for the interview.
- Prepare for the interview by compiling a list of questions that will help elicit information. Avoid asking questions that can be answered with a yes or no.
- During the interview, follow the sequence of prepared questions, but be flexible—pursue unexpected information.
- If possible, tape-record the interview with permission of the interviewee and transcribe it later.

OBJECTIVE
(3) INSTRUCT

Changes in the Southern Economy

▶ ***Discussing Key Ideas***
- Freed slaves want their own land.
- The planter class seeks to restore the plantation system.
- Economic necessity forces many former slaves to become sharecroppers.

ELECTRONIC LIBRARY OF PRIMARY SOURCES
from An Address on Reconstruction by Thaddeus Stevens

HISTORY FROM VISUALS
The Sharecropper Cycle of Poverty

Reading the Chart When and where in the chart does the cycle of sharecropping begin? *Possible Responses: When the landowner gives the sharecropper land and seed, at the top of the chart.*

Extension Have students create a similar chart for tenant farming. Ask them to begin their cycle with a sharecropper who has saved enough money to purchase tools and a horse or mule, and rent some land. *Possible items in cycle: Purchases tools and mule; rents land; buys seed; buys food and clothing, some on credit; plants crop; harvests crop; sells crop; pays rent and debts; saves a little if possible.*

CRITICAL THINKING TRANSPARENCIES
CT46, Agricultural Production in the South: 1850–1900

GEOGRAPHY TRANSPARENCIES
G12, The Barrow Plantation, 1860, 1881

Changes in the Southern Economy

Most former slaves strongly desired to own property. Few, however, had enough money to buy land. Those who did have cash were frequently frustrated by whites' refusal to sell property to them.

40 ACRES AND A MULE In January 1865, General Sherman had promised the former slaves who followed his army 40 acres per family and the use of army mules. Soon afterward, about 40,000 freed persons settled on 400,000 acres in coastal Georgia and South Carolina. The freed African Americans farmed their plots until August 1865, when President Johnson ordered that the original landowners be allowed to reclaim their land.

Many newly free African Americans asserted that they deserved part of the planters' land. Thaddeus Stevens agreed, calling for the government to redistribute part of the land to former slaves. However, his plan failed because most Republicans considered private property a basic American right. As a result, Congress either rejected land-reform proposals or set aside land for former slaves that was unsuitable for farming.

THINK THROUGH HISTORY
F. Making Inferences *Thaddeus Stevens believed that giving land to former slaves was more important than giving them the vote. Why do you think he held this belief?*

F. Answer Because freed persons needed their own land in order to gain economic independence; the vote meant little without economic independence.

RESTORATION OF PLANTATIONS While African Americans and poor whites wanted to own small farms, the planter class wanted to restore the plantation system. To make the system work, planters claimed that they needed to have almost complete control over their laborers. However, many African Americans refused to work in the fields after they were freed. Some worked in mills or on railroad construction crews. Others tried to support themselves by growing food for their own families. To stop this trend, white planters were determined to keep the former slaves from acquiring their own land.

SHARECROPPING AND TENANT FARMING Without their own land, freed African Americans could not grow crops to sell or to use to feed their families. Therefore, economic necessity forced many former slaves to become share-

Skillbuilder Answer The system was rigged so they had little or no money left at the end of the year.

SKILLBUILDER
INTERPRETING CHARTS
How did the sharecropping system make it hard for small farmers to improve their standard of living?

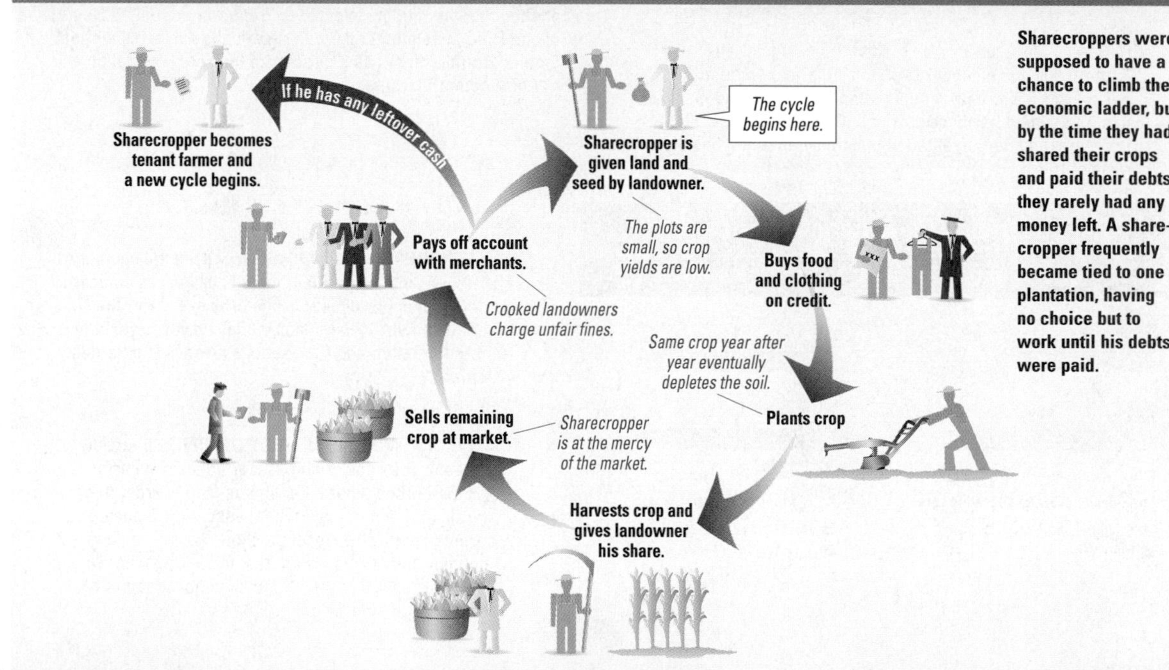
The Sharecropper Cycle of Poverty
The cycle begins here.
Sharecropper is given land and seed by landowner.
The plots are small, so crop yields are low.
Buys food and clothing on credit.
Same crop year after year eventually depletes the soil.
Plants crop
Harvests crop and gives landowner his share.
Sharecropper is at the mercy of the market.
Sells remaining crop at market.
Crooked landowners charge unfair fines.
Pays off account with merchants.
If he has any leftover cash
Sharecropper becomes tenant farmer and a new cycle begins.

Sharecroppers were supposed to have a chance to climb the economic ladder, but by the time they had shared their crops and paid their debts, they rarely had any money left. A sharecropper frequently became tied to one plantation, having no choice but to work until his debts were paid.

TEACHING OPTION

Exploring Themes

Constitutional Concerns Have students read together the Fifth Amendment on page 100. Then have them focus on this excerpt: "No person shall be . . . deprived of life, liberty, or property, without due process of law; nor shall private property be taken for public use, without just compensation."

Have students discuss the issue of each person's right to private property. Ask students to explain why the government did not simply take away land from large plantation owners and give it to former slaves. *Possible Response: It would be a violation of the Fifth Amendment because the government would be confiscating private property.*

Ask students what the government might have done to protect the right to private property for both plantation owners and freedmen. *Possible Responses: President Johnson could have kept General Sherman's promise of "40 acres and a mule" for former slaves; since as slaves they had been deprived of their right to own land, freedmen should have been compensated by the government.*

croppers. In the system of **sharecropping,** landowners divided their land and gave each head of household a few acres, along with seed and tools. Sharecroppers kept a small portion of their crops and gave the rest to the landowners. The chart on page 198 shows the sharecropping system in detail. (See *poverty* on page 937 in the Economics Handbook.)

In theory, "croppers" who saved a little could become tenants and rent land for cash in a system known as **tenant farming.** Eventually they might move up the economic ladder to become outright owners of their farms. However, very few farmers managed to do this.

The Collapse of Reconstruction

Most white Southerners swallowed whatever resentment they felt over African-American suffrage and participation in government. Some whites expressed their feelings by refusing to register to vote. Others, however, frustrated by their loss of political power and by the South's economic stagnation, formed vigilante groups and used violence to intimidate African Americans.

OPPOSITION TO RECONSTRUCTION The most notorious and widespread of the Southern vigilante groups was the **Ku Klux Klan.** The Klan's goals were to destroy the Republican Party, to throw out the Reconstruction governments, to aid the planter class, and to prevent African Americans from exercising their political rights. To achieve these goals, the Klan and other secret groups killed several thousand men, women, and children. Although some of the victims were whites who had tried to help African Americans, the vast majority of Klan victims were African Americans.

While the Klan operated in secret, some Southern Democrats openly used violence to intimidate Republicans and frighten African Americans away from the polls. More frequently, though, white Southerners used nonviolent economic pressure to force former slaves to work for whites as wage laborers or sharecroppers. Some white Southern employers and merchants also refused to hire or do business with African Americans who voted Republican. The fear of economic reprisals kept many former slaves from voting for Republicans or from going to the polls at all.

To curtail Klan violence and Democratic intimidation, Congress passed a series of Enforcement Acts in 1870 and 1871. One act provided for the federal supervision of elections in Southern states. Another act gave the president the power to use federal troops in areas where the Klan was active.

Although Congress seemed to shore up Republican power with the Enforcement Acts, it soon passed legislation that severely weakened the power of the Republican Party in the South. In May 1872, Congress passed the Amnesty Act, which returned the right to vote and the right to hold federal and state offices to about 160,000 former Confederates. In the same year Congress allowed the Freedmen's Bureau to expire. These actions allowed Southern Democrats to regain political power.

SCANDALS AND MONEY CRISES HURT REPUBLICANS As Republicans struggled to maintain their hold on Reconstruction governments in the South, widespread political corruption in the Grant administration weakened their party. Scandals diverted public attention in the North away from conditions in the South.

President Grant, who was elected for a second term in 1872, was never found guilty of any wrongdoing. However,

"The Klan . . . whipped me three hours or more and left me for dead."

ABRAM COLBY,
AFRICAN AMERICAN WHO SERVED ON THE GEORGIA LEGISLATURE

Although Klan members disguised themselves, the results of their terrorism were unmistakable.

OBJECTIVE
④ INSTRUCT

The Collapse of Reconstruction

▶ ***Discussing Key Ideas***
- The Ku Klux Klan terrorizes African Americans.
- Scandals in Grant's administration and bank failures weaken the Republican Party.
- Supreme Court decisions undermine the Fourteenth and Fifteenth Amendments.
- Democrats regain control of the South.

IN-DEPTH RESOURCES: UNIT 1
Primary Source: *from* An Inquiry on the Condition of the South, p. 112

GROLIER MULTIMEDIA ENCYCLOPEDIA
excerpt from Grant's memoirs

Issues for the 21st Century

Breaking the Cycle of Poverty

Connect the experience of poverty during Reconstruction with the experience of poverty today by having students read pages 896–899. Then have them answer these questions.

1. What role did discrimination play in maintaining the cycle of poverty during Reconstruction? *Many white Southerners used economic pressure to keep former slaves dependent.*
2. What steps have state and federal welfare programs taken to break the cycle of poverty today? *States have enacted their own welfare reforms. Federal programs offer incentives and limit payments.*

TEACHING OPTIONS

Exploring Themes

Civil Rights Discuss with students the devastating effect of the Ku Klux Klan's actions on African Americans' civil rights. Point out that the Klan tried to prevent blacks from exercising both their political and economic rights. Ask students what steps the government took to protect the civil rights of African Americans. *Congress passed a series of Enforcement Acts to curtail the intimidation.* Why weren't these laws very effective? *Congress also passed legislation that weakened the power of the Republican Party in the South.*

Making Connections Across the Curriculum

Writing Freed slaves were bitterly disappointed that white leaders were not more vocal in their opposition to the Klan. "One short letter (from a prominent former North Carolina governor) could put down all these outrages," one black legislator insisted. Have students write a short letter from the point of view of a white Southern leader condemning the terrorist acts of the Klan. Remind the students that their audience will be Klan members who have participated in violence or who have supported it. Ask students to construct persuasive arguments that would be convincing to such an audience.

MORE ABOUT . . .
The Breakdown of Republican Unity

Disgusted with the graft and corruption in the Grant administration, a group of Missouri Republicans banded together to form the Liberal Republican Party in 1872. In the 1872 presidential election, the Liberal Republicans held a separate convention and nominated Horace Greeley as their candidate. The Democrats also nominated Greeley—even though he had once called them "murderers . . . drunkards, cowards, liars, thieves." Nevertheless, Greeley lost the election to Grant by a wide margin. Physically exhausted by his rigorous campaign, Greeley died a few weeks after the election.

GROLIER MULTIMEDIA ENCYCLOPEDIA

Horace Greeley and the Penny Press

POINT/COUNTERPOINT
Reconstruction

▶ ***Starting with the Student***
Have students vote, based on what they learned in this chapter, on whether they think Reconstruction was a success or a failure.

▶ ***Discussing Key Ideas***
- Reconstruction governments cannot guarantee the rights of former slaves.
- Former slaves experience ongoing poverty and discrimination.
- For a time, African Americans become involved at all levels of government.
- They establish families, schools, and churches, and achieve some independence in Southern society.

CRITICAL THINKING TRANSPARENCIES

CT12, Reconstruction

POINT

"Reconstruction was a failure."

Reconstruction governments were charged with the responsibility of securing hard-won rights guaranteed to former slaves by constitutional amendments, but they failed to make these guarantees stick.

- **State Republican parties could not keep together black-white voter coalitions that would enable them to stay in power and continue political reform.**
- **Radical Republican governments were unable to enact land reform or to provide former slaves with the economic resources needed to break the "cycle of poverty." African Americans who continued to work the land wound up as sharecroppers or tenant farmers rather than as landowners.**
- **Racial bias was a national, not a regional, problem. After the Panic of 1873, Northerners were more concerned with economic problems than with the problems of former slaves.**

At the end of Reconstruction, former slaves found themselves once again in a subordinate position in society. The historian Eric Foner concludes, "Whether measured by the dreams inspired by emancipation or the more limited goal of securing blacks' rights as citizens, . . . Reconstruction can only be judged a failure."

COUNTERPOINT

"Reconstruction was a success."

Reconstruction was an attempt to create a social and political revolution despite economic collapse and the opposition of a large portion of the white South. Under these conditions its accomplishments were extraordinary.

- **African Americans only a few years removed from slavery participated at all levels of government.**
- **State governments had some success in solving social problems; for example, they funded public school systems open to all citizens.**
- **African Americans established institutions that had been denied them during slavery: schools, churches, and families.**
- **The breakup of the plantation system led to some redistribution of land, from which African Americans benefited.**

W. E. B. Du Bois summarized the achievements of the period this way: "It was Negro loyalty and the Negro vote alone that restored the South to the Union; established the new democracy, both for white and black."

Despite their loss of ground during the period that followed Reconstruction, African Americans were successful in carving out a measure of independence within Southern society.

INTERACT WITH HISTORY

1. **COMPARING AND FORMING OPINIONS** What are the two major arguments made by each side over whether Reconstruction was a success? Which perspective do you agree with, and why?

 SEE SKILLBUILDER HANDBOOK, PAGES 909 AND 919.

2. **RESEARCHING RECONSTRUCTION'S LEGACY** One historian has referred to Reconstruction as "America's Unfinished Revolution." Is the United States still dealing with issues left over from that period? Use newspaper stories, magazine articles, or other sources of information to back your arguments. Make a short presentation in class.

Grant's appointees frequently turned out to be dishonest. Scandals involving his vice-president, private secretary, and secretary of war shattered Republican unity. The breakdown of Republican unity made it even harder for the Radicals to continue to impose their Reconstruction plan on the South.

As if political scandals were not enough for the country to deal with, a series of bank failures known as the Panic of 1873 triggered a five-year depression. The depression fueled a dispute over currency. Many financial experts advocated withdrawing the paper money that had been issued during the war and returning the country to a currency backed by gold. Farmers and manufacturers, on the other hand, wanted the government to issue even more paper money to help them pay off their debts. (See *gold standard* on page 935 in the Economics Handbook.)

As the economy improved in 1879, the controversy died down. However, the debate over the money question in the 1870s was one of many factors that drew the attention of voters and politicians away from Reconstruction.

JUDICIAL AND POPULAR SUPPORT FADES The Supreme Court also began to undo some of the social and political changes that the Radicals had made. During the 1870s, the Court issued a series of decisions that undermined both the Fourteenth and Fifteenth Amendments. In one ruling, for example, the Court stated that the Fifteenth Amendment did not "confer the right of suffrage on anyone" but merely listed grounds on which states could not deny suffrage.

THINK THROUGH HISTORY
G. *Analyzing Issues* *How did the scandals in the Grant administration and the economic problems of the 1870s affect Northern attitudes toward Reconstruction?*

G. Answer They commanded the attention of Northern voters and made them care less about what was happening in the South.

TEACHING OPTIONS

Comparing and Forming Opinions

Possible Responses: *Those saying that Reconstruction was a failure may argue that former slaves were not much better off at the end of Reconstruction: they were still in a subordinate position; they had lost many rights that had been guaranteed through constitutional amendments; racial bias continued.*

Those saying that Reconstruction was a success may argue that African Americans were able to become more independent in Southern society: they participated in government; they established schools and churches; they owned some land.

2. Researching Reconstruction's Legacy

You may wish to give students the following suggestions to help them find sources and organize information for their reports:

- Begin research in the library. Ask the librarian where to find specialized reference books on the topic.
- Check the *Readers' Guide to Periodical Literature* or Infotrak, a computer database of periodicals, for articles on the topic.
- Search for specialized books such as Eric Foner's *America's Reconstruction: People and Politics After the Civil War.*
- Check the Internet for sites dealing with the Civil War and Reconstruction.

THINK THROUGH HISTORY
H. THEME Civil Rights *How did the Supreme Court fail to defend former slaves' civil rights?*

H. Answer The Court issued a series of decisions that undermined the Fourteenth and Fifteenth Amendments.

At the same time, Northern support for congressional Reconstruction began to fade. Weary of the "Negro question" and "sick of carpet-bag government," many Northern voters shifted their attention to national concerns. In addition, a desire for reconciliation between the regions spread through the North. Although political violence continued in the South and African Americans were denied civil and political rights, Republicans slowly retreated from the policies of Reconstruction.

"We obey laws, others make them."

CHARLES HARRIS, AN AFRICAN-AMERICAN UNION ARMY VETERAN

DEMOCRATS "REDEEM" THE SOUTH As the Republicans' hold on the South loosened, Southern Democrats began to regain control of the region. As a result of "redemption"—as the Democrats called their return to power—and a political deal made during the national election of 1876, congressional Reconstruction came to an end.

In 1876, the Republicans nominated Governor **Rutherford B. Hayes,** of Ohio, for the presidency. The Democratic candidate, Governor Samuel J. Tilden of New York, carried the popular vote. However, he fell one short of the number of electoral votes needed to win. Congress appointed a commission to deal with the problem. The commission, which had a Republican majority, gave the election to Hayes. Republican leaders, meanwhile, struck a deal with Southern Democrats to prevent them from delaying Congressional approval of Hayes.

The price Southern Democrats demanded included the withdrawal of federal troops from Louisiana and South Carolina—two of the three Southern states that Republicans still governed. In the Compromise of 1877, Republican leaders agreed to the demands, and Hayes was peacefully inaugurated. The acceptance of this compromise meant the end of Reconstruction in the South.

Although President Hayes united the North and the South, his presidency marked the end of newly won political and civil rights for former slaves.

I. Answer Possible Responses: Many of their newly gained rights will not be enforced; Republicans will withdraw their support; white Southerners will attempt to institutionalize racism.

THINK THROUGH HISTORY
I. Making Predictions *What do you think will be the effect of the end of Reconstruction on African Americans in the South?*

Reconstruction ended without much real progress in the battle against discrimination. Congress did not adequately protect the rights of African Americans, and the Supreme Court undermined them. But congressional Reconstruction was not a complete failure. The Thirteenth, Fourteenth, and Fifteenth Amendments remained part of the Constitution. In the 20th century, these amendments provided the necessary constitutional foundation for important civil rights legislation.

Moreover, for many years after the end of Reconstruction, the African-American community proudly looked back on the period as a time when they voted, held political office, and made important achievements. In contrast, after 1877, most white Americans put the memory of Reconstruction behind them. They turned their attention to other matters, such as expansion into the western frontier.

Section 4 Assessment

1. TERMS & NAMES
Identify:
- Andrew Johnson
- Reconstruction
- Fourteenth Amendment
- Fifteenth Amendment
- scalawag
- carpetbagger
- sharecropping
- tenant farming
- Ku Klux Klan
- Rutherford B. Hayes

2. SUMMARIZING List five problems facing the South after the Civil War, and at least one attempted solution for each one. Use a table such as this one.

Problem	Attempted Solution

3. FORMING GENERALIZATIONS How did the Civil War weaken the Southern economy? Give examples to support your viewpoint.

THINK ABOUT
- the devastation of the war
- economic conditions
- changes in agriculture

4. FORMING OPINIONS Do you think the political deal to settle the election of 1876 was an appropriate solution? Explain why or why not.

THINK ABOUT
- the causes of the conflict over the election
- other possible solutions to the controversy
- the impact of the settlement

ANSWERS

1. TERMS & NAMES
Andrew Johnson, p. 192
Reconstruction, p. 192
Fourteenth Amendment, p. 193
Fifteenth Amendment, p. 194
scalawag, p. 195
carpetbagger, p. 195
sharecropping, p. 199
tenant farming, p. 199
Ku Klux Klan, p. 199
Rutherford B. Hayes, p. 201

2. SUMMARIZING
Possible Responses:
Reuniting North and South/congressional Reconstruction; physical devastation of the South/public works programs; former slaves need assistance/Freedmen's Bureau established; Former slaves need land/40 acres and a mule plan; vigilante groups arise/Enforcement Acts.

3. FORMING GENERALIZATIONS
Possible Responses:
Devastation of population; devaluation of property; increased taxes; decline in demand for cotton; lack of land for freedmen.

4. FORMING OPINIONS
Possible Responses:
Appropriate—The deal showed how a democracy can settle conflict with compromise. **Inappropriate**—The deal was a sign of corruption, not democracy, because it did not acknowledge the popular vote. It also ended federal efforts to help African Americans in the South.

MORE ABOUT . . .
Rutherford B. Hayes
Rutherford B. Hayes (1822–1893) was described by others as studious and good-natured. Born in Delaware, Ohio, he was the son of a store owner and graduated from Harvard Law School. First nominated for Congress while serving in the Union Army, he was elected even though he refused to campaign. Hayes also served three terms as governor of Ohio.

ASSESS & RETEACH

Section 4 Assessment
Have students answer question 1 by themselves. Then have them work with a partner to answer questions 2, 3, and 4.

Self-Assessment
Have students select two answers they feel they could improve. Ask them to rewrite the answers to make them more complete and coherent.

Section Quiz
FORMAL ASSESSMENT
Section Quiz, p. 57

Reteach
Review the arguments in the Point Counterpoint feature on page 200 to help consolidate students' understanding of Reconstruction's legacy.

CLOSE

Congress and the Radical Republicans control Reconstruction. African Americans begin to exercise freedoms denied to them during their enslavement. However, continued opposition to Reconstruction in the South and economic problems in the North bring the process to an end in 1877.

REVIEW CHAPTER 4
ASSESSMENT ANSWERS

REVIEWING THE CHAPTER

TERMS & NAMES

1. Underground Railroad, p. 166
2. Harriet Beecher Stowe, p. 167
3. Dred Scott, p. 170
4. Bull Run, p. 177
5. Emancipation Proclamation, p. 179
6. Clara Barton, p. 183
7. Gettysburg, p. 185
8. William Tecumseh Sherman, p. 187
9. Fifteenth Amendment, p. 194
10. Ku Klux Klan, p. 199

MAIN IDEAS

11. It allowed California to be admitted as a free state and Utah and New Mexico to decide about slavery, and it prevented the abolition of slavery within the District of Columbia without the consent of its residents. It also included a tougher fugitive slave law.
12. Because of its opposition to slavery in the territories; the Whigs and Know-Nothings split over slavery.
13. Both opposed slavery in the territories. Lincoln thought the federal government should ban it; Douglas relied on popular sovereignty.
14. North—Blockade Southern ports; split the Confederacy; capture Richmond. South—Ward off Union invasion.
15. Some slaves began to resist their owners, while others sought freedom behind the lines of the Union army. Southern bread riots broke out in 1863. Many white male workers went on labor strikes.
16. Farmers' resentment toward unfair tax policies; mass desertion of Confederate soldiers; peace movements.
17. Rifles, minié balls, hand grenades, land mines, ironclad ships.
18. They thought he was obstructing Reconstruction efforts.
19. They traveled to find jobs; organized schools, colleges, universities, and churches; and participated in politics.
20. Some regained power through terror, others by the compromise over the election of 1876.

Review Chapter  Assessment

REVIEWING THE CHAPTER

TERMS & NAMES For each term below, write a sentence explaining its connection to the growing controversy over slavery, to the Civil War, or to Reconstruction. For each person named below, explain his or her role in the particular period.

1. **Underground Railroad**
2. **Harriet Beecher Stowe**
3. **Dred Scott**
4. **Bull Run**
5. **Emancipation Proclamation**
6. **Clara Barton**
7. **Gettysburg**
8. **William Tecumseh Sherman**
9. **Fifteenth Amendment**
10. **Ku Klux Klan**

MAIN IDEAS

SECTION 1 *(pages 164–173)*

The Divisive Politics of Slavery

11. What were the major terms of the Compromise of 1850?
12. Why did the Republican Party grow as the Whig and Know-Nothing parties declined in the 1850s?
13. Compare and contrast Abraham Lincoln's and Stephen A. Douglas's views about slavery in the territories.

SECTION 2 *(pages 176–183)*

The Civil War Begins

14. What were the military strategies of the North and the South at the onset of the Civil War?
15. What acts of protest or resistance occurred in both the North and South because of economic and social changes during the war?

SECTION 3 *(pages 184–191)*

The North Takes Charge

16. Cite events that illustrate the South's deteriorating morale after defeats at Gettysburg and Vicksburg.
17. Give examples of new military machinery and technologically improved weapons used during the Civil War.

SECTION 4 *(pages 192–201)*

Reconstruction and Its Effects

18. Why did the Radicals want to impeach Andrew Johnson?
19. In what ways did emancipated slaves exercise their freedom?
20. How did Southern whites regain political power during Reconstruction?

THINKING CRITICALLY

1. **NATIONAL ELECTIONS** Re-create the chart shown below on your paper. Then list the results and significance of the national elections of 1856, 1860, 1866, 1868, 1872, and 1876.

Year	Results	Significance

2. **PRESERVING THE UNION** Reread the quote by Abraham Lincoln on page 162. How might Stephen Douglas, John Brown, William Tecumseh Sherman, Andrew Johnson, or Thaddeus Stevens have answered Lincoln's question? Use details from the chapter to support your response.
3. **GEOGRAPHY OF BATTLE** Compare the maps on pages 177 and 188. What do they tell you about the progress of the Civil War from 1861 to 1865? What do they show about the geography of the land where many battles were fought? Explain your answer.
4. **CIVIL WAR FIRSTS** On a scale of 1 to 5, rank the following groundbreaking events related to the Civil War era from most historically significant to least historically significant. Give reasons to support your rankings.
   - first U.S. president assassinated
   - first draft law passed
   - one of the first modern wars
   - first time women employed in government jobs
   - first time U.S. government collected income tax
5. **TRACING THEMES** **CIVIL RIGHTS** What might Americans today learn from the civil rights experiences of African Americans during Reconstruction?
6. **ANALYZING PRIMARY SOURCES** Toby, a slave in South Carolina, was held in servitude by his former master even after receiving his freedom. After four years, Toby escaped and headed for Texas with Govie, who became his wife. This is how he described their lives.

> **I don't know as I 'spected nothing from freedom, but they turned us out like a bunch of stray dogs, no homes, no clothing, no nothing, not 'nough food to last us one meal. After we settles on that place, I never seed man or women 'cept Govie, for six years, cause it was a long ways to anywhere. All we had to farm with was sharp sticks. We'd stick holes and plant corn, and when it come up we'd punch up the dirt round it. We didn't plant cotton, 'cause we wouldn't eat that. I made bows and arrows to kill wild game with, and we never went to a store for nothing. We made our clothes out of animal skins.**
>
> **TOBY,** quoted in *The Black Americans: A History in Their Own Words*

Summarize the problems Toby faced on becoming free. In your opinion, what might the federal government have done to help former slaves economically?

THINKING CRITICALLY

1. NATIONAL ELECTIONS
Possible Responses: 1856—James Buchanan wins but Republican candidate has strong showing—Buchanan is indecisive and plagued by slavery issues; 1860—Lincoln wins but receives no electoral votes from the South—distrust of Lincoln prompts eleven Southern states to secede; 1866—Republicans win large majority—Congress able to override presidential vetoes; 1868—Grant wins with small margin in the popular vote—shows importance of African-American votes; 1872—Grant reelected president—Republican unity shattered; 1876—Hayes wins presidential election—end of Reconstruction in the South.

2. PRESERVING THE UNION
Possible Responses: Most students may suggest that Douglas and Johnson would respond in a moderate way, while Brown, Sherman, and Stevens would probably exclaim that such a situation could not continue.

3. GEOGRAPHY OF BATTLE
Possible Responses: Maps show that the Union occupied many more states between 1863 and 1865. The end of the war—final battles and surrender at Appomattox—took place very near the site of the Seven Days' Battle in the early days of the war. Geography shows that many battles were fought in hilly regions where the terrain must have been rugged and fighting difficult, especially if enemy troops were in the hills above.

Bridge to Chapter 5

Review Chapter 4

SECTIONAL DIFFERENCES In the 1850s, the controversy over slavery in the territories sharply divided the North and the South. As slavery increasingly dominated politics, many Northerners joined the newly organized Republican Party.

The election of Republican Abraham Lincoln in 1860 pushed the country to the brink of war. Within months after his election, seven Southern states seceded from the Union. By February 1861, the Confederate States of America had declared their independence.

THE CIVIL WAR In 1861, Confederate forces fired on Fort Sumter, igniting a war between the states. Heavy casualties in the early battles shattered both sides' illusions that the war would end swiftly.

Lincoln ennobled the Civil War in 1863 when he issued the Emancipation Proclamation. The proclamation did not free any slaves immediately, but it gave the war a high moral purpose.

The war ended with Lee's surrender at Appomattox in April 1865. Lincoln was faced with the difficult task of reunifying, or reconstructing, the nation. Unfortunately, Lincoln was assassinated before he could implement his plans.

RECONSTRUCTION The weakness of Lincoln's successor, Andrew Johnson, allowed the Republicans to dominate Reconstruction. Sweeping social changes occurred as former slaves gained mobility and the right to attend school and organize churches.

However, many white Southerners opposed African-American freedom. Some groups used violence to terrorize African Americans. Others used economic pressure to exert their control.

Political scandals and the Panic of 1873 weakened the Republicans. Finally, Rutherford B. Hayes won the election of 1876 through a compromise in which Republicans agreed to halt Reconstruction.

Preview Chapter 5

During and after Reconstruction, Americans continued expanding westward. This expansion caused many crises for Native Americans, the growth of a new cattle industry and society on the Great Plains, and a reform movement known as populism. You will learn about these significant developments in the next chapter.

ALTERNATIVE ASSESSMENT

1. **REPORTING ABOUT THE CIVIL WAR**
   How were battles of the Civil War fought? Who were the leaders? the soldiers? What were war conditions like?
   - Acting as a reporter for an international newspaper, write an eyewitness account of a battle in the American Civil War.
     CD-ROM Use the CD-ROM *Fateful Lightning* and other reference materials to research the events of a specific battle, including information on key players and details about the setting.
   - Think about the information you would share with a foreign audience living in the days before radio, television, or film. Include details about people, places, and events, as well as relevant historical background, to enhance your account.
   - Conclude your report with a prediction of which side will win and how America might change as a result of the war.
2. **LEARNING FROM MEDIA**
   VIDEO View the videos for Chapter 4, *War Outside My Window* and *Teacher of a Freed People.* Discuss the following questions in small groups; then do the cooperative learning activity.
   - What is your overall impression of Mary Chesnut?
   - What, if anything, surprised you about the diary entries?
   - What was Robert Fitzgerald's experience in the Civil War?
   - Which experiences in Fitzgerald's life helped foster his passion for learning and teaching?
   - How did Fitzgerald respond to the difficulties he faced?
   - **Cooperative Learning** Imagine that Mary Chesnut and Robert Fitzgerald met to discuss their beliefs. As a group, write a dialogue that might have taken place between the two. Take turns role-playing the pair to establish their personalities and clarify their ideas.
3. **PORTFOLIO PROJECT**
   Use the Living History activity to expand your portfolio.

LIVING HISTORY

WRITING YOUR BIOGRAPHY

Use the materials you have collected about a Civil War or Reconstruction figure to write a biography of that person. Show how

- experiences during early life affected the person
- experiences during the Civil War or Reconstruction affected the person
- the person expressed his or her beliefs

Give your first draft to another student to read. Make changes based on the feedback you get. Add your biography to your American history portfolio.

ALTERNATIVE ASSESSMENT

1. REPORTING ABOUT THE CIVIL WAR

Standards for Evaluation

A strong eyewitness account should meet the following criteria.

- Focuses on one specific battle from the Civil War.
- Shows evidence of research from a variety of sources.
- Includes descriptive details, personal observations, and facts.
- Creates a sense of immediacy.

2. LEARNING FROM MEDIA

Answers will vary. Possible answers follow.

- Intelligent, feisty, articulate, sensitive, insightful.
- Mary Chesnut's insights into the politics of war; her access to Jefferson Davis; her account of the outrageous prices of staple items during the war.
- Union soldier who fought at the Battle of Petersburg, Virginia, in 1864.
- Experiences at Lincoln University inspired him to become a teacher in the Freedmen's Bureau.
- Raised a family and continued to teach.

3. PORTFOLIO PROJECT

LIVING HISTORY

Standards for Evaluation

A biography should meet the following criteria.

- Clearly identifies and describes the person.
- Explains what makes the person a significant Civil War or Reconstruction figure.
- Uses specific examples to show how the war or Reconstruction influenced the person.
- Uses quotations and anecdotes whenever possible to illustrate the person's life.
- Supports statements with evidence from a variety of sources.

IN-DEPTH RESOURCES: UNIT 1
See the form for scoring this activity on page 119.

THINKING CRITICALLY

4. CIVIL WAR FIRSTS
Rankings will vary widely, but should be well supported with reasons.

5. TRACING THEMES CIVIL RIGHTS
Possible Responses: The federal government needs to help people protect their rights; we have to be vigilant so that civil rights laws or amendments do not become diminished by newer laws; reliance on the government can fail because of bias, corruption, or lack of leadership.

6. ANALYZING PRIMARY SOURCES
Possible Responses: The government could have provided former slaves with fertile farmland, money, or tools. The government could have passed a law making planters give either money or land to freedmen for their past work. However, these efforts might have simply angered whites even more and caused more terrorism.

OBJECTIVES

1. To explain how migration and immigration shaped the early United States.
2. To describe changing U.S. roles in world affairs between 1792 and 1877.
3. To analyze the impact of diverse cultures on American life.
4. To discuss the constitutional issues facing the nation between 1792 and 1877.
5. To analyze the civil rights issues that emerged during the Civil War and Reconstruction.
6. To describe the growth of democracy in the United States before 1877.
7. To identify the changes in women's roles between 1792 and 1877.
8. To analyze the changes in the American economy in the 19th century.
9. To determine how science and technology affected American life in the 1800s.
10. To define the American dream.

CRITICAL THINKING

- Recognizing effects, pp. 204, 208
- Drawing conclusions, p. 205
- Identifying problems, p. 206
- Analyzing issues, p. 206
- Developing historical perspective, p. 207
- Comparing and contrasting, pp. 207, 209

FOCUS & MOTIVATE

5-MINUTE WARM-UP

Making Judgments

To reflect on the themes, have students look over pages 204–209, and then answer the following questions.

1. Which of these themes do you think played the most important role in American history up to 1877?
2. Which of these themes might play the most important role in the 20th century?

WARM-UP TRANSPARENCY THEMATIC REVIEW

Thematic Review of Unit 1

Beginnings Through Reconstruction

To help you make sense of the formative years of the American republic, the next six pages provide a review that is organized around the ten historical themes that are woven into *The Americans.* This Thematic Review will help you focus on the major issues that had emerged in American history by the end of Reconstruction in 1877.

Immigrants arrive in New York harbor in the mid-1800s.

Immigration and Migration

The movement of people has been an important force shaping American history. Most anthropologists believe that the first humans migrated to the Americas about 40,000 years ago, crossing a land bridge that connected Asia to Alaska. Over the centuries, these people spread throughout North and South America.

In 1492, Columbus completed his first voyage to this New World. People from several countries soon started colonies there. The English settled along the Atlantic Coast, in Jamestown (1607), Plymouth Colony (1620), and Massachusetts Bay Colony (1630). The Dutch settled in New Amsterdam (now New York) in 1625. The French established a settlement to the north, in Quebec City.

The Spanish built a fort at St. Augustine, on the Florida coast, and established a capital in the Southwest at Santa Fe, New Mexico. A number of Spanish missions arose in New Mexico and in California.

After centuries of isolation, Native Americans had no defenses against European diseases. They died by the thousands, making it more difficult for them to resist European expansion. Another group that suffered terribly from immigration were the millions of Africans who were forcibly brought to the colonies as enslaved people.

After the colonies won their independence from England, the United States continued to attract new immigrants. Groups already settled in the United States did not always welcome newcomers. But the stream of immigrants—primarily Irish and Germans—continued. By the 1840s, many of these immigrants joined native-born Americans moving west. They drove their long wagon trains as far as the Pacific Coast, where they met thousands of Chinese immigrants who had come to California to work on railroads and in the mines. Americans had spread from coast to coast.

THINK THROUGH HISTORY
A. ***Recognizing Effects*** *In what ways did immigration and migration shape the early United States?*

THEMATIC REVIEW RESOURCES

PRINT RESOURCES

IN-DEPTH RESOURCES: UNIT 1
Activities, p. 120

ACCESS FOR STUDENTS ACQUIRING ENGLISH
Activities (Spanish), p. 78

FORMAL ASSESSMENT
Essay Questions, p. 66

ALTERNATIVE ASSESSMENT BOOK
See forms for supporting and scoring alternative activities.

TECHNOLOGY RESOURCES

INTERNET http://www.mlushistory.com

America in the World

The European settlement of North America began as part of a contest for empire. The British pushed the Dutch out of what is now New York. Then, in 1763, they drove the French from North America. Just 15 years later, though, the British colonies rebelled. The French and Spanish helped them win their independence by supplying money, soldiers, and ships.

England, France, and Spain still held much of the continent, but that changed in the next few decades. First, France sold the United States the Louisiana Territory, doubling the nation's size. Soon, though, conflict with Native Americans and anger over British actions led to the War of 1812, which brought no clear victory but did produce a surge of nationalist feeling.

More confident, the United States began to flex its muscles. Mexico and Spain's other colonies in Latin America gained their own independence. With the Monroe Doctrine, the United States warned European powers to stay out of the Western Hemisphere.

The United States began to act on the idea of "manifest destiny," or the belief that the country should expand to the Pacific coast. Americans in Texas proclaimed a new republic, removing that region from Mexican control. Soon the United States annexed Texas, which led to the War with Mexico. After a swift victory by U.S. forces, the Treaty of Guadalupe Hidalgo gave California and the Southwest to the United States. Shortly thereafter, the Gadsden Purchase completed the boundaries of the lower 48 states. The former English and Spanish colonies were now joined together.

In summary, international relations in the nation's early years were marked by two major achievements: establishment of the United States on the world stage and expansion of its territory.

The French Revolution was partly inspired by the colonists' revolt against the British in North America.

THINK THROUGH HISTORY
B. *Drawing Conclusions* *What was the most important change in the U.S. involvement in foreign affairs from 1789 to 1877?*

B. Answer Possible Response: The country's growing confidence and assertiveness on the world stage.

Cultural Diversity

The United States developed a diverse population. For centuries, Native American groups had followed many different ways of life, each suited to a particular environment. While adopting some aspects of European culture, they passed on parts of their own culture. English settlers did not respect Native American culture, but adopted many native terms and agricultural practices. In the Spanish colonies, settlers and native peoples interacted closely.

Settlers brought different cultures to different regions. In fact, the diversity of the populations and the unequal status of the different cultures caused tension. Dutch New Amsterdam and Quaker Pennsylvania showed more tolerance of religious differences than Puritan New England did. German and Scots-Irish immigrants settled from New Netherlands to as far south as the Carolinas. The Southwest and California reflected the culture of the Spanish settlers and the cowboy.

Over time, the Northern and Southern regions of the United States developed distinct cultures. A key feature of Southern culture was slavery. African Americans maintained their traditions of dance, music, and crafts, which helped shape Southern culture.

The mission system played a vital role in the development of the Southwest.

THINK THROUGH HISTORY
C. *Drawing Conclusions* *What impact did the different cultures in North America have on the United States?*

C. Answer Possible Responses: English—law, customs, driving away of native peoples; Spanish—language; African-American—traditional dance, music, and crafts; Dutch—greater tolerance of religious differences.

▶Starting with the Student
Invite students to record in their journals the themes they find in their own lives. Then ask them how themes can help them understand historical events.

OBJECTIVE
 **INSTRUCT**

Immigration and Migration

▶Discussing Key Ideas
- People first migrate to the Americas about 40,000 years ago.
- European settlers bring diseases and displace Native Americans.
- African Americans are brought to the colonies as slaves.
- Immigrants continue to come to the United States in the 19th century.

OBJECTIVE
 **INSTRUCT**

America in the World

▶Discussing Key Ideas
- European nations compete for control of North America.
- The colonies rebel and establish a new nation.
- The United States expands through war and diplomacy.

OBJECTIVE
 **INSTRUCT**

Cultural Diversity

▶Discussing Key Ideas
- European settlers bring European cultures to

(continued on next page)

Block Schedule TEACHING OPTION **Time Needed: 20 Minutes**

Cooperative Activity: Exhibiting Immigrant Experiences

Task: Small groups of students will prepare multimedia exhibits on immigrant experiences in America.

Purpose: To help students understand the reasons immigrants came to the United States as well as the immigrants' experiences in their new homes.

Activity: Each of the students in the group should complete one task in preparing the exhibit. One student could interview immigrants about their experiences. Another student could conduct historical research to explain the historical context of the immigration experiences of these people. A third student could research photos or other images for the report. A fourth student might design a layout for the exhibit.

Building a Portfolio: Students should save their exhibits for their portfolios.

ALTERNATIVE ASSESSMENT BOOK
Standards for Evaluating a Cooperative Activity

Standards for Evaluation
Exhibits should . . .
- show evidence of research in a variety of sources and media
- provide a clear connection between the experiences of the immigrants and the historical context

(continued from page 205)

North America and displace Native American societies and their cultures.
- In the young United States, people in different regions develop diverse cultures.

OBJECTIVE

④ INSTRUCT

Constitutional Concerns

▶ ***Discussing Key Ideas***
- The Constitution creates a strong central government that is balanced by the individual liberties protected in the Bill of Rights.
- The issue of slavery leads to a debate over the power of the federal government versus the power of the states that culminates in the Civil War.

OBJECTIVE

⑤ INSTRUCT

Civil Rights

▶ ***Starting with the Student*** The Fourteenth and Fifteenth Amendments promised equality to African Americans but did not deliver it. Ask students whether African Americans have achieved equality yet.

▶ ***Discussing Key Ideas***
- The Southern states maintain and expand the institution of slavery.
- In 1857, the Supreme Court declares in the Dred Scott case that slaves are property.
- The Fourteenth and Fifteenth Amendments recognize African Americans as citizens and give them full voting rights, but complete equality is not achieved.

D. Answer Possible Responses: States' rights vs. federal power; large states vs. small states; freedom vs. the maintenance of order; strict interpretation vs. loose interpretation of the Constitution.

E. Answer The 14th and 16th amendments banned slavery and extended citizenship, as did the Civil Rights Act. However, Reconstruction did not ensure full participation by blacks. The North lost interest in reforming the racial structure in the South.

Constitutional Concerns

From the start, the English colonists enjoyed varying degrees of self-government. But by the 1770s, the feeling had grown that the colonists' rights would not be secure so long as they remained subject to Great Britain. They fought the Revolutionary War to win their independence.

The new nation's leaders set out to construct a framework for the new government, moving from the Articles of Confederation to the Constitution. Several leaders expressed alarm at the strong central government that the Constitution created. Only with the promise of passing several amendments that guaranteed individual freedoms—the Bill of Rights—did the framers win approval of the Constitution.

Questions about the relative power of state and national governments still remained. South Carolina threatened to nullify, or disallow, a federal law in the 1830s, but the crisis was defused. The issue of slavery, though, threatened to tear the Union apart. The Civil War was the greatest constitutional crisis the country faced. The war settled the matter of secession, but the balance between states' rights and federal power continued to be an important constitutional issue.

New Yorkers celebrate the new Constitution with a parade featuring the "Ship of State" float in 1788.

THINK THROUGH HISTORY
D. *Identifying Problems* *What was the most important constitutional conflict in the United States between 1789 and 1877? How was this played out, and how did it get resolved?*

Civil Rights

Slavery came to British North America in the 17th century. Racism, labor shortages, and the establishment of plantation agriculture had led to the entrenchment of slavery in the South during the early 19th century. African-American slaves had few rights. The Constitution had stipulated that banning the slave trade could not be considered until 1808, but opposition to the institution grew throughout the North—and became more vocal and more violent.

Southerners feared that the North would increase its power in Congress and abolish slavery. They pushed to extend the institution to new territories.

In the pivotal 1857 *Dred Scott* decision, the Supreme Court declared that slaves were not people, but property, and thus had no rights.

Less than ten years later, the nation fought a bloody civil war that ended slavery. The Fourteenth Amendment to the Constitution recognized African Americans as citizens, and they briefly enjoyed full civil rights. Even when those rights were later denied, the Constitution then included the Fifteenth Amendment, which banned the denial of voting rights on the basis of race or color. These amendments, along with the Civil Rights Act of 1964, would become powerful tools in the quest for equality in the 1950s and the 1960s.

THINK THROUGH HISTORY
E. *Analyzing Issues* *What were the successes and failures of the Civil War and Reconstruction in extending civil rights to African Americans?*

This former slave family welcomed the passage of the Thirteenth Amendment, which abolished slavery.

TEACHING OPTIONS

Teaching Gifted and Talented Students

Writing an Essay Have students read about the themes dealing with constitutional concerns and civil rights on page 206. Then have them write a one-page essay discussing how these two themes were related between the ratification of the Constitution and the end of Reconstruction.

Making Connections Across the Curriculum

Civics The issue of slavery raised important questions that relate to the two themes dealing with constitutional concerns and civil rights. Discuss with students why this was the case. Point out that the framers of the Constitution tried to avoid the issue of slavery but that the issue divided the nation and eventually led to the Civil War. Students should also understand that slavery was an institution defined by law, which stated that slaves were property. Controlled by the slaveowners, slaves enjoyed few, if any, civil rights.

Democracy in America

This period was critical to the establishment of a stable constitutional democracy in the United States. The Constitution and the Bill of Rights were ratified. The important democratic institutions—Congress, the Presidency, the Supreme Court, and political parties—were firmly established.

During the 1800s, the right to vote was gradually broadened to include more members of society. In the 1820s, state governments enlarged the voter base by easing voter requirements, such as property qualifications. These new voters were critical to the election of Andrew Jackson in 1828 and 1832.

While growing numbers of white males had won the right to vote, women were still denied that right. Elizabeth Cady Stanton led other women to push for this right and other reforms to give women equal status with men. Their efforts were often met with scorn.

Democratic rights were extended to African Americans after the Civil War, when the Fifteenth Amendment gave them the right to vote. Within a few years, though, Southern states instituted harsh new laws against blacks—called black codes. When courts upheld these laws, African Americans lost their rights. Northerners, tired of decades of conflict over slavery and its aftermath, turned their attention away from the status of former slaves and toward other matters.

Campaign flags of the 1800s often emphasized the candidate's patriotism.

THINK THROUGH HISTORY
F. *Developing Historical Perspective* *In the period from 1789 until 1877, what were the signs that the United States had developed a stable constitutional democracy?*

F. Answer Some indications were the establishment of stable institutions, such as the presidency. Easing of voter requirements was another sign of stability.

Women in America

Beginning in colonial times, women in America confronted many limits, including lack of suffrage. Laws in some colonies prohibited them from owning property. Laws in others said that only single women or widows could run their own businesses.

During the American Revolution, women expanded their roles by filling in for their husbands on the farms and in the shops and, occasionally, taking up arms. In the new nation, however, the concept of republican motherhood emphasized the role of women in preparing the next generation of citizens.

In the early 1800s, many women became more socially active. Reformers such as Elizabeth Cady Stanton and Lucretia Mott pushed for women's rights. Others, like Harriet Beecher Stowe and Sojourner Truth, spoke out against slavery. Women worked to advance the temperance movement against alcohol and to improve health and education.

Many women were swept up in the massive population movement to the West. With spirit and determination, frontier women overcame tremendous hardships to help carve a new life from the land.

Women endured much during the Civil War, whether they lived in the North or the South. Many lost their fathers and husbands. Many, too, gained strength by meeting new demands placed on them. With hundreds of thousands of men serving in armies and out of the work force, women filled the void by serving as laborers in farms and factories.

THINK THROUGH HISTORY
G. *Comparing and Contrasting* *Compare and contrast women's roles in the United States in 1877 with those in 1789.*

G. Answer In the 1800s, women expanded their roles by being active in many reform movements. They took an equal role with men in the movement west and increased their economic roles by joining the work force in greater numbers. But women still had no official political role, because they did not have the vote.

Molly Pitcher was only one example of the women who took a strong role in creating a new nation.

OBJECTIVE
(6) INSTRUCT

Democracy in America

▶***Starting with the Student***
Ask students to brainstorm a list of rights and institutions that ensure democracy in America today.

▶***Discussing Key Ideas***
- The easing of voting requirements in the 1820s enlarges the voter base.
- Institutions such as Congress, the Supreme Court, the presidency, and political parties help maintain a stable democracy.
- Women and African Americans continue to face discrimination and political inequality.

OBJECTIVE
(7) INSTRUCT

Women in America

▶***Discussing Key Ideas***
- In 1792, women do not have the right to vote. Many women are prohibited from owning property or running a business.
- During the 1800s, women become active in social reform movements.
- Women are among the pioneers of the West, and they meet the new demands placed on them during the Civil War.

TEACHING OPTIONS

Making Connections Across Time

Democracy in America Discuss with students how the issues that affect U.S. democratic processes today relate to the issues of expanding democracy in the early 19th century. Ask students if they feel low voter turnout or campaign finance scandals pose a serious threat to democracy. Do they think the obstacles to democracy were greater in the 19th century than they are today? Ask them to explain the reasons for their answers.

Making Connections Across Time

Women in America Discuss with students how the issues that shaped the lives of women in the early 19th century relate to the issues that shape women's lives today. Ask them to consider whether the right to own property has helped women achieve economic equality with men. Discuss the ways in which women participate in modern reform movements. Ask students to discuss women's roles in modern wars. How have these roles evolved since the 19th century?

OBJECTIVE

8 INSTRUCT

Economic Opportunity

▶ ***Starting with the Student*** Ask students where they believe the greatest economic opportunities are today.

▶ ***Discussing Key Ideas***
- The lure of economic success helps fuel immigration and migration.
- The Industrial Revolution and the Civil War accelerate industrial growth in the North while an agricultural economy remains dominant throughout the South.
- Legally free, many African Americans remain economically dependent as a result of the sharecropping system.

OBJECTIVE

9 INSTRUCT

Science and Technology

▶ ***Starting with the Student*** Name a recent invention. Then ask students how it affects the lives of Americans today.

▶ ***Discussing Key Ideas***
- New inventions in the 1800s produce wide-ranging economic and social effects.

Economic Opportunity

Slater's Mill—the first successful mechanized textile factory in America—became a model for the many factories built in the Northeast.

The promise of wealth first attracted Europeans to the New World. Seeing the vast riches that the Spanish had won in conquering native empires, other European nations scrambled to begin their own colonies. Early settlements were created by companies of investors hoping to strike it rich in the new land. The lure of the land and the hope of economic success continued to fuel immigration to the United States—and the movement of people within the country.

Regional differences developed in the American economy during the colonial period. The North focused on farming and some industry. New transportation routes, such as the Erie Canal, brought increased trade among Northern states. As the Industrial Revolution took hold in the early 1800s, factories sprung up throughout the Northern states and farming declined. After this, the rich farmlands of the Midwest became the breadbasket of the nation. The Civil War accelerated economic growth in the North and Midwest. Industry boomed. Farm output grew as well.

A plantation economy geared to raising cash crops for export arose early in the South. At first, planters grew tobacco, rice, and indigo. Beginning in the 1800s, the main crop was cotton. Cotton was called "king," and a small group of large landowners dominated the Southern economy and society. They became wealthy and powerful by exploiting the labor of masses of African-American slaves.

With the end of the Civil War, slaves gained their freedom and finally had a chance for economic opportunity. The Congress decided not to redistribute the land, however. Though legally free, many blacks became economically controlled by landowners—mostly whites—through tenant farming or sharecropping.

H. Answer Possible Responses: Industrial Revolution—movement from farms to factories; movement to Midwest—wealthier farms; growth of cotton—increased use of slave labor; emancipation of slaves—rise of sharecropping.

THINK THROUGH HISTORY

H. *Recognizing Effects* *What was one important economic development in the United States between the colonial period and 1877? How did this development affect the everyday lives of Americans?*

Science and Technology

During the 1800s, the United States established itself as highly innovative and quick to find commercial applications for technological advances. For instance, the cotton gin—invented by a Northerner, Eli Whitney—speeded up the processing of cotton and spurred a cotton boom. The boom in cotton led, in turn, to the renewed growth of slavery. Cotton growers spread the practice to new areas, including Mississippi, Alabama, and Louisiana.

The cotton was shipped to the North, where in the mid-19th century entrepreneurs built new factories that turned it into cloth. New shoemaking and sewing machines sped up clothing manufacture. These changes affected Northern society. Skilled artisans gave way to factory workers skilled in the techniques of mass production. Feeling powerless compared with the factory owners, workers tried to organize labor unions.

Samuel F. B. Morse's telegraph made instant communication possible.

As the nation expanded, inventors created new technologies that improved transportation and communication. Pioneers traveled over roads and trails to reach the frontier. The Erie Canal brought food from the Midwest to the ports of the east, helping to make New York City a major commercial center. Steamboats sped up and down rivers, increasing trade. Railroads linked cities. With the completion of the transcontinental railroad in 1869, rails stretched from sea to sea. Telegraph lines allowed people to send messages instantly over vast distances.

I. Answer Possible Responses: Sewing machine—cheaper clothing, but good quality; cotton gin—boosted slavery; railroads—improved mobility, boosted factories.

THINK THROUGH HISTORY

I. *Recognizing Effects* *What was one innovation that affected how Americans worked and lived? What were the effects of this innovation?*

TEACHING OPTIONS

Teaching Less Proficient Readers

Organizing Information To help students understand the effects of an invention such as the cotton gin, draw the following organizer on the chalkboard and help students fill in the missing information.

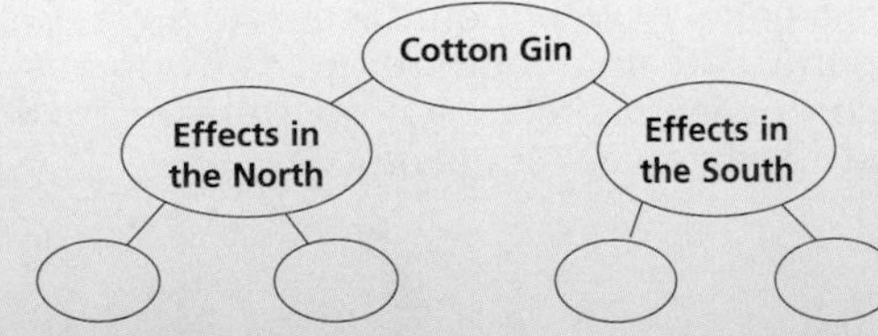

Making Connections Across the Curriculum

Science Amateur surveyors decided how the Erie Canal would be built. There were many engineering challenges. The route included large ascents and descents, most notably the 688-foot ascent from Rochester to Buffalo. Basic hydraulic engineering principles, some of which were discovered long ago by Leonardo da Vinci, were used to construct 83 locks to raise and lower water levels. To keep water flowing gently over varying levels, a complex system of feeders drew water from lakes and streams. Another engineering feat was making the east-west canal cross the north-south rivers—this was achieved through the construction of aqueducts.

The American Dream

What is the American dream? For two centuries, it has been the hope that kept the American people going. It was the Native Americans' longing to retain the lands on which they had lived for so long. It was the Puritans' desire to find religious freedom and tolerance. It was the patriots' wish to found a new republic that guaranteed the rights of its citizens. It was the reformers' call for a better society. It was the pioneers' or immigrants' hunger for a better life. It was the slaves' yearning for freedom while escaping slavery on the Underground Railroad.

The American dream was all these hopes and desires—and more. All nations evolve over time, and the superb ideals on which the United States was founded were increasingly implemented. Strengthened by these ideals, colonists survived the starving time of Jamestown. Bolstered by their dreams, African Americans lived through the horrors of the Middle Passage and the injustice of the plantation. Americans kept their faith through the hard labor of clearing the wilderness, through war and the division caused by the Civil War, and through the assassination of a beloved president. Sustained by their visions of the future, they built a new nation that embodied the different visions of a wide variety of people.

For the Pilgrims, the American dream meant religious freedom that they had been denied in England.

THINK THROUGH HISTORY
J. *Comparing and Contrasting* *Compare and contrast the American dream during the colonial period with the American dream in 1877. How did it stay the same? How did it change?*

J. Answer In the colonies, the dream included the desire for religious freedom and for land. With immigration, the American dream is still economically based, but also includes a hope for reform and justice—for inclusion in the body politic.

LIVING HISTORY

COURSE–LONG PORTFOLIO PROJECT

Choose one of the ten themes that you find most interesting or about which you want to learn more. Build a portfolio about that theme as you continue your study of American history. Here are some ideas to think about:

- Explore the availability of possible resources you might use during your research. Find out what references are available in your school and local library—including encyclopedias, historical journals, U.S. government statistical abstracts, and access to the Internet.
- Develop a bibliography of scholarly articles and books—secondary sources—that relate to the theme you have chosen. Consider adding annotations to each bibliographic entry that explain how the source relates to the theme you are exploring.
- Collect readings, letters, and diary entries—primary sources—as well as your own personal writing related to that theme.
- Create a time line of the major events in U.S. history that relate to the theme. Add dates and events to the time line as you bring your study of American history to the present day.
- Gather images—or create your own—that illustrate the theme. Use such resources as this textbook, books of fine art that portray events in American history, and historical magazines.

PORTFOLIO PROJECT
Keep the materials you gather about the theme in a folder. At the end of the course, you will create a written and visual presentation in which you explain the significance of the theme for the nation's past and for its future.

OBJECTIVE
10 INSTRUCT

The American Dream

Discussing Key Ideas
- The American dream takes many forms.
- Strengthened by their dreams, Americans have survived many ordeals.

ASSESS & RETEACH

Thematic Review Assessment
Have students form small groups to discuss the Think Through History questions.

Self-Assessment
Ask students to choose a theme and create an essay question about it. Then have students trade questions with a partner and write responses.

FORMAL ASSESSMENT
Essay Questions, p. 66

PORTFOLIO PROJECT
LIVING HISTORY

Standards for Evaluation
This is an ongoing project. (See page 875 for a final evaluation of this project.) In its early stages the theme portfolio should meet the following criteria.
- Focuses on one theme.
- Includes the beginning of a bibliography.
- Includes at least one primary source.
- Begins to develop a time line of major events.
- Presents images that illustrate the theme.

IN-DEPTH RESOURCES: UNIT 1
See worksheet and standards for evaluation, pp. 121, 122.

Block Schedule TEACHING OPTION **Time Needed: 20 Minutes**

Cooperative Activity: Writing About the American Dream

Task: To define the American dream and give an example of people who have achieved it.

Purpose: To show the different ways in which people understand the American dream as well as the different ways in which they have pursued it.

Activity: Ask each group of three or four students to agree on a definition of the American dream. Then each member of the group should research various individuals throughout American history who have achieved this definition of the American dream. Have students write an essay on how the person they researched fulfilled the American dream. Then have the group reexamine its definition of the American dream and consider whether the definition needs to be revised.

Building a Portfolio: Students should add their essay to their history portfolio.

ALTERNATIVE ASSESSMENT BOOK
Standards for Evaluating a Cooperative Activity

Standards for Evaluation
Essays should . . .
- include a definition of the American dream
- describe different American dreams
- demonstrate how people strive to achieve the American dream

UNIT OVERVIEW

Bridge to the 20th Century

HISTORY AND ART

The intersection of Orchard and Hester Streets in New York's Lower East Side

Oil over a photograph by unknown artist (1905).

Art Note
By the turn of the century, lithographs and woodcuts had largely been replaced by photographs as the most-used medium for prints aimed at the mass market. Though color film had not yet been developed, photo studios could still provide color images. Skilled workers hand-tinted the photographs.

▶ ***Previewing the Unit***
Unit 2 describes how the United States transforms itself from a mostly rural, agricultural society to an urban, industrial one. Farmers, miners, and ranchers settle all regions of the West, costing Native Americans their land. Large businesses begin to dominate the economy. Providing much of the labor for these huge new concerns are millions of immigrants who stream to the major cities of the North and East. New manufacturing and selling techniques begin to create mass consumer markets for goods and services.

UNIT 2

1877–1917

Bridge to the 20th Century

"People are the common denominator of progress."
JOHN KENNETH GALBRAITH

1 Lower East Side
New York's Lower East Side became home to hundreds of thousands of immigrants, especially those from southern and eastern Europe around the turn of the century. The population density was estimated at 500 to 1,000 people per acre—among the highest in the world.

2 Street peddlers
About a quarter of the immigrants who settled in New York—and high proportions in other cities as well—worked as street peddlers. Licenses were cheap, as were the goods they sold. Selling gave immigrants a chance to interact with others who spoke their language.

3 Horse-drawn carts
In 1905, when this photo was taken, horse-drawn carts were still the main means of transportation. Electric-powered elevated railways or subways provided mass transit. The automobile had only just started to become available.

211

Discussing the Quotation

In the nearly 40 years from 1876 to 1914, millions of immigrants came to the United States. This great influx of people was a key element in what Galbraith calls "progress."

FOR DISCUSSION:

- Why did people come?
- How did they contribute to the economy?
- How did their arrival shape American society?
- What was the "common denominator" for the residents of the Lower East Side, who had immigrated from so many different countries?

Discussing the Image

Photographs can document more accurately than a painting the appearance and atmosphere of a time and place. The people and objects captured on film tell us much about how people once lived.

FOR DISCUSSION:

- What goods are being sold in stores and by peddlers? What does this say about New York in 1905?
- What kinds of people are pictured and what are they doing?
- How are the people dressed, and how does that compare with today?

4 Tenements

The Lower East Side was full of tenements—apartment buildings that often had one family per room. Reformers passed laws that limited buildings in size to leave some open space; limited the number of people in a unit; required that all rooms have access to fresh air; and required running water and toilet facilities. Still, the buildings were crowded. Many families used their units not only to live but also to work. One building on Orchard Street today is home to the Lower East Side Tenement Museum.

5 Street signs

The city in 1905 was poised between its past and its future. Signs marking streets, paved streets, and manhole covers *(lower right)* show some features that we would recognize today. But note the absence of traffic signs, traffic lights, and streetlights.

CHAPTER 5

PLANNING GUIDE

Changes on the Western Frontier

	Key Ideas	COPYMASTERS	ASSESSMENT
SECTION 1 Native American Cultures in Crisis **pp. 214–221**	*Pursuit of economic opportunity leads settlers to push westward, forcing confrontation with established Native American cultures.*	***In-Depth Resources: Unit 2*** • Guided Reading, p. 1 • Primary Source: The Battle of the Little Bighorn, p. 9 • American Lives: Chief Joseph, p. 15 ***Lesson Plans,*** pp. 45–46	PE ***Section 1 Assessment,*** p. 221 TE ***Self-Assessment,*** p. 221 ***Formal Assessment*** • Section Quiz, p. 68 ***Alternative Assessment Book*** • Standards for Evaluating a Cooperative Activity
SECTION 2 The Growth of the Cattle Industry **pp. 222–227**	*The cattle industry thrives as the culture of the Great Plains Indians declines, and a new worker—the cowboy—appears on the scene.*	***In-Depth Resources: Unit 2*** • Guided Reading, p. 2 • Skillbuilder Practice: Creating Graphs, p. 5 ***Lesson Plans,*** pp. 47–48	PE ***Section 2 Assessment,*** p. 227 TE ***Self-Assessment,*** p. 227 ***Formal Assessment*** • Section Quiz, p. 69 ***Alternative Assessment Book*** • Standards for Evaluating a Cooperative Activity
SECTION 3 Settling on the Great Plains **pp. 230–234**	*The promise of cheap, fertile land draws thousands of settlers westward to seek their fortunes as farmers.*	***In-Depth Resources: Unit 2*** • Guided Reading, p. 3 • Geography Application: Land Regions of the West, p. 7 • Primary Source: Letter from a Woman Homesteader, p. 10 • Literature: from *My Ántonia* by Willa Cather, p. 12 ***Lesson Plans,*** pp. 49–50	PE ***Section 3 Assessment,*** p. 234 TE ***Self-Assessment,*** p. 234 ***Formal Assessment*** • Section Quiz, p. 70 ***Alternative Assessment Book*** • Standards for Evaluating a Cooperative Activity
SECTION 4 Farmers and the Populist Movement **pp. 235–239**	*Farmers band together to address their economic problems, giving rise to the Populist movement.*	***In-Depth Resources: Unit 2*** • Guided Reading, p. 4 • Skillbuilder Practice: Interpreting Charts, p. 6 • Primary Source: *from* William Jennings Bryan's "Cross of Gold" Speech, p. 11 • American Lives: Mary Elizabeth Lease, p. 16 ***Lesson Plans,*** pp. 51–52	PE ***Section 4 Assessment,*** p. 239 TE ***Self-Assessment,*** p. 239 ***Formal Assessment*** • Section Quiz, p. 71 ***Alternative Assessment Book*** • Standards for Evaluating a Cooperative Activity
CHAPTER RESOURCES	**Chapter Overview** *In the late 1800s, growing numbers of white settlers move to the West, and Native Americans lose their lands. Railroads cross the nation, and both the cattle kingdom and Populism rise and fall.*	***In-Depth Resources: Unit 2*** • Living History Project: Worksheet, p. 17; Standards, p. 18 ***Telescoping the Times*** • Chapter Summary, pp. 9–10 ***Planning for Block Schedules***	PE ***Chapter Assessment,*** pp. 242–243 PE ***Alternative Assessment,*** p. 243 ***Formal Assessment*** • Chapter Test, forms A and B, pp. 72–77 ***Test Generator*** ***Alternative Assessment Book*** See explanation and forms for different kinds of alternative assessments including portfolio assessment.

KEY
- PE Pupil's Edition
- TE Teacher's Edition
- http://www.mlushistory.com

TECHNOLOGY

Warm-Up Transparency 5

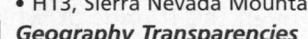

Humanities Transparencies
- H13, Sierra Nevada Mountains

Geography Transparencies
- G13, Railroad Land Grants, 1871

Electronic Library of Primary Sources
- On the Use of English in Indian Schools

Grolier Multimedia Encyclopedia
- Indian Wars

AMERICAN STORIES video series
- *"A Walk in Two Worlds"*

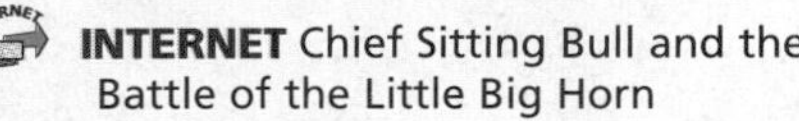

INTERNET Chief Sitting Bull and the Battle of the Little Big Horn

Warm-Up Transparency 5

Grolier Multimedia Encyclopedia
- Cattle Raising

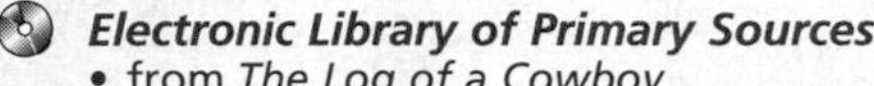

Electronic Library of Primary Sources
- from *The Log of a Cowboy*

INTERNET Interact with History p. 229 (PE)

Warm-Up Transparency 5

Critical Thinking Transparencies
- CT13, Transcontinental Railroad
- CT47, Population Changes in the West, 1850–1900

Electronic Library of Primary Sources
- from *Letters of a Woman Homesteader*

INTERNET Sod houses and home-steading

Warm-Up Transparency 5

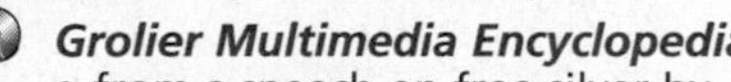

Grolier Multimedia Encyclopedia
- from a speech on free silver by William Jennings Bryan
- Overview of the Populist Party

INTERNET William McKinley

American Portfolio: A Videodisc for U.S. History, user's guide, pp. 121–129, 132–133, 135–139, 157, 160

Chapter Summary Audiotapes
- Unit 2, Chapter 5

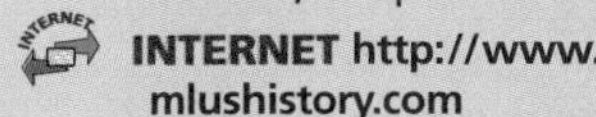

INTERNET http://www.mlushistory.com

Block Scheduling (90 MINUTES)

Day 1

Section 1, pp. 214–221

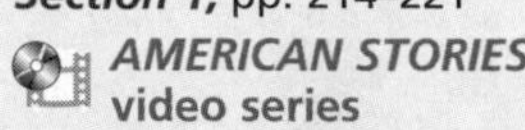

AMERICAN STORIES video series
"A Walk in Two Worlds"

Section 2, pp. 222–227

Section Assessments, pp. 221, 227

Daily Life: Mining, pp. 228–229

COOPERATIVE ACTIVITIES
- Cross-Cultural Debate, p. 216 (TE)
- Composing Boarding School Journals, p. 220 (TE)
- Researching Cowboy Music, p. 226 (TE)

Day 2

Section 3, pp. 230–234

Section Assessment, p. 234

COOPERATIVE ACTIVITY
- Advertising Agricultural Inventions, p. 233 (TE)

Day 3

Section 4, pp. 235–239

American Literature: Literature of the West, pp. 240–241

Chapter Assessment, pp. 242–243

COOPERATIVE ACTIVITIY
- Researching Populist Reforms, p. 237 (TE)

YEARLY PACING ***Chapter 5 Total:*** 3 days ***Yearly Total:*** 85 days

See *Planning for Block Schedules* for special activities and pacing strategies.

Customizing for Special Populations

Students Acquiring English

Access for Students Acquiring English: Spanish Translations
- Guided Reading for Sections 1–4, pp. 81–84
- Chapter Summary, pp. 79–80
- Skillbuilder Practice: Creating Graphs, p. 85; Interpreting Charts, p. 86
- Geography Application: Land Regions of the West, p. 87

Spanish Reading Study Guide, pp. 57–66

Translations of Chapter Summaries, Hmong, Cantonese, Vietnamese, and Cambodian

Chapter Summary Audiotapes in Spanish
Unit 2, Chapter 5

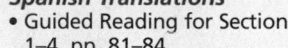

AMERICAN STORIES video series
- "A Walk in Two Worlds" (Spanish track)

INTERNET The Diverse Classroom

Gifted and Talented Students

In-Depth Resources: Unit 2
- Primary Sources: The Battle of the Little Bighorn, p. 9; Letter from a Woman Homesteader, p. 10; *from* William Jennings Bryan's "Cross of Gold" Speech, p. 11
- American Lives: Chief Joseph, p. 15; Mary Elizabeth Lease, p. 16

Less Proficient Readers

In-Depth Resources: Unit 2
- Guided Reading for Sections 1–4, pp. 1–4
- Skillbuilder Practice: Creating Graphs, p. 5; Interpreting Charts, p. 6
- Geography Application: Land Regions of the West, p. 7

Reading Study Guide
- pp. 57–66

Telescoping the Times
- Chapter Summary, pp. 9–10

Chapter Summary Audiotapes, Unit 2, Chapter 5

Connections to Literature READINGS FOR STUDENTS

In-Depth Resources: Unit 2
- **from *My Ántonia* by Willa Cather,** p. 12

Enrichment Reading
- **Willa Cather**
  O Pioneers!
  New York: Penguin, 1994.
  O Pioneers! is the story of Alexandra Bergson, the daughter of Swedish immigrants whose devotion to the land sustains her against the hardships and suffering of prairie life.
- **Ole Edvart Rolvaag**
  Giants in the Earth.
  New York: HarperCollins, 1991.
  This heroic tale focuses on Norwegian settlers in the plains of South Dakota. This has been called one of the "most powerful novels that has been written about pioneer life in America."

McDougal Littell *The Language of Literature*
American Literature
- **White Thunder, Black Elk, Paul Robert Walker,** pp. 511–512
- **Black Elk, told through John G. Neihardt, "High Horse's Courting," from *Black Elk Speaks,*** p. 521
- **Chief Joseph, "I Will Fight No More Forever,"** p. 527
- **Elinore Pruitt Stewart, from *Letters of a Woman Homesteader,*** p. 551

McDougal Littell *Literature Connections*

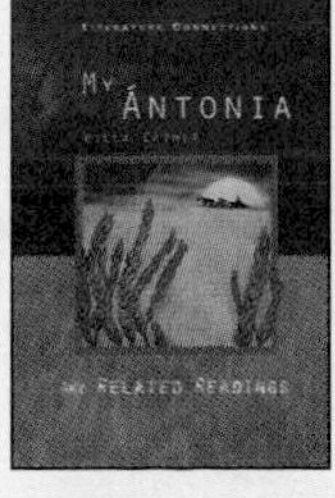

- **Willa Cather,**
  My Ántonia
  In this novel about a woman of the Nebraska prairie, Willa Cather writes with passion and truth about the land and characters she remembered from her childhood.

CHAPTER 5

OVERVIEW

Changes on the Western Frontier

▶ ***Accessing Prior Knowledge***
Ask students what the word *frontier* means to them. Have them describe the images that come to mind when they think of the Western frontier. Then ask them what frontiers they think are left today.

▶ ***Predicting Outcomes***
Ask students to look at the photos in Chapter 5. Based on these photos, have students predict what changes would come to the Western frontier.

MORE ABOUT . . .
Chief Joseph

Chief Joseph (1840?–1904) was joint leader of a Nez Perce band. He agreed to have his people leave their homeland in the Wallowa Valley in Oregon. After warriors killed some settlers, the band was pursued for more than 1,700 miles. Chief Joseph surrendered and later died without being allowed to return to his homeland.

CHAPTER 5

Changes on the Western Frontier

SECTION 1

Native American Cultures in Crisis

Pursuit of economic opportunity leads settlers to push westward, forcing confrontation with established Native American cultures.

SECTION 2

The Growth of the Cattle Industry

The cattle industry thrives as the culture of the Plains Indians declines, and a new worker—the cowboy—appears on the scene.

SECTION 3

Settling on the Great Plains

The promise of cheap, fertile land draws thousands of settlers westward to seek their fortunes as farmers.

SECTION 4

Farmers and the Populist Movement

Farmers band together to address their economic problems, giving rise to the Populist movement.

"My people have always been the friends of white men. Why are you in such a hurry?"

Chief Joseph of the Nez Perce to U.S. Army general O. O. Howard, 1877

Passengers aboard railroad cars shoot buffalo for sport.

THE UNITED STATES

- 1870 — Red Cloud, chief of the Oglala Sioux, states his people's case in Washington, D.C.
- 1871 — Long cattle drive enjoys its heyday.
- 1876 — George A. Custer and his troops are killed at Little Bighorn.
- 1879 — Thomas A. Edison invents the light bulb.

THE WORLD

- 1870 — Impressionism becomes an influential art movement in France.
- 1872 — Secret ballot is adopted in Great Britain.

1880

THEMES IN CHAPTER 5

The American Dream

The dreams of Native Americans and those of white settlers and immigrants conflicted, and violent confrontations often resulted.

See Teacher's Edition note, p. 217.

Cultural Diversity

Cowboys were a melting pot of diverse cultures—whites, African Americans, Mexicans, and Native Americans. These diverse groups lived and worked together harmoniously, despite cultural clashes in the society at large.

See Teacher's Edition note, p. 225.

Economic Opportunity

A major lure of the frontier was economic opportunity. The government contributed to economic development by financing the building of railroads and making land available to settlers at little or no cost. Economic opportunity was influenced by currency issues and economic panic.

See Teacher's Edition notes, pp. 224 and 236.

Women in America

Pioneer women played a crucial role on the frontier. Despite isolation and loneliness, they worked on the land and provided food, clothing, emotional support, and even medical care for their families.

See Teacher's Edition note, p. 232.

LIVING HISTORY

COMPILING A WESTERN TRAVEL GUIDE

Write a travel guide for Western travelers in the 1870s, based on what you learn in this chapter and on additional research. First decide who your readers are—settlers, cowboys, miners, or farmers. Then write your guide in parts, providing such information as:

- what to bring (e.g., 400 lb. of flour per person)
- how to get there (e.g., what transportation and route to take and where to stop along the way)
- how to avoid dangers (e.g., snakes, swollen rivers, lightning, and bandits)

Add visual material, such as maps, to your guide to make it more useful.

PORTFOLIO PROJECT Keep the guide in a folder for your American history portfolio. You will revise and present your guide at the end of the chapter.

Wearing shirts like this Arapaho one, Native Americans inspired by the Paiute prophet Wovoka perform the Ghost Dance in the hope of reclaiming their lands.

1881 — French occupy Tunisia.

1885 — Karl Benz builds the first automobile powered by internal-combustion engine.

Berlin Conference divides Africa among European nations.

1887 — Worst blizzard in American history causes a great "die-up" of cattle on the plains.

1889 — Buffalo Bill tours the United States and Europe with his Wild West Show.

1890

1893 — Collapse of railroads triggers the Panic of 1893.

1894 — Sino-Japanese War is fought.

1896 — William Jennings Bryan runs for president, calling for free coinage of silver.

1899 — Boer War in South Africa begins.

1900

ALTERNATIVE ASSESSMENT

LIVING HISTORY

COMPILING A WESTERN TRAVEL GUIDE

Help students plan their travel guides by making the following suggestions:

- Make a list of questions your readers would want answered before setting out on a trip west.
- Decide what section of the West you will cover in your guide.
- Consider the sections you will include. For each section, list the main ideas you will cover and where to find the information.
- Decide how to illustrate your guide. You can either photocopy maps and pictures from source material or draw your own.

Travel Guide Decision Tree

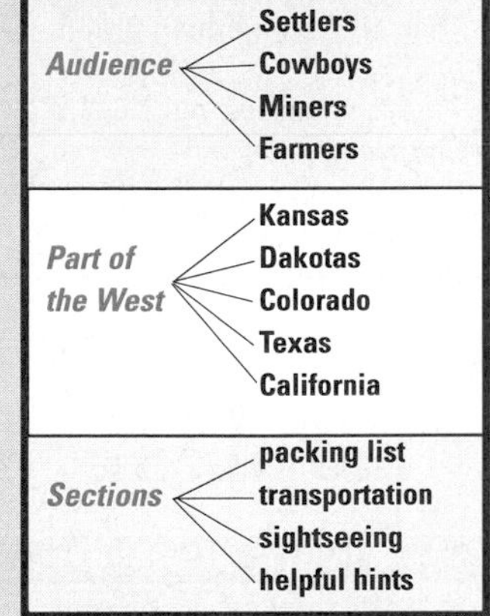

Audience
Settlers
Cowboys
Miners
Farmers
Part of the West
Kansas
Dakotas
Colorado
Texas
California
Sections
packing list
transportation
sightseeing
helpful hints

IN-DEPTH RESOURCES, UNIT 2
See worksheet and standards for evaluation, pp. 17, 18.

RECOMMENDED RESOURCES

Books for the Teacher

Brown, Dee. *Bury My Heart at Wounded Knee.* New York: Bantam, 1970. A Native American view of the West.

Josephy, Alvin M., Jr. *The Indian Heritage of America.* Boston: Houghton, 1991.

Ward, Geoffrey C. *The West: An Illustrated History.* New York: Little, 1996.

Books for the Student

Freeman, Russell. *Cowboys of the Wild West.* New York: Scholastic, 1985.

Jeffrey, Julie. *Frontier Women.* New York: Hill and Wang, 1979.

Stratton, Joanne L. *Pioneer Women.* New York: Simon, 1981.

Videos

How the West Was Lost (3 tapes), *How the West Was Lost II* (4 tapes). Discovery Channel Home Video.

The West. 9-part series. Produced by Stephen Ives and Ken Burns. Time-Life Video, 1996.

Software

500 Nations. CD-ROM. Microsoft, 800-555-4512.

The Wild West. CD-ROM. Educational Software Institute, 800-955-5570.

Section 1 Overview

OBJECTIVES

1. To describe the culture of Native Americans living on the Great Plains.
2. To contrast the cultures of Native Americans and white settlers and to explain why white settlers moved west.
3. To identify restrictions imposed by the government on Native Americans and to describe the consequences.
4. To summarize the continuing conflict between Native Americans and settlers moving west.
5. To identify the government's policy of assimilation.
6. To summarize the causes and effects of the Battle of Wounded Knee.

SKILLBUILDERS

- Understanding geography: location, movement, p. 217
- Interpreting charts, p. 220

CRITICAL THINKING

- Theme: The American Dream, p. 215
- Analyzing causes, pp. 216, 218, 221
- Clarifying, p. 217
- Recognizing effects, pp. 219, 221
- Making inferences, pp. 220, 221
- Summarizing, p. 221

FOCUS & MOTIVATE

5-MINUTE WARM-UP

Inferring Main Idea

To gain insight into the conflict between Native Americans and white settlers, have students read A Personal Voice on page 218 and answer these questions.

1. What does the quotation refer to?
2. According to the quotation, what is the basic conflict between Native Americans and white settlers?

WARM-UP TRANSPARENCY 5

▶ ***Starting with the Student*** Watch the video "A Walk in Two Worlds" to find out how a young Native American's life was affected by white settlement of the Western frontier.

1 Native American Cultures in Crisis

TERMS & NAMES
- Great Plains
- Homestead Act
- exoduster
- Sand Creek Massacre
- Sitting Bull
- George A. Custer
- assimilation
- Dawes Act
- Ghost Dance
- Battle of Wounded Knee

LEARN ABOUT the Native Americans' and settlers' ways of life ***TO UNDERSTAND*** the conflicts that occurred during settlement of the Western frontier.

ONE AMERICAN'S STORY

Zitkala-Ša was born into a Sioux tribe in 1876. As she grew up on the Great Plains, she learned the ways of her people and explored the world around her, which seemed alive with spirits. "I grew sober with awe and was alert to hear a long-drawn-out whistle rise from the roots of [the plum tree] . . . this strange whistle of departed spirits." When she was eight years old, she had a chance to go to a Quaker missionary school in Indiana. Though her mother warned her of the "white men's lies," Zitkala-Ša was eager to see "the wonderful Eastern land." She was not prepared, however, for the loss of dignity and identity she experienced, which was symbolized by the cutting of her hair.

A PERSONAL VOICE

I cried aloud, shaking my head all the while until I felt the cold blades of the scissors against my neck, and heard them gnaw off one of my thick braids. Then I lost my spirit. Since the day I was taken from my mother I had suffered extreme indignities. . . . And now my long hair was shingled like a coward's! In my anguish I moaned for my mother, but no one came to comfort me. . . . Now I was only one of many little animals driven by a herder.

ZITKALA-ŠA, quoted in *The School Days of an Indian Girl*

Zitkala-Ša

Zitkala-Ša experienced firsthand the clash of two very different cultures that occurred as ever-growing numbers of white settlers moved onto the Great Plains, where Native Americans had lived for thousands of years. In the resulting struggle, the Native American way of life was changed forever.

A WALK IN TWO WORLDS
The Education of Zitkala-Ša, a Sioux

The Culture of the Plains Indians

Like most Native Americans in the West, Zitkala-Ša knew very little about the world east of the Mississippi River. Most Easterners knew equally little about the West, picturing a vast desert occupied by savage tribes. That view was quite inaccurate. In fact, two distinct and highly developed Native American ways of life existed on the **Great Plains,** the grassland extending through the west-central portion of the United States (see map on page 217).

On the eastern side, near the lower Missouri River, tribes such as the Osage and Iowa planted crops and lived in small villages. Farther west, in what is now Nebraska and South Dakota, nomadic tribes such as the Sioux and Cheyenne gathered wild foods and hunted buffalo.

This Yankton Sioux coup stick was intricately carved.

THE IMPORTANCE OF THE HORSE AND THE BUFFALO After the Spanish brought horses to New Mexico in 1598, the Native American way of life began to change. As the native peoples acquired horses—and then guns—they were able to travel farther and hunt more efficiently. By the 1700s, almost all the tribes on the Great Plains had abandoned their farming villages to roam the plains and hunt buffalo.

SECTION 1 RESOURCES

PRINT RESOURCES

IN-DEPTH RESOURCES: UNIT 2
Guided Reading, p. 1
Primary Source: The Battle of the Little Bighorn, p. 9
American Lives: Chief Joseph, p. 15

READING STUDY GUIDE, p. 57

ACCESS FOR STUDENTS ACQUIRING ENGLISH
Guided Reading (Spanish), p. 81

SPANISH READING STUDY GUIDE, p. 57

FORMAL ASSESSMENT
Section Quiz, p. 68

ALTERNATIVE ASSESSMENT BOOK
See forms for supporting and scoring alternative activities.

TECHNOLOGY RESOURCES

HUMANITIES TRANSPARENCIES
H13, Sierra Nevada Mountains

GEOGRAPHY TRANSPARENCIES
G13, Railroad Land Grants, 1871

CD-ROM *Grolier Multimedia Encyclopedia*
Electronic Library of Primary Sources

VIDEO *American Stories* video series; *American Portfolio: A Videodisc for U.S. History,* user's guide, pp. 121–124, 126, 128, 132–133

INTERNET http://www.mlushistory.com

A Sioux encampment near the South Dakota–Nebraska border appears peaceful, but a portrait of a Sioux man and woman shows their defiance.

This increased mobility often led to war when hunters in one tribe trespassed on other tribes' hunting grounds. For the young men of a tribe, taking part in war parties and raids was a way to win prestige. But a Plains warrior gained more honor by "counting coup," or touching a live enemy and escaping unharmed, than by killing. Moreover, it was not unusual for warring tribes to call a truce so that they could trade goods, share news, or enjoy harvest festivals.

While the horse gave Native Americans increased mobility, the buffalo provided many of their basic needs. Native Americans made tepees from buffalo hides and also used the skins for clothing, shoes, and blankets. Buffalo meat was dried into jerky or mixed with berries and fat to make a staple food called pemmican. Buffalo sinews were used to make thread and bowstrings; buffalo bones and horns, to make tools and toys. The buffalo, like the horse, had become central to life on the plains.

THINK THROUGH HISTORY
A. THEME ***The American Dream*** *How did the horse and the buffalo influence Native American life on the Great Plains?*

A. Answer The horse gave them increased mobility, extending their hunting territory and promoting clashes with other tribes. They hunted the buffalo, using it for food, clothing, shelter, and tools.

FAMILY LIFE Native Americans on the plains usually lived in small extended family groups with ties to other bands that spoke the same language. The men went on hunting or raiding parties to obtain food and supplies, sharing what they had obtained with the group. The women helped butcher the game and prepared the hides that the men brought back to the camp.

Despite their communal way of life, however, the people of the plains valued individualism. Young men trained to become hunters and warriors; young women sometimes chose their own husbands. The Plains Indian tribes believed that powerful spirits controlled the events in the natural world, and men or women who demonstrated particular sensitivity to the spirits became medicine men, or shamans.

Children learned proper behavior and culture through stories and myths, games, and good examples. No individual was allowed to dominate the group; the leaders of a tribe ruled by counsel rather than by force. Land was held in common for the use of the whole tribe.

Settlers Push Westward

The culture of the white settlers differed in many ways from that of the Native Americans on the plains. Unlike Native Americans, who believed that land could not be owned, the settlers defined a better life and prosperity in terms of private property. Owning land and a house, making a mining claim, or starting a business would give them a stake in the country. Prospectors, settlers, and ranchers alike argued that the Native Americans had forfeited their rights to the land because they hadn't settled down to "improve" it. Concluding that the plains were "unsettled," settlers streamed westward to claim the land.

AMERICAN STORIES **video series**
"A Walk in Two Worlds"
Videocassette: Volume 1

Videodisc: Disc 1, Side B, Chapter 2

OBJECTIVE
① INSTRUCT

The Culture of the Plains Indians

▶ ***Discussing Key Ideas***
- The horse and the buffalo are central to the nomadic life of the Plains Indians.
- Plains Indians live communally in small groups that value individualism.

IN-DEPTH RESOURCES: UNIT 2
Guided Reading, p. 1

ACCESS FOR STUDENTS ACQUIRING ENGLISH
Guided Reading (Spanish), p. 81

OBJECTIVE
② INSTRUCT

Settlers Push Westward

▶ ***Starting with the Student***
Have students contrast the culture of the white settlers with that of the Plains Indians by adding a column to their charts.

	Plains Indians	White Settlers
Settled/Nomadic		
Food		

▶ ***Discussing Key Ideas***
- White settlers move westward to claim land, to farm, or to mine for gold.
- The Homestead Act of 1862 offers free land to settlers.

TEACHING OPTIONS

Teaching Less Proficient Readers

Main Ideas and Supporting Details Have students work in pairs to identify the main ideas of the section and the details that support them. Suggest they follow these steps:

1. Read pages 214–216 of the text together.
2. Individually list the main ideas (e.g., the importance of the buffalo) and details that support the main ideas (e.g., the uses of the buffalo).
3. Compare lists and agree on one statement of main ideas and supporting details.

Making Connections Across Cultures

Other Frontier Experiences The United States is only one of many countries—Canada, Brazil, Australia, Russia, and South Africa, for example—that were shaped by frontier experiences. Here is a comparison of the American and South African experiences. "The North American and southern African frontiers . . . were products of the same general process: the expansion of Europe and of capitalism. . . . Frontier zones successively closed and came under white control and new zones opened up, as whites moved westward in North America and north and east in southern Africa."

MORE ABOUT . . .
Homesteaders

Many settlers were farmers from the Midwest. Foreign immigrants—especially from Germany, Britain, and Canada—also took advantage of the availability of cheap, fertile land.

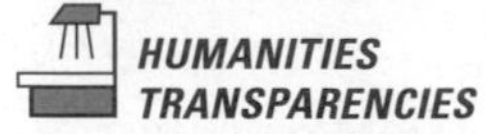

HUMANITIES TRANSPARENCIES
H13, Sierra Nevada Mountains

MORE ABOUT . . .
The Railroads

The U.S. railroads had expected completion of the transcontinental line to facilitate shipment of goods between Europe and the Far East. However, about the same time that the Union Pacific and Central Pacific lines met in Utah in 1869, the Suez Canal—which linked European ports to Asian ports—was also completed. Faced with the need to find new business, the railroads intensified their efforts to attract settlers.

GEOGRAPHY TRANSPARENCIES
G13, Railroad Land Grants, 1871

OBJECTIVE
③ INSTRUCT

The Government Restricts Native Americans

▶ ***Starting with the Student***
Ask students to think of current local or world events in which two strong cultures clashed. Students might cite a local situation, such as urban renewal that displaced families in the community, or an international conflict, such as between Arabs and Israelis in Israel.

(continued on next page)

THE LURE OF SILVER AND GOLD The prospect of striking it rich was one powerful attraction of the West. The gold fever that had flared in California in 1849 never really died out, and the discovery of gold in Colorado in 1858 drew tens of thousands of miners to the region.

The glitter of gold must have blinded prospective miners to other concerns, because most mining camps and tiny frontier towns had filthy, ramshackle living quarters. Rows of tents and shacks with dirt "streets" and wooden sidewalks had replaced unspoiled streams and picturesque landscapes. Fortune seekers of every description—including Irish, German, Swedish, Polish, Chinese, and African-American men—crowded the camps and boomtowns. A few hardy, business-minded women tried their luck too, working as laundresses, freight haulers, or even miners. Cities such as Virginia City, Nevada, and Helena, Montana, originated as mining camps on Native American land.

FARMING THE GREAT PLAINS Another powerful attraction of the West was the land itself. In 1862, Congress passed the **Homestead Act,** offering 160 acres of land free to anyone who would live on and cultivate it for five years. From 1862 to 1900, between 400,000 and 600,000 families took advantage of the government's offer. They came from the South and from New England, eager to exchange their worn-out fields for more fertile land farther west. Some German and Scandinavian farmers unable to earn a living in their native lands were lured to America by public relations campaigns sponsored by the railroad companies. Several thousand settlers were **exodusters**—African Americans who moved from the post-Reconstruction South to Kansas in a great exodus. Free land alone was not enough to lure farmers onto the Great Plains, however. They also needed a reliable way to get there and a way to ship their crops to growing urban markets.

Many settlers traveled west in prairie schooners, sturdy descendants of the Conestoga wagon. The white canvas tops made the wagons look like ships sailing across the open plains.

In 1862, Congress passed the Pacific Railroad Act, which granted government loans and huge tracts of land to the Union Pacific and Central Pacific Railroads. The Central Pacific began laying track at Sacramento in 1863. The Union Pacific began near Omaha in 1865. Both companies hired thousands of immigrants, many Chinese among them, to build bridges, dig tunnels, and lay track.

Before the railroads came west, hardy travelers rode west on horseback or in wagon trains that were cold in winter, hot in summer, and vulnerable to attack by Native Americans and outlaws. Until the completion of a transcontinental route in 1869, long-distance travel was dangerous, uncomfortable, and slow. After 1869, however, people could ride from coast to coast in ten days or less. Still, the railroads were not for everyone. A "bargain" fare from Omaha to Sacramento was about $40—more than a month's pay for the average person. Yet the trains were relatively luxurious. All of them had indoor toilets, and most of the cars were heated. For $75, a traveler could ride on a padded seat. For another $4 per night, he or she could reserve a berth in a Pullman sleeping car. Instead of heading west at the rate of 15 miles a day in a covered wagon, aspiring settlers could speed along at 50 miles an hour.

B. Answer Government acts and railroad lines made it easier for white settlers to take advantage of mining and farming opportunities in the West.

THINK THROUGH HISTORY
B. Analyzing Causes *Why did white settlers suddenly flood the Great Plains?*

The Government Restricts Native Americans

While allowing more settlers to move westward, the railroads also influenced the government's policy toward the Native Americans who lived on the plains. In 1834, the federal government had passed an act that designated the entire Great Plains as one enormous reservation, or land set aside for Native American tribes. In response to the increasing stream of settlers in the 1850s, however, the government changed its policy. In order to open up more land for white settlers, it began signing treaties that created definite boundaries for each tribe.

Block Schedule TEACHING OPTION **Time Needed: 20 Minutes**

Cooperative Activity: Cross-Cultural Debate

Task: Students will write statements of belief about settlement of the West and will stage a debate between a white settler and a Native American.

Purpose: To help students understand the clashes of beliefs and aims that occurred during the settlement of the West.

Activity: Assign small groups of students to represent either the Native Americans' or the settlers' point of view. Groups will prepare statements of their beliefs about settlement, addressing the meaning of the land itself and the methods used in settling it. The groups should present their statements as a debate.

Building a Portfolio: Students who add their statements to their portfolios should attach a note indicating their contribution to the statement.

ALTERNATIVE ASSESSMENT BOOK
Standards for Evaluating a Cooperative Activity

Standards for Evaluation
Statements should . . .

- clearly present the group's beliefs about settlement of the West
- address opposing arguments
- include supporting details and examples

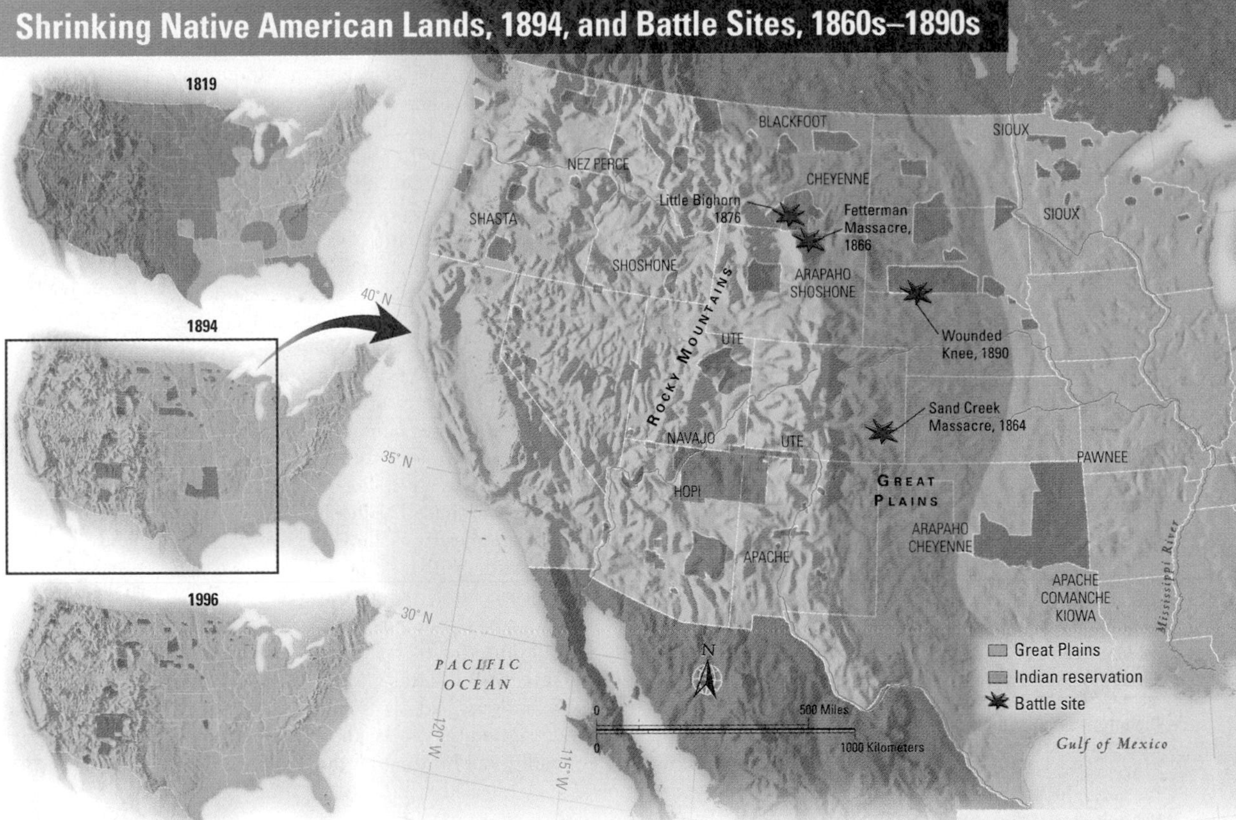

THINK THROUGH HISTORY
C. Clarifying
What was the government's policy toward Native American land?

C. Answer The government wanted to restrict all Native Americans to designated areas.

Most Native Americans did not agree to sign treaties with the government, though, and many of the "chiefs" who did sign did not represent their tribes. Many tribes, including the Cheyenne and the Sioux, continued to hunt on their traditional lands, clashing with settlers and miners—with tragic results.

MASSACRE AT SAND CREEK One of the most tragic events occurred in 1864. The Cheyenne, who had been forced into a barren area of the Colorado Territory known as the Sand Creek Reserve, began raiding nearby trails and settlements for food and supplies. The territorial governor, John Evans, ordered the militia to attack the raiders but urged the Cheyenne who did not want to fight to report to Fort Lyon, near the reserve, where they would be safe from harm. Most of the Cheyenne moved back to Sand Creek for the winter, flying both the American flag and a white flag as a sign of their peaceful intentions.

General S. R. Curtis, U.S. army commander in the West, sent a telegram to militia colonel John Chivington that read, "I want no peace till the Indians suffer more." In response, Chivington and his troops descended on the 500 Cheyenne camped at Sand Creek at dawn on November 29, 1864. Chivington had his own reasons to want revenge on Native Americans, because they had killed his family. Without warning, Chivington and his men attacked the sleeping village. The exhausted warriors and terrified women and children never had a chance to defend themselves. Chivington's soldiers killed about 200 inhabitants, mostly women and children, and mutilated the bodies. After the **Sand Creek Massacre,** as this battle came to be called, Chivington was treated as a hero in his hometown, Denver.

DEATH ON THE BOZEMAN TRAIL Another tribe, the Sioux, was angered by white settlement along the Bozeman Trail, which had been opened during the

GEOGRAPHY SKILLBUILDER
LOCATION
Which battles took place on Native American land?
MOVEMENT
About what percentage of Native American lands had the government taken over by 1894? About what percentage had Native Americans recovered by 1996?

Skillbuilder Answers
Location: Little Bighorn, Wounded Knee.
Movement: 1894—about 90%; 1996—less than 1%.

(continued from page 216)

▶ *Discussing Key Ideas*
- The government sets aside land for Native Americans but later reverses its policy and limits the land occupied by individual tribes.
- Some tribes that attempt to remain on their lands are slaughtered by U.S. Army troops.
- The government forces the Sioux to sign the Treaty of 1868, which restricts them to a reservation.

HISTORY FROM VISUALS
Shrinking Native American Lands, 1894, and Battle Sites, 1860s–1890s

Reading the Map Make sure students understand that the small maps indicate changes in the buffalo population over time and that the large map is a blowout—or more detailed version—of the central small map.

Extension Have students work in pairs to find out how the land of a particular reservation shown on the map is used today.

TEACHING OPTIONS

Making Connections Across the Curriculum

Geography Have students consult an atlas to determine the quality of the land set aside for Native Americans by 1895. They should consider if the land was agricultural, if it contained mining resources, or if it was barren and nonproductive. Ask students what conclusions they draw from their research. *Possible Response: The most desirable land was given or sold to white settlers or to mining companies. Much of the land that Native Americans received was poor for farming and contained few natural resources.*

Exploring Themes

The American Dream Discuss the dreams Native Americans might have had for their life in the United States. Ask students to consider how the dreams of white settlers and immigrants conflicted with those of the Native Americans. *Possible Answer: Both groups wanted to use Western land and its resources.* Discuss provisions that might have been made to enable both groups to realize their dreams. *Possible Answer: Lands might have been set aside for the Native Americans and the resources (including the buffalo) left untouched so the people could pursue their way of life.*

KEY PLAYER
Sitting Bull

Critical Thinking: Analyzing Character Ask students to describe the attributes suggested by the name Sitting Bull. How might those character traits be useful to a warrior, a tribal leader, and a representative of his people? *Possible Answer: The strength, determination, and even stubbornness suggested by Sitting Bull's name might enable him to be a stalwart supporter of his people's cause.*

OBJECTIVE

4 INSTRUCT

Bloody Battles Continue

▶ ***Discussing Key Ideas***

- Conflict escalates as settlement continues and Native Americans resist restriction to reservations.
- The Black Hills—sacred Sioux territory—become a contested area as the government tries to secure its gold resources.
- Custer's defeat shocks white Americans and leads to increased army raids and the defeat of the Sioux.

GROLIER MULTIMEDIA ENCYCLOPEDIA
Indian wars

MORE ABOUT . . .
Gall

Gall was a leader of the Hunkpapa Sioux. Remembering the U.S. Army bullets that wiped out his family, Gall fought at the battle of the Little Bighorn armed only with a hatchet.

KEY PLAYER

SITTING BULL
1831–1890

As a child, Sitting Bull was known as Hunkesni, or Slow; he earned the name Tatanka Yotanka (Sitting Bull) after a fight with the Crow Indians, a traditional enemy of the Sioux.

Sitting Bull led his people by the strength of his character and purpose. He was a warrior, counselor, and medicine man, and he was determined that whites should leave Sioux territory. His most famous fight was at the Little Bighorn River. About his opponent, George Armstrong Custer, he said, "They tell me I murdered Custer. It is a lie. . . . He was a fool and rode to his death."

After Sitting Bull's surrender to the federal government in 1881, his dislike of whites did not change, although he loved to shake hands, learned to sign his name, and took drawing lessons from a German artist. He was killed by Native American police at Standing Rock Reservation on December 15, 1890.

Civil War. This major transportation route ran directly through the favorite hunting grounds of the Sioux, in the Bighorn Mountains. Their chief, Red Cloud (Mahpiua Luta), appealed to the government to stop settlers from using the trail, but soldiers continued to build forts along it. When talking proved futile, Sioux, Arapaho, and Cheyenne warriors began a guerrilla war, sending small bands on surprise raids to harass the troops. On December 21, 1866, Crazy Horse and several other warriors lured Captain William J. Fetterman and his company of soldiers into an ambush at Lodge Trail Ridge. The warriors surrounded the soldiers and killed them all. Native Americans called this fight the Battle of the Hundred Slain. Whites called it the Fetterman Massacre.

Skirmishes followed for about a year, until the government agreed to close the Bozeman Trail. In return, the Sioux signed the historic Treaty of Fort Laramie in 1868, in which they agreed to live on a reservation along the Missouri River. The terms of this treaty resembled those of the 1867 treaties. In these treaties, the southern Kiowa, Comanche, Cheyenne, and Arapaho promised to live on large reservations in return for protection and supplies from the U.S. government.

Conflicts between whites and Native Americans continued despite these treaties. Several factors contributed to the ongoing hostilities. Promised supplies often arrived late and were of poor quality and insufficient quantity. In addition, the Treaty of Fort Laramie had been forced on the Sioux. **Sitting Bull** (Tatanka Yotanka), a medicine man and leader of the Hunkpapa Sioux, had never signed it. Although the Oglala and Brulé Sioux had signed the treaty, they expected to be able to continue using their traditional hunting grounds and to come and go on the reservation as they pleased.

D. Answer It had been forced on some of the Sioux, and Native Americans were not given adequate protection or supplies.

THINK THROUGH HISTORY
D. *Analyzing Causes* *Why was the Treaty of Fort Laramie ineffective?*

Bloody Battles Continue

The Treaty of Fort Laramie provided only a temporary halt to warfare. The conflict between the two cultures continued as settlers moved westward and Native American tribes resisted the restrictions of the reservations. A Sioux warrior explained why.

A PERSONAL VOICE

[We] have been taught to hunt and live on the game. You tell us that we must learn to farm, live in one house, and take on your ways. Suppose the people living beyond the great sea should come and tell you that you must stop farming, and kill your cattle, and take your houses and lands, what would you do? Would you not fight them?

GALL, a Hunkpapa Sioux, quoted in *Bury My Heart at Wounded Knee*

RAIDS BY THE KIOWA AND COMANCHE In late 1868, war broke out yet again, this time on the southern plains, as Kiowa and Comanche refused to move to a reservation in the Texas Panhandle. They began a raiding spree that continued for six years and finally led to the Red River War of 1874–1875. The U.S. Army responded to the Native Americans' guerrilla warfare by herding the friendly tribespeople onto reservations and opening fire on all others. General Philip Sheridan, a Union Army veteran, gave orders "to destroy their villages and ponies, to kill and hang all warriors, and to bring back all women and children."

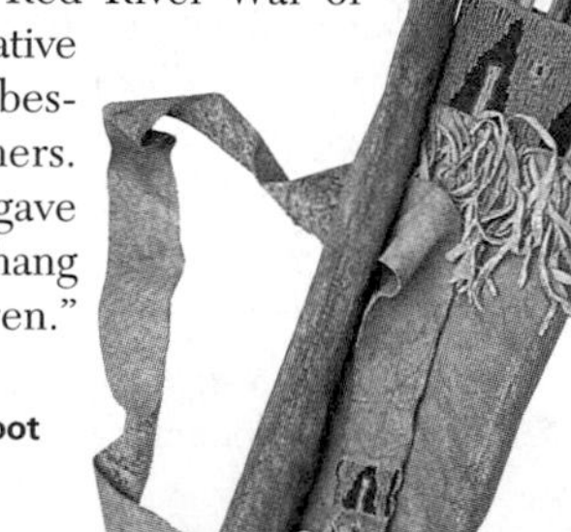

The Sioux war bow was accurate up to 100 yards and could shoot arrows more rapidly than a single-shot rifle could fire bullets.

TEACHING OPTIONS

Teaching Gifted and Talented Students

Analyzing Gall's Speech Have students analyze the effectiveness of Gall's speech. Ask them to consider the following points.

- In what person is Gall's speech given?
- What persuasive techniques, such as parallel structure and direct questions, does he use?

Suggest that students rewrite the speech omitting these techniques, and compare its effectiveness to that of the original.

Making Connections Across Time

Current Reparations for Broken Treaties Discuss with students the rise in political activism among Native Americans in the 1960s, which coincided with civil rights movements among other minorities, including African Americans, Hispanics, and women. Ask students what they know about Native Americans' efforts to seek reparations from Congress for broken treaties. Point out that native peoples in other parts of the world are also making claims for settlements of broken treaties. In 1996, for example, the Maori settled a land and cash claim with the New Zealand government that totaled $117 million.

With these tactics, the army crushed the resistance on the southern plains.

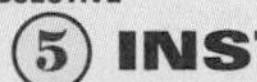

GOLD RUSH Within four years of the Treaty of Fort Laramie, miners began flooding into the Black Hills to search for gold. The Sioux, Cheyenne, and Arapaho protested—to no avail. By 1874, the rumor of gold had grown so strong that the army sent **George Armstrong Custer,** a Civil War hero and colonel in the Seventh Cavalry, to investigate and send back a report.

When Custer reported that the Black Hills had gold "from the grass roots down," a gold rush was on. Red Cloud and Spotted Tail, another Sioux chief, appealed again to government officials in Washington, who responded with an offer to purchase the land. When the Sioux refused to sell their sacred ground, the stage was set for the last battles of the plains wars.

The Winchester '76 rifle, which was widely used by government troops, had a large loading slot and could fire 16 bullets without reloading.

CUSTER'S LAST STAND In early June 1876, the Sioux and Cheyenne held a sun dance, during which Sitting Bull had a vision of soldiers and some Native Americans falling from their horses. He interpreted the vision as a sign that victory would come for his people. Soon after, a successful battle with the Seventh Cavalry at Rosebud Creek in south central Montana prepared the tribes for the military's next move. When Lieutenant Colonel Custer and his troops reached the Little Bighorn River, the Native Americans were ready for them.

On June 25, Custer rode out in search of glory. He expected to pit his disciplined regiment against 1,500 warriors. Custer's plan had several flaws, however. First, despite warnings from Indian scouts, he underestimated the number of Native American warriors. Between 2,000 and 3,000 awaited his attack. Second, his men and horses were exhausted. Third, he split up his regiment and attacked with barely 200 men. Led by Crazy Horse, the warriors—in warpaint and bonnets and with raised spears and rifles—outflanked and overpowered Custer's troops. Within 20 minutes, Custer and all of his men were dead.

E. Answer Death of Custer and all his men, demand for revenge by American people, continued raids on Native American camps.

THINK THROUGH HISTORY
E. *Recognizing Effects* *What were the results of Custer's last stand?*

The American people were shocked and angered at Custer's defeat. Many criticized him for his bad judgment, but the nation as a whole demanded revenge. The army continued to raid Native American camps and to slaughter the buffalo. By late 1876, the Sioux were beaten. Sitting Bull and a few followers took refuge in Canada, where they remained until 1881.

Eventually, to prevent his people's starvation, even the proud Sitting Bull was forced to surrender. Later, in 1885, he became an attraction in William F. "Buffalo Bill" Cody's Wild West Show.

"Stripped of the beautiful romance with which we have been so long willing to envelop him . . . the Indian forfeits his claim to the [name] 'noble red man.' "

GEORGE A. CUSTER

The Government Supports Assimilation

The Native Americans still had supporters in the United States, and debate over the treatment of Native Americans continued. The well-known writer Helen Hunt Jackson, for example, exposed the government's many broken promises in her 1881 book *A Century of Dishonor*: "It makes little difference . . . where one opens the record of the history of the Indians; every page and every year has its dark stain."

Sometimes, the "friends" of the Native Americans were not much more helpful than their enemies. Many sympathizers were supporters of **assimilation,** a plan under which Native Americans would give up their beliefs and way of life and become part of the white culture. Although the Native Americans had lost much land and their means of independent living, they did not want to lose their culture as well.

FAILURE OF THE DAWES ACT In 1887, in an effort to make assimilation the official government policy, Congress passed the **Dawes Act.** The aim was to "Americanize" the Native Americans by cultivating in them the desire to own property and to farm. The Dawes Act broke up the reservations and distributed some of the reservation land—160 acres for farming or 320 acres for grazing—

MORE ABOUT . . .
George Armstrong Custer

Lt. Col. Custer (1839–1876) went to the West after a distinguished career in the Civil War. Although he was last in his class at West Point, he became, at age 23, the youngest general in the Union Army. (He was later demoted.) Native Americans called him Yellow Hair, because he wore his blond hair in long ringlets.

IN-DEPTH RESOURCES: UNIT 2
Primary Source: The Battle of the Little Bighorn, p. 9

OBJECTIVE
(5) INSTRUCT

The Government Supports Assimilation

▶ ***Discussing Key Ideas***

- Some Americans propose that Native Americans be assimilated into the dominant white culture.
- The Dawes Act is an attempt to provide Native American families with individual plots of former reservation land, but much of the best land is sold to speculators.
- Native American children are taken away from their families and educated in boarding schools in the "white man's ways."
- Buffalo hunters, tourists, and fur traders destroy the very basis of the Great Plains culture—the buffalo.

TEACHING OPTIONS

Making Connections Across Time

Reservations Today Ask students to research life on the reservations today. Students might find out about the problems facing Native Americans who live there, such as unemployment and low-paying jobs, a higher infant mortality rate and a lower life expectancy than the general U.S. population. Students should also find out about the successes and gains made by Native Americans, such as protecting tribal interests in the use of natural resources found on reservations.

Teaching Less Proficient Readers

Identifying Supporting Details Help students understand how the government tried to assimilate Native Americans to white culture. Point out that the heading "The Government Supports Assimilation" states the main idea of the material that follows. Tell students to change the heading into a question *(How did the government support assimilation?)*. Tell them to read the material under the heading, on pages 219-220, to answer the question. Point out that finding answers to the question will provide them with details that support the main idea.

MORE ABOUT . . .

Carlisle Indian School

Discipline was harsh at this off-reservation boarding school. Students—some as young as five years old—were punished if they even whispered in their native languages, or danced, or sang native songs. Their hair was cut off, their native costumes and belongings were taken from them, and they were dressed like white people.

ELECTRONIC LIBRARY OF PRIMARY SOURCES
On the Use of English in Indian Schools

HISTORY FROM VISUALS

The Legend of the Buffalo

Reading the Chart Make sure students understand that, in addition to the uses of the buffalo listed at the right of the chart, the meat was a major source of food. Also, bring to their attention the similarities between the sequence of three maps here and the one on page 217.

Extension Have students research the policies and programs that enabled the buffalo population to increase between 1865 and 1996.

to each adult head of a Native American family. The government would sell the remainder of the reservations to settlers, and the resulting income would be used by Native Americans for farm implements. But the Native Americans received nothing from the sale of these lands. By 1934, whites had taken about two-thirds of the territory that had been set aside for Native Americans. Speculators, who bought land to sell at a profit, grabbed most of the best land. Much of the land that remained was useless for farming.

EDUCATING THE NATIVE AMERICANS While the Dawes Act addressed the physical assimilation of Native Americans, education addressed their minds and spirits. Off-reservation boarding schools, like the one attended by Zitkala-Ša, flourished. Among the reformers was Richard H. Pratt, who founded the Carlisle boarding school in Pennsylvania to "kill the Indian and save the man." The Carlisle school and others like it taught Native American children that their traditional ways were backward and superstitious. The teachers promoted the values of white civilization and then returned the "educated" children to the reservations, where the skills they had learned were useless. What resulted was a generation of Native American young people caught in a tragic conflict between the culture of their parents and that of their teachers. They didn't fit in on the reservations, yet they faced discrimination when they tried to live in the white world.

F. Answer
Assimilation was forced on an unwilling population, and well-meaning measures were corrupted by unscrupulous agents and fortune seekers.

THINK THROUGH HISTORY
F. *Making Inferences* *How did the assimilation policy affect Native Americans?*

THE DESTRUCTION OF THE BUFFALO Perhaps the most significant blow to tribal life on the plains was the destruction of the buffalo. Railroad companies like the Kansas Pacific hired buffalo hunters to accompany the workers and supply them with meat as they laid track westward, often in violation of treaties. Working for the railroads, the hunter William F. Cody killed nearly 4,300 bison in eight months, earning himself the nickname Buffalo Bill. Trappers, who had already destroyed beaver and other wildlife, now turned to the buffalo as a source of income. "Wherever the Whites are established," a Sioux chief bitterly observed, "the buffalo is gone, and the red hunters must die of hunger."

Tourists and fur traders also shot buffalo for sport from speeding railroad trains. General Sheridan noted with approval that buffalo hunters were destroying the Plains Indians' main source of food, clothing, shelter, and fuel. In 1800, approximately 15 million buffalo roamed the plains; by 1886, fewer than 600 remained. In 1900, the United States sheltered, in Yellowstone National Park, a single wild herd of buffalo.

Skillbuilder Answer
They are roughly parallel, though buffalo herds have increased through conservation and breeding programs.

SKILLBUILDER
INTERPRETING CHARTS ***Look at the maps on page 217. What connections can you draw between the loss of Native American lands and the decline of buffalo populations?***

The Legend of the Buffalo
1800 15,000,000
1870 1,000
1996 200,000
The buffalo provided the Plains Indians with more than just a high-protein food source.
THE SKULL of the buffalo was considered sacred and was used in many Native American rituals.
THE HIDE was by far the most precious part of the buffalo. Native American clothing, tepees, and even arrow shields were made from buffalo hide.
THE BONES of the buffalo were made into hide scrapers, tool handles, sled runners, and hoe blades. The hoofs were ground up and used as glue.
THE HORNS were carved into bowls and spoons.

Block Schedule TEACHING OPTION **Time Needed: 30 Minutes**

Cooperative Activity: Composing Boarding School Journals

Task: Students will research off-reservation boarding schools and then compose journal entries Native American students might have written when they first arrived at school.

Purpose: To better understand what life was like for many Native American children.

Activity: Working in small groups, students should read several descriptions of boarding schools, paying particular attention to the children's own words. The video "A Walk in Two Worlds: The Education of Zitkala-Ša, a Sioux," is an excellent source. Students should discuss how the Native American children might have felt and then collaborate on their journal entries.

Building a Portfolio: Students who add journal entries to their portfolios should attach a note pointing out their contribution.

ALTERNATIVE ASSESSMENT BOOK
Standards for Evaluating a Cooperative Activity

Standards for Evaluation
Journal entries should . . .

- be factually correct
- use specific details to support the writer's observations and feelings
- exhibit a personal voice and an informal, diary style

The Battle of Wounded Knee

Although some people tried to improve the lives of Native Americans, the Sioux continued to suffer reduced rations, increased restrictions, and the loss of their cattle to disease. In desperation, they turned to Wovoka, a Paiute prophet who had had a vision in which Native American lands were restored, the buffalo returned, and the whites disappeared. Wovoka promised that if the Sioux performed a ritual called the **Ghost Dance,** this vision would be realized.

The Ghost Dance movement spread rapidly among the 25,000 Sioux on the Dakota reservation. Its popularity alarmed military leaders and the local reservation agent, who decided to arrest Sitting Bull. On a drizzly December morning in 1890, about 40 Indian policemen were sent to arrest him. As two of the policemen pulled Sitting Bull out of his cabin, Sitting Bull's bodyguard, Catch-the-Bear, shot one of them. The policemen returned fire, killing Sitting Bull. A free-for-all resulted.

As the shots rang out, Sitting Bull's horse abruptly sat down and began performing the tricks it had learned in the Wild West Show with Buffalo Bill. For a moment, at least, it seemed to observers that the horse was performing the outlawed Ghost Dance.

The army wasn't satisfied with the death of Sitting Bull. On December 29, 1890, the Seventh Cavalry—Custer's old regiment that had been defeated at Little Bighorn—rounded up about 350 starving and freezing Sioux and took them to a camp at Wounded Knee Creek in South Dakota. The soldiers demanded that the Native Americans give up all their weapons. One Native American resisted this order and fired his rifle. The soldiers fired back with deadly cannons.

Within minutes, the Seventh Cavalry slaughtered 300 unarmed Native Americans, including several children. The soldiers left the corpses to freeze on the ground. This event, the **Battle of Wounded Knee,** brought the Indian wars—and an entire era—to a bitter end.

G. Answer Spread of the Ghost Dance movement, killing of Sitting Bull.

THINK THROUGH HISTORY
G. Analyzing Causes *What events led to the Battle of Wounded Knee?*

A PERSONAL VOICE

I did not know then how much was ended. When I look back now from this high hill of my old age, I can still see the butchered women and children lying heaped and scattered all along the crooked gulch as plain as when I saw them with eyes still young. And I can see that something else died there in the bloody mud, and was buried in the blizzard. A people's dream died there. It was a beautiful dream.

BLACK ELK, quoted in *Black Elk Speaks*

NOW & THEN

HOMECOMING

"I never thought I'd see the day," said Earl (Taz) Conner, a direct descendant of the best known of the Nez Perce, Chief Joseph. Forced off their tribal lands in Wallowa County, Oregon, in 1877, the Nez Perce in the United States, now numbering 4,000, are returning almost 120 years later.

When hard times hit during the 1990s, Wallowa community leaders saw a chance to bring money to the area by taking advantage of people's growing interest in Native Americans. They obtained a grant and asked for contributions to develop a Nez Perce cultural center, which they hope will be a big tourist draw. In the words of Soy Redthunder, another tribe member, "The whites may look at it as an economic plus, but we look at it as homecoming."

Section 1 Assessment

1. TERMS & NAMES

Identify:
- Great Plains
- Homestead Act
- exoduster
- Sand Creek Massacre
- Sitting Bull
- George A. Custer
- assimilation
- Dawes Act
- Ghost Dance
- Battle of Wounded Knee

2. SUMMARIZING Fill in supporting details about the culture of the Plains Indians.

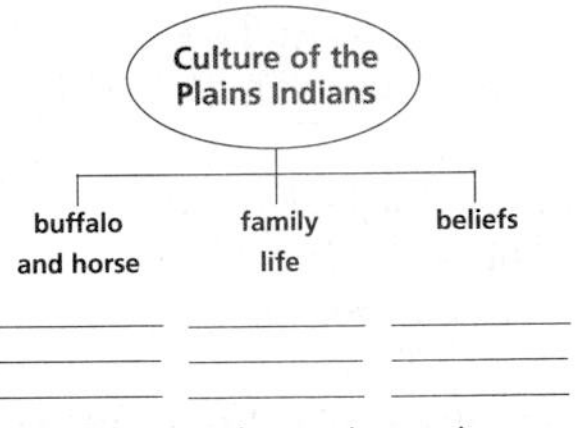

Which was changed most by white settlement?

3. RECOGNIZING EFFECTS This section says that the destruction of the buffalo was "perhaps the most significant blow to tribal life." Explain why you agree or disagree with this statement.

THINK ABOUT
- how Native Americans used the buffalo
- how Native Americans viewed ownership of land

4. MAKING INFERENCES Why do you think the assimilation policy of the Dawes Act failed? Support your opinion with information from the text.

THINK ABOUT
- the experience of Native Americans such as Zitkala-Ša
- the attitudes of many white leaders toward Native Americans
- the merits of owning property
- the importance of people's cultural heritage

NOW & THEN
Homecoming

Critical Thinking: Predicting Outcomes
Discuss how the return of the native inhabitants might benefit both the Nez Perce and Wallowa County.

IN-DEPTH RESOURCES: UNIT 2
American Lives: Chief Joseph, p. 15

OBJECTIVE **6 INSTRUCT**

The Battle of Wounded Knee

Discussing Key Ideas
- Prophets claim the Ghost Dance will cause the return of the buffalo.
- White people fear violence.
- Misunderstandings and fear lead to the death of Sitting Bull and the massacre at Wounded Knee.

ASSESS & RETEACH

Section 1 Assessment
Assign pairs of students to answer questions together.

Self-Assessment
Have students determine if questions in the Section 1 Assessment that they could not answer have anything in common.

Section Quiz

FORMAL ASSESSMENT
Section Quiz, p. 68

Reteach
Have a volunteer read Black Elk's statement on page 221 aloud. Then have students discuss the Native Americans' dream and its conversion into a nightmare.

CLOSE

As the westward migration of white settlers destroyed the Native American way of life, the era of the cowboy dawned.

ANSWERS

1. TERMS & NAMES

Great Plains, p. 214
Homestead Act, p. 216
exoduster, p. 216
Sand Creek Massacre, p. 217
Sitting Bull, p. 218
George A. Custer, p. 219
assimilation, p. 219
Dawes Act, p. 219
Ghost Dance, p. 221
Battle of Wounded Knee, p. 221

2. SUMMARIZING

buffalo and horse:
buffalo—source of food, clothes, shelter
horse—source of transportation
family life:
communal property and government
individualism valued
beliefs:
world inhabited by spirits
focus on the present, not the future

3. RECOGNIZING EFFECTS

Answers will vary but should be supported by examples from the text. ***Possible support:*** **Agree**—The buffalo was central to Native American culture, providing shelter, clothing, and food. **Disagree**—Loss of land was more significant because Native Americans might have adapted their culture to the loss of buffalo, but settlers seized their land.

4. MAKING INFERENCES

Answers will vary but should be supported by examples. Possible reasons for the failure include lack of support by the government, abuses of the act by white opportunists, and resistance by Native Americans.

Section 2 Overview

OBJECTIVES

1 To trace the development of the cattle industry.
2 To describe both the myth and the reality of the American cowboy.
3 To explain the end of cattle ranching on the open plains.

SKILLBUILDER

- Understanding geography: region, place, p. 224

CRITICAL THINKING

- Theme: Cultural Diversity, p. 223
- Theme: Economic Opportunity, p. 224
- Contrasting, p. 225
- Forming opinions, p. 226
- Synthesizing, p. 227
- Summarizing, p. 227
- Comparing and contrasting, p. 227

FOCUS & MOTIVATE

5-MINUTE WARM-UP

Describing Setting
To describe the conditions of the cowboys' life, ask students to look at the painting on page 223 and answer these questions.

1. What does the title of the painting refer to?
2. Using the painting, write a list of words that describes the setting in which a cowboy lived.

WARM-UP TRANSPARENCY 5

▶ Starting with the Student
Have students answer the following questions and save their answers to reexamine after reading the section.

- What are students' images of cowboys?
- How have movies and novels influenced those images?
- How true do students think those images are to the reality of life on the open range?

2 The Growth of the Cattle Industry

TERMS & NAMES
- longhorn
- James Butler "Wild Bill" Hickok
- Martha Jane Cannary (Calamity Jane)
- long drive

LEARN ABOUT the cowboy's life and work
TO UNDERSTAND the difference between the myth and the reality of the cowboy.

ONE AMERICAN'S STORY

The cowboy G. D. Burrows remembered his life on the trails as one of "going hungry, getting wet and cold, riding sore-backed horses, going to sleep on herd and losing cattle, getting 'cussed' by the boss [and] scouting for 'gray-backs' (body lice)." Yet Burrows claimed that his memory of the discomforts faded whenever he delivered a herd and rode into town.

He would put on new high-heeled boots and striped pants and sit through performance after performance of local entertainment. After a few days, having gone broke, he would borrow money and head back to the ranch for the winter.

A PERSONAL VOICE

I would put in the fall and winter telling about the big things I had seen up North. The next spring I would have the same old trip, the same old things would happen in the same old way, and with the same old wind-up. I put in 18 or 20 years on the trail, and all I had in the final outcome was the high-heeled boots, the striped pants, and about $4.80 worth of other clothes.

G. D. BURROWS, quoted in *The Trail Drivers of Texas*

A group of cowboys take a well-earned rest before heading back out on the trail.

By taking over Native American lands and eliminating the buffalo, whites opened up a vast stretch of western land that would soon be transformed by a new way of life—cattle ranching—and a new American hero—the cowboy. Over a century after his heyday, this independent, but often overworked and lonely, figure still captures the American imagination.

The Cattle Industry Becomes Big Business

As the great herds of buffalo disappeared, horses and cattle flourished on the plains. Before long, cattle were plentiful and ranching had become big business from Texas to Kansas.

THE FIRST COWBOYS Horses and cattle had been introduced to the New World by Spanish explorers. Among the small, quick horses brought to Mexico in 1519 by Hernán Cortés was the piebald pinto, which added a variety of color to the endless plains. The **longhorn** cattle brought by the Spaniards, first to the West Indies and then to Mexico, were sturdy, long-horned, short-tempered breeds that were accustomed to the dry grasslands of Andalusia, in southern Spain. The Spanish settlers used the horses as work animals and the cattle for food.

The Spanish herds thrived on the grassy Mexican plains, with some ranches eventually including as many as 150,000 head of cattle. To help them with these herds, the Spaniards employed their native Aztec prisoners as vaqueros, or cowboys. At first, most of the vaqueros worked on foot. But as the herds grew, the vaqueros learned to use horses to manage the cattle. These first cowboys quickly became expert riders skilled in the use of *la reata*, or "the lariat," which they used to rope and control the herds.

SECTION 2 RESOURCES

PRINT RESOURCES

IN-DEPTH RESOURCES: UNIT 2
Guided Reading, p. 2
Skillbuilder Practice: Creating Graphs, p. 5

READING STUDY GUIDE, p. 59

ACCESS FOR STUDENTS ACQUIRING ENGLISH
Guided Reading (Spanish), p. 82
Skillbuilder Practice: Creating Graphs (Spanish), p. 85

SPANISH READING STUDY GUIDE, p. 59

FORMAL ASSESSMENT
Section Quiz, p. 69

ALTERNATIVE ASSESSMENT BOOK
See forms for supporting and scoring alternative activities.

TECHNOLOGY RESOURCES

CD-ROM *Grolier Multimedia Encyclopedia*
Electronic Library of Primary Sources

VIDEO *American Portfolio: A Videodisc for U.S. History,* user's guide, pp. 125, 127, 128

INTERNET http://www.mlushistory.com

When silver was discovered in northern Mexico, the Spanish ranchers and their vaqueros herded their cattle north to provide food for the miners. In 1598, some of the ranchers drove their herds into what is now New Mexico, where they taught the Pueblo Indians how to ride and rope.

About a hundred years later, other Spaniards crossed the Rio Grande and settled in Texas, on the southern Great Plains. Over the years, thousands of cows and many horses escaped or strayed on the open range and gathered in wild herds. These herds flourished in the United States as they had in Mexico.

THE INFLUENCE OF MEXICAN CULTURE As American as the cowboy seems today, his way of life stemmed directly from that of those first Spanish ranchers in Mexico. The American settlers had never managed large herds on an open range, and they learned from their Mexican neighbors how to round up, rope, brand, and care for the animals. Even the animals themselves, the Texas longhorns that came to symbolize the West, were descendants of Spanish cattle.

The American cowboy's clothes, food, and vocabulary were also heavily influenced by his Mexican forerunner. The Mexican vaquero was the first to wear spurs, which he attached with straps to his bare feet and used to control his horse. His *chaparreras,* or leather overalls, became known as chaps. He ate *charqui,* or "jerky"—dried strips of meat. The Spanish *caballo bronco,* or "rough horse" that ran wild, became known as a bronco or bronc. The strays that the vaquero called *mesteños,* were the same mustangs that the American cowboy tamed and prized. The Mexican *rancho* became the model for the American ranch. Finally, the English words *corral* and *rodeo* were borrowed directly from Spanish. In his skills, dress, and vocabulary, the Mexican vaquero was the true forerunner of the American buckaroo.

A. Answer Mexicans taught American cowboys how to rope and ride. They greatly influenced cowboys' language, clothes, and activities.

The American cowboy, of course, added his own signature to his adopted way of life. Cowboy boots were designed with pointed toes to fit inside stirrups and with high heels to keep the feet from sliding through. Chaps were padded with wool or fur to offer protection against the cold northern climate. The bandanna became such an all-purpose necessity that it was once proposed as the official flag of the open range. This cowboy trademark served as a sun screen, tourniquet, dust mask, washcloth, strainer for muddy water, face covering for dead cowboys, noose for hanging horse thieves, and blindfold for skittish horses. Then there was the six-shooter—the gun that could fire six shots without reloading and that came to symbolize not only the cowboy but the entire Old West.

THINK THROUGH HISTORY
A. THEME ***Cultural Diversity*** *What does the American cowboy tradition owe to the Mexican vaquero?*

THE IMPORTANCE OF THE RAILROADS Despite the plentiful herds of cattle in Texas and throughout the West, cowboys were not in great demand until the railroads reached the Great Plains.

Before the Civil War, ranchers for the most part didn't stray far from their homesteads with their cattle. They sold some hides and animal fat, or tallow, to Western markets along the coast of the Gulf of Mexico but generally just watched their herds increase. There were, of course, some exceptions. During

The cowboy's days, like the line of longhorns he herded, seemed to stretch endlessly. William Henry David Koerner captured this feeling in his painting *And So, Unemotionally, There Began One of the Wildest and Strangest Journeys Ever Made in Any Land.*

OBJECTIVE

 **INSTRUCT**

The Cattle Industry Becomes Big Business

▶ ***Discussing Key Ideas***

- Spanish explorers introduce horses and cattle into the Southwest.
- Many aspects of cowboy culture—food, clothing, vocabulary—are borrowed from Spanish ranchers in Mexico.
- The growth of the railroads provides a market for the booming cattle industry.

IN-DEPTH RESOURCES: UNIT 2
Guided Reading, p. 2

ACCESS FOR STUDENTS ACQUIRING ENGLISH
Guided Reading (Spanish), p. 82

MORE ABOUT . . .
The Cowboy Hat

A cowboy could tell a lot about another cowboy by looking at his hat. If the hat had a wide brim and a high crown, the wearer was from the Southwest, where he needed extra protection from the sun. If the hat had a narrow brim and a low crown, the hat's owner was probably from the northern plains, where it was very windy. A hat did more than cover a cowboy's head, though. It served as a pillow, a bucket to carry water, a fan to start a fire, and a paddle to slap a steer and control a stampede.

TEACHING OPTION

Teaching Less Proficient Readers

Using Graphic Organizers Pair less proficient readers with proficient readers, and Spanish-speaking students with non-Spanish speakers. Ask a Latino student to pronounce the Spanish words in the text, and then pronounce the English equivalent yourself, emphasizing the similarity in sound. Then have students read pages 222 and 223 together and keep in mind how each item was used. Ask them to create a table such as the one shown on the right, listing the Spanish name, the English name, and the use of each item.

Spanish term	English term	Use
chaparreras	chaps	to protect riders' legs when riding through the brush
charqui	jerky	"fast food" for the trail
—	pointed boots	to fit through stirrups

HISTORY FROM VISUALS

Cattle Trails and the Railroads, 1870s–1890s

Reading the Map Have students locate the beginnings of the cattle trails and follow the arrows to their termination at railroad junctions.

Extension Have students work in pairs to plot three possible routes from ranch to meatpacking center. Ask them to use the map scale to measure the distances the cattle traveled on foot and by train.

MORE ABOUT . . .

Joseph McCoy

This entrepreneur was a real showman, and may have been the source of the term "the real McCoy." To advertise Abilene as a shipping center, he hired cowboys to capture large buffalo, one of which weighed over 2,300 pounds. He sent three of these buffalo by train to Chicago, exhibiting them at every stop along the way. This promotion was so successful that cattle buyers thronged to Abilene before the hotel was ready, and McCoy had to house them in several large tents.

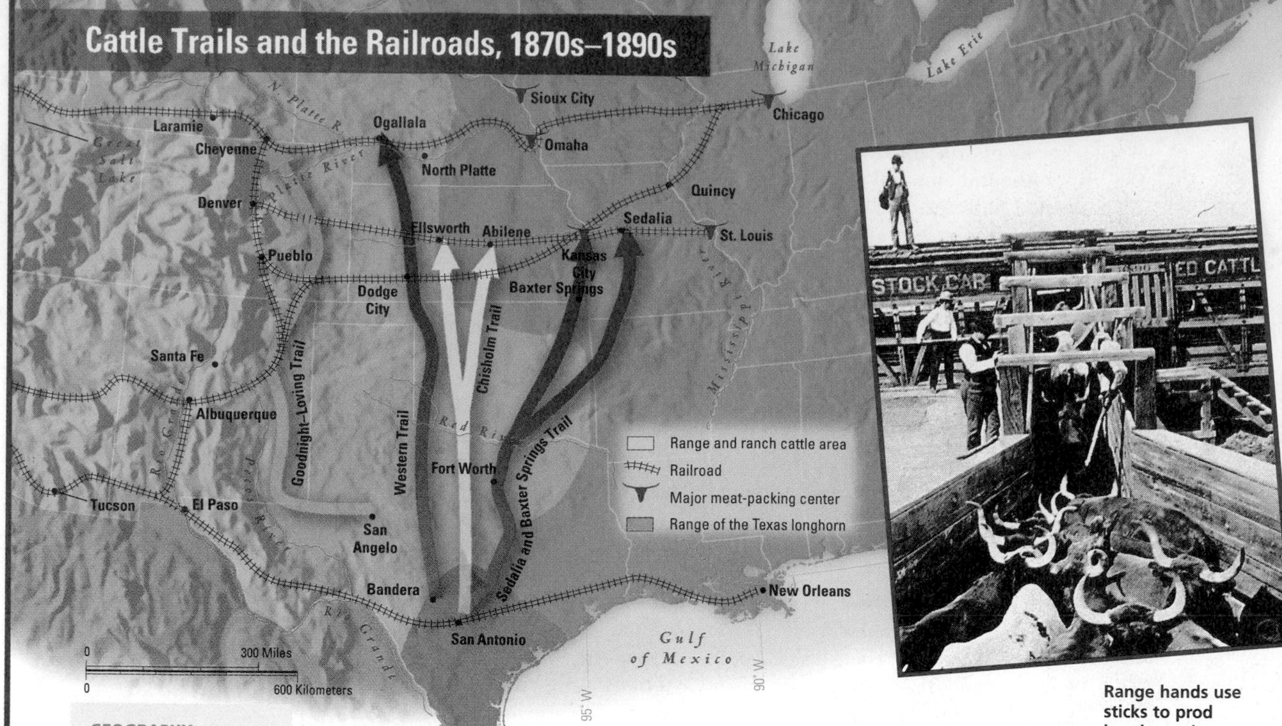

Range hands use sticks to prod longhorns into railcars. This work earned them the nickname "cowpokes."

GEOGRAPHY SKILLBUILDER

REGION *At what towns did the cattle trails and the railroads intersect to form cattle-shipping centers?*

PLACE *Which cities were served by the most railroads?*

Skillbuilder Answer

Region: Abilene, Kansas; Ellsworth, Kansas; Sedalia, Missouri; Kansas City, Missouri; Ogallala, Nebraska; Cheyenne, Wyoming.

Place: Cheyenne, Wyoming; Denver, Colorado; Pueblo, Colorado; Albuquerque, New Mexico.

the California gold rush in 1849, some hardy cattlemen on horseback braved a long trek, or drive, through Apache country and across the desert to collect $25 to $125 a head for their cattle. Others suffered through quicksand and hazardous swamps to reach the market in New Orleans. In 1854, two ranchers even drove their cattle 700 miles to Muncie, Indiana, where they loaded them on stock cars bound for New York City. When the cattle were unloaded in New York, the stampede that followed caused a panic on Third Avenue. Parts of the country were obviously not ready for the mass transportation of animals.

CITY DWELLERS DEMAND MORE BEEF After the Civil War, however, the demand for beef skyrocketed. There was a large market for beef in cities, where the population continued to grow. After the Chicago Union Stock Yards opened on Christmas Day, 1865, Texas cattlemen heard rumors that their longhorns would be worth $40 a head there. By spring 1866, the railroads had reached Sedalia, Missouri. From the railhead at Sedalia, ranchers could ship their cattle to Chicago and markets throughout the East. Unfortunately, they found that the route to Sedalia was riddled with obstacles: hostile weather, such as thunderstorms; rough land and rain-swollen rivers; and farmers who did not want cattle trampling their crops and spreading disease. In 1866, angry farmers blockaded cattle in Baxter Springs, Kansas, and prevented them from reaching Sedalia. As a result, some herds had to be sold at cut-rate prices, and others died of starvation.

B. Answer Expanded rail lines and increased demand for beef after the Civil War.

THINK THROUGH HISTORY

B. THEME ***Economic Opportunity*** *What developments led to the rapid growth of the cattle industry?*

The next year, the cattlemen found a more convenient route, thanks to cattle dealer Joseph McCoy of Springfield, Illinois. McCoy approached several Western towns with plans to create a shipping yard where the trails and rail lines came together. St. Louis, Missouri, turned down McCoy's plan, but the tiny Kansas town of Abilene agreed enthusiastically.

McCoy purchased grassy land around Abilene and built pens to hold the cattle for shipping. He also built a three-story hotel downtown. He helped survey the Chisholm Trail—the major cattle route from San Antonio, Texas, through

TEACHING OPTIONS

Exploring Themes

Economic Opportunity The railroads directly influenced major meatpacking centers such as Chicago and Omaha, as well as shipping centers such as Abilene and Sedalia. This economic development occurred at the expense of Native Americans, however. Ask students about the government's attitude towards the railroads, the ranchers, and the Native Americans. *Students might say that the government was sympathetic to ranchers and meat producers because they benefited the economy. These sympathies emerged in the government's repressive policy toward Native Americans.*

Making Global Connections

Ranching in Argentina Horses and cattle introduced from Spain into Mexico and then north into the American West also spread south and found a natural home on the pampas, or grassy plains, of Argentina. A cowboy culture similar to the one of the American West developed there and spread rapidly. Argentina continues to be one of the world's largest exporters of beef and other cattle products.

Oklahoma to Kansas. Thirty-five thousand head of cattle were shipped out of the yard in Abilene during its first year in operation. The following year, business more than doubled, to 75,000 head. Soon ranchers began hiring cowboys to drive their cattle to Abilene. Within a few years, the Chisholm Trail was worn wide and deep. An American legend was born.

The Truth About Cowboys

The meeting of the Chisholm Trail and the railroad in Abilene ushered in the heyday of the cowboy. As many as 55,000 worked the plains between 1866 and 1885. Although novels, folklore, and picture postcards depicted the cowboy as Anglo-American, about 25 percent of cowboys were African American and about 12 percent Mexican. The highly romanticized American cowboy of myth rode the open range, fighting and shooting villains. Meanwhile, the real-life cowboy was doing real work.

"I was at all times along with the men when there was excitement or adventure to be had. . . . When I joined Custer I donned the uniform of a soldier."

THE COWBOYS' LIFE A cowboy generally worked 10 to 14 hours a day on a ranch and 18 or more on the trail, alert at all times for dangers that might harm or upset the herds. The average cowboy was a wiry young man of 24, bowlegged from a life in the saddle. Some cowboys were as young as 15; most were broken-down by the time they were 40. A cowboy owned his saddle, but his trail horse belonged to his boss. He was an expert rider and roper. If he did carry a gun, he probably never shot anyone. A cowboy knew how to calm cattle and head off stampedes, but he probably never headed off—or even saw—a holdup. Prairie fires and lightning worried him more than Indians, and he was more likely to die from a riding accident or pneumonia than in an ambush by outlaws.

MARTHA JANE CANNARY (CALAMITY JANE)

The ordinary cowboy worked hard all summer for cattlemen who often banned drinking, gambling, and cursing. When winter came, he lived off his savings or rambled from ranch to ranch, doing odd jobs for a meal and a bed. Legendary figures like **James Butler "Wild Bill" Hickok** and **Martha Jane Cannary (Calamity Jane),** although serving as models for the Western hero, never dealt with cows. Their fame had more to do with stories in popular dime novels than with real cowboy life.

C. Answer The cowboy's life was hard, boring, and unromantic, unlike the romanticized myth of exciting gunfights and adventure.

THINK THROUGH HISTORY
C. *Contrasting* *How did the cowboy's life differ from the myth about it?*

Hickok served as a scout and a spy during the Civil War and, later, as a marshal in Abilene, Kansas. He was a violent man who was shot and killed while holding a pair of aces and a pair of eights in a poker game, a hand still known as the "dead man's hand." Calamity Jane was an expert markswoman who dressed like a man. She spread exaggerated stories about herself, and some historians believe she actually may have been a scout for Colonel George Custer. Wild Bill and Calamity Jane had also been entertainers—Hickok on the stage in a play called *Scouts of the Prairie* and Calamity Jane in Wild West shows. Although the shows drew large audiences, they bore little resemblance to the real life of the West.

ROUNDUP The cowboy's season began with a spring roundup, in which he and other hands from the ranch rode the open range and chased all the longhorns they could find into a large corral. They kept the herd penned there for several days, until the cattle were so hungry that they preferred grazing to running away. Then the cowboys sorted through the herd, claiming the cattle that were marked with the brand of their ranch and calves that still needed to be branded. Branding cattle required both brute force and riding and roping skill. A cowboy first had to separate a calf from its protective mother, rope it, and then drop it to the ground. Then he held the struggling animal while searching the ranch's emblem into its hide with a hot branding iron.

OBJECTIVE
② INSTRUCT

The Truth About Cowboys

▶ ***Starting with the Student***
Have students create a chart listing myths and truths about cowboys. Their charts might look like this:

Myth	Truth
Good guys wore white hats.	Cowboys wore hats of different colors.

▶ ***Discussing Key Ideas***
- The ordinary cowboy's life differed greatly from the popular conception of it.
- Cattle herds were rounded up in the spring and were driven many miles to railroad shipping centers.

ELECTRONIC LIBRARY OF PRIMARY SOURCES
from *The Log of a Cowboy*

GROLIER MULTIMEDIA ENCYCLOPEDIA
Cattle raising

MORE ABOUT . . .
Calamity Jane
The myths about Calamity Jane—many of which she perpetuated herself—are difficult to separate from the truth. She was born in Missouri in 1852 and, she claimed, was already an expert markswoman and rider when she arrived in the West with her family at age 13. She may have been a scout for George A. Custer, a Pony Express rider, and a nurse. Some say she got her nickname because calamity awaited anyone who offended her.

TEACHING OPTIONS

Exploring Themes

Cultural Diversity Discuss with students the cultural diversity of the cowboys—whites, African Americans, Mexicans, and Native Americans. A few women even rode the range. Ask students why such diverse people seemed to be able to get along with one another in those circumstances and not in others. *Students might note that cowboys developed their own subculture. A cowboy's worth was measured by his skill at riding and roping. Cooperation, dependability, and a level head in situations such as a flood or stampede were far more important than a person's ancestry.*

Making Connections Across the Curriculum

Art Much of the romantic myth about cowboys has been spread in paintings, sculpture, and popular art, such as magazine illustrations and cigarette advertisements. Ask students to break into small groups. Have each group select the works of an artist, such as Frederic Remington, or a broader medium, such as advertisements, to research. Have students analyze the image of cowboys that the art suggests and, if appropriate, how that image helps promote a product or service.

HISTORY FROM VISUALS

A Cowboy's Day on the Long Drive

Reading the Chart Have students examine the sequence of images and determine how long the cowboy's day might be. *When he had night duty, a cowboy might put in a 20-hour day.*

Extension Have students consult an almanac to determine about how many hours a cowboy was in his saddle, from dawn to dusk, if the long drive took place in the early summer.

OBJECTIVE

③ INSTRUCT

The End of the Cattle Frontier

▶ ***Starting with the Student*** Ask students what events might cause major physical changes on the earth or social changes in people's ways of life. *Students might mention factors such as severe weather, diseases, migration and immigration, depletion of natural resources, and technological inventions.*

▶ ***Discussing Key Ideas***
- Overgrazing combined with a series of natural disasters brings an end to the cattle frontier.
- The invention of barbed wire transforms the open plains into fenced-in ranches and farms.

A Cowboy's Day on the Long Drive

No self-respecting cowboy ever went far on foot. He lived his life in the saddle, protected from sun and rain by his hat, chaps, bandanna, and boots. On his saddle he carried a lariat, a bedroll, and anything else he might need at a moment's notice.

4:12 A.M. A cowboy slept outdoors in all kinds of weather. The chuck wagon was the meeting place for the trail crew every workday before dawn.

11:18 A.M. One of the tasks the cowboy liked least was crossing rivers. Cattle were often swept away in the swift current.

THE LONG DRIVE After the herd was gathered and branded, the trail boss chose a crew for the **long drive** to Abilene or another shipping yard. This overland transport of the animals often lasted about three months. A typical drive included one cowboy for every 250 to 300 head of cattle; a cook who drove the chuck wagon, set up camp, and fixed the meals; and a wrangler who cared for the extra horses. The trail boss earned $100 or more a month for supervising the drive and negotiating with settlers and Indians. The cook's monthly salary was between $35 and $50. Although the wrangler usually earned less than a dollar a day, he had few expenses and his wages equaled what he could earn at other jobs.

During the long drive, the cowboy was in the saddle from dawn to dusk. He drank coffee and ate beans, bacon, bread, and, if he was lucky, dried fruit. He slept on the ground and bathed in rivers. He risked death every day of the drive, especially at river crossings, where cattle often hesitated and were swept away. Because lightning was a constant danger, cowboys piled their spurs, buckles, and other metal objects at the edge of their camp to avoid attracting lightning bolts. Thunder, or even a sneeze, could cause a stampede of runaway cattle.

A PERSONAL VOICE

We went back to look for him, and we found him among the prairie dog holes, beside his horse. The horse's ribs [were] scraped bare of hide, and all the rest of horse and man was mashed into the ground as flat as a pancake. The only thing you could recognize was the handle of his six-shooter. We tried to think the lightning hit him, and that was what we wrote his folks down in Henrietta, Texas. But we couldn't really believe it ourselves. I'm afraid it wasn't the lightning. I'm afraid his horse stepped into one of them holes and they both went down before the stampede.

TEDDY BLUE ABBOTT, quoted in *The American West*

After three months or more of long days on the trail, the cowboy would hear a train whistle or glimpse some chimney smoke. He would break into cheers and song, deliver the cattle, and celebrate in town. After a bath and a shave, a good meal and a card game or two, he would head back to the ranch to collect his pay.

D. Answer Students might respond that the romanticized cowboy's independence, strength, and style are traits Americans admire.

THINK THROUGH HISTORY
D. Forming Opinions *Why do you think the romantic myth of the American cowboy has proved to be so enduring?*

The End of the Cattle Frontier

Almost as quickly as cattle herds had multiplied and ranching had become big business, the cattle frontier met its end. Overgrazing of the land, extended bad weather, and the invention of barbed wire were largely responsible.

NATURAL DISASTERS The promise of great profits to be had on the plains drew increasing numbers of ranchers. Herds of cattle crowded the plains and destroyed the grass. Sheepherders also invaded in great numbers, sparking range wars with cattlemen, who complained that "everything in front of a sheep is eaten and everything behind is killed." Then, in 1883, drought struck the

Block Schedule TEACHING OPTION **Time Needed: 30 Minutes**

Cooperative Activity: Researching Cowboy Music

Task: Small groups of students will research cowboy music and select one song for analysis. They will write a report and prepare it for presentation to the class.

Purpose: To explore the importance of music and its message about the cowboy's life.

Activity: Students should research how cowboys used music as entertainment and as a means of communication. They should select one song and should prepare a written report and presentation that includes the song (tape-recorded, sung, or read) and an analysis of how it reflects cowboy life.

Building a Portfolio: Students who add their reports to their portfolios should attach a note indicating their own contribution to the report and perhaps commenting on the reaction of the class.

ALTERNATIVE ASSESSMENT BOOK
Standards for Evaluating a Cooperative Activity

Standards for Evaluation
Reports should
- demonstrate evidence of research
- include specific details about the song to support the analysis
- show good organization

2:34 P.M. Capturing strays was part of the job. The cowboy had to master the "art of the lariat," or roping and handling the cattle.

7:19 P.M. The cowboy's greatest fear was a stampede. Controlling a runaway herd tested all his skills.

1:00 A.M. Some cowboys didn't sleep much. Each night a few men patrolled the herd for rustlers, and they often sang songs to calm the cattle.

Great Plains. Water holes and streams dried up. Prairie fires blazed, and at least one desperate rancher fought a fire with blood from slaughtered longhorns. Another drought three years later turned the overgrazed land to rock-hard desert. Temperatures soared to 115 degrees, leading Texans to claim that their potatoes were coming up cooked and ready to eat.

The dry, blazing heat was followed by the worst blizzard in American history. On January 28, 1887, temperatures fell to 68 degrees below zero and winds reached 60 miles an hour. For three days and nights, snow fell at the rate of an inch an hour. Hundred-foot ravines filled with snow and trapped cattlemen and their herds. Ranchers lost from 40 to 90 percent of their livestock. Granville Stuart, the cattleman who had introduced longhorns into Montana, recalled his despair: "I never wanted to own again an animal that I couldn't feed or shelter."

BARBED WIRE After the "die-up" of 1887, as it was called, most ranchers turned to smaller herds of high-grade stock that would yield more meat per animal. Unlike the hardy, free-grazing longhorns, however, high-grade cattle needed care and feeding throughout the year. Ranchers bought or rented large tracts of land so that they could raise hay for their herds. To keep the cattle from straying or trampling the crops, ranchers fenced the land with barbed wire, which had been invented by an Illinois farmer, Joseph Glidden, to keep dogs out of his wife's garden. It was cheap and easy to use, and it caught on fast. In his first year in business, 1874, Glidden sold 10,000 pounds of barbed wire. In 1878, he sold almost 27 million pounds.

This simple invention of twisted wire became a major factor in transforming the open plains into a series of fenced-in ranches and farms. The era of the wide-open West was over.

E. Answer Drought, a blizzard, and the invention of barbed wire.

THINK THROUGH HISTORY
E. Synthesizing *What events led to the end of the cattle frontier?*

HISTORICAL SPOTLIGHT

THE WILD WEST SHOW

In 1889, William F. Cody toured the country with a show called Buffalo Bill's Wild West. The show featured trick riding and roping exhibitions, and it thrilled audiences with mock battles between cowboys and Indians. A command performance of the show was even given for Queen Victoria in London on June 26, 1892. In her journal, she wrote,

> There were Cow Boys, Red Indians, Mexicans, Argentinos taking part, and then a wonderful riding display by Cossacks, accompanied by curious singing, and a war dance by the Indians. . . . The whole was a very pretty wild sight.

Wild Bill Hickok, Annie Oakley, Calamity Jane, and even Sitting Bull toured the country in Wild West shows. Their performances helped make Western life a part of American mythology.

Section 2 Assessment

1. TERMS & NAMES

Identify:
- longhorn
- James Butler "Wild Bill" Hickok
- Martha Jane Cannary (Calamity Jane)
- long drive

2. SUMMARIZING In a diagram similar to the one below, identify the reasons for the rise and the decline of the cattle frontier.

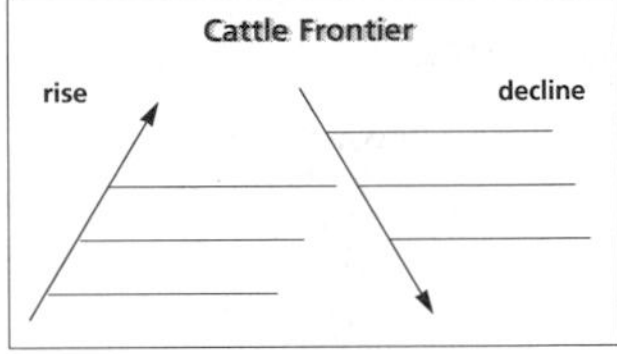

How might the decline of the cattle frontier have been prevented?

3. COMPARING AND CONTRASTING How were cowboys in the United States similar to and different from Mexican vaqueros?

THINK ABOUT
- their reasons for working
- the skills required
- the equipment they used
- their ethnic backgrounds

4. SYNTHESIZING Write a monologue in which someone from this section, such as a typical cowboy, discusses life on the cattle frontier. Prepare to present the monologue to your class.

THINK ABOUT
- how the person knows about the cattle frontier
- the person's attitude toward the frontier
- how the person might express his or her attitude

ANSWERS

1. TERMS & NAMES

longhorn, p. 222

James Butler "Wild Bill" Hickok, p. 225

Martha Jane Cannary (Calamity Jane), p. 225

long drive, p. 226

2. SUMMARIZING

Rise of the Cattle Frontier:
- Mexican culture
- railroads
- growth of Eastern cities

Decline of the Cattle Frontier:
- overgrazing
- natural disasters
- invention of barbed wire

3. COMPARING AND CONTRASTING

Vaqueros were sometimes prisoners, while cowboys were usually hired workers. Both used similar skills—horse riding, roping, and handling cattle—and similar equipment, such as chaps, spurs, and lariats. Most vaqueros were Mexicans, while about two-thirds of cowboys were Anglo Americans, another quarter were African Americans.

4. SYNTHESIZING

In the monologue, students should present the unromanticized reality of the cattle frontier.

HISTORICAL SPOTLIGHT

The Wild West Show

Critical Thinking: Recognizing Stereotypes
Discuss with students how the Wild West show might have helped perpetuate the myths about cowboys and Native Americans.

ASSESS & RETEACH

Section 2 Assessment
Assign pairs of students to ask each other the questions and find supporting evidence in the text.

Self-Assessment
Have students look back at the questions they answered about cowboys at the beginning of the section. Ask them to note new information they learned from their reading and discuss how their ideas have changed.

Section Quiz

FORMAL ASSESSMENT
Section Quiz, p. 69

Reteach
Use the map on page 224 and the visual at the top of pages 226 and 227 to help students review the main ideas about the cattle industry and cowboys.

CLOSE

Overgrazing, a series of natural disasters, and the fencing of the open range brought an end to the domination of cattle ranching in the West. The land became available for farming, but farmers faced hardships of their own.

Daily Life 1849–1900

OBJECTIVES

1. To summarize the role of gold in luring people to the American West.
2. To describe people's experiences in their often fruitless efforts to find gold.

FOCUS & MOTIVATE

▶ ***Starting with the Student***

- Students might be interested to know that the phrase *strike it rich* originated during the American gold rush of 1849. The term was later generalized to include other sources of quick wealth.
- Discuss natural resources other than gold that figure in modern American dreams of striking it rich. *Students might mention oil and precious stones, such as diamonds.*

MORE ABOUT . . .

Placer Mining

The word *placer* (pronounced plăs′ər) comes not from the English word *place,* but from the Spanish word *placer,* which means "sandbar," one of the places that placer deposits are found. Placer deposits are created when gold-bearing rock is eroded and the particles are washed downstream. Because gold is heavier than other minerals, it is deposited more quickly, often in places like sandbars, where the current of the stream slows down.

DAILY LIFE
1849–1900

Mining: Some Struck It Rich—Most Struck Out

GOLD! Between the Civil War and the turn of the century, this precious metal was discovered in scattered sites from the Black Hills of Dakota and Cripple Creek, Colorado, to Nome, Alaska. The dream of riches lured hundreds of thousands of hopeful prospectors into territories that were previously inhabited only by Native Americans. The fortune seekers came from all walks of life: grizzled veterans from the gold rush of 1849, young men seeking adventure, middle-class professionals, and even some families.

A FAMILY AFFAIR
This early placer, or surface, mine at Cripple Creek attracted many women and children. It grew out of the vision of a young rancher, Bob Womack. He had found gold particles washed down from higher land and was convinced that the Cripple Creek area was literally a gold mine.

But because Womack was unreliable and generally disliked, the community ignored him. When a German count struck gold there, however, business boomed. Womack died penniless—but the mines produced a $400 million bonanza.

SLUICES AND ROCKERS
In 1898, prospectors like this mother and son in Fairbanks, Alaska, found sluicing to be more efficient than panning, since it could extract gold from soil. They would shovel soil into a sluice—a trough through which water flowed—and the water would carry off lightweight materials. The gold sank to the bottom, where it was caught in wooden ridges called cleats. A rocker was a portable sluice that combined the mobility of panning with the efficiency of sluicing.

RECOMMENDED RESOURCES

Books

London, Jack. *Novels and Stories.* New York: Viking, 1982. *The Call of the Wild, White Fang,* "Klondike," "To Build a Fire," and other tales of the North.

Marks, Paula Mitchell. *Precious Dust.* New York: William Morrow, 1994. Mining and prospecting in the gold rush.

Seelye, John, ed. *Stories of the Old West.* New York: Penguin, 1994. Tales of mining and cattle ranches.

Time-Life Books. *The Miners.* New York: Time-Life Books, 1976. Illustrated history of mining in the West.

Twain, Mark. *Roughing It.* Berkeley: U of California P, 1996. Twain's witty 1872 account of his experiences in the mining camps and towns of the West after the Civil War.

Ward, Geoffrey. *The West: An Illustrated History.* Boston: Little, 1996. Companion volume to the 1996 PBS series.

Videos

Had You Lived Then: Life in a Gold Mining Camp. AIMS.

The Way West. PBS Video, 1994. A 6-hour miniseries from the California Gold Rush to the Battle of Wounded Knee.

The West. Time-Life Video, 1996. A look at the American West.

Software

America Goes West. Queue. Mountain men, placer gold, ranch life, and other aspects of the American West.

Yukon Trail. MECC. Students venture back to the Klondike Gold Rush of 1896.

IN THE BOWELS OF THE EARTH

Although surface gold could be extracted by panning and sluicing, most gold was located in veins in underground rock. Mining these deposits involved digging tunnels along the veins of gold and breaking up tons of ore—hard and dangerous work. Tunnels often collapsed, and miners who weren't killed were trapped in utter darkness for days.

Heat was a problem, too. As miners descended into the earth, the temperature inside the mine soared. At a depth of about 2,000 feet, the temperature of the water that invariably flooded the bottom of a mine could be 160°F. One miner who fell into such water up to his hips lost all the skin from his legs and eventually died.

Cave-ins and hot water weren't the only dangers that miners faced. The pressure in the underground rock sometimes became so intense that it caused deadly explosions. There were freak accidents, too. In one mine, a dog that attempted to jump over an open shaft missed and fell 300 feet. It landed on two miners and killed them.

PANNING FOR GOLD

At the start of a gold rush, prospectors usually looked for easily available gold—particles eroded from rocks and washed downstream. Panning for it was easy—even children could do it. They scooped up mud and water from the streambed in a flat pan and swirled it. The circular motion of the water caused the sand to wash over the side and the remaining minerals to form layers according to weight. Gold, which is heavier than most other minerals, sank to the bottom.

DATA FILE

Boom to Bust

This old signpost from Gleeson, Nevada, illustrates how a gold-rush town that had mushroomed overnight could die just as quickly when the gold ran out.

Long Odds

These statistics for the Klondike gold rush, from 1896 to 1899, show the incredible odds against striking it rich.

100,000 people set out for the Klondike.

40,000 make it.

20,000 stake claims.

4,000 prospectors find gold.

200 become rich.

Deadly Digging

An estimated 7,500 people died while digging for gold and silver during the Western gold rushes—more than the total number of people who died in the Indian wars.

Ongoing Gold Rush

In 1996, entrepreneurs advertised on the Internet a map showing likely places for prospecting. They claimed, "In the winter of 1995, abnormally high levels of snow blanketed the California Sierra-Nevada Mountains. The runoff of snow melt will provide unprecedented opportunities for the discovery of newly deposited placer GOLD!!!"

INTERACT WITH HISTORY

1. **CREATING GRAPHS** Use the Data File to create a bar graph that shows the percentage of people who set out for the Klondike who did not get there, got there, staked claims, found gold, and became rich.

SEE SKILLBUILDER HANDBOOK, PAGE 931.

2. **RESEARCHING GHOST TOWNS** Research the history of a ghost town from boom to bust. Present a short report on life in the town and its attempts to survive beyond the gold rush.

INTERNET Visit http://www.mlushistory.com for more about gold mining.

INSTRUCT

▶ *Discussing Key Ideas*

- In the second half of the 19th century, the possibility of finding gold draws many people to the American West.
- Few succeed in this dangerous pursuit of wealth.

HISTORY FROM VISUALS

Reading the Images

- Ask students what they think life would be like in the Cripple Creek placer mining camp. What aspects of the photograph suggest this to them?
- Have any students been inside a mine? What was the experience like? Do they think they would be able to tolerate the dangers, heat, poor air, and close quarters in the bowels of the earth?
- Bring in a pan such as the one shown at the bottom of page 229. Fill it with sand and water and give students a chance to try panning.

MORE ABOUT . . .

Mining Hazards

In very deep mines, the pressure within the rock built to such levels that the rock itself sometimes exploded, killing miners with flying debris. Miners were also notoriously careless with the copper blasting caps they used to set off dynamite. When children found the caps, their attempts to explore the inside of a mine could set off an explosion. In some mining camps, an average of one boy a week lost fingers in such mishaps.

INTERACT WITH HISTORY

1. Skillbuilder Mini-Lesson: Creating Graphs

Explaining the Skill Tell students that bar graphs are useful for comparing related information. Point out that bar graphs should include a title and labeled vertical and horizontal axes.

Applying the Skill Have students complete #1 in "Interact With History," comparing the categories under "Long Odds." First, students should figure out how many people did not make it to the Klondike. Then suggest to them that they calculate the percentages by dividing the total number of people in each category by 100,000 (the total number of people who set out).

IN-DEPTH RESOURCES: UNIT 2
Skillbuilder Practice: Creating Graphs, p. 5

2. Researching Ghost Towns

Standards for Evaluation
Reports should
- focus on a single town
- trace the town's experience in chronological order
- explain how discovery of gold established or expanded the town
- discuss the town's attempts to survive beyond the gold rush

Section 3 Overview

OBJECTIVES

1. To explain the rapid settlement of the Great Plains after they were opened for homesteading.
2. To describe how early settlers met the challenges of surviving on the plains and transformed them into profitable farm land.

SKILLBUILDERS

- Interpreting charts, pp. 233, 234

CRITICAL THINKING

- Synthesizing, p. 231
- Recognizing effects, pp. 231, 234
- Finding main ideas, p. 232
- Theme: Women in America, p. 233
- Summarizing, p. 234
- Sequencing history, p. 234
- Generalizing, p. 234
- Evaluating, p. 234

FOCUS & MOTIVATE

5-MINUTE WARM-UP

Making Judgments
To gain insight into the reasons for rapid settlement of the Great Plains, refer students to the poster on page 231. Have them answer these questions.

1. What was the purpose of the poster?
2. Do you think moving westward was a good move for a person? Why do you think so?

WARM-UP TRANSPARENCY 5

▶ ***Starting with the Student***
Ask the class to think about the students who set the trends in their school and what qualities they have in common.

OBJECTIVE ① **INSTRUCT**

Settlers Flock Westward to Farm

▶ ***Discussing Key Ideas***
- Transcontinental railroads open up the West for settlement.

(continued on next page)

3 Settling on the Great Plains

TERMS & NAMES
- homesteader
- soddy
- Morrill Land Grant Acts
- bonanza farm

LEARN ABOUT the life of farmers on the Great Plains
TO UNDERSTAND how the settlers endured hardships and transformed the land.

Plains settlers, like this one depicted in Harvey Dunn's painting *Pioneer Woman,* had to be strong and self-reliant. They also had to have a clear vision of the future for their families on the prairie.

ONE AMERICAN'S STORY

When Esther Clark Hill was a girl on the Kansas prairie, her father often left the family to go on hunting or trading expeditions. His trips left Esther's mother, Allena Clark, alone on the farm with her children, crops, and sheep. One spring, when the sheep got stuck on the wrong side of the river, Esther watched her mother drive the family wagon back and forth through the rising water until all the sheep were safe.

Esther also remembered her mother holding on to the reins of a runaway mule team, "her black hair tumbling out of its pins and over her shoulders, her face set and white, while one small girl clung with chattering teeth to the sides of the rocking wagon." The men in the settlement spoke admiringly about "Leny's nerve," but Esther thought that daily life itself presented a greater challenge than either of those crises.

A PERSONAL VOICE
I think, as much courage as it took to hang onto the reins that day, it took more to live twenty-four hours at a time, month in and out, on the lonely and lovely prairie, without giving up to the loneliness.
ESTHER CLARK HILL, quoted in *Pioneer Women*

As the railroads penetrated the frontier and the days of the free-ranging cowboy ended, hundreds of thousands of families migrated west, lured by vast tracts of cheap, fertile land. In their effort to establish a new life, they endured extreme hardships and loneliness.

Settlers Flock Westward to Farm

It took 263 years—from the first settlement at Jamestown until 1870—to turn 400 million acres of forests and prairies into flourishing farms. Settling the second 400 million acres took only 30 years, from 1870 to 1900. Federal land policy and the completion of transcontinental railroad lines made this rapid settlement possible.

RAILROADS OPEN THE WEST From 1850 to 1871, the federal government made huge land grants to the railroads—170 million acres, worth half a billion dollars—for laying track in the West. In one grant, both the Union Pacific and the Central Pacific received 10 square miles of public land for every mile of track laid in a state and 20 square miles of land for every mile of track laid in a territory.

In 1867, the two companies began a race to lay track. The Central Pacific moved eastward from Sacramento, and the Union Pacific moved westward from Omaha. They hired Civil War veterans, Irish and Chinese immigrants, African Americans, and Mexican Americans to do the grueling labor. During

SECTION 3 RESOURCES

PRINT RESOURCES

IN-DEPTH RESOURCES: UNIT 2
Guided Reading, p. 3
Geography Application: Land Regions of the West, p. 7
Primary Source: Letter from a Woman Homesteader, p. 10
Literature: from *My Ántonia* by Willa Cather, p. 12

READING STUDY GUIDE, p. 61

ACCESS FOR STUDENTS ACQUIRING ENGLISH
Guided Reading (Spanish), p. 83
Geography Application: Land Regions of the West (Spanish), p. 87

SPANISH READING STUDY GUIDE, p. 61

FORMAL ASSESSMENT
Section Quiz, p. 70

ALTERNATIVE ASSESSMENT BOOK
See forms for supporting and scoring alternative activities.

TECHNOLOGY RESOURCES

CRITICAL THINKING TRANSPARENCIES
CT13, Transcontinental Railroad
CT47, Population Changes in the West, 1850–1900

CD-ROM Electronic Library of Primary Sources

VIDEO *American Portfolio: A Videodisc for U.S. History,* user's guide, pp. 126–129, 135–139

INTERNET http://www.mlushistory.com

the winter of 1868, workers for the Union Pacific cut their way through the solid rock of the mountains, laying up to eight miles of track a day. Both companies had reached Utah by the spring of 1869, and their lines met at Promontory on May 10. They marked the completion of the first transcontinental track with a ceremony and a golden spike. Fifteen years later, the country boasted four transcontinental railroads, and the East and West Coasts were linked.

The railroad companies sold some of their land to farmers for two to ten dollars an acre. Some companies sent agents to Europe to recruit buyers. Many Europeans came, hoping to escape wars, overpopulation, and lack of economic opportunity. By 1880, 44 percent of the settlers in Nebraska and more than 70 percent of those in Minnesota and Wisconsin were immigrants.

THINK THROUGH HISTORY
A. *Synthesizing* *How did the railroads help open the West?*

A. Answer They made it possible for people to travel quickly and also recruited settlers.

GOVERNMENT SUPPORT FOR SETTLEMENT By 1900, more than 400,000 families had taken advantage of the Homestead Act of 1862, which offered 160 acres of land free to anyone who would cultivate it for five years. Despite the massive response by **homesteaders,** or settlers on this free land, the legislation didn't always work exactly as the federal government had planned. For example, private speculators and railroad and state government agents used the law for their own gain. Cattlemen fenced and claimed open lands, while miners and woodcutters claimed national resources. Railroad companies held land to sell later instead of building promised extensions of their lines. Only about 10 percent of the land was actually settled by the families for whom it was intended. In addition, not all plots of land were of equal value. Although 160 acres could provide a decent living in the fertile soil of Iowa or Minnesota, settlers on drier Western land required larger plots to make farming worthwhile.

Because settlement of the West became a goal for the government, it strengthened the Homestead Act and passed additional legislation to encourage settlers. Thousands of African Americans responded to Kansas governor John P. St. John's offer to settle in his state. In 1889, a major land giveaway in what is now Oklahoma attracted thousands of people. In less than 24 hours, land-hungry settlers claimed 2 million acres in a massive land rush. Some of them took possession of the land before the government officially declared it open. Because these settlers claimed land sooner than they were supposed to, Oklahoma came to be known as the Sooner State. Although speculators and businesses continued to buy land intended for individual families, the land-grant acts did continue to draw people westward.

B. Answer By making land available cheaply through various land grants.

THINK THROUGH HISTORY
B. *Recognizing Effects* *In what ways did government policies encourage settlement of the West?*

Ho for Kansas!
Brethren, Friends, & Fellow Citizens:
I feel thankful to inform you that the
REAL ESTATE
AND
Homestead Association,
Will Leave Here the
15th of April, 1878,
In pursuit of Homes in the Southwestern Lands of America, at Transportation Rates, cheaper than ever was known before.
For full information inquire of
Benj. Singleton, better known as old Pap,
NO. 5 NORTH FRONT STREET.
Beware of Speculators and Adventurers, as it is a dangerous thing to fall in their hands.
Nashville, Tenn., March 18, 1878.

Posters like the one shown above drew hundreds of thousands of settlers to the West. Among the settlers were thousands of exodusters—freed slaves who left the South to seek land and better lives.

(continued from page 230)

- The government encourages settlement by offering free land.
- In response to the rapid disappearance of open land, the government sets aside some public land to preserve the wilderness.

IN-DEPTH RESOURCES: UNIT 2
Guided Reading, p. 3

ACCESS FOR STUDENTS ACQUIRING ENGLISH
Guided Reading (Spanish), p. 83

MORE ABOUT . . .
Building the Railroads

On the Central Pacific line, over 90 percent of the labor force, about 12,000, were Chinese. They labored under extremely difficult conditions—including avalanches and 40-foot snowdrifts—for as little as $35 a month. White workers often received $40 to $60 a month—plus board and lodging.

CRITICAL THINKING TRANSPARENCIES
CT13, Transcontinental Railroad

HISTORY FROM VISUALS
Reading the Photo Ask students what they can tell about the people in the photograph. Have them think about

- the way they are dressed
- their posture and expressions
- the setting

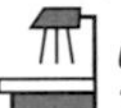

CRITICAL THINKING TRANSPARENCIES
CT47, Population Changes in the West, 1850–1900

TEACHING OPTION

Teaching Less Proficient Readers

Previewing and Visualizing Preview the text on page 231, "Government Support for Settlement," before asking students to read it. Point out that the Homestead Act of 1862 didn't work out exactly as the government had hoped and only 10 percent of the land was actually homesteaded. The rest was swallowed up by speculators, cattlemen, miners, lumber companies, and railroads. To remedy this situation, the government passed additional legislation regulating the provision of land. After students read the text, have them organize the information in a concept web such as that shown on the right.

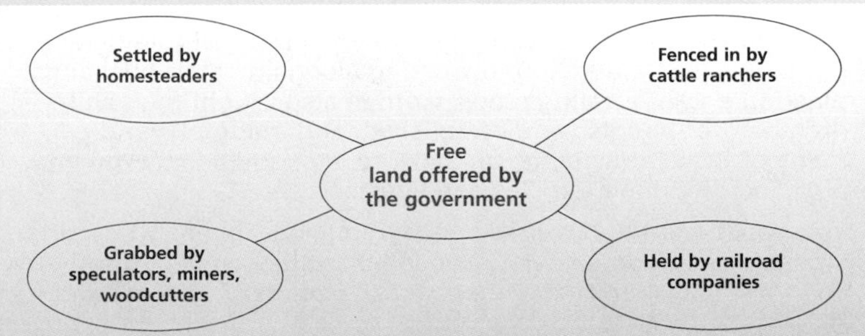

MORE ABOUT . . .
Yellowstone National Park

Fueled by General Washburn's enthusiasm for the natural wonders near the Yellowstone River, Congress created the country's first national park there in 1872. Four more national parks were created in the 1890s—Yosemite, Sequoia, and General Grant (now Kings Canyon) in California and Mount Rainier in Washington. The Army controlled Yellowstone National Park from 1886 until 1916, when the National Park Service was established.

IN-DEPTH RESOURCES: UNIT 2
Geography Application: Land Regions of the West, p. 7

OBJECTIVE
② INSTRUCT

Settlers Meet the Challenges of the Plains

▶ ***Discussing Key Ideas***
- The settlers' first task is to provide shelter for themselves on the treeless prairies.
- Pioneer women do much of the work of feeding, clothing, and sustaining their families.
- New technology and farming methods help tame the prairie.
- Many farmers go into debt investing in technology and transporting their grain to market.

IN-DEPTH RESOURCES: UNIT 2
Primary Source: Letter from a Woman Homesteader, p. 10

ELECTRONIC LIBRARY OF PRIMARY SOURCES
from *Letters of a Woman Homesteader*

THE CLOSING OF THE FRONTIER As settlers gobbled up Western land, the government decided to take action to protect and preserve the wilderness. In 1870, General Henry D. Washburn, who was surveying land near the Yellowstone River in northwestern Wyoming for the Northern Pacific Railroad, was overwhelmed by the area's geysers and bubbling springs, "objects new in experience . . . and possessing unlimited grandeur and beauty."

Instead of claiming the area for the railroad, he asked Congress to help protect it from settlement. In 1872, the federal government set aside land to create Yellowstone National Park. Seven years later, the Department of the Interior forced railroads to give up their claim to Western land holdings that were equal in area to New York, New Jersey, Pennsylvania, Delaware, Maryland, and Virginia combined. Still, a great deal of public land had been claimed. By 1880, individuals had bought more than 19 million acres of government-owned land.

The Western frontier was fast disappearing, although it continued to influence, and even define, the American spirit. In an 1893 essay entitled "The Significance of the Frontier in American History," the historian Frederick Jackson Turner declared that the frontier had ceased to exist.

A PERSONAL VOICE

The existence of an area of free land, its continuous recession, and the advance of American settlement westward, explain American development. . . . Now, four centuries from the discovery of America, at the end of a hundred years of life under the Constitution, the frontier has gone and with its going has closed the first period of American history.

FREDERICK JACKSON TURNER, "The Significance of the Frontier in American History"

C. Answer That it had ceased to exist.

THINK THROUGH HISTORY
C. Finding Main Ideas *What was Turner's view of the American frontier in 1893?*

Turner's argument was very influential during the late 19th century. It was incorrect in two ways, however. Much uninhabited land still remained. Turner also ignored Native Americans, African Americans, and Latinos. But he did express how important the idea of the frontier was to Americans.

Settlers Meet the Challenges of the Plains

The settlers who had been drawn to the frontier faced extreme hardships—droughts, floods, fires, blizzards, locust plagues, and occasional raids by outlaws and Native Americans. Probably two-thirds of the settlers stayed, however. The number of people living west of the Mississippi River grew from 1 percent of the nation's population in 1850 to almost 30 percent by the turn of the century.

A pioneer family stands in front of their soddy near Coburg, Nebraska, in 1887.

DUGOUTS AND SODDIES Settlers had to provide shelter for themselves before they could even begin to prepare their land for farming. Since trees were scarce on the Western plains, most settlers built their homes from the land itself. Many pioneers dug their homes into the sides of ravines or small hills. A stovepipe jutting from the ground was often the only clear sign of such a dugout home.

Those who moved to the broad, flat plains often made freestanding houses by stacking blocks of prairie turf. Like a dugout, a sod home, or **soddy,** was warm in winter and cool in summer, and it was an island of color when wildflowers bloomed on its roof. Soddies were small, however, and offered little light or air. They were havens for snakes, insects, and other pests. Although they were fireproof, they leaked continuously when it rained.

TEACHING OPTIONS

Exploring Themes

Women in America Women played an essential role in taming the plains. In addition to working alongside their husbands planting and harvesting crops, women also taught their children before schools were established, and made by hand many of the products the family wore, ate, and used. Women also doctored their families and livestock.

You might want to have students write a journal entry describing a pioneer woman's day. Suggest that they consult the chart of the cowboy's day on pages 226 and 227 as a guide.

Making Connections Across the Curriculum

Geography Have students break into small groups and prepare a report on an aspect of the geography of the Great Plains. Groups may choose to report on topics such as vegetation, average rainfall and temperature range, dust storms, prairie fires, thunderstorms, blizzards, or insect devastation. Ask groups to present their reports to the class. After all the reports have been presented, you might want to lead a discussion in which students draw connections and consolidate what they have learned about the geography of the Great Plains.

WOMEN'S WORK Rain was the least of the worries that the families who inhabited these makeshift houses had to contend with. Virtually alone on the flat, endless prairie, they had to be almost superhumanly self-sufficient. Women were especially burdened. They did much of the work of feeding and clothing their families. They often worked beside the men in the fields, plowing the land and planting and harvesting the predominant crop, wheat. They raised cows, hogs, sheep, chickens—and children. They milked the cows, skimmed cream, churned butter, and made cheese. They sheared the sheep, carded wool, and sewed or knit clothes for their families. They hauled water from wells that they had helped to dig, made soap and candles from tallow, did laundry by hand, and ironed clothes with a heavy flatiron. They milled the grain, baked bread, and cooked meals over an open fire. At harvest time, they canned fruits and vegetables and made sausages and jam. They doctored their families—and often other people—for everything from cradle cap to snakebites. "With a razor as a lance and a pair of embroidery scissors," a pioneer woman "once removed three fingers from the crushed hand of a railroad brakeman." They also sponsored schools and churches in an effort to provide for the future.

THINK THROUGH HISTORY
D. THEME ***Women in America*** *How were women central to the homesteading process?*

D. Answer Women helped work the land and handled a multitude of household chores, including raising children.

TECHNICAL AND EDUCATIONAL SUPPORT FOR FARMERS Establishing a homestead was challenging work. Once that was accomplished, however, farming the prairie year in and year out became an ongoing and sometimes overwhelming task. The thick prairie sod broke wooden plows, and reaping wheat by hand with a scythe was slow, backbreaking work. In 1837, John Deere had invented a steel plow that could slice through heavy soil. And in 1847, Cyrus McCormick had begun to mass-produce and aggressively market a reaping machine he had patented in 1834. A mass market for these devices didn't fully develop, however, until the last quarter of the century, with the migration of farmers onto the plains.

New and improved devices quickly followed, such as the spring-tooth harrow to prepare the soil (1869), the grain drill to plant the seed, and barbed wire to fence the land (1874). The first successful harvester, the cord binder, was patented in 1878. Then came a reaper that could cut and thresh wheat in one pass. By 1890, more than 900 manufacturers of farm equipment had sprung up. In 1830, it had taken about 183 minutes to produce a bushel of grain; by 1900, with the use of these machines, it took only 10 minutes. These inventions made more grain available and meant more money for farmers.

The federal government supported farmers by financing agricultural education. The **Morrill Land Grant Acts** of 1862 and 1890 gave federal land to the states to help finance agricultural colleges, and the Hatch Act of 1887

Skillbuilder Answer **Problem:** Crop dehydration. **Invention:** Answers will vary.

SKILLBUILDER
INTERPRETING CHARTS ***What farming problem did the steel windmill solve? Which invention do you think had the greatest impact on Western agriculture? Why?***

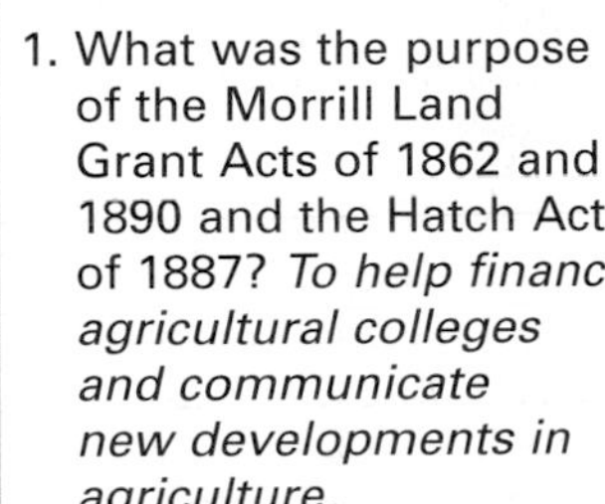

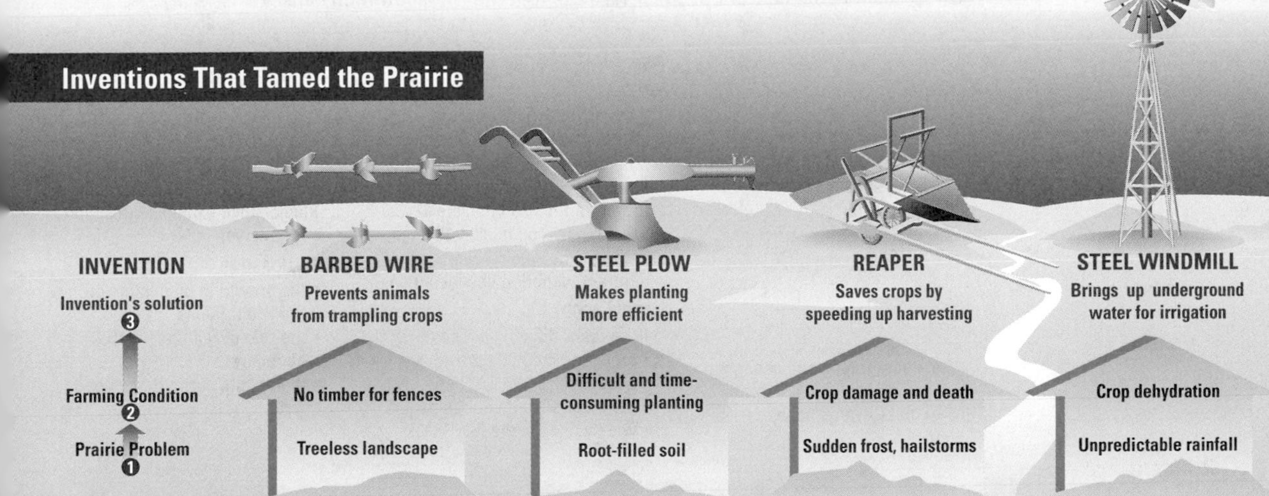

Inventions That Tamed the Prairie

INVENTION	BARBED WIRE	STEEL PLOW	REAPER	STEEL WINDMILL
Invention's solution ❸	Prevents animals from trampling crops	Makes planting more efficient	Saves crops by speeding up harvesting	Brings up underground water for irrigation
Farming Condition ❷	No timber for fences	Difficult and time-consuming planting	Crop damage and death	Crop dehydration
Prairie Problem ❶	Treeless landscape	Root-filled soil	Sudden frost, hailstorms	Unpredictable rainfall

HISTORY FROM VISUALS
Inventions That Tamed the Prairie

Reading the Chart Make sure students understand that they should read the chart from the bottom to the top—that each prairie problem led to a difficult farming condition, which, in turn, was solved by a particular invention.

Extension Have students research the types of agricultural technology used today, such as computer-controlled operations, fertilizers, and insecticides.

Issues for the 21st Century

Exploring Education Today

Connect education in the 1800s to education today by having students read pages 888-891. Then have them answer these questions.

1. What was the purpose of the Morrill Land Grant Acts of 1862 and 1890 and the Hatch Act of 1887? *To help finance agricultural colleges and communicate new developments in agriculture.*
2. Why was education for farmers an issue in the United States in the 1800s? *Farmers had to learn ways to farm the Great Plains.*
3. What issues in education does the United States face today? *How to improve quality, school finance, and affirmative action.*

Block Schedule TEACHING OPTION **Time Needed: 40 Minutes**

Cooperative Activity: Advertising Agricultural Inventions

Task: Student groups will write advertisements for one of the agricultural inventions pictured on this page.

Purpose: To help students understand the importance of the inventions in cultivating the plains.

Activity: Assign groups of three or four students to plan, write, and illustrate advertising posters or leaflets for barbed wire, the steel plow, the reaper, or the steel windmill. The advertisements should be directed at new settlers. Students may wish to include the history of the invention and a diagram showing how it is used.

Building a Portfolio: Students who add their advertisements to their portfolios should attach a note indicating their contribution to the advertisement.

ALTERNATIVE ASSESSMENT BOOK
Standards for Evaluating a Cooperative Activity

Standards for Evaluation
Advertisements should . . .

- indicate knowledge of the importance and use of the invention
- show awareness of the audience for whom they are intended
- demonstrate creativity and effectiveness

MORE ABOUT . . .
Bonanza Farms
The labor needed to plow and harvest the bonanza farms was seasonal. A farm that required only a few hands most of the year might need 150 men for the April plowing and 400 men for the fall harvesting. Harvesting crews moved from one farm to another, from south to north, during the summer. According to the writer Hamlin Garland, "They reached our neighborhood in July, arriving like a flight of alien unclean birds, and vanished into the north as mysteriously as they had appeared."

ASSESS & RETEACH

Section 3 Assessment
Have pairs of students split the four questions. Each student should present the answers for his or her two questions to the other for discussion and modification, if necessary.

Self-Assessment
Have students review the questions they could not answer. Ask them to find the answer in the text and then to write an additional question to test their understanding of the problematic concept.

Section Quiz

FORMAL ASSESSMENT
Section Quiz, p. 70

Reteach
Use the chart on page 233 to review the farming problems that faced settlers on the plains. Ask students to add to this list the social and psychological problems settlers—especially women—had to contend with.

CLOSE

Although many farmers successfully met the challenges of the plains, they lost money in the process. They needed to organize to solve common problems.

established agricultural experiment stations to communicate new developments in agriculture to farmers in every state. The work of agricultural researchers began to pay off when they developed grains for arid soil and techniques for dry farming, which helped the land to retain moisture. These innovations enabled the dry eastern plains to flourish and become "the breadbasket of the nation."

THINK THROUGH HISTORY
E. *Summarizing* *How did new inventions change farming in the West?*

E. Answer Inventions such as barbed wire, the steel plow, and the reaper helped farmers increase production and led to the development of massive bonanza farms.

FARMERS IN DEBT But elaborate machinery was expensive, and farmers often had to borrow money to buy it. When prices for wheat were high, farmers could usually repay their loans. When wheat prices fell, however, farmers needed to raise more crops to make ends meet. This situation gave rise to a new type of farming in the late 1870s. Railroad companies and investors such as George Cass and Oliver Dalrymple created massive **bonanza farms,** enormous single-crop spreads of 10,000 acres or more. The Cass-Cheney-Dalrymple farm near Fargo, North Dakota, for example, covered 24 square miles. By 1900, even the average farmer had nearly 150 acres under cultivation. Some farmers mortgaged their land to buy more property, and as farms grew bigger, so did farmers' debts. Between 1885 and 1890 much of the plains experienced drought, and the large single-crop operations couldn't compete with smaller farmers, who could be more flexible in the crops they grew. The bonanza farms slowly folded, and by 1896 Dalrymple, the "bonanza king," was bankrupt.

Bonanza farms like this one required the labor of hundreds of men and horses. They brought in big money for their owners when times were good and overwhelming debts when drought struck in the late 1880s.

Farmers also felt pressure from the rising cost of shipping grain. Railroads charged Western farmers a higher fee than they did farmers in the East. Also, the railroads sometimes charged more for short hauls, for which there was no competing transportation, than for long hauls. The railroads claimed that they were merely doing business, but farmers resented being taken advantage of. "No other system of taxation has borne as heavily on the people as those extortions and inequalities of railroad charges," said Henry Demarest Lloyd in an article in the March 1881 edition of *Atlantic Monthly.*

F. Answer By charging more than they did to Eastern farmers and by charging more for short hauls than for long hauls.

THINK THROUGH HISTORY
F. *Recognizing Effects* *How did the railroads take advantage of farmers?*

Many farmers found themselves growing as much grain as they could grow, on as much land as they could acquire, for the doubtful privilege of going further into debt. But they were not defeated by these conditions. Instead, these challenging conditions drew farmers together in a common cause.

Section 3 Assessment

1. TERMS & NAMES
Identify:
- homesteader
- soddy
- Morrill Land Grant Acts
- bonanza farm

2. SEQUENCING HISTORY Create a time line of at least four events that shaped the settling of the Great Plains.

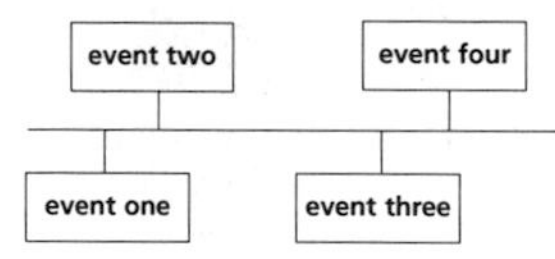

Write a paragraph speculating on how history would be different if one of these events hadn't happened.

3. GENERALIZING Review the changes in technology that influenced the life of settlers on the Great Plains in the late 1800s. Explain how you think settlement of the plains would have been different without these inventions.
THINK ABOUT
- the tasks done by the settlers
- tools and methods previously used
- the inventions that became widely used in the late 1800s

4. EVALUATING How successful were government efforts to promote settlement of the Great Plains? Give examples to support your answer.
THINK ABOUT
- the growth in population on the Great Plains
- the role of railroads in the economy
- the results of the Homestead Act

ANSWERS

1. TERMS & NAMES
homesteader, p. 231
soddy, p. 232
Morrill Land Grant Acts, p. 233
bonanza farm, p. 234

2. SEQUENCING HISTORY
Possible Answers:
1862—Homestead Act
1869—Completion of the first transcontinental railroad
1874—Development of barbed wire
1889—Oklahoma land rush
1893—Turner's essay on the frontier

3. GENERALIZING
Answers will vary, but students should include support from the text.

4. EVALUATING
Answers will vary, but should include supporting examples.
Possible Support:
Success—Increased miles of railroad track and population helped settle the plains.
Failure—Only about 10 percent of the land was actually settled by the families for whom it was intended; the railroads subsidized by the government became overly powerful.

4 Farmers and the Populist Movement

TERMS & NAMES
- Oliver Kelley
- Grange
- Populism
- bimetallism
- William McKinley
- William Jennings Bryan
- "Cross of Gold" speech

LEARN ABOUT pressures that made farming increasingly unprofitable
TO UNDERSTAND the rise and fall of the Populist movement.

ONE AMERICAN'S STORY

Mary Elizabeth Lease—daughter of Irish immigrants—had always had an independent streak. As a young adult in the early 1870s, Mary left her family home in Pennsylvania to become a schoolteacher on the Kansas plains. After she married Charles Lease and moved to a farm, she joined the growing Farmers' Alliance movement and soon began speaking on issues of concern to farmers. Lease joked that her tongue was "loose at both ends and hung on a swivel," but her golden voice and deep blue eyes hypnotized her listeners.

A PERSONAL VOICE

What you farmers need to do is to raise less corn and more *Hell!* We want the accursed foreclosure system wiped out. . . . We will stand by our homes and stay by our firesides by force if necessary, and we will not pay our debts to the loan-shark companies until the Government pays its debts to us.

MARY ELIZABETH LEASE, quoted in "The Populist Uprising"

Although farmers had endured great hardships in helping to transform the plains from the "Great American Desert" into the "breadbasket of the nation," every year they reaped less and less of the bounty they had sowed with their sweat.

Mary Elizabeth Lease

Farmers Unite to Address Common Problems

In the late 1800s, many farmers were trapped in a vicious economic cycle. The prices for crops were falling, and farmers often mortgaged their farms so that they could buy more land and produce more crops in an attempt to break even. Good farming land was becoming scarce, though, and banks were foreclosing on the mortgages of increasing numbers of farmers who couldn't make payments on their loans. Moreover, the railroads were taking advantage of farmers by charging them excessive prices for shipping and storage.

THE DEMAND FOR CHEAPER MONEY The troubles of the farmers were part of a larger economic problem that was affecting the entire nation. The period after the Civil War was marked by deflation, which meant that the amount of money in circulation decreased and the value of every dollar therefore increased. As a result, the cost of goods and services fell. This was good news for consumers because their dollars bought more products. It was bad news for farmers, however, because they received less money for their crops. They also had to repay loans on their property with dollars that were worth more than the ones they had borrowed. In effect, they lost money at every turn.

A. Answer It would increase prices for their products.

THINK THROUGH HISTORY
A. Analyzing Motives *Why did farmers think that an increased money supply would help solve their economic problems?*

The farmers thought the only solution to their problem was to force prices up by increasing the money supply. During a period of inflation—the opposite of deflation—the value of each dollar falls because there are more dollars in circulation. The result is what is called "cheap money." When money is cheap, the prices of goods and services tend to rise.

When the Civil War ended, the farmers tried to persuade the government to increase the money supply by printing more greenbacks—the paper currency issued during the war. When the government refused, the farmers demanded

Section 4 Overview

OBJECTIVES

1. To identify the problems farmers faced and their cooperative efforts to solve them.
2. To explain the rise and fall of the Populist Party.

SKILLBUILDERS

- Interpreting political cartoons, p. 236
- Interpreting charts, p. 238

CRITICAL THINKING

- Analyzing motives, p. 235
- Analyzing causes, pp. 236, 237, 239
- Making inferences, p. 236
- Analyzing issues, p. 238
- Analyzing causes and effects, p. 239
- Applying, p. 239
- Forming an opinion, p. 239

FOCUS & MOTIVATE

5-MINUTE WARM-UP

Drawing Conclusions
To discuss the problems facing farmers, have students read One American's Story on page 235 and answer these questions.

1. Who was Mary Lease?
2. What problems did Lease believe the farmers had to face?

 ***WARM-UP TRANSPARENCY 5***

▶***Starting with the Student***
Have students read the biography of Mary Elizabeth Lease and discuss how she might have come to be such a vocal promoter of the farmers' cause.

IN-DEPTH RESOURCES: UNIT 2
American Lives: Mary Elizabeth Lease, p. 16

OBJECTIVE
1 INSTRUCT

Farmers Unite to Address Common Problems

▶***Discussing Key Ideas***
- Farmers go into debt because of deflation and

(continued on next page)

SECTION 4 RESOURCES

 **PRINT RESOURCES**

IN-DEPTH RESOURCES: UNIT 2
Guided Reading, p. 4
Skillbuilder Practice: Interpreting Charts, p. 6
Primary Source: *from* William Jennings Bryan's "Cross of Gold" speech, p. 11
American Lives: Mary Elizabeth Lease, p. 16

READING STUDY GUIDE, p. 63

ACCESS FOR STUDENTS ACQUIRING ENGLISH
Guided Reading (Spanish), p. 84
Skillbuilder Practice: Interpreting Charts (Spanish), p. 86

SPANISH READING STUDY GUIDE, p. 63

FORMAL ASSESSMENT
Section Quiz, p. 71

ALTERNATIVE ASSESSMENT BOOK
See forms for supporting and scoring alternative activities.

TECHNOLOGY RESOURCES

CD-ROM *Grolier Multimedia Encyclopedia*

VIDEO *American Portfolio: A Videodisc for U.S. History,* user's guide, pp. 157, 160

INTERNET http://www.mlushistory.com

(continued from page 235)

- high shipping costs and demand monetary reform.
- Farmers form organizations to address their common problems.

IN-DEPTH RESOURCES: UNIT 2
Guided Reading, p. 4

ACCESS FOR STUDENTS ACQUIRING ENGLISH
Guided Reading (Spanish), p. 84

HISTORY FROM VISUALS
Political Cartoons

Reading the Cartoon Make sure students understand that the people who form the railroad ties are businessmen and bankers who supported the railroad interests.

Extension Have students write a title or a caption for the cartoon.

HISTORICAL SPOTLIGHT
The Colored Farmers' National Alliance

Critical Thinking: Analyzing Discuss why landowners and suppliers were more hostile to black farmers than to white farmers.

OBJECTIVE
② INSTRUCT

The Rise and Fall of Populism

▶ ***Discussing Key Ideas***
- The Populist Party provides a political power base for the farmers' alliances.

(continued on next page)

SKILLBUILDER
INTERPRETING POLITICAL CARTOONS *How does this cartoon illustrate the plight of the farmers?*

Skillbuilder Answer
They're at the mercy of the railroads, and their warnings are being ignored by businessmen and industrialists.

unlimited coinage of silver. That tactic also failed. After the passage of the Bland-Allison Act in 1878, from $2 million to $4 million was added to the silver supply each month, but that amount wasn't enough to produce the cheaper money the farmers wanted.

PROBLEMS WITH THE RAILROADS Meanwhile, farmers paid outrageously high prices to transport grain. It sometimes cost as much to ship a bushel of grain as they received for it. Because of the lack of competition among the railroads, it might cost more to ship grain from the Dakotas to Minneapolis by rail than from Chicago to England by boat. What's more, railroads made secret agreements with middlemen—grain brokers and merchants—that allowed the railroads to control grain storage prices and to influence the market price of crops.

Farmers who were short of cash mortgaged their crops or their farms for credit with which to buy seed and supplies. Suppliers charged high rates of interest and sometimes even charged more for items bought on credit than they did for cash purchases. Farmers got caught in a cycle of credit that meant longer hours and more debt every year. Clearly, it was time for reform.

B. Answer Deflation, high railroad rates, cycle of mortgage and debt.

THINK THROUGH HISTORY
B. *Analyzing Causes* *What were some of the causes of farmers' economic problems?*

THE FARMERS' ALLIANCES But to push effectively for reforms, farmers needed to organize. In 1867, a farmer named **Oliver Kelley** started the Patrons of Husbandry, an organization for farmers that became popularly known as the **Grange.** Its original purpose was to provide a social outlet and an educational forum for isolated farm families. By the 1870s, however, Grange members spent most of their time and energy fighting the railroads. The Grange's battle plan included teaching its members how to organize, how to set up farmers' cooperatives, and how to sponsor state legislation to regulate railroads.

HISTORICAL SPOTLIGHT

THE COLORED FARMERS' NATIONAL ALLIANCE

A white Baptist missionary, R. M. Humphrey, organized the Colored Farmers' National Alliance in 1886 in Houston, Texas. By 1891, the organization claimed a membership of more than a million, though it was more likely about a fourth of that. Like their counterparts in the white alliances, members of the local colored farmers' alliances promoted cooperative buying and selling. Unlike white organizations, however, the black alliances had to work mostly in secret to avoid racially motivated violence at the hands of angry landowners and suppliers.

The Grange gave rise to other organizations, such as Farmers' Alliances. These organizations included teachers, preachers, newspaper writers and editors, and others who sympathized with farmers. Alliances sent lecturers from town to town throughout the 1880s to educate people about lower interest rates on loans, government control over railroads and banks, an increase in the money supply, and high tariffs to protect farmers from foreign grain markets. Spellbinding speakers such as Mary Elizabeth Lease helped get the message across.

Membership grew to more than 4 million men and women—mostly in the South and the West. The Southern Alliance, which included white Southern farmers, was the largest. Approximately 250,000 African Americans in 16 states belonged to the Colored Farmers' National Alliance. Some alliance members even promoted cooperation between black and white alliances. But most members feared being branded as supporters of racial mingling and accepted the separation of the organizations.

C. Answer These organizations provided farmers with ways to organize and to respond to social and political problems.

THINK THROUGH HISTORY
C. *Making Inferences* *How did the Grange and the Farmers' Alliances pave the way for the Populist Party?*

The Rise and Fall of Populism

Leaders of the alliance movement realized that to make far-reaching changes, they would need to build a base of political power. **Populism**—the movement of the people—was born with the founding of the Populist, or People's, Party, in 1892.

TEACHING OPTIONS

Making Connections Across Cultures

Organizations for Minorities Ask students to consider the positive and negative aspects of organizations with restricted membership based on race, gender, politics, or religion. *Students may reply that such organizations give minority groups representation and power. Such restricted organizations might not have adequate membership to be effective politically, however. Often, several such special-interest groups join to help one another achieve their goals.*

Exploring Themes

Economic Opportunity Discuss the concept of "cheap money" and its meaning for the economy by pointing out two factors that determine the value of money—how long it takes to earn it and how much it can buy. Then discuss the relation between the time to earn a dollar, how "cheap" it is, and its buying power. *Answer: The less time it takes to earn a dollar, the "cheaper" it is and the less buying power it has.*

THE POPULIST PARTY On July 4, 1892, in a spirit harking back to the founding of the nation, a Populist Party convention in Omaha, Nebraska, demanded reforms to lift the burden of debt from farmers and other workers and to give the people a greater voice in their government.

The economic reforms they proposed included an increase in the money supply, which would produce a rise in prices received for goods and services; a graduated income tax, which would tax high incomes more heavily than low incomes; and a federal loan program. The proposed governmental reforms included the election of U.S. senators by popular vote, single terms for the president and the vice-president, and a secret ballot to end vote fraud. Finally, to represent labor as well as farming interests, the Populists called for an eight-hour workday and restrictions on immigration.

Most Americans considered these reforms to be radical at the time they were proposed. Yet the proposed changes were so attractive to struggling farmers and desperate laborers that in 1892 the Populist presidential candidate won more than a million votes—almost 10 percent of the total vote. In the West, the People's Party elected five senators, three governors, and about 1,500 state legislators. While the Populists lacked the power of the two major parties, they clearly had become a force in the political life of the country. Their programs eventually became the platform of the Democratic Party and kept alive the concept that the government is responsible for reforming social injustices.

THE PANIC OF 1893 Then, in 1893, political issues were forced aside by economic concerns. During the 1880s, the economy had grown too fast. Farmers and businesspeople had overextended themselves with debts and loans. Railroad construction had expanded faster than markets. In February 1893, the Philadelphia and Reading Railroad went bankrupt. The Erie Railroad failed in July, followed by the Northern Pacific, the Union Pacific, and the Santa Fe. Related industries, such as iron and steel, were the first to be affected. A general business collapse was not far behind. The stock market collapsed and banks stopped giving loans. The government's gold reserves fell as people panicked and traded paper money for gold. The price of silver also dropped dramatically, causing silver mines to close. By the fall, more than 8,000 businesses, 156 railroads, and 400 banks had failed. By the end of the year, about 15,000 businesses and 600 banks had folded.

D. Answer Overexpansion of key industries, especially the railroads, and a shrinking federal gold reserve.

THINK THROUGH HISTORY ***D. Analyzing Causes*** *What caused the Panic of 1893?*

Investments declined, and consumer purchases, wages, and prices also fell. Panic deepened into depression as 3 million people lost their jobs. By December 1894, a fifth of the work force was unemployed. In New York City alone, some 20,000 people were not only jobless but homeless as well. In Detroit, the mayor turned vacant lots over to the poor so that they could grow food. Some farm families, like the Orcutts of Kansas, suffered from both agricultural problems and unemployment. Susan Orcutt expressed the experience of many Americans.

> A PERSONAL VOICE
>
> I take my Pen In hand to let you know that we are Starving to death It is Pretty hard to do without any thing to Eat hear in this God for saken country we would have had Plenty to Eat if the hail hadent cut our rye down and ruined our corn and Potatoes. . . . My Husband went a way to find work and came home last night and told me that we would have to Starve he has bin in ten countys and did not Get no work.
>
> **SUSAN ORCUTT,** quoted in *Making America*

ECONOMIC BACKGROUND

BOOM OR BUST?

The cycle of prosperity and depression—boom and bust—that the U.S. economy went through during the 19th century was not peculiar to this country or to that century. All industrialized societies experience this cycle.

A boom occurs during industrial expansion, when it seems that business profits will continue to expand as well. As production increases, so does the demand for raw materials, machinery, and labor. Prices and wages rise—and business profits decrease.

As profits decrease, companies slow their expansion. The need for raw materials, machinery, and labor decreases correspondingly. With a decline in production and an increase in unemployment, people give up looking for work. Production decreases even more, and the unemployment lines grow longer. If the situation continues, a panic or a depression sets in. (See *business cycle* on page 933 in the Economics Handbook.)

FREE SILVER The Populist Party had done well in the elections of 1892 and 1894, and economic conditions had not improved as the 1896 presidential campaign approached. Populists watched as the two major parties became deeply divided

(continued from page 236)

- The Populist Party proposes financial and governmental reforms.
- Farmers suffer increasingly as a general business collapse deepens into an economic depression.
- The metal backing paper currency becomes a major issue in the 1896 presidential campaign.
- The Populist Party and Democrats both back William Jennings Bryan, who favors a bimetal policy.
- Bryan is defeated and the Populist Party collapses.

GROLIER MULTIMEDIA ENCYCLOPEDIA
Overview of the Populist Party

ECONOMIC BACKGROUND

Boom or Bust?

Critical Thinking: Summarizing Ask students to diagram the boom and bust cycle. Their diagram might look like this:

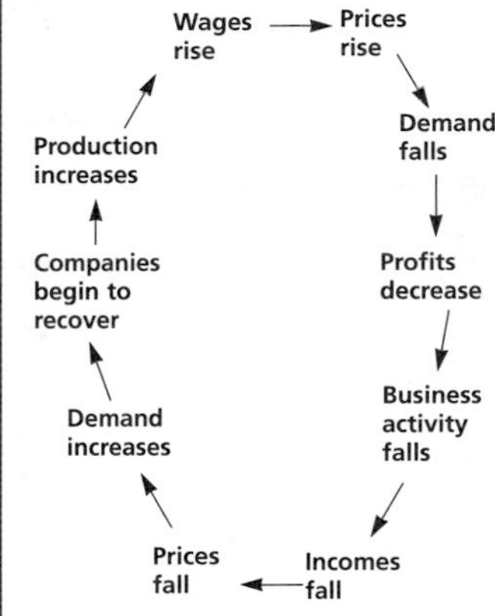

Block Schedule TEACHING OPTION **Time Needed: 40 Minutes**

Cooperative Activity: Researching Populist Reforms

Task: Small groups of students research and write a report on the outcome of the reforms promoted by the Populist Party.

Purpose: To help students understand the Populist platform and recognize that minor political parties can have far-reaching effects.

Activity: Student groups will use history texts, encyclopedias, or the Internet to research one of the platform planks of the Populist Party mentioned on page 237. They should determine if the reform has subsequently been enacted, if the issue is still being debated, or if it has now been forgotten. Finally, they will write a report on the issue to be shared with the class.

Building a Portfolio: Students who decide to add reports to their portfolios should attach a note describing their contribution to the report and indicating their personal stand on the reform issue.

ALTERNATIVE ASSESSMENT BOOK
Standards for Evaluating a Cooperative Activity

Standards for Evaluation
Reports should . . .

- clearly state the reform proposed by the Populists
- show evidence of appropriate research
- explain the outcome of the issue and give supporting details

MORE ABOUT . . .
U.S. Currency

The U.S. monetary system was established by the Coinage Act of 1792. It was a bimetallic system in which both gold and silver were used as legal tender. The government began issuing paper currency during the Revolutionary War, but it printed so much that the money became almost worthless. It was not until the 1860s that the government again issued paper money, "greenbacks," that could not be exchanged for gold or silver. Paper currency is no longer backed by any metal.

KEY PLAYER
William Jennings Bryan

Critical Thinking: Synthesizing Ask students to consider the paradox of Bryan's fame as an orator while many of the causes he supported did not succeed.

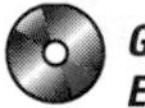
GROLIER MULTIMEDIA ENCYCLOPEDIA
from a speech on free silver by William Jennings Bryan

HISTORY FROM VISUALS
Gold Bugs and Silverites

Reading the Chart Suggest to students that they first read the chart vertically to understand how the Gold Bug and Silverite positions may lead respectively to deflation and inflation. Then have them read it horizontally to compare characteristics of the two positions.

Extension Ask students to consider categories they might add to the chart.

KEY PLAYER

WILLIAM JENNINGS BRYAN
1860–1925

William Jennings Bryan might be considered a patron saint of lost causes, largely because he let beliefs, not politics, guide his actions. He resigned his position as secretary of state (1913–1915) under Woodrow Wilson, for example, to protest the president's movement away from neutrality regarding the war in Europe. Near the end of his life, he appeared as the chief witness for the state of Tennessee in the famous Scopes "monkey trial," contesting the teaching of evolution in public schools. He is perhaps best characterized by a quote from his own "Cross of Gold" speech: "The humblest citizen of all the land, when clad in the armor of a righteous cause, is stronger than all the hosts of Error."

in a struggle between different regions and economic interests. The businessmen and bankers of the industrialized Northeast were Republicans, and the farmers and laborers of the agrarian South and West were Democrats.

The central issue of the campaign was which metal would be the basis of the nation's monetary system. On one side were the "free silverites," who favored **bimetallism,** a policy in which the government would give people either gold or silver in exchange for paper currency or checks. On the other side were the "gold bugs," who favored the gold standard—backing dollars solely with gold.

The backing of currency was such an important campaign issue because people regarded paper money as worthless if it could not be turned in for gold or silver. Because silver was more plentiful than gold, backing currency with both metals, as the free silverites advocated, would make more currency (with less value per dollar) available—cheap money. Supporters of bimetallism hoped that this measure would stimulate the stagnant economy. Retaining the gold standard would provide a more stable, but expensive, currency.

E. Answer Because people thought that paper currency had value only if it could be turned in for precious metals, such as gold or silver.

THINK THROUGH HISTORY
E. *Analyzing Issues* *Why was the metal that backed paper currency such an important issue in the 1896 presidential campaign?*

BRYAN AND THE "CROSS OF GOLD" Stepping into the debate, the People's Party called for bimetallism and free coinage of silver. Yet their strategy was undecided: should they join forces with sympathetic candidates in the major parties and risk losing their political identity, or should they nominate their own candidates and risk losing the election?

As the 1896 campaign progressed, the Republican Party stated its firm commitment to the gold standard and nominated **William McKinley,** a conservative Ohioan, for president. After a heated debate, the Democratic Party came out in favor of a combined gold and silver standard, including unlimited coinage of silver. While the party was trying to settle on a candidate at the Democratic convention, **William Jennings Bryan,** a former member of Congress from Nebraska and the editor of the Omaha *World-Herald,* delivered an impassioned address to the assembled delegates. An excerpt of what has become known as the **"Cross of Gold" speech** follows.

Skillbuilder Answer **Farmers:** They would get more money for their crops. **City Dwellers:** Probably gold bugs, because many were bankers and businessmen, who would benefit from stable money.

SKILLBUILDER **INTERPRETING CHARTS** *How would farmers benefit from inflation? Do you think city dwellers would be gold bugs or silverites? Why?*

Gold Bugs and Silverites

	GOLD BUGS	SILVERITES
Who They Were	bankers and businessmen	farmers and laborers
What They Wanted	gold standard "tight money" (less money in circulation)	bimetallism "cheap money" (more money in circulation)
Why	loans would be repaid in stable money	products would be sold at higher prices
Effects	DEFLATION • prices fall • value of money increases • fewer people have money	INFLATION • prices rise • value of money decreases • more people have money

TEACHING OPTION

Skillbuilder Mini-Lesson: Interpreting Charts

Explaining the Skill Charts such as the one on this page can be used to compare groups of people and movements. When information is presented in chart form, the comparisons can be seen at a glance. The information in the chart on this page is arranged in columns and rows. Students should study the labels for each row and column to understand the information that the chart presents.

Applying the Skill Ask students to explain what information is presented in each column and row. Then ask the following questions:

1. What was the difference between what the gold bugs wanted and what the silverites wanted? *Gold bugs wanted the gold standard to be the basis of the nation's monetary system and wanted less money in circulation; silverites supported bimetallism and wanted more money in circulation.*
2. What would be the result of the policies favored by the gold bugs? by the silverites? *gold bugs—deflation; silverites—inflation*

IN-DEPTH RESOURCES: UNIT 2
Skillbuilder Practice: Interpreting Charts, p. 6

A PERSONAL VOICE

You come to us and tell us that the great cities are in favor of the gold standard; we reply that the great cities rest upon our broad and fertile prairies. Burn down your cities and leave our farms, and your cities will spring up again as if by magic; but destroy our farms and the grass will grow in the streets of every city in the country. . . . Having behind us the producing masses of this nation and the world, supported by the commercial interests, the laboring interests, and the toilers everywhere, we will answer their demand for a gold standard by saying to them: You shall not press down upon the brow of labor this crown of thorns, you shall not crucify mankind upon a cross of gold.

WILLIAM JENNINGS BRYAN, Democratic convention speech, Chicago, July 8, 1896

A cartoon about William Jennings Bryan's "Cross of Gold" speech

Bryan's speech won him a full hour of wild applause—and the Democratic nomination. Still, the People's Party was hesitant to accept him as its candidate, since the Democratic Party had nominated for vice-president a wealthy banker from Maine named Arthur Sewall—who showed no sympathy for the farmers. Yet the Populists feared splitting the anti-McKinley vote between Bryan and a third candidate. After much debate, the People's Party nominated Bryan for president and Populist Thomas E. Watson of Georgia, an important figure in the Southern alliance movement, for vice-president. In this way, the Populists hoped both to retain their party identity and platform and to back a presidential candidate who could win.

THE END OF POPULISM Even with the support of the Populists, however, Bryan faced a difficult campaign. His free-silver stand had led gold bug Democrats to nominate their own candidate. It also weakened his support in cities, where consumers feared inflation because it would make goods more expensive. In addition, Bryan's meager funds could not match the millions backing McKinley.

Bryan attempted to make up for his lack of funds by spreading himself widely. He campaigned in 27 states, covering 18,000 miles, and sometimes made as many as 20 speeches a day. McKinley, on the other hand, campaigned from the front porch of his home in Canton, Ohio, while thousands of well-known people toured the country speaking on his behalf.

When the returns were in, McKinley had approximately 7 million votes and Bryan about 6.5 million. As expected, McKinley carried the East, while Bryan carried the South and the farm vote of the Middle West. The voters of the industrial Middle West and the voters of the growing middle class, with their fear of inflation, brought McKinley into office.

With McKinley's election, Populism collapsed, burying the hopes of the farmers. The movement left two powerful legacies, however: a message that the downtrodden could organize and have political impact, and an agenda of reforms, many of which would be enacted in the 20th century.

F. Answer It collapsed because it did not appeal to urban laborers and because it became too focused on the issue of free silver.

THINK THROUGH HISTORY
F. *Analyzing Causes* *Why did the Populist movement collapse?*

Section 4 Assessment

1. TERMS & NAMES
Identify:
- Oliver Kelley
- Grange
- Populism
- bimetallism
- William McKinley
- William Jennings Bryan
- "Cross of Gold" speech

2. ANALYZING CAUSES AND EFFECTS Identify the causes of the rise of the Populist Party and the effects the party had.

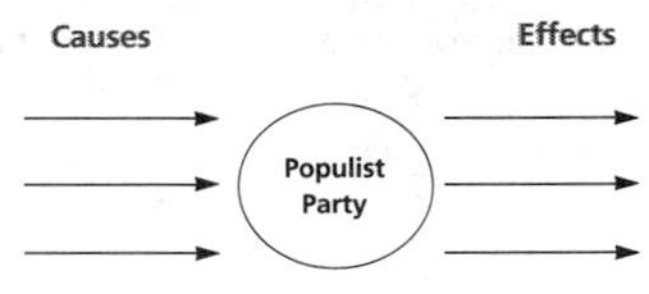

Which effect has the most influence today?

3. APPLYING Rank the following four factors in order of the impact you think they had on bringing an end to the Populist Party:
- support for free silver
- lack of wealthy backers
- advocating a greater voice in government
- third-party status

4. FORMING AN OPINION Who do you think was most to blame for the Panic of 1893: (1) farmers and businesspeople, (2) railroads and banks, or (3) government? Support your answer with information from the text.

THINK ABOUT
- the actions of each group prior to the Panic of 1893
- the causes of the panic
- the business cycle

ANSWERS

1. TERMS & NAMES

Oliver Kelley, p. 236
Grange, p. 236
Populism, p. 236
bimetallism, p. 238
William McKinley, p. 238
William Jennings Bryan, p. 238
"Cross of Gold" speech, p. 238

2. ANALYZING CAUSES AND EFFECTS

Causes:
Falling prices for crops
Inability to repay loans
High railroad rates
Effects:
New ideas that later became law
Political forum for addressing special interests
Message of hope to downtrodden

3. APPLYING

Rankings will vary but should be supported with examples from the text.

4. FORMING AN OPINION

Answers will vary but should include support from the text.
Possible Reasons:
Farmers and businesspeople—because they overextended themselves.
Railroads and banks—because they expanded so rapidly.
Government—because it did not regulate borrowing or take measures to rescue the economy.

HISTORY FROM VISUALS
Political Cartoon

Reading the Cartoon Make sure students recognize the central symbols in the cartoon—*the crown of thorns and the cross of gold referred to in Bryan's speech.*

Extension Have students discuss the religious meaning of the crown of thorns and the cross. Then have them write one or two sentences explaining how Bryan adapted this meaning to suit his political purposes.

ASSESS & RETEACH

Section 4 Assessment

Have students answer the questions, then exchange papers to assess their answers.

Self-Assessment

Have students identify two incorrect or weak answers they had given and discuss those questions with their classmates. Then ask them to revise their answers.

Section Quiz

FORMAL ASSESSMENT
Section Quiz, p. 71

Reteach

Make a problem-solution chart on the board and ask students to fill it in with the problems that farmers faced and the solutions they proposed to solve them. Then discuss how effective those solutions were.

CLOSE

Although the Populist Party collapsed with McKinley's election as president, efforts to remedy both social and political problems continued into the 20th century.

American Literature

OBJECTIVES

1. To learn how the literature of the West reflected its diverse population.
2. To learn views of the American frontier expressed in works of literature.

FOCUS & MOTIVATE

▶ ***Starting with the Student*** Ask students what books they have read and films they have seen about the American West, especially the American West of the second half of the nineteenth century. Ask how the West and its people are portrayed in these works.

MORE ABOUT . . .
The Diverse Literature of the West

The years following the Civil War brought an explosion of life, movement, and progress. In the West, the novel and short story continued to develop. Native Americans produced not only oratory but had a long tradition of myths, tales, and poetry. Among settlers, a wave of poetry, song, and folk tales burst forth, recreating the lives and tales of lumberjacks, miners, railroad workers, cowboys, and outlaws. Songs like "The Old Chisholm Trail" and "Git Along, Little Dogies" as well as tales of Paul Bunyan are all expressions of the West.

AMERICAN LITERATURE

Literature of the West

After gold was discovered in California, Americans came to view the West as a region of unlimited possibility. Those who could not venture there in person enjoyed reading about the West in colorful tales by writers such as Mark Twain (Samuel Clemens) and Bret Harte. Dime novels, cheaply bound adventure stories that sold for a dime, were also enormously popular in the second half of the 19th century.

Since much of the West was Spanish-dominated for centuries, Western literature includes legends and songs of Hispanic heroes and villains. It also includes the haunting words of Native Americans whose lands were taken and cultures threatened as white pioneers moved west.

THE CELEBRATED JUMPING FROG OF CALAVERAS COUNTY

The American humorist Samuel Clemens—better known as Mark Twain—was a would-be gold and silver miner who penned tales of frontier life. "The Celebrated Jumping Frog of Calaveras County" is set in a California mining camp. Most of the tale is told by Simon Wheeler, an old-timer given to exaggeration.

"Well, Smiley kep' the beast in a little lattice box, and he used to fetch him downtown sometimes and lay for a bet. One day a feller—a stranger in the camp, he was—come acrost him with his box, and says:

"'What might it be that you've got in the box?'

"And Smiley says, sorter indifferent-like, 'It might be a parrot, or it might be a canary, maybe, but it ain't—it's only just a frog.'

"And the feller took it, and looked at it careful, and turned it round this way and that, and says, 'H'm—so 'tis. Well, what's *he* good for?'

"'Well,' Smiley says, easy and careless, 'he's good enough for *one* thing, I should judge—he can outjump any frog in Calaveras County.'

"The feller took the box again, and took another long, particular look, and give it back to Smiley, and says, very deliberate, 'Well,' he says, 'I don't see no p'ints about that frog that's any better'n any other frog.'

"'Maybe you don't,' Smiley says. 'Maybe you understand frogs and maybe you don't understand 'em; maybe you've had experience, and maybe you ain't only a amature, as it were. Anyways, I've got *my* opinion, and I'll resk forty dollars that he can outjump any frog in Calaveras County.'"

MARK TWAIN, "The Celebrated Jumping Frog of Calaveras County" (1865)

RECOMMENDED RESOURCES

Books

Bierhorst, John, Ed. In the *Trail of the Wind: American Indian Poems and Ritual Orations.* New York: Farrar, Strauss, and Giroux, 1971. Also contains a bibliography.

Cather, Willa. *O Pioneers!* New York: Book-of-the-Month Club, 1995. Cather's first farm novel depicts pioneer life in Nebraska.

Muir, John. *The Mountains of California.* San Francisco: Sierra Club Books, 1989. Early travel and description by America's premier naturalist explorer.

Norris, Frank. *McTeague: A Story of San Francisco.* New York: Modern Library, 1996. Characters struggle with the American dream of success.

Velie, Alan R., ed. *American Indian Literature.* Norman: University of Oklahoma Press, 1979. Anthology that includes songs, tales, memoirs, oratory, poetry, and fiction.

Sound Recordings

Black Elk Speaks. Berkeley, Ca: Audio Literature, 1991. Recording of Black Elk as told to John G. Neihardt, abridged from the book of the same title.

Grey, Zane. *Riders of the Purple Sage.* Prince Frederick, Md.: Recorded Books, 1990. Unabridged recording of an adventure novel by the acknowledged creator of the genre known as the western.

Videos

Call of the Wild. Carlsbad, Ca: Bridgestone Multimedia, 1994. Motion picture drama based on Jack London's tale of wilderness survival in Alaska.

CHIEF SATANTA'S SPEECH AT THE MEDICINE LODGE CREEK COUNCIL

Known as the Orator of the Plains, Chief Satanta represented the Kiowa people in the 1867 Medicine Lodge Creek negotiations with the U.S. government. The speech from which this excerpt is taken was delivered by Satanta in Spanish but was translated into English and widely published in leading newspapers of the day.

Chief Satanta

All the land south of the Arkansas belongs to the Kiowas and Comanches, and I don't want to give away any of it. I love the land and the buffalo and will not part with it. I want you to understand well what I say. Write it on paper. Let the Great Father [U.S. president] see it, and let me hear what he has to say. I want you to understand also, that the Kiowas and Comanches don't want to fight, and have not been fighting since we made the treaty. I hear a great deal of good talk from the gentlemen whom the Great Father sends us, but they never do what they say. I don't want any of the medicine lodges [schools and churches] within the country. I want the children raised as I was. When I make peace, it is a long and lasting one—there is no end to it. . . . A long time ago this land belonged to our fathers; but when I go up to the river I see camps of soldiers on its banks. These soldiers cut down my timber; they kill my buffalo; and when I see that, my heart feels like bursting; I feel sorry. I have spoken.

CHIEF SATANTA, speech at the Medicine Lodge Creek Council (1867)

THE BALLAD OF GREGORIO CORTEZ

In the border ballads, or *corridos,* of the American Southwest, few figures are as famous as the Mexican vaquero, Gregorio Cortez. This excerpt from a ballad about Cortez deals with a confrontation between Cortez and a group of Texas lawmen. Although he is hotly pursued, Cortez has an amazingly long run before being captured.

And in the county of Kiansis
They cornered him after all;
Though they were more than three hundred
He leaped out of their corral.

Then the Major Sheriff said,
As if he was going to cry,
"Cortez, hand over your
weapons;
We want to take you alive."

Then said Gregorio Cortez,
And his voice was like a bell,
"You will never get my weapons
Till you put me in a cell."

Then said Gregorio Cortez,
With his pistol in his hand,
"Ah, so many mounted Rangers
Just to take one Mexican!"

ANONYMOUS, "The Ballad of Gregorio Cortez," translated by Américo Paredes

Vaquero (modeled 1980/cast 1990), Luis Jiménez. National Museum of American Art/Art Resource, New York.

INTERACT WITH HISTORY

1. **COMPARING AND CONTRASTING** Compare and contrast the views these selections give of the American frontier in the second half of the 19th century. Use details from the selections to help explain your answer.

SEE SKILLBUILDER HANDBOOK, PAGE 909.

2. **PREPARING A DISPLAY** From the gauchos of the Argentine pampas to the workers on Australian sheep stations, many nations have had their own versions of the cowboys of the American West. Choose one such nation and prepare a bulletin-board display that shows the similarities and differences between Western cowboys and their counterparts in that country.

INTERNET Visit http://www.mlushistory.com for more about the literature of the West.

INSTRUCT

▶ *Starting with the Student*

- Have students comment on what role they think stories, tales, yarns, songs, and ballads served in the changing West.
- Have students brainstorm a list of the types of heroes, plain folk, and problems depicted in the literature of the West.

▶ *Discussing Key Ideas*

- Oratory was a highly respected art among Native Americans and an attribute of leadership. Many fine examples of oratory reveal clear thoughts expressed in eloquent words and phrases.
- The theme of one against many, as well as man against nature, were common in the literature of the West. The individual, whether outlaw, cowboy, or explorer, was often a hero who faced and overcame great odds.

HISTORY FROM VISUALS

Reading the Images

Ask students to look at the art on the page.

- What does the magazine cover on the far left show? *Possible Responses: A young Mark Twain is astride the famous jumping frog as it leaps over a country gate; his hand is holding a cup in which to collect the profits from the tale.*
- What words would you use to describe the image of the cowboy? *Possible Responses: Strong, daring, dominant.*

INTERACT WITH HISTORY

1. Comparing and Contrasting

Possible Answers: *The selection from Twain shows a male world in which men live in camps, finding their amusement where they can. Ownership seems to be important, and betting appears to be a recreation. Chief Satanta's speech reflects the changing frontier, as Native American lands are consistently encroached upon by whites, no matter what treaty is made. The passage suggests settlement and the transformation of wild places into "tamed" ones. "The Ballad of Gregorio Cortez" shows the outsized figure of the outlaw, the single man on the American frontier who can stand up to three hundred seemingly lesser men.*

2. Preparing a Display

Standards for Evaluation

Displays should . . .

- spotlight the cowboys of a single country other than the United States
- offer several comparisons with and contrasts between the selected cowboy and the cowboy of the American West
- contain strong visual images
- include brief captions or labels that clearly name each image and provide additional information as needed
- be logically arranged so that comparisons and contrasts can be easily understood

CHAPTER 5 ASSESSMENT ANSWERS

REVIEWING THE CHAPTER

TERMS & NAMES

1. Homestead Act, p. 216
2. Sitting Bull, p. 218
3. George A. Custer, p. 219
4. assimilation, p. 219
5. James Butler "Wild Bill" Hickok, p. 225
6. Martha Jane Cannary (Calamity Jane), p. 225
7. Morrill Land Grant Acts, p. 233
8. Populism, p. 236
9. William McKinley, p. 238
10. William Jennings Bryan, p. 238

MAIN IDEAS

11. Native Americans—hunters and gatherers; settlers—farmers. Native Americans—communal property; settlers—individual property. Native Americans—migratory; settlers—settled.
12. The Native Americans' successful fight for the closing of the Bozeman Trail was followed by the breaking of the treaty by the U.S. government.
13. It was a failure.
14. With the growth of cities, the market for beef increased. The development of railways provided a link between the cattle frontier and the cities.
15. Over one-third were non-white—mostly African American or Mexican.
16. While cowboy myths focused on excitement and on the dangers of confrontations with Native Americans or outlaws, cowboys actually led a hard, often boring life.
17. The Homestead Act and the Morrill Land Grant Acts.
18. They were self-reliant and strong, building houses in the sides of hills or out of sod and working long, hard hours.
19. High railroad rates, crop failures, and the inability to repay loans.
20. They hoped that backing the dollar with both gold and silver and increasing the coinage of silver by putting more money in circulation would raise prices and allow farmers to get out of debt.

Chapter 5 Assessment

REVIEWING THE CHAPTER

TERMS & NAMES For each term below, write a sentence explaining its connection to the late 1800s and changes on the Great Plains. For each person below, explain how he or she influenced life on the Great Plains.

1. **Homestead Act**
2. **Sitting Bull**
3. **George A. Custer**
4. **assimilation**
5. **James Butler "Wild Bill" Hickok**
6. **Martha Jane Cannary (Calamity Jane)**
7. **Morrill Land Grant Acts**
8. **Populism**
9. **William McKinley**
10. **William Jennings Bryan**

MAIN IDEAS

SECTION 1 *(pages 214–221)*

Native American Cultures in Crisis

11. Identify three significant differences between the cultures of the Native Americans and the culture of the white settlers on the Great Plains.

12. How did the conflict over the Bozeman Trail symbolize the difficulties Native Americans faced?

13. How effective was the Dawes Act in promoting the assimilation of Native Americans into white culture?

SECTION 2 *(pages 222–227)*

The Growth of the Cattle Industry

14. Why did the cattle industry become a big business in the late 1800s?

15. How did cowboy culture reflect the ethnic diversity of the United States?

16. How did the real life of cowboys differ from the myths about them?

SECTION 3 *(pages 230–234)*

Settling on the Great Plains

17. What measures did the government take to support settlement of the frontier?

18. How did settlers overcome the challenges of living on the Great Plains?

SECTION 4 *(pages 235–239)*

Farmers and the Populist Movement

19. What economic problems confronted American farmers in the 1890s?

20. According to farmers and other supporters of free silver, how would bimetallism help the economy?

THINKING CRITICALLY

1. BREADBASKET OF THE NATION Create a cause-and-effect diagram identifying the reasons that agricultural output from the Great Plains increased during the late 1800s.

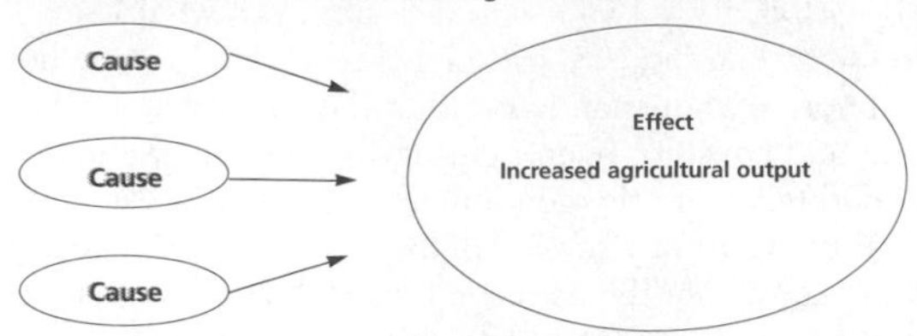

2. WESTWARD HO In the quotation on page 212, Chief Joseph says, "My people have always been the friends of white men. Why are you in such a hurry?" Why do you think white people were in such a hurry to settle the West and had so little regard for the Native Americans who inhabited the land? Give evidence to support your position.

3. TRACING THEMES ECONOMIC OPPORTUNITY Imagine you are a miner in Colorado in 1887. Tell about events in your daily life that would encourage or discourage a friend living in New York City who is considering joining you.

4. GEOGRAPHY AND SETTLEMENT Look back at the map on page 224. Near what kind of geographical feature were most cities located? How do you think the railroads changed this pattern of settlement?

5. COWBOY STEREOTYPES Explain why you think the myth of the cowboy had such a powerful hold on the American imagination, even though it was an inaccurate portrayal of real life.

6. ANALYZING PRIMARY SOURCES Read the following excerpt from a speech given by Red Cloud in 1870, during a visit to Washington, D.C. Then answer the question below.

> The Great Father [U.S. president] may be good and kind but I can't see it. . . . [He] has sent his people out there and left me nothing but an island. Our nation is melting away like the snow on the sides of the hills where the sun is warm, while your people are like the blades of grass in the spring when the summer is coming.
>
> **RED CLOUD,** quoted in *Bury My Heart at Wounded Knee*

How does Red Cloud compare the Native Americans and the settlers? Explain whether you agree or disagree with his assessment of the Great Father.

THINKING CRITICALLY

1. BREADBASKET OF THE NATION
Possible Answers: **Causes:** Increased land in production, resulting from various government programs to encourage settlement.
Population growth.
New technology, including the steel plow, the McCormick mowing and reaping machine, barbed wire, the spring-tooth harrow, the grain drill, and the cord binder.
New methods and crops, such as grains suitable for dry soil and techniques for dry farming.

2. WESTWARD HO
Answers will vary, but students might mention greed, the pioneering spirit, and the belief that Native Americans were savages.

3. TRACING THEMES ECONOMIC OPPORTUNITY
Lists should include details about the miner's daily life, such as the tedium of panning and sluicing for gold, the discomfort of the mining towns, the hazards of the mines, the hard work, and the difficulty of finding large amounts of gold.

ALTERNATIVE ASSESSMENT

1. **PROJECT FOR CITIZENSHIP**
   The Populist Party held a convention in Omaha, Nebraska, in July 1892, calling for reforms to help farmers and other workers. The party also called for reforms to provide people with a greater voice in government.

   Imagine that you are a member of the Populist Party and a supporter of the party's reform proposals. You have decided to lobby for—convince government officials to support—one of the reform proposals. Create a plan for lobbying. Use the following steps to guide you. (See "Understanding How to Lobby" on page 115 in Projects for Citizenship.)

   - Choose one of the Populist reforms to lobby for.
   - Identify the people you want to influence. Gather information about the reform proposal you chose to help support your case.
   - Encourage other people to write to the government officials to convince them to support your proposal.
   - Write a speech that you could present to an official to influence him or her to enact your reform proposal into law.

2. **LEARNING FROM MEDIA**
   VIDEO View the video for Chapter 5, *A Walk in Two Worlds.* Discuss the following questions in small groups.

   - What options did Native Americans have as white settlers threatened their life on the plains?
   - How might the American government have acted differently toward the Native Americans?
   - How did Zitkala-Ša react to life in the boarding school?
   - In what ways did Zitkala-Ša benefit from her education?
   - What lessons about clashes of cultures did you learn from Zitkala-Ša's experiences walking in two worlds?
   - How might people make interactions with other cultures a positive, rather than a negative, experience?

3. **PORTFOLIO PROJECT**
   Use the Living History activity to expand your portfolio.

LIVING HISTORY

REVISING YOUR TRAVEL GUIDE

After you have written the parts of your travel guide, ask a friend to read it and to answer the following questions:

- Is the guide helpful for the intended reader?
- What illustrations, maps, charts, or other visual materials would make the guide more interesting?

Make changes based on your friend's suggestions, and add a cover to your book. Then share your guidebook or display it in your classroom before adding it to your American history portfolio.

Bridge to Chapter 6

Review Chapter 5

NATIVE AMERICANS Between the 1850s and 1890s, settlers flocked to the West in search of gold and land. In the process, they nearly destroyed the traditional cultures of the Native Americans living on the Great Plains. Competition for land often led to bloody conflicts, including the Sand Creek Massacre (1864), Custer's last stand (1876), and the Battle of Wounded Knee (1890).

THE CATTLE INDUSTRY As the settlers took over the Native American lands, they developed a thriving cattle industry. Learning skills and borrowing terminology from Mexicans, cowboys drove cattle to be shipped by railroad to the growing cities in the East. The cowboy became one of America's most romantic figures. By the 1880s, however, droughts, blizzards, and the introduction of barbed wire ended the cattle frontier.

SETTLING ON THE GREAT PLAINS The government actively promoted the settlement of the Great Plains by subsidizing the construction of railways, providing free land, and sponsoring agricultural research. Settlers on the Great Plains often lived in dugouts or soddies, and they struggled to survive inclement weather and isolation. In the 1880s, many farmers suffered from growing debts and rising railroad rates.

THE POPULIST MOVEMENT In an attempt to deal with their economic troubles, farmers organized to demand changes. The Grange and various Farmers' Alliances became active in politics. Building on farmers' discontent, the Populist movement grew rapidly, particularly after the Panic of 1893. In 1896, the Populist Party nominated the noted orator William Jennings Bryan for president. After Bryan's loss to conservative William McKinley, though, the Populist Party lost its momentum.

Preview Chapter 6

The changes that led to the decline of the frontier were just the beginning of widespread economic and social developments that ushered in a whole new way of life at the end of the 19th century. The availability of natural resources, new inventions, and a receptive market combined to fuel an industrial boom. Large businesses grew larger, and workers united to demand higher pay, shorter hours, and safer working conditions. You will learn about these significant developments in the next chapter.

ALTERNATIVE ASSESSMENT

1. PROJECT FOR CITIZENSHIP
Standards for Evaluation
The plan for lobbying should meet the following criteria:

- Reflects a specific Populist reform.
- Indicates the audience from whom student will seek additional support for the chosen reform.
- Includes a well-organized speech that effectively uses information and statistics to influence an official to enact the reform proposal into law.

2. LEARNING FROM MEDIA
Answers to the questions:

- They could have either fought to retain their lands or accepted their loss.
- The government might have upheld Native Americans' claims to Western lands and restricted settlement by farmers and prospectors.
- She resisted the loss of her native identity.
- She gained the skills necessary to function in the white world and to fight for the cause of her people.
- Cultural values cannot be imposed on people without their consent.
- People could respect those with different values and ways and embrace interaction as a way to expand their own understanding.

3. PORTFOLIO PROJECT
LIVING HISTORY
Standards for Evaluation
A travel guide should meet the following criteria:

- Shows awareness of the needs and knowledge of the target audience.
- Presents appropriate and detailed information in an organized format.
- Includes lively visual materials that engage readers' interest and enhance the usefulness of the guide.

IN-DEPTH RESOURCES: UNIT 2
See the form for scoring this activity on page 18.

THINKING CRITICALLY

4. GEOGRAPHY AND SETTLEMENT
Rivers. ***Possible Answer:*** Railroads converted rivers from pathways into barriers to cross. Cities such as Abilene, Kansas, grew because of their position on the railroad rather than on a river. The shift from river to rails gave people greater flexibility in establishing trade routes, businesses, and cities.

5. COWBOY STEREOTYPES
The romance of the independent, hardworking man pitting himself against the elements has a powerful attraction for people of all times whose lives are boring and dependent on others.

6. ANALYZING PRIMARY SOURCES
Red Cloud's nation is disappearing like melting snow; the settlers are increasing like growing grass. Some students may agree that the president deserved blame, citing the ill treatment Native Americans received. Others may argue that the president was less at fault for abuses to the Native Americans than were the settlers and the military.

CHAPTER 6

PLANNING GUIDE
A New Industrial Age

	Key Ideas	COPYMASTERS	ASSESSMENT
SECTION 1 The Expansion of Industry *pp. 246–249*	*Industry booms as natural resources, creative ideas, and growing markets fuel technological development.*	***In-Depth Resources: Unit 2*** • Guided Reading, p. 19 • Geography Application: The Changing Labor Force, p. 24 • Primary Source: The Birth of the Telephone, p. 26 ***Lesson Plans,*** pp. 53–54	PE ***Section 1 Assessment,*** p. 249 TE ***Self-Assessment,*** p. 249 ***Formal Assessment*** • Section Quiz, p. 80 ***Alternative Assessment Book*** • Standards for Evaluating a Cooperative Activity
SECTION 2 The Age of the Railroads *pp. 252–256*	*The growth and consolidation of the railroads benefit the nation but lead to corruption and regulation.*	***In-Depth Resources: Unit 2*** • Guided Reading, p. 20 • Literature: *from* "The Bride Comes to Yellow Sky" by Stephen Crane, p. 30 ***Lesson Plans,*** pp. 55–56	PE ***Section 2 Assessment,*** p. 256 TE ***Self-Assessment,*** p. 256 ***Formal Assessment*** • Section Quiz, p. 81 ***Alternative Assessment Book*** • Standards for Evaluating a Cooperative Activity
SECTION 3 Big Business Emerges *pp. 257–261*	*The expansion of industry in the North results in the growth of big business and the development of a new social philosophy.*	***In-Depth Resources: Unit 2*** • Guided Reading, p. 21 • Skillbuilder Practice: Forming Opinions, p. 23 • Primary Sources: *from* "Wealth and Its Uses" by Andrew Carnegie, p. 27; from *The History of the Standard Oil Company,* p. 28 • American Lives: Andrew Carnegie, p. 33 ***Lesson Plans,*** pp. 57–58	PE ***Section 3 Assessment,*** p. 261 TE ***Self-Assessment,*** p. 261 ***Formal Assessment*** • Section Quiz, p. 82 ***Alternative Assessment Book*** • Standards for Evaluating a Cooperative Activity
SECTION 4 Workers of the Nation Unite *pp. 262–269*	*Laborers form unions to better their working conditions and pay. Despite some success, they eventually lose ground against government-supported business interests.*	***In-Depth Resources: Unit 2*** • Guided Reading, p. 22 • Primary Source: Labor Poster, p. 29 • American Lives: Mary Harris "Mother" Jones, p. 34 ***Lesson Plans,*** pp. 59–60	PE ***Section 4 Assessment,*** p. 269 TE ***Self-Assessment,*** p. 269 ***Formal Assessment*** • Section Quiz, p. 83 ***Alternative Assessment Book*** • Standards for Evaluating a Cooperative Activity
CHAPTER RESOURCES	**Chapter Overview** *Technological innovations and the growth of the railroad industry help fuel an industrial boom. Some business leaders follow corrupt practices, and workers, suffering harsh working conditions, try to organize.*	***In-Depth Resources: Unit 2*** • Living History Project: Worksheet, p. 35; Standards, p. 36 ***Telescoping the Times*** • Chapter Summary, pp. 11–12 ***Planning for Block Schedules***	PE ***Chapter Assessment,*** pp. 270–271 PE ***Alternative Assessment,*** p. 271 ***Formal Assessment*** • Chapter Test, forms A and B, pp. 84–89 ***Test Generator*** ***Alternative Assessment Book*** See explanation and forms for different kinds of alternative assessments including portfolio assessment.

KEY
- PE Pupil's Edition
- TE Teacher's Edition
- http://www.mlushistory.com

TECHNOLOGY

Warm-Up Transparency **6**

Geography Transparencies
- G14, Mining and Industry

Critical Thinking Transparencies
- CT14, Industrial Growth

Grolier Multimedia Encyclopedia
- Edison and Bell

Electronic Library of Primary Sources
- How Women Are Treated by the Pullman Company

AMERICAN STORIES video series
- "Gusher!"

INTERNET Interact with History p. 251 (PE)

Warm-Up Transparency **6**

Grolier Multimedia Encyclopedia
- The Growth of Railroads

INTERNET George Pullman and railroads

Warm-Up Transparency **6**

Critical Thinking Transparencies
- CT48, Horizontal Consolidation and Vertical Integration

Humanities Transparencies
- H35, "The Bosses of the Senate": American antitrust cartoon

Electronic Library of Primary Sources
- "The Two Acre Lot" by Horatio Alger

Our Times
- Freedom and Free Enterprise

INTERNET Andrew Carnegie

Warm-Up Transparency **6**

Humanities Transparencies
- H14, *The Gun Foundry* by John Ferguson Weir

Electronic Library of Primary Sources
- *from* "141 Die in Factory Fire"
- On the Goals of Trade Unions by Samuel Gompers

INTERNET The Haymarket riot

American Portfolio: A Videodisc for U.S. History, user's guide, pp. 135–139, 141–142, 148, 160, 166

Chapter Summary Audiotapes
- Unit 2, Chapter 6

INTERNET http://www.mlushistory.com

Block Scheduling (90 MINUTES)

Day 1	Day 2	Day 3
Section 1, pp. 246–249 *Geography Spotlight: Industry Changes the Environment,* pp. 250–251 *Section 2,* pp. 252–256 *Section Assessments,* pp. 249, 256 **COOPERATIVE ACTIVITIES** • Tracking the Growth of Steel, p. 247 (TE) • Debating Company Towns, p. 255 (TE)	*Section 3,* pp. 257–261 *Section Assessment,* p. 261	*Section 4,* pp. 262–269 *Section Assessment,* p. 269 *Chapter Assessment,* pp. 270–271 **COOPERATIVE ACTIVITY** • Reporting on Union Goals, p. 267 (TE)

YEARLY PACING *Chapter 6 Total:* 3 days *Yearly Total:* 85 days

See *Planning for Block Schedules* for special activities and pacing strategies.

Customizing for Special Populations

Students Acquiring English

Access for Students Acquiring English: Spanish Translations
- Guided Reading for Sections 1–4 , pp. 91–94
- Chapter Summary, pp. 89–90
- Skillbuilder Practice: Forming Opinions, p. 95
- Geography Application: The Changing Labor Force, p. 96

Spanish Reading Study Guide, pp. 67–76

Translations of Chapter Summaries, Hmong, Cantonese, Vietnamese, and Cambodian

Chapter Summary Audiotapes in Spanish Unit 2, Chapter 6

AMERICAN STORIES video series
- "Gusher!" (Spanish track)

INTERNET The Diverse Classroom

Gifted and Talented Students

In-Depth Resources: Unit 2
- Primary Sources: The Birth of the Telephone, p. 26; from "Wealth and Its Uses" by Andrew Carnegie, p. 27; from *The History of the Standard Oil Company,* p. 28; Labor Poster, p. 29
- American Lives: Andrew Carnegie, p. 33; Mary Harris "Mother" Jones, p. 34

Less Proficient Readers

In-Depth Resources: Unit 2
- Guided Reading for Sections 1–4, pp. 19–22
- Skillbuilder: Forming Opinions, p. 23
- Geography Application: The Changing Labor Force, p. 24

Reading Study Guide
- pp. 67–76

Telescoping the Times
- Chapter Summary, pp. 11–12

Chapter Summary Audiotapes, Unit 2, Chapter 6

Connections to Literature READINGS FOR STUDENTS

In-Depth Resources: Unit 2
- ***from* "The Bride Comes to Yellow Sky" by Stephen Crane,** p. 30

Enrichment Reading
- **Dee Brown**
  Hear That Lonesome Whistle Blow.
  New York: Simon and Schuster, 1994.
  By the end of the 19th century, the Iron Horse had conquered the West—railroads linked the two coasts of the United States. In Hear That Lonesome Whistle Blow, *Dee Brown tells the story of this extraordinary undertaking.*
- **Paul Goble**
  Death of the Iron Horse.
  New York: Aladdin Books, 1993.
  A group of Cheyenne braves derail and raid a freight train in 1867 as an act of defiance against the white man's encroachment on their land.

McDougal Littell ***The Language of Literature*** American Literature
- **Mark Twain, from *The Autobiography of Mark Twain,*** p. 531

- **Mary Harris "Mother" Jones**
  The Autobiography of Mother Jones.
  Chicago: Kerr, 1990.
  This self-portrait by the feisty union activist is a fascinating account of one woman's activism.
- **Liston Leyendecker**
  Palace Car Prince.
  Nivot, Colo.: UP of Colorado, 1992.
  The flamboyant story of George Pullman is told in this detailed biography.

CHAPTER 6

OVERVIEW

A New Industrial Age

▶ ***Accessing Prior Knowledge***
Ask students to identify industries that are important today. Have them discuss problems faced by these industries and how people seek to solve these problems.

▶ ***Predicting Outcomes***
Ask students what images the phrase "A New Industrial Age" brings to mind. Then ask students to read the quotation from Mother Jones and to study the time line. Based on the quotation and the time line, what do they think the people would fight for during the new industrial age?

MORE ABOUT . . .
"Mother" Jones
Mary Harris "Mother" Jones (1830–1930) worked tirelessly during most of her long life to win decent working conditions and adequate pay for laborers. She particularly supported miners and railroad workers.

CHAPTER 6

A New Industrial Age

SECTION 1
The Expansion of Industry
Industry booms as natural resources, creative ideas, and growing markets fuel technological development.

VIDEO
GUSHER!

SECTION 2
The Age of the Railroads
The growth and consolidation of the railroads benefit the nation but lead to corruption and regulation.

SECTION 3
Big Business Emerges
The expansion of industry in the North results in the growth of big business and the development of a new social philosophy.

SECTION 4
Workers of the Nation Unite
Laborers form unions to better their working conditions and pay. Despite some success, they eventually lose ground against government-supported business interests.

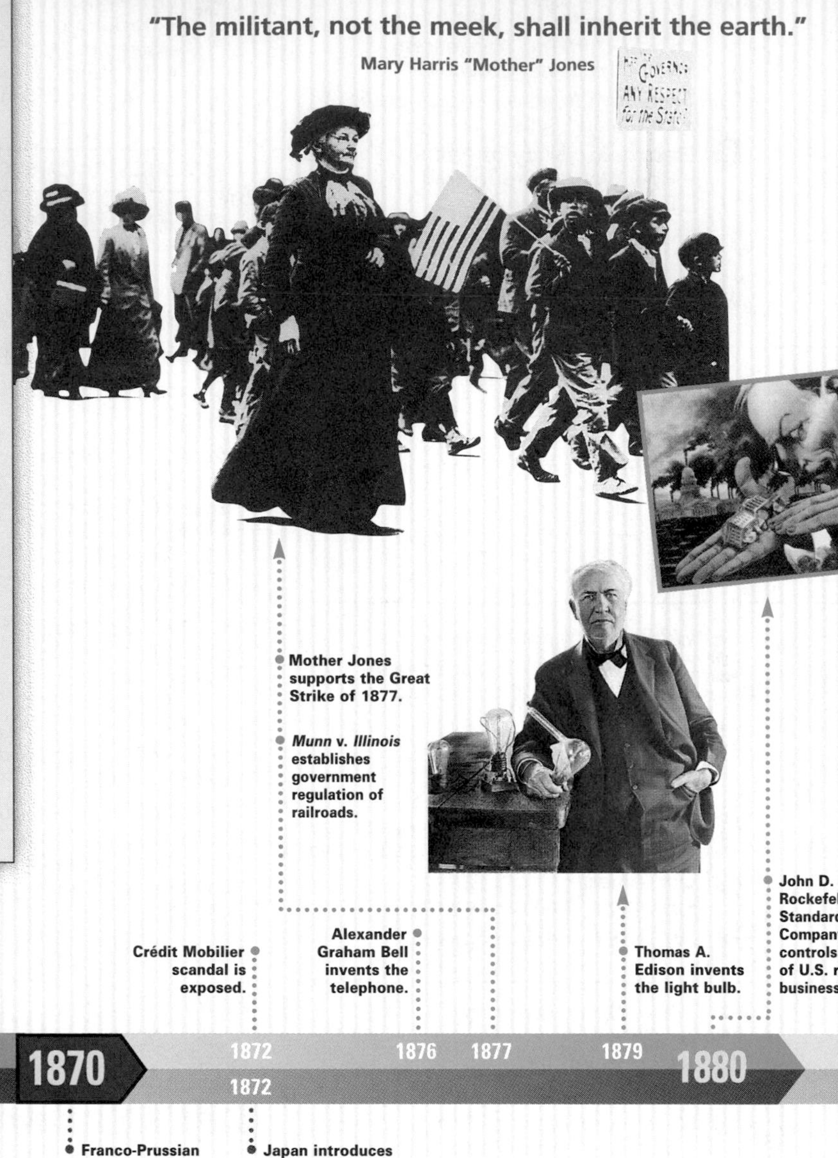
"The militant, not the meek, shall inherit the earth."
Mary Harris "Mother" Jones
Mother Jones supports the Great Strike of 1877.
Munn v. *Illinois* establishes government regulation of railroads.
Crédit Mobilier scandal is exposed.
Alexander Graham Bell invents the telephone.
Thomas A. Edison invents the light bulb.
John D. Rockefeller's Standard Oil Company controls 90% of U.S. refini[ng] business.
THE UNITED STATES
THE WORLD
1870
1872
1876
1877
1879
1880
1872
Franco-Prussian War is fought.
Japan introduces universal military service.

THEMES IN CHAPTER 6

Science and Technology
The rapid expansion of the railroads from coast to coast and the development of new inventions and improved technologies ushered in a new age for America and Americans. All aspects of life—where people lived, how they worked, what they ate, and how they spent their leisure time—were changed forever.
See Teacher's Edition note, p. 254.

The American Dream
Newcomers to this country and settlers who crowded the frontier pursued the American dream of opportunity to create a good life for themselves and their families. For some, however—men, women, and children who toiled long hours for low pay—the dream remained out of reach.
See Teacher's Edition notes, pp. 258 and 263.

Women in America
Industrialization enabled women to enter the labor force in great numbers. They played a significant role in the labor movement and worked tirelessly to improve working conditions for themselves and their children. They wanted recognition for their contributions, however, and "Equal pay for equal work" became their rallying cry.
See Teacher's Edition note, p. 268.

LIVING HISTORY

WRITING SCIENCE FICTION

Write a science fiction story in which a society like mid-19th-century American society does not undergo industrialization. On the basis of what you learn in this chapter, decide why your fictional society does not become industrialized: lack of natural resources, no creative ideas, or sparse population, for example. Then describe daily life in that society, including

- where people live
- how they provide food and shelter for their families
- what kinds of social and cultural activities they engage in

PORTFOLIO PROJECT You might want to present your story in a creative form, such as a letter or a newsreel. Keep your story in a folder for your American history portfolio. You will revise your story at the end of the chapter.

- **1881** France institutes freedom of the press.
- **1883** Railroad time goes into effect across the country.
- **1883** Germany becomes the first nation to provide national health insurance.
- **1885** Adult males gain the vote in Great Britain.
- **1885** Indian National Congress is established.
- **1886** Haymarket riot turns public sentiment against unions.
- **1887** Interstate Commerce Act is passed.
- **1890** Congress passes the Sherman Antitrust Act.
- **1890** Colonization of sub-Saharan Africa reaches its peak.
- **1894** President Cleveland sends federal troops to Illinois to end the Pullman strike.
- **1896** First modern Olympic Games are held in Athens, Greece.
- **1900**

ALTERNATIVE ASSESSMENT

LIVING HISTORY

WRITING SCIENCE FICTION

Suggest to students the following strategies for creating a work of science fiction:

- Decide on your audience and identify their interests and knowledge.
- Consider the setting of your story. What conditions will be different from those in the mid-19th century?
- Choose one or two main characters to focus on.

Project Planning Guide

Who?	**Who are the main characters?**
What?	**What happens in the story?**
Where?	**Where does the story take place?**
When?	**What details will show that the time is the mid-19th century?**
Why?	**What prevents the society from becoming industrialized?**
How?	**How does the society develop?**

IN-DEPTH RESOURCES: UNIT 2

See worksheet and standards for evaluation, pp. 35, 36.

RECOMMENDED RESOURCES

Books for the Teacher

Dulles, Foster Rhea. *Labor in America: A History.* New York: Harlan Davidson, 1993.

Foner, Philip Sheldon. *Women and the American Labor Movement.* New York: Free Press, 1979.

Josephson, Matthew. *The Robber Barons.* San Diego: Harcourt, 1995.

Books for the Student

Alger, Horatio, Jr. *Struggling Upward and Other Works.* New York: Crown, 1945.

Brown, Dee. *The Year of the Century.* New York: Scribner's, 1966.

Carnegie, Andrew. *Autobiography of Andrew Carnegie.* Boston: Houghton, 1986.

Videos

American History: The Game of Monopoly. MasterVision, 969 Park Avenue South, New York, NY 10028.

Labor's Struggle. RMI Media, 800-745-5480.

Andrew Carnegie: The Original Man of Steel. Videodisc. American Lifestyle Series. Educational Software Institute, 800-955-5570.

Software

The Industrial Revolution in America. CD-ROM. Educational Software Institute, 800-955-5570.

Section 1 Overview

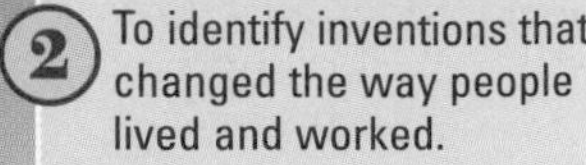

OBJECTIVES

1. To explain how the abundance of natural resources, new recovery and refining methods, and new uses for them led to intensive industrialization.
2. To identify inventions that changed the way people lived and worked.

SKILLBUILDER

- Understanding geography: human-environment interaction, location, p. 247

CRITICAL THINKING

- Analyzing causes, p. 247
- Recognizing effects, pp. 248, 249
- Theme: Science and Technology, p. 249
- Clarifying, p. 249
- Summarizing, p. 249
- Making inferences, p. 249

FOCUS & MOTIVATE

5-MINUTE WARM-UP

Interpreting Diagrams
To gain insight into the increase of inventions that occurred in the 1800s, ask students to examine the time line on pages 248–249.

1. What energy source made most inventions in the 1870s possible?
2. Do you think that the title "Technological Explosion" is a good title for this time line? Why or why not?

WARM-UP TRANSPARENCY 6

▶ ***Starting with the Student***
Have students watch the video "Gusher!" to learn about Pattillo Higgins and the beginning of the Texas oil boom.

***AMERICAN STORIES* video series**
"Gusher!"
Videocassette: Volume 2

Videodisc: Disc 1, Side B, Chapter 3

1 The Expansion of Industry

TERMS & NAMES
- Edwin L. Drake
- Bessemer process
- Thomas Alva Edison
- Christopher Sholes
- Alexander Graham Bell

LEARN ABOUT new technological processes and inventions
TO UNDERSTAND the developments that fueled industrialization.

ONE AMERICAN'S STORY

Pattillo Higgins

One day, Pattillo Higgins noticed bubbles in the springs around Spindletop, a hill near Beaumont in eastern Texas. He stuck his cane into the ground and lit the gases that were released. Further examination of the area convinced him that oil was underground. He figured that if he could find oil, it could serve as a fuel source around which a vibrant industrial city would develop.

But Higgins, who had been a mechanic and a lumber merchant, couldn't convince geologists or investors that oil was present. In fact, one member of the Texas Geological Society published an article in 1898, telling people not to invest in Higgins's dream.

Higgins didn't give up, however. He placed an ad in a magazine to find someone to drill for oil and got one response—from Captain Anthony F. Lucas, an experienced prospector who also believed that there was oil at Spindletop. For a while even Lucas couldn't find investors, but Higgins kept his faith, not only in Spindletop, but in Lucas.

A PERSONAL VOICE
Captain Lucas, . . . these experts come and tell you this or that can't happen because it has never happened before. You believe there is oil here . . . , and I think you are right. I know there is oil here in greater quantities than man has ever found before.
PATTILLO HIGGINS, quoted in *Spindletop*

Finally the two men's perseverance paid off. In 1900 they found investors, and they began to drill that autumn. Months of hard, and often frustrating, work followed. But on the morning of January 10, 1901, oil gushed from the well, and the Texas oil boom had begun. The oil that exploded from the dirt of eastern Texas helped fuel the industrial revolution in America.

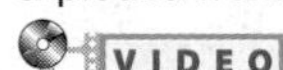
GUSHER!
Pattillo Higgins and the Great Texas Oil Boom

Natural Resources Fuel Industrialization

After the Civil War, the United States was still largely an agricultural nation. By the 1920s—a mere 60 years later—it had become the leading industrial power in the world. This immense industrial boom was due to three major factors: a wealth of natural resources, an explosion of inventions, and a growing urban population that provided markets for new products.

BLACK GOLD Though eastern Native American tribes had made fuel and medicine from crude oil long before Europeans arrived on the continent, early American settlers had little use for it. In 1840, however, the Canadian geologist Abraham Gesner realized that kerosene could be used to light lamps and discovered how to distill it from oil or coal.

It wasn't until 1859, however, when **Edwin L. Drake** successfully used a steam engine to drill for oil near Titusville, Pennsylvania, that removing it from beneath the earth's surface became practical. This breakthrough started an oil boom that spread to Kentucky, Ohio, Illinois, and Indiana. Petroleum-refining industries arose in Cleveland and Pittsburgh as entrepreneurs rushed to transform the oil into kerosene. Gasoline, a byproduct of the refining process,

SECTION 1 RESOURCES

PRINT RESOURCES

IN-DEPTH RESOURCES: UNIT 2
Guided Reading, p. 19
Geography Application: The Changing Labor Force, p. 24
Primary Source: The Birth of the Telephone, p. 26

READING STUDY GUIDE, p. 67

ACCESS FOR STUDENTS ACQUIRING ENGLISH
Guided Reading (Spanish), p. 91
Geography Application: The Changing Labor Force (Spanish), p. 96

SPANISH READING STUDY GUIDE, p. 67

FORMAL ASSESSMENT
Section Quiz, p. 80

ALTERNATIVE ASSESSMENT BOOK
See forms for supporting and scoring alternative activities.

TECHNOLOGY RESOURCES

GEOGRAPHY TRANSPARENCIES
G14, Mining and Industry

CRITICAL THINKING TRANSPARENCIES
CT14, Industrial Growth

CD-ROM *Grolier Multimedia Encyclopedia*
Electronic Library of Primary Sources

VIDEO *American Stories* video series; *American Portfolio: A Videodisc for U.S. History,* user's guide, pp. 137, 139, 142

INTERNET http://www.mlushistory.com

Natural Resources and the Birth of a Steel Town, 1886–1906

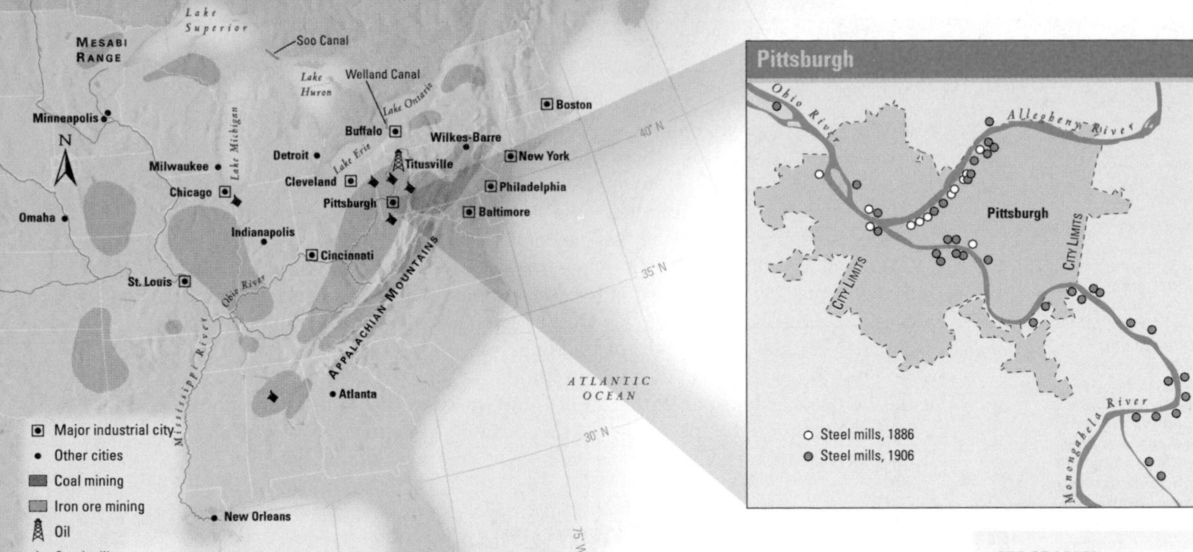

originally was thrown away. But after the automobile became popular, gasoline became the most important form of oil.

BESSEMER STEEL PROCESS Oil was not the only natural resource that was plentiful in the United States. There were also abundant deposits of coal and iron to make steel. In 1887, prospectors discovered iron ore deposits more than 100 miles long and up to 3 miles wide in the Mesabi Range of Minnesota. At the same time, coal production was skyrocketing—from 33 million tons in 1870 to more than 250 million tons in 1900.

Iron is a strong metal, but it is heavy and tends to break and rust. It also generally contains other elements, such as carbon. Removing the carbon from iron produces a lighter, more flexible, rust-resistant metal—steel. The raw materials needed to make steel were readily available; all that was needed was a cheap and efficient manufacturing process. The **Bessemer process,** developed independently by the British manufacturer Henry Bessemer and the American ironmaker William Kelly around 1850, soon became widely used. This technique involved injecting air into molten iron to remove the carbon and transform it into steel. By 1880, manufacturers were using the new method to produce more than 90 percent of the nation's steel. In this age of rapid change and innovation, even the successful Bessemer process was bettered by 1886. It was eventually replaced by the open-hearth process, with which manufacturers could produce quality steel from scrap metal as well as from raw materials.

THINK THROUGH HISTORY
A. *Analyzing Causes* *How did the availability of raw materials influence industrialization?*

A. Answer Inexpensive, readily available raw materials gave inventors and entrepreneurs the means they needed to develop and implement new products and methods.

NEW USES FOR STEEL The railroads, with their thousands of miles of track, became the biggest customers for steel, but inventors soon found additional uses for it. Joseph Glidden's barbed wire and McCormick's and Deere's farm machines helped transform the plains into the food producer of the nation.

Steel changed the face of the country as well, as it made innovative construction possible. One of the most remarkable structures was the Brooklyn Bridge. Completed in 1883, it spanned 1,595 feet of the East River in New York City. Its

GEOGRAPHY SKILLBUILDER
HUMAN-ENVIRONMENT INTERACTION *Steel mills generally were built in regions of the country rich in what natural resource?*
LOCATION *What connection can you draw between the location of natural resources (including water) and the development of steel mills in Pittsburgh?*

Skillbuilder Answer
Human-Environment Interaction: Coal.
Location: Pittsburgh is located near coal and iron deposits and at a junction of rivers that provide transportation routes.

OBJECTIVE
① INSTRUCT

Natural Resources Fuel Industrialization

▶ ***Starting with the Student*** Ask students what components they think are required for industrialization to occur. Organize their responses as shown:

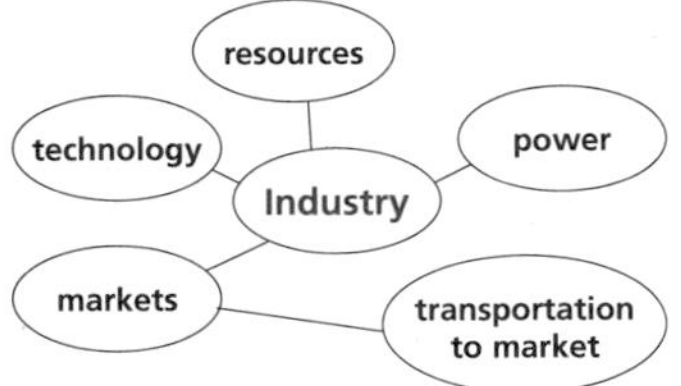

▶ ***Discussing Key Ideas***

- New methods of recovering and refining oil touch off an oil boom.
- Abundance of iron and coal fuel steel production.
- New uses for steel emerge.

IN-DEPTH RESOURCES: UNIT 2
Guided Reading, p. 19

ACCESS FOR STUDENTS ACQUIRING ENGLISH
Guided Reading (Spanish), p. 91

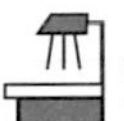
GEOGRAPHY TRANSPARENCIES
G14, Mining and Industry

HISTORY FROM VISUALS

Natural Resources and the Birth of a Steel Town, 1886–1906

Reading the Maps Remind students that the map of Pittsburgh is projected out from the United States map.

Extension Have students choose a city other than Pittsburgh and identify the nearest coal and iron deposits and waterway.

Block Schedule TEACHING OPTION **Time Needed: 40 Minutes**

Cooperative Activity: Tracking the Growth of Steel

Task: Groups of students will research topics related to the production and uses of steel and will organize their information into a class time line.

Purpose: To recognize the importance of steel and the interrelatedness of science, technology, and daily life.

Activity: Working in small groups, students will research a topic related to the production or uses of steel, such as the Bessemer process. Each group will provide illustrations and text for their topic, and one group will design, coordinate, and produce the class time line.

Building a Portfolio: Students who add their time-line entries to their portfolios should attach a note pointing out their contribution to the entry and include a short statement evaluating the overall impact of steel on society.

ALTERNATIVE ASSESSMENT BOOK
Standards for Evaluating a Cooperative Activity

Standards for Evaluation
Time-line entries should . . .

- show evidence of research from appropriate sources
- demonstrate an understanding of chronology
- include vivid details and examples

HISTORY FROM VISUALS
The Technological Explosion

Reading the Time Line Ask students how much time elapsed between the invention of the steam engine used in trains and the internal combustion engine used in cars. *170 years.* How much time between the combustion engine and the airplane? *43 years.*

OBJECTIVE
② **INSTRUCT**

Inventions Promote Change

▶ ***Starting with the Student*** Discuss with students how their lives would be made more difficult without electricity. Have them make a chart listing ways they use electricity and nonelectrical alternatives. The chart might look like this:

Electricity

Use	Substitute
Pencil sharpener	Knife or mechanical sharpener
Clothes dryer	Outdoor clothesline

▶ ***Discussing Key Ideas***
- The harnessing of electricity transforms American business.
- A profusion of inventions promotes rapid change.
- New products affect people at home and at work.

IN-DEPTH RESOURCES: UNIT 2
Primary Source: The Birth of the Telephone, p. 26

GROLIER MULTIMEDIA ENCYCLOPEDIA
Edison and Bell

The Technological Explosion

6000 B.C. | 5000 B.C. Plow | 3500 B.C. Wheel | 1000 B.C. Sundial | A.D. 1000 | A.D. 1100 Magnetic Compass | 1200

steel cables were supported by towers higher than any man-made structure except the pyramids of Egypt. Like those ancient marvels, the completed bridge was called a wonder of the world. Nonetheless, many people were skeptical about its structural soundness. P. T. Barnum—the flamboyant showman—helped dispel their doubts when he drove a herd of elephants across the bridge.

At about this time, setting the stage for a new era of expansion upward as well as outward, William Le Baron Jenney designed the first skyscraper with a steel frame—the Home Insurance Building in Chicago. Before Jenney had his pioneering idea, the weight of buildings was supported entirely by their walls. This meant that the taller the building, the thicker the walls had to be, so the height was limited. With a steel frame to support the building, however, architects could build as high as they wanted. As structures soared into the air, not even the sky seemed to limit what Americans could achieve.

Most great inventions went through painstaking development. Shown below is the first light bulb, along with patent drawings of it and the telephone—just two of more than 51,000 patents issued between 1876 and 1880.

Inventions Promote Change

By capitalizing on natural resources and their own ingenuity, inventors changed more than the physical shape of life. Their inventions affected the very way people lived and worked.

THE POWER OF ELECTRICITY In 1876, **Thomas Alva Edison** became a pioneer on the new industrial frontier when he established the world's first research laboratory in Menlo Park, New Jersey. Edison perfected the incandescent light bulb there and followed up his invention with an entire system for producing and distributing electrical power. Another inventor, George Westinghouse, added innovations that made electricity safer and less expensive. Edison's company established power plants across the country, while Westinghouse encouraged scientists to create applications for the new source of energy.

The harnessing of electricity completely changed the nature of business in America. By 1890, electric power ran numerous machines, ranging from fans to printing presses. This inexpensive, convenient source of energy soon became available in homes and spurred the invention of increasing numbers of appliances. Electric streetcars made travel cheap and efficient and also promoted the outward spread of cities.

More important, electricity allowed manufacturers to locate their plants wherever they wanted—not just near sources of power. This enabled industry to grow as never before. Huge operations, such as the meatpacking plants of Armour and Swift, and the efficient processes that they used became the models for new consumer industries.

THINK THROUGH HISTORY
B. *Recognizing Effects* *How did electricity change American life?*

B. Answer It changed the nature of business, made the invention of new appliances possible, and helped cities and industries grow.

INSPIRED INVENTIONS Edison's incandescent light bulb, patented in 1880, was only one of several revolutionary developments. Another upheaval in the workplace took place after **Christopher Sholes** invented the typewriter in 1867 and James Densmore improved and marketed it in 1873. Next to the light bulb, however, perhaps the most dramatic invention was the telephone, unveiled by **Alexander Graham Bell** and Thomas Watson in 1876. Although coast-to-coast phone service did not

TEACHING OPTION

Teaching Less Proficient Readers

Using a Chart Pair less proficient readers with more able ones. After students read pages 248 and 249, have each pair create a chronological chart listing the date and the inventor for each invention mentioned. Completed invention charts might look like this:

Date	Inventor	Invention
1867	Christopher Sholes	Typewriter
1873	James Densmore	Improved typewriter
1876	Alexander Graham Bell and Thomas Watson	Telephone
1880	Thomas Alva Edison	Incandescent light bulb

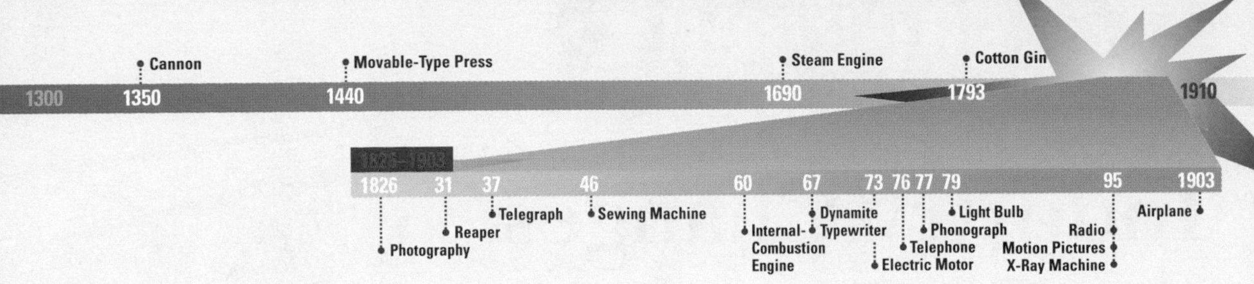

THINK THROUGH HISTORY
C. THEME Science and Technology *What caused the explosion of inventions in the late 19th century?*

C. Answer Development of natural resources and a growing, receptive market.

begin until 1915 and was initially slow and expensive, this invention laid the groundwork for a worldwide communications network.

NEW PRODUCTS AND LIFESTYLES The country's expanding urban population provided a potential market for new inventions and products. What people may not have foreseen, however, is how much their everyday lives would change as a result of the innovations of the industrial age.

Inventions such as the typewriter and the telephone particularly affected office work and opened up new jobs for women. Although women made up less than 5 percent of all office workers in 1870, by 1910 they accounted for nearly 40 percent of the clerical work force. Most of these approximately 500,000 working women were single, white, native-born, and between 15 and 24.

New inventions also had a tremendous impact on factory work, as well as on jobs that traditionally had been done at home. Whereas most women had previously hand-sewn their families' clothes, for example, the invention of the sewing machine created a demand for professional garment workers. These laborers—men, women, and children—worked long hours, often under unhealthy conditions. Although machinery freed other factory workers from backbreaking labor, many, realizing that they were easily replaceable, felt a loss of self-worth and pride.

While some workers lost power in the workplace as a result of industrialization, they gained some power back as consumers in the marketplace. New industries arose to advertise and promote consumer goods. Companies like American Tobacco, for example, offered trading cards, premiums, and prizes with their products. The consumer had become an important new force in American business.

D. Answer They created new jobs and made factory work easier but contributed to workers' loss of self-esteem.

THINK THROUGH HISTORY
D. Clarifying *How did new inventions affect the nation's workers?*

Overall, industrialization contributed to an improved standard of living. By 1890, the average workweek had been reduced by about ten hours. Goods such as phonographs, bicycles, and cameras provided new opportunities for recreation. Industrialization changed American society forever.

HISTORICAL SPOTLIGHT

ILLUMINATING THE LIGHT BULB

Shortly after moving into a long wooden shed at Menlo Park, Edison and his associates set to work to develop the perfect incandescent bulb. Arc lamps already lit some city streets and shops, but these lamps used an electric current passing between two sticks of carbon, and they were glaring and inefficient.

Edison and his team hoped to create a long-lasting lamp with a soft, steady glow, and they began searching for a filament that would burn slowly and stay lit. Edison tried wires, sticks, blades of grass, and even hairs from his assistants' beards. Finally, a piece of carbonized bamboo from Japan did the trick. Edison's company used bamboo filaments until 1911, when it began using tungsten filaments, which are still in use today.

Section 1 Assessment

1. TERMS & NAMES
Identify:
- Edwin L. Drake
- Bessemer process
- Thomas Alva Edison
- Christopher Sholes
- Alexander Graham Bell

2. SUMMARIZING List several technological breakthroughs and explain their impact on society.

Technological Breakthrough	Impact

Write a paragraph that explains the impact of one of these breakthroughs.

3. MAKING INFERENCES Do you think that consumers gained power as industry expanded in the late 19th century? Why or why not?

THINK ABOUT
- how consumers can influence manufacturers
- efforts 19th-century businesses made to win customers

4. RECOGNIZING EFFECTS Which invention or development described in this section had the greatest impact on society? Give reasons to justify your choice.

THINK ABOUT
- the applications of inventions
- the impact of inventions on people's daily lives
- the effect of inventions on the workplace

ANSWERS

1. TERMS & NAMES
Edwin L. Drake, p. 246
Bessemer process, p. 247
Thomas Alva Edison, p. 248
Christopher Sholes, p. 248
Alexander Graham Bell, p. 248

2. SUMMARIZING
Possible Answers:
oil drill—initiated oil boom
Bessemer steel process—made steel production cheaper and more efficient
barbed wire and farm machines—increased farmers' output
light bulb—made artificial light widely available
telephone—revolutionized communications

3. MAKING INFERENCES
Possible Responses: Agree—Availability of products and increase in promotional gimmicks.
Disagree—Low incomes and increasing dependence on manufactured (rather than home-made) products.

4. RECOGNIZING EFFECTS
Possible Responses: Some students will cite electricity as the invention with the greatest impact because it changed the nature of business, of travel, and of home and social life. Others will cite the telephone and the Bessemer steel process for similar reasons.

HISTORICAL SPOTLIGHT

Illuminating the Light Bulb

Critical Thinking: Clarifying Share with students Thomas Edison's definition of genius: "1 percent inspiration and 99 percent perspiration." Ask them to discuss how his search for the perfect lamp filament illustrates this definition.

IN-DEPTH RESOURCES: UNIT 2
Geography Application: The Changing Labor Force, p. 24

ELECTRONIC LIBRARY OF PRIMARY SOURCES
How Women Are Treated by the Pullman Company

ASSESS & RETEACH

Section 1 Assessment

Have students create questions on the material in the chapter, then separate into teams and test each other in a game-show format.

Self-Assessment.

Have students mark the questions on the Section 1 Assessment that they could not answer. Ask them to find the answers in the text.

Section Quiz

FORMAL ASSESSMENT
Section Quiz, p. 80

Reteach

Use the chart in Critical Thinking Transparency 14 to review the causes and effects of industrial growth.

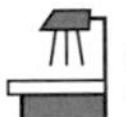

CRITICAL THINKING TRANSPARENCIES
CT14, Industrial Growth

CLOSE

An industrial explosion created a demand for shipping routes for both raw materials and finished products and increased the demand for rail networks. Technological advances in the production of steel made rapid expansion of the railroads possible.

Geography Spotlight

OBJECTIVES

1. To trace the environmental effects of industrialization in Cleveland, Ohio.
2. To generalize the effects of industrialization on the environment.

FOCUS & MOTIVATE

▶ ***Starting with the Student***
Have students consider environmental problems affecting their city or region.

- What are the causes of the problems?
- What is being done, or should be done, to correct them?

MORE ABOUT . . .
Cleveland, Ohio

Founded in 1796 by Moses Cleaveland, for whom the city is named, Cleveland, Ohio, began to grow appreciably after the Erie Canal opened in New York State in 1825. The canal completed an all-water route from the Atlantic Ocean to Lake Erie. More canals—and then railroads—made Cleveland a shipping hub in the Great Lakes area and prompted John D. Rockefeller to found the Standard Oil Company there. For a time Cleveland's Euclid Avenue was one of America's most luxurious addresses, lined with the mansions of wealthy industrialists.

GEOGRAPHY SPOTLIGHT

Industry Changes the Environment

By the mid-1870s, industrialization was well on the way to changing almost every aspect of American life. Cleveland, Ohio, located on the shores of Lake Erie and not far from raw materials, was an industrial city waiting to be born. What no one could have predicted at the time was the dark side of its rapid development and technological progress.

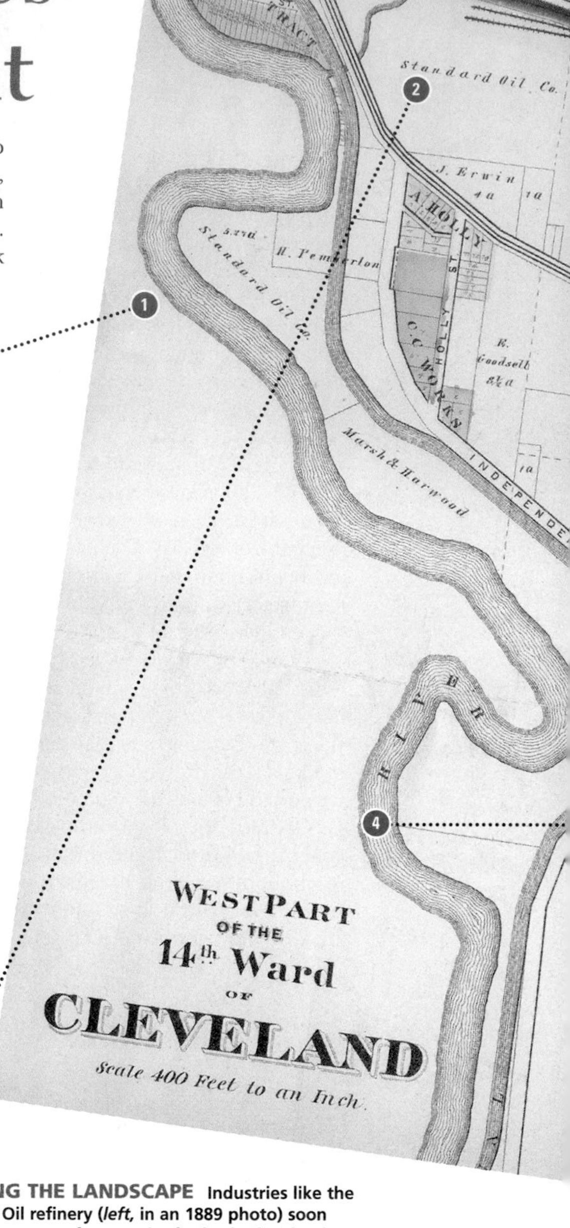

1 FROM HAYSTACKS TO SMOKESTACKS In 1874, parts of Cleveland were still rural, with farms like the one pictured below dotting the landscape. The smokestacks of the Standard Oil refinery in the distance, however, indicate that industrialization had begun.

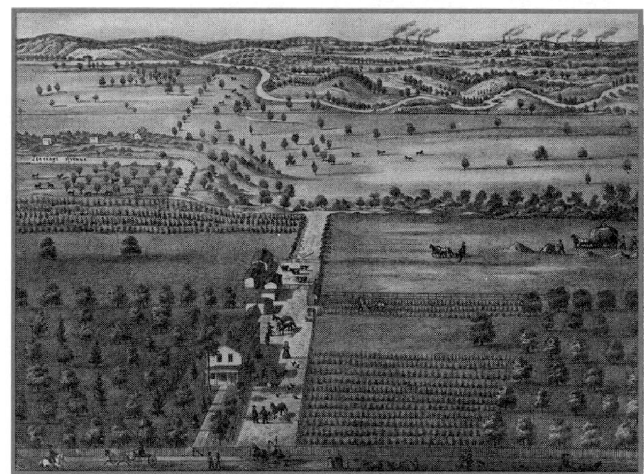

2 REFINING THE LANDSCAPE Industries like the Standard Oil refinery (*left*, in an 1889 photo) soon became a source of prosperity for both Cleveland and the entire country. The pollution they belched into the atmosphere, however, was the beginning of an ongoing problem—how to balance industrial production and environmental concerns.

RECOMMENDED RESOURCES

Books

Burns, Noel M. *Erie: The Lake That Survived.* Totowa, NJ: Rowman & Allanheld, 1985. How cleanup efforts helped Lake Erie recover from pollution.

Miggins, Edward M., and Thomas F. Campbell. *The Birth of Modern Cleveland.* Cranbury, NJ: Associated UP, 1988. A history of the city from 1865 to 1930.

Schuyler, David. *The New Urban Landscape.* Baltimore: Johns Hopkins UP, 1986. Environmental aspects of the growth of American cities in the 19th century.

Tarbell, Ida M. *The History of the Standard Oil Company.* Mattituck, NY: Amereon, 1993.

Videos

Great Lakes, Fragile Seas. National Geographic and WQED, 1991. Past pollution and present efforts to correct it.

The Rise of the American City. Encyclopaedia Britannica. The growth of cities and consequent problems they face.

U.S. Cities. Encyclopaedia Britannica. Focus on industrial development.

Software

Balance of the Planet. CD-ROM. Broderbund. Students must find ways to sustain industry but protect the environment.

Planetary Manager. National Geographic. Impact of fossil fuels, solid-waste management, and water pollution.

Pollution Patrol. Entrex. The city of Misery is plagued by pollution.

3 LIFE IN THE BIG CITY Although the serenity and slow pace of preindustrial life were becoming a thing of the past, urban growth improved people's daily lives in many ways. Factories were built near transportation centers, and working-class housing sprang up for the laborers. Rail lines carried the lifeblood of the city, and electric streetcars made urban travel faster and more pleasant than ever before.

4 A RIVER OF FIRE Industrial pollution would affect not only the air people breathed but also the water they drank. Refineries and steel mills discharged so much oil into the Cuyahoga River that major fires broke out on the water in 1936, 1952, and 1969. The 1952 blaze pictured above destroyed three tugboats, three buildings, and the ship-repair yards. In the decade following the 1969 fire, changes in the way industrial plants operated, along with the creation of wastewater treatment plants, helped restore the quality of the water.

INTERACT WITH HISTORY

1. **ANALYZING ISSUES** What impact did Cleveland's industrial development have on its environment?

 SEE SKILLBUILDER HANDBOOK, PAGE 916.

2. **RESEARCHING AN URBAN ENVIRONMENT** Use library resources or the Internet to learn about the steps Cleveland has taken in recent years to improve its environment. Report your findings to the class.

INTERNET Visit http://www.mlushistory.com for more about Cleveland.

INSTRUCT

▶ *Starting with the Student*
Discuss with students positive and negative effects eliminating environmental hazards might have on the local economy. *Possible Responses: Positive—Revitalizing industries such as fishing and boating, making it safer to ship goods, making the area more attractive for businesses to settle or remain there; Negative—Forcing industries to update their equipment and finance cleanup costs, possibly leading to layoffs, relocation, or even bankruptcy.*

▶ *Discussing Key Ideas*

- Expanding industry rapidly turns rural Cleveland into a booming city in the second half of the 19th century.
- Industrial expansion helps improve the lives of urban workers but also creates pollution that endangers their health and safety.

HISTORY FROM VISUALS

Reading the Images

- Why might John D. Rockefeller have chosen the location he did for his Standard Oil company? *Possible Responses: The accessibility of both railroad lines and water transportation in the form of the Cuyahoga River and canals.*
- Discuss with students the irony of a river on fire and the incredible quantities of oil that must have accumulated to cause the Cuyahoga to go up in flames three times.

INTERACT WITH HISTORY

1. Analyzing Issues

Possible Answer: *Industrial development led to a transformation of a rural landscape to a mostly urban one. As a result, some aspects of people's lives such as transportation and housing, improved, but the overall pace of life increased, with possible effects on their health. In addition, industrialization created noise and polluted both air and water.*

2. Researching an Urban Environment

Standards for Evaluation
Reports should . . .

- include up-to-date information from recent books and periodicals, reliable Internet sources, government agencies, or environmental organizations
- present information in a logical order
- include visual materials, such as charts, graphs, or photographs

The Age of the Railroads

TERMS & NAMES
- transcontinental railroad
- George M. Pullman
- Crédit Mobilier
- *Munn* v. *Illinois*
- Interstate Commerce Act

LEARN ABOUT the growth and consolidation of the railroads
TO UNDERSTAND their influence on the expansion of industry.

Section 2 Overview

OBJECTIVES

1. To identify the role of the railroads in unifying the country.
2. To list positive and negative effects of railroads on the nation's economy.
3. To summarize reasons for, and outcomes of, the demand for railroad reform.

SKILLBUILDERS

- Understanding geography: location, p. 254
- Interpreting political cartoons, p. 256

CRITICAL THINKING

- Analyzing issues, p. 253
- Making predictions, p. 254
- Analyzing motives, p. 255
- Summarizing, pp. 255, 256
- Clarifying, p. 256
- Analyzing causes, p. 256
- Making decisions, p. 256
- Synthesizing, p. 256

FOCUS & MOTIVATE

5-MINUTE WARM-UP

Describing Mood

To explore the impact of the railroad on life in the United States, have students read Historical Spotlight on page 253 and look at the picture on page 255. Then have them answer these questions.

1. Why do you think railroads became a part of American culture in the late 1800s?
2. What mood about railroad travel does the picture on page 255 express?

WARM-UP TRANSPARENCY 6

▶ ***Starting with the Student***

- What name might students give the present age? *Possible Response: "The Age of the Car" or "The Age of the Computer."* In formulating their answers, have them consider the technology that exerts the most influence on all aspects of American life.
- Do they think the railroads may have played a similar role in American life in the late 19th century? Why or why not?

ONE AMERICAN'S STORY

In October 1884, the economist Richard Ely visited the town of Pullman, Illinois, just south of Chicago, to write about it for *Harper's* magazine. At first, Ely was impressed with the atmosphere of order, planning, and well-being in the town George M. Pullman had designed for the employees of his railroad-car factory. But after talking at length with a dissatisfied company officer, Walter E. Burrows, Ely concluded that the town had a fatal flaw: it restricted its residents. Pullman employees were compelled to obey rules in which they had no say. Ely concluded that "the idea of Pullman is un-American."

The town of Pullman was carefully laid out and strictly controlled.

A PERSONAL VOICE

It is benevolent, well-wishing feudalism [a medieval social system], which desires the happiness of the people, but in such a way as shall please the authorities. . . . If free American institutions are to be preserved, we want no race reared as underlings. . . . [The town should include] cooperative features [that would] awaken in the residents an interest and pride in Pullman.

RICHARD T. ELY, "Pullman: A Social Study"

As the railroads grew, their influence extended to every facet of American life, including, as in the town of Pullman, the personal lives of the country's citizens. They determined the time standard of the country and influenced the growth of towns and communities. The unchecked power of railroad companies led to widespread abuses, however, which spurred citizens to demand and win federal regulation of the industry.

Railroads Span Time and Space

Chinese laborers did dangerous work, blasting through the Sierra Nevada to lay track for the Central Pacific Railroad.

Railroads had captured the imagination of Americans ever since the 1830s, when Horatio Allen imported the first steam locomotive from Britain. The iron horse could cross vast distances and terrains that exhausted horses and excluded riverboats. Rails made local transit reliable and westward expansion possible for business as well as for people. Realizing how important railroads were to the settlement of the West and the development of the country, the government made huge land grants and loans to the railroad companies.

A NATIONAL NETWORK By 1856, the railroads extended west to the Mississippi River, and three years later, they crossed the Missouri. A decade later, crowds across the United States cheered as the Central Pacific and Union Pacific Railroads met at Promontory, Utah, on May 10, 1869. A golden spike marked the spanning of the nation by the first **transcontinental railroad.** Other transcontinental lines followed, and regional lines multiplied as well. At the start of the Civil War, the nation had had about 30,000 miles of track. By 1890, that figure was nearly seven times greater.

ROMANCE AND REALITY The railroads lent romance to long-distance travel by bringing the dreams of unsettled land, adventure, and a fresh start within the

SECTION 2 RESOURCES

PRINT RESOURCES

IN-DEPTH RESOURCES: UNIT 2
Guided Reading, p. 20
Literature: *from* "The Bride Comes to Yellow Sky" by Stephen Crane, p. 30

READING STUDY GUIDE, p. 69

ACCESS FOR STUDENTS ACQUIRING ENGLISH
Guided Reading (Spanish), p. 92

SPANISH READING STUDY GUIDE, p. 69

FORMAL ASSESSMENT
Section Quiz, p. 81

ALTERNATIVE ASSESSMENT BOOK
See forms for supporting and scoring alternative activities.

TECHNOLOGY RESOURCES

CD-ROM *Grolier Multimedia Encyclopedia*

VIDEO *American Portfolio: A Videodisc for U.S. History,* user's guide, pp. 135–137

INTERNET http://www.mlushistory.com

grasp of many Americans. This romance was made possible, however, only at the expense of the railroad workers, whose lives were stark and harsh. The Central Pacific Railroad employed thousands of Chinese immigrants, and the Union Pacific hired Irish immigrants and desperate, out-of-work Civil War veterans to lay track across treacherous terrain. Accidents and pneumonia and other diseases disabled and killed thousands of men each year. In 1888, when the first railroad statistics were published, the casualties totaled more than 2,000 employees killed and 20,000 injured.

All railroad workers—whether surveyors, track layers, or engineers, firemen, and brakemen—faced difficult conditions and numerous hazards for very little pay. As an employee of the Baltimore and Ohio Railroad complained, "We eat our hard bread and tainted meat two days old on sooty cars up the road, and when we come home, find our children gnawing on bones and our wives complaining that they cannot even buy hominy and molasses for food."

Although the railroads paid all their employees poorly, Asians and African Americans usually earned less than whites. The average pay for whites working a ten-hour day was $40 to $60 a month plus free meals. Chinese immigrants hired by the Central Pacific performed similar tasks from dawn to dusk for about $35 a month—and they had to supply their own food. The immigrants' working conditions were miserable as well. In 1866, for example, the railroad hired them to dig a tunnel through a granite mountain. For five months of that year, the Chinese lived and worked in camps surrounded by 40 feet of snow. Hundreds of the men were buried in avalanches or later found frozen, still clutching their shovels or picks.

THINK THROUGH HISTORY

A. Analyzing Issues *What were the positive and negative aspects of railroad expansion?*

A. Answer **Positive:** Reliable local transportation and westward expansion. **Negative:** Harsh, dangerous conditions and low pay for railroad workers.

RAILROAD TIME In spite of these difficult working conditions, the railroad laborers helped to transform the country from a collection of individual localities into a united nation. Though linked in space, each community still operated on its own time, with noon when the sun was overhead. The time in Boston, for example, was almost 12 minutes later than the time in New York. Illinois had 27 different local times, and Wisconsin had 38. Travelers riding from Maine to California had to reset their watches at least 20 times.

In 1870, to remedy this problem, Professor C. F. Dowd proposed that the earth's surface be divided into 24 time zones, one for each hour of the day. Under his plan, the United States would contain four zones: Eastern, Central, Mountain, and Pacific. The railroad companies endorsed Dowd's plan enthusiastically, and many towns followed suit.

Finally, on November 18, 1883, railroad crews and towns across the country synchronized their watches. In 1884, an international conference set worldwide

HISTORICAL SPOTLIGHT

RAILROAD LORE

As the railroads expanded, they left a lasting mark on American culture as well as on its economy. People hung pictures of famous trains on their walls and adopted railroad phrases such as "working up a full head of steam" and "getting sidetracked."

The songs that railroad laborers sang as they worked, such as "I've Been Working on the Railroad" and "The Wabash Cannonball," soon gained widespread popularity. Tall tales, anecdotes, and romantic lore about hoboes who rode the rails spread faster than the lines themselves.

Even the railroad companies got into the game. The Erie Railroad printed so many anecdotes, verses, and jokes on its timetables that passengers began calling it the Erie Joke Book.

Railroad workers in Armstrong, Kansas, show off their "iron horses" like prize thoroughbreds in a stable.

OBJECTIVE

① **INSTRUCT**

Railroads Span Time and Space

▶ ***Starting with the Student*** Discuss with students what they know about railroads. What are the advantages and disadvantages of railroads compared with other forms of transportation?

▶ ***Discussing Key Ideas***
- The government facilitates the expansion of the railroads through land grants and loans.
- Transcontinental railroads link American coasts.
- The railroads promote a sense of adventure.
- Railroad workers endure hardships and danger for low pay.
- The importance of the railroads spurs adoption of a standardized time system.

IN-DEPTH RESOURCES: UNIT 2
Guided Reading, p. 20

ACCESS FOR STUDENTS ACQUIRING ENGLISH
Guided Reading (Spanish), p. 92

HISTORICAL SPOTLIGHT

Railroad Lore

Critical Thinking: Comparing and Contrasting Have students write sentences comparing the meaning of the railroad phrases mentioned as they relate to the railroads and to everyday life.

GROLIER MULTIMEDIA ENCYCLOPEDIA
The Growth of Railroads

TEACHING OPTIONS

Making Connections Across the Curriculum

Music You might want to mention that railroad songs often include rhythms or sounds that mimic the motion or whistles of trains. Ask students to think of examples from the songs mentioned in the text or from other traditional railroad songs, such as "The Atchison, Topeka, and the Santa Fe," and of modern songs, such as "The City of New Orleans." Consider asking student volunteers to bring in a tape or songbook and to play the tape or perform a song for the class.

Teaching Less Proficient Readers

Using Prior Knowledge To help students understand the difference between local time and standardized time zones, ask them how individual communities might determine when it was noon, for example. *When the sun was directly overhead.* Help them see that this calculation of local time could differ by several minutes even in different parts of one state. Have them consider the advantages and disadvantages of each system of reckoning time. *Local time is in sync with nature; standardized time zones are in sync with the rest of the world.*

HISTORY FROM VISUALS

Major Railroad Lines, 1870–1890

Reading the Map Have students study the distribution of railroads throughout the country and the land forms associated with various regions. What connections can they draw? *Possible Answer: The greatest concentration of railroads is in the relatively flat Midwest.*

Extension Have students trace possible railroad routes from Boston to Sacramento, from Cleveland to Los Angeles, or from Seattle to Omaha.

OBJECTIVE

② **INSTRUCT**

Opportunities and Opportunists

▶ ***Discussing Key Ideas***

- The growth of railroad lines promotes trade and interdependence among cities and leads to the development of new markets.
- Communities of workers spring up, including company-managed, planned towns.
- Some corrupt industrialists make huge profits at the expense of workers and stockholders.

ANOTHER PERSPECTIVE

On the Wrong Track

Critical Thinking: Analyzing Motives Ask students why people might resist change. Have them write a paragraph objecting to a modern development, such as supersonic air travel, e-mail, or cellular telephones.

Major Railroad Lines, 1870–1890

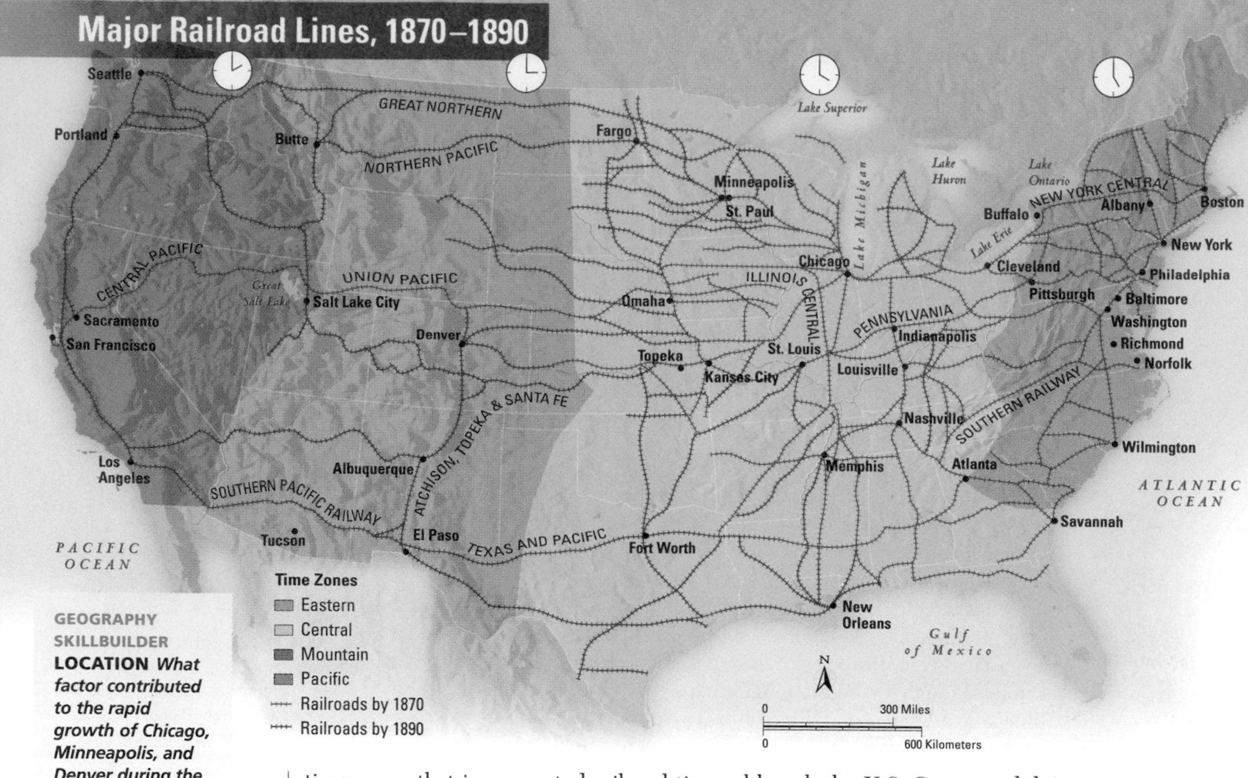

GEOGRAPHY SKILLBUILDER

LOCATION *What factor contributed to the rapid growth of Chicago, Minneapolis, and Denver during the 1870s and 1880s?*

LOCATION *In which zones had only one railroad been built before 1870?*

Skillbuilder Answer
Location: Their location as rail hubs. **Location:** Mountain and Pacific.

time zones that incorporated railroad time, although the U.S. Congress didn't officially adopt railroad time as the standard for the nation until 1918.

A PERSONAL VOICE

The sun will be requested to rise and set by railroad time. . . . People will have to marry by railroad time and die by railroad time. Ministers will be required to preach by railroad time, banks will open and close by railroad time; in fact, the Railroad Convention has taken charge of the time business, and the people may as well set about adjusting their affairs in accordance with its decree.

Editorial in the *Indianapolis Sentinel*, November 1883

As strong a unifying force as the railroads were, however, they also opened the way for abuses that led to social and economic unrest.

THINK THROUGH HISTORY

B. *Making Predictions* *How might the development of industry have been affected if the railroads had not existed?*

B. Answer
Industry would have developed more slowly, and most businesses would probably have been smaller and more local.

ANOTHER PERSPECTIVE

ON THE WRONG TRACK

While the railroads captured the imagination of most 19th-century Americans, there were those who didn't get on the bandwagon. The writer Herman Melville raged against the smoke-belching iron horse and the waves of change it set in motion as vehemently as his character Captain Ahab raged against the white whale and the sea in *Moby-Dick.* "Hark! here comes that old dragon again—that gigantic gadfly . . . snort! puff! scream! Great improvements of the age," Melville fumed. "Who wants to travel so fast? My grandfather did not, and he was no fool."

Opportunities and Opportunists

The growth of the railroads influenced not only Americans' concepts of time and space but also the industries and businesses in which Americans worked. Iron, coal, steel, lumber, and glass industries grew rapidly as they tried to keep pace with the railroads' demand for materials and parts. The rapid spread of railroad lines also fostered the growth of towns, helped establish new markets, and offered rich opportunities for both visionaries and profiteers.

NEW TOWNS AND MARKETS By linking previously isolated cities, towns, and settlements, the railroads promoted trade and interdependence. As part of a nationwide network of suppliers and markets, individual towns began to specialize in particular products. Chicago soon became known for its stockyards and Minneapolis for its grain industries, and these cities prospered by selling mass quantities of their products to the entire country. New towns and communities also grew

TEACHING OPTIONS

Making Connections Across Time

Railroads Today Ask students the reasons for and the effects of current cutbacks in railroad service. *Railroads can't accommodate the fast pace of modern life, and they have lost passengers to both airlines and high-speed interstate buses. Also, tracks have not been properly maintained, leading to slowdowns and accidents. The railroads now serve mainly as middlemen—piggy-back freight haulers that transport containers loaded directly from ships to connecting points where they are unloaded, connected to cabs, and trucked the rest of their journey by road.*

Exploring Themes

Science and Technology The new technology that contributed to the rapid growth of the railroads and, in turn, benefitted from them had negative as well as positive effects on society. Ask students to consider the effects on different groups of people, such as farmers, ranchers, Native Americans, settlers, and business owners. Based on these negative effects, what lessons can be learned from the rapid growth of the railroads? *Possible Answer: New technology brings not only opportunity but breeds opportunists, individuals who seize the opportunity to profit at the expense of others.*

up along the railroad lines. Cities as diverse as Abilene, Kansas; Flagstaff, Arizona; Denver, Colorado; and Seattle, Washington, owed their prosperity, if not their very existence, to the railroads.

Pullman cars brought luxury to the rails, as shown in this advertisement from about 1890.

PULLMAN The railroads helped cities not only grow up but branch out as well. In 1880, for example, **George M. Pullman** built a factory for manufacturing sleepers and other railroad cars on the prairie miles from the center of Chicago. Since increasing demand for the Pullman company's cars required a large and steady work force, he built a town nearby for his employees. In 1881, the first resident moved in.

Pullman's idea of a company town for his employees was inspired in part by New England textile manufacturers, who had traditionally provided housing for their workers. Pullman was a model town, providing clean, well-constructed brick houses and apartment buildings with at least one window in every room—a luxury for city dwellers. In addition, the town offered its residents medical and legal offices, shops, a church, a library, a theater, and an athletic field.

C. Answer They resented having their personal lives controlled by their employer.

THINK THROUGH HISTORY
C. *Analyzing Motives* *Why did the residents of Pullman resent their employer?*

As Richard Ely observed, however, the town of Pullman remained firmly under company control. For example, residents were not allowed to loiter on their front steps or to drink alcohol. Pullman hoped that his tightly controlled environment would ensure a stable work force. The widespread dissatisfaction of employees like Walter Burrows proved Pullman wrong, however. The dissatisfaction grew and led to a violent strike in 1894.

CRÉDIT MOBILIER The desire for control and profit that led Pullman to create his company town—and that enraged many of his employees—was common among industrialists. Some railroad magnates, or powerful and influential industrialists, carried it even further, into self-serving corruption. In one of the most infamous schemes, stockholders in the Union Pacific Railroad formed, in 1864, a construction company called **Crédit Mobilier** that enabled them to skim off railroad money for themselves. They gave this company a contract to lay track at two to three times the actual cost—and pocketed the profits. To prevent government meddling, they donated shares of stock to about 20 representatives in Congress in 1867.

D. Answer By charging too much for railroad construction, keeping the extra money for themselves, and paying off government officials.

THINK THROUGH HISTORY
D. *Summarizing* *How did railroad owners use the Crédit Mobilier company to make huge undeserved profits?*

A congressional investigation of the company, spurred by reports in the *New York Sun,* eventually found that the officers of the Union Pacific had pocketed up to $23 million in stocks, bonds, and cash. Testimony implicated such well-known and respected federal officials as Vice-President Schuyler Colfax, House Speaker James G. Blaine, and Congressman James Garfield, who later became president. Although these public figures made off with their profits scot-free, the reputation of the Grant administration and the Republican Party was tarnished.

The Grange and the Railroads

The corruption in the railroads further enraged the people who relied on this means of transport for their living. Farmers were especially affected, and the Grangers began demanding government control over the railroads.

RAILROAD ABUSES Farmers were angry with railroad companies for a host of reasons. They were upset by misuse of government land grants, which the railroads sold to other businesses rather than to settlers as the government intended. The railroads also entered into formal agreements to fix prices and keep farmers in their debt. In addition, they charged different customers different rates, often demanding more for short hauls—for which there was no alternative carrier—than they did for long hauls.

OBJECTIVE
③ **INSTRUCT**

The Grange and the Railroads

▶ ***Starting with the Student*** Remind students what they learned in Chapter 5 about the problems farmers had with the railroads. List some of those complaints on the board: *high prices to ship goods to market; railroads' attempts to control prices for the sale and storage of grain.*

▶ ***Discussing Key Ideas***
- Farmers resent abuses inflicted on them by the railroads.
- The Grangers take political action against the railroads.
- Controversy arises over regulation of the railroads.
- The Supreme Court rules that railroads are involved in interstate commerce and should be federally regulated.
- The financial breakdown of many railroads triggers a national economic collapse.
- Railroads begin consolidating—a trend that other businesses follow.

Block Schedule TEACHING OPTION **Time Needed: 30 Minutes**

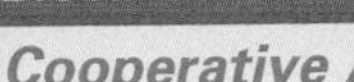

Cooperative Activity: Debating Company Towns

Task: Students will debate the pros and cons of towns owned and operated by companies for their workers and will write evaluations of the debate.

Purpose: To understand how individual points of view on a historical issue can differ widely.

Activity: Small groups of students will choose lots to determine their position on the issue. Groups will then research their position, considering why companies built the towns, why workers chose to live there, advantages and disadvantages to both the company and the workers, and alternatives for both parties. Groups should take turns debating one another, with the rest of the class evaluating the outcome of the debate.

Building a Portfolio Students who add their materials to their portfolios should indicate their contribution to the debate and include an evaluation of their group's performance.

ALTERNATIVE ASSESSMENT BOOK
Standards for Evaluating a Cooperative Activity

Standards for Evaluation
Debates should . . .
- use sound research and logical presentation
- employ oral skills and use of persuasive techniques
- include specific details to support arguments

HISTORY FROM VISUALS

Political Cartoon

Reading the Cartoon What do the strings that are attached to the trains suggest about how these tycoons controlled the railroads?

Extension Have students write a caption for the cartoon that helps the reader understand it.

ASSESS & RETEACH

Section 2 Assessment

Have students work in small groups to answer the questions. Have them indicate the portion of the text that best substantiates each answer.

Self-Assessment

Have students write one or two sentences about the most surprising thing they learned in this section.

Section Quiz

FORMAL ASSESSMENT
Section Quiz, p. 81

Reteach

Have a small group of students volunteer to present a summary of the main ideas of the section to the class.

CLOSE

The growth of the railroads affected every facet of American life. Their eventual consolidation inaugurated the age of big business.

GRANGER LAWS In response to these abuses by the railroads, the Grangers took political action. They sponsored state and local political candidates, elected legislators, and pressed for laws to protect their interests. In 1871, as a result of their pressure, Illinois authorized a commission "to establish maximum freight and passenger rates and prohibit discrimination." In the wake of this success, Grangers throughout the West convinced state legislators to pass similar laws.

The Grangers also set up a fund to help citizens sue for violations of these Granger laws. The railroads fought back, challenging the constitutionality of the regulatory laws. In 1877, however, in the case of ***Munn* v. *Illinois*,** the Supreme Court upheld the Granger laws by a vote of seven to two. The states thus won the right to regulate the railroads for the benefit of farmers and consumers. The Grangers also helped establish an important principle—the federal government's right to regulate private industry to serve the public interest.

INTERSTATE COMMERCE ACT The Grangers' triumph was short-lived, however. In 1886, the Supreme Court ruled that a state could not set rates on interstate commerce—railroad traffic that either came from or was going to another state. In response to public outrage, Congress passed the **Interstate Commerce Act** in 1887. This act reestablished the right of the federal government to supervise railroad activities and established a five-member Interstate Commerce Commission (ICC) for that purpose. The ICC had difficulty regulating railroad rates because of a long legal process and resistance from the railroads. The final blow to the Commission came in 1897, when the Supreme Court ruled that it could not set maximum railroad rates. Not until 1906, when President Theodore Roosevelt began his campaign for railroad regulation, did the ICC gain the power it needed to be effective.

SKILLBUILDER

INTERPRETING POLITICAL CARTOONS ***What does this cartoon—featuring the railroad "giants" William Vanderbilt (top), Cyrus W. Field (bottom left), and Jay Gould (bottom right)—imply about the railroad trusts?***

Skillbuilder Answer They exerted total control over the nation's railroad system.

E. Answer The farmers took united political action and pressed legislators to enact laws to protect them.

THINK THROUGH HISTORY
E. *Clarifying* *How did the Grangers, who were largely poor farmers, do battle with the giant railroad companies?*

THE PANIC OF 1893 Although the ICC presented few problems for the railroads, corporate abuses, mismanagement, overbuilding, and competition pushed many railroads to the brink of bankruptcy. Because the railroads were so crucial to the nation's economy, their financial problems played a major role in a nationwide economic collapse. The Panic of 1893 was the worst depression up to that time: by the end of 1893, 600 banks and 15,000 businesses had failed, and 3 million people had lost their jobs. By the middle of 1894, a quarter of the nation's railroads had been taken over by banks. Large firms such as J. P. Morgan & Company and entrepreneurs such as Cornelius Vanderbilt and his son William seized many of the railroads. As the 20th century dawned, seven powerful companies held sway over two-thirds of the nation's railroad tracks.

Businesses of all kinds soon followed the path of consolidation that the railroads had blazed. The age of big business had begun.

F. Answer Corporate abuses and mismanagement, overbuilding, and intense competition.

THINK THROUGH HISTORY
F. *Analyzing Causes* *What were the causes of the Panic of 1893?*

Section 2 Assessment

1. TERMS & NAMES
Identify:
- transcontinental railroad
- George M. Pullman
- Crédit Mobilier
- *Munn* v. *Illinois*
- Interstate Commerce Act

2. SUMMARIZING Re-create the web below on your paper and fill in effects of the rapid growth of railroads.

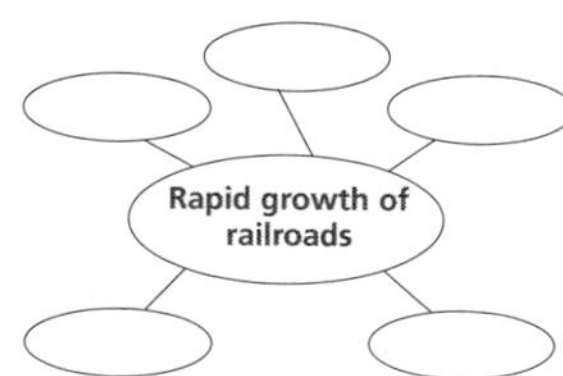

3. MAKING DECISIONS Do you think the government and private citizens could have done more to curb the corruption and power of the railroads? Give examples to support your opinion.

THINK ABOUT
- the reasons that the railroads had power
- the rights of railroad customers and workers
- the scope of government regulations

4. SYNTHESIZING Do you agree with Herman Melville's opinion of the railroads as expressed in "Another Perspective"? Why or why not?

THINK ABOUT
- effects of the railroads on business and industry
- effects of the railroads on daily life
- aspects of life before the growth of railroads

ANSWERS

1. TERMS & NAMES

transcontinental railroad, p. 252
George M. Pullman, p. 255
Crédit Mobilier, p. 255
Munn v. *Illinois*, p. 256
Interstate Commerce Act, p. 256

2. SUMMARIZING

Possible Responses: Governmental regulation of private industry; growth of towns and cities; creation of nationwide market; greed and corruption; consolidation of railroads.

3. MAKING DECISIONS

Possible Responses: **Yes**—Consumer boycotts, greater government regulation, and prosecution of corrupt officials. **No**—*Munn* v. *Illinois* broke new ground in government's regulation of industry; enacting additional regulation would take a long time.

4. SYNTHESIZING

Possible Responses: Some students will say that Melville's opposition to change was stubborn and old-fashioned. Others may agree that the noise and social changes brought by the railroads were unpleasant.

3 Big Business Emerges

TERMS & NAMES
- Andrew Carnegie
- vertical integration
- horizontal consolidation
- Social Darwinism
- monopoly
- holding company
- John D. Rockefeller
- trust
- Sherman Antitrust Act

LEARN ABOUT Social Darwinism and the rise of industry
TO UNDERSTAND the government's attempts to regulate big business.

ONE AMERICAN'S STORY

Born in Scotland to penniless parents, **Andrew Carnegie** came to this country in 1848, at age 13. He worked 12 hours a day, six days a week, in a cotton mill. Several years later, he became a messenger for a telegraph service and worked his way up to become a skilled telegrapher and head of the messenger service. Impressed by the boy's energy, Thomas A. Scott, the local superintendent of the Pennsylvania Railroad, hired him as a private secretary. He was glad he did.

One evening when Scott was out, Carnegie single-handedly relayed messages that unsnarled a tangle of freight and passenger trains. Scott repaid him by giving him a chance to buy stock in a promising company. Since Carnegie had no money saved, his mother mortgaged the family home to make the purchase possible. Soon Carnegie received his first dividend, or share of the profits.

A PERSONAL VOICE

One morning a white envelope was lying upon my desk, addressed in a big John Hancock hand to "Andrew Carnegie, Esquire." . . . All it contained was a check for ten dollars upon the Gold Exchange Bank of New York. I shall remember that check as long as I live. . . . It gave me the first penny of revenue from capital—something I had not worked for with the sweat of my brow. "Eureka!" I cried, "Here's the goose that lays the golden eggs."

ANDREW CARNEGIE, *Autobiography of Andrew Carnegie*

Andrew Carnegie

Andrew Carnegie was one of the first industrial moguls to make his own fortune. His rise from rags to riches, along with his passion for giving his fortune away to charities and other noble causes, made him a model of the American success story.

Carnegie's Innovations

Carnegie was so inspired by his first investment experience that he continued buying stock in new companies and inventing new business practices. By 1865, he had earned so much money in dividends that he was able to leave his job at the Pennsylvania Railroad. He entered the steel business in 1873, shortly after touring a British steel mill and witnessing the awesome spectacle of the Bessemer process in operation. By 1899, the Carnegie Steel Company manufactured more steel than all the factories in Great Britain.

A. Answer Efficient production methods, quality control, cost tracking, and encouraged competition among competent workers.

THINK THROUGH HISTORY
A. *Summarizing* *What were Andrew Carnegie's management techniques?*

MANAGEMENT TECHNIQUES Carnegie's success was due in part to management practices that he initiated and that soon became widespread. First, he continually searched for ways to make better products more cheaply. He incorporated new techniques and machinery in his plants and hired chemists and metallurgists to improve the quality of his steel. Detailed accounting systems enabled him to track the precise cost of each process and every item. Second, he attracted talented people to his operations. He hired topnotch assistants, offered them stock in the company, and encouraged competition among them to increase production and cut costs.

Section 3 Overview

OBJECTIVES

1. To identify management and business strategies that contributed to the success of business tycoons such as Andrew Carnegie.
2. To explain Social Darwinism and its effects on society.
3. To cite methods used by ruthless businessmen to eliminate free competition.
4. To describe the reasons for the slow industrialization of the south.

SKILLBUILDER

- Interpreting political cartoons, p. 260

CRITICAL THINKING

- Summarizing, pp. 257, 259, 261
- Theme: The American Dream, p. 258
- Recognizing effects, p. 258
- Forming opinions, p. 260
- Evaluating, p. 261
- Analyzing, p. 261

FOCUS & MOTIVATE

5-MINUTE WARM-UP

Drawing Conclusions
To gain insight into the people who contributed to big business, have students read the Key Player on page 259 and answer these questions.

1. What company was John D. Rockefeller the head of?
2. What does the quote by Rockefeller's associate suggest about Rockefeller's character?

WARM-UP TRANSPARENCY 6

▶***Starting with the Student***
Ask students what qualities they think a poor person would need to become a billionaire in today's world.

SECTION 3 RESOURCES

PRINT RESOURCES

IN-DEPTH RESOURCES: UNIT 2
Guided Reading, p. 21
Skillbuilder Practice: Forming Opinions, p. 23
Primary Sources: *from* "Wealth and Its Uses" by Andrew Carnegie, p. 27; from *The History of the Standard Oil Company,* p. 28
American Lives: Andrew Carnegie, p. 33

READING STUDY GUIDE, p. 71

ACCESS FOR STUDENTS ACQUIRING ENGLISH
Guided Reading (Spanish), p. 93
Skillbuilder Practice: Forming Opinions (Spanish), p. 95

SPANISH READING STUDY GUIDE, p. 71

FORMAL ASSESSMENT
Section Quiz, p. 82

ALTERNATIVE ASSESSMENT BOOK
See forms for supporting and scoring alternative activities.

TECHNOLOGY RESOURCES

HUMANITIES TRANSPARENCIES
H35, "The Bosses of the Senate"

CRITICAL THINKING TRANSPARENCIES
CT48, Horizontal Consolidation and Vertical Integration

CD-ROM *Our Times*
Electronic Library of Primary Sources

VIDEO *American Portfolio: A Videodisc for U.S. History,* user's guide, p. 138

INTERNET http://www.mlushistory.com

OBJECTIVE
1 INSTRUCT

Carnegie's Innovations

▶***Discussing Key Ideas***
- Andrew Carnegie uses new management

(continued on next page)

(continued from page 257)

techniques to improve the quality and cut the cost of producing steel.
- New business strategies enable Carnegie to control the steel industry.

IN-DEPTH RESOURCES: UNIT 2
Guided Reading, p. 21
American Lives: Andrew Carnegie, p. 33

ACCESS FOR STUDENTS ACQUIRING ENGLISH
Guided Reading (Spanish), p. 93

CRITICAL THINKING TRANSPARENCIES
CT48, "Horizontal Consolidation and Vertical Integration"

OBJECTIVE
② INSTRUCT

▶Social Darwinism and Business

Discussing Key Ideas
- Economists apply Darwin's theory of natural selection to the marketplace.
- This theory implies no government regulation of business and leads to the notion that people deserve their lot in life.
- Stories of rags-to-riches success become popular.

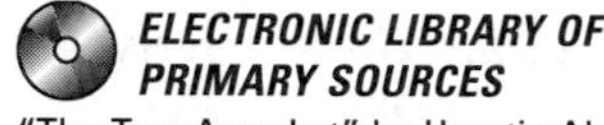

"The Two Acre Lot" by Horatio Alger

BUSINESS STRATEGIES In addition to improving his own manufacturing operation, Carnegie attempted to control the entire steel industry as much as possible. He did this mainly by a process known as **vertical integration,** in which he bought out all his suppliers—coal and iron mines, ore freighters, and railroad lines. Controlling the raw materials, transportation systems, and every stage of the manufacturing process gave him total power over the quality and cost of his product.

Carnegie also attempted to buy out competing steel producers in a process known as **horizontal consolidation.** In this process, companies producing similar products merge. Having gained control over both his suppliers and his competition, Carnegie almost monopolized the steel industry. By the time he sold his business in 1901, the Carnegie Steel Company was producing 80 percent of the nation's steel.

THINK THROUGH HISTORY
B. THEME ***The American Dream*** *How did Andrew Carnegie's life symbolize the American success story?*

Social Darwinism and Business

Carnegie explained his extraordinary success by pointing to his hard work, shrewd investments, and innovative business practices. Late-19th-century social philosophers, on the other hand, thought that Carnegie's achievement could be explained by a new theory—Social Darwinism.

Herbert Spencer

PRINCIPLES OF SOCIAL DARWINISM The philosophy of **Social Darwinism** grew out of the English biologist Charles Darwin's theory of biological evolution, which appeared in the *Origin of Species* in 1859. Darwin had observed not only that individuals of a particular species differ but also that some individuals flourish and pass their traits along to the next generation, while others do not. He explained this as a process of natural selection, which he claimed weeded out weaker individuals and enabled the strongest to survive.

Darwin's biological theories captured the interest of economists, who used his ideas to justify the doctrine of laissez faire (a French term meaning "allow to do"). In practice, this doctrine translated into an absence of regulation in the marketplace. In his 1862 book *First Principles,* the British philosopher Herbert Spencer spelled out the principles of Social Darwinism—that free competition in the economy, like natural selection in the biological arena, would ensure survival of the fittest. A political science professor at Yale University, William Graham Sumner, went even further, saying that success and failure in business were actually governed by natural law and that no one—particularly the government—had the right to intervene.

THINK THROUGH HISTORY
C. *Recognizing Effects* *How did Darwin's theory of evolution affect 19th-century economic policy?*

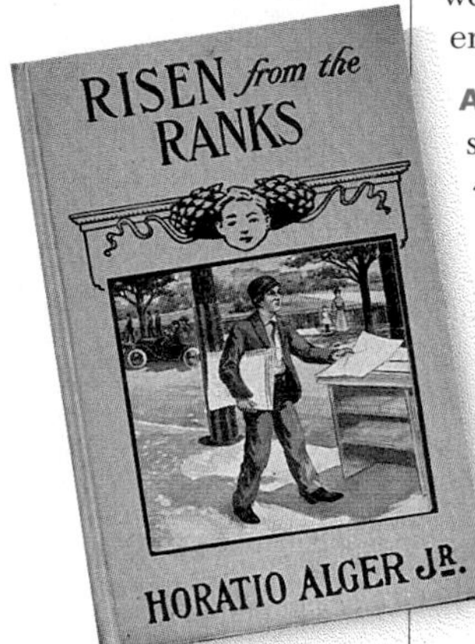

Horatio Alger's books promoted the possibility of rags-to-riches success for anyone willing to work hard.

A NEW DEFINITION OF SUCCESS In providing support for the survival and success of the most capable, Social Darwinism naturally made sense to the 4,000 millionaires who had emerged since the Civil War. However, because the theory supported the notion of individual responsibility and blame, it also appealed to the Protestant work ethic of many Americans. Social Darwinism supported the belief that riches were simply a sign of God's favor and that the poor must be lazy or inferior people who deserved their lot in life.

Popular literature reinforced the emerging cult of the individual. Horatio Alger was one of the most successful writers of the time, and readers gobbled up his inspirational stories. His 135 novels, which sold millions of copies each, often featured an orphan or street urchin who rose to good fortune through model behavior. Though Alger's characters were often extraordinarily lucky, their virtue made them deserve their good fortune. While Alger's stories supported the work ethic, they implied that there was no shame in humble or lowly beginnings. Instead, they focused on the opportunities that awaited those who were upright, energetic, and smart, and popularized the idea of "pulling yourself up by your own bootstraps."

TEACHING OPTIONS

Exploring Themes

The American Dream In the late 19th century, the theory of Social Darwinism helped vitalize the American dream. The prevailing climate of optimism suggested that with perseverance, hard work, and intelligence, anyone might rise from humble beginnings to good fortune. Have students find similarities between the dreams achieved by Andrew Carnegie and by the fictional heroes of Horatio Alger's stories.

IN-DEPTH RESOURCES: UNIT 2
Primary Source: *from* "Wealth and Its Uses" by Andrew Carnegie, p. 27

Making Connections Across the Curriculum

Writing Have students write a scene from a rags-to-riches story. They could base the scene on an incident from Andrew Carnegie's life, or create imaginary characters. Remind students that business opportunities for women were extremely limited at that time but certainly not impossible. Their scenes should be set in the late 19th century and should include description as well as dialogue.

Fewer Control More

Although some economists and businessmen endorsed the "natural law" of competition in theory, they did not give themselves over to it wholeheartedly in practice. In fact, some entrepreneurs actually did everything they could do to control or eliminate the competition that threatened the growth of their business empires.

GROWTH AND CONSOLIDATION Many industrialists took the approach "If you can't beat them, join them." That approach set the stage for the rise of an oligopoly—a market in which only a few sellers provided a particular product. An oligopoly was formed when businesses producing similar products joined together. This horizontal consolidation often took the form of mergers. A merger usually occurred when one corporation bought out the stock of another. A firm that managed to buy out all its competitors could achieve a **monopoly,** or complete control over its industry's production, quality, wages paid, and prices charged. (See *monopoly* on page 937 in the Economics Handbook.)

One way to create a monopoly was to set up a **holding company,** a corporation that did nothing but buy out the stock of other companies. Headed by banker J. P. Morgan, United States Steel was one of the most successful holding companies. In 1901, when it bought the largest manufacturer, Carnegie Steel, for almost $500 million, it became the world's largest business organization.

Corporations such as the Standard Oil Company, established by **John D. Rockefeller,** took a different approach to mergers and joined with competing companies in trust agreements. Participants in a **trust** turned their stock over to a group of trustees—people who ran the separate companies as one large corporation. (See *trust* on page 940 in the Economics Handbook.) In return, the companies received certificates that entitled them to dividends on profits earned by the trust. Trusts were not legal mergers, however. Rockefeller made the most of this legal gray area to gain total control of the oil industry in America.

THINK THROUGH HISTORY
D. *Summarizing* *What strategies enabled big businesses to eliminate competition?*

D. Answer Horizontal and vertical mergers and the creation of monopolies, holding companies, and trusts.

ROCKEFELLER AND THE ROBBER BARONS Rockefeller's achievement was remarkable. In 1870, the Standard Oil Company of Ohio processed two or three percent of the country's crude oil. Within a decade it controlled 90 percent of the refining business. Rather than passing savings along to employees or consumers, however, Rockefeller reaped large profits. He paid his employees extremely low wages and drove his competitors out of business by selling his oil at a lower price than it cost to produce it. Then, when he had control of the market, he hiked prices far above their original level to gain back his money. Rockefeller's agents also used their clout to win rebates on railroad shipping costs and kickbacks from the higher fees railroads charged to other firms.

Alarmed at the ruthless tactics of industrialists, critics began to call them robber barons, after the feudal lords who had owned estates in Europe during the Middle Ages. Men such as Rockefeller, Morgan, and Carnegie defended their wealth by pointing to the charities they sponsored and the philanthropy in which they engaged. Indeed, they often gave away fortunes that others could only dream about. Although Rockefeller held onto most of his wealth, he still gave away over $500 million, establishing the Rockefeller Foundation, providing $80 million to found the University of Chicago, and creating a medical institute that helped stamp out yellow fever.

Andrew Carnegie actually gave away less money than Rockefeller did—a mere $325 million—but he was a fiery evangelist for his self-

KEY PLAYER

JOHN D. ROCKEFELLER
1839–1937

At the height of John Davison Rockefeller's power as head of the Standard Oil Company, an associate commented that he "always sees a little farther than the rest of us—and then he sees around the corner."

Rockefeller's vision began at home, where he was raised by a hard-working, God-fearing mother and a father who was a flashy peddler of phony cancer cures with a unique approach to raising children. "I cheat my boys every chance I get," Rockefeller's father boasted. "I trade with the boys and skin 'em and I just beat 'em every time I can. I want to make 'em sharp."

It seems that this approach succeeded with the oldest son, John D., who was sharp enough to land a job as an assistant bookkeeper at the age of 16. At the end of his life, Rockefeller revealed how many corners he had turned when he referred not to his millions but to his own son, John D., Jr., as "my greatest fortune."

OBJECTIVE
(3) INSTRUCT

Fewer Control More

▶ ***Starting with the Student*** Discuss with students the advantages and disadvantages of free competition, in which the best competitor wins, and the handicap system, in which allowances are made to give all competitors an equal chance. Point out that, in the business world, the first system is equivalent to laissez faire and the second to government regulation.

▶ ***Discussing Key Ideas***
- Consolidation of companies eliminates competition and concentrates power in the hands of a few business tycoons.
- Because of their ruthless business tactics, some industrialists are called "robber barons," although many are also generous philanthropists.
- To protect free competition the government passes the Sherman Antitrust Act, but it proves difficult to enforce.

KEY PLAYER
John D. Rockefeller

Critical Thinking: Comparing and Contrasting Have students compare the attitudes of Rockefeller and of his father toward their children. Some students may wish to research the contributions to society made by Rockefeller's five sons and his grandson, John D. IV.

IN-DEPTH RESOURCES: UNIT 2
Primary Source: from *The History of the Standard Oil Company,* p. 28

TEACHING OPTION

Skillbuilder Mini-Lesson: Forming Opinions

Explaining the Skill Much of the study of history involves forming opinions about historical events and people. Referring to facts, examples, and historical parallels can help people form and support opinions. For example, after watching games and examining football statistics, a fan might form the opinion that a specific person is the best quarterback in professional football. The fan would then use those statistics to support that opinion in conversations with other fans.

Applying the Skill: John D. Rockefeller Ask students to form an opinion of John D. Rockefeller based on the information on this page. Have them list three statements from the text that support their opinion. *Possible Answers: Rockefeller was a good man and businessman—he built a small business into a monopoly; he gave generously to charities; he called his son his "greatest fortune." He was ruthless—he paid low wages to employees, charged high prices, and kept most of his wealth.*

IN-DEPTH RESOURCES: UNIT 2
Skillbuilder Practice: Forming Opinions, p. 23

HISTORY FROM VISUALS

Political Cartoon

Reading the Cartoon Ask students what the relative sizes of Rockefeller and the government buildings mean. What do the smokestacks coming out of the Capitol building in the background signify?

Extension Have students summarize the meaning of the cartoon in two or three sentences.

 ***HUMANITIES TRANSPARENCIES***

H35, "The Bosses of the Senate"

POINT/COUNTERPOINT

Robber Barons or Captains of Industry?

▶ ***Starting with the Student***
Ask students to discuss what they know about business tycoons. What personal characteristics do they have? What kinds of business practices do they use? Do students look up to them or reject their values?

▶ ***Discussing Key Ideas***
- Some people think business tycoons are robber barons because they exploit their workers and the public.
- These people point to the tycoons' unscrupulous business practices.
- Others see the tycoons as captains of industry because they revolutionize business.
- They also give generously to social causes and provide a model for others to emulate.

OUR TIMES
Freedom and Free Enterprise

"WHAT A FUNNY LITTLE GOVERNMENT!"

SKILLBUILDER
INTERPRETING POLITICAL CARTOONS *How does this cartoon depict the power of Rockefeller's Standard Oil empire?*

styled "gospel of wealth." He believed that people should be allowed to make as much money as they could but then should pass it along to worthy causes. Carnegie's donations—90 percent of the wealth he accumulated during his lifetime—helped fund Carnegie Hall in New York City, the Carnegie Foundation, and 3,000 libraries across the nation. His fortune still supports the arts and learning today. "It will be a great mistake for the community to shoot the millionaires," he said, "for they are the bees that make the most honey, and contribute most to the hive even after they have gorged themselves full."

E. Answer Answers will vary, but should be supported with valid reasons.

THINK THROUGH HISTORY
E. Forming Opinions *Do you agree with Carnegie's defense of millionaires? Why or why not?*

SHERMAN ANTITRUST ACT Despite Carnegie's defense of millionaires, the government took a stand against monopolies. In 1890, concerned that expanding corporations would stifle free competition, Congress passed the **Sherman Antitrust Act.** The act stated that any attempt to interfere with free trade between states or internationally by forming a trust was illegal.

Enforcement of the Sherman act proved to be nearly impossible, however. Because the act didn't clearly define terms such as *trust,* prosecuting companies

Skillbuilder Answer As even greater than the power of the federal government.

POINT

"The tycoons of the late 19th century were ruthless robber barons."

Some historians and journalists charge that 19th-century industrialists built their great fortunes at the expense of competitors, customers, and workers. They point to the monopolies and combinations that guaranteed industrialists cheap labor and allowed them to set their own prices.

The critics also point out that the industrialists made hundreds of millions of dollars, while the average industrial worker earned $350 a year. The novelist Edward Bellamy noted that "the individual laborer, who had been relatively important to the small employer, was reduced to insignificance and powerlessness against the great corporation."

The manufacturer George Rice, who was forced out of business by the Standard Oil Company, struck out bitterly against that industrial giant. He declared, "There is no crime in the calendar—save possibly murder—of which it is not guilty or capable. It is the blue-ribbon enemy of everything moral."

The journalist Ida Tarbell agreed about the industrialists. "I never objected to their corporate form. I was willing that they should combine and grow as big and rich as they could, but by legitimate means. But they never played fair."

COUNTERPOINT

"The tycoons of the late 19th century were effective captains of industry."

Many prominent industrialists defended their wealth and achievements in both words and deeds. Some contributed generously to educational and cultural institutions, and they justified their techniques as good business practice. John D. Rockefeller, for example, declared, "I believe in the spirit of combination and cooperation when properly conducted. . . . It helps to reduce waste, and waste is a dissipation of power."

The historian Joseph Pusateri has since noted that Standard Oil "transformed an industry marked by chronic excess capacity, instability, and general aimlessness, into one of the cutting edges of an enormous American economic expansion."

Another historian, H. Wayne Morgan, went even further when he stated, "The stereotype of the Robber Baron is much overdrawn. It must be balanced with the fuller picture, showing the new technology he often brought to his industry, the wealth and resources he developed for the economy in general, [and] the social good he sometimes did with his money." The captain of industry, Morgan suggested, should be a model for every working person. Anyone, he implied, could become another Rockefeller or Carnegie.

INTERACT WITH HISTORY

1. **ANALYZING ISSUES** On which points do critics and admirers of the tycoons agree? With which side do you agree?
   SEE SKILLBUILDER HANDBOOK, PAGE 916.
2. **WRITING A DIALOGUE** Research the points of view of industrialists and workers and write a dialogue between characters representing the two points of view. For additional support for the arguments, use library resources.

INTERACT WITH HISTORY

1. Analyzing Issues

Possible Answers:

- *Industrialists made huge fortunes by applying effective business practices.*
- *Some students may say that the good the industrialists did with their money justified their business practices. Others may say that their exploitation of workers and the public was unjustified.*

2. Writing a Dialogue

You may want to suggest that students use a chart to organize the two sides of the arguments for their dialogues. The framework of their charts may look like this:

Robber Barons or Captains of Industry?

	Industrialists	Workers
Personal gain		
Effective business practices		
Model for working people		
Contribution to society		

was not easy. In addition, if firms such as Standard Oil felt pressure from the government, they simply dissolved their trusts and reorganized into single corporations. The Supreme Court also refused to support the act and threw out seven of the eight cases the federal government brought against trusts. Eventually, the government stopped trying to enforce the Sherman Antitrust Act, and the consolidation of businesses continued.

Business Boom Bypasses the South

The industrialization that fueled this growth and controversy was concentrated in the North, where natural and urban resources were plentiful. The South, on the other hand, was still trying to recover from the physical devastation it had suffered in the Civil War. Its economic growth was also hindered by a lack of capital—money for investment—and by a scarcity of large cities.

ECONOMIC CAUSES Before the Civil War, several banks served the South, providing capital for some business and educational ventures. This situation changed after the war, however, when people with capital were unwilling to invest in what they considered to be a poor risk. Northern businesses already owned 90 percent of the stock in the most profitable Southern enterprise, the railroads, thereby keeping Southerners in a stranglehold. The Southern economy remained basically agricultural, with farmers at the mercy of railroad rates. The few brave business entrepreneurs suffered not only from excessive transportation costs, but also from high tariffs on raw materials and manufactured goods that they needed to import. The post-Reconstruction South seemed to have no way to climb out of the pit of economic stagnation.

SOCIAL CAUSES In addition to economic obstacles to industrial growth, social factors were just as powerful. Southern businesses had to compete with well-established Northern companies not only for capital and markets but also for skilled workers. One Southern businessman complained, "The shops north owe their success largely to the mechanics in their employ. . . . Down here anybody who can pull a monkey wrench and pound his machine with a hammer and cuss the builder for making such a machine is called a mechanic." Growth did take place rapidly, though, in Southern industries such as forestry and mining, and in the tobacco, furniture, and textile industries. This regional growth did change and improve the lives of millions of Americans.

F. Answer Post-Civil War devastation and Northern ownership of the railroads made it hard for the South to grow economically.

THINK THROUGH HISTORY
F. Synthesizing *How did economic factors limit industrialization in the South?*

Although the North preceded the South in entering the industrial age, Northern wage earners were not much better off than Southern laborers. Low pay and poor working conditions drew American workers together in a nationwide labor movement to demand their rights.

Section 3 Assessment

1. TERMS & NAMES
Identify:
- Andrew Carnegie
- vertical integration
- horizontal consolidation
- Social Darwinism
- monopoly
- holding company
- John D. Rockefeller
- trust
- Sherman Antitrust Act

2. SUMMARIZING Compare the lives and beliefs of Andrew Carnegie and John D. Rockefeller, using a Venn diagram.

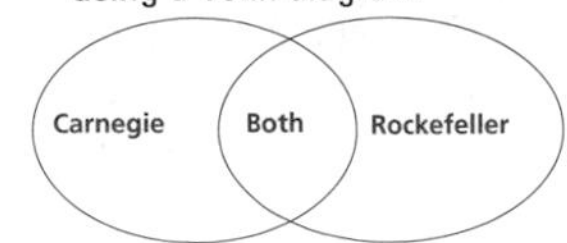

Write a paragraph defending or criticizing these tycoons' accomplishments.

3. EVALUATING Do you agree or disagree with the principles of Social Darwinism? Support your opinion.

THINK ABOUT
- why some people succeed and others don't
- the responsibility individuals have for one another in a society
- the role of government in its citizens' lives

4. ANALYZING If you were a business consultant at the end of the 19th century, what advice would you have offered the people of the South to help them boost their economy?

THINK ABOUT
- differences between the North and the South
- the impact of industrialization on the North
- why the South experienced slow economic development

ANSWERS

1. TERMS & NAMES

Andrew Carnegie, p. 257
vertical integration, p. 258
horizontal consolidation, p. 258
Social Darwinism, p. 258
monopoly, p. 259
holding company, p. 259
John D. Rockefeller, p. 259
trust, p. 259
Sherman Antitrust Act, p. 260

2. SUMMARIZING

Entries on the Venn diagram may include the following:
Carnegie: Born in Scotland; steel magnate; used vertical integration to expand; gave away 90 percent of his wealth.
Both: Leaders of business; extremely wealthy; philanthropists.
Rockefeller: Oil magnate; formed trusts; used ruthless tactics; paid low wages; kept most of his wealth.

3. EVALUATING

Possible Responses: **Agree**—In society, as in nature, the strongest or most powerful survive and succeed; **Disagree**—People should cooperate and take responsibility for others, which means sharing the fruits of their success with the less fortunate.

4. ANALYZING

Possible Responses: Southern investors could invest in northern enterprises, turning profits back to the South; Northerners could be asked to open branches of their businesses in the South; Southern businessmen could write proposals for new businesses and ask for loans from Northern banks; people might try to start cottage industries.

OBJECTIVE
④ **INSTRUCT**

Business Boom Bypasses the South

Discussing Key Ideas
- The post-Civil War South is mainly agricultural.
- Northerners are unwilling to invest in Southern businesses but own major industries such as the railroads.
- Southern entrepreneurs are handicapped by high transportation costs and tariffs.

ASSESS & RETEACH

Section 3 Assessment

Assign pairs of students to discuss the questions and formulate joint responses.

Self-Assessment

Have students list three new facts that they learned and one misconception that was corrected as they read this section.

Section Quiz

FORMAL ASSESSMENT
Section Quiz, p. 82

Reteach

Have students review the Geography Spotlight on page 250, the Point-Counterpoint feature on page 260, and their answers to the Interact with History questions; then discuss the positive and negative effects of industrialization.

CLOSE

As businesses consolidated and industrialists became richer and richer, individual workers continued to work long hours in unhealthy conditions for low pay. They eventually followed the lead of merging companies and united in a nationwide labor movement to demand their rights.

Section 4 Overview

OBJECTIVES

1. To describe the exploitation of workers.
2. To summarize the emergence and growth of unions.
3. To identify the various types of unions.
4. To explain the violent reactions of industry and government to union strikes.
5. To identify the influence of women in the labor movement.
6. To describe the role of the government in opposing union activity.

SKILLBUILDER

- Interpreting charts, p. 266

CRITICAL THINKING

- Analyzing issues, p. 263
- Contrasting, p. 265
- Summarizing, p. 266
- Recognizing effects, p. 267
- Clarifying, p. 268
- Theme: Women in America, p. 269
- Identifying causes, p. 269
- Sequencing history, p. 269
- Evaluating, p. 269
- Hypothesizing, p. 269

FOCUS & MOTIVATE

5-MINUTE WARM-UP

Recognizing Facts and Details

Have students look at the photos on pages 262 and 263 and answer these questions.

1. What kinds of work are shown in the photos?
2. What were the conditions under which women and children worked?

WARM-UP TRANSPARENCY 6

▶ ***Starting with the Student***
Ask students how they would convince school officials to change a policy.

OBJECTIVE ① **INSTRUCT**

Workers Are Exploited

▶ ***Discussing Key Ideas***

- Laborers work long hours with no benefits.

(continued on next page)

④ Workers of the Nation Unite

TERMS & NAMES

- Samuel Gompers
- American Federation of Labor (AFL)
- collective bargaining
- Eugene V. Debs
- socialism
- Industrial Workers of the World (IWW)
- scab
- Mary Harris "Mother" Jones

LEARN ABOUT the conditions that led workers to form unions
TO UNDERSTAND the struggles between labor and management.

ONE AMERICAN'S STORY

Aurora Phelps, a seamstress, had experienced firsthand the changes brought about by industrialization. Like other girls and women in her trade, Phelps saw new production methods reduce the job of a garment worker to a dull, repetitive, and unskilled task. Although these production techniques lowered costs for consumers and increased profits for business owners, they did nothing to improve working conditions for Phelps and other laborers in 1869.

A PERSONAL VOICE

When I was younger, girls learned full trades, now they do not—one stitches seams, another makes buttonholes, and another sews on the buttons. Once girls learned to do all these, and then they learned to cut garments and carried on business. . . . [Now] you can see them in those shops, seated in long rows, crowded together in a hot, close atmosphere, working at piecework, 30, 40, 60 or 100 girls crowded together, working at 20 and 25 cents a day.

AURORA PHELPS, quoted in *The Revolution*

Women do tedious piecework in a New York hat factory about 1900.

Workers were tired of seeing their lives grow more difficult and less rewarding as businesses grew bigger and richer during the last half of the 19th century. They decided that they needed to band together to demand better pay and better conditions.

Workers Are Exploited

Industrial innovations angered Aurora Phelps because they diminished workers' skills and sense of accomplishment. The working conditions of the time also included long hours for low pay under substandard conditions.

LONG HOURS AND DANGER Seamstresses, like factory workers in most industries, worked 12 or more hours a day, six days a week. One of the largest employers, the steel mills, often demanded a seven-day workweek. Employees were not entitled to vacation, sick leave, unemployment compensation, or reimbursement for injuries suffered on the job.

Yet injuries were commonplace. In 1882, an average of 675 laborers were killed in work-related accidents each week. In 1890, the fatality rate for railroad workers was 1 in 300. Many of these were brakemen, who had to balance on the icy roofs of speeding railroad cars. Hazardous working conditions abounded in other industries as well. Factories often were dirty, poorly ventilated, and poorly lit; workers had to perform repetitive, mind-dulling tasks hour after hour, often with dangerous or faulty equipment.

WOMEN AND CHILDREN Workers had little choice but to put up with the deplorable conditions in sweatshops. In addition, wages were so low that most families could not survive unless everyone held a job. Between 1890 and 1910,

SECTION 4 RESOURCES

PRINT RESOURCES

IN-DEPTH RESOURCES: UNIT 2
Guided Reading, p. 22
Primary Source: Labor Poster, p. 29
American Lives: Mary Harris "Mother" Jones, p. 34

READING STUDY GUIDE, p. 73

ACCESS FOR STUDENTS ACQUIRING ENGLISH
Guided Reading (Spanish), p. 94

SPANISH READING STUDY GUIDE, p. 73

FORMAL ASSESSMENT
Section Quiz, p. 83

ALTERNATIVE ASSESSMENT BOOK
See forms for supporting and scoring alternative activities.

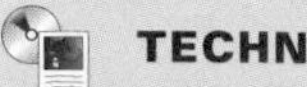

TECHNOLOGY RESOURCES

HUMANITIES TRANSPARENCIES
H14, *The Gun Foundry* by John Ferguson Weir

CD-ROM Electronic Library of Primary Sources

VIDEO *American Portfolio: A Videodisc for U.S. History,* user's guide, pp. 141, 148, 160, 166

INTERNET http://www.mlushistory.com

for example, the number of women working for wages doubled, from 4 million to more than 8 million. Twenty percent of the boys and 10 percent of the girls under age 15—some as young as five years old—also held full-time jobs. Many of these children worked from dawn to dusk, wasted by hunger and exhaustion that made them prone to crippling accidents. With little time or energy left for school, child laborers forfeited their futures to help their families make ends meet. The reformer Jacob Riis described the conditions faced by "sweaters" in tenement workshops.

Many young girls wasted their youth and health in sweatshops such as this North Carolina cotton mill.

A PERSONAL VOICE

The bulk of the sweater's work is done in the tenements, which the law that regulates factory labor does not reach. . . . In [them] the child works unchallenged from the day he is old enough to pull a thread. There is no such thing as a dinner hour; men and women eat while they work, and the "day" is lengthened at both ends . . . far into the night.

JACOB RIIS, *How the Other Half Lives*

Most of the work available to women and children was tedious and required few skills; not surprisingly, these jobs paid the lowest wages—often as little as 27 cents for a child's 14-hour day. In 1899, for example, women earned an average of $269 a year, nearly half men's average pay of $498. The very next year Andrew Carnegie made $23 million—with no income tax.

Labor Unions Emerge

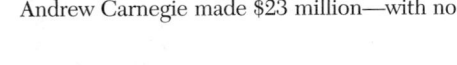

THINK THROUGH HISTORY
A. *Analyzing Issues* *How did industrial working conditions contribute to the growth of the labor movement?*

A. Answer Poor working conditions and low wages forced workers to organize into unions to demand fair treatment.

Laborers thought they at least deserved fair wages and decent working conditions. Business leaders were merging and consolidating their forces, so it seemed reasonable for workers to do the same. Laborers of all types—skilled and unskilled, female and male, black and white—joined together in unions to try to improve their lot.

NATIONAL LABOR UNION The concept of labor unions wasn't a new one. Skilled workers had had small local unions since the early 1800s. The first large-scale national organization of laborers, the National Labor Union (NLU), was formed in 1866 by an ironworker named William H. Sylvis. The NLU consisted of about 300 local unions in 13 states.

To make the union as representative and effective as possible, Sylvis urged local chapters to admit women and African Americans. Although carpenters and cabinetmakers agreed to open their locals to African Americans, other unions refused, leading to the creation of the Colored National Labor Union (CNLU). Nevertheless, NLU membership grew to 640,000; and in 1868, the NLU persuaded Congress to legalize an eight-hour day for government workers. The union gained enough momentum to form its own political party—the Labor Reform Party—and to run its own candidate in the 1872 presidential election.

KNIGHTS OF LABOR While NLU organizers concentrated mainly on linking existing local unions, Uriah Stephens focused his attention on individual workers and, in 1868, organized the Noble Order of the Knights of Labor. Its motto was "An injury to one is the concern of all."

Membership in the Knights of Labor was officially open to all workers, regardless of race, gender, or degree of skill. Like the NLU, the Knights supported an eight-hour workday and advocated "equal pay for equal work" by men and women. They saw strikes, or refusals to work, as a last resort and instead advocated arbitration, or settlement of disagreements by an impartial person.

HISTORICAL SPOTLIGHT

AFRICAN AMERICANS IN THE LABOR MOVEMENT

In 1869, delegates at a national convention of African Americans were so angered by their exclusion from the NLU that they formed the Colored National Labor Union (CNLU). Led by Isaac Meyers (*above*), a caulker from Baltimore, the CNLU vigorously avoided strikes and preached cooperation between management and labor. It was committed to political reform and staunchly supported the Republican Party.

The CNLU disbanded in the early 1870s, but many African-American laborers did find a home in the Knights of Labor, the first union to bring blacks into the growing white labor movement.

Despite the union activities of African Americans, management often used them as strikebreakers. Some white union members then retaliated with violence in black communities. Clearly, the union movement was divided along racial lines.

(continued from page 262)

- Many women and children work at tedious jobs that require little skill and pay low wages to help their families survive.

IN-DEPTH RESOURCES: UNIT 2
Guided Reading, p. 22
Primary Source: Labor Poster, p. 29

ACCESS FOR STUDENTS ACQUIRING ENGLISH
Guided Reading (Spanish), p. 94

Issues for the 21st Century

Breaking the Cycle of Poverty
Connect poverty in the late 1800s to poverty today by having students read pages 896–899. Then have them answer these questions.

1. What group constitutes a major part of the American poor today? *Children.*
2. What conditions did child laborers face in the late 1800s? *Long hours, unsafe conditions.*
3. Many people in the late 1800s faced poverty even though they were working. How does this situation compare to the situation today? *The working poor make up a large group of people in poverty today.*

OBJECTIVE
② **INSTRUCT**

Labor Unions Emerge

▶***Discussing Key Ideas***
- Several local unions merge into national organizations.

(continued on next page)

TEACHING OPTIONS

Making Connections Across Time

Do Sweatshops Exist Today? Discuss with students whether or not sweatshops exist today. Ask under what conditions they would most likely be found. *Possible Answer: Sweatshops are illegal today, and public awareness and disdain run high. They are most likely to be found where legal regulations are difficult to enforce. Public outcry has also been raised against products made in foreign sweatshops and sold in this country.*

Exploring Themes

The American Dream The necessity of working in sweatshops destroyed many women's and children's dreams. This work not only destroyed their health, but children often dropped out of school or neglected their studies, which handicapped them the rest of their lives. In the assembly-line system that existed in many women learned only a limited skill, which prevented them from getting better jobs. Discuss how people might maintain their dreams in the face of such hardships.

(continued from page 263)

- Unions use different tactics—some favoring strikes and others, arbitration.

ELECTRONIC LIBRARY OF PRIMARY SOURCES
On the Goals of Trade Unions by Samuel Gompers

HISTORICAL SPOTLIGHT
African Americans in the Labor Movement
Critical Thinking: Drawing Conclusions Why might the CNLU have preferred to negotiate rather than to strike? *Possible Response: Because its membership was small, strikes might not have been effective.*

OBJECTIVE
(3) **INSTRUCT**

Union Movements Diverge

▶ ***Discussing Key Ideas***
- Craft unions bring together workers who do similar jobs in different industries.
- Industrial unions include all workers in a specific industry.
- Agricultural workers in the West and Southwest also organize into unions.

Membership in the Knights of Labor grew slowly until Terence V. Powderly, a mechanic from Scranton, Pennsylvania, became its head in 1881. Under Powderly's leadership, the Knights expanded from 28,000 members in 1880 to about 700,000 in 1886. Although the Knights of Labor declined rapidly after the failure of a series of strikes, other unions continued to organize.

Union Movements Diverge

As labor activism spread, it diversified, and factions within the union movement emerged. Two major types of unions made great gains under forceful leaders. The labor movement also received support from socialists and social reformers.

CRAFT UNIONISM AND SAMUEL GOMPERS One approach to the organization of labor was craft unionism, which included all skilled workers from many

NOW & THEN

Underage and on the Job

Is working a good thing? Many American teenagers seem to think so. Three out of four high school juniors and seniors work at least part-time, in the evenings and on weekends.

Most do so to earn spending money or to save for college. Typically, they work in low-wage service jobs—at fast-food restaurants or discount stores, for example. Some teenagers work long hours out of economic necessity. Some neglect their schoolwork in the process, but most manage to balance work with educating themselves for the future and enjoying their youth.

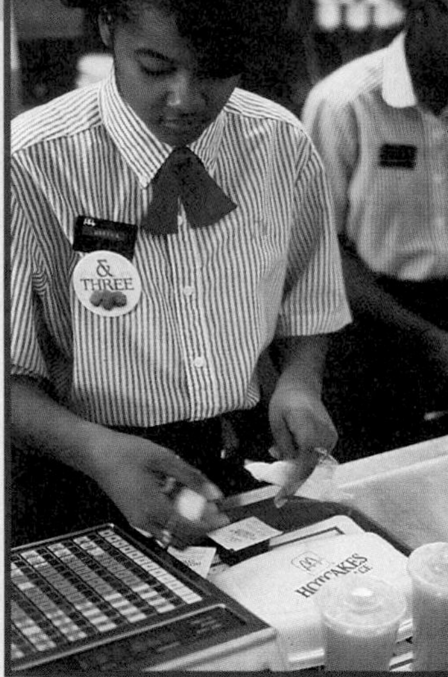

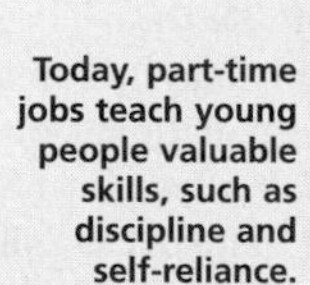

Today, part-time jobs teach young people valuable skills, such as discipline and self-reliance.

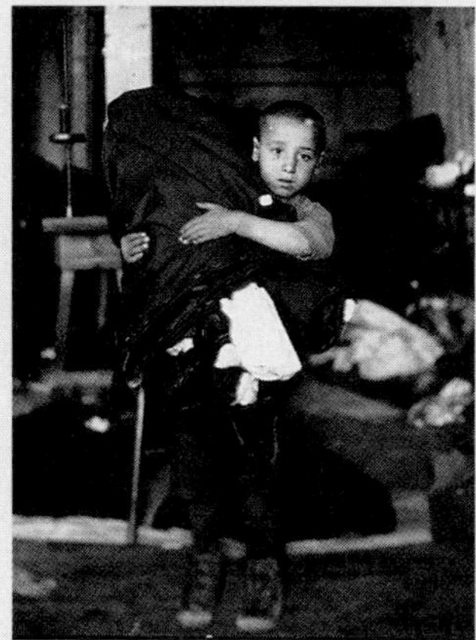

1885
In the late 19th and early 20th centuries, many urban teenagers and children went to work full-time out of necessity. Factory wages were so low that children often had to work to help support their families. Forced to take on adult responsibilities at an early age, child laborers barely experienced their youth. Going to school to prepare for a brighter future was a luxury these underage workers rarely enjoyed.

1889
The long hours and horrendous working conditions for children like these Pennsylvania coal miners eventually provoked a public outcry. Though it took many years and great effort, state legislatures finally passed laws banning or restricting child labor. In 1938, the federal government followed suit with the Fair Labor Standards Act. This law banned most employment for children under 16 and prohibited employment in hazardous occupations for those under 18.

INTERACT WITH HISTORY

1. Contrasting

Possible Answers: *Most teenagers who work today do so voluntarily to earn extra money for expenses or for college, not to support their families. They generally work part-time so they can pursue both their education and a social life. The Fair Labor Standards Act protects the abuse of child labor, although violations of the law are on the rise.*

2. Writing a Proposal

You may wish to suggest that students organize their proposals by following an outline such as this:

I. Thesis statement—summary of ways that work can enhance schooling
II. Most important enhancement—main idea and supporting details
III. Next most important enhancement—main idea and supporting details
IV. Least important enhancement—main idea and supporting details
V. Summary—restatement of thesis

B. Answer A craft union included skilled workers from many different industries; an industrial union included skilled and unskilled workers in a specific industry.

THINK THROUGH HISTORY
B. Contrasting *How did craft unionism and industrial unionism differ?*

different industries. Under leaders such as **Samuel Gompers,** the Cigar Makers' International Union joined with other trade and craft unions in 1886 to form the **American Federation of Labor (AFL).** With Gompers as its president, the AFL focused on **collective bargaining,** or group negotiations, to reach written agreements between workers and employers. Unlike the Knights of Labor, the AFL used strikes as a major tactic, rather than as a last resort, to achieve its aims. Successful strikes helped the AFL win higher wages and shorter workweeks for skilled workers. Between 1890 and 1915, the average weekly wages in unionized industries rose from $17.50 to $24, and the average workweek fell from almost 54.5 hours to just under 49 hours.

INDUSTRIAL UNIONISM AND EUGENE DEBS Some labor leaders felt that the strength of unions lay in reaching beyond skilled workers to include all laborers—skilled and unskilled—who worked in a specific industry. This concept captured the imagination of **Eugene V. Debs,** who made the first major attempt to form such an industrial union—the American Railway Union (ARU). Most of the new union's members were unskilled and semiskilled laborers, but skilled engineers and firemen joined too. In 1894, the new union won a strike for higher wages. Within two months, its membership climbed to 150,000, dwarfing the 90,000 enrolled in the four skilled railroad brotherhoods. Though the ARU, like the Knights of Labor, never recovered from the losses suffered in a major strike, it had its effect.

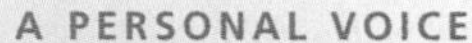

A PERSONAL VOICE

Brothers of the American Railway Union, even in defeat, our rewards are grand beyond expression. . . . The American Railway Union . . . espoused the cause of justice. It furrowed the land deeper with the plows of Truth and Courage than had fallen to the lot of any labor organization since time began, and the seeds of emancipation which it sowed . . . are germinating and a new era is destined to dawn upon labor.

EUGENE V. DEBS, "Proclamation to American Railway Union," 1895

SOCIALISM AND THE IWW Eugene Debs and some other labor activists eventually came to believe that the problems faced by workers were symptoms of an underlying problem with the American capitalist system. They believed that the principles on which the economy was based—private ownership of business and free competition—made the rich richer and the poor poorer. These activists turned to **socialism,** an economic and political system based on government control of business and property and equal distribution of wealth. Socialism had obvious appeal for the downtrodden workers, whom it would empower. But it threatened the wealthy, whose wealth it would confiscate.

Socialism, carried to its extreme form—communism, as advocated by the German philosopher Karl Marx—would result in the overthrow of the capitalist system. Most socialists in late-19th-century America drew back from this goal, however,

"Show me the country in which there are no strikes, and I will show you that country in which there is no liberty."

SAMUEL GOMPERS

INTERACT WITH HISTORY

CONTRASTING How have times changed for working teens? Support your answer.

SEE SKILLBUILDER HANDBOOK, PAGE 909.

WRITING A PROPOSAL With a group of classmates, discuss the value of work experience for young people. How might work be used to enhance, rather than limit, future opportunities? Write a short proposal summarizing your ideas.

1995

Despite legal restrictions, however, the illegal use of underage labor is on the rise. According to the Labor Department, between 1980 and 1992 the number of child-labor violations doubled, to more than 19,000 a year. Many of these underage workers are immigrants working in the fields or in sweatshops or other makeshift factories, where wages are low and health and safety conditions are often appalling. Although most young people are better off than they were a century ago, for some of them, times haven't changed much.

NOW & THEN
Underage and on the Job

▶ *Starting with the Student* Ask students if any of them work after school or on weekends. What benefits have they gained from working? What, if any, negative effects has working had on their academic performance and social life?

▶ *Discussing Key Ideas*
- Many modern teenagers hold part-time jobs while going to school.
- In the late 19th and early 20th centuries, many children worked out of necessity.
- Public outcry against the horrendous effects of child labor led to a legal ban.
- Increasing numbers of children still work illegally.

MORE ABOUT . . .
Samuel Gompers

With the exception of 1895, Samuel Gompers (1850–1924) remained president of the AFL until his death. He became the first registered member of the Cigar Makers' International Union at age 14, and continued to work in cigar shops for 20 years, even after he became active in union activities.

MORE ABOUT . . .
The Union Label

The AFL was an early user of the union label, which was put on products to identify them as having been made in union shops. Union supporters were encouraged to look for the union label in products they bought.

TEACHING OPTIONS

Making Connections Across Cultures

The European Roots of Socialism Socialism came into its own as a social, political, and economic system in the early 19th century in response to the problems brought about by the industrial revolution in western Europe. Although some European immigrants brought their socialist ideas to America with them, the movement never developed the following it had in Europe. Discuss with students why this might be the case. *Students might respond that the United States offered greater opportunities than Europe, even to the poor. They might say that the American dream of individual opportunity and incentive worked against socialist ideals.*

Making Connections Across Time

The Socialist Party in the United States Ask students what they know about the Socialist Party in the United States today. You might want to tell them that the most important leader of the Socialist Party after Eugene Debs's death was Norman Thomas. Thomas ran as a third-party candidate in every presidential election from 1928 to 1948. You might want to have students use the Internet to research Socialist Party candidates currently running for local, state, or national offices.

HISTORY FROM VISUALS

The Growth of Union Membership, 1878–1904

Reading the Graph Have students trace the lines showing the development of each union. Ask them when AFL membership and total union membership in the nation were essentially the same. *About 1897.*

Extension Have students research the membership of the AFL today. *13,200 as of 1993.* You might also ask them to identify other influential unions, such as the Teamsters Union.

MORE ABOUT . . .

The Sugar Beet and Farm Laborers' Union of Oxnard

When the Sugar Beet and Farm Laborers' Union of Oxnard applied to the AFL for a charter, Samuel Gompers informed the union secretary, a Mexican, that Chinese and Japanese workers must be excluded from membership. The farm laborers rejected Gompers's conditions.

OBJECTIVE

④ **INSTRUCT**

Strikes Turn Violent

▶ ***Starting with the Student*** Discuss with students the circumstances that can breed violence. *Possible Answer: When groups with conflicting goals clash, especially when one group feels powerless or fears the other.*

▶ ***Discussing Key Ideas***

- Riots erupt as workers in various industries strike.

(continued on next page)

SKILLBUILDER

INTERPRETING GRAPHS *Which strike did not lead to a decline in union membership?*

Skillbuilder Answer The Wabash Railroad strike.

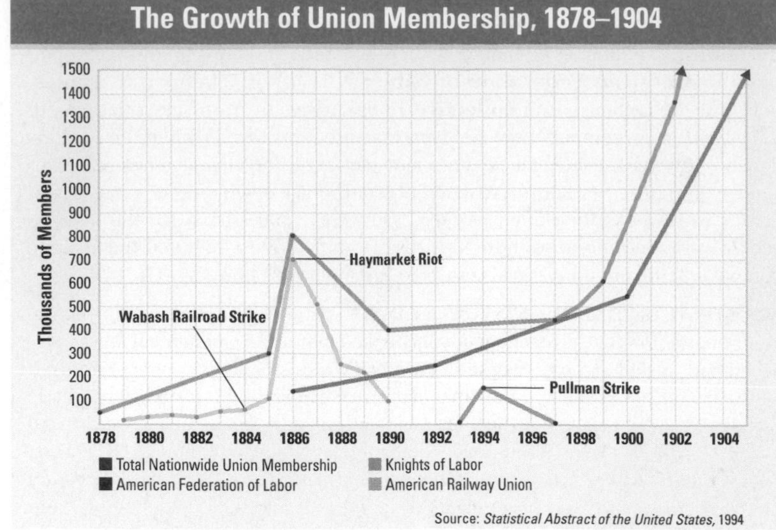

and worked within the labor movement to achieve better conditions for workers. In 1905, a group of radical unionists and socialists in the West organized the **Industrial Workers of the World (IWW),** or the Wobblies. Headed by William "Big Bill" Haywood, the Wobblies included miners, lumberers, and cannery and dock workers. Unlike the ARU, the IWW welcomed women and African Americans, but membership never topped 150,000. Its only major strike victory occurred in 1912. Yet the Wobblies, like the ARU, gave dignity and a sense of solidarity to unskilled workers barred from other groups.

THINK THROUGH HISTORY

C. *Summarizing* *How did socialists work within the labor movement?*

C. Answer They joined unions, such as the IWW, to strike for fair treatment.

OTHER LABOR ACTIVISM IN THE WEST Asian and Mexican agricultural workers in the West and Southwest also organized unions. In April 1903, about 1,000 Japanese and Mexican workers organized a successful strike in the sugar-beet fields of Ventura County, California. In the wake of their victory, they formed the Sugar Beet and Farm Laborers' Union of Oxnard. In Wyoming, the State Federation of Labor supported a union of Chinese and Japanese miners who sought the same wages and treatment as other union miners. These small, independent unions increased the overall strength of the labor movement and helped fuel the increasing tension between labor and management.

Strikes Turn Violent

As union members took action to reduce long hours and to end wage cuts, industry and government acted forcefully to put down the strikes, which they saw as a threat to the entire capitalist system.

THE GREAT STRIKE OF 1877 A turning point in labor history took place in July 1877. Workers for the Baltimore and Ohio Railroad (B&O) went on strike to protest their second wage cut in several months. This strike spread quickly to every railroad line east of the Mississippi and then to the Missouri Pacific and other Western lines. For more than a week, most freight and even some passenger traffic covering over 50,000 miles stopped in its tracks. Riots erupted in Baltimore, Pittsburgh, Chicago, St. Louis, and San Francisco. Some industrialists feared a socialist revolution.

B&O president John Garret wired President Rutherford B. Hayes, urging him to stop the strikes because the strikers were impeding interstate commerce. Hayes agreed and ordered troops to clear the way. The strikers retreated, and by August 2, the trains were running again.

TEACHING OPTIONS

Teaching Gifted and Talented Students

Joe Hill and the Wobblies Although it had relatively few members, the IWW spoke out loudly for the underdogs of the labor movement—women, ethnic minorities, and unskilled laborers. Interested students may wish to investigate the legacy of idealistic social activism left by the Wobblies. Suggest that they begin by researching the life of Joe Hill, who was immortalized in a ballad popular with labor groups.

Making Connections Across Time

Agricultural Activism Today Discuss with students union activities among agricultural workers today. You might want to mention Cesar Chavez, who founded the National Farm Workers Association in 1962, and ask what they know about the strategies he pioneered in the late 1960s. *Chavez appealed to consumers across the nation to boycott the sale of nonunion grapes. Later he used the same strategy to put pressure on nonunion lettuce growers.*

THE HAYMARKET AFFAIR Encouraged by the strike's major impact, labor leaders continued to press for change. On the evening of May 4, 1886, 1,200 people gathered at Chicago's Haymarket Square to protest the killing of a striker by police at the McCormick Harvester plant the day before. Rain began to fall at about 10 o'clock, and the crowd was dispersing when police arrived. Then someone tossed a bomb into the police line. As the confrontation veered out of control, police fired into the crowd. Seven police officers and several workers died in the riot. No one ever learned who threw the bomb, but the three speakers and five other radicals were charged with inciting a riot. All eight men were convicted; four were hanged and one committed suicide in prison. As a result of the Haymarket violence, the public began to turn against the labor movement.

THINK THROUGH HISTORY
D. *Recognizing Effects* *What was one major effect of the Haymarket affair?*

D. Answer Public hostility to the labor movement.

THE HOMESTEAD STRIKE This violence against strikers and rising public anger did not stop workers from fighting against unfair treatment. The Carnegie Steel Company's Homestead plant in Pennsylvania, for example, was ripe for a strike. The writer Hamlin Garland described conditions at the plant.

> A PERSONAL VOICE
> The streets of the town were horrible; the buildings were poor; the sidewalks were sunken and full of holes. Everywhere groups of pale, lean men slouched in faded garments, grimy with the soot and grease of the mills. . . . The mill itself was hell: A roar of a hundred lions, a thunder as of cannons . . . jarring clang of falling iron, burst of fluttering flakes of fire, scream of terrible saws, shifting of mighty trucks with hiss of Steam!
>
> **HAMLIN GARLAND,** quoted in *McClure's Magazine*

The steelworkers finally called a strike on July 6, 1892, after the company president, Henry Clay Frick, announced his plan to cut wages. Frick hired armed guards from the Pinkerton Detective Agency to protect the plant so that he could hire **scabs,** or strikebreakers, to keep it operating. In a battle that left three detectives and six workers dead, the steelworkers ousted the Pinkertons and kept the plant closed until the Pennsylvania National Guard arrived on July 12. At that time, Frick reopened the plant. The strike continued until November, but by then the union had lost much of its support and gave in to the company. It would take 40 years for steelworkers to mobilize once again.

THE PULLMAN STRIKE Strikes continued in other industries, however. During the Panic of 1893 and the economic depression that followed, the Pullman company laid off 3,000 of its 5,800 employees and cut the wages of the rest by 25 to 40 percent. But the company did not cut the cost of its employee housing, and after paying rent, most workers took home less than $6 a week. One man with a grim sense of humor framed a two-cent check.

After the depression lifted and business improved, the Pullman company hired back 2,000 workers, but it failed to restore wages or decrease rents. Outraged and desperate, the workers called for a strike in the spring of 1894. Eugene Debs asked for arbitration, but Pullman refused to negotiate with the strikers; so the ARU began boycotting Pullman trains.

Striking Pullman workers lash out at armed deputies accompanying an engine out of the rail yard in Blue Island, Illinois, in 1894.

(continued from page 266)

- Management appeals to the government to stop striking railroad workers.
- Many companies retaliate against striking workers.

MORE ABOUT . . .
The Haymarket Affair

The three surviving men of the eight convicted of the Haymarket bombings were pardoned by the governor of Illinois, John Peter Altgeld. He justified the pardon because he believed that the accused had not received a fair trial. Altgeld was a staunch supporter of labor, and in 1894, he opposed President Grover Cleveland's decision to send federal troops into Pullman to stop striking railroad workers.

HUMANITIES TRANSPARENCIES
H14, *The Gun Foundry* by John Ferguson Weir

Block Schedule TEACHING OPTION **Time Needed: 30 Minutes**

Cooperative Activity: Reporting on Union Goals

Task: Small groups of students will research the goals of a union and write a report indicating if and when those goals were met.

Purpose: To help students understand the causes and effects of union activity.

Activity: Each group of students should research the history of a particular union. Groups should identify the main goals established by the union and determine which goals were met and when. They should write a report for presentation to the class accompanied by visual aids such as time lines or charts.

Building a Portfolio: Students who decide to add reports to their portfolios should attach a note indicating their contribution to the report.

ALTERNATIVE ASSESSMENT BOOK
Standards for Evaluating a Cooperative Activity

Standards for Evaluation
Reports should . . .

- show evidence of research from a variety of sources
- identify union goals and indicate whether they have been achieved
- include visuals

OBJECTIVE

(5) INSTRUCT

Women in the Labor Movement

▶ ***Starting with the Student*** Ask students why they think many unions did not include women in their ranks, despite their prominence in the work force. *Possible Answer: Traditional prejudice against women, belief that their place was in the home, and the fact that they generally didn't work in skilled trades.*

▶ ***Discussing Key Ideas***
- Women play significant roles in unions that admit them.
- Public exposure of dangerous and unhealthy working conditions for children leads to the passage of laws banning child labor.
- After the tragic Triangle Shirtwaist Factory fire, New York state passes strict fire codes and other reforms.

KEY PLAYERS

Eugene V. Debs

Critical Thinking: Synthesizing Have students write a paragraph describing the relationship between Debs's labor activism and his belief in socialism.

Mother Jones

Critical Thinking: Analyzing Motives Ask students to consider what might have driven Mary Harris to become the "Mother" of union activism. Have them support their opinion in a short paragraph.

IN-DEPTH RESOURCES: UNIT 2
American Lives: Mary Harris "Mother" Jones, p. 34

ELECTRONIC LIBRARY OF PRIMARY SOURCES
from "141 Die in Factory Fire"

KEY PLAYERS

EUGENE V. DEBS
1855–1926

Eugene V. Debs realized his true calling while he was in prison following the Pullman strike in 1894. The failure of the strike and Debs's disillusionment with the conditions of workers under capitalism turned him into a fervent socialist. He became a spokesperson for the Socialist Party of America and was its candidate for president five times. In 1912, he won 900,000 votes—an amazing 6 percent of the total. "I say now," Debs vowed, "that while there is a lower class, I am in it; while there is a criminal element, I am of it; while there is a soul in prison, I am not free."

MOTHER JONES
1830–1930

Mary Harris "Mother" Jones—born in Ireland and raised in Canada—became a leading figure in the American labor movement after her husband and children died of yellow fever in 1867. According to a reporter who followed "the mother of the laboring class" on her children's march in 1903, "She fights their battles with a Mother's Love"—and she continued fighting them until her death at age 100. Maternal as she was, Mother Jones was definitely not the kind of woman admired by John D. Rockefeller and other industrialists. "God almighty made women," she declared, "and the Rockefeller gang of thieves made ladies."

At Debs's urging, both the strike and the boycott remained peaceful—until Pullman hired strikebreakers. Violence broke out, and President Grover Cleveland sent in federal troops to end the strike. In the bitter aftermath, Debs was jailed, Pullman fired most of the strikers, and the railroads blacklisted many others, so they could never again get railroad jobs.

THINK THROUGH HISTORY
E. *Clarifying* *In what ways did strikes threaten industry?*

E. Answer Strikes challenged the power of employers to control conditions, wages, and their own profits.

Women in the Labor Movement

Although women were barred from many unions, they were not silent onlookers in labor struggles. United behind powerful leaders, they raised their voices to demand better working conditions, equal pay for equal work, and an end to child labor.

MINES, MILLS, AND MOTHER JONES Perhaps the most prominent organizer in the women's labor movement was **Mary Harris "Mother" Jones.** Daughter of an Irish union activist, Jones supported the Great Strike of 1877 and later joined the United Mine Workers of America (UMW). She endured death threats and jail with the coal miners, who gave her the nickname Mother Jones.

Not one to stand aside while others took risks, Mother Jones often led the miners in strikes. She advised them to stay home and avoid violence and persuaded their wives instead to march to the mine entrances, where they banged pots and pans to scare the strikebreakers. She also led mill women in sympathy strikes and encouraged them to shame their strikebreaking husbands into joining unions. In 1903, to expose the cruelties of child labor, she led 80 mill children—many with hideous deformities and injuries—on a march to the home of President Theodore Roosevelt. Their crusade gained widespread publicity and influenced the passage of child labor laws.

In the searing heat of the Triangle fire, the fire escape twisted away from the building, hurling panicked women to the brick courtyard nine floors below.

PAULINE NEWMAN AND THE GARMENT WORKERS Other organizers also achieved significant gains for women laborers. In 1909, at age 16, Pauline Newman became the first female organizer of the International Ladies' Garment Workers' Union (ILGWU). A garment worker from the age of eight, Newman also joined the Women's Trade Union League (WTUL) and supported the "Uprising of the 20,000." This massive 1909 strike by the makers of tailored women's blouses, also known as shirtwaists, won labor agreements for some strikers but did nothing to change their deplorable working conditions.

The public could no longer ignore the deadly reality of those conditions after a fire broke out at the Triangle Shirtwaist Factory in New York City on March 25, 1911. The fire spread swiftly through the oil-soaked machines and piles of cloth, and engulfed the seventh, eighth, and ninth floors of the building. As the women tried to flee, they discovered that the company had locked all but one of the exit doors to prevent theft by the workers and to keep out union organizers.

TEACHING OPTIONS

Exploring Themes

Women in America Women played a crucial role in the labor movement. Point out that the Knights of Labor included as one of its goals "equal pay for equal work." Discuss with students whether this goal has been achieved. Make sure they are aware that activists are still fighting for passage of the Equal Rights Amendment, and that equal work still brings women less pay than it does men.

Making Connections Across the Curriculum

Mathematics Have students make a bar graph showing the relative annual earnings of men and women. Have them use these figures and research and add others, if desired:

1899: women $ 267; men $ 498
1904: women $ 289; men $ 540
1909: women $ 339; men $ 631

Graphs might look like this:

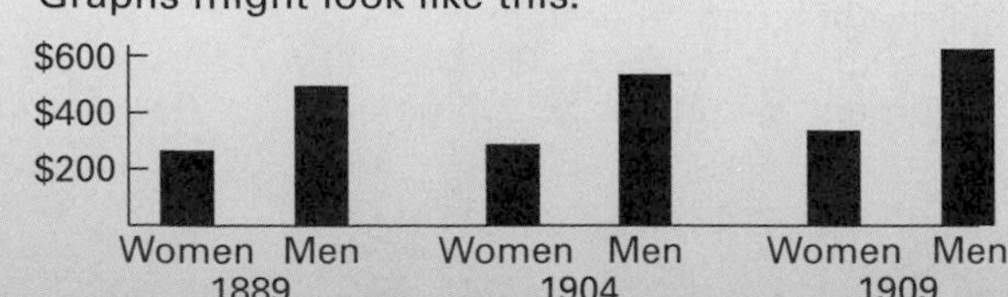

F. Answer They struck in support of mine, mill, and garment workers and won improved conditions for women and children.

THINK THROUGH HISTORY
F. THEME *Women in America* *What tactics did women organizers use to achieve labor reforms?*

The unlocked door was blocked by fire. The factory had no sprinkler system, and the single fire escape collapsed almost immediately. Many of the 500 workers were trapped inside the building, and 145 died. Some were found huddled with their faces raised to a small window. Others jumped to their deaths on the sidewalk or were impaled on the spikes of a fence.

Public outrage flared in the aftermath of the fire, especially when a jury acquitted the factory owners of manslaughter. In response, the state of New York set up a task force to study factory working conditions. The task force finally convinced the New York legislature to establish strict fire codes, a 54-hour maximum work-week for women and minors, a prohibition of Sunday work, and the abolition of labor by children under the age of 14 years.

Difficult Decisions IN HISTORY

STRIKE! MANAGEMENT OR LABOR?

The decision to strike or not to strike was not—and is not—an easy one. Because many workers faced poor conditions for terribly low wages, they protested by withholding their most valuable resource—their labor. In the words of the leader of the Women's Trade Union League, Rose Schneiderman, "It is up to the working people to save themselves."

Management, on the other hand, felt that workers were under contract to provide their labor. In the eyes of employers, strikers not only violated that contract but kept companies from providing essential services. A newspaper editorial applauded President Cleveland's action in stopping the Pullman strike in 1894, "nominally for the expedition of the mails, but really for the preservation of society."

1. Think about the basic goals and values behind labor's and management's positions in the Pullman strike. Which side would you have supported?
2. If you had been called in to arbitrate in the strike, how would you have attempted to reach a settlement? Explain why you would have used that approach.

INTERNET Visit http://www.mlushistory.com for more about labor unions.

Government Pressure on Unions

Despite these gains, union members faced growing opposition from industrialists, who enlisted the help of the federal government to put down strikers.

LEGAL ACTION AGAINST STRIKERS The more powerful the unions became, the more employers came to fear them. Management took steps to weaken labor's influence by refusing to recognize or negotiate with unions as representatives of the workers. Many employers forbade union meetings, fired union members, and forced new employees to sign "yellow-dog contracts," swearing that they would not join a union or take part in a strike.

Finally, industrial leaders, with the helpful rulings of the courts, turned the Sherman Antitrust Act against labor. All a company had to do was say that a strike, picket line, or boycott would hurt interstate trade, and the state or federal government would issue an injunction, or court order, prohibiting the labor action.

G. Answer Court decisions based on the Sherman Antitrust Act, which made unions less effective; negative public opinion; economic hardship; and prejudice against many potential members.

THINK THROUGH HISTORY
G. *Identifying Causes* *Why did labor unions start to decline in the 1890s?*

ORGANIZING BECOMES MORE DIFFICULT These legal limitations made it more and more difficult for unions to be effective. In addition, although the public was generally sympathetic to workers, they became angry when strikes caused shortages of goods. Many feared disorder, chaos, and even socialist revolution. The unions were also losing members: in 1910, only 8.3 percent of industrial workers and 5 percent of the general working population belonged to unions. Ongoing prejudice against minorities and immigrants also kept many willing laborers from helping to form what WTUL activist Rose Schneiderman called "a strong working class movement" that would enable "the working people to save themselves."

Section 4 Assessment

1. **TERMS & NAMES**
   Identify:
   - Samuel Gompers
   - American Federation of Labor (AFL)
   - collective bargaining
   - Eugene V. Debs
   - socialism
   - Industrial Workers of the World (IWW)
   - scab
   - Mother Jones

2. **SEQUENCING HISTORY** Create a time line of major events in labor activism between 1876 and 1911.

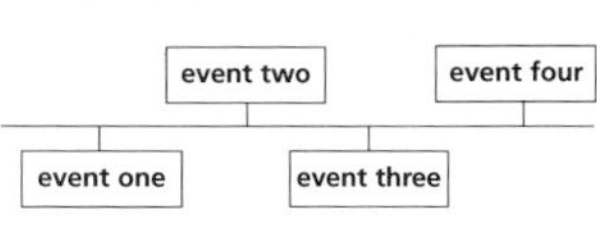

   Write a news report describing the most important event you listed.

3. **EVALUATING** Do you think workers were wise to organize unions in the late 19th century? Why or why not?
   THINK ABOUT
   - working conditions in the late 19th century
   - how unions presented their demands
   - management efforts to oppose unions

4. **HYPOTHESIZING** If the government had supported unions instead of management in the late 19th century, how might the lives of workers have been different?
   THINK ABOUT
   - the strength of management
   - the issues behind labor disputes
   - the government's actions and power

ANSWERS

1. TERMS AND NAMES
Samuel Gompers, p. 265
American Federation of Labor (AFL), p. 265
collective bargaining, p. 265
Eugene V. Debs, p. 265
socialism, p. 265
Industrial Workers of the World (IWW), p. 266
scab, p. 267
Mary Harris "Mother" Jones, p. 268

2. SEQUENCING HISTORY
Possible events:
1866 NLU organized
1868 KOL organized
1869 CNLU organized
1877 The Great Strike
1886 Haymarket Affair
1886 AFL organized
1892 Steelworkers go on strike
1894 The Pullman Strike
1905 IWW organized
1911 The Triangle Shirtwaist Factory fire

3. EVALUATING
Possible Responses: Some students will say that workers had to organize unions despite opposition because working conditions were so dreadful. Others will point out that union activity often resulted in worse conditions and loss of jobs and so was ultimately unwise.

4. HYPOTHESIZING
Possible Responses: Labor relations would have been more peaceful; unions would have grown; management might not have been able to fire union members; the Haymarket affair might not have happened; workers might have won higher pay and better working conditions; industries' profits might have been somewhat lower.

OBJECTIVE
⑥ INSTRUCT

Government Pressure on Unions

Discussing Key Ideas
- Employers fear the power of unions, and ask the government for help.
- The courts use the Sherman Antitrust Act against labor.
- The public withdraws support from unions, whose membership declines.

DIFFICULT DECISIONS IN HISTORY
Strike! Management or Labor?
Critical Thinking: Identifying Problems
Have students make a chart listing the problems workers faced and the solutions other than strikes they might have tried.

ASSESS & RETEACH

Section 4 Assessment
Ask students to discuss questions 3 and 4 and answer them as a group.

Self-Assessment
Have students determine if incorrect answers were related to content or to critical thinking skills and review the appropriate material.

Section Quiz
FORMAL ASSESSMENT
Section Quiz, p. 83

Reteach
Draw a time line from 1876 to 1911 on the board and have students fill in major events in labor activism.

CLOSE

Low wages and poor working conditions compelled workers to form unions and to press for changes. Some reforms were achieved, but when industrialists joined forces with the federal government, the effectiveness of unions began to decline.

CHAPTER 6
ASSESSMENT ANSWERS

REVIEWING THE CHAPTER

TERMS & NAMES
1. Thomas Alva Edison, p. 248
2. Alexander Graham Bell, p. 248
3. George M. Pullman, p. 255
4. Interstate Commerce Act, p. 256
5. Social Darwinism, p. 258
6. Sherman Antitrust Act, p. 260
7. Samuel Gompers, p. 265
8. American Federation of Labor (AFL), p. 265
9. Eugene V. Debs, p. 265
10. Mary Harris "Mother" Jones, p. 268

MAIN IDEAS
11. Steel created demand for coal and iron ore; it was used extensively in the railroad, agriculture, food, and construction industries.
12. They opened up new jobs for women, drew people to the cities, and made jobs less technically demanding.
13. Railroads linked distant places, making them more interdependent, and they created a uniform time system for the country.
14. Railroads were very powerful and often corrupt.
15. The long legal process and resistance from the railroads hampered implementation of the Interstate Commerce Act.
16. They supported the cult of the individual and the work ethic.
17. They used ruthless tactics to amass great wealth.
18. The South had fewer natural and urban resources and less capital for investment.
19. Workers realized that they needed to unite to protect themselves and to improve their pay, shorten their hours, and improve their working conditions.
20. Government support of management; the use of violence and scabs to break strikes.

Chapter 6 Assessment

REVIEWING THE CHAPTER

TERMS & NAMES For each term below, write a sentence explaining its connection to the industrialization of the late 19th century. For each person below, explain his or her role in industrialization.

1. **Thomas Alva Edison**
2. **Alexander Graham Bell**
3. **George M. Pullman**
4. **Interstate Commerce Act**
5. **Social Darwinism**
6. **Sherman Antitrust Act**
7. **Samuel Gompers**
8. **American Federation of Labor (AFL)**
9. **Eugene V. Debs**
10. **Mary Harris "Mother" Jones**

MAIN IDEAS

SECTION 1 *(pages 246–249)*

The Expansion of Industry

11. How did the growth of the steel industry influence the development of other industries?
12. How did inventions and developments in the late 19th century change the way people worked?

SECTION 2 *(pages 252–256)*

The Age of the Railroads

13. How did railroads help unify the United States?
14. Why did people, particularly farmers, demand regulation of the railroads in the late 19th century?
15. Why were attempts at railroad regulation often unsuccessful?

SECTION 3 *(pages 257–261)*

Big Business Emerges

16. How did Horatio Alger's stories reflect the doctrines of Social Darwinism?
17. Why were business leaders such as John D. Rockefeller called robber barons?
18. Why did the South industrialize more slowly than the North did?

SECTION 4 *(pages 262–269)*

Workers of the Nation Unite

19. Why did workers form unions in the late 19th century?
20. What factors limited the success of unions?

THINKING CRITICALLY

1. **INDUSTRIALIZATION: PRO AND CON** What do you think were the overall costs and benefits of industrialization? Summarize your ideas in a chart such as the one below.

Industrialization

Costs	Benefits

2. **UNIONS TODAY** Consider the problems that workers faced in the late 19th century and those that workers face today. On the basis of what you know about unions, how important do you think they are for workers today? Give reasons to support your answer.
3. **INHERITING THE EARTH** Reread the quotation by Mother Jones on page 244. Do you agree that people will be rewarded more if they fight for their rights than if they meekly accept their lot? Support your opinion with information from the text.
4. **TRACING THEMES** **SCIENCE AND TECHNOLOGY** Look at the map on page 254. How do you think the expansion of the railroads influenced the growth of cities in the Midwest and the West?
5. **INDUSTRY AND NATURE** How do you think the growth of industry affected people's connection to nature? Consider factors such as where people worked and whether people became more or less dependent on natural resources.
6. **ANALYZING PRIMARY SOURCES** After Rutherford B. Hayes left the presidency in 1881, he often expressed concern over the growing concentration of wealth in the country.

> No man, however benevolent, liberal, and wise, can use a large fortune so that it will do half as much good in the world as it would if it were divided into moderate sums and in the hands of workmen who had earned it by industry and frugality.
>
> RUTHERFORD B. HAYES, *Diary and Letters of Rutherford Birchard Hayes*

Consider how men like Carnegie and Rockefeller got their wealth and how they used it. Do you agree with Rutherford B. Hayes's statement? Explain and support your opinion.

THINKING CRITICALLY

1. INDUSTRIALIZATION: PRO AND CON
Costs: Increased power of big business; corruption; labor-management conflicts; dangerous jobs; loss of pride in work; Social Darwinism.
Benefits: Better transportation; new methods of communication; less isolation for communities; opportunities for women; new concepts in buildings.

2. UNIONS TODAY
Some students may say that unions are not as important today because most workers have less hazardous jobs; others may support the need for modern unions and emphasize the ongoing conflicts between workers and managers.

3. INHERITING THE EARTH
Those who agree may cite the positive results of social protest, such as safer working conditions, shorter work days, and no child labor; those who disagree may mention the death and injury that can result from militant protest.

ALTERNATIVE ASSESSMENT

1. **REPORTING ABOUT UNIONS**
   How did workers stand up for their rights in the face of dangerous and exploitative working conditions in the new industrial economy of 1870 to 1890?

   Acting as a reporter for a television news magazine, report on and explain a particular labor situation of the time.

   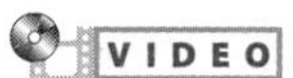
   Use the CD-ROM *Grolier Multimedia Encyclopedia* and other reference materials to research labor strikes and union organizing in this period.

   - Research different types of unions and strikes in the period (the issues, as well as the responses of corporations and the government to striking workers).
   - Choose one incident of labor unrest and report on it to your class, comparing and contrasting it with other incidents. Give the background of the event; tell what happened, including the results; and add your own commentary about the situation.

2. **LEARNING FROM MEDIA**

   View the video for Chapter 6, *Gusher!* Discuss the following questions.

   - Why did Pattillo Higgins believe that he could find oil in a hill near Beaumont, Texas?
   - Why were the first attempts at drilling oil on Big Hill by the Gladys City company not successful?
   - What were the effects of the discovery of oil at Spindletop?
   - How did Higgins influence his great-granddaughter?
   - What lessons can people learn from Pattillo Higgins?

3. **PORTFOLIO PROJECT**
   Use the Living History activity to expand your portfolio.

LIVING HISTORY

REVISING YOUR SCIENCE FICTION STORY

You have written a science fiction story about a society that does not undergo industrialization. Now ask one of your classmates to read the story and give you feedback that will help you improve it.

- Does the story have a conflict, and is the conflict resolved by the end?
- Does the story have a setting that is not industrialized?
- Does the story make clear how the characters obtain food and shelter?
- Does the story show the characters in social and cultural activities?

After you have revised your story, publish it as part of a class collection. Then add it to your American history portfolio.

Bridge to Chapter 7

Review Chapter 6

INVENTIONS AND INDUSTRIALIZATION In the late 19th century, the harnessing of abundant natural resources and an explosion of inventions radically changed industry and daily life in the United States. Drake's oil well, Bessemer's steel-making process, Edison's light bulb, and Bell's telephone were only some of these revolutionary developments. New industries flourished, creating new products and jobs for both men and women.

THE AGE OF THE RAILROADS Railroads, one of the growing industries, provided great benefits, but at a high cost. While railroads linked towns and cities across the country, the workers who built them faced low pay and dangerous conditions. Corrupt management, demonstrated in the Crédit Mobilier scandal, abounded and angered the public. Demands by farmers for regulation resulted in the formation of the Interstate Commerce Commission but did not prevent railroads from becoming a powerful political and economic force.

THE POWER OF BUSINESS Like the railroads, other large corporations exerted increasing power in government and in society. Andrew Carnegie, John D. Rockefeller, and others accumulated tremendous personal fortunes, often using ruthless tactics. Many justified their actions by citing the doctrine of Social Darwinism—that the wealthy deserved their success and the poor deserved their poverty.

LABOR RESPONDS Workers responded to the growing power of business by joining together in unions. Labor activists fought for better working conditions and adequate pay through strikes and protests. However, the government supported management in its attack on unions and weakened the power of labor.

Preview Chapter 7

Industrialization created new job opportunities, mostly in cities. To fill the jobs, migrants from rural parts of the United States and immigrants—primarily from southern and eastern Europe—flocked to urban areas. This rapid urban growth created ongoing challenges for cities. You will learn about these significant developments in the next chapter.

ALTERNATIVE ASSESSMENT

1. REPORTING ABOUT UNIONS

Standards for Evaluation
An effective report should meet the following criteria:

- Provides adequate background information and a clear description of the labor situation.
- Compares and contrasts the situation with other labor incidents.
- Indicates the outcome of the event and offers a personal response to it.

2. LEARNING FROM MEDIA

Answers to the questions:

- The sour smell of nearby springs, the seepage of natural gas, and other indications.
- The drillers did not drill below 1,000 feet, as Higgins insisted.
- There was a new respect for the scientific search for oil; new oil companies developed, breaking the monopoly of Standard Oil; companies developed oil fields around the world; people gained confidence that oil was a reliable and plentiful resource.
- Higgins inspired her to overcome her disability and attain her dream.
- Answers will vary, but students might indicate that people should set goals for themselves and persevere in attaining them, even when facing great odds.

3. PORTFOLIO PROJECT

LIVING HISTORY

Standards for Evaluation
A science fiction story should meet the following criteria:

- Depicts a society in which the effects of industrialization do not play a part.
- Clearly describes the setting.
- Provides detailed information about people's daily lives.
- Introduces and resolves a conflict.

IN-DEPTH RESOURCES: UNIT 2
See the form for scoring this activity on page 36.

THINKING CRITICALLY

4. TRACING THEMES SCIENCE AND TECHNOLOGY
Railroads expanded urban areas at railroad hubs, enabled movement of goods into and out of central points, allowed people to relocate, and connected remote or inaccessible areas to the rest of the nation.

5. INDUSTRY AND NATURE
People became more dependent on resources such as iron ore and coal, moved off farms and into cities, but didn't consider the effects of pollution on the environment.

6. ANALYZING PRIMARY SOURCES
Students should support their opinions of Hayes's statement with examples from the text.

CHAPTER 7

PLANNING GUIDE

Immigrants and Urbanization

	Key Ideas	COPYMASTERS	ASSESSMENT
SECTION 1 **The New Immigrants** ***pp. 274–279***	*New immigrants from southern and eastern Europe, Asia, the Caribbean, and Mexico face culture shock and prejudice—as well as the opportunity for a better life—in the United States.*	***In-Depth Resources: Unit 2*** • Guided Reading, p. 37 • Skillbuilder Practice: Interpreting Graphs, p. 41 • Primary Source: Artifacts from Ellis Island, p. 46 • Literature: from *Call It Sleep* by Henry Roth, p. 50 ***Lesson Plans,*** pp. 61–62	PE ***Section 1 Assessment,*** p. 279 TE ***Self-Assessment,*** p. 279 ***Formal Assessment*** • Section Quiz, p. 92 ***Alternative Assessment Book*** • Standards for Evaluating a Cooperative Activity
SECTION 2 **The Problems of Urbanization** ***pp. 282–287***	*The rapid growth of cities creates many problems: how to provide adequate housing, transportation, water, and sanitation and how to fight fire and crime. The search for solutions begins.*	***In-Depth Resources: Unit 2*** • Guided Reading, p. 38 • Geography Application: Industry and Urban Growth, p. 42 • Outline Map: The Urbanization of America, p. 44 • Primary Sources: from *How the Other Half Lives* by Jacob Riis, p. 47; from *Twenty Years at Hull-House* by Jane Addams, p. 48 • American Lives: Jane Addams, p. 53 ***Lesson Plans,*** pp. 63–64	PE ***Section 2 Assessment,*** p. 287 TE ***Self-Assessment,*** p. 287 ***Formal Assessment*** • Section Quiz, p. 93 ***Alternative Assessment Book*** • Standards for Evaluating a Cooperative Activity
SECTION 3 **The Emergence of the Political Machine** ***pp. 288–290***	*The political machine emerges as cities attempt to deal with the problems of rapid urbanization.*	***In-Depth Resources: Unit 2*** • Guided Reading, p. 39 • Primary Source: from *The Shame of the Cities* by Lincoln Steffens, p. 49 • American Lives: William Marcy Tweed, p. 54 ***Lesson Plans,*** pp. 65–66	PE ***Section 3 Assessment,*** p. 290 TE ***Self-Assessment,*** p. 290 ***Formal Assessment*** • Section Quiz, p. 94 ***Alternative Assessment Book*** • Standards for Evaluating a Cooperative Activity
SECTION 4 **Politics in the Gilded Age** ***pp. 291–293***	*Local and national political corruption during the Gilded Age leads to a call for reform.*	***In-Depth Resources: Unit 2*** • Guided Reading, p. 40 ***Lesson Plans,*** pp. 67–68	PE ***Section 4 Assessment,*** p. 293 TE ***Self-Assessment,*** p. 293 ***Formal Assessment*** • Section Quiz, p. 95 ***Alternative Assessment Book*** • Standards for Evaluating a Cooperative Activity
CHAPTER RESOURCES	**Chapter Overview** *The population rises as immigrants supply a willing workforce for urban industrialization and a political base for many urban politicians. Abuses in local and national government prompt calls for reform.*	***In-Depth Resources: Unit 2*** • Living History Project: Worksheet, p. 55; Standards, p. 56 ***Telescoping the Times*** • Chapter Summary, pp. 13–14 ***Planning for Block Schedules***	PE ***Chapter Assessment,*** pp. 294–295 PE ***Alternative Assessment,*** p. 295 ***Formal Assessment*** • Chapter Test, forms A and B, pp. 96–101 ***Test Generator*** ***Alternative Assessment Book*** See explanation and forms for different kinds of alternative assessments including portfolio assessment.

KEY
- PE Pupil's Edition
- TE Teacher's Edition
- INTERNET http://www.mlushistory.com

TECHNOLOGY

Warm-Up Transparency 7

Geography Transparencies
- G15, Where the Foreign-Born Lived, 1900

Electronic Library of Primary Sources
- *from* Chinese Exclusion Act of 1882
- Twelve Hundred More
- from *The Days of Our Years* by Israel Kasovich

AMERICAN STORIES video series
- "From China to Chinatown"

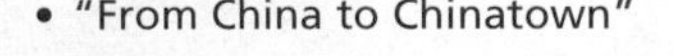

INTERNET Ellis Island and Angel Island

Warm-Up Transparency 7

Humanities Transparencies
- H15, *Cliff Dwellers*

Critical Thinking Transparencies
- CT15, Urban Growth
- CT49, From Country to City, 1870–1920

Electronic Library of Primary Sources
- "The Modern City" by Jane Addams

Our Times
- San Francisco earthquake and fire

INTERNET Jane Addams and the San Francisco earthquake

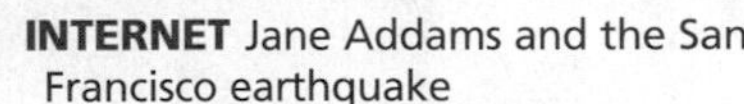

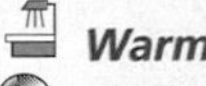

Warm-Up Transparency 7

Grolier Multimedia Encyclopedia
- Thomas Nast and a history of editorial and political cartoons

INTERNET Thomas Nast

Warm-Up Transparency 7

INTERNET Chester A. Arthur and Benjamin Harrison

American Portfolio: A Videodisc for U.S. History, user's guide, pp. 146–155, 157

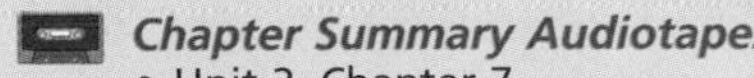

Chapter Summary Audiotapes
- Unit 2, Chapter 7

INTERNET http://www.mlushistory.com

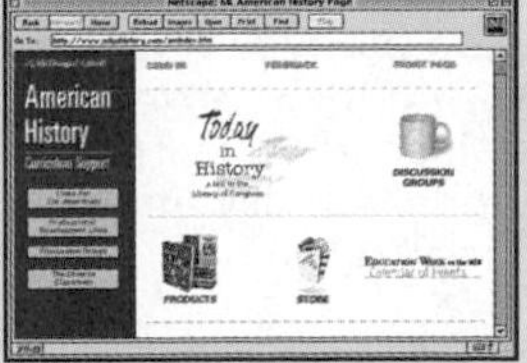

Block Scheduling (90 MINUTES)

Day 1

Section 1, pp. 274–279

AMERICAN STORIES video series
"From China to Chinatown"

Tracing Themes: The American Dream, pp. 280–281

Section 2, pp. 282–287

Section Assessments, pp. 279, 287

COOPERATIVE ACTIVITIES
- Writing Letters or Poems About Immigrant Experiences, p. 277 (TE)
- Researching Catastrophes, p. 285 (TE)

Day 2

Section 3, pp. 288–290

Section Assessment, p. 290

Chapter Assessment, pp. 294–295

COOPERATIVE ACTIVITY
- Creating Political Cartoons, p. 289 (TE)

Day 3

Section 4, pp. 291–293

Section Assessment, p. 293

Chapter Assessment, pp. 294–295

YEARLY PACING *Chapter 7 Total:* 3 days *Yearly Total:* 85 days

See *Planning for Block Schedules* for special activities and pacing strategies.

Customizing for Special Populations

Students Acquiring English

Access for Students Acquiring English: Spanish Translations
- Guided Reading for Sections 1–4), pp. 100–103
- Chapter Summary, pp. 98–99
- Skillbuilder Practice: Interpreting Graphs, p. 104
- Geography Application: Industry and Urban Growth, p. 105
- Outline Map: The Urbanization of America, p. 107

Spanish Reading Study Guide, pp. 77–86

Translations of Chapter Summaries, Hmong, Cantonese, Vietnamese, and Cambodian

Chapter Summary Audiotapes in Spanish
Unit 2, Chapter 7

AMERICAN STORIES video series
- "From China to Chinatown" (Spanish Track)

INTERNET The Diverse Classroom

Gifted and Talented Students

In-Depth Resources: Unit 2
- Primary Sources: Artifacts from Ellis Island, p. 46; from *How the Other Half Lives* by Jacob Riis, p. 47; from *Twenty Years at Hull-House* by Jane Addams, p. 48; from *The Shame of the Cities* by Lincoln Steffens, p. 49
- American Lives: Jane Addams, p. 53; William Marcy Tweed, p. 54

Less Proficient Readers

In-Depth Resources: Unit 2
- Guided Reading for Sections 1–4, pp. 37–40
- Skillbuilder: Interpreting Graphs, p. 41
- Geography Application: Industry and Urban Growth, p. 42
- Outline Map: The Urbanization of America, p. 44

Reading Study Guide
- pp. 77–86

Telescoping the Times
- Chapter Summary, pp. 13–14

Chapter Summary Audiotapes, Unit 2, Chapter 7

Connections to Literature READINGS FOR STUDENTS

In-Depth Resources: Unit 2
- **from *Call It Sleep* by Henry Roth,** p. 50

Enrichment Reading
- **Theodore Dreiser**
  Sister Carrie.
  New York: Bantam, 1993
  Dreiser transforms the conventional "fall-en woman" story into a study of the persistent idealism and the grasping and seductive materialism of the American culture.
- **Anzia Yezierska**
  Bread Givers.
  New York: Persea Books, 1975
  This touching tale tells the story of Jewish immigrants trying to find their way in America and the conflict between a father of the old world and a daughter of the new world.

McDougal Littell *Literature Connections*

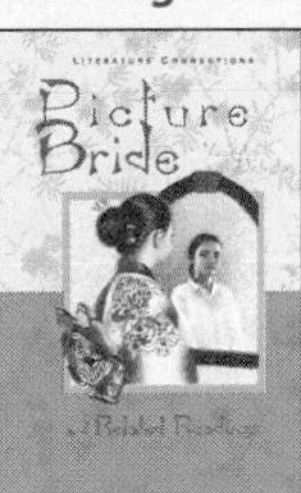

- **Yoshiko Uchida,**
  Picture Bride *(with related readings). This novel follows the experiences of a Japanese woman who comes to America in 1917 to marry a man she has never met. The story ends in a Japanese internment camp in Utah in 1943.*

McDougal Littell *The Language of Literature*
American Literature
- **Américo Paredes, "The Legend of Gregorio Cortez,"** p. 556
- **Hisaye Yamamoto, "Seventeen Syllables,"** p. 628
- **Anzia Yezierska, "America and I,"** p. 703
- **Bernard A. Weisberger, from *A Nation of Immigrants,*** p. 713
- **Gish Jen, "In the American Society,"** p. 717

OVERVIEW

Immigrants and Urbanization

▶ ***Accessing Prior Knowledge***
Ask students to share experiences of family members or family friends who immigrated to the United States, either recently or generations ago. Ask what the basic reason for immigration was.

▶ ***Predicting Outcomes***
Ask students what Horace Greeley meant by his quotation. Ask them what problems they think new immigrants to the United States in the late 1800s might face.

MORE ABOUT . . .
The Statue of Liberty
The Statue of Liberty was a gift from France commemorating that country's alliance with the United States during the American Revolution. The statue's pedestal is inscribed with a poem by Emma Lazarus that ends with the words: " 'Give me your tired, your poor, / Your huddled masses yearning to breathe free, / . . . I lift my lamp beside the golden door!' "

CHAPTER 7

Immigrants and Urbanization

SECTION 1
The New Immigrants
New immigrants from southern and eastern Europe, Asia, the Caribbean, and Mexico face culture shock and prejudice—as well as the opportunity for a better life—in the United States.

FROM CHINA TO CHINATOWN

SECTION 2
The Problems of Urbanization
The rapid growth of cities creates many problems: how to provide adequate housing, transportation, water, and sanitation and how to fight fire and crime. The search for solutions begins.

SECTION 3
The Emergence of the Political Machine
Political machines emerge as cities attempt to deal with the problems of rapid urbanization.

SECTION 4
Politics in the Gilded Age
Local and national political corruption during the Gilded Age leads to a call for reform.

"We cannot all live in the city, yet nearly all seem determined to do so."
Horace Greeley

THE UNITED STATES
- 1871 Boss Tweed is indicted for fraud and forgery.
- 1877 Rutherford B. Hayes becomes president.
- 1880 James A. Garfield is elected president.
- 1881 Chester A. Arthur succeeds to presidency after Garfield is assassinated.
- 1884 Grover Cleveland is elected president.
- 1886 Statue of Liberty is dedicated.

1870 **1880**

THE WORLD
- 1871 Otto von Bismarck unifies the new German Empire.
- 1876 Porfirio Díaz seizes power in Mexico.
- 1886 Gold is discovered in South Africa.

THEMES IN CHAPTER 7

America in the World
Like the United States, other countries also experienced a marked increase of immigrants to their land. These immigrants came in search of freedom, to escape political persecution, or to find economic opportunities.
See Teacher's Edition note, p. 276.

Immigration and Migration
The settlers' quest for rich farmland, the California gold rush, the Homestead Act, the transcontinental railroad, and the Great Depression all contributed to migration within the United States. The nation remains highly mobile today.
See Teacher's Edition note, p. 278.

Cultural Diversity
Immigrants arrived with their own religious beliefs, language, and social customs. In the cities, many immigrants took advantage of the abundant opportunities to enrich their lives. They went to museums, theaters, and concerts.
See Teacher's Edition note, p. 288.

The American Dream
Free public education has long been a part of the American dream. Such public education enabled many immigrants to enter into their new world. In school, children learned about democracy and civic responsibility.
See Teacher's Edition note, p. 284.

LIVING HISTORY

TRACING THE GROWTH OF A TOWN

Write a biography of your town or neighborhood. Using what you learn in this chapter about how cities grow and why people immigrate, discuss some of the following:

- the town's or neighborhood's founders
- major ethnic groups, including when they arrived and what they have contributed to the area
- the problems created by growth and the way that the problems were solved
- what the future of the town/neighborhood might be

Include maps, photos, and newspaper stories about interesting local events.

PORTFOLIO PROJECT Keep these materials in a folder for your American history portfolio. You will present the biography to the class at the end of the chapter.

1888 — Benjamin Harrison is elected president.

1890 — Immigration by Europeans, such as these Dutch children, soars.

1892 — Grover Cleveland is elected president for a second term.

1895 — X-rays are discovered by Wilhelm Roentgen.

1896 — William McKinley is elected president.

1897 — First electric subway is opened in Boston.

1898 — Hawaii is annexed by the United States.

1900 — Tenements abound in New York City.

1901 — Commonwealth of Australia is created.

1903 — Wright brothers make the first successful airplane flight.

1908 — Conspicuous spending by Mrs. Jay Gould and other wives of wealthy industrialists characterizes the era.

1912 — Qing Dynasty in China is overthrown.

1914 — Panama Canal opens.

ALTERNATIVE ASSESSMENT

LIVING HISTORY

TRACING THE GROWTH OF A TOWN

Discuss the following ways of gathering information for a biography of a town or neighborhood:

- Use the local newspaper, library, or museum to find books, maps, and other information.
- Prepare questions and then interview older members of the community, tape-recording their comments.
- Get permission to visit schools, places of worship, the Chamber of Commerce, and other sites of interest.
- Check your own family's sources for photographs and memorabilia.

Project Planning Guide

Step 1	Students prepare a list of persons and places to visit.
Step 2	Students gather information from the persons and places they have listed in Step 1.
Step 3	Students organize the data they have collected.
Step 4	Students write a summary of the town's past and predict the town's future.

IN-DEPTH RESOURCES: UNIT 2
See worksheet and standards for evaluation on pp. 55, 56.

RECOMMENDED RESOURCES

Books for the Teacher

Higham, John. *Strangers in the Land.* New York: Atheneum, 1965. Immigrants and nativists.

McCullough, David. *The Great Bridge.* New York: Simon, 1972. Building Brooklyn Bridge.

Takaki, Ronald. *A Different Mirror.* Boston: Little, 1993. Hispanic and Asian experience.

Books for the Student

Callow, Alexander B. *The Tweed Ring.* New York: Oxford UP, 1966. Story of the most notorious political machine.

Kessler-Harris, Alice. *Out to Work.* New York: Oxford UP, 1982. Women in the industrialized workplace.

Ratzel, Friedrich. *Sketches of Urban and Cultural Life in America.* New Brunswick, NJ: Rutgers UP, 1988. German traveler describes American society.

Videos

The Brooklyn Bridge. Direct Cinema, 1982. Building the bridge.

The Great San Francisco Earthquake. PBS Home Video, 1988. 800-424-7963. Documentary.

Journey to America. PBS Home Video, 1988. 800-424-7963.

Journey to Freedom: The Immigrant Experience. Videodisc.

Ragtime. Dir. Milos Forman. 1981. Paramount Home Video, 1989.

Software

Who Built America? CD-ROM. Voyager, 800-446-2001.

Section 1 Overview

OBJECTIVES

1. To summarize the various parts of the world from which immigrants came to the "golden door."
2. To describe the journey immigrants endured and how they passed through the immigration stations.
3. To explain the kinds of discrimination immigrants faced and the actions taken by nativists.

SKILLBUILDER

- Understanding geography: movement, p. 275

CRITICAL THINKING

- Summarizing, pp. 275, 279
- Theme: America in the World, p. 276
- Theme: Immigration and Migration, p. 277
- Clarifying, p. 278
- Making inferences, p. 279
- Forming opinions, p. 279
- Synthesizing, p. 279

FOCUS & MOTIVATE

5-MINUTE WARM-UP

Making Inferences

To learn what immigrating to the United States meant to the immigrants, ask students to read A Personal Voice on page 276 and answer these questions.

1. What country did Rosa Cavalleri come from?
2. What words would describe how she felt about immigrating to the United States?

WARM-UP TRANSPARENCY 7

▶ ***Starting with the Student*** Have students watch the video "From China to Chinatown" to learn about American attitudes toward Chinese immigrants.

AMERICAN STORIES **video series**

"From China to Chinatown"

Videocassette: Volume 2

Videodisc: Disc 1, Side B, Chapter 4

1 The New Immigrants

TERMS & NAMES
- Ellis Island
- Angel Island
- culture shock
- melting pot
- Chinese Exclusion Act
- Gentlemen's Agreement

LEARN ABOUT why people emigrate and the challenges they face ***TO UNDERSTAND*** the impact of immigration on the United States in the late 19th and early 20th centuries.

ONE AMERICAN'S STORY

In 1871, 14-year-old Fong See came from China to "Gold Mountain"—the United States—to search for his father and brothers, who had emigrated here. Fong See found his father in Sacramento, and when his father returned to China, Fong See stayed, worked at menial jobs, and saved enough money to buy a business. Despite widespread restrictions against the Chinese, he became a very successful and influential importer and was able to marry, move to Los Angeles, and sponsor many other Chinese who wanted to enter the United States. Fong See had achieved the American dream. However, as his great-granddaughter Lisa See recalls, he was not satisfied.

Fong See *(second from left)* and family, 1901

A PERSONAL VOICE

He had been trying to achieve success ever since he had first set foot on the Gold Mountain. His dream was very "American." He wanted to make money, have influence, be respected, have a wife and children who loved him. In 1919, when he traveled to China, he could look at his life and say he had achieved his dream. But once in China he suddenly saw his life in a different context. In America, was he really rich? Could he live where he wanted? . . . Did *Americans* care what he thought? . . . The answers played in his head—no no no.

LISA SEE, *On Gold Mountain*

Despite Fong See's success in America and his standing as a leader in the Chinese-American community, he could not, upon his death in 1957, be buried next to his Caucasian wife because California cemeteries were still segregated.

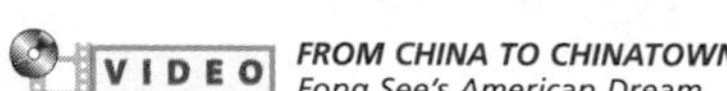
FROM CHINA TO CHINATOWN
Fong See's American Dream

Through the "Golden Door"

Millions of immigrants like Fong See entered the United States in the late 19th and early 20th centuries because they were lured by the promise of a better life. Some of these immigrants sought to escape difficult conditions—such as poverty, famine, land shortages, or religious or political persecution—in their native countries. Others, known as "birds of passage," intended to immigrate temporarily in order to make money and then return to their homelands.

IMMIGRANTS FROM EUROPE Between 1870 and 1920, approximately 20 million Europeans arrived in the United States. Before 1890, most immigrants came from countries in western and northern Europe, including Great Britain, Ireland, and Germany. Beginning in the 1890s, however, increasing numbers came from southern and eastern Europe, especially Italy, Austria-Hungary, and Russia. In 1905 alone, about a million people arrived from these countries through the "golden door" to the land of opportunity.

Many of these new immigrants left their homelands to escape religious persecution. Whole villages of Jews—businesspeople, intellectuals, workers, and farmers —were driven out of Russia by pogroms. These were organized anti-Semitic

SECTION 1 RESOURCES

PRINT RESOURCES

IN-DEPTH RESOURCES: UNIT 2
Guided Reading, p. 37
Skillbuilder Practice: Interpreting Graphs, p. 41
Primary Source: Artifacts from Ellis Island, p. 46
Literature: from *Call It Sleep* by Henry Roth, p. 50

READING STUDY GUIDE, p. 77

ACCESS FOR STUDENTS ACQUIRING ENGLISH
Guided Reading (Spanish), p. 100
Skillbuilder Practice: Interpreting Graphs (Spanish), p. 104

SPANISH READING STUDY GUIDE, p. 77

FORMAL ASSESSMENT
Section Quiz, p. 92

ALTERNATIVE ASSESSMENT BOOK
See forms for supporting and scoring alternative activities.

TECHNOLOGY RESOURCES

GEOGRAPHY TRANSPARENCIES
G15, Where the Foreign-Born Lived, 1900

CD-ROM Electronic Library of Primary Sources

VIDEO *American Stories* video series
American Portfolio: A Videodisc for U.S. History user's guide, pp. 149–152

INTERNET http://www.mlushistory.com

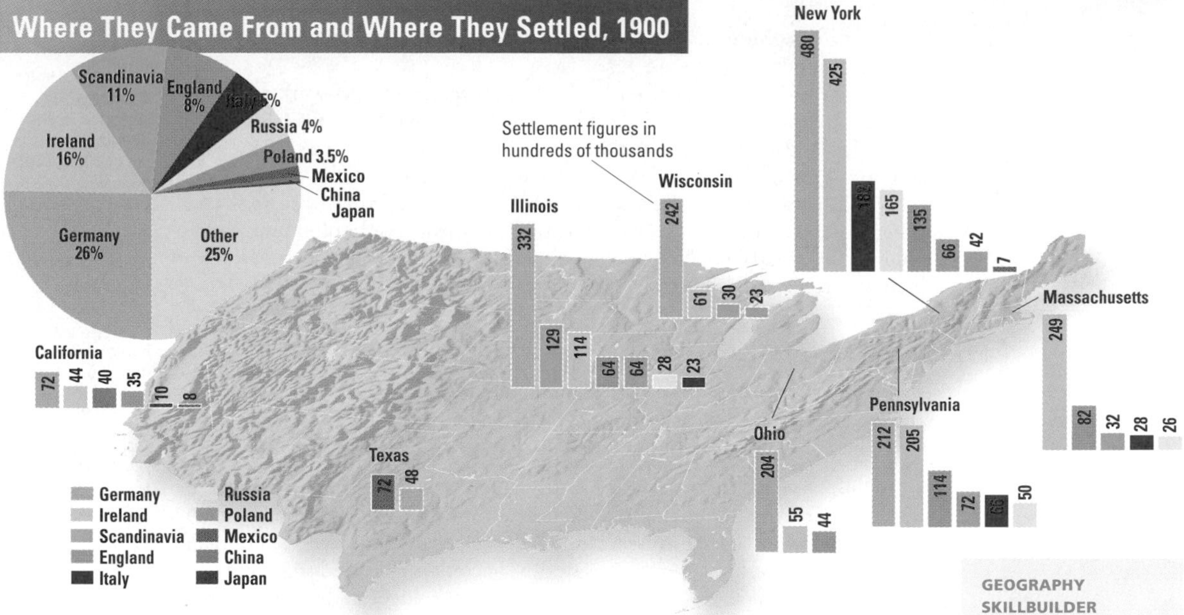

GEOGRAPHY SKILLBUILDER

MOVEMENT

Where did the greatest number of Italian immigrants settle? Which two states combined had about the same number of Irish immigrants as Illinois?

Skillbuilder Answer
Italians: New York.
Irish: Ohio and Wisconsin.

campaigns that led to the massacre of Jews during the early 1880s and early 1900s.

Other Europeans left because of rising population. Between 1800 and 1900, the population in Europe more than doubled, reaching 432 million. This population explosion resulted in a scarcity of land for farming. Farmers as well as laborers often found themselves competing for too few industrial jobs. Some emigrated to the United States, where jobs were supposedly plentiful.

Finally, there was a spirit of reform and revolt in Europe, especially after the political disturbances in France, Germany, Italy, and elsewhere in the late 1840s. Many young European men and women who were influenced by the spirit of these movements sought to start independent lives in the United States.

IMMIGRANTS FROM CHINA AND JAPAN While waves of Europeans arrived on the shores of the East Coast, Chinese immigrants came to the West Coast in smaller numbers. Between 1851 and 1883, about 200,000 Chinese arrived. Many came to seek their fortunes after the discovery of gold in 1848 sparked the California gold rush. The Chinese helped build the nation's first transcontinental railroad as well as other railroads in the West. When the railroads were completed, they turned to farming, mining, and domestic service. Chinese immigration was sharply limited by a congressional act in 1882.

In 1884, the Japanese government allowed Hawaiian planters to recruit Japanese workers, and a Japanese emigration boom began. When the United States annexed Hawaii in 1898, Japanese emigration to the West Coast increased. As word of comparatively high American wages spread in Japan, the number of Japanese who entered the United States each year reached about 10,000. By 1920, more than 200,000 Japanese lived on the West Coast.

A. Answer Mainly from eastern and southern Europe, Asia, and Mexico.

THINK THROUGH HISTORY
A. *Summarizing* *Where did the new immigrants come from?*

IMMIGRANTS FROM THE WEST INDIES AND MEXICO Between 1880 and 1920, about 260,000 immigrants arrived in the eastern and southeastern United States from the West Indies. They came from Jamaica, Cuba, Puerto Rico, and other islands. Many West Indians left their homelands because jobs were scarce.

The Mexican population in the United States also increased. Unlike the Europeans, Asians, and West Indians, however, some Mexicans became U.S. residents without even leaving home. As a result of the annexation of Texas in 1845 and the treaty with Mexico in 1848, the United States acquired vast

OBJECTIVE
① **INSTRUCT**

Through the "Golden Door"

Discussing Key Ideas

- Immigrants come from Europe, Japan, China, the West Indies, and Mexico.
- Some emigrate because of overpopulation, famine, or religious or political persecution.

IN-DEPTH RESOURCES: UNIT 2
Guided Reading, p. 37

ACCESS FOR STUDENTS ACQUIRING ENGLISH
Guided Reading (Spanish), p. 100

ELECTRONIC LIBRARY OF PRIMARY SOURCES
from *The Days of Our Years* by Israel Kasovich

HISTORY FROM VISUALS

Where They Came From and Where They Settled, 1900

Reading the Map Show students that the map, bar graph, and pie chart present essentially the same information in different ways in order to make the material easier to understand. Tell them, for example, that green is used on the pie chart to represent the Irish and that it is used again on the bar graphs to show Irish immigrants.

Extension Ask students to use a world almanac to find the latest U.S. immigration figures. Then have them prepare a bar graph showing the percentage of immigrants from each continent.

GEOGRAPHY TRANSPARENCIES
G15, Where the Foreign-Born Lived, 1900

TEACHING OPTION

Skillbuilder Mini-Lesson: Interpreting Graphs

Explaining the Skill Graphs offer illustrations of statistics and often make numerical information and relationships easier to grasp. Visual features such as color and size as well as verbal labels and measurements on a graph all help clarify the information presented.

Applying the Skill: Where They Came From Have students study the graphs on this page, noting how the colors and the relative sizes of the bars and the pie-graph wedges communicate information. Then ask,

1. Which state has the most countries represented in its immigrant population? *New York.* The fewest? *Texas.*
2. Which states have Scandinavian populations? *Illinois, Wisconsin, New York, Massachusetts.*
3. What similarities and differences in foreign settlement do you see between the eastern states and California? *Both have sizable German and Irish populations. No significant Italian or Russian population in California, but that state has more Chinese and Japanese than the eastern states.*

IN-DEPTH RESOURCES: UNIT 2
Skillbuilder Practice: Interpreting Graphs, p. 41

OBJECTIVE

② INSTRUCT

Life in the New Land

▶ ***Starting with the Student***
Ask students to describe the most difficult journey they have ever undertaken.

- Ask them how it compares with the kind of journey immigrants faced.
- Have students tell what hardships endured by immigrants were similar to hardships they faced on their journey.

▶ ***Discussing Key Ideas***

- Immigrants endure a frightening and uncomfortable journey in crowded, unsanitary quarters.
- Immigrants on both coasts have to pass a physical exam, prove they are literate in a language, meet legal requirements, and have at least $25.
- The newcomers seek out people of their own native culture.

MORE ABOUT . . .
The Transatlantic Journey
Toward the end of the 1800s, the price for a steerage ticket across the Atlantic was only $15, considerably less than it had been at the start of the 1800s. Why the cheaper fare? Toward the end of the century, the United States was exporting to Europe bulky raw materials, such as cotton, timber, tobacco, and wheat. On the return trip, the ships carried less bulky luxury items, such as china, linens, and wines. That left plenty of room for passengers.

territories from Mexico. Many of the residents of these territories chose to become American citizens.

Other Mexicans immigrated to the United States to find work or to flee political turmoil. As a result of the 1902 National Reclamation Act (also known as the Newlands Act), which encouraged the irrigation of arid land, new farmland was created in many Western states, including Texas, Arizona, and California. This farmland drew Mexican farm workers northward to seek jobs. After 1910, political and social upheavals in Mexico prompted even more immigration. Nearly a million people—7 percent of the population of Mexico at the time—came to the United States over the next 20 years.

THINK THROUGH HISTORY
B. THEME ***America in the World*** *What reasons did people from other parts of the world have for leaving their countries to immigrate to the United States?*

B. Answer The desire to escape intolerable conditions such as land shortages, famine, and political or religious persecution; the prospect of jobs, cheap land, or higher wages.

Life in the New Land

No matter what part of the globe immigrants came from, they faced many adjustments. Having left behind all that was familiar, they were plunged into an alien—and often unfriendly—culture.

A DIFFICULT JOURNEY By the 1870s, almost all immigrants traveled by steamship. The trip across the Atlantic Ocean from Europe took approximately one week, while the Pacific crossing from Asia took nearly three weeks. For many immigrants, the long sea journey was stormy, uncomfortable, and frightening.

Many immigrants traveled in steerage or in the cargo holds below a ship's waterline. Rarely allowed on deck, immigrants spent most of the trip crowded together in the gloom, unable to exercise or catch a breath of fresh air. They often had to sleep in louse-infested bunks and share toilet facilities with many other passengers. Under these conditions, diseases spread quickly, and some immigrants died before they reached their destination. For those who survived, like Rosa Cavalleri from Italy, the first glimpse of America could be breathtaking.

A PERSONAL VOICE

America! . . . We were so near it seemed too much to believe. Everyone stood silent—like in prayer. . . . Then we were entering the harbor. The land came so near we could almost reach out and touch it. . . . Everyone was holding their breath. Me too. . . . Some boats had bands playing on their decks and all of them were tooting their horns to us and leaving white trails in the water behind them.

ROSA CAVALLERI, quoted in *Rosa: The Life of an Italian Immigrant*

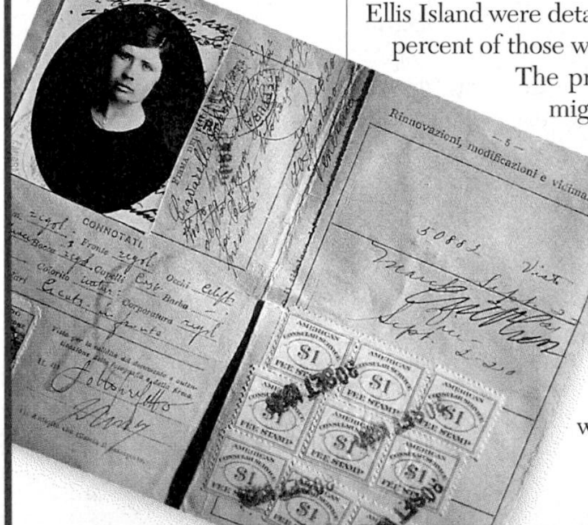

Many foreign governments issued passports to their citizens who were planning to emigrate. In this way they could control the number of trained professionals and young men of military age who left the country.

ELLIS ISLAND After initial moments of excitement, the immigrants faced loneliness, homesickness, and the anxiety of not knowing whether they would be admitted to the United States. They had to pass inspection at immigration stations, such as the one at Castle Garden in New York, which was later moved to **Ellis Island** in New York Harbor. About 20 percent of the immigrants who arrived at Ellis Island were detained for a day or more before being inspected. Only about 2 percent of those who reached Ellis Island had to return home, however.

The processing of immigrants on Ellis Island was an ordeal that might take five hours or more. First, they had to pass a physical examination by a doctor. Any who were found to have a serious health problem or a contagious disease, such as tuberculosis, were promptly sent home. Those who passed the medical exam then reported to a government inspector. The inspector checked documents and questioned immigrants to determine whether they met the legal requirements for entering the United States. The requirements included passing a literacy test in their native language, proving that they were able to work, and showing that they had at least $25.

TEACHING OPTIONS

Exploring Themes

America in the World Immigration to other nations of the world was also at an increase during the late 1800s and early 1900s. Between 1850 and 1930, about 6 1/2 million people immigrated to Canada. Most came from Great Britain and the United States. In the late 1800s, Chinese immigrants were brought into Canada to work on the construction of the Canadian railroad. About 5 million immigrants arrived in Latin America between 1850 and 1930. Most of these immigrants came from Italy, Spain, and Portugal. After gold was discovered in Australia in the 1850s, many non-British immigrants arrived in Australia as well as New Zealand.

Making Connections Across Cultures

Cultural Heritage One of the fascinating exhibits at the Ellis Island Museum is a display of items immigrants brought with them from their countries of origin. Since passengers in steerage were allowed only a hundred pounds of goods, immigrants had to be very selective in what they took. Among the cherished items on display are musical instruments, pieces of lace finery, cobblers' tools, books, religious items, family pictures, and handmade quilts. Ask students why each of these objects would have been treasured by its owner.

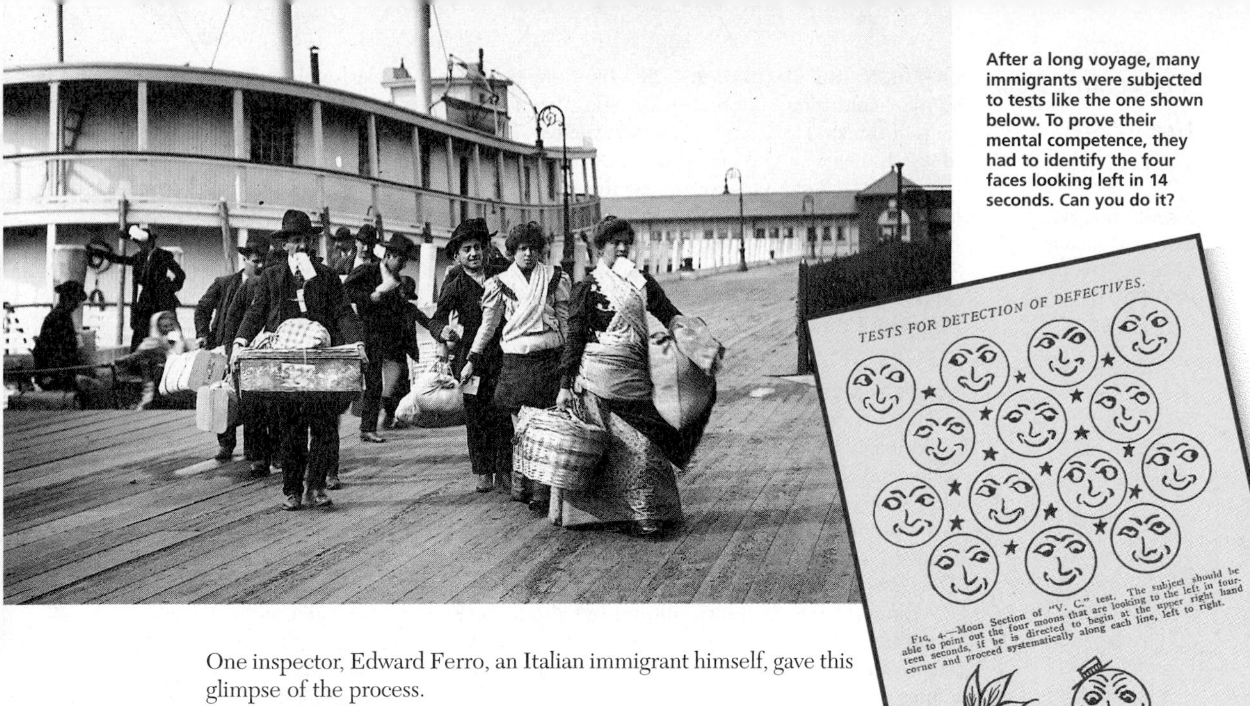

TESTS FOR DETECTION OF DEFECTIVES.
FIG. 4.—Moon Section of "V. C." test. The subject should be able to point out the four moons that are looking to the left in fourteen seconds, if he is directed to begin at the upper right hand corner and proceed systematically along each line, left to right.
A.
B.
C.
D.
E.
FIG. 5.—The Key Section of the "V. C." test. The time
has not been worked out for this section, but it is hardly
valuable. "A" is shown the subject and he is asked to
nearest like it in Fig. 1, "B" is shown and he is asked to
in Fig. 3, "C" is shown and he is asked to find it in Fig.
is shown and he is asked to find it in Fig. 2, and "E"
and he is asked to find it in Fig. 4.

After a long voyage, many immigrants were subjected to tests like the one shown below. To prove their mental competence, they had to identify the four faces looking left in 14 seconds. Can you do it?

One inspector, Edward Ferro, an Italian immigrant himself, gave this glimpse of the process.

A PERSONAL VOICE

The language was a problem of course, but it was overcome by the use of interpreters. We had interpreters on the island who spoke practically every language.

It would happen sometimes that these interpreters—some of them—were really softhearted people and hated to see people being deported, and they would, at times, help the aliens by interpreting in such a manner as to benefit the alien and not the government.

EDWARD FERRO, quoted in *I Was Dreaming to Come to America*

From 1892 to 1943, Ellis Island was the chief immigration station in the United States. More than 16 million immigrants passed through its noisy, bustling facilities. During the peak immigration years from 1905 to 1907, as many as 11,000 immigrants a day hurried down the long staircase leading to the ferry that would take them to New York City and their new lives.

ANGEL ISLAND While European immigrants arriving on the East Coast passed through Ellis Island, Asians—primarily Chinese—arriving on the West Coast gained admission at **Angel Island** in San Francisco Bay. Between 1910 and 1940, about 50,000 Chinese immigrants entered the United States through Angel Island. In contrast to the procedure at Ellis Island, processing at Angel Island included harsh questioning and a long detention while government officials decided whether to admit or reject an immigrant.

The Angel Island facility consisted of filthy, ramshackle buildings in which Chinese immigrants were confined like prisoners. To protest these terrible conditions, some immigrants rioted in 1919. Others expressed their feelings by composing poems, which they wrote on the walls. Some of these poems express the difficulties of the journey, anger at being detained, and disappointment with their new home. One immigrant summarized it this way: "Everyone says travelling to North America is / a pleasure. / I suffered misery on the ship and sadness in / the wooden building. / After several interrogations, still I am not / done."

An Angel Island "wall poem" expresses the feelings of a Chinese immigrant.

C. Answer Medical and administrative inspections and, on Angel Island, harsh questioning and detention.

THINK THROUGH HISTORY
C. THEME ***Immigration and Migration*** *What difficulties did immigrants face in gaining admission to the United States?*

MORE ABOUT . . .
Ellis Island

The buildings on Ellis Island were restored in the 1980s, and the Ellis Island Immigration Museum opened in 1990. Have students compare Ellis Island in New York Harbor with Angel Island in San Francisco Bay by making a chart listing similarities and differences between the two places.

	Similarities	Differences
Ellis Island and Angel Island		

IN-DEPTH RESOURCES: UNIT 2
Primary Source: Artifacts from Ellis Island, p. 46

Block Schedule TEACHING OPTION **Time Needed: 30 Minutes**

Cooperative Activity: Writing Letters or Poems About Immigrant Experiences

Task: Students will write letters or poems based on an imagined immigrant experience.

Purpose: To sensitize students to the difficulties faced by newcomers in a strange land.

Activity: Ask each group of three or four students to select a particular immigrant experience. The group should create a letter or poem expressing one immigrant's feelings, observations, and ways of dealing with the problems of being a newcomer. One student might be the recorder, a second the facilitator, another the timekeeper, and a fourth the presenter of the group's letter or poem.

Building a Portfolio: Students adding a letter or poem to their portfolios should attach a note pointing out their own contribution to the work.

ALTERNATIVE ASSESSMENT BOOK
Standards for Evaluating a Cooperative Activity

Standards for Evaluation
Letters or poems should . . .

- reflect the background and feelings of the writer
- give adequate details about the setting and the events
- be written using appropriate form and style

OBJECTIVE

3 INSTRUCT

Immigration Restrictions

▶ ***Discussing Key Ideas***

- As increasing numbers of immigrants enter the country, anti-immigrant sentiment grows.
- Asians are discriminated against more than whites, and from 1882 until 1943 most Chinese immigration is banned.
- The Gentlemen's Agreement limits Japanese immigration.

ELECTRONIC LIBRARY OF PRIMARY SOURCES

from Chinese Exclusion Act of 1882; Twelve Hundred More (a popular anti-Chinese song)

Issues for the 21st Century

The Debate over Immigration

Connect immigration in the late 1800s with immigration today by having students read pages 880–883. Then have them answer these questions.

1. What factor contributed to the rise of nativism in the 1800s? *Suspicion of growing numbers of immigrants.*
2. What has been the trend in the admission of immigrants to the United States since 1940? *Steady increase.*
3. Compare the arguments against immigration to the United States today with the arguments used in the 1800s. *They are similar.*

"There she lies, the great Melting Pot."

ISRAEL ZANGWILL,
BRITISH AUTHOR AND COINER OF THE TERM "MELTING POT"

EXPERIENCING CULTURE SHOCK Immigrants also had to deal with **culture shock**—confusion and anxiety resulting from immersion in a culture whose ways of thinking and acting they didn't understand. Some con men and thieves took advantage of the newcomers' bewilderment and stole their money and possessions. Most immigrants faced the ongoing nightmare of finding a place to live, getting a job, and dealing with the problems of daily life while trying to understand an alien language and customs.

Many immigrants reacted to culture shock by seeking out people who shared their cultural values, practiced their religion, and spoke their native language. Ethnic communities sprang up in areas that had large concentrations of immigrants.

COOPERATION FOR SURVIVAL The ethnic communities were life rafts for immigrants, who often clung to them fiercely. People pooled their money to build neighborhood churches or synagogues. They formed social clubs where young and old could meet to share experiences, offer mutual support, and enjoy one another's company. Groups of immigrants set up aid societies that furnished medical treatment for members and helped with medical costs. They founded orphanages and old people's homes and established cemeteries. They even published newspapers in their own languages.

D. Answer They helped one another, forming ethnic enclaves, social clubs, and aid societies.

THINK THROUGH HISTORY
D. *Clarifying* *How did immigrants deal with the challenges they faced?*

Committed to their own cultures but also trying hard to grow into their new identities, many immigrants came to think of themselves as "hyphenated" Americans. As hard as they tried to fit in, these new Polish- and Italian- and Chinese-Americans felt increasing friction as they rubbed shoulders with people born and raised in the United States. Native-born people often disliked the immigrants' unfamiliar customs and languages and viewed them as a threat to the American way of life.

Residents of San Francisco's Chinatown survey their adopted country from a doorway in Rag Alley.

Immigration Restrictions

At the turn of the century, many native-born Americans thought of their country as a **melting pot,** a mixture of people of different cultures and races who blended together by abandoning their native languages and customs. Many new immigrants, however, refused to give up their cultural identities in order to merge into American society. As growing numbers of immigrants entered the country, strong anti-immigrant feelings emerged, and the government reacted by passing legislation that restricted immigration.

THE RISE OF NATIVISM One response to the growth in immigration was nativism, or overt favoritism toward native-born Americans. Nativist sentiments gave rise to anti-immigrant groups and led to a demand for immigration restrictions. Some nativists did not mind immigrants from the "right" countries—identified by one observer as "British, German, and Scandinavian stock, historically free, energetic, progressive." The problem, they thought, was immigrants from the "wrong" countries—"Slav, Latin, and Asiatic races, historically down-trodden . . . and stagnant."

Nativism gained support as suspicion and fear of foreigners grew. For example, many native-born Americans, the majority of whom were Protestants, feared the growing influence of the Roman Catholics and Jews who were emigrating from Europe in increasing numbers. Nativist groups like the American Protective Association, founded in 1887, launched vicious anti-Catholic attacks, and many colleges, businesses, and social clubs refused to admit Jews.

Some Americans believed that Anglo-Saxons—the Germanic ancestors of the English—were superior to other ethnic groups, an idea widespread in the 19th century. Acting on that belief, the Immigration Restriction

TEACHING OPTIONS

Exploring Themes

Immigration and Migration Americans have been on the move since the founding of the nation. Many early settlers stayed along the coast, but others moved westward in search of rich farmland. Southerners moved west, to Kentucky and Tennessee, when their land began to erode. The California gold rush and the offer of free land through the Homestead Act of 1862 spurred more migration from east to west, as did the building of the transcontinental railroad. The Great Depression and drought of the 1930s put Americans on the move again.

Making Connections Across Time

Relations with Russia and Japan In mediating an end to the Russo-Japanese War in 1905, President Theodore Roosevelt was interested in restricting the power of two nations that had the potential to become great international powers. In the closing days of World War II, Japan was America's archenemy. Although an ally in 1945, Russia—then known as the Soviet Union—was soon to become America's nemesis in the Cold War. Today, Japan is one of America's most important trading partners, and Russia is struggling with change as it develops closer ties to the West.

League, a nativist group founded in Boston in 1894, campaigned to keep out "undesirable classes" from southern and eastern Europe. In 1896, at the league's urging, Congress passed a bill that required a literacy test for these new immigrants. Although President Cleveland vetoed the bill, it was a powerful statement of public sentiment.

ANTI-ASIAN SENTIMENT On the West Coast, prejudice against Asians was first directed at the Chinese. This sentiment was particularly strong because the Chinese, in addition to having a "strange" language and unfamiliar customs, looked markedly different from most native-born Americans. In the 1800s and early 1900s, most Chinese men wore their hair in a long braid, called a queue, and dressed in a quilted cotton jacket, broad cotton pants, and a wide-brimmed hat.

THINK THROUGH HISTORY
E. *Making Inferences* *Why do you think Asians received such harsh treatment in California?*

E. Answer Their unfamiliar appearance and languages provoked racial and cultural prejudice and fear; they provided competition in the job market.

The depression of 1873 intensified anti-Chinese sentiment in California. Jobs were scarce, and native-born workers feared that work would go to Chinese immigrants, who would accept lower wages. Violent anti-Chinese riots erupted, and labor groups exerted political pressure on the government to restrict Asian immigration. Terence V. Powderly, the head of the Knights of Labor, spoke forcefully for general restrictions on the Chinese. The founder of the Workingmen's Party, Denis Kearney, headed the anti-Chinese movement in California. He made hundreds of speeches throughout the state, each ending with the message "The Chinese must go!"

In 1882, Congress slammed the door on Chinese immigration for ten years by passing the **Chinese Exclusion Act.** This act banned entry to all Chinese except students, teachers, merchants, tourists, and government officials. In 1892, Congress extended the law for another ten years. In 1902, Chinese immigration was prohibited indefinitely; the law was not repealed until 1943.

THE GENTLEMEN'S AGREEMENT The fears that had led to anti-Chinese agitation were extended to Japanese and other Asian people in the early 1900s. In 1906, the local board of education in San Francisco segregated all Chinese, Japanese, and Korean children and put them in special Asian schools. Anti-American riots erupted in Japan in response to this segregation, prompting President Theodore Roosevelt to intervene. He persuaded San Francisco authorities to withdraw the segregation order. In exchange, under the **Gentlemen's Agreement** of 1907–1908, Japan's government agreed to limit emigration to the United States.

Although doorways for immigrants had been all but closed to Asians on the West Coast, cities in the East and the Midwest teemed with European immigrants—and with urban opportunities and challenges.

ON THE WORLD STAGE

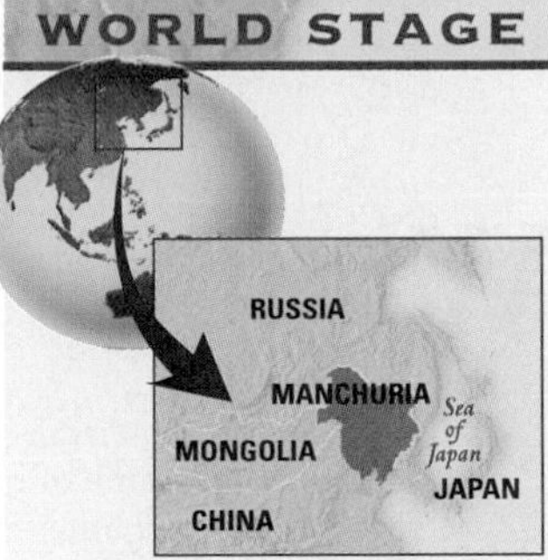

RUSSO–JAPANESE WAR

As the United States turned its back on Chinese immigrants at the end of the 19th century, a nationalistic group in China—the Boxers—was attempting to drive all foreigners from the country. In 1900, Russia occupied Manchuria, a northern Chinese province, in order to intervene in the Boxer Rebellion. Four years later, when Russia had not retreated, the Japanese invaded the region, sparking the Russo-Japanese War. Japan won striking victories, but as its resources dwindled, it turned to President Theodore Roosevelt to mediate the conflict. Roosevelt agreed, reasoning that it was in America's interest to contain both Russia and Japan. Japan's show of power inspired distrust of the island nation and increased the level of anti-Japanese feeling in the United States.

Section 1 Assessment

1. TERMS & NAMES

Identify:
- Ellis Island
- Angel Island
- culture shock
- melting pot
- Chinese Exclusion Act
- Gentlemen's Agreement

2. SUMMARIZING Create a diagram such as the one below. List two or more causes of each effect.

Causes →	Effect
1. 2. 3.	Immigrants leave their home countries.
1. 2. 3.	Immigrants face hardships in the United States.
1. 2. 3.	Some nativists want to restrict immigration.

3. FORMING OPINIONS Which group of immigrants faced the greatest challenges in the United States? Why?

THINK ABOUT
- the difficulties of travel to the United States
- where the immigrants settled
- the opportunities open to each immigrant group

4. SYNTHESIZING What arguments can you make against nativism and anti-immigrant feeling?

THINK ABOUT
- the personal qualities of immigrants
- the reasons for anti-immigrant feeling
- the contributions of immigrants to the United States

ANSWERS

1. TERMS & NAMES

Ellis Island, p. 276
Angel Island, p. 277
culture shock, p. 278
melting pot, p. 278
Chinese Exclusion Act, p. 279
Gentlemen's Agreement, p. 279

2. SUMMARIZING

Possible Responses:
Leaving home countries: Poverty; religious persecution; shortage of agricultural land; lack of industrial jobs; spirit of reform.
Facing hardships in U.S.: New, unfamiliar culture; harsh interrogation and detention; prejudice and discrimination; problems of urban life; culture shock.
Nativists wanting to restrict immigration: Growing immigration; suspicion and fear of differences; religious intolerance; racial prejudice; economic depression.

3. FORMING OPINIONS

Possible Response: Many students may say that the Chinese faced the most prejudice, because of their different appearance and customs, and because of the fear that they would take jobs away from native-born workers.

4. SYNTHESIZING

Possible Responses: Immigrants were brave and willing to work hard; there is cultural value in being exposed to many customs and ways of life; nativists themselves were descendants of immigrants.

ON THE WORLD STAGE

Russo-Japanese War

Critical Thinking: Analyzing Issues Ask students to distinguish between mediating a foreign dispute and intervening in such a dispute. Have them suggest recent instances in which American presidents have mediated or intervened. *President Carter mediated the dispute between Israel and Egypt; President Clinton has intervened in Haiti and in Bosnia by sending in American soldiers.*

ASSESS & RETEACH

Section 1 Assessment

Have groups of students divide up the questions and work together to find the answers.

Self-Assessment

Have students develop an analogy between the controversy surrounding immigration in 1870–1920 and the controversy surrounding immigration today.

Section Quiz

FORMAL ASSESSMENT
Section Quiz, p. 92

Reteach

Show the video "From China to Chinatown" again and discuss the immigration issues raised in the film.

AMERICAN STORIES **video series**
"From China to Chinatown"

CLOSE

European immigrants, eager to find work and new opportunities, poured into the cities of the East and the Midwest. Anti-Asian sentiment led the United States to ban Chinese immigration for over 60 years and to limit Japanese immigration.

Tracing Themes

OBJECTIVES

1. To explore Americans' different definitions of the American dream.
2. To recognize the role of the American dream in inspiring immigration to and migration within America.

FOCUS & MOTIVATE

▶ ***Starting with the Student***
The phrase "the American dream" recurs in political discussions. Ask students what the term means to them. Then ask whether they think the meaning is the same for every generation.

MORE ABOUT . . .
The American Dream for African Americans
African-American leaders have often defined the American dream as one of equal rights and opportunities for all Americans. Martin Luther King, Jr., described it in his famous "I Have a Dream" speech, delivered at the Lincoln Memorial in Washington, D.C., in 1963. Two years earlier, at Lincoln University in Pennsylvania, King delivered a commencement address entitled "The American Dream," in which he told his audience: "America is essentially a dream, a dream as yet unfulfilled. It is a dream of a land where men of all races, of all nationalities and of all creeds can live together as brothers."

TRACING THEMES
THE AMERICAN DREAM

What Is the American Dream?

What is the American dream? A 17th-century colonist's setting sail in search of religious freedom? An 18th-century revolutionary's fighting for political independence? A 19th-century African-American freedman's farming his own plot of land in Kansas? A 20th-century couple's buying their first home or car? It is all of these—and more. The American dream has as many faces as there are Americans. And it's still being dreamed.

European and Asian Immigrants Immigrants, hoping to escape religious persecution or to explore new economic opportunities, left their homelands by the thousands in pursuit of a chance for a better life.

1890
CHANGING FRONTIERS

As immigrants flooded onto both coasts of the United States and white settlers pushed westward, many competing dreams collided.

1620
THE PILGRIMS

A group of people who wanted the freedom to practice their religion risked a treacherous voyage across the Atlantic to build a colony in an unknown land.

African Americans
After the Civil War, many emancipated African Americans in the South became sharecroppers or tenant farmers. Others later moved north and west, looking for work and for opportunities for their children.

RECOMMENDED RESOURCES

Books

Hearn, Charles R. *The American Dream in the Great Depression.* Westport, CT: Greenwood, 1977. How hard times affected the American dream.

Hochschild, Jennifer L. *Facing Up to the American Dream.* Princeton, NJ: Princeton UP, 1995. How race and class differences affect the American dream.

Terkel, Studs. *American Dreams, Lost and Found.* New York: Pantheon, 1980. Interviews with average Americans presenting their views of the American dream.

Videos

The American Dream Contest. Pyramid, 1989. Twelve winners in a contest in which Americans aged 9 to 17 created concepts for short films on the American dream.

The American Dream: Myth or Reality? Guidance Associates. The evolution of the American dream in 19th-century America.

The Promised Land. Discovery and BBC. The expectations and discoveries of African Americans who migrated from the rural South to urban Chicago in the 20th century; narrated by Morgan Freeman.

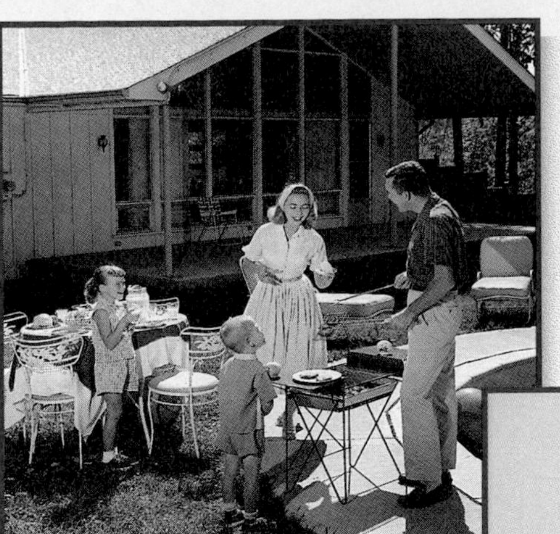

1950
LIFE IN THE SUBURBS

After World War II, many people believed that their troubles were behind them. The American dream blossomed in the form of a new home, a big car, and a nuclear family.

1990
THE RECURRING DREAM

As America moved toward the millennium, minorities and other Americans—like this Latino owner of a tortilla factory in Texas—continued to overcome obstacles and hardships to realize their dreams. In the words of President Bill Clinton, "The American Dream that we were all raised on is a simple but powerful one—if you work hard and play by the rules, you should be given a chance to go as far as your God-given abilities will take you."

Native Americans
The Native Americans on the Great Plains had their dream—the traditional life they had led for centuries. Until the coming of the white settlers, they thrived on the land, free to move about or to cultivate its bounty.

INTERACT WITH HISTORY

1. **ANALYZING ISSUES** Think about the competing dreams mentioned under "1890—Changing Frontiers." What factors might determine whether an individual's American dream is realized?

    SEE SKILLBUILDER HANDBOOK, PAGE 916.

2. **LIVING THE DREAM** What is your American dream for the 21st century? How do you plan to fulfill it? What conflicts or obstacles might you have to overcome? Write down your thoughts and save them in a folder for your American history portfolio. Revisit and revise your dream periodically.

INSTRUCT

▶ *Starting with the Student*
- Ask students what additions they would make to the chronological sequence on pages 280–281.
- Have students share their reactions to President Clinton's definition of the American dream in the 1990s. Ask them what they think the president means by "rules."

▶ *Discussing Key Ideas*
- The American dream has inspired generations of Americans.
- Its definition has varied for different Americans at different times.

HISTORY FROM VISUALS
Reading the Images

Ask students to study the pictures that illustrate the changing American dream.

- Have them list adjectives to describe their impressions of each scene. *Example: The central image of the parents and child looking at the Statue of Liberty suggests hope, ambition, and a dream of a better life.*
- Have students tell which scenes they find especially moving, and why.

INTERACT WITH HISTORY

1. Analyzing Issues

Possible Answers: *Personality, expectations, education, racial or ethnic group, economic conditions, luck, attitude toward future generations, willingness to work hard and play by the rules.*

2. Living the Dream

To organize their thoughts about their American dream for the 21st century, students should think about

- technological advances
- social justice
- the environment
- education
- family life
- their personal careers

Section 2 Overview

OBJECTIVES

1 To describe the movement of immigrants to cities and the opportunities they found there.

2 To explain how cities dealt with problems related to housing, transportation, water supply, sanitation, and fire and police protection.

3 To describe some of the organizations and people who offered help to urban immigrants.

SKILLBUILDER

- Understanding geography: place, movement, p. 283

CRITICAL THINKING

- Theme: Cultural Diversity, p. 283
- Contrasting, p. 283
- Identifying problems, p. 284
- Recognizing effects, pp. 285, 287
- Theme: The American Dream, p. 286
- Analyzing causes, p. 287
- Summarizing, p. 287
- Evaluating leadership, p. 287

FOCUS & MOTIVATE

5-MINUTE WARM-UP

Drawing Conclusions

To discuss the problems facing cities in the late 1800s, have students look at the photos on pages 282, 285, and 286 and answer these questions.

1. What problems of urban life are shown in the photo on page 282?
2. What other problems might result from the situation shown in the photo on page 285?

WARM-UP TRANSPARENCY 7

▶ ***Starting with the Student***
Ask students to suggest ways of helping a newly arrived foreign student adjust to school. Have them tell how the suggestions would help the newcomer to solve some of his or her problems.

IN-DEPTH RESOURCES: UNIT 2
Primary Source: from *How the Other Half Lives* by Riis, p. 47

2 The Problems of Urbanization

TERMS & NAMES
- urbanization
- Americanization movement
- row house
- dumbbell tenement
- Social Gospel movement
- settlement house
- Jane Addams

LEARN ABOUT the rapid growth of American cities in the late 1800s and early 1900s
TO UNDERSTAND the promise and problems of urbanization.

ONE AMERICAN'S STORY

In 1870, at age 21, Jacob Riis left his native Denmark and arrived penniless in the United States. Like many other immigrants, he experienced hunger, homelessness, and life in the slums. Riis overcame the challenges of living in a new country, however, and eventually became a journalist and a tireless reformer. He used his talents to expose the conditions in which he had grown up—the overcrowded, airless, filthy tenements that still housed New York City's poor.

As many as 12 people slept in rooms such as this one in New York City, photographed by Jacob Riis about 1889. The rent was five cents per night.

A PERSONAL VOICE

Be a little careful, please. The hall is dark and you might stumble over the children pitching pennies back there. Not that it would hurt them; kicks and cuffs are their daily diet. They have little else. . . . Close [stuffy]? Yes! What would you have? All the fresh air that enters these stairs is from the hall-door that is forever slamming. . . . Here is a door. Listen! That short hacking cough, that tiny helpless wail—what do they mean? . . . The child is dying with measles. With half a chance it might have lived; but it had none. That dark bedroom killed it.

JACOB RIIS, *How the Other Half Lives*

Making a living in the late 19th and early 20th centuries was not easy. Natural and economic disasters had hit farmers hard, both in Europe and in the United States, and the promise of industrial jobs drew millions of people to American cities. The urban population exploded, jumping from 10 million to 54 million between 1870 and 1920. This rapid urban growth not only revitalized the cities but also created serious problems. As Jacob Riis observed firsthand, these problems had a powerful impact on the new urban poor.

Urban Opportunities

The lure that drew people to the cities was largely the same one that had attracted settlers to the West and immigrants to America—opportunity. The technological boom in the 19th century not only revolutionized age-old occupations, such as farming, but also contributed to the growing industrial strength of the United States. While many settlers were pushing westward to start new lives on the frontier, thousands of other people were drawn to the Northeast and Midwest. The result was rapid **urbanization,** or growth of cities, in those regions.

IMMIGRANTS SETTLE IN CITIES Most of the immigrants who streamed into the United States in the late 19th century became city dwellers because cities were the cheapest and most convenient places to live. Cities also offered unskilled laborers steady jobs in mills and factories and provided the social support of other immigrant families. By 1890, there were twice as many Irish residents in New York City as in Dublin, Ireland, and the world's largest Polish population was not in Warsaw, Poland, but in Chicago. By 1910, immigrant families made up more than half the total population of 18 major American cities.

SECTION 2 RESOURCES

PRINT RESOURCES

IN-DEPTH RESOURCES: UNIT 2
Guided Reading, p. 38
Geography Application: Industry and Urban Growth, p. 42
Outline Map: The Urbanization of America, p. 44
Primary Sources: from *How the Other Half Lives* by Riis, p. 47; from *Twenty Years at Hull-House* by Addams, p. 48
American Lives: Jane Addams, p. 53

READING STUDY GUIDE, p. 79

ACCESS FOR STUDENTS ACQUIRING ENGLISH
Guided Reading (Spanish), p. 101
Geography Application: Industry and Growth (Spanish), p. 105
Outline Map: Urbanization (Spanish), p. 107

SPANISH READING STUDY GUIDE, p. 79

FORMAL ASSESSMENT
Section Quiz, p. 93

ALTERNATIVE ASSESSMENT BOOK
See forms for supporting and scoring alternative activities.

TECHNOLOGY RESOURCES

HUMANITIES TRANSPARENCIES
H15, *Cliff Dwellers* by George Bellows, 1913

CRITICAL THINKING TRANSPARENCIES
CT15, Urban Growth; CT49, From Country to City, 1870–1920

CD-ROM *Our Times*; Electronic Library of Primary Sources

VIDEO *American Portfolio: A Videodisc for U.S. History* user's guide, pp. 146–149

INTERNET http://www.mlushistory.com

Immigrants often clustered in ethnic neighborhoods with others from the same country—or even from the same province or village. Living among people who shared their background enabled the newcomers to speak their own language and practice their customs and religion.

At the same time newcomers were able to learn about their new home through a program of education known as the **Americanization movement.** Schools and voluntary associations provided programs aimed at teaching immigrants the English language as well as American history and government—subjects that were necessary to help the newcomers become citizens. The movement also included the teaching of other subjects, such as cooking and social etiquette, designed to assist the immigrants in assimilating into American culture.

Unfortunately, many native-born Americans felt threatened by these mushrooming ethnic communities and expressed their fear by becoming hostile. Overcrowding soon became a problem as well, one that was intensified by the arrival of new urbanites from America's rural areas.

A. Answer For mutual support.

THINK THROUGH HISTORY
A. THEME *Cultural Diversity* *Why did immigrants tend to group together in the cities?*

Ethnic Enclaves in New York City, 1910

Austrian
German
Irish
Italian
Russian
Scandinavian

Light tint indicates at least 20% of population.
Darker tint indicates 40% of population or more.

Nonresidential
No group with more than 20% of population
Boundary between Brooklyn and Queens

BRONX
MANHATTAN
QUEENS
BROOKLYN

GEOGRAPHY SKILLBUILDER
PLACE *What general pattern of settlement do you notice in this map of ethnic neighborhoods in New York City in 1910?*

Skillbuilder Answer Immigrants often settled near others of similar backgrounds.

MIGRATION FROM COUNTRY TO CITY The rapid improvements in farming technology during the second half of the 19th century were good news for some farmers but bad news for others. Inventions such as the McCormick reaper and the steel plow made farming more efficient but meant that fewer laborers were needed to work the land. As use of the new equipment spread across the country, farms merged, and many rural people could not find jobs in agriculture. They left their land and agricultural way of life and made their way to cities to find whatever jobs they could.

Many of the Southern farmers who lost their jobs were African Americans. Other African Americans in the rural South also became aware of the opportunities in large cities. Between 1890 and 1910, about 200,000 African Americans moved north and west, to cities such as Chicago and Detroit, in an effort to escape racial violence, economic hardship, and political oppression. Many found conditions in the cities only somewhat better than those they had left behind. Because of racial prejudice and their inadequate education, they were often forced to take low-paying factory jobs or to work as domestic servants.

B. Answer Both groups had to find jobs. African-American farm workers faced the additional challenge of racial prejudice.

THINK THROUGH HISTORY
B. *Contrasting* *How was the experience of moving to cities similar and different for African-American farm workers and other farm workers?*

URBAN CULTURAL OPPORTUNITIES Although people moved to cities for economic reasons, cultural opportunities offered an additional attraction. In contrast to the relatively slow-paced life in both immigrants' native villages and American rural communities, life in a city was varied and exciting. Each city had a personality all its own. In New York City, you had an opportunity to see the first moving pictures. In Chicago, you could join your neighbors on an outing to the Columbian Exposition or to Buffalo Bill's Wild West Show. In

OBJECTIVE
① INSTRUCT

Urban Opportunities

▶*Discussing Key Ideas*
- Most new immigrants settle in cities because cities are the cheapest and most convenient places to live.
- New technology makes farming more efficient, resulting in the loss of jobs for some farmworkers, who move to cities.
- Cities offer diverse cultural opportunities.

IN-DEPTH RESOURCES: UNIT 2
Guided Reading, p. 38
Geography Application: Industry and Urban Growth, p. 42
Outline Map: The Urbanization of America, p. 44

ACCESS FOR STUDENTS ACQUIRING ENGLISH
Guided Reading (Spanish), p. 101

CRITICAL THINKING TRANSPARENCIES
CT15, Urban Growth
CT49, From Country to City, 1870–1920

HISTORY FROM VISUALS
Ethnic Enclaves in New York City, 1910

Reading the Map Point out that each ethnic group is represented by two colors.

Extension Ask students to review the map and answer the following question:
- In what ways was the building of bridges an important improvement? *People and businesses had better access to areas away from the port; it was easier to commute to work and to visit family.*

TEACHING OPTIONS

Making Connections Across Time

Immigrants and the Economy Most immigrants coming into the United States today start by taking low-paying jobs as domestics, unskilled workers, or workers in the burgeoning service industries, such as fast-food restaurants, laundries, car washes, and dry cleaners. An immigrant's income may be subsidized by state or local funds until the immigrant becomes self-supporting. Such government welfare was not available for earlier immigrants, although charitable organizations, both religious and secular, offered assistance. Today's immigrants provide revenue to the government by paying sales and income taxes, neither of which existed in the 19th century.

Teaching Gifted and Talented Students

Making a Map of Your Town or City Ask students to do some research in the library and on the Internet to discover what ethnic groups have played an important role in the history of their community. Have them use the results of their research to make a map, similar to "Ethnic Enclaves in New York City, 1910," that shows what groups lived in their community, and where, at a specific time. They might use the year 1910, or they might show the ethnic makeup of their community at a later time.

OBJECTIVE

② **INSTRUCT**

Urban Problems

▶ ***Starting with the Student*** Ask students to list reasons they might want to live in a city. Then ask them to make a list of problems related to urban living.

▶ ***Discussing Key Ideas***
- As the urban population increases, cities struggle with many problems.
- Among the problems cities face are overcrowded, unsanitary housing; mass transportation needs; lack of a fresh water supply; and fires and crime.

HUMANITIES TRANSPARENCIES

H15, *Cliff Dwellers* by George Bellows, 1913

HISTORICAL SPOTLIGHT

Streetcar Suburbs

Critical Thinking: Cause and Effect Use the diagram in this feature to discuss with students how better transportation after 1880 improved the lives of the people living in urban and suburban settings.

MORE ABOUT . . .

Row-House Living

Living in a row house was comfortable. Each room had a brass fixture for gas jets or electric bulbs. The furnace fire glowed all night, so people did not wake up shivering with cold. A gas flame heated the water in the water tank and fueled the stove. And every house had a bathroom with running water and an indoor toilet.

Boston, you could travel to the ball park and watch the hometown Boston Nationals battle their way to a championship. Cultural attractions such as these sometimes made up for the hardships that life in the city presented.

Urban Problems

As the urban population skyrocketed, city governments faced serious problems, such as how to provide adequate housing, transportation, water, and sanitation and how to deal effectively with fire and crime.

HOUSING When the industrial age began, housing options for working-class families in major cities were few and far from satisfactory. A family could buy a house on the outskirts of town, but its members would have to commute to work on often inadequate public transportation. A family could also rent rooms in a boardinghouse in the central city, sharing kitchen and dining-room facilities with other families. As the urban population increased, however, new types of housing were designed to eliminate some disadvantages of these options. For example, **row houses**—single-family dwellings that shared side walls with other similar houses—packed many single-family residences onto a single block.

After working-class families moved away from the central city, immigrants often took over their old housing, sometimes with two or three families occupying a one-family residence. As Jacob Riis noted, these multifamily dwellings, called tenements, were overcrowded and unsanitary.

In 1879, to improve such slum conditions, New York City passed a law that set minimum standards for plumbing and ventilation in apartment buildings. To meet these standards, landlords began building **dumbbell tenements**—long, narrow, five- or six-story buildings that were shaped like barbells. The central part was indented on either side to allow for an air shaft and, thus, an outside window for each room.

C. Answer Overcrowding and unsanitary conditions.

THINK THROUGH HISTORY
C. Identifying Problems *What housing problems did urban working-class families face?*

Since garbage was picked up infrequently, people sometimes dumped it into the air shafts, where it attracted rats and vermin. To keep out the stench, residents nailed windows shut. Though established with good intent, dumbbell tenements soon became even worse places to live than the converted single-family residences.

TRANSPORTATION Getting around a city safely and efficiently was as much of a problem as finding a steady job and a decent place to live. Before industrialization, people went on foot or in horse-drawn vehicles. But innovations in mass transit enabled large numbers of workers to go to and from jobs more easily. Street cars attached to moving underground cables were introduced in San Francisco in 1873. In 1888, the first practical electric streetcar line began operating in Richmond, Virginia. In addition, new modes of transportation were developed to take advantage of space available above and below street level. In Boston, for example, electric subways began running underneath the city's busy streets in 1897. By the early 20th century, mass-transit networks in many urban areas linked city neighborhoods to one another and outlying communities to the central business district and other focal points. As urban populations kept expanding, cities were hard-pressed to keep old transportation systems in good repair and to build new ones to meet the growing demand.

STREETCAR SUBURBS

By the late 19th century, electric streetcars were carrying more than 2 billion fares a year in cities throughout the United States. This new mode of transportation changed not only the way people traveled but also where they lived. As streetcar lines extended outward from the heart of the city, people who were not wealthy were no longer limited to living within walking distance of the workplace. Modest single-family homes and multifamily dwellings sprang up in the urban outskirts served by these lines. These streetcar suburbs offered middle- and working-class families an attractive alternative to inner-city life.

CITY CENTER — Pedestrian city 2 miles — 1880 Horse-drawn streetcar 3.5 miles — 1900 Electric streetcar 6 miles

TEACHING OPTIONS

Exploring Themes

Cultural Diversity In 1900, the average annual income of American workers was about $500. Many workers who lived in cities, however, were able to enrich their drab existence by taking advantage of the many cultural activities that were offered. Places such as Hull House in Chicago and the Henry Street Settlement House in New York offered classes in art, music, and drama. Museums offered free days, and ethnic groups, such as the Yiddish theater in New York, provided reasonably priced entertainment in a particular group's native language.

Exploring Themes

The American Dream To many new immigrants, free public education was a miracle. One immigrant recalled her father had "brought his children to school as if it were an act of consecration." At schools, the children learned about democracy, voting, and civic responsibility. They also gained language proficiency and a background in American history. Many immigrant parents who worked during the day attended night school, where they, too, learned the English language, American history, and how democracy works.

WATER Cities also faced the problem of supplying fresh water that was safe to drink. Before industrialization, many people bought water for drinking and cooking from vendors on horse-drawn carts. As the urban population grew in the 1840s and 1850s, cities such as New York and Cleveland built public waterworks to handle the increasing demand. As late as the 1860s, however, the residents of many cities had grossly inadequate water mains and piped water—or none at all. Even in large cities like New York, homes seldom had indoor plumbing, and residents had to collect water in pails from faucets on the street and heat it for bathing. The necessity of improving water quality to control diseases such as cholera and typhoid fever was obvious. To make city water safer, chlorination was introduced in 1893 and filtration in 1908. These innovations spread slowly, however. In the early 20th century, many city dwellers still had no access to safe water.

Sanitation problems in big cities were overwhelming. It was not unusual to see a dead horse in the street.

SANITATION As the cities grew, so did the challenge of keeping them clean. In most, unsanitary conditions were all too widespread. Horse manure piled up on the streets, sewage flowed through open gutters, and factories spewed foul smoke into the air. Without a dependable system of trash removal, people dumped their garbage into alleys and streets. Although private contractors called scavengers were hired to sweep the streets, collect garbage, and clean outhouses, they often did not do the jobs they were paid to do. Sewer lines and sanitation departments, which many cities had instituted by 1900, helped somewhat in keeping cities clean, but the task of providing healthful urban living conditions was an ongoing challenge for urban leaders.

D. Answer Lack of fresh water and inadequate sanitation created health hazards.

THINK THROUGH HISTORY
D. Recognizing Effects *How did conditions in cities affect people's health?*

FIRE The limited water supply in many cities contributed to another menace: the spread of fires. Major fires occurred in almost every large American city during the 1870s and 1880s. In addition to lacking water with which to combat blazes once they started, most cities were packed with wooden dwellings, which were like kindling waiting to be ignited. The use of candles and kerosene

Fire: Enemy of the City

THE GREAT CHICAGO FIRE OCTOBER 8, 1871	THE SAN FRANCISCO EARTHQUAKE APRIL 18, 1906
The fire burned for 29 hours.	The quake lasted 28 seconds; fires burned for 4 days.
An estimated 300 people died.	An estimated 478 people died.
100,000 were left homeless.	250,000 were left homeless.
More than 3 square miles of the central city was destroyed.	Fire swept through 5 square miles of the city.
Property loss was estimated at $200 million.	Property loss was estimated at $500 million.
17,500 buildings were destroyed.	28,000 buildings were destroyed.

HISTORY FROM VISUALS
Fire: Enemy of the City

Reading the Chart Point out to students that this graphic makes comparisons. They could make charts of their own with the following headings: number of deaths, number left homeless, square miles destroyed, estimated property loss, number of buildings destroyed.

Extension Ask students what measures experts might use today to prevent or contain damage from fires and earthquakes. *They now design earthquake-proof buildings, and use the Richter scale to measure the magnitude of quakes. Experts know how to fire-proof buildings and use asbestos for firefighting gear.*

OUR TIMES San Francisco earthquake and fire

MORE ABOUT . . .
Transportation

In the 1800s, the streets of most American cities were not paved, making them dusty in summer and muddy in winter. Improvements were slow to be made, and there was controversy over what paving material to use. Asphalt was smooth, long-lasting, and easy to clean but very expensive. By the end of the 1800s, however, engineers had developed a cheaper way to make asphalt, and it became widely used in paving city streets.

Block Schedule TEACHING OPTION **Time Needed: 30 Minutes**

Cooperative Activity: Researching Catastrophes

Task: Students will research the San Francisco earthquake of 1906 and the Great Chicago Fire and then write short reports comparing the two disasters.

Purpose: To understand the impact of both catastrophes and to learn about measures taken to contain similar disasters in the future.

Activity: Form teams of three or four students, and ask groups to choose, by lottery, one of the following topics to research:

- Which of the two cities recovered more quickly? Why?
- What effects did each disaster have on long-range city planning?
- What are some of the important differences between the San Francisco earthquake of 1906 and the Great Chicago Fire?

Building a Portfolio: Students adding a research report to their portfolio should attach a note pointing out their own contribution to the project.

ALTERNATIVE ASSESSMENT BOOK
Standards for Evaluating a Cooperative Activity

Standards for Evaluation
Reports should . . .

- show evidence of careful research, based on the use of two or more sources
- include concrete details and examples to illustrate the catastrophes
- be clear and organized

MORE ABOUT . . .
The Great Chicago Fire

The Great Chicago Fire was preceded by a succession of small fires that broke out during the first week of October 1871. At that time, the city was particularly susceptible to fires because there had been almost no rain for three months. On the night of October 8, so the story goes, a wagon driver named Daniel "Peg Leg" Sullivan was drinking whiskey in the barn of his neighbor, Mrs. Catherine O'Leary, as he often did. That night, Sullivan apparently took one nip too many and dropped a kerosene lamp into a pile of hay. Mrs. O'Leary's barn caught fire—and the rest is history. The fire was so destructive that even Chicago's marble courthouse, which had just been built for $1 million and had been considered fireproof, collapsed in the blaze.

OBJECTIVE
③ INSTRUCT

Reformers Mobilize

▶ ***Starting with the Student*** Ask students the following questions:

- If you could start an organization to help some group less fortunate than you, what kind of organization would it be?
- How would you go about setting up such an organization?

(continued on next page)

heaters was also a fire hazard. In San Francisco, deadly fires often broke out in the aftermath of earthquakes. Jack London described the fires that broke out during the San Francisco earthquake of 1906.

A PERSONAL VOICE

On Wednesday morning at a quarter past five came the earthquake. A minute later the flames were leaping upward. In a dozen quarters south of Market Street, in the working-class ghetto, and in the factories, fires started. There was no opposing the flames. . . . The streets were humped into ridges and depressions; . . . steel rails were twisted into perpendicular and horizontal angles. And the great water mains had burst. All the shrewd contrivances and safeguards of man had been thrown out of gear by thirty seconds twitching of the earthcrust.

JACK LONDON, *The Story of an Eyewitness*

At first, most firefighters were volunteers and not always available when their services were needed. Cincinnati, Ohio, tackled this problem when it established the nation's first paid fire department in 1853. By 1900, most cities had full-time professional fire departments. The invention of the automatic fire sprinkler in 1874 and the replacement of many wooden buildings with structures made of brick, stone, and concrete also made cities safer. Despite these various improvements, however, blazes still got out of control. John R. Chapin, an artist for *Harper's Weekly,* described the destruction done by the Great Chicago Fire of 1871: "[The blaze] was devouring the most stately and massive buildings as though they had been the cardboard playthings of a child. . . . One after another they dissolved, like snow on a mountain."

CRIME As the populations of cities increased, so did crime. Pickpockets and thieves flourished in urban crowds, and con men fooled non-English-speaking immigrants and naive country people with clever scams. Crime-ridden areas of certain cities, which were controlled by gangs of young toughs, became known as Murderers' Alleys or Robbers' Roosts. Although New York City organized the first full-time, salaried police force in 1844, it and most other city law enforcement units were too small to adequately protect residents from rising crime and violence.

E. Answer Possible Answers: Overcrowding, lack of affordable housing, health problems, fire, crime, and prejudice toward new immigrants.

THINK THROUGH HISTORY
E. THEME *The American Dream* *Which of the problems facing late-19th-century city dwellers remain problems today?*

Reformers Mobilize

As problems in cities mounted, some Americans worked to find solutions. Social reformers—mostly young, educated men and women from the middle class—established programs to aid the poor and to improve urban life.

Jane Addams helped children who might otherwise have turned to crime leave the streets and improve their lives.

TEACHING OPTIONS

Making Connections Across Time

Gangs Then and Now From the 1850s on, in such cities as Boston, New York, and Chicago, some young immigrants formed gangs for mutual protection and survival. From acts of petty crime, scams against new immigrants, and theft, gangs moved into politics, electioneering, and the stuffing of ballot boxes. Today, gangs still flourish in the major cities and even in suburbia. Some deal in petty crime, others in drug trafficking, big-time gambling, and counterfeiting.

Teaching Less Proficient Readers

Clarifying Ideas To help students clarify the problems in the cities in the late 1800s, copy this chart onto the chalkboard and have students fill it in.

Problems	Causes	Solutions
Housing		
Transportation		
Water		
Sanitation		
Fire		
Crime		

THE SOCIAL GOSPEL MOVEMENT Social welfare reformers targeted their efforts at relieving the poverty of immigrants and other city dwellers. An early reform program, the **Social Gospel movement,** preached salvation through service to the poor. Social Gospel ministers such as Walter Rauschenbusch of New York City and Washington Gladden of Columbus, Ohio—who called his teachings Applied Christianity— inspired followers to erect churches in poor communities and persuaded some business leaders to treat workers more fairly.

THE SETTLEMENT HOUSE MOVEMENT Inspired by the message of the Social Gospel movement, many 19th-century reformers responded to the call to help the urban poor. In the late 1800s, a few reformers established **settlement houses,** community centers in slum neighborhoods that provided assistance and friendship to local men, women, and children—especially immigrants. Many settlement workers lived at the houses so that they could learn firsthand about the problems caused by urbanization and help create solutions.

Run largely by middle-class, college-educated women, settlement houses provided educational, cultural, and social services. They provided classes in such subjects as English, health, crafts, drama, music, and painting, and offered college extension courses. They sponsored reading circles in which volunteers read books aloud to help educate the illiterate. Settlement houses also sent visiting nurses into the homes of the sick and provided whatever aid was needed to secure "support for deserted women, insurance for bewildered widows, damages for injured operators, furniture from the clutches of the installment store."

F. Answer Both movements focused on social problems that the urban poor faced, such as isolation and exploitation. The Social Gospel movement promoted social consciousness, and the settlement houses provided actual aid to the poor.

THINK THROUGH HISTORY
F. Analyzing Causes *How did the Social Gospel and settlement-house movements help the urban poor meet the challenges of city life?*

Early settlement houses in the United States, founded by Charles Stover and Stanton Coit, opened in New York City in 1886. **Jane Addams** and Ellen Gates Starr founded Chicago's Hull House in 1889, and Lillian D. Wald established New York's Henry Street Settlement House in 1893. In 1890, Janie Porter Barrett founded Locust Street Social Settlement in Hampton, Virginia—the first settlement house for African Americans. By 1910, about 400 settlement houses were operating in cities across the country.

The Social Gospel and settlement-house movements firmly established the need for social responsibility toward the urban poor and provided means of addressing some of the ongoing problems of urbanization. A new type of political structure also developed in response to these urban issues. But it soon created problems of its own.

KEY PLAYER

JANE ADDAMS
1860–1935

Jane Addams was a community worker, a champion of organized labor, and a peace advocate. She believed that in all things the best approach to problem solving was to "learn from life itself."

During a trip overseas, she visited England's Toynbee Hall, the first settlement house. She viewed the problems of urban life firsthand—and resolved to do something about them. She co-founded Hull House in Chicago, where she began working to solve neighborhood problems. In time her concerns expanded. She became an antiwar activist, a spokesperson for racial justice, and an advocate for quality-of-life issues, from infant mortality to better care for the aged. In 1931 she was a co-winner of the Nobel Peace Prize.

Until the end of her life, Addams insisted that she was just a "very simple person." But many who know what she accomplished consider her a source of continuing inspiration.

Section 2 Assessment

1. TERMS & NAMES
Identify:
- urbanization
- Americanization movement
- row house
- dumbbell tenement
- Social Gospel movement
- settlement house
- Jane Addams

2. SUMMARIZING Re-create the spider map below on your paper. Write three urban problems on the vertical lines. Fill in details about attempts that were made to solve each problem.

3. RECOGNIZING EFFECTS What effects did the migration from rural areas to the cities in the late 19th century have on urban society?

THINK ABOUT
- the reasons people moved to cities
- the problems caused by rapid urban growth
- the impact of urban growth on rural areas

4. EVALUATING LEADERSHIP Do you think the Social Gospel reformers and those who started settlement houses had realistic goals? Why or why not?

THINK ABOUT
- the motives of the reformers
- the types of reforms they supported
- the impact of their reforms

ANSWERS

1. TERMS & NAMES

urbanization, p. 282

Americanization movement, p. 283

row house, p. 284

dumbbell tenement, p. 284

Social Gospel movement, p. 287

settlement house, p. 287

Jane Addams, p. 287

2. SUMMARIZING

Students should choose three problems.
inadequate housing—dumbbell tenements, row houses; inadequate transportation—new streetcar lines, subways; unsafe water—public waterworks, chlorination, filtration; poor sanitation—sewer lines, sanitation departments; frequent fires—full-time fire departments, replacement of wooden buildings with brick, stone, and concrete ones; high crime—improved police protection.

3. RECOGNIZING EFFECTS

Possible Responses: Overcrowding; competition for jobs.

4. EVALUATING LEADERSHIP

While some students might criticize the reformers and their efforts as unrealistic, others might defend their accomplishments. Students' opinions should be supported with adequate reasons.

(continued from page 286)

Discussing Key Ideas
- Reform-minded church leaders inspire the building of churches in poor neighborhoods and espouse efforts to help the indigent.
- Settlement houses are established in slum areas.

KEY PLAYER
Jane Addams

Critical Thinking: Drawing Conclusions After students have read the information about Jane Addams, have them discuss on what basis they think Addams qualified for the Nobel Peace Prize. *Possible Response: She was a peace advocate, an antiwar activist, and a fighter for racial justice.*

IN-DEPTH RESOURCES: UNIT 2
American Lives: Jane Addams, p. 53
Primary Source: from *Twenty Years at Hull-House* by Addams, p. 48

ELECTRONIC LIBRARY OF PRIMARY SOURCES
"The Modern City and the Municipal Franchise for Women" by Jane Addams

ASSESS & RETEACH

Section 2 Assessment
Have students answer the questions and then note the pages on which the answers can be found.

Self-Assessment
Ask students to choose one of the urban problems discussed in this section and write a one-paragraph solution to the problem.

Section Quiz

FORMAL ASSESSMENT
Section Quiz, p. 93

Reteach
Survey students to find out what part of this section was difficult for them. Use the graphic on page 283 as a discussion starter.

CLOSE

Rapid population growth revitalized the cities but also brought new problems.

Section 3 Overview

OBJECTIVES

1. To explain the role of political machines and political bosses.
2. To describe how politicians' greed and fraud cost taxpayers millions of dollars.

SKILLBUILDERS

- Interpreting cartoons, p. 290
- Interpreting charts, p. 290

CRITICAL THINKING

- Summarizing, pp. 289, 290
- Analyzing motives, p. 289
- Comparing, p. 290
- Generalizing, p. 290
- Analyzing causes, p. 290

FOCUS & MOTIVATE

5-MINUTE WARM-UP

Recognizing Purpose
To gain insight into the workings of political bosses in the nineteenth century, ask students to study the cartoon on page 288 and answer these questions.

1. What does the figure in the cartoon represent?
2. What does the cartoon attempt to show?

WARM-UP TRANSPARENCY 7

▶ ***Starting with the Student***
Ask students if they have ever given someone a gift with the intention of getting something in return. Then ask them if they believe that such a practice is common among politicians today.

3 The Emergence of the Political Machine

TERMS & NAMES
- graft
- political machine
- kickback
- Tammany Hall
- Tweed Ring
- Thomas Nast

LEARN ABOUT the emergence of political machines in American cities in the 19th century
TO UNDERSTAND the role that politics played in shaping urban life.

ONE AMERICAN'S STORY

George Washington Plunkitt was born in 1842 to Irish immigrants in New York City. He quit school when he was 11 years old and went to work in a butcher's shop. Despite a lack of formal education, Plunkitt became a shrewd leader in Tammany Hall, New York City's Democratic political machine. He worked his way up the political ladder from precinct captain to ward boss to state senator. In the process, he became a millionaire, largely through **graft,** or the illegal use of political influence for personal gain.

A PERSONAL VOICE
There's an honest graft, and I'm an example of how it works. . . . My party's in power in the city, and it's goin' to undertake a lot of public improvements. Well, I'm tipped off, say, that they're going to lay out a new park at a certain place. . . . I see my opportunity and I take it. I go to that place and I buy up all the land I can. . . . There's a rush to get my land, which nobody cared particular for before. . . . Ain't it perfectly honest to charge a good price and make a profit on my investment and foresight? Of course it is. Well, that's honest graft.
GEORGE WASHINGTON PLUNKITT, quoted in *The Bosses*

A corrupt 19th-century political boss robs the city treasury by easily cutting through the red tape that bogs the government down.

"Honest" or not, graft and corruption not only lined the pockets of political bosses like Plunkitt but also oiled the workings of the emerging urban political machines.

Political Machines Run the Cities

In the late 19th century, cities were in trouble. Rapid growth, inefficient government, and a climate of Social Darwinism opened the way for a new power structure, the political machine, and a new politician, the city boss.

THE POLITICAL MACHINE A **political machine** was an organized group that controlled the activities of a political party in a city and offered services to voters and businesses in exchange for political or financial support. In the decades after the Civil War, political machines seized control of local government in major cities such as Baltimore, New York, Philadelphia, Boston, and San Francisco.

The political machine was organized like a pyramid. At the pyramid's base were local precinct workers and captains, who worked to gain voters' support on a city block or in a neighborhood and who reported to a ward boss. At election time, the ward boss worked to secure the vote in all the precincts in the ward, or electoral district. In return for their votes, people received city jobs, contracts, or political appointments. Ward bosses helped the poor and gained their votes by doing favors or providing services. As Martin Lomasney, elected ward boss of Boston's West End in 1885, explained, "There's got to be in every ward a guy that any bloke can go to . . . and get help—not justice and the law, but help."

At the top of the pyramid was the city boss. The boss controlled the activities of the political party throughout the city. Like a finely tuned machine,

SECTION 3 RESOURCES

PRINT RESOURCES

IN-DEPTH RESOURCES: UNIT 2
Guided Reading, p. 39
Primary Source: from *The Shame of the Cities* by Lincoln Steffens, p. 49
American Lives: William Marcy Tweed, p. 54

READING STUDY GUIDE, p. 81

ACCESS FOR STUDENTS ACQUIRING ENGLISH
Guided Reading (Spanish), p. 102

SPANISH READING STUDY GUIDE, p. 81

FORMAL ASSESSMENT
Section Quiz, p. 94

ALTERNATIVE ASSESSMENT BOOK
See forms for supporting and scoring alternative activities.

TECHNOLOGY RESOURCES

CD-ROM *Grolier Multimedia Encyclopedia*

VIDEO *American Portfolio: A Videodisc for U.S. History* user's guide, p. 149

INTERNET http://www.mlushistory.com

THINK THROUGH HISTORY
A. Summarizing *In what form was a political machine organized?*

A. Answer Like a pyramid—precinct workers and captains formed the base; the city boss was at the top.

precinct captains, ward bosses, and the city boss worked together to elect their candidates and guarantee the success of the machine.

THE ROLE OF THE POLITICAL BOSS A city boss controlled thousands of municipal jobs, including those in the police, fire, and sanitation departments. Whether or not the boss officially served as mayor, he controlled business licenses and inspections and influenced the courts and other municipal agencies. Bosses like Roscoe Conkling in New York used their power to build parks, sewer systems, and waterworks and gave money to schools, hospitals, and orphanages. Bosses could also provide government support for new businesses, a service for which they were often paid extremely well.

It was not only money that gave city bosses the drive to deal with urban issues. By solving problems, bosses could reinforce voters' loyalty, win additional political support, and extend their influence.

IMMIGRANTS AND THE POLITICAL MACHINE Immigrants received sympathetic understanding from the political machines and in turn became loyal supporters. Many political bosses were first-generation or second-generation immigrants who had been raised in poverty. Few were educated beyond grammar school. They entered politics early and worked their way up from the bottom. They could speak to immigrants in their own language and understood the challenges that newcomers faced. The bosses not only understood the immigrants' problems but were able to provide solutions. The machines helped immigrants become naturalized, find places to live, and get jobs—the newcomers' most pressing needs. In return, the immigrants provided what the political bosses needed most—votes.

THINK THROUGH HISTORY
B. Analyzing Motives *Why did immigrants support political machines?*

B. Answer Because the machines helped them adjust to life in America.

"Big Jim" Pendergast, an Irish-American saloonkeeper, worked his way up from precinct captain to Democratic city boss in Kansas City by aiding Italian, African-American, and Irish voters in his ward. By 1900, he controlled Missouri state politics as well, because he effectively gathered political support.

A PERSONAL VOICE

I've been called a boss. All there is to it is having friends, doing things for people, and then later on they'll do things for you. . . . You can't coerce people into doing things for you—you can't make them vote for you. I never coerced anybody in my life. Wherever you see a man bulldozing anybody he don't last long.

JAMES PENDERGAST, quoted in *The Pendergast Machine*

"All there is to it is . . . doing things for people, and then later on they'll do things for you."

JAMES PENDERGAST

Municipal Graft and Scandal

Although the well-oiled political machines provided city dwellers with vital services, many political bosses fell victim to greed and corruption as their power and influence grew.

ELECTION FRAUD AND GRAFT Since the power of political machines and the loyalty of voters were not always enough to carry an election, some political machines turned to fraud. They padded the lists of eligible voters with the names of dogs, children, and people who had died. Then, under those names, they cast as many votes as were needed to win. In a Philadelphia election, for example, a precinct with 100 registered voters returned 252 votes.

Once a political machine got its candidates into office, it could take advantage of numerous opportunities for graft. For example, after hiring a person to work on a construction project for the city, a political machine could ask the worker to turn in a bill that was higher than the actual cost of materials and labor. The worker then "kicked back" a portion of the earnings to the machine. Taking these **kickbacks,** or illegal payments, for their services made many political machines—and individual politicians—very wealthy.

OBJECTIVE
① INSTRUCT

Political Machines Run the Cities

▶ ***Discussing Key Ideas***

- In major cities, political machines provide services to voters in exchange for political or financial support.
- Political bosses control thousands of municipal jobs and regulate business licenses and inspections.
- Many of the bosses are immigrants who have worked their way up through the political system.

IN-DEPTH RESOURCES: UNIT 2
Guided Reading, p. 39

ACCESS FOR STUDENTS ACQUIRING ENGLISH
Guided Reading (Spanish), p. 102

OBJECTIVE
② INSTRUCT

Municipal Graft and Scandal

▶ ***Discussing Key Ideas***

- To maintain their power and to make money, some political machines turn to election fraud, bribery, and graft.
- The efforts of political cartoonist Thomas Nast help bring down Boss Tweed and Tammany Hall, New York City's powerful Democratic machine.

IN-DEPTH RESOURCES: UNIT 2
Primary Source: from *The Shame of the Cities* by Lincoln Steffens, p. 49

Block Schedule TEACHING OPTION **Time Needed: 40 Minutes**

Cooperative Activity: Creating Political Cartoons

Task: Students will produce one or more cartoons or graphics reflecting the urban political scene in the late 1800s.

Purpose: To understand the way political cartoonists can have an impact on politics through pictures rather than words.

Activity: Ask students to work in pairs to produce one or two political cartoons showing one of the following:

1. How the pyramid design of a political machine (described on page 288) operates
2. How a political machine uses graft
3. How political bosses provide services to immigrants in exchange for votes
4. How a political machine affects taxpayers

Building a Portfolio: Students adding cartoons to their portfolio should attach a note describing their contribution to the work.

ALTERNATIVE ASSESSMENT BOOK
Standards for Evaluating a Cooperative Activity

Standards for Evaluation
Cartoons should . . .

- make a clear point about political machines or political bosses
- be focused on one idea
- include an appropriate caption
- be carefully drawn

HISTORY FROM VISUALS

"The Tammany Tiger Loose"

Viewing the Cartoon Ask students to answer the following questions:

- *Who are the onlookers?*
- *Why are they allowing the tiger to attack the victim?*

Extension Ask students to tell what cartoon they would draw to convey the same idea.

HISTORY FROM VISUALS

Boss Tweed's City Hall

Reading the Chart Have students look closely at Boss Tweed's picture. Ask them why they think his picture is included on the bar graph.

Extension Have students discuss the connection between the Nast cartoon on this page and the chart. *In both, Tweed is in control and the public pays.*

IN-DEPTH RESOURCES: UNIT 2
American Lives: William Marcy Tweed, p. 54

GROLIER MULTIMEDIA ENCYCLOPEDIA
Thomas Nast and a history of editorial and political cartoons

ASSESS & RETEACH

Section 3 Assessment

Have students focus on item 2, which provides a good overview of the section.

Self-Assessment

Ask students to review what they wrote for item 4.

Section Quiz

FORMAL ASSESSMENT
Section Quiz, p. 94

Reteach

Use the political cartoons to review political corruption.

CLOSE

In the late 19th century, political machines ran the major cities.

"THE TAMMANY TIGER LOOSE"

SKILLBUILDER
INTERPRETING POLITICAL CARTOONS ***Who watches from the stands as the Tammany Hall tiger destroys the principles of truth and justice the nation was founded on?***

Skillbuilder Answer
The public.

Other ways that political machines made money were by granting favors to businesses in return for cash and by accepting bribes to allow illegal activities, such as gambling, to flourish. Politicians were able to get away with shady dealings because the police rarely interfered. Until about 1890, police forces were hired and fired by political bosses. Eventually, however, most cities removed from the hands of political bosses the responsibility for hiring police and established more impartial hiring procedures.

THE TWEED RING SCANDAL William Marcy Tweed, one of the earliest and most powerful bosses, became head of **Tammany Hall,** New York City's powerful Democratic political machine, in 1868. Between 1869 and 1871, the **Tweed Ring,** a group of corrupt politicians led by Boss Tweed, pocketed as much as $200 million from the city in kickbacks and payoffs. One scheme involving extravagant graft was the construction of the New York County Courthouse, which cost taxpayers $11 million. The actual construction cost was $3 million; the rest of the money went into the pockets of Tweed and his followers.

The widespread, profound graft practiced by Tammany Hall under Boss Tweed's leadership gradually aroused public outrage. **Thomas Nast,** a political cartoonist, ridiculed Tweed in the *New York Times* and in *Harper's Weekly.* Nast's work particularly angered Tweed, who reportedly said, "I don't care what the papers write about me—my constituents can't read; but . . . they can see pictures!"

The Tweed Ring was finally broken in 1871. Tweed was indicted on 120 counts of fraud and extortion, and in 1873 he was sentenced to 12 years in jail. After serving two years of his sentence, Tweed escaped. He was later captured in Spain when Spanish officials identified him from a Thomas Nast cartoon. By that time, corruption had become an issue in national politics.

C. Answer Both amassed huge fortunes—not always legally—but also did some social good.

THINK THROUGH HISTORY
C. *Comparing* *How were politicians like Boss Tweed similar to industrial magnates like Carnegie and Rockefeller?*

Boss Tweed's City Hall

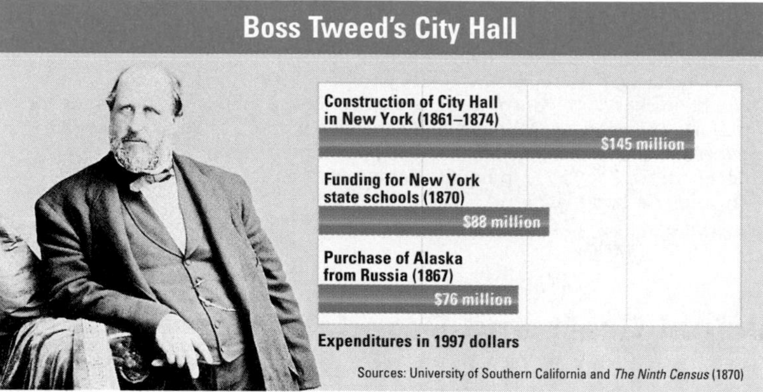

Sources: University of Southern California and *The Ninth Census* (1870)

Skillbuilder Answer
Almost two.

SKILLBUILDER
INTERPRETING CHARTS ***How many Alaskas could have been purchased with the funds used to build Tweed's City Hall?***

Section 3 Assessment

1. TERMS & NAMES
Identify:
- graft
- political machine
- kickback
- Tammany Hall
- Tweed Ring
- Thomas Nast

2. SUMMARIZING In a two-column chart, list at least three advantages and three disadvantages of political machines.

Advantages	Disadvantages

Write an editorial defending or condemning the political machines.

3. GENERALIZING Read the quotation from James Pendergast on page 289. Explain whether you agree or disagree that machine politicians did not coerce people.

THINK ABOUT
- the types of power exerted by political machines
- the consequences of failing to support a machine
- the ways citizens in a democracy can influence the government

4. ANALYZING CAUSES Why do you think corruption such as that practiced by the Tweed Ring was able to flourish in the late 19th century?

THINK ABOUT
- the trends in business during that era
- the problems faced by cities
- the way machine politicians won the support of voters

ANSWERS

1. TERMS & NAMES
graft, p. 288
political machine, p. 288
kickback, p. 289
Tammany Hall, p. 290
Tweed Ring, p. 290
Thomas Nast, p. 290

2. SUMMARIZING
Advantages: Provided people with jobs; provided public services; helped immigrants become citizens.
Disadvantages: Engaged in election fraud; collected kickbacks; controlled the police; granted favors to businesses.

3. GENERALIZING
Students might focus on the meaning of *coerce.* Although machine politicians may not have threatened people with violence, they could have caused them great hardship.

4. ANALYZING CAUSES
Answers should be supported with reasons. Possible point: The rapid economic growth of large cities meant that decisions by local governments could provide people with the opportunity to make large amounts of money.

4 Politics in the Gilded Age

TERMS & NAMES
- patronage
- civil service
- Rutherford B. Hayes
- Stalwarts
- James A. Garfield
- Chester A. Arthur
- Pendleton Act
- Grover Cleveland
- Benjamin Harrison

LEARN ABOUT the national effects of political corruption in the late 19th century
TO UNDERSTAND why Americans wanted reform.

ONE AMERICAN'S STORY

The writer Mark Twain not only observed the transformation of 19th-century America by industrialization but also took advantage of the opportunities it offered. Twain invested in many projects, most of them—including a publishing company and an unworkable typesetting machine—resounding failures. Perhaps those experiences spurred him to collaborate with the journalist and writer Charles Dudley Warner on a satirical novel about their time, *The Gilded Age.* That title has since come to represent the period from the 1870s to the 1890s, when the external glitter of wealth concealed a corrupt political core and reflected a growing gap between the very few rich and the many poor.

A PERSONAL VOICE

In a state where there is no fever of speculation, no inflamed desire for sudden wealth, where the poor are all simple-minded and contented, and the rich are all honest and generous, where society is in a condition of primitive purity, and politics is the occupation of only the capable and the patriotic, there are necessarily no materials for such a history as we have constructed.

MARK TWAIN and CHARLES DUDLEY WARNER, *The Gilded Age*

Although the Gilded Age, like Twain and Warner's fictional era, was a time of unrestricted corruption, it was also a time of movement toward political reform.

Glaring inequalities—such as this luxurious apartment house rising behind a New York City shantytown in 1889—characterized the Gilded Age.

Civil Service Replaces Patronage

The desire for power and money that made local politics corrupt in the industrial age also infected national politics.

PATRONAGE AND THE SPOILS SYSTEM SPUR REFORM Since the beginning of the 19th century, presidents had complained about the problem of **patronage,** or the giving of government jobs to people who had helped a candidate get elected. The theory was that winning candidates deserved the spoils, or the benefits to be seized after a victory. This method of rewarding political supporters existed as far back as Andrew Jackson's presidency and was known as the spoils system.

People from cabinet members to workers who scrubbed the steps of the Capitol owed their jobs to patronage. As might be expected, some government employees were not qualified for the positions they filled. Moreover, political appointees, whether qualified or not, sometimes used their positions for personal gain.

The spoils system not only led to incompetence and fraud but also interfered with the daily functioning of government. With each change of administration, thousands of positions had to be filled. Instead of addressing important national issues, politicians distributed government jobs.

Reformers began to press for a federal merit system to replace the spoils system. Under the merit system, jobs in **civil service**—government administration—would go to the most qualified persons, no matter what political views

A. Answer By allowing people to be hired for government jobs on the basis of political beliefs rather than competence, and by making possible opportunities for misuse of influence.

THINK THROUGH HISTORY
A. Recognizing Effects *How did the spoils system contribute to government incompetence and fraud?*

Section 4 Overview

OBJECTIVES

1. To describe measures taken by Presidents Hayes, Garfield, and Arthur to reform the spoils system.
2. To explain the positions taken by presidents Cleveland, Harrison, and McKinley on the tariff issue.

CRITICAL THINKING

- Recognizing effects, pp. 291, 292
- Analyzing motives, p. 292
- Analyzing causes, p. 293
- Summarizing, p. 293
- Hypothesizing, p. 293
- Forming an opinion, p. 293

FOCUS & MOTIVATE

5-MINUTE WARM-UP

Predicting Outcomes
Ask students to read the definitions of patronage and civil service on pages 291–292 and answer these questions.

1. What are the meanings of *patronage* and *civil service*?
2. Why do you think some people in the late 1800s might have been opposed to the civil service system?

WARM-UP TRANSPARENCY 7

▶***Starting with the Student***
Ask students to discuss how they would go about getting a job. Ask them whether or not they would get help from a friend or a friend's parent. Then have them discuss whether they think it is fair to use "connections."

SECTION 4 RESOURCES

PRINT RESOURCES

IN-DEPTH RESOURCES: UNIT 2
Guided Reading, p. 40

READING STUDY GUIDE, p. 83

ACCESS FOR STUDENTS ACQUIRING ENGLISH
Guided Reading (Spanish), p. 103

SPANISH READING STUDY GUIDE, p. 83

FORMAL ASSESSMENT
Section Quiz, p. 95

ALTERNATIVE ASSESSMENT BOOK
See forms for supporting and scoring alternative activities.

TECHNOLOGY RESOURCES

VIDEO *American Portfolio: A Videodisc for U.S. History* user's guide, pp. 153, 154, 155, 157

INTERNET http://www.mlushistory.com

OBJECTIVE
1 INSTRUCT

Civil Service Replaces Patronage

▶***Discussing Key Ideas***
- Patronage results in incompetence and fraud in government.

(continued on next page)

(continued from page 291)

- Hayes takes measures to reform civil service.
- Garfield wins the 1880 election but is assassinated the following year.
- With Arthur's civil service reform, Congress passes the Pendleton Act in 1883.

IN-DEPTH RESOURCES: UNIT 2
Guided Reading, p. 40

ACCESS FOR STUDENTS ACQUIRING ENGLISH
Guided Reading (Spanish), p. 103

MORE ABOUT . . .
Chester A. Arthur

Before moving into the White House, President Arthur had it completely cleaned out and refurnished. He managed to fill 24 wagons with items that had accumulated over the years, including a hat that had belonged to John Quincy Adams and a pair of trousers worn by Abraham Lincoln. These and other items were sold at auction. Ironically, a sideboard that the Women's Christian Temperance Union had presented to Mrs. Rutherford Hayes—nicknamed "Lemonade Lucy," because she had refused to serve liquor in the White House—was bought by a Washington saloonkeeper, who installed it in his barroom.

The Presidency Takes Its Toll

"Nobody ever left the presidency with less regret . . . than I do."
Rutherford B. Hayes (1877–1881)

"Assassination can be no more guarded against than death by lightning."
James A. Garfield (1881)

"There doesn't seem to be anything else for an ex-president to do but . . . raise big pumpkins."
Chester A. Arthur (1881–1885)

they held or who recommended them. Civil servants would keep their jobs as long as their work was satisfactory.

HAYES LAUNCHES REFORM About a month after being declared the winner of the 1876 election, President **Rutherford B. Hayes** wrote in his diary, "Now for Civil-Service Reform." Hayes could not get legislative support for his ideas, so he used other means.

Hayes began by naming independents to his cabinet. One of these officials took the unheard-of step of firing clerks who had no work to do. Hayes also set up a commission to investigate the nation's customhouses, which were notoriously corrupt. On the basis of the commission's report, Hayes fired the two top officials of New York City's customhouse, where all of the more than 1,000 employees had spent most of their time working for the Republican Party. These firings enraged the Republican New York senator and political boss Roscoe Conkling and his supporters, the Stalwarts.

GARFIELD CONTINUES REFORM Hayes decided not to run for reelection in 1880. At the Republican convention, a free-for-all broke out between the **Stalwarts**—who opposed changes in the spoils system—and reformers. The reformers themselves were split. One group, the Mugwumps, wanted civil service reform, while the other, the Half-Breeds, wanted reform but were loyal to the party. Since neither Stalwarts nor reformers could win a majority of delegates, the convention settled on an independent presidential candidate, Ohio congressman **James A. Garfield.**

Garfield had ties to reformers, however, so to balance the ticket, the Republicans nominated for vice-president one of Conkling's supporters, **Chester A. Arthur.** Arthur, in fact, was one of the two New York customhouse officials Hayes had fired. Despite Arthur's inclusion on the ticket, Garfield gave reform Republicans most of his patronage jobs once he was elected. The Stalwarts were furious.

On July 2, 1881, as President Garfield walked through the Washington, D.C., train station, two gunshots were fired, both wounding the president. His attacker, a mentally unbalanced lawyer named Charles Guiteau, whom Garfield had turned down for a job, shouted, "I did it and I will go to jail for it. I am a Stalwart and Arthur will be president." Garfield finally died from his wounds on September 19, killed, some say, not so much by the bullets as by his doctors' blundering. In any case, Guiteau was convicted of murder and was hanged.

B. Answer Because they thought his antireform views would balance presidential candidate James A. Garfield's belief in civil-service reform.

THINK THROUGH HISTORY
B. *Analyzing Motives* *Why did the Republicans choose Chester Arthur as their vice-presidential candidate for the 1880 election?*

ARTHUR TURNS REFORMER AND SUPPORTS CIVIL SERVICE Despite his ties to Conkling and the Stalwarts, Chester Arthur turned reformer when he became president. His first message to Congress urged legislators to pass a civil service law.

The resulting **Pendleton Act** of 1883 authorized a bipartisan civil service commission to make appointments to federal jobs through the merit system—that is, on the basis of performance on an examination. By 1901, more than 40 percent of all federal jobs had been classified as civil service positions. Today, the merit system covers about 90 percent of all federal jobs.

The Pendleton Act had mixed consequences. On the one hand, increasing numbers of federal jobs were held by qualified people, and public administration became more honest and efficient. On the other hand, because officials could no longer pressure government employees for campaign contributions, politicians had to find other sources of funds. Since the most obvious source was wealthy business owners, the alliance between government and big business became stronger than ever.

C. Answer **Positive:** More competent and honest federal workers. **Negative:** Closer ties between government and big business.

THINK THROUGH HISTORY
C. *Recognizing Effects* *What were the positive and the negative effects of the Pendleton Act?*

TEACHING OPTIONS

Making Connections Across the Curriculum

Economics In "A Personal Voice" on page 293, President Grover Cleveland confesses his ignorance of a basic economic concept, the tariff. A tariff is a tax imposed by a government on imported or exported goods. The issue of tariffs has been important throughout American history. Manufacturing interests have tended to support tariffs on imports because they keep the prices for imported goods high, so that it is cheaper for consumers to buy domestic goods. Consumers, on the other hand, have tended to oppose tariffs because they add to the cost of imported goods.

Teaching Less Proficient Readers

Use the chart below to help students summarize some advantages and disadvantages of high and low tariffs.

	High Tariffs	Low Tariffs
Advantages	protect domestic industry	keep down the cost of goods
Disadvantages	cause prices to rise	discourage domestic industry

Efforts to Regulate Tariffs Fail

Political reformers also addressed another issue—the tariff. Most Americans agreed that tariffs were necessary to protect domestic industries from foreign competition. But they did cause prices to rise. The question was how high tariffs should be.

HARRISON AND HIGH TARIFFS—1; CLEVELAND—0 In 1884, the Democratic Party captured the presidency for the first time in 28 years with the election of **Grover Cleveland.** Carl Schurz, a former secretary of the interior, recalled a conversation he'd had with the newly elected president.

A PERSONAL VOICE

[Cleveland asked] what big question he ought to take up when he got into the White House. I told him . . . the tariff. The man bent forward and buried his face in his hands. . . . After two or three minutes he straightened up and . . . said to me, "I am ashamed to say it, but the truth is I know nothing about the tariff."

CARL SCHURZ, quoted in *The Politicos*

Cleveland learned fast, though, and tried to lower tariff rates, but Congress refused to support him.

In 1888, Cleveland ran for reelection on a low-tariff platform against the former Indiana senator **Benjamin Harrison,** the grandson of President William Henry Harrison. Harrison's campaign was financed by large contributions from companies that wanted tariffs even higher than they were. Although Cleveland won about 100,000 more popular votes than Harrison, Harrison took a majority of the electoral votes and the presidency. Once in office, he won passage of the McKinley Tariff Act of 1890, which raised tariffs to their highest level ever.

D. Answer Because of political pressure exerted by companies that benefited from the tariff.

THINK THROUGH HISTORY
D. Analyzing Causes *Why do you think tariff reform failed?*

CLEVELAND TRIES AGAIN In 1892, Cleveland was elected again—the only president to serve two nonconsecutive terms. He supported a bill for lowering the McKinley Tariff but refused to sign it because it provided for a federal income tax. The Wilson-Gorman Tariff became law in 1894 without the president's signature. In 1897, William McKinley was inaugurated president and raised tariffs once again.

The attempt to reduce the tariff had failed, but the spirit of reform was not dead. New developments in areas ranging from technology and education to mass culture and social policy helped redefine American society as the United States moved into the 20th century.

NOW & THEN

TARIFFS VERSUS NAFTA

Since 1789, when the United States first placed a tariff on certain foreign goods, the issue of tariffs has been hotly debated. In 1993, Congress passed the North American Free Trade Agreement (NAFTA). This agreement eliminated most trade barriers between the United States, Canada, and Mexico.

While critics believed that NAFTA would cost some American workers their jobs because companies would hire cheap Mexican labor, supporters argued that this agreement would create new jobs as Mexican markets opened up to American products. The results remain to be seen.

Section 4 Assessment

1. TERMS & NAMES

Identify:
- patronage
- civil service
- Rutherford B. Hayes
- Stalwarts
- James A. Garfield
- Chester A. Arthur
- Pendleton Act
- Grover Cleveland
- Benjamin Harrison

2. SUMMARIZING In a chart similar to the one below, list three politicians mentioned in this section. Give the position of each and his stand on a major issue, such as civil service reform or lowering tariffs.

Leader	Position	Stand

Which one would you have voted for and why?

3. HYPOTHESIZING How do you think politics in the United States would have been different if the Pendleton Act had not been passed?

THINK ABOUT
- the act's impact on federal workers
- the act's impact on political fundraising
- conflicts within the Republican Party at the time

4. FORMING AN OPINION If you had been running for Congress in 1892, would you have supported a reduction in tariffs? Why or why not?

THINK ABOUT
- the needs of the voters in your state
- the economic impact of reducing tariffs
- the social consequences of a reduction in tariffs

ANSWERS

1. TERMS & NAMES

patronage, p. 291
civil service, p. 291
Rutherford B. Hayes, p. 292
Stalwarts, p. 292
James A. Garfield, p. 292
Chester A. Arthur, p. 292
Pendleton Act, p. 292
Grover Cleveland, p. 293
Benjamin Harrison, p. 293

2. SUMMARIZING

Leader	Position	Stand
Rutherford B. Hayes	president ('77–'81)	for civil service reform
Roscoe Conkling	NY senator	against civil service reform
Chester A. Arthur	president ('81–'85)	supported Pendleton Act
Grover Cleveland	president ('85–'89, '93–'97)	supported lower tariffs
Benjamin Harrison	president ('89–'93)	supported higher tariffs

3. HYPOTHESIZING

Possible Response: Federal employment would have continued to be dominated by politics, politicians would have been less dependent on big business for campaign funds, and a key issue would have continued dividing the Republicans.

4. FORMING AN OPINION

Responses should reflect awareness that high tariffs might help businesses at the expense of consumers.

OBJECTIVE 2 **INSTRUCT**

Efforts to Regulate Tariffs Fail

▶ ***Discussing Key Ideas***
- Cleveland runs on a low-tariff platform and loses the presidency to Harrison, who raises tariffs.
- In his second term, Cleveland fails to lower tariffs.

NOW & THEN
Tariffs Versus NAFTA

Critical Thinking: Synthesizing Have students write an editorial about tariffs. Some topics that might be dealt with include jobs and the cost of goods.

ASSESS & RETEACH

Section 4 Assessment

Have students work individually to answer the questions; then have them share with the class the charts they drew up for item 2.

Self-Assessment

Ask students to review what they wrote for item 3. As they give their opinions about the Pendleton Act, ask students what new ideas they have.

Section Quiz

FORMAL ASSESSMENT
Section Quiz, p. 95

Reteach

Survey students to find out what material in the section was the most difficult for them. Then review that material with students.

CLOSE

In the Gilded Age, political reformers began to replace the evils of patronage with a civil service system. They did not have the same success in reducing the high tariffs that protected American industry.

CHAPTER 7
ASSESSMENT ANSWERS

REVIEWING THE CHAPTER

TERMS & NAMES
1. melting pot, p. 278
2. Gentlemen's Agreement, p. 279
3. urbanization, p. 282
4. Jane Addams, p. 287
5. graft, p. 288
6. political machine, p. 288
7. Thomas Nast, p. 290
8. patronage, p. 291
9. Chester A. Arthur, p. 292
10. Pendleton Act, p. 292

MAIN IDEAS
11. Poverty, famine, shortage of land, lack of jobs, religious or political persecution, and a spirit of rebellion and independence.
12. Culture shock, the negative effects of nativism, and the struggle to make a living.
13. Industrialization, new technology, and an influx of workers.
14. The need to provide adequate housing, transportation, water, and sanitation, and to fight fire and crime.
15. Efforts to help alleviate poverty of immigrants and other city dwellers; building churches in poor neighborhoods.
16. The growing need for city services and the large number of immigrants required a new power structure.
17. Tweed took the corruption practiced by many other city bosses to unprecedented heights.
18. Inefficiency, fraud, and incompetence.
19. Increased efficiency, decreased fraud, and closer ties between government and big business.
20. Cleveland wanted to reduce tariffs; Harrison wanted to keep them high.

Chapter 7 Assessment

REVIEWING THE CHAPTER

TERMS & NAMES For each term below, write a sentence explaining its connection to immigration and urbanization in the late 19th century. For each person below, explain his or her role in these developments.

1. **melting pot**
2. **Gentlemen's Agreement**
3. **urbanization**
4. **Jane Addams**
5. **graft**
6. **political machine**
7. **Thomas Nast**
8. **patronage**
9. **Chester A. Arthur**
10. **Pendleton Act**

MAIN IDEAS

SECTION 1 *(pages 274–279)*

The New Immigrants

11. What trends or events in other countries prompted people to move to the United States in the late 19th and early 20th centuries?
12. What difficulties did many of these new immigrants face?

SECTION 2 *(pages 282–287)*

The Problems of Urbanization

13. Why did cities in the United States grow rapidly in the decades following the Civil War?
14. What problems did this rapid growth pose for cities?
15. What solutions to urban problems did supporters of the Social Gospel propose?

SECTION 3 *(pages 288–290)*

The Emergence of the Political Machine

16. Why did machine politics become common in big cities in the late 19th century?
17. How was Boss Tweed similar to and different from other big city bosses?

SECTION 4 *(pages 291–293)*

Politics in the Gilded Age

18. What government problems arose as a result of the spoils system?
19. What effects did the Pendleton Act have on the running of the federal government?
20. Summarize the views of Grover Cleveland and Benjamin Harrison on tariffs.

THINKING CRITICALLY

1. **RESULTS AND REACTIONS** Create a diagram similar to the one below, showing one result of and one reaction against (a) the increase in immigration and (b) the increase in machine politics.

	Result	Reaction
Increased Immigration →	______ →	______
Increased Machine Politics →	______ →	______

2. **POLITICS TODAY** Compare the current system of politics with the political machines described in this chapter. Which system is more effective? Explain your opinion.
3. **TRACING THEMES THE AMERICAN DREAM** In the opening quotation of this chapter, on page 272, Horace Greeley indicated that everyone seemed to want to live in the city. Why do you think this was true at the end of the 19th century? Do you think it is still true today? Why or why not?
4. **GEOGRAPHY OF PEOPLE AND POLITICS** How do you think immigration and migration influenced the development of American political power structures in the late 19th century? Explain your answer.
5. **POWER OF THE PENCIL** Why do you think political cartoons such as Thomas Nast's had such an impact during the late 19th century?
6. **ANALYZING PRIMARY SOURCES** Read the following introduction by the journalist Lincoln Steffens to his collection of articles exposing horrible urban conditions and political corruption. Then answer the questions below.

> **Democracy with us may be impossible and corruption inevitable, but these articles, if they have proved nothing else, have demonstrated beyond doubt that we can stand the truth; that there is pride in the character of American citizenship; and that this pride may be a power in the land.**
>
> LINCOLN STEFFENS, *The Shame of the Cities*

Do you agree with Steffens that democracy is impossible and corruption inevitable in American politics? How might the pride of American citizens become a powerful voice for a better American government and way of life?

THINKING CRITICALLY

1. RESULTS AND REACTIONS
Possible Answers:
Increase in immigration
Result: growth of urban populations
Reaction: growth of nativism
Increase in machine politics
Result: widespread corruption
Reaction: support for civil service reform

2. POLITICS TODAY
Students might note that politicians still give out patronage jobs and that governmental fraud and incompetence have not been eliminated. They should give solid reasons to support their opinion regarding which system is more effective.

3. TRACING THEMES THE AMERICAN DREAM
At the end of the 19th century, cities offered jobs and other economic opportunities. Regarding the situation today, students might mention the current exodus from the cities or the status of cities as centers of business and industry.

ALTERNATIVE ASSESSMENT

1. **MAKING DECISIONS**
   Review the information in Sections 1 and 2, paying particular attention to the reasons for immigration, the problems facing immigrants in the United States in the late 1800s, and the conditions in southern and eastern European countries at that time. Imagine that you are living in one of these countries and that some of your family members and friends have gone to the United States to seek other opportunities. They are urging you to join them. What will you do? Use the following steps to help you make a decision:
   - Identify the situation that needs a decision.
   - Gather necessary information to help you make a decision. How would leaving your country improve your situation?
   - Identify your options. What are your choices in this situation?
   - Predict the consequences of each option. What would be the consequences of leaving your country? What would be the consequences of staying in your country?
   - Take action. What is your decision about migrating to the United States?

2. **LEARNING FROM MEDIA**
   VIDEO View the video for Chapter 7, *From China to Chinatown.* Discuss the following questions with a small group of your classmates.
   - How did Fong See overcome the difficulties that faced Asian immigrants in America in the late 19th and early 20th centuries?
   - What motivated him to return to China?
   - What did Lisa See learn about living in a multicultural society from her great-grandfather's experience?
   - How are immigrants treated in America today?
   - What lessons does Fong See's story have for present-day Americans?

3. **PORTFOLIO PROJECT**
   Use the Living History activity to expand your portfolio.

LIVING HISTORY

REVISING YOUR TOWN BIOGRAPHY

After completing the biography of your town or neighborhood, ask a friend or two to read it and to answer the following questions. If possible, choose one reader who is familiar with the town and one who is not.

- What interested you most about my biography?
- What would you like to know more about?
- Do you agree with my prediction about the future of my town or neighborhood? Why or why not?

Make changes based on your friends' suggestions, and finalize your biography for your American history portfolio. You also might consider making an oral presentation to your class or to an audience at the local library or community center.

Bridge to Chapter 8

Review Chapter 7

IMMIGRATION INCREASES In the late 19th and early 20th centuries, millions of people from Europe, China, Japan, the Caribbean, and Mexico fled poverty and persecution in their homelands and moved to the United States. Many immigrants endured prejudice and culture shock in their new home as they strove to build a better life for themselves and their children.

CHALLENGES OF THE CITIES Most immigrants settled in cities, where they joined millions of newcomers from rural communities in the United States. While cities offered jobs in growing factories and mills, they were overcrowded, dirty, and unsafe. In response to urban problems, reformers such as Washington Gladden and Jane Addams worked to help the urban poor.

THE POLITICAL MACHINE As cities and their problems grew, a new power structure emerged—the political machine. Machine bosses often were notoriously corrupt and got rich from graft, kickbacks, and bribes, but they also provided jobs, legal assistance, and support that many poor people needed. Among the most famous machine politicians was New York's Boss Tweed, who was jailed in 1873.

NATIONAL POLITICS IN THE GILDED AGE In national politics, two main issues emerged—civil service reform and the tariff. The passage of the Pendleton Act of 1883 marked a victory for those who wanted to reform the patronage system of hiring federal employees. In 1888, the Democratic president Grover Cleveland, a supporter of low tariffs, was defeated by the high-tariff candidate, Republican Benjamin Harrison.

Preview Chapter 8

In addition to forces such as immigration, industrialization, and urbanization, developments in science and technology helped reshape life in the United States in the late 19th century. These developments—from the skyscraper to the amusement park—affected many aspects of life in cities, from education and the role of women to leisure activities. Despite these advances, however, social problems, such as racial segregation and discrimination, continued to plague society. You will learn about these significant developments in the next chapter.

ALTERNATIVE ASSESSMENT

1. MAKING DECISIONS
Standards for Evaluation
The process for deciding the action should meet the following criteria:

- Identifies the situation that needs a decision.
- Includes information to help make the decision.
- Identifies options that can be taken in making a final decision.
- Shows an understanding of the consequences of each option.

2. LEARNING FROM MEDIA
Answers to the questions:

- Fong See came to America to search for his father.
- Fong See overcame difficulties by a combination of hard work and clever business tactics.
- Fong See returned to China to see his family and share with them the wealth he had earned in America.
- Lisa See learned from her great-grandfather's experience that hard work and perseverance are necessary when living in a multicultural society.
- Accept all reasonable responses.
- Accept all reasonable responses.

3. PORTFOLIO PROJECT
LIVING HISTORY
Standards for Evaluation
A biography should meet the following criteria:

- Includes information about the town's founders.
- Describes the town's major ethnic groups.
- Discusses the problems created by growth.
- Predicts the future of the town.
- Includes maps, photos, or other illustrations about local events.

IN-DEPTH RESOURCES: UNIT 2
See the form for scoring this activity on page 56.

THINKING CRITICALLY

4. GEOGRAPHY OF PEOPLE AND POLITICS
The growth of cities resulting from immigration and migration led to the need for vital services, and the political machines stepped in to provide them. Also, more representatives in Congress came from cities, which gave urban areas increased national influence.

5. POWER OF THE PENCIL
Students might mention that the cartoons could be understood even by people who couldn't read English or that the political bosses' corruption was so glaring that satirical cartoons were the perfect vehicle for fueling public outrage.

6. ANALYZING PRIMARY SOURCES
Students should give solid reasons to support their opinion regarding the possibility of democracy. They might suggest that pride in America might be translated into participation in government at many levels.

CHAPTER 8

PLANNING GUIDE

Life at the Turn of the Century

	Key Ideas	COPYMASTERS	ASSESSMENT
SECTION 1 **Science and Urban Life** *pp. 298–302*	*Advances in science and technology address urban problems, including lack of space and inadequate systems of transportation and communication.*	***In-Depth Resources: Unit 2*** • Guided Reading, p. 57 • Geography Application: New York's Central Park, p. 62 • Primary Sources: *from* Orville Wright's Diary, p. 64; Advertisement, p. 65 ***Lesson Plans,*** pp. 69–70	PE ***Section 1 Assessment,*** p. 302 TE ***Self-Assessment,*** p. 302 ***Formal Assessment*** • Section Quiz, p. 104 ***Alternative Assessment Book*** • Standards for Evaluating a Cooperative Activity
SECTION 2 **Education and Culture** *pp. 303–308*	*The impulses of moral uplift and economic necessity spur changes in education, a rise in national literacy, and the promotion of high culture.*	***In-Depth Resources: Unit 2*** • Guided Reading, p. 58 • Primary Source: *from* "The Talented Tenth" by W. E. B. Du Bois, p. 66 • American Lives: W. E. B. Du Bois, p. 71 ***Lesson Plans,*** pp. 71–72	PE ***Section 2 Assessment,*** p. 308 TE ***Self-Assessment,*** p. 308 ***Formal Assessment*** • Section Quiz, p. 105 ***Alternative Assessment Book*** • Standards for Evaluating a Cooperative Activity
SECTION 3 **Segregation and Discrimination** *pp. 309–313*	*African Americans lead the fight against institutionalized racism in the form of voting restrictions and Jim Crow laws.*	***In-Depth Resources: Unit 2*** • Guided Reading, p. 59 • Skillbuilder Practice: Finding Main Ideas, p. 61 • Primary Source: *from* "Lynching and the Excuse for It" by Ida B. Wells, p. 67 ***Lesson Plans,*** pp. 73–74	PE ***Section 3 Assessment,*** p. 313 TE ***Self-Assessment,*** p. 313 ***Formal Assessment*** • Section Quiz, p. 106 ***Alternative Assessment Book*** • Standards for Evaluating a Cooperative Activity
SECTION 4 **Dawn of Mass Culture** *pp. 314–321*	*Americans have more time for leisure activities and a modern mass culture emerges, especially through newspapers and retail advertising.*	***In-Depth Resources: Unit 2*** • Guided Reading, p. 60 • Literature: from *Ragtime* by E. L. Doctorow, p. 68 • American Lives: Lillian Gish, p. 72 ***Lesson Plans,*** p. 75–76	PE ***Section 4 Assessment,*** p. 321 TE ***Self-Assessment,*** p. 321 ***Formal Assessment*** • Section Quiz, p. 107 ***Alternative Assessment Book*** • Standards for Evaluating a Cooperative Activity
CHAPTER RESOURCES	**Chapter Overview** *As the twentieth century begins, American culture changes due to new technological advances, cultural forms, and mass media. Some Americans, though, protest discrimination that denies them rights.*	***In-Depth Resources: Unit 2*** • Living History Project: Worksheet, p. 73; Standards, p. 74 ***Telescoping the Times*** • Chapter Summary, pp. 15–16 ***Planning for Block Schedules***	PE ***Chapter Assessment,*** pp. 324–325 PE ***Alternative Assessment,*** p. 325 ***Formal Assessment*** • Chapter Test, forms A and B, pp. 108–113 ***Test Generator*** ***Alternative Assessment Book*** See explanation and forms for different kinds of alternative assessments including portfolio assessment.

KEY
PE Pupil's Edition
TE Teacher's Edition
INTERNET **http://www.mlushistory.com**

TECHNOLOGY

 *Warm-Up Transparency* 8
Geography Transparencies
- G16, Telephone Long Distance Lines: 1890–1917

Electronic Library of Primary Sources
- from "Automobiles: The Other Side of the Shield" by Frederick Dwight
- From *A Visit to the World's Columbian Exposition* by Charles E. Bolton

 **INTERNET** Louis Sullivan and Eastman Kodak

 *Warm-Up Transparency* 8
Critical Thinking Transparencies
- CT16, Expansion of Education
- CT50, Increasing School Enrollment: 1870–1920

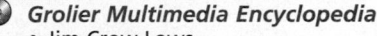

 *Grolier Multimedia Encyclopedia*
- from *The Souls of Black Folk* by W.E.B. Du Bois
- Thomas Eakins

 **INTERNET** W.E.B. Du Bois and Mark Twain

 *Warm-Up Transparency* 8
Grolier Multimedia Encyclopedia
- Jim Crow Laws

Electronic Library of Primary Sources
- from *The Autobiography of Ida B. Wells*

 **INTERNET** Jim Crow laws, Ida B. Wells, and the Chinese Exclusion Act

 *Warm-Up Transparency* 8
 *Humanities Transparencies*
- H16, *Washington Square North* by Ferdinand Lundgren

Electronic Library of Primary Sources
- *from* "The Base-Ball Season" in *Harper's Weekly*
- from *The Movies, Mr. Griffith, and Me* by Lillian Gish

 **INTERNET** Interact with History p. 323 (PE)

 *American Portfolio: A Videodisc for U.S. History,* user's guide, pp. 142, 146–148, 151, 155, 158, 160, 162, 166–167, 178

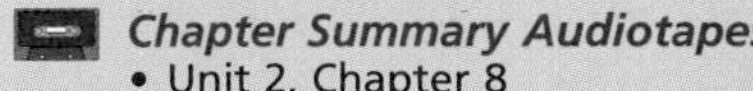 *Chapter Summary Audiotapes*
- Unit 2, Chapter 8

 **INTERNET http://www. mlushistory.com**

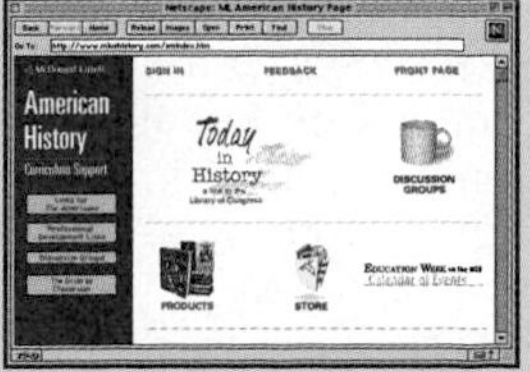

Block Scheduling (90 MINUTES)

Day 1
Section 1, pp. 298–302
Section 2, pp. 303–308
Section Assessments, pp. 302, 308

 **COOPERATIVE ACTIVITIES**
- Planning Ideal Cities, p. 300 (TE)
- Reforming Public Education, p. 304 (TE)

Day 2
Section 3, pp. 309–313
Section Assessment, p. 313

 **COOPERATIVE ACTIVITY**
- Debating Discrimination, p. 312 (TE)

Day 3
Section 4, pp. 314–321
Daily Life: New Ways to Play, pp. 322–323
Section Assessment, p. 321
Chapter Assessment, pp. 324–325

COOPERATIVE ACTIVITIES
- Writing Sports History, p. 316 (TE)
- Critiquing Historical Films, p. 318 (TE)

YEARLY PACING ***Chapter 8 Total:*** 3 days ***Yearly Total:*** 85 days

See *Planning for Block Schedules* for special activities and pacing strategies.

Customizing for Special Populations

Students Acquiring English
Access for Students Acquiring English: Spanish Translations
- Guided Reading for Sections 1–4, pp. 111–114
- Chapter Summary, pp. 109–110
- Skillbuilder Practice: Finding Main Ideas, p. 115
- Geography Application: New York's Central Park, p. 116

Spanish Reading Study Guide, pp. 87–96
Translations of Chapter Summaries, Hmong, Cantonese, Vietnamese, and Cambodian

Chapter Summary Audiotapes in Spanish Unit 2, Chapter 8

INTERNET The Diverse Classroom

Gifted and Talented Students
In-Depth Resources: Unit 2
- Primary Sources: *from* Orville Wright's Diary, p. 64; Advertisement, p. 65; *from* "The Talented Tenth" by W.E.B. Du Bois, p. 66; *from* "Lynching and the Excuse for It" by Ida B. Wells, p. 67
- American Lives: W.E.B. Du Bois, p. 71; Lillian Gish, p. 72

Less Proficient Readers
In-Depth Resources: Unit 2
- Guided Reading for Sections 1–4, pp. 57–60
- Skillbuilder: Finding Main Ideas, p. 61
- Geography Application: New York's Central Park, p. 62

Reading Study Guide
- pp. 87–96

Telescoping the Times
- Chapter Summary, pp. 15–16

Chapter Summary Audiotapes, Unit 2, Chapter 8

Connections to Literature READINGS FOR STUDENTS

In-Depth Resources: Unit 2
- **from *Ragtime* by E. L. Doctorow,** p. 68

Enrichment Reading
- **Sherwood Anderson**
  Winesburg, Ohio.
  New York: Penguin, 1996
  In this modern classic, Anderson mixes his memories of his childhood in Clyde, Ohio, with his observations of life in turn-of-the-century Chicago. In the book, the inhabitants of Winesburg confide their disappointed dreams and dashed hopes to a young reporter. This deeply honest portrait of life in small-town America was a shock to many readers at the time.
- **Louise Erdrich**
  Tracks.
  New York: HarperCollins, 1989
  This novel, third in a cycle, tells the story of a group of Chippewa and their culture under siege in a white man's world.

McDougal Littell *The Language of Literature* American Literature
- **Carl Sandburg, "Chicago,"** p. 668
- **Edgar Lee Masters, "Lucinda Matlock,"** p. 668
- **Edwin Arlington Robinson, "Richard Cory,"** p. 675
- **Paul Laurence Dunbar, "We Wear the Mask,"** p. 675

McDougal Littell *Literature Connections*

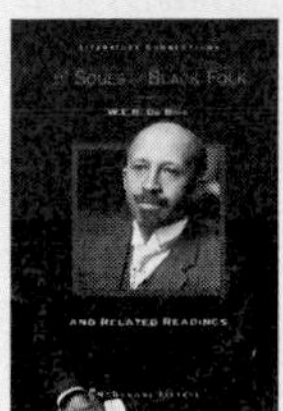

W.E.B. Du Bois,
The Souls of Black Folk *(with related readings). In this collection of essays, Du Bois considers the condition of African Americans in the early 1900s. Among the ideas discussed in the book is Du Bois's famous assertion: "The problem in the Twentieth Century is the problem of the color line."*

OVERVIEW

Life at the Turn of the Century

▶ ***Accessing Prior Knowledge***
Ask students what they know about American life a hundred years ago. How did Americans work and play? What new inventions were changing people's ways of life?

▶ ***Predicting Outcomes***
Ask students to read the quotation on this page and have them look at the photos in the chapter. Ask students to make a list of what they think would be the best and worst of life at the turn of the century.

MORE ABOUT . . .
James Weldon Johnson
The first African American to be accepted to the Florida bar, Johnson later served as a U.S. consul in Venezuela. He had a varied career in the arts, composing and performing for a song-and-dance act with his brother John, editing anthologies of African-American verse and spirituals, and penning fine prose and poetry of his own.

CHAPTER 8

Life at the Turn of the Century

SECTION 1
Science and Urban Life
Advances in science and technology alleviate urban problems, including lack of space and inadequate systems of transportation and communication.

SECTION 2
Education and Culture
The impulses of moral uplift and economic necessity spur changes in education, a rise in national literacy, and the promotion of high culture.

SECTION 3
Segregation and Discrimination
African Americans lead the fight against institutionalized racism in the form of voting restrictions and Jim Crow laws.

SECTION 4
Dawn of Mass Culture
Americans have more time for leisure activities, and a modern mass culture emerges, especially through newspapers and retail advertising.

"Every nation should be judged by the best it has been able to produce, not by the worst."
James Weldon Johnson

THE UNITED STATES / THE WORLD — 1877

1879 — F. W. Woolworth opens his first "five-and-ten-cent" store.
1883 — Construction of the Brooklyn Bridge is completed.
1884 — Mark Twain publishes *The Adventures of Huckleberry Finn*.
1891 — James Naismith invents basketball.
1891 — Ida B. Wells crusades against lynching.

1878 — Bicycle touring club is founded in Europe.
1882 — Triple Alliance of Italy, Austria-Hungary, and Germany is formed.
1884 — Fifteen nation conference on the division of Africa convenes in Berlin.
1889 — Barnum & Bailey Circus opens in London.

THEMES IN CHAPTER 8

Science and Technology
Technology helped cities grow upward with skyscrapers and outward with better roads, bridges, subways, and streetcars to accommodate the influx of immigrants and rural migrants to the urban areas.
See Teacher's Edition note, p. 299.

Immigration and Migration
Education was a vital tool for assimilating the millions of immigrants who came to America. Besides schools, employers, labor unions, and political organizations helped immigrants assimilate.
See Teacher's Edition note, p. 305.

Civil Rights
Booker T. Washington and W. E. B. Du Bois struggled for African-American equality, although they differed on tactics. Washington stressed a gradual approach that would lead to economic independence. Du Bois demanded immediate assimilation.
See Teacher's Edition note, p. 310.

Women in America
Women's lifestyles in the United States continued to evolve. Women expanded their educational and occupational opportunities. Some traditional restrictions on female behavior loosened, as seen in the changing clothing styles and leisure activities.
See Teacher's Edition note, p. 315.

LIVING HISTORY

CATALOGING MASS CULTURE

The mass culture that emerged at the turn of the century was a product of advancements in technology and the expansion of educational and cultural opportunities. Create your own version of a catalog displaying objects, places, and events that contributed to the formation of American mass culture. Consider these guidelines:

- Keep notes as you read about changes in the American landscape.
- Think about people and events that caused change.

PORTFOLIO PROJECT Keep your catalog in a folder. At the end of this chapter, you will add illustrations to the catalog, display it, and add it to your American history portfolio.

- **1894** African kingdom of Uganda becomes a British protectorate.
- **1895** Coney Island amusement park opens in New York.
- **1899** German psychoanalyst Sigmund Freud publishes *The Interpretation of Dreams.*
- **1900** William McKinley is reelected.
- **1901** McKinley is assassinated.
- **1901** Theodore Roosevelt becomes president.
- **1903** Wright brothers successfully complete the first airplane flight at Kitty Hawk, North Carolina.
- **1903** W. E. B. Du Bois publishes *The Souls of Black Folk.*
- **1904** Theodore Roosevelt is elected president.
- **1904** Russo-Japanese War breaks out.
- **1907** Ringling Bros. and Barnum & Bailey circuses merge.
- **1908** William H. Taft is elected president.
- **1910** Japan annexes Korea.
- **1912** Woodrow Wilson is elected president.
- **1914** World War I begins in Europe.
- **1915** D. W. Griffith's epic film *The Birth of a Nation* is released.
- **1916** Woodrow Wilson is reelected.
- **1917**

ALTERNATIVE ASSESSMENT

LIVING HISTORY

CATALOGING MASS CULTURE

Show the class some catalogs from an art or natural history museum. Point out how they are organized. Then help students determine the items to include in their catalogs. They might follow these steps:

- Prepare a list of possible methods for illustrating the changes, events, and people. Consider creating original art, taking photographs, and copying photos from periodicals or books.
- Use a chart to help determine which events, people, and places are the most important and easily illustrate mass culture and social change. Then include them in the catalog.
- Do additional research if necessary to write the catalog descriptions of each item, event, or person included.

Item	Reason why important to include

IN-DEPTH RESOURCES: UNIT 2
See worksheet and standards for evaluation, pp. 73, 74.

RECOMMENDED RESOURCES

Books for the Teacher

Ayers, Edward L. *The Promise of the New South: Life after Reconstruction.* New York: Oxford UP, 1992.

Schlereth, Thomas J. *Victorian America: Transformations in Everyday Life, 1876–1915.* New York: Harper, 1991.

Books for the Student

Bryson, Bill. *Made in America.* New York: Morrow, 1994.

Du Bois, W. E. B. *The Souls of Black Folk.* New York: Signet, 1995.

McCullough, David. *The Great Bridge.* New York: Simon, 1972. A lively account of the building of the Brooklyn Bridge.

Videos

Baseball. Dir. Ken Burns. PBS Home Video, 1994. "Inning 1" discusses the origins of professional baseball.

Booker T. Washington's Tuskegee America. AIMS Media, 1987.

Coney Island. Direct Cinema, 800-525-0000.

Hollywood: A Celebration of the American Silent Film. Dir. David Gill and Kevin Brownlow. Image Entertainment, 1990.

Mr. Sears's Catalogue. PBS Home Video, 800-424-7963.

Section 1 Overview

OBJECTIVES

1. To describe technological advances and urban planning and their effects on turn-of-the-century city life.
2. To summarize turn-of-the-century advances in communications.

CRITICAL THINKING

- Theme: Science and Technology, p. 299
- Summarizing, pp. 301, 302
- Clarifying, p. 301
- Synthesizing, p. 302
- Forming opinions, p. 302

FOCUS & MOTIVATE

5-MINUTE WARM-UP

Making Judgments
To discuss the technological advances of the turn of the century, have students look at the photos in this section and answer these questions.

1. What are the technological advances shown in the photos?
2. Which of these advances do you think had the greatest impact on life at the turn of the century? Why do you think so?

WARM-UP TRANSPARENCY 8

▶ ***Starting with the Student***
Ask students what changes could be made in modern American cities to make them more livable.

OBJECTIVE
① **INSTRUCT**

Technology and City Life

▶ ***Discussing Key Ideas***
- Technology helps cities grow both upward and outward.

(continued on next page)

1 Science and Urban Life

TERMS & NAMES
- Louis Sullivan
- Frederick Law Olmsted
- Central Park
- Daniel Burnham
- Orville and Wilbur Wright
- web-perfecting press
- Linotype machine
- George Eastman

LEARN ABOUT developments in architecture, transportation, and communication
TO UNDERSTAND how technological changes at the turn of the century affected American cities.

ONE AMERICAN'S STORY

The 1,595-foot-long Brooklyn Bridge, connecting Brooklyn to the island of Manhattan in New York City, was called the eighth wonder of the world when it opened in 1883. Workers took 14 years to build what was then the world's largest suspension bridge. Each day the laborers working on the foundation descended to work in a caisson, or watertight chamber, that lay deep beneath the East River.

Within the chamber, the warm air dripped with mist. E. F. Farrington, a mechanic who worked on the bridge, described the working conditions.

New Yorkers celebrated the opening of the Brooklyn Bridge with a huge fireworks display, but a herd of P. T. Barnum's circus elephants had to cross the bridge before people trusted its safety.

A PERSONAL VOICE

Inside the caisson everything wore an unreal, weird appearance. There was a confused sensation in the head, like "the rush of many waters." The pulse was at first accelerated, then sometimes fell below the normal rate. The voice sounded faint, unnatural, and it became a great effort to speak. What with the flaming lights, the deep shadows, the confusing noise of hammers, drills, and chains, the half-naked forms flitting about . . . one might, if of a poetic temperament, get a realizing sense of Dante's Inferno.

E. F. FARRINGTON, quoted in *The Great Bridge*

Although Farrington claimed that working beneath the water made conditions difficult, the bridge was a huge success. Within a year of its completion, the bridge carried 37,000 commuters daily. Four years later, trains across the bridge ran 24 hours a day and carried more than 30 million travelers each year. This section explores the impact of innovations, such as the Brooklyn Bridge, that laid the groundwork for modern American life.

Technology and City Life

Many people crossed the Brooklyn Bridge each day on their way to and from work. After all, it was the increasing number of industrial jobs more than any other factor that drew people to America's cities. By 1890, Chicago and Philadelphia claimed more than a million residents. By 1900, New York boasted a population of 3.5 million people.

In 1870, only 25 American cities had populations of 50,000; by 1890, 58 cities could make that claim. Four out of ten Americans made their homes in cities by the turn of the century. As rural and immigrant people entered the cities, one enthusiastic city dweller hailed the "mighty streams of human beings that forever flow up and down the thoroughfares."

To accommodate these streams of people, cities needed to expand upward as well as outward. Technological advances, like the ones that contributed to the construction of the Brooklyn Bridge, soon began to meet the urbanizing nation's needs for space, transportation, and communication. One remedy for the ever-shrinking space for new residents was to build upward.

SECTION 1 RESOURCES

PRINT RESOURCES

IN-DEPTH RESOURCES: UNIT 2
Guided Reading, p. 57
Geography Application: New York's Central Park, p. 62
Primary Sources: *from* Orville Wright's Diary, p. 64; Advertisement, p. 65

READING STUDY GUIDE, p. 87

ACCESS FOR STUDENTS ACQUIRING ENGLISH
Guided Reading (Spanish), p. 111
Geography Application: New York's Central Park (Spanish), p. 116

SPANISH READING STUDY GUIDE, p. 87

FORMAL ASSESSMENT
Section Quiz, p. 104

ALTERNATIVE ASSESSMENT BOOK
See forms for supporting and scoring alternative activities.

TECHNOLOGY RESOURCES

GEOGRAPHY TRANSPARENCIES
G16, Telephone Long Distance Lines, 1890–1917

CD-ROM Electronic Library of Primary Sources

VIDEO *American Portfolio: A Videodisc for U.S. History* user's guide, pp. 142, 146–148

INTERNET http://www.mlushistory.com

SKYSCRAPERS Architects were able to design taller buildings than ever before because of two factors: the invention of elevators and the development of internal steel skeletons to bear the weight of buildings. In 1890, the architectural pioneer **Louis Sullivan** designed the ten-story Wainwright Building in St. Louis, which he called a "proud and soaring thing." The tall building's appearance was graceful because its steel framework supported both floors and walls. The unusual form of another skyscraper, the Flatiron Building, seemed perfect for its location at one of New York's busiest intersections. Daniel Burnham designed this slender 285-foot tower in 1902.

THINK THROUGH HISTORY
A. THEME ***Science and Technology*** *Explain how new technologies made the building of skyscrapers practical.*

A. Answer The elevator made tall buildings usable; steel frames could bear the weight of tall buildings.

The skyscraper soon became America's greatest contribution to architecture, "a new thing under the sun" according to the architect Frank Lloyd Wright, who studied under Sullivan. Skyscrapers solved the practical problem of how to make the best use of limited and expensive space. The buildings also served as towering symbols of a rich and optimistic society.

ELECTRIC TRANSIT As skyscrapers expanded upward, changes in transportation allowed cities to spread outward. Before the Civil War, horses had drawn the earliest streetcars over iron rails embedded in city streets. In some cities during the 1870s and 1880s, underground moving cables powered streetcar lines. Electricity, however, transformed urban transportation.

In 1888, Richmond, Virginia, became the first American city to electrify its urban transit. After Richmond installed streetcars driven by electric motors powered by an overhead wire, other cities installed electric streetcars. By the turn of the century, intricate networks of electric streetcar lines carried the residents of outlying neighborhoods to downtown department stores, offices, banks, and factories. In Kansas City in 1891, a journalist named William Allen White exclaimed that the city's streetcars were "marvels." The small "walking city," whose limits depended on how far people's legs could carry them, soon gave way to a sprawling metropolis crisscrossed with mass transit lines.

The Flatiron Building, shown here under construction in 1903, stands at the intersection of Fifth Avenue and 23rd Street in New York City.

New railroad lines also fed the growth of suburbs, whose residents could now commute to downtown jobs. By 1890, 70,000 suburban commuters made the daily trip to Chicago. New York's northern suburbs alone supplied 100,000 commuters each day to the central business district.

Faced with congestion on their streets, a few large cities moved their streetcars above street level, creating elevated or "el" trains. Other cities, like New York, built subways by moving their rail lines underground. These streetcars, elevated trains, and subways enabled cities to annex suburban developments that mushroomed along the advancing transportation routes. Indeed, many suburbs wanted to be annexed by the larger cities so that the train lines would reach them. Between 1860 and 1890, Boston grew from 5 square miles to 39 square miles. At the same time, Chicago expanded from 17 square miles to 178 square miles.

Steel-cable suspension bridges, of which the Brooklyn Bridge proved the most spectacular example, also brought cities' sections closer together. Sometimes these bridges even provided recreational opportunities. In his design for the Brooklyn Bridge, for example, John Augustus Roebling provided an elevated promenade whose "principal use will be to allow people of leisure, and old and young invalids, to promenade over the bridge on

(continued from page 298)

- The growth of cities prompts the new science of urban planning.

IN-DEPTH RESOURCES: UNIT 2
Guided Reading, p. 57

ACCESS FOR STUDENTS ACQUIRING ENGLISH
Guided Reading (Spanish), p. 111

ELECTRONIC LIBRARY OF PRIMARY SOURCES
from "Automobiles: The Other Side of the Shield" by Frederick Dwight

HISTORY FROM VISUALS
The Flatiron Building

Reading the Image Ask what urban improvements are visible in this picture. *Possible Responses: A skyscraper with steel construction, streetcars, and sidewalks.*

Extension Ask why the Flatiron Building has a triangular shape. *Possible Responses: To make the best use of space between two streets that meet in a V; to win fame and tenants; to be different; to create exotic tapered-corner offices for higher rent.*

MORE ABOUT . . .
The Brooklyn Bridge

Like most of the workers who built the bridge, John Roebling immigrated to America, arriving from Prussia (Germany) in 1831. A few weeks after his bridge plans won approval, he died of tetanus, which he contracted when his toes were crushed by a boat docking near the bridge site. His son Washington supervised the actual construction but was eventually bedridden from repeated bouts of "caisson disease," or the bends.

TEACHING OPTIONS

Exploring Themes

Science and Technology Technology helped cities spread both upward and outward. New construction methods created ever-taller skyscrapers as well as better roads and bridges to connect the downtown with outlying areas. Streetcars, subways, and other new means of rapid transit also promoted urban sprawl. Faster ships brought increasing numbers of immigrants to America, most of whom settled first in their ports of entry. Improved agricultural technologies allowed more and more children of farm families to leave rural America for the economic opportunities of the cities.

Making Connections Across Time

Mass Transit Today Encourage students to discuss recent advances in public transportation as well as some of the problems that plague mass transit today. *Recent advances include monorails, magnetic and "bullet" (very fast) trains, and supersonic aircraft; problems include funding shortages, decaying infrastructure, overcrowding, crime, and graffiti.*

ON THE WORLD STAGE
The Garden City

Critical Thinking: Comparing Ask students to discuss why nature and wildlife might be important to city life and to identify a city, town, or neighborhood that they feel displays aspects of Howard's plan.

MORE ABOUT . . .
Central Park

The call to preserve a piece of park land on the island of Manhattan was made as early as 1844 by poet and editor William Cullen Bryant and echoed by eminent landscape designer Andrew Jackson Downing. The campaign took twelve years, but in 1856 the city purchased most of the park's 840 acres with $5 million in state funds. The unappetizing land had a garbage dump, a bone-boiling works, and many shacks and squatters' farms.

IN-DEPTH RESOURCES: UNIT 2
Geography Application: New York's Central Park, p. 62

HISTORY FROM VISUALS
The Chicago Plan

Reading the Art Ask students to consider the patterns of the streets in Burnham's plan. Why would someone plan streets set on a grid bisected by diagonals? *The grid makes the city easy to navigate. Streets running into the city center help create a unified city.*

Extension Ask students what aspects of urban planning they can identify in their own (or the nearest) city or town.

ON THE WORLD STAGE

THE GARDEN CITY

Urban planning in the United States had European counterparts. For example, in *Tomorrow: A Peaceful Path to Social Reform* (1898), the British city planner Ebenezer Howard described a planned residential community called a garden city.

Howard set out to combine the benefits of urban life with easy access to nature. He designed a city plan based on concentric circles—with a town at the center and a wide circle of rural or agricultural land on the perimeter. The town center included a garden, concert hall, museum, theater, library, and hospital. The circle around the town center included a park, a shopping center, a conservatory, a residential area, and industry. Six wide avenues radiated out from the town center.

Howard's plan, first executed in 1903 at Letchworth, England, has served as a model for other planned towns well into the 20th century.

fine days, in order to enjoy the beautiful views and the pure air." This need for open spaces in the midst of crowded commercial cities inspired the emerging science of urban planning.

THE SCIENCE OF URBAN PLANNING Even before skyscrapers and advances in transportation began to make life in the cities more comfortable, city planners in several cities sought to restore a measure of serenity to the urban environment by designing parks and recreational areas. **Frederick Law Olmsted**—farmer, surveyor, and journalist—spearheaded the movement for planned urban parks.

In 1858, Olmsted teamed with the English architect Calvert Vaux to draw up a plan for "Greensward," which became **Central Park,** in New York. Olmsted envisioned the park as a rustic haven in the center of the busy city. The finished park featured boating and tennis facilities, a zoo, and bicycle paths, with curved roadways that provided a pleasing contrast to the straight-line grid of New York's streets. Olmsted hoped that the park's beauty would soothe the city's inhabitants and let them enjoy a "natural" setting.

A PERSONAL VOICE

> The main object and justification [of the park] is simply to produce a certain influence in the minds of people and through this to make life in the city healthier and happier. The character of this influence is a poetic one and it is to be produced by means of scenes, through observation of which the mind may be more or less lifted out of moods and habits into which it is, under the ordinary conditions of life in the city, likely to fall.
>
> FREDERICK LAW OLMSTED, quoted in *Frederick Law Olmsted's New York*

In the 1870s, Olmsted planned landscaping for Washington, D.C., and St. Louis. He also drew the initial designs for the Fenway, Boston's park system. Boston's Back Bay area, originally a 450-acre swamp, was drained and developed into an area of elegant streets and cultural attractions.

The Chicago Plan

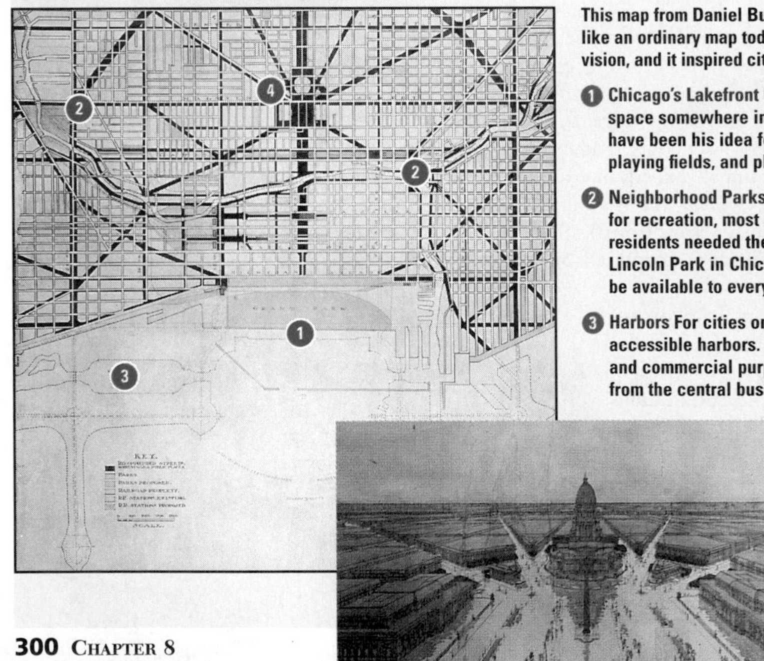

This map from Daniel Burnham's original plan of Chicago looks deceptively like an ordinary map today. But at the time, it was almost revolutionary in its vision, and it inspired city planners to draft plans for cities all over the country.

1 Chicago's Lakefront Urban planners attempted to preserve recreational space somewhere in each city. Burnham's greatest legacy to Chicago may have been his idea for a lakefront park system, complete with beaches, playing fields, and playgrounds.

2 Neighborhood Parks Though not all cities could claim a lakefront vista for recreation, most cities sprinkled neighborhood parks where their residents needed them. Urban planners provided for local parks—such as Lincoln Park in Chicago—so that "the sweet breath of plant life" would be available to everyone.

3 Harbors For cities on the Great Lakes, the shipping business depended on accessible harbors. Burnham saw the advantage of harbors for recreation and commercial purposes, but he advocated moving the harbors away from the central business districts to free space for public use.

4 The City Center Burnham redesigned the street pattern to create a group of long streets that would converge on a grand plaza, a practice reflected in other American cities. The convergence of major thoroughfares at a city's center helped create a unified city from a host of neighborhoods.

Block Schedule TEACHING OPTION **Time Needed: 40 Minutes**

Cooperative Activity: Planning Ideal Cities

Task: Groups of students will create plans of ideal cities for today or for future decades.

Purpose: To understand the achievements of turn-of-the-century urban planners.

Activity: Groups of four or five students should brainstorm for imaginative ideas to solve specific urban problems, such as overcrowding, affordable housing, efficient transportation, economic development, and recreation. Each student should focus on one topic, and then each group should incorporate these ideas into plans for an ideal city. Students' plans should include economic zones, roads, civic institutions, parks, schools, and housing units.

Building a Portfolio: Students should polish their plans and save them for their portfolio.

Standards for Evaluation
Final plans should . . .

- demonstrate careful consideration of the services needed by urban residents
- clearly label business and industrial districts, parks, schools, and housing units
- be drawn to a reasonable scale

By contrast, Chicago, with its explosive growth from 30,000 people in 1850 to 300,000 in 1870, represented a nightmare of unregulated expansion. As Rudyard Kipling complained of the city, "Having seen it, I urgently desire never to see it again." Fortunately for the growing city, the Chicago architect **Daniel Burnham** was intrigued by the prospect of remaking the city. Burnham's motto was "Make no little plans. They have no magic to stir men's blood." He oversaw the transformation of a swampy area near Lake Michigan into a glistening White City for Chicago's 1893 Columbian Exposition. Majestic exhibition halls, statues, and a lagoon greeted 27 million visitors who came to the city.

THINK THROUGH HISTORY
B. *Summarizing* *List three major changes in cities near the turn of the century. What effect did each have?*

"Make no little plans."
DANIEL BURNHAM

Many urban planners saw in Burnham's White City glorious visions of future cities. Burnham, however, left Chicago an even more important legacy: an overall plan for the city, crowned by elegant parks strung along Lake Michigan. As a result, Chicago's lakefront today features curving banks of grass and sandy beaches instead of a jumbled mass of piers and warehouses.

New Technologies Transform Communications

B. Answer *Possible Answers:* Skyscrapers conserved space by allowing cities to grow upward; new transportation systems and bridges drew neighborhoods closer together; urban planning put parks into cities.

While science and technology pushed American cities upward and outward, new developments in communications brought people closer together in time. In addition to a railroad network that now spanned the nation, advances in aviation, printing, and photography helped to speed the transmission of information.

AIRPLANES AND MAIL DELIVERY During the early 20th century, **Orville and Wilbur Wright,** two brothers who manufactured bicycles in Dayton, Ohio, experimented with new engines powerful enough to keep "heavier-than-air" craft aloft. The Wright brothers began by building a glider. Eventually they built their own four-cylinder internal combustion engine, chose a propeller, and designed a biplane with a 40-foot wingspan. Their first successful flight—on December 17, 1903, at Kitty Hawk, North Carolina—covered 120 feet and lasted 12 seconds.

When the Wright brothers tested their airplane, Orville, the pilot, had to position himself on the lower wing, next to the motor, to steer the plane.

The public paid little attention to the Wright brothers' achievement. Only a few newspapers in the country even bothered to print the story. The rest probably shared the "national suspicion that the sky was a place only for birds, angels, and fools." Within two years, however, the Wright brothers were making flights of 24 miles. By 1908, the pioneer aviators had attracted the interest of the U.S. government.

THINK THROUGH HISTORY
C. *Clarifying* *How did the use of mail planes bring people in different regions of the country closer together?*

Convinced of the great potential of flight, the government established the first transcontinental airmail service in 1920. At first, it took a day and a half for mail to travel between New York and San Francisco. The mail planes flew only in the daytime; at night the mail continued by train. By 1925, however, 61 of the 96 planes flying the mail could fly at night.

C. Answer Mail planes made it faster and easier for people in different regions to communicate.

A REVOLUTION IN PRINTING Thanks to better public education, the literacy rate in the United States had risen to nearly 90 percent by 1890. As Americans demonstrated an increased interest in reading, publishers turned out ever-increasing numbers of books, magazines, and newspapers to meet the demand. A series of technological advances in printing aided their efforts.

Less expensive paper and better printing presses helped lower the cost of printing. After chemists discovered that wood pulp could be used to make paper, American mills began to produce huge quantities of cheap paper. The new paper proved durable enough to withstand high-speed presses like the one invented by William Bullock. His electrically powered **web-perfecting press** printed on both sides of a continuous paper roll, rather than on just one side,

MORE ABOUT . . .
The Columbian Exposition

Celebrating the 400th anniversary of Columbus's landing in America, the 1893 World's Columbian Exposition was held in Chicago after cities across the nation competed to be the site. The White City sported the latest in electric lighting. President Grover Cleveland opened the fair by flicking a switch in Washington, D.C., to turn on the lights in Chicago.

ELECTRONIC LIBRARY OF PRIMARY SOURCES
from *A Visit to the World's Columbian Exposition* by Charles E. Bolton

OBJECTIVE
(2) INSTRUCT

New Technologies Transform Communications

▶***Discussing Key Ideas***
- Pioneered by the Wright brothers, airplanes revolutionize communications as well as transportation.
- Advances in paper and printing spur the publication of newspapers, books, and magazines, while better photography greatly enhances journalism.

IN-DEPTH RESOURCES: UNIT 2
Primary Source: *from* Orville Wright's Diary, p. 64

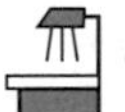
GEOGRAPHY TRANSPARENCIES
G16, Telephone Long Distance Lines, 1890–1917

TEACHING OPTIONS

Teaching Less Proficient Readers

Visual Learners Students who learn better visually than verbally may benefit from drawing a two-column chart that lists the technological developments that improved urban life at the turn of the century and their applications.

Technological Improvements	Uses
electricity	streetcars, elevated trains and subways
steel construction	suspension bridges, skyscrapers
internal combustion engines	automobiles, airplanes

Making Connections Across the Curriculum

Science Have interested students research and write a brief report on the Wright brothers' experiments with the principles of aerodynamics, such as lift and drag, that led to the invention of the airplane.

Students might give their final reports orally with accompanying illustrations, via computer with appropriate graphics, or in a special exhibit or bulletin-board display.

KEY PLAYER

George Eastman

Critical Thinking: Evaluating Ask students why Eastman's slogan and other sales methods were so effective with consumers. *Possible Responses: Sold good products to begin with; slogan stressed ease of use, made company seem helpful; simple operating instructions got good word of mouth; sending new film back made people feel that they were getting value for their money.*

IN-DEPTH RESOURCES: UNIT 2
Primary Source: Advertisement, p. 65

ASSESS & RETEACH

Section 1 Assessment

Have students work in small groups to answer the questions. For item 2, students may select one of the diagrams and then share their answers with other groups.

Self-Assessment

Ask students to list the impact of technology that most surprised them and to tell why it was surprising.

Section Quiz

FORMAL ASSESSMENT
Section Quiz, p. 104

Reteach

Have students create a list of the major technological advancements presented in the section. Then review the list to see how Americans addressed some of their social problems at the turn of the century.

CLOSE

Turn-of-the-century technological advances spurred the growth of America's cities and improved both transportation and communications.

then cut, folded, and counted the pages as they came down the line. Faster production and lower costs made newspapers and magazines more affordable. People could now buy newspapers for a penny a copy, and the price of most magazines plunged from about 25 cents to a nickel.

New inventions also sped the tedious process of typesetting. The **Linotype machine,** which was invented by Ottmar Mergenthaler and first used by a newspaper in 1886, streamlined the process of setting type. Illustration also became easier in the 1880s, when the process of chemical engraving enabled printers to reproduce paintings and photographs cheaply and accurately. As a result, illustrations filled newspapers, magazines, and books and became even more commonplace as photography improved.

KEY PLAYER

GEORGE EASTMAN
1854–1932

In 1877, a bank clerk named George Eastman took up photography as a hobby. For one day's outing, he had to lug more than 100 pounds of equipment, including heavy glass plates. To lighten his load, Eastman replaced the glass plates with film that could be rolled onto a spool.

In 1888, Eastman sold his first roll-film camera. The purchase price of $25 included a 100-picture roll of film. After taking the pictures, the photographer would send the camera back to Eastman's Rochester, New York, factory. For $10, the pictures were developed and returned with the camera loaded with a brand-new roll of film.

Eastman called his new camera the Kodak, because the made-up name was short, memorable, and easy to pronounce. It came with simple operating instructions, popularized by the slogan "You press the button—we do the rest."

D. Answer New printing methods sped production and lowered the cost of newspapers. New techniques in photography made it possible for reporters to photograph events as they happened.

THINK THROUGH HISTORY
D. *Synthesizing* *How did advances in printing and photography change newspapers?*

PHOTOGRAPHY FOR EVERYONE Before the 1880s, photography was a professional activity, difficult for the casual hobbyist. Because of the time required to take a picture and the weight of the equipment, a photographer could not shoot a moving object. In addition, photographers had to develop their shots immediately.

New techniques eliminated the need to develop pictures right away. **George Eastman** developed a paper-based film as an alternative to the heavy glass plates previously used. Now, instead of carrying their darkrooms around with them, photographers could send their film to a studio for processing. When professional photographers were slow to begin using the new film, Eastman decided to aim his product at the masses.

In 1888, Eastman introduced his Kodak camera. Easily held and operated, the Kodak prompted millions of Americans to become amateur photographers. The camera also helped to create the field of photojournalism. Reporters could now photograph events as they occurred. When the Wright brothers first flew their simple airplane at Kitty Hawk, an amateur photographer captured the first successful flight on film.

Transformations in communication, transportation, and the use of space reshaped the American landscape toward the end of the 19th century. At the same time, developments in education changed the American lifestyle.

Section 1 Assessment

1. TERMS & NAMES
Identify:
- Louis Sullivan
- Frederick Law Olmsted
- Central Park
- Daniel Burnham
- Orville and Wilbur Wright
- web-perfecting press
- Linotype machine
- George Eastman

2. SUMMARIZING Create three diagrams like this one and label each with one of these types of urban changes: city design, transportation, and communication. Fill in examples for each category.

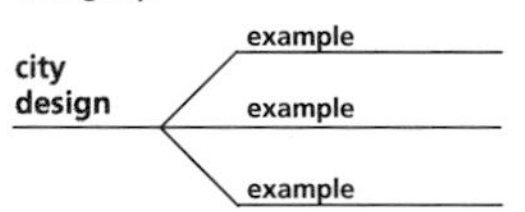

Choose one of the categories and create a poster showing changes that occurred.

3. FORMING OPINIONS Which scientific or technological development described in this section had the greatest impact on American culture? Use details from the text to justify your choice.

THINK ABOUT
- short-term and long-term effects of each development
- how each development affected the attitudes and lives of people at the time

4. SYNTHESIZING If you had been an urban planner at the turn of the century, what new ideas would you have included in your plan for the ideal city?

THINK ABOUT
- Olmsted's plans for Central Park and the Fenway
- Burnham's ideas for Chicago
- the concept of the garden city

ANSWERS

1. TERMS & NAMES

Louis Sullivan, p. 299
Frederick Law Olmsted, p. 300
Central Park, p. 300
Daniel Burnham, p. 301
Orville and Wilbur Wright, p. 301
web-perfecting press, p. 301
Linotype machine, p. 302
George Eastman, p. 302

2. SUMMARIZING

Student diagrams might include these:

City design: Suspension bridges; skyscrapers; urban planning; parks.

Urban transportation: Street cars; commuter trains; el trains; subways.

Communications: Web-perfecting press; Linotype machine; photography; airplanes.

3. FORMING OPINIONS

Possible Answer: Students should cite reasons, such as the long-term impact of air travel or the widespread influence of low-cost printing, to support their opinions.

4. SYNTHESIZING

Possible Response: Students' plans might mention additional recreational facilities or increased numbers of parks, or other personal preferences.

2 Education and Culture

TERMS & NAMES
- W. E. B. Du Bois
- Booker T. Washington
- Thomas Eakins
- Mark Twain

LEARN ABOUT changes in education and the promotion of high culture
TO UNDERSTAND how these developments affected America's changing identity.

ONE AMERICAN'S STORY

William Torrey Harris was an educational reformer who saw the public schools as a great instrument "to lift all classes of people into . . . civilized life." As superintendent of schools in St. Louis from 1868 to 1880 and U.S. commissioner of education from 1889 to 1906, Harris advised teachers to "lift" students by enforcing strict discipline. "The pupil," he preached, "must have his lessons ready at the appointed time, must rise at the tap of the bell, move to the line, return; in short, go through all the evolutions with equal precision." Such discipline, according to Harris, would properly prepare students for responsible citizenship.

A PERSONAL VOICE

We believe that a child can easily learn the lesson of willing obedience to lawful authority. We would, therefore, place him upon the basis upon which he must stand when he leaves our care; under such circumstances alone we can predict that those whose school record is good will make useful citizens.

WILLIAM TORREY HARRIS, quoted in *Public Schools and Moral Education*

Compulsory-school-attendance laws, though slow to be enforced, expanded school enrollments and filled classrooms like this one at the turn of the century.

Many other middle-class reformers agreed with Harris and viewed the public schools as training grounds for employment and citizenship. People believed that economic development depended on scientific and technological knowledge. As a result, they viewed education as a key to greater security and social status. Others saw the public schools as the best opportunity to assimilate the millions of immigrants entering American society. Most people also believed that education was necessary for a stable and prosperous democratic nation.

Expanding Public Education

Although most states had established public schools by the Civil War, many school-age children still received no formal schooling at all. In the South, only North Carolina had a public school system by the 1860s. Throughout the nation, the majority of students who went to school left within four years, and few went to high school.

These facts alarmed educational reformers like Harris. They argued that without a proper education, young Americans would not have the knowledge or skills needed to take part in civic affairs or to get good jobs in an industrial society. In the 1870s, reformers worked to extend schooling to more children, to increase the number of years of mandatory school attendance, and to lengthen the school year.

SCHOOLS FOR CHILDREN Between 1865 and 1895, 31 states passed laws requiring 12 to 16 weeks a year of school attendance by children between the ages of 8 and 14. By 1900, almost three-quarters of American children between those ages attended school, mostly in the cities. Students studied a curriculum that emphasized reading, writing, and arithmetic.

Section 2 Overview

OBJECTIVES

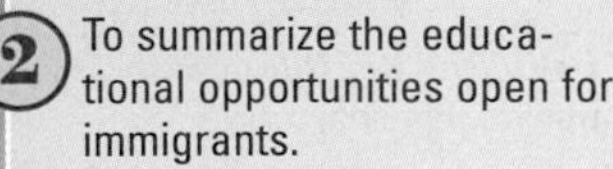

1. To trace the expansion of public education at the turn of the century.

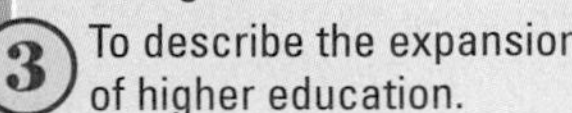

2. To summarize the educational opportunities open for immigrants.

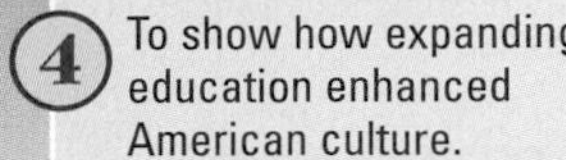

3. To describe the expansion of higher education.
4. To show how expanding education enhanced American culture.

SKILLBUILDER
- Interpreting graphs, p. 304

CRITICAL THINKING
- Making inferences, p. 304
- Theme: Immigration and Migration, p. 305
- Recognizing effects, p. 306
- Synthesizing, p. 307
- Summarizing, p. 308
- Developing historical perspective, p. 308
- Making predictions, p. 308

FOCUS & MOTIVATE

5-MINUTE WARM-UP

Making Generalizations

To recognize the changes in education, have students study the graph on page 304 and answer these questions.

1. What two trends does the graph show?
2. What generalization can you make about education or illiteracy between 1870 and 1920?

 ***WARM-UP TRANSPARENCY 8***

▶***Starting with the Student***

Ask students how an educational system might help a nation meet its social needs.

SECTION 2 RESOURCES

 **PRINT RESOURCES**

IN-DEPTH RESOURCES: UNIT 2
Guided Reading, p. 58
Primary Source: *from* "The Talented Tenth" by W. E. B. Du Bois, p. 66
American Lives: W. E .B. Du Bois, p. 71

READING STUDY GUIDE, p. 89

ACCESS FOR STUDENTS ACQUIRING ENGLISH
Guided Reading (Spanish), p. 112

SPANISH READING STUDY GUIDE, p. 89

FORMAL ASSESSMENT
Section Quiz, p. 105

ALTERNATIVE ASSESSMENT BOOK
See forms for supporting and scoring alternative activities.

 **TECHNOLOGY RESOURCES**

CRITICAL THINKING TRANSPARENCIES
CT16, Expansion of Education
CT50, Increasing School Enrollment: 1870–1920

CD-ROM *Grolier Multimedia Encyclopedia*

VIDEO *American Portfolio: A Videodisc for U.S. History* user's guide, pp. 151, 158, 166, 167

INTERNET http://www.mlushistory.com

OBJECTIVE
1 INSTRUCT

Expanding Public Education

▶***Discussing Key Ideas***
- States try to improve and expand public education to produce good citizens and skilled workers.

(continued on next page)

(continued from page 303)

- High schools emerge as industrial work demands more educated workers.
- Discriminatory educational policies deny most African Americans equal educational opportunities.

IN-DEPTH RESOURCES: UNIT 2
Guided Reading, p. 58

ACCESS FOR STUDENTS ACQUIRING ENGLISH
Guided Reading (Spanish), p. 112

HISTORY FROM VISUALS

Expanding Education/ Decreasing Illiteracy

Reading the Graph Remind the students that each stick figure in the graph equals 2 million students. Therefore, the six stick figures in the top row (1870) equal 12 million students.

CRITICAL THINKING TRANSPARENCIES
CT16, Expansion of Education
CT50, Increasing School Enrollment: 1870–1920

Issues for the 21st Century

Exploring Education Today

Connect education in the late 1800s to education today by having students reread pages 888–891. Then have them answer these questions.

1. What problems in education existed in the 1800s? *Poor quality teachers, poor teaching methods.*
2. What do you think are the most serious issues facing education in the United States today? *Improving quality, financing.*

Expanding Education/Decreasing Illiteracy

YEAR	SCHOOL-AGE POPULATION (5 TO 18 YEARS OF AGE)	ILLITERACY (% OF TOTAL POPULATION)
1870	12,000,000	20.0%
1880	15,065,767	17.0%
1890	18,543,201	13.0%
1900	21,404,322	10.7%
1910	24,360,888	7.7%
1920	27,728,788	6.0%

= 2,000,000 students

Sources: *Statistical Abstract of the United States, 1921; Historical Statistics of the United States*

SKILLBUILDER
INTERPRETING GRAPHS ***How much did the illiteracy rate drop from 1870 to 1920? Does the number of immigrants arriving during this period make the reduction in illiteracy more or less impressive? Why?***

Skillbuilder Answer
Rate: 14%.
Immigrants: *Possible Answer:* More impressive, because millions of immigrants could not read when they arrived in America.

However, the emphasis on rote memorization and the uneven quality of teachers drew criticism. Joseph Mayer Rice, a New York pediatrician, visited 36 cities and interviewed 1,200 teachers. He observed numerous problems, including teachers who focused more on their students' posture than on their mastery of academic subjects. At many schools, strict rules and physical punishment made students miserable. One 13-year-old boy explained to a Chicago school inspector why he hid in a warehouse basement instead of going to school.

A PERSONAL VOICE

They hits ye if yer don't learn, and they hits ye if ye whisper, and they hits ye if ye have string in yer pocket, and they hits ye if yer seat squeaks, and they hits ye if ye don't stan' up in time, and they hits ye if yer late, and they hits ye if ye ferget the page.

ANONYMOUS, quoted in *The One Best System*

Despite such problems, children began attending school at a younger age. Kindergartens, which had been created outside the public school system to offer childcare for employed mothers, became increasingly popular. The number of kindergartens surged from 200 in 1880 to 3,000 in 1900, and public school systems began to add kindergartens to their programs.

Although the pattern in public education during this era was one of growth, opportunities differed sharply for white and black students. In 1880, about 62 percent of white children attended elementary school, compared to only 34 percent of African-American children. Not until the 1940s would public school education become available to the majority of black children living in the South.

A. Answer Public schools provided the skills people needed to obtain good jobs, as well as the knowledge they needed to take part in civic affairs.

THE GROWTH OF HIGH SCHOOLS In the new industrial age, people realized that the economy demanded advanced technical and managerial skills. Moreover, business leaders like Andrew Carnegie pointed out that keeping workers loyal to capitalism required society to "provide ladders upon which the aspiring can rise."

The number of public high schools jumped from 800 in 1878 to 5,500 in 1898. Whereas fewer than 72,000 students had attended high school in 1870, more than half a million students attended by the turn of the century. The high school curriculum expanded to include courses in science, civics, home economics, history, and literature. In addition, new vocational courses helped prepare male graduates for industrial jobs in drafting, carpentry, and mechanics, and female graduates for work as secretaries and bookkeepers.

THINK THROUGH HISTORY
A. *Making Inferences* *Explain why many people saw public schools as "ladders upon which the aspiring can rise."*

This boys' track meet was typical of high school athletics at the turn of the century.

Block Schedule TEACHING OPTION **Time Needed: 20 Minutes**

Cooperative Activity: Reforming Public Education

Task: Groups of students will form a school reform committee and create a plan to reform public schools at the turn of the century.

Purpose: To understand the methods and goals of turn-of-the-century educational reformers.

Activity: Groups of five or six students will act as a school board at the turn of the century. They are to devise a plan to reform their school district to address an influx of new immigrants, increasing school age populations, and new industrial jobs available in their area.

Building a Portfolio: Students should save their reform plans and place them in their portfolio.

Standards for Evaluation
Reform plans should . . .

- address the cultural issues that might arise from a large immigrant population
- provide adequate school capacity for increased population
- devise a curriculum that creates skilled workers
- propose a reasonable funding plan

RACIAL DISCRIMINATION Although white enrollment in public high schools surged after 1880, African Americans for the most part were excluded from public secondary education. In 1890, fewer than 1 percent of black teenagers attended high school. Two out of three of these students went to private schools, which received no government financial support. By 1910, about 3 percent of African Americans between the ages of 15 and 19 attended high school, but most of these students still attended private schools.

Education for Immigrants

Unlike African Americans, immigrants were not locked out of schools. In fact, they were encouraged to go to school. Of the 10 million European immigrants settled in the United States between 1860 and 1890, many were Jewish people fleeing poverty and oppression in eastern Europe to pursue economic and educational opportunities in America. Years after she became a citizen, the Russian Jewish immigrant Mary Antin recalled the large numbers of non-English-speaking immigrant children. By the end of the school year, they could recite "patriotic verses in honor of George Washington and Abraham Lincoln, with a foreign accent, indeed, but with plenty of enthusiasm."

Most immigrants sent their children to America's free public schools, where they quickly became "Americanized." Others were dismayed by the prospect. Some people resented the suppression of their native languages in favor of English.

Catholics were especially concerned because many public school systems had mandatory readings from the (Protestant) King James Version of the Bible and refused to observe holidays in honor of Catholic saints. Instead of sending their children to such schools, Catholic communities often set up parochial schools to give their children a Catholic education.

Thousands of adult immigrants attended night school to learn English and to qualify for American citizenship. Employers, too, offered daytime programs to Americanize their workers. At his Model T plant in Highland Park, Michigan, Henry Ford established a "Sociology Department." It sent caseworkers into immigrants' homes because "men of many nations must be taught American ways, the English language, and the right way to live."

Ford's idea about the "right way to live" was not universally accepted, however. Labor activists often protested that Ford's educational goals were aimed at weakening the trade union movement by teaching workers not to confront management.

B. Answer Public schools and adult classes, which taught English to the immigrants, and places of employment, which offered programs to Americanize them.

THINK THROUGH HISTORY
B. THEME ***Immigration and Migration*** *What institutions encouraged European immigrants to become assimilated?*

Expanding Higher Education

Although the number of students attending high school had increased by the turn of the century, only a minority of Americans had high school diplomas. At the same time, an even smaller minority—only 2.3 percent—of America's young people attended colleges and universities.

With few exceptions, college students came from middle-class or wealthy families. College prepared well-to-do young men for successful careers in business or the professions. Between 1880 and 1900, more than 150 new colleges were founded. Between 1880 and 1920, college enrollments more than quadrupled. In addition, colleges instituted major changes in curricula and admission policies.

CHANGES IN UNIVERSITIES Through most of the 19th century, the traditional college curriculum was focused on the study of Greek and

"I believe that the motion picture is destined to revolutionize our educational system."

THOMAS EDISON, 1922

NOW & THEN

TECHNOLOGY AND SCHOOLS

In 1922, Thomas Alva Edison wrote, "I believe that the motion picture is destined to revolutionize our educational system and that in a few years it will supplant . . . the use of textbooks." Today's high schools show that the brilliant inventor was mistaken.

Recently, some people have predicted that computers will replace traditional classrooms and texts. According to a 1995 survey, three-quarters of the nation's schools plan on installing at least two computers per classroom.

Computers allow video course-sharing, in which students in many schools view the same instructors. Students also use computers to access up-to-the-minute scientific data, such as weather information.

For many teens, though, the lure of using computers to access the Internet is more social than educational. One small study revealed that only one-quarter of teens' e-mail messages related to schoolwork—most of their messages were social.

OBJECTIVE
② INSTRUCT

Education for Immigrants

▶ ***Starting with the Student*** Ask students to consider how they might assimilate to new schools and lifestyles if they immigrated to a different country.

▶ ***Discussing Key Ideas***
- Public schools and employers attempt to Americanize immigrants.
- Some immigrants resist the pressure to abandon their native cultures.

NOW & THEN
Technology and Schools
Critical Thinking: Evaluating Have students discuss the value of computers in the classroom. Do they think computers are overrated as an educational tool or that computer skills are essential in today's world?

OBJECTIVE
③ INSTRUCT

Expanding Higher Education

▶ ***Discussing Key Ideas***
- Higher education greatly expands at the turn of the century, drawing students mainly from upper- and middle-class backgrounds.
- The college curriculum changes to suit the new technological age.
- African Americans establish colleges of their own to overcome their exclusion from most white schools.

TEACHING OPTIONS

Exploring Themes

Immigration and Migration Note that education was a vital tool for assimilating the millions of immigrants who came to America from 1880 to 1920. Not only did immigrant children attend school by day, but their parents often took adult education courses at night or went through Americanization programs at work. Immigrants were also indirectly assimilated on the job through the labor unions and political organizations that many of them joined. Encourage students to offer their own definitions of Americanization and to discuss its importance.

Teaching Less Proficient Readers

Guided Reading Suggest that students focus their reading by turning each heading and subheading into a question and then reading the material below it to find the answer. For example, the headings and subheadings on pages 304 and 305 could be turned into these questions:

- Why did high schools grow?
- What group faced discrimination and in what ways?
- What education was provided for immigrants?
- How was higher education expanded?

HISTORICAL SPOTLIGHT
Stanford University

Critical Thinking: Analyzing Motives Point out to students that Leland Stanford wanted the education programs at the university "to qualify students for personal success and direct usefulness in life." Ask students why they think Stanford established this objective.

MORE ABOUT . . .
W. E. B. Du Bois

Du Bois (often *DuBois;* pronounced *doo bois'*) attended Fisk University in Nashville before going to graduate school at Harvard. Although his doctorate was in history, he was really more of a sociologist who devoted his scholarship to fighting racism. Du Bois used statistical evidence to disprove racist myths that were used to support segregation. Among his early writings with this goal was *The Philadelphia Negro* (1899), the first case study of an African-American community.

IN-DEPTH RESOURCES: UNIT 2
Primary Source: *from* "The Talented Tenth" by W. E. B. Du Bois, p. 66
American Lives: W. E. B. Du Bois, p. 71

GROLIER MULTIMEDIA ENCYCLOPEDIA
from *The Souls of Black Folk* by W. E. B. Du Bois

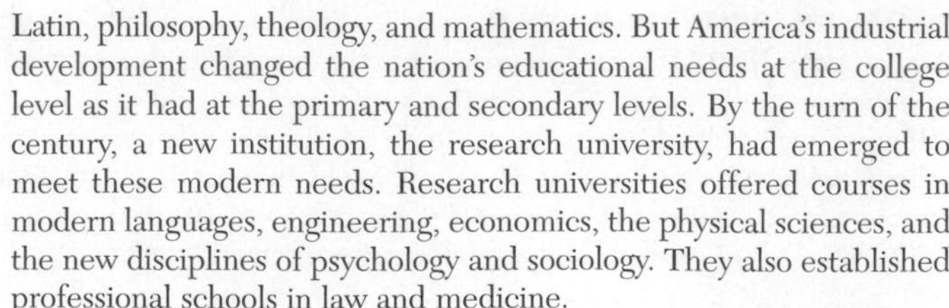

HISTORICAL SPOTLIGHT

STANFORD UNIVERSITY

After Leland Stanford and Jane Lathrop Stanford's only child died from typhoid fever in 1884, Stanford told his wife, "The children of California shall be our children." With these words, the idea of Stanford University, in Palo Alto, California, took shape. The Stanfords chose the landscape architect Frederick Law Olmsted—the designer of Central Park in New York City—to develop the general plans for the university, which included building designs similar to California mission architecture.

Leland Stanford Junior University, now known as Stanford University, opened in 1891 to about 500 students. From the beginning the university was coeducational and nondenominational. The university's programs reflected the objectives that had been established by Stanford, which included "to qualify students for personal success and direct usefulness in life."

Latin, philosophy, theology, and mathematics. But America's industrial development changed the nation's educational needs at the college level as it had at the primary and secondary levels. By the turn of the century, a new institution, the research university, had emerged to meet these modern needs. Research universities offered courses in modern languages, engineering, economics, the physical sciences, and the new disciplines of psychology and sociology. They also established professional schools in law and medicine.

Some research universities were founded by wealthy capitalists who wanted to ensure an ample supply of engineers and scientists. In Palo Alto, California, Leland Stanford and his wife, Jane Lathrop Stanford, donated $21 million to open Stanford University in memory of their son. In 1891, the University of Chicago was founded with gifts totaling $34 million from John D. Rockefeller. By the end of his life, Rockefeller had given the university more than $80 million.

During this period, private colleges and universities required entrance exams. State universities in the Midwest and California, however, began to admit students without requiring an exam, using the high school diploma as the entrance requirement.

Higher education also changed because of developments in medicine. During the Civil War, wounds killed only half as many soldiers as infections caused by doctors who, ignorant of the effects of germs, failed to wash their hands. After the war, American medical professionals who had been trained in Germany and France restructured American medical education to include basic hygiene, laboratory experience, and courses in biology, chemistry, and physics. By the turn of the century, medical education was set on a firm course. Professional programs in architecture, engineering, and law also benefited from reforms.

THINK THROUGH HISTORY
C. ***Recognizing Effects*** *How did the Civil War affect medical education?*

C. Answer
Because of the number of deaths from infection during the war, reformers sought changes in medical schools to ensure a rigorous education for doctors.

HIGHER EDUCATION FOR AFRICAN AMERICANS After the Civil War, thousands of freed African Americans pursued higher education, despite their exclusion from white colleges and universities. All-black schools soon opened to educate merchants, ministers, physicians, dentists, and teachers. With the help of the Freedmen's Bureau and Northern groups like the American Missionary Association, African Americans founded Howard, Atlanta, and Fisk Universities and Hampton Institute, all of which opened between 1865 and 1868.

White and black charitable organizations that supported black colleges could not, however, financially support or educate a sufficient number of black college graduates to provide enough doctors, lawyers, and teachers to meet the needs of the segregated communities. By 1900, out of 9.2 million African Americans, only 3,880 had graduated from colleges or professional schools. In 1910, 5 percent of the white population attended college, compared to less than one-third of 1 percent of the African-American community.

W. E. B. Du Bois became, in 1895, the first African American to receive a doctorate from Harvard. "The honor, I assure you," the confident Du Bois said, "was Harvard's." Born to a middle-class family in Massachusetts, Du Bois believed that blacks should seek a liberal arts education so that the African-

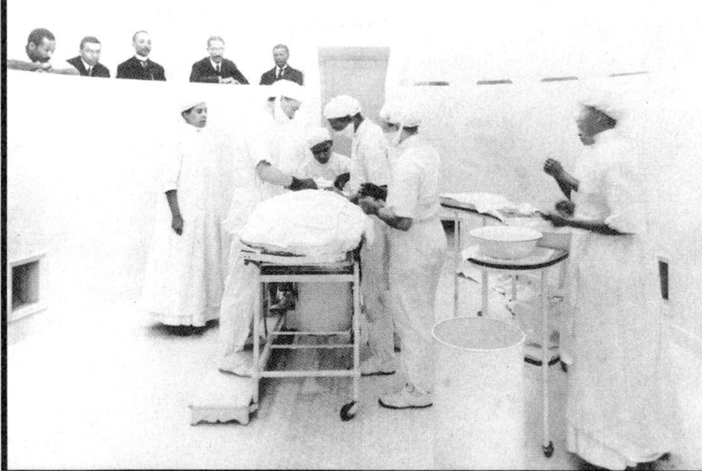

Medical students and their professors work in the operating theater of the Moorland-Spingarn Research Center at Howard University.

TEACHING OPTIONS

Making Connections Across Time

Trends in Education At the turn of the century, public-school education typically consisted of eight years of grade school and four years of high school. Some educators believed that middle-grade students would learn and socialize better in a different format, and the junior high school was born. More recent trends include block scheduling, the increased use of video and computer technologies, and preschool training.

Encourage students to discuss new ideas in education, such as the voucher system, charter schools, and Americorps.

Making Connections Across Cultures

Campus Diversity Until the late 19th century, most American college students were wealthy white males. Throughout the 20th century, however, the number of women, minorities, and international students has climbed. These groups of people brought fresh perspectives to the intellectual and cultural aspects of campus life that have expanded the focus of scholarship and created new departments and programs (such as Afro-American Studies). Sometimes this diversity results in tensions, and campus groups have come into conflict over issues like speech codes (rules regulating potentially offensive language).

American community would have well-educated leaders. Toward this end, Du Bois proposed that a group of educated blacks, the most "talented tenth" of the African-American community, attempt to achieve immediate inclusion into mainstream American life. "We are Americans, not only by birth and by citizenship," Du Bois argued, "but by our political ideals. . . . And the greatest of those ideals is that ALL MEN ARE CREATED EQUAL."

D. Answer All-black colleges and universities opened, but only a tiny percentage of African Americans received a college education.

THINK THROUGH HISTORY
D. Synthesizing *Describe the state of higher education for African Americans at the turn of the century.*

Another prominent African American, **Booker T. Washington,** believed that racism would end once African Americans acquired useful labor skills and proved their economic value to society. Washington, who was born a slave in Virginia, graduated from Hampton Institute after his emancipation. In 1881, he opened his own school in Alabama, the Tuskegee Normal and Industrial Institute. Tuskegee aimed to enable its black graduates to teach and to do agricultural, domestic, or mechanical work. "No race," Washington said, "can prosper till it learns that there is as much dignity in tilling a field as in writing a poem."

Education Influences Culture

As increasing numbers of Americans attended school and learned to read, the cultural vistas of ordinary Americans expanded. Art galleries, libraries, books, and museums also brought new cultural opportunities to more people.

PROMOTING FINE ARTS Public schools and colleges were not the only sources of education for Americans. By 1900, at least one art gallery graced every large city. Often, wealthy patrons established art galleries and museums to share the art treasures they had acquired for their palatial houses.

In the late 19th century, some American artists, including **Thomas Eakins,** began to embrace realism, an artistic school that aimed at portraying real life even in its grittier forms. Eakins filled his canvases with muscular rowers who looked especially lifelike because of his study of anatomy and experience in dissecting bodies at a medical school. In his drawing classes at the Pennsylvania Academy of Fine Arts, Eakins employed nude models, which led wealthy Philadelphians to call for his dismissal. The same wealthy patrons had already been offended by Eakins's realist approach to portrait painting.

The realist movement in American art is exemplified in *The Champion Single Sculls (Max Schmitt in a Single Scull)* (1871) by Thomas Eakins.

Americans' preoccupation with the problems and prospects of their cities found expression in the works of artists such as Robert Henri in the early 20th century. Henri and like-minded artists became known as the ashcan school because of their portrayals of urban poverty and working-class people.

Both Eakins and the ashcan school artists soon were challenged by the European development known as abstract art, a shocking nonrepresentational form of modernist expression that most people found difficult to understand. When an exhibit of European modernists opened at the National Guard Armory in New York in 1913, half a million people eagerly viewed the works of Pablo Picasso, Henri Matisse, and others.

OBJECTIVE
4 INSTRUCT

Education Influences Culture

▶ ***Starting with the Student***
- Ask students to discuss what kinds of topics, issues, and activities (such as music, literature, film, or other hobbies) that education has helped them appreciate.

▶ ***Discussing Key Ideas***
- The expansion of education broadens Americans' cultural horizons, with art galleries, libraries, and museums making culture available to more people.
- Many turn-of-the-century artists and writers embrace social realism, attempting to portray life as it is really lived.
- Increased literacy boosts sales of "dime novels" and other light fiction.

MORE ABOUT
Thomas Eakins

Except for four years in Europe, when he studied art in France and viewed the masterpieces of Spain, Eakins spent virtually his entire life in the city of his birth, Philadelphia. His pioneering efforts in realism at first met with scorn. *The Gross Clinic,* the realistic depiction of a surgery, now deemed his masterpiece, was rejected for display at the Centennial Exposition held in Philadelphia in 1876.

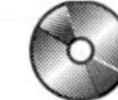

GROLIER MULTIMEDIA ENCYCLOPEDIA
Thomas Eakins with an example of his work

TEACHING OPTIONS

Making Global Connections

Technology and Culture Stress that improved communications and transportation made culture far more international, enabling successful Americans to travel overseas and more foreign art and artists to visit America. Mark Twain satirized foreign sights and ways through the supposedly naive American world traveler in *The Innocents Abroad,* a narrative based on his own experiences on a tour of Mediterranean Europe and the Holy Land. Painter Mary Cassatt and authors Henry James, Edith Wharton, and Stephen Crane are just a few of the many turn-of-the-century American artists and intellectuals who spent extensive time in Europe.

Making Connections Across the Curriculum

Art Note that the Ashcan (often *Ash Can)* School got its name because its paintings portrayed urban life with gritty realism. Artists Robert Henri, Everett Shinn, John Sloan, Arthur B. Davies, Ernest Lawson, Maurice Prendergast, George Luks, and William Glackens opposed New York's conservative exhibit rules in 1907 and together displayed their work at a 1908 exhibit. They later became a part of the Ashcan School, of which Edward Hopper was also a member.

Have students examine and critique paintings by Ashcan School artists. Ask them what aspects of turn-of-the-century urban life the paintings portray.

MORE ABOUT . . .
Mark Twain

Clemens grew up in the Mississippi River town of Hannibal, Missouri, and took his pen name from a riverboat pilot's cry, "Mark twain!"—which meant the water was two fathoms deep, or safe for the boat to cross. Twain's satirical pen gave late 19th-century America its nickname, the Gilded Age, which was the title of a novel he coauthored with Charles Dudley Warner. A pioneer work of American realism, *The Adventures of Huckleberry Finn* is usually cited as Twain's masterpiece. "All modern American literature," Ernest Hemingway once said, "comes from one book by Mark Twain called *Huckleberry Finn.*"

ASSESS & RETEACH

Section 2 Assessment

Students might work in pairs to respond to the questions.

Self-Assessment

To assess what they have learned, students might write their own questions, exchange them with a partner, and try to answer their partner's questions.

Section Quiz

FORMAL ASSESSMENT
Section Quiz, p. 105

Reteach

Ask students to consider the three most important changes in education at the turn of the century and give the reasons they occurred.

CLOSE

Education, which expanded to train the work force and teach good American citizenship, also led to new cultural achievements.

In many cities, inhabitants could walk from the new art gallery to the new public library, sometimes called "the poor man's university." Recalling his boyhood yearning for books, the wealthy industrialist Andrew Carnegie donated $60 million to build public libraries all over the country. The cities that built the libraries provided the land and levied taxes to buy books and pay librarians. By 1900, free circulating libraries in America numbered in the thousands.

The highly popular dime novels often featured adventure stories.

POPULAR FICTION As literacy rates rose, intellectual leaders debated the role of literature in society. Some felt that literature should uplift America's literary tastes, which tended toward crime tales and Western adventures. Editors at *The Nation, Atlantic Monthly,* and *North American Review* combed their publications to remove sexual or anti-Christian material, slang, and tragic endings.

Others wanted a more realistic portrayal of American life. Samuel Langhorne Clemens, the novelist and humorist better known as **Mark Twain,** inspired a host of other young authors when he declared his independence of "literature and all that bosh." Though some critics of the day felt Twain's work to be little better than mild amusement, some of his books have become classics of American literature. *The Adventures of Huckleberry Finn,* for example, remains famous for its realistic rendering of American life along the Mississippi River.

In *The Country of the Pointed Firs* (1896), Sarah Orne Jewett, known as a regionalist for her realistic portrayals of the dialect and detail of New England village life, captured the simplicity of life in South Berwick, Maine. Other writers of the era—Theodore Dreiser, Stephen Crane, Jack London, and Willa Cather, for example—portrayed characters less polished than the upper-class men and women of Henry James's and Edith Wharton's novels.

Most people, however, preferred to read light fiction. Harlan F. Halsey churned out one popular novel after another and sometimes produced a book a day. Such books sold for a mere ten cents, hence their name, "dime novels." Dime novels typically told glorified adventure tales of the West and featured heroes like Edward Wheeler's Deadwood Dick. Wheeler published his first Deadwood Dick novel in 1877 and in less than a decade produced over 30 more.

E. Answer New printing technologies and America's growing literacy rate.

THINK THROUGH HISTORY
E. Summarizing *What factors contributed to the popularity of dime novels?*

Although art galleries and libraries attempted to raise cultural standards, many Americans had scant interest in high culture—and others did not have access to it. African Americans, for example, were excluded from visiting museums and other white-controlled cultural institutions. They and other racial and ethnic groups struggled against this discrimination and enforced segregation in all parts of the country.

Section 2 Assessment

1. TERMS & NAMES
Identify:
- W. E. B. Du Bois
- Booker T. Washington
- Thomas Eakins
- Mark Twain

2. SUMMARIZING In a chart like the one below, list at least three developments in education at the turn of the century and their major results.

Development	Result
1.	
2.	
3.	

Write a paragraph explaining which educational development you think was most important.

3. DEVELOPING HISTORICAL PERSPECTIVE Compare the impact of museums, libraries, and other cultural institutions on early-20th-century society with their impact on today's society. Are these institutions more or less important today than they were then?

THINK ABOUT
- the audiences museums and libraries reached then and now
- the role of museums and libraries in mass culture then and now

4. MAKING PREDICTIONS How might the economy and culture of the United States have been different without the expansion of public schools?

THINK ABOUT
- the goals of public schools and whether those goals have been met
- why people supported expanding public education
- the impact of public schools on the development of private schools

ANSWERS

1. TERMS & NAMES

W. E. B. Du Bois, p. 306
Booker T. Washington, p. 307
Thomas Eakins, p. 307
Mark Twain, p. 308

2. SUMMARIZING

Students might include some of the following entries:

- Compulsory education laws: Literacy increased.
- Increase in number of kindergartens: Immigrants became "Americanized."
- Growth of high schools: College enrollments increased.
- Discrimination against African Americans: All-black colleges founded.
- New curricula: Advances in science and medicine.

Students' paragraphs will vary but should include reasons for their choices.

3. DEVELOPING HISTORICAL PERSPECTIVE

Possible Answer: Students may note that in the early 20th century, cultural institutions promoted high culture, rather than the mass culture that was emerging. Today, museums and libraries are more integrated into the modern mass culture and reach larger audiences.

4. MAKING PREDICTIONS

Possible Answer: Without public schools, economic growth, the adapting of immigrants to American life, and the growth of high culture might have slowed. However, private schools might have developed more rapidly.

3 Segregation and Discrimination

TERMS & NAMES
- Ida B. Wells
- literacy test
- poll tax
- grandfather clause
- Jim Crow laws
- segregation
- *Plessy* v. *Ferguson*
- debt peonage

LEARN ABOUT racial tensions in the late 19th century
TO UNDERSTAND the persistence of racial discrimination in America.

ONE AMERICAN'S STORY

African Americans clutched at their dreams of equality in the years following Reconstruction. In both the South and the North, though, a system of segregation and discrimination prevented equal access to schools, jobs, and housing. **Ida B. Wells** refused to accept this system.

Born into slavery shortly before emancipation, Wells was raised in a well-respected and politically active African-American family. The death of her parents in a yellow fever epidemic rushed her into an adulthood that included caring for her younger siblings. In the early 1880s, she moved to Memphis to work as a teacher, and she later became an editor of a local paper.

Racial justice was a persistent theme in Wells's reporting, but the events of 1892 turned that theme into a crusade. On March 9, three of Wells's friends were lynched. The men had opened a store called the People's Grocery, that successfully competed with a nearby white-owned store. The competition escalated into violence, and the three black proprietors were arrested. Later a white mob formed, grabbed the three men from the jail and killed them. Wells recognized lynching for what it was.

Ida B. Wells

A PERSONAL VOICE

Thomas Moss, Calvin McDowell, and Lee Stewart had been lynched in Memphis . . . [where] no lynching had taken place before. . . . This is what opened my eyes to what lynching really was. An excuse to get rid of Negroes who were acquiring wealth and property and thus keep the race terrorized.

IDA B. WELLS, quoted in *Crusade for Justice*

As Wells denounced the lynching, the local white press in Memphis called for her to be lynched. She decided she was no longer safe in Memphis and moved to the North, where she continued her fight against lynching by writing, lecturing, and organizing for civil rights.

The racial hostility Wells encountered in Memphis was common in late-19th-century America. All African Americans faced constant threats to their civil rights—as workers, as consumers, and as citizens—throughout the United States. Nor were African Americans the only group to experience oppression. Native Americans, Chinese immigrants, and Mexican residents also encountered bitter forms of discrimination in the American West.

African Americans Fight Legal Discrimination

As African Americans exercised their newly won political and social rights during Reconstruction, they faced hostile, and often violent, opposition from whites. After the federal government lifted military authority over the Southern states in 1877, white Southern Democrats reclaimed control over their state governments and quickly instituted laws to subject African Americans to second-class citizenship. African Americans eventually fell victim to laws restricting their civil rights but never stopped fighting for equality.

VOTING RESTRICTIONS For at least ten years after the end of Reconstruction in 1877, African Americans in the South continued to vote and occasionally to

SECTION 3 RESOURCES

PRINT RESOURCES

IN-DEPTH RESOURCES: UNIT 2
Guided Reading, p. 59
Skillbuilder Practice: Finding Main Ideas, p. 61
Primary Source: *from* "Lynching and the Excuse for It" by Ida B. Wells, p. 67

READING STUDY GUIDE, p. 91

ACCESS FOR STUDENTS ACQUIRING ENGLISH
Guided Reading (Spanish), p. 113
Skillbuilder Practice: Finding Main Ideas (Spanish), p. 115

SPANISH READING STUDY GUIDE, p. 91

FORMAL ASSESSMENT
Section Quiz, p. 106

ALTERNATIVE ASSESSMENT BOOK
See forms for supporting and scoring alternative activities.

TECHNOLOGY RESOURCES

CD-ROM *Grolier Multimedia Encyclopedia*
Electronic Library of Primary Sources

VIDEO *American Portfolio: A Videodisc for U.S. History* user's guide, pp. 151, 155, 160, 174

INTERNET http://www.mlushistory.com

Section 3 Overview

OBJECTIVES

1. To trace the development of legal discrimination against African Americans in the South and their struggle against it.
2. To summarize turn-of-the-century race relations in the North and in the South.
3. To identify discrimination against nonwhites in the American West.

SKILLBUILDER

- Interpreting charts, p. 310

CRITICAL THINKING

- Theme: Civil Rights, p. 311
- Finding main ideas, p. 311
- Contrasting, p. 313
- Summarizing, p. 313
- Identifying problems, p. 313

FOCUS & MOTIVATE

5-MINUTE WARM-UP

Recognizing Point of View
To gain insight into different views on African-American equality, have students read the Historical Spotlight on page 311 and answer these questions.

1. How did Washington believe equality should be gained?
2. How did Du Bois's view differ from Washington's?

WARM-UP TRANSPARENCY 8

▶ ***Starting with the Student***
You might ask students whether they have ever been unfairly discriminated against.

OBJECTIVE
(2) INSTRUCT

African Americans Fight Legal Discrimination

▶ ***Discussing Key Ideas***
- White Southerners institute voting restrictions

(continued on next page)

(continued from page 309)

and segregation laws, reducing African Americans to second-class citizenship.

- In *Plessy* v. *Ferguson* in 1896, the Supreme Court made "separate but equal" the law of the land. In practice, the separation was enforced, but the equality was not.

IN-DEPTH RESOURCES: UNIT 2
Guided Reading, p. 59

ACCESS FOR STUDENTS ACQUIRING ENGLISH
Guided Reading (Spanish), p. 113

MORE ABOUT . . .
Jim Crow

Thomas Dartmouth ("Daddy") Rice was the father of American minstrel shows, musical entertainment in which blacks, or whites in blackface, poked fun at the singing and dancing of African-American slaves. Winning fame as a "Negro impersonator," Rice created the character of Jim Crow in an 1828 minstrel routine that conveyed the stereotype of the simple, happy-go-lucky black who loves to dance and sing for "de white folks." Minstrel shows became hugely popular by mid-century when companies like the Virginia Minstrels and Bryant's Minstrels went on tour and the most famous of all, the Christy Minstrels, performed Stephen Foster songs on Broadway in New York City.

GROLIER MULTIMEDIA ENCYCLOPEDIA
Jim Crow Laws

hold political office. By the end of the century, however, Southern states had adopted a broad system of legal policies of racial discrimination and devised methods to weaken African-American political power.

All Southern states imposed new voting restrictions. The Supreme Court generally refused to view such legislation as a violation of the Thirteenth, Fourteenth, and Fifteenth Amendments, and thus these new laws denied legal equality to African Americans. For example, some states required that prospective voters be literate. To enforce that requirement, voter registration officials administered a **literacy test.** Registrars often asked blacks more difficult questions than they asked whites, or gave them a test in a foreign language. The officials administering the test could pass or fail applicants as they wished.

Another requirement was the **poll tax,** an annual tax that had to be paid to gain access to the voting booth. Black as well as white sharecroppers, who usually lacked the cash to pay the tax, were frequently unable to vote.

To reinstate white voters who may have failed the literacy test or could not pay the poll tax, several Southern states added **grandfather clauses** to their constitutions. Louisiana was the first to do so, in 1898. The clause stated that even if a man failed the literacy test or could not afford the poll tax, he was still entitled to vote if he, his father, or his grandfather had been eligible to vote before January 1, 1867. The date is important because before that time freed slaves did not have the right to vote. The grandfather clause therefore did not allow them to vote.

During the 1870s and 1880s, the Supreme Court failed to overturn these laws—even though the laws undermined all federal protections for African Americans' civil rights. For example, in *United States* v. *Reese* in 1876, the Supreme Court argued that the Fifteenth Amendment did not automatically give the vote to anyone. It simply made it illegal to use a person's race as a reason for denying the right to vote. Since laws establishing poll taxes and literacy tests said nothing about race, the Supreme Court allowed them to stand.

JIM CROW LAWS At the same time that African Americans lost voting rights, Southern state and local governments passed laws to separate white and black people in public and private facilities. These laws came to be known as **Jim Crow laws** after a minstrel-show character who sang a comic song ending in the words "Jump, Jim Crow." By the early 20th century, the word ***segregation*** was used to describe this system of separating people on the basis of race. Racial segregation developed in schools, hospitals, parks, and transportation systems throughout the South.

PLESSY V. FERGUSON Eventually a legal case reached the U.S. Supreme Court to test the constitutionality of segregation. Homer A. Plessy, classified as a black man in Louisiana because he was one-eighth African American, had been denied a seat in a railroad car reserved for white passengers. Plessy

SKILLBUILDER
INTERPRETING CHARTS
What do you think Justice Brown meant when he said that the Constitution could not put people "on the same plane"? How did Justice Harlan oppose Brown's opinion?

Skillbuilder Answer
Possible Answer: Brown meant that laws could not make people equal. Harlan wrote a dissenting opinion and argued that it was wrong to have laws that distinguished people solely on the basis of race.

Plessy v. *Ferguson*

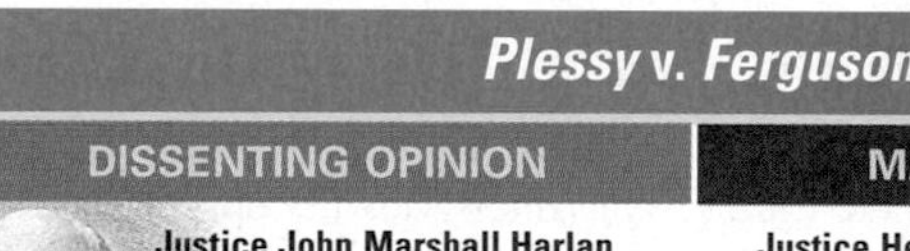

DISSENTING OPINION	MAJORITY OPINION
Justice John Marshall Harlan	**Justice Henry P. Brown**
"The thin disguise of 'equal' accommodations for passengers in railroad coaches will not mislead any-one nor atone for the wrong this day done."	**"If one race be inferior to the other socially, the Constitution of the United States cannot put them upon the same plane."**

TEACHING OPTIONS

Teaching Gifted and Talented Students

Legal Briefs Encourage interested students to research the arguments and decisions in *Plessy* v. *Ferguson* or another famous Supreme Court case in the history of civil rights, such as the Dred Scott decision of 1857 or *Brown* v. *Board of Education of Topeka* (1954). Final reports may consist of written briefs or dramatizations in which small groups of students present each case to classmates.

Exploring Themes

Civil Rights Note that W. E. B. Du Bois and Booker T. Washington were both pioneers in the struggle for African-American rights, although their approaches differed. Washington stressed a gradual approach through education and suggested that African Americans focus on developing skills that would lead to economic independence. Du Bois demanded more rapid change and insisted on an immediate end to segregation. Washington's approach was more acceptable to many progressive whites who argued for greater social equality but feared Du Bois's approach was too radical.

challenged the Louisiana law that required railroad companies to segregate white and black passengers. He contended that the law denied him his rights under Louisiana's constitution, and he took the issue to court. The railroad argued that the separate facilities for black people were just as good as the ones for whites.

A. Answer The Supreme Court decision opened the door for the legal segregation of almost all public facilities.

THINK THROUGH HISTORY
A. THEME *Civil Rights* *How did the* Plessy v. Ferguson *ruling affect the civil rights of African Americans?*

The Supreme Court sided with the railroad. In 1896, in ***Plessy* v. *Ferguson,*** the Court ruled that the separation of races in public accommodations was legal and did not violate the Fourteenth Amendment. The decision established the doctrine of "separate but equal," which allowed states to maintain segregated facilities for blacks and whites as long as they provided equal service. The decision permitted legalized racial segregation for almost 60 years. Unfortunately for African Americans, the "separate" part of the law was enforced far more often than the "equal" part, and facilities labeled "colored" rapidly declined in quality.

Turn-of-the-Century Race Relations

B. Answer He believed it was best not to emphasize legal equality but to concentrate on creating economic opportunities for African Americans instead.

THINK THROUGH HISTORY
B. *Finding Main Ideas* *What were Booker T. Washington's views about establishing racial equality?*

African Americans faced not only formal discrimination but also informal rules and customs, called racial etiquette, that regulated relationships between whites and blacks. Usually, these customs belittled and humiliated African Americans, affirming their second-class status.

African Americans had to show deference to whites, including children, and endure humiliating treatment. For example, blacks and whites never shook hands, since shaking hands would have implied equality. Blacks had to yield the sidewalk to white pedestrians, and black men always had to remove their hats for whites.

Some moderate reformers, like Booker T. Washington, advocated gradual improvements for African Americans. Washington thought it best to avoid demands for legal equality, which most whites staunchly opposed, and concentrate on creating economic opportunities. Washington earned support from whites because he tacitly accepted segregation while he suggested whites and blacks work together for social progress.

A PERSONAL VOICE

To those of the white race . . . I would repeat what I say to my own race, "Cast down your bucket where you are." . . . Cast down your bucket among these people who have, without strikes and labor wars, tilled your fields, cleared your forests, builded your railroads and cities, and brought forth treasures from the bowels of the earth, and helped make possible this magnificent representation of the progress of the South. . . . In all things that are purely social we can be as separate as the fingers, yet one as the hand in all things essential to mutual progress.

BOOKER T. WASHINGTON, Atlanta Exposition address, 1895

HISTORICAL SPOTLIGHT

WASHINGTON AND DU BOIS DEBATE

Booker T. Washington's Atlanta Exposition address won the applause of whites throughout the country. Arguing for a gradual approach to racial equality, Washington suggested that "it is at the bottom of life we must begin, and not at the top."

Ten years later, W. E. B. Du Bois denounced this view of gradual equality and belittled it as the "Atlanta Compromise." Demanding full social and economic equality for African Americans, Du Bois founded the Niagara Movement in 1905 and announced that "persistent manly agitation is the way to liberty."

In 1909 the Niagara Movement became the National Association for the Advancement of Colored People (NAACP), with Du Bois as the editor of its journal, *The Crisis.* He wrote, "We refuse to surrender . . . leadership . . . to cowards and trucklers. We are men; we will be treated as men."

Improving the economic skills of African Americans, Washington hoped, would pave the way for long-term gains. People like Ida B. Wells and W. E. B. Du Bois, however, thought that the problems of inequality were too urgent to ignore.

VIOLENCE African Americans who did not follow the racial etiquette could face severe punishment. Minor breaches might be overlooked, or met with a mild reprimand, but serious violations could provoke serious, and often violent, response. If the offended white person complained to the African American's employer, the employee could lose his or her job.

All too often, African Americans who were accused of violating the etiquette were lynched. Between 1885 and 1900, more than 2,500 African-American men

OBJECTIVE **2 INSTRUCT**

Turn-of-the-Century Race Relations

▶ ***Starting with the Student***
- Ask students how they would have reacted to the Jim Crow laws described on page 310.
- Ask how such laws could have been fought.

▶ ***Discussing Key Ideas***
- African Americans face segregation, especially in the South, and discrimination everywhere.
- In the struggle for equality, Booker T. Washington urges a gradual approach, while W. E. B. Du Bois demands full equality immediately.
- Crusaders like Ida Wells fight against the violence that confronts African Americans accused of violating the racial etiquette.

IN-DEPTH RESOURCES: UNIT 2
Primary Source: *from* "Lynching and the Excuse for It" by Ida B. Wells, p. 67

ELECTRONIC LIBRARY OF PRIMARY SOURCES
from *The Autobiography of Ida B. Wells*

HISTORICAL SPOTLIGHT
Washington and Du Bois Debate

Critical Thinking: Interpreting Ask students why Du Bois may have used the phrase "Atlanta Compromise." *Possible Responses: To convey his view that Washington merely accommodated the white status quo; to remind people of the inadequacies of the Missouri Compromise decades earlier.*

TEACHING OPTION

Skillbuilder Mini-Lesson: Finding Main Ideas

Explaining the Skill Finding the main idea means choosing the sentence or making a statement that sums up what a particular selection is about. To find the main idea of a selection, decide what main idea each fact or example in the selection supports or how the facts or examples are related.

Applying the Skill Have students read the information under "African Americans Fight Legal Discrimination." Then ask students to identify the sentence in the selection that reflects the main idea of the selection. Students should identify "Southern states had adopted a broad system of legal policies of racial discrimination and devised methods to weaken African-American political power," the second sentence on page 310.

Then ask students to list examples from the selection that support the main idea. Students might list the literacy test, poll tax, the grandfather clause, and Jim Crow laws.

IN-DEPTH RESOURCES: UNIT 2
Skillbuilder Practice: Finding Main Ideas, p. 61

MORE ABOUT . . .
Segregated Neighborhoods

The most famous African-American neighborhood was probably Harlem in New York City. Even before the subway line opened along Harlem's Lenox Avenue in 1901, real-estate speculators began building fine apartment houses there, anticipating a middle-class influx. When the middle class did not arrive, African-American developer Philip A. Payton stepped in, promising high rents to landlords who would allow African-American tenants. Soon, despite inflated costs, African Americans from all over began moving to Harlem, which offered far better accommodations than most other areas where blacks were permitted to live.

OBJECTIVE
③ INSTRUCT

Discrimination in the West

▶ ***Discussing Key Ideas***
- In the West, nonwhite immigrants such as the Mexicans and Chinese fall victim to discrimination.
- Mexican workers are sometimes forced into debt peonage, or involuntary servitude, until the Supreme Court declared it unconstitutional in 1911.
- Prejudice against the Chinese is so great that in 1882 Congress passed the Chinese Exclusion Act, which restricted Chinese immigration and suspended naturalization for those already present.

and women were shot, burned, or hanged without trial in the South. Lynching—illegal execution, without a trial, carried out by a mob—peaked in the 1880s and 1890s but continued well into the 20th century.

Like the three friends of Ida B. Wells, blacks were often targeted for lynching if they showed signs of becoming successful. They were also in danger if someone accused them of showing too little respect for whites, especially white women.

Crusaders like Ida B. Wells fought a nationwide struggle to remove impediments to racial equality. Although most African Americans lived in the segregated South, those in the North also faced discrimination in housing, education, and work.

DISCRIMINATION IN THE NORTH By 1900, a small but growing number of African Americans lived in Northern cities. Many African Americans, who believed legends of harmonious race relations in the North, migrated to Northern cities in search of better-paying jobs and social equality. But after their arrival, the African Americans experienced racial discrimination similar to that in the South.

African Americans found themselves forced into segregated neighborhoods, since local residents and realtors prevented them from moving into white neighborhoods. Blacks also faced discrimination in the workplace. Labor unions often denied them membership, and employers hired them only as a last resort and fired them before white employees.

Sometimes the competition between African Americans and working-class whites became violent, as in the New York City race riot of 1900. Violence erupted after a young black man, Arthur J. Harris, believing that his wife was being mistreated by a white policeman, killed the policeman. Word of the killing spread, and whites demanded revenge. As one local reporter noted, "Men and women poured by the hundreds from the neighboring tenements" and attacked blacks wherever they found them. Northern blacks, however, were not alone in facing such discrimination. Nonwhites in the West also faced oppression.

Discrimination in the West

White Americans were not the only people to populate the West. Native Americans continued to live in the Western territories claimed by the United States. Asian immigrants traveled to America's Pacific Coast in search of wealth and work. Mexicans continued to inhabit the American Southwest. African Americans were also present, especially in former slave-holding areas, such as Texas. Many Western communities were culturally diverse, with people of differing ethnic and racial backgrounds working and living side by side. Still, racial tensions often made life uncomfortable for nonwhites.

MEXICAN WORKERS Mexicans in the Southwest often faced difficult conditions because of racial discrimination. In the 1880s and 1890s, the Southern Pacific and Santa Fe Railroads hired more Mexicans than members of any other ethnic group to construct rail lines in Arizona, southern California, Nevada, and New Mexico. Railroad managers hired Mexicans not only because they were accustomed to the Southwest's hot, dry climate but also because they could be made to work for less money than members of other ethnic groups.

Mexican workers were also vital to the development of mining and agriculture in the Southwest. When the 1902 National Reclamation Act (also called the Newlands Act) provided government assistance for irrigation projects, many desert areas in the Southwest bloomed. Raising grapes, lettuce, citrus fruits, and cotton required manual labor, and Mexicans, who had worked so well for the railroads, provided a major source of agricultural labor.

Block Schedule TEACHING OPTION **Time Needed: 40 Minutes**

Cooperative Activity: Debating Discrimination

Task: Students will research and then debate issues of racial and ethnic discrimination at the turn of the century.

Purpose: To understand the ways that racism affected American society at the turn of the century.

Activity: Groups of four or five students should research specific topics of race relations at the turn of the century (such as *Plessy* v. *Ferguson,* the passage of Jim Crow laws, debt peonage, and the segregation of African Americans in Northern cities). Then they should divide into two sub-groups and debate these issues from a turn-of-the-century perspective.

Building a Portfolio: Students should make a transcript of their debates and save those transcripts in their history portfolio.

Standards for Evaluation
Transcripts should . . .
- refer to the major participants and issues of turn-of-the-century discrimination
- show an understanding of turn-of-the-century racial attitudes

These Mexican workers sometimes found themselves reduced to **debt peonage,** a system of involuntary servitude in which the laborer is forced to work off a debt. After slavery was abolished, some Mexicans, as well as African Americans in the territories of New Mexico and Arizona, were forced into debt peonage. Not until 1911 did the U.S. Supreme Court declare involuntary peonage to be a violation of the Thirteenth Amendment.

Anti-Chinese feeling was so strong that attacks on the Chinese by mobs were not uncommon.

EXCLUDING THE CHINESE Between 1850 and 1880, the Chinese immigrant population in the United States grew from 7,520 to more than 100,000. The Chinese had come to the United States to work and formed a major part of the labor force in the West. They helped to build the transcontinental railroad, and they were indispensable to important industries in California, where more than half of all shoemakers, more than four-fifths of all cigar makers, and roughly one-third of all woolen-mill operators were Chinese immigrants.

With so many Chinese people working, a growing group of whites feared losing out in job competition with them. Consequently, Chinese people often found themselves pushed into segregated schools and neighborhoods. Strong opposition to Chinese immigration developed, and not only in the West. In 1882, Congress overwhelmingly passed the Chinese Exclusion Act. The act prohibited almost all further immigration of Chinese to the United States and suspended naturalization for those who were already present.

C. Answer African Americans faced segregation and lynchings. Mexicans faced debt peonage. Chinese faced segregation and obstacles to immigration.

THINK THROUGH HISTORY
C. Contrasting *Compare the ways African Americans, Mexicans, and Chinese immigrants were discriminated against in the United States.*

While racial discrimination posed terrible legal and economic problems for nonwhites throughout the United States, that was not the whole story of turn-of-the-century America. Because of rapid industrialization and improvements that made daily life and work easier, more people, especially whites, had leisure time for new recreational activities, as well as money to spend on a growing array of consumer products. These Americans began to be drawn to fads and fashions—and a mass culture was born.

Section 3 Assessment

1. TERMS & NAMES

Identify:
- Ida B. Wells
- literacy test
- poll tax
- grandfather clause
- Jim Crow laws
- segregation
- *Plessy* v. *Ferguson*
- debt peonage

2. SUMMARIZING Use a cluster like this one to identify people, places, legal issues, and events related to discrimination at the turn of the century.

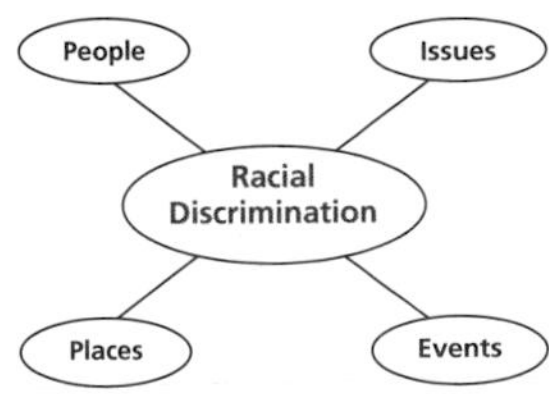

3. IDENTIFYING PROBLEMS Explain how segregation and discrimination affected the lives of African Americans at the turn of the century. Use details from the section to support your explanation.

4. CONTRASTING How did the challenges and opportunities for Mexicans in the United States differ from those for African Americans? Give examples to support your viewpoint.

THINK ABOUT
- the types of work each group did
- the wages paid each group
- the effects of government policies on each group

MORE ABOUT . . .
The Chinese Exclusion Act of 1882

The Chinese Exclusion Act of 1882 emerged not simply as an example of American racism. The act was part of a broader social concern over class tensions in an industrial society. At first, the act only restricted the immigration of Chinese laborers for ten years, in order to protect the jobs of white workers and reduce the kinds of tensions that led to events like the Railroad Strike of 1877. Nevertheless, the act expanded to include "all persons of the Chinese race" in 1888. It was then extended another ten years in 1892 and made indefinite in 1902.

ASSESS & RETEACH

Section 3 Assessment

You might have a student volunteer lead a class discussion of question 2.

Self-Assessment

Have students make a two-column chart about turn-of-the-century segregation and discrimination. In the left column, they should list what they already knew; in the right, what they learned in the section.

Section Quiz

FORMAL ASSESSMENT
Section Quiz, p. 106

Reteach

Look through the section for references to American regions (South and West, for example) and review regional variations of race relations.

ANSWERS

1. TERMS & NAMES

Ida B. Wells, p. 309
literacy test, p. 310
poll tax, p. 310
grandfather clause, p. 310
Jim Crow laws, p. 310
segregation, p. 310
Plessy v. *Ferguson,* p. 311
debt peonage, p. 313

2. SUMMARIZING

Entries for student diagrams might include the following:

People: Ida B. Wells; Booker T. Washington; W. E. B. Du Bois.

Places: The Southwest (Mexican peonage); California (the Chinese).

Legal Issues: Literacy tests; poll tax; Jim Crow laws; segregated schools; *Plessy* v. *Ferguson.*

Events: Lynchings; Wells's anti-lynching campaign.

3. IDENTIFYING PROBLEMS

Possible Answer: African Americans were the victims of voting restrictions and Jim Crow laws, and were forced to adhere to a racial etiquette. They faced discrimination in jobs and housing, and were forced to accept separate schools and other facilities.

4. CONTRASTING

Possible Answer: Both faced discrimination in employment. While both were not treated as well as white workers, African Americans had more conflicts with whites. The Newlands Reclamation Act created work for Mexicans, while Jim Crow laws harmed African Americans.

CLOSE

African Americans faced legal segregation in the South and de facto segregation in the North, while Mexican Americans and Chinese Americans, mostly in the West, also faced severe discrimination.

4 Dawn of Mass Culture

TERMS & NAMES
- vaudeville
- ragtime
- Joseph Pulitzer
- William Randolph Hearst
- department store
- mail-order catalog
- rural free delivery

LEARN ABOUT transformations in leisure activities, shopping, and advertising
TO UNDERSTAND the emergence of modern mass culture.

ONE AMERICAN'S STORY

Along the Brooklyn seashore, on a narrow sandbar just nine miles from busy Manhattan, rose the most famous urban amusement center in the world: Coney Island. In 1886, its principal developer, George Tilyou, bragged, "If Paris is France, then Coney Island, between June and September, is the world." Indeed, tens of thousands of visitors mobbed Coney Island after work each evening and on Sundays and holidays. When Luna Park, a Coney Island amusement park, opened in May 1903, a reporter described the scene that greeted 45,000 people.

A PERSONAL VOICE

[Inside the park was] an enchanted, storybook land of trellises, columns, domes, minarets, lagoons, and lofty aerial flights. And everywhere was life—a pageant of happy people; and everywhere was color—a wide harmony of orange and white and gold. . . . It was a world removed—shut away from the sordid clatter and turmoil of the streets.

BRUCE BLEN, quoted in *Amusing the Million*

The sprawling amusement center at Coney Island became a model for other urban amusement parks.

Couples at Coney Island cuddled in the Tunnel of Love, tested their luck at games of chance, and enjoyed exciting new rides. A schoolteacher who walked fully dressed into the ocean explained her unusual behavior by saying, "It has been a hard year at school, and when I saw the big crowd here, everyone with the brakes off, the spirit of the place got the better of me." Leisure opportunities like Coney Island offered Americans a few hours of escape from the hard workweek.

The end of the century saw the rise of a "mass culture" in the United States. New recreational activities, as well as the rise of a consumer culture and nationwide advertising campaigns, began to obliterate regional differences. Middle-class Americans from all over the country shared experiences and identities.

American Leisure

"EIGHT HOURS FOR WORK, EIGHT HOURS FOR REST, AND EIGHT HOURS FOR WHAT WE WILL" declared a popular slogan of the carpenters' union in Worcester, Massachusetts, in 1889. Eight hours of "what we will" often meant leisure activities. As the century drew to a close, many urban Americans escaped the congested cities and dull industrial work to enjoy amusement parks, bicycling, tennis, and spectator sports.

AMUSEMENT PARKS To meet the needs of city dwellers for recreational activities, Chicago, New York, and other cities began setting aside precious green space for their residents' outdoor enjoyment. Many cities distributed small playgrounds and playing fields throughout their neighborhoods so that most citizens had park space for public recreation.

Some cities constructed amusement parks on their outskirts. Often built by trolley-car companies that sought more passengers, these parks boasted picnic

Section 4 Overview

OBJECTIVES

1. To give examples of turn-of-the-century popular sports and other leisure activities.
2. To describe turn-of-the-century trends in music and the performing arts.
3. To summarize the growing circulation of newspapers.
4. To describe turn-of-the-century innovations in marketing and advertising.

SKILLBUILDER

- Interpreting political cartoons, p. 319

CRITICAL THINKING

- Theme: Women in America, p. 315
- Developing historical perspective, p. 315
- Analyzing motives, p. 316
- Synthesizing, pp. 318, 321
- Summarizing, pp. 319, 321
- Forming opinions, p. 321

FOCUS & MOTIVATE

5-MINUTE WARM-UP

Making Generalizations
To understand the attraction of vaudeville to the American public, ask students to find the definition of vaudeville and read A Personal Voice on page 317 and answer these questions.

1. What was vaudeville?
2. Why was vaudeville so popular at the turn of the century?

WARM-UP TRANSPARENCY 8

▶ ***Starting with the Student***
- Ask students about their favorite leisure activities.
- Ask how some or all of these activities affect American life in general.

OBJECTIVE
1 **INSTRUCT**

American Leisure

▶ ***Discussing Key Ideas***
- Playgrounds, playing fields, and amusement parks help provide vital outdoor activity to city dwellers.

(continued on next page)

SECTION 4 RESOURCES

PRINT RESOURCES

IN-DEPTH RESOURCES: UNIT 2
Guided Reading, p. 60
Literature: from *Ragtime* by E. L. Doctorow, p. 68
American Lives: Lillian Gish, p. 72

READING STUDY GUIDE, p. 93

ACCESS FOR STUDENTS ACQUIRING ENGLISH
Guided Reading (Spanish), p. 114

SPANISH READING STUDY GUIDE, p. 93

FORMAL ASSESSMENT
Section Quiz, p. 107

ALTERNATIVE ASSESSMENT BOOK
See forms for supporting and scoring alternative activities.

TECHNOLOGY RESOURCES

HUMANITIES TRANSPARENCIES
H16, *Washington Square North* by Ferdinand Lundgren

CD-ROM Electronic Library of Primary Sources

VIDEO *American Portfolio: A Videodisc for U.S. History* user's guide, pp. 142, 146–147, 162

INTERNET http://www.mlushistory.com

grounds and a variety of rides to amuse visitors. The first roller coaster drew daredevil customers to Coney Island in 1884, and the first Ferris wheel turned in Chicago at the World's Fair in 1893. Loop-the-Loop, another Coney Island roller coaster, took passengers on a terrifying upside-down ride. The writer Albert Bigelow Paine described the sensation.

A PERSONAL VOICE

A fierce upward rush of air, a wild grip at a loosening hat, and an instant later the shock. We were on the loop. We were shooting upward as a billow that breaks against the cliff; we were curling over as the wave curls backward; we were darting down to inevitable annihilation!

ALBERT BIGELOW PAINE, quoted in *Coney Island*

A. Answer The attire women adopted for bicycle riding soon became popular for daily wear. The bicycle also freed women from always having to have a chaperone with them.

B. Answer Leisure activities provided Americans with relief from crowded urban life and occupied their increased time outside of work.

Clearly, many Americans were ready for new and innovative forms of entertainment—and a whole panorama of recreational activities soon became available.

BICYCLING AND OTHER CRAZES At the turn of the century, new pastimes such as bicycling entertained women as well as men. With their huge front wheels and solid rubber tires, the first American bicycles, manufactured by Colonel Albert A. Pope in the 1870s, challenged their brave riders. Because a bump might toss the cyclist over the handlebars, bicycling began as a male-only sport. The 1885 introduction of the "safety bicycle" with its smaller wheels and air-filled tires made the activity safer, and the Victor safety bicycle with a dropped frame and no crossbar appealed to women.

Abandoning their tight corsets, women bicyclists donned shirtwaists (tailored blouses) and "split" skirts in order to cycle more comfortably. This attire soon became popular for daily wear. The bicycle also freed women from the scrutiny of the ever-present chaperone. The suffragist Susan B. Anthony declared, "I think [bicycling] has done more to emancipate women than anything else in the world. It gives women a freedom and self-reliance." Fifty thousand men and women had taken to cycles by 1888. Two years later 312 American firms turned out 10 million bikes.

THINK THROUGH HISTORY **A.** THEME *Women in America How did bicycle riding change women's lives?*

Americans took up the sport of tennis as enthusiastically as they had taken up cycling. The modern version of this sport originated in England in 1873. A year later, the United States saw its first tennis match. The socialite Florence Harriman recalled that in the 1880s her father returned from England with one of New York's first tennis sets. At first, neighbors thought the elder Harriman had installed the nets to catch birds. Before tennis caught on with his neighbors, Harriman taught the game to his footman so the servant could participate as a fourth for doubles.

THINK THROUGH HISTORY **B.** *Developing Historical Perspective Why do you think leisure activities became so popular in the late 1800s?*

Hungry or thirsty after tennis or cycling? Turn-of-the-century enthusiasts turned to new snacks with recognizable brand names. They could munch on a

SKATES TO BLADES

The fastest-growing sport in the country, in-line skating, had captured 22 million enthusiasts by the end of 1994. The national craze for in-line skating parallels an earlier enthusiasm for roller-skating, invented by the New Yorker James Plimpton in 1863. By the 1880s, America boasted 3,000 hard maple rinks for roller skaters.

A roller, or "quad," skate has two wheels on each side. In-line skates, invented by the Minnesotan Scott Olson in 1979, feature wheels running in a straight line from front to back.

In-line skating attracts equal numbers of males and females from every economic bracket, ethnic group, geographic region, and age group, though the majority of skaters are under the age of 17. In New York's Central Park, a 6.2-mile paved loop attracts large crowds of skaters each day.

Bicycling could be done alone or in groups—though it was rare to find a whole group on one bicycle!

(continued from page 314)

- Bicycle riding and tennis become popular crazes that help liberate women from corsets and less tangible confinements.
- Sports like boxing and the evolving game of baseball draw crowds of spectators.

IN-DEPTH RESOURCES: UNIT 2
Guided Reading, p. 60

ACCESS FOR STUDENTS ACQUIRING ENGLISH
Guided Reading (Spanish), p. 114

HUMANITIES TRANSPARENCIES
H16, *Washington Square North* by Ferdinand Lundgren

MORE ABOUT . . .
Albert Bigelow Paine

Best-known for editing Mark Twain's letters and writing his authorized biography, Paine also penned works of his own, including the play *The Great White Way* (1901), a title that became the nickname for New York City's theater district.

NOW & THEN
Skates to Blades

Critical Thinking: Evaluating Have students imagine they are comparative shoppers deciding between "quad" and in-line skates. What qualities would they consider? *Possible Responses: Stability, speed, price, appearance, maneuverability, ease of learning, stylishness.*

TEACHING OPTIONS

Making Global Connections

International Bicycling The development of the bicycle was a truly international affair. As early as 1818 people began developing different bicycle models. Pierre Michaux and his son Ernest introduced the modern bicycle in 1860s France. Their mechanic, Pierre Lallement, immigrated to America in 1866 and joined James Carroll of Ansonia, Connecticut, in taking out the first U.S. bicycle patent. English designers also made useful modifications, and perhaps the most important innovation came from John Boyd Dunlop, a Northern Irish veterinarian, who introduced the pneumatic tire.

Exploring Themes

Women in America Explain that bicycle riding was an example of changing opportunities for women at the turn of the century. During this time, the ideal model for female beauty was the "Gibson girl"—as drawn by *Life* magazine artist Charles Dana Gibson—a beautifully dressed woman with an hourglass figure shaped by corsets. Bicycle riding and the abandonment of corsets symbolized a new freedom that many women could enjoy. Even before World War I, the sleekly dressed, corsetless, "flapper" had arrived on the scene, especially among working-class women.

MORE ABOUT . . .
Turn-of-the-Century Health Foods

Several well-known foods were originally sold for dubious health purposes. John Harvey Kellogg spent years trying to create the cereal that eventually became corn flakes. In addition, Quaker Oats and Fleischmann's Yeast both claimed to curb nervousness and constipation.

MORE ABOUT . . .
Boxing

Like horse racing, boxing was enormously popular among 18th-century English gentlemen. Then fought without gloves, it was extremely brutal until boxer Jack Broughton introduced a set of rules in 1743. In the 1860s the Marquis of Queensberry sponsored new rules that, among other things, required boxers to wear gloves. Though American boxing star John L. Sullivan was a bare-knuckle champion, he began fighting under the Marquis of Queensberry rules when he found that many U.S. towns and cities would legalize boxing only if gloves were worn.

ELECTRONIC LIBRARY OF PRIMARY SOURCES
"The Base-Ball Season" in *Harper's Weekly*

Hershey chocolate bar, first sold in 1900, and wash down the chocolate with a Coca-Cola® or a Pepsi-Cola®. An Atlanta pharmacist named John S. Pemberton formulated Coca-Cola as a cure for headaches in 1886. He and his partner settled on that name in order to advertise that the ingredients included extracts from Peruvian coca leaves as well as African cola nuts. Ten years later, Calab D. Bradham of New Bern, North Carolina, introduced Coca-Cola's main competitor, Pepsi-Cola.

SPECTATOR SPORTS American men and women not only participated in sports such as tennis and cycling but also became avid fans of spectator sports, especially boxing and baseball. Though these two sports had begun as popular informal activities, by the turn of the century they had become profitable businesses. Fans who couldn't attend an important boxing match jammed barber shops and hotel lobbies to listen to telegraphed transmissions of the contest's highlights.

When John L. Sullivan, the first great heavyweight boxer, captured his title in 1882, he fought most of his bouts with bare knuckles. The Great John L. traveled the country, offering up to $10,000 to anyone who could survive four rounds in the ring with him. Finally, in 1892, James J. "Gentleman Jim" Corbett knocked him out in the 21st round. For his victory Corbett relied on fast footwork and diligent practice and followed the new Marquis of Queensberry rules for the sport.

In the first World Series, the Boston Pilgrims defeated the Pittsburgh Pirates on the Huntington Avenue baseball grounds in Boston *(above).* Johnny Evers *(right)* was part of a famous Chicago Cubs infield.

BASEBALL New rules also transformed baseball into a professional sport. In 1845, a group of wealthy New Yorkers set down regulations that combined aspects of two children's games that English immigrants had brought to the United States. Fifty baseball clubs had sprung up by 1850, and New York alone boasted 12 clubs in the mid-1860s.

In 1869, a professional team named the Cincinnati Red Stockings toured the country. Other clubs soon took to the road, which led to the formation of the National League in 1876 and the American League in 1901. In the first World Series, held in 1903, the Boston Pilgrims beat the Pittsburgh Pirates. African-American baseball players, who were excluded from both leagues because of racial discrimination, formed their own clubs and two leagues—the Negro National League and the Negro American League.

Summer afternoon baseball games drew a wide variety of people to the bleachers and grandstands. More than 51,000 fans attended an 1887 championship series between St. Louis and Detroit. The novelist Mark Twain raved that baseball was "the very symbol . . . and visible expression of the drive and push and rush and struggle of the raging, tearing, booming nineteenth century." An 1886 article in *Harper's Weekly* noted that the new national pastime had "seized upon the American people, irrespective of age, sex, or other condition." By the 1890s, baseball resembled today's sport, with a published game schedule, official rules, and a standard-sized diamond.

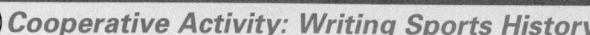

C. Answer Sports offered one way to fill increased leisure time. Americans could participate directly in sports like bicycling or indirectly in spectator sports like baseball.

THINK THROUGH HISTORY
C. Analyzing Motives *Why do you think sports were so popular among Americans at the end of the century?*

Block Schedule TEACHING OPTION **Time Needed: 20 Minutes**

Cooperative Activity: Writing Sports History

Task: Groups of students will write historical articles about sports.

Purpose: To describe American sports at the turn of the century.

Activity: Groups of three or four students will write historical articles about particular sports that existed in turn-of-the-century America. Different groups could write on different sports, such as basketball, football, tennis, or boxing. Some might write about Olympic sports, women's sports, or on variations of a sport such as baseball, softball, cricket, and stickball. Students should do additional research if necessary.

Building a Portfolio: Have students collect their histories for their portfolio.

Standards for Evaluation
Articles should . . .

- show how the particular sports developed and evolved during the era
- include information on where these sports were most popular and who played or watched them

Going to the Show

Like sports, other forms of entertainment attracted audiences of working people with leisure time to fill. Two other advances fostered the new mass entertainment: improved railroad transportation and new media technology, such as motion pictures. Enterprising companies now formed traveling groups of entertainers who brought live performances to cities and small towns around the country.

LIVE PERFORMANCES The companies that booked talent typically featured stars, popular performers who could attract large audiences and compensate for the less-talented supporting actors. Three popular female stars guaranteed a full house wherever they performed—the "divine" Sarah Bernhardt, a French actress; the actress Lillie Langtry of Great Britain; and the singer Jenny Lind, "the Swedish Nightingale."

Audiences could choose serious drama, exciting melodrama, or vaudeville shows. To many audiences, serious drama meant a Shakespearean tragedy, with the talented Edwin Booth playing the lead. Melodramas, such as *Under the Gaslight,* featured improbable plots in which seemingly doomed heroes and heroines nonetheless managed to evade disaster at the last minute. **Vaudeville** performances included song, dance, slapstick comedy, and sometimes even chorus lines of female performers. Promoters sought large audiences with varied backgrounds. Writing in *Scribner's Magazine* in October 1899, actor Edwin Milton Royle hailed vaudeville theater as "an American invention" that offered something to attract nearly everyone.

"It [the circus] was the embodiment of all that was skillful and beautiful in human action."

HAMLIN GARLAND, WRITER

A PERSONAL VOICE

[Vaudeville] appeals to the businessman, tired and worn, who drops in for half an hour on his way home; to the person who has an hour or two before a train goes, or before a business appointment; to the woman who is wearied of shopping; to the children who love animals and acrobats; to the man with his sweetheart or sister, to the individual who wants to be diverted but doesn't want to think or feel; to the American of all grades and kinds who wants a great deal for his money.

EDWIN MILTON ROYLE, quoted in *Victorian America*

The biggest spectacle of all was often the annual visit of the Barnum & Bailey Circus, which its founders, P. T. Barnum and Anthony Bailey, touted as "The Greatest Show on Earth." Established in 1881, the circus arrived by railroad train and gathered trapeze artists, acrobats, lion tamers, clowns, elephants, and stallions under a big tent. There, the daring performers delighted audiences of adults and children alike.

P. T. Barnum earned his reputation as a hustler. His traveling circus sideshows often claimed to feature two-headed animals or humans who were well over 100 years old.

Until the 1890s, African-American performers filled roles mainly in minstrel shows that featured exaggerated imitations of African-American music and dance and reinforced racist stereotypes of blacks. By the turn of the century, however, minstrel shows had largely been replaced by more sophisticated musicals, and many black performers had entered vaudeville shows.

RAGTIME At the same time, an exciting new form of music called **ragtime** began to draw hoards of listeners. A blending of African-American spirituals and European musical forms, ragtime had originated in the 1880s in the saloons of the South. The strains of ragtime had impressed the African-American

OBJECTIVE

② INSTRUCT

Going to the Show

▶ ***Discussing Key Ideas***

- In their leisure hours, many turn-of-the-century Americans watch circuses, vaudeville shows, melodramas and other plays, as well as famous acting and singing stars on tour.
- Minstrel shows give way to musicals and vaudeville, and ragtime—which blended African-American and European music and paved the way for jazz—becomes popular.
- Soon after the turn of the century, movies emerge as popular entertainment, and by 1914 the American public idolizes its first generation of movie stars.

MORE ABOUT . . .

Hamlin Garland

Garland was a turn-of-the-century writer strongly influenced by the local-color movement—an offshoot of realism that stressed the accurate portrayal of a particular region or people. Garland's region was the American Midwest—or "Middle Border," as he often called it. Drawn from personal experience, his short stories, in anthologies such as *Main-Travelled Roads* (1891) and *Prairie Folks* (1893), focused on the hardships of Midwestern farm life.

TEACHING OPTIONS

Making Connections Across Cultures

Modern American Music Around the turn of the century, modern American music—jazz, blues, and country—emerged in the South. Much of this music developed within the context of cultural exchange between African Americans and Southern whites who borrowed instruments, lyrics, and styles from each other. There were also international influences (such as Hawaiian steel guitars and Alpine singers) appropriated from acts which toured many American towns in the North as well as the South. Almost all current popular American music—including rock— traces its roots to the original forms of jazz, blues, and country.

Making Connections Across the Curriculum

Performing Arts Note that vaudeville had its origins in 18th-century France, where the national drama group, the Comédie Française, held a monopoly on all acting. To get around that monopoly, other entertainers performed in pantomime, song, and dance in shows that came to be called vaudeville. In America, vaudeville drew on earlier, coarser variety shows geared to all-male audiences on the frontier. It was pioneered as family entertainment by singer Tony Pastor, who opened a New York City theater in 1881. By the 1890s vaudeville had become hugely popular in theaters across the nation.

MORE ABOUT . . .
Scott Joplin

Known as the "king of ragtime," Joplin studied piano as a child in Texas and then traveled the Midwest performing, including a stint at Chicago's Columbian Exposition in 1893. After receiving further musical training at Missouri's George R. Smith College for Negroes, he began creating his own compositions, winning fame for classic piano "rags" like "Maple Leaf Rag" and "The Entertainer." He spent his final years in New York City, working mainly on a three-act opera called *Treemonisha.*

NOW & THEN
Going to the Movies

▶ ***Discussing Key Ideas***
- By 1903 the first modern films emerge, and theater owners realize that movies are more profitable than vaudeville.
- Sound is added to films in 1927, and majestic movie palaces are built.
- The popularity of television in the 1950s causes a decline in movie attendance by 1960, but theater owners combat this with outdoor drive-in movies.
- Although the number of movie screens in the United States increases in the 1990s, movie attendance remains flat due to cable TV, satellite dishes, and videos.

IN-DEPTH RESOURCES: UNIT 2
American Lives: Lillian Gish, p. 72

ELECTRONIC LIBRARY OF PRIMARY SOURCES
from *The Movies, Mr. Griffith, and Me* by Lillian Gish

pianist and composer Scott Joplin on his tours through black communities from New Orleans to Chicago. Joplin's first ragtime composition, "Maple Leaf Rag," made him famous in the first decade of the 20th century, when a rage for ragtime seized the country. Ragtime became an important element in the development of American jazz.

THE SILVER SCREEN Early in the 20th century, live entertainment began to get competition from motion pictures. The first films, one-reel 10-minute sequences, consisted mostly of vaudeville skits or faked newsreels. Early audiences found plenty to marvel at in random scenes of galloping horses and runaway trains. In 1903, *The Great Train Robbery* increased the popularity of movies that told a story.

Like the melodramas of the stage, popular movie serials featured heroes and heroines who narrowly evaded one disaster after another. One popular serial was *The Perils of Pauline,* starring Pearl White in the title role. Pauline, a headstrong heiress seeking adventure, fought off Indians, fell off cliffs, and was tied to a railroad track in front of an oncoming train. To the relief of her amazed audience, though, her courageous boyfriend always saved her just in the nick of time.

D. W. Griffith's epic three-hour film *The Birth of a Nation* (1915) made movie history by pioneering bold new techniques, such as close-ups, fade-outs, and blockbuster scenes. The story the film told, however, inflamed racial prejudice by glorifying the Ku Klux Klan and portraying African Americans as a threat to white morality. The National Association for the Advancement of Colored People (NAACP), founded in 1909, organized protests against the film's racist portrayal of Reconstruction.

By 1914, the typical film was a two-hour silent feature with a famous star, such as Mary Pickford, Lillian Gish, or Charlie Chaplin. These beloved stars soon received more adoration than the stars of the theater had ever won. Movies' low admission price of just a nickel ensured their continuing popularity among all classes of people. Unlike live performances, movies could be shown all over the country at the same time and spread the current ideas and trends that contributed to the formation of a mass culture.

D. Answer Popular entertainment usually was melodramatic, exciting, and featured popular stars.

THINK THROUGH HISTORY
D. Synthesizing *List a few characteristics of the types of entertainment that appealed to people at the turn of the century.*

NOW & THEN

Going to the Movies

Perhaps the most popular form of entertainment among Americans in the 1990s continues to be the motion picture. While seven out of ten households own videocassette recorders (VCRs), modern theaters lure audiences by showing big-screen blockbuster films—highly advertised movies that often include popular stars and sophisticated special effects.

1903

The first modern film—an eight-minute silent feature called *The Great Train Robbery*—debuts in five-cent theaters called nickelodeons. Entrepreneurs quickly see that by showing a film as often as 16 times a day, they can generate greater profits than by presenting a costly vaudeville or stage production. By 1907, an estimated 3,000 nickelodeons dot the country.

1927

Films become more popular when sound is added to them in 1927 and color soon afterward. Huge audiences fill larger and grander theaters with names like Majestic, Ritz, and Palace. Movie palaces, like the one shown above, boast beautiful lobbies, promenades with elaborate artwork, and graceful staircases. Weekly movie attendance doubles from 40 million in 1922 to 80 million in 1930.

Block Schedule TEACHING OPTION **Time Needed: 20 Minutes**

Cooperative Activity: Critiquing Historical Films

Task: Small groups of students will hold critics' round tables discussing their criteria for films about historical topics (such as *Glory, Patton,* and *All the President's Men),* listing the three best films, and giving brief explanations of their decisions.

Purpose: To develop and defend critical opinions.

Activity: Ask students to decide which are their favorite historical films and why. Students could use *Past Imperfect: History According to the Movies,* edited by Mark C. Carnes (New York: Holt, 1995) as a guide. In the ensuing critics' round table, each group should create a list of the criteria that they feel make a historical film superior or memorable and the three films they feel best fulfill those criteria.

Building a Portfolio: Students should save their lists of criteria and best historical movies and place them in their portfolio.

Standards for Evaluation
The criteria should . . .
- demonstrate a thoughtful awareness of film as an art form
- show sensitivity to questions of historical accuracy

Mass Circulation Newspapers

Americans increasingly found coverage of their favorite new sports or shows in newspapers that looked for ways to captivate the masses of readers. Instead of headlines like "POLITICS IN ALBANY," newspapers began using sensational headlines. For example, to introduce its story about the horrors of the Johnstown, Pennsylvania, flood of 1889, in which more than 2,000 people lost their lives, one newspaper used the headline "THE VALLEY OF DEATH."

Newspapers also devised promotional stunts. In 1889, for example, the *New York World* sent the reporter Nellie Bly around the world in imitation of a fictional character in Jules Verne's novel *Around the World in Eighty Days.* After reporting from exotic locales, Bly returned to her starting place in just over 72 days.

E. Answer By printing lurid headlines, devising promotional stunts, making up news, and instituting Sunday editions, comics and coverage of sports and women's news.

THINK THROUGH HISTORY
E. ***Summarizing*** *How did the* World *and the* Journal *lure readers?*

Joseph Pulitzer, a Hungarian immigrant who had bought the *World* in 1883, pioneered popular innovations, such as a large Sunday edition, comics, sports coverage, and women's news. Pulitzer's paper emphasized "sin, sex, and sensation" in an attempt to surpass his main competitor, **William Randolph Hearst,** who had purchased the *New York Morning Journal* in 1895. The wealthy Hearst, who already owned the *San Francisco Examiner,* sought to outdo Pulitzer by filling the *Journal* with exaggerated tales of personal scandals, cruelty, hypnotism, and even an imaginary conquest of Mars.

The escalation of their circulation war drove both papers to even more sensational news coverage. By 1898, the circulation of each paper had reached more than 1 million copies a day.

SKILLBUILDER
INTERPRETING POLITICAL CARTOONS
According to the cartoonist, where were Pulitzer and Hearst leading American journalism?

Skillbuilder Answer
Possible Answer: Pulitzer and Hearst were leading journalism to probable destruction.

New Ways to Sell Goods

Along with enjoying new leisure activities, Americans also changed the way they shopped. The combination of concentrated urban markets and vast quantities of reasonably priced manufactured goods encouraged city merchants to look for new sales methods. Americans at the turn of the century witnessed the beginnings of the shopping center, the development of department and chain stores, and the birth of modern advertising.

1950s

Movie attendance plummets from 60 million per week in 1950 to 40 million per week by 1960. Because of the enormous popularity of television, fewer people go to the movies; but the new drive-in theaters bring some of them back—especially young suburban families and teenagers with driver's licenses. The drive-in's popularity peaks in 1958, when outdoor theaters in the United States number 4,000.

1990s

The popularity of videocassette recorders and of network and cable TV continues to threaten the movie industry. Nevertheless, developers anchor shopping malls with huge multiplex theaters showing many films at the same time. Between 1980 and 1991, the number of screens in the United States increases by 62 percent, but movie attendance remains flat, largely because VCRs and satellite dishes keep movies at Americans' fingertips.

INTERACT WITH HISTORY

1. **ANALYZING CAUSES** Explain the factors that have affected movie-theater attendance since the emergence of motion pictures.

SEE SKILLBUILDER HANDBOOK, PAGE 908.

2. **COMPARING MEDIA** Contrast the experiences of watching a movie on television and seeing a movie in a theater. Consider factors such as cost, comfort, convenience, privacy, and enjoyment in analyzing the two experiences.

Visit http://www.mlushistory.com for more about movies.

OBJECTIVE
③ **INSTRUCT**

Mass Circulation Newspapers

▶ ***Discussing Key Ideas***
- Turn-of-the-century newspapers are widely read by an increasingly literate public.
- Publishing moguls Joseph Pulitzer's and William Randolph Hearst's newspapers grow more and more sensational.

MORE ABOUT . . .
William Randolph Hearst

After acquiring the *Morning Journal,* Hearst raided Pulitzer's *World* for some of its best employees, including Richard F. Outcault, the inventor of color comics. The son of a U.S. senator, Hearst extended his sensationalism into politics—the frenzy against Spain whipped up in his newspapers is often cited as a cause of the Spanish-American-Cuban War.

OBJECTIVE
④ **INSTRUCT**

New Ways to Sell Goods

▶ ***Discussing Key Ideas***
- The growth of cities prompts new sales venues such as urban arcades, department stores, and chain stores.
- Advertising and brand names become vital parts of the popular culture.
- Mail-order catalogs blossom as rural free delivery allows packages to be sent to all parts of America.

INTERACT WITH HISTORY

1. Analyzing Causes

Possible Responses: *Factors that increased attendance in the 1920s included the advent of sound and the grandness of movie theaters; factors that decreased it in the 1950s–1990s included television, VCRs, and home satellite dishes.*

2. Comparing Media

To help students complete this assignment, ask them to create a form comparing their experiences when they watch a movie in the theater with watching a video at home. The form may include these items:

	Home	Theater
1. Cost		
2. Comfort		
3. Convenience		
4. Privacy		
5. Enjoyment		

ECONOMIC BACKGROUND
Brand Names

Critical Thinking: Evaluating Have students discuss the importance they or their families place on brand names. What brand-name products do they find reliable? For what kinds of products do they find the different brands indistinguishable?

MORE ABOUT . . .
Marshall Field's

Marshall Field's became the world's biggest department store, serving as many as 250,000 customers a day by 1900. Helping Field in his efforts was Harry Selfridge, a Wisconsin native who began working at Field's as a stock boy in 1879. Selfridge's innovations included gift certificates, annual sales, the bargain basement, and the practice of reminding customers how many days were left for Christmas shopping.

MORE ABOUT . . .
F. W. Woolworth

Frank Winfield Woolworth opened his first "five-and-ten" (or "five-and-dime") variety stores in Utica, New York, and Lancaster, Pennsylvania, in 1879. The Utica store failed, but the Lancaster store was so successful that he opened 21 like it in the next decade. In 1909, he successfully expanded into Great Britain and Ireland.

URBAN SHOPPING As cities grew, their populations made promising targets for enterprising manufacturers and merchants. The nation's first shopping center opened in Cleveland, Ohio, in 1890. A glass-topped arcade contained four levels of jewelry, leather goods, and stationery shops. The arcade also provided band music on Sundays so that middle-class Cleveland residents could spend their Sunday afternoons strolling through the arcade and gazing at the inviting window displays.

The growth of cities led to specialization, with separate districts within the city housing financial services, hotels and entertainment, light manufacturing, and trade. Financial districts in the largest cities contained banks, insurance companies, and the headquarters of large corporations. Nearby hotel and entertainment areas provided services to the cities' visitors. An adjoining district of light manufacturing might include clothing and printing factories. Nearby wholesale trade districts consisted of warehouses and wholesalers' offices.

Retail shopping districts formed in the middle of cities, where public transportation could easily bring shoppers from outlying areas. To anchor these retail shopping districts, ambitious merchants established something completely different, the modern department store.

ECONOMIC BACKGROUND
BRAND NAMES

In the past, a manufacturer usually marketed its products by distributing them through a wholesaler, who sold the goods of many firms to retailers. This method of marketing almost disappeared in some industries in the early 20th century, when national advertising made household words out of brand names such as Jell-O. After advertising created a demand for products made by specific companies, customers, rather than retailers, began to choose the brands they wanted.

People who had been persuaded to want "The Skin You Love to Touch" demanded Woodbury Soap at their neighborhood stores. They also demanded Kodak cameras, Arrow collars, and Campbell's soups because these brand names were widely advertised. To please customers, many retailers began to order directly from the national manufacturers and reduced their reliance on wholesaling companies. (See *supply and demand* on page 939 in the Economics Handbook.)

THE DEPARTMENT STORE Marshall Field of Chicago pioneered the concept of the **department store.** At the beginning of his career, Field worked as a salesclerk in a dry goods store and discovered that paying close attention to each woman customer could increase sales considerably. In 1865, Field decided to open his own store, using as his motto "Give the lady what she wants." Field's store allowed women to take merchandise home on approval and return it if it didn't satisfy them. Marshall Field himself advised the head of his upholstery department never to forget that "we are the servants of the public."

Advertising directed at women appeared in such specialized publications as the *Chicago Magazine of Fashion.* A lavish, colorful two-page spread in the magazine's premiere issue featured Field's "Fashion Specials." Field's pioneered the bargain basement, which sold bargain goods that were "less expensive but reliable," and opened a restaurant where women shoppers might lunch at their leisure.

THE CHAIN STORE While department stores like Marshall Field's prided themselves on offering a variety of personal services, new chain stores—groups of stores under the same ownership—advertised the bargains they could offer by buying in quantity and limiting personal service. In the 1870s, F. W. Woolworth found that if he offered an item at a very low price, "the consumer would purchase it on the spur of the moment" because "it was only a nickel." Woolworth didn't raise the nickel or dime price of items at his "five-and-dime store" until 1932. By 1911, the chain boasted 596 stores and sold more than a million dollars in merchandise a week.

The popularity of the five-and-ten-cent store chain matched that of the chain grocery stores. The chains didn't carry the variety of items today's shoppers expect, but they employed modern sales methods, such as offering brand names, standardized packaging, and high-volume, low-cost sales.

TURN-OF-THE-CENTURY ADVERTISING An explosion in advertising also heralded modern consumerism. Expenditures for advertising were under $10 million a year in 1865 but increased tenfold, to $95 million, by 1900, partly because of improvements in printing pictures.

TEACHING OPTIONS

Teaching Less Proficient Readers

Clarifying In reading pages 314–321, less proficient readers might use the SQ3R study method, as follows:

1. **Survey** the pages by skimming for headings and topic sentences.
2. **Question** the information by jotting down questions about turn-of-the-century mass culture and leisure activities.
3. **Read** the pages, looking for answers to these questions.
4. **Recite** or record any answers that are found.
5. **Review** the information to answer any questions that remain.

Making Connections Across Time

Demise of the Department Store Note that in recent decades, many department stores have closed their doors, especially in urban areas. For example, New York City alone has seen the demise of such well-known stores and chains as B. Altman's, Ohrbach's, Alexander's, May's, Abraham & Strauss (A & S), and Gimbel's. Discuss the factors contributing to these closings. *Possible factors include high rents, crime, and lack of parking in urban areas, and competition from large discount outlets like Wal-Mart and K-Mart.*

Though few American magazines carried advertising before the 1870s, by 1900 a host of magazines contained ads for new products.

Patent medicines grabbed the largest number of advertising lines. Next came soaps, followed by baking powders, cereals such as Cream of Wheat and Quaker Oats, the Eastman Kodak Company, and clothing makers. In addition to newspapers and magazines, advertisers used other ingenious methods to push products. Passengers riding the train between New York and Philadelphia in the 1870s might look up to see signs for Dr. Drake's Plantation Bitters on barns, houses, billboards, and even rocks.

MAIL-ORDER CATALOGS **Mail-order catalogs** from Montgomery Ward and Sears Roebuck brought department store merchandise to farmers and residents of small towns. Taking advantage of printing improvements, Ward's catalog, launched in 1872, provided instructions in ten languages to help customers order products. Richard Sears, who started his company in 1886, brought out what he called a consumer's guide twice a year. Early catalogs came with a letter from Sears, reassuring customers that the company received "hundreds of orders every day from young and old who never [before] sent away for goods." Customers needn't be afraid of making a mistake in their order. "Tell us what you want, in your own way," cajoled Sears, "written in any language, no matter whether good or poor writing, and your goods will be sent promptly to you." By 1910, about 10 million Americans shopped by mail.

THINK THROUGH HISTORY
F. Synthesizing *How did American methods of selling goods change at the turn of the century?*

F. Answer New department stores allowed women to take merchandise home on approval and offered bargain goods; shoppers used rural free delivery to shop by mail.

RURAL FREE DELIVERY The United States Post Office boosted mail-order businesses in 1896 by starting a **rural free delivery** (RFD) system that brought packages directly to every home. Now the catalogs could advise consumers to "give the letter and money to the mail carrier and he will get the money order at the post office and mail it in the letter for you." In 1913, the initiation of parcel post made it possible to send a 50-pound package from Chicago to any location in the country.

At the turn of the century, Americans experienced tremendous changes—most of which were positive—in their lives. However, the nation's growing industrial sector created problems that some believed the federal government should address. The spirit of progressive reform brought about lasting changes in the role of government in Americans' lives.

NOW & THEN

CATALOGS TODAY

Though catalogs were quite a novelty when Sears and Montgomery Ward arrived on the scene, in 1996 more than 13 billion catalogs filled American mailboxes—an average of nearly two per household each week—and mail-order buying continues to increase. Catalog sales grew over 40 percent between 1991 and 1997, when they were expected to reach $71 billion.

What do today's consumers order? Clothing ranks first, and home furnishings second.

Many retailers use mail-order catalogs for advertising because they know that catalog customers will shop in their stores as well. In fact, 20 percent of women will subsequently visit a store that has sent them a catalog, thereby boosting its walk-in business.

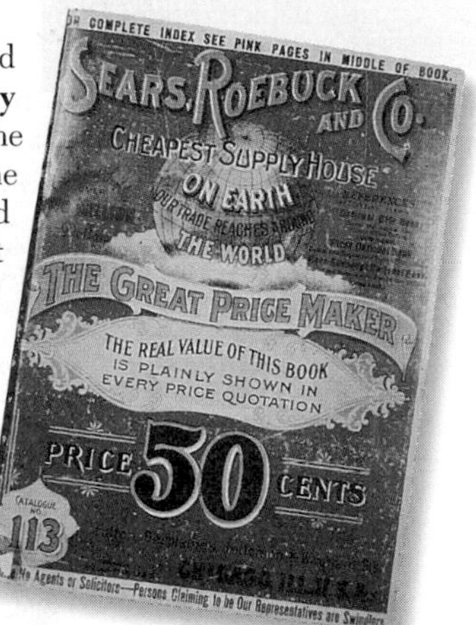

Section 4 Assessment

1. TERMS & NAMES
Identify:
- vaudeville
- ragtime
- Joseph Pulitzer
- William Randolph Hearst
- department store
- mail-order catalog
- rural free delivery

2. SUMMARIZING Recreate the spider diagram below on your paper. Label the diagonals "Leisure" and "Shopping," and add examples to each.

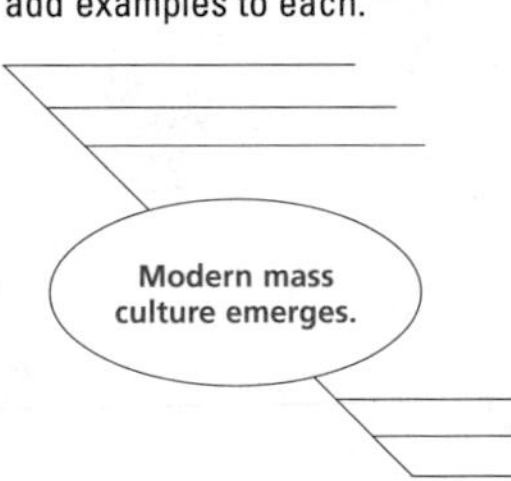

3. SYNTHESIZING Write an advertisement for one of the leisure activities described in this section.

THINK ABOUT
- the audience you are trying to appeal to
- the image you want to create
- the place or publication in which your advertisement will appear

4. FORMING OPINIONS Do you think the publication of sensational stories in newspapers is justified? Why or why not?

THINK ABOUT
- the reasons Hearst and Pulitzer included such stories
- the effect that adding sensational stories had on newspapers' circulation
- the purpose that you believe newspapers should serve

ANSWERS

1. TERMS & NAMES

vaudeville, p. 317
ragtime, p. 317
Joseph Pulitzer, p. 319
William Randolph Hearst, p. 319
department store, p. 320
mail-order catalog, p. 321
rural free delivery, p. 321

2. SUMMARIZING

Students may include the following entries:

Leisure: Amusement parks; bicycling; tennis; boxing; baseball; theater; vaudeville; ragtime music; movies.

Shopping: Shopping centers; department stores; chain stores; advertising; mail-order catalogs.

3. SYNTHESIZING

Advertisements should use creativity to appeal to the growing number of middle-class consumers.

4. FORMING OPINIONS

Students may indicate that including sensational stories is justified, because the public can always choose not to purchase a newspaper with such stories. Some might argue that such stories are dishonest and have no place on the pages of a newspaper.

NOW & THEN
Catalogs Today

Critical Thinking: Analyzing Causes Have students consider why catalog shopping has become so popular. *Possible Responses: More women are juggling work and family and have little time to shop in stores; more people living in rural areas because they can work or run a business from home are too far from the cities and suburbs where most stores are; crime has dissuaded some shoppers from visiting department stores and malls; catalog retailers have grown more sophisticated in offering the right goods to the right customers.*

ASSESS & RETEACH

Section 4 Assessment

Have students work in small groups to discuss the questions and review one another's responses.

Self-Assessment

Have students create a two-column chart on which they compare their own responses to the section assessment (column 1) with the portions of the text that best answer each question (column 2).

Section Quiz

FORMAL ASSESSMENT
Section Quiz, p. 107

Reteach

Use the Guided Reading Worksheet for Section 4 to help review the main ideas of this section.

IN-DEPTH RESOURCES: UNIT 2
Guided Reading, p. 60

CLOSE

From movies to shopping to advertising, the turn of the century saw the birth of the American mass culture that has dominated 20th-century life.

Daily Life

OBJECTIVES

1. To explain how the shift to an urban, industrial economy spurred Americans to seek outdoor leisure activities.
2. To identify sites and activities that turn-of-the-century Americans enjoyed in their leisure time.

FOCUS & MOTIVATE

▶ ***Starting with the Student*** Have students imagine that they have a dull job that keeps them indoors during the workweek.

- What kinds of places would they want to spend their leisure time?
- What kinds of leisure activities would they want to do?

MORE ABOUT . . .
The Bicycle Craze

Though bicycles developed gradually, it was not until the closing decades of the 19th century that they became popular. At the Centennial Exhibition in Philadelphia in 1876, a British firm displayed an "ordinary English bicycle" that caught the attention of manufacturer Albert A. Pope, who soon converted his Massachusetts air-pistol factory into a bicycle works. Within a decade, America had over 50,000 cyclists, with just about every big city sporting a bicycle club. By the turn-of-the-century bicycle manufacturing had grown into a $60 million business in America alone.

DAILY LIFE
1877–1917

New Ways to Play

As Americans moved from rural areas to cities, they developed new urban lifestyles. Unlike agricultural work schedules, which varied from season to season (heavy during harvest and planting, light during winter), urban work schedules remained essentially the same throughout the year. Because the urban residents worked weekdays indoors, they wanted to spend their weekend and evening leisure time outdoors.

In most cities in the mid-19th century, children had only the streets to play in. But as streets became more crowded with traffic and commerce, they became dangerous places for children. Jacob Riis proposed a series of parks for New York so that children and families could have pleasant and safe places to play or relax. For the many Americans who could not afford expensive toys and fancy vacations, new urban parks, like New York's Central Park, provided safe spaces and affordable facilities for outdoor leisure.

CENTRAL PARK

Built between 1857 and 1876, Central Park covers 840 acres in the middle of Manhattan Island in New York City. In 1857, the New York state legislature paid $5 million for the land, which was occupied by farms, livestock, and some open sewers.

The park's terrain was shaped by workers following a design, by Frederick Law Olmsted and Calvert Vaux, that included flat, grassy areas, rolling hills, woods, and ravines.

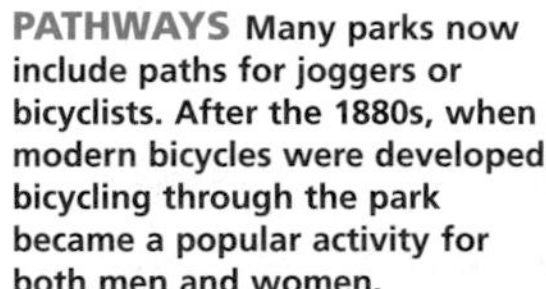

1

PATHWAYS **Many parks now include paths for joggers or bicyclists. After the 1880s, when modern bicycles were developed, bicycling through the park became a popular activity for both men and women.**

Many people enjoyed taking long walks through the park. Others took carriage rides or sat on benches and watched the passersby.

The Picnic Grounds (1906–1907), John Sloan

RECOMMENDED RESOURCES

Books

Hall, Lee. *Olmsted's America.* Boston: Little, 1995. The landscape designer's vision for urban America.

Kinkead, Eugene. *Central Park, 1857–1995.* New York: Norton, 1990. The birth, decline, and renewal of New York City's best-known park.

Nasaw, David. *Going Out.* New York: Basic, 1993. A history of American leisure and public amusements.

Rogers, Elizabeth Barlow. *Frederick Law Olmsted's New York.* New York: Praeger, 1972. A book published with the input of the Whitney Museum of American Art in New York City.

Videos

The Innocent Years. From America: A Look Back series. Social Studies, School Services, 800-421-4246.

New Beginnings (1895–1904). AIMS Media. Educational Software Institute, 800-955-5570. America at the turn of the century.

Olmsted and Central Park. Dir. Philip Gittelman. NVC Arts, 1983. Part of the home video collection of New York's Metropolitan Museum of Art.

Turn-of-the-Century America. Guidance Associates. An exploration of American society and everyday life.

2 **BOATING** Although most people did not have the money to own a boat, Central Park had a number of lakes and lagoons where people could rent one and go for a row.

Along the banks, one could see women holding parasols to protect themselves from the summer sun. Picnickers with wicker baskets searched for a grassy place to spread a blanket.

3 **ICE-SKATING** Even in the middle of winter, people would find enjoyable outdoor activities. Frozen ponds and lakes provided perfect settings for people to ice-skate.

In the 1850s, E. W. Bushnell had designed and produced a skate with a steel blade to replace the wooden skates with iron blades—turning skating into a speedier, more graceful form of exercise that became popular with all social classes.

DATA FILE

Changes in the U.S. Workweek

YEAR	HOURS PER WEEK
1860	66
1890	60
1920	47

A LOOK AT THE FACTS:

A shorter workweek allowed many Americans more time for leisure activities, and they certainly took advantage of it.

- In 1890, an average of 60,000 fans attended professional baseball games daily.
- In 1893, a crowd of 50,000 attended the Princeton-Yale football game.
- *A Trip to Chinatown,* one of the popular new musical comedies, ran for an amazing 650 performances in the 1890s.
- In 1900, 3 million phonograph records of Broadway-produced musical comedies were sold.
- The love of the popular musicals contributed to the sale of $42 million worth of musical instruments in 1900.
- By 1900, almost 500 men's social clubs existed. Nine hundred college fraternity and sorority chapters had over 150,000 members.

Public Parks

Between 1902 and 1919, the number of public parks in the United States grew dramatically.

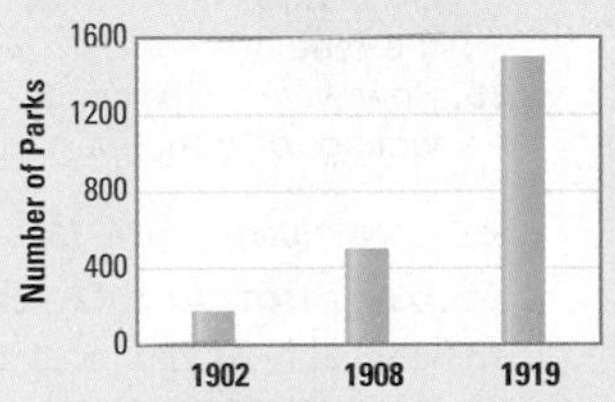

Source: Robert Lewis,"Well-Directed Play," *Impressions of a Gilded Age,* eds. Marc Chenetier and Rob Kroes (Amsterdam: U of Amsterdam P, 1983)

INTERACT WITH HISTORY

1. **INTERPRETING CHARTS AND GRAPHS** Study the statistics in the Data File. What summary statements about the culture and attitudes of this time period can you make? Is this a period of history that you would have liked to have witnessed? Why or why not?

   SEE SKILLBUILDER HANDBOOK, PAGES 928 AND 929.

2. **DESIGNING A MURAL** Work with a partner to design for your classroom a mural that expresses the nature of American life at the turn of the century. Use details from this chapter to help you depict the many changes that were taking place.

INSTRUCT

▶ *Starting with the Student*

- Ask students what parks, beaches, or other outdoor recreational sites are near their homes.
- What kinds of public recreational facilities do students frequently use?
- How does their use of these facilities compare with the use of Central Park described in the feature?

▶ *Discussing Key Ideas*

- A shorter workweek gives Americans more leisure time.
- Cities establish parks for outdoor recreation, and activities like bicycle riding, ice-skating, boating, and watching sports become more popular.

HISTORY FROM VISUALS

Reading the Images

Ask students the following:

- Based on the central illustration, describe the impression Olmsted and Vaux hoped to achieve with Central Park.
- Based on the data file, what other leisure activities did Americans pursue at the turn of the century? How could they afford all this leisure while working fewer hours? *Possible Responses: Americans went to the theater, bought records, and joined social clubs. They could afford this because industrialization was creating more higher-paying jobs, more leisure time, and affordable goods.*

INTERACT WITH HISTORY

1. Interpreting Charts and Graphs

Possible Responses: *There was a flowering of popular culture and a better life for many, but not all, Americans. There was also a shift from rural to urban living.*

Students' opinions about life at the turn of the century will vary, but should be supported with facts from the text.

2. Designing a Mural

Students should review their class materials for ideas of items to include in their murals.

- They should incorporate details about turn-of-the-century American life as described in this feature and the rest of the chapter.
- They could portray a variety of people, events, activities, or things—Ida B. Wells, the first flight at Kitty Hawk, bicycling, or the Brooklyn Bridge—including one from each section.

CHAPTER 8
ASSESSMENT ANSWERS

REVIEWING THE CHAPTER

TERMS & NAMES

1. Louis Sullivan, p. 299
2. Orville and Wilbur Wright, p. 301
3. W. E. B. Du Bois, p. 306
4. Booker T. Washington, p. 307
5. Mark Twain, p. 308
6. Ida B. Wells, p. 309
7. Jim Crow laws, p. 310
8. *Plessy* v. *Ferguson*, p. 311
9. vaudeville, p. 317
10. rural free delivery, p. 321

MAIN IDEAS

11. Skyscrapers allowed for cities to grow upward, and electric trains allowed cities to expand outward.
12. Paper and printing became less expensive, photography became widespread, and airplanes came into use to deliver mail.
13. The number of schools and students in them increased, and new subjects were added.
14. They did not like how schools Americanized their children, particularly in matters of religion.
15. Both portrayed a more realistic, less genteel, world than did works by earlier painters and writers.
16. The Supreme Court upheld the constitutionality of segregation and state voting restrictions, and Congress passed the Chinese Exclusion Act.
17. They helped build the railroads and provided labor for the growing agricultural industry.
18. The growing number of people in cities escaped from the hard workweek with many of the same leisure activities. They also used more mass-produced, widely advertised, brand-name goods.
19. ***Possible Responses:*** Visiting amusement parks, riding bicycles, watching sports, going to the circus or show, reading magazines and novels.
20. Shopping centers, department stores, chain stores, modern advertising, and mail-order catalogs developed in this period.

Chapter 8 Assessment

REVIEWING THE CHAPTER

TERMS & NAMES For each term below, write a sentence explaining its connection to American life at the turn of the 19th century. For each person below, explain his or her significance during this period.

1. Louis Sullivan
2. Orville and Wilbur Wright
3. W. E. B. Du Bois
4. Booker T. Washington
5. Mark Twain
6. Ida B. Wells
7. Jim Crow laws
8. *Plessy* v. *Ferguson*
9. vaudeville
10. rural free delivery

MAIN IDEAS

SECTION 1 *(pages 298–302)*

Science and Urban Life

11. How did new technology promote urban growth around the turn of the century?

12. In what ways did methods of communication improve in the late 19th and early 20th centuries?

SECTION 2 *(pages 303–308)*

Education and Culture

13. How did public schools change during the late 19th century?

14. Why did some immigrants oppose sending their children to public schools around the turn of the century?

15. How were the paintings of Thomas Eakins and the writings of Mark Twain similar?

SECTION 3 *(pages 309–313)*

Segregation and Discrimination

16. In what ways was racial discrimination reinforced by the federal government's actions and policies?

17. How did Mexicans help make the Southwest prosperous in the late 19th century?

SECTION 4 *(pages 314–321)*

Dawn of Mass Culture

18. Why did a mass culture develop in the United States in the late 19th century?

19. What leisure activities flourished at the turn of the century?

20. What innovations in retail methods changed the way Americans shopped during this time period?

THINKING CRITICALLY

1. CULTURAL CHANGE Create a table similar to the one shown, listing at least six major trends at the turn of the century, along with a major impact of each.

Trend	Impact
1.	
2.	
3.	
4.	
5.	
6.	

2. THE AMERICAN PROMISE Reread the quotation by James Weldon Johnson on page 296. On the basis of your reading about life at the turn of the century, what would you identify as the "best" and "worst" aspects of that time period? Explain your response, using details from the chapter.

3. TRACING THEMES SCIENCE AND TECHNOLOGY How had changes in technology affected urban life by the turn of the century?

4. EVALUATING DAILY LIFE Considering the changes occurring around the turn of the century, do you think daily life for a typical American was getting better or worse?

5. ANALYZING PRIMARY SOURCES The historian Henry Steele Commager claimed that the decade of the 1890s was "the watershed of American history."

> On the one side lies an America predominantly agricultural; . . . an America still in the making, physically and socially; an America on the whole self-confident, self-contained, self-reliant, and conscious of its unique character and of a unique destiny. On the other side lies the modern America, predominantly urban and industrial; inextricably involved in world economy and politics; . . . experiencing profound changes in population, social institutions, economy, and technology; and trying to accommodate its traditional institutions and habits of thought to conditions new and in part alien.
>
> HENRY STEELE COMMAGER, quoted in *The American Mind*

Explain whether you agree with Commager that the 1890s marked a significant turning point in American history.

THINKING CRITICALLY

1. CULTURAL CHANGE
Possible student entries include the following trends and impacts:

Skyscrapers: Cities grew upward.

Improved printing: Cost of newspapers and magazines decreased.

Expansion of public education: Literacy increased.

Research universities: A modern curriculum developed.

Voting restrictions: Voting by African Americans declined.

Jim Crow laws: Segregation expanded in the South.

Increased leisure time: Spectator sports and other forms of entertainment became popular.

New ways to sell goods: Consumers had greater choices.

2. THE AMERICAN PROMISE
Possible Responses: Students may say that the best aspects include new technologies to deal with urban problems, expanded educational opportunities, and new leisure activities. The worst aspects of the era would include legalized segregation and discrimination, lynching, and Jim Crow laws.

ALTERNATIVE ASSESSMENT

1. **CREATING AN ADVERTISEMENT**
   How did innovations in manufacturing and retailing affect people's lives between 1900 and 1915?
   Create a magazine or newspaper advertisement for one product of the years 1900–1915.
   CD-ROM Use the CD-ROM *Our Times* and other reference materials to research new inventions and products of this period. You might choose to advertise a new invention or a product related to a new trend in transportation, communication, or leisure activities.
   - Think about the best way to entice your audience to buy your product.
   - Find pictures or create your own images. Write the advertising copy, including the price and relevant information about the product. Create and polish your advertisement.
   - Combine your advertisement with those of your classmates to create a class booklet.
2. **BRINGING HISTORY TO LIFE**
   Select a book, play, movie, or song that was popular at the turn of the century. For possible selections, look in literature anthologies, songbooks, and histories of popular culture. Then choose one of these avenues for sharing your selection with your classmates:
   - Prepare an oral presentation about the selection you've chosen, in which you discuss its history and significance to the time period.
   - Create a poster or other visual, displaying the selection and providing annotations that highlight points of interest.
   - **Cooperative Learning** With a partner, create a short theatrical presentation based upon the pieces you each selected. Discuss differences between the attitudes portrayed in the selections and those of people today.
3. **PORTFOLIO PROJECT**
   Use the Living History activity to expand your portfolio.

LIVING HISTORY

PRESENTING YOUR CATALOG

After you have written your catalog entries, ask a friend to look through the catalog and to answer the following questions:

- Does the catalog accurately reflect the culture of the era?
- What other catalog entries should be added?

When you have made changes based on your friend's suggestions, add illustrations and display the catalog in your classroom. Then add it to your American history portfolio.

Bridge to Chapter 9

Review Chapter 8

TECHNOLOGICAL ADVANCEMENTS Innovations in science and technology around the turn of the century provided the foundation for modern American life. Skyscrapers, electric streetcars, and urban planning shaped rapidly growing American cities. The web-perfecting press, the Linotype machine, and the mail plane brought Americans closer together through improved communication.

EXPANDING EDUCATION Public schools and a growing number of colleges provided the educated work force that businesses needed. Immigrant populations entered schools and faced gradual "Americanization." As the number of educated people grew, so did the demand for literature, libraries, and art museums.

DISCRIMINATION IN AMERICA Few African Americans benefited from the expanding educational system. In education, voting rights, and other areas of life, discrimination and segregation became more firmly entrenched. In *Plessy* v. *Ferguson,* the Supreme Court supported Jim Crow laws that imposed rigid segregation throughout the South. Worse, the lynching of African Americans became commonplace. Mexicans in the Southwest and Chinese immigrants in the West also had to deal with prejudice.

MASS CULTURE EMERGES The growing urban population turned to new forms of recreation. Amusement parks, bicycle riding, tennis, boxing, baseball, vaudeville, ragtime music, and movies all attracted large followings. With the development of mass culture came high-circulation newspapers and new methods of selling goods. Shopping centers, department stores, chain stores, and modern advertising provided consumers with greater selection and lower prices than ever before.

Preview Chapter 9

Rapid changes in American life were accompanied by increased poverty, changing moral standards, and corruption in government. Reformers who initiated the progressive movement demanded that more attention be paid to social justice, moral values, and clean government. You will learn about these developments in the next chapter.

ALTERNATIVE ASSESSMENT

1. CREATING AN ADVERTISEMENT
Standards for Evaluation
An effective advertisement should meet the following criteria:

- Clearly identifies the product in a memorable way.
- Gives the audience reasons to use the product, including information about its price and how it works.
- Uses attractive design features to gain and hold viewers' attention.

2. BRINGING HISTORY TO LIFE
Standards for Evaluation
An oral presentation should meet the following criteria:

- Clearly places the book, play, movie, or song in its proper historical context.
- Uses reviews from the era to support the significance of the piece to the time period.

A visual presentation should meet the following criteria:

- Uses clear and concise annotations.
- Accurately reflects the main point of the piece.
- Uses visual images that reflect the era that the piece came from.

A theatrical presentation should meet the following criteria:

- Incorporates both items chosen by the students.
- Focuses on one significant issue that emerged during the era.
- Gives historically accurate portrayals of turn-of-the-century people and issues.

3. PORTFOLIO PROJECT
LIVING HISTORY
Standards for Evaluation
An effective catalog should meet the following criteria:

- Is organized around categories or themes of mass culture.
- Provides a balanced representation of people and events from the era.
- Uses visuals that are both appropriate and appealing.
- Includes written captions that explain the visuals.

IN-DEPTH RESOURCES: UNIT 2
See the form for scoring this activity on page 74.

THINKING CRITICALLY

3. TRACING THEMES SCIENCE AND TECHNOLOGY
The invention of the elevators and the development of internal steel skeletons to bear the weight of buildings led to the design of skyscrapers. This expanded cities upward and addressed the cities' need for space. Changes in transportation—electric streetcars, new railroad lines, elevated trains, steelcabled suspension bridges—allowed cities to spread outward.

4. EVALUATING DAILY LIFE
Some students might mention that greater choice of goods, greater educational opportunity, and new forms of recreation made life better for many people. Others might point out that life was not better for many minorities and that rapid economic change often disrupts the lives of many people.

5. ANALYZING PRIMARY SOURCES
Most students might say that this time period did mark a turning point in American history, noting the significant changes in technology, education, and leisure activities. Students should support their responses with references to the text.

UNIT OVERVIEW

Modern America Emerges

HISTORY AND ART

Parade of suffragists in New York City

Tinted photograph by unknown artist (1912).

Art Note
Photographs like this one became an increasingly important part of newspaper coverage in the early 1900s. New printing processes allowed papers to reproduce photos more clearly, and their use became increasingly popular.

▶ ***Previewing the Unit***
Unit 3 describes how the modern United States begins taking shape in the first two decades of the 1900s. Americans embrace the progressive movement, which leads to greater government involvement in many aspects of life. Starting with the move to gain colonies overseas and ending with efforts to make peace after World War I, America also plays a greater role in world affairs than ever before.

UNIT 3

1890–1920

Modern America Emerges

"Far better it is to dare mighty things, to win glorious triumphs, than to take rank with those poor spirits who neither enjoy much nor suffer much."

THEODORE ROOSEVELT

326 UNIT 3

1 Action photography
By the time this photograph was taken in 1912, technical improvements had enhanced the power of photography. This photo captures the women in the middle of their march. Some faces—like this woman's—are quite expressive.

2 Parades
A New York group, the Equality League, held the first suffrage parade in 1910. The League was formed and led by Harriot Stanton Blatch, daughter of Elizabeth Cady Stanton. The parade became an annual spring event in New York and spread throughout the country.

3 All walks of life
The suffragist parades included women from all walks of life—professional women, industrial workers, waitresses and maids, and mothers with children. Writing about a 1912 parade, a reporter said "all marched with an intensity of purpose that astonished the crowds that lined the street."

Discussing the Quotation

The Theodore Roosevelt quotation comes from a speech he gave in 1899, when he was governor of New York. Within two years, he became president and was in a position to "dare mighty things" himself.

FOR DISCUSSION:

- What do Roosevelt's words say about the attitudes of American leaders in the early 1900s?
- What changes to society might Americans in 1900 have wanted?
- How did the suffragists exemplify Roosevelt's desire to "dare mighty things"?

Discussing the Image

Woman suffrage seemed to many to be a radical departure for American society. To make their goal more acceptable, suffragists tried to show that they fit squarely within American tradition. The banner reads, "We demand equal representation for equal taxation."

FOR DISCUSSION:

- How does the slogan on the banner help the cause?
- How would parading with children help the cause of suffragists?

4 Formality
The years leading up to World War I were a period marked by formality of dress. The parading women wear long skirts, and many wear hats and gloves.

5 Wide streets
The suffragists' New York parades proceeded up Fifth Avenue, a major street in the city. By using one of the city's most important streets, they gave their parade greater visibility. The tactic would be adopted by leaders of other protest movements later in the century.

6 Patriotic symbols
The suffragists helped promote their cause by using patriotic symbols. Many carried flags. Stars decorated the red sashes that many wore. This marcher sports a patriotic red, white, and-blue hat.

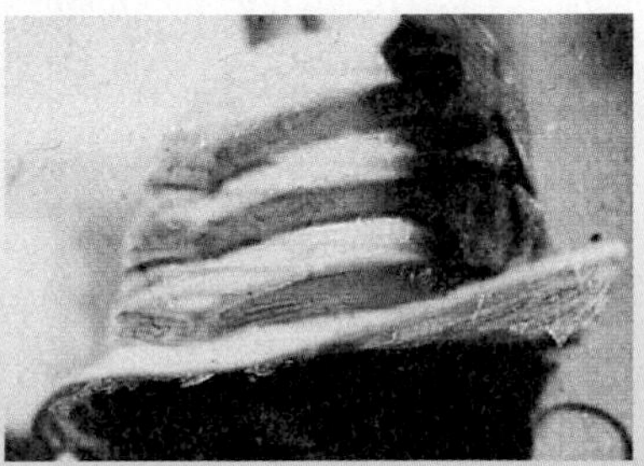

CHAPTER 9

PLANNING GUIDE

The Progressive Era

	Key Ideas	COPYMASTERS	ASSESSMENT
SECTION 1 The Origins of Progressivism *pp. 330–336*	*Social and economic changes during the late 19th century create broad reform movements in American society.*	***In-Depth Resources: Unit 3*** • Guided Reading, p. 1 • Skillbuilder Practice: Forming Generalizations, p. 6 • Primary Sources: Declaration of the WCTU, p. 9; Child Labor in the Coal Mines, p. 10 • American Lives: Robert M. La Follette, p. 16 ***Lesson Plans,*** pp. 77–78	PE ***Section 1 Assessment,*** p. 336 TE ***Self-Assessment,*** p. 336 ***Formal Assessment*** • Section Quiz, p. 116 ***Alternative Assessment Book*** • Standards for Evaluating a Cooperative Activity
SECTION 2 Women in Public Life *pp. 337–340*	*Many of the social and economic changes giving rise to progressivism lead women into public life as reformers and workers.*	***In-Depth Resources: Unit 3*** • Guided Reading, p. 2 • Primary Sources: Political Poster, p. 11; *from* "The Status of Woman" by Susan B. Anthony, p. 12 ***Lesson Plans,*** pp. 79–80	PE ***Section 2 Assessment,*** p. 340 TE ***Self-Assessment,*** p. 340 ***Formal Assessment*** • Section Quiz, p. 117 ***Alternative Assessment Book*** • Standards for Evaluating a Cooperative Activity
SECTION 3 Teddy Roosevelt's Square Deal *pp. 341–347*	*Theodore Roosevelt pursues a reform agenda known as the Square Deal. His energetic style contributes to the emergence of the modern presidency.*	***In-Depth Resources: Unit 3*** • Guided Reading, p. 3 • Literature: from *The Jungle* by Upton Sinclair, p. 13 ***Lesson Plans,*** pp. 81–82	PE ***Section 3 Assessment,*** p. 347 TE ***Self-Assessment,*** p. 347 ***Formal Assessment*** • Section Quiz, p. 118 ***Alternative Assessment Book*** • Standards for Evaluating a Cooperative Activity
SECTION 4 Progressivism Under Taft *pp. 350–353*	*William H. Taft pursues a more cautious progressive program during his one term as president.*	***In-Depth Resources: Unit 3*** • Guided Reading, p. 4 ***Lesson Plans,*** pp. 83–84	PE ***Section 4 Assessment,*** p. 353 TE ***Self-Assessment,*** p. 353 ***Formal Assessment*** • Section Quiz, p. 119 ***Alternative Assessment Book*** • Standards for Evaluating a Cooperative Activity
SECTION 5 Wilson's New Freedom *pp. 354–359*	*Woodrow Wilson claims the presidency as a progressive leader and establishes a strong reform agenda.*	***In-Depth Resources: Unit 3*** • Guided Reading, p. 5 • Geography Application: The Movement Toward Woman Suffrage, p. 7 • American Lives: Carrie Chapman Catt, p. 17 ***Lesson Plans,*** pp. 85–86	PE ***Section 5 Assessment,*** p. 359 TE ***Self-Assessment,*** p. 359 ***Formal Assessment*** • Section Quiz, p. 120 ***Alternative Assessment Book*** • Standards for Evaluating a Cooperative Activity
CHAPTER RESOURCES	**Chapter Overview** *In the first two decades of the 1900s, Americans embrace the progressive movement and many of its reforms.*	***In-Depth Resources: Unit 3*** • Living History Project: Worksheet, p. 18; Standards, p. 19 ***Telescoping the Times*** • Chapter Summary, pp. 17–18 ***Planning for Block Schedules***	PE ***Chapter Assessment,*** pp. 360–361 PE ***Alternative Assessment,*** p. 361 ***Formal Assessment*** • Chapter Test, forms A and B, pp. 121–126 ***Test Generator*** ***Alternative Assessment Book*** See explanation and forms for different kinds of alternative assessments including portfolio assessment.

KEY
PE Pupil's Edition
TE Teacher's Edition
INTERNET http://www.mlushistory.com

TECHNOLOGY

Warm-Up Transparency **9**
Geography Transparencies
• G17, Continental United States in 1900
Critical Thinking Transparencies
• CT51, Child Labor, 1890–1930
Electronic Library of Primary Sources
• On the Need for Child Labor Laws
• On Prohibition and Liberty
• The Taylor System
AMERICAN STORIES video series
• "A Child on Strike"
INTERNET Hull House and Prohibition

Warm-Up Transparency **9**
Electronic Library of Primary Sources
• from *The United States of America* v. *Susan B. Anthony*
INTERNET Susan B. Anthony and the suffrage movement

Warm-Up Transparency **9**
Electronic Library of Primary Sources
• *from* "Whatever Is, Is Wrong" by E. W. Scripps
Our Times
• Upton Sinclair
INTERNET Theodore Roosevelt and W. E. B. Du Bois

Warm-Up Transparency **9**
Humanities Transparencies
• H36, "I Must Have Been Dozing"
Grolier Multimedia Encyclopedia
• Conservation in the United States
• Bull Moose Party
INTERNET Gifford Pinchot and William H. Taft

Warm-Up Transparency **9**
Critical Thinking Transparencies
• CT17, Progressive Movement
Grolier Multimedia Encyclopedia
• from a speech on the rights of labor by William H. Taft
• Multimedia map of woman suffrage
INTERNET Woodrow Wilson and Carrie Chapman Catt

American Portfolio: A Videodisc for U.S. History, user's guide, pp.155, 159, 165–175
Chapter Summary Audiotapes
• Unit 3, Chapter 9
INTERNET http://www. mlushistory.com

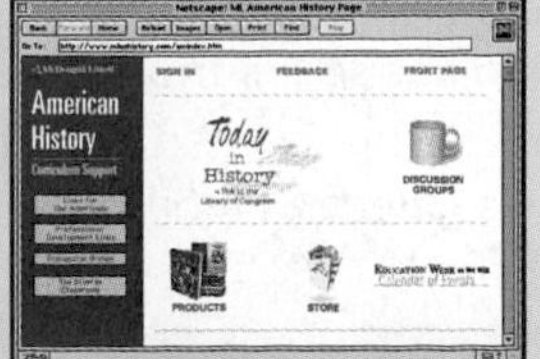

Block Scheduling (90 MINUTES)

Day 1
Section 1, pp. 330–336
AMERICAN STORIES video series "A Child on Strike"
Section Assessment, p. 336
COOPERATIVE ACTIVITY
• Learning About Muckrakers, p. 333 (TE)

Day 2
Section 2, pp. 337–340
Section 3, pp. 341–347
Section Assessments, pp. 340, 347
COOPERATIVE ACTIVITIES
• Creating Political Placards, p. 339 (TE)
• Creating Political Cartoons, p. 343 (TE)

Day 3
Section 4, pp. 350–353
Section Assessment, p. 353
American Literature: The Muckrakers, pp. 348–349
COOPERATIVE ACTIVITY
• Reporting Election Results, p. 352 (TE)

Day 4
Section 5, pp. 354–359
Section Assessment, p. 359
Chapter Assessment, pp. 360–361
COOPERATIVE ACTIVITY
• Writing Letters to the Editor, p. 357 (TE)

YEARLY PACING ***Chapter 9 Total:*** 4 days ***Yearly Total:*** 85 days

See *Planning for Block Schedules* for special activities and pacing strategies.

Customizing for Special Populations

Students Acquiring English
Access for Students Acquiring English: Spanish Translations
• Guided Reading for Sections 1–5, pp. 120–124
• Chapter Summary, pp. 118–119
• Skillbuilder Practice: Forming Generalizations, p. 125
• Geography Application: The Movement Toward Woman Suffrage, p.126
Spanish Reading Study Guide, pp. 97–108
Translations of Chapter Summaries, Hmong, Cantonese, Vietnamese, and Cambodian

Chapter Summary Audiotapes in Spanish
Unit 3, Chapter 9
AMERICAN STORIES video series
• "A Child on Strike" (Spanish track)
INTERNET The Diverse Classroom

Gifted and Talented Students
In-Depth Resources: Unit 3
• Primary Sources: Declaration of the WCTU, p. 9; Child Labor in the Coal Mines, p. 10; Political Poster, p. 11; *from* "The Status of Woman" by Susan B. Anthony, p. 12
• American Lives: Robert M. La Follette, p. 16; Carrie Chapman Catt, p. 17

Less Proficient Readers
In-Depth Resources: Unit 3
• Guided Reading for Sections 1–5, pp. 1–5
• Skillbuilder Practice: Forming Generalizations, p. 6
• Geography Application: The Movement Toward Woman Suffrage, p. 7
Reading Study Guide
• pp. 97–108
Telescoping the Times
• Chapter Summary, pp. 17–18
Chapter Summary Audiotapes, Unit 3, Chapter 9

Connections to Literature READINGS FOR STUDENTS

In-Depth Resources: Unit 3
• **from *The Jungle* by Upton Sinclair,** p. 13

Enrichment Reading

John Dos Passos
U.S.A.
New York: Penguin Books, 1996.
The three separate novels of U.S.A. *sharply satirize 20th-century America in every region and at every social level.*

N.A. Perez
Breaker
Boston: Houghton, 1988.
After his father's death, 14-year-old Pat is forced to work in the coal mines in his Pennsylvania town. He becomes involved in the big mine workers' strike of 1902.

Carl Sandburg
Chicago Poems
New York: Dover, 1994.
This is Sandburg's first book of poetry. These free-verse poems celebrate the voices of the people and are concerned with themes of injustice and the effects of industrialization on humanity.

McDougal Littell *The Language of Literature* American Literature
• **Charlotte Perkins Gilman, "The Yellow Wallpaper,"** p. 605
• **Barbara Ehrenreich and Deirdre English, from *Complaints and Disorders: The Sexual Politics of Sickness,*** p. 619
• **Kate Chopin, "The Story of an Hour,"** p. 623

CHAPTER 9 OVERVIEW

The Progressive Era

▶ *Accessing Prior Knowledge*

Ask students to give examples of people they know in their school or community who have worked hard to reform a bad condition. Students should explain what the person's goal was and how he or she went about making the reform.

▶ *Predicting Outcomes*

Ask the students what Wilson meant when he said democracy "releases the energies" of people. What does the release of energy suggest to students about what might happen during the progressive era?

MORE ABOUT...
Woodrow Wilson

Woodrow Wilson (1856–1924) became president in 1912, when the progressive movement was well underway. Believing he had been elected with a mandate for continued social reform, Wilson asserted, "We stand in the presence of a revolution whereby America will insist upon recovering in practice those ideals which she has always professed."

CHAPTER 9

The Progressive Era

SECTION 1
The Origins of Progressivism
Social and economic changes during the late 19th century create broad reform movements in American society.

VIDEO *A CHILD ON STRIKE*

SECTION 2
Women in Public Life
Many of the social and economic changes giving rise to progressivism lead women into public life as reformers and workers.

SECTION 3
Teddy Roosevelt's Square Deal
Theodore Roosevelt pursues a reform agenda known as the Square Deal. His energetic style contributes to the emergence of the modern presidency.

SECTION 4
Progressivism Under Taft
William H. Taft pursues a more cautious progressive program during his one term as president.

SECTION 5
Wilson's New Freedom
Woodrow Wilson claims the presidency as a progressive leader and establishes a strong reform agenda.

"I believe in democracy because it releases the energies of every human being."
Woodrow Wilson

THE UNITED STATES

- **1890** Suffragists unite behind the National American Woman Suffrage Association (NAWSA).
- **1890** Congress passes the Sherman Antitrust Act.
- **1892** Grover Cleveland is elected president for a second term.
- **1893** Illinois Factory Act prohibits child labor.
- **1895** Anti-Saloon League is founded.
- **1896** William McKinley is elected president.
- **1900** William McKinley is reelected.
- **1901** McKinley is assassinated.
- **1901** Theodore Roosevelt becomes president.

THE WORLD

- **1891** Construction of the Trans-Siberian railroad across Russia begins.
- **1895** Italian Guglielmo Marconi invents radio telegraphy.
- **1901** Com of A creat

THEMES IN CHAPTER 9

Economic Opportunity

The progressive movement responded to a growing public demand for government involvement to curb big business and to deal with the nation's economic issues.

See Teacher's Edition note, p. 332.

Women in America

Women entered the work force in increasing numbers. Though usually paid less than their male counterparts, their increasing visibility in the public arena helped spur the movement toward woman suffrage.

During the progressive era, woman suffrage finally was achieved, brought about in part because of the increased role of women in public life due to the beginning of World War I. Ratification of the Nineteenth Amendment took place in 1920.

See Teacher's Edition notes, pp. 338, 356.

Constitutional Concerns

Theodore Roosevelt changed the role of the president, using the White House as a "bully pulpit" to influence public policy and expanding the responsibilities of the office. His actions helped shape the modern presidency.

See Teacher's Edition note, p. 342.

LIVING HISTORY

PLANNING A SUFFRAGE CAMPAIGN

Suppose that suffragists—those who worked to win women the right to vote—had been able to use today's communications media to win support for their argument. Follow these guidelines to plan your own campaign for woman suffrage:

- Consider how you might use television, the Internet, and other modern devices to convince the public and the government to pass an amendment giving women the right to vote.
- Work with a partner or group to plan in detail your TV ads and other campaign strategies.

PORTFOLIO PROJECT Keep your ideas in a folder. At the end of the chapter, you will present your campaign to the class and add it to your American history portfolio.

1904 National Child Labor Committee is formed.

1904 Theodore Roosevelt is elected president.

1905 Niagara Convention advocates the militant pursuit of African-American rights.

1905 Albert Einstein publishes papers on the special theory of relativity and the particle theory of light.

1906 Upton Sinclair publishes *The Jungle.*

1908 William H. Taft is elected president.

1909 National Association for the Advancement of Colored People (NAACP) is founded.

1909 Payne-Aldrich Tariff is passed.

1910

1911 Membership in the Woman's Christian Temperance Union grows to 245,000.

1912 Woodrow Wilson is elected president.

1913 Seventeenth Amendment provides for direct election of senators.

1914 World War I begins in Europe.

1916 Woodrow Wilson is reelected.

1916 Followers of the Mexican revolutionary Pancho Villa raid Columbus, New Mexico.

1917 Congress passes the Eighteenth Amendment, outlawing alcoholic beverages.

1917 U.S. enters World War I.

1919 Congress passes the Nineteenth Amendment, which grants women the vote.

1920 Olympic Games are held in Antwerp, Belgium.

ALTERNATIVE ASSESSMENT

LIVING HISTORY

PLANNING A SUFFRAGE CAMPAIGN

Discuss these ideas for conducting the suffrage campaigns:

- Discuss the overall strategy for the campaign: What message about suffrage do students want to convey?
- Have groups sketch a diagram or write an outline that summarizes their campaign strategy.
- Have students develop effective slogans to use for their campaigns.

Project Planning Guide	
Step 1	Student teams outline a strategy to achieve suffrage.
Step 2	Student groups assign members to handle various aspects of the campaign.
Step 3	Students complete the elements chosen as part of their campaign strategies.
Step 4	Students assemble the pieces of their campaign in their folders.

IN-DEPTH RESOURCES: UNIT 3

See worksheet and standards for evaluation, pp. 18, 19.

RECOMMENDED RESOURCES

Books for the Teacher

Schlereth, Thomas J. *Victorian America: Transformations in Everyday Life, 1876–1915.* New York: Harper, 1991. A useful overview of the period.

Woloch, Nancy. *Women and the American Experience.* New York: Knopf, 1984. An introduction to the history of American women.

Books for the Student

Addams, Jane. *Twenty Years at Hull House.* Urbana: U of Illinois P, 1990. Addams's story of the settlement house.

Schneir, Miriam, ed. *Feminism: The Essential Historical Writings.* New York: Random, 1972. A collection of primary-source materials.

Wilson, Dorothy Clarke. *Bright Eyes: The Story of Susette La Flesche, an Omaha Indian.* New York: McGraw, 1974. A readable account.

Videos

One Woman, One Vote. Prod. Ruth Pollak. PBS Home Video, 1995. Final drive for woman suffrage.

Theodore Roosevelt: Roughrider to Rushmore. Prod. Arthur Drooker. A&E Home Video, 1996. Bold life of an energetic president.

TR, the Story of Theodore Roosevelt. Prod. David Grubin. PBS Home Video, 1996. Four-hour biography.

Software

Her Heritage. CD-ROM. Pilgrim New Media, 1994. Biographical profiles of famous American women.

Social Reform Movements. CD-ROM. Educational Software Institute.

U.S. History: Government, Part 2. CD-ROM. Educational Software Institute.

Section 1 Overview

OBJECTIVES

1. To explain the four goals of progressivism.
2. To summarize progressive efforts to clean up local government.
3. To identify progressive efforts to clean up state government, protect workers, and reform elections.

CRITICAL THINKING

- Summarizing, pp. 331, 336
- Forming generalizations, pp. 332, 336
- Contrasting, p. 333
- Finding main ideas, p. 334
- Recognizing effects, p. 335
- Theme: Constitutional Concerns, p. 336
- Forming opinions, p. 336

FOCUS & MOTIVATE

5-MINUTE WARM-UP

Recognizing Facts and Details

To explore the conditions of child labor, have students look at the photo on page 335 and answer these questions.

1. What is the age group of these factory workers? How are they dressed?
2. What details do you notice about the factory and the machinery?

WARM-UP TRANSPARENCY 9

▶***Starting with the Student***

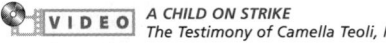

Watch the video "A Child on Strike" to learn how a young girl injured in a woolen mill is affected by progressivism.

- Using the *Teacher's Resource Book* as a guide, discuss Camella Teoli's experience in the mill. Use extension activities, including primary sources, to help students understand the use of child labor.

***AMERICAN STORIES* video series**

"A Child on Strike"

Videocassette: Volume 2

Videodisc: Disc 2, Side A, Chapter 2

1 The Origins of Progressivism

TERMS & NAMES
- progressive movement
- Florence Kelley
- prohibition
- muckraker
- scientific management
- Robert M. La Follette
- initiative
- referendum
- recall
- Seventeenth Amendment

LEARN ABOUT the political, economic, and moral roots of progressivism ***TO UNDERSTAND*** how progressive reforms changed modern America.

ONE AMERICAN'S STORY

Angry crowds confront the militia at the Lawrence mill workers' strike in 1912.

In 1900, three-year-old Camella Teoli and her family came from Italy to join Camella's father, who had immigrated earlier to work in the textile mills of Lawrence, Massachusetts. To help support the family, Teoli's wife and his older children all went to work in the mills. Camella began working at the Washington Woolen Mill when she was about 12 years old. On July 9, 1909, a machine used for twisting cotton into thread tore off part of the girl's scalp, sending her to the hospital for seven months. A six-inch scar marked the injury for the rest of Camella's life.

In 1912, more than 20,000 Lawrence mill workers went on strike over wage cuts. The mill owners had responded to a Massachusetts law reducing hours for women and children by cutting all workers' salaries and increasing the work pace. The striking workers, who could barely get by on an average of about $9 per week, refused to accept less.

Prominent supporters of the strike arranged for a group of Washington Woolen Mill workers, including Camella Teoli, to testify before a congressional committee. Camella's shocking story soon made headlines across the United States. When asked why she had gone on strike, Camella answered simply, "Because I didn't get enough to eat at home." She explained to the committee how she had gone to work before reaching the legal age of 14.

A PERSONAL VOICE

I used to go to school, and then a man came up to my house and asked my father why I didn't go to work, so my father says I don't know whether she is 13 or 14 years old. So, the man say you give me $4 and I will make the papers come from the old country [Italy] saying that you are 14. So my father gave him the $4, and in one month came the papers that I was 14. I went to work, and about two weeks later got hurt in my head.

CAMELLA TEOLI, at congressional hearings, March 1912

The Lawrence workers held out for nine weeks and won the sympathy of the nation as well as a 10 percent pay raise. Stories like Camella's set off a national investigation of labor conditions. As reformer Mary Heaton Vorse said, "What we saw in Lawrence affected us so strongly that this moment in time in Lawrence changed life for us." Indeed, across the country, people organized to address the problems of industrialization.

A CHILD ON STRIKE
The Testimony of Camella Teoli, Mill Girl

Four Goals of Progressivism

At the dawn of the new century, middle-class reformers addressed many of the problems that had contributed to the social upheavals of the 1890s. Journalists and writers exposed the unsafe conditions that factory workers, including women and children, often faced. Intellectuals questioned the dominant role of large corporations in American society. Political reformers struggled to make government more responsive to the people. Together, these reform efforts formed the **progressive movement,** which aimed to return control of the government to the people, restore economic opportunities, and correct injustices in American life.

SECTION 1 RESOURCES

PRINT RESOURCES

IN-DEPTH RESOURCES: UNIT 3
Guided Reading, p. 1
Skillbuilder Practice: Forming Generalizations, p. 6
Primary Sources: Declaration of the WCTU, p. 9; Child Labor in the Coal Mines, p. 10
American Lives: Robert M. La Follette, p. 16

READING STUDY GUIDE, p. 97

ACCESS FOR STUDENTS ACQUIRING ENGLISH
Guided Reading (Spanish), p. 120
Skillbuilder Practice: Forming Generalizations (Spanish), p. 125

SPANISH READING STUDY GUIDE, p. 97

FORMAL ASSESSMENT
Section Quiz, p. 116

ALTERNATIVE ASSESSMENT BOOK
See forms for supporting and scoring alternative activities.

TECHNOLOGY RESOURCES

GEOGRAPHY TRANSPARENCIES
G17, Continental United States in 1900

CRITICAL THINKING TRANSPARENCIES
CT51, Child Labor, 1890–1930

CD-ROM Electronic Library of Primary Sources

VIDEO *American Stories* video series
American Portfolio: A Videodisc for U.S. History user's guide, pp. 159, 172, 173

INTERNET http://www.mlushistory.com

Unlike populism, the political movement that started with dissatisfied farmers, the progressive movement attracted middle-class city dwellers, who included writers, teachers, and scholars. Even though they never completely agreed on the problems or the solutions, these progressives sought to cure the many social problems caused by industrialization. For example, some progressives believed that business required stricter regulation, while others threw their energy into reforming city governments, making laws to protect workers, or closing saloons. However, every progressive reform movement had at least one of the following four goals:

- protecting social welfare
- promoting moral improvement
- creating economic reform
- fostering efficiency

PROTECTING SOCIAL WELFARE Many social welfare reformers strove to relieve urban problems. The Social Gospel and settlement-house movements had begun as efforts to soften some of the harsh effects of industrialization. These efforts continued during the progressive era and inspired even more reform activities.

The Young Men's Christian Association (YMCA), for example, opened libraries, sponsored classes, and built swimming pools and handball courts. The Salvation Army fed poor people in soup kitchens, cared for children in nurseries, and sent "slum brigades" to convert poor immigrants to the middle-class values of hard work and temperance.

Settlement houses inspired social activism on the part of many women reformers. **Florence Kelley,** for example, a newly divorced mother of three young children, moved into Jane Addams's Hull House in Chicago. There, Kelley became an advocate for improving the lives of women and children. Eventually, Governor John P. Altgeld appointed her chief inspector of factories for Illinois after she had helped to win passage of the Illinois Factory Act in 1893. The act, which prohibited child labor and limited women's working hours, soon became a model for other states.

THINK THROUGH HISTORY
A. *Summarizing* *What was Florence Kelley's role in the progressive reform movement?*

A. Answer Kelley worked for child labor laws and shorter working days for women.

PROMOTING MORAL REFORM Other reformers felt that morality, not the workplace, held the key to improving the lives of poor people. Reformers offered a host of programs to uplift immigrants and poor city dwellers by improving personal behavior. **Prohibition,** the banning of alcoholic beverages, was one such program.

The Woman's Christian Temperance Union (WCTU), founded in Chicago in 1873, promoted the goal of prohibition. Members advanced their cause by entering saloons, singing, praying, and urging saloonkeepers to stop selling alcohol.

In 1879, Frances Willard, who had been the president of Evanston (Illinois) College for Ladies, transformed the WCTU from a small midwestern religious group into a powerful national organization with a variety of reformist goals. With 245,000 members in 1911, the WCTU became the largest women's group in the nation's history. Willard was a skillful organizer with a talent for political slogans. A WCTU member, according to Willard, must be ready to "bless and brighten every place she enters and enter every place."

Willard also told her members to "do everything." WCTU members followed their leader's dictum, opening kindergartens for immigrants, visiting inmates in prisons and asylums, and working for suffrage. The WCTU

KEY PLAYER

FLORENCE KELLEY
1859–1932

Florence Kelley was born into privilege as the daughter of an antislavery Republican congressman from Pennsylvania. She became a social reformer whose sympathies clearly lay with the powerless, especially working women and children. During a long career, Kelley, whom one colleague admiringly called a guerrilla warrior, pushed the government to solve America's social problems.

In 1899, Kelley became general secretary of the National Consumers' League, where she lobbied to improve factory conditions. "Why," Kelley pointedly asked while campaigning for a federal child-labor law, "are seals, bears, reindeer, fish, wild game in the national parks, buffalo, [and] migratory birds all found suitable for federal protection, but not children?"

In the 1890s, Carry Nation worked for prohibition by walking into saloons, scolding the customers, and using her hatchet to destroy the bottles of liquor.

OBJECTIVE ① **INSTRUCT**

Four Goals of Progressivism

▶***Starting with the Student*** Have students create a concept map like this one to identify the four goals.

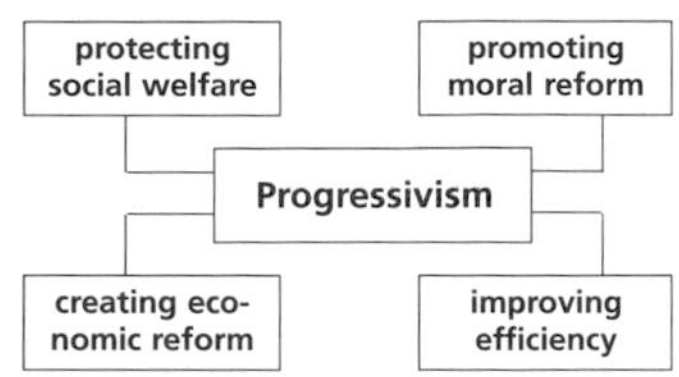

▶***Discussing Key Ideas***

- Progressivism aims to protect social welfare.
- Progessives promote moral and economic reform.
- Progressive reformers improve workplace efficiency.

IN-DEPTH RESOURCES: UNIT 3
Guided Reading, p. 1
Primary Source: Declaration of the WCTU, p. 9

ACCESS FOR STUDENTS ACQUIRING ENGLISH
Guided Reading (Spanish), p. 120

GEOGRAPHY TRANSPARENCIES
G17, Continental United States in 1900

KEY PLAYER
Florence Kelley
Critical Thinking: Analyzing Ask what the term "guerrilla warrior" suggests about Kelley.
Possible Responses: Is a dedicated fighter; knows the political landscape well; harasses those she opposes in an effort to undermine their authority.

TEACHING OPTIONS

Making Global Connections

British Roots of Social Welfare Some U.S. social-welfare organizations began in Britain as part of Victorian liberalism. The YMCA was founded in 1844 by a London draper named George Williams, who sought "improvement of the spiritual condition" of young workers. The Salvation Army grew out of a mission founded in 1865 by itinerant preacher William Booth in the Whitechapel slum district of London. Also in Whitechapel was Toynbee Hall, a settlement house named for social reformer Arnold Toynbee and used by Jane Addams as the model for Hull House.

Teaching Less Proficient Readers

Reviewing Concepts Remind students that they may already have read about the Social Gospel and settlement house movements in Chapter 7. Make sure they understand that the Social Gospel movement applied the beliefs and practices of the church in providing social services in urban communities. Briefly discuss Jane Addams, her role in creating Hull House, and the community needs that the settlement house fulfilled. Remind students that Addams also worked to establish juvenile courts, regulations for tenement housing, and an eight-hour work day for women.

HISTORICAL SPOTLIGHT
Anti-Saloon League

Critical Thinking: Analyzing Motives Allow students to debate the goals and methods of the Anti-Saloon League. Then ask what specific reasons the League may have had for trying to ban alcohol. *Possible Responses: Religious convictions; problem behavior induced by drinking, such as job loss and spouse or child abuse.*

ELECTRONIC LIBRARY OF PRIMARY SOURCES
On Prohibition and Liberty by Percy Andreae

MORE ABOUT . . .
Edward Bellamy

Son of a Baptist minister, Bellamy developed a deep concern for the urban poor. Soon after studying law and passing the bar, he became a journalist, but his greatest fame came from a novel, *Looking Backward.* Published in 1888, the novel describes a socialist utopia in what for Bellamy and his readers was the distant future—the year 2000.

MORE ABOUT . . .
Eugene Debs

Debs was only 14 years old when he left home to work for the railroads, and by age 20 he had become a union organizer. In 1895, he was jailed for helping to direct the famous Pullman strike a year earlier. After William Jennings Bryan, whom Debs supported, lost the presidential election of 1896, Debs led the founding of the Socialist Party of America. He ran as its presidential candidate in 1900, 1904, 1908, 1912, and 1920.

HISTORICAL SPOTLIGHT

ANTI–SALOON LEAGUE

Progressive women in particular denounced alcohol, which they called Demon Rum. Whereas early temperance efforts, dating back to the 1820s, had asked individuals to change their ways, turn-of-the century reformers sought the government's help in controlling alcohol consumption. Quietly founded in 1895, the Anti-Saloon League called itself "the Church in action against the saloon."

The league endorsed politicians who opposed Demon Rum, no matter which party they belonged to or where they stood on other issues. The Anti-Saloon League also organized statewide referenda to ban alcohol. Between 1900 and 1917, voters in nearly half of the states—mostly in the South and the West—prohibited the sale, production, or use of alcohol. Individual towns, city wards, and rural areas also voted themselves "dry."

reform activities, like those of the settlement-house movement, provided women with expanded public roles, which they used to justify giving women voting rights. A woman's right to vote, Willard believed, would offer "the most potent means of social and moral reform."

The most prominent reform pushed by the WCTU, however, was prohibition. Sometimes efforts at prohibition led to tension with immigrant groups, whose customs often included the consumption of alcohol. The Anti-Saloon League, founded in 1895, angered many immigrants when its members attacked saloons, which filled several roles in many immigrant communities. The saloons served inexpensive meals, cashed paychecks, and provided rooms for any purpose, from wedding receptions to political meetings to union headquarters. Prohibitionist groups feared that alcohol was undermining American culture and democracy. By concentrating on closing saloons, the league became a model for other single-issue interest groups that set out to reform American culture and government.

THINK THROUGH HISTORY
B. *Forming Generalizations* *What goals did the WCTU have in common with other progressive organizations?*

B. Answer The WCTU worked for social welfare, moral improvement, and economic reform by opening kindergartens, promoting prohibition and suffrage, and expanding roles for women in public life.

CREATING ECONOMIC REFORM As moral reformers sought to change individual behavior, a severe economic panic in 1893 prompted some Americans to question the capitalist economic system. (See *free enterprise* on page 935 in the Economics Handbook.) Writers like Henry George and Edward Bellamy, for example, criticized the laissez-faire theory—the belief that government should leave the economy alone. Bellamy called the capitalist ideal of competition a "brutal and cowardly slaughter of the unarmed and overmatched by bullies in armor."

Some Americans, especially workers, embraced socialism. (See *socialism* on page 938 in the Economics Handbook.) The labor leader Eugene V. Debs helped organize the American Socialist Party in 1900. Debs commented on the uneven balance among big business, government, and ordinary people under the free-market system of capitalism.

A PERSONAL VOICE

Competition was natural enough at one time, but do you think you are competing today? Many of you think you are competing. Against whom? Against Rockefeller? About as I would if I had a wheelbarrow and competed with the Santa Fe [railroad] from here to Kansas City.

EUGENE DEBS, *Debs: His Life, Writings and Speeches*

Though most progressives distanced themselves from socialism, they saw the truth of many of Debs's criticisms. Indeed, big business often received favorable treatment from government officials and politicians.

Journalists who wrote about the corrupt side of business and public life in mass circulation magazines during the early 20th century became known as **muckrakers.** (The term refers to John Bunyan's *Pilgrim's Progress,* in which a character is so busy using a rake to clean up the muck of this world that he does not raise his eyes to heaven.) In her *History of the Standard Oil Company,* a monthly serial in *McClure's Magazine,* the muckraking writer Ida M. Tarbell described the company's cutthroat methods of eliminating competition. "Mr. Rockefeller has systematically played with loaded dice," Tarbell charged, "and it is doubtful if there has been a time since 1872 when he has run a race with a competitor and started fair."

FOSTERING EFFICIENCY While muckrakers fought corporate and government corruption, other reformers tried to increase the efficiency of American society. Frederick Winslow Taylor popularized the concept of **scientific management,** the effort to improve efficiency in the workplace by applying scientific principles

TEACHING OPTIONS

Exploring Themes

Economic Opportunity The more complex economies of the industrial age experienced far greater economic disturbances than had occurred in the past. Especially severe in the 19th century were the panics or depressions of 1837, 1857, 1873, and 1893. The progressive movement was in part a response to what its proponents saw as a growing need for government involvement to try to curb the devastation of the widespread bank failures, job losses, and bankruptcies that characterized these periods of economic chaos.

Making Connections Across the Curriculum

Economics When a 19th-century panic occurred, a depression followed. For example, the Panic of 1893 ushered in a four-year depression. In general, economists make these distinctions:

- panic: a period of acute financial disturbance that usually begins a depression
- recession: a slowdown in the business cycle when declining production and employment lead to declining incomes and purchasing
- depression: a period of drastic economic decline characterized by sharply reduced business activity, falling prices and wages, and widespread unemployment

to make tasks simpler and easier. As a result, workers became more productive and the amount of goods and services available to the people increased.

In *Principles of Scientific Management* (1911), Taylor declared, "Time studies of work forms the basis of modern management." Followers of Taylor studied factory operations to see just how quickly each task could be performed. Armed with the results, bosses like the Lawrence mill owners raised the speed of their machines and increased laborers' workloads to match.

One problem was that some people worked more quickly than others. In response, the Ford Motor Company tried introducing an assembly line in its Highland Park, Michigan, plant in 1913. The assembly line moved the automobile parts at a steady speed. Following that experiment, time-and-motion studies led to an expanded assembly line. By 1914, three lines were in full operation at the plant, where workers turned out 1,212 chassis assemblies every eight hours.

Workers at the Ford flywheel factory cope with the demanding pace of the assembly line to earn $5 a day—a good wage before the First World War.

C. Answer Scientific management reformers worked to improve efficiency and productivity, while other reformers aimed at improving individual behavior or addressing economic inequality.

THINK THROUGH HISTORY
C. *Contrasting* *Contrast the goals and effects of scientific management with other progressive reforms.*

Such assembly lines led to a huge increase in production, but the system required people to work like machines. The result was a high worker turnover, often due to injuries suffered by exhausted workers. As one steelworker complained in 1910, "It's simply a killing pace in the steelworks."

To keep his assembly line workers happy and to prevent strikes, Henry Ford reduced the workday to eight hours and paid workers five dollars a day, twice as much as other industrial workers earned at the time. The "Five-Dollar Day" attracted thousands of job seekers. For their money, though, workers on Ford's assembly line exhausted themselves. As one homemaker mildly complained in a letter to Henry Ford in 1914, "That $5 a day is a blessing—a bigger one than you know but oh they earn it."

Such efforts at improving efficiency, an important part of progressivism, targeted not only industry, but government as well.

> ***"When I'm through everybody will be able to afford [a car], and about everyone will have one."***
>
> HENRY FORD, 1909

Cleaning Up Government

Cities posed some of the most obvious social problems of the new industrial age. In many large cities, political bosses rewarded their supporters with jobs and kickbacks and openly bought votes with favors and bribes. Efforts to reform city politics stemmed in part from the desire to make government more efficient and responsive to its constituents. But those efforts also grew from distrust of immigrants' participation in politics.

REFORMING LOCAL GOVERNMENT Natural disasters sometimes played an important role in prompting reform of city governments. In 1900, for example, a hurricane and tidal wave swept out of the Gulf of Mexico and almost demolished Galveston, Texas. The politicians on the city council botched the huge relief and rebuilding job so badly that the Texas legislature appointed a five-member commission of experts to take over. Each expert took charge of a different city department. The commission soon rebuilt Galveston, prompting the city to adopt the commission idea as a form of government. By 1917, some 500 cities had followed Galveston's example and replaced city councils with commissions.

MORE ABOUT . . .
Ford and the Automobile

Henry Ford applied the assembly line on a much larger scale than ever before. He also sped up production by sticking to the basics: "You can have any color you want as long as it's black," he joked. His innovations cut production time of his Model T cars from 14 man-hours in 1910 to two man-hours in 1913, making them more affordable.

HISTORY FROM VISUALS
Ford Factory Workers

Reading the Image Ask what the picture reveals about what it would be like to work on an assembly line. *Possible Responses: Exhausting; crowded; tedious; noisy.*

ELECTRONIC LIBRARY OF PRIMARY SOURCES
The Taylor System by Frederick W. Taylor

OBJECTIVE
② **INSTRUCT**

Cleaning Up Government

▶ ***Starting with the Student***
- Have students discuss what the saying "You can't fight city hall" means.
- Ask whether they think the saying is usually true.

▶ ***Discussing Key Ideas***
- Incompetent handling of natural disasters like hurricanes and floods prompts local reform.
- Progressive mayors such as Hazen Pingree of Detroit work to reform local government.

Block Schedule TEACHING OPTION **Time Needed: 30 Minutes**

Cooperative Activity: Learning About Muckrakers

Task: Student groups will research various muckrakers writing during the progressive era and present reports about the muckrakers and the subjects they exposed.

Purpose: To help students understand the muckrakers' role in exposing corruption.

Activity: Assign small groups of students to identify one or more prominent muckrakers of the time period, such as Upton Sinclair or Ida Tarbell. Groups will research that individual and try to locate examples of his or her articles. Each student should write up his or her findings. Groups should present their information to the class.

Building a Portfolio: Students adding their findings to their portfolio should include a statement about why they feel this is an example of their strongest work.

ALTERNATIVE ASSESSMENT BOOK
Standards for Evaluating a Cooperative Activity

Standards for Evaluation
Presentations should . . .
- name one or more prominent muckrakers from the progressive era
- provide examples of the muckrakers' writing
- explain the impact the muckrakers had on life and politics of the time

MORE ABOUT . . .
Hazen Pingree

As Detroit's reform mayor, Pingree's most famous innovation was providing gardens for the unemployed, which became known as "Pingree's Potato Patches." Pingree went on to serve as Michigan's governor from 1897 to 1901.

OBJECTIVE

INSTRUCT

Reform at the State Level

▶ ***Discussing Key Ideas***

- Progressive governors such as Wisconsin's La Follette help reform state government.
- States pass laws to end child labor and improve work conditions.
- States introduce election reforms that pave the way for the Seventeenth Amendment, which provides for direct election of U.S. senators.

MORE ABOUT . . .
Robert M. La Follette

La Follette became famous when he revealed that Philetus Sawyer, Wisconsin's Republican boss, had tried to bribe him. La Follette planned to run as the Progressive Party's 1912 presidential candidate but was ousted by Roosevelt. He did run in 1924 and received about a sixth of the vote.

IN-DEPTH RESOURCES: UNIT 3
American Lives: Robert M. La Follette, p. 16

Another natural disaster, a flood in Dayton, Ohio, in 1913, led to the widespread adoption of the council-manager form of government. Staunton, Virginia, had already pioneered this system, in which people elected a city council to make laws. The council in turn appointed a manager, typically a person with training and experience in public administration, to run the city's departments. By 1925, managers were administering nearly 250 cities.

Cleveland mayor Tom Johnson *(center)* tried to make city government more responsive to citizens' needs.

REFORM MAYORS In some cities, mayors introduced progressive reforms without changing how government was organized. Hazen Pingree, mayor of Detroit, Michigan (1890–1897), and Tom Johnson, mayor of Cleveland, Ohio (1901–1909), gained national reputations as progressive mayors.

Pingree concentrated on economic issues. He instituted a fairer tax structure, lowered fares for public transportation, and rooted out corruption. Under his administration, city workers built schools, parks, and a municipal lighting plant. Detroit lowered gas rates and set up a system of work relief for unemployed people. Tom Johnson, a socialist, believed that citizens should play a more active role in city government. Toward that end, he held meetings in a large circus tent and invited citizens to question officials about how the city was managed. Like Pingree, Johnson appointed competent, honest people to city jobs and reassessed property values to achieve a fairer tax structure.

Johnson was only one of 19 socialist mayors who worked to institute progressive reforms in America's cities. In general, these mayors practiced "gas and water socialism," focusing on dismissing corrupt and greedy private owners of utilities—such as gasworks, waterworks, and transit lines—and converting the utilities to publicly owned enterprises.

THINK THROUGH HISTORY
D. *Finding Main Ideas* *What new types of city government emerged during the progressive era?*

D. Answer
The commission system, in which a commission runs city services, and the council-manager system, in which a council appoints a city manager.

Reform at the State Level

Local reforms coincided with progressive efforts at the state level. Spurred by progressive governors, many states passed laws to regulate railroads, mines, mills, telephone companies, and other large businesses.

REFORM GOVERNORS Under the leadership of **Robert M. La Follette,** Wisconsin led the way in regulating big business. Leader of the progressive wing of the Republican Party in Wisconsin, "Fighting Bob" La Follette served three terms as governor before he entered the U.S. Senate in 1906. He explained that, as governor, he did not mean to "smash corporations, but merely to drive them out of politics, and then to treat them exactly the same as other people are treated."

Governor La Follette made the railroad industry his major target. He taxed railroad property at the same rate as other business property, set up a commission to regulate rates, and forbade railroads to issue free passes to state officials.

Other reform governors who attacked big business interests included Charles B. Aycock of North Carolina, Albert B. Cummins of Iowa, Joseph W. Folk of Missouri, and James S. Hogg of Texas.

PROTECTING WORKERS In addition to lobbying for political reforms that would protect consumers against dishonest business practices, progressives also lobbied for regulations to protect workers and especially to end child labor.

Many Americans were outraged by the effects of industrial labor upon young people. The number of children under the age of 15 who worked in industrial jobs for wages climbed from 1.5 million in 1890 to 2 million in 1910. Businesses liked to hire children because they performed unskilled jobs for lower wages than adults, and children's small hands made them more adept at handling small parts

TEACHING OPTIONS

Making Connections Across Time

Political Reform Mayors Hazen Pingree and Tom Johnson, and Wisconsin Governor Robert La Follette were frontrunners of activism for political reform on the state and local levels. Point out to students that efforts to reform government and the political process continue today. Have students debate the pros and cons of one or more current efforts, such as the term-limits movement, the idea of returning power and funds from federal to state or local governments, or various proposals to achieve campaign finance reform.

Making Connections Across the Curriculum

Biology and Medicine The occupational illness known as black lung is common among coal miners, who acquire it by repeatedly inhaling coal dust over a period of years. People suffering from black lung are prone to other respiratory diseases, such as tuberculosis, bronchitis, and emphysema. Ask students what other occupational illnesses or conditions they have heard about. *Possible Responses: Divers can get the bends; typists or keyboardists can get carpal tunnel syndrome; bartenders and others who stand a great deal can get varicose veins.*

and tools. Immigrants and rural migrants often sent their children to work, or worked alongside them, because they viewed their children as part of the family economy. Often wages were so low for adults that every family member needed to work to pull the family out of poverty.

But as children worked in industrial settings, they began to develop serious health problems. Many child laborers were underweight. Some suffered from stunted growth or curvature of the spine. Those who worked near coal dust developed respiratory diseases, like bronchitis and tuberculosis. Children were also more prone than adults to accidents caused by physical and mental fatigue. Furthermore, some progressive reformers were alarmed by the bad habits—smoking, drinking, and cursing—acquired by many child laborers.

In 1904, a group of progressive reformers organized the National Child Labor Committee to end child labor. They sent teams of investigators to gather evidence of children working in harsh conditions and then organized exhibitions with photographs and statistics to dramatize the plight of these children. They were joined by labor union members who argued that child labor lowered wages for all workers. These groups pressured national politicians to pass the Keating-Owen Act in 1916. The act prohibited the transportation of goods produced with child labor across state lines.

Three years later, however, the Supreme Court declared the act unconstitutional because it interfered with interstate commerce. Later efforts to pass national legislation met a similar fate. Although they lost at the national level, reformers succeeded in forcing legislation banning child labor and setting maximum hours in nearly every state. By 1920, the number of child laborers was nearly half of what it had been in 1910.

THINK THROUGH HISTORY
E. *Recognizing Effects* *What changes did reformers bring about in the area of child labor?*

E. Answer They won the passage of legislation banning child labor at the state level.

EFFORTS TO LIMIT WORKING HOURS Despite the Supreme Court's opposition to a federal child-labor law, the courts sometimes took a more sympathetic view of the plight of workers. In 1908, the Supreme Court decided in the case of *Muller* v. *Oregon* that a state could legally limit the working hours of women. In the past the Court had held that such limits interfered with freedom of contract. This time, however, the lawyer Louis D. Brandeis—assisted by Florence Kelley and Josephine Goldmark—persuasively argued that poor working women were much more economically insecure than large corporations. Asserting that women required the state's protection against powerful employers, Brandeis convinced the Court to uphold an Oregon law limiting women to a ten-hour workday. Other states responded by enacting or strengthening laws to reduce

JAMES S. HOGG, TEXAS GOVERNOR

Among the most colorful of the reform governors was James S. Hogg of Texas. After being orphaned at 11 and leaving school in his mid-teens, Hogg held a series of jobs that taught him about the problems faced by ordinary people. Eventually he studied law and joined the bar. He entered state government as attorney general in 1866 and served as governor from 1891 to 1895. A compelling speaker, he always drew a crowd.

Hogg helped to drive illegal insurance companies from the state and championed antitrust legislation. His chief interest, however, was in regulating the railroads. He pointed out abuses in rates—noting, for example, that it cost more to ship lumber from East Texas to Dallas than to ship it all the way to Nebraska. A railroad commission, established largely as a result of his efforts, helped increase milling and manufacturing in Texas by lowering freight rates.

Spindle boys work at a spinning frame in a Macon, Georgia, cotton mill in 1909.

335

HISTORICAL SPOTLIGHT

James S. Hogg

Critical Thinking: Analyzing Motives Ask students how James Hogg's childhood and early background might have contributed to his progressive attitudes as an official in the Texas government. *Possible Response: Hogg understood the problems of working people and had a natural empathy for the disadvantaged because he was orphaned at the age of 11 and had to go to work.*

HISTORY FROM VISUALS

Child Labor at Textile Mills

Reading the Image Ask what is unusual about the spindle boys' dress. *Possible Responses: Caps; bare feet.*

Extension Ask whether or not bare feet would be allowed today, and why. *Possible Responses: Students may suggest that since bare feet pose a danger to the boy and a possible health hazard to others, regulations today would require shoes.*

IN-DEPTH RESOURCES: UNIT 3
Primary Source: Child Labor in the Coal Mines, p. 10

ELECTRONIC LIBRARY OF PRIMARY SOURCES
On the Need for Child Labor Laws by Florence Kelley

CRITICAL THINKING TRANSPARENCIES
CT51, Child Labor, 1890–1930

TEACHING OPTION

Skillbuilder Mini-Lesson: Forming Generalizations

Explaining the Skill People form generalizations when they make broad judgments based on information in a text or in other sources. It is important for a generalization to be valid. The generalization has to be based on evidence. It also has to be consistent with all the information that is given.

Applying the Skill: Child Labor Have students review the material under "Protecting Workers." Ask them to form a generalization about the effects of industrialization on young people. Suggest that students begin by listing statements that address the effects. Then have them note what information the statements have in common. *Possible generalization: Industrialization had harmful physical, mental, and social effects on young people.*

IN-DEPTH RESOURCES: UNIT 3
Skillbuilder Practice: Forming Generalizations, p. 6

ON THE WORLD STAGE
Australian Ballot
Critical Thinking: Analyzing Ask why a secret ballot would help end threats or intimidation from opposing political parties.
Possible Responses: Since in a secret ballot no one knows how an individual votes, that person can say he or she is voting one way and actually vote another; in an open ballot, others could observe or hear a person's vote and make vocal protests or start fights.

ASSESS & RETEACH

Section 1 Assessment

Students might work in pairs or small groups to respond to the questions.

Self-Assessment

To show how students' understanding of progressivism has increased, have them create a cluster diagram or list in which they identify five key characteristics of the progressive era.

Section Quiz

FORMAL ASSESSMENT
Section Quiz, p. 116

Reteach

Replay the video "A Child on Strike," and discuss the reform issues raised by the film.

***AMERICAN STORIES* video series**
"A Child on Strike"

CLOSE

Progressivism prompted new laws, political cleanups, and other changes aimed at protecting social welfare, promoting moral and economic reform, and improving industrial efficiency.

ON THE WORLD STAGE

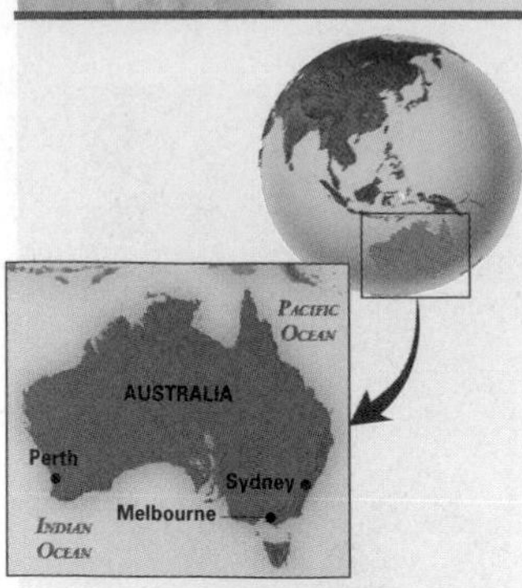

AUSTRALIAN BALLOT

During the Gilded Age, American voters often faced threats from opposing political parties fighting for votes. The Australian ballot is a system in which voters mark secret ballots in walled or curtained booths. This voting system gained rapid popularity in the United States after Louisville, Kentucky, adopted it in 1888 in order to protect voters from being intimidated.

In many parts of Australia, the secret ballot had been law since the late 1850s. England adopted the Australian ballot in 1872, after a hearing during which an Australian government member testified in favor of the system. He said, "Before the ballot was in operation our elections were exceedingly riotous." Canada, Belgium, Luxembourg, Italy, and then the United States soon followed the example of Australia and England.

women's hours of work. A similar Brandeis brief in *Bunting* v. *Oregon* in 1917 persuaded the Court to uphold a ten-hour workday for men.

Progressives also succeeded in winning workers' compensation to aid the families of workers who were hurt or killed on the job. Beginning with Maryland in 1902, one state after another passed legislation requiring employers in dangerous occupations to pay benefits to injured employees.

REFORMING ELECTIONS In some cases, ordinary citizens, rather than legislators or governors, won state reforms. In Oregon, William S. U'Ren prompted his state to adopt the secret ballot (also called the Australian ballot), the initiative, the referendum, and the recall. The initiative and referendum gave citizens the power to create laws. Citizens could petition to place an **initiative**—a bill originated by the people rather than lawmakers—on the ballot. Then voters, instead of the legislature, accepted or rejected the initiative by **referendum,** a vote on the initiative. The **recall** enabled voters to remove public officials from elected positions by forcing them to face another election before the end of their term if enough voters asked for it. By 1920, 20 states had adopted at least one of these procedures. (See "Understanding How to Lobby" on page 115 in Projects for Citizenship.)

Wisconsin became the first state to adopt another democratic reform, the direct primary, in 1903. A direct primary meant that voters, instead of political machines, would choose candidates for public office through a special popular election. About two-thirds of the states had adopted some form of direct primary by 1915.

DIRECT ELECTION OF SENATORS The success of the direct primary paved the way for the **Seventeenth Amendment** to the Constitution. Before 1913, state legislatures had chosen United States senators, a process that put even more power in the hands of party bosses and wealthy corporation heads. To force senators to be more responsive to the public, progressives pushed for the popular election of senators. The Senate at first refused to go along with the idea. Gradually, however, more and more states began allowing voters to nominate senatorial candidates in direct primaries. As a result, Congress approved the amendment in 1912. Its ratification in 1913 made direct election of senators the law of the land.

Government reform—including efforts to give Americans more of a voice in electing their legislators and creating laws—drew increased numbers of women into public life and focused renewed attention on the issue of woman suffrage.

F. Answer It called for the direct election of senators, so that members of the Senate would no longer be appointed by state legislators—over whom special interests had influence—but would be elected by a direct vote of the people.

THINK THROUGH HISTORY
F. THEME *Constitutional Concerns* *How did the Seventeenth Amendment broaden constitutional provisions for democratic representation?*

Section 1 Assessment

1. TERMS & NAMES
Identify:
- progressive movement
- Florence Kelley
- prohibition
- muckraker
- scientific management
- Robert M. La Follette
- initiative
- referendum
- recall
- 17th Amendment

2. SUMMARIZING Draw this web on your paper. Fill it in with examples of political organizations or professional groups that campaigned for the reforms shown.

Progressive Reforms: Economic, Moral, Political, Social Welfare

Which group was most effective?

3. FORMING GENERALIZATIONS In what ways might Illinois, Wisconsin, and Oregon all be considered trailblazers in progressive reform? Support your answer with reasons.

THINK ABOUT
- legislative and election reforms at the state level
- the leadership of William U'Ren and Robert La Follette
- Governor Altgeld's appointment of Florence Kelley as chief inspector of factories for Illinois

4. FORMING OPINIONS Imagine you are a muckraking journalist in the early 1900s. A magazine publisher has asked you to submit a list of story ideas for upcoming issues. What wrongdoings would you like to probe?

THINK ABOUT
- Ida M. Tarbell's articles on the Standard Oil Company
- the targets of political, economic, and moral reformers
- topics that might require government reform

ANSWERS

1. TERMS & NAMES
progressive movement, p. 330
Florence Kelley, p. 331
prohibition, p. 331
muckraker, p. 332
scientific management, p. 332
Robert M. La Follette, p. 334
initiative, p. 336
referendum, p. 336
recall, p. 336
17th Amendment, p. 336

2. SUMMARIZING
Possible Answers:
Social Welfare—YMCA; Salvation Army.
Moral—WCTU; Anti-Saloon League.
Economic—American Socialist Party; muckrakers.
Political—National Consumers' League; National Child Labor Committee.
Students should give reasons for their choice of the most effective group.

3. FORMING GENERALIZATIONS
Possible Responses: Reforms first instituted in Illinois, Wisconsin, and Oregon soon spread to other states. Illinois—prohibition of child labor and limit of women's working hours; Wisconsin—regulation of big business, especially railroads, and adoption of the direct primary; Oregon—adoption of the secret ballot, the initiative, the referendum, and the recall.

4. FORMING OPINIONS
Possible Responses: The effects of urban poverty on an immigrant family; city saloons; political bosses' kickbacks and bribes; election fraud; public utility owners' corruption; child labor; health problems; hazardous working conditions in factories.

2 Women in Public Life

TERMS & NAMES
- Maria Mitchell
- NACW
- suffrage
- Susan B. Anthony
- NAWSA

LEARN ABOUT women's growing participation in work, education, politics, and reform
TO UNDERSTAND how women's lives changed in the early 20th century.

Section 2 Overview

OBJECTIVES

1. To trace women's growing presence in the turn-of-the-century work force.

2. To summarize women's leadership in reform movements and the effort to achieve woman suffrage.

CRITICAL THINKING
- Analyzing causes, p. 338
- Recognizing effects, p. 339
- Summarizing, p. 340
- Analyzing issues, p. 340
- Analyzing motives, p. 340

ONE AMERICAN'S STORY

Susette La Flesche, a young Native American woman, traveled east in 1879 to translate into English the sad words of Chief Standing Bear, whose Ponca people had been forcibly removed from their homeland. Calling her Bright Eyes, an English translation of La Flesche's Native American name, one newspaper gushed, "No such interesting squaw has appeared since Pocahontas. . . . Bright Eyes has taken sober Boston captive."

La Flesche was born in 1854, the year her own Omaha people were forced by treaty to give up their territory in Nebraska. Raised on a small reservation, she later attended a women's seminary, the Elizabeth Institute, in New Jersey. When the Ponca's removal occurred in 1877, La Flesche was teaching in a government school on her reservation. A sympathetic Omaha journalist convinced Chief Standing Bear and La Flesche to go on a lecture tour to draw attention to the Ponca's situation. La Flesche's words were fierce.

A PERSONAL VOICE

> We are thinking men and women. We have a right to be heard in whatever concerns us. Your government has driven us hither and thither like cattle. . . . Your government has no right to say to us, Go here, or Go there, and if we show any reluctance, to force us to do its will at the point of the bayonet. . . . Do you wonder that the Indian feels outraged by such treatment and retaliates, although it will end in death to himself?
>
> SUSETTE LA FLESCHE, quoted in *Bright Eyes*

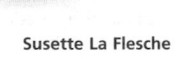

Susette La Flesche

Susette La Flesche later testified before congressional committees and helped win passage of the Dawes Act of 1887, which allowed individual Native Americans to claim reservation land and citizenship rights. La Flesche's activism was an example of a new role for American women, who were expanding their participation in public life.

Women in the Work Force

Before the Civil War, a "cult of domesticity" had prevailed. Married women were expected to devote their time to the care of their homes and families. By the late 19th century, however, only middle-class and upper-class women could afford to put all their energies into their homes. Poorer women usually had no choice but to work in order to contribute to the family income.

FARM WOMEN On farms in the South and the Midwest, women and children remained a critical part of the economic structure of the family in the early 20th century. Their roles had not changed substantially since the previous century. Besides performing domestic tasks like cooking, cleaning, and sewing, they handled a host of other chores. If their husbands were ill or absent, farm women had to plow and plant the fields and harvest the crops in addition to performing their own duties.

DOMESTIC WORKERS Many women without formal education or industrial skills contributed to the economic survival of their families by doing domestic work. After almost 2 million African-American women were freed from

FOCUS & MOTIVATE

5-MINUTE WARM-UP

Recognizing Main Ideas
To introduce women's rights at the beginning of the 20th century, ask students to read One American's Story on page 337 and answer these questions.

1. How did Susette La Flesche become a spokesperson for the Ponca?
2. What sentence in One American's Story states the main idea about La Flesche?

WARM-UP TRANSPARENCY 9

▶ ***Starting with the Student***
- Ask students whether they think boys and girls have the same opportunities open to them.
- Ask them if they think men and women share equal rights in public life, and why.

OBJECTIVE 1 INSTRUCT

Women in the Work Force

▶ ***Discussing Key Ideas***
- African-American and immigrant women often work as domestics.
- More women, especially immigrants, work in industry, where they are paid only about half as much as men doing equivalent jobs.

(continued on next page)

SECTION 2 RESOURCES

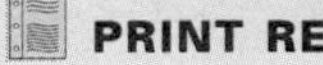

PRINT RESOURCES

IN-DEPTH RESOURCES: UNIT 3
Guided Reading, p. 2
Primary Sources: Political Poster, p. 11; *from* "The Status of Woman" by Susan B. Anthony, p. 12

READING STUDY GUIDE, p. 99

ACCESS FOR STUDENTS ACQUIRING ENGLISH
Guided Reading (Spanish), p. 121

SPANISH READING STUDY GUIDE, p. 99

FORMAL ASSESSMENT
Section Quiz, p. 117

ALTERNATIVE ASSESSMENT BOOK
See forms for supporting and scoring alternative activities.

TECHNOLOGY RESOURCES

CD-ROM Electronic Library of Primary Sources

VIDEO *American Portfolio: A Videodisc for U.S. History* user's guide, pp. 155, 165, 167, 174

INTERNET http://www.mlushistory.com

(continued from page 337)

- More women take white-collar jobs as teachers, typists, and bookkeepers.

IN-DEPTH RESOURCES: UNIT 3
Guided Reading, p. 2

ACCESS FOR STUDENTS ACQUIRING ENGLISH
Guided Reading (Spanish), p. 121

NOW & THEN
Telephone Operators
Critical Thinking: Analyzing Causes and Effects Ask students how the gap between men's and women's salaries drew more women into the work force. *Possible Response: Women's salaries were lower than men's, prompting businesses to hire them to save expenses.*

OBJECTIVE
② **INSTRUCT**

Women's Leadership in Reform

▶ ***Starting with the Student***
Students might begin a time line of important dates in the suffrage movement.

1848	First women's rights convention in Seneca Falls

▶ ***Discussing Key Ideas***
- Colleges for women open.
- Female reformers work to improve social welfare, public morals, and race relations.
- Susan B. Anthony helps lead the struggle for woman suffrage.

NOW & THEN

TELEPHONE OPERATORS
Today, when Americans use the telephone, an automated voice often greets them with instructions about which buttons to press. This computerized approach to modern communication is only one of many modifications of Alexander Graham Bell's 1876 invention, the telephone.

Young men, the first telephone operators, proved unsatisfactory. Patrons complained that the male operators used profane language and talked back to callers. Because of their willingness to accept a ten-dollar weekly salary, women soon largely replaced men as telephone operators.

Department stores advertised shopping by telephone as a convenience. One ad in the Chicago telephone book of 1904 declared, "Every [telephone] order, inquiry, or request will be quickly and intelligently cared for." The ad pictured a line of female telephone operators.

slavery, poverty quickly drove nearly half of them into the work force. In 1890, about 1 million African-American women held jobs. While 38 percent labored on farms, 46 percent toiled as domestic workers. African-American women migrated by the thousands to cities to work as cooks, laundresses, scrubwomen, and maids.

Unmarried immigrant women also did domestic labor, especially when they first arrived in the United States. Many middle-class homes in the Northeast, for example, provided domestic employment for young Irish women. Typically, married immigrant women contributed to the family income by taking in piecework or caring for boarders at home.

In 1870, roughly 70 percent of American working women worked as servants. As better-paying opportunities started to open up, however, women began to take jobs in offices, stores, classrooms, and factories.

WOMEN IN INDUSTRY At the turn of the century, one out of five American women worked; 25 percent of them held jobs in manufacturing. Working women who spent up to 12 hours a day sewing, folding, packing, or bottling came primarily from the ranks of young, white city dwellers. Most had been born in a foreign country or were the children of immigrants.

In tobacco factories, nearly 40 percent of the employees were women. Women also worked in canneries, bookbinderies, packing plants, and commercial laundries. However, the garment trade claimed about half of all women industrial workers. Women in the work force often performed jobs, such as sewing, that resembled the work they might have done at home. Typically they held the least skilled positions and received the lowest pay. Even when they did the same work, women received only about half as much money as their male counterparts did. This was because many working women were single and were assumed to be supporting only themselves, while men were assumed to be supporting families.

As business opportunities expanded, women began to fill new jobs in offices, stores, and classrooms. White-collar positions as stenographers, typists, bookkeepers, and teachers beckoned women who had never worked before. These jobs required a high school education, and by 1890 women high school graduates outnumbered men. Moreover, new business schools were preparing bookkeepers and stenographers as well as training female typists to operate the new machines.

THINK THROUGH HISTORY
A. *Analyzing Causes* *What kinds of job opportunities prompted more women to complete high school?*
A. Answer White-collar positions as stenographers, typists, and teachers.

Women's Leadership in Reform

Many middle-class and upper-class women became involved in activities outside their homes by joining women's clubs to discuss art or literature. Indeed, by 1910, nearly 800,000 women belonged to women's clubs, which sometimes became reform groups that addressed such issues as temperance or the abolition of child labor. Women like Susette La Flesche entered the public sphere, demanded increased opportunities for women in higher education, and campaigned for the right to vote.

TEACHING OPTIONS

Exploring Themes

Women in America Women were entering the work force in increasing numbers. Unlike domestics and industrial workers, the white-collar female worker was becoming something of a glamorous stereotype. "The average American woman of the middle-classes," said a visiting Englishman in 1914, "is incomparably the smartest, most elegant and beautiful thing that exists under Heaven. It is not of the women of fashion I speak. . . . It is the ordinary, everyday-go-to-work girl who takes her lunch at Child's . . . and patronizes what you call the cinematograph theatre and she calls the 'movies.'"

Making Connections Across Cultures

Native American Women Susette La Flesche's role in public life was remarkable, because she was both a woman and a Native American. The role of women varied among Native American cultures. Among the Navaho, for example, males were the heads of households and could even take multiple wives—though females played their part in the agricultural economy. The Iroquois tribes, on the other hand, were matrilineal and matrilocal societies in which descent was traced in the female line, young families moved into their mothers'—not fathers'—homes, and women enjoyed major property rights.

WOMEN IN HIGHER EDUCATION Many of the women who became active in public life in the late 19th century had attended the new women's colleges. Vassar College—with a faculty of 8 men and 22 women—accepted its first students in 1865. Smith and Wellesley Colleges followed in 1875. In the South, Randolph-Macon Women's College opened in 1891. Though Columbia, Brown, and Harvard Colleges refused to admit women, each university established a separate college for women. Barnard opened in 1889, Pembroke in 1891, and Radcliffe in 1894.

Women's colleges sought to grant women an excellent education, but female graduates were still expected to fulfill traditional domestic roles. Indeed, in her will, Smith College's founder, Sophia Smith, made her goals clear.

A PERSONAL VOICE

[It is my desire] to furnish for my own sex means and facilities for education equal to those which are afforded now in our College to young men. . . . It is not my design to render my sex any the less feminine, but to develop as fully as may be the powers of womanhood & furnish women with the means of usefulness, happiness, & honor now withheld from them.

SOPHIA SMITH, quoted in *Alma Mater*

THINK THROUGH HISTORY
B. Recognizing Effects *What social and economic effects did higher education have on women?*

B. Answer Women who attended college no longer relied on marriage as their only option; some pursued professional careers, while others did volunteer reform work.

Now that more women attended college, marriage no longer was a woman's only alternative. Indeed, almost half of college-educated women in the late 19th century never married. Instead, many educated women began to apply their skills to needed social reforms.

WOMEN AND REFORM The participation of educated women often strengthened existing reform groups and provided leadership for new ones. Because women were not allowed to vote or run for office, women reformers strove to improve conditions at work and home. In what historians call "social housekeeping," women targeted unsafe factories and labor abuses and promoted housing reform, educational improvement, and food and drug laws.

In 1896, African-American women founded the National Association of Colored Women (**NACW**) by merging two earlier organizations. The NACW managed nurseries, reading rooms, and kindergartens. Josephine Ruffin, a prominent African-American woman from Boston, identified as the mission of the African-American women's club movement "the moral education of the race with which we are identified."

THE FIGHT FOR THE VOTE Winning **suffrage,** the right to vote, had been a focus of women reformers since the Seneca Falls convention of 1848. During Reconstruction, the Fourteenth and Fifteenth Amendments, which granted African-American men the right to vote, had split the women's movement. Feeling that this was "the Negro's hour," some women supported the amendments. Others opposed the amendments because they excluded women. **Susan B. Anthony,** a leader in the woman suffrage movement, said that she "would sooner cut off my right hand than ask the ballot for the black man and not for women." By 1890, however, suffragists had united in the National American Woman Suffrage Association (**NAWSA**). Prominent leaders of the suffrage crusade included Anthony, Elizabeth Cady Stanton, Lucy Stone, and Julia Ward Howe, the author of "The Battle Hymn of the Republic."

A THREE-PART STRATEGY FOR SUFFRAGE The leaders of the suffrage movement tried three different approaches to achieve their objective. First, they tried to convince state legislatures to grant women the right to vote. They

HISTORICAL SPOTLIGHT

VASSAR'S MARIA MITCHELL

As a child on Nantucket Island, Massachusetts, **Maria Mitchell** (1818–1889) observed the heavens with her father, who made his living in celestial observation. Years later—on October 1, 1847—Mitchell discovered a new comet, using a two-inch telescope. Mitchell's discovery won her election to the American Academy of Arts and Sciences in Boston. She was the first woman to be so honored.

Matthew Vassar, who had founded a women's college in Poughkeepsie, New York, convinced Mitchell to teach at his school by offering her the use of a 12-inch telescope, then the country's third largest. Though she herself had never attended college, Mitchell became one of Vassar's greatest teachers.

Mitchell demanded that her students learn science from observation, just as she had. "Nature made woman an observer. . . . So many of the natural sciences are well fitted for woman's power of minute observation that it seems strange that the hammer of the geologist is not seen in her hand or the tin box of the botanist."

HISTORICAL SPOTLIGHT

Vassar's Maria Mitchell

Critical Thinking: Evaluating Have students discuss Matthew Vassar's decision to offer Mitchell a teaching post at Vassar even though she had not attended college. *Possible Responses: Some students may feel that degrees are not the only indicator of knowledge or that a college degree could not be expected in an age when higher education for females was so rare.*

Issues for the 21st Century

Women and the Glass Ceiling

Connect the economic problems faced by women in the early 1900s to those faced in the present by having students read pages 894–895. Then have them answer these questions.

1. How did women's actions in the early 20th century help them to make economic progress? *Education at women's colleges, taking the lead in the reform movement, and fighting for the vote prepared women to compete in the workplace.*
2. What economic problems do women continue to face today? *Lower salaries than men; balancing work and home; slow to be promoted in management.*

IN-DEPTH RESOURCES: UNIT 3
Primary Sources: Political Poster, p. 11
from "The Status of Woman" by Susan B. Anthony, p. 12

Block Schedule TEACHING OPTION **Time Needed: 30 Minutes**

Cooperative Activity: Creating Political Placards

Task: Groups of students will create placards or signs that demonstrators in favor of woman suffrage might carry.

Purpose: To understand the background and goals of the woman suffrage movement.

Activity: Tell students to imagine that the time is about 1900 and that they are about to attend a rally to bring the issue of woman suffrage to the public eye. Divide students into small groups to create at least five placards for marchers to carry. Each group member should develop a list of possible slogans for the signs—such as "Votes for Women"—using their textbook as a source or doing additional research. After the group chooses among the slogans, placards can be lettered by the more artistic members of the group. Bring the class together for a review of the placards, perhaps asking students to vote on the most effective slogan.

ALTERNATIVE ASSESSMENT BOOK
Standards for Evaluating a Cooperative Activity

KEY PLAYER
Susan B. Anthony
Critical Thinking: Evaluating Ask students what they think of Anthony's outrage when only African-American males—and not women, black or white—were granted the right to vote after the Civil War.
Possible Responses: Some students may sympathize with her outrage. Others may feel that such divisions foster prejudice or split and weaken the progressive cause.

ELECTRONIC LIBRARY OF PRIMARY SOURCES
from *The United States of America* v. *Susan B. Anthony*

ASSESS & RETEACH

Section 2 Assessment
Have students answer the section assessment questions. Then ask them to form pairs and compare their responses to item 2.

Self-Assessment
Have students reread Woodrow Wilson's quote on page 328. Ask them to demonstrate their understanding of women's roles in public life at the turn of the century by writing a paragraph explaining how the concept of "release of energies" applies to events in this section.

Section Quiz
FORMAL ASSESSMENT
Section Quiz, p. 117

Reteach
Use the Guided Reading Worksheet for Section 2 to help review the main ideas of the section.

IN-DEPTH RESOURCES: UNIT 3
Guided Reading, p. 2

CLOSE
As more and more women entered the work force and led the movements for progressive reform, they also pressed for the right to vote.

KEY PLAYER

SUSAN B. ANTHONY
1820–1906

Like her peers in the women's rights movement, Susan B. Anthony endured hostile audiences who taunted her when she lectured on temperance, abolition, and women's rights.

In 1851, Anthony met Elizabeth Cady Stanton, with whom she founded the National Woman Suffrage Association (NWSA) in 1869. (The NWSA later merged with another organization to become the NAWSA.)

Along with her three sisters and several other women, Anthony voted illegally in the presidential election of 1872. At her trial, which she described in her diary as "the greatest outrage History ever witnessed," she was fined $100. "Not a penny shall go to this unjust claim," declared the defiant Anthony. The judge didn't press the issue, and the case was closed.

Susan B. Anthony died 14 years before the Nineteenth Amendment finally granted women the vote in 1920. A one-dollar coin, minted in 1979 and 1980, bears her picture.

achieved a victory in 1869, when the territory of Wyoming granted the vote to women. By the 1890s Utah, Colorado, and Idaho had enfranchised women, but after 1896, efforts in other states failed.

Second, women pursued court cases to test the Fourteenth Amendment, which declared that states denying their male citizens the right to vote would lose congressional representation. Weren't women citizens, too? In 1871 and 1872, Susan B. Anthony and other women attempted to get the Supreme Court to answer that question by making at least 150 attempts to vote in 10 states and the District of Columbia. When the Supreme Court ruled in 1875 on the relationship between the Fourteenth Amendment and woman suffrage, the justices agreed that women were indeed citizens—but citizenship did not automatically confer the right to vote.

C. Answer Trying to convince state legislatures to grant woman suffrage, testing the Fourteenth Amendment in court, and working for a constitutional amendment giving women the vote.

THINK THROUGH HISTORY
C. Summarizing *What three approaches did women try in order to win the vote?*

Third, women pushed for a national constitutional amendment that would grant women the vote. In 1878, Anthony persuaded Senator Aaron Sargent of California to introduce an amendment that read, "The right of citizens of the United States to vote shall not be denied or abridged by the United States or by any state on account of sex." Although a Senate committee killed the Anthony amendment, women activists lobbied for the next 18 years to have it reintroduced. On the rare occasions when the bill reached the floor for a vote, the senators invariably rejected it.

Despite this three-pronged approach, the campaign for woman suffrage achieved only modest success. After the turn of the century, however, other women's reform efforts paid off in improvements in the treatment of workers and safer food and drug products—all part of President Theodore Roosevelt's own plans for reforming business, labor, and the environment.

Suffragists campaign for the vote.

Section 2 Assessment

1. TERMS & NAMES
Identify:
- Maria Mitchell
- NACW
- suffrage
- Susan B. Anthony
- NAWSA

2. SUMMARIZING Re-create the diagram below on your paper and fill it in with details about working women in the late 1800s.

What generalizations can you make about women workers at this time?

3. ANALYZING ISSUES What women and movements during the progressive era helped dispel the stereotype of submissive, nonpolitical women? Support your answers with evidence from the text.

THINK ABOUT
- new work and educational opportunities for women
- new roles women played in public life
- the suffrage movement

4. ANALYZING MOTIVES Explain why women might have participated in each of the following reform movements: improving education, promoting housing reform, correcting labor abuses, pushing for food and drug laws, winning the right to vote.

THINK ABOUT
- the problems that each movement was trying to remedy
- how women benefited from each

ANSWERS

1. TERMS & NAMES
Maria Mitchell, p. 339
NACW, p. 339
suffrage, p. 339
Susan B. Anthony, p. 339
NAWSA, p. 339

2. SUMMARIZING
Possible Answers:
Farmwomen—domestic work and farm labor
Domestic workers—servants, cooks, laundresses, maids; often African Americans or immigrants
Factory workers—tobacco workers, garment trade, manufacturing; often immigrants or children of immigrants
White-collar workers—stenographers, typists, bookkeepers, teachers; required high school or business degree; white, native-born, middle-class women
Generalizations will vary but should make connections among the types of workers.

3. ANALYZING ISSUES
Possible Responses: New college opportunities for women, new jobs in factories and offices, and women speaking out on reform subjects, including Susan B. Anthony, Elizabeth Cady Stanton, Lucy Stone, and Julia Ward Howe.

4. ANALYZING MOTIVES
Possible Responses: Women pushed for education reform so that more women could enter higher education and get better jobs. They fought for improved housing and stricter food and drug laws to protect their families, and for labor reform to improve conditions at work. Winning the right to vote would give women a voice in governing.

3 Teddy Roosevelt's Square Deal

TERMS & NAMES
- Upton Sinclair
- *The Jungle*
- Theodore Roosevelt
- Square Deal
- Meat Inspection Act
- Pure Food and Drug Act
- conservation
- NAACP

LEARN ABOUT Theodore Roosevelt's domestic agenda and policies *TO UNDERSTAND* the reforms of Roosevelt's administration.

ONE AMERICAN'S STORY

In November 1904, the muckraking journalist **Upton Sinclair** visited Chicago to do research for a novel. For seven weeks, he lived in a neighborhood called Packingtown, where he interviewed workers, lawyers, doctors, saloonkeepers, and social workers. Sinclair intended his novel to reveal "the breaking of human hearts by a system which exploits the labor of men and women for profit."

What shocked readers in Sinclair's book ***The Jungle*** (1906), however, was the sickening conditions in the meatpacking industry. The author admitted that the public's reaction to his exposé had surprised him. "I aimed at the nation's heart," he said, "but by accident I hit it in the stomach." Sinclair's graphic descriptions of the filthy conditions turned the stomachs of the nation and the world.

Upton Sinclair poses with his son at the time of the writing of *The Jungle*.

A PERSONAL VOICE

> There would be meat that had tumbled out on the floor, in the dirt and sawdust, where the workers had tramped and spit uncounted billions of consumption [tuberculosis] germs. There would be meat stored in great piles in rooms; . . . and thousands of rats would race about on it. . . . A man could run his hand over these piles of meat and sweep off handfuls of the dried dung of rats. These rats were nuisances, and the packers would put poisoned bread out for them; they would die, and then rats, bread, and meat would go into the hoppers together. . . . There were things that went into the sausage in comparison with which a poisoned rat was a tidbit.
>
> UPTON SINCLAIR, *The Jungle*

The sensational book sold 25,000 copies in one week alone. Like many other readers, President Theodore Roosevelt lost his taste for meat, reportedly crying, "I'm poisoned," after reading the book. The nauseated president invited the author to visit him at the White House, where Roosevelt promised that "the specific evils you point out shall, if their existence be proved, and if I have the power, be eradicated."

A Rough-Riding President

Theodore Roosevelt was not supposed to be president. In fact, the political bosses of New York who found the young governor impossible to control had hatched a familiar scheme: kick Roosevelt upstairs, where he could do no harm. The plot to nominate Roosevelt as McKinley's vice-president in 1900 worked, but while "Boss" Platt of New York gloated about Roosevelt's becoming vice-president, the Republican political organizer and senator Mark Hanna immediately realized something that Platt did not. Roosevelt, the man Hanna derided as a "cowboy," stood a heartbeat away from becoming president. Indeed, President McKinley had served barely six months of his second term before he was assassinated. The man who had been kicked upstairs now became the most powerful person in the government.

SECTION 3 RESOURCES

PRINT RESOURCES

IN-DEPTH RESOURCES: UNIT 3
Guided Reading, p. 3
Literature: from *The Jungle* by Upton Sinclair, p. 13

READING STUDY GUIDE, p. 101

ACCESS FOR STUDENTS ACQUIRING ENGLISH
Guided Reading (Spanish), p. 122

SPANISH READING STUDY GUIDE, p. 101

FORMAL ASSESSMENT
Section Quiz, p. 118

ALTERNATIVE ASSESSMENT BOOK
See forms for supporting and scoring alternative activities.

TECHNOLOGY RESOURCES

CD-ROM *Our Times*
Electronic Library of Primary Sources

VIDEO *American Portfolio: A Videodisc for U.S. History*
user's guide, pp. 166, 170, 171, 175

INTERNET http://www.mlushistory.com

Section 3 Overview

OBJECTIVES

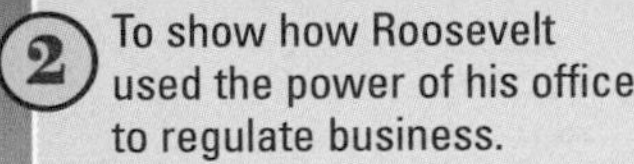

1. To trace the events of Theodore Roosevelt's presidency.
2. To show how Roosevelt used the power of his office to regulate business.
3. To identify laws passed to protect citizens' health and preserve the environment.
4. To summarize Roosevelt's stand on civil rights.

SKILLBUILDERS

- Interpreting political cartoons, p. 343
- Understanding geography: location, human-environment interaction, p. 345

CRITICAL THINKING

- Synthesizing, pp. 342
- Recognizing effects, p. 343
- Developing historical perspective, p. 345
- Summarizing, pp. 345, 346, 347
- Forming generalizations, p. 347
- Drawing conclusions, p. 347

FOCUS & MOTIVATE

5-MINUTE WARM-UP

Making Inferences
Ask students to look at the photo on page 342 and answer these questions.

1. What is President Roosevelt doing in the photo?
2. What can you infer about his character and personality from the photo?

WARM-UP TRANSPARENCY 9

▶ ***Starting with the Student***
- Ask students what constitutes a "square," or fair, deal in bargaining with their friends.

OBJECTIVE 1 **INSTRUCT**

A Rough-Riding President

▶ ***Discussing Key Ideas***
- Theodore Roosevelt becomes president when President McKinley is assassinated in 1901.

(continued on next page)

(continued from page 341)

- Roosevelt rises through political offices and wins acclaim in the Battle of San Juan Hill.
- Roosevelt's belief in a strong federal government helps define the modern presidency.

IN-DEPTH RESOURCES: UNIT 3
Guided Reading, p. 3

ACCESS FOR STUDENTS ACQUIRING ENGLISH
Guided Reading (Spanish), p. 122

MORE ABOUT . . .
Teddy Roosevelt

"For unflagging interest and enjoyment, a household of children, if things go reasonably well, certainly makes all other forms of success and achievement lose their importance by comparison," Roosevelt once remarked. He himself had six children, making for what one staff member called "the wildest scramble in the history of the White House." In addition to sports, the Roosevelt children played often with their pets: dogs, rabbits, flying squirrels, a badger named Josiah, a macaw called Eli, and a small bear.

OBJECTIVE
② INSTRUCT

Using Federal Power

▶ ***Discussing Key Ideas***

- Roosevelt intervenes in a 1902 coal strike and sets a precedent for federal arbitration.
- The president sets out to control or break up trusts and to regulate the railroads.

Teddy Roosevelt enjoyed an active lifestyle, as this 1902 photo reveals.

ROOSEVELT'S RISE Born into a wealthy New York family, young Theodore Roosevelt suffered from asthma. "Teedie" was so frail that he had to sleep propped up in order to breathe. Fighting asthma for the rest of his life, Roosevelt drove himself to accomplish demanding physical feats. As a teenager, he mastered marksmanship and horseback riding. At Harvard College, Roosevelt boxed and wrestled. In the 1880s, after his beloved first wife died, he recovered from his grief on a Dakota ranch.

The ambitious Roosevelt, however, would not stay away from New York politics. After serving three terms in the New York State Assembly, he became New York City's police commissioner and then assistant secretary of the U.S. Navy. The aspiring politician grabbed national attention during the war with Spain in 1898. The Rough Riders, Roosevelt's volunteer cavalry brigade, won public acclaim for its role in the battle at San Juan Hill in Cuba. Roosevelt returned a hero and soon won election to the governorship of New York and then the vice-presidency.

THE MODERN PRESIDENCY When McKinley's assassination thrust Roosevelt into the presidency in 1901, he became—at 42 years old—the youngest person ever to hold that office. Unlike previous presidents, Roosevelt soon dominated the news with his many exploits. While president, Roosevelt boxed with professionals, one of whom blinded him in the left eye. On another day, he galloped 100 miles on horseback, merely to prove the feat possible. When the president spared a bear cub on a hunting expedition, a toymaker marketed a popular new product, the Teddy Bear. To young people the brash Roosevelt said, "In life, as in a football game, the principle to follow is: Hit the line hard."

In politics, as in sports, Roosevelt acted boldly. Indeed, his leadership and publicity campaigns helped create the modern presidency, making him a model by which all future presidents would be measured. Before Roosevelt, presidents had rarely stood out among national politicians in terms of personality. Roosevelt was different. He used his dynamic personality and popularity to advance his programs. Citing federal responsibility for the national welfare, Roosevelt thought the government should assume control whenever states proved incapable of dealing with problems. He explained, "It is the duty of the President to act upon the theory that he is the steward of the people, and . . . to assume that he has the legal right to do whatever the needs of the people demand, unless the Constitution or the laws explicitly forbid him to do it."

Roosevelt saw the presidency as a "bully pulpit," from which he could influence the news media and shape legislation. If big business victimized workers, then President Roosevelt would see to it that the common people received what he called a **Square Deal.** This term was used to describe the various progressive reforms sponsored by the Roosevelt administration.

A. Answer Roosevelt was an active, forceful, and energetic executive; he used his position to shape legislation and influence the media.

THINK THROUGH HISTORY
A. Synthesizing *What actions and characteristics of Roosevelt's contributed to his reputation as the first modern president?*

Using Federal Power

Roosevelt's study of history—he wrote the first of his 30 books at the age of 24—convinced him that modern America required a powerful federal government. "A simple and poor society can exist as a democracy on the basis of sheer individualism," Roosevelt declared, "but a rich and complex society

TEACHING OPTIONS

Exploring Themes

Constitutional Concerns After Theodore Roosevelt's presidency, the office of the chief executive would never be the same. Roosevelt expanded the responsibilities and prerogatives of the office on a variety of fronts, including the establishment of a federal government role in arbitrating labor disputes and in regulating business. Roosevelt declared, "Wherever it is practicable we propose to preserve competition; but where . . . competition has been eliminated and cannot be successfully restored, then the Government must step in and itself supply the needed control."

Making Connections Across Time

Federal Power Theodore Roosevelt, from the progressive wing of the Republican party, pushed for a stronger federal government that would regulate business excesses. A number of politicians today, including many in the Republican party, have argued for less government regulation and a smaller federal government, with more power returned to state and local authorities. Allow students to argue these issues in a formal or informal debate, perhaps modeled on a TV political show.

cannot so exist." The young president soon met the first challenge to his assertion of federal power.

1902 COAL STRIKE When 140,000 coal miners in Pennsylvania went on strike and demanded a 20 percent raise, a 9-hour day, and the right to organize a union, the mine operators refused to bargain or even to meet with the labor leaders. George Baer, a multimillionaire mine owner and the president of the Reading Railroad, felt a religious duty to defeat the strikers. He stated, "The rights and interests of the laboring men will be protected and cared for—not by labor agitators, but by the Christian men to whom God in his infinite wisdom has given control of the property interests of this country." President Roosevelt denounced Baer's claim as arrogant.

Five months into the strike, winter threatened and coal reserves ran low. Schools and factories shut down, and patients shivered in icy hospitals. Instead of calling out the troops, Roosevelt called both sides to the White House to talk. Irked by the "extraordinary stupidity and bad temper" of the mine operators, he later confessed that only the dignity of the presidency had kept him from taking one owner "by the seat of his breeches" and tossing him out of the window.

FEDERAL ARBITRATION Faced with Roosevelt's threat to take over the mines, the opposing sides finally agreed to submit their differences to an arbitration commission. Such a commission works with both sides to mediate the dispute and thus settle the strike. In 1903, the commission issued its findings. In the compromise settlement, the miners won a 10 percent pay hike and a shorter, 9-hour day but gave up their demand for a closed shop—in which all workers must belong to the union—and their right to strike during the next three years.

President Roosevelt's actions had demonstrated a new principle. From then on, when a strike threatened the public welfare, the federal government was expected to intervene. In addition, Roosevelt's actions reflected the progressive belief that disputes could be settled in an orderly way with the help of experts, such as those on the arbitration commission.

THINK THROUGH HISTORY
B. *Recognizing Effects* *What was significant about the way the 1902 Pennsylvania coal strike was settled?*

B. Answer From that point on, the federal government played a more active role in settling labor disputes.

TRUSTBUSTING Roosevelt also used his mediation skills to deal with the problem of trusts. (See *trust* on page 940 in the Economics Handbook.) By 1900, trusts controlled about four-fifths of the industries in the United States. Some trusts, like Standard Oil, had earned poor reputations with the American public by using unfair business practices. Many trusts lowered their prices to drive competitors out of the market and then took advantage of the lack of competition to jack prices up even higher. In 1890, Congress had passed the Sherman Antitrust Act. The act's vague language, however, made enforcement difficult; nearly all the suits filed against the trusts under the Sherman act were ineffective.

President Roosevelt did not believe that all trusts were harmful. "Good" trusts had a conscience, while "bad" trusts greedily abused the public. He sought to curb trusts when their actions hurt the public interest, but he also maintained that only big business could ensure national greatness. Explaining his cautious approach to trustbusting, Roosevelt said, "The man who advocates destroying the trusts by measures which would paralyze the industries of the country is at least a quack, and at worst an enemy to the Republic."

The president concentrated his efforts on filing suits under the Sherman Antitrust Act. In 1902,

"In life, as in a football game, the principle to follow is: Hit the line hard."

THEODORE ROOSEVELT

Skillbuilder Answer
Cartoonist's view: *Possible Answer:* The cartoonist views Roosevelt as a fearless lion tamer who has tamed the trusts, which are as fierce and powerful as lions. **Lions:** *Possible Answer:* Wall Street was the location of the country's most powerful financial interests.

SKILLBUILDER
INTERPRETING POLITICAL CARTOONS
How does the cartoonist seem to view Theodore Roosevelt? Why are all the lions in the cartoon coming out of a door labeled "Wall St."?

THE LION-TAMER

MORE ABOUT . . .
George Baer

Baer worked as a printer's apprentice before becoming owner of a Pennsylvania newspaper. After studying law, he rose from legal counsel to president of the Philadelphia & Reading (pronounced "Redding") Railroad. His mining and railroading interests were connected: the Philadelphia & Reading—later just called the Reading Railroad—developed mainly as a means of transporting coal from the mines of Pennsylvania, and in fact became America's largest carrier of anthracite coal. An associate of multimillionaire financier J. P. Morgan, Baer himself left an estate of $15 million when he died.

HISTORY FROM VISUALS
Political Cartoon

Reading the Cartoon
Have a student explain what the character of Theodore Roosevelt appears to be doing in the cartoon. *Using a whip to keep the lions, or trusts, in control.* Then ask whether students think this is a positive or negative portrayal of Roosevelt. *Possible Responses: Most students may indicate that the ordinary citizen would see this as a positive portrayal of Roosevelt, while business interests would see it as negative.*

Extension Ask students to discuss whether the relationship today between the U.S. president and big business interests would be portrayed in the same way.

Block Schedule TEACHING OPTION **Time Needed: 40 Minutes**

Cooperative Activity: Creating Political Cartoons

Task: Groups of students will design and create four or five political cartoons on a single subject.

Purpose: To discover how humor and exaggeration can effectively convey political ideas.

Activity: Tell students that their collections should focus on a single national, regional, or local issue—perhaps a school-related matter, such as conditions in the cafeteria or problems with school funding. The entire group should brainstorm for ideas. Then one artistically inclined group member can do the drawings and another can add any captions, labels, or speech bubbles required. Remaining group members can arrange the cartoons for presentation.

Building a Portfolio: Have students attach notes to the cartoons indicating their own contributions to the project.

ALTERNATIVE ASSESSMENT BOOK
Standards for Evaluating a Cooperative Activity

Standards for Evaluation
Cartoons should . . .
- communicate a message visually rather than just through words
- make their subjects clear
- use humor or exaggeration to make their points

OBJECTIVE

③ INSTRUCT

Protecting Citizens and the Environment

▶ ***Starting with the Student*** Have students make a chart like this one to detail Roosevelt's reforms.

Law	Date	Details
Meat Inspection Act	1906	strict cleanliness for meatpackers

▶ ***Discussing Key Ideas***
- In 1906 Congress passes the Meat Inspection Act and the Pure Food and Drug Act.
- Roosevelt supports conservation.

MORE ABOUT . . .
Upton Sinclair

The Jungle was rejected by many publishers, and Sinclair himself finally paid for its publication. When it proved a bestseller, he used the proceeds to found a cooperative-living community that he was forced to abandon when it burned down. In 1934, he lost a bid to become governor of California.

HISTORY FROM VISUALS
Meat Inspection

Reading the Image Ask which details show the attempt to make meat safer. *Possible Responses: Sign for government inspector; butcher's clean smock.*

OUR TIMES
Upton Sinclair

ELECTRONIC LIBRARY OF PRIMARY SOURCES
from "Whatever Is, Is Wrong" by E. W. Scripps

Roosevelt made newspaper headlines as a trustbuster when he ordered the Justice Department to sue the Northern Securities Company, which had established a monopoly over Northwestern railroads. In 1904, the Supreme Court ordered the dissolution of the Northern Securities Company. Roosevelt also sued the beef trust, the oil trust, and the tobacco trust.

In all, the Roosevelt administration filed 44 antitrust suits. The government won a number of cases and broke up some of the trusts, but it was unable to slow the merger movement in business. Indeed, though Roosevelt won a reputation as a trustbuster, his real goal was federal regulation.

> ***"We recognize and are bound to war against the evils of today."***
>
> THEODORE ROOSEVELT

RAILROAD REGULATION Roosevelt was more successful in railroad regulation. In 1887, Congress had passed the Interstate Commerce Act, which prohibited "pools" in which wealthy railroad owners divided the business in a given area and shared the profits. The act set up the Interstate Commerce Commission (ICC) to enforce the new law. Before Roosevelt's administration, however, the Interstate Commerce Commission had had little power. Railroad owners could bypass the ICC by appealing its decisions to federal courts, which could delay a finding for as long as ten years. With Roosevelt's urging, Congress put some teeth into the ICC. The Elkins Act of 1903 made it illegal for railroad officials to give, and shippers to receive, rebates—that is, discounts or refunds for using particular railroads. The act also specified that once a railroad had set rates, it could not change them without notifying the public.

The Hepburn Act of 1906 strictly limited the distribution of free railroad passes, a common form of bribery. It also gave the ICC power to set maximum railroad rates, subject to court approval, whenever shippers complained. Within two years, the commission had received thousands of complaints and lowered many rates. To win passage of the act, Roosevelt had to compromise with conservative senators who opposed it. In its final form the act did not completely satisfy Wisconsin's Senator Robert La Follette and other reformers, but it nevertheless boosted the government's power to regulate the railroads.

Protecting Citizens and the Environment

Government workers inspected meat as it moved through the packinghouse.

President Roosevelt also promoted laws to protect citizens from unsafe food and drugs and to protect the environment from pollution by businesses. Armed with progressive ideals, Roosevelt advocated a two-pronged approach to solve these problems. He wrote, "We recognize and are bound to war against the evils of today. The remedies are partly economic and partly spiritual, partly to be obtained by laws, and in greater part to be obtained by individual and associated effort." Roosevelt's enthusiasm and his considerable skill at compromise led to policies that benefited both public health and the environment.

PROTECTING HEALTH After reading *The Jungle* by Upton Sinclair, Roosevelt listened to the public's clamor for action. He appointed a commission of experts to investigate the meatpacking industry. The commission issued a scathing report that backed up Sinclair's description of "potted ham" as a hash whose disgust-

TEACHING OPTIONS

Making Connections Across the Curriculum

Economics Clarify that a trust was a monopoly, or a supplier offering a product or service exclusively, with no market competition. Then have students discuss the benefits and drawbacks of monopolies. Point out that drawbacks include the ability to charge very high prices or produce an inferior product, since the buyer cannot switch to a competitor; benefits include efficiency in meeting market needs or in consolidating the different areas of service and production (which could lead to lower prices).

Teaching Gifted and Talented Students

Influential Books Encourage students to read and report on *The Jungle* or another influential turn-of-the-century book encouraging social reform. Possibilities include these:

- *Looking Backward* by Edward Bellamy
- *The Octopus* by Frank Norris
- *The Shame of the Cities* by Lincoln Steffens
- *An American Tragedy* by Theodore Dreiser
- *The History of the Standard Oil Company* by Ida M. Tarbell

Students' reports should include a summary of the book, information about its author, and an explanation of its impact at the time.

ing ingredients included ground rope and pigskin. True to his word, in 1906 Roosevelt pushed for passage of the **Meat Inspection Act,** which dictated strict cleanliness requirements for meatpackers and created the program of federal meat inspection that was in use until it was replaced with more sophisticated techniques in the 1990s.

THINK THROUGH HISTORY
C. *Developing Historical Perspective* *How did the publication of* The Jungle *in 1906 affect the safety of the meat that people eat today?*

C. Answer The Meat Inspection Act, passed in 1906 as a direct result of Sinclair's book, established a system of meat inspection that was in place into the 1990s.

Like the Hepburn Act, the Meat Inspection Act supported the progressive principle of government regulation. The compromise that won the act's passage, however, left the government paying for the inspections and did not require companies to label their canned goods with date-of-processing information. The compromise also granted meatpackers the right to appeal negative decisions in court.

PURE FOOD AND DRUG ACT That same year, Congress passed the **Pure Food and Drug Act,** which halted the sale of contaminated foods and medicines and called for truth in labeling. Credit for the Pure Food and Drug Act belongs largely to Dr. Harvey Washington Wiley, chief chemist at the Department of Agriculture. In lectures across the country, Wiley criticized manufacturers for adding harmful preservatives to food—chemicals such as coal-tar dye and borax in sausage and formaldehyde in canned pork and beans.

Before passage of the Pure Food and Drug Act, manufacturers had advertised that their products accomplished everything from curing cancer to growing hair. In addition, popular children's medicines often contained opium, cocaine, or alcohol. Colden's Liquid Beef Tonic, recommended for "treatment of the alcohol habit," itself packed a walloping dose of 26.5 percent alcohol.

D. Answer The administration secured the passage of the Pure Food and Drug Act and the Meat Inspection Act in 1906.

THINK THROUGH HISTORY
D. *Summarizing* *What actions did the Roosevelt administration take to regulate food and medicines?*

By 1906, however, the largest food and medicine manufacturers were eager to regain public confidence by supporting increased federal regulation. The Pure Food and Drug Act did not ban harmful products outright. Nevertheless, its requirement of truthful labels reflected the progressive belief that given accurate information, people would act wisely.

NOW & THEN

MEAT INSPECTION

During the progressive era, people worried about the kinds of things that might fall—or walk—into a batch of meat being processed. Today, Americans worry more about meat contaminated by unseen dangers, such as *E. coli* bacteria, and meat from animals that have been treated with antibiotics or other chemicals that may pose long-range health risks to people.

Despite changes in technology that have permitted more thorough inspection of meat for bacteria, over the years meat inspectors have continued to rely on "observing, poking, and sniffing" to determine food safety.

In July 1996, Congress passed the most extensive changes in standards for meat inspection since the Meat Inspection Act of 1906. The new, more scientific methods of meat inspection will cost companies $80 to $100 million per year. When passed on to consumers, these costs amount to about a tenth of a penny per pound of meat.

CONSERVATION AND NATURAL RESOURCES Before Roosevelt's presidency, the federal government had paid very little attention to the nation's natural resources. Despite the establishment of the U.S. Forest Bureau in 1887 and the subsequent withdrawal from public sale of 45 million acres of timberlands for a

Skillbuilder Answer **Location:** California. **Human/Environment Interaction:** *Possible Answer:* Roosevelt helped establish a strong conservation movement in the United States.

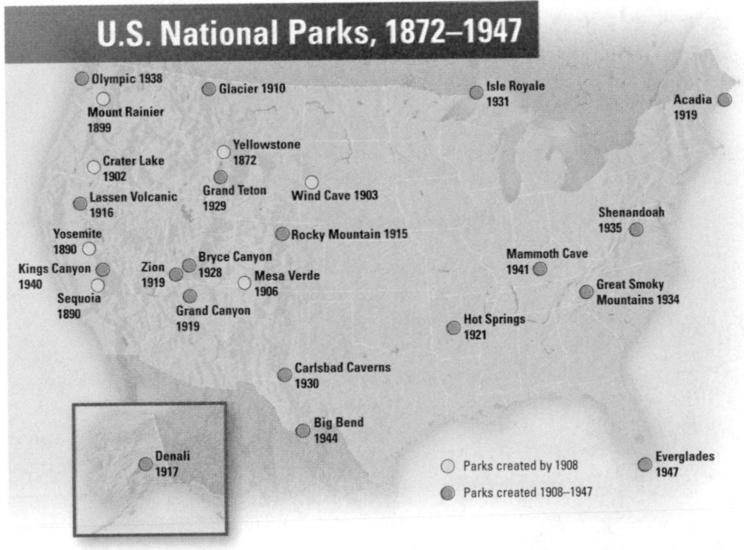

GEOGRAPHY SKILLBUILDER
LOCATION *Which state had the most parks in 1947?*
HUMAN-ENVIRONMENT INTERACTION *What does the growth of the national park system after 1908 suggest about Roosevelt's impact on conservation?*

MORE ABOUT . . .
Harvey Washington Wiley

Indiana native Harvey Washington Wiley attended a log schoolhouse. He went on to study chemistry at Purdue University and began working for the U.S. Department of Agriculture in 1883. Before his campaign, pure food and drug laws were impossible to enforce because they varied from state to state and did not clearly define what was "pure." The 1906 law that he helped get passed was further strengthened by the Federal Food, Drug, and Cosmetic Act of 1938.

NOW & THEN
Meat Inspection

Critical Thinking: Evaluating Ask students' opinions of the new regulations. Note that the food industry generally supported the new regulations, which were drawn up with their participation.

HISTORY FROM VISUALS
U.S. National Parks, 1872–1947

Reading the Map Ask students to identify the oldest national park and the number of national parks east of the Mississippi River. *Yellowstone; six.*

Extension Ask students why they think so many of the parks are west of the Mississippi. *Possible Responses: The area east of the river was already built up, with much of its wilderness destroyed, when the nation began engaging in preservation efforts.*

TEACHING OPTIONS

Teaching Less Proficient Readers

Clarifying Ideas As students read about conservation, make sure they understand the distinction between the various interpretations of the term *conservation* held by Muir, Pinchot, Roosevelt, and Western business interests.

Ask students to read the subsection "Conservation and Natural Resources." Then have them make a chart listing the names above. Next to each name have the students jot down notes indicating whether that person advocated complete conservation of the wilderness, partial conservation, or the indiscriminate selling of wilderness land to business interests.

Making Connections Across the Curriculum

Science Ingestion of the *E. coli* bacteria induces grave illness and sometimes death. The bacteria can be killed by high heat; many of the outbreaks of *E. coli* come from rare or undercooked meat. Several *E. coli* cases in 1996 were traced to unpasteurized gourmet apple juice—pasteurization, which uses heat, would have killed the bacteria, though it also would have made the juice taste less rich and natural.

MORE ABOUT . . .
John Muir

A Scottish native, Muir immigrated to Wisconsin as a boy. He worked as an industrial inventor until sustaining an eye injury, then turned to a career as a naturalist. Settling in California, he spent his time growing fruit trees, traveling throughout the western states and Alaska, and campaigning for government preservation of western forests. His efforts helped establish Sequoia and Yosemite national parks in 1890. Muir was founder of the Sierra Club, an environmental group still active today.

HISTORICAL SPOTLIGHT
Yosemite National Park

Critical Thinking: Using the Internet Have students "visit" Yosemite National Park on the Internet. Ask them to report their findings to the class and indicate the most interesting aspect of their visit.

http://www.mlushistory.com

OBJECTIVE
④ **INSTRUCT**

Roosevelt and Civil Rights

▶ ***Discussing Key Ideas***
- Roosevelt does little for civil rights in general but sometimes champions the rights of individual African Americans.
- W. E. B. Du Bois joins others in the Niagara Movement, which in 1909 evolves into the National Association for the Advancement of Colored People (NAACP).

national forest reserve, the government stood by while private interests gobbled up the shrinking wilderness.

Americans had shortsightedly exploited their natural environment. Pioneer farmers leveled the forests and plowed up the prairies. Ranchers allowed their cattle to overgraze the Great Plains. Coal companies cluttered the land with spoil dumps. Lumber companies ignored the effect of their logging operations on flood control and neglected to plant trees to replace those they had cut down. Cities dumped untreated sewage and industrial wastes into rivers, poisoning the streams and creating health hazards.

Roosevelt condemned the view that America's resources were endless. In fact, on assuming the presidency, Roosevelt deemed forest and water problems a vital concern for the country. He proceeded to attack environmental problems with his characteristic zeal, even banning Christmas trees in the White House in 1902. John Muir, a naturalist and writer with whom Roosevelt camped in California's Yosemite National Park in 1903, persuaded the president to set aside 148 million acres of forest reserves. Roosevelt also set aside 1.5 million acres of water-power sites and another 80 million acres of land that experts from the U.S. Geological Survey would explore for mineral and water resources. To help preserve the "beautiful and wonderful wild creatures whose existence was threatened by greed," Roosevelt established more than 50 wildlife sanctuaries and several national parks.

HISTORICAL SPOTLIGHT

YOSEMITE NATIONAL PARK

The naturalist John Muir visited the Yosemite region of central California in 1867 and made it his home base for a period of six years while he traveled throughout the West. He was the first to suggest that Yosemite's spectacular land formations had been shaped by glaciers. Today the great U-shaped valley and flat meadows—first carved into lakes, then filled with sediment—draw sports enthusiasts and tourists in all seasons.

Made famous by the black-and-white photographs of Ansel Adams, the park today can be "visited" on the Internet. There you can find out about today's weather in Yosemite and see photographs that are taken every 15 minutes.

GIFFORD PINCHOT True to the progressive belief in using experts, in 1905 the president named Gifford Pinchot, a professional conservationist, as head of the U.S. Forest Service. Armed with administrative skill as well as the latest scientific and technical information, Pinchot advised Roosevelt to conserve forest and grazing lands by keeping large tracts of federal land exempt from private sale.

Conservationists like Roosevelt and Pinchot, however, did not share the views of Muir, who advocated complete preservation of the wilderness. Instead, **conservation** meant that some wilderness areas would be preserved while others would be developed for the common good. Indeed, Roosevelt's federal water projects transformed some dry wilderness areas to make agriculture possible. Under the National Reclamation Act of 1902, known as the Newlands Act, money from the sale of public lands in the West funded large-scale irrigation projects, such as the Roosevelt Dam in Arizona and the Shoshone Dam in Wyoming. The Newlands Act established the precedent that the federal government would manage the precious water resources in the West. However, this was quite a different position from Muir's, who wanted to preserve the wilderness as it was.

E. Answer Roosevelt worked for conservation, among other things setting aside 148 million acres of forest reserves.

THINK THROUGH HISTORY
E. *Summarizing* *Summarize Roosevelt's approach to environmental problems.*

Civil rights leaders gathered at the 1905 Niagara Falls conference.

Roosevelt and Civil Rights

Roosevelt's care for the land and its inhabitants was not matched in the area of civil rights. Though Roosevelt's father had been a Northern abolitionist, his mother, Mittie, may well have been the model for the Southern belle Scarlett O'Hara in Margaret Mitchell's famous novel *Gone with the Wind.* In almost two terms as president, Roosevelt—like most other progressives—was no supporter of civil rights for African Americans. He did, however, support a few individual African Americans.

TEACHING OPTIONS

Making Connections Across the Curriculum

Geography Muir once walked all the way from Indianapolis, Indiana, to the Gulf of Mexico, keeping a nature journal that he later published. Have students write their own journal entries about a real or imagined visit to a national or state park in your area. Students who need to research their details might consult travel books, newspaper and magazine articles, and free travel brochures from the park in question.

Making Connections Across Time

Environmental Controversy The debate between conservation and preservation continues today. In September 1996 President Clinton, a Democrat, created the Grand Staircase-Escalante National Monument in southern Utah, placing 1.7 million acres of red-rock cliffs and canyons off limits to coal mining and other development. The decision, praised by environmental groups, sparked controversy among Utah's mostly Republican politicians, who felt that portions of the area should be considered for development that would enhance Utah's economy. Have a panel of students debate this or similar environmental controversies.

Roosevelt appointed an African American as head of the Charleston, South Carolina, customhouse, for example, despite opposition from whites. In another instance, when some whites demanded that he dismiss the black postmistress of a Mississippi post office, he chose to close the station rather than to comply. In 1906, however, Roosevelt angered many African Americans when he dismissed without question an entire regiment of African-American soldiers accused of rioting in Brownsville, Texas.

As a symbolic gesture, Roosevelt invited the African-American leader Booker T. Washington to dinner at the White House. At the time, no African American enjoyed more respect from powerful whites than Washington, who was head of an all-black training school, the Tuskegee Institute. However, Washington faced opposition from African Americans for his accommodation of segregationists.

Persistent in his criticism of Washington's ideas, W. E. B. Du Bois renewed his demands for immediate social and economic equality for African Americans. In his 1903 book *The Souls of Black Folk,* Du Bois wrote of his opposition to Washington's position.

A PERSONAL VOICE

So far as Mr. Washington preaches Thrift, Patience, and Industrial Training for the masses, we must hold up his hands and strive with him. . . . But so far as Mr. Washington apologizes for injustice, North or South, does not rightly value the privilege and duty of voting, belittles the emasculating effects of caste distinctions, and opposes the higher training and ambition of our brighter minds—so far as he, the South, or the Nation, does this,—we must unceasingly and firmly oppose them.

W. E. B. DU BOIS, *The Souls of Black Folk*

Du Bois and other advocates of equality for African Americans were deeply upset by the apparent progressive indifference to racial injustice. They held a conference at Niagara Falls in 1905. In 1909, a number of African Americans joined with prominent white reformers in New York to found the National Association for the Advancement of Colored People **(NAACP)**, which had about 6,000 members by 1914. The NAACP aimed for nothing less than full equality among the races. That goal, however, found little support in the progressive movement, which focused on the needs of middle-class whites. The two presidents who followed Roosevelt also did little to advance the goal of racial equality.

KEY PLAYER

W. E. B. DU BOIS
1868–1963

W. E. B. Du Bois's establishment of the NAACP in 1909—and his role as its publicity and research director—put him at the forefront of the early U.S. civil rights movement. However, in the 1920s, he faced a power struggle with the NAACP's executive secretary, Walter White.

Ironically, Du Bois had retreated to a position others saw as dangerously close to that of Booker T. Washington. Arguing for a separate economy for African Americans, Du Bois made a distinction between enforced and voluntary segregation that White rejected. By mid-century, Du Bois was outside the mainstream of the civil rights movement. His work remained largely ignored until the 1960s. Du Bois died in 1963.

Section 3 Assessment

1. TERMS & NAMES

Identify:
- Upton Sinclair
- *The Jungle*
- Theodore Roosevelt
- Square Deal
- Meat Inspection Act
- Pure Food and Drug Act
- conservation
- NAACP

2. SUMMARIZING Create a diagram like this one to show how these problems were solved during Roosevelt's presidency: (a) 1902 coal strike, (b) Northern Securities Company's monopoly, (c) unsafe meat processing, and (d) exploitation of the environment.

Problem → Solution

Write headlines announcing the solutions.

3. FORMING GENERALIZATIONS In what ways do you think the progressive belief in using experts played a role in shaping Roosevelt's reforms? Refer to details from the text.

THINK ABOUT
- Roosevelt's use of experts to help him tackle political, economic, and environmental problems
- how experts' findings affected legislative actions

4. DRAWING CONCLUSIONS How did Theodore Roosevelt expand the role of the federal government? Refer to specific passages in the chapter in your response.

ANSWERS

1. TERMS & NAMES

Upton Sinclair, p. 341
The Jungle, p. 341
Theodore Roosevelt, p. 341
Square Deal, p. 342
Meat Inspection Act, p. 345
Pure Food and Drug Act, p. 345
conservation, p. 346
NAACP, p. 347

2. SUMMARIZING

Possible Answers:
(a) federal arbitration, (b) Supreme Court's dissolution of the Northern Securities Company, (c) passage of the Meat Inspection Act, (d) legislation passed to protect the environment
Students' headlines will vary.

3. FORMING GENERALIZATIONS

Possible Responses: Roosevelt used an arbitration commission to mediate the 1902 coal strike. Roosevelt appointed experts to verify the accuracy of Sinclair's *The Jungle* and thus helped the passage of the Meat Inspection Act. Dr. Wiley, chief chemist of the Department of Agriculture, helped get the Pure Food and Drug Act passed. Gifford Pinchot, a professional conservationist, headed the U.S. Forest Service.

4. DRAWING CONCLUSIONS

Possible Responses: Roosevelt used the presidency as a "bully pulpit" to shape public opinion. He established the precedent of federal arbitration for strikes. Roosevelt regulated big business and strengthened the Interstate Commerce Commission. He promoted laws protecting the public from unsafe food and drugs, and the environment from abuse.

KEY PLAYER
W. E. B. Du Bois

Critical Thinking: Analyzing Motives Refer students to Chapter 8 for more on W. E. B. Du Bois and Booker T. Washington. Ask students why they think Du Bois may have changed from advocating immediate change to a more gradual approach.
Possible Responses: First stance not getting anywhere; new approach gets more white support; becomes more conservative as he grows older.

ASSESS & RETEACH

Section 3 Assessment

You might have a student volunteer lead a class discussion of the questions and answers.

Self-Assessment

Have students make a two-column chart about Teddy Roosevelt's presidency. In the left column, they should list facts or ideas they had already associated with Roosevelt; in the right, the new facts and ideas they learned in the section.

Section Quiz

FORMAL ASSESSMENT
Section Quiz, p. 118

Reteach

Based on what they have learned from this section, have students develop and compare lists of words and phrases that describe progressivism as embodied by Theodore Roosevelt.

CLOSE

Defining the modern presidency, the dynamic Theodore Roosevelt enhanced the president's leadership role and helped expand federal power to curb business excesses and to protect citizens' health and the environment.

American Literature

OBJECTIVES

1. To learn the subjects and goals of the muckrakers.
2. To understand the effects of exposés dealing with both business and government corruption.

FOCUS & MOTIVATE

▶ ***Starting with the Student***

- Ask students to define the term *muckraker.* You might begin with the meaning of the word *muck,* and ask under what circumstances a journalist might be regarded as someone who rakes up muck.
- Ask students which present-day writers might be called muckrakers.

MORE ABOUT . . .
McClure's *Magazine*

Perhaps the most politically influential single issue of a magazine ever published was the January 1903 edition of *McClure's.* The issue contained three carefully documented muckraking articles: "The Shame of Minneapolis" by Lincoln Steffens, "The Right to Work: The Story of the Non-Striking Miners" by Ray Stannard Baker, and "The Oil War of 1872," a chapter from Ida M. Tarbell's Standard Oil history. Rival magazines such as *Collier's* and *Cosmopolitan* immediately began to publish similar types of articles, and the "literature of exposure" soon became commonplace.

AMERICAN LITERATURE

The Muckrakers

The tradition of the investigative reporter uncovering corruption was established early in the 20th century by the writers known as muckrakers. Coined by President Theodore Roosevelt, the term *muckraker* alludes to the English author John Bunyan's famous 17th-century religious allegory *The Pilgrim's Progress,* which features a character too busy raking up the muck to see a heavenly crown held over him. The originally negative term soon was applied to many writers whose reform efforts Roosevelt himself supported. The muckraking movement spilled over from journalism into fiction, particularly among novelists, such as Upton Sinclair, who had worked as journalists.

THE HISTORY OF THE STANDARD OIL COMPANY

Ida M. Tarbell's *The History of the Standard Oil Company* exposed the ruthlessness with which John D. Rockefeller had turned his oil business into an all-powerful monopoly. Her writing added force to the trustbusting reforms of the early 20th century. Here Tarbell describes how Standard Oil used lower transportation rates to drive out smaller refineries, such as Hanna, Baslington and Company.

Ida M. Tarbell

Mr. Hanna had been refining since July, 1869. . . . Some time in February, 1872, the Standard Oil Company asked [for] an interview with him and his associates. They wanted to buy his works, they said. "But we don't want to sell," objected Mr. Hanna. "You can never make any more money, in my judgment," said Mr. Rockefeller. "You can't compete with the Standard. We have all the large refineries now. If you refuse to sell, it will end in your being crushed." Hanna and Baslington were not satisfied. They went to see . . . General Devereux, manager of the Lake Shore road. They were told that the Standard had special rates; that it was useless to try to compete with them. General Devereux explained to the gentlemen that the privileges granted the Standard were the legitimate and necessary advantage of the larger shipper over the smaller. . . . General Devereux says they "recognised the propriety" of his excuse. They certainly recognised its authority. They say that they were satisfied they could no longer get rates to and from Cleveland which would enable them to live, and "reluctantly" sold out. It must have been reluctantly, for they had paid $75,000 for their works, and had made thirty per cent. a year on an average on their investment, and the Standard appraiser allowed them $45,000.

IDA M. TARBELL, *The History of the Standard Oil Company* (1904)

RECOMMENDED RESOURCES

Books

Denevi, Donald P. and Friend, Helen M. *Muckrakers and Robber Barons.* Danville, CA: Consensus, 1973. Includes an introduction that explores the phenomenon of muckraking as well as facsimiles of original articles from *McClure's* and other magazines.

Kaplan, Justin. *Lincoln Steffens: A Biography.* New York: Simon, 1974. Detailed account of the life of a central figure in the history of muckraking.

Sinclair, Upton. *Boston.* Cambridge, MA: Robert Bentley, 1978. Facts document and fiction recreates the injustice of the Sacco-Vanzetti case.

Sinclair, Upton. *The Jungle.* Urbana: U of Illinois P, 1988. With introduction by historian James R. Barrett to place the book in historical context.

Steffens, Lincoln. *The Autobiography of Lincoln Steffens.* New York: Harcourt, 1931. Steffens's immensely successful own story.

Steffens, Lincoln. *The Shame of the Cities.* New York: Hill, 1963. Groundbreaking exposé of political corruption in municipal governments.

Tarbell, Ida M. *The History of the Standard Oil Company.* New York: Norton, 1969. A briefer version of the original exposé.

THE SHAME OF THE CITIES

Lincoln Steffens is usually named as the leader of the muckraking movement. He published exposés of business and government corruption in *McClure's* and other magazines. These articles were then collected in *The Shame of the Cities* and two other volumes. Below is a section from an article Steffens wrote to expose voter fraud in Philadelphia.

The police are forbidden by law to stand within thirty feet of the polls, but they are at the box and they are there to see that the [Republican political] machine's orders are obeyed and that repeaters whom they help to furnish are permitted to vote without "intimidation" on the names they, the police, have supplied. The editor of an anti-machine paper who was looking about for himself once told me that a ward leader who knew him well asked him into a polling place. "I'll show you how it's done," he said, and he had the repeaters go round and round voting again and again on the names handed them on slips. . . . The business proceeds with very few hitches; there is more jesting than fighting. Violence in the past has had its effect; and is not often necessary nowadays, but if it is needed the police are there to apply it.

LINCOLN STEFFENS, *The Shame of the Cities* (1904)

Lincoln Steffens

THE JUNGLE

Upton Sinclair's chief aim in writing *The Jungle* was to expose the shocking conditions that immigrant workers endured. The public, however, reacted even more strongly to the novel's revelations of unsanitary conditions in the meatpacking industry. Serialized in 1905 and published in book form one year later, *The Jungle* prompted a federal investigation that resulted in passage of the Meat Inspection Act in 1906.

Jonas had told them how the meat that was taken out of pickle would often be found sour, and how they would rub it up with [baking] soda to take away the smell, and sell it to be eaten on free-lunch counters; also of all the miracles of chemistry which they performed, giving to any sort of meat, fresh or salted, whole or chopped, any color and any flavor and any odor they chose. . . .

It was only when the whole ham was spoiled that it came into the department of Elzbieta. Cut up by the two-thousand-revolutions-a-minute flyers, and mixed with half a ton of other meat, no odor that ever was in a ham could make any difference. There was never the least attention paid to what was cut up for sausage; there would come all the way back from Europe old sausage that had been rejected, and that was moldy and white—it would be dosed with borax and glycerine, and dumped into the hoppers, and made over again for home consumption.

UPTON SINCLAIR, *The Jungle* (1906)

INTERACT WITH HISTORY

1. **FINDING MAIN IDEAS** State the main idea of each of these selections. What role do details play in making the passages convincing?

SEE SKILLBUILDER HANDBOOK, PAGE 911.

2. **WRITING AN ARTICLE** Do some research on a local or national issue in today's world. Report your findings in a nonfiction exposé for your school or local newspaper.

INTERNET Visit http://www.mlushistory.com for more about the muckrakers.

INSTRUCT

▶ *Starting with the Student*

- Have students talk about investigative reporting, such as the type that uncovered Watergate and other recent political scandals.
- Ask students to supply theories about why muckraking occurred with such prominence during the progressive era.

▶ *Discussing Key Ideas*

- By the second half of the nineteenth century, individuals seem to get lost in the expansion of the country, government, and business.
- The progressive era includes determined reformers who want to increase the power of the individual once again.
- Muckraking reaches its height at a time of rapidly multiplying trusts and monopolies and corruption among politicians.

HISTORY FROM VISUALS

Reading the Image

- Ask students to tell what they see on the cover of *The Jungle* and what they can infer about the kind of working conditions meatpackers faced.
- Steffens wrote, "I have seen the future and it works" to a friend in 1919, just after returning from a trip to Petrograd in Russia. Although Steffens never identified with a party or doctrine, his leanings were socialist, and he supported many Communist activities.

INTERACT WITH HISTORY

1. Finding Main Ideas

Possible Responses: The History of the Standard Oil Company: *Although Hanna and Baslington did not want to sell their business, they sold out to Standard Oil Company at a huge loss because they would be crushed if they did not. Details about the sale price of the business help convince the reader that Hanna and Baslington had no choice but to sell.* The Shame of the Cities: *At the polls, the police actually assist "repeaters," or people who vote more than one time. Details about the ward leader demonstrating the process of illegal voting help to make the idea of political corruption convincing.* The Jungle: *Even meat that had gone bad was treated chemically or processed so that it could be sold. Details about the ham and sausage, as well as descriptive words such as moldy, make the process of treating bad meat more revolting to the reader.*

2. Writing an Article

Standards for Evaluation
Articles should . . .

- spotlight a local or national issue
- be aimed at readers of a school or local newspaper
- present the main ideas clearly
- back up main ideas with supporting details
- be clearly and persuasively written

Section 4 Overview

OBJECTIVES

1. To summarize the Taft presidency.

2. To trace the division in the Republican party.
3. To describe the election of 1912.

CRITICAL THINKING

- Contrasting, pp. 351, 353
- Analyzing issues, p. 351
- Summarizing, pp. 352, 353
- Making predictions, p. 353
- Forming opinions, p. 353

FOCUS & MOTIVATE

5-MINUTE WARM-UP

Recognizing Facts and Details

To gain insight into William Howard Taft as president, ask students to read the Key Player on page 352 and answer these questions.

1. What did Theodore Roosevelt have to do with William Howard Taft's becoming president?
2. What did Taft say about his years as president?

WARM-UP TRANSPARENCY 9

▶ ***Starting with the Student***

- Have students tell about a time when they had to give an oral report just after a classmate had given a great one, or when they followed a terrific athlete in a sport in which they don't excel.

OBJECTIVE

① INSTRUCT

Taft Becomes President

▶ ***Discussing Key Ideas***

- Refusing a third term, Roosevelt handpicks his successor.
- William Howard Taft angers his party's progressive wing.

IN-DEPTH RESOURCES: UNIT 3
Guided Reading, p. 4

ACCESS FOR STUDENTS ACQUIRING ENGLISH
Guided Reading (Spanish), p. 123

4 Progressivism Under Taft

TERMS & NAMES
- Gifford Pinchot
- William Howard Taft
- Payne-Aldrich Tariff
- Bull Moose Party
- Woodrow Wilson

LEARN ABOUT the policies of the Taft administration
TO UNDERSTAND the growing conflict between progressive reform and business interests.

ONE AMERICAN'S STORY

Early in the 20th century, American interest in the preservation of the country's wilderness areas intensified. Popular writers sang the praises of America's vistas, while newly founded groups like the Girl Scouts provided city children with an escape from their urban environment. Preservationists, however, faced off against groups with business interests that favored the land's unrestricted development. Conservationists like **Gifford Pinchot** staked a middle ground. Head of the U.S. Forest Service under President Roosevelt, Pinchot believed that wilderness areas could be scientifically managed to yield public enjoyment while allowing private development.

Gifford Pinchot

A PERSONAL VOICE

The American people have evidently made up their minds that our natural resources must be conserved. That is good, but it settles only half the question. For whose benefit shall they be conserved—for the benefit of the many, or for the use and profit of the few? . . . There is no other question before us that begins to be so important, or that will be so difficult to straddle, as the great question between special interest and equal opportunity, between the privileges of the few and the rights of the many, between government by men for human welfare and government by money for profit.

GIFFORD PINCHOT, *The Fight for Conservation*

Pinchot's multi-use land program suited his friend and fellow conservationist, Theodore Roosevelt. When Roosevelt left office in 1908, however, Pinchot's approach came under increasing pressure from business people who favored unrestricted commercial development.

Taft Becomes President

As soon as Roosevelt won election in 1904, he pledged not to run for reelection in 1908. Popular enough to designate a successor, Roosevelt hand-picked his secretary of war, **William Howard Taft,** to carry out his policies.

For the third time, the Democrats nominated William Jennings Bryan, who campaigned on the slogan of "Let the people rule." The people, however, ignored Bryan's call for a federal income tax, a lower tariff, and new antitrust laws. "Vote for Taft this time," the Republicans said, "You can vote for Bryan any time." And vote for Taft the people did. The gigantic man—6 feet tall and 350 pounds—captured an easy victory.

TAFT STUMBLES As president, Taft pursued a cautiously progressive agenda, but received little credit for his accomplishments. While the so-called trustbuster, Roosevelt, had noisily busted 44 trusts in 7½ years in office, Taft busted 90 trusts in a 4-year term. However, Taft's legal victories did not bolster his popularity. Indeed, the new president confessed in a letter to Roosevelt that he never felt like the president. "When I am addressed as 'Mr. President,'" Taft wrote, "I turn to see whether you are not at my elbow."

SECTION 4 RESOURCES

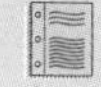
PRINT RESOURCES

IN-DEPTH RESOURCES: UNIT 3
Guided Reading, p. 4

READING STUDY GUIDE, p. 103

ACCESS FOR STUDENTS ACQUIRING ENGLISH
Guided Reading (Spanish), p. 123

SPANISH READING STUDY GUIDE, p. 103

FORMAL ASSESSMENT
Section Quiz, p. 119

ALTERNATIVE ASSESSMENT BOOK
See forms for supporting and scoring alternative activities.

TECHNOLOGY RESOURCES

HUMANITIES TRANSPARENCIES
H36, "Goodness Gracious, I Must Have Been Dozing"

CD-ROM *Grolier Multimedia Encyclopedia*

VIDEO *American Portfolio: A Videodisc for U.S. History* user's guide, pp. 169, 171

INTERNET http://www.mlushistory.com

THINK THROUGH HISTORY
A. *Contrasting* *Contrast President Taft with Theodore Roosevelt.*

A. Answer Unlike Roosevelt, Taft was cautious and unable to unify his own party. He did not use his position to shape public opinion.

The cautious Taft hesitated to use the presidential bully pulpit to arouse public opinion. Nor could he subdue troublesome members of his own party. Tariffs and conservation posed his first problems.

THE PAYNE–ALDRICH TARIFF Taft had campaigned on a platform of lowering tariffs, a staple of the progressive agenda. (See *tariff* on page 939 in the Economics Handbook.) The House duly passed the Payne bill, which would lower rates on many manufactured goods. In the Senate, however, conservative Republicans eliminated most of the cuts. Amid cries of betrayal from the progressive wing of his party, Taft signed the **Payne-Aldrich Tariff.**

The president made his difficulties worse by clumsily attempting to defend the tariff. Before a hostile audience of grain growers in Winona, Minnesota, Taft asserted that the new law was "the best [tariff] bill the Republican party ever passed." Later, he tried to repair the damage but only made matters more difficult when he explained that he had dictated the speech hurriedly between two railroad stations without bothering to reread it.

DISPUTING PUBLIC LANDS Next, Taft angered conservationists by appointing as his secretary of the interior Richard A. Ballinger. Ballinger was a wealthy Seattle lawyer who disapproved of conservationist controls on western lands. The new secretary removed 1 million acres of forest and mining lands from the reserved list and approved the sale to Seattle businesses of several million acres of coal-rich land in Alaska. These businesses then sold their holdings to a group of New York bankers, including J. P. Morgan, who for many Americans symbolized the power of money. However, Ballinger's decisions delighted Western entrepreneurs.

B. Answer Ballinger didn't approve of conservationist controls on western lands; he permitted the sale of reserved lands to business interests.

When a Department of the Interior official was fired for protesting Ballinger's actions, the fired worker published a muckraking article against Ballinger in *Collier's Weekly* magazine. Then, in congressional testimony in January 1910, Pinchot added his voice and accused Ballinger of letting commercial interests exploit the natural resources that rightfully belonged to the public.

THINK THROUGH HISTORY
B. *Analyzing Issues* *How did Taft's appointee Richard Ballinger anger conservationists?*

As a result, President Taft reluctantly fired Pinchot from the U.S. Forest Service. Retaliating in a book called *The Fight for Conservation,* Pinchot wrote, "The more successful the Forest Service has been in preventing land-grabbing and the absorption of water power by the special interests, the more ingenious, the more devious, and the more dangerous these attacks have become."

Difficult Decisions IN HISTORY

CONTROLLING RESOURCES

The question of what to do with wilderness areas became more urgent in the 1990s with the spotted owl controversy in the Pacific Northwest. Loggers protested that laws to safeguard the owl's habitat would deprive them of the opportunity to make a living.

Historically, conservationists such as Gifford Pinchot have stood for the balanced use of natural resources, preserving some and using others for private industry. Free-market advocates like Richard Ballinger pressed for the private development of wilderness areas. Preservationists such as John Muir have advocated preserving all remaining wilderness.

1. Examine the pros and cons of each position. With which do you agree? What other factors, if any, do you think should influence decisions about America's wilderness areas?
2. If you'd been asked in 1902 to decide whether to develop or preserve America's wilderness areas, what would you have decided?

William Howard Taft

The Republican Party Splits

Taft's cautious nature made it impossible for him to hold together the two wings of the Republican Party: progressives who sought change and conservatives who did not. Roosevelt had asserted, "I believe in a strong executive," but Taft followed a course of presidential restraint. While Taft remained above the fray, the Republican Party began to fragment.

PROBLEMS WITHIN THE PARTY Republican conservatives and progressives split over Taft's support of the political boss Joseph Cannon, Speaker of the House of Representatives. A poker-playing, rough-talking, tobacco-chewing politician, "Uncle Joe" not only disregarded seniority in filling committee slots but also anointed himself head of the Committee on Rules, which decided what bills Congress would consider. Under Cannon's virtual dictatorship, the House often ignored or weakened progressive bills.

DIFFICULT DECISIONS IN HISTORY
Controlling Resources

1. Factors may include job loss, health concerns, unknown results of upsetting the balance of nature, and the danger of letting potentially useful species become extinct.
2. Some students will indicate that the wilderness should be preserved at all costs. Others may suggest that, in 1902, the need to develop the West may have seemed vital—and, at that time, the resources of the West may still have seemed inexhaustable.

 ***GROLIER MULTIMEDIA ENCYCLOPEDIA***
History of Conservation in the United States

OBJECTIVE
② **INSTRUCT**

The Republican Party Splits

▶ ***Discussing Key Ideas***
- Taft's support of Republican boss Joe Cannon further alienates progressive Republicans.
- The party splits, and Roosevelt becomes leader of the Bull Moose Party.

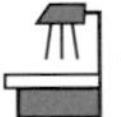 ***HUMANITIES TRANSPARENCIES***
H36, Goodness Gracious, I Must Have Been Dozing

TEACHING OPTIONS

Making Connections Across the Curriculum

Economics A tariff is a tax on imports that the public pays indirectly when its costs are passed along to consumers. A protectionist trade policy uses tariffs to protect domestic industry (and jobs), keeping out foreign goods or making their prices too high to compete with equivalent domestic products. A free-trade policy allows foreign goods to enter the country with lower or no tariffs so that consumers benefit from lower prices. Since nations usually reciprocate in tariff policies, lowering tariffs in one country encourages foreign countries to lower their tariffs on exports from that country.

Making Connections Across Time

Party Turmoil and the Elections of 1912 and 1992 The split in the Republican Party that preceded the 1912 presidential election would be echoed in the election of 1992—though not to the same degree. In 1992, third-party candidate Ross Perot, like Roosevelt, was a former Republican who split from the party and ran on a reform platform. The elections were also similar in other ways. An incumbent Republican, George Bush, had succeeded a more popular one, Ronald Reagan, and a Democrat, Bill Clinton, won with just over 40 percent of the vote.

MORE ABOUT . . .
Joseph Cannon

After being elected speaker in 1903, "Uncle Joe" began changing House rules to benefit Republicans—a process known as "cannonizing." Ousted as head of the Rules Committee by a coalition of Democrats and Republican progressives, he remained in the House until 1913 and then returned to serve in 1917, when he was in his eighties.

KEY PLAYER
William Howard Taft

Critical Thinking: Interpreting Ask what the nickname "Big Lub" suggests about Taft. *Possible Responses: Large; awkward; held in affection.*

GROLIER MULTIMEDIA ENCYCLOPEDIA
Bull Moose Party

OBJECTIVE
③ **INSTRUCT**

The Election of 1912

▶ ***Starting with the Student*** Students might list the section's main details in a chart like this one.

The Election of 1912

Candidate	Party	States Won
Woodrow Wilson		
William Howard Taft		
Theodore Roosevelt		
Eugene V. Debs		

▶ ***Discussing Key Ideas***
- Democrat Woodrow Wilson wins the election of 1912.
- The real winner is reform, with 75 percent of the vote going to reform candidates.

KEY PLAYER

WILLIAM HOWARD TAFT
1857–1930

William Howard Taft never wanted to be president. After he was designated by Roosevelt to inherit the Republican nomination in 1908, Taft served only one term. Having spent the first 20 years of his career as a lawyer and judge, he eventually spent his happiest years as a Supreme Court justice.

After leaving the White House, which Taft called "the lonesomest place in the world," he taught constitutional law at Yale for eight years. In 1921, President Harding named Taft chief justice of the Supreme Court. The man whose family had nicknamed him "Big Lub" called this appointment the highest honor he had ever received. As chief justice, Taft wrote that "in my present life I don't remember that I ever was President."

However, Americans remember Taft for, among many other things, initiating in 1910 the popular presidential custom of throwing out the first ball of the major league baseball season.

A group of reform-minded Republicans decided that their only alternative was to strip Cannon of his power. With the help of Democrats, they finally succeeded in March 1910. George W. Norris of Nebraska presented a resolution—adopted after hours of stormy debate—that called for the entire House to elect the Committee on Rules.

By the midterm elections of 1910, the Republican Party was in a shambles, with the progressives on one side and the "old guard" on the other. Voters voiced concern over the rising cost of living, which they blamed on the Payne-Aldrich Tariff. They also believed Taft to be against conservation. When the Republicans lost the election, the Democrats gained control of the House of Representatives for the first time in 18 years.

THINK THROUGH HISTORY
C. *Summarizing* *Over what issues did the Republican Party split during the Taft administration?*

C. Answer Conservatives and progressives divided over eliminating the power of Joe Cannon, the Speaker of the House; they also divided over Taft's support of the Payne-Aldrich Tariff.

THE BULL MOOSE PARTY After Taft's election, Roosevelt had gone to Africa to shoot big game. He returned in 1910 to a hero's welcome. People sang "When Rough and Ready Teddy Dashes Home" and "Mr. Roosevelt, Our Country Calls for You." Roosevelt responded by delivering a rousing speech and declaring that the country needed a "New Nationalism," under which the federal government would exert its power for "the welfare of the people."

By 1912, Roosevelt had decided to run for a third term as president. Taft, however, had the advantage of being the incumbent—that is, the holder of the office. At the Republican convention in June 1912, Taft's supporters refused to seat Roosevelt delegates and renominated Taft on the first ballot. Screaming "fraud," Roosevelt's supporters stormed out and held their own convention in August. There they formed a new third party, the Progressive Party, and nominated Roosevelt for president in an atmosphere of near hysteria. "We stand at Armageddon," Roosevelt proclaimed, invoking the biblical battle between good and evil. "We battle for the Lord."

The Progressive Party became known as the **Bull Moose Party,** after Roosevelt's boast that he was "as strong as a bull moose." The Bull Moose platform called for the direct election of senators and the adoption in all states of the initiative, referendum, and recall. It also advocated woman suffrage, national workmen's compensation, an eight-hour workday, a minimum wage for women, a federal law against child labor, and a federal trade commission to regulate business.

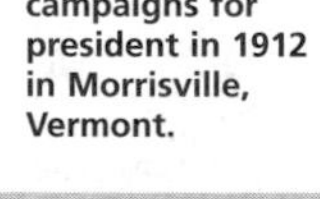

Roosevelt campaigns for president in 1912 in Morrisville, Vermont.

The split in the Republican ranks between the Bull Moose Party and Taft's conservative Republicans handed the Democrats their first real chance at the White House since the election of Grover Cleveland in 1892. In the 1912 presidential election, they put forward as their candidate a reform governor of New Jersey named **Woodrow Wilson.**

The Election of 1912

Under Governor Woodrow Wilson's leadership, the previously conservative New Jersey legislature had passed a host of reform measures. Now, as the Democratic presidential nominee, Wilson endorsed a progressive platform, called the New Freedom, that demanded even stronger antitrust legislation, banking reform, and reduced tariffs.

The split between Taft and Roosevelt, former Republican allies, turned nasty during the fall campaign. Taft labeled Roosevelt a "dangerous egotist," while Roosevelt

Block Schedule TEACHING OPTION **Time Needed: 40 Minutes**

Cooperative Activity: Reporting Election Results

Task: Groups of students will create a newspaper edition covering the results of the election of 1912.

Purpose: To understand a presidential election in which more than two parties claim a substantial amount of the vote.

Activity: Students' newspapers should include a variety of articles. One student might write a news article on election results, another might report on candidates' reactions, and a third might write a human-interest article based on interviewing voters as they leave the polls. Other students in the group might edit, create graphics, or put the paper together.

Building a Portfolio: Students can add the newspaper to their portfolio, along with a statement indicating which articles are theirs or what their role has been in creating the newspaper.

ALTERNATIVE ASSESSMENT BOOK
Standards for Evaluating a Cooperative Activity

Standards for Evaluation
Newspapers should . . .
- reflect the election with reasonable accuracy
- tell who, what, where, when, how, and why
- use catchy headlines
- include graphics and several different types of articles

branded Taft a "fathead" with the brain of a "guinea pig." Wilson stayed above the political feud, quietly gloating, "Don't interfere when your enemy is destroying himself."

The election offered voters several choices: Wilson's New Freedom, Taft's conservatism, Roosevelt's progressivism, or the Socialist Party policies of Eugene V. Debs. Both Roosevelt and Wilson supported a stronger government role in economic affairs but differed over strategies. Roosevelt supported government action to supervise big business but did not oppose all business monopolies. Wilson supported small business and free-market competition, and characterized all business monopolies as evil. In a speech in which Wilson declared that America stood for "a free field and no favor," he explained why he felt that all business monopolies were a threat.

D. Answer Taft favored business; Roosevelt supported government control of some big businesses; Wilson supported small businesses and thought monopolies were evil; Debs thought the national wealth should be distributed more equally.

THINK THROUGH HISTORY
D. *Contrasting* *Contrast the attitudes toward big business of the four major candidates for president in 1912.*

Election of 1912

ELECTORAL AND POPULAR VOTES

Party	Candidate	Electoral votes	Popular vote
Democratic	Woodrow Wilson	435	6,296,547
Progressive	Theodore Roosevelt	88	4,118,571
Republican	William H. Taft	8	3,486,720
Socialist	Eugene V. Debs	0	900,672

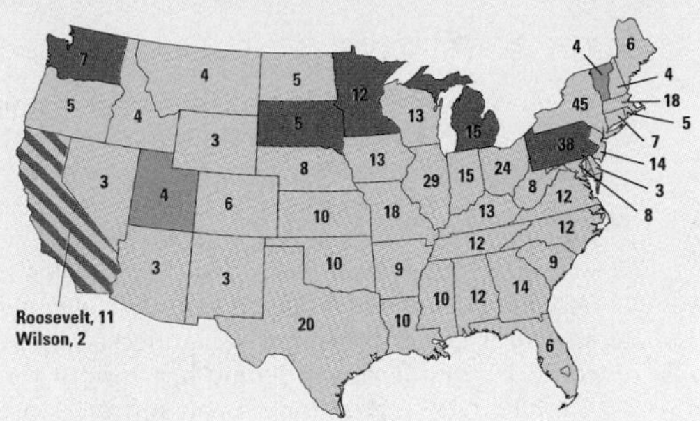

A PERSONAL VOICE

If the government is to tell big business men how to run their business, then don't you see that big business men have to get closer to the government even than they are now? Don't you see that they must capture the government, in order not to be restrained too much by it? . . . I don't care how benevolent the master is going to be, I will not live under a master. That is not what America was created for. America was created in order that every man should have the same chance as every other man to exercise mastery over his own fortunes.

WOODROW WILSON, quoted in *The New Freedom*

Debs, who won over 900,000 popular votes (6 percent of the total), went further than Wilson and Roosevelt, and called for an end to capitalism. He wanted to use the government not only to regulate business and bust trusts but also to distribute national wealth more equally among the people.

Although Wilson captured only 42 percent of the popular vote, he won an electoral victory and a Democratic majority in Congress. As a third-party candidate, Roosevelt defeated Taft in both popular and electoral votes. But reform claimed the real victory, with 75 percent of the vote going to the reform candidates, Wilson, Roosevelt, and Debs. In victory, Wilson could claim a mandate to break up trusts and to expand the government's role in social reform.

Section 4 Assessment

1. TERMS & NAMES
Identify:
- Gifford Pinchot
- William Howard Taft
- Payne-Aldrich Tariff
- Bull Moose Party
- Woodrow Wilson

2. SUMMARIZING Re-create the chart below on your paper. Then fill in the causes Taft supported that made people question his leadership.

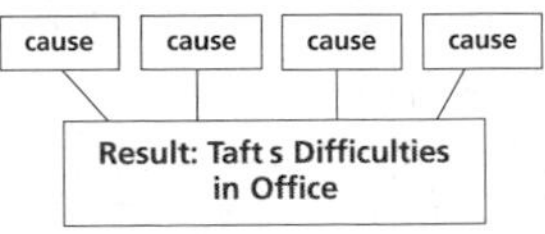

Which causes do you think would offend most people today? Explain.

3. MAKING PREDICTIONS What if Roosevelt had won another term in office in 1912? Speculate on how this might have affected the future of progressive reform. Support your answer.

THINK ABOUT
- Roosevelt's policies that Taft did not support
- the power struggles within the Republican Party
- Roosevelt's perception of presidential leadership

4. FORMING OPINIONS Both Roosevelt and Taft resorted to mudslinging during the 1912 presidential campaign. Do you approve or disapprove of negative campaign tactics? Support your opinion.

THINK ABOUT
- Roosevelt's and Taft's name-calling
- how you've reacted to negative campaign ads you've seen on television

ANSWERS

1. TERMS & NAMES

Gifford Pinchot, p. 350
William Howard Taft, p. 350
Payne-Aldrich Tariff, p. 351
Bull Moose Party, p. 352
Woodrow Wilson, p. 352

2. SUMMARIZING

Possible Answers: Signed Payne-Aldrich Tariff amid public outcry; returned reserved land to public sale; fired Pinchot; supported Joseph Cannon, Speaker of the House of Representatives; contributed to split in the Republican Party.
Students' responses about offending causes will vary but should include an explanation of their opinions.

3. MAKING PREDICTIONS

Possible Responses: Unlike Taft, Roosevelt would probably not have caved in to the conservatives in the Republican Party, his reform policies would have been strong. Roosevelt would probably have undone Taft's more conservative, less progressive policies and decisions in an attempt to restore a stronger government role in public affairs.

4. FORMING OPINIONS

Possible Responses: Students who approve might say that negative campaign tactics often help candidates win votes and that these tactics can get to the heart of key issues, especially the candidate's character. Students who disapprove might say that negative campaign tactics can alienate the public and cause candidates to lose votes and that these tactics can encourage dishonesty.

HISTORY FROM VISUALS
Election of 1912

Reading the Map Point out to students that if Roosevelt had not run—and if his votes had gone to Taft—Taft would have won over 50 percent of the vote in enough states to win the election.

ASSESS & RETEACH

Section 4 Assessment

Have students work individually to answer the questions. Then have them hold an informal debate on negative campaign tactics based on their answers to item 4.

Self-Assessment

Have students identify specific passages from the section that helped them answer each assessment question.

Section Quiz

FORMAL ASSESSMENT
Section Quiz, p. 119

Reteach

Ask students to share their responses to the Difficult Decisions questions on page 351. Students should draw on material in the text to support their opinions.

CLOSE

When Taft could not hold together the conservative and progressive wings of the Republican Party, the party split, allowing Democrat Woodrow Wilson to win the presidency in 1912.

Section 5 Overview

OBJECTIVES

1. To describe Woodrow Wilson's background and the progressive reforms of his presidency.
2. To explain the steps leading to woman suffrage.
3. To sum up the limits of Wilson's progressivism.

SKILLBUILDER

- Interpreting graphs, p. 356

CRITICAL THINKING

- Comparing and contrasting, p. 355
- Theme: Economic Opportunity, p. 356
- Summarizing, pp. 357, 359
- Theme: Women in America, p. 358
- Recognizing effects, p. 358
- Drawing conclusions, p. 359
- Developing historical perspective, p. 359

FOCUS & MOTIVATE

5-MINUTE WARM-UP

Drawing Conclusions
To draw conclusions about Wilson's progressive ideals, have students preview the section's key terms and answer these questions.

1. What types of reform were important to Wilson?
2. What did Wilson think should be the relationship between government and business?

WARM-UP TRANSPARENCY 9

▶ ***Starting with the Student***

- Ask students who the "movers and shakers" in their school or community are.
- Have students discuss the qualities that effective people share. Ask if they think those qualities would be found in a person described as "born halfway between the Bible and the dictionary."

IN-DEPTH RESOURCES: UNIT 3
American Lives: Carrie Chapman Catt, p. 17

5 Wilson's New Freedom

TERMS & NAMES
- Carrie Chapman Catt
- Clayton Antitrust Act
- Federal Trade Commission
- Federal Reserve System
- Nineteenth Amendment

LEARN ABOUT Woodrow Wilson and his approach to reform
TO UNDERSTAND the victories and defeats for progressivism during his administration.

ONE AMERICAN'S STORY

When Woodrow Wilson arrived in Washington for his inauguration on March 3, 1913, he looked in vain for the cheering crowds. In fact, many Washingtonians had disappeared to watch a woman suffrage parade, in which 5,000 women marched through a hostile crowd on Pennsylvania Avenue. Alice Paul and Lucy Burns, the parade's organizers, were radical young members of the National American Woman Suffrage Association (NAWSA). As police failed to restrain the rowdy gathering and embarrassed congressmen demanded an investigation, Burns and Paul could see momentum building in the fight for suffrage.

Indeed, the battle for woman suffrage entered a bold new phase during the Wilson administration. By the time Wilson began his campaign for a second term, the NAWSA's president, **Carrie Chapman Catt,** saw victory on the horizon. Catt expressed her optimism in a letter to her friend Maud Wood Park.

Carrie Chapman Catt

A PERSONAL VOICE

I do feel keenly that the turn of the road has come. . . . I really believe that we might pull off a campaign which would mean the vote within the next six years if we could secure a Board of officers who would have sufficient momentum, confidence and working power in them. . . . Come! My dear Mrs. Park, gird on your armor once more.

CARRIE CHAPMAN CATT, letter to Maud Wood Park, August 30, 1916

Catt called an emergency suffrage convention in September 1916, at which Wilson cautiously supported suffrage. He told the convention, "There has been a force behind you that will . . . be triumphant and for which you can afford to wait." They did have to wait, but within four years, the passage of the suffrage amendment became the capstone of the progressive movement.

Progressive Reform Under Wilson

Like Theodore Roosevelt, Woodrow Wilson claimed progressive ideals. Although both presidents certainly believed in a strong executive, Wilson pictured a different role for the federal government than the one Roosevelt had favored. The new president didn't think that trusts should be regulated; he thought they should be broken up. He didn't think government should get bigger; he thought business should be made smaller. Wilson earned his progressive credentials by attacking large concentrations of power in an effort to give greater freedom to average citizens. However, the prejudices of his Southern background prevented him from using federal power to fight off attacks directed at the civil rights of African Americans.

WILSON'S BACKGROUND The son, grandson, and nephew of Presbyterian ministers, Wilson spent his youth in the South during the Civil War and Reconstruction. There he received a strict moral upbringing. In fact, a critic once said that the pious and scholarly Wilson had been "born halfway between the Bible and the dictionary and never got away from either." Though Wilson prac-

SECTION 5 RESOURCES

PRINT RESOURCES

IN-DEPTH RESOURCES: UNIT 3
Guided Reading, p. 5
Geography Application: The Movement Toward Woman Suffrage, p. 7
American Lives: Carrie Chapman Catt, p. 17

READING STUDY GUIDE, p. 105

ACCESS FOR STUDENTS ACQUIRING ENGLISH
Guided Reading (Spanish), p. 124
Geography Application: The Movement Toward Woman Suffrage (Spanish), p. 126

SPANISH READING STUDY GUIDE, p. 105

FORMAL ASSESSMENT
Section Quiz, p. 120

ALTERNATIVE ASSESSMENT BOOK
See forms for supporting and scoring alternative activities.

TECHNOLOGY RESOURCES

CRITICAL THINKING TRANSPARENCIES
CT17, Progressive Movement

CD-ROM *Grolier Multimedia Encyclopedia*

VIDEO *American Portfolio: A Videodisc for U.S. History* user's guide, pp. 168, 169, 171, 172

INTERNET http://www.mlushistory.com

ticed law for a short time after graduating from the College of New Jersey (which in 1896 became known as Princeton University), he much preferred his position as a political science professor. In 1902, Wilson became the president of Princeton University, where his reforms earned national praise.

New Jersey's Democratic political machine tapped Wilson to run for governor in 1910. Wilson declared his independence of the party machine shortly after he took office. As governor, he sponsored legislation to adopt such progressive programs as a direct primary, workmen's compensation, and regulation of public utilities and railroads. As America's newly elected president, Wilson moved to enact his program, the "New Freedom," and planned his attack on what he called the triple wall of privilege: the trusts, tariffs, and high finance.

THINK THROUGH HISTORY
A. Comparing and Contrasting *Compare and contrast Wilson's background with Roosevelt's.*

A. Answer Roosevelt was born into a wealthy family; he made up for his asthma with rigorous physical activities. Wilson had a strict upbringing, becoming a lawyer and professor. Both became reform governors with progressive reputations; both had reputations as scholars.

Woodrow Wilson continued Roosevelt s and Taft s antitrust effort.

CLAYTON ANTITRUST ACT "Freedom today," Wilson said, "is something more than being let alone. Without the watchful . . . resolute interference of the government, there can be no fair play between individuals and such powerful institutions as the trust." (See *trust* on page 940 in the Economics Handbook.) Congress enacted two key antitrust measures during Wilson's administration, the Federal Trade Act and the **Clayton Antitrust Act.** The Clayton Act of 1914 sought to strengthen the Sherman Antitrust Act of 1890 by declaring certain business practices illegal. For example, a corporation could no longer acquire the stock of another corporation if doing so would create a monopoly. In addition, if a company violated the law, its officers could be prosecuted.

Conservative courts had been treating trade unions as monopolies under the Sherman Antitrust Act. The Clayton Act specified that labor unions and farm organizations not only had a right to exist but also would no longer be subject to antitrust laws. Now strikes, peaceful picketing, boycotts, and the collection of strike benefits became legal. Furthermore, injunctions against strikers were prohibited unless the strikers threatened "irreparable injury to property"—that is, damage that could not be remedied. Recognizing the Clayton Act's value to workers, Samuel Gompers, president of the American Federation of Labor (AFL), called the act a Magna Carta for labor, referring to the English document, signed in 1215, in which the English king recognized that he was under the law and that the law granted rights to his subjects.

The Federal Trade Act of 1914 set up a five-member "watchdog" agency called the **Federal Trade Commission** (FTC), with the power to investigate possible violations of regulatory statutes, to require periodic reports from corporations, and to put an end to unfair business competition and unfair business practices, such as inaccurate labeling. If the FTC discovered a corporation to be engaging in illegal activity, the commission could hand down a cease-and-desist order, as it did almost 400 times during Wilson's administration.

A NEW TAX SYSTEM Wilson believed that high tariff rates created monopolies by reducing competition. Early in 1913, the new president summoned Congress to a special session and established a precedent by delivering the State of the Union message in person rather than sending it to be read by a clerk.

Drawing on his experience as a professor, Wilson defended and helped secure passage of the Underwood Tariff of 1913, which substantially reduced tariff rates for the first time since the Civil War. Senate passage had appeared unlikely because manufacturing lobbyists—people hired by manufacturers to present their case to

NOW & THEN

DEREGULATION

In recent years railroads, airlines, and the telecommunications industries have all been deregulated, or permitted to compete without government control, in an effort to improve their efficiency and lower prices. As one supporter of deregulation said, "There will be no turning back from a more competitive, more efficient, and more pro-consumer industry."

During the progressive era, reformers viewed regulation as a necessary role of government to ensure safety and fairness for consumers as well as industrial competitors. Opponents of regulation, however, believed that government regulation caused inefficiency and high prices.

Modern critics of deregulation argue that deregulated businesses may simply ignore hard-to-serve populations, such as elderly, poor, or disabled people, while competing for more profitable customers.

OBJECTIVE
① INSTRUCT

Progressive Reform Under Wilson

▶ ***Starting with the Student*** Have students use a cluster diagram similar to this one to organize Wilson administration policies.

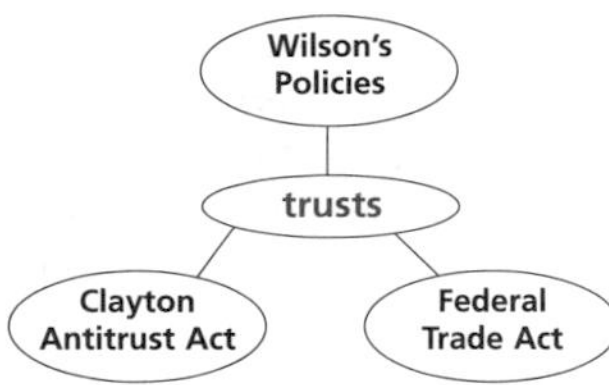

▶ ***Discussing Key Ideas***
- Woodrow Wilson attacks the trusts with the Federal Trade Act and Clayton Antitrust Act.
- Wilson lowers tariffs, making up for revenue losses with the new income tax.
- Wilson establishes the Federal Reserve System.

IN-DEPTH RESOURCES: UNIT 3
Guided Reading, p. 5

ACCESS FOR STUDENTS ACQUIRING ENGLISH
Guided Reading (Spanish), p. 124

GROLIER MULTIMEDIA ENCYCLOPEDIA
from a speech on the rights of labor by William H. Taft

NOW & THEN
Deregulation
Critical Thinking: Analyzing Ask students if they or their families have felt the effects of deregulation. Discuss such topics as airfare wars, media mergers, and the Telecommunications Act of 1996, which removed some of the restrictions of those mergers.

TEACHING OPTIONS

Teaching Less Proficient Readers

Clarifying To clarify Wilson's antitrust measures, ask students to identify some key parts of the antitrust laws and list them on the board. Then ask students to make up examples of such laws in action. For example:

1. Monopolies: A business cannot buy another business if that purchase would create a monopoly. *Example: There cannot be only one telephone company or steel company or oil company.*
2. Unions: Unions have a right to exist and are not subject to antitrust laws. *Example:* ___________.
3. Watchdog agencies: The Federal Trade Commission has the power to investigate business practices. *Example:* _______.

Making Connections Across the Curriculum

Economics Have a student explain how a high tariff might create a monopoly by reducing competition, as Wilson believed. *Possible Response: The tariff would keep out foreign competition.* Then allow interested students to debate the effects of the Clayton Antitrust Act on labor unions. What do students think of the right to strike?

HISTORY FROM VISUALS

Tax Revenue, 1915–1995

Reading the Graph Ask what the data presented on the graph suggests about the nation and the federal government from 1915 to 1995. *Possible Response: U.S. residents were making more money and being taxed at a higher percent, and the federal government grew far richer.*

Extension Ask what students would guess about inflation in the United States from 1915 to 1995. *Possible Response: Judging from the increases in taxes collected, there was probably a high level of inflation.*

OBJECTIVE

② **INSTRUCT**

Voting Rights for Women

▶ ***Discussing Key Ideas***

- Women press for the vote, winning some local battles.
- Carrie Chapman Catt succeeds Susan B. Anthony as head of NAWSA.
- In 1920, women finally win the right to vote through ratification of the Nineteenth Amendment.

MORE ABOUT . . .

Suffrage in Wyoming

While still a territory, Wyoming granted women the right to vote, hold office, and serve on juries in a law passed on December 10, 1869—the first of its kind in the nation.

IN-DEPTH RESOURCES: UNIT 3
Geography Application: The Movement Toward Woman Suffrage, p. 7

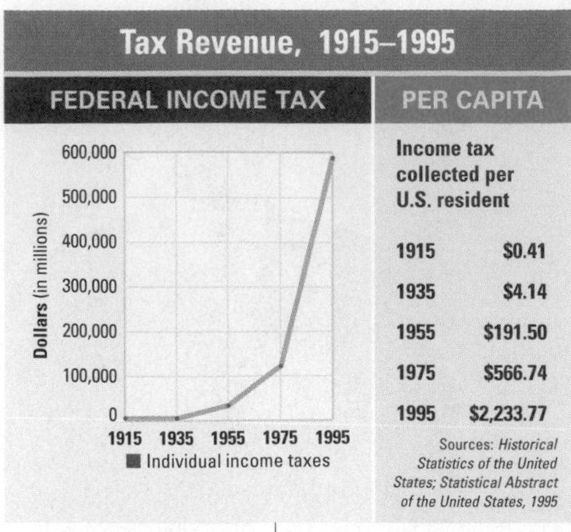

SKILLBUILDER
INTERPRETING GRAPHS ***About what year did income tax revenues first begin to rise sharply? About how much revenue did the income tax bring into the federal government in 1995?***

Skillbuilder Answer
Year: About 1955.
Revenue: Just under $600 billion.

government officials—had descended on the capital to urge senators to vote no. Wilson denounced the lobbyists and urged voters to monitor their senators' votes. Because of the new president's use of the bully pulpit, the Senate cut tariff rates even more deeply than the House version had done.

FEDERAL INCOME TAX Overall, tariff rates dropped from about 40 percent to under 30 percent. Lowering tariffs, however, meant that the federal government had to replace the revenue that tariffs had previously supplied. The Sixteenth Amendment, which was ratified in 1913, legalized a graduated federal income tax, which provided revenue by taxing individual earnings and corporate profits. (See *taxation* on page 939 in the Economics Handbook.)

The graduated tax, which taxed larger incomes at higher rates than smaller incomes, began with a modest tax on incomes over $4,000. Almost all factory workers and farmers were exempt from this tax, since their incomes were far less than that figure. The tax then ranged from 1 percent to a maximum of 6 percent on incomes over $500,000. At the time, few congressmen realized the revenue-generating potential of the income tax. By 1917, however, the government was receiving more money from the income tax than it had ever gained from tariffs, even though the amount was small by today's standards. Currently, income taxes on corporations and individuals represent the federal government's main source of revenue.

FEDERAL RESERVE SYSTEM After tackling tariff reform, Wilson turned his attention to financial reform. Both liberals and conservatives agreed that the nation needed a way to make credit more easily available outside the financial centers of New York City and Boston. The nation also needed a way to quickly adjust the amount of money in circulation. Both credit availability and money supply had to keep pace with the economy.

Wilson solved both of these problems by establishing a decentralized private banking system under federal control. The Federal Reserve Act of 1913 divided the nation into 12 districts. Each district had a federal reserve bank with which all the national banks within the district were affiliated. State banks within the district could join if they met certain requirements.

The federal reserve banks had the power to issue new paper currency in emergency situations. The member banks could use the new currency to make loans to their customers. Federal reserve banks could transfer funds to member banks that ran into trouble, saving the banks from closing and protecting the savings of customers. By 1923, roughly 70 percent of the nation's banking resources were part of the **Federal Reserve System.** The Federal Reserve System, which still serves as the basis of the nation's banking system, is one of the most enduring achievements of the Wilson administration.

B. Answer
Wilson's tariff reform cut tariff rates and reduced the likelihood of monopolies controlling competition. The Federal Reserve System made it possible for credit availability and the money supply to be responsive to the state of the economy.

THINK THROUGH HISTORY
B. THEME
Economic Opportunity *Why were tariff reform and the Federal Reserve System important?*

Voting Rights for Women

While Wilson pushed hard for reform of trusts, tariffs, and banking, determined women intensified their push for the vote. The educated, native-born, middle-class women who had been active in progressive movements had grown increasingly impatient about not being allowed to vote, especially when they saw male immigrants granted suffrage automatically upon achieving citizenship. In 1910, women had federal voting rights only in Wyoming, Utah, Colorado, and Idaho.

TEACHING OPTIONS

Making Connections Across the Curriculum

Economics Discuss the difference between a flat tax, which takes the same percentage of income from everyone, and a graduated tax, which takes a higher percentage from those who earn more. For example, a person earning $10,000 has barely enough on which to live. If you take away 10 percent in taxes, he or she has only $9,000, clearly cutting into necessities. On the other hand, someone earning $100,000 can probably afford to pay 10 percent in taxes without suffering any hardship. Note that a tariff is an indirect flat tax since it is passed along equally, like a sales tax, to rich and poor alike.

Exploring Themes

Women in America Underscore the role of World War I in ensuring women the right to vote at last. It was not until so many women filled the shoes of men off fighting the war that women achieved suffrage. Note that the ratification of the Nineteenth Amendment, which granted woman suffrage, took place in 1920, over 70 years after Lucretia Mott and Elizabeth Cady Stanton led the first women's rights convention in Seneca Falls, New York.

Suffragists parading in New York City carry a banner that quotes President Wilson s support of the movement.

Despite disappointing failures in California and New York, determined suffragists persisted in their campaign. Three new developments finally brought success within reach: the increased activism of local groups, the use of bold new strategies to build enthusiasm for the movement, and the rebirth of the national movement under Carrie Chapman Catt.

LOCAL SUFFRAGE BATTLES Growing numbers of young, college-educated women helped breathe new life into the woman suffrage movement. Two Massachusetts organizations, the Boston Equal Suffrage Association for Good Government and the College Equal Suffrage League, initiated door-to-door campaigns to reach potential supporters. Founded by the Radcliffe graduate Maud Wood Park, the Boston group spread the message of suffrage to poor and working-class women, who did not attend suffrage meetings. Women who belonged to these groups also took trolley tours. At each stop, a suffragist would speak to the crowds that gathered to watch the unusual sight of a woman speaking in public.

Many wealthy young women who visited Europe as part of their education became involved in the suffrage movement in Britain. Led by Emmeline Pankhurst, British suffragists used increasingly strident tactics, such as heckling government officials, to advance their cause. Inspired by such bold activism, American women returned to the United States ready to try similar approaches in their own campaigns for suffrage.

THINK THROUGH HISTORY
C. *Summarizing* *Summarize the strategies women used in their fight for suffrage.*

C. Answer Grassroots, state-by-state efforts of the NAWSA and local groups; militant efforts, such as heckling officials.

"How long must women wait for liberty?"

NAWSA PICKET SIGN

CATT AND THE NATIONAL MOVEMENT On the national level, Susan B. Anthony's retirement from the presidency of the National American Woman Suffrage Association (NAWSA) in 1900 pushed Carrie Chapman Catt into prominence. Catt became president of NAWSA, a post she held until 1904 and returned to in 1915. In the years between her tenures as NAWSA president, Catt organized New York's Woman Suffrage Party, which narrowly lost its first referendum in 1915. Within two days, the women raised $100,000 for the next campaign, announcing that with "undiminished courage we are again in the field of action." When Catt returned to the NAWSA presidency in 1915, she concentrated on (1) painstaking organization; (2) close ties between local, state, and national workers; (3) establishing a wide base of support; (4) cautious lobbying; and (5) gracious, ladylike behavior.

The energy of local groups and the NAWSA's example of careful grassroots organization won victories in Washington, California, Kansas, Oregon, and Arizona between 1910 and 1912. During the same period, however, failures in Michigan, Ohio, and Wisconsin turned some suffragists to more militant

HISTORY FROM VISUALS
Women March for Suffrage

Reading the Image Ask students to discuss details from the photograph that they find interesting, such as the women's clothing and the message on the banner.

Extension Note that Wilson's support for woman suffrage was tepid and vague, and ask why the women might nevertheless carry this banner. *Possible Responses: To force his hand; to shame him into stronger support; to mislead the public into thinking his support is stronger.*

GROLIER MULTIMEDIA ENCYCLOPEDIA
Multimedia map of women's suffrage

MORE ABOUT . . .
Maud Wood Park

After the death of her first husband, Park married a theatrical agent named Robert Hunter but kept the marriage quiet while she campaigned for woman suffrage. A Boston native, she founded the College Equal Suffrage League with Inez Haynes Gillmore Irwin in 1901 and was the first president of the League of Women Voters, founded in 1919. In later years Park led the Women's Joint Congressional Committee and wrote a book about her experiences in Washington.

Block Schedule TEACHING OPTION **Time Needed: 30 Minutes**

Cooperative Activity: Writing Letters to the Editor

Task: Groups of students will write letters expressing opinions about woman suffrage.

Purpose: To understand historical attitudes toward woman suffrage.

Activity: Ask students to imagine that they are writing letters to the editor of a newspaper or magazine during the presidency of Woodrow Wilson. Each group member should write a brief letter expressing an opinion on woman suffrage. Students should pool their ideas before writing the letters, including ideas for imaginary background details about the letters' writers, and should make sure that various viewpoints are expressed. Final letters might be printed or posted.

Building a Portfolio Students who choose to add their letter to their portfolio should include an explanation of their own contribution to the letter.

ALTERNATIVE ASSESSMENT BOOK
Standards for Evaluating a Cooperative Activity

Standards for Evaluation
Letters should . . .

- reflect historical facts accurately
- express a view on woman suffrage
- contain details about their imaginary authors
- use correct business-letter form

MORE ABOUT . . .
Alice Paul

Raised in a Quaker family, Paul attended Swarthmore College and later trained as a lawyer. In London she worked in a settlement house and was jailed for her activities in the suffrage movement. In 1913, she helped found the Congressional Union for Woman Suffrage, later part of the National Woman's Party, which she chaired in the 1940s. After World War II, she helped ensure that the U.N. charter included equal rights provisions for women.

ON THE WORLD STAGE
Emmeline Pankhurst

Critical Thinking: Evaluating Have students give their opinions of Pankhurst's tactics. *Possible Responses: Some may feel that her tactics earned needed publicity and advanced a cause. Others may feel that she antagonized too many people.*

OBJECTIVE
③ INSTRUCT

The Limits of Progressivism

▶ ***Starting with the Student***
- Have students discuss how they feel when someone breaks a promise.
- Ask them if they think similar feelings apply when a politician breaks a campaign promise.

▶ ***Discussing Key Ideas***
- Wilson retreats on civil rights.
- Reform moves to the back burner as America enters World War I.

ON THE WORLD STAGE

EMMELINE PANKHURST

American women struggling for suffrage received valuable tutoring in effective tactics from their English counterparts, whose bold maneuvers had captured media coverage.

The noted British suffragist Emmeline Pankhurst, who helped found the National Women's Social and Political Union, often engaged in radical tactics. Pankhurst and other suffragists staged parades, organized protest meetings, endured hunger strikes, heckled candidates for Parliament, and spit on policemen who tried to quiet them. They were often imprisoned for their activities, before Parliament granted them their right to vote in 1928.

methods. Meanwhile, other suffragists focused on securing a constitutional amendment to achieve their goals in one broad sweep.

Lucy Burns and Alice Paul had recently returned from England infused with the bold tactics of the British movement. At first, Burns and Paul worked with NAWSA, but the pair broke off in 1914 to form their own more radical organization, the Congressional Union, and its successor, the National Woman's Party. Impatient with NAWSA's careful state-by-state approach, the National Woman's Party sought instead to pressure the federal government to pass a suffrage amendment. While NAWSA tried to enlist lawmakers from both parties, the National Woman's Party openly blamed "the party in power"—the Democrats—for women's failure to win suffrage.

In 1916, delegates to the Democratic convention faced hostile women who were wearing yellow sashes and holding signs and banners demanding the right to vote. By 1917, Paul had organized her followers to mount a round-the-clock picket line around the White House, whose occupant, Wilson, had issued only a lukewarm endorsement of suffrage. Some of the picketers were arrested, jailed, and even force-fed when they attempted a hunger strike.

The untiring efforts of these groups and America's involvement in World War I finally made suffrage inevitable. Patriotic American women who headed committees, knitted socks for soldiers, and sold liberty bonds now claimed their overdue reward for supporting the war effort. In 1919, Congress passed the **Nineteenth Amendment,** granting women the right to vote. The amendment won final ratification in August 1920—72 years after women had first convened and demanded the vote at the Seneca Falls convention in 1848.

D. Answer *Possible Response:* A combination of factors, including women's growing experience in the public realm—which increased their economic and social power—and their importance in the war effort.

THINK THROUGH HISTORY
D. THEME ***Women in America*** *Why do you think women won the right to vote in 1920, after earlier efforts had failed?*

The Limits of Progressivism

Despite Wilson's successes at instituting progressive economic and political reforms, he disappointed progressives who favored social reform. For example, he opposed a federal child-labor law because he considered such a ban unconstitutional. On racial matters, Wilson appeased conservative Southern Democratic voters but disappointed his Northern white and black supporters. He placed segregationists in charge of federal agencies, thereby expanding racial segregation in the federal government, the military, and Washington, D.C.

WILSON AND CIVIL RIGHTS Like Roosevelt and Taft, Wilson seemed to retreat on civil rights once in office. During the presidential campaign of 1912, he won the support of the NAACP's black intellectuals and white liberals by promising to treat blacks equally and to speak out against lynching.

As president, however, Wilson opposed federal antilynching legislation, arguing that these crimes fell under state jurisdiction. In addition, the Capitol and the federal offices in Washington, D.C., which had been desegregated during Reconstruction, resumed the practice of segregating the races shortly after Wilson's election.

Wilson appointed to his cabinet fellow white Southerners who extended segregation. Secretary of the Navy Josephus Daniels, for example, proposed at a cabinet meeting to do away with common drinking fountains and towels in his department. According to an entry in Daniels's diary, President Wilson agreed because he had "made no promises in particular to negroes, except to do them justice." Segregated facilities, in the president's mind, were just.

African Americans and their liberal white supporters in the NAACP felt betrayed. Oswald Garrison Villard, a grandson of the abolitionist William Lloyd Garrison, wrote to Wilson in dismay, "The colored men who voted and worked for

E. Answer Wilson opposed anti-lynching legislation, did not continue desegregation in the federal government, and appointed to his cabinet white Southerners who supported segregation.

THINK THROUGH HISTORY
E. *Recognizing Effects* *What actions by Wilson disappointed civil rights advocates?*

TEACHING OPTIONS

Teaching Gifted and Talented Students

Amending the Constitution Have interested students research and report on these different constitutional amendments passed in the progressive era:

- Sixteenth Amendment, authorizing the income tax.
- Seventeenth Amendment, establishing a direct popular vote for U.S. senators.
- Eighteenth Amendment, prohibiting the manufacture, sales, or transportation of liquor (later repealed).
- Nineteenth Amendment, granting women the vote.

Making Connections Across Cultures

Civil Rights One of the ironies of the progressive movement was that, for political reasons if not personal preference, it remained rather unprogressive on the issue of African-American civil rights. Wilson's ultimate betrayal despite campaign promises points to a regional division in the Democratic Party that would plague it for several decades. In telling Villard he was acting "in the interest of the negroes," Wilson went on to explain that he had segregated several Washington departments to help allay friction and safeguard the holding of offices by "negroes."

you in the belief that their status as Americans was safe in your hands are deeply cast down." Wilson's response—that he had acted "in the interest of the negroes" and "with the approval of some of the most influential negroes I know"—only widened the rift between the president and some of his former supporters.

The president's reception of an African-American delegation on November 12, 1914, brought the confrontation to a bitter climax. William Monroe Trotter, editor-in-chief of an African-American Boston newspaper called the *Guardian*, led the delegation. Trotter complained that African Americans from 38 states had asked the president to reverse the segregation of government employees, but that segregation had since increased. Trotter then commented on Wilson's inaction.

A PERSONAL VOICE

Only two years ago you were heralded as perhaps the second Lincoln, and now the Afro-American leaders who supported you are hounded as false leaders and traitors to their race. . . . As equal citizens and by virtue of your public promises we are entitled at your hands to freedom from discrimination, restriction, imputation, and insult in government employ. Have you a "new freedom" for white Americans and a new slavery for your "Afro-American fellow citizens"? God forbid!

WILLIAM MONROE TROTTER, address to President Wilson, November 12, 1914

"There's no chance of progress and reform in an administration in which war plays the principal part."

WOODROW WILSON

Wilson found Trotter's tone infuriating. After an angry Trotter shook his finger at the president to emphasize a point, the furious Wilson demanded that the delegation leave. Wilson's refusal to extend civil rights to African Americans pointed to the limits of progressivism under his administration. The specter of American involvement in the war raging in Europe would soon reveal more weaknesses.

THE TWILIGHT OF PROGRESSIVISM After taking office in 1913, Wilson had said, "There's no chance of progress and reform in an administration in which war plays the principal part." The outbreak of World War I in Europe in 1914 demanded America's involvement. Meanwhile, distracted Americans and their legislators allowed reform efforts to stall. As the pacifist and reformer Jane Addams mournfully reflected, "The spirit of fighting burns away all those impulses . . . which foster the will to justice."

But international conflict was destined to be part of Wilson's presidency. During the early years of his administration, Wilson had dealt with issues of imperialism that had roots in the late 19th century. However, World War I dominated most of his second term as president.

Section 5 Assessment

1. TERMS & NAMES

Identify:
- Carrie Chapman Catt
- Clayton Antitrust Act
- Federal Trade Commission
- Federal Reserve System
- Nineteenth Amendment

2. SUMMARIZING Create a time line of key events relating to progressivism during Wilson's first term. Use the dates already plotted on the time line below as a guide.

1913 1914 1915 1916

Write a paragraph explaining which event you think best demonstrates progressive reform.

3. DRAWING CONCLUSIONS Wilson said, "Without the watchful . . . resolute interference of the government, there can be no fair play between individuals and . . . the trust." How does this statement reflect Wilson's approach to reform? Support your answer.

THINK ABOUT
- government's responsibility to the public
- the passage of two key antitrust measures during Wilson's administration

4. DEVELOPING HISTORICAL PERSPECTIVE If you were a suffragist in the early 1900s, which organization would you have joined—the National American Woman Suffrage Association or the National Woman's Party?

THINK ABOUT
- Catt's strategy to win the vote
- Alice Paul's approach to achieving suffrage
- the National Woman's Party's protest at the 1916 Democratic convention

ANSWERS

1. TERMS & NAMES

Carrie Chapman Catt, p. 354
Clayton Antitrust Act, p. 355
Federal Trade Commission, p. 355
Federal Reserve System, p. 356
Nineteenth Amendment, p. 358

2. SUMMARIZING

Possible Answers:
1913—NAWSA protests on Wilson's inauguration day; Federal Reserve Act divides nation into 12 regions, each headed by a federal reserve bank.
1914—Federal Trade Act sets up Federal Trade Commission to investigate unfair business practices; Clayton Antitrust Act strengthens the Sherman Antitrust Act; African-American delegation confronts Wilson on his segregation policies.
1916—Suffragists picket the Democratic Party convention.
Students' paragraphs will vary.

3. DRAWING CONCLUSIONS

Possible Responses: Wilson believed that the unbridled growth of big business threatened the freedom of individuals—the consumers and workers—who alone were powerless to curb the exploitative practices of trusts. He thought that government had the responsibility to step in to represent individuals' concerns and rights and to safeguard public welfare.

4. DEVELOPING HISTORICAL PERSPECTIVE

Possible Answers: Students who would prefer to join the NAWSA might say that the organization's focus on persuasion, rather than coercion, is a more effective approach because it is less likely to provoke confrontation. Students who would prefer to join the National Woman's Party might say that suffragists needed to be more confrontational and use militant tactics to achieve their goals.

MORE ABOUT . . .
William Monroe Trotter

A Harvard graduate, Trotter opposed Booker T. Washington's accommodation and instead helped found the Niagara Movement with W. E. B. Du Bois. On finding that the NAACP was still too moderate in its timetable, he established the National Equal Rights League to protest discrimination. The nonviolent protest Trotter advocated was later adopted by Martin Luther King, Jr., and others in the civil rights movement.

ASSESS & RETEACH

Section 5 Assessment

Have students work in small groups to discuss the questions and share their responses.

Self-Assessment

Have students create a two-column chart on which they compare their own responses to the section assessment (column 1) with the portions of the text that best answer each question (column 2).

Section Quiz

FORMAL ASSESSMENT
Section Quiz, p. 120

Reteach

Use the critical thinking transparency on the progressive era to review concepts.

CRITICAL THINKING TRANSPARENCIES
CT17, Progressive Movement

CLOSE

Although Wilson initiated progressive economic and political reforms, his record on social reforms disappointed progressives. Women won the vote with little real help from him, and his record on civil rights was poor.

CHAPTER 9
ASSESSMENT ANSWERS

REVIEWING THE CHAPTER

TERMS & NAMES

1. progressive movement, p. 330
2. muckraker, p. 332
3. suffrage, p. 339
4. Susan B. Anthony, p. 339
5. Theodore Roosevelt, p. 341
6. NAACP, p. 347
7. Gifford Pinchot, p. 348
8. Woodrow Wilson, p. 352
9. Clayton Antitrust Act, p. 355
10. Federal Reserve System, p. 356

MAIN IDEAS

11. Protecting social welfare, promoting moral reform, creating economic reform, and fostering efficiency.

12. Laws setting minimum age, limiting work hours, and providing workers' compensation.

13. Many African-American and immigrant women who lacked education or skills worked as domestic workers.

14. The NACW, promoted the moral education of African Americans. The NAWSA was committed to winning women's right to vote.

15. Sinclair's descriptions of the meatpacking industry's corrupt practices disgusted both the public and Roosevelt, who pushed Congress to pass the Meat Inspection Act.

16. When a strike threatened public welfare, the federal government was expected to intervene, with arbitration.

17. Taft was a more cautious progressive than Roosevelt but did break up more trusts than Roosevelt had.

18. Though Wilson himself captured only 42 percent of the popular vote, 75 percent of the popular vote did go to reform candidates.

19. It recognized the legality of labor unions, strikes, peaceful picketing, boycotts, and strike benefits; it limited the use of injunctions in court disputes.

20. Child labor laws, because he felt they were unconstitutional; federal antilynching laws, because he contended such crimes fell under state jurisdictions.

Chapter 9 Assessment

REVIEWING THE CHAPTER

TERMS & NAMES For each item below, write a sentence explaining its connection to the progressive era. For each person named below, explain his or her role in events during this period.

1. progressive movement	**6. NAACP**
2. muckraker	**7. Gifford Pinchot**
3. suffrage	**8. Woodrow Wilson**
4. Susan B. Anthony	**9. Clayton Antitrust Act**
5. Theodore Roosevelt	**10. Federal Reserve System**

MAIN IDEAS

SECTION 1 *(pages 330–336)*

The Origins of Progressivism

11. What were the four goals that various progressive reform movements struggled to achieve?
12. What kinds of state labor laws resulted from progressives' lobbying to protect workers?

SECTION 2 *(pages 337–340)*

Women in Public Life

13. In the 1890s, what job opportunities were available to uneducated women without industrial skills? Who typically filled these positions?
14. Give two examples of women's national organizations committed to social activism, and briefly describe their progressive missions.

SECTION 3 *(pages 341–347)*

Teddy Roosevelt's Square Deal

15. What scandalous practices did Upton Sinclair expose in his novel *The Jungle?* How did the American public, Roosevelt, and Congress respond?
16. What precedent did Roosevelt set when he helped mediate the 1902 coal strike?

SECTION 4 *(pages 350–353)*

Progressivism Under Taft

17. As a progressive, how did Taft compare with Roosevelt, his predecessor?
18. Why could Wilson claim a mandate to broaden the government's role in social reform, based on the popular vote in the 1912 presidential election?

SECTION 5 *(pages 354–359)*

Wilson's New Freedom

19. How did the Clayton Antitrust Act benefit labor?
20. Cite two examples of social welfare legislation that Wilson opposed during his presidency and the arguments he used to defend his position.

THINKING CRITICALLY

1. PRESIDENTIAL AGENDAS Create a Venn diagram to show some of the similarities and differences between Roosevelt's Square Deal and Wilson's New Freedom.

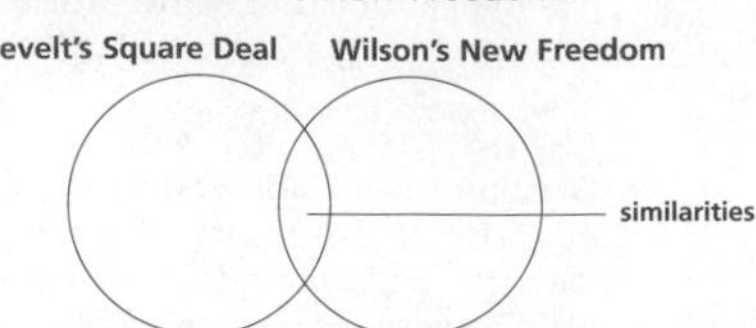

2. TRENDS IN AMERICAN SOCIETY What social, political, and economic trends in American life do you think caused the reform impulse during the progressive era? Support your answer with details from the text.

3. PROGRESSIVISM AND DEMOCRACY Reread Woodrow Wilson's words on page 328. How does the quotation show the progressive point of view? Whose energies were released during the progressive era?

4. GEOGRAPHY OF NATIONAL PARKS Review the map on page 345. Notice how many more parks there are in the West than in the East and the Midwest. Do you think that if the government had not saved those lands in the years 1872–1947, the West today would have as few parks as the East? Give reasons for your opinion.

5. TRACING THEMES WOMEN IN AMERICA What methods used by women reformers of the progressive era are still methods of modern-day reform and social protest movements? Support your answer with examples.

6. ANALYZING PRIMARY SOURCES Read the following excerpt from the naturalist John Muir's book *Our National Parks,* published in 1901. Then answer the questions below.

> So far our government has done nothing effective with its forests, though the best in the world, but is like a rich and foolish spendthrift who has inherited a magnificent estate in perfect order, and then has left his fields and meadows, forests and parks, to be sold and plundered and wasted at will, depending on their inexhaustible abundance. Now it is plain that the forests are not inexhaustible, and that quick measures must be taken if ruin is to be avoided. . . .
>
> Just now, while protective measures are being deliberated languidly, destruction and use are speeding on faster and faster every day. The axe and the saw are insanely busy, chips are flying thick as snowflakes and every summer thousands of acres of priceless forests . . . are vanishing away in clouds of smoke. . . .
>
> **JOHN MUIR,** "The American Forests," in *Our National Parks*

Whose actions do you think Muir criticized in this excerpt? Why might his concerns about the forests be justified? Cite evidence from the text to support your answers.

THINKING CRITICALLY

1. PRESIDENTIAL AGENDAS
Possible Responses: Similarities: both promoted a strong executive branch and the president's use of the bully pulpit; both claimed progressive ideals; both tackled the problems of trusts; both excluded the cause of civil rights for African Americans from their progressive agendas. Differences: Roosevelt favored regulating trusts, while Wilson favored breaking them up; Roosevelt thought the federal government should get bigger, Wilson believed it should get smaller; Wilson's attacks on trusts were more aggressive than Roosevelt's.

2. TRENDS IN AMERICAN SOCIETY
Possible Responses: Urbanization and its related problems, especially poverty and industrialization; the spread of the Social Gospel; increase in the number of college-educated women; exploitative practices and shabby ethics of big business; rise of socialism; widespread popularity of muckraking magazines; corruption in politics.

3. PROGRESSIVISM AND DEMOCRACY
Possible Responses: Progressives believed in using action to solve existing problems; they were an energetic group who believed that a democracy required everyone to take responsibility. Examples in the chapter include women involved in all kinds of reforms from child labor to suffrage; novelists and journalists (muckrakers); government officials, including conservationists, governors, mayors, and laborers; and African-American civil-rights activists.

ALTERNATIVE ASSESSMENT

1. **CREATING AN EXHIBIT**
   How are artists influenced by events of their time? How does art help explain the past?
   Research and create a poster or display that explores how artists in the years 1890–1920 reflected progressive ideals.
   CD-ROM Use the CD-ROM *Our Times* and other resources to research a turn-of-the-century musician, writer, artist, designer, or director of your choice.
   - Create a time line of events from this artist's working years.
   - Create an exhibit of images, audiotape samples, or videotape samples of the artist's work. Write or tape an explanation of how the work reflects the progressive era.
   - Share your exhibit with the class.

2. **LEARNING FROM MEDIA**
   VIDEO View the McDougal Littell video for Chapter 9, *A Child on Strike.* Discuss these questions in small groups; then do the cooperative learning activity.
   - What was your reaction to Camella Teoli's accident?
   - What labor practices do you take for granted today that a person living in 1910 could not have taken for granted?
   - **Cooperative Learning** What coverage might the 1912 congressional hearing have received in newspapers of the time? In your group, imagine yourselves as news reporters in 1912 and write two articles—one that objectively reports on the findings of the hearing, and one that has a bias in favor of businesses such as the Washington Woolen Mill. Share the articles with the class, and analyze the ways in which language can affect the reporting of information.

3. **PORTFOLIO PROJECT**
   Use the Living History activity to expand your portfolio.

LIVING HISTORY

PRESENTING YOUR CAMPAIGN

Choose the best part of your woman suffrage campaign—whether a TV or magazine ad, a speech, or an Internet plan—to present to the class. Polish that section of your plan for presentation. Ask your classmates to answer the following questions:

- Is the campaign an effective way to get action on the issue?
- Would the modern methods have made passage of the Nineteenth Amendment occur earlier or more easily?

Include your entire campaign plan as well as the presentation in your American history portfolio.

Bridge to Chapter 10

Review Chapter 9

PROGRESSIVE MOVEMENT The social upheavals of the 1890s sparked reform efforts called the progressive movement. Moral reformers focused on improving personal behavior; muckraking journalists exposed corruption. Experts increased efficiency in both industry and government.

Progressives worked for state and local government reforms. Most progressives also supported reforms to protect consumers against dishonest business practices and to protect workers, especially child laborers, against abuse by employers. Many women reformers targeted unsafe factories and labor abuses and promoted housing reform, educational improvement, and the passage of food and drug laws. Women also waged a tough campaign for woman suffrage. Finally, in 1920, the Nineteenth Amendment, which granted women the vote, was ratified.

PROGRESSIVISM UNDER ROOSEVELT AND TAFT As president, Theodore Roosevelt increased federal power, mediated the 1902 coal strike, regulated trusts and the railroad, pushed for legislation to protect consumers, and called for new conservation measures. William Howard Taft, Roosevelt's successor, was a more cautious progressive. Taft signed a bill for higher tariffs and went against the conservation issues Roosevelt promoted. Taft's policies resulted in a split in the Republican Party, which contributed to the Democrat Woodrow Wilson's victory in the 1912 presidential election.

PROGRESSIVISM UNDER WILSON Like Roosevelt, Wilson believed in a strong executive branch. Wilson pushed for antitrust laws that benefited labor and for legislation that lowered tariffs. He also took bold steps in instituting financial reforms. Wilson's weak stand on civil rights for African Americans marred his record.

Preview Chapter 10

As progressives worked for reforms, others pushed for U.S. expansion overseas. This goal was achieved when the United States gained colonial possessions in both the Caribbean and the Pacific. You will learn about these and other significant developments in the next chapter.

ALTERNATIVE ASSESSMENT

1. CREATING AN EXHIBIT
Standards for Evaluation
The display should meet the following criteria:

- Focuses on a musician, writer, artist, designer, or director from the appropriate time period.
- Displays a variety of examples of the artist's work that convey his or her style.
- Includes a concise explanation of how the artist reflects progressive ideals.

2. LEARNING FROM MEDIA
Answers to the questions:

- Many students will express outrage at Camella's scalping. The entire incident might seem hard to believe.
- Answers will vary. Among practices they take for granted, students might mention the 40-hour work week, insurance benefits, child labor laws, minimum wage, and equal opportunity regardless of gender, race, or disability.

Standards for Articles on the Hearing Evaluation
An effective article should meet the following criteria:

- Includes fictional details from the hearing.
- Uses language to make the article either objective or biased.
- Accurately reflects the result of the hearing.

3. PORTFOLIO PROJECT
LIVING HISTORY
Standards for Evaluation
A campaign should meet the following criteria:

- Maintains a consistent position on the issue.
- Includes a variety of approaches, such as ads and speeches.
- Conveys a clear message.
- Appeals to a wide audience.
- Gives an effective display or delivery of part of the campaign.

IN-DEPTH RESOURCES: UNIT 3
See the form for scoring this activity on page 19.

THINKING CRITICALLY

4. GEOGRAPHY OF NATIONAL PARKS
Possible Responses: Had the government not protected the lands, they might have been exploited as the eastern United States was; the gold rush showed how quickly lands in the West could be ruined. On the other hand, the West is more open, was not developed as early as the East and Midwest were, and the lands are harder to develop because of deserts and mountains.

5. TRACING THEMES WOMEN IN AMERICA
Possible Responses: Lecture tours; civil disobedience; organizing statewide referenda; hunger strikes; picketing political events, such as presidential conventions; forming grassroots and national organizations to advocate a cause; using publicity; lobbying; door-to-door campaigns to reach potential supporters.

6. ANALYZING PRIMARY SOURCES
Possible Responses: Muir criticizes the government's slowness in passing laws to protect the forests, as well as blaming the logging operations. Despite the establishment of the Forest Bureau and the withdrawal of timberlands for a national forest preserve, the government allowed private interests to gobble up the wilderness. Muir's concern is justified; logging companies neglected to replant trees to replace those they cut down.

CHAPTER 10

PLANNING GUIDE

America Claims an Empire

	Key Ideas	COPYMASTERS	ASSESSMENT
SECTION 1 **Imperialism and America** *pp. 364–367*	*Economic and cultural factors convince U.S. policymakers to join the competition for new markets in territories overseas, including Hawaii.*	***In-Depth Resources: Unit 3*** • Guided Reading, p. 20 • Literature: from *Hawaii* by James Michener, p. 33 ***Lesson Plans,*** pp. 87–88	PE ***Section 1 Assessment,*** p. 367 TE ***Self-Assessment,*** p. 367 ***Formal Assessment*** • Section Quiz, p. 129 ***Alternative Assessment Book*** • Standards for Evaluating a Cooperative Activity
SECTION 2 **The Spanish-American-Cuban War** *pp. 370–374*	*The United States goes to war with Spain over Cuban independence and emerges with colonies in Guam, Puerto Rico, and the Philippine Islands.*	***In-Depth Resources: Unit 3*** • Guided Reading, p. 21 • Primary Sources: Newspaper Front Page, p. 29; from *The Rough Riders* by Theodore Roosevelt, p. 30; In Favor of Imperialism, p. 31 • American Lives: José Martí, p. 36; William Randolph Hearst, p. 37 ***Lesson Plans,*** pp. 89–90	PE ***Section 2 Assessment,*** p. 374 TE ***Self-Assessment,*** p. 374 ***Formal Assessment*** • Section Quiz, p. 130 ***Alternative Assessment Book*** • Standards for Evaluating a Cooperative Activity
SECTION 3 **Acquiring New Lands** *pp. 375–381*	*The United States encounters continuing conflict in Puerto Rico, Cuba, and the Philippines, as well as in its attempt to expand trade with China.*	***In-Depth Resources: Unit 3*** • Guided Reading, p. 22 ***Lesson Plans,*** pp. 91–92	PE ***Section 3 Assessment,*** p. 381 TE ***Self-Assessment,*** p. 381 ***Formal Assessment*** • Section Quiz, p. 131 ***Alternative Assessment Book*** • Standards for Evaluating a Cooperative Activity
SECTION 4 **America as a World Power** *pp. 382–387*	*Presidents Theodore Roosevelt and Woodrow Wilson continue to use American military power in territories around the world, including Panama and Mexico.*	***In-Depth Resources: Unit 3*** • Guided Reading, p. 23 • Skillbuilder Practice: Creating Maps, p. 24 • Geography Application: Geography of the Panama Canal, p. 25 • Outline Map: America Becomes a World Power, p. 27 • Primary Source: Building the Panama Canal, p. 32 ***Lesson Plans,*** pp. 93–94	PE ***Section 4 Assessment,*** p. 387 TE ***Self-Assessment,*** p. 387 ***Formal Assessment*** • Section Quiz, p. 132 ***Alternative Assessment Book*** • Standards for Evaluating a Cooperative Activity
CHAPTER RESOURCES	**Chapter Overview** *To compete with other powers, America gains colonies overseas, although some Americans object.*	***In-Depth Resources: Unit 3*** • Living History Project: Worksheet, p. 38; Standards, p. 39 ***Telescoping the Times*** • Chapter Summary, pp. 19–20 ***Planning for Block Schedules***	PE ***Chapter Assessment,*** pp. 390–391 PE ***Alternative Assessment,*** p. 391 ***Formal Assessment*** • Chapter Test, forms A and B, pp. 133–138 ***Test Generator*** ***Alternative Assessment Book*** See explanation and forms for different kinds of alternative assessments including portfolio assessment.

KEY
- PE Pupil's Edition
- TE Teacher's Edition
- INTERNET http://www.mlushistory.com

TECHNOLOGY

Warm-Up Transparency 10

Grolier Multimedia Encyclopedia
- Hawaii

INTERNET Age of imperialism

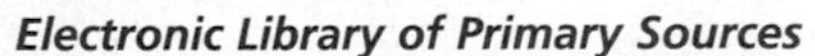

Warm-Up Transparency 10

Electronic Library of Primary Sources
- from *The "Maine": An Account of Her Destruction* by Captain Charles D. Sigsbee
- from *The Strenuous Life* by Theodore Roosevelt

INTERNET José Martí and Cuba

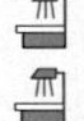

Warm-Up Transparency 10

Humanities Transparencies
- H17, *Athletic Contest*
- H37, Declined with Thanks

Critical Thinking Transparencies
- CT18, Overseas Expansion

Electronic Library of Primary Sources
- On the War in the Philippines
- The Anti-Imperialist League platform

INTERNET Boxer Rebellion

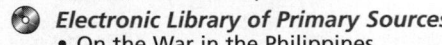

Warm-Up Transparency 10

Geography Transparencies
- G18, United States Interventions

Critical Thinking Transparencies

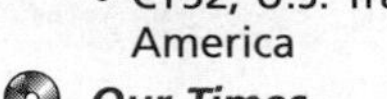

- CT52, U.S. Trade with Central America

Our Times
- The Rise of Theodore Roosevelt

INTERNET Interact with History pp. 385 and 389 (PE)

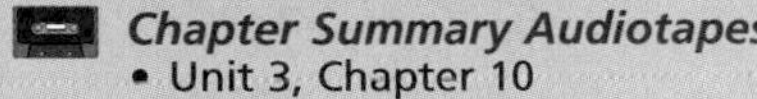

American Portfolio: A Videodisc for U.S. History, user's guide, pp. 175–179

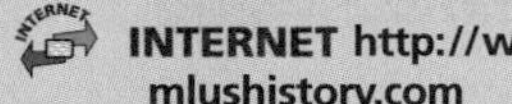

Chapter Summary Audiotapes
- Unit 3, Chapter 10

INTERNET http://www.mlushistory.com

Block Scheduling (90 MINUTES)

Day 1

Section 1, pp. 364–367

Section 2, pp. 370–374

Section Assessments, pp. 367, 374

COOPERATIVE ACTIVITIES
- Considering the Annexation of Hawaii, p. 366 (TE)
- Covering the Rough Riders, p. 373 (TE)

Day 2

Section 3, pp. 375–381

Section Assessment, p. 381

COOPERATIVE ACTIVITY
- Writing Letters to Uncle Sam, p. 378 (TE)

Day 3

Section 4, pp. 382–387

Geography Spotlight: The Panama Canal, pp. 388–389

Section Assessment, p. 387

Chapter Assessment, pp. 390–391

COOPERATIVE ACTIVITY
- Debating Wilson's Missionary Diplomacy, p. 386 (TE)

YEARLY PACING *Chapter 10 Total:* 3 days *Yearly Total:* 85 days

See *Planning for Block Schedules* for special activities and pacing strategies.

Customizing for Special Populations

Students Acquiring English

Access for Students Acquiring English: Spanish Translations
- Guided Reading for Sections 1–4, pp. 130–133
- Chapter Summary, pp. 128–129
- Skillbuilder Practice: Creating Maps, p. 134
- Geography Application: Geography of the Panama Canal, p. 135
- Outline Map: America Becomes a World Power, p. 137

Spanish Reading Study Guide, pp. 109–118

Translations of Chapter Summaries, Hmong, Cantonese, Vietnamese, and Cambodian

Chapter Summary Audiotapes in Spanish Unit 3, Chapter 10

INTERNET The Diverse Classroom

Gifted and Talented Students

In-Depth Resources: Unit 3
- Primary Sources: Newspaper Front Page, p. 29; from *The Rough Riders* by Theodore Roosevelt, p. 30; In Favor of Imperialism, p. 31; Building the Panama Canal, p. 32
- American Lives: José Martí, p. 36; William Randolph Hearst, p. 37

Less Proficient Readers

In-Depth Resources: Unit 3
- Guided Reading for Sections 1–4, pp. 20–23
- Skillbuilder Practice: Creating Maps, p. 24
- Geography Application: Geography of the Panama Canal, p. 25
- Outline Map: America Becomes a World Power, p. 27

Reading Study Guide
- pp. 109–118

Telescoping the Times
- Chapter Summary, pp. 19–20

Chapter Summary Audiotapes, Unit 3, Chapter 10

Connections to Literature READINGS FOR STUDENTS

In-Depth Resources: Unit 3
- **from *Hawaii* by James Michener,** p. 33

Enrichment Reading

- **Rosario Ferré**
  The House on the Lagoon.
  New York: Farrar, 1995.
  Nominated for a National Book Award, this novel is about the history of a Puerto Rican family whose secrets and conflicts add up to the larger story of Puerto Rico itself.

- **Cristina Garcia**
  Dreaming in Cuban.
  New York: Ballantine, 1993.
  Set in Havana, Brooklyn, and the Cuban seaside, this novel is a lively and funny account of three generations of a Cuban family divided by conflicting loyalties over the long history of Cuban politics.

- **Deborah Iida**
  Middle Son.
  Chapel Hill, NC: Algonquin Books, 1996.
  The narrator of this novel tells the story of his Japanese-American family who were sugar-cane cutters in Hawaii working for the huge corporations that controlled the business. The richness and tragedy of their family life and the narrator's final communion with his mother make this novel memorable.

OVERVIEW

America Claims an Empire

▶ *Accessing Prior Knowledge*

Ask students how they would react if the United States took over another country. For students who say they oppose it under any circumstances, ask them why. For students who say it might be all right under certain circumstances, ask what those circumstances are.

▶ *Predicting Outcomes*

Have students read the section overviews and the quotation by Secretary of State John Hay. Ask students to restate the basis of American dealings with other nations and to predict what the response from other countries might be.

MORE ABOUT . . . *John Hay*

As a young lawyer in Springfield, Illinois, John Hay met Abraham Lincoln. He accompanied Lincoln to Washington and served as assistant private secretary to the President. Hay later co-authored a ten-volume biography of Abraham Lincoln. In addition to serving as secretary of state under Presidents McKinley and Roosevelt, Hay also served as a diplomat in France, Spain, Austria, and Britain.

CHAPTER 10

America Claims an Empire

SECTION 1

Imperialism and America

Economic and cultural factors convince U.S. policymakers to join the competition for new markets in territories overseas, including Hawaii.

SECTION 2

The Spanish-American-Cuban War

The United States goes to war with Spain over Cuban independence and emerges with colonies in Guam, Puerto Rico, and the Philippine Islands.

SECTION 3

Acquiring New Lands

The United States encounters continuing conflict in Puerto Rico, Cuba, and the Philippines, as well as in its attempt to expand trade with China.

SECTION 4

America as a World Power

Presidents Theodore Roosevelt and Woodrow Wilson continue to use American military power in territories around the world, including Panama and Mexico.

"In the field of trade and commerce, we shall be the keen competitors of the richest and greatest powers, and . . . we shall bring the sweat to their brows."

Secretary of State John Hay, 1899

THE UNITED STATES

- 1890 — Alfred T. Mahan's *The Influence of Sea Power upon History, 1660–1783* is published.
- 1893 — Ferris wheel makes its debut at the World's Fair in Chicago.
- 1893 — Hawaiian revolution overthrows Queen Liliuokalani.
- 1898 — Spanish-American-Cuban War is fought.
- 1898 — U.S.S. *Maine* explodes and sinks.
- 1899 — John Hay issues the first Open Door notes, calling for equal trading opportunities in China.
- 1899 — United States annexes the Philippine Islands.
- 1900 — Luis Muñoz Rivera begins his 16-year campaign for Puerto Rican independence.

THE WORLD

- 1895 — Sino-Japanese War ends in Japanese victory over China.
- 1900 — Boxer Rebellion begins in China.

THEMES IN CHAPTER 10

Science and Technology

Technological advances helped fuel U.S. imperialism at the turn of the 20th century. First, improved equipment helped increase agricultural and factory output. These changes produced a surplus of goods and prompted the need for overseas markets.

Second, engineering know-how and advances in disease control made it possible for the United States to construct the Panama Canal and thus facilitate trade within its growing empire.

See Teacher's Edition notes, pp. 365, 384.

Constitutional Concerns

Two constitutional concerns arose during America's age of imperialism. The first involved the press. The second concern involved the rights of people in lands acquired by the United States.

See Teacher's Edition notes, pp. 371, 376.

America in the World

The late 1800s are often referred to as the "Age of Imperialism." During this time, several European nations had taken over much of Africa and parts of Asia and the Pacific. The United States joined in the pursuit of colonies.

See Teacher's Edition note, p. 372.

LIVING HISTORY

WRITING A HISTORICAL MONOLOGUE

Many of the historical figures of the United States in the years 1890–1920 were colorful individuals. Choose from this chapter a figure whom you find particularly interesting. As you read, take notes about that person, paying close attention to personal details and his or her political role and views. Write a monologue, or first-person narrative, from that person's point of view. As you draft your monologue, try to

- use language that reflects how the person talked
- refer to situations and events that reveal the person's feelings and concerns

PORTFOLIO PROJECT Save your monologue in a folder for your American history portfolio. You will present your historical monologue to your classmates at the end of the chapter.

- 1901 President McKinley is assassinated.
- 1901 Theodore Roosevelt becomes president.
- 1903 Republic of Panama is formed.
- 1904 Theodore Roosevelt is elected president.
- 1904 Russo-Japanese War begins.
- 1908 William H. Taft is elected president.
- 1910 Mexican Revolution begins.
- 1912 Woodrow Wilson is elected president.
- 1914 Panama Canal opens.
- 1914 U.S. troops invade Mexico.
- 1915 Venustiano Carranza assumes power in Mexico.
- 1916 Woodrow Wilson is reelected.
- 1917 Puerto Ricans become U.S. citizens.
- 1920

ALTERNATIVE ASSESSMENT

LIVING HISTORY

WRITING A HISTORICAL MONOLOGUE

Students should create their monologue using the following guidelines:

- ***Select a person.*** Students might brainstorm to select a list of people from the text and then select the one they find the most interesting.
- ***Focus on a time and place.*** After students position their speakers—the White House on Inauguration Day 1909, for example—they can still mention other key people, events, and situations that are likely to reveal character.
- ***Reveal the character through word choice.*** Tell students to bring out the speaker's personality through word choice. For example, the professorial Woodrow Wilson might use more elegant and formal language than might Theodore Roosevelt.

IN-DEPTH RESOURCES: UNIT 3
See worksheet and standards for evaluation, pp. 38, 39.

RECOMMENDED RESOURCES

Books for the Teacher

Marks, George P., ed. *The Black Press Views American Imperialism.* New York: Arno, 1971. Unusual perspective on imperialism.

O'Toole, G. J. A. *The Spanish War.* New York: Norton, 1984. Popular, readable history.

Wagenheim, Kal. *The Puerto Ricans: a Documentary History.* New York: Praeger, 1973.

Books for the Student

McCullough, David G. *The Path Between the Seas: the Creation of the Panama Canal, 1870–1914.* New York: Simon, 1977.

Rydell, Robert W. *All the World's a Fair: Visions of Empire at American International Expositions: 1876–1916.* Chicago: U of Chicago P, 1984.

Videos

The Big Stick. 1991. RMI Media, 800-745-5480. U.S. foreign policy in Latin America.

The Hunt for Pancho Villa. PBS Home Video, 1993. 800-424-7963.

The 1890s. 1994. Video Knowledge, 516-367-4250. U.S. Imperialism.

Software

American History: Becoming a World Power. World Associates, 3226 Robincrest Drive, Northbrook, IL 60062.

Section 1 Overview

OBJECTIVES

1. To summarize the causes and effects of European and Asian imperialism.
2. To identify factors that influenced American imperialism.
3. To explain how the United States acquired Hawaii.

SKILLBUILDER

- Interpreting graphs, p. 366

CRITICAL THINKING

- Recognizing effects, p. 364
- Analyzing causes, p. 365
- Theme: Constitutional Concerns, p. 366
- Identifying problems, p. 367
- Summarizing, p. 367
- Developing historical perspective, p. 367
- Finding main ideas, p. 367

FOCUS & MOTIVATE

5-MINUTE WARM-UP

Making Inferences
To introduce the conflict between the United States and Hawaii, ask students to read One American's Story on page 364 and answer these questions.

1. How did Queen Liliuokalani know her influence had come to an end?
2. How did Queen Liliuokalani feel about the U.S. takeover of the Hawaiian government?

WARM-UP TRANSPARENCY 10

▶ ***Starting with the Student***
- How does a person behave when he or she feels superior to others?
- Ask students if governments might act in a similar fashion. Why or why not?

1 Imperialism and America

TERMS & NAMES
- Queen Liliuokalani
- imperialism
- Alfred T. Mahan
- Sanford B. Dole

LEARN ABOUT the economic and cultural factors that shaped American foreign policy at the turn of the century
TO UNDERSTAND why the United States became an imperial power.

ONE AMERICAN'S STORY

Queen Liliuokalani realized that her influence had come to an end. More than 160 U.S. sailors and marines stood ready to aid the *haoles* (white foreigners) who planned to overthrow the Hawaiian monarchy. The group included some of her own cabinet members, who had refused to sign the constitution that would help achieve her goal of preserving Hawaii for Hawaiians. In an eloquent statement of protest, the proud monarch surrendered only to the superior force of the United States.

A PERSONAL VOICE

I, Liliuokalani, . . . do hereby solemnly protest against any and all acts done against myself and the constitutional government of the Hawaiian Kingdom. . . . Now, to avoid any collision of armed forces and perhaps the loss of life, I do under this protest . . . yield my authority until such time as the Government of the United States shall . . . undo the action of its representatives and reinstate me in the authority which I claim as the constitutional sovereign of the Hawaiian Islands.

QUEEN LILIUOKALANI, quoted in *Those Kings and Queens of Old Hawaii*

Hawaii's "Queen Lil" announced that if restored to power, she would behead those who had conspired to depose her.

U.S. ambassador John L. Stevens informed the State Department, "The Hawaiian pear is now fully ripe, and this is the golden hour for the United States to pluck it." The annexation of Hawaii was only one of the goals of America's empire builders.

Global Imperialism

Americans had always sought to expand the size of their nation, and throughout the 19th century they extended their control over much of the North American continent. By the 1880s, policymakers had become convinced that the United States should join the imperialist powers of Europe and establish colonies overseas, such as the Hawaiian Islands. **Imperialism—**the policy in which stronger nations extend their economic, political, or military control over weaker territories—was a global trend.

EUROPEAN IMPERIALISM European nations had been establishing colonies for centuries. By the late 19th century, Africa had emerged as a prime target of European expansionism. Britain, France, Belgium, Italy, Germany, Portugal, and Spain competed for African raw materials and markets. These ambitious nations carved up Africa and distributed control of the pieces among themselves.

By the early 20th century, only Ethiopia and Liberia remained independent. The rest of Africa had been divided into European colonies. Americans watched keenly as Great Britain acquired territory not only in Africa but in Asia and the Pacific as well. Soon the expression "The sun never sets on the British Empire" became astonishingly accurate. During the reign of Queen Victoria (1837–1901), Britain built an empire that included a quarter of the world's land and people.

A. Answer Only two African nations remained independent; the rest of the continent was divided up among the European nations.

THINK THROUGH HISTORY
A. *Recognizing Effects* *How did European imperialism affect Africa?*

SECTION 1 RESOURCES

PRINT RESOURCES

IN-DEPTH RESOURCES: UNIT 3
Guided Reading, p. 20
Literature: from *Hawaii* by James Michener, p. 33

READING STUDY GUIDE, p. 109

ACCESS FOR STUDENTS ACQUIRING ENGLISH
Guided Reading (Spanish), p. 130

SPANISH READING STUDY GUIDE, p. 109

FORMAL ASSESSMENT
Section Quiz, p. 129

ALTERNATIVE ASSESSMENT BOOK
See forms for supporting and scoring alternative activities.

TECHNOLOGY RESOURCES

CD-ROM *Grolier Multimedia Encyclopedia*

VIDEO *American Portfolio: A Videodisc for U.S. History* user's guide, p. 178

INTERNET http://www.mlushistory.com

ASIAN IMPERIALISM Imperialism also surfaced in parts of Asia during this period. In its late-19th-century reform era, Japan replaced its old feudal order with a central government modeled on the bureaucracies of Western nations. Hoping that military strength would bolster industrialization, Japan joined European nations in their imperialist competition in China in the 1890s. Although the United States did not seek colonies in Asia, it did compete with other nations to expand trading opportunities with China.

American Imperialism

Most Americans gradually warmed to the idea of expansion overseas. With a belief in manifest destiny, they already had pushed the U.S. border to the Pacific Ocean. Three factors fueled the new American imperialism: (1) economic competition among industrial nations; (2) political and military competition, including the creation of a strong naval force; and (3) a belief in the racial and cultural superiority of people of Anglo-Saxon (English) descent, especially in comparison with nonwhite people.

A THIRST FOR NEW MARKETS In the United States, imperialism had economic roots, just as it did in Europe and Japan. Advances in technology enabled American farms and factories to produce far more than American citizens could consume. Now the United States needed raw materials for its factories and new markets for its manufactured goods. Imperialists viewed foreign trade as the solution to overproduction and the related problems of unemployment and economic depression. Indiana senator Albert J. Beveridge, a staunch imperialist, defended the pursuit of new territories on economic grounds.

> A PERSONAL VOICE
>
> Fate has written our policy for us; the trade of the world must and shall be ours. . . . We will establish trading-posts throughout the world as distributing-points for American products. . . . Great colonies governing themselves, flying our flag and trading with us, will grow about our posts of trade.
>
> ALBERT J. BEVERIDGE, quoted in *Beveridge and the Progressive Era*

B. Answer The United States produced more goods than Americans needed. To keep business growing, the nation had to gain foreign markets.

THINK THROUGH HISTORY **B. Analyzing Causes** *How did U.S. economic prosperity lead it to pursue a policy of imperialism?*

By the turn of the century, the United States had started to fulfill Beveridge's goals. American exports, which had totaled $234 million at the end of the Civil War, rose to $1.5 billion by 1900. By achieving a favorable balance of trade (exporting more than it imported), the United States had become a leading economic power.

DESIRE FOR MILITARY STRENGTH Seeing that other nations were establishing a global military presence, American foreign-policy experts advised that the United States build up its own military strength. Admiral **Alfred T. Mahan,** president of the Naval War College in Newport, Rhode Island, had become one of the most outspoken advocates of American military expansion.

ON THE WORLD STAGE

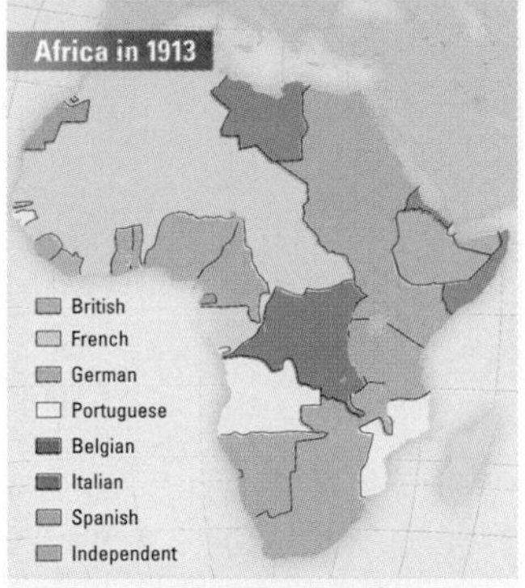

CARVING UP AFRICA

Europeans avoided war by carving up Africa through diplomatic agreements. Nations staked out their claims to colonies and signed treaties to reserve those colonies for their own use.

In the mid-1880s, Germany and France called for a conference to discuss competition for African land. Fourteen European nations and the United States met in Berlin in 1884. The nations agreed to respect established colonies in Africa and proposed some ground rules for future colonization.

The Berlin Conference left many questions unsettled, but it was the first international agreement on imperialism in Africa.

Admiral Mahan's efforts eventually led to the development of the "Great White Fleet" of the U.S. Navy.

OBJECTIVE ① INSTRUCT

Global Imperialism

▶ ***Discussing Key Ideas***

- European nations carve Africa into colonies.
- Britain's empire includes a quarter of the world's land and people.
- Japan joins European nations in imperialist competition in China.

IN-DEPTH RESOURCES: UNIT 3
Guided Reading, p. 20
Literature: from *Hawaii* by James Michener, p. 33

ACCESS FOR STUDENTS ACQUIRING ENGLISH
Guided Reading (Spanish), p. 130

ON THE WORLD STAGE
Carving Up Africa
Critical Thinking: Analyzing Have students create a flow chart showing causes and effects of imperialism in Africa. The chart might look like this:

OBJECTIVE ② INSTRUCT

American Imperialism

▶ ***Discussing Key Ideas***

- American imperialists seek more markets for U.S. goods.
- The United States develops a modern fleet and plans to acquire naval bases abroad.
- Some Americans argue that their culture is superior and should be spread to other nations.

TEACHING OPTIONS

Exploring Themes

Science and Technology Between 1860 and 1900, new and better farm machinery greatly improved grain production in the United States. For example, plows, harrows, grain drills, reapers, and threshing machines increased the nation's corn harvest by 264 percent and the wheat harvest by 252 percent. Faced with such a surplus of farm products, the United States increased its foreign trade, as it sought new markets for these goods. Have students research the inventions of the late 19th century that helped spur the production of farm goods, and then have them prepare a time line of these inventions.

Making Connections Across Time

Balance of Trade in the 1990s Throughout the late 20th century, the United States has endured an unfavorable balance of trade—in which imports exceed exports. The nation's trade deficit peaked at $152.2 billion in 1987 and has since fluctuated. Although the country's trade deficit dipped to $66.7 billion in 1991, it had grown again to $105.1 billion by 1995. Experts attribute the trade deficit to, among other things, a heavy domestic demand for foreign goods and economic stagnation abroad, which reduces demand for American goods.

Issues for the 21st Century

Foreign Policy After the Cold War

Connect foreign policy in 1900 to today's policies by having students read pages 878–879. Then have them answer these questions.

1. When did the Cold War end? *1992.*
2. How do America's foreign policy goals after the Cold War compare with American foreign policy around 1900? *Earlier: New markets, military strength. Later: Promote democracy, protect human rights, open markets.*

OBJECTIVE

③ INSTRUCT

The United States Takes Hawaii

▶ ***Discussing Key Ideas***

- American sugar planters gain control of Hawaii's government and economy.
- White business groups depose Queen Liliuokalani.
- The United States annexes Hawaii.

HISTORY FROM VISUALS

Hawaii's Changing Population, 1853–1920

Reading the Graph Tell students to note that the graph depicts shifts in the percentage of Hawaii's total population and does not address numbers of persons.

Extension Discuss with students what the changes in Hawaii's population say about the effects of imperialism on weaker countries.

In *The Influence of Sea Power upon History, 1660–1783* (1890), Mahan argued for a strong U.S. navy to defend the peacetime shipping lanes essential to American economic growth. He said the nation also needed strategically located bases where its fleets could refuel. Mahan urged the United States to develop a modern fleet, establish naval bases in the Caribbean, construct a canal across the Isthmus of Panama, and acquire Hawaii and other Pacific islands.

The United States built nine steel-hulled cruisers between 1883 and 1890. The construction of modern battleships such as the *Maine* and the *Oregon* transformed the country into the world's third largest naval power. With a modern fleet, the United States set out to accomplish the protectionist goals Mahan had recommended.

BELIEF IN ANGLO-SAXON SUPERIORITY Cultural factors also helped to justify imperialism. Some Americans combined the philosophy of Social Darwinism—a belief that free-market competition would lead to the survival of the fittest—with a belief in the racial superiority of Anglo-Saxons. They argued that the United States had a responsibility to spread Christianity and civilization to the world's "inferior" peoples. This viewpoint was highly racist, because it defined civilization according to the standards of only one culture.

Skillbuilder Answer
Possible Answer:
The percentage of Native Hawaiians declined from about 98% in 1853 to about 16% in 1920. The percentage of other non-Caucasians (mostly Asian) increased from about 1% in 1853 to about 62% in 1920.

ANTI-IMPERIALISM While some Americans believed that the notion of ethnic superiority justified imperialism, others saw imperialism as a threat to Americans' Anglo-Saxon heritage. Anti-imperialists also objected to U.S. imperialism on moral and practical grounds. Many believed that nothing justified domination of other countries by the United States. Some objected when territories claimed by the United States were not given U.S. constitutional protections. Others argued that the costs of maintaining a military force large enough to enforce U.S. claims abroad were prohibitive. In any case, certain countries overseas were vulnerable to empire builders looking for potential conquests, and Hawaii was a tempting target for the United States.

THINK THROUGH HISTORY
C. THEME ***Constitutional Concerns*** *Why do you think some people were concerned that the United States did not extend constitutional protections to its territories?*

C. Answer
Probably because this suggested that U.S. citizens were superior to the residents of the territory—an assertion inconsistent with the values expressed in the Constitution.

Hawaii's Changing Population, 1853–1920

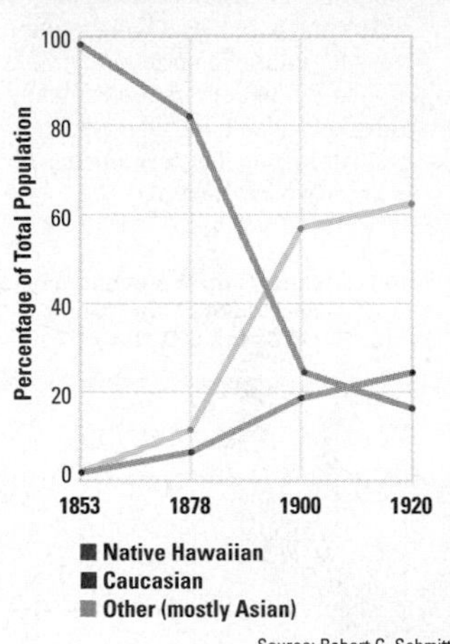

Source: Robert C. Schmitt, *Demographics of Hawaii, 1778–1965*

SKILLBUILDER
INTERPRETING GRAPHS
Which groups experienced the most dramatic changes in their percentages of the total Hawaiian population between 1853 and 1920? What were these changes?

The United States Takes Hawaii

The Hawaiian Islands had been economically important to the United States for nearly a century. Since the 1790s, American merchants had stopped there on their way to China and East India. In the 1820s, Yankee missionaries founded Christian schools and churches on the islands. Next came sugar merchants, who eventually changed the Hawaiian economy.

HAWAII'S ECONOMY In the mid-19th century, American-owned sugar plantations accounted for about three-quarters of the islands' wealth. Plantation owners imported thousands of laborers from Japan, Portugal, and China. By 1900, foreigners and immigrant laborers outnumbered native Hawaiians about three to one.

White planters profited from close ties with the United States. An 1875 treaty allowed the sale of Hawaiian sugar in the United States without a duty. In 1887, white business leaders in Hawaii forced King Kalakaua to change Hawaii's constitution to grant voting rights only to wealthy landowners. This change basically gave control of Hawaii's government to the American businessmen. Also in 1887, the United States strong-armed Hawaii into signing a treaty allowing the construction of an American naval base at Pearl Harbor.

The McKinley Tariff of 1890 provoked a crisis by eliminating the duty-free status of Hawaiian sugar. (See *tariff* on page 939 in the Economics Handbook.) As a result, Hawaiian sugar growers faced competition in the American market,

Block Schedule — TEACHING OPTION — Time Needed: 30 Minutes

Cooperative Activity: Considering the Annexation of Hawaii

Task: Student groups will write position papers representing different interests in Hawaii.

Purpose: To recognize different viewpoints regarding the annexation of Hawaii.

Activity: Assign the following roles to small groups of students: American planters, native Hawaiians, contract laborers, Queen Liliuokalani, U.S. ambassador John L. Stevens, President Cleveland, and President McKinley. Instruct each group to write a position paper representing the assigned viewpoint regarding annexation of Hawaii. Encourage students to use quotes from the text and other sources. Provide time for groups to share their work.

Building a Portfolio: Students adding a position paper to their portfolios should highlight their own contribution to the paper.

ALTERNATIVE ASSESSMENT BOOK
Standards for Evaluating a Cooperative Activity

Standards for Evaluation
Position papers should. . .

- identify the viewpoint of the person or group represented
- clearly state reasons supporting the position
- provide concrete details to support the reasons

THINK THROUGH HISTORY
D. *Identifying Problems* *What problems did the McKinley Tariff cause for American sugar growers in Hawaii?*

D. Answer It forced them to compete with other foreign growers and enabled U.S. growers to undersell them. As a result, they faced economic ruin.

especially from Cuban sugar. American planters in Hawaii called for the United States to annex the islands so they wouldn't have to pay the duty.

Sanford B. Dole, (pictured here with his wife, Anna) helped to engineer the deposing of Queen Liliuokalani, who would be Hawaii's last monarch.

THE QUEEN IS DEPOSED When King Kalakaua died in 1891, his sister, Liliuokalani, became queen. Liliuokalani proposed a new constitution that would remove property qualifications for voting. This change would have restored political power over the islands to native Hawaiians.

To prevent this from happening, business groups—with the help of U.S. ambassador John L. Stevens—organized a revolution against the queen. On the night of January 16, 1893, the U.S.S. *Boston* appeared in Honolulu harbor. Following Stevens's orders, American marines moved ashore, supposedly to protect American lives and property. At the same time, volunteer troops took over the government building, imprisoned the queen in her palace, and established a provisional government with **Sanford B. Dole** as president.

"The Hawaiian pear is now fully ripe, and this is the golden hour . . . to pluck it."

JOHN L. STEVENS

REPUBLIC OF HAWAII Stevens immediately recognized the provisional government, which sent a commission to Washington, D.C., and asked that the islands be annexed. After a U.S. special investigator blamed Stevens for the revolution, President Cleveland directed that the queen be restored to her throne. When Dole refused to surrender power, Cleveland—unwilling to use force—formally recognized the Republic of Hawaii, but he refused to consider annexation unless a majority of Hawaiians favored it.

In 1897, William McKinley, who favored annexation, succeeded Cleveland as president. On August 12, 1898, Congress proclaimed Hawaii an American territory, without Hawaiians having had the chance to vote on annexation. At the same time, Cuba, an island much closer to the U.S. mainland, attracted U.S. attention.

Section 1 Assessment

1. TERMS & NAMES

Identify:
- Queen Liliuokalani
- imperialism
- Alfred T. Mahan
- Sanford B. Dole

2. SUMMARIZING Copy this web on your paper and fill it in with events and concepts that illustrate the idea in the center.

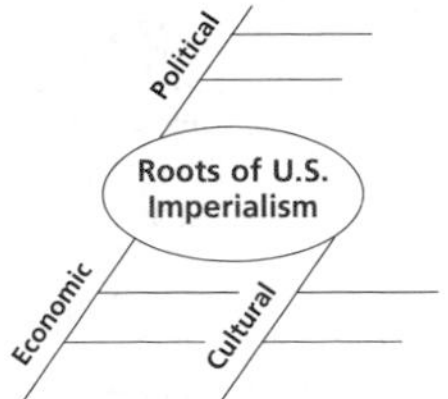

Choose one event to further explain in a paragraph.

3. DEVELOPING HISTORICAL PERSPECTIVE To what extent might the mid-19th-century belief in manifest destiny have set the stage for the new American imperialism at the end of the century? Support your answers with evidence from the text.

THINK ABOUT
- why westward expansion might inspire overseas expansion
- justifications for imperialism
- Senator Beveridge's remark that "fate has written our policy for us."

4. FINDING MAIN IDEAS Why did the United States want to annex Hawaii? Use specific references to the chapter to support your response.

ANSWERS

1. TERMS & NAMES

Queen Liliuokalani, p. 364
imperialism, p. 364
Alfred T. Mahan, p. 365
Sanford B. Dole, p. 367

2. SUMMARIZING

Possible Responses: Political—political and military rivalry with other imperialist powers; construction of a modern naval fleet. Economic—foreign trade as the solution to overproduction, unemployment, and economic depression; economic competition among industrial nations. Cultural—combining the philosophies of Social Darwinism with Anglo-Saxon superiority; missionary impulse to spread Christianity.

3. DEVELOPING HISTORICAL PERSPECTIVE

Possible Response: Some students might say that manifest destiny was the guiding force behind the annexation of western territories and that leaders believed cultural superiority justified racial prejudice toward Native Americans. These patterns of western expansion seemed to influence the United States to join the race for overseas expansion.

4. FINDING MAIN IDEAS

Possible Response: U.S. businessmen operated numerous sugar plantations on the islands. Also, there was a U.S. naval base in Hawaii.

MORE ABOUT . . .
Sanford B. Dole

The son of an American missionary, Dole was born in Hawaii and educated in the United States. He returned to Hawaii to practice law and was twice elected to the Hawaii Legislature. An opponent of King Kalakaua's policies, Dole led an opposition party against the king and eventually helped engineer the overthrow of his sister. After the United States annexed Hawaii, Dole served as first territorial governor.

GROLIER MULTIMEDIA ENCYCLOPEDIA
Hawaii

ASSESS & RETEACH

Section 1 Assessment

Have the students work in small groups to answer the questions. Have each group share their answers to question 3 with the class.

Self-Assessment

Ask students to write two paragraphs, one which summarizes what they knew about Hawaii before reading this section, the other summarizing what they now know.

Section Quiz

FORMAL ASSESSMENT
Section Quiz, p. 129

Reteach

Have students work in groups to outline one of the three subsections of Section 1. They should use the boldfaced titles as main ideas and fill in supporting details.

CLOSE

The United States joined European and Asian countries in political and economic competition for colonies. A belief in Anglo-Saxon superiority provided additional incentive for imperialism. These factors led to annexation of Hawaii.

Tracing Themes

OBJECTIVES

1. To examine ways in which America has asserted itself in world affairs over the last one hundred years.
2. To analyze motives for getting involved in, or staying out of, various conflicts.

FOCUS & MOTIVATE

▶ ***Starting with the Student***
Ask students to think about a place in the world where war or conflict is raging now.

- What are the reasons the United States should become involved in this conflict?
- What are the reasons the United States should stay out of this conflict?
- If the United States were to become involved in this conflict, what type of support might it give, and to whom?

INSTRUCT

▶ ***Starting with the Student***
Ask students to characterize the current administration's foreign policy positions by placing them on a continuum from "Isolationism" to "Active Military Involvement." To support their choices, have students cite specific conflicts and responses to them.

(continued on next page)

TRACING THEMES
AMERICA IN THE WORLD

America in World Affairs

"Steer clear of permanent alliances," George Washington cautioned Americans in his Farewell Address of 1796. Washington's warning to the young nation became a theme of government policy for the next hundred years, as domestic issues dominated Americans' attention.

In the late 1800s, however, Americans began to look outward to the larger world. The country had matured, reaching from ocean to ocean across the continent. The Western frontier was closed. A century after Washington had issued his warning, popular sentiment carried the country into the Spanish-American-Cuban War. This involvement, at the very end of the 19th century, marked the emergence of a modern America—a country taking its place among the chief powers of the world.

1823–1898
THE UNITED STATES AND LATIN AMERICA

Throughout the 19th century, the United States expanded its influence in the Western Hemisphere. The Monroe Doctrine was intended to diminish European interference. After the Civil War, American trade with Latin America, including the Spanish colony of Cuba, grew. In fact, the United States traded more heavily with Cuba than Spain did.

When the Cubans rebelled against Spain, Americans sympathized with the rebels. After the U.S. battleship *Maine* sank in the Cuban harbor of Havana, Americans blamed the Spanish, and Congress declared war. After defeating the Spanish, the United States expanded its influence in territories such as Puerto Rico, Panama, and Mexico. A new expansionist era had begun.

DESTRUCTION OF THE U.S. BATTLESHIP MAINE
IN HAVANA HARBOR FEBY 15TH 1898.

1930s
ISOLATIONISM

The United States joined World War I in 1917, determined to "make the world safe for democracy." However, President Woodrow Wilson's plans to ensure a lasting peace through the League of Nations collapsed. The dictators Benito Mussolini and Adolf Hitler came to power in Italy and in Germany, menacing other European countries.

Americans were sharply divided in their responses. Many promoted isolationism, arguing that the best way to preserve American democracy was to stay out of war in Europe. In this climate, President Franklin D. Roosevelt gave material support to Britain but did not commit troops. It took Japan's attack on Pearl Harbor, Hawaii, in 1941 to force the United States into the war.

RECOMMENDED RESOURCES

Books

Barnet, Richard J. *The Rockets' Red Glare: When America Goes to War: The Presidents and the People.* New York: Simon, 1990.

Beschloss, Michael R. *At the Highest Levels: The Inside Story of the End of the Cold War.* Boston: Little, 1993.

Brands, H. W. *The Devil We Knew: Americans and the Cold War.* New York: Oxford UP, 1993.

Lord, Mary and Martha L. McCoy, eds. *In Harm's Way: When Should We Risk American Lives in World Conflicts?* Washington, D.C.: ACCESS, 1994.

O'Toole, G. I. A. *The Spanish War.* New York: Norton, 1984. A narrative history of how the war started, what happened, and where it led.

Williams, William A. *The Tragedy of American Diplomacy.* New York: Norton, 1988. Long-range view of American foreign policy.

Videos

Vietnam: A Television History. WGBH-TV Boston, 1983. Thirteen one-hour videotapes tell the story of the conflict.

Headline Stories of the Century: A Newsreel Library of World War II. Questar Video, 1992. Presents 84 edited newsreels showing combat.

Software

The War in Vietnam. CD-ROM. Macmillan Digital USA, 1995. Includes articles, photos, broadcast clips, maps, and a searchable database.

1945–1991
THE COLD WAR

Tensions between the United States and the Soviet Union and Communist China rose quickly in the late 1940s. The Cold War that resulted from these tensions lasted for nearly 50 years.

During the Cold War, the United States opposed communism around the globe. One result of this effort was the war in Vietnam. Although Communists eventually won control of Vietnam in 1975, it was the Soviet Union that could not survive the Cold War. Economic troubles decimated the Soviet empire. Small nations like Latvia reclaimed their independence and destroyed the relics of Communist rule, like the statue above of Vladimir I. Lenin, the leader of the 1917 Russian Revolution.

1939–1945
INVOLVEMENT IN EUROPE

As the United States became a leading world economic power, it became more closely linked with Europe through trade and finance. Americans also respected democratic nations, like Great Britain and France.

When the fascist threat to democracy became too great to ignore, the United States joined the Allies in fighting the Second World War. After the war, most Americans came to believe that the world was too small for the United States to ignore world affairs. Americans took an active role in rebuilding Europe after the war through programs like the Marshall Plan. The United States also stayed involved with Europe militarily during the Cold War as a member of the North Atlantic Treaty Organization (NATO).

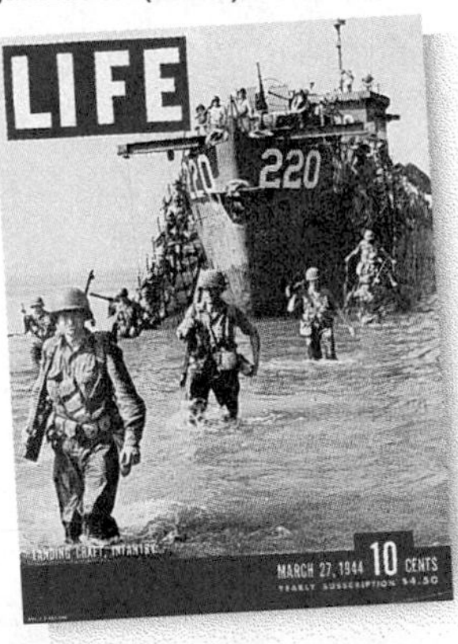

INTERACT WITH HISTORY

1. **ANALYZING MOTIVES** What were America's motives for getting involved in each of the wars described on these two pages? Why do you think the efforts of isolationists have generally not prevailed over the forces promoting involvement?

SEE SKILLBUILDER HANDBOOK, PAGE 907.

2. **WRITING ABOUT WARTIME EXPERIENCE** Imagine that you are a reporter writing about one of the wars in the 20th century. Interview someone you know—or look for information in the library or on the Internet—to find out how an individual soldier, nurse, cook, sailor, or pilot spent each day as part of the war effort. Write a feature article for a local newspaper, quoting that person.

INTERNET Visit http://www.mlushistory.com for more information about American involvement overseas.

(continued from page 368)

▶ *Discussing Key Ideas*

- Involvement in the Spanish-American-Cuban War marked the beginning of America's role as a world power.
- Although protests against war and calls for isolationism have recurred, America has followed a course of involvement.
- After World War II, military victory became more complex and elusive.

MORE ABOUT . . .
The Spanish-American-Cuban War

When the *Maine* exploded on February 15, 1898, a naval court of inquiry convened two days later to investigate it. But even before the court had reached its conclusion, Teddy Roosevelt, then assistant secretary of the Navy, made a bold decision. He ordered a U.S. squadron to Hong Kong, so that it would be ready for offensive operations in the Philippines. Roosevelt, like many other Americans, did not credit the theory suggested by several naval officers and ordnance experts. They suggested that the explosion was the result of coal bunker fires, just as similar explosions had been in the past.

INTERACT WITH HISTORY

1. Analyzing Motives

Possible Responses:

Spanish-American-Cuban War—Motives ranged from imperialism, to protection of American economic interests in Cuba, to sympathy for the Cuban people in their quest for independence from Spain.

World War II—Motives centered on fear and outrage directed at Japan and Germany. Some also felt sympathy for Britain and other allies, and economic and political interests did appear to hang in the balance.

The Vietnam War—Motives centered on fear of Communism and its spread via the domino effect.

2. Writing About Wartime Experience

Standards for Evaluation Feature articles should . . .

- identify the war and the individual's wartime role
- detail the daily life of the individual by focusing on the various activities that made up a typical day
- create interest in the individual
- provide insight into the lives of those who participated in a specific war

Students might share their accounts by obtaining permission to submit them to a local newspaper, offer them on a web site, or include them in a class collection.

Section 2 Overview

OBJECTIVES

1. To contrast American opinions regarding the Cuban revolt against Spain.
2. To identify events that escalated conflict between the United States and Spain.
3. To describe the course of the Spanish-American-Cuban War and its results.

SKILLBUILDERS

- Interpreting political cartoons, p. 371
- Understanding geography: location, p. 372
- Understanding geography: movement, place p. 373

CRITICAL THINKING

- Analyzing motives, pp. 371, 374
- Clarifying, p. 371
- Summarizing, pp. 372, 374
- Making inferences, pp. 373, 374
- Forming opinions, p. 374

FOCUS & MOTIVATE

5-MINUTE WARM-UP

Interpreting Maps
To gain insight into the war between the United States and Spain, refer students to the maps on pages 372 and 373.

1. In what parts of the world did battles between the United States and Spain take place?
2. In what places was the Spanish fleet destroyed?

WARM-UP TRANSPARENCY 10

▶ ***Starting with the Student***
- Ask students if they ever have been shocked or angered by something they read or heard. How did it make them want to act?

OBJECTIVE
① **INSTRUCT**

American Interest in Cuba

▶ ***Discussing Key Ideas***
- Investments in sugar plantations give Americans an economic interest in Cuba.

(continued on next page)

② The Spanish-American-Cuban War

TERMS & NAMES
- José Martí
- Valeriano Weyler
- yellow journalism
- U.S.S. *Maine*
- George Dewey
- Rough Riders
- San Juan Hill

LEARN ABOUT the causes and course of the Spanish-American-Cuban War
TO UNDERSTAND how and why the United States gained control of Spain's former colonial possessions.

ONE AMERICAN'S STORY

Early in 1896, James Creelman traveled to Cuba as a *New York World* correspondent, covering the second Cuban war for independence from Spain. Although Spanish officials ordered him to leave, he remained in Havana and continued to write articles about the war.

A PERSONAL VOICE

No man's life, no man's property is safe [in Cuba]. American citizens are imprisoned or slain without cause. American property is destroyed on all sides. . . . Wounded soldiers can be found begging in the streets of Havana. . . . Cuba will soon be a wilderness of blackened ruins. . . . The horrors of a barbarous struggle for the extermination of the native population are witnessed in all parts of the country. Blood on the roadsides, blood in the fields, blood on the doorsteps, blood, blood, blood! The old, the young, the weak, the crippled—all are butchered without mercy. . . . Is there no nation wise enough, brave enough to aid this blood-smitten land?

JAMES CREELMAN, *New York World*, May 17, 1896

Creelman's articles reached Americans who were beginning to understand the implications of imperialism—and to be intrigued by the prospect of the United States as a world player. His descriptions of Spanish atrocities aroused sympathy for Cubans. Newspapers often exaggerated stories like Creelman's to boost their sales as well as to provoke American intervention in Cuba.

Cuban rebels burned the town of Jaruco in March 1896.

American Interest in Cuba

By 1825, Spain—once the most powerful colonial nation on earth—had lost most of its overseas possessions. It retained only the Philippines, the island of Guam, a few outposts in Africa, and Cuba and Puerto Rico in the Americas.

However, the United States had long had an interest in Cuba. In 1854, diplomats had recommended to President Franklin Pierce that the United States buy Cuba from Spain. In 1860, the Democratic Party's national platform called for the admission of Cuba to the Union as a slave state. Toward the end of the century, events in Cuba drew the United States into war with Spain.

CUBAN POLITICAL AND ECONOMIC INSTABILITY Both Puerto Rico and Cuba had strong cultural ties with Spain, but Cuba also had a history of rebellion. From 1868 to 1878, Cubans fought their first war for independence. They forced Spain to abolish slavery in 1886 but failed to achieve independence.

After the emancipation of Cuba's slaves, American capitalists began investing millions of dollars in large sugar cane plantations on the island. Cuba's economy depended on sugar, and the United States now became Cuba's main market. In 1884, the United States had abolished its tariff on Cuban sugar, causing sugar production to skyrocket. But when a high tariff on Cuban sugar was restored in 1894, the Cuban economy was ruined.

SECOND WAR FOR INDEPENDENCE Anti-Spanish sentiment in Cuba soon erupted into a second war for independence. **José Martí,** a Cuban poet and

SECTION 2 RESOURCES

PRINT RESOURCES

IN-DEPTH RESOURCES: UNIT 3
Guided Reading, p. 21
Primary Sources: Newspaper Front Page, p. 29; from *The Rough Riders* by Theodore Roosevelt, p. 30; In Favor of Imperialism, p. 31
American Lives: José Martí, p. 36; William Randolph Hearst, p. 37

READING STUDY GUIDE, p. 111

ACCESS FOR STUDENTS ACQUIRING ENGLISH
Guided Reading (Spanish), p. 183

SPANISH READING STUDY GUIDE, p. 111

FORMAL ASSESSMENT
Section Quiz, p. 130

ALTERNATIVE ASSESSMENT BOOK
See forms for supporting and scoring alternative activities.

TECHNOLOGY RESOURCES

CD-ROM Electronic Library of Primary Sources

VIDEO *American Portfolio: A Videodisc for U.S. History* user's guide, pp. 175–178, 179

INTERNET http://www.mlushistory.com

journalist in exile in New York, launched a revolution in 1895. Martí organized Cuban resistance against Spain, using an active guerrilla campaign and deliberately destroying property, especially American-owned sugar mills and plantations. Martí counted on provoking U.S. intervention to help the rebels achieve *Cuba Libre!*—a free Cuba.

THINK THROUGH HISTORY
A. Analyzing Motives *Why did José Martí destroy American-owned sugar mills and plantations in Cuba?*

Public opinion in the United States was split. Many businesspeople wanted the government to support Spain in order to protect their investments. Other Americans, however, were enthusiastic about the rebel cause. The cry *"Cuba Libre!"* was, after all, similar to Patrick Henry's "Give me liberty or give me death!"

The Threat of War Escalates

A. Answer Martí hoped to provoke the United States into intervening to help free Cuba from Spain.

In 1896, Spain responded to the Cuban revolt by sending General **Valeriano Weyler** to Cuba to restore order. Believing that regular military methods would not work against guerrilla tactics—in which small bands of local fighters attack by surprise—Weyler moved the entire rural population of central and western Cuba into concentration camps. An estimated 300,000 Cubans filled these camps, where thousands of them died from hunger and disease within two years.

YELLOW JOURNALISM Weyler's actions fueled a war over newspaper circulation that had developed between the American newspaper tycoons William Randolph Hearst and Joseph Pulitzer. To lure readers, Hearst's *New York Journal* and Pulitzer's *New York World* printed exaggerated accounts—by reporters such as James Creelman—of "Butcher" Weyler's brutality. Stories of poisoned wells and of children being thrown to the sharks deepened American sympathy for the rebels. Legitimate reports of Cuban suffering mixed with these sensationalized stories became known as **yellow journalism**—reporting that exaggerates the news to lure new readers.

B. Answer Denied access to combat areas, reporters created false and misleading accounts, which they presented as true; they exaggerated the brutality of the fighting.

Spanish authorities restricted the freedom of the reporters that Hearst and Pulitzer sent to Cuba and prevented them from entering combat areas. Some American correspondents claimed to have communicated with Cuban rebels secretly. Others gathered in Havana's bars and made up reports of battles that never took place. Hearst sent the artist Frederic Remington, famous for his landscapes of the American West, to Cuba to illustrate reporters' stories. When Remington informed the publisher that a war between the United States and Spain seemed unlikely, Hearst reportedly replied, "You furnish the pictures and I'll furnish the war."

THINK THROUGH HISTORY
B. Clarifying *How did yellow journalism distort coverage of the Cuban revolt?*

THE DE LÔME LETTER Many Americans sympathized with the Cuban rebels. When President William McKinley took office in 1897, demands for American intervention in Cuba were increasing. Preferring to avoid war with Spain, McKinley tried diplomatic means to resolve the crisis. At first, his efforts appeared to succeed. Spain recalled General Weyler, modified the policy regarding concentration camps, and offered Cuba limited self-government.

In February 1898, however, the *New York Journal* published a private letter written by Enrique Dupuy de Lôme, the Spanish minister to the United States. A Cuban rebel had stolen the letter from a Havana post office and leaked it to the newspaper, which was thirsty for scandal. The de Lôme letter criticized President McKinley, calling him "weak" and "a bidder for the admiration of the crowd."

KEY PLAYER

JOSÉ MARTÍ
1853–1895

The Cuban political activist José Martí dedicated his life to achieving independence for Cuba. Expelled from Cuba at the age of 16 because of his revolutionary activities, Martí earned a master's degree and a law degree and eventually settled in the United States.

Wary of the U.S. role in the Cuban struggle against the Spanish, Martí warned, "I know the Monster, because I have lived in its lair." His fears of U.S. imperialism turned out to have been well-founded: U.S. troops occupied Cuba on and off from 1906 until 1922.

Martí died fighting for Cuban independence in 1895. He is revered today in Cuba as a hero and martyr.

SKILLBUILDER
INTERPRETING POLITICAL CARTOONS
What images do you think the cartoonist wanted the viewer to see in this drawing? What was the cartoonist's view of U.S. involvement in Cuba?

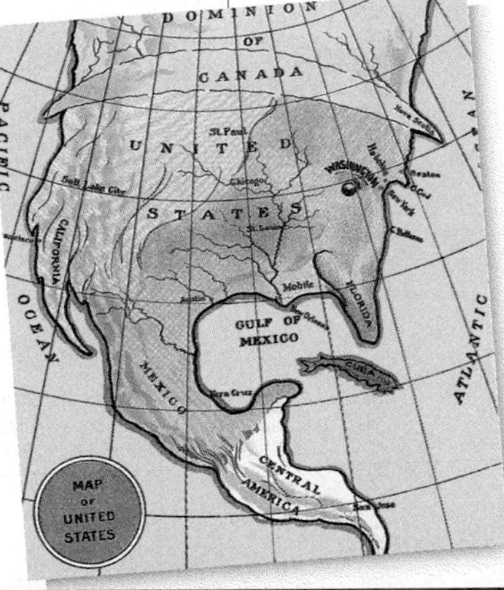

Skillbuilder Answer
Images: *Possible Answer:* The map forms the head of Uncle Sam about to swallow Cuba, which has the appearance of a small fish. **U.S. Involvement:** The artist viewed it as a powerful country's attempt to dominate a smaller country.

(continued from page 370)

- Some Americans support Spanish control of Cuba, while others sympathize with Cuban rebels.

IN DEPTH RESOURCES: UNIT 3
Guided Reading, p. 21

ACCESS FOR STUDENTS ACQUIRING ENGLISH
Guided Reading (Spanish), p. 131

KEY PLAYER
José Martí
Critical Thinking: Analyzing Issues Ask students to explain why Martí sought U.S. intervention in Cuba yet was wary of a U.S. presence in Cuba. *Martí felt that U.S. help was needed to overthrow the Spanish, but he was worried about the United States' imperialistic tendencies.*

IN-DEPTH RESOURCES, UNIT 3
American Lives: José Martí, p. 36

OBJECTIVE
② INSTRUCT

The Threat of War Escalates

▶ ***Discussing Key Ideas***
- Spanish leaders employ harsh tactics in an attempt to crush the Cuban revolt.
- Yellow journalism arouses American sympathy for Cuban rebels.

HISTORY FROM VISUALS
Reading the Cartoon
Who represents the United States in the cartoon? *Uncle Sam.* What does he appear to be on the verge of doing to Cuba? *Swallowing the country.*

IN-DEPTH RESOURCES, UNIT 3
Primary Source: In Favor of Imperialism, p. 31

TEACHING OPTIONS

Exploring Themes

Constitutional Concerns The nation's press, whose freedom and independence are derived from the Constitution, strengthens America's democracy by keeping its citizens well informed and by holding the government accountable for its actions. However, the tactics employed in yellow journalism raise questions about the responsibilities and limits of a free press. Discuss with students the possible dangers to society of unrestrained news media and under what circumstances, if any, constraints should be placed on the media in a democracy.

Teaching Less Proficient Readers

Reexamining Quotes Rereading aloud and interpreting quotes may help less proficient readers to better understand the material. Have those students follow these steps:

1. Read aloud the quotations from Hearst, the de Lôme letter, and Theodore Roosevelt on pages 371 and 372.
2. Discuss the general meaning of each quotation.
3. Have students restate the ideas in their own words. *Example: Roosevelt thought that McKinley was a coward.*

MORE ABOUT . . .
Yellow Journalism

One of Hearst's gimmicks to boost newspaper sales was a color comic strip. The term *yellow journalism* comes from the comic strip's main character, "The Yellow Kid." Hearst's and Pulitzer's role in sensationalizing events such as the sinking of the *Maine* prompted this response from the editor of the New York *Evening Post:* "Nothing so disgraceful . . . has been known in the history of American journalism."

IN-DEPTH RESOURCES: UNIT 3
Primary Source: Newspaper Front Page, p. 29
American Lives: William Randolph Hearst, p. 37

ELECTRONIC LIBRARY OF PRIMARY SOURCES
from *The "Maine": An Account of Her Destruction*

OBJECTIVE
③ INSTRUCT

War Breaks Out

▶ ***Discussing Key Ideas***
- The United States defeats Spanish forces in the Philippines and in Cuba.
- As a result of the Treaty of Paris of 1898, Cuba becomes independent and the United States annexes the Philippines.

HISTORY FROM VISUALS
War in the Philippines, 1898

Reading the Map Refer students to the globe to help them understand the location of the Philippines.

"You furnish the pictures and I'll furnish the war."
WILLIAM RANDOLPH HEARST TO ARTIST FREDERIC REMINGTON

De Lôme's judgment of McKinley was actually much milder than Theodore Roosevelt's. Roosevelt, assistant secretary of the navy, considered McKinley "a white-livered cur" with "no more backbone than a chocolate eclair!" Although some Americans agreed with de Lôme's opinion of McKinley, they resented this criticism of their president by a Spanish official. Before an indignant State Department could demand his recall, de Lôme resigned.

THE U.S.S. *MAINE* EXPLODES Only a few days after publication of the de Lôme letter, American resentment toward Spain turned to outrage. Early in 1898, President McKinley had ordered the **U.S.S. *Maine*** to Cuba to protect American lives and property. On February 15, 1898, an explosion sent the ship's ammunition up in flames, and the *Maine* sank. More than 260 of the 350 American officers and crew aboard lost their lives.

No one really knows what caused the explosion that destroyed the *Maine.* At the time, a naval court of inquiry reported that the ship had hit a mine, while a 1976 study by Admiral Hyman G. Rickover determined that an internal explosion in the ship's coal bunkers had caused the initial blast. In 1898, however, the yellow journalists held Spain responsible. The *Journal's* headline read "THE WARSHIP MAINE WAS SPLIT IN TWO BY AN ENEMY'S SECRET INFERNAL MACHINE." Hearst's paper offered a reward of $50,000 for the capture of the Spaniards who supposedly had committed the outrage.

THINK THROUGH HISTORY
C. Summarizing *What events increased the tensions between the United States and Spain?*

C. Answer
Publication of the de Lôme letter, which criticized President McKinley, and the explosion of the U.S.S. *Maine,* which many Americans blamed on Spain.

War Breaks Out

Now there was no holding back the forces that wanted war. "Remember the *Maine!*" became the rallying cry for U.S. intervention in Cuba. It made no difference that the Spanish government agreed, on April 9, to almost everything the United States demanded, including a six-month cease-fire.

War in the Philippines, 1898

GEOGRAPHY SKILLBUILDER LOCATION ***How far did Admiral Dewey travel to reach the Philippines?*** **LOCATION** ***How did the location of the Philippine Islands make them important to the United States?***

Despite the Spanish concessions, public opinion favored war. On April 11, McKinley asked Congress for authority to use force against Spain in order to bring peace to Cuba. After a week of debate, Congress agreed, and on April 20 the United States went to war with Spain.

THE PHILIPPINES Although American attention focused on Cuba, the first battle of the war took place on the other side of the world—in the Philippine Islands. In February 1898, Roosevelt had ordered the Pacific fleet to sail for the Philippines in case war with Spain broke out. A Spanish colony for over 300 years, the Philippines had repeatedly rebelled against Spanish rule.

On May 1, **George Dewey,** the American naval commander in the Pacific, steamed into Manila Bay and then destroyed

Skillbuilder Answer
Location: About 600 miles.
Location: *Possible Answer:* The Philippines were well-placed for naval bases to protect sea lanes to China and the rest of eastern Asia.

TEACHING OPTIONS

Exploring Themes

America in the World The United States wanted to take over the Philippines for a number of reasons. For one thing, the U.S. government wanted to forestall Germany and other imperialist countries. Many people believed that an independent Philippine Republic would lead to a scramble for territory by several European countries. The United States also needed new markets for its exports and believed that China, with its vast population, would be a promising choice. The Philippines would provide a commercial base in that part of the world.

Teaching Gifted and Talented Students

Writing an Editorial Ask students to review the information on pages 370–373. Then ask them to imagine that they are the editor of a major newspaper during the time of the Spanish-American-Cuban War. Their assignment is to write an editorial expressing the newspaper's viewpoint about the government's actions. Encourage students to include specific reasons for their viewpoints. Call on students to read their editorials to the class.

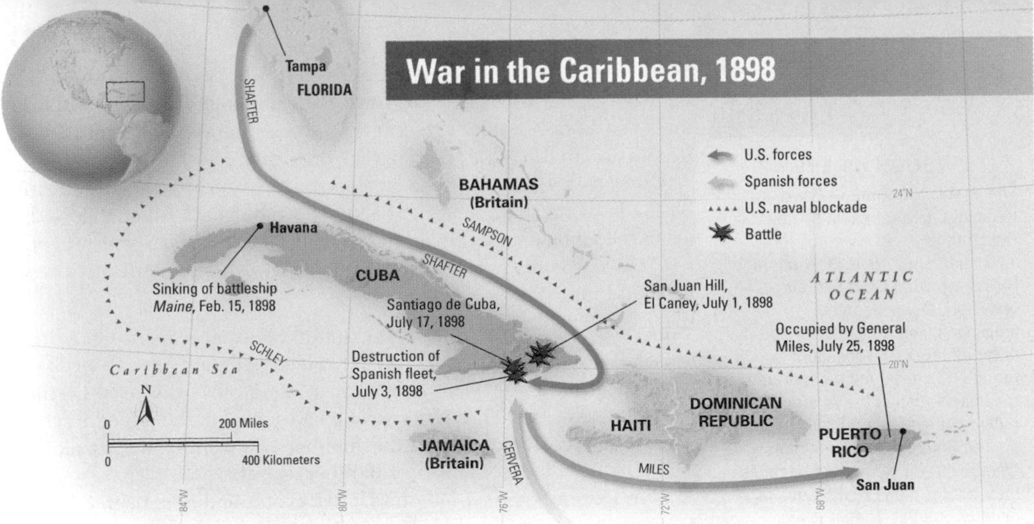

GEOGRAPHY SKILLBUILDER **MOVEMENT** ***Besides Cuba and Puerto Rico, what countries were affected by the U.S. naval blockade in the Caribbean?*** **PLACE** ***What important event took place in the harbor of Santiago de Cuba?***

Skillbuilder Answer **Movement:** Haiti and the Dominican Republic. **Place:** The destruction of the Spanish fleet in July 1898.

the Spanish fleet nearby. Spain lost 381 men, while the United States lost only one sailor, who collapsed from the heat. Dewey's victory allowed U.S. troops to land in the Philippines. Over the next two months, 11,000 Americans joined forces with Filipino rebels led by Emilio Aguinaldo. In August, Spanish troops in Manila surrendered to Americans rather than to the Filipinos, who had been fighting for freedom since 1896.

U.S. FORCES INVADE CUBA Back in the Caribbean, hostilities began with a naval blockade of Cuba. Admiral William T. Sampson effectively sealed the Spanish fleet up in the harbor of Santiago de Cuba. Meanwhile, American troops organized to invade the island.

Dewey's victory had demonstrated the superiority of U.S. naval forces. In contrast, the U.S. Army maintained only a small professional force, supplemented by a larger inexperienced and ill-prepared volunteer force. About 125,000 Americans had volunteered to fight. However, the new soldiers were sent to training camps that lacked adequate supplies and effective leaders. Moreover, there were not enough modern guns to go around, and the troops were outfitted with heavy woolen uniforms that were unsuitable for Cuba's tropical climate. In addition, the officers—most of whom were Civil War veterans—had a tendency to spend their time recalling their war experiences rather than training the volunteers.

THINK THROUGH HISTORY **D.** ***Making Inferences*** *Why do you think U.S. troops were so poorly prepared for war?*

D. Answer The poor training of the volunteer soldiers and the lack of supplies suggest that the army had not been well funded since the Civil War, possibly because the government had other priorities and the navy had a stronger advocate.

ROUGH RIDERS Despite these handicaps, American forces landed in Cuba in June 1898 and began to converge on the port city of Santiago. The army of 17,000 included four African-American regiments of the regular army and the **Rough Riders,** a volunteer cavalry under the command of Leonard Wood and Theodore Roosevelt.

The most famous land battle in Cuba took place near Santiago on July 1. The first part of the battle, on nearby Kettle Hill, featured a gallant uphill charge by the Rough Riders and two African-American regiments, the Ninth and

This lithograph of Roosevelt leading the Rough Riders at San Juan Hill shows the men on horseback, though they actually fought on foot.

HISTORY FROM VISUALS
War in the Caribbean, 1898

Reading the Map Point out to students that the row of small triangles indicates the extent of the U.S. naval blockade.

Extension Remind students of Alfred T. Mahan's argument for a strong navy in his book, *The Influence of Sea Power upon History 1660–1783* (p. 366). Discuss how Mahan's philosophy played a role in the U.S. victory in the Caribbean. Have students list the possible effects of a naval blockade on a surrounded country using the following chart:

Effects of a Blockade
1.
2.
3.
4.

MORE ABOUT . . .
Battle of San Juan Hill

Twenty years after the battle, Roosevelt stated, "San Juan was the great day of my life." He believed that he deserved the Congressional Medal of Honor for his part in the war, but the award was denied him.

IN-DEPTH RESOURCES: UNIT 3 from *The Rough Riders* by Theodore Roosevelt, p. 30

ELECTRONIC LIBRARY OF PRIMARY SOURCES from *The Strenuous Life* by Theodore Roosevelt

Block Schedule TEACHING OPTION **Time Needed: 40 Minutes**

Cooperative Activity: Covering the Rough Riders

Task: Students will role-play reporters and members of the Rough Riders and together craft a news article about the key battles of the war in Cuba.

Purpose: To help students to better understand the major battles of the Spanish-American-Cuban War and the reasons why the United States won.

Activity: Students should pair off and do further research through the use of various library resources or the Internet on the Rough Riders, as well as on the battles of Kettle Hill and San Juan Hill. One student then will play a reporter, while the other plays a member of the Rough Riders. The reporter will interview the Rough Rider about his or her experiences in the war and write a brief article based on the interview. The students who played the reporter should read their articles aloud to the class.

Building a Portfolio: Encourage students to place their news article in their portfolio if they feel it is one of their stronger works.

Standards for Evaluation
News articles should . . .

- be written in a clear and concise manner
- show evidence of research from more than one source
- include the key aspects of an event, as well as relevant quotes

HISTORICAL SPOTLIGHT
Rough Riders

Critical Thinking: Analyzing Discuss the characteristics of the Rough Riders. Then ask students to imagine that a movie is being made about this regiment. Whom would they cast in leading roles? Why?

ASSESS & RETEACH

Section 2 Assessment

Divide students into four groups and assign one of the questions to each group to answer. Then form new groups of four, consisting of one student from each original group. Students should share and discuss their answers.

Self-Assessment

Have pairs of students use the Think Through History Questions to review main ideas in this section. Students should find the portion of the text that helps answer each question.

Section Quiz

FORMAL ASSESSMENT
Section Quiz, p. 130

Reteach

Use the Guided Reading Worksheet for Section 2 to help review the main ideas of this section.

IN-DEPTH RESOURCES: UNIT 3
Guided Reading, p. 21

CLOSE

The Spanish-American-Cuban War demonstrated the superiority of U.S. naval forces and added Puerto Rico, Guam, and the Philippines to America's empire.

HISTORICAL SPOTLIGHT

ROUGH RIDERS

The First U.S. Volunteer Cavalry Regiment, better known as the Rough Riders, consisted of about 1,200 men aged 16 to 69. The Rough Riders included cowboys, clerks, New York City policemen, musicians, and polo players and other athletes. The regiment existed for only 133 days, but it captured the imagination of the American public and won the public's respect.

The Rough Riders trained as cavalry but fought on foot because their horses didn't reach Cuba in time for combat. They had the highest casualty rate of any American unit in the war. Among those who survived were future governors, members of Congress, and Theodore Roosevelt, who later became president of the United States.

Tenth Cavalries. Their victory cleared the way for an infantry attack on the strategically important **San Juan Hill.** Although Roosevelt and his units played only a minor role in the second victory, American newspapers declared him the hero of San Juan Hill.

Two days later, the Spanish fleet tried to escape the American blockade of the harbor at Santiago. The naval battle that followed, along the Cuban coast, ended in the destruction of the Spanish fleet. On July 17, Santiago surrendered, and on July 25, American troops invaded Puerto Rico.

TREATY OF PARIS OF 1898 The United States and Spain signed an armistice on August 12, ending what Secretary of State John Hay called "a splendid little war." The fighting had lasted only 16 weeks. Of the approximately 300,000 Americans who had served in the armed forces, about 5,400 lost their lives. Of this number, 379 were battle casualties, while the rest died from diseases or other causes.

On December 10, 1898, the United States and Spain agreed in a treaty that (1) Cuba would become independent, (2) Spain would give Puerto Rico and the Pacific island of Guam to the United States, and (3) the United States would pay Spain $20 million for the annexation of the Philippine Islands.

ANNEXATION OF THE PHILIPPINES The Treaty of Paris touched off great debate in the United States. Arguments centered on the annexation of the Philippines, but imperialism was the real issue. President McKinley told a group of Methodist ministers that he had prayed for guidance on Philippine annexation and had concluded "that there was nothing left for us to do but to take them all [the Philippine Islands], and to educate the Filipinos, and uplift and Christianize them." McKinley's imperialist beliefs must have clouded his memory—most Filipinos had been Christian for centuries.

Other prominent Americans presented a variety of arguments—political, moral, and self-serving—against annexation. Some felt that the treaty violated the Declaration of Independence by denying self-government to the newly acquired territories. The African-American educator Booker T. Washington argued that the United States should settle race-related issues at home before taking on social problems elsewhere. The labor leader Samuel Gompers feared that Filipino immigrants would compete for American jobs.

On February 6, 1899, the annexation question was settled with the Senate's approval of the Treaty of Paris. The United States now had an empire. The next question Americans faced was how and when the United States would add to its dominion.

E. Answer Imperialists justified annexation as a means to educate and civilize Filipinos.

THINK THROUGH HISTORY
E. *Analyzing Motives* *What justifications were used by Americans who favored annexing the Philippines?*

Section 2 Assessment

1. TERMS & NAMES
Identify:
- José Martí
- Valeriano Weyler
- yellow journalism
- U.S.S. *Maine*
- George Dewey
- Rough Riders
- San Juan Hill

2. SUMMARIZING Write newspaper headlines explaining the significance of each of the following dates related to the Spanish-American-Cuban War:

February 15, 1898
April 20, 1898
May 1, 1898
July 25, 1898
August 12, 1898
February 6, 1899

Write the first paragraph of the newspaper article for one of the headlines.

3. MAKING INFERENCES What do you think were the unstated editorial policies of the yellow press? Support your answer with evidence from the text.

THINK ABOUT
- James Creelman's account of Spanish atrocities against Cubans (page 370)
- Hearst's remark to Remington.
- the *Journal's* headline about the explosion of the battleship *Maine*

4. FORMING OPINIONS If you had been a member of Congress in 1898, would you have voted to declare war on Spain? Why or why not?

THINK ABOUT
- events that fueled the U.S. conflict with Spain
- the public's opinion of the war
- the success of McKinley's diplomatic measures in resolving the crisis
- the debate in Congress before the declaration of war

ANSWERS

1. TERMS & NAMES

José Martí, p. 370

Valeriano Weyler, p. 371

yellow journalism, p. 371

U.S.S. *Maine*, p. 372

George Dewey, p. 372

Rough Riders, p. 373

San Juan Hill, p. 374

2. SUMMARIZING

Possible Responses: February 15, 1898: Battleship *Maine* Mysteriously Explodes and Sinks Near Cuban Coast; Over 260 Americans Die. April 20, 1898: U.S. Goes to War with Spain. May 1, 1898: Admiral Dewey Steams into Manila Bay and Destroys Spanish Fleet. July 25, 1898: U.S. Troops Invade Puerto Rico. August 12, 1898: War Over! U.S. and Spain Sign Armistice. February 6, 1899: Senate Passes Treaty of Paris.

3. MAKING INFERENCES

Possible Responses: To create news rather than to document it; to sensationalize events by distorting the truth; to exploit the public's fears; to manipulate the public's perceptions of events; to write articles that sell newspapers; to advance the newspaper publisher's political views.

4. FORMING OPINIONS

Possible Responses: Yes—the war was a humanitarian effort to stop Spanish atrocities against Cubans and to ensure Cubans' independence; it was important to represent public opinion that supported war; belief in imperialism meant supporting aggressive foreign policies. No—the yellow press was spreading war fever; belief in anti-imperialism meant supporting cautious foreign policies.

3 Acquiring New Lands

TERMS & NAMES
- Platt Amendment
- protectorate
- Emilio Aguinaldo
- John Hay
- Open Door notes
- Boxer Rebellion

LEARN ABOUT U.S. relations with Cuba, Puerto Rico, and the Philippines
TO UNDERSTAND how American imperialism developed across the globe.

ONE AMERICAN'S STORY

On May 5, 1916, Luis Muñoz Rivera stood before the U.S. House of Representatives to discuss the future of his homeland, Puerto Rico. For more than a quarter of a century, he had fought to secure self-government for the people of Puerto Rico, first from Spain and then from the United States. In 1891, as the editor of *La Democracia,* Muñoz Rivera had published a series of articles proposing self-government for Puerto Rico.

In 1897, after the Puerto Ricans and Cubans rebelled against Spain, Spanish authorities agreed to self-government for Puerto Rico. On July 17, 1898, the new Puerto Rican legislature met. Eight days, later, however, American troops landed on the island as part of their campaign against the Spanish. The Americans opposed Puerto Rican attempts at self-government, but Muñoz Rivera did not give up. Between 1900 and 1916, he led a campaign for Puerto Rican self-government in the United States as well as in Puerto Rico. Finally, in 1916, the U.S. Congress, facing possible war in Europe and wishing to settle the issue of Puerto Rico, invited Muñoz Rivera to speak before it.

A PERSONAL VOICE

You, citizens of a free fatherland, with its own laws, its own institutions, and its own flag, can appreciate the unhappiness of the small and solitary people that must await its laws from your authority. . . . When you acquire the certainty that you can found in Puerto Rico a republic like that founded in Cuba and Panama . . . give us our independence and you will stand before humanity as . . . a great creator of new nationalities and a great liberator of oppressed peoples.

LUIS MUÑOZ RIVERA, quoted in *The Puerto Ricans*

Luis Muñoz Rivera

Muñoz Rivera returned to Puerto Rico, where he died in November 1916. Three months later, the United States made Puerto Ricans American citizens. They were not granted independence.

For nearly two decades before the First World War, the U.S. government viewed its colonies' demands for autonomy with suspicion. Only when America felt threatened by international calamity—World War I—did it bend to the wishes of its colonial populations.

U.S. Involvement in Puerto Rico

Not all Puerto Ricans wanted independence, as Muñoz Rivera did. Some wanted statehood, while others hoped for some measure of local self-government as an American territory. As a result, the United States gave Puerto Ricans no promises regarding independence after the Spanish-American-Cuban War.

AMERICANS IN PUERTO RICO When American military forces landed on the island in July 1898, the commanding officer, General Nelson A. Miles, issued a statement assuring Puerto Ricans that the Americans were there to "bring you protection, not only to yourselves but to your property, to promote your prosperity, and to bestow upon you the immunities and blessings of the liberal institutions of our government." Other American officers were openly insulting. For example, General Guy V. Henry, military governor of the island, doubted that Puerto Ricans could govern themselves. He argued that "they

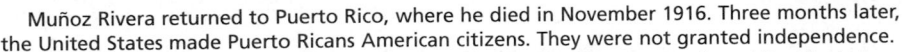

SECTION 3 RESOURCES

PRINT RESOURCES

IN-DEPTH RESOURCES: UNIT 3
Guided Reading, p. 22

READING STUDY GUIDE, p. 113

ACCESS FOR STUDENTS ACQUIRING ENGLISH
Guided Reading (Spanish), p. 132

SPANISH READING STUDY GUIDE, p. 113

FORMAL ASSESSMENT
Section Quiz, p. 131

ALTERNATIVE ASSESSMENT BOOK
See forms for supporting and scoring alternative activities.

TECHNOLOGY RESOURCES

HUMANITIES TRANSPARENCIES
H17, *Athletic Contest* by Max Weber
H37, Declined with Thanks

CRITICAL THINKING TRANSPARENCIES
CT18, Overseas Expansion

CD-ROM Electronic Library of Primary Sources

VIDEO *American Portfolio: A Videodisc for U.S. History* user's guide, p. 179

INTERNET http://www.mlushistory.com

Section 3 Overview

OBJECTIVES

1. To describe U.S. involvement in Puerto Rico.
2. To explain how the United States maintained political control over Cuba.
3. To identify causes and effects of the Philippine-American War.
4. To explain the purpose of the Open Door Policy in China.
5. To summarize views regarding U.S. imperialism.

SKILLBUILDERS

- Interpreting political cartoons, p. 377
- Understanding geography: human-environment interaction, p. 380
- Interpreting graphs, p. 381

CRITICAL THINKING

- Drawing conclusions, p. 376
- Synthesizing, p. 377
- Contrasting, p. 378
- Analyzing motives, p. 379
- Theme: America in the World, p. 381
- Summarizing, p. 381
- Analyzing issues, p. 381
- Forming opinions, p. 381

FOCUS & MOTIVATE

5-MINUTE WARM-UP

Making Generalizations
To make generalizations about American imperialism, have students study the cartoon on page 377 and answer these questions.

1. What do the territories listed on the menu have in common?
2. What does the cartoon suggest about the methods the United States would use to acquire new lands?

WARM-UP TRANSPARENCY 10

Starting with the Student
- How do students convince their parents to give them more independence?
- How do students think colonial populations convinced the United States to grant them self-government?

OBJECTIVE
① **INSTRUCT**

U.S. Involvement in Puerto Rico

▶ ***Discussing Key Ideas***
- Puerto Ricans resent U.S. control of their government.
- Congress passes the Foraker Act, which denies U.S. citizenship to Puerto Ricans and gives the president control over Puerto Rico's government.

IN-DEPTH RESOURCES: UNIT 3
Guided Reading, p. 22

ACCESS FOR STUDENTS ACQUIRING ENGLISH
Guided Reading (Spanish), p. 132

NOW & THEN
Puerto Rico as Commonwealth

Critical Thinking: Drawing Conclusions Have students make a chart comparing pros and cons of statehood for Puerto Rico. Then ask them to write a paragraph stating how they would vote on a national referendum on statehood if they were living in Puerto Rico.

OBJECTIVE

② **INSTRUCT**

Cuba Becomes a Protectorate

▶ ***Discussing Key Ideas***
- The Treaty of Paris ensures Cuban independence, but the U.S. Army steps in.
- As a result of the Platt Amendment, the United States maintains control over Cuba.

NOW & THEN

PUERTO RICO AS COMMONWEALTH

Today, some Puerto Ricans argue in favor of statehood for Puerto Rico, and others support independence. However, in 1993, Puerto Ricans narrowly voted to remain a U.S. commonwealth, a status given the island in 1952.

As a commonwealth, Puerto Rico is allowed to make its own laws and handle its own finances, while the United States controls defense and sets tariffs. In addition, as commonwealth citizens, Puerto Ricans can move freely between their island and the United States—there are no immigration restrictions.

As a commonwealth, Puerto Rico enjoys a tax-exempt status that encourages corporations to build factories there. As a state, it would gain representation in Congress, the right to vote in presidential elections, and opportunities for federal aid—but it would lose its tax-exempt status.

are still children, each one has a different idea and they don't really know what they want." Henry limited Puerto Ricans' access to alcoholic beverages and tobacco, tried to Americanize the Puerto Ricans by teaching them English, and limited freedom of the press, especially after being criticized by Muñoz Rivera.

PUERTO RICAN ATTITUDES TOWARD INDEPENDENCE Many Puerto Ricans at first welcomed U.S. intervention, seeing it as an improvement over control by Spain. Following General Henry's heavy-handed tactics in 1899, however, large numbers of Puerto Ricans came to fear the "Yankee Peril." Even those who supported U.S. control became disillusioned with the military government and its attitude of superiority toward the Puerto Ricans. Some, like Muñoz Rivera, campaigned for an end to military government and requested U.S. citizenship and full local self-government. They believed that after Puerto Rico demonstrated the ability to govern itself, it should become a state. Still others felt that Puerto Ricans should be allowed to choose between statehood and complete independence from the United States.

CITIZENSHIP FOR PUERTO RICANS Although Puerto Ricans had dreams of independence or statehood, the United States had a different agenda for the island's future. Puerto Rico was strategically important to the United States, both for maintaining a U.S. presence in the Caribbean and for protecting a future canal that some American leaders wanted to build across the Isthmus of Panama. In 1900, Congress passed the Foraker Act, which denied U.S. citizenship to Puerto Ricans and gave the president the power to appoint Puerto Rico's governor and members of the upper house of its legislature. Puerto Ricans could elect only the members of the legislature's lower house.

In 1901, in the Insular Cases, the U.S. Supreme Court ruled that the Constitution did not automatically apply to people in acquired territories. Congress, however, retained the right to extend U.S. citizenship, and it granted that right to Puerto Ricans in 1917. It also gave them the right to elect both houses of their legislature.

THINK THROUGH HISTORY
A. Drawing Conclusions *How did the Foraker Act benefit the United States?*

A. Answer It allowed the president to appoint Puerto Rico's governor and part of its legislature, thus enabling the United States to maintain control.

Cuba Becomes a Protectorate

The war resolution against Spain in 1898 had included the Teller Amendment, which said that the United States did not intend to annex or control Cuba. After all, Spanish oppression of Cubans was the United States' main argument for waging war. Consequently, the Treaty of Paris of 1898 guaranteed Cuba the independence that its nationalist leaders had been demanding for years. Still, for four years following the war, the U.S. Army governed Cuba.

José Martí had feared that the United States would merely replace Spain and dominate Cuban politics. In some ways, Martí's prediction came true. Under American occupation, the same officials who had served Spain remained in office. Cubans who protested this policy were imprisoned or exiled.

On the other hand, the American military government provided food and clothing for thousands of families, helped farmers put land back into cultivation, and organized elementary schools. Through improvement of sanitation and medical research, the military government eliminated yellow fever, a disease that had killed hundreds of Cubans each year.

PLATT AMENDMENT In 1900 the newly formed Cuban government wrote a constitution, one that did not specify the relationship between Cuba and the United States. Consequently, in 1901, the United States insisted that Cuba

TEACHING OPTIONS

Exploring Themes

Constitutional Concerns In 1788, as the United States ratified its Constitution, probably few Americans dreamed of acquiring other countries. For that reason, the U.S. Constitution does not explicitly address the rights of people in acquired territories. Instead, the Supreme Court had to step in and rule on the matter. Discuss with students the Supreme Court's ruling that the rights granted by the Constitution do not automatically apply to persons in territories acquired by the United States. Ask students to offer reasons why they agree or disagree.

Making Connections Across Cultures

Puerto Ricans in the United States Throughout the 20th century, native Puerto Ricans and their ancestors have made notable contributions to U.S. society. In 1970, Herman Badillo became the first Puerto Rican to win election to the U.S. Congress. The writer William Carlos Williams, whose mother was born in Puerto Rico, won the Pulitzer Prize in poetry in 1963. Throughout the 1960s, Roberto Clemente starred as an outfielder for the Pittsburgh Pirates. During his 18-year career, Clemente won four National League batting titles. He eventually was elected to baseball's Hall of Fame.

add to its constitution several provisions, known as the **Platt Amendment,** stating that

1. Cuba could not make treaties that might limit its independence or permit a foreign power to control any part of its territory
2. the United States reserved the right to intervene in Cuba to preserve independence and maintain order
3. Cuba was not to go into debt
4. the United States could buy or lease land on the island for naval and coaling stations

The United States made it clear that the army would not withdraw until Cuba adopted the Platt Amendment. In response, a torchlight procession marched on the residence of Governor-General Leonard Wood to protest the provisions. Some protesters even called for a return to arms to defend their national honor against this American insult. The U.S. government stood firm, though, and Cubans reluctantly ratified the new constitution. In 1903, the Platt Amendment became part of a treaty between the two nations, and it remained in effect for 31 years. Cuba became a U.S. **protectorate,** a country whose affairs are partially controlled by a stronger power.

THINK THROUGH HISTORY
B. *Synthesizing* *How did the United States maintain political control over Cuba?*

B. Answer The United States refused to withdraw troops until Cuba agreed to the Platt Amendment, which gave the United States partial control over Cuba's affairs.

PROTECTING AMERICAN BUSINESS INTERESTS The most important reason for the United States to maintain a strong political presence in Cuba was to protect its economic interests. American corporations had invested heavily in the island's sugar, tobacco, and mining industries, as well as in its railroads and public utilities. American investments in Cuba soared from $50 million in 1898 to $220 million by 1913. Although many businesspeople were convinced that political control of colonies was necessary in order to protect the large profits to be found there, some were concerned about colonial entanglements. The industrialist Andrew Carnegie argued that a policy of imperialism was unnecessary.

A PERSONAL VOICE

The exports of the United States this year [1898] are greater than those of any other nation in the world. Even Britain's exports are less, yet Britain "possesses" . . . a hundred "colonies" . . . scattered all over the world. The fact that the United States has none does not prevent her products and manufactures from invading . . . all parts of the world in competition with those of Britain.

ANDREW CARNEGIE, quoted in *Distant Possessions*

The U.S. Department of State, however, continued to push for control of its Latin American neighbors. American troops withdrew from Cuba in 1902 but later returned three times to intervene in Cuban affairs. Marines occupied the island to quell popular uprisings against conservative leaders from 1906 to 1909, briefly in 1912, and again from 1917 to 1922. The United States also established a naval base at Guantánamo Bay, which it still maintains.

HISTORICAL SPOTLIGHT

DR. CARLOS FINLAY AND YELLOW FEVER

Yellow fever is a dangerous disease that damages many body tissues, especially the liver. It was once widespread in Central and South America, and almost 800 people per year died of yellow fever in Havana alone.

In 1881, the Cuban physician Carlos Finlay suggested that yellow fever was carried by mosquitoes. When an epidemic swept Cuba in 1900, a team of U.S. Army surgeons led by Dr. Walter Reed went to Havana to find the cause. The army doctors conducted experiments that proved Finlay's theory was correct.

Clearing out the mosquitoes' breeding places helped eliminate yellow fever in Cuba within a year. Dr. Finlay served as chief sanitary officer of Cuba from 1902 to 1909.

SKILLBUILDER
INTERPRETING POLITICAL CARTOONS
Who is the waiter taking Uncle Sam's order for dinner? What seems to be Uncle Sam's attitude toward the offerings on the menu?

WELL, I HARDLY KNOW WHICH TO TAKE FIRST!

Skillbuilder Answer
Waiter: President McKinley.
Attitude: *Possible Answer:* Uncle Sam seems very smug, as if all the menu items (territories) were his for the asking.

Filipinos Rebel

In the Philippines, the native population was intent on independence. Even more than the Cubans, Filipinos reacted with outrage to American annexation of their

HISTORICAL SPOTLIGHT
Dr. Carlos Finlay and Yellow Fever

Several members of the team of U.S. Army surgeons in Cuba actually volunteered to be infected with deadly yellow fever virus to track the course of the disease. Fortunately, they all survived. Have students find out about other scientists and physicians who conquered life-threatening viruses.

HISTORY FROM VISUALS
Political Cartoon

Reading the Cartoon What territories are listed on the bill of fare? *Cuba, Puerto Rico, the Philippines, the Sandwich Islands (Hawaii).*

Extension Tell students to review the cartoon on page 371. Discuss in what ways these two cartoons represent similar views.

CRITICAL THINKING TRANSPARENCIES
CT18, Overseas Expansion

OBJECTIVE
3 INSTRUCT

Filipinos Rebel

▶ ***Starting with the Student*** Have students create a chart like this to show events in the Philippines from its annexation to its independence.

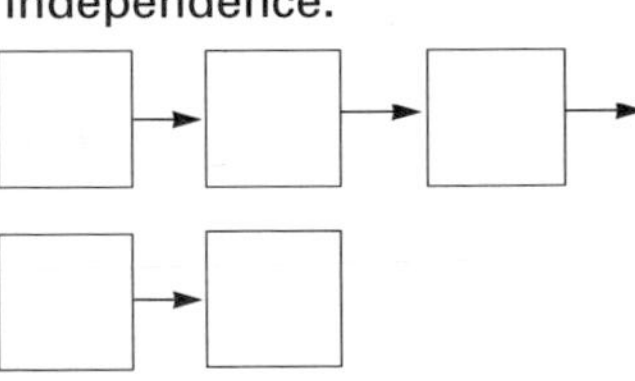

(continued on next page)

TEACHING OPTIONS

Making Global Connections

Yellow Fever Epidemics While the deadly yellow fever virus wreaked much havoc in Central and South America, it also spread misery throughout North America. In 1853, yellow fever killed more than 11,000 people in New Orleans. In 1878, about 5,000 residents of Memphis, Tennessee, died of the disease. While the disease knew no national boundaries, conquering it also took on a global dimension. In addition to the work of Carlos Finlay and Dr. Walter Reed, Dr. Max Theiler, a South African research physician, developed a vaccine in 1937 to prevent yellow fever.

Making Connections Across the Curriculum

Economics Although nations strive for a favorable balance of trade, in which they export more than they import, economists stress that imports are an important part of a healthy economy. Imports help create jobs, from the dock workers who unload the merchandise, to the truckers who deliver the goods to the store, to the retailers who sell the products to the public. Imports also add greatly to the supply of consumer goods, which reduces their prices. Ask students to consider what things they own—shoes, CD players, clothes—that might be imported.

(continued from page 377)

▶ ***Discussing Key Ideas***
- The Filipinos revolt against U.S. rule, and U.S. forces brutally crush the rebellion.
- Under U.S. rule, the Philippines gradually achieve independence.

MORE ABOUT . . .
Philippine-American War
The process of Americanization of the Philippines included making English the official language and introducing basketball. However, the Moros—Muslim Filipinos on the island of Mindanao—refused to submit to American rule. They finally surrendered in 1906 after 600 of them, including many women and children, died in the Battle of Bud Dajo.

ELECTRONIC LIBRARY OF PRIMARY SOURCES
On the War in the Philippines by Albert J. Beveridge

OBJECTIVE
4 INSTRUCT

China and the Open Door Policy

▶ ***Discussing Key Ideas***
- European powers and Japan establish spheres of influence in China.
- John Hay proposes that European nations share their trading rights in China with the United States.
- The United States and other imperialist powers put down a rebellion against foreign influences in China.

U.S. military action in the Philippines resulted in suffering for Filipino civilians. About 200,000 people died as a result of malnutrition, disease, and such guerrilla tactics as the burning of villages.

homeland. The rebel leader **Emilio Aguinaldo** believed that the United States had promised independence and that it had betrayed the Filipinos after helping them win freedom from Spain. Resentment over the 1898 Treaty of Paris erupted in rebellion.

PHILIPPINE–AMERICAN WAR In January 1899, Aguinaldo proclaimed the Philippines an independent republic and drafted a constitution. But the presence of American soldiers reinforced U.S. control over the islands. In February, the Filipinos, led by Aguinaldo, rose in armed revolt. The United States assumed the role that Spain had played and imposed its authority on a colony that was fighting for freedom. When Aguinaldo turned to guerrilla tactics, the United States resorted to forcing Filipinos to live in designated zones, where poor sanitation, starvation, and disease killed thousands. This was the very same practice that Americans had condemned Spain for using in Cuba.

White American soldiers looked down on the Filipinos because of their skin color. However, many of the 70,000 U.S. troops sent to the Philippines were African Americans. When African-American newspapers questioned why blacks were helping to spread racial prejudice to the Philippines, some African-American soldiers deserted to the Filipino side and developed bonds of friendship with the Filipinos.

The Philippine-American War lasted three years. American forces captured Aguinaldo in 1901, but the rebellion continued until mid-1902. About 20,000 Filipino rebels died fighting for independence. The war claimed 4,000 American lives and cost $400 million—20 times the price the United States had paid for the islands.

THINK THROUGH HISTORY
C. *Contrasting* *What were the aims of the Filipinos? of the Americans?*

C. Answer Filipinos wanted independence. The United States wanted to take over the role that Spain had played in governing the Philippines.

AFTERMATH OF THE WAR After suppressing the rebellion, the United States set up a government for the Philippines similar to the one it had established for Puerto Rico. The U.S. president would appoint a governor, who would then appoint the upper house of the legislature. Filipinos would elect the lower house. From 1901 to 1904, William Howard Taft served as governor of the islands. He established programs to build schools and hospitals and improve sanitation.

One of Taft's programs brought American college graduates to the islands to improve education. The 540 young Americans who sailed to Manila aboard the U.S.S. *Thomas* became known as Thomasites. They settled throughout the islands, trained Filipino teachers, and conducted classes. The number of Filipino students attending elementary school increased from 5,000 in 1898 to more than 1 million in 1920. Under American rule, the Philippines moved gradually toward independence and finally became an independent republic on July 4, 1946.

China and the Open Door Policy

U.S. imperialists saw the Philippines as a gateway to the rest of Asia, particularly China. The United States did not want to seek colonies on the Asian mainland or risk another war like the one in the Philippines. China, however, was seen as a vast potential market for American products. It also presented American investors with opportunities for large-scale railroad construction.

Block Schedule TEACHING OPTION **Time Needed: 30 Minutes**

Cooperative Activity: Writing Letters to Uncle Sam

Task: Student groups will write letters to the United States government expressing Cuban, Puerto Rican, Filipino, and Chinese attitudes toward American imperialism.

Purpose: To better understand the effects of imperialism on colonial peoples.

Activity: Divide students into groups of four and have each group represent one of the following countries: Puerto Rico, Cuba, the Philippines, and China. The group should write a letter to the United States (addressing it to Uncle Sam) expressing how U.S. imperialism affects the country which they represent. Allow time for the group to share its letter with the class.

Building a Portfolio: Students wishing to add the assignment to their portfolios should highlight their contribution to the letter.

ALTERNATIVE ASSESSMENT BOOK
Standards for Evaluating a Cooperative Activity

Standards for Evaluation
Letters should . . .
- include specific examples of the positive and negative effects of American imperialism in the assigned country
- accurately reflect information from the textbook and other references
- use appropriate letter form and style

Weakened by war and foreign intervention, China had become the "sick man of Asia" by the early 20th century. As China's 250-year-old Qing Dynasty began to crumble, European powers and Japan demanded trading rights and other concessions. Under pressure from American business leaders, who feared they might be squeezed out of China, the United States took action.

JOHN HAY'S OPEN DOOR NOTES By 1899, France, Germany, Britain, Japan, and Russia not only had established prosperous settlements along the coast of China but also had spheres of influence, or exclusive rights to railroad construction and mining development, in the nation's interior.

The United States had no wish for territory in China. Its access to China's ports was protected by treaties that trading nations had signed decades earlier. But the growing struggle among countries for control of China's resources caused American leaders to fear that the United States might lose access to China's ports as the result of a war or a takeover.

To protect American interests, and also to help the Chinese, U.S. Secretary of State **John Hay** issued a series of policy statements called the **Open Door notes.** These statements were sent to officials of Great Britain, Germany, France, Italy, Japan, and Russia. In them the United States called for open access to China's coastal ports, the elimination of special privileges for any of the trading nations, and the maintenance of China's independence. Other nations reluctantly accepted these proposals, which remained in effect until after World War II.

THINK THROUGH HISTORY
D. *Analyzing Motives* *Why did John Hay propose an Open Door policy in China?*

D. Answer To protect American access to Chinese markets and to help the Chinese maintain their independence.

REBELLION IN CHINA In 1900, events in China brought the United States and other imperial powers together to stop a rebellion. At that time, many Chinese opposed the spread of Western influence in their country. A secret society, known as the Boxers, rose in revolt to drive out the "foreign devils." The Boxers killed hundreds of missionaries and other foreigners, as well as Chinese converts to Christianity. In August 1900, troops from Britain, France, Germany, and Japan joined about 2,500 American soldiers and marched on the Chinese capital. Within two months, the international forces put down the **Boxer Rebellion.** Thousands of Chinese people died during the fighting.

ON THE WORLD STAGE

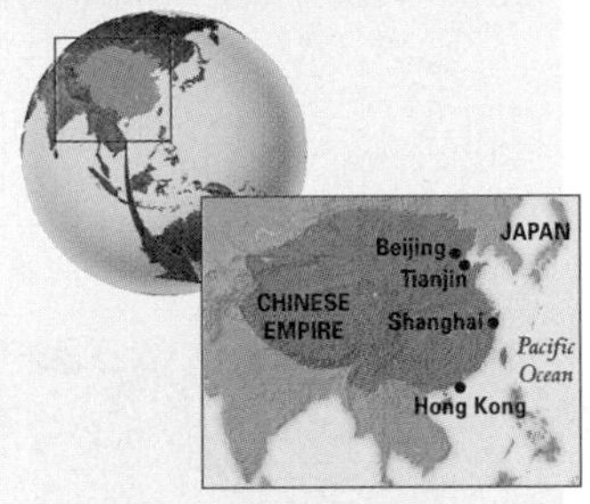

THE BOXER PROTOCOL

On September 7, 1901, China and 11 other nations signed the Boxer Protocol—a final settlement of the Boxer Rebellion.

The Qing government agreed to execute some Chinese officials, to punish others, and to pay about $332 million in damages. The United States was awarded a settlement of $24.5 million. It used about $4 million to pay American citizens for actual losses incurred during the rebellion. In 1908, the U.S. government returned the rest of the money to China to be used for the purpose of educating Chinese students in their own country and in the United States.

U.S. Army troops attack the walls of Beijing while invading the city during the rebellion of the Righteous and Harmonious Fists, or Boxers, in 1900.

MORE ABOUT . . .

The Boxers

The real name of the group known as the Boxers was the Righteous and Harmonious Fists. Westerners referred to the organization as the Boxers because its members practiced Chinese exercises that resembled boxing.

ON THE WORLD STAGE

The Boxer Protocol

Critical Thinking: Analyzing Motives Why did the U.S. government want the money it returned to China to be used for educating Chinese students in China and the United States? *Possible Responses: To foster good will; to introduce Chinese students to Western influences; to exercise some control over Chinese use of the money.*

HUMANITIES TRANSPARENCIES
H17, *Athletic Contest* by Max Weber

TEACHING OPTIONS

Teaching Gifted and Talented Students

Investigating the Life and Rule of Cixi Empress Cixi (also spelled Tz'u-hsi), who ruled China during the Boxer Rebellion, is considered to be one of the most powerful women in the history of China. Like the Boxers, Cixi detested foreign influence in China. "The foreigners are like fish in the stewpan," she said. "For forty years have I . . . eaten bitterness because of them." Have students research and report on Empress Cixi's reign and her role in the Boxer Rebellion. Why did she endorse and then eventually condemn the rebellion? How did she maintain power after western nations put down the uprising?

Making Connections Across Time

China Reclaims Hong Kong On July 1, 1997, Hong Kong once again became part of China. In 1898, China had leased the small peninsula along its southern coast to Britain for 99 years. During that time Hong Kong became a major port for British trade with Asia and grew into a prosperous center of international trade and finance. In reclaiming the land, Communist China vowed to allow Hong Kong a "high degree of autonomy" for the next fifty years. However, observers fear that China's rulers will bring with them their repressive ways, and many Hong Kong residents are bracing for an end to their democratic freedoms.

OBJECTIVE

5 INSTRUCT

The Impact of U.S. Territorial Gains

▶ ***Discussing Key Ideas***
- Imperialism forces Americans to expand their knowledge of the world.
- Some Americans continue to oppose imperialism for economic and moral reasons.

MORE ABOUT . . .

William Jennings Bryan

In one anti-imperialist speech, Bryan declared that the famous words of Patrick Henry applied not only to Americans, but all peoples of the world. "When he uttered that passionate appeal, 'Give me liberty or give me death,' he expressed a sentiment which still echoes in the hearts of men."

ELECTRONIC LIBRARY OF PRIMARY SOURCES

Platform of the Anti-Imperialist League

HISTORY FROM VISUALS

U.S. Imperialism, 1885–1910

Reading the Map Point out that the date next to each flag indicates when the United States gained that territory.

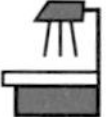

HUMANITIES TRANSPARENCIES

H37, Declined with Thanks

The United States then took additional steps to prevent the imperial powers from carving up China.

John Hay issued a second series of Open Door notes, announcing that the United States would "safeguard for the world the principle of equal and impartial trade with all parts of the Chinese Empire." This policy paved the way for greater American influence in Asia and was used not only to open foreign markets but also to try to establish a strong presence in each of the markets.

The Open Door policy reflected three deeply held American beliefs about the U.S. industrial capitalist economy. First, Americans believed that the growth of the U.S. economy depended on exports. Second, they felt the United States had a right to intervene abroad to keep foreign markets open. Third, they feared that the closing of an area to American products, citizens, or ideas threatened U.S. survival. These beliefs were the bedrock of American foreign policy.

The Impact of U.S. Territorial Gains

William McKinley's reelection in 1900 seemed to indicate that many Americans favored his policies over those of his anti-imperialist opponent, William Jennings Bryan. McKinley stated, "The expansion of our trade and commerce is the pressing problem." The United States enjoyed unprecedented economic prosperity, but some Americans agreed with Bryan, who insisted, "It is not necessary to own people to trade with them."

Skillbuilder Answer

Mediator: The Algeciras and Congo conferences.

Status: *Possible Answer:* It shows the growing power and prestige of the United States, because other powerful nations chose the U.S. to help settle their disputes.

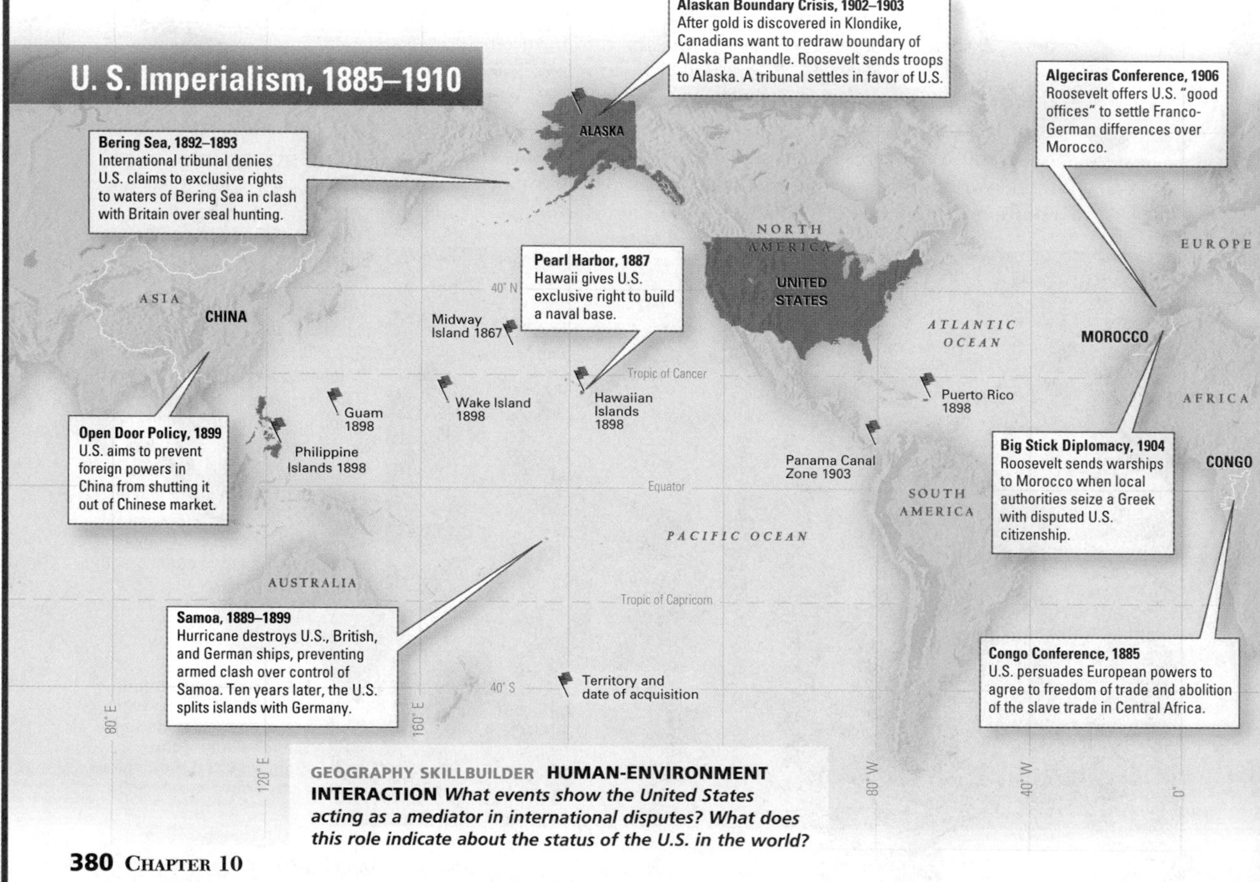

U. S. Imperialism, 1885–1910
Alaskan Boundary Crisis, 1902–1903
After gold is discovered in Klondike, Canadians want to redraw boundary of Alaska Panhandle. Roosevelt sends troops to Alaska. A tribunal settles in favor of U.S.
Algeciras Conference, 1906
Roosevelt offers U.S. "good offices" to settle Franco-German differences over Morocco.
Bering Sea, 1892–1893
International tribunal denies U.S. claims to exclusive rights to waters of Bering Sea in clash with Britain over seal hunting.
ALASKA
NORTH AMERICA
UNITED STATES
EUROPE
Pearl Harbor, 1887
Hawaii gives U.S. exclusive right to build a naval base.
ASIA
CHINA
Midway Island 1867
40° N
ATLANTIC OCEAN
MOROCCO
Tropic of Cancer
Wake Island 1898
Hawaiian Islands 1898
Puerto Rico 1898
AFRICA
Guam 1898
Philippine Islands 1898
Open Door Policy, 1899
U.S. aims to prevent foreign powers in China from shutting it out of Chinese market.
Panama Canal Zone 1903
Big Stick Diplomacy, 1904
Roosevelt sends warships to Morocco when local authorities seize a Greek with disputed U.S. citizenship.
CONGO
Equator
SOUTH AMERICA
PACIFIC OCEAN
AUSTRALIA
Tropic of Capricorn
Samoa, 1889–1899
Hurricane destroys U.S., British, and German ships, preventing armed clash over control of Samoa. Ten years later, the U.S. splits islands with Germany.
40° S
Territory and date of acquisition
Congo Conference, 1885
U.S. persuades European powers to agree to freedom of trade and abolition of the slave trade in Central Africa.
80° E
120° E
160° E
80° W
40° W
0°

GEOGRAPHY SKILLBUILDER **HUMAN-ENVIRONMENT INTERACTION** ***What events show the United States acting as a mediator in international disputes? What does this role indicate about the status of the U.S. in the world?***

TEACHING OPTIONS

Making Connections Across the Curriculum

Composition Ask students to list the arguments for and against imperialism. Then have them choose one point of view and write an essay supporting that view using the arguments from their list. Students should take into account the economic, military, paternalistic and moral factors regarding U.S. imperialism, as well as the views of countries that have come under U.S. control. Provide time for students to share their work.

Teaching Less Proficient Readers

Understanding Satire Some students may have difficulty understanding the true meaning of satirical statements, that employ irony and subtle wit to attack policies or ideas. Have these students reread Mark Twain's quote on page 381. Discuss with them Twain's use of irony and sarcasm in making some of his points. *For instance, when Twain refers to other peoples of the world as "our Brother who Sits in Darkness," he is ridiculing the belief that anyone who has not yet acquired American culture lives an unfulfilled and backward existence.*

JUSTIFYING U.S. IMPERIALISM Prior to the Spanish-American-Cuban War, many Americans, including President McKinley, did not even know where the Philippines were located. Acquiring an empire had forced Americans to expand their knowledge of distant lands and people. In the United States, world's fairs provided a perfect opportunity for Americans to do this while demonstrating how imperialism profited everyone.

Between 1900 and 1910, the United States held five international expositions. Nearly 20 million visitors flocked to the 1904 Louisiana Purchase Exposition, which included a Philippine "reservation." About 1,200 people were brought from the Philippines to live in villages on a 47-acre site on the fairgrounds. The ethnic groups included in the exhibit represented only a small number of the diverse Filipino cultures. They were carefully chosen to create the impression that some Filipinos were capable of cultural advancement under American influence but that others were "primitive savages."

U.S. Exports, 1880–1910

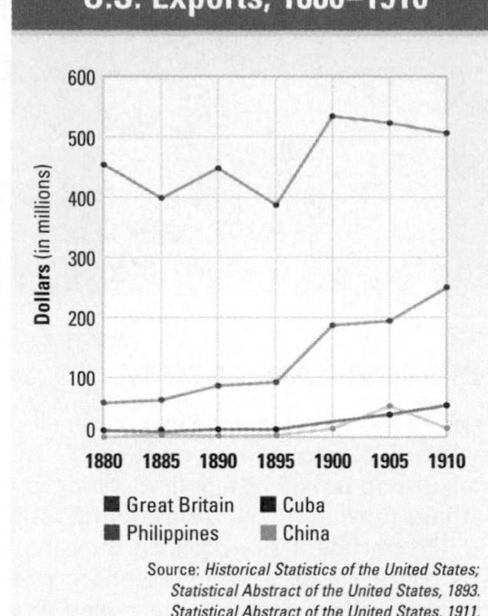

Source: *Historical Statistics of the United States; Statistical Abstract of the United States, 1893. Statistical Abstract of the United States, 1911.*

SKILLBUILDER
INTERPRETING GRAPHS
Which market saw the greatest increase in U.S. exports between 1900 and 1905? To which country did the United States export the most during this time period?

Skillbuilder Answer
Increase: China.
Most: Great Britain.

E. Answer The U.S. did not need colonies in order to trade with other nations; the expense of maintaining an empire outweighed the economic benefits; the imperative to spread Anglo-Saxon culture was just an excuse to exploit people.

THINK THROUGH HISTORY
E. THEME ***America in the World*** *How would you summarize the arguments of those who opposed American imperialism?*

OPPOSING IMPERIALISM The exhibit disseminated the pro-imperialist notions that the Philippines were economically valuable to the United States and that Filipinos were racially inferior and incapable of governing themselves. But not all Americans believed these arguments. The politician Carl Schurz, for example, warned that the expense of maintaining an American empire would outweigh any economic benefits. The novelist Mark Twain questioned the motives for imperialism in a satirical piece written in 1901.

A PERSONAL VOICE

Shall we go on conferring our Civilization upon the peoples that sit in darkness, or shall we give those poor things a rest? . . . Extending the Blessings of Civilization to our Brother who Sits in Darkness has been a good trade and has paid well, on the whole; and there is money in it yet . . . but not enough, in my judgment, to make any considerable risk advisable.

MARK TWAIN, quoted in *To the Person Sitting in Darkness*

Twain, however, did not determine American foreign policy. In the early 20th century, Presidents Theodore Roosevelt and Woodrow Wilson continued to exert American power around the globe.

Section 3 Assessment

1. TERMS & NAMES
Identify:
- Platt Amendment
- protectorate
- Emilio Aguinaldo
- John Hay
- Open Door notes
- Boxer Rebellion

2. SUMMARIZING Create a time line of key events relating to U.S relations with Cuba, Puerto Rico, and the Philippines. Use the dates already plotted on the time line below as a guide.

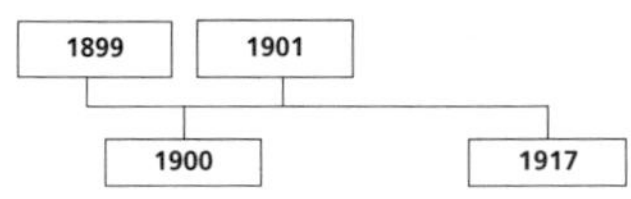

Which event do you think was most significant? Why?

3. ANALYZING ISSUES
How did U.S. foreign policy at the turn of the century affect actions taken by the United States toward China?

THINK ABOUT
- why the United States wanted access to China's markets
- the purpose of the Open Door notes

4. FORMING OPINIONS Do you think that America was justified in its policy of overseas expansion? Why or why not?

THINK ABOUT
- Andrew Carnegie's comment about U.S. exports
- economic advantages of imperialism for the United States
- William Jennings Bryan's comment
- Carl Schurz's warnings about the expense of imperialism

ANSWERS

1. TERMS & NAMES
Platt Amendment, p. 377
protectorate, p. 377
Emilio Aguinaldo, p. 378
John Hay, p. 379
Open Door notes, p. 379
Boxer Rebellion, p. 379

2. SUMMARIZING
Possible Responses: **1899**—Aguinaldo's armed revolt sparks Philippine-American War. **1900**—Foraker Act denies U.S. citizenship to Puerto Ricans and gives the U.S. president partial control of their government; McKinley is reelected as president. **1901**—Platt Amendment authorizes U.S. intervention in Cuba. **1917**—Congress grants U.S. citizenship to Puerto Ricans.

3. ANALYZING ISSUES
Possible Answers: Students should suggest that the United States government believed that the growth of the U.S. economy depended on exports and that the nation had the right to intervene to keep foreign markets open to the United States. The Open Door notes were a nonmilitary attempt to secure U.S. trading rights in China.

4. FORMING OPINIONS
Possible Responses: Yes—seizing control of overseas territories was essential to maintaining a favorable balance of trade and ensuring economic growth. No—keeping foreign markets open was not contingent on acquiring overseas territories; Bryan raised an important moral issue about whether the U.S. had the right to dominate people in foreign countries.

HISTORY FROM VISUALS

U.S. Exports, 1880–1910

Reading the Graph Tell students that the graph shows the values of U.S. exports to each of the four countries represented by the colored lines. For example, the value of U.S. exports to the Philippines in 1895 was about $100 million.

Extension Discuss whether U.S. trade patterns seemed to justify or contradict the economic arguments in favor of imperialism.

ASSESS & RETEACH

Section 3 Assessment

Ask students to work in small groups to answer the questions. Have one student from each group read the group's answer to question 4 before the class. (If the group formed two opinions, have two students read.)

Self-Assessment

Have students work in study groups to discuss answers and resolve differences by verifying information in the text.

Section Quiz

FORMAL ASSESSMENT
Section Quiz, p. 131

Reteach

Have students work in groups to summarize the main ideas under each boldfaced heading in this section. Groups should share their summaries with the class.

CLOSE

U.S. involvement in Puerto Rico, Cuba, the Philippines, and China spread American political and economic influence around the world. While many in the United States endorsed American imperialism, many Americans opposed it.

Section 4 Overview

OBJECTIVES

1. To explain how Theodore Roosevelt's foreign policy promoted American power around the world.
2. To describe how Woodrow Wilson's missionary diplomacy ensured U.S. dominance in Latin America.

CRITICAL THINKING

- Analyzing motives, pp. 383, 386
- Finding main ideas, p. 383
- Theme: Science and Technology, p. 384
- Comparing, p. 385
- Summarizing, p. 387
- Comparing and contrasting, p. 387
- Forming opinions, p. 387

FOCUS & MOTIVATE

5-MINUTE WARM-UP

Predicting Outcomes
To describe Teddy Roosevelt's view of the United States as a naval power, ask students to read the quote on page 384 and answer these questions.

1. What do you think Roosevelt might have meant by "speak softly and carry a big stick; you will go far"?
2. How do you think Roosevelt's belief would change America's role in the world?

WARM-UP TRANSPARENCY 10

▶ ***Starting with the Student***
- Ask student how they would resolve a conflict between two friends. How might the United States try to resolve a conflict between two countries?

OBJECTIVE
① **INSTRUCT**

Teddy Roosevelt and the World

▶ ***Starting with the Student***
Theodore Roosevelt was one of the most colorful figures in U.S. history. Ask students

(continued on next page)

4 America as a World Power

TERMS & NAMES
- Panama Canal
- Roosevelt Corollary
- dollar diplomacy
- Francisco "Pancho" Villa
- John J. Pershing

LEARN ABOUT American involvement in the Russo-Japanese War, the building of the Panama Canal, and the Mexican Revolution
TO UNDERSTAND how and why Presidents Roosevelt and Wilson used American military and economic power around the world.

ONE AMERICAN'S STORY

Joseph Bucklin Bishop, a small, grouchy-looking man with a pointed gray beard, played an important role in the building of the Panama Canal. Bishop served as a policy adviser to the chief engineer, George Goethals, starting in 1907. President Roosevelt had directed Bishop to send him confidential reports on the canal project. Bishop became editor of the *Canal Record,* a weekly newspaper that provided Americans with updates on the project as well as reports on social life, sports, and other general-interest topics. In one account, Bishop described a frustrating problem the workers encountered.

Workers digging the Panama Canal faced hazardous landslides and death from disease.

A PERSONAL VOICE
The Canal Zone was a land of the fantastic and the unexpected. No one could say when the sun went down what the condition of the Cut would be when [the sun] rose. For the work of months or even years might be blotted out by an avalanche of earth or the toppling over of a mountain of rock. It was a task to try men's souls; but it was also one to kindle in them a joy of combat . . . and a faith in ultimate victory which no disaster could shake.
JOSEPH BUCKLIN BISHOP, quoted in *The Impossible Dream*

The building of the Panama Canal reflected America's new role as a world power. As a marvelous technological accomplishment, not unlike the Brooklyn Bridge, the canal represented a confident nation's refusal to let any physical obstacle stand in its way. As a project conducted completely on foreign soil, the canal reflected the determination of American leaders, such as Theodore Roosevelt, not to let any political obstacle block their path.

Teddy Roosevelt and the World

The assassination of William McKinley in 1901 thrust Vice-President Theodore Roosevelt into the role of a world leader. Roosevelt was unwilling to allow the imperial powers of Europe to control the world's political and economic destiny without American participation. In 1905, building on the Open Door notes to increase American influence in East Asia, Roosevelt mediated a settlement in the war between Russia and Japan.

RUSSO-JAPANESE WAR In 1904, tension between Japan and Russia over Korea escalated to full-scale war. After the Boxer Rebellion, the Russians controlled Manchuria, the northernmost province of China, and set their sights on Korea. The Japanese, who had taken Korea from China in 1895 and set it up as an independent state, suggested that they and the Russians should respect each other's spheres of influence. When Russia refused, Japan gave Russia "a last and earnest warning" not to press the issue.

In February 1904, the Japanese attacked the Russian Pacific fleet. To everyone's surprise, Japan destroyed it and then destroyed the Russian European fleet, which had been ordered to Asia to replace the Pacific fleet. Through a series of land battles in China, Japan secured firm control over Korea as well as a foothold in Manchuria.

SECTION 4 RESOURCES

PRINT RESOURCES

IN-DEPTH RESOURCES: UNIT 3
Guided Reading, p. 23
Skillbuilder Practice: Creating Maps, p. 24
Geography Application: Geography of the Panama Canal, p. 25
Outline Map: America Becomes a World Power, p. 27
Primary Source: Building the Panama Canal, p. 32

READING STUDY GUIDE, p. 115

ACCESS FOR STUDENTS ACQUIRING ENGLISH
Guided Reading (Spanish), p. 133
Geography Application: Geography of the Panama Canal (Spanish), p. 135
Outline Map: America Becomes a World Power (Spanish), p. 137

SPANISH READING STUDY GUIDE, p. 115

FORMAL ASSESSMENT
Section Quiz, p. 132

ALTERNATIVE ASSESSMENT BOOK
See forms for supporting and scoring alternative activities.

TECHNOLOGY RESOURCES

GEOGRAPHY TRANSPARENCIES
G18, United States Interventions

CRITICAL THINKING TRANSPARENCIES
CT52, U.S. Trade with Central America

CD-ROM *Our Times*

VIDEO *American Portfolio: A Videodisc for U.S. History* user's guide, p. 179

INTERNET http://www.mlushistory.com

ROOSEVELT THE PEACEMAKER Japan's victories, however, cost a great deal of money, so the Japanese, hoping to end the economic drain, asked Roosevelt to mediate the conflict. He agreed, and in 1905, Russian and Japanese delegates convened in Portsmouth, New Hampshire.

The first meeting took place on the presidential yacht. Roosevelt had a charming way of greeting people with a grasp of the hand, a broad grin, and a hearty "*Dee*-lighted." Soon the opposing delegates began to relax and cordially shook hands.

The Japanese, who were in the driver's seat, wanted Sakhalin Island, off the coast of Siberia, and a large sum of money from Russia. Russia refused. Roosevelt persuaded Japan to accept half the island and forgo the cash payment. In exchange, Russia agreed to let Japan take over its interests in Manchuria and Korea. As a result of his efforts in negotiating the Treaty of Portsmouth, Roosevelt won the 1906 Nobel Peace Prize.

THINK THROUGH HISTORY
A. *Analyzing Motives* *Why did the Japanese decide on mediation in their conflict with Russia?*

A. Answer Japan lacked the money to continue the war.

RELATIONS WITH JAPAN As U.S. and Japanese interests expanded in East Asia, the two nations continued their diplomatic talks. In later agreements, they pledged to respect each other's possessions and interests in East Asia and the Pacific.

In 1907, after building up the U.S. Navy, Roosevelt sent 16 gleaming white battleships on a world tour to demonstrate U.S. naval power. The "Great White Fleet" was warmly received by the Japanese, who were so impressed by the American navy that they began to build a bigger navy of their own.

PANAMA CANAL When Roosevelt became president, the United States had already achieved three of Admiral Mahan's four recommendations for becoming a world power. The nation had a modern navy and naval bases in the Caribbean and Hawaii. Roosevelt set out to accomplish the fourth goal—building a canal through Central America. Such a canal would greatly reduce travel time for commercial and military ships by providing a shortcut between the Atlantic and Pacific oceans. As early as 1850, the United States and Britain had agreed to share the rights to such a canal. In the Hay-Pauncefote Treaty of 1901, however, Britain gave the United States exclusive rights to build and control a canal through Central America.

THINK THROUGH HISTORY
B. *Finding Main Ideas* *Why did the United States want a canal through the Isthmus of Panama?*

B. Answer A canal through Panama would greatly reduce the time it took commercial and military ships to travel between the Atlantic and Pacific oceans.

Engineers identified two possible routes for the proposed canal. One, through Nicaragua, posed fewer obstacles because much of it crossed a large lake. The other, through Panama (then a province of Colombia), was shorter but was beset with mountains and swamps. Shortly before Congress voted to choose a route, Philippe Bunau-Varilla, chief engineer of and investor in the New Panama Canal Company, sent all U.S. senators a Nicaraguan stamp that pictured an erupting volcano. He hoped that the stamp would weaken Congress's confidence in the practicability of the Nicaraguan route. The Senate approved the route through Panama, and the United States began negotiations over

Panama Canal locks, like this one under construction, lift ships a total of 85 feet.

THEODORE ROOSEVELT
1858–1919

Rimless glasses, a bushy mustache, and prominent teeth made Roosevelt easy for cartoonists to caricature. His great enthusiasm for the strenuous life—boxing, tennis, swimming, horseback riding, and hunting—provided cartoonists with additional material. Some cartoons portrayed Roosevelt with the toy teddy bear that he inspired.

Roosevelt had six children, who became notorious for their rowdy antics. Their father once sent a message through the War Department, ordering them to call off their "attack" on the White House. Roosevelt thrived on the challenges of the presidency. He wrote, "I do not believe that anyone else has ever enjoyed the White House as much as I have."

(continued from page 382)

to share their impressions of him.

▶ ***Discussing Key Ideas***

- President Roosevelt helps negotiate an end to the Russo-Japanese War.
- During Roosevelt's administration, the United States begins constructing the Panama Canal.
- The Roosevelt Corollary strengthens U.S. dominance in Latin America.

IN-DEPTH RESOURCES: UNIT 3
Guided Reading, p. 23

ACCESS FOR STUDENTS ACQUIRING ENGLISH
Guided Reading (Spanish), p. 133

KEY PLAYER
Theodore Roosevelt

Critical Thinking: Drawing Conclusions Ask students to brainstorm a list of adjectives describing Theodore Roosevelt. Then discuss how Roosevelt's personality and leadership style affected the image of the United States.

OUR TIMES
The Rise of Theodore Roosevelt

MORE ABOUT . . .
Roosevelt and the Canal

Roosevelt considered the Panama Canal the greatest accomplishment of his presidency. He denied any role in planning the revolution that freed Panama from Colombia. Yet he later claimed, "I took the canal zone and let Congress debate, and while the debate goes on the canal does also."

IN-DEPTH RESOURCES: UNIT 3
Primary Source: Building the Panama Canal, p. 32

TEACHING OPTIONS

Making Connections Across Cultures

Japanese Immigration While it did not approach the number of Europeans, a sizable group of Japanese journeyed to the United States during the great wave of immigration at the turn of the 20th century. By 1920, more than 200,000 Japanese lived on the nation's West Coast. Unlike most other emigrants, Japanese emigrants actually had to seek permission to leave their shores. Japanese officials, concerned about their country's image around the world, screened prospective emigrants to ensure they were healthy, literate, and would "maintain Japan's national honor" abroad.

Making Connections Across the Curriculum

Geography Have students examine a physical map of Central America and compare the two possible routes for the proposed canal: through Nicaragua and through Panama. Have them make a chart like the one below listing advantages and disadvantages of each route.

	Advantages	Disadvantages
Nicaragua		
Panama		

NOW AND THEN
U.S. Intervention

▶ ***Starting with the Student*** Have students imagine they are the president of the United States. Ask them under what circumstances they would send U.S. troops into another country. Have them explain the reasons for their decisions.

▶ ***Discussing Key Ideas***
- Although isolationism is a recurrent theme in U.S. history, so too is intervention into the affairs of other nations.
- The overriding reasons for U.S. intervention abroad are to protect its economic interests, oppose aggression, and provide humanitarian relief.
- The United States intervened in Cuba to halt Spain's aggression and expand its empire, while its main interest in sending troops to Nicaragua was economic.
- America acted in the Persian Gulf to protect its economic interests and stop aggression, while U.S. troops entered Somalia to provide humanitarian relief.

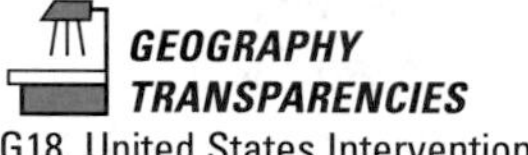
GEOGRAPHY TRANSPARENCIES
G18, United States Interventions

Panama with Colombia. When these negotiations broke down, Bunau-Varilla helped organize a Panamanian rebellion against Colombia. Nearly a dozen U.S. warships were present as Panama declared its independence. The United States negotiated a treaty that guaranteed Panama's independence and at the same time gave the United States perpetual control of a ten-mile-wide canal zone.

CONSTRUCTING THE CANAL Construction of the **Panama Canal** ranks as one of the world's greatest engineering feats. Builders fought diseases—such as yellow fever and bubonic plague—and soft volcanic soil that was difficult to remove. Work began in 1904 with the clearing of brush and draining of swamps. By 1913, the height of the construction, more than 43,400 workers were employed. Some had come from Italy and Spain; three-quarters were blacks from the British West Indies. More than 5,600 workers on the canal died from accidents or disease. The total cost to the United States was about $380 million.

On August 15, 1914, the canal opened for business, and more than 1,000 merchant ships passed through during its first year. U.S.–Latin American relations, however, had been damaged by the takeover of Panama. The resulting ill will lasted for decades, despite Congress's paying Colombia $25 million in 1921 to compensate the country for its lost territory.

C. Answer He recommended that the United States build up the navy with new ships and equipment; he also recommended building a canal across Central America, which required great technological expertise.

THINK THROUGH HISTORY
C. THEME ***Science and Technology*** *In what ways did Admiral Mahan's plans for making the United States a world power depend upon technology?*

"Speak softly and carry a big stick; you will go far."

THEODORE ROOSEVELT, QUOTING A WEST AFRICAN PROVERB

THE ROOSEVELT COROLLARY Financial factors drew the United States further into Latin American affairs. In the late 19th century, many Latin American nations had borrowed huge sums from European banks to build railroads and develop industries. Roosevelt feared that if these nations defaulted on their loans, Europeans might intervene in the Western Hemisphere. He was determined to make the United States the predominant power in the Caribbean and Central America.

Roosevelt based his Latin American policy on a West African proverb that said, "Speak softly and carry a big stick; you will go far." In his December 1904 message to Congress, Roosevelt defined his "big stick" diplomacy, the **Roosevelt Corollary** to the Monroe Doctrine. He not only argued that European powers must not intervene in the Western Hemisphere but warned that disorder in Latin America might "force the United States . . . to the exercise of an international police power" in order to protect U.S. economic interests.

During the next decade, the United States exercised its police power on several occasions. For example, when a 1911 rebellion in Nicaragua left the nation near bankruptcy, President William H. Taft, Roosevelt's successor, arranged for American bankers to loan Nicaragua enough money to pay its debts. In return, the bankers were given the right to recover their money by collecting Nicaragua's customs duties. The U.S. bankers also gained control of Nicaragua's state-owned railroad system and its national bank. When Nicaraguan citizens heard about this deal, they revolted

NOW & THEN

U.S. Intervention

Although isolationism is a recurrent theme in U.S. history, the United States has often intervened in the affairs of other nations. In the decades prior to the First World War, the United States joined the imperialist powers of Europe in the scramble for colonies like Puerto Rico and Hawaii. Following World War II, Americans supported numerous interventions to prevent the expansion of communism, as in Korea and Vietnam.

Since the passing of the Cold War, the United States has continued to project power abroad to protect its economic interests, oppose aggression, and provide humanitarian relief.

Cuba, 1898
In April 1898, the United States declares war on Spain to support the Cuban struggle for independence. President McKinley expresses concern about the threat Cuba's unrest poses to America. Imperialists view the war as an opportunity for the United States to expand its empire into the Pacific.

TEACHING OPTIONS

Exploring Themes

Science and Technology Building the Panama Canal involved much more than moving earth. Developers relied heavily on American advances in engineering and medicine to construct the canal. In response to the changing water elevation along the course of the canal, engineers constructed locks along necessary points of the canal to help ships move from one level of water to the next. In addition, U.S. doctors, armed with improved methods of disease control, wiped out the deadly yellow fever virus that had run rampant in the Canal Zone.

Making Connections Across Time

U.S. Relations with Panama The United States has had several dealings with Panama in the late 20th century—one of which was peaceful, while another involved military force. In 1977, the United States and Panama signed two treaties regarding the Panama Canal. One provided for Panama to take control of the canal on December 31, 1999. The other gave the United States the right to defend the canal's neutrality. In 1990, U.S. troops ousted Panama's ruler, and accused drug trafficker, Manuel Noriega. Noriega stood trial in the United States. In 1992, he was convicted on several drug charges and sentenced to 40 years in prison.

against President Adolfo Díaz. To prop up Díaz's government, some 2,000 marines were sent to Nicaragua. The revolt was put down, but some marine detachments remained in the country until 1933.

THINK THROUGH HISTORY
D. *Comparing* *How were big stick diplomacy and dollar diplomacy alike?*

The Taft administration followed the policy of using the U.S. government to guarantee loans made to foreign countries by American businesspeople. This policy was called **dollar diplomacy** by its critics and was often used to justify keeping European powers out of the Caribbean.

Woodrow Wilson's Missionary Diplomacy

D. Answer Both were intended to ensure U.S. dominance in Latin America.

The original Monroe Doctrine, issued by President James Monroe in 1823, warned other nations against expanding their influence in Latin America. The Roosevelt Corollary asserted that the United States had a right to exercise international police power in the Western Hemisphere. In 1913, President Woodrow Wilson gave the Monroe Doctrine a moral tone.

According to Wilson's "missionary diplomacy," the United States had a moral responsibility to deny recognition to any Latin American government it viewed as oppressive, undemocratic, or hostile to U.S. interests. Until that time, the United States had recognized any government that controlled a nation, regardless of its policies or how it had come to power. Wilson's policy pressured

Nicaragua, 1926

In Central America and the Caribbean, the United States seeks to protect its economic interests by supporting conservative governments, training local national guards to keep order, and occasionally resorting to military invasion.

In 1926, American troops invade Nicaragua, where a brutal civil war rages. Between 1927 and 1932, guerrilla nationalist forces under Augusto Sandino successfully fight both the conservative government and the American forces. Sandino promises to rid Nicaragua of every last American soldier. When American troops finally pull out of Nicaragua in 1933, however, the national guard leader Anastasio Somoza seizes power, assassinates Sandino, and acts as dictator until his own assassination in 1956.

Persian Gulf, 1991

Following the Cold War, when U.S. policy is dominated by anti-communism, the United States stands as the nation most capable of protecting international stability. When Iraq invades oil-rich Kuwait in 1990, it threatens to take control of 40 percent of the world's oil. President George Bush builds an international coalition and asks Congress for a declaration of war. A six-week air attack in 1991 transfixes U.S. TV viewers, leaves at least 100,000 Iraqis dead, and paves the way for an infantry attack. It takes only 100 hours for the American infantry to crush Iraqi resistance.

The World near the Year 2000

Unlike the Iraqi invasion of Kuwait in 1990, many international problems result from natural catastrophes, factional fighting, or ethnic strife. As in the 1992 American effort to deliver humanitarian relief to Somalia, U.S. leaders closely monitor such potential emergencies as drought conditions in Africa, human rights violations in Bosnia and China, conflicts between Israel and the Palestinians, and the disposal of nuclear weapons in the former Soviet Union.

INTERACT WITH HISTORY

1. **DRAWING CONCLUSIONS** What purposes did U.S. intervention serve in Cuba, Nicaragua, and the Persian Gulf?

SEE SKILLBUILDER HANDBOOK, PAGE 920.

2. **RESEARCHING U.S. ROLES** Choose an intervention described here, or another example, such as U.S. involvement in Vietnam. List effects of the intervention.

Visit http://www.mlushistory.com for more about the Persian Gulf War.

OBJECTIVE
② INSTRUCT

Woodrow Wilson's Missionary Diplomacy

▶ ***Discussing Key Ideas***

- Wilson's policy of missionary diplomacy pressures nations in the Western Hemisphere to establish democratic governments.
- Wilson refuses to recognize governments that come to power through violence.
- U.S. intervention in Mexico increases anti-American feelings there.

MORE ABOUT . . .
Woodrow Wilson

President Wilson was less of an economic imperialist than his predecessors, stating that "The force of America is the force of moral principle. . . . There is nothing else that she loves, and . . . there is nothing else for which she will contend." However, Wilson firmly believed in imparting his moral values to other countries, particularly in Latin America. He once declared, "I am going to teach the South American republics to elect good men."

INTERACT WITH HISTORY

1. Drawing Conclusions

Possible Responses:

Cuba: The U.S. intervened to halt Spanish aggression and possibly to expand its own empire.

Nicaragua: The U.S. sent in troops to keep order and thus protect its economic interest in the country.

Persian Gulf: The U.S. acted to repel Iraq's aggression, as well as to protect its interest in the region's rich oil supply.

2. Researching U.S. Roles

Strategies for completing this activity might first include brainstorming for topics. In addition to Vietnam, students could research U.S. involvement in Lebanon, Haiti, or Bosnia.

After choosing a topic, students should list effects of U.S. intervention by category. Some examples include:

1. the well-being of U.S. troops
2. U.S. public opinion
3. the stability of the country in which the United States has intervened

nations in the Western Hemisphere to establish democratic governments. The Mexican Revolution put Wilson's policy to the test almost immediately.

THE MEXICAN REVOLUTION Between 1876 and 1911, President Porfirio Díaz dominated Mexico as a military dictator. He suppressed internal opposition and welcomed foreign investment. Americans had invested heavily in Mexican oil wells, mines, railroads, and ranches. Wealthy landowners, the church, and the military supported Díaz, but peasants and workers finally revolted against him in 1910. In 1911, he fled Mexico City as it was occupied by revolutionaries.

The leader of the rebellion, Francisco Madero, became president of Mexico in 1911. A wealthy landowner and reformer, he proved unable to satisfy the conflicting demands of landowners, peasants, factory workers, and the urban middle class. After two years, General Victoriano Huerta took over the government and executed Madero. Americans with business interests in Mexico urged Wilson to recognize the Huerta government. But Wilson was committed to his policy of missionary diplomacy, and he refused to recognize "a government of butchers."

A PERSONAL VOICE

We can have no sympathy with those who seek to seize the power of government to advance their own personal interests or ambition. We are the friends of peace, but we know that there can be no lasting or stable peace in such circumstances. As friends, therefore, we shall prefer those who act in the interest of peace and honor, who protect private rights, and respect the restraints of constitutional provision.

WOODROW WILSON, statement on Latin America, March 11, 1913

Wilson adopted a plan of "watchful waiting," looking for an opportunity to act against Huerta. The opportunity came in April 1914, when Mexican officials arrested a small group of American sailors in Tampico, on Mexico's eastern shore. The Mexicans quickly released them and apologized, but Wilson used the incident as an excuse to intervene in Mexico and ordered U.S. marines to occupy Veracruz. Nineteen Americans and at least 200 Mexicans died during the invasion.

The incident brought the United States and Mexico close to war. Argentina, Brazil, and Chile stepped in to mediate the conflict. They proposed that Huerta step down and that U.S. troops withdraw without paying Mexico for damages. Mexico rejected the plan, and Wilson refused to recognize a government that had come to power as a result of violence. The Huerta regime soon collapsed, however, and Venustiano Carranza, a nationalist leader, became president in 1915. Wilson withdrew the troops and formally recognized the Carranza government.

THINK THROUGH HISTORY
E. *Analyzing Motives* *Why did President Wilson refuse to recognize Huerta's government?*

E. Answer Huerta had taken Mexico's government by force and had executed the previous leader. Wilson refused to recognize a government that came to power through violence.

PERSHING PURSUES VILLA Turmoil in Mexico continued, as Emiliano Zapata and **Francisco "Pancho" Villa** led revolts against Carranza. Zapata was an Indian dedicated to land reform. Villa was an anti-Carranza revolutionary. Angry over Wilson's recognition of Carranza's government, Villa threatened reprisals against the United States. In January 1916, Carranza invited a group of American engineers to operate abandoned mines in northern Mexico. Before they reached the mines, however, Villa's men took the Americans off a train and shot them. Two months later, some of Villa's followers raided Columbus, New Mexico, and killed 17 Americans. Americans held Villa responsible.

Carranza reluctantly agreed to let Wilson send U.S. troops into Mexico to try to capture Villa. General **John J. Pershing** led an expeditionary force of about 15,000 soldiers in pursuit of Villa. For almost a year, Villa eluded Pershing's forces. Wilson then called out 150,000 National Guardsmen and stationed them along the Mexican border. In the meantime, the Mexicans grew angrier over the U.S. invasion of their land. In June 1916, U.S. troops clashed

MORE ABOUT . . .
Wilson's Foreign Policy

In addition to intervening in Mexico, Wilson dispatched U.S. troops to several other Latin American countries. In 1915, he sent U.S. marines to put down revolts in Haiti and the Dominican Republic. American forces controlled the Dominican Republic until 1924 and Haiti until 1934. However, President Wilson did not always seek solutions to foreign problems through military means. His administration also negotiated thirty treaties that promoted arbitration of international disputes.

IN-DEPTH RESOURCES: UNIT 3
Outline Map: America Becomes a World Power, p. 27

MORE ABOUT . . .
Pancho Villa

Despite his disdain for the United States, Villa was fond of American automobiles—and it was while driving one that the former rebel leader met his death. On a July day in 1923—three years after he "retired" from fighting—Villa was driving around his small town in his Dodge sedan. A pedestrian shouted his name, and Villa slowed down to acknowledge him. The shout was actually a signal to gunmen hiding in a house along the road. The assassins opened fire and gunned down Villa.

Block Schedule TEACHING OPTION **Time Needed: 40 Minutes**

Cooperative Activity: Debating Wilson's Missionary Diplomacy

Task: Student groups will debate whether the United States is within its right to try to impose its morals and beliefs on other nations and cultures.

Purpose: To discuss what role morality and human rights play in foreign affairs.

Activity: Divide the class into groups of three or four students and have them research the arguments either for or against the philosophy of "missionary diplomacy." In addition to researching Wilson's involvement in Mexico, students could investigate more recent or current situations, such as the United States' struggle with China over human rights abuses and the yearly debate over whether to grant China most-favored- nation trading status. Groups holding positions for and against missionary diplomacy will debate each other.

ALTERNATIVE ASSESSMENT BOOK
Standards for Evaluating a Cooperative Activity

Pancho Villa directs a column of his troops through northern Mexico in 1914. U.S. troops never captured Villa, who continued his raids until Carranza was overthrown in 1920. Three years later, Villa was assassinated.

with Carranza's army, resulting in deaths on both sides. Carranza demanded the withdrawal of U.S. troops, but Wilson refused.

Pershing's pursuit of Villa intensified anti-American feelings in Mexico. In 1917, as the United States faced possible war in Europe, Wilson withdrew U.S. troops. Later that year, Mexico adopted a constitution that gave the government control of the nation's oil and mineral resources and placed strict regulations on foreign investors.

U.S. intervention in Mexican affairs provided a clear model of American imperialist attitudes in the early years of the 20th century. Americans believed in the superiority of their political and economic institutions, and attempted to extend the reach of these economic and political systems, even through armed intervention. Few Americans, however, wanted to go so far as to annex territory, as had been the pattern of the Europeans and Japanese.

Nevertheless, the United States pursued and achieved several foreign policy goals in the early 20th century. First, it expanded its access to foreign markets in order to ensure the continued growth of the domestic economy. Second, the United States built a modern navy to protect its interests abroad. Third, the United States exercised its international police power to ensure American dominance in Latin America.

For better or worse, imperialism had drawn the United States deeper into world affairs. At the same time, imperialism pushed Europeans toward the most destructive war they had yet experienced—a war the United States could not avoid.

ANOTHER PERSPECTIVE

INTERVENTION IN MEXICO

Most U.S. citizens supported American intervention in Mexico. Edith O'Shaughnessy, wife of an American diplomat in Mexico City, had another perspective. After touring Veracruz, O'Shaughnessy wrote to her mother:

> "I think we have done a great wrong to these people; instead of cutting out the sores with a clean, strong knife of war, . . . we have only put our fingers in each festering wound and inflamed it further."

Section 4 Assessment

1. **TERMS & NAMES** *Identify:*
   - Panama Canal
   - Roosevelt Corollary
   - dollar diplomacy
   - Francisco "Pancho" Villa
   - John J. Pershing

2. **SUMMARIZING** In a two-column chart, list ways Teddy Roosevelt and Woodrow Wilson used American power around the world during their presidencies.

Using American Power	
Roosevelt	Wilson

Choose one example and discuss its impact with your classmates.

3. **COMPARING AND CONTRASTING** What do you think were the similarities and differences between Roosevelt's big stick diplomacy and Wilson's missionary diplomacy? Use evidence from the text to support your response.

   THINK ABOUT
   - the goals of each of these foreign policies
   - how they defined the role of U.S. intervention in international affairs
   - how they were applied

4. **FORMING OPINIONS** In your opinion, should the United States have become involved in the affairs of Colombia, Nicaragua, and Mexico during the early 1900s? Support your answer with details.

   THINK ABOUT
   - the effect of the Roosevelt Corollary
   - the implication of Wilson's missionary diplomacy
   - the results of dollar diplomacy

ANSWERS

1. TERMS & NAMES

Panama Canal, p. 384
Roosevelt Corollary, p. 384
dollar diplomacy, p. 385
Francisco "Pancho" Villa, p. 386
John J. Pershing, p. 386

2. SUMMARIZING

Possible Responses: **Roosevelt:** helped mediate the settlement in Russo-Japanese War; launched construction of Panama Canal; formulated the Roosevelt Corollary to the Monroe Doctrine. **Wilson:** formulated "missionary diplomacy"; ordered U.S. military occupation of Veracruz; sent General Pershing and expeditionary forces to pursue Pancho Villa.

3. COMPARING AND CONTRASTING

Possible Responses: Both were foreign policies that broadened the Monroe Doctrine; both addressed situations in Latin American countries that could be potentially troublesome to the United States. "Big stick" diplomacy cast the U.S. in the role of international police officer and had an economic focus; "missionary diplomacy" cast the U.S. in the role of judge and had a moral focus.

4. FORMING OPINIONS

Possible Responses: Yes—Americans felt the Roosevelt Corollary justified intervention; the United States needed to protect its various economic interests in Latin America; the United States felt morally bound to protect democracy in Latin America. No—the United States's belief in its own superiority led to the use of excessive military force against those countries; those countries had the right to choose their own governments.

ANOTHER PERSPECTIVE

Intervention in Mexico

Critical Thinking: Evaluating Why do you think Edith O'Shaughnessy's opinion might be more valid than that of others? *Possible Response: Because she was an eyewitness to the effects of U.S. intervention in Mexico.*

Clarifying Have students restate O'Shaughnessy's letter in their own words.

ASSESS & RETEACH

Section 4 Assessment

Assign pairs of students to help each other answer the questions.

Self-Assessment

Have students write their impressions of Roosevelt's and Wilson's foreign policy in two brief paragraphs.

Section Quiz

FORMAL ASSESSMENT
Section Quiz, p. 132

Reteach

Have several students read their answer to question 4 before the class, making sure both opinions are expressed. Then discuss further the arguments for and against U.S involvement in Latin America.

CLOSE

Theodore Roosevelt defined America's role as a world power by making the United States dominant in Latin America. Woodrow Wilson added a moral dimension to American foreign policy by making the United States responsible for enforcing democratic values in other nations.

Geography Spotlight

OBJECTIVES

1. To summarize the development of the Panama Canal.
2. To identify the benefits of building the canal.

FOCUS & MOTIVATE

▶ ***Starting with the Student*** Have students imagine they are workers on the Panama Canal and discuss what characteristics they would need to see them through the job. *Possible Responses: Patience, physical strength, the ability to work as part of a team.*

MORE ABOUT . . .
The Panama Canal

In 1882, the French had tried to carve out a canal through Panama. Heading up the project was Ferdinand Marie De Lesseps, who had directed the construction of Egypt's Suez Canal—which opened in 1869. The Panama endeavor quickly ran into problems. A group of dishonest politicians who supported De Lesseps stole large amounts of money from the canal company. French engineers lacked the proper tools to complete the huge digging job. In addition, scientists did not yet know how to combat the region's deadly viruses. De Lessep's company went bankrupt in 1889 and shortly thereafter abandoned the canal project.

GEOGRAPHY SPOTLIGHT

The Panama Canal: Funnel for Trade

Trade has always fueled exploration. European nations gradually evolved a system of mercantilism, in which they sought new colonies and established a favorable balance of trade by exporting more than they imported. America was born into world trade and rapidly matured into an economic leader in the world's marketplace.

By the late 19th century, the U.S. position in the pattern of global trade was firmly established. A glance at the world map revealed the trade advantages of cutting through the world's great landmasses at two strategic points. The first cut, through the Isthmus of Suez, was completed in 1869 and was a spectacular success. One more cut, this one through Central America, would be especially advantageous to the United States because it would substantially reduce the sailing time between the nation's Atlantic and Pacific ports.

It took the United States ten years, from 1904 to 1914, to build the Panama Canal. By 1996, more than 700,000 vessels, flying the flags of about 70 nations, had passed through its locks.

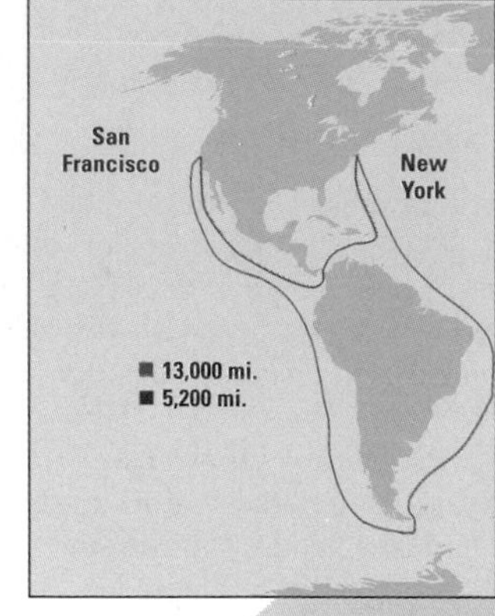

NUMBERS TELL THE STORY A ship sailing from New York to San Francisco by going around South America travels 13,000 miles; the canal shortens the journey to 5,200 miles.

San Francisco

to Asia

INTERCOASTAL TRADE The first boat through the canal, shown here, heralded the arrival of increased trade between the Atlantic and Pacific ports of the United States.

1 PANAMA is a narrow isthmus that connects North and South America. In building the canal, engineers took advantage of natural waterways like Gatun Lake. Moving ships through the mountains of the Continental Divide required the use of massive locks, such as the Miraflores Locks (see map at left). These locks allow a section of the waterway to be closed off so that the water level can be raised or lowered.

PANAMA CANAL CROSS-SECTION

Gold Hill
Gaillard Cut 85 feet above sea Level
Continental Divide
Pacific Ocean
Atlantic Ocean
Miraflores Locks
Pedro Miguel Locks
Gatun Lake
Gatun Locks
0 Miles 5 10 15 20 25 30 35 40 45 50 Miles

RECOMMENDED RESOURCES

Books

Chidsey, Donald Barr. *The Panama Canal.* New York: Crown, 1970. An informal history.

Fast, Howard. *Goethals and the Panama Canal.* New York: Julian Messner, 1942. A popular account of George Washington Goethals, the canal's builder.

Keller, Ulrich. *The Building of the Panama Canal in Historic Photographs.* New York: Dover, 1983. An interesting pictorial history.

McCullough, David G. *The Path Between the Seas.* New York: Simon, 1977. A well-known account of the creation of the Panama Canal.

Videos

A Man, A Plan, a Canal: Panama. Coronet, 1988. A history of the canal and its construction, produced with Boston PBS channel WGBH.

Americans Build the Panama Canal. Agency for Instructional Technology (AIT), 1991. Construction of the canal from 1901 to 1914.

Panama Canal. A&E Home Video, 1994. A historical documentary in the Modern Marvels series.

Software

Who Built America? Voyager. Teddy Roosevelt digging the Panama Canal is among the ample historical video, audio, images, and documents in this program for grades 10–12.

2 NEW YORK CITY and other U.S. Atlantic ports accounted for about 60 percent of the traffic using the Panama Canal in the early decades of its existence.

OCEANGOING VESSELS like this one must be of a certain dimension in order to fit through the canal's locks. These container ships must be no more than 106 feet across and 965 feet in length, with a draft (the depth of the vessel below the water line when fully loaded) of no more than 39.5 feet. Each ship pays a toll based on its size, its cargo, and the number of passengers it carries.

3 NEW ORLEANS, since its founding in 1718, has served as a major port for the produce of the areas along the Mississippi River. In 1914, the Panama Canal brought Pacific markets into its orbit.

INTERACT WITH HISTORY

1. **CLARIFYING** Before the Panama Canal opened, what route did ships follow to sail from New York City to San Francisco?
2. **CREATING A MAP** Imagine that you are a farmer in the U.S. Midwest. Sketch this map and trace the route(s)—through the Panama Canal—along which your grain might be transported to markets abroad. Note what methods of transportation would take the grain to the port cities.

SEE SKILLBUILDER HANDBOOK, PAGES 905 AND 932.

Visit http://www.mlushistory.com for more about the Panama Canal.

INSTRUCT

▶ Discussing Key Ideas

- Cutting nearly 8,000 miles off the sea journey from New York to San Francisco, the Panama Canal greatly enhanced world trade and America's role in it.
- The difficult construction of the Panama Canal took a decade and was completed in 1914.

IN-DEPTH RESOURCES: UNIT 3
Geography Application: Geography of the Panama Canal, p. 25

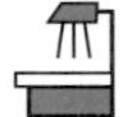
CRITICAL THINKING TRANSPARENCIES
CT52, U.S. Trade with Central America

HISTORY FROM VISUALS

Reading the Images

- Have students examine the main map and then briefly identify some other routes that could probably have been included in red.
Possible Responses: A route from Europe or Africa through the canal to the west coast of North America and vice versa; a route from Europe or Africa through the canal to Asia and vice versa; a route from the east coast of South America through the canal to the west coast of North America or Asia and vice versa.

INTERACT WITH HISTORY

1. Clarifying

Ships leaving New York City would have to make the roughly 13,000-mile trip around the continent of South America in order to reach San Francisco.

2. Skillbuilder Mini-Lesson: Creating Maps

Explaining the Skill Tell students that creating a map involves representing geographical data. It is easiest to work from an existing map.

Applying the Skill Have students complete question 2 in "Interact with History." Students' maps should depict a route from a midwestern site to at least two foreign destinations. They should indicate one or more means of inland transport by which goods will travel from the midwestern site to the appropriate U.S. port or ports. They should also indicate clear travel lines that run through the Panama Canal.

IN-DEPTH RESOURCES: UNIT 3
Skillbuilder Practice: Creating Maps, p. 24

CHAPTER 10
ASSESSMENT ANSWERS

REVIEWING THE CHAPTER

1. Queen Liliuokalani, p.364
2. imperialism, p. 364
3. José Martí, p. 370
4. yellow journalism, p. 371
5. U.S.S. *Maine*, p. 372
6. protectorate, p. 377
7. Open Door notes, p. 379
8. Boxer Rebellion, p. 379
9. Panama Canal, p. 384
10. Roosevelt Corollary, p. 384

MAIN IDEAS

11. Economic competition; political and military competition; a belief in the racial and cultural superiority of Anglo-Saxons.
12. She wanted to preserve Hawaii for Hawaiians, while American imperialists sought to annex the island chain.
13. U.S. businessmen sided with Spain because they wanted to protect their investments. Other Americans, however, sympathized with the Cuban demand for independence.
14. Cuba's independence; Spain's relinquishing of Puerto Rico and Guam to the United States; U.S. payment for annexation of the Philippines.
15. Puerto Rico was strategically important to the United States as a way to assert its presence in the Caribbean and as a base for protecting a possible canal through the Isthmus of Panama.
16. The Boxers staged a military campaign to expel foreigners. In retaliation, several nations joined forces to crush the rebellion.
17. U.S. economy's dependence on exports to ensure growth; U.S. right to intervene abroad to keep foreign markets open; closing an area to American products threatened U.S. survival.
18. A dispute over Korea.
19. A modern navy, naval bases in the Caribbean, and the acquisition of Hawaii.
20. The U.S. had a moral responsibility to deny recognition of a Latin American government it considered undemocratic.

Chapter 10 Assessment

REVIEWING THE CHAPTER

TERMS & NAMES For each item below, write a sentence explaining its significance in U.S. foreign affairs between 1890 and 1920. For each person below, explain his or her role in the events of this period.

1. **Queen Liliuokalani**
2. **imperialism**
3. **José Martí**
4. **yellow journalism**
5. **U.S.S. *Maine***
6. **protectorate**
7. **Open Door notes**
8. **Boxer Rebellion**
9. **Panama Canal**
10. **Roosevelt Corollary**

MAIN IDEAS

SECTION 1 *(pages 364–367)*

Imperialism and America

11. What three factors spurred the new American imperialism?
12. How did Queen Liliuokalani's goal conflict with one of the American imperialists' goals?

SECTION 2 *(pages 370–374)*

The Spanish-American-Cuban War

13. Why was American opinion about Cuban independence divided?
14. Briefly describe the terms of the Treaty of Paris of 1898.

SECTION 3 *(pages 375–381)*

Acquiring New Lands

15. Why was the United States interested in events in Puerto Rico?
16. What sparked the Boxer Rebellion in 1900, and how was it crushed?
17. What three key beliefs about America's industrial capitalist economy were reflected in the Open Door policy?

SECTION 4 *(pages 382–387)*

America as a World Power

18. What conflict triggered the war between Russia and Japan?
19. Which of Admiral Mahan's recommendations for making the United States a world power were achieved before Roosevelt became president in 1901?
20. Explain Woodrow Wilson's missionary diplomacy.

THINKING CRITICALLY

1. **REBEL LEADERS** Create a Venn diagram like the one below to show some of the similarities and differences between José Martí of Cuba and Emilio Aguinaldo of the Philippines.

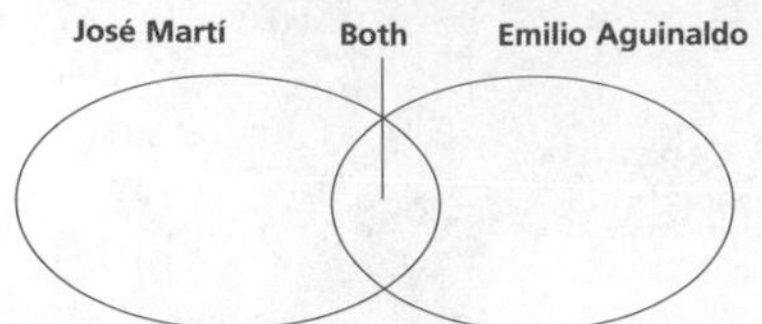

2. **KEEN COMPETITORS** Reread the quotation from Secretary of State John Hay on page 362. What attitudes of the era do you think his statement reflects?
3. **TRACING THEMES AMERICA IN THE WORLD** Look carefully at the Caribbean map on page 373 and the world map on page 380. Why do you think American naval bases in the Caribbean and the Pacific were beneficial to the United States?
4. **U.S. INTERVENTION** Would Cuba have won its independence in the late 19th century if the United States had not intervened there at that time? Support your opinion with details from the text.
5. **ANALYZING PRIMARY SOURCES** Read the following excerpt from an editorial written by Walter Hines Page, the editor of *Atlantic Monthly* magazine, soon after Admiral Dewey's victory in Manila Bay. Then answer the questions that follow.

> Are we yet the same race of Anglo-Saxons, whose restless energy in colonization, in conquest, in trade, in "the spread of civilization," has carried their speech into every part of the world, and planted their habits everywhere?
>
> Within a week such a question . . . has been put before us by the first foreign war [Spanish-American-Cuban War] that we have had since we became firmly established as a nation. Before we knew the meaning of foreign possessions in a world growing ever more jealous, we have found ourselves the captors of islands in both great oceans; and from our home-staying policy of yesterday we are brought face to face with world-wide forces in Asia as well as in Europe. . . . The news from Manila sets every statesman and soldier in the world to thinking new thoughts about us, and to asking new questions.
>
> **WALTER HINES PAGE,** "The War with Spain and After," *Atlantic Monthly,* June 1898

How does Page explain the significance of the Spanish-American-Cuban War? Which of his points do you find most meaningful and why?

THINKING CRITICALLY

1. REBEL LEADERS
Possible Responses: José Martí—Born in Cuba; expelled from Cuba at age 16; earned a master's degree and law degree; settled in United States; worked as journalist and poet; died fighting for Cuban independence in 1895; revered today as hero.

Both—His country of origin was a former Spanish colony; feared that the United States would dominate his country's politics as Spain had done; was a political activist and rebel leader; staged revolts for independence; used guerrilla tactics.

Emilio Aguinaldo—His native country was the Philippines; felt betrayed by U.S. government in Treaty of Paris; proclaimed the Philippines an independent republic; drafted a constitution; in February 1899 led the Filipinos in armed revolt; was captured by American forces in 1901.

2. KEEN COMPETITORS
Belief in American superiority; belief in the righteousness of American imperialism; the desire to conquer other nations; belief in American economic and military strength; belief in Anglo-Saxon superiority; belief in the greatness of the United States and the weakness of "inferior nations."

3. TRACING THEMES
AMERICA IN THE WORLD
Possible Responses: The nearness of Cuba to the southern tip of Florida meant that the United States could better defend its Southern coast; bases on the islands in

ALTERNATIVE ASSESSMENT

1. **PRESENTING A PERSUASIVE SPEECH**
In the late 19th and early 20th centuries, the United States began to exercise military and economic authority over countries in the Western Hemisphere. What were some of the arguments made for and against American imperialism?

Write a persuasive speech that takes a stand on American imperialism between 1895 and 1920.

Use the CD-ROM *Electronic Library of Primary Sources* and other resources to research opinions on imperialism between 1895 and 1920.

- Choose a document, incident, or piece of writing about imperialism. Decide if you will support it or argue against it. Write a speech that presents your position.
- Decide how you will make your arguments clear and convincing while also addressing opposing concerns. Practice your speech aloud and then present it to the class.

2. **PROJECT FOR CITIZENSHIP**
Prepare to debate the proposition "Resolved: The United States is justified in intervening in the affairs of foreign countries." With the class divided into two teams, have each team select two or three debaters to represent its position. (See "Debating an Issue" on page 114 in Projects for Citizenship.) Each team should prepare as follows:

- List incidents of U.S. intervention in foreign countries during the period from 1885 to 1920.
- Review the chapter to find details about each.
- Create arguments that support your position, pro or con.
- Prepare rebuttals to arguments that will be presented.

Hold the debate in class, with nondebating members acting as members of the press. Following the debate, have the press members write articles evaluating the outcome.

3. **PORTFOLIO PROJECT**
Use the Living History activity to expand your portfolio.

LIVING HISTORY

PRESENTING YOUR HISTORICAL MONOLOGUE

You have written your monologue. Now think about how you can present it dramatically.

- Find suitable clothing and props to help you imitate the person's outward appearance.
- Practice reading your monologue for a friend.

Present your monologue to the class. Add your monologue and a tape recording of your presentation to your American history portfolio.

Bridge to Chapter 11

Review Chapter 10

IMPERIALISM AND AMERICA In the late 1800s, the U.S. drive to acquire new territories, to secure foreign markets for trade, and to boost its naval power mirrored the global trend of imperialism. Joining the competition for overseas expansion, the United States annexed Hawaii, prized for its commercial value and strategic location, in 1898.

WAR WITH SPAIN In 1895, Spain's brutal treatment of Cubans during a revolt outraged the American public. The publication of a Spanish diplomat's letter criticizing President McKinley and the explosion of the battleship *Maine* pushed Congress to declare war on Spain in 1898. U.S. naval forces swiftly defeated the Spanish fleet. After the fall of Santiago de Cuba, U.S. troops invaded Puerto Rico. The ensuing peace treaty granted Cuba its independence and gave the United States colonial possessions in both the Caribbean and the Pacific.

ACQUIRING NEW LANDS Following the war, the United States reorganized the government in Puerto Rico, established a protectorate over Cuba, and crushed a revolt in the Philippines, setting up a government similar to Puerto Rico's there. The Philippines gave U.S. investors greater access to China. In 1900, the Open Door policy established American trading rights in China.

AMERICA AS A WORLD POWER As presidents, both Roosevelt and Wilson exerted U.S. military and economic power worldwide. Roosevelt's achievements included initiating plans for the Panama Canal and asserting the right of the United States to exercise international police power in the Western Hemisphere. Wilson's policy pressured nations in the Western Hemisphere to establish democratic governments.

Preview Chapter 11

Complex causes, including a spirit of nationalism and economic competition for overseas empires, led to the First World War. President Wilson at first defended neutrality, but in 1917 he asked Congress to declare war. American forces helped secure an Allied victory. You will learn about these and other developments in the next chapter.

ALTERNATIVE ASSESSMENT

1. PRESENTING A PERSUASIVE SPEECH
Standards for Evaluation
A persuasive speech should meet the following criteria:

- Clearly states the speaker's position.
- Uses well-researched and documented evidence to support the position.
- Anticipates and answers opposing arguments.
- Concludes with a strong call for action or with a forceful appeal for agreement.

2. PROJECT FOR CITIZENSHIP
Standards for Evaluation
The debate should meet the following criteria:

- Includes incidents of U.S. intervention in foreign countries during the designated period.
- Provides details for each incident.
- Includes arguments that support either the chosen pro or con position.
- Presents rebuttal arguments.

3. PORTFOLIO PROJECT
LIVING HISTORY
Standards for Evaluation
A historical monologue should meet the following criteria:

- Focuses on a specific person at a particular place and time.
- Conveys a consistent point of view.
- Brings out the speaker's true personality with appropriate word choice.
- Accurately reflects the speaker's stance on the subject he or she is addressing.

IN-DEPTH RESOURCES: UNIT 3
See the form for scoring this activity on p. 39.

THINKING CRITICALLY

the Pacific would afford the United States strategic defensive and offensive military positions; bases on the Pacific Islands could provide stops for trade ships; bases on the Pacific islands would spread U.S. influence halfway across the world.

4. U.S. INTERVENTION
Possible Response: Spain might have kept Cuba from achieving independence at first, but since Cuba had a history of rebellion, it probably would have won independence eventually, although probably not before the turn of the century.

5. ANALYZING PRIMARY SOURCES
Possible Responses: Significance—Page thinks the Spanish-American-Cuban War links Americans to the long history of Anglo-Saxon conquest; he sees the United States leaving isolationism behind and becoming a world power while Americans question the meaning of U.S. involvement. Points—his link to Anglo-Saxon conquest because he puts the war in context of imperialism and shows how people have still not learned to respect people of different cultures; his view of Americans as "captors of islands" because it labels Americans as imperialists who subjugated others.

PLANNING GUIDE

CHAPTER 11

The First World War

	Key Ideas	COPYMASTERS	ASSESSMENT
SECTION 1 World War I Begins *pp. 394–401*	*Long-term tensions erupt into a devastating war among European nations, while the United States tries to remain neutral.*	***In-Depth Resources: Unit 3*** • Guided Reading, p. 40 • Skillbuilder Practice: Evaluating Alternative Courses of Action, p. 44 • Primary Source: The Zimmermann Note, p. 47 • American Lives: Jeannette Rankin, p. 54 • Literature: from *A Son at the Front* by Edith Wharton, p. 51 ***Lesson Plans,*** pp. 95–96	PE ***Section 1 Assessment,*** p. 401 TE ***Self-Assessment,*** p. 401 ***Formal Assessment*** • Section Quiz, p. 141 ***Alternative Assessment Book*** • Standards for Evaluating a Cooperative Activity
SECTION 2 American Power Tips the Balance *pp. 402–408*	*American forces, though poorly equipped at the outset, tip the balance decisively in favor of the Allies.*	***In-Depth Resources: Unit 3*** • Guided Reading, p. 41 • Primary Source: Patriotic Song, p. 48 • Literature: *from* "In Another Country" by Ernest Hemingway, p. 53 ***Lesson Plans,*** pp. 97–98	PE ***Section 2 Assessment,*** p. 408 TE ***Self-Assessment,*** p. 408 ***Formal Assessment*** • Section Quiz, p. 142 ***Alternative Assessment Book*** • Standards for Evaluating a Cooperative Activity
SECTION 3 The War at Home *pp. 409–416*	*The war unleashes a series of disruptions in American society as the U.S. government attempts to meet the demands of modern warfare.*	***In-Depth Resources: Unit 3*** • Guided Reading, p. 42 • Primary Sources: Liberty Bond Poster, p. 49; "Returning Soldiers" by W. E. B. Du Bois, p. 50 • American Lives: Oliver Wendell Holmes, Jr., p. 55 ***Lesson Plans,*** pp. 99–100	PE ***Section 3 Assessment,*** p. 416 TE ***Self-Assessment,*** p. 416 ***Formal Assessment*** • Section Quiz, p. 143 ***Alternative Assessment Book*** • Standards for Evaluating a Cooperative Activity
SECTION 4 Wilson Fights for Peace *pp. 417–421*	*President Wilson's plans for peace are modified by Allied leaders in Europe and by Americans who are eager to free the country from foreign entanglements.*	***In-Depth Resources: Unit 3*** • Guided Reading, p. 43 • Geography Application: A New Look for Europe, p. 45 ***Lesson Plans,*** pp. 101–102	PE ***Section 4 Assessment,*** p. 421 TE ***Self-Assessment,*** p. 421 ***Formal Assessment*** • Section Quiz, p. 144 ***Alternative Assessment Book*** • Standards for Evaluating a Cooperative Activity
CHAPTER RESOURCES	**Chapter Overview** *After the United States enters World War I and helps to defeat Germany, President Wilson tries to fashion a lasting peace.*	***In-Depth Resources: Unit 3*** • Living History Project: Worksheet, p. 56; Standards, p. 57 ***Telescoping the Times*** • Chapter Summary, pp. 21–22 ***Planning for Block Schedules***	PE ***Chapter Assessment,*** pp. 424–425 PE ***Alternative Assessment,*** p. 425 ***Formal Assessment*** • Chapter Test, forms A and B, pp. 145–150 ***Test Generator*** ***Alternative Assessment Book*** See explanation and forms for different kinds of alternative assessments including portfolio assessment.

KEY
PE Pupil's Edition
TE Teacher's Edition
INTERNET http://www.mlushistory.com

TECHNOLOGY

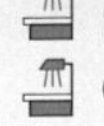
Warm-Up Transparency 11
Geography Transparencies
- G19, Europe Goes to War

Critical Thinking Transparencies
- CT19, World War I

Electronic Library of Primary Sources
- Request for a Declaration of War by Woodrow Wilson

INTERNET World War I and Jeannette Rankin

Warm-Up Transparency 11
Humanities Transparencies
- H18, *Oppy Wood* by John Nash

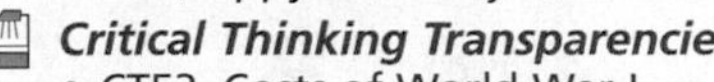
Critical Thinking Transparencies
- CT53, Costs of World War I

Electronic Library of Primary Sources
- *From Harlem to the Rhine*

Grolier Multimedia Encyclopedia
- *John Pershing*

Our Times
- George M. Cohan and "Over There"

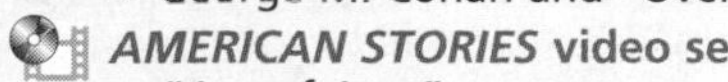
AMERICAN STORIES **video series**
- *"Ace of Aces"*

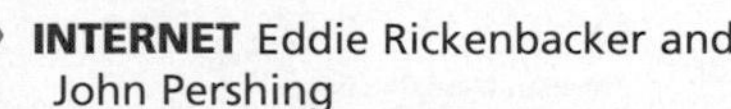
INTERNET Eddie Rickenbacker and John Pershing

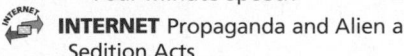

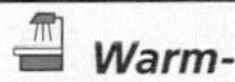
Warm-Up Transparency 11
Electronic Library of Primary Sources
- Four-Minute Speech

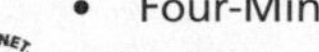
INTERNET Propaganda and Alien and Sedition Acts

Warm-Up Transparency 11
Humanities Transparencies
- H38, Senate Opposes the League of Nations

Electronic Library of Primary Sources
- On the Terms of Peace by Henry Cabot Lodge
- Why a League of Nations Is Necessary by Woodrow Wilson

INTERNET League of Nations and the Treaty of Versailles

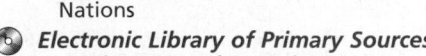

American Portfolio: A Videodisc for U.S. History, user's guide, pp. 181–189

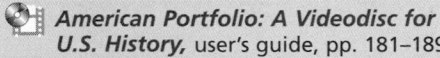

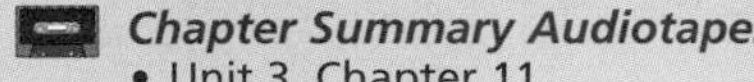
Chapter Summary Audiotapes
- Unit 3, Chapter 11

INTERNET http://www.mlushistory.com

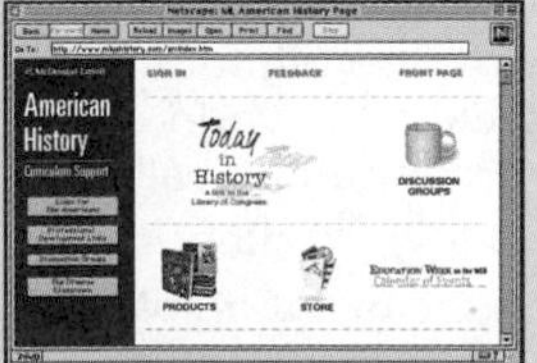

Block Scheduling (90 MINUTES)

Day 1
Section 1, pp. 394–401
Section Assessment, p. 401

COOPERATIVE ACTIVITY
- Creating Wartime Propaganda, p. 399 (TE)

Day 2
Section 2, pp. 402–408
Section Assessment, p. 408

AMERICAN STORIES **video series**
- *"Ace of Aces"*

COOPERATIVE ACTIVITY
- Letters from Conscientious Objectors and the Draft Board, p. 405 (TE)

Day 3
Section 3, pp. 409–416
Section Assessment, p. 416

COOPERATIVE ACTIVITY
- Creating a Wartime Ad Campaign, p. 411 (TE)

Day 4
Section 4, pp. 417–421
Tracing Themes: Immigration and Migration, pp. 422–423
Section Assessment, p. 421
Chapter Assessment, pp. 424–425

COOPERATIVE ACTIVITY
- Debating the League of Nations, p. 420 (TE)

YEARLY PACING ***Chapter 11 Total:*** 4 days ***Yearly Total:*** 85 days

See *Planning for Block Schedules* for special activities and pacing strategies.

Customizing for Special Populations

Students Acquiring English
Access for Students Acquiring English: Spanish Translations
- Guided Reading for Sections 1–4, pp. 141–144
- Chapter Summary, pp. 139–140
- Skillbuilder Practice: Evaluating Alternative Courses of Action, p. 145
- Geography Application: A New Look for Europe, p. 146

Spanish Reading Study Guide, pp. 119–128
Translations of Chapter Summaries, Hmong, Cantonese, Vietnamese, and Cambodian

Chapter Summary Audiotapes in Spanish
Unit 3, Chapter 11

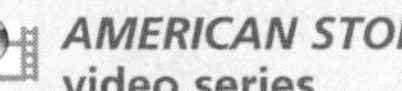
AMERICAN STORIES **video series**
- "Ace of Aces" (Spanish track)

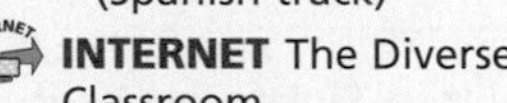
INTERNET The Diverse Classroom

Gifted and Talented Students
In-Depth Resources: Unit 3
- Primary Sources: The Zimmermann Note, p. 47; Patriotic Song, p. 48; Liberty Bond Poster, p. 49; "Returning Soldiers" by W. E. B. Du Bois, p. 50
- American Lives: Jeannette Rankin, p. 54; Oliver Wendell Holmes, Jr., p. 55

Less Proficient Readers
In-Depth Resources: Unit 3
- Guided Reading for Sections 1–4, pp. 40–43
- Skillbuilder: Evaluating Alternative Courses of Action, p. 44
- Geography Application: A New Look for Europe, p. 45

Reading Study Guide
- pp. 119–128

Telescoping the Times
- Chapter Summary, pp. 21–22

Chapter Summary Audiotapes, Unit 3, Chapter 11

Connections to Literature READINGS FOR STUDENTS

In-Depth Resources: Unit 3
- **from *A Son at the Front* by Edith Wharton,** p. 51
- ***from* "In Another Country" by Ernest Hemingway,** p. 53

Enrichment Reading
- **Mark Helprin**
  A Soldier of the Great War
  New York: Avon, 1992
  An old professor recalls his adventures as a soldier, a hero, a prisoner, a deserter, and a wanderer in the hell of World War I, as he tells the story of his life to an illiterate factory worker in Italy. The horror of war and the triumph of love are central themes of the novel.
- **Ernest Hemingway**
  A Farewell to Arms
  New York: Scribners, 1987
  The brutality and confusion of World War I dominate this story of a volunteer ambulance driver and an English nurse who fall in love.

McDougal Littell *Literature Connections*

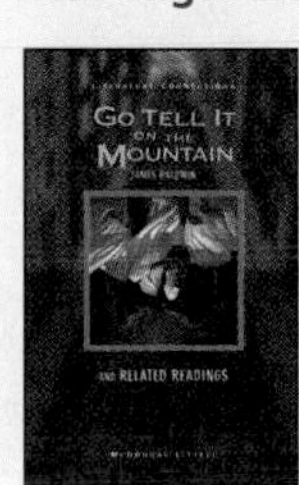

- **James Baldwin,**
  Go Tell It on the Mountain
  (with related readings). Baldwin's novel, set in a storefront church in Harlem, brings the black experience vividly to life in a story that has been called "brutal, objective, and compassionate." Dealing with characters who came north during the Great Migration, the novel focuses on a 14-year-old boy whose family history reveals the complexities of the human heart.

CHAPTER 11 OVERVIEW

The First World War

▶ *Accessing Prior Knowledge*

Ask students what they have read or heard about World War I. Ask them what movies or television programs they have seen about the war. Discuss with them how both sides in the conflict were portrayed.

▶ *Predicting Outcomes*

Have students read President Wilson's quotation on this page. Ask students to predict what they think might happen to make the world "safe for democracy."

MORE ABOUT . . .
War Posters

American artists created various kinds of posters during the war in addition to the recruiting poster that appears on page 393. Some artists painted Liberty Loan posters, urging Americans to help finance the war. Charles Dana Gibson, known for his drawings of beautiful girls, portrayed workers in shipyards.

CHAPTER 11

The First World War

SECTION 1
World War I Begins
Long-term tensions erupt into a devastating war among European nations, while the United States tries to remain neutral.

SECTION 2
American Power Tips the Balance
American forces, though poorly equipped at the outset, tip the balance decisively in favor of the Allies.

VIDEO *ACE OF ACES*

SECTION 3
The War at Home
The war unleashes a series of disruptions in American society as the U.S. government attempts to meet the demands of modern warfare.

SECTION 4
Wilson Fights for Peace
President Wilson's plans for peace are modified by Allied leaders in Europe and by Americans who are eager to free the country from foreign entanglements.

"The world must be made safe for democracy."
President Woodrow Wilson, 1917

THE UNITED STATES

- Aug. 1914: Panama Canal officially opens.
- May 1915: German U-boats sink the British liner *Lusitania*, and 1,198 people, including 128 Americans, die.
- June 1915: Secretary of State William Jennings Bryan resigns because he believes the United States has not remained neutral.

THE WORLD

- June 1914: Archduke Franz Ferdinand of Austria and his wife are assassinated in Sarajevo.
- Aug. 1914: Germany declares war on Russia and France. Great Britain declares war on Germany and Austria-Hungary.
- April 1915: Germans use poison gas as a weapon at the Battle of Ypres.
- Jan. 1916: Allies withdraw from the Dardanelles after suffering more than 200,000 casualties.

THEMES IN CHAPTER 11

Women in America	*Democracy in America*	*Immigration and Migration*	*America in the World*
During the war, many women worked in factories, while others served as nurses and ambulance drivers. After the war, women were expected to give up their jobs and return to traditional domestic roles. See Teacher's Edition notes, pp. 395 and 415.	Although discrimination existed in the U.S. military, the army had a more progressive attitude toward African Americans than society at large did. See Teacher's Edition note, p. 403.	During the war years, many Southern African Americans moved to cities in the North in search of jobs, equal treatment, and greater opportunities. See Teacher's Edition note, p. 414.	At the war's end, Wilson wanted to help spread democratic reform throughout the world by creating a world peacekeeping organization, called the League of Nations. See Teacher's Edition note, p. 418.

LIVING HISTORY

CHARTING THE EFFECTS OF WORLD WAR I

The First World War brought about many changes in the United States and the rest of the world. As you read the chapter, compile a chart in which you list the effects of the war in the following categories:

- military methods
- American society
- world politics

Then, using information from your chart and outside sources, write a report in which you explain the impact of the war in one of the categories.

PORTFOLIO PROJECT Keep your chart and report in a folder for your American history portfolio. At the end of the chapter you will present your report to your classmates.

I WANT YOU FOR U.S. ARMY
NEAREST RECRUITING STATION

Nov. 1916 ● Woodrow Wilson is reelected.

1917

Jan. ● Germany resumes unrestricted submarine warfare.

March ● Provisional government replaces the czarist regime in Russia.

April ● America enters the First World War.

May ● Selective Service Act sets up compulsory military service—the draft.

1918 ● Flu epidemic afflicts millions of Americans.

1918 ● Vladimir I. Lenin and the Bolsheviks establish a Communist regime in Russia.

Jan. ● President Wilson proposes the League of Nations.

May ● Congress passes the Sedition Act.

1919

June ● Germany signs the Treaty of Versailles.

Oct. ● President Wilson suffers a stroke.

1920 ● Nineteenth Amendment, granting woman suffrage, is ratified.

1920 ● Warren G. Harding is elected president.

ALTERNATIVE ASSESSMENT

LIVING HISTORY

CHARTING THE EFFECTS OF WORLD WAR I

Encourage students to compile information in a chart like the one below. You might also suggest that students list the page number for each item they add to the chart.

Category	Effects
Military Methods	
American Society	
World Politics	

After students have finished the chapter and their charts, have them follow these steps as they write their reports:

- Read the material in the chart and decide which category or topic is of most interest.
- Freewrite to come up with questions to answer about the topic.
- Research to find answers to the questions.

IN-DEPTH RESOURCES: UNIT 3
See worksheet and standards for evaluation, pp. 56, 57.

RECOMMENDED RESOURCES

Books for the Teacher

Haythornthwaite, Philip J. *The World War I Sourcebook.* London: Arms and Armour, 1996. Encyclopedia covers all aspects of the war.

Tuchman, Barbara. *The Guns of August.* New York: Ballantine, 1992. Dramatic account of the early months of the war.

Wall, Richard and Jay Winter, eds. *The Upheaval of War.* New York: Cambridge UP, 1988. Essays on the consequences of the war.

Books for the Student

Ellis, Edward Robb. *Echoes of Distant Thunder.* New York: Coward, 1978. Society between 1914 and 1918.

Schachtman, Tom. *Edith and Woodrow.* New York: Putnam's, 1981. Joint biography of the Wilsons.

Winter, J. M. *The Experience of World War I.* New York: Oxford, 1995. Illustrated description of military and home life.

Videos

America: The Second Century: World War I. GPN, 402-472-2007. The U.S. role in the war.

The Great War and the Shaping of the 20th Century. PBS Home Video, 1996. Eight-hour documentary.

Sergeant York. Dir. Howard Hawks. 1941. Twentieth Century Fox Video, 1982. Hollywood story of war hero.

Software

World War I: An Interactive Documentary. CD-ROM. First Electronic Publishing, 211 Congress Street, Boston, MA 02110, 617-338-6820.

Section 1 Overview

OBJECTIVES

1. To identify the four long-term causes of the First World War.
2. To explain the circumstances that led to the war.
3. To describe the slaughter of the first two years of the war.
4. To summarize public opinion about the war in the United States.
5. To explain why the United States entered the war.

SKILLBUILDERS

- Understanding geography: location, p. 395
- Understanding geography: location, movement, p. 397
- Interpreting graphs, p. 398

CRITICAL THINKING

- Summarizing, pp. 395, 401
- Recognizing effects, pp. 396, 399
- Analyzing causes, p. 399
- Theme: Democracy in America, p. 401
- Making predictions, p. 401
- Analyzing issues, p. 401

FOCUS & MOTIVATE

5-MINUTE WARM-UP

Interpreting Charts

To understand the scope of World War I, refer students to the chart on page 395. Then have them answer these questions.

1. What two groups made up the warring powers in 1915?
2. Why do you think the war was called World War I?

WARM-UP TRANSPARENCY 11

▶ ***Starting with the Student***

- What do students do when someone insults their friends? Do they defend them? How?
- What do they think a country should do when one of its allies is atacked?

IN-DEPTH RESOURCES: UNIT 3
American Lives: Jeannette Rankin, p. 54

1 World War I Begins

TERMS & NAMES

- militarism
- Allies
- Central Powers
- Archduke Franz Ferdinand
- no man's land
- trench warfare
- *Lusitania*
- Zimmermann note

LEARN ABOUT the international politics that led to war in Europe
TO UNDERSTAND why the United States finally became involved in the world war.

ONE AMERICAN'S STORY

It was about 1:00 A.M. on April 6, 1917, and the members of the U.S. House of Representatives were tired. For the past 15 hours they had been debating President Wilson's request for a declaration of war against Germany. At last the roll call began. When the clerk came to the name of Jeannette Rankin of Montana, the first woman elected to Congress, there was a breathless hush. Suddenly Representative Rankin, contrary to precedent, stood up and declared, "I want to stand by my country but I cannot vote for war. I vote no." In later years she reflected on her action.

A PERSONAL VOICE

I believe that the first vote I cast was the most significant vote and a most significant act on the part of women, because women are going to have to stop war. I felt at the time that the first woman [in Congress] should take the first stand, that the first time the first woman had a chance to say no to war she should say it.

JEANNETTE RANKIN, quoted in *Jeannette Rankin: First Lady in Congress*

Both the House and the Senate voted overwhelmingly in favor of U.S. entry into World War I, thus abandoning American neutrality three years after hostilities first began. And even then, there was considerable debate as to whether the United States should join the fight. Woodrow Wilson had won a second term in 1916 on the antiwar slogan "He Kept Us Out of War." What, then, made the United States change its mind in 1917?

Jeannette Rankin was the only member of the House to vote against entering both World War I and World War II.

Long-Term Causes of World War I

The First World War began on August 4, 1914, when German troops poured into Belgium. Although many Americans wanted to stay out of the war, several factors made American neutrality difficult to maintain. As an industrial and imperial power, the United States felt many of the same pressures that had led the nations of Europe into devastating warfare. Historians generally cite four long-term causes of the First World War: nationalism, imperialism, militarism, and the formation of a system of alliances.

NATIONALISM Nationalism—the belief that national interests and national unity should be placed ahead of global cooperation and that a nation's foreign affairs should be guided by its own self-interest—grew in Europe throughout the 19th century. Often, it was expressed as competitiveness with, and even antagonism toward, other nations.

France and Germany jockeyed for European leadership. France still smarted over its loss of parts of the provinces of Alsace and Lorraine in the Franco-Prussian War of 1871. Germany, which had been created after the Prussian victory over France, wanted to protect its newly industrializing economy by ensuring open markets in Europe and access to overseas territories.

Russia regarded itself as the protector of Europe's Slavic peoples, no matter which government they lived under. Among these were the Serbs.

SECTION 1 RESOURCES

PRINT RESOURCES

IN-DEPTH RESOURCES: UNIT 3
Guided Reading, p. 40
Skillbuilder Practice: Evaluating Courses of Action, p. 44
Primary Source: The Zimmermann Note, p. 47
Literature: from *A Son at the Front* by Edith Wharton, p. 51
American Lives: Jeannette Rankin, p. 54

READING STUDY GUIDE, p. 119

ACCESS FOR STUDENTS ACQUIRING ENGLISH
Guided Reading (Spanish), p. 141
Skillbuilder Practice: Evaluating Courses of Action (Spanish), p. 145

SPANISH READING STUDY GUIDE, p. 119

FORMAL ASSESSMENT
Section Quiz, p. 141

ALTERNATIVE ASSESSMENT BOOK
See forms for supporting and scoring alternative activities.

TECHNOLOGY RESOURCES

GEOGRAPHY TRANSPARENCIES
G19, Europe Goes to War

CRITICAL THINKING TRANSPARENCIES
CT19, World War I

CD-ROM Electronic Library of Primary Sources

VIDEO *American Portfolio: A Videodisc for U.S. History* user's guide, p. 181

INTERNET http://www.mlushistory.com

Serbia—located in the Balkans—was an independent nation at the time, but millions of ethnic Serbs lived under the rule of Austria-Hungary. As a result, Russia and Austria-Hungary were rivals for influence over Serbia.

In addition, various ethnic groups resented domination by others and hoped to create nations of their own. Poland, for example, had been divided among Germany, Austria-Hungary, and Russia. Poles wanted to reunite as an independent Polish nation. The Czechs were restless under the domination of Austria-Hungary, which would not let them use their own language.

IMPERIALISM Nationalist competition often worsened imperial conflicts among the major powers of Europe. To some degree, industrialization and imperialism were closely linked. As Germany industrialized, it competed with France and Britain in the contest for colonies, which supplied imperial powers with raw materials such as cotton, oil, and rubber, as well as markets for manufactured goods. Colonies also added to the imperialist nations' prestige.

The late 19th and early 20th centuries witnessed several quarrels and small wars over colonies. The Russo-Japanese War was an imperial war over Korea and Manchuria. France and Britain nearly went to war over Africa.

MILITARISM Empires were expensive to build and to defend. The growth of nationalism and imperialism caused military budgets to rise. Because each nation wanted its armed forces to be stronger than those of any potential enemy, the imperial powers followed a policy of **militarism**—the development of armed forces and their use as a tool of diplomacy.

A. Answer Nationalism and imperialism caused each country in Europe to look out for its own interests and to begin a deadly competition for power.

THINK THROUGH HISTORY
A. Summarizing *Summarize the role that nationalism and imperialism played in worsening the conflict in Europe.*

By 1890 the strongest nation on the European continent was Germany, which had set up an army reserve system that drafted young men, trained them, and returned them to civilian life until they were needed. At first Great Britain was not concerned about Germany's military buildup. An island nation, Great Britain had always relied on its navy for defense and protection of its shipping routes—and the British navy was the strongest in the world. However, in 1897, Wilhelm II, Germany's kaiser, or emperor, decided that his nation should also become a major sea power in order to compete more successfully against the British. Soon British and German shipyards competed to build the largest battleships and destroyers. France, Italy, Japan, and the United States quickly joined the naval arms race.

ALLIANCE SYSTEM All these mutual hostilities, jealousies, fears, and desires led the nations of Europe to sign treaties of assistance that committed them to support one another if they faced attack. By 1914 there were two major

Skillbuilder Answer
Possible Answer: The Allies bordered the Central Powers on both the east and the west.

The Warring Powers, 1915

ALLIES

Although not all of the following countries sent troops into the war, they all joined the war on the Allied side at various times.

Australia	India
Belgium	Italy
British Colonies	Japan
Canada & Newfoundland	Montenegro
	New Zealand
France	Portugal
French North Africa & French Colonies	Romania
	Russia
	Serbia
Great Britain	South Africa
Greece	United States

CENTRAL POWERS

Austria-Hungary
Bulgaria
Germany
Ottoman Empire

GEOGRAPHY SKILLBUILDER LOCATION *Considering the geographical location of the Allies, what military advantage might the Allies have had over the Central Powers?*

OBJECTIVE

① INSTRUCT

Long-Term Causes of World War I

▶ ***Discussing Key Ideas***

- A growing sense of nationalism and imperialism fuels competitiveness and antagonism in Europe.
- The growth of nationalism and imperialism leads to military buildups in many powerful nations.
- The fears and jealousies among these nations results in the creation of two major defense alliances, the Allies and the Central Powers.

IN-DEPTH RESOURCES: UNIT 3
Guided Reading, p. 40

ACCESS FOR STUDENTS ACQUIRING ENGLISH
Guided Reading (Spanish), p. 141

HISTORY FROM VISUALS

The Warring Powers, 1915

Reading the Map Ask students to examine the borders of the European countries on the map and to tell why France and Russia might have felt particularly threatened by the Central Powers nations. *Possible Response: Because they shared borders with Central Powers countries.*

Extension Have small groups of students compare this map with the current world political map on pages 940–941 to see how the region has changed over time.

TEACHING OPTIONS

Exploring Themes

Women in America Jeannette Rankin served as a role model to other independent American women. During the First World War, many women assumed traditionally male jobs in factories. They also served overseas as nurses and ambulance drivers. In 1920, after the war was over, the Nineteenth Amendment was ratified, giving women the right to vote. Ask students why women demanded and gained this right after the war. *Possible Response: After filling male roles, women felt entitled to share men's rights and privileges.*

Teaching Less Proficient Readers

Analyzing Causes Some students might have difficulty understanding the four major causes of the First World War. Have these students create an outline listing each cause mentioned on pages 394–396. In the outline, students should:

- list the countries discussed under the heading for each cause
- briefly explain the factors that fueled the situation in each country

Encourage students to use the outline during class discussion of the section.

OBJECTIVE

② INSTRUCT

An Assassination Leads to War

▶ ***Discussing Key Ideas***

- The Balkan Peninsula is a "powder keg."
- The assassination of Archduke Franz Ferdinand sparks the First World War.
- The alliance system forces many nations into the war.

GEOGRAPHY TRANSPARENCIES
G19, Europe Goes to War

CRITICAL THINKING TRANSPARENCIES
CT19, World War I

NOW & THEN
Crisis in Bosnia
Critical Thinking: Evaluating Have groups of students research the situation in the Balkans today. Ask each group to concentrate on the situation from the point of view of the Serbs, the Croats, or the Muslims. Have students discuss their findings in class. Ask them whether they think the Balkan Peninsula is still a powder keg.

OBJECTIVE

③ INSTRUCT

The Fighting Starts

▶ ***Discussing Key Ideas***

- Germany invades Belgium.
- Armies use trench warfare to fight for small areas of land.
- Fighting is deadlocked for two years.

mutual-defense alliances. The Triple Entente, later known as the **Allies,** consisted of France, Great Britain, and Russia. (Russia also had a separate treaty with Serbia.) The Triple Alliance consisted of Germany, Austria-Hungary, and Italy. (In 1915, Italy would join the Allies in return for promised territorial gains.) Germany and Austria-Hungary, together with the Ottoman Empire—an empire of mostly Middle Eastern lands controlled by the Turks—were later known as the **Central Powers.** The alliances provided a measure of international security because nations were reluctant to disturb the balance of power. As it turned out, though, a spark set off a major conflict.

An Assassination Leads to War

That spark flared in the Balkan Peninsula. The peninsula—bounded by the Black Sea, the Adriatic Sea, the Mediterranean Sea, and the Aegean Sea—was known as "the powder keg of Europe." Most of the continent's leading powers had interests there. Russia wanted to gain an outlet to the Mediterranean Sea. Germany wanted to extend the railroad between itself and the Ottoman Empire. Austria-Hungary—which had annexed Bosnia in 1908—objected to Serbia's role in encouraging Bosnians to reject the rule of Austria-Hungary. The "powder keg" was ready to explode.

On June 28, 1914, the streets of Sarajevo, the capital of Bosnia, were jammed with people who had gathered to see **Archduke Franz Ferdinand.** A nephew of Emperor Franz Joseph, the archduke was heir to the Austrian throne. He and his wife, Sophie, waved gaily to the crowd as their automobile moved along. Suddenly a young man leaped toward them from the curb. Before the guards could react, he fired a series of shots, killing the archduke and his wife.

The teenage assassin, Gavrilo Princip, turned out to be a member of a secret society called the Black Hand. The society's aim was to unite all Serbs, including those living in Bosnia, under one government. The assassination immediately touched off a diplomatic crisis. Austria-Hungary hoped to make an example of Serbia once and for all and to squelch the possibility of nationalist uprisings within Austria-Hungary. On July 28, Austria-Hungary declared what it expected to be a "bright, brisk little war" against Serbia.

The alliance system pulled one nation after another into the conflict. To help its ally Serbia, Russia ordered full mobilization of its armies on July 29. On August 1, Germany, obligated by treaty to support Austria-Hungary, declared war on Russia. On August 3, Germany declared war on Russia's ally France. Great Britain, linked by treaty to France, declared war on Germany and Austria-Hungary. The Great War had begun.

NOW & THEN

CRISIS IN BOSNIA

Ethnic and religious strife have haunted the Balkans for centuries.

After World War I, Bosnia became part of the new multiethnic nation of Yugoslavia. In 1991, Yugoslavia began to break apart, and Bosnia declared its independence. Serbs in Bosnia wanted Bosnia to remain part of Yugoslavia, which was now dominated by the Serbs. If Bosnia became independent, they thought, the government might fall into the hands of non-Serbs—Croats, Muslims, or both.

Soon a civil war raged in Bosnia. As the Serbs conquered more territory, they pushed out all non-Serbs in a process called ethnic cleansing. At first the Croats and the Muslims united to resist the Serbs. After a few months, however, they were fighting each other as well.

In 1995, the United States helped negotiate a cease-fire agreement among the Serbs, Croats, and Muslims. It also sent some 20,000 American soldiers as part of a multinational force to Bosnia to keep the peace. Most observers feared that without the presence of foreign troops, the civil war might resume or the country would split.

THINK THROUGH HISTORY
B. *Recognizing Effects* *Why did European nations mobilize so quickly after the archduke's assassination?*

B. Answer European nations were bound by a system of mutual defense alliances to come to the aid of any ally attacked.

The Fighting Starts

Germany began its war offensive by invading Belgium on August 4, 1914. The Germans followed a strategy that Count Alfred von Schlieffen, chief of the German General Staff, had planned in 1905. The Schlieffen Plan called for a holding action against Russia, combined with a quick drive through the Belgian lowlands to Paris. Then, after France had fallen, the two German armies would join to defeat the Russian czar. As German troops swept across Belgium, thousands of refugees fled in terror. The American war correspondent Richard Harding Davis described the Belgians' reaction as the troops entered the capital, Brussels.

TEACHING OPTIONS

Making Connections Across the Curriculum

Geography Tell students that the topography of the land through which a country launches its war offensive can be as important as its military strength. In the First World War, Germany's initial goal was France. The quickest route to France was through the flat lowland region of Belgium. Although Belgium was neutral, Germany declared war on the country on August 4th. By August 16th, the German army had leveled much of the Belgian countryside. Ask students why Germany didn't march through Switzerland, another neutral nation. *Switzerland is protected by mountains.*

Making Connections Across Time

World War II Strategies Tell students that at the beginning of World War II, Germany once again used the northern route through the lowlands to reach France. The German army pushed through Holland and Belgium, decimating both countries. This time, Germany took Paris. Hitler had accomplished in four weeks what Kaiser Wilhelm's armies had failed to achieve in four years. Belgium and Holland would not be liberated until 1944, when the Germans were forced to retreat following the Battle of the Bulge.

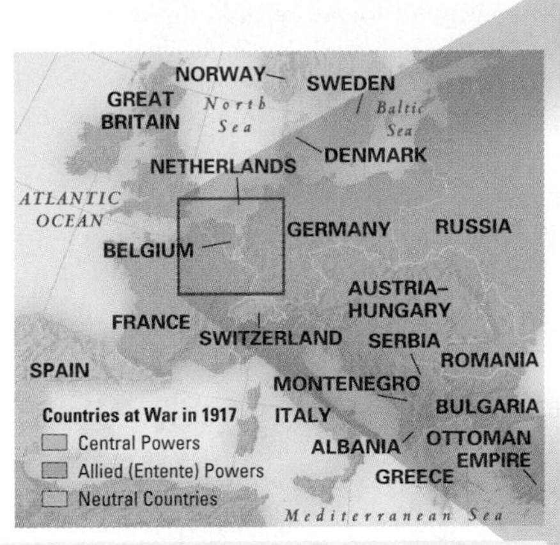

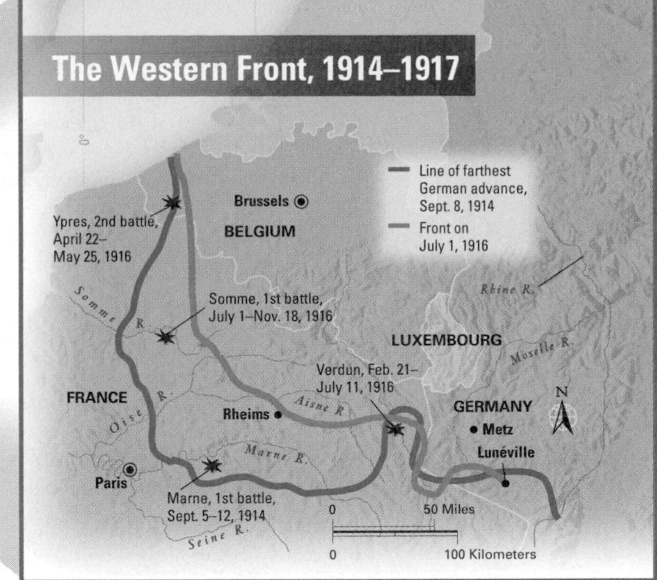

GEOGRAPHY SKILLBUILDER LOCATION *What were the northwestern and southwestern limits of the western front?* **MOVEMENT** *About how many miles separated the city of Paris from German forces at the point of their closest approach?*

Skillbuilder Answer
Location: The Belgian coast and the Rhine River in southwestern Germany.
Movement: About 10 miles.

A PERSONAL VOICE

[We] found the side streets blocked with their carts. Into these they had thrown mattresses, or bundles of grain, and heaped upon them were families of three generations. Old men in blue smocks, white-haired and bent, old women in caps, the daughters dressed in their one best frock and hat, and clasping in their hands all that was left to them, all that they could stuff into a pillow-case or flour-sack. . . . Heart-broken, weary, hungry, they passed in an unending caravan.

RICHARD HARDING DAVIS, quoted in *Hooray for Peace, Hurrah for War*

Unable to save Belgium, the British and French retreated to the Marne River in France, where they managed to stop the German advance in September 1914. By the spring of 1915, two lines of deep, rat-infested trenches zigzagged across northern and eastern France. German soldiers occupied one line, Allied soldiers the other line. Between them lay **"no man's land"**—a barren expanse of mud pockmarked with shell craters and filled with barbed wire entanglements. Every once in a while, the soldiers would climb out of their trenches and try to overrun enemy lines, while machine guns blazed and poison gas filled the air.

The slaughter was unbelievable. For example, during the First Battle of the Somme—which began on July 1, 1916, and lasted until mid-November—the British lost 60,000 men the first day alone. Final casualties totaled about 1.2 million—650,000 Germans, 420,000 British, and nearly 200,000 French. Yet only seven miles of ground changed hands. This bloody **trench warfare,** in

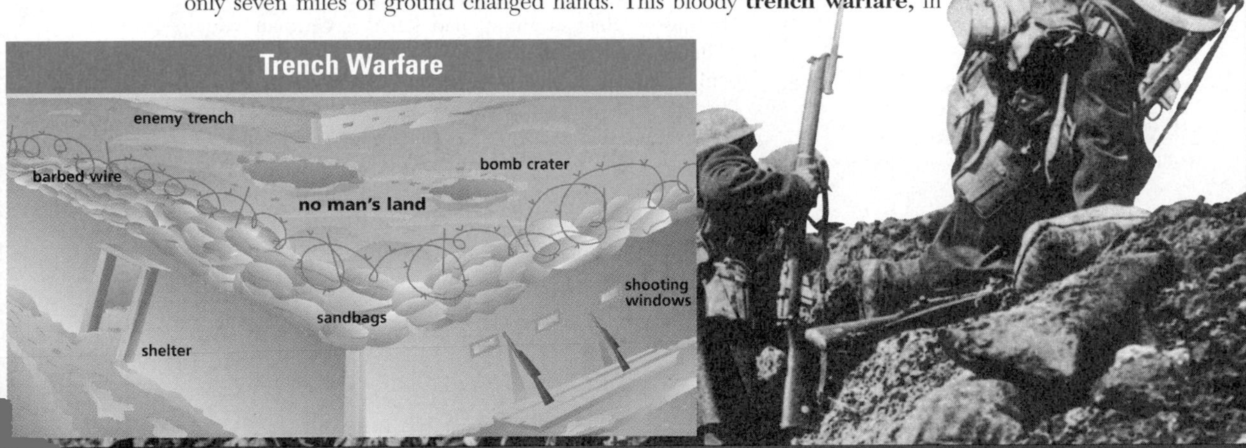

Soldiers climb out of a trench and charge an enemy position.

HISTORY FROM VISUALS
The Western Front, 1914–1917

Reading the Map
Ask students to explain how the boxed area on the smaller map corresponds to the larger map. *It shows the Western Front in relation to the rest of Europe.*

Extension Ask students what took place at the points where the two lines on the larger map overlap. *Possible Response: The Allies and the Central Powers both gained and lost small areas of ground as they won and lost battles.*

MORE ABOUT . . .
Trench Warfare

Life in the trenches was bleak and uncomfortable. Trenches were only wide enough for two people to pass and provided little shelter from the elements. This is how one soldier described the trenches: "Nothing to see but bare mud walls, nowhere to sit but on a wet muddy ledge; no shelter of any kind against the weather except the clothes you are wearing; no exercise you can take in order to warm yourself." Life in the trenches was also boring. Most activity occurred at night, when soldiers could repair their dugouts under cover of darkness. Attacks usually came before dawn, when most soldiers going "over the top" were mowed down by enemy fire. Above all, life in the trenches seemed hopeless. As one soldier said, "There doesn't seem the slightest chance of leaving except in an ambulance."

TEACHING OPTION

Making Connections Across Time

Poison Gas Warfare In the middle of the 19th century, a British admiral suggested the use of poison gas as a weapon of war. However, the committees that examined the proposal concluded that poison gas "was so hideous that . . . any power that used [it] would inevitably be branded as beyond the pale of civilization for all time." Nonetheless, the Germans used poison gas at Ypres in April 1915. Many of the Allied soldiers who survived the battle but had been enveloped by gas spent the rest of their lives in veterans' hospitals. The British retaliated by using poison gas, and the horrifying casualties continued.

In reaction to the devastation caused by poison gas, an international document was signed in 1925 banning the use of toxic gas and biological weapons. Though gas was not used during battle in World War II, toxic gases have been used by various countries since then. For example, Iraq used poison gas during its war with Iran in the 1980s.

OBJECTIVE

④ **INSTRUCT**

American Neutrality

▶ ***Discussing Key Ideas***

- Although most Americans oppose entering the war, public opinion about the war is strongly divided.
- Economic and cultural ties with Britain plus reports of German atrocities gain American sympathy for the Allies.

Ask students to create a Venn diagram like the one shown below to compare and contrast American public opinion on the war.

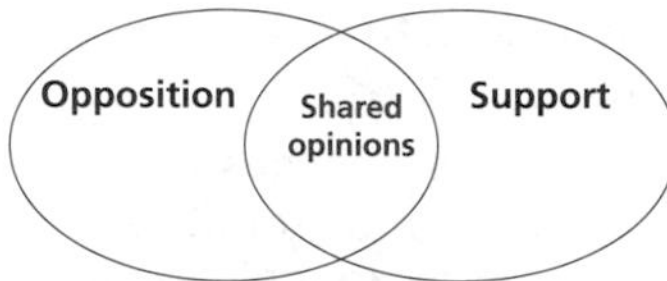

HISTORY FROM VISUALS

U.S. Exports to Europe, 1910–1915

Reading the Graph Ask students to use the graph to determine which country received the most American exports in 1915 and which country received the least. *Great Britain received the most, and Austria-Hungary received the least.*

Extension Ask students to speculate about the kinds of goods that were exported to Britain and France in 1914 and 1915. *Possible Response: War supplies.*

which armies fought and died for mere yards, continued for more than three years. Elsewhere, the fighting was equally devastating and equally inconclusive. On the Eastern Front, Russian and German armies advanced and retreated in turn. The Italian Front, between Austria-Hungary and Italy, was likewise deadlocked. The Allied assault on the Dardanelles, part of the waterway between the Black Sea and the Mediterranean, ended after almost a year of trench warfare. In Africa, German and British troops were stalemated after two years of battle. It seemed as if neither side would be able to gain a decisive victory.

American Neutrality

In 1914, most Americans saw no reason to join a struggle 3,000 miles away. The war did not threaten American lives or property. Whether or not the Allies beat the Central Powers did not seem a matter of national concern. This does not mean, however, that individual Americans were indifferent to who would win the war. Public opinion was strong—but divided.

OPPOSITION TO THE WAR Millions of naturalized U.S. citizens followed the war closely because they still had ties to the nations from which they had emigrated. For example, many Americans of German descent sympathized with Germany. Americans of Irish descent remembered the centuries of British oppression in Ireland and saw the war as a chance for Ireland to gain its independence.

Socialists criticized the war as an imperialist struggle between German and English businessmen to control raw materials and markets in China, Africa, and the Middle East. Pacifists, such as William Jennings Bryan, believed that war was evil, and that the United States should set an example of peace to the world. Bryan asserted, "If civilization is to advance, the day must come when a nation will feel no more obligated to accept a challenge to war than an American citizen now feels obligated to accept a challenge to fight a duel."

Many Americans simply did not want their sons to experience the horrors of warfare, as a hit song of 1915 conveyed.

> I didn't raise my boy to be a soldier,
> I brought him up to be my pride and joy.
> Who dares to place a musket on his shoulder,
> To shoot some other mother's darling boy?

SYMPATHY FOR THE ALLIES Despite the widespread opposition to the war, a general feeling of sympathy for Great Britain and France emerged. Many Americans felt close to England because of a common ancestry, language, and literature, as well as similar democratic institutions and legal systems.

Germany's aggressive sweep through Belgium also increased American sympathy for the Allies. On one occasion, for example, the Germans leveled the town of Louvain because a Belgian sniper had killed a German soldier. They charged hundreds of civilians, including women and children, with armed resistance and shot them without trial. They destroyed cathedrals, libraries, and even hospitals. Some atrocity stories—distributed in British propaganda—later proved to be false, but enough proved true that within a month after the war broke out, one magazine referred to Germany as "the bully of Europe."

More important, America's economic ties with the Allies were far stronger than its ties with the Central Powers. Before the war began, America had traded with Great Britain and France more than twice as much as with Germany. During the first two years of the war, America's

Skillbuilder Answer
France: They more than tripled—from just over $100 million to almost $400 million. **Taking Sides:** *Possible Answer:* U.S. exports to the two major Allied powers increased dramatically, probably because of exports of war-related materials. Exports to the two major Central Powers dropped sharply.

SKILLBUILDER
INTERPRETING GRAPHS
By how much did U.S. exports to France increase between 1910 and 1915? What does the pattern of U.S. exports show about which side the U.S. took in the European war?

U.S. Exports to Europe, 1910–1915

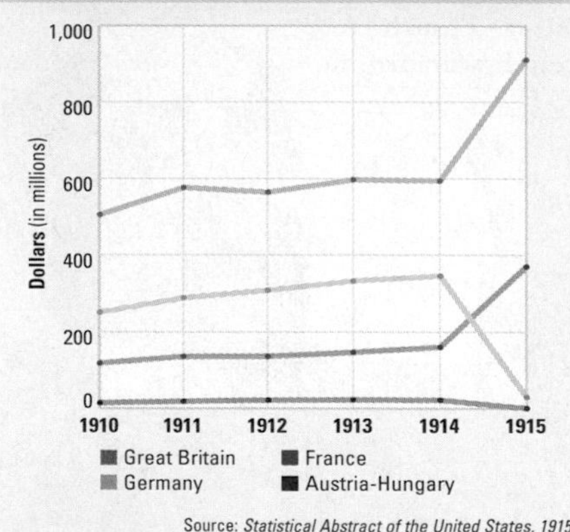

Source: *Statistical Abstract of the United States, 1915*

TEACHING OPTIONS

Teaching Gifted and Talented Students

Analyzing Switzerland's Neutrality Tell students that unlike the United States, Switzerland remained neutral throughout World War I. In fact, Switzerland has managed to maintain an armed neutrality since 1815. Have students research Swiss neutrality by answering these questions:

- How has Switzerland managed to remain the only European country to preserve its neutrality through two world wars?
- What role, if any, did Switzerland play in the two wars?
- How did the people of other European countries benefit from Switzerland's neutrality?

Making Connections Across Time

German Retaliation in World War II Tell students that German soldiers often exacted a high price in lives and property when they retaliated against their enemies during World War II. One such retaliation was similar to that avenged on the town of Louvain during the First World War. In 1942, after Czech fighters assassinated Reinhard Heydrich, the chief planner of the Nazi program to kill all European Jews, the Germans wiped out the Czech village of Lidice in revenge. All the men in the village were killed, all the women were sent to labor camps, and all the children were sent to Germany.

THINK THROUGH HISTORY
C. *Analyzing Causes* *Why did the United States tend to favor Britain and France?*

transatlantic trade became even more lopsided, as the Allies flooded American manufacturers with orders for all sorts of war supplies, including TNT, cannon powder, submarines, copper wire and tubing, and armored cars. The United States shipped millions of dollars of war supplies to the Allies, but requests kept coming. By 1915, the nation was experiencing a labor shortage.

The United States Enters the War

C. Answer The United States favored Britain and France because it traded extensively with them and because Germany was the aggressor.

Although the majority of Americans favored victory for the Allies rather than the Central Powers, they did not want to join the Allies' fight. By 1917, however, Americans had mobilized for war against the Central Powers for two reasons: to ensure Allied repayment of debts to the United States and to prevent the Germans from threatening U.S. shipping.

THE BRITISH BLOCKADE As fighting on land continued without any resolution, Great Britain began to make more use of its naval strength. It set up a blockade along the German coast to prevent contraband—or weapons and other military goods—from getting through. However, the British expanded the definition of contraband to include food. They also extended the blockade to neutral ports and mined the entire North Sea.

The results were twofold. First, American ships carrying goods for Germany refused to challenge the blockade and seldom reached their destination. Second, Germany found it increasingly difficult to import foodstuffs and chemical fertilizers. Since it had to use its available nitrates to produce munitions, it could not produce fertilizers of its own. Without fertilizers, German farmers could not grow enough food. By 1917, famine stalked the country. An estimated 750,000 Germans starved to death as a result of the British blockade.

GERMAN U-BOAT RESPONSE Germany responded to the British blockade with a counterblockade by U-boats (from *Unterseeboot*, the German word for a submarine). The kaiser announced that all cargoes headed for Great Britain would be considered contraband. Any ship found in the waters around Britain would be sunk—and it would not always be possible to warn crews and passengers in advance of an attack.

ECONOMIC BACKGROUND

THE COSTS OF NEUTRALITY

Although Woodrow Wilson hoped to keep Americans neutral in the First World War, neutrality proved difficult for those who had a great deal of money invested in the Allies. Some warned that drained treasuries would force European nations to cut their purchases of food and war material from the United States, which in turn would slow down the booming U.S. war industries. Secretary of the Treasury William McAdoo argued that to maintain American prosperity, the United States must finance the war.

By 1917 American banks had loaned $2.3 billion to the Allies but only $27 million to the Central Powers. Furthermore, U.S. trade with the Allies quadrupled while trade with the Central Powers fell drastically between 1914 and 1917. A major reason that U.S. leaders backed the Allies was that only an Allied victory would assure repayment of the American loans. (See *trade* on page 940 in the Economics Handbook.)

D. Answer Because the U-boat campaign killed Americans and destroyed American property, it turned American public opinion against Germany and helped bring the United States into the war.

The German blockade turned out to be far less destructive than the British blockade. All told, about 75,000 people lost their lives from German submarine warfare, about one-tenth of the number of Germans who died of starvation. However, the effects of the British blockade were only visible inside Germany. U-boat attacks, on the other hand, were spectacular events, easily exploited in the propaganda reaching the United States from Britain, which had cut the transatlantic cable between Germany and the United States. News of the European front that flashed around the world from London carried accounts of sinking ships and drowning victims.

THINK THROUGH HISTORY
D. *Recognizing Effects* *How did the German U-boat campaign affect U.S. public opinion and actions?*

As a result, Americans who had been angry at Great Britain's blockade, which threatened freedom of the seas and prevented American goods from reaching German ports, became outraged with Germany because of the loss of life. American public opinion toward Germany and the Central Powers rapidly became negative.

One of the worst disasters occurred on May 7, 1915, when a U-boat sank the British liner ***Lusitania*** off the southern coast of Ireland. Of the 1,198 persons killed, 128 were Americans. The Germans defended their action on the grounds that the liner carried ammunition and explosives. But most Americans agreed with the New York minister who thundered from his pulpit, "This sinking . . . is

OBJECTIVE
5 INSTRUCT

The United States Enters the War

▶ ***Discussing Key Ideas***

- The British naval blockade creates terrible food shortages in Germany.
- German U-boats sink British ships, including passenger liners, and turn American public opinion against Germany.
- Wilson is reelected in 1916 on a platform of neutrality, but events soon prompt the president to declare war.

ECONOMIC BACKGROUND

The Costs of Neutrality

Critical Thinking: Speculating Discuss the economic motivation for American entry into the war. Ask students whether they think the United States would have backed the Central Powers if Americans had invested more money in those countries. Would the United States have entered the war if American banks had not loaned money to either side?

Block Schedule TEACHING OPTION **Time Needed: 30 Minutes**

Cooperative Activity: Creating Wartime Propaganda

Task: Groups of four to five students will create a piece of propaganda designed to promote sympathy for one side in the First World War.

Purpose: To help students understand the power of propaganda during a war.

Activity: Students should create a poster that exaggerates the villainy of the enemy and the righteousness of their own side. Some students might want to illustrate a U-boat sinking to influence public opinion against Germany. Others might illustrate action on the part of the Allies that can be shown in a negative manner. Students should include a caption or slogan that effectively captures the poster's message. Collect the finished posters, display them, and discuss them in class.

Building a Portfolio: Students who decide to add their posters to their portfolios should attach a note describing how the poster is intended to influence public opinion.

ALTERNATIVE ASSESSMENT BOOK
Standards for Evaluating a Cooperative Activity

Standards for Evaluation
Posters should . . .

- exaggerate the villainy of one side and the goodness of the other
- include a caption or catchy slogan that summarizes the message
- appeal to the intended audience's emotions

DIFFICULT DECISIONS IN HISTORY

Should the United States Enter the War?

Critical Thinking: Forming Opinions Engage students in a debate on the question raised in the feature. Divide students on both sides into smaller groups. Then have pairs of opposing groups discuss whether the United States should have entered the war. Remind students to use sound reasons and logic to support their arguments.

MORE ABOUT . . .

Hughes and the 1916 Election

Hughes took part in various political stunts on the campaign trail in an attempt to counter his reputation as a cold, reserved man. In Reno, Nevada, he attended a rodeo and shook hands with all the cowboys. In Butte, Montana, he went down into a copper mine to shake hands with the miners. In Detroit, he jumped on top of the Tigers' dugout to shake hands with Ty Cobb and other baseball players. Hughes's biggest mistake took place in California, where he failed to visit Governor Hiram Johnson. Insulted, Johnson refused to campaign for Hughes, who consequently lost the state by fewer than 4,000 votes.

NOTICE!

TRAVELLERS intending to embark on the Atlantic voyage are reminded that a state of war exists between Germany and her allies and Great Britain and her allies; that the zone of war includes the waters adjacent to the British Isles; that, in accordance with formal notice given by the Imperial German Government, vessels flying the flag of Great Britain, or of any of her allies, are liable to destruction in those waters and that travellers sailing in the war zone on ships of Great Britain or her allies do so at their own risk.

IMPERIAL GERMAN EMBASSY
WASHINGTON, D. C., APRIL 22, 1915.

Notices like the one above were printed in American newspapers, warning passengers not to travel by sea. The 1915 painting of an American transport sunk by a German U-boat *(right)* shows how serious that warning was.

not war; it is . . . organized murder and no language is too strong for it. . . . It is getting to be too much to ask America to keep out when Americans are drowned as part of a European war."

THE UNITED STATES REMAINS NEUTRAL Despite this provocation, Wilson ruled out a military response. However, he protested sharply to Germany. Two months later, in July 1915, a U-boat sank another British liner, the *Arabic*, drowning two Americans. Again the United States protested, and this time Germany agreed not to sink any more liners. But in March 1916 Germany broke its promise and torpedoed an unarmed French passenger steamer, the *Sussex*. The *Sussex* did not sink, but about 80 passengers, including Americans, were killed or injured. Once again the United States warned that it would break off diplomatic relations unless Germany changed its tactics. Again Germany agreed, but there was a string attached: if the United States could not persuade Britain to lift its blockade against food and fertilizers, Germany said, it would consider renewing unrestricted submarine warfare.

Difficult Decisions IN HISTORY

SHOULD THE UNITED STATES ENTER THE WAR?

Though President Wilson urged Americans to be "neutral in fact as well as in name," many wanted to join the war on the Allied side. Secretary of State Robert Lansing, for example, undercut Wilson's peace initiatives with Britain and France, hoping Germany would resume unrestricted U-boat attacks and thus pull America into the war.

As a pacifist, Jane Addams worked hard to keep the United States out of the war altogether, and she endured criticism for her efforts. Senator George Norris argued against the war resolution in Congress, charging that millions would suffer and die "all because we want to preserve the commercial right of American citizens to deliver munitions of war to belligerent nations."

1. In your opinion, which side had the stronger argument—those who backed the Allies or those who favored staying out of the war?
2. In your opinion, should the United States have entered the war?

THE 1916 ELECTION In November 1916 came the U.S. presidential election. The Democrats renominated Wilson, and the Republicans nominated Supreme Court Justice Charles Evans Hughes. Wilson campaigned on the slogan "He Kept Us Out of War." Hughes pledged to uphold America's right to freedom of the seas but also promised not to be too severe on Germany.

The election returns shifted from hour to hour. In fact, Hughes went to bed believing he had been elected. When a reporter tried to reach him with the news of Wilson's victory, an aide said, "The President can't be disturbed." "Well," replied the reporter, "when he wakes up, tell him he's no longer President."

NEUTRALITY COLLAPSES Following the election, Wilson tried to end the war by calling upon both sides to state the terms on which they would be willing to stop fighting. The attempt failed. In a speech before the Senate on January 22, 1917, the president called for "a peace without victory . . . a peace among equals" in which neither side would impose harsh terms on the other. Instead, all nations would join in a "league for peace" that would work to extend democracy, maintain freedom of the seas, and reduce armaments.

Nine days later the Germans responded. Germany's leaders felt they had a good chance to knock out Great Britain by resuming unrestricted

TEACHING OPTION

Skillbuilder Mini-Lesson: Evaluating Alternative Courses of Action

Explaining the Skill In order to understand historical decisions, historians often look at the alternative courses of action that were available to people at the time. Evaluating such alternatives involves analyzing the pros and cons of each alternative based on the conditions, expectations, and values of the times, and on the information that was available then.

Applying the Skill Have students read the feature on this page, Difficult Decisions in History, and review the events leading up to the U.S. entrance into World War I. Then ask what alternatives President Wilson had in responding to Germany and how effective each alternative might have been. *Possible Responses: Stay out entirely, which didn't seem to be working, since Germany kept threatening American lives and property; continue to try to negotiate with Germany, which also didn't seem to work, because Germany kept breaking agreements; enter the war, as Wilson did after Germany promised to help Mexico regain lands that were part of the U.S.*

IN-DEPTH RESOURCES: UNIT 3
Skillbuilder Practice: Evaluating Alternative Courses of Action, p. 44

submarine warfare. On January 31 the kaiser announced that U-boats would sink all ships in British waters—hostile or neutral—on sight. Wilson was stunned. The German decision meant the United States would have to go to war. However, the president held back, saying that he would wait for "actual overt acts" before breaking diplomatic relations.

The overt acts came. First was the **Zimmermann note,** a telegram sent by the German foreign minister to the German ambassador in Mexico and intercepted by British agents. The telegram suggested an alliance between Mexico and Germany and promised that if war with the United States broke out, Germany would support Mexico in recovering "the lost territory in Texas, New Mexico, and Arizona." Next came the sinking of four unarmed American merchant ships, with a loss of 36 lives. Moreover, in March the Russians overthrew their repressive czarist regime and replaced it with a representative government. Now supporters of entry into the war could claim that the war against the Central Powers was a war of democracies against brutal monarchies.

THINK THROUGH HISTORY
E. *Summarizing* *What events finally prompted Wilson to ask for a declaration of war?*

E. Answer The Zimmermann note, the sinking of four merchant ships, and the overthrow of the Russian czar made it possible to justify the war on moral grounds.

A light drizzle fell on Washington on April 2, 1917, as senators, representatives, ambassadors, members of the Supreme Court, and other guests crowded into the Capitol building to hear President Wilson deliver his war resolution.

A PERSONAL VOICE

Property can be paid for; the lives of peaceful and innocent people cannot be. The present German submarine warfare against commerce is a warfare against mankind. . . . We are glad . . . to fight . . . for the ultimate peace of the world and for the liberation of its peoples . . . for the rights of nations great and small and the privilege of men everywhere to choose their way of life. . . . The world must be made safe for democracy. . . . We have no selfish ends to serve. We desire no conquest, no dominion. We seek no indemnities. . . . It is a fearful thing to lead this great peaceful people into war. . . . But the right is more precious than peace.

WOODROW WILSON, quoted in *American Voices*

THINK THROUGH HISTORY
F. THEME **Democracy in America** *How did the German offensives threaten democracy?*

F. Answer The Germans would not allow people to choose their own "way of life"; although the United States was not attacked directly, it saw itself as protecting democracy elsewhere.

The Senate passed the resolution on April 4, and the House of Representatives did so on April 6. With the illusion of neutrality finally shattered, U.S. troops would follow the stream of American money and munitions that had been heading to the Allies throughout the war. But Wilson's desire to make the world "safe for democracy" wasn't just political rhetoric. Indeed, Wilson and many Americans truly believed that the United States must join the war to pave the way for a future order of peace and freedom. A resolved but anxious nation held its breath as the United States prepared for war.

ON THE WORLD STAGE

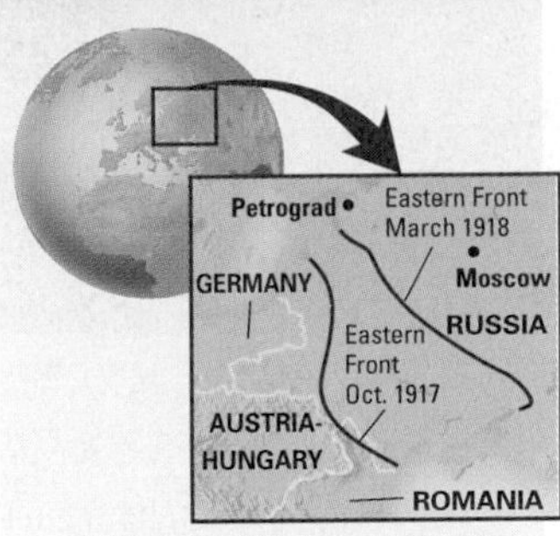

WAR ON THE EASTERN FRONT

The Russian army surprised the Germans by mobilizing rapidly in the early months of the war. Russian troops advanced quickly into German territory. The Germans turned the Russians back, however, at the Battle of Tannenberg in August 1914.

Throughout 1915, the Russians suffered successive defeats and continued to fall back into their own territory. By the end of 1915 they had suffered about 2.5 million casualties. Beyond the casualties, the war also caused massive bread shortages within Russia.

Demanding bread and peace, revolutionaries ousted the czar in March 1917 and established a provisional government led by Alexander Kerensky, who refused to pull Russia out of the war. In November, the Bolsheviks, led by Vladimir Lenin and Leon Trotsky, overthrew the Kerensky government. They then set up a Communist state and sought peace with the Central Powers.

Section  1 Assessment

1. TERMS & NAMES
Identify:
- militarism
- Allies
- Central Powers
- Archduke Franz Ferdinand
- no man's land
- trench warfare
- *Lusitania*
- Zimmermann note

2. SUMMARIZING In a chart like the one shown, list events or reasons that promoted and slowed the entrance of the United States into World War I.

The U.S. Entrance into World War I	
Promoted	Slowed

Choose a reason or an event to explain orally to your class.

3. MAKING PREDICTIONS If Archduke Franz Ferdinand had not been assassinated, do you think World War I would still have occurred? Give reasons to support your viewpoint.

THINK ABOUT
- the long-term causes of World War I
- the reason for the archduke's assassination
- the multinational interest in the Balkans

4. ANALYZING ISSUES Why do you think Germany responded to Wilson's call for "peace without victory" by escalating its U-boat attacks?

THINK ABOUT
- Germany's military buildup
- its reputation as "the bully of Europe"
- its reason for using submarine warfare

ANSWERS

1. TERMS & NAMES
militarism, p. 395
Allies, p. 396
Central Powers, p. 396
Archduke Franz Ferdinand, p. 396
"no man's land," p. 397
trench warfare, p. 397
Lusitania, p. 399
Zimmermann note, p. 401

2. SUMMARIZING
Possible Answer: **Promoted:** cultural links with Great Britain and France; British propaganda; economic ties with Allies; anger at U-boat attacks; Zimmermann note. **Slowed:** ethnic ties of German and Irish Americans; charges of imperialism; pacifism; Wilson's slogan in 1916 campaign. **Explanation:** British propaganda—Americans knew about U-boat attacks but didn't know thousands of Germans were starving.

3. MAKING PREDICTIONS
Possible Responses: **Yes**—Long-term forces were pushing Europe into war; the alliances were ready and waiting to defend their groups; Germany's military buildup foretold war. **No**—At least not at that time, because nations did not want to upset the balance of power in the alliances; militarism resulted in an arms race, but war might not have followed.

4. ANALYZING ISSUES
Possible Response: The Germans had been slowly building their military power and were preparing for a show of strength, so peace without victory would have been meaningless; Germany thought it could defeat Britain with unrestricted submarine warfare before the Americans could mobilize for war.

ON THE WORLD STAGE
War on the Eastern Front

Critical Thinking: Analyzing Ask students why the Russian people were unwilling to fight against the Central Powers for the czar or for the Kerensky government.
Possible Response: The people felt no allegiance to either the repressive czarist regime or the new government.

ASSESS & RETEACH

Section 1 Assessment
Have pairs of students divide the questions and then share their answers.

Self-Assessment
Have students jot down what they found most interesting, most surprising, and most challenging in the section.

Section Quiz
FORMAL ASSESSMENT
Section Quiz, p. 141

Reteach
Use the map on page 397 to review the progress of the fighting during the early years of the war.

CLOSE

After the assassination of Archduke Franz Ferdinand, the alliance system drew many of the world's nations into war. In the face of the savage fighting, Wilson resolved to maintain American neutrality. However, German submarine warfare and economic concerns caused Wilson to make a declaration of war in April 1917. Anxiously, the United States prepared for war.

IN-DEPTH RESOURCES: UNIT 3
Primary Source: The Zimmermann Note, p. 47

 ***ELECTRONIC LIBRARY OF PRIMARY SOURCES***
Request for a Declaration of War by Woodrow Wilson

Section 2 Overview

OBJECTIVES

1. To describe how the United States mobilized for war.
2. To summarize American success on the war front.
3. To identify the new weapons and the medical problems faced in World War I.
4. To assess the impact of the war on the key participating nations.

SKILLBUILDERS

- Understanding geography: movement, region, p. 405
- Interpreting graphs, p. 408

CRITICAL THINKING

- Clarifying, p. 403
- Summarizing, pp. 404, 405, 408
- Recognizing effects, p. 407
- Evaluating, p. 408
- Making predictions, p. 408

FOCUS & MOTIVATE

5-MINUTE WARM-UP

Describing Mood

To describe the mood in the United States during World War I, ask students to study the poster on page 403 and the quote on page 406 and answer these questions.

1. How does the poster stir feelings of patriotism?
2. What mood do you think the song was intended to inspire?

WARM-UP TRANSPARENCY 11

▶ ***Starting with the Student***

- How would students react if their country went to war? Would they volunteer to serve? Would they refuse to go? Would they protest the country's involvement in the conflict?

AMERICAN STORIES **video series**
"Ace of Aces"

Videocassette: Volume 3

Videodisc: Disc 2, Side A, Chapter 3

2 American Power Tips the Balance

TERMS & NAMES

- Eddie Rickenbacker
- Selective Service Act
- convoy system
- Alvin York
- conscientious objector
- mechanized warfare

LEARN ABOUT the American experience fighting in the First World War
TO UNDERSTAND how the United States contributed to Allied victory.

ONE AMERICAN'S STORY

Captain **Eddie Rickenbacker** became one of the most celebrated American heroes of World War I. Born in Columbus, Ohio, Rickenbacker grew up to be a racecar driver and set a world speed record before the war—134 miles per hour.

His daring served him well in the military, where he began as a driver for General John J. Pershing but soon entered a pioneer flight organization, the 94th Aero Pursuit Squadron. As a pilot in the 94th, also called the Hat-in-the-Ring Squadron, Rickenbacker engaged in more than 130 air battles and downed 26 enemy planes. In the following passage from his autobiography, Rickenbacker described his daily flight experiences.

A PERSONAL VOICE

> I put in six or seven hours of flying time each day. I would come down, gulp a couple of cups of coffee while the mechanics refueled the plane and patched the bullet holes and take off again. . . . In my 134 air battles, my narrowest escape came at a time when I was fretting over the lack of action. . . . Guns began barking behind me, and sizzling tracers zipped by my head. I was taken completely by surprise. At least two planes were on my tail. They had me cold. They had probably been watching me for several minutes and planning this whole thing.
>
> They would expect me to dive. Instead I twisted upward in a corkscrew path called a "chandelle." I guessed right. As I went up, my two attackers came down, near enough for me to see their faces. I also saw the red noses on those [German] Fokkers. I was up against the Flying Circus again.
>
> EDDIE RICKENBACKER, *Rickenbacker*

Eddie Rickenbacker

Again and again, Rickenbacker came up against the dreaded Flying Circus—a German air squadron under the leadership of Manfred von Richthofen, also known as the Red Baron. Eventually, Rickenbacker shot down enough enemy planes to earn the title that went to the pilot with the most victories—"American ace of aces."

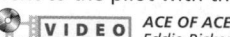

ACE OF ACES
Eddie Rickenbacker and the First World War

American Military Mobilization

Before Rickenbacker and other Americans could make their contributions to the war effort, however, the United States needed to build up its armed forces through recruitment. When war was declared, only about 200,000 men were in service. Few officers had combat experience. Almost all of the army's weapons were out of date, and the whole U.S. air corps consisted of 55 small planes and 130 pilots.

The country responded to the lack of manpower with a draft. Also called conscription, a draft requires men to register with the government so that some of them can be selected for compulsory service. Many members of Congress initially opposed the draft, arguing that conscription would produce a "sulky, unwilling, indifferent army." But after weeks of debate, Congress passed the **Selective Service Act** in May 1917. By the end of 1918, the number of men registered under the act had reached 24 million. Of this number, almost 3 million, chosen by lottery, were called up. About 2 million troops reached Europe before the armistice was signed, and three-fourths of them saw actual combat. The ages of the inductees (those entering the service) ranged from 18 to 45. However, since

SECTION 2 RESOURCES

PRINT RESOURCES

IN-DEPTH RESOURCES: UNIT 3
Guided Reading, p. 41
Primary Source: Patriotic Song, p. 48
Literature: *from* "In Another Country" by Hemingway, p. 53

READING STUDY GUIDE, p. 121

ACCESS FOR STUDENTS ACQUIRING ENGLISH
Guided Reading (Spanish), p. 142

SPANISH READING STUDY GUIDE, p. 121

FORMAL ASSESSMENT
Section Quiz, p. 142

ALTERNATIVE ASSESSMENT BOOK
See forms for supporting and scoring alternative activities.

TECHNOLOGY RESOURCES

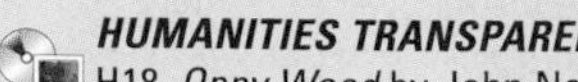

HUMANITIES TRANSPARENCIES
H18, *Oppy Wood* by John Nash

CRITICAL THINKING TRANSPARENCIES
CT53, Human and Financial Costs of World War I

CD-ROM *Our Times*
Grolier Multimedia Encyclopedia
Electronic Library of Primary Sources

VIDEO *American Stories* video series
American Portfolio: A Videodisc for U.S. History user's guide, pp. 183–188

INTERNET http://www.mlushistory.com

married men and those with dependents were generally excused, the overseas army consisted primarily of men between 21 and 23. Most had not attended high school, and about one in five was foreign-born.

The training period lasted for nine months, partly in the United States and partly in Europe. During this time the men put in 17-hour days on target practice, bayonet drill, kitchen duty, and cleaning up the grounds. Since real weapons were in short supply, they often drilled with imaginary ones—rocks instead of hand grenades, wooden poles instead of rifles. To keep up morale, volunteer organizations provided the recruits with movies, books, and vaudeville shows. After nine months, they were moved to wherever the fighting was hottest.

THINK THROUGH HISTORY
A. Clarifying *How did the United States raise an army for the war?*
A. Answer Congress passed the Selective Service Act, which caused 24 million men to register for the draft.

Women were not drafted. The army also refused to let them enlist, but the navy accepted them for noncombat positions. Accordingly, some 13,000 women served in the navy and marines as nurses, secretaries, and telephone operators, with full military rank. Although the army reluctantly accepted women in the Army Corps of Nurses, it denied them army rank, pay, and benefits.

James Montgomery Flagg's portrayal of Uncle Sam in *I Want You* became the most famous recruiting poster in American history.

The proportion of African Americans in service was double their proportion in the general population. As in earlier wars, black soldiers served in segregated units and were excluded from the navy and marines. They had separate living quarters and separate recreational facilities. Although most officers were white, the army for the first time trained some black officers and placed them in command of black troops. Most African Americans were assigned to noncombat duties, but not all. The all-black 369th Infantry Regiment saw more continuous duty on the front lines than any other American regiment. Two soldiers of the 369th, Henry Johnson and Needham Roberts, were among the first Americans to receive the French military honor of the Croix de Guerre, the "cross of war."

American Success in Combat

The next task facing the United States was to transport its troops overseas, along with food and equipment sufficient for them and for America's allies. It was an immense task, made more difficult by Germany's unrestricted submarine warfare, which by early 1917 had sunk twice as much ship tonnage as the Allies had built.

BUILDING THE "BRIDGE TO FRANCE" The United States immediately began constructing ships to expand its fleet. For decades American manufacturers had relied mostly on foreign ships to carry their products overseas. In addition, the draft reduced the number of skilled shipyard workers.

To overcome these obstacles, the U.S. government took four critical steps. First, it either exempted shipyard workers from the draft or gave them a "deferred" classification, delaying their participation in the draft. Second, the government and the U.S. Chamber of Commerce cooperated in a public relations campaign to emphasize the importance of shipyard work. They distributed service flags to families of shipyard workers, just like the flags given to families of soldiers and sailors. An official of the Chamber of Commerce went around the country, urging automobile owners to give shipyard employees rides to and

A convoy of American ships heads toward Britain.

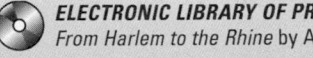

OBJECTIVE
① INSTRUCT

American Military Mobilization

▶ ***Discussing Key Ideas***
- Although some members of Congress fear that a draft will produce an unwilling army, almost 10 million men register for combat under the Selective Service Act.
- Women are not drafted, but some fill noncombat positions.
- Black soldiers serve in segregated units, and some are assigned to fight on the front lines.

IN-DEPTH RESOURCES: UNIT 3
Guided Reading, p. 41

ACCESS FOR STUDENTS ACQUIRING ENGLISH
Guided Reading (Spanish), p. 142

OBJECTIVE
② INSTRUCT

American Success in Combat

▶ ***Discussing Key Ideas***
- The United States constructs ships to expand its fleet for the war effort.
- Using the convoy system, the Allies break the German blockade.
- General Pershing insists on having American soldiers fight as an independent force.
- With Americans fighting in large numbers, the United States helps turn the tide against the Central Powers by October 1918.

TEACHING OPTIONS

Making Connections Across Cultures

African Americans in World War I Discuss the treatment of African-American soldiers during World War I. Tell students that the NAACP and black leader W. E. B. Du Bois urged African Americans to join the fight for world democracy. Ask students why many African Americans wanted to fight for a country that failed to grant them equal rights. *Possible Response: They hoped that fighting for world democracy might ensure fairer treatment at home.*

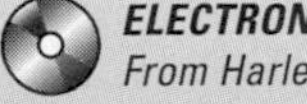
ELECTRONIC LIBRARY OF PRIMARY SOURCES
From Harlem to the Rhine by Arthur Little

Exploring Themes

Democracy in America Tell students that although many of the army's practices were discriminatory, the decision to train black officers revealed a more progressive attitude toward minorities than that prevalent in society in general. Point out that the army has frequently been at the vanguard in according African Americans and other minorities democratic rights. Ask students why the army, particularly during times of war, has often granted minorities more rights, freedoms, and opportunities than society has. *Possible Responses: War is a great equalizer; war inspires feelings of brotherhood.*

MORE ABOUT . . .
Arthur Taber

In a sense, Taber began training for battle in childhood. When he was eight years old and on summer vacation, he would swim for half an hour a day in an ice-cold lake. When he was bitten by a snake in his early teens, he did not flinch. Nor did he complain when he had to undergo nine operations for a wrenched knee. He carried out an experiment in a Western desert to see how long he could survive without water. Before enlisting in the U.S. Army, he spent part of a year as a volunteer driver with the American Field Ambulance Service in France. After the war ended, he remained in France to test-fly planes and to observe the peace conference at Versailles "from the front-row, so to speak." Sadly, after surviving the war, Taber was killed in February 1919 while test-flying an army plane. He was buried in a military cemetery outside Paris.

from work, since streetcars were so crowded. Third, shipyards developed a new construction technique called fabrication. Instead of building an entire ship in the yard, they had standardized parts built elsewhere and merely assembled them at the yard. This method reduced construction time substantially. As a result, on just one day—July 4, 1918—the United States was able to launch 95 ships. Fourth, the government took over ships being constructed for private owners and ones designed for use on the Great Lakes and converted them for transatlantic war use.

THINK THROUGH HISTORY
B. *Summarizing* *What four steps did the U.S. government take to build a naval fleet quickly?*

B. Answer It let shipyard workers out of the draft, used a public relations campaign to stress the importance of shipbuilding, used a new construction technique called fabrication, and took control of ships built for private owners or use on the Great Lakes for transatlantic duty.

BREAKING THE BLOCKADE The goal of building a navy was to reduce the shipping losses caused by German U-boat attacks on merchant ships trying to cross the Atlantic. Rear Admiral William S. Sims persuaded the British that the best way to defeat the U-boats was the **convoy system,** in which merchant vessels would travel in a large group with a guard of circling destroyers and cruisers. The British agreed, and by midsummer of 1917 shipping losses had been cut in half. Eventually the United States put 100 submarine chasers and 500 airplanes into the anti–U-boat campaign.

The U.S. Navy also helped lay down a 230-mile barrier of mines across the North Sea from Scotland to Norway. The barrier was designed to bottle up the U-boats that sailed from German ports and keep them out of the Atlantic Ocean.

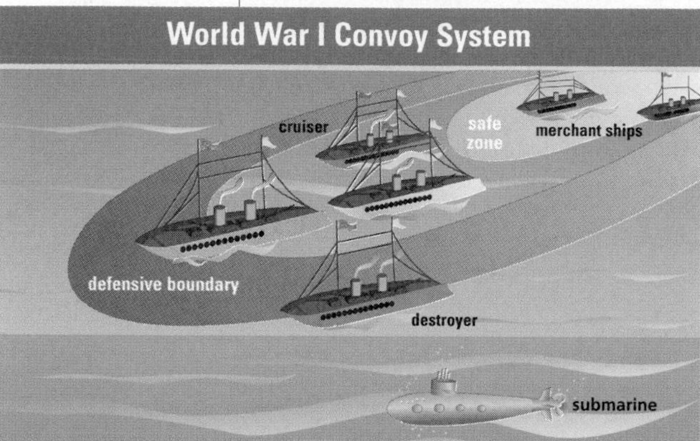

The convoy system helped equip Britain with crucial supplies.

By the first months of 1918 the Allies had overcome the U-boat threat. Days and even weeks went by without the loss of a single Allied vessel. Moreover, as U-boat losses mounted, the Germans found it increasingly difficult to replace their losses and to man their fleet with trained submariners. Of the almost 2 million Yanks who sailed to Europe during the war, only 100 were lost to U-boats, when the transport *Tuscania* was torpedoed in the English Channel.

FIGHTING IN EUROPE One of the main contributions that American troops made to the Allied war effort, apart from their numbers, was their freshness and enthusiasm. Unlike the British, French, and Germans, American troops had not endured three years of exhausting warfare. They were determined to hit the Germans hard. Arthur "Archie" Taber, a university student who left Princeton University to enlist in the air force, enthusiastically described his experiences as a fledgling pilot in a letter to his father.

A PERSONAL VOICE

The most extraordinary piece of good luck has suddenly fallen from the skies. I . . . have been appointed as a "ferry" pilot, which means that I shall fly all over France. . . . I shall have to take planes up to the front to any point along the line where our squadrons are. . . . Of course this will be great fun; but the reason I am so enthusiastic over this job is that it gives unparalleled training in cross-country flying, the experience of flying in all kinds of machines, and the valuable foundation for any kind of work, of *time in the air*. . . . Also you can appreciate that in such a job as this, one will have to be able to fly everything from a monoplane to a triplane, from the smallest to the largest and from the fastest to the slowest!

ARTHUR TABER, quoted in *Hooray for Peace, Hurrah for War*

Taber's only regret was that he would have to wait several months, if not more, before he could hope to be assigned to "the very best pilot's job, chasing German planes over the front line trenches."

TEACHING OPTIONS

Making Connections Across the Curriculum

Economics Tell students that during the war, the United States mobilized the economy as well as the military. About one-fourth of all American production was diverted to the war effort. Agriculture and many industries experienced a boom in sales and profits. However, as demand exceeded supply, prices skyrocketed and inflation resulted. Have students discuss who reaped the greatest economic benefits from the war. What groups of Americans probably suffered the most?

Making Connections Across Time

Remembering Lafayette Tell students that after the American troops joined the Allies in France, the saying "Lafayette, we are here!" became popular. The comment is usually attributed to General Pershing. In fact, it was delivered at an address at the grave of Lafayette in Paris on July 4, 1917, by Colonel C. E. Stanton. The statement reminded Americans that French troops under the Marquis de Lafayette had aided Washington and the cause of the American Revolution. The landing of American soldiers in World War I represented America's repayment of its debt to France.

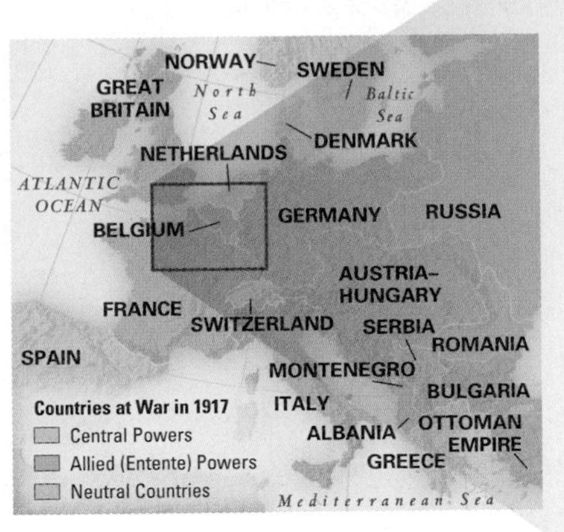

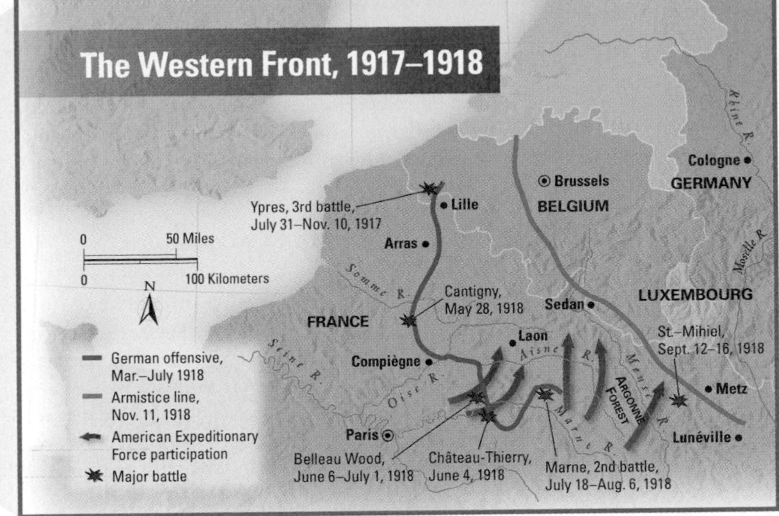

General John J. Pershing commanded the American Expeditionary Force (AEF). At first the Americans served mostly as replacements for Allied casualties. The American infantrymen were nicknamed doughboys, apparently because of the white belts they wore, which they cleaned with pipe clay, or "dough." Pershing, however, kept insisting that they should fight as a separate army. "We came American," he said. "We shall remain American and go into battle with Old Glory over our heads. I will not parcel out American boys!"

Pershing believed in aggressive combat and felt that three years of trench warfare had made the Allies too defensive. In addition, he wanted the United States to have a strong voice at the peace table. This was most likely to occur if the AEF remained distinct and separate. Accordingly, after April 1918, American soldiers fought as an independent force, under the overall direction of French marshal Ferdinand Foch, commander of all Allied forces in Europe.

GEOGRAPHY SKILLBUILDER

MOVEMENT *Across which rivers did American troops attack German forces?* **REGION** *What territory captured by Germany after the beginning of the war lay on the German side of the Armistice line?*

Skillbuilder Answer
Movement: The Marne, Aisne, and Meuse rivers. **Region:** Parts of Belgium and eastern France.

THE TIDE TURNS By then the Germans had succeeded in knocking Russia out of the war and had shifted their armies from the eastern front in Russia to the western front in France. By May their spring offensive had smashed to within 50 miles of Paris. The Americans began to fight in large numbers just in time. They helped stop the German advance at Cantigny in France. Several weeks later they played a major role in throwing back German attacks at Château-Thierry and Belleau Wood. In July and August, they helped win the Second Battle of the Marne. In September, they mounted offensives against the Germans at Saint-Mihiel and in the Meuse-Argonne area. All told, the United States lost 48,000 men in battle, with an additional 62,000 dying of disease. More than 200,000 Americans were wounded. But by October it was clear that the tide had definitely turned against the Central Powers.

THINK THROUGH HISTORY
C. *Summarizing* *How did the United States contribute to the Allied victory?*

C. Answer The United States helped break the German blockade and helped defeat Germany on the western front in France.

It was during the fighting in the Meuse-Argonne area that one of America's greatest war heroes, **Alvin York,** became famous. A redheaded mountaineer and blacksmith from Tennessee, York became a born-again Christian in 1915. When war came, he sought exemption as a **conscientious objector,** a person who opposes warfare on moral grounds, pointing out to his draft board that the Bible says, "Thou shalt not kill." The board denied his appeal and sent him to a training camp in Georgia. There Captain E. C. B. Danforth presented to York a different Biblical quotation: "I bring you not peace but a sword. . . . He that hath no sword, let him sell his garment and buy one."

York eventually decided that it was morally acceptable to fight if the cause was just. On October 8, 1918, armed only with a rifle and a revolver, Corporal

HISTORY FROM VISUALS

The Western Front, 1917–1918

Reading the Map Point out that the smaller map shows the location of the Western Front in relation to the rest of Europe. Then ask students what countries lie to the west of the Armistice line. What countries lie to the east?

Extension Ask students why the American Expeditionary Force was launched from the places shown by the red arrows. *To help prevent the German offensive from invading Paris.*

HUMANITIES TRANSPARENCIES
H18, *Oppy Wood* by John Nash

MORE ABOUT . . .

Conscientious Objectors

About 1,400 conscientious objectors refused to cooperate with the military in any way. Many were court-martialed and imprisoned. Some were even physically tortured. While these men held fast to their convictions, many suffered from feelings of isolation. One man sentenced to a 20-year prison term wrote to his brother: "The comradeship one must give up, the being part of the fun and hardship of all this, yes of fighting and maybe dying along with the rest of your fellows on both sides in this huge tragedy makes my stand seem so terribly aloof, so terribly unhuman."

Block Schedule TEACHING OPTION **Time Needed: 30 Minutes**

Cooperative Activity: Letters from Conscientious Objectors and the Draft Board

Task: Student groups will write letters explaining the position of conscientious objectors and of the draft board on the war.

Purpose: To help students understand different points of view on the war.

Activity: Have small groups of students take turns representing a conscientious objector and a draft board official. As conscientious objectors, students should write letters explaining why they are opposed to the war and what, if anything, they propose to do to aid the war effort. As draft board officials, students should explain why participation in the war is so important.

Building a Portfolio: Students who wish to add the letters to their portfolios should attach a note telling which side they found more sympathetic and whether the activity changed their minds about pacifism.

ALTERNATIVE ASSESSMENT BOOK
Standards for Evaluating a Cooperative Activity

Standards for Evaluation
Letters should . . .

- state clearly the position
- give detailed reasons to support the position
- use persuasive techniques to help convince readers
- use appropriate letter form and style

OBJECTIVE

③ INSTRUCT

Fighting "Over There"

▶ ***Discussing Key Ideas***
- New, terrifying weapons change the face of warfare.
- Medical services cannot keep up with the physical and emotional wounds suffered by the soldiers.

MORE ABOUT . . .

Soldiers' Nicknames

Before George M. Cohan popularized the use of the name Yanks for American soldiers, U.S. troops had tried several other names. The *Cleveland Press* coined the name Sammies, after Uncle Sam, but American soldiers disliked the term and it soon disappeared. The French at first referred to Americans as Teddies, after Theodore Roosevelt, but stopped using the name when General Pershing said it had no national significance. Other Allied fighting men also bore distinctive nicknames. Australians were called Aussies, the British were called Tommies, and New Zealanders were called Kiwis, after a native bird.

York killed 25 Germans and—with six other doughboys—captured 132 prisoners. General Pershing called him the outstanding soldier of the AEF, while Marshal Foch described his feat as "the greatest thing accomplished by any private soldier of all the armies of Europe." For his heroic acts, York was promoted to sergeant and became a celebrity when he returned to the United States.

Fighting "Over There"

For Sergeant York, as for many other members of the AEF, going abroad was an eye-opening experience. Most doughboys had never ventured outside the farms or small towns where they lived, and the sights and sounds of Paris made a vivid impression. Sergeant York, for example, saw his first subway there. Then, too, the AEF included men from widely separated parts of the country. Living and fighting together, they developed a better sense of what it meant to be an American. Nevertheless, the war experience was devastating in many ways, especially in view of the new weapons soldiers used.

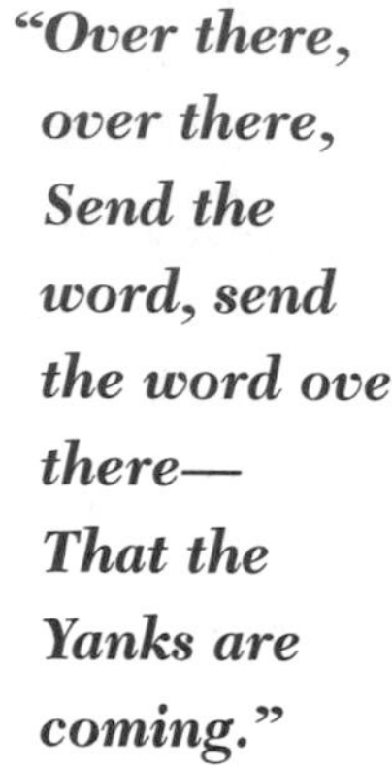

"Over there, over there, Send the word, send the word over there— That the Yanks are coming."

GEORGE M. COHAN, FROM THE SONG "OVER THERE," 1917

NEW WEAPONS One terrifying weapon was a German cannon that could hurl an 1,800-pound shell a distance of 75 miles. Allied soldiers called it Big Bertha—after Bertha Krupp, the wife of the German munitions king Gustav Krupp. Another new weapon was the zeppelin, a gas-filled airship that enabled Germans to drop bombs on English coastal cities. However, zeppelins were so easy to shoot down that the Germans abandoned their use within two years. Far deadlier was the machine gun, which sprayed 600 rounds of ammunition per minute. And there were tubes that spewed poison gas rather than bullets. Their first large-scale use occurred at the Battle of Ypres in April 1915. The Germans discharged a greenish-yellow fog of chlorine that suffocated two entire French divisions and left a four-mile-wide gap in the battle line. Gas masks soon became standard equipment for everyone.

The two most innovative weapons were the tank and the airplane. Together, they inaugurated **mechanized warfare,** or warfare that relies on machines powered by gasoline and diesel engines.

Tanks ran on caterpillar treads and were built of steel so that bullets bounced off. The British, who developed the tank, first used them during the 1916 Battle of the Somme, but not very effectively. By 1917, the British had learned how to gather large numbers of tanks and drive them through barbed wire defenses against the enemy, clearing a path for the infantry.

The early airplanes were so flimsy that at first both sides limited their use to scouting. After a while, the two sides used tanks to fire at enemy planes that were gathering information. Early dogfights, or individual air combats, resembled duels. Pilots sat in their open cockpits and shot at each other with pistols. Because it was hard to fly a plane and shoot a pistol at the same time, planes began carrying mounted machine guns. But the planes' propeller blades kept

New Weapons in World War I

POISON GAS
- First large-scale use was in 1915.
- Gas masks became standard equipment.

MACHINE GUNS
- Firepower increased from several rounds per minute to 600 rounds per minute.

TANKS
- Tanks were first developed by the British.
- They were used in formations to clear a path for the infantry.

406

TEACHING OPTION

Making Connections Across the Curriculum

Music Tell students that many American songs helped keep up the soldiers' spirits and voiced the typical reaction to various aspects of the First World War. For example, thousands of men volunteered for combat to the sound of the popular song "Johnny Get Your Gun." Tunes like "Over There" by George M. Cohan were played by warships leaving for Europe. Irving Berlin's "Oh! How I Hate to Get Up in the Morning" reflected every soldier's dread of the morning bugle call. Other songs recognized the eye-opening effect of the war on young, naive soldiers. As the song title asks, "How 'Ya Gonna Keep 'Em Down on the Farm, After They've Seen Paree?" Still other songs, such as "There's a Long, Long Trail A-Winding," expressed the homesickness experienced by most of those in service.

IN-DEPTH RESOURCES: UNIT 3
Primary Source: Patriotic Song, p. 48

OUR TIMES
George M. Cohan and "Over There"

getting in the way of the bullets. Then a Dutchman who was working for Germany invented an interrupter gear that permitted the stream of bullets to avoid the whirring blades.

THINK THROUGH HISTORY
D. *Recognizing Effects* *How did the tank and the airplane change warfare?*

D. Answer They inaugurated mechanized warfare, which made fighting speedier, deadlier, more expensive, and more dependent on gasoline.

Meanwhile, airplanes became faster and able to carry heavy bomb loads. By 1918 the British had built up a strategic bomber force of 22,000 planes with which to attack German war plants and army bases.

Observation balloons were used extensively by both sides in the war in Europe. As Eddie Rickenbacker noted in his autobiographical account of air battles, "From an altitude of two thousand feet on a clear day an observer with a telescope, comfortable in his wicker basket slung from the balloon, could see many miles into the enemy's rear." What is more, the observer was connected to the command headquarters by telephone, so the observer could make a report without taking the time to land, as airplane pilots could not. Balloons were so important strategically that they were often protected by aircraft hovering above them, and they became prime targets for Rickenbacker and other ace pilots.

MEDICAL CARE DURING THE WAR As in all wars, the fighting men suffered greatly. They were surrounded by filth, lice, rats, and polluted water that caused dysentery. They smelled the stench of poison gas and the reek of decaying bodies. They suffered from lack of sleep. Bombardments that continued for hours often led to battle fatigue and "shell shock"—a complete emotional collapse.

Another problem was a disease called trench foot, caused by standing in wet trenches for long periods of time without changing into dry socks or boots. First the soldier's toes would turn red or blue, then they would become numb, and finally they would start to rot. The only solution was to amputate the foot. A painful infection of the gums and throat, called trench mouth, was also common among the soldiers.

Red Cross ambulances, often staffed by American volunteers, carried the wounded from the battlefield to the hospital. An American nurse named Florence Bullard recounted her experience in a hospital near the front in 1918.

KEY PLAYER

JOHN J. PERSHING
1860–1948

Pershing became head of the American Expeditionary Force after many years in the military. A West Point graduate in 1886, he helped to put down Apache and Sioux uprisings in the 1880s and 1890s. He acquired the nickname Black Jack because he had led a unit of African-American soldiers.

He led more African-American troops in Cuba during the Spanish-American-Cuban War and later served in the Philippines. In 1916–1917, he led the expedition against Francisco "Pancho" Villa in Mexico.

At first, fellow officers thought that calling him Black Jack might offend Pershing, but it didn't. He was proud of the name because his men were top-notch soldiers. Both Pershing's superiors and those he commanded respected him greatly for his courage, his fairness, and his administrative ability.

A PERSONAL VOICE

The Army is only twelve miles away from us and only the wounded that are too severely injured to live to be carried a little farther are brought here. . . . Side by side I have Americans, English, Scotch, Irish, and French, and a part in the corners are Boche [Germans]. They have to watch each other die side by side. I am sent for everywhere—in the . . . operating room, the dressing-room, and back again to the rows of men. . . . The cannon goes day and night and the shells are breaking over and around us. . . . I have had to write many sad letters to American mothers. I wonder if it will ever end.

FLORENCE BULLARD, quoted in *Over There*

In fact, the end was near.

The Collapse of Germany

On November 3, 1918, the German admiralty—its naval leadership—ordered the Grand Fleet to leave its naval base at Kiel and set out to sea. But the admiralty was shocked when the sailors and marines refused to man the ships. There was no use in fighting any longer, they said.

The mutiny spread quickly. Everywhere in Germany, groups of soldiers and workers organized revolutionary councils. On November 9, the people of Berlin rose in rebellion, and socialist leaders in the capital proclaimed the

KEY PLAYER
John J. Pershing

Critical Thinking: Drawing Conclusions Have students review Pershing's personality traits. Discuss with them why these traits would be important ones for a military leader.

GROLIER MULTIMEDIA ENCYCLOPEDIA
John Pershing

MORE ABOUT . . .
Eddie Rickenbacker

Rickenbacker continued his adventures during World War II, where he was a civilian inspector of American air bases abroad. In 1942, during an inspection trip, Rickenbacker's plane was forced down over the Pacific Ocean. For 24 days he and six other people survived on the ocean on rubber rafts before rescue arrived.

Between the two wars, Rickenbacker worked with various automobile companies and was a co-owner of the Indianapolis Speedway. He was also the president of Eastern Airlines from 1938 to 1959.

OBJECTIVE
(4) INSTRUCT

The Collapse of Germany

▶ ***Discussing Key Ideas***

- Soon after the German people rebel against the war and the kaiser, Germany agrees to an armistice on November 11, 1918.
- The toll of the war on human life is staggering.

TEACHING OPTION

Making Connections Across the Curriculum

Science Tell students that at the time of the First World War, psychiatry was a relatively new science. Nonetheless, military doctors recognized that thousands of their patients were suffering from the same mental illness. Doctors called the illness war neurosis, or war psychosis, but almost everyone else called it shell shock. For many of the soldiers whose nervous systems had been shattered by noisy shelling, a treatment of rest, exercise, and counseling proved successful. Others, who had been exposed to the sounds of especially intense and prolonged explosives, suffered persistent anxiety and disorientation, which made it difficult for them to live normal lives.

Before the war, mental illness was generally misunderstood and carried a stigma of shame. The First World War helped educate the public about mental illness and the importance of psychiatry. As a result of the war, most people understood that like diseases of the body, mental illness required treatment. After the war was over, psychiatrists who had treated shell-shock victims used their experience to improve care for the mentally ill at home.

HISTORY FROM VISUALS

World War I Casualties

Reading the Graph Point out that the graph provides the data needed to compare casualties among the countries involved in the war. Then ask students to calculate the percentage of casualties in the total war effort. *About 46 percent.*

Extension Have students draw conclusions about the relationship between the number of troops employed and the number of casualties suffered on each side.

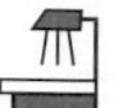

CRITICAL THINKING TRANSPARENCIES

CT53, Human and Financial Costs of World War I

ASSESS & RETEACH

Section 2 Assessment

Have gifted students work with less proficient readers to answer the questions.

Self-Assessment

Have students use a chart to explore how their understanding of the First World War has developed. In the first column, students should list what they knew about the war before reading Section 2. In the second column, they should list what they have learned.

Section Quiz

FORMAL ASSESSMENT
Section Quiz, p. 142

Reteach

Review the section by creating a time line of events, beginning with American mobilization and ending with the armistice.

CLOSE

The American infusion of fresh troops, ships, and military know-how helped achieve an Allied victory. On November 11, 1918, the world rejoiced at the war's end. However, many people found that the war had forever changed their lives.

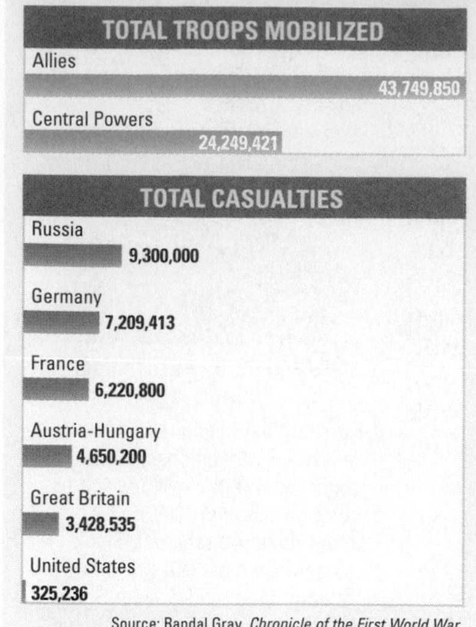

SKILLBUILDER
INTERPRETING GRAPHS
Which country suffered the greatest number of military casualties in World War I? What might account for the relatively low number of American casualties in World War I?

Skillbuilder Answer
Greatest Casualties: Russia. **American Casualties:** *Possible Answer:* The U.S. entered the war three years after it started.

establishment of a German republic. The kaiser abdicated the throne and took refuge in the Netherlands.

Although there were no Allied soldiers on German territory and no truly decisive battle had been fought, the German war machine and war economy were too exhausted to continue. So at the eleventh hour, on the eleventh day, in the eleventh month of 1918, Foch stopped the fighting after Germany agreed to a cease-fire that ended the war. (Austria-Hungary and the Ottoman Empire had surrendered several days earlier.)

The final toll of the war was staggering. It had lasted four years and involved more than 30 nations. It was the bloodiest war in history to that time. Deaths numbered about 26 million, half of them civilians who died as a result of disease, starvation, or exposure. In addition, 20 million more people were wounded, and an additional 10 million became refugees. Historians estimate the direct economic costs of the war to have been about $350 billion.

For the Allies, news of the armistice brought great relief. Eddie Rickenbacker flew over the trenches on the day of the armistice and later described what had happened when the guns fell silent.

A PERSONAL VOICE

On both sides of no-man's land, the trenches erupted. Brown-uniformed men poured out of the American trenches, gray-green uniforms out of the German. From my observer's seat overhead, I watched them throw their helmets in the air, discard their guns, wave their hands. Then all up and down the front, the two groups of men began edging toward each other. . . . Hesitantly at first, then more quickly, each group approached the other. Suddenly gray uniforms mixed with brown. I could see them hugging each other, dancing, jumping. Americans were passing out cigarettes and chocolate. I flew up to the French sector. There it was even more incredible. After four years of slaughter and hatred, they were not only hugging each other but kissing each other on both cheeks as well.

EDDIE RICKENBACKER, quoted in *Hooray for Peace, Hurrah for War*

Across the Atlantic, American civilians also rejoiced at the war's end. Many hoped the world would go on much as it had before the war. However, the war had unleashed powerful forces at home, and people found their lives changed almost as much as the lives of those who fought in Europe.

Section 2 Assessment

1. TERMS & NAMES
Identify:
- Eddie Rickenbacker
- Selective Service Act
- convoy system
- Alvin York
- conscientious objector
- mechanized warfare

2. SUMMARIZING Create a web, similar to the one shown, illustrating problems Americans faced as they prepared for and participated in World War I.

Which problem do you think created the most difficulties for Americans?

3. EVALUATING In your opinion, did the U.S. government use fair methods in selecting people to serve in the military? Explain.

THINK ABOUT
- the exemptions to the draft
- the role played by women
- the treatment of African Americans

4. MAKING PREDICTIONS How might the events and outcome of World War I have been different if the United States had not sent troops to Europe? Explain your answer.

THINK ABOUT
- the results of battles before the United States entered the war
- the role of American soldiers in the fighting
- the emotional impact of American troops' arrival

ANSWERS

1. TERMS & NAMES

Eddie Rickenbacker, p. 402
Selective Service Act, p. 402
convoy system, p. 404
Alvin York, p. 405
conscientious objector, p. 405
mechanized warfare, p. 406

2. SUMMARIZING

Possible Answers: Developing an army; transporting troops overseas; building ships; building fighter planes; avoiding U-boats; using tanks, airplanes, and machine guns; dealing with Big Bertha; fighting in trenches; dealing with poison gas; fighting diseases. Most difficulties: trench warfare, because it took so many lives, extended the length of the war, and resulted in the spread of diseases.

3. EVALUATING

Possible Responses: **Yes**—Exemptions and the lottery were fair, and discrimination against women and African Americans merely reflected attitudes of the time. **No**—The government placed unfair burdens on young, single males; not enough opportunities were offered to African Americans; the army should have given women rank, pay, and benefits.

4. MAKING PREDICTIONS

Possible Responses: The Allies might not have withstood the 1918 German offensive without the boost from American troops; The stalemate might have continued until both sides were so exhausted and depleted that they may have reached a compromise settlement; The Allies might still have won without American troops if America had provided supplies and medical help.

❸ The War at Home

TERMS & NAMES
- War Industries Board
- Bernard M. Baruch
- George Creel
- Espionage and Sedition Acts
- Great Migration

LEARN ABOUT the political, social, and economic forces unleashed by the war ***TO UNDERSTAND*** how the war changed American society.

ONE AMERICAN'S STORY

In the summer of 1918, after President Wilson had ordered 7,000 troops to Russia, leaflets condemning the action hit the streets of Manhattan. Some local residents, in the midst of their war-era patriotic fervor, were infuriated by the tone of the leaflets and tipped off local and federal authorities about the source of the literature.

Police quickly targeted and arrested five Russian immigrant anarchists—people who opposed any and all forms of government—for distributing literature that violated the newly passed Sedition Act. The law made it illegal to use "disloyal, profane, scurrilous, or abusive" descriptions of American leaders or institutions. While the five anarchists—Jacob Abrams, Hyman Lachowsky, Samuel Lipman, Mollie Steimer, and Jacob Schwartz—sat in jail awaiting trial, Schwartz died, possibly because of a beating by the police. The remaining four were found guilty and sentenced to serve 15 to 20 years in prison. Their appeal went before the Supreme Court, which ruled 7–2 against the defendants. One of the dissenting justices, Oliver Wendell Holmes, Jr., explained his position.

Justice Oliver Wendell Holmes, Jr.

A PERSONAL VOICE

[In this case] sentences of twenty years imprisonment have been imposed for the publishing of two leaflets that I believe the defendants have as much right to publish as the Government has to publish the Constitution. . . . When men have realized that time has upset many fighting faiths, they may come to believe that . . . the best test of truth is the power of the thought to get itself accepted in the competition of the market, and that truth is the only ground upon which their wishes safely can be carried out.

JUSTICE OLIVER WENDELL HOLMES, JR., dissenting opinion in *Abrams* v. *United States*

Abrams, Lachowsky, Lipman, and Steimer never served their full sentences. Instead, they were deported to Russia in 1921. But their experiences in the United States were not uncommon at a time when Americans were trying to sort out their reactions to events overseas.

Congress Gives Power to Wilson

The political forces that brought the *Abrams* case to the forefront were unleashed by the war. Concerns over patriotism arose as Americans tried to eliminate any possible internal enemies. Often those efforts resulted in American citizens' attacking immigrants who were uncomfortable with the English language and who might secretly still have loyalties to distant homelands.

The war economy likewise caused far-reaching changes in American lives. Many people, especially African Americans, moved from one region to another, lured by promises of higher wages. And women, who usually had limited roles in the nation's industrial economy, filled many positions left open by men who had joined the armed forces, providing the hardware those men needed to fight.

Winning the war was not a job for American soldiers alone. As Secretary of War Newton Baker said, "War is no longer Samson with his shield and spear and sword, and David with his sling. It is the conflict of smokestacks now, the combat of the driving wheel and the engine." In other words, it was necessary to mobilize the entire economy, to shift from producing consumer goods to

Section 3 Overview

OBJECTIVES

1. To explain how business and government cooperated during the war.
2. To show how the government promoted the war.
3. To describe the attacks on civil liberties that occurred.
4. To summarize the social changes that occurred among African Americans and women.

SKILLBUILDER

- Interpreting graphs, p. 411

CRITICAL THINKING

- Recognizing effects, p. 410
- Summarizing, pp. 412, 416
- Clarifying, p. 414
- Theme: Immigration and Migration, p. 415
- Theme: Women in America, p. 416
- Forming opinions, p. 416
- Synthesizing, p. 416

FOCUS & MOTIVATE

5-MINUTE WARM-UP

Recognizing Propaganda

Ask students to study the poster on page 411 and answer these questions.

1. What images and details in the poster suggest that German soldiers are inhuman?
2. Why would the poster help sell Liberty Bonds?

WARM-UP TRANSPARENCY 11

▶***Starting with the Student***
- Are people who voice their opposition to the government's policies during wartime disloyal or unpatriotic?

OBJECTIVE ① **INSTRUCT**

Congress Gives Power to Wilson

▶***Discussing Key Ideas***
- The War Industries Board is established to regulate the economy in the interests of the war effort.

(continued on next page)

SECTION 3 RESOURCES

PRINT RESOURCES

IN-DEPTH RESOURCES: UNIT 3
Guided Reading, p. 42
Primary Sources: Liberty Bond Poster, p. 49; "Returning Soldiers" by W. E. B. Du Bois, p. 50
American Lives: Oliver Wendell Holmes, Jr., p. 55

READING STUDY GUIDE, p. 123

ACCESS FOR STUDENTS ACQUIRING ENGLISH
Guided Reading (Spanish), p. 143

SPANISH READING STUDY GUIDE, p. 123

FORMAL ASSESSMENT
Section Quiz, p. 143

ALTERNATIVE ASSESSMENT BOOK
See forms for supporting and scoring alternative activities.

TECHNOLOGY RESOURCES

CD-ROM Electronic Library of Primary Sources

VIDEO *American Portfolio: A Videodisc for U.S. History* user's guide, pp. 181–184, 189

INTERNET http://www.mlushistory.com

(continued from page 409)

- Profits for farmers and war-related industries rise during the war, while prices soar.
- The country unites in the effort to help produce and conserve food.

IN-DEPTH RESOURCES: UNIT 3
Guided Reading, p. 42

ACCESS FOR STUDENTS ACQUIRING ENGLISH
Guided Reading (Spanish), p. 143

KEY PLAYER
Bernard M. Baruch

Critical Thinking: Analyzing Ask students how Baruch's personality traits might have helped him carry out his duties as leader of the War Industries Board. *Possible Responses: His decision-making ability helped him make quick, informed choices. His imagination helped him find creative solutions to problems. His consideration of others earned him loyal friends and workers.*

MORE ABOUT . . .
Bernard Baruch

Baruch had trouble dealing with the steel industry, led by U.S. Steel's board chairman, Elbert Gary. U.S. Steel made enormous wartime profits. In September 1917, Baruch threatened to take over U.S. Steel unless the company agreed to lower its prices. When Gary sneeringly said that the government wasn't capable of running the company, Baruch replied that he would get a second lieutenant to do the job and added, "If those mill towns find out why we've taken over, they'll present you with your mills—brick by brick." Gary lowered his prices.

KEY PLAYER

BERNARD M. BARUCH
1870–1965

Bernard M. "Barney" Baruch became a millionaire before he was 30 by speculating in the stock market. His ability to amass large amounts of information, as well as his friendship with numerous business leaders, made him a natural choice to head the War Industries Board (WIB). In addition, he was energetic, decisive, imaginative, and considerate. Observers remarked that whenever he entered the room, President Wilson became noticeably more serene.

It was Wilson who gave Baruch his nickname Dr. Facts—a name that proved accurate, as Baruch quickly assembled, coordinated, and distributed information about war materials and production techniques. Several of the executives whom Baruch brought into the government reappeared during the 1930s, when the New Deal again mobilized American industry.

producing weapons, ammunition, and other war supplies. This was too complicated and important a job for private industry to handle on its own, so business and government cooperated in the effort. Congress gave President Wilson direct control over much of the economy, including the power to fix prices and to regulate—even to nationalize—certain war-related industries.

WAR INDUSTRIES BOARD The main regulatory body was the **War Industries Board** (WIB). It was established in 1917 and reorganized in 1918 under the leadership of **Bernard M. Baruch.** The board encouraged companies to use mass-production techniques to increase efficiency and urged them to eliminate waste by standardizing products—for instance, by making only 5 colors of typewriter ribbons instead of 150. The WIB set production quotas and allocated raw materials. It also conducted psychological testing to help people find the right jobs.

Under the WIB, industrial production in the United States increased by about 20 percent. However, the WIB applied price controls only at the wholesale level. As a result, retail prices soared, and in 1918 they were almost double what they had been before the war. Corporate profits soared as well, especially in such industries as chemicals, copper, lumber, meatpacking, oil, and steel.

The activities of the WIB had several side effects, including changes in women's clothing. For example, Baruch pointed out that corsets required 8,000 tons of steel a year, which could be better employed in building two battleships. Accordingly, women stopped buying corsets with steel ribs. Tall leather shoes, which were fashionable but not functional, disappeared, and the extra leather went into soldiers' boots. Hemlines rose, and the fabric that had formerly gone into long skirts went into military uniforms instead.

The WIB was not the only federal agency to regulate the economy in the interests of the war effort. The Railroad Administration controlled the nation's railroads, and the Fuel Administration monitored coal supplies and rationed gasoline and heating oil. In addition, many people voluntarily adopted "gasless Sundays" and "lightless nights" to help conserve fuel. In March 1918, the Fuel Administration introduced another conservation measure: daylight-saving time, which had first been proposed by Benjamin Franklin in the 1770s as a way to take advantage of the longer days of summer.

THINK THROUGH HISTORY
A. *Recognizing Effects* *What effects did the WIB have on the economy?*

A. Answer The WIB encouraged business to use mass-production techniques and to standardize products. Its pricing policies resulted in soaring corporate profits.

WAR ECONOMY Wages in some industries—especially the metal trades, shipbuilding, and meatpacking—rose during the war years by as much as 20 percent. By contrast, white-collar workers, like clerks, managers, and lawyers, lost about 35 percent of their purchasing power because of inflation. As a result of the uneven treatment of workers, union membership climbed from about 2.5 million in 1916 to more than 4 million in 1919, and more than 6,000 strikes broke out during the war months in protest against stagnant wages at a time of rising prices.

"Work or fight."

NATIONAL WAR LABOR BOARD

In 1918, President Wilson established the National War Labor Board to deal with disputes between management and labor. Employers warned workers who were reluctant to go along with board decisions that they would lose their exemption from the draft. "Work or fight," they were told. However, the War Labor Board did try to improve working conditions. It pushed for the eight-hour day and urged factory owners to allow safety inspections. It also pressured all manufacturers to observe the federal ban on child labor.

To help produce and conserve food, President Wilson set up the Food Administration and placed Herbert Hoover in charge. Hoover's entire staff,

TEACHING OPTION

Making Connections Across the Curriculum

Economics Discuss the state of the economy during the First World War. Tell students that many workers benefited from full-time employment and increased earnings during the war. However, most people saw little improvement in their buying power, due to the sharp rise in prices during the war years. The cost of clothing tripled, for example, while food prices more than doubled. A quart of milk cost 9 cents in 1914 and 17 cents in 1920. The price of fuel also rose. The value of coal jumped fully 100 percent.

The government, meanwhile, did little to control this inflation. It fixed prices on most raw materials but not on the finished products. That meant that companies could determine their own prices for their goods. Since demand exceeded supply, the companies could get away with inflated prices. Even the price of some raw materials, such as cotton, was left unregulated. By bowing to political pressure from the South, the government allowed the price of cotton to skyrocket.

except for clerks, consisted of volunteers. Instead of rationing food, he organized a tremendous publicity campaign that called on people to follow the "gospel of the clean plate." He declared one day a week "meatless," another "sweetless," two days "wheatless," and two other days "porkless." Restaurants removed sugar bowls from the table and served bread only after the first course. Since Europeans were accustomed to eating wheat, Hoover urged Americans to eat corn so that they could send their wheat abroad.

Homeowners planted "victory gardens" in their yards. There was even a victory garden in one corner of the White House lawn. Schoolchildren joined the United States School Garden Army and spent their after-school hours growing tomatoes and cucumbers in public parks. As a result of these and similar efforts, American food shipments to the Allies tripled. Hoover also set a high government price on wheat and other staples. Farmers responded by putting an additional 40 million acres into production. In the process, they increased their income by almost 30 percent.

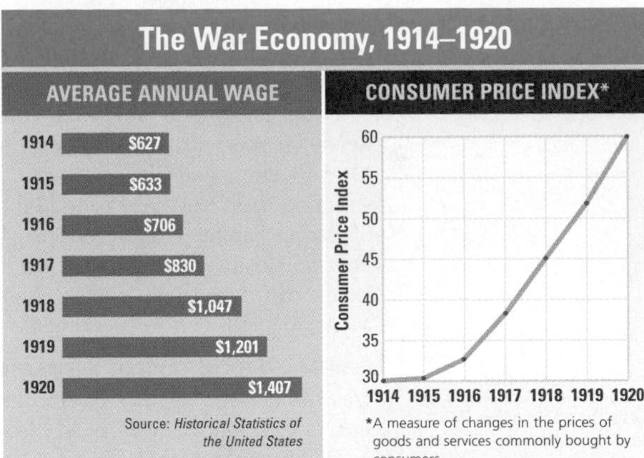

SKILLBUILDER
INTERPRETING GRAPHS
Which one-year period between 1914 and 1920 saw the least growth in the Consumer Price Index? How did the rise in wages compare with the rise in prices from 1914 to 1920?

Skillbuilder Answer
Least Growth: 1914–1915.
Comparison: The price index doubled in that period, while wages more than doubled.

The wartime need for labor brought over a million more women into the work force. The suffragist Harriot Stanton Blatch visited a munitions plant in New Jersey and described with pride what she saw.

> A PERSONAL VOICE
> The day I visited the place, in one of the largest shops women had only just been put on the work, but it was expected that in less than a month they would be found handling all of the twelve hundred machines under that one roof alone. The skill of the women staggers one. After a week or two they master the operations on the "turret," gauging and routing machines. The best worker on the "facing" machine is a woman. She is a piece worker, as many of the women are. . . . This woman earned, the day I saw her, five dollars and forty cents. She tossed about the fuse parts, and played with that machine, as I would with a baby. Perhaps it was in somewhat the same spirit—she seemed to love her toy.
>
> **HARRIOT STANTON BLATCH,** quoted in *We, the American Women*

The woman Blatch described was unusual: she was paid at the same rate as men. Although President Wilson called for equal pay for equal work, most women in war plants received less than men—and almost all of them lost their jobs when the war ended.

Some World War I government posters scared Americans into buying Liberty Bonds by portraying the Germans as bloodthirsty barbarians.

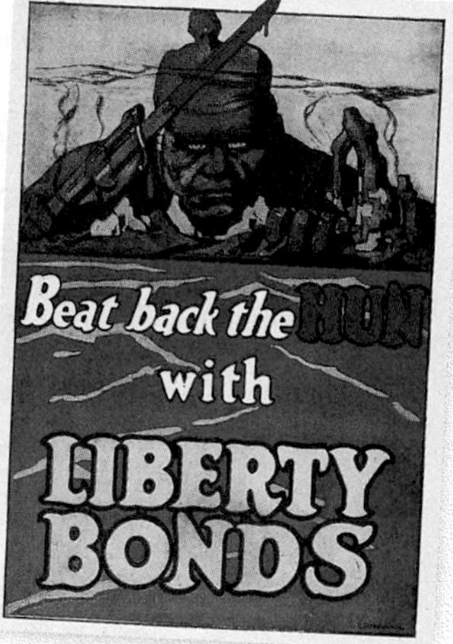

Selling the War

"It is not an army we must shape and train for war," argued President Wilson; "it is a nation." Not only did soldiers need to learn to fight, but civilians needed to learn how to sacrifice for the war effort. Since the war was not universally popular, the government embarked on a massive propaganda campaign to justify civilian sacrifices and sell the war to the public. The campaign had two aspects. On one hand, it promoted patriotism. On the other hand, it manufactured hate.

WAR FINANCING The United States spent about $33 billion directly on the war effort. The government raised about one-third of this amount through taxes, including a steeper income tax (which taxed high incomes at a higher rate than low incomes), a war-profits

HISTORY FROM VISUALS
The War Economy, 1914–1920

Reading the Graph Have students compare the graph of average wages with that showing the consumer price index. Ask them what happened to prices as wages increased. *Prices also increased.*

Extension Ask students why wages and prices continued to rise after the war. *Possible Response: Because inflation continued to cause both to spiral out of control.*

MORE ABOUT . . .
Food Restrictions

Hoover's directions about conserving food provoked many jokes and satires. *Life* magazine, for example, wrote: "Do not permit your child to take a bite or two from an apple and throw the rest away; nowadays even children must be taught to be patriotic to the core."

OBJECTIVE
② INSTRUCT

Selling the War

▶ ***Discussing Key Ideas***
- The government finances the war by raising income and excise taxes and by promoting the sale of war bonds.
- The government sets up the nation's first propaganda agency to popularize the war.

IN-DEPTH RESOURCES: UNIT 3
Primary Source: Liberty Bond Poster, p. 49

Block Schedule TEACHING OPTION **Time Needed: 30 Minutes**

Cooperative Activity: Creating a Wartime Ad Campaign

Task: Groups of three to four students will design an ad campaign to urge people to help produce and conserve food for the war effort.

Purpose: To help students understand the sacrifices and fervor stimulated by war.

Activity: Students should first decide what they want to publicize. Some may want to design an ad campaign illustrating an idea suggested by the text, such as "meatless" days or victory gardens. Others may want to come up with their own ideas for persuading the public to conserve or produce food. Students should present their ads on a poster and include a catchy slogan. Display the posters and discuss their persuasive power in class.

Building a Portfolio: Students who believe their poster represents some of their best work may wish to add it to their portfolio.

ALTERNATIVE ASSESSMENT BOOK
Standards for Evaluating a Cooperative Activity

Standards for Evaluation
Ads should . . .
- encourage the audience to conserve and produce food for the war effort
- suggest that this activity supports a noble cause
- include a catchy slogan that helps the audience remember the ad

MORE ABOUT . . .

Wartime Propaganda

To aid the war effort, Hollywood turned out both patriotic and hate films. Among the former were *Pershing's Crusaders* and *Under Four Flags.* Hate films included *To Hell with the Kaiser* and *The Beast of Berlin.* Advertisements for the latter film showed a hanged effigy of the kaiser. Another hate film portrayed mad German scientists training millions of houseflies to bring germs into the United States.

ELECTRONIC LIBRARY OF PRIMARY SOURCES

Four-Minute Speech

OBJECTIVE

③ INSTRUCT

Attacks on Civil Liberties

▶ ***Discussing Key Ideas***

- The main targets of anti-immigrant hysteria are immigrants from Germany and Austria-Hungary.
- Clearly violating the spirit of the First Amendment, the Espionage and Sedition Acts allow people to be arrested for any antiwar activities.

IN-DEPTH RESOURCES: UNIT 3

American Lives: Oliver Wendell Holmes, Jr., p. 55

tax, and higher excise taxes on tobacco, liquor, and luxury goods. (See *taxation* on page 000 in the Economics Handbook.) It raised the rest through public borrowing by selling war bonds.

The government sold bonds through tens of thousands of volunteers who never received any sales commission. Movie stars such as Douglas Fairbanks, Mary Pickford, and Charlie Chaplin spoke at rallies in factories, in schools, and on street corners. Newspapers and billboards carried advertisements for bonds free of charge. Salesmen delivered speeches between theater acts and film screenings. Towns held war-bond parades. All told, the government ran four great "Liberty Loan" drives and one "Victory Loan" drive. As Treasury Secretary William G. McAdoo put it, only "a friend of Germany" would refuse to buy war bonds.

COMMITTEE ON PUBLIC INFORMATION To directly popularize the war, the government set up the nation's first propaganda agency, the Committee on Public Information. The head of the CPI was a former muckraking journalist named **George Creel.**

Some wartime posters encouraged Americans to help the war effort by saving resources—in this case, food.

Food *is* Ammunition-
Don't waste it.

An imaginative individual, Creel mobilized the nation's artists and advertising people, who created thousands of paintings, posters, cartoons, and sculptures promoting the war. He persuaded choirs, social clubs, and religious institutions to join "the world's greatest adventure in advertising." He recruited some 75,000 men to serve as "Four Minute Men" who would deliver a speech anytime, any place. The Four Minute Men spoke about everything relating to the war: the draft, rationing, bond drives, victory gardens, and topics such as "Why We Are Fighting," "Maintaining Morals and Morale," and "The Meaning of America." It is estimated that by the end of the war, the Four Minute Men had delivered more than 7.5 million speeches to 314 million listeners.

Nor did Creel neglect the written word. He ordered a printing of almost 7 million copies of "How the War Came to America"—which included Wilson's war message—not just in English but also in Swedish, Polish, Italian, Spanish, Czech, and Portuguese. He distributed some 60 million pamphlets, booklets, and leaflets, many with the enthusiastic help of the Boy Scouts. He did not convince everyone, but he certainly succeeded in reaching them.

THINK THROUGH HISTORY
B. *Summarizing* *What methods did the CPI use to popularize the war?*

B. Answer The CPI used posters and other visual means, public speakers, and written pamphlets to promote the war.

Attacks on Civil Liberties

Early in 1917, President Wilson expressed some apprehension about U.S. attitudes toward the war.

A PERSONAL VOICE

Once lead this people into war and they'll forget there ever was such a thing as tolerance. To fight you must be brutal and ruthless, and the spirit of the ruthless brutality will enter into the very fiber of our national life, infecting Congress, the courts, the policeman on the beat, the man in the street. Conformity would be the only virtue, and every man who refused to conform would have to pay the penalty.

WOODROW WILSON, quoted in *Cobb of "The World"*

The president's prediction was correct. As soon as war was declared, conformity indeed became the order of the day. Attacks on civil liberties, both unofficial and official, erupted.

ANTI–IMMIGRANT HYSTERIA The main targets of the drive for conformity were Americans who had emigrated from other nations, especially those from Germany and Austria-Hungary. The most bitter attacks were directed against the 2 million Americans who had been born in Germany, but other foreign-born persons and native-born Americans of German descent suffered as well.

TEACHING OPTIONS

Teaching Less Proficient Readers

Predicting Help students make predictions when they read. After students read Wilson's quotation on page 412, have them choose a partner and do the following:

1. Discuss any words or phrases that they don't understand, such as "ruthless" and "the very fiber of our national life."
2. Express the quotation's main idea in their own words.
3. Jot down any predictions they can make based on the quotation.
4. After reading pages 412–414, check to see how many of their predictions were correct.

Making Connections Across Time

Anti-Immigrant Hysteria During World War II Tell students that during World War II, Japanese Americans became the targets of anti-immigrant hysteria. Many Japanese Americans on the West Coast were rounded up and put in internment camps. For the duration of the war, they lived behind barbed wire and were guarded by soldiers. Nevertheless, about 17,000 Japanese Americans enlisted in the army and served in segregated units. The most famous of these was the 442nd Regiment, which earned more decorations than any other combat unit.

As part of anti-immigrant hysteria, New York immigrants were forced to register with the authorities during the war.

Many Americans with German-sounding names lost their jobs. Orchestras refused to play the music of Mozart, Bach, Beethoven, and Brahms. Some towns with German names changed them. (One exception was Berlin, New Hampshire, whose citizens voted 933 to 566 to keep their town's original name.) Schools stopped teaching the German language, and librarians removed books by German authors from the shelves. People even resorted to physical violence against German-Americans, flogging them or smearing them with tar and feathers. A mob in Collinsville, Illinois, wrapped a German flag around a German-born miner named Robert Prager and lynched him. A jury later cleared the mob's leaders.

Finally, in a burst of anti-German fervor, Americans changed the name of German measles to "liberty measles." Hamburger—named after the German city of Hamburg—became "Salisbury steak" or "liberty sandwich," depending on whether you were buying it in a store or eating it in a restaurant. Sauerkraut was renamed "liberty cabbage," and dachshunds turned into "liberty pups."

> *"Nobody can say we aren't loyal now."*
>
> JURY MEMBER, UPON CLEARING ROBERT PRAGER'S ALLEGED MURDERERS

ESPIONAGE AND SEDITION ACTS In June 1917 Congress passed the Espionage Act, and in May 1918 it passed the Sedition Act. Under the **Espionage and Sedition Acts** a person could be fined up to $10,000 and sentenced to 20 years in jail for interfering with the draft, obstructing the sale of government bonds, or saying anything disloyal, profane, or abusive about the government or the war effort.

Like the Alien and Sedition Acts of 1798, these laws clearly violated the spirit of the First Amendment. Their passage led to some 6,000 arrests for loosely defined antiwar activities and 1,500 convictions, including the five anarchists of the *Abrams* case. One man, Walter Mathey, was imprisoned for attending an antiwar meeting and contributing 25 cents. The Reverend Clarence Waldron received 15 years in the penitentiary for telling a Bible class that Christians should not take part in the war.

Other results of the laws included the loss of mailing privileges for newspapers and magazines that opposed the war or criticized any of the Allies. By 1918 even mainstream publications like the *New York Times* and *The Saturday Evening Post* had lost their mailing privileges, at least temporarily. The House of Representatives refused to seat Victor Berger, a socialist congressman from Wisconsin, because of his antiwar views. Columbia University fired a distinguished psychologist from its faculty because he too opposed the war. A colleague who supported the war thereupon resigned in protest, saying, "If we have to suppress everything we don't like to hear, this country is resting on a pretty wobbly basis."

MORE ABOUT . . .
The Espionage and Sedition Acts

Robert Goldstein of Los Angeles was convicted of sedition under the Espionage and Sedition Acts for making a film called *The Spirit of '76.* In addition to showing Thomas Jefferson signing the Declaration of Independence, the film depicted a massacre in which British redcoats bayoneted American colonists. The film was historically accurate. However, because the film showed the British—one of America's allies—in an unflattering light, Goldstein received a ten-year prison sentence.

Issues for the 21st Century

Crime and Public Safety

To link issues of public safety during World War I to issues today, have students read pages 884–887. Then have them answer these questions.

1. Why did the U.S. government pass the Espionage and Sedition Acts? *To discourage antiwar and antigovernment speech and activities.*
2. How do the government's efforts to protect public safety in the 1990s compare to its efforts in 1918? *In 1918, the government sought to control unpatriotic attitudes; in the 1990s, the government focused on preventing crimes against people and property.*

TEACHING OPTIONS

Teaching Gifted and Talented Students

Conducting a Trial Have a group of interested students get together and conduct a trial of an American citizen accused of committing antiwar activities. Each student in the group should assume one of the following roles:

- judge
- jury members
- prosecuting attorney and defense attorney
- defendant
- witnesses

Have students present the trial to the rest of the class.

Making Global Connections

The Red Scare Tell students that after the Bolshevik Revolution in 1917, some of the Allies' hatred of Germany was transferred to Communist Russia. In 1918, Wilson sent troops to northern Russia and to Siberia in an unacknowledged attempt to put down the Bolshevik government. The American soldiers were joined by troops sent by the European Allies and by Japan. France and Great Britain feared the spread of Bolshevism across Europe. Japan was anxious to protect its influence in Asia.

MORE ABOUT . . .
The End of the IWW

The government dealt the death blow to the IWW on September 29, 1917, when federal agents arrested more than 1,000 Wobblies throughout the country. A mass trial of 101 defendants began on April 1, 1918. Presiding at the trial was Judge Kenesaw Mountain Landis, who later became the nation's first baseball commissioner. Although the trial lasted five months, it took the jury less than one hour to reach a guilty verdict. After Judge Landis handed out jail terms to all 101 Wobblies, Ben Fletcher, head of the Philadelphia dockworkers and the only African-American defendant, said wryly, "Judge Landis has been using bad English today. His sentences are too long."

OBJECTIVE
(4) INSTRUCT

Social Changes During the War

▶ ***Starting with the Student*** Have students create a chart similar to the one below to list some of the causes and effects of the Great Migration.

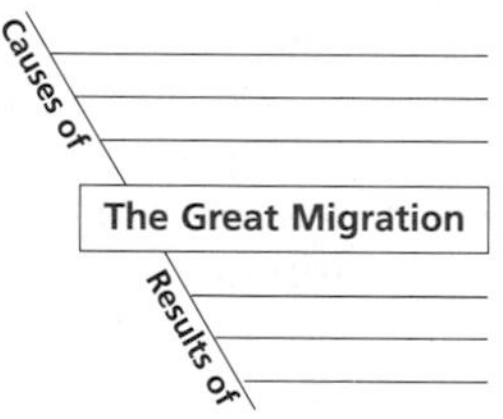

(continued on next page)

The Espionage and Sedition Acts targeted socialists and labor leaders. Eugene V. Debs was handed a ten-year prison sentence for delivering a speech in which he discussed the economic causes of the war, but he was pardoned by President Warren G. Harding after serving only three years. The anarchist "Red Emma" Goldman received a two-year sentence and a $10,000 fine for organizing the No Conscription League. When she left jail, the authorities deported her to Russia. "Big Bill" Haywood and other leaders of the Industrial Workers of the World were accused of sabotaging the war effort because they urged workers to strike for better conditions and higher pay. Haywood received 30 years, while most of the other Wobblies received 5 to 10. Under such federal pressure, the IWW faded away. On the whole, the civil liberties record of the Wilson administration was not one to make Americans proud.

THINK THROUGH HISTORY
C. *Clarifying* *What was the original purpose of the Espionage and Sedition Acts?*

C. Answer The original purpose was to prevent interference with the war effort. The government, however, began applying the acts to peaceful expressions of antiwar opinion.

Social Changes During the War

Wars often unleash powerful social forces. The period of World War I was no exception, and important changes occurred among African Americans and women. The war also contributed to one of the worst epidemics in history—the 1918 flu epidemic.

AFRICAN AMERICANS AND THE WAR Black public opinion about the war was divided. On one side were people like W. E. B. Du Bois, who editorialized in *The Crisis*, the NAACP newspaper, that blacks should support the war effort. Du Bois recognized the German imperial threat.

A PERSONAL VOICE

That which the German power represents today spells death to the aspirations of Negroes and all darker races for equality, freedom and democracy. . . . Let us, while this war lasts, forget our special grievances and close our ranks shoulder to shoulder with our own white fellow citizens and the allied nations that are fighting for democracy.

W. E. B. DU BOIS, "Close Ranks"

Du Bois believed that it made sense for African Americans to cooperate with the Wilson administration because African-American support for the war would lend strength to calls for racial justice.

On the other side were people like William Monroe Trotter, founder and editor of the *Boston Guardian*, who believed that victims of racism should not support a racist government. Trotter condemned Du Bois's accommodationist approach and favored protest instead. Nevertheless, despite grievances over continued racial inequality in the United States, most African Americans backed the war.

A panel from the mural series *The Migration of the Negro* by Jacob Lawrence shows three of the most common destinations for African Americans leaving the South.

THE GREAT MIGRATION In concrete terms, the greatest effect of the First World War on African Americans' lives was that it accelerated the **Great Migration,** the large-scale movement of hundreds of thousands of Southern blacks to cities in the North. As early as the late 19th century, African Americans had trickled northward to escape

TEACHING OPTIONS

Exploring Themes

Immigration and Migration Discuss why so many African Americans took part in the great exodus to the North. Then tell students that the Great Migration greatly increased the black population in many Northern cities. In Detroit, for example, the black population grew by more than 600 percent between 1910 and 1920. Ask students what effects this enormous influx of people had on these cities. *Possible Responses: Housing shortages, unemployment.* Discuss how these problems were aggravated by the racism African Americans encountered in the Northern cities.

Making Connections Across Cultures

The African-American Migration to the North Tell students that most of the migrants were young, unmarried black men who were skilled or semiskilled workers. To finance the move, some families pooled their savings, while others sold their possessions. Although black migrants faced many problems, employment in the North did help them escape sharecropping, boll weevil infestations, floods, lynchings, and political disenfranchisement. One man wrote to a friend back in Mississippi: "I just begin to feel like a man. . . . I don't have to humble to no one. I have registered. Will vote in the next election."

the Jim Crow South, but in the decade between 1910 and 1920, the trickle became a tidal wave.

Several factors caused the tremendous growth in black migration. First, many African Americans sought to escape the racial discrimination in the South, which made it hard to make a living and often threatened their lives. Also, a boll weevil infestation, aided by floods and droughts, had ruined much of the South's cotton fields by 1916. In the meantime, Henry Ford had opened his automobile assembly line to black workers in 1914. Then the outbreak of World War I and the drop in European immigration increased job opportunities for African Americans in steel mills, munitions plants, and stockyards. Northern manufacturers sent recruiting agents with free railroad passes through the South. In addition, Robert S. Abbott, publisher of the *Chicago Defender*, bombarded Southern blacks with articles contrasting Dixieland lynchings with the prosperity of Northern African Americans.

THINK THROUGH HISTORY
D. THEME ***Immigration and Migration*** *What were the causes of the Great Migration?*

D. Answer Causes included the destruction of the South's cotton economy by the boll weevil; the demand for labor by Northern manufacturers, caused partly by a slowdown in immigration; newspaper articles; and other recruitment efforts.

So Southern blacks boarded trains and moved away from the South. Between 1910 and 1930, hundreds of thousands of African Americans migrated to such cities as Chicago, New York, and Philadelphia. The migration was heaviest from about 1915 to 1925. The author Richard Wright described the great exodus.

A PERSONAL VOICE

We are bitter no more; we are leaving! We are leaving our homes, pulling up stakes to move on. We look up at the high southern sky and remember all the sunshine and all the rain and we feel a sense of loss, but we are leaving. We look out at the wide green fields which our eyes saw when we first came into the world and we feel full of regret, but we are leaving. We scan the kind black faces we have looked upon since we first saw the light of day, and, though pain is in our hearts, we are leaving. We take one last furtive look over our shoulders to the Big House—high upon a hill beyond the railroad tracks—where the Lord of the Land lives, and we feel glad, for we are leaving.

RICHARD WRIGHT, quoted in *12 Million Black Voices*

Black migrants faced many problems in their new surroundings. They lived in crowded ghettos, often in one-room kitchenettes for which they had to pay exorbitant rents. Unskilled whites resented them, not only because of racial prejudice, but also because African Americans competed for jobs and Northern companies often used them as strikebreakers.

At the same time, however, the concentration of African Americans in particular areas encouraged them to set up their own commercial institutions. Some were in businesses that provided personal services, such as hairdressing and undertaking. Others entered areas of finance that whites considered too risky—such as insuring blacks' lives and property or arranging credit for them. African Americans established thousands of such enterprises in Northern communities.

HISTORICAL SPOTLIGHT

RACE RIOTS

Racial prejudice against African Americans in the North sometimes took violent forms. The press of new migrants to Northern cities caused overcrowding and intensified racial hatred. In July 1917, a race riot exploded in East St. Louis, Illinois, when white workers, furious over the hiring of African Americans as strikebreakers at a munitions plant, rampaged through the streets. Forty blacks and nine whites died.

Another bloody riot erupted in July 1919 in Chicago. The riot was sparked when a 17-year-old African American swam from the water off a "black beach" to the water off a "white beach." There, white bathers threw rocks at him until he drowned.

In retaliation, African Americans on shore attacked whites with bottles and fists, and within a few hours mobs were fighting throughout several neighborhoods in the city. State troopers finally restored order after three days of violence that involved about 10,000 persons. Thirty-eight people lost their lives (23 blacks and 15 whites), and 520 were injured (342 blacks and 178 whites).

WOMEN IN THE WAR While African Americans carved new lives for themselves in unfamiliar places, women increasingly found themselves filling unfamiliar social roles as they moved into jobs that had formerly been held exclusively by men. Women began driving cabs and delivery trucks. They became railroad workers, cooks, dockworkers, and bricklayers. They even mined coal and took part in shipbuilding. At the same time, women continued to fill more traditional jobs as nurses, clerks, and teachers.

Many women worked as volunteers, serving at Red Cross facilities and encouraging the sale of bonds and the planting of victory gardens. In contrast, other women were active in the peace movement. For example, Jane Addams

(continued from page 414)

Discussing Key Ideas

- The war accelerates the movement of Southern blacks to Northern cities.
- The war provides more job opportunities for women, who are praised for their contribution to the war effort.
- About 500,000 Americans die from an international flu epidemic.

IN-DEPTH RESOURCES: UNIT 3
Primary Source: "Returning Soldiers" by W. E. B. Du Bois, p. 50

HISTORICAL SPOTLIGHT
Race Riots

Discuss the relationship between racial groups today. Ask students how the relationship has improved. In what ways do the race riots of 1917 and 1919 reflect the current relationship between blacks, whites, and other racial groups?

MORE ABOUT . . .
Women in the War

Many women who were industrial workers during the war found that their male co-workers resented them. The men objected to the women's rate of productivity and willingness to work for lower pay. They were also angered by the women's independent spirit. Women in a Vermont machine-tool company wrote the following verse to express their reactions to the men's complaints: "We're independent now you see, / Your bald head don't appeal to me, / I love my overalls; / And I would rather polish steel / Than get you up a tasty meal. / Or go with you to balls."

TEACHING OPTION

Exploring Themes

Women in America Discuss the contributions women made to the war effort and the new opportunities that opened up to them. Then tell students that once the war was over, women discovered that society's attitude toward them had really changed very little. Working women were still expected to shoulder all of the responsibilities at home, including housework, meal preparation, and child care. Tired from working all day, most women had little energy to devote to this domestic work. As a result, husbands felt resentful, blaming their wives' employment for a disruption of home life. In addition, many married and unmarried women were forced to give up their jobs to men returning from overseas. They observed this treatment with bitterness. As one woman remarked, "During the war they called us heroines, but they throw us on the scrapheap now."

MORE ABOUT . . .
The Flu Epidemic
The flu epidemic was one of the worst plagues in history, second only to the Black Plague of 1347–1351, which killed one out of every three Europeans, or about 75 million people. In the absence of medical knowledge, Americans came up with all sorts of ways to treat the flu. Some people recommended snuff, while others suggested chewing tobacco. Even doctors proposed some far-fetched treatments, including removing the flu patients' tonsils, extracting all their teeth, and sprinkling sulfur in their shoes.

ASSESS & RETEACH

Section 3 Assessment
Have students work in small groups to answer the questions.

Self-Assessment
To document what students have learned in Section 3, have them make a list of the economic and social changes brought about in the United States by the First World War.

Section Quiz

FORMAL ASSESSMENT
Section Quiz, p. 143

Reteach
Use the Section Quiz to help students understand the section's key concepts.

CLOSE

World War I brought about many political, social, and economic changes in American life. While dealing with these changes, Americans were also faced with a deadly flu epidemic. After the war and the epidemic ended, the people looked to Wilson to obtain a peace settlement that would put an end to war for all time.

Women worked in a variety of jobs during the war. Here women assemble an aircraft wing.

E. Answer They served in noncombat positions in the military; altered clothing fashions to free up steel, leather, and fabric needed in the war effort; planted victory gardens and conserved foodstuffs; and filled roles normally held by men in factories and businesses.

helped found the Women's Peace Party in 1915 and remained a pacifist even after the United States entered the war.

In general, women made notable contributions to the nation's war effort. As President Wilson acknowledged, "The services of women during the supreme crisis have been of the most signal usefulness and distinction; it is high time that part of our debt should be acknowledged." While acknowledgment of that debt did not include equal pay for equal work, it did help bolster public support for woman suffrage. In 1919, Congress finally passed the Nineteenth Amendment, and the states ratified it the following year.

THINK THROUGH HISTORY
E. THEME ***Women in America*** *In what ways did women contribute to the war effort at home and overseas?*

THE FLU EPIDEMIC In the fall of 1918, the United States suffered a home-front crisis that affected both men and women, white and black alike. An international flu epidemic gripped the nation. It apparently came from France, to which it had been brought by Chinese war workers. About one-quarter of the U.S. population fell ill with high fever, headaches, and aching muscles, often followed by pneumonia.

The effect of the epidemic on the economy was devastating. Mines shut down, telephone service was cut in half, and factories and offices staggered working hours to avoid contagion. Cities ran short of coffins, and the corpses of poor people lay unburied as long as a week. Doctors did not know what to do, other than to recommend cleanliness and quarantine. One epidemic survivor recalled that "so many people died from the flu they just rang the bells; they didn't dare take [corpses] into the church."

In all, about 500,000 Americans perished before the epidemic disappeared in 1919. Historians believe that the influenza virus killed as many as 40 million people worldwide.

Like the flu epidemic, the war ended, and Americans across the country hoped that this "war to end all wars" would do just that. Their hopes rested on the peace settlement, and President Wilson traveled to Europe to ensure it.

New York City street cleaners wore masks in an effort to avoid catching influenza.

Section 3 Assessment

1. TERMS & NAMES
Identify:
- War Industries Board
- Bernard M. Baruch
- George Creel
- Espionage and Sedition Acts
- Great Migration

2. SUMMARIZING Create a diagram like the one shown, in which you present examples of ways U.S. civilians supported the war effort.

Civilians Support the War

	Social	Economic
1.		
2.		
3.		

Write a paragraph in which you explain which effort you think was most significant and why.

3. FORMING OPINIONS Why do you think civil liberties were so easily violated by the people and government of the United States during the First World War? Explain your opinion.

THINK ABOUT
- the effect of the Committee on Public Information
- the diverse ethnic backgrounds of Americans
- the reasons for the Espionage and Sedition Acts

4. SYNTHESIZING Were changes in the American economy during World War I beneficial to the country overall? Give examples to support your opinion.

THINK ABOUT
- the effect on various groups of workers
- the impact on African Americans
- changes in the role of the government

416 CHAPTER 11

ANSWERS

1. TERMS & NAMES
War Industries Board, p. 410
Bernard M. Baruch, p. 410
George Creel, p. 412
Espionage and Sedition Acts, p. 413
Great Migration, p. 414

2. SUMMARIZING
Possible Answer: Social—women's clothing changed; gas and heating oil rationed; daylight-saving time began; gasless Sundays and lightless nights adopted; victory gardens planted. Economic—war bonds purchased; higher income and excise taxes paid; Liberty and Victory Loan drives took place; women joined work force.

3. FORMING OPINIONS
Possible Response: The Committee on Public Information propagandized the American people into thinking that the war was right and dissenters were disloyal or criminal. Because so many nations were involved in the war and the U.S. had immigrants from these nations, Americans distrusted one another.

4. SYNTHESIZING
Possible Response: Students answering yes might cite the rise in union membership; rise in wages; expanded jobs and business opportunities for African Americans and women. Students answering no might say that inflation and shortages were problems; that government regulation of industry was excessive; that price controls brought huge profits for corporations but raised prices.

4 Wilson Fights for Peace

TERMS & NAMES
- **Fourteen Points**
- **League of Nations**
- **Treaty of Versailles**
- **reparations**
- **war-guilt clause**
- **Henry Cabot Lodge**

LEARN ABOUT the Treaty of Versailles and President Wilson's attempts to create a League of Nations
TO UNDERSTAND the consequences of Wilson's efforts.

ONE AMERICAN'S STORY

In December 1918, President and Mrs. Wilson sailed for Europe. At the magnificent Palace of Versailles outside Paris, Wilson tried to persuade the Allies to construct a just and lasting peace. His main hope for achieving this goal was a League of Nations, whose members would be bound to protect any nation that was attacked by another. One evening, after delivering a speech in favor of the League, Wilson got into the presidential car with his wife to return to their hotel. Edith Wilson recalled her husband's comments.

A PERSONAL VOICE

He took off his high hat and leaned back in the car. "Are you so weary?" I asked. "Yes," he answered, "I suppose I am, but how little one man means when such vital things are at stake." Then, continuing: "This is our first real step forward, for I now realize, more than ever before, that once established the League can arbitrate and correct mistakes which are inevitable in the Treaty we are trying to make at this time. . . . One by one the mistakes can be brought to the League for readjustment, and the League will act as a permanent clearinghouse where every nation can come, the small as well as the great."

EDITH BOLLING GALT WILSON, quoted in *Hooray for Peace, Hurrah for War*

Edith Bolling Galt Wilson

As matters turned out, Wilson's idealism ran into practical politics. The leaders of the European Allies, vengeful toward their defeated enemy after four years of warfare, rejected most of his peace program. The Senate, skeptical about continued U.S. involvement abroad, rejected the Treaty of Versailles mostly because it established the League of Nations.

Wilson at Versailles

Rejection was probably the last thing Wilson anticipated when he arrived in Europe. Everywhere he went, people gave him a hero's welcome. Italians displayed his picture in their windows; Parisians strewed the road with flowers. Representatives of one group after another—Armenians, Jews, Ukrainians, and Poles—appealed to him for help in setting up independent nations for themselves. Even the normally restrained British showed their regard as men removed their hats and women bowed and waved as he passed.

FOURTEEN POINTS Even before the war was over, Wilson presented his plan for world peace. On January 18, 1918, he delivered his famous **Fourteen Points** speech before Congress. The points were divided into three groups. The first five points addressed issues that Wilson believed had caused the war:

1. Nations should engage only in open covenants (agreements) openly arrived at. There should be no secret treaties among nations.
2. Freedom of the seas should be maintained for all.
3. Tariffs and other economic barriers among nations should be lowered or abolished in order to foster free trade.
4. Arms should be reduced "to the lowest point consistent with domestic safety" in order to lessen militaristic impulses during diplomatic crises.
5. Colonial policies should consider the interests of the colonial peoples as well as the interests of the imperialist powers.

SECTION 4 RESOURCES

PRINT RESOURCES

IN-DEPTH RESOURCES: UNIT 3
Guided Reading, p. 43
Geography Application: A New Look for Europe, p. 45

READING STUDY GUIDE, p. 125

ACCESS FOR STUDENTS ACQUIRING ENGLISH
Guided Reading (Spanish), p. 144
Geography Application: A New Look for Europe (Spanish), p. 146

SPANISH READING STUDY GUIDE, p. 125

FORMAL ASSESSMENT
Section Quiz, p. 144

ALTERNATIVE ASSESSMENT BOOK
See forms for supporting and scoring alternative activities.

TECHNOLOGY RESOURCES

HUMANITIES TRANSPARENCIES
H38, Senate Opposes the League of Nations

CD-ROM Electronic Library of Primary Sources

VIDEO *American Portfolio: A Videodisc for U.S. History* user's guide, pp. 187–188

INTERNET http://www.mlushistory.com

Section 4 Overview

OBJECTIVES

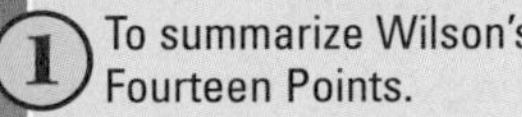
1. To summarize Wilson's Fourteen Points.

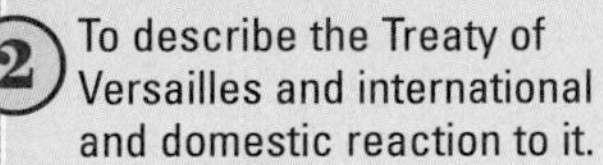
2. To describe the Treaty of Versailles and international and domestic reaction to it.

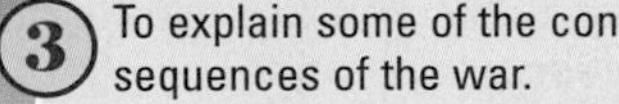
3. To explain some of the consequences of the war.

SKILLBUILDER

- Understanding geography: region, p. 420

CRITICAL THINKING

- Summarizing, pp. 418, 421
- Analyzing motives, p. 420
- Hypothesizing, p. 421
- Evaluating decisions, p. 421
- Forming opinions, p. 421

FOCUS & MOTIVATE

5-MINUTE WARM-UP

Making Inferences
Have students read the quote from John J. Pershing on page 421 and answer these questions.

1. According to General Pershing, how did the Germans feel after World War I?
2. What did General Pershing mean when he said, "It will have to be done all over again"?

WARM-UP TRANSPARENCY 11

Starting with the Student
- Ask students if they think that people and governments can resolve their differences without war.

OBJECTIVE

1 INSTRUCT

Wilson at Versailles

Discussing Key Ideas
- Wilson delivers his Fourteen Points—his plan for world peace—to Congress.
- The Allies reject most of Wilson's plan.

IN-DEPTH RESOURCES: UNIT 3
Guided Reading, p. 43

ACCESS FOR STUDENTS ACQUIRING ENGLISH
Guided Reading (Spanish), p. 144

OBJECTIVE

② INSTRUCT

Treaty of Versailles

▶ ***Starting with the Student*** Have students create a chart in which they list the provisions of the Treaty of Versailles and the results of these provisions. The chart might look like this:

Provision	Result
1.	
2.	
3.	
4.	

▶ ***Discussing Key Ideas***

- The Treaty of Versailles weakens hopes for a lasting peace in Europe.
- Several groups in the United States oppose the treaty because they believe that it is too harsh.
- Domestic opposition to the treaty centers on the League of Nations.

IN-DEPTH RESOURCES: UNIT 3
Geography Application: A New Look for Europe, p. 45

MORE ABOUT . . .
The Hall of Mirrors
In 1871, following France's defeat in the Franco-Prussian War, the Hall of Mirrors in the palace of Versailles was where the kaiser's grandfather was proclaimed head of the new German Empire, also known as the Second Reich. The French felt the hall was an appropriate place to sign a treaty marking Germany's defeat in World War I and the end of the Second Reich.

The next eight points dealt with specific boundary changes. Wilson based these provisions on the principle of self-determination "along historically established lines of nationality." In other words, national groups who claimed distinct ethnic identities were to decide for themselves what nations they would belong to.

The fourteenth point called for the creation of an international organization to address diplomatic crises like those that had sparked the war. This **League of Nations** would provide a forum for nations to discuss and settle their grievances without having to resort to war.

THINK THROUGH HISTORY
A. *Summarizing* *Summarize Wilson's Fourteen Points.*
A. Answer Open covenants openly arrived at, freedom of the seas, lower tariffs, arms reductions, consideration of the interests of colonized peoples, the League of Nations, and the redrawing of national boundaries.

THE ALLIES REJECT WILSON'S PLAN Wilson's naiveté about the political aspects of securing a peace treaty showed itself in his failure to grasp the anger felt by the Allied leaders. The French premier, Georges Clemenceau, had lived through two German invasions of France and was determined to prevent future invasions. The British prime minister, David Lloyd George, had just won reelection on the slogan "Make Germany Pay." The Italian prime minister, Vittorio Orlando, wanted control of Austrian territory.

Contrary to custom, the peace conference did not include the defeated Central Powers. Nor did it include Russia or the smaller Allied nations. Instead, the "Big Four"—Wilson, Clemenceau, Lloyd George, and Orlando—worked out the treaty's details among themselves. Wilson conceded on most of his Fourteen Points in return for the establishment of the League of Nations.

Treaty of Versailles

On June 28, 1919, the Big Four and the leaders of the defeated nations gathered in the Great Hall of the Palace of Versailles to sign the treaty. After four years of devastating warfare, everyone hoped that the treaty would create stability for a rebuilt Europe. Instead, anger held sway.

PROVISIONS OF THE TREATY The **Treaty of Versailles** established nine new nations—including Poland, Czechoslovakia, and Yugoslavia—and shifted the boundaries of other nations. It carved four areas out of the Ottoman Empire and gave them to France and Great Britain as mandates, or temporary colonies. The two Allies were to administer their respective mandates until the areas were ready for self-rule and then independence. The mandates included Iraq, Syria, Lebanon, and Palestine (now Israel and Jordan).

The treaty demilitarized Germany, stripping it of its air force and most of its navy and reducing its army to 100,000 men. The treaty also required Germany to return Alsace-Lorraine to France and to pay **reparations,** or war damages, in the amount of $33 billion to the Allies. Furthermore, the treaty contained a **war-guilt clause** that forced Germany to acknowledge that it alone was responsible for World War I.

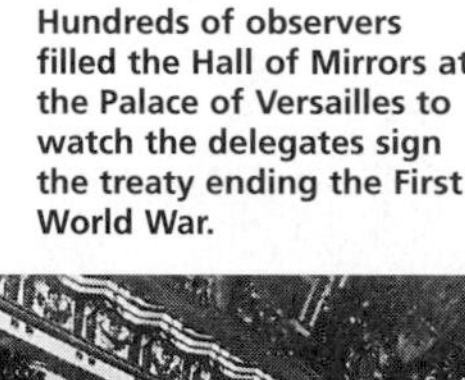

Hundreds of observers filled the Hall of Mirrors at the Palace of Versailles to watch the delegates sign the treaty ending the First World War.

THE TREATY'S WEAKNESSES Such treatment of Germany weakened the ability of the Treaty of Versailles to serve as the basis of a lasting peace in Europe. Three basic weaknesses provided the seeds of postwar international problems that eventually led to the Second World War.

TEACHING OPTIONS

Exploring Themes

America in the World Discuss Wilson's Fourteen Points. Tell students that Wilson hoped to create a new world order through democratic reform. Ask students whether they believe Wilson's plan was practical. Then point out that today the United Nations (UN) serves much the same purpose as Wilson's proposed League of Nations. Would Wilson have been satisfied with the organization? Has the UN been successful in providing a forum for nations and preventing war?

Making Connections Across Time

Provisions of the World War II Treaty Tell students that at the end of the Second World War, the victorious nations recalled the lessons learned from the Treaty of Versailles. They sought to draft a treaty that was fair to the victors but that did not completely devastate the losers. At the Yalta Conference in February 1945, the Allied leaders met to discuss the problems of postwar Europe. Among other points, the leaders agreed to establish a world peacekeeping organization—which would become the United Nations. They also agreed to reestablish order in Europe and help the defeated countries create democratic governments.

First, the treaty humiliated Germany. Although German militarism had played a major role in igniting the war, other European nations had been no less guilty in provoking diplomatic crises before the war. The war-guilt clause caused Germans of all political viewpoints to detest the treaty. Furthermore, there was no way Germany could pay the huge financial reparations demanded by the Allies.

Second, the Bolshevik government in Russia felt that the Big Four ignored its needs. For three years the Russians had fought with the Allies, suffering higher casualties than any other nation. However, Russia was excluded from the peace conference. Consequently, Russia lost more territory than Germany did. The Union of Soviet Socialist Republics (or Soviet Union), as Russia was officially called after 1922, became determined to regain its former territory.

The third issue that contributed to international instability resulted from decisions about what should be done with colonial territories. Germany was stripped of its colonial possessions in the Pacific, which might have helped it pay its reparations bill. Also, the treaty ignored the claims of colonized people for self-determination, as in the case of Southeast Asia.

In the early 20th century, much of Southeast Asia was a French colony called French Indochina. For decades, nationalist movements for independence had developed in what is now Vietnam. At Versailles, a young Vietnamese man later known as Ho Chi Minh appealed to President Wilson for help. Ho Chi Minh wanted a constitutional government that would give the Vietnamese people the same civil and political rights as the French. Wilson refused to consider Ho Chi Minh's proposal. Ho Chi Minh later founded the Indochina Communist Party and led the Vietnamese fight against French, and later American, forces until his death in 1969.

POINT

"The League of Nations was the world's best hope for lasting peace."

President Wilson campaigned for the League of Nations as "necessary to meet the differing and unexpected contingencies" that could threaten world peace. Besides creating a forum where nations could talk through their disagreements, the League, Wilson believed, would provide collective security, in which nations would "respect and preserve as against external aggression the territorial integrity and existing political independence of all members of the League," and thereby prevent devastating warfare.

Critics complained that membership in the League would limit American independence in international affairs, but Wilson argued that League membership included "a moral, not a legal, obligation" that would leave Congress free to decide its own course of action. Wilson tried to assure Congress as well as the general public that the League was "not a straightjacket, but a vehicle of life" and "a definite guarantee . . . against the things that have just come near bringing the whole structure of civilization into ruin."

COUNTERPOINT

"The League of Nations posed a threat to U.S. self-determination."

Senator William Borah was one of the foremost critics of the Treaty of Versailles because he objected to U.S. membership in the League of Nations. Borah feared that membership in the League "would draw America away from her isolation and into the internal affairs and concerns of Europe" and involve the United States in foreign wars. "Once having surrendered and become a part of the European concerns," Borah wondered, "where, my friends, are you going to stop?"

Many opponents also believed that the League would nullify the Monroe Doctrine by limiting American self-determination, "the right of our people to govern themselves free from all restraint, legal or moral, of foreign powers." Although Wilson argued that the League of Nations codified moral—not legal—obligations, and that the League would have no such power of restraint, Borah was unconvinced. He responded to Wilson's argument by asking, "What will your League amount to if it does not contain powers that no one dreams of giving it?"

INTERACT WITH HISTORY

1. **SUMMARIZING** Both supporters and opponents of the League hoped to preserve peace. What did each group propose as a means to secure peace for the United States?

SEE SKILLBUILDER HANDBOOK, PAGE 905.

2. **PROPOSING A NEW TREATY** Research the debates between Wilson and the opponents of the League of Nations. Then make a series of suggestions for a treaty agreement that would have satisfied both sides. In one or two paragraphs, defend your version of the treaty.

POINT COUNTERPOINT
The League of Nations

▶ *Starting with the Student*
Have students create a chart like the one below to organize the information in the feature. In the first column, students should list the arguments in favor of U.S. membership in the League of Nations. In the second column, they should list the reasons against joining the league.

Pro	Con

▶ *Discussing Key Ideas*
- Wilson believes that the League of Nations will provide a forum for nations to talk through their problems and offer collective security.
- Wilson assures critics that the league will not limit American independence in international affairs but will help achieve world peace.
- Critics fear that membership in the league will involve the United States in foreign wars and limit American self-determination.
- Opponents believe that the league's emphasis on moral rather than legal obligations will weaken its powers and render the organization useless.

ELECTRONIC LIBRARY OF PRIMARY SOURCES
Why a League of Nations Is Necessary by Woodrow Wilson

INTERACT WITH HISTORY

1. Summarizing

Possible Response:

American supporters believed that the league members would respect and preserve each other's boundaries and independence and work together to secure peace.

American opponents of the League of Nations believed that the United States could best preserve peace by maintaining a policy of isolation.

2. Proposing a New Treaty

Before students begin making suggestions for a new treaty, encourage them to do the following:

- Pinpoint the precise weaknesses of the old treaty.
- Make a list of the goals of those on both sides.
- Make a list of the objections raised by opponents of the treaty.
- Address each objection and decide what compromises could be made. Keep in mind that the compromises should satisfy both sides and respect the spirit of their goals.

HISTORY FROM VISUALS

Postwar Europe, 1919

Reading the Map Tell students that they can use the map's colors and boundaries to determine what new nations were created in postwar Europe and where they are located in relation to other countries. Then ask students which new nations were created from territory that once belonged to Germany. *Poland and Czechoslovakia.*

Extension Ask students which of the nations created after the First World War have since been dissolved. *Yugoslavia and Czechoslovakia.* What new nations have replaced them? *Bosnia, Croatia, Macedonia, Slovenia, and a smaller Yugoslavia; Czech Republic, Slovakia.*

MORE ABOUT . . .

Henry Cabot Lodge

Henry Cabot Lodge served as a member of the House of Representatives for three terms before being elected to the Senate in 1892, where he remained until 1924. Lodge intensely disliked Wilson, whom he described as "shifty" and "not a scholar in the true sense of the word." Wilson returned the feeling, calling Lodge "contemptible," "narrow," and "selfish."

ELECTRONIC LIBRARY OF PRIMARY SOURCES
On the Terms of Peace by Henry Cabot Lodge

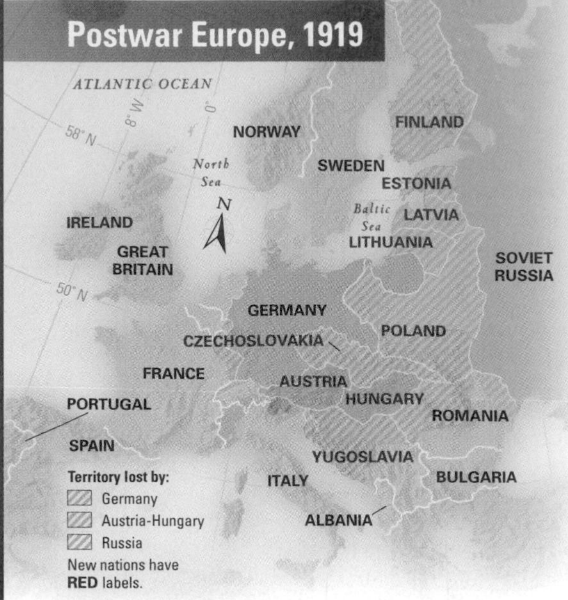

GEOGRAPHY SKILLBUILDER
REGION ***Which country was awarded the largest amount of German territory?***
REGION ***What was an unusual feature of the territory left to Germany after World War I?***

Skillbuilder Answer
Region: Poland. **Region:** *Possible Answer:* Germany was divided into two parts—with the smaller, eastern part surrounded by Polish territory.

OPPOSITION TO THE TREATY When Wilson returned to the United States, he found several groups opposed to the treaty. Some people, including Herbert Hoover, believed it was too harsh. Hoover noted, "The economic consequences alone will pull down all Europe and thus injure the United States." Others considered the treaty a sellout to imperialism that simply exchanged one set of colonial rulers for another.

Some ethnic groups objected to the treaty because the new national boundaries it established did not satisfy their particular demands for self-determination. For example, before the war many Poles had been under German rule. Now many Germans were under Polish rule. Furthermore, Wilson hadn't tried to obtain Ireland's independence from Great Britain.

DEBATE OVER THE LEAGUE OF NATIONS The main domestic opposition, however, centered on the issue of the League of Nations. A few opponents believed that the League threatened the U.S. foreign policy of staying clear of European entanglements. Conservative senators, headed by **Henry Cabot Lodge,** were suspicious of the provision for joint economic and military action against aggression, even though it was voluntary. They wanted the constitutional right of Congress to declare war also included in the treaty.

THINK THROUGH HISTORY
B. ***Analyzing Motives*** *Why did many senators oppose the Treaty of Versailles?*

B. Answer
They feared that the League of Nations would infringe on America's independence and force a change in America's policy of avoiding entanglements in Europe.

Wilson could have smothered these concerns if he had chosen the membership of the American delegation more carefully. Accompanying the president were his personal aide, Colonel Edward M. House; Secretary of State Robert Lansing; General Tasker H. Bliss; and the diplomat Henry White. Only one of the four, White, was a Republican, although the 1918 congressional campaign had given the Republicans a majority in both houses. None was a senator, although the Senate would have to ratify the peace treaty.

Also, if Wilson had been more willing to accept a compromise on the League, it is quite likely that the Senate would have approved the treaty. Wilson, however, was exhausted from his efforts at Versailles. As a result, he became more cold, aloof, and rigid than ever.

Realizing that the Senate might not approve the treaty, Wilson decided to appeal directly to the people. Despite warnings from friends and doctors that his health was fragile, he set out in September 1919 on an 8,000-mile tour. He delivered 35 speeches in 22 days, explaining why the United States should join the League of Nations. On October 2, he collapsed and was rushed back to the White House. Wilson had suffered a stroke (a blood clot in the brain) and lay partially paralyzed for more than two months. He could not even meet with his cabinet, and his once-powerful voice was no more than a thick whisper.

"That evil thing with the holy name"

HENRY CABOT LODGE, DESCRIBING THE LEAGUE OF NATIONS

When the treaty came up for a vote in the Senate in November 1919, Senator Lodge introduced a number of amendments, the most important of which qualified the terms under which the United States would enter the League of Nations. Lodge and a large group of senators feared that U.S. membership in the League would force the United States to form its foreign policy in accord with other members of the League. Most Americans opposed such limitations on American action. Although the Senate rejected the amendments, it also failed to ratify the treaty.

Wilson, however, refused to compromise with Lodge and other senators over their reservations about the League. "I will not play for position," Wilson

Block Schedule TEACHING OPTION **Time Needed: 40 Minutes**

Cooperative Activity: Debating the League of Nations

Task: Groups of four to five students will debate the following hypothesis: The U.S. Senate was correct in not approving the plan to join the League of Nations.

Purpose: To understand in depth the arguments of both supporters and opponents of the League of Nations.

Activity: After choosing a position through a lottery, students should research the arguments for and against the League of Nations. Students should take notes on the logical reasons used to defend their own position. They should also list the reasons offered by the opposition and decide which ones they should concede and which ones they can attack with counter arguments. After students have prepared their arguments, pair opposing groups and have them conduct their debate.

ALTERNATIVE ASSESSMENT BOOK
Standards for Evaluating a Cooperative Activity

HUMANITIES TRANSPARENCIES
H38, Senate Opposes the League of Nations

THINK THROUGH HISTORY
C. *Hypothesizing* *What might Wilson have done to encourage Senate approval of the Treaty of Versailles?*

proclaimed, "This is not a time for tactics. It is a time to stand square. I can stand defeat; I cannot stand retreat from conscientious duty." The treaty came up again in March 1920. The Senate again rejected the Lodge amendments—and again failed to muster enough votes for ratification.

The United States finally signed a separate treaty with Germany in 1921, after Wilson was no longer president. The United States never joined the League of Nations, but it maintained an unofficial observer at League meetings.

"This is not a time for tactics. It is a time to stand square."

PRESIDENT WILSON

The Legacy of the War

C. Answer He might have included one or more senators in the peace delegation; he might have accepted some of Lodge's amendments to the treaty.

In 1923, General Pershing delivered a speech in which he complained about the aftermath of the war.

A PERSONAL VOICE

We never really let the Germans know who won the war. They are being told that their army was stabbed in the back, betrayed, that their army had not been defeated. The Germans never believed that they were beaten. It will have to be done all over again.

GENERAL JOHN J. PERSHING, quoted in *Over Here and Over There*

Pershing believed that, because the kaiser's government had censored newspapers during the war, most Germans were unaware that the Allies had been pushing their soldiers back or that the German General Staff itself had demanded an end to the war. Many Germans were shocked by the armistice and incensed at the Treaty of Versailles.

To make matters worse, postwar economic conditions—although bad all over Europe—were especially desperate in Germany. A severe depression developed in 1923, and millions of workers lost their jobs. The mark, the German currency unit, was nearly worthless. People burned paper money for fuel and carted baskets of marks with them when they went grocery shopping.

Circumstances in Germany drove many Germans to search for scapegoats. One former Austrian corporal, Adolf Hitler, blamed German problems on Jews and socialists in the Weimar Republic, the government in Germany following World War I. In 1933, Hitler and his Nazi Party won control of the German government and embarked on a militaristic policy that led directly to the Second World War.

In the 1920s, most Americans did not want to be bothered with the future of Europe. The war had strengthened their desire to stay out of European affairs. Most desired a "return to normalcy."

Domestic Consequences of World War I

- **Accelerated America's emergence as the world's greatest industrial power**
- **Contributed to the movement of Americans, especially African Americans, to Northern cities**
- **Focused anti-immigrant and antiradical sentiments among middle-class Americans**

Section 4 Assessment

1. TERMS & NAMES
Identify:
- Fourteen Points
- League of Nations
- Treaty of Versailles
- reparations
- war-guilt clause
- Henry Cabot Lodge

2. SUMMARIZING Re-create the web diagram below on your paper. Then fill it in with details about the provisions and weaknesses of the Treaty of Versailles and opposition to it.

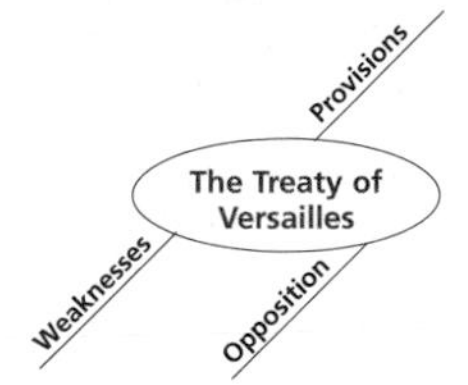

3. EVALUATING DECISIONS If you had been a member of the United States Senate in 1919, would you have supported or opposed ratification of the Treaty of Versailles? Provide reasons for your decision.

THINK ABOUT
- the provisions of the treaty regarding Germany
- the impact of new boundaries in Europe
- the significance of membership in the League of Nations

4. FORMING OPINIONS What do you think were the most important reasons that Wilson failed to persuade the United States to join the League of Nations?

THINK ABOUT
- the attitudes of Europeans at Versailles
- American attitudes about the League
- Wilson's tactics for getting the League adopted

ANSWERS

1. TERMS & NAMES

Fourteen Points, p. 417
League of Nations, p. 418
Treaty of Versailles, p. 418
reparations, p. 418
war-guilt clause, p. 418
Henry Cabot Lodge, p. 420

2. SUMMARIZING

Possible Response: **Provisions:** Established nine new countries; shifted boundaries of many countries; punished Germany. **Weaknesses:** Humiliated Germany; ignored Russia; ignored self-determination for colonized people. **Opposition:** Hoover and others considered it too harsh; some considered it a sellout to imperialism; some ethnic groups objected to new boundaries.

3. EVALUATING DECISIONS

Possible Responses: **Supporting:** The treaty provided needed postwar changes; it promoted peace; it established new nations; it provided for independence of smaller nations; it demilitarized Germany; it ordered reparations. **Opposing:** The treaty was unduly harsh; it promoted American involvement in European affairs; it was undiplomatic in humiliating Germany; it did not consider all nations equally.

4. FORMING OPINIONS

Possible Response: Many students will suggest that the main reason for Wilson's failure was the American desire to avoid foreign involvement after a lengthy war. Some will refer to Wilson's poor selections for the American delegation.

OBJECTIVE

 **INSTRUCT**

The Legacy of the War

▶ ***Discussing Key Ideas***
- Many Germans are shocked by the armistice and the terms of the Treaty of Versailles.
- Desperate economic conditions in Germany help foster the rise of Hitler and his Nazi Party.
- After the war, the United States emerges as the world's greatest industrial power.

ASSESS & RETEACH

Section 4 Assessment

Have students discuss the questions in class.

Self-Assessment

Have students make a two-column chart. In the first column, students should list what they knew about the Treaty of Versailles, the League of Nations, and the legacy of the First World War before they read the section. In the second column, they should jot down what they've learned.

Section Quiz

FORMAL ASSESSMENT
Section Quiz, p. 144

Reteach

Use the Point Counterpoint feature on page 419 to review the debate over the League of Nations.

CLOSE

The Allies rejected Wilson's Fourteen Points and instead drew up their own provisions in the Treaty of Versailles. At home, the Senate voted down U.S. membership in the League of Nations. Most Americans did not want any more involvement in European affairs. However, the treaty had sown the seeds of the Second World War.

Tracing Themes

OBJECTIVES

1. To explain how war and other factors affected immigration to and migration within the United States.
2. To describe the consequences of different waves of immigration and migration.

FOCUS & MOTIVATE

▶ ***Starting with the Student***

- Do students think the United States should open its borders to all immigrants? Or do they think the government should impose some restrictions on immigration?
- Should immigrants be required to learn English and observe the customs of the majority culture? Or should immigrants be encouraged to observe only their home customs?

MORE ABOUT . . .

Anti-Immigrant Feelings

Many prominent people voiced prejudices against the "new" immigrants of the early 1900s. Senator Henry Cabot Lodge, for example, felt that the immigrants were inferior peoples. Francis A. Walker, president of the Massachusetts Institute of Technology, theorized that the new immigrants were "beaten men from beaten races; representing the worst failures in the struggle for existence."

TRACING THEMES
IMMIGRATION AND MIGRATION

Immigration, Migration, and War

Some people who have moved to various regions of the United States have felt "pushed" away from their homes because of poverty or oppression. Others have felt "pulled" to a new land and the opportunities it promised. These push-and-pull feelings have been a major factor in making the United States a nation of immigrants and migrants.

Wars have often created these push-and-pull feelings among immigrants and migrants. Sometimes they have pushed people away from fighting or pulled them to regions where there was work. At other times, war has affected migrants by forcing them to adjust to cultural change in their new homes. Many immigrants discovered that war unleashed forces that affected their lives in unpredictable ways. As wars forced American society to evolve, immigrants and migrants created new roles for themselves as Americans and helped shape the way America would change.

1840s
MIGRATING TO THE WEST

Throughout the 19th century, Americans continued their movement westward to the Pacific Ocean. Victory in the War with Mexico in 1848 greatly increased the amount of land under American control, and thousands of Americans were pulled to the West to take advantage of it.

Two important consequences emerged from this movement. First, following the discovery of gold in California, hundreds of thousands of people from around the world rushed in to strike it rich. Within a year, there were enough people in California to qualify it for statehood. Second, Americans disagreed over whether the new lands should be open to slavery. That disagreement culminated in the Civil War.

1910s
ANTI-IMMIGRANT FEELINGS

The new immigrants of the early 20th century—unlike the "old-stock" Americans who traced their ancestry to northern and western Europe—came mostly from southern and eastern Europe, and they often did not speak English. Many old-stock Americans feared that the new immigrants posed a threat to American culture. As a result, old-stock Americans tried to "Americanize" the new immigrants by encouraging them to abandon their old customs and teaching them American ones.

During World War I, when anti-immigrant sentiment increased, the Committee on Public Information (CPI) was concerned that new immigrants were not loyal to the United States. The CPI therefore set up Loyalty Leagues in immigrant communities to foster American patriotism. George Creel, head of the CPI, claimed that there was "not a pin dropped in the home of any one with a foreign name, but that it ran like thunder on the inner ear of some listening sleuth."

RECOMMENDED RESOURCES

Books

Chermayeff, Ivan et al. *Ellis Island: An Illustrated History of the Immigrant Experience.* New York: Macmillan, 1991. Text by Mary J. Shapiro.

Orth, Samuel Peter. *Our Foreigners.* New Haven: Yale UP, 1920. A period account of immigration.

Pan, Lynn. *Sons of the Yellow Emperor.* Boston: Little, 1990. A history of the Chinese diaspora.

Portes, Alejandro. *Immigrant America: A Portrait.* Berkeley: U of California P, 1990. A study of immigrants and the process of their Americanization.

Videos

Ellis Island: Gateway to America. Sterling Educational Media, 1991. History of Ellis Island.

The Immigrant Experience: The Long, Long Journey. Dir. Joan M. Silver. Coronet/MTI Film and Video, 1972. Experiences of one turn-of-the-century immigrant family.

Old World, New World. Thames Television, 1977. Media Guild. Late-19th-century European immigration to the United States.

Software

Ellis Island. Diskette. Educational Activities, 1994. Students role-play an Italian teenager who immigrates to America in 1892.

1970s
IN SEARCH OF A NEW LIFE

In 1964, only 603 Vietnamese lived in the United States. A decade later, as the Vietnam War ended, hundreds of thousands of refugees, mostly South Vietnamese who had been allies of the United States during the war, fled their country. They used boats, braving stormy seas and pirates, to reach Thailand or Cambodia. There they lived in refugee camps for months before moving to other nations, including the United States. By 1985, there were 643,200 Vietnamese living across the United States.

Although many of the hundreds of thousands of Vietnamese pushed from their homes in Vietnam have faced discrimination in the United States, most have overcome it. Chased from Vietnam by Communist dictators, many Vietnamese have become successful entrepreneurs. In San Jose, California, for example, 40 percent of the downtown retail businesses are Vietnamese-owned, bringing new commercial vitality to the area.

1940s
MIGRATING FOR JOBS

Throughout the 20th century, African Americans responded to push-and-pull feelings as they moved across the United States. In the Great Migration of the early 20th century, they felt pushed out of their homes in the rural South by racial discrimination and the arrival of mechanized farming. Of the millions of African Americans who left, most moved to cities, usually in the North.

The Second Migration, sparked by World War II, was an important part of this movement because it allowed African Americans to take industrial jobs—many formerly held by whites—to support the war effort. This migration also had important consequences for the civil rights movement. Many African Americans who remained in the South moved to Southern cities, where they developed organizations that helped them fight against segregation.

INTERACT WITH HISTORY

1. **SYNTHESIZING** Based on what you have read about immigration, what generalizations can you make about the way war has affected immigrants and migrants in the United States?

    SEE SKILLBUILDER HANDBOOK, PAGE 921.

2. **EXPLORING YOUR COMMUNITY** Interview family members and people in your community to find out about the history of immigration and migration—where people came from and what their reasons for coming were. Try to record specific stories of people and events. Share your findings with the class.

INSTRUCT

▶*Starting with the Student*
- Ask students to describe how immigrants have influenced and enriched their community. What stores or other businesses have immigrants established? What holidays, sports, or beliefs have students learned about?
- Discuss whether immigrants and migrants are entitled to education, health care, and other rights of American citizens.

▶*Discussing Key Ideas*
- Often in the face of prejudicial treatment, immigrants and migrants create new roles for themselves as Americans.
- Immigrants and migrants help shape American history.

HISTORY FROM VISUALS

Reading the Images Have students study the four illustrations on these pages.
- What view of the immigrants or migrants does each illustration evoke? *Possible Responses: 1840s—rugged, courageous; 1910s—naive, hopeful; 1940s—poor, hard working; 1970s—uncertain, bleak.*
- Which picture presents the most accurate portrait of the group of immigrants or migrants?

INTERACT WITH HISTORY

1. Synthesizing

Possible Answers: *War has impelled people to leave their homeland and flee the threat of violence. People have been constrained to uproot themselves and find new homes after their own have been destroyed. New economic opportunities resulting from war have caused people to relocate to find new jobs.*

2. Exploring Your Community

Suggestions for Interviews
- Ask to see any photos or other mementos of the people's relatives or home culture.
- Discuss the holidays celebrated in the home culture. Ask what customs are observed during the holidays, what foods are eaten, and what songs are sung.
- Ask the people to describe their first impressions when they arrived in their new home.
- Ask the people what they hoped to find or achieve in their new home and whether these hopes were fulfilled.

CHAPTER 11
ASSESSMENT ANSWERS

REVIEWING THE CHAPTER

TERMS & NAMES

1. Archduke Franz Ferdinand, p. 396
2. trench warfare, p. 397
3. *Lusitania,* p. 399
4. Selective Service Act, p. 402
5. Alvin York, p. 405
6. George Creel, p. 412
7. Great Migration, p. 414
8. Fourteen Points, p. 417
9. League of Nations, p. 418
10. Treaty of Versailles, p. 418

MAIN IDEAS

11. Nationalism, imperialism, militarism, and alliances were long-term causes; Archduke Franz Ferdinand's assassination set off the immediate diplomatic crisis that led to war.
12. In Belgium; the Germans defeated British and French forces.
13. The German threat contained in the Zimmermann note and the sinking of four unarmed American merchant ships.
14. The United States started a draft, created a nine-month training program, and took steps to increase ship production.
15. Larger cannons, poison gas, machine guns, tanks, and fighter planes.
16. The government advertised and sold war bonds; the Committee on Public Information popularized the war through a massive propaganda campaign.
17. Americans with German-sounding names suffered loss of jobs and violence due to anti-immigrant hysteria; the Espionage and Sedition Acts repressed freedom of speech.
18. It created international problems that would eventually lead to World War II: it humiliated Germany; it provoked Russia's determination to regain former Russian territory; it ignored the claims of colonized people for self-determination.
19. Many senators objected to the provision calling for the league, yet Wilson was unwilling to compromise on it.
20. Germans were shocked by the armistice and angered at the Treaty of Versailles; desperate economic conditions prevailed in Europe; Germany suffered a severe depression.

Chapter 11 Assessment

REVIEWING THE CHAPTER

TERMS & NAMES For each term below, write a sentence explaining its connection to World War I. For each person below, explain his role in the events before, during, or after the war.

1. **Archduke Franz Ferdinand**
2. **trench warfare**
3. ***Lusitania***
4. **Selective Service Act**
5. **Alvin York**
6. **George Creel**
7. **Great Migration**
8. **Fourteen Points**
9. **League of Nations**
10. **Treaty of Versailles**

MAIN IDEAS

SECTION 1 *(pages 394–401)*

World War I Begins

11. What were the long-term and immediate causes of World War I?
12. Where did Germany begin its war offensive, and what happened there?
13. What overt acts caused the United States to enter World War I in 1917?

SECTION 2 *(pages 402–408)*

American Power Tips the Balance

14. How did the United States mobilize a strong military during World War I?
15. What new weapons made fighting in World War I deadlier than fighting in previous wars?

SECTION 3 *(pages 409–416)*

The War at Home

16. What methods did the U.S. government use to sell the war to the nation?
17. What events during World War I undermined Americans' civil liberties?

SECTION 4 *(pages 417–421)*

Wilson Fights for Peace

18. What were the major effects of the Treaty of Versailles?
19. How did Wilson's support for the League of Nations stand in the way of Senate support for the Treaty of Versailles?
20. What were the major international consequences of World War I?

THINKING CRITICALLY

1. **WAR AND PEACE** In a chart like the one shown, provide causes for the listed effects of World War I.

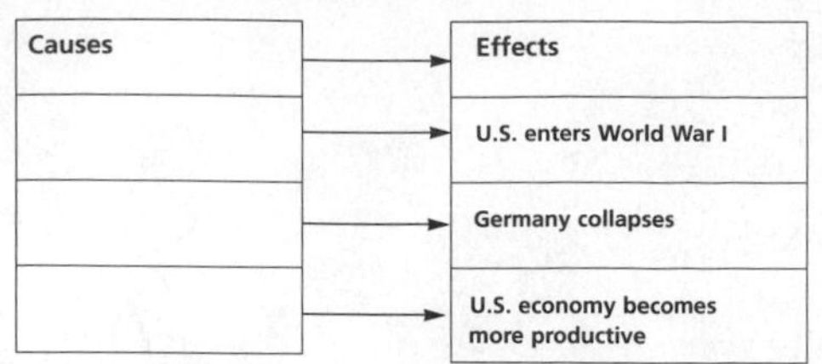

2. **AMERICA'S ROLE** Between 1914 and 1920, Americans debated the role their country should have in world affairs. What might Americans have learned about intervention in the affairs of other nations from the events of World War I?
3. **TRACING THEMES DEMOCRACY IN AMERICA** Reread the quotation from President Woodrow Wilson on page 392. How does his statement reflect issues of the time? Explain.
4. **GEOGRAPHY OF POSTWAR EUROPE** Compare the maps on pages 395 and 420. Describe the changes in national boundaries after the Versailles peace settlement.
5. **DOMESTIC EFFECT OF WAR** In your opinion, what was the major domestic effect of World War I? Support your opinion with specific details from the chapter.
6. **ANALYZING PRIMARY SOURCES** When Congress declared war in 1917, the settlement-house worker Mary Simkhovitch expressed the view of many Americans who desired peace.

> There were two great evils facing us in 1917. One was to go into the war, and the other was to stay out. Whatever the outcome, war was bound to bring in its train not only the loss of life and the destruction of property, but also new social alignments, a re-evaluating of customs, habits and outlooks, a redistributing of wealth and power. Gradually, step by step, we slipped into war in the presidency of Wilson, who won his second term with the slogan "He kept us out of war."
>
> **MARY SIMKHOVITCH,** *Neighborhood: My Story of Greenwich House*

Summarize Simkhovitch's account of the effects of going to war and of staying out. Do you agree that both entering the war and staying out of it were evil? Explain.

THINKING CRITICALLY

1. WAR AND PEACE
Possible Response: **U.S. enters WWI:** Germany resumed unrestricted submarine warfare; Zimmermann note intercepted; four American merchant ships sunk. **Germany collapses:** German war machine and war economy too exhausted to keep fighting; German sailors and marines refused orders to man their ships. **U.S. economy becomes more productive:** wages in metal trades, meatpacking, and shipbuilding rose; farmers increased crop production; women joined work force.

2. AMERICA'S ROLE
Possible Response: To pay closer attention to international situations, such as extreme nationalism or militarism, that could lead to crises; the importance of nations' helping one another in global affairs; the importance of diplomacy in drawing up treaties so as not to unduly punish or cast blame on offending nations; the importance of listening to and helping smaller nations.

3. TRACING THEMES DEMOCRACY IN AMERICA
Possible Response: He mentions safety, which was a key issue of the time, since so many nations were threatened by invasion from Germany. He mentions democracy, which was a timely issue in Russia in 1917, when the Russians overthrew their czarist regime; that overthrow helped the democratic Allied nations feel that they were defending democracy in fighting the monarchies of the Central Powers.

ALTERNATIVE ASSESSMENT

1. **MAKING DECISIONS**
Imagine that you have just immigrated from Germany to the United States when World War I breaks out in Europe. Americans are hotly debating whether the United States should enter the war. Use the Difficult Decisions feature on page 400 and the following list to help you write an essay explaining what position you would take.
   - What major choices would you need to make about entry into the war?
   - What information would you want to gather in order to make your choices?
   - What options would each choice present to you?
   - What would be the consequences of each of the options?
   - What actions would you take to implement your final decisions?

2. **LEARNING FROM MEDIA**
VIDEO View the McDougal Littell video for Chapter 11, *Ace of Aces.* Discuss these questions in small groups; then do the cooperative learning activity.
   - What is your impression of Eddie Rickenbacker? What words would you use to describe him?
   - How did Rickenbacker adapt his skills and talents to wartime?
   - Do you think a soldier who received the Congressional Medal of Honor for bravery on the battlefield today would receive a hero's welcome from the public? Why or why not?
   - **Cooperative Learning** What would have happened if Eddie Rickenbacker and the Red Baron had engaged in an air battle? Discuss the encounter in your group. What emotions would the two fighter pilots experience during the battle? What would each want to prove to the other? Who would win? Write a film script that dramatizes the encounter. Then enact the scene before the class.

3. **PORTFOLIO PROJECT**
Use the Living History activity to expand your portfolio.

LIVING HISTORY

PRESENTING YOUR CHART

You have completed a chart and report on the effects of World War I. Now share your work in an oral presentation. Select the portion of your chart that corresponds with the subject matter of your report, and prepare it as a large-format visual aid. Before your presentation, ask yourself these questions:

- Is my report clearly written and informative?
- Have I quoted from and/or cited my sources?
- Does my visual aid support my report?

Add your chart and report to your American history portfolio.

Bridge to Chapter 12

Review Chapter 11

THE WAR ABROAD Shortly after the assassination of Archduke Franz Ferdinand in 1914, Great Britain, France, Russia, and their allies were at war with Germany, Austria-Hungary, and their allies. The fighting continued for the next three years, despite deaths in the millions.

AMERICANS AND THE WAR In 1914, most Americans wanted to stay out of the fighting. However, economic and cultural ties to the Allies, and anger at Germany's submarine warfare, brought the United States into the war in April 1917. American soldiers fought under General John J. Pershing, using improved weapons that made World War I deadlier than any earlier war. About 26 million people died before the fighting ended on November 11, 1918.

The war brought dramatic changes to the United States. The government took a more active role in the economy and helped boost industrial production by 20 percent. Millions of African Americans moved to cities in the North to take jobs in factories. Anti-immigrant hysteria erupted and was directed particularly at German Americans. Laws such as the Espionage and Sedition Acts limited freedom of speech and fed an atmosphere of suspicion.

AFTERMATH OF WAR Toward the end of the war, a great flu epidemic swept the globe, killing 40 million people, including 500,000 Americans. Leaders met in Paris to negotiate the Treaty of Versailles, which created nine new nations and redrew the boundaries of many others. However, the treaty's harsh treatment of Germany helped lead to World War II. The United States never ratified the treaty, primarily because of opposition to Wilson's League of Nations.

Preview Chapter 12

After World War I, many Americans wished to return to the peaceful time before the war. During the 1920s, Americans focused on building economic prosperity. You will learn about these significant developments in the next chapter.

ALTERNATIVE ASSESSMENT

1. MAKING DECISIONS
Standards for Evaluation
An essay should meet the following criteria:
- Identifies the decision made.
- Cites reasons that support the position taken.
- Discusses the probable consequences of the decision.

2. LEARNING FROM MEDIA
Answers to the questions:
- Rickenbacker was a natural leader, had a good sense of humor, was brave and adventurous, patient and determined.
- He used his skills as a public speaker to urge U.S. entry into the war, as a race-car driver to become a pilot and fly dangerous missions, and as a leader to head the 94th Squadron.
- *Possible Response:* Whether a winner of the Congressional Medal of Honor received a hero's welcome would probably depend upon the popularity of the conflict.
- *Possible Response:* The two aviators would have been very competitive. Film scripts should show the pilots' excitement, determination, and bravery, and portray logical outcomes.

3. PORTFOLIO PROJECT
LIVING HISTORY
Standards for Evaluation
An oral report should meet the following criteria:
- Presents information clearly and logically.
- Includes research from a variety of sources.
- Uses quotations and refers to specific sources.
- Makes logical connections between the chart and main topics in the report.

IN-DEPTH RESOURCES: UNIT 3
See the form for scoring this activity on page 57.

THINKING CRITICALLY

4. GEOGRAPHY OF POSTWAR EUROPE
Possible Answer: From land formerly belonging to Russia, Germany, and Austria-Hungary, new nations appeared such as Latvia, Lithuania, Poland, Czechoslovakia, and Yugoslavia; Serbia became part of Yugoslavia.

5. DOMESTIC EFFECT OF WAR
Possible Responses: The wartime need for labor provided job opportunities for African Americans and women; government propaganda created an atmosphere of intolerance; the nation grew in economic power; many African Americans permanently moved from the South to take jobs in cities in the North; the concentration of African Americans in the North provided new economic opportunities and allowed many to set up their own businesses.

6. ANALYZING PRIMARY SOURCES
Possible Response: No matter who won, the war would result in destruction, death, and social change. Students agreeing might argue that going to war would contribute to deaths, diseases, and destruction of lands, but not going might have meant that the Allies would lose the war. Some students disagreeing might argue that not fighting Germany and not helping the Allies would have been wrong; others might argue that the war accomplished nothing significant but loss of life and that it was wrong to fight.

UNIT OVERVIEW

The Twenties and the Great Depression

HISTORY AND ART

Drouth Stricken Area

Oil painting by Alexandre Hogue (1934).

Art Note
Hogue grew up in West Texas, part of the area that became the Dust Bowl. He was part of the regionalist movement, in which artists rejected European influences in an attempt to forge a uniquely American art. Hogue painted many distinctive landscapes of Texas and other parts of the Southwest. In this painting he used his distinctive style to depict the devastating effects of drouth (more commonly spelled *drought*).

▶ ***Previewing the Unit***
Unit 4 covers the vast changes that touch the United States from 1920 to 1940, as people feel a clash between the values of a traditional, rural society and those of a growing urban culture. Underlying economic problems are obscured by apparent prosperity until a long, deep economic slowdown causes widespread suffering. In response, President Franklin Roosevelt experiments with various approaches to rebuild the economy.

UNIT 4

1920–1940

The Twenties and the Great Depression

"This great nation will endure as it has endured, will revive and will prosper."

FRANKLIN D. ROOSEVELT

426 UNIT 4

1 Shapes and colors
Hogue's use of strong lines and vivid colors echoes techniques associated with folk art. Many regionalist artists of the 1930s used such techniques. Here, the shapes and colors also help stress the harshness of the landscape.

2 Lonely house
The starkness of the scene is emphasized by the absence of people. The vast distance between this farmhouse and the one in the background emphasizes the loneliness of life on the Great Plains.

3 Starving cow
The devastation of the Dust Bowl is evident in the skeletal cow. Underscoring the misery of the scene, it looks forlornly at the well that has no water.

4

7

5

6

427

Discussing the Quotation

Franklin Roosevelt gave many inspirational speeches to the American people. The quotation comes from his first inaugural address. The next sentence in the speech contains Roosevelt's most famous statement: "The only thing we have to fear is fear itself."

FOR DISCUSSION:

- Why might people in the 1930s want to hear such speeches?
- What else, beyond reassuring words, would people need?
- How could anyone convince the owners of this farm that they will recover and prosper?

Discussing the Image

Hogue adopted Native American ideas about the land, ideas that he had encountered in his youth. He came to believe that plowing the land broke a sacred bond owed to it. He felt that the farmers deserved some of the blame for the Dust Bowl because of their farming methods.

FOR DISCUSSION:

- Where are the people?
- What feeling does the blue tone in the painting convey?
- Suggest some adjectives to describe the feeling in the painting.

4 Broken windmill
The useless windmill shows the power of nature in two ways. The sail has been broken by the Plains wind—and remains unrepaired apparently because the owners have fled. The spout seems to have produced not life-giving water but death-bringing dust.

5 Dunes
The destruction is evident in the mound of dust that has partially engulfed the house.

6 Vulture
To remove any doubt about the fate of the cow—and of the way of life on the plains—Hogue includes the waiting vulture.

7 No relief
The scene contains no sign of relief. The dust-filled sky contains one cloud that seems unlikely to bring rain. The other birds in the sky may be circling vultures.

CHAPTER 12

PLANNING GUIDE

Politics of the Roaring Twenties

	Key Ideas	COPYMASTERS	ASSESSMENT
SECTION 1 Americans Struggle with Postwar Issues *pp. 430–435*	*The Russian Revolution brings a Communist government to power. Many Americans fear that a similar revolution will occur in the United States. Political radicals and labor activists meet with increasing opposition.*	***In-Depth Resources: Unit 4*** • Guided Reading, p. 1 • Primary Sources: *from* Bartolomeo Vanzetti's Speech to the Jury, p. 7; *from* Report on the Steel Strike of 1919, p. 9 • Literature: from *The Big Money* by John Dos Passos, p. 11; "Justice Denied in Massachusetts" by Edna St. Vincent Millay, p. 13 ***Lesson Plans,*** pp. 103–104	PE ***Section 1 Assessment,*** p. 435 TE ***Self-Assessment,*** p. 435 ***Formal Assessment*** • Section Quiz, p. 153 ***Alternative Assessment Book*** • Standards for Evaluating a Cooperative Activity
SECTION 2 "Normalcy" and Isolationism *pp. 436–440*	*The Republicans return to isolationism and the kind of policies that had characterized the period before the reforms of the progressive era.*	***In-Depth Resources: Unit 4*** • Guided Reading, p. 2 • Skillbuilder Practice: Summarizing p. 4 • American Lives: Ernesto Galarza, p. 14 ***Lesson Plans,*** pp. 105–106	PE ***Section 2 Assessment,*** p. 440 TE ***Self-Assessment,*** p. 440 ***Formal Assessment*** • Section Quiz, p. 154 ***Alternative Assessment Book*** • Standards for Evaluating a Cooperative Activity
SECTION 3 The Business of America *pp. 441–445*	*During the prosperous 1920s, the automobile industry and other industries flourish. Americans' standard of living rises to new heights.*	***In-Depth Resources: Unit 4*** • Guided Reading, p. 3 • Geography Application: The Automobile Industry, p. 5 • Primary Source: Advertisement, p. 10 • American Lives: Henry Ford, p. 15 ***Lesson Plans,*** pp. 107–108	PE ***Section 3 Assessment,*** p. 445 TE ***Self-Assessment,*** p. 445 ***Formal Assessment*** • Section Quiz, p. 155 ***Alternative Assessment Book*** • Standards for Evaluating a Cooperative Activity
CHAPTER RESOURCES	**Chapter Overview** *Americans lash out at those who are different while they enjoy prosperity and new conveniences produced by American businesses.*	***In-Depth Resources: Unit 4*** • Living History Project: Worksheet, p. 16; Standards, p. 17 ***Telescoping the Times*** • Chapter Summary, pp. 23–24 ***Planning for Block Schedules***	PE ***Chapter Assessment,*** pp. 448–449 PE ***Alternative Assessment,*** p. 449 ***Formal Assessment*** • Chapter Test, forms A and B, pp. 156–161 ***Test Generator*** ***Alternative Assessment Book*** See explanation and forms for different kinds of alternative assessments including portfolio assessment.

KEY
- PE Pupil's Edition
- TE Teacher's Edition
- http://www.mlushistory.com

TECHNOLOGY

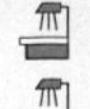

- *Warm-Up Transparency* 12
- *Humanities Transparencies*
  - H19, *The Passion of Sacco and Vanzetti* by Ben Shahn
- *Electronic Library of Primary Sources*
  - Instructions Regarding Conduct on Raids
- *Our Times*
  - Sacco-Vanzetti case

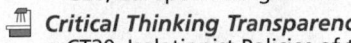

- **INTERNET** Sacco and Vanzetti and the Russian Revolution

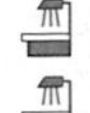

- *Warm-Up Transparency* 12
- *Humanities Transparencies*
  - H39, Looking Backward

- *Geography Transparencies*
  - G20, European Emigration
- *Critical Thinking Transparencies*
  - CT20, Isolationist Policies of the 1920s
- *Electronic Library of Primary Sources*
  - *from* A Letter Regarding Immigration Restrictions
  - Teapot Dome

- **INTERNET** Harding

- *Warm-Up Transparency* 12
- *Critical Thinking Transparencies*
  - CT54, Consumer Spending Power
- *Electronic Library of Primary Sources*
  - from *Middletown* by Robert S. and Helen Merrell Lynd
- *Grolier Multimedia Encyclopedia*
  - History of aviation

- *Our Times*
  - 1925 Listerine advertisement

- **INTERNET** Interact with History p. 447 (PE)

- *American Portfolio: A Videodisc for U.S. History,* user's guide, pp. 193–194, 196, 198–199

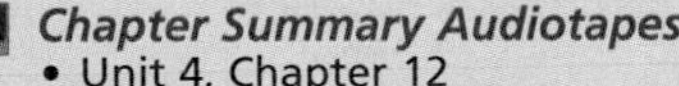

- *Chapter Summary Audiotapes*
  - Unit 4, Chapter 12

- **INTERNET http://www.mlushistory.com**

Block Scheduling (90 MINUTES)

Day 1

Section 1, pp. 430–435

Section 2, pp. 436–440

Section Assessments, pp. 435, 440

COOPERATIVE ACTIVITIES
- Staging a Fair Trial for Sacco and Vanzetti, p. 432 (TE)
- Researching Immigration Issues, p. 438 (TE)

Day 2

Section 3, pp. 441–445

Tracing Themes Economic Opportunity: Consumer Spending, pp. 446–447

Section Assessment, p. 445

Chapter Assessment, pp. 448–449

COOPERATIVE ACTIVITY
- Creating a 1920s Automobile Newsletter, p. 442 (TE)

YEARLY PACING *Chapter 12 Total:* 2 days *Yearly Total:* 85 days

See *Planning for Block Schedules* for special activities and pacing strategies.

Customizing for Special Populations

Students Acquiring English

Access for Students Acquiring English: Spanish Translations
- Guided Reading for Sections 1–3, pp. 150–152
- Chapter Summary, pp. 148–149
- Skillbuilder Practice: Summarizing, p. 153
- Geography Application: The Automobile Industry, pp. 154–155

Spanish Reading Study Guide, pp. 129–136

Translations of Chapter Summaries, Hmong, Cantonese, Vietnamese, and Cambodian

Chapter Summary Audiotapes in Spanish Unit 4, Chapter 12

INTERNET The Diverse Classroom

Gifted and Talented Students

In-Depth Resources: Unit 4
- Primary Sources: *from* Bartolomeo Vanzetti's Speech to the Jury, p. 7; *from* Report on the Steel Strike of 1919, p. 9; Advertisement, p. 10
- American Lives: Ernesto Galarza, p. 14; Henry Ford, p. 15

Less Proficient Readers

In-Depth Resources: Unit 4
- Guided Reading for Sections 1–3, pp. 1–3
- Skillbuilder: Summarizing, p. 4
- Geography Application: The Automobile Industry, p. 5

Reading Study Guide
- pp. 129–136

Telescoping the Times
- Chapter Summary, pp. 23–24

Chapter Summary Audiotapes, Unit 4, Chapter 12

Connections to Literature READINGS FOR STUDENTS

In-Depth Resources: Unit 4
- **from *The Big Money* by John Dos Passos,** p. 11
- **"Justice Denied in Massachusetts" by Edna St. Vincent Millay,** p. 13

Enrichment Reading
- **Dashiell Hammett**
  Red Harvest
  New York: Vintage Books, 1989
  This superb crime novel depicts gang war and labor organization. It is a classic exploration of corruption and violence in 1920s America.
- **Sinclair Lewis**
  Main Street
  New York: Bantam, 1996
  A small midwestern prairie town in the 1920s is the setting of this famous novel. The story is about a city girl who marries the town doctor and attempts to bring culture to the village. Her efforts are met with gossip, greed, and bigotry resulting in a horrifying picture of small town life.
- **Katherine Anne Porter**
  The Never-Ending Wrong
  Boston: Little, Brown, 1977
  This brief memoir by a noted writer details her protests during the Sacco-Vanzetti case.
- **Upton Sinclair**
  Boston
  Cambridge, MA: Bentley, 1978
  Written in a white heat in the aftermath of the Sacco-Vanzetti case, this novel skillfully mixes fiction and real life with vividly realized characters of the principal actors in the case that aroused great passion and controversy.
- **Upton Sinclair**
  Oil!
  Cambridge, MA: Bentley, 1981
  Based on the oil scandals of the Harding administration, especially the Teapot Dome affair, the story tells of the struggles of two independent oil operators against the encroachments of monopoly.

CHAPTER 12 OVERVIEW

Politics of the Roaring Twenties

▶ ***Accessing Prior Knowledge***

Ask students what images come to mind when they think about the 1920s. Discuss why the decade is called the Roaring Twenties. Then have students suggest a nickname for the 1990s.

▶ ***Predicting Outcomes***

Have students read the quotation on page 428 and look at the images on the time line. Then have them make predictions about the impact business might have on Americans in the twenties and about the relationship between owners and workers.

MORE ABOUT . . .
Calvin Coolidge

Coolidge was usually so taciturn that people called him "Silent Cal" and told dozens of anecdotes about his reluctance to speak. On one occasion, a dinner partner informed Coolidge that she had bet a friend that she could get him to say more than two words. "You lose," he replied and then kept his mouth shut the entire evening. When he died in 1933, writer Dorothy Parker asked wryly: "How can they tell?"

CHAPTER 12

Politics of the Roaring Twenties

SECTION 1

Americans Struggle with Postwar Issues

The Russian Revolution brings a Communist government to power. Many Americans fear that a similar revolution will occur in the United States. Political radicals and labor activists meet with increasing opposition.

SECTION 2

"Normalcy" and Isolationism

The Republicans return to isolationism and the kind of policies that had characterized the period before the reforms of the progressive era.

SECTION 3

The Business of America

During the prosperous 1920s, the automobile industry and other industries flourish. Americans' standard of living rises to new heights.

"The business of America is business."

President Calvin Coolidge

THE UNITED STATES

1920

- John L. Lewis is president of the United Mine Workers.
- Nineteenth Amendment is ratified.
- Warren G. Harding is elected president.

1921

- Sacco and Vanzetti are convicted.
- Federal-Aid Highway Act funds a national highway system.

1922

- Miners leave a Scranton, Pennsylvania, mine at the beginning of a strike.

1923

- President Harding dies and Calvin Coolidge becomes president.

THE WORLD

1921

- Chinese Communist Party is founded in Shanghai.
- Vladimir Ilich Lenin adopts the New Economic Policy.

1922

- Benito Mussolini is appointed prime minister of Italy.

1923

- Adolf Hitler's putsch in Germany fails.

THEMES IN CHAPTER 12

Economic Opportunity	America in the World	Science and Technology
During World War I, workers were not allowed to strike because the government wouldn't let anything interfere with the war effort. After the war, union membership increased and workers went on strike for higher wages and better working conditions. The U.S. government played an important role in ending these strikes. See Teacher's Edition note, p. 433.	After World War I, the United States pursued an isolationist foreign policy. At the same time, the government sought to protect American business from foreign competition. As a result, the government raised taxes on imports, which made it difficult for America's Allies to repay their war debts. See Teacher's Edition note, p. 437.	In the 1920s, many people were able to buy automobiles. The widespread purchase and popularity of cars changed the face of the American landscape, economy, and way of life. See Teacher's Edition note, p. 443.

LIVING HISTORY

PUTTING THE TWENTIES ON DISPLAY

Create a floor plan for a museum exhibit that highlights some of the accomplishments, trends, or events of the 1920s that are presented in this chapter. Consider the following categories as you choose your topic:

- political groups and factions
- relationships between workers and management
- the growth of business
- industrial and technological advances
- the Emergency Quota Act of 1921
- the consumer economy

PORTFOLIO PROJECT Keep your plans in a folder for your American history portfolio. At the end of the chapter, you will share your exhibit ideas with others.

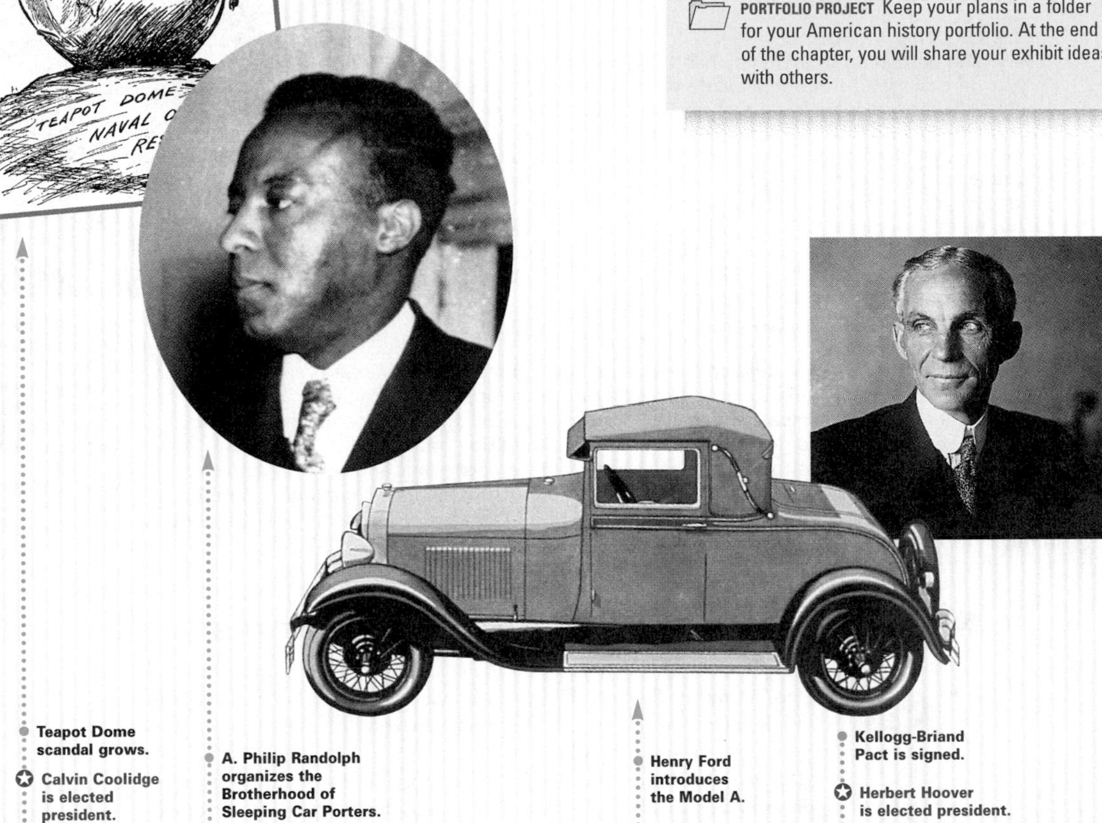

1924
- Teapot Dome scandal grows.
- Calvin Coolidge is elected president.
- Vladimir Ilich Lenin, founder of the Soviet Union, dies.

1925
- A. Philip Randolph organizes the Brotherhood of Sleeping Car Porters.

1926
- British laborers declare a national strike.
- Hirohito becomes emperor of Japan.

1927
- Henry Ford introduces the Model A.

1928
- Kellogg-Briand Pact is signed.
- Herbert Hoover is elected president.
- Joseph Stalin launches the first five-year plan in the USSR.

1929
- Institutional Revolutionary Party is organized in Mexico.

ALTERNATIVE ASSESSMENT

LIVING HISTORY

PUTTING THE TWENTIES ON DISPLAY

Discuss sources for materials that could be used in the exhibit.

- Review the chapter for references to objects that could be used as historical artifacts.
- Look for visuals in reference books, in periodicals, and on the Internet.
- Create graphs and charts that illustrate some aspect of the topic.
- If possible, borrow relevant pictures or other objects from friends or family members.

Encourage students to consider how to arrange their exhibit materials in a logical, interesting manner. Students may wish to arrange their materials in chronological order using a diagram like the one below.

Relations Between Workers and Management
↓
Items illustrating relations during the war
↓
Items illustrating 1919 strikes
↓
Items illustrating union membership in 1920
↓
Items illustrating declining union membership after 1920

IN-DEPTH RESOURCES: UNIT 4
See worksheet and standards for evaluation, pp. 16, 17.

RECOMMENDED RESOURCES

Books for the Teacher

Boyer, Richard O., and Herbert M. Morais. *Labor's Untold Story.* New York: United Electrical, Radio, and Machine Workers of America, 1982. History of the labor movement, includes the story of the strikes in the early 1920s.

Daniels, Roger. *Coming to America.* New York: Harper, 1990. History of immigration; discusses nativism in the 1920s.

Nye, David E. *Electrifying America.* Cambridge, MA: MIT P, 1995. How electricity changed life in Muncie, Indiana.

Books for the Student

Allen, Frederick Lewis. *Only Yesterday.* New York: Harper, 1964. Society in the 1920s.

Koral, April. *An Album of the Great Wave of Immigration.* New York: Watts, 1992. A pictorial history of American immigration from the 1880s through the 1920s.

Parrish, Michael A. *Anxious Decades.* New York: Norton, 1992. Concerns in the 1920s.

Videos

Los Mineros. PBS Home Video, 1990. Documentary of Mexican American miners.

Reds. Dir. Warren Beatty. Paramount, 1981. Lives of American radicals and Communists.

Route 66. Dir. Robert Townsend. PBS Video, 1996.

Software

American Chronicle Series: Between the Wars (1918–1939). CD-ROM. AIMS Media.

The Model T Man from Michigan. American Lifestyle Series. Educational Software Institute, 800-955-5570.

Wall Street On-Line: An Investment Simulation. Educational Software Institute, 800-955-5570.

1 Americans Struggle with Postwar Issues

TERMS & NAMES
- communism
- A. Mitchell Palmer
- anarchist
- Sacco and Vanzetti
- Calvin Coolidge
- John L. Lewis

LEARN ABOUT postwar conditions in America
TO UNDERSTAND how fear of communism affected civil liberties and the labor movement.

Section 1 Overview

OBJECTIVES

1. To summarize the reaction in the United States to the perceived threat of communism.
2. To describe some of the conflicts between labor and management after the war.

SKILLBUILDER

- Interpreting graphs, p. 434

CRITICAL THINKING

- Analyzing motives, p. 431
- Drawing conclusions, p. 432
- Analyzing issues, p. 433
- Summarizing, p. 434
- Theme: Economic Opportunity, p. 435
- Sequencing, p. 435
- Forming opinions, p. 435
- Analyzing, p. 435

FOCUS & MOTIVATE

5-MINUTE WARM-UP

Making Inferences
To explore the impact of the Sacco and Vanzetti case, have students look at the painting and caption on page 432 and answer these questions.

1. The man standing beside Sacco and Vanzetti is Governor Fuller of Massachusetts. Why has the artist made Fuller so much smaller than the other two?
2. Do you think the artist feels more sympathy for Sacco and Vanzetti or for their accusers? Why?

WARM-UP TRANSPARENCY 12

▶ ***Starting with the Student***
- How do students react to others who look different or who hold views that differ from the majority of those in the classroom? Do they ignore them? Try to make friends with them? Try to antagonize them?
- How are such people treated in society? Do these people inspire fear in the majority? If so, why?

ONE AMERICAN'S STORY

During the 1920s and 1930s, Irving Fajans sold merchandise from behind the counters of several of New York City's large department stores. When he wasn't selling goods, he was trying to persuade fellow workers to join the Department Store Employees Union. He described some of the techniques he and other union organizers used.

A PERSONAL VOICE

Everything pertaining to the union had to be on the q.t. [quiet]. If you were caught distributing leaflets or other union literature around the job you were instantly fired. We thought up ways of passing leaflets without the boss being able to pin anybody down. Sometimes we'd insert the leaflets into the sales ledgers after closing time. In the morning every clerk would find a pink sheet saying: "Good morning, how's everything . . . and how about coming to a union meeting tonight?" . . . We swiped the key to the toilet-paper dispenser in the washroom, took out the paper, and substituted printed slips of just the right size! We got a lot of new members that way—it appealed to their sense of humor.

IRVING FAJANS, quoted in *The Jewish Americans*

Irving Fajans worked actively to organize department store workers in their efforts to gain better pay and working conditions during the 1920s.

As Fajans's words indicate, tensions between labor and management rose dramatically after World War I. As a result, America experienced a rash of labor strikes in the early 1920s. The public, though, was not sympathetic to striking workers. After the sacrifices of the war, most people wanted to return to normal, peaceful living. In addition, many people feared that behind workers' unrest was the specter of **communism**—an economic and social system that advocated a single political party and state ownership of property. (See *communism* on page 933 in the Economics Handbook.) A violent revolution had created a Communist government in Russia in 1917.

Revolution Abroad and Reaction at Home

World War I left much of the American public exhausted. Many Americans had died or been injured in the war. The debate over the League of Nations had deeply divided the nation. Then, too, the progressive era had caused numerous wrenching changes in American life.

After the war, Americans yearned to return to what President Warren G. Harding described as "normalcy." During the 1920s, three trends in American society resulted from this desire:

- Renewed isolationism, in which the United States pulled away from involvement in world affairs
- A resurgence of nativism, or suspicion of foreign-born people
- A trend toward political conservatism that caused a turning away from the governmental activism of the progressive era

Immediately after the war, Americans were especially concerned about a new threat to normalcy—the threat of communism.

SECTION 1 RESOURCES

PRINT RESOURCES

IN-DEPTH RESOURCES: UNIT 4
Guided Reading, p. 1
Primary Sources: *from* Bartolomeo Vanzetti's Speech to the Jury, p. 7; *from* Report on the Steel Strike of 1919, p. 9
Literature: from *The Big Money* by John Dos Passos, p. 11; "Justice Denied in Massachusetts" by Edna St. Vincent Millay, p. 13

READING STUDY GUIDE, p. 129

ACCESS FOR STUDENTS ACQUIRING ENGLISH
Guided Reading (Spanish), p. 150

SPANISH READING STUDY GUIDE, p. 129

FORMAL ASSESSMENT
Section Quiz, p. 153

ALTERNATIVE ASSESSMENT BOOK
See forms for supporting and scoring alternative activities.

TECHNOLOGY RESOURCES

HUMANITIES TRANSPARENCIES
H19, *The Passion of Sacco and Vanzetti* by Ben Shahn

CD-ROM *Our Times*
Electronic Library of Primary Sources

INTERNET http://www.mlushistory.com

THE RUSSIAN REVOLUTION By 1917, conditions in Russia had become desperate. Czar Nicholas II seemed unable to cope with the crises at home and abroad. His reign had been fatally weakened by the great loss of life and resources in World War I. People from all classes were clamoring for change and for an end to the war. There were food riots in many cities. Soldiers mutinied, deserted, or ignored orders. Faced with massive opposition, the czar abdicated his throne on March 15, 1917.

A provisional representative government replaced the czarist regime. Then, in November 1917, a group of revolutionaries, who called themselves Bolsheviks ("the majority"), led by Vladimir I. Lenin, seized power and eventually established a state based on the social and economic system of communism. Two years after the revolution, in March 1919, the Third Communist International meeting was held in Moscow. Under the banner of their symbolic revolutionary red flag, Communist speakers advocated worldwide revolution—the overthrow of the capitalist system and the abolition of free enterprise and private property.

THE RED SCARE IN THE UNITED STATES In response to that Communist call for international revolution, about 70,000 radicals joined the newly formed Communist Party in the United States. This U.S. branch of the Communist Party included members of the Industrial Workers of the World (IWW), as well as radicals from many walks of life.

In total, less than one-tenth of 1 percent of Americans joined the party. But the Communist talk about abolishing private property and substituting government ownership of factories, railroads, and other businesses frightened the public.

Adding to this fear was the mailing of several dozen bombs to government and business leaders, including the postmaster general and John D. Rockefeller. The nation panicked in its fear that "Reds," or Communists, would take over America. Attorney General **A. Mitchell Palmer** decided to take action to combat this "Red Scare."

Palmer had had a distinguished career as a Democratic member of the House of Representatives and had served in the government during World War I before being appointed attorney general in 1919. His ambitions extended to the presidency, leading some people to believe he was looking for a campaign issue for the 1920 election. Palmer was convinced that radicals were undermining American values.

A PERSONAL VOICE

The blaze of revolution was sweeping over every American institution of law and order . . . eating its way into the homes of the American workman, its sharp tongues of revolutionary heat . . . licking at the altars of the churches, leaping into the belfry of the school bell, crawling into the sacred corners of American homes, . . . burning up the foundations of American society.

A. MITCHELL PALMER

A. Answer He believed that a Communist revolution was imminent in the United States, and he needed an issue on which to campaign for the 1920 Democratic presidential nomination.

THINK THROUGH HISTORY

A. Analyzing Motives *Why did Attorney General A. Mitchell Palmer launch a series of raids against suspected Communists?*

THE PALMER RAIDS In August 1919, Palmer appointed J. Edgar Hoover to head the new antiradical division in the Justice Department—the division that later became the Federal Bureau of Investigation. Palmer sent government agents to hunt down suspected Communists, socialists, and **anarchists**—people who opposed any and all forms of government. In their zeal, the agents ran roughshod over people's civil rights, invading private homes, meeting halls, and offices without search warrants. They jailed suspects for weeks at a time without allowing them to see lawyers, and they arrested those who came to visit the suspects. The government deported hundreds of foreign-born radicals without trying them in courts.

ECONOMIC BACKGROUND

ROOTS OF COMMUNISM

In 1917, a small group headed by Vladimir I. Lenin led a successful revolution in Russia and set up a Communist government based on the teachings of Karl Marx and Friedrich Engels. In 1848, these two had published a pamphlet called *The Communist Manifesto,* in which they presented a theory of class struggle. According to their theory, a social class that has economic power also has political and social power. Marx and Engels asserted that opposing economic classes—the "haves" and the "have-nots"—have struggled for control throughout history. In ancient times, they said, the conflict was between free and enslaved people. In the Middle Ages, it was between lords and peasants.

Now, during the Industrial Revolution, they believed, the struggle was between the capitalists who owned the means of production—land, capital (or, money for investment), and machines—and the workers in mines and factories, who owned only their labor.

Marx and Engels urged workers to seize political power and the means of production. The Communist Party would lead the way in organizing workers and overthrowing capitalism through violent revolution. The party would then control a nation's government and plan all its economic activities. (See *communism* on page 933 in the Economics Handbook.)

OBJECTIVE

(1) INSTRUCT

Revolution Abroad and Reaction at Home

▶ ***Discussing Key Ideas***

- After the Russian Revolution, the newly formed Communist Party in the United States attracts some members.
- In response to the widespread Red Scare, the government hunts down suspected Communists, socialists, and anarchists.
- Sacco and Vanzetti, two anarchists and Italian immigrants, are executed for a crime they may not have committed.
- Groups such as the Ku Klux Klan use anticommunism as an excuse to harass ethnic and religious minorities.

IN-DEPTH RESOURCES: UNIT 4

Guided Reading, p. 1

ACCESS FOR STUDENTS ACQUIRING ENGLISH

Guided Reading (Spanish), p. 150

ELECTRONIC LIBRARY OF PRIMARY SOURCES

Instructions Regarding Conduct on Raids

ECONOMIC BACKGROUND

Roots of Communism

Critical Thinking: Analyzing Issues Discuss the theory that the "haves" and the "have-nots" constantly struggle for economic control. Ask students whether these economic classes exist in American society. Do they think communism can bridge the gap between the classes?

TEACHING OPTIONS

Making Connections Across Time

The Red Scare in the 1950s Tell students that the Cold War, which developed between the United States and the Soviet Union after the Second World War, once again awakened the public's fear of communism. In the 1950s, Senator Joseph McCarthy launched widely publicized attacks on suspected Communists in the U.S. government. Congressional committees also investigated possible Communist influence outside the government, particularly in the movie and entertainment industry. In this atmosphere of fear, millions of Americans were forced to take loyalty oaths and undergo investigation. Many lost their jobs.

Making Connections Across the Curriculum

Economics Discuss the theory of class struggle proposed by Marx and Engels. Tell students that Marx's ideas were, in part, a reaction to the hardships endured by many workers in Europe during the Industrial Revolution. They worked long hours for little pay under unhealthful and sometimes dangerous conditions. Marx believed that the working class would eventually rise up, overthrow capitalism, and seize control of industry and of government. He taught that society continued to develop as it advanced from one stage to the next. Marx believed that communism was the final stage of this development.

MORE ABOUT . . .
Sacco and Vanzetti

Worldwide protest erupted following the verdict against Sacco and Vanzetti. Some of these protests were violent. In Paris, a bomb exploded at the house of the American ambassador, and crowds menaced the American embassy in Rome. Other protests were peaceful. In Uruguay, people mounted a general strike and a boycott of American goods, while newspapers from Mexico to Algeria carried numerous editorials condemning the verdict.

IN-DEPTH RESOURCES: UNIT 4
Primary Sources: *from* Bartolomeo Vanzetti's Speech to the Jury, p. 7

OUR TIMES
Sacco-Vanzetti case

MORE ABOUT . . .
The Art of Ben Shahn

The painting reproduced on this page is the work of Ben Shahn. His family came to the United States from Lithuania when he was eight years old. As Jews, they had suffered persecution in their homeland, and Shahn grew up with a strong devotion to justice and fair play. When he became a painter, he decided to devote his art to helping create a more just society. Horrified by the Sacco and Vanzetti case, Shahn produced a series of 23 paintings, including the one shown here. Sacco and Vanzetti are pictured with a diminutive image of Governor Fuller, indicating his weakness as a leader.

HUMANITIES TRANSPARENCIES
H19, *The Passion of Sacco and Vanzetti* by Ben Shahn

Bartolomeo Vanzetti *(center)* and Nicola Sacco *(right)* were both executed after a trial that caused worldwide controversy.

Palmer's raids, however, failed to turn up evidence of a revolutionary conspiracy. Agents discovered no explosives, and they found only three pistols in their search for weapons. Then Palmer warned the nation of a Communist plot to overthrow the government on May 1, 1920, which was May Day, the international workers' holiday. When the day passed without incident, the public decided that Palmer didn't know what he was talking about.

SACCO AND VANZETTI Although short-lived, the Red Scare fed people's suspicions of foreigners and immigrants, sometimes leading to ruined reputations and wrecked lives. The two most infamous victims were **Nicola Sacco** and **Bartolomeo Vanzetti,** a shoemaker and a fish peddler. Both men were Italian immigrants, and both were anarchists who had evaded the draft during World War I.

In April 1920, at the height of the Red Scare, a crime took place in South Braintree, Massachusetts. Two men shot and killed a factory paymaster and his guard, grabbed the $15,000 payroll, jumped into an automobile, and made their getaway. Witnesses said the murderers appeared to be Italians. Three weeks later, the police arrested Sacco and Vanzetti and charged them with the crime. The accused provided alibis, the evidence was circumstantial, and the presiding judge made several prejudicial remarks. Nevertheless, the jury found them guilty and sentenced them to death. In spite of protests and demonstrations in the United States, Europe, and Latin America, the two men died in the electric chair on August 23, 1927. Before he was executed, Vanzetti made a statement.

THINK THROUGH HISTORY
B. *Drawing Conclusions*
What do you think the handling of the Sacco and Vanzetti case shows about the 1920s?

B. Answer That they were years of suspicion and fear.

A PERSONAL VOICE

In all my life I have never stole, never killed, never spilled blood.. . . We were tried during a time . . . when there was hysteria of resentment and hate against the people of our principles, against the foreigner. . . . I am suffering because I am a radical and indeed I am a radical; I have suffered because I was an Italian and indeed I am an Italian. . . . If you could execute me two times, and if I could be reborn two other times, I would live again to do what I have done already.

BARTOLOMEO VANZETTI, quoted in *The National Experience*

In 1925, nearly 60,000 Ku Klux Klan members marched along Pennsylvania Avenue in Washington, D.C., to demonstrate the organization's new strength and determination.

Block Schedule TEACHING OPTION **Time Needed: 40 Minutes**

Cooperative Activity: Staging a Fair Trial for Sacco and Vanzetti

Task: Students will research the Sacco and Vanzetti case and stage a fair trial for the accused.

Purpose: To explore the Sacco and Vanzetti case in depth.

Activity: The entire class can take part in a single trial, or you might have two large groups conduct two different trials. All students should research the entire case but should find detailed information about the person or role they will play in the trial. Roles in the trial should be divided by lottery or by selection. The roles should include the following: judge, members of the jury, Sacco, Vanzetti, defense attorney, prosecuting attorney, and witnesses for both sides. Remind students that, although they are attempting to give Sacco and Vanzetti a fair trial, they should be aware of the period in which the trial took place and address some of the general public's fears and prejudices. After the trial, have students discuss the proceedings and the verdict.

ALTERNATIVE ASSESSMENT BOOK
Standards for Evaluating a Cooperative Activity

In 1961, new ballistics tests showed that the pistol found on Sacco was in fact the one used to murder the guard. However, there was no proof that Sacco had actually pulled the trigger. On August 23, 1977, exactly 50 years after the executions, Massachusetts governor Michael Dukakis declared that Sacco and Vanzetti had not been given a fair trial.

THE KLAN RISES AGAIN As a result of the Red Scare and anti-immigrant feelings, different groups of bigots used anticommunism as an excuse to harass anyone unlike themselves. One such group was the Ku Klux Klan (KKK). Although it had been somewhat inactive since the 1870s, the Klan revived in 1915 and really strengthened in the early 1920s. This revived Klan was devoted to "100 percent Americanism." By 1924 it boasted a membership of 4.5 million "white male persons, native-born gentile citizens" who believed in keeping blacks "in their place," destroying saloons, opposing unions, and driving Roman Catholics, Jews, and foreign-born people out of the country. It also opposed union organizers and helped enforce prohibition.

The Klan's appeal did not rest on its ideas alone. Members dressed up in hooded robes and used an elaborate secret language and rituals. Then, too, Edward Clarke, of the sales organization known as the Southern Publicity Association, created an incentive program under which KKK salesmen, known as kleagles, kept four dollars of the ten-dollar initiation fee for each new Klan member they recruited. As one historian put it, "Kleagling became one of the profitable industries of the decade."

THINK THROUGH HISTORY
C. *Analyzing Issues* *What were the main goals of the Ku Klux Klan at this time?*

C. Answer To keep America under the control of white, native-born males; to get rid of other groups, including Roman Catholics, Jews, foreign-born people, and radicals; to oppose union organizers; to help enforce prohibition.

Klan members, as Grand Wizard Hiram Evans explained, were "plain people . . . the everyday, not highly cultured, not overly intellectualized, but entirely unspoiled . . . citizens of the old stock." In other words, they were people who felt threatened by changes occurring in American society. Klan members resented the small advances made by African Americans during World War I. They also felt that their moral values were being attacked by urban intellectuals, and they feared job competition from immigrants. They were convinced that foreigners were going to overthrow the American way of life.

Klan members vented some of their frustrations through racial violence. They also tried to influence national, state, and local politics. At times during the 1920s, the Klan dominated state politics in Arkansas, California, Indiana, Ohio, Oklahoma, Oregon, and Texas. Crimes committed by Klan leaders in Indiana resulted in a major decrease in the Klan's power nationwide by the end of the 1920s.

A Time of Labor Unrest

Another severe postwar conflict formed between labor and management. During the war, workers had not been allowed to strike, because the government would allow nothing to interfere with the war effort. However, 1919 saw more than 3,000 strikes, during which some 4 million workers walked off the job at one time or another.

Employers did not want to give their employees raises, nor did they want their employees to join unions. Some employers, either out of sincere belief or because they saw a way to keep wages down, attempted to show that union members were planning revolution. Newspaper headlines screamed "Crimes Against Society," "Conspiracies Against the Government," and "Plots to Establish Communism." Three strikes in particular grabbed public attention. (See *strike* on page 938 in the Economics Handbook.)

Women tailors formed picket lines during a strike for improved working conditions.

MORE ABOUT . . .
The Ku Klux Klan

The Ku Klux Klan was well-organized and replete with titles. Its leader was known as the Imperial Wizard. The chief organizer became the Imperial Kleagle. Local units were called Domains and were headed by Grand Goblins. Several Domains made up a Realm, which was led by a King Kleagle.

OBJECTIVE
(2) INSTRUCT

A Time of Labor Unrest

▶ ***Starting with the Student***
Have students create a chart like the one shown below to list the outcome of the three strikes discussed on pages 433–435.

Strike	Outcome
Boston police	
Steel mill	
Coal miners	

▶ ***Discussing Key Ideas***
- Conflict between labor and management erupts after the war.
- In 1919, workers go on more than 3,000 strikes, but fear of communism turns the public against the strikers.
- Labor union membership declines in the 1920s largely because of the movement's association with Communist ideals.

IN-DEPTH RESOURCES: UNIT 4
Primary Source: *from* Report on the Steel Strike of 1919, p. 9

TEACHING OPTIONS

Exploring Themes

Economic Opportunity Discuss the factors that fostered labor unrest after the war. Ask students why workers had not been allowed to strike during the war. *Possible Response: Because nothing was allowed to interfere with the war effort.* Why did so many strikes occur after the war? *Possible Response: Because wages had not kept pace with rising prices.* Ask students whether they think labor unions harmed or helped the workers' cause. Then ask them to evaluate the U.S. government's role during the 1919 strikes.

Teaching Less Proficient Readers

Cause and Effect Help students identify the causes and effects of labor unrest after the First World War. Have them read pages 433–435 and follow these steps:

1. Create a two-column chart on a piece of paper. Label one column *Causes,* label the other column *Effects.*
2. List the causes of labor unrest in the first column. Some causes include low wages and poor working conditions. List the effects of labor unrest in the second column.
3. In the next row, list causes and effects of the decline in union membership.

HISTORY FROM VISUALS

Union Activity, 1920–1929

Reading the Graph Point out that, although the bar format is the same for both graphs, the grids are different. One graph expresses numbers in thousands, the other in millions. Ask students why different numbering systems are used to count labor strikes and union membership. *Possible Response: Each year, millions of people belonged to unions. However, the number of strikes between 1920 and 1929 never numbered much more than 3,000.*

Extension Ask students to explain why union membership stabilized after 1923. *Possible Response: Few new unions were formed, but such unions as the Brotherhood of Sleeping Car Porters and the United Mine Workers of America were successful in improving the conditions of their workers.*

THE BOSTON POLICE STRIKE The police of Boston were angry. They had not had a raise since the beginning of World War I, and between then and 1919 the cost of living had doubled. The police sent representatives to the police commissioner to ask for what they considered a living wage. The commissioner promptly fired everyone in the group, and the remaining police responded by going out on strike. After Massachusetts governor **Calvin Coolidge** called out the National Guard to restore order, the police called off the strike.

The police commissioner, however, refused to allow the men to return to their jobs. Instead, he hired new men for his police force, who, ironically, received everything the strikers had asked for. Months later, the president of the American Federation of Labor (AFL), Samuel Gompers, appealed to Coolidge on behalf of the fired men. The governor replied, "There is no right to strike against the public safety by anyone, anywhere, any time." People praised Coolidge for saving Boston, if not the nation, from communism and anarchy. In the 1920 election he became Warren G. Harding's running mate.

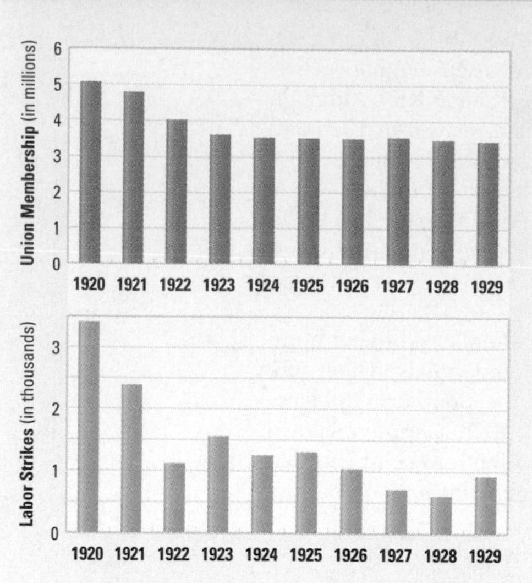

SKILLBUILDER
INTERPRETING GRAPHS
After sharp declines from 1920 to 1923, what was the trend in union membership during the rest of the 1920s? What factors do you think might explain the sharp drop in the number of strikes during the 1920s?

Skillbuilder Answer
Pattern: It remained fairly stable at around 3.5 million. **Drop:** *Possible Answers:* Increasing public disapproval of unions and strikes; reduced union membership; booming prosperity and rising wages during this period.

THINK THROUGH HISTORY
D. Summarizing *What was Governor Coolidge's position on the Boston police strike?*

D. Answer That the police had no right to strike against the public safety.

THE STEEL MILL STRIKE If the Boston police strike outraged the public, the strike that began at the U.S. Steel Corporation in September 1919 was even more upsetting. Working conditions in the steel industry were extremely difficult and dangerous. Many laborers worked seven 12-hour days a week in hot and noisy foundries. When the company refused to meet with union representatives, 350,000 workers walked off the job. They demanded the right, as organized workers, to bargain with their employer for shorter working hours and a living wage. One steel-strike leader, William Z. Foster, had worked in several industries before joining the IWW and becoming a militant labor organizer. At the time of the steel strike of 1919, Foster was a leader of the AFL. His participation in the strike caused management to claim that labor activities were led by radicals.

Steel companies hired strikebreakers and used force. U.S. Steel security police, state militias, and federal troops killed 18 workers and wounded or beat hundreds more. The companies also instituted a widespread propaganda campaign, seeking to link the strikers to Communists.

In October 1919, a vote on three collective-bargaining resolutions produced a deadlock. Then President Woodrow Wilson made a written plea to the combative conference members.

A PERSONAL VOICE

At a time when the nations of the world are endeavoring to find a way of avoiding international war, are we to confess that there is no method to be found for carrying on industry except in the spirit and with the very method of war? . . . Are our industrial leaders and our industrial workers to live together without faith in each other, constantly struggling for advantage over each other, doing naught but what is compelled?

WOODROW WILSON, quoted in *Labor in Crisis*

The president's plea did not resolve the issues, but the steel strike was finally broken in January 1920. The fact that AFL leader William Foster later joined the Communist Party did not help the image of labor unions.

At first the public was relieved that another threat by "un-American elements" had been turned back. Then, in 1923, a Protestant interfaith committee

TEACHING OPTIONS

Teaching Gifted and Talented Students

Arbitrating Strikes Have groups of interested students work together to settle one of the strikes described on pages 434 and 435. Students should:

- Select one of the strikes and do research to find out more about it.
- Divide the roles among group members. Half the students should represent the labor union. The other half should represent management.
- Make a list of goals and demands. Each side should state its position and be willing to compromise.

Making Connections Across Cultures

African Americans in the Labor Movement The Pullman Company was the largest private employer of black workers in the United States when A. Philip Randolph organized a labor union for sleeping car porters. As a result, many African-American leaders advised black workers to support management rather than the union. Randolph advocated what he called "manhood rights" for African Americans. He insisted that joining the union was a continuation of the fight against slavery. Randolph said: "[Frederick] Douglass fought for the abolition of chattel slavery, and today we fight for economic freedom."

published a report on the harsh working conditions in the steel mills. The report shocked the public, and the steel companies agreed to establish an eight-hour day. However, the steelworkers remained without a union.

THE COAL MINERS' STRIKE Unionism was more successful in America's coalfields. In 1919, the United Mine Workers, organized since 1890, got a new president—**John L. Lewis.** In protest of low wages and long workdays, Lewis called his union's members out on strike on November 1, 1919. Attorney General Palmer obtained a court order sending the miners back to work. Lewis then declared the strike over, but he quietly gave the word for the strike to continue.

In defiance of the court order, the mines stayed closed another month. Then President Wilson appointed an arbitrator, or judge, to decide the outstanding issues between the miners and the mine owners. In due course, the coal miners received a 27 percent wage increase, and John L. Lewis became a national figure. The miners, however, did not achieve a shorter workday and a five-day workweek until the 1930s.

KEY PLAYER

JOHN LLEWELLYN LEWIS
1880–1969

John L. Lewis was born in the little mining town of Lucas, Iowa. His family had traditionally been concerned with labor rights and benefits.

Lewis grew up with a fierce determination to fight for what he believed companies owed their employees: decent working conditions and a fair salary. As he said years later, "I have pleaded your case not in the tones of a feeble mendicant [beggar] asking alms but in the thundering voice of the captain of a mighty host, demanding the rights to which free men are entitled."

LABOR MOVEMENT LOSES APPEAL In spite of the gains by the coal miners, the 1920s hurt the labor movement badly. Membership in unions declined for several reasons: (1) much of the work force consisted of immigrants who were willing to work in poor conditions, (2) since immigrants spoke a multitude of languages, unions had difficulty trying to organize them, (3) farmers who had migrated to cities to find factory jobs were used to relying on themselves, and (4) most unions excluded African Americans. The thousands of African Americans who had migrated from the South to take factory jobs in the North were likely candidates for unionization, but only about 82,000 African Americans—or less than 1 percent of their total in the population—held union memberships by 1929. By contrast, just over 3 percent of all whites were union members.

E. Answer Immigrants and farmers were difficult to organize; most of the unions rejected African Americans.

THINK THROUGH HISTORY
E. THEME ***Economic Opportunity*** *Why did union membership drop in the twenties?*

The exceptions to this discrimination were provided by the mine workers', longshoremen's, and railroad porters' unions. An important step in organizing African Americans into unions occurred in 1925, when A. Philip Randolph founded the Brotherhood of Sleeping Car Porters to help African Americans gain a fair wage. During the decade, however, union membership dropped from more than 5 million to around 3.5 million, as shown by the graph on page 434.

During the twenties, many Americans changed their attitudes not only toward unions but also toward immigrants and America's role in the world.

Section 1 Assessment

1. TERMS & NAMES

Identify:
- communism
- A. Mitchell Palmer
- anarchist
- Sacco and Vanzetti
- Calvin Coolidge
- John L. Lewis

2. SEQUENCING Create a time line of the major events involving labor unions between 1917 and 1929, using a form like the one below.

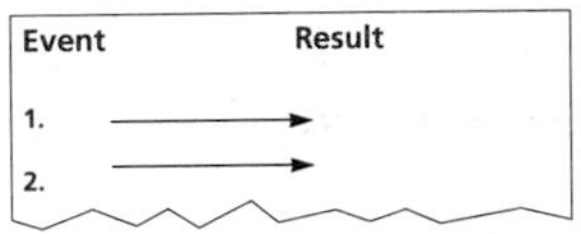

What event do you think was the most significant? Explain your choice.

3. FORMING OPINIONS Do you think Americans were justified in their fear of radicals and foreigners in the decade following World War I? Explain your answer.

THINK ABOUT
- the goals of the leaders of the Russian Revolution
- the impact of radicals in the United States
- the challenges facing the United States

4. ANALYZING What factors led union organizers to call so many strikes in 1919?

THINK ABOUT
- economic factors
- labor leaders' determination to fight for workers' rights

KEY PLAYER
John Llewellyn Lewis

Critical Thinking: Analyzing Character Ask students to discuss the elements in Lewis's background and the personality traits that helped him be a successful union leader in the 1920s.

ASSESS & RETEACH

Section 1 Assessment

Have small groups of students work together to answer and discuss the questions.

Self-Assessment

Have students make a list of three or four of the key people discussed in Section 1 and the roles they played in dealing with such postwar issues as the Red Scare and labor unrest.

Section Quiz

FORMAL ASSESSMENT
Section Quiz, p. 153

Reteach

Use the bar graphs on page 434 to review the origins and outcomes of labor unrest in postwar America.

CLOSE

After the end of the First World War, most Americans wanted to return to normalcy. However, fear of communism and labor unrest seemed to threaten this desired stability. As a result, attitudes toward immigrants and America's role in the world began to change.

ANSWERS

1. TERMS & NAMES

communism, p. 430
A. Mitchell Palmer, p. 431
anarchist, p. 431
Sacco and Vanzetti, p. 432
Calvin Coolidge, p. 434
John L. Lewis, p. 435

2. SEQUENCING

Possible Answers: Students may include the following events on their time lines:
1919 Boston police strike begins
1919 Steel strike begins under William Z. Foster
1919 Coal strike begins under John L. Lewis
1920 Steel strike broken
1925 A. Philip Randolph organizes the Brotherhood of Sleeping Car Porters

3. FORMING OPINIONS

Possible Responses: Students saying yes may argue that radicals and immigration threatened American traditions and that the Communists' desire to overthrow capitalism and abolish private property posed a threat to the American way of life. Those saying no may point out that radical movements in this country were small, membership in the Communist Party was minimal, and the country had enough room to absorb immigrants.

4. ANALYZING

Possible Responses: Students might point out that workers had not received wage increases since the beginning of World War I, that working conditions were difficult and dangerous in some industries, and that labor leaders were determined to secure better wages and shorter workdays for union members.

❷ "Normalcy" and Isolationism

LEARN ABOUT the policies of the Harding administration
TO UNDERSTAND the development of postwar isolationism and the immigration quota system.

TERMS & NAMES
- Warren G. Harding
- Kellogg-Briand Pact
- isolationist
- Fordney-McCumber Tariff
- quota system
- Charles Evans Hughes
- Ohio gang
- Albert B. Fall
- Teapot Dome scandal

ONE AMERICAN'S STORY

In the 1920s, when Ernesto Galarza was a little boy, his family came to California from Mexico to earn a better living. When they reached Sacramento, they went immediately to its barrio, the city neighborhood inhabited by Spanish-speaking people. There they looked for jobs and for an affordable place to live. In his old age, Galarza recalled his barrio experience.

A PERSONAL VOICE

Ours was a neighborhood of leftover houses. The cheapest rents were in the back quarters of the rooming houses, the basements, and the run-down clapboard rentals in the alley. . . . *Barrio* people, when they first came to town, had no furniture of their own. They rented it with their quarters or bought a piece at a time from the second-hand stores, the *segundas*, where we traded. . . . Beds and meals were provided [to newcomers] . . . on trust, until the new *Chicano* found a job. On trust and not on credit, for trust was something between people who had plenty of nothing, and credit was between people who had something of plenty.

ERNESTO GALARZA, quoted in *The Hispanic Americans*

Hispanic-American men gather in a park in California in the 1920s.

Galarza and his family were able to enter the United States only because they were from Mexico. Potential immigrants from outside the Western Hemisphere could not legally enter the country because of new restrictions on immigration. These restrictions reflected a new attitude that emerged after World War I. Seeking a return to the "normalcy" of prewar days, Americans wanted less government control over business and much less international involvement. "Keep America for Americans" became the prevailing attitude.

A Return to "Normalcy"

As the Republicans gathered in Chicago in the summer of 1920 to nominate their presidential candidate, they wanted to retake the White House. The American public seemed tired of the push for reform that had marked the progressive era—particularly the administration of President Woodrow Wilson.

None of the Republican candidates, however, could gather enough support to win the nomination. Finally the party leaders turned to Senator **Warren G. Harding** of Ohio. Although his judgment turned out to be poor, he was a good-natured man who, according to one of his followers, "looked like a president ought to look," and the public loved his soothing speeches.

A PERSONAL VOICE

America's present need is not heroics, but healing; not nostrums, but normalcy; not revolution, but restoration; not agitation, but adjustment; not surgery, but serenity; not the dramatic, but the dispassionate; . . . not submergence in internationality, but sustainment in triumphant nationality.

WARREN G. HARDING, quoted in *The Rise of Warren Gamaliel Harding*

At election time, Harding and his running mate, Calvin Coolidge, swamped their Democratic opponents, James M. Cox and Franklin D. Roosevelt, 16 mil-

Section 2 Overview

OBJECTIVES

1. To describe Harding's efforts to return the United States to normalcy after the progressive era reforms.
2. To summarize the immigration policy pursued by the United States in the 1920s.
3. To identify the scandals that plagued Harding's administration.

SKILLBUILDERS

- Interpreting graphs, p. 438
- Interpreting political cartoons, p. 440

CRITICAL THINKING

- Theme: America in the World, p. 437
- Summarizing, pp. 437, 440
- Developing historical perspective, p. 439
- Drawing conclusions, p. 439
- Making inferences, p. 440
- Forming generalizations, p. 440
- Evaluating, p. 440

FOCUS & MOTIVATE

5-MINUTE WARM-UP

Making Generalizations
To explore the experience of Mexican immigrants in the 1920s, have students read One American's Story on page 436 and answer these questions.

1. What challenges did most Mexican immigrants face when they came to the United States?
2. How did the inhabitants of the *barrios* treat newcomers?

WARM-UP TRANSPARENCY 12

▶ ***Starting with the Student***
Have students think about the period following a holiday or some other disruptive event.

- Are they glad to get back to a normal, everydav routine?
- Or do they prefer life to be unpredictable and unsettled?

SECTION 2 RESOURCES

PRINT RESOURCES

IN-DEPTH RESOURCES: UNIT 4
Guided Reading, p. 2
Skillbuilder Practice: Summarizing, p. 4
American Lives: Ernesto Galarza, p. 14

READING STUDY GUIDE, p. 131

ACCESS FOR STUDENTS ACQUIRING ENGLISH
Guided Reading (Spanish), p. 151
Skillbuilder Practice: Summarizing (Spanish), p. 153

SPANISH READING STUDY GUIDE, p. 131

FORMAL ASSESSMENT Section Quiz, p. 154

ALTERNATIVE ASSESSMENT BOOK
See forms for supporting and scoring alternative activities.

TECHNOLOGY RESOURCES

HUMANITIES TRANSPARENCIES
H39, Looking Backward

GEOGRAPHY TRANSPARENCIES
G20, European Emigration: 1820–1920

CRITICAL THINKING TRANSPARENCIES
CT20, Isolationist Policies of the 1920s

CD-ROM Electronic Library of Primary Sources

VIDEO *American Portfolio: A Videodisc for U.S. History* user's guide, pp. 193–194, 196

INTERNET http://www.mlushistory.com

lion votes to 9 million. The electoral count was even more of a landslide: 404 to 127. In his campaign speeches, Harding had promoted a "return to normalcy" on the domestic front. He wanted to return America to the simpler days before progressive reforms.

WORKING FOR PEACE In the aftermath of World War I, problems surfaced relating to war debts, arms control, and the reconstruction of war-torn countries. In 1921, President Harding invited four major naval powers and four smaller nations with interests in the Far East to a conference in Washington, D.C. Russia was conspicuously left out because of its Communist government. In his welcoming speech, the president appealed resoundingly for peace: "I can speak officially only for our United States. Our hundred millions frankly want less of armament and none of war."

Warren G. Harding looked respectably presidential—but he is considered by historians to have been one of the least successful presidents.

Then Secretary of State Charles Evans Hughes took the floor and urged that no more warships be built for ten years. In addition, he suggested that the five major naval powers—the United States, Great Britain, Japan, France, and Italy—scrap a significant proportion of their existing battleships, cruisers, and aircraft carriers. Conference delegates cheered, wept, threw their hats into the air—and adopted the proposal. It was the first time in history that such powerful nations had agreed to disarm.

THINK THROUGH HISTORY
A. THEME ***America in the World*** *Do you think the goal of the Kellogg-Briand Pact was unrealistic?*

A. Answer Possible response: It was unrealistic because the pact provided no means for enforcement.

Eventually, the United States succeeded in urging 64 nations, or almost all the nations then in existence, to sign the **Kellogg-Briand Pact,** which basically renounced war as an instrument of national policy. Americans were jubilant. However, there was no way to enforce the pact, because it made no provision for the use of military or economic force against any nation that violated the agreement.

HIGH TARIFFS AND REPARATIONS Behind the international glow of the Washington Naval Conference and the Kellogg-Briand Pact, the Harding administration was actually pursuing an **isolationist** foreign policy. Nevertheless, the United States was trying to head off trouble in Asia and to reduce the amount of money spent on armaments.

At the same time, it was not retreating from its stand on war debts. Britain and France had borrowed more than $10 billion from American bankers during World War I and now were having trouble repaying the loans while rebuilding their economies. They could raise the money in only two ways: by exporting more goods to the United States or by collecting the reparations that Germany owed to the Allies for war damages.

B. Answer Possible responses: Their economies had been weakened in the war; they were unable to raise money they needed to make payments because exports to the U.S. were sharply limited by high tariffs; Germany failed to pay them expected reparations.

THINK THROUGH HISTORY
B. *Summarizing* *What were the reasons European countries were not paying their war debts?*

Neither alternative worked. For one thing, in 1922 the United States adopted the **Fordney-McCumber Tariff,** which raised the tax on imports to its highest level ever—almost 60 percent. (See *tariff* on page 939 in the Economics Handbook.) The act was designed to protect American businesses, especially chemical and metal industries, from foreign competition. As a result of the high tariff, Britain and France were unable to sell their goods in the United States and could not earn the revenue to repay their debts.

The two nations then demanded that Germany pay its promised reparations, but the economically ruined Germans defaulted on (failed to make) their payments. At the end of 1922, French troops marched into Germany's industrial Ruhr Valley. To avoid a new war, the United States sent the American banker Charles G. Dawes, soon to be President Coolidge's vice-president, to negotiate loans to Germany from American investors. Through the Dawes Plan, U.S. banks loaned Germany $2.5 billion, which Germany was able to use to pay reparations to Britain and France. Those countries then turned around and made payments on their war debts to the United States. Thus, the United States, in effect, arranged to be repaid with its own money.

This solution caused bad feelings all around. Britain and France considered the United States a miser for not paying a fair share of the costs of World War I.

OBJECTIVE
① INSTRUCT

A Return to "Normalcy"

▶ ***Discussing Key Ideas***

- Harding vows to return the United States to the simpler days before the progressive era reforms.
- Most of the world's nations agree to disarm and sign the Kellogg-Briand Pact, but there is no way to enforce the pact.
- The Harding administration raises taxes on imports and demands that Britain and France pay their war debts.

IN-DEPTH RESOURCES: UNIT 4
Guided Reading, p. 2

ACCESS FOR STUDENTS ACQUIRING ENGLISH
Guided Reading (Spanish), p. 151

MORE ABOUT . . .
Warren G. Harding

Harding liked to deliver long speeches, but they were filled with grammatical mistakes. He also loved to use alliteration, the repetition of initial consonant sounds in two or more consecutive words. Writer H. L. Mencken believed Harding spoke the worst English he had ever heard: "It reminds me of a string of wet sponges; it reminds me of tattered washing on the line; it reminds me of stale bean soup, of college yells, of dogs barking idiotically through endless nights. It is so bad that a sort of grandeur creeps into it."

TEACHING OPTIONS

Exploring Themes

America in the World Discuss the Harding administration's decision to raise taxes on imports. Ask students why the government chose to do this. *To protect American business from foreign competition.* Then ask them what effect the raise had on Britain and France. *The countries were unable to sell their products in the United States and so were unable to repay their war debts.* Do students think the U.S. government's stand was fair? Should the government have assumed a greater share of the costs of World War I? Or was the government right to insist on repayment?

Making Connections Across the Curriculum

Economics Remind students that a tariff is a tax that one nation imposes on goods imported from another country. Many nations use tariffs to help protect their industries from foreign competition. Tariffs encourage domestic production of goods. They also make foreign goods more expensive. Many nations have commercial treaties that include a most-favored-nation clause. This clause requires the application of a nation's lowest tariff rate to all countries that sign the treaty. A country may also levy an even lower tariff to favor imports from less developed countries.

OBJECTIVE

② INSTRUCT

Limiting Immigration

▶ ***Discussing Key Ideas***

- Nativist attitudes arise because of economic competiton and racist ideas.
- Congress sets up a quota system limiting immigration.

CRITICAL THINKING TRANSPARENCIES
CT20, Isolationist Policies of the 1920s

ELECTRONIC LIBRARY OF PRIMARY SOURCES
from A Letter Regarding Immigration Restrictions by Louis Marshall

HISTORY FROM VISUALS

U.S. Patterns of Immigration, 1921 and 1929

Reading the Graph Point out the relationship between the colors of the bars and the colors of the countries on the maps below the bars. Then discuss the numbering system used in the graph.

Extension Ask students why they think the number of German immigrants increased between 1921 and 1929. *Possible Response: Many Germans wanted to leave their devastated country after the war.*

IN-DEPTH RESOURCES: UNIT 4
American Lives: Ernesto Galarza, p. 14

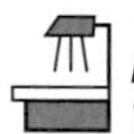

HUMANITIES TRANSPARENCIES
H39, Looking Backward

GEOGRAPHY TRANSPARENCIES
G20, European Emigration, 1820–1920

Their people had died while America had profited! At the same time, the United States considered the two nations financially irresponsible for being unwilling to repay their debts. As President Calvin Coolidge, who succeeded Harding, reportedly remarked, "They hired the money, didn't they?"

Limiting Immigration

Nativist, or anti-immigrant, attitudes had been growing in the United States ever since the 1880s, when new immigrants began arriving from southern and eastern Europe. Nativist feelings were fueled by the fact that some of the people involved in postwar labor disputes were immigrant anarchists and socialists, who many Americans believed were actually revolutionary radicals and Communists.

In addition, the demand for unskilled labor in the United States decreased after World War I, especially in industries such as coal mining and the production of steel and textiles. Immigrants had generally filled these jobs, and with fewer unskilled jobs available, nativists reasoned, fewer immigrants should be allowed into the United States. Also, racist ideas like those expressed by Madison Grant, an anthropologist at the American Museum of Natural History in New York City, had an influence on attitudes toward immigration.

Skillbuilder Answer Five **Groups:** Italy; Portugal, Spain, and Greece; Yugoslavia, Austria, Hungary, and Czechoslovakia; USSR and Baltic states; Great Britain. **Increase:** Germany and Mexico.

A PERSONAL VOICE

The result of unlimited immigration is showing plainly in the rapid decline in the birth rate of native Americans . . . [who] will not bring children into the world to compete in the labor market with the Slovak, the Italian, the Syrian and the Jew. The native American is too proud to mix socially with them.

MADISON GRANT, quoted in *United States History: Ideas in Conflict*

SKILLBUILDER

INTERPRETING GRAPHS

Which five geographical areas show the sharpest decline in immigrants coming to the U.S. between 1921 and 1929? What are the only areas to register an increase in immigrants to the U.S.?

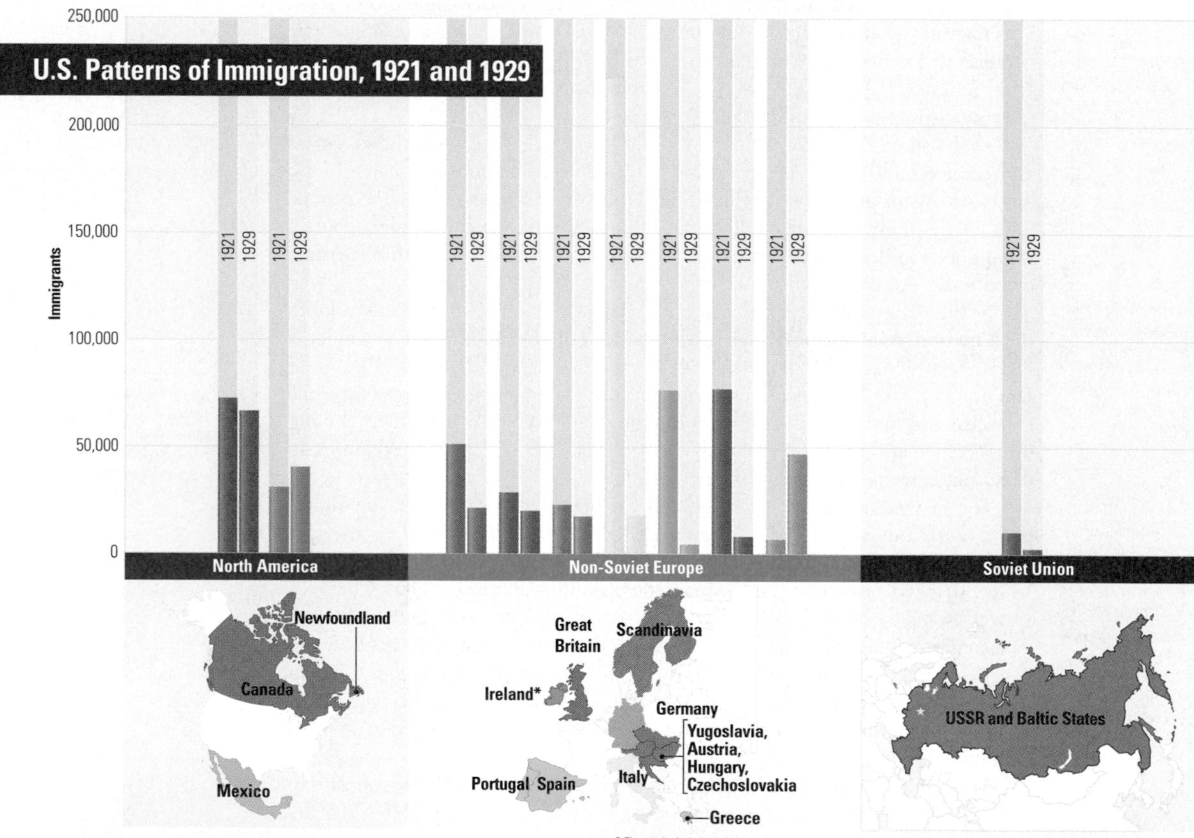

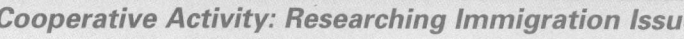

* Figures include both Northern Ireland and the Republic of Ireland. Source: *Historical Statistics of the United States*

Block Schedule — TEACHING OPTION — Time Needed: 30 Minutes

Cooperative Activity: Researching Immigration Issues

Task: Groups of four or five students will research and report on immigration issues in the 1920s or in the 1990s.

Purpose: To explore some of the controversies surrounding U.S. immigration.

Activity: Assign half the groups to research immigration issues in the 1920s. Have the other half research issues in the 1990s. Each student in a group should study immigration from one country and research such issues as the causes and effects of immigration and the immigrants' experience with housing and employment. Group members should compile their findings into one report that can be shared with the rest of the class.

Building a Portfolio: Students who add their reports to their portfolios should attach a note identifying their contribution to the project.

ALTERNATIVE ASSESSMENT BOOK
Standards for Evaluating a Cooperative Activity

Standards for Evaluation
Reports should . . .

- discuss the causes and effects of the immigration
- describe the immigrants' experiences
- use specific details to support ideas
- include photos to enhance information

THE QUOTA SYSTEM In 1919, the number of immigrants was a modest 141,000, but by 1921 the number had shot up to 805,000. Congress, in response to nativist pressure, decided that the time had come to limit immigration from Europe. The Emergency Quota Act of 1921 set up a **quota system.** This system established the maximum number of people who could enter the United States from each foreign country. As amended in 1924, the law limited immigration from each European nation to 2 percent of the number of its nationals living in the United States in 1890. This provision discriminated against people from eastern and southern Europe—mostly Roman Catholics and Jews—who had not started coming in large numbers until after 1890. Later, the National Origins Act of 1929 shifted the base year to 1920, but it reduced the total number of persons to be admitted in any one year to 150,000.

C. Answer The number of immigrants increased sharply, and many Americans did not want people from foreign countries entering the nation, since some of them were anarchists and socialists and some were believed to be Communists.

In addition, the law excluded Japanese altogether, causing much ill will between the two nations. Japan—which had faithfully kept the Gentlemen's Agreement to limit emigration to the United States, negotiated by Theodore Roosevelt in 1907—expressed anger over the insult.

THINK THROUGH HISTORY
C. Developing Historical Perspective *Why did Congress make changes in immigration laws during the 1920s?*

The national-origins quota system did not apply to immigrants from the Western Hemisphere. During the 1920s, about a million Canadians and at least 500,000 Mexicans crossed the nation's borders.

The goal of the quota system was to sharply cut European immigration to the United States. As the chart on page 438 shows, the system achieved that goal.

HISTORICAL SPOTLIGHT

JAPANESE IMMIGRATION

The pattern of Japanese immigration differed from that of other countries, like China, in that it included more women. In 1908, Japan entered into the Gentlemen's Agreement to limit the number of Japanese migrating to the United States. However, although this agreement prohibited Japanese "laborers" from entering the United States, it permitted Japanese women to enter as family members. Women were therefore able to come in greater numbers than they would have as workers.

Women tended to be open to the idea of immigration. In Japan, education for girls was promoted, and the curriculum included learning about other countries. English was taught in middle school. Some women came as "picture brides" in a long-distance version of the traditional arranged marriage. By 1920, 46 percent of the Japanese population in Hawaii and 35 percent in California consisted of women.

Scandal Hits Harding's Administration

Harding opposed government interference in business affairs, and he disapproved of most social reforms. However, he did set up the Bureau of the Budget to help run the government more efficiently, and he urged U.S. Steel to abandon the 12-hour day. He also made some excellent cabinet appointments.

HARDING'S CABINET Harding appointed **Charles Evans Hughes** as secretary of state. Hughes later went on to become chief justice of the Supreme Court. The president made Herbert Hoover the secretary of commerce. Hoover had done a masterful job handling food distribution and refugee problems during World War I. Andrew Mellon, one of the country's wealthiest men, became secretary of the treasury and set about reducing the national debt. By 1923 the national debt had fallen by about one-third.

THINK THROUGH HISTORY
D. Drawing Conclusions *What do Harding's appointments indicate about his judgment?*

D. Answer That although he made some good appointments, his appointment of cronies from his home state showed poor judgment.

However, the cabinet also included the so-called **Ohio gang,** the president's rowdy, poker-playing cronies from back home. Attorney General Harry M. Daugherty, a lobbyist for tobacco and meatpacking companies, and Interior Secretary **Albert B. Fall,** a close friend of various oil executives, would soon cause Harding—and the country—a great deal of embarrassment.

SCANDALS PLAGUE HARDING The president's main problem was that he didn't understand many things he had to deal with. He admitted as much to a secretary after listening to advisers discuss a federal money problem.

A PERSONAL VOICE

John, I can't make a . . . thing out of this tax problem. I listen to one side and they seem right, and then . . . I talk to the other side and they seem just as right. I know somewhere there is an economist who knows the truth, but I don't know where to find him and haven't the sense to know him and trust him when I find him. . . . What a job!

WARREN G. HARDING, quoted in *Only Yesterday*

HISTORICAL SPOTLIGHT

Japanese Immigration

Critical Thinking: Evaluating Decisions Ask students why they think so many Japanese women were willing to come to the United States in the early 1900s. *Possible Response: The United States might have been represented to women as a land of opportunity.*

Issues for the 21st Century

The Debate over Immigration

Connect immigration in the 1920s to immigraton today. Have students read pages 880–883. Then have them answer these questions.

1. Why have immigrants been drawn to the United States? *Economic opportunity, religious freedom, and political asylum.*
2. Compare the arguments against immigration in the 1920s with those used today. *Similar: lack of jobs. Different: 1920s—fear of anarchists; Today—amount of government support needed.*

OBJECTIVE
(3) INSTRUCT

Scandal Hits Harding's Administration

▶ ***Discussing Key Ideas***
- Members of Harding's cabinet use their offices to become wealthy.
- Harding's administration is plagued by scandals.
- Harding avoids disgrace but dies in office.

TEACHING OPTION

Skillbuilder Mini-Lesson: Summarizing

Explaining the Skill Restating an idea or a written passage in one's own words can help to clarify the meaning of the material. To summarize means to restate and condense a passage by stating only the main ideas using words that are different from those in the original version. A summary that uses the same words as the original source without giving credit to that source would be seen as plagiarism.

Applying the Skill: Immigration Quotas Have students read about the Emergency Quota Act on this page and identify the main points as if they were preparing to write a summary of the passage. These points include the following:

1. The act limited the number of immigrants allowed from each foreign country except Western Hemisphere nations.
2. The goal was to cut European immigration to the U.S.
3. The provisions discriminated especially against Roman Catholics and Jews.
4. The act outlawed Japanese immigration entirely, angering Japan.

IN-DEPTH RESOURCES: UNIT 4
Skillbuilder Practice: Summarizing, p. 4

HISTORY FROM VISUALS

Political Cartoon

Reading the Cartoon Ask students how the cartoonist places blame for the scandal on the Republicans without actually naming them. *By drawing the elephant in the shape of a teapot; by labeling the teapot GOP.*

Extension Have students draw a cartoon representing Harding's reaction to the Teapot Dome scandal.

ELECTRONIC LIBRARY OF PRIMARY SOURCES

Senate Demands Information on Teapot Dome

ASSESS & RETEACH

Section 2 Assessment

Have students answer the questions individually. Then ask them to share the evaluations they wrote for item 2 with the class.

Self-Assessment

Have students make a time line of events in Harding's administration.

Section Quiz

FORMAL ASSESSMENT
Section Quiz, p. 154

Reteach

Review the graphs on page 438 to initiate a discussion of U.S. policy on immigration during the 1920s.

CLOSE

Harding promised the American people a return to normalcy. To that end, his administration pursued an isolationist foreign policy and created an immigration quota system. Although scandals plagued Harding's administration, Coolidge restored people's faith in government with his pro-business spirit.

As a result of Harding's inadequacies, his administration began to unravel. He had the same problem Grant had had nearly 50 years before: his corrupt friends used their offices to become wealthy through graft.

Charles R. Forbes, the head of the Veterans Bureau, allowed operators of veterans' hospitals to overcharge the government by some $250 million. In exchange for bribes, the head of the Office of Alien Property, Colonel Thomas W. Miller, took German chemical patents the government had seized during the war and sold them for far less than their worth.

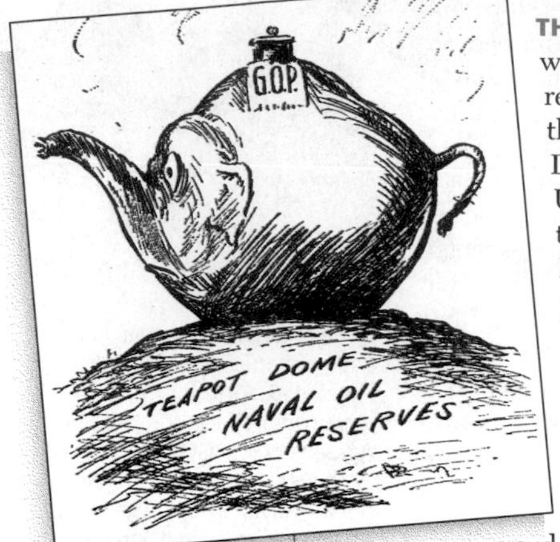

SKILLBUILDER
INTERPRETING POLITICAL CARTOONS
The elephant is the symbol of the Republican Party (Grand Old Party). Why is the elephant shaped like a teapot? What point was the cartoonist making?

Skillbuilder Answer The elephant is shaped like a teapot because of the Teapot Dome scandal. The cartoonist was making the point that the Republicans are responsible for the scandal.

THE TEAPOT DOME SCANDAL The most spectacular wrongdoing, however, was the **Teapot Dome scandal.** As a result of the conservation movement of the progressive era, the government had set aside oil-rich public lands at Teapot Dome, Wyoming, and Elk Hills, California, for use by the U.S. Navy. Secretary of the Interior Albert B. Fall managed to get the oil reserves transferred from the navy to the Interior Department, since it seemed sensible to place all public reserves under the control of the same department.

Once the transfer was completed, however, Fall secretly leased the land to two private oil companies: Harry Sinclair's Mammoth Oil Company at Teapot Dome and Edward L. Doheny's Pan-American Petroleum and Transport Company at Elk Hills. Although Fall claimed that these contracts were in the government's interest, he suddenly became the owner of $325,000 in bonds and cash, as well as several ranches and some prize livestock.

By the summer of 1923, Harding realized corruption existed in his administration, but he himself managed to avoid public disgrace and humiliation. A hurt and confused man, he declared, "I have no trouble with my enemies. . . . But my damned friends . . . they're the ones that keep me walking the floor nights!" At that point he left on a goodwill tour to Alaska. Returning from Alaska to San Francisco, he became ill; and he died on August 2, 1923, probably from a heart attack or the bursting of a blood vessel in his brain.

The American people sincerely mourned their good-natured president. Vice-President Calvin Coolidge became president upon Harding's death. The crimes of the Harding administration were coming to light just as Coolidge, a respected man of integrity, helped to restore people's faith in their government and in the Republican Party. He was elected president in 1924.

E. Answer The government lost revenue when veterans' hospitals overcharged it and patents were sold for less than their worth; in the Teapot Dome scandal, public oil reserves were leased for private gain.

THINK THROUGH HISTORY
E. *Making Inferences* *How did the scandals of the Harding administration hurt the country economically?*

Section 2 Assessment

1. TERMS & NAMES
Identify:
- Warren G. Harding
- Kellogg-Briand Pact
- isolationist
- Fordney-McCumber Tariff
- quota system
- Charles Evans Hughes
- Ohio gang
- Albert B. Fall
- Teapot Dome scandal

2. SUMMARIZING List and evaluate five significant events from this section, using a table like the one shown. In the "Evaluation" column, enter + if an event benefited the country, 0 if it had a mixed impact, or – if it harmed the country. Share your evaluations with the class.

Event	Evaluation
1.	
2.	

Which event do you think benefited the country the most? Why do you think so?

3. FORMING GENERALIZATIONS How do you think the Harding administration viewed the role of America in world affairs? Support your response with examples from the text.

THINK ABOUT
- policies on trade and tariffs
- efforts to enforce peace
- attitudes toward immigrants

4. EVALUATING How successful was Harding in fulfilling his campaign pledge of returning the country to "normalcy"? Support your opinion with specific examples.

THINK ABOUT
- events in foreign relations
- changes in immigration laws
- scandals during Harding's administration

ANSWERS

1. TERMS & NAMES

Warren G. Harding, p. 436
Kellogg-Briand Pact, 437
isolationist, p. 437
Fordney-McCumber Tariff, p. 437
quota system, p. 439
Charles Evans Hughes, p. 439
Ohio gang, p. 439
Albert B. Fall, p. 439
Teapot Dome scandal, p. 440

2. SUMMARIZING

Possible Answers: Tables might include:
election of Harding
naval disarmament agreement
Kellogg-Briand Pact signed
Fordney-McCumber Tariff passed
Dawes Plan implemented
increase in immigration in 1921
immigration quotas created
Teapot Dome scandal uncovered

3. FORMING GENERALIZATIONS

Possible Responses: Some students may think that the Harding administration wanted limited global involvement. The refusal to enforce international agreements, the passage of high tariffs, and the implementation of immigration restrictions could be considered isolationist. Other students may think the administration viewed itself as a peacemaker, urging international disarmament.

4. EVALUATING

Possible Responses: Some students may say that high tariffs, immigration restrictions, and government corruption created an atmosphere of distrust that was hardly normal. Others may cite the Kellogg-Briand Pact as a somewhat successful attempt by the administration to promote postwar "normalcy."

❸ The Business of America

TERMS & NAMES
- urban sprawl
- installment plan

LEARN ABOUT the impact of automobiles, electric power, advertising, and installment buying on the American consumer
TO UNDERSTAND how consumer goods became the foundation of the business boom of the 1920s.

ONE AMERICAN'S STORY

In 1927, the last Model T Ford—number 15,077,033—rolled off the assembly line. On December 2, some 1 million New Yorkers mobbed show rooms to view the new Model A. A striking difference between the two models was that customers could order the Model A in such colors as "Arabian sand" and "Niagara blue," the old Model T had come only in black. A Ford spokesman explained some additional advantages of the new automobile.

A PERSONAL VOICE
Good-looking as that car is, its performance is better than its appearance. We don't brag about it, but it has done seventy-one miles an hour. It will ride along a railroad track without bouncing, and you can drive across the rails, if you can find a place to do it, without pitching. It's the smoothest thing you ever rode in.
A FORD SALESMAN, quoted in *Flappers, Bootleggers, and "Typhoid Mary"*

The automobile became the backbone of the American economy in the 1920s (and remained such until the 1970s). The automobile profoundly altered the American landscape and American society, but it was only one of several factors in the country's business boom of the 1920s.

The Model A was a more luxurious car than the Model T. It was introduced at $495, whereas the Model T had cost $290.

America's Standard of Living Soars

The new president, Calvin Coolidge, fit into the probusiness spirit of the 1920s very well. It was he who said, "The chief business of America is business. . . . The man who builds a factory builds a temple—the man who works there worships there." Both Coolidge and his Republican successor, Herbert Hoover, favored government policies that would keep taxes down and business profits up. Their goal was to keep government interference in business to a minimum and to allow private enterprise to flourish. For most of the 1920s, the approach seemed to work, as the years from 1920 to 1929 were prosperous ones for the United States. Americans owned around 40 percent of the world's wealth, and that wealth changed the way most Americans lived, worked, and consumed.

Skillbuilder Answer The sharp rise of automobile ownership in the 1920s indicates a strong economy; the leveling off of automobile ownership in the 1930s indicates a weakening economy.

THE IMPACT OF THE AUTOMOBILE The automobile literally changed the American landscape. Its most visible effect was the construction of paved roads suitable for driving in all weather. Architectural styles changed, as new houses typically came equipped with a garage or carport and a driveway—and a smaller lawn as a result. The

Automobile Registrations, 1900–1990

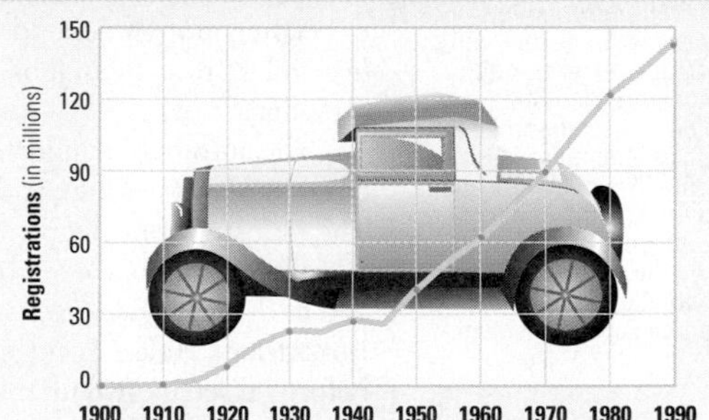

Source: *Historical Statistics of the United States; Statistical Abstract of the United States, 1975, 1994, 1995;* The American Automobile Association.

SKILLBUILDER **INTERPRETING GRAPHS** *Car ownership often reflects the strength of the economy. How strong do you think the economy was during the 1920s? the 1930s?*

SECTION 3 RESOURCES

PRINT RESOURCES

IN-DEPTH RESOURCES: UNIT 4
Guided Reading, p. 3
Geography Application: The Automobile Industry, p. 5
Primary Source: Advertisement, p. 10
American Lives: Henry Ford, p. 15

READING STUDY GUIDE, p. 133

ACCESS FOR STUDENTS ACQUIRING ENGLISH
Guided Reading (Spanish), p. 152
Geography Application: The Automobile Industry (Spanish), pp. 154–155

SPANISH READING STUDY GUIDE, p. 133

FORMAL ASSESSMENT
Section Quiz, p. 155

ALTERNATIVE ASSESSMENT BOOK
See forms for supporting and scoring alternative activities.

TECHNOLOGY RESOURCES

CRITICAL THINKING TRANSPARENCIES
CT54, Consumer Spending Power

CD-ROM *Our Times*
Electronic Library of Primary Sources
Grolier Multimedia Encyclopedia

VIDEO *American Portfolio: A Videodisc for U.S. History* user's guide, pp. 193, 198–199

INTERNET http://www.mlushistory.com

Section 3 Overview

OBJECTIVES

1. To summarize the impact of the automobile and other consumer goods on the lifestyle of Americans.
2. To explain in what ways the country's prosperity was superficial.

SKILLBUILDERS

- Interpreting graphs, p. 441
- Understanding geography, place, p. 442
- Interpreting political cartoons, p. 444

CRITICAL THINKING

- Theme: Science and Technology, p. 442
- Recognizing effects, p. 443
- Analyzing issues, p. 445
- Summarizing, p. 445
- Interpreting, p. 445
- Drawing conclusions, p. 445

FOCUS & MOTIVATE

5-MINUTE WARM-UP

Recognizing Facts and Details
To understand the relationship between government and big business in the 1920s, have students look at the political cartoon on page 444 and answer these questions.

1. Who represents big business in the cartoon?
2. What details suggest that the federal government is less powerful than big business?

WARM-UP TRANSPARENCY 12

▶ ***Starting with the Student***
- What products help students save time? What products encourage them to waste time?

OBJECTIVE
① **INSTRUCT**

America's Standard of Living Soars

▶ ***Discussing Key Ideas***
- The automobile changes American life.

(continued on next page)

(continued from page 441)

- The airplane industry takes off.
- Electricity and electrical conveniences become more widespread.
- Business relies on advertising to sell products.

IN-DEPTH RESOURCES: UNIT 4
Guided Reading, p. 3
Geography Application: The Automobile Industry, p. 5

ACCESS FOR STUDENTS ACQUIRING ENGLISH
Guided Reading (Spanish), p. 152

HISTORY FROM VISUALS

Automobile Registrations, 1900–1990

Reading the Graph Point out that car registrations in the graph on page 441 are numbered in millions. Then ask students how many cars were registered in the United States in 1980. *About 120 million.*

Extension Discuss why automobile registration began to soar in the 1950s.

HISTORY FROM VISUALS

Route 66

Reading the Map Have students trace Route 66 with their pencil erasers, paying attention to the plains and mountains along the way. Then have students use the map to determine where the town of Claremore is located. *In Oklahoma.*

Extension Ask students to discuss how Route 66 and other highways affected the American landscape.

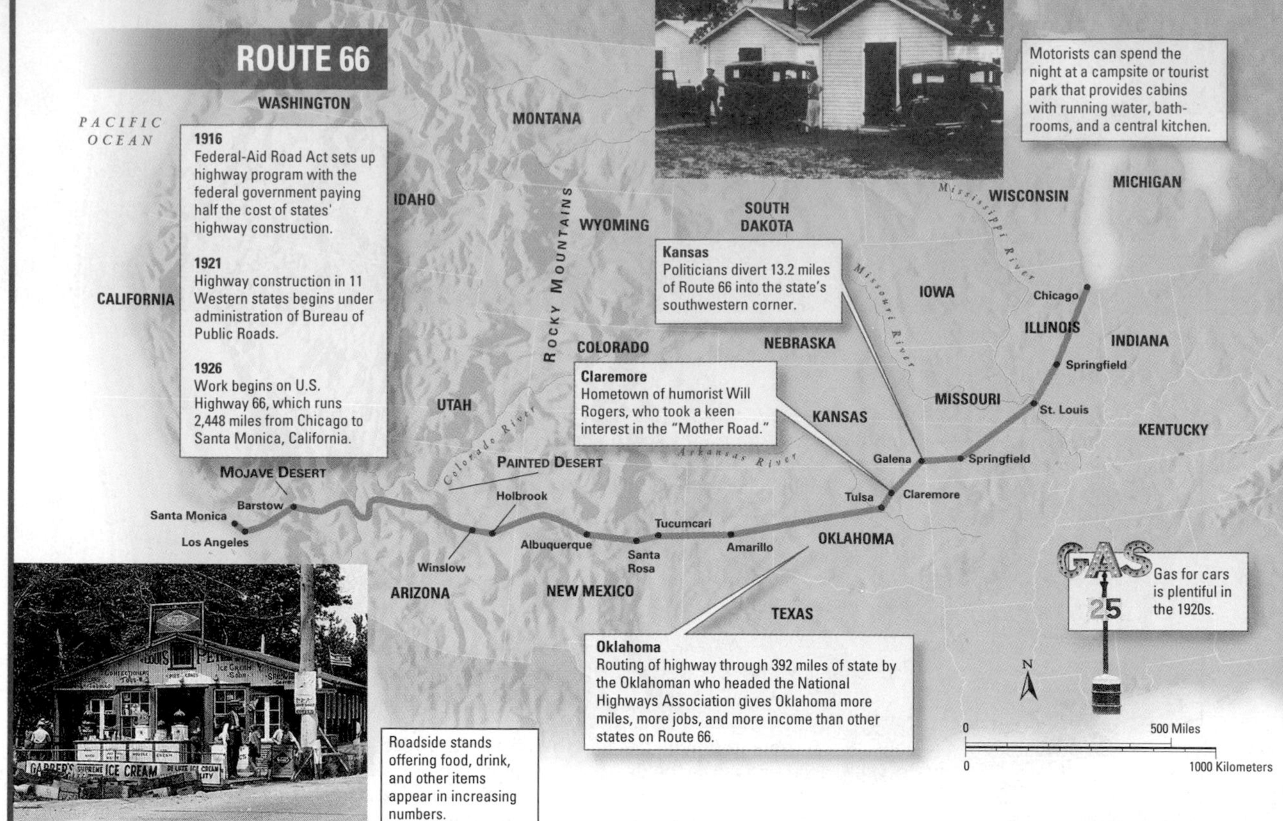

GEOGRAPHY SKILLBUILDER
PLACE ***What do you think were some of the reasons government officials decided to build Route 66 through the Southwest rather than straight west from Chicago?***

Skillbuilder Answer
Possible Answers: With a Southwestern route, engineers did not have to build a road across the Rocky Mountains. Also, Route 66 would help open up the sparsely populated Southwest to the rest of the country and thus spur population growth and economic development.

automobile also launched the rapid construction of gasoline stations, repair shops, public garages, motels, tourist camps, and shopping centers. The first automatic traffic signals began blinking in Detroit in the early 1920s. The Holland Tunnel, the first underwater tunnel designed specifically for motor vehicles, opened in 1927 to connect New York City and Jersey City, New Jersey. The Woodbridge Cloverleaf, the first cloverleaf intersection, sprouted in New Jersey in 1928.

The automobile liberated the isolated rural family, who could now travel to the city for shopping and entertainment, and it gave families the opportunity to vacation in new and faraway places. It allowed both women and young people to become more independent through increased mobility. It allowed workers to live miles from their jobs, resulting in **urban sprawl** as cities spread in all directions.

The automobile industry also provided an economic underpinning for such cities as Akron in Ohio, and Detroit, Dearborn, Flint, and Pontiac in Michigan. The industry drew people to such oil-producing states as California and Texas.

The automobile even became a status symbol—both for individual families and to the world at large. In their 1920's work *Middletown,* the social scientists Robert and Helen Lynd noted one woman's comment: "I'll go without food before I'll see us give up the car." Another woman said, "We don't have no fancy clothes when we have the car to pay for."

The auto industry symbolized the success of the free enterprise system. Nowhere else in the world could people with little money own their own transportation and go wherever they wanted. By the late 1920s, around 80 percent of all registered motor vehicles in the world were in the United States—about one automobile for every five people. The comedian Will Rogers remarked to

A. Answer Roads were paved, and shopping centers and other services for cars were built; people commuted to work, and urban sprawl developed; regional differences diminished.

THINK THROUGH HISTORY
A. THEME ***Science and Technology*** *How did the widespread use of the automobile affect the environment and the lives of Americans?*

Block Schedule TEACHING OPTION **Time Needed: 30 Minutes**

Cooperative Activity: Creating a 1920s Automobile Newsletter

Task: Groups of four to five students will create a newsletter containing information about automobiles in the 1920s.

Purpose: To help students understand the impact of the automobile on the United States in the 1920s.

Activity: Students should decide what topics to cover in their newsletter. Topics might include highways, safety concerns, lifestyle changes, and new businesses. Groups should research and write brief essays on each topic. Encourage students to include ads and pictures to add interest to the selections. Have groups print their newsletters and share them with the class.

Building a Portfolio: Students may wish to print their favorite newsletter selections and add them to their portfolios.

ALTERNATIVE ASSESSMENT BOOK
Standards for Evaluating a Cooperative Activity

Standards for Evaluation
Newsletters should . . .

- contain well-researched information on a variety of topics
- include visuals that convey the excitement inspired by the automobile
- be clear, well organized, and engaging

Henry Ford, "It will take a hundred years to tell us whether you have helped us or hurt us, but you certainly didn't leave us like you found us."

THE YOUNG AIRPLANE INDUSTRY At the same time, the airplane industry began its growth by carrying mail for the government. Although the first such flight in 1918 was a disaster, soon afterward a number of successful flights established the airplane as a useful peacetime means of transportation. With the development of weather forecasting, planes began carrying radios and navigational instruments. Henry Ford made a trimotor airplane in 1926. In 1927, the Lockheed Company produced a single-engine plane, the Vega. The Ford plane could carry ten passengers, and the Vega could carry six. They were two of the most popular transport airplanes of the late 1920s.

Flight attendants train for an early United Airlines flight. When commercial airline flights began, all flight attendants were female and white.

ELECTRICAL CONVENIENCES Gasoline powered much of the economic boom of the 1920s, but electricity also turned on the nation. American factories used electricity to run their machines. Also, the development of an alternating electrical current made it possible to distribute electric power by means of a transformer. Now electricity was no longer restricted to central cities but could be transmitted to outlying suburbs. The number of electrified households grew, although most farms still lacked power. Americans used all sorts of electrical appliances. Eunice Fuller Barnard listed some of them in a magazine article she wrote in 1928.

Goods and Prices in 1928		Goods and Prices in 1900	
1 radio	$75		
1 phonograph	50		
1 washing machine	150	wringer and washboard	$5
1 vacuum cleaner	50	brushes and brooms	5
1 sewing machine (electric)	60	sewing machine (mechanical)	25
other electrical equipment	25		
	$410		$35

B. Answer It encouraged consumers to consider many more items necessities rather than luxuries.

THINK THROUGH HISTORY
B. Recognizing Effects *How did the use of electricity affect Americans' lifestyle?*

By the end of the 1920s, more and more homes had electric irons, while well-to-do families used electric refrigerators, electric cooking ranges, and toasters. These electrical appliances made the lives of housewives easier, freed them for other community and leisure activities, and coincided with an increase in the number of women working outside the home.

The prevalence of electrical appliances, store-bought clothes and foods, and mass cultural activities (such as miniature golf, marathon dancing, moviegoing, sports, and newspapers) resulted in a lifestyle that seemed conformist. In Sinclair Lewis's famous 1922 novel *Babbitt,* the title character describes Zenith, his fictional hometown in a way that satirizes this conformity.

> I tell you, Zenith and her sister-cities are producing a new type of civilization. There are many resemblances between Zenith and these other burgs [cities], and I'm darn glad of it! The extraordinary, growing, and sane standardization of stores, offices, streets, hotels, clothes, and newspapers throughout the United States shows how strong and enduring a type is ours.
>
> SINCLAIR LEWIS, *Babbitt*

"I look forward to the day when transatlantic flying will be a regular thing."

CHARLES A. LINDBERGH

MORE ABOUT . . .
Charles Lindbergh

"Lucky Lindy" made the first solo nonstop flight across the Atlantic Ocean in 1927. After his historic flight, Americans and Europeans adored the shy, slim young Lindbergh and showered him with honors. His life was not always so happy, however. In 1932, Lindbergh's 20-month-old son was kidnapped and eventually murdered. The long, difficult trial that followed the arrest of the alleged kidnapper became known as the "trial of the century." During World War II, Lindbergh was criticized for his isolationist beliefs. After the war, he avoided publicity until the 1960s, when he began to support conservation efforts.

GROLIER MULTIMEDIA ENCYCLOPEDIA
History of aviation

MORE ABOUT . . .
Will Rogers

Will Rogers was a popular American humorist of the 1920s and 1930s. He began his career as a cowboy and gained international fame as an author, lecturer, and star of motion pictures and radio. Known as the "Cowboy Philosopher," Rogers poked fun at the political and social figures of his day. He died in a plane crash in 1935. A memorial to Rogers in his Oklahoma hometown bears the statement for which he is most remembered: "I never met a man I didn't like."

TEACHING OPTIONS

Exploring Themes

Science and Technology Discuss Will Rogers's remark to Henry Ford: "It will take a hundred years to tell us whether you have helped us or hurt us, but you certainly didn't leave us like you found us." Ask students how the automobile has improved life. *Possible Responses: Given people more freedom; made travel easier and faster.* Then ask them what harm, if any, has been caused by the invention. *Possible Responses: Resulted in a high rate of deaths and injuries from car accidents; causes pollution.*

IN-DEPTH RESOURCES: UNIT 4
American Lives: Henry Ford, p. 15

Making Connections Across the Curriculum

Literature Tell students that both *Main Street* and *Babbitt* by Sinclair Lewis focus on the limitations of American culture. In *Main Street,* Lewis satirizes the smug self-satisfaction of a small American town. In *Babbitt,* he focuses on the efforts of the central character to break free from the restrictions of middle-class life. Ask students what writers today criticize the limitations and values of American society.

ELECTRONIC LIBRARY OF PRIMARY SOURCES
from *Middletown* by Robert S. and Helen Merrell Lynd

ANOTHER PERSPECTIVE
The Needy

Critical Thinking: Making Predictions Discuss the quotation: "Depressions are farm led and farm fed." What do students predict might happen by the end of the 1920s? *There will be a depression.*

HISTORY FROM VISUALS
Political Cartoon

Reading the Cartoon Tell students that big business is dressed like a flapper, a young woman of the 1920s who flaunted convention. She is dancing the Charleston, a dance that epitomized the wild abandon of the period.

Extension Ask students to discuss how big business and Coolidge are represented in the cartoon.

OBJECTIVE
(2) INSTRUCT

A Superficial Prosperity

▶ ***Starting with the Student*** Have students use a word web like the one below to list the effects of buying on the installment plan.

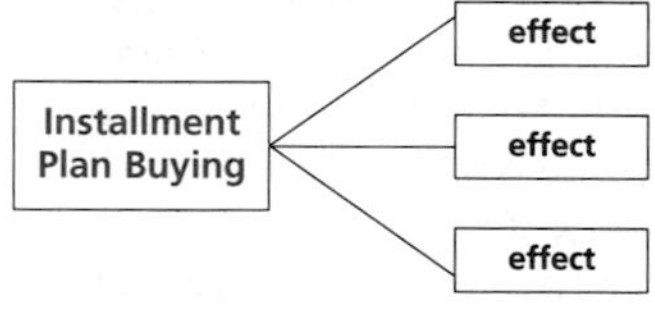

▶ ***Discussing Key Ideas***

- Although many businesses expand during the 1920s, others suffer losses.
- The installment plan lures many American consumers into buying more goods than they can afford.

ANOTHER PERSPECTIVE

THE NEEDY

While income rose for many Americans in the 1920s, it did not rise for everyone. Industries such as textile and steel manufacturing made very little profit. Mining and farming actually suffered losses. Farmers were deeply in debt because they had borrowed heavily to buy land and machinery so that they could produce more crops during World War I. When European agriculture bounced back after the war, prices fell, and before long there were U.S. farm surpluses.

Many American farmers suffered because they could not make their loan and mortgage payments. As one South Dakota farmer, Emil Loriks, remarked, "Farm prices collapsed. . . . There's a saying: 'Depressions are farm led and farm fed.'" Many farmers lost their purchasing power, their equipment, and their farms.

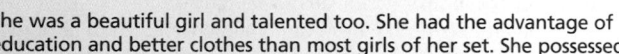

THE DAWN OF MODERN ADVERTISING With new goods flooding the market, business relied increasingly on advertising to sell the products. Advertising people no longer limited themselves to informing the public about products and prices. Instead, they hired psychologists to study how to appeal to buyers. What colors were best for what size packages? What was the most effective way to take advantage of people's worship of youth, beauty, health, and wealth?

Results were impressive. The slogan "Say it with flowers" doubled florists' business between 1912 and 1924. "Reach for a Lucky instead of a sweet" lured weight-conscious Americans to cigarettes and away from candy. Some variation of "Even your best friend won't tell you" helped sell a great deal of mouthwash, deodorants, dandruff shampoos, and cures for athlete's foot. Brand names became familiar from coast to coast, and items that people had formerly considered luxuries now seemed necessities.

American consumers in the 1920s could purchase the latest household electrical appliances, such as a refrigerator, for as little as a dollar down and a dollar a week.

One of those necessities was Listerine mouthwash. A 1923 Listerine advertisement made it seem so. The ad aimed to convince readers that without Listerine a person ran the risk of having halitosis—bad breath. The results could be a disaster—as the advertisement clearly stated, while revealing the 1920s attitude toward women.

> She was a beautiful girl and talented too. She had the advantage of education and better clothes than most girls of her set. She possessed that culture and poise that travel brings. Yet in the one pursuit that stands foremost in the mind of every girl and woman—marriage—she was a failure.
>
> LISTERINE ADVERTISEMENT

Businesspeople extended the advertising mentality into other areas of American life. Every week, in cities and towns across the land, they met for lunch with fellow members of such service organizations as Rotary, Kiwanis, and the Lions. As one observer noted, they sang songs, raised money for various charities, and boosted the image of the businessman "as a builder, a doer of great things, yes, and a dreamer whose imagination was ever seeking out new ways of serving humanity." Many Americans idolized business during these prosperous times.

Skillbuilder Answer The Coolidge administration and big business got along very well together.

SKILLBUILDER
INTERPRETING POLITICAL CARTOONS
Calvin Coolidge plays a saxophone as big business dances the Charleston. What does this cartoon tell you about the Coolidge administration and big business?

A Superficial Prosperity

During the 1920s, most Americans believed that prosperity would go on forever. After all, wasn't the average factory worker producing 50 percent more at the end of the decade than at its start? Hadn't national income grown from $58 billion in 1921 to $83 billion in 1929? Weren't most major corporations making fortunes? Wasn't the stock market reaching new heights?

PRODUCING GREAT QUANTITIES OF GOODS As productivity increased, businesses expanded in size. There were numerous mergers of companies that

TEACHING OPTIONS

Making Connections Across Time

Advertising Today Point out to students that, in the 1920s, advertisers began to study how best to persuade consumers to buy products. Then tell students that, today, advertising has become much more adept at appealing to an audience. Ask how advertisers use language to manipulate teenagers.

IN-DEPTH RESOURCES: UNIT 4
Primary Source: Advertisement, p. 10

OUR TIMES
1925 Listerine advertisement

Teaching Less Proficient Readers

Identifying Supporting Details Help students understand why the 1920s was a time of superficial prosperity. Tell them that the heading on page 444 states this main idea. The next page contains details that support the idea. Help students identify these details by following these steps:

1. Read pages 444 and 445, starting with the head "A Superficial Prosperity."
2. Create an outline, using the main idea as its heading.
3. Reread the pages and list details that explain why people weren't really prosperous, including the plight of farmers and miners and the widespread use of the installment plan.

manufactured automobiles, steel, and electrical equipment and that provided public utilities. Chain stores sprouted, selling groceries, drugs, shoes, and clothes. Five-and-dime stores like Woolworth's also spread rapidly. Banks invented branch banking. But as the number of businesses grew, so did the income gap between workers and managers. There were a number of other clouds in the blue sky of prosperity. The iron and railroad industries, among others, really weren't prosperous, and mining and farming concerns suffered losses.

BUYING MANY GOODS ON CREDIT In addition to advertising, industry provided another solution to the problem of luring consumers to purchase the mountain of goods produced each year: easy credit, or "a dollar down and a dollar forever." The **installment plan,** as it was then called, enabled people to buy goods over an extended period, without having to put down much money at the time of purchase. Banks provided the money at low interest rates, while advertisers pushed the idea with such slogans as "You furnish the girl, we'll furnish the home" and "Enjoy while you pay."

Some economists and business owners worried that installment buying might be getting out of hand and that it was really a sign of a careless and superficial prosperity. One business owner even wrote to President Coolidge and related a conversation he had overheard on a train.

THINK THROUGH HISTORY
C. *Analyzing Issues* *What were the advantages and disadvantages of buying on credit?*

C. Answer **Advantages:** People could buy many goods over a period of time with little money down at low interest. **Disadvantages:** People easily went into too much debt without really thinking about it.

A PERSONAL VOICE

"Have you an automobile yet?"
"No, I talked it over with John and he felt we could not afford one."
"Mr. Budge who lives in your town has one and they are not as well off as you are."
"Yes, I know. Their second installment came due, and they had no money to pay it."
"What did they do? Lose the car?"
"No, they got the money and paid the installment."
"How did they get the money?"
"They sold the cook-stove."
"How could they get along without a cook-stove?"
"They didn't. They bought another on the installment plan."

BUSINESS OWNER, quoted in *In the Time of Silent Cal*

Still, most Americans focused their attention on the present, with little concern for the future. What could possibly go wrong with the nation's economy? The decade of the 1920s had brought about many technological and economic changes. Life definitely seemed easier and more enjoyable for hundreds of thousands of Americans.

HISTORICAL SPOTLIGHT

THE STANLEY STEAMER

In 1897, the twin brothers Francis and Freeland Stanley went into the automobile business. Instead of gas, they used steam as their power source. The Stanley Steamer ran on any burnable fuel and was easy to start: all you had to do was light the boiler and wait for the water to boil. The Steamer was also very fast: in 1906 it reached the unheard-of speed of 127.66 miles an hour. The country's first police car was a Stanley Steamer purchased by the Boston Police Department.

The Stanley brothers charged $2,000 for the Steamer and produced just 1,000 cars a year. They weren't interested in increasing volume or in improving the model. When the electric self-starter made the internal-combustion engine efficient, Henry Ford began mass-producing cars. He sold them for under $500—and by the middle of the 1920s, the Stanley Steamer had disappeared from the country's roads.

Section 3 Assessment

1. TERMS & NAMES
Identify:
- urban sprawl
- installment plan

2. SUMMARIZING Re-create the web below on your paper and fill it in with events that illustrate the center idea.

Choose one event from the web and explain its significance in the 1920s.

3. INTERPRETING Do you agree with President Coolidge's statement "The man who builds a factory builds a temple—the man who works there worships there"? Explain your answer.

THINK ABOUT
- the goals of business and of religion
- the American idolization of business
- the difference between workers and management

4. DRAWING CONCLUSIONS Do you think the changes in the 1920s gave Americans more control over their lives? Explain.

THINK ABOUT
- the impact of new technology
- the influence of advertising
- the results of installment buying

ANSWERS

1. TERMS & NAMES

urban sprawl, p. 442

installment plan, p. 445

2. SUMMARIZING

Possible Answers: Development of the automobile industry; expansion of the airline industry; invention of new electrical appliances; spread of modern advertising; use of the installment plan.

3. INTERPRETING

Possible Responses: Students may agree with Coolidge that a business and a religion both serve important needs. They might disagree with him and argue that a business is organized for the financial gain of its owners while a religious institution serves the spiritual needs of its members. They might also point out that while business owners in the 1920s profited, most workers did not.

4. DRAWING CONCLUSIONS

Possible Responses: Students might emphasize different issues. While automobiles gave people more mobility and appliances gave people more free time, advertising lured them to buy more, and the use of the installment plan encouraged them to go into debt.

HISTORICAL SPOTLIGHT

The Stanley Steamer

Critical Thinking: Analyzing Discuss why the Stanley Steamer was displaced by Ford's mass-produced cars. Then ask students what advantages the Steamer had over Ford's cars. *Possible Responses: The Steamer did not pollute the air; its high price would have limited the number sold and hence the number of vehicles on the road.*

ASSESS & RETEACH

Section 3 Assessment

After students have answered the questions, discuss item 4 in class.

Self-Assessment

To document what students have learned, have them create a cluster diagram listing five characteristics of American business in the 1920s.

Section Quiz

FORMAL ASSESSMENT
Section Quiz, p. 155

Reteach

Use the list of goods and prices on page 443 to review the role of business and consumer goods in the 1920s.

CLOSE

Automobiles, electrical appliances, and other consumer goods flooded the market as America's standard of living soared in the 1920s. Although not everyone took part in the general prosperity, many Americans embraced the present and enjoyed life.

CRITICAL THINKING TRANSPARENCIES
CT54, Consumer Spending Power

Tracing Themes

OBJECTIVES

1. To examine trends in American consumer spending over 150 years.
2. To explain how shopping methods have changed to suit technology and lifestyle changes.

FOCUS & MOTIVATE

▶ ***Starting with the Student*** Ask students to think about the methods of shopping available to them now.

- Which methods are easiest to use? Most fun? Most challenging? What are the drawbacks of each method?
- Do Americans spend too much time shopping? What, if anything, does excessive consumer spending say about Americans?

MORE ABOUT . . .
Early Department Stores

The first department stores provided an unprecedented array of products. Shoppers who couldn't afford mink coats, perfume, or other luxuries could examine these items in the store and get a glimpse of elegant living. Department stores also provided a new level of comfort and convenience. Almost from the beginning, the stores included restaurants, tea rooms, and restrooms. With all their needs covered, shoppers could spend a whole day in the department store—a luxury in itself.

TRACING THEMES
ECONOMIC OPPORTUNITY

Consumer Spending

Ask people in the United States what one of their favorite activities is, and many will answer "shopping." Shopping has become one of America's favorite leisure activities. During the 1920s, when people had a little extra money and a little more free time in which to spend it, the consumer economy really began to flourish. As more products became available, companies faced increasing competition, so they hired advertising firms to create ads appealing to people's desire for status, comfort, luxury, and style. Today, the story continues. For many people, "Shop till you drop!" has become much more than just a T-shirt slogan.

1800s
VARIETY STORES

Mid-1800s: General Stores At a general store, such as the one pictured at the right, one could purchase almost anything, from dry goods (cloth and clothing), crockery, silverware, pots and pans, and small farming equipment to medicines and ointments.

Department Stores Department stores were larger than general stores and carried a wider variety and a greater supply of goods. They organized their merchandise in separate departments, such as home furnishings and women's clothing.

Chain Stores In the mid-1800s, chain stores—retail stores under the same ownership and dealing in the same merchandise—spread across the nation. The Great Atlantic & Pacific Tea Company sold groceries. The F. W. Woolworth's five-and-ten-cent chain sold numerous items at very reasonable prices.

1870s: Mail-Order Catalogs During the 1870s, Montgomery Ward and Sears, Roebuck and Company began to produce and distribute mail-order catalogs displaying an enormous array of products that consumers could order through the mail and have delivered directly to their door. Using this new method, people purchased everything from trousers to beds to farm tools.

1920s
MORE PRODUCTS; MORE STORES

The 1920s saw an enormous increase in the number and kinds of goods available. Automobiles were the biggest item, but there were also many small electrical appliances, such as vacuum cleaners and radios. Drugstores like the one shown above stocked not only medicines and grooming supplies but many kinds of other items, including electrical appliances.

This drugstore also had a soda fountain, where one could sit and enjoy a cup of coffee for 10 cents, a lemon phosphate for 5 cents, or a slice of cake for 5 cents.

RECOMMENDED RESOURCES

Books

Hendrickson, Robert. *The Grand Emporiums.* New York: Stein, 1979. An illustrated history of America's great department stores.

Kowinski, William Severini. *The Malling of America.* New York: Morrow, 1985. An inside look at the consumerism of the 1980s.

Roberts, Bruce. *American Country Stores.* Chester, CT: Globe, 1991. A photographic history.

Sears, Roebuck & Company. *1897 Sears Roebuck Catalogue.* New York: Chelsea, 1976. A period piece reissued.

Wendt, Lloyd. *Give the Lady What She Wants!* Chicago: Rand, 1952. The story of Marshall Field & Company.

Videos

Mr. Sears' Catalogue. PBS Video, 1989. A look at the Sears catalog and its significance in rural America.

Supermarket Savvy. Family Experiences Productions, 1987. Guidance in modern shopping.

Software

Consumer Shopping. Education Associates. Orients users about where to shop and how to shop wisely.

1990s
TV SHOPPING NETWORKS

Cable television ushered in home shopping networks. Consumers can shop from home and pay with a credit card for any item that is being displayed or demonstrated on TV.

1940s
SHOPPING CENTERS

The growth of suburbs resulted in the building of many shopping centers—large groups of stores surrounded by parking lots. Sometimes the stores were arranged around an open or enclosed area for pedestrians, known as a mall. A shopping center usually had dozens of specialty stores, each selling just one kind of merchandise—such as home appliances, as pictured here. It also often had one or more department stores. Although the first shopping center reportedly opened in Baltimore, Maryland, in 1896, such centers did not become widely popular until 1945.

INTERACT WITH HISTORY

1. **COMPARING** Weigh the pros and cons of each method of shopping available to consumers over the last 150 years. Which method do you imagine might be used in the future? Why do you think so?

SEE SKILLBUILDER HANDBOOK, PAGE 909.

2. **WINDOW-SHOPPING ON THE INTERNET** Browse the Internet to investigate the kinds of things that are available. How could one purchase these goods? How would one pay for them? What is the value of shopping on the Internet? What are the dangers? In what ways is this kind of shopping different from and similar to other ways of shopping, both in the past and today? Report your findings to the class.

Visit http://www.mlushistory.com for more about Internet commerce.

INSTRUCT

▶ *Starting with the Student*

- Ask students to share any shopping innovations they have witnessed or heard about.
- Discuss the trend toward home shopping—via TV, the Internet, telephone, and mail. Ask students to explain whether this trend suggests that Americans are experiencing an increase or a decrease in leisure time.

▶ *Discussing Key Ideas*

- Shopping has increasingly become a leisure-time activity.
- Shopping methods have changed to accommodate changing times and consumer needs.

HISTORY FROM VISUALS

Reading the Images

Have students examine the illustrations on these pages.

- What impressions are the displays in the photographs intended to convey? *Possible Responses: Size, quality, variety, efficiency, good service, modernity.*
- Which one do you find the most impressive?

INTERACT WITH HISTORY

1. Comparing

***Possible Answers:** 1800s: Pros—more personal service; Cons—limited goods; 1920s: Pros—more goods available; Cons—required shopping at many different stores; 1940s: Pros—one-stop shopping; Cons—wide array of stores enticed people to spend more than they intended; 1990s: Pros—allowed people to shop from home; Cons—didn't allow people to see merchandise before purchasing it.*

The home shopping network will be used more in the future because people will have less and less time for shopping.

2. Window-Shopping on the Internet

Students should provide accurate information about Internet sites, printing out Internet pages if possible to support their answers. Possible value of Internet shopping: saves time, no crowds, reduces some kinds of crime, shopper can live far from population centers/stores. Possible dangers: requires giving private information (such as credit card numbers) over Internet, shopper can't examine merchandise. Similarities: Internet shopping is similar to using mail-order catalogs and the Home Shopping Network because all three can be done at home. Differences: Unlike shopping in stores, Internet shopping provides no human contact.

CHAPTER 12
ASSESSMENT ANSWERS

REVIEWING THE CHAPTER

TERMS & NAMES

1. A. Mitchell Palmer, p. 431
2. Sacco and Vanzetti, p. 432
3. Calvin Coolidge, p. 434
4. John L. Lewis, p. 435
5. Warren G. Harding, p. 436
6. Kellogg-Briand Pact, p. 437
7. isolationist, p. 437
8. quota system, p. 439
9. Teapot Dome scandal, p. 440
10. installment plan, p. 445

MAIN IDEAS

11. About 70,000 Americans joined the Communist Party, which indirectly led to the Red Scare.
12. All three events reflected fear of immigrants and radical movements.
13. Boston police who went on strike were fired; security forces killed 18 striking steelworkers; the government ordered an end to the coal miners' strike.
14. Harding wanted to get America back to the simpler days before the progressive era reforms.
15. The conference to lessen nations' dependence on armaments; U.S. efforts to get nations to sign the Kellogg-Briand Pact; the Fordney-McCumber Tariff; U.S. efforts to solve the reparations problem; the policy to limit immigration.
16. The system reduced immigration from eastern and southern Europe, and excluded the Japanese.
17. The scandal was about corruption in the leasing of government oil reserves to private companies; one cabinet member received bonds, cash, and ranches in exchange for oil contracts.
18. The automobile prompted the building of new roads, gave people more mobility, and created jobs; airplanes improved transportation and communication; electrical appliances freed up time for other activities.
19. Advertisers hired psychologists to study how to appeal to buyers; brand names became familiar; slogans popularized items; businesspeople used service organizations to boost their own image.
20. The income gap between workers and managers was growing; some industries were stagnant or losing money; people were increasing their debt.

Chapter 12 Assessment

REVIEWING THE CHAPTER

TERMS & NAMES For each term below, write a sentence explaining its connection to the decade following World War I. For each person below, explain his role in the events of the period.

1. **A. Mitchell Palmer**
2. **Sacco and Vanzetti**
3. **Calvin Coolidge**
4. **John L. Lewis**
5. **Warren G. Harding**
6. **Kellogg-Briand Pact**
7. **isolationist**
8. **quota system**
9. **Teapot Dome scandal**
10. **installment plan**

MAIN IDEAS

SECTION 1 *(pages 430–435)*

Americans Struggle with Postwar Issues

11. What impact did the Russian Revolution have on the United States?
12. Explain how the Red Scare, the Sacco and Vanzetti case, and the rise of the Ku Klux Klan reflected concerns held by many Americans.
13. What evidence suggests that strikes were a risky activity for workers during the 1920s?

SECTION 2 *(pages 436–440)*

"Normalcy" and Isolationism

14. What did Harding want to do to return America to "normalcy"?
15. What evidence shows that the United States was pursuing an isolationist foreign policy?
16. Describe the primary goal of the immigration quota system established in 1921.
17. Summarize the Teapot Dome scandal.

SECTION 3 *(pages 441–445)*

The Business of America

18. How did changes in technology in the 1920s influence American life?
19. Describe the new methods used by advertisers beginning in the 1920s.
20. What evidence suggests that the prosperity of the 1920s was not on a firm foundation?

THINKING CRITICALLY

1. **RETURN TO "NORMALCY"** Create a cause-and-effect web, similar to the one shown, in which you give several causes for the declining power of labor unions in the 1920s and give examples of the unions' decline.

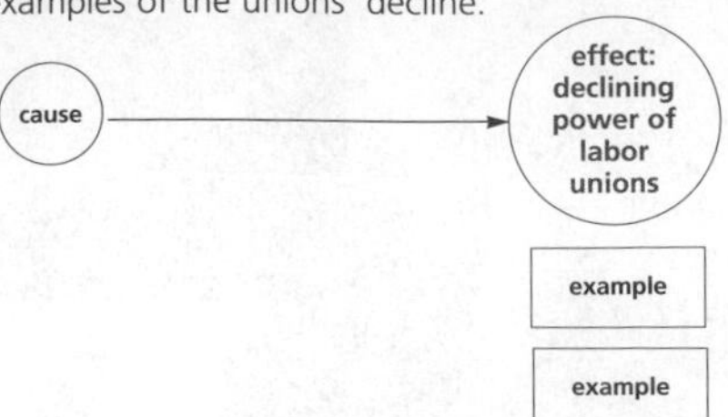

2. **COMPARING CONCERNS** Do you think Americans today are as worried about immigration and radical movements as they were in the 1920s? Explain why or why not.
3. **THE ROLE OF BUSINESS** Reread the quotation from Calvin Coolidge on page 428. What events and trends of the 1920s support Coolidge's statement?
4. **GEOGRAPHY OF ROUTE 66** Look at the path of Route 66 in the map on page 442. What factors may have influenced where and why the highway was built? Explain your answer.
5. **TRACING THEMES ECONOMIC OPPORTUNITY** Compare and contrast the types of shopping and goods described in the Tracing Themes feature on pages 446–447. What characteristics of American culture are evident in this feature? Give examples to support your opinion.
6. **ANALYZING PRIMARY SOURCES** William Ashdown, a banker in a small town, considered himself a careful and thrifty man. In 1925, he wrote a magazine article describing how the purchase of a car changed his life.

> Having a quick method of locomotion, it was easy to run out into the country on a Sunday for dinner, or on an evening for a drive and a "bite." Then, too, my friends expected me to do the honors, as chauffeur and host, and this added to the mounting costs. But I had started something that I could not stop gracefully or consistently. My thrift habits were steadily giving way to spendthrift habits.
>
> After eight years of experience I find that the psychological processes of car-owners are much alike. First you want a car; then you conclude to buy it. Once bought, you must keep it running. . . . Therefore you spend and keep on spending. . . . The result upon the individual is to break down his sense of values. . . . Whether he will or no, he must spend money at every turn.
>
> **WILLIAM ASHDOWN,** quoted in *The Twenties: Fords, Flappers, and Fanatics*

Do you agree with Ashdown that automobile ownership—and materialism in general—contributes to spending and undermines values? Explain why or why not.

THINKING CRITICALLY

1. RETURN TO "NORMALCY"

Possible Responses: Cause—Association of unions with radicalism; difficulty organizing immigrants who tolerated poor working conditions and spoke other languages. Examples—New membership declines; strikers are fired in Boston; troops prevent picketing; public perception of unions turns negative.

2. COMPARING CONCERNS

Possible Responses: Students answering no might mention that concerns about a Communist revolution in the United States no longer exist. Students answering yes might point to the spread of antigovernment militia groups and of legislation to discourage any government help for illegal immigrants.

3. THE ROLE OF BUSINESS

Possible Responses: America's standard of living went up during the 1920s; 80 percent of all registered motor vehicles were in the United States; the number of electrified households and the use of electrical appliances in the United States greatly increased; advertising grew; credit increased demand for American goods.

ALTERNATIVE ASSESSMENT

1. **GRAPHING STATISTICS**
How were American lives changed by the social, political, and economic events of the 1920s? Create a graphic—a pie chart, bar or line graph, or circle graph—that uses statistics to illustrate one aspect of these changes.

CD-ROM Use the CD-ROM *Our Times,* the Internet, your textbook, and other sources to gather statistics about incomes, prices, employment levels, divorce rates, or other areas in which figures show how people were affected by the events of the 1920s.

- Present the statistics in a graph to show their impact. Clearly label the parts of the graph.
- Research and find statistics that show comparable information for today. Create another graph, comparing today's statistics with those of the 1920s.

2. **PROJECT FOR CITIZENSHIP: BECOMING A CITIZEN**
Imagine that you are planning to come to the United States from Italy, France, Great Britain, Ireland, Germany, or Spain. Try to determine what your chances would be of being admitted to the United States in 1921, in 1924, and in 1929. (See "Learning the Process of Becoming a Citizen" on page 112 in Projects for Citizenship.) Use these steps to guide you in your research:
   - Learn about the Emergency Quota Act of 1921, its amendment in 1924, and the National Origins Act of 1929.
   - Find out how many people from your country there were in the United States at the time specified by each law and what percentage of that number would be permitted to enter the United States from your country each year.
   - Discover whether there were other barriers placed on immigration during the period.
   - Estimate your chances of being admitted.

3. **PORTFOLIO PROJECT**
Use the Living History activity to expand your portfolio.

LIVING HISTORY

PRESENTING YOUR EXHIBIT

Explain your floor plan to a small group of classmates. Then ask the group to evaluate the exhibit's success, using these criteria:

- Does the exhibit present important facts and details?
- Is the exhibit interesting and entertaining?
- Is the floor plan clearly and thoughtfully arranged?

Save your exhibit descriptions and floor plan in your American history portfolio.

Bridge to Chapter 13

Review Chapter 12

In the years following the end of World War I, Americans felt frightened by the Communist victory in the 1917 Russian Revolution. Signs of fear were widespread. Federal agents jailed or deported radicals. Two anarchists who immigrated from Italy, Nicola Sacco and Bartolomeo Vanzetti, were executed for murder despite the weakness of the evidence against them. Labor unions lost several key strikes, as well as membership. The Ku Klux Klan reemerged and grew steadily until outrageous acts by Klan members led to its decline.

In politics, voters expressed their desire to return to the "normalcy" of pre–World War I society. In 1920, they elected Republican Warren G. Harding in a landslide.

REJECTING GLOBAL CONCERNS Under Harding and his vice-president and successor, Calvin Coolidge, the United States tried to isolate itself from world affairs even as it promoted disarmament. The country refused involvement in international efforts to maintain peace, passed high tariffs that reduced international trade, and limited immigration from eastern and southern Europe and Japan.

CORRUPTION AND PROSPERITY For many Americans, the 1920s were years of prosperity. A few attempted to gain wealth illegally, including Harding's secretary of the interior, who accepted bribes in the Teapot Dome scandal. Most people, though, prospered as the economy grew. Many found work building, selling, and servicing automobiles and the new electrical appliances that were revolutionizing everyday life. Consumers fueled economic growth by responding to new forms of advertising and to the installment plan with increased spending. The country seemed headed for ever-increasing wealth.

Preview Chapter 13

Changes in politics and in the economy during the 1920s contributed to a variety of cultural developments. Heated debates over religion, dramatic shifts in the roles of women and African Americans, and the rapid expansion of the entertainment industry made the 1920s a period of tension and debate. You will learn about these significant developments in the next chapter.

ALTERNATIVE ASSESSMENT

1. GRAPHING STATISTICS
Standards for Evaluation
A graph should meet the following criteria.

- Presents statistics in a readable, accessible form.
- Clearly labels headings, parts, or grids.
- Uses statistics in an area that illustrates how people were affected by the events of the 1920s.
- Includes another, similar graph that compares today's statistics in the same field with those of the 1920s.

2. PROJECT FOR CITIZENSHIP: BECOMING A CITIZEN
Standards for Evaluation
A research paper should meet the following criteria.

- Clearly identifies the immigrant country.
- Compares the impact of immigration legislation on the country in 1921, 1924, and 1929.
- Discusses the barriers placed on immigration from the country.
- Contains an informed estimation of the possibility of being admitted to the United States from the country.

3. PORTFOLIO PROJECT
LIVING HISTORY
Standards for Evaluation
An exhibit should meet the following criteria.

- Is arranged thoughtfully and logically.
- Provides important information on the topic.
- Presents information in an entertaining and visually exciting manner.
- Engages and informs the audience.

IN-DEPTH RESOURCES: UNIT 4
See the form for scoring this activity on page 17.

THINKING CRITICALLY

4. GEOGRAPHY OF ROUTE 66

Possible Responses: The road was built through the Southwest so it didn't have to go through the Rocky Mountains; the road was meant to promote vacation travel and regional growth.

5. TRACING THEMES ECONOMIC OPPORTUNITY

Possible Responses: Americans have always loved to shop. The American economy is dependent on consumer spending; businesses have tried to make shopping easier—through mail order, malls, computer networks, chain stores—to encourage more spending; if shopping is made a cultural experience as it is in America, consumerism becomes entrenched in society. This is clearly seen in Americans' purchase of ready-to-wear clothing, ready-to-eat foods, ready-to-assemble housing, and many other goods.

6. ANALYZING PRIMARY SOURCES

Possible Responses: Students who agree may cite Americans' infatuation with buying and how it causes people to seek happiness in material things; how the overuse of automobiles has caused pollution; how materialism causes us to admire people for what they have, not for who they are. Others may emphasize that individuals determine their own values and that merely buying things need not alter these values.

CHAPTER 13

PLANNING GUIDE

The Roaring Life of the 1920s

	Key Ideas	COPYMASTERS	ASSESSMENT
SECTION 1 **Changing Ways of Life** *pp. 452–457*	*Americans experience cultural conflicts as customs and values change in the United States during the 1920s.*	***In-Depth Resources: Unit 4*** • Guided Reading, p. 18 • Primary Sources: Political Cartoon, p. 25; *from* The Scopes Trial, p. 26 • Literature: from *Inherit the Wind* by Jerome Lawrence and Robert E. Lee, p. 29 ***Lesson Plans,*** pp. 109–110	PE ***Section 1 Assessment,*** p. 457 TE ***Self-Assessment,*** p. 457 ***Formal Assessment*** • Section Quiz, p. 164 ***Alternative Assessment Book*** • Standards for Evaluating a Cooperative Activity
SECTION 2 **The Twenties Woman** *pp. 458–461*	*American women of the 1920s pursue new lifestyles and assume new jobs and different roles in society.*	***In-Depth Resources: Unit 4*** • Guided Reading, p. 19 ***Lesson Plans,*** pp. 111–112	PE ***Section 2 Assessment,*** p. 461 TE ***Self-Assessment,*** p. 461 ***Formal Assessment*** • Section Quiz, p. 165 ***Alternative Assessment Book*** • Standards for Evaluating a Cooperative Activity
SECTION 3 **Education and Popular Culture** *pp. 464–469*	*The mass media, movies, and spectator sports play important roles in the popular culture of the 1920s.*	***In-Depth Resources: Unit 4*** • Guided Reading, p. 20 • Skillbuilder Practice: Drawing Conclusions, p. 22 • Geography Application: From Coast to Coast, p. 23 • Primary Source: *from* An Interview with Charles A. Lindbergh, p. 27 • American Lives: Georgia O'Keeffe, p. 32 ***Lesson Plans,*** pp. 113–114	PE ***Section 3 Assessment,*** p. 469 TE ***Self-Assessment,*** p. 469 ***Formal Assessment*** • Section Quiz, p. 166 ***Alternative Assessment Book*** • Standards for Evaluating a Cooperative Activity
SECTION 4 **The Harlem Renaissance** *pp. 470–475*	*African-American ideas, politics, art, literature, and music flourish in Harlem and elsewhere in the United States.*	***In-Depth Resources: Unit 4*** • Guided Reading, p. 21 • Primary Source: *from* "When the Negro Was in Vogue" by Langston Hughes, p. 28 • American Lives: Louis Armstrong, p. 33 ***Lesson Plans,*** pp. 115–116	PE ***Section 4 Assessment,*** p. 475 TE ***Self-Assessment,*** p. 475 ***Formal Assessment*** • Section Quiz, p. 167 ***Alternative Assessment Book*** • Standards for Evaluating a Cooperative Activity
CHAPTER RESOURCES	**Chapter Overview** *During the 1920s, rural America clashes with a faster-paced urban culture. Women's attitudes and roles change, influenced in part by the mass media. Many African Americans join in the new urban culture.*	***In-Depth Resources: Unit 4*** • Living History Project: Worksheet, p. 34; Standards, p. 35 ***Telescoping the Times*** • Chapter Summary, pp. 25–26 ***Planning for Block Schedules***	PE ***Chapter Assessment,*** pp. 478–479 PE ***Alternative Assessment,*** p. 479 ***Formal Assessment*** • Chapter Test, forms A and B, pp. 168–173 ***Test Generator*** ***Alternative Assessment Book*** See explanation and forms for different kinds of alternative assessments including portfolio assessment.

KEY
PE Pupil's Edition
TE Teacher's Edition
INTERNET http://www.mlushistory.com

TECHNOLOGY

Warm-Up Transparency 13

Geography Transparencies
- G21, Prohibition: 1890 and 1915

Critical Thinking Transparencies
- CT21, Prohibition

Our Times
- Scopes Trial

Electronic Library of Primary Sources
- from "My Bootlegger" by Samuel H. Adams

INTERNET Al Capone and speakeasies

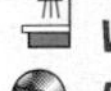
Warm-Up Transparency 13

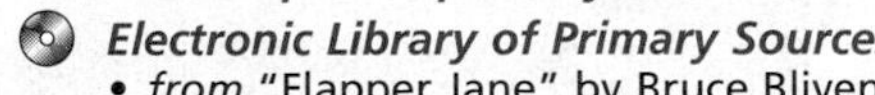
Electronic Library of Primary Sources
- *from* "Flapper Jane" by Bruce Bliven

INTERNET Interact with History p. 463 (PE)

Warm-Up Transparency 13

Humanities Transparencies
- H20, *Automat* by Edward Hopper

Our Times
- Charles Lindbergh, Sinclair Lewis, and F. Scott Fitzgerald

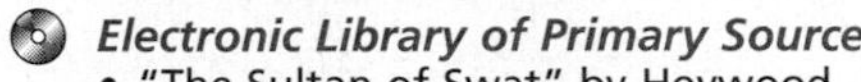
Electronic Library of Primary Sources
- "The Sultan of Swat" by Heywood Broun

INTERNET Babe Ruth and F. Scott Fitzgerald

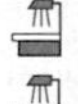
Warm-Up Transparency 13

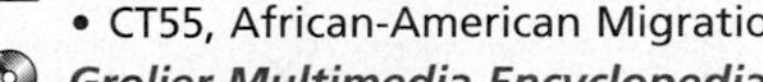
Critical Thinking Transparencies
- CT55, African-American Migration

Grolier Multimedia Encyclopedia
- African-American Literature

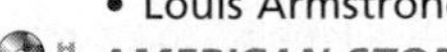
Our Times
- Louis Armstrong

AMERICAN STORIES video series
- "Jump at the Sun"

INTERNET Interact with History p. 477 (PE)

American Portfolio: A Videodisc for U.S. History, user's guide, pp. 192, 195–200

Chapter Summary Audiotapes
- Unit 4, Chapter 13

INTERNET http://www. mlushistory.com

Block Scheduling (90 MINUTES)

Day 1
Section 1, pp. 452–457

Section 2, pp. 458–461

Daily Life: Youth in the Roaring Twenties, pp. 462–463 (TE)

Section Assessments, pp. 457, 461

COOPERATIVE ACTIVITIES
- Creating a Dictionary of 1920s Slang, p. 455 (TE)
- Analyzing Changes in Women's Roles, p. 460 (TE)

Day 2
Section 3, pp. 464–469

Section Assessment, p. 469

COOPERATIVE ACTIVITY
- Presenting Art, p. 468 (TE)

Day 3
Section 4, pp. 470–475

American Literature: Literature in the Jazz Age, pp. 476–477

Section Assessment, p. 475

AMERICAN STORIES video series
- "Jump at the Sun"

Chapter Assessment, pp. 478–479

COOPERATIVE ACTIVITY
- Celebrating African-American culture, p. 473 (TE)

YEARLY PACING *Chapter 13 Total:* 3 days *Yearly Total:* 85 days

See *Planning for Block Schedules* for special activities and pacing strategies.

Customizing for Special Populations

Students Acquiring English

Access for Students Acquiring English: Spanish Translations
- Guided Reading for Sections 1–4, pp. 158–161
- Chapter Summary, pp. 156–157
- Skillbuilder Practice: Drawing Conclusions, p. 162
- Geography Application: From Coast to Coast, p. 163

Spanish Reading Study Guide, pp. 137–146

Translations of Chapter Summaries, Hmong, Cantonese, Vietnamese, and Cambodian

Chapter Summary Audiotapes in Spanish
Unit 4, Chapter 13

AMERICAN STORIES video series
- "Jump at the Sun" (Spanish track)

INTERNET The Diverse Classroom

Gifted and Talented Students

In-Depth Resources: Unit 4
- Primary Sources: Political Cartoon, p. 25; *from* The Scopes Trial, p. 26; *from* An Interview with Charles A. Lindbergh, p. 27; *from* "When the Negro Was in Vogue" by Langston Hughes, p. 28
- American Lives: Georgia O'Keeffe, p. 32; Louis Armstrong, p. 33

Less Proficient Readers

In-Depth Resources: Unit 4
- Guided Reading for Sections 1–4, pp. 18–21
- Skillbuilder: Drawing Conclusions, p. 22
- Geography Application: From Coast to Coast, p. 23

Reading Study Guide
- pp. 137–146

Telescoping the Times
- Chapter Summary, pp. 25–26

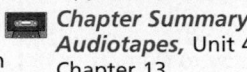

Chapter Summary Audiotapes, Unit 4, Chapter 13

Connections to Literature READINGS FOR STUDENTS

In-Depth Resources: Unit 4
- **from *Inherit the Wind* by Jerome Lawrence and Robert E. Lee,** p. 29

McDougal Littell *The Language of Literature*
American Literature

- **F. Scott Fitzgerald, "Winter Dreams,"** p. 680
- **Langston Hughes, Alain Locke, Louis Armstrong, Carl Van Doren, Marcus Garvey, *Voices from the Times,*** p. 763
- **Langston Hughes, "I, Too,"** p. 766; **"The Weary Blues,"** p. 768
- **James Weldon Johnson, "My City,"** p. 772
- **Countee Cullen, "Any Human to Another,"** p. 774
- **Claude McKay, "If We Must Die,"** p. 777
- **Arna Bontemps, "A Black Man Talks of Reaping,"** p. 779
- **Zora Neale Hurston, "How It Feels to Be Colored Me,"** p. 782
- **Alice Walker, *from Zora Neale Hurston: A Cautionary Tale and a Partisan View,*** p. 787
- **Ernest Hemingway, "The End of Something,"** p. 827
- **Dorothy Parker, "Here We Are,"** p. 835
- **T. S. Eliot, "The Love Song of J. Alfred Prufrock,"** p. 845
- **Richard Wright, "The Man Who Was Almost a Man,"** p. 853
- **Thornton Wilder, *The Long Christmas Dinner,*** p. 866

CHAPTER 13 OVERVIEW

The Roaring Life of the 1920s

▶ ***Accessing Prior Knowledge***
Ask students to name the music, dances, and other forms of entertainment they associate with the 1920s. Do students think the current era emphasizes play over work?

▶ ***Predicting Outcomes***
Ask students what Westbrook Pegler could have meant when he said the 1920s was an "era of wonderful nonsense." Have students read the section heads and then make predictions about the kinds of "wonderful nonsense" Pegler might have had in mind.

MORE ABOUT . . .
Westbrook Pegler
From copy boy to Pulitzer Prize–winning columnist, Westbrook Pegler had a career that spanned 40 years. He served as a war correspondent during World War I and during the 1920s began writing a syndicated newspaper column on national affairs. Pegler was noted for his scathing attacks on just about everything.

CHAPTER 13

The Roaring Life of the 1920s

SECTION 1
Changing Ways of Life
Americans experience cultural conflicts as customs and values change in the United States during the 1920s.

SECTION 2
The Twenties Woman
American women of the 1920s pursue new lifestyles and assume new jobs and different roles in society.

SECTION 3
Education and Popular Culture
The mass media, movies, and spectator sports play important roles in the popular culture of the 1920s.

SECTION 4
The Harlem Renaissance
African-American ideas, politics, art, literature, and music flourish in Harlem and elsewhere in the United States.

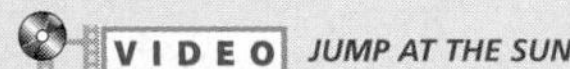
VIDEO JUMP AT THE SUN

"The Era of Wonderful Nonsense"
Westbrook Pegler

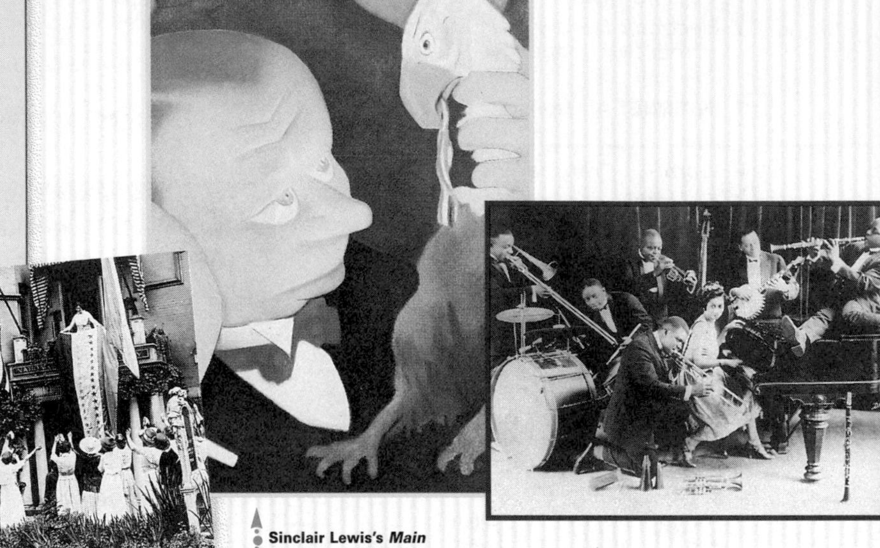

THE UNITED STATES

1920
- National Woman's Party celebrates the ratification of the Nineteenth Amendment.
- Sinclair Lewis's *Main Street* is published.
- Pittsburgh radio station KDKA is the first to begin commercial broadcasting.
- First of the Negro baseball leagues is founded.

1921
- Andrew Mellon is named secretary of the treasury.

1922
- Louis Armstrong plays for King Oliver's Creole Jazz Band in Chicago.
- Harlem Renaissance flourishes.

1923
- Publication of *Time* magazine begins.
- Supreme Court strikes down a minimum wage law for women.

THE WORLD

1920
- Pan-African movement gains strength.

1921
- Irish civil war begins.

1922
- King Tut's tomb is discovered in Egypt.

1923
- Kemal Ataturk begins the modernization of Turkey.

THEMES IN CHAPTER 13

Constitutional Concerns
Federal enforcement of prohibition was inefficient, and some states stopped trying to enforce the Eighteenth Amendment. Disregard for the amendment convinced legislators to repeal it.
See Teacher's Edition note, p. 454.

Women in America
Women's role in society changed significantly in the 1920s. Young women, especially, became more assertive and independent in their quest for equality. The flapper reflected the changing image of women in America.
See Teacher's Edition note, p. 459.

Science and Technology
The first scheduled radio broadcast took place in 1920. By the end of the decade, more than 10 million American families had radios in their homes. The mass media revolutionized communication and created a shared national experience.
See Teacher's Edition note, p. 465.

Immigration and Migration
By the end of the 1920s, more than a third of all African Americans lived in cities. The migration to cities marked the beginning of a new era in African-American history. It also sparked a wave of violence in many northern cities.
See Teacher's Edition note, p. 471.

LIVING HISTORY

MAKING A DISPLAY

A number of social issues deeply affected Americans during the 1920s. Many of these issues continue to challenge society today. As you read each section of this chapter, think about social issues of the 1920s that you think relate directly to concerns of today. Create a now-and-then storyboard that visually presents these parallel issues. Consider the following topics as you organize your ideas:

- the impact of technology
- the struggle for equal rights
- attempts to solve social problems
- attempts to accommodate the educational needs of diverse groups

PORTFOLIO PROJECT Keep your notes and your storyboard in a folder for your American history portfolio. At the end of the chapter, you will be asked to present your storyboard to others.

1924
- Native Americans receive full citizenship.
- American swimmer Gertrude Ederle is the first woman to swim the English Channel.
- Greece is proclaimed a republic.

1925
- F. Scott Fitzgerald's *The Great Gatsby* is published.
- Scopes trial takes place in Tennessee.
- Physicist R. A. Millikan discovers cosmic rays in the upper atmosphere.
- Alain Locke publishes *The New Negro.*
- Adolf Hitler publishes the first volume of *Mein Kampf.*

1926
- Ernest Hemingway's *The Sun Also Rises* is published.

1927
- Charles Lindbergh makes the first solo transatlantic flight.
- First sound movie, *The Jazz Singer,* is released.
- Babe Ruth hits 60 home runs in one season.
- Duke Ellington's band opens at the Cotton Club.
- Leon Trotsky is expelled from the Soviet Union's Communist Party.

1928
- George Gershwin's *An American in Paris* has its premiere in New York.
- Herbert Hoover is elected president.
- President Alvaro Obregón of Mexico is assassinated.

1929
- William Faulkner's *The Sound and the Fury* is published.

ALTERNATIVE ASSESSMENT

LIVING HISTORY

MAKING A DISPLAY

Help students create their now-and-then displays.

- Students should make a list of questions the viewers of the now-and-then storyboard would want answered about parallel social issues of the 1920s and today.
- Taking into account students' artistic ability and interests, suggest ways in which they might present the social parallels visually on their storyboards. Color photocopies, sketches, maps, charts, and graphs are some possibilities.
- Put on the chalkboard a chart of additional topics and ask students to suggest appropriate parallels between the 1920s and today.

Project Planning Guide

Topic	Parallels
Substance abuse	
Organized crime	
Religious fundamentalism	
Sports heroes	

IN-DEPTH RESOURCES: UNIT 4
See worksheet and standards for evaluation, pp. 34, 35.

RECOMMENDED RESOURCES

Books for the Teacher

Anderson, Jervis. *This Was Harlem.* New York: Farrar, 1982. Engaging social history covers Harlem Renaissance.

Clarke, John Henrik., ed. *Marcus Garvey and the Vision of Africa.* New York: Random, 1974. Garvey's words and those of others.

Lewis, Thomas. *Empire of the Air.* New York: Burlingame, 1991. Early radio.

Books for the Student

Huggins, Nathan Irvin., ed. *Voices from the Harlem Renaissance.* New York: Oxford UP, 1976. Readings.

This Fabulous Century: 1920–1930. New York: Time-Life, 1969.

Torrence, Bruce. *Hollywood, the First Hundred Years.* New York: New York Zoetrope, 1982. Rise of movie industry.

Videos

The Age of Ballyhoo. Dir. David Shepard. Republic Pictures Home Video, 1973. Society and culture.

Amelia Earhart. Dir. Nancy Porter. PBS Video, 1993. Documentary.

Lindbergh. Dir. Stephen Ives. PBS Video, 1990. Documentary about aviator's triumph and subsequent difficult life.

Midnight Ramble. Dir. Bestor Cram and Pearl Bowser. PBS Video, 1994. African-American film industry in 1920s.

Software

Cultural Contributions of Black Americans. CD-ROM. Available from Educational Software Institute, 800-955-5570.

History of Jazz. CD-ROM. CLEARVUE/eav, 800-253-2788.

Section 1 Overview

OBJECTIVES

1. To explain how urbanization created a new way of life that often clashed with the values of the traditional American rural society.
2. To describe the controversy over the role of science and religion in American education and society in the 1920s.

CRITICAL THINKING

- Contrasting, p. 453
- Theme: Constitutional Concerns, p. 455
- Recognizing effects, p. 455
- Analyzing issues, p. 457
- Summarizing, p. 457
- Analyzing, p. 457
- Forming opinions, p. 457

FOCUS & MOTIVATE

5-MINUTE WARM-UP

Perceiving Cause and Effect

To recognize some of the causes and effects of prohibition, have students read the chart on page 455 and answer these questions.

1. What beliefs led reformers to support prohibition?
2. What was the primary result of prohibition?

WARM-UP TRANSPARENCY 13

▶ ***Starting with the Student***

- What differences do students think exist between urban and rural lifestyles today?

MORE ABOUT . . . *Billy Sundav*

William Ashley "Billy" Sunday was born in Ames, Iowa, in 1862. As a young man, Sunday played major-league baseball in Chicago, Pittsburgh, and Philadelphia. In 1903, after giving up his baseball career, he became a Presbyterian minister. He reportedly preached to over 100 million people before his death in 1935.

1 Changing Ways of Life

TERMS & NAMES
- speakeasy
- bootlegger
- fundamentalism
- Clarence Darrow
- Scopes trial

LEARN ABOUT life in the cities, Prohibition, and the outcome of the Scopes trial
TO UNDERSTAND how the "twenties" reflected conflicts and tensions in American culture.

ONE AMERICAN'S STORY

As the 1920s dawned, social reformers who hoped to ban alcohol—and the evils associated with it—rejoiced. The Eighteenth Amendment to the Constitution, banning the manufacture, sale, and transportation of alcohol, took effect in January of 1920. Billy Sunday, an evangelist who preached against the evils of drinking, predicted a new age of virtue and religion.

A PERSONAL VOICE

The reign of tears is over! The slums will soon be only a memory. We will turn our prisons into factories and our jails into storehouses and corncribs. Men will walk upright now, women will smile and the children will laugh. Hell will be forever for rent!

BILLY SUNDAY, quoted in *How Dry We Were: Prohibition Revisited*

Sunday's dream of a new age of morality and sobriety was not to be realized in the 1920s. By the end of the decade, the effort to outlaw alcohol had failed because too many people disagreed with the law to make it enforceable. The failure of prohibition reflected the changing values that marked the period of the 1920s. These changes produced clashes between small-town residents and big-city dwellers, between Americans who opposed the use of alcohol and those who used alcohol as part of their daily lives, and between religious believers who thought science and religion were incompatible and others who thought the two could coexist.

These cultural conflicts became most evident in the nation's cities. Lured by jobs and by the challenge and freedom that the city represented, millions of people—including returning World War I soldiers, who had seen the great cities of Europe—rode excitedly out of America's rural past and into its urban future.

Evangelist Billy Sunday

Rural and Urban Differences

The agricultural world that millions of Americans left behind was largely unchanged from the 19th century—a world of small towns and farms bound together by conservative moral values and close social relationships. Established, well-to-do families set a community's social standards. The church defined morality, and parents enforced the church's teachings. Out of the hard lives of rural dwellers emerged the American middle-class values of thriftiness, moderation, and respectability. Before the widespread use of cars, small towns were self-contained places. The people on the streets were friends and neighbors, and county fairs and church socials provided entertainment.

But America changed dramatically in the years before 1920, as was revealed in the 1920 census. That year, the figures showed, 51.4 percent of Americans lived in communities with populations of 2,500 to more than 1 million. America had become a more urban nation. Between 1922 and 1929, migration to the cities accelerated, with nearly 2 million people leaving farms and towns each year. "Cities were the place to be, not to get away from," said

SECTION 1 RESOURCES

PRINT RESOURCES

IN-DEPTH RESOURCES: UNIT 4
Guided Reading, p. 18
Primary Sources: Political Cartoon, p. 25; *from* The Scopes Trial, p. 26
Literature: from *Inherit the Wind* by Jerome Lawrence and Robert E. Lee, p. 29

READING STUDY GUIDE, p. 137

ACCESS FOR STUDENTS ACQUIRING ENGLISH
Guided Reading (Spanish), p. 158

SPANISH READING STUDY GUIDE, p. 137

FORMAL ASSESSMENT
Section Quiz, p.164

ALTERNATIVE ASSESSMENT BOOK
See forms for supporting and scoring alternative activities.

TECHNOLOGY RESOURCES

GEOGRAPHY TRANSPARENCIES
G21, Prohibition: 1890 and 1915

CRITICAL THINKING TRANSPARENCIES
CT21, Prohibition

CD-ROM *Our Times*
Electronic Library of Primary Sources

VIDEO *American Portfolio: A Videodisc for U.S. History* user's guide, pp. 195–196

INTERNET http://www.mlushistory.com

New York Street Scene (1920), Joaquín Torres-García.

one historian. Small-town attitudes began to lose their hold on the American mind as the city rose to prominence.

THE NEW URBAN SCENE At the beginning of the 1920s, New York, with a population of 5.6 million people, topped the list of big cities. Next came Chicago, with nearly 3 million, and Philadelphia, with nearly 2 million. Another 65 cities claimed populations of 100,000 or more, and they grew more crowded by the day. Life in these booming cities was far different from the slow-paced, intimate life in America's small towns. Chicago, for instance, was an industrial powerhouse, home to native-born whites and African Americans and immigrant Poles, Irish, Russians, Italians, Swedes, Arabs, French, and Chinese. The city's skyline sparkled with 163 skyscrapers. Each day, an estimated 300,000 workers, 150,000 cars and buses, and 20,000 trolleys poured into the pulsing downtown. Speculators made fortunes on the stock market. At night, stylish Chicagoans crowded ornate movie theaters and vaudeville houses offering live variety shows.

A. Answer Small towns were bound by traditional morals and close ties of family, friends, and religion. Cities offered varied perspectives and additional options because of their large, mixed populations; cultural variety; and greater tolerance of worldly values and ideas.

THINK THROUGH HISTORY
A. Contrasting *How did small-town life and city life differ?*

For small-town migrants, adapting to the urban environment demanded changes in thinking as well as in everyday living. The city was a world of competition and change. City dwellers took in new ideas at museums and art exhibits, plays and sports events, and nightclubs and movies. They read and argued about current scientific and social ideas. They judged one another by accomplishment more often than by background. City dwellers also tolerated drinking, gambling, and casual dating—worldly behaviors considered shocking and sinful in small towns.

For all its color and challenge, though, the city could be impersonal and frightening. Streets were filled with strangers, not friends and neighbors. Life was fast-paced, not leisurely. Social standards and values were hard to pin down in a world populated by brash businessmen, where foreign cultures mingled and many people pursued wealth and pleasure. The city demanded endurance, as a foreign visitor to Chicago observed.

A PERSONAL VOICE

It is not for nothing that the predominating color of Chicago is orange. It is as if the city, in its taxicabs, in its shop fronts, in the wrappings of its parcels, chose the color of flame that goes with the smoky black of its factories. It is not for nothing that it has repelled the geometric street arrangement of New York and substituted . . . great ways with names that a stranger must learn if he can. . . . He is in a [crowded] city, and if he has business there, he tells himself, "If I weaken I shan't last long."

WALTER L. GEORGE, *Hail Columbia!*

"How ya gonna keep 'em down on the farm, after they've seen Paree?"

POPULAR SONG OF THE 1920s

OBJECTIVE
① INSTRUCT

Rural and Urban Differences

▶ ***Starting with the Student*** Ask students to imagine themselves moving from a rural community to a large city or vice versa.

- How might their life change?
- How might they feel about their old friends? How might their friends feel about them?
- Do they think differences in lifestyles can cause conflicts between people? Why or why not?

▶ ***Discussing Key Ideas***

- The growth of cities results in new urban lifestyles that conflict with traditional values.
- Supporters of prohibition clash with those who ignore the law.

IN-DEPTH RESOURCES: UNIT 4
Guided Reading, p. 18

ACCESS FOR STUDENTS ACQUIRING ENGLISH
Guided Reading (Spanish), p. 158

MORE ABOUT . . .
Walter L. George

A son of British parents, Walter L. George was born in Paris in 1882. He became a special correspondent to several European newspapers, and in 1920 he traveled extensively in the United States. *Hail Columbia!* reports his impressions of America. According to George, the "true America" was to be found in the Midwest.

TEACHING OPTIONS

Making Connections Across Cultures

Immigration Throughout the 1920s Congress passed legislation that restricted immigration. A quota system limited the number of immigrants that could be admitted from each country annually. This system severely decreased the numbers of immigrants arriving from eastern and southern Europe.

- What attitudes did these laws reflect? *Discrimination against certain ethnic groups.*
- Why would these laws have affected cities more than rural areas? *Most immigrants settled in cities.*

Making Connections Across the Curriculum

Literature As the 1920s dawned, many of America's best writers set out to record the powerful forces reshaping the nation, including the pull of the cities. Sherwood Anderson, for example, ended his famous collection of stories *Winesburg, Ohio* with George Willard, the main character, leaving his provincial hometown for the big city—a "young man, going out of his town to meet the adventure of life." Throughout the 1920s millions of small-town men and women like George Willard streamed into New York, Los Angeles, and America's other booming cities.

DIFFICULT DECISIONS IN HISTORY

To Prohibit Alcohol or Not?

Critical Thinking: Compare and Contrast Have students create charts in which they list the pros and cons of prohibition. Then have them use their completed charts to answer the three questions in the feature.

MORE ABOUT . . .

Federal Agents

Izzy Einstein and Moe Smith were among the most colorful and most successful of the prohibition agents. They were masters of disguise, once posing as gravediggers to bust a moonshine operation in a New York City cemetery. During their service as prohibition agents, the two reportedly brought in 20 percent of all prohibition cases tried in New York City.

IN-DEPTH RESOURCES: UNIT 4
Primary Source: Political Cartoon, p. 25

Issues for the 21st Century

Crime and Public Safety

Connect crime in the Prohibition era with crime today. Have students read pages 884–887. Then have them answer these questions.

1. Why did prohibition trigger a rise in organized crime during the 1920s? *Underworld gangs made and sold liquor for huge profits.*
2. What factors led to an increase in crime in the 1980s? *The spread of crack-cocaine abuse.*

Difficult Decisions IN HISTORY

TO PROHIBIT ALCOHOL OR NOT?

The question of whether to outlaw alcohol divided Americans. Many reformers and religious groups thought drinking was sinful, unhealthy, and devastating to families. They believed that the government should protect the public's health and morals by making alcohol illegal.

Other Americans, including liberals, conservatives, intellectuals, and immigrant groups, did not believe alcohol consumption to be sinful or dangerous in moderation. They believed that consuming alcohol was a personal, not a government, decision and resisted any group's trying to tell them how to live.

1. Examine the pros and cons of each position. Which do you agree with? What other factors, if any, do you think would influence your position?
2. If you had been a legislator asked to vote for the Eighteenth Amendment, what would you have said? Explain.
3. What issues might the experiment of prohibition relate to today? Should the government attempt to prohibit immoral behavior?

INTERNET Visit http://www.mlushistory.com for more about prohibition and its repeal.

In the city, lonely migrants from the country often ached for home. Throughout the 1920s, Americans found themselves caught in a tug between the rural and urban cultures—a tug that pitted what seemed to be a safe, small-town world of close ties, hard work, and strict morals against a big-city world of anonymous crowds, moneymakers, and pleasure seekers.

THE PROHIBITION EXPERIMENT One vigorous clash between small-town and big-city Americans began in earnest in January 1920, when the Eighteenth Amendment went into effect. This amendment, which prohibited the manufacture, sale, and transportation of alcoholic beverages, launched the era known as Prohibition.

Reformers had long considered liquor a prime cause of corruption. They thought that too much drinking led to crime, wife and child abuse, accidents on the job, and other serious social problems. The church-affiliated Anti-Saloon League had led the drive to pass the prohibition amendment. The Woman's Christian Temperance Union, which considered drinking a sin, had helped push the measure through. Even before the amendment was ratified, certain areas of the country had established prohibition through state law. Most support for prohibition came from the rural South and West, areas with large populations of native-born Protestants who opposed alcohol consumption.

At first, saloons closed their doors, and arrests for drunkenness declined. But the effort to stop Americans from drinking was as doomed as "trying to dry up the Atlantic with a post-office blotter," according to one New Yorker. In the aftermath of World War I, many Americans were tired of making sacrifices; they wanted to enjoy life. Most immigrant groups did not consider drinking a sin but a natural part of socializing, and they resented government meddling.

Ironically, prohibition's fate was sealed by the government, which failed to budget enough men and money to enforce the law. The Volstead Act established a Prohibition Bureau in the Treasury Department in 1919, but the agency was underfunded. The job of enforcement involved patrolling 18,700 miles of coastline as well as inland borders, tracking down illegal stills (equipment for distilling liquor), monitoring highways for truckloads of illegal alcohol, and overseeing all the industries that legally used alcohol to be sure none was siphoned off for illegal purposes. The task fell to just 1,550 poorly paid federal agents and local police—clearly an impossible job.

SPEAKEASIES AND BOOTLEGGERS Drinkers went underground, flocking to hidden saloons and nightclubs known as **speakeasies** (so called because when inside, one spoke quietly—"easily"—to avoid detection), where liquor was sold illegally. Speakeasies could be found everywhere—in penthouses, cellars, office buildings, rooming houses, tenements, hardware stores, and tearooms. To be admitted to a speakeasy, one had to use a password, such as "Joe sent me," or present a special card. Inside, one would find a mix of fashionable middle-class and upper-middle-class men and women.

A young woman demonstrates one of the means used to conceal alcohol—hiding it in containers strapped to one's legs.

TEACHING OPTIONS

Exploring Themes

Constitutional Concerns Discuss reasons for the widespread violation of the Eighteenth Amendment. *Some people simply refused to obey a law they disagreed with; by 1932 some states had stopped enforcing prohibition.*

- Did violations of the Eighteenth Amendment indicate a lack of respect for the Constitution? *Many people thought that the Eighteenth Amendment violated their personal freedom, and it was poorly enforced, so the lack of respect for this amendment did not necessarily imply lack of respect for the Constitution as a whole.*

Teaching Less Proficient Readers

Recognizing Cause and Effect Help students use the following methods to recognize cause-effect relationships:

1. Look for key words, such as *because, therefore,* and *as a result.* (Example, p. 456: "As a result, they did not want evolutionary theory taught to their children.")
2. Look for statements indicating that a list of causes or effects will follow. (Example, p. 455: "Prohibition not only generated disrespect for the law but had other harmful effects.")

Before long, people grew bolder in getting around the law. Hardware stores sold cheap stills, and books and magazines explained how to distill liquor from apples, from watermelon—even from potato peelings. Since alcohol was allowed for medicinal and religious purposes, prescriptions for alcohol and sales of sacramental wine (intended for church services) skyrocketed. People also bought liquor from **bootleggers** (named for a smuggler's practice of carrying liquor in the legs of boots), who smuggled it in from Canada, Cuba, and the West Indies. They sold the liquor from ships anchored in international waters off the Atlantic coast. Then they bribed policemen and judges to let them operate freely. "The business of evading [the law] and making a mock of it has ceased to wear any aspects of crime and has become a sort of national sport," wrote the journalist H. L. Mencken, and he was right. Americans bought liquor and hid it cleverly—in false books, in hot-water bottles, in high boots, in containers strapped to their legs.

THINK THROUGH HISTORY
B. THEME ***Constitutional Concerns*** *Why do you think the Eighteenth Amendment failed to eliminate alcohol consumption?*

B. Answer *Possible Responses:* The consumption of alcohol was a traditional part of many cultures; the government failed to provide sufficient manpower and resources to enforce the law; the means of manufacturing, selling, and transporting liquor were many and could easily be concealed.

ORGANIZED CRIME Prohibition not only generated disrespect for the law but had other harmful effects as well. Most serious was the flow of money out of lawful businesses and into fast-growing organized crime. In nearly every major city, underworld gangs seized the opportunity to make and sell liquor and pocket huge profits. Chicago became notorious as the home of Al Capone, a gangster whose bootlegging empire netted over $60 million a year. Capone took control of the Chicago liquor business by killing off his competition. During the 1920s, headlines reported 522 bloody gang killings and made the image of flashy Al Capone part of the folklore of the period. In 1940, the writer Herbert Asbury recalled the Capone era in Chicago.

A PERSONAL VOICE

The famous seven-ton armored car with the pudgy gangster lolling on silken cushions in its darkened recesses, a big cigar in his fat face, and a $50,000 diamond ring blazing from his left hand, was one of the sights of the city; the average tourist felt that his trip to Chicago was a failure unless it included a view of Capone out for a spin. The mere whisper: "Here comes Al," was sufficient to stop traffic and to set thousands of curious citizens craning their necks along the curbing.

HERBERT ASBURY, *Gem of the Prairies*

HISTORICAL SPOTLIGHT

AL CAPONE

By age 28, Al Capone had built a criminal empire in Chicago, which he controlled through the use of bribes and violence. From 1925 to 1929, Capone bootlegged whiskey from Canada, operated illegal breweries in Chicago, and ran a network of 10,000 speakeasies. In 1927 alone, the "Big Fellow," as he liked to be called, made $105 million, writing himself into the *Guinness Book of World Records* as the private citizen who had made the most money in a single year.

The end came quickly for Capone, though. In 1931, the gangster chief was arrested for tax evasion and went to jail. That was the only crime of which the authorities were ever able to convict him. Capone was later released from jail, but he died several years later at age 48.

Al Capone built a criminal empire based on bootlegging.

By the mid-1920s, only 19 percent of Americans supported prohibition. The rest, who wanted the amendment changed or repealed, pointed to a rise in crime and lawlessness that they considered worse than the problem prohibition had set out to fix. Rural Protestant Americans, however,

THINK THROUGH HISTORY
C. *Recognizing Effects* *How did criminals take advantage of prohibition?*

C. Answer Criminals broke the law by smuggling, as well as by making alcohol and selling it for profit.

Prohibition, 1920–1933

SOME CAUSES	SOME EFFECTS
• Various religious groups thought drinking alcohol was sinful.	• Disrespect for the law developed.
• Reformers believed that government should protect the public's health.	• An increase in lawlessness, such as smuggling and bootlegging, was evident.
• Reformers believed that alcohol led to crime, wife and child abuse, and accidents on the job.	• Criminals found a new source of income.
• During World War I, native-born Americans developed a hostility to German-American brewers and toward other immigrant groups that used alcohol.	• Organized crime grew.

HISTORICAL SPOTLIGHT

Al Capone

Critical Thinking: Evaluating

- Why do students think people remain fascinated with Al Capone? *Possible Responses: Colorful figure, media attention, movies and TV shows.*
- Ask students to write editorials for a Chicago newspaper in answer to the following question: Should Chicagoans continue to promote fascination with Capone through museums, memorabilia, and tours of gangland sites?

ELECTRONIC LIBRARY OF PRIMARY SOURCES
from "My Bootlegger" by Samuel Hopkins Adams

HISTORY FROM VISUALS

Prohibition, 1920–1933

Reading the Chart Make sure students understand that the causes and effects in this chart are not linked to each other. The chart lists some important causes and effects of prohibition, but each cause did not produce the effect listed across from it.

Extension Have each student choose one of the effects listed in this chart (such as disrespect for the law) and then give examples of that effect.

CRITICAL THINKING TRANSPARENCIES
CT21, Prohibition

GEOGRAPHY TRANSPARENCIES
G21, Prohibition: 1890 and 1915

Block Schedule TEACHING OPTION **Time Needed: 20 Minutes**

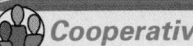

Cooperative Activity: Creating a Dictionary of 1920s Slang

Task: Student groups will define and illustrate 1920s slang terms for a dictionary.

Purpose: To investigate how popular culture affects language.

Activity: Assign the following 1920s slang terms to groups of students: *bathtub gin, bee's knees, bootlegger, cement overshoes, cheaters, flapper, gatecrasher, heebie-jeebies, jake, jalopy, lounge lizard, main drag.* Instruct students to find the meanings of the terms, write definitions in a dictionary format, and draw illustrations to accompany the definitions. Groups should combine their work to create a classroom dictionary of 1920s slang.

Building a Portfolio: Students may choose to add their illustrated definitions to their portfolios.

ALTERNATIVE ASSESSMENT BOOK
Standards for Evaluating a Cooperative Activity

Standards for Evaluation
Definitions should . . .
- state the meanings of the slang terms clearly and concisely
- give examples of the use of the terms
- be accompanied by appropriate illustrations

OBJECTIVE

2 INSTRUCT

Science and Religion Clash

▶ ***Discussing Key Ideas***

- Fundamentalists believe that the biblical account of creation is true.
- Many others believe in the scientific theory of evolution.
- The opposing values clash in the Scopes trial, which questions the roles of science and religion in public schools.

IN-DEPTH RESOURCES: UNIT 4
Primary Source: *from* The Scopes Trial, p. 26

NOW & THEN

Evolution, Creationism, and Education

Critical Thinking: Contrasting Have students make Venn diagrams to contrast evolutionist and creationist arguments. A diagram might look like the one below.

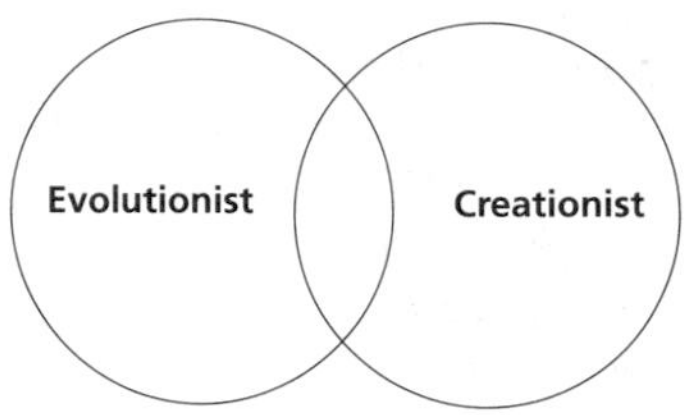

Then ask students what arguments, if any, might serve as support for both points of view. Have them write these arguments in the overlapping section of their diagrams.

Students might also find newspaper or magazine articles dealing with the teaching of evolution in public schools.

defended a law that they felt strengthened moral values. The Eighteenth Amendment remained in force until 1933, when it was repealed by the Twenty-first Amendment.

Science and Religion Clash

Another bitter controversy highlighted the growing rift between traditional and modern ideas during the 1920s. This battle raged between fundamentalist religious groups and secular thinkers over the truths of science.

AMERICAN FUNDAMENTALISM **Fundamentalism** was a Protestant movement grounded in a literal, or nonsymbolic, interpretation of the Bible. Since the late 19th century, many Protestants had gradually adapted to a society marked by a growing trust in science and by an acceptance of the different religious faiths practiced by immigrants. Protestant fundamentalists resisted this trend. They were skeptical of scientific knowledge and argued that all important knowledge could be found in the Bible. They believed that the Bible was inspired by God, and therefore its stories in all their details were true.

Their beliefs led fundamentalists to reject the theory of evolution advanced by Charles Darwin in the 19th century—a theory stating that plant and animal species had developed and changed over millions of years. They pointed instead to the Bible's account of creation, in which God made the world in six days and then created Adam and Eve. To deny the truth of this story, fundamentalists said, was to deny the Scriptures and to blaspheme God. As a result, they did not want evolutionary theory taught to their children in school.

NOW & THEN

EVOLUTION, CREATIONISM, AND EDUCATION

There is still great controversy today over the teaching of evolution in the public schools. Some people believe that creationism should be taught as a theory of the origin of life, along with evolution. Creationism argues that the account of the creation of the universe given in Genesis—the first book of the Bible—is literally true.

The issue of what should be taught about the origin of life—and who should decide this issue—continues to stir up debate. Some moderates have suggested that science and religion are not necessarily incompatible and that a theory of the origin of life can accommodate both the scientific theory of evolution and religious beliefs.

Fundamentalism expressed itself in several ways. In the South and West, preachers led religious revivals based on the authority of the Scriptures. One of the most powerful revivalists was Billy Sunday, a baseball player turned preacher who staged emotional meetings across the South. In Los Angeles, Aimee Semple McPherson, a theatrical woman who dressed in flowing white satin robes, used Hollywood showmanship to preach the word to throngs of homesick Midwestern migrants. In the 1920s, fundamentalists also began to win political power and to call for laws prohibiting the teaching of evolution. Moderate Protestants and liberal thinkers viewed this trend with deep concern.

The evangelist Aimee Semple McPherson, who won thousands of devoted followers with her broadcasts from the Angelus Temple in Los Angeles, founded the International Church of the Foursquare Gospel.

THE SCOPES TRIAL In March 1925, Tennessee passed the nation's first law that made it a crime to teach evolution. Immediately, the American Civil Liberties Union (ACLU) promised to defend any teacher who would challenge the law. The ACLU had been founded in 1920—the time of the Red Scare and of routine violence against African Americans—as a public-interest law firm defending rights, such as freedom of speech, protected under the Constitution. John T. Scopes, a young biology teacher in Dayton, Tennessee, accepted the challenge. In his biology class, Scopes read this passage from *Civic Biology:* "We have now learned that animal forms may be arranged so as to begin with the simple one-celled forms and culminate with a group which includes man himself." Scopes was promptly arrested, and his trial was set for July.

The ACLU hired **Clarence Darrow,** the most famous trial lawyer of the day, to defend Scopes. William Jennings Bryan, three-time Democratic candidate for president and a devout fundamentalist, served as a special prosecutor.

TEACHING OPTIONS

Making Connections Across the Curriculum

Literature The Scopes trial has been the subject of several books, including *Six Days or Forever?* by Ray Ginger. The play *Inherit the Wind* by Jerome Lawrence and Robert E. Lee (made into a motion picture in 1960) also concerns the Scopes trial. Have students examine *Six Days or Forever?* and *Inherit the Wind* (and view the movie version of the latter if they can). Then suggest that they compare the characterizations of Darrow and Bryan in the different versions of the story.

Teaching Gifted and Talented Students

Interpreting Points of View Have interested students work in pairs to present dramatic readings of the courtroom exchanges between Darrow and Bryan. They might locate a transcript of the trial or portions of the trial (such as are provided in Leslie H. Allen's *Bryan and Darrow at Dayton* and in *Six Days or Forever?*). If students have trouble finding a transcript of the trial, they might get a copy of *Inherit the Wind* at the library. Then have them look for passages in the play that they would like to present to the class in their dramatic readings. Ask the class to summarize each man's point of view on the basis of the readings.

There was no real question of guilt or innocence: Scopes was honest about his action. The **Scopes trial** was a fight over evolution and the role of science and religion in public schools and in American society.

Almost overnight, the trial became a national sensation. Throngs of big-city reporters filed daily stories from Dayton, and Chicago's WGN radio covered the drama live. When the proceedings opened on July 10, 1925, a steamy summer day, Darrow appeared coatless, wearing a tan shirt and a white string tie. The aging, heavyset Bryan dressed in a white pleated shirt and bow tie and carried a palm-leaf fan and a jug of water. When he entered the courtroom, the audience burst into applause.

Clarence Darrow speaks at the Scopes trial in Dayton, Tennessee, in 1925.

BRYAN TAKES THE WITNESS STAND Darrow called Bryan as an expert on the Bible. This was the contest that everyone had been waiting for. To handle the throngs of Bryan supporters, Judge Raulston moved the court outside, to a platform built under the maple trees. There, before a crowd of 2,000, Darrow relentlessly questioned Bryan about his beliefs. Bryan stood firm, a smile on his face, claiming he believed in the Bible.

A PERSONAL VOICE

Mr. Darrow—Do you claim that everything in the Bible should be interpreted literally?

Mr. Bryan—I believe everything in the Bible should be accepted as it is given there. Some of the Bible is given illustratively. For instance: "Ye are the salt of the earth." I would not insist that man was actually salt, or that he had flesh of salt, but it is used in the sense of salt as saving God's people.

CLARENCE DARROW AND WILLIAM JENNINGS BRYAN, quoted in *Bryan and Darrow at Dayton*

D. Answer Fundamentalists believed that God created the world in six days, whereas evolutionists argued that modern species developed from earlier forms of life over millions of years.

THINK THROUGH HISTORY
D. Analyzing Issues *What was the conflict between fundamentalists and those who accepted evolution?*

Darrow asked Bryan if he agreed with Bishop James Ussher's calculation that according to the Bible, Creation happened in 4004 B.C. Bryan said he did. Had every living thing on earth appeared since that time? Did Bryan know that ancient civilizations had thrived before 4004 B.C.? Did he know the age of the earth? Bryan grew edgy but stuck to his guns. Finally, Darrow asked Bryan, "Do you think the earth was made in six days?" Cornered by the questions, Bryan answered, "Not six days of 24 hours." People sitting on the lawn gasped.

With this answer, Bryan admitted that the Bible might be interpreted in different ways. But in spite of this admission, Scopes was found guilty and fined $100. The Tennessee Supreme Court later changed the verdict on a technicality, but the law outlawing the teaching of evolution stayed on the books after the trial.

This clash over evolution, the prohibition experiment, and the emerging urban scene all were evidence of the changes and conflicts occurring during the 1920s. During that period, women also experienced conflict as they redefined their roles and pursued new lifestyles.

Section 1 Assessment

1. TERMS & NAMES
Identify:
- speakeasy
- bootlegger
- fundamentalism
- Clarence Darrow
- Scopes trial

2. SUMMARIZING Create two diagrams like the one below, showing how government attempted to deal with (a) prohibition and (b) the teaching of evolution.

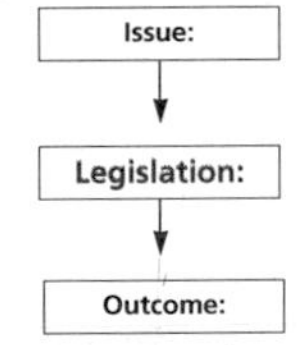

Write a paragraph stating your position on one of these issues.

3. ANALYZING How might the overall atmosphere of the 1920s have contributed to the failure of prohibition?

THINK ABOUT
- changing values
- changing lifestyles
- fashions of the time

4. FORMING OPINIONS Do you think the passage of the Volstead Act and the verdict in the Scopes trial represented genuine triumphs for traditional values? Why or why not?

THINK ABOUT
- changes in urban life in the 1920s
- the effects of prohibition
- the legacy of the Scopes trial

MORE ABOUT . . .
Clarence Darrow

The most famous American lawyer of the early 1900s, Clarence Darrow, gained his fame as a defender of labor interests. Darrow was nearly 70 years old when he tried his most famous criminal cases. In 1924 he defended Nathan Leopold and Richard Loeb, two young men who admitted kidnapping and murdering a 14-year-old boy. To keep them from receiving the death penalty, Darrow successfully argued that they were mentally ill.

OUR TIMES
the Scopes trial

ASSESS & RETEACH

Section 1 Assessment

Assign pairs of students to answer alternate questions. Then have them share their answers.

Self-Assessment

Have each student use the Think Through History questions to review the main ideas of this section. Students should verify their answers in the text.

Section Quiz

FORMAL ASSESSMENT
Section Quiz, p. 164

Reteach

Use the Guided Reading Worksheet for Section 1 to reinforce understanding.

IN-DEPTH RESOURCES: UNIT 4
Guided Reading, p. 18

CLOSE

The shift to a predominantly urban society brought about many changes during the 1920s. New lifestyles of city dwellers and new ideas in education challenged traditional values.

ANSWERS

1. TERMS & NAMES

speakeasy, p. 454
bootlegger, p. 455
fundamentalism, p. 456
Clarence Darrow, p. 456
Scopes trial, p. 457

2. SUMMARIZING

Issue: prohibition
Legislation: The Eighteenth Amendment banned the manufacture, sale, and transportation of alcohol.
Outcome: Many Americans broke the law.
Issue: teaching evolution
Legislation: A Tennessee state law made it a crime to teach evolution.
Outcome: Biology teacher John Scopes broke the law, was arrested, and was convicted.

3. ANALYZING

Possible Responses: People living in cities felt freer and less bound by traditional values; immigrants brought their own cultures, habits, and religious values.

4. FORMING OPINIONS

Possible Responses: Students answering yes might say that these events raised people's awareness and have had a lasting influence, since today legislators and some religious groups work to solve the problems of alcoholism and the teaching of evolution still provokes legal controversy. Those answering no might say that the Volstead Act not only did not stop people from drinking alcohol but caused the growth of organized crime and that the conviction of John Scopes failed to discredit Charles Darwin's theory.

Section 2 Overview

OBJECTIVES

1. To explain how the image of the flapper embodied the changing values and attitudes of young women in the 1920s.
2. To identify the causes and results of the changing roles of women in the 1920s.

SKILLBUILDER

- Interpreting graphs, p. 460

CRITICAL THINKING

- Theme: Women in America, p. 459
- Recognizing effects, pp. 460, 461
- Summarizing, p. 461
- Analyzing, p. 461
- Forming opinions, p. 461

FOCUS & MOTIVATE

5-MINUTE WARM-UP

Interpreting Graphs
To gain insight into women's employment between 1910 and 1930, have students study the graphs on page 460 and answer these questions.

1. Between 1910 and 1920, which type of work registered the greatest increase? Which type of work registered the greatest decrease?
2. Which type of work in all three periods employed the most women? Which type of work employed the fewest?

WARM-UP TRANSPARENCY 13

▶ ***Starting with the Student***
Discuss how students' tastes in music and clothing differ from their parents' tastes.

- Why do students think young people's attitudes toward life differ from those of the preceding generation?

2 The Twenties Woman

TERMS & NAMES
- flapper
- double standard

LEARN ABOUT changes in lifestyles, jobs, and families during the 1920s
TO UNDERSTAND how women's roles changed.

ONE AMERICAN'S STORY

One January day in 1922, the psychologist G. Stanley Hall was strolling down the street when he encountered a young woman. She was about 16, "comely, happy, innocent," and Hall took the "liberty to look at her . . . carefully."

A PERSONAL VOICE

She wore a knitted hat, with hardly any brim, of a flame or bonfire hue; a henna scarf; two strings of Betty beads, of different colors, twisted together; an open short coat, with ample pockets; a skirt with vertical stripes so pleated that, at the waist, it seemed very dark, but the alternate stripes of white showed progressively downward, so that, as she walked, it gave something of what . . . psychologists call a flicker effect. On her right wrist were several bangles; on her left, of course, a wrist watch. Her shoes were oxfords, with a low broad heel. Her stockings were woolen and of brilliant hue. But most noticeable of all were her high overshoes, or galoshes. One seemed to be turned down at the top and entirely unbuckled, while the other was fastened below and flapped about her trim ankle in a way that compelled attention.

G. STANLEY HALL, "Flapper Americana Novissima," *Atlantic Monthly,* June 1922

So noteworthy was this young woman—and millions of others like her—that Hall wrote a long article about the twenties woman. In her fashions, manners, and lifestyle, she represented a gathering social revolution.

This flapper models a stylish summer outfit in June 1920. The dress is made of silk piqué, with a jacket of checked crepe.

Young Women Change the Rules

By the 1920s, the experiences of World War I, the pull of cities, and changing attitudes had opened up a new world for many young Americans. These "wild young people," wrote one of them (John F. Carter, Jr., in a 1920 issue of *Atlantic Monthly*), were experiencing a world unknown to their parents: "We have seen man at his lowest, woman at her lightest, in the terrible moral chaos of Europe. We have been forced to question, and in many cases to discard, the religion of our fathers. . . . We have been forced to live in an atmosphere of 'to-morrow we die,' and so, naturally, we drank and were merry." In the rebellious, pleasure-loving atmosphere of the twenties, many women began to assert their independence and demand the same freedoms as men.

THE FLAPPER During the twenties, a new ideal emerged for some women: the **flapper,** an emancipated young woman who embraced the new fashions and urban attitudes of the day. Even though many young women donned the new outfits and flouted tradition, the flapper was more of an image of rebellious youth than a widespread reality. Even so, the casual, boyish fashions of the 1920s reflected this image of a new, sophisticated woman. Prewar clothes disappeared into attics and trash bins—all those dark and prim ankle-length dresses, whalebone corsets, petticoats, black stockings, and high-laced shoes.

Out of the shopping bags came close-fitting felt hats, bright waistless dresses an inch above the knees, skin-toned silk stockings, sleek pumps, strings

SECTION 2 RESOURCES

PRINT RESOURCES

IN-DEPTH RESOURCES: UNIT 4
Guided Reading, p. 19

READING STUDY GUIDE, p. 139

ACCESS FOR STUDENTS ACQUIRING ENGLISH
Guided Reading (Spanish), p. 159

SPANISH READING STUDY GUIDE, p. 139

FORMAL ASSESSMENT
Section Quiz, p. 165

ALTERNATIVE ASSESSMENT BOOK
See forms for supporting and scoring alternative activities.

TECHNOLOGY RESOURCES

CD-ROM Electronic Library of Primary Sources

VIDEO *American Portfolio: A Videodisc for U.S. History* user's guide, pp. 192, 199–200

INTERNET http://www.mlushistory.com

of beads, and bracelets. Flappers clipped their long hair into boyish bobs and dyed it jet black. The finishing touches were rouge on the cheeks and "kissproof" lipstick on the lips. "The prevailing feminine ideal was a type that suggested criminality—not an unnatural reflection of the speakeasy life introduced by prohibition," said a writer for *Life* magazine.

The new fashions reflected a new attitude. Some women in the 1920s acted differently, too, as G. Stanley Hall noticed in the young woman he observed that day in January 1922.

A PERSONAL VOICE

We were on a long block that passed a college campus, where the students were foregathering for afternoon sports. She was not chewing gum, but was occasionally bringing some tidbit from her pocket to her mouth, taking in everything in sight, and her gait was swagger and superior. 'Howdy, Billy,' she called to a youth whom I fancied a classmate; and 'Hello, boys,' was her greeting to three more a little later.

G. STANLEY HALL, "Flapper Americana Novissima," *Atlantic Monthly,* June 1922

Like the young woman Hall observed, many young twenties females became more assertive. In their bid for equal status with men, some began smoking cigarettes and drinking in public, actions that would have ruined their reputations not many years before. They danced the fox trot, camel walk, tango, lindy hop, and shimmy with abandon. Early in the decade, young women who still wore corsets left them behind when they went to dances for fear that they might be called "ironsides" or spend the evening as a wallflower. Some women learned to play golf and competed with men on the fairways.

Attitudes toward marriage changed as well. Many middle-class men and women began to view marriage as more of an equal partnership, although both agreed that housework and child-rearing were a woman's job.

THE DOUBLE STANDARD Magazines, newspapers, and advertisements promoted the image of the flapper, and young people openly discussed relationships in ways that scandalized their elders. However, the image of the flapper did not reflect the attitudes and values of many young people. During the 1920s, morals loosened only so far. Traditionalists in churches and schools protested the new casual dances and women's acceptance of smoking and drinking.

In the years before World War I, when men "courted" women, they pursued only women they intended to marry. In the 1920s, however, casual dating became increasingly accepted. Even so, a **double standard**—a set of principles granting greater sexual freedom to men than to women—required women to observe stricter standards of behavior than men did. As a result, many women were pulled back and forth between the old standards and the new.

This stylized rendition of the flapper appeared on the cover of *McClure's,* a popular magazine of the time.

NOW & THEN

THE MISS AMERICA PAGEANT

"There she is, Miss America; there she is, your ideal." These are the opening words to the song that came to represent the Miss America pageant.

This tradition began in 1921 in Atlantic City, New Jersey. Hotel owners had dreamed up the bathing-beauty pageant in 1920 to attract tourists to the city after Labor Day. The first Miss America was Margaret Gorman, a petite 16-year-old from Washington, D.C. The second was 15-year-old Mary Katherine Campbell from Columbus, Ohio, a straight-A high school student with red hair and tiny, size-three feet. Campbell recalled her road to the title:

"I was pretty naive when I was starting. . . . Mercy, after all I was only fifteen. You were supposed to be sixteen, so I was sixteen, but I was really only fifteen in May. I came home and told my mother, 'I was chosen Miss Columbus, and they said it's because of my figure. Mother, what's a figure?' My mother said: 'It's none of your business.'"

THINK THROUGH HISTORY

A. THEME ***Women in America*** *How was the flapper like and unlike women of today?*

A. Answer Flappers used clothing, hairstyles, and behavior to claim a new freedom; today's women use the same means of self-expression, but social, political, and economic changes have made rebellion a less necessary means of gaining recognition.

OBJECTIVE

① **INSTRUCT**

Young Women Change the Rules

▶ ***Starting with the Student*** Have each student write a paragraph describing a fashionable young woman of today.

- What style of clothing does she wear? What colors are most popular?
- What are her hairstyle, makeup, and jewelry and other accessories like?
- How do these styles reflect American society today?

▶ ***Discussing Key Ideas***

- The flapper represents a new ideal for young women.
- A double standard requires women to abide by stricter standards of behavior than men.

IN-DEPTH RESOURCES: UNIT 4
Guided Reading, p. 19

ACCESS FOR STUDENTS ACQUIRING ENGLISH
Guided Reading (Spanish), p. 159

ELECTRONIC LIBRARY OF PRIMARY SOURCES
from "Flapper Jane" by Bruce Bliven

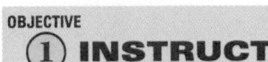

NOW & THEN
The Miss America Pageant

Critical Thinking: Evaluating The opening words of the Miss America theme song describe the winner as "your ideal."

- In what sense is Miss America an ideal for young women?
- Do students think the ideal has changed since the 1920s? If so, how?

TEACHING OPTIONS

Exploring Themes

Women in America Discuss how styles have reflected changing images of American women through history. What image did the whalebone corsets and ankle-length dresses of the early 1900s reflect? How did the flapper styles of the 1920s change that image? *Early 1900s women were prim and proper; 1920s women were freer, more independent.*

- What influences women's styles today?
- What images of women do styles such as "grunge" and "cute" reflect?

Making Connections Across Time

Miss America Pageant In the 1920s, Atlantic City tourists objected to the Miss America pageant, claiming that it was immoral for young women to parade in bathing suits. In recent years, women's groups have criticized the pageant's bathing-suit competition for portraying women as "objects" rather than as people.

- How do the recent criticisms of the pageant differ from the 1920s objections? *1920s objections were based on what women should and should not do; recent criticisms are based on how people should regard women.*

OBJECTIVE

② INSTRUCT

Women Shed Old Roles at Home and at Work

▶ ***Starting with the Student***

- Ask students if they think opportunities for women in the workplace are greater today than in the 1920s.
- Have students create flow charts, listing causes and effects of the changing roles of women in the 1920s. A chart might look like the one below.

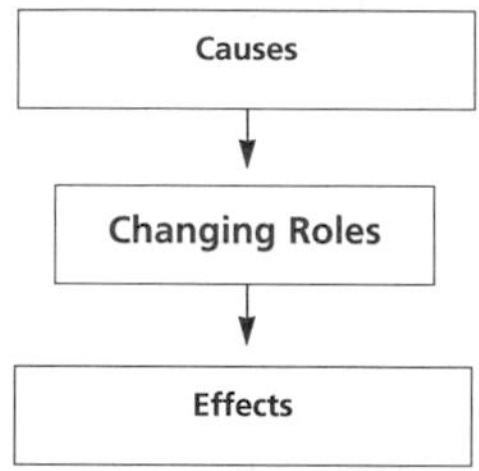

▶ ***Discussing Key Ideas***

- Women assume new roles in the workplace.
- Technological advances simplify household tasks.
- Married women remain responsible for housework and child care.

HISTORY FROM VISUALS

Women's Changing Employment, 1910–1930

Reading the Graphs Tell students to note the time span of the pie graphs. The first graph deals with a year (1910) before the time period of this chapter to provide background.

Extension Ask students to check an almanac or a statistical abstract to find the percentages of women employed in these ways today.

Women Shed Old Roles at Home and at Work

The fast-changing world of the 1920s produced new roles for women in the workplace and new trends in family life. A booming industrial economy opened new work opportunities for women in offices, factories, stores, and professions. The same economy churned out time-saving appliances and products that reshaped the roles of housewives and mothers.

A young woman in 1920 works as an expert typesetter in a publishing house.

NEW WORK OPPORTUNITIES The wartime trend of women's seeking employment continued into the twenties, but opportunities for women changed with growing mechanization and the return of men to the work force. In the 1920s, nearly 1 million female college graduates moved into the "women's professions" of teaching and nursing, and thousands more became librarians and social workers. The number of women bankers, lawyers, police officers, and probation officers rose, too.

Big businesses required extensive correspondence and record keeping, creating a huge demand for clerical workers. Two million women took jobs as typists, filing clerks, secretaries, stenographers, and office-machine operators. In addition, about 800,000 became clerks in stores, and about 2 million took jobs on assembly lines. A handful of women broke the old stereotypes by doing work once reserved for men, such as flying airplanes, driving taxis, and drilling oil wells.

By 1930, 10 million women were earning wages; however, they made up only 24 percent of American workers. The battle for equality in the workplace had just begun. Medical schools imposed a 5 percent quota on female admissions. Consequently, the number of women doctors actually declined between 1910 and 1920. Few women rose to managerial jobs, and wherever they worked, women earned less than men. Fearing female competition for well-paying jobs, men argued that women were just temporary workers whose real job was at home. Between 1900 and 1930, the patterns of discrimination and inequality for women in the business world were established.

B. Answer Although big business and industry produced time-saving appliances that freed women from some household chores, and although business growth also created jobs for millions of women, most women were confined to traditional jobs.

THINK THROUGH HISTORY
B. *Recognizing Effects* *How did the growth of business and industry affect women?*

Skillbuilder Answer
Decline: Agriculture.
Increase: Clerical.

SKILLBUILDER
INTERPRETING GRAPHS
According to the pie graphs, in which area of work did the percentage of women decline the most between 1910 and 1930? In which area did the percentage of women increase the most?

THE CHANGING FAMILY Widespread social and economic changes reshaped the family. The birthrate had been declining for several decades, and it dropped at a slightly faster rate in the 1920s. This decline was due in part to the wider availability of birth-control information. Margaret Sanger, who had opened the first birth-control clinic in the United States in 1916, founded the American Birth Control League in 1921 and fought for the legal rights of physicians to give birth-control information to their patients.

At the same time, social and technological innovations simplified household labor and family life. Stores overflowed with ready-made clothes, sliced bread,

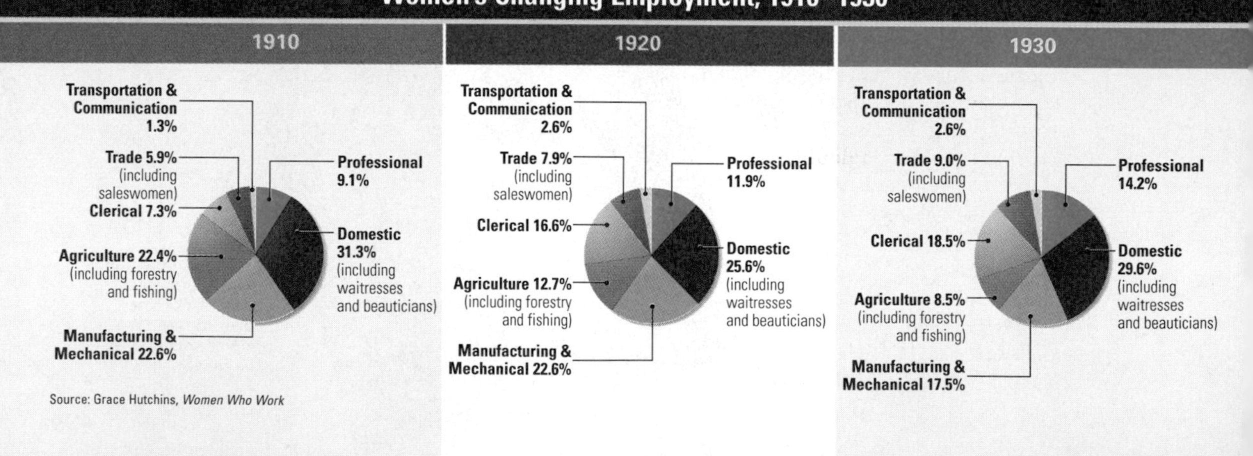

Block Schedule TEACHING OPTION **Time Needed: 30 Minutes**

Cooperative Activity: Analyzing Changes in Women's Roles

Task: Student groups will depict ways that the behavior, work, and attitudes of American women changed in the 1920s.

Purpose: To synthesize information about women's changing roles in the 1920s and present this information to the class.

Activity: Assign topics—such as fashion, manners, housework, family, and jobs—to groups of three to four students. Instruct the groups to depict the ways in which women's lives changed in these areas during the 1920s. Students might find or draw pictures, perform skits, or create models to contrast American women of the 1920s with those of an earlier time period. Assign a role to each student: one might be a recorder; another, a facilitator; another, a timekeeper; and another, a presenter. Provide time for groups to share their work with the class.

ALTERNATIVE ASSESSMENT BOOK
Standards for Evaluating a Cooperative Activity

and canned foods. Public agencies provided services for the elderly, public health clinics served the sick, and workers' compensation assisted those who could no longer work. These institutions had the effect of freeing homemakers from some of their traditional family responsibilities. Many middle-class housewives, the main shoppers and money managers, focused their attention on their homes, husbands, children, and pastimes. "I consider time for reading clubs and my children more important than . . . careful housework and I just don't do it," said an Indiana woman in the 1920s.

As women's spheres of activity and influence expanded, they experienced greater equality in marriage. Marriages were based increasingly on romantic love and companionship. Children, no longer thrown together with adults in factory work, farm labor, and apprenticeships, spent most of their days at school and in organized activities with others their own age. This meant that peer groups became relatively more important. At the same time, parents began to rely more heavily on manuals of child care and the advice of experts.

Despite these changes, however, the vast majority of married women remained homemakers. For one thing, a woman's going to work might be seen as evidence that her husband had failed as a breadwinner. Nevertheless, many women worked from necessity. Working-class or college educated, women quickly discovered the pressure of juggling work and family, but the strain on working-class women was more severe. Helen Wright, who worked for the Women's Bureau in Chicago, recorded the struggle of an Irish mother of two.

"You younger women have a harder task than ours. You will want equality in business, and it will be even harder to get than the vote."

ANNA HOWARD SHAW,
VETERAN SUFFRAGIST

A PERSONAL VOICE

She worked in one of the meat-packing companies, pasting labels from 7 A.M. to 3:30 P.M. She had entered the eldest child at school but sent her to the nursery for lunch and after school. The youngest was in nursery all day. She kept her house "immaculately clean and in perfect order," but to do so worked until eleven o'clock every night in the week and on Saturday night she worked until five o'clock in the morning. She described her schedule as follows: on Tuesday, Wednesday, Thursday, and Friday she cleaned one room each night; Saturday afternoon she finished the cleaning and put the house in order; Saturday night she washed; Sunday she baked; Monday night she ironed.

HELEN WRIGHT, quoted in *Wage-Earning Women*

C. Answer The birthrate dropped; household labor was simplified by technology; children spent all day in school; the divorce rate increased; adolescent rebelliousness increased.

THINK THROUGH HISTORY
C. Recognizing Effects *What were some of the changes that affected the family in the 1920s?*

As women adjusted to changing roles, some also struggled with rebellious adolescents, who put an unprecedented strain on families. Teens in the 1920s studied and socialized with other teens and spent less time with their families. As peer pressure intensified, some adolescents resisted parental control.

This theme of adolescent rebelliousness can be seen in much of the popular culture of the 1920s. Education and entertainment reflected the conflict between traditional attitudes and modern ways of thinking.

Section 2 Assessment

1. TERMS & NAMES
Identify:
- flapper
- double standard

2. SUMMARIZING Copy the concept web shown below and add to it examples that illustrate the concepts.

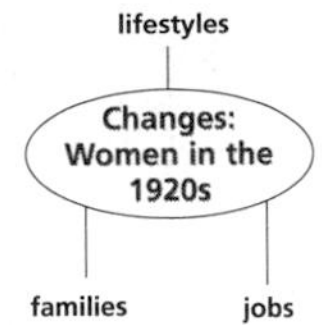

Write a paragraph explaining how you think women's lives changed most dramatically in the 1920s.

3. ANALYZING During the 1920s, a double standard required women to observe stricter codes of behavior than men. Do you think that some women of this decade made real progress toward placing both genders on an equal footing? Support your answer with evidence from the text.

THINK ABOUT
- G. Stanley Hall's observations on pages 458 and 459
- the flapper's style and image
- changing views of marriage

4. FORMING OPINIONS Today the term "glass ceiling" refers to the barriers women and minorities encounter in seeking higher career positions. In your opinion, could this term be applied to women's job opportunities during the 1920s? Cite evidence to support your answer.

THINK ABOUT
- technology's impact on jobs
- women's battle for equality
- roadblocks to professional success for women

MORE ABOUT . . .
The American Homemaker

In the 1920s women shopped for items they had formerly made by hand. National chain stores expanded rapidly to meet the needs of American homemakers. Piggly Wiggly pioneered the concept of self-service grocery stores. By offering prepackaged national brands at low prices, the Piggly Wiggly chain grew from 500 stores in 1920 to 2,500 stores in 1929.

ASSESS & RETEACH

Section 2 Assessment

Assign the questions as homework or as a class activity.

Self-Assessment

Ask students to review the answers they wrote for item 4 in the Section Assessment. As they gave their opinions about applying the term "glass ceiling" to women's job opportunities in the 1920s, what new ideas did they have?

Section Quiz

FORMAL ASSESSMENT
Section Quiz, p. 165

Reteach

Have each student write a set of questions based on the main topics in this section, then answer the questions on a separate sheet of paper. Have pairs of students answer each other's questions and work together to verify the answers.

ANSWERS

1. TERMS & NAMES

flapper, p. 458

double standard, p. 459

2. SUMMARIZING

Possible Responses: **Lifestyles**—wearing new clothing styles, wearing more makeup, playing golf, dancing. **Families**—decline in birthrate, more leisure time for housewives because of labor-saving devices, more pressure on working-class women, rebellious adolescents. **Jobs**—teachers, nurses, librarians, social workers, clerical workers, store clerks, factory workers.

3. ANALYZING

Possible Responses: Students answering yes might say that women laid the foundation for equality when they smoked and drank in public, became more open and assertive in communicating with men their age, dated casually, dressed nontraditionally, and viewed marriage as an equal partnership. Students answering no may say that new ways of dressing, smoking in public, and casual dating were basically superficial changes.

4. FORMING OPINIONS

Possible Responses: Students answering yes may say that medical schools had 5-percent admission quotas for women, that women were paid lower wages than their male counterparts, that few women were promoted to management positions, and that jobs were labeled as male or female. Students answering no may say that a glass ceiling is almost invisible but barriers to advancement in the 1920s were all too visible.

CLOSE

The flapper symbolized the new, more independent, and sometimes flamboyant role of women in the 1920s. In spite of new opportunities in the workplace, women earned less than men and continued to be primarily responsible for the home and child care.

Daily Life

OBJECTIVES

1. To describe the popular culture of the 1920s.
2. To explain why the youth-dominated decade came to be called the Roaring Twenties.

FOCUS & MOTIVATE

▶ ***Starting with the Student***
Have students think about some of the hallmarks of contemporary American popular culture.

- What are some of the fads and fashions of today's pop culture?
- What impact do fads and fashions have on the young?

MORE ABOUT . . .
Pop Figures of the 1920s
In the 1920s Americans loved contests of all sorts. Some of their biggest heroes were sports figures—like baseball's Babe Ruth, who hit a record-breaking 60 home runs in 1927, and Gertrude Ederle, the 19-year-old American who was the first woman to swim the English Channel. Other sports stars of the 1920s included football's Red Grange and Knute Rockne, the heavyweight boxers Jack Dempsey and Gene Tunney, the golfer Bobby Jones, the tennis champ Bill Tilden, and the thoroughbred racehorse Man O'War, who won all of his starts but one, which he lost to a horse named Upset.

DAILY LIFE 1920–1929

Youth in the Roaring Twenties

The decade known as the Roaring Twenties was a celebration of youth and its culture. Fads, crazy and frenetic dances, silly songs, and radically new styles of clothing captured the public's fancy. This was an especially liberating period for women, who received the right to vote in 1920. Many women also opted for a liberating change of fashion—short skirts and short hair—as well as the freedom to smoke and drink in public.

During this period of relative prosperity, many people questioned the values of the past and were willing to experiment with new values and behavior as well as with new fashions. Among the fads were the ukulele, the game of mahjong, the crossword puzzle, and water skiing. A favorite song of the day asked, "In the morning, in the evening, ain't we got fun?"

FLAGPOLE SITTING
One of the more bizarre fads of the 1920s was flagpole sitting. The fad began in 1924 as a publicity stunt to attract viewers to movie theaters. The sitter would climb to the top of a flagpole, set up a small platform, and remain sitting on it for days at a time.

The most famous flagpole sitter was "Shipwreck" Kelly (at left, waving from high above a movie theater in Union City, New Jersey). In 1929, for a total of 145 days, Kelly took up residence atop various flagpoles throughout the country. Imitators, of course, followed. At one point that year, Baltimore had at least 17 boys and 3 girls sitting atop 18-foot hickory poles, with their friends and families cheering them on.

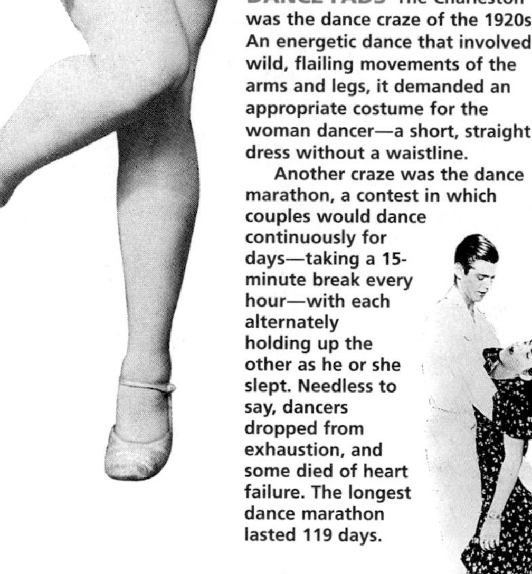

DANCE FADS The Charleston was the dance craze of the 1920s. An energetic dance that involved wild, flailing movements of the arms and legs, it demanded an appropriate costume for the woman dancer—a short, straight dress without a waistline.

Another craze was the dance marathon, a contest in which couples would dance continuously for days—taking a 15-minute break every hour—with each alternately holding up the other as he or she slept. Needless to say, dancers dropped from exhaustion, and some died of heart failure. The longest dance marathon lasted 119 days.

RECOMMENDED RESOURCES

Books

Andrist, Ralph K., ed. *The American Heritage History of the '20's & '30's.* New York: American Heritage, 1970. A profusely illustrated account.

Stevenson, Elizabeth. *Babbitts and Bohemians.* New York: Macmillan, 1967. America in the Roaring Twenties.

This Fabulous Century: 1920–1930. New York: Time-Life, 1969. A fascinating pictorial history.

Videos

The Jazz Age. Time-Life Video, 1990. Newsreels and vintage photos capture the 1920s; part of the series America: A Look Back.

Lowell Thomas Remembers: The Roaring Twenties. Blackhawk, 1975. Three videocassettes covering the Roaring Twenties.

The Roaring '20s. Guidance Associates, 1990. Social and political changes of the era.

The Twenties. PBS Video, 1988. Part of the acclaimed PBS series *A Walk Through the 20th Century with Bill Moyers.*

The Twenties: From Illusion to Disillusion. Dir. Mirea Alexandresso and Henri Torrent. Films for the Humanities and Sciences, 1991.

BESSIE SMITH was "Empress of the Blues." In 1923, she sold a million recordings of "Down Hearted Blues."

MAHJONG is a game of Chinese origin that became wildly popular in the 1920s. It is usually played by four people using tiles resembling dominoes and bearing various designs.

BOBBED HAIR In keeping with the liberating influence of their new clothing, women bobbed their hair—that is, they had it cut much shorter—freeing themselves of the long tresses that had been fashionable for years. The woman shown is having her hair cut at a barber shop.

GENTLEMEN'S FASHIONS Gentlemen, not to be outdone by the ladies, enjoyed some outrageous fashions of their own. This young man, with the aid of two flappers, displays the latest fashion—extra-wide, floppy trousers, sometimes called Oxford bags. He also sports a popular men's hairstyle of the day—"patent-leather hair," parted on the side or in the middle and slicked down close to the head.

DATA FILE

School Days, School Days

During the 1920s, children studied reading, writing, and arithmetic in elementary school. In high school, students also studied history and literature and had vocational training. Girls learned cooking and sewing, and boys learned woodworking.

Slang Expressions

crush—an infatuation with someone
gatecrasher—someone who attends an event without paying or without an invitation
keen–attractive or appealing
ritzy—elegant
scram—to leave in a hurry
screwy—crazy
the bee's knees—a superb person or thing

Radio

- KDKA, Pittsburgh, the first commercial radio station, went on the air on November 2, 1920. It was owned by Westinghouse.
- In 1922, 500 radio stations were in operation in the United States.
- In 1924, over 3 million radios were in use throughout the United States. By the end of the 1920s, over 10 million radios were in use. Popular radio shows included *Amos 'n' Andy* and *Jones and Hare.*

Song Titles

"Baby Face"
"Barney Google"
"Blue Skies"
"Bye Bye Blackbird"
"Button Up Your Overcoat"
"Charleston"
"Crazy Rhythm"
"If You Knew Susie"
"I Want to Be Happy"
"Let a Smile Be Your Umbrella"
"Makin' Whoopee"
"My Blue Heaven"
"My Heart Stood Still"
"Show Me the Way to Go Home"
"Singin' in the Rain"
"Tea for Two"

INTERACT WITH HISTORY

1. **COMPARING** With a small group, listen to several of the songs listed above or to several others from the period. Discuss the lyrics and the melodies of the songs, and compare them with those of popular songs today. What can you learn about the 1920s from this music? Report your findings to the class.

SEE SKILLBUILDER HANDBOOK, PAGE 909.

2. **RESEARCHING CLOTHING STYLES** Find out more about the clothing styles just before the flapper era. How severe were the changes in fashion in the 1920s? How do you think parents of flappers reacted to these changes? If you had lived at this time, would you have chosen to wear the new styles? Why or why not?

Visit http://www.mlushistory.com for more about life in the 1920s.

INSTRUCT

▶ *Starting with the Student*
- Have students consider what role World War I may have played in shaping the attitudes of the Roaring Twenties. *Possible Responses: War brought disillusionment, which prompted cynicism and hedonism in the young; having witnessed death and destruction, Americans now turned to play; postwar American isolationism led to a concentration on domestic issues.*

▶ *Discussing Key Ideas*
- During the 1920s a youth-dominated popular culture that questions the values of the past emerges in America.
- New styles and crazes sweep the nation during the decade often called the Roaring Twenties.

HISTORY FROM VISUALS

Reading the Images Have students examine the illustrations and captions on these pages.
- On the basis of these details, how would students describe American youth in the 1920s? What conclusions can students draw from the Data File? *Possible Responses: Radical, liberated, aiming to shock, hedonistic, self-absorbed, frivolous, experimental.*

INTERACT WITH HISTORY

1. Comparing

Provide recordings for students, if possible, or suggest that they borrow recordings from libraries, relatives, or friends. Point out that they can look for collections of 1920s songs or hunt for songs individually; for example, "Stardust" and "Blue Skies" appear on the Willie Nelson CD *Stardust;* "My Blue Heaven," on *Fats Domino's Greatest Hits.* If necessary, students might use music-store or on-line music catalogs or library music references, such as those published by the Schwann Group, to locate CDs or cassettes containing specific songs.

2. Researching Clothing Styles

Students might examine references on the history of fashion or books containing photographs of the 1900–1920 period (such as the first two volumes of Time-Life's *This Fabulous Century*) for more on clothing just before the Roaring Twenties. After comparing the more conservative clothing of earlier years, they may speculate that many parents of flappers were shocked or outraged by their children's dress. Descriptions of what students themselves would have chosen to wear will vary, but they should offer reasons for their choices.

Section 3 Overview

OBJECTIVES

1. To explain how schools and mass media influenced American culture in the 1920s.
2. To identify the athletes, celebrities, artists, and writers who contributed to American popular culture in the 1920s.

SKILLBUILDER

- Understanding geography: location, place, p. 467

CRITICAL THINKING

- Theme: Science and Technology, p. 465
- Forming opinions, pp. 466, 469
- Making inferences, p. 467
- Analyzing causes, p. 469
- Summarizing, p. 469
- Synthesizing, p. 469

FOCUS & MOTIVATE

5-MINUTE WARM-UP

Drawing Conclusions
To introduce students to writers of the 1920s, have them read the excerpt from Sinclair Lewis's *Babbitt* on page 468 and answer these questions.

1. What tone does Lewis use to describe Babbitt?
2. What conclusions can you draw about Babbitt's character from the excerpt?

WARM-UP TRANSPARENCY 13

▶ ***Starting with the Student***
Ask students to name three well-known Americans whom they consider heroes—people worthy of respect. List their suggestions on the chalkboard and ask them to identify the field in which each is famous. Then ask students these questions.

- What kinds of people do you consider heroes?
- Why do you admire these people?

3 Education and Popular Culture

LEARN ABOUT the growth of schools, movies, mass media, and spectator sports ***TO UNDERSTAND*** how America developed a popular culture in the 1920s—a culture that many artists and writers criticized.

TERMS & NAMES
- Babe Ruth
- Gertrude Ederle
- Charles A. Lindbergh
- George Gershwin
- Georgia O'Keeffe
- Sinclair Lewis
- F. Scott Fitzgerald
- Edna St. Vincent Millay
- Ernest Hemingway

ONE AMERICAN'S STORY

On September 22, 1927, approximately 50 million Americans sat listening to their radios as Graham McNamee, radio's most popular announcer, breathlessly called the boxing match between the former heavyweight champ Jack Dempsey and the current titleholder, Gene Tunney.

A PERSONAL VOICE

Good evening Ladies & Gentlemen of the Radio Audience . . . this is a big night. Three million dollars worth of boxing bugs are gathered around a ring at Soldier Field, Chicago. Burning down at us are 44 1,000-watt lamps over the ring. All is darkness in the muttering mass of crowd beyond the spotlight. The crowd is thickening in the seats . . . it's like the Roman Coliseum. . . .

Here comes Jack Dempsey, climbing through the ropes . . . white flannels, long bathrobe. . . . Here comes Tunney. . . . He's got on blue trunks with red trimmings. They're getting the gloves out of a box tied with pretty blue ribbon . . . The announcer shouting in the ring . . . trying to quiet 150,000 people. . . . Robes are off. . . . The Bell.

GRAHAM McNAMEE, *Time* magazine, October 3, 1927

Gene Tunney, down for the "long count," went on to defeat Jack Dempsey in their epic 1927 battle.

Punches flew for six rounds. Tunney went down in the seventh, but the referee didn't start his ten-second count for the knockout until Dempsey got back to his corner. The slow count gave Tunney time to get up, continue punching, and defeat the legendary Dempsey. So suspenseful was the brutal match that a number of radio listeners died of heart failure. The "fight of the century" was just one of a host of spectacles and events that transformed American popular culture in the 1920s.

Schools and the Mass Media Shape Culture

Not every change in popular culture had the immediate drama of the Dempsey-Tunney fight. Nevertheless, developments in the areas of education and news coverage had a powerful impact on the nation during the 1920s. Throughout the period, schools and the mass media worked to shape American minds.

SCHOOL ENROLLMENTS In 1914, approximately 1 million American students attended high school. By 1926, that number had risen to 4 million, a fourfold increase sparked by prosperous times and by the higher educational standards demanded for jobs in industry.

The modern high school emerged during this period of expanding education. Before the 1920s, most high schools had catered to college-bound students. In contrast, the new high schools offered courses for a broad range of students, including vocational training for those interested in industrial jobs and home economics for future homemakers.

The public schools met another special challenge in the 1920s—teaching the children of new immigrant families. While this job wasn't a new one for American schools, it became a bigger one. The years before World War I had seen the largest stream of immigrants in the nation's history—close to 1 million

SECTION 3 RESOURCES

PRINT RESOURCES

IN-DEPTH RESOURCES: UNIT 4
Guided Reading, p. 20
Skillbuilder Practice: Drawing Conclusions, p. 22
Geography Application: From Coast to Coast, p. 23
Primary Source: *from* An Interview with Charles A. Lindbergh, p. 27
American Lives: Georgia O'Keeffe, p. 32

READING STUDY GUIDE, p. 141

ACCESS FOR STUDENTS ACQUIRING ENGLISH
Guided Reading (Spanish), p. 160
Skillbuilder Practice: Drawing Conclusions (Spanish), p. 162
Geography Application: From Coast to Coast (Spanish), p. 163

SPANISH READING STUDY GUIDE, p. 141

FORMAL ASSESSMENT
Section Quiz, p. 166

ALTERNATIVE ASSESSMENT BOOK
See forms for supporting and scoring alternative activities.

TECHNOLOGY RESOURCES

HUMANITIES TRANSPARENCIES
H20, *Automat* by Edward Hopper

CD-ROM *Our Times*
Electronic Library of Primary Sources

VIDEO *American Portfolio: A Videodisc for U.S. History* user's guide, pp. 191–193, 196–197, 199–200

INTERNET http://www.mlushistory.com

newcomers a year. Unlike the earlier English and Irish immigrants, many of the new immigrants spoke no English. By the 1920s their children filled city classrooms. Determined teachers met the challenge and created a large pool of literate Americans.

As the demands placed on public schools grew, taxes to finance the schools increased as well. School costs doubled between 1913 and 1920, then doubled again by 1926. The total cost of American education in the mid-1920s amounted to $2.7 billion a year.

EXPANDING NEWS COVERAGE Widespread education increased literacy in America, but it was the growing mass media that shaped a mass culture. Newspaper circulation rose as writers and editors learned how to hook readers by imitating the sensational stories in the tabloids. The success of tabloids, such as those founded by William Randolph Hearst, revealed the public's appetite for the details of one big event after another. Mass-circulation magazines, appealing to readers around the country, also flourished during the 1920s. Many of these magazines summarized the week's news, both foreign and domestic.

A. Answer More widespread education produced a nationwide pool of readers. Mass media created a popular culture by enabling people nationwide to experience the same entertainment and information.

"All I know is what I read in the papers."

WILL ROGERS,
HUMORIST

RADIO COMES OF AGE Although major magazines and newspapers reached big audiences, radio was the most powerful communications medium to emerge in the 1920s. Americans added terms such as "airwaves," "radio audience," and "tune in" to their everyday speech. As radio networks emerged, they invested heavily in market research to find out what people wanted to hear. They became successful by programming to satisfy the public's interests. By the end of the decade, the radio networks had created something new in the United States—the shared national experience of hearing the news as it happened. The wider world had opened up to Americans, who could hear the voice of their president or listen to the World Series live. The announcer Graham McNamee received thousands of letters a year

THINK THROUGH HISTORY
A. THEME *Science and Technology* *What changes took place in public education and the mass media in the 1920s?*

The Mass Media, 1920s

NEWSPAPERS

- By the mid-1920s, about 36 million Americans read newspapers, an increase of 8 million from prewar years.
- Since 1914, about 600 local newspapers had shut down, and 230 others had been swallowed up by 55 huge newspaper chains.
- During the 1920s, most Americans stopped getting news only from local writers. They began reading more news stories, columns, editorials, sports articles, and features in newspapers distributed from the big-city headquarters of the newspaper chains.
- Tabloids such as the *Daily News* and the *Daily Mirror* in New York City featured sensational stories of murders, kidnappings, gangsters, and entertainers, using bold photographs and large headlines to scream the news.

Lou Tellegen Wed; Pola Negri Bride Suspect
DAILY MIRROR
COLLINS DEAD IN CAVE; ROCK HOLDS BODY FAST

MAGAZINES

- In 1923, Henry Luce cofounded *Time*, a weekly newsmagazine that interpreted the news it presented.
- In 1921, DeWitt and Lila Wallace founded *Reader's Digest*, a magazine that condensed articles originally published in other magazines and periodicals.
- By the end of the 1920s, ten American magazines—including *Time*, the *Saturday Evening Post*, *Collier's*, and *Reader's Digest*—boasted a circulation of more than 2 million each.
- Other popular magazines of the age were *Life*, *Smart Set*, *American Mercury*, and *The New Yorker*.
- Many of these magazines featured a blend of fiction, cartoons, and articles. Others focused on tales of crime and "true confessions."

RADIO

- In 1921, New York's WEAF broadcast a regular news program with the announcer H. V. Kaltenborn; in 1922, the same station broadcast the first commercially sponsored program.
- In 1926, three corporations—General Electric (GE), Westinghouse, and the Radio Corporation of America (RCA)—formed the first radio network, the National Broadcasting Corporation (NBC); the Columbia Broadcasting System (CBS) was formed in 1927.
- In 1929, Americans spent $850 million on radio equipment, and NBC was charging advertisers $10,000 to sponsor an hour-long program.
- By 1930, 40 percent of U.S. households had radios.

OBJECTIVE
① INSTRUCT

Schools and the Mass Media Shape Culture

▶ ***Starting with the Student*** Make a list of students' favorite TV shows. Point out that in the late 1920s, Americans regularly listened to variety shows and comedy series, such as *Amos 'n' Andy* and *The Smith Family.*

▶ ***Discussing Key Ideas***
- Public high schools take on new roles in preparing students for the future.
- Expanded news coverage and the development of radio give Americans shared experiences.

IN-DEPTH RESOURCES: UNIT 4
Guided Reading, p. 20

ACCESS FOR STUDENTS ACQUIRING ENGLISH
Guided Reading (Spanish), p. 160

HISTORY FROM VISUALS
The Mass Media, 1920s

Reading the Chart Remind students that the term *mass media* refers to all the means of public communication that reach a large audience.

Extension Have students draw up a list of mass media that have become important since the 1920s.

MORE ABOUT . . .
The Tabloids

Only about half the size of ordinary newspapers, tabloids were easier to handle on crowded subway trains.

TEACHING OPTIONS

Exploring Themes

Science and Technology Radio created a shared national experience for Americans in the 1920s. As people all over the nation listened to the same news and entertainment, a sense of community and shared values was created.

Ask students to discuss the positive and negative effects of a shared national experience. *Possible Response: Positive—unity; Negative—lack of individuality.*

Teaching Gifted and Talented Students

Radio Broadcasts of the 1920s Have students work in groups to present radio broadcasts like those of the 1920s. They may choose to report on sports events, political events, or news or to present entertainment shows. Encourage them to make the broadcasts as authentic as possible by copying the styles of the times. As part of their research, they can listen to recordings of old radio shows in order to gain a sense of what such broadcasts were like.

OBJECTIVE

2 INSTRUCT

America Chases New Heroes and Old Dreams

▶ ***Starting with the Student***
- Which of students' activities or interests might be considered fads?
- Compare today's fads with those of the 1920s.

▶ ***Discussing Key Ideas***
- Sports heroes, movie stars, and Charles Lindbergh inspire Americans.
- Writers, artists, and composers experiment with new styles.
- Much of the decade's literature expresses a clash of values within society.

IN-DEPTH RESOURCES: UNIT 4
American Lives: Georgia O'Keeffe, p. 32

HUMANITIES TRANSPARENCIES
H20, *Automat* by Edward Hopper

ELECTRONIC LIBRARY OF PRIMARY SOURCES
"The Sultan of Swat Steals a World Series Show" by Heywood Broun

ON THE WORLD STAGE

The 1924 Winter Olympics

Critical Thinking: Evaluating Ask students if they think, on the basis of what they know about the Olympics in recent years, that including winter games was a good decision. Have them give reasons to support their opinions.

from radio fans. One from a hospital worker summed up a national feeling: "The hospital is really a home for some eight hundred patients. . . . Their little Main Street is quite narrow, and the radio is bringing the world to their feet."

America Chases New Heroes and Old Dreams

During the 1920s, many people had money and the leisure time to enjoy it. In 1929, Americans spent $4.5 billion on entertainment, much of it on ever-changing fads. Early in the decade, Americans engaged in new leisure pastimes such as working crossword puzzles and playing mahjong, a Chinese game whose playing pieces resemble dominoes. In 1922, after explorers opened the dazzling tomb of the Egyptian pharaoh Tutankhamen, consumers mobbed stores for pharaoh-inspired accessories, jewelry, and furniture. In the mid-1920s, people turned to flagpole sitting, six-day bike races, and dance marathons. They also flooded athletic stadiums to see sports stars, who were glorified as superheroes by the mass media.

ON THE WORLD STAGE

FRANCE
Chamonix

THE 1924 WINTER OLYMPICS

In the early 1920s, sports enthusiasts began to clamor for Olympic competition in skiing, skating, and other winter sports. The International Olympic Committee hesitated; the original Olympics, it pointed out, featured summer sports. But in 1924, the committee gave in and staged the first Winter Olympics in Chamonix, France. The round of events that year featured ice hockey, figure skating, skiing, speed skating, and bobsledding. Norwegian and Finnish athletes dominated the games; but Canada won the ice hockey competition, and an American took the gold medal in the 500-meter skating race.

B. Answer Students might mention sports heroes, such as Michael Jordan, who are as hugely popular as Babe Ruth was.

THINK THROUGH HISTORY
B. Forming Opinions *Is there an athlete today to whom you would compare Babe Ruth?*

SPORTS HEROES OF THE 1920s Although the media hyped sports heroes, the Golden Age of Sports reflected common aspirations. As athletes in nearly every sport set new records, they inspired masses of ordinary Americans. When poor, unknown athletes rose to national fame and fortune, they restored Americans' belief in the power of the individual to improve his or her life.

Baseball's legendary star was New York Yankees slugger **Babe Ruth.** Through the 1920s, the paunchy, hard-drinking Ruth smashed home run after home run, earning himself such nicknames as Sultan of Swat and Colossus of Clout. When Ruth hit a record 60 home runs for the Yankees in 1927, America went wild. The *New York Times* writer John Kiernan exclaimed, ". . . I'll stand and shout till the last man's out: There never was a guy like Ruth!"

The Negro National League, founded in 1920, was the first of a series of black baseball leagues that played in the Northern cities to which many blacks had moved from the South. Featuring such players as Josh Gibson—credited with hitting 89 home runs in a single season—and Leroy "Satchel" Paige, these leagues held their own world series, but they declined in the 1940s after Paige and others followed Jackie Robinson into the major leagues.

Boxing's biggest star was the heavyweight champion Jack Dempsey. Seemingly unbeatable, Dempsey defended his championship many times and turned boxing into a legitimate sport. He was finally defeated by Gene Tunney in 1926 and again in 1927. When the fighters met for their second match, a record crowd of some 150,000 people paid approximately $2,650,000 to watch.

Red Grange, nicknamed the Galloping Ghost, boosted enthusiasm for college football with his feats as a University of Illinois running back. Between 1918 and 1930, the Fighting Irish of Notre Dame, led by coach Knute Rockne, were wildly popular because of their five undefeated seasons and 105 victories.

Tennis greats Big Bill Tilden and Helen Wills became household names. The public devoured stories of Atlanta's Bobby Jones, the only golfer ever to win the British and American open and amateur championships in one year. They also cheered for **Gertrude Ederle,** who in 1926 became the first woman to swim the English Channel.

Helen Wills won the singles title at the U.S. Open seven times and the Wimbledon title eight times. Her nickname was Little Miss Poker Face.

TEACHING OPTIONS

Teaching Less Proficient Readers

Identifying Main Ideas Demonstrate the following technique for identifying main ideas in the text:

1. Read the heading on page 466: "America Chases New Heroes and Old Dreams." Then restate the heading as a question or series of questions: Who were the new heroes of the 1920s? What were the dreams of the age? How does America "chase" heroes and dreams?
2. Skim the text under that heading to find the answers to the questions. The answers generally state the main ideas. Have students practice the technique with other headings.

Making Global Connections

Charles Lindbergh The historic flight from New York to Paris made Lindbergh a hero on two continents. In December 1927 the U.S. government sent Lindbergh to Latin America as a goodwill ambassador.

- What qualities made Charles Lindbergh a popular hero? *Honesty, bravery, ambition, and skill.*
- How did the United States benefit from Lindbergh's popularity? *Possible Response: People in other countries associated Lindbergh's positive qualities with America.*

IN-DEPTH RESOURCES: UNIT 4
Primary Source: *from* An Interview with Charles A. Lindbergh, p. 27

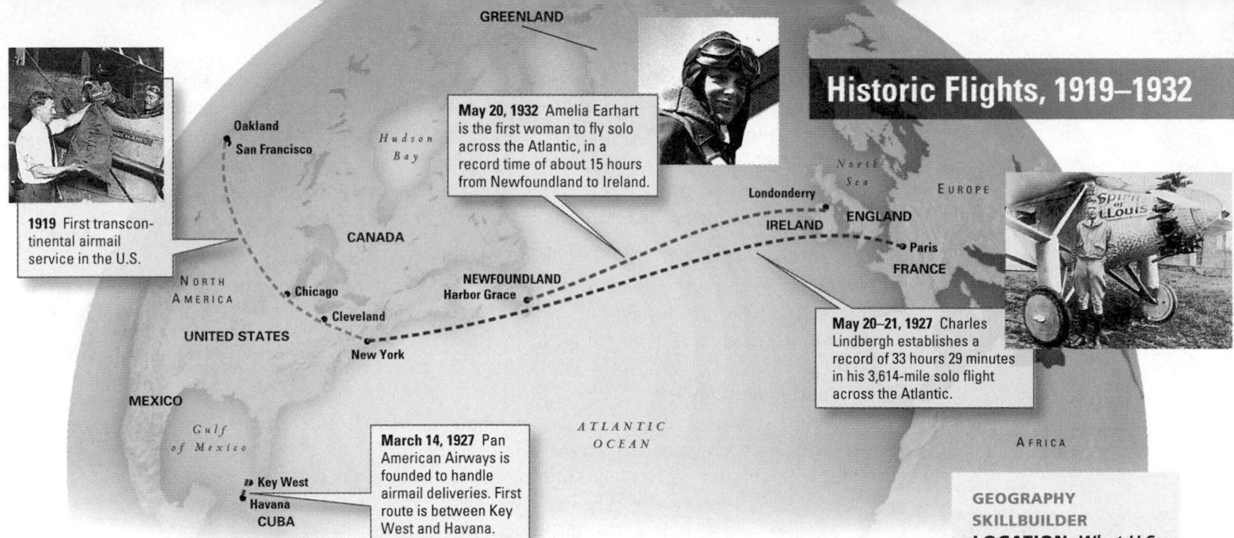
Historic Flights, 1919–1932
GREENLAND
Oakland
San Francisco
Hudson Bay
CANADA
May 20, 1932 Amelia Earhart is the first woman to fly solo across the Atlantic, in a record time of about 15 hours from Newfoundland to Ireland.
1919 First transcontinental airmail service in the U.S.
North America
Chicago
Cleveland
UNITED STATES
New York
NEWFOUNDLAND
Harbor Grace
Londonderry
IRELAND
ENGLAND
Paris
FRANCE
Europe
North Sea
May 20–21, 1927 Charles Lindbergh establishes a record of 33 hours 29 minutes in his 3,614-mile solo flight across the Atlantic.
MEXICO
Gulf of Mexico
ATLANTIC OCEAN
March 14, 1927 Pan American Airways is founded to handle airmail deliveries. First route is between Key West and Havana.
Key West
Havana
CUBA
Africa

GEOGRAPHY SKILLBUILDER
LOCATION *What U.S. cities were among the stops on the first transcontinental airmail route?*
PLACE *What would be the advantage of beginning a transatlantic flight in Newfoundland, as Amelia Earhart did, rather than in New York, as Lindbergh did?*

Skillbuilder Answer **Location:** New York, Cleveland, Chicago, and San Francisco. **Place:** *Possible Answer:* Newfoundland lies farther east than other parts of North America; leaving from there would shorten the flight distance across the ocean.

LINDBERGH'S FLIGHT America's most beloved hero of the time, however, wasn't an athlete but a small-town pilot named **Charles A. Lindbergh,** who made the first nonstop solo flight across the Atlantic. A handsome, modest Minnesotan, Lindbergh decided to go after a $25,000 prize for the first solo transatlantic flight. On May 20, 1927, he took off from New York City in the *Spirit of St. Louis,* flew up the coast to Newfoundland, and headed over the Atlantic. The weather was so bad, Lindbergh recalled, that "the average altitude for the whole . . . second 1,000 miles of the [Atlantic] flight was less than 100 feet." After 33 hours and 29 minutes, Lindbergh set down at Le Bourget airfield outside of Paris, France, amid beacons, searchlights, and mobs of enthusiastic French people.

Paris threw a huge party. New York showered Lindbergh with ticker tape, the president received him at the White House, and America made him its idol. In an age of sensationalism, excess, and crime, Lindbergh stood for the honesty and bravery the nation seemed to have lost. The novelist F. Scott Fitzgerald, a fellow Minnesotan, caught the essence of Lindbergh's fame.

A PERSONAL VOICE
In the spring of 1927, something bright and alien flashed across the sky. A young Minnesotan who seemed to have nothing to do with this generation did a heroic thing, and for a moment people set down their glasses in country clubs and speakeasies and thought of their old best dreams.

F. SCOTT FITZGERALD, quoted in *The Lawless Decade*

C. Answer Movie stars provided excitement and romance through a medium that was new and changing; they offered vicarious adventure to people whose lives were taken up mostly with earning a living.

Lindbergh's success spurred others to greatness. In the next decade, Amelia Earhart was to undertake many brave aerial exploits, inspired by Lindbergh's example.

MOVIES Despite the feats of real-life heroes, America's yearning for excitement and romance seemed unquenchable in the 1920s. Movies tapped into this national craving. By 1925, filmmaking had become the nation's fourth-largest industry, and more than 20,000 movie houses did a steady business nationwide.

Hollywood, just outside Los Angeles, established itself as America's movie capital and produced a host of silent films. Among the stars of these films was Charlie Chaplin, who played the comical, warm-hearted Little Tramp. Tom Mix rose to fame in Westerns. Theda Bara, the "vamp," and Clara Bow, the "It Girl," reflected society's infatuation with physical attractiveness and freedom. But most famous of all was Rudolph Valentino, the dark, seductive leading man in *The Sheik,* who melted women's hearts.

THINK THROUGH HISTORY
C. *Making Inferences* *Why were Americans so entranced with movie stars in the 1920s?*

Charlie Chaplin was one of the most famous stars in movie history.

HISTORY FROM VISUALS
Historic Flights, 1919–1932

Reading the Map Have students list in chronological order the flights mentioned on the map.

Extension Students might do some research in order to add dates of other historic flights during this period (1919–1932), or they might add dates of later historic flights.

IN-DEPTH RESOURCES: UNIT 4
Geography Application: From Coast to Coast, p. 23

MORE ABOUT . . .
Charlie Chaplin

The famous movie star Charlie Chaplin was born in London in 1889. He began touring the United States as a music-hall performer in 1910. He first appeared on film as the Little Tramp in 1914, and five years later he joined with others in the movie industry to form the United Artists film company. Chaplin gained complete control over the production of his films. He wrote and directed almost all of them, and he composed music for those with sound. In 1972 Chaplin received an honorary Academy Award for "the incalculable effect he has had in making motion pictures the art form of this century."

TEACHING OPTION

Skillbuilder Mini-Lesson: Drawing Conclusions

Explaining the Skill Drawing conclusions about a historical event or condition means forming an opinion or making an inference based on facts and available evidence. In the process of drawing conclusions, historians also consider evidence in the light of what they know to be true from past experience.

Applying the Skill Have students read about Lindbergh's flight. Then direct their attention to the quotation from F. Scott Fitzgerald. Ask students to draw conclusions about Fitzgerald's opinion of the flight and of the lifestyles of the 1920s. Have students support their conclusions with specific evidence from the text. *Students might say that Fitzgerald admired Lindbergh's accomplishment, had contempt for the lifestyles of his time, and felt that earlier times were more praiseworthy. Specific supporting evidence includes information in the second paragraph on this page and Fitzgerald's words: "who seemed to have nothing to do with this generation" and "people set down their glasses . . . and thought of their old best dreams."*

IN-DEPTH RESOURCES: UNIT 4
Skillbuilder Practice: Drawing Conclusions, p. 22

MORE ABOUT . . .
Mickey Mouse

Steamboat Willie was the first cartoon to use sound synchronized with the movements of animated characters. Walt Disney pioneered this technique. The high-pitched voice that Disney himself provided for Mickey soon became famous around the world.

MORE ABOUT . . .
Writers of the 1920s

Dorothy Parker, Robert Benchley, and Robert Sherwood worked together as writers and editors at *Vanity Fair* and *The New Yorker*—popular magazines of the period. Their lunches at the nearby Algonquin Hotel became the famous Round Table that attracted some of the most brilliant writers and artists of the time. The members called themselves the Vicious Circle because of their practice of insulting others and enjoying laughs at others' expense.

OUR TIMES
Charles Lindbergh, Sinclair Lewis, F. Scott Fitzgerald

In 1927, Hollywood released *The Jazz Singer* starring Al Jolson—the first major film with sound. A year later, the young Walt Disney produced *Steamboat Willie,* the first sound movie starring the cartoon character Mickey Mouse. With the coming of "talkies," movie attendance doubled. By 1930, millions of Americans were going to the movies every week. Along with the mass media and spectator sports, movies bound Americans even more tightly into a national family.

Walt Disney's Mickey Mouse first talked on screen in the 1928 film *Steamboat Willie.* Disney himself provided the voice for Mickey.

THEATER, MUSIC, AND ART While movies provided a romantic escape, the arts gave Americans fresh perspectives. Before this era, most plays in American theaters had imitated European melodrama. All that changed with Eugene O'Neill, the first American playwright to win a Nobel Prize in literature. O'Neill's plays, such as *The Hairy Ape* (1922), forced Americans to reflect on modern isolation, confusion, and family conflict.

Composers of concert music also began breaking away from European traditions in the 1920s. **George Gershwin's** *Rhapsody in Blue* and *Concerto in F* brought him instant fame. They were among the first classical works to combine American jazz with traditional musical forms. Soon thereafter Aaron Copland extended this identifiably American influence in his symphonic *Music for the Theater* and *Piano Concerto.*

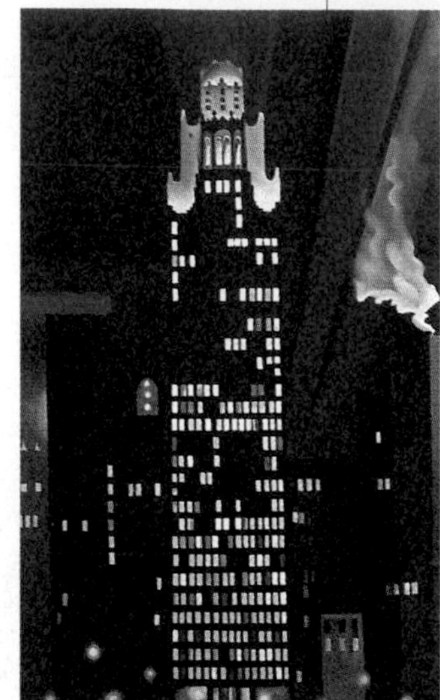

***Radiator Building—Night, New York* (1927), Georgia O'Keeffe.**

American painters recorded an America of dreams and realities. Edward Hopper caught the loneliness of American life in his canvases of empty streets, stark storefronts, and solitary people. He was part of the "ashcan school" of painting—known for its honest look at everyday realities—that had emerged in the first decade of the 20th century. Another painter, **Georgia O'Keeffe**—who later became famous for her paintings of the Southwest—produced intensely colored canvases that captured the grandeur of New York: dark buildings thrusting into the sky, glaring sun reflected from sky-high windows, nighttime streets forming ribbons of orange light in the blackness. "One can't paint New York as it is," O'Keeffe once told a friend, "but rather as it is felt."

WRITERS OF THE 1920s Many of America's gifted writers were alienated by the values and lifestyles of the 1920s. They criticized what they felt to be the strait-laced culture of small towns and the shallowness and vulgarity of business culture. Much of the work they produced was despairing or critical of a society with few ideals or avenues to personal fulfillment. Even so, this outpouring of fresh, insightful writing made the 1920s one of the richest eras in the country's literary history.

Sinclair Lewis, the first American to win a Nobel Prize in literature, was among the era's most outspoken critics. In *Main Street* and *Babbitt,* his two most famous novels, Lewis took aim at the shallow, stifling existence of middle-class America. Lewis used the character of George F. Babbitt, a real-estate salesman in a medium-sized town, to ridicule Americans for their conformity and materialism.

> A sensational event was changing from the brown suit to the gray the contents of his pockets. He was earnest about these objects. They were of eternal importance, like baseball or the Republican Party. They included a fountain pen and a silver pencil . . . which belonged in the righthand upper vest pocket. Without them he would have felt naked. On his watch-chain were a gold pen-knife, silver cigar-cutter, seven keys . . . and incidentally a good watch. . . . Last, he stuck in his lapel the Booster's Club button. With the conciseness of great art the button displayed two words: "Boosters—Pep!"
>
> SINCLAIR LEWIS, *Babbitt*

The Baltimore journalist H. L. Mencken, coeditor of the *American Mercury,* was equally scornful of modern America. A scathing critic, Mencken ridiculed virtually every American institution, from the church and public schools to social workers, politicians, and the middle class.

Block Schedule TEACHING OPTION **Time Needed: 20 Minutes**

Cooperative Activity: Presenting Art

Task: Student groups will research the work of famous artists of the period (playwrights, musicians, painters, or writers) and then collaborate on presentations of the artists' work to the class.

Purpose: To better understand the variety of artistic achievement in the 1920s.

Activity: Instruct each group of three or four students to choose a particular artist, do research on the artist's work, and then present their findings about the artist to the class. A group's presentation might include examples of the artist's writing, music, or paintings, as well as the artist's own statements about what he or she was trying to achieve.

Building a Portfolio: Students adding a presentation to their portfolio should attach a note pointing out their contribution.

ALTERNATIVE ASSESSMENT BOOK
Standards for Evaluating a Cooperative Activity

Standards for Evaluation
Presentations should . . .

- draw on the artists' own words
- provide examples of the artists' work
- show evidence of research into a variety of sources
- be clear and well organized

The novelist **F. Scott Fitzgerald** coined the term "Jazz Age" to describe the 1920s. In *This Side of Paradise* and *The Great Gatsby,* he revealed the negative side of the period's gaiety and freedom, portraying wealthy and attractive people leading imperiled lives in gilded surroundings. In New York City, a brilliant group of writers routinely lunched together at the Algonquin Hotel's "Round Table." Among the best-known of them was Dorothy Parker, a short story writer, poet, and essayist. Parker was famous for her wisecracking wit, expressed in such lines as "I was the toast of two continents—Greenland and Australia."

Many writers also met important issues head on. In *The Age of Innocence,* Edith Wharton dramatized the clash between traditional and modern values that had undermined high society 50 years earlier. The Southern novelist Ellen Glasgow criticized the constricting morals of the South in *Barren Ground.* Willa Cather celebrated the simple, dignified lives of such people as the immigrant farmers of Nebraska (in *My Ántonia*) and the first Catholic bishop of New Mexico (in *Death Comes for the Archbishop*). **Edna St. Vincent Millay** wrote poems celebrating youth and a life of independence and freedom from traditional constraints.

Some writers were so soured by American culture that they settled in Europe, mostly in Paris. Socializing in the city's cafes, they formed a group that the writer Gertrude Stein called the Lost Generation. These writers included Fitzgerald, Ernest Hemingway, and John Dos Passos. Other American writers were already living in Europe. The poet Ezra Pound lived in London, Paris, and Italy. T. S. Eliot, who later won a Nobel Prize in literature, lived in London. Eliot's most famous poem, *The Waste Land,* was an agonized view of a society that seemed stripped of humanity.

D. Answer Many writers found American culture shallow and materialistic, with few ideals for people to strive for and few paths that people could follow to personal fulfillment.

THINK THROUGH HISTORY
D. Analyzing Causes *Why did many American writers reject their culture and its values?*

Several writers saw action in World War I, and their early books denounced war. John Dos Passos's novel *Three Soldiers* attacked war as a machine designed to crush human freedom. Later, Dos Passos turned to social and political themes, using modern techniques to capture the mood of city life and the losses that came with success. **Ernest Hemingway,** wounded in the First World War, became the best-known expatriate author. In his novels *The Sun Also Rises* and *A Farewell to Arms,* he criticized the glorification of war. He also introduced a tough, simplified style of writing that set a new literary standard, using sentences a *Time* reporter compared to "round stones polished by rain and wind."

During this rich literary era, vital developments were also taking place in African-American society. Black Americans of the 1920s began to voice pride in their heritage, and black artists and writers revealed the richness of African-American culture.

KEY PLAYERS

ZELDA FITZGERALD 1899–1948
F. SCOTT FITZGERALD 1896–1940

F. Scott Fitzgerald and his vivacious wife, Zelda, married in 1920 after Fitzgerald's novel *This Side of Paradise* became an instant hit. Fitzgerald said of this time in his life: "Riding in a taxi one afternoon between very tall buildings under a mauve and rosy sky, I began to bawl because I had everything I wanted and knew I would never be so happy again."

Flush with money, the couple plunged into a wild social whirl and outspent their incomes. Although Fitzgerald continued to write, the alcoholism he had long battled took its toll. As Zelda struggled to establish a career as a dancer and writer, she suffered repeated mental breakdowns. Fitzgerald ended his career in Hollywood, where he struggled to stay afloat as a screenwriter.

Section 3 Assessment

1. TERMS & NAMES
Identify:
- Babe Ruth
- Gertrude Ederle
- Charles A. Lindbergh
- George Gershwin
- Georgia O'Keeffe
- Sinclair Lewis
- F. Scott Fitzgerald
- Edna St. Vincent Millay
- Ernest Hemingway

2. SUMMARIZING Create a time line of key events relating to 1920s popular culture. Use the dates below as a guide.

In a sentence or two, explain which of these events interests you the most and why.

3. FORMING OPINIONS Do you think the popular heroes of the 1920s were heroes in a real sense? Why or why not?

THINK ABOUT
- how you define heroism
- the media hyping of sports stars during the 1920s
- the accomplishments of Babe Ruth, Jack Dempsey, Gertrude Ederle, and Charles Lindbergh

4. SYNTHESIZING In what ways do you think the mass media and mass culture helped Americans create a sense of community in the 1920s? Support your answer with details from the text.

THINK ABOUT
- the content and readership of newspapers and magazines
- attendance at sports events and movie theaters
- the scope of radio broadcasts

ANSWERS

1. TERMS & NAMES

Babe Ruth, p. 466
Gertrude Ederle, p. 466
Charles A. Lindbergh, p. 467
George Gershwin, p. 468
Georgia O'Keeffe, p. 468
Sinclair Lewis, p. 468
F. Scott Fitzgerald, p. 469
Edna St. Vincent Millay, p. 469
Ernest Hemingway, p. 469

2. SUMMARIZING

Possible Responses:
1920—first scheduled radio broadcast
1923—founding of *Time*
1926—Gertrude Ederle's historic swim across the English Channel
1927—Tunney-Dempsey boxing match, Lindbergh's solo flight to Paris, Babe Ruth's record-breaking 60 home runs, *The Jazz Singer*
1928—Production of *Steamboat Willie,* the first animated talkie

3. FORMING OPINIONS

Possible Responses: Students answering yes might say that ordinary Americans, such as athletes and aviators, could epitomize lofty human virtues and the exceptional power of the individual. Students answering no may say that sports stars, such as Babe Ruth and Gertrude Ederle, were not true heroes because their achievements had no enduring social value.

4. SYNTHESIZING

Possible Responses: Radio audiences heard news and sports events as they took place; radio networks geared shows to public interests. Sports fans in stadiums cheered together for favorite athletes or teams. Filmgoers from diverse backgrounds sat together in theaters and escaped into the fantasy world of movies. Major newspapers and national magazines reached broad audiences.

KEY PLAYERS
The Fitzgeralds

Critical Thinking: Drawing Conclusions
- How did F. Scott and Zelda Fitzgerald epitomize the Jazz Age? *They had a fast-paced, extravagant lifestyle that masked their problems and desperation.*

ASSESS & RETEACH

Section 3 Assessment

Assign students to study groups and have them help one another answer the questions.

Self-Assessment

Have each student create a six-column chart in which he or she lists important figures of this period in the fields of sports, movies, theater, music, painting, and literature.

Section Quiz

FORMAL ASSESSMENT
Section Quiz, p. 166

Reteach

On the chalkboard create a web diagram like the one below. Ask students to list examples of ways in which each group of people contributed to the popular culture of the 1920s.

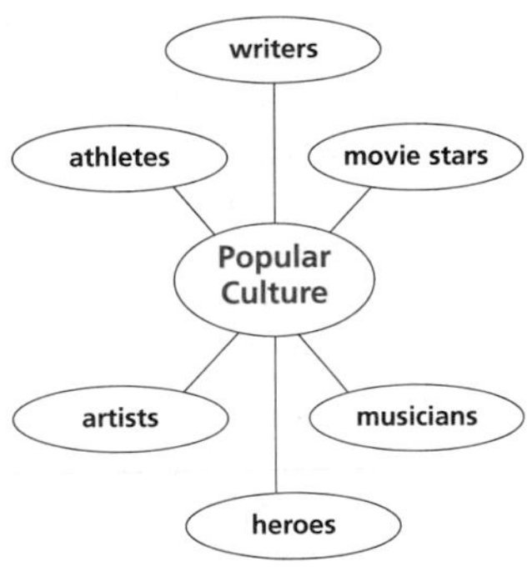

CLOSE

The mass media, spectator sports, and movies created a shared popular culture in the 1920s. The art and literature of the decade reflected the disillusionment of many Americans.

Section 4 Overview

OBJECTIVES

1. To identify the causes and results of the migration of African Americans to Northern cities in the early 1900s.
2. To describe the outburst of African-American artistic activity that became known as the Harlem Renaissance.

CRITICAL THINKING

- Theme: Immigration and Migration, p. 471
- Summarizing, pp. 472, 474, 475
- Synthesizing, p. 473
- Drawing conclusions, p. 475
- Analyzing causes, p. 475
- Forming generalizations, p. 475

FOCUS & MOTIVATE

5-MINUTE WARM-UP

Making Inferences
To make inferences about Zora Neale Hurston, have students read the One American's Story on page 470 and answer these questions.

1. What effect did Hurston's early reading have on her?
2. What do you think the oyster knife represented to Hurston?

WARM-UP TRANSPARENCY 13

▶ ***Starting with the Student***
Watch the video "Jump at the Sun" to find out about Zora Neale Hurston and the Harlem Renaissance.

- Using the *Teacher's Resource Book* as a guide, explore the background of Hurston in Eatonville, Florida; discuss her participation in the Harlem Renaissance; and engage in extension activities using key primary sources.

***AMERICAN STORIES* video series**
"Jump at the Sun"

Videocassette: Volume 3

Videodisc: Disc 2, Side A, Chapter 4

4 The Harlem Renaissance

TERMS & NAMES
- Zora Neale Hurston
- James Weldon Johnson
- Marcus Garvey
- Harlem Renaissance
- Claude McKay
- Langston Hughes
- Paul Robeson
- Louis Armstrong
- Duke Ellington
- Bessie Smith

LEARN ABOUT the efforts of the NAACP, Marcus Garvey's movement, and the Harlem Renaissance
TO UNDERSTAND why the 1920s were a crucial era in African-American history.

ONE AMERICAN'S STORY

When the spirited **Zora Neale Hurston** was a girl in Eatonville, Florida, in the early 1900s, she loved to read adventure stories and myths. The powerful tales struck a chord. They made the young, talented Hurston yearn for a wider world.

A PERSONAL VOICE
My soul was with the gods and my body in the village. People just would not act like gods. . . . Raking back yards and carrying out chamber-pots, were not the tasks of Thor. I wanted to be away from drabness and to stretch my limbs in some mighty struggle.
ZORA NEALE HURSTON, quoted in *The African American Encyclopedia*

In 1915, Hurston left home and eked out a living as a nanny and housekeeper. She attended Howard University, where she began writing and publishing fiction, then moved north to New York. She struggled to the top of African-American literary society by hard work, flamboyance, and, above all, grit. "I have seen that the world is to the strong regardless of a little pigmentation more or less," Hurston wrote later. "I do not weep at [being Negro]—I am too busy sharpening my oyster knife."

Hurston's success set her apart from most African Americans of the 1920s, but she also shared many of their experiences. Hurston was on the move, like millions of others. And, like them, she went after the pearl in the oyster—the good life in America.

JUMP AT THE SUN: Zora Neale Hurston and the Harlem Renaissance

Zora Neale Hurston

African-American Voices in the 1920s

During the 1920s, African Americans set new goals for themselves as they moved north to the nation's cities. Their migration was an expression of their changing attitude toward themselves—an attitude perhaps best captured in a phrase first used around this time, "Black is beautiful."

THE MOVE NORTH Between 1910 and 1920, in a movement known as the Great Migration, hundreds of thousands of African Americans had uprooted themselves from their homes in the South and moved north to the big cities in search of jobs. They left the South because of racial violence and economic discrimination. In addition, in 1915 and 1916, floods, droughts, and the destruction of cotton crops by an insect called the boll weevil had brought economic disaster to the South and had provided low-paid sharecroppers and field hands with an incentive to move north. Zora Neale Hurston documented the departure of some of these African Americans.

A PERSONAL VOICE
Some said goodbye cheerfully . . . others fearfully, with terrors of known dangers in their mouths . . . others in their eagerness for distance said nothing. The daybreak found them gone. The wind said North.
ZORA NEALE HURSTON, quoted in *Sorrow's Kitchen: The Life and Folklore of Zora Neale Hurston*

SECTION 4 RESOURCES

PRINT RESOURCES

IN-DEPTH RESOURCES: UNIT 4
Guided Reading, p. 21
Primary Source: *from* "When the Negro Was in Vogue" by Langston Hughes, p. 28
American Lives: Louis Armstrong, p. 33

READING STUDY GUIDE, p. 143

ACCESS FOR STUDENTS ACQUIRING ENGLISH
Guided Reading (Spanish), p. 161

SPANISH READING STUDY GUIDE, p. 143

FORMAL ASSESSMENT
Section Quiz, p. 167

ALTERNATIVE ASSESSMENT BOOK
See forms for supporting and scoring alternative activties.

TECHNOLOGY RESOURCES

CRITICAL THINKING TRANSPARENCIES
CT55, African-American Migration from the South, 1890–1930

CD-ROM *Our Times*
Grolier Multimedia Encyclopedia

VIDEO *American Stories* video series
American Portfolio: A Videodisc for U.S. History user's guide, pp. 193, 196–197

INTERNET http://www.mlushistory.com

THINK THROUGH HISTORY
A. THEME *Immigration and Migration* How did the influx of African Americans change Northern cities?

A. Answer The movement of millions of African Americans to Northern cities greatly increased their black populations, heightening racial tensions and sometimes resulting in discrimination and violence.

During the 1920s, the number of African Americans in New York, Chicago, and Detroit doubled. Other destinations included Cleveland, Indianapolis, Philadelphia, St. Louis, Cincinnati, and Pittsburgh. By the end of the decade, 4.8 million of the nation's 12 million African Americans—some 40 percent—lived in cities.

In general, Northern cities did not welcome the massive influx of African Americans. Tensions had escalated in the years prior to 1920, culminating, in the summer of 1919, in more than 25 urban race riots.

AFRICAN-AMERICAN GOALS The race riots shocked and alarmed African Americans. In response, the National Association for the Advancement of Colored People (NAACP), which had been founded in 1909, urged African Americans to aggressively protest such racial violence. W. E. B. Du Bois, a founding member of the NAACP, led a parade of 10,000 African-American men down New York's Fifth Avenue to protest all violence against African Americans. The men marched quietly beneath fluttering banners that read "Thou Shalt Not Kill." Du Bois also used the NAACP's official magazine, *The Crisis,* which he edited, as a platform for leading a struggle for civil rights. In 1919, as African-American veterans returned from the war, he wrote, "We return. / We return from fighting. / We return fighting."

By 1920, the NAACP's membership had doubled. From 1919 through the 1920s, the organization fought, by means of legislation, to protect African-American rights, and it made antilynching laws one of its main priorities. **James Weldon Johnson,** poet, lawyer, and NAACP executive secretary, led the fight. In 1919, three antilynching bills were introduced in Congress. One bill finally passed the House but was stopped in the Senate. However, the NAACP continued its campaign through antilynching organizations that had been established earlier by Ida B. Wells. Gradually, the number of lynchings dropped. The NAACP represented the new, more militant voice of African Americans seeking a better place in a changing America.

MARCUS GARVEY AND THE UNIA Many African Americans found their voice in the NAACP. But African Americans still faced daily threats and discrimination, and a different, more radical message of black pride aroused their hopes.

The man behind this message was **Marcus Garvey,** a Jamaican immigrant who believed that African Americans should build a separate society. In 1914, he had founded, in his native Jamaica, a black nationalist group called the Universal Negro Improvement Association (UNIA). Two years later, he moved the UNIA to New York City and opened offices in urban ghettos in order to recruit followers.

By the mid-1920s, Garvey had mobilized more than 500,000 African Americans with a combination of spellbinding oratory, mass meetings, parades, and a message of pride.

A PERSONAL VOICE

In view of the fact that the black man of Africa has contributed as much to the world as the white man of Europe, and the brown man and yellow man of Asia, we of the Universal Negro Improvement Association demand that the white, yellow, and brown races give to the black man his place in the civilization of the world. We ask for nothing more than the rights of 400 million Negroes.

MARCUS GARVEY, speech at Liberty Hall, New York City, 1922

KEY PLAYER

JAMES WELDON JOHNSON
1871–1938

James Weldon Johnson worked as a school principal, newspaper editor, and lawyer in Florida. In 1900, he wrote the lyrics for "Lift Every Voice and Sing," the song that became known as the Black national anthem. The first stanza begins as follows:

Lift every voice and sing
Till earth and heaven ring,
Ring with the harmonies of
Liberty;
Let our rejoicing rise
High as the listening skies,
Let it resound loud as the
rolling sea.

In the 1920s, Johnson straddled the worlds of politics and art. He served as executive secretary of the NAACP, spearheading the fight against lynching. In addition, he wrote well-known works, such as *God's Trombones,* a series of sermon-like poems, and *Black Manhattan,* a look at black cultural life in New York during the Roaring Twenties.

OBJECTIVE ① **INSTRUCT**

African-American Voices in the 1920s

▶ ***Discussing Key Ideas***
- Racial violence, economic discrimination, and natural disasters in the South cause many African Americans to move to Northern cities.
- Tensions resulting from the influx of African Americans erupt in race riots.
- African-American leaders propose different ways of responding to discrimination and violence.

IN-DEPTH RESOURCES, UNIT 4
Guided Reading, p. 21

ACCESS FOR STUDENTS ACQUIRING ENGLISH
Guided Reading (Spanish), p. 161

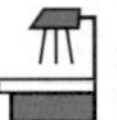

CRITICAL THINKING TRANSPARENCIES
CT55, African-American Migration from the South, 1890–1930

KEY PLAYER
James Weldon Johnson
Critical Thinking: Analyzing
How might James Weldon Johnson's success as a writer have made him an effective leader in the fight to protect African-American rights? *Possible Responses: He was well-known; his works helped white people understand the African-American experience.*

TEACHING OPTIONS

Exploring Themes

Immigration and Migration Have students discuss the push-and-pull factors that led to the Great Migration. *Push—racial violence, economic discrimination, and natural disasters in the South; pull—job opportunities and better pay in the North.*

- Do you think most African Americans achieved their goals by moving to Northern cities? Why or why not? *They encountered discrimination and violence; many urban neighborhoods were overcrowded; poverty existed in the North as well as in the South.*

Making Connections Across Time

African-American Demonstrations Have students compare the "Silent Protest Parade" led by W. E. B. Du Bois in New York City with the "Million Man March" led by Louis Farrakhan in Washington, D.C., in 1995.

- How were the two events similar? *They demonstrated African-American unity.*
- How did they differ? *Silent Protest Parade focused on violence against African Americans; the Million Man March appealed to African Americans to restore black pride and end violence.*

OBJECTIVE
② INSTRUCT

The Harlem Renaissance Flowers in New York

▶ ***Starting with the Student***
Ask students if they listen to rap music. Are they aware that rap started as part of African-American street culture in New York City in the 1980s? Point out that jazz started in New Orleans in the early 1900s and spread to Chicago, where it revolutionized popular music in the 1920s.

▶ ***Discussing Key Ideas***
- African-American writers explore and celebrate their heritage.
- African-American performers and musicians popularize their culture by appealing to a wide audience.

GROLIER MULTIMEDIA ENCYCLOPEDIA
Overview of African-American literature

MORE ABOUT . . .
Harlem
African Americans began to move into New York's Harlem neighborhood in the early 1900s. Whites became alarmed and left the community, but vacant apartments soon were filled by blacks who migrated from the South or moved from nearby neighborhoods. The transition took place without violence.

Marcus Garvey designed this uniform of purple and gold, complete with feathered hat, for his role as "Provisional President of Africa."

Garvey also lured followers with practical plans, especially his program to promote African-American businesses. Through the Negro Fortunes Corporation, he set up grocery stores, laundries, millinery stores, tailor shops, and a successful newspaper called *The Negro World.* Shareholders in the corporation received health and death benefits.

Furthermore, Garvey preached that African Americans needed an independent nation. He encouraged his followers to return to Africa, help native people throw off white colonial oppressors, and build a mighty nation. His idea struck a chord in many African Americans, as well as in blacks in the Caribbean and Africa. As part of his plan to colonize Africa, Garvey founded a steamship company, the Black Star Line, to carry blacks to Africa. His steamship line later went bankrupt.

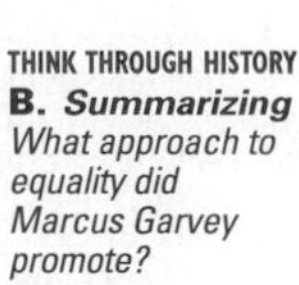
THINK THROUGH HISTORY
B. *Summarizing* *What approach to equality did Marcus Garvey promote?*

B. Answer Garvey believed that African Americans should build a separate society; he preached a message of self-pride and he promoted African-American businesses.

Despite the appeal of Garvey's movement, support for it declined in the mid-1920s, when he was convicted of mail fraud and jailed. Deported to Jamaica after his release from jail, he continued to lead the UNIA from his homeland; but his followers in the United States lost influence, and the movement dwindled. Even so, Garvey left behind a powerful legacy of newly awakened black pride, economic independence, and reverence for Africa.

The Harlem Renaissance Flowers in New York

Many African Americans who migrated north moved to Harlem, a neighborhood on the upper west side of New York's Manhattan Island. In the 1920s, Harlem became the world's largest black urban community. During that decade, its population soared from about 152,000 to nearly 330,000 as newcomers from the South, the West Indies, Cuba, Puerto Rico, and Haiti crowded into handsome old brownstone apartments. The result was a highly diverse mix of cultures. James Weldon Johnson described Harlem as the capital of black America.

A PERSONAL VOICE
Harlem is not merely a Negro colony or community, it is a city within a city, the greatest Negro city in the world. It is not a slum or a fringe, it is located in the heart of Manhattan and occupies one of the most beautiful . . . sections of the city. . . . It has its own churches, social and civic centers, shops, theaters, and other places of amusement. And it contains more Negroes to the square mile than any other spot on earth.
JAMES WELDON JOHNSON, "Harlem: The Culture Capital"

Like many other urban neighborhoods, Harlem suffered from overcrowding, unemployment, and poverty. But its problems in the 1920s were eclipsed by a flowering of African-American creativity called the **Harlem Renaissance,** a literary and artistic movement celebrating African-American culture.

AFRICAN-AMERICAN WRITERS Above all, the Harlem Renaissance was a literary movement led by well-educated, middle-class African Americans. Caught up in the rebellious spirit of the 1920s, these young writers expressed a new pride in the African-American experience. They explored and celebrated their African heritage and their people's folklore. They wrote with defiance and poignancy about the trials of being black in a white world. W. E. B. Du Bois and James Weldon Johnson helped these young talents along, as did the Harvard-educated former Rhodes scholar Alain Locke. In 1925, Locke published *The New Negro*, a landmark collection of works by many promising young African-American writers.

The poet **Claude McKay,** a Jamaican immigrant, was a major figure in the Harlem Renaissance. His militant verses urged African Americans to resist prejudice and discrimination. His poems also expressed the pain of life in the

TEACHING OPTIONS

Making Connections Across Cultures

African-American Heritage The Harlem Renaissance celebrated the African-American heritage. Writers incorporated the stories, expressions, rhythms, and experiences of African Americans into their works. This celebration of African-American culture spread to the white community in the 1920s, primarily through the work of African-American performers who became popular with white audiences.

Making Connections Across the Curriculum

Literature Zora Neale Hurston grew up in the South, where she was exposed to African-American oral traditions, such as the "lying" sessions in which people told exaggerated folk tales that featured talking animals. In addition to writing her own stories, Hurston toured the South to collect black folk tales, which she preserved in a collection titled *Mules and Men.* Some students might examine Hurston's book to find examples of the influence of folk tales on her work. You might also have students read other African-American folk tales, such as the Uncle Remus stories.

black ghettos of the 1920s and the strain of being black in a world dominated by whites. "Your door is shut against my tightened face, / And I am sharp as steel with discontent," he wrote in his poem "White Houses."

Another gifted writer of the Harlem Renaissance was Jean Toomer. His experimental book *Cane* (1923), a mix of poems and sketches about blacks in the North and the South, was among the first full-length literary publications of the Harlem Renaissance. The book probed the meaning of African-American life, an issue the movement would go on to explore in depth.

Missouri-born **Langston Hughes** was the movement's best-known poet. Many of Hughes's 1920s poems described the difficult everyday lives of working-class African Americans. Some moved to the tempo of jazz and the blues. (See "Literature in the Jazz Age," pages 476–477.)

The Harvard-educated writer Countee Cullen gained fame for his 1925 volume of poems titled *Color.* Unlike Hughes and others who wove African-American expressions and rhythms into their work, Cullen used a classical style to capture the black struggle. "Yet I do marvel at this curious thing: / To make a poet black and make him sing!" he wrote of the conflicts of the black artist in his most famous poem.

The most accomplished African-American woman writer of the era was Zora Neale Hurston. In many of her novels, books of folklore, poems, and short stories, Hurston portrayed the lives of poor, unschooled Southern blacks—in her words, "the greatest cultural wealth of the continent." Much of her work celebrated what she called the common person's art form—the simple folkways and values of people who had survived slavery through their ingenuity and strength. Hurston's finest novel, *Their Eyes Were Watching God,* told the story of a strong woman's battle to assert herself and win personal freedom.

Many other talented writers added their voices to the Harlem Renaissance. The novelist and short story writer Nella Larsen won fame for "Quicksand" and "Passing," despairing stories of black women who struggled to seize control of their lives and fortunes. Boston-born Dorothy West wrote poignant stories about people trapped in a web of racism and sexism. West also founded *Challenge,* a magazine of African-American writing..

Alain Locke, the champion of many of the best African-American writers of the 1920s, looked back on the Harlem Renaissance from the vantage point of the Great Depression—ten years after the publication of *The New Negro.* In the interval, his point of view had changed: "The rosy enthusiasm and hopes of

"And I am sharp as steel with discontent."

CLAUDE McKAY

THINK THROUGH HISTORY
C. *Synthesizing* *In what ways did writers of the Harlem Renaissance celebrate a "rebirth"?*

C. Answer They expressed their pride in the African-American experience; they celebrated their heritage and folklore.

The painting ***Black Belt*** by Archibald J. Motley, Jr., records the lively street life in an urban African-American neighborhood. The phrase "black belt" was sometimes used to describe an area having a predominantly African-American population.

MORE ABOUT . . .
The Harlem Renaissance

In the Harlem Renaissance, African Americans created their own distinctive culture in the United States. The writers and artists of the Harlem Renaissance celebrated their culture, but few of them addressed the problems that most African Americans faced in the 1920s. The Harlem Renaissance was brief, but it remains a lasting tribute to the artistic creativity of African Americans.

Now have students fill in a chart, similar to the one below, comparing themes of major Harlem Renaissance writers.

	Themes
McKay	pain of life in black ghettos
Toomer	
Hughes	
Hurston	
West	

IN-DEPTH RESOURCES: UNIT 4
Primary Source: *from* "When the Negro Was in Vogue" by Langston Hughes, p. 28

Block Schedule TEACHING OPTION **Time Needed: 30 Minutes**

Cooperative Activity: Celebrating African-American Culture

Task: Groups of students will develop presentations honoring writers, performers, and musicians of the Harlem Renaissance.

Purpose: To recognize the impact of the Harlem Renaissance on American culture.

Activity: Divide students into three groups representing writers, performers, and musicians. Each group should develop a presentation celebrating the work of the African-American artists they represent. Presentations might include recordings of music, posters advertising performances, book reviews, dramatic readings, and role-playing. Provide time for the groups to share their presentations with the class.

Building a Portfolio: If students create a product as part of their presentation, they should add a note describing their contribution to the project.

ALTERNATIVE ASSESSMENT BOOK
Standards for Evaluating a Cooperative Activity

Standards for Evaluation
Presentations should . . .

- give examples of artists' works
- suggest the nature of the artists' achievements
- show the relationship between the artists and the Harlem Renaissance

HISTORY FROM VISUALS

The Hot Five

Viewing the Photograph Point out to students the instruments in the picture. Armstrong at the piano holds a trumpet. The other instruments on display are a banjo, a saxophone, a clarinet, and a trombone. In this group, Lil Hardin was the pianist.

Extension Bring in and play for students some recordings of the Hot Five to give them a sense of how the music of the period sounded.

MORE ABOUT . . .

Louis Armstrong

As a teenager in New Orleans, Louis Armstrong was arrested for firing a gun on New Year's Eve and sent to a home for boys. In that institution, Armstrong first learned to play the cornet. He continued to develop the talent that eventually made him one of the most influential jazz musicians of all time and an internationally known performer. Once, when asked to define jazz, Armstrong replied, "Man, if you gotta ask, you'll never know."

IN-DEPTH RESOURCES: UNIT 4
American Lives: Louis Armstrong, p. 33

OUR TIMES
Louis Armstrong

1925 were cruelly deceptive mirages. [The Depression] revealed a Harlem that the social worker knew all along, but had not been able to dramatize. There is no cure or saving magic in poetry and art for precarious marginal employment, high mortality rates and civic neglect."

The Hot Five included *(from left)* Louis Armstrong, Johnny St. Cyr, Johnny Dodds, Kid Ory, and Lil Hardin.

AFRICAN-AMERICAN PERFORMERS The spirit and talent of the Harlem Renaissance reached far beyond the world of African-American writers and intellectuals. In fact, some observers, including Langston Hughes, thought the movement was launched with *Shuffle Along,* a black musical comedy popular in 1921.

> A PERSONAL VOICE
> *Shuffle Along* was a honey of a show. Swift, bright, funny, rollicking and gay, with a dozen danceable, singable tunes. . . . It gave just the proper push to that Negro vogue of the '20s that spread to books, African sculpture, music, and dancing.
>
> **LANGSTON HUGHES,** *The Big Sea*

Several songs in *Shuffle Along,* including "Love Will Find a Way," won popularity among white audiences. The show also spotlighted the talents of several black performers, including the singers Florence Mills, Josephine Baker, and Mabel Mercer.

During the 1920s, African Americans in the performing arts won large followings. The tenor Roland Hayes rose to stardom as a concert singer, and the singer and actress Ethel Waters debuted on Broadway in the musical *Africana.* **Paul Robeson,** the son of a runaway slave, became a major dramatic actor. After a brilliant record as a student and athlete at Rutgers University, Robeson went on to Columbia University Law School. His magnificent bass voice and commanding presence brought him early fame as an actor. In 1924, he created the title role in Eugene O'Neill's play *The Emperor Jones.* His performance in Shakespeare's *Othello,* first in London and later in New York City, was widely acclaimed. Subsequently, the racism Robeson experienced in the United States and the indignities inflicted upon him because of his support of the Soviet Union and the Communist Party made him take up residence abroad, and he lived for a time in England and the Soviet Union. (See Historical Spotlight on page 620.)

AFRICAN AMERICANS AND JAZZ Jazz was born in the early 20th century in New Orleans, where musicians blended instrumental ragtime and vocal blues into an exuberant new sound. In 1919, Joe "King" Oliver and his Creole Jazz Band traveled north to Chicago, carrying jazz with them. Joining Oliver's group in 1922 was a young trumpet player named **Louis Armstrong,** whose talent rocketed him to stardom in the jazz world. Famous for his astounding sense of rhythm and his ability to improvise, Armstrong made personal expression a key part of jazz. After two years in Chicago, in 1924 he joined Fletcher Henderson's band, the most important big jazz band in New York City. Armstrong went on to become the single most important and influential musician in the history of jazz. At the end of his life, he talked about his anticipated funeral.

> A PERSONAL VOICE
> They're going to blow over me. Cats will be coming from everywhere to play. I had a beautiful life. When I get to the Pearly Gates I'll play a duet with Gabriel. We'll play "Sleepy Time Down South." He wants to be remembered for his music just like I do.
>
> **LOUIS ARMSTRONG,** quoted in *The Negro Almanac*

THINK THROUGH HISTORY
D. Summarizing *In what other areas besides writing did African Americans of the 1920s achieve remarkable results?*

D. Answer African Americans were outstanding in the performing arts.

TEACHING OPTIONS

Making Global Connections

The European Tour In 1932 Louis Armstrong appeared at the London Palladium, and he toured Europe in 1933–1935. Duke Ellington also performed in Europe during the early 1930s. Both men were to return to Europe with their bands on musical tours throughout their careers. Discuss how jazz musicians helped spread American culture to other parts of the world.

Making Connections Across the Curriculum

Music Provide opportunities for students to listen to recordings of jazz artists of the 1920s. Some of the most important African-American musicians of the period were Louis Armstrong, King Oliver, Duke Ellington, Cab Calloway, and Bessie Smith. Point out the key elements of jazz: improvisation (the ability to create music spontaneously) and syncopation (the use of irregular rhythms and accents). Some students might be interested in tracing the development of jazz since the 1920s.

Jazz quickly spread from Chicago to Kansas City, Los Angeles, and New York City, and it became the most popular music for dancing. During the 1920s, Harlem pulsed to the sounds of jazz, which lured throngs of whites to the showy, exotic nightclubs there, including the famed Cotton Club. In the late 1920s, **Edward Kennedy "Duke" Ellington,** a jazz pianist and composer, led his ten-piece orchestra at the Cotton Club. In a 1925 essay titled "The Negro Spirituals," Alain Locke seemed almost to predict the career of the talented Ellington.

A PERSONAL VOICE
Up to the present, the resources of Negro music have been tentatively exploited in only one direction at a time–melodically here, rhythmically there, harmonically in a third direction. A genius that would organize its distinctive elements in a formal way would be the musical giant of his age.
ALAIN LOCKE, quoted in *Afro-American Writing: An Anthology of Prose and Poetry*

Through the 1920s and 1930s, Ellington won renown as one of America's greatest composers, with pieces such as "Mood Indigo" and "Sophisticated Lady."

Cab Calloway, a talented drummer, saxophonist, and singer, formed another important jazz orchestra, which played at Harlem's Savoy Ballroom and the Cotton Club, alternating with Duke Ellington. Along with Louis Armstrong, Calloway popularized "scat," or jazz singing using sounds instead of words.

Bessie Smith, a female blues singer, was perhaps the outstanding vocalist of the decade. She recorded on black-oriented labels produced by the major record companies. She achieved enormous popularity and in 1927 became the highest-paid black artist in the world.

Many African-American musical artists achieved great celebrity in Europe. The most popular was Josephine Baker, who lived and worked in Paris. A dancing, singing, and comedy star for 40 years, Baker, known for walking her pet leopards, was outrageously stylish. During World War II, however, Baker volunteered for the Red Cross and spied for the French underground. After the war, the French government awarded her the Legion of Honor.

The Harlem Renaissance represented a portion of the great social and cultural changes that swept America in the 1920s. The period was characterized by economic prosperity, new ideas, changing values, and personal freedom, as well as important developments in art, literature, and music. Most of the social changes were lasting. The economic boom, however, was short-lived.

E. Answer The Harlem Renaissance helped nurture African Americans' pride in their unique culture. It also contributed great literature, drama, and music to American culture.

THINK THROUGH HISTORY
E. *Drawing Conclusions* *What did the Harlem Renaissance contribute to both black and general American history?*

KEY PLAYER

DUKE ELLINGTON
1899–1974

Edward Kennedy "Duke" Ellington, one of the greatest composers of the 20th century, was largely a self-taught musician. He developed his skills by playing at family socials. He wrote his first song, "Soda Fountain Rag," at 15 and started his first band when he was 21.

During the five years Ellington played at Harlem's glittering Cotton Club, he set a new standard, playing mainly his own stylish compositions. Within two years, the Duke Ellington Orchestra reached a nationwide audience through radio and the movie *Black and Tan.* Billy Strayhorn, Ellington's long-time arranger and collaborator, said, "Ellington plays the piano, but his real instrument is his band."

Many critics say that Ellington's orchestra reached its peak in the 1940s, when it premiered his suite *Black, Brown and Beige,* a musical history of African Americans. Ellington continued composing, playing, and touring until the 1970s.

Section 4 Assessment

1. TERMS & NAMES
Identify:
- Zora Neale Hurston
- James Weldon Johnson
- Marcus Garvey
- Harlem Renaissance
- Claude McKay
- Langston Hughes
- Paul Robeson
- Louis Armstrong
- Duke Ellington
- Bessie Smith

2. SUMMARIZING Copy the tree diagram shown below, and fill it in with three areas of artistic achievement in the Harlem Renaissance. For each area of achievement, write the name of two outstanding African-American artists.

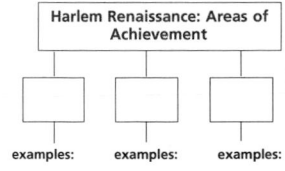

Harlem Renaissance: Areas of Achievement

examples: examples: examples:

3. ANALYZING CAUSES Speculate on why an African-American renaissance flowered during the 1920s. Support your answer.

THINK ABOUT
- racial discrimination in the South
- campaigns for equality in the North
- the diverse cultures that made up Harlem's soaring population
- the changing culture of all Americans

4. FORMING GENERALIZATIONS What were some of the most important ideas, opinions, and beliefs expressed in African-American literature of the 1920s? Support your answer with examples from the text.

THINK ABOUT
- the experience of writers such as Langston Hughes and Zora Neale Hurston
- what 1920s society was like
- the flowering of the Harlem Renaissance in all the arts

KEY PLAYER
Duke Ellington

Critical Thinking: Synthesizing Have students commemorate Duke Ellington's contributions to American culture by designing memorials to honor him. Students might work individually or in pairs. Possible kinds of memorials are postage stamps, plaques, statues, poems, songs, and pictures.

ASSESS & RETEACH

Section 4 Assessment
Use the Section 4 Assessment as an oral pretest for the section quiz. As volunteers answer the questions in class, have other students take note of any questions they could not answer.

Self-Assessment
As a homework assignment, students should write answers to the questions they could not answer in the oral pretest.

Section Quiz

FORMAL ASSESSMENT
Section Quiz, p. 167

Reteach
Repeat the video "Jump at the Sun" and discuss the African-American experience, with particular reference to the Harlem Renaissance.

***AMERICAN STORIES* video series**
"Jump at the Sun"

CLOSE

The migration of African Americans to Northern cities in the 1920s marked a period of changing attitudes and goals. African-American leaders differed in their approaches to dealing with discrimination and violence. Harlem Renaissance writers and artists celebrated their unique culture.

ANSWERS

1. TERMS & NAMES
Zora Neale Hurston, p. 470
James Weldon Johnson, p. 471
Marcus Garvey, p. 471
Harlem Renaissance, p. 472
Claude McKay, p. 472
Langston Hughes, p. 473
Paul Robeson, p. 474
Louis Armstrong, p. 474
Duke Ellington, p. 475
Bessie Smith, p. 475

2. SUMMARIZING
Possible Responses:
Writers—Langston Hughes, Zora Neale Hurston
Performers—Paul Robeson, Ethel Waters
Musicians—Bessie Smith, Louis Armstrong

3. ANALYZING CAUSES
Possible Responses: After suffering economic disadvantage and racial prejudice in the South, African Americans migrated to the North, especially to urban areas like Harlem, where the community supported the arts and had its own cultural institutions and theaters. The mingling of Caribbean peoples with Southern and Northern blacks in Harlem may have created a unique cultural interchange and served as a source of inspiration for works of art.

4. FORMING GENERALIZATIONS
Possible Responses: African-American writers expressed black pride and black identity, protested racial discrimination, told of the struggles of African Americans in a white-dominated society, celebrated their African heritage, and celebrated the strength and ingenuity of African Americans.

American Literature

OBJECTIVES

1. To describe the role of American literature in the 1920s.
2. To recognize three 1920s literary icons and give examples of their works.

FOCUS & MOTIVATE

▶ ***Starting with the Student***
Have students think about celebrated Americans today.

- Which of these people do students think best captures the spirit of the time?
- Whom would students name as contemporary America's greatest living writers? Students should cite achievements to support their opinions.

MORE ABOUT . . .
Langston Hughes

Hughes was an unknown figure employed as a busboy when the eminent poet Vachel Lindsay came into the Washington, D.C., restaurant where he worked. Hoping for recognition, Hughes left some of his poems beside Lindsay's plate. Later that day Lindsay read them and was so impressed that he praised them to reporters. Hughes's name appeared in newspapers the next day, and not long afterward Alfred A. Knopf published Hughes's first poetry collection, *The Weary Blues.*

AMERICAN LITERATURE

Literature in the Jazz Age

After World War I, American literature—like American jazz—moved to the vanguard of the international artistic scene. Many American writers remained in Europe after the war, some settling in London but many more joining the expatriate community on the Left Bank of the Seine River in Paris, where they could live cheaply.

Back in the United States, such cities as Chicago and New York were magnets for America's young artistic talents. The sweeping popularity of jazz helped spur the Harlem Renaissance, a blossoming of African-American culture named for the New York City neighborhood where many African-American writers and artists settled. Further downtown, the artistic community of Greenwich Village drew literary talents such as the poets Edna St. Vincent Millay and E. E. Cummings and the playwright Eugene O'Neill.

F. SCOTT FITZGERALD

The foremost chronicler of the Jazz Age was the Minnesota-born writer F. Scott Fitzgerald, who in Paris, New York, and later Hollywood rubbed elbows with other leading American writers of the day. In the following passage from Fitzgerald's novel *The Great Gatsby*, the narrator describes a fashionable 1920s party thrown by the title character at his Long Island estate.

By seven o'clock the orchestra has arrived, no thin five-piece affair, but a whole pitful of oboes and trombones and saxophones and viols and cornets and piccolos, and low and high drums. The last swimmers have come in from the beach now and are dressing upstairs; the cars from New York are parked five deep in the drive, and already the halls and salons and verandas are gaudy with primary colors, and hair shorn in strange new ways, and shawls beyond the dreams of Castile. The bar is in full swing, and floating rounds of cocktails permeate the garden outside, until the air is alive with chatter and laughter, and casual innuendo and introductions forgotten on the spot, and enthusiastic meetings between women who never knew each other's names.

The lights grow brighter as the earth lurches away from the sun, and now the orchestra is playing yellow cocktail music, and the opera of voices pitches a key higher. Laughter is easier minute by minute, spilled with prodigality, tipped out at a cheerful word. The groups change more swiftly, swell with new arrivals, dissolve and form in the same breath; already there are wanderers, confident girls who weave here and there among the stouter and more stable, become for a sharp, joyous moment the center of a group, and then, excited with triumph, glide on through the sea-change of faces and voices and color under the constantly changing light.

Suddenly one of these gypsies, in trembling opal, seizes a cocktail out of the air, dumps it down for courage and, moving her hands like Frisco, dances out alone on the canvas platform. A momentary hush; the orchestra leader varies his rhythm obligingly for her, and there is a burst of chatter as the erroneous news goes around that she is Gilda Gray's understudy from the *Follies*. The party has begun.

F. Scott Fitzgerald, *The Great Gatsby* (1925)

RECOMMENDED RESOURCES

Books

Cheney, Anne. *Millay in Greenwich Village.* University: U of Alabama P, 1975. A biography of the young Millay.

Cowley, Malcolm. *Exile's Return.* New ed. New York: Viking, 1951. A famous literary history of the 1920s.

Fitzgerald, F. Scott. *The Great Gatsby.* New York: Scribner, 1925. Fitzgerald's masterpiece.

Hughes, Langston. *The Langston Hughes Reader.* New York: Braziller, 1958. A good sampling of his work.

Lewis, David L. *When Harlem Was in Vogue.* New York: Knopf, 1981. A well-known account of the Harlem Renaissance.

Millay, Edna St. Vincent. *Collected Poems.* New York: Harper, 1956. All the famous lyrics and sonnets.

Videos

Against the Odds. PBS Video, 1994. Describes artists of the Harlem Renaissance.

The Great Gatsby. Dir. Jack Clayton. Paramount, 1974. Fitzgerald's novel on screen.

Langston Hughes: Poet. Dir. Rhonda Fabian and Jerry Baber. Schlessinger Video Productions, 1994. Part of the Black Americans of Achievement Video Collection.

Langston Hughes: The Poet in Our Hearts. Chip Taylor Communications, 1994. Readings of several of Hughes's poems.

EDNA ST. VINCENT MILLAY

In the 1920s, Edna St. Vincent Millay was the quintessential modern young woman, a celebrated poet living a bohemian life in New York's Greenwich Village. The following quatrain memorably proclaims the exuberant philosophy of the young and fashionable in the Roaring Twenties.

My candle burns at both ends;
It will not last the night;
But ah, my foes, and oh, my friends—
It gives a lovely light!

EDNA ST. VINCENT MILLAY, "First Fig,"
From *A Few Figs from Thistles* (1920)

LANGSTON HUGHES

A towering figure of the Harlem Renaissance, Langston Hughes often imbued his poetry with the rhythms of jazz and blues. In the poem "Dream Variations," for example, the two stanzas resemble improvised passages played and varied by a jazz musician. The dream of freedom and equality is a recurring symbol in Hughes's verse and has appeared frequently in African-American literature since the 1920s, when Hughes penned this famous poem.

To fling my arms wide
In some place of the sun,
To whirl and to dance
Till the white day is done.
Then rest at cool evening
Beneath a tall tree
While night comes on gently,
Dark like me—
That is my dream!

To fling my arms wide
In the face of the sun,
Dance! Whirl! Whirl!
Till the quick day is done.
Rest at pale evening . . .
A tall, slim tree . . .
Night coming tenderly
Black like me.

LANGSTON HUGHES, "Dream Variations,"
from *The Weary Blues* (1926)

INTERACT WITH HISTORY

1. **COMPARING AND CONTRASTING** What does each selection reveal about life in 1920s America? Cite details to help explain your answers.

SEE SKILLBUILDER HANDBOOK, PAGE 909.

2. **CREATING A BIBLIOGRAPHY** Draw up an annotated bibliography of American literature of the 1920s, perhaps grouping titles by genre (poetry, drama, and so on) before arranging them alphabetically by the authors' surname. The annotation, or brief description, for each work you list should include information on the work's relevance to the period and on its place in American letters.

Visit http://www.mlushistory.com for more about literature in the 1920s.

INSTRUCT

▶ *Starting with the Student*

- Ask students if there is a term—like *Jazz Age, Roaring Twenties,* or *Harlem Renaissance*—that could be applied to the 1990s.
- Have interested students read more works by one of the three writers and share their impressions in panel discussions.

▶ *Discussing Key Ideas*

- Many American writers of the 1920s lived overseas—especially in Paris—or in large U.S. cities, such as Chicago and New York.
- Important 1920s writers included F. Scott Fitzgerald, the best-known chronicler of the age; the poet Edna St. Vincent Millay, whose bohemian lifestyle caught the public's imagination; and Langston Hughes, a towering figure of the Harlem Renaissance.

HISTORY FROM VISUALS

Reading the Images Have students study the art and selections.

- What feelings does the *Great Gatsby* book cover convey? *Possible Responses: Sadness, bleakness, mystery, glamour, romantic yearning.*
- What double meanings does the language in the two poems contain? *Possible Responses: "My candle burns at both ends" suggests living life fully but also burning oneself out; Hughes's "white," "dark," and "black" refer to day and night but also to white and black Americans.*

INTERACT WITH HISTORY

1. Comparing and Contrasting

Possible Answers: *The Fitzgerald selection reveals the excess, shallowness, emphasis on fashion, and frenzied modernity of the age; the Millay quatrain conveys the youthful exuberance, emphasis on self-expression, and self-destructiveness of the time; the Hughes poem illustrates the desire for self-expression, the dreams and plight of African Americans, and the influence of jazz and blues.*

2. Creating a Bibliography

Standards for Evaluation
Bibliographies should . . .

- list works of the 1920s by noted American authors
- provide accurate publication dates and other information
- include brief annotations describing each work and its significance
- use an acceptable and consistent bibliographic form, perhaps grouping entries by place of publication or by genre before arranging them alphabetically by author

CHAPTER 13
ASSESSMENT ANSWERS

REVIEWING THE CHAPTER

TERMS & NAMES

1. bootlegger, p. 455
2. fundamentalism, p. 456
3. flapper, p. 458
4. Babe Ruth, p. 466
5. Charles A. Lindbergh, p. 467
6. F. Scott Fitzgerald, p. 469
7. Zora Neale Hurston, p. 470
8. Harlem Renaissance, p. 472
9. Langston Hughes, p. 473
10. Paul Robeson, p. 474

MAIN IDEAS

Answers will vary.

11. Government had to patrol coastlines and inland borders for alcohol smugglers, monitor highways for trucks carrying illegal alcohol, oversee industries that used alcohol.
12. Scopes broke a Tennessee law that made teaching evolution a crime. He was found guilty, but a higher court later set aside the verdict.
13. A boyish haircut, long beads, bangle bracelets, close-fitting hat, short, waistless dress.
14. Birthrate declined; more married women worked; labor-saving devices provided more leisure.
15. Broadened curriculums to meet the needs of a wide range of students, offered vocational training and home economics, and taught English to immigrants.
16. Crossword puzzles; mahjong; flagpole sitting; bike races; dance marathons.
17. Conformity; materialism; vulgarity of business culture; shallowness of middle-class values; constricting morals; glorification of war.
18. Desire of African Americans to escape inequality and poverty, fight injustice, improve their lives.
19. Pride; racial justice; equality; richness of folklore.
20. Claude McKay, Langston Hughes, and Zora Neale Hurston were outstanding writers; Josephine Baker, Paul Robeson, Louis Armstrong, and Duke Ellington were outstanding performers and musicians.

Chapter 13 Assessment

REVIEWING THE CHAPTER

TERMS & NAMES For each term below, write a sentence explaining its historical significance during the 1920s. For each person listed, write a sentence explaining his or her role in events of this period.

1. **bootlegger**
2. **fundamentalism**
3. **flapper**
4. **Babe Ruth**
5. **Charles A. Lindbergh**
6. **F. Scott Fitzgerald**
7. **Harlem Renaissance**
8. **Langston Hughes**
9. **Zora Neale Hurston**
10. **Paul Robeson**

MAIN IDEAS

SECTION 1 *(pages 452–457)*

Changing Ways of Life

11. Why was heavy funding needed to enforce the Volstead Act?
12. Explain the circumstances and outcome of the trial of the biology teacher John Scopes.

SECTION 2 *(pages 458–461)*

The Twenties Woman

13. Describe the appearance of the typical flapper, including her hairstyle, clothing, and fashion accessories.
14. What key social, economic, and technological changes of the 1920s affected women's marriages and family life?

SECTION 3 *(pages 464–469)*

Education and Popular Culture

15. How did high schools change during the 1920s?
16. What fads gained popularity during the 1920s?
17. Cite examples of the flaws in American society that some famous 1920s authors attacked in their writing.

SECTION 4 *(pages 470–475)*

The Harlem Renaissance

18. What do the Great Migration and the growth of the NAACP and UNIA reveal about the African-American experience in this period?
19. What were some of the important themes treated by African-American writers in the Harlem Renaissance?
20. What were some important African-American achievements in the arts during this period?

THINKING CRITICALLY

1. **CULTURAL TRENDS OF THE ROARING TWENTIES** Create a concept web similar to the one below, and fill it in with trends in popular culture that emerged in the 1920s and continue to influence American society today.

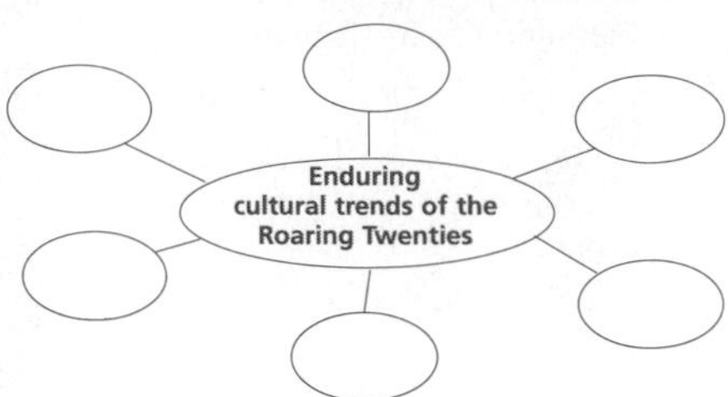

2. **TRACING THEMES IMMIGRATION AND MIGRATION** Do you think the Harlem Renaissance would have occurred without the movement of African Americans from the South to Northern cities during the early part of the century? Why or why not?
3. **DESCRIBING THE 1920s** Reread the quotation from Westbrook Pegler on page 450. Do you think his comment accurately sums up the 1920s? Support your opinion.
4. **ALL THAT JAZZ** In "Literature in the Jazz Age," on pages 476–477, you read excerpts from works written in the 1920s by F. Scott Fitzgerald, Edna St. Vincent Millay, and Langston Hughes. How might a phrase current at the time—"flaming youth"—be an appropriate and accurate phrase to describe the young people and voices in these excerpts?
5. **ANALYZING PRIMARY SOURCES** Read the following excerpt from a 1931 essay in which F. Scott Fitzgerald reflects on the Roaring Twenties. Then answer the question below.

> It was an age of miracles, it was an age of art, it was an age of excess, and it was an age of satire. . . . Scarcely had the staider citizens of the republic caught their breaths when the wildest of all generations, the generation which had been adolescent during the confusion of the War, brusquely shouldered my contemporaries out of the way and danced into the limelight. This was the generation whose girls dramatized themselves as flappers, the generation that corrupted its elders and eventually overreached itself less through lack of morals than through lack of taste. . . . Charm, notoriety, mere good manners, weighed more than money as a social asset. This was rather splendid, but things were getting thinner and thinner as the eternal necessary human values tried to spread over all that expansion.
>
> F. SCOTT FITZGERALD, "Echoes of the Jazz Age"

What does F. Scott Fitzgerald praise and what does he criticize about the young people of the 1920s? Support your opinion.

THINKING CRITICALLY

1. CULTURAL TRENDS OF THE ROARING TWENTIES
Possible Responses: Media hyping of sensational trials; public's fascination with scandalous stories in tabloid newspapers; hero worship of sports celebrities; popularity of spectator sports and movies; popularity of African-American music; novels of social protest; poetry with political messages; fashion as a statement of rebellion.

2. TRACING THEMES IMMIGRATION AND MIGRATION
Possible Responses: Students answering yes may say that the celebration of African-American culture was a natural response to the desire for increased freedom and could have occurred in the South. Those answering no may say that the participants in the Harlem Renaissance needed to break free from the South—both physically and psychologically—in order to give full rein to their artistic expression.

3. DESCRIBING THE 1920S
Possible Responses: Students answering yes may say that the era is known for frivolity, citing its fashions, the growth of popular culture, and the emphasis on movie and sports heroes. Those answering no may say that the era offered much more than nonsense; they may cite new roles for women, the growth of schools, advances in civil-rights awareness, the flowering of African-American culture, and the creation of new literature by gifted writers.

ALTERNATIVE ASSESSMENT

1. **CREATING AN AUDIO SAMPLER**
   What was popular culture like during the 1920s?

   Cooperative Learning Working with a small group, tape-record an audio sampler that reflects American culture and society during that decade.

    Expand your understanding of the period by using the CD-ROM *Our Times*, your textbook, and additional sources.

   - Gather a wide variety of sources, including excerpts from vintage radio broadcasts and popular music; selections of literature, comedy, and drama of the day; excerpts from news, sports, and fashion articles in periodicals of the time; and first-person accounts from oral histories.
   - For each selection, tape-record a brief explanation that identifies its source and its significance.
   - Share the tape with the rest of your class.

2. **LEARNING FROM MEDIA**
   VIDEO View the McDougal Littell video for Chapter 13, *Jump at the Sun.* Discuss the following questions with a small group of classmates, and then do the cooperative-learning activity:

   - What effect did World War I have on the attitudes of African Americans?
   - What effect might growing up in Eatonville, Florida, have had on Zora Neale Hurston?
   - How did Hurston connect the study of anthropology with the world of her youth?
   - **Cooperative Learning** With your group, make a collage that depicts Zora Neale Hurston's dramatic life. Search through books, magazines, and encyclopedias for pictures that seem to capture Hurston's spirit and life. Make copies of the pictures, and then put them together in a collage inspired by Zora Neale Hurston.

3. **PORTFOLIO PROJECT**
   Use the Living History activity to expand your portfolio.

LIVING HISTORY

PRESENTING YOUR DISPLAY

Display your now-and-then storyboard with those of your classmates. Then, with your classmates, discuss the impact the storyboards had on you. Consider these questions during your discussion:

- How closely do 1920s issues parallel today's issues?
- What conclusions, if any, can be drawn from these parallels?
- On which issues do you think our country has made the most progress? Why?

Add your storyboard to your American history portfolio.

Bridge to Chapter 14

Review Chapter 13

CULTURAL CLASHES Changes in lifestyles during the 1920s resulted in clashes between the conservative values of rural Americans and the more liberal values of urban Americans. Small towns, firmly entrenched in traditional moral and religious beliefs, embraced prohibition, while the ethnically diverse cities rejected the ban on alcohol. Difficulties in enforcing prohibition led to an increase in lawlessness. The Scopes trial brought to the forefront another divisive issue, as the attorney Clarence Darrow defended the teaching of evolution.

TWENTIES WOMEN The emancipated young flapper emerged as a new ideal for some women, while her rebelliousness and bold fashions shocked others. Many women during this time cast themselves in other new roles—as more equal partners to their husbands and as valuable employees in the business and professional worlds. However, the majority of married women remained homemakers.

POPULAR CULTURE The growing mass media shaped a mass culture during the 1920s. Major newspapers, magazines, and radio reached broad audiences, who consequently became better informed about many events, including sports. While the media hyped real-life stories of heroic accomplishments, the movies' make-believe stories thrilled theater audiences. Gifted writers, composers, and artists expressed their unique visions of the American scene.

AFRICAN-AMERICAN VOICES Responding to the urban race riots of 1919, African-American leaders became more vocal in denouncing racial violence and injustice. The NAACP represented a new, more militant political voice, which was echoed by the literary voices of many African-American writers during the Harlem Renaissance. The writers, performers, and musicians who were part of this movement displayed extraordinary artistic talents.

Preview Chapter 14

As the Roaring Twenties came to a close, the downturn in the economy signaled the end of an era. The stock market crash of 1929 marked the beginning of the Great Depression. This economic collapse brought enormous suffering to Americans in all walks of life. You will learn about these and other developments in the next chapter.

ALTERNATIVE ASSESSMENT

1. CREATING AN AUDIO SAMPLER
Standards for Evaluation
An audio sampler should meet the following criteria.

- Presents a wide variety of sources.
- Reflects American culture during the 1920s.
- Explains the significance of each selection.

2. LEARNING FROM MEDIA
Answers to the questions.

- African Americans who fought to defend democracy in the war were bitter when they encountered discrimination at home.
- She grew up with a love for the town, its people, and their stories, but she wanted to enter the wider world.
- Her study convinced her that the African-American stories she had heard in her childhood were a vital part of American culture.

COLLAGE ON ZORA NEALE HURSTON
Standards for Evaluation
A collage should meet the following criteria.

- Includes pictures that illustrate Hurston's life.
- Includes pictures from a variety of sources, including books, magazines, and encyclopedias.
- Is well organized and neatly put together.

3. PORTFOLIO PROJECT
LIVING HISTORY
Standards for Evaluation
A strong display should meet the following criteria.

- Presents important issues.
- Shows a clear parallelism between the 1920s and today.
- Presents clear conclusions based on comparisons between now and then.

IN-DEPTH RESOURCES: UNIT 4
See the form for scoring this activity on page 35.

THINKING CRITICALLY

4. ALL THAT JAZZ
Possible Responses: The images of bright lights, parties, dancing, whirling, and candles all seem to belong to a world of fast living and brief but luminous existence that suggests youthful exuberance.

5. ANALYZING PRIMARY SOURCES
Possible Responses: He praises them for their art, their flamboyance, and their breaking away from tradition. He faults them for lack of good taste, for corrupting the older generation, for going too far, and for losing sight of necessary human values.

CHAPTER 14

PLANNING GUIDE

The Great Depression Begins

	Key Ideas	COPYMASTERS	ASSESSMENT
SECTION 1 **The Nation's Sick Economy** ***pp. 482–489***	*Economic problems affecting industries, farmers, and consumers lead to the Great Depression.*	***In-Depth Resources: Unit 4*** • Guided Reading, p. 36 • Primary Sources: The Stock Market Crash, p. 42; Political Cartoon, p. 43 • American Lives: Gordon Parks, p. 49; Alfred E. Smith, p. 50 ***Lesson Plans,*** pp. 117–118	PE ***Section 1 Assessment,*** p. 489 TE ***Self-Assessment,*** p. 489 ***Formal Assessment*** • Section Quiz, p. 176 ***Alternative Assessment Book*** • Standards for Evaluating a Cooperative Activity
SECTION 2 **Hardship and Suffering During the Depression** ***pp. 490–494***	*The Great Depression brings suffering of many kinds and degrees to people from all walks of life.*	***In-Depth Resources: Unit 4*** • Guided Reading, p. 37 • Skillbuilder Practice: Formulating Historical Questions, p. 39 • Geography Application: The Great Depression Takes Its Toll, p. 40 • Primary Source: Letter from a Dust Bowl Survivor, p. 44 • Literature: from *In the Beginning* by Chaim Potok, p. 46 ***Lesson Plans,*** pp. 119–120	PE ***Section 2 Assessment,*** p. 494 TE ***Self-Assessment,*** p. 494 ***Formal Assessment*** • Section Quiz, p. 177 ***Alternative Assessment Book*** • Standards for Evaluating a Cooperative Activity
SECTION 3 **Hoover Struggles with the Depression** ***pp. 495–499***	*President Hoover tries to restore confidence and halt the Depression, but his actions are ineffective.*	***In-Depth Resources: Unit 4*** • Guided Reading, p. 38 • Primary Source: Attack on the Bonus Army, p. 45 ***Lesson Plans,*** pp. 121–122	PE ***Section 3 Assessment,*** p. 499 TE ***Self-Assessment,*** p. 499 ***Formal Assessment*** • Section Quiz, p. 178 ***Alternative Assessment Book*** • Standards for Evaluating a Cooperative Activity
CHAPTER RESOURCES	**Chapter Overview** *The economic boom of the 1920s collapses in 1929 as the United States enters a deep economic depression. Millions of Americans lose their jobs, and President Hoover is unable to end the downslide.*	***In-Depth Resources: Unit 4*** • Living History Project: Worksheet, p. 51; Standards, p. 52 ***Telescoping the Times*** • Chapter Summary, pp. 27–28 ***Planning for Block Schedules***	PE ***Chapter Assessment,*** pp. 500–501 PE ***Alternative Assessment,*** p. 501 ***Formal Assessment*** • Chapter Test, forms A and B, pp. 179–184 ***Test Generator*** ***Alternative Assessment Book*** See explanation and forms for different kinds of alternative assessments including portfolio assessment.

KEY
PE Pupil's Edition
TE Teacher's Edition
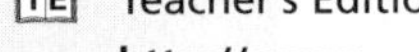
http://www. mlushistory.com

TECHNOLOGY

***Warm-Up Transparency* 14**

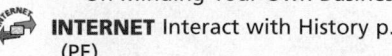

Geography Transparencies
- G22, Growth of Electricity, 1918, 1933

Critical Thinking Transparencies
- CT22, The Great Depression
- CT56, Investing in Stock

Grolier Multimedia Encyclopedia
- campaign speech by Herbert Hoover

Electronic Library of Primary Sources
- "On Minding Your Own Business"

INTERNET Interact with History p. 487 (PE)

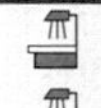

***Warm-Up Transparency* 14**

Humanities Transparencies
- H21, Dust Storm. Arthur Rothstein

Electronic Library of Primary Sources
- "Beans, Bacon, and Gravy"
- Childhood During the Depression by Cesar Chavez

AMERICAN STORIES **video series**
- "Broke but Not Broken"

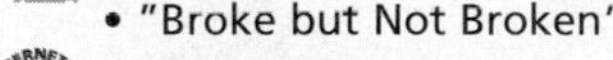

INTERNET Dust Bowl and the Great Depression

***Warm-Up Transparency* 14**

Electronic Library of Primary Sources
- *from* A Report on the Employment of Federal Troops by General Douglas MacArthur
- from *B. E. F.: The Whole Story of the Bonus Army* by W. W. Waters

INTERNET Herbert Hoover and Boulder Dam

American Portfolio: A Videodisc for U.S. History, user's guide, pp. 201–206

Chapter Summary Audiotapes
- Unit 4, Chapter 14

INTERNET http://www.mlushistory.com

Block Scheduling (90 MINUTES)

Day 1

Section 1, pp. 482–489

Section 2, pp. 490–494

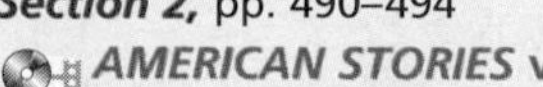

AMERICAN STORIES video series
"Broke but Not Broken"

Section Assessments, pp. 489, 494

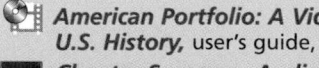

COOPERATIVE ACTIVITIES
- Creating a TV Special About the Stock Market Crash, p. 486 (TE)
- Compiling an Oral History of the Depression, p. 493 (TE)

Day 2

Section 3, pp. 495–499

Section Assessment, p. 499

Chapter Assessment, pp. 500–501

COOPERATIVE ACTIVITY
- Debating the Bonus Army March, p. 498 (TE)

YEARLY PACING *Chapter 14 Total:* 2 days *Yearly Total:* 85 days

See *Planning for Block Schedules* for special activities and pacing strategies.

Customizing for Special Populations

Students Acquiring English

Access for Students Acquiring English: Spanish Translations
- Guided Reading for Sections 1–3, pp. 167–169
- Chapter Summary, pp. 165–166
- Skillbuilder Practice: Formulating Historical Questions, p. 170
- Geography Application: The Great Depression Takes Its Toll, p. 171

Spanish Reading Study Guide, pp. 147–154

Translations of Chapter Summaries, Hmong, Cantonese, Vietnamese, and Cambodian

Chapter Summary Audiotapes in Spanish Unit 4, Chapter 14

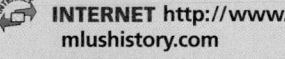

AMERICAN STORIES video series
- "Broke but Not Broken" (Spanish track)

INTERNET The Diverse Classroom

Gifted and Talented Students

In-Depth Resources: Unit 4
- Primary Sources: The Stock Market Crash, p. 42; Political Cartoon, p. 43; Letter from a Dust Bowl Survivor, p. 44; Attack on the Bonus Army, p. 45
- American Lives: Gordon Parks, p. 49; Alfred E. Smith, p. 50

Less Proficient Readers

In-Depth Resources: Unit 4
- Guided Reading for Sections 1–3, pp. 36–38
- Skillbuilder: Formulating Historical Questions, p. 39
- Geography Application: The Great Depression Takes Its Toll, p. 40

Reading Study Guide
- pp. 147–154

Telescoping the Times
- Chapter Summary, pp. 27–28

Chapter Summary Audiotapes, Unit 4, Chapter 14

Connections to Literature READINGS FOR STUDENTS

In-Depth Resources: Unit 4
- **from *In the Beginning* by Chaim Potok,** p. 46

Enrichment Reading
- **Zora Neale Hurston**
  Their Eyes Were Watching God.
  New York: Harper & Row, 1990
  First published in 1937, this novel focuses on a proud, independent African-American woman's search for identity. In a journey that takes her through three marriages and back to her roots, this story powerfully affirms and celebrates African-American culture.
- **John Steinbeck**
  Of Mice and Men.
  New York, Penguin Books, 1994
  In depression-era California, two migrant workers dream of better days until an act of unintentional violence leads to tragedy.

McDougal Littell *Literature Connections*

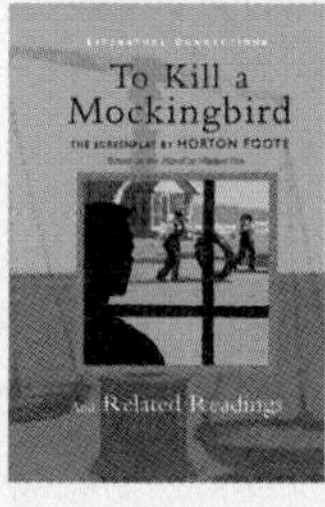

- **Horton Foote**
  ***To Kill a Mockingbird* (the screenplay)** *(with related readings) Adapted from the Pulitzer-prize winning novel by Harper Lee, this screenplay is constructed as a series of episodes concerning the trial of an unjustly accused black man. It examines the consequences of ignorance, prejudice, and hate, and the values of courage, honor, and decency.*

McDougal Littell *The Language of Literature* American Literature
- **William Faulkner, "A Rose for Emily,"** p. 392

CHAPTER 14 OVERVIEW

The Great Depression Begins

▶ *Accessing Prior Knowledge*

Ask students what they already know about the Great Depression. Have they ever discussed the Depression with a relative who lived through it? If so, what did that relative say?

▶ *Predicting Outcomes*

Have students look at the photo of unemployed men on page 481. Based on the photo, ask students to discuss the ways in which the Depression would affect the American people. What do students think the mood of the country would be?

MORE ABOUT . . .
Robert M. La Follette, Jr.

La Follette (1895–1953) was a member of a prominent political family in Wisconsin. As a U.S. senator from that state, La Follette vigorously supported government action to deal with the Depression. He condemned Hoover's economic program and charged the president with trying to "minimize the seriousness of the Depression."

CHAPTER 14

The Great Depression Begins

SECTION 1
The Nation's Sick Economy
Economic problems affecting industries, farmers, and consumers lead to the Great Depression.

SECTION 2
Hardship and Suffering During the Depression
The Great Depression brings suffering of many kinds and degrees to people from all walks of life.

BROKE BUT NOT BROKEN

SECTION 3
Hoover Struggles with the Depression
President Hoover tries to restore confidence and halt the Depression, but his actions are ineffective.

"The illusory prosperity and feverish optimism which marked preceding years have given way to fearful economic insecurity and to widespread despair."
Senator Robert M. La Follette, Jr., 1931

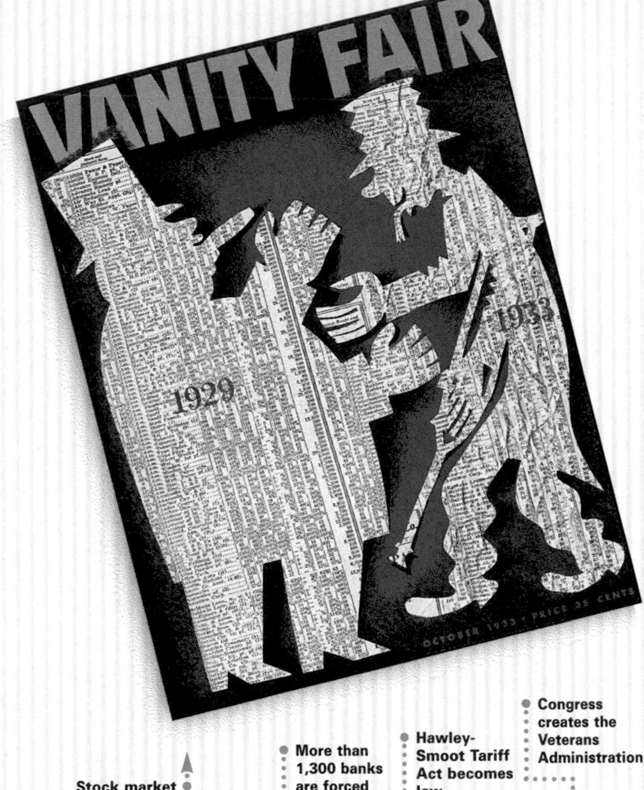

VANITY FAIR
1929
1933
OCTOBER 1933 · PRICE 35 CENTS

THE UNITED STATES

- 1929, March: Herbert Hoover is inaugurated.
- 1929, October: Stock market crashes.
- 1930: More than 1,300 banks are forced to close.
- 1930, June: Hawley-Smoot Tariff Act becomes law.
- 1930, July: Congress creates the Veterans Administration.

THE WORLD

- 1929: Albert Einstein publishes articles on a unified field theory.
- 1930: Army officers led by José Uriburu seize control of the government of Argentina.

THEMES IN CHAPTER 14

Economic Opportunity

The lack of economic opportunity was the dominant theme of the Great Depression. In the years before and during the Depression, many Americans called on the government to create more economic opportunity for its citizens. However, Presidents Coolidge and Hoover were reluctant to do so. Coolidge, for example, refused to support the McNary-Haugen bill, which would have helped boost the farming industry, whose crop prices had fallen due to years of overproduction.

See Teacher's Edition note, p. 483.

Immigration and Migration

The effects of the Great Depression and dust storms forced many farm families to leave their land. Their mass migration to the nation's urban areas further transformed the U.S. from an agricultural to an urban society.

See Teacher's Edition note, p. 492.

The American Dream

The Great Depression undermined the notion of the American dream. As millions of families watched their livelihoods slip away, many viewed the future with despair. Some Americans even began to reject the ideas of democracy and capitalism.

See Teacher's Edition note, p. 497.

LIVING HISTORY

CREATING A COLLAGE

You will encounter a number of compelling personal voices in this chapter, voices telling stories about people's hardship and suffering during the Great Depression.

- Plan a collage of images that will tell the stories of the people you meet in this chapter.
- For each personal voice, choose from a magazine, a newspaper, or another source an image that you think fairly represents the person's experience.
- If you can't find an existing image, make one of your own.

PORTFOLIO PROJECT Keep the images that you gather in a folder for your American history portfolio. At the end of the chapter, you will finish, present, and display your collage.

1931
- Hoover proposes a one-year delay in repayment of war debts and reparations.
- Between 4 million and 5 million Americans are unemployed.
- Austria suffers economic collapse.

May — Empire State Building opens in New York City.

September — Japan occupies Manchuria.

December — Jane Addams wins the Nobel Peace Prize.

1932
- Reconstruction Finance Corporation is established.
- Ibn Saud becomes king of Saudi Arabia.
- More than 13 million Americans are unemployed.

May — Bonus Army arrives in Washington, D.C.

September — From prison, Mohandas K. Gandhi leads a protest against British policies in India.

November — Franklin Delano Roosevelt is elected president.

1933
- Century of Progress world's fair begins.
- Average annual income drops to $1,500 per family.
- Adolf Hitler comes to power.
- Japan withdraws from the League of Nations.

ALTERNATIVE ASSESSMENT

LIVING HISTORY

CREATING A COLLAGE

Give students these strategies for gathering material for the collage:

- Choose the personal stories that most appeal to you and write down the images that each of those stories brings to mind.
- Look for pictures that best illustrate these images in news or art magazines and newspapers.
- Create your own image if you can't find the one you have in mind. Use color to convey the proper mood.
- Decide how you want to organize the pictures in your collage. You may, for example, want to build your collage around a central image.

Project Planning Guide

Step 1	**Students choose stories that most appeal to them.**
Step 2	**Students find images that correspond with their feelings about each story.**
Step 3	**Students organize the images into a collage.**

IN-DEPTH RESOURCES: UNIT 4

See worksheet and standards for evaluation, pp. 51, 52.

RECOMMENDED RESOURCES

Books for the Teacher

Bendiner, Robert. *Just Around the Corner.* New York: Dutton, 1968. Amusing "selective history" of life in the 1930s.

Bulosan, Carlos. *America Is in the Heart.* Seattle: University of Washington Press, 1973. Filipino Americans in 1930s California.

McIlvaine, Robert S. *The Great Depression.* New York: Times Books, 1993. Overview of the Depression.

Books for the Student

Allen, Frederick Lewis. *Since Yesterday.* New York: Bantam, 1961. Society in the 1930s.

Graubert, Judah, and Alice Graubert, eds. *Decade of Destiny.* Chicago: Contemporary, 1978. Reminiscences of the Depression.

Terkel, Studs. *Hard Times.* New York: Pantheon, 1970. Oral history of the Depression.

Videos

America: The Second Century: The Depression. GPN, 402-472-2007. Documentary.

Brother, Can You Spare a Dime? Dir. Philippe Mora. VCI Home Video, 1975. Life during the Great Depression.

Herbert Hoover. Dir. Alan Landsburg. Coronet/MTI Film & Video, 1962. The life and presidency of Herbert Hoover.

Sounder. Dir. Martin Ritt. Paramount Pictures, 1972. The struggles of an African-American sharecropper family.

The Great Depression. WGBH-TV, 1993. Videocassette series.

Software

U.S. History: The Great Depression. CD-Rom. Clearview. Educational Software Institute, 800-955-5570.

Section 1 Overview

OBJECTIVES

1. To summarize some of the problems threatening the American economy in the late 1920s.
2. To describe the causes of the stock market crash and of the Great Depression.
3. To explain how the Great Depression affected the economy in the United States and throughout the world.

SKILLBUILDERS

- Interpreting graphs, pp. 483, 485, 488

CRITICAL THINKING

- Analyzing causes, pp. 483, 487, 489
- Theme: Economic Opportunity, p. 483
- Drawing conclusions, pp. 484, 489
- Forming opinions, p. 486
- Recognizing effects, p. 488
- Summarizing, p. 489

FOCUS & MOTIVATE

5-Minute Warm-Up

Drawing Conclusions
To understand the economic impact of the Great Depression, have students look at the poster on page 488 and answer these questions.

1. What economic troubles are suggested by the term "smokeless chimneys" and by the image of the men?
2. Why did the artist include the picture of the mother and children in the poster?

WARM-UP TRANSPARENCY 14

▶ ***Starting with the Student***

- Ask students whether they have ever felt tempted to spend more money than they actually had. When?
- What do students think happens when industries or governments exceed their budgets?

1 The Nation's Sick Economy

TERMS & NAMES

- price support
- credit
- Alfred E. Smith
- speculation
- buying on margin
- Black Tuesday
- Great Depression
- Dow Jones Industrial Average
- Hawley-Smoot Tariff Act

LEARN ABOUT economic problems affecting industries, farmers, and consumers at home and abroad
TO UNDERSTAND the causes of the Great Depression.

ONE AMERICAN'S STORY

Gordon Parks, who would later become a well-known photographer, author, and filmmaker, was 16 years old during the fall of 1929. He attended high school in St. Paul, Minnesota, and supported himself as a bellboy at the exclusive Minnesota Club. Observing the prosperous club members, Parks saw people who were confident in the economy. Parks felt that he too could look forward to a bright future. Then came the stock market crash of October 1929, and everything seemed to fall apart. In his autobiography, Parks recalled his feelings at the time.

Gordon Parks

A PERSONAL VOICE

I couldn't imagine such financial disaster touching my small world; it surely concerned only the rich. But by the first week of November I too knew differently; along with millions of others across the nation, I was without a job. All that next week I searched for any kind of work that would prevent my leaving school. Again it was, "We're firing, not hiring.". . . Finally, on the seventh of November I went to school and cleaned out my locker, knowing it was impossible to stay on. A piercing chill was in the air as I walked back to the rooming house. The hawk had come. I could already feel his wings shadowing me.

GORDON PARKS, *A Choice of Weapons*

The crash of 1929, and the Depression that followed, dealt a crushing blow to the hopes and dreams of millions of Americans. The high-flying prosperity of the 1920s was over. Hard times had begun.

Economic Troubles on the Horizon

As the 1920s advanced, it grew increasingly clear that serious problems threatened economic prosperity. Though some Americans were becoming wealthy, many more could not earn a decent living. Important industries were in trouble. Farmers produced more food than they could sell at a profit. In hopes of finding wealth, Americans gambled on the stock market. As the decade drew to a close, slippages in the economy signaled the end of an era.

INDUSTRIES IN TROUBLE The superficial prosperity of the late 1920s hid troubling weaknesses that would ultimately lead to the Great Depression of the 1930s. A number of key basic industries, such as textiles, steel, and railroads, barely made a profit. Railroads lost business to new forms of transportation (trucks, buses, and private automobiles), while textile mills faced competition from foreign producers in Japan, India, China, and Latin America.

Mining and lumbering, which had expanded to supply wartime needs during World War I, faced diminished demand for their goods in peacetime. Coal mining was especially hard-hit, in part due to stiff competition from new forms of energy, including hydroelectric power, fuel oil, and natural gas. By the early 1930s, these sources supplied more than half the energy that had once come from coal.

SECTION 1 RESOURCES

PRINT RESOURCES

IN-DEPTH RESOURCES: UNIT 4
Guided Reading, p. 36
Primary Sources: The Stock Market Crash, p. 42; Political Cartoon, p. 43
American Lives: Gordon Parks, p. 49; Alfred E. Smith, p. 50

READING STUDY GUIDE, p. 147

ACCESS FOR STUDENTS ACQUIRING ENGLISH
Guided Reading (Spanish), p. 167

SPANISH READING STUDY GUIDE, p. 147

FORMAL ASSESSMENT
Section Quiz, p. 176

ALTERNATIVE ASSESSMENT BOOK
See forms for supporting and scoring alternative activities.

TECHNOLOGY RESOURCES

GEOGRAPHY TRANSPARENCIES
G22, Growth of Electricity, 1918, 1933

CRITICAL THINKING TRANSPARENCIES
CT22, The Great Depression
CT56, Investing in Stock

CD-ROM *Grolier Multimedia Encyclopedia*
Electronic Library of Primary Sources

VIDEO *American Portfolio: A Videodisc for U.S. History* user's guide, p. 201

INTERNET http://www.mlushistory.com

Even the boom industries of the 1920s—automobiles, construction, and consumer goods—began to weaken. The construction of new houses, for example, fell steadily after peaking in 1925. Between 1925 and 1929, applications for new building permits declined by approximately 25 percent. Housing starts—or the number of new dwellings beginning construction—are an important economic indicator, because house construction has spinoff effects on other industries. New houses require building materials, new furnishings, new equipment, and new appliances. Construction also creates jobs.

THINK THROUGH HISTORY
A. *Analyzing Causes* *What industrial weakness signaled a declining economy in the 1920s?*

A. Answer The older industries, such as textiles, steel, and railroads, which were basic to the fundamental well-being of the economy, were barely profitable.

When housing began to decline, so did other businesses that depended on construction. Furniture companies that had expected an expanding market produced too many goods and cut their labor forces to reduce inventories. The story was similar for makers of household appliances.

Skillbuilder Answer
Price: From the 1927 price of about $1.15, it dropped to a low of about 35 cents in 1932. **How Many Times:** A little more than three times greater. **Factors:** *Possible Answers:* The Depression forced almost all prices down. People had less money to buy products made from wheat, so the price went down to attract buyers. Wheat production went up in 1931 (to 942 million bushels), which caused the price to fall even further.

FARMERS NEED A LIFT Perhaps more than any other part of the economy, agriculture suffered in the 1920s. During World War I, international demand for crops such as wheat and corn had soared, causing prices to rise. Farmers had planted more crops and taken out loans to buy land and equipment. After the war, demand for farm products fell, and crop prices declined by 50 percent or more. (See *supply and demand* on page 939 in the Economics Handbook.)

To compensate for falling prices, farmers boosted production in the hope of selling more crops, but this only depressed prices further. Between 1919 and 1921, annual farm income declined from $10 billion to just over $4 billion. Farmers who had gone into debt had difficulty in paying off their loans. Many lost their farms when banks foreclosed and seized the property as payment for the debt. As farmers began to default on their loans, many rural banks began to fail.

THINK THROUGH HISTORY
B. THEME *Economic Opportunity* *What were some of the basic difficulties faced by farmers in the 1920s?*

B. Answer During World War I, the demand for crops had caused prices to rise. Farmers had planted more crops and taken out loans to buy land and equipment. After the war, however, demand for farm products declined, and prices fell.

U.S. Wheat Production and Wheat Prices

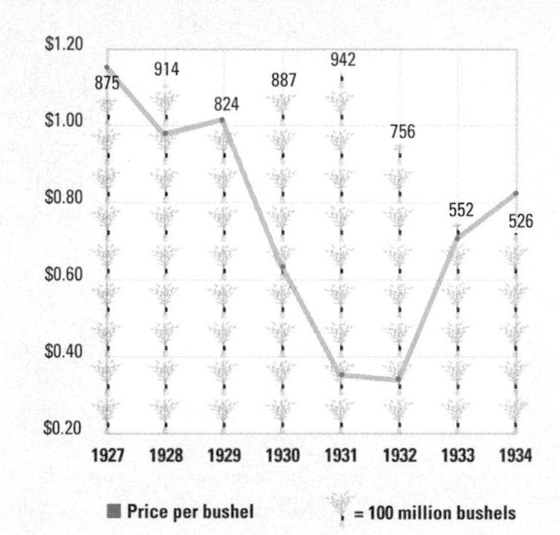

Source: *Historical Statistics of the United States*

SKILLBUILDER
INTERPRETING GRAPHS ***How far did the price per bushel of wheat drop in the years after 1927? How many times greater than the lowest price was the highest price? What factors do you think contributed to this drop?***

To prop up the farm sector, members of Congress proposed a complicated piece of legislation called the McNary-Haugen bill. This proposal called for federal **price supports**—the support of certain price levels at or above market values by the government—for key products. The bill had three major provisions:

- The government would buy surplus crops, such as wheat, corn, cotton, and tobacco, at guaranteed prices that were higher than the market rate.
- The government would then sell these crops on the world market for the lower prevailing prices.
- To make up for losses caused by buying high and selling low, the government would place a tax on domestic food sales, thus passing the cost of the farm program along to consumers.

Congress passed the bill twice, in 1927 and 1928, but each time President Coolidge vetoed it. At one point, the president commented, "Farmers have never made money. I don't believe we can do much about it." Farm prices remained low, and farmers continued to struggle.

CONSUMERS HAVE LESS MONEY TO SPEND As farmers' incomes fell, they bought fewer goods and services. Without money to spend, rural families could not buy the products of American industry. The same problem was evident among American consumers as a whole.

OBJECTIVE
① INSTRUCT

Economic Troubles on the Horizon

▶ ***Discussing Key Ideas***
- Businesses and farmers face diminished demands for goods in the 1920s.
- As incomes fall, many Americans pile up debts and cut back on spending.
- The country elects Herbert Hoover in 1928 because most Americans believe the nation is prospering.

IN-DEPTH RESOURCES: UNIT 4
Guided Reading, p. 36
American Lives: Gordon Parks, p. 49

ACCESS FOR STUDENTS ACQUIRING ENGLISH
Guided Reading (Spanish), p. 167

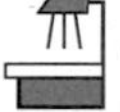
GEOGRAPHY TRANSPARENCIES
G22, Growth of Electricity, 1918, 1933

HISTORY FROM VISUALS

U.S. Wheat Production and Wheat Prices

Reading the Graph Alert students to the dual information on the graph. The green line represents the shift in price of a bushel of wheat. The rows of wheat stalks indicate the amount of wheat the nation produced each year.

Extension Discuss with students the concept of supply and demand. *If supply is great, then the demand, and prices, go down, and vice versa.* Then ask how the graph conveys this concept. *The abundance of wheat led to a decrease in demand, and thus a drop in price. When supply fell, demand increased, which raised the price.*

TEACHING OPTIONS

Teaching Less Proficient Readers

Analyzing Causes and Effects To help students understand why the U.S. economy began to weaken in the 1920s, have them complete the following list of signs of weakness in the economy:

1. Key basic industries began losing out to advanced machinery and foreign competition.
2. The coal mining industry suffered due to . . .
3. New home construction fell steadily, which led to . . .
4. The farming industry grew weak when . . .
5. More Americans began living on credit because . . .
6. The country's uneven distribution of income led to . . .

Exploring Themes

Economic Opportunity Discuss the federal price supports proposed by Congress to aid farmers. Ask students what effect the provisions might have had on farmers. What effect, if any, do students think the bill might have had on the course of the Great Depression? *Possible Responses: The bill might have helped farmers, who in turn would have spent more money and aided industry; on the other hand, the bill might have had little effect because the world agricultural market was weak and consumers could not the pay the higher sales tax for which the plan called.*

MORE ABOUT . . .
Living on Credit

Purchasing goods through credit remains a highly popular practice with American consumers, as well as with shoppers around the world. The producers of one of the most widely used credit cards, for example, announced that consumers worldwide had charged a record $630.6 billion on their cards in 1994—a 22 percent increase from the year before. The number of the company's cards in use also surged that year, from 333 million to 391 million worldwide.

MORE ABOUT . . .
Alfred E. Smith

Smith was a political associate and friend of Franklin Roosevelt. It was Roosevelt who bestowed upon Smith his nickname, "the Happy Warrior," from a William Wordsworth poem. After Roosevelt became president, however, their friendship deteriorated. Smith openly criticized Roosevelt's Great Depression policies as socialist. "Unless they are stopped," Smith said about the president and his advisers, "you and I may never live to see the time when this country will get back to the fundamental principles it was founded on."

IN-DEPTH RESOURCES: UNIT 4
American Lives: Alfred E. Smith, p. 50

GROLIER MULTIMEDIA ENCYCLOPEDIA
audio excerpt of a campaign speech by Herbert Hoover

By the late 1920s, Americans were buying less—mainly because of rising prices, stagnant wages, unbalanced distribution of income, and overbuying on credit in the preceding years—even as American farms and factories were producing more. Production expanded much faster than wages, resulting in an ever-widening gap between the rich and the poor.

LIVING ON CREDIT Although many Americans appeared prosperous during the 1920s, in fact they were living beyond their means. They often bought goods on **credit**—an arrangement in which consumers agreed to buy now and pay later for purchases, often on an installment plan (usually in monthly payments) that included interest charges.

By making credit easily available, businesses encouraged Americans to pile up a large consumer debt. Many people then had trouble paying off their growing debts. Faced with debt, consumers cut back on spending.

THINK THROUGH HISTORY
C. *Drawing Conclusions* *What did the experience of industry, farmers, and consumers at this time suggest about the health of the economy?*

C. Answer Beneath the surface prosperity of the 1920s, the economy was in trouble.

UNEVEN DISTRIBUTION OF INCOME Consumers also spent less because their incomes were not rising fast enough. During the 1920s, nearly half the nation's families earned less than $1,500 per year, then considered the minimum amount needed for a decent standard of living. Even families earning twice that much could not afford many of the household products that manufacturers produced. Economists estimate that the average man or woman bought a new outfit of clothes only once a year. Scarcely half the homes in many cities had electric lights or a furnace for heat. Only one city home in ten had an electric refrigerator.

In contrast, rich Americans did very well. Between 1920 and 1929, the income of the wealthiest 1 percent of the population rose by 75 percent, compared with a 9 percent increase for Americans as a whole. In 1929, the wealthiest 5 percent of American families took in nearly a third of the nation's income, while the poorest 40 percent of the population earned just over a tenth of the national income.

This unequal distribution of income meant that most Americans could not participate fully in the economic advances of the 1920s. Many people did not have the money to consume the flood of goods that factories produced. The prosperity of the era rested on a fragile foundation.

A NEW PRESIDENT Although economic disaster was around the corner, the election of 1928 took place in a national mood of apparent prosperity. This election pitted Republican candidate Herbert Hoover against Democrat **Alfred E. Smith.** The two men could hardly have been more different. Hoover, the secretary of commerce under Harding and Coolidge, was a mining engineer from Iowa who had never run for public office.

"We in America are nearer to the final triumph over poverty than ever before."
HERBERT HOOVER

Smith, in contrast, was a career politician who had served four terms as governor of New York. Unlike the formal and reserved Hoover, Smith was witty and outgoing. Both men came from poor families and had worked hard to succeed, but Hoover felt uncomfortable in the limelight, whereas Smith relished it.

Hoover had one major advantage: he could point to years of prosperity under Republican administrations since 1920. Many Americans believed Hoover when he declared, "We in America are nearer to the final triumph over poverty than ever before. . . . The poorhouse is vanishing among us."

Although Smith ran a spirited campaign, he could not overcome the Republican advantage. In addition, Smith's heavy Brooklyn accent, his opposition to prohibition, and his religion (Roman Catholicism) counted heavily against him. In the election, Hoover captured 58 percent of the popular vote and won 444 electoral votes to Smith's 87. The message was clear: most Americans were happy with the course of the nation and its Republican leadership.

TEACHING OPTIONS

Making Connections Across the Curriculum

Economics A depression is a rare phase in what is known as the business cycle. The business cycle is a series of periods of growing and shrinking economic activity measured by increases or decreases in a country's GDP—gross domestic product. Since World War II, the business cycle has consisted of two overall phases: expansion and recession. A recession is defined as two or more consecutive fiscal quarters of declining GDP. A depression occurs when the cycle of economic slowdown and high unemployment continues for a long time.

Making Global Connections

The World Stock Exchange The daily flurry of trading activity at the New York Stock Exchange has earned it the nickname "the nation's marketplace." However, the New York Stock Exchange is not the only stock exchange in the world, nor is it the oldest. The first European stock exchange, for example, was established in Antwerp, Belgium, in 1531. Today, major stock exchanges operate in a number of major cities in the United States and in many foreign capitals, including Tokyo, Paris, and Mexico City.

The Stock Market Comes Tumbling Down

By 1929, some economists were warning of serious weaknesses in the economy. Most Americans, however, remained unaware of these problems and continued to have confidence in the nation's economic health. Those who could afford to invest in the stock market did so in increasing numbers. In fact, the stock market had become the most visible symbol of an American economy that seemed to be producing wonderful products in the years after World War I.

DREAMS OF RICHES IN THE STOCK MARKET Through most of the 1920s, stock prices rose steadily. (See *stock market* on page 938 in the Economics Handbook.) Eager to take advantage of this "bull market"—period of rising stock prices—many Americans rushed to buy stocks and bonds. One observer wrote, "It seemed as if all economic law had been suspended and a new era opened up in which success and prosperity could be had without knowledge or industry." By 1929, about 4 million Americans—or 3 percent of the nation's population—owned stocks. Many of these investors were already wealthy, but others were average Americans who hoped to strike it rich.

As stock prices rose, several problems became evident. More and more investors were engaging in **speculation**—that is, they bought stocks and bonds on the chance that they might make a quick or a large profit, ignoring the risks. Their unrestrained buying and selling fueled the market's upward spiral. As prices rose, wealth was generated on paper, but it bore little relation to the real worth of companies or the goods that they produced. The price of stocks had little relationship to the dividends the stocks paid.

Furthermore, many investors began **buying on margin**—paying a small percentage of a stock's price as a down payment and borrowing the rest. With stockbrokers willing to lend buyers up to 75 percent of a stock's purchase price, buying on margin became the rule. This system worked as long as prices continued to rise, since investors could sell their inflated stocks to make a profit and pay off their debt. If stocks declined, however, there was no way to pay off the loan.

BLACK TUESDAY In early September 1929, stock prices peaked and began to decline. Confidence in the market started to waver, and some investors sold their stocks and pulled out. On October 24, the market took a plunge, as panicked investors unloaded their shares. But the worst was yet to come.

On October 29—known as **Black Tuesday**—the bottom fell out of the market. People and corporations alike frantically tried to sell their stocks before prices plunged even lower. The individual investors who had bought stocks on credit acquired huge debts as the prices plummeted. Other investors, who had put most of their savings into the market, lost huge portions of their nest eggs. The number of shares dumped that day was a record 16 million. Additional millions of

This cartoon by James N. Rosenberg, which shows Wall Street crumbling on October 29, 1929, is titled *Dies Irae*, Latin for "day of wrath."

ECONOMIC BACKGROUND

AMERICA'S DECLINING WEALTH

As the following chart demonstrates, the yearly income and spending per person declined after 1929, the year of the stock market crash. (See *depression* on page 934 in the Economics Handbook.)

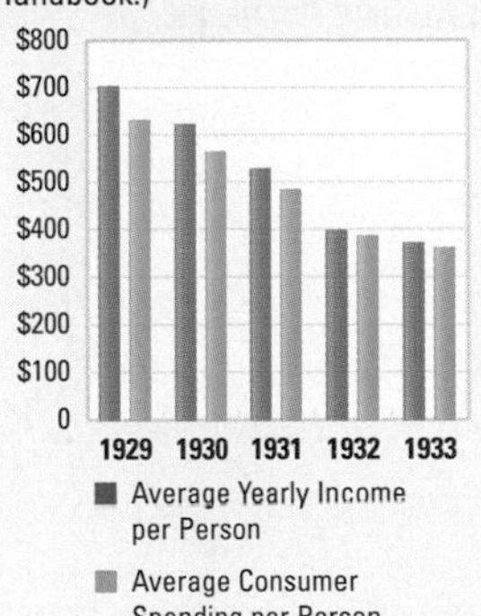

Source: *Historical Statistics of the United States*

SKILLBUILDER

INTERPRETING GRAPHS ***What happened to the difference between yearly income and consumer spending in the years 1929–1931? What do you think this change meant to Americans?***

Skillbuilder Answer
Possible Answer: Each year, the difference between the two grew smaller, which probably meant that people were spending more of their income and saving less.

OBJECTIVE
② INSTRUCT

The Stock Market Comes Tumbling Down

▶ ***Starting with the Student***
Have students create a chart to list the causes and effects, as discussed in the text, of several events that prompted the onset of the Great Depression.

Onset of the Great Depression	
Cause	Effect
1.	
2.	
3.	
4.	

▶ ***Discussing Key Ideas***
- On October 29, 1929, the market crashes as stock prices plunge.
- The stock market crash hastens the Great Depression, which is caused by a number of economic and social factors.

IN-DEPTH RESOURCES: UNIT 4
Primary Source: The Stock Market Crash, p. 42

ELECTRONIC LIBRARY OF PRIMARY SOURCES
"On Minding Your Own Business" from the *New York Times*

ECONOMIC BACKGROUND
America's Declining Wealth
Critical Thinking: Analyzing Ask students why, by 1933, Americans were spending nearly as much as they were earning. *Possible Response: Americans were earning so much less on average by 1933 that they could not afford to save any money.*

TEACHING OPTIONS

Teaching Gifted and Talented Students

Create a Crash Cartoon Discuss with students the cartoon on page 485. Then encourage interested students to create their own cartoon illustrating some aspect of the stock market crash: its effect on business, on business people, on farmers, or on consumers. Cartoons should . . .

- illustrate the effects of the crash
- convey the sense of fear and shock inspired by the crash
- include a caption or title that captures the essential spirit of the illustration

Making Connections Across Time

The Crash of 1987 On October 19, 1987—almost exactly 58 years after Black Tuesday—the American stock market experienced the greatest single-day decline in its history. On what became known as Black Monday, the market fell 508 points. As in 1929, the crash was preceded by a prosperous economy and a stock market boom. Experts blamed the '87 crash on several factors, including rising interest rates, the U.S. bombing of oil platforms in Iran, and conflict among U.S. trading partners. Unlike in 1929, stock prices quickly recovered after the '87 crash and continued to rise over the next couple of years.

NOW & THEN

The Dow Jones Averages

▶ ***Starting with the Student*** Have students interview someone who invests in the stock market. Interview questions might include: What are the pros and cons of investing in the market? How does one make investments? What advice should a new investor follow?

▶ ***Discussing Key Ideas***

- In 1882, Charles H. Dow, Edward Jones, and Charles M. Bergstresser start a company that distributes copies of stock market reports to business customers in New York City.
- In 1896, Charles Dow creates the Dow Jones Industrial Average by choosing 12 major companies and averaging the prices of their stocks.
- Through the years, the Dow fluctuates between sudden, sometimes disastrous, drops and steady increases.
- Throughout the Dow's history, the stocks that compose it have changed to reflect the times. Today, the group of 30 companies includes McDonald's and Walt Disney.

CRITICAL THINKING TRANSPARENCIES
CT56, Investing in Stock

"Wall Street Lays an Egg"
HEADLINE, *VARIETY,* OCTOBER 1929

shares could not even find buyers. By mid-November, investors had lost $30 billion, an amount equal to American spending in World War I. The stock market bubble had finally burst. One eyewitness to these events, Frederick Lewis Allen, described the resulting situation.

A PERSONAL VOICE

The Big Bull Market was dead. Billions of dollars' worth of profits—and paper profits—had disappeared. The grocer, the window cleaner, and the seamstress had lost their capital [savings]. In every town there were families which had suddenly dropped from showy affluence into debt. . . . With the Big Bull Market gone and prosperity going, Americans were soon to find themselves living in an altered world which called for new adjustments, new ideas, new habits of thought, a new order of values.

FREDERICK LEWIS ALLEN, *Only Yesterday*

THINK THROUGH HISTORY
D. Forming Opinions *What role did greed play in the stock market crash?*

D. Answer Students may say that some investors bought large amounts of stock on margin because the rise in stock prices had made them greedy.

CAUSES OF THE GREAT DEPRESSION The stock market crash signaled the beginning of the **Great Depression**—the period from 1929 to 1941, in which the economy was in severe decline and millions of people were out of work. The crash alone did not cause the Great Depression, but it hastened the collapse of the economy and made the Depression more severe.

Although historians and economists differ on the main causes of the Great Depression, most cite a common set of factors. Among these causes were the following:

NOW & THEN

The Dow Jones Averages

Television and radio news programs report the Dow Jones Industrial Average many times during the workweek. "The Dow closed 20 points higher today at 5672." "The Dow Jones passed the 8000 mark." What is the Dow Jones Industrial Average?

1882
Charles H. Dow, Edward Jones, and Charles M. Bergstresser start a company that distributes copies of stock market reports to business customers in New York City. The first reports are handwritten and distributed by messenger boys. In 1889, the reports, plus additional editorials, become known as the *Wall Street Journal.*

Charles H. Dow (*left*); a trading floor in the 1920s (*above*); and a modern trading floor (*right*).

1896
Charles H. Dow creates the Dow Jones Industrial Average by choosing 12 major American companies and averaging the prices of their stocks. The twelve original companies are:

American Cotton Oil	Laclede Gas
American Sugar	National Lead
American Tobacco	North American
Chicago Gas	Tennessee Coal & Iron
Distilling & Cattle Feeding	U.S. Leather
General Electric	U.S. Rubber

Block Schedule — TEACHING OPTION — Time Needed: 30 Minutes

Cooperative Activity: Creating a TV Special About the Stock Market Crash

Task: Student groups will investigate one aspect of the stock market crash and write a script for a television program about the crash.

Purpose: To explore in depth different aspects of the stock market crash.

Activity: Have each group research a different aspect of the stock market crash. Topics might include the panicked events of Black Tuesday, the crash's effects on banks and business, Hoover and the government's response to the crash, or a profile of an investor or investors who lost everything. After researching the topic, the group should write a television script based on its research and then present it to the class.

Building a Portfolio: Students may wish to add a copy of the script to their portfolio.

ALTERNATIVE ASSESSMENT BOOK
Standards for Evaluating a Cooperative Activity

Standards for Evaluation
News scripts should . . .

- contain well-researched information
- be presented in a clear, well-organized, and objective manner
- use quotations to personalize the story

E. Answer Decaying industrial base; farm crisis; unequal distribution of income; falling demand for consumer goods; low interest rates, which encouraged borrowing.

THINK THROUGH HISTORY
E. *Analyzing Causes* *What were some of the causes of the Great Depression?*

- an old and decaying industrial base—outmoded equipment made some industries less competitive
- a crisis in the farm sector—farmers produced more than they were able to sell, especially after the end of World War I and the disappearance of markets that the war had opened to them
- the availability of easy credit—many people went into debt by buying goods on the installment plan
- an unequal distribution of income—there was too little money in the hands of working people, who were the vast majority of consumers.

These factors in turn led to falling demand for consumer goods, even as newly mechanized factories produced more products. The federal government contributed to the crisis by keeping interest rates low, thereby allowing companies and individuals to borrow easily and build up large debts. Some of this borrowed money was used to buy stocks, but the government did little to discourage such buying or to regulate the market.

At first people found it hard to believe that economic disaster had struck the country. In November 1929, President Hoover encouraged Americans to remain confident about the future of the economy. Yet despite the comforting words, the most severe depression in American history was well on its way.

Then, as now, the **Dow Jones Industrial Average** was the most widely used barometer of the stock market's health. The Dow is a measure based on the stock prices of 30 representative large firms trading on the New York Stock Exchange. Just prior to the crash of 1929, the Dow reached a high of 381 points, nearly 300

October 28–29, 1929
The Dow loses nearly one-fourth of its value over a two-day period as the stock market crashes.

1982–1987
During the Reagan presidency, the Dow Jones Industrial Average moves steadily upward, from 776.92 in August 1982 to a peak of 2722.42 in August 1987.

January 8, 1987
The Dow breaks the 2000 mark for the first time.

October 19, 1987
The Dow falls 508 points, to 1738.74, on what has been called Black Monday.

100TH BIRTHDAY

1997
Through the years, the stocks that make up the Dow Jones Industrial Average have changed to reflect the times. The group of 30 stocks now includes McDonald's, Walt Disney, and American Express as well as industrial companies, such as Caterpillar Inc. There are also averages of 20 transportation companies, of 15 utility companies, and of the 65 stocks together. In 1997, the Dow Jones Industrial Average exceeds the 8000 mark for the first time.

INTERACT WITH HISTORY

1. **ANALYZING ISSUES** On the basis of what you have read, do stocks seem to be a good investment? If you had invested in stocks in 1990, would you probably have lost money or made a profit since then?

SEE SKILLBUILDER HANDBOOK, PAGE 916.

2. **STUDYING THE MARKET** Look at a newspaper to see what the Dow Jones Industrial Average is on a given day. Did the average go up or down on that day?

Visit http://www.mlushistory.com for more about the Dow Jones Industrial Average.

MORE ABOUT . . .
Charles H. Dow and Edward Jones

Although Dow and Jones were partners, they had little in common. Dow grew up on a farm and was an austere, reserved man. Jones came from a fairly well-to-do family and was passionate and hot tempered. Richard Stillman, who wrote a book about the Dow Jones Industrial Average, characterized Jones as "excitable, emotional and you never knew when [he] might explode." Dow did not approve of his partner's lifestyle, particularly his choice of friends—the pool operators and wheeler-dealers of Wall Street. Jones often hung out with these men after work in saloons, seeking tips for his newsletter. Perhaps sensing his partner's disapproval, Jones left the newsletter in 1899 to work in the world he had covered—Wall Street.

INTERACT WITH HISTORY

1. Analyzing Issues

Possible Responses:

Yes—The rise in the stock market seems steady and predictable. For example, the Dow Jones Industrial Average steadily increased between 1982 and 1987. No—The stock market seems too unpredictable. It appears hard to tell when the market might crash. In 1987, for example, it had been climbing to record heights before it suddenly plummeted.

Investments since 1990 would likely have returned a profit, for since that time the average has steadily increased. In 1997, it exceeded the 8000 mark for the first time.

2. Studying the Market

The business section of most daily newspapers lists the previous day's activity of individual stocks as well as the Dow Jones Industrial Average. The Dow's overall increase or decrease usually appears before the listing of the individual stocks. To determine the activity of an individual stock, students should locate the stock on the page and check the number in the last column of its line, which usually represents the stock's daily activity.

HISTORY FROM VISUALS

Depression Indicators in the United States, 1928–1933

Reading the Graphs Remind students that the figures on the unemployment graph are in millions, while the figures on the bank and business failures graphs are in thousands.

Extension Discuss with students in what way the three depression indicators may be related. *Possible Response: When banks fail, many businesses have to close down, which in turn causes unemployment to rise.*

OBJECTIVE

INSTRUCT

Financial Collapse

▶ ***Discussing Key Ideas***

- As the economy collapses, banks and businesses fail and millions of Americans lose their jobs.
- Countries all over the world suffer the effects of the Great Depression.
- The drastic decrease in world trade during the Depression further reduces overall economic activity.

IN-DEPTH RESOURCES: UNIT 4
Primary Source: Political Cartoon, p. 43

Depression Indicators in the United States, 1928–1933

UNEMPLOYMENT | BANK FAILURES | BUSINESS FAILURES

Source: *Historical Statistics of the United States*

SKILLBUILDER **INTERPRETING GRAPHS** ***In what year did the biggest jump in bank failures occur? What measure on the graphs seems to indicate an improvement in the U.S. economy during the Depression?***

Skillbuilder Answer **Bank Failures:** 1932–1933. **Improvement:** *Possible Answer:* Business failures dropped significantly in 1932–1933.

points higher than it had been five years earlier. On October 28 and 29, Black Monday and Black Tuesday, the Dow fell dramatically, and it continued to fall until 1932.

Financial Collapse

After the crash, many Americans panicked and withdrew their money from banks, forcing some banks to close. Many banks could not cover their customers' withdrawals, because the banks had invested and lost money in the stock market, just as individuals had. As a result, 659 banks shut their doors in 1929. By 1933, around 6,000 banks—one-fourth of the nation's total—had failed. Because the federal government did not protect or insure bank accounts, these bank failures wiped out around 9 million individual savings accounts. People who went to the bank to retrieve their savings came home with nothing.

This British election poster shows that the Great Depression was a global event.

The Great Depression hit other businesses equally hard. Between 1929 and 1932, the gross national product—the nation's total output of goods and services—was cut nearly in half, from $104 billion to $59 billion. Some 85,000 businesses went bankrupt. Among these failed enterprises were some of the automobile companies that had prospered during the 1920s, including Pierce-Arrow and Bearcat. Railroad companies controlling one-third of the nation's track mileage had gone bankrupt by the early 1930s.

As the economy plunged into a tailspin, millions of workers lost their jobs. Unemployment leaped from 3 percent of the work force (1.6 million workers) in 1929 to 25 percent in 1933 (13 million workers). One out of every four workers was without a job. The workers who managed to hold on to their jobs often had to accept pay cuts and reduced hours.

THINK THROUGH HISTORY

F. *Recognizing Effects* *What happened to ordinary workers during the Great Depression?*

F. Answer As the economy collapsed, millions of workers lost their jobs. Without jobs, they had to cut back on their spending, further deepening the economic downturn. Many workers who had jobs had to accept pay cuts.

TEACHING OPTION

Making Connections Across the Curriculum

Music The Great Depression touched many aspects of American society, including its music. Many of the songs of the Great Depression reflected the nation's despair. For example, the lyrics of the popular Depression song "Brother, Can You Spare a Dime?" tell the story of a man's abrupt decline: "Once I built a railroad, I made it run / I made it race against time / Once I built a railroad, now it's done / Brother, can you spare a dime?" On the other hand, lavish motion picture musicals were also popular during the Great Depression. Musicals such as *Gold Diggers of 1933* portrayed optimistic characters singing light, cheerful songs. Many musicals of the time also featured spectacular costumes, sets, and dance routines. Ask students why they think such musicals were popular during the Great Depression. *Possible Response: People wanted to see light, frivolous shows to escape the misery of the Depression.*

"Brother, Can You Spare a Dime?" by E. Y. Harburg and J. Gorney, copyright © Warner Bros., Inc.

Not everyone fared so badly, of course. In the months before the crash, some stock market speculators had begun to unload their stocks and take the profits. Bernard Baruch was one who did so. Joseph P. Kennedy, the father of future president John F. Kennedy, was another. Most people, however, were not so lucky or shrewd.

WORLDWIDE SHOCK WAVES The United States was not the only country gripped by the Great Depression. Much of Europe, for example, had suffered throughout the 1920s. European countries trying to recover from the ravages of World War I faced high debt payments. In addition, Germany had to pay war reparations—payments to compensate the Allies for the damage Germany had caused. The Great Depression compounded these problems by limiting America's ability to import European goods. This made it difficult to sell American farm products and manufactured goods abroad.

In 1930, Congress made a bad situation worse by passing the **Hawley-Smoot Tariff Act,** which established the highest protective tariff in United States history. (See *tariff* on page 939 in the Economics Handbook.) This act—designed to help American farmers and manufacturers by protecting their products from foreign competition—had the opposite effect. By reducing the flow of goods into the United States, the tariff prevented other countries from earning American currency to buy American exports. In this way, the tariff made unemployment worse in industries that could no longer export goods to Europe. Many countries retaliated by raising their own tariffs. Within a few years, world trade had fallen more than 40 percent—a severe reduction in overall economic activity.

The problem was complicated by the effects of World War I on currency and the gold standard. (See *gold standard* on page 935 in the Economics Handbook.) Not only had vast amounts of property in Europe been destroyed, but European nations also faced heavy debts. This made them reduce their purchases of American goods even more. In order to encourage European nations to purchase American goods, Hoover proposed a moratorium, or postponement, on payments of Allied war debts and German reparations. Before anyone could agree to this plan, however, Britain and other European countries went off the gold standard—that is, their paper money could no longer be exchanged for gold. As a result, gold dropped in value, so that Europeans would be buying American goods and repaying American loans in cheaper currency. All these economic troubles caused a tremendous amount of suffering for people throughout the world as they adjusted to the harsh realities of the Depression.

G. Answer World trade fell; many European countries went off the gold standard; unemployment increased.

THINK THROUGH HISTORY
G. *Summarizing* *How did the Great Depression affect the world economy?*

ON THE WORLD STAGE

GLOBAL EFFECTS OF THE DEPRESSION

The Great Depression was a worldwide phenomenon, in large part because many industries depended on worldwide sources of raw materials and foreign markets. After World War I, European firms needed capital to rebuild their factories. Suppliers of raw materials in Asia, Africa, and Latin America needed to export their products to the industrialized nations.

As the American economy collapsed, other nations suffered as well. Austria's main bank failed in May 1931. Germany imposed currency controls in July. Great Britain went off the gold standard in September of the same year. Throughout the world, many banks and businesses failed, and rates of joblessness skyrocketed.

Section 1 Assessment

1. TERMS & NAMES
Identify:
- price support
- credit
- Alfred E. Smith
- speculation
- buying on margin
- Black Tuesday
- Great Depression
- Dow Jones Industrial Average
- Hawley-Smoot Tariff Act

2. SUMMARIZING In a diagram like this, record the causes of the 1929 stock market crash.

When you have finished, add effects of the crash to the bottom of the diagram.

3. ANALYZING CAUSES How did the economic trends of the 1920s help cause the Great Depression?

THINK ABOUT
- what happened in industry
- what happened in agriculture
- what happened with consumers

4. DRAWING CONCLUSIONS Judging from the events of the late 1920s and early 1930s, how important do you think public confidence is to the health of the economy? Explain.

THINK ABOUT
- what happened when overconfidence in the stock market led people to speculate and buy on margin
- what happened when lack of confidence caused people to sell stocks and close bank accounts

ON THE WORLD STAGE
Global Effects of the Depression

Hypothesizing Ask students how the worldwide depression might have contributed to the onset of World War II. *Possible Response: The atmosphere of economic despair and uncertainty allowed movements such as fascism—which promised to restore economic stability—to gain strength.*

ASSESS & RETEACH

Section 1 Assessment

Break students into small groups and have them work together to answer the questions. Have a member from each group read the group's answer to question 4 before the class. Discuss the varying conclusions the groups drew.

Self-Assessment

To document what students have learned, have them create a two-column chart. In the first column, students should list what they knew about the causes of the Great Depression before reading Section 1. In the second column, students should list what they've learned.

Section Quiz

FORMAL ASSESSMENT
Section Quiz, p. 176

Reteach

Use Critical Thinking Transparency 22 to review the causes of the Great Depression.

CRITICAL THINKING TRANSPARENCIES
CT22, The Great Depression

ANSWERS

1. TERMS & NAMES
price support, p. 483
credit, p. 484
Alfred E. Smith, p. 484
speculation, p. 485
buying on margin, p. 485
Black Tuesday, p. 485
Great Depression, p. 486
Dow Jones Industrial Average, p. 487
Hawley-Smoot Tariff Act, p. 489

2. SUMMARIZING
Possible Answers:

Causes
speculation
buying on margin
falling stock prices
loss of confidence

Effects
loss of savings
bank failures
bankrupt businesses
high unemployment
worldwide depression

3. ANALYZING CAUSES
Possible Responses: The economy slowed because industries found less demand for their goods in peacetime than in wartime, and unbalanced income distribution meant that most consumers had little to spend. International demand for crops fell, and many farmers went bankrupt, causing rural banks to fail. Too many people lived on credit, burdening themselves with debt that proved disastrous when the banks failed.

4. DRAWING CONCLUSIONS
Possible Response: Public confidence has a big effect on the economy. Too much confidence can lead people to make unwise decisions, committing themselves to more debt than they can repay. Too little confidence can lead individuals to pull money out of the stock market and banks—triggering a panic that endangers the entire economy.

CLOSE

The stock market crash of 1929 and the Great Depression that followed created grave economic problems for the United States and the world.

Section 2 Overview

OBJECTIVES

1. To describe how people struggled to survive during the Depression.
2. To explain how the Depression affected men, women, and children.

SKILLBUILDER

- Understanding geography: region, movement, p. 492

CRITICAL THINKING

- Recognizing effects, pp. 491, 494
- Theme: Immigration and Migration, p. 492
- Analyzing causes, p. 493
- Theme: The American Dream, p. 494
- Summarizing, p. 494
- Comparing and contrasting, p. 494

FOCUS & MOTIVATE

5-MINUTE WARM-UP

Making Inferences
To gain insight into the African-American view of the Depression, have students read Another Perspective on page 491 and answer these questions.

1. Why did the man quoted in the feature claim, "The Negro was born in depression"?
2. Why do you think the man said that the Great Depression "only became official when it hit the white man"?

WARM-UP TRANSPARENCY 14

▶ ***Starting with the Student***

- Watch the video "Broke but Not Broken" to examine how a young woman and her family coped with the Dust Bowl.
- Using the *Teacher's Resource Book* as a guide, hold class discussions about the effects of the Dust Bowl and Great Depression on farming families, and engage in extension activities using key primary sources.

(continued on next page)

❷ Hardship and Suffering During the Depression

TERMS & NAMES
- Dust Bowl
- shantytown
- soup kitchen
- bread line
- direct relief

LEARN ABOUT living conditions during the Great Depression
TO UNDERSTAND how people coped with hard times.

ONE AMERICAN'S STORY

Ann Marie Low lived with her parents on their North Dakota farm when the stock market crashed and the Great Depression struck. In her diary entry of November 9, 1929, she wrote, "There seems to be quite a furor in the country over a big stock market crash that wiped a lot of people out. We are ahead of them." Like many farm families in the 1920s, Ann's family had already experienced hard times. Things would get worse, however. During the early 1930s, several years of drought ravaged the Great Plains, destroying crops and leaving the earth dry and cracked. Then the wind began to blow. On April 25, 1934, Ann wrote an account of the conditions.

Ann Marie Low

A PERSONAL VOICE

Last weekend was the worst dust storm we ever had. We've been having quite a bit of blowing dirt every year since the drouth [drought] started, not only here, but all over the Great Plains. Many days this spring the air is just full of dirt coming, literally, for hundreds of miles. It sifts into everything. After we wash the dishes and put them away, so much dust sifts into the cupboards we must wash them again before the next meal. . . . Newspapers say the deaths of many babies and old people are attributed to breathing in so much dirt.

ANN MARIE LOW, *Dust Bowl Diary*

The dust storms in North Dakota, South Dakota, Nebraska, Kansas, Oklahoma, and Texas were so severe that this region of the Great Plains became known as the **Dust Bowl.** The dust storms were one of the greatest hardships—but only one of many—that Americans faced during the Great Depression.

BROKE BUT NOT BROKEN: *Ann Marie Low Remembers the Dust Bowl*

The Depression Devastates People's Lives

Statistics such as the unemployment rate tell only part of the story of the Great Depression. More important was the impact that it had on people's lives: the Depression brought hardship and suffering to millions of Americans. In cities as well as rural areas, it turned people's lives into a grim struggle for survival, marked by homelessness and hunger.

Unemployed people built shacks on a vacant lot in New York City in 1932.

THE DEPRESSION IN THE CITIES In cities across the country, from New York City to Los Angeles, people who lost their jobs found that they could no longer pay their rent or mortgage. Many were evicted from their homes and ended up living in the streets. Some slept in parks or sewer pipes, wrapped in newspapers to fend off the cold. Others built makeshift shacks out of scrap materials. Before long, large **shantytowns**—little towns consisting largely of shacks—sprang up on the outskirts of cities. Years later, an observer recalled one such settlement.

SECTION 2 RESOURCES

PRINT RESOURCES

IN-DEPTH RESOURCES: UNIT 4
Guided Reading, p. 37
Skillbuilder Practice: Formulating Historical Questions, p. 39
Geography Application: The Great Depression Takes Its Toll, p. 40
Primary Source: Letter from a Dust Bowl Survivor, p. 44
Literature: from *In the Beginning* by Chaim Potok, p. 46

READING STUDY GUIDE, p. 149

ACCESS FOR STUDENTS ACQUIRING ENGLISH
Guided Reading (Spanish), p. 168
Skillbuilder Practice: Formulating Historical Questions (Spanish), p. 170
Geography Application: The Great Depression Takes Its Toll (Spanish), p. 171

SPANISH READING STUDY GUIDE, p. 149

FORMAL ASSESSMENT
Section Quiz, p. 177

ALTERNATIVE ASSESSMENT BOOK
See forms for supporting and scoring alternative activities.

TECHNOLOGY RESOURCES

HUMANITIES TRANSPARENCIES
H21, Dust Storm. Arthur Rothstein

CD-ROM Electronic Library of Primary Sources

VIDEO *American Stories* video series

INTERNET http://www.mlushistory.com

A PERSONAL VOICE

Here were all these people living in old, rusted-out car bodies. . . . There were people living in shacks made of orange crates. One family with a whole lot of kids were living in a piano box. . . . People living in whatever they could junk together.

VISITOR TO A SHANTYTOWN OUTSIDE OKLAHOMA CITY, quoted in *Hard Times*

Every day the urban poor could be seen scrounging for food, digging in garbage cans or begging on street corners. **Soup kitchens** (places where food is offered free to the needy) and **bread lines** (lines of people waiting to receive food provided by charitable organizations or public agencies) became a common sight in many cities. One man noted the condition of people waiting for free food in New York City.

A PERSONAL VOICE

Two or three blocks along Times Square, you'd see these men, silent, shuffling along in a line. Getting this handout of coffee and doughnuts, dealt out from great trucks. . . . I'd stand and watch their faces, and I'd see that flat, opaque, expressionless look which spelled, for me, human disaster. On every corner, there'd be a man selling apples. Men . . . who had responsible positions. Who had lost their jobs, lost their homes, lost their families. And worse than anything else, lost belief in themselves. They were destroyed men.

HERMAN SHUMLIN, quoted in *Hard Times*

People stand in a bread line outside a soup kitchen in Chicago in 1930.

THE IMPACT ON AFRICAN AMERICANS AND LATINOS Conditions for African Americans and Latinos in the cities were especially difficult. The unemployment rates for both groups were higher than for most other Americans, and the jobs these groups held tended to bring the lowest pay. The Depression years also saw an increase in racial violence against African Americans by unemployed whites competing for the same jobs. Twenty-four African Americans died by lynching in 1933.

Latinos—mainly Mexicans and Mexican Americans living in the Southwest—were also the targets of hostility. Unemployed whites, angered at losing their jobs, demanded that Latinos be deported to Mexico, even though many Latinos were native-born Americans. By the late 1930s, hundreds of thousands of people of Mexican descent had returned to Mexico. Some left voluntarily, and some were deported by the federal government.

A. Answer Many city people were evicted from their homes; shantytowns sprang up in cities; people begged and scrounged for food. Some farmers lost their farms; others traveled from place to place in search of work.

THINK THROUGH HISTORY
A. *Recognizing Effects* *How did the Great Depression affect the lives of ordinary people in cities and towns and on farms?*

THE DEPRESSION IN RURAL AREAS Life in rural areas during the Great Depression was hard, but it did have one advantage over city life: most farmers could manage to grow some food to feed their families. Crop prices kept falling, however, and farmers continued to lose their land when they couldn't pay their debts. Between 1929 and 1932, about 400,000 farms were lost through foreclosure—the process in which a mortgage holder takes over property on which an occupant has failed to make mortgage payments. Many farmers had no choice but to turn to tenant farming and barely scrape out a living.

THE DUST BOWL In addition, the drought that began in the early 1930s wreaked havoc on the Great Plains. During the previous decade, farmers from Texas to North Dakota—the region that became known as the Dust Bowl—had used tractors to break up the grasslands and plant millions of acres of new farmland. Then they exhausted the land through overproduction of crops, and the grasslands became unsuitable for

ANOTHER PERSPECTIVE

AN AFRICAN-AMERICAN VIEW OF THE DEPRESSION

Although the suffering of the 1930s was severe for many people, it was especially grim for African Americans. Hard times were already a fact of life for blacks, as one African-American man noted:

"The Negro was born in depression. It didn't mean too much to him, The Great American Depression. . . . The best he could be is a janitor or a porter or shoeshine boy. It only became official when it hit the white man."

Nonetheless, the African-American community was very hard hit by the Great Depression. In 1932, the unemployment rate among African Americans stood at over 50 percent, while the overall unemployment rate was approximately 25 percent.

(continued from page 490)

***AMERICAN STORIES* video series**
"Broke but Not Broken"

Videocassette: Volume 3
Videodisc: Disc 2, Side B, Chapter 2

OBJECTIVE ① **INSTRUCT**

The Depression Devastates People's Lives

▶***Discussing Key Ideas***

- The Great Depression forces people in cities to live in shacks and stand in bread lines.
- Racial tensions rise as whites compete for scarce jobs with African Americans and Latinos.
- The Dust Bowl in the Great Plains forces many farmers to leave their land.

IN-DEPTH RESOURCES: UNIT 4
Guided Reading, p. 37

ACCESS FOR STUDENTS ACQUIRING ENGLISH
Guided Reading (Spanish), p. 168

ELECTRONIC LIBRARY OF PRIMARY SOURCES
"Beans, Bacon, and Gravy,"
Childhood During the Depression
by Cesar Chavez

ANOTHER PERSPECTIVE
An African-American View of the Depression
Critical Thinking: Analyzing Ask students to describe the tone of the man's comments. Why would unemployment rates for African Americans have been particularly high during the Depression?

TEACHING OPTION

Skillbuilder Mini-Lesson: Formulating Historical Questions

Explaining the Skill Asking probing questions about what they find in primary sources helps historians learn about historical events and conditions and the people who influenced or were affected by them. The kinds of questions news reporters ask to flesh out a news story—*who, what, when, where, why,* and *how*—also lead historians to a deeper understanding of the past.

Applying the Skill: A Personal Voice Suggest that students might better understand conditions of the Great Depression if they ask historical questions about the primary sources on this page. Have them read the two quotations labeled "A Personal Voice" and study the photograph. Then on the chalkboard, write the categories Who, What, When, Where, Why, How, and Other. As a class, for each category list questions about the primary sources. Sample questions: Who were the victims most affected by the Depression? What was it like to stand in line for handouts of bread? When was the worst time for these people? Where did they spend their days? Why couldn't people find work? How did homeless families manage to cook, wash, or go to school?

IN-DEPTH RESOURCES: UNIT 4
Skillbuilder Practice: Formulating Historical Questions, p. 39

HISTORY FROM VISUALS

The Dust Bowl, 1933–1936

Reading the Map Tell students to note that the perforated line on the map encompasses an area struck by a major dust storm in May of 1934.

HUMANITIES TRANSPARENCIES

H21, Dust Storm, 1936, Arthur Rothstein.

IN-DEPTH RESOURCES: UNIT 4

Geography Application: The Great Depression Takes Its Toll, p. 40

Primary Source: Letter from a Dust Bowl Survivor, p. 44

HISTORICAL SPOTLIGHT

Early Conservation Efforts in Texas

Critical Thinking: Analyzing Ask students why the conservation efforts begun in 1910 did not prevent the Dust Bowl from extending to Texas. *Possible Response: World War I began several years after 1910. The demand during the war for agricultural products caused most farmers to grow as much as they could.*

OBJECTIVE

② INSTRUCT

Effects on the American Family

▶ ***Discussing Key Ideas***

- During the Depression, some men abandon their families.
- Some women, ashamed of their condition, starve to death, while many children suffer from poor health.
- The Depression has long-lasting psychological consequences for those who live through it.

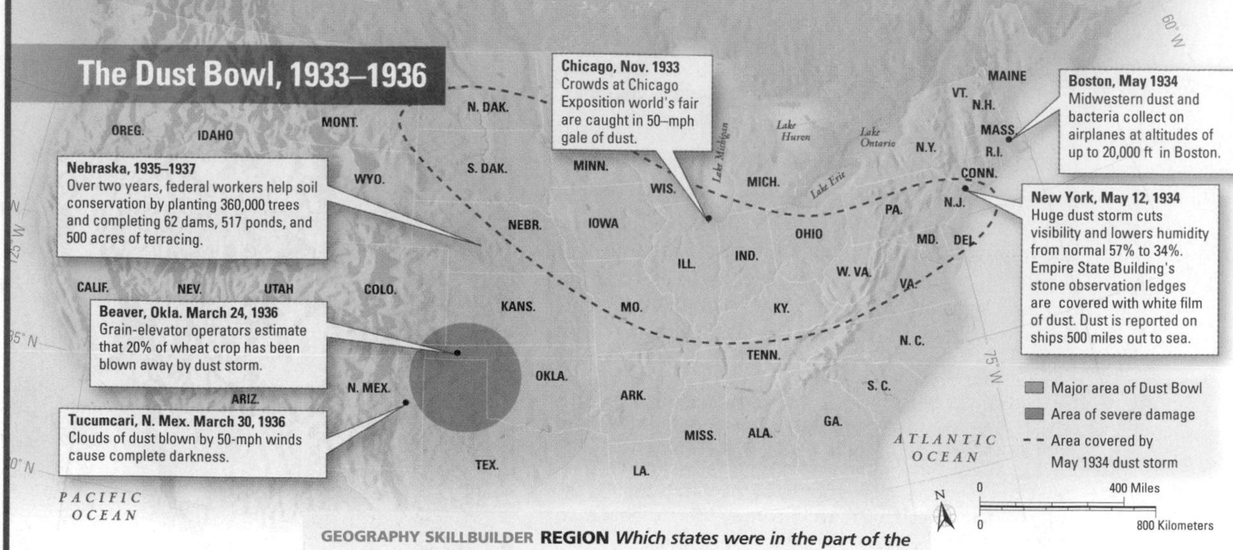

The Dust Bowl, 1933–1936
Chicago, Nov. 1933
Crowds at Chicago Exposition world's fair are caught in 50-mph gale of dust.
Boston, May 1934
Midwestern dust and bacteria collect on airplanes at altitudes of up to 20,000 ft in Boston.
Nebraska, 1935–1937
Over two years, federal workers help soil conservation by planting 360,000 trees and completing 62 dams, 517 ponds, and 500 acres of terracing.
New York, May 12, 1934
Huge dust storm cuts visibility and lowers humidity from normal 57% to 34%. Empire State Building's stone observation ledges are covered with white film of dust. Dust is reported on ships 500 miles out to sea.
Beaver, Okla. March 24, 1936
Grain-elevator operators estimate that 20% of wheat crop has been blown away by dust storm.
Tucumcari, N. Mex. March 30, 1936
Clouds of dust blown by 50-mph winds cause complete darkness.
OREG.
IDAHO
MONT.
N. DAK.
S. DAK.
MINN.
WYO.
NEBR.
IOWA
WIS.
MICH.
CALIF.
NEV.
UTAH
COLO.
KANS.
MO.
ILL.
IND.
OHIO
ARIZ.
N. MEX.
OKLA.
ARK.
KY.
TENN.
W. VA.
VA.
TEX.
LA.
MISS.
ALA.
GA.
S.C.
N.C.
PA.
N.Y.
MD.
DEL.
N.J.
CONN.
R.I.
MASS.
VT.
N.H.
MAINE
Lake Huron
Lake Ontario
Lake Erie
Lake Michigan
PACIFIC OCEAN
ATLANTIC OCEAN
Major area of Dust Bowl
Area of severe damage
Area covered by May 1934 dust storm
0 400 Miles
0 800 Kilometers
N

GEOGRAPHY SKILLBUILDER **REGION** *Which states were in the part of the Dust Bowl where damage was most severe?* **MOVEMENT** *Why might most of the migrants who left the Dust Bowl have traveled west?*

Skillbuilder Answer **Region:** Kansas, Colorado, New Mexico, Texas, Oklahoma. **Movement:** The prevailing winds carried the dust storms to the east, and therefore migrants may have traveled west to avoid them.

farming. When the drought and winds began in the early 1930s, little grass and few trees were left on the plains to hold the soil down. As you learned from the excerpt from Ann Marie Low's diary on page 490, the dust traveled hundreds of miles. One windstorm in 1934 picked up millions of tons of dust from the plains and carried it to East Coast cities. Even ships far out in the Atlantic Ocean reported dust settling on their decks.

The southern plains, including Kansas, Oklahoma, and Texas, were hardest hit. Plagued by dust storms and evictions, thousands of farmers and sharecroppers left their land behind. They packed up their families and their few belongings and headed west, following Route 66 to California. Some of these migrants—known as Okies (a term that originally referred to Oklahomans but came to be used negatively for all the migrants)—found work as farm hands. But others continued to wander in search of work. By the end of the 1930s, the population of California had grown by more than a million.

HISTORICAL SPOTLIGHT

EARLY CONSERVATION EFFORTS IN TEXAS

The potential for soil erosion in Texas had been recognized long before the 1930s, and efforts had been made to combat it. As early as 1910, the forerunner of today's Texas Agricultural Extension Service had begun to educate farmers about the problem of soil erosion.

Texas cooperated with federal conservation programs during the 1930s, and in 1939 the state legislature enacted a law enabling each landowner to establish a soil conservation district. This meant that they could take full advantage of federal programs. By the 1940s, the Dust Bowl region of Texas had largely recovered as a result of newly planted windbreaks and the restoration of native grasses.

THINK THROUGH HISTORY

B. THEME ***Immigration and Migration*** *How did the drought and dust storms affect migration and population distribution in the United States?*

B. Answer They ruined farmland; thousands of farmers and sharecroppers left their land in the Great Plains and headed west; the population of California swelled.

Effects on the American Family

In the face of the suffering caused by the Great Depression, the family stood as a source of strength for most Americans. Although some people feared that hard times would undermine moral values, those fears were largely unfounded. In general, Americans believed in traditional values and emphasized the importance of family unity. At a time when money was tight, many families entertained themselves by staying at home playing board games, such as Monopoly (invented in 1933), and listening to the radio. Nevertheless, the economic difficulties of the Great Depression put severe pressure on family life. Making ends meet was a daily struggle and, in some cases, families broke apart under the strain.

MEN IN THE STREETS AND ON THE RAILS Many men had difficulty coping with unemployment because they were accustomed to working and supporting their families. Every day, they would set out to walk the streets in search of jobs. As Frederick Lewis Allen noted in *Since Yesterday*, "Men who have

TEACHING OPTIONS

Exploring Themes

Immigration and Migration The thousands of families that fled their drought-plagued Midwest farms prompted a significant demographic shift in the United States. While some of the families who journeyed to California gravitated to the state's fruit farms, many others traveled to Los Angeles. They eventually settled there, finding work in the many factories that expanded with the onset of World War II. Many of the farm families that fled elsewhere also settled in cities. This mass migration played a key role in the United States's continuing transformation from a mostly rural to a mostly urban society.

Making Connections Across Cultures

Mexican Americans and the Depression At the onset of the Great Depression, about 1.5 million Mexican Americans, or Chicanos, lived in the United States. The largest group of Mexican Americans—roughly 100,000—lived in Los Angeles. Between 1931 and 1934, as a result of racism and the struggle for scarce jobs, Los Angeles County officials deported nearly 13,000 Mexicans Americans to Mexico. However, as journalist Carey McWilliams noted, many of the deportees eventually returned to Los Angeles after "having had a trip to Mexico at the expense of the county."

THINK THROUGH HISTORY
C. Analyzing Causes *Why did so many men leave their homes during the Depression?*

C. Answer Many men were depressed by their inability to support their families, and so abandoned them. Others hoped to find work and send money home to their families.

been sturdy and self-respecting workers can take unemployment without flinching for a few weeks, a few months, even if they have to see their families suffer; but it is different after a year . . . two years . . . three years." Some men became so discouraged that they simply stopped trying. Some even abandoned their families.

During the Great Depression, approximately 2 million men wandered the country, hitching rides on railroad boxcars and sleeping under bridges. These hoboes of the 1930s would occasionally turn up at homeless shelters in big cities. The novelist Thomas Wolfe described a group of these men in New York City.

A PERSONAL VOICE

These were the wanderers from town to town, the riders of freight trains, the thumbers of rides on highways, the uprooted, unwanted male population of America. They drifted across the land and gathered in the big cities when winter came, hungry, defeated, empty, hopeless, restless, driven by they knew not what, always on the move, looking everywhere for work, for the bare crumbs to support their miserable lives, and finding neither work nor crumbs.

THOMAS WOLFE, *You Can't Go Home Again*

During the early years of the Great Depression, there was no federal system of **direct relief**—cash payments or food provided by the government to the poor. Some cities and charity services did offer relief to those who needed it, but the benefits were meager. In New York City, for example, the weekly payment was just $2.39 per family. This was the most generous relief offered by any city, but it was still well below the amount needed to feed a family.

WOMEN AND CHILDREN STRUGGLE TO SURVIVE Women worked hard to help their families survive adversity during the Great Depression. Many women canned food and sewed clothes. They also carefully managed household budgets. Jeane Westin, the author of *Making Do: How Women Survived the '30s*, recalled, "Those days you did everything to save a penny. . . . My next door neighbor and I used to shop together. You could get two pounds of hamburger for a quarter, so we'd buy two pounds and split it—then one week she'd pay the extra penny and the next week I'd pay."

Many women also worked outside the home, though they usually received less money than men did. As the Depression wore on, however, working women became the targets of enormous resentment. Some people believed that women, especially married women, had no right to work when men were unemployed. In the early 1930s, some cities refused to hire married women as schoolteachers.

Many Americans assumed that women were having an easier time than men during the Depression because few were seen begging or standing in bread lines. As a matter of fact, many women were starving to death in cold attics and rooming houses. As one writer pointed out, women were often too ashamed to reveal their hardship.

A PERSONAL VOICE

I've lived in cities for many months, broke, without help, too timid to get in bread lines. I've known many women to live like this until they simply faint in the street. . . . A woman will shut herself up in a room until it is taken away from her, and eat a cracker a day and be as quiet as a mouse. . . . [She] will go for weeks verging on starvation, . . . going through the streets ashamed, sitting in libraries, parks, going for days without speaking to a living soul, shut up in the terror of her own misery.

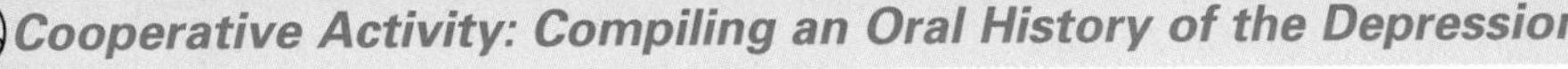

MERIDEL LE SEUER, *America in the Twenties*

NOW & THEN

HOMELESSNESS

Today, thousands of homeless people wander the streets of American cities, just as they did during the Great Depression. The main causes of homelessness in the 1930s were economic and social changes that left many people without work and with few prospects for the future.

The causes of the problem today are less clear, although economic dislocation is still one of the factors. Others are the closing down of large institutions for mentally ill people, urban renewal that led to the destruction of cheap hotels and boarding houses, fewer jobs for unskilled workers, and rising rents in the cities.

There are key differences between now and the 1930s as far as treatment of homeless people is concerned. More services for homeless people—such as emergency medical treatment, temporary shelter, food, and psychological counseling—are available today. However, there is also probably a greater stigma attached to homelessness today, during a period of general prosperity, than there was during the 1930s, when a larger percentage of the population was out of work.

UNEMPLOYED
BUY
APPLES
5 EACH

Congressman Fred Hartley *(left)* buys an apple from an unemployed man in Washington, D.C.

NOW & THEN
Homelessness

Discuss with students the differences between homelessness in the Great Depression and today, and then have students suggest possible solutions to the problem of homelessness in the present-day United States.

MORE ABOUT . . .
Women in the Depression

While the Great Depression made victims of many women, it also moved others to action. In 1935, Margaret Bourke-White, a commercial photographer accustomed to privilege, photographed the Dust Bowl region for *Fortune* magazine. The experience changed her life. "I had never seen people caught helpless like this in total tragedy," she wrote. "For me this was the turning point. . . . I felt I could never again face a shiny automobile stuffed with vapid smiles." Bourke-White abandoned her glamorous lifestyle and began making photographic documentaries to promote social change. In the late 1930s, she helped produce the documentary, *You Have Seen Their Faces,* about sharecropping life in the South. After World War II broke out, she worked as a war photojournalist in Europe.

Block Schedule TEACHING OPTION **Time Needed: 30 Minutes**

Cooperative Activity: Compiling an Oral History of the Depression

Task: Groups of four or five students will interview relatives and friends who lived through the Great Depression and combine the results of their interviews into an oral history.

Purpose: To understand the effects of the Great Depression on the people who survived it.

Activity: Have students make a list of persons they know who experienced the Depression. Before the interview, group members should work together to prepare a list of questions. Instruct students to use a tape recorder during the interview, as well as take notes. Students should transcribe their taped notes and combine their pages with those of the rest of the group. Allow time for each group to read its oral history before the class.

Possible Interview Questions: Students might ask their interview subjects the following questions: How did the Depression affect you and your family? What specific things did you do to cope with the Depression? What long-term effects did the Depression have on you?

ALTERNATIVE ASSESSMENT BOOK
Standards for Evaluating a Cooperative Activity

MORE ABOUT . . .
Suicides

While their numbers probably have been exaggerated, some stock investors distraught over losing everything during the crash of 1929 did choose to kill themselves. In one case, a vice-president with the Earl Radio Corporation, having lost $124,000, climbed out onto the ledge of his 11th-floor hotel window and jumped to his death. "We are broke," read part of his suicide note.

ASSESS & RETEACH

Section 2 Assessment

Have students work in pairs to answer the assessment questions. Draw the chart for question 2 on the board and work as a class to fill in the possible answers.

Self-Assessment

To show what students have learned, have them write down four or five facts they learned about living conditions during the Depression.

Section Quiz

FORMAL ASSESSMENT
Section Quiz, p. 177

Reteach

Replay the video "Broke but Not Broken" to help review the impact of the Dust Bowl.

AMERICAN STORIES
video series
"Broke but Not Broken"

CLOSE

Millions of people coped with the hardships brought about by the Great Depression. In the cities, many people lived in shacks and depended on charity. In the rural areas of the Great Plains, terrible dust storms forced farmers to leave their homes.

Children also suffered great hardship during the 1930s. Poor diets and a lack of money for health care led to serious health problems. Milk consumption declined across the country, and clinics and hospitals reported a dramatic rise in malnutrition and diet-related diseases, such as rickets and pellagra. At the same time, child-welfare programs were slashed as cities and states cut their budgets in the face of dwindling resources.

Falling tax revenues also caused school boards to shorten the school year and even close schools. By 1933, some 2,600 schools across the nation had shut down, leaving more than 300,000 students out of school. Many children went to work instead; they often labored in sweatshops under horrendous conditions.

This Ozark sharecropper family was photographed in Arkansas during the 1930s by the artist Ben Shahn.

D. Answer Many women had to tightly manage household budgets; women encountered opposition in holding jobs outside the home; many children suffered from poor diets and inadequate health care; many child-welfare programs and even schools were shut down.

THINK THROUGH HISTORY
D. *Recognizing Effects* *How did the Great Depression affect women and children?*

SOCIAL AND PSYCHOLOGICAL EFFECTS The hardships of the Great Depression had a tremendous social and psychological impact. Some people were so demoralized by hard times that they lost their will to survive. Between 1928 and 1932, the suicide rate rose by nearly 30 percent. Three times as many people were admitted to state mental hospitals as in normal times.

The economic problems forced many Americans to accept compromises and make sacrifices that affected them for the rest of their lives. Adults stopped going to the doctor or dentist because they couldn't afford it. Young people gave up their dreams of going to college. Others put off getting married, raising large families, or having children at all.

For many people, the stigma of poverty and of having to scrimp and save never disappeared completely. For some, achieving financial security became the primary focus in life. As one woman recalled, "Ever since I was twelve years old there was one major goal in my life . . . one thing . . . and that was to never be poor again."

During the Great Depression many people showed great kindness to strangers who were down on their luck. People often gave food, clothing, and a place to stay to the needy. Families helped other families and shared resources and strengthened the bonds within their communities. In addition, many people developed habits of saving and thriftiness—habits they would need to see themselves through the dark days ahead as the nation and President Hoover struggled with the Great Depression. These habits shaped a whole generation of Americans.

E. Answer The Depression took away homes, jobs, and the chance of higher education; it caused people to delay marrying and having children; it led to mental illness, despair, and suicide.

THINK THROUGH HISTORY
E. THEME *The American Dream* *In what ways did the Great Depression prevent or delay the fulfillment of the American Dream for many people?*

Section 2 Assessment

1. TERMS & NAMES
Identify:
- Dust Bowl
- shantytown
- soup kitchen
- bread line
- direct relief

2. SUMMARIZING In a chart, list at least three groups of people and the effects that the Great Depression had on them.

Group	Effects of Depression

3. COMPARING AND CONTRASTING How was what happened to city dwellers during the Great Depression similar to and different from what happened to farmers?

THINK ABOUT
- what happened to each group's livelihood
- what happened to their homes
- what help was available to them

4. RECOGNIZING EFFECTS How did Dust Bowl conditions affect the entire country?

THINK ABOUT
- the effect on farmers on the plains
- the effect on California and other states where Okies resettled
- the effect on the East

ANSWERS

1. TERMS & NAMES

Dust Bowl, p. 490

shantytown, p. 490

soup kitchen, p. 491

bread line, p. 491

direct relief, p. 493

2. SUMMARIZING

Possible Answers:

urban poor—lived in shantytowns, ate in soup kitchens or bread lines

African Americans—experienced increased discrimination

Latino Americans—experienced increased discrimination

farmers—lost land and headed west

unemployed men—wandered country looking for work

women—cut back on household spending, lost jobs, some starved

children—experienced malnutrition and health problems, left school to work

3. COMPARING AND CONTRASTING

Possible Responses: Both in cities and on farms, people lost their jobs and their homes. Both urban and rural populations were dislocated. In cities, there was a slightly higher chance of receiving charity or government aid.

4. RECOGNIZING EFFECTS

Possible Responses: Farmers experienced crop failure, lost their land, and had to move. Eastern cities and even ships at sea were covered with dirt blown from the plains. California's population swelled, which increased unemployment there.

3 Hoover Struggles with the Depression

TERMS & NAMES
- Herbert Hoover
- Boulder Dam
- Federal Home Loan Bank Act
- Reconstruction Finance Corporation
- Bonus Army

LEARN ABOUT President Hoover's response to the Great Depression
TO UNDERSTAND why the Hoover administration lost public support.

ONE AMERICAN'S STORY

Oscar Ameringer was a newspaper editor in Oklahoma City during the Great Depression. In 1932, he traveled around the country for several months to gather information on economic and social conditions. Testifying in congressional hearings on unemployment that same year, Ameringer described a population of poor, desperate people who were losing patience with the government. "Unless something is done for them and done soon," he asserted, "you will have a revolution on hand." At the hearings, Ameringer told the following story.

During the Great Depression, a family from Arkansas walks through Texas, looking for work in the cotton fields along the Rio Grande.

A PERSONAL VOICE
The roads of the West and Southwest teem with hungry hitchhikers. . . . Between Clarksville and Russellville, Ark., I picked up a family. The woman was hugging a dead chicken under a ragged coat. When I asked her where she procured the fowl, first she told me she had found it dead in the road, and then added in grim humor, "They promised me a chicken in the pot, and now I got mine."

OSCAR AMERINGER, quoted in *The American Spirit*

The woman was recalling President Hoover's 1928 campaign pledge: "A chicken in every pot and two cars in every garage." That pledge turned out to be an empty promise. Many Americans were now highly critical of Hoover and called on the government to do more to ease their suffering.

Hoover Tries to Reassure the Nation

After the stock market crash of October 1929, President **Herbert Hoover** tried to reassure Americans that the nation's economy was on a sound footing. "Any lack of confidence in the economic future . . . is foolish," he declared. The important thing was for Americans to remain optimistic and to go about their business as usual.

Americans had traditionally believed depressions to be a normal part of the business cycle. (See *business cycle* on page 933 in the Economics Handbook.) According to this theory, periods of rapid economic growth were naturally followed by periods of economic contraction, or depression. The best course of action in such a slump, many experts believed, was to do nothing and let the economy fix itself.

Most officials in the Hoover administration echoed that economic view, including Secretary of the Treasury Andrew Mellon. A strong advocate of the "do-nothing" approach, Mellon advised President Hoover to "let the slump liquidate [end] itself. Liquidate labor, liquidate stocks, liquidate the farmers, liquidate real estate. . . . It will purge the rottenness out of the system."

Hoover took a different position. Although he believed that the economy should be allowed to function with minimal intervention, he also felt that government could play a role in helping to solve economic problems. The key, in his view, was to limit that role and prevent government from taking too much power.

Section 3 Overview

OBJECTIVES

1. To explain Hoover's initial response to the Depression.
2. To describe some of the measures Hoover took to help the economy and ease people's suffering.

SKILLBUILDER

- Interpreting political cartoons, p. 497

CRITICAL THINKING

- Summarizing, pp. 496, 499
- Forming opinions, p. 497
- Evaluating decisions, p. 498
- Making inferences, p. 499
- Analyzing issues, p. 499
- Clarifying, p. 499

FOCUS & MOTIVATE

5-MINUTE WARM-UP

Making Generalizations
To make generalizations about Herbert Hoover, have students study the political cartoon on page 497 and answer these questions.

1. Why are all the figures in the cartoon pointing at Hoover?
2. What does Hoover's characterization suggest about his attitude toward his accusers?

WARM-UP TRANSPARENCY 14

▶***Starting with the Student***
Have students imagine they are living a hand-to-mouth existence during the Depression. Would they want the government to control the economy to help end the Depression?

OBJECTIVE
(1) **INSTRUCT**

Hoover Tries to Reassure the Nation

▶***Discussing Key Ideas***
- Hoover believes people should help themselves during the Depression rather than depend on government handouts.

(continued on next page)

SECTION 3 RESOURCES

PRINTING RESOURCES

IN-DEPTH RESOURCES: UNIT 4
Guided Reading, p. 38
Primary Source: Attack on the Bonus Army, p. 45

READING STUDY GUIDE, p. 151

ACCESS FOR STUDENTS ACQUIRING ENGLISH
Guided Reading (Spanish), p. 169

SPANISH READING STUDY GUIDE, p. 151

FORMAL ASSESSMENT
Section Quiz, p. 178

ALTERNATIVE ASSESSMENT BOOK
See forms for supporting and scoring alternative activities.

TECHNOLOGY RESOURCES

CD-ROM Electronic Library of Primary Sources

VIDEO *American Portfolio: A Videodisc for U.S. History* user's guide, pp. 205, 206

INTERNET http://www.mlushistory.com

(continued from page 495)

• Hoover takes cautious and largely ineffective steps to remedy the Depression.

IN-DEPTH RESOURCES: UNIT 4
Guided Reading, p. 38

ACCESS FOR STUDENTS ACQUIRING ENGLISH
Guided Reading (Spanish), p. 169

KEY PLAYER
Herbert Hoover

Critical Thinking: Analyzing Ask students how Hoover's early life might have affected his belief in rugged individualism. *Possible Response: As a poor orphan, Hoover was probably forced to rely on his own resources and initiative.*

MORE ABOUT . . .
Herbert Hoover

As the Depression wore on, Hoover's popularity continued to plummet. Near the end of the 1932 presidential campaign—which Hoover lost to Franklin Roosevelt—Americans showed their disgust with their president in the most public of ways. On its way through Wisconsin, Hoover's train was forced to stop after officials found a man pulling up spikes on the track. During a campaign stop in Nevada, protesters pelted Hoover's car with rotten eggs, and the state's governor refused to appear publicly with him. One constituent sent Hoover a telegram suggesting that he "vote for Roosevelt and make it unanimous."

HOOVER'S PHILOSOPHY OF GOVERNMENT Herbert Hoover was a man of strong principles. As an engineer, he had great faith in the power of reason to solve problems. Hoover was also a humanitarian who believed in helping others, as he made clear in one of his first speeches after becoming president.

A PERSONAL VOICE

Our first objective must be to provide security from poverty and want. We want security in living for every home. We want to see a nation built of home owners and farm owners. We want to see their savings protected. We want to see them in steady jobs. We want to see more and more of them insured against death and accident, unemployment and old age. We want them all secure.

HERBERT HOOVER

KEY PLAYER

HERBERT HOOVER
1874–1964

Born to a Quaker family in Iowa, Herbert Hoover was the first president born west of the Mississippi River. He was orphaned at an early age, and his life was a real rags-to-riches story. He worked his way through Stanford University and later made a fortune as a mining engineer and consultant in China, Australia, Europe, and Africa. During and after World War I, he coordinated U.S. relief efforts in Europe, earning a reputation for efficiency and humanitarian ideals.

As president, Hoover took steps reflecting his belief that social problems were best solved locally, through private initiatives. He asserted, "Every time we find solutions outside of government, we have not only strengthened character, but we have preserved our sense of real government."

Hoover was not a career politician, however, and found it difficult to make political compromises. Inflexible by nature, he had a hard time adjusting his attitudes and actions to fit the nation's changing and increasingly desperate circumstances.

Hoover believed that one of government's chief functions was to foster cooperation between competing groups and interests in society. If business and labor were in conflict, for example, government should step in and help them find a solution that served their mutual interest. In Hoover's view, this cooperation should be voluntary rather than forced. Government's proper role, he believed, was to encourage and facilitate cooperation, not to control it.

Hoover also believed strongly in "rugged individualism"—the idea that people should succeed through their own efforts. They should take care of themselves and their families, rather than depend on the government to bail them out. As a supporter of rugged individualism, Hoover opposed any form of federal welfare, or direct relief to the needy. He believed that direct federal handouts would weaken people's self-respect and undermine the nation's moral fiber.

Hoover's answer to the sufferings of the needy was that individuals, charities, and local organizations should pitch in to help care for the less fortunate. The federal government should direct relief measures, but not through a vast federal bureaucracy. Such a bureaucracy, he said, would be too expensive and would stifle individual liberties.

THINK THROUGH HISTORY
A. *Summarizing* *What were some of Hoover's key convictions about government?*

A. Answer Hoover believed that reason could solve problems; that government should foster cooperation between competing groups; and that individuals, charities, and private organizations should help care for the less fortunate.

HOOVER TAKES CAUTIOUS STEPS Hoover's political philosophy caused him to take a cautious approach to the depression. Soon after the stock market crash, he called together key leaders in the fields of business, banking, and labor. He urged them to work together to find solutions to the nation's economic woes and to act in ways that would not make a bad situation worse. For example, he asked employers not to cut wages or lay off workers, and he asked labor leaders not to demand higher wages or to strike. He also created a special organization to help private charities generate contributions for the poor.

However, none of these steps made much of a difference. A year after the crash, the economy was still shrinking, and unemployment was still rising. More companies went out of business, soup kitchens became a common sight, and the general misery of ordinary people continued to grow. Shantytowns arose in every city, and hoboes roamed the cities and the countryside.

DEMOCRATS WIN IN 1930 CONGRESSIONAL ELECTIONS As the country's economic difficulties increased, the political tide turned against Hoover and the Republicans. In the 1930 congressional elections, the Democrats took advantage of anti-Hoover sentiments to win more seats in Congress. As a result of

TEACHING OPTIONS

Making Connections Across Cultures

Hoover and African Americans While his name will always be synonymous with the Great Depression, Hoover was also a reform-minded president who worked to improve the lives of African Americans. Hoover appointed more blacks to mid-level federal positions than his two predecessors combined. He also pushed to increase minority employment on public works, and he sponsored a federal program aimed at eradicating illiteracy among blacks. In addition, he continually sought support for a plan enabling both white and black sharecroppers to buy the land they worked.

Making Connections Across Time

Welfare Today Federal welfare remains a controversial issue in the United States. In 1996, President Clinton signed a new welfare bill reversing a policy begun under Franklin D. Roosevelt that guaranteed federal assistance to the nation's poor. The new law hands most welfare authority to the states and imposes work requirements on welfare recipients, as well as a five-year lifetime limit on welfare. Clinton said the measure would help make welfare "what it was meant to be: a second chance, not a way of life." Critics argued it would only increase poverty. The bill's signing represents a "moment of shame," said one opponent.

that election, the Republicans lost control of the House of Representatives and saw their majority in the Senate dwindle to one vote.

As Americans grew more and more frustrated by the Depression, they expressed their anger in a number of ways. Farmers stung by low crop prices burned their corn and wheat and dumped their milk on highways rather than sell it at a loss. Some farmers even declared a "farm holiday" and refused to work their fields. A number blocked roads to prevent food from getting to market, hoping that food shortages would raise prices. Some farmers also used force to prevent authorities from foreclosing on farms.

By 1930, people were calling the shantytowns in American cities Hoovervilles—a direct slap at the president's policies. To keep warm, homeless people wrapped themselves in newspapers, which they called Hoover blankets. Empty pockets turned inside out were Hoover flags. Many Americans who had hailed Hoover as a great humanitarian a few years earlier, now saw him as a cold and heartless leader.

Despite public criticism, Hoover continued to hold firm to his principles. He refused to support direct relief or other forms of federal welfare. Some Americans were going hungry, and many blamed Hoover for their plight. Criticism of the president and his policies continued to grow. An anonymous ditty of the time was widely repeated.

> Mellon pulled the whistle
> Hoover rang the bell
> Wall Street gave the signal
> And the country went to hell.

B. Answer Answers will vary, but some students will probably say that Americans look to their leaders for results, and Hoover wasn't getting results.

THINK THROUGH HISTORY
B. Forming Opinions *Why do you think people blamed Hoover for the nation's difficulties?*

SKILLBUILDER
INTERPRETING POLITICAL CARTOONS
In this cartoon, various segments of American society point their fingers at a beleaguered President Hoover. What does the cartoon suggest about Hoover's chances for reelection?
Skillbuilder Answer The cartoon suggests that Hoover's chances for reelection were not good.

Hoover Takes Action

Hoover, however, was sensitive to suffering and started listening to the criticism. As time went on and the Depression deepened, he gradually softened his position on government intervention in the economy and took a more activist approach to the nation's economic troubles. By 1930, he was directing federal funds into projects—such as the construction of **Boulder Dam**—designed to jump-start the economy and add jobs.

This mural, entitled *Construction of a Dam*, shows the building of the Boulder Dam. It was painted in 1937 by William Gropper for the Department of the Interior building in Washington, D.C.

HISTORY FROM VISUALS
Political Cartoon

Reading the Cartoon Ask students who is pictured in the middle of the cartoon. *Herbert Hoover.* What is everyone blaming Hoover for? *The Depression.*

OBJECTIVE
(2) INSTRUCT

Hoover Takes Action

Discussing Key Ideas
- Hoover initiates several relief projects, but the measures are too little, too late.
- Hoover approves the use of force to disperse World War I veterans protesting for increased benefits.

Issues for the 21st Century

Breaking the Cycle of Poverty

Connect the Great Depression to poverty today by having students read pages 896–899. Then have them answer these questions.

1. What actions did Hoover take to help end the Depression? *Boulder Dam and other government projects.*
2. Compare the experience of the poor during the Depression with that of the poor today. *Similar: Homeless and dependent on the government. Different: During the Depression, people helped each other more.*

TEACHING OPTIONS

Exploring Themes

The American Dream The Great Depression seriously tested the notion of the American dream. Many Americans believed that hard work, coupled with the ideals of democracy and capitalism, would lead them to prosperity. However, the Depression, and the apparent failure of capitalism, caused many citizens to question the very foundations upon which their country was built. During the 1930s, the ideas of socialism and communism gained increasing popularity in the United States. The Communist Party/USA , for example, claimed 25,000 members and about 500,000 "sympathizers" by 1934.

Teaching Less Proficient Readers

Clarifying As students read pages 497 and 498, have the less proficient readers create a chart like the one below listing the actions Hoover took to combat the Depression, and the purpose of each act.

Hoover's Actions to Confront Depression	
Action	Purpose
1.	
2.	
3.	
4.	

DIFFICULT DECISIONS IN HISTORY

Hoover and Federal Projects

Possible Responses:

1. Yes—Hoover's limited intervention was appropriate, for too much government control of people's lives would undermine democracy. No—The severity of the Depression demanded that the government do more to provide relief.

2. Some students might answer that they would have acted as Hoover did, while others might say they would have increased the number of government work projects and instituted a federal welfare program.

MORE ABOUT . . .

Gassing the Bonus Army

Hoover actually wanted MacArthur to proceed more peacefully in disbanding the Bonus Army. However, MacArthur, sensing "incipient revolution in the air," ignored the president's command. While Hoover reproached his general in private, he declined to challenge MacArthur's insubordination in public. Nearly 20 years later, MacArthur again challenged the authority of a president, crossing Harry Truman over his war strategy in Korea. Truman took a different course than Hoover had. He fired MacArthur.

IN-DEPTH RESOURCES: UNIT 4

Primary Source: Attack on the Bonus Army, p. 45

ELECTRONIC LIBRARY OF PRIMARY SOURCES

from a Report on the Employment of Federal Troops by General Douglas MacArthur

from *B.E.F.: The Whole Story of the Bonus Army* by W. W. Waters

Difficult Decisions IN HISTORY

HOOVER AND FEDERAL PROJECTS

On the one hand, President Hoover opposed federal welfare and intervention in the economy. On the other, he felt that government had a duty to help solve problems and ease suffering. The question was, What kind of assistance would be proper and effective?

1. Consider the pros and cons of Hoover's actions during the Depression. Did he do enough to try to end the Depression? Why or why not?
2. If you had been president during the Great Depression, what and policies would you have supported? Explain the approach you would have taken.

BOULDER DAM AND OTHER GOVERNMENT PROJECTS One of Hoover's first major initiatives was a public-works program to build roads, dams, and other large project, in an effort to stimulate business and provide jobs for unemployed workers. Congress approved $800 million for these projects, which included the giant Boulder Dam (now called Hoover Dam), on the Colorado River between Arizona and Nevada.

Hoover also backed the creation of the Federal Farm Board. This organization was designed to raise crop prices by helping farm cooperatives buy crops and keep them off the market temporarily. In addition, Hoover tried to prop up the banking system by persuading the nation's largest banks to establish the National Credit Corporation. This organization loaned money to smaller banks, which helped them stave off bankruptcy.

By late 1931, however, many people could see that these measures had failed to turn the economy around. With a presidential election looming, Hoover decided to take more serious action. He appealed to Congress to pass a series of measures to reform banking, provide mortgage relief, and funnel more federal money into business investment. Congress responded in 1933 with the Glass-Steagall Banking Act, which increased bank reserves and made bank loans easier to get. Congress also passed the **Federal Home Loan Bank Act,** which lowered mortgage rates for homeowners and allowed farmers to refinance their farm loans and avoid foreclosure.

C. Answer: Public works program to build roads and dams; Federal Farm Board; National Credit Corporation; Federal Home Loan Bank Act; Reconstruction Finance Corporation. These projects and measures were not able to turn the economy around.

THINK THROUGH HISTORY
C. ***Evaluating Decisions*** *What were some of the projects proposed by Hoover, and how effective were they?*

Hoover's most ambitious economic measure, however, was the **Reconstruction Finance Corporation** (RFC), approved by Congress in January 1932 and authorized to provide emergency financing to banks, life insurance companies, railroads, and other large businesses. This financing—up to $2 billion worth—was intended to pump new life into the economy by fueling business expansion. Hoover believed that the money would trickle down to the average citizen through job growth and higher wages. Many critics questioned this approach; they argued that the program would benefit only corporations and that the poor still needed direct relief. Hungry people could not wait for the benefits to trickle down to their tables.

Initially, the RFC did provide substantial assistance to industry. In its first five months of operation, the agency loaned more than $805 million to large corporations, but business failures continued. The RFC was an unprecedented example of federal involvement in a peacetime economy, but in the end it was too little, too late.

Members of the Bonus Army march to the Capitol Building from the Washington Monument in July 1932.

GASSING THE BONUS ARMY In 1932, an incident further damaged Hoover's image and public morale. That spring, between 10,000 and 20,000 World War I veterans and their families arrived in Washington, D.C., from various parts of the country. They called themselves the Bonus Expeditionary Force, or the **Bonus Army.**

Led by Walter Waters, an unemployed cannery worker from Oregon, the Bonus Army came to the nation's capital to support a bill under debate in

Block Schedule — TEACHING OPTION — Time Needed: 40 Minutes

Cooperative Activity: Debating the Bonus Army March

Task: Student groups will debate each other on different issues surrounding the Bonus Army's march on Washington.

Purpose: To explore the Bonus Army incident in depth.

Activity:

1. Divide the class in half. One half will debate the merits of the Patman Bill; the other half will debate the decision to forcibly disband the Bonus Army.
2. Have the half that is debating the Patman Bill divide into two groups. One group will support the bill, while the other will oppose it. Each group should do further research to support its position. The two groups should then debate each other.
3. Have the half that is debating the removal of the Bonus Army also divide into two groups. One group will support the forcible removal of the army, while the other will oppose it. Each group should do further research to support its position. The two groups should then debate each other.

ALTERNATIVE ASSESSMENT BOOK

Standards for Evaluating a Cooperative Activity

Congress. The Patman Bill authorized the government to pay a bonus to World War I veterans who had not been compensated adequately for their wartime service. This bonus, which Congress had approved in 1924, was supposed to be paid out in 1945 in the form of a life insurance policy, but Congressman Wright Patman believed that the money—an average of $500 per soldier—should be paid immediately.

Although Hoover opposed the legislation, he respected the veterans' right to peaceful assembly. He even provided food and supplies so that they could erect a shantytown within sight of the Capitol. On June 17, however, the Senate voted down the Patman Bill. Hoover then called on the Bonus Army marchers to leave, and although most did, approximately 2,000, still hoping to meet with the president, refused to budge.

Nervous that the angry group could become violent, President Hoover decided that the Bonus Army should be disbanded. On July 28, a force of 1,000 soldiers under the command of General Douglas MacArthur and his aide, Major Dwight D. Eisenhower, came to roust the veterans. A government official watching from a nearby office recalled what happened next.

A PERSONAL VOICE

The 12th infantry was in full battle dress. Each had a gas mask and his belt was full of tear gas bombs. . . . At orders, they brought their bayonets at thrust and moved in. The bayonets were used to jab people, to make them move. Soon, almost everybody disappeared from view, because tear gas bombs exploded. The entire block was covered by tear gas. Flames were coming up, where the soldiers had set fire to the buildings to drive these people out. . . . Through the whole afternoon, they took one camp after another.

A. EVERETTE MCINTYRE, quoted in *Hard Times*

D. Answer He approved the use of force against veterans who had served their country with honor; the government response seemed excessive and hardhearted.

THINK THROUGH HISTORY **D. *Making Inferences*** *Why was the Bonus Army incident so damaging to Hoover's image?*

In the course of the operation, the infantry gassed more than 1,000 people, including an 11-month-old baby, who died, and an 8-year-old boy, who was partially blinded. Two people were shot and many were injured. Most Americans were stunned and outraged at the government's treatment of the veterans.

Once again, President Hoover's image suffered, and now an election was nearing. In November, Hoover would face a formidable opponent, the Democratic candidate Franklin Delano Roosevelt. When Roosevelt heard about the attack on the Bonus Army, he said to his friend Felix Frankfurter, "Well, Felix, this will elect me." The downturn in the economy and Hoover's inability to effectively deal with the Depression had sealed his political fate.

HISTORICAL SPOTLIGHT

CENTURY OF PROGRESS EXPOSITION

In 1893, Chicago hosted the World's Columbian Exposition, which celebrated the 400th anniversary of Columbus's voyage to America. Forty years later—in 1933, at the height of the Great Depression—another great world's fair the Century of Progress Exposition, opened along the Chicago lakefront.

This fair, which commemorated the 100th anniversary of the founding of Chicago, celebrated modern advances in science and industry. The fair highlighted how far the city had come in the last century and promised a better tomorrow. It was one of the most financially successful world's fairs in history. During its two seasons of operation, in 1933 and 1934, there were approximately 39 million paid admissions.

Section 3 Assessment

1. TERMS & NAMES

Identify:
- Herbert Hoover
- Boulder Dam
- Federal Home Loan Bank Act
- Reconstruction Finance Corporation
- Bonus Army

2. SUMMARIZING In a cluster diagram, record what Hoover said and did in response to the Depression.

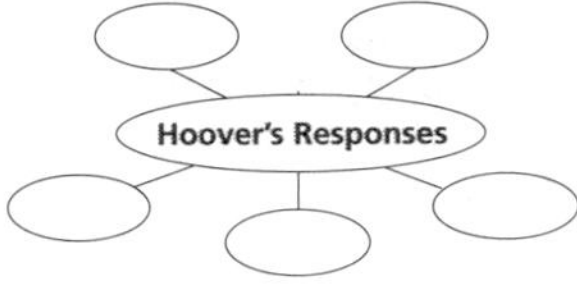

Put a plus sign by the response you think was most helpful and a minus sign by the one you think was least helpful.

3. ANALYZING ISSUES How did Hoover's belief in "rugged individualism" shape his policies during the depression?

THINK ABOUT
- what that belief implies about government action
- Hoover's policies
- whether those policies were consistent with his beliefs

4. CLARIFYING When Franklin Delano Roosevelt heard about the attack on the Bonus Army, why was he so certain that Hoover was going to lose?

THINK ABOUT
- the American public's impression of Hoover
- Hoover's actions to alleviate the Depression
- how people judged Hoover after the attack

HISTORICAL SPOTLIGHT
Century of Progress Exposition

Critical Thinking: Analyzing Ask students why they think so many people paid to see the exposition during a time when money was so tight. *Possible Responses: It gave them the opportunity to escape from the misery and dreariness of the Depression; it may have given them hope that life would return to normal someday.*

ASSESS & RETEACH

Section 3 Assessment

Have students work in small groups to answer the questions. Have each group share its answer to question 3 with the class.

Self-Assessment

Have students state in a paragraph or two their impressions of Herbert Hoover's response to the Depression and what he might have done differently.

Section Quiz

FORMAL ASSESSMENT
Section Quiz, p. 178

Reteach

Use the Guided Reading worksheet for Section 3 to help review the section's main ideas.

IN-DEPTH RESOURCES: UNIT 4
Guided Reading, p. 38

CLOSE

Herbert Hoover, who espoused the virtue of self-reliance, took little action to combat the Depression. The plans that Hoover did implement were viewed as too little, too late. Hoover's reluctance to act, as well as his role in gassing the Bonus Army, cost him a great deal of public support and, consequently, his chance for reelection.

ANSWERS

1. TERMS & NAMES

Herbert Hoover, p. 495

Boulder Dam, p. 497

Federal Home Loan Bank Act, p. 498

Reconstruction Finance Corporation, p. 498

Bonus Army, p. 498

2. SUMMARIZING

The cluster diagram might include the following words and phrases:

"Any lack of confidence in the economic future . . . is foolish"; "rugged individualism"; public-works programs; Boulder Dam; Federal Farm Board; Federal Home Loan Bank Act; Reconstruction Finance Corporation; sending of troops against Bonus Army

3. ANALYZING ISSUES

Possible Responses: Some students may say that Hoover's belief in "rugged individualism" implied limited government intervention and prompted him to take a cautious approach. For example, he allowed the government to hire unemployed people for public-works programs, but he would not give them direct aid. Others may say that the public-works programs show that he stopped believing in rugged individualism.

4. CLARIFYING

Possible Responses: Some students may say that the public wanted a warm, generous leader who would act to relieve its suffering and that the attack made Hoover seem uncaring and cruel. Others may mention that the public was already blaming Hoover for all its suffering, and the attack just confirmed that negative impression of him.

CHAPTER 14
ASSESSMENT ANSWERS

REVIEWING THE CHAPTER

TERMS & NAMES

1. credit, p. 484
2. speculation, p. 485
3. buying on margin, p. 485
4. Black Tuesday, p. 485
5. Great Depression, p. 486
6. Dow Jones Industrial Average, p. 487
7. Dust Bowl, p. 490
8. direct relief, p. 493
9. Herbert Hoover, p. 495
10. Bonus Army, p. 498

MAIN IDEAS

11. During the 1920s, farmers faced decreased demand for their products and lower crop prices. Those who were in debt could not repay loans, and rural banks failed. This pattern repeated itself in other sectors of the economy during the Depression.
12. Because a small number of people controlled a large percentage of the nation's wealth, most consumers could not afford the products the nation was producing—a trend that threatened economic growth.
13. The stock market crash triggered bank and business failures, high unemployment, and worldwide depression.
14. It hurt the U.S. economy because it lowered the income of foreign nations and reduced their spending on American goods.
15. Shantytowns consisted of makeshift housing built by the homeless, and soup kitchens and bread lines were places where charitable organizations handed out food to the hungry.
16. Some unemployed whites were angered by job competition from minorities.
17. Unemployment reduced household income. Some families lost homes. Many adults lost the ability to provide for their families.
18. Mellon believed that depressions were a normal part of the business cycle and the economy would eventually fix itself.
19. The harshness of the attack on the veterans and their families damaged Hoover's reputation.
20. He started public-works programs and backed the Federal Farm Board, Federal Home Loan Bank Act, and the RFC.

Chapter 14 Assessment

REVIEWING THE CHAPTER

TERMS & NAMES For each term below, write a sentence explaining its connection to the period 1929–1933. For the person below, explain his role in the events of the period.

1. **credit**
2. **speculation**
3. **buying on margin**
4. **Black Tuesday**
5. **Dow Jones Industrial Average**
6. **Great Depression**
7. **Dust Bowl**
8. **direct relief**
9. **Herbert Hoover**
10. **Bonus Army**

MAIN IDEAS

SECTION 1 *(pages 482–489)*

The Nation's Sick Economy

11. How did what happened to farmers during the 1920s foreshadow events of the Great Depression?
12. Why was uneven distribution of income bad for the economy?
13. What were some of the effects of the stock market crash in October 1929?
14. What effect did the Hawley-Smoot Tariff Act have on the economy and why?

SECTION 2 *(pages 490–494)*

Hardship and Suffering During the Depression

15. How were shantytowns, soup kitchens, and bread lines a response to the Depression?
16. Why did minorities often experience an increase in discrimination during the Great Depression?
17. What pressures did the American family experience during the Depression?

SECTION 3 *(pages 495–499)*

Hoover Struggles with the Depression

18. Why did Secretary of the Treasury Andrew Mellon believe that the government should do nothing about the Depression?
19. How did Hoover's treatment of the Bonus Army affect his standing with the public?
20. In what ways did Hoover try to use the government to relieve the Depression?

THINKING CRITICALLY

1. **THE GREAT DEPRESSION** Create a cause-and-effect web for the Great Depression, using a graphic similar to the one shown.

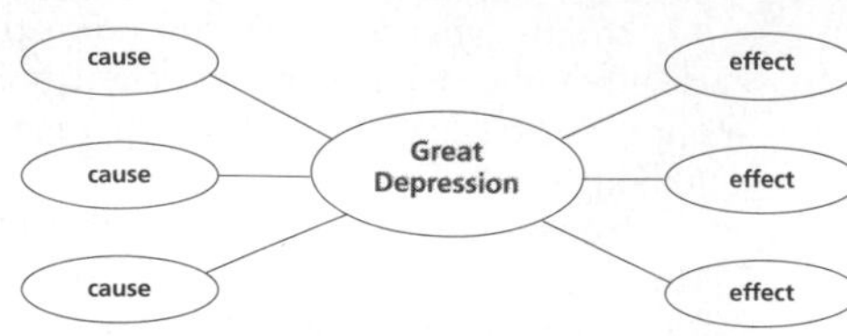

2. **TRACING THEMES ECONOMIC OPPORTUNITY** Do you think it would have been difficult for individuals to recover financially during the Depression without the entire economy's recovering? Why or why not?
3. **ECONOMIC DESPAIR** Reread the quotation from Senator La Follette on page 480. Do you think he accurately summarized the change in the mood of the nation? What words or phrases do you find especially accurate or especially misleading?
4. **GEOGRAPHY OF THE DUST BOWL** Look carefully at the map on page 492. What generalizations can you make about the topography, or surface features, of the land where the Dust Bowl was? How might that topography have contributed to the problem? Remember that the prevailing winds blew the dust from west to east.
5. **THE DOW JONES AVERAGE** Review the Now & Then feature on pages 486–487, and compare the stocks that made up the Dow Jones Industrial Average in 1896 with the stocks that made it up in 1997. What can you conclude about the way the economy changed during the 20th century?
6. **ANALYZING PRIMARY SOURCES** Read the following excerpt from Oscar Ameringer's testimony before the U.S. Congress in 1932. Then answer the questions below.

> **Personally, and as a lifelong student of political economy [economics], I am of the opinion that all this talk about speedy recovery and prosperity being just around the corner is bosh and nonsense. What we are confronted with is not a mere panic like those of 1873 and 1883 but a worldwide economic catastrophe that may spell the end of the capitalistic era—for the cause of it is production for profit instead of production for consumption. The masses cannot buy what they have themselves produced; and unless ways and means are found to make cash customers out of some 20 million of unemployed wage earners and bankrupt farmers, there can be no recovery.**
>
> **OSCAR AMERINGER,** testimony before a subcommittee of the House Committee on Labor

Judging from what you read in this section, do you agree with Ameringer's assessment that recovery from the Great Depression would be difficult? Did his prediction that the Depression would end the capitalistic era come true? Explain.

THINKING CRITICALLY

1. THE GREAT DEPRESSION
Possible Answers: **Causes:** decaying industrial base, farm crisis, failure of rural banks, uneven distribution of income, consumers' overdependence on credit, stock market speculation.

Effects: widespread bank failures, bankrupt businesses, high unemployment, decrease in worldwide trade, increasing numbers of homeless persons, widespread hunger and illness.

2. TRACING THEMES ECONOMIC OPPORTUNITY
Possible Responses: Students answering yes may say that individuals can't recover financially if the banks, businesses, and people around them do not also recover. Students answering no may say that individuals can sell necessary goods or services that do not depend on outside agencies.

3. ECONOMIC DESPAIR
Possible Responses: Students answering yes might say that "illusory prosperity" describes the 1920s well and "widespread despair" describes the 1930s well. Students answering no might say the quotation overgeneralizes; for example, farmers and minority groups in the 1920s did not feel "feverish optimism."

Bridge to Chapter 15

Review Chapter 14

PROSPERITY TURNS TO PANIC Unresolved economic problems of the 1920s led to the Great Depression. Industries and farmers faced reduced demand, most people could not earn an adequate income, and many went deeply into debt. Dreams of wealth had led people to take risks in the stock market, and when stock prices fell, panicked investors sold their shares, causing a market crash. Mass withdrawals of savings closed banks. All sorts of businesses went bankrupt, throwing millions out of work.

HOMELESSNESS AND HUNGER Many unemployed people lost their homes and had to live on the streets or in shantytowns. Many farmers lost their farms, especially in the area of the Great Plains known as the Dust Bowl. Hoping to work as migrants, thousands of these headed for California. Two million unemployed men wandered the country looking for work. The families they left behind struggled to survive despite poverty, hunger, and illness.

A CAUTIOUS PRESIDENT President Hoover believed that people should succeed through their own efforts and that government should not intervene much in the economy. Yet he was a humanitarian who believed in helping others, so he supported public-works programs to create jobs. He also made a few financial reforms. However, the public thought he was not doing enough to ease their suffering. When Hoover used troops against the Bonus Army, he lost the last of his popular support.

Preview Chapter 15

In 1932, Americans rejected President Hoover in favor of the Democrat Franklin Delano Roosevelt. To relieve suffering and spark the economy, Roosevelt began programs to provide financial reform, works projects, and direct relief. The Depression influenced popular culture as Americans sought to forget their trouble by listening to the radio and attending movies. You will learn about these and other significant developments in the next chapter.

ALTERNATIVE ASSESSMENT

1. **MAKING DECISIONS**
Imagine you are a Kansas farmer in the 1930s. Use the following list to help you decide whether you would uproot your family and move farther west, or remain where you are.
   - What major choices would you need to make about moving?
   - What information would you want to gather in order to make your choices?
   - What options would each choice present to you?
   - What would be the consequences of each of the options?
   - What actions would you take to implement your final decisions?

2. **LEARNING FROM MEDIA**

VIDEO View the McDougal Littell video for Chapter 14, *Broke but Not Broken.* Discuss the following questions in small groups, then do the cooperative-learning activity:
   - According to Ann Marie Low, how did the farmers contribute to their own ruin?
   - What choices did Ann Marie Low's family make during the Depression? Do you agree with their choices?
   - What did you learn about the relationship between the government and the farmers?
   - What did the older Ann Marie Low's comments add to your understanding of the Great Depression?
   - **Cooperative Learning** With your group, compile a list of questions that you still have about the experience of living in the Dust Bowl. Then write a letter to Ann Marie Low, asking for more information. Share your letter with the class.

3. **PORTFOLIO PROJECT**
Use the Living History activity to expand your portfolio.

LIVING HISTORY

DISPLAYING YOUR COLLAGE

Finish, present, and display your collage depicting the stories of people who lived through the Great Depression.

- Review the images you have assembled. If any seem weak, find or create a replacement.
- Experiment with different ways of grouping the images. Your groupings may emphasize either similarities or differences in the personal stories.
- When you have an arrangement you like, make your collage permanent by affixing the images to poster board.

Be prepared to present your collage in class and to answer any questions about why you chose the images and whom each one represents. Display your collage in the classroom, then add it to your American history portfolio.

ALTERNATIVE ASSESSMENT

1. MAKING DECISIONS
Standards for Evaluation
A well-reasoned decision should meet the following criteria.

- Realistically evaluates the changes and adjustments involved in a major move.
- Weighs the available options.
- Considers the consequences of the action taken.
- Details the steps to take to implement the decision.

2. LEARNING FROM MEDIA
Answers to the questions.

- They overfarmed the land and ruined the topsoil, thus leaving nothing to hold down the dust.
- The Low family remained on their farm as others fled. Possible Responses: Yes, they had worked too long and hard at building the farm to leave. No, they should have left and sought better opportunities.
- The relationship was marked by tension and mistrust.
- Students may point to a better understanding of the farmers' plight during the Depression.

Standards for Evaluation
A letter to Ann Marie Low should meet the following criteria.

- Asks questions about issues not covered in the video.
- Makes the questions clear and specific.
- Uses appropriate letter form and style.

3. PORTFOLIO PROJECT
LIVING HISTORY
Standards for Evaluation:
A collage should meet the following criteria.

- Builds upon descriptive details and viewpoints expressed in the personal voices about the Great Depression.
- Presents an accurate visual representation of Depression-era issues.

IN-DEPTH RESOURCES: UNIT 4
See the form for scoring this activity on page 52.

THINKING CRITICALLY

4. GEOGRAPHY OF THE DUST BOWL
Possible Responses: The land is very flat; there were no obstructions to reduce the wind that blew the topsoil away.

5. THE DOW JONES AVERAGE
Possible Response: Heavy industry has grown less important to the economy. Important sectors of today's economy include software production, television broadcasting, and legal services.

6. ANALYZING PRIMARY SOURCES
Possible Responses: Agree—Ameringer points out the unequal distribution of income, the farm crisis, and the worldwide impact. Disagree—Production for profit is not necessarily different from production for consumption. False—The United States is still a capitalist nation. True—The United States no longer has such a capitalistic economy—the government is heavily involved in the economy.

CHAPTER 15

PLANNING GUIDE
The New Deal

	Key Ideas	COPYMASTERS	ASSESSMENT
SECTION 1 **A New Deal Fights the Depression** *pp. 504–510*	*President Roosevelt takes many actions to combat the Depression.*	***In-Depth Resources: Unit 4*** • Guided Reading, p. 53 • Skillbuilder Practice: Analyzing Issues, p. 58 • Primary Source: *from* Father Coughlin's Anti-New Deal Speech, p. 63 • American Lives: Huey Long, p. 70 ***Lesson Plans,*** pp. 123–124	PE ***Section 1 Assessment,*** p. 510 TE ***Self-Assessment,*** p. 510 ***Formal Assessment*** • Section Quiz, p. 187 ***Alternative Assessment Book*** • Standards for Evaluating a Cooperative Activity
SECTION 2 **The Second New Deal Takes Hold** *pp. 511–516*	*The Second New Deal institutes new programs to extend federal aid and stimulate the nation's economy.*	***In-Depth Resources: Unit 4*** • Guided Reading, p. 54 ***Lesson Plans,*** pp. 125–126	PE ***Section 2 Assessment,*** p. 516 TE ***Self-Assessment,*** p. 516 ***Formal Assessment*** • Section Quiz, p. 188 ***Alternative Assessment Book*** • Standards for Evaluating a Cooperative Activity
SECTION 3 **The New Deal Affects Many Groups** *pp. 517–522*	*New Deal policies and actions affect Americans in all walks of life. The Democratic Party forms a new political coalition.*	***In-Depth Resources: Unit 4*** • Guided Reading, p. 55 • Primary Source: The Memorial Day Massacre, p. 64 • Literature: from *Waiting for Lefty* by Clifford Odets, p. 67 • American Lives: Mary McLeod Bethune, p. 71 ***Lesson Plans,*** pp. 127–128	PE ***Section 3 Assessment,*** p. 522 TE ***Self-Assessment,*** p. 522 ***Formal Assessment*** • Section Quiz, p. 189 ***Alternative Assessment Book*** • Standards for Evaluating a Cooperative Activity
SECTION 4 **Society and Culture** *pp. 523–528*	*Motion pictures, radio, art, and literature all blossom during the period of the New Deal.*	***In-Depth Resources: Unit 4*** • Guided Reading, p. 56 • Primary Sources: WPA Posters, p. 65; from *Let Us Now Praise Famous Men* by James Agee and Walker Evans, p. 66 ***Lesson Plans,*** pp. 129–130	PE ***Section 4 Assessment,*** p. 528 TE ***Self-Assessment,*** p. 528 ***Formal Assessment*** • Section Quiz, p. 190 ***Alternative Assessment Book*** • Standards for Evaluating a Cooperative Activity
SECTION 5 **The Impact of the New Deal** *pp. 529–533*	*The New Deal affects American society not only in the 1930s but also in the decades that follow.*	***In-Depth Resources: Unit 4*** • Guided Reading, p. 57 • Geography Application: Decade of the Democrats, p. 59 • Outline Map: Anatomy of the Tennessee Valley Authority, p. 61 ***Lesson Plans,*** pp. 131–132	PE ***Section 5 Assessment,*** p. 533 TE ***Self-Assessment,*** p. 533 ***Formal Assessment*** • Section Quiz, p. 191 ***Alternative Assessment Book*** • Standards for Evaluating a Cooperative Activity
CHAPTER RESOURCES	**Chapter Overview** *President Roosevelt launches a program aiming to end the Depression. The Depression and Roosevelt's New Deal have profound effects on the nation.*	***In-Depth Resources: Unit 4*** • Living History Project: Worksheet, p. 72; Standards, p. 73 ***Telescoping the Times*** • Chapter Summary, pp. 29–30 ***Planning for Block Schedules***	PE ***Chapter Assessment,*** pp. 536–537 PE ***Alternative Assessment,*** p. 537 ***Formal Assessment*** • Chapter Test, forms A and B, pp. 192–197 ***Test Generator*** ***Alternative Assessment Book*** See explanation and forms for different kinds of alternative assessments including portfolio assessment.

KEY
- PE Pupil's Edition
- TE Teacher's Edition
- **http://www.mlushistory.com**

TECHNOLOGY

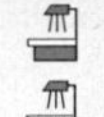
Warm-Up Transparency 15

Humanities Transparencies
- H40, Nine Old Men

Geography Transparencies
- G23, P. W. A. in Action

Electronic Library of Primary Sources
- Speeches of Franklin D. Roosevelt

INTERNET FDR and Huey Long

Warm-Up Transparency 15

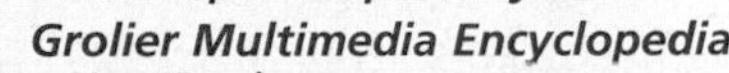
Grolier Multimedia Encyclopedia
- New Deal

INTERNET WPA Projects and Dorothea Lange

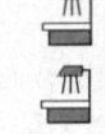
Warm-Up Transparency 15

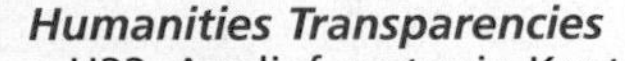
Humanities Transparencies
- H22, A relief center in Kentucky

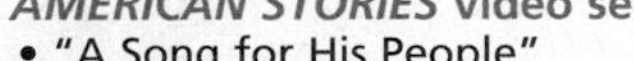
AMERICAN STORIES video series
- "A Song for His People"

Electronic Library of Primary Sources
- Bethune-Cookman College
- Eleanor Roosevelt

INTERNET CIO and Mary McLeod Bethune

Warm-Up Transparency 15

INTERNET Richard Wright, the Marx Brothers, John Steinbeck, and Grant Wood

Warm-Up Transparency 15

Critical Thinking Transparencies
- CT23, The New Deal
- CT57, The U.S. Economic Indicators: 1929–1939

Grolier Multimedia Encyclopedia
- Tennessee Valley Authority

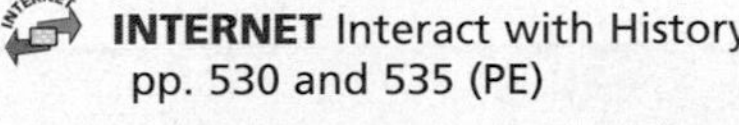
INTERNET Interact with History pp. 530 and 535 (PE)

American Portfolio: A Videodisc for U.S. History, user's guide, pp. 203, 206–207

Chapter Summary Audiotapes
- Unit 4, Chapter 15

INTERNET http://www.mlushistory.com

Block Scheduling (90 MINUTES)

Day 1
Section 1, pp. 504–510
Section 2, pp. 511–516
Section Assessments, pp. 510, 516

COOPERATIVE ACTIVITIES
- Delivering a Fireside Chat, p. 506 (TE)
- Creating a New Deal Poster, p. 515 (TE)

Day 2
Section 3, pp. 517–522
AMERICAN STORIES video series
- "A Song for His People"

Section Assessment, p. 522

COOPERATIVE ACTIVITY
- Researching Treatment of Women and Minorities, p. 519 (TE)

Day 3
Section 4, pp. 523–528
Section Assessment, p. 528

COOPERATIVE ACTIVITY
- Producing a Depression-Era Radio Program, p. 525 (TE)

Day 4
Section 5, pp. 529–533
Geography Spotlight: The Tennessee Valley Authority, pp. 534–535
Section Assessment, p. 533
Chapter Assessment, pp. 536–537

COOPERATIVE ACTIVITY
- Debating the New Deal, p. 531 (TE)

YEARLY PACING *Chapter 15 Total:* 4 days *Yearly Total:* 85 days

See *Planning for Block Schedules* for special activities and pacing strategies.

Customizing for Special Populations

Students Acquiring English
Access for Students Acquiring English: Spanish Translations
- Guided Reading for Sections 1–5, pp. 175–179
- Chapter Summary, pp. 173–174
- Skillbuilder Practice: Analyzing Issues, p. 180
- Geography Application: Decade of the Democrats, p. 181
- Outline Map: Anatomy of the Tennessee Valley Authority, p. 183

Spanish Reading Study Guide, pp. 155–166

Translations of Chapter Summaries, Hmong, Cantonese, Vietnamese, and Cambodian

Chapter Summary Audiotapes in Spanish
Unit 4, Chapter 15

AMERICAN STORIES video series
- "A Song for His People" (Spanish Track)

INTERNET The Diverse Classroom

Gifted and Talented Students
In-Depth Resources: Unit 4
- Primary Sources: *from* Father Coughlin's Anti-New Deal Speech, p. 63; The Memorial Day Massacre, p. 64; WPA Posters, p. 65; from *Let Us Now Praise Famous Men* by James Agee and Walker Evans, p. 66
- American Lives: Huey Long, p. 70; Mary McLeod Bethune, p. 71

Less Proficient Readers
In-Depth Resources: Unit 4
- Guided Reading for Sections 1–5, pp. 53–57
- Skillbuilder: Analyzing Issues, p. 58
- Geography Application: Decade of the Democrats, p. 59
- Outline Map: Anatomy of the Tennessee Valley Authority, p. 61

Reading Study Guide
- pp. 155–166

Telescoping the Times
- Chapter Summary, pp. 29–30

Chapter Summary Audiotapes, Unit 4, Chapter 15

Connections to Literature READINGS FOR STUDENTS

In-Depth Resources: Unit 4
- **from *Waiting for Lefty* by Clifford Odets,** p. 67

Enrichment Reading
- **Robert Penn Warren**
  All the King's Men
  New York: Harcourt Brace, 1985
  Winner of the Pulitzer Prize in 1947, this novel tells the story of Willie Stark, a Southern politician whose character is based on Governor Huey Long of Louisiana. Through appeals to the common man and by playing dirty politics, Stark is a successful leader but at a price that eventually costs him his life. The mixture of good and evil in the novel adds up to a lyrical and painful story of idealism, politics, and personal history.

James T. Farrell
Studs Lonigan
New York: Vanguard Press, 1978
This novel about ordinary people expressing their opinions and struggling with issues of family and work is told with extraordinary honesty. The sad, funny, and ultimately tragic story brings the 1920s and 1930s vividly to life.

McDougal Littell ***The Language of Literature***
American Literature
- **Tillie Olsen, "I Stand Here Ironing,"** p. 642
- **Julia Alvarez, "Ironing Their Clothes,"** p. 650

CHAPTER 15

OVERVIEW

The New Deal

▶ *Accessing Prior Knowledge*

Ask students to discuss government programs that have a direct impact on their lives. What programs have a positive impact? Which ones have a negative impact? What new programs do students think the government should initiate for teenagers?

▶ *Predicting Outcomes*

Have students look on page 503 at the *Vanity Fair* cover, which shows President Roosevelt riding a bucking bronco in the shape of the United States. What might this image suggest about Roosevelt's role as president during the 1930s?

MORE ABOUT . . .
Franklin Delano Roosevelt

After FDR developed polio in 1921, many people thought his political career was over. But they underestimated Roosevelt's spirit. When a friend visited him in the hospital, FDR struck the man hard in the chest and said, "You thought you were coming to see an invalid, but I can knock you out in any bout."

CHAPTER 15

The New Deal

SECTION 1

A New Deal Fights the Depression

President Roosevelt takes many actions to combat the Depression.

SECTION 2

The Second New Deal Takes Hold

The Second New Deal institutes new programs to extend federal aid and stimulate the nation's economy.

SECTION 3

The New Deal Affects Many Groups

New Deal policies and actions affect Americans in all walks of life. The Democratic Party forms a new political coalition.

A SONG FOR HIS PEOPLE

SECTION 4

Society and Culture

Motion pictures, radio, art, and literature all blossom during the period of the New Deal.

SECTION 5

The Impact of the New Deal

The New Deal affects American society not only in the 1930s but also in the decades that follow.

"The only thing we have to fear is fear itself."

Franklin Delano Roosevelt

THE UNITED STATES

1933
- Franklin Delano Roosevelt is inaugurated.
- Congress creates the TVA.

1934
- Indian Reorganization Act is passed.
- Congress creates the SEC.

1935
- Huey Long is assassinated.
- Supreme Court declares the NIRA unconstitutional.
- CIO is organized.
- Congress passes the Social Security Act.
- Women wait in line for New Deal relief.

THE WORLD

1933
- Hitler and the Nazi Party come to power in Germany.
- Fulgencio Batista y Zaldívar seizes control of the Cuban government.

1934
- Chinese Communists engage in the Long March.
- Lázaro Cárdenas becomes president of Mexico.

1935
- Italy invades Ethiopia.
- British Parliament passes the Government of India Act.

THEMES IN CHAPTER 15

Economic Opportunity

The Roosevelt administration dealt with some major economic issues through legislation and policymaking during the New Deal. For example, the administration initiated policies that supported and regulated agriculture and industry. It also passed legislation that greatly improved labor conditions and gave more power to unions. Some of the programs begun under the New Deal—for example, the FDIC, the SEC, and Social Security—continue to help soften the economic impact of recessions.

See Teacher's Edition notes, pp. 507, 514, 532.

Cultural Diversity

Although discrimination remained widespread in the 1930s, the New Deal created some new opportunities for women and minority groups. The Indian Reorganization Act of 1934, for example, was created to help Native Americans.

See Teacher's Edition note, p. 520.

Science and Technology

Motion pictures and radio programs helped people escape the hard realities of life in the 1930s. Today, televisions and computers serve a similar function when they are used for entertainment purposes.

See Teacher's Edition note, p. 524.

LIVING HISTORY

WRITING A NEW DEAL DIARY

Imagine that you are a worker who has been laid off from his or her job during the Great Depression. You eventually get work through one of the New Deal agencies, such as the CWA, CCC, or WPA. Use your textbook and other sources to gather information about the agency. Then write diary entries about your experiences over two or three weeks or more. Be sure to include information about the following:

- any training you receive
- the kind of work you do
- the tools you use
- the pay you receive

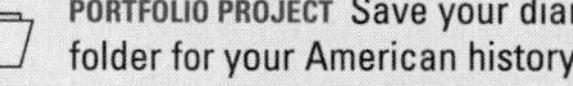

PORTFOLIO PROJECT Save your diary entries in a folder for your American history portfolio.

1936
- President Roosevelt is reelected.
- Civil War begins in Spain.
- Soviet dictator Joseph Stalin purges the Communist Party and government leadership.

1937
- Labor unions begin using sit-down strikes.
- *Snow White and the Seven Dwarfs* is released.
- Japan invades China.
- Early international radio broadcast reports the *Hindenburg* disaster.

1938
- Fair Labor Standards Act passes.
- Mexico nationalizes oil wells.

1939
- Marian Anderson sings at the Lincoln Memorial.
- John Steinbeck publishes *The Grapes of Wrath.*
- Germany invades Poland.

1940
- President Roosevelt is elected a third time.

ALTERNATIVE ASSESSMENT

LIVING HISTORY

WRITING A NEW DEAL DIARY

Discuss with students the following process of gathering material and writing the diary entries:

- Choose the agency they want to work for.
- Do some research to find out more about the agency. Pay particular attention to first-person statements from those who actually worked under the agency.
- Specifically identify the work they will be doing. Think about the training and tools they will need and the pay they'll receive.
- Write their diary entries. Describe what they hope to gain from the job. They should try to write from the point of view of someone who lived through the Depression.

Project Planning Guide

Step 1	**Select an agency.**
Step 2	**Conduct research to learn about the agency.**
Step 3	**Decide what work they will do and think through the details.**
Step 4	**Write the diary entries and place them in their folder.**

IN-DEPTH RESOURCES: UNIT 4
See worksheet and standards for evaluation, pp. 72, 73.

RECOMMENDED RESOURCES

Books for the Teacher

Goodwin, Doris Kearns. *No Ordinary Time.* New York: Simon, 1995. Lives of Franklin and Eleanor Roosevelt.

Williams, T. Harry. *Huey Long.* New York: Knopf, 1969. Biography of Long.

Books for the Student

Aptheker, Herbert, ed. *A Documentary History of the Negro People in the United States.* New York: Carol, 1992. From New Deal to World War II.

Banks, Ann, ed. *First-Person America.* New York: Knopf, 1980. Lives of 80 Americans, collected by Federal Writers' Project.

Videos

Eleanor Roosevelt: A Restless Spirit. Dir. Harry Rasky. A&E Home Video, 1994.

FDR. PBS Home Video, 1994. Four-hour documentary.

The New Deal. Republic Pictures Home Video, 1986. The TVA, the WPA, and other New Deal projects of the 1930s.

Software

FDR. CD-ROM. Corbis Publishing, 1996.

U.S. History: The Great Depression. CD-ROM. Clearvue. Educational Software Institute, 800-955-5570.

Section 1 Overview

OBJECTIVES

1. To summarize some of the steps Roosevelt took early in his presidency to reform banking and finance.
2. To describe New Deal programs that provided relief to farmers and other workers.
3. To identify critics of Roosevelt and his New Deal policies.

SKILLBUILDERS

- Interpreting political cartoons, pp. 506, 509

CRITICAL THINKING

- Summarizing, pp. 505, 510
- Evaluating decisions, p. 506
- Finding main ideas, p. 507
- Theme: Economic Opportunity, p. 508
- Comparing, pp. 509, 510
- Analyzing issues, p. 509
- Interpreting, p. 510
- Analyzing, p. 510

FOCUS & MOTIVATE

5-MINUTE WARM-UP

Recognizing Main Idea
To introduce the New Deal, have students read One American's Story on page 504 and answer these questions.

1. Why did receiving a CWA paycheck make people so happy?
2. Why did New Deal programs like the CWA raise the hopes of the American people?

WARM-UP TRANSPARENCY 15

▶ ***Starting with the Student***

- Ask students if they think the government should have no control, some control, or total control of education, including their school.
- Ask them if they think the president should be given more power in times of crisis. Then ask them what could happen if the president is given too much power.

1 A New Deal Fights the Depression

TERMS & NAMES
- Franklin Delano Roosevelt
- New Deal
- Glass-Steagall Banking Act of 1933
- Federal Securities Act
- Agricultural Adjustment Act
- Civilian Conservation Corps
- National Industrial Recovery Act
- Huey Long

LEARN ABOUT the early actions taken by the Roosevelt administration ***TO UNDERSTAND*** how the New Deal tried to combat the Depression.

ONE AMERICAN'S STORY

Hank Oettinger was working as a printing press operator in a small town in northern Wisconsin when the Great Depression began. He lost his job in 1931, and he was unemployed for the next two years. In 1932, however, Americans elected a new president, Franklin Delano Roosevelt. Once in office, Roosevelt created work programs to provide jobs for the unemployed. Through one of these programs, the Civil Works Administration (CWA), Oettinger went back to work in 1933. As he later recalled, the CWA was cause for great celebration in his town.

A PERSONAL VOICE

I can remember the first week of the CWA checks. It was on a Friday. That night everybody had gotten his check. The first check a lot of them had in three years. . . . I never saw such a change of attitude. Instead of walking around feeling dreary and looking sorrowful, everybody was joyous. Like a feast day. They were toasting each other. They had money in their pockets for the first time.

HANK OETTINGER, quoted in *Hard Times*

Programs like the CWA raised the hopes of the American people and sparked great enthusiasm for the new president. As Oettinger put it, "If Roosevelt had run for president the next day, he'd have gone in by a hundred percent." To many Americans, it appeared as if the country had turned a corner and was beginning to emerge from the nightmare of the Great Depression.

Civil Works Administration workers prepare to participate in a parade for workers in San Francisco in 1934.

New Deal Actions

In 1932, the presidential election showed that Americans were clearly ready for a change. Because of the Depression, people were suffering from lack of work, lack of food, and lack of hope.

ELECTING FRANKLIN DELANO ROOSEVELT Although the Republicans renominated President Hoover as their candidate, they recognized that he had little chance of winning. Too many Americans blamed Hoover for doing too little about the Depression and wanted a new president in the White House.

The Democrats pinned their hopes on **Franklin Delano Roosevelt,** known popularly as FDR, the two-term governor of New York and a distant cousin of Theodore Roosevelt. As governor, Franklin Roosevelt had proved an effective, reform-minded leader. He pushed a series of new measures through the New York legislature to combat the problems of unemployment and poverty. Unlike Hoover, Roosevelt projected an air of friendliness and confidence that

SECTION 1 RESOURCES

PRINT RESOURCES

IN-DEPTH RESOURCES: UNIT 4
Guided Reading, p. 53
Skillbuilder Practice: Analyzing Issues, p. 58
Primary Source: *from* Father Coughlin's Anti-New Deal Speech, p. 63
American Lives: Huey Long, p. 70

READING STUDY GUIDE, p. 155

ACCESS FOR STUDENTS ACQUIRING ENGLISH
Guided Reading (Spanish), p. 175
Skillbuilder Practice: Analyzing Issues (Spanish), p. 180

SPANISH READING STUDY GUIDE, p. 155

FORMAL ASSESSMENT
Section Quiz, p. 187

ALTERNATIVE ASSESSMENT BOOK
See forms for supporting and scoring alternative activities.

TECHNOLOGY RESOURCES

HUMANITIES TRANSPARENCIES
H40, Nine Old Men

GEOGRAPHY TRANSPARENCIES
G23, P. W. A. in Action

CD-ROM Electronic Library of Primary Sources

VIDEO *American Portfolio: A Videodisc for U.S. History* user's guide, pp. 203, 206, 208, 212–213

INTERNET http://www.mlushistory.com

attracted voters. Though practical at heart, he had a creative, adventurous side that allowed him to take risks that others might avoid. As he once said, "It is common sense to take a method and try it. If it fails, admit it frankly and try another. But above all, try something." This "can-do" attitude appealed to a public that regarded Hoover, rightly or wrongly, as a "do-nothing" president.

Roosevelt won an overwhelming victory, capturing 23 million votes to Hoover's 16 million and carrying the South, the West, and all but six states in the Northeast. In the Senate, Democrats claimed a nearly two-thirds majority. In the House, they won almost three-fourths of the seats, their greatest victory since before the Civil War.

WAITING FOR ROOSEVELT TO TAKE OVER Four months would elapse between Roosevelt's victory in November and his inauguration as president in March 1933. The Twentieth Amendment, which moved presidential inaugurations to January, was not ratified until February 1933 and did not apply to the 1932 election. Americans waited anxiously to find out what plans their new president had for solving the nation's problems. Meanwhile, the economy continued to worsen. Industrial production fell; more businesses and banks shut down; and more people lost their jobs, their homes, and their farms.

FDR was not idle during this waiting period, however. He worked with his team of carefully picked advisers—a select group of professors, lawyers, and journalists known as the brain trust. Roosevelt began to formulate a set of policies for his new administration. This program, designed to alleviate the problems of the Great Depression, became known as the **New Deal,** from a phrase in a campaign speech in which Roosevelt had promised "a new deal for the American people." New Deal policies focused on three general goals: relief for the needy, economic recovery, and financial reform.

KEY PLAYERS

FRANKLIN D. ROOSEVELT 1882–1945

Born into an old, wealthy New York family, Franklin Delano Roosevelt entered politics as a state senator in 1910 and later became assistant secretary of the navy. In 1921, he was stricken with polio and paralyzed from the waist down. He struggled to regain the use of his legs, and he eventually learned to stand with the help of heavy leg braces. Roosevelt became governor of New York in 1928, and because he "would not allow bodily disability to defeat his will," he went on to the White House in 1933. Always interested in people, Roosevelt gained greater compassion for others as a result of his own physical handicap.

ELEANOR ROOSEVELT 1884–1962

A niece of Theodore Roosevelt and a distant cousin of her husband, Franklin, Eleanor Roosevelt lost her parents at an early age. She was raised by a strict grandmother.

As first lady, she often urged the president to take stands on controversial issues. She became known for speaking out against economic and social injustice. In presenting a booklet on human rights to the United Nations in 1958, she said, "Where, after all, do human rights begin? . . . [In] the world of the individual person: the neighborhood . . . the school . . . the factory, farm or office where he works."

THINK THROUGH HISTORY
A. *Summarizing* *What plans did Roosevelt make in the four months while he waited to take office?*

A. Answer He began to formulate a set of policies to alleviate the problems of the Depression.

On taking office, the Roosevelt administration launched into a period of intense activity, known as the Hundred Days, lasting from March 9 to June 16, 1933. During this period, Congress passed more than 15 major pieces of New Deal legislation. These laws, and others that followed, significantly expanded the federal government's role in the nation's economy.

REFORMING BANKING AND FINANCE Roosevelt's first step as president was to carry out reforms in banking and finance. By 1933, widespread bank failures had caused most Americans to lose faith in the banking system. On March 5, one day after taking office, Roosevelt declared a bank holiday and closed all banks to prevent further withdrawals. Then he persuaded Congress to pass the Emergency

OBJECTIVE
① INSTRUCT

New Deal Actions

▶ ***Discussing Key Ideas***
- Roosevelt easily wins the presidency in 1932 and immediately begins to formulate a set of policies that become known as the New Deal.
- During the Hundred Days in Roosevelt's first term, the president reforms banking and finance.
- In his fireside chats, Roosevelt explains his policies to the American people.

IN-DEPTH RESOURCES: UNIT 4
Guided Reading, p. 53

ACCESS FOR STUDENTS ACQUIRING ENGLISH
Guided Reading (Spanish), p. 175

ELECTRONIC LIBRARY OF PRIMARY SOURCES
from Acceptance Speech by Franklin Delano Roosevelt
from First Inaugural Address by Franklin Delano Roosevelt

KEY PLAYERS
Franklin and Eleanor Roosevelt

Critical Thinking: Summarizing Ask students to create a two-column chart in which they summarize the achievements and legacies of Franklin and Eleanor Roosevelt. Have them jot down in the first column words that describe FDR, and in the second column, words that describe Eleanor Roosevelt.

TEACHING OPTION

Making Connections Across Time

Unconventional First Ladies Tell students that Eleanor Roosevelt was frequently criticized for her active role as First Lady. During her husband's presidency, she made lecture tours, worked with children and the underprivileged, and fought for equal rights for minority groups. Although beloved by many, Roosevelt angered some Americans, who felt that she should pursue a more traditional role as wife and mother. In the 1990s, Hillary Rodham Clinton, wife of President Bill Clinton, was similarly criticized for the role she played in her husband's administration. A strong influence on her husband, Hillary Clinton was given a leadership role in the effort to reform health care. Some Americans felt that she had been given too much power. The First Lady admitted that at times, when she had felt overwhelmed by her critics, she had sought strength by looking to her role model—Eleanor Roosevelt.

HISTORY FROM VISUALS

Political Cartoon

Reading the Cartoon Ask students who the "patient" is. *Uncle Sam.* Ask them what he represents. *Possible Response: He represents the nation's sick economy.*

Extension Have students describe how Roosevelt and Congress are depicted in the cartoon. *Possible Response: Roosevelt is depicted as a trusted doctor, and Congress as a docile nurse.* Then ask them what the depictions suggest about the relationship between the president and Congress. *Possible Response: Congress was willing to pass anything Roosevelt proposed.*

OBJECTIVE

(2) INSTRUCT

Helping the American People

▶ ***Discussing Key Ideas***

- The Roosevelt administration establishes programs to provide relief to farmers, create jobs for other workers, and foster regional development.
- The National Industrial Recovery Act seeks to establish codes of fair practice for individual industries and promote industrial growth.
- Other New Deal programs focus on helping homeowners.

Banking Relief Act, which authorized the Treasury Department to inspect the country's banks. Those that were sound could reopen at once; those that were insolvent—unable to pay their debts—would remain closed. Those that needed help could receive loans. This measure revived public confidence in banks, since customers now had greater faith that the open banks were in good financial shape.

AN IMPORTANT FIRESIDE CHAT On March 12, the day before the first banks were to reopen, President Roosevelt boosted confidence further through the first of his many fireside chats. These were radio talks that Roosevelt gave occasionally about issues of public concern, explaining in clear, simple language his New Deal measures. Informal and relaxed, these talks made Americans feel as if the president were talking directly to them. In his first chat, President Roosevelt explained why the nation's welfare depended on public support of the government and the banking system. "We have provided the machinery to restore our financial system," he said. "It is up to you to support and make it work." This is how he explained the banking system.

SKILLBUILDER
INTERPRETING POLITICAL CARTOONS
What do you think was meant by Roosevelt's remark concerning New Deal remedies?

Skillbuilder Answer If one proposal or remedy didn't work, he would try another.

A PERSONAL VOICE

When you deposit money in a bank, the bank does not put the money into a safe deposit vault. It invests your money. . . . A comparatively small part of the money you put into the bank is kept in currency—an amount which in normal times is wholly sufficient to cover the cash needs of the ordinary citizen.

FRANKLIN DELANO ROOSEVELT

The president then explained that when too many people demanded their savings in cash, banks would fail. This did not mean that the banks were weak, because even strong banks could not meet such heavy demands.

Over the next few weeks, many Americans returned their savings to banks. Congress took another step to reorganize the banking system by passing the **Glass-Steagall Banking Act of 1933.** Among other provisions, this law established the Federal Deposit Insurance Corporation (FDIC), which provided federal insurance for individual bank accounts of less than $5,000. The Glass-Steagall Banking Act reassured millions of bank customers that their money was safe.

THINK THROUGH HISTORY
B. *Evaluating Decisions* *Why did bank customers return their savings to banks?*

B. Answer President Roosevelt explained that the banks weren't weak, and Congress established the Federal Deposit Insurance Corporation.

Congress and the president also took steps to regulate the stock market, which had suffered a tremendous loss of credibility in the crash of 1929. The **Federal Securities Act,** passed in May 1933, required corporations to provide complete information on all stock offerings and made them liable for any misrepresentations. The following year, in June 1934, Congress created the Securities and Exchange Commission (SEC) to regulate the stock market. One of the goals of this commission was to prevent people with inside information about companies from "rigging" the stock market, causing prices to go up or down for their own profit, regardless of the real value of the stocks.

In addition, Roosevelt persuaded Congress to approve a bill allowing the manufacture and sale of some alcoholic beverages. This bill included an alcohol tax designed to raise government revenues. By the end of 1933, the passage of the Twenty-first Amendment had repealed prohibition altogether.

Helping the American People

While working on banking and financial matters, the Roosevelt administration implemented programs to provide relief to farmers. It also aided other workers and attempted to stimulate economic recovery.

Block Schedule TEACHING OPTION **Time Needed: 30 Minutes**

Cooperative Activity: Delivering a Fireside Chat

Task: Groups of four to five students will write and record a Roosevelt-style radio talk that explains a New Deal program.

Purpose: To explore a New Deal program.

Activity: Groups of students should get together to choose the New Deal program they want to discuss in a fireside chat. Each student in a group should research and write about one aspect of the program—for example, its purpose, the people who benefited from it, the drawbacks of the program, and its results. Students should then compile their reports and tape-record the talk. Play the audiotapes in class and discuss them.

Building a Portfolio: Students may wish to add a transcript of their fireside chat to their portfolio.

ALTERNATIVE ASSESSMENT BOOK
Standards for Evaluating a Cooperative Activity

Standards for Evaluation
Fireside chats should . . .

- cover a New Deal program in depth
- be given in clear, simple language
- be delivered in a relaxed, informal manner that inspires confidence

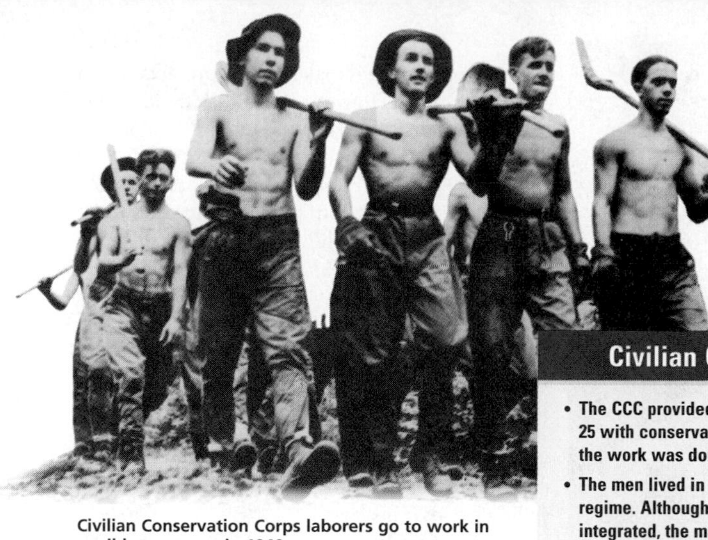

Civilian Conservation Corps laborers go to work in a wilderness area in 1940.

Civilian Conservation Corps

- The CCC provided unemployed men between 18 and 25 with conservation work and job training. Much of the work was done in U.S. national parks.
- The men lived in work camps under a military-like regime. Although some of the camps were integrated, the majority were segregated.
- The CCC provided almost 3 million men with work and wages between 1933 and 1942.
- Many New Deal agencies did little to give opportunities to African Americans. By 1938, however, the CCC had an 11 percent African-American enrollment.

ASSISTING FARMERS The **Agricultural Adjustment Act** (AAA) sought to raise crop prices by lowering production, which the government achieved by paying farmers to leave a certain amount of every acre of land unseeded. The theory was that reduced supply would boost prices. (See *supply and demand* on page 939 in the Economics Handbook.) In some cases crops were too far advanced for the acreage reduction to take effect. As a result, the government paid cotton growers $200 million to plow under 10 million acres of their crop. It also paid hog farmers to slaughter 6 million pigs. This policy upset many Americans, who protested the destruction of food when many people were going hungry. It did, however, help raise farm prices and put more money in farmers' pockets.

PROVIDING WORK PROJECTS The administration also established programs to provide relief through work projects and cash payments. One important program, the **Civilian Conservation Corps** (CCC), put young men, aged 18 to 25, to work building roads, developing parks, planting trees, and helping in soil-erosion and flood-control projects. The CCC paid a small wage, $30 a month, of which $25 was automatically sent home to the worker's family. It also supplied free food and uniforms. By the time the program ended in 1942, almost 3 million young men had passed through the CCC. Many of the camps were located on the Great Plains, where, within a period of eight years, the men of the CCC planted more than 200 million trees. This tremendous reforestation program was aimed at preventing another Dust Bowl.

Another program, the Federal Emergency Relief Administration (FERA), was funded with $500 million to provide direct relief for the needy. Half of the money was given to the states as direct grants-in-aid to help furnish food and clothing to the unemployed, the aged, and the ill. An additional $250 million was distributed on the basis of one federal dollar for every three state dollars contributed. Harry Hopkins, who headed this program, believed that money helped people buy food, but work enabled them to gain confidence and self-respect.

THINK THROUGH HISTORY
C. Finding Main Ideas *In what two ways did the New Deal attempt to assist the unemployed?*

C. Answer By providing jobs and direct relief.

The Public Works Administration (PWA), created in June 1933, provided money to states to create jobs. These were chiefly in the construction of schools and other community buildings. When these programs failed to make a sufficient dent in unemployment, President Roosevelt established the Civil Works Administration (CWA) in November 1933. It provided 4 million immediate jobs during the winter of 1933–1934. Some critics of the CWA claimed that

> *"Eighteen million Americans are so poor of this world's goods that they are on relief."*
>
> HARRY HOPKINS

HISTORY FROM VISUALS
Civilian Conservation Corps

Reading the Chart Point out to students how the chart and the photograph complement each other. As the chart reveals, the CCC provided unemployed men with work and wages. This work made the men feel better about themselves, a mood that the picture seems to capture.

Extension Have students create a chart to keep track of the New Deal programs listed on pages 507 and 508. Students should name each program and list its purpose and results. The chart might look like this:

Program	Purpose	Results

MORE ABOUT . . .
Harry L. Hopkins

Hopkins was a loyal FDR supporter who once declared, "There is a new day, and this is it, and Roosevelt is its leader." As head of FERA, Hopkins worked to promote his relief program and quiet skeptics. Above all, he tried to impress his audience with the magnitude of the crisis—18 million people in need of relief.

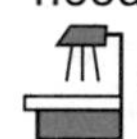

GEOGRAPHY TRANSPARENCIES
G23, P. W. A. in Action

TEACHING OPTIONS

Exploring Themes

Economic Opportunity Discuss the federal government's role in supporting and regulating agriculture and industry under the New Deal. Ask students the following questions:

- Why did the government take the measures it did?
- Was the government justified in taking them?
- Do you think the Roosevelt administration went too far or did not go far enough?
- How much control does the government have today over agriculture and industry?

Making Connections Across Cultures

The New Deal for African Americans Discuss the fact that many New Deal agencies provided few opportunities for African Americans and that discrimination was still widespread. Then tell students that in spite of the discrimination, most African Americans supported Roosevelt because New Deal agencies, particularly at the state level, gave them more assistance than they had ever received before. For example, between 1933 and 1936, the PWA spent four times as much on black schools and hospitals as had been spent by governments in the previous 30 years.

MORE ABOUT . . .
FDR's Handicap
Throughout his presidency, Roosevelt was rarely photographed in his wheelchair. Although people knew that he had been crippled by polio, Roosevelt wished to appear as a strong, healthy man. In public, Roosevelt walked and stood, supported on either side by his aides. Every movement cost him great pain and fatigue, but he always grinned and waved energetically to the crowds. In March 1945, just about a month before his death, Roosevelt made a rare public reference to his physical disability as he spoke before Congress: "I hope that you will pardon me for this unusual posture of sitting down, . . . but . . . it makes it a lot easier for me not to have to carry about 10 pounds of steel around at the bottom of my legs."

OBJECTIVE
 **INSTRUCT**

The New Deal Comes Under Attack

▶ ***Discussing Key Ideas***
- Both conservative and liberal critics oppose New Deal policies.
- After the Supreme Court strikes down two of Roosevelt's new programs, the president proposes a bill that would allow him to appoint six new justices to the Court.
- Charles Coughlin, Francis Townsend, and Huey Long are among Roosevelt's toughest critics.

Franklin D. Roosevelt was fond of spending time at Hyde Park, New York, his birthplace on the bank of the Hudson River. Here, he is holding his dog Fala and talking to a young family friend.

the programs were "make-work" projects and a waste of money. However, the CWA built 40,000 schools and paid the salaries of more than 50,000 schoolteachers in America's rural areas. It also built more than half a million miles of roads.

Another major initiative of the Roosevelt administration was the **National Industrial Recovery Act** (NIRA), passed in June 1933. This act sought to promote industrial growth by establishing codes of fair practice for individual industries. It created the National Recovery Administration (NRA), which set prices of many products to ensure fair competition, and established standards for working hours and a ban on child labor. The aim of the NRA was to promote recovery by interrupting the trend of wage cuts, falling prices, and layoffs.

Competing businesses met with representatives of workers and consumers to draft the codes of fair competition. These codes both limited production and established prices. Because businesses were given new concessions, workers made demands. Congress met their demands by passing a section of the NIRA guaranteeing workers' right to unionize and to bargain collectively.

THINK THROUGH HISTORY
D. THEME
Economic Opportunity
How did the New Deal support labor organizations?
D. Answer It guaranteed workers' right to unionize and to bargain collectively.

Many businesses and politicians were critical of the NRA. Charges arose that the codes served large business interests. There were also charges of increasing code violations. The economist Gardiner C. Means, however, stated the goal of industrial planning.

A PERSONAL VOICE
The National Recovery Administration [was] created in response to an overwhelming demand from many quarters that certain elements in the making of industrial policy . . . should no longer be left to the market place and the price mechanism but should be placed in the hands of administrative bodies.
GARDINER C. MEANS, *The Making of Industrial Policy*

Finally, the Roosevelt administration undertook an especially ambitious program of regional development. The Tennessee Valley Authority (TVA), established on May 18, 1933, focused on the badly depressed Tennessee River valley. The TVA renovated five existing dams and constructed 20 new ones in the Tennessee Valley. It created thousands of jobs and provided flood control, hydroelectric power, and other benefits to an impoverished region.

HELPING PEOPLE WITH HOUSING A number of New Deal programs concerned housing and home mortgage problems. The Home Owners Loan Corporation (HOLC) provided government loans to homeowners who faced foreclosure because they couldn't meet their loan payments. In addition, the National Housing Act created the Federal Housing Administration (FHA). This agency continues to furnish loans for home mortgages and repairs today.

The New Deal Comes Under Attack

At the end of the Hundred Days, President Roosevelt could look back on some major accomplishments. Together with Congress, his administration had moved decisively to implement a series of programs designed to provide benefits for millions of Americans. In general, public confidence in the nation's future had rebounded.

TEACHING OPTION

Making Connections Across Time

The TVA Today Tell students that the TVA was a highly controversial program for many years. Private power companies opposed what they viewed as the government's interference in private business. State and local agencies in Tennessee feared that the federal government would take over their functions in the region. In spite of its rocky beginnings, the TVA has greatly benefited the Tennessee Valley. Over the years, the TVA has built dams, created electric power, deepened rivers for shipping, planted new forests and protected existing ones, and developed highly effective fertilizers. The TVA has helped individuals by providing low-interest loans to homeowners and businesses. It has also provided inexpensive power to people in the region—one of the program's original goals. A consumer of TVA power today still pays about one-third less per kilowatt-hour than the average American consumer.

Nevertheless, opposition to the New Deal grew among some parts of the population. Liberal critics argued that the New Deal did not go far enough to help the poor and to reform the nation's economic system. Conservative critics argued just the opposite: that Roosevelt spent too much on direct relief and used New Deal policies to control business and socialize the economy. Conservatives were particularly angered by laws such as the Agricultural Adjustment Act and the National Industrial Recovery Act, which they believed gave the federal government too much control over agriculture and industry. Many New Deal critics thought the Roosevelt administration was going too far in its attempt to regulate the production and supply of goods and to control prices. They believed the New Deal interfered with the workings of a free market economy.

THINK THROUGH HISTORY
E. *Comparing* *How did liberal and conservative critics differ in their opposition to the New Deal?*

E. Answer Liberal critics thought the New Deal did not go far enough in helping the poor and in reforming the nation's economic system; conservative critics believed the New Deal spent too much money on direct relief and was trying to control business and socialize the economy.

THE SUPREME COURT REACTS By the mid-1930s, conservative opposition to the New Deal had received a boost from two Supreme Court decisions. In 1935, the Court struck down the NIRA as unconstitutional, declaring that the law gave legislative powers to the executive branch. It also argued that the enforcement of industry codes within states went beyond the federal government's constitutional powers, which are limited to the regulation of interstate commerce. The next year, the Supreme Court struck down the AAA on the grounds that agriculture is a local matter and should be regulated by the states rather than the federal government.

THAT COMPASS DOESN'T POINT THE WAY I WANT TO GO. CHANGE IT. NOW!
FDR
SUPREME
CONGRESS

SKILLBUILDER
INTERPRETING POLITICAL CARTOONS
What "compass" did Roosevelt want to change, and why?
Skillbuilder Answer FDR wanted to change the Supreme Court compass because the Court had ruled that some of his actions were unconstitutional.

President Roosevelt was dismayed by these rulings. Fearing that further Court decisions might dismantle the New Deal, in February 1937 he proposed that Congress enact a court-reform bill that would reorganize the federal judiciary and allow him to appoint six new Supreme Court justices. Although Roosevelt argued that the bill would make the judiciary more effective, it was clearly designed to create a Supreme Court more sympathetic to New Deal programs. Quickly labeled the "court-packing bill," Roosevelt's proposal aroused a storm of protest in Congress and the press. Many people believed that the president was violating principles of judicial independence and the separation of powers. The bill damaged the president's public image. Then events that the president could not have foreseen led to changes in the Court. Rulings of the Court began to shift in favor of the New Deal, and, without reorganizing the judiciary, President Roosevelt managed to appoint new justices who supported the New Deal. Because of resignations, the president was able to appoint seven new justices in the next four years.

F. Answer Because Roosevelt, as the head of the executive branch, was trying to exercise too much influence over the judiciary, another branch of government; the branches are supposed to remain independent of each other.

THINK THROUGH HISTORY
F. *Analyzing Issues* *Why did people regard FDR's court-packing scheme as a threat to the separation of powers?*

THREE FIERY CRITICS In 1934, some of the strongest conservative opponents of the New Deal banded together to form an organization called the American Liberty League. This group was largely made up of wealthy business leaders. It also included important political leaders: Al Smith and John W. Davis, both former Democratic presidential candidates. The American Liberty League opposed New Deal measures that it believed violated respect for the rights of individuals and property. The group accused President Roosevelt of trying to establish a dictatorship. Perhaps the toughest critics the president faced, however, were three men who expressed views that appealed to poor Americans: Charles Coughlin, Francis Townsend, and Huey Long.

HISTORY FROM VISUALS
Political Cartoon

Reading the Cartoon Ask students what uniform Roosevelt is wearing in the cartoon. *A ship captain's uniform.* Ask them what the ship represents. *The country; the government.* Then ask them what figure represents Congress. *A sailor.* Have them tell what the cartoon is referring to. *FDR's efforts to pack the Supreme Court.*

Extension Have students compare the depiction of Roosevelt and Congress in this cartoon with the depiction in the cartoon on page 506. Ask them how the apparent relationship between FDR and Congress differs in the two cartoons. *Possible Response: In the other cartoon, Congress seems to be deferring to the president. In this cartoon, Congress seems shocked by a power-mad FDR.* Then ask students what they think might account for the change. *Possible Response: FDR's attempts to pack the Supreme Court suggested to many people that the president had too much power.*

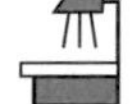
HUMANITIES TRANSPARENCIES
H40, Nine Old Men

TEACHING OPTION

Skillbuilder Mini-Lesson: Analyzing Issues

Explaining the Skill An issue is a matter of debate or of public concern. Typically, issues in history are economic, social, political, or moral in nature. Examples of such issues are the desirability of balancing the national budget, the effectiveness of various welfare programs, the desirability of campaign finance reforms, and the extent to which a nation has responsibilities to other nations. Analyzing such an issue involves defining the central problem and examining differing points of view.

Applying the Skill: Think Through History Question To answer the question about the Supreme Court on this page, students will need to identify the following aspects of the issue:

1. The central problem (President Roosevelt's attempt to change and control the makeup of the Supreme Court)
2. The different points of view on the issue (Roosevelt wanted a Court that would be sympathetic to his New Deal programs. His opponents feared that presidential control over the Court would influence justices to side with the president rather than the Constitution.)

IN-DEPTH RESOURCES: UNIT 4
Skillbuilder Practice: Analyzing Issues, p. 58

ANOTHER PERSPECTIVE
Townsend's Pension Plan
Critical Thinking: Analyzing Ask students why they think Townsend stipulated that recipients of the pension spend all the money within 30 days.
Possible Response: He wanted the money to be recirculated in the economy.

IN-DEPTH RESOURCES: UNIT 4
Primary Source: *from* Father Coughlin's Anti-New Deal Speech, p. 63
American Lives: Huey Long, p. 70

ASSESS & RETEACH

Section 1 Assessment
Have pairs of students work together to answer the questions.

Self-Assessment
Students can document what they have learned in Section 1 by creating a cluster diagram in which they list each New Deal program and its goals.

Section Quiz

FORMAL ASSESSMENT
Section Quiz, p. 187

Reteach
Use the Section Quiz to help students review the section's main ideas.

CLOSE

When Franklin Roosevelt took office in 1933, he immediately launched the first of his New Deal programs, which focused on relief for the needy, economic recovery, and financial reform. Many Americans approved of the New Deal measures, but others criticized them—some for doing too little, some for doing too much. Roosevelt responded to those who felt he could do more by extending his programs in the Second New Deal—the next phase of his program.

ANOTHER PERSPECTIVE

TOWNSEND'S PENSION PLAN

Francis Townsend devised his pension plan after being laid off at age 67 with only $100 in savings. His plan called for all Americans over age 60 to receive a monthly pension of $200, on the condition that they spend the money within 30 days. Townsend claimed that his plan would stop poverty among the elderly and end the Depression by pumping money into the economy. Although his plan was financially unrealistic, it did draw attention to the needs of the elderly.

One of President Roosevelt's most vocal critics was Father Charles Coughlin, a Roman Catholic priest from a suburb of Detroit. Every Sunday, Father Coughlin broadcast radio sermons that combined economic, political, and religious ideas. Initially a supporter of the New Deal, Coughlin soon turned against Roosevelt. He favored a guaranteed annual income and the nationalization of banks. At the height of his popularity, Father Coughlin claimed a radio audience of some 40 million people, but his increasingly anti-Semitic (anti-Jewish) views eventually cost him support.

Another critic of New Deal policies was Dr. Francis Townsend, a physician and health officer in Long Beach, California. He believed that Roosevelt wasn't doing enough to help the poor and elderly, so he devised a pension plan that would provide monthly benefits to the aged. The plan was too expensive to work, but it found strong backing among the elderly, and it undermined their support for President Roosevelt.

Perhaps the most serious challenge to the New Deal came from Senator **Huey Long** of Louisiana. Long was a former traveling salesman, but he had studied law and become a persuasive spokesman for the poor. He was elected governor of Louisiana in 1928 and later served in the United States Senate.

Like Coughlin, Long was an early supporter of the New Deal, but he soon turned against Roosevelt. Eager to win the presidency for himself, Long proposed a nationwide social program called Share Our Wealth. Under the banner "Every Man a King," he promised something for everyone.

A PERSONAL VOICE

> We owe debts in America today, public and private, amounting to $252 billion. That means that every child is born with a $2,000 debt tied around his neck. . . . We propose that children shall be born in a land of opportunity, guaranteed a home, food, clothes, and the other things that make for living, including the right to education.
>
> **HUEY LONG,** *Record, 74 Congress, Session 1.*

Long's program for sharing the nation's wealth was so popular that by 1935, he boasted of having over 27,000 Share-Our-Wealth clubs with around 7.5 million members. In 1935, however, at the height of his popularity, Long was assassinated by a lone gunman.

As the initial impetus of the New Deal began to wane, President Roosevelt started to look ahead. He knew that a lot more needed to be done to help the people and to solve the nation's economic problems.

Senator Huey Long emphasizes a point during a 1935 speech in Des Moines, Iowa.

G. Answer They said that the New Deal didn't go far enough in helping the poor and elderly. It didn't provide a guaranteed annual income or other benefits.

THINK THROUGH HISTORY
G. Comparing *What did Charles Coughlin, Francis Townsend, and Huey Long dislike about the New Deal?*

Section 1 Assessment

1. TERMS & NAMES
Identify:
- Franklin Delano Roosevelt
- New Deal
- Glass-Steagall Banking Act of 1933
- Federal Securities Act
- Agricultural Adjustment Act
- Civilian Conservation Corps
- National Industrial Recovery Act
- Huey Long

2. SUMMARIZING In a two-column chart, list problems that Franklin Roosevelt confronted as president and how he tried to solve them.

Problem	Solution

Write a paragraph telling which problem you think was most critical, and why.

3. INTERPRETING Of the New Deal programs discussed in this section, which do you consider the most important? Explain your choice.

THINK ABOUT
- the type of assistance offered by each program
- the scope of each program
- the impact of each program

4. ANALYZING Do you think Roosevelt's most vocal critics had reasonable objections?

THINK ABOUT
- the American Liberty League's beliefs regarding violation of rights
- Father Coughlin's calls for nationalization
- Huey Long's slogan "Every Man a King"

510 Chapter 15

ANSWERS

1. TERMS & NAMES
Franklin Delano Roosevelt, p. 504
New Deal, p. 505
Glass-Steagall Banking Act of 1933, p. 506
Federal Securities Act, p. 506
Agricultural Adjustment Act, p. 507
Civilian Conservation Corps, p. 507
National Industrial Recovery Act, p. 508
Huey Long, p. 510

2. SUMMARIZING
Possible Responses: **Problem:** lack of confidence in banks. **Solution:** bank holiday, Treasury inspection of banks, deposit insurance. **Problem:** little confidence in stock market. **Solution:** regulation of stock market. **Problem:** low farm prices. **Solution:** paying farmers not to raise crops. **Problem:** massive unemployment. **Solution:** federal jobs programs. **Problem:** poverty in Tennessee River Valley. **Solution:** build dams. **Problem:** mortgage foreclosures. **Solution:** government loans to homeowners.

3. INTERPRETING
Possible Responses: The FDIC, because it boosted confidence in banks; the CCC, because it provided badly needed jobs, raised morale, and helped the environment; the NRA, because it helped workers of the 1930s.

4. ANALYZING
Possible Responses: **Yes:** Programs such as the NIRA and AAA should have been curtailed when they infringed on the rights of free enterprise and gave excessive control to government. **No:** Few of the critics' solutions were practical. They might have made things worse.

2 The Second New Deal Takes Hold

TERMS & NAMES
- Eleanor Roosevelt
- Works Progress Administration
- National Youth Administration
- Wagner Act
- Social Security Act

LEARN ABOUT the second phase of New Deal policies
TO UNDERSTAND how the Roosevelt administration tried to extend its relief, recovery, and reform programs.

ONE AMERICAN'S STORY

Dorothea Lange was a photographer whose pictures documented American life during the Great Depression and the era of the New Deal. One famous picture, entitled *Migrant Mother,* shows a woman and her children in a migrant labor camp in California in the winter of 1936. In her biography, Lange recalled the circumstances of that photograph.

A PERSONAL VOICE

I saw and approached the hungry and desperate mother, as if drawn by a magnet. I do not remember how I explained my presence or my camera to her, but I do remember she asked me no questions. . . . She told me her age, that she was 32. She said that they had been living on frozen vegetables from the surrounding fields, and birds that the children killed. She had just sold the tires from her car to buy food. There she sat in that lean-to tent with her children huddled around her, and seemed to know that my pictures might help her, and so she helped me. There was a sort of equality about it.

DOROTHEA LANGE, quoted in *Dorothea Lange: A Photographer's Life*

Much of Lange's work was funded by a federal agency, the Farm Security Administration, which was established to alleviate rural poverty. Lange's photographs helped draw attention to the desperate conditions in rural America and to underscore the need for direct relief.

Dorothea Lange's photograph *Migrant Mother* captures the concern of a weary mother for her children.

The Second Hundred Days

By 1935, the Roosevelt administration was seeking ways to build on the programs established during the Hundred Days. Although the economy had improved during FDR's first two years in office, the gains were not as great as he had expected. Unemployment remained high despite government work programs, and production still lagged behind the levels of the 1920s.

Nevertheless, the New Deal enjoyed widespread popularity. In the 1934 midterm election, the Democrats increased their majority in both houses of Congress. The Democrats now held 319 seats in the House and 69 in the Senate, while the Republicans held just 103 House seats and 25 Senate seats.

Buoyed by these results, President Roosevelt launched a second burst of activity, often called the Second New Deal or the Second Hundred Days. During this phase, the president called on Congress to provide more extensive relief for both farmers and workers. He encouraged them to help the "forgotten man," as he called the poor and dispossessed at the bottom of society. The president was prodded in this direction by his wife, **Eleanor Roosevelt,** a social reformer who combined her deep humanitarian impulses with great political skills.

SECTION 2 RESOURCES

PRINT RESOURCES

IN-DEPTH RESOURCES: UNIT 4
Guided Reading, p. 54

READING STUDY GUIDE, p. 157

ACCESS FOR STUDENTS ACQUIRING ENGLISH
Guided Reading (Spanish), p. 176

SPANISH READING STUDY GUIDE, p. 157

FORMAL ASSESSMENT
Section Quiz, p. 188

ALTERNATIVE ASSESSMENT BOOK
See forms for supporting and scoring alternative activities.

TECHNOLOGY RESOURCES

CD-ROM *Grolier Multimedia Encyclopedia*

VIDEO *American Portfolio: A Videodisc for U.S. History* user's guide, pp. 207–209

INTERNET http://www.mlushistory.com

Section 2 Overview

OBJECTIVES

1. To describe the purpose of the Second New Deal.
2. To summarize Second New Deal programs that helped farmers.
3. To describe Second New Deal programs that helped youths and professionals.
4. To summarize labor and economic reforms under the Second New Deal.

CRITICAL THINKING

- Analyzing, pp. 513, 516
- Forming opinions, p. 513
- Finding main ideas, p. 514
- Summarizing, p. 516
- Evaluating, p. 516

FOCUS & MOTIVATE

5-MINUTE WARM-UP

Recognizing Facts and Details
To understand the suffering caused by the Depression, have students study the photo on page 511 and answer these questions.

1. How are the mother and children dressed? What does their appearance suggest?
2. What emotions does the woman's expression convey?

WARM-UP TRANSPARENCY 15

▶ ***Starting with the Student***
- What do students do to earn money?
- What would students do if they couldn't find a job? Would they expect the government to help?

OBJECTIVE

1 INSTRUCT

The Second Hundred Days

▶ ***Discussing Key Ideas***
- Although FDR's programs do not bring economic gains as great as expected, the New Deal enjoys widespread popularity.

(continued on next page)

(continued from page 511)

- Roosevelt launches the Second New Deal and seeks to help the "forgotten man."
- The 1936 election results in an overwhelming victory for Roosevelt and the Democrats in Congress.

IN-DEPTH RESOURCES: UNIT 4
Guided Reading, p. 54

ACCESS FOR STUDENTS ACQUIRING ENGLISH
Guided Reading (Spanish), p. 176

OBJECTIVE
 **INSTRUCT**

Helping Farmers

▶ ***Discussing Key Ideas***
- Under the Second New Deal, Congress passes legislation to help farmers.
- The Second New Deal seeks to help sharecroppers and migrant workers.

MORE ABOUT . . .
The Grapes of Wrath

John Steinbeck's novel *The Grapes of Wrath,* which focuses on the plight of migrant farm workers in the 1930s, won the 1939 Pulitzer Prize in fiction. The novel was made into a film in 1940. The movie won Academy Awards for its director, John Ford, and for actress Jane Darwell. Henry Fonda was nominated for best actor, and the film itself was nominated for best picture.

Eleanor Roosevelt traveled the country tirelessly, observing social conditions and helping to shape New Deal policies. She candidly and almost continuously reminded the president about the suffering of the nation's people. She also reminded him to appoint women to government positions. As a great advocate of rights for poor people, women, and minorities, she gave a caring, human face to the Roosevelt administration.

REELECTING FDR The Second New Deal was under way by the time of the 1936 presidential election. The Republicans nominated Alfred Landon, the governor of Kansas. Although Landon criticized FDR, he didn't suggest that the entire New Deal be scrapped. The Democrats, of course, nominated President Roosevelt for a second term. The president assailed his critics. He asked the crowds of people, "Are you better off than you were four years ago?" The crowds roared back, "Yes."

The election resulted in an overwhelming victory for the Democrats. FDR carried every state except two: Maine and Vermont. His popular vote was 27.7 million to Landon's 16.6 million, and he received 523 electoral votes to Landon's 8. The Democrats achieved a congressional majority of 331 to 89 in the House and 76 to 16 in the Senate. This great Democratic victory marked the first time that most African Americans had voted Democratic rather than Republican. It was also the first time that labor unions gave united support to a presidential candidate instead of dividing their votes between two major parties. The 1936 election represented a vote of confidence in FDR and the New Deal.

Helping Farmers

One important goal of the Second New Deal was to help the nation's farmers. In the mid-1930s, rural areas continued to suffer some of the most difficult social and economic conditions in the United States. Nevertheless, recovery in the farm area had begun, partly as a result of the Agricultural Adjustment Act.

When the Supreme Court struck down the AAA early in 1936, Congress passed another law to replace it: the Soil Conservation and Domestic Allotment Act. This act paid farmers for cutting production of soil-depleting crops like cotton and wheat. It also rewarded farmers for practicing good soil conservation methods. Two years later, in 1938, Congress approved a second Agricultural Adjustment Act that brought back many features of the first AAA. The second AAA did not include a processing tax to pay for farm subsidies, a provision of the first AAA that the Supreme Court had declared unconstitutional.

In the mid-1930s, two of every five farms in the United States were mortgaged. As the Depression deepened, thousands of small farmers lost their farms. The land went to the mortgage holders—insurance companies and banks. In time, many small farms became part of large mechanized farms or were destroyed as the land was cleared for new development. The novelist John Steinbeck described the experience of one tenant farmer and his family.

A poster promotes the movie adaptation of John Steinbeck's novel *The Grapes of Wrath.*

A PERSONAL VOICE

Across the dooryard the tractor cut, and the hard, foot-beaten ground was seeded field, and the tractor cut through again; the uncut space was ten feet wide. And back he came. The iron guard bit into the house-corner, crumbled the wall, and wrenched the little house from its foundation so that it fell sideways, crushed like a bug. . . . The tractor cut a straight line on, and the air and ground vibrated with its thunder. The tenant man stared after it, his rifle in his hand. His wife was beside him, and the quiet children behind. And all of them stared after the tractor.

JOHN STEINBECK, *The Grapes of Wrath*

TEACHING OPTIONS

Teaching Less Proficient Readers

Clarifying Ideas To enable students to understand the Second New Deal measures to help farmers (pages 512–513), have them follow these steps:

1. Read the section, a paragraph at a time.
2. List the program described, including its former name, if applicable.
3. List the purpose of the program and the people who benefited from it.
4. Add to the list as you read about other New Deal programs.

Teaching Gifted and Talented Students

See with a Photographer's Eye Encourage students to take photographs that capture a segment of society. Have students do the following:

- Select a group to study, such as children, teenagers, or the elderly.
- Take photos of people in the group, capturing their strengths, weaknesses, energy, despair—whatever you want to convey.
- Write captions for the photos.
- Assemble the photos in an album.

The Second New Deal also attempted to help sharecroppers, migrant workers, and many other poor farmers. In May 1935, Congress created the Resettlement Administration to loan money to small farmers to buy land. It was hoped that this agency would help tenant farmers and sharecroppers resettle on more productive farmland. In 1937, this agency was replaced by the Farm Security Administration (FSA), which loaned more than $1 billion to help tenant farmers become landholders. The FSA also established a network of camps for migrant farm workers, who had traditionally lived in squalid housing.

THINK THROUGH HISTORY
A. *Analyzing* *How did the Second New Deal help sharecroppers, migrant workers, and other poor farmers?*

Another activity of the FSA was making a pictorial record that showed the difficult situation of people in rural America. The agency sent photographers such as Dorothea Lange, Ben Shahn, Walker Evans, Arthur Rothstein, and Carl Mydans to take many pictures of rural towns and farms and their inhabitants.

Helping Youth, Professionals, and Others

A. Answer It established agencies to loan money to small farmers to buy land, and it set up a network of camps for migrant farm workers.

Farmers weren't the only Americans who received direct assistance during the Second New Deal. The Roosevelt administration and Congress also set up a series of programs to help youths, professionals, and other workers. One of the largest programs begun under the New Deal was the **Works Progress Administration** (WPA), headed by Harry Hopkins, the former chief of the Federal Emergency Relief Administration.

The WPA set out to create as many jobs as possible as quickly as possible. It received a budget of $5 billion, the largest sum any nation had ever spent for public welfare at one time. Between 1935 and 1943, it employed more than 8 million persons. WPA workers, most of them unskilled, built 850 airports throughout the country. They constructed or repaired 651,000 miles of roads and streets. They put up 110,000 libraries, schools, and hospitals. Sewing groups, in which most of the WPA's female workers were employed, made 300 million garments for the needy. Some people criticized the WPA, as they had the CWA, as a "make-work" program that created jobs just to provide workers with a paycheck. Nevertheless, the WPA did produce public works of lasting value to the nation, and it gave working people a sense of hope and purpose that had been sorely lacking. As one man recalled, "It was really great. You worked, you got a paycheck, and you had some dignity. Even when a man raked leaves, he got paid, he had some dignity."

Unemployed workers sit on a street in an Oklahoma town, in a 1936 photograph by Dorothea Lange.

The WPA also employed many professionals—including teachers, writers, artists, actors, and musicians. These professionals were hired to create music, art, and scholarly studies. They wrote guides to cities, collected historical slave narratives, painted murals on the walls of schools and other public buildings, and performed in theater troupes around the country. At the urging of Eleanor Roosevelt, the WPA made special efforts to help women, minorities, and young people.

B. Answer Some students may say that they were valid, since they provided income to people in need, while producing public works. Other students may say that private business, rather than the federal government, should provide jobs.

THINK THROUGH HISTORY
B. *Forming Opinions* *Do you think work programs like the WPA were a valid use of federal money? Why or why not?*

Another program, the **National Youth Administration** (NYA), was

OBJECTIVE
③ INSTRUCT

Helping Youth, Professionals, and Others

Discussing Key Ideas
- The WPA offers direct assistance by creating new jobs.
- The NYA is created specifically to provide aid and employment to young people.

MORE ABOUT . . .
The WPA

Some people objected to the WPA's giving assistance to writers and artists. Art, they claimed, was not real work. The program's critics probably didn't anticipate that the work produced then by many of the artists would be worth far more today than any wages they received from the WPA. One artist recalled the WPA's Federal Art Project: "The total cost of the Federal Art Project was only $23 million. Many of these paintings, sculptures, and prints were given to museums, courthouses, public buildings. . . . I think that today those in museums alone are worth about $100 million." He may be right. The abstract expressionist painter Jackson Pollock received $7,800 from the WPA. In 1996, his WPA-funded paintings were valued at more than half a million dollars.

TEACHING OPTIONS

Making Connections Across the Curriculum

Literature Tell students that some people who received assistance from the WPA went on to become successful writers. For example, Pulitzer Prize–winning author Saul Bellow got his first literary job under the WPA's Federal Writers' Project. The project also enabled African-American author Richard Wright to write his highly acclaimed first novel, *Native Son.* The WPA produced the American Guide Series, which was written in collaboration with local groups. Volumes in this series were produced for all the states as well as for outlying territories. They included comprehensive descriptions of each place.

Making Connections Across the Curriculum

Art Tell students that many of the WPA-funded murals and paintings still decorate public buildings throughout the United States. Encourage students to look in the library for books containing reproductions of these works. Ask students to bring the books to class and discuss the artwork. Point out to students the existence of any WPA murals or paintings in their community. Post offices and schools are two likely locations for such works. If any murals or paintings are located, you might assign groups of students to research them and report on them to the class.

OBJECTIVE

④ INSTRUCT

Labor and Other Reforms

▶ *Starting with the Student* Have students create a cluster diagram, similar to the one below, to organize information on the reforms enacted by the Second New Deal. As students read this section, they should list the main reforms under each category.

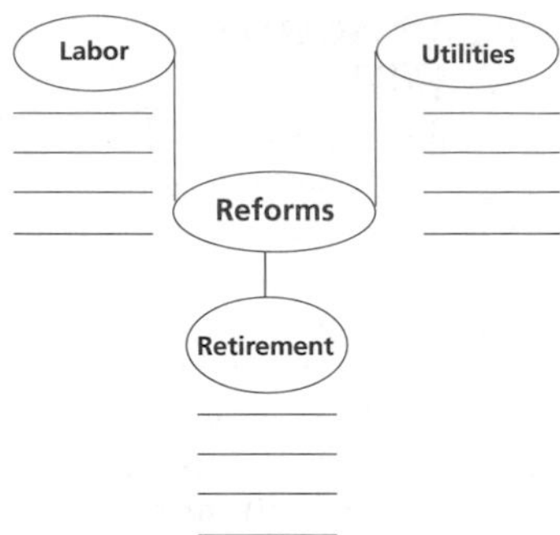

▶ *Discussing Key Ideas*

- Congress passes labor reforms proposed by the Roosevelt administration that establish maximum hours and minimum wages.
- The Social Security system provides economic security for retired workers and financial benefits for millions of other Americans.
- The Second New Deal promotes rural electrification and seeks to regulate public utilities.

created specifically to help young people. The project was highly successful in providing aid and employment to young Americans. More than 2 million high school and college students worked in part-time clerical positions at their schools. One participant later described her experience.

> A PERSONAL VOICE
>
> I lugged . . . drafts and reams of paper home, night after night. . . . Sometimes I typed almost all night and had to deliver it to school the next morning. . . . This was a good program. It got necessary work done. It gave teenagers a chance to work for pay. Mine bought me clothes and shoes, school supplies, some movies and mad money. Candy bars, and big pickles out of a barrel. It gave my mother relief from my necessary demands for money.
>
> **HELEN FARMER,** quoted in *The Great Depression*

In 1936, more than 200,000 students received aid and assistance through the NYA. It also provided work-relief programs for hundreds of young adults.

Labor and Other Reforms

During the Second New Deal, the Roosevelt administration moved beyond relief to enact sweeping reforms. (See the chart on page 515.) In a speech to Congress in January 1935, the president declared, "When a man is getting over an illness, wisdom dictates not only cure of the symptoms but removal of their cause." With the help of Congress, Roosevelt brought about important reforms in the areas of labor relations and economic security for retired workers.

IMPROVING LABOR CONDITIONS One of the first reforms of the Second New Deal was prompted by the Supreme Court's declaring the NIRA unconstitutional in 1935. In addition to setting industry standards, the National Recovery Administration had provided some protections for workers, such as a 40-hour week and a ban on child labor.

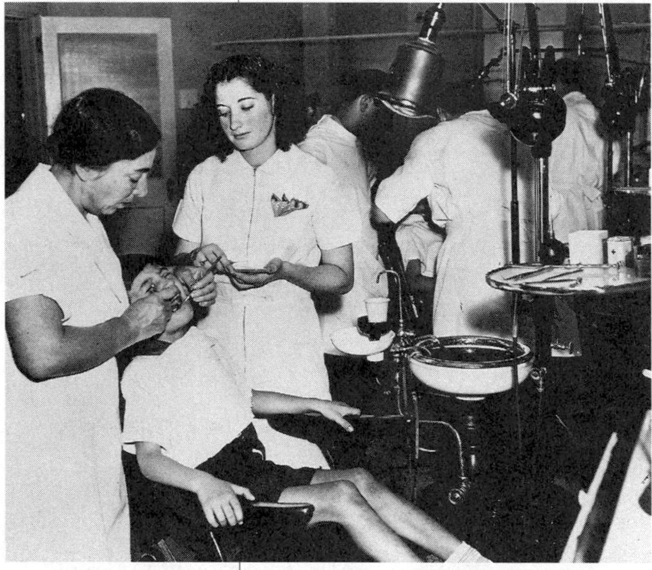

The National Youth Administration helped young people, such as this dental assistant *(third from left)*, receive training and job opportunities.

After the Supreme Court declared the NIRA unconstitutional, Congress passed the National Labor Relations Act, more commonly called the **Wagner Act,** after its sponsor, Senator Robert F. Wagner of New York. The act reestablished the NIRA provision involving collective bargaining. The federal government now supported the right of workers to join unions and to engage in collective bargaining with employers.

In addition, the Wagner Act listed unfair labor practices that companies could not use. Among these were threatening workers, firing union members, and interfering with union organizing efforts. The act also set up the National Labor Relations Board (NLRB) to hear testimony about unfair practices and to hold elections among workers to find out if they wanted union representation.

Congress later passed the Fair Labor Standards Act in 1938 to establish maximum hours and minimum wages. The hours and wages standards set by the National Recovery Administration had been invalidated when the Supreme Court declared the NIRA unconstitutional. The Fair Labor

C. Answer It reversed the position of the federal government from favoring employers to supporting workers.

THINK THROUGH HISTORY
C. Finding Main Ideas *Why was the Wagner Act significant?*

TEACHING OPTIONS

Exploring Themes

Economic Opportunity Discuss the impact of the Wagner Act on labor conditions. Point out that the act gave more power to unions—including the support of the federal government. Ask students what this support meant for workers. *Possible Response: Labor would have more leverage in disputes.* Then ask them how the act affects labor and labor unions today. *Possible Response: Today labor unions are powerful, politically influential institutions.*

Making Connections Across Time

Social Security Today Tell students that today the Social Security system continues to pay benefits to retired workers. Then tell them that when the program was established in 1935, the number of retirees was relatively small. Point out that this number will begin to increase in 2010 when members of the baby-boom generation (those born between 1946 and 1964) begin to retire. Tell them that the government predicts that because retirees will increasingly outnumber workers, Social Security funds might run out before 2040.

Standards Act, for the first time, set a national minimum hourly rate for wages: 25 cents an hour at first, 40 cents an hour by 1945. It also established a national maximum workweek: 44 hours to begin, followed by 40 hours in two years. In addition, the act banned factory labor for workers under the age of 16 (or 18 if the work was hazardous).

THE SOCIAL SECURITY ACT One of the most important achievements of the New Deal was creating the Social Security system. The **Social Security Act,**

New Deal Programs

EMPLOYMENT PROJECTS	PURPOSE
1933 Civilian Conservation Corps (CCC)	Provided jobs for single males on conservation projects.
1933 Federal Emergency Relief Act (FERA)	Helped states to provide aid for the unemployed.
1933 Civil Works Administration (CWA)	Provided work in federal jobs.
1933 Public Works Administration (PWA)	Created jobs on government projects increasing workers' buying power and stimulating the economy.
1935 Works Progress Administration (WPA)	Quickly created as many jobs as possible—from construction jobs to positions in symphony orchestras.
1935 National Youth Administration (NYA)	Provided job training for unemployed young people and part-time jobs for needy students.
BUSINESS ASSISTANCE AND REFORM	
1933 Emergency Banking Relief Act (EBRA)	Regulated bank transactions in credit, currency, gold and silver, and foreign exchange.
1933 Federal Deposit Insurance Corporation (FDIC)	Protected bank deposits up to $5,000. (Today, accounts are protected up to $100,000.)
1933 National Recovery Administration (NRA)	Established codes of fair competition and voluntary guidelines for minimum wage and 40-hour workweek.
1934 Securities and Exchange Commission (SEC)	Supervised the country's Stock Commission Exchanges and eliminated dishonest practices.
1935 Banking Act of 1935	Created a seven-member board to regulate the nation's money supply and the interest rates on loans.
1938 Food, Drug and Cosmetic Act	Required manufacturers to list ingredients in foods, drugs, and cosmetic products.
FARM RELIEF AND RURAL DEVELOPMENT	
1933 Agricultural Adjustment Administration (AAA)	Aided farmers and regulated crop production.
1933 Tennessee Valley Authority (TVA)	Developed the resources of the Tennessee Valley.
1935 Rural Electrification Administration (REA)	Provided cheap electricity for isolated rural areas.
HOUSING	
1933 Home Owners Loan Corporation (HOLC)	Loaned money at low interest to homeowners who could not meet mortgage payments.
1934 Federal Housing Administration (FHA)	Insured loans for building and repairing homes.
1937 United States Housing Authority (USHA)	Provided federal loans for a national home-improvement program.
LABOR RELATIONS	
1935 National Labor Relations Act (Wagner Act of 1935)	Defined "unfair labor practices" and established the National Labor Relations Board (NLRB) to settle disputes between employers and employees.
1938 Fair Labor Standards Act	Established a minimum hourly wage and a maximum number of hours in the workweek for the entire country. Prohibited children under the age of 16 from working in factories.
RETIREMENT	
1935 Social Security Act	Provided a pension for retired workers and their spouses and aided people with disabilities.

HISTORY FROM VISUALS

New Deal Programs

Reading the Chart
Emphasize to students that each program and act listed in the left-hand column of the chart aligns with a purpose in the right-hand column.

Extension Ask students which programs they think provided relief only during the Depression, and why. *Possible Response: The employment projects, because they were established to create jobs and weren't needed once the economy began to thrive again.* Ask them which programs they think continue to influence the economy today, and why. *Possible Response: Most of the other programs, because they produced fundamental reforms in banking, housing, and labor.*

GROLIER MULTIMEDIA ENCYCLOPEDIA
New Deal

Block Schedule TEACHING OPTION **Time Needed: 20 Minutes**

Cooperative Activity: Creating a New Deal Poster

Task: Groups of four to five students will create a poster advertising and promoting a New Deal program.

Purpose: To visually convey the purpose of a New Deal program.

Activity: Groups should select the New Deal program they want to advertise in a poster. Group members should then research the program and discuss how its purpose could be conveyed in a poster. They should also write a slogan that will distinguish the program and catch the reader's attention. To get ideas, students can study the posters illustrating the chart on page 515. After the posters are completed, display them around the room and discuss them in class.

ALTERNATIVE ASSESSMENT BOOK
Standards for Evaluating a Cooperative Activity

Issues for the 21st Century

Tough Choices About Entitlements

Connect the Social Security Act to entitlements today by having students read pages 900–901. Then have them answer these questions.

1. What was the original purpose of the Social Security Act? *To provide a base for a worker's retirement.*
2. What factors threaten the future of Social Security? *Retiring baby boomers, longer life spans, slow growth in the rate of employment.*
3. What can be done today to save Social Security? *Tax hikes, benefit cuts, invest funds in stocks.*

ASSESS & RETEACH

Section 2 Assessment

Have small groups of students work together to answer the questions.

Self-Assessment

Have students locate portions of the text that contain information for any questions they were not able to answer.

Section Quiz

FORMAL ASSESSMENT
Section Quiz, p. 188

Reteach

Use the chart on page 515 to review the New Deal programs discussed in Section 2.

CLOSE

Under the Second New Deal, the Roosevelt administration launched more programs to provide relief to farmers and other workers. The administration also spurred Congress to enact the Social Security system and reforms in labor and public utilities.

"We have undertaken a new order of things, yet we progress to it under the framework and in the spirit and intent of the American Constitution."

FRANKLIN DELANO ROOSEVELT

passed in 1935, was created by a committee chaired by Secretary of Labor Frances Perkins. The act had three major parts:

- *Old-age insurance for retirees 65 or older and their spouses.* The insurance was not a complete retirement plan but a supplement to a person's private retirement plan. The initial payments ranged from $10 to $85 a month, depending on the amount a worker paid into the system. This amount came half from the worker and half from the employer. Some groups were excluded from the system: domestic servants, farm workers, many hospital workers, and many restaurant workers.
- *Unemployment compensation system.* The unemployment system was funded by a federal tax on employers. It was administered at the state level. The initial payments ranged from $15 to $18 per week.
- *Aid to families with dependent children and the disabled.* The aid was paid for by federal funds made available to the states. It assisted the blind, the crippled, the needy elderly, and mothers with dependent children.

D. Answer It helped retirees and their spouses, the unemployed, families with dependent children, and the disabled.

THINK THROUGH HISTORY
D. *Summarizing* *Whom did Social Security help?*

Although the Social Security Act was not a total pension system or a complete welfare system, it did provide substantial benefits to millions of Americans.

EXPANDING AND REGULATING UTILITIES The Second New Deal also included laws to promote rural electrification and to regulate public utilities. The Roosevelt administration took steps to extend electricity to rural areas nationwide. At the time, only about 30 percent of American farms had electricity.

At President Roosevelt's urging, Congress established the Rural Electrification Administration (REA). The REA created, financed, and worked with rural and farm electrical cooperatives to bring electricity to previously isolated areas. By 1945, 45 percent of America's farms and rural homes had electricity. That figure rose to 90 percent by 1951. By making electricity widely available, the REA had a tremendous impact on rural life.

The Public Utilities Holding Company Act of 1935 took aim at financial corruption in the public utility industry. It outlawed the ownership of utilities by multiple holding companies—a practice known as the pyramiding of holding companies. Lobbyists for the holding companies fought the law fiercely, and it proved extremely difficult to enforce.

As the New Deal struggled to help farmers and other workers, it assisted many different groups in the nation, including women, African Americans, Latinos, and Native Americans.

Many WPA posters were created to promote New Deal programs—in this case the Rural Electrification Administration.

Section 2 Assessment

1. TERMS & NAMES
Identify:
- Eleanor Roosevelt
- Works Progress Administration
- National Youth Administration
- Wagner Act
- Social Security Act

2. SUMMARIZING Create a cluster diagram similar to the one below, showing how groups such as farmers, the unemployed, youth, and retirees were helped by Second New Deal programs.

Which group do you think benefited the most from the Second New Deal? Explain.

3. ANALYZING Do you think the Second New Deal could have succeeded without the WPA? Why or why not?

THINK ABOUT
- the millions of people the WPA employed
- criticism of the WPA as a "make-work" program
- the many other New Deal reform and recovery programs

4. EVALUATING Why might the Social Security Act be considered the most important achievement of the New Deal?

THINK ABOUT
- the types of relief needed in the 1930s
- alternatives to government assistance to the elderly, the unemployed, and the disabled
- the scope of the act

ANSWERS

1. TERMS & NAMES

Eleanor Roosevelt, p. 511
Works Progress Administration, p. 513
National Youth Administration, p. 513
Wagner Act, p. 514
Social Security Act, p. 515

2. SUMMARIZING

Possible Responses: Farmers: second Agricultural Adjustment Act, Farm Security Administration, Rural Electrification Administration. Unemployed: Works Progress Administration, National Youth Administration, Social Security Act. Youth: National Youth Administration, Works Progress Administration. Labor: Wagner Act, Fair Labor Standards Act. Retirees: Social Security Act.

3. ANALYZING

Possible Responses: Yes: The farm recovery acts and labor and utilities reforms created changes that had a significant impact both in the short term and over time; the WPA provided only for short-term "welfare," not long-term recovery. No: The WPA gave more than 8 million people immediate relief and provided them with a sense of dignity; nothing else worked quite as quickly in producing returns for communities.

4. EVALUATING

Possible Responses: It showed that the Roosevelt administration wanted to ensure that some of the problems of the 1930s would not recur; it provided a safety net for many people—the unemployed, the elderly, the disabled, and families with dependent children—who needed help in times of crisis; it had the largest scope of the New Deal programs, affecting thousands of people over a great many years

3 The New Deal Affects Many Groups

TERMS & NAMES
- Frances Perkins
- Mary McLeod Bethune
- John Collier
- New Deal Coalition
- Congress of Industrial Organizations

LEARN ABOUT how New Deal policies affected various social and ethnic groups
TO UNDERSTAND how the Democratic Party forged a new political coalition.

ONE AMERICAN'S STORY

Pedro J. González came to this country from Mexico in 1924 and later became a United States citizen. González soon was involved in the music business, both as a performer and as the first Spanish-language disc jockey in Los Angeles. During the 1930s, González used his radio program to condemn discrimination against Mexicans and Mexican Americans, who were often made scapegoats for social and economic problems during the Depression. For his efforts, González was arrested, jailed, and deported on trumped-up charges. Late in life, he reflected on his experiences.

A PERSONAL VOICE

Seeing how badly they treated Mexicans back in the days of my youth, I could have started a rebellion. But now there could be a cultural understanding so that without firing one bullet, we might understand each other. We [Mexicans] were here before they [Anglos] were, and we are not, as they still say, "undesirables" or "wetbacks." They say we come to this land and it's not our home. Actually, it's the other way around.

PEDRO J. GONZÁLEZ, quoted in the *Los Angeles Times*, December 9, 1984

Because of his stand against discrimination, Pedro J. González became a hero to many Mexican Americans and a symbol of Mexican cultural pride. He criticized the prejudice displayed by a large number of people in the United States toward Mexican Americans who sought jobs. He also criticized government actions to round up people in Mexican-American neighborhoods to send them back to Mexico. His life reflected some of the difficulties faced by Mexicans and other minority groups in the United States during the New Deal era.

Pedro J. González

A SONG FOR HIS PEOPLE:
Pedro J. González and the Fight for Mexican-American Rights

New Opportunities for Women

In some ways, the New Deal represented an important opportunity for minorities and women. Some New Deal programs and their administrators made a conscious effort not to discriminate in hiring or in distributing benefits. The Roosevelt administration appointed a number of women and African Americans to key positions in the government, and it welcomed their input on important issues.

Nevertheless, gains for women and minorities during the New Deal were limited. Long-standing patterns of prejudice and discrimination continued to plague these groups and to prevent their full and equal participation in national life.

WOMEN MAKE THEIR MARK One of the most notable changes during the New Deal was the naming of several women to important official positions. For the first time, a woman, **Frances Perkins,** became a cabinet member. As secretary of labor, she played a major role in the creation of

Frances Perkins was the New York state industrial commissioner in 1933.

SECTION 3 RESOURCES

PRINT RESOURCES

IN-DEPTH RESOURCES: UNIT 4
Guided Reading, p. 55
Primary Source: The Memorial Day Massacre, p. 64
Literature: from *Waiting for Lefty* by Clifford Odets, p. 67
American Lives: Mary McLeod Bethune, p. 71

READING STUDY GUIDE, p. 159

ACCESS FOR STUDENTS ACQUIRING ENGLISH
Guided Reading (Spanish), p. 177

SPANISH READING STUDY GUIDE, p. 159

FORMAL ASSESSMENT
Section Quiz, p. 189

ALTERNATIVE ASSESSMENT BOOK
See forms for supporting and scoring alternative activities.

TECHNOLOGY RESOURCES

HUMANITIES TRANSPARENCIES
H22, A relief center in Louisville, Kentucky, 1937. Margaret Bourke-White

CD-ROM Electronic Library of Primary Sources

VIDEO *American Stories* video series
American Portfolio: A Videodisc for U.S. History user's guide, pp. 205, 207

INTERNET http://www.mlushistory.com

Section 3 Overview

OBJECTIVES

1. To describe how New Deal programs affected women.

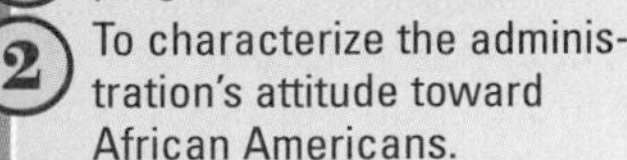

2. To characterize the administration's attitude toward African Americans.

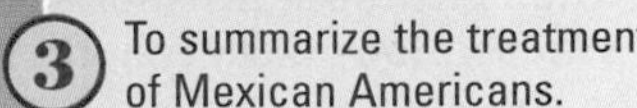

3. To summarize the treatment of Mexican Americans.

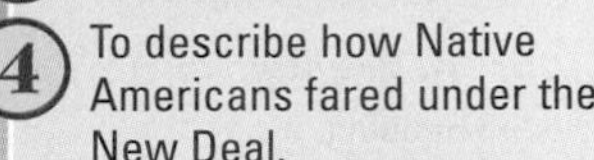

4. To describe how Native Americans fared under the New Deal.

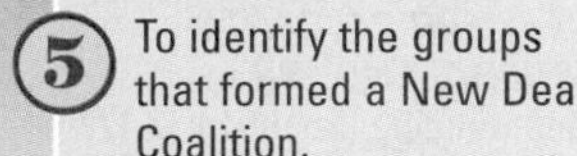

5. To identify the groups that formed a New Deal Coalition.

CRITICAL THINKING

- Theme: Cultural Diversity, p. 518
- Evaluating decisions, p. 519
- Analyzing causes, p. 520
- Recognizing effects, p. 520
- Analyzing, p. 521
- Summarizing, p. 522
- Forming generalizations, p. 522
- Forming opinions, p. 522

FOCUS & MOTIVATE

5-MINUTE WARM-UP

Interpreting Graphs
To explore the growth of the labor movement in the 1930s, have students study the graph on page 521 and answer these questions.

1. What trend characterized union membership between 1931 and 1933? between 1936 and 1940?
2. How did the New Deal affect union membership in the late 1930s?

WARM-UP TRANSPARENCY 15

▶ ***Starting with the Student***
Have students watch the video "A Song for His People" to learn about Pedro J. González and his fight for Mexican-American rights.

AMERICAN STORIES
video series
"A Song for His People"

Videocassette: Volume 4
Videodisc: Disc 2, Side B, Chapter 3

OBJECTIVE
① INSTRUCT

New Opportunities for Women

▶ ***Discussing Key Ideas***
- Roosevelt appoints women to government positions.
- Women face discrimination in the workplace.

IN-DEPTH RESOURCES: UNIT 4
Guided Reading, p. 55

ACCESS FOR STUDENTS ACQUIRING ENGLISH
Guided Reading (Spanish), p. 177

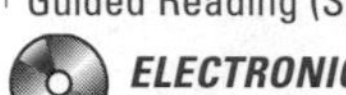
ELECTRONIC LIBRARY OF PRIMARY SOURCES
from Women Must Learn to Play the Game as Men Do by Eleanor Roosevelt

OBJECTIVE
② INSTRUCT

New Opportunities for African Americans

▶ ***Discussing Key Ideas***
- Bethune helps organize Roosevelt's "Black Cabinet."
- Eleanor Roosevelt plays a key role in opening doors for African Americans.
- Although Roosevelt fails to support civil rights, most African Americans support the president.

IN-DEPTH RESOURCES: UNIT 4
American Lives: Mary McLeod Bethune, p. 71

HUMANITIES TRANSPARENCIES
H22, A relief center in Louisville, Kentucky, 1937. Margaret Bourke-White

ELECTRONIC LIBRARY OF PRIMARY SOURCES
How Bethune-Cookman College Began by Mary McLeod Bethune

the Social Security system and in the crafting of labor legislation. President Roosevelt also appointed the first female ambassador and a number of female federal judges.

In making these appointments, President Roosevelt hoped to appeal to female voters. He also received a strong push from his wife, Eleanor, and from the head of the Democratic Party's women's division, Molly Dewson. During the 1936 presidential campaign, Dewson had mobilized 15,000 women to go door to door, distributing leaflets promoting New Deal programs. Though a feminist at heart, Dewson did not push a strong women's rights agenda. She was, however, especially proud of the advances made by women. As she said, "The change from women's status in government before Roosevelt is unbelievable."

In general, however, women continued to struggle for equal rights during the New Deal era. They faced ongoing discrimination in the workplace. Male workers persisted in their belief that women took jobs from men, especially when so many men were out of work. In fact, a Gallup poll taken in 1936 reported that 82 percent of Americans said that a wife should not work if her husband had a job.

New Deal laws yielded mixed results regarding women. In fact, the codes established by the National Recovery Administration set wage levels lower for women than for men. In addition, the Federal Emergency Relief Administration and the Civil Works Administration hired far fewer women than men, only about one in ten. The Civilian Conservation Corps hired only men. These hiring practices were very much in line with those pursued by business and industry in the 1930s.

In spite of these barriers, women continued their movement into the workplace. Although the overall percentage of women working for wages increased only slightly during the 1930s, the percentage of married women in the workplace grew from 11.7 percent in 1930 to 15.6 percent in 1940. In short, widespread criticism of working women did not halt the long-term trend of women working outside the home.

New Opportunities for African Americans

An important African American in the Roosevelt administration was **Mary McLeod Bethune.** She was an educator who dedicated herself to promoting opportunities for young African Americans. The president named her to head a special department of the National Youth Administration, the Office of Minority Affairs. In this post, Bethune worked to ensure that the NYA hired African-American administrators and provided job training and other benefits to minority students.

Bethune also helped organize a "Black Cabinet" of influential African Americans to advise the Roosevelt administration on racial issues. Included in this group were African-American lawyers, journalists, and specialists on housing, labor, and other issues. Among these figures were William H. Hastie and Robert C. Weaver, both appointees to Roosevelt's Interior Department. Never before had so many African Americans had a voice in the White House.

Mary McLeod Bethune, a close friend of Eleanor Roosevelt, was a strong supporter of the New Deal.

William H. Hastie was appointed by President Roosevelt to the Interior Department.

A. Answer It gave President Roosevelt valuable advice on racial issues and provided African Americans with a voice, for the first time, at the highest levels of government.

THINK THROUGH HISTORY
A. THEME ***Cultural Diversity*** *Why was the "Black Cabinet" important to the Roosevelt administration?*

TEACHING OPTION

Making Connections Across Time

Women in the Workplace Today Tell students that the percentage of women in the workplace rose from 28 percent in 1940 to 59 percent in 1994. Tell them that the women's movement of the 1960s and 1970s helped bring about many gains for working women. The Equal Pay Act of 1963 required equal pay for men and women performing the same job. Among other stipulations, the Civil Rights Act of 1964 prohibited job discrimination on the basis of sex. Nonetheless, in the 1990s, women still lagged behind men in job opportunities and earnings. Although some women pursued careers in fields traditionally reserved for men, most women still worked in such "women's" jobs as nursing, teaching, retail sales, and secretarial work. Because these jobs remained low paying, women continued to earn less than men. In the mid 1990s women earned, on the average, only about three-fourths of what men earned.

Eleanor Roosevelt played a key role in opening doors for African Americans in government. She also was instrumental in bringing about one of the most dramatic cultural events of the period: a performance of the African-American singer Marian Anderson in 1939. When the Daughters of the American Revolution chose not to allow Anderson to perform in their concert hall in Washington, D.C., because of her race, Eleanor Roosevelt arranged for Anderson to perform at the Lincoln Memorial on Easter Sunday. Mrs. Roosevelt also resigned from the Daughters of the American Revolution. At the concert, Walter White, an official of the NAACP, noticed one girl in the crowd.

Marian Anderson sang from the steps of the Lincoln Memorial on April 9, 1939.

A PERSONAL VOICE

Her hands were particularly noticeable as she thrust them forward and upward, trying desperately . . . to touch the singer. They were hands which despite their youth had known only the dreary work of manual labor. Tears streamed down the girl's dark face. Her hat was askew, but in her eyes flamed hope bordering on ecstasy. . . . If Marian Anderson could do it, the girl's eyes seemed to say, then I can, too.

WALTER WHITE, *A Man Called White*

THE PRESIDENT FAILS TO SUPPORT CIVIL RIGHTS Despite efforts to promote racial equality, the president himself was never committed to full civil rights for African Americans. He was afraid of upsetting Southern whites, an important segment of Democratic voters. For this reason, he refused to support a federal antilynching law and an end to the poll tax, two key goals of the civil rights movement. Furthermore, although as many as a million African-American families benefited from WPA work relief, a number of New Deal programs, including the FHA, the CCC, and the TVA, clearly discriminated against African Americans. They favored white Americans when providing direct relief and New Deal jobs. African Americans were segregated from whites and often received lower wages.

Recognizing the need to fight for their own rights, African Americans took steps to improve conditions in areas that the New Deal ignored. In 1934, they helped organize the Southern Tenant Farmers' Union, which sought to protect the rights of tenant farmers and sharecroppers, both white and black. In the North, the union created tenants' groups and launched campaigns to increase job opportunities. When discriminatory hiring practices continued to deprive African Americans of their fair share of jobs, they organized the March on Washington Movement in 1941.

In general, however, African Americans supported the Roosevelt administration and the New Deal, and they abandoned their traditional allegiance to the Republican Party. Although segregation and racial violence remained shameful features of American life, African Americans generally regarded the New Deal and President Roosevelt as their best hope for the future. As one man recalled, "Roosevelt touched the temper of the black community. You did not look upon him as being white, black, blue, or green. He was President Roosevelt."

B. Answer President Roosevelt was not committed to full civil rights for African Americans. He did not support a federal antilynching law and an end to poll taxes. Many African-American families benefited from work relief, but some New Deal programs discriminated against African Americans.

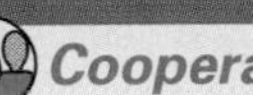

THINK THROUGH HISTORY
B. *Evaluating Decisions* *Evaluate the actions and policies of the Roosevelt administration on civil rights.*

HISTORICAL SPOTLIGHT

THE SCOTTSBORO CASE

In April 1931, nine African-American men were brought to trial in Scottsboro, Alabama, for raping a white woman on a train. That day they met their court-appointed lawyer for the first time. An all-white jury convicted the men, despite medical evidence that no rape had taken place. All were sentenced to death except the youngest, who was 12 years old.

In 1932, in *Powell* v. *Alabama*, the Supreme Court overturned the convictions on the grounds that the men had not been given adequate legal counsel. Over the next several years, the men were retried and reconvicted. In 1935, the Supreme Court overturned one conviction in *Norris* v. *Alabama*, stating that the systematic exclusion of blacks from the jury meant that the defendant had not received equal protection under the law. These Supreme Court decisions have had far-reaching effects on the provision of legal counsel and the balance of juries.

MORE ABOUT . . .
Marian Anderson

Conductor Arturo Toscanini claimed that a voice like Marian Anderson's was "heard once in a hundred years." Anderson did not always receive such high praise, however. When the contralto gave a recital in New York's Town Hall in 1925, she received very unfavorable reviews. Her poor performance may have been due to her voice teacher's having attempted to raise her voice a full octave. Following the disastrous recital, Anderson vowed never to sing again. She broke that vow, however, and eventually won wide praise for her concert singing. In 1955, she became the first black soloist to sing with the Metropolitan Opera of New York City.

HISTORICAL SPOTLIGHT
The Scottsboro Case

Critical Thinking: Evaluating Decisions
Have students discuss the Supreme Court decision in *Norris* v. *Alabama*. Why did the Court decide that the exclusion of blacks from the jury was unfair?
Possible Responses: The Constitution guarantees defendants a jury of their peers. An all-white jury may have been swayed by prejudice.

Block Schedule TEACHING OPTION **Time Needed: 30 Minutes**

Cooperative Activity: Researching Treatment of Women and Minorities

Task: Groups of three students will research, write, and present a report on the New Deal's treatment of women and minorities.

Purpose: To explore in depth the treatment of women and minorities during the FDR administration.

Activity: Each group should focus on the treatment of one of the following: women, African Americans, Mexican Americans, or Native Americans. One student might do the research, another might write the report, and the third student might present the report to the class. Students should include as many anecdotes, illustrations, and first-person statements as possible.

Building a Portfolio: Students who add the report to their portfolio should include a note identifying their work on the project.

ALTERNATIVE ASSESSMENT BOOK
Standards for Evaluating a Cooperative Activity

Standards for Evaluation
Reports should . . .

- provide an in-depth look at the treatment of women and minorities
- include anecdotes, illustrations, and first-person statements
- be clear and well organized

OBJECTIVE
③ INSTRUCT

Mexican-American Fortunes

▶ *Discussing Key Ideas*
- Mexican Americans support the New Deal, even though they receive fewer benefits than African Americans.

HISTORICAL SPOTLIGHT
Deportation of Mexican Americans
Critical Thinking: Analyzing Ask students why many Mexican-American migrant workers were treated with hostility during the Depression. *Because they took jobs away from white workers.* Ask them why the white workers didn't want these jobs during good times. *Possible Response: Because during good times, whites could get better jobs and were content to leave the low-paying ones to minorities.*

OBJECTIVE

④ INSTRUCT

Native American Gains

▶ *Discussing Key Ideas*
- Native Americans receive strong support under the New Deal.

HISTORICAL SPOTLIGHT

DEPORTATION OF MEXICAN AMERICANS

Many Mexican Americans were long-time residents or citizens of the United States. Others came during the 1920s to work on farms in Texas, California, and Arizona. Valued for their low-cost labor during good times, these migrant workers became the target of hostility during the Great Depression. Many returned to Mexico willingly, while others were deported by the United States government. During the 1930s, as many as half a million persons of Mexican descent, many of them U.S. citizens, were deported to Mexico.

Mexican-American Fortunes

Mexican Americans also tended to support the New Deal, even though they received even fewer benefits than African Americans did. Large numbers of Mexican Americans had come to the United States during the 1920s, settling mainly in the Southwest. Most found work laboring on farms, an occupation that was essentially unprotected by state and federal laws. During the Depression, farm wages fell to as little as nine cents an hour. Farm workers who tried to unionize often met with violence from employers and government authorities. Although the CCC and WPA helped some Mexican Americans, these agencies also discriminated against them by disqualifying from their programs migrant workers who had no permanent address.

THINK THROUGH HISTORY
C. *Analyzing Causes* *Why was life difficult for farm laborers?*

C. Answer Farm laborers were essentially unprotected by state and federal laws.

Native American Gains

Native Americans received strong government support from the New Deal. In 1924, Native Americans had received full citizenship by law. In 1933, President Roosevelt appointed **John Collier** as commissioner of Indian affairs. A strong advocate of Native American rights, Collier helped create the Indian Reorganization Act of 1934.

John Collier talks with Chief Richard, one of several Native American chiefs attending the Four Nation Celebration held at Niagara Falls, New York, in September 1934.

This act strengthened Native American land claims by prohibiting the government from taking over unclaimed reservation lands and selling them to people other than Native Americans. Thus, the 1934 act was able to restore some reservation lands to tribal ownership. Some Native Americans who valued their tribal traditions hailed the act as an important step forward. Those who had become more "Americanized" as individual landowners under the previous Dawes Act, however, objected that the act would make it harder for Native Americans to improve their economic conditions and participate fully in mainstream American life.

A New Deal Coalition

Although New Deal policies had mixed results for minorities, these groups generally backed President Roosevelt against his Republican rivals. In fact, one of FDR's great achievements was to create a **New Deal Coalition**—an alignment of diverse groups dedicated to supporting the Democratic Party. The coalition included Southern whites, various urban groups, African Americans, and unionized industrial workers. This new voting bloc enabled the Democrats to dominate national politics throughout the 1930s and 1940s.

LABOR UNIONS FLOURISH Organized labor was a critical element of the New Deal coalition. As a result of the Wagner Act and other prolabor legislation passed during the New Deal, union members enjoyed better working conditions and increased bargaining power. In their eyes, President Roosevelt was a "friend of labor." Labor unions donated money to Roosevelt's reelection campaigns, and union workers pledged their votes to him.

During the 1930s, and particularly after passage of the Wagner Act, the number of unionized workers soared. Between 1933 and 1941, union membership grew from 3 million to more than 8 million. Unionization especially affected coal miners and workers in mass-production industries, such as the

D. Answer New Deal labor laws gave unions greater power to organize and negotiate with employers. As a result, unions grew in size and joined with other groups in the New Deal coalition.

THINK THROUGH HISTORY
D. *Recognizing Effects* *How did New Deal policies affect organized labor?*

TEACHING OPTIONS

Exploring Themes

Cultural Diversity Discuss the dissent among Native Americans regarding the Indian Reorganization Act of 1934. Ask students to explain why some Native Americans favored the act and others did not. Ask them how some Native Americans became Americanized. *Possible Response: By adopting aspects of white mainstream culture.* Then ask students if they think minorities have a better chance of succeeding when they adopt the dominant culture, or if they think minorities should retain their traditions.

Making Connections Across Cultures

Mexican Americans During the Depression Tell students that as a radio-show host in Los Angeles in the 1930s, Pedro González once announced to his Latino listeners that workers were needed to clear some land in the city. Soon thereafter, hundreds of Mexican-American workers arrived at the site, ready for work with picks and axes. However, the police, fearing that the people were armed for a riot, arrested many of them. Ask students what the response of the police reveals about relations between whites and Mexican Americans during the Depression.

automobile, rubber, and electrical industries. It was in these industries, too, that conflicts began to develop within the labor movement.

Traditionally, organized labor had been largely restricted to the craft unions—carpenters, plumbers, electricians, and so on—that made up the American Federation of Labor (AFL). The AFL opposed industrywide unions: unions that represented all the workers in a given industry, such as automobile manufacturing.

Frustrated by this position, several key labor leaders, including John L. Lewis of the United Mine Workers and Walter Reuther of the United Automobile Workers, formed the Committee for Industrial Organization to organize industrial unions. The committee signed up unskilled and semiskilled workers rapidly, and within two years it succeeded in gaining union recognition in the steel and automobile industries. In 1938, the Committee for Industrial Organization completed its break with the AFL by officially separating from the AFL and changing its name to the **Congress of Industrial Organizations** (CIO). This split lasted until 1955.

E. Answer They brought results because factory owners had to negotiate with the workers to end the strike so they could begin production again.

THINK THROUGH HISTORY
E. Analyzing *Why were sit-down strikes an effective bargaining tool?*

One of the main bargaining tactics of the labor movement in the 1930s was the sit-down strike. (See *strike* on page 938 in the Economics Handbook.) Instead of walking off their jobs, workers remained inside their plants, but they did not work. This prevented the factory owners from carrying on production with strikebreakers, or scabs. Some Americans disapproved of the sit-down strike, calling it a violation of private property. But it proved to be an effective bargaining tool.

Not all labor disputes in the 1930s were peaceful. For example, a sit-down strike that began in 1936 at the General Motors (GM) automobile plant in Flint, Michigan, turned violent. GM called in the police, who used tear gas to try to disperse the strikers. Then the strikers turned on the plant's water hoses to douse the police. A series of bloody encounters also erupted between striking

The Growing Labor Movement, 1933–1940

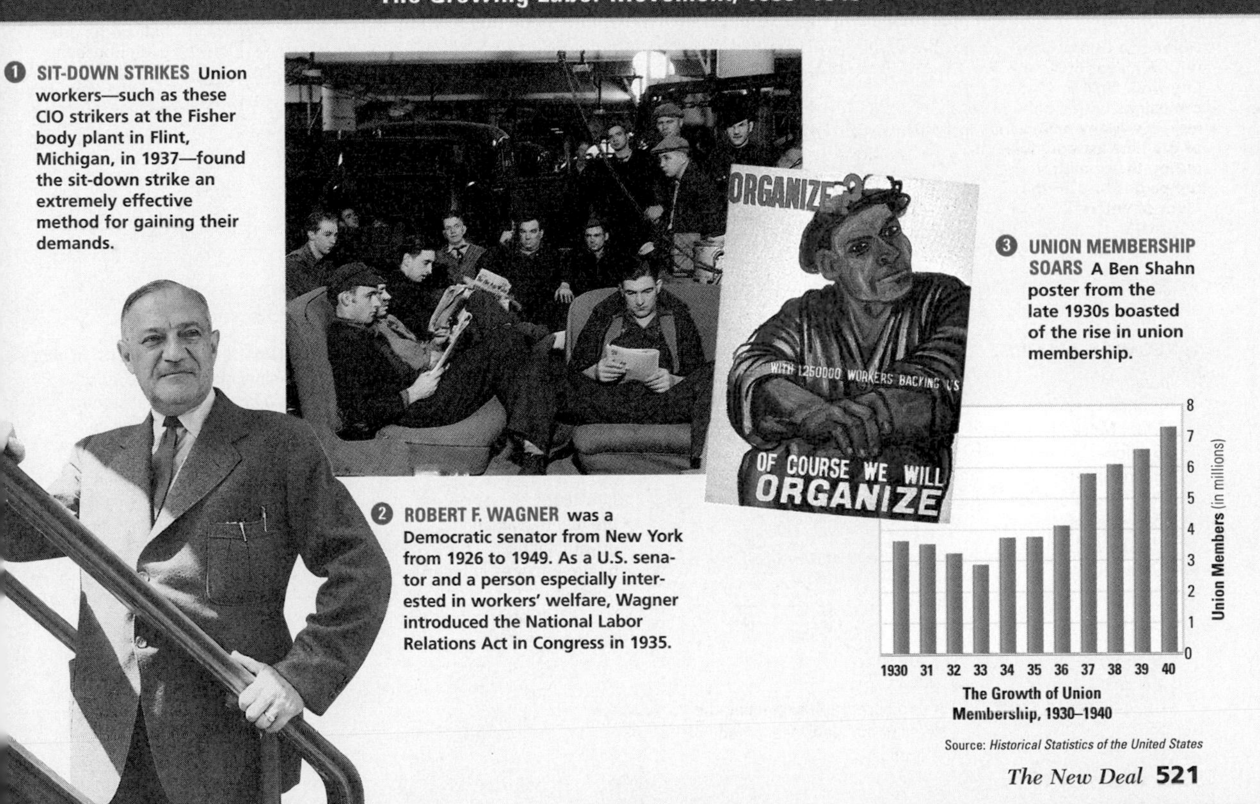

❶ **SIT-DOWN STRIKES** Union workers—such as these CIO strikers at the Fisher body plant in Flint, Michigan, in 1937—found the sit-down strike an extremely effective method for gaining their demands.

❷ **ROBERT F. WAGNER** was a Democratic senator from New York from 1926 to 1949. As a U.S. senator and a person especially interested in workers' welfare, Wagner introduced the National Labor Relations Act in Congress in 1935.

❸ **UNION MEMBERSHIP SOARS** A Ben Shahn poster from the late 1930s boasted of the rise in union membership.

The Growth of Union Membership, 1930–1940

Source: *Historical Statistics of the United States*

OBJECTIVE
⑤ **INSTRUCT**

A New Deal Coalition

Discussing Key Ideas
- Labor unions flourish under the New Deal.
- The growing labor movement results in disputes that are not always settled peacefully.
- The urban population supports FDR.

HISTORY FROM VISUALS
The Growing Labor Movement, 1933–1940

Reading the Graph Point out to students that the bar graph makes it easier to see that there was a decline in union membership from 1930 through 1933, a big increase in 1934, and an even bigger increase in 1937.

Extension Have students create a two-column chart in which they list the different groups of workers who belonged to the AFL and to the CIO.

IN-DEPTH RESOURCES: UNIT 4
Primary Source: The Memorial Day Massacre, p. 64

TEACHING OPTION

Making Connections Across Time

Labor Movements in the 1960s and 1970s Tell students that in the 1960s and 1970s, farm workers and federal employees became unionized for the first time. A Mexican American named Cesar Chavez organized farm workers during the 1960s and eventually established the United Farm Workers of America, a union of migrant workers and other farm laborers. Early in the 1960s, federal employees were given the right to organize and bargain collectively, but they could not strike. Over time, the laws began to change. These laws allowed public employees to strike and encouraged the growth of unionism among the workers. By the 1970s, strikes by teachers and other government employees had affected many cities. The American Federation of State, County, and Municipal Employees, a union of public employees, became the fastest-growing labor group in the country. Union membership among women and minority groups also increased during these decades.

ASSESS & RETEACH

Section 3 Assessment

Have students focus on item 2, which gives an especially good overview of the section.

Self-Assessment

Have students cite a quotation in this section that they think sums up an important idea. They should look at the quotations under the label "A Personal Voice" as well as other quotations in the text.

Section Quiz

FORMAL ASSESSMENT
Section Quiz, p. 189

Reteach

Survey the students to discover what topics in this section were difficult for them. Then review the relevant material.

CLOSE

Although discrimination remained a fact of life for many people, the New Deal created some new opportunities for women and minority groups. With organized labor, these groups forged a new political coalition dedicated to supporting the Democratic Party. The New Deal had a great influence on workers from all walks of life.

employees of the Ford Motor Company and hoodlums hired by Ford's management. Perhaps the most dramatic incident, however, was the clash at the Republic Steel plant in Chicago on Memorial Day, 1937. Police attacked striking steelworkers outside the plant. One striker, an African-American man, recalled the experience.

A PERSONAL VOICE

I began to see people drop. There was a Mexican on my side, and he fell; and there was a black man on my side and he fell. Down I went. I crawled around in the grass and saw that people were getting beat. I'd never seen police beat women, not white women. I'd seen them beat black women, but this was the first time in my life I'd seen them beat white women—with sticks.

JESSE REESE, quoted in *The Great Depression*

Fiorello La Guardia, the reform mayor of New York City from 1934 to 1945, campaigns with a baby in his arms. Many politicians of the time kissed babies during their political campaigns to gain the favor of voters.

Ten people were killed and dozens wounded in this incident, which became known as the Memorial Day Massacre. Shortly afterward, the National Labor Relations Board stepped in and required the head of Republic Steel, Tom Girdler, to negotiate with the union. This and other actions helped labor gain strength during the 1930s.

THE URBAN POPULATION SUPPORTS FDR Urban voters were another important component of the New Deal Coalition. Support for the Democratic Party surged, especially in large Northern cities, such as New York, Boston, Philadelphia, and Chicago. These and other cities had powerful city political organizations that provided services, such as jobs, in exchange for votes. Support for President Roosevelt came from various religious and ethnic groups—Roman Catholics, Jews, Italians, Irish, and Polish and other Slavic peoples—as well as from African Americans.

President Roosevelt's appeal to these groups was based on New Deal labor laws and work-relief programs, which aided the urban poor. The president also made direct and persuasive appeals to urban voters at election time. At presidential campaign stops in Northern cities, throngs of supporters came out to cheer the president. In the 1936 election, President Roosevelt carried the nation's 12 largest cities. To reinforce his support, he also appointed many officials of urban-immigrant backgrounds, particularly Roman Catholics and Jews, to important government positions.

Women, African Americans, Mexican Americans, Native Americans, and workers from all walks of life were greatly affected by the New Deal. It also had a tremendous influence on American society and culture.

F. Answer New Deal labor and relief programs helped the urban poor. Roosevelt also made direct appeals to these groups.

THINK THROUGH HISTORY
F. *Summarizing* *Why did urban voters support Roosevelt?*

Section 3 Assessment

1. TERMS & NAMES

Identify:
- Frances Perkins
- Mary McLeod Bethune
- John Collier
- New Deal Coalition
- Congress of Industrial Organizations

2. SUMMARIZING Using a web diagram like the partial one shown here, note the effects of New Deal policies on American women, African Americans, Mexican Americans, Native Americans, unionized workers, and urban Americans.

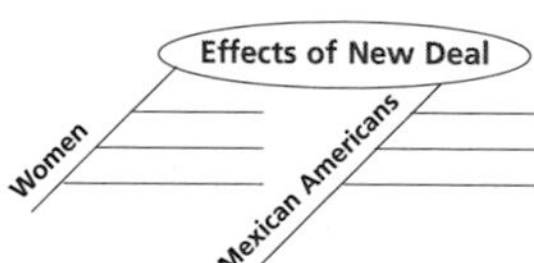

Write a paragraph explaining the effects of the New Deal on one of the groups.

3. FORMING GENERALIZATIONS Do you think women made significant progress toward equality during the 1930s? Support your answer with evidence from the text.

THINK ABOUT
- the role of women in government
- hiring practices in federal programs
- women's opportunities in business and industry

4. FORMING OPINIONS In your opinion, did organized labor become too powerful in the 1930s? Explain your answer.

THINK ABOUT
- why workers joined unions
- how unions organized workers
- the role of unions in politics

ANSWERS

1. TERMS & NAMES

Frances Perkins, p. 517

Mary McLeod Bethune, p. 518

John Collier, p. 520

New Deal Coalition, p. 520

Congress of Industrial Organizations, p. 521

2. SUMMARIZING

Possible Responses: **Women:** Appointment to key government positions; welcoming of women's input on issues. **African Americans:** Role of Mary McLeod Bethune and the "Black Cabinet." **Mexican Americans:** Help from the CCC and the WPA. **Native Americans:** Passage of the Indian Reorganization Act of 1934. **Unionized workers:** Passage of the Wagner Act. **Urban voters:** Appeal of work-relief programs.

3. FORMING GENERALIZATIONS

Possible Responses: Students answering yes might cite Roosevelt's appointments of women and the increase in the percentage of women employed, and they might say that the growth of employment reflected greater opportunity for women. Students answering no might point to lower wage levels for women and to discrimination in the workplace and in federal programs.

4. FORMING OPINIONS

Possible Responses: Students answering yes might argue that strikes, especially sit-down strikes, interfered with business and that labor disputes sometimes resulted in violence, as in Chicago and Flint, Michigan. Students answering no might argue that union membership was finally open to industrial workers and that union members enjoyed better working conditions and increased bargaining power.

4 Society and Culture

TERMS & NAMES
- *Gone with the Wind*
- Orson Welles
- Grant Wood
- Richard Wright
- *The Grapes of Wrath*

LEARN ABOUT arts, entertainment, and literature during the 1930s
TO UNDERSTAND how the Great Depression and New Deal influenced American culture.

ONE AMERICAN'S STORY

Don Congdon, editor of the book *The Thirties: A Time to Remember,* was a high school student when the New Deal began. He recalls "the air of excitement that pervaded the country. People spoke out freely and were willing to fight for what they believed in." During the 1930s, many artists and writers produced works that reflected the important issues of the day. It was the movies and radio, however, that most clearly captured the public imagination. Congdon remembers the role movies played at the time.

A PERSONAL VOICE

Lots of us enjoyed our leisure at the movies. The experience of going was like an insidious [tempting] candy we could never get quite enough of; the visit to the dark theater was an escape from the drab realities of Depression living, and we were entranced by the never-ending variety of stories. Hollywood, like Scheherazade [the storyteller] in *The Thousand and One Nights,* supplied more the next night, and the next night after that.

DON CONGDON, *The Thirties: A Time to Remember*

During the Great Depression, movies provided a window on a different, more exciting world. Despite economic hardship, many people gladly paid the 25 cents it cost to go to the movies. Along with radio, motion pictures became an increasingly dominant feature of American life.

People line up to get into a movie theater during the Great Depression.

The Lure of Motion Pictures and Radio

Although the 1930s were a difficult time for many Americans, they were a golden age for the motion-picture and radio industries. Statistics tell part of the story. By late in the decade, as many as 75 million people—around 65 percent of the population—were attending the movies once a week. The nation boasted over 15,000 movie theaters, more than the number of banks and double the number of hotels. Sales of radios also greatly increased during the 1930s, from just over 10 million at the beginning of the decade to around 30 million by the end. Nearly 90 percent of American households owned a radio. Clearly, movies and radio had taken the country by storm.

MOVIES ARE A HIT A wide variety of movies were made during the New Deal years. Wacky comedies, lavish musicals, tender love stories, and tough gangster films all vied for the attention of the moviegoing public. The movies introduced a new set of Hollywood stars, including Greta Garbo, Clark Gable, Marlene Dietrich, and James Cagney. These stars, who emerged following the end of

SECTION 4 RESOURCES

PRINT RESOURCES

IN-DEPTH RESOURCES: UNIT 4
Guided Reading, p. 56
Primary Sources: WPA Posters, p. 65; from *Let Us Now Praise Famous Men* by James Agee and Walker Evans, p. 66

READING STUDY GUIDE, p. 161

ACCESS FOR STUDENTS ACQUIRING ENGLISH
Guided Reading (Spanish), p. 178

SPANISH READING STUDY GUIDE, p. 161

FORMAL ASSESSMENT
Section Quiz, p. 190

ALTERNATIVE ASSESSMENT BOOK
See forms for supporting and scoring alternative activities.

TECHNOLOGY RESOURCES

VIDEO *American Portfolio: A Videodisc for U.S. History* user's guide, pp. 202, 207

INTERNET http://www.mlushistory.com

Section 4 Overview

OBJECTIVES

1. To describe the entertainment provided by motion pictures and radio.
2. To identify some of the artists and writers of the New Deal era.

CRITICAL THINKING

- Theme: Science and Technology, p. 524
- Analyzing causes, pp. 525, 528
- Analyzing issues, p. 527
- Synthesizing, p. 528
- Summarizing, p. 528
- Making predictions, p. 528

FOCUS & MOTIVATE

5-MINUTE WARM-UP

Making Inferences
To explore radio's impact on Depression America, have students read the Historical Spotlight on page 525 and answer these questions.

1. Why do you think Orson Welles chose to broadcast "The War of the Worlds" on October 31?
2. What did the public's reaction to the broadcast suggest about radio in the 1930s?

WARM-UP TRANSPARENCY 15

▶ ***Starting with the Student***
Ask students what kinds of movies they like best—action films, comedies, dramas, musicals.

OBJECTIVE
1 INSTRUCT

The Lure of Motion Pictures and Radio

▶ ***Discussing Key Ideas***
- During the Depression, people flock to the movies.

(continued on next page)

(continued from page 523)

- Most families spend several hours a day listening to their favorite radio programs.

IN-DEPTH RESOURCES: UNIT 4
Guided Reading, p. 56

ACCESS FOR STUDENTS ACQUIRING ENGLISH
Guided Reading (Spanish), p. 178

MORE ABOUT . . .
"The War of the Worlds"

During this golden age of entertainment, one of the most dramatic events was the radio broadcast of "The War of the Worlds" (described on page 525). The panic generated by the broadcast demonstrated the power of radio during the 1930s. When a voice cut into a musical program with the announcement "Ladies and gentlemen, we interrupt our program of dance music to bring you a special bulletin from the Intercontinental Radio News," thousands of listeners were convinced the reported Martian invasion was real. Some people ran out to the street, their mouths covered with handkerchiefs. One woman, fearful of being seized by Martians, almost took poison. When the electricity went out in a Washington town, many of the residents thought that the Martians were responsible. A woman who was a teenager at the time recalls her own experience: "My two girl friends and I were crying and holding each other and everything seemed so unimportant in the face of death. We felt it was terrible we should die so young."

Clark Gable and Vivien Leigh embrace in a scene from the popular film *Gone with the Wind.*

silent films and the rise of "talking" pictures, helped launch a new era of glamour and sophistication in Hollywood.

Some films made during the 1930s offered pure escape from the hard realities of the Depression by presenting visions of wealth, romance, and good times. Perhaps the most famous film of the era, and one of the most popular of all time, was ***Gone with the Wind*** (1939). This sweeping drama about life among Southern plantation owners during the Civil War starred Clark Gable and Vivien Leigh.

Another film, *Flying Down to Rio* (1933), was a light romantic comedy featuring Fred Astaire and Ginger Rogers, who went on to make many movies together, becoming America's favorite dance partners. The lavish musical *Gold Diggers of 1933,* with its theme song "We're in the Money," expressed many Americans' dream of a life of comfort and affluence. Other notable movies made during the 1930s include *The Wizard of Oz* (1939), a classic American film starring Judy Garland, and *Snow White and the Seven Dwarfs* (1937), which showcased the dazzling animation of Walt Disney.

COMEDIES AND HEROES ENTERTAIN Americans also flocked to see comedies on the silver screen. The most famous movie comedians of the time, the Marx Brothers, made a series of films that captured their zany humor. In one scene from *Duck Soup* (1933), Groucho Marx plays the prime minister of Freedonia, a fictional country. He holds up a document and says to his advisers, "Why, a four-year-old child could understand this report." Then, whispering to his brother Zeppo, he says, "Run out and find me a four-year-old child. I can't make head or tail out of it."

Other movies combined escapist appeal with more realistic plots and settings that conveyed a truer sense of Depression America. Often, these films showed heroes grappling with problems and rising above their circumstances. One type of realistic movie that was especially popular was the gangster film. Gangster films presented images of urban America—dark, gritty streets and looming skyscrapers. These movies featured hard-bitten characters, played by stars such as James Cagney and Edward G. Robinson, struggling to succeed in a harsh environment. Although these characters were often on the wrong side of the law, they faced difficulties that Depression-era audiences could easily understand. Notable films in this genre include *Little Caesar* (1930) and *The Public Enemy* (1931).

One of the first worldwide radio broadcasts was about the *Hindenburg,* a German zeppelin (rigid-frame dirigible balloon). The *Hindenburg* caught fire while landing in Lakehurst, New Jersey, on May 6, 1937. Thirty-six lives were lost in the fire.

In addition, several films made between 1934 and 1936 presented the social and political accomplishments of the New Deal in a positive light. *Mr. Deeds Goes to Town* (1936) and *Mr. Smith Goes to Washington* (1939), by director Frank Capra, portrayed honest, kindhearted people winning out over those with greedy special interests. In much the same way, the New Deal seemed to represent the interests of average Americans in relation to the wealthy and powerful.

RADIO ENTERTAINS Even more than movies, radio embodied the democratic spirit of the times. Almost every home had a radio, and families typically spent several

A. Answer
People attended movies in record numbers and saw realistic portrayals as well as escapist comedies and romances, all of which helped them cope with Depression reality.

THINK THROUGH HISTORY
A. THEME
Science and Technology
What were the cultural effects of technological advances in film?

TEACHING OPTIONS

Exploring Themes

Science and Technology Discuss the effect of motion pictures and radio on society during the Depression. Ask students to explain the appeal of movies and radio programs during this period. *Possible Response: They made people laugh, forget their own problems, and imagine a better world.* Ask them how technology serves a similar function in today's society. *Possible Response: Today, movies, television, and computer games provide entertainment and escape.*

Making Connections Across Time

Movies Today Tell students that action films with spectacular special effects attract large audiences today. Films featuring such effects—for example, *Star Wars* (1977, re-released in 1997), *E.T.: The Extra-Terrestrial* (1983), *Jurassic Park* (1993), and *Independence Day* (1996)—are among the most successful films in history. Some of the special effects are spaceships, aliens, dinosaurs, and images of mass destruction. Ask students to compare the effects used in *The Wizard of Oz* with those in a modern film. Ask them how the special effects are similar and how they differ.

hours a day gathered together, listening to their favorite programs. It's no surprise that President Roosevelt chose radio as the medium for his "fireside chats." It was the most direct means of access to the American people.

Like movies, radio programs offered great variety: news, comedies, dramas, soap operas, and children's shows. Soap operas—so named because they were usually sponsored by soap companies—tended to play early in the afternoon. These "real-life" dramas, which included *The Romance of Helen Trent* and *The Guiding Light,* typically featured women characters with romantic difficulties. Homemakers, the prime audience for these shows, found that the stories and characters gave them an outlet for their imagination during days filled with housework. Children's programs, such as *The Green Hornet* and *The Lone Ranger,* generally aired later in the afternoon, when children were home from school.

NETWORKS PROVIDE GREAT DRAMA AND COMEDY In the evening, radio networks offered excellent dramas and variety programs, featuring such stars as Bob Hope, Jack Benny, George Burns and Gracie Allen, and **Orson Welles.** Welles, an actor, director, and producer, created one of the most renowned radio broadcasts of all time, "The War of the Worlds." Later he directed movie classics such as *Citizen Kane* (1941) and *A Touch of Evil* (1958). Comedians Hope, Benny, and Burns and Allen performed routines that have stood the test of time. After making their reputation in radio, these stars later moved on to work in television and movies.

The comedy couple George Burns and Gracie Allen delighted NBC radio audiences for years, and their popularity continued on television.

HISTORICAL SPOTLIGHT

WAR OF THE WORLDS

On October 30, 1938, radio listeners were stunned by a special announcement: Martians had invaded Earth! Panic set in as many Americans became convinced that the world was coming to an end. Of course, the story wasn't true: it was a radio drama based on H. G. Wells's novel *The War of the Worlds.*

In his book, Wells describes the canisters of gas fired by the Martians as releasing "an enormous volume of heavy, inky vapour . . . and the touch of that vapour, the inhaling of its pungent wisps, was death to all that breathes." The broadcast, produced by Orson Welles, revealed the power of radio at a time when many Americans received fast-breaking news over the airwaves.

Art and Literature in Depression America

In contrast to the radio and movie productions of the 1930s, much of the art and literature of the time was more sober and serious. Many writers and artists depicted the real conditions of Depression America. Identifying with the struggles of working people, these artists and writers produced paintings, plays, novels, and poetry that focused on the hardships faced by average Americans.

Some of this artistic work was grim and somber, but much of it conveyed a more uplifting message about the strength of character and the democratic values of the American people. A number of artists and writers embraced the spirit of social and political change fostered by the New Deal, and many received direct support through New Deal work programs.

Although some people argued that the government should not be in the business of funding art projects, New Deal officials thought that art played an important role in national life. They also believed that artists deserved work relief as much as other unemployed Americans. As the head of the WPA, Harry Hopkins, put it, "They've got to eat just like other people."

B. Answer New Deal officials believed that art played an important role in the life of the American people. They also believed that artists deserved work relief just as other unemployed Americans did.

THINK THROUGH HISTORY
B. *Analyzing Causes* *Why did the New Deal fund art projects?*

ARTISTS DECORATE AMERICA The Federal Art Project, a branch of the WPA, paid artists a living wage to produce public art. It also had two other functions: to increase public appreciation of art and to promote positive images of American society. Artists created posters, taught art in the schools, and painted murals on the walls of public buildings. These murals, inspired in part by the revolutionary work of Mexican muralists such as Diego Rivera, typically portrayed the dignity

HISTORICAL SPOTLIGHT
War of the Worlds

Critical Thinking: Analyzing Ask students how the Depression might have made listeners more liable to believe that the Martian invasion was real. *Possible Response: The Depression was a terrible calamity and to many people it probably seemed to have happened without warning. The Depression and its consequences may have led people to believe anything could happen.*

OBJECTIVE
(2) INSTRUCT

Art and Literature in Depression America

▶ ***Starting with the Student*** Have students create a chart to help them organize the information in this section. Students should list each artist and writer and his or her work and briefly describe the subject.

Artist/Writer	Work	Subject

▶ ***Discussing Key Ideas***
- During the New Deal era, some American artists produce outstanding works of art.
- Writers produce works depicting both the dark side of life and the positive values of American culture.

IN-DEPTH RESOURCES: UNIT 4
Primary Source: WPA Posters, p. 65

Block Schedule TEACHING OPTION **Time Needed: 30 Minutes**

Cooperative Activity: Producing a Depression-Era Radio Program

Task: Groups of four or five students will collaborate on an outline for a 1930s-style radio program.

Purpose: To understand the power and appeal of radio during the Depression.

Activity: Have groups get together to decide what type of radio program they want to plan: a comedy, drama, soap opera, or children's show. Students should then discuss ideas and collaborate on an outline. The outline should include full descriptions of the characters to be featured. Outlines should also include directions for sound effects.

Building a Portfolio: Students who add a copy of the outline to their portfolio should attach a note explaining their contribution.

ALTERNATIVE ASSESSMENT BOOK
Standards for Evaluating a Cooperative Activity

Standards for Evaluation
Outlines should . . .
- include full character descriptions
- describe voices, music, and sound effects to help listeners visualize the story
- suggest a clear plan for a radio broadcast

NOW & THEN
The Coit Tower Murals
Critical Thinking: Evaluating Ask students why they think the murals in Coit Tower—and many of those in other public buildings—deal with work and workers. *Possible Response: During the Depression, people were consumed with the idea of returning to work and a normal life.* Then point out that today there has been renewed interest in the murals. Why do students think this is so? *Possible Responses: The Depression is studied as a historical event. The artistic merit of the murals has been recognized.*

of ordinary Americans at work. One artist, Robert Gwathmey, recalled the importance of these efforts.

NOW & THEN

THE COIT TOWER MURALS

One of the best-preserved WPA mural projects can be seen in San Francisco's Coit Tower. Twenty-five artists and many assistants worked on the paintings, which cover the lobby walls. Their style, called social realism, created some controversy, because it used the depiction of everyday life to criticize the conditions under which people lived and worked.

A sense of the dignity and importance of work—as well as its strenuousness and monotony—is typical of murals painted by WPA artists on public buildings across the country. You can see this in the rich, subdued colors and the somber expressions of the subjects in the Coit Tower murals.

A PERSONAL VOICE

The director of the Federal Art Project was Edward Bruce. He was a friend of the Roosevelts—from a polite family—who was a painter. He was a man of real broad vision. He insisted there be no restrictions. You were a painter: Do your work. You were a sculptor: Do your work. You were a printmaker: Do your work. . . . That was a very free and happy period. Social comment was in the wind.

ROBERT GWATHMEY, in an interview with Studs Terkel

During the New Deal era, a number of American artists produced outstanding works of art. Edward Hopper, a New York painter, continued to depict scenes of urban life in a striking, highly realistic style. Other artists, such as Thomas Hart Benton of Missouri, helped create a regional style of painting that drew on Midwestern cultural roots. One of the most notable of these regional artists, Iowa's **Grant Wood,** liked to say that his best ideas "came while milking a cow." His work includes the famous painting *American Gothic,* which shows two stern-faced farmers, a father and daughter, standing stiffly in front of their farmhouse.

Some artists also worked for the Federal Theater Project, which was part of the WPA. Artists hired for this project provided stage sets and props for theater productions that played around the country. By 1939,

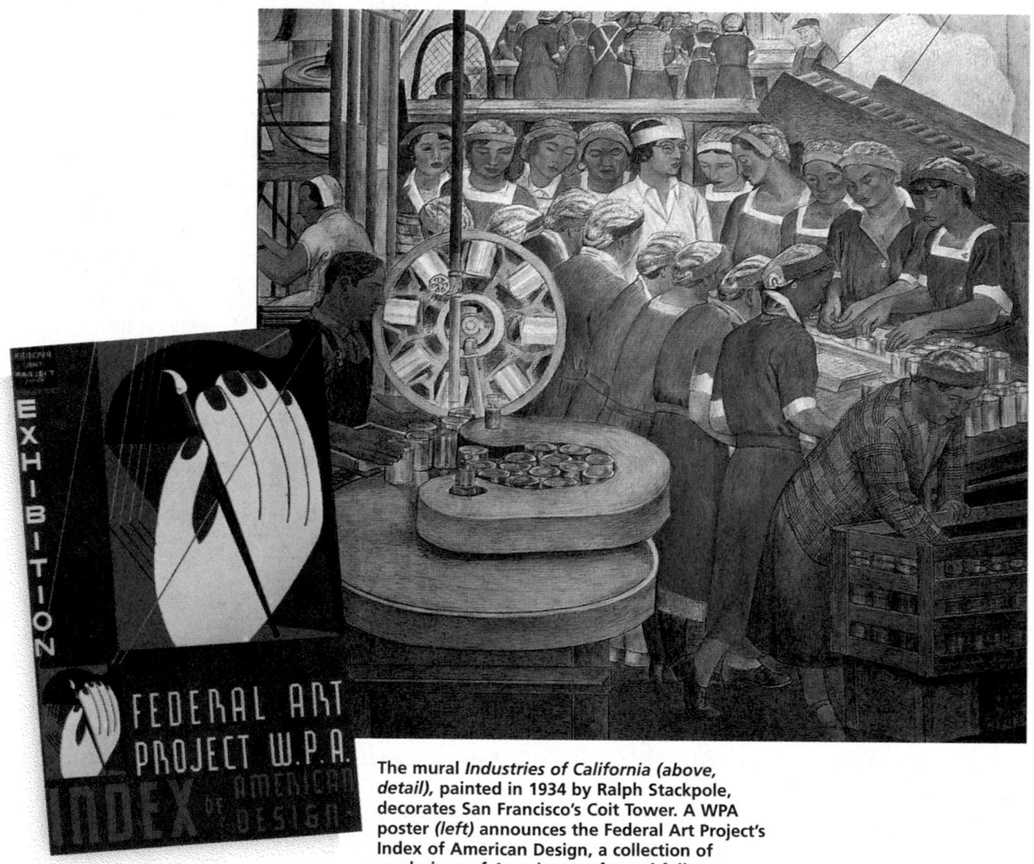

The mural *Industries of California (above, detail),* painted in 1934 by Ralph Stackpole, decorates San Francisco's Coit Tower. A WPA poster *(left)* announces the Federal Art Project's Index of American Design, a collection of renderings of American crafts and folk arts.

TEACHING OPTIONS

Making Connections Across the Curriculum

Art Tell students that painters such as Grant Wood and Edward Hopper wanted to create a completely American style of painting. In Wood's *American Gothic,* for instance, the artist depicts the people, landscape, and architecture of the Midwest. Edward Hopper, on the other hand, found many of his subjects in urban settings. Paintings of his such as *Nighthawks* or *Early Sunday Morning* convey the loneliness and isolation of modern life.

Making Connections Across the Curriculum

Art Jackson Pollock achieved fame in the 1940s as an artist of the abstract expressionist school. Earlier, from 1929 to 1931, he had studied with the regional artist Thomas Hart Benton in New York City while receiving financial support from the WPA. In his later work, Pollock moved away from regional themes and began painting in a new style, using symbols and abstract images.

Grant Wood's painting *American Gothic* (1930) became one of the most famous portrayals of America's rural life during the Great Depression.

an estimated 30 million people had seen WPA theater programs, which featured such noted actors as John Houseman and Arlene Francis. The Federal Theater Project also subsidized the work of important American playwrights, including Clifford Odets, whose play *Waiting for Lefty* (1935) dramatized the labor struggles of the 1930s.

WRITERS DEPICT AMERICAN LIFE Many writers received relief support through yet another WPA program, the Federal Writers' Project (FWP). The FWP hired unemployed writers to produce a series of state and city guides and to write histories of ethnic and immigrant groups, including a major study of Southern slavery. This project also gave the future Pulitzer Prize winner Saul Bellow his first writing job and helped **Richard Wright,** an African-American author, complete his acclaimed novel *Native Son* (1940). Wright's novel depicts the difficulties faced by a young man trying to survive in a racist world. Zora Neale Hurston wrote a stirring novel with FWP assistance—*Their Eyes Were Watching God* (1937), about a young woman growing up in rural Florida.

C. Answer Writers depicted the difficulties of the Depression Era, such as the Dust Bowl, working-class life, violence and poverty, small-town life in New England, and life in urban America.

THINK THROUGH HISTORY
C. Analyzing Issues *How did the literature of the time reflect issues of the Depression?*

One of this country's most famous authors, John Steinbeck, also received assistance from the Federal Writers' Project. Eventually, Steinbeck was able to publish his epic novel ***The Grapes of Wrath*** (1939), which reveals the lives of Oklahomans who left the Dust Bowl and ended up in California, where their hardships continued. Before his success, however, Steinbeck had endured the difficulties of the Depression like most other writers. In an essay, he recalled his experience.

A PERSONAL VOICE

Being without a job, I went on writing—books, essays, short stories. Regularly they went out and just as regularly came back. Even if they had been good, they would have come back because publishers were hardest hit of all. When people are broke, the first things they give up are books. . . . It's not easy to go on writing constantly with little hope that anything will come of it. But I do remember it as a time of warmth and mutual caring. If [a friend] got hurt or ill or in trouble, the others rallied with what they had. Everyone shared bad fortune as well as good.

JOHN STEINBECK, "I Remember the Thirties"

MORE ABOUT . . .
John Steinbeck and the Depression

When the Depression began, Steinbeck didn't lose any money. As an unemployed writer, he claimed, "I had been practicing for the Depression a long time." Fortunately for Steinbeck, his father owned a small home along the coast of northern California. The home provided Steinbeck with a place to live, and the location enabled him to obtain plenty of food. "Given the sea," he wrote, "a man must be very stupid to starve." Only one thing frightened Steinbeck—illness. "You have to have money to be sick—or did then. And dentistry also was out of the question, with the result that my teeth went badly to pieces. Without dough, you couldn't have a tooth filled."

IN-DEPTH RESOURCES: UNIT 4
Primary Source: from *Let Us Now Praise Famous Men* by James Agee and Walker Evans, p. 66

TEACHING OPTIONS

Making Connections Across the Curriculum

Literature Have groups of students select and read a work of fiction or nonfiction written during the Depression. Books they might read include *The Grapes of Wrath* by John Steinbeck, *Native Son* by Richard Wright, a volume from James T. Farrell's Studs Lonigan trilogy, or a volume from John Dos Passos's trilogy, *U.S.A.* Then have group members engage in a discussion of the book to prepare for an oral report. The group discussion should produce a number of points about the book that can be presented to the class.

Making Connections Across Cultures

The African-American Experience Point out that African-American authors, such as Richard Wright and Zora Neale Hurston, wrote about the racial injustice of the 1930s and 1940s. During this time, discrimination was openly practiced and instances of lynchings were on the rise. In *Native Son,* Wright suggested that an environment of injustice and racial hatred could force young African Americans into a life of crime.

ASSESS & RETEACH

Section 4 Assessment

Have students answer the questions and then note which ones gave them the most trouble.

Self-Assessment

To document what they have learned, students should list the insights they've gained on the impact of motion pictures, radio, art, and literature during the 1930s.

Section Quiz

FORMAL ASSESSMENT
Section Quiz, p. 190

Reteach

Use the graphic in item 2 of the Section Assessment to review the material. Copy the graphic onto the chalkboard, and ask students to volunteer names to fill in the chart.

CLOSE

During the Depression, motion pictures and radio programs were highly popular forms of entertainment—and escape. The art and the literature of the time, on the other hand, were more serious, depicting the real conditions of Depression America.

Walker Evans took this photograph of a sharecropper for the influential book *Let Us Now Praise Famous Men.*

Other books and authors also examined the difficulties of life during the 1930s. James T. Farrell's Studs Lonigan trilogy (1932–35) provides a bleak picture of working-class life in an Irish neighborhood of Chicago. A three-part work by John Dos Passos, *U.S.A.* (1930–36), draws a detailed portrait of 20th-century American history. In Dos Passos's view, much of the country's promise was being destroyed by a small class of rich and powerful people driven by selfish interests, without regard for the nation as a whole. Jack Conroy's novel *The Disinherited* (1933) portrays the violence and poverty of the Missouri coalfields, where Conroy's own father and brother died in a mine disaster.

While some writers focused on the dark side of American life, others found hope in the positive values of American culture. The writer James Agee and the photographer Walker Evans collaborated on a book about Alabama sharecroppers, *Let Us Now Praise Famous Men* (1941). Though it deals with the difficult lives of poor farmers, this book portrays the dignity and strength of character in the people it presents. The play *Our Town* (1938), by Thornton Wilder, captures the warmth and beauty of small-town life in New England. William Saroyan's play *The Time of Your Life* (1939) offers a tender look at a diverse assortment of characters in urban America.

By the late 1930s, artists such as Horace Pippin and Anna "Grandma" Moses—along with writers such as Margaret Mitchell, who wrote the novel *Gone with the Wind,* and the poet Carl Sandburg—had embraced a cultural nationalism. Although these intellectuals recognized that the United States had its flaws, they also praised the virtues of American life and took pride in the nation's cultural traditions and accomplishments. These artists and writers contributed positively to the New Deal legacy.

D. Answer It did both. Some books revealed the seamy side of American society, while others extolled the virtues of American culture. On the whole, however, most writers seemed to appreciate the underlying strength of American life.

THINK THROUGH HISTORY
D. *Synthesizing* *Did literature during the 1930s present a positive or a negative view of American society? Explain.*

Section 4 Assessment

1. TERMS & NAMES

Identify:
- *Gone with the Wind*
- Orson Welles
- Grant Wood
- Richard Wright
- *The Grapes of Wrath*

2. SUMMARIZING Using a four-column chart, such as the one below, list three important movie stars, radio performers, painters, and writers from the 1930s.

Movie Stars	Radio Stars	Painters	Writers
1. 2. 3.	1. 2. 3.	1. 2. 3.	1. 2. 3.

What contribution did each group make?

3. MAKING PREDICTIONS What type of movies do you think might have been produced if the government had supported moviemaking as part of the New Deal? Use evidence from the chapter to support your response.

THINK ABOUT
- the role entertainment played in the 1930s
- the variety of movies made during the New Deal years
- the subject matter of New Deal literature and art

4. ANALYZING CAUSES In your opinion, what were the main benefits of government support for art and literature in the 1930s? Support your response with details from the text.

THINK ABOUT
- the experiences of Americans in the Great Depression
- the writers who got their start through the FWP
- the subject matter of WPA murals and other New Deal art

ANSWERS

1. TERMS & NAMES

Gone with the Wind, p. 524
Orson Welles, p. 525
Grant Wood, p. 526
Richard Wright, p. 527
The Grapes of Wrath, p. 527

2. SUMMARIZING

Possible Answers: **Movie Stars:** Greta Garbo, Clark Gable, Marlene Dietrich, James Cagney, Vivien Leigh, Fred Astaire, Ginger Rogers, Edward G. Robinson. **Radio Stars:** George Burns, Gracie Allen, Bob Hope, Jack Benny. **Painters:** Edward Hopper, Thomas Hart Benton, Grant Wood. **Writers:** Richard Wright, Zora Neale Hurston, James T. Farrell, John Steinbeck, John Dos Passos, Thornton Wilder.

3. MAKING PREDICTIONS

Possible Responses: Perhaps more films that focused on social and political accomplishments such as *Mr. Smith Goes to Washington;* perhaps documentary films about the Depression or the Dust Bowl, or about difficulties faced by African Americans (such as those Richard Wright wrote about); perhaps films that incorporated New Deal ideals with popular film techniques.

4. ANALYZING CAUSES

Possible Responses: It allowed writers to produce serious literature that told about the difficulties endured by people in the 1930s; it left a written and pictorial legacy of the 1930s that enabled future generations to understand what happened then; it gave a gift to all Americans by providing great writers and artists the opportunity to create; it made the arts available to everyone.

5 The Impact of the New Deal

TERMS & NAMES
- deficit spending
- National Labor Relations Board
- parity
- Securities and Exchange Commission
- Federal Deposit Insurance Corporation
- Tennessee Valley Authority

LEARN ABOUT the effects of New Deal reforms
TO UNDERSTAND the short-term and long-term impact of the New Deal on American society.

Section 5 Overview

OBJECTIVES

1. To summarize opinions about the effectiveness of the New Deal.
2. To describe the legacies of the New Deal.

SKILLBUILDER

- Interpreting graphs, p. 531

CRITICAL THINKING

- Analyzing, p. 529
- Recognizing effects, pp. 531, 533
- Contrasting, p. 532
- Summarizing, p. 533
- Forming opinions, p. 533
- Evaluating, p. 533

ONE AMERICAN'S STORY

George Dobbin staunchly supported Franklin Delano Roosevelt and his New Deal policies. A cotton-mill worker, Dobbin was interviewed at age 67 for a book compiled by the Federal Writers' Project. This book, entitled *These Are Our Lives,* presents the experiences of ordinary Americans during the Depression. In the interview, Dobbin explained his feelings about President Roosevelt.

A PERSONAL VOICE

I do think that Roosevelt is the biggest-hearted man we ever had in the White House. . . . It's the first time in my recollection that a President ever got up and said, "I'm interested in and aim to do somethin' for the workin' man." Just knowin' that for once . . . [there] was a man to stand up and speak for him, a man that could make what he felt so plain nobody could doubt he meant it, has made a lot of us feel a sight [lot] better even when . . . [there] wasn't much to eat in our homes.

GEORGE DOBBIN, quoted in *These Are Our Lives*

Although not all people shared Dobbin's opinion of FDR, the president was extremely popular among working-class Americans. Far more important than his personal popularity, however, was the impact of the policies he initiated. Even today, reforms begun under the New Deal continue to influence American politics and society.

A coal miner, Zeno Santinello, shakes hands with Franklin D. Roosevelt as he campaigns in Elm Grove, West Virginia, in 1932.

New Deal Reforms That Endure

During his second term in office, President Roosevelt hinted at plans to launch a Third New Deal to build on the achievements of his first four years in office. In his inaugural address, the president exclaimed, "I see millions of families trying to live on incomes so meager that the pall of family disaster hangs over them day by day. I see one-third of a nation ill-housed, ill-clad, ill-nourished."

Nevertheless, by 1937, the economy had improved enough to convince many Americans that the Depression was finally ending. Industrial production had returned to 1929 levels, and unemployment had fallen to 14 percent—still high, but much lower than in the early 1930s. Although economic troubles still plagued the nation, President Roosevelt faced rising pressure from Congress to scale back on New Deal programs, and he did. As a result, industrial production dropped again, and the number of unemployed rose from about 7 million early in 1937 to 11 million early in 1938. FDR did not like **deficit spending**—spending more money than the government receives in revenue. (See *deficit spending* on page 934 in the Economics Handbook.) Therefore, he never launched a third reform era. By 1939, the New Deal was effectively over and Roosevelt was increasingly concerned with events in Europe—particularly Hitler's rise to power in Germany.

THINK THROUGH HISTORY
A. Analyzing *Why did industrial production drop again and unemployment go up again in 1938?*
A. Answer Because, in response to pressure from Congress, FDR cut back on New Deal programs.

SUPPORTERS AND CRITICS OF THE NEW DEAL Over time, opinions about the New Deal have ranged from harsh criticism to high praise. Most conservatives think President Roosevelt's policies made the federal government too large and too powerful by involving government agencies in the nation's finances, agriculture, industries, and housing. They believe that the government has stifled free enterprise and individual initiative. Liberal critics, in contrast, argue that President

FOCUS & MOTIVATE

5-MINUTE WARM-UP

Evaluating Judgments
To understand FDR's popularity, have students read One American's Story on page 529 and answer these questions.

1. Why was President Roosevelt popular among working-class Americans?
2. How did Roosevelt's personality bolster his popularity?

WARM-UP TRANSPARENCY 15

▶***Starting with the Student***
Ask students what effect, if any, they think government policies have on them. Then ask them if they think government should do more to help people or should do less.

SECTION 5 RESOURCES

PRINT RESOURCES

IN-DEPTH RESOURCES: UNIT 4
Guided Reading, p. 57
Geography Application: Decade of the Democrats, p. 59
Outline Map: Anatomy of the Tennessee Valley Authority, p. 61

READING STUDY GUIDE, p. 163

ACCESS FOR STUDENTS ACQUIRING ENGLISH
Guided Reading (Spanish), p. 179
Geography Application: Decade of the Democrats (Spanish), p. 181
Outline Map: Anatomy of the Tennessee Valley Authority (Spanish), p. 183

SPANISH READING STUDY GUIDE, p. 163

FORMAL ASSESSMENT
Section Quiz, p. 191

ALTERNATIVE ASSESSMENT BOOK
See forms for supporting and scoring alternative activities.

TECHNOLOGY RESOURCES

CRITICAL THINKING TRANSPARENCIES
CT23, The New Deal
CT57, The U.S. Economic Indicators: 1929–1939

CD-ROM *Grolier Multimedia Encyclopedia*

VIDEO *American Portfolio: A Videodisc for U.S. History* user's guide, p. 207

INTERNET http://www.mlushistory.com

OBJECTIVE
① INSTRUCT

New Deal Reforms That Endure

▶***Discussing Key Ideas***
- Opinions about the New Deal range from harsh criticism to high praise.

(continued on next page)

(continued from page 529)

- New Deal policies have a lasting effect on labor, agriculture, and banking and finance.

IN-DEPTH RESOURCES: UNIT 4
Guided Reading, p. 57
Geography Application: Decade of the Democrats, p. 59

ACCESS FOR STUDENTS ACQUIRING ENGLISH
Guided Reading (Spanish), p. 179

POINT/COUNTERPOINT
The New Deal

▶ ***Starting with the Student***
Ask students to name a recent controversy in the news about the usefulness of a particular government program (such as welfare, affirmative action, or Social Security).

- Have students benefited from any government programs?
- Do they think government is the problem, the solution, or neither?

▶ ***Discussing Key Ideas***

- Supporters of the New Deal believe it helped the nation recover from economic crisis and established a necessary role for government in ensuring the economic stability of the nation.
- Conservative critics of the New Deal believe it made government's role in the economy too intrusive, whereas liberal critics say the New Deal didn't go far enough in establishing economic and social equality.

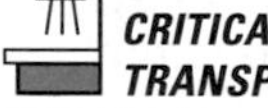
CRITICAL THINKING TRANSPARENCIES
CT23, The New Deal
CT57, The U.S. Economic Indicators: 1929–1939

Roosevelt didn't do enough to socialize the economy and to eliminate social and economic inequalities. The nation still had only a few very rich people and an enormous number of poor people. Supporters of the New Deal contend, however, that the president struck a reasonable balance between two extremes—unregulated capitalism and overregulated socialism—and helped the country recover from its economic difficulties. Rexford Tugwell, one of Roosevelt's top advisers, made this assessment of the president's goals.

A PERSONAL VOICE

He had in mind a comprehensive welfare concept, infused with a stiff tincture of morality. . . . He wanted all Americans to grow up healthy and vigorous and to be practically educated. He wanted business men to work within a set of understood rules. Beyond this he wanted people free to vote, to worship, to behave as they wished so long as a moral code was respected; and he wanted officials to behave as though office were a public trust.

REXFORD TUGWELL, quoted in *Redeeming the Time*

POINT

"The New Deal . . . transformed the way American government works."

Supporters of the New Deal believe that it was successful. Many historians and journalists make this judgment by using the economic criterion of creating jobs. The editors of *The New Republic*, for example, noted in an editorial published in 1940 that the shortcomings of the WPA "are insignificant beside the gigantic fact that it has given jobs and sustenance to a minimum of 1,400,000 and a maximum 3,300,000 persons for five years."

Some historians stress that the New Deal was more than a temporary solution to a crisis. Professor David Bennett claims about the New Deal that "beyond . . . its relief and recovery programs lay its larger achievement, the recognition that social and economic problems in this great nation required national political solutions and national political responsibility, that the old order would not and could not work any more." Professor A. A. Berle states that "human beings cannot indefinitely be sacrificed by millions to the operation of economic forces."

The historian William E. Leuchtenburg argues that the New Deal "should be recognized as a series of imaginative initiatives and programs that helped innumerable Americans during the Great Depression and transformed the way American government works."

The Pulitzer Prize–winning historian Allan Nevins sums up the importance of New Deal measures by pointing out that "the resourcefulness of the New Deal marks a fundamental shift in which the government assumed a greater responsibility for ensuring economic prosperity for all Americans."

COUNTERPOINT

"Many more problems have been created than solved by the New Deal."

Critics of the New Deal believe that it failed to reach its goals. Reporting on the New Deal when it was implemented, the journalists Benjamin Stolberg and Warren Jay Vinton accused the government of "trying to right the unbalance of our economic life by strengthening all its contradictions." They went on to claim that "in trying to move in every direction at once the New Deal betrays the fact that it has no policy."

The historian Barton J. Bernstein accepted the goals of the New Deal but declared that they were never met. To him, the New Deal "failed to raise the impoverished, it failed to redistribute income, [and] it failed to extend equality."

In Senator Robert A. Taft's opinion, "many more problems have been created than solved" by the New Deal. He maintained that "whatever else has resulted from the great increase in government activity . . . it has certainly had the effect of checking private enterprise completely. This country was built up by the constant establishment of new business and the expansion of old businesses. . . . In the last six years this process has come to an end because of government regulation and the development of a tax system which penalizes hard work and success." Senator Taft claimed that "government competition with private industry should be confined to its present limits. . . . The government should gradually withdraw from the business of lending money and leave that function to private capital under proper regulation." Taft insisted that he was "convinced that we can restore prosperity. . . . It can be done, but it cannot be done by government regulation of agriculture and commerce and industry."

INTERACT WITH HISTORY

1. **COMPARING AND CONTRASTING** In what ways did the New Deal succeed? In what ways did it fail? Reread the article and summarize the main points.

SEE SKILLBUILDER HANDBOOK, PAGE 909.

2. **RESEARCHING THE WPA** Research the various programs of the WPA and draft a proposal for a WPA-type program that would especially benefit your community.

Visit http://www.mlushistory.com for more about the New Deal.

INTERACT WITH HISTORY

1. Comparing and Contrasting

Possible Responses:

The New Deal succeeded in creating jobs; it gave national government a greater role in solving social and economic problems; it took measures to help ensure economic prosperity.

The New Deal failed because it created more problems than it solved; it gave government too intrusive a role in economic matters; it did not redistribute income, reduce poverty, or extend equality.

2. Researching the WPA

Standards for Evaluation
Proposals should . . .

- present details and examples of a specific program
- identify ways in which the program would benefit the community
- list various kinds of public works
- make practical suggestions for addressing problems in the community
- be well organized and clearly written

EXPANDING GOVERNMENT'S ROLE IN THE ECONOMY The Roosevelt administration expanded the power of the federal government, giving it—and particularly the president—a more active role in shaping the economy. It did this by infusing the nation's economy with millions of dollars, by creating federal jobs, by attempting to regulate supply and demand, and by increasing the government's active participation in settling labor and management disputes. The federal government also established agencies, such as the Federal Deposit Insurance Corporation and the Securities and Exchange Commission, to regulate banking and investment activities. Although the New Deal did not end the Great Depression, it did help reduce the suffering of thousands of men, women, and children by providing them with jobs, food, and money. It also gave people hope and helped them to regain a sense of dignity.

The federal government had to go deeply in to debt to provide jobs and aid to the American people. As the graph on this page shows, the federal deficit increased to $3.3 billion in the fiscal year ending June 30, 1934. As a result of the cutbacks in federal spending made in 1937–1938, the deficit dropped to $100 million. The next year it rose again, to $2.9 billion. What really ended the Depression was the massive amount of spending by the federal government for guns, tanks, ships, airplanes, and all the other equipment and supplies the country needed for the World War II effort. During the war, the deficit reached a high of about $54 billion, in 1943.

THINK THROUGH HISTORY
B. Recognizing Effects *What impact did the New Deal have on the federal government?*

B. Answer It increased the size of government and its power in many areas of American life.

THE LABOR FRONT One of the areas in which New Deal policies have had a lasting effect is the protection of workers' rights. Before the New Deal, workers were typically on their own when seeking a fair contract from employers. Indeed, the government tended to side with the interests of business against the interests of labor. New Deal legislation, such as the Wagner Act and the Fair Labor Standards Act, changed that pattern by setting standards for wages and hours, banning child labor, and ensuring the right of workers to organize and bargain collectively with employers. Today, the **National Labor Relations Board,** created under the Wagner Act, continues to act as a mediator in labor disputes between unions and employers.

ECONOMIC BACKGROUND

DEFICIT SPENDING

John Maynard Keynes, an influential British economist, promoted the idea of deficit spending to stimulate economic recovery. In his view, a country in the grip of a depression should spend its way out of it by putting money into the hands of consumers. This would make it possible for them to buy goods and services and thus fuel economic growth. Therefore, even if a government has to go deeply into debt, it should spend great amounts of money to help get the economy growing again.

Although President Roosevelt agreed a policy of deficit spending, he did so with great reluctance. FDR was a firm believer in balanced budgets. He regarded deficit spending as a necessary evil to be used only at a time of great economic crisis. (See *deficit spending* on page 934 and *Keynesian economics* on page 936 in the Economics Handbook.)

Federal Deficit and Unemployment, 1933–1945

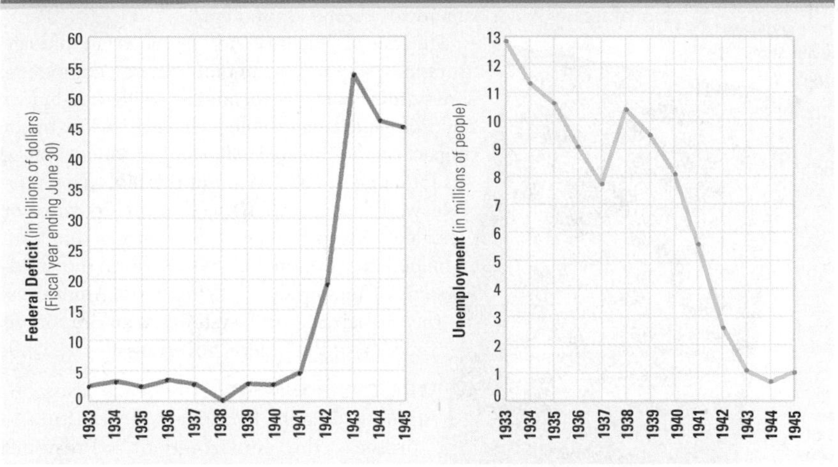

SKILLBUILDER **INTERPRETING GRAPHS** *What was the peak year of the deficit? What relationship does there seem to be between deficit spending and unemployment? Why do you think this is so?*

Skillbuilder Answer **Peak Year** 1943. **Relationship:** Unemployment increases when there is less deficit spending and decreases when there is more deficit spending, perhaps because the deficit spending stimulates the creation of jobs.

ECONOMIC BACKGROUND
Deficit Spending

Critical Thinking: Analyzing Ask students whether they think the Roosevelt administration was justified in using deficit spending to stimulate the economy. If they say it wasn't justified, ask them what other measures the government should have taken to end the Depression.

MORE ABOUT . . .
John Maynard Keynes

In Herbert Hoover's indictment of his successor's New Deal, he wrote: "I vetoed the idea of recovery through stupendous spending to prime the pump. That was born of a British professor." The British professor Hoover referred to was John Maynard Keynes. Keynes was one of the most influential economists of the first half of the 20th century.

HISTORY FROM VISUALS
Federal Deficit and Unemployment, 1933–1945

Reading the Graphs Help students to see the inverse relationship between deficit spending and unemployment—as deficit spending goes up, the unemployment rate goes down.

Extension Have students draw these graphs on a sheet of paper, superimposing one on top of the other to emphasize the point that as the deficit went up, the unemployment rate went down.

Block Schedule TEACHING OPTION **Time Needed: 40 Minutes**

Cooperative Activity: Debating the New Deal

Task: Teams of four to five students will take a stand on the effectiveness of the New Deal and engage in a debate with teams who support the opposing viewpoint.

Purpose: To express an informed opinion about the effectiveness of New Deal policies.

Activity: Have students form teams to investigate the effectiveness of the New Deal. Team members should first research material on both sides of the issue. Then they should have a brainstorming session in which they decide which side of the argument they want to make. Next, they should prepare an argument defending their case. Students should use sound reasoning, facts, and examples to support their argument. They should also be prepared to counter or concede valid points raised by the opposition. Pair opposing teams and conduct the debates in class.

ALTERNATIVE ASSESSMENT BOOK
Standards for Evaluating a Cooperative Activity

NOW & THEN
Social Security
Critical Thinking: Evaluating Ask students whether they think the Social Security system should be changed, and if so, how.

OBJECTIVE
② INSTRUCT

Continuing Benefits

▶ ***Starting with the Student*** Have students create a three-column chart showing the continuing benefits of the New Deal. Students should compare FDR's original policies on Social Security, the environment, and labor with the policies pursued today. Students might list the information in a chart like this:

	Then	Now
Social Security		
Environment		
Labor		

▶ ***Discussing Key Ideas***
- Under the New Deal, the federal government assumes some responsibility for the social welfare of its citizens.
- The New Deal promotes policies designed to protect the environment.

IN-DEPTH RESOURCES: UNIT 4
Outline Map: Anatomy of the Tennessee Valley Authority, p. 61

GROLIER MULTIMEDIA ENCYCLOPEDIA
History of the Tennessee Valley Authority

THE RURAL SCENE New Deal policies also had a significant impact on the nation's agriculture. New Deal farm legislation set quotas on the production of crops such as wheat to control surpluses. Under the second Agricultural Adjustment Act, passed in 1938, farmers stored their crops until prices reached **parity**—a price equal to what farmers had received in the years between 1910 and 1914. Establishing price supports for farmers set a precedent of federal aid to farmers that continued into the 1990s. Other government programs, such as electrification, helped to improve conditions in rural America.

By subsidizing farmers and setting minimum wages for workers, New Deal legislation had a very important effect on the nation's economy: more people had more money to spend, so the economy began to recover.

BANKING AND FINANCE New Deal programs established new policies in the area of banking and finance. The **Securities and Exchange Commission** (SEC), created in 1934, continues to monitor the stock market and enforce laws regarding the sale of stocks and bonds. The **Federal Deposit Insurance Corporation** (FDIC), created by the Glass-Steagall Banking Act of 1933, has shored up the banking system by reassuring individual depositors that their savings are protected against loss in the event of a bank failure. Today, individual accounts in United States federal banks are insured by the Federal Deposit Insurance Corporation for up to $100,000.

NOW & THEN

SOCIAL SECURITY

Today the Social Security system continues to rely on mandatory contributions. These contributions are paid both by workers, through payroll deductions, and by employers. The money is invested in a trust fund, from which retirement benefits are later paid. Several problems, however, have surfaced. One problem is that Americans are now living longer than they did in 1935. Also, the ratio of workers to retirees is shrinking: fewer people are contributing to the system relative to the number who are receiving benefits. In addition, benefits under Social Security have been expanded. Today, the system includes Medicare benefits, which provide health care for the elderly.

The long-range payment of benefits may be in jeopardy because of the large number of recipients. Many people believe that the system should be reexamined and probably changed.

A Social Security poster proclaims the benefits of the system for those who are 65 or older.

Continuing Benefits

New Deal economic and financial reforms, including creation of the FDIC, the SEC, and Social Security, have helped to stabilize the nation's finances and economy. Although the nation still experiences economic downturns, known as recessions, people's savings are insured and they can receive unemployment compensation if they lose their jobs.

SOCIAL SECURITY One of the most important legacies of the New Deal has been that the federal government has assumed some responsibility for the social welfare of its citizens. This philosophy represented a major departure from the traditional attitude that churches and private charities were the only institutions that should help care for the needy. Under President Roosevelt, the government undertook the creation of a Social Security system that would help a large number of needy Americans receive some assistance.

The Social Security Act provides an old-age insurance program, an unemployment compensation system, and aid to families with dependent children and the disabled. It has had a major impact on the lives of millions of Americans since its founding in 1935. Without this aid, many people would have experienced severe poverty or neglect. The payments to laid-off workers have helped to cushion individuals from the hardships of unemployment. For most Americans, the Social Security system is an important function of the federal government.

C. Answer The government began accepting responsibility for providing assistance to needy members of society, whereas the traditional attitude was that private institutions should take care of those in need.

THINK THROUGH HISTORY
C. Contrasting *How did the Social Security system represent a change from past policies?*

THE ENVIRONMENT Americans also continue to benefit from New Deal efforts to protect the environment. President Roosevelt was highly committed to conservation and promoted policies designed

TEACHING OPTIONS

Exploring Themes

Economic Opportunity Tell students that recessions are part of the business cycle, the continual rise and fall in business activity. Tell them that a recession is caused by a decline in business activity. Point out that during a recession, people buy and sell less and unemployment rises. Discuss with students how some of the programs established under the New Deal, such as the FDIC, the SEC, and Social Security, have helped to soften the economic impact of recession on the lives of people. Ask them if they think government should play a role in protecting citizens from the economic impact of a recession.

Teaching Less Proficient Readers

Clarifying Ideas To help less proficient readers understand the main ideas in this section, pair them with more proficient readers and have the pairs follow these steps:

1. Read pages 532–533 together.
2. After students finish reading, have them make a list of the continuing benefits of the New Deal.
3. List what they want to find out about these continuing benefits.
4. Review pages 532–533 and write down what they have found out about each benefit.

to protect the nation's natural resources. As a result, the Civilian Conservation Corps planted trees, created hiking trails, and built fire lookout towers. Also, the Soil Conservation Service taught farmers how to conserve the soil through contour plowing, terracing, and crop rotation. Congress also passed the Taylor Grazing Act in 1934 to help reduce grazing on public lands. Such grazing had contributed to the erosion that brought about the dust storms of the 1930s.

Paul Sample, an artist who received funding from the WPA, painted the Tennessee Valley Authority's Norris Dam in 1935.

D. Answer They benefited the environment with new trees, hiking trails, fire lookouts, soil conservation, flood control, national parks, wildlife refuges, and wilderness areas. They harmed it with air, water, and land pollution.

THINK THROUGH HISTORY
D. *Recognizing Effects* *How did New Deal programs benefit and harm the environment?*

The **Tennessee Valley Authority** harnessed water power to generate electricity and to help prevent disastrous floods in the Tennessee Valley. During the New Deal, the government also added to the national park system. Olympic National Park in Washington and Shenandoah National Park in Virginia were added to the national park system during the 1930s, as were Carlsbad Caverns in New Mexico, Isle Royale in Michigan, and the Great Smoky Mountains in North Carolina and Tennessee. The New Deal also established new wildlife refuges and set aside large wilderness areas.

The New Deal, however, did not have a spotless record on the environment. The Roosevelt administration contributed to air, water, and land pollution. For example, the TVA polluted the Tennessee Valley region by engaging in strip mining to get coal for its coal-burning generators. The strip mining caused soil erosion, and the burning of the coal increased air pollution. The TVA also caused water pollution by dumping untreated sewage and toxic chemicals from its strip-mining operations into the region's rivers and streams.

The New Deal legacy has many dimensions. It has brought hope and gratitude from some people for the benefits they receive. It has also brought anger and criticism from those who believe that it has taken more of their money in taxes and curtailed their freedom through increased government regulations. The deficit spending necessary to fund New Deal programs grew immensely as the nation entered World War II.

Section 5 Assessment

1. TERMS & NAMES
- deficit spending
- National Labor Relations Board
- parity
- Securities and Exchange Commission
- Federal Deposit Insurance Corporation
- Tennessee Valley Authority

2. SUMMARIZING In a cluster diagram like the one below, show long-term benefits of the New Deal.

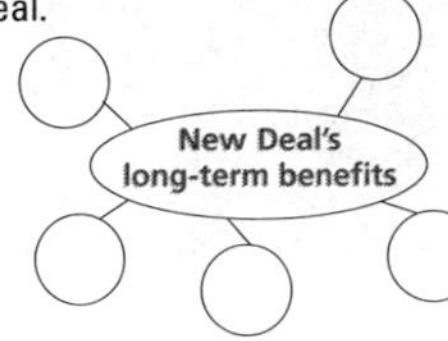

Which long-term benefit do you think has had the most impact? Why?

3. FORMING OPINIONS Some critics have charged that the New Deal was antibusiness and anti–free enterprise. Explain why you agree or disagree with this charge.

THINK ABOUT
- the expanded power of the federal government
- the New Deal's effect on the economy
- the New Deal's effect on the American people

4. EVALUATING How successful do you think Franklin Roosevelt was as a president? Support your answer with details from the text.

THINK ABOUT
- the condition of the country when he took office
- the short- and long-term impact of his policies
- his popularity with working-class Americans

ASSESS & RETEACH

Section 5 Assessment
Have students answer the questions and then compare their answers with each other.

Self-Assessment
To document what they have learned, students should list the insights they've gained regarding the impact of New Deal policies and reforms on society today.

Section Quiz
FORMAL ASSESSMENT
Section Quiz, p. 191

Reteach
Use the Point/Counterpoint feature on page 530 to review the central issue of the New Deal legacy—the role of government in people's lives.

CLOSE

New Deal policies have had long-term effects on labor, banking and finance, social welfare, and the environment. However, opinion is divided on the success of the New Deal. Some people praised the New Deal's creation of jobs and the greater role of government in solving problems, while others denounced the deficit spending used to fund its programs—spending that would increase even more during World War II.

ANSWERS

1. TERMS & NAMES
deficit spending, p. 529

National Labor Relations Board, p. 531

parity, p. 532

Securities and Exchange Commission, p. 532

Federal Deposit Insurance Corporation, p. 532

Tennessee Valley Authority, p. 533

2. SUMMARIZING
Possible Responses: National Labor Relations Board still mediates labor disputes; Federal Deposit Insurance Corporation insures accounts up to $100,000; Securities and Exchange Commission continues to monitor the stock market; Social Security still provides assistance to senior citizens, people with disabilities, families with dependent children, and the unemployed; the New Deal protected wilderness areas.

3. FORMING OPINIONS
Possible Responses: **Agree:** Students might argue that the New Deal weakened free enterprise and business profits by increasing regulations, taxes, union membership, and wages. **Disagree:** Students might argue that increased government spending, the improved economy, the resurgence of hope, and more prosperous consumers all aided free enterprise and helped businesses prosper.

4. EVALUATING
Possible Responses: Students might argue that Roosevelt's spirit, vision, array of programs, and concern for common people helped him deal with the problems of the Depression and made him a success. Others may criticize him for not having given strong support to minorities and the very poor. Still others may say that his increasing the size of the federal government had negative long-term consequences.

Geography Spotlight

OBJECTIVES

1. To describe the federal government's role and achievement in establishing the Tennessee Valley Authority.
2. To summarize benefits of the TVA to the Tennessee Valley region.

FOCUS & MOTIVATE

▶ ***Starting with the Student***
Ask students whether the electric power they use in their homes is produced by a private utility or by a government corporation such as the TVA. Then ask these questions:

- What role does electric power play in their daily life.
- How might improving electric power benefit an area economically?

MORE ABOUT . . .
The Tennessee River
Before the creation of the TVA, the Tennessee River was subject to periodic flooding and could not be navigated in the area around Muscle Shoals, Alabama. The dams of the TVA project helped control flooding, saving lives and crops and curbing soil erosion while at the same time generating hydroelectric power vital to industrial development. Damming also created "the Great Lakes of the South," which provided new recreational opportunities.

GEOGRAPHY SPOTLIGHT

The Tennessee Valley Authority

The Tennessee Valley Authority (TVA) is a federal corporation that was established in 1933 to construct dams and power plants along the Tennessee River and its tributaries. The Tennessee River basin is one of the largest river basins in the United States, and people who live in this area have a number of common concerns. The TVA has helped the region in various ways: through flood and navigation control, the conservation of natural resources, and the generation of electric power, as well as through agricultural and industrial development.

The Tennessee Valley covers parts of seven states. Thus, the TVA became an enormous undertaking, eventually comprising dozens of major dams, each with associated power plants, recreational facilities, and navigation aids.

Citizens in the Guntersville, Alabama area, for example, decided to take advantage of the tremendous electrical power that the local dam was capable of producing. They decided to build a harbor, develop Guntersville Lake's recreational possibilities, and attract new industry with the abundant power that would be available.

❶ **ART AND THE TVA** Charles Sheeler's 1939 painting ***Suspended Power*** gives an awe-inspiring view of a huge turbine about to be lowered into place.

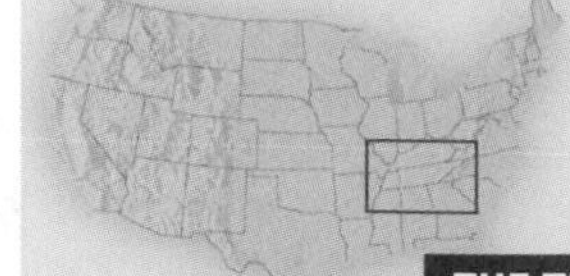

THE TENNESSEE VALLEY

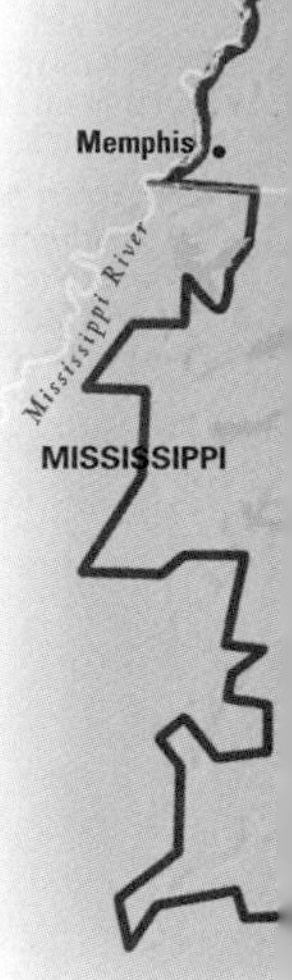

❷ **THE TVA** applied the regional concept to the generation of electricity. Before the 1930s, the supplying of electricity was conceived in local terms, with each generating station producing power only for its vicinity. The TVA, in contrast, was a network of stations feeding power into a grid.

RECOMMENDED RESOURCES

Books

Davidson, Donald. *The Tennessee.* New York: Rinehart, 1946–48. A two-volume history of the Tennessee River, the Tennessee Valley, and the TVA.

Duffus, R. L. *The Valley and Its People.* New York: Knopf, 1944. The story of the Tennessee Valley Authority, written not long after it was established.

A History of the Tennessee Valley Authority. Knoxville: TVA Information Office, 1983. A history put out by the organization itself.

Hubbard, Preston J. *Origins of the TVA.* Nashville: Vanderbilt UP, 1961. The Tennessee Valley Authority and the Muscle Shoals controversy that helped create it.

Videos

The Electric Valley. Dir. Ross Spears. The James Agee Film Project, 1984. The 50-year history of the Tennessee Valley Authority.

FDR. Dir. John Alan Kane. A&E Home Video, 1995.

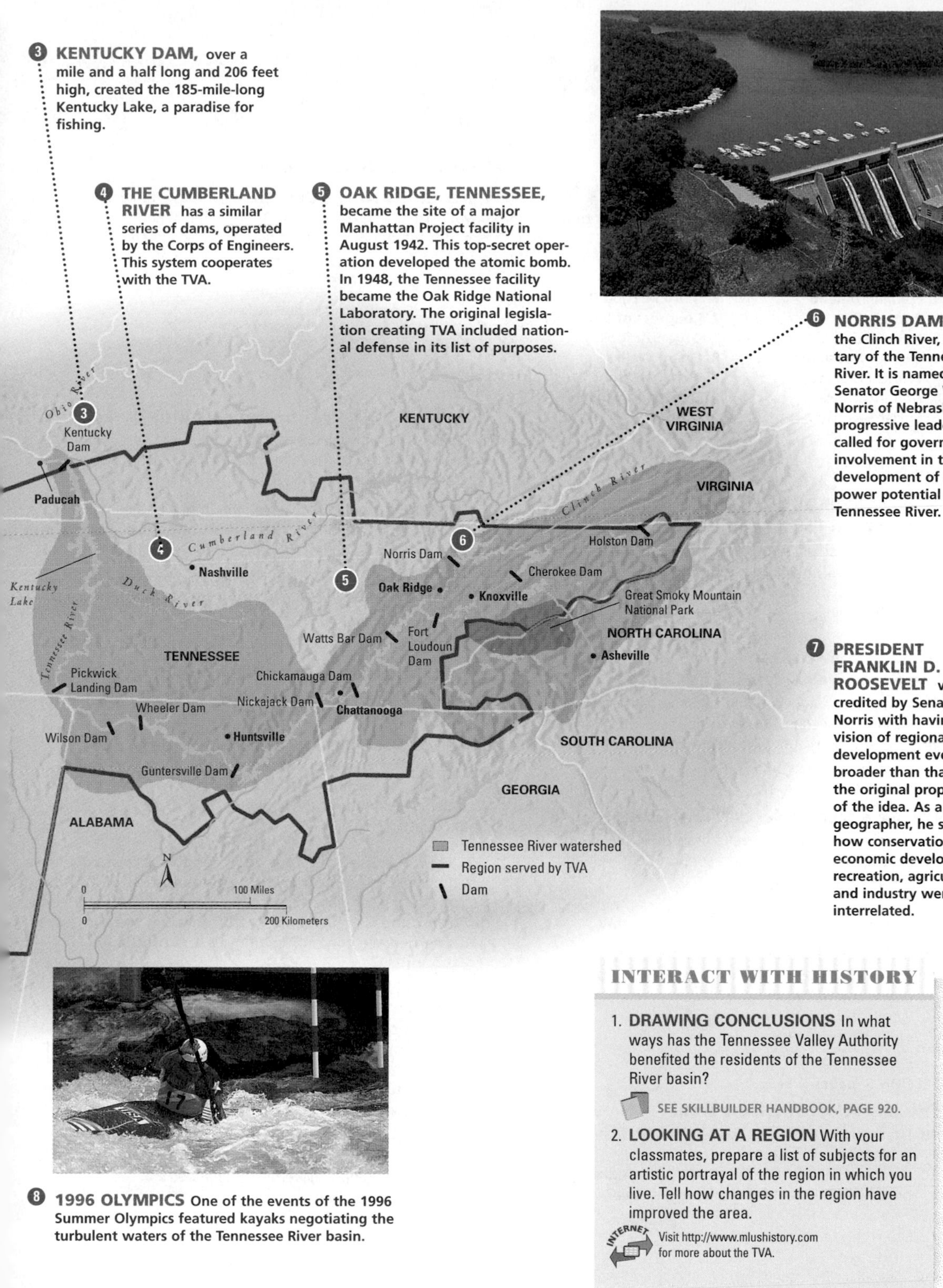

3 KENTUCKY DAM, over a mile and a half long and 206 feet high, created the 185-mile-long Kentucky Lake, a paradise for fishing.

4 THE CUMBERLAND RIVER has a similar series of dams, operated by the Corps of Engineers. This system cooperates with the TVA.

5 OAK RIDGE, TENNESSEE, became the site of a major Manhattan Project facility in August 1942. This top-secret operation developed the atomic bomb. In 1948, the Tennessee facility became the Oak Ridge National Laboratory. The original legislation creating TVA included national defense in its list of purposes.

6 NORRIS DAM is on the Clinch River, a tributary of the Tennessee River. It is named after Senator George W. Norris of Nebraska, a progressive leader who called for government involvement in the development of the power potential of the Tennessee River.

7 PRESIDENT FRANKLIN D. ROOSEVELT was credited by Senator Norris with having a vision of regional development even broader than that of the original proponents of the idea. As a good geographer, he saw how conservation, economic development, recreation, agriculture, and industry were interrelated.

8 1996 OLYMPICS One of the events of the 1996 Summer Olympics featured kayaks negotiating the turbulent waters of the Tennessee River basin.

INTERACT WITH HISTORY

1. **DRAWING CONCLUSIONS** In what ways has the Tennessee Valley Authority benefited the residents of the Tennessee River basin?

   SEE SKILLBUILDER HANDBOOK, PAGE 920.

2. **LOOKING AT A REGION** With your classmates, prepare a list of subjects for an artistic portrayal of the region in which you live. Tell how changes in the region have improved the area.

INTERNET Visit http://www.mlushistory.com for more about the TVA.

INSTRUCT

▶ *Starting with the Student*

- Ask students if there is a federal corporation similar to the Tennessee Valley Authority in their area.
- Ask students whether government should have a role in such areas as flood control, protection of the environment, and disaster relief.

▶ *Discussing Key Ideas*

- The Tennessee Valley Authority, a federal corporation, is established in 1933 to build dams and power plants in the Tennessee River Valley.
- The TVA vastly improves industry, agriculture, navigation, recreation, electric power, and conservation in the Tennessee Valley region.

HISTORY FROM VISUALS

Viewing the Images

Have students study the map and accompanying information.

- List the seven states into which the TVA reached. *Alabama, Georgia, Kentucky, Mississippi, North Carolina, Tennessee, Virginia.*
- Identify three tributaries of the Tennessee River. *Possible Responses: Cumberland River, Duck River, Clinch River.*

INTERACT WITH HISTORY

1. Drawing Conclusions

Possible Answers *The TVA built power plants along with dams to generate electric power, thereby enhancing living standards and attracting industry to the area; dams and other improvements to control flooding saved lives and crops, created recreational opportunities, and aided in conservation; improvements to develop ports and make rivers navigable further enhanced recreational and industrial opportunities.*

2. Looking at a Region

Some items that might be listed include rivers, mountains, lakes, cities, towns, villages, plains, valleys, marshes, swamps, forests, coasts, and islands. Changes that have improved the region might include environmental regulations, dams, power plants, recreational facilities, agricultural development, and economic development. Students may wish to list changes that they think have made the region worse.

CHAPTER 15
ASSESSMENT ANSWERS

REVIEWING THE CHAPTER

TERMS & NAMES

1. Franklin Delano Roosevelt, p. 504
2. New Deal, p. 505
3. Eleanor Roosevelt, p. 511
4. Works Progress Administration, p. 513
5. Social Security Act, p. 515
6. Mary McLeod Bethune, p. 518
7. Congress of Industrial Organizations, p. 521
8. Orson Welles, p. 525
9. Richard Wright, p. 527
10. Tennessee Valley Authority, p. 533

MAIN IDEAS

11. He expanded its role in the economy through programs designed to restore confidence and provide jobs.
12. Some said it made the federal government too powerful, and others said it didn't go far enough.
13. Second Agricultural Adjustment Act, Farm Security Administration, and Rural Electrification Administration.
14. It supported the rights of workers to join unions and to bargain.
15. He appointed African Americans to office; he did not support anti-lynching laws or an end to the poll tax.
16. The Democrats supported labor legislation and work-relief programs that helped the urban poor.
17. They allowed people to escape from the grim realities of the Depression.
18. The Federal Art Project, the Federal Theater Project, and the Federal Writers' Project.
19. Possible Responses: Federal Deposit Insurance Corporation, Securities and Exchange Commission, National Labor Relations Board, Social Security system, Tennessee Valley Authority.
20. It provided flood control, hydroelectric power, jobs, conservation, recreational facilities, and navigation aids. Strip mining caused soil erosion; coal-burning generators caused air pollution; toxic chemicals from strip mining polluted rivers.

Chapter 15 Assessment

REVIEWING THE CHAPTER

TERMS & NAMES For each term below, write a sentence explaining its relationship to the policies of the Roosevelt administration. For each person below, explain his or her role in the 1930s.

1. **Franklin Delano Roosevelt**
2. **New Deal**
3. **Eleanor Roosevelt**
4. **Works Progress Administration**
5. **Social Security Act**
6. **Mary McLeod Bethune**
7. **Congress of Industrial Organizations**
8. **Orson Welles**
9. **Richard Wright**
10. **Tennessee Valley Authority**

MAIN IDEAS

SECTION 1 *(pages 504–510)*

A New Deal Fights the Depression

11. How did Franklin Roosevelt change the role of the federal government during the Hundred Days?
12. Summarize the reasons why some people opposed the New Deal.

SECTION 2 *(pages 511–516)*

The Second New Deal Takes Hold

13. What federal agencies and acts assisted farmers during the Second New Deal?
14. How did the Wagner Act help working people?

SECTION 3 *(pages 517–522)*

The New Deal Affects Many Groups

15. Explain President Roosevelt's policies on civil rights.
16. Why did many urban voters support Roosevelt and the Democratic Party?

SECTION 4 *(pages 523–528)*

Society and Culture

17. What purpose did movies and radio programs serve during the Great Depression?
18. Which New Deal programs supported artists and writers in the 1930s?

SECTION 5 *(pages 529–533)*

The Impact of the New Deal

19. List five New Deal agencies or programs that are still in place today.
20. What benefits did the Tennessee Valley Authority provide? What negative impact did it have?

THINKING CRITICALLY

1. **REACTING TO THE DEPRESSION** Copy the web below on your paper and fill it in with actions that Americans took to end the economic crisis of the 1930s.

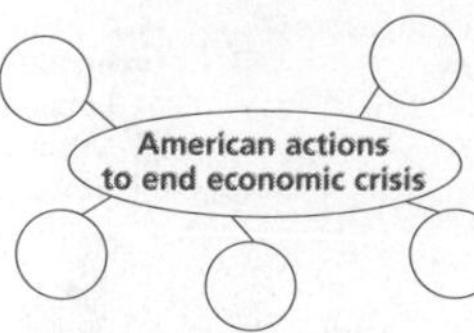

2. **TRACING THEMES ECONOMIC OPPORTUNITY** What federal programs instituted in the 1930s and later discontinued might be of use to the nation today? Explain and support your opinion.
3. **CONFRONTING FEAR** Reread the quotation from Franklin Delano Roosevelt on page 502. What do you think his comment reveals about his approach to the problems of the 1930s?
4. **GEOGRAPHY OF THE TENNESSEE VALLEY** Look at the map on pages 534–535. Describe the landforms and water bodies of the Tennessee Valley. How might the geography of the area have been different if dams had not been built?
5. **EVALUATING THE NEW DEAL** In your opinion, did the New Deal have major failings? Support your answer with details from the text.
6. **ANALYZING PRIMARY SOURCES** Read the following excerpt from *This Was America* by the French writer André Maurois, in which he describes his impressions of the United States after a tour of the country in the 1930s. Then answer the questions that follow.

> A curious unity of habits and thoughts is created by the movies, the magazines, the radio, advertising, and the newspaper chains. . . . Americans who never meet each other and who live under different skies come to have innumerable common memories and brotherly thoughts.
>
> Little by little the American federation is transforming itself into a union, marked by the growth in importance of the role of the federal capital. In the beginning, the United States had only a small federal bureaucracy. Today the central administration is powerful and rich.
>
> **ANDRÉ MAUROIS,** *This Was America*

What effect has popular culture had on the American people? How has the federal government changed?

THINKING CRITICALLY

1. REACTING TO THE DEPRESSION
Possible Responses: Voters elected Franklin Roosevelt as president; the federal government expanded its role in the economy to aid banks, farmers, workers, and the unemployed.

2. TRACING THEMES ECONOMIC OPPORTUNITY
Possible Responses: A type of NYA could help low-income students afford college; a type of WPA could be used for people who otherwise would be on welfare; the government might think about reinstituting a CCC to help deal with environmental problems, to educate people about environmental concerns, and to employ young people.

3. CONFRONTING FEAR
Possible Responses: That he is optimistic; that he will aggressively move the nation forward; that without fear, many things are possible; that if all Americans work together and are not afraid, problems will be solved; that with a bold, brave approach, the nation will have nothing to fear.

ALTERNATIVE ASSESSMENT

1. **MUSIC OF THE 1930s**
CD-ROM The Great Depression, the New Deal, Franklin Roosevelt, movies, and radio all inspired popular songs in the 1930s. Use the CD-ROM *Our Times*, your textbook, and other sources to make a collection of five to ten songs that reflect economic, political, or cultural events of the decade. Write a short essay explaining the significance of each song.
   - Your collection of songs might include the written lyrics or recordings of performances.
   - Possible sources of music include anthologies of folk songs, protest songs, and union songs; books on songwriters such as Woody Guthrie, Huddie Ledbetter, Alfred Hayes, and Irving Berlin; and histories of culture in the 1930s.
   - In your essay, analyze how each song relates to events or personalities of the 1930s.

   Save your collection of songs and your essay in your American history portfolio.

2. **LEARNING FROM MEDIA**
VIDEO View the video for Chapter 15, *A Song for His People.* Then discuss the following questions with a small group of classmates:
   - Why did Mexican immigration to the United States increase in the early 1920s?
   - Why were thousands of Mexicans in the United States sent back to Mexico in the 1930s?
   - Why did Pedro J. González become a hero to many Mexican Americans and a symbol of Mexican cultural pride?

3. **PORTFOLIO PROJECT**
Use the Living History activity to expand your portfolio.

LIVING HISTORY

PRESENTING YOUR NEW DEAL DIARY

You have written diary entries about your imaginary New Deal experiences. Now, consider the following points as you review and assess your entries:

- Do they use vivid description?
- Do they use details that recreate the feel of the era?
- Do they provide a personal viewpoint?

Select a few diary entries to present to the class. Choose interesting passages in which you use vivid description and details to illuminate some aspect of the New Deal. Then add your diary entries to your American history portfolio.

Bridge to Chapter 16

Review Chapter 15

A NEW DEAL FIGHTS THE DEPRESSION After his landslide election in 1932, Franklin Roosevelt took office in March 1933. During the so-called Hundred Days, he pushed a series of bills through Congress to restore confidence in the county's financial system, to help farmers and the needy, and to provide work for the unemployed. He faced opposition from the Supreme Court and from many critics.

THE SECOND NEW DEAL TAKES HOLD During the Second New Deal, Congress passed additional measures to boost the economy. The second Agricultural Adjustment Act and other measures aided farmers. The Works Progress Administration created jobs for unskilled laborers and for professionals. The Wagner Act supported the right of workers to organize unions and engage in collective bargaining. The Social Security Act of 1935 provided old age insurance, unemployment compensation, and aid to families with dependent children and to people with disabilities.

THE NEW DEAL AFFECTS MANY GROUPS The New Deal brought limited progress in the struggle for equality. Although Roosevelt selected women and African Americans as key advisers, he did not push for equality in the administration of New Deal programs. Nevertheless, his popularity created a powerful political coalition for the Democrats.

SOCIETY AND CULTURE The Depression, the New Deal, and new technology changed how people lived, played, and thought in the 1930s. The increasing popularity of movies and radio programs, along with government-supported art and writing, made the decade a productive era in American culture.

THE IMPACT OF THE NEW DEAL The greatest impact of the New Deal was on the federal government. Since the 1930s, the government has played a significant role in the nation's economy, and some programs started in the 1930s, such as Social Security, continue to play an important role in the nation today.

Preview Chapter 16

While the United States worked to overcome the Great Depression, military conflicts were breaking out in Europe and Asia. The United States attempted to stay out of these conflicts but was eventually pulled into World War II. You will learn about the beginnings of World War II in the next chapter.

ALTERNATIVE ASSESSMENT

1. MUSIC OF THE 1930s
Standards for Evaluation
A collection of songs and an accompanying essay should meet the following criteria.
- Provide 5–10 songs that reflect the economic, political, or cultural events of the 1930s.
- Include written lyrics or recordings.
- Explain the significance of each song.
- Connect each song to the period of the 1930s.

2. LEARNING FROM MEDIA
Answers to the questions.
- Millions of Mexicans were fleeing the violence of the Mexican Revolution, which left the economy in ruins.
- A panic for jobs during the Great Depression led to a movement to deport Mexican immigrants.
- Because of his radio show, he was a strong voice for the Mexican-American community. He dedicated his life to the struggle for justice and equality.

3. PORTFOLIO PROJECT
LIVING HISTORY
Standards for Evaluation
Diary entries should meet the following criteria.
- Use vivid description.
- Use details that help to bring the era alive.
- Provide a personal viewpoint about being gainfully employed.
- Provide details about the work experience.

IN-DEPTH RESOURCES: UNIT 4
See the form for scoring this activity on page 73.

THINKING CRITICALLY

4. GEOGRAPHY OF THE TENNESSEE VALLEY
Possible Responses: The darkest area in the center is the lowest land, the Tennessee River watershed; to the right are mountains; there are several rivers in the region; the largest rivers on the map are the Mississippi and the Ohio; some smaller rivers are the Cumberland, Duck, Tennessee, and Clinch. Without the dams, the Tennessee River would flow faster and Kentucky Lake would not have been formed.

5. EVALUATING THE NEW DEAL
Possible Responses: **Yes:** It should have instituted programs to improve civil rights and economic opportunity for African Americans and Mexican Americans; it should have ensured that the TVA's toxic wastes would not pollute the waters. **No:** It achieved important reforms in the nation's financial system, it provided relief for millions of unemployed people, and it built needed dams and other public works.

6. ANALYZING PRIMARY SOURCES
Possible Responses: Popular culture has lessened regional differences and helped to create a more uniform way of life. The federal government has grown from a small bureaucracy to a powerful and rich central government.

UNIT OVERVIEW

World War II and Its Aftermath

HISTORY AND ART

Corpsman on Saipan Helps Wounded Marine

Photograph by unknown photographer (1944).

Art Note
Working for the military services or for news organizations, photographers often risked their lives to take pictures of all aspects of World War II. The war was also covered by film crews who shot footage for the military and for newsreel companies.

▶ ***Previewing the Unit***
Unit 5 describes how militaristic dictators in Europe and Japan start a worldwide war that forces the United States to fight on two fronts. Victory leads to an uneasy peace with the Soviet Union, with the threat of nuclear war looming over the world. The economic expansion brought on by the war and the return to peace fuels a postwar economic boom and the spread of a suburb-based consumer culture.

UNIT 5

1931–1960 World War II and Its Aftermath

"Never in the field of human conflict was so much owed by so many to so few."
WINSTON CHURCHILL

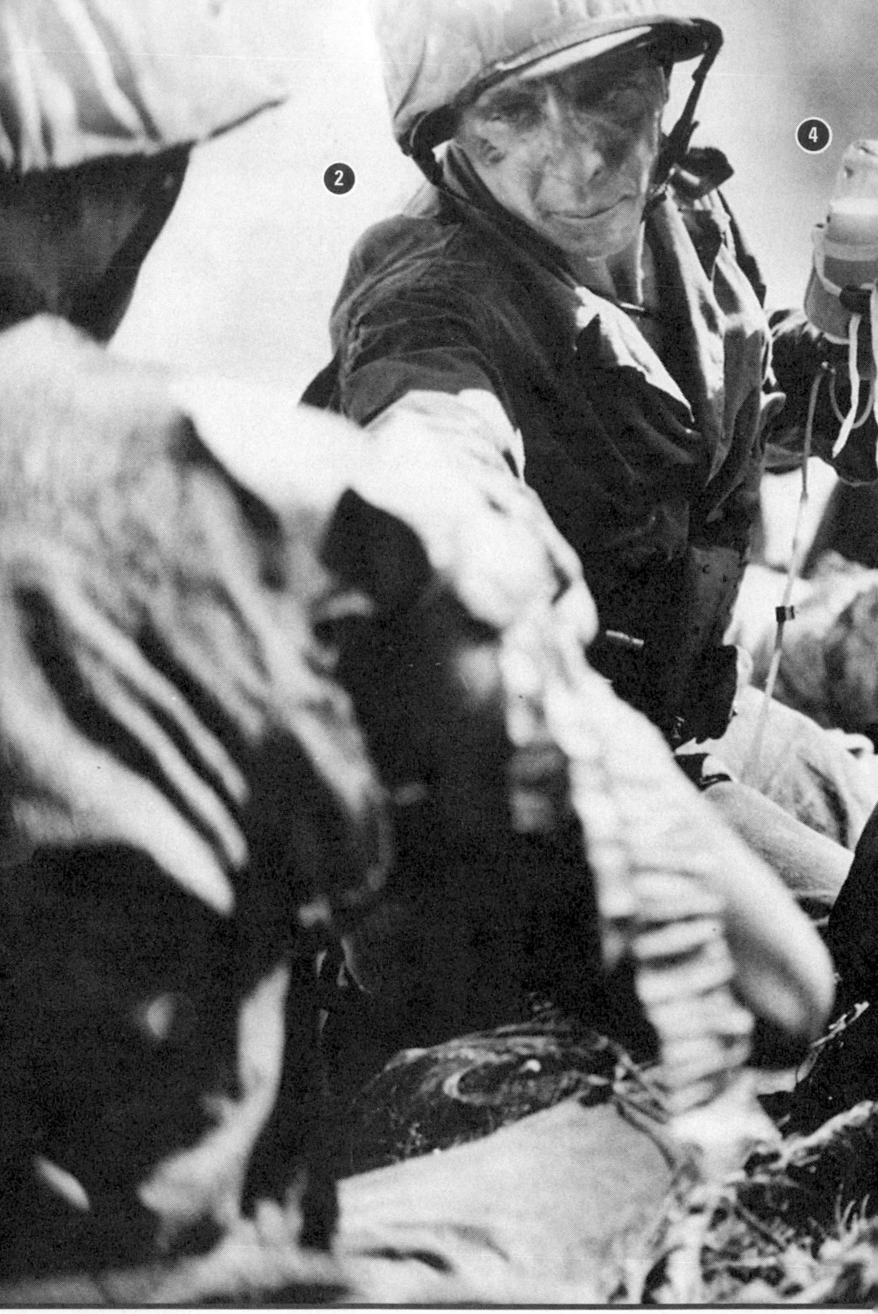

538 Unit 5

1 Saipan
The battle of Saipan was fought in late June 1944 in the Mariana Islands, about 1,700 miles south of Tokyo —just a few weeks after the Normandy invasion in Europe. While U.S. marines and soldiers fought on land, the navy destroyed three Japanese aircraft carriers and hundreds of planes, crippling the Japanese Navy. Taking Saipan gave the Americans an island from which to launch bombing raids on Japan. Japanese prime minister Tojo called the battle a "great national crisis" and resigned. The new government began to accept the possibility of Japanese defeat.

2 Field medicine
Medical advances and improved methods of treatment saved tens of thousands of soldiers' lives. In World War I, only 4 of every 100 wounded soldiers lived. In World War II, the number rose to 50 of every 100.

3 Combat photography
Combat photographers, working at the front lines, were in just as much danger as soldiers. During the invasion of Guam, just weeks after Saipan, four marine combat photographers were killed and one was wounded.

Discussing the Quotation
Churchill's words are from a speech about the fierce efforts of the Royal Air Force to save England from a German invasion, but the sentiments could apply to the entire war effort.

FOR DISCUSSION:
- Who are the "many" and the "few" in the quotation?
- Corpsmen like the one shown in this picture did not fight. Was anything "owed" to them?

Discussing the Image
Compare this photograph with the Civil War photographs in Chapter 4. The inaction of the early photographs contrasts with the intense moment captured in this dramatic image. By World War II, photographic equipment had improved greatly, allowing photographers to take more compelling pictures.

FOR DISCUSSION:
- What do the expressions on the two visible faces reveal?
- What is the overall impression conveyed by this photograph?

4 Plasma
The effectiveness of using plasma in blood transfusions was discovered in 1939. Whole blood could not be dried without destroying red blood cells. Because plasma could be dried, it could be more easily stored and transported, making it a vital tool in battlefield medicine. Plasma is the fluid portion of blood, in which blood cells are suspended.

5 Casualties
Amphibious invasions—like that of Saipan—had higher casualties than other operations. As much as 25 percent of a landing force could be killed or wounded.

6 Camouflage
Helmet covers had green and brown coloring to hide soldiers in the jungle foliage.

7 The jungle
The fighting in the Pacific was of two kinds. Large-scale naval battles— fought primarily by aircraft carriers—took place on the high seas. Marines and army soldiers conducted a campaign of island-hopping that brought Allied forces closer and closer to Japan.

PLANNING GUIDE

CHAPTER 16

World War Looms

	Key Ideas	COPYMASTERS	ASSESSMENT
SECTION 1 **Dictators Threaten World Peace** ***pp. 542–547***	*The United States remains isolated from world affairs as economic and political factors lead to the rise of nationalist leaders in the Soviet Union, Germany, and Italy.*	***In-Depth Resources: Unit 5*** • Guided Reading, p. 1 • Primary Source: *from* Franklin D. Roosevelt's "Quarantine Speech," p. 8 ***Lesson Plans,*** pp. 133–134	PE ***Section 1 Assessment,*** p. 547 TE ***Self-Assessment,*** p. 547 ***Formal Assessment*** • Section Quiz, p. 200 ***Alternative Assessment Book*** • Standards for Evaluating a Cooperative Activity
SECTION 2 **War in Europe** ***pp. 548–553***	*A series of bold moves by Adolf Hitler—and weak countermoves by other leaders—triggers World War II in Europe.*	***In-Depth Resources: Unit 5*** • Guided Reading, p. 2 • Skillbuilder Practice: Developing Historical Perspective, p. 5 ***Lesson Plans,*** pp. 135–136	PE ***Section 2 Assessment,*** p. 553 TE ***Self-Assessment,*** p. 553 ***Formal Assessment*** • Section Quiz, p. 201 ***Alternative Assessment Book*** • Standards for Evaluating a Cooperative Activity
SECTION 3 **The Holocaust** ***pp. 554–558***	*Hitler's plans for conquering the world include the killing of Jews and other ethnic groups, which is carried out with frightening determination and success.*	***In-Depth Resources: Unit 5*** • Guided Reading, p. 3 • Literature: from *Sophie's Choice* by William Styron, p. 12 • American Lives: Elie Wiesel, p. 15 ***Lesson Plans,*** pp. 137–138	PE ***Section 3 Assessment,*** p. 558 TE ***Self-Assessment,*** p. 558 ***Formal Assessment*** • Section Quiz, p. 202 ***Alternative Assessment Book*** • Standards for Evaluating a Cooperative Activity
SECTION 4 **America Moves Toward War** ***pp. 559–565***	*The United States provides aid to nations resisting Hitler and enters World War II after the bombing of Pearl Harbor.*	***In-Depth Resources: Unit 5*** • Guided Reading, p. 4 • Geography Application: Japanese Aggression, p. 6 • Primary Sources: The Bombing of Pearl Harbor, p. 9; War Poster, p. 11 • American Lives: Charles A. Lindbergh, p. 16 ***Lesson Plans,*** pp. 139–140	PE ***Section 4 Assessment,*** p. 565 TE ***Self-Assessment,*** p. 565 ***Formal Assessment*** • Section Quiz, p. 203 ***Alternative Assessment Book*** • Standards for Evaluating a Cooperative Activity
CHAPTER RESOURCES	**Chapter Overview** *An imperfect peace leads to the rise of dictators who brutally suppress opponents and innocent people at home and attack their neighbors. Soon the United States is plunged into worldwide war.*	***In-Depth Resources: Unit 5*** • Living History Project: Worksheet, p. 17; Standards, p. 18 ***Telescoping the Times*** • Chapter Summary, pp. 31–32 ***Planning for Block Schedules***	PE ***Chapter Assessment,*** pp. 566–567 PE ***Alternative Assessment,*** p. 567 ***Formal Assessment*** • Chapter Test, forms A and B, pp. 204–209 ***Test Generator*** ***Alternative Assessment Book*** See explanation and forms for different kinds of alternative assessments including portfolio assessment.

KEY
- PE Pupil's Edition
- TE Teacher's Edition
- INTERNET **http://www.mlushistory.com**

TECHNOLOGY

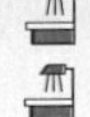
Warm-Up Transparency 16
Humanities Transparencies
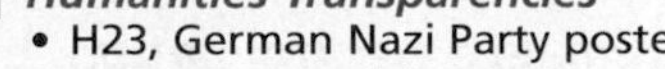
- H23, German Nazi Party poster

INTERNET Joseph Stalin and Benito Mussolini

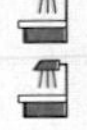
Warm-Up Transparency 16
Geography Transparencies
- G24, Aggression in Europe, 1936–1939

Our Times
- Edward R. Murrow's Christmas Eve radio broadcast from London

Electronic Library of Primary Sources
- Letter to Roosevelt by Winston Churchill

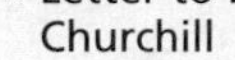
INTERNET Winston Churchill and Charles de Gaulle

Warm-Up Transparency 16
AMERICAN STORIES video series
- "Escaping the Final Solution"

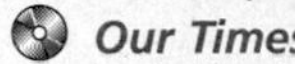
Our Times
- the Holocaust in Hungary and the Warsaw ghetto uprising
- excerpt of *The Diary of Anne Frank*
- Kristallnacht

INTERNET The Holocaust

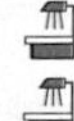
Warm-Up Transparency 16
Critical Thinking Transparencies
- CT24 World War II Begins in Europe
- CT58, Time Line of Events Leading to World War II

Electronic Library of Primary Sources
- from "Let Us Face the Truth" from the *New York Times*
- "Are We Being Led Into War?" by George A. Dondero
- On the Declaration of War by Franklin Delano Roosevelt

INTERNET U-boats and Pearl Harbor

American Portfolio: A Videodisc for U.S. History, user's guide, pp. 209–210, 216–217, 221, 223

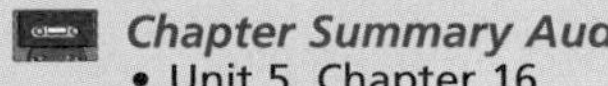
Chapter Summary Audiotapes
- Unit 5, Chapter 16

INTERNET http://www. mlushistory.com

Block Scheduling (90 MINUTES)

Day 1
Section 1, pp. 542–547
Section Assessment, p. 547

COOPERATIVE ACTIVITY
- Writing a Newspaper Editorial, p. 546 (TE)

Day 2
Section 2, pp. 548–553
Section Assessment, p. 553

COOPERATIVE ACTIVITY
- Creating a Radio Broadcast, p. 552 (TE)

Day 3
Section 3, pp. 554–558

AMERICAN STORIES video series
- "Escaping the Final Solution"

Section Assessment, p. 548

COOPERATIVE ACTIVITY
- Exploring Literature of the Holocaust, p. 556 (TE)

Day 4
Section 4, pp. 559–565
Section Assessment, p. 565
Chapter Assessment, pp. 566–567

COOPERATIVE ACTIVITY
- Creating a Political Cartoon, p. 563 (TE)

YEARLY PACING ***Chapter 16 Total:*** 4 days ***Yearly Total:*** 85 days

See *Planning for Block Schedules* for special activities and pacing strategies.

Customizing for Special Populations

Students Acquiring English
Access for Students Acquiring English: Spanish Translations
- Guided Reading for Sections 1–4 (Spanish), pp. 187–190
- Chapter Summary (Spanish), pp. 185–186
- Skillbuilder Practice: Developing Historical Perspective (Spanish), p. 191
- Geography Application: Japanese Aggression (Spanish), p. 192

Spanish Reading Study Guide, pp. 167–176

Translations of Chapter Summaries, Hmong, Cantonese, Vietnamese, and Cambodian

Chapter Summary Audiotapes in Spanish Unit 5, Chapter 16

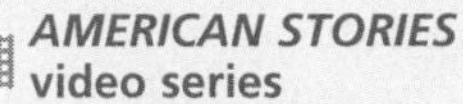
AMERICAN STORIES video series
- "Escaping the Final Solution" (Spanish track)

INTERNET The Diverse Classroom

Gifted and Talented Students
In-Depth Resources: Unit 5
- Primary Sources: *from* Franklin D. Roosevelt's "Quarantine Speech," p. 8; The Bombing of Pearl Harbor, p. 9; War Poster, p. 11
- American Lives: Elie Wiesel, p. 15; Charles A. Lindbergh, p. 16

Less Proficient Readers
In-Depth Resources: Unit 5
- Guided Reading for Sections 1–4, pp. 1–4
- Skillbuilder: Developing Historical Perspective, p. 5
- Geography Application: Japanese Aggression, p. 6

Reading Study Guide
- pp. 167–176

Telescoping the Times
- Chapter Summary, pp. 31–32

Chapter Summary Audiotapes, Unit 5, Chapter 16

Connections to Literature READINGS FOR STUDENTS

In-Depth Resources: Unit 5
- **from *Sophie's Choice* by William Styron,** p. 12

Enrichment Reading
- **Ernest Hemingway**
  For Whom the Bell Tolls
  New York: Scribner, 1996
  On the eve of World War II, this major American classic tells the story of the impending death of an American in the Spanish Civil War. A deeply felt and timeless story of love and loss, of courage and commitment, the novel reflects Hemingway's passionate feelings about the nature of war and the meaning of loyalty.
- **Katherine Anne Porter**
  Ship of Fools
  New York: Little, Brown, 1984
  Porter's belief that "evil is always done with the collusion of good" is played out in this moral allegory about the voyage of life. A variety of people, mostly Germans on the eve of Hitler's rise to power, travel on the Vera, a passenger freighter, from Mexico to Germany during 27 days of 1931.
- **Yoshiko Uchida**
  Journey to Topaz
  New York: Scribner, 1971
  After the attack on Pearl Harbor, an eleven-year old Japanese-American girl and her family are forced into an internment camp called Topaz in the Utah desert.

CHAPTER 16 OVERVIEW

World War Looms

▶ *Accessing Prior Knowledge*

Ask students what impressions they have about World War II. They might create a list of terms or issues that they associate with the war era and explain where they got these impressions.

▶ *Predicting Outcomes*

In the quotation on page 540, President Roosevelt predicts that the United States "will remain a neutral nation." Predict whether or not his prediction might be accurate and explain why or why not.

MORE ABOUT . . .
Franklin Delano Roosevelt

On the same day that Franklin Delano Roosevelt (1882–1945) took the oath of office in 1933, Japanese troops marched into China. On the following day, Germans went to the polls and brought Adolf Hitler to power. Roosevelt recognized the threat these events posed to world peace and order. But he had to balance his recognition with Americans' strongly isolationist views.

CHAPTER 16

World War Looms

SECTION 1
Dictators Threaten World Peace

The United States remains isolated from world affairs as economic and political factors lead to the rise of nationalist leaders in the Soviet Union, Germany, and Italy.

SECTION 2
War in Europe

A series of bold moves by Adolf Hitler—and weak countermoves by other leaders—triggers World War II in Europe.

SECTION 3
The Holocaust

Hitler's plans for conquering the world include the killing of Jews and other ethnic groups, which is carried out with frightening determination.

ESCAPING THE FINAL SOLUTION

SECTION 4
America Moves Toward War

The United States provides aid to nations resisting the Axis powers and enters World War II after the bombing of Pearl Harbor.

"This nation will remain a neutral nation, but I cannot ask that every American remain neutral in thought as well."

President Franklin D. Roosevelt, August 24, 1939

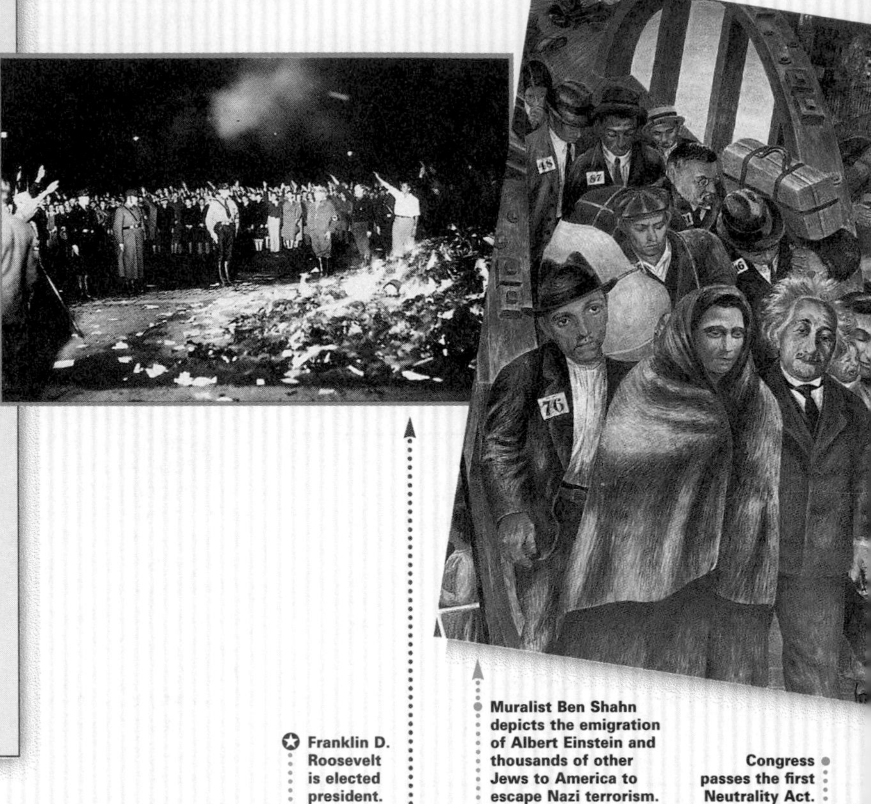

THE UNITED STATES / THE WORLD — 1931

1931 — Japan invades Manchuria.

1932 — Franklin D. Roosevelt is elected president.

1933 (U.S.) — Muralist Ben Shahn depicts the emigration of Albert Einstein and thousands of other Jews to America to escape Nazi terrorism.

1933 (World) — Hitler becomes chancellor of Germany, and his followers honor him by burning 20,000 "non-Aryan" books.

1935 (U.S.) — Congress passes the first Neutrality Act.

1935 (World) — Mussolini invades Ethiopia.

THEMES IN CHAPTER 16

Cultural Diversity	Science and Technology	Immigration and Migration	Constitutional Concerns
One of the recurring themes in Adolf Hitler's *Mein Kampf* was an intense hostility toward different racial and cultural groups. African Americans were among the first Americans to appreciate this threat.	The 1939 German blitzkrieg in Poland revealed the destructive potential of two military weapons first used in World War I: the aerial bomber and the tank. Together these two weapons would revolutionize modern warfare.	During the 1930s, thousands of refugees from Nazi Germany and other totalitarian regimes entered the United States as immigrants each year. Their numbers, however, were limited by the quotas imposed by the Immigration Act of 1924.	The election of Franklin Roosevelt to a third term in 1940 broke the unwritten two-term rule of presidential politics, eventually leading to the passage of the 22nd Amendment, which limits presidents to two terms.
See Teacher's Edition note, p. 545.	See Teacher's Edition note, p. 551.	See Teacher's Edition note, p. 555.	See Teacher's Edition note, p. 560.

LIVING HISTORY

COMPILING AN ORAL HISTORY

Interview a relative or a friend of the family who lived through the period prior to America's entry into World War II. Before the interview, prepare a list of questions to ask the person, based on specific information in this chapter. Include general questions such as the following:

- How did you feel about the cautious response of the United States to events in Europe?
- How did events between 1931 and 1941 affect your life?

PORTFOLIO PROJECT Keep the records of your interview in a folder. You will use these records to create an oral history for your American history portfolio at the end of the chapter.

Hostilities Declared by

1936
- President Franklin Roosevelt is reelected.
- Spanish Civil War begins.
- Germany occupies the Rhineland.

1937
- President Roosevelt delivers his anti-isolationist "Quarantine Speech."
- Japan invades China.

1938
- Germany annexes Austria.
- Hitler unleashes aggression against Jews on *Kristallnacht*.

1939
- Germany invades Poland, starting World War II.
- Nazis begin to convert labor camps into extermination camps for Jews and other ethnic groups.

1940
- President Franklin Roosevelt is elected to a third term.
- Britain and Germany fight the Battle of Britain.
- Japan, Germany, and Italy sign the Tripartite Pact.

1941
- President Roosevelt signs the Lend-Lease Act, and U.S. industry begins mass production of war materiel.
- United States enters the war after the Japanese attack on Pearl Harbor.
- Germany invades the Soviet Union.
- Japanese attack Pearl Harbor.

ALTERNATIVE ASSESSMENT

LIVING HISTORY

COMPILING AN ORAL HISTORY

You might give students these strategies for finding subjects and conducting interviews:

- If you don't have friends or family members who lived through World War II, ask a local senior-citizens center to suggest someone to interview.
- Prepare a list of questions in advance. Include open-ended questions that will encourage your interviewee to share detailed information.
- Take notes during the interview and, if your interviewee agrees, use a tape recorder.
- Save your notes and the audiotape to write your oral history. Include a description of your interviewee.

Project Planning Guide

Step 1	Identify interviewee.
Step 2	Prepare interview questions.
Step 3	Conduct interview.
Step 4	Save notes and audiotapes as a source to write the oral history.

IN-DEPTH RESOURCES: UNIT 5
See worksheet and standards for evaluation, pp. 17, 18.

RECOMMENDED RESOURCES

Books for the Teacher

Churchill, Winston. *The Gathering Storm.* Boston: Houghton, 1986.

Hitler, Adolf. *Mein Kampf.* Boston: Houghton, 1973. Presentation of the basic beliefs of Nazism.

Levin, Nora. *The Holocaust.* New York: Crowell, 1968. Comprehensive history of the Holocaust.

Shirer, William. *The Rise and Fall of the Third Reich.* New York: Simon, 1990.

Books for the Student

Persico, Joseph E. *Nuremberg.* New York: Penguin, 1994. Discussion of the war crimes trials.

Time-Life Books, *World War II.* Englewood Cliffs, NJ: Prentice, 1989.

Wiesel, Elie. *Night.* New York: Bantam, 1982. Survivor's moving account of the Holocaust.

Videos

Hitler: The Whole Story. Dir. Christian Herrendoerfer. Discovery Communications, 1991.

Schindler's List. Dir. Steven Spielberg. Amblin Entertainment: Universal, 1994. Rated "R."

Shoah. Dir. Claude Lanzmann. Aleph/ Historia, 1985.

Software

American Chronicle Series: Seeds of Discord (1933–1936), Prelude to War (1935–1939), Darkest Hour (1939–1941). CD-ROM. AIMS Media, 800-367-2467

Causes of World War II. CD-ROM. ZCI Publishing, 1950 Stemmons, Suite 4044, Dallas, TX 75207-3109, 214-800-6000

The Holocaust. CD-ROM. Quanta Press, 1313 Fifth St., SE, Minneapolis, MN 55414, 612-379-3956

Section 1 Overview

OBJECTIVES

1. To characterize the governments that took power in Russia, Italy, Germany, and Japan after World War I.
2. To describe America's return to isolationism in the 1930s.

SKILLBUILDERS

- Understanding geography: region, location, p. 543
- Interpreting charts, p. 545
- Understanding geography: movement, p. 546
- Interpreting political cartoons, p. 547

CRITICAL THINKING

- Identifying problems, p. 543
- Summarizing, pp. 544, 547
- Theme: Cultural Diversity, p. 544
- Analyzing motives, pp. 545, 547
- Forming generalizations, p. 546
- Analyzing causes, p. 547

FOCUS & MOTIVATE

5-MINUTE WARM-UP

Making Generalizations
To understand the sources of political instability in the 1920s and 1930s, have students read "Failures of the World War I Peace Settlement" on pages 542–543 and then answer these questions.

1. Why did the Germans dislike the Treaty of Versailles?
2. What happened to the democratic governments created by the treaty?

WARM-UP TRANSPARENCY 16

▶ ***Starting with the Student***
- What kind of people become bullies?
- How do bullies influence other people?
- What is likely to happen when bullies gain control of a country?

1 Dictators Threaten World Peace

TERMS & NAMES
- **Joseph Stalin**
- **totalitarian**
- **Benito Mussolini**
- **fascism**
- **Adolf Hitler**
- **Nazism**
- **Neutrality Acts**

LEARN ABOUT the rise of totalitarian dictatorships in Europe and Asia
TO UNDERSTAND the challenge they posed to the U.S. policy of neutrality.

ONE AMERICAN'S STORY

Martha Gellhorn arrived in Madrid, Spain, in the spring of 1937 with a knapsack, less than $50, and a letter identifying her as a special correspondent for *Collier's Weekly.* The young American writer had come to Madrid to cover the brutal civil war that had broken out in Spain the year before. There she met the writer Ernest Hemingway, whom she later married. To Gellhorn, the Spanish Civil War was a deadly struggle between tyranny and democracy. For the people of Madrid, it was also a daily struggle for survival.

A PERSONAL VOICE

You would be walking down a street, hearing only the city noises of streetcars and automobiles and people calling out to one another, and suddenly, crushing it all out, would be the huge stony deep booming of a falling shell, at the corner. There was no place to run, because how did you know that the next shell would not be behind you, or ahead, or to the left or right? And going indoors was fairly silly too, considering what shells can do to a house.

MARTHA GELLHORN, *The Face of War*

A French journalist escapes from Spain t[o] France with a child h[e] rescued from a street battle. But fighting would soon engulf not only France, but the rest of Europe and Asia.

Less than two decades after the end of World War I—"the war to end all wars"—brutal fighting erupted again, not only in Europe but also in Asia. As Americans read about distant battles, they hoped that these deadly conflicts would remain on the other side of the world.

Nationalism Threatens Europe and Asia

A German homemaker, about to cook her family's breakfast, lights a fire with money made nearly worthless by high inflation following World War I.

The seeds of new conflicts had been sown in World War I. For many nations, peace had brought not prosperity but revolution caused by economic unrest. It also brought the rise of leaders driven by dreams of national greatness and territorial expansion.

FAILURES OF THE WORLD WAR I PEACE SETTLEMENT Contrary to the hopes of President Woodrow Wilson, the Treaty of Versailles that ended World War I did not create a "just and secure peace." Germans saw nothing fair in a treaty that blamed them for starting the war. Nor did they find much security in a settlement that stripped their country of territories they had long seen as German. Similarly, the Soviets resented the carving away of parts of Russia to create an independent Poland and the nations of Finland, Estonia, Lithuania, and Latvia.

In addition, the peace settlement did not make the world "safe for democracy," as Wilson had hoped. At the end of the war, new democratic governments did emerge in many European nations, including Germany, Austria, Italy, Czechoslovakia, Bulgaria, Romania, and Greece. Most of these nations lacked democratic traditions, though, and their newly elected leaders needed to show that democracy could improve people's lives economically. However, the Versailles treaty did nothing to help the war-torn nations of Europe rebuild. Instead, many of the new democracies were

SECTION 1 RESOURCES

PRINT RESOURCES

IN-DEPTH RESOURCES: UNIT 5
Guided Reading, p. 1
Primary Source: *from* Franklin D. Roosevelt's "Quarantine Speech," p. 8

READING STUDY GUIDE, p. 167

ACCESS FOR STUDENTS ACQUIRING ENGLISH
Guided Reading (Spanish), p. 187

SPANISH READING STUDY GUIDE, p. 167

FORMAL ASSESSMENT
Section Quiz, p. 200

ALTERNATIVE ASSESSMENT BOOK
See forms for supporting and scoring alternative activities.

TECHNOLOGY RESOURCES

HUMANITIES TRANSPARENCIES
H23, German Nazi Party poster

VIDEO *American Portfolio: A Videodisc for U.S. History* user's guide, pp. 209–210

INTERNET http://www.mlushistory.com

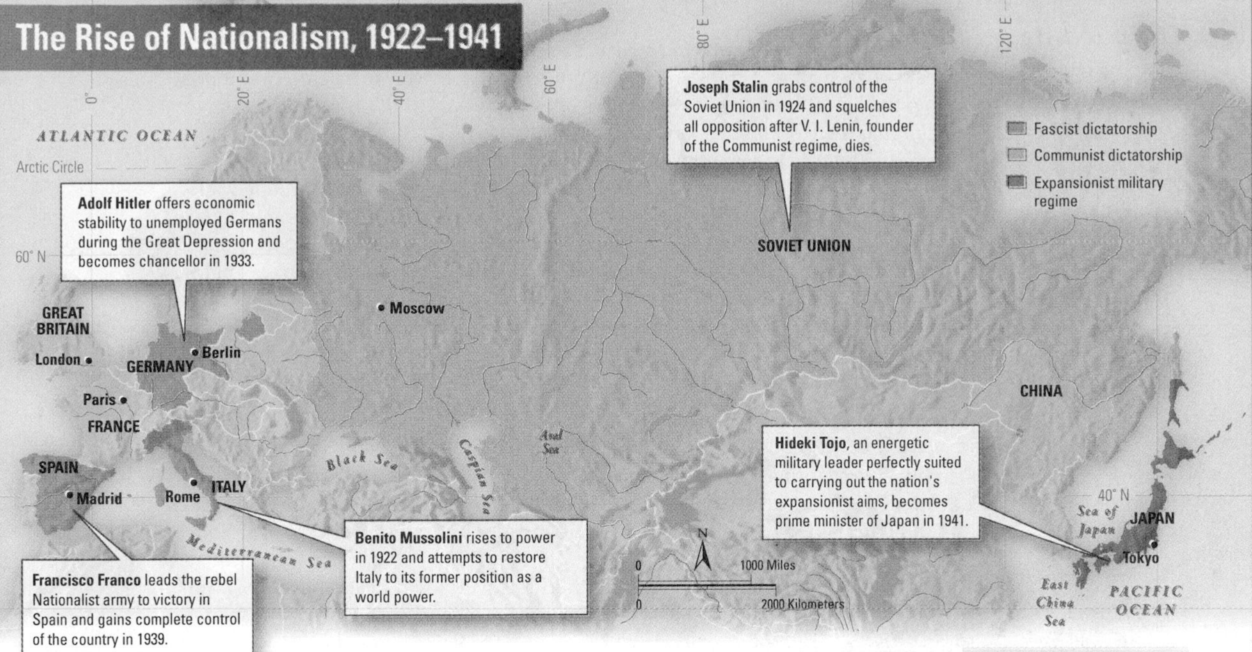

The Rise of Nationalism, 1922–1941
ATLANTIC OCEAN
Arctic Circle
60° N
0°
20° E
40° E
60° E
80° E
120° E
Joseph Stalin grabs control of the Soviet Union in 1924 and squelches all opposition after V. I. Lenin, founder of the Communist regime, dies.
Fascist dictatorship
Communist dictatorship
Expansionist military regime
Adolf Hitler offers economic stability to unemployed Germans during the Great Depression and becomes chancellor in 1933.
SOVIET UNION
GREAT BRITAIN
Moscow
London
GERMANY
Berlin
Paris
FRANCE
CHINA
SPAIN
Madrid
Rome
ITALY
Black Sea
Caspian Sea
Aral Sea
Mediterranean Sea
Hideki Tojo, an energetic military leader perfectly suited to carrying out the nation's expansionist aims, becomes prime minister of Japan in 1941.
40° N
Sea of Japan
JAPAN
Tokyo
Benito Mussolini rises to power in 1922 and attempts to restore Italy to its former position as a world power.
N
0
1000 Miles
0
2000 Kilometers
Francisco Franco leads the rebel Nationalist army to victory in Spain and gains complete control of the country in 1939.
East China Sea
PACIFIC OCEAN

THINK THROUGH HISTORY
A. *Identifying Problems* *What problems did European countries face after World War I?*

A. Answer The failure of the Treaty of Versailles and economic devastation.

expected to pay off huge war debts while trying to deal with widespread hunger, homelessness, and unemployment.

Unable to cope with these problems, several new democracies collapsed and dictators seized power. Some of these dictators were content simply to collect taxes and keep order. A few, however, had far grander ambitions.

JOSEPH STALIN TRANSFORMS THE SOVIET UNION In Russia, hopes for democracy gave way to civil war, resulting in the establishment of a Communist state, the Soviet Union, in 1922. When V. I. Lenin, the first leader of the Soviet Union, died in 1924, **Joseph Stalin** took control of the country. Stalin, whose last name meant "man of steel," was as iron-willed as his name implied. Once he decided on a goal, Stalin let nothing stand in his way, no matter what the costs. In contrast to Lenin, who had seen the Russian Revolution as only part of a worldwide uprising by the working class, Stalin focused on creating a model Communist state in the Soviet Union. In doing so, he began an agricultural and industrial restructuring that trampled the rights of—and brought great suffering to—his people.

In 1927, Stalin launched his massive drive to transform the Soviet Union into a truly socialist country, which meant stamping out private enterprise—especially private farming. He began by ordering the collectivization of Soviet agriculture—that is, the organization of production under collective, or state, control. He forced Russia's peasants to give up their small plots of land so that they could be combined into large state-owned farms. They were then expected to work on the collective farms as wage earners.

Meanwhile, Stalin turned to his second great goal, the transformation of the Soviet Union from a backward rural nation into a great industrial power. In 1928, the Soviet dictator issued his first "five-year plan," a campaign to build massive state-owned factories, steel mills, and power plants. A second five-year plan followed in 1933 (which was completed in only four years), and a third in 1937. By 1939, the Soviet Union had become the world's third largest industrial power, surpassed in overall production by only the United States and Germany.

The human costs of this transformation, however, were enormous. To accomplish his ambitious goals, the "man of steel" turned the Soviet Union into

GEOGRAPHY SKILLBUILDER
REGION *In which countries did nationalistic leaders come to power? Who were the leaders?*
LOCATION *What geographic features might have led Japan to expand?*

Skillbuilder Answer
Region: Germany—Adolf Hitler; Spain—Francisco Franco; Italy—Benito Mussolini; Soviet Union—Joseph Stalin; Japan—Hideki Tojo.
Location: Its status as an island nation.

OBJECTIVE
① INSTRUCT

Nationalism Threatens Europe and Asia

▶ ***Starting with the Student*** Have students use a three-column chart—with one column labeled Italy, one Germany, and one Japan—to take notes on the countries' beliefs and actions during their leaders' rise to power.

Italy	Germany	Japan

▶ ***Discussing Key Ideas***
- After World War I totalitarian governments take root in Russia, Italy, and Germany.
- Militarists dreaming of territorial expansion gain control of Japan.
- The League of Nations proves helpless in the face of aggression by Japan and Italy.

IN-DEPTH RESOURCES: UNIT 5
Guided Reading, p. 1

ACCESS FOR STUDENTS ACQUIRING ENGLISH
Guided Reading (Spanish), p. 187

HISTORY FROM VISUALS
The Rise of Nationalism, 1922–1941

Reading the Map Have students identify the Fascist, Communist, and expansionist military regimes. *Fascist—Germany, Italy, and Spain; Communist—Soviet Union; expansionist military—Japan.*

TEACHING OPTIONS

Making Connections Across the Curriculum

Economics Explain to students that economists describe the Soviet Union under Stalin as a "command economy," meaning one in which almost all economic decisions are controlled and directed by the government. Discuss with students how a capitalist economy differs from a command economy. *In a capitalist economy, most economic decisions are not made by the government but by individuals, who decide how to spend or invest their own money.*

Making Connections Across Time

The Russian Economy Today Ask students what they know about the Russian economy today and how it has changed since Stalin's time. Discuss with them Russia's difficult transition from a command to a capitalist economic system. Point out that under communism, the Soviet Union lacked many basic features of a capitalist system, such as private property and the right to own or make a profit from a business.

MORE ABOUT . . .
Stalin's Purges

Despite the mass terror created by Stalin's purges, the Soviet people never lost their sense of humor. Here is one of the jokes told by Russians in the 1930s.

Polish rabbit: Why have you fled to Poland?
Russian rabbit: Because Stalin is preparing a bear hunt.
Polish rabbit: But you're not a bear.
Russian rabbit: No, but I can't prove it.

MORE ABOUT . . .
Hitler's Propaganda Techniques

In *Mein Kampf,* Adolf Hitler described one of the Nazi Party's major propaganda tools—the "big lie." Hitler wrote that "the great masses of the people . . . more easily fall a victim to a big lie than to a little one, since they themselves lie in little things, but would be ashamed of lies that were too big. Such a falsehood will never enter their heads, and they will not be able to believe in the possibility of such monstrous effrontery and infamous misrepresentation in others."

HUMANITIES TRANSPARENCIES
H23, German Nazi Party poster

"Italy wants peace, work, and calm. I will give these things with love if possible, with force if necessary."

BENITO MUSSOLINI

a vast police state—a state in which no one was safe from the prying eyes and ears of government spies and secret police. Anyone even suspected of criticizing the Soviet leader or his goals was arrested and shipped off to a forced labor camp in the frozen wastelands of Siberia.

In his drive to purge, or rid, the Soviet Union of people who disagreed with the government's policies, Stalin did not spare even his most faithful supporters. During the Great Purge of the 1930s, tens of thousands of Communist Party officials, bureaucrats, and army officers were branded "enemies of the people" and were executed. While the final toll will never be known, historians estimate that Stalin was responsible for the deaths of 8 million to 13 million people. Millions more died in famines caused by the restructuring of Soviet society.

By 1939, Stalin had established a centralized **totalitarian** government, one that maintained complete control over its citizens. In a totalitarian state, individuals have no rights, and the government suppresses all opposition.

THINK THROUGH HISTORY
B. ***Summarizing*** *What are the characteristics of a totalitarian state?*

B. Answer Complete control over citizens and ruthless suppression of opposition.

THE RISE OF FASCISM IN ITALY While Stalin was consolidating his power in the Soviet Union, **Benito Mussolini** was establishing a totalitarian regime in Italy. In 1919, Mussolini had begun his rise to power by advertising for war veterans to fight the politicians, who, in Mussolini's view, were destroying Italy. This mobilization was the beginning of **fascism,** a new political movement that consisted of a strong, centralized government headed by a powerful dictator. Fascism was rooted in the nationalism that had reshaped Europe over the past century. Mussolini dreamed of making Italy a great power in the world.

Unlike Stalin's Communist regime, Mussolini's Fascist state did not attempt to control farms and factories. In fact, many discontented veterans, jobless youth, and businesspeople greatly feared the spread of communism to Italy. These people became firm supporters of Mussolini. In 1921, Mussolini established the Fascist Party, which then won 35 seats in the Italian parliament. A year later, after Mussolini staged a march on Rome with thousands of his black-shirted followers, the Italian king allowed him to form a new government.

Calling himself *Il Duce,* or "the chief," Mussolini gradually extended Fascist control to every aspect of Italian life. Tourists marveled that *Il Duce* had even "made the trains run on time." Mussolini achieved this efficiency, however, by crushing all opposition and by making Italy a totalitarian state.

THE NAZIS TAKE OVER GERMANY In Germany, **Adolf Hitler** had followed a path to power similar to Mussolini's. At the end of World War I, Hitler had been a jobless soldier drifting around Germany. In 1919, he joined a struggling group called the National Socialist German Workers' Party, better known as the Nazi Party. Despite the word *Socialist* in its name, this party had no ties to socialism and in fact hated it. Soon Hitler became the tiny party's führer, or leader.

Hitler laid out the basic beliefs of **Nazism** in his book *Mein Kampf* ("My Struggle"), published in two volumes in 1925 and 1927. A type of fascism, Nazism was based on extreme nationalism. Hitler, who had been born in Austria, dreamed of uniting all German-speaking people in a great German empire. To this element of nationalism, Hitler added his theories about race. In his view, Germans—especially blue-eyed, blond-haired "Aryans"—formed a "master race" that was destined to rule the world. "Inferior races," such as Jews, Slavs, and nonwhites, were fit only to serve Aryans.

C. Answer Although racism has existed in the United States, especially among slaveholders, arguments for the superiority of any race have become increasingly indefensible.

THINK THROUGH HISTORY
C. THEME ***Cultural Diversity*** *Compare and contrast the racial attitudes expressed in* Mein Kampf *with racial attitudes in the United States?*

A third element of Nazism was national expansion. Hitler believed that for Germany to thrive, it needed more lebensraum, or living space. One of the Nazis' aims, as Hitler wrote in *Mein Kampf,* was "to secure for the German people the land and soil to which they are entitled on this earth," even if this could be accomplished only by "the might of a victorious sword."

TEACHING OPTION

Teaching Less Proficient Readers

Previewing Foreign Terms Before less proficient readers begin reading pages 544 and 545, help them preview the foreign terms they will encounter.

fascism: (făsh'ĭz ĕm) A system of government marked by centralization of authority under a dictator. This term, first used by Mussolini in 1919, comes from the Latin word *fasces,* a bundle of sticks bound to an ax, an object which symbolized unity and authority.

Il Duce: (ēl do͞o'chā) Italian for "the leader" or "chief"

führer: (fyo͝or'ər) German for "leader" or "guide"

Nazism: (nät'sĭz əm) A political movement based on extreme nationalism and racism. The term *Nazi* is a shortened form of the German word *Nationalsozialist.*

lebensraum: (lā'bəns-roum) German for "living room," or "space for a growing population"

Reich: (rīk) German for "kingdom," "empire," or "realm"

The Faces of Totalitarianism

FASCIST ITALY	NAZI GERMANY	COMMUNIST SOVIET UNION
• Extreme nationalism • Militaristic expansionism • Charismatic leader • Private property with strong government controls • Anti-Communist	• Extreme nationalism and racism • Militaristic expansionism • Forceful leader • Private property with strong government controls • Anti-Communist	• Create a sound communist state and wait for world revolution • Revolution by workers • Eventual rule by working class • State ownership of property

SKILLBUILDER **INTERPRETING CHARTS** *How did fascism in Italy differ from communism in the Soviet Union?*

The Great Depression helped the Nazis come to power. By 1932, some 6 million Germans were unemployed. Many of these desperate people turned to Hitler as their last hope. In elections held in March 1932, the Nazis won more votes than any other party, though not a majority. In January 1933, Hitler was appointed chancellor (prime minister).

Once in power, the Führer quickly dismantled Germany's democratic Weimar Republic. In its place he established what he called the Third Reich, or Third German Empire. Like the first German empire (the Holy Roman Empire established by Charlemagne), and unlike the short-lived second empire established by Bismarck in the 19th century, the Third Reich, according to Hitler, would be a "Thousand-Year Reich."

MILITARISTS GAIN CONTROL IN JAPAN Halfway around the world from Germany, nationalistic military leaders in Japan were trying to take control of their government. These leaders shared Hitler's belief in the need for more "living space" for a growing population. Ignoring the protests of more moderate Japanese officials, the militarists launched a surprise invasion of the Chinese province of Manchuria in 1931. Within several months, Japanese troops controlled the entire province, a resource-rich area nearly as large as Alaska.

THINK THROUGH HISTORY
D. ***Analyzing Motives*** *Why did Japan invade Manchuria?*

As you read in Chapter 11, the League of Nations had been established after World War I to prevent such aggressive acts. In this first test of its power, the League sent representatives to Manchuria to investigate the situation. Their report condemned Japan, which simply quit the League. Meanwhile, the success of the Manchurian invasion put the militarists firmly in control of Japan's government.

AGGRESSION IN EUROPE The failure of the League of Nations to take action against Japan did not escape the notice of Europe's dictators. In 1933, Hitler felt bold enough to pull Germany out of the League. In 1935, he began a military buildup in violation of the Versailles treaty. A year later, he sent troops into the Rhineland, a German region bordering France and Belgium which was demilitarized as a result of the Versailles treaty. He also signed the Rome-Berlin Axis Pact, which established a formal alliance between Germany and Italy. The League did nothing to stop Hitler.

Meanwhile, Mussolini began building his new Roman Empire. His first target was Ethiopia, Africa's only remaining independent country. By the fall of 1935, tens of thousands of Italian soldiers stood ready to advance on Ethiopia. The League of Nations reacted with brave talk of "collective resistance to all acts of unprovoked aggression."

HISTORICAL SPOTLIGHT

AFRICAN AMERICANS STAND BY ETHIOPIANS

When Mussolini invaded Ethiopia, many Europeans and Americans—especially African Americans—were outraged. Almost overnight, African Americans organized to raise money for medical supplies, and a few went to fight in Ethiopia. Years later, the Ethiopian emperor Haile Selassie said of these efforts,

> "We can never forget the help Ethiopia received from Negro Americans during the terrible crisis. . . . It moved me to know that Americans of African descent did not abandon their embattled brothers, but stood by us."

HISTORY FROM VISUALS
The Faces of Totalitarianism

Reading the Chart Suggest that students first read down each column of the chart to learn the basic characteristics of each totalitarian government. Then have them read across to compare and contrast the totalitarian systems.

Extension Ask students to predict on the basis of this chart which of these nations might become allies and which enemies. *Possible Response: Italy and Germany might become allies because of their shared fascist beliefs. The Soviet Union might regard both Italy and Germany as enemies because of their hostility to communism.*

HISTORICAL SPOTLIGHT
African Americans Stand by Ethiopians

Critical Thinking: Analyzing Motives Ask students to consider what motivated African Americans to mobilize on behalf of Ethiopia in 1935. You may want to remind students that Ethiopia was one of the few independent black nations in the world in 1935, and that, for African Americans, its defeat might symbolize the victory of whites over blacks.

TEACHING OPTION
Exploring Themes

Cultural Diversity African Americans were among the first Americans to condemn the rise of Nazism and racism in Germany. Some had read *Mein Kampf* and were deeply offended by Hitler's view that blond, blue-eyed Germans constituted a "master race." Others were awakened to the Nazi threat during the 1936 summer Olympics, which were held in the German capital of Berlin. During the games, African-American track star Jesse Owens stole the show by winning four gold medals. Hitler regarded Owens's victories as a threat to his racial theories, and walked out of the Olympic stadium rather than congratulate a black athlete. In his extraordinary performance, Owens tied the Olympic record in the 100-meter run (10.3 seconds). He also broke the Olympic and world records in the 200-meter run (20.7 seconds) and the running broad jump (26 feet 5¼ inches). After he retired from competitive sports, Owens made goodwill visits to India and East Asia on behalf of the U.S. Department of State.

HISTORY FROM VISUALS

Aggressive Acts, 1931–1936

Reading the Map Be sure that students understand the relationship between the two detailed maps and the globe. Point out that the maps show the relative location of Italy and Japan to the countries they invaded. The globe shows the relative location of these two hot spots on opposite sides of the world.

Extension Ask students to speculate what effects Italy's and Japan's actions might have on America. *Students might say that these countries are so far away that the actions would have no effect.*

The United States Responds Cautiously

▶ ***Starting with the Student***
- Ask students what they would do if they saw a fight break out on the far side of the schoolyard and they didn't know any of the people involved.
- Discuss how this situation compares with the dilemma facing Americans in the 1930s as they watched Ethiopia and China.

▶ ***Discussing Key Ideas***
- After World War I, the United States returns to a policy of isolationism.
- Congress passes the Neutrality Acts to keep the United States out of war.
- Many Americans find it hard to remain neutral.

IN-DEPTH RESOURCES: UNIT 5
Primary Source: *from* Franklin D. Roosevelt's "Quarantine Speech," p. 8

Aggressive Acts, 1931–1936

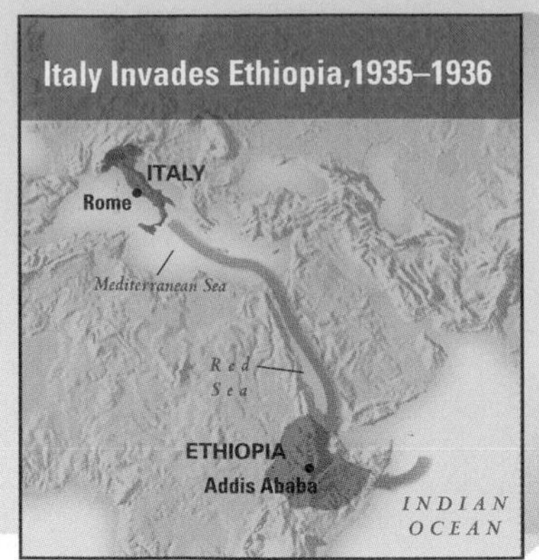

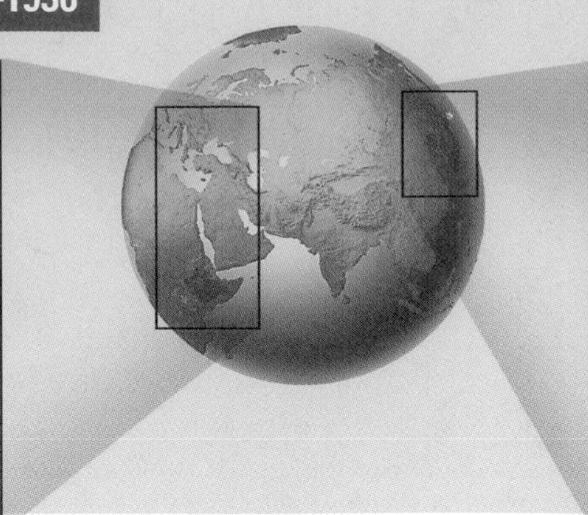

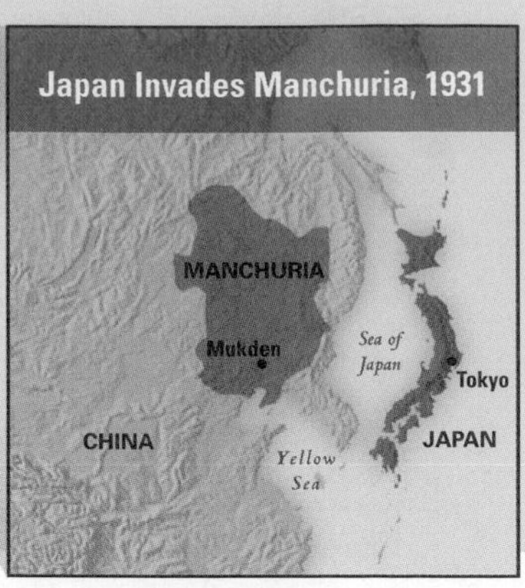

GEOGRAPHY SKILLBUILDER

MOVEMENT ***Notice the size and location of Italy and of Japan with respect to the country each invaded. What similarities do you see?***

Skillbuilder Answer
They were both small nations that invaded larger countries by sea.

When the invasion began, however, the League's response was an ineffective economic boycott—little more than a slap on Italy's wrist. By June 1936, Ethiopia had fallen. In desperation, Haile Selassie, the ousted Ethiopian emperor, appealed to the League for assistance. Nothing was done. "It is us today," he told them. "It will be you tomorrow."

The United States Responds Cautiously

As disturbing as these events in Europe and Asia were to Americans, most believed that the United States should not get involved. In 1928, the United States had joined 61 other nations in signing the Kellogg-Briand Pact, in which they pledged never to make war again. But this agreement still permitted defensive war and did not provide for using economic or military force against nations that broke the pact.

CLINGING TO ISOLATIONISM In the early 1930s, a flood of books argued that the United States had been dragged into World War I by greedy bankers and arms dealers. Public outrage led to the creation of a congressional committee, chaired by North Dakota senator Gerald Nye, that held hearings on these charges. The Nye committee fueled the controversy by documenting the large profits that banks and manufacturers made during the war.

The furor over these "merchants of death" made Americans more determined than ever to avoid war. A poll taken in 1937 revealed that fully 70 percent of Americans believed that the United States should not have entered World War I. Antiwar feeling was so strong that the Girl Scouts of America changed the color of its uniforms from khaki to green to appear less militaristic. Across the country, college students staged antiwar rallies with banners proclaiming "Scholarships, not battleships."

Americans' growing isolationism eventually had an impact on President Roosevelt's foreign policy. When he had first taken office in 1933, Roosevelt had felt comfortable reaching out to the world in several ways. He officially recognized the Soviet Union in 1933 and agreed to exchange ambassadors with Moscow. He continued the policy of nonintervention in Latin America, begun by Presidents Coolidge and Hoover, with his Good Neighbor policy and withdrew armed forces stationed there. In 1934, Roosevelt pushed the Reciprocal Trade Agreement Act through Congress. This act lowered trade barriers by giving the president the power to make trade agreements with other nations and was aimed at reducing tariffs by as much as 50 percent.

Beginning in 1935, however, Congress passed a series of **Neutrality Acts** in an effort to keep the United States out of future wars. The first two acts outlawed

E. Answer
Evidence that large profits had been made by banks and arms industries during World War I; regret over having been involved in that war; hatred of militarism.

THINK THROUGH HISTORY
E. ***Forming Generalizations*** *What factors contributed to Americans' growing isolationism?*

Block Schedule TEACHING OPTION **Time Needed: 20 Minutes**

Cooperative Activity: Writing a Newspaper Editorial

Task: Student groups will write a newspaper editorial about President Roosevelt's "Quarantine Speech."

Purpose: To help students appreciate the difficulties Roosevelt faced in trying to promote world peace.

Activity: Assign small groups of students to serve as editorial boards of newspapers in the 1930s. Students will determine the editorial response of their newspaper to President Roosevelt's "Quarantine Speech" of October 5, 1937, and then write a short editorial explaining why their paper approves or disapproves of his call for action. Groups should read their editorials to the class.

Building a Portfolio: Students who add the editorial to their portfolio should attach a note indicating their contribution.

ALTERNATIVE ASSESSMENT BOOK
Standards for Evaluating a Cooperative Activity

Standards for Evaluation
Editorials should . . .
- take a clear position for or against President Roosevelt's "Quarantine Speech"
- give detailed reasons supporting that position
- use appropriate editorial form and style

arms sales or loans to nations at war. The third act was passed in response to fighting that broke out in Spain in 1936, between the troops of the Fascist general Francisco Franco and forces loyal to the country's elected government. This act extended the ban on arms sales and loans to nations undergoing civil wars.

NEUTRALITY BREAKS DOWN Despite congressional efforts to legislate neutrality, many Americans found it difficult not to take sides in the Spanish Civil War. When Hitler and Mussolini came to Franco's aid early in the war, some 3,000 volunteers from the United States responded by forming the Abraham Lincoln Brigade and traveling to Spain to fight Franco. "We knew, we just *knew*," recalled Martha Gellhorn, "that Spain was the place to stop fascism." Among the volunteers were African Americans still bitter about Mussolini's invasion of Ethiopia the year before.

Such limited aid was not sufficient to stop the spread of fascism, however. Hitler and Mussolini, who saw the conflict as a testing ground for their military power, supported Franco with troops, weapons, tanks, and fighter planes. The Western democracies, fearful of triggering a larger war, sent only food and clothing to the anti-Fascist forces. In early 1939, after a loss of 600,000 lives and at a cost of more than $15 billion, the resistance to Franco had collapsed. Europe now had yet another totalitarian government.

Roosevelt himself found it impossible to remain neutral when Japan launched a new attack on China in July of 1937. Since Japan had not formally declared war against China, the president refused to enforce the Neutrality Acts. The United States continued sending arms and supplies to China.

A few months later, Roosevelt spoke out strongly against isolationism in a speech delivered in Chicago. He called on peace-loving nations to "quarantine," or isolate, aggressor nations in order to stop the spread of war.

THINK THROUGH HISTORY
F. *Analyzing Motives* *What events caused Roosevelt to take a strong stand against isolationism?*

F. Answer The Spanish Civil War and Japan's attack on China.

A PERSONAL VOICE

> The peace, the freedom, and the security of 90 percent of the population of the world is being jeopardized by the remaining 10 percent who are threatening a breakdown of all international law and order. Surely the 90 percent who want to live in peace under law and in accordance with standards that have received almost universal acceptance through the centuries, can and must find some way . . . to preserve peace.
>
> FRANKLIN DELANO ROOSEVELT, "Quarantine Speech," October 5, 1937

SKILLBUILDER
INTERPRETING POLITICAL CARTOONS
What does Uncle Sam's turning his back to Europe show about American attitudes in the late 1930s?

Skillbuilder Answer The United States didn't want to become involved in the war in Europe.

At last Roosevelt seemed ready to take a stand against aggression—that is, until isolationist newspapers exploded in protest and letters flooded the White House accusing the president of leading the nation into war. Roosevelt backed off. For the moment the conflicts remained "over there."

Section  Assessment

1. TERMS & NAMES
Identify:
- Joseph Stalin
- totalitarian
- Benito Mussolini
- fascism
- Adolf Hitler
- Nazism
- Neutrality Acts

2. SUMMARIZING List the main ambition of each dictator in a graphic like the one shown.

Ambitions of European Dictators

Stalin	Mussolini	Hitler

What ambitions did the dictators have in common?

3. ANALYZING CAUSES How did the Treaty of Versailles sow the seeds of instability in Europe?

THINK ABOUT
- effects of the treaty on Germany and the Soviet Union
- effects of the treaty on national pride
- the economic legacy of the war

4. ANALYZING MOTIVES Why do you think Hitler found widespread support among the German people? Support your answer with details from the text.

THINK ABOUT
- Germans' postwar resentment and bitterness
- Germany's economic situation before Hitler's rise to power
- the appeal of Hitler's views

ANSWERS

1. TERMS & NAMES

Joseph Stalin, p. 543
totalitarian, p. 544
Benito Mussolini, p. 544
fascism, p. 544
Adolf Hitler, p. 544
Nazism, p. 544
Neutrality Acts, p. 546

2. SUMMARIZING

Possible Responses:
Stalin—To create a model Communist state and to transform the Soviet Union into a great industrial power.
Mussolini—To make Italy a great world power.
Hitler—To unite the German "master race" into an empire destined to rule the world.

3. ANALYZING CAUSES

Possible Responses:
Germany's and Russia's resentment of the treaty's harsh terms contributed to their renouncing democratic values; the treaty did not halt the rise of totalitarian governments or help nations rebuild their postwar economies.

4. ANALYZING MOTIVES

Possible Responses:
They were disheartened by the effects of World War I, were suffering from widespread unemployment, and responded positively to Hitler's Nazi doctrine, which restored their national pride.

HISTORY FROM VISUALS
"It Ain't What it Used to Be"

Reading the Cartoon Have students identify the symbols used in the cartoon. *Uncle Sam and the U.S. map—the United States; the symbolic "war clouds" looming ominously over Europe.* What is Uncle Sam referring to in his statement? *The width of the Atlantic Ocean.*

Extension Discuss with students why the Atlantic Ocean seemed to have shrunk in the late 1930s. *The war clouds over Europe and Africa were fast approaching America.*

FOCUS & MOTIVATE

Section 1 Assessment

Have students work in groups of three to answer the questions. In question 2, have each student fill in the column for a different dictator and then discuss the question as a group.

Self-Assessment

Have each group compare its answers with those of another group. If the answers disagree, have students work together to formulate a mutually acceptable response.

Section Quiz

FORMAL ASSESSMENT
Section Quiz, p. 200

Reteach

Review the political cartoon on page 547 to help students understand the issues facing the United States as it tried to maintain neutrality.

CLOSE

After World War I, aggressive dictators and military leaders took power in Russia, Italy, Germany, Japan, and Spain. Meanwhile, the United States adopted a policy of isolation and neutrality.

Section 2 Overview

OBJECTIVES

1. To explain Germany's motives for expansion and the timid response of France and Britain.
2. To describe Germany's blitzkrieg tactics against Poland.
3. To summarize the first battles of World War II.

SKILLBUILDER

- Understanding geography: region, location, p. 552

CRITICAL THINKING

- Summarizing, p. 549
- Analyzing motives, p. 550
- Theme: Science and Technology, p. 551
- Comparing, p. 551
- Finding main ideas, p. 552
- Contrasting, p. 553
- Following chronological order, p. 553
- Forming generalizations, p. 553
- Making decisions, p. 553

FOCUS & MOTIVATE

5-MINUTE WARM-UP

Evaluating Judgments

To investigate the origins of the Second World War, have students read "Bargaining for the Sudetenland" on pages 549–550 and answer the following questions.

1. Did Neville Chamberlain do the right thing in signing the Munich agreement?
2. How might history have been different if he had refused to sign it?

WARM-UP TRANSPARENCY 16

▶ ***Starting with the Student***

- Ask students what they would do if someone came up to them and demanded their jacket. Give up the jacket and hope the person goes away? Try to persuade the person to leave them alone? Fight?
- Would their decision be different if the other person was a lot bigger and stronger than they are?

2 War in Europe

TERMS & NAMES

- **Neville Chamberlain**
- **Winston Churchill**
- **appeasement**
- **nonaggression pact**
- **blitzkrieg**
- **Charles de Gaulle**

LEARN ABOUT the weak response of world leaders to Germany's aggressive moves in the late 1930s
TO UNDERSTAND how Germany started World War II.

William Shirer

ONE AMERICAN'S STORY

A warm June sun bathed the little clearing in the Forest of Compiègne where, 22 years earlier, defeated German generals had signed the armistice ending World War I. It was now 1940, and CBS correspondent William Shirer was standing in the clearing, waiting for Adolf Hitler to deliver *his* armistice terms to a defeated France. Shirer watched as Hitler walked up to the monument and slowly read the inscription: "Here on the eleventh of November 1918 succumbed the criminal pride of the German empire . . . vanquished by the free peoples it tried to enslave." Later that day, Shirer wrote a diary entry describing the Führer's reaction.

A PERSONAL VOICE

I have seen that face many times at the great moments of his life. But today! It is afire with scorn, anger, hate, revenge, triumph. He steps off the monument and contrives to make even this gesture a masterpiece of contempt. . . . He glances slowly around the clearing, and now, as his eyes meet ours, you grasp the depth of his hatred. But there is triumph there too—revengeful, triumphant hate.

WILLIAM SHIRER, *Berlin Diary: The Journal of a Foreign Correspondent, 1934–1941*

Again and again Shirer had heard Hitler proclaim that "Germany needs peace . . . Germany wants peace." The hatred and vengefulness that drove the dictator's every action, however, drew Germany ever closer to war.

Austria and Czechoslovakia Fall

On November 5, 1937, Hitler met with his most trusted military advisers for a top-secret briefing. The Third Reich's future, he told them, depended on solving the need for lebensraum. Where would new living space come from? Not from overseas colonies, he declared, but from those nations nearest Germany—Austria and Czechoslovakia. When someone protested that annexing those countries could provoke war, Hitler replied, "Germany's problems can be solved only by means of force, and this is never without risk."

UNION WITH AUSTRIA In fact, the risk turned out to be less than Hitler's advisers feared. The following February, Hitler invited Austrian chancellor Kurt von Schuschnigg to meet with him at his villa at Berchtesgaden, high in the Bavarian Alps. When the Austrian chancellor began making polite conversation about the view and the lovely day, Hitler snapped, "We did not gather here to speak of the fine view or of the weather."

For the next few hours, Hitler pounded the table and demanded that Schuschnigg appoint Austrian Nazis to key government posts. By the end of the meeting, Hitler had bullied Schuschnigg into signing an agreement to bring Austrian Nazis into his government. On returning home, Schuschnigg

SECTION 2 RESOURCES

PRINT RESOURCES

IN-DEPTH RESOURCES: UNIT 5
Guided Reading, p. 2
Skillbuilder Practice: Developing Historical Pespective, p. 5

READING STUDY GUIDE, p. 169

ACCESS FOR STUDENTS ACQUIRING ENGLISH
Guided Reading (Spanish), p. 188
Skillbuilder Practice: Developing Historical Pespective (Spanish), p. 191

SPANISH READING STUDY GUIDE, p. 169

FORMAL ASSESSMENT
Section Quiz, p. 201

ALTERNATIVE ASSESSMENT BOOK
See forms for supporting and scoring alternative activities.

TECHNOLOGY RESOURCES

GEOGRAPHY TRANSPARENCIES
G24, Aggression in Europe, 1936–39

CD-ROM *Our Times*
Electronic Library of Primary Sources

VIDEO *American Portfolio: A Videodisc for U.S. History* user's guide, pp. 209–210

INTERNET http://www.mlushistory.com

had second thoughts about the agreement and informed Hitler. Hitler was furious. On March 12, 1938, German troops marched into Austria unopposed, forcing Schuschnigg to resign. Two days later, Germany announced that its Anschluss, or "union," with Austria was complete. The United States and the rest of the world did nothing.

BARGAINING FOR THE SUDETENLAND Hitler then turned to Czechoslovakia. When the Austro-Hungarian Empire was broken up at the end of World War I, the Sudetenland, a mountainous region inhabited by 3 million German-speaking people, had been joined to Czechoslovakia. In the spring of 1938, Hitler charged that the Czechs were abusing the Sudeten Germans, and he began massing troops on the Czech border. The American correspondent William Shirer, then stationed in Berlin, wrote in his diary: "The Nazi press [is] full of hysterical headlines. All lies. Some examples: 'Women and Children Mowed Down by Czech Armored Cars,' or 'Bloody Regime—New Czech Murders of Germans.'"

Early in the crisis, both France and Great Britain promised to protect Czechoslovakia. Then, just when war seemed inevitable, Hitler invited French premier Edouard Daladier and British prime minister **Neville Chamberlain** to meet with him in Munich. When they arrived, the Führer declared that the Sudetenland would be his "last territorial demand." In their eagerness to avoid war, Daladier and Chamberlain chose to believe him. On September 30, 1938, they signed the Munich Pact, which turned the Sudetenland over to Germany without a shot being fired.

THINK THROUGH HISTORY
A. ***Summarizing*** *What moves did Germany make in its quest for lebensraum?*

A. Answer Annexation of Austria and the Sudetenland.

Chamberlain returned home to wildly cheering crowds. Waving a copy of the Munich agreement, he proclaimed: "My friends, . . . there has come back from Germany peace with honor. I believe it is peace in our time." The crowd joyously responded by chanting "Good old Neville" and singing "For he's a jolly good fellow."

These sentiments were not shared by **Winston Churchill,** Chamberlain's political rival for the leadership of Great Britain. In Churchill's view, by signing the Munich Pact, Daladier and Chamberlain had adopted a shameful policy of **appeasement,** or giving up

KEY PLAYER

ADOLF HITLER
1889–1945

"All great world-shaking events have been brought about not by written matter, but by the spoken word!" declared Adolf Hitler. A shy and awkward speaker at first, Hitler rehearsed carefully. He even had photos taken of his favorite gestures so that he could study them and make changes to produce exactly the desired effect. Hitler's extraordinary power as a speaker, wrote Otto Strasser, stemmed from an intuitive ability to sense "the vibration of the human heart . . . telling it what it most wants to hear."

Hitler whips a million supporters into a frenzy of smiles and salutes at a Harvest Day celebration in 1937.

OBJECTIVE
① INSTRUCT

Austria and Czechoslovakia Fall

▶ ***Starting with the Student***
Ask students to create a time line to track German expansion from 1937 to the end of 1940. Their time lines might look like this:

1937 — 1938 — 1939 — 1940

Students should add to their time lines the names of countries taken over by Germany during this period.

▶ ***Discussing Key Ideas***
- Once in power, Hitler begins a policy of territorial expansion, starting with Austria and Czechoslovakia.
- France and Britain prefer a policy of appeasement toward Germany to one of armed confrontation.

IN-DEPTH RESOURCES: UNIT 5
Guided Reading, p. 2

ACCESS FOR STUDENTS ACQUIRING ENGLISH,
Guided Reading (Spanish), p. 188

KEY PLAYER
Adolf Hitler

Critical Thinking: Drawing Conclusions Ask students to speculate about the emotions or attitudes Hitler was trying to communicate to audiences with each of the gestures shown in the photographs. Would his style of speaking work well on television today? Why or why not?

TEACHING OPTION

Skillbuilder Mini-Lesson: Developing Historical Perspective

Explaining the Skill Historical perspective is a way of looking at events, conditions, decisions, and leaders of the past in the context of their own times, rather than judging them based on what we now know. For example, we might now see a historical figure as a cruel, ruthless dictator. At the time, however, some of his policies may have seemed to be exactly what his country needed to settle disputes or to feed the people.

Applying the Skill: The Munich Pact Point out to students that, in light of what we know now, many historians believe that Chamberlain should not have bargained with Hitler. Ask students to identify reasons for the cheering crowds that greeted Chamberlain when he returned to England from Munich and proclaimed "peace with honor."

The people had been through one terrible war recently and did not want another one. The public, and many leaders, did not then know that Hitler was filled with hate and that he would ignore his promises.

IN-DEPTH RESOURCES: UNIT 5
Skillbuilder Practice: Developing Historical Perspective, p. 5

MORE ABOUT . . .
Hitler on His Critics

Annoyed by criticism of the Munich agreement by Churchill and others, Hitler replied, "We would like to give these gentlemen the advice that they should busy themselves with their own affairs and leave us in peace."

The German Offensive Begins

▶ ***Starting with the Student*** Have students continue filling in their time lines on German expansion as they read this section.

▶ ***Discussing Key Ideas***
- Germany and the Soviet Union sign a nonaggression pact, encouraging Hitler to invade Poland.
- German troops overrun Poland quickly using a military strategy known as the blitzkrieg.
- The Polish blitzkrieg is followed by an eerie period of calm nicknamed the "phony war."

HISTORY FROM VISUALS
The Tactics of the Blitzkrieg

Reading the Diagram Point out that the numbered drawings show the order of attack in the blitzkrieg. The right column gives detailed information about the key player in the aerial bombardment.

Extension Have students compare and contrast the advantages and disadvantages of the blitzkrieg and more traditional battle strategies.

"Hitler and Mussolini are madmen who respect force and force alone."

FRANKLIN D. ROOSEVELT, 1939

principles to pacify an aggressor. As Churchill bluntly put it, "Britain and France had to choose between war and dishonor. They chose dishonor. They will have war." Nonetheless, the House of Commons approved Chamberlain's policy toward Germany by a vote of 366 to 144. Churchill responded with a warning.

A PERSONAL VOICE

We have passed an awful milestone in our history. . . . And do not suppose that this is the end. This is only the first sip, the first foretaste of a bitter cup which will be proffered to us year by year unless, by a supreme recovery of moral health and martial vigor, we arise again and take our stand for freedom as in the olden time.

WINSTON CHURCHILL, speech to the House of Commons, quoted in *The Gathering Storm*

THINK THROUGH HISTORY
B. ***Analyzing Motives*** *What was appeasement, and why did Churchill oppose it so strongly?*

B. Answer An attempt to do whatever was necessary to pacify Hitler; Churchill saw it as an abandonment of moral principles that would lead to a war and national disaster.

The German Offensive Begins

Contrary to his promise at Munich, Hitler was not finished expanding the Third Reich. As dawn broke on March 15, 1939, German troops poured into what remained of Czechoslovakia. At nightfall Hitler gloated, "Czechoslovakia has ceased to exist." After that, the German dictator turned his land-hungry gaze toward Germany's eastern neighbor, Poland.

THE SOVIET UNION DECLARES NEUTRALITY Like Czechoslovakia, Poland had a sizable German-speaking population. In the spring of 1939, Hitler began his familiar routine, charging that Germans in Poland were mistreated by the Poles and needed his protection. Some people thought that this time Hitler must be bluffing. After all, an attack on Poland might bring Germany into conflict with the Soviet Union, Poland's eastern neighbor. At the same time, such an attack would most likely provoke a declaration of war from France and

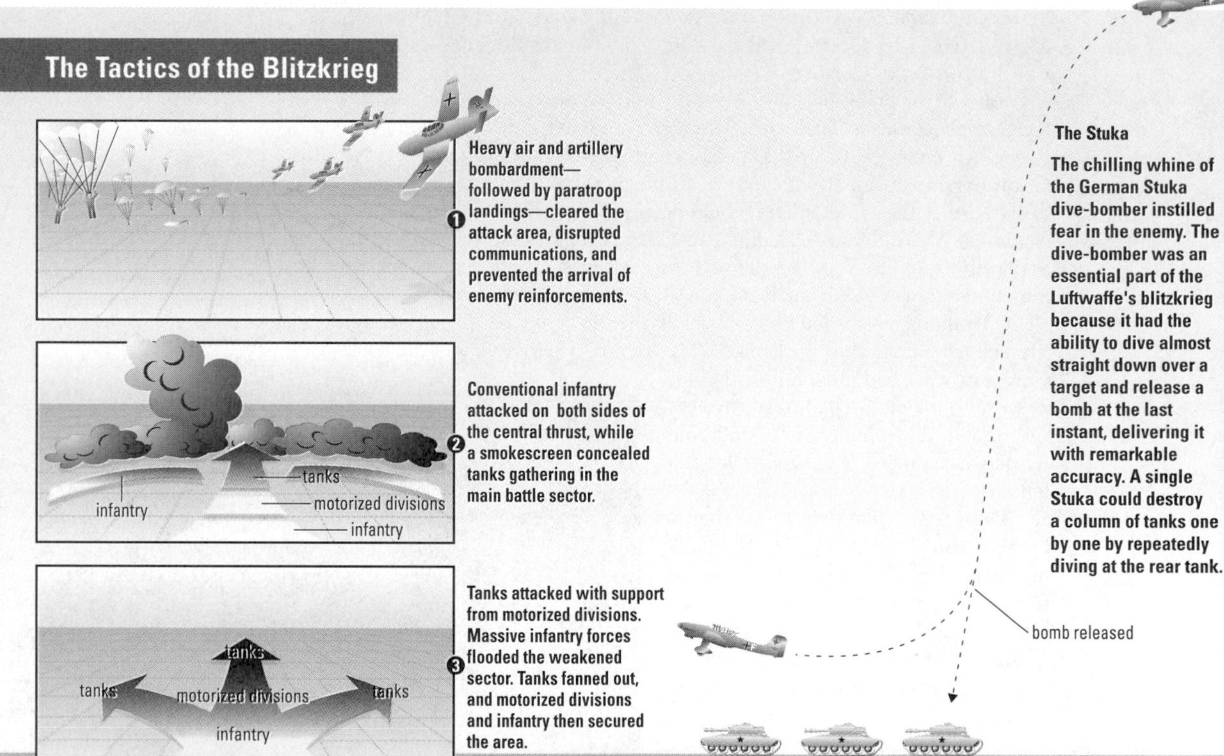

The Tactics of the Blitzkrieg
1 Heavy air and artillery bombardment—followed by paratroop landings—cleared the attack area, disrupted communications, and prevented the arrival of enemy reinforcements.
2 Conventional infantry attacked on both sides of the central thrust, while a smokescreen concealed tanks gathering in the main battle sector.
tanks
motorized divisions
infantry
infantry
3 Tanks attacked with support from motorized divisions. Massive infantry forces flooded the weakened sector. Tanks fanned out, and motorized divisions and infantry then secured the area.
tanks
tanks
motorized divisions
tanks
infantry
The Stuka
The chilling whine of the German Stuka dive-bomber instilled fear in the enemy. The dive-bomber was an essential part of the Luftwaffe's blitzkrieg because it had the ability to dive almost straight down over a target and release a bomb at the last instant, delivering it with remarkable accuracy. A single Stuka could destroy a column of tanks one by one by repeatedly diving at the rear tank.
bomb released

TEACHING OPTION

Connections Across Time

Czechoslovakia and the Czech Republic Czechoslovakia was one of the new nations created after World War I as part of President Woodrow Wilson's Fourteen Points. Czechoslovakia began as a Western-style democratic republic, with a parliamentary form of government, universal suffrage, and firm guarantees for human rights. In 1939, however, Germany occupied the country. By 1945, the Soviets had liberated the country and had signed a treaty of cooperation with Czechoslovakia. In the 1946 national elections, Communists received more votes than any other party, and they took over the government in 1948.

The Communists held sway until 1989, when widespread demonstrations forced the resignation of the old guard and led to the election of a non-Communist regime. In 1992, in a major move away from the Communist system, the government took steps to institute a free-market economy. On January 1, 1993, the country split along ethnic lines into two republics—the Czech Republic and Slovakia.

Britain—both of whom had promised military aid to Poland. The result would be a two-front war. Fighting on two fronts had exhausted Germany in World War I. Surely, many thought, Hitler would not be foolish enough to repeat that mistake.

Hitler took the chance, though, and his luck held. As tensions rose over Poland, Stalin, despite his deep dislike and distrust of the Nazis, decided he had more to lose than to gain in a war against Germany. On August 23, 1939, the Soviet Union and Germany signed a **nonaggression pact,** in which they agreed not to fight each other. They also signed a second, secret pact, agreeing to divide Poland between them. With the danger of a two-front war eliminated, the fate of Poland was sealed.

Pillbox bunkers such as these had been designed to provide effective defense along the Maginot Line, which was supposed to protect France. But the Germans just bypassed these fortifications.

BLITZKRIEG IN POLAND As day broke on September 1, 1939, German warplanes roared over Poland, raining bombs on military bases, airfields, railroads, and cities. At the same time, German tanks rumbled across the Polish countryside, spreading terror and confusion. This invasion was the first test of Germany's newest military strategy, the **blitzkrieg,** or lightning war. The new tactics enabled the Germans to take the enemy by surprise and then quickly crush all opposition with overwhelming force. Britain and France declared war on Germany on September 3.

THINK THROUGH HISTORY
C. THEME ***Science and Technology*** *How did German blitzkrieg tactics rely on new military technology?*

C. Answer The development of improved tanks and airplanes had made blitzkrieg tactics effective.

The blitzkrieg tactics worked perfectly, however. The fighting was over in three weeks, long before France, Britain, and their allies could respond. In the last week of fighting, the Soviet Union attacked Poland from the east, grabbing some of its territory. The portion Germany annexed contained almost two-thirds of Poland's population. By the end of the month, Poland had ceased to exist—and World War II had begun.

THE PHONY WAR Or had it? For the next few months, an eerie calm settled over Europe. Bored French and British troops on the Maginot Line, a system of fortifications along France's eastern border, sat staring into Germany, waiting for something to happen. Equally bored German troops sitting on the Siegfried Line a few miles away stared back. The blitzkrieg had given way to what the Germans called the *sitzkrieg* ("sitting war"), and the English called the phony war. To fight the tedium, French officer Denis Barlone made sure that his men were well fed.

A PERSONAL VOICE

Throughout the day the squeals of doomed pigs and poultry can be heard, while the men go off to thrash the walnut trees, . . . unearth the spuds, uproot the salads. My men feed sumptuously, pastry cooks make flans with the flour, found in abundance, and butter made in the dairy. This is the land of milk and honey.

DENIS BARLONE, *A French Officer's Diary*

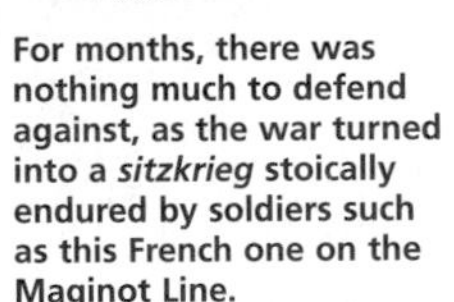

For months, there was nothing much to defend against, as the war turned into a *sitzkrieg* stoically endured by soldiers such as this French one on the Maginot Line.

This deceptive peace was first broken not by Germany but by the Soviet Union. After occupying eastern Poland, Stalin began annexing other regions that the Soviet Union had lost at the end of World War I. The Baltic states of Estonia, Latvia, and Lithuania fell with little struggle. However, Finland—a country that journalist William Shirer admired as "the most decent and workable little democracy in Europe"—resisted. Late in 1939, Stalin sent his Soviet army into Finland. After three months of fierce winter fighting, the outnumbered Finns surrendered. Shirer wrote in his diary, "Stalin reveals himself of the same stamp as Hitler."

D. Answer Both were willing to use secret agreements, armed force, and intimidation to gain the territories they wanted.

THINK THROUGH HISTORY
D. *Comparing* *In what way were Stalin and Hitler alike by 1940?*

MORE ABOUT . . .
Stalin and the Nonaggression Pact

Stalin was well aware that by signing a nonaggression pact with Germany in 1939, he had freed Hitler from the threat of a two-front war, thus opening the way for a German invasion of Poland and the start of World War II. Stalin counted on remaining neutral in the ensuing conflict. He planned to use that time to consolidate his control over Eastern Europe while the Fascists and Western democracies fought each other to exhaustion. Once a stalemate had been reached, the Soviets would be in a strong position to intervene and decide the outcome of the war.

MORE ABOUT . . .
The Phony War

During "the phony war" French, British, and German troops often worked and rested in plain sight of each other on opposite sides of the Siegfried line. The mood of the British troops was expressed in these lyrics from a popular song: "We're gonna hang out the washing on the Siegfried Line—if the Siegfried Line's still there."

TEACHING OPTIONS

Exploring Themes

Science and Technology It was largely advances in military technology that made the German blitzkrieg so effective. These developments included specialized military aircraft, such as the Stuka dive-bomber, the use of the parachute to drop troops where land vehicles couldn't penetrate, and use of the tank as a rapid-moving attack weapon.

Ask students what psychological impact they think this advanced warfare might have on a civilian population. *Possible Responses: It was likely to leave people stunned, disorganized, and demoralized by what seemed to be overwhelming force.*

Making Connections Across the Curriculum

Language Arts / Foreign Languages Have students read the excerpt from Denis Barlone's *A French Officer's Diary.* Then ask them to write their own diary entries describing what it might have been like to be a soldier on the Maginot or Siegfried Line during the *sitzkrieg.* Encourage them to give details about the countryside, the weather, the food, and their daily activities. You might also suggest that they create dialogues between soldiers on opposing sides. Students who are studying French or German might like to write their entries in that language and provide accompanying translations.

OBJECTIVE

③ INSTRUCT

France and Britain Fight On

▶ ***Discussing Key Ideas***

- The phony war ends in a second blitzkrieg that leads to the fall of France.
- By the end of 1940, Britain faces the Nazis alone.
- The Luftwaffe fails to wrest control of the skies from the Royal Air Force during the Battle of Britain.

OUR TIMES
Edward R. Murrow

HISTORY FROM VISUALS

World War II: German Advances, 1939–1941

Reading the Map Remind students to use the color key to help them identify the four categories of nations shown on the map.

Extension Ask students what German advances meant to Great Britain by the end of 1941. *Possible Answer: Great Britain was essentially cut off from the rest of Europe.*

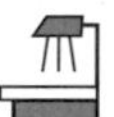
GEOGRAPHY TRANSPARENCIES
G24, Aggression in Europe, 1936–39

MORE ABOUT . . .

Charles de Gaulle

As head of France's government-in-exile, Charles de Gaulle commanded a military force known as the Free French. The Free French played a prominent role in the North African invasion in 1942 and in the invasion of southern France. They were the first troops to enter liberated Paris in 1944.

On April 7, 1940, a leading German newspaper announced, "Germany is ready. Eighty million pairs of [German] eyes are turned upon the Führer." Two days later, the rest of the world stared, unbelieving, as Hitler launched a surprise invasion of Denmark and Norway. Germany said this action was necessary in order "to protect [those countries'] freedom and independence." Next, the German blitzkrieg was turned against the Netherlands, Belgium, and Luxembourg, which were overrun by the end of May. The phony war had suddenly become painfully real.

THINK THROUGH HISTORY
E. *Finding Main Ideas* *How did Hitler rationalize the German invasion of Denmark and Norway?*
E. Answer
As a way of protecting their independence.

France and Britain Fight On

Before the war, France had built the massive fortifications of the Maginot Line on its border with Germany. With the invasion of Belgium, however, Germany threatened to bypass the line. French and British troops were sent north into Belgium. Hitler's generals had anticipated this reaction and sent their tanks slicing through the Ardennes, a region of wooded ravines in northeast France that the Allies thought was impassable.

THE FALL OF FRANCE Suddenly, the Allied forces in the north were cut off. Outnumbered, outgunned, and pounded from the air, they fled to the beaches of Dunkirk, on the English Channel. In less than a week, a makeshift fleet of fishing trawlers, tugboats, river barges, pleasure craft, and almost anything else that would float ferried 330,000 British troops to safety across the Channel.

A few days later, Italy entered the war on the side of Germany and invaded France from the south as the Germans closed in on Paris from the north. On June 17, 1940, Marshal Henri Pétain, an aged military commander and World War I hero, told his country, "We must stop fighting." Four days later, at Compiègne, as William Shirer and the rest of the world watched, Hitler handed French officers his terms of surrender. Germans would occupy the northern part of France, and a Nazi-controlled puppet government, headed by Marshal Pétain, would be set up at Vichy, in southern France.

Skillbuilder Answer
Region: Austria, Yugoslavia, Bulgaria, Greece, Romania, Slovakia, Hungary, Poland, Lithuania, Latvia, Estonia, Finland, Norway, France, Denmark, the Netherlands, Belgium, and the Soviet Union.
Location: It was centrally located.

GEOGRAPHY SKILLBUILDER
REGION *Which European countries did Germany invade?*
LOCATION *How was Germany's geographic location an advantage?*

World War II: German Advances, 1939–1941

Battle of Britain Aug. 1940–June 1941

Paris Falls June 21, 1940

VICHY FRENCH GOVERNMENT (Unoccupied zone)

Axis powers
Axis-controlled by Dec. 1941
Allied territory, Dec. 1941
Neutral countries
German troop movements
Farthest German advance, as of Dec. 1941
Boundaries shown as of Sep. 1, 1939

Block Schedule TEACHING OPTION **Time Needed: 30 Minutes**

Cooperative Activity: Creating a Radio Broadcast

Task: Students will research, write, and present a radio newscast from Dunkirk during the Allied evacuation of late May 1940.

Purpose: To explore and report on an event in depth.

Activity: Groups of students will research the events during the rescue of Allied troops from Dunkirk. They will then prepare newscasts featuring interviews with people involved—an Allied soldier awaiting evacuation, a volunteer on one of the rescue vessels, and a Luftwaffe pilot, for example. You might want to have groups choose one or more of these people to interview so that all sides of the event are presented in the class newscasts.

Building a Portfolio: Students who add their newscasts to their portfolios should include a note indicating their contribution.

ALTERNATIVE ASSESSMENT BOOK
Standards for Evaluating a Cooperative Activity

Standards for Evaluation
Newscasts should . . .

- show evidence of research from reliable sources
- present the point of view of a participant in the rescue
- include vivid details that describe the setting and emotions of the participants

Children watch with wonder and fear as the battling British and German air forces set the skies of London aflame.

After France fell, a French general named **Charles de Gaulle** fled to England, where he set up a government-in-exile. De Gaulle proclaimed defiantly, "France has lost a battle, but France has not lost the war."

THE BATTLE OF BRITAIN "The final German victory over England is only a matter of time," wrote a German general after the fall of France. In the summer of 1940, the Germans began to assemble an invasion fleet along the French coast. Because its naval power could not compete with that of Britain, however, Germany launched an air war at the same time. The Luftwaffe, or German air force, began making bombing runs over Britain. Its goal was to gain total control of the skies by destroying Britain's Royal Air Force (RAF). Hitler had 2,600 planes at his disposal. On a single day—August 15—1,000 of his planes ranged over Britain. Every night for two solid months, bombers pounded London.

The Battle of Britain raged on through the summer and the fall. Night after night, up to a thousand German planes pounded British targets. At first the Luftwaffe concentrated on airfields and aircraft factories. Next it targeted cities. Londoner Len Jones was just 18 years old when bombs fell on his East End neighborhood.

A PERSONAL VOICE

After an explosion of a nearby bomb, you could actually feel your eyeballs being sucked out. I was holding my eyes to try to stop them going. And the suction was so vast, it ripped my shirt away, and ripped my trousers. Then I couldn't get my breath, the smoke was like acid and everything around me was black and yellow.

LEN JONES, quoted in *London at War*

F. Answer France had been defeated and partly occupied by the Germans; Britain remained undefeated, although under nightly air attack by the Luftwaffe.

THINK THROUGH HISTORY
F. *Contrasting* *How did the situations of France and Britain differ by the fall of 1940?*

The RAF fought back brilliantly. With the help of a new technological device called radar—which accurately plotted the flight paths of German planes, even in darkness—British pilots unleashed deadly air strikes against the enemy. On September 15, the RAF shot down 56 German planes. They lost only 26 aircraft. Two days later, the Führer called off the invasion of Britain indefinitely. "Never in the field of human conflict," said Churchill in praise of the RAF pilots, "was so much owed by so many to so few."

KEY PLAYER

WINSTON CHURCHILL 1874–1965

Possibly Britain's greatest weapon as that nation faced the Nazis was its wartime leader, Winston Churchill. A born fighter, Churchill became prime minister in May 1940 and used his gift as a speaker to arouse Britons and unite them:

"We shall defend our island, whatever the cost may be. We shall fight on the beaches, we shall fight on the landing-grounds, we shall fight in the fields and in the streets, we shall fight in the hills. We shall never surrender."

Section 2 Assessment

1. TERMS & NAMES

Identify:
- Neville Chamberlain
- Winston Churchill
- appeasement
- nonaggression pact
- blitzkrieg
- Charles de Gaulle

2. FOLLOWING CHRONOLOGICAL ORDER Arrange the following events on a time line in the order that they occurred: Germany's invasion of Poland, Germany's annexation of Austria, signing of the nonaggression pact, signing of the Munich Pact.

event one | event two | event three | event four

3. FORMING GENERALIZATIONS To what extent do you think lies and deception played a role in Hitler's tactics? Support your answer with examples.

THINK ABOUT
- William Shirer's diary entry about headlines in the Nazi newspapers
- Soviet-German relations
- Hitler's justifications for military aggression

4. MAKING DECISIONS If you had been a member of the British House of Commons in 1938, would you have voted for or against the Munich Pact? Support your decision.

THINK ABOUT
- Hitler's credibility
- the British public's fear of being involved in another war
- Churchill's opinion of the appeasement policy

ANSWERS

1. TERMS & NAMES

Neville Chamberlain, p. 509
Winston Churchill, p. 509
appeasement, p. 509
nonaggression pact, p. 551
blitzkrieg, p. 551
Charles de Gaulle, p. 553

2. FOLLOWING CHRONOLOGICAL ORDER

(1) Hitler's annexation of Austria, (2) signing of the Munich Pact, (3) signing of the nonaggression pact, (4) Germany's invasion of Poland.

3. FORMING GENERALIZATIONS

Possible Response: Hitler falsely charged the Czechs with abusing Sudeten Germans and lied when he said that the Sudetenland was "his last territorial demand." He falsely accused Poles of brutalizing Germans in Poland and signed a secret pact with the Soviet Union agreeing to divide Poland between them. He also falsely justified the surprise invasion of Denmark and Norway as necessary "to protect [their] freedom and independence."

4. MAKING DECISIONS

Possible Responses: For—Appeasement would help avert war; compromise is not a sign of weakness; Against—Appeasement would feed Hitler's military aggression; Great Britain should defend its honor by declaring war.

KEY PLAYER
Winston Churchill

Critical Thinking: Summarizing Churchill has sometimes been described as a bulldog. Ask students to read Churchill's words and study his photograph and then come up with their own one-word description of Britain's wartime leader.

ELECTRONIC LIBRARY OF PRIMARY SOURCES
Letter to Roosevelt by Winston Churchill

FOCUS & MOTIVATE

Section 2 Assessment
Have students answer the questions independently. Then have them compare answers with a partner and discuss any discrepancies.

Self-Assessment
Have students review their understanding of the events leading up to World War II by asking them to identify the key steps in Hitler's drive to expand the German Reich between 1937 and 1940. Ask them to note any events they omit from their summaries.

Section Quiz

FORMAL ASSESSMENT
Section Quiz, p. 201

Reteach
Ask a volunteer to put the time line he or she generated in question 2 on the board. Then ask students to add events to create a complete class summary of events leading up to World War II.

CLOSE

After taking power in Germany, the Nazis undertook an aggressive policy of territorial expansion that led to the outbreak of World War II.

Section 3 Overview

OBJECTIVES

1. To explain the reasons behind the Nazis' persecution of Jews and the problems facing Jewish refugees.
2. To describe the Nazis' "final solution" to the Jewish problem and the horrors of the Holocaust.

CRITICAL THINKING

- Identifying problems, p. 554
- Theme: Immigration and Migration, p. 555
- Summarizing, p. 557
- Analyzing causes, p. 558
- Forming opinions, p. 558
- Developing historical perspective, p. 558

FOCUS & MOTIVATE

5-MINUTE WARM-UP

Interpreting Graphs
To understand the effects of the Holocaust, have students look at the graph and images on pages 556–557 and answer the following questions.

1. What reaction do you think people had when they saw images like these for the first time?
2. What percent of Holocaust victims were Jews?

WARM-UP TRANSPARENCY 16

▶ ***Starting with the Student***
Watch the video "Escaping the Final Solution" to find out how the Holocaust affected two German Jews.

- Discuss with students what they already know about the Holocaust and how the information in the video enhanced their understanding.
- Use the *Teacher's Resource Book* as a guide to focus on students' questions.

***AMERICAN STORIES* video series**
"Escaping the Final Solution"
Videocassette: Volume 4

Videodisc: Disc 3, Side A, Chapter 2

3 The Holocaust

TERMS & NAMES
- Holocaust
- *Kristallnacht*
- genocide
- concentration camp

LEARN ABOUT Nazi plans for the German "master race"
TO UNDERSTAND the fate of Jews and other "enemies" of the Third Reich.

ONE AMERICAN'S STORY

In September 1939, Gerda Weissmann was a carefree girl of 15 who had just returned to her home in Bielsko, Poland, after a summer vacation. A few days later, invading German troops overran Bielsko and Gerda's world was shattered. Because the Weissmanns were Jews, they were forced to give up their home to a German family. In 1942, Gerda and her parents, along with the rest of Poland's Jews, were sent to labor camps. Gerda never forgot the day when members of Hitler's elite SS (*Schutzstaffel*, or "security squadron") came for the Jews.

A PERSONAL VOICE

> We had to form a line and an SS man stood there with a little stick. I was holding hands with my mother and . . . he looked at me and said, "How old?" And I said, "eighteen," and he sort of pushed me to one side and my mother to the other side. . . . And shortly thereafter, some trucks arrived—open trucks; with sort of a gate behind it and we were loaded onto the trucks. I heard my mother's voice from very far off ask, "Where to?" and I shouted back, "I don't know."
>
> GERDA WEISSMANN KLEIN, quoted in the film *One Survivor Remembers*

Gerda Weissmann Klein

When the American lieutenant Kurt Klein, who would later become Gerda Weissmann's husband, liberated her from the Nazis in 1945—just one day before her 21st birthday—she weighed 68 pounds and her hair was white. Even so, Gerda could count herself fortunate. Of all her family and friends, she alone had survived the Nazi's campaign to exterminate Europe's Jews.

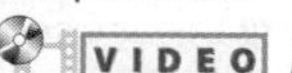
ESCAPING THE FINAL SOLUTION
Kurt Klein and Gerda Weissmann Klein Remember the Holocaust

The Persecution Begins

German streets were strewn with shattered glass in the aftermath of *Kristallnacht*.

On April 4, 1933, barely three months after Hitler took power in Germany, he ordered all "non-Aryans" to be removed from government jobs. This order was one of the first moves in a campaign for racial purity that would become the **Holocaust**—the systematic murder of 11 million people across Europe, more than half of whom were Jews.

THINK THROUGH HISTORY
A. *Identifying Problems* *What problems did German Jews face in Nazi Germany from 1935 to 1938?*
A. Answer Deciding whether to try to survive under the hostile Nazi government or to escape from Germany.

WHY THE JEWS? Although Jews were not the only victims of the Holocaust, they were the center of the Nazis' target. Anti-Semitism, or hatred of Jews, had deep roots in European history. For decades, many Germans looking for a scapegoat, or someone to blame for their failures and frustrations, had targeted the Jews. As a result, when Hitler blamed the Jews for Germany's defeat in World War I and for its economic problems following the war, many Germans were more than ready to support him.

As the Nazis tightened their hold on Germany, their persecution of Jews increased. In 1935, the Nuremberg Laws stripped Jews of their civil rights and property if they tried to leave Germany. To make identification easier, Jews over the age of six had to wear a bright yellow Star of David on their clothing.

SECTION 3 RESOURCES

PRINT RESOURCES

IN-DEPTH RESOURCES: UNIT 5
Guided Reading, p. 3
Literature: from *Sophie's Choice* by William Styron, p. 12
American Lives: Elie Wiesel, p. 15

READING STUDY GUIDE, p. 171

ACCESS FOR STUDENTS ACQUIRING ENGLISH
Guided Reading (Spanish), p. 189

SPANISH READING STUDY GUIDE, p. 171

FORMAL ASSESSMENT
Section Quiz, p. 202

ALTERNATIVE ASSESSMENT BOOK
See forms for supporting and scoring alternative activities.

TECHNOLOGY RESOURCES

CD-ROM *Our Times*

VIDEO *American Stories* video series
American Portfolio: A Videodisc for U.S. History user's guide, pp. 221, 223

INTERNET http://www.mlushistory.com

Worse was to come. On November 9, 1938, a night that came to be known as ***Kristallnacht,*** or "crystal night"—the night of broken glass—gangs of Nazi storm troopers attacked Jewish homes, businesses, and synagogues across Germany. An American who witnessed the violence in Leipzig wrote, "Jewish shop windows by the hundreds were systematically and wantonly smashed. . . . The main streets of the city were a positive litter of shattered plate glass." Afterward, the Nazis blamed the Jews for the destruction. More than 20,000 Jews were arrested and sent to concentration camps. At the same time, a German official announced, "The Jews will pay a collective fine of one billion marks, 20 percent of their property."

Dutch Jews were forced to wear this yellow Star of David to make them easily identifiable.

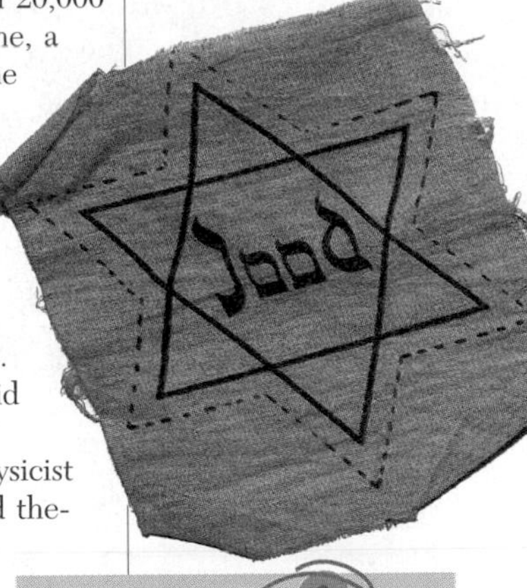

THE PLIGHT OF JEWISH REFUGEES Beginning in 1933, tens of thousands of Jews fled Germany each year. After *Kristallnacht,* the Nazis tried to speed Jewish emigration but encountered difficulty. France already had 40,000 Jewish refugees and did not want more. The British, who were already admitting about 500 Jewish refugees a week, worried about fueling anti-Semitism if that number were to increase. Late in 1938, Germany's foreign minister observed, "We all want to get rid of our Jews. The difficulty is that no country wishes to receive them."

About 60,000 refugees—including such distinguished people as physicist Albert Einstein, author Thomas Mann, architect Walter Gropius, and theologian Paul Tillich—fled to the United States. More could have come if the United States had been willing to relax its strict immigration quotas. This was not done, partly because of widespread anti-Semitism among Americans and partly because many Americans feared that letting in more refugees during the Great Depression would mean competition for scarce jobs.

THINK THROUGH HISTORY
B. THEME ***Immigration and Migration*** *How did the United States respond to Jewish refugees?*
B. Answer The United States refused to loosen immigration restrictions to allow more Jews to immigrate to the United States.

After war broke out in Europe in 1939, Americans also feared that opening the door to refugees from Germany would allow "enemy agents" to enter the United States. President Roosevelt said that while he sympathized with the Jews, he would not "do anything which would conceivably hurt the future of present American citizens."

Official indifference to the plight of Germany's Jews was so strong that when the *St. Louis*—a German luxury liner filled with refugees—passed Miami in 1939, the Coast Guard followed it to prevent the passengers from attempting to leave the ship for the United States. This decision was made even though 740 of the liner's 943 passengers had U.S. immigration papers. Passenger Liane Reif-Lehrer, who was just four years old at the time, recalled, "My mother and brother and I were among the passengers who survived, about a fourth of those on the ship. We were sent back to Europe and given haven in France, only to find the Nazis on our doorstep again a few months later."

ANOTHER PERSPECTIVE

DENMARK'S RESISTANCE

In 1942, the Nazis began pressuring occupied Denmark to enforce the Nuremberg Laws against its Jews. The Danes resisted fiercely. Denmark's aged king, Christian X, is reported to have said,

> "The Jews are part of the Danish nation. We have no Jewish problem. . . . If the Jews are forced to wear the yellow star, I and my whole family shall wear it as a badge of honor."

Not only the royal family but thousands of Danes from all walks of life did just that.

The Final Solution

Unable to rid Germany of its Jews by forcing them to emigrate, the Nazis adopted a new approach following *Kristallnacht.* Jews healthy enough to work were sent to labor camps to perform slave labor. The rest would be sent to extermination camps. This horrifying plan amounted to **genocide,** or the deliberate and systematic killing of an entire people.

THE CONDEMNED The Nazis' "final solution" rested on their belief that "Aryans" were a superior people and that the strength and purity of this "master race" must be preserved. To accomplish this, the Nazis condemned to slavery and death not only the Jews but other groups that they viewed as inferior or unworthy or as "enemies of the state."

OBJECTIVE ① **INSTRUCT**

The Persecution Begins

▶ ***Discussing Key Ideas***
- Once in power, the Nazis begin to persecute Jews and others in a campaign to achieve racial purity.
- Many Jews try to escape Germany but few countries will accept them.

IN-DEPTH RESOURCES: UNIT 5
Guided Reading, p. 3

ACCESS FOR STUDENTS ACQUIRING ENGLISH
Guided Reading (Spanish), p. 189

OUR TIMES
Kristallnacht

ANOTHER PERSPECTIVE
Denmark's Resistance
Critical Thinking: Analyzing Motives Ask students to consider why the Danes resisted the Nuremberg Laws while most Germans accepted them. *Possible Responses: Denmark lacked Germany's history of anti-Semitism. Danes resented Germans telling them how to treat Jews.*

OBJECTIVE ② **INSTRUCT**

The Final Solution

▶ ***Discussing Key Ideas***
- The Nazis' aim to eliminate Jews and other "enemies of the state."
- The Nazis systematically murder Jews or send them to labor camps.

(continued on next page)

TEACHING OPTIONS

Exploring Themes

Immigration and Migration The United States has a long and proud tradition of offering asylum to victims of religious and political persecution. In the 1930s, that tradition ran into direct conflict with the quota system imposed by the Immigration Act of 1924. Few Americans called for a change in the quota system, however. Even many who were sympathetic to the plight of German Jews opposed admitting more refugees while millions of workers remained jobless in the United States. As a result, for every Jewish refugee who came to this country, many more who could have been saved died in the Nazi's death camps.

Making Connections Across Cultures

German Jews Before the Nazis took power, Germany was home to a large and vital population of about 500,000 Jews. By 1939, fewer than half these Jews remained in Germany. The majority of those left were either too old to emigrate or were married to non-Jews. In the years that followed, most of Germany's remaining Jews perished in Nazi death camps along with millions of other Jews from across Europe. Today only about 30,000 Jews make their homes in Germany.

(continued from page 555)

- The Nazis build huge death camps equipped with gas chambers and crematoriums.

Issues for the 21st Century

The Debate over Immigration

Connect the debate over immigration in the 1930s to today by having students read pages 880–883. Then have them answer these questions.

1. Do immigrants to the United States today face similar human rights abuses as the Jewish refugees of the 1930s? *Possible Response: Some people in places like Bosnia and China face similar problems.*
2. Does the United States have an obligation to offer political asylum to the victims of oppression? *Possible Responses: Some will say that the United States has a moral obligation to help people who face oppression. Others might say that those problems can only be addressed in the abusive countries.*

HISTORY FROM VISUALS

Holocaust Victims, 1939–1945

Reading the Graph Have students add up the numbers of victims shown in the graph to get a rough total of those killed in the Holocaust. *About 10 million.*

OUR TIMES
The Holocaust
The Diary of Anne Frank

Holocaust Victims, 1939–1945

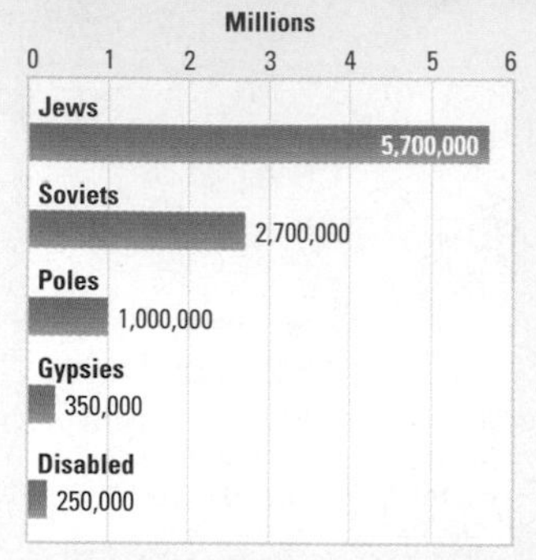

Source: U.S. Holocaust Memorial Museum

After taking power in 1933, the Nazis had concentrated on silencing their political opponents—Communists, Socialists, liberals, and anyone else who spoke out against the government. Once the Nazis had eliminated these enemies, they turned against other groups in Germany. In addition to Jews, these groups included

- Gypsies—whom the Nazis believed to be an "inferior race"
- Freemasons—whom the Nazis charged to be supporters of the "Jewish conspiracy" to rule the world
- Jehovah's Witnesses—who refused to join the army or salute Hitler

The Nazis also targeted other Germans whom they found unfit to be part of the "master race," such as homosexuals, the mentally retarded, the insane, the disabled, and the incurably ill. Beginning in 1939, the German government rounded up these individuals and shipped them off to "special treatment" centers, where they were "accorded a mercy death." By 1941, children near one of these centers had become so used to seeing the special buses that were used to transport victims that they would call out to each other, "Look, there's the murder box coming again."

As the Nazis moved eastward, they added Poles, Ukrainians, and Russians to their growing list of *Untermenschen,* or "subhumans," who were standing in the way of the expanding "master race." After the invasion of Poland, for example, hundreds of thousands of Poles were killed or shipped to Germany to perform slave labor. The emptied Polish towns and farms were resettled with Germans seeking lebensraum.

CONCENTRATION CAMPS The Nazis began implementing their "final solution" in Poland. Nazi murder squads were assigned to round up Jews, strip them of their clothing, and then shoot them in cold blood. Other Jews were herded into dismal ghettos, or Jewish sections, in Polish cities and were left to starve or die from disease. Still others were dragged from their homes and herded into trains and trucks for shipment to **concentration camps.** In this process, families were often separated, sometimes—like the Weissmanns—forever.

Life in the camps was a cycle of hunger, humiliation, and work that only ended with death. The prisoners were crammed into crude wooden barracks that held up to a thousand people each. They shared their crowded quarters—as well as their meager meals of thin soup and occasional scraps of bread or potato—with hordes of rats and fleas. Hunger was so intense, recalled one survivor, "that if a bit of soup spilled over, prisoners would converge on the spot, dig their spoons into the mud and stuff the mess into their mouths."

Block Schedule TEACHING OPTION **Time Needed: 20 Minutes**

Cooperative Activity: Exploring Literature of the Holocaust

Task: Students will read literary works dealing with the Holocaust, write book reviews, and present them to the class.

Purpose: To help students deepen their understanding of the Holocaust.

Activity: Small groups of students will choose a firsthand account of the Holocaust to review. They can read short works in their entirety or excerpts from longer works. Authors they might consider include Elie Wiesel, Anne Frank, Etty Hillesum, and Binjamin Wilkomirski. Students will then work together to write a book review and prepare it for presentation to the class. The class as a whole should then discuss the similarities and differences among the works.

Building a Portfolio: Students who add their book reviews to their portfolios should include a note indicating their contribution.

ALTERNATIVE ASSESSMENT BOOK
Standards for Evaluating a Cooperative Activity

Standards for Evaluation

Book reviews should . . .

- exhibit careful reading of the literary work
- cite vivid details to explain the author's experience
- indicate the aspects of the book that had the greatest effect on the reader and why

The prisoners worked from dawn to dusk, seven days a week, until they collapsed. Those too weak to work were killed. Some, like Rudolf Reder, endured. He was one of only two Jews to survive the camp at Belzec, Poland.

Inmates at the Ebensee concentration camp in the Alps *(top)* seem beyond all emotion; Women prisoners at the Belsen concentration camp in Germany *(above)* use the boots of their dead comrades for fuel.

A PERSONAL VOICE

The brute Schmidt was our guard; he beat and kicked us if he thought we were not working fast enough. He ordered his victims to lie down and gave them 25 lashes with a whip, ordering them to count out loud. If the victim made a mistake, he was given 50 lashes. . . . Thirty or 40 of us were shot every day. A doctor usually prepared a daily list of the weakest men. During the lunch break they were taken to a nearby grave and shot. They were replaced the following morning by new arrivals from the transport of the day. . . . It was a miracle if anyone survived for five or six months in Belzec.

RUDOLF REDER, quoted in *The Holocaust*

EXTERMINATION As deadly as overwork, starvation, beatings, and bullets were, they did not kill fast enough to satisfy the Nazis. Late in 1941, the Germans built six death camps in Poland. Each camp had several huge gas chambers in which as many as 6,000 lives could be snuffed out daily.

When prisoners arrived at Auschwitz, the largest of the death camps, they had to parade by several SS doctors. With a wave of the hand, the doctors separated those strong enough to work from those who would die that day. Both groups were told to leave all their belongings behind, with a promise that they would be returned later. Those destined to die were then led into a room outside the gas chamber and were told to undress for a shower. To complete the deception, they were even given pieces of soap. Finally, they were led into the chamber and poisoned with cyanide gas that spewed from vents in the walls. This orderly mass extermination was sometimes carried out to the accompaniment of cheerful music played by an orchestra of camp inmates who had temporarily been spared execution.

C. Answer Extermination of European Jews in death camps.

THINK THROUGH HISTORY
C. *Summarizing* *What was the goal of the Nazis' "final solution," and how was that goal nearly achieved?*

At first the bodies were buried in huge pits. At Belzec, Rudolf Reder was part of a 500-man death brigade that labored all day, he said, "either at grave digging or emptying the gas chambers." But the decaying corpses gave off a stench that could be smelled for miles around. Worse yet, mass graves left evidence of the mass murder. At some camps, to try to cover up the evidence of their slaughter, the Nazis installed

After stripping their victims of life and dignity, the Nazis hoarded whatever articles of value the victims had possessed, such as wedding rings and gold fillings from teeth.

HISTORY FROM VISUALS

Images of the Holocaust

Critical Thinking: Synthesizing Have students examine the images on pages 556 and 557 carefully. Ask them to describe their emotional responses to the pictures, beginning with the faces that run across the top of the pages and moving on to the women prisoners and the tray of hoarded wedding rings. If they find it difficult to put their reactions into words, explain that part of the horror of the Holocaust is that it defies logic and language.

MORE ABOUT . . .

Rudolf Reder

Rudolf Reder was a soap manufacturer from Lvov in the Soviet Union. He was on one of the first trains carrying deportees from Lvov and arrived at the concentration camp in Belzec on August 11, 1942. This is his description of his gruesome work at the camp: "I heard the doors being locked, the moaning, shouting and cries of despair in Polish and Jewish; the crying of the children and women which made the blood run cold in my veins. Then came one last terrible shout . . . and I, together with all the others left over from the previous transports, began our work. We pulled out the corpses of those who were alive only a short time ago, we pulled them using leather belts to the huge mass graves while the camp orchestra played; played from morning 'till night."

TEACHING OPTIONS

Teaching Less Proficient Readers

Following Chronological Order To help less proficient readers understand the sequence of events perpetrated by the Nazis during the Holocaust, draw a time line, which students can fill in as they read. Time lines might look like this:

1933	1935	1938	1939
Removal of non-Aryans from government	Nuremberg Laws	*Kristallnacht*	Institution of final solution

Teaching Gifted and Talented Students

Researching and Designing Holocaust Memorials Ask students to consider how they would design a memorial to commemorate the victims of the Holocaust. What type of architecture would be appropriate? What audio and visual materials would they include? Then have them use the Internet or library resources to research existing memorials. Learning about those in Washington, D.C., Miami, Florida, and at former concentration camps such as Auschwitz, Buchenwald, and Dachau, for example, may give them ideas on which to base their designs.

NOW & THEN

Genocide or "Ethnic Cleansing"?

Critical Thinking: Analyzing Issues Ask students to search the World Wide Web for current information about ethnic cleansing or genocide in Bosnia or elsewhere in the world. Have them compile and organize the information and report their findings to the class.

IN-DEPTH RESOURCES: UNIT 5
American Lives: Elie Wiesel, p. 15

ASSESS & RETEACH

Section 3 Assessment

Have students work in small groups to answer the questions. Have them discuss questions 3 and 4 with others in their group before answering.

Self-Assessment

Have students write a personal reflection on the Holocaust to test their understanding of the events involved.

Section Quiz

FORMAL ASSESSMENT
Section Quiz, p. 202

Reteach

Create a class chart on the board listing the acts against Jews during the Holocaust and their impact. Base the chart on the ones the students prepared individually as they read the section.

CLOSE

After taking power in 1933, the Nazis began a campaign to rid Germany of Jews and other "subhumans." The result was the Holocaust—the destruction of about 10 million human beings in the worst genocide in human history.

NOW & THEN

GENOCIDE OR "ETHNIC CLEANSING"?

In 1992, a civil war broke out in Bosnia between that country's ethnic Serbs and its non-Serb Muslims and Croats. Soon, reports from Bosnia told alarming stories of Serbian terrorism directed at non-Serbs living in Serb-controlled areas.

The list of horrors included the destruction of villages, systematic rape, death camps, random slaughter, and assaults on refugees fleeing for their lives. Bosnian Serbs called their campaign to drive more than 2 million Muslims and Croats from Serbian areas "ethnic cleansing." To the rest of the world, it looked like genocide.

huge crematoriums, or ovens in which to burn the dead. At other camps, the bodies were simply thrown into a pit and set on fire.

Gassing was not the only method of extermination used in the camps. Prisoners were also shot, hanged, or injected with poison. Still others died as a result of horrible medical experiments carried out by camp doctors. Some of these victims were injected with deadly germs in order to study the effect of disease on different groups of people. Others were forced to exist only on seawater in experiments to determine how long shipwrecked seamen could survive. Many more were used to test methods of sterilization, a subject of great interest to some Nazi doctors in their search for ways to improve the "master race."

THE SURVIVORS Six million Jews died in the death camps and in Nazi massacres. But some miraculously escaped the worst of the Holocaust. Many had help from ordinary people who were appalled by the Nazis' treatment of Jews. These people risked death by hiding Jews in their homes or by helping them escape to neutral countries such as Sweden and Switzerland.

Some Jews even survived the horrors of the concentration camps. In Gerda Weissmann Klein's view, survival depended as much on one's spirit as on getting enough to eat. "I do believe that if you were blessed with imagination, you could work through it," she wrote. "If, unfortunately, you were a person that faced reality, I think you didn't have a chance." Those who did come out of the camps alive were forever changed by what they had witnessed. For survivor Elie Wiesel, who entered Auschwitz in 1944 at the age of 14, the sun had set forever.

"Never shall I forget these things. . . . Never."

ELIE WIESEL

A PERSONAL VOICE

Never shall I forget that night, the first night in the camp, which has turned my life into one long night. . . . Never shall I forget the little faces of the children, whose bodies I saw turned into wreaths of smoke beneath a silent blue sky. Never shall I forget those flames which consumed my faith forever. Never shall I forget that nocturnal silence which deprived me, for all eternity, of the desire to live. Never shall I forget those moments which murdered my God and my soul and turned my dreams to dust. Never shall I forget these things, even if I am condemned to live as long as God Himself. Never.

ELIE WIESEL, *Night*

Elie Wiesel

Section 3 Assessment

1. **TERMS & NAMES**
   Identify:
   - Holocaust
   - *Kristallnacht*
   - genocide
   - concentration camp

2. **ANALYZING CAUSES** List at least four events that led to the Holocaust.

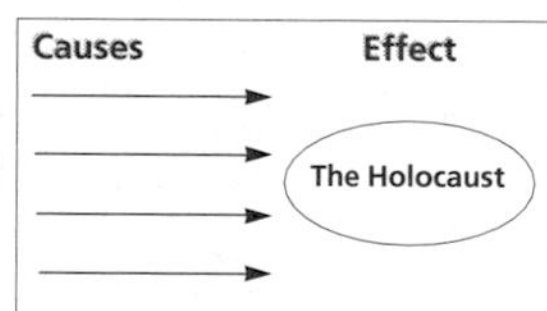

Write a paragraph summarizing one of the events that you listed.

3. **FORMING OPINIONS** Do you think that the United States was justified in not allowing more Jewish refugees to immigrate? Why or why not?

   THINK ABOUT
   - the views of isolationists in the United States
   - some Americans' prejudices and fears
   - the incident on the German luxury liner *St. Louis*

4. **DEVELOPING HISTORICAL PERSPECTIVE** Why do you think the Nazi program of systematic genocide was so brutally effective? Support your answer with details from the text.

   THINK ABOUT
   - the long German history of anti-Semitism
   - the secrecy and lies of the Nazis
   - the scope and organization of the Nazis' genocidal plans

ANSWERS

1. TERMS & NAMES

Holocaust, p. 554
Kristallnacht, p. 555
genocide, p. 555
concentration camp, p. 556

2. ANALYZING CAUSES

Possible Responses: The removal of non-Aryans from government jobs; Nuremberg Laws stripping Jews of their civil rights and property; *Kristallnacht* — Nazi storm troopers' attack on Jewish homes, businesses, and synagogues; "final solution"—systematic genocide of Jews, gypsies, and other groups that Nazis considered "subhuman." Paragraphs will vary.

3. FORMING OPINIONS

Possible Responses: **Justified**—The United States had to protect the national security and the welfare of its own citizens, including their job security during the Depression; **Not justified**—The United States was obligated to provide political asylum for victims of prejudice and mass murder.

4. DEVELOPING HISTORICAL PERSPECTIVE

Possible Responses: The Nazis lied about and covered up many of their activities. People had difficulty believing the evidence. A basic element in human nature made people tend to cling tenaciously to hope.

4 America Moves Toward War

TERMS & NAMES
- Axis powers
- Lend-Lease Act
- Atlantic Charter
- Allies
- Hideki Tojo

LEARN ABOUT the American response to aggression in Europe and Asia
TO UNDERSTAND how the United States entered World War II.

ONE AMERICAN'S STORY

In late August 1939, President Franklin D. Roosevelt had sent a cable to Hitler, urging him to settle his differences with the Polish people peacefully. In answer, Hitler invaded Poland on September 1. "Hitler is a madman," Roosevelt had said after the Nazis took power in Germany, "and his counselors, some of whom I personally know, are even madder than he is." Now those same madmen had unleashed their insanity on the world. Two days after the invasion of Poland, Roosevelt spoke reassuringly to Americans about the outbreak of war in Europe.

A PERSONAL VOICE
Let no man or woman thoughtlessly or falsely talk of America sending its armies to European fields. . . . This nation will remain a neutral nation, but I cannot ask that every American remain neutral in thought as well. Even a neutral has a right to take account of facts. Even a neutral cannot be asked to close his mind or his conscience. . . . I have said not once, but many times, that I have seen war and I hate war. . . . As long as it is in my power to prevent, there will be no blackout of peace in the United States.
FRANKLIN DELANO ROOSEVELT, radio speech, September 3, 1939

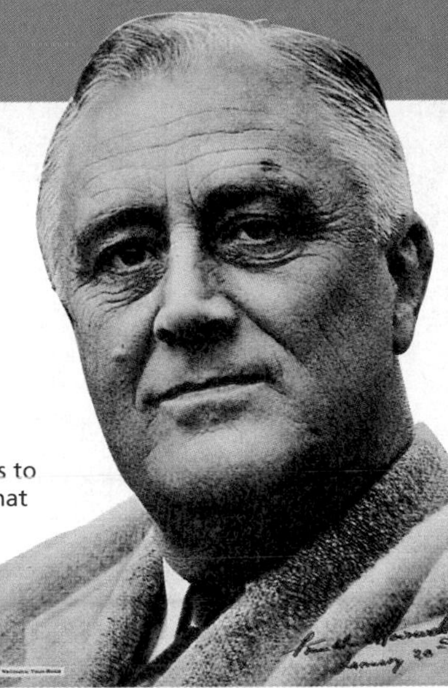
Franklin D. Roosevelt

At that time, Roosevelt knew that Americans were still deeply committed to staying out of war. In his heart, however, he also knew that there could be no peace in a world controlled by dictators.

The United States Musters Its Forces

As German tanks thundered across Poland, Roosevelt issued an official proclamation of neutrality as required by the Neutrality Acts. At the same time, he began to prepare the nation for the struggle he feared lay just ahead.

A. Answer Because they thought that providing arms to nations at war would make America a participant in the war.

THINK THROUGH HISTORY ***A. Making Inferences*** *Why did some Americans object to the cash-and-carry policy?*

MOVING CAUTIOUSLY AWAY FROM NEUTRALITY On September 8, 1939, Roosevelt announced that he was calling a special session of Congress to revise the Neutrality Acts. When Congress met two weeks later, the president asked for a "cash-and-carry" provision, which would permit nations to buy American arms as long as they paid cash and carried the goods home in their own ships. Providing the arms that would help France and Britain defeat Hitler, Roosevelt argued, was the best way to keep America out of the war.

Isolationists in Congress, such as Senator Arthur Vandenberg, argued just the opposite, however. "I do not believe that we can become an arsenal for one belligerent without becoming a target for another," Vandenberg said. After six weeks of heated debate, Congress passed the Neutrality Act of 1939, and cash-and-carry went into effect.

"I have seen war and I hate war."
FRANKLIN D. ROOSEVELT, 1939

THE AXIS THREAT Over the next few months, America's cash-and-carry policy began to look like too little, too late. By the summer of 1940, France had fallen and Britain was under siege by the German Luftwaffe. Then, in September, Americans were jolted by the news that Japan, Germany, and Italy had signed a mutual defense treaty, the Tripartite Pact. The three nations became known as the **Axis powers.**

Section 4 Overview

OBJECTIVES

1. To describe the response of the United States to the outbreak of war in Europe in 1939.
2. To show how Roosevelt assisted the Allies without declaring war.
3. To summarize the events that brought the United States into armed conflict with Germany.
4. To characterize the American response to the Japanese attack on Pearl Harbor.

SKILLBUILDERS

- Interpreting political cartoons, p. 560
- Understanding geography: movement, p. 564

CRITICAL THINKING

- Making inferences, p. 559
- Recognizing effects, p. 560
- Theme: Constitutional Concerns, p. 560
- Analyzing motives, p. 561
- Summarizing, pp. 562, 565
- Analyzing causes, p. 562
- Analyzing issues, p. 563
- Making predictions, p. 565
- Forming opinions, p. 565
- Clarifying, p. 565

FOCUS & MOTIVATE

5-MINUTE WARM-UP

Recognizing Point of View To understand President Roosevelt's efforts at maintaining American neutrality, have students read One American's Story on page 559 and answer these questions.

1. What reasons did President Roosevelt offer for wanting to remain neutral?
2. Did he think it would be easy to maintain that neutrality?

WARM-UP TRANSPARENCY 16

▶ ***Starting with the Student*** Discuss with students the circumstances under which they would support America's entry into a war.

SECTION 4 RESOURCES

PRINT RESOURCES

IN-DEPTH RESOURCES: UNIT 5
Guided Reading, p. 4
Geography Application: Japanese Aggression, p. 6
Primary Sources: The Bombing of Pearl Harbor, p. 9; War Poster, p. 11
American Lives: Charles A. Lindbergh, p. 16

READING STUDY GUIDE, p. 173

ACCESS FOR STUDENTS ACQUIRING ENGLISH
Guided Reading (Spanish), p. 190
Geography Application: Japanese Aggression (Spanish), p. 192

SPANISH READING STUDY GUIDE, p. 173

FORMAL ASSESSMENT
Section Quiz, p. 203

ALTERNATIVE ASSESSMENT BOOK
See forms for supporting and scoring alternative activities.

TECHNOLOGY RESOURCES

CRITICAL THINKING TRANSPARENCIES
CT24, World War II Begins in Europe
CT58, Time Line of Events Leading to World War II

CD-ROM Electronic Library of Primary Sources

VIDEO *American Portfolio: A Videodisc for U.S. History* user's guide, pp. 210, 216–217

INTERNET http://www.mlushistory.com

OBJECTIVE

① INSTRUCT

The United States Musters Its Forces

▶ ***Discussing Key Ideas***

- The United States moves cautiously to help the Allies.
- The United States faces the prospect of a two-ocean war if it becomes involved in the conflict.
- The U.S. begins building its defenses and reelects Roosevelt.

IN-DEPTH RESOURCES: UNIT 5
Guided Reading, p. 4

ACCESS FOR STUDENTS ACQUIRING ENGLISH
Guided Reading (Spanish), p. 190

HISTORY FROM VISUALS

Carving Up the World

Reading the Cartoon Have students compare the caricatures of Hitler, Mussolini, and Tojo in this cartoon with the photographs of these three leaders in the chapter. What characteristics has the cartoonist focused on?

HISTORICAL SPOTLIGHT

The Election of 1940

Critical Thinking: Forming Opinions Roosevelt told voters during the campaign, "Your boys are not going to be sent into any foreign wars." Have students consider why he made this promise.

SKILLBUILDER
INTERPRETING POLITICAL CARTOONS
What are the Axis leaders—Hitler, Mussolini, and Tojo—greedily carving up?
Skillbuilder Answer The world.

The Tripartite Pact was clearly aimed at keeping the United States out of the war. Under the treaty, each Axis nation agreed to come to the defense of the others in case of attack. This meant that if the United States were to declare war on any one of the Axis powers, it would face its worst military nightmare—a two-ocean war, with fighting in both the Atlantic and the Pacific.

Hoping to avoid this situation, Roosevelt scrambled to provide the British with "all aid short of war." In June 1940, he sent Britain 500,000 rifles and 80,000 machine guns to help replace those lost at Dunkirk. In September, the United States traded 50 old destroyers for leases on British military bases in the Caribbean and Newfoundland. Even British prime minister Winston Churchill later called this deal "a decidedly unneutral act."

BUILDING AMERICA'S DEFENSES Meanwhile, Roosevelt asked Congress to increase spending for national defense. After years of isolationism, the United States was militarily weak. Critics pointed out that 18 countries had larger armies, that the navy could hardly protect the Panama Canal, and that Italy's air force had more firepower than that of the United States.

In response, Congress dramatically boosted defense spending in 1940. It also passed the nation's first peacetime military draft. Under the Selective Training and Service Act, 16 million men between the ages of 21 and 35 were registered. Of these, 1 million were to be drafted for one year. Roosevelt himself drew the first draft numbers. "This is a most solemn ceremony," he told a national radio audience. "It is accompanied by no fanfare—no blowing of bugles or beating of drums. There should be none."

B. Answer Revision of the Neutrality Acts; dramatically increased defense spending; institution of the nation's first peacetime draft.

THINK THROUGH HISTORY
B. *Recognizing Effects* *What impact did the outbreak of war in Europe have on U.S. foreign and defense policy?*

HISTORICAL SPOTLIGHT

THE ELECTION OF 1940

War was the key issue in the 1940 presidential election. At the Democratic convention, isolationists inserted a plank in the party platform that read, "We will not participate in foreign wars. We will not send our armed forces to fight in lands across the seas." This was wording Roosevelt could not accept. No one, he argued, could say where Americans might have to fight if the nation's survival was at stake. His solution was to add five words to the no-war plank: "except in case of attack."

Again and again during the campaign, Roosevelt reassured voters by saying, "This country is not going to war." In his mind, however, he qualified that promise with the same five words, "except in case of attack."

ROOSEVELT'S REELECTION That same year, Roosevelt decided to break the tradition of a two-term presidency, begun by George Washington, and to run for reelection. To the great disappointment of isolationists, Roosevelt's Republican opponent, a public utilities executive named Wendell Willkie, supported Roosevelt's policy of aiding Britain. At the same time, both Willkie and Roosevelt promised to keep the nation out of war. Because there was so little difference between the candidates, the majority of voters chose the one they knew best. Roosevelt was reelected with nearly 55 percent of the votes cast.

THINK THROUGH HISTORY
C. THEME *Constitutional Concerns* *How might FDR's reelection in 1940 have affected the Constitution?*

C. Answer It gave him a third term and inspired the movement to pass the 22nd Amendment, limiting presidents to two terms.

"The Great Arsenal of Democracy"

Not long after the election, President Roosevelt held another of his fireside chats on the radio. There was no hope of negotiating a peace with Hitler, he told the nation. "No man can tame a tiger into a kitten by stroking it." He also warned that if Britain fell, the Axis powers would be left unchallenged to conquer the world, at which point, he said, "all of us in all the Americas would be living at the point of a gun." To prevent such a situation, the United States had to help defeat the Axis threat by turning itself into "the great arsenal of democracy."

THE LEND-LEASE PLAN By late 1940, however, Britain had no more cash to spend in the arsenal of democracy. Consequently, Roosevelt suggested replacing cash-and-carry with a new plan that he called lend-lease. Under this plan, the president would lend or lease arms and other supplies to "any country whose defense was vital to the United States."

Even though the isolationists were losing the support of the American public, they argued bitterly against lend-lease. Congress finally passed the

TEACHING OPTIONS

Exploring Themes

Constitutional Concerns The "no-third-term tradition" for American presidents dates back to George Washington. After Roosevelt broke this unwritten rule by winning a third term in 1940, and then a fourth in 1944, the tradition was made part of the Constitution. The Twenty-second Amendment, adopted in 1951, states, "No person shall be elected to the office of President more than twice." Discuss with students whether they think this is a wise limitation, especially considering the circumstances under which Roosevelt was elected to his third term in 1940.

Making Connections Across Time

Current Limitations on Legislative Terms Today only the president is constitutionally limited to two terms. Many states, however, are seeking to limit representatives and senators to a fixed number of terms in office. Ask students to research the current status of term-limiting legislation or initiatives in their state. Interested students could research the situations in other states and create a chart like this summarizing their findings:

Term Limitations

State	Senators	Representatives	Pending Legislation

POINT

"The United States should not become involved in European wars."

Still recovering from World War I and struggling with the Great Depression, many Americans believed their country should remain strictly neutral in the war in Europe.

Representative James F. O'Connor voiced the country's reservations when he asked, "Dare we set America up and commit her as the financial and military blood bank of the rest of the world when the proportion of want in this country is still so great that by doing this our country would become a victim of financial and military pernicious anemia?" O'Connor maintained that the United States could not "right every wrong" or "police [the] world."

The widely admired aviator Charles Lindbergh risked his reputation by stating his hope that "the future of America . . . not be tied to these eternal wars in Europe." Lindbergh asserted that "Americans [should] fight anybody and everybody who attempts to interfere with our hemisphere." However, he went on to say, "Our safety does not lie in fighting European wars. It lies in our own internal strength, in the character of the American people and American institutions." Like many isolationists, Lindbergh asserted that democracy would not be saved "by the forceful imposition of our ideals abroad, but by example of their successful operation at home."

COUNTERPOINT

"The United States must protect democracies throughout the world."

As the conflict in Europe deepened, interventionists embraced President Franklin D. Roosevelt's declaration that "when peace has been broken anywhere, peace of all countries everywhere is in danger." Roosevelt emphasized the global character of 20th-century commerce and communication by noting, "Every word that comes through the air, every ship that sails the sea, every battle that is fought does affect the American future."

Roosevelt and other political leaders also appealed to the nation's conscience. Secretary of State Cordell Hull noted that the world was "face to face . . . with an organized, ruthless, and implacable movement of steadily expanding conquest." In the same vein, Undersecretary of State Sumner Welles called Hitler "a sinister and pitiless conqueror [who] has reduced more than half of Europe to abject serfdom."

After the war expanded into the Atlantic, Roosevelt declared, "It is time for all Americans . . . to stop being deluded by the romantic notion that the Americas can go on living happily and peacefully in a Nazi-dominated world." He added, "Let us not ask ourselves whether the Americas should begin to defend themselves after the first attack . . . or the twentieth attack. The time for active defense is now."

INTERACT WITH HISTORY

1. **ANALYZING ASSUMPTIONS** How did isolationists' and interventionists' opinions differ regarding America's responsibility to other nations?

SEE SKILLBUILDER HANDBOOK, PAGE 917.

2. **WRITING AN EDITORIAL** Do research to find out more about Charles Lindbergh's antiwar activities. Then write an editorial supporting or criticizing Lindbergh's arguments.

Lend-Lease Act in 1941 and supported it with $7 billion. In all, the United States eventually spent $50 billion under the act.

Britain was not the only nation to receive lend-lease aid. On June 22, 1941, Hitler ignored his peace treaty with Stalin and invaded the Soviet Union with 3 million troops. The Führer confidently predicted victory within six weeks. But the Soviets resisted fiercely. As they pulled back from the Nazi advance, they employed a scorched-earth policy, destroying everything that might be of use to the invaders. Six weeks stretched into six months. Then, as the bitter Russian winter set in, the German invasion ground to a halt.

THINK THROUGH HISTORY
D. *Analyzing Motives* *Why did Roosevelt take one "unneutral" step after another to assist Britain and the Soviet Union in 1941?*

D. Answer Roosevelt believed that the best way to stop the Axis powers was to help their opponents—mainly Britain and the Soviet Union.

Meanwhile, Roosevelt began sending lend-lease supplies to the Soviet Union. Some Americans opposed providing aid to Stalin. They even argued that Hitler was doing the United States a favor by attacking the Communists. But Roosevelt agreed with Winston Churchill, who once remarked that "if Hitler invaded Hell," the British would be prepared to work with the devil himself.

GERMAN WOLF PACKS For lend-lease aid to be of any use to Britain and the Soviet Union, supply lines had to be kept open across the Atlantic Ocean. To prevent delivery of lend-lease shipments, Hitler deployed hundreds of German submarines—or U-boats—in the North Atlantic. There, groups of 15 to 20 submarines, known as wolf packs, searched shipping lanes for cargo ships.

During five weeks in April and May 1941, the Germans sank 1.2 million tons of British shipping. They were sinking ships faster than the British could replace them. Something had to be done to protect cargo ships, supporters of

OBJECTIVE ② INSTRUCT

"The Great Arsenal of Democracy"

▶ ***Discussing Key Ideas***
- Roosevelt supplies the Allies with war equipment.
- German U-boat attacks threaten Roosevelt's lend-lease program.

POINT/COUNTERPOINT
Isolationism

▶ ***Starting with the Student***
- Have students create a chart listing the advantages and disadvantages of involvement or isolationism. Their charts might look like this:

	Pros	Cons
Involvement		
Isolation		

▶ ***Discussing Key Ideas***
- Isolationists believe that America should not police the world.
- Interventionists respond that a breach of peace anywhere in the world affects everyone and that not to act is to accept tyranny.

IN-DEPTH RESOURCES: UNIT 5
American Lives: Charles A. Lindbergh, p. 16

ELECTRONIC LIBRARY OF PRIMARY SOURCES
from "Let Us Face the Truth" from the New York Times
from "Are We Being Led Into War?" by George A. Dondero

INTERACT WITH HISTORY

1. Analyzing Assumptions

Possible Answers:

Isolationists: America's responsibilities consisted of bolstering its own strength and conducting its internal affairs in a way that would serve as a model to other nations. Democratic principles could not be forcibly imposed on other nations.

Interventionists: America, as a leading member of the global community, was obligated to offer all possible assistance to help stop the conquest of Europe and the defeat of democratic ideals by Hitler.

2. Writing an Editorial

Standards for Evaluation
Editorials should meet the following criteria:
- State clearly students' position on Lindbergh's isolationism.
- Support that opinion with details about his antiwar activities and speeches.
- Include specific quotations from Lindbergh to increase the effectiveness of their editorials.

MORE ABOUT . . .
The U-Boats

After the fall of France in 1940, Germany controlled a 2,500-mile coastline from which to launch his submarines against Allied shipping. With the threat of invasion keeping British warships close to home, the U-boats enjoyed excellent hunting. During the summer and fall of 1940, each U-boat sank an average of eight ships per month, leading German submariners to call this period their "Happy Time." The U-boats did so well, in fact, that Hitler refused to step up Germany's production of submarines, despite the urging of his top naval commander. This decision would turn out to be a crucial mistake.

OBJECTIVE
③ INSTRUCT

Planning for War

▶ ***Starting with the Student*** Ask students to recall what they learned about Woodrow Wilson's Fourteen Points. Remind them that Roosevelt served in Wilson's administration as the assistant secretary of the navy and was very familiar with Wilson's views on war and peace.

▶ ***Discussing Key Ideas***
- Roosevelt and Churchill meet in mid-1941 and declare their war aims in a statement known as the Atlantic Charter.
- German attacks on U.S. naval vessels bring the United States into an undeclared war against the German wolf packs.

The German mother ship *Saar* and her brood of U-boats wait in Bremen harbor in Germany for orders to attack.

lend-lease argued. Otherwise, the United States might just as well dump its lend-lease shipments into the ocean.

In June 1941, Roosevelt ordered the U.S. Navy to protect lend-lease shipments as far east as Iceland. He also gave American warships permission to attack German U-boats in self-defense.

Planning for War

With each step Roosevelt took against the Axis powers, the roar of the isolationists grew louder. In August 1941, they voiced their opposition to a bill that would extend the draft for another 18 months. Congress passed the draft-extension bill, but only by a razor-thin margin of 203 to 202 in the House of Representatives. Roosevelt was not discouraged by this narrow victory, however. With the army provided for, he began planning for the war he thought was certain to come.

THE ATLANTIC CHARTER While Congress voted on the draft extension, Roosevelt and Churchill met secretly aboard a warship off the coast of Newfoundland. Churchill had come hoping for a military commitment from the United States. Instead, he settled for a declaration of principles called the **Atlantic Charter.** In this document, the two leaders spelled out the causes for which World War II was fought—even before the United States officially entered the conflict. The charter pledged both Great Britain and the United States to (1) seek no territorial expansion, (2) pursue no territorial changes without the consent of the inhabitants, (3) respect the right of people to choose their own form of government, (4) promote free trade among nations, (5) encourage international cooperation to improve peoples' lives, (6) build a secure peace based on freedom from want and fear, (7) work for disarmament of aggressors, and (8) establish a "permanent system of general security."

Later in 1941, the Atlantic Charter became the basis of a new document called "A Declaration by the United Nations." The term "United Nations" was suggested by Roosevelt to express the common purpose of the **Allies,** those nations that had joined together to fight the Axis powers. The declaration was signed by 26 nations, including the Soviet Union and China. Together, observed Churchill, these nations represented "four-fifths of the human race."

THINK THROUGH HISTORY
E. *Summarizing* *Why was the Atlantic Charter important?*

E. Answer It set forth the war aims of the Allies.

THE SHOOTING BEGINS "How near is the United States to war?" That was the question Churchill asked rhetorically after his August 1941 meeting with Roosevelt. For the moment, the answer still seemed to be "not very." Then, on September 4, a German U-boat fired two torpedoes at the U.S. destroyer *Greer.* President Roosevelt responded with the announcement that the U.S. Navy had been ordered to fire on German ships on sight. "When you see a rattlesnake poised to strike," the president explained, "you do not wait until he has struck before you crush him. These Nazi submarines and raiders are the rattlesnakes of the Atlantic."

Two weeks later, the *Pink Star,* an American merchant ship, was sunk off Greenland. Its lost cargo included machine tools, evaporated milk, and enough cheddar cheese to feed more than 3.5 million British laborers for a week. In mid-October, the U.S. destroyer *Kearny* was torpedoed near Iceland and 11 lives were lost. "America has been attacked," Roosevelt announced grimly. "The shooting has started. And history has recorded who fired the first shot." A few days later, German U-boats sank the U.S. destroyer *Reuben James* in the same waters, killing at least 100 sailors.

F. Answer German U-boats were attacking American ships.

THINK THROUGH HISTORY
F. *Analyzing Causes* *Why did the United States enter into an undeclared shooting war with Germany in the fall of 1941?*

TEACHING OPTION

Teaching Less Proficient Readers

Translating Abstract Concepts into Concrete Ideas Less proficient readers may not appreciate the remarkable ideas set forth in the Atlantic Charter. You can help all students better understand these abstract principles by dividing the class into eight groups of mixed-ability readers. Assign one of the principles to each group and have groups complete the following steps:

- Read the assigned principle.
- Determine the meaning of the principle.
- Create a concrete example of the principle at work.
- Decide on the best way to communicate this example to other students clearly and vividly.
- Prepare a presentation on the principle for the class.

For example, the group presenting principle 7, "Work for disarmament of aggressors," may want to do a skit in which a student representing a peaceful nation tries to mediate the disagreement between students representing two warring nations. The presentation might include charts comparing rising casualties with declining agricultural production and props such as drawings or models of a tank and a family sedan.

As the death toll mounted, the Senate finally repealed the ban against arming merchant ships. The vote was so close, however, that Roosevelt knew that something far more dramatic than German attacks on U.S. ships would be needed to persuade Congress to declare war. Churchill knew this as well, advising his impatient war cabinet to "have patience and trust to the tide which is flowing our way, and to events."

Japan Attacks the United States

The tide pushing the United States toward war was flowing much faster than either leader knew. To almost everyone's surprise, however, the attack that brought the United States into the war came from an unexpected country—not from Germany but from Japan.

JAPAN'S AMBITIONS In Japan, expansionists had long dreamed of creating a vast colonial empire that would stretch from Manchuria and China south to Thailand and Indonesia. This dream had motivated Japan's invasion of Manchuria in 1931 and of China in 1937. South of China, though, Japan's ambitions for expansion brought them into conflict with other colonial powers. These powers included France (in French Indochina), the Netherlands (in the Dutch East Indies), Britain (in Burma, India, and Malaya), and the United States (in Guam and the Philippines). By 1941, France and the Netherlands had fallen to Germany, and the British were too busy fighting Hitler to block Japanese expansion. Only the United States and its Pacific islands remained in Japan's way.

The Japanese began their southward push in July of 1941 by taking over French military bases in Indochina (now Vietnam, Cambodia, and Laos). The United States protested this new act of aggression by cutting off trade with Japan. The embargoed goods included the one thing Japan could not live without—oil to fuel its war machine. Japanese military leaders warned that, without oil, Japan could be defeated without its enemies ever striking a blow. The leaders declared that Japan must either persuade the United States to end its oil embargo or seize the oil fields in the Dutch East Indies.

THINK THROUGH HISTORY
G. *Analyzing Issues* *How was oil a source of conflict between Japan and the United States?*

G. Answer Japan needed oil, and the United States had placed an embargo on it to protest Japanese aggression in Indochina.

In October, the militant Japanese general **Hideki Tojo** became the new prime minister of Japan. Shortly after taking office, Tojo met Japan's revered emperor, Hirohito. At that meeting, Tojo promised the emperor that the government would make a final attempt to preserve peace with the Americans. If the peace talks failed, Japan would have no choice but to go to war. But on November 5, 1941, the very day that Tojo's special "peace" envoy flew to Washington for talks, the prime minister ordered the Japanese navy to prepare for an attack on the United States.

The U.S. military had broken Japan's secret communication codes and knew that Japan was preparing for a strike. What it didn't know was where the attack would come. Late in November, Roosevelt sent out a "war warning" to military commanders in Hawaii, Guam, and the Philippines. If war could not be avoided, the warning said, "the United States desires that Japan commit the first overt act." And the nation waited.

The peace talks went on for a month. Then, late on December 6, 1941, the president received a decoded message that had been intercepted. This message instructed Japan's peace envoy to reject all American peace proposals. "This means war," Roosevelt told his friend and adviser Harry Hopkins. "It's too bad we can't strike first and prevent a surprise," Hopkins replied. "No, we can't do that," Roosevelt

KEY PLAYER

HIDEKI TOJO
1884–1948

Who was Hideki Tojo? Information in the world press when Tojo took power in 1941 suggested that the answer depended on who was responding. American newspapers described Tojo as "smart, hardboiled, resourceful, [and] contemptuous of theories, sentiments, and negotiations." The Nazi press in Germany praised Tojo as "a man charged with energy, thinking clearly and with a single purpose." To a British paper, Tojo was "the son of Satan" whose single purpose was "unleashing all hell on the Far East." In Japan, however, Tojo was looked up to as a man whose "decisive leadership was a signal for the nation to rise and administer a great shock to the anti-Axis powers."

MORE ABOUT . . .
The Sinking of the Reuben James

The sinking of the *Reuben James* inspired folk singer Woody Guthrie to write a ballad in memory of the men who served and died in America's undeclared war in the Atlantic. At the end of the refrain was the line "Did you have a friend on the good *Reuben James?*"

OBJECTIVE
④ INSTRUCT

Japan Attacks the United States

▶***Discussing Key Ideas***
- The expansionist ambitions of Japan put it on a collision course with the United States.
- Japan's surprise attack on Pearl Harbor in 1941 precipitates America's formal entry into World War II.

IN-DEPTH RESOURCES: UNIT 5
Primary Sources: The Bombing of Pearl Harbor, p. 9; War Poster, p. 11
Geography Application: Japanese Aggression, p. 6

KEY PLAYER
Hideki Tojo

Critical Thinking: Synthesizing Ask students to look for clues about the character of Hideki Tojo in his photograph. *Possible Responses: Tojo appears to be a much-decorated military officer. His array of medals suggests that he may have had strong leadership qualities as well as courage and intelligence.*

Block Schedule TEACHING OPTION **Time Needed: 20 Minutes**

Cooperative Activity: Creating a Political Cartoon

Task: Student groups will create a political cartoon supporting or opposing the entry of the United States into World War II after the bombing of Pearl Harbor.

Purpose: To help students communicate ideas visually.

Activity: Small groups of students will create a political cartoon on America's response to Japan's attack on Pearl Harbor. The cartoon should clearly support or oppose entry into the war. After the group brainstorms for ideas, one student might do the research, another do the drawing, and another write the caption. Groups should share their completed cartoons with the class.

Building a Portfolio: Students who add the cartoons to their portfolios should attach a note indicating their contribution to the cartoon and explaining its meaning.

Standards for Evaluation
Cartoons should . . .
- take a clear position for or against America's involvement in World War II
- communicate that position using images and minimal words
- be easily understood

ECONOMIC BACKGROUND

War and the Depression

Critical Thinking: Analyzing Issues Discuss with students the long-debated question of whether war is "good for business." If so, does this mean that bankers and business leaders promote wars for their own profit, as so many Americans believed in the 1930s?

MORE ABOUT . . .

John Garcia's War

John Garcia lost a number of friends during the attack on Pearl Harbor, including his girlfriend, whose home in Honolulu was hit by an American shell. He tried to join the military, only to be refused because his work was considered essential to the war effort. A letter to President Roosevelt got Garcia into the military at age 17.

HISTORY FROM VISUALS

The Attack on Pearl Harbor, Dec. 7, 1941

Reading the Maps Make sure students understand how to follow the arrows from the globe to the inset map of the Hawaiian Islands to the map of Oahu to the boxed map of Pearl Harbor.

Extension Ask students what information the map of Oahu conveys. What additional information does the map of Pearl Harbor convey? *Possible Responses: Oahu map—The Japanese attack came in two waves. Japanese planes hit targets other than the Pearl Harbor naval base. Pearl Harbor map—Three different types of aircraft were involved in the assault.*

ECONOMIC BACKGROUND

WAR AND THE DEPRESSION

The approach of war did what the "alphabet soup" of New Deal programs could not do—end the Great Depression. As defense spending skyrocketed in 1940, long-idle factories came back to life. A merry-go-round company began producing gun mounts; a stove factory made lifeboats; a famous New York toy maker made compasses; a pinball-machine company made armor-piercing shells. With factories hiring again, the nation's unemployment rolls began shrinking rapidly—by 400,000 in August 1940 and by another 500,000 in September. By the time the Japanese attacked Pearl Harbor, America was heading back to work. (See *Keynesian economics* on page 936 in the Economics Handbook.)

---

reportedly responded. "We are a democracy of peaceful people. We have a good record. We must stand on it."

THE ATTACK ON PEARL HARBOR Early the next morning, a Japanese dive-bomber swooped low over the U.S. naval base at Pearl Harbor—the largest U.S. naval base in the Pacific. The bomber was followed by more than 180 Japanese warplanes launched from six aircraft carriers. As the first Japanese bombs found their targets, a radio operator flashed this message: "Air raid on Pearl Harbor. This is not a drill."

For an hour and a half, the Japanese planes were barely disturbed by American antiaircraft guns and blasted target after target. By the time the last plane soared off around 9:30 A.M., the devastation was appalling. John Garcia, a pipe fitter's apprentice, was there.

> A PERSONAL VOICE
>
> It was a mess. I was working on the U.S.S. *Shaw.* It was on a floating dry dock. It was in flames. I started to go down to the pipe fitter's shop to get my toolbox when another wave of Japanese came in. I got under a set of concrete steps at the dry dock where the battleship *Pennsylvania* was. An officer came by and asked me to go into the *Pennsylvania* and try to get the fires out. A bomb had penetrated the marine deck, and . . . three decks below. Under that was the magazines: ammunition, powder, shells. I said "There ain't no way I'm gonna go down there." It could blow up any minute. I was young and 16, not stupid.
>
> **JOHN GARCIA,** quoted in *The Good War*

For Japan, the attack on Pearl Harbor was a stunning victory. The Japanese navy all but crippled the entire U.S. Pacific Fleet in one blow. Its own casualties numbered only 29 planes. In Tokyo, the elated Tojo visited a shrine to thank the spirits of his ancestors for this favorable opening of Japan's campaign to rule East Asia.

In Washington, the mood ranged from outrage to panic. At the White House, Eleanor Roosevelt watched closely as her husband, with a "deadly calm,"

Skillbuilder Answer
Scatter the ships to make them more difficult targets.

The Attack on Pearl Harbor, Dec. 7, 1941

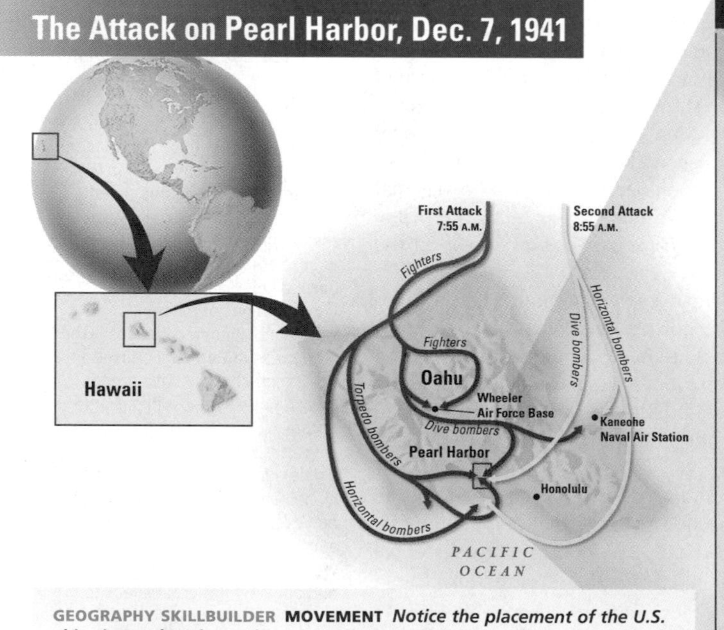

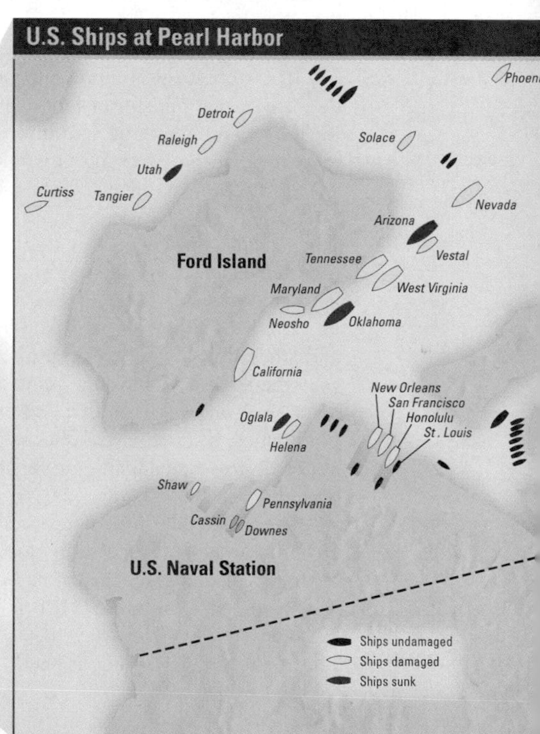

GEOGRAPHY SKILLBUILDER MOVEMENT ***Notice the placement of the U.S. ships in Pearl Harbor. What might the navy have done differently to minimize damage from a surprise attack?***

TEACHING OPTION

Making Connections Across Cultures

Pearl Harbor After the Japanese attack in 1941, Pearl Harbor was quickly restored to become what it is still today, the headquarters of most of the U.S. naval operations in the Pacific.

Pearl Harbor is also the site of a monument to all of the service personnel who were killed during the attack on December 7, 1941. The U.S.S. *Arizona,* one of three U.S. warships destroyed during the raid, sank with a loss of 1,177 sailors. Most of those men are still entombed within the *Arizona*'s sunken hull. The memorial is a striking white concrete and steel structure that spans the U.S.S. *Arizona*'s 608-foot-long hull. The entire ship is visible from the memorial's viewing platform. Since the memorial's dedication in 1962, it has attracted visitors from around the world.

If any of your students have visited the U.S.S. *Arizona* Memorial, ask them to report on that experience. You might also want to lead a general discussion about the meaning of war memorials to those who lived through the war and to later generations.

absorbed the news from Hawaii, "each report more terrible than the last." The surprise raid had sunk or badly damaged 18 ships. About 350 planes had been destroyed or severely damaged. Some 2,400 people had died, and another 1,178 had been wounded. These losses constituted more damage than the U.S. Navy had suffered in all of World War I.

H. Answer The attack would make Americans so angry that it would be easy for Roosevelt to unify public support behind the war effort, but it would cripple the fleet needed to fight the war.

Beneath the president's calm, Eleanor could see how worried he was. "I never wanted to have to fight this war on two fronts," Roosevelt told his wife. "We haven't the Navy to fight in both the Atlantic and the Pacific . . . so we will have to build up the Navy and the Air Force and that will mean that we will have to take a good many defeats before we can have a victory."

THINK THROUGH HISTORY
H. *Making Predictions* *What problem would the Japanese attack on Pearl Harbor solve for Roosevelt? What new problems would it create?*

The next day, President Roosevelt addressed Congress. "Yesterday, December 7, 1941, a date which will live in infamy," he said, ". . . the Japanese launched an unprovoked and dastardly attack on American soil." He asked for a declaration of war against Japan, which Congress quickly approved. Three days later, Germany and Italy declared war on the United States.

For all the damage done at Pearl Harbor, perhaps the greatest was to the cause of isolationism. "The only thing now to do," said the isolationist senator Burton Wheeler after the attack, "is to lick the hell out of them."

Casualties of the Japanese attack on Pearl Harbor included the U.S.S. *California (above)*, which was hit by two torpedoes and a bomb. Also hit were about 350 aircraft, such as those shown here *(above left)* in their flaming graveyard.

Section  4 Assessment

1. TERMS & NAMES
Identify:
- Axis powers
- Lend-Lease Act
- Atlantic Charter
- Allies
- Hideki Tojo

2. SUMMARIZING Create a time line of key events leading to America's entry into World War II. Use the dates already plotted on the time line below as a guide.

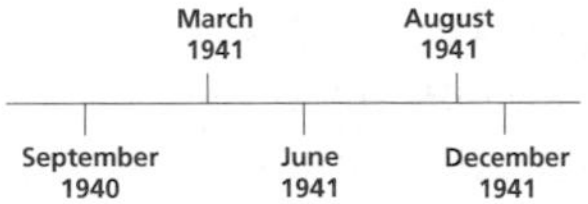

Which of the events that you listed was most influential in bringing the United States into the war? Why?

3. FORMING OPINIONS Do you think that the United States should have waited to be attacked before declaring war?

THINK ABOUT
- the reputation of the United States
- the influence of the isolationists
- the destruction of Pearl Harbor

4. CLARIFYING Although the U.S. Congress was still unwilling to declare war early in 1941, Churchill told his war cabinet, "We must have patience and trust to the tide which is flowing our way, and to events." What do you think Churchill meant by this remark? Support your answer.

THINK ABOUT
- Roosevelt's series of "unneutral" steps to assist Great Britain in its war efforts
- the Atlantic Charter
- Churchill's view of Hitler

ANSWERS

1. TERMS & NAMES

Axis powers, p. 559
Lend Lease Act, p. 561
Atlantic Charter, p. 562
Allies, p. 562
Hideki Tojo, p. 563

2. SUMMARIZING

Possible Answers:
September 1940—Japan, Germany, and Italy sign the Tripartite Pact
March 1941—Congress passes Lend-Lease Act.
June 1941—Germany invades Soviet Union; Roosevelt orders U.S. Navy to protect lend-lease shipments.
August 1941—Roosevelt and Churchill draw up Atlantic Charter.
December 1941—Japan bombs Pearl Harbor.

3. FORMING OPINIONS

***Possible Answers:* Should have waited**—An attack by Japan would swing public opinion away from isolationism and allow Roosevelt to enter the war with the strong commitment of Americans. **Should not have waited**—An earlier declaration of war might have prevented the attack on Pearl Harbor.

4. CLARIFYING

Possible Answers: Churchill believed that the United States's entry into World War II was inevitable; the United States was edging closer and closer to war.

MORE ABOUT . . .
Declaration of War

Stunned by the attack on Pearl Harbor, the Senate voted unanimously for war. In the House, a single dissenting vote was cast by Montana representative Jeannette Rankin, a life long pacifist. Rankin was the first woman elected to the House and the only member of Congress to oppose the entry of the United States into both world wars.

ELECTRONIC LIBRARY OF PRIMARY SOURCES
On the Declaration of War by Franklin Delano Roosevelt

CRITICAL THINKING TRANSPARENCIES
CT24, World War II Begins in Europe
CT58, Time Line of Events Leading to World War II

ASSESS & RETEACH

Section 4 Assessment

Have students answer the questions individually, then compare answers with a partner.

Self-Assessment

Have students note the questions they had trouble answering or answered incorrectly. Have them look for patterns that emerge in the types of questions they find difficult.

Section Quiz

FORMAL ASSESSMENT
Section Quiz, p. 203

Reteach

Stage a class debate on isolationism based on the material presented in the Point Counterpoint feature on page 561.

CLOSE

After the outbreak of war in Europe, the United States abandoned its neutrality to become increasingly involved in the war effort. It finally entered the war after Japan's surprise attack on Pearl Harbor.

CHAPTER 16
ASSESSMENT ANSWERS

REVIEWING THE CHAPTER

TERMS & NAMES
1. fascism, p. 544
2. Adolf Hitler, p. 544
3. Nazism, p. 544
4. Winston Churchill, p. 549
5. appeasement, p. 549
6. Charles de Gaulle, p. 553
7. Holocaust, p. 554
8. genocide, p. 555
9. Axis powers, p. 559
10. Allies, p. 562

MAIN IDEAS

11. To make the Soviet Union socialist by ending private enterprise; to transform it into a great industrial power by building state-owned factories and power plants.
12. The failure of the League of Nations to take action against Japan sent a message to European dictators, that they could behave more aggressively without fear of reprisal.
13. Hitler and Mussolini's military support helped Franco take power in Spain.
14. It surprised the enemy and then crushed it with overwhelming force.
15. German occupation of northern France and the establishment of a Nazi-controlled puppet government in southern France; de Gaulle fled to England and set up a government-in-exile.
16. Jews, gypsies, homosexuals, people with mental or physical disabilities, Poles, Ukrainians, and Russians.
17. Many Danish citizens wore the yellow Star of David; some people risked death by hiding Jews in their homes or helping them to escape to neutral countries.
18. Japan, Germany, and Italy; if the United States declared war on any one of the Axis powers, it would have to fight on two oceans.
19. Increased defense spending, peacetime draft, Lend-Lease Act, and an end to the ban against arming merchant ships.
20. Because the Japanese bombed Pearl Harbor.

Chapter 16 Assessment

REVIEWING THE CHAPTER

TERMS & NAMES For each item below, write a sentence explaining its historical significance in the years leading up to World War II. For each person below, explain his role in the events of this period.

1. fascism
2. Adolf Hitler
3. Nazism
4. Winston Churchill
5. appeasement
6. Charles de Gaulle
7. Holocaust
8. genocide
9. Axis powers
10. Allies

MAIN IDEAS

SECTION 1 *(pages 542–547)*

Dictators Threaten World Peace

11. What were Stalin's goals and what steps did he take to achieve them?
12. What actions taken by the League of Nations revealed its inability to control the aggressive moves of Japan, Germany, and Italy?
13. How did Germany's and Italy's involvement affect the outcome of the Spanish Civil War?

SECTION 2 *(pages 548–553)*

War in Europe

14 Why was the blitzkrieg an effective military strategy?
15. What terms of surrender did Hitler demand of the French after the fall of France in 1940? What was General Charles de Gaulle's reaction?

SECTION 3 *(pages 554–558)*

The Holocaust

16. What groups did Nazis deem unfit to belong to the Aryan "master race"?
17. How did some Europeans show their resistance to Nazi persecution of the Jews?

SECTION 4 *(pages 559–565)*

America Moves Toward War

18. Which nations formed the Axis powers? What were the military implications of the Tripartite Pact for the United States?
19. What congressional measures paved the way for the entry of the United States into World War II?
20. Why did the United States enter World War II?

THINKING CRITICALLY

1. **WAR OR PEACE?** At what points do you think France, Great Britain, and their allies might have stopped Hitler and prevented World War II? Plot these events on a time line like the one below. Support your answers with reasons.

   1933—Hitler is appointed chancellor of Germany.
   1939—Great Britain and France declare war on Germany.

2. **THE POWER OF SPEECH** Compare and contrast the ways in which Hitler, Churchill, and Roosevelt used their powers as gifted speakers to accomplish their political aims during World War II. Support your answer with details from the text.
3. **TRACING THEMES AMERICA IN THE WORLD** Reread the quotation from President Roosevelt on page 540. What message do you think he was conveying to the American public? Explain.
4. **GEOGRAPHY OF EUROPE AND THE SOVIET UNION** Look at the map of German advances on page 552. How might Poland's location have influenced the secret pact that Germany and the Soviet Union signed on August 23, 1939?
5. **THE FACES OF TERROR** What similarities and differences do you see between the terrorism of Stalin's Great Purge of the 1930s and Hitler's policy of genocide? Support your answer with details from the text.
6. **ANALYZING PRIMARY SOURCES** Read the following excerpt from the British writer Jessica Mitford's autobiography, in which she comments on Germany's attack on the Netherlands and other European countries in 1940. Then answer the question below.

> On the 9th of May [1940], a month after Chamberlain had looked into his clouded crystal ball, there to find that Hitler had "missed the bus" and was no longer capable of waging aggressive war, the Germans struck. . . . Within hours the Germans had swept through Holland . . . and the French front was reported to be in mortal danger, perhaps already lost.
>
> Out of the wild confusion of these first few days of the attack . . . the real nature of the danger confronting Europe had exposed for all to see and understand the criminal stupidity of the years of shabby deals and accommodation to Hitler's ambitions. Overnight, the appeasement policy was buried forever.
>
> **JESSICA MITFORD,** *Hons and Rebels*

Do you agree or disagree with Mitford's view of Chamberlain's appeasement policy? Why or why not?

THINKING CRITICALLY

1. WAR OR PEACE?
Possible Answers:
1936: Germany occupies the Rhineland. (Force might have stopped Hitler.)
March 1938: Germany annexes Austria. (Military action might have undermined Hitler's authority.)
Spring 1938: Munich Pact gives Sudetenland to Germany. (If France and England had joined forces with the Czechs, they might have defeated the Germans.)
September 1939: German troops occupy the remainder of Czechoslovakia. (Probably the last chance to avert war.)

2. THE POWER OF SPEECH
Possible Responses: All three motivated their audiences to embrace certain beliefs and fostered national unity. Hitler spread a message of hate and nationalism. Churchill aroused and united Britons to defeat the Nazis. Roosevelt informed Americans about his policies and underscored his beliefs in democratic ideals.

3. TRACING THEMES AMERICA IN THE WORLD
Possible Responses: Though Roosevelt did not take any actions that violated U.S. neutrality, he would not discourage Americans in believing in the cause of the Allies.

ALTERNATIVE ASSESSMENT

1. MAKING DECISIONS

Imagine that you are a member of President Roosevelt's cabinet. Write a policy brief to advise him on the official position that the United States should take with regard to the war in Europe. Use the following guidelines to help you decide on your advice:

- Identify the policy options that you can offer the president.
- Consider what goals you want to achieve with your policies (for example, saving American lives, protecting commerce, or opposing aggression).
- Decide which course of action will achieve your goals.
- Predict the consequences that will result if President Roosevelt takes your advice.

2. LEARNING FROM MEDIA

VIDEO View the video for Chapter 16, *Escaping the Final Solution.* Discuss the following questions with a small group of classmates.

- How did life change for Gerda Weissmann and her family when the Nazis invaded Poland?
- How did Kurt Klein's family respond to the Nazi threat?
- What conditions that Gerda faced in the forced-labor factory would be most difficult for you to endure? Why?
- How did Kurt's and Gerda's lives finally come together?
- What lessons can people learn from the Holocaust to help prevent such an event from recurring?

3. PORTFOLIO PROJECT

Use the Living History activity to expand your portfolio.

LIVING HISTORY

WRITING YOUR ORAL HISTORY

Using your interview as a source, create an oral history of the pre–World War II period. Use your interviewee's own words to express what it was like to live through the time. Since most oral histories also include some biographical information, write a paragraph giving important facts about your source's life, as an introduction to your oral history.

In revising your oral history, ask yourself the following questions:

- Is the oral history informative and interesting?
- Does the history give a personal glimpse of the country's mood before the war?

Add your oral history to your American history portfolio.

Bridge to Chapter 17

Review Chapter 16

DICTATORSHIPS EMERGE The failings of World War I peace settlements, economic instability, and political unrest set the stage for the rise of totalitarian dictators in Russia, Italy, and Germany. Nationalistic military leaders took power in Japan. Although many Americans were disturbed by Japan's attacks on China in 1931 and 1937, Italy's invasion of Ethiopia in 1935, and Germany's occupation of the Rhineland in 1936, most supported neutrality.

OUTBREAK OF WORLD WAR II A series of bold moves by Adolf Hitler—and weak countermoves by other leaders—triggered World War II in Europe. Germany annexed Austria and then occupied all of Czechoslovakia. When Nazi forces invaded Poland in 1939, Britain and France declared war on Germany. The following year Hitler overran the Netherlands, Belgium, Luxembourg, and France. Facing the Nazis alone, Britain vowed that it would never surrender.

THE HOLOCAUST The European crisis became grimmer as Nazis began persecuting Jews. The Nuremberg Laws stripped Jews of their civil rights and property in 1935, and in 1938, on *Kristallnacht,* Nazi storm troopers attacked Jewish homes, businesses, and synagogues. Late in 1941, the Nazis built death camps and began the systematic killing of millions of Jews.

AMERICA'S PREPARATION FOR WAR In response to the events in Europe, Congress boosted defense spending, passed the nation's first peacetime draft and the Lend-Lease Act, and repealed the ban on the arming of merchant ships. President Roosevelt and Prime Minister Churchill spelled out their war aims in the Atlantic Charter. On December 7, 1941, the Japanese attacked Pearl Harbor. The next day Roosevelt asked Congress to declare war on Japan.

Preview Chapter 17

After Pearl Harbor, the United States mobilized for war. Americans enlisted to fight the Axis powers in North Africa, Europe, Asia, and the Pacific, and hundreds of thousands died. The war ended when Japan surrendered after the United States dropped atomic bombs on Hiroshima and Nagasaki. You will learn about these and other significant developments in the next chapter.

ALTERNATIVE ASSESSMENT

1. MAKING DECISIONS

Standards for Evaluation

An effective brief should meet the following criteria:

- state clearly the goals that the policy is meant to achieve.
- consider the potential of other options to achieve those goals.
- explain clearly which policy is best and why.
- logically predict the consequences of this policy.

2. LEARNING FROM MEDIA

Answers to the questions.

- The Weissmanns' rights and activities were progressively curtailed and they were deported to Nazi death camps.
- The Kleins sent their three children to the United States to protect them from the Nazis.
- Answers will vary, but should be supported with details from the video and well-supported explanations.
- Kurt was a soldier in the U.S. army division that liberated Gerda and other prisoners from the bicycle factory in Volary in which they had been held.
- Answers will vary, but might include lessons such as being aware of world events and speaking out and taking action against injustice.

3. PORTFOLIO PROJECT

LIVING HISTORY

Standards for Evaluation

An oral history should meet the following criteria:

- Presents well-chosen information about the subject that makes him or her come alive.
- Includes only relevant information.
- Shows clear organization.
- Creates a vivid impression of life in America before its entry into World War II.

IN-DEPTH RESOURCES: UNIT 5

See the form for scoring this activity on page 18.

THINKING CRITICALLY

4. GEOGRAPHY OF EUROPE AND THE SOVIET UNION

Possible Responses: Poland shared its western border with Germany and its eastern border with the Soviet Union. When Germany and the Soviet Union agreed not to fight each other, Germany was spared a two-front war after it invaded Poland. In their secret pact, the two countries agreed to split Poland between them.

5. THE FACES OF TERROR

Possible Responses: **Similarities**—Stalin executed from 8 million to 13 million "enemies of the people"—Nazis executed more than 11 million "enemies of the state" (over half of them Jews). Both terrorist purges were carried out under totalitarian dictatorships. **Differences**—Stalin did not choose most of his victims based on ethnicity, while the Nazis did. The implementation of the Nazis' "final solution" relied on technology (gas chambers) and was more systematic than Stalin's purges.

6. ANALYZING PRIMARY SOURCES

Possible Responses: **Agree**—Appeasement policy allowed Hitler to pursue his ambitions of territorial expansion. **Disagree**—Appeasement represented the British public's desire to avoid war.

CHAPTER 17

PLANNING GUIDE

The United States in World War II

	Key Ideas	COPYMASTERS	ASSESSMENT
SECTION 1 Mobilization on the Home Front *pp. 570–577*	*The United States enters the war and mobilizes its citizens and resources to give its allies unprecedented military and industrial support.*	***In-Depth Resources: Unit 5*** • Guided Reading, p. 19 • Skillbuilder Practice: Analyzing Bias, p. 23 • Primary Sources: from *Farewell to Manzanar,* p. 28; War Ration Stamps, p. 29 • Literature: from *Snow Falling on Cedars* by David Guterson • American Lives: Oveta Culp Hobby, p. 35 ***Lesson Plans,*** pp. 141–142	PE ***Section 1 Assessment,*** p. 577 TE ***Self-Assessment,*** p. 577 ***Formal Assessment*** • Section Quiz, p. 212 ***Alternative Assessment Book*** • Standards for Evaluating a Cooperative Activity
SECTION 2 The War for Europe and North Africa *pp. 578–585*	*The United States, Great Britain, and the Soviet Union cooperate in the fight to defeat Germany and its allies.*	***In-Depth Resources: Unit 5*** • Guided Reading, p. 20 • Geography Application: Thunderclap, p. 24 • Outline Map: Crisis in Europe, p. 26 • Primary Source: War Dispatch from Ernie Pyle, p. 30 • American Lives: George S. Patton, p. 36 ***Lesson Plans,*** pp. 143–144	PE ***Section 2 Assessment,*** p. 585 TE ***Self-Assessment,*** p. 585 ***Formal Assessment*** • Section Quiz, p. 213 ***Alternative Assessment Book*** • Standards for Evaluating a Cooperative Activity
SECTION 3 The War in the Pacific *pp. 586–593*	*America wages an aggressive military campaign against Japan in the Pacific islands and finally ends the war.*	***In-Depth Resources: Unit 5*** • Guided Reading, p. 21 • Primary Source: The Bombing of Nagasaki, p. 31 ***Lesson Plans,*** pp. 145–146	PE ***Section 3 Assessment,*** p. 593 TE ***Self-Assessment,*** p. 593 ***Formal Assessment*** • Section Quiz, p. 214 ***Alternative Assessment Book*** • Standards for Evaluating a Cooperative Activity
SECTION 4 The Impact of the War *pp. 596–601*	*Americans begin to adjust to new economic opportunities and continuing social problems after World War II.*	***In-Depth Resources: Unit 5*** • Guided Reading, p. 22 ***Lesson Plans,*** pp. 147–148	PE ***Section 4 Assessment,*** p. 601 TE ***Self-Assessment,*** p. 601 ***Formal Assessment*** • Section Quiz, p. 215 ***Alternative Assessment Book*** • Standards for Evaluating a Cooperative Activity
CHAPTER RESOURCES	**Chapter Overview** *In the first two decades of the 1900s, Americans embrace the Progressive movement and many of its reforms.*	***In-Depth Resources: Unit 5*** • Living History Project: Worksheet, p. 37; Standards, p. 38 ***Telescoping the Times*** • Chapter Summary, pp. 33–34 ***Planning for Block Schedules***	PE ***Chapter Assessment,*** pp. 602–603 PE ***Alternative Assessment,*** p. 603 ***Formal Assessment*** • Chapter Test, forms A and B, pp. 216–221 ***Test Generator*** ***Alternative Assessment Book*** See explanation and forms for different kinds of alternative assessments including portfolio assessment.

KEY
- PE Pupil's Edition
- TE Teacher's Edition
- http://www.mlushistory.com

TECHNOLOGY

Warm-Up Transparency **17**

Electronic Library of Primary Sources
- "What Can I Do?" by the Office of Civilian Defense
- Japanese-American Testimony from the National Defense Migration Hearings

INTERNET Pearl Harbor and Japanese-American internment

Warm-Up Transparency **17**

Humanities Transparencies
- H24, Flying Fortresses

Geography Transparencies
- G25, Battle of the Bulge

Grolier Multimedia Encyclopedia
- "The World at War"

Electronic Library of Primary Sources
- George S. Patton

Our Times
- Dispatch by Ernie Pyle

INTERNET D-Day

Warm-Up Transparency **17**

Grolier Multimedia Encyclopedia
- video of an atomic blast

Electronic Library of Primary Sources
- Statement on the Atomic Bomb by Harry S. Truman

Our Times
- excerpt of Truman's V-J speech
- testimony from the Nuremberg trials

INTERNET Harry S. Truman and the Yalta Conference

Warm-Up Transparency **17**

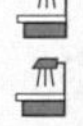

Critical Thinking Transparencies
- CT25, U.S. Joins the Allies in World War II
- CT59, Human Cost of World War II

INTERNET Interact with History p. 600 (PE)

American Portfolio: A Videodisc for U.S. History, user's guide, pp. 216–232

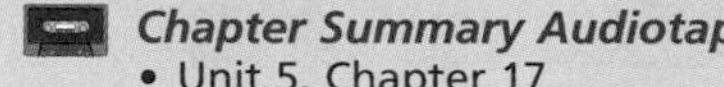

Chapter Summary Audiotapes
- Unit 5, Chapter 17

INTERNET http://www.mlushistory.com

Block Scheduling (90 MINUTES)

Day 1

Section 1, pp. 570–577

Section Assessments, p. 577

COOPERATIVE ACTIVITY
- Creating a War Poster, p. 576 (TE)

Day 2

Section 2, pp. 578–585

Section Assessment, p. 585

COOPERATIVE ACTIVITY
- Planning a D-Day Memorial Tour, p. 583 (TE)

Day 3

Section 3, pp. 586–593

Section Assessment, p. 593

COOPERATIVE ACTIVITY
- Writing Memos to Truman About Use of the Atomic Bomb, p. 591 (TE)

Day 4

Section 4, pp. 596–601

Section Assessment, p. 601

Tracing Themes: Science and Technology pp. 594–595

Chapter Assessment, pp. 602–603

COOPERATIVE ACTIVITY
- Creating a Political Cartoon, p. 599 (TE)

YEARLY PACING ***Chapter 17 Total:*** 4 days ***Yearly Total:*** 85 days

See *Planning for Block Schedules* for special activities and pacing strategies.

Customizing for Special Populations

Students Acquiring English

Access for Students Acquiring English: Spanish Translations
- Guided Reading for Sections 1–4 (Spanish), pp. 196–199
- Chapter Summary (Spanish), pp. 194–195
- Skillbuilder Practice: Analyzing Bias (Spanish), p. 200
- Geography Application: Thunderclap (Spanish), p. 201
- Outline Map: Crisis in Europe (Spanish), p. 203

Spanish Reading Study Guide, pp. 177–186

Translations of Chapter Summaries, Hmong, Cantonese, Vietnamese, and Cambodian

Chapter Summary Audiotapes in Spanish Unit 5, Chapter 17

INTERNET The Diverse Classroom

Gifted and Talented Students

In-Depth Resources: Unit 5
- Primary Sources: from *Farewell to Manzanar,* p. 28; War Ration Stamps, p. 29; War Dispatch of Ernie Pyle, p. 30; The Bombing of Nagasaki, p. 31
- American Lives: Oveta Culp Hobby, p. 35; George S. Patton, p. 36

Less Proficient Readers

In-Depth Resources: Unit 5
- Guided Reading for Sections 1–4, pp. 19–22
- Skillbuilder: Analyzing Bias, p. 23
- Geography Application: Thunderclap, p. 24
- Outline Map: Crisis in Europe, p. 26

Reading Study Guide
- pp. 177–186

Telescoping the Times
- Chapter Summary, pp. 33–34

Chapter Summary Audiotapes, Unit 5, Chapter 17

Connections to Literature READINGS FOR STUDENTS

In-Depth Resources: Unit 5
- **from *Snow Falling on Cedars* by David Guterson, p. 32**

McDougal Littell *The Language of Literature* American Literature

- **Diane Mei Lin Mark, "Suzie Wong Doesn't Live Here,"** p. 252
- **Studs Terkel, from "The Good War,"** p. 909
- **Randall Jarrell, "The Death of the Ball Turret Gunner,"** p. 922
- **John Steinbeck, "Why Soldiers Won't Talk,"** p. 924
- **Joan Didion, "Letter from Paradise,"** p. 929

McDougal Littell *Literature Connections*

- **Jeanne Wakatsuki Houston and James D. Houston** ***Farewell to Manzanar*** *(with related readings) The true story of a Japanese-American family's confinement in California's Manzanar internment camp.*

- **John Knowles** ***A Separate Peace*** *(with related readings) Consistently hailed as a modern classic, this story of two friends at an elite boarding school during the early years of World War II is a deeply moving novel of the confusions of adolescence. Despite the personal tragedy encountered by the two friends caused by circumstance and war, the novel is ultimately life-affirming.*

OVERVIEW

The United States in World War II

▶ ***Accessing Prior Knowledge***

Ask students to give examples of the ways that previous wars have affected American society. Students should refer specifically to the Civil War and the First World War and recall these wars' economic, social, and political effects.

▶ ***Predicting Outcomes***

Based on the effects of previous wars, ask students what effects they believe will result from the Second World War.

CHAPTER 17

The United States in World War II

SECTION 1

Mobilization on the Home Front

The United States enters the war and mobilizes its citizens and resources to give its allies unprecedented military and industrial support.

SECTION 2

The War for Europe and North Africa

The United States, Great Britain, and the Soviet Union cooperate in the fight to defeat Germany and its allies.

SECTION 3

The War in the Pacific

America wages an aggressive military campaign against Japan in the Pacific and finally ends the war.

SECTION 4

The Impact of the War

Americans begin to adjust to new economic opportunities and continuing social problems after World War II.

"We are now in this war. We are all in it—all the way."

Franklin D. Roosevelt

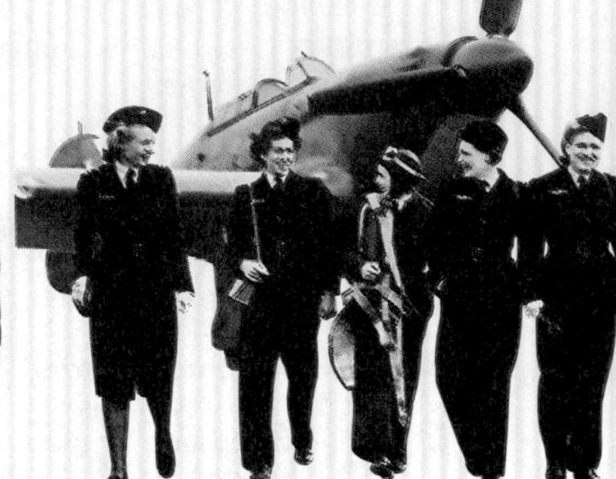

African-American air corps in Tuskegee, Alabama, certifies its first group of combat pilots. These "Tuskegee Airmen" gain fame for their skill and courage.

Office of Scientific Research and Development is created to bring scientists into the war effort.

Female service divisions are established, allowing women like these Ladybirds to serve

A. Philip Randolph demands that African Americans be allowed to work and fight for their country.

Japan bombs Pearl Harbor, and the United States declares war on Japan.

President Roosevelt signs an order forcing Japanese Americans into internment camps.

THE UNITED STATES

THE WORLD

1941

1942

1942

Germany invades Greece and Yugoslavia.

Germany invades the Soviet Union.

Nazis develop "final solution" for exterminating Jews.

Battle of Mi[dway] rages in the Pacific.

THEMES IN CHAPTER 25

Women in America	Civil Rights	Immigration and Migration	The American Dream
As American men marched off to war, both the armed services and defense industries turned to women to meet their "manpower" needs. Women proved they could handle almost any job. See Teacher's Edition note, p. 571.	For America's minorities, the war meant a struggle for equal treatment in the workplace and in the military. The government trampled the civil rights of Japanese Americans by sending them to internment camps. See Teacher's Edition note, p. 572.	The war put unprecedented numbers of Americans on the move. Young men left home for military training and service overseas. As towns and cities with defense plants boomed to the bursting point, workers moved in to take jobs. See Teacher's Edition note, p. 597.	The war brought renewed opportunity for Americans to forge their dreams of the good life. The GI Bill of Rights promised to help returning veterans keep that dream alive after the war. See Teacher's Edition note, p. 598.

LIVING HISTORY

WRITING AN ALTERNATIVE HISTORY

Write an alternative history of the Second World War predicting how the outcome would have been different if a historical event happened differently. Follow these steps in writing your alternative history:

- Develop a "what if" question about a significant event in the war (for example, "What if President Roosevelt had never supported lend-lease?").
- Write an essay predicting how the history of the war would have been changed by the alternative event.

PORTFOLIO PROJECT Save your essay in a folder for your American history portfolio. You will share it with the class at the end of the chapter.

1943

- "Zoot-suit" riots rock Los Angeles.
- Allies, reinforced by armor like this battle-scarred Sherman tank, force Italy to surrender.
- Hitler orders attack on Stalingrad.
- Allies invade North Africa.
- German soldiers surrender to Soviets at Stalingrad.

1944

- GI Bill of Rights is passed.
- President Roosevelt is elected to a fourth term.
- Allies invade occupied Europe on June 6, D-Day.
- Allied soldiers begin to liberate survivors of Nazi death camps.

1945

- U.S. Marines take Iwo Jima.
- Harry S. Truman becomes president after President Roosevelt dies.
- United States drops atomic bombs on Hiroshima and Nagasaki.
- V-E Day signals the end of the war in Europe.
- Nazi retreat begins after the Battle of the Bulge.
- Roosevelt, Churchill, and Stalin meet at Yalta.

ALTERNATIVE ASSESSMENT

LIVING HISTORY

WRITING AN ALTERNATIVE HISTORY

The following steps might help students outline and write their alternative histories:

- Have students make a chronological chart that shows the causes and consequences of the event they have chosen.
- Then have them decide how changes in the central event would have changed the consequences.
- Students should make a list of the new consequences that shows which were most important.
- Before writing their essay, have each student create an outline that highlights the central argument of their alternative history essay.

Project Planning Guide

Step 1	Choose an event.
Step 2	Create chronological chart.
Step 3	Decide on changed consequences.
Step 4	Make list of important consequences.
Step 5	Make outline for essay.

IN-DEPTH RESOURCES: UNIT 5
See worksheet and standards for evaluation, pp. 37, 38.

RECOMMENDED RESOURCES

Books for the Teacher

Goodwin, Doris K. *No Ordinary Time: Franklin & Eleanor Roosevelt—The Home Front in World War II.* New York: S&S Trade, 1994.

Hess, Gary R. *The United States at War, 1941–1945.* Arlington Heights, IL: Harlan, 1986.

Leckie, Robert. *Delivered from Evil.* New York: Harper, 1987. Narrative history of World War II.

Books for the Student

Nichols, David, ed. *Ernie's War: The Best of Ernie Pyle's World War II Dispatches.* New York: Random, 1986.

Sulzberger, C. L. *The American Heritage Picture History of World War II.* New York: Random, 1987.

Terkel, Studs. *The "Good War."* New York: Pantheon, 1984. Oral histories of World War II.

Videos

America, the Way We Were: The Home Front. International Video Network, 1989. A three-tape series on behavior, attitudes, and popular culture.

Eisenhower. PBS Home Video, 1993. 800-424-7963. Documentary biography.

Zoot Suit. MCA Universal Home Video, 1981. Mexican and Anglo cultures clash in 1940s California.

Software

D-Day: 100 Days of Destiny. Educorp, 7434 Trade Street, San Diego, CA 92121, 800-843-9497.

Powers of Persuasion: The Art of Propaganda in World War II. Fife and Drum Software, 316 Soapstone Lane, Silver Spring, MD 20905.

World War II. CD-ROM. Flag Tower, 1995. Interactive documentary.

Section 1 Overview

OBJECTIVES

1 To explain how the United States expanded its armed forces in response to America's entry into World War II.

2 To describe the wartime mobilization of industry, labor, scientists, and the media.

3 To characterize the efforts of the federal government to control the economy and deal with alleged subversion.

SKILLBUILDER

- Interpreting charts, p. 575

CRITICAL THINKING

- Contrasting, p. 570
- Theme: Women in America, p. 571
- Theme: Civil Rights, p. 572
- Forming generalizations, p. 573
- Summarizing, pp. 574, 577
- Analyzing motives, p. 575, 577
- Identifying problems, p. 576
- Forming opinions, p. 577

FOCUS & MOTIVATE

5-MINUTE WARM-UP

Making Judgments
To explore the major events of the Second World War, have students look at the time line on pages 568–569 and answer the following questions.

1. What event during the war do you think had the most impact on the United States?
2. What do you think was the most important world event that occurred during the war?

WARM-UP TRANSPARENCY 17

▶ ***Starting with the Student***
Have students imagine that Japan has attacked Pearl Harbor, and President Roosevelt has asked Congress to declare war on the Axis Powers.

- Do students support the declaration of war?
- How do they think war will change their lives?
- What sacrifices are students willing to make to help their country?

1 Mobilization on the Home Front

TERMS & NAMES
- George Marshall
- A. Philip Randolph
- Nisei
- Office of Price Administration (OPA)
- War Production Board (WPB)
- rationing

LEARN ABOUT how the United States mobilized for war following the attack on Pearl Harbor
TO UNDERSTAND the issues and problems the nation faced in fighting the Second World War.

ONE AMERICAN'S STORY

Charles Swanson looked all over his army base for a tape recorder on which to play the tape his wife had sent him for Christmas. "In desperation," he later recalled, "I had it played over the public-address system. It was a little embarrassing to have the whole company hear it, but it made everyone long for home."

A PERSONAL VOICE
Merry Christmas, honey. Surprised? I am so glad I have a chance to say hello to you this way on our first Christmas apart. . . . About our little girl . . . she is just big enough to fill my heart and strong enough to help Mommy bear this ache of loneliness. . . . Her dearest treasure is her daddy's picture. It's all marked with tiny handprints, and the glass is always cloudy from so much loving and kissing. I'm hoping you'll be listening to this on Christmas Eve, somewhere over there, your heart full of hope, faith and courage, knowing each day will bring that next Christmas together one day nearer. Lynne and I are . . . praying for that tomorrow and for all the daddies in the world to come home.
MRS. CHARLES SWANSON, quoted in *We Pulled Together . . . and Won!*

Mrs. Charles Swanson and her daughter, Lynne, with a picture of her husband

As the United States began to mobilize for war, the Swansons, like most Americans, had few illusions as to what lay ahead. It would be a long time, they knew—a time filled with hard work and hope, with sacrifice and sorrow—before all the families in the world would be reunited.

Americans Join the War Effort

The Japanese had attacked Pearl Harbor with the expectation that once Americans had experienced Japan's power, they would shrink from further conflict. The day after the raid, the *Japan Times* boasted that the United States, now reduced to a third-rate power, was "trembling in her shoes." But if Americans were trembling, it was with rage, not fear. Uniting under the battle cry "Remember Pearl Harbor," they set out to prove Japan wrong.

SELECTIVE SERVICE AND THE GI After Pearl Harbor, eager young Americans jammed the recruiting offices. "I wanted to be a hero, let's face it," admitted Roger Tuthrup. "I was havin' trouble in school. . . . The war'd been goin' on for two years. I didn't wanna miss it. . . . I was an American. I was seventeen."

Even the 5 million who volunteered for military service, however, were not enough to face the challenge of an all-out war on two global fronts—Europe and the Pacific. The Selective Service System expanded the draft and eventually provided another 10 million soldiers to meet the armed forces' needs. Richard Leacock, a filmmaker who came to America from the Canary Islands to go to Harvard, recalls, "You couldn't volunteer unless you were a citizen. . . . When they drafted me in my senior year I was delighted. . . . I can't say that going to Harvard is a democratic process. Going into the army certainly was."

A. Answer The Japanese expected American discouragement, not outrage and total support of the war effort.

THINK THROUGH HISTORY
A. *Contrasting* *How did Americans' response to the Japanese raid on Pearl Harbor differ from Japanese expectations?*

SECTION 1 RESOURCES

PRINT RESOURCES

IN-DEPTH RESOURCES: UNIT 5
Guided Reading, p. 19
Skillbuilder Practice: Analyzing Bias, p. 23
Primary Sources: from *Farewell to Manzanar,* p. 28; War Ration Stamps, p. 29
Literature: from *Snow Falling on Cedars* by David Guterson, p. 32
American Lives: Oveta Culp Hobby, p. 35

READING STUDY GUIDE, p. 177

ACCESS FOR STUDENTS ACQUIRING ENGLISH
Guided Reading (Spanish), p. 196
Skillbuilder Practice: Analyzing Bias (Spanish), p. 200

SPANISH READING STUDY GUIDE, p. 177

FORMAL ASSESSMENT
Section Quiz, p. 212

ALTERNATIVE ASSESSMENT BOOK
See forms for supporting and scoring alternative activities.

TECHNOLOGY RESOURCES

CD-ROM Electronic Library of Primary Sources

VIDEO *American Portfolio: A Videodisc for U.S. History* user's guide, pp. 216–217, 226–229, 232

INTERNET http://www.mlushistory.com

The volunteers and draftees reported to military bases around the country for eight weeks of basic training. In this short period, seasoned sergeants did their best to turn raw recruits into disciplined, battle-ready GIs. (The initials *GI*—meaning "Government Issue"—were first applied to government-issued uniforms, weapons, and supplies but soon it was used to describe soldiers as well.) According to Sergeant Deb Myers, however, there was more to basic training than teaching a recruit how to stand at attention, march in step, handle a rifle, and follow orders.

A PERSONAL VOICE

The civilian went before the Army doctors, took off his clothes, feeling silly; jigged, stooped, squatted, wet into a bottle; became a soldier. He learned how to sleep in the mud, tie a knot, kill a man. He learned the ache of loneliness, the ache of exhaustion, the kinship of misery. He learned that men make the same queasy noises in the morning, feel the same longings at night; that every man is alike and that each man is different.

SERGEANT DEB MYERS, quoted in *The GI War*

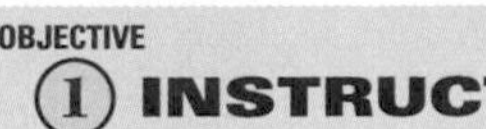

HISTORICAL SPOTLIGHT

TEXAS MILITARY BASES

It takes an enormous amount of organization and training to create an effective military. During World War II, Texas, with its strong military tradition and warm climate, became a prime location for military bases.

A few Texas cities became U.S. Army headquarters. For much of the war, San Antonio was the site of the headquarters of the Third Army, which General George Patton commanded in Europe. Fort Sam Houston was the headquarters for the Southern Defense Command, which guarded the Gulf Coast.

As air power became ever more critical to the war effort, Texas became the nation's most active aviation-training region. Several fields, like Kelly Field near San Antonio and Ellington Field near Houston, were expanded or rebuilt, and new ones were also built. Meanwhile, the headquarters of the American Air Force Training Command was established in Fort Worth.

WOMEN IN THE MILITARY The military's manpower needs were so great that early in 1942 Army Chief of Staff General **George Marshall** pushed for the formation of a Women's Auxiliary Army Corps (WAAC). "There are innumerable duties now being performed by soldiers that can actually be done better by women," Marshall said in support of a bill to establish the WAAC. Under this bill, women volunteering for the army would not receive the same rank, pay, or benefits as men doing the same jobs, nor could they expect to make the army a career.

Even so, the bill ran into fierce opposition in Congress. "Take women into the armed services . . . ," asked one congressman, "[and] who then will do the cooking, the washing, the mending?" Another representative scorned the bill as "the silliest piece of legislation" he had ever seen. "A woman's army to defend the United States of America," he raged. "Think of the humiliation. What has become of the manhood of America, that we have to call on our women to do what has ever been the duty of men?"

Despite this opposition, the bill establishing the WAAC became law on May 15, 1942. When Oveta Culp Hobby, a Texas newspaper executive and the first director of WAAC, put out a call for recruits a few weeks later, more than 13,000 women applied on the first day applications were available. In all, some 250,000 women served in this and other auxiliary branches during the war.

THINK THROUGH HISTORY
B. THEME ***Women in America*** *Why did some congressmen oppose admitting women to the military?*

B. Answer They thought war was men's work and would take women away from their place in the home.

MINORITIES IN THE ARMED SERVICES For many minority groups—especially African Americans, Native Americans, Mexican Americans, and Asian Americans—the war created new dilemmas. Restricted to racially segregated neighborhoods and reservations and denied basic citizenship rights, some members of these groups questioned whether this was their war to fight. "Why die for democracy for some foreign country when we don't even have it here?" asked an editorial in an African-American newspaper. On receiving his draft notice, an African American responded unhappily, "Just carve on my tombstone, 'Here lies a black man killed fighting a yellow man for the protection of a white man.'"

Two privates in the Fifth Army sit at the entrance to an air-raid shelter at Anzio, Italy, where they held the beachhead against the Nazis.

OBJECTIVE
① INSTRUCT

Americans Join the War Effort

Discussing Key Ideas

- The Selective Service System helps meet U.S. manpower needs.
- Many women and minorities serve in the military.

IN-DEPTH RESOURCES: UNIT 5
Guided Reading, p. 19

ACCESS FOR STUDENTS ACQUIRING ENGLISH
Guided Reading (Spanish), p. 196

HISTORICAL SPOTLIGHT
Texas Military Bases

Critical Thinking: Hypothesizing Ask students to consider which states had characteristics similar to those of Texas that might have made them good places for bases. *Other states in the South and Southwest.* Have these places attracted military bases and spending since the Second World War ended? *Yes.*

MORE ABOUT . . .
The WAACs

In 1942, the army decided to send WAACs into combat areas. WAAC director Oveta Culp Hobby flew to a training center in Daytona Beach, Florida, to speak to 300 women selected to go overseas. She told them how dangerous such assignments could be and that only volunteers would be sent abroad. Every one of the women signed up. From that point on, WAACs followed the troops, with more than 8,000 women

(continued on next page)

TEACHING OPTIONS

Exploring Themes

Women in America While most women who served in World War II were in the WAAC, many joined the navy's auxiliary corps, the WAVE, and the Coast Guard's auxiliary, the SPAR. Female pilots served in the Women's Auxiliary Ferrying Squadron (WAFS) and the Women's Air Force Service Pilots (WASP). The performance of these women led General Dwight D. Eisenhower to admit that "when this project [women in the military] was proposed . . . like most old soldiers, I was violently against it. . . . Every phase of the record they compiled during the war convinced me of the error of my first reaction."

Making Global Connections

Military Service in Israel Israel is surrounded by hostile Arab states and has been almost continually at war since its founding in 1948. This nation of 4.75 million has a militia—army, navy, and air force—of about 141,000 citizens. To provide for its military defense, it drafts both men and women into the armed forces at age 18. Men serve for three years and women for two. After their compulsory service, men and childless women also undergo annual reserve training and service.

(continued from page 571)
serving in Africa and Europe and about 5,000 in Asia. More than 500 women earned combat decorations for their courage under enemy attack in the war in the Pacific.

IN-DEPTH RESOURCES: UNIT 5
American Lives: Oveta Culp Hobby, p. 35

OBJECTIVE
 **INSTRUCT**

Life on the Home Front

▶ ***Discussing Key Ideas***

- American industry quickly converts to war production in 1942.
- The growth of war industries creates new job opportunities for women and minorities.
- Scientists aid the war effort by developing new military technologies, weapons, and wonder drugs.
- The mass media expand as they deliver war news and patriotic messages as well as escapist entertainment.

 ***ELECTRONIC LIBRARY OF PRIMARY SOURCES***
"What Can I Do?" by the Office of Civilian Defense

Still, minorities knew that no matter how badly they had been treated in the past, they were likely to be worse off under Axis control. "We know that under Nazism we should have no rights at all; we should be used as slaves," declared a Native American. The Congreso del Pueblo de Habla Espanola (Spanish Speaking Congress) agreed, proclaiming that "our liberties, our homes, and our lives [are] directly threatened by Fascism. . . . We are also children of the United States. We will defend her."

In response, at least a half million Mexican Americans joined the armed forces. All-Latino units saw heavy action both in Europe and in Asia. While Mexican Americans in Los Angeles made up only a tenth of the city's population, they suffered a fifth of the city's wartime casualties.

More than a million African Americans also served in the military. Black soldiers lived and worked in segregated units and were mostly limited to noncombat roles. When 3,000 black troops were asked in 1943 if "Negroes are being given a fair chance to do as much as they want to do to help win the war," more than half answered "No!" After much protest, African Americans did finally see combat in the last year of the war.

Asian Americans took part in the struggle as well. More than 13,000 Chinese Americans, or about one of every five adult males, joined the armed forces. In addition, 33,000 Japanese Americans put on uniforms. Of these, several thousand volunteered to serve as spies and interpreters in the Pacific war. "During battles," wrote an admiring officer, "they crawled up close enough to be able to hear [Japanese] officers' commands and to make verbal translations to our soldiers."

Some 25,000 Native Americans enlisted in the armed services too, including 800 women. Their willingness to serve led *The Saturday Evening Post* to comment, "We would not need the Selective Service if all volunteered like Indians." For many Native Americans, the war provided their first opportunity to leave the reservation and meet non-Indians. A Chippewa wrote a poem describing his experience fighting with soldiers from very different backgrounds: "We bind each other's wounds and eat the same ration. / We dream of our loved ones in the same nation."

C. Answer They'd be worse off under Nazism; they were citizens and wanted to do their duty; they had essential skills.

THINK THROUGH HISTORY
C. THEME Civil Rights *What reasons did minority Americans give for joining the armed services?*

Life on the Home Front

Early in February 1942, newspapers reported the end of automobile production in the United States. The last car to roll off an automaker's assembly line was a gray sedan with "victory trim,"—that is, without chrome-plated parts. This was just one more sign that the war would affect almost every aspect of life on the home front.

Women inspect mass-produced propellers in America's stepped-up war industry.

THE INDUSTRIAL RESPONSE Within weeks of the shutdown in production, the nation's automobile plants had been retooled to produce tanks, planes, boats, and command cars. They were not alone. Across the nation, factories were quickly converted to war production. A maker of mechanical pencils turned out bomb parts. A bedspread manufacturer made mosquito netting. A soft-drink company converted from filling bottles with liquid to filling shells with explosives.

TEACHING OPTIONS

Making Connections Across Cultures

Native American Stereotypes While Native Americans were widely praised for their enthusiastic response to World War II, some of that praise reflected old stereotypes of Indian warriors. "The red soldier is tough," wrote *American Legion Magazine.* "Usually he has lived outdoors all his life, and lived by his senses; he is a natural Ranger. He takes to commando fighting with gusto. Why not? His ancestors invented it. . . ." Ironically, however, most Native Americans were struggling to live in the white man's world, in which their native traditions and ancestral pride had been stripped from them.

Exploring Themes

Civil Rights In 1942, sociologist Rose Hum Lee wrote an article on Chinese-American participation in the war effort. In it she noted that the Chinese exclusion laws still banned immigration from China to the United States and that Chinese immigrants already in America were not allowed to become naturalized citizens. "To be fighting for freedom and democracy in the Far East . . . and to be denied equal opportunity in the greatest of democracies, seems the height of irony."

This irony was not lost on President Roosevelt, who persuaded Congress to repeal the Chinese exclusion laws in 1943.

Meanwhile, shipyards and defense plants expanded with dizzying speed. By the end of 1942, industrialist Henry J. Kaiser had built seven massive new shipyards that turned out Liberty ships (cargo carriers), tankers, troop transports, and "baby" aircraft carriers at an astonishing rate. Late that year, Kaiser invited reporters to Way One in his Richmond, California, shipyard to watch as his workers assembled *Hull 440,* a Liberty ship, in a record-breaking four days. Writer Alyce Mano Kramer described the first day and night of construction.

A PERSONAL VOICE

At the stroke of 12, Way One exploded into life. Crews of workers, like a champion football team, swarmed into their places in the line. Within 60 seconds, the keel was swinging into position. . . . *Hull 440* was going up. The speed of [production] was unbelievable. At midnight, Saturday, an empty way—at midnight Sunday, a full-grown hull met the eyes of graveyard workers as they came on shift.

ALYCE MANO KRAMER, quoted in *Home Front, U.S.A.*

"THE GIRL HE LEFT BEHIND" IS STILL BEHIND HIM
She's a WOW

This World War II poster reinforces the message that the home front was an important part of the battlefield.

Three days later, 25,000 amazed spectators watched as *Hull 440* slid into the water. How could such a ship be built so fast? Kaiser used prefabricated, or factory-made, parts that could be quickly assembled at his shipyards. Equally important were his workers, who had learned new skills and performed jobs at record speeds.

LABOR'S CONTRIBUTION When the war began, defense contractors warned the Selective Service System that the nation did not have enough manpower to meet both its military and its industrial needs. They were wrong. By 1944, despite the draft, nearly 18 million workers were laboring in war industries, three times as many as in 1941.

More than 6 million of these new workers were women. At first, war industries feared that most women lacked the necessary stamina for factory work and were reluctant to hire them. But once women proved they could wield welding torches or riveting guns as well as men, employers could not hire enough of them—especially since women earned only about 60 percent as much as men doing the same jobs.

Boys using pots and pans as helmets and drums encourage New Yorkers to donate aluminum to the war effort.

Defense plants also hired more than 2 million minority workers during the war years. Like women, minorities faced strong prejudice at first. Before the war, 75 percent of defense contractors simply refused to hire African Americans, while another 15 percent employed them only in menial jobs. "Negroes will be considered only as janitors," declared the general manager of North American Aviation. "It is the company policy not to employ them as mechanics and aircraft workers."

THINK THROUGH HISTORY
D. *Forming Generalizations* *What difficulties did women and minorities face in the wartime work force?*

D. Answer Both faced job and pay discrimination.

To protest such discrimination both in the military and in industry, **A. Philip Randolph,** president of the Brotherhood of Sleeping Car Porters and the nation's leading African-American labor leader, organized a march on Washington. Randolph called on blacks everywhere to come to the capital on July 1, 1941, and to march under the banner "We Loyal Colored Americans Demand the Right to Work and Fight for Our Country."

Fearing that the march might provoke white resentment or violence, President Roosevelt called Randolph to the White House and asked him to back down. "I'm sorry Mr. President," the labor leader said, "the march cannot be called off." Roosevelt then asked, "How many people do you plan to bring?" Randolph replied, "One hundred thousand, Mr. President." Roosevelt was stunned. Even half that number of black protesters would be far more than Washington—still a very segregated city—could feed, house, and transport.

MORE ABOUT . . .

Henry J. Kaiser

The industrialist Henry John Kaiser (1882–1967) first proved his organizational prowess as the head of construction of the Boulder, Bonneville, and Grand Coulee dams. During World War II, Kaiser took over management of West Coast shipyards and revolutionized ship construction. By 1945 Kaiser, who had earned the nickname "Sir Launchalot," was launching one cargo ship a day from his busy shipyards.

MORE ABOUT . . .

A. Philip Randolph

American labor leader Asa Philip Randolph (1889–1979) was born in Crescent City, Florida, the son of an African Methodist Episcopal minister. During his youth, Randolph worked as a section hand on a railroad, learning firsthand how African Americans were treated by railroad companies. After attending college in New York, he organized the Brotherhood of Sleeping Car Porters in 1925. It was the first union composed mostly of black workers to be granted a charter by the American Federation of Labor. In 1957, Randolph was elected a vice-president of the American Federation of Labor and Congress of Industrial Organizations. He was also one of the organizers of the March on Washington in 1963.

TEACHING OPTION

Skillbuilder Mini-Lesson: Analyzing Bias

Explaining the Skill A biased, or prejudiced, point of view often appears in primary sources and other historical materials. Bias can be for or against something. One way to detect bias is by looking at the words and visual images to see if they give a one-sided, idealized, or unrealistic view of the subject.

Applying the Skill: The Girls Left Behind Have students look at the poster reproduced on this page. Then ask:

1. What is the meaning of the words on the poster? *The women—wives, girlfriends—that soldiers left behind when they went to war are supporting the soldiers by working in factories that support the war effort.*
2. What words or phrases show bias or stereotypes? *"Girl" instead of "woman"; "he left behind" and "behind him" imply that her work supports him instead of supporting the nation, as his does.*
3. What stereotype of women does the image convey? *They are young, white, slender, and loyal.*

IN-DEPTH RESOURCES: UNIT 5
Skillbuilder Practice: Analyzing Bias, p. 23

HISTORICAL SPOTLIGHT

Hollywood and the War

Critical Thinking: Forming Opinions Ask students to think about the importance of propaganda for a nation's war effort. Do they think that propaganda is necessary in order for a nation to effectively mobilize for war? How does their position on propaganda relate to their views on censorship?

The Federal Government Takes Control

Discussing Key Ideas

- After Pearl Harbor, the federal government orders the internment of 110,000 Japanese Americans living on the West Coast.
- The government institutes broad economic controls to contain wartime inflation and to ensure that war industries and the military have the supplies they need to win the war.

In the end it was Roosevelt, not Randolph, who backed down. In return for Randolph's promise to cancel the march, the president issued an executive order calling on employers and labor unions "to provide for the full and equitable participation of all workers in defense industries, without discrimination because of race, creed, color, or national origin."

MOBILIZATION OF SCIENTISTS That same year, Roosevelt created the Office of Scientific Research and Development (OSRD) to bring scientists into the war effort. The OSRD spurred improvements in both radar and sonar, a new technology for locating submarines underwater. It encouraged the use of pesticides like DDT to fight insects. As a result, U.S. soldiers were probably the first in history to be relatively free from body lice. The OSRD also pushed the development of "miracle drugs," such as penicillin, that saved countless lives on and off the battlefield.

The greatest scientific achievement of the OSRD, though, was the secret development of a new weapon, the atomic bomb. Interest in such a weapon began in 1939, after German scientists succeeded in splitting uranium atoms, releasing an enormous amount of energy. This news prompted physicist and German refugee Albert Einstein to write a letter to President Roosevelt, warning that the Germans could use their discovery to construct a weapon of enormous destructive power.

Roosevelt responded by creating a National Committee on Uranium to study the new discovery. In 1941, the committee reported that it would take from three to five years to build an atomic bomb. Hoping to shorten that time, the OSRD set up a crash program in 1942 to develop a bomb as quickly as possible. Because its offices were located in New York City, the atomic bomb program came to be known as the Manhattan Project.

THINK THROUGH HISTORY
E. *Summarizing* *Why did President Roosevelt create the OSRD, and what did it do?*
E. Answer To bring scientists into the war effort; it oversaw improvements in radar and sonar, the use of pesticides and "miracle drugs," and the Manhattan Project to create an atomic bomb.

CHANGES IN ENTERTAINMENT The war not only put Americans back to work but also put money in their pockets. As a result, spending on entertainment more than doubled between 1941 and 1945.

From 60 million to 100 million Americans (out of a total population of 135 million) went to the movies each week. In the aftermath of Pearl Harbor, Hollywood churned out war-oriented propaganda films. Heroic movies like *Mission to Moscow* and *Song of Russia* glorified America's new wartime ally, the Soviet Union. "Hiss-and-boo" films with titles like *Hitler, Beast of Berlin* stirred up hatred against the enemy. As the war dragged on, however, people grew tired of propaganda and war themes. Hollywood responded with musicals, romances, comedies, and other escapist fare designed to take filmgoers away from the grim realities of war, if only for an hour or two.

Meanwhile, public hunger for war news spurred a boom in the publishing and radio industries. Magazines such as *Life, Look,* and *Time,* which covered the war in both words and pictures, saw their circulation soar. Radio audiences also reached record levels as people tuned in the latest war reports. Between newscasts, listeners could follow the radio soap operas' tales of love gone wrong, or they could escape wartime concerns by laughing at comedians such as Jack Benny and Fanny Brice.

HISTORICAL SPOTLIGHT

HOLLYWOOD AND THE WAR

Hollywood took up the war effort like the rest of the nation. In addition to films like *Mission to Moscow,* in which fictional tales were used to support the war effort, moviemakers also turned out informational films. The most important of these films—the Why We Fight series—were made by the great director Frank Capra.

Sworn into the army as a major the day after the attack on Pearl Harbor, Capra was assigned to the Signal Corps, the army's communications branch. Capra's task was to create informational and training films for enlistees.

Capra set up his headquarters in California, where he convinced many of his Hollywood friends to help him staff and supply a studio to make his films. Within three months Capra produced *Prelude to War,* the first film in the Why We Fight series and one of the greatest propaganda films ever made. It used brilliantly edited footage, diagrams, and music to dramatically show how aggression by the Axis powers had led to war. When President Roosevelt saw it, he proclaimed, "Every man, woman, and child in the world must see this film."

The Federal Government Takes Control

In addition to instituting the draft and supporting war industries, the federal government took vigorous social and economic measures to ensure that events on the home front went smoothly.

TEACHING OPTIONS

Making Connections Across the Curriculum

Biology The development of the first antibiotic drugs on the eve of World War II signaled a revolution in the treatment of infectious diseases. Although penicillin had been discovered by British bacteriologist Alexander Fleming in 1928 and a method of extraction and purification in the late 1930s, a means of producing large quantities of the drug was not found until 1943. That same year, the American bacteriologist Selman A. Waksman discovered another powerful antibiotic, streptomycin.

Making Connections Across Cultures

Children and the War Effort In 1942, the government launched the Schools at War Program. Children brought dimes and quarters to school to buy defense stamps; one sixth-grade class in Kansas donated enough to buy one submachine gun, one tent, four field telephones, five steel helmets, and nine entrenching tools. Both boys and girls knit afghans, sweaters, mittens, and socks for service people. They turned schoolyards into victory gardens. In 1944 Congress recognized the efforts of the nation's children in a resolution thanking them for their "contribution to the victory effort."

INTERNMENT OF JAPANESE AMERICANS After the bombing of Pearl Harbor, many Americans questioned the loyalty of Japanese Americans living in Hawaii and on the West Coast. They feared that these Asian Americans were part of Japan's master plan for destroying the United States, although no evidence existed that any of them were spies. Early in 1942, the War Department called for the mass evacuation of all Japanese Americans from Hawaii. General Delos Emmons, the military governor of Hawaii, resisted the order because 37% of the people in Hawaii were Japanese Americans. To remove them would have destroyed the islands' economy and hindered U.S. military operations there. However, he was eventually forced to order the internment, or confinement, of 1,444 Japanese Americans, 1 percent of Hawaii's Japanese-American population.

On the West Coast, however, panic and prejudice ruled the day. In California, only 1 percent of the people were Japanese, but they constituted a minority large enough to focus the prejudice of many whites, without being large enough to effectively resist internment. Newspapers whipped up anti-Japanese sentiment by running ugly stories attacking Japanese Americans daily.

On February 19, 1942, President Roosevelt signed an order requiring the removal of people of Japanese ancestry from California and parts of Washington, Oregon, and Arizona. He justified this step as necessary for national security. In the following weeks, the army rounded up some 110,000 Japanese Americans and shipped them to ten hastily constructed internment camps. About two-thirds were **Nisei,** or Japanese Americans who had been born in this country and were thus American citizens. Thousands of Nisei had already been drafted into the armed forces, and to Ted Nakashima, an architectural draftsman from Seattle, the evacuation seemed utterly senseless.

THINK THROUGH HISTORY
F. Analyzing Motives *Why did President Roosevelt order the internment of Japanese Americans?*

F. Answer Because some people perceived them as a threat to American security.

A PERSONAL VOICE

[There are] electricians, plumbers, draftsmen, mechanics, carpenters, painters, farmers—every trade—men who are able and willing to do all they can to lick the Axis. . . . What really hurts is the constant reference to [us] evacuees as "Japs." "Japs" are the guys we are fighting. We're on this side and we want to help. Why won't America let us?

TED NAKASHIMA, *New Republic* magazine, June 15, 1942

The Government Takes Control of the Economy, 1942–1945

AGENCIES AND LAWS	WHAT THE REGULATIONS DID
National War Labor Board (NWLB)	• Limited wage increases. • Allowed negotiated benefits, such as paid vacations, pensions, and medical insurance. • Kept unions stable by forbidding workers to change unions.
Office of Price Administration (OPA)	• Fought inflation by freezing wages, prices, and rents. • Rationed foods such as meat, butter, cheese, vegetables, sugar, and coffee.
War Production Board (WPB)	• Rationed fuel and materials vital to the war effort, such as gasoline, heating oil, metals, rubber, and plastics.
Department of the Treasury	• Issued war bonds to raise money for the war effort and to fight inflation.
Revenue Act of 1942	• Raised the top personal-income-tax rate to 90%. • Added lower- and middle-income Americans to the income-tax rolls.
Smith-Connally Labor Disputes Act (1943)	• Limited the right to strike in industries crucial to the war effort. • Gave the president power to take over striking plants.

SKILLBUILDER
INTERPRETING CHARTS
What was the overall aim of these economic regulations?

Skillbuilder Answer To provide maximal resources for the war effort.

MORE ABOUT . . .

Japanese Americans in Hawaii after Pearl Harbor

So few of the 150,000 Japanese Americans living in Hawaii were interned after Pearl Harbor because they made up more than a third of Hawaii's population. Any effort to intern them all would have devastated the island's economy. In addition, Hawaii's wartime leaders promoted a reasoned response to fears of Japanese subversion. "No person, be he citizen or alien, need worry, provided he is not connected with subversive elements," declared General Delos Emmons after the attack.

IN-DEPTH RESOURCES: UNIT 5
Primary Source: *Farewell to Manzanar*, p. 28

ELECTRONIC LIBRARY OF PRIMARY SOURCES
Japanese-American Testimony from the National Defense Migration Hearings

HISTORY FROM VISUALS

The Government Takes Control of the Economy, 1942–1945

Reading the Chart Suggest that students read this chart horizontally, first noting the federal agency or law in the left column and then reading the regulations it was responsible for in the right column.

Extension Ask students which regulations would have created the greatest hardship for them.

IN-DEPTH RESOURCES: UNIT 5
Primary Source: War Ration Stamps, p. 29

TEACHING OPTIONS

Making Connections Across Time

Reparations to Interned Japanese Americans After World War II was over, Japanese Americans formed the Japanese American Citizen League (JACL) and pressed the federal government to compensate their people for property lost during internment. In 1965, Congress allocated $38 million in compensation—less than 10 percent of the losses actually suffered by Japanese Americans. The JACL was not satisfied with this gesture and kept lobbying the government. Their efforts finally paid off in 1988—nearly 50 years after internment—when Congress voted to pay $20,000 to every Japanese American who had been sent to a relocation camp during World War II.

Teaching Less Proficient Readers

Understanding the Effects of Government Regulations To help less proficient readers understand how the economic regulations listed in the chart affected the lives of Americans, you might want to group them with more adept readers and ask the groups to list the effects of each regulation on employers, workers, and consumers.

	Regulation	Effect
Employers		
Workers		
Consumers	WPB rationing	Less food and fuel

HISTORY FROM VISUALS

The War Fought at Home

Reading the Images Make sure students understand that each image or cluster of images represents a specific aspect of civilian life that was affected by America's involvement in World War II. There is no hierarchy of importance implied by their position on the page. Ask students what new or surprising information they learned from the images.

Extension Ask students to suggest other fronts on which the war at home might have been fought. *Possible Responses: Housing, jobs, radio and television programming, literature, and music.*

The War Fought at Home

When you ride ALONE you ride with Hitler!
Join a Car-Sharing Club TODAY!

TRANSPORTATION With oil, gas, and rubber in short supply, many Americans car-pooled or rode their bicycles.

FOOD Each month the ration board gave consumers stamps for canned goods and perishables such as meat and butter. Sometimes unanticipated shortages made it difficult to find some foods, so many Americans grew "victory gardens" everywhere from abandoned lots to flower beds.

FASHION The armed forces' demand for textiles led to shortages of wool and rayon, causing fashion changes back home. The War Production Board banned ruffles, pleats, and patch pockets, favoring the single-breasted, vestless "victory suit" over the baggy "zoot suit" in vogue at the time. To conserve silk, women painted seams up the backs of their legs to make it seem as if they were wearing stockings.

ECONOMIC CONTROLS Another problem for the federal government was preventing inflation from skyrocketing, as it had during World War I. With incomes rising and the production of consumer goods falling, prices were bound to soar.

Congress responded to this threat by passing legislation to create the **Office of Price Administration (OPA).** The OPA fought inflation by freezing prices on most goods. Congress also raised income-tax rates and extended the tax to millions of people who had never paid it before. The higher taxes reduced consumer demand on scarce goods by leaving workers with less to spend. In addition, the government encouraged Americans to use their extra cash to buy war bonds. As a result of these measures, inflation remained below 30 percent—about half that of World War I—for the entire period of World War II. (See *taxation* on page 939 in the Economics Handbook.)

Besides controlling inflation, the government needed to ensure that the armed forces and war industries received the resources they needed to win the war. The **War Production Board (WPB)** assumed that responsibility. The WPB decided which companies would convert from peacetime to wartime production and allocated raw materials to key industries. The WPB also organized nationwide drives to collect scrap iron, tin cans, paper, rags, and cooking fat for recycling into war goods. Across America, children scoured attics, cellars, garages, vacant lots, and back alleys, looking for useful junk. During one five-month-long paper drive in Chicago, schoolchildren collected 36 million pounds of old paper—about 65 pounds per child.

In addition, the OPA set up a system for **rationing,** or establishing fixed allotments of goods deemed essential for the military. Under this system, households received ration books with coupons to be used for buying such scarce goods as meat, shoes, sugar, coffee, and gasoline. Gas rationing was particularly hard on those who lived in Western regions, where driving was the only way to get around. Eleanor Roosevelt sympathized with their complaints. "To tell the people in the West not to use their cars," she observed,

G. Answer Controlling inflation, managing shortages, and making sure that the armed forces and war industries got the resources they needed.

THINK THROUGH HISTORY
G. *Identifying Problems* *What basic problems were the OPA and WPB created to solve?*

Block Schedule — TEACHING OPTION — Time Needed: 20 Minutes

Cooperative Activity: Creating a War Poster

Task: Student groups will create a poster designed to encourage civilian participation in the war effort.

Purpose: To help students understand the climate of opinion in America in the early 1940s and the power of visual media in shaping public attitudes and behavior.

Activity: Assign small groups of students to create a poster to encourage the public either to buy war bonds or to accept and comply with rationing.

Before students begin their own posters, discuss the poster at the top of this page and, if possible, other World War II posters, and consider what makes each one effective.

You might suggest that students discuss the concept for their poster as a group and then divide the following individual tasks: creating a rough sketch of the poster; writing the headlines, captions, and other text that will appear on the poster; producing the final poster.

ALTERNATIVE ASSESSMENT BOOK
Standards for Evaluating a Cooperative Activity

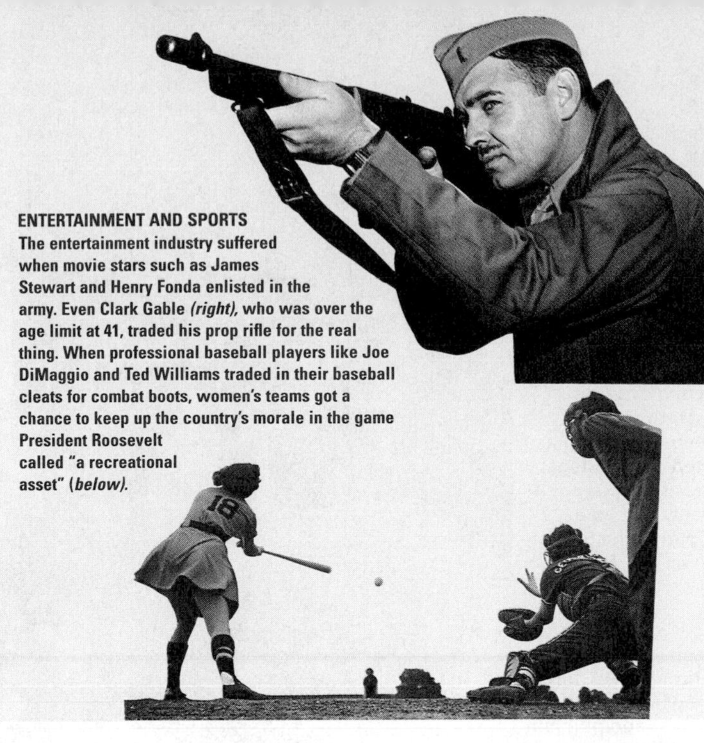

ENTERTAINMENT AND SPORTS The entertainment industry suffered when movie stars such as James Stewart and Henry Fonda enlisted in the army. Even Clark Gable *(right)*, who was over the age limit at 41, traded his prop rifle for the real thing. When professional baseball players like Joe DiMaggio and Ted Williams traded in their baseball cleats for combat boots, women's teams got a chance to keep up the country's morale in the game President Roosevelt called "a recreational asset" *(below)*.

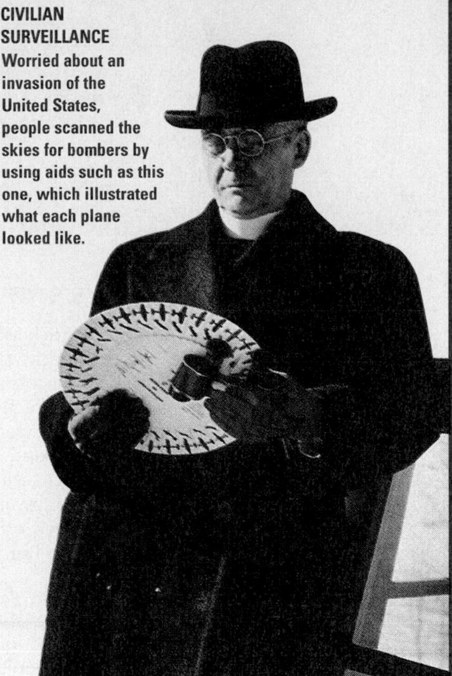

CIVILIAN SURVEILLANCE Worried about an invasion of the United States, people scanned the skies for bombers by using aids such as this one, which illustrated what each plane looked like.

"means that these people may never see another soul for weeks and weeks nor have a way of getting a sick person to a doctor."

Most Americans accepted rationing as a personal contribution to the war effort. Workers car-pooled or rode bicycles. Families coped with shortages of everything from tires to toys. Inevitably, some cheated by hoarding scarce goods or by purchasing them through the "black market," where rationed items could be bought illegally without coupons at inflated prices.

In 1943, the WPB hired Harvard professor Thomas North Whitehead to tour the nation and find out how Americans were reacting to rationing and controls. He reported that "the good temper and common sense of most people under restrictions and vexations was really impressive. . . . My own observation is that most people are behaving like patriotic, loyal citizens."

While people tightened their belts at home, millions of other Americans put their lives on the line for their country in air, sea, and land battles on the other side of the world.

Section 1 Assessment

1. TERMS & NAMES

Identify:
- George Marshall
- A. Philip Randolph
- Nisei
- Office of Price Administration (OPA)
- War Production Board (WPB)
- rationing

2. SUMMARIZING Re-create the web below on your paper, and fill in ways that America prepared for war.

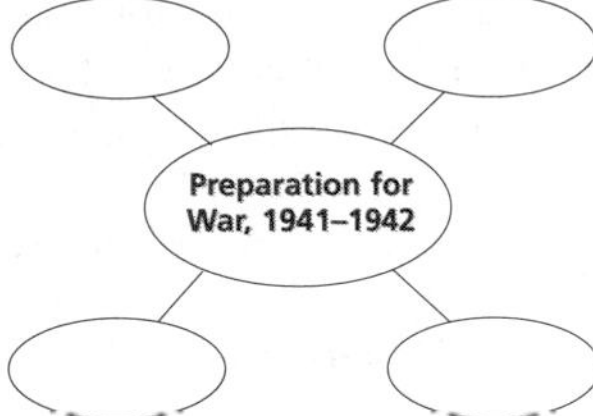

3. ANALYZING MOTIVES Why do you think President Roosevelt gave in to A. Philip Randolph's demands for equal African-American participation in the war effort?

THINK ABOUT
- the impact a large demonstration in Washington would have on Roosevelt's popularity
- the relationship between blacks and whites in 1941

4. FORMING OPINIONS Do you think that President Roosevelt should have ordered the internment of Japanese Americans living on the West Coast? Support your opinion.

THINK ABOUT
- the founding principles of the United States
- the human costs of internment
- the behavior of Japanese Americans
- the risks Japanese Americans posed to U.S. security

ANSWERS

1. TERMS & NAMES

George Marshall, p. 571

A. Philip Randolph, p. 573

Nisei, p. 575

Office of Price Administration (OPA), p. 576

War Production Board (WPB), p. 576

rationing, p. 576

2. SUMMARIZING

Possible Answers: Selective Service draft, conversion of industries to wartime production, employment of women in the war industry, creation of OSRD, establishment of OPA.

3. ANALYZING MOTIVES

Possible Response: Roosevelt might have feared violence between whites and blacks or the disruption of transportation and other activities in the nation's capital.

4. FORMING OPINIONS

Possible Response: No—Internment violated the Constitution, and Japanese Americans had shown no signs of disloyalty. Yes—Internal dangers had to be reduced during a war, and Japanese Americans might have been attacked by suspicious whites if they had remained in their communities.

MORE ABOUT . . .
Baseball in World War II

In response to the shortage of baseball players during World War II, more than 40 Latin Americans joined major-league teams. In 1943, Chicago Cubs owner Philip Wrigley founded the All-American Girls' Professional Baseball League, which operated until 1954. The tradition of playing the national anthem prior to games also began during the war as a means of promoting patriotism.

ASSESS & RETEACH

Section 1 Assessment

Have students work in pairs to answer the questions. One student should work on questions 1 and 3 and the other on questions 2 and 4.

Self-Assessment

Have students exchange papers and discuss how they would modify each other's answers to make them more complete.

Section Quiz

FORMAL ASSESSMENT
Section Quiz, p. 212

Reteach

Create a class web on the board indicating the ways that America prepared for war in 1940–1941. Use students' answers to question 2 as the basis for the web.

CLOSE

Once the United States entered World War II, Americans in all walks of life mobilized for the struggle ahead. The war brought new opportunities for women and for some minorities, but not for many Japanese Americans, who faced years of internment.

Section 2 Overview

OBJECTIVES

1. To summarize the Allies' plans for winning the war.
2. To identify events in the war in Europe.
3. To describe the liberation of Europe.

SKILLBUILDERS

- Understanding geography: place, movement, p. 579
- Understanding geography: location, region, p. 583

CRITICAL THINKING

- Finding main ideas, p. 579
- Making inferences, p. 580
- Synthesizing, p. 581
- Summarizing, p. 581
- Recognizing effects, p. 582
- Analyzing causes, pp. 584, 585
- Following chronological order, p. 585
- Making predictions, p. 585
- Forming opinions, p. 585

FOCUS & MOTIVATE

5-MINUTE WARM-UP

Recognizing Facts and Details

To explore the terrors of combat, have students read One American's Story on page 578 and answer the following questions.

1. Where was John Patrick McGrath when he had his combat flashback?
2. What happened to his buddy during the battle?

 ***WARM-UP TRANSPARENCY 17***

▶ ***Starting with the Student***

- Have students ever been in a situation in which they thought they might die? How did they react?
- How do they think their reactions compare with those of soldiers facing battle for the first time?

② The War for Europe and North Africa

LEARN ABOUT how the Allies coordinated the war effort ***TO UNDERSTAND*** how they defeated Germany and Italy.

TERMS & NAMES
- Dwight D. Eisenhower
- D-Day
- George Patton
- Harry S. Truman
- Battle of the Bulge
- V-E Day

ONE AMERICAN'S STORY

It was 1951 and John Patrick McGrath was just finishing his second year in drama school. For an acting class, his final exam was to be a performance of a death scene. McGrath knew his lines perfectly. But as he began the final farewell, he broke out in a sweat and bolted off the stage. "A cold winter freeze crackled through me as we played that scene," McGrath later recalled. Suddenly he had a flashback to a frozen meadow in Belgium during the Battle of the Bulge in 1945. Three German tanks were spraying his platoon with machine-gun fire.

A PERSONAL VOICE

Only a few feet away, one of the men in my platoon falls. Red blood spatters the pristine snow at his feet. He calls out to me. "Don't leave me. Don't. . . ." The tanks advance, one straight for me. I grab my buddy by the wrist and pull him across the snow. . . . Barren bush is all I can find to hide behind. The tank nearest to us is on a track to run us down. . . . I fire several rounds from my rifle with no effect. . . . When the German tank is but 15 yards away, I grab my buddy by the wrist and feign a lurch to my right. The tank follows the move. Then I lurch back to my left. The German tank clamors by, only inches away. . . . It speeds away with the other two tanks, satisfied with the damage inflicted. In their wake the meadow is strewn with casualties. I turn to tend my fallen comrade. He is dead.

JOHN PATRICK MCGRATH, *A Cue for Passion*

Like countless other soldiers, McGrath would never forget both the heroism and the horrors he witnessed while fighting to free Europe.

Private John P. McGrath fought at both Anzio, Italy, and the Battle of the Bulge. He carried the bullet-riddled letter (*above left*) in a pack that saved his life. In 1990, he visited Anzio, where the rest of his company is buried (*top*).

The United States and Britain Join Forces

"Now that we are, as you say, 'in the same boat,'" British prime minister Winston Churchill wired President Roosevelt two days after the Pearl Harbor attack, "would it not be wise for us to have another conference . . . and the sooner the better." Roosevelt responded with an invitation for Churchill to come at once. So began a remarkable alliance between the two nations.

WAR PLANS Prime Minister Churchill arrived at the White House on December 22, 1941, and spent the next three weeks working out war plans with President Roosevelt. Their first major decision was to make the defeat of Germany the Allies' top priority. There were several reasons for this policy:

- Roosevelt had always considered Adolf Hitler the number one enemy of the United States.
- Joseph Stalin, whose Soviet Union was now one of the Allies, was desperate for help against invading German forces.
- Only after Germany was defeated could the United States look to Britain and the Soviet Union for help in defeating Japan.

SECTION 2 RESOURCES

PRINT RESOURCES

IN-DEPTH RESOURCES: UNIT 5
Guided Reading, p. 20
Geography Application: Thunderclap, p. 24
Outline Map: Crisis in Europe, p. 26
Primary Source: War Dispatch from Ernie Pyle, p. 30
American Lives: George S. Patton, p. 36

READING STUDY GUIDE, p. 179

ACCESS FOR STUDENTS ACQUIRING ENGLISH
Guided Reading (Spanish), p. 197
Geography Application: Thunderclap (Spanish), p. 201
Outline Map: Crisis in Europe (Spanish), p. 203

SPANISH READING STUDY GUIDE, p. 179

FORMAL ASSESSMENT
Section Quiz, p. 213

ALTERNATIVE ASSESSMENT BOOK
See forms for supporting and scoring alternative activities.

TECHNOLOGY RESOURCES

HUMANITIES TRANSPARENCIES
H24, War and Peace: Flying Fortresses Taking Off, by Peter Hurd

GEOGRAPHY TRANSPARENCIES
G25, Battle of the Bulge

CD-ROM *Our Times*
Grolier Multimedia Encyclopedia
Electronic Library of Primary Sources

VIDEO *American Portfolio: A Videodisc for U.S. History*
user's guide, pp. 219–224, 231–232

INTERNET http://www.mlushistory.com

A second important decision the two leaders made was to accept only the unconditional surrender of the Axis powers. Some historians have criticized this decision, arguing that it led Germany and Japan to fight longer and more desperately than they might otherwise have done. The Allied leaders, however, were united in their belief that "complete victory . . . [was] essential to defend life, liberty, and religious freedom, and to preserve human rights and justice in their own lands as well as in other lands."

THINK THROUGH HISTORY
A. Finding Main Ideas *Why was the defeat of Germany the Allies' top priority?*

A. Answer Hitler was the United States' prime enemy; Stalin needed help in defeating the Germans; the Allies couldn't help the U.S. fight Japan until Germany had been defeated.

By the end of their meeting, Roosevelt and Churchill had formed, in Churchill's words, "a very strong affection, which grew with our years of comradeship." When Churchill reached London, he found a message from the president waiting for him. "It is fun," Roosevelt wrote, "to be in the same decade with you."

THE BATTLE OF THE ATLANTIC After the attack on Pearl Harbor, Hitler ordered submarine raids against ships along America's East Coast. Unprotected American ships proved to be easy targets. In the first four months of 1942, the Germans sank 87 U.S. ships off the Atlantic shore. Seven months into the year, German wolf packs had destroyed a total of 681 Allied ships in the Atlantic. Something had to be done or the war would be lost at sea.

The Allies responded by organizing their cargo ships into convoys, or groups for mutual protection, as they had done in the First World War. The convoys were escorted across the Atlantic by destroyers equipped with sonar for detecting submarines underwater and by airplanes that used radar to spot U-boats on the ocean's surface. With this improved tracking, the Allies were able to find and destroy German U-boats faster than the Germans could build them. In May 1943, Admiral Karl Doenitz, the commander of the German U-boat offensive, reported that his losses had "reached an unbearable height."

At the same time, the United States launched a crash shipbuilding program. Between 1939 and 1940, the United States had built only 102 ships.

Skillbuilder Answer
Place: Sweden, Switzerland, Turkey, Spain, Ireland, Saudi Arabia, Portugal. **Movement:** It positioned them a short distance from Sicily.

GEOGRAPHY SKILLBUILDER
PLACE *Which countries were neutral in 1942?*
MOVEMENT *How did establishing a foothold in North Africa enable the Allies to attack Italy?*

World War II: Europe and Africa, 1942–1943

Axis and Axis controlled
Allies
Neutral countries
Axis forces
Allied forces
Major battles

Nov. 4, 1942
Operation Torch

November 1942
Farthest Axis Advance

May 19, 1943
Axis surrender of North Africa

579

OBJECTIVE
① **INSTRUCT**

The United States and Britain Join Forces

▶ ***Discussing Key Ideas***
- Early in the war, Churchill and Roosevelt agree to make the defeat of Germany the top priority of the Allies.
- Winning the Battle of the Atlantic turns the tide in favor of the Allies in 1943.

IN-DEPTH RESOURCES: UNIT 5
Guided Reading, p. 20

ACCESS FOR STUDENTS ACQUIRING ENGLISH
Guided Reading (Spanish), p. 197

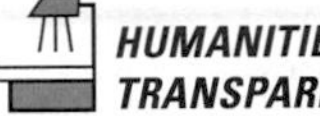
HUMANITIES TRANSPARENCIES
H24, War and Peace: Flying Fortresses Taking Off by Peter Hurd

HISTORY FROM VISUALS
World War II: Europe and Africa, 1942–1943

Reading the Map Remind students to use the key to help them interpret the map. Ask them what the situation of the Soviet Union was in 1942 and 1943. *Most of the Soviet Union west of Moscow was under Nazi control.*

Extension Discuss with students how Stalin was likely to feel about the decision of his Allies to invade North Africa, rather than western Europe, in 1942.

IN-DEPTH RESOURCES: UNIT 5
Outline Map: Crisis in Europe, p. 26

GROLIER MULTIMEDIA ENCYCLOPEDIA
"The World at War"

TEACHING OPTIONS

Teaching Gifted and Talented Students

The Enigma Machine The German Enigma cipher machine was an electromechanical coder that was produced commercially in the 1920s and became the standard code machine of the German military and secret police. Ask one or two mathematically gifted students to research the story of how Alan Turing and other British cryptanalysts unlocked the secrets of the Enigma machine and helped turn the tide of the war in favor of the Allies. Have the students describe the machine and explain their findings to the class.

Making Connections Across the Curriculum

Physics Have a student studying physics do research and report on the critical role of the "huff-duff" (from *HF/DF,* or "high-frequency direction finding") network of radio-transmission detection stations in the Battle of the Atlantic. Using this network, the Allies were able to pinpoint the location of German submarines by triangulating on their radio transmissions. Once the U-boats were located, they were targeted and destroyed by Allied subhunters.

OBJECTIVE

② INSTRUCT

The Eastern Front and the Mediterranean

▶ *Discussing Key Ideas*
- The Battle of Stalingrad marks a turning point in the war on Germany's eastern front.
- The Allies wrest control of North Africa from the Axis Powers in1943.
- The Allied invasion of Italy in 1943 triggers a long and bloody campaign for control of the Italian peninsula.

OUR TIMES
Dispatch by Ernie Pyle from the Sicilian campaign

MORE ABOUT . . .
Stalingrad
Stalingrad was originally known as Tsaritsyn, or "the tsarina's city." Tsaritsyn had been an important defensive stronghold and trading center since it was founded in the late 1500s on the Volga River and along trade routes leading into the Caucasus Mountains. In 1918, Stalin led the defense of the city against White Guard troops, after which the city was renamed Stalingrad in his honor. By the time the Germans attacked in 1942, Stalingrad had grown into an industrial city of nearly half a million people. Of particular importance to the Soviet war effort were the city's steel industry, tractor plant, and gun factory.

By early 1943, though, 140 Liberty ships alone were being produced each month. For the first time in the war, launchings of Allied cargo ships began to outnumber sinkings.

By mid-1943, the tide of the Battle of the Atlantic had turned in the Allies' favor. A happy Churchill reported to the House of Commons that June "was the best month [at sea] from every point of view we have known in the whole 46 months of the war."

THINK THROUGH HISTORY
B. *Making Inferences* *Why had the tide turned in the Battle of the Atlantic by mid-1943?*

B. Answer
The Allies had succeeded in using convoys, with destroyers and planes that sank U-boats; the U.S. had greatly increased production of cargo ships.

The Eastern Front and the Mediterranean

By the summer of 1943, the Allies began to see victories on land as well. The first great turning point came in the Battle of Stalingrad.

THE BATTLE OF STALINGRAD The initial German push into the Soviet Union had stalled in front of Moscow and Leningrad (now St. Petersburg) in early 1942. (See the map on page 579.) With the German war machine running low on oil, Hitler changed his tactics. He sent his Sixth Army south with two objectives: (1) to seize the rich Soviet oil fields in the Caucasus Mountains, and (2) to capture Stalingrad (now Volgograd), a major industrial center on the Volga River. Once the Germans controlled Stalingrad, they could cut the movement of military supplies along the Volga River to Moscow.

The German army confidently approached Stalingrad in midsummer. "To reach the Volga and take Stalingrad is not so difficult for us," one German soldier wrote home. "Victory is not far away." The Luftwaffe—the German air force—prepared the way with nightly bombing raids over the city. Nearly every wooden building in Stalingrad was set ablaze. One night the flames were so bright that it was possible to read a newspaper 40 miles away. The situation looked so desperate that Soviet officers in Stalingrad recommended blowing up its factories and abandoning the city. A furious Stalin ordered them to defend his namesake city no matter what the cost. "Not a step back" became the motto of Stalingrad's defenders.

For three months the Germans pressed in on Stalingrad, conquering it house by house in brutal hand-to-hand combat. By the end of September, they controlled nine-tenths of the city—or what was left of it. A German officer described the devastation in his diary.

A PERSONAL VOICE
Stalingrad is no longer a town. By day it is an enormous cloud of burning, blinding smoke; it is a vast furnace lit by the reflection of the flames. And when night arrives, one of those scorching, howling, bleeding nights, the dogs plunge into the Volga and swim desperately to gain the other bank. The nights of Stalingrad are a terror for them. Animals flee this hell; the hardest stones cannot bear it for long; only man endures.
LIEUTENANT WEINER, quoted in *199 Days: The Battle for Stalingrad*

Dazed, starved, and freezing, these German soldiers were taken prisoner after months of struggle. But they were the lucky ones. More than 230,000 of their comrades died in the Battle of Stalingrad.

TEACHING OPTION

Teaching Less Proficient Readers

Utilizing Different Learning Styles To help less proficient readers understand the sequence of events in the Battle of Stalingrad, you might want to capitalize on visual as well as verbal learning strategies. First, enlarge the map on page 579 or another map of eastern Europe and the Soviet Union and post it in the front of the classroom. Then divide the battle into segments—perhaps summer and fall of 1942 and winter of 1943—and divide the class into the same number of mixed-ability groups. Ask each group to present its battle segment to the class, with some members describing the action orally and others tracing it on the map. Suggest that students follow these steps.

- As a group, discuss the events of the battle as presented on pages 580 and 581.
- Decide which members of the group will do the verbal presentation and which will do the visual.
- Rehearse the presentation to make sure the verbal and visual elements are coordinated.
- Meet with the other groups to make sure all aspects of the battle are covered.

In November, the Soviets launched a massive counterattack. Hitler's military advisers begged him to order a retreat before the Sixth Army was trapped. The Führer, every bit as stubborn as Stalin, refused, shouting, "I won't go back from the Volga." The Germans were ordered to stand and fight to the last man.

The fighting continued as winter turned Stalingrad into a frozen wasteland. "We just lay in our holes and froze, knowing that 24 hours and 48 hours later we should be shivering precisely as we were now," wrote a German soldier, Benno Zieser. "But there was now no hope whatsoever of relief, and that was the worst thing of all." On February 2, 1943, Zieser and some 91,000 other frost-bitten, lice-ridden, half-starved German troops surrendered. They were all that was left of the army of 330,000 that had come to Stalingrad what seemed like a lifetime ago.

THINK THROUGH HISTORY
C. *Synthesizing* *What two key decisions determined the final outcome at Stalingrad?*

C. Answer Stalin's decision to defend the city and Hitler's decision to besiege it no matter what the cost.

In defending Stalingrad, the Soviets lost a total of 1,250,000 soldiers and civilians—more than all American casualties during the entire war. Despite the staggering death toll, the Soviets' victory on the Volga marked a turning point in the war in the east. From that point on, the Soviet army began to move steadily westward toward Germany.

THE NORTH AFRICAN FRONT While the battle of Stalingrad raged, Stalin pressured Britain and America to open a "second front" in western Europe. He argued that an invasion across the English Channel would force Hitler to divert troops from the Soviet front. Churchill and Roosevelt didn't think the Allies had enough troops. Instead, they launched Operation Torch, an invasion of Axis-controlled North Africa, commanded by American general **Dwight D. Eisenhower.** (See the map on page 579.)

In November 1942, some 107,000 Allied troops, the great majority of them Americans, landed in Casablanca, Oran, and Algiers in North Africa. From there they sped eastward, chasing the Afrika Korps led by General Erwin Rommel, the legendary Desert Fox. After months of heavy fighting, the last of the Afrika Korps surrendered in May 1943. British general Harold Alexander sent a message to Churchill, reporting that "All enemy resistance has ceased. We are masters of the North African shores." American war correspondent Ernie Pyle caught the mood of the victorious troops.

THINK THROUGH HISTORY
D. *Summarizing* *What was the outcome of the North African campaign?*

D. Answer The defeat of German troops.

A PERSONAL VOICE

The colossal German surrender has done more for American morale here than anything that could possibly have happened. Winning in battle is like winning at poker or catching a lot of fish. . . . As a result, the hundreds of thousands of Americans in North Africa are now happy men.

ERNIE PYLE, "German Supermen Up Close," May 8, 1943

KEY PLAYER

DWIGHT D. EISENHOWER
1890–1969

When Army Chief of Staff George Marshall chose modest Lieutenant General Dwight David Eisenhower to become the Supreme Commander of U.S. forces in Europe, he knew what he was doing: people liked Ike. "He looks sort of like the guys you know at home," observed an American soldier.

More important, Eisenhower had an uncommon ability to work with all kinds of people, even competitive and temperamental allies. After V-E Day, a grateful Marshall wrote to Ike, saying, "You have been selfless in your actions, always sound and tolerant in your judgments and altogether admirable in the courage and wisdom of your military decisions. You have made history, great history for the good of mankind."

THE ITALIAN CAMPAIGN Even before the battle in North Africa was won, Roosevelt, Churchill, and their commanders met in Casablanca to decide where to strike next. The Americans argued that the best approach to victory was to assemble a massive invasion fleet in Britain and to launch it across the English Channel, through France, and into the heart of Germany. Churchill, however, thought it would be safer to first attack Italy, "the soft underbelly of the Axis." The Allies compromised. They would push ahead with plans for the cross-channel invasion; meanwhile, Allied troops would invade Italy.

The Italian campaign got off to a good start with the capture of Sicily in the summer of 1943. By then, the Italians were weary of war. On July 25, 1943, King Victor Emmanuel III summoned the Fascist dictator and prime minister Benito Mussolini to his palace and stripped him of power. "At this moment," the king

KEY PLAYER
Dwight D. Eisenhower

Critical Thinking: Formulating Historical Questions Have students imagine they are war correspondents interviewing General Eisenhower shortly after the liberation of Paris. What questions would they want to ask him? After students have compiled their questions, pair students to research and answer each other's inquiries.

IN-DEPTH RESOURCES: UNIT 5
Primary Source: War Dispatch of Ernie Pyle, p. 30

MORE ABOUT . . .
The Last Letters from Stalingrad

In January 1943, the last Nazi plane flew out of Stalingrad. Its cargo included seven bags of soldiers' letters, none of which was delivered. Instead the army seized the letters, hoping to use them to demonstrate soldiers' support for Hitler's regime. Most letters were hardly supportive, however, and they were buried in German army archives until 1954. Here are some excerpts:

"Around me everything is collapsing, a whole army is dying, day and night are on fire. . . . I don't know much about war. . . . But I know this much: the other side would never show such a lack of understanding for its men."

"I was shocked when I saw the map. . . . Hitler has left us in the lurch. If the airfield is still in our possession, this letter may still get out. . . . When Stalingrad has fallen, you'll hear and read it. And then you'll know that I shall not come back."

TEACHING OPTION

Making Connections Across Time

Stalingrad Then and Now The Battle of Stalingrad left that city empty and in ruins. In May 1943, just four months after the German surrender, rebuilding began. By September, about 210,000 people were once again living in Stalingrad. By the time World War II ended, the city's industrial capacity had returned to 90 percent of its prewar level. Stalingrad was renamed Volgograd in 1961, eight years after the death of Stalin. Today Volgograd is one of Russia's major industrial centers, with shipyards, oil refineries, steel and aluminum mills, and a population of more than a million people.

While the ruins left by the Battle of Stalingrad have long been rebuilt, reminders of that conflict still appear from time to time on the plains around the city in the form of bleached human bones. These are the last remains of German soldiers who froze to death in the cruel winter of 1942–1943 and, in the confusion of war, were never properly buried.

OBJECTIVE

③ **INSTRUCT**

The Allies Liberate Europe

▶ ***Discussing Key Ideas***

- D-Day marks the beginning of the Allied advance into Germany.
- The Battle of the Bulge is Germany's last effort to avoid defeat and force a negotiated peace.
- Allied troops liberate Nazi death camps in Poland and Germany, finding nightmarish horrors.
- A week after a defeated Hitler commits suicide, Germany surrenders unconditionally to the Allies, and the war in Europe ends.

IN-DEPTH RESOURCES: UNIT 5
Geography Application: Thunderclap, p. 24

HISTORY FROM VISUALS

Normandy Invasions, June 6, 1944

Reading the Map Instruct students to first look at the small inset map on page 582, which shows the overall location and plan of the D-Day invasions. Then have them examine the large map, which shows the movements of specific invasion forces.

Extension Why might General Eisenhower have invaded France at Normandy, rather than at Calais, which was closer to Great Britain? *Possible Response: The wide expanse of beach at Normandy allowed for a convergence of troops from several British bases on multiple landing points in France.*

told *Il Duce,* "you are the most hated man in Italy." As he left the palace, Mussolini was arrested, and Italians began celebrating the end of the war.

But their cheers were premature. Hitler responded by seizing control of Italy, reinstalling Mussolini as its leader, and ordering German troops to dig in and hold firm. It took 18 months of miserable fighting in the mud and mountains for the Allies to drive the Germans from Italian soil. One of the hardest battles the Allies encountered in Europe was fought less than 40 miles from Rome. This battle, "Bloody Anzio," lasted four months—until the end of May 1944—and left about 25,000 Allied and 30,000 Axis soldiers dead. In this grim struggle, the Allies were aided by 50,000 Italian partisans—members of underground resistance movements. The partisans harassed the Germans by cutting telephone wires, derailing trains, and dynamiting bridges and roads.

On April 28, 1945, partisans who had ambushed a Nazi convoy found Mussolini disguised as a German soldier in one of the trucks. The next day, they shot *Il Duce* and hung his body in a Milan square. At the time of his arrest in 1943, Mussolini had prophetically described his own fate: "From dust to power and from power back to dust."

E. Answer The taking of Italy by the Allies, tens of thousands of deaths, Mussolini's assassination.

THINK THROUGH HISTORY
E. *Recognizing Effects* *What were the results of the Italian campaign?*

The Allies Liberate Europe

As Allied troops pushed northward through Italy, the Soviet army moved westward into Poland. Meanwhile, in England, General Eisenhower organized Operation Overlord, the planned invasion of Hitler's "fortress Europe."

D-DAY For two years the United States and Britain had been building an invasion force of ships, landing craft, and nearly 3 million troops to attack Axis forces on the other side of the English Channel. Eisenhower hoped to take the Axis by surprise and pinpointed the relatively lightly fortified Normandy peninsula as the focus of

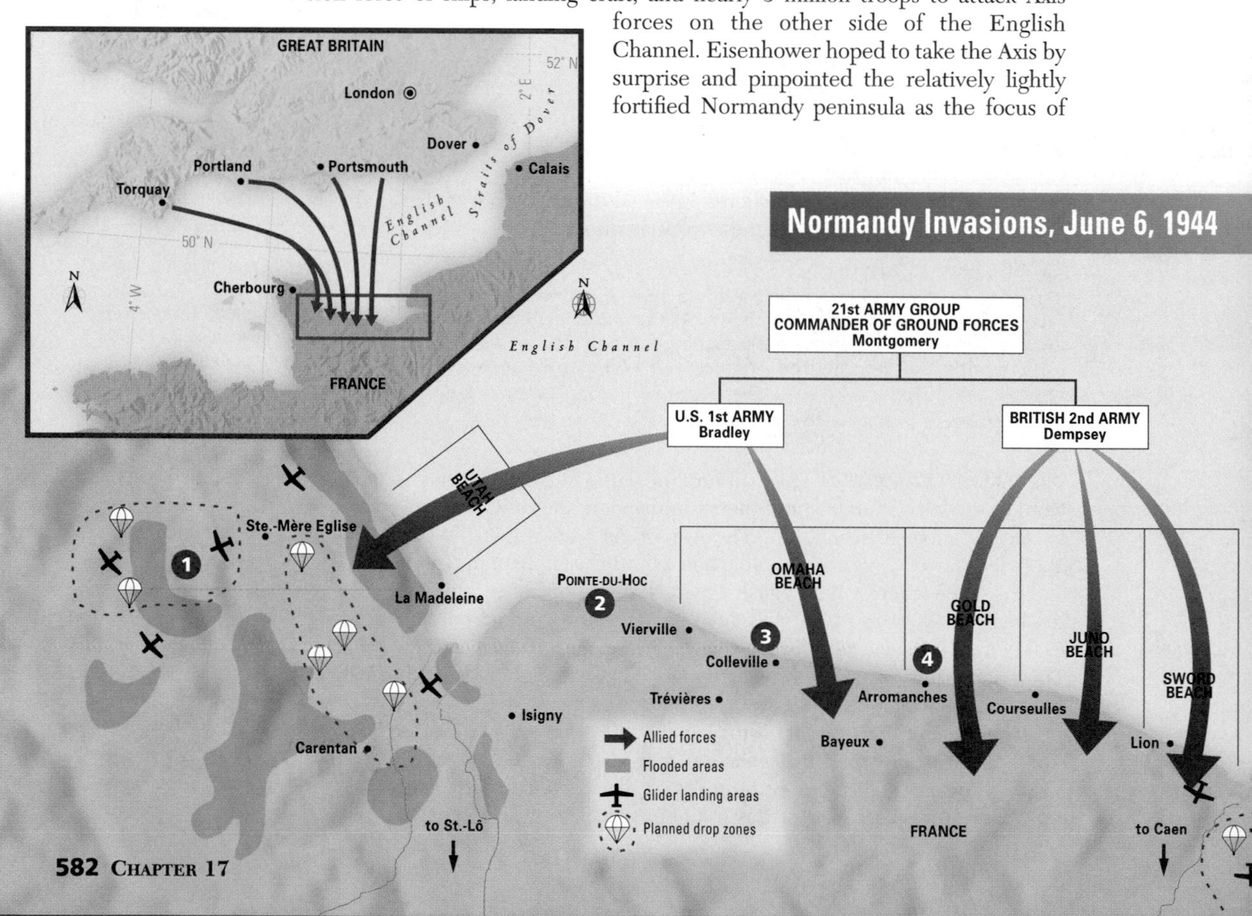

TEACHING OPTION

Making Connections Across Time

The Parachute World War II was the first war in which parachutes were used extensively for a variety of purposes, including landing troops and supplies in isolated or otherwise inaccessible places. On the night before D-Day, some 10,000 American paratroopers were scattered behind the Normandy beaches. The result, writes historian David Howarth, was a "gigantic . . . game of hide-and-seek" in which "the Americans knew what was happening, but few of them knew where they were; the Germans knew where they were, but none of them knew what was happening."

After World War II, parachuting, or skydiving, emerged as a popular sport. Early parachuting competitions were limited to accuracy in landing. Later, as skydivers learned to control their bodies in free fall, they added style events that involved performing aerobatic maneuvers before opening their parachutes. In the most popular form of competition, teams of skydivers form geometric patterns, racing to make as many patterns as they can. Today, teams from more than 30 countries participate in world skydiving championships.

the assault. To make reinforcement of the German forces more difficult once the invasion began, the Allies bombed northern France's supply routes—roads, bridges, and rail lines—for a month and a half before the planned assault.

D-Day, the day of the invasion, had originally been set for June 5, but bad weather forced a delay. Banking on a forecast for clearing skies, Eisenhower gave the go-ahead for the next day—and June 6, 1944, became a day that will live in history.

Three divisions parachuted down behind German lines during the night, and British, American, and Canadian troops fought their way ashore at five points along the 60-mile stretch of beach. With 156,000 troops, 4,000 landing craft, 600 warships, and 11,000 planes, it was the largest land-sea-air operation in history. Despite the massive air and sea bombardment by the Allies before the invasion, German retaliation was brutal, particularly at Omaha Beach. "People were yelling, screaming, dying, running on the beach, equipment was flying everywhere, men were bleeding to death, crawling, lying everywhere, firing coming from all directions," soldier Felix Branham wrote of the scene there. "We dropped down behind anything that was the size of a golf ball."

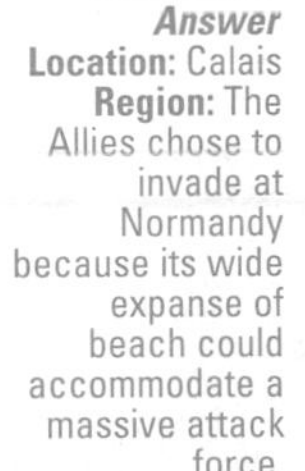
Skillbuilder Answer
Location: Calais
Region: The Allies chose to invade at Normandy because its wide expanse of beach could accommodate a massive attack force.

Despite heavy casualties, the Allies held the beachheads. Within a month, they had landed a million troops, 567,000 tons of supplies, and 170,000 vehicles in France. On July 25, General Omar Bradley unleashed massive air and land bombardment against the enemy at St.-Lô, giving General **George Patton** and his Third army the gap they needed to advance. On August 23, they reached the Seine River south of Paris. Two days later, French resistance troops and American troops liberated the French capital from four years of German

Men of the 1st Airlanding Brigade load a jeep into a glider. Cheap, easy to make, and noiseless in the air, gliders were a key part of the Allied attack.

Prior to the full-scale invasion, 225 U.S. Rangers scaled the 100-foot cliffs at Pointe-du-Hoc to knock out the massive German guns positioned there.

The first wave of troops to land on Omaha Beach takes shelter behind barriers designed by the Germans and built to keep amphibious craft from landing.

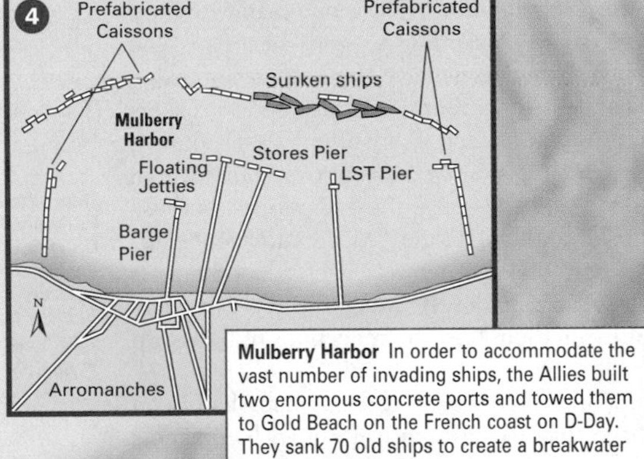

Mulberry Harbor In order to accommodate the vast number of invading ships, the Allies built two enormous concrete ports and towed them to Gold Beach on the French coast on D-Day. They sank 70 old ships to create a breakwater for the artificial harbor.

GEOGRAPHY SKILLBUILDER **LOCATION** ***What other spot on the French coast might the Germans have expected the Allies to attack?*** **REGION** ***What natural geographical features of the region affected the Allied strategy in the D-Day invasion?***

MORE ABOUT . . .
George Patton

George S. Patton is considered one of the greatest United States generals of World War II, but also one of the most controversial. His reckless, outspoken manner gained him both admirers and critics. In 1942 and 1943, Patton led American troops in Morocco, Tunisia, and Sicily. In Sicily, while touring an evacuation hospital, the hotheaded general provoked enormous criticism when he slapped a shell-shocked soldier and called him "yellow." Patton later publicly apologized for the incident.

Patton's career peaked when he was given command of the Third Army for Operation Overlord. In a campaign marked by ruthless drive and a brilliant disregard for classic military strategy, Patton quickly led his troops through the German lines at Normandy and then across France into Germany. His toughness on his enemies, as well as his own troops, led his admirers to call him "Old Blood and Guts."

ELECTRONIC LIBRARY OF PRIMARY SOURCES
from Instructions to the Third United States Army by George S. Patton

IN-DEPTH RESOURCES: UNIT 5
American Lives: George S. Patton, p. 36

Block Schedule TEACHING OPTION **Time Needed: 30 Minutes**

Cooperative Activity: Planning a D-Day Memorial Tour

Task: Student groups will research and plan a trip to Great Britain and France to commemorate the Normandy invasions.

Purpose: To help students appreciate the historic significance of D-Day.

Activity: Assign small groups of students to create an itinerary and map for a D-Day memorial tour. The tour plan should include visits to museums, cemeteries, and beaches associated with the D-Day operation. One student might research points of interest, another compile the itinerary, and a third create a map that traces the tour and locates points of interest.

Building a Portfolio: Students who decide to add their D-Day tour itineraries and maps to their portfolios should include a statement indicating their contribution to the project.

ALTERNATIVE ASSESSMENT BOOK
Standards for Evaluating a Cooperative Activity

Standards for Evaluation
D-Day tour plans should . . .

- present a realistic and feasible itinerary of visits to points of interest
- include a map tracing the tour route and locating each point of interest

HISTORICAL SPOTLIGHT

Audie Murphy

Critical Thinking: Distinguishing Fact from Opinion Is it a fact or an opinion that Murphy was the most decorated American soldier of the war? *Fact.* Is it a fact or opinion that he was the bravest soldier of the war? Opinion.

MORE ABOUT . . .

The Battle of the Bulge

Hitler committed 250,000 troops to the German counteroffensive in this battle. Among them were 33 English-speaking German commandos who, dressed in American uniforms and driving captured American jeeps and trucks, infiltrated Allied lines and caused great confusion before the deception was discovered. As a result, suspicious American sentries questioned everyone who moved. "Three times I was ordered to prove my identity by cautious GIs," recalled American general Omar Bradley. "The first time by identifying Springfield as the capital of Illinois (my questioner held out for Chicago); the second by locating the guard between the center and tackle on a line of scrimmage; the third time by naming the then-current spouse of a blonde [movie star] named Betty Grable. Grable stopped me, but the sentry did not. Pleased at having stumped me, he nevertheless passed me on."

GEOGRAPHY TRANSPARENCIES

G25, Battle of the Bulge

occupation. Patton announced this joyous event to his commander in a message that read, "Dear Ike: Today I spat in the Seine."

By September 1944, the Allies had freed France, Belgium, Luxembourg, and much of the Netherlands. This good news—and the American people's desire not to "change horses in midstream"—helped elect Roosevelt to an unprecedented fourth term in November, along with his new moderate running mate, Senator **Harry S. Truman**.

HISTORICAL SPOTLIGHT

AUDIE MURPHY

Near the end of the Second World War, Audie Murphy became famous as the most decorated American soldier of the war. He received 24 medals from the United States—including the Congressional Medal of Honor. He was also awarded three medals by France and one more by Belgium.

Born in Kingston, Texas, Murphy enlisted in the army in 1942. He served in North Africa and Europe, and in 1944 he rose to the rank of second lieutenant. His most impressive act of bravery occurred in January 1945 near Colmar, France, when in the midst of a furious German attack, he jumped onto a burning tank destroyer and killed about 50 Axis troops with its machine gun. Although wounded in the leg, he rallied his troops to retake the ground the Germans had gained earlier in the day.

THE BATTLE OF THE BULGE In October 1944, Americans captured their first German town, Aachen. Hitler responded with a surprising counterattack. He ordered his troops to break through the Allied lines and to recapture the Belgian port of Antwerp. This bold move, the Führer hoped, would disrupt the enemy's supply lines and demoralize the Allies.

On December 16, under cover of dense fog, eight German tank divisions broke through weak American defenses along an 80-mile front. The resulting dent in the Allied lines gave this desperate last-ditch offensive its name, the **Battle of the Bulge.** As the Germans swept westward, they captured 120 American GIs near Malmédy. Elite German troops—the SS troopers—herded the prisoners into a field and mowed them down with machine guns and pistols. Private Homer Ford was one of the 43 who somehow survived.

A PERSONAL VOICE

Men were lying around moaning and crying. When the Germans came over, they would say, "Is he breathing?" and would either shoot or hit [him] with the butt of their guns. . . . After they fired at us, I . . . could feel the blood oozing out. I was [lying] in the snow, and I got wet and started to shiver, and I was afraid they would see me shivering, but they didn't.

HOMER FORD, quoted in *The GI War*

American troops led by Brigadier General Anthony McAuliffe made a heroic stand at the Belgian town of Bastogne. Surrounded and badly outnumbered, McAuliffe received a surrender demand from the Germans. His reply was just one word: "Nuts!"

The initial success of the German offensive was due mainly to their ability to keep the Allies off guard. According to some historians, the Allies unknowingly helped the Germans achieve this goal by not taking intelligence reports seriously. Since September, British code breakers had been deciphering messages indicating that Hitler was planning a major campaign. Military strategists—not taking into account whom they were dealing with—chose not to believe these messages, because they thought that such a move would be insane. "Allied intelligence had committed the most grievous sin of which [an intelligence operation] is capable," observed the historian Charles B. MacDonald. "They had looked in a mirror for the enemy and seen there only the reflections of their own intentions."

THINK THROUGH HISTORY

F. *Analyzing Causes* *Why was the German offensive in the Battle of the Bulge initially successful?*

F. Answer It caught the Allies off guard.

The battle raged for a month. When it was over, the Germans had been pushed back and little seemed to have changed. But, in fact, things had taken a decisive turn. The Germans had lost 120,000 troops, 600 tanks and assault guns, and 1,600 planes in the Battle of the Bulge—men and weapons they could not replace. From that point on, the Nazis could do little but retreat.

LIBERATION OF THE DEATH CAMPS Meanwhile, Allied troops pressed eastward into the German heartland, and the Soviet army pushed westward across Poland toward Berlin. Soviet troops were the first to come upon one of the Nazi death camps, in July 1944. As the Soviets drew near a camp called Majdanek in Poland, SS guards worked feverishly to bury and burn all evidence of their

TEACHING OPTIONS

Making Connections Across the Curriculum

Language Arts: Creative Writing Before Jews were gassed at the death camps, the SS confiscated their money and belongings. Among other things, this pillage yielded mountains of shoes. Some of those shoes were distributed to inmates of other concentration camps. Some were burned by the SS. But some shoes survived to be displayed in Holocaust museums and memorials in Germany and Israel and in the United States Holocaust Museum in Washington, D.C. Ask students to write a poem or short story based on the history of one of these confiscated shoes.

Making Connections Across Cultures

Multicultural Liberation Forces Among the soldiers entering the concentration camps were Japanese Americans who had left their families in internment camps at home. African-American units also helped liberate the German camps. "Something happened when I walked through the gates," recalled African-American soldier Leon Bass. "I came into that camp an angry black soldier. Angry at my country and justifiably so. . . . But I came to realize that human suffering is not just relegated to me and mine. I now knew that human suffering could touch us all."

crimes. But they ran out of time. When the Soviets entered Majdanek, they found a thousand "living corpses," the world's largest crematorium, and a storehouse containing 800,000 shoes. "This is not a concentration camp," reported a stunned Soviet war correspondent, "it is a gigantic murder plant." The Americans who later liberated death camps in Germany were equally overwhelmed.

> A PERSONAL VOICE
> We started smelling a terrible odor and suddenly we were at the concentration camp at Landsberg. Forced the gate and faced hundreds of starving prisoners. . . . We saw emaciated men whose thighs were smaller than wrists, many had bones sticking out thru their skin. . . . Also we saw hundreds of burned and naked bodies. . . . That evening I wrote to my wife that "For the first time I truly realized the evil of Hitler and why this war had to be waged."
>
> ROBERT T. JOHNSON, quoted in *Voices: Letters from World War II*

UNCONDITIONAL SURRENDER By April 25, 1945, the Soviet army had stormed Berlin. As Soviet shells burst overhead, the city panicked. "Hordes of soldiers stationed in Berlin deserted and were shot on sight or hanged from the nearest tree," wrote Claus Fuhrmann, a Berlin clerk. "On their chests they had placards reading, 'We betrayed the Führer.'"

In his underground headquarters in Berlin, Hitler prepared for the end. On April 29, he married Eva Braun, his longtime companion. The same day, he wrote out his last address to the German people. In it he blamed the Jews for starting the war and his generals for losing it. "I myself and my wife choose to die in order to escape the disgrace of . . . capitulation [surrender]," he said. "I die with a happy heart aware of the immeasurable deeds of our soldiers at the front." The next day Hitler shot himself while his new wife swallowed poison. In accordance with Hitler's orders, the two bodies were carried outside, soaked with gasoline, and burned.

The historian Alan Bullock later wrote of the Führer's extraordinary farewell, "Word for word, Hitler's final address to the German nation could be taken from almost any of his early speeches of the 1920s or from the pages of *Mein Kampf*. Twenty-odd years had changed and taught him nothing."

A week later, General Eisenhower accepted the unconditional surrender of the Third Reich. On May 8, 1945, the Allies celebrated **V-E Day**—Victory in Europe Day. The first part of the war was finally over.

G. Answer Because of their endurance and dedication, the entry of American troops into the war, the help of partisans, and the Nazis' massive loss of equipment and troops in the Soviet Union.

THINK THROUGH HISTORY
G. *Analyzing Causes* *Why were the Allies finally able to win the war in Europe?*

New Yorkers celebrate V-E Day with a massive party that began in Times Square and went on for days at sites throughout the city.

Section 2 Assessment

1. TERMS & NAMES
Identify:
- Dwight D. Eisenhower
- D-Day
- George Patton
- Harry S. Truman
- Battle of the Bulge
- V-E Day

2. FOLLOWING CHRONOLOGICAL ORDER
Create a time line of the major events influencing the fighting in Europe and North Africa.

event one — event two — event three — event four

Write a paragraph indicating how any two of these events are related.

3. MAKING PREDICTIONS
What do you think might have happened if the Nazis had defeated the Soviets at Stalingrad?

THINK ABOUT
- the military significance of a German victory
- the psychological impact of a Soviet loss

4. FORMING OPINIONS Do you agree with the decision by Roosevelt and Churchill to require unconditional surrender by the Axis powers? Why or why not?

THINK ABOUT
- the advantages of defeating a foe decisively
- the advantages of ending a war quickly
- how other conflicts, such as the Civil War and World War I, ended

MORE ABOUT . . .
Survivors of Concentration Camps

Israel Lau was just eight years old when an American Jewish chaplain, smiling and weeping, embraced him in Buchenwald on April 11, 1945. "'How old are you, my child?' he asked. 'What difference does it make. I'm older than you,' I answered. 'Why do you think you are older than me?' he asked. 'Because you cry and laugh as a child. And I stopped laughing and I can't even cry. So I must be older than you.'"

ASSESS & RETEACH

Section 2 Assessment
Divide the class in half. Have the groups compete to answer questions 1 and 2 in the shortest time with the fewest errors. Then have the groups work on questions 3 and 4 cooperatively.

Self-Assessment
Have students write short narratives following a fictional American soldier through the events of World War II in North Africa and Europe between 1942 and 1944.

Section Quiz
FORMAL ASSESSMENT
Section Quiz, p. 213

Reteach
Use the maps on pages 579 and 582–583 to review the events leading up to the liberation of Europe during World War II.

CLOSE

More than three years after Roosevelt and Churchill agreed to make the defeat of Nazi Germany the Allies' top priority, the Third Reich surrendered.

ANSWERS

1. TERMS & NAMES
Dwight D. Eisenhower, p .581
D-Day, p. 583
George Patton, p. 583
Harry S. Truman, p. 584
Battle of the Bulge, p. 584
V-E Day, p. 585

2. FOLLOWING CHRONOLOGICAL ORDER
Possible Answers:
December 22, 1941: Churchill and Roosevelt meet.
February 2, 1943: Germans surrender at Stalingrad.
May 1943: Last of Afrika Korps surrenders.
May 1944: Battle of Anzio ends.
June 6, 1944: Allies invade Normandy.
July 1944: Russians liberate first death camp.
January 1945: Germany loses Battle of the Bulge.
April 1945: Hitler commits suicide.
May 8, 1945: Germany surrenders.

3. MAKING PREDICTIONS
Possible Response: Students might argue that even if the Germans had captured Stalingrad, their heavy losses would have led to a Soviet triumph. Others might argue that a German victory would have allowed Germany to concentrate on its western front and achieve greater victories in Europe.

4. FORMING OPINIONS
Possible Response: **Agree**—Hitler had to be crushed completely so that he would not have the opportunity to rebuild his army. **Disagree**—The sooner the bloodshed stopped, the fewer Allied soldiers would be killed.

Section 3 Overview

OBJECTIVES

1 To identify key turning points in the war in the Pacific.
2 To explain the development of and the debates concerning use of the atomic bomb.
3 To describe the challenges faced by the Allies in building a just and lasting postwar peace.

SKILLBUILDER

- Understanding geography: movement, region, p. 588

CRITICAL THINKING

- Comparing, p. 587
- Drawing conclusions, pp. 589, 590, 593
- Analyzing issues, p. 591
- Summarizing, pp. 592, 593
- Analyzing motives, p. 593
- Forming opinions, p. 593

FOCUS & MOTIVATE

5-MINUTE WARM-UP

Using Sequential Order
To understand the course of the war in the Pacific, have students look at the map on page 588 and answer these questions.

1. List the major battles of the war in the Pacific chronologically.
2. What was the last battle fought before the dropping of the atomic bomb on Hiroshima?

WARM-UP TRANSPARENCY 17

Starting with the Student

- Have students study the Pacific region on a world map or globe. About how much of the earth does the Pacific Ocean cover? *One-third.*
- What does the vastness of this region suggest about fighting a war in the Pacific? What kind of war would it be? *Possible Response: A war fought on many islands at once or on one island after another over an extended period of time.*

3 The War in the Pacific

LEARN ABOUT U.S. strategy in the Pacific
TO UNDERSTAND how the Allies defeated Japan and ended World War II.

TERMS & NAMES
- Douglas MacArthur
- Chester Nimitz
- kamikaze
- Manhattan Project
- J. Robert Oppenheimer
- Hiroshima
- Nagasaki
- Yalta Conference
- United Nations (UN)
- Nuremberg trials

ONE AMERICAN'S STORY

The writer William Manchester left college after Pearl Harbor to join the marines. He was so skinny that he had to stuff himself with bananas and milk to pass the recruits' weight test. Manchester says that, as a child, his "horror of violence had been so deep-seated that I had been unable to trade punches with other boys." On a Pacific island, he would have to confront that horror the first time he killed a man in face-to-face combat. Manchester's target was a Japanese sniper firing on his buddies from a fisherman's shack.

American soldiers on Leyte help retake the Philippine Islands in late 1944.

A PERSONAL VOICE

My mouth was dry, my legs quaking, and my eyes out of focus. Then my vision cleared. I unlocked the safety of my Colt [handgun], kicked the door with my right foot, and leapt inside. My horror returned. I . . . saw him as a blur to my right. . . . My first shot missed him, embedding itself in the straw wall, but the second caught him dead on in the femoral artery. A wave of blood gushed from the wound. . . . He dipped a hand in it and listlessly smeared his cheek red. . . . I kept firing, wasting government property. . . . His eyes glazed over. Almost immediately a fly landed on his left eyeball. . . . A feeling of disgust and self-hatred clotted darkly in my throat, gagging me.

WILLIAM MANCHESTER, *Goodbye Darkness: A Memoir of the Pacific War*

The Pacific war was a savage conflict fought with raw courage on heaving seas, barren beaches, and jungle-covered hillsides. Few who took part in that fearsome struggle would return home unchanged.

The Allies Stem the Japanese Tide

While the Allies agreed that the defeat of the Nazis was their first priority, the United States did not wait until V-E Day to move against Japan. Fortunately, the Japanese attack on Pearl Harbor in 1941 had missed the Pacific Fleet's submarines. Even more importantly, the attack had missed the fleet's aircraft carriers, which were at sea at the time. In addition, almost all of the sunk or damaged ships were repaired and returned to service.

JAPANESE ADVANCES In the first six months after Pearl Harbor, the Japanese conquered an empire that dwarfed Hitler's Third Reich. On the Asian mainland, Japanese troops overran Hong Kong, French Indochina, Malaya, Burma, Thailand, and half of China. They also swept south and east across the Pacific, conquering Formosa, the Dutch East Indies, Guam, Wake Island, the Solomon Islands, and countless other dots in the ocean, including two islands in the Aleutian chain, which were part of Alaska.

SECTION 3 RESOURCES

PRINT RESOURCES

IN-DEPTH RESOURCES: UNIT 5
Guided Reading, p. 21
Primary Source: The Bombing of Nagasaki, p. 31

READING STUDY GUIDE, p. 181

ACCESS FOR STUDENTS ACQUIRING ENGLISH
Guided Reading (Spanish), p. 198

SPANISH READING STUDY GUIDE, p. 181

FORMAL ASSESSMENT
Section Quiz, p. 214

ALTERNATIVE ASSESSMENT BOOK
See forms for supporting and scoring alternative activities.

TECHNOLOGY RESOURCES

CD-ROM *Our Times*
Grolier Multimedia Encyclopedia
Electronic Library of Primary Sources

VIDEO *American Portfolio: A Videodisc for U.S. History*
user's guide, pp. 216–219, 224–226, 231–232

INTERNET http://www.mlushistory.com

In the Philippines, 80,000 American and Filipino troops commanded by General **Douglas MacArthur** held out against 200,000 invading Japanese troops for four months on the Bataan Peninsula and for another month on the island of Corregidor at the entrance to Manila Bay. Hunger, disease, and bombardments took a terrible toll—14,000 killed and 48,000 wounded. Finally MacArthur was ordered to abandon the Philippines. As he left, he pledged to the many thousands of his men who did not make it out, "I shall return."

An American LCI (Landing Craft Infantry) fires shells in an assault on the Philippines.

Japan's admirals and generals were dazzled by their success. Not only had they surpassed the Allies militarily, but they had also destroyed the myth of white supremacy in Asia. Emperor Hirohito, who had suddenly acquired 150 million new subjects spread over one-seventh of the globe, wondered, on the other hand, if "the fruits of war are tumbling into our mouths almost too quickly."

U.S. RETALIATION On April 18, 1942, 16 B-52 bombers, led by Colonel James Doolittle, took off from the aircraft carrier *Hornet.* Hours later they swept in from the sea over Tokyo and four other Japanese cities, blasting factories, steel mills, oil tanks, and other military targets before vanishing. The next day America awoke to headlines proclaiming "Tokyo Bombed! Doolittle Do'od It." Seeing the U.S. pull off a Pearl Harbor–style air raid over Japan lifted Americans' sunken spirits. At the same time, it dampened spirits in Japan. "We started to doubt," recalled a Japanese civilian later, "that we were invincible."

Early in May, a combined American and Australian fleet intercepted a Japanese strike force aimed at Australia. This confrontation, the Battle of the Coral Sea, established a new type of naval warfare. All the fighting was done by carrier-based airplanes; the opposing ships never saw one another or exchanged gunfire. The Allies lost more ships than the Japanese, so that the Japanese were able to declare victory. But the real triumph belonged to the Allies. By the end of the battle, the Japanese fleet was too short of fuel to continue on to Australia. For the first time since Pearl Harbor, a Japanese invasion had been stopped and turned back.

THE BATTLE OF MIDWAY In June, Admiral **Chester Nimitz,** the commander of American naval forces in the Pacific, learned from intercepted messages that a Japanese invasion force of well over 110 ships—the largest assemblage of naval power in history—was heading toward Midway, a strategic island in the Pacific. From there, the invasion force planned to move on to Hawaii to finish the destruction of American naval power started at Pearl Harbor.

Even though he was outnumbered four to one in ships and planes, Nimitz prepared a surprise reception for the Japanese at Midway. As the enemy drew near, he ordered his carrier planes into the air again and again, with orders "to inflict maximum damage on the enemy." The results were devastating. By the end of the Battle of Midway, the Japanese had lost four irreplaceable aircraft carriers, a cruiser, and 322 planes. In the words of a Japanese official, at Midway the Americans had "avenged Pearl Harbor."

A. Answer *Both were surprise naval attacks that resulted in substantial damage to the enemy's fleet.*

THINK THROUGH HISTORY
A. ***Comparing*** *In what ways were the American victory at Midway and the Japanese triumph at Pearl Harbor alike?*

ISLAND HOPPING The Pacific war was one of vast distances. Japanese troops were dug in on hundreds of islands scattered across thousands of miles of ocean. To storm each one, MacArthur argued, would have been "a long and costly effort." Instead, he wanted to leapfrog, or bypass, Japanese strongholds. MacArthur seized less-well-fortified islands, built

HISTORICAL SPOTLIGHT

NAVAJO CODE TALKERS

On each of the Pacific islands that American GIs stormed in World War II, the Japanese heard a "strange language gurgling" in their radio headsets. The code seemed to have Asian overtones, but it baffled everyone who heard it. In fact, the language was Navajo, which was spoken only in the American Southwest and had no alphabet or other written symbols. Its "hiddenness" made it a perfect candidate for a code language.

Though the Navajo had no words for combat terms, they developed terms such as *chicken hawk* for airplane and *war chief* for commanding general, and 200 Navajo were recruited into the Marine Corps as code talkers. Their primary duty was transmitting telephone and radio messages.

Throughout the Pacific campaign—from Midway to Iwo Jima—the code talkers were considered indispensable to the war effort. They finally received national recognition at a ceremony in Chicago in 1969.

OBJECTIVE
① INSTRUCT

The Allies Stem the Japanese Tide

▶***Starting with the Student*** Have students begin a time line of events in the Pacific war, which they will fill in as they read Section 3. Initial entries might look like this:

1942
January–April
Japan conquers Formosa, Guam, the Philippines, and other Pacific islands.

May
Allies turn back Japan in Battle of the Coral Sea.

▶***Discussing Key Ideas***
- Japan conquers 150 million people.
- Americans surprise Japan in an air raid over Tokyo and in the Battle of the Coral Sea.
- The Battle of Midway halts Japan's westward expansion.
- The United States adopts an "island-hopping" strategy against Japan.

IN-DEPTH RESOURCES: UNIT 5
Guided Reading, p. 21

ACCESS FOR STUDENTS ACQUIRING ENGLISH
Guided Reading (Spanish), p. 198

HISTORICAL SPOTLIGHT
Navajo Code Talkers
Critical Thinking: Hypothesizing Ask students to speculate why it took so long for the Navajo Code Talkers to receive national recognition.
Possible Response: Because of their minority status and general invisibility in mainstream American life.

TEACHING OPTIONS

Making Connections Across the Curriculum

Writing Divide the class in half and designate one group as war correspondents for an American newspaper and the other as correspondents for the Japanese press. Ask both groups to write brief news accounts of the Battle of the Coral Sea. Have each group choose a representative to "broadcast" its report to the class. Discuss with students differences between the two accounts. Why do they think reports of the same events differ? What consequences do they think such differences have for achieving peace and understanding among warring nations?

Teaching Gifted and Talented Students

Researching the Bataan Death March Have gifted students research the Bataan Death March. Then have them compile a summary flow chart of major events, indicating their causes and effects. Based on their flow chart, ask them to propose a film treatment for a motion picture based on those events. Challenge the students to present a balanced view of this 60-mile trek, in which about half of the prisoners rode in trucks in relative comfort, while others were forced to walk and suffered inhumane tortures. Have them present their film concept to the class.

HISTORY FROM VISUALS

War in the Pacific and in Europe

Critical Thinking: Synthesizing Point out to students the battles that were fought simultaneously on two fronts—in Europe and in the Pacific—between 1941 and 1945. Discuss the strategic and logistic problems this two-front war presented for the Allies.

HISTORY FROM VISUALS

World War II: Japan's Defeat, 1942–1945

Reading the Map Help students understand that the large map is a detailed version of the area enclosed in the square on the globe. Have them trace the extent of Japan's empire, outlined by the red line. Then have them follow the arrow-tipped blue lines that show the American forces' island hopping.

Extension Ask students what special problems Japan faced in defending its vast, widespread empire. *Possible Responses: Long supply lines, troops spread thinly over many islands, dependence on air and sea transport, difficulty of predicting where the enemy would strike next.*

War in the Pacific and in Europe

PACIFIC
- Dec 1941: U.S. declares war on Japan.
- Apr 1942: U.S. surrenders in the Philippines.
- May 1942: Allies turn back Japanese fleet in Battle of the Coral Sea.
- Jun 1942: Allies defeat Japan in Battle of Midway.
- Aug 1942: U.S. marines land on Guadalcanal.

1941 | Apr | Jun | Dec | 1942 | Apr | May | Jun | Aug | Nov | 1943 | Feb | May

EUROPE
- Apr 1941: Germany invades Greece and Yugoslavia.
- Jun 1941: Germany invades the Soviet Union.
- Dec 1941: Germany and Italy declare war on the United States.
- Aug 1942: Hitler orders attack on Stalingrad.
- Nov 1942: Allies land in North Africa.
- Feb 1943: Germans surrender at Stalingrad.
- May 1943: Axis forces surrender in Africa.

airfields on them, and then used air power to cut supply lines to enemy troops in the area. As a result, a Japanese intelligence officer later reported, "Our strong points were gradually starved out."

The Americans' first land offensive of the war began in August 1942, when 19,000 marines stormed Guadalcanal in the Solomon Islands. By the time the Japanese finally abandoned Guadalcanal six months later, they called it the Island of Death. To war correspondent Ralph Martin and the GIs who fought there, nearly a third of whom became battle casualties, it was simply "hell."

Skillbuilder Answer
Movement: Guam.
Region: It made preparing and executing battle plans very difficult.

A PERSONAL VOICE

Hell was red furry spiders as big as your fist, giant lizards as long as your leg, leeches falling from trees to suck blood, armies of white ants with bites of fire, scurrying scorpions inflaming any flesh they touched, enormous rats and bats everywhere, and rivers with waiting crocodiles. Hell was the sour, foul smell of the squishy jungle, humidity that rotted a body within hours, . . . stinking wet heat of dripping rain forests that sapped the strength of any man.

RALPH G. MARTIN, from *The GI War*

Guadalcanal marked Japan's first defeat on land, but not its last. The Americans continued leapfrogging across the Pacific toward Japan, and in October 1944, some 178,000 Allied troops and 738 ships converged on Leyte Island in the Philippines. General MacArthur, who had left the American colony two years earlier, waded ashore and announced, "People of the Philippines: I have returned."

GEOGRAPHY SKILLBUILDER

***MOVEMENT** Which island served as a jumping-off point for several Pacific battles?*

***REGION** How do you think the distances between the Pacific islands affected U.S. naval strategy?*

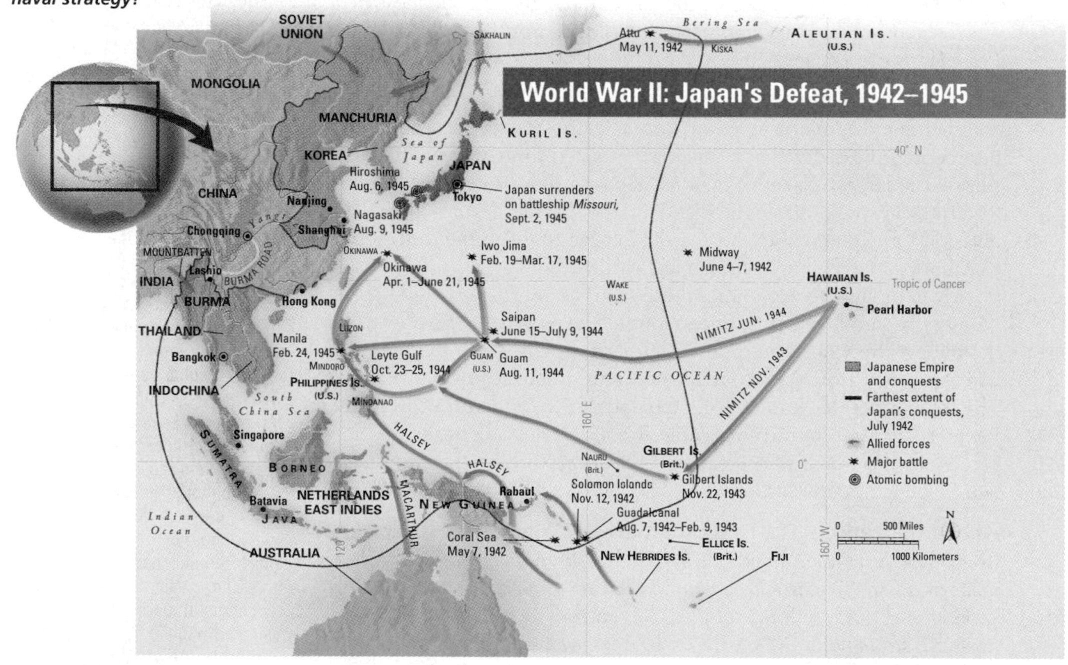

TEACHING OPTION

Making Connections Across Time

Guadalcanal Today From offshore, Guadalcanal looked far more like a South Seas "Isle of Enchantment" than a green hell. The American landing, the first big amphibious assault undertaken by the United States, went remarkably well. On August 7, 1942, approximately 10,000 marines swept ashore virtually unopposed. Convinced that the Americans would quickly tire of jungle warfare, however, the Japanese responded by sending their toughest, best-trained infantry and artillery units to the island. These soldiers seemed to disappear in the jungle, moving silently by day and then screaming out of the darkness in wild suicide attacks by night. This gruesome battle went on for six months. By the time the last enemy sniper was silenced, 24,000 Japanese had perished on Guadalcanal. The American dead numbered 1,752.

Today, Guadalcanal has regained its status as a tropical paradise. Fast-flowing streams cascade down lush green mountains to mangrove swamps on the coast. A population of over 80,000 makes its living mainly from fishing; growing coconuts, fruit, cocoa, and timber; and working the gold and silver found in the island's rivers.

Jul 1943 Sep | 1944 May Jun Jul Aug Oct Dec | 1945 Mar Apr May Jun Aug Sep | 1946

- Jul: Allies invade Sicily.
- Sep: Italy secretly surrenders to Allies.
- May: "Bloody Anzio" ends.
- Jun: Allies invade Europe on D-Day.
- Jun: Allies win Battle of the Philippine Sea.
- Jul: Soviets liberate first death camps.
- Aug: Allies liberate Paris.
- Oct: Allies win Battle of Leyte Gulf.
- Dec: Germans attack Allies in Battle of the Bulge.
- Mar: Allies capture Iwo Jima.
- Apr: Italians assassinate Mussolini.
- Apr: Hitler commits suicide.
- May: V-E Day ends the war in Europe.
- Jun: Allies capture Okinawa.
- Aug: U.S. drops atomic bombs on Hiroshima and Nagasaki.
- Sep: Japan surrenders.

The Japanese threw their entire fleet into the battle for Leyte Gulf. They also tested a new tactic, the **kamikaze,** or suicide-plane, attack in which Japanese pilots crashed their bomb-laden planes into Allied ships. (*Kamikaze* means "divine wind" and refers to a legendary typhoon that saved Japan in 1281 by destroying a Mongol invasion.) In the Philippines, 424 kamikaze pilots embarked on suicide missions, sinking 16 ships and damaging another 80.

Japanese kamikaze pilots receive a briefing on the mission that would be their last.

B. Answer After it, the Japanese navy no longer posed a major threat to Allied advances.

THINK THROUGH HISTORY
B. Drawing Conclusions *Why was the Battle of Leyte Gulf so crucial to the Allies?*

Americans watched these terrifying attacks with "a strange admixture of respect and pity" according to Vice Admiral Charles Brown. "You had to admire the devotion to country demonstrated by those pilots," recalled Seaman George Marse. "Yet, when they were shot down, rescued and brought aboard our ship, we were surprised to find the pilots looked like ordinary, scared young men, not the wide-eyed fanatical 'devils' we imagined them to be."

Despite the damage done by the kamikazes, the Battle of Leyte Gulf was a disaster for Japan. In three days of battle, it lost 3 battleships, 4 aircraft carriers, 13 cruisers, and almost 400 planes. From then on, the Imperial Navy played only a minor role in the defense of Japan.

After retaking the Philippines and liberating the American prisoners of war there, the Allies turned to Iwo Jima, an island William Manchester later described as "an ugly, smelly glob of cold lava squatting in a surly ocean." Iwo Jima was critical to the United States as a base from which heavily loaded bombers could reach Japan. It was also perhaps the most heavily defended spot on earth, with 20,700 Japanese troops entrenched in tunnels and caves. More than 6,000 marines died taking this desolate island, the greatest number in any battle in the Pacific to that point. Only 200 Japanese survived. Just one obstacle now stood between the Allies and a final assault on Japan—the island of Okinawa.

The Atomic Bomb Ends the War

Roosevelt did not live to see the final battles of the Pacific war. On April 12, 1945, while posing for a portrait in Warm Springs, Georgia, the president had a stroke and died. That night, Harry S. Truman became the nation's president.

Grieving crowds lined the tracks as the president's body was brought by train back to Washington. Betty Conrad was among the servicewomen who escorted his casket from Union Station to the White House. "The only sound was that of the hoofbeats of the riderless horse and the sobs of mourners," she observed. "The body in the casket was not only our leader but the bodies of all the men and women who had given their lives for freedom. They must not and will not have died in vain."

THE BATTLE FOR OKINAWA As the world mourned Roosevelt's death, an inexperienced Truman began to grapple with his new job as president and commander in chief of the armed forces. By then the war in Europe was winding down. In the Pacific, however, a ferocious battle would soon rage on

MORE ABOUT . . .
Japan's Kamikaze Pilots

At first, young Japanese airmen considered it a great honor to volunteer for suicide missions. The pilots' farewell letters were filled with passionate patriotism. One young man told his family, "Think kindly of me and consider it my good fortune to have done something praiseworthy." Another left this final entry in his diary: "Like cherry blossoms / In the spring / Let us fall / Clean and radiant."

As the kamikaze campaign continued, however, the Allies developed effective tactics to combat the suicide planes. At the same time, fewer and fewer young Japanese volunteered for suicide duty. Even so, before the Japanese surrendered, the kamikaze corps had damaged more than 300 U.S. ships and caused about 15,000 casualties.

OBJECTIVE
② INSTRUCT

The Atomic Bomb Ends the War

▶***Discussing Key Ideas***
- The top-secret Manhattan Project produces the world's first atomic bomb and tests it in July 1945.
- Scientists involved in the project debate how the weapon should be used.
- In August of 1945, President Truman orders the dropping of two atomic bombs on Japan, forcing its unconditional surrender.

TEACHING OPTION

Making Connections Across Cultures

Attitudes Toward Suicide Most Allied sailors who witnessed Japanese kamikaze missions found them shocking, even incomprehensible. Such reactions reflect widespread Western attitudes and beliefs regarding suicide. Suicide was then, and still is, illegal in many American states and in other Western nations and is condemned as a sin by the Roman Catholic Church. Many Westerners see suicide as at best a desperate act of a depressed mind and, at worst a shameful moral failure.

On the other hand, some societies have traditionally honored certain kinds of suicide. In the past, the Japanese respected acts of hara-kiri, a suicide ritual in which shamed individuals made amends for failure or desertion of duty by disemboweling themselves with a knife. During World War II, Japanese kamikaze pilots considered it an honor to perform their aerial suicide missions.

KEY PLAYER

Douglas MacArthur

Critical Thinking: Synthesizing Ask students to develop their own definition of a hero. Does MacArthur qualify as a hero under that definition? Why or why not? Interested students also might like to research the military career of Darius the Great and evaluate the accuracy of John Gunther's comparison between MacArthur and that ancient leader.

MORE ABOUT . . .

Germany and the Atomic Bomb

Germany came terrifyingly close to developing its own atomic bomb during World War II. In 1939, the German physicist Otto Hahn and his associates became the first scientists to split the uranium atom. German physicists led by Werner Heisenberg attempted to take the next step—creating a rapid chain reaction that would produce an explosion. This effort might have succeeded if Hitler had not decided to cut back on nuclear research and concentrate on Germany's rocketry program. The result was the development of the powerful V-1 and V-2 long-range liquid-fuel rockets, which rained destruction on London and Antwerp, Belgium, late in the war. But as advanced as these rockets were, they did not change the course of the war for Germany.

KEY PLAYER

DOUGLAS MACARTHUR
1880–1964

Douglas MacArthur was too arrogant and prickly to be considered a "regular guy" by his troops. But he was arguably the most brilliant strategist of World War II. For every American soldier killed in his campaigns, the Japanese lost ten.

He was considered a real hero of the war, both by the military and by the prisoners on the Philippines whom he freed. "MacArthur took more territory with less loss of life," observed journalist John Gunther, "than any military commander since Darius the Great [king of Persia, 522–486 B.C.]."

Okinawa, Japan's last defensive outpost. The Japanese unleashed more than 1,900 kamikaze attacks on the Allies during the Okinawa campaign, sinking 30 ships, damaging more than 300 more, and killing almost 5,000 seamen.

Once ashore, the Allies faced even fiercer opposition than on Iwo Jima. By the time the fighting ended on June 22, 1945, more than 7,600 Americans had died. But the Japanese paid a still ghastlier price—110,000 lives—in defending Okinawa. This total includes two generals who chose ritual suicide over the shame of surrender. A witness to this ceremony described their end: "A simultaneous shout and a flash of the sword . . . and both generals had nobly accomplished their last duty to their Emperor."

The Battle for Okinawa was a chilling foretaste of what the Allies imagined the final invasion of Japan's home islands would be like. Although many historians now think the projected toll was vastly overestimated, Winston Churchill predicted that the cost would be a million American lives, and half that number of British.

THINK THROUGH HISTORY
C. *Drawing Conclusions* *Why was Okinawa a significant island in the war in the Pacific?*

C. Answer It was the last defensive position held by the Japanese outside of Japan itself.

THE MANHATTAN PROJECT Not long after Truman took office, Secretary of War Henry Stimson handed him a memo that began, "Within four months we shall in all probability have completed the most terrible weapon ever known in human history, one bomb of which could destroy a whole city."

Over the next hour, the president learned that the **Manhattan Project** was not only the most ambitious scientific enterprise in history but also the best-kept secret of the war. At its peak, more than 600,000 Americans were involved in the project, although few of them knew its ultimate purpose—the creation of an atomic bomb.

Work on the atomic bomb had begun in 1942, after a group of scientists under the direction of physicist Enrico Fermi successfully achieved a controlled nuclear reaction at the University of Chicago. General Leslie Groves, the organizer of the Manhattan Project, had two gigantic atomic reactors built at Oak Ridge, Tennessee, and another at Hanford, Washington, to produce uranium 235, a rare form of the element, along with the even rarer element plutonium, to fuel the explosive device. Meanwhile, a group of brilliant American, British, and European-refugee scientists headed by **J. Robert Oppenheimer** worked in a secret laboratory in Los Alamos, New Mexico, to build the actual bomb.

Not yet fully aware of the effects of nuclear fallout, J. Robert Oppenheimer and General Leslie Groves survey a nuclear test site, wearing plastic bags to protect their feet.

As the time to test the bomb drew near, the air around Los Alamos crackled with rumors and fears. At one end of the scale were fears that the bomb wouldn't work at all or, if it did, would not produce enough punch to amount to much. At the other end was the prediction that the explosion would set fire to the atmosphere, which would mean the end of the earth.

On the night of July 16, 1945, the first atomic bomb was detonated in an empty expanse of desert near Alamogordo, New Mexico. A blinding flash, which was visible 180 miles away, was followed by a deafening roar as a tremendous shock wave rolled across the trembling desert. Otto Frisch, a scientist on the project, described the huge mushroom cloud that rose over the desert as "a red-hot elephant standing balanced on its trunk." The bomb not only worked, but it was more powerful than most had dared hope.

TO BOMB OR NOT TO BOMB In spite of this success, many of the scientists who had worked on the bomb, as well as many military leaders and civilian policymakers, had doubts about using it. A petition drawn up by Leo Szilard, a leading physicist in the Manhattan Project, and signed by 70 other scientists argued that it would be immoral to drop an atomic bomb on Japan without fair warning. Others supported staging a demonstration of the bomb for Japanese

TEACHING OPTIONS

Teaching Gifted and Talented Students

Theoretical Science and Social Responsibility Development of the atomic bomb represented not only a triumph of theoretical science but also a technological application of unprecedented destructive power. Have gifted and talented students consider the responsibility of scientists for the practical results of their investigations. Ask the following questions: How can scientists pursue "pure" knowledge if they must be alert for possible negative applications of their discoveries? Who should take responsibility for the application of theoretical knowledge?

Teaching Less Proficient Readers

Evaluating Alternative Courses of Action To help less proficient readers understand the agonizing decisions that President Truman faced over the atomic bomb, pair such students with more able readers. Suggest that each pair make a pro-and-con chart to help them evaluate Truman's options.

	Pros	Cons
Drop the bomb on Japan	Would end the war and save lives.	Would kill civilians.
Don't drop the bomb	Would set a precedent of nuclear restraint.	Americans would continue dying.

leaders, perhaps by exploding one on a deserted island near Japan, to convince them to surrender.

These objections were discussed in detail on May 31, 1945, by a newly formed advisory body, the Interim Committee. At that meeting, Oppenheimer outlined the problems with a test explosion: (1) nothing less than dropping a bomb on a city would convince the Japanese to surrender; (2) the test might be a dud; (3) the Japanese might shoot down the delivery plane or move American prisoners of war into the test area. Swayed by these arguments, the committee recommended that the bomb be used against military targets in Japan, and that it be dropped without warning.

Many scientists working on the bomb agreed with this recommendation—even more so as the heavy casualty figures from Iwo Jima and Okinawa sank in. "Are we to go on shedding American blood when we have available means to a steady victory?" they asked in a petition. "No! If we can save even a handful of American lives, then let us use this weapon—now!" But other scientists remained firmly opposed.

D. Answer For—The bomb would hasten the surrender of Japan, save American and British lives, and give the United States an advantage over the Soviet Union. Against—It was immoral to drop such a terrible weapon on civilians without warning the Japanese and allowing them to surrender.

THINK THROUGH HISTORY
D. *Analyzing Issues* *What were the main arguments for and against dropping the atomic bomb on Japanese cities in 1945?*

Saving American lives, however, was not the only consideration. Two other concerns pushed Americans to use the bomb. One was that the weapon needed to be used to justify the cost of building it. Some people feared that if the bomb were not dropped, the project might be viewed as a gigantic waste of money. The second consideration involved the Soviet Union. Tension and distrust were already developing between the Western Allies and the Soviets. Some American officials believed that a successful use of the atomic bomb would give the United States a powerful advantage over the Soviets in shaping the postwar world.

Truman did not hesitate. On July 25, 1945, he ordered the military to make final plans for dropping the only two atomic bombs then in existence on Japanese targets. A day later, the United States warned Japan that it faced "prompt and utter destruction" unless it surrendered at once. Japan refused. Truman later wrote, "The final decision of where and when to use the atomic bomb was up to me. Let there be no mistake about it. I regarded the bomb as a military weapon and never had any doubt that it should be used."

HIROSHIMA AND NAGASAKI On August 6, a B-29 bomber named *Enola Gay* released an atomic bomb, code-named Little Boy, over **Hiroshima,** an important Japanese military center. Forty-three seconds later, almost every building in the city collapsed into dust. Hiroshima had ceased to exist. Still Japan's leaders hesitated to surrender. Three days later a second bomb, code-named Fat Man, was dropped on **Nagasaki,** leveling half the city. By the end of the year, an estimated 200,000 people had died as a result of injuries and radiation poisoning caused by the atomic blasts. Yamaoko Michiko was 15 years old and living near the center of Hiroshima when the first bomb hit.

A PERSONAL VOICE

They say temperatures of 7,000 degrees centigrade hit me. . . . Nobody there looked like human beings. . . . Humans had lost the ability to speak. People couldn't scream, "It hurts!" even when they were on fire. . . . People with their legs wrenched off. Without heads. Or with faces burned and swollen out of shape. The scene I saw was a living hell.

YAMAOKO MICHIKO, quoted in *Japan at War: An Oral History*

In the aftermath of the bombing of Nagasaki, a mushroom cloud hides the sun, and a dazed mother and child clutch rice balls provided by rescue parties.

Emperor Hirohito was horrified by the death and destruction wrought by the bomb. "I cannot bear to see my innocent people suffer any longer," he told

MORE ABOUT . . .
J. Robert Oppenheimer and the First Atomic Bomb Test

"A few people laughed, a few people cried, most people were silent," J. Robert Oppenheimer recalled after the first atomic bomb exploded into a fireball over the New Mexican desert. As Oppenheimer watched the awesome spectacle, he recalled two passages from the ancient Hindu epic *Bhagavad-Gita.* First this passage came to mind: "If the radiance of a thousand suns were to burst into the sky, that would be the splendor of the Mighty One." But then he recalled this one: "I am become Death, the shatterer of worlds."

GROLIER MULTIMEDIA ENCYCLOPEDIA
video of an atomic blast

MORE ABOUT . . .
The Firebombing of Tokyo

Just after midnight on March 10, 1945, 334 American B-29 bombers left Guam, Saipan, and the Tinian islands and headed for Tokyo. Within half an hour, fires started by the bombardment had been whipped by high winds into an immense firestorm. A Japanese reporter wrote of the scene, "The city was as bright as at sunrise. . . . We thought the whole of Tokyo was reduced to ashes." The firebombing of Tokyo left 97,000 people dead, 125,000 wounded, and 1.2 million homeless—damage more extensive than that done by the atomic blasts that leveled Hiroshima and Nagasaki five months later.

Block Schedule TEACHING OPTION **Time Needed: 30 Minutes**

Cooperative Activity: Writing Memos to Truman About Use of the Atomic Bomb

Task: Student groups will write a memo to President Truman advising him on what to do with the first two atomic bombs.

Purpose: To help students understand the arguments for and against using the atomic bomb against Japan.

Activity: Assign small groups of students to determine if they believe Truman should use the two atomic bombs being readied in Los Alamos. They will write up their recommendations in a one-page memo to the president along with their reasons for advocating that course of action. Groups should read their completed memos to the class.

Building a Portfolio: Students who decide to add the memo to their portfolios should attach a note indicating their contribution.

ALTERNATIVE ASSESSMENT BOOK
Standards for Evaluating a Cooperative Activity

Standards for Evaluation
Memos should . . .

- make a clear recommendation about what should be done with the bombs
- support the recommendation with reasons
- state all reasons clearly and succinctly

OBJECTIVE
③ INSTRUCT

Rebuilding Begins

▶ ***Starting with the Student*** Have students consider how they treat someone they have had a fight or a disagreement with once the issue is resolved.

- Are they more considerate than usual, more belligerent, or more withdrawn and cautious?

▶ ***Discussing Key Ideas***
- As the end of the war nears, the Allies pursue plans to create a new international peacekeeping organization, the United Nations.
- Trials are held in Germany, Japan, and elsewhere to prosecute individuals guilty of crimes against humanity during the war.
- U.S. forces occupy Japan and help rebuild it as a democratic nation.

OUR TIMES
excerpt of Truman's V-J speech

DIFFICULT DECISIONS IN HISTORY
Agonizing Over the A-Bomb

Critical Thinking: Formulating Historical Questions Have students work in small groups to create a list of questions that will guide their research and help them evaluate President Truman's decision to drop the atomic bombs on Japan.

ELECTRONIC LIBRARY OF PRIMARY SOURCES
Statement on the Atomic Bomb by Harry S. Truman

Japan's leaders tearfully. Then he ordered them to draw up papers "to end the war." On September 2, formal surrender ceremonies took place on the U.S. battleship *Missouri* in Tokyo Bay. "Today the guns are silent," said General MacArthur in a speech marking this historic moment. "The skies no longer rain death—the seas bear only commerce—men everywhere walk upright in the sunlight. The entire world is quietly at peace."

Rebuilding Begins

With Japan's surrender, the Allies turned to the challenge of rebuilding a war-torn world. Even before the last guns fell silent, they began thinking about principles that would govern the postwar world.

Difficult Decisions IN HISTORY

AGONIZING OVER THE A-BOMB

It was 1945. The war in the Pacific dragged on. After only 116 days in office, President Truman had to decide whether to use the atomic bomb against the Japanese cities of Hiroshima and Nagasaki, whose combined population was 540,000.

Secretary of War Henry Stimson said yes because it would bring an end to the war, save American lives, and provide a threat to the Soviets, who stood ready to invade Japan themselves. "The face of war is the face of death," he proclaimed.

On the other hand, General Dwight D. Eisenhower maintained that "dropping the bomb was completely unnecessary" to save American lives and that Japan was already defeated.

1. Think about the pros and cons of each position. What additional information do you need to evaluate them fully?
2. If you had been in President Truman's position in August 1945, would you have used the A-bomb against Japan? Why or why not?

PREPARATION FOR PEACE In February 1945, Roosevelt had met with Churchill and Stalin at the Soviet city of Yalta on the Black Sea. At the **Yalta Conference,** the three leaders made a number of important decisions about the future. They agreed to move ahead in creating a new international peacekeeping body, the **United Nations (UN),** based on the principles in the Atlantic Charter. In exchange for Japan's Kuril and Sakhalin islands, Stalin promised to enter the war against Japan after the surrender of Germany. He also promised "free and unfettered elections" in Poland and in other Soviet-occupied Eastern European countries.

THINK THROUGH HISTORY
E. *Summarizing* *What decisions did Roosevelt, Churchill, and Stalin make at the Yalta Conference?*
E. Answer That the United Nations should be established; that the Soviet Union would enter the war against Japan after Germany surrendered and would allow free elections in Poland and other Soviet-occupied countries.

The following April, representatives of 50 nations met in San Francisco to establish the United Nations. By June they had agreed on a charter. The charter created the General Assembly, which was made up of all member nations and was expected to function as a "town meeting of the world." The charter also set up administrative, judicial, and economic governing bodies.

An 11-member Security Council held the real power, though. The five main wartime Allies—the United States, Great Britain, the Soviet Union, France, and China—were given permanent seats on the Security Council. At the insistence of the Soviet Union and the United States, each permanent member had the power to veto any council action. The other six seats rotated to countries elected by the General Assembly. As the charter was signed, hopes were high that the Security Council would be far more effective than the League of Nations at keeping world peace.

In July 1945, President Truman met with Churchill and Stalin at Potsdam in defeated Germany. In addition to drawing up a blueprint for disarming Germany and eliminating the Nazi regime, the Allies agreed that "stern justice shall be meted out to all war criminals, including those who have visited cruelties on our prisoners."

THE NUREMBERG WAR TRIALS In accordance with decisions made at Potsdam, Germany was divided into four zones, or sectors. The United States, Great Britain, France, and the Soviet Union each occupied and administered one zone. Germany's capital, Berlin, although within the Soviet zone, was also divided into four sectors, each administered by one of the occupying powers.

During the next year, in an unprecedented move, an international tribunal representing 23 nations tried Nazi war criminals in Nuremberg, Germany. Twenty-two Nazi leaders were tried at the first of the **Nuremberg trials.** They included Hitler's most trusted party officials, government ministers, military leaders, and powerful industrialists. As the trial began, U.S. Supreme Court justice Robert Jackson explained the significance of the event.

TEACHING OPTION

Making Global Connections

The United Nations The United Nations was established in San Francisco and is headquartered in New York City. Nonetheless, it has become a truly global organization. Under the UN's charter, membership is open to all "peace-loving" states that accept the obligations of the organization. Since 1945, UN membership has more than tripled, mainly with the admission of many new African and Asian countries that were formerly European colonies. UN peacekeeping forces have been active around the world. The UN has also spearheaded action on a wide range of global issues, including arms control, global warming, hunger, population growth, and economic development. After more than 40 years of international discussion, the UN in 1993 established the post of high commissioner for human rights to monitor worldwide respect for fundamental human rights. Although the United Nations is not a world government, it has become a flexible institution through which nations can cooperate to solve mutual problems.

F. Answer To hold German and Japanese leaders responsible for starting the war and for committing atrocities against both soldiers and civilians; to make it clear that even in wartime "crimes against humanity" would not be tolerated in a civilized society.

THINK THROUGH HISTORY
F. Analyzing Motives *Why did the Allies hold war crimes trials after World War II?*

A PERSONAL VOICE

The wrongs which we seek to condemn and punish have been so calculated, so malignant and so devastating, that civilization cannot tolerate their being ignored because it cannot survive their being repeated.... It is hard now to perceive in these miserable men ... the power by which as Nazi leaders they once dominated much of the world and terrified most of it. Merely as individuals, their fate is of little consequence to the world. What makes this inquest significant is that these prisoners represent sinister influences that will lurk in the world long after their bodies have returned to dust. They are living symbols of racial hatreds, of terrorism and violence, and of the arrogance and cruelty of power.... Civilization can afford no compromise with the social forces which would gain renewed strength if we deal ambiguously or indecisively with the men in whom those forces now precariously survive.

ROBERT JACKSON, from opening address to the Nuremberg War Crimes Trial

War Criminals on Trial, 1945–1949

Each defendant at the Nuremberg trials was accused of one or more of the following crimes:

- **Crimes Against the Peace**—planning and waging an aggressive war
- **War Crimes**—acts against the customs of warfare, such as the killing of hostages and prisoners, the plundering of private property, and the destruction of towns and cities
- **Crimes Against Humanity**—the murder, extermination, deportation, or enslavement of civilians

Twelve of the 22 defendants were sentenced to death, and most of the rest to prison. In later trials of lesser leaders, nearly 200 more Nazis were found guilty of war crimes. For the first time in history a nation's leaders had been held legally responsible for their actions during wartime.

THE OCCUPATION OF JAPAN Japan was occupied by U.S. forces under the command of General Douglas MacArthur. In the early months of the occupation, more than 1,100 Japanese, from former prime minister Hideki Tojo to lowly prison guards, were arrested and put on trial. Seven, including Tojo, were sentenced to death. In the Philippines, in China, and in other Asian battlegrounds, additional Japanese officials were tried for atrocities against civilians or prisoners of war.

G. Answer Government reform and economic recovery under MacArthur.

THINK THROUGH HISTORY
G. Summarizing *What were the most significant results of the U.S. occupation of Japan?*

During the six-year American occupation, MacArthur reformed Japan's economy by introducing free-market practices that led to a remarkable economic recovery. MacArthur also worked to transform Japan's government. He called for a new constitution that would provide for woman suffrage and guarantee basic freedoms. In the United States, Americans followed these changes with interest. The *New York Times* reported that "General MacArthur . . . has swept away an autocratic regime by a warrior god and installed in its place a democratic government presided over by a very human emperor and based on the will of the people as expressed in free elections." The Japanese apparently agreed. To this day, their constitution is known as the MacArthur Constitution.

Having taken care of responsibilities to its allies and its enemies, America was ready to begin rebuilding at home.

Section 3 Assessment

1. TERMS & NAMES
Identify:
- Douglas MacArthur
- Chester Nimitz
- kamikaze
- Manhattan Project
- J. Robert Oppenheimer
- Hiroshima
- Nagasaki
- Yalta Conference
- United Nations (UN)
- Nuremberg trials

2. SUMMARIZING Using a diagram such as the one below, describe the significance of key military actions in the Pacific during World War II.

Military Action	Significance
1.	
2.	
3.	
4.	
5.	

3. DRAWING CONCLUSIONS Explain how the United States was able to defeat the Japanese in the Pacific war.

THINK ABOUT
- the geography of the region
- the role of technology in the battles
- the strategies used by each side

4. FORMING OPINIONS Do you think that it is legitimate to hold people accountable for crimes committed during wartime? Why or why not?

THINK ABOUT
- the laws that govern society
- the likelihood of conducting a fair trial
- the behavior of soldiers, politicians, and civilians during war

MORE ABOUT . . .
The War Crimes Trials

After the first Nuremberg trial, 12 more trials were held across Germany. Those indicted included doctors who had conducted medical experiments on concentration-camp inmates and POWs, judges who had misused their power to commit murder and other crimes, industrialists who had looted occupied countries and used slave labor, and SS officials who had run the concentration camps.

OUR TIMES testimony from the Nuremberg trials

ASSESS & RETEACH

Section 3 Assessment

Have students work in small groups to answer the questions. If individuals disagree, they should locate the text that supports their responses.

Self-Assessment

Have students review the time line on pages 588–589. They should be able to describe the significance of each event in the war in the Pacific.

Section Quiz

FORMAL ASSESSMENT
Section Quiz, p. 214

Reteach

Have students read the selection from "The Bombing of Nagasaki." Then discuss the events that led up to that incident.

IN-DEPTH RESOURCES: UNIT 5
Primary Source: The Bombing of Nagasaki, p. 31

ANSWERS

1. TERMS & NAMES

Douglas MacArthur, p. 587
Chester Nimitz, p. 587
kamikaze, p. 589
Manhattan Project, p. 590
J. Robert Oppenheimer, p. 590
Hiroshima, p. 591
Nagasaki, p. 591
Yalta Conference, p. 592
United Nations (UN), p. 592
Nuremberg trials, p. 592

2. SUMMARIZING

Possible Answers:
Philippines/Japanese victory destroyed myth of white supremacy in Asia.
Tokyo/American bombing lifted American spirits.
Midway/Americans damaged Japanese air power by destroying aircraft carriers.
Leyte Gulf/Reduced Japanese Navy to minor role.
Okinawa/American victory allowed attack on Japan.
Hiroshima/America became first country to use atomic bomb.
Nagasaki/Caused Japan to surrender.

3. DRAWING CONCLUSIONS

Possible Answer: The United States could replace damaged ships more easily than Japan could, had new technology such as the atomic bomb, and had a strategy—island hopping—that conserved its power.

4. FORMING OPINIONS

Possible Response:
Legitimate—People should be prosecuted for committing atrocities. **Not legitimate**—War is such an unusual situation that ordinary laws do not apply.

CLOSE

The brutal Pacific battles of World War II finally ended when the United States dropped atomic bombs on Hiroshima and Nagasaki in Japan. The Allies then began the process of rebuilding a more peaceful world.

Science and Technology

OBJECTIVES

1. To explain the connection between military technology and subsequent civilian technological developments.
2. To describe civilian applications of selected military technologies.

FOCUS & MOTIVATE

▶ ***Starting with the Student***
Ask students to name technological inventions that have an impact on their daily lives. Have them speculate about the origins of these inventions.

MORE ABOUT . . .
The Shrinking World
The Internet grew out of the Cold War. In the 1960s, the U.S. Department of Defense recognized the value of linking computers to communicate in the event of a nuclear attack. The result was ARPANET, the first of several early U.S. computer networks. Meanwhile, similar work in Britain resulted in networks like JANET, the Joint Academic Network, which in 1979 was linked to U.S. computers on a transatlantic cable shared with NASA. In the 1980s, new software, supercomputers, fiber-optic cables, and other improvements allowed the Internet to circle the globe. By January 1997, the number of Internet web sites had passed the million mark, with over 100 million estimated users.

TRACING THEMES
SCIENCE AND TECHNOLOGY

From the Frontlines to Your Back Yard

Radar, guided missiles, nuclear submarines, reconnaissance satellites, atomic bombs—the inventions of the 20th century seems to have been mainly intended for war, with the usual dreaded results. But these technological developments have also had far-reaching applications in peacetime. Because the innovations were originally intended for the battlefield, they were developed quickly and with a narrow purpose. However, their peaceful applications have led to life-enhancing benefits that will extend far into the 21st century.

1939

WORLD WAR II (1939–1945) ATOM BOMBS TO BRAIN SCANS

Faced with alarming rumors of work on a German atomic bomb, America mobilized some of the finest scientific minds in the world to create its own atomic bomb. The energy released by its nuclear reaction was enough to kill hundreds of thousands of people, as it did at Hiroshima and Nagasaki. But the resulting ability to harness the atom's energy also led to new technologies for diagnosing and treating human diseases. Techniques such as positron emission tomography (PET) now reveal the inner workings of the human brain itself.

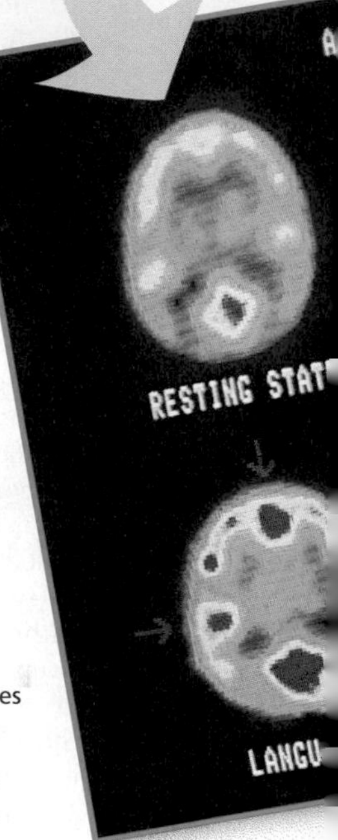

1914

WORLD WAR I (1914–1918) FIGHTER PLANES TO COMMUTER FLIGHTS

Airplanes were first used to gather military information but were soon put to work as fighters and bombers. The Sopwith Camel, shown above, was one of the most successful British fighter planes and brought down almost 1,300 enemy aircraft during World War I. The development of flight technology eventually led to sophisticated supersonic aircraft. Today, planes smash the barriers of time and space and enable people to travel faster than the speed of sound.

RECOMMENDED RESOURCES

Books

Buderi, Robert. *The Invention That Changed the World.* New York: Simon, 1996. Radar launches a technological revolution.

Campbell-Kelly, Martin. *Computer: A History of the Information Machine.* New York: Basic, 1996. Story of the machine that revolutionized modern life.

Elder, Donald C. *Out from Behind the Eight-Ball.* San Diego: American Astronautical Society, 1995. A history of Project Echo, a landmark in the development of satellite communications.

Watson-Watt, Sir Robert Alexander. *The Pulse of Radar.* New York: Dial, 1959. An autobiographical account by a British pioneer of radar.

Videos

A Is for Atom. Coronet/MTI. An exploration of nuclear energy and how science harnessed it.

The Age of Flight. MPI Home Video, 1991. A history of aviation.

Distant Voices. BBC and Time-Life, 1979. Part 3 of the *Connections* series explores technological changes in warfare and related developments.

Echoes of War. Vestron Video, 1989. An episode from PBS's *Nova* series tracing the development of radar in World War II.

Wings: The Jet Age. Pacific Arts Video, 1989. The evolution of civil and military jets from World War II to the late 1980s.

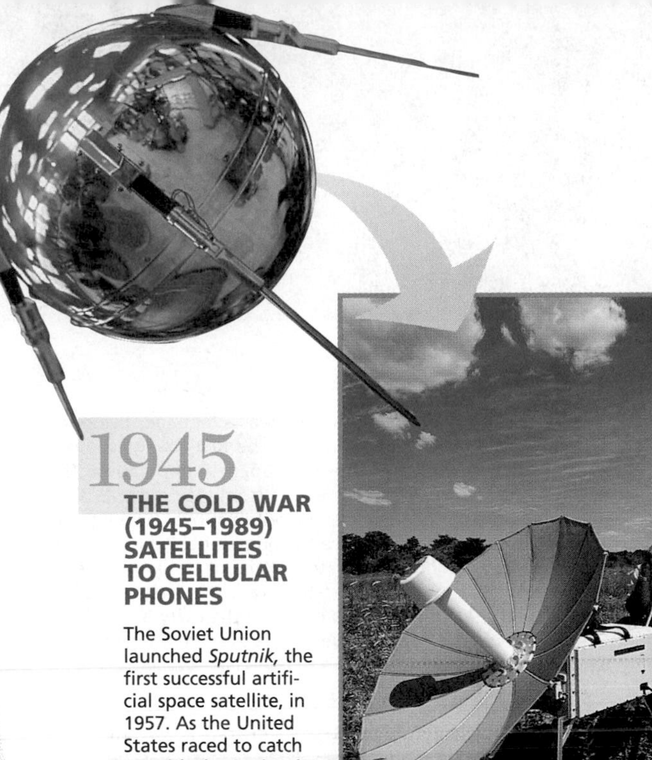

1945

THE COLD WAR (1945–1989) SATELLITES TO CELLULAR PHONES

The Soviet Union launched *Sputnik*, the first successful artificial space satellite, in 1957. As the United States raced to catch up with the Soviets in space, both countries eventually produced satellites that have improved life for people around the world. Satellites now not only track weather patterns and control air traffic but also link the continents in a vast communications network.

Other Applications of World War II Technology

TECHNOLOGY	MILITARY USE	PEACETIME USE
Semi-conductors	Navigation	Transistors, radios, electronics
Computers	Code breaking	Software programs, video games
Freeze-dried food	Soldiers' rations	TV dinners, space-shuttle rations
Synthetic materials	Parachutes, weapons parts, tires	Telephones, automobile fenders, pacemakers
Infrared technology	Night tracking	TV remote controls, police surveillance, medical treatment
Radar	Tracking and surveillance	Weather tracking, air traffic control, archaeological digs, microwave ovens

INTERACT WITH HISTORY

1. **HYPOTHESIZING** Do you think that peacetime technologies would have been developed without the stimulus provided by war? Support your answer.

 SEE SKILLBUILDER HANDBOOK, PAGE 915.

2. **RECOGNIZING TECHNOLOGICAL IMPACT** What invention or technological breakthrough do you think has had the greatest impact on American society? Write a paragraph to explain your answer. Stage a debate with your classmates in which you defend your choice.

INSTRUCT

▶ *Starting with the Student*

- Ask students to evaluate the importance of the inventions and applications discussed on pages 594 and 595. Then have the class rank the developments based on their usefulness.
- Discuss additional civilian applications of the technologies discussed on pages 594 and 595. *Possible Responses: Airplane—crop dusting, cloud seeding; nuclear power—generation of electricity; satellites—satellite TV, the Internet.*

▶ *Discussing Key Ideas*

- Much of the funding and research for 20th-century technology is for war and defense purposes.
- This military technology has valuable peacetime applications.

HISTORY FROM VISUALS

Reading the Images

Have students study the illustrations and chart.

- Which image or idea was most surprising to them? Why?
- What additions might students make to these pages? *Possible Responses: Sonar, lasers, CD-ROM.*

INTERACT WITH HISTORY

1. Hypothesizing

Possible Response: *Students who say the technologies would have been developed anyway may point to peacetime inventions of the past or may mention the motives played by profit, fame, and the desire to benefit humanity. Those who say that the technologies may not have been developed may say that the funding for and/or drive to do the research arose only because of wartime emergencies, Cold War competition, and threats to the nation's survival.*

2. Recognizing Technological Impact

Standards for Evaluation
Paragraphs should . . .

- identify a specific invention or technological breakthrough
- explain why it is important
- support opinions with accurate facts and examples

Debates may be conducted between pairs of students, in small groups, or by the entire class.

Section 4 Overview

OBJECTIVES

1. To describe the economic and social changes that reshaped American life during World War II.
2. To summarize the opportunities and the discrimination American minorities experienced during the war.

SKILLBUILDER

- Understanding geography: movement, p. 597

CRITICAL THINKING

- Theme: Immigration and Migration, p. 597
- Recognizing effects, p. 597
- Theme: The American Dream, p. 598
- Analyzing causes, p. 599
- Evaluating decisions, p. 601
- Summarizing, p. 601
- Drawing conclusions, p. 601
- Making inferences, p. 601

FOCUS & MOTIVATE

5-MINUTE WARM-UP

Recognizing Facts and Details

To understand the economic effects of the war, have students read "Economic Gains" on pages 596–597 and answer these questions.

1. How much did Americans' average weekly pay rise during the war?
2. How many women entered the work force during the war?

WARM-UP TRANSPARENCY 17

▶ ***Starting with the Student*** Discuss with students the impact World War II had on their families. How was their community affected?

OBJECTIVE

① **INSTRUCT**

Opportunity and Adjustment

▶ ***Discussing Key Ideas***

- The war brings prosperity to millions of workers.
- The growth of the defense industry sparks the largest

(continued on next page)

4 The Impact of the War

TERMS & NAMES
- **GI Bill of Rights**
- **James Farmer**
- **Congress of Racial Equality (CORE)**
- **Japanese American Citizens League (JACL)**

LEARN ABOUT the impact of the war on life at home ***TO UNDERSTAND*** the social and economic changes that helped reshape postwar America.

TWICE A PATRIOT!
EX-PRIVATE OBIE BARTLETT LOST LEFT ARM—PEARL HARBOR—RELEASED: DEC., 1941—NOW AT WORK WELDING IN A WEST COAST SHIPYARD...

Like many minority veterans, Obie Bartlett was twice a patriot—and was still regarded as a second-class citizen.

ONE AMERICAN'S STORY

The writer and poet Maya Angelou was a teenager living in San Francisco when World War II began. The first change she noticed was the disappearance of the city's Japanese population. The second was an influx of war workers from the South. "The Japanese shops," she recalled, "were taken over by enterprising Negro businessmen. . . . Where the odors of tempura, raw fish and *cha* [tea] had dominated, the aroma of chitlings, greens, and hamhocks now prevailed." San Franciscans, she noted, maintained that there was no racism in their city by the bay. But Angelou, who had seen her Nisei schoolmates vanish, knew differently.

A PERSONAL VOICE

A story went the rounds about a San Francisco white matron who refused to sit beside a Negro civilian on the streetcar, even after he made room for her on the seat. Her explanation was that she would not sit beside a draft dodger who was a Negro as well. She added that the least he could do was fight for his country the way her son was fighting on Iwo Jima. The story said that the man pulled his body away from the window to show an armless sleeve. He said quietly and with great dignity, "Then ask your son to look around for my arm, which I left over there."

MAYA ANGELOU, *I Know Why the Caged Bird Sings*

America welcomed its heroic troops home from the war with ticker-tape parades and joyous celebration. But after the confetti settled, returning veterans—even those who weren't disabled—had to begin dealing with the very real issues of reentry and adjustment to a society that offered many opportunities but still had many unsolved problems.

Opportunity and Adjustment

In contrast to the Great Depression, World War II was a time of opportunity for millions of Americans. Jobs abounded, and despite rationing and shortages, there was money to spend again. The war was America's shining moment, and the nation emerged as the world's dominant economic and military power.

ECONOMIC GAINS The war years were good ones for working people. As defense industries boomed, unemployment fell to a low of 1.2 percent in 1944. Even with price and wage controls, average weekly paychecks rose 70 percent during the war. And although workers complained about long hours, overtime, and night shifts, they were also able to save money for the future. Some workers invested up to half their paychecks in war bonds.

Farmers also prospered during the war. Unlike the depression years, when farmers had battled dust storms and floods, the early 1940s had good weather for growing crops. Farmers also benefited from improvements in farm machinery and fertilizers and reaped the profits from rising crop prices. As a result, crop production increased by 50 percent, and farm income tripled. Before the war ended, many farmers could pay off their mortgages.

SECTION 4 RESOURCES

PRINT RESOURCES

IN-DEPTH RESOURCES: UNIT 5
Guided Reading, p. 22

READING STUDY GUIDE, p. 183

ACCESS FOR STUDENTS ACQUIRING ENGLISH
Guided Reading (Spanish), p. 199

SPANISH READING STUDY GUIDE, p. 183

FORMAL ASSESSMENT
Section Quiz, p. 215

ALTERNATIVE ASSESSMENT BOOK
See forms for supporting and scoring alternative activities.

TECHNOLOGY RESOURCES

CRITICAL THINKING TRANSPARENCIES
CT25, U.S. Joins the Allies in World War II
CT59, Human Cost of World War II

VIDEO *American Portfolio: A Videodisc for U.S. History* user's guide, p. 230

INTERNET http://www.mlushistory.com

Women also enjoyed employment gains during the war, although many lost their jobs when the war ended. Over 6 million women entered the work force for the first time, boosting the percentage of women in the total work force to 35 percent. A third of those jobs were in defense plants, which offered women more challenging work and better pay than such traditional female jobs as waitressing, clerking, and domestic service. With men away at war, many women also took advantage of openings in journalism and other professions. "The war really created opportunities for women," said Winona Espinosa, a wife and mother who became a riveter and bus driver during the war. "It was the first time we got a chance to show that we could do a lot of things that only men had done before."

The range of jobs taken on by women was impressive. Aircraft maker Glenn Martin reported, "We have women helping design our planes in the Engineering Department, building them on the production line, operating almost every conceivable type of machinery, from rivet guns to giant stamp presses." Late in 1942, *Newsweek* reported that "depending on the industry, women today make up from 10 percent to 88 percent of total personnel in most war plants." Strato Equipment, a company that researched and designed high-altitude pressure suits for pilots, had no men at all—just a department-store dummy.

The war gave women the chance to prove they could be just as productive as men. But their pay usually did not reflect their productivity.

POPULATION SHIFTS In addition to revamping the economy, the war triggered one of the greatest mass migrations of American history. Not only were millions of servicemen and women sent to places all over the world, but civilians were on the move as well. Americans whose families had lived for decades in one place suddenly uprooted themselves to seek war work elsewhere. States with military bases and defense industries, such as Connecticut, Delaware, Maryland, Michigan, Florida, and the Pacific Coast states, all experienced large population gains. More than a million newcomers poured into California between 1941 and 1944. Towns with defense industries saw their populations double and even triple, sometimes almost overnight.

A. Answer In search of jobs, people moved from rural areas to cities, and many Southerners, black and white alike, moved to the North and the West.

THINK THROUGH HISTORY
A. THEME ***Immigration and Migration*** *How did World War II cause shifts in U.S. population?*

African-American Migration, 1940–1950

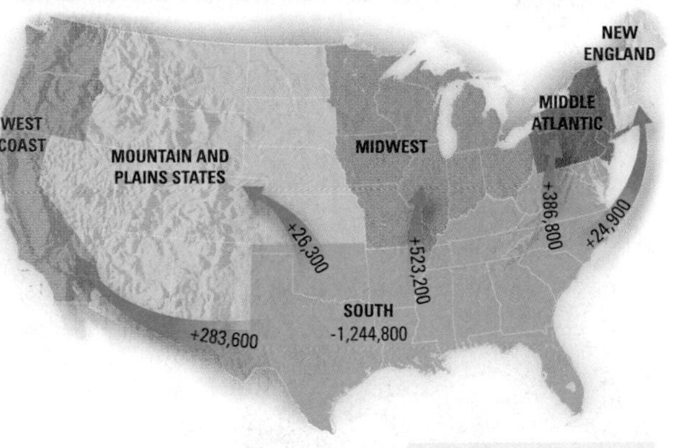

GEOGRAPHY SKILLBUILDER
MOVEMENT ***To which geographic region did the greatest number of African Americans migrate?***

Skillbuilder Answer The Midwest.

Elkton, Maryland, for example, had been a sleepy farming community until an ammunition plant was built there. Its population quickly surged from 6,000 to 12,000, of whom 80 percent were young women. Burbank, California, the home of a major aircraft company, grew from 12,000 to 60,000 people in the first two years of the war. The populations of some major cities—including Washington, D.C., Los Angeles, San Francisco, Portland, Seattle, San Antonio, and Dallas—jumped by a third or more.

The inevitable result of such population booms was an acute housing shortage. Even though workers had money for rent, many were virtually homeless. They camped out in tents, old cars, trailer parks, rented garages, and overcrowded rooming houses. Food was a problem as well. Many workers had no place to cook, yet because of food rationing, there were not enough restaurants to feed them. In Elkton, according to one observer, food was so scarce and expensive that "many girls [went] through the day on a cup of coffee and a piece of toast."

B. Answer The war created new jobs, all but eliminated unemployment, raised wages, uprooted workers, created housing shortages, and opened up new types of employment to women and minority workers.

THINK THROUGH HISTORY
B. *Recognizing Effects* *How did the war affect working Americans?*

SOCIAL ADJUSTMENTS Families adjusted to the changes brought on by war as best they could. With millions of fathers in the armed forces, mothers struggled to rear their children alone. Young children got used to being left with

(continued from page 596)

migration in American history.
- Families struggle with separations and changing roles.

IN-DEPTH RESOURCES: UNIT 5
Guided Reading, p. 22

ACCESS FOR STUDENTS ACQUIRING ENGLISH
Guided Reading (Spanish), p. 199

Issues for the 21st Century

Women and the Glass Ceiling

Connect working women in the 1940s with working women today by having students read pages 894–895. Then have them answer these questions.

1. What problems did women workers face during World War II that they no longer face? *Possible Response: More women today have industrial or professional experience.*
2. How might women's work experiences during the Second World War have laid the groundwork for women's economic roles today? *Possible Response: Women gained new work experiences and valued the economic independence jobs provided.*

HISTORY FROM VISUALS

African-American Migration, 1940–1950

Reading the Map Remind students that the positive numbers in the arrows represent regional gains in African-American populations; the negative number

(continued on next page)

TEACHING OPTION

Exploring Themes

Immigration and Migration The American character had always been marked by restlessness, but the country's entry into World War II triggered a nationwide upheaval. In addition to the mass African-American migration from the South, thousands of young men left home for military training in other parts of the country and then for service overseas. The rapid growth of defense industries further changed American demographics as workers pulled up roots to follow the job opportunities.

To give students a perspective on the ongoing impact of immigration and migration on the United States, remind them of other major population movements in American history, such as the arrival of the colonists in 1620, the displacement of Native Americans in the 1830s, the settling of the Great Plains in the 1880s, the mass influx of European, Asian, and Mexican immigrants in the late 19th and early 20th centuries, and the immigration of Asian refugees after the Vietnam War. Discuss similarities and differences in these population movements.

(continued from page 597)

represents the loss in the South. Have them verify that the South's loss equals the North's gain by adding the positive numbers and comparing that sum with the total.

MORE ABOUT . . .
The Marriage Boom

The World War II marriage boom actually began before Pearl Harbor, mainly for economic reasons. Millions of couples who had postponed marriage during the Depression were the first to rush to the altar. Once the United States entered the war, the boom continued as young men and women facing uncertain futures looked for someone to live for. Have students use the following figures to graph the number of marriages per 1,000 unmarried women over age 14 from the Depression through World War II.

1929—75.5; 1932—56.0

1938—69.9; 1940—82.8

1942—93.0; 1944—76.5

1946—118.1

Students might present the data on a line graph like this:

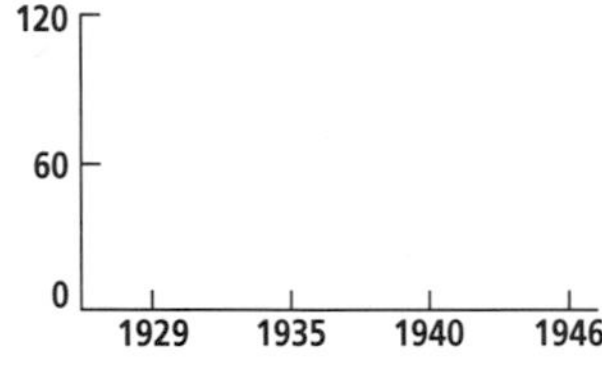

OBJECTIVE

② INSTRUCT

Discrimination and Reaction

▶ ***Discussing Key Ideas***

- African Americans in the military fight segregation

(continued on next page)

neighbors or relatives or in child-care centers as more and more mothers went to work. Teenagers left at home without parents sometimes drifted into juvenile delinquency. And when fathers finally did come home, there was often a painful period of readjustment as families got to know one another again.

The war helped create new families, too, as it triggered a huge marriage boom. Longtime sweethearts—as well as couples who barely knew each other—rushed to marry before the soldier or sailor was shipped overseas. In booming towns like Seattle, the number of marriage licenses issued went up by as much as 300 percent early in the war. A New Yorker observed in 1943, "On Fridays and Saturdays, the City Hall area is blurred with running soldiers, sailors, and girls hunting the license bureau, floral shops, ministers, [and] blood-testing laboratories."

Many of these romances did not survive the long separation, though. For numerous servicemen, the bad news came in much-dreaded "Dear John" letters—letters from their wife or sweetheart, saying that she had found someone new. In 1945, there were 502,000 divorces in the United States, or 31 for every 100 marriages. This was double the prewar total and enough to give the United States the highest divorce rate in the world.

In 1944, to help ease the transition of returning servicemen to civilian life, Congress passed the Servicemen's Readjustment Act, better known as the **GI Bill of Rights.** This bill provided education and training for veterans, paid for by the federal government. Just over half the returning soldiers, or about 7.8 million veterans, attended colleges and technical schools under the GI Bill. The act also provided federal loan guarantees to veterans buying homes or farms or starting businesses. Because of this act, millions who would otherwise never have been able to afford a college education or a house went to school, became homeowners, and improved their economic prospects after the war.

THINK THROUGH HISTORY
C. THEME ***The American Dream*** *What provisions did the GI Bill make for returning veterans?*

C. Answer Education, training, and federal loan guarantees.

Discrimination and Reaction

Despite the opportunities that opened up for women and minorities during the war, old prejudices and policies persisted, both in the military and at home.

Pilots of the all-black 99th Fighter Squadron—the Tuskegee Airmen—served in North Africa and Italy. Several of them are shown here, with the flight helmet and goggles that became their trademark.

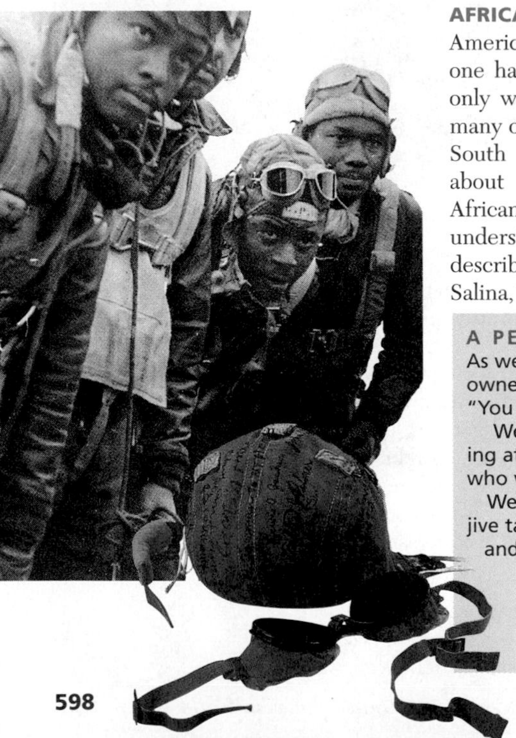

AFRICAN AMERICANS IN THE MILITARY For African Americans, World War II was a turning point of sorts. On the one hand, segregation remained the rule in the military. Not only were African Americans assigned to all-black units, but many of them were assigned to rigidly segregated camps in the South for their training. "My comrades did not understand about segregation," Southerner Preston McNeil said of his African-American buddies from the North. "They couldn't understand the sign that says, 'Colored,' 'White.'" Lloyd Brown described his experience with segregation in a lunchroom in Salina, Kansas.

A PERSONAL VOICE

As we entered, the counterman hurried to the rear to get the owner, who hurried out front to tell us with urgent politeness: "You boys know we don't serve colored here." . . .

We ignored him, and just stood there inside the door, staring at what we had come to see—the German prisoners of war who were having lunch at the counter. . . .

We continued to stare. This was really happening. It was no jive talk. The people of Salina would serve these enemy soldiers and turn away black American G.I.'s. . . .

If we were *untermenschen* [inferior people] in Nazi Germany, they would break our bones. As "colored" men in Salina, they only break our hearts. . . .

LLOYD BROWN, quoted in *V Was for Victory*

598

TEACHING OPTIONS

Exploring Themes

The American Dream The GI Bill of Rights made the American dream a reality for millions of World War II veterans by providing them with unemployment and education allowances and home, farm, and business loans. The GI Bill program currently also covers men and women who served in the armed forces between 1955 and 1976. Ask students to talk with family members or adult friends who have taken advantage of these benefits about how the GI Bill affected their lives. Have students share their anecdotes with the class.

Making Connections Across Cultures

African Americans in the Military The discrimination African Americans experienced in the military embittered them even more when they saw how well prisoners of war were treated. At Camp Hood, outside Killeen, Texas, for example, German prisoners were assigned to clean up the base grounds. Soldier E. G. McConnell noted, however, "They didn't pick up the black area. We had to do that ourselves."

On the other hand, under great pressure from civil rights organizations, the military no longer restricted its all-black units to menial tasks. Many black units distinguished themselves in combat, including the famous 92nd Infantry Division, nicknamed the Buffaloes. In just six months of fighting in Europe, the Buffaloes won 7 Legion of Merit awards, 65 Silver Stars, and 162 Bronze Stars for courage under fire. The 99th Fighter Squadron, better known as the Tuskegee Airmen, won two Distinguished Unit Citations (the military's highest commendation) for its outstanding aerial combat against the German Luftwaffe.

AFRICAN AMERICANS AT HOME African Americans also made some progress on the home front. During the war, about 330,000 blacks left the South. The majority moved to the West Coast. There they found not only jobs, but good jobs. Between 1940 and 1944, the percentage of blacks working in skilled or semiskilled jobs rose from 16 to 30 percent.

Wherever African Americans moved, however, discrimination followed. In 1942, civil rights leader **James Farmer** founded an interracial organization called the **Congress of Racial Equality (CORE)** to confront urban segregation in the North. That same year, CORE staged its first sit-in at a segregated Chicago restaurant.

As new black migrants moved into already overcrowded cities, tensions rose. In 1943, a tidal wave of racial violence swept across the country. The worst conflict erupted in Detroit on a hot Sunday afternoon in June. What started as a tussle between blacks and whites at a beach on the Detroit River mushroomed into a riot when white sailors stationed nearby joined the fray. The fighting raged for three days, fueled by false rumors that whites had murdered a black woman and her child and that black rioters had killed 17 whites. By the time President Roosevelt sent federal troops into the city to restore order, 9 whites and 25 blacks lay dead or dying.

The violence of 1943 revealed to many Americans—black and white alike—just how serious racial tensions had become in the United States. By 1945, more than 400 communities had formed committees to improve race relations. Progress was slow, but African Americans were determined not to give up the gains they had made.

THINK THROUGH HISTORY
D. *Analyzing Causes* *What caused the race riots in the 1940s?*

D. Answer Discrimination, racism, and the rising population of minorities in cities.

MEXICAN AMERICANS IN WARTIME Mexican Americans also experienced both progress and prejudice during the war years. In the military, most served in segregated units. Mexican-American soldiers distinguished themselves in combat, with 17 being awarded the Medal of Honor. An all-Chicano infantry unit—Company E of the 141st Regiment, 36th Division—became one of the most decorated of the war.

But while Mexican Americans were defending democracy overseas, they also had to defend themselves against racism at home. In the violent summer of 1943, Los Angeles exploded in anti-Mexican "zoot-suit" riots. The zoot suit was a style of dress adopted by Mexican-American youths as a symbol of their rebellion against tradition. It consisted of a knee-length jacket and pleated pants nipped in at the cuff. Broad-brimmed hats were often worn with the suits.

The riots began when 11 sailors in Los Angeles reported that they had been attacked by Mexican Americans. This charge triggered two nights of violence involving thousands of servicemen and civilians. Mobs poured into Mexican neighborhoods and grabbed any zoot-suiters they could find. The attackers ripped off their victims' clothes and beat them senseless. The city's response was to outlaw the wearing of zoot suits.

Despite such unhappy experiences with racism, many Mexican Americans believed that their sacrifices during wartime would lead to a better future.

The exaggerated style of the zoot suits that many Mexican-American young men wore expressed their rebellion and made them easy targets for racial violence.

(continued from page 598)
and discrimination as well as the Axis Powers.
- African-American gains on the home front are accompanied by racial unrest.
- Despite prejudice, Mexican Americans make gains during the war.
- During and after the war, interned Japanese Americans struggle first for their freedom, then for justice.

MORE ABOUT . . .
Mexican Americans in Los Angeles

By 1940, Los Angeles had the largest urban population of people of Mexican descent outside Mexico City. It also had a shameful record of discrimination in jobs, housing, education, and recreation. A public swimming pool, for example, was only open to Mexican Americans (and African Americans) on Wednesdays. After that, the pool was drained and cleaned before being reopened for whites. During the war, many young Mexican Americans dressed in zoot suits to show their rejection of Anglo society and its prejudices. The city's mainstream press characterized the "zooters" as draft dodgers and dope addicts, exacerbating already strained relations.

Block Schedule TEACHING OPTION **Time Needed: 20 Minutes**

Cooperative Activity: Creating a Political Cartoon

Task: Student groups will create a political cartoon commenting on race riots during World War II.

Purpose: To help students recognize and communicate the sad irony of Americans fighting each other at home while fighting a war abroad.

Activity: Small groups of students should create a political cartoon explaining the impact of either the Detroit race riot or the Los Angeles "zoot suit" riot on the war effort. Students could discuss the concept of their cartoon as a group and then divide the tasks of drawing the cartoon, writing the caption, and compiling the finished product.

Building a Portfolio: Students who add the cartoons to their portfolios should attach a note indicating their contribution.

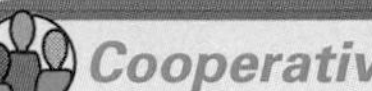

ALTERNATIVE ASSESSMENT BOOK
Standards for Evaluating a Cooperative Activity

Standards for Evaluation
Cartoons should . . .
- express a clear position on the impact of home-front riots on the war effort
- communicate that position with pictures and minimal words
- be easily understood

MORE ABOUT . . .
Life in the Internment Camps

The ten internment camps set up for Japanese Americans were mostly located in remote desert areas of the West. The internees were housed in barracks, with each family allotted one 20-foot-square room. The adults did what they could to bring a semblance of normality into this abnormal setting. Children began school each day by saluting the flag and singing "My country, 'tis of thee, sweet land of liberty." But they didn't have to look far to see armed guards and barbed wire fences.

POINT/COUNTERPOINT
Japanese-American Internment

▶ ***Starting with the Student***
Have students create a chart to help them organize the arguments for and against the internment:

Japanese-American Internment

Necessary	Racist

▶ ***Discussing Key Ideas***
- Some Americans feel threatened by the attack on Pearl Harbor.
- They fear that Japanese Americans will aid the enemy.
- Some justify internment as a way of protecting Japanese Americans.
- No Japanese Americans are known to have committed acts of disloyalty or sabotage.
- Many criticize internment as a racist act.

A PERSONAL VOICE

This war . . . is doing what we in our Mexican-American movement had planned to do in one generation. . . . It has shown those "across the tracks" that we all share the same problems. It has shown them what the Mexican American will do, what responsibility he will take and what leadership qualities he will demonstrate. After this struggle, the status of the Mexican Americans will be different.

MANUEL DE LA RAZA, quoted in *A Different Mirror: A History of Multicultural America*

JAPANESE AMERICANS IN THE WAR EFFORT For Japanese Americans locked up in U.S. internment camps, the war was a daily struggle to maintain their dignity in the face of injustice. Many young men escaped the camps by volunteering for military service. As William Hosokawa explained, they "felt it was their obligation to volunteer and go into service and do what they could to demonstrate that they were indeed loyal, and the government was wrong in putting them into camps."

At the urging of General Delos Emmons, the army created the 100th Battalion, which consisted of 1,400 Hawaiian Nisei. The 100th fought in North Africa and Italy, where it saw brutal combat, becoming known as the Purple

POINT

"Japanese-American internment was necessary for national defense."

The United States was still reeling from the Japanese attack on Pearl Harbor that had brought it into World War II—a threat, some felt, to its very existence. Tom Clark, assistant to the commanding general of the U.S. Army's Western Defense Command and later associate justice of the Supreme Court, offered a justification for internment. "Soon after Pearl Harbor I was deluged by demands that, regardless of citizenship, every person of Japanese descent must be removed from the West Coast," he explained. "The threatening public attitude . . . would permit nothing less than total mass relocation."

Chief Justice Earl Warren pointed out that many Japanese Americans held dual citizenship and had been educated in both Japan and the United States. "Their affiliation in time of war worried us," he explained.

War correspondent Walter Lippman offered more concrete reasons. "It is the fact that the Japanese navy has been reconnoitering the Pacific Coast. . . . It is the fact that communication takes place between the enemy at sea and the enemy agents on land."

Historians Donald Pike and Roger Olmsted observed that only Japan among the Axis nations had attacked the United States and "suddenly the Japanese . . . threatened our very national existence."

COUNTERPOINT

"Japanese-American internment was an unnecessary and a racist act."

"Our unjust imprisonment was the result of two closely related emotions: racism and hysteria," says Edison Tomimaro Uno, a former internee. According to Uno, the claim that Japanese Americans were relocated for their own protection was "sheer hypocrisy," since Japanese Americans posed no national security threat. Instead, he calls the relocation a crime attributable to "racism [and] economic and political opportunism."

"War makes for harsh measures," noted the historian Cary McWilliams, "but we cannot justify the evacuation even as a war measure. No such measure was taken against German or Italian nationals."

Another historian, Henry Steele Commager commented, "It is sobering to recall that the record does not disclose a single case of Japanese disloyalty or sabotage during the whole war." In fact, 33,000 Japanese Americans served in the armed forces during the war, and the one all-Nisei regiment received more decorations than any comparable army unit.

For many, relocation left a legacy of shame. Chief Justice Earl Warren confessed in his autobiography that he "deeply regretted" his testimony in favor of internment. Tom Clark said, "It was a sad day in our constitutional history."

INTERACT WITH HISTORY

1. **FORMING OPINIONS** Do you believe that internment of Japanese Americans was necessary? Give reasons to support your opinion.

SEE SKILLBUILDER HANDBOOK, PAGE 919.

2. **RESEARCHING INTERNMENT** Use library resources or the Internet to research the experience of a specific Japanese American in an internment camp. Present your findings as a diary entry or a report.

INTERNET Visit http://www.mlushistory.com for more about Japanese-American internment.

INTERACT WITH HISTORY

1. Forming Opinions

Possible Responses:

Internment was necessary—Japanese Americans posed a security threat to the United States due to their dual allegiance.

Internment was unnecessary—There was no evidence that Japanese Americans had committed any acts that posed a threat to the United States. Their internment was motivated by racism.

2. Researching Internment

Suggest that students use the books *And Justice for All* by John Tateishi and *A Different Mirror: A HIstory of Multicultural America* by Ronald Takaki as sources of eyewitness accounts of internment. Their presentations of this information should meet the following criteria:

- Gives a brief biography of the person and his or her family.
- Includes specific details about the person's life before, during, and after internment.
- Uses direct quotations from the person whenever possible.

Japanese Americans were finally released from U.S. internment camps at the end of the war.

Heart Battalion because 300 of its soldiers were killed and another 650 were wounded.

Later the 100th was merged into the all-Nisei 442nd Regimental Combat Team, whose slogan was "Go for Broke." It became the most decorated combat unit of the war. The 442nd took heavy casualties—more than one fourth of the unit—in the Italian campaign and then was ordered to France, where the Nisei captured the town of Bruyères in house-to-house fighting. After that they were sent to rescue the "Lost Battalion"—a unit of 211 Americans surrounded by the Germans in the Vosges Mountains. One Nisei soldier described the campaign, "If we advanced a hundred yards, that was a good day's job. . . . We'd dig in again, move up another hundred yards, and dig in. . . . It took us a whole week to get to the Lost Battalion. It was a tree-to-tree fight." When the soldiers of the Lost Battalion caught sight of their rescuers, they sobbed for joy. In 1946, President Truman welcomed the 442nd home with these words: "You fought not only the enemy, you fought prejudice—and you won."

Japanese Americans also fought for justice, both in the courts and in Congress. The initial results were discouraging. In 1944, the Supreme Court decided, in *Korematsu* v. *United States,* that the government's policy of evacuating Japanese Americans to camps was justified on the basis of "military necessity." After the war, however, the **Japanese American Citizens League (JACL)** pushed the government to compensate those sent to the camps for their lost property. In 1965, Congress authorized the spending of $38 million for that purpose—less than a tenth of Japanese Americans' actual losses. In 1942 the Federal Reserve Bank in San Francisco estimated that the relocation had cost evacuees $400,000,000.

America would barely have time to deal with the aftermath of war and to adjust to peace, however, before it found itself mobilizing against a new enemy without and within—the threat of communism.

E. Answer To acknowledge the injustice done to Japanese Americans during the war.

THINK THROUGH HISTORY
E. *Evaluating Decisions* *Why did Congress award compensation to Japanese Americans years after the war ended?*

HISTORICAL SPOTLIGHT

REPARATIONS FOR INTERNMENT

The JACL did not give up its quest for justice in 1965. In 1978 it called for the payment of reparations, or restitution, to each individual that suffered internment. A decade later, Congress passed, and President Ronald Reagan signed, a bill that promised $20,000 to every Japanese American sent to a relocation camp.

When the checks were sent in 1990, a letter from President George Bush accompanied them, in which he stated, "We can never fully right the wrongs of the past. But we can take a clear stand for justice and recognize that serious injustices were done to Japanese Americans during World War II."

Section  Assessment

1. TERMS & NAMES
Identify:
- GI Bill of Rights
- James Farmer
- Congress of Racial Equality (CORE)
- Japanese Americans Citizens League (JACL)

2. SUMMARIZING List the advances and problems in the economy and in civil rights during World War II.

	Advances	Problems
Economy		
Civil Rights		

Which of these advances and problems do you think had the most far-reaching effect?

3. DRAWING CONCLUSIONS What effect do you think World War II had on the traditional attitudes and beliefs of Americans?

THINK ABOUT
- the role of women in families and the economy
- the relationship between the races
- the impact of the federal government on society

4. MAKING INFERENCES How were the experiences of African Americans, Mexican Americans, and Japanese Americans similar during World War II?

THINK ABOUT
- the role of each group in the military
- government actions toward each group
- wartime changes that affected minority groups

ANSWERS

1. TERMS & NAMES

GI Bill of Rights, p. 598

James Farmer, p. 599

Congress of Racial Equality (CORE), p. 599

Japanese American Citizens League (JACL), p. 601

2. SUMMARIZING

Possible Answers:
Economy Advances: Low unemployment, rising crop prices, opportunity for women. **Problems:** Shortages of housing and food.
Civil Rights—Advances: More equality in the military, founding of CORE. **Problems:** Segregation, discrimination, race riots in Detroit and Los Angeles, internment of Japanese Americans.

3. DRAWING CONCLUSIONS

Possible Responses: Some students may say the war broke down traditions as it drew women into the workplace and gave African Americans more opportunities in the military. Others may argue that riots and the Korematsu decision strengthened the tradition of discrimination.

4. MAKING INFERENCES

Possible Response: Despite service in the military, members of all three groups suffered from discrimination backed by government action.

MORE ABOUT . . .
America's Debt to Japanese Americans

Several thousand Japanese Americans served as interpreters and translators in the U.S. Military Intelligence Service during the war. These Nisei soldiers gleaned invaluable information from captured documents and battle plans and from intercepted radio transmissions. General Charles Willoughby, chief of military intelligence in the Pacific, estimated that the contributions of Japanese Americans shortened the war by two years.

ASSESS & RETEACH

Section 4 Assessment

Have students work in groups of four, with each student answering one question.

Self-Assessment

Have students note the changes made in their answers during group discussion. Ask them how they could improve their answers next time.

Section Quiz

FORMAL ASSESSMENT
Section Quiz, p. 215

Reteach

Use the poster of Obie Bartlett on page 596 as the basis of a class discussion of the social impact of World War II on various groups of Americans.

CLOSE

World War II had a wide-ranging impact on American society. People became more affluent and mobile as job opportunities arose; marriage—and divorce—rates soared; and minorities became increasingly militant in their opposition to discrimination and injustice.

 ***CRITICAL THINKING TRANSPARENCIES***
CT25, U.S. Joins the Allies in World War II
CT59, Human Cost of World War II

CHAPTER 17
ASSESSMENT ANSWERS

REVIEWING THE CHAPTER

TERMS & NAMES

1. A. Philip Randolph, p. 573
2. Nisei, p. 575
3. Dwight D. Eisenhower, p. 581
4. D-Day, p. 583
5. V-E Day, p. 585
6. Douglas MacArthur, p. 587
7. Manhattan Project, p. 590
8. Hiroshima, p. 591
9. GI Bill of Rights, p. 598
10. Congress of Racial Equality (CORE), p. 599

MAIN IDEAS

11. It included large numbers of whites, African Americans, Native Americans, Mexican Americans, and Asian Americans.
12. Factories converted to military production, civilians took jobs in military industries, scientists worked on military research, and the entertainment industry produced propaganda films.
13. It drafted civilians, interned Japanese Americans, and established a system of rationing and other economic controls.
14. They used the convoy system and an accelerated shipbuilding program.
15. Soviets stopped Germany's eastward expansion, destroyed the German Sixth Army, and prevented the Germans from focusing on the western front.
16. Germany could not replace the men and weapons it lost, and could only retreat.
17. The United States avoided attacking Japanese strongholds and used its air power to cut off supplies to them.
18. The United States wanted to avoid the casualties resulting from an invasion of Japan and to end the war quickly.
19. Unemployment decreased, more women took factory jobs, and both housing and food were in short supply.
20. Race riots in Detroit, the zoot suit riots in Los Angeles, and the internment of Japanese Americans.

Chapter 17 Assessment

REVIEWING THE CHAPTER

TERMS & NAMES For each term below, write a sentence explaining its connection to World War II. For each person below, explain his or her role in the war.

1. **A. Philip Randolph**
2. **Nisei**
3. **Dwight D. Eisenhower**
4. **D-Day**
5. **V-E Day**
6. **Douglas MacArthur**
7. **Manhattan Project**
8. **Hiroshima**
9. **GI Bill of Rights**
10. **Congress of Racial Equality (CORE)**

MAIN IDEAS

SECTION 1 *(pages 570–577)*

Mobilization on the Home Front

11. How did the U.S. military reflect the diversity of American society during World War II?
12. How did World War II affect life on the home front?
13. How did the federal government's actions influence civilian life during World War II?

SECTION 2 *(pages 578–585)*

The War for Europe and North Africa

14. How did the Allies win control of the Atlantic Ocean between 1941 and 1943?
15. What was the significance of the Battle of Stalingrad?
16. How did the Battle of the Bulge signal the beginning of the end of World War II in Europe?

SECTION 3 *(pages 586–593)*

The War in the Pacific

17. What strategy did the United States use in fighting the Japanese in the Pacific?
18. Why did President Truman decide to use atomic weapons on Hiroshima and Nagasaki?

SECTION 4 *(pages 596–601)*

The Impact of the War

19. How did the U.S. economy change during World War II?
20. What events show the persistence of racial tension during World War II?

THINKING CRITICALLY

1. **HEADLINE EVENTS** List the five most important political and military events and the five most important social and economic changes during World War II.

World War II

Political and Military Events	Social and Economic Changes
1.	1.
2.	2.
3.	3.
4.	4.
5.	5.

2. **NUCLEAR DECISION** Nuclear weapons are vastly more powerful now than they were in 1945. Would you support the use of nuclear weapons today, and if so, under what circumstances?
3. **TRACING THEMES WOMEN IN AMERICA** Do you think the opportunities that opened up for women during World War II would have arisen if the United States hadn't entered the war? Explain your answer.
4. **UPDATING DECISIONS** Reread the quotation from President Roosevelt on page 568. Then reread his statement on page 540. What hints, if any, in his first statement indicate that he might reverse his position on neutrality?
5. **GEOGRAPHY OF MILITARY EXPANSION** Study the map on page 579. What geographic features might have slowed expansion by the Axis countries? What features—or lack of features—emphasize the significance of the Soviet defense of Stalingrad?
6. **ANALYZING PRIMARY SOURCES** Ernie Pyle, probably the most popular journalist who covered World War II, believed that the war changed how soldiers viewed the world:

> Our men, still thinking of home, are impatient with the strange peoples and customs of the countries they now inhabit. They say that if they ever get home they never want to see another foreign country. But I know how it will be. The day will come when they'll look back and brag about how they learned a little Arabic, and how swell the girls were in England, and how pretty the hills of Germany were. Every day their scope is broadening despite themselves, and once they all get back with their global yarns and their foreign-tinged views, I cannot conceive of our nation ever being isolationist again.
>
> **ERNIE PYLE,** *Here Is Your War*

Summarize the shift in attitudes that Pyle describes. Explain whether you agree or disagree with the conclusion he draws.

THINKING CRITICALLY

1. HEADLINE EVENTS
Possible Responses: **Political and military events**—The attack on Pearl Harbor, the Battle of Midway, the Soviet defense of Stalingrad, the D-Day invasion, the bombing of Hiroshima, and the Nuremberg trials. **Economic and social changes**—The proposed march on Washington, the internment of Japanese Americans, new roles for women, and the movement of people to new communities.

2. NUCLEAR DECISION
Possible Responses: **Pro**—Use of nuclear weapons is justified to respond to an enemy attack or to stop another country from using them. **Con**—Using atomic weapons is never justifiable because they kill and maim so massively and indiscriminately.

3. TRACING THEMES WOMEN IN AMERICA
Possible Responses: **Yes**—Change would have come anyway, but more gradually. **No**—Only a dramatic event such as World War II could break down a strongly held traditions such as keeping women in the home.

ALTERNATIVE ASSESSMENT

1. **PROJECT FOR CITIZENSHIP**
   Volunteers played a vital role in the American war effort. Ordinary citizens volunteered their time, resources, and expertise to ensure victory.

   Cooperative Activity With a group of three to five classmates, imagine that you are serving on a board to organize volunteers in your community during World War II. Create a guide for volunteers wanting to help in the war effort. For ideas, see "Volunteering in Your Community" on page 115 in Projects for Citizenship.

   CD-ROM Conduct research, using the CD-ROM *Our Times*, your textbook, and other resources, such as the Internet or library books. Find out what kinds of activities people volunteered to do during the war in your community and elsewhere.

- Create a list of all the services needed in the war effort. Then set up volunteer organizations to meet those needs.
- Establish rules, guidelines, or schedules for volunteers participating in each of the organizations. Consider how much personal sacrifice people could make, and take that into account when you create your guidelines.
- Use the materials you have gathered to write a pamphlet that describes the services organized by your board.

2. **PICTURING HISTORY**
   Create a visual history of World War II, using photocopies of 10 to 20 pictures taken during the war. As you select your pictures, consider the story you want to tell about the war and the images that best convey that story. For each picture, write a caption that explains the image and its significance. Finally, write an introduction to your photo essay, briefly explaining the message you want to get across. Save your materials in your American history portfolio.

3. **PORTFOLIO PROJECT**
   Use the Living History activity to expand your portfolio.

LIVING HISTORY

ASSESSING YOUR ALTERNATIVE HISTORY

Read your alternative history essay to the class. Have other students evaluate your essay, using the following criteria:

- Does the "what if" question address a significant event in the history of the Second World War?
- Does the essay logically consider how World War II would have been different in the alternative situation?
- Does the essay realistically predict the ways in which the outcome of the war would be affected?

Write a short evaluation and add it and your essay to your history portfolio.

Bridge to Chapter 18

Review Chapter 17

MOBILIZATION FOR WAR After the Japanese attack on Pearl Harbor, the United States mobilized to defeat the Axis powers. The 5 million volunteers and 10 million draftees included men and women of all ethnic and racial groups. Industries, workers, and scientists all contributed to the war effort. The government relocated Japanese Americans and instituted economic controls to promote military production and to prevent inflation.

FIGHTING IN EUROPE The United States, along with its allies, won control of the Atlantic Ocean in the middle of 1943. A heroic defense of Stalingrad by the Soviet Union, along with Allied victories in North Africa and Italy and the D-Day invasion on June 6, 1944, led to a retreat by German forces. Finally, on May 8, 1945, Germany surrendered.

WAR IN THE PACIFIC By the middle of 1942, the United States had stopped Japanese expansion with victories at the Coral Sea and Midway. Island hopping allowed the United States to avoid direct attacks on Japanese strongholds. Some of the bloodiest fighting in the Pacific occurred on Iwo Jima and Okinawa. When the atomic bomb became available, President Truman ordered that it be dropped on the Japanese cities of Hiroshima and Nagasaki. With the Japanese surrender on September 2, 1945, the war in the Pacific ended. War criminals from both Germany and Japan were tried by international tribunals.

THE IMPACT World War II resulted in great economic gains for the United States. During the war, unemployment decreased, many women found jobs, and millions of Americans relocated. With these growing opportunities, though, came an increase in racial and ethnic tensions. Riots in Detroit and Los Angeles, and the internment of Japanese Americans reflected the seriousness of these tensions.

Preview Chapter 18

After World War II ended, a new conflict emerged between two former allies—the United States and the Soviet Union. This conflict dominated America's politics and its foreign policy, leading to a war in Korea, a crisis in the Middle East, and widespread suspicion of disloyalty at home. You will learn about these significant developments in the next chapter.

ALTERNATIVE ASSESSMENT

1. PROJECT FOR CITIZENSHIP

Standards for Evaluation
A news broadcast should meet the following criteria:

- Includes a wide variety of volunteer activities for many different citizens to perform.
- Ensures that the volunteer activities listed were necessary and important to the war effort.
- Demonstrates a clear understanding of the types of volunteer activities that actually existed during the Second World War.

2. PICTURING HISTORY

Standards for Evaluation
A pictorial history should meet the following criteria:

- Tells a coherent story about World War II.
- Presents images in a logical sequence.
- Includes captions that concisely identify and enhance the images.
- Has a concise introduction that explains the intent of the presentation.

3. PORTFOLIO PROJECT

LIVING HISTORY

Standards for Evaluation
An alternative history should meet the following criteria:

- Addresses a critical event in the history of the Second World War.
- Draws logical conclusions about the consequences of changing that event.
- Makes realistic predictions about how the outcome of the war would be affected.

IN-DEPTH RESOURCES: UNIT 5
See the form for scoring this activity on page 38.

THINKING CRITICALLY

4. UPDATING DECISIONS

Possible Response: Roosevelt's statement that he could not ask Americans to be neutral in thought might have indicated that he was not totally committed to neutrality in his own thoughts.

5. GEOGRAPHY OF MILITARY EXPANSION

Possible Response: Expansion might have been difficult west across the Atlantic Ocean, south across the Sahara, and north into the Arctic. No geographic feature slowed expansion eastward into the Soviet Union.

6. ANALYZING PRIMARY SOURCES

Pyle believed that World War II destroyed isolationism because it opened many Americans' minds to the larger world. Opinions will vary but should be supported with reasons.

CHAPTER 18

PLANNING GUIDE

Cold War Conflicts

	Key Ideas	COPYMASTERS	ASSESSMENT
SECTION 1 Origins of the Cold War *pp. 606–612*	*The Allied coalition falls apart as the United States and the Soviet Union find themselves in conflict with each other.*	***In-Depth Resources: Unit 5*** • Guided Reading, p. 39 • Skillbuilder Practice: Analyzing Motives, p. 43 • Geography Application: The Marshall Plan, p. 44 • Primary Source: *from* Harry S. Truman's Letter to His Daughter, p. 46 ***Lesson Plans,*** pp. 149–150	PE ***Section 1 Assessment,*** p. 612 TE ***Self-Assessment,*** p. 612 ***Formal Assessment*** • Section Quiz, p. 224 ***Alternative Assessment Book*** • Standards for Evaluating a Cooperative Activity
SECTION 2 The Cold War Heats Up *pp. 613–618*	*U.S. containment policies and Communist successes in China and North Korea lead to the Korean War.*	***In-Depth Resources: Unit 5*** • Guided Reading, p. 40 • Primary Source: *from* Douglas MacArthur's Farewell to Congress, p. 47 • American Lives: Douglas MacArthur, p. 53 ***Lesson Plans,*** pp. 151–152	PE ***Section 2 Assessment,*** p. 618 TE ***Self-Assessment,*** p. 618 ***Formal Assessment*** • Section Quiz, p. 225 ***Alternative Assessment Book*** • Standards for Evaluating a Cooperative Activity
SECTION 3 The Cold War at Home *pp. 619–624*	*The Cold War kindles a fear of Communist influence in the United States.*	***In-Depth Resources: Unit 5*** • Guided Reading, p. 41 • American Lives: Margaret Chase Smith, p. 54 ***Lesson Plans,*** pp. 153–154	PE ***Section 3 Assessment,*** p. 624 TE ***Self-Assessment,*** p. 624 ***Formal Assessment*** • Section Quiz, p. 226 ***Alternative Assessment Book*** • Standards for Evaluating a Cooperative Activity
SECTION 4 Two Nations Live on the Edge *pp. 625–629*	*Tension mounts between the United States and the Soviet Union as both try to spread their influence around the world.*	***In-Depth Resources: Unit 5*** • Guided Reading, p. 42 • Primary Source: *from* Dwight D. Eisenhower's Statement on the U-2 Incident, p. 49 • Literature: from *The Nuclear Age* by Tim O'Brien, p. 50 ***Lesson Plans,*** pp. 155–156	PE ***Section 4 Assessment,*** p. 629 TE ***Self-Assessment,*** p. 629 ***Formal Assessment*** • Section Quiz, p. 227 ***Alternative Assessment Book*** • Standards for Evaluating a Cooperative Activity
CHAPTER RESOURCES	**Chapter Overview** *After World War II, tensions between the United States and the Soviet Union lead to a war without direct military confrontation–a Cold War*	***In-Depth Resources: Unit 5*** • Living History Project: Worksheet, p. 55; Standards, p. 56 ***Telescoping the Times*** • Chapter Summary, pp. 35–36 ***Planning for Block Schedules***	PE ***Chapter Assessment,*** pp. 632–633 PE ***Alternative Assessment,*** p. 633 ***Formal Assessment*** • Chapter Test, forms A and B, pp. 228–233 ***Test Generator*** ***Alternative Assessment Book*** See explanation and forms for different kinds of alternative assessments including portfolio assessment.

KEY
PE Pupil's Edition
TE Teacher's Edition
http://www.mlushistory.com

TECHNOLOGY

Warm-Up Transparency **18**

Geography Transparencies
- G26, The Berlin Airlift: 1948–49

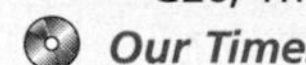
Our Times
- The Creation of NATO

Electronic Library of Primary Sources
- The Truman Doctrine

INTERNET Truman and the Marshall Plan

Warm-Up Transparency **18**

Electronic Library of Primary Sources
- Frustration in Korea by Douglas MacArthur

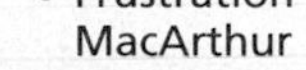
INTERNET Korean War and Douglas MacArthur

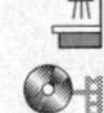
Warm-Up Transparency **18**

AMERICAN STORIES video series
- "The Cold War Comes Home"

Electronic Library of Primary Sources
- Statement on Civil Liberties in America by Paul Robeson

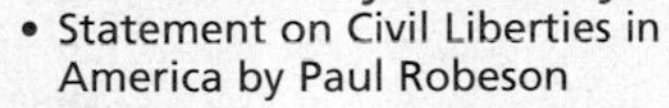

INTERNET Interact with History, p. 623 (PE)

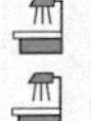
Warm-Up Transparency **18**

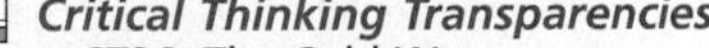
Critical Thinking Transparencies
- CT26, The Cold War
- CT60, The Space Race

Humanities Transparencies
- H25, California bomb shelter, 1951
- H41, Political Cartoon

Electronic Library of Primary Sources
- Life in a Shelter by Thamar E. Dufwa

Grolier Multimedia Encyclopedia
- The Cold War
- Soviet-Russian manned spaceflight

INTERNET *Sputnik* and the U-2

American Portfolio: A Videodisc for U.S. History, user's guide, pp. 234–241

Chapter Summary Audiotapes
- Unit 5, Chapter 18

INTERNET http://www.mlushistory.com

Block Scheduling (90 MINUTES)

Day 1
Section 1, pp. 606–612
Section Assessment, p. 612

COOPERATIVE ACTIVITIES
- Letters from Truman and Stalin, p. 607 (TE)
- Researching the Berlin Airlift, p. 611 (TE)

Day 2
Section 2, pp. 613–618
Section Assessment, p. 618

COOPERATIVE ACTIVITY
- Debating Containment, p. 615 (TE)

Day 3
Section 3, pp. 619–624
Section Assessment, p. 624

AMERICAN STORIES video series
- "The Cold War Comes Home"

COOPERATIVE ACTIVITIES
- Examining the Rosenberg Case, p. 621 (TE)
- Investigating Witch Hunts, p. 623 (TE)

Day 4
Section 4, pp. 625–629
Section Assessment, p. 629
American Literature: Science Fiction Reflects Cold War Realities, pp. 630–631
Chapter Assessment, pp. 632–633

COOPERATIVE ACTIVITY
- Creating a Political Cartoon, p. 627 (TE)

YEARLY PACING *Chapter 18 Total:* 4 days *Yearly Total:* 85 days

See *Planning for Block Schedules* for special activities and pacing strategies.

Customizing for Special Populations

Students Acquiring English
Access for Students Acquiring English: Spanish Translations
- Guided Reading for Sections 1–4 (Spanish), pp. 207–210
- Chapter Summary (Spanish), pp. 205–206
- Skillbuilder Practice: Analyzing Motives (Spanish), p. 211
- Geography Application: The Marshall Plan (Spanish), p. 212

Spanish Reading Study Guide, pp. 187–196

Translations of Chapter Summaries, Hmong, Cantonese, Vietnamese, and Cambodian

Chapter Summary Audiotapes in Spanish
Unit 5, Chapter 18

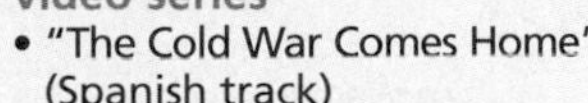
AMERICAN STORIES video series
- "The Cold War Comes Home" (Spanish track)

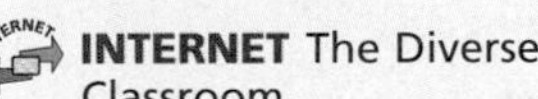
INTERNET The Diverse Classroom

Gifted and Talented Students
In-Depth Resources: Unit 5
- Primary Sources: *from* Harry S. Truman's letter to his daughter, p. 46; *from* MacArthur's Farewell Address to Congress, p.47; *from* Dwight D. Eisenhower's Statement on the U-2, p. 49
- American Lives: Douglas MacArthur, p. 53; Margaret Chase Smith, p. 54

Less Proficient Readers
In-Depth Resources: Unit 5
- Guided Reading for Sections 1–4, pp. 39–42
- Skillbuilder Practice: Analyzing Motives, p. 43
- Geography Application: The Marshall Plan, p. 44

Reading Study Guide
- pp. 187–196

Telescoping the Times
- Chapter Summary, pp. 35–36

Chapter Summary Audiotapes, Unit 5, Chapter 18

Connections to Literature READINGS FOR STUDENTS

In-Depth Resources: Unit 5
- **from *The Nuclear Age* by Tim O'Brien,** pp. 50–52

McDougal Littell *Literature Connections*

- **George Orwell**
1984 *(with related readings). Originally published in 1949, this startling, futuristic indictment of the totalitarian state was the original "big brother."*

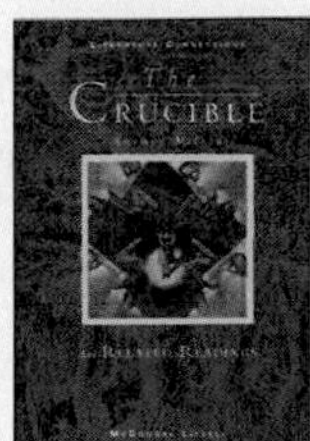

- **Arthur Miller**
The Crucible *(with related readings). A witch hunt in Puritan New England with overtones of McCarthyism.*

- **Ray Bradbury**
Fahrenheit 451 *(with related readings). Set in a future where the government burns books to keep people from thinking or rebelling, this chilling story, first published in 1953, has powerful meaning today.*

- **George Orwell**
Animal Farm *(with related readings). An animal fable satirizing communism and warning against the dangers of totalitarianism.*

CHAPTER 18

OVERVIEW

Cold War Conflicts

▶ *Accessing Prior Knowledge*

Ask students to speculate about ways in which the Cold War was "cold." Then discuss the opening quotation with them.

▶ *Predicting Outcomes*

Ask the students why the wartime alliance between the United States and the Soviet Union might fall apart. What do the students think could be the ultimate consequences of that division?

MORE ABOUT . . .

J. Robert Oppenheimer

J. Robert Oppenheimer (1904–1967) is known as the father of the atomic bomb because of his work directing the development of the first A-bomb in Los Alamos, New Mexico, from 1943 to 1945. After the war, he served as an adviser for the newly formed Atomic Energy Commission and for the U.S. Department of Defense. He also worked to establish international control of nuclear energy.

CHAPTER 18

Cold War Conflicts

SECTION 1

Origins of the Cold War

The Allied coalition falls apart as the United States and the Soviet Union find themselves in conflict with each other.

SECTION 2

The Cold War Heats Up

U.S. containment policies and Communist successes in China and North Korea lead to the Korean War.

SECTION 3

The Cold War at Home

The Cold War kindles a fear of Communist influence in the United States.

VIDEO

THE COLD WAR COMES HOME

SECTION 4

Two Nations Live on the Edge

Tension mounts between the United States and the Soviet Union as both try to spread their influence around the world.

"We may be likened to two scorpions in a bottle, each capable of killing the other, but only at the risk of his own life."

J. Robert Oppenheimer, speaking of the buildup of atomic weapons by the United States and the Soviet Union, 1953

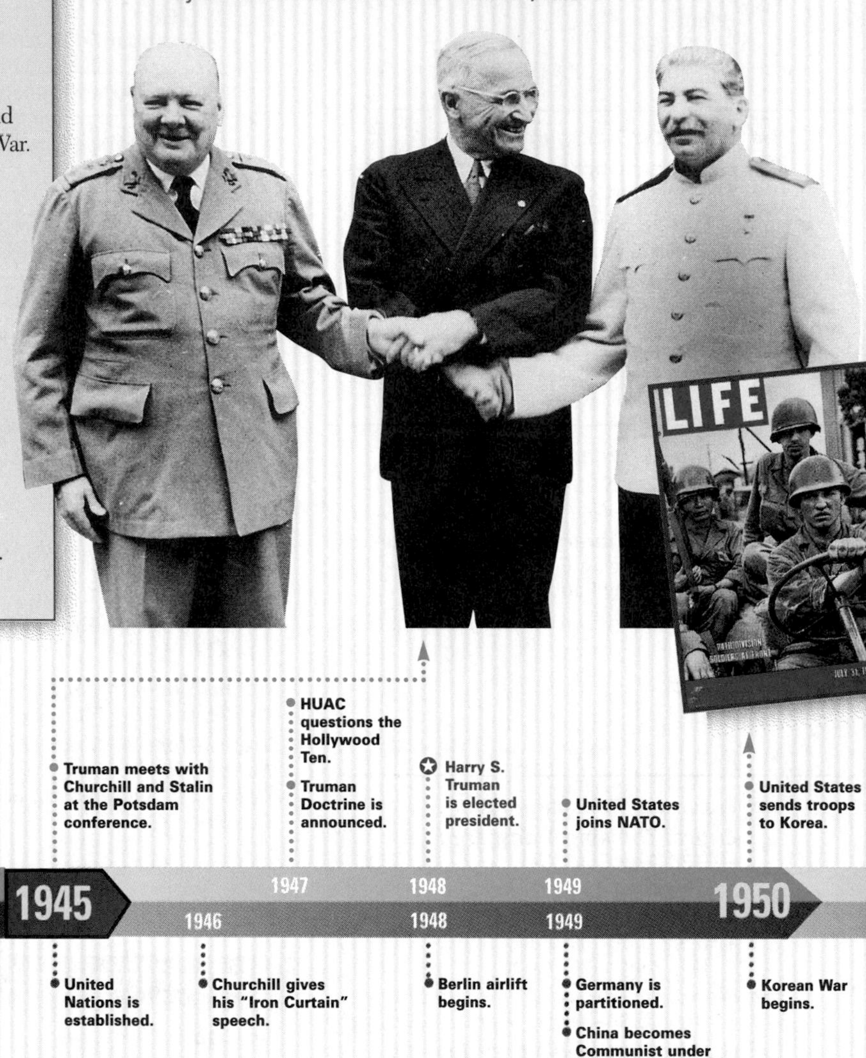
LIFE
THE UNITED STATES
THE WORLD
1945
Truman meets with Churchill and Stalin at the Potsdam conference.
United Nations is established.
1946
Churchill gives his "Iron Curtain" speech.
1947
HUAC questions the Hollywood Ten.
Truman Doctrine is announced.
1948
Harry S. Truman is elected president.
1948
Berlin airlift begins.
1949
United States joins NATO.
1949
Germany is partitioned.
China becomes Communist under Mao Zedong.
1950
United States sends troops to Korea.
Korean War begins.

THEMES IN CHAPTER 18

Economic Opportunity	*America in the World*	*Constitutional Concerns*	*Science and Technology*
After World War II, the United States converted to a peacetime economy. It faced the monumental tasks of supplying jobs for returning soldiers and meeting civilians' demand for goods that were unavailable in wartime. See Teacher's Edition note, p. 608.	The United States intervened in the Korean War as part of a UN contingent. It has done this regularly in other conflicts since the end of the Cold War. See Teacher's Edition note, p. 617.	Senator Joseph McCarthy posed a constitutional threat when he attempted to eliminate suspected Communists from the country. This "witch hunt" trampled Americans' civil liberties of free speech and assembly. See Teacher's Edition note, p. 620.	The scientific achievements that led to the creation of the atomic and hydrogen bombs also cast a shadow of impending nuclear holocaust over the 1950s. Despite this fear, many peaceful applications of nuclear energy resulted. See Teacher's Edition note, p. 628.

LIVING HISTORY

CONDUCTING TWO INTERVIEWS

Conduct two interviews—one with a person who was a teenager during the period 1945–1960 and another with someone who was an adult during that period. The topic of the interviews should be the people's memories of the Cold War and its effects on Americans. Possible questions to ask include

- What do you remember as your greatest fear during the Cold War?
- What do you recall as important conflicts during that time?

PORTFOLIO PROJECT Keep the records of your interviews in a folder. At the end of this chapter, you will compile and present the interviews and add them to your American history portfolio.

1952 — United States explodes the first hydrogen bomb.

1952 — Dwight D. Eisenhower is elected president.

1953 — Rosenbergs are executed as spies.

1953 — Soviets explode their first hydrogen bomb.

1953 — Korean War cease-fire is agreed to.

1954 — Senator Joseph McCarthy (shown with Roy Cohn) alleges Communist involvement in the U.S. Army.

1954 — French are defeated in Vietnam.

1955

1956 — President Eisenhower is reelected.

1957 — Soviets launch *Sputnik*.

1959 — Fidel Castro comes to power in Cuba.

1960 — Francis Gary Powers's U-2 spy plane is shot down by the Soviets.

1960 — John F. Kennedy is elected president.

ALTERNATIVE ASSESSMENT

LIVING HISTORY

CONDUCTING TWO INTERVIEWS

Suggest interviewing strategies that students can use.

- Look for people who are from about 55 to 75 years old to interview—family members, family friends, neighbors, or teachers.
- Compile some biographical information about the interviewees to help your audience understand the interview.
- Prepare a list of questions in advance.
- During the interviews, take notes and, with the permission of the interviewees, use a tape recorder.
- Note physical details of the interviewees to include in your presentation.

Interview Planning Guide

Step 1	**Students choose the people they are going to interview.**
Step 2	**Students prepare interview questions.**
Step 3	**Students conduct their interviews.**
Step 4	**Students compile their interview tapes and other relevant information in their folders.**

IN-DEPTH RESOURCES: UNIT 5
See worksheet and standards for evaluation, pp. 55, 56.

RECOMMENDED RESOURCES

Books for the Teacher

Bundy, McGeorge. *Danger and Survival: The Political History of the Nuclear Weapon.* New York: Random House, 1989.

McCullough, David. *Truman.* New York: Simon, 1992.

Paterson, Thomas. *On Every Front.* New York: Norton, 1979.

Winik, Jay. *On the Brink.* New York: Simon, 1996.

Books for the Student

Miller, Merle. *Plain Speaking: An Oral Biography of Harry S. Truman.* New York: Berkley, 1986.

Rovere, Richard. *Senator Joseph McCarthy.* New York: Harper, 1973.

Videos

Are We Winning, Mommy? America and the Cold War. First Run Features, 153 Waverly Place, New York, NY 10014

Atomic Cafe. Archives Project, New York, 1982. History of atomic bomb.

Fat Man and Little Boy. Paramount, 1990. The development of the first two atomic bombs.

Korea: The Unknown War. WGBH-Boston

On the Beach. Dir. Stanley Kramer. MGM/UA, 1959.

McCarthy: Death of a Witch Hunter. Film Archives, The Cinema Center, Botsford, CT 06404, 800-366-1920

Software

Trinity and Beyond: A History of Nuclear Weapons. Heizer Software, P.O. Box 232019, Pleasant Hill, CA 94523

Section 1 Overview

OBJECTIVES

1. To explain the breakdown of relations between the United States and the Soviet Union after World War II.
2. To summarize the steps the United States took to contain Soviet influence as tensions increased.
3. To describe how the Truman Doctrine and the Marshall Plan further defined and deepened the Cold War in Europe.
4. To explain how conflicts over Germany increased fears of Soviet aggression.

SKILLBUILDERS

- Interpreting charts, p. 608
- Understanding geography: location, human-environment interaction, p. 609
- Interpreting graphs, p. 610
- Understanding geography: location, place, p. 612

CRITICAL THINKING

- Analyzing causes, p. 608
- Analyzing motives, p. 609
- Theme: Economic Opportunity, p. 610
- Recognizing effects, p. 611
- Summarizing, p. 612
- Evaluating, p. 612
- Making inferences, p. 612

FOCUS & MOTIVATE

5-MINUTE WARM-UP

Using Sequential Order
To explore the chronological order of the origins of the Cold War, have students look at the time line on pages 604–605 and answer these questions.

1. Which occurred first—the Hollywood Ten hearings or the Army–McCarthy hearings?
2. Who was the American president when the Soviets launched Sputnik?

WARM-UP TRANSPARENCY 18

▶***Starting with the Student***

- What happens when two people, such as two students, stop being friendly because of conflicting

(continued on next page)

1 Origins of the Cold War

LEARN ABOUT economic and political differences between the United States and the Soviet Union
TO UNDERSTAND the Cold War and how it began.

TERMS & NAMES
- satellite nation
- containment
- Cold War
- Truman Doctrine
- Marshall Plan
- Berlin airlift
- North Atlantic Treaty Organization (NATO)

ONE AMERICAN'S STORY

Private Joseph Polowsky was 70 miles south of Berlin, part of a patrol of American soldiers who were scouting for signs of the Soviet army, which was advancing from the east. As the soldiers neared the Elbe River, they saw lilacs in bloom. Polowsky later said the sight of the flowers filled them with the "exaltation of being alive, after all those days trapped in a trench war."

On the other side of the Elbe, the Americans spotted Soviet soldiers, who signaled for them to cross over. When the Americans reached the other bank, their joy turned to shock. They saw to their horror that the bank was covered with dead civilians, victims of bombing raids.

32
USA
U.S. and Soviets link up at Elbe River, April 1945

American and Soviet soldiers meet *(top)* at the Elbe River in Germany near the end of World War II. A 1996 postage stamp *(above)* commemorates the historic meeting.

A PERSONAL VOICE

Here we are, tremendously exhilarated, and there's a sea of dead. . . . [The platoon leader] was much moved. . . . He said, "Joe, lets make a resolution with these Russians here and also the ones on the bank: this would be an important day in the lives of the two countries." . . . It was a solemn moment. There were tears in the eyes of most of us. . . . We embraced. We swore never to forget.

JOSEPH POLOWSKY, quoted in *The Good War*

The Soviet and U.S. soldiers believed that their encounter would serve as a symbol of peaceful relations between their two countries. Unfortunately, such hopes were soon dashed. After World War II, the United States and the Soviet Union emerged as rival superpowers, each strong enough to greatly influence world events.

Former Allies Clash

Although the American and Soviet soldiers hoped for friendship between their countries, problems had been building between the Soviet Union and the United States before and during the war. The two countries' economic and political systems were incompatible, and they had built up resentments toward each other over previous events.

In the Soviet system of communism, the state controlled all property and economic activity, while in the capitalistic American system, private citizens controlled almost all property and economic activity. In the American democratic system, the people elected a president and a congress from competing political parties; in the Soviet Union, the Communist Party established a totalitarian government in which no opposing parties were allowed to exist. The Soviets were deeply resentful that the United States had not recognized their Communist government until 16 years after the revolution.

In addition, the United States was furious that Joseph Stalin—the leader of the Soviet Union—had signed a nonaggression pact with Hitler in 1939. Although Hitler had broken the agreement two years later and the United

SECTION 1 RESOURCES

PRINT RESOURCES

IN-DEPTH RESOURCES: UNIT 5
Guided Reading, p. 39
Skillbuilder Practice: Analyzing Motives, p. 43
Geography Application: The Marshall Plan, p. 44
Primary Source: Harry S. Truman's Letter to His Daughter, p. 46

READING STUDY GUIDE, p. 187

ACCESS FOR STUDENTS ACQUIRING ENGLISH
Guided Reading (Spanish), p. 207
Skillbuilder Practice: Analyzing Motives (Spanish), p. 211
Geography Application: The Marshall Plan (Spanish), p. 212

SPANISH READING STUDY GUIDE, p. 187

FORMAL ASSESSMENT
Section Quiz, p. 224

ALTERNATIVE ASSESSMENT BOOK
See forms for supporting and scoring alternative activities.

TECHNOLOGY RESOURCES

GEOGRAPHY TRANSPARENCIES
G26, The Berlin Airlift: 1948–49

CD-ROM *Our Times*
Electronic Library of Primary Sources

VIDEO *American Portfolio: A Videodisc for U.S. History* user's guide, p. 235

INTERNET http://www.mlushistory.com

States and the Soviet Union had become allies during World War II, their leaders often hadn't seen eye to eye. Stalin had wanted the other Allies to invade Europe earlier than 1944, and their delay in doing so fed Stalin's distrust of them. Relations worsened after Stalin learned that the United States had kept its development of the atomic bomb secret from the Soviets.

In spite of these problems, hopes for world peace were high at the end of the war. The most visible symbol of these hopes was the United Nations (UN). On April 25, 1945, the representatives of 50 nations met in San Francisco to establish this new international peacekeeping body. After two months of debate, on June 26, 1945, the delegates signed the charter establishing the UN. The UN headquarters was built in New York City.

Ironically, even though the UN was intended to promote peace, it soon became an arena where the two superpowers competed. Both the United States and the Soviet Union used the UN as a forum to spread their influence over other nations.

TRUMAN BECOMES PRESIDENT For the United States, the key figure in the early years of conflict with the Soviets was President Harry S. Truman. Thirteen days before the UN conference convened, Truman had suddenly become president when Franklin Roosevelt died. In many ways he was unprepared for the responsibilities of national and world leadership. Before becoming vice-president, he had been a hard-working, well-liked senator but had had very little power. In the 82 days he was vice-president, he met with the president only twice. Roosevelt not only left him uninformed about military matters and peace negotiations—he did not even tell Truman that the United States was developing an atomic bomb!

Many Americans doubted Truman's abilities because they knew very little about him and he was very different from Roosevelt. Whereas Roosevelt had been a wealthy, handsome, sophisticated New Yorker, Truman was a self-educated, plain-spoken Missourian, whose only business venture had ended in failure. On the plus side, however, Truman had honesty, self-confidence, and a willingness to make tough decisions—qualities that he would need desperately in the first few months of his presidency. As the war ended, not only would he have to make difficult military decisions, but he would also have to deal with world leaders of vastly greater experience—such as Stalin and Churchill.

THE POTSDAM CONFERENCE Truman's first meeting with those two leaders came at the final wartime conference of the Big Three (the leaders of Great

KEY PLAYERS

HARRY S. TRUMAN
1884–1972

Young Harry S. Truman, the son of a Missouri livestock trader and his wife, did not seem destined for greatness. When he graduated from high school in 1901, he drifted from job to job—drugstore clerk, newspaper mailroom clerk, timekeeper, bank clerk, bookkeeper, farmer, World War I soldier. After the war, he invested in a men's clothing store; but the business failed, and he spent the next 15 years paying off business debts.

Discouraged by his business failure, Truman sought a career in politics. As a politician, his blunt and outspoken style won loyal friends and bitter enemies. As president, his decisiveness and willingness to accept responsibility for his decisions ("The Buck Stops Here" read a sign on his desk) earned him respect that has grown in the decades following his presidency.

JOSEPH STALIN
1879–1953

As a young revolutionary, Iosif Vissarionovich Dzhugashvili took the name Stalin, which means "man of steel."

His father was a failed shoemaker and an alcoholic. His mother helped support the family as a washerwoman. Following her wishes, Stalin entered a seminary, but he was eventually expelled for revolutionary activism.

Stalin is credited with turning the Soviet Union into a world power, but at a terrible cost to its citizens. He ruled with terror and brutality and saw "enemies" everywhere, even among friends and supporters. He subdued the population with the use of secret police and labor camps, and he is believed to have been responsible for the murder of millions of people in the Soviet Union.

(continued from page 606)

ideas or personalities?
- Could the same situation happen between two countries? Explain.

OBJECTIVE
① INSTRUCT

Former Allies Clash

▶ ***Discussing Key Ideas***
- The United States and the Soviet Union have incompatible economic and political systems.
- Both feel resentments over political slights.

IN-DEPTH RESOURCES: UNIT 5
Guided Reading, p. 39

ACCESS FOR STUDENTS ACQUIRING ENGLISH
Guided Reading (Spanish), p. 207

KEY PLAYERS
Truman and Stalin

Critical Thinking: Comparing and Contrasting Ask students to create a chart comparing Truman and Stalin on criteria such as family history, early life, education, political career, and character.

IN-DEPTH RESOURCES: UNIT 5
Primary Source: *from* Truman's Letter to His Daughter, p. 46

MORE ABOUT . . .
Joseph Stalin

Joseph Stalin amazed everyone who met him—this dictator of over 180 million people in a nation covering one-sixth of the earth; commander of huge, victorious armies; ruler by terror and murder—because he was physically small, standing about 5 feet 5. "A little bit of a squirt," Truman described him.

Block Schedule TEACHING OPTION **Time Needed: 20 Minutes**

Cooperative Activity: Letters from Truman and Stalin

Task: Student groups will write letters from Truman to Stalin and from Stalin to Truman protesting specific political actions.

Purpose: To help students understand the underlying tensions and resentments that contributed to Cold War conflicts.

Activity: Assign small groups of students to represent either Truman or Stalin. Groups will write letters protesting specific actions, such as Stalin's refusal to allow elections in Poland or the U.S. secrecy about the atomic bomb. The letters should urge changes in policy. Groups should read completed letters to the class.

Building a Portfolio: Students who add letters to their portfolios should attach a note indicating their contribution to the letter.

ALTERNATIVE ASSESSMENT BOOK
Standards for Evaluating a Cooperative Activity

Standards for Evaluation
Letters should . . .
- name at least one specific political action
- give detailed reasons for objecting to the action
- make a clear proposal for changing the policy
- use appropriate letter form and style

OBJECTIVE
② INSTRUCT

Tension Mounts

▶ ***Starting with the Student*** Ask students to think about how parents or teachers try to block what they believe are negative influences on teenagers, such as television or cigarette advertisements. Have students consider similar actions the United States might have taken to block, or contain, harmful Soviet influence in Europe.
- How do parental containment policies compare with the postwar containment policies of the U.S. government?

▶ ***Discussing Key Ideas***
- The Americans and Soviets want different political systems in Europe.
- The two countries have completely different economic systems.
- The Soviets take control of several European countries after World War II.
- The U.S. wants to block Soviet influence.

HISTORY FROM VISUALS
U.S. Aims Versus Soviet Aims in Europe

Reading the Chart Remind students to repeat the column head before reading each of the bulleted items: For example: *"The United States wanted to* encourage democracy . . ."

Extension Have pairs of students each write three sentences. One student will write a sentence summarizing a U.S. aim; the other will write a sentence summarizing the corresponding Soviet aim. Then the students will collaborate on a sentence explaining the incompatibility of the aims.

Britain, the United States, and the Soviet Union) at Potsdam, Germany, in July 1945. The participants at Potsdam differed from those at Yalta. Truman now took Roosevelt's place. Clement Atlee replaced Churchill in mid-conference, because Atlee's Labor Party won a national election.

At Yalta, the United States and Great Britain had insisted that the Soviets allow free, open elections in Poland and other Eastern European nations after the war. Stalin had agreed, but he had kept his language vague. Then, in 1945, the Soviets prevented free elections in Poland and banned democratic parties, leaving Poland in the hands of a pro-Soviet government. Stalin said that Poland was "not only a question of honor for Russia, but one of life and death."

To Truman, the Soviets' refusal to allow free and open elections in Poland and other Eastern European nations was a clear violation of those nations' right of self-determination. Consequently, at Potsdam, Truman pushed Stalin to allow free elections, but the Soviet dictator refused. With the Soviet army occupying the Eastern European nations in question, the West could do little.

THINK THROUGH HISTORY
A. Analyzing Causes *What did Stalin do to make President Truman distrust him?*

A. Answer Stalin would not allow free elections in Eastern Europe.

Tension Mounts

Stalin's refusal to allow free elections in Poland convinced Truman that U.S. and Soviet aims were deeply at odds. Truman's objective in demanding free elections in Eastern Europe was to spread democracy to nations that had been under Nazi rule. He and his advisers believed that the best way to avoid a third world war was to create a new world order in which all nations had the right of self-determination, guaranteed by free elections.

Truman also feared giving in too much to Stalin's demands for territory and war reparations. For example, Stalin wanted to strip all of Germany of its industry, using the plundered equipment to rebuild the war-torn economy of the Soviet Union. The United States and Great Britain opposed his demands, but it was agreed at Potsdam that each of the Allies could take reparations from the part of Germany that it occupied.

Truman also felt that the United States had a large economic stake in spreading democracy and free trade across the globe. In contrast to the war-ravaged countries of Europe and Asia, the United States had no ruined factories or bombed-out cities. U.S. industry boomed during the war, making the United States the economic leader of the world. To continue growing, American businesses wanted access to raw materials in Eastern Europe, and they wanted to be able to sell goods to Eastern European countries.

SOVIETS TIGHTEN THEIR GRIP ON EASTERN EUROPE On the other hand, the Soviet Union felt justified in staying in Eastern Europe. The Soviets had suf-

U.S. Aims Versus Soviet Aims in Europe

THE UNITED STATES WANTED TO	THE SOVIETS WANTED TO
• encourage democracy in other countries to help prevent the rise of new totalitarian governments	• encourage communism in other countries as part of the worldwide struggle between workers and the wealthy
• gain access to raw materials and markets for its booming industries	• transfer the industrial equipment of Eastern Europe to the Soviet Union to help rebuild its war-ravaged economy
• rebuild European governments to ensure stability and to create new markets for American goods	• control Eastern Europe to balance the U.S. influence in Western Europe
• reunite Germany, believing that Europe would be more secure if Germany were productive and less bitter about defeat	• keep Germany divided and weak, since the Germans had waged war against Russia twice in 30 years and had caused most of the 20 million Soviet deaths in World War II

SKILLBUILDER **INTERPRETING CHARTS** *Which U.S. aims involved economic growth? Which Soviet aims involved self-protection? How did the differences in these aims lead to the Cold War?*

Skillbuilder Answer **U.S. Aims:** Gaining access to raw materials and markets, rebuilding European governments. **Soviet Aims:** Controlling Eastern Europe, keeping Germany divided and weak. **Differences in Aims:** They were incompatible.

TEACHING OPTIONS

Teaching Less Proficient Readers

Clarifying Ideas Pair less proficient readers with more proficient ones to clarify the main ideas in this section. Have the student pairs follow these steps:

1. Read pages 608 and 609 of the text together.
2. Make a list of the causes of tension between the United States and the Soviet Union.
3. List unanswered questions they have about the tensions.
4. Review the pages and write answers to the questions.

Exploring Themes

Economic Opportunity Economic considerations strongly influenced U.S. foreign policy after World War II. The U.S. government wanted to promote a healthy world economy by making it possible for Europe to rebuild and by encouraging capitalism. At the same time, the United States was creating markets for its goods and materials.

Ask students if they think economic considerations continue to influence U.S. foreign policy today. *Possible Response: A potential market of more than one billion consumers is one reason the United States wants good relations with China today.*

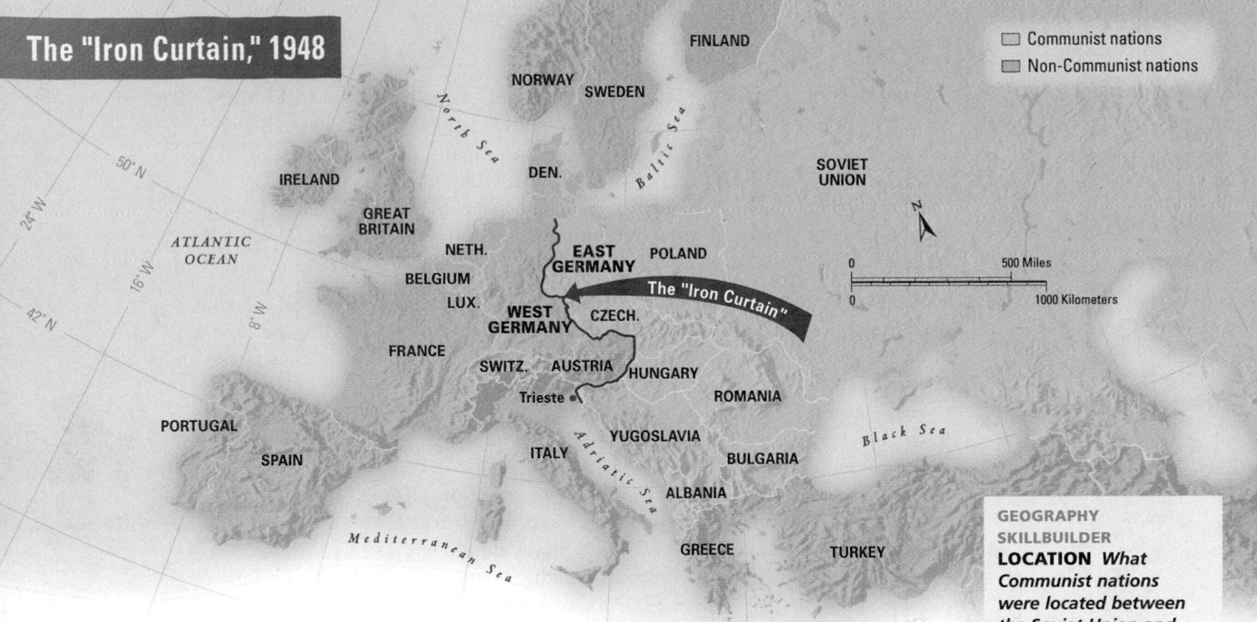

GEOGRAPHY SKILLBUILDER

LOCATION ***What Communist nations were located between the Soviet Union and the Iron Curtain?***

HUMAN-ENVIRONMENT INTERACTION ***Why did the Soviet Union want to control these nations?***

Skillbuilder Answer
Location: East Germany, Czechoslovakia, Poland, Hungary, Romania, Yugoslavia, Bulgaria, Albania.
Human-Environment Interaction: Stalin wanted a buffer between the Soviet Union and Western Europe.

fered more than 20 million deaths and extensive damage during World War II and felt vulnerable to attack from the west. They needed friendly neighbors—Communist countries that they could control.

B. Answer To create satellite nations on the Soviet Union's western border.

THINK THROUGH HISTORY
B. *Analyzing Motives* *What was Stalin's goal in supporting Communist governments in Eastern Europe?*

Stalin installed or propped up Communist governments in Albania, Bulgaria, Czechoslovakia, Hungary, Romania, and Poland. These countries became known as **satellite nations,** countries dependent upon and dominated by the Soviet Union. In addition, Stalin seized the industrial assets, such as factory equipment, of these countries to rebuild the Soviet Union. In early 1946, Stalin gave a speech announcing that communism and capitalism were incompatible—and that another war was inevitable. Therefore, he said, the Soviet Union would concentrate on producing weapons rather than consumer goods. The United States interpreted this speech as virtually a declaration of war.

THINK THROUGH HISTORY
C. *Analyzing Motives* *What were Truman's goals in establishing the policy of containment?*

C. Answer To stop the spread of Soviet influence.

UNITED STATES ESTABLISHES A POLICY OF CONTAINMENT Faced with the Soviet threat, American officials decided it was time, in Truman's words, to stop "babying the Soviets." In February 1946, George F. Kennan, an American diplomat in Moscow, proposed a policy of **containment**—an effort to block the Soviets' attempts to spread their influence by creating alliances and supporting weaker countries. This policy began to guide the Truman administration's foreign policy.

A few weeks later, in March 1946, Winston Churchill traveled to the United States and gave a speech that described the situation in Europe.

A PERSONAL VOICE

A shadow has fallen upon the scenes so lately lighted by the Allied victory. . . . From Stettin in the Baltic to Trieste in the Adriatic, an iron curtain has descended across the continent. Behind that line lie all the capitals of the ancient states of Central and Eastern Europe. . . . All these famous cities and the populations around them lie in the Soviet sphere and all are subject in one form or another, not only to Soviet influence but to a very high and increasing measure of control from Moscow.

WINSTON CHURCHILL, "Iron Curtain" speech in Fulton, Missouri

"An iron curtain has descended across . . . Europe."

WINSTON CHURCHILL

When Stalin heard about the speech, he declared in no uncertain terms that Churchill's words were a "call to war."

HISTORY FROM VISUALS

The "Iron Curtain," 1948

Reading the Map Have students examine the topographical features of the map, especially east of the iron curtain. What inference can they draw about the Soviet Union's vulnerability to attack? *Possible Response: Much of the land was flat and provided little protection against invasion from Western Europe.*

Extension Ask how the satellite nations functioned as a buffer zone for the Soviets. *Possible Response: Only about 500 miles separated the Soviet Union from the border of West Germany. By controlling nations on their border, the Soviets gained protection.*

Issues for the 21st Century

Foreign Policy After the Cold War

Connect U.S. Cold War policies to U.S. foreign policy today by having students read pages 878–879. Then have them answer these questions.

1. Did the U.S. response toward the Soviet Union at the end of the Cold War reflect greater interest in opposing aggression or opening markets? *Answers will vary.*
2. What do you think has replaced the Soviet Union as the main threat to American security? *Possible Responses: Terrorism, unfair trade, nuclear proliferation.*

TEACHING OPTION

SkillBuilder Mini-Lesson: Analyzing Motives

Explaining the Skill To analyze something is to separate it into its constituent parts. Analysis can be applied to almost anything—a math problem, a sports outcome, or the reasons behind political actions. Analyzing a motive involves separating the event into parts and then examining the emotions or needs that caused persons or groups to take the action.

Applying the Skill: Analyzing Motives To answer the Think Through History questions on this page, which ask students to analyze motives, suggest that they separate the subjects into the following parts:

Question B:
- need for buffers against invasion
- destruction to the Soviet Union during World War II
- industrial assets needed for rebuilding

Question C:
- Soviet actions after World War II
- differing ideologies of capitalism and communism

IN-DEPTH RESOURCES: UNIT 5
Skillbuilder Practice: Analyzing Motives, p. 43

OBJECTIVE

③ INSTRUCT

Cold War in Europe

▶ ***Starting with the Student*** Have students analyze the impact of the Truman Doctrine and the Marshall Plan by making charts listing the actions of the United States under each plan and the results of those actions.

	Action	Results
Truman Doctrine		
Marshall Plan		

▶ ***Discussing Key Ideas***

- The Truman Doctrine authorizes foreign aid to help prevent the spread of communism.
- The Marshall Plan enables Europe to rebuild and helps create markets for U.S. goods.

ELECTRONIC LIBRARY OF PRIMARY SOURCES
"The Truman Doctrine" by Harry S. Truman

HISTORY FROM VISUALS

The Marshall Plan

Reading the Graph Ask what factors students think determined the amount of aid each nation received. *Possible Response: Its involvement in and damage incurred by the war.*

IN-DEPTH RESOURCES: UNIT 5
Geography Application: The Marshall Plan, p. 44

Cold War in Europe

Bags of sugar arrive in Istanbul, Turkey, courtesy of the Marshall Plan.

The conflicting U.S. and Soviet aims in Eastern Europe led to the **Cold War**—the state of hostility short of direct military confrontation that developed between the two superpowers. The Cold War would dominate global affairs—and U.S. foreign policy—until the breakup of the Soviet Union in 1991.

During the Cold War, the United States and the Soviet Union tried to spread their political and economic influence wherever they could. Eventually the Cold War spread to Asia, Africa, and Latin America.

THE TRUMAN DOCTRINE The United States first tried to contain Soviet influence in Greece and Turkey. After the war, Britain was sending economic and military support to both nations to prevent Communist takeovers. However Britain's economy had been badly hurt by the war, and the formerly wealthy nation could no longer afford to give the aid. It asked the United States to take over the responsibility.

On March 12, 1947, Truman asked Congress for $400 million in economic and military aid for Greece and Turkey. The president also declared that the United States should support free peoples throughout the world who were resisting takeovers by "armed minorities" or "outside pressures." This statement, known as the **Truman Doctrine,** caused great controversy. Some of its opponents objected to interfering in the internal affairs of other nations. Others argued that U.S. power would be spread too thin if the country carried on a global crusade against communism. Still others opposed helping any dictators, even if they were anti-Communist.

Congress, though, agreed with Truman and decided that the doctrine was essential to keeping Soviet influence from spreading in Europe. So between 1947 and 1950, the United States sent over $400 million in aid to Turkey and Greece, greatly reducing the danger of Communists' taking over those nations.

The Marshall Plan

Country	Millions of Dollars
Great Britain	2,826
France	2,445
Italy	1,316
West Germany	1,297
Holland	877
Austria	561
Belgium /Lux.	547
Greece	515
Denmark	257
Norway	237
Turkey	153
Ireland	146
Sweden	119
Portugal	51
Yugoslavia	33
Iceland	29
Other	350

0 500 1000 1500 2000 2500
Millions of Dollars

Source: *Problemes Économiques*, No. 306

SKILLBUILDER
INTERPRETING GRAPHS ***Which country received the most aid from the U.S.? Why do you think that country received so much aid?***

THE MARSHALL PLAN Like postwar Greece, Western Europe was in economic chaos. Most of its factories had been bombed or looted. Many Europeans could not find work, and many turned to the black market and theft in order to survive. Millions of people were living in refugee camps while European governments tried to figure out where to resettle them.

To make matters worse, the winter of 1946–1947 was the bitterest in several centuries, with below-zero temperatures and record-breaking snow. The weather severely damaged crops and froze rivers, cutting off water transportation and causing a fuel shortage. In Britain, people could use electricity only a few hours each day, and food rations were even lower than during the war.

In June 1947, Secretary of State George Marshall proposed that the United States provide aid to all European nations that needed it, saying that this move was directed "not against any country or doctrine but against hunger, poverty, desperation, and chaos." However, in keeping with U.S. economic goals, the nations receiving aid had to remove trade barriers and to cooperate economically with one another.

Congress debated the **Marshall Plan** for several months. Many people opposed giving away $12.5 billion. Then, in February 1948, Soviet tanks rumbled into Czechoslovakia and took over the country. This invasion dramatized to Congress the need for strong, stable governments in Europe to resist communism, so it quickly approved the Marshall Plan.

D. Answer The financial aid helped pull the weak European economies out of their postwar problems.

THINK THROUGH HISTORY
D. THEME ***Economic Opportunity*** *How did the Marshall Plan contribute to growth in Europe?*

Skillbuilder Answer **Country:** Great Britain. **Reason:** *Possible Answer:* It was the staunchest U.S. ally.

TEACHING OPTIONS

Making Connections Across Time

Relations with Former Soviet Republics Today Ask students what they know about current relations between the United States and the former Soviet republics. Discuss with them the struggles these countries—and other former Communist countries such as Poland and Czechoslovakia—have had in making the transition to capitalism. You might want to mention that the United States has provided business and educational assistance to these countries through organizations such as the Peace Corps.

Making Connections Across the Curriculum

Economics Ask why the United States was the only large country in the world with a healthy economy after World War II. *Students may say that the U.S. mainland was never bombed. U.S. factories, farms, railroads, and cities were untouched by the war, while most European countries and Japan suffered devastating damage.*

How did the Marshall Plan help both the European and the U.S. economy? *Students may point out that the credit the plan provided allowed Europeans to purchase goods from U.S. manufacturers. These new markets created a demand for U.S. goods, which stimulated the American economy.*

The plan was a great success both economically and politically. Nutrition improved. Industry grew. By 1952, Western Europe was flourishing, and Communist parties had lost much of their appeal to voters.

Superpowers Struggle over Germany

As Europe began to get back on its feet, the United States and its allies clashed with the Soviet Union over German reunification. At the end of World War II, Germany had been divided into four zones, occupied by the United States, Great Britain, and France in the west and the Soviet Union in the east. The Soviet Union wanted to keep Germany weak and divided. In contrast, the other three nations believed that Europe would be more stable if German industry were productive and the German people were not agitating for unity. In 1948, they decided to recombine the three western zones into one nation.

THE BERLIN AIRLIFT The Soviet Union retaliated by holding West Berlin hostage. Although Berlin lay deep within the Soviet zone of Germany, it was also divided into four zones. (See the map on the next page.) When the three western zones of Germany reunified, the Soviet Union cut off all highway, water, and rail traffic into the western zones of Berlin. No supplies could get in, so the city faced starvation. Stalin believed this threat would force the Western nations either to give up the idea of a reunified Germany or to surrender control of Berlin.

The resulting situation was dire. West Berlin's 2.1 million inhabitants would run out of food and fuel in about five weeks. In an attempt to break the blockade, American and British officials started the **Berlin airlift** to fly food and supplies into West Berlin. For 327 days, planes took off and landed every few minutes, around the clock. In 277,000 flights, they brought in 2.3 million tons of supplies—everything from food, fuel, and medicine to Christmas presents that the planes' crews bought with their own money.

E. Answer It broke the Soviet blockade, increased U.S. prestige, and reduced Soviet prestige.

THINK THROUGH HISTORY
E. *Recognizing Effects* *What were the effects of the Berlin airlift?*

West Berlin survived because of the airlift. In addition, the mission to aid Berlin gave a large boost to American prestige around the world, while causing Soviet prestige to drop. By May 1949, the Soviet Union realized it was beaten and lifted the Berlin blockade.

In the same month voters in the western part of Germany approved a constitution. By fall the Federal Republic of Germany, commonly called West Germany, had been established, with Bonn as its capital. The Soviet Union

> *"Democracy alone can supply the vitalizing force to stir the peoples of the world into triumphant action."*
>
> HARRY S. TRUMAN

Planes bringing tons of food and other supplies to West Berlin landed every three minutes.

OBJECTIVE
④ INSTRUCT

Superpowers Struggle over Germany

▶ ***Starting with the Student*** Ask students to imagine their city divided by an impassable wall. How would their daily lives be affected by the division?

▶ ***Discussing Key Ideas***
- The United States and its allies try to reunify Germany.
- The Soviet Union retaliates by holding West Berlin hostage.
- An airlift of supplies to Berlin by the United States and Britain enables the city's residents to survive.
- Western European nations form a military alliance—NATO—to counter possible Soviet aggression.

MORE ABOUT . . .
The Berlin Airlift

The Berlin airlift was an important political event, but it also had a human side. One German child recalled later, "The Americans remembered, as they had many times before, to make the children happy. . . . In the afternoon came the surprise. A transport machine landed, and a living camel got out." The camel was part of a "Camel Caravan" organized to collect food and gifts from families in West Germany for the children of Berlin.

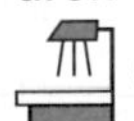

GEOGRAPHY TRANSPARENCIES
G26, The Berlin Airlift: 1948–49

Block Schedule TEACHING OPTION **Time Needed: 40 Minutes**

Cooperative Activity: Researching the Berlin Airlift

Task: Pairs of students will research the Berlin airlift and then collaborate on short reports describing the dangers and challenges of the airlift for the U.S. soldiers and for the people of Berlin.

Purpose: To explore an event in depth.

Activity: Students should decide how they will allot the tasks of researching and writing their reports. One student could do the research and the other the writing, or they could do both tasks collaboratively. They should examine books, articles, and newspaper stories, and collect anecdotes and quotations to use in their reports.

Building a Portfolio: Students who add reports to their portfolios should include a note specifying their contribution to the finished product.

ALTERNATIVE ASSESSMENT BOOK
Standards for Evaluating a Cooperative Activity

Standards for Evaluation
Reports should . . .
- show evidence of careful research using a variety of sources
- use specific details to support statements
- be clear and well organized

HISTORY FROM VISUALS

Postwar Germany, 1949

Reading the Map Point out that the squares on this map are called "areas of detail" and that each square conveys a different level of information. In a way, the series of maps functions like a series of enlarged snapshots.

Extension Discuss what students know about Berlin today. On November 9, 1989, the wall was breached as the East German Communist regime collapsed. After German reunification in October 1990, the parliament voted to make Berlin the capital of united Germany.

OUR TIMES The Creation of NATO

ASSESS & RETEACH

Section 1 Assessment

Assign pairs of students to help each other answer the questions.

Self-Assessment

Have students mark those questions on the Section 1 Assessment that they could not answer. Ask them to locate the portions of the text that best answer each question.

Section Quiz

FORMAL ASSESSMENT
Section Quiz, p. 224

Reteach

On the board, create a blank chart like the one on page 608. Have students fill in the aims of the Soviet Union and the United States as a way of testing their comprehension of the material.

CLOSE

Although the United States and the Soviet Union tried to forge friendly relations, the two countries soon clashed over ideology and territory. The resulting Cold War affected the policies of each country for many years.

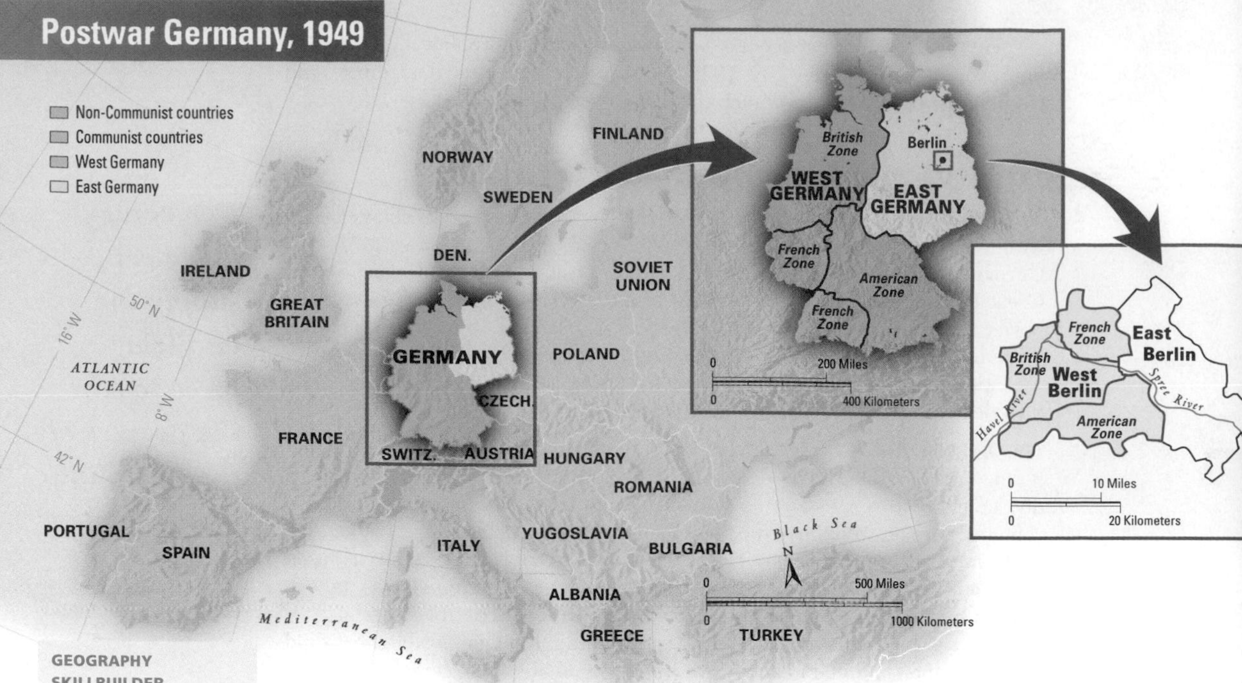

GEOGRAPHY SKILLBUILDER

LOCATION ***In which part of Germany was Berlin located?***

PLACE ***What effects might the division of Berlin have had on its citizens?***

Skillbuilder Answer
Location: East Germany.
Place: *Possible Answer:* It separated families, made travel between the zones difficult, and created economic problems.

turned its zone into the German Democratic Republic, commonly called East Germany, with East Berlin as its capital.

THE NATO ALLIANCE The Berlin blockade increased Western European fear of Soviet aggression. In response, ten Western European nations—Belgium, Denmark, France, Great Britain, Iceland, Italy, Luxembourg, the Netherlands, Norway, and Portugal—joined with the United States and Canada on April 4, 1949, to form a defensive military alliance called the **North Atlantic Treaty Organization (NATO).** All member countries promised that an attack on one would be regarded as an attack on all—which they would resist with armed force if necessary. Although Ohio senator Robert Taft spoke for several Republican senators in opposing the treaty, for fear that it would stimulate an arms race and massive American military aid to Europe, the Senate approved it overwhelmingly. For the first time in its history, the United States entered into a military alliance with other nations during peacetime. The Cold War had ended U.S. isolationism.

Section 1 Assessment

1. TERMS & NAMES
Identify:
- satellite nation
- containment
- Cold War
- Truman Doctrine
- Marshall Plan
- Berlin airlift
- North Atlantic Treaty Organization (NATO)

2. SUMMARIZING In a two-column chart, list the Soviet and U.S. actions that contributed most to the beginning of the Cold War.

U.S. Actions	Soviet Actions

Write a paragraph explaining which country was more responsible and why you think so.

3. EVALUATING Former aides of Franklin Roosevelt worried that Truman was not qualified to handle world leadership. Considering what you learned in this section, evaluate Truman as a world leader.

THINK ABOUT
- his behavior toward Stalin
- his economic support of European nations
- his support of West Berlin

4. MAKING INFERENCES Which of the two superpowers do you think was more successful in achieving its aims during the period 1945–1949? Support your answer by referring to historical events.

THINK ABOUT
- events in Eastern Europe
- the Truman Doctrine and the Marshall Plan
- the conflicts over Berlin and the rest of Germany

ANSWERS

1. TERMS & NAMES

satellite nation, p. 609

containment, p. 609

Cold War, p. 610

Truman Doctrine, p. 610

Marshall Plan, p. 610

Berlin airlift, p. 611

North Atlantic Treaty Organization (NATO), p. 612

2. SUMMARIZING

Possible Responses: U.S. actions—Marshall Plan, aid to Greece and Turkey, Truman Doctrine, Berlin airlift

Soviet actions—refusal of free elections in Poland, control of countries in Eastern Europe, invasion of Czechoslovakia

3. EVALUATING

Possible Responses: Most students will probably think Truman was a good leader because he took firm actions to contain the spread of Soviet influence, and he supported the Marshall Plan and the Berlin airlift.

Some may think he overreacted and was too belligerent toward Stalin.

4. MAKING INFERENCES

Some may say the Soviets were more successful, because they imposed their influence on nations along their border even though they failed to take over West Berlin. Others will say the United States was more successful in protecting West Berlin and in rebuilding Europe.

2 The Cold War Heats Up

TERMS & NAMES
- Mao Zedong
- Chiang Kai-shek
- Taiwan (Formosa)
- 38th parallel
- Korean War

LEARN ABOUT how Communist governments were established in Asia
TO UNDERSTAND why the United States became involved in the Korean War.

ONE AMERICAN'S STORY

First Lieutenant Philip Day, Jr., vividly remembers his first taste of battle in Korea. On the morning of July 5, 1950, Day spotted a column of eight enemy tanks moving toward his company. The Americans fired on the rapidly advancing enemy, but their bombardment had little effect. The enemy tanks kept on coming.

A PERSONAL VOICE

I was with a 75-mm recoilless-rifle team. "Let's see," I shouted, "if we can get one of those tanks." We picked up the gun and moved it to where we could get a clean shot. I don't know if we were poorly trained, . . . but we set the gun on the forward slope of the hill. When we fired, the recoilless blast blew a hole in the hill which instantly covered us in mud and dirt. The effect wasn't nearly as bad on us as it was on the gun. It jammed and wouldn't fire until we'd cleaned the whole damn thing. When we were ready again, we moved the gun to a better position and began banging away. I swear we had some hits, but the tanks never slowed down. . . . In a little less than two hours, 30 North Korean tanks rolled through the position we were supposed to block as if we hadn't been there.

PHILIP DAY, JR., quoted in *The Korean War: Pusan to Chosin*

American infantry soldiers fire heavy mortars at Communist strongholds near Mundung-ni in Korea.

Only five years after World War II ended, the United States became embroiled in a war in Korea. The policy of containment had led the United States into battle to halt Communist expansion. In this conflict, however, the enemy was North Korea and China.

Civil War in China

American involvement in Korea grew out of events that took place during World War II and the early years of the Cold War. When the Japanese had occupied China in 1937, Chinese Communists and Nationalists had temporarily interrupted their long civil war and joined in the common cause against the invader. The Communists under **Mao Zedong** led the struggle in the north. The Nationalists under China's president, **Chiang Kai-shek** (Jiang Jieshi), fought in the south. During the war the United States sent the Nationalists approximately $3 billion in aid.

Many Americans were impressed by Chiang Kai-shek and admired the courage and determination that the Chinese Nationalists showed in resisting the Japanese. However, U.S. military and State Department officials who dealt with Chiang held a different view of him. They found his government dictatorial, inefficient, and hopelessly corrupt.

Furthermore, the political and economic policies of Chiang's government undermined the Nationalists' support in the Chinese countryside. For example, the Nationalists collected a grain tax from farmers even during the famine of

SECTION 2 RESOURCES

PRINT RESOURCES

IN-DEPTH RESOURCES: UNIT 5
Guided Reading, p. 40
Primary Source: *from* Douglas MacArthur's Farewell Address to Congress, p. 47
American Lives: Douglas MacArthur, p. 53

READING STUDY GUIDE, p. 189

ACCESS FOR STUDENTS ACQUIRING ENGLISH
Guided Reading, (Spanish), p. 208

SPANISH READING STUDY GUIDE, p. 189

FORMAL ASSESSMENT
Section Quiz, p. 225

ALTERNATIVE ASSESSMENT
See forms for supporting and scoring alternative activities.

TECHNOLOGY RESOURCES

CD-ROM Electronic Library of Primary Sources

VIDEO *American Portfolio: A Videodisc for U.S. History* user's guide, pp. 234–235

INTERNET http://www.mlushistory.com

Section 2 Overview

OBJECTIVES

1. To explain how Communists came to power in China and how the United States reacted.
2. To summarize the events of the Korean War.
3. To explain the conflict between President Truman and General MacArthur.

SKILLBUILDERS
- Interpreting charts, p. 614
- Understanding geography: movement, location, p. 616

CRITICAL THINKING
- Analyzing causes, pp. 614, 615
- Recognizing effects, pp. 615, 617
- Summarizing, p. 618
- Following chronological order, p. 618
- Hypothesizing, p. 618
- Forming an opinion, p. 618

FOCUS & MOTIVATE

5-MINUTE WARM-UP

Predicting Outcomes
To predict some of the issues that might arise from the Chinese civil war, ask students to answer these questions.

1. Who led the Communists and Nationalists during the civil war in China?
2. What might the Communist victory in China mean for U.S.–Chinese relations?

WARM-UP TRANSPARENCY 18

Starting with the Student
Ask students what they know about the Korean War from relatives or friends or from movies or television programs such as *M*A*S*H*. What experiences did people have? How did they feel about the Korean War?

OBJECTIVE
1 INSTRUCT

Civil War in China

Discussing Key Ideas
- The Communists and the Nationalists break into

(continued on next page)

(continued from page 613)

open conflict when the Japanese occupation ends.
- Civil war in China ends with a Communist victory.
- Conservatives attack the Truman administration for "losing" China.

IN-DEPTH RESOURCES: UNIT 5
Guided Reading, p. 40

ACCESS FOR STUDENTS ACQUIRING ENGLISH
Guided Reading (Spanish), p. 208

HISTORY FROM VISUALS

Nationalists Versus Communists

Reading the Chart Suggest that students read the chart horizontally, comparing each bulleted characteristic of the Nationalists with the corresponding characteristic of the Communists across from it.

Extension Tell students that in 1949, about 95 percent of the more than 450 million Chinese people were farmers. Ask how this situation may have influenced the outcome of the civil war. *Possible Response: The farmers, many of whom wanted change and supported the Communists, vastly outnumbered the Nationalists.*

Nationalists Versus Communists

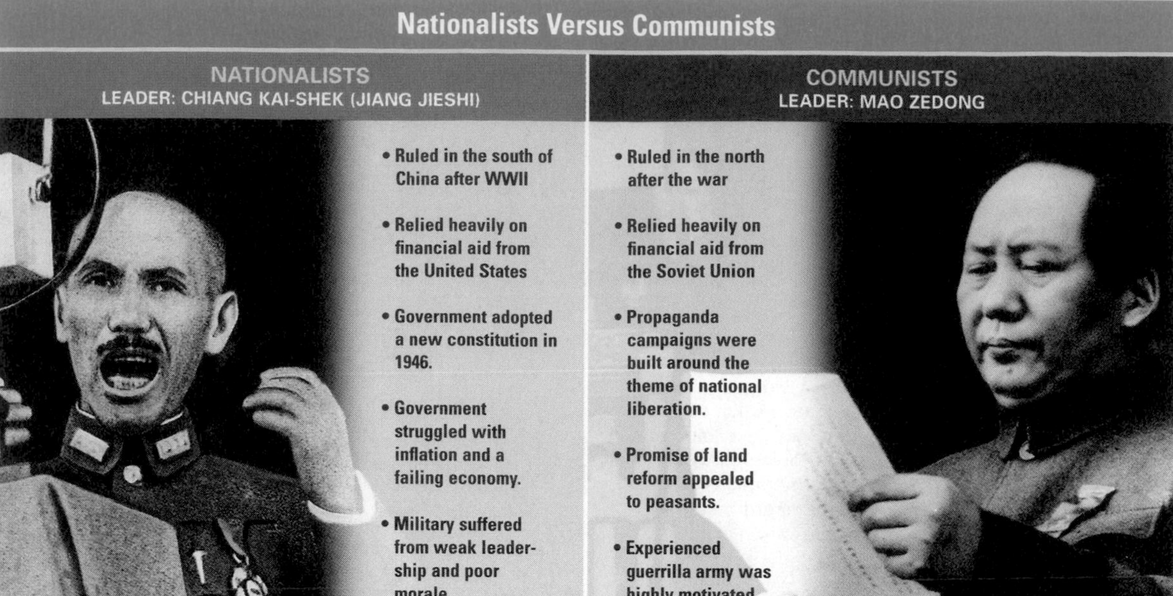

NATIONALISTS LEADER: CHIANG KAI-SHEK (JIANG JIESHI)	COMMUNISTS LEADER: MAO ZEDONG
• Ruled in the south of China after WWII	• Ruled in the north after the war
• Relied heavily on financial aid from the United States	• Relied heavily on financial aid from the Soviet Union
• Government adopted a new constitution in 1946.	• Propaganda campaigns were built around the theme of national liberation.
• Government struggled with inflation and a failing economy.	• Promise of land reform appealed to peasants.
• Military suffered from weak leadership and poor morale.	• Experienced guerrilla army was highly motivated.

SKILLBUILDER **INTERPRETING CHARTS** *What problems did the Nationalists have after World War II? How did the Communists appeal to the peasants?*

Skillbuilder Answer
Nationalists: Inflation, failing economy, weak military leadership, poor morale.
Communists: With promises of national liberation and land reform.

1944. When city dwellers demonstrated against a 10,000 percent increase in the price of rice that had occurred over a three-year period, Chiang's secret police opened fire on them.

In contrast, the Communists proved to be more skillful in winning the support of peasants. For instance, after the Communists took over an area, they redistributed land to peasants and reduced rents. (In the 1950s, the Chinese Communist government would force these peasants to work on collective farms.) As a result, Chinese popular support for the Communists grew.

FIGHTING BREAKS OUT As soon as the defeated Japanese left China at the end of World War II, cooperation between the Nationalists and the Communists ceased. Civil war erupted between the two groups. In spite of the problems in the Nationalist regime, American policy favored the Nationalists because they opposed communism.

From 1944 to 1947, the United States played peacemaker between the two groups, while still supporting the Nationalists. However, U.S. officials repeatedly failed to negotiate peace. Truman refused to commit American soldiers to back up the Nationalists, although the United States did send $2 billion worth of military equipment and supplies to China.

The aid wasn't enough to save the Nationalists, whose weak military leadership and corrupt, abusive practices drove the peasants to the Communist side. In May 1949, Chiang and the remnants of his demoralized government and army fled to **Taiwan** (or **Formosa**), an island to the east of mainland China.

THINK THROUGH HISTORY
A. ***Analyzing Causes*** *What factors led to the Communist takeover in China?*

A. Answer The corruption of the Nationalist government and the weakness of its military.

AMERICA REACTS TO COMMUNIST TAKEOVER The American public was stunned that China had become Communist. Containment had failed! In Congress, conservative Republicans and Democrats attacked the Truman administration for supplying only limited aid to Chiang. If containing communism was important in Europe, they asked, why was it not equally important in Asia?

The State Department replied by saying that what had happened in China was a result of internal forces. The United States had failed in its attempts to

TEACHING OPTIONS

Making Global Connections

The United States and China After the Communist Party gained control of China in 1949, contacts between China and the West were minimal for more than 20 years. However, in 1971, Taiwan lost its seat in the United Nations, and China joined the Security Council. In a breakthrough visit in 1972, President Richard M. Nixon became the first U.S. president to visit China. Nixon's China policy later contributed to improved relations with the Soviet Union and the thawing of the Cold War.

Making Connections Across Time

Relations with Taiwan Today Tell students that for many years the United States has tried to balance historical ties with the Chinese Nationalist government in Taiwan with the desire to establish a diplomatic and trade relationship with the People's Republic of China.

China claims the right to govern Taiwan, but the Taiwanese wish to maintain as much independence as possible. When China conducted military exercises close to the coast of Taiwan in 1996, the U.S. government sent ships to the area as a show of support for Taiwan.

B. Answer Their fear of communism spun out of control.

THINK THROUGH HISTORY
B. *Recognizing Effects* *How did Americans react when the Communists came to power in China?*

influence these forces, such as Chiang's inability to retain the support of his people. Trying to do more would only have started a war in Asia—a war that the United States wasn't prepared to fight.

Most Americans accepted the State Department's arguments, but some conservatives rejected them as lame excuses. They claimed that the United States had "lost" China and should have provided greater support to the Nationalists. They also charged that the American government was riddled with Communist agents. Like wildfire, American fear of communism began to burn out of control, and the flames were fanned even further by the events in Korea in the following year.

Koreans Go to War

Japan had taken over Korea in 1910 and ruled it until August 1945. As World War II ended, Japanese troops north of the 38th parallel surrendered to the Soviets. (The **38th parallel** is an imaginary line that bisects Korea at 38 degrees north latitude.) Japanese troops south of the parallel surrendered to the Americans. The 38th parallel was not intended as a permanent boundary, since it artificially divided the country's resources—industry in the north and agriculture in the south—making it difficult for either of the two regions to prosper. Nevertheless, as in Germany, two nations developed, one Communist and one not.

In 1948 the Republic of Korea, usually called South Korea, was established in the zone that had been occupied by the United States. Its government, headed by Syngman Rhee, was based in Seoul, Korea's traditional capital. Simultaneously, the Communists formed the Democratic People's Republic of Korea in the north. Kim Il Sung led its government, which was based in Pyongyang. By 1949, both the United States and the Soviet Union had withdrawn their troops, leaving the two new nations glaring at each other across the 38th parallel. Each government claimed the sole right to rule all of Korea.

HISTORICAL SPOTLIGHT

NSC-68

In 1947, Congress created the National Security Council to advise the president on national security issues. In April 1950, the 68th paper issued by the council (NSC-68) argued that the only way to prevent the Soviet Union from dominating the world was containment and a massive increase in defense spending.

At first, the administration doubted whether Americans would be willing to pay the additional tax dollars that an increase in defense spending would require. However, when North Korea invaded South Korea in June 1950, the administration had the justification it needed to spend more defense money to contain communism.

NORTH KOREA ATTACKS SOUTH KOREA On June 25, 1950, North Korean troops started the **Korean War** by invading South Korea. The invasion alarmed Americans: yet another Asian country was about to fall to communism. Was the United States going to sit back and let it happen? When news of the invasion reached President Truman, he decided to take military action.

A PERSONAL VOICE

What the Communists, the North Koreans, were doing was nothing new. . . . Hitler and Mussolini and the Japanese were doing exactly the same thing in the 1930s. . . . Nobody had stood up to them. And that is what led to the Second World War.

PRESIDENT TRUMAN

THINK THROUGH HISTORY
C. *Analyzing Causes* *Why did the U.S. support South Korea?*

C. Answer South Korea was seen as a barrier to Chinese and North Korean Communist expansion.

Accordingly, Truman ordered naval and air support for South Korea. When his action was announced, Congress stood up and cheered. Only Republican senator Robert Taft of Ohio, the staunchly conservative son of President William Howard Taft, objected that the president, by acting on his own, had wrongfully taken over Congress's power to declare war.

On June 27, 1950, the UN Security Council adopted an American resolution calling on member nations to help the Republic of South Korea. Ironically, the Soviet Union was boycotting the UN because of the UN's refusal to recognize Communist China and was not present to veto the resolution. In all, 16 nations sent some 520,000 troops to assist South Korea; just over 90 percent of these troops were American. South Korean troops numbered an additional 590,000. The combined UN and South Korean forces were placed under the command of General Douglas MacArthur.

OBJECTIVE

② INSTRUCT

Koreans Go to War

▶ ***Discussing Key Ideas***

- After World War II, Korea is divided into two separate countries.
- The policy of containing communism leads the U.S. to provide military support for South Korea when it is invaded by the North.

HISTORICAL SPOTLIGHT
NSC-68

Critical Thinking: Analyzing Motives You might tell students about the domino theory, which hypothesizes that if one country in a region becomes Communist, other countries nearby will become Communist as well, like a line of falling dominos. Ask students to apply the domino theory in analyzing the motivation behind NSC-68.

Extension Ask students to consider how the failure of appeasement after the Munich agreement of 1938 might have shaped the policy of containment. *Possible Response: American leaders believed that the only way to prevent aggression, like that of Hitler or Stalin, was through strong, military opposition.*

Block Schedule TEACHING OPTION **Time Needed: 20 Minutes**

Cooperative Activity: Debating Containment

Task: Student groups will debate the wisdom of sending ground troops to support another country against invasion.

Purpose: To understand the underlying reasons for U.S. involvement in the Korean War and to apply that understanding to situations today.

Activity: After choosing a position through a lottery, groups of three to four students will research the arguments either for or against ground troop involvement in the Korean War and in conflicts today. Students should consider the global situation at the time of the Korean War as well as public opinion at home. Each group should also investigate a recent or current situation involving U.S. foreign policy such as Iraq's invasion of Kuwait, China's desire to control Taiwan, and the ongoing situation with Cuba. Groups holding positions for and against involvement will debate each other.

ALTERNATIVE ASSESSMENT BOOK
Standards for Evaluating a Cooperative Activity

OBJECTIVE

③ **INSTRUCT**

The United States Fights in Korea

▶ ***Starting with the Student*** Ask students to create a flow chart of events of the Korean War as they read this section.

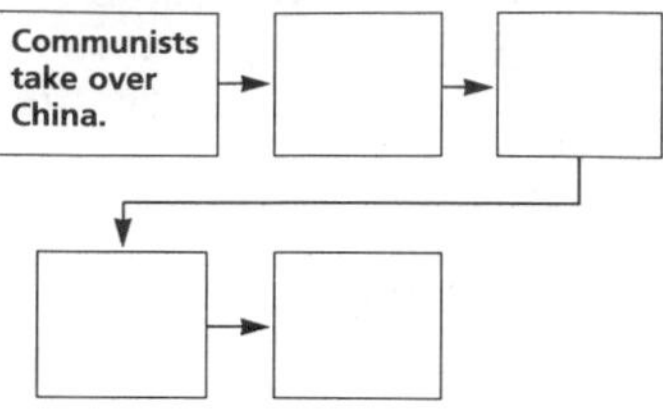

Communists take over China.

▶ ***Discussing Key Ideas***

- MacArthur achieves a brilliant military victory over North Korea.
- China enters the Korean War.
- President Truman fires General MacArthur.
- The Korean War ends in a stalemate.

ANOTHER PERSPECTIVE

India's Viewpoint

Critical Thinking: Interpreting Have students discuss the various reasons for India's neutrality. *Possible Response: By not choosing sides between the two super powers, India avoids the risk of domination by either one.*

HISTORY FROM VISUALS

The War in Korea, 1950–1953

Reading the Map Tell students that the series of small maps shows the development of the war over time.

(continued on next page)

The United States Fights in Korea

ANOTHER PERSPECTIVE

INDIA'S VIEWPOINT

Nonaligned nations, such as India, were on neither side of the Cold War and had their own perspectives on it. In 1951, the prime minister of India, Jawaharlal Nehru, had this to say about the Korean War:

> "This great struggle between the United States and Soviet Russia is hardly the proper role in this world for those great powers. . . . Their role should be to function in their own territories and not be a threat to others."

At first, North Korean armored units seemed unstoppable. Driving steadily south, they captured Seoul. After a month of bitter combat, the North Koreans had forced UN and South Korean troops into a small defensive zone around Pusan, in the southeastern corner of the peninsula.

MACARTHUR'S MIRACLE COUNTERATTACK Then MacArthur launched a counterattack with tanks, heavy artillery, and fresh troops from the United States. On September 15, 1950, his troops made an amphibious landing behind enemy lines at Inchon, on Korea's west coast. Other troops moved north from Pusan. Trapped between the two attacking forces, about half of the North Korean troops surrendered; the rest fled back across the 38th parallel.

MacArthur's phenomenal success made him a hero to the American public. Experts called his plan one of the most brilliant military strategies in history. However, the sudden military triumph posed a political problem. MacArthur and his troops had achieved their objective of chasing the invaders out of South Korea. What should happen now? If UN and South Korean forces crossed the 38th parallel, the war would change from a defensive one to an offensive one. On the other hand, the Allies had agreed at Potsdam that Korea should be unified.

On October 7, 1950, the UN General Assembly recommended that MacArthur cross the 38th parallel and reunite Korea. However, days earlier, Communist China's foreign minister, Zhou Enlai, had warned that his country would not stand idly by and "let the Americans come to the border"—meaning

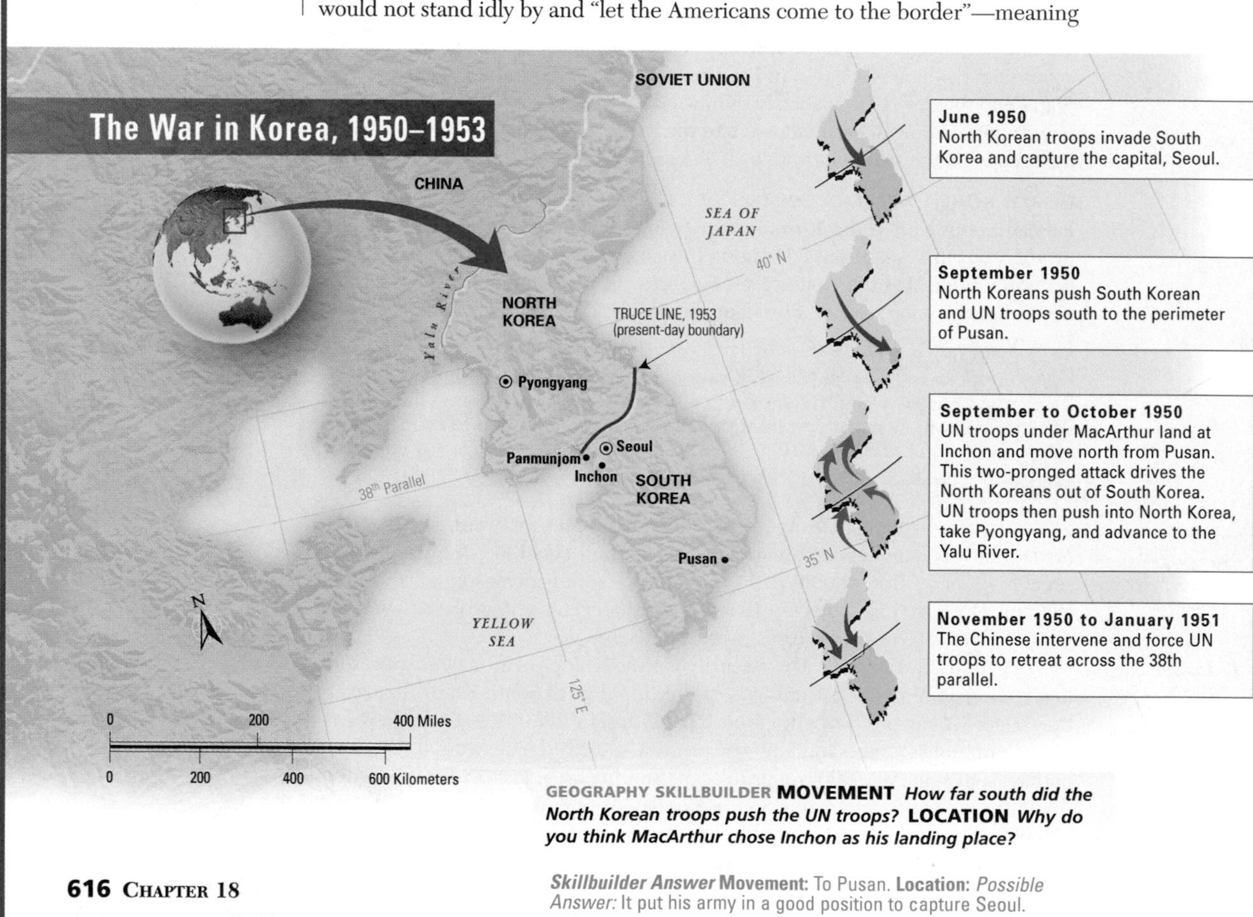

The War in Korea, 1950–1953
SOVIET UNION
CHINA
SEA OF JAPAN
40° N
Yalu River
NORTH KOREA
TRUCE LINE, 1953 (present-day boundary)
Pyongyang
Seoul
Panmunjom
Inchon
SOUTH KOREA
38th Parallel
Pusan
35° N
YELLOW SEA
125° E
0 200 400 Miles
0 200 400 600 Kilometers
June 1950
North Korean troops invade South Korea and capture the capital, Seoul.
September 1950
North Koreans push South Korean and UN troops south to the perimeter of Pusan.
September to October 1950
UN troops under MacArthur land at Inchon and move north from Pusan. This two-pronged attack drives the North Koreans out of South Korea. UN troops then push into North Korea, take Pyongyang, and advance to the Yalu River.
November 1950 to January 1951
The Chinese intervene and force UN troops to retreat across the 38th parallel.

GEOGRAPHY SKILLBUILDER **MOVEMENT** *How far south did the North Korean troops push the UN troops?* **LOCATION** *Why do you think MacArthur chose Inchon as his landing place?*

Skillbuilder Answer Movement: To Pusan. Location: *Possible Answer:* It put his army in a good position to capture Seoul.

TEACHING OPTION

Making Connections Across Cultures

Integration In 1948, President Truman ordered the integration of the armed services, making Korea the first war in which African-American soldiers lived and fought side by side with white soldiers. At first, the services were slow to comply with the presidential order, but as the Korean War dragged on, black soldiers became the replacements in white units and the army slowly became integrated.

First Lieutenant Bev Scott, an African-American officer, said, "There was no better institution in American life . . . than the army for the black man in the forties and fifties. . . . You had more leverage in the army. You always had somebody you could go to and complain about bad treatment. A black man couldn't do that in civilian life. Especially in the South. . . . "Officer Candidate School . . . was my first experience with meeting white people on a person-to-person basis. Previous to that all my experience with whites had been adversarial. Growing up in rural North Carolina, . . . I was always subjected to insults and names."

the Yalu River, the boundary between North Korea and Manchuria, a region of northeast China. He repeated his warning again and again during the first weeks of October. When Truman asked MacArthur about the threat of Chinese involvement, the general dismissed the possibility. MacArthur boasted that the war would be over by Thanksgiving and that he'd have American troops back in Tokyo by Christmas.

THE CHINESE FIGHT BACK The advance into North Korea went on, pressing ever closer to the Yalu River. Then, on the evening of November 25, some 300,000 Chinese soldiers poured across the Yalu River into Korea, forcing the UN and South Korean forces moving toward the river to retreat. By Christmas, the North Koreans and Chinese had driven the UN and South Korean troops 75 to 100 miles below the 38th parallel. Seoul was lost for the second time on January 4, 1951.

For two years, the two sides fought bitterly to obtain strategic positions in the Korean hills, but neither side was able to make important advances.

A PERSONAL VOICE

Shortly after this we moved to Heartbreak Ridge. . . . Our trenches in that sector were only about 20 meters in front of theirs. We were eyeball to eyeball. Just 20 meters of no man's land between us. We couldn't move at all in the daytime without getting shot at. Machine-gun fire would come in, grenades, small-arms fire, all from within spitting distance. It was like World War I. We lived in a maze of bunkers and deep trenches. . . . There were bodies strewn all over the place. Hundred of bodies frozen in the snow. We could see the arms and legs sticking up. Nobody could get their dead out of there.

BEV SCOTT, quoted in *No Bugles, No Drums: An Oral History of the Korean War*

First Lieutenant Bev Scott in 1951, at age 20

MACARTHUR RECOMMENDS ATTACKING CHINA To halt the bloody stalemate, in early 1951 MacArthur called for an extension of the war into China. He wanted to blockade the Chinese coast and use atomic bombs on China. He also wanted to use Chiang Kai-shek's troops to invade southern China.

Truman rejected MacArthur's requests. The president did not want the United States involved in a massive land war in Asia. As General Omar N. Bradley, chairman of the Joint Chiefs of Staff, said, an all-out conflict with China would be "the wrong war, at the wrong place, at the wrong time, and with the wrong enemy." Also, the Soviet Union had a mutual-assistance pact with China. Attacking China could set off World War III.

THINK THROUGH HISTORY
D. ***Recognizing Effects*** *How did the involvement of Communist China affect the course of the Korean War?*

Instead of attacking China, the UN and South Korean forces began to advance once more, using the U.S. Eighth Army, led by Matthew B. Ridgway, as a spearhead. By March 1951, Ridgway had retaken Seoul and had moved back up to the 38th parallel. The situation was just what it had been before the fighting began.

D. Answer It prevented the UN troops from overrunning all of North Korea and forced a stalemate in which North Korea remained Communist and South Korea remained non-Communist.

MACARTHUR VERSUS TRUMAN Not satisfied with the recapture of South Korea, MacArthur continued to urge the waging of a full-scale war against China. Every time he raised the issue, the president or the Joint Chiefs of Staff told him that he was expected to fight only a limited war. Finding this intolerable, and certain that his views were correct, MacArthur tried to go over the president's head. He spoke and wrote privately to newspaper and magazine publishers and, especially, to Republican leaders.

Finally, Truman decided he could no longer tolerate MacArthur's insubordination. "Mr. Prima Donna, Brass Hat, Five Star MacArthur," as Truman had called him years earlier, could not be allowed to wrest control from the

"Mr. Prima Donna, Brass Hat, Five Star MacArthur."
HARRY S. TRUMAN

General MacArthur

(continued from page 616)

Extension Draw an outline map of Korea on the chalkboard. Have students take turns marking *x's* in different colors to show the advances and retreats of the two armies.

MORE ABOUT . . .
The Chinese in Korea

On October 25, 1950, South Korean troops encountered Chinese soldiers wearing North Korean uniforms. Not possible, said American general Walker. The Chinese are not involved in the Korean War—General MacArthur said so. A month later, 300,000 Chinese soldiers convinced even General Walker.

MORE ABOUT . . .
Beverly Scott

After his tour in Korea, Beverly Scott continued to serve the U.S. Army in duty stations around the world. In 1968, he served in yet another war—on the staff of the Army Inspector General in Vietnam.

MORE ABOUT . . .
The Firing of MacArthur

The firestorm of protest that swept the country when MacArthur was dismissed included an editorial in the *Chicago Tribune:* "President Truman must be impeached and convicted. . . . [He] is unfit, morally and mentally, for his high office."

IN-DEPTH RESOURCES: UNIT 5
American Lives: Douglas MacArthur, p. 53

ELECTRONIC LIBRARY OF PRIMARY SOURCES
Frustration in Korea by Douglas MacArthur

TEACHING OPTIONS

Exploring Themes

America in the World The Korean War was America's first major military action with the UN. Throughout the Cold War, the United States and Soviet Union used their respective veto powers to prevent the other from controlling UN policy. Since the collapse of the Soviet Union, however, the United States and Russia have used the UN to cooperate in international affairs—as in the UN role in the former Yugoslavia. While some Americans see the UN as a tool to create international consensus, others fear that the UN poses a threat to American sovereignty.

Teaching Gifted and Talented Students

Analyzing MacArthur's Farewell Address to Congress Ask students to read MacArthur's address to Congress and to analyze its skillful use of rhetorical devices. Tell them to look for the use of repetition, alliteration, and emotional appeals. Also ask students to evaluate the accuracy of statements in the speech. For example, MacArthur's claim that the Joint Chiefs of Staff "fully shared" his views was not true. What other statements were exaggerated or fake?

IN-DEPTH RESOURCES, UNIT 5
Primary Source: *from* Douglas MacArthur's Farewell Address to Congress, p. 47

NOW & THEN
The Two Koreas
Critical Thinking: Comparing Ask students to compare the situation in Korea in 1953 with the situation in that country today. Discuss conditions under which the two countries might be united?

ASSESS & RETEACH

Section 2 Assessment
Have students answer the questions and then compare answers with another student. Ask the student pairs to find text passages to support their answers.

Self-Assessment
Have students make a time line of events of the Korean War to illustrate what they learned. Have them compare these time lines with the ones they created as they read the selection and note any omissions or discrepancies.

Section Quiz
FORMAL ASSESSMENT
Section Quiz, p. 225

Reteach
Review the map on page 616 to reinforce students' understanding of the Korean War.

CLOSE
A Communist victory in China caused deep concern in the United States over Communist influence around the world. When North Korea invaded South Korea, therefore, the U.S. sent ground troops, a military presence that would last more than 40 years.

constitutionally designated commander in chief. On April 11, 1951, with the unanimous approval of the Joint Chiefs of Staff, he relieved MacArthur of his command.

Many Americans were outraged over their hero's downfall. A public opinion poll showed that 69 percent of the American public backed General MacArthur. When MacArthur returned to the United States, he gave an address to Congress, an honor usually awarded only to heads of government. New York City honored him with a ticker-tape parade. Trying to gain sympathy, MacArthur said, "Old soldiers never die, they just fade away."

Throughout the fuss, Truman stayed in the background. After MacArthur's moment of public glory passed, the Truman administration began to make its case. Before a congressional committee investigating MacArthur's dismissal, a parade of witnesses argued the case for a limited war. The committee agreed with them. As a result, the public swung around to the view that Truman had done the right thing. As a political figure, MacArthur did indeed fade away.

E. Answer MacArthur wanted to use nuclear weapons and wage full-scale war; Truman wanted to limit the war.

THINK THROUGH HISTORY
E. *Summarizing* *How did Truman and MacArthur differ over strategy in the Korean War?*

NOW & THEN

THE TWO KOREAS
Korea is still split into North Korea and South Korea, even after 50 years. South Korea is booming economically, while North Korea, still Communist, is struggling with shortages of food and energy.

Periodically, discussions about reuniting the two countries resume, but economic and political differences continue to keep them apart. In fact, in 1996 North Korea sent troops into the demilitarized zone, threatening South Korea's border. The United States still has 37,000 troops stationed in South Korea.

SETTLING FOR STALEMATE As the MacArthur controversy died down, the Soviet Union unexpectedly suggested a cease-fire on June 23, 1951. Truce talks began in July 1951. By the following spring, the opposing sides had agreed on two points: the location of the cease-fire line at the existing battle line and the establishment of a demilitarized zone between the opposing sides. Negotiators spent another year wrangling over the exchange of prisoners. Finally, in July 1953, the two sides signed an armistice ending the war.

At best, the agreement was a stalemate. On the one hand, the North Korean invaders had been pushed back, and communism had been contained without a world war and without the use of atomic weapons, although America's threat to use them helped break the deadlock. On the other hand, Korea was still two nations rather than one.

Back on the home front, the war had affected the lives of ordinary Americans in many ways. It had cost 54,000 American lives between $20 billion and $22 billion in expenditures. The high cost of this unsuccessful war was one of many factors leading Americans to reject the Democratic Party in 1952 and to elect a Republican administration under Dwight D. Eisenhower. In addition, the Korean War increased fear of Communist aggression and prompted a hunt for spies on whom to blame Communist gains.

Section 2 Assessment

1. **TERMS & NAMES**
   Identify:
   - Mao Zedong
   - Chiang Kai-shek
   - Taiwan (Formosa)
   - 38th parallel
   - Korean War

2. **FOLLOWING CHRONOLOGICAL ORDER** Create a time line of the major events of the Korean War, using a form such as the one below.

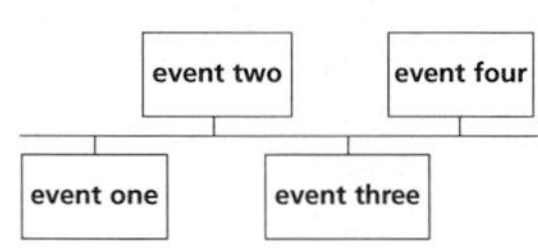

   Choose two events on your time line and explain how one event led to the other.

3. **HYPOTHESIZING** If the Communists had lost the Chinese civil war, how might later events in Korea have been different?
   THINK ABOUT
   - how North Korean plans might have been different
   - how American public opinion might have been different
   - what might have happened when MacArthur's troops neared the North Korea–China border

4. **FORMING OPINIONS** Many Americans have questioned whether fighting the Korean War—a bloody war that ended in a stalemate—was worthwhile. What is your opinion? Why?
   THINK ABOUT
   - what the war cost in lives and material goods
   - what might have happened if UN troops had stayed out of the conflict
   - what might have happened if UN troops had waged full-scale war against China

ANSWERS

1. TERMS AND NAMES
Mao Zedong, p. 613
Chiang Kai-shek, p. 613
Taiwan (Formosa), p. 614
38th parallel, p. 615
Korean War, p. 615

2. FOLLOWING CHRONOLOGICAL ORDER
1. 1948 Korea is split into two nations.
2. June 1950: North Korea invades South Korea.
3. June 1950: U.S. supports South Korea
4. Sept. 1950: North Korea captures most of Korea
5. Oct.1950: UN counterattack succeeds
6. Nov. 1950: Chinese troops enter war
7. July 1953: Armistice signed

3. HYPOTHESIZING
Possible Responses:
- North Korea, lacking a nearby supporter, might have been less aggressive.
- Americans might have been less worried about Communist expansion.
- China might have been less worried about an invasion.

4. FORMING OPINIONS
Possible Responses: Some students may say that the war was not worthwhile because of the financial cost and the lost lives. Others may say that the United States had to prevent the spread of communism. Without the presence of UN troops, North Korea might have conquered the South. War against China might have brought Russia into the conflict and resulted in another world war.

❸ The Cold War at Home

LEARN ABOUT the Hollywood Ten, two famous spy cases, and Senator Joseph McCarthy
TO UNDERSTAND how and why fear of communism swept the nation.

TERMS & NAMES
- HUAC
- Hollywood Ten
- blacklist
- Alger Hiss
- Ethel and Julius Rosenberg
- Senator Joseph McCarthy
- McCarthyism

Section 3 Overview

OBJECTIVES

1. To summarize government efforts to investigate the loyalty of U.S. citizens.
2. To explain the spy cases of Alger Hiss and Ethel and Julius Rosenberg.
3. To describe the efforts of Joseph McCarthy to purge the nation of communism.

SKILLBUILDERS

- Interpreting political cartoons, pp. 623, 624
- Interpreting charts, p. 624

CRITICAL THINKING

- Analyzing causes, pp. 619, 620, 623
- Theme: Constitutional Concerns, p. 620
- Summarizing, p. 624
- Making decisions, p. 624
- Role-playing history, p. 624

ONE AMERICAN'S STORY

Tony Kahn made the neighbors uncomfortable because they thought his father, Gordon Kahn, was a Communist. In 1947, Gordon Kahn had been a successful screenwriter for almost 20 years. However, when a congressional committee began to investigate Communists in Hollywood, Kahn was blacklisted—named as too dangerous to hire. Later, in 1951, he was scheduled to testify before the committee himself.

To save himself, Kahn simply had to name others as Communists, but he refused. Rather than face the congressional committee, he fled to Mexico. Not only was Kahn's career ruined, but his wife and sons suffered from his being blacklisted for the next 25 years. Tony Kahn remembers how the Cold War hurt him and his family.

A PERSONAL VOICE

The first time I was called a Communist, I was four years old. . . . I'll never forget the look in our neighbors' eyes when I walked by. I thought it was hate. I was too young to realize it was fear.

TONY KAHN, from *The Cold War Comes Home*

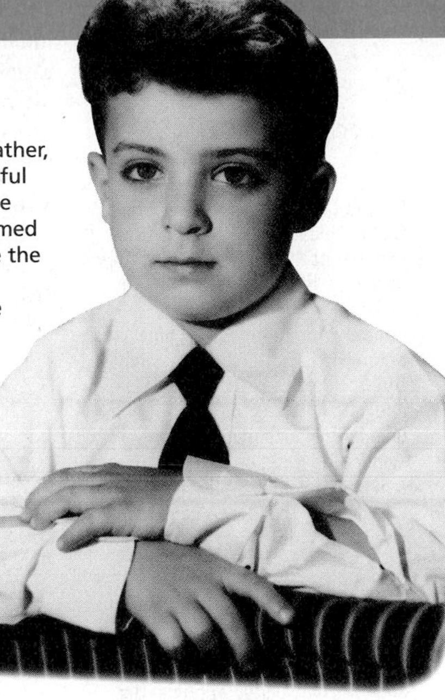
Tony Kahn

The members of the Kahn family were among thousands of victims of the anti-Communist hysteria that gripped this country in the late 1940s and early 1950s. At first, only those in potentially influential positions were accused of being "Reds," or Communists. However, by the end of the period that some historians call the Great Fear, no one was safe from false charges.

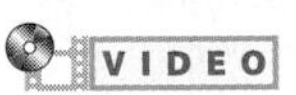
THE COLD WAR COMES HOME
Hollywood Blacklists the Kahn Family

Fear of Communist Influence

In the early years of the Cold War, many Americans believed that there was good reason to be concerned about the security of the United States. The Soviet domination of Eastern Europe and the Communist takeover of China shocked the American public, fueling a fear that communism would spread around the world.

In addition, several factors contributed to a growing suspicion of Communist influence within the United States. At the height of World War II, about 80,000 Americans claimed membership in the Communist Party; some people feared that these Communists' first loyalty was to the Soviet Union. In 1945, federal officials discovered that two State Department workers and one naval intelligence officer had stolen classified documents and passed them to a pro-Communist magazine. In the same year, a clerk at the Soviet embassy in Ottawa, Canada, defected to the West, bringing documents showing that a spy had been giving the Soviet Union secret information about the atomic bomb.

A. Answer The Soviet domination of Eastern Europe, the "loss" of China to communism.

THINK THROUGH HISTORY
A. *Analyzing Causes* *What were causes of the fear of communism in the U.S.?*

As such incidents came to light, strongly anti-Communist Republicans began to accuse the Truman administration of being soft on communism. Personally, Truman thought that his critics were making too much of what one reporter called the "Communist bugaboo," but he recognized the need to answer them.

FOCUS & MOTIVATE

5-MINUTE WARM-UP

Making Inferences
To discuss the effects of the Cold War at home, ask students to read One American's Story on page 619 and answer these questions.

1. In the postwar period, did most Americans think it was a good thing or a bad thing to be a Communist?
2. What kinds of things happened to people suspected of being Communists?

WARM-UP TRANSPARENCY 18

▶ ***Starting with the Student***
Watch the video "The Cold War Comes Home" to find out how Cold War suspicions and fears affected a young boy and his family when his father was branded a Communist.

- Using the *Teacher's Resource Book* as a guide, explore the background of the Kahn family and hold a class discussion about the phenomenon of mass hysteria and paranoia.

(continued on next page)

SECTION 3 RESOURCES

PRINT RESOURCES

IN-DEPTH RESOURCES: UNIT 5
Guided Reading, p. 41
American Lives: Margaret Chase Smith, p. 54

READING STUDY GUIDE, p. 191

ACCESS FOR STUDENTS ACQUIRING ENGLISH
Guided Reading (Spanish), p. 209

SPANISH READING STUDY GUIDE, p. 191

FORMAL ASSESSMENT
Section Quiz, p. 226

ALTERNATIVE ASSESSMENT BOOK
See forms for supporting and scoring alternative activities.

TECHNOLOGY RESOURCES

CD-ROM Electronic Library of Primary Sources

VIDEO *American Stories* video series: "The Cold War Comes Home"
American Portfolio: A Videodisc for U.S. History user's guide, p. 237

INTERNET http://www.mlushistory.com

(continued from page 619)

***AMERICAN STORIES* video series**
"The Cold War Comes Home"
Videocassette: Tape 4

Videodisc: Disc 3. Side A, Chapter 3

OBJECTIVE
① **INSTRUCT**

Fear of Communist Influence

▶ ***Discussing Key Ideas***
- The Loyalty Review Board and HUAC begin investigations of U.S. citizens.
- Witnesses from the film industry refuse to testify.
- Blacklists destroy many careers.

IN-DEPTH RESOURCES: UNIT 5
Guided Reading, p. 41

ACCESS FOR STUDENTS ACQUIRING ENGLISH
Guided Reading (Spanish), p. 209

HISTORICAL SPOTLIGHT
Paul Robeson

Critical Thinking: Comparing Ask students to read an account of Paul Robeson's life in a book such as *Paul Robeson Speaks* by Philip S. Foner and then summarize Robeson's strong social and political activism. What parallels do students see in the lives of Gordon Kahn and Paul Robeson?

ELECTRONIC LIBRARY OF PRIMARY SOURCES
Statement on Civil Liberties in America by Paul Robeson

HISTORICAL SPOTLIGHT

PAUL ROBESON

Paul Robeson was an all-American football player and Phi Beta Kappa member at Rutgers University. After earning a law degree in 1923, he entered on a distinguished international career as a singer and actor. (He is shown here playing Othello.) He was a vocal civil rights activist and a supporter of left-wing union activities, and he was sympathetic to the Soviet culture and political philosophy.

In 1950, when he refused to sign an affidavit indicating whether he had ever been a member of the Communist Party, the State Department revoked his passport for seven years. During that time, he was unable to perform abroad and was blacklisted at home. His income fell from $150,000 to $3,000 a year.

LOYALTY REVIEW BOARD Consequently, in March 1947, President Truman issued an executive order setting up the Federal Employees Loyalty and Security Program, which included the Loyalty Review Board. Its purpose was to investigate government employees and to dismiss those who were found to be disloyal to the U.S. government. Exactly what constituted "disloyalty" was never clearly defined. The U.S. attorney general drew up a list of 91 "subversive" organizations; membership in any of these groups was grounds for suspicion.

From 1947 to 1951, government loyalty boards investigated 3.2 million employees and dismissed 212 as security risks. Another 2,900 resigned because they did not want to be investigated or felt that the investigation violated their constitutional rights. Individuals under investigation were not allowed to see the evidence against them—or even to know who had accused them of being disloyal.

B. Answer Yes, it didn't clearly define disloyalty, and people accused of being disloyal didn't get to see the evidence against them.

THINK THROUGH HISTORY
B. THEME ***Constitutional Concerns*** *Did the Loyalty Review Board pose a threat to civil liberties?*

THE HOUSE COMMITTEE ON UN-AMERICAN ACTIVITIES Other agencies investigated possible Communist influence, both inside and outside the U.S. government. One of the most famous of these was the House Committee on Un-American Activities **(HUAC),** which developed from a congressional committee created to search out disloyalty before World War II. HUAC first made headlines in 1947, when it began to investigate Communist influence in the movie industry.

Hollywood did contain a substantial number of Communists, former Communists, and socialists. Furthermore, since the Soviet Union had been a U.S. ally during World War II, Hollywood studios had produced several pro-Soviet films. After 1945, when this wartime alliance cooled, some argued that such films proved that subversives were spreading Soviet propaganda. HUAC wanted to rid Hollywood of these suspected Communist influences.

THINK THROUGH HISTORY
C. ***Analyzing Causes*** *Why was Hollywood a target of anti-Communist investigations by Congress?*

C. Answer Hollywood contained a number of Communists and other left-wingers, and its studios had produced several pro-Soviet movies during World War II.

THE HOLLYWOOD TEN For these reasons, HUAC subpoenaed 43 witnesses from the Hollywood film industry in September 1947. Many of the witnesses were "friendly," supporting the accusation that Communists had infiltrated the film industry. For example, the movie star Gary Cooper said he had "turned down quite a few scripts because I thought they were tinged with Communistic ideas." However, when asked which scripts he meant, Cooper couldn't remember their titles.

Protesters demonstrate in support of the Hollywood Ten.

TEACHING OPTIONS

Exploring Themes

Constitutional Concerns HUAC's attempts to remove persons with "un-American" views from the entertainment industry raised significant constitutional issues. The investigations by HUAC and later by Senator Joseph McCarthy seemed to clash with constitutional rights to freedom of speech and freedom of assembly, and of accused persons to be fully informed of the nature of accusations against them. The investigations continued despite protests by the Hollywood Ten and other prominent Americans.

Making Connections Across the Curriculum

U.S. Government Either house of Congress can set up a select committee, a group established for a specific, and often limited, purpose. The House Committee on Un-American Activities, like other select committees of Congress, did have investigative powers. Another famous select committee was formed to investigate the presidential campaign of Richard M. Nixon in 1972. Known as the Watergate Committee, its investigations were every bit as sensational as those of HUAC and resulted in the only presidential resignation in U.S. history.

Ten "unfriendly" witnesses eventually testified. These men, known as the **Hollywood Ten,** decided not to cooperate with the committee because they believed that the hearings were unconstitutional. Because the Hollywood Ten refused to answer the committee's questions, they were sent to prison.

In response to the hearings, Hollywood executives instituted a **blacklist,** a list of people whom they in effect condemned for having a Communist background. People who were blacklisted—approximately 500 actors, writers, producers, and directors—had their careers ruined because they could no longer work in films.

THE MCCARRAN ACT As Hollywood tried to rid itself of Communists, Congress decided that Truman's Loyalty Review Board did not go far enough in protecting the nation's security. In 1950, it passed the McCarran Internal Security Bill. This made it unlawful to plan any action that might lead to the establishment of a totalitarian dictatorship in the United States. Truman vetoed the bill, saying, "In a free country, we punish men for the crimes they commit, but never for the opinions they hold." But Congress enacted the law over Truman's veto.

Spy Cases Stun the Nation

Two spy cases added to fear that was spreading like an epidemic across the country. One case involved a former State Department official named **Alger Hiss.**

ALGER HISS In 1948, a former Communist spy, Whittaker Chambers, accused Hiss of spying for the Soviet Union. To support his charges, Chambers produced microfilm of government documents that he claimed had been typed on Hiss's typewriter. Too many years had passed for government prosecutors to charge Hiss with espionage, but a jury convicted him of perjury—for lying about passing the documents—and sent him to jail. A young conservative Republican congressman named Richard Nixon gained fame for pursuing the charges against Hiss. Within four years of the highly publicized case, Nixon was elected vice-president of the United States.

Hiss claimed that he was innocent and that Chambers had forged the documents used against him. However, in the 1990s, Soviet cables released by the National Security Agency seemed to prove Hiss's guilt.

NOW & THEN

SPIES

Spying is still an active business in both the United States and Russia. In February 1994, Aldrich Ames was arrested for spying. Ames was a "mole" within the CIA who turned over to the Russians the names of all the important U.S. spies at work in Russia, causing ten CIA agents to be executed and others to be imprisoned. Ames was convicted and sentenced to life in prison.

THE ROSENBERGS Another spy case rocked the nation even more than the Hiss case, partially because of international events occurring about the same time. On September 23, 1949, Americans learned that the Soviet Union had exploded an atomic bomb. Most American experts had predicted that it would take the Soviets three to five more years to figure out how to make the bomb, and people began to wonder if the Soviets had stolen the secret of the bomb.

This second spy case seemed to confirm that suspicion. In 1950, the British physicist Klaus Fuchs admitted giving the Soviet Union information about America's atomic bomb. The information probably enabled Soviet scientists to develop their own atomic bomb 18 months earlier than they would have otherwise. Implicated in the Fuchs case were **Ethel and Julius Rosenberg,** minor activists in the American Communist Party.

Ethel and Julius Rosenberg were executed in June 1953 despite numerous pleas to spare their lives.

The Rosenbergs denied the charges against them and pleaded the Fifth Amendment, choosing not to incriminate themselves, when asked if they were Communists. They claimed they were being persecuted both for being Jewish and for holding radical beliefs. The Rosenbergs were found guilty and given the

OBJECTIVE ② **INSTRUCT**

Spy Cases Stun the Nation

▶ ***Discussing Key Ideas***
- Alger Hiss and Ethel and Julius Rosenberg are convicted of spying for the Soviet Union.
- The Rosenbergs are put to death in the face of worldwide protests.

NOW & THEN
Spies

Critical Thinking: Synthesizing Spying is an ancient occupation. Ask students to investigate the activities of famous spies in history, such as Nathan Hale, Mata Hari, Francis Walsingham, and Allan Pinkerton. Have students share their findings with the class.

MORE ABOUT . . .
Alger Hiss

A Soviet intelligence cable from March 1945 was released by the U.S. National Security Agency in March 1996, about six months before Hiss died. The cable supports the claim that he was a Soviet agent. It points out that because Hiss was a member of the American delegation to Yalta as an aide to the U.S. secretary of state, he was especially valuable to the Soviets. Hiss maintained his innocence until the end of his life, however.

Block Schedule TEACHING OPTION **Time Needed: 40 Minutes**

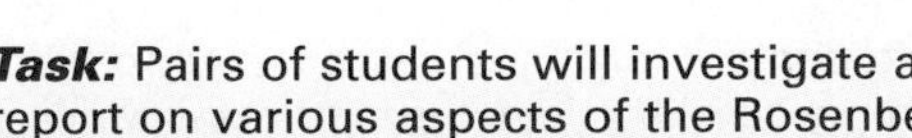

Cooperative Activity: Examining the Rosenberg Case

Task: Pairs of students will investigate and report on various aspects of the Rosenberg case.

Purpose: To make students aware of the powerful effect of public opinion on the government and the justice system.

Activity: Create a grab bag of questions to guide students' examination of the Rosenberg case. You might include questions such as these: What was the case against the Rosenbergs? What defense did they use? What was the political climate at the time? Why was the punishment so severe? Have students draw a question and research and write their answers in the form of a report. They can collaborate on the tasks or divide the research and writing. Have students present their reports in an order that sets the stage for and follows the development of the case.

Building a Portfolio: Students who add reports to their portfolios should include a note indicating their contribution.

ALTERNATIVE ASSESSMENT BOOK
Standards for Evaluating a Cooperative Activity

Standards for Evaluation
Reports should . . .
- show clear understanding of the question being answered
- use several sources for information
- use concrete examples from the Rosenberg case to support ideas

NOW & THEN
Television: Making the News

▶ ***Starting with the Student***
Ask students to name a recent major news story that has been carried by network news for at least several days.

- What pictures accompanied the story?
- If pictures had been unavailable, do students think the networks would have carried the story? Why or why not?
- What effect do they think television coverage might have on the outcome of the story?

▶ ***Discussing Key Ideas***

- Television news reporting sometimes plays an active role in shaping events that it covers.
- Political conventions are increasingly produced for television.
- Television news powerfully revealed Senator McCarthy's tactics, the daily brutality of the Vietnam War, and President Nixon's possible involvement in a cover-up of criminal activities.

death penalty. In pronouncing their sentence, Judge Irving Kaufman declared their crime "worse than murder." To him, they were directly responsible for one of the deadliest clashes of the Cold War.

A PERSONAL VOICE
I believe your conduct in putting into the hands of the Russians the A-bomb years before our best scientists predicted Russia would perfect the bomb has already caused, in my opinion, the Communist aggression in Korea.
IRVING KAUFMAN, quoted in *The Unquiet Death of Julius and Ethel Rosenberg*

People from all over the world appealed for clemency. Many considered the evidence and the testimony too weak to be used to deprive two people of their lives. The case was appealed to the U.S. Supreme Court, but the Court

NOW & THEN

Television: Making the News

Since the 1950s, television not only has become a major vehicle for reporting the news but has increasingly helped to create it. In fact, TV networks themselves made news at the Republican National Convention in August 1996. The networks chose to limit their coverage because they thought that fuller coverage would merely constitute an extended advertisement for the party, which had already chosen its candidates. The shift away from news to "infotainment" that the networks were protesting is a sign of the fierce competition among a bewildering variety of network and cable alternatives. This "media muddle" promises to blur even further the already indistinct line between reporting the news and making it.

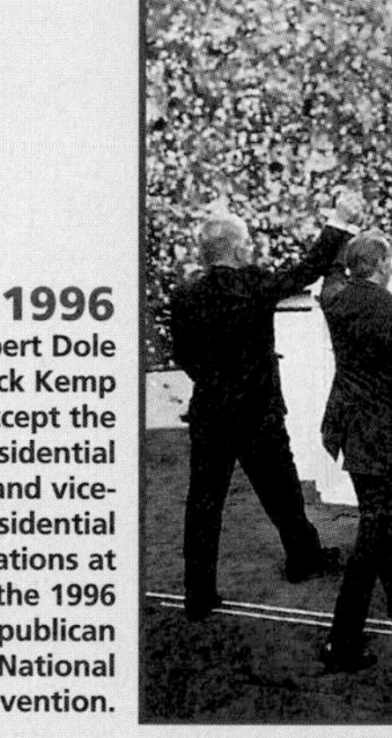
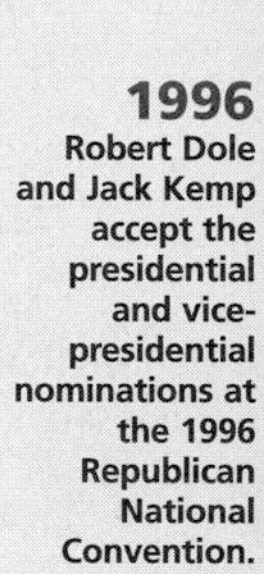

1996
Robert Dole and Jack Kemp accept the presidential and vice-presidential nominations at the 1996 Republican National Convention.

1954
The power of television not only to report the news but actually to make it became apparent in 1954. In that year the Communist-hunting senator Joseph McCarthy, in U.S. Senate hearings that were televised live, accused the U.S. Army of coddling Communists. As many as 20 million Americans watched the combative senator bully witnesses and slander people who had no chance to defend themselves. McCarthy's televised antics had finally thrust him into the villain's role.

1967
By 1967, with a television set in virtually every household in America, nightly news broadcasts had become established as a powerful influence on public opinion. For example, American support for the Vietnam War plummeted as millions of viewers saw Vietnamese civilians mutilated by U.S. bombs and chemical sprays. When Walter Cronkite, a CBS newscaster, announced in 1968 the likelihood that the "bloody experience of Vietnam" would end in a stalemate, President Lyndon Johnson admitted, "If I've lost Walter, then it's over."

INTERACT WITH HISTORY

1. Drawing Conclusions

Possible Answers:

1954: Television coverage exposed McCarthy's tactics and helped end his power.
1967: Television revealed the brutality of war, and support for U.S. involvement in Vietnam plummeted.
1974: Live television coverage convinced many Americans of President Nixon's involvement in Watergate.
1996: National political parties shape their messages into pat slogans for national audiences.

2. Tracking the Media

You may wish to give students a form such as this one to help them organize their comparison of television and newspaper coverage of a media event:

	TV	Newspaper
Extent of coverage		
Focus of story		
Main points presented		
Visuals included		

THINK THROUGH HISTORY
D. Analyzing Causes *Why did the cases of Alger Hiss and the Rosenbergs heighten the anti-Communist mood of Americans?*

refused to overturn the conviction. Julius and Ethel Rosenberg died in the electric chair in June 1953, leaving behind two sons. They became the first U.S. civilians executed for espionage. Many of those who formerly believed in their innocence have been convinced of their guilt by evidence contained in the same Soviet cables that implicated Hiss.

McCarthy Launches His "Witch Hunt"

D. Answer They added to the impression that the United States was being betrayed by Communist spies.

The most famous anti-Communist activist was **Senator Joseph McCarthy,** a Republican from Wisconsin. During his first three years in the Senate, he had acquired a reputation for being an ineffective legislator. By January 1950, he realized that he was going to need a winning issue in order to be reelected in 1952. Looking for such an issue, McCarthy charged that Communists were taking over the government.

"IT'S OKAY – WE'RE HUNTING COMMUNISTS."

SKILLBUILDER
INTERPRETING POLITICAL CARTOONS
What does this cartoon imply about the methods and tactics of HUAC?

Skillbuilder Answer
Possible Answer: That the committee was reckless and displayed little concern that innocent people might be harmed.

INTERACT WITH HISTORY

1. **DRAWING CONCLUSIONS** In each example shown, how did television influence the outcome of events?

SEE SKILLBUILDER HANDBOOK, PAGE 920.

2. **TRACKING THE MEDIA** Watch an evening news show for three or four evenings. How does it cover its lead stories? With interviews? With videotapes? Read newspaper reports of the same events and compare them with the TV coverage. Which is more comprehensive?

INTERNET Visit http://www.mlushistory.com for more about television broadcast news.

1974
The Watergate scandal that toppled Richard Nixon's presidency in 1974 played to a rapt TV audience. During the Senate hearings in 1973, the televised testimony of John Dean, the president's counsel, had convinced two out of three Americans that the president had committed a crime by planning or covering up the Watergate break-in. The House Judiciary Committee delayed its final deliberations on Nixon's impeachment until prime TV time, allowing the maximum number of people to watch.

MCCARTHY'S TACTICS Taking advantage of people's concerns about communism, McCarthy made one unsupported accusation after another. These attacks on suspected communists in the early 1950s became known as **McCarthyism.** Since that time, McCarthyism has referred to the unfair tactic of accusing people of disloyalty without providing evidence. At various times McCarthy claimed to have in his hands the names of 57, 81, and 205 Communists in the State Department. (He never actually produced even a single name.) He also charged that the Democratic Party was guilty of "20 years of treason" for allowing Communist infiltration into the government. Whenever he was challenged, he would respond with another accusation. However, he was always careful to do his name-calling only in the Senate, where he had legal immunity that protected him from being sued for slander.

The Republicans did little to stop McCarthy's attacks because they believed they would win the 1952 presidential election if the public saw them purging the nation of Communists. But, one small group of six senators did speak out, led by Senator Margaret Chase Smith of Maine.

A PERSONAL VOICE
I speak as a Republican. I speak as a woman. I speak as a United States Senator. I speak as an American. . . . I am not proud of the way in which the Senate has been made a publicity platform for irresponsible sensationalism. I am not proud of the reckless abandon in which unproved charges have been hurled from this side of the aisle.

MARGARET CHASE SMITH, "Declaration of Conscience"

MCCARTHY'S DOWNFALL Finally, in 1954, McCarthy made accusations against the U.S. Army, which resulted in a nationally televised

OBJECTIVE 3 INSTRUCT

McCarthy Launches His "Witch Hunt"

▶ ***Discussing Key Ideas***
- Senator Joseph McCarthy makes widely publicized attacks on suspected Communists in the U.S. government.
- Televised coverage of his bullying tactics leads to his downfall.

HISTORY FROM VISUALS
Political Cartoon

Reading the Cartoon Ask students why the HUAC car is driving over pedestrians. *The committee showed no regard for citizens' rights.*

Extension Ask students how they might illustrate the same idea.

MORE ABOUT . . .
Joseph McCarthy

McCarthy's executive secretary was Mary Brinkley Driscoll, sister of David Brinkley, the television news commentator. Years later, David Brinkley asked his sister what McCarthy was holding when he made his famous accusation that 205 Communists were working for the State Department. Mary replied, "He had a few scribbled notes to use in his speech. Nothing about Communists." She confirmed that McCarthy made up the number to get publicity.

IN-DEPTH RESOURCES: UNIT 5
American Lives: Margaret Chase Smith, p. 54

Block Schedule TEACHING OPTION **Time Needed: 40 Minutes**

Cooperative Activity: Investigating Witch Hunts

Task: Groups of three to four students will investigate either Senator McCarthy's crusade against Communists in the 1950s or the witch trials in Salem, Massachusetts, in 1692. Each group will report their findings to the class.

Purpose: To explore the impact of widespread public fears and hysteria on the lives of people and institutions.

Activity: Each group of students will research the assigned topic through the use of various library resources or the Internet. Reports should include a description of the actual events of the time, the accusations made, the type of evidence presented, and a description of the witch trials or of the Senate hearings. Students should draw conclusions about why waves of fear in these cases swept away reason and what could be done to prevent such situations in the future.

ALTERNATIVE ASSESSMENT BOOK
Standards for Evaluating a Cooperative Activity

HISTORY FROM VISUALS

Causes and Effects of McCarthyism

Reading the Chart Show students that the chart lists general causes and effects and does not imply links between them.

Extension Ask students to suggest possible links between the causes and effects listed.

HISTORY FROM VISUALS

Political Cartoon

Reading the Cartoon Who is the person pictured in the cartoon? *Senator McCarthy.* What does the web he is entangled in represent? *The accusations and lies that were his downfall.*

Extension Have students draw their own cartoons about McCarthy.

ASSESS & RETEACH

Section 3 Assessment

Ask students to work in pairs or small groups to answer the questions.

Self-Assessment

Have students explore their understanding of anti-Communist feelings by creating a two-column chart in which they list the actions taken against suspected Communists and the results of those actions.

Section Quiz

FORMAL ASSESSMENT
Section Quiz, p. 226

Reteach

Repeat the video "The Cold War Comes Home," and discuss the Cold War issues raised by the film.

***AMERICAN STORIES* video series**
"The Cold War Comes Home"

CLOSE

As communism spread around the world, spy cases and election-year politicking led to rising anti-Communist fears in the U.S. The resulting investigations damaged careers and silenced responsible debate.

Causes and Effects of McCarthyism

CAUSES

- Soviets successfully establish Communist regimes in Eastern Europe after World War II.
- Soviets develop the atomic bomb more quickly than expected.
- Korean War ends in a stalemate.
- Republicans gain politically by accusing Truman and Democrats of being soft on communism.

EFFECTS

- Millions of Americans are forced to take loyalty oaths and undergo loyalty investigations.
- Activism by labor unions goes into decline.
- Many people are hesitant to speak out on public issues for fear they will be accused of having Communist leanings.
- Anticommunism continues to drive U.S. foreign policy.

SKILLBUILDER **INTERPRETING CHARTS** ***How did world events help lead to McCarthyism? How did McCarthyism affect the behavior of individual Americans?***

I CAN'T DO THIS TO ME!

SKILLBUILDER
INTERPRETING POLITICAL CARTOONS
What does this cartoon suggest about McCarthy's downfall?

Skillbuilder Answer
Possible Answer: That he caused his own downfall.

Senate investigation. McCarthy's bullying of witnesses alienated the audience and cost him public support. The Senate condemned him for improper conduct that tended "to bring the Senate into disrepute." Three years later McCarthy died a broken man, suffering from alcoholism.

OTHER ANTI-COMMUNISTS Others besides Joseph McCarthy made it their mission to root communism out of American society. By 1953, 39 states had passed laws making it illegal to advocate the violent overthrow of the government, even though such laws clearly violated the constitutional right of free speech. Across the nation, cities and towns passed similar laws.

At times, the fear of communism seemed to have no limits. In Indiana, professional wrestlers had to take a loyalty oath. In experiments run by newspapers, pedestrians on the street refused to sign petitions that quoted the Declaration of Independence because they were afraid the ideas were Communist. The government investigated union leaders, librarians, newspaper reporters, and scientists. It seemed that no profession was safe from the Red hunt. The FBI even interviewed a Washington, D.C., bootblack 70 times before deciding he could shine shoes in the Pentagon.

During this era many Americans tried so hard to root out communism that they were sometimes willing to compromise their own freedom. But even those measures did not stop the escalation of the Cold War.

Skillbuilder Answer
World Events: Soviet success in Europe, the Soviet development of the atomic bomb, and the Korean War stalemate heightened fear of communism.
Behavior: McCarthyism led to mandatory loyalty oaths, hesitancy to speak out on issues, and decreased activism by labor unions.

Section 3 Assessment

1. TERMS & NAMES
Identify:
- HUAC
- Hollywood Ten
- blacklist
- Alger Hiss
- Ethel and Julius Rosenberg
- Senator Joseph McCarthy
- McCarthyism

2. SUMMARIZING Re-create the web below on your paper and fill in events that illustrate the main idea in the center.

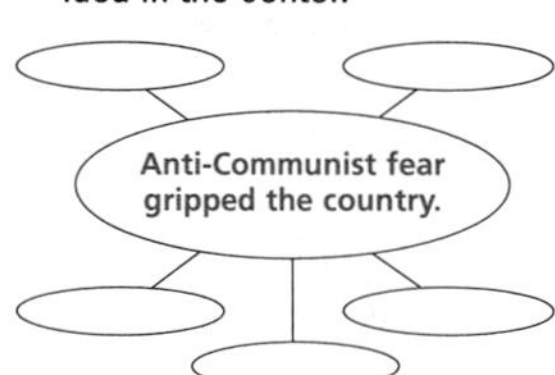

3. MAKING DECISIONS If you had lived in this period and been accused of being a Communist, what would you have done?

THINK ABOUT
- the Hollywood Ten, who refused to answer questions
- the Rosenbergs, who pleaded the Fifth Amendment
- those who informed on others to save themselves

4. ROLE-PLAYING HISTORY Get together with three classmates, with each group member playing one of the following roles: Harry Truman, a member of HUAC, Judge Irving Kaufman, and Joseph McCarthy. As the person you have chosen, explain your motivation for opposing communism.

ANSWERS

1. TERMS & NAMES

HUAC, p. 620
Hollywood Ten, p. 621
blacklist, p. 621
Alger Hiss, p. 621
Ethel and Julius Rosenberg, p. 621
Senator Joseph McCarthy, p. 623
McCarthyism, p. 623

2. SUMMARIZING

Events
1. HUAC investigated "un-American" activity in Hollywood.
2. Congress passes the McCarran Act.
3. Spy cases increase fears.
4. McCarthy arouses fears of a Communist conspiracy.

3. MAKING DECISIONS

Possible Responses: Some students may say they might have refused to name others because that is the honorable thing to do. Others may say they would have shown their loyalty to the government by answering the committee's questions.

4. ROLE-PLAYING HISTORY

Possible Responses: Although motivations will vary, the basic reasons offered for opposing communism during this period were the aggression of the Soviet Union in taking over countries in Eastern Europe and in the fact that Soviet leaders were opposed to democracy.

4 Two Nations Live on the Edge

LEARN ABOUT the arms race, the spread of the Cold War, and the U-2 incident
TO UNDERSTAND how tensions grew between the United States and the Soviet Union.

TERMS & NAMES
- H-bomb
- Dwight D. Eisenhower
- John Foster Dulles
- brinkmanship
- CIA
- Warsaw Pact
- Nikita Khrushchev
- Eisenhower Doctrine
- Francis Gary Powers
- U-2 incident

ONE AMERICAN'S STORY

Annie Dillard was one of thousands of children who grew up in the 1950s with the chilling knowledge that nuclear war could obliterate their world in an instant. Dillard recalls practicing what to do in case of a nuclear attack.

A PERSONAL VOICE

At school, we had air-raid drills. We took the drills seriously; surely Pittsburgh, which had the nation's steel, coke, and aluminum, would be the enemy's first target. . . . When the air-raid siren sounded, our teachers stopped talking and led us to the school basement. There the gym teachers lined us up against the cement walls and steel lockers, and showed us how to lean in and fold our arms over our heads. . . . The teachers stood in the middle of the room, not talking to each other. We tucked against the walls and lockers. . . . We folded our skinny arms over our heads, and raised to the enemy a clatter of gold scarab bracelets and gold bangle bracelets.

ANNIE DILLARD, *An American Childhood*

The fear of nuclear attack was a direct result of the Cold War. After the Soviet Union developed its atomic bomb, the two superpowers embarked on an arms race that enormously increased both the number and the destructive power of weapons.

A father helps his daughter practice getting into a bomb shelter.

Brinkmanship Rules U.S. Policy

Although air-raid drills were not common until the Eisenhower years (1953–1961), the nuclear arms race began during Truman's presidency. When the Soviet Union exploded its first atomic bomb in 1949, President Truman had to make a terrible decision—whether to develop an even more horrifying weapon.

RACE FOR THE H-BOMB The scientists who had developed the atomic bomb, in which atoms were split, had suspected since 1942 that it was possible to create a hydrogen, or thermonuclear, bomb in which atoms would be fused. They estimated that such a bomb would have the force of 1 million tons of TNT (67 times the power of the bomb dropped on Hiroshima). But they argued vehemently about the morality of creating such a destructive weapon. J. Robert Oppenheimer, head of the atomic-bomb team, opposed the new project. Referring to his role in creating the weapon used on Japan, Oppenheimer told Truman, "Mr. President, I have blood on my hands."

However, political forces soon affected the decision. The Soviet Union's successful explosion of an atomic bomb took away the U.S. nuclear advantage. Politicians and military leaders pressed for a more powerful weapon, warning that the United States had to develop one before the Soviets did. On January 31, 1950, Truman authorized work on the hydrogen bomb, or **H-bomb.**

On November 1, 1952, the United States exploded the first thermonuclear device. The blast far exceeded initial estimates, delivering a force equal to 10.4 million tons of TNT. However, the new American advantage lasted less than a year, for in August 1953 the Soviets exploded their own thermonuclear weapon.

SECTION 4 RESOURCES

PRINT RESOURCES

IN-DEPTH RESOURCES: UNIT 5
Guided Reading, p. 42
Primary Source: *from* Dwight D. Eisenhower's Statement on the U-2 Incident, p. 49
Literature: from *The Nuclear Age* by Tim O'Brien, p. 50

READING STUDY GUIDE, p. 193

ACCESS FOR STUDENTS ACQUIRING ENGLISH
Guided Reading (Spanish), p. 210

SPANISH READING STUDY GUIDE, p. 193

FORMAL ASSESSMENT
Section Quiz, p. 227

ALTERNATIVE ASSESSMENT

See forms for supporting and scoring alternative activities.

TECHNOLOGY RESOURCES

HUMANITIES TRANSPARENCIES
H25, California bomb shelter, 1951
H41, Political Cartoon

CRITICAL THINKING TRANSPARENCIES
CT26, The Cold War
CT60, The Space Race

CD-ROM *Grolier Multimedia Encyclopedia*
Electronic Library of Primary Sources

VIDEO *American Portfolio: A Videodisc for U.S. History,* user's guide, pp. 234–241

INTERNET http://www.mlushistory.com

Section 4 Overview

OBJECTIVES

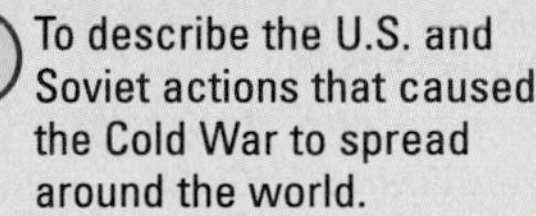

1. To explain the policy of brinkmanship.
2. To describe the U.S. and Soviet actions that caused the Cold War to spread around the world.
3. To summarize the impact of *Sputnik* and the U-2 incident on the United States.

SKILLBUILDERS
- Understanding geography: region, p. 627
- Interpreting graphs, p. 628

CRITICAL THINKING
- Analyzing causes, p. 626
- Summarizing, pp. 626, 627, 629
- Theme: Science and Technology, p. 628
- Hypothesizing, p. 629
- Evaluating Decisions, p. 629
- Analyzing Cause, p. 629

FOCUS & MOTIVATE

5-MINUTE WARM-UP

Recognizing Facts and Details

To explore some of the issues that arose during the Cold War, have students read "Race for the H-Bomb" on page 625 and answer these questions.

1. On what date did Truman authorize work on the H-Bomb?
2. How much force was delivered by the first H-Bomb?

WARM-UP TRANSPARENCY 18

▶ ***Starting with the Student***
- Ask students how they react when they feel threatened? Do they think those same reactions apply to nations? Explain.

OBJECTIVE ① **INSTRUCT**

Brinkmanship Rules U.S. Policy

▶ ***Discussing Key Ideas***
- In a nuclear race with the Soviet Union, the United

(continued on next page)

(continued from page 625)
States develops a hydrogen bomb.
- The U.S. policy of brinkmanship further accelerates the Cold War.

IN-DEPTH RESOURCES: UNIT 5
Guided Reading, p. 42

ACCESS FOR STUDENTS ACQUIRING ENGLISH
Guided Reading (Spanish), p. 227

HUMANITIES TRANSPARENCIES
H25, California bomb shelter, 1951

ELECTRONIC LIBRARY OF PRIMARY SOURCES
Life in a Shelter by Thamar E. Dufwa

OBJECTIVE
② **INSTRUCT**

The Cold War Spreads Around the World

▶ ***Starting with the Student***
Have students do a concept web to explore what they know about the CIA.

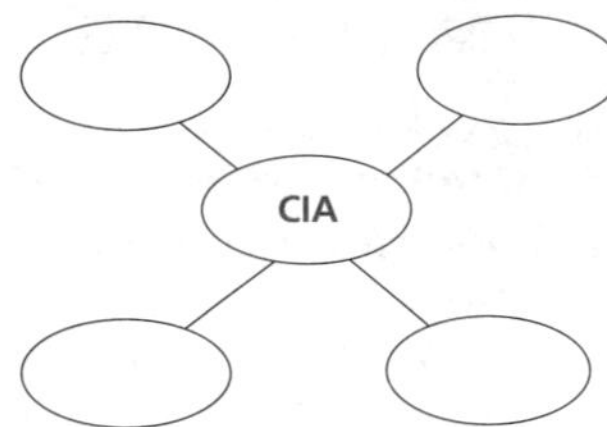

▶ ***Discussing Key Ideas***
- The CIA uses covert actions against governments unfriendly to the United States.
- Eisenhower and Soviet leaders meet in Geneva, kindling hope of better U.S.–Soviet relations.
- Crises in the Middle East and Hungary keep tensions high.
- The Eisenhower Doctrine commits the president to use force against armed aggression in the Middle East.

"You have to take chances for peace, just as you must take chances in war. . . . If you are scared to go to the brink, you are lost."

JOHN FOSTER DULLES

THE POLICY OF BRINKMANSHIP By the time both countries had the H-bomb, **Dwight D. Eisenhower** was president. His secretary of state, **John Foster Dulles,** was staunchly anti-Communist. He also viewed compromise as immoral. Winston Churchill once said of him, "Mr. Dulles makes a speech every day, holds a press conference every other day, and preaches on Sunday."

Dulles proposed a new policy, based on threats of massive retaliation. The United States would, in effect, keep the peace by promising to use all its force, including nuclear weapons, against any aggressor nation. This willingness to go to the brink, or edge, of war became known as **brinkmanship.** Because Dulles's policy required greater dependence on nuclear weapons and the airplanes that delivered them, the United States trimmed its army and navy but beefed up its air force and produced massive numbers of nuclear weapons.

The arms race began in earnest when the Soviet Union answered this development by also producing huge quantities of nuclear bombs. As a result, many American citizens became convinced that Soviet weapons were aimed directly at their cities. Schoolchildren like Annie Dillard practiced air-raid procedures, and some families built underground fallout shelters in their back yards. Fear of nuclear war became a constant in American life for 30 years.

A. Answer By developing more powerful weapons, including the H-bomb.

THINK THROUGH HISTORY
A. *Analyzing Causes* *How did the U.S. and the Soviet Union start an arms race?*

The Cold War Spreads Around the World

As the nation shifted to a dependence on nuclear arms, the Eisenhower administration began to rely heavily on the recently formed Central Intelligence Agency **(CIA)** for information. The CIA used spies to gather information abroad. The CIA also began to carry out covert actions, or secret operations, to weaken or overthrow governments unfriendly to the United States.

THINK THROUGH HISTORY
B. *Summarizing* *What was the role of the CIA in the Cold War?*

B. Answer To gather intelligence and to carry out secret operations against unfriendly governments.

COVERT ACTIONS IN THE MIDDLE EAST AND LATIN AMERICA The Eisenhower administration believed that the struggle against communism was similar to the fight against totalitarian governments in World War II. The leader of the Soviet Union, an absolute dictator, ordered secret operations against his enemies. Eisenhower feared that the United States would be at a disadvantage if it did not also carry out covert actions.

One of the CIA's first covert actions took place in the Middle East. In 1951, Iran's prime minister, Mohammed Mossadegh, placed the oil industry under the government's control. To protest, the Western nations stopped buying Iranian oil. As the Iranian economy faltered, the United States feared that Mossadegh might turn to the Soviets for help. In 1953, the CIA persuaded the shah, the monarch of Iran, to replace Mossadegh with someone more favorable to the West. The people remained loyal to the shah, and the prime minister fled.

In 1954, the CIA also took covert actions in Guatemala, a Central American country just south of Mexico. Eisenhower believed that Guatemala's government, headed by Jacobo Arbenz Guzmán, had Communist sympathies because it had given more than 200,000 acres of American-owned land to peasants. In response, the CIA trained an army, which invaded Guatemala and captured Arbenz Guzmán and his forces. The army's leader, Carlos Castillo Armas, became dictator of the country.

A SUMMIT IN GENEVA In spite of the growing tension between the superpowers, U.S.-Soviet relations seemed to thaw following the death of Joseph Stalin in 1953. The Soviets recognized West Germany and concluded peace treaties with Austria and Japan. However, in 1955, when West Germany was allowed to rearm and join NATO, the Soviet Union grew fearful. It formed its own military alliance, called the **Warsaw Pact,** with the Eastern European satellite nations under its control.

In July 1955, Eisenhower traveled to Geneva, Switzerland, to meet with Soviet leaders in the first East-West summit conference since World War II.

TEACHING OPTIONS

Making Connections Across Cultures

Iran Iran, or Persia, as it was called for hundreds of years, is the home of some of the world's most ancient settlements, dating to about 4000 B.C. For centuries it has been a crossroads for migration because of its long borders with Russia, Iraq, Turkey, Pakistan, and Afghanistan. Its culturally diverse population is religiously unified under Islam. Iran's rich cultural heritage includes some of the world's most magnificent mosques and palaces decorated with jewel-like mosaics in bright colors.

Teaching Less Proficient Readers

To help students clarify the events of the Cold War, put this chart on the chalkboard and have students fill in the blanks.

Event	Result
The U.S. is suspicious of the Soviet Union.	CIA operates covertly to support non-Communist governments.
U.S. and Soviet leaders hold summit meeting.	Meeting goes nowhere.
U.S. and Great Britain withdraw offer to build dam in Egypt.	
Hungarians ask for more freedoms.	
U.S. worries about Soviet aggression.	

Skillbuilder Answer **Region:** NATO—Portugal, Great Britain, France, Belgium, the Netherlands, Luxembourg, West Germany, Denmark, Norway, Italy, Greece, Turkey. Warsaw Pact—Soviet Union, Poland, East Germany, Czechoslovakia, Hungary, Romania, Bulgaria, Albania. **Region:** Ireland, Spain, Switzerland, Austria, Yugoslavia, Sweden, Finland.

There Eisenhower put forth an "open skies" proposal. The United States and the Soviet Union would allow flights over each other's territory to guard against surprise nuclear attacks. The Soviet Union rejected this proposal, fearing it was a U.S. trick to learn where the Soviets were keeping their weapons.

The summit accomplished nothing specific, but the world hailed the "spirit of Geneva" that seemed to promise movement toward peace. However, hope that the Cold War was easing was short-lived, as the Soviet Union turned aggressor a year later.

The Warsaw Pact and NATO, 1955

Warsaw Pact countries
NATO members, 1955
Nonaligned nations

GEOGRAPHY SKILLBUILDER
***REGION** Which nations shown on the map belonged to NATO, and which to the Warsaw Pact?*
***REGION** Which nations shown on the map belonged to neither defense alliance?*

CRISIS IN THE MIDDLE EAST Although the United States and the Soviet Union had agreed on establishing the nation of Israel in 1948, the Cold War affected the Middle East as well as Europe. In 1955, Great Britain and the United States agreed to help Egypt finance construction of a dam at Aswan on the Nile River. When Gamal Abdel Nasser, the head of Egypt, began to strengthen his ties with Communist countries, the United States and Great Britain withdrew their offer. Angered, Nasser seized the Suez Canal, which is located in Egypt but was owned by France and Great Britain.

The British and the French were furious. Israel was also angry at Egypt, which had been making terrorist raids into its territory. Joining forces, Great Britain, France, and Israel invaded Egypt, the Soviets' ally, in October 1956. When the Soviets threatened to use missiles against Britain and France, the United States warned that it would not tolerate such action. Direct confrontation with the Soviet Union was avoided when the UN imposed a cease-fire. The canal reopened in April 1957 under Egyptian management.

SOVIET AGGRESSION IN HUNGARY In February 1956, **Nikita Khrushchev,** head of the Soviet Communist Party, publicly criticized his predecessor, Stalin, for having committed crimes against the Soviet people. Such open criticism of the previous regime made people around the world wonder if the Soviet Union was becoming a less repressive country. Some Eastern European nations began to dream of breaking free of Soviet control.

One such nation, Hungary, had experienced several years of unrest as the country's leaders clashed over how much freedom to grant Hungarians. The Soviets had occupied the country, and Hungarians had made several efforts to oust them. In October 1956, students and workers tried to force the more repressive leaders out of office. Khrushchev agreed that the reform-minded leader Imre Nagy should be premier.

After the Soviet army had been forced to leave the country, the Hungarians demanded other liberties, including the right to leave the Warsaw Pact. Moscow responded brutally. In November 1956, Soviet tanks rolled into Hungary and killed approximately 30,000 Hungarian protesters. Thousands of refugees fled, many to the United States. Eisenhower provided no military aid, but protested the invasion, sent Hungary $20 million for food and medicine, authorized another $5 million to go to the UN to aid Hungarian refugees, and allowed more Hungarians to enter the country.

C. Answer Khrushchev's allowing Imre Nagy to become premier led to protests and other demands.

THINK THROUGH HISTORY
C. *Summarizing* *How did Hungary become a Cold War trouble spot?*

ON THE WORLD STAGE

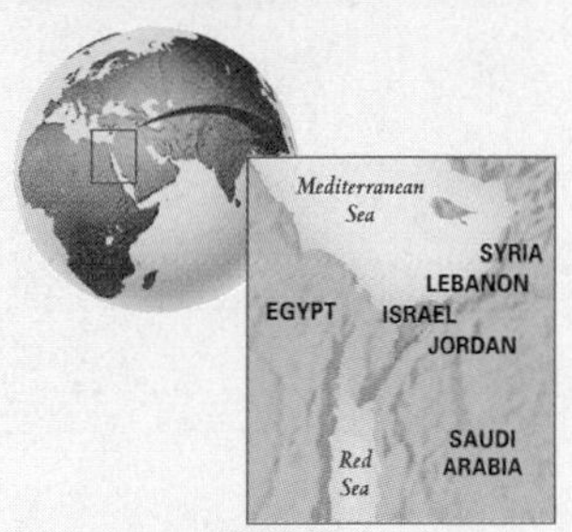

ISRAEL

On May 14, 1948, the United Nations created the nation of Israel by partitioning Palestine into two states, one Jewish and one Arab. Thousands of Jews had immigrated to Palestine from Europe before and during World War II, and Israel became the "promised land" they had been seeking since biblical times. The creation of Israel was one of the few issues that the United States and the Soviet Union agreed on, as the world reacted uniformly to the horror that had befallen the Jews in the Holocaust.

HISTORY FROM VISUALS
The Warsaw Pact and NATO, 1955

Reading the Map Tell students to note the positions of countries in NATO and the Warsaw Pact. Which members of NATO seem isolated? *Greece and Turkey.*

Extension Discuss with students why Greece and Turkey belong to NATO instead of the Warsaw Pact. *After World War II, the U.S. supported Greece and Turkey with millions in aid under the Truman Doctrine. The two countries thus came under Western influence.*

ON THE WORLD STAGE
Israel

Critical Thinking: Summarizing The ancient land of Palestine has a long and turbulent history. Ask students to do some outside reading about this area and to write brief summaries of the positions of the Israelis and the Palestinians on the current conflicts there.

Block Schedule TEACHING OPTION **Time Needed: 20 Minutes**

Cooperative Activity: Creating a Political Cartoon

Task: Students will research U.S. attitudes toward the Soviet Union in the 1950s and then create political cartoons that capture the anxiety of the time.

Purpose: To help students understand U.S. motivations in pursuing the Cold War.

Activity: Have groups of three to four students read newspaper and magazine accounts of the Suez crisis, the invasion of Hungary, the launch of *Sputnik*, or the downing of the U-2. They can then brainstorm together to create a political cartoon showing some aspect of the U.S. response to a specific event. They might consider "Flopnik," the fear of *Sputnik* as an all-seeing spy, or the U-2 incident, for example.

Building a Portfolio: Students who add cartoons to their portfolios should attach a note describing their contribution to the cartoon.

ALTERNATIVE ASSESSMENT BOOK
Standards for Evaluating a Cooperative Activity

Standards for Evaluation
Political cartoons should . . .

- make a clear point about the U.S. reaction to Soviet actions
- focus on one idea
- include an appropriate caption
- be carefully drawn

OBJECTIVE
③ **INSTRUCT**

The Cold War Takes to the Skies

▶ ***Starting with the Student***
The launching of *Sputnik* resulted in improved science education in the U.S. Do students think their science courses today reflect a national push for strong science education? Why or why not?

▶ ***Discussing Key Ideas***
- Soviet success in launching the first space satellite shocks the United States.
- The United States successfully launches a space satellite and improves science education.
- Relations between the United States and the Soviet Union worsen after the Soviets down a U.S. spy plane.

GROLIER MULTIMEDIA ENCYCLOPEDIA
Soviet-Russian manned spaceflight

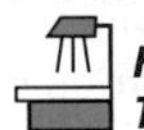
HUMANITIES TRANSPARENCIES
H41, Political Cartoon

HISTORY FROM VISUALS
U.S. Budget, 1940–1990

Reading the Graphs
Remind students that the second and third graphs cover the early Cold War period. The first and last ones provide comparisons.

Extension Ask students to check an almanac or a statistical abstract to find a more recent figure for defense spending. How does it compare with other figures in the graph? *1996—16.9% (estimated).*

THE EISENHOWER DOCTRINE The Soviet Union's prestige in the Middle East rose because of its support for Egypt. To counterbalance this development, President Eisenhower issued a warning in January 1957. This warning, known as the **Eisenhower Doctrine,** said that the United States would defend the Middle East against attack by any Communist country. In March, Congress officially approved the doctrine. It gave the president authority to use American forces, at his discretion, against armed aggression in the Middle East by any nation "controlled by international communism."

The Cold War Takes to the Skies

The Cold War was not limited to political matters; it also affected science and education. The United States began 1957 confident that it was ahead of the Soviets in military technology. It had guided missiles that could deliver nuclear warheads with great accuracy at distances of 1,500 to 3,000 miles. Then, in August 1957, the Soviets announced that they had developed a rocket capable of traveling much greater distances—a true ICBM, or intercontinental ballistic missile.

U.S. Budget, 1940–1990

PERCENTAGE SPENT ON DEFENSE

Year	Percentage
1940	18%
1950	32%
1960	52%
1990	24%

Source: Historical Tables, Budget of the United States Government, Fiscal Year 1997

SKILLBUILDER
INTERPRETING GRAPHS ***By how much did the percentage of the federal budget spent on defense increase between 1950 and 1960? Why do you think it increased that much?***

Skillbuilder Answer
Budget: By 20%. **Reason:** *Possible Answer:* The arms race with the Soviet Union.

SPUTNIK LAUNCHES THE SPACE RACE The real shock came on October 4, when the Soviets used an ICBM to push the first unmanned artificial satellite above the friction of the earth's atmosphere. There the satellite, the first Sputnik, traveled around the earth at 18,000 miles per hour, circling the globe every 96.2 minutes. Its weight of nearly 200 pounds indicated that 1.1 million pounds of thrust had been used to lift it into orbit—more than enough to deliver a nuclear warhead from the Soviet Union to any target in the world.

The launching of *Sputnik I* made many Americans feel inferior to the Soviets and vulnerable to nuclear attack. The United States seemed to be falling behind in science and technology. To try to solve the apparent problem, the United States made changes in its educational system. Schools sought to improve their science, mathematics, and foreign-language courses.

In addition, U.S. scientists worked frantically to catch up to the Soviets. The first attempt at an American satellite launch was a humiliating failure, with the rocket toppling to the ground. The press labeled it "Flopnik" and "Stayputnik." However, on January 31, 1958, the United States successfully launched its first satellite. The race to launch bigger satellites—and develop better weapons-delivery systems—was on.

THINK THROUGH HISTORY
D. THEME
Science and Technology *What effect did the Cold War have on space exploration?*

D. Answer It accelerated the pace of exploration.

A U-2 IS SHOT DOWN Following the rejection of Eisenhower's "open skies" proposal at the 1955 Geneva summit conference, the CIA began making secret high-altitude flights over Soviet territory. The plane used for these missions, the U-2, was designed to fly higher than Soviet fighter planes and beyond the reach of antiaircraft fire. As a U-2 passed over the USSR, its infrared cameras took detailed photographs.

By 1960, however, many U.S. officials were nervous about the U-2 program. First, the existence and purpose of the U-2 was an open secret among some members of the American press. Second, the Soviets had been aware of the flights since 1958, as **Francis Gary Powers,** a U-2 pilot, explained.

A PERSONAL VOICE

> We . . . knew that the Russians were radar-tracking at least some of our flights. . . . We also knew that SAMs [surface-to-air missiles] were being fired at us, that some were uncomfortably close to our altitude. But we knew too that the Russians had a control problem in their guidance system. . . . We were concerned, but not greatly.
>
> FRANCIS GARY POWERS, *Operation Overflight: The U-2 Spy Pilot Tells His Story for the First Time*

TEACHING OPTIONS

Exploring Themes

Science and Technology The brilliant scientific achievements that led to the creation of the atomic and hydrogen bombs also cast a shadow of impending nuclear holocaust over the 1950s. Misunderstanding and mistrust between the United States and the Soviet Union escalated into an arms race that drained national economies and instilled fear in people all over the world. Americans built bomb shelters, and air-raid drills became part of the school curriculum. Scientists, however, continued to develop peaceful applications of nuclear energy, such as computer tomography and magnetic resonance imaging.

Making Connections Across the Curriculum

Science In 1666, Isaac Newton imagined firing a cannonball from the top of a giant mountain. The faster the cannonball went, the farther it would travel before hitting the ground. At a high enough speed, the cannonball, which travels in a natural arc, wouldn't hit the ground at all because of the curvature of the earth. Discuss how scientists applied Newton's theory to the launching of satellites. *In the first stage of a satellite launch, the rocket is thrust high enough to escape the earth's gravitational pull. When it reaches a speed that counterbalances gravity, it is oriented to follow the curvature of the earth.*

Finally, Eisenhower himself wanted the flights discontinued. He and Khrushchev were going to hold another summit conference on the arms race on May 15, 1960. "If one of these aircraft were lost when we were engaged in apparently sincere deliberations, it could . . . ruin my effectiveness," he told an aide. However, Dulles persuaded him to authorize one last flight.

That flight took place on May 1, and the pilot was Francis Gary Powers. Four hours after Powers entered Soviet airspace, a Soviet pilot, Igor Mentyukov, brought down his plane. The United States issued a false story that a plane had disappeared while on a weather mission. Khrushchev announced that the U-2 had been brought down 1,300 miles inside the Soviet Union by a Soviet rocket and that Powers had been captured alive and had confessed his activities. This was the official line for 38 years. But in 1996, Mentyukov revealed the true story and explained that the Soviets had covered up the truth to make their missile defenses appear more advanced than they really were.

The CIA had supplied Francis Gary Powers with a special pin, laced with enough poison to kill him within 90 seconds, to use in case of capture. Shown here *(clockwise from top)* are the plane, the pin, and the pilot.

KHRUSHCHEV DENOUNCES EISENHOWER It was a bad moment for the United States. President Eisenhower frankly owned up to the charge and took full personal responsibility for authorizing the flight. The admission angered Khrushchev, who interpreted it as a sign not of honesty but of contempt. He felt that the incident made him look bad in the Soviet Union, where hard-liners disapproved of his willingness to negotiate with the Americans. To regain prestige back home, Khrushchev used the beginning of the summit conference to denounce the United States and then left. As Eisenhower feared, the U-2 had put an end to his effectiveness as a peacemaker. The Soviet Union tried Powers for espionage and sentenced him to ten years in prison. After 17 months, however, he was returned to the United States in exchange for a Soviet spy, Colonel Rudolf Abel.

E. Answer *Possible Answers:* Without a confrontation to expose covert actions, Cold War tensions might have eased. Peace talks could have been pursued without a breach in trust.

Because of the **U-2 incident,** the 1960s opened with tension between the two superpowers as high as ever. The few hopeful events of the 1950s—such as the Geneva summit and the Soviet Union's turn away from Stalinism—had been eclipsed by aggression, competitiveness, and mutual suspicion. The Cold War would continue into the next decade, with an enormous effect on U.S. policies toward Cuba—and ultimately toward Vietnam.

THINK THROUGH HISTORY
E. *Hypothesizing* *How might the Cold War have progressed if the U-2 incident had never occurred?*

Section 4 Assessment

1. TERMS & NAMES
Identify:
- H-bomb
- Dwight D. Eisenhower
- John Foster Dulles
- brinkmanship
- CIA
- Warsaw Pact
- Nikita Khrushchev
- Eisenhower Doctrine
- Francis Gary Powers
- U-2 incident

2. SUMMARIZING Skim this section for information about Cold War troubles in Guatemala, Iran, Egypt, and Hungary. For each, write a newspaper headline that summarizes the U.S. role and the outcome of the situation.

Trouble Spot	Headline

Choose one headline and write a paragraph about that trouble spot.

3. EVALUATING DECISIONS Do you think that the United States should have taken each of the following actions? Why or why not?

THINK ABOUT
- the development of the H-bomb
- the adoption of a policy of massive retaliation
- covert actions, including those in Iran and Guatemala and the U-2 flights

4. ANALYZING CAUSES Which of the two superpowers do you think contributed more to Cold War tensions during the 1950s?

THINK ABOUT
- U.S. decisions during this period
- each country's participation in the arms race
- the Soviet Union's invasion of Hungary

ANSWERS

1. TERMS & NAMES

H-bomb, p. 625
Dwight D. Eisenhower, p. 626
John Foster Dulles, p. 626
brinkmanship, p. 626
CIA, p. 626
Warsaw Pact, p. 626
Nikita Khrushchev, p. 627
Eisenhower Doctrine, p. 628
Francis Gary Powers, p. 628
U-2 incident, p. 629

2. SUMMARIZING

Possible Response: **Guatemala:** CIA-Trained Army Topples Guatemalan Ruler or CIA Keeps Communism Out of Guatemala
Iran: U.S. Prevents Iranian-Soviet Alliance or U.S. Engineers Iranian Chaos
Egypt: U.S. Urges Peaceful Suez Solution
Hungary: U.S. Protests Soviet Invasion

3. EVALUATING DECISIONS

Possible Responses: Some students will feel that the development of the H-bomb, massive retaliation, and covert actions were understandable because of the fear of communism.
Other students may feel that the United States was too aggressive and had no right to meddle in the affairs of other countries.

4. ANALYZING CAUSES

Possible Responses: Students may find both countries equally at fault. Some students may find the U.S. more at fault and cite the U-2 incident, the Eisenhower Doctrine, and the involvement in Guatemala and Iran. Others may say the Soviet Union was more to blame because they invaded Hungary and made threats during the Suez Canal crisis.

MORE ABOUT . . .
The U-2 Incident

The U-2 was actually brought down when Mentyukov caught Powers's plane in the slipstream of his Sukhoi Su-9. The U-2 flipped over and the wings broke off. Mentyukov's great skill as a pilot was never acknowledged because of the official cover-up.

IN-DEPTH RESOURCES: UNIT 5
Primary Source: *from* Dwight D. Eisenhower's Statement on the U-2, p. 49

ASSESS & RETEACH

Section 4 Assessment

Have students work individually to answer the questions; then have them share the headlines they wrote for question 2 with the class.

Self-Assessment

Ask students to review their answers for question 3 on the section assessment. What did they learn from evaluating U.S. actions?

Section Quiz

FORMAL ASSESSMENT
Section Quiz, p. 227

Reteach

Use the cause-and-effect transparency to review the actions and reactions of the two superpowers during the Cold War.

CRITICAL THINKING TRANSPARENCIES
CT26, The Cold War

GROLIER MULTIMEDIA ENCYCLOPEDIA
The Cold War

CLOSE

A nuclear arms race between the United States and the Soviet Union infected the 1950s with widespread fear of a nuclear holocaust. Covert activities, hostile actions in Egypt and Hungary, and the Soviet launch of an unmanned space satellite raised mutual suspicion to new levels.

American Literature

OBJECTIVES

1. To explain how science fiction of the 1950s reflected the anxieties of the age.
2. To identify the messages of three science fiction excerpts.

FOCUS & MOTIVATE

▶ ***Starting with the Student***
Ask students to discuss science fiction films they have seen recently.

- What was the general feeling conveyed in the film?
- How might today's films differ from films in the 1950s, other than in their use of special effects?
- Do students think science fiction films generally convey social or political messages, or are they simply entertainment?

MORE ABOUT . . .
Ray Bradbury

Because Bradbury rarely writes about space hardware and gadgetry, some critics have been reluctant to call him a true science fiction writer. Bradbury himself says, "If you're too good a scientist, you're not a good writer." He goes on to say, "I write for fun. . . . I have fun with ideas. I play with them. I approach my craft with enthusiasm and respect. If my work sparks serious thought, fine. But I don't write with that in mind. I'm not a serious person, and I don't like serious people."

AMERICAN LITERATURE

Science Fiction Reflects Cold War Realities

Many writers of science fiction draw on the scientific and social trends of the present to describe future societies that might arise if those trends continued. Nuclear proliferation, the space race, early computer technology, and the pervasive fear of known and unknown dangers during the Cold War were the realities that prompted a boom in science fiction during the 1950s and 1960s.

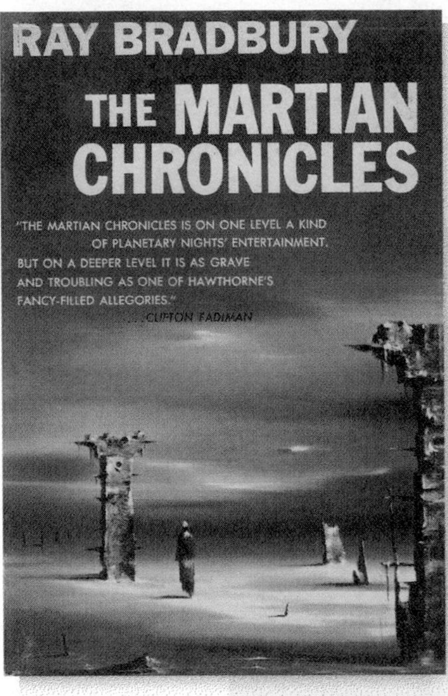

THE MARTIAN CHRONICLES

In *The Martian Chronicles,* Ray Bradbury describes how earthlings who have colonized Mars watch helplessly as their former planet is destroyed by nuclear warfare.

They all came out and looked at the sky that night. They left their suppers or their washing up or their dressing for the show and they came out upon their now-not-quite-as-new porches and watched the green star of Earth there. It was a move without conscious effort; they all did it, to help them understand the news they had heard on the radio a moment before. There was Earth and there the coming war, and there hundreds of thousands of mothers or grandmothers or fathers or brothers or aunts or uncles or cousins. . . .

At nine o'clock Earth seemed to explode, catch fire, and burn.

The people on the porches put up their hands as if to beat the fire out. . . .

But nobody moved. Late dinners were carried out onto the night lawns and set upon collapsible tables, and they picked at these slowly until two o'clock and the light-radio message flashed from Earth. They could read the great Morse-code flashes which flickered like a distant firefly:

AUSTRALIAN CONTINENT ATOMIZED IN PREMATURE EXPLOSION OF ATOMIC STOCKPILE. LOS ANGELES, LONDON BOMBED. WAR. COME HOME. COME HOME. COME HOME.

Ray Bradbury, *The Martian Chronicles* (1950)

RECOMMENDED RESOURCES

Books

Benét, Stephen Vincent. "By the Waters of Babylon," in *Selected Works of Stephen Vincent Benét.* New York: Farrar, 1942. A famous coming-of-age story set in New York City long after its total destruction.

Bradbury, Ray. *Fahrenheit 451.* New York: Ballantine, 1953. A repressive society controls its citizens by burning books.

Clark, Walter van Tilburg. "The Portable Phonograph," in *The Watchful Gods and Other Stories.* New York: New American, 1961. Survivors of a nuclear war fight over their meager remaining possessions.

Videos

Fahrenheit 451. Dir. François Truffaut, MCA Universal Home Video, 1966.

Invasion of the Body Snatchers. Dir. Don Siegel. Republic Pictures Home Video, 1956. Chillingly paranoid McCarthy-era classic.

The Martian Chronicles, Parts 1 and 2. Dir. Jack Gold. Fries Home Video, 1979. Made for television.

Planet of the Apes. Dir. Franklin J. Schaffner. CBS/Fox Video, 1967. A popular film with a fine surprise ending.

Ray Bradbury Theater, Buena Vista Home Video, 1985. Adaptations of Bradbury tales. "The Playground" is especially famous and creepy.

THE BODY SNATCHERS

Written in 1954 at the height of the Great Fear, Jack Finney's *The Body Snatchers* (on which the movies *Invasion of the Body Snatchers* were based) tells of giant seedpods from outer space that descend on the inhabitants of a California town. The pods create perfect physical duplicates of them that lack only one thing—human souls.

"It's him, Wilma. It's your uncle, all right."

She just nodded, as though expecting exactly that answer. "It's not," she murmured, but she said it quietly—not arguing, just asserting a fact.

"Well," I said, leaning my head back against the pillar, "let's take this a little at a time. After all, you could hardly be fooled; you've lived with him for years. How do you know he isn't Uncle Ira, Wilma? How is he different?"

For a moment her voice shot up, high and panicky. "That's just *it!*" But she quieted down instantly, leaning toward me. "Miles, there *is* no difference you can actually see....

"Miles, he looks, sounds, acts, and remembers exactly like Ira. On the outside. But *inside* he's different. His responses"—she stopped, hunting for the word—"aren't *emotionally* right, if I can explain that. He remembers the past, in detail, and he'll smile and say, 'You were sure a cute youngster, Willy. Bright one, too,' just the way Uncle Ira did. But there's something *missing*...."

JACK FINNEY, *The Body Snatchers* (1955)

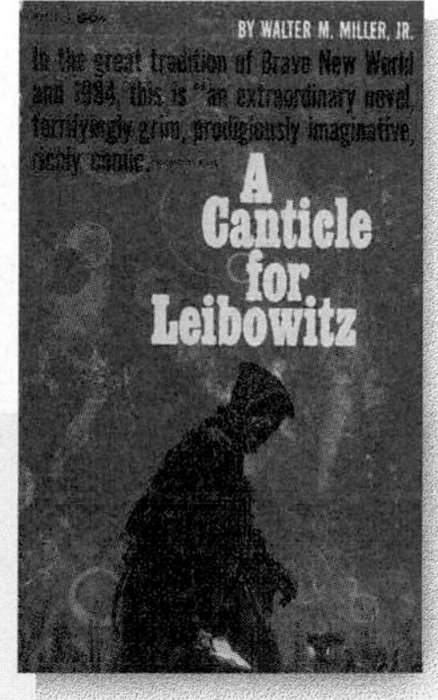

A CANTICLE FOR LEIBOWITZ

In *A Canticle for Leibowitz,* Walter M. Miller, Jr., portrays the centuries after a nuclear holocaust as a new dark age for humanity on earth.

He had been wandering for a long time. The search seemed endless, but there was always the promise of finding what he sought across the next rise or beyond the bend in the trail. When he had finished fanning himself, he clapped the hat back on his head and scratched at his bushy beard while blinking around at the landscape. There was a patch of unburned forest on the hillside just ahead. It offered welcome shade, but still the wanderer sat there in the sunlight and watched the curious buzzards....

Pickings were good for a while in the region of the Red River; but then out of the carnage, a city-state arose. For rising city-states, the buzzards had no fondness, although they approved of their eventual fall. They shied away from Texarkana and ranged far over the plain to the west. After the manner of all living things, they replenished the Earth many times with their kind.

Eventually it was the Year of Our Lord 3174.

There were rumors of war.

WALTER M. MILLER, JR., *A Canticle for Leibowitz* (1959)

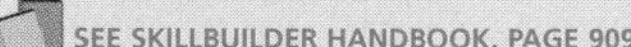

INTERACT WITH HISTORY

1. **COMPARING** What themes, or general messages about life or humanity, do you think these three books convey? How might readers' interpretations of these messages today differ from readers' interpretations during the Cold War?

SEE SKILLBUILDER HANDBOOK, PAGE 909.

2. **PLOTTING THE FUTURE** Working alone or with a partner, outline a plot for a work of science fiction that reflects a concern in today's world—computer viruses or a danger to the environment, for example. Include brief descriptions of characters and settings, as well as of major events in the story.

visit http://www.mlushistory.com For more about science fiction.

INSTRUCT

▶ *Starting with the Student*

- To help students explore the science fiction of the 1950s, you might bring to class copies of the three books and allow students to borrow them.
- Suggest that students rent one of the videos listed below for home viewing. Ask interested students to share their reactions to the film with the class.

▶ *Discussing Key Ideas*

- The science fiction of the 1950s often reflects the fears and confusion of the time.
- *The Martian Chronicles, The Body Snatchers,* and *A Canticle for Leibowitz* offer chilling glimpses of a bleak future dominated by powerful technologies.

HISTORY FROM VISUALS

Reading the Images Ask students to write quickly four or five words that express mood that each book cover or film advertisement creates. *Possible Responses: fear, horror, desolation, loneliness, alienation, anger.* Discuss how each image reflects the content of the story.

Extension Have students look for various printings of these stories and trace how the book covers have changed over time.

INTERACT WITH HISTORY

1. Comparing

Possible Answers: The Martian Chronicles: *even life on Mars is simple, ordinary; people are helpless and sad in the face of nuclear destruction; life goes on.*

The Body Snatchers: *As technology advances, we may be in danger of losing our souls.*

A Canticle for Leibowitz: *Life in the future may be desolate and violent, filled with scavengers and sadness.*

Critical Thinking: Comparing *Readers during the Cold War would have interpreted these works as dire warnings of a terrible future. Readers today would be less afraid of a nuclear holocaust and would treat the works more as adventure stories.*

2. Plotting the Future

Standards for Evaluation
Plot outlines should . . .

- describe the setting in enough detail so that readers will know the time, place, general environment, and circumstances of the story
- name and describe each character and show how the characters relate to one another
- list the major events of the story and show how the events are related to one another
- give enough realism to imagined events to capture readers' interest

CHAPTER 18
ASSESSMENT ANSWERS

REVIEWING THE CHAPTER

TERMS & NAMES

1. containment, p. 609
2. North Atlantic Treaty Organization (NATO), p. 612
3. Mao Zedong, p. 613
4. Korean War, p. 615
5. McCarthyism, p. 623
6. John Foster Dulles, p. 626
7. brinkmanship, p. 626
8. CIA, p. 626
9. Nikita Khrushchev, p. 627
10. U-2 incident, p. 629

MAIN IDEAS

11. To encourage democracy; to gain access to raw materials and markets; to rebuild Europe; to contain Soviet expansion.

12. A policy of helping countries resist Communist takeover; basically supported by Americans, especially after the Soviets invaded Czechoslovakia.

13. To prevent Soviet aggression.

14. Communist victory in China; North Korea's attack on South Korea.

15. Truman wanted a limited war; MacArthur wanted to bomb and invade mainland China.

16. Pushed back the North Korean invaders and contained communism without a world war and without using nuclear weapons; failed to unite Korea.

17. McCarthy's allegation of Communists in the State Department and in the armed services; national hearings in the Senate.

18. Rosenberg case involved transfer of nuclear secrets to the Soviets; Americans feared Soviet influence in America and possession of nuclear weapons.

19. By sponsoring covert actions to overthrow governments unfriendly to the U.S.

20. Development of atomic bomb and H-bomb, space flights, intercontinental ballistic missiles, and high-altitude aircraft.

Chapter 18 Assessment

REVIEWING THE CHAPTER

TERMS & NAMES For each term below, write a sentence explaining its significance in the 1950s and the Cold War. For each name below, explain the person's role in Cold War events.

1. containment
2. NATO
3. Mao Zedong
4. Korean War
5. McCarthyism
6. John Foster Dulles
7. brinkmanship
8. CIA
9. Nikita Khrushchev
10. U-2 incident

MAIN IDEAS

SECTION 1 *(pages 606–612)*

Origins of the Cold War

11. What were the goals of U.S. foreign policy during the Cold War?
12. Explain the Truman Doctrine and describe how Americans reacted to it.
13. What was the purpose of the NATO alliance?

SECTION 2 *(pages 613–618)*

The Cold War Heats Up

14. What global events helped to bring about U.S. involvement in Korea?
15. What issue of military strategy led to a disagreement between General Douglas MacArthur and President Truman, eventually costing MacArthur his job?
16. What goals did the United States achieve by fighting in Korea? What goals did it fail to achieve?

SECTION 3 *(pages 619–624)*

The Cold War at Home

17. What actions of Joseph McCarthy worsened the national hysteria about communism?
18. How did the spy case of the Rosenbergs feed anti-Communist sentiment in America?

SECTION 4 *(pages 625–629)*

Two Nations Live on the Edge

19. By what means did the U.S. government, including the CIA, fight the Cold War around the world?
20. What technological developments during the 1950s contributed to an arms race that would last for more than 30 years?

THINKING CRITICALLY

1. CONTAINMENT Create a cause-and-effect diagram, similar to the one shown, for each of these events: (a) the United States' adoption of a policy of containment and (b) the beginning of the nuclear arms race between the United States and the Soviet Union.

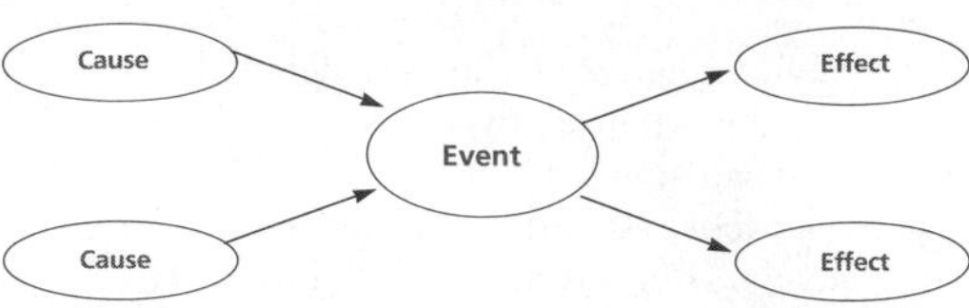

2. TRACING THEMES CONSTITUTIONAL CONCERNS What government actions in response to widespread anti-Communist sentiment do you think conflicted with the individual freedoms guaranteed in the Bill of Rights? Which of these actions were justified?

3. COLD WAR CONFLICTS Reread the quotation from J. Robert Oppenheimer on page 604. Do you agree with his assessment of the U.S.-Soviet conflict during the Cold War? Explain your opinion.

4. GEOGRAPHY OF THE SOVIET UNION Look carefully at the map on page 609. How did the absence of a natural barrier on the western border of the Soviet Union affect post–World War II Soviet foreign policy? Explain your answer.

5. AMERICAN LITERATURE: SCIENCE FICTION Which of the science fiction works quoted on pages 630–631 do you think best exemplifies the concerns of the Cold War? Why?

6. ANALYZING PRIMARY SOURCES Read the following excerpt from a memorandum President Truman wrote in 1953, explaining his refusal to use the atomic bomb during the Korean War. Then answer the questions below.

> In 1945 I had ordered the A Bomb dropped on Japan at two places devoted almost exclusively to war production. We were at war. We were trying to end it in order to save the lives of our soldiers and sailors. . . . We stopped the war and saved thousands of casualties on both sides.
>
> In Korea we were fighting a police action with sixteen allied nations to support the World Organization which had set up the Republic of Korea. We had held the Chinese after defeating the North Koreans and whipping the Russian Air Force.
>
> I just could not make the order for a Third World War. I know I was *right.*
>
> **PRESIDENT TRUMAN,** *Off the Record: The Private Papers of Harry S. Truman*

How does Truman explain the difference between using the atomic bomb against Japan and using it against China? Do you agree or disagree with Truman's reasons? Why?

THINKING CRITICALLY

1. CONTAINMENT
Possible Responses: **(a)** *Event:* containment. *Cause:* Soviet aggression in Europe. *Effect:* Truman Doctrine. *Cause:* Soviets hold Berlin hostage. *Effect:* Berlin airlift. *Cause:* North Koreans invade South Korea. *Effect:* U.S. enters Korean War. **(b)** *Event:* nuclear arms race. *Cause:* Soviets explode an atomic bomb. *Effect:* U.S. develops an H-bomb. *Cause:* U.S. tests an H bomb. *Effect:* Soviets develop an H-bomb. *Cause:* U.S. builds large numbers of nuclear weapons. *Effect:* Soviets build large numbers of nuclear weapons.

2. TRACING THEMES CONSTITUTIONAL CONCERNS
Possible Response: Loyalty Review Board, HUAC, McCarran Act, McCarthy's accusations; students may say that none of the actions was justified, or that a government may investigate spying if the investigation is done fairly.

3. COLD WAR CONFLICTS
Possible Response: Students who agree with Oppenheimer may say that because both countries were fully armed with nuclear weapons, an attack on one would bring instant retaliation from the other. Such nuclear attacks would destroy the world. Students who disagree may say that it is possible to have winners and losers even in a nuclear war and that the first country to attack would be the winner.

ALTERNATIVE ASSESSMENT

1. REPORTING WORLD NEWS

What was happening around the world while the United States was concentrating on the Cold War?

Prepare a script and a plan for visuals for a television news segment that summarizes one international news event that happened during the 1950s.

 To identify and research the international event that interests you, use the CD-ROM *Our Times* and other resources.

- Use a storyboard format to plan your visuals—sketches of people and events you would show, perhaps graphs or maps—and figure out what the narrator will say as each picture is shown.
- In your script, narrate the highlights of the event and analyze its effect on U.S. foreign-policy decisions.

2. LEARNING FROM MEDIA

VIDEO View the McDougal Littell video for Chapter 18, *The Cold War Comes Home.* Discuss the following questions with a small group of classmates, and then do the cooperative learning activity:

- How was Gordon Kahn caught up in events beyond his control?
- What alternatives did Gordon Kahn have? Do you think he chose the right path? Explain your opinion.
- From whose point of view is the story told? How does that viewpoint affect your opinion of the events?
- Gordon Kahn is portrayed as a victim in the video. How could he have been portrayed differently?
- **Cooperative Learning** With your group, create a report card to evaluate the video. Decide what criteria you will use to evaluate it, and come up with a grade for each criterion. Share and defend your final report card.

3. PORTFOLIO PROJECT

Use the Living History activity to expand your portfolio.

LIVING HISTORY

PRESENTING YOUR INTERVIEWS

Write and present to your class your two interviews with people who have memories of the Cold War era.

- Review the interviews. Has your study of the Cold War suggested any other questions that you would like to ask? If so, try to contact your interviewees again to ask the questions.
- Make a written transcript of each complete interview.
- Decide what you will present from each interview. If you omit some parts, use ellipses (. . .) to mark your omissions.
- Write an introduction for each interview. The introduction should include the interviewee's name and a description of what he or she was doing during the Cold War era.

Save your interviews, along with the tapes and transcripts you used in preparing them, in your American history portfolio.

Bridge to Chapter 19

Review Chapter 18

ORIGINS OF THE COLD WAR After World War II ended, the differing global economic and political goals of the United States and the Soviet Union resulted in a nonmilitary conflict known as the Cold War. The United States provided aid to European nations through the Marshall Plan and joined the defensive alliance known as the North Atlantic Treaty Organization (NATO).

THE COLD WAR HEATS UP In China the Communists defeated the Nationalists in 1949. Starting in 1950, the United States and other UN countries fought a war in Korea to keep South Korea from being overrun by North Korean Communists. The fighting ended in 1953, with Korea still divided into two countries.

THE COLD WAR AT HOME Anti-Communist sentiment gripped the United States in the late 1940s and the 1950s, causing the government to investigate the loyalty of millions of its employees. Alger Hiss was sent to prison, and Ethel and Julius Rosenberg were executed as Communist spies. Senator Joseph McCarthy accused hundreds of people of being Communists, and his unfounded accusations ruined many lives.

TWO NATIONS LIVE ON THE EDGE Throughout the 1950s people lived in fear of nuclear destruction as the United States and the Soviet Union engaged in a nuclear arms race. The Soviet leader Nikita Khrushchev sent tanks to crush a reform movement in Hungary in 1956. The Eisenhower Doctrine warned that the United States would defend the Middle East against Communist aggression. The launching of the first Sputnik satellite in 1957 spurred a space race between the two superpowers, and the United States sent U-2 spy planes into Soviet airspace. In May 1960, the Soviets shot down a U-2 plane and convicted the pilot, Francis Gary Powers, of espionage.

Preview Chapter 19

Although the Cold War had an enormous impact on domestic affairs in the 1950s, many Americans experienced the decade as a time of prosperity rather than a time of anti-Communist fear. Popular culture celebrated the growing middle class and its suburban lifestyle, although many minorities and poor people were excluded from economic gains. You will learn about these significant developments in the next chapter.

ALTERNATIVE ASSESSMENT

1. REPORTING WORLD NEWS

Standards for Evaluation

The TV script and plan for visuals should meet the following criteria:

- Focuses on one international event from the 1950s and shows how it affected U.S. foreign policy.
- Cites at least four references from a variety of research sources.
- Includes appropriate and effective visuals.
- Integrates the visuals appropriately into the script.

2. LEARNING FROM MEDIA

Answers to the questions:

- He was implicated in the anti-Communist hysteria that led to blacklisting.
- He could have answered questions about the alleged Communist activities of his colleagues and of himself. Opinions will vary.
- The story is told from the point of view of Gordon Kahn's son, probably making students more sympathetic to Kahn.
- As a principled man who chose to take the consequences of his beliefs.

Standards for Evaluation

Report Card on the Video

The report card should meet the following criteria:

- Establishes detailed criteria for evaluating the video.
- Expresses the criteria clearly.
- Gives a letter grade for each criterion.
- Supports each grade with an example from the video.

3. PORTFOLIO PROJECT

LIVING HISTORY

Standards for Evaluation

An effective interview should meet the following criteria:

- Maintains a consistent focus.
- Makes use of open-ended questions that elicit varied information.
- Includes follow-up questions.
- Shows good organization.
- Provides an introduction containing relevant biographical information about the interviewees.
- Includes a clear, coherent tape or written transcript of the interview.

IN-DEPTH RESOURCES: UNIT 5

See the form for scoring this activity on page 23.

THINKING CRITICALLY

4. GEOGRAPHY OF THE SOVIET UNION

Possible Response: Some students may say that the lack of a natural barrier caused the Soviets to create buffer nations between themselves and Western Europe. Other students may argue that the Soviets would have created buffer nations even with natural protection.

5. AMERICAN LITERATURE: SCIENCE FICTION

In their answers students should support their ideas by pointing out details from the text they chose.They may point to such Cold War concerns as nuclear world destruction, pervasive fear of the unknown, or despair that accompanies loss of control over one's life.

6. ANALYZING PRIMARY SOURCES

Possible Response: Bombing Japan would end the war quickly and would save American lives. Bombing China would simply start World War III. **Agree**—Truman had no choice in World War II; other measures were working in Korea. **Disagree**—Truman should have used any means at his disposal to end the Korean War.

CHAPTER 19

PLANNING GUIDE
The Postwar Boom

	Key Ideas	COPYMASTERS	ASSESSMENT
SECTION 1 **Postwar America** *pp. 636–642*	*As Americans try to put the nightmare of World War II behind them and begin rebuilding their lives, the economy booms and the country becomes conservative.*	***In-Depth Resources: Unit 5*** • Guided Reading, p. 57 • Primary Source: Cartoon, p. 64 • American Lives: Jackie Robinson, p. 71 ***Lesson Plans,*** pp. 157–158	PE ***Section 1 Assessment,*** p. 642 TE ***Self-Assessment,*** p. 642 ***Formal Assessment*** • Section Quiz, p. 236 ***Alternative Assessment Book*** • Standards for Evaluating a Cooperative Activity
SECTION 2 **The American Dream in the Fifties** *pp. 643–649*	*Many Americans find their dream of material comfort and economic prosperity realized. But some find the cost too high.*	***In-Depth Resources: Unit 5*** • Guided Reading, p. 58 • Geography Application: The Baby Boom, p. 62 • Primary Source: from *The Organization Man* by William H. Whyte, Jr., p. 65 • Literature: from *The Man in the Gray Flannel Suit* by Sloan Wilson, p. 68 ***Lesson Plans,*** pp. 159–160	PE ***Section 2 Assessment,*** p. 649 TE ***Self-Assessment,*** p. 649 ***Formal Assessment*** • Section Quiz, p. 237 ***Alternative Assessment Book*** • Standards for Evaluating a Cooperative Activity
SECTION 3 **Popular Culture** *pp. 652–657*	*Mass popular culture booms, largely because of television. While the media generally reflect mainstream middle-class values, a vital counterculture flourishes.*	***In-Depth Resources: Unit 5*** • Guided Reading, p. 59 • Skillbuilder Practice: Primary Sources, p. 61 • Literature: from *1959* by Thulani Davis, p. 70 • American Lives: Milton Berle, p. 72 ***Lesson Plans,*** pp. 161–162	PE ***Section 3 Assessment,*** p. 657 TE ***Self-Assessment,*** p. 657 ***Formal Assessment*** • Section Quiz, p. 238 ***Alternative Assessment Book*** • Standards for Evaluating a Cooperative Activity
SECTION 4 **The Other America** *pp. 660–663*	*Many Americans suffer from poverty and racial discrimination, despite unprecedented economic prosperity in the nation.*	***In-Depth Resources: Unit 5*** • Guided Reading, p. 60 • Primary Source: from *The Other America* by Michael Harrington, p. 66; The Voluntary Relocation Program, p. 67 ***Lesson Plans,*** pp. 163–164	PE ***Section 4 Assessment,*** p. 663 TE ***Self-Assessment,*** p. 663 ***Formal Assessment*** • Section Quiz, p. 239 ***Alternative Assessment Book*** • Standards for Evaluating a Cooperative Activity
CHAPTER RESOURCES	**Chapter Overview** *Postwar America experiences an economic boom fueled by consumer spending that is spurred by the mass media, especially television. But many find themselves mired in poverty and stifled by discrimination.*	***In-Depth Resources: Unit 5*** • Living History Project: Worksheet, p. 73; Standards, p. 74 ***Telescoping the Times*** • Chapter Summary, pp. 37–38 ***Planning for Block Schedules***	PE ***Chapter Assessment,*** pp. 664–665 PE ***Alternative Assessment,*** p. 665 ***Formal Assessment*** • Chapter Test, forms A and B, pp. 240–245 ***Test Generator*** ***Alternative Assessment Book*** See explanation and forms for different kinds of alternative assessments including portfolio assessment.

KEY
- PE Pupil's Edition
- TE Teacher's Edition
- INTERNET **http://www.mlushistory.com**

TECHNOLOGY

 ***Warm-Up Transparency* 19**

Electronic Library of Primary Sources
- Desegregation at Central High School by Melba Pattillo Beals
- Desegregation at Central High School by Craig Rains

 **INTERNET** Truman and Eisenhower

---

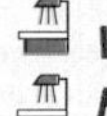 ***Warm-Up Transparency* 19**

Humanities Transparencies
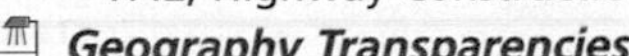
- H42, Highway Construction

Geography Transparencies
- G27, Highway Systems, 1950 and 1987

Critical Thinking Transparencies
- CT61, Urban-Suburban Growth Rates

Electronic Library of Primary Sources
- from *The Feminine Mystique*

INTERNET Polio vaccine and fads and fashions

 ***Warm-Up Transparency* 19**

Our Times
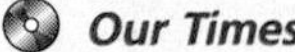
- *TV Guide* listings from June 1956

INTERNET Interact with History p. 659 (PE)

 ***Warm-Up Transparency* 19**

Humanities Transparencies

- H26, "Her World" by Philip Evergood

 ***Critical Thinking Transparencies***
- CT27, Postwar Boom

 ***Electronic Library of Primary Sources***
- from *The Other America* by Michael Harrington

 **INTERNET** Youth in the fifties.

 ***American Portfolio: A Videodisc for U.S. History,*** user's guide, pp. 235–239, 241

 ***Chapter Summary Audiotapes***
- Unit 5, Chapter 19

 **INTERNET http://www.mlushistory.com**

Block Scheduling (90 MINUTES)

Day 1

Section 1, pp. 636–642

Section 2, pp. 643–649

Section Assessments, pp. 642, 649

Geography Spotlight: The Road to Suburbia, pp. 650–651

 **COOPERATIVE ACTIVITIES**
- Exploring Postwar Life, p. 637 (TE)
- Developing Commercials, p. 648 (TE)

Day 2

Section 3, pp. 652–657

Section Assessment, p. 657

Daily Life: The Emergence of the Teenager, pp. 658–659

 **COOPERATIVE ACTIVITY**
- Creating a TV Program Guide, p. 654 (TE)

Day 3

Section 4, pp. 660–663

Section Assessment, p. 663

Chapter Assessment, pp. 664–665

 **COOPERATIVE ACTIVITY**
- Preparing a Family Budget, p. 661 (TE)

YEARLY PACING ***Chapter 19 Total:*** 3 days ***Yearly Total:*** 85 days

See *Planning for Block Schedules* for special activities and pacing strategies.

Customizing for Special Populations

Students Acquiring English

Access for Students Acquiring English: Spanish Translations
- Guided Reading for Sections 1–4 (Spanish), pp. 216–219
- Chapter Summary (Spanish), pp. 214–215
- Skillbuilder Practice: Primary Sources (Spanish), p. 220
- Geography Application: The Baby Boom (Spanish), p. 221

Spanish Reading Study Guide, pp. 197–206

Translations of Chapter Summaries, Hmong, Cantonese, Vietnamese, and Cambodian

 ***Chapter Summary Audiotapes in Spanish***
Unit 5, Chapter 19

INTERNET The Diverse Classroom

Gifted and Talented Students

In-Depth Resources: Unit 5
- Primary Sources: Cartoon, p. 64; from *The Organization Man* by William H. Whyte, Jr., p. 65; from *The Other America* by Michael Harrington, p. 66; The Voluntary Relocation Program, p. 67
- American Lives: Jackie Robinson, p. 71; Milton Berle, p. 72

Less Proficient Readers

In-Depth Resources: Unit 5
- Guided Reading for Sections 1–4, pp. 57–60
- Skillbuilder: Primary Sources, p. 61
- Geography Application: The Baby Boom, p. 62

Reading Study Guide
- pp. 197–206

Telescoping the Times
- Chapter Summary, pp. 37–38

Chapter Summary Audiotapes, Unit 5, Chapter 19

Connections to Literature READINGS FOR STUDENTS

In-Depth Resources: Unit 5
- **from *The Man in the Gray Flannel Suit* by Sloan Wilson, p. 68**
- **from *1959* by Thulani Davis, p. 70**

Enrichment Reading
- **Annie Dillard**
  An American Childhood
  New York: HarperPerennial, 1993
  This outstanding autobiography traces the author's development from preschool through her teenage years. It is filled with joyful and humorous memories of growing up in the 1950s.
- **Oscar Hijuelos**
  The Mambo Kings Play Songs of Love
  New York: Farrar, 1989
  Brothers Cesar and Nestor Castillo come to New York City from Cuba as they follow the example of their heroes Xavier Cugat and Desi Arnaz. They dream of becoming stars. Their lush, sensuous music earns them the title Mambo Kings, and they appear in the 1950s hit TV series "I Love Lucy." The novel won a Pulitzer Prize in 1990.

McDougal Littell *Literature Connections*

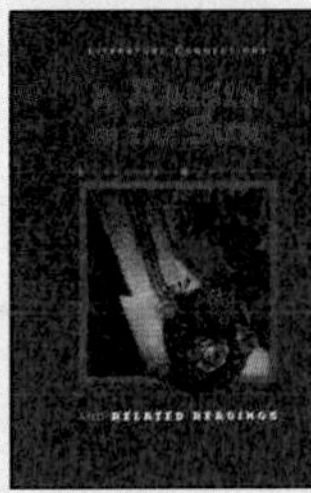

- **Lorraine Hansberry**
  A Raisin in the Sun *(with related readings). Set in Chicago in the 1950s, this three-act play explores the struggles of an African-American family who dream of owning a house. The racism they encounter and their own family tensions and anger lead them to examine what is truly important in their lives.*

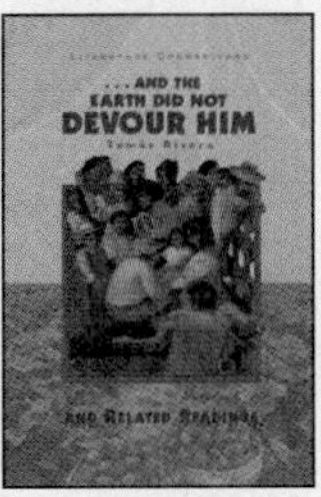

- **Tomás Rivera**
  . . . And The Earth Did Not Devour Him
  A classic of Chicano literature, this novel offers impressions of a community of South Texas migrant workers who go north to pick crops after World War II.

CHAPTER 19

OVERVIEW

The Postwar Boom

▶ Accessing Prior Knowledge

Ask students to list their impressions of the 1950s under headings such as People, Events, Popular Culture, Fashions, or Problems. Ask the following questions:

- On what sources did you base your impressions of the 1950s?
- Which sources do you think are most accurate? Why?

▶ Predicting Outcomes

Ask the students to read the section summaries on page 634. What issues might run through most of the chapter? Did these issues effect all Americans in the same way?

MORE ABOUT . . . *Prosperity*

Several publications in the early 1950s echoed the sentiments expressed in the opening quotation from *Life* magazine. In October 1956, *Fortune* magazine reported, "Never has a whole people spent so much money on so many expensive things in such an easy way as Americans are doing today."

CHAPTER

19 The Postwar Boom

SECTION 1

Postwar America

As Americans try to put World War II behind them and begin rebuilding their lives, the economy booms and American society becomes more conservative.

SECTION 2

The American Dream in the Fifties

Many Americans find their dream of material comfort and economic prosperity realized. But some find the cost too high.

SECTION 3

Popular Culture

Popular culture flourishes, largely because of television. While the media generally reflect mainstream middle-class values, a vital counterculture emerges.

SECTION 4

The Other America

Many Americans suffer from poverty and racial discrimination, despite unprecedented economic prosperity in the nation.

"Never before so much for so few."

Life magazine, 1954

THE UNITED STATES

- 1946: American families joyfully welcome their GIs home, as depicted in this Norman Rockwell painting; but reentry is not always easy.
- 1947: Congress passes the Taft-Hartley Act.
- 1948: Southern Democrats called Dixiecrats form the States' Rights Democratic Party.
- 1948: Harry S. Truman is elected president.
- 1949: National Housing Act calls for urban renewal.
- 1950: Television begins its reign as the center of home entertainment
- 195[1]: Disc jockey Alan Freed is the first to use the term "rock 'n' roll" on the air.

THE WORLD

- 1948: UN mandates the creation of the nation of Israel.
- 1948: Mahatma Gandhi is assassinated in India.
- 1949: Communists under Mao Zedong take power in China.
- 1950: Korean War begins.

THEMES IN CHAPTER 19

Economic Opportunity

The economic boom of the postwar years brought prosperity to millions of Americans. However, the nation experienced a recession in 1957–1958, and the national debt was rising.

See Teacher's Edition note, p. 638.

Women in America

The ideal woman of the 1950s was wife, mother, and homemaker. Many suburban housewives, however, felt dissatisfied and bored with their lack of identity.

See Teacher's Edition note, p. 646.

Science and Technology

The rapid rise of television in the 1950s affected many aspects of American life. Television provided entertainment and information, but critics objected to the stereotypes and violence it presented.

See Teacher's Edition note, p. 653.

Democracy in America

Thousands of Mexican Americans and Native Americans fought for the United States in World War II. After the war, these citizens faced discrimination in a society that ignored the rights of minorities.

See Teacher's Edition note, p. 662.

LIVING HISTORY

PLANNING A FIFTIES PARTY

Plan a 1950s party for your classmates and friends. To recreate the time as authentically as possible, use the information in the chapter and additional research or interviews to learn the following about fifties teenagers:

- how they dressed
- what they did for entertainment
- what music they listened to
- what they liked to eat

PORTFOLIO PROJECT Create an invitation that tells guests what to wear and what they can expect to hear, see, taste, and do at the party. Keep a copy of the invitation in a folder. At the end of the chapter, you will write a radio advertisement for your party and add it to your American history portfolio.

1952 Dwight D. Eisenhower is elected president.

1954 *Brown v. Board of Education of Topeka* ruling orders the desegregation of public schools.

1955 Ray Kroc opens the first McDonald's franchise.

1956 Elvis Presley appears on *The Ed Sullivan Show.*

1956 President Eisenhower is reelected.

1957 President Eisenhower backs the integration of public schools with federal troops, as depicted in this painting by Norman Rockwell.

1960 The familiar greeting "It's Howdy Doody time" is heard for the last time on TV sets in 45 million American homes.

1960 John F. Kennedy is elected president.

1952 Mau Mau Revolt shakes Kenya.

1954 USSR opens the world's first nuclear power station.

1956 Soviets suppress the Hungarian uprising.

1959 Fidel Castro comes to power in Cuba.

1960 War begins in the Congo.

ALTERNATIVE ASSESSMENT

LIVING HISTORY

PLANNING A FIFTIES PARTY

Discuss possible sources of information about the 1950s and the various tasks involved in planning a party:

- Students can use the library to locate magazines and newspapers from the 1950s.
- Suggest that students ask adults who were teenagers in the 1950s for ideas for the party.
- Students can watch videos or reruns of television programs set in the 1950s.

Project Planning Guide

Step 1	**Students choose aspects of the 1950s to research.**
Step 2	**Students use the library and the Internet to locate and gather information about the decade.**
Step 3	**Students interview people who were teenagers during the 1950s.**
Step 4	**Students compile information from interviews and research, and plan music and other aspects of the party.**

IN-DEPTH RESOURCES: UNIT 5

See worksheet and standards for evaluation, pp. 73, 74.

RECOMMENDED RESOURCES

Books for the Teacher

Goldman, Eric F. *The Crucial Decade—and After.* New York: Knopf, 1965. Readable history of political and social changes.

Halberstam, David. *The Fifties.* New York: Villard, 1993. A fascinating study of all aspects of American life and culture.

Katz, Donald. *Home Fires.* New York: Harper, 1992. An account of a real family's adjustment to postwar life and beyond.

Books for the Student

Barnouw, Erik. *Tube of Plenty.* 2nd ed. New York: Oxford UP, 1990. History of television and its impact.

Kytle, Elizabeth, ed. *Willa Mae.* Athens: U of Georgia P, 1993. An African-American woman recalls segregation.

This Fabulous Century: 1950–1960. New York: Time-Life, 1970. Visual collection on life during the 1950s.

Videos

Avalon. Dir. Barry Levinson. RCA/Columbia Pictures Home Video, 1991. Several generations of immigrants move from poverty to prosperity and adapt to the world changes around them.

The Best Years of Our Lives. Dir. William Wyler. 1946. HBO Home Video. Gripping story of GIs returning home.

Elvis '56. Dir. Alan and Susan Raymond. Music Media, 1987. Documentary about early career and impact.

Software

American Chronicles Series: Age of Anxiety (1952–1958) and *Fragile Balance (1955–1961).* CD-ROM. AIMS Media.

Section 1 Overview

OBJECTIVES

1. To identify economic and social problems Americans faced after World War II.
2. To explain how the desire for economic stability led to political conservatism.
3. To describe causes and effects of social unrest in the postwar period.
4. To contrast domestic policy under Truman and Eisenhower.

SKILLBUILDERS

- Interpreting graphs, p. 638
- Understanding geography: region, p. 640

CRITICAL THINKING

- Identifying problems, p. 637
- Theme: Economic Opportunity, p. 638
- Clarifying, p. 640
- Summarizing, pp. 641, 642
- Developing historical perspective, p. 642
- Drawing conclusions, p. 642
- Making decisions, p. 642

FOCUS & MOTIVATE

5-MINUTE WARM-UP

Inferring Main Idea

To discuss some of the difficulties of postwar adjustment, have students read Now & Then on page 637 and answer these questions.

1. What is the main idea of this feature?
2. What examples are given to support the main idea?

WARM-UP TRANSPARENCY 19

▶ ***Starting with the Student***

- Have students discuss the choices they will face when they graduate from high school and from college.
- Ask them whether they think soldiers returning from World War II faced similar choices.

1 Postwar America

TERMS & NAMES
- GI Bill of Rights
- suburb
- Harry S. Truman
- Dixiecrat
- Fair Deal

LEARN ABOUT the social, economic, and political readjustment of the United States following World War II
TO UNDERSTAND the new prosperity and rising conservatism.

ONE AMERICAN'S STORY

Sam Gordon had been married less than a year when he was shipped overseas in July 1943. As a sergeant in the United States Army, he fought in Belgium and France during World War II. Arriving back home in November 1945, Sam nervously anticipated a reunion with his family. A friend, Donald Katz, reported Sam's reactions.

A PERSONAL VOICE

Sam bulled through the crowd and hailed a taxi. The cab motored north through the warm autumn day as he groped for feelings appropriate to being back home alive from a terrible war. . . . [He was] nearly panting under the weight of fear. *Back home alive . . . married to a girl I haven't seen since 1943 . . . father of a child I've never seen at all.*

DONALD KATZ, quoted in *Home Fires*

GIs returned home to their families after World War II with new hope, but also new problems.

Sam Gordon met his daughter, Susan, for the first time the day he returned home from the war, and he went to work the next morning. Like many other young couples, the Gordons began to put the nightmare of the war behind them and to return to normality.

Readjustment and Recovery

By the summer of 1946, about 10 million men and women had been released from the armed forces. Veterans like Sam Gordon—along with the rest of American society—settled down to rebuild their lives.

THE IMPACT OF THE GI BILL To help ease veterans' return to civilian life, Congress passed the Servicemen's Readjustment Act, or the **GI Bill of Rights,** in 1944. In addition to encouraging veterans to get an education, and paying part of their tuition, the GI Bill guaranteed them a year's unemployment benefits while they looked for jobs. It also offered low-interest, federally guaranteed loans. Millions of young families used these benefits to buy homes and farms or to establish businesses. As a Veterans Administration official said, "I've talked to hundreds and hundreds of these kids. . . .They like the idea of making more money but they like even more the idea . . . of 'getting to be somebody.'"

HOUSING CRISIS In 1945 and 1946, returning veterans at first faced a severe housing shortage. Many families lived in cramped apartments or moved in with relatives. Some veterans resorted to living in cars or in coal sheds. Others lived in grain silos that were turned into apartments or in old streetcars that were converted into homes.

In response to this housing crisis, developers like William Levitt and Henry Kaiser used efficient assembly-line methods to mass-produce houses. Levitt, who bragged that his company could build a house in 16 minutes, offered homes in small residential communities surrounding cities, or **suburbs,** for less than $8,000. His first postwar development—rows of standardized homes built on treeless lots—was located on New York's Long Island and named Levittown.

SECTION 1 RESOURCES

PRINT RESOURCES

IN-DEPTH RESOURCES: UNIT 5
Guided Reading, p. 57
Primary Source: Cartoon, p. 64
American Lives: Jackie Robinson, p. 71

READING STUDY GUIDE, p. 197

ACCESS FOR STUDENTS ACQUIRING ENGLISH
Guided Reading (Spanish), p. 216

SPANISH READING STUDY GUIDE, p. 197

FORMAL ASSESSMENT
Section Quiz, p. 236

ALTERNATIVE ASSESSMENT BOOK
See forms for supporting and scoring alternative activities.

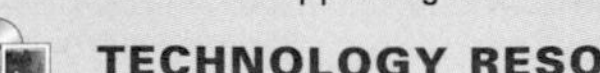

TECHNOLOGY RESOURCES

CD-ROM Electronic Library of Primary Sources

VIDEO *American Portfolio: A Videodisc for U.S. History* user's guide, pp. 235, 236

INTERNET http://www.mlushistory.com

A tree was planted every 28 feet, and all the streets curved at the same angle. Levitt standardized not only the houses themselves but also the way they were built: "Convoys of trucks moved over the pavements, tossing out prefabricated sidings at 8:00 A.M., toilets at 9:30, sinks and tubs at 10:00, sheetrock at 10:45, flooring at 11:00." Within days, several hundred identical houses were ready for occupancy.

These homes looked exactly alike, and certain rules ensured that they would stay the same. Residents were required to mow their lawns regularly and were forbidden to put up fences. They could hang laundry to dry on Mondays, but not Sundays. They could choose the door chimes they wanted, but they couldn't install bells or buzzers. Nevertheless, the planned suburbs that sprang up around the country offered the friendliness of small towns. With the help of the GI Bill, many veterans moved in and cultivated a new lifestyle.

A PERSONAL VOICE

We were all in the same boat. . . . We shared everything; we shared tools and cars, minded each other's kids, passed play-pens and high-chairs from house to house—everything.

It was—at least to us—a Paradise.

MRS. KLERK, quoted in *Expanding the American Dream*

The suburbs were a mass phenomenon, even on moving day.

REDEFINING THE FAMILY Tension created by changes in men's and women's roles after the war led to a high divorce rate. Traditionally, men were the breadwinners and heads of households, while women were expected to care for the family. During the war, however, about 6 million women, 75 percent of whom were married, entered the paid work force. These women supported their families, paid the bills, and made important household decisions. Many were reluctant to give up their newfound independence when their husbands returned. By 1950, more than a million war marriages had ended in divorce.

ECONOMIC READJUSTMENT After World War II, the United States converted from a wartime to a peacetime economy. The government immediately canceled war contracts totaling $35 billion. Within ten days of Japan's surrender, more than a million defense workers were laid off. Unemployment increased as veterans joined laid-off defense workers in the search for jobs. At the peak of postwar unemployment, in March 1946, nearly 3 million people were seeking work. (See *unemployment rate* on page 940 in the Economics Handbook.)

Rising unemployment was not the nation's only postwar economic problem, however. During the war, the Office of Price Administration (OPA) had halted inflation by imposing maximum prices on goods. When these controls ended on June 30, 1946, prices skyrocketed. In the next two weeks, the cost of consumer products soared 25 percent, double the increase of the previous three years. The price of pork chops, for example, jumped from 48 cents to 72 cents a pound; the price of margarine, from 28 cents to 41 cents a pound. At the same time, items such as beef, men's suits, and nylon stockings became unavailable. In some cities, consumers stood in long lines, hoping to buy scarce items, such as sugar, coffee, and beans. Prices continued to rise for the next two years until the supply of goods caught up with the demand. (See *inflation* on page 936 in the Economics Handbook.)

While prices spiraled upward, many American workers also earned less than they had earned during the war. To halt runaway inflation and to help the nation convert to a peacetime economy, Congress eventually reestablished controls similar to the wartime controls on prices, wages, and rents.

A. Answer Housing shortages, unemployment, readjustment to family life, rising inflation and lower wages, and shortages of goods.

THINK THROUGH HISTORY
A. Identifying Problems *What problems did Americans face after World War II?*

NOW & THEN

THE ONGOING COSTS OF WAR

"War is a contagion," observed Franklin D. Roosevelt. And the aftermath can be as devastating as the disease itself. Following World Wars I and II, many returning soldiers suffered from shell shock or battle fatigue. They were sensitive to noise and easily irritated, and their sleep was disturbed by dreams of battle. In the 1970s, similar symptoms—with the updated name "posttraumatic stress disorder"—plagued many veterans of the Vietnam War as they tried to readjust to postcombat life.

Today, many veterans of the Persian Gulf War, fought in 1991, suffer from unexplained illnesses, sometimes referred to collectively as Gulf War syndrome. Several thousand veterans—and a few spouses and civilian employees—complain of fatigue, skin rashes, headaches, muscle and joint pain, and sleep disturbances. Researchers continue to hunt for the causes of these symptoms, which may have included the veterans' exposure to chemical weapons, harmful bacteria, harsh living conditions, and the smoke of 605 oil-well fires that were ignited by the retreating Iraqis.

OBJECTIVE 1 **INSTRUCT**

Readjustment and Recovery

▶ ***Discussing Key Ideas***

- The GI bill enables veterans to attend college, establish businesses, and buy homes.
- Americans face housing shortages, unemployment, and rising prices.
- Increased demand for consumer goods creates economic prosperity.

IN-DEPTH RESOURCES: UNIT 5
Guided Reading, p. 57
Primary Source: Cartoon, p. 64

ACCESS FOR STUDENTS ACQUIRING ENGLISH
Guided Reading (Spanish), p. 216

NOW & THEN
The Ongoing Costs of War

Critical Thinking: Compare and Contrast
Have students identify similarities among the symptoms experienced by war veterans. *Possible Responses: fatigue, sleep disturbances, emotional stress.*

MORE ABOUT . . .
Levittown

Levitt & Sons' first development consisted of 2,000 homes, which the company rented to married veterans for $65 a month. These homes had two bedrooms and a bathroom; a kitchen equipped with refrigerator, stove, and washing machine; a living room with a fireplace and built-in TV; and an attic that could be made into additional bedrooms.

Block Schedule TEACHING OPTION **Time Needed: 30 Minutes**

Cooperative Activity: Exploring Postwar Life

Task: Student groups will create one of the following items for an exhibit about postwar issues: a song, essay, letter, series of fictional journal entries, cartoon, or news report.

Purpose: To understand U.S. social and economic problems after World War II.

Activity: Have groups choose one of the following topics: GI bill, housing shortage, family roles, or economic problems. Each group should use one of the formats described above to represent the impact of that topic on American society in the late 1940s. Students' contributions to the exhibit should include both a visual and a written component.

Building a Portfolio: Students who wish to include their exhibit as part of their portfolio should submit a written description of the exhibit, along with a statement indicating their contribution to the project.

ALTERNATIVE ASSESSMENT BOOK
Standards for Evaluating a Cooperative Activity

Standards for Evaluation
Exhibit items should . . .

- relate clearly to the assigned topic
- indicate understanding of readjustment in the postwar period
- include appropriate symbols, labels, and/or captions

HISTORY FROM VISUALS

A Dynamic Economy, 1950–1960

Reading the Graphs Ask students to identify the years each indicator grew the most quickly and most slowly (or fell).
Homes: quickly 1950–56; slowly 1956–60.
Autos: quickly 1952–54; slowly 1954–56.
Incomes: quickly 1950–52; slowly 1952–54 or 1956–58.
Savings: quickly 1960–62; slowly 1958–60.

Extension Ask students to research the consumer price index from 1950 or 1960 to determine how much median income and savings grew relative to price increases.

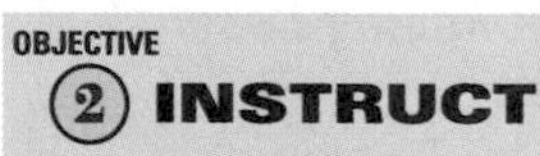

Economic Challenges

▶ ***Starting with the Student***
- Ask students what "passing the buck" means. *Possible Response: Putting responsibility on others.*
- Discuss the leadership quality indicated by Truman's motto, "The Buck Stops Here." *Possible Response: Willingness to accept responsibility for one's actions.*

▶ ***Discussing Key Ideas***
- Truman intervenes to end strikes by miners and railroad workers.
- Economic problems and strikes cause voters to elect a conservative Republican Congress in 1946.

A Dynamic Economy, 1950–1960

HOME OWNERSHIP — Millions of Homeowners (20–35), 1950 1952 1954 1956 1958 1960

AUTOMOBILE REGISTRATIONS — Millions of Registrations (40–70), 1950 1952 1954 1956 1958 1960

MEDIAN FAMILY INCOME — Income in Dollars (3000–6000), 1950 1952 1954 1956 1958 1960

SAVINGS ACCOUNTS — Billions of Dollars (0–25), 1950 1952 1954 1956 1958 1960 1962

Source: *Historical Statistics of the United States*

SKILLBUILDER
INTERPRETING GRAPHS
From 1950 to 1960, by what percentage did each of the economic indicators shown above increase?

Skillbuilder Answer
Home ownership—38%; Automobile registrations—50%; Income—75%; Savings—400%.

REMARKABLE RECOVERY Although most economists pessimistically forecast a postwar depression, they were wrong. They had failed to consider consumers' pent-up accumulation of needs and wants.

People had lived on shoestring budgets during the Great Depression of the 1930s and had lived without luxuries during the years of wartime shortages. In the late 1940s, with more than $135 billion in savings from defense work, service pay, and investments in war bonds, Americans suddenly had money to spend. They snatched up automobiles and appliances. Houses and apartment buildings could not be built fast enough. After a brief period of postwar economic readjustment, the American economy boomed as the demand for goods and services outstripped the supply, and increased production fostered new jobs. For the next 25 years, many Americans prospered in what the economist John Kenneth Galbraith called "the affluent society."

The Cold War also contributed to economic growth. Concern over Soviet expansion kept American defense spending high and people employed. Between 1950 and 1955, the number of Americans in the military increased from about 1.5 million to almost 3 million. Foreign-aid programs, such as the Marshall Plan provided another boost to American economy. By helping nations in Western Europe recover from the war, the United States also helped itself by creating strong foreign markets for American exports.

THINK THROUGH HISTORY
B. THEME ***Economic Opportunity*** *What factors contributed to the American postwar economic boom?*

B. Answer The GI bill, which offered veterans low-interest loans and education benefits; wage, price, and rent controls; the Cold War military buildup; foreign-aid programs, such as the Marshall Plan; savings, and a desire for consumer products.

Economic Challenges

Despite an impressive recovery, Americans faced a number of economic problems. Americans' lives had been in turmoil throughout the war, and a desire for stability made the country more conservative.

TRUMAN'S INHERITANCE When **Harry S. Truman** abruptly became president after Franklin D. Roosevelt's death in 1945, he asked Roosevelt's widow, Eleanor, whether there was anything he could do for her. She replied, "Is there anything *we* can do for *you*? For you are the one in trouble now." In many ways, Truman *was* in trouble.

A PERSONAL VOICE
I don't know whether you fellows ever had a load of hay or a bull fall on you, but when they told me yesterday [about Roosevelt's death], I felt like the moon, the stars, and all the planets had fallen on me.
HARRY S. TRUMAN, in a speech, April 13, 1945

Despite his lack of preparation for the job, Truman was honorable, direct, down-to-earth, and self-confident. Perhaps most important of all, he had the ability to make difficult decisions and to accept full responsibility for them. As the plaque on his desk at the White House read, "The Buck Stops Here." Truman faced two huge challenges: dealing with the rising threat of communism, as discussed in Chapter 18, and restoring the American economy to a strong footing.

TRUMAN FACES STRIKES One economic problem that President Truman had to address was strikes. Facing higher prices and lower wages, 4.5 million discontented workers went on strike in 1946. No sooner had 750,000 steelworkers returned to their jobs after an 80-day strike than 400,000 coal miners hit the picket lines. Eighteen days later, two railroad unions announced that they would go on strike in a month and stop rail traffic throughout the nation.

Although he generally supported organized labor, Truman refused to let strikes cripple the nation. He threatened to draft the striking workers and to order them as soldiers to stay on the job. He had the federal government seize the mines, and he threatened to take control of the railroads. Appearing before a

TEACHING OPTIONS

Making Connections Across the Curriculum

Economics Help students understand supply and demand by reviewing the basics: Supply is the quantity of a good or service producers are willing and able to sell at specific prices. Demand is the quantity of a good or service consumers are willing and able to purchase at specific prices. Point out that the things people want most—in this case, products such as new cars and appliances—are always scarce. During the postwar period, the demand for these new products led to a dramatic increase in jobs and incomes. Have students sketch flow charts to illustrate the relationships among economic factors.

Exploring Themes

Economic Opportunity Postwar economic changes brought to the United States a standard of living higher than the world had ever experienced. The increasing demand for consumer goods and services, combined with heavy government spending, led to a 50 percent increase in the country's gross national product during the 1950s. However, two economic issues surfaced to mar the decade's prosperity: a brief recession in 1957–1958 (with an increase in the U.S. unemployment rate) and the rising national debt, which by the end of the decade was roughly $290 billion.

special session of Congress, Truman asked for authority to draft the striking workers into the army. Before he could finish his speech, the unions gave in. (See *strike* on page 938 in the Economics Handbook.)

"HAD ENOUGH?" Disgusted by shortages, rising inflation, and labor strikes, Americans were ready for a change. The Republicans asked the public, "Had enough?" Voters gave their answer at the polls: in the 1946 congressional elections, the Republican Party won control of both the Senate and the House of Representatives for the first time since 1928. The new 80th Congress ignored Truman's domestic proposals. In 1947, Congress passed the antiunion Taft-Hartley Act over his veto.

Social Unrest Persists

Problems arose not only in the economy but in the very fabric of society. After World War II, a wave of racial violence erupted in the South. Many African Americans, particularly those who had served in the armed forces during the war, demanded their rights as citizens.

TRUMAN SUPPORTS CIVIL RIGHTS Truman put his career on the line for civil rights. "I am asking for equality of opportunity for all human beings," he said, ". . . and if that ends up in my failure to be reelected, that failure will be in a good cause." In September 1946, President Truman met with African-American leaders to find out what they considered their top priorities. They asked for the following:

- a federal antilynching law (Authorities in Southern states usually looked the other way when mobs took violent action against African Americans.)
- abolition of the poll tax as a voting requirement (This tax was often used to prevent African Americans from voting.)
- establishment of a permanent body to prevent racial discrimination in hiring (The wartime Fair Employment Practices Commission [FEPC] was due to expire that year.)

When Congress would not pass these measures, Truman appointed a biracial Committee on Civil Rights in December 1946 to investigate race relations. In its 1947 report, *To Secure These Rights,* the committee reaffirmed the earlier recommendations and added several more: in addition to the antilynching, poll-tax, and FEPC measures, the report recommended the establishment of a permanent civil rights commission, the passage of federal legislation to eliminate discrimination in voting, and the integration of the armed forces.

When Congress again failed to act, Truman himself took action. In July 1948, he issued an executive order for integration of the armed forces, calling for "equality of treatment and opportunity without regard to race, color, religion, or national origin." In addition, he ordered an end to discrimination in the hiring of

HISTORICAL SPOTLIGHT

JACKIE ROBINSON

Jackie Robinson took a brave step when he turned the Brooklyn Dodgers into an integrated baseball team in 1947. But he—and the country—had a long way to go to enjoy interracial harmony. Unhappy fans hurled insults at Robinson from the stands. Some players on opposing teams tried to hit him with pitches or to injure him with the spikes on their shoes. He even received death threats. But he endured this abuse with poise and restraint, saying,

> "Plenty of times I wanted to haul off when somebody insulted me for the color of my skin. But I had to hold to myself. I knew I was kind of an experiment."

And the experiment was successful. In 1949, Robinson was voted the National League's most valuable player. He later became the first African American inducted into the Baseball Hall of Fame. By 1959, every major-league team had become integrated.

African-American baseball teams like the 1939 Negro League All-Stars *(right)* often played against teams from the all-white major leagues in exhibition games. But in 1947, Jackie Robinson *(far right)* joined the Brooklyn Dodgers, angering some fans but winning the hearts, and respect, of many others.

OBJECTIVE ③ **INSTRUCT**

Social Unrest Persists

▶ ***Starting with the Student*** Ask students to name some prominent people from the fields of business, politics, professional sports, or entertainment. List names on the chalkboard. How many of these people are African Americans? Point out that in postwar society African Americans were denied equal rights in all of these areas.

▶ ***Discussing Key Ideas***
- President Truman takes measures to secure civil rights for African Americans.
- The Democratic Party splits over civil rights issues in the 1948 election.
- Truman's Fair Deal provides some social and economic reforms but meets with strong opposition in Congress.

HISTORICAL SPOTLIGHT
Jackie Robinson

Critical Thinking: Analyzing Effects Jackie Robinson once said, "A life is not important except in the impact it has on other lives." Have students discuss Jackie Robinson's impact on professional sports. Ask them whether they think Robinson's response to discrimination influenced American attitudes toward civil rights.

IN-DEPTH RESOURCES: UNIT 5
American Lives: Jackie Robinson, p. 71

TEACHING OPTIONS

Making Connections Across Cultures

Desegregation of the Military Racial violence and social unrest marked the postwar period as African-American veterans began to demand equal rights at home. When Congress failed to enact civil rights legislation, President Truman issued an executive order ending segregation in the armed forces. Executive Order 9981 also banned discrimination in federal hiring.

Making Connections Across the Curriculum

Composition Have students research and write brief biographies of other African-American athletes whose contributions helped break down racial barriers in the late 1940s and 1950s. Some possibilities include Jim Brown from the Cleveland Browns (football), Bill Russell or Chuck Cooper, both from the Boston Celtics (basketball), and Willie Mays, Hank Aaron, or Roy Campanella (baseball). After they have completed their biographies, students might create a hall of fame—with photographs of the athletes and biographical information—to recognize the achievements of these athletes.

MORE ABOUT . . .
Strom Thurmond

The Dixiecrat candidate failed to win a majority of Southern votes in spite of his attempt to preserve white supremacy. Thurmond later changed his views and supported some civil rights legislation. He served as governor of South Carolina from 1947 to 1951. In 1964, he withdrew from the Democratic Party and became a Republican.

HISTORY FROM VISUALS
Election of 1948

Reading the Map Students can use the colors on the chart to determine which states each candidate carried. The numbers on the map indicate each state's total electoral votes.

Extension Investigate reasons the Republicans lost the election in spite of Dewey's comfortable lead in the polls. *Possible Responses: Truman's whistle-stop campaign; farmers and laborers backed Democrats; the polls were inaccurate because of bad survey methods.*

***Wipe Out Discrimination* (1949), by Milton Ackoff, depicts the civil rights consciousness that caused the Dixiecrats to leave the Democratic Party.**

government employees. The Supreme Court also ruled that the courts could not bar African Americans from residential neighborhoods. These actions represented the beginnings of a federal commitment to dealing with racial issues.

THE 1948 ELECTION Although many Americans blamed Truman for the nation's inflation and labor unrest, the Democrats nominated him for president in 1948. Truman insisted that the party platform include a strong civil rights plank. Southern delegates to the national convention—who became known as **Dixiecrats**—opposed civil rights and sought to protect "the Southern way of life" against the interference of the federal government. To protest Truman's emphasis on civil rights, they walked out of the convention, formed the States' Rights Democratic Party, and nominated their own presidential candidate, Governor Strom Thurmond of South Carolina.

Discontent reigned at the far left of the Democratic spectrum as well. Former vice-president Henry A. Wallace led his supporters out of mainstream Democratic ranks to form a more liberal Progressive Party.

As the election approached, opinion polls gave the Republican candidate, New York governor Thomas E. Dewey, a comfortable lead. But they overlooked one thing: Truman's fighting spirit. He had stepped into Roosevelt's shoes to end the war with Japan and shepherd the nation into a peacetime economy and was now determined to be elected on his own.

Truman developed a winning strategy. First, he called the Republican-dominated Congress into a special session. He challenged it to pass laws supporting such elements of the Democratic Party platform as public housing, federal aid to education, a higher minimum wage, and extended Social Security coverage. Not one law was passed. Then he took his campaign to the people. He traveled from one end of the country to the other by train, speaking from the rear platform in a sweeping "whistlestop campaign." Day after day, people heard the president denounce the "do-nothing, good-for-nothing 80th Congress." Commenting on the success of this strategy, he said, "I met the people face to face, and I convinced them, and they voted for me."

STUNNING UPSET Truman's "Give 'em hell, Harry" campaign worked. Even though the headline of the early edition of the *Chicago Tribune* read "Dewey Defeats Truman," it was clear the morning after the election that Dewey had lost in one of the

GEOGRAPHY SKILLBUILDER **REGION**
In what regions of the country did Truman carry states? Dewey? Thurmond?

Election of 1948

ELECTORAL AND POPULAR VOTES

Party	Candidate	Electoral votes	Popular vote
Democratic	Harry S. Truman	303	24,179,000
Republican	Thomas E. Dewey	189	21,991,000
States' Rights	J. Strom Thurmond	39	1,176,000
Progressive	Henry A. Wallace	--	1,157,000

* Tennessee — 11 for Truman, 1 for Thurmond

Truman surprised experts and newspapers alike with the greatest presidential-election upset in the nation's history.

THINK THROUGH HISTORY
C. Clarifying *How did Truman use his executive power to advance civil rights?*

C. Answer Truman issued an executive order integrating the military after Congress refused to act.

Skillbuilder Answer Truman—the West, the Midwest, and the South; Dewey—the Northwest, the Northeast, and the Midwest; Thurmond—the South.

TEACHING OPTIONS

Making Connections Across Time

Election Polls The most famous example of incorrectly predicted election results is the *Chicago Tribune's* report of the Truman-Dewey contest of 1948. Pollsters had failed to take into account the effectiveness of Truman's campaign and confidently announced a Dewey victory. Their predictions stemmed in part from poorly conducted telephone polls, which reached more rich people than poor, more Republicans than Democrats. Today's polling involves sophisticated research methods that produce more reliable data about the candidates.

Making Connections Across the Curriculum

U.S. Government Discuss with students the role that minor parties have played in presidential elections. Explain that minor parties are sometimes categorized into three groups: splinter parties (those that split from a major party), such as the States' Rights Democratic Party in 1948; single-issue parties (those that concentrate on one public policy matter), such as the Free-Soil Party in the mid-19th century, which opposed extending slavery into the territories; or ideological parties (those based on a set of beliefs), such as today's Libertarian Party, which opposes most forms of government regulation.

nation's most stunning, and narrow, political upsets ever—24 million popular votes (49.5 percent) went to Truman while 22 million (45.1 percent) went to Dewey. Wallace and Thurmond each received about a million votes. The Democrats gained control of Congress as well, even though they suffered losses in the South, which had been solidly Democratic since Reconstruction.

D. Answer He led the U.S. to final victory in World War II, dealt with labor disputes, and supported social programs and civil rights legislation.

THE FAIR DEAL After his victory, Truman began trying to implement an ambitious economic program. Truman's **Fair Deal,** an extension of Roosevelt's New Deal, included proposals for a nationwide system of compulsory health insurance and a crop-subsidy system to provide a steady income for farmers. In Congress, some Northern Democrats joined Southern Democrats and Republicans in defeating both measures.

THINK THROUGH HISTORY
D. *Summarizing* *What were some of Truman's achievements as president?*

In other instances, however, Truman's ideas prevailed. Congress raised the hourly minimum wage from 40 cents to 75 cents, extended Social Security coverage to about 10 million more people, and initiated flood control and irrigation projects. Congress also provided financial support for cities to clear out slums and build 810,000 housing units for low-income families.

Republicans Take the Middle Road

Despite these social and economic victories, Truman's approval rating sank to an all-time low of 23 percent in 1951. The stalemate in the Korean War and the rising tide of McCarthyism, which cast doubt on the loyalty of some federal employees, became overwhelming issues. As the 1952 presidential election neared, Truman decided not to run for reelection. The Democrats nominated the intellectual and articulate governor Adlai Stevenson of Illinois to run against the Republican candidate, General Dwight D. Eisenhower.

I LIKE IKE! During the campaign, the Republicans accused the Democrats of "plunder at home and blunder abroad." To fan the anti-Communist hysteria that was sweeping over the country, Republicans raised the specter of the rise of communism in China and Eastern Europe. They also criticized the growing power of the federal government and the alleged bribery and corruption among Truman's political allies. In addition, the Korean War had set off another round of inflation, leading to more strikes and labor unrest. Above all, negotiations for a Korean armistice had been dragging on for over a year. Many voters felt that the country needed a change after two decades of Democratic leadership.

Buoyed by these sentiments, Eisenhower took the lead. But his campaign hit a snag when newspapers accused his running mate, California senator Richard M. Nixon, of profiting from a secret fund set up by wealthy supporters. Nixon decided to reply to the charges. In an emotional presentation to an audience of 58 million, now known as the "Checkers speech," he exhibited masterful use of a new medium—television. Nixon denied any wrongdoing, but he did admit accepting a gift from a political supporter.

Whimsical campaign accessories expressed voters' desire for a positive political change.

A PERSONAL VOICE

You know what it was? It was a little cocker spaniel dog in a crate that he [the political supporter] sent all the way from Texas. Black and white spotted. And our little girl—Tricia, the six-year-old—named it Checkers. And you know the kids love that dog and I just want to say this right now, that regardless of what they say about it, we're going to keep it.

RICHARD M. NIXON, "Checkers speech," September 23, 1952

OBJECTIVE
④ **INSTRUCT**

Republicans Take the Middle Road

▶ ***Starting with the Student***
Have students create a chart comparing Truman and Eisenhower. Bases of comparison might include those listed below:

	Truman	Eisenhower
Leadership style		
Domestic policy		
Accom-plishments		

▶ ***Discussing Key Ideas***
- Truman loses public support and decides not to run for reelection in 1952.
- Eisenhower brings a conservative style of leadership to the presidency.
- Americans endorse Republican leadership by reelecting Eisenhower in 1956.

TEACHING OPTIONS

Teaching Less Proficient Readers

Analyzing Issues Make sure students understand the reasons for the shift in popularity from the Democrats to the Republicans. Ask students to identify reasons and list them on the board for general classroom discussion. *Possible Responses: Stalemate in the Korean War; questions of loyalty of federal employees rising from the McCarthy witchhunt; the rise of communism in China and eastern Europe and the implications for the United States; alleged corruption among Truman's political allies; problems with the economy, including inflation; strikes and general labor unrest.*

Making Connections Across Time

Television and Politics The same medium that Nixon used masterfully in 1952 proved his undoing in 1960. During the first televised debates between presidential candidates, Nixon fared poorly against John Kennedy. Nixon perspired heavily and appeared pale and haggard in contrast to his tanned, youthful-looking opponent. Radio listeners thought Nixon won the debates, but television viewers proclaimed Kennedy the better candidate.

MORE ABOUT . . .
Little Rock

In September 1957, Arkansas governor Orval Faubus mobilized the National Guard to prevent integration of Little Rock Central High School. Eisenhower took no action until a federal judge ordered Faubus to withdraw the troops. Fearing violence, Eisenhower sent 1,000 U.S. paratroopers to Little Rock and put the Arkansas National Guard under federal command. Troops patrolled the school for the rest of the year.

ELECTRONIC LIBRARY OF PRIMARY SOURCES

Desegregation at Central High School by Melba Pattillo Beals

Desegregation at Central High School by Craig Rains

ASSESS & RETEACH

Section 1 Assessment

Have students form groups to share and discuss their answers to all questions.

Self-Assessment

Have students write down the five most interesting things they learned from this section. Then have them compare their lists with those of other classmates.

Section Quiz

FORMAL ASSESSMENT
Section Quiz, p. 236

Reteach

Use the Guided Reading Worksheet for Section 1 to help review the main ideas of the section.

IN-DEPTH RESOURCES: UNIT 5
Guided Reading, p. 57

CLOSE

A booming economy enabled many returning veterans to pursue the American dream. Civil rights issues caused social unrest and divided voters. Eisenhower pursued "middle-of-the-road" policies during his tenure.

> ***"I don't believe you can change the hearts of men with laws or decisions."***
> **DWIGHT D. EISENHOWER**

Nixon's speech saved his place on the Republican ticket. In November 1952, "Ike," as Eisenhower was commonly called, won 55 percent of the popular vote, and the Republicans narrowly captured Congress.

WALKING THE MIDDLE OF THE ROAD President Eisenhower's style of governing differed from that of the Democrats. He kept a low public profile and believed in working behind the scenes to get things done. His approach, which he called "dynamic conservatism," called for government to be "conservative when it comes to money and liberal when it comes to human beings."

Although Eisenhower followed a middle-of-the-road course and avoided many controversial issues, he could not completely sidestep a persistent domestic issue—civil rights—that gained national attention due to judicial rulings and civil disobedience in the mid-1950s. The most significant judicial action occurred in 1954, when the Supreme Court ruled in *Brown* v. *Board of Education of Topeka* that public schools should be racially integrated. In a landmark act of civil disobedience a year later, a black seamstress named Rosa Parks refused to give up her seat on a bus to a white man. Her arrest sparked a boycott of the entire Montgomery, Alabama, bus system. The civil rights movement had entered a new era.

Eisenhower believed that the federal government should not be involved in desegregation, and he privately disagreed with the *Brown* ruling. He insisted, "I don't believe you can change the hearts of men with laws or decisions." But he upheld the law. When the governor of Arkansas tried to keep blacks out of an all-white high school in Little Rock in September 1957, Eisenhower sent federal troops to see to it that black students were allowed to attend classes.

Although Eisenhower did not assume leadership on civil rights issues, he accomplished much on the domestic scene. During his terms, Alaska and Hawaii became the 49th and 50th states to enter the Union. Ike's administration also raised the minimum wage, extended Social Security and unemployment benefits, increased funding for public housing, and backed the creation of interstate highways. His popularity soared.

In general, the mid-1950s, like the post–World War I 1920s, were a time of "peace, progress, and prosperity." Pleased that "everything's booming but the guns," voters flocked to the polls in 1956 and reelected Eisenhower over Adlai Stevenson by the greatest majority since Franklin D. Roosevelt's in 1936. To many of the nation's citizens, the American dream had finally come within reach.

Linda Brown's case prompted the Supreme Court to begin the process of desegregating U.S. public schools in 1954.

E. Answer The Cold War caused many Americans to seek security in traditional conservative values, and Eisenhower's approach had brought progress and prosperity.

THINK THROUGH HISTORY
E. *Developing Historical Perspective* *Why do you think most Americans went along with Eisenhower's conservative approach to domestic policy?*

Section 1 Assessment

1. TERMS & NAMES
Identify:
- GI Bill of Rights
- suburb
- Harry S. Truman
- Dixiecrat
- Fair Deal

2. SUMMARIZING Create a time line of key events relating to postwar America. Use the dates below as a guide.

1946 — 1947 — 1948 — 1949 — 1952

Write a paragraph describing the effects of one of these events.

3. DRAWING CONCLUSIONS Do you think Eisenhower's actions reflected his philosophy of dynamic conservatism? Why or why not?

THINK ABOUT
- the definition of *dynamic conservatism*
- Eisenhower's civil rights policies
- Eisenhower's accomplishments on other domestic issues

4. MAKING DECISIONS If you had voted in the 1952 presidential election, would you have cast your ballot for Adlai Stevenson or Dwight D. Eisenhower? Support your choice with reasons.

THINK ABOUT
- each candidate's background and political experience
- the previous presidents
- Republicans' criticisms of Democrats
- Eisenhower's running mate

ANSWERS

1. TERMS & NAMES

GI Bill of Rights, p. 636

suburb, p. 636

Harry S. Truman, p. 638

Dixiecrat, p. 640

Fair Deal, p. 641

2. SUMMARIZING

Possible Answers:
1946—Postwar unemployment peaks; strikes break out; Republican Party controls the House and Senate; Truman appoints Committee on Civil Rights.
1947—Congress passes anti-union Taft-Hartley Act.
1948—Truman integrates the armed forces; Dixiecrats form States' Rights Democratic Party; Truman wins presidency.
1949—Jackie Robinson voted National League's Most Valuable Player.
1952—Eisenhower wins presidency.

3. DRAWING CONCLUSIONS

Possible Answers: Yes—He raised the minimum wage, extended social security and unemployment benefits, and increased funding for public housing. No—He did little to support civil rights.

4. MAKING DECISIONS

Possible Answers: Stevenson—has more political experience than Eisenhower; would be a good decision-maker and communicator; would continue Truman's policies, especially with civil rights; Nixon, Eisenhower's running mate, might not be trustworthy. Eisenhower—his military experience would help him negotiate the Korean War armistice; is a strong leader; the country needs a change after two decades of Democrats in the White House.

❷ The American Dream in the Fifties

TERMS & NAMES
- conglomerate
- franchise
- baby boom
- Dr. Jonas Salk
- consumerism
- planned obsolescence

LEARN ABOUT the material comforts that many Americans enjoyed in the 1950s
TO UNDERSTAND the benefits and the costs of pursuing the American dream.

ONE AMERICAN'S STORY

Settled into her brand new house near San Diego, California, Carol Freeman felt very fortunate. Her husband Mark had his own law practice, and when her first baby was born, she became a full-time homemaker. She was living the American dream, yet Carol felt dissatisfied—as if there were "something wrong" with her because she was not happy.

A PERSONAL VOICE

As dissatisfied as I was, and as restless, I remember so well this feeling [you] had at the time that the world was going to be your oyster. You were going to make money, your kids were going to go to good schools, everything was possible if you just did what you were supposed to do. The future was rosy. There was a tremendous feeling of optimism. . . . Much as I say it was hateful, it was also hopeful. It was an innocent time.

CAROL FREEMAN, quoted in *The Fifties: A Women's Oral History*

After World War II ended, Americans turned their attention to their families and jobs. The economy prospered. New technologies and business ideas created fresh opportunities for many, and by the end of the decade Americans were enjoying the highest standard of living in the world. The American dream of a happy and successful life seemed within the reach of many people.

The dream woman of the 1950s could brown a turkey to perfection for her family's dinner. However, she could also feel starved of meaning and fulfillment in her own life.

The Organization and the Organization Man

During the 1950s, businesses expanded rapidly. By 1956, the majority of Americans no longer held blue-collar, or industrial, jobs. Instead, more people worked in higher-paid, white-collar positions—clerical, managerial, or professional occupations. Unlike blue-collar workers, who manufactured goods for sale, white-collar workers tended to perform services in fields like sales, advertising, insurance, and communications.

CONGLOMERATES Many white-collar workers performed their services in large corporations or government agencies. Some of these organizations continued expanding by forming conglomerates. (A **conglomerate** is a major corporation that includes a number of smaller companies in unrelated industries.) For example, one conglomerate, International Telephone and Telegraph (ITT), whose original business was communications, bought car-rental companies, insurance companies, and hotel and motel chains. Through this diversification, or investment in various areas of the economy, ITT tried to protect itself from declines in individual industries. Other huge corporations included American Telephone and Telegraph, Xerox, and General Electric.

FRANCHISES In addition to diversifying, another strategy for business expansion—franchising—developed at this time. A **franchise** is a company that offers similar products or services in many locations. (*Franchise* is also used to

Section 2 Overview

OBJECTIVES

1. To explain how changes in business affected workers.
2. To describe the suburban lifestyle of the 1950s.
3. To identify causes and effects of the automobile industry boom.
4. To explain the increase in consumerism in the 1950s.

CRITICAL THINKING

- Comparing, p. 644
- Recognizing effects, pp. 644, 645, 649
- Theme: Women in America, p. 646
- Analyzing causes, pp. 647, 649
- Analyzing issues, p. 648
- Summarizing, p. 649
- Forming opinions, p. 649

FOCUS & MOTIVATE

5-MINUTE WARM-UP

Using Visual Stimuli for Writing

To discuss the lifestyles of the 1950s, have students scan the pictures on pages 643–649. Then have them respond to one of the following items.

1. Write a paragraph that describes the central theme expressed by the pictures.
2. Write a paragraph based on these images that discusses how America has changed since the 1950s.

WARM-UP TRANSPARENCY 19

▶ ***Starting with the Student***
Ask volunteers to describe the American dream. Do students think their version of the dream differs from that of their parents? If so, how?

OBJECTIVE
① INSTRUCT

The Organization and the Organization Man

▶ ***Discussing Key Ideas***
- By the mid-1950s, blue-collar jobs no longer

(continued on next page)

SECTION 2 RESOURCES

 **PRINT RESOURCES**

IN-DEPTH RESOURCES: UNIT 5
Guided Reading, p. 58
Geography Application: The Baby Boom, p. 62
Primary Source: from *The Organization Man* by William H. Whyte Jr., p. 65
Literature: from *The Man in the Gray Flannel Suit* by Sloan Wilson, p. 68

READING STUDY GUIDE, p. 199

ACCESS FOR STUDENTS ACQUIRING ENGLISH
Guided Reading (Spanish), p. 217
Geography Application: The Baby Boom (Spanish), p. 221

SPANISH READING STUDY GUIDE, p. 199

FORMAL ASSESSMENT
Section Quiz, p. 237

ALTERNATIVE ASSESSMENT BOOK
See forms for supporting and scoring alternative activities.

TECHNOLOGY RESOURCES

HUMANITIES TRANSPARENCIES
H42, Highway Construction

GEOGRAPHY TRANSPARENCIES
G27, Highway Systems, 1950 and 1987

CD-ROM Electronic Library of Primary Sources

VIDEO *American Portfolio: A Videodisc for U.S. History* user's guide, pp. 238, 239, 241

INTERNET http://www.mlushistory.com

(continued from page 643)

employ the majority of Americans.
- American business expands by diversifying and franchising.
- Conformity replaces individuality among workers.

IN-DEPTH RESOURCES: UNIT 5
Guided Reading, p. 58
Primary Source: from *The Organization Man* by William H. Whyte, Jr., p. 65

ACCESS FOR STUDENTS ACQUIRING ENGLISH
Guided Reading (Spanish), p. 217

MORE ABOUT. . .
Social Conformity

In a popular song titled "Little Boxes," folk singer Malvina Reynolds satirized social conformity:

"And they all play on the golf course
And drink their martinis dry,
And they all have pretty children
And the children go to school,
And the children go to summer camp
And then to the university,
Where they are put in boxes
And they come out all the same."

OBJECTIVE
(2) INSTRUCT

The Suburban Lifestyle

▶ ***Starting with the Student*** Have students discuss the relationships between family members in TV shows from the 1950s and the 1990s. Ask, Do you think these shows accurately depict American families in the 1950s and the 1990s? Why or why not?

(continued on next page)

refer to the right, sold to an individual, to do business using the parent company's name and the system that the parent company developed.)

Fast-food restaurants developed some of the first and most successful franchises. McDonald's, for example, had its start when the McDonald brothers developed unusually efficient service, based on assembly-line methods, at their small drive-in restaurant in San Bernardino, California. They simplified the menu, featured 15-cent hamburgers, and mechanized their kitchen. They used blenders, called multimixers, that could make five milkshakes at a time—and they had eight of these machines!

In 1954, Ray Kroc paid the McDonalds $2.7 million for the franchise rights to their hamburger drive-in. In April 1955, he opened his first McDonald's in Des Plaines, Illinois, where he further improved the assembly-line process and introduced the golden arches that are now familiar all over the world.

A. Answer Both were successful business entities that grew rapidly. The conglomerate grew by diversifying; franchises grew by opening identical stores in new locations.

THINK THROUGH HISTORY
A. Comparing *How were conglomerates and franchises alike and different?*

A PERSONAL VOICE

It requires a certain kind of mind to see the beauty in a hamburger bun. Yet is it any more unusual to find grace in the texture and softly curved silhouette of a bun than to reflect lovingly on the . . . arrangements and textures and colors in a butterfly's wings? . . . Not if you view the bun as an essential material in the art of serving a great many meals fast.

RAY KROC, quoted in *The Fifties*

SOCIAL CONFORMITY While franchises like McDonald's helped standardize what people ate, some American workers found themselves becoming standardized as well. Employees who were well paid and held secure jobs in thriving companies sometimes paid a price for economic advancement: a loss of their individuality. In general, businesses did not want creative thinkers, rebels, or anyone who would rock the corporate boat.

In *The Organization Man,* a classic 1956 study of suburban Park Forest, Illinois, and other communities, William H. Whyte described how the new, large organizations created "company people." Companies would give personality tests to people applying for jobs to make sure they would "fit in" the corporate culture. Furthermore, according to Whyte, "in about 25 percent of the country's corporations, the [personality] tests are used not merely to help screen applicants for The Organization but to check up on people already in it." Companies rewarded employees for teamwork, cooperation, and loyalty and so contributed to the growth of conformity, which Whyte called "belongingness."

The "organization man" had to step lively to keep up with the Joneses.

Large workplaces could be very cold and impersonal. Sociologist C. Wright Mills satirized the modern office in which "rows of blank-looking girls" sat "with blank, white folders in their blank hands, all blankly folding blank papers."

The writer Sloan Wilson also criticized this conformity in his 1955 autobiographical novel *The Man in the Gray Flannel Suit.* The title character, Tom, is the typical businessman, who wears a dark suit, a white shirt, and a conservative tie and shoes. He and his wife have three children and a house in the suburbs, and he commutes to a good job in Manhattan. Despite their success, however, the couple feels dissatisfied. Like the novel's fictional couple, some Americans questioned whether pursuing the American dream exacted too high a price, as conformity replaced individuality.

B. Answer Some became dissatisfied with the emphasis on conformity and the impersonal corporate atmosphere.

THINK THROUGH HISTORY
B. Recognizing Effects *What effects did the climate in many corporations have on workers?*

The Suburban Lifestyle

Though achieving job security did take a psychological toll on Americans who resented having to repress their own personalities, it also enabled many people to provide their families with the good things in life. Most Americans worked

TEACHING OPTIONS

Making Connections Across Time

Dressing for Success Conformity during the 1950s was not just a matter of living in identical suburban houses or buying the same cars and consumer goods as one's neighbors. Conformity was an issue at work, too. Corporate conformity for men in the 1950s included wearing a dark suit, white shirt, and conservative tie. Women in business were similarly expected to adhere to formal business attire. Have students contrast the image of the successful corporate employee of the 1950s with the "business casual" image of corporate America in the 1990s.

Making Connections Across the Curriculum

Sociology The emphasis on conformity in all avenues of life during the 1950s had a profound impact on the workplace. Sociologist David Riesman described the change in worker attitudes from being "inner-directed"—that is, relying on the principles and practices that a person internalized as a child—to being "other-directed"—guided by social pressure and others' expectations rather than one's own values and ethics. Discuss with students worker attitudes today: Do people they know seem more inner-directed or other-directed?

in cities, but fewer and fewer of them lived there. New highways and the availability and affordability of automobiles and gasoline made commuting possible. By the early 1960s, every large city in the United States was surrounded by suburbs. Of the 13 million new homes built in the 1950s, 85 percent were suburban. For many people, the suburbs embodied the American dream of an affordable single-family house, good schools, a safe, healthy environment for children, and congenial neighbors just like themselves.

At the peak of the baby boom, an American was born every seven seconds.

THE BABY BOOM As soldiers returned from World War II and settled into family life, they contributed to an unprecedented population explosion known as the **baby boom.** Between 1946 and 1964, the birthrate (number of births per 1,000 population) in the United States soared. At the height of the baby boom, in 1957, one American infant was born every seven seconds—a total of 4,254,784. The result was the largest generation in the nation's history.

Contributing to the size of the baby-boom generation were many factors, including the following:

- reunion of families after the war
- decreasing marriage age
- desirability of large families
- confidence in continued economic prosperity
- advances in medicine

Among the medical advances that saved hundreds of thousands of children's lives were the discovery of drugs to fight and prevent childhood diseases, such as diphtheria and typhoid fever, and the development by **Dr. Jonas Salk,** of a vaccine for the crippling disease poliomyelitis.

DR. SPOCK'S BABIES Suburban family life revolved around children, and many of them were raised according to guidelines devised by the author and pediatrician Dr. Benjamin Spock. His *Common Sense Book of Baby and Child Care,* published in 1946, sold nearly 10 million copies during the 1950s. He advised parents not to spank or scold children and encouraged families to hold meetings in which children could express themselves. He considered it so important for mothers to be at home with their children that at one point he suggested that the government pay mothers to stay home.

C. Answer Creation of youth-centered culture; increased demand for consumer goods and jobs related to rearing and educating children.

THINK THROUGH HISTORY
C. *Recognizing Effects* *How did the baby boom affect American life in the 1950s?*

The baby boom had a tremendous impact not only on child care but on the American economy and the educational system as well. Financial expert Sylvia F. Porter wrote in her popular newspaper column, "Take the 3,548,000 babies born in 1950. . . . Just imagine how much these extra people, these new markets, will absorb—in food, [in] clothing, in gadgets, in housing, in services. Our factories must expand just to keep pace." In 1958, toy sales alone reached $1.25 billion. During the decade, 10 million new students entered the elementary schools. The sharp increase in enrollment caused overcrowding and teacher shortages in many parts of the country. In California, a new school opened every seven days.

WOMEN'S ROLES During the 1950s, the role of homemaker and mother was glorified in popular magazines, movies, and TV programs such as *Father Knows Best* and *The Adventures of Ozzie and Harriet. Time* magazine described the homemaker as "the key figure in all

KEY PLAYER

JONAS SALK 1914–1995

One of the most feared childhood diseases in the 1950s was poliomyelitis—polio, the disease that had disabled President Franklin D. Roosevelt. Polio afflicted 58,000 American children in 1952, killing some and making others reliant on crutches, wheelchairs, or iron lungs (machines that helped people with paralyzed chest muscles to breathe). Mothers kept their children inside during hot summers, fearful that they would catch the highly contagious infection in swimming pools or other public places.

In the early 1950s, Dr. Jonas Salk *(at right in photo above)* developed an effective vaccine to prevent the disease, and the government sponsored a free inoculation program for children. The vaccine was extremely effective, and in 1958 only 5,700 new cases of the disease were reported. In 1974, thanks to Salk's vaccine and an oral vaccine developed in 1961 by Albert Sabin, there were only seven polio cases in the country.

(continued from page 644)

Discussing Key Ideas

- Affluence, automobiles, and highways help many Americans achieve the dream of owning a home in the suburbs.
- The postwar baby boom creates a youth-centered culture and a demand for products related to children.
- Many American women become dissatisfied with the role of homemaker.

IN-DEPTH RESOURCES: UNIT 5
Geography Application: The Baby Boom, p. 62

CRITICAL THINKING TRANSPARENCIES
CT61, Urban-Suburban Growth Rates

KEY PLAYER
Jonas Salk

Critical Thinking: Recognizing Effects Ask students to discuss how the Salk vaccine contributed to the well-being of the baby boom generation. Students might write a tribute to Jonas Salk, reflecting the impact of his work on wiping out a crippling disease.

Issues for the 21st Century

Curing the Health Care System

Connect health care issues of the 1950s to today by having students read pages 892–893. Then have them answer the following questions.

1. What might be the consequences if uninsured children lacked access to vaccines such as Salk's polio vaccine? *Answers will vary.*
2. What percentage of the uninsured people in America are children? *About 25 percent.*

TEACHING OPTIONS

Making Connections Across Time

Baby Boomers Today The largest generation in U.S. history continued to influence American society as its members grew into adulthood. In 1996, the first of the boomers turned 50. Discuss with students the impact of the aging baby boom generation on American society today. Consider these questions:

- What are the needs of growing numbers of people in their fifties?
- How do these needs affect the economy?
- How does the aging of the boomers impact your generation?

Making Global Connections

Wiping Out Polio By the mid-1990s, the World Health Organization (WHO) officially declared that polio had been eliminated from the Western Hemisphere. Although worldwide cases of polio declined by 80 percent between 1988 and 1994, the disease remained a serious problem in some parts of the world, especially in the Indian subcontinent. A program funded by Rotary International pledged to eradicate polio worldwide by the year 2000.

MORE ABOUT . . .
Betty Friedan

Assigned to write an article for her 15th college reunion in 1957, Betty Friedan prepared a questionnaire for the Smith College graduates of 1942. Responses to the questionnaire led Friedan to do the research that resulted in her landmark book, *The Feminine Mystique.* In a 1960 article for *Good Housekeeping* magazine, Friedan asked, "Who knows what women can be when they finally are free to become themselves?"

ELECTRONIC LIBRARY OF PRIMARY SOURCES

from *The Feminine Mystique* by Betty Friedan

MORE ABOUT . . .
Comic Books

Although comic books had been around for a few years, the advent of *Superman* comic books in 1939 helped promote a steady increase in the popularity of comic books in general. By the mid-1950s, comic book publishers cranked out over 600 titles and 90 to 100 million dollar sales each month. Critics argued that comic books were partly responsible for a rise in juvenile delinquency.

"Is this all?"

BETTY FRIEDAN, QUOTING A DISSATISFIED 1950s HOMEMAKER

suburbia, the thread that weaves between family and community—the keeper of the suburban dream." In contrast to the ideal portrayed in the media, however, some women, like Carol Freeman, were not happy with their roles and felt isolated, bored, and unfulfilled. According to one survey in the 1950s, more than one-fifth of suburban wives were dissatisfied with their lives. Betty Friedan, author of the groundbreaking 1963 study of women and society *The Feminine Mystique,* described the problem.

A PERSONAL VOICE

For the first time in their history, women are becoming aware of an identity crisis in their own lives, a crisis which . . . has grown worse with each succeeding generation. . . . I think this is the crisis of women growing up—a turning point from an immaturity that has been called femininity to full human identity.

BETTY FRIEDAN, *The Feminine Mystique*

Some women did have lives outside the confines of suburbia, though, and the number of women working outside the home rose steadily during the decade. By 1960, almost 40 percent of women with children between the ages of 6 and 17 held jobs. Some of these women worked because they were single, divorced, or widowed and had to support themselves and their families. Others worked to supplement their husbands' incomes or to seek personal fulfillment.

D. Answer Most 1950s women were homemakers and had fewer educational and career opportunities than women have today.

But having a job didn't necessarily contribute to a woman's happiness. A woman's career opportunities tended to be limited to fields such as nursing, teaching, and office support, which paid less than other professional and business positions did. Women also earned less than men for comparable work. Although increasing numbers of women attended four-year colleges, they generally received little financial, academic, or psychological encouragement to pursue their goals.

THINK THROUGH HISTORY
D. THEME **Women in America** *How did women's roles and opportunities in the 1950s differ from women's roles today?*

Many people in the 1950s pursued their recreation—like their work—in lock step with their neighbors.

LEISURE IN THE FIFTIES Most Americans of the 1950s had more leisure time than ever before. Employees worked a 40-hour week and earned several weeks' vacation. People owned more labor-saving devices, like washing machines, clothes dryers, dishwashers, vacuum cleaners, and power lawn mowers, which decreased the time it took to do chores. *Fortune* magazine reported that in 1953 Americans spent more than $30 billion on leisure goods and activities.

Americans enjoyed a wide variety of recreational pursuits—both active and passive. Millions of Americans participated in such sports as fishing, bowling, hunting, boating, and golf. More people than ever attended baseball, basketball, and football games, and others watched professional sports on television.

Americans also became avid readers. They devoured books about cooking, religion, do-it-yourself projects, and homemaking. They also read mysteries, romance novels, and fiction by popular writers, such as Ernest Hemingway, John Steinbeck, Daphne du Maurier, and J. D. Salinger. Book sales doubled, due in part to a thriving paperback market. The circulation of popular magazines like *Reader's Digest* and *Sports Illustrated* steadily rose, increasing from about 148 million to more than 190 million readers. Sales of comic books also reached a peak in the mid-1950s.

Activities geared to youth also grew rapidly. Membership in Brownies and Girl Scouts soared from

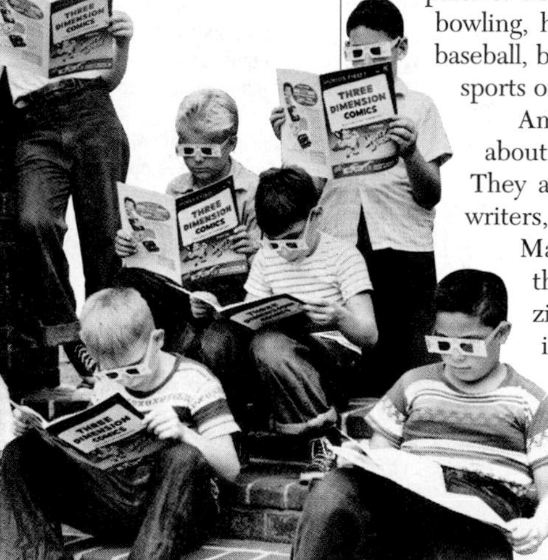

3-D comics were just one of many fads that mesmerized the nation in the 1950s.

TEACHING OPTIONS

Exploring Themes

Women in America In the 1950s, most women put their husband's success above their own achievement. The percentage of women college students was smaller in the 1950s than in the 1920s. In a 1962 Gallup Poll of 2,300 women, however, 90 percent hoped that their daughters would be better educated and would not lead the same lives as they had led. Have the class discuss the social factors that influenced women's attitudes toward higher education in the 1950s. Ask them for evidence that suggests that women did not find complete fulfillment in the role of homemaker.

Teaching Gifted and Talented Students

Women's Goals Have selected students conduct a panel discussion or a simulated television talk show focusing on women's attitudes and goals today, as compared with those of women in the 1950s. Assign another student to act as the facilitator or "host" to keep the conversation moving. The rest of the class can be members of the audience who generate questions for the panel members. Pose these questions to get the discussion started:

- What would you say is the legacy of women in the 1950s?
- Do you think their daughters and granddaughters find life more fulfilling than they did? Why or why not?

1.8 million to 4 million between 1950 and 1960; the number of Cub Scouts jumped from about 770,000 to almost 2.5 million. Little League baseball, founded in 1939, became a fixture in most suburban communities.

The Automobile Culture

During World War II, the U.S. government had rationed gasoline to curb inflation and conserve supplies. After the war, however, an abundance of both imported and domestically produced petroleum—the raw material from which gasoline is made—led to inexpensive, plentiful fuel for consumers. Easy credit terms and extensive advertising persuaded Americans to buy cars in record numbers. "You auto buy now!" one slogan urged. In response, new car sales rose from 6.7 million in 1950 to 7.9 million in 1955. The total number of private cars on the road jumped from 40 million in 1950 to 60 million in 1960.

E. Answer Cars were necessary for life in the suburbs, Americans loved cars, and the positive economic factors allowed Americans to buy cars.

THINK THROUGH HISTORY
E. *Analyzing Causes* *Why did auto sales surge in the 1950s?*

AUTOMANIA Suburban living made owning a car a necessity. Most of the new suburbs, built in formerly rural areas, did not offer public transportation, and people had to drive to their jobs in the cities. In addition, many of the schools, stores, synagogues, churches, and doctors' and dentists' offices were not within walking distance of suburban homes. Many families owned not one, but two cars—one for commuting to work and the other, often a station wagon, for doing local errands and taking the children to their activities.

THE INTERSTATE HIGHWAY SYSTEM The more cars there were, the more roads were needed. "Automania" spurred local and state governments to construct roads that would connect schools, shopping centers, and workplaces to residential suburbs. The Interstate Highway Act, which President Eisenhower signed in 1956, authorized the building of a nationwide highway network—41,000 miles of expressways. The new roads, in turn, encouraged the development of new suburbs farther and farther from the cities.

Interstate highways also made high-speed, long-haul trucking possible, which contributed to a decline in the commercial use of railroads. Towns along the new highways prospered, while towns along the older, smaller roads experienced hard times. The system of highways also helped unify and homogenize the nation. As John Keats observed in his 1958 book *The Insolent Chariots,* "Our new roads,

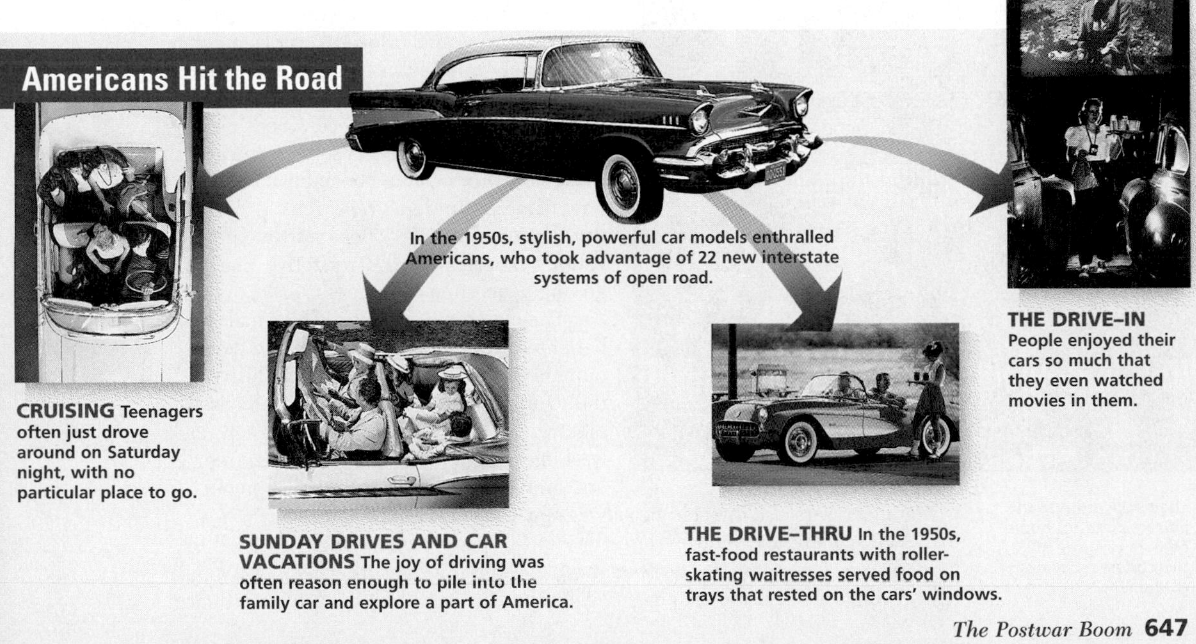

Americans Hit the Road

In the 1950s, stylish, powerful car models enthralled Americans, who took advantage of 22 new interstate systems of open road.

CRUISING Teenagers often just drove around on Saturday night, with no particular place to go.

SUNDAY DRIVES AND CAR VACATIONS The joy of driving was often reason enough to pile into the family car and explore a part of America.

THE DRIVE-THRU In the 1950s, fast-food restaurants with roller-skating waitresses served food on trays that rested on the cars' windows.

THE DRIVE-IN People enjoyed their cars so much that they even watched movies in them.

OBJECTIVE
③ INSTRUCT

The Automobile Culture

▶ *Starting with the Student*
- Discuss whether students think today's automobile culture differs from that of the 1950s.

▶ *Discussing Key Ideas*
- Americans buy cars in record numbers in the 1950s.
- Access to cars and an interstate highway system make Americans mobile.
- The car industry creates opportunities and problems.

HISTORY FROM VISUALS

Americans Hit the Road

Reading the Graphic
Have students identify the activities that automobiles made possible. *Possible Responses: Cruising, drive-in movies, eating at fast-food restaurants, vacations.* Poll the class to see how many students have experienced a car vacation or a drive-in movie.

Extension Have students create a chart comparing the positive and negative effects of automania.

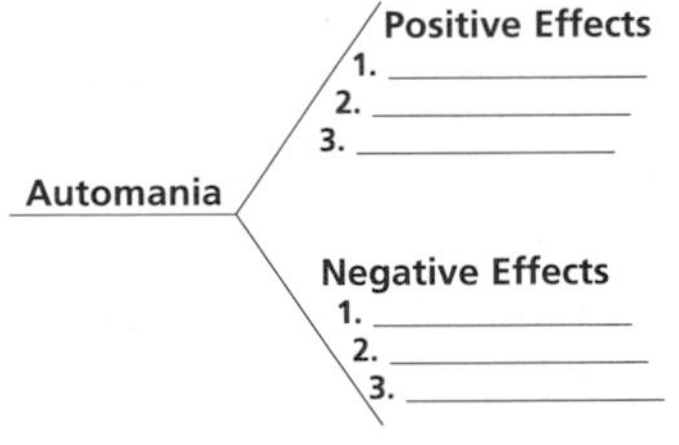

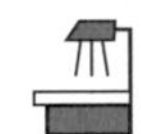
GEOGRAPHY TRANSPARENCIES
G27, Highway Systems, 1950–1987

HUMANITIES TRANSPARENCIES
H42, Highway Construction

TEACHING OPTIONS

Making Connections Across the Curriculum

Geography Suburban living made car ownership a necessity. Developers lured home buyers farther and farther from cities. Subdivision names that included "park," "grove," "field," "forest," or "wood" emphasized the contrast between suburbs and cities. Discuss with students the qualities of suburban living that made it attractive to many Americans in the 1950s.

Making Connections Across Time

Automobile Culture In the mid-1950s, automakers promoted sales by featuring long, low cars with lots of chrome, tail fins, bright colors, and plush interiors. One industry official observed that "a square foot of chrome sells ten times more cars than the best safety-door latch." Ask students to brainstorm a list of adjectives that today's car dealers use to capture the imagination—and money—of millions of Americans. Discuss the differences between what made cars appealing to potential buyers in the 1950s and what makes them appealing today.

NOW & THEN
Southern California and the Automobile

Critical Thinking: Analyzing Causes What factors contributed to the growth of the automobile culture in California? *Suburban lifestyle of the region, freedom of movement offered by autos.*

OBJECTIVE

④ **INSTRUCT**

Consumerism Unbound

▶***Discussing Key Ideas***
- In the 1950s, Americans buy more consumer goods than ever before.
- To encourage spending, manufacturers create new products planned to become obsolete in a short time.
- To increase sales of consumer goods, advertisers appeal to Americans' desire for status and conformity.

HISTORY FROM VISUALS
Suburban Backyards

Reading the Illustration Point out details such as the bicycle, clothesline, and lawn furniture that illustrate aspects of suburban lifestyles. Note similarities and differences among neighbors' backyards and activities.

Extension Have students compare and contrast the backyards shown in the illustration and their own (or someone else's) backyard today, either in a written paragraph or in a sketch of their yard.

NOW & THEN

SOUTHERN CALIFORNIA AND THE AUTOMOBILE

No state has exemplified American automania more than California. By the mid-1990s, Californians owned more cars, held more drivers' licenses, and traveled more miles on their roads than the people of any other state. The center of this automobile culture is the city of Los Angeles. Angelenos own more than 5 million cars, and the city has more than 650 miles of freeways.

One factor that contributes to the importance of the automobile in southern California is the suburban lifestyle of the region—even within the city limits of Los Angeles. In fact, Los Angeles has been described as "a hundred suburbs in search of a city."

This dependence on cars has contributed to problems of air pollution and traffic jams. But Californians have begun to address these problems by reviving public transportation systems, requiring catalytic converters to reduce pollution, and encouraging the increased use of electric cars that produce no pollution.

with their ancillaries, the motels, filling stations, and restaurants advertising Eats, have made it possible for you to drive from Brooklyn to Los Angeles without a change of diet, scenery, or culture." With access to cars, affordable gas, and new highways, more and more Americans hit the road. They flocked to mountains, lakes, national parks, historic sites, and amusement parks for family vacations. Disneyland, which opened in California in July 1955, attracted 3 million visitors the next year.

MOBILITY TAKES ITS TOLL As the automobile industry boomed, it stimulated production and provided jobs in other industries, such as drive-in movies and restaurants and shopping malls. Yet cars also created new problems for both society and the environment. Noise and exhaust polluted the air. Automobile accidents claimed more lives every year. Traffic jams raised people's stress levels, and heavy use damaged the roads. Because cars made it possible for Americans to live in suburbs, many upper-class and middle-class whites left the crowded cities. Jobs and businesses eventually followed them to the suburbs. Public transportation declined, and poor people in the inner cities were often left without jobs and vital services. As a result, the economic gulf between suburban and urban dwellers and between the middle class and the poor widened.

F. Answer Positive—growth of suburbs, increased mobility. Negative—pollution, deterioration of public transportation.

THINK THROUGH HISTORY
F. *Analyzing Issues* *What positive and negative effects did the mass availability of the automobile have on American life in the 1950s?*

Consumerism Unbound

By the mid-1950s, nearly 60 percent of Americans were members of the middle class, about twice as many as before World War II. They wanted, and had the money to buy, increasing numbers of products. **Consumerism,** buying material goods, came to be equated with success.

NEW PRODUCTS One new product after another appeared in the marketplace, as various industries responded to consumer demand. *Newsweek* magazine reported in 1956 that "hundreds of brand-new goods have become commonplace overnight."

The chemical industry, for example, produced several polyester fabrics—rayon, dacron, and orlon—to replace cotton, wool, and silk. It also developed Teflon, a nonstick coating for cookware, as well as plastics that replaced wood, glass, and metal. The materials for many of these new products had been developed in government-funded research projects during World War II. These wartime innovations quickly found a receptive market among peacetime consumers.

The electronics industry, which had also benefited from military research and development, became the fifth largest industry in the United States. Consumers purchased electric household appliances—such as washing machines, dryers, blenders, freezers, and dishwashers—in record numbers. Manufacturers also invested heavily in new electrical equipment.

The back yard was the perfect place for homeowners to show off their latest recreational equipment.

With more and more leisure time to fill, people increasingly invested in recreational equipment. They bought televisions, tape recorders, and the new hi-fi (high-fidelity) record players. They bought casual clothing to suit their

Block Schedule TEACHING OPTION **Time Needed: 20 Minutes**

Cooperative Activity: Developing Commercials

Task: Student groups will prepare one-minute television commercials for consumer goods of the 1950s.

Purpose: To help students recognize social and economic factors that contributed to consumerism in the 1950s.

Activity: Assign one of the following categories of products to small groups of students: household appliances, recreational equipment, clothing, or cars. Each group should prepare a 1950s-style TV commercial to market a product in its assigned category. Within each group, students should choose from the following roles: director, scriptwriter, graphic designer (to plan the visual element of the commercial), and music researcher. Groups should present their commercials to the class.

Discuss the marketing techniques each commercial uses. Examples include appeal to Americans' desire for status, social conformity, or family values.

ALTERNATIVE ASSESSMENT BOOK
Standards for Evaluating a Cooperative Activity

suburban lifestyles and rotary lawn mowers, barbecue equipment, swimming pools, and lawn decorations for their suburban homes. In 1960, Americans spent more than $145 million on lawn and patio furniture alone.

PLANNED OBSOLESCENCE In addition to creating new products, manufacturers began using a marketing strategy called **planned obsolescence.** In order to encourage consumers to purchase more goods, manufacturers purposely designed products to become obsolete—that is, to wear out or become outdated—in a short period of time. Carmakers brought out new models every year, urging consumers to stay up-to-date. Because of planned obsolescence, Americans came to expect new and better products, and they began to discard items that were sometimes barely used. Some observers commented that American culture was on the way to becoming a "throwaway society."

BUY NOW, PAY LATER Many Americans made their purchases with credit and therefore did not have to pay for them right away. The Diner's Club issued the first credit card in 1950, and the American Express card came along in 1958. In addition, people bought large items on the installment plan and made regular payments over a fixed time. Home mortgages (loans for buying a house) and automobile loans worked the same way. During the decade, the total private debt grew from $73 billion to $179 billion. Instead of saving money, Americans were spending it, confident that prosperity would continue.

THE ADVERTISING AGE The advertising industry capitalized on this runaway consumerism by encouraging even more spending. Ads were everywhere—in newspapers and magazines, on radio and television, and on billboards along the highways—prompting people to buy goods that ranged from cars to cereals to cigarettes. Advertisers spent about $6 billion in 1950; by 1955, the figure was up to $9 billion. During this time, businesses dedicated more money to advertising every year than the country spent on its public schools. Since most Americans had satisfied their basic needs, advertisers tried to convince them to buy things they really didn't need. Advertisers appealed to people's desire for status and "belongingness" and to associate their products with those values.

Television became a powerful new advertising tool. The first one-minute TV commercial was produced in 1941 at a cost of $9. In 1960, advertisers spent $1.6 billion for television ads. Television had become not only the medium for mass transmission of cultural values, but a symbol of popular culture itself.

Advertisers promised a world in which labor that was once difficult could be done by a machine at the touch of a button.

G. Answer Rising standard of living; success equated with material possessions; successful advertising campaigns.

THINK THROUGH HISTORY
G. *Analyzing Causes* *What factors contributed to the rapidly growing demand for consumer goods in the 1950s?*

MORE ABOUT . . .
Advertising

In the 1957 bestseller *The Hidden Persuaders,* author Vance Packard exposed advertising techniques that appealed to values. For example, Cadillac ads appealed to the desire for status, and mouthwash ads held the promise of social acceptance.

ASSESS & RETEACH

Section 2 Assessment

Have students locate parts of the text that answer each question. Discuss answers in class and clarify understandings.

Self-Assessment

Have students synthesize their understanding of this section by writing a paragraph describing the American dream in the 1950s.

Section Quiz

FORMAL ASSESSMENT
Section Quiz, p. 237

Reteach

Have students write one question for each main heading in Section 2. Then have them exchange questions with another student. Partners should answer each other's questions, then work together to verify information.

CLOSE

Many Americans achieved their dream by acquiring homes, cars, and material goods. In spite of these comforts, however, many Americans became dissatisfied with a lifestyle based on social conformity.

Section 2 Assessment

1. **TERMS & NAMES**
Identify:
- conglomerate
- franchise
- baby boom
- Dr. Jonas Salk
- consumerism
- planned obsolescence

2. **SUMMARIZING** In a graphic organizer like the one below, list examples of specific goals that characterized the American dream for suburbanites in the 1950s.

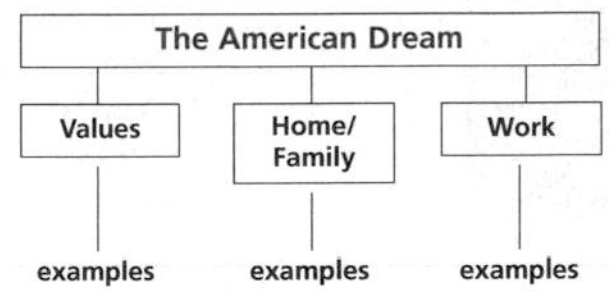

3. **FORMING OPINIONS** Do you think that the life of a typical suburban homemaker during the 1950s was more like a dream come true or a living nightmare? Support your answer.
THINK ABOUT
- Carol Freeman's remarks on page 643
- Betty Friedan's comments on page 646
- the homemaker's responsibilities
- job opportunities for women

4. **RECOGNIZING EFFECTS** In what ways do you think current environmental consciousness is related to the "throwaway society" of the 1950s? Support your answer.
THINK ABOUT
- the purchasing habits of 1950s consumers
- the effects of planned obsolescence
- today's emphasis on recycling

ANSWERS

1. TERMS & NAMES

conglomerate, p. 643
franchise, p. 643
baby boom, p. 645
Dr. Jonas Salk, p. 645
consumerism, p. 648
planned obsolescence, p. 649

2. SUMMARIZING

Possible Answers: Values—conformity, material goods implied success; Home/Family—two or three children, close family ties, single-family home in suburbia, one or two cars, television; Work—man is the breadwinner who works at a white-collar job; woman takes care of home and children.

3. FORMING OPINIONS

Possible Answers: Dream—had a husband to support her, a home in the suburbs, a car, children, material comforts, and did not have to work outside the home; Nightmare—was a slave to her home and family and had no time or encouragement to develop her own interests.

4. RECOGNIZING EFFECTS

Possible Answer: Today's common practices of recycling discarded items and trash, reusing empty food and product containers, and buying products with long-term warranties might be seen as necessary steps to reverse the "throwaway" trend of the 1950s and its resulting environmental problems.

Geography Spotlight

OBJECTIVES

1. To trace the growth of American suburbs after World War II.
2. To describe details about one representative suburb.

FOCUS & MOTIVATE

▶ ***Starting with the Student*** Have students contrast urban, rural, and suburban life.

- What are the main lifestyle differences in urban, suburban, and rural areas?
- If students could live in any of the three areas, which would they prefer, and why?

MORE ABOUT . . .

Postwar Suburbs

Like Park Forest, Illinois, Levittown was another preplanned American suburb. Built from 1946 to 1951 by the development firm of Levitt and Sons, Inc., the first Levittown was located in Nassau County on Long Island, New York. It contained shopping centers, schools, playgrounds, swimming pools, and community centers as well as thousands of low-cost homes. In part because of its proximity to the media center of New York City, Levittown came to represent all the suburbs developed in postwar America.

GEOGRAPHY SPOTLIGHT

The Road to Suburbia

"Come out to Park Forest where small-town friendships grow—and you still live so close to a big city." Advertisements like this one for a scientifically planned Chicago suburb captured the lure of the suburbs for thousands of growing families in the 1950s—affordable housing, congenial neighbors, fresh air and open spaces, good schools, and easy access to urban jobs and culture. Good transportation was the lifeline of suburban growth a half a century ago, and it continues to spur expansion today.

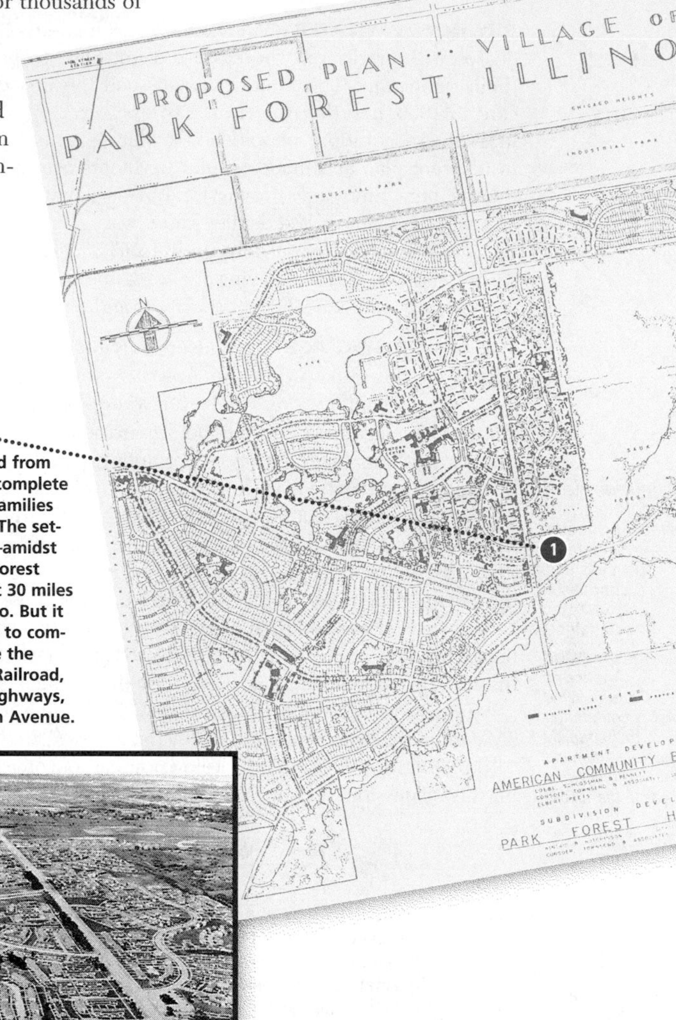

❶ **WHERE THE 'BURBS ARE** Park Forest, Illinois, was planned from its conception in 1945 to be a "complete community for middle-income families with children." The setting was rural—amidst cornfields and forest preserves about 30 miles south of Chicago. But it was convenient to commuter lines, like the Illinois Central Railroad, and to major highways, such as Western Avenue.

1947

1952

SHARED PRIVACY By 1952, development had expanded to include both low-cost rental units and single-family homes. All the streets were curved to slow traffic, present a pleasing sweep of space, and give residents maximum privacy and space for yards.

RECOMMENDED RESOURCES

Books

Arnold, Eve. *The Fifties.* New York: Pantheon, 1985. A social history in photographs, introduced by John Chancellor.

Baldassare, Mark. *Trouble in Paradise.* New York: Columbia UP, 1986. The suburban transformation in America.

Gans, Herbert J. *The Levittowners.* New York: Pantheon, 1967. A study of life and politics in a then-new suburban community.

Halberstam, David. *The Fifties.* New York: Villard, 1993. A noteworthy recent account of the era.

Jackson, Kenneth T. *Crabgrass Frontier.* New York: Oxford UP, 1985. The suburbanization of the U.S.A.

Marling, Karal Ann. *As Seen on TV: The Visual Culture of Everyday Life in the 1950s.* Cambridge: Harvard UP, 1994. Fifties America through the eyes of television.

Wood, Robert Coldwell. *Suburbia: Its People and Their Politics.* Boston: Houghton, 1958. A contemporaneous account.

Videos

Suburbs, Arcadia for Everyone. Dir. Murray Grigor. Films for the Humanities, 1986. The evolution of the suburban ideal in 20th-century America.

❷ THE COMMUTER CRUSH AND JUNGLE GYMS Men commuted to work on the IC railroad, while their wives usually stayed home to take care of the children, who thrived in Park Forest's safe, wholesome family environment. The school system struggled to keep pace with the ongoing baby boom.

❸ SHOP TILL YOU DROP Consumerism was a major driving force in the 1950s, and Park Forest kept up with the trend. The central shopping center served the community well until the late 1960s.

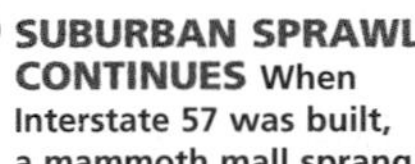

❹ SUBURBAN SPRAWL CONTINUES When Interstate 57 was built, a mammoth mall sprang up just off the highway, and the local shopping area withered. Park Forest is still struggling to revive its central shopping area.

INTERACT WITH HISTORY

1. **SYNTHESIZING** How did the availability of transportation influence the creation and ongoing development of Park Forest?

   SEE SKILLBUILDER HANDBOOK, PAGE 921.

2. **CREATING A DATABASE** Collect statistics about changes in population, living patterns, income, and economic development in a suburb near you. Use those statistics to create a database about the growth of the suburb.

INSTRUCT

▶ *Starting with the Student*

- Have students discuss drawbacks to living in the suburbs. *Possible Responses: Commuting, less variety of people and activities, fewer cultural activities, new developments not always scenic, homes sometimes poorly constructed.*
- Have students discuss why the suburbs might have been so appealing to so many postwar Americans. *Possible Responses: Affordable housing, less congested, less polluted, status symbol, more privacy and independence, home an investment, better schools, less crime, many like to live closer to nature.*

▶ *Discussing Key Ideas*

- In the baby-boom years after World War II, many American families move to the suburbs.
- Good transportation helps make suburban development possible.

HUMANITIES TRANSPARENCIES

H42, Highway Construction

HISTORY FROM VISUALS

Reading the Images

Have students study the graphics.

- Where is Park Forest in relation to the downtown part of Chicago known as the Loop? *South.*
- In addition to the IC, or Illinois Central, railroad, how might suburbanites have commuted to work in downtown Chicago? *Driving on Route 1 or 54.*

INTERACT WITH HISTORY

1. Synthesizing

Possible Answers: *Good transportation was necessary to both the creation and ongoing development of the suburb. Commuters had to have a convenient way to get to and from work. Commuter railroad lines such as the Illinois Central Railroad provided reliable transportation to and from the city.*

2. Creating a Database

Students might perform this activity in small groups. In addition to visiting the community's school (including college, if any) or public library, students may find information through local real-estate firms, development housing offices, and/or organizations such as the Chamber of Commerce. Encourage students to discuss how their database might be used when it is complete.

Section 3 Overview

OBJECTIVES

1. To explain how television programs in the 1950s reflected middle-class values.
2. To explain how the beat movement and rock 'n' roll music clashed with middle-class values.
3. To describe ways that African-American entertainers integrated the media in the 1950s.

SKILLBUILDER

- Interpreting charts, p. 653

CRITICAL THINKING

- Theme: Science and Technology, p. 653
- Forming opinions, pp. 654, 657
- Clarifying, pp. 655, 657
- Analyzing causes, p. 655
- Recognizing effects, p. 656
- Summarizing, p. 657
- Comparing and contrasting, p. 657

FOCUS & MOTIVATE

5-MINUTE WARM-UP

Interpreting Graphs
To explore the growth of television viewing in America, have students look at the graphs on page 653 and then answer the following questions.

1. What was the percentage increase in daily hours of viewing from 1950 to 1990?
2. How do you explain the virtually constant rise in both charts?

WARM-UP TRANSPARENCY 19

▶ ***Starting with the Student***
Ask students if they listen to recordings of hit songs from the 1950s on the radio or watch reruns of 1950s programs on television.

- Ask, Why do these examples of 1950s culture remain popular today? *Possible Responses: They represent nostalgia to baby boomers; they reach a new audience.*

3 Popular Culture

TERMS & NAMES
- **mass media**
- **Federal Communications Commission (FCC)**
- **beat movement**
- **beatnik**
- **rock 'n' roll**

LEARN ABOUT television, radio, movies, literature, and music in the 1950s
TO UNDERSTAND how mass popular culture reflected middle-class values and how some subcultures dissented from those values.

ONE AMERICAN'S STORY

Popular music thrived in the 1950s. Singers like Frank Sinatra, Nat "King" Cole, Tony Bennett, Lena Horne, and Perry Como crooned love songs, and silly tunes like Patti Page's "The Doggie in the Window" topped the charts. But in the middle of the decade, spurred by the growth of radio stations and live tours aimed at African-American audiences, record sales of hard-driving rhythm and blues began to take off. A 14-year-old saxophone player, who later became a music producer, described the first time he saw the rhythm-and-blues performer Richard Wayne Penniman, better known as Little Richard.

A PERSONAL VOICE

He'd just burst onto the stage from anywhere, and you wouldn't be able to hear anything but the roar of the audience. . . . He'd be on the stage, he'd be off the stage, he'd be jumping and yelling, screaming, whipping the audience on. . . . Then when he finally did hit the piano and just went into di-di-di-di-di-di-di, you know, well nobody can do that as fast as Richard. It just took everybody by surprise.

H. B. BARNUM, quoted in *The Rise and Fall of Popular Music*

Little Richard

Born poor, Little Richard wore flashy clothes on stage, curled his hair, and shouted his songs. As one writer observed, "In two minutes [he] used as much energy as an all-night party." He distinctly did not fit the gray-flannel-suit-and-station-wagon, suburban middle-class values of the 1950s. His wild individualism appealed strongly to many young people who felt constrained by the mass conformity. Although much of America's popular culture, especially television, reflected those mainstream values—secure jobs, material success, well-behaved children, and general conformity—Little Richard became a popular idol only when he appeared on the TV show *American Bandstand.*

New Era of the Mass Media

Compared with other **mass media**—means of communication that reach large audiences—television developed with lightning speed. First widely available in 1948, television had reached 9 percent of American homes by 1950 and 55 percent of homes by 1954. In 1960, almost 90 percent—45 million—of American homes had television sets. Clearly, TV was the entertainment and information marvel of the postwar years.

THE RISE OF TELEVISION Early television sets were small boxes with round screens. Programming was meager, and broadcasts were in black and white. The first regular broadcasts, beginning in 1949, reached only a small part of the East Coast and offered only two hours of programs per week. Post–World War II innovations such as microwave relays, which could transmit television waves over long distances, sent the television industry soaring.

At first, the **Federal Communications Commission (FCC)**—the government agency that regulates and licenses television, telephone, telegraph, radio, and other communications industries—was very cautious about allowing television stations to open. It imposed a freeze on new stations between 1948 and 1952 to give the industry time to plan for expansion and to solve problems

SECTION 3 RESOURCES

PRINT RESOURCES

IN-DEPTH RESOURCES: UNIT 5
Guided Reading, p. 59
Skillbuilder Practice: Primary Sources, p. 61
Literature: from *1959* by Thulani Davis, p. 70
American Lives: Milton Berle, p. 72

READING STUDY GUIDE, p. 201

ACCESS FOR STUDENTS ACQUIRING ENGLISH
Guided Reading (Spanish), p. 218
Skillbuilder Practice: Primary Sources (Spanish), p. 220

SPANISH READING STUDY GUIDE, p. 201

FORMAL ASSESSMENT
Section Quiz, p. 238

ALTERNATIVE ASSESSMENT BOOK
See forms for supporting and scoring alternative activities.

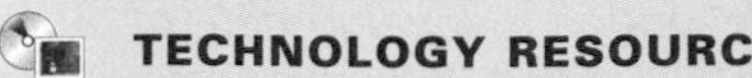

TECHNOLOGY RESOURCES

CD-ROM *Our Times*

VIDEO *American Portfolio: A Videodisc for U.S. History* user's guide, pp. 238, 239

INTERNET http://www.mlushistory.com

Glued to the Set, 1950–1995

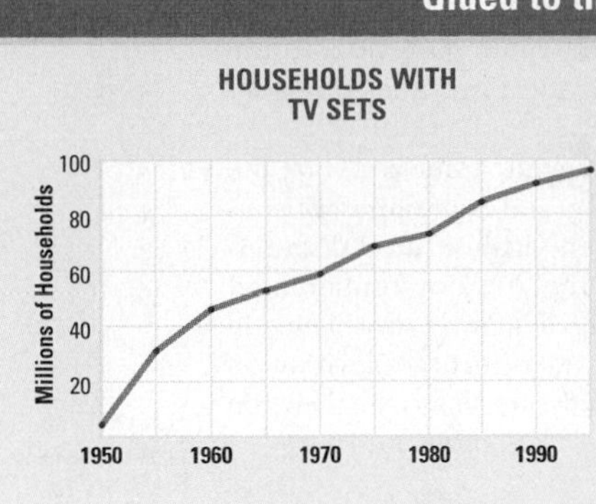

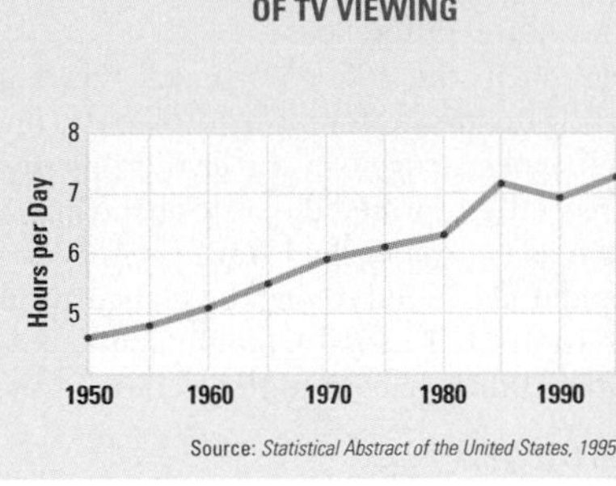

SKILLBUILDER INTERPRETING CHARTS *During which decade did the number of households with TV sets increase the most?*

Audrey Meadows and Jackie Gleason starred in the wildly popular TV series *The Honeymooners,* which was still being rerun in the late 1990s.

Skillbuilder Answer 1950–1960.

that interfered with reception. After the freeze ended, the number of stations jumped from 108 in 1952 to almost 500 in 1956.

This period of rapid expansion was the "golden age" of television entertainment—and entertainment in the 1950s often meant comedy. Programs were usually broadcast live, with mistakes and bloopers intact. Milton Berle attracted huge audiences with *The Texaco Star Theater,* and Lucille Ball and Desi Arnaz's early situation comedy, *I Love Lucy,* began its enormously popular run in 1951.

At the same time, veteran radio broadcaster Edward R. Murrow introduced two innovations: on-the-scene reporting, with his program *See It Now* (1951–1958), and interviewing, with *Person to Person* (1953–1959). Westerns, sports events, and original dramas shown on *Playhouse 90* and *Studio One* offered entertainment variety. The introduction of videotape technology in 1956 took some of the risks out of broadcasting. After that, producers could prerecord and edit programs and broadcast them anytime. Television thus gained flexibility but lost some of its early spontaneity.

A. Answer More households used television for entertainment and people spent an increasing number of hours watching TV. More varied shows were broadcast, and TV dinners were invented to accommodate viewers.

THINK THROUGH HISTORY
A. THEME ***Science and Technology*** *How did the emergence of television affect American culture in the 1940s and 1950s?*

American businesses took advantage of the opportunities offered by the new television industry. Advertising expenditures on TV, which were $170 million in 1950, reached $1 billion in 1955 and nearly $2 billion in 1960.

Children's programs, such as *The Mickey Mouse Club* and *The Howdy Doody Show,* attracted loyal young fans who wanted to buy the products associated with the programs. Inspired by television advertising, TV heroes (like the actor who portrayed Davy Crockett), and TV coverage of the latest fads, children badgered their parents to buy coonskin caps, whiffle balls, Hula-Hoops, and Silly Putty.

Sales of *TV Guide,* introduced in 1953, quickly outpaced sales of other magazines. In 1954, the food industry introduced a new convenience item, the frozen TV dinner. Complete, ready-to-heat individual meals on disposable aluminum trays, TV dinners made it easy for people to eat without missing their favorite shows.

STEREOTYPES AND GUNSLINGERS Not everyone was thrilled with television, though. Critics objected to its effects on children and its stereotypical portrayal of women and minorities.

Women did, in fact, appear in stereotypical roles, such as the ideal mothers of *Father Knows Best* and *The Adventures of Ozzie and Harriet.* Male characters outnumbered women characters three to

HISTORICAL SPOTLIGHT

TV QUIZ SHOWS

Beginning with *The $64,000 Question* in 1955, television created hit quiz shows by adopting a popular format from radio and adding big cash prizes. Two contestants squared off over topics ranging from Shakespeare to boxing.

The quiz show *Twenty-One* made a star of a shy English professor named Charles Van Doren. He rode a wave of fame and fortune until 1958, when a former contestant revealed that, to heighten the dramatic impact, producers had been giving some of the contestants the right answers. Van Doren stated:

> "I was almost able to convince myself that it did not matter what I was doing because it was having such a good effect on the national attitude toward teachers, education, and the intellectual life."

A scandal followed when a congressional subcommittee investigated and confirmed the charges. Former contestants faced trial for perjury, and most of the quiz shows left the air.

OBJECTIVE ① **INSTRUCT**

New Era of the Mass Media

▶ ***Discussing Key Ideas***
- TV provides information and entertainment.
- Americans object to TV stereotypes and violence.
- Radio and movies work to maintain their share of the mass media market.

IN-DEPTH RESOURCES: UNIT 5
Guided Reading, p. 59
American Lives: Milton Berle, p. 72

ACCESS FOR STUDENTS ACQUIRING ENGLISH
Guided Reading (Spanish), p. 218

HISTORY FROM VISUALS
Glued to the Set, 1950–1995

Reading the Graphs Point out that data for the midpoint of each decade is available on both graphs, even though only the decade dates are shown.

Extension Ask students to track their family's TV habits for one week on a graph like the one below:

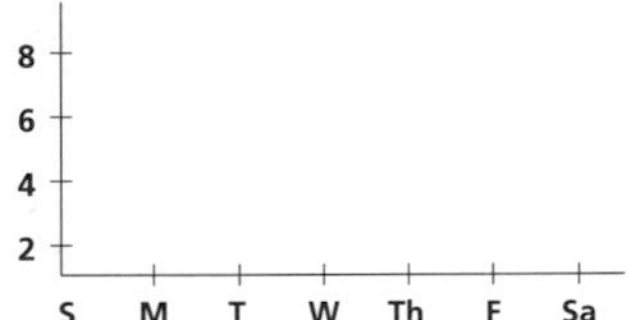

HISTORICAL SPOTLIGHT
TV Quiz Shows

Critical Thinking: Analyzing Effects Ask students why a TV quiz show might have had a positive effect on national attitudes toward education. *Possible Response: Showed benefits of knowledge.*

TEACHING OPTIONS

Exploring Themes

Science and Technology Television, according to some critics, was a vast wasteland. To commentator Bill Moyers, however, television held great potential for good: "Once I thought the most important political statement we could make about television was to turn it off. But television can instruct, inform, and inspire, as well as distract, distort, and demean. And turning it off rejects the good with the bad." Have students discuss the positive and negative effects of television.

Teaching Gifted and Talented Students

Polling the Community Have students expand their tracking of TV viewing time to a larger population. Interested students can devise a survey to give to students, teachers, family members, and others in their communities. Questions might focus on hours of television viewing, the age and educational level of the respondent, and the kind of programs watched. Students should come up with a way to compile their data in a clear and coherent manner and then share their findings in a report to the class or in an article written for the school newspaper.

MORE ABOUT . . .
Newton Minow and the FCC

The FCC cannot interfere directly with television programming. Under Minow's leadership, however, the agency refused to renew licenses for stations whose programming did not meet the standards promised in their original applications. In his "vast wasteland" speech, Minow told broadcasters, "For every hour the people give you—you owe them something. I intend to see that your debt is paid with service. . . ."

MORE ABOUT . . .
James Dean

Movie actor James Dean starred in only three films. In his most famous movie, *Rebel Without a Cause,* he played a teenager fighting against conformity. To American teenagers, Dean became a symbol of their own frustrations with society. James Dean died in an automobile crash at the age of 24.

"Television is . . . a vast wasteland."

NEWTON MINOW

one. African Americans and Latinos rarely appeared in television programs at all. A 1959 episode of *Father Knows Best* provided a rare positive portrayal of a racial minority when a Latino gardener taught the town a lesson about accepting cultural differences.

Television in the 1950s portrayed an idealized white America. For the most part, it omitted references to poverty, diversity, and contemporary conflicts, such as the struggle of the civil rights movement against racial discrimination. Instead, it glorified the historical conflicts of the Western frontier in hit shows such as *Gunsmoke* and *Have Gun, Will Travel.* The level of violence in these popular shows led to ongoing concerns about the effect of television on children. In 1961, Federal Communications Commission chairman Newton Minow voiced this concern to the leaders of the television industry.

THINK THROUGH HISTORY
B. *Forming Opinions* *Do you think the rise of television had a positive or a negative effect on Americans? Explain.*

B. Answer *Possible Answers:* Positive—informing and entertaining; reinforcing cultural values. Negative—promoting stereotypes of minorities and women; exposing children to images of violence.

A PERSONAL VOICE

When television is bad, nothing is worse. I invite you to sit down in front of your television set when your station goes on the air . . . and keep your eyes glued to that set [until] the station signs off. I can assure you that you will observe a vast wasteland.

NEWTON MINOW, speech to the National Association of Broadcasters, Washington, D.C., May 9, 1961

RADIO AND MOVIES In the early days of television, reaction to the new medium was mixed. Some predicted that it would never catch on, while others feared that TV would eclipse all competing forms of entertainment. Although TV turned out to be wildly popular, radio and movies survived. But instead of competing with television's mass market for drama and variety shows, radio stations turned to local programming of news, weather, music, and community issues. The strategy paid off. During the decade, radio advertising rose by 35 percent, and the number of stations increased by 50 percent.

From the beginning, television cut into the profitable movie market. In 1948, 18,500 movie theaters had drawn nearly 90 million paid admissions per week. As more people stayed home to watch TV, the number of moviegoers decreased by nearly half. By 1960, one-fifth of the nation's movie theaters had been converted into bowling alleys or supermarkets, or they simply stood empty. As early as 1951, producer David Selznick worried about Hollywood: "It'll never come back. It'll just keep on crumbling until finally the wind blows the last studio prop across the sands."

The young actor James Dean, seen here in the movie *Giant,* had a self-confident indifference that made him the idol of teenagers in the fifties. He became a legend, although he appeared in only three films. He died in a car accident at age 24.

But Hollywood did not crumble and blow away. Instead, it capitalized on the advantages that movies still held over television—size, color, and stereophonic sound. Stereophonic sound, which surrounded the viewer, was introduced in 1952, and by 1954, more than 50 percent of movies were in color. By contrast, color television, which became available that year, did not become widespread until the next decade. In 1953, 20th Century Fox introduced CinemaScope, which projected a wide-angle image on a broad screen. The industry also tried novelty features: Smell-O-Vision and Aroma-Rama piped smells into the theaters to coincide with events shown on the

Block Schedule TEACHING OPTION **Time Needed: 30 Minutes**

Cooperative Activity: Creating a TV Program Guide

Task: Student groups will create a program guide of popular 1950s TV shows.

Purpose: To investigate the images and values portrayed in popular programs of the 1950s.

Activity: Groups may choose a category of program, such as comedies, westerns, or dramas. Two students should be researchers, using the library, the Internet, rental videos, or cable TV to learn which shows were popular and why. One or two students can sketch images to include in the guide. Another student can write descriptions of the shows to accompany the images. The group as a whole should compile the entries.

Building a Portfolio: Students who add their guide to their portfolio should indicate their contribution to the project.

ALTERNATIVE ASSESSMENT BOOK
Standards for Evaluating a Cooperative Activity

OUR TIMES
TV Guide listings from June 1956

Standards for Evaluation
A program guide should . . .

- represent TV shows from the appropriate era
- include brief descriptions of the nature of the shows
- identify actors and actresses in the shows
- use appropriate form and style

screen. Three-dimensional images, viewed through special glasses supplied by the theaters, appeared to leap into the audience.

The availability of the wide screen and stereophonic sound inspired the creation of spectacular epic movies, such as the award-winning *Around the World in Eighty Days* and *The Ten Commandments.* The film director Alfred Hitchcock sounded a different, more ominous note with his eerie, suspenseful masterpieces—*Rear Window, The Man Who Knew Too Much, Vertigo,* and *North by Northwest*—all made between 1954 and 1959.

THINK THROUGH HISTORY
C. *Clarifying* *How did radio and movies maintain their appeal in the 1950s?*

A Subculture Emerges

Although the mass media found a wide audience for their portrayals of mostly white popular culture, dissenting voices rang out throughout the 1950s. The messages of the beat movement in literature, and of rock 'n' roll in music, clashed with the tidy suburban view of life and set the stage for the counterculture that would burst forth in the 1960s.

C. Answer They concentrated on what they did best—local news, weather, and music programming on radio and size, color, and stereophonic sound in movies.

THE BEAT MOVEMENT Centered in San Francisco, Los Angeles, and New York City's Greenwich Village, the **beat movement** expressed the social and literary nonconformity of artists and poets. The word *beat* originally meant "weary" but came to refer as well to a musical beat.

Followers of this movement, called beats or **beatniks,** lived nonconformist lives and cared little for material goods. Many of the men wore sandals and beards; the women, black leotards and no lipstick. They picked up the "hip" language of jazz musicians—a vocabulary that included words such as *bread* for money and *pad* for apartment. They tended to shun regular work and to live in inexpensive, sparsely furnished rooms. They sought a higher consciousness through Zen Buddhism, music, and, sometimes, drugs.

Many beat poets and writers believed in imposing as little structure as possible on their artistic works, which often had a free, open form. They read their poetry aloud in coffeehouses and gathering places, such as poet and publisher Lawrence Ferlinghetti's City Lights Bookstore in San Francisco. Works that capture the essence of this era include Allen Ginsberg's long, free-verse poem *Howl,* published in 1956, and Jack Kerouac's novel of the movement, *On the Road,* published in 1957. This novel describes a nomadic search across America for authentic experiences, people, and values.

The beat generation marched to the tune of nonconformists like Jack Kerouac.

D. Answer Teenagers looking for alternatives to the conformity and consumerism of their parents found a celebration of poverty, nonconformity, and art that reflected immediate, sensory experience.

A PERSONAL VOICE

The only people for me are the mad ones, the ones who are mad to live, mad to talk, mad to be saved . . . the ones who never yawn or say a commonplace thing, but burn, burn, burn like fabulous yellow roman candles exploding like spiders across the stars.

JACK KEROUAC, *On the Road*

Many mainstream Americans found this lifestyle less enchanting. *Look* magazine proclaimed, "There's nothing really new about the beat philosophy. It consists merely of the average American's value scale—turned inside out. The goals of the Beat are *not* watching TV, *not* wearing gray flannel, *not* owning a home in the suburbs, and especially—*not* working." Although the beats' rebellion against consumerism and suburban living left many Americans cold, the beatnik attitudes, way of life, and literature attracted the attention of the media and fired the imaginations of many college students. *On the Road* sold half a million copies, and Ferlinghetti's *A Coney Island of the Mind* hundreds of thousands of copies—extraordinary sales for a book of poetry.

THINK THROUGH HISTORY
D. *Analyzing Causes* *Why do you think young Americans were attracted to the beat movement?*

ROCK 'N' ROLL While beats expressed themselves in unstructured literature, musicians in the 1950s added electronic instruments to traditional blues music,

OBJECTIVE
② INSTRUCT

A Subculture Emerges

▶ ***Starting with the Student***

- Pose this question to students: How do teenagers today express a lack of conformity with the social values of their parents? *Possible Responses: Through music, clothing styles, pierced body parts and tattoos, hair styles.*
- Ask students to identify values they think teenagers and young adults of the 1950s might have rejected. *Possible Responses: Social conformity, materialism, superficiality.*

▶ ***Discussing Key Ideas***

- The beat movement expresses social and literary nonconformity.
- Rock 'n' roll represents nonconformity in music.
- Radio disc jockeys, television, and movies bring rock 'n' roll into the mainstream of popular culture.

MORE ABOUT . . .
Jack Kerouac

The son of French-Canadian parents, Jack Kerouac was born in Massachusetts. He attended Columbia University and served in the navy. Kerouac's wanderings throughout the United States, Mexico, and Europe provided the background for his novels. *On the Road,* which he wrote in three weeks, tells of several beatniks who travel across the United States in search of personal fulfillment.

TEACHING OPTION

Skillbuilder Mini-Lesson: Analyzing Primary Sources

Explaining the Skill Works created by a member of a historical movement can tell historians much about the movement and about the society in which it developed. Such sources often reflect the person's strong feelings and attitudes. Therefore, identifying the writer or speaker of the material and investigating his or her attitudes helps historians assess the value of the source.

Applying the Skill Have students read about the beat movement and look at "A Personal Voice" on this page. Then ask these questions:

1. Is Jack Kerouac a good source for information about the beat movement? Why or why not? *Most will say yes, because he was a leader of the movement and felt passionately about it. He is not objective, but one should not expect him to be.*
2. What does Kerouac mean by the word *mad*? *Passionate, excited.*
3. What is Kerouac's message in this passage? *Possible Response: Kerouac is bored with traditional society and likes people who feel passion about life.*

IN-DEPTH RESOURCES: UNIT 5
Skillbuilder Practice: Primary Sources, p. 61

MORE ABOUT . . .
Elvis Presley

Ed Sullivan once condemned Elvis as "unfit for a family audience." In 1956, however, Sullivan hired Presley for three performances on his popular Sunday-night variety show. Sullivan paid Elvis an unprecedented $50,000, but he insisted that the gyrating performer be shown only from the waist up.

OBJECTIVE
③ INSTRUCT

African Americans and Popular Culture

▶ ***Starting with the Student***

- Ask students to identify the most popular African-American performers today.
- Discuss how those performers influence popular culture.
- Ask, Do you think there is enough integration in the media today?

▶ ***Discussing Key Ideas***

- Some African-American performers pave the way for minority representation in white-dominated entertainment.
- African-American radio stations appeal to black audiences.
- Throughout the 1950s, African Americans remain segregated from the dominant culture.

Jukeboxes in diners and other public places helped spread rock 'n' roll music to every part of the country.

creating rhythm and blues. In 1951, a Cleveland, Ohio, radio disc jockey, Alan Freed, was among the first to play this music, which was usually produced by African-American musicians for his mostly white audience. His listeners responded enthusiastically, and he gave the new music that grew out of rhythm and blues the name that has lasted: **rock 'n' roll.**

In the next few years, Little Richard, Chuck Berry, Bill Haley and the Comets, and especially Elvis Presley brought rock 'n' roll to a frantic pitch of popularity among the newly affluent teens who bought their records. The music's heavy rhythm, simple melodies, and lyrics—featuring love, cars, and the problems of being young—captivated teenagers across the country.

Elvis Presley, the King of Rock 'n' Roll, learned his music by singing in church and listening to country and blues music on the radio in Memphis, Tennessee. His mother gave him a guitar, and he paid four dollars of his own money to record two songs in 1953. Sam Phillips, a rhythm-and-blues producer, discovered Presley and produced his first records, which sold well. In 1955, Phillips sold Presley's contract to RCA for $35,000.

Presley's live appearances were immensely popular, and 45 of his records sold over a million copies, including "Heartbreak Hotel," "Hound Dog," "All Shook Up," "Don't Be Cruel," and "Burning Love." In 1956, he created a sensation on TV shows hosted by Steve Allen and Ed Sullivan and began his movie career by starring in *Love Me Tender.* Although *Look* magazine dismissed him as "a wild troubadour who wails rock 'n' roll tunes, flails erratically at a guitar, and wriggles like a peep-show dancer," Presley's rebellious style captivated young audiences. Girls screamed and fainted, and boys tried to imitate him.

Not surprisingly, many adults condemned rock 'n' roll. They believed that the new music would lead to teenage delinquency and immorality. In a few cities, rock 'n' roll concerts were banned. Citizens' groups tried to keep the records out of stores, and disc jockeys around the United States were fired or punished for playing the music. But despite this controversy, television and radio exposure helped bring rock 'n' roll into the mainstream, and it became more acceptable by the end of the decade. The long-running TV show *American Bandstand,* hosted by Dick Clark, featured wholesome rock 'n' roll singers and showed well-dressed, middle-class teenagers dancing to the music. Record sales, which were 189 million in 1950, grew with the popularity of rock 'n' roll, reaching 600 million in 1960.

E. Answer Radio disc jockeys played rock 'n' roll; TV variety shows promoted the stars and the music; movies featured Elvis Presley.

THINK THROUGH HISTORY
E. Recognizing Effects *How did radio, TV, and the movies contribute to the rise of rock 'n' roll?*

African Americans and Popular Culture

Many of the decade's great performers in all categories of popular culture were African American. Singers Nat Cole and Lena Horne, singer and actor Harry Belafonte, actor Sidney Poitier, and many others paved the way for minority representation in white-dominated fields. In 1956, CBS ran an all-black soap opera called *The Story of Ruby Valentine,* set in New York City's Harlem. Musicians Miles Davis, Sonny Rollins, Charlie Parker, Dizzy Gillespie, and Thelonius Monk entertained audiences of all races.

TEACHING OPTIONS

Making Connections Across the Curriculum

Music Much of the rock 'n' roll music of the 1950s has regained its popularity today. Have students listen to several rock 'n' roll hits of the 1950s, such as "Blue Suede Shoes," "Jailhouse Rock," or some favorites of their own. Ask the class to discuss the characteristics these songs have in common. *Possible Responses: Strong beat; simple melody; most feature electric guitar, drums, and piano; repetitive lyrics.* Ask, Why do you think this style appealed to teenagers? *Possible Responses: Easy to dance to; lyrics are about teenage interests and problems.*

Making Connections Across Cultures

African-American Influence Rock 'n' roll grew out of African-American music known as rhythm and blues, or "R&B." Echoing the rhythmic songs of Southern sharecroppers, rhythm and blues gained recognition in the early 1900s with such songs as "St. Louis Blues" by W. C. Handy. Just as jazz had been adapted for white audiences, during the 1950s musicians transformed black rhythm and blues into rock 'n' roll songs for teenagers. Have students discuss African-American influence on popular music of the 1990s.

But true integration in the media was slow in coming. Nat Cole, the first African American to have a weekly half-hour series on national television, observed, "There's a lot more integration in the actual life of the U.S. than you'll find on TV. But I notice that they always have integration in the prison scenes on television." Dick Clark integrated his popular *American Bandstand* in a pioneer 1957 broadcast. For the first time, black teenage couples joined white couples on the dance floor—and not one of the 15,000 letters Clark received every week complained. However, it was not until the middle of the next decade, when Duke Ellington's granddaughter performed with a mixed dance group, that professional dance on television was integrated.

Before integration reached radio audiences, popular African-American culture thrived on separate stations. By 1954, there were 250 radio stations nationwide aimed specifically at African-American listeners. Over 700 black DJs and a few white ones, including Alan Freed, played music by black artists like Amos Milburn, Little Esther, and a doo-wop group called the Orioles. These performers regularly reached the African-American top ten list, and their records sold upwards of 150,000 copies.

African-American stations were part of radio's attempt to counter the mass popularity of television by targeting specialized audiences. These stations also served advertisers, who wanted to reach a large African-American audience. But it was the black listeners—who had fewer television sets than whites and did not find themselves reflected in mainstream programming—who appreciated the stations most. Thulani Davis, a poet, journalist, and playwright, expressed the feelings of one listener about African-American radio (or "race radio" as the character called it) in her novel *1959*.

The Drifters' smooth, synchronized movements and mellow harmony helped win them a wide audience that included both blacks and whites.

F. Answer They reached receptive African Americans who didn't have TVs and were interested in enjoying their own culture.

THINK THROUGH HISTORY
F. Clarifying *How did radio stations help African-American performers gain wide audiences?*

A PERSONAL VOICE

Billie Holiday died and I turned twelve on the same hot July day. The saddest singing in the world was coming out of the radio, race radio that is, the radio of the race. The white stations were on the usual relentless rounds of Pat Boone, Teresa Brewer, and anybody else who couldn't sing but liked to cover songs that were once colored. . . . White radio was honest at least—they knew anybody in the South could tell Negro voices from white ones, and so they didn't play our stuff.

THULANI DAVIS, *1959*

At the end of the 1950s, African Americans were still largely segregated from the dominant culture. This ongoing segregation—and the racial tensions it fed—would become a powerful force for change in the turbulent 1960s.

Section 3 Assessment

1. TERMS & NAMES

Identify:
- mass media
- Federal Communications Commission (FCC)
- beat movement
- beatnik
- rock 'n' roll

2. SUMMARIZING Create a "Who's Who" chart of popular culture idols of the 1950s. Identify the art form each person was associated with and his or her major accomplishments.

Personality	Art Form	Accomplishments

3. COMPARING AND CONTRASTING In what ways were the rock 'n' roll musicians and the beat poets of the 1950s similar and different? Support your answer with details from the text.

THINK ABOUT
- the values the musicians and poets believed in
- people's reactions to them

4. FORMING OPINIONS From what you have learned about television of the 1950s, do you agree with Newton Minow's statement, on page 654, that it was "a vast wasteland"? Support your answer with details from the text.

THINK ABOUT
- the graphs on page 653
- the types of shows that appeared on television
- the way characters were portrayed and the values they expressed

MORE ABOUT . . .
Thulani Davis

In her novel *1959,* Thulani Davis describes life in a small Southern town at the start of the civil rights movement. In addition to writing poetry, prose, and plays, Davis also wrote the libretto for the opera *X: The Life and Times of Malcolm X.*

ASSESS & RETEACH

Section 3 Assessment

Have students work in study groups to locate the passage in the text that answers each question.

Self-Assessment

Have students reinforce their understanding of this section by writing two or three sentences summarizing each subsection.

Section Quiz

FORMAL ASSESSMENT
Section Quiz, p. 238

Reteach

Have students form small groups to compare their "Who's Who" charts of culture idols from Item 2 in the section assessment.

CLOSE

Popular culture of the 1950s reflected the values of white middle-class Americans. The beat movement and rock 'n' roll expressed nonconformity that appealed to young people. African-American performers influenced popular culture but generally remained excluded from it.

ANSWERS

1. TERMS & NAMES

mass media, p. 652

Federal Communications Commission (FCC), p. 652

beat movement, p. 655

beatnik, p. 655

rock 'n' roll, p. 656

2. SUMMARIZING

Possible Responses:
Lucille Ball/television/star of *I Love Lucy*; Edward R. Murrow/television/host of *Person to Person;* Alfred Hitchcock/movies/director of thrillers; Sidney Poitier/movies/actor; Elvis Presley/music/rock 'n' roll star; Jack Kerouac/ literature/beat novelist and author of *On the Road.*

3. COMPARING AND CONTRASTING

Possible Answers: Both were rebellious, spontaneous, experimental, and innovative; often wore nonconformist clothing; attracted the young as well as alienated older, middle-class Americans; and performed for live audiences. Rock 'n' roll performers probably had a wider popular audience, due to their promotion in the mass media.

4. FORMING OPINIONS

Possible Answers: Agree—TV provided mass appeal by addressing mainstream America. Programs presented idealized white values and ignored the problems and realities of minorities. Disagree—TV programs provided needed entertainment and escape for many people and also portrayed the ideal family life that many valued.

Daily Life

OBJECTIVES

1. To describe the broader role of teenagers in postwar America.
2. To explain how teenagers' new social and economic significance helped shape American popular culture.

FOCUS & MOTIVATE

▶ ***Starting with the Student***
Have students compare and contrast American popular music of their generation with that of their parents' or guardians' generation.

- What is similar and different about the music?
- What role, if any, does dancing play in the music's popularity?

MORE ABOUT . . .
Rock 'n' Roll

Early in the 1950s, young white audiences seeking something to dance to turned increasingly to rhythm and blues, a lively form of music popular with black musicians. White performers brought to the mix an infusion of country music, and rock 'n' roll was born. Its early stars were both black (Chuck Berry, Little Richard, Fats Domino) and white (Buddy Holly, Elvis Presley, Jerry Lee Lewis, Bill Haley and the Comets). The term *rock 'n' roll* was popularized by Cleveland disc jockey Alan Freed in his radio show "Moondog Rock 'n' Roll Party."

The Emergence of the Teenager

Life after World War II brought changes in the family. For the first time, the teenage years were recognized as an important and unique developmental stage between childhood and adulthood. The booming postwar economy made it possible for teenagers to stay in school instead of working to help support their families and allowed their parents to give them generous allowances. American business, particularly the music and movie industries, rushed to court this new consumer group. Ads, like this one for the soft drink Seven-Up, used clever slogans about the latest trends to influence teens' decisions about which products to buy.

Slumber party? Gee, that's dandy!
Look your sharpest, everyone!
Snappy PJ's come in handy–
"Fresh up" parties sure are fun!
"Fresh up" with Seven-Up!
THE ALL-FAMILY DRINK! Enjoy sparkling, crystal-clear 7-Up . . . often. Seven-Up is so pure, so good, so wholesome that everybody—from tiny tots to grandmas and all ages in between—may "fresh up" to his heart's content. And 7-Up makes food taste extra good. So have a Stackwich with chilled 7-Up. Buy 7-Up wherever you see those bright 7-Up signs.
You like it ... it likes you!

1 THE TEEN MOVIE SCENE
Teenagers with money in their pockets often found themselves at the movies. Hollywood responded by producing films especially for them, like *The Blackboard Jungle*. This film tells the story of the confrontation between an idealistic young teacher and a gang of delinquents.

RECOMMENDED RESOURCES

Books

Breines, Wini. *Young, White, and Miserable.* Boston: Beacon, 1992. One person's experience of growing up female in 1950s America.

Crenshaw, Marshall. *Hollywood Rock.* New York: Harper, 1994. This guide to rock 'n' roll in films covers most of the movies geared to teens.

Gillett, Charlie. *The Sound of the City.* New York: Da Capo, 1996. The rise of rock 'n' roll.

Horsley, E. M. *The 1950s.* New York: Mallard, 1990. A pictorial history.

Tobler, John. *30 Years of Rock.* New York: Exeter, 1985. The story of rock music by a noted rock historian.

Videos

American Graffiti. Dir. George Lucas. 1973. MCA Universal Home Video, 1991. This award-winning PG-rated film vividly captures the pastimes and music of teens in the early 1960s.

The Blackboard Jungle. Dir. Richard Brooks. 1955. MGM/UA Home Video, 1989. Based on an Evan Hunter novel, this famous film about troubled youth played Bill Haley's "Rock Around the Clock" during the opening credits—the first major use of rock 'n' roll in a movie.

History of Rock 'n' Roll. Warner Home Video, 1995. A ten-part series, with the first two parts focusing on fifties music.

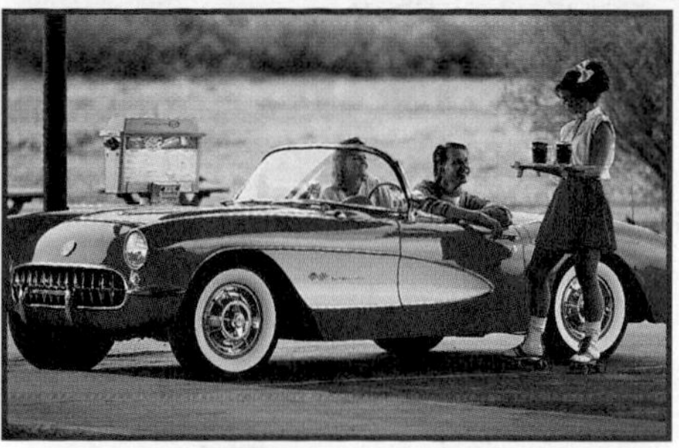

❷ TEENS AS CONSUMERS
Pimple creams and lipsticks were just a few of the products aimed at teenagers with money to spend. Teens even dreamed of buying their own cars. This 1953 Corvette was simply "the rage."

❸ ROCKING TO A NEW BEAT
Teenagers seeking an identity found it in rock 'n' roll, a fresh form of music that delighted teenagers and enraged their parents. Elvis Presley (*right*), the King of Rock 'n' Roll, helped create the new sound by blending country, gospel, and the African-American rhythm and blues sung by performers such as B. B. King (*below*). The songs' insistent beat underscored themes of alienation and unhappiness in love.

DATA FILE

U.S. School Enrollments, 1950–1990

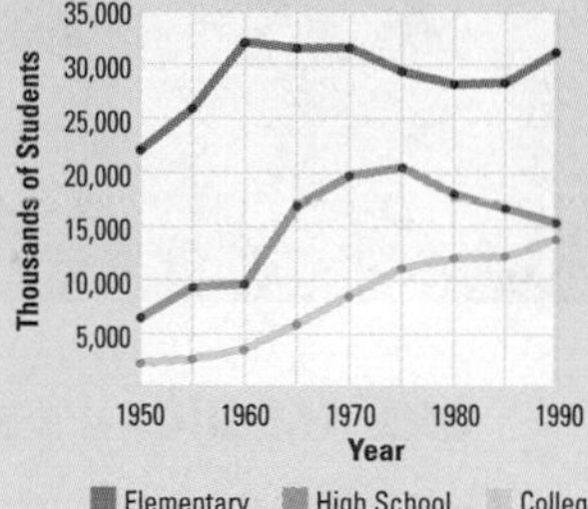

Source: *Statistical Abstract of the United States, 1995*

Teenagers and Employment, 1950–1990

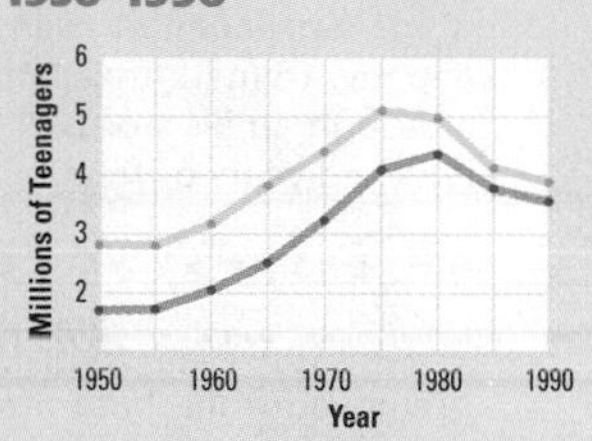

Source: *Statistical Abstract of the United States, 1995*

Teenage Tidbits

- A *Life* magazine survey showed that, during the 1950s, teenagers spent $20 million on lipstick alone.
- In 1956, a total of 42,000 drive-in movie theaters—heavily frequented by teenagers—took in one-quarter of the year's total box-office receipts.
- College enrollments more than doubled between 1946 and 1960.
- Weekly credit payment for record player—$1.00

INTERACT WITH HISTORY

1. **INTERPRETING DATA** What were the causes of the emergence of the teenage market in the 1950s? To answer the question, review the entire feature, including the Data File.
2. **ANALYZING MOVIES TODAY** What types of movies do American movie studios make for the teenage market today? How do these movies differ from those made in the 1950s?

Visit http://www.mlushistory.com for more about youth in the 1950s.

INSTRUCT

▶ *Starting with the Student*
- Have students share what they know about teenage lifestyles in the 1950s.
- If possible, bring in and play a few recordings by fifties rockers such as Elvis Presley and Little Richard. Then have students discuss their reactions to the music.

▶ *Discussing Key Ideas*
- New attitudes and affluence give postwar American teenagers more influence than ever before.
- Teenage consumers affect product development, advertising, and aspects of popular culture such as music and films.

HISTORY FROM VISUALS

Reading the Images
Have students examine the illustrations.
- Ask them to jot down adjectives to describe the car shown near the top of page 659. *Possible Responses: Shiny, colorful, antique, snazzy, old fashioned.*
- Ask, What is your reaction to the Seven-Up ad? Why? *Possible Responses: Students who find the ad pleasant or effective may mention the smiling faces, bright colors, and relaxed attitudes. Those who find it corny or old-fashioned may mention outdated slang, such as "Gee, that's dandy!"*

INTERACT WITH HISTORY

1. Interpreting Data

Possible Answers: *New social attitudes placed more significance on the teen years and distinguished teenagers from both children and adults; economic affluence allowed parents to give teenagers an allowance, enabled more teenagers to remain in school instead of leaving early to help support the family, and provided part-time and summer jobs for those who wished to work; the resulting increase in teens' spending money made them a potent new consumer group, prompting product manufacturers and pop culture to cater to the teen market; advertising whetted that market's appetite.*

2. Analyzing Movies Today

In identifying types of movies made today, students may mention action films, horror films, science fiction, films with popular music scores, and films with popular young stars, among other things. In comparing the movies of today with those of the fifties, students might mention more sophisticated special effects, few black-and-white films, less about fifties subjects like the Cold War, different slang and other dialogue, and changes in viewing venues (home viewing on videotape, few drive-ins). Accept all reasonable responses, and encourage students to pool their ideas orally or on group lists.

Section 4 Overview

OBJECTIVES

1. To explain how the white migration to suburbs created an urban crisis.
2. To describe attempts of minorities to relieve poverty and gain equal rights.

CRITICAL THINKING

- Recognizing effects, p. 660
- Analyzing causes, p. 661
- Theme: Democracy in America, p. 663
- Summarizing, p. 663
- Forming opinions, p. 663
- Drawing conclusions, p. 663

FOCUS & MOTIVATE

5-MINUTE WARM-UP

Recognizing Point of View
To examine the lives of people who did not benefit from the prosperity of the 1950s, have students read One American's Story on page 660 and answer these questions.

1. Did James Baldwin offer a pessimistic or optimistic view of America in the 1950s?
2. Why do you think he held this point of view?

 ***WARM-UP TRANSPARENCY 19***

▶ ***Starting with the Student***
- Ask students to think of a time when they felt overlooked or invisible.

OBJECTIVE
① **INSTRUCT**

The Urban Poor

▶ ***Discussing Key Ideas***
- In the wake of white flight, poor whites and minorities move to cities.
- Many Americans remain unaware of urban poverty.
- Urban renewal fails to provide adequate housing for the urban poor.

IN-DEPTH RESOURCES: UNIT 5
Guided Reading, p. 60
Primary Source: from *The Other America*, p. 66

ACCESS FOR STUDENTS ACQUIRING ENGLISH
Guided Reading (Spanish), p. 219

4 The Other America

TERMS & NAMES
- urban renewal
- bracero
- termination policy

LEARN ABOUT the existence of poverty in the United States in the 1950s
TO UNDERSTAND the other side of the American dream.

ONE AMERICAN'S STORY

James Baldwin was born in New York City, the eldest of nine children, and grew up in the poverty of the Harlem ghetto. As a novelist, essayist, and playwright, he eloquently portrayed the struggles of African Americans against racial injustice and discrimination. He believed that blacks inhabited a country other than that of whites in mainstream America—a country without rights, privileges, or even hope. He wrote a letter to his young nephew to mark the 100th anniversary of emancipation, although, in his words, "the country is celebrating one hundred years of freedom one hundred years too soon."

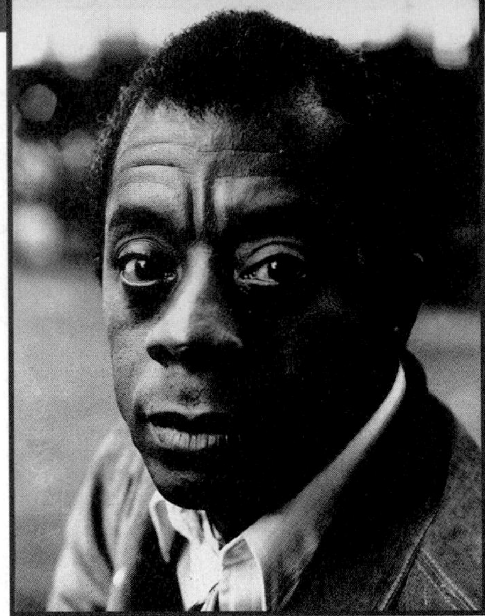
James Baldwin

A PERSONAL VOICE

These innocent and well-meaning people, your countrymen, have caused you to be born under conditions not very far removed from those described for us by Charles Dickens in the London of more than a hundred years ago. . . . This innocent country set you down in the ghetto in which, in fact, it intended that you should perish. . . . You were born where you were born and faced the future that you faced because you were black and *for no other reason.*

JAMES BALDWIN, *The Fire Next Time*

For many Americans, the 1950s were a time of unprecedented prosperity. But not everyone experienced this well-being. In the "other" America, about 40 million people lived in poverty, untouched by the economic boom.

The Urban Poor

Despite the portrait painted by popular culture, life in postwar America was not the "nifty fifties" for all Americans. In 1962, nearly one out of every four Americans was living below the poverty level. Many of these poor were elderly people, single women with children, or members of minority groups, including African Americans, Latinos, and Native Americans.

WHITE FLIGHT In the 1950s, millions of middle-class white Americans left the cities for the suburbs, taking with them precious economic resources and isolating themselves from other races and classes. At the same time, the rural poor migrated to the inner cities. Between the end of World War II and 1960, for example, nearly 5 million African Americans moved from the rural South to urban areas.

The urban crisis prompted by the "white flight" had a direct impact on poor whites and nonwhites. The cities lost not only people and businesses but also the property and income taxes they had paid. City governments could no longer afford to properly maintain or improve schools, public transportation, and police and fire departments—and the urban poor suffered. As one urban planner observed, "We turned our cities into doughnuts with all the dough [or money] around the center and nothing in the middle."

A. Answer Loss of people and income, leading to decaying ghettos.

THINK THROUGH HISTORY
A. Recognizing Effects *What effect did white flight have on America's cities?*

SECTION 4 RESOURCES

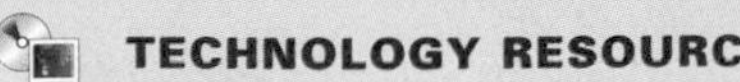

PRINT RESOURCES

IN-DEPTH RESOURCES: UNIT 5
Guided Reading, p. 60
Primary Sources: from *The Other America* by Michael Harrington, p. 66; The Voluntary Relocation Program, p. 67

READING STUDY GUIDE, p. 203

ACCESS FOR STUDENTS ACQUIRING ENGLISH
Guided Reading (Spanish), p. 219

SPANISH READING STUDY GUIDE, p. 203

FORMAL ASSESSMENT
Section Quiz, p. 239

ALTERNATIVE ASSESSMENT BOOK
See forms for supporting and scoring alternative activities.

TECHNOLOGY RESOURCES

HUMANITIES TRANSPARENCIES
H26, *Her World* by Philip Evergood

CRITICAL THINKING TRANSPARENCIES
CT27, Postwar Boom

CD-ROM Electronic Library of Primary Sources

VIDEO *American Portfolio: A Videodisc for U.S. History* user's guide, pp. 236, 237

INTERNET http://www.mlushistory.com

THE INNER CITIES While poverty grew rapidly in the decaying inner cities, many suburban Americans remained unaware of it. Some even refused to believe that poverty could exist in the richest, most powerful nation on the earth. And the urban poor had few advocates to call attention to their segregated ghettos. Many politicians, economists, and journalists advanced the belief that poverty in America was on the road to extinction. An article in *Fortune* magazine, for example, declared in 1960 that poverty in the United States would be eliminated by the end of the decade.

After living among the nation's poor across America, however, Michael Harrington published a shocking account that starkly illuminated the issue of poverty. In *The Other America: Poverty in the United States* (1962), he not only confirmed that widespread poverty existed but also exposed its brutal reality.

B. Answer Because the building boom primarily took place in the suburbs; because of lack of jobs, discrimination, and the impact of white flight.

THINK THROUGH HISTORY
B. ***Analyzing Causes*** *Why were poor people unable to find decent housing, despite the building boom in the 1950s?*

A PERSONAL VOICE

The poor live in a culture of poverty. . . .The poor get sick more than anyone else in the society. . . . When they become sick, they are sick longer than any other group in the society. Because they are sick more often and longer than anyone else, they lose wages and work, and find it difficult to hold a steady job. And because of this, they cannot pay for good housing, for a nutritious diet, for doctors . . . [and] their prospect is to move to an even lower level . . . toward even more suffering.

MICHAEL HARRINGTON, *The Other America*

URBAN RENEWAL Although millions of new homes were built in the suburbs in the 1950s, few of them were available to the nation's poor. Most African Americans, Native Americans, and Latinos not only could not afford homes in the suburbs but also were rarely welcome there. Instead, they were forced to live in dirty, crowded urban slums. A Texas newspaper described how almost 200,000 Mexican Americans in a San Antonio barrio lived like penned cattle in a stockyard "with roofed-over corrals for homes and chutes for streets."

One proposed solution to the housing problem in inner cities was **urban renewal.** The National Housing Act of 1949 was passed to provide "a decent home and a suitable living environment for every American family." This act called for tearing down rundown neighborhoods and constructing low-income housing.

Although dilapidated areas were razed, parking lots, shopping centers, highways, parks, and factories were constructed on some of the cleared land, and there was seldom enough new housing built to accommodate all the displaced people. For example, a barrio in Los Angeles was torn down to make way for Dodger Stadium, and poor people who were displaced from their homes simply moved from one ghetto to another. Some critics of urban renewal claimed that it had merely become urban *removal.*

ECONOMIC BACKGROUND

WHERE IS THE POVERTY LINE?

The poverty line, calculated each year by the federal government, is the minimum amount of annual income that an individual or a family needs in order to survive in the United States. In 1959, the poverty line for a family of four was $2,973; in 1996, it was $15,600.

Originally, the poverty line was based on a food budget that provided just enough nutrition to maintain decent health. This number was multiplied by three because a third of a family's total household budget was typically spent on food.

Since 1969, however, the government has determined the poverty line by simply readjusting the previous year's figure to take inflation into account. (See *poverty* on page 936 in the Economics Handbook.)

Poverty Thresholds for a Family of Four

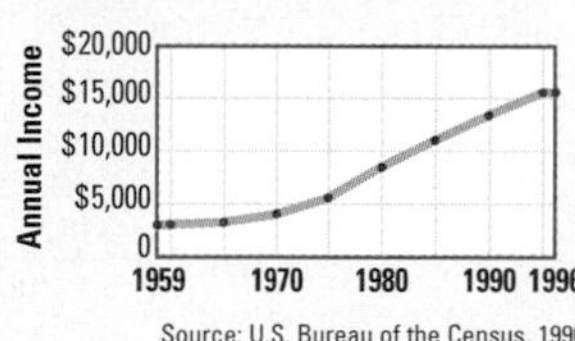

Source: U.S. Bureau of the Census, 1996

Mexican Americans and Native Americans

Despite ongoing poverty, during the 1950s African Americans began to make significant strides toward the reduction of racial discrimination and segregation. (See Chapter 21.) Inspired by the African-American civil rights movement, other minorities also began to develop a deeper political awareness and a voice. Mexican-American activism gathered steam after veterans returned from World War II, and a drastic change in government policy under Eisenhower's administration fueled Native American protest.

MEXICAN-AMERICAN ACTIVISM Many Mexicans had become citizens during the 19th century, when the United States had annexed the Southwest after

ECONOMIC BACKGROUND

Where is the Poverty Line?

Critical Thinking: Evaluating Ask students to discuss the reason the government established a poverty line. *Possible Response: To determine who is eligible for welfare.*

HUMANITIES TRANSPARENCIES
H26, *Her World* by Philip Evergood

ELECTRONIC LIBRARY OF PRIMARY SOURCES
from *The Other America* by Michael Harrington

Issues for the 21st Century

Breaking the Cycle of Poverty

Connect poverty in the 1950s with poverty today by having students read pages 896–899. Then have them answer these questions.

1. Is poverty a worse problem today than it was in the 1950s? *Answers will vary.*
2. Does discrimination still contribute to poverty as it did in the 1950s? *Answers will vary.*
3. How is welfare reform likely to affect poverty in America today? *Answers will vary.*

OBJECTIVE

② INSTRUCT

Mexican Americans and Native Americans

▶ ***Discussing Key Ideas***

• Mexican Americans play a

(continued on next page)

Block Schedule TEACHING OPTION **Time Needed: 20 Minutes**

Cooperative Activity: Preparing a Family Budget

Task: Student groups will prepare a basic budget for a family of four (earning $15,600 a year), based on average costs in their community.

Purpose: To understand the difficulty in managing income to cover expenses.

Activity: Three student groups will calculate expenses for food, shelter, and other necessities (clothing, utilities, transportation, medical care). Each group will have $5,200—one third of the family's income—to budget. Students should use local newspaper ads to determine costs. Have students compile data to create the family budget for one year, using a chart similar to the one shown.

One Year's Budget

Food		Transportation	
Shelter		Medical care	
Clothing		Other	
Utilities			

Based on this budget, discuss whether a family with this income—at the poverty level—could provide for its needs.

ALTERNATIVE ASSESSMENT BOOK
Standards for Evaluating a Cooperative Activity

(continued from page 661)

major role in the development of the Southwest yet continue to confront racism and discrimination.

- An insult to the memory of Felix Longoria, a World War II hero, prompts some Mexican Americans to organize.
- Native Americans establish the National Congress of American Indians to work for civil rights for Native Americans.
- The federal government adopts the termination policy, which halted the reservation system for Native Americans and eventually proves to be a failure.

MORE ABOUT . . .
Braceros

After World War II, an increase in agricultural land, due to irrigation, created demand for cheap farm labor. In 1951, Congress enacted a temporary work program that permitted braceros to enter the United States for seasonal work. In 1962, braceros came under the minimum wage law. In 1965, the braceros program ended.

MORE ABOUT . . .
Native American Culture

A Seminole petition to President Eisenhower expressed Native American attitudes toward the government policy of assimilation: ". . . we are not White Men but Indians, do not wish to become White Men but wish to remain Indians, and have an outlook on all things different from the outlook of the White Man."

IN-DEPTH RESOURCES: UNIT 5
Primary Source: The Voluntary Relocation Program, p. 67

"[The braceros were a] highly regimented and effective labor force."

ERASMO GAMBOA, HISTORIAN

the War with Mexico. Large numbers of Mexicans had also crossed the border to work in the United States during and after World War I. Most of them were miners, railroad workers, or migrant workers employed temporarily.

When the United States entered World War II, the shortage of agricultural laborers spurred the federal government to initiate, in 1942, a program in which Mexican **braceros,** or hired hands, were allowed into the United States to harvest crops. More than 200,000 braceros entered the United States on a short-term basis between 1942 and 1947. When their employment was ended, the braceros were expected to return to Mexico. However, many remained in the United States illegally.

In addition to the braceros who remained past their work contracts, hundreds of thousands of Mexicans entered the country illegally to escape poor economic conditions in Mexico. To stop the flow of illegal migrants, in 1954 the United States launched Operation Wetback, a federal program designed to find illegal aliens and return them to Mexico. (Many Mexicans swam across the Rio Grande to reach the United States illegally, and were labeled with the derogatory name *wetbacks.*) Between 1953 and 1955, the United States government deported more than 2 million illegal aliens.

Although Mexican Americans had played a major role in the economic growth of the Southwest, they still encountered prejudice and discrimination. Change occurred after World War II, in which almost 350,000 Mexican Americans had fought for democracy. Returning to civilian life, they were determined to keep fighting for democracy at home—to remedy poor living conditions and wage discrimination. Many were hampered by poor job skills and lack of fluency in English, but they wanted opportunities to become well educated and to earn a decent living.

The body of Felix Longoria was buried in Arlington National Cemetery after a Texas undertaker refused to bury him.

THE LONGORIA INCIDENT Some Mexican Americans were shocked into organized action by an insult to the family of Felix Longoria. Longoria was a Mexican-American World War II hero who had been killed in the Philippines. The only undertaker in his hometown in Texas refused to let the Longoria family use his funeral home because they were "Mexicans." To protest this and other injustices, Mexican-American veterans organized the American G.I. Forum in 1948.

Soon after the Longoria incident, Ignacio Lopez founded the Unity League of California to register Mexican-American voters and to promote candidates who would represent them. In response to league actions, California outlawed segregated classrooms for Mexican Americans. Similar voter-registration groups developed in Arizona and Texas. The Asociación Nacional México-Americana and the League of United Latin American Citizens coordinated efforts to end discrimination, giving Mexican Americans a nationwide political voice.

NATIVE AMERICANS CONTINUE THEIR STRUGGLE Native Americans also continued to fight for their rights and identity. From the passage of the Dawes Act in 1887 until 1934, the policy of the federal government toward Native Americans had been one of "Americanization" and assimilation. In 1924, all Native Americans were made citizens of the United States, but they remained second-class citizens.

In 1934, the Indian Reorganization Act moved official policy away from assimilation and toward Native American autonomy. Its passage signaled a change in federal policy. In addition, because the government was reeling from the Great Depression, it didn't want to continue subsidizing the Native Americans. The act mandated changes in three areas—economic, cultural, and political:

TEACHING OPTIONS

Teaching Less Proficient Readers

Context Clues Ask students to list words in this section that are unfamiliar to them. Then use the word *advocates* on p. 661 to demonstrate the following steps for using context clues to decode unfamiliar words:

1. Read the sentence that contains the word, as well as the sentence before and after it.
2. Determine the general meaning of the text.
3. Substitute familiar words in the sentence to see if they make sense. *(defenders, supporters, promoters)*

Have students follow these steps to decode other difficult words.

Exploring Themes

Democracy in America During the 1950s, one third of the Mexican Americans in the United States lived below the poverty level. Native Americans remained the poorest minority. These groups were part of the invisible poor—on the other side of the American dream. Have student groups act as advocates for Mexican Americans and Native Americans in the 1950s. Ask them to write petitions listing grievances and suggesting solutions.

C. Answer Mexican Americans and Native Americans formed organizations to register voters and protest discrimination.

THINK THROUGH HISTORY
C. THEME ***Democracy in America*** *How did Mexican Americans and Native Americans work to increase their political participation?*

- economic—Native American lands were no longer to be broken up into individual farms, but would belong to a tribe as a whole.
- cultural—the number of boarding schools for Native American children was cut back, and children could attend day schools on the reservations.
- political—Native American tribes were given permission to elect tribal councils to govern their reservations.

Native Americans also took the initiative to improve their own lives. In 1944, they established the National Congress of American Indians. The organization eventually included some 90 tribes—two-thirds of all the Native Americans in the nation. The congress had two main goals: (1) to ensure for Native Americans the same civil rights that white Americans had, and (2) to enable Native Americans on reservations to retain their own customs.

During World War II, some 65,000 Native Americans left their reservations for military service and war work. As a result, they became very aware of discrimination. When the war ended Native Americans stopped receiving family allotments and wages. Outsiders also grabbed control of tribal lands, primarily to exploit their deposits of minerals, oil, and timber.

Native Americans like the man shown here received job training sponsored by the Bureau of Indian Affairs to help them settle in urban areas.

THE TERMINATION POLICY In 1953, the federal government announced that it would give up its responsibility for Native American tribes. This new approach, known as the **termination policy,** eliminated federal economic support, discontinued the reservation system, and distributed tribal lands among individual Native Americans. Between 1954 and 1960, the federal government withdrew financial support from 61 reservations. But the states—not the tribal leaders—maintained authority over civil and criminal cases on the reservations, and thousands of acres of tribal lands were sold to developers.

In response to the termination policy, the Bureau of Indian Affairs began a voluntary relocation program to help Native Americans resettle in cities. The bureau helped them find a place to live, paid moving costs and living expenses, and helped them find work and adjust to their new communities.

The termination policy was a dismal failure, however. Although the Bureau of Indian Affairs helped relocate 35,000 Native Americans to urban areas during the 1950s, they were often unable to find jobs in their new homes because of poor training and racial prejudice. They were also left without access to medical care when federal programs were abolished. And the number of Native Americans on state welfare rolls soared. In 1963, the termination policy was abandoned.

By the early 1960s, contrary to the optimistic prophecies of *Fortune* magazine, poverty had not disappeared. In fact, the poor had become more visible than ever. The other America could no longer be ignored.

Section  Assessment

1. TERMS & NAMES

Identify:
- urban renewal
- bracero
- termination policy

2. SUMMARIZING In overlapping circles like the one below, fill in the common problems that African Americans, Mexican Americans, and Native Americans faced during the 1950s.

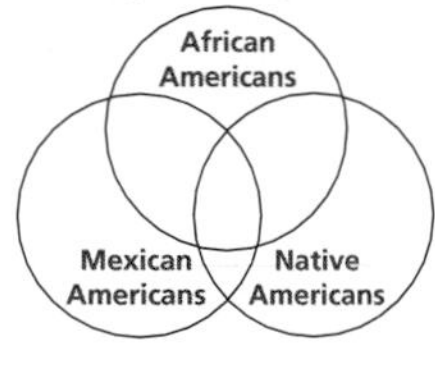

3. FORMING OPINIONS Do you think that urban renewal was an effective approach to the housing problem in inner cities? Why or why not?

THINK ABOUT
- the goals of the National Housing Act of 1949
- the claims made by some critics of urban renewal

4. DRAWING CONCLUSIONS Which major population shift—"white flight," migration from Mexico, or relocation of Native Americans—do you think had the greatest impact on society? Why?

THINK ABOUT
- the impact of "white flight"
- the outcome of Operation Wetback
- the effects of the termination policy

ANSWERS

1. TERMS & NAMES

urban renewal, p. 661

bracero, p. 662

termination policy, p. 663

2. SUMMARIZING

Possible Responses: Poverty, inadequate housing, uphill struggle to end discrimination and social injustice, limited job opportunities, limited social mobility, harsh or ineffective government policies, few advocates among mainstream public, second-class citizenship, exclusion from the American dream.

3. FORMING OPINIONS

Possible Responses: Effective—Its ultimate goal was to construct affordable housing for the poor, and it did tear down many bad areas and put up some new housing. Ineffective—It did not provide enough new housing and displaced many poor people when old housing was torn down.

4. DRAWING CONCLUSIONS

Possible Responses: White flight—It caused polarization of rich and poor and suburban and urban cultures. Migration of Mexicans—Mexican immigrants met with opposition because they provided job competition. Native American relocation—It displaced an entire group of people without providing an effective alternative way of life and put a strain on urban resources.

MORE ABOUT . . .
Native American Relocation

Between 30 and 70 percent of the Native Americans who relocated to cities returned to reservations. Lack of economic opportunity was an important factor. Many people also cited the need to preserve their Native American identity as a reason for returning to tribal lands.

ASSESS & RETEACH

Section 4 Assessment

Assign questions as homework or a class activity.

Self Assessment

Hold an informal debate in which students take the positions they took in their answer to Item 4 in the section assessment. Make sure they use references to the text to support their positions.

Section Quiz

FORMAL ASSESSMENT
Section Quiz, p. 239

Reteach

Have students review main understandings of this section by creating a chart comparing minority groups with middle-class white Americans in the 1950s. Bases of comparison might include living conditions, employment opportunities, and quality of life.

 ***CRITICAL THINKING TRANSPARENCIES***
CT27, Postwar Boom

CLOSE

While white middle-class Americans pursued the American dream, the "other" Americans lived in a culture of poverty. African Americans, Mexican Americans, and Native Americans were among the groups who were largely excluded from the economic prosperity of the 1950s.

CHAPTER 19
ASSESSMENT ANSWERS

REVIEWING THE CHAPTER

TERMS & NAMES

1. suburb, p. 636
2. Dixiecrat, p. 640
3. Fair Deal, p. 641
4. conglomerate, p. 643
5. baby boom, p. 645
6. mass media, p. 652
7. beat movement, p. 655
8. rock 'n' roll, p. 656
9. urban renewal, p. 661
10. bracero, p. 662

MAIN IDEAS

11. Tuition reimbursements provided an incentive for education; a year's unemployment benefits gave financial support for job searches; loans helped them buy homes, buy farms, or establish businesses.

12. The Korean War stalemate, the rise of McCarthyism, the threat of communism, the expanding power of the federal government, alleged corruption among Truman's political allies, inflation, and labor unrest.

13. An increase in the minimum wage, expanded social security coverage, increased funding for low-income housing.

14. By 1956, the majority of Americans held white-collar jobs.

15. Suburbia offered affordable single-family houses, good schools, a safe environment for children, and neighbors like themselves.

16. Local programming of news, weather, music, and community issues; targeting specific audiences, such as African Americans.

17. Beatniks shunned the conformity, the planning for the future, and the materialism that characterized mainstream American values.

18. They became actors and singers, and their music greatly influenced rock 'n' roll.

19. Many white families moved to the suburbs and the rural poor moved into the cities, which contributed to the economic decline of many large cities.

20. Racial prejudice, poor training, lack of work, and no access to medical care.

Chapter 19 Assessment

REVIEWING THE CHAPTER

TERMS & NAMES For each item below, write a sentence explaining its historical significance in the 1950s. For each person below, explain his role in that period.

1. **suburb**
2. **Dixiecrat**
3. **Fair Deal**
4. **conglomerate**
5. **baby boom**
6. **mass media**
7. **beat movement**
8. **rock 'n' roll**
9. **urban renewal**
10. **bracero**

MAIN IDEAS

SECTION 1 *(pages 636–642)*

Postwar America

11. How did the GI Bill of Rights help World War II veterans make the transition to civilian life?
12. What domestic and foreign issues concerned voters during the 1952 presidential election?
13. What similar legislative measures did Presidents Truman and Eisenhower push through Congress?

SECTION 2 *(pages 643–649)*

The American Dream in the Fifties

14. What shift in employment trends had occurred by the mid-1950s?
15. How did life in the suburbs provide the model for the American dream?

SECTION 3 *(pages 652–657)*

Popular Culture

16. What strategies did radio stations use to counteract the mass popularity of television?
17. How did the values of the beatniks differ from those of mainstream America of the 1950s?
18. How did African-American performers influence American popular culture in the 1950s?

SECTION 4 *(pages 660–663)*

The Other America

19. How did many major cities change in the 1950s?
20. What obstacles to improving their lives did Native Americans face in the 1950s?

THINKING CRITICALLY

1. **TECHNOLOGICAL BREAKTHROUGHS** Create a web like the one below to show the four postwar technological breakthroughs that you consider to be most influential.

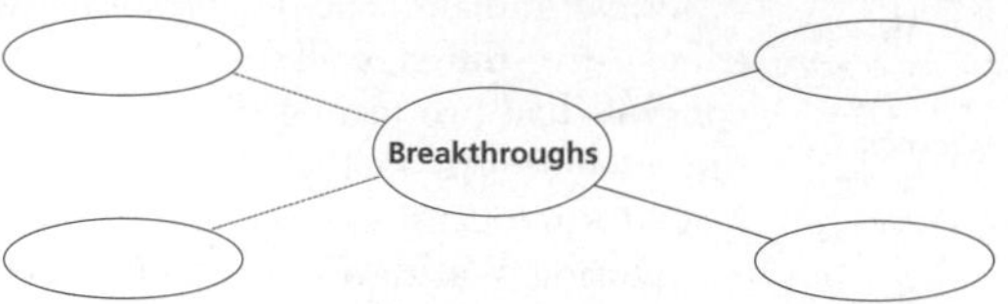

2. **FASTER, FARTHER, HIGHER** In what way do you think the fast pace of American life today had its origins in the 1950s? Support your answer with examples.
3. **MORE FOR FEWER** Do you agree or disagree with the quotation from *Life* magazine on page 634? Support your answer with evidence from the chapter.
4. **TRACING THEMES CULTURAL DIVERSITY** Why do you think many middle-class Americans tended to have little awareness and appreciation of cultural diversity during the 1950s?
5. **FROM INDIVIDUALIST TO ORGANIZATION MAN** During the first two centuries of America's history, the national character was marked by pioneering individualism. Why do you think that conformity became the norm during the 1950s?
6. **ANALYZING PRIMARY SOURCES** Read the following excerpt from *The Hidden Persuaders* by Vance Packard, about the psychology of advertising during the 1950s. Then answer the questions.

> On May 18, 1956, *The New York Times* printed a remarkable interview with a young man named Gerald Stahl, executive vice-president of the Package Designers Council. He stated: "Psychiatrists say that people have so much to choose from that they need help—they will like the package that hypnotizes them into picking it." He urged food packers to put more hypnosis into their package designing, so that the housewife will stick out her hand for it rather than one of many rivals.
>
> Mr. Stahl found that it takes the average woman exactly twenty seconds to cover an aisle in a supermarket if she doesn't tarry; so a good package design would hypnotize the woman like a flashlight waved in front of her eyes.
>
> **VANCE PACKARD,** *The Hidden Persuaders*

How are women shoppers of the 1950s portrayed in this excerpt? Do you think this description applies to shoppers today? Support your answer with reasons.

THINKING CRITICALLY

1. TECHNOLOGICAL BREAKTHROUGHS
Possible Responses: Hi-fidelity record players; television sets; Teflon-coated cookware; polyester fabrics; various plastic products; electric household appliances; frozen TV dinners.

2. FASTER, FARTHER, HIGHER
Possible Responses: Evidence of the emphasis on speed and efficiency in the 1950s included construction of the interstate highway system, mass production of communities like Levittown, the rise of fast-food franchises, and an explosion of labor-saving devices. These trends have continued, resulting in today's instant foods, microwave ovens, automated teller machines, computer technology, and pay-per-view television.

3. MORE FOR FEWER
Possible Responses: Agree—Many elderly people, single women with children, and members of minority groups lived in poverty, untouched by the general economic boom. Disagree—The 1950s was a time of unprecedented prosperity for growing numbers of Americans, and by the end of the decade, America had the highest standard of living in the world.

ALTERNATIVE ASSESSMENT

1. **PRESENTING AN INTERNATIONAL NEWS SHOW**
In the 1950s, many Americans turned their sights inward and settled down to rebuild civilian lives and enjoy the economic benefits that followed World War II. What was happening on the other sides of the oceans during the postwar period?

Prepare a script and notes about visuals to be used in a television news show on one international event that took place during the 1950s.

CD-ROM Use the CD-ROM *Our Times,* your textbook, and other resources to identify and research an international event that interests you.

- Use a storyboard format to plan the visuals you will include—people, places, maps, graphs—and indicate what the narrator will say as each picture is shown. Be sure to explain the highlights of the event and to analyze its effects on U.S. foreign and domestic policy.
- **Cooperative Activity** Talk with the other students in your class to identify those who chose events from the same time period as yours. Then work with those students to plan a summary news broadcast about world events that year.

2. **CREATING A 1950s–STYLE TV QUIZ SHOW**
Cooperative Activity With a small group of classmates, plan and stage a quiz show in which student-contestants answer questions based on information in this chapter. Discuss with group members what the name and format of your show will be and how you will categorize the questions.

Then present your quiz show to the class, using volunteer class members as contestants.

3. **PORTFOLIO PROJECT**
Use the Living History activity to expand your portfolio.

LIVING HISTORY

ADVERTISING YOUR FIFTIES PARTY

Working with a partner, create a radio advertisement for the party. Decide which elements of each person's invitation you will include, and think of a 1950s song to use as background music.

Make an audiotape of your radio spot to play for the class. Class members should write an evaluation of each ad, based on the following criteria:

- Did the ad capture your attention?
- Could you visualize what the party would be like?
- How would you rate the overall effectiveness of the ad?

Save your audiotape and evaluations in your American history portfolio.

Bridge to Chapter 20

Review Chapter 19

POSTWAR TRANSITIONS After World War II, Americans faced social, economic, and political readjustments. With the help of the GI Bill, veterans began to rebuild their civilian lives. For minority veterans, this rebuilding included seeking full rights as citizens. The transition from wartime to peacetime brought temporary rises in unemployment and inflation. But the economy soon stabilized as the demand for goods and services exceeded the supply, and increased production created new jobs. Eisenhower's two-term presidency ushered in an era of new prosperity and rising political conservatism.

THE AMERICAN DREAM An economic boom in the 1950s made the American dream possible—an affordable suburban house in a safe neighborhood with good schools. Yet this lifestyle also had its negative side. Many businesspeople had to repress their individuality in white-collar corporate jobs, and homemakers sometimes felt bored, isolated, and unfulfilled, despite their comfortable surroundings.

POPULAR CULTURE By 1960, almost every American home had a television set. Programming reflected and reinforced the mainstream values of white America—a secure job, a suburban home, material success, well-behaved children, and general conformity. In contrast, the rebellious messages of the beat movement in literature and of rock 'n' roll in music clashed with the tidy suburban view of life.

THE PLIGHT OF THE POOR The idealized image of postwar America expressed in popular culture did not encompass the plight of minorities and the nation's poor. Despite increased economic prosperity, African Americans, Mexican Americans, and Native Americans still faced racial discrimination. They all formed organizations to improve their conditions and chance of realizing the American dream.

Preview Chapter 20

In the early 1960s, the mood of the country dramatically shifted as the new Democratic president, John F. Kennedy, faced some of the most dangerous Soviet-American confrontations of the nuclear age. After Kennedy's assassination in 1963, President Lyndon B. Johnson launched a campaign against poverty and racial discrimination. You will learn about these and other significant developments in the next chapter.

ALTERNATIVE ASSESSMENT

1. PRESENTING AN INTERNATIONAL NEWS SHOW
Standards for Evaluation
A script with notes about visuals should meet the following criteria:

- Focuses on one international event from the 1950s.
- Examines how that event affected U.S. foreign and domestic policy.
- Includes clear visuals that support the narrator's text.
- Uses a variety of research sources.

2. CREATING A 1950s-STYLE TV QUIZ SHOW
Standards for Evaluation
A quiz show should meet the following criteria:

- Identifies the name and purpose of the show.
- Uses interesting and thought-provoking questions.
- Is conducted in an organized and orderly fashion.
- Gives each group member a role in the project.

3. PORTFOLIO PROJECT LIVING HISTORY
Standards for Evaluation
A radio advertisement should meet the following criteria:

- Includes lively music as a background.
- Identifies the time and place of the party clearly.
- Uses catchy slogans and sound effects.
- Presents a clear tape recording of the radio ad.

IN-DEPTH RESOURCES: UNIT 5
See the form for scoring this activity on page 74.

THINKING CRITICALLY

4. TRACING THEMES CULTURAL DIVERSITY
Possible Responses: Suburbs were homogeneous communities that did not welcome minority residents; television portrayed an idealized white America and ignored cultural diversity or presented minorities in stereotyped roles; minorities did not yet have a powerful political voice or accepted programs for social activism.

5. FROM INDIVIDUALIST TO ORGANIZATION MAN
Possible Responses: The unsettling effects of the Great Depression and World War II made Americans long for stability and sameness; the business world rejected creative thinkers and rebels and fostered an environment that rewarded employees who "fit in"; the rapid growth of cookie-cutter communities encouraged conformity.

6. ANALYZING PRIMARY SOURCES
Women shoppers are portrayed as easily manipulated by advertising tactics, such as package design, and as making somewhat mindless, rather than informed, purchasing decisions. ***Possible Responses:*** Opinions will vary, but should be supported with reasons and details.

UNIT OVERVIEW

Living with Great Turmoil

HISTORY AND ART

March from Selma to Montgomery, Alabama

Photograph by Ivan Massar (1965).

Art Note
The photographer Ivan Massar studied with Roy Stryker, who had organized a massive photographic documentation of the United States during the Depression. Massar made his living as a freelance photographer, taking news and documentary photos for magazines and books.

▶ *Previewing the Unit*
Unit 6 describes the social changes in American society from the 1950s through the mid-1970s. During this time Congress passes many new laws in an effort to create a "great society." African Americans launch a powerful movement that gains civil rights and spurs Hispanics, women, and Native Americans to push for rights for themselves. U.S. military involvement in Vietnam sharply divides American society.

UNIT 6

"Struggle is a never-ending process. Freedom is never really won. You earn it and win it in every generation."
CORETTA SCOTT KING

1954–1975

Living with Great Turmoil

❶
Selma march
In March 1965, police assaulted hundreds of African Americans marching from Selma to Montgomery, Alabama, in support of voting rights. The violence spurred President Lyndon Johnson to urge Congress to pass a voting rights law. On March 21, 1965, Martin Luther King, Jr., led more than 3,000 people, black and white, on a successful subsequent march.

❷ **A. Philip Randolph**
Since the 1920s, the head of a labor union with mostly African-American membership, Randolph was the dean of civil rights leaders. He organized the 1963 march on Washington that featured King's "I have a dream" speech.

❸ **Dr. Ralph Abernathy**
Abernathy was a close aide to King. He headed the Southern Christian Leadership Conference after King's death in 1968.

❹ **Ralph Bunche**
Working for the U.S. State Department, Bunche helped write the United Nations charter. He then joined the UN staff. His diplomatic success in arranging an end to a Middle East war won him the 1950 Nobel Peace Prize.

Discussing the Quotation

As Coretta King notes, the movement for civil rights is a continuing struggle. John Lewis, who joined in this part of the struggle, recalled his feelings as the Selma marchers reached Montgomery:

> "I think we all walked those days with a sense of pride and with a sense of dignity. . . . It was more than an ordinary march. . . . It was the sense of community moving there."

FOR DISCUSSION:

- Why does King say the struggle has to be won in each generation?
- How are King's and Lewis's quotations related?
- What struggles for equality remain today?

Discussing the Image

News coverage of the civil rights movement had great impact on public opinion. Images of policemen beating civil rights activists aroused outrage. And the peaceful, dignified behavior of the civil rights marchers themselves contrasted sharply with their treatment.

FOR DISCUSSION:

- What words best describe these marchers?
- Why have some marchers linked arms?
- Why do the marchers carry American flags?

5 Singing
This marcher and many others appear to be singing. When President Johnson announced his aim to push for a voting rights bill and full civil rights for African Americans, he used the words of an old spiritual that had often been part of civil rights marches: "We shall overcome."

6 Martin Luther King, Jr.
In a speech he gave to the marchers when they reached Montgomery, King said that the day of victory for the civil rights movement was near. "How long? Not long, because the arm of the moral universe is long but it bends toward justice."

7 Coretta Scott King
Coretta King has remained active in the movement for civil rights. Just four days after her husband was shot in 1968, she led a march for peace and nonviolence. She founded and heads the Martin Luther King Jr. Center for Nonviolent Social Change.

PLANNING GUIDE

CHAPTER 20 The New Frontier and the Great Society

	Key Ideas	COPYMASTERS	ASSESSMENT
SECTION 1 Kennedy and the Cold War *pp. 670–676*	*Foreign affairs dominate the presidential campaign of 1960 and the administration of John F. Kennedy. Kennedy faces some of the most dangerous Soviet-American confrontations of the Cold War.*	***In-Depth Resources: Unit 6*** • Guided Reading, p. 1 • Skillbuilder Practice: Making Predictions, p. 4 • Geography Application: Divided Germany and the Berlin Wall, p. 5 • Primary Sources: John F. Kennedy's Inaugural Address, p. 7; Political Cartoon, p. 9 ***Lesson Plans,*** pp. 165–166	PE ***Section 1 Assessment,*** p. 676 TE ***Self-Assessment,*** p. 676 ***Formal Assessment*** • Section Quiz, p. 248 ***Alternative Assessment Book*** • Standards for Evaluating a Cooperative Activity
SECTION 2 The New Frontier *pp. 677–682*	*With the stirring phrase the "New Frontier," Kennedy outlines a broad vision for progress, but Congress enacts few of his initiatives. His efforts are ended by his tragic assassination.*	***In-Depth Resources: Unit 6*** • Guided Reading, p. 2 • American Lives: Alan Shepard, p. 14 • Literature: from *Paper Wings* by Marly Swick, p. 11 ***Lesson Plans,*** pp. 167–168	PE ***Section 2 Assessment,*** p. 682 TE ***Self-Assessment,*** p. 682 ***Formal Assessment*** • Section Quiz, p. 249 ***Alternative Assessment Book*** • Standards for Evaluating a Cooperative Activity
SECTION 3 The Great Society *pp. 683–691*	*Lyndon B. Johnson drives the most ambitious legislative agenda through Congress since the New Deal. The landmark decisions of the Supreme Court under Chief Justice Earl Warren reflect the era of liberal activism.*	***In-Depth Resources: Unit 6*** • Guided Reading, p. 3 • Primary Source: from *Unsafe at Any Speed,* p. 10 • American Lives: Rachel Carson, p. 15 ***Lesson Plans,*** pp. 169–170	PE ***Section 2 Assessment,*** p. 691 TE ***Self-Assessment,*** p. 691 ***Formal Assessment*** • Section Quiz, p. 250 ***Alternative Assessment Book*** • Standards for Evaluating a Cooperative Activity
CHAPTER RESOURCES	**Chapter Overview** *President Kennedy survives major confrontations with the Soviet Union but cannot get his domestic policies past Congress. President Johnson succeeds him and launches an era of liberal activity with a wide-ranging program of new laws.*	***In-Depth Resources: Unit 6*** • Living History Project: Worksheet, p. 16; Standards, p. 17 ***Telescoping the Times*** • Chapter Summary, pp. 39–40 ***Planning for Block Schedules***	PE ***Chapter Assessment,*** pp. 692–693 PE ***Alternative Assessment,*** p. 693 ***Formal Assessment*** • Chapter Test, forms A and B, pp. 251–256 ***Test Generator*** ***Alternative Assessment Book*** See explanation and forms for different kinds of alternative assessments including portfolio assessment.

KEY
- PE Pupil's Edition
- TE Teacher's Edition
- INTERNET **http://www.mlushistory.com**

TECHNOLOGY

 *Warm-Up Transparency* **20**

Grolier Multimedia Encyclopedia
- President Kennedy's address on the Nuclear Test Ban

Our Times
- Bay of Pigs and the Berlin Wall

 **INTERNET** John F. Kennedy and Nikita Khrushchev

---

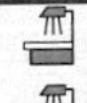 *Warm-Up Transparency* **20**

Humanities Transparencies
- H43, The Nation Mourns

Geography Transparencies
- G28, Influence of Alliance for Progress

Electronic Library of Primary Sources
- On the Space Program by John F. Kennedy and Lyndon B. Johnson
- from "That Day in Dallas"

 **INTERNET** Peace Corps and JFK assassination

---

 *Warm-Up Transparency* **20**

Humanities Transparencies
- H44, Johnson Rag

Critical Thinking Transparencies
- CT28, The Great Society
- CT62, Federal Budget: 1952–1968

 *Electronic Library of Primary Sources*
- from *Citizens' Guide to the Civil Rights Act of 1964*
- *from* Civil Rights Act of 1964

 **INTERNET** Interact with History pp. 689 and 690 (PE)

 *American Portfolio: A Videodisc for U.S. History,* user's guide, pp. 239–240, 243–245, 248

 *Chapter Summary Audiotapes*
- Unit 6, Chapter 20

 **INTERNET http://www.mlushistory.com**

Block Scheduling (90 MINUTES)

Day 1	Day 2	Day 3
Section 1, pp. 670–676	*Section 2,* pp. 677–682	*Section 3,* pp. 683–691
Section Assessment, p. 676	*Section Assessment,* p. 682	*Section Assessment,* p. 691
		Chapter Assessment, pp. 692–693
COOPERATIVE ACTIVITY • Keeping a Journal During the Cuban Missile Crisis, p. 674 (TE)	 **COOPERATIVE ACTIVITY** • Writing an Advertisement for the Peace Corps, p. 679 (TE)	 **COOPERATIVE ACTIVITY** • Outlining Provisions for a Great Society Program, p. 687 (TE)

YEARLY PACING ***Chapter 20 Total:*** 3 days ***Yearly Total:*** 85 days

See *Planning for Block Schedules* for special activities and pacing strategies.

Customizing for Special Populations

Students Acquiring English

Access for Students Acquiring English: Spanish Translations
- Guided Reading for Sections 1–3, pp. 225–227
- Chapter Summary, pp. 223–224
- Skillbuilder Practice: Making Predictions, p. 228
- Geography Application: Divided Germany and the Berlin Wall, p. 229

Spanish Reading Study Guide, pp. 207–214

Translations of Chapter Summaries, Hmong, Cantonese, Vietnamese, and Cambodian

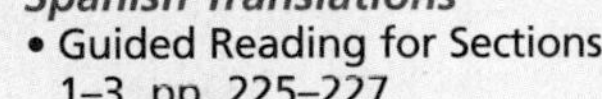

Chapter Summary Audiotapes in Spanish Unit 6, Chapter 20

INTERNET The Diverse Classroom

Gifted and Talented Students

In-Depth Resources: Unit 6
- Primary Sources: John F. Kennedy's Inaugural Address, p. 7; Political Cartoon, p. 9; from *Unsafe at Any Speed* by Ralph Nader, p. 10
- American Lives: Alan Shepard, p. 14; Rachel Carson, p. 15

Less Proficient Readers

In-Depth Resources: Unit 6
- Guided Reading for Sections 1–3, pp. 1–3
- Skillbuilder: Making Predictions, p. 4
- Geography Application: Divided Germany and the Berlin Wall, p. 5

Reading Study Guide
- pp. 207–214

Telescoping the Times
- Chapter Summary, pp. 39–40

Chapter Summary Audiotapes, Unit 6, Chapter 20

Connections to Literature READINGS FOR STUDENTS

In-Depth Resources: Unit 6
- **from *Paper Wings* by Marly Swick,** p. 11

Enrichment Reading
- **Joyce Carol Oates**
  Because It Is Bitter, and Because It Is My Heart
  New York: Plume, 1991
  This novel is a realistic retelling of life in America during the 1950s and 1960s. Issues of race and family dominate this gritty, realistic story.
- **Maria Thomas**
  Antonia Saw the Oryx First
  New York: Soho Press, 1987
  The experiences of a Peace Corps volunteer in Africa are at the center of this story of a richly complex community, unusual personalities, cultural confusions, and the powerful African landscape.
- **Tom Wolfe**
  The Right Stuff
  New York: Farrar, Straus, and Giroux, 1991
  This is the true story of the first seven men—Alan Shepard, Gus Grissom, John Glenn, Scott Carpenter, Walter Schirra, Gordon Cooper, and Deke Slayton—chosen for the U.S. space program. The novel follows them through their selection, training, and daily routines.

McDougal Littell *The Language of Literature* American Literature
- **Robert Frost, "Acquainted with the Night,"** p. 821
- **Robert Frost, "Mending Wall,"** p. 822
- **Robert Frost, "Out, Out—,"** p. 824

CHAPTER 20 OVERVIEW

The New Frontier and the Great Society

▶ ***Accessing Prior Knowledge***

Ask students to discuss some of the books they've read and films they've seen about John F. Kennedy and Lyndon B. Johnson. Ask students what images come to mind when they think about either president.

▶ ***Predicting Outcomes***

Have students read the quotation on this page from Kennedy's inaugural address. Then have them use the time line to predict some of the actions people would take in the 1960s to benefit their country.

MORE ABOUT . . .
John F. Kennedy

The White House received many letters pointing out the fact that President Kennedy always seemed to walk a few steps ahead of his wife. "Jackie will just have to walk faster," he said once. Actually, protocol dictated that the President precede everyone. Early in his presidency, Kennedy held the door open for Eleanor Roosevelt, who hung back. "No, you go first," she said. "You are the President." Kennedy laughingly replied, "I keep forgetting." "But you must never forget," Mrs. Roosevelt said gently.

CHAPTER 20 The New Frontier and the Great Society

SECTION 1
Kennedy and the Cold War

Foreign affairs dominate the presidential campaign of 1960 and the administration of John F. Kennedy. Kennedy faces some of the most dangerous Soviet-American confrontations of the Cold War.

SECTION 2
The New Frontier

With the stirring phrase the "New Frontier," Kennedy outlines a broad vision for progress, but Congress enacts few of his initiatives. His efforts are ended by his tragic assassination.

SECTION 3
The Great Society

Lyndon B. Johnson drives the most ambitious legislative agenda through Congress since the New Deal. The landmark decisions of the Supreme Court under Chief Justice Earl Warren reflect the era of liberal activism.

"Ask not what your country can do for you—ask what you can do for your country."
John F. Kennedy

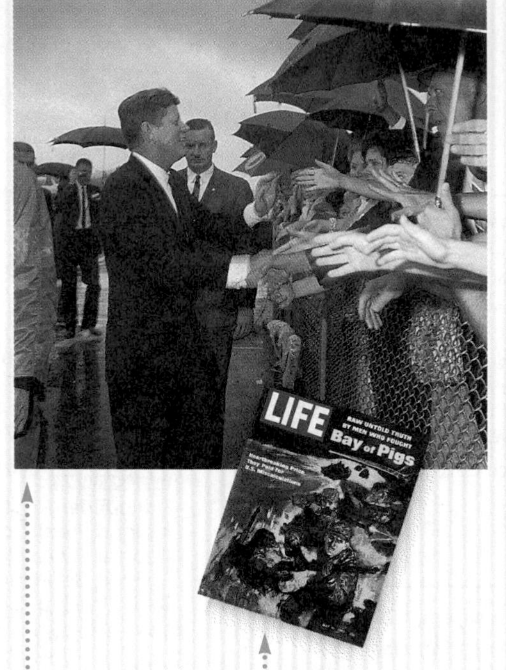

THE UNITED STATES

1960 — John F. Kennedy is elected president.

1961 — U.S. launches the Bay of Pigs invasion. Peace Corps is established.

1962 — U.S. and USSR face off in the Cuban missile crisis. John Glenn is the first American to orbit the earth.

1963 — Lyndon B. Johnson becomes president upon the assassination of John F. Kennedy.

THE WORLD

1960 — Seventeen African countries gain independence.

1961 — Berlin Wall is erected. Soviet cosmonaut Yuri Gagarin becomes the first human in outer space.

1962 — The drug thalidomide is proved responsible for thousands of birth defects in Europe.

THEMES IN CHAPTER 20

Science and Technology

By the early 1960s, the United States and the Soviet Union had built up a stockpile of nuclear weapons. During periods of crisis, including the Cuban missile crisis, the American people feared that these powerful weapons would be used.

The United States and Soviet Union also competed in the space race. After the Soviet Union successfully launched the first human into space in 1961, President Kennedy announced America's goal of sending a man to the moon by the end of the decade.

See Teacher's Edition notes, pp. 672, 680.

Economic Opportunity

With the legislative agenda of the Great Society, Johnson sought to aid the poor and others in need. The Economic Opportunity Act provided funds for jobs training, education, and the war on poverty.

See Teacher's Edition note, p. 685.

Immigration and Migration

The Great Society brought profound changes to the nation's immigration laws with the Immigration Act of 1965. The act allowed many non-European immigrants to settle in the United States.

See Teacher's Edition note, p. 686.

ALTERNATIVE ASSESSMENT

LIVING HISTORY

PLANNING A CAMPAIGN COMMERCIAL

Discuss ways of gathering information and ideas for a commercial:

- Choose a candidate and research the important issues of his or her day.
- Select an important issue that can be addressed visually.
- In an election year, study the style and content of current campaign commercials.
- Keep a file on commercials and take notes on elements students admire or wish to imitate.

Encourage students to freewrite to determine the setting, content, and tone of their commercials. Students might use a cluster diagram like the one below when they freewrite:

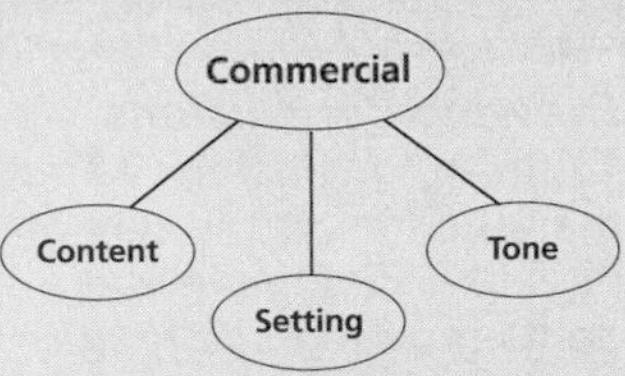

IN-DEPTH RESOURCES: UNIT 6
See worksheet and standards for evaluation, pp. 16, 17.

LIVING HISTORY

PLANNING A CAMPAIGN COMMERCIAL

During the 1960 presidential election, television assumed a major role in American politics. Since then, candidates have relied heavily on TV commercials to reach and persuade the voters.

Gather ideas and write a script for your own TV political ad. You may choose to make a commercial for a real candidate from the past or present, or you might present yourself as a candidate. In any case, focus the ad on one or more issues that were or are important to voters and to you.

PORTFOLIO PROJECT Save your ideas and written work in a folder. You will prepare and present your commercial at the end of the chapter and add it to your American history portfolio.

1964
- Congress passes a major tax cut, the Economic Opportunity Act, and the Civil Rights Act.
- Lyndon B. Johnson is elected president.
- Nikita Khrushchev is ousted from power in the Soviet Union.

1965
- Edward White II takes the first spacewalk by an American.
- Congress begins passing Great Society legislation.
- Ferdinand Marcos becomes president of the Philippines.

1966
- Supreme Court rules in *Miranda* that criminal suspects must be read their rights before questioning.
- Indira Gandhi becomes prime minister of India.
- France withdraws from NATO.

1967
- Thurgood Marshall becomes the first African-American justice on the Supreme Court.
- Israel wins Arab territories in the Six-Day War.

1968
- Martin Luther King, Jr., and Robert Kennedy are assassinated.
- Richard M. Nixon is elected president.
- Tet offensive by the North Vietnamese begins.
- Warsaw Pact troops invade Czechoslovakia.

RECOMMENDED RESOURCES

Books for the Teacher

Schlesinger, Arthur. *A Thousand Days.* New York: Fawcett, 1965. An account of JFK's presidency.

Unger, Irwin. *The Best of Intentions.* New York: Doubleday, 1996. Assessment of the Great Society.

Books for the Student

Morrison, Joan, and Robert K. Morrison, eds. *From Camelot to Kent State.* New York: Times, 1987. Remembrances of the 1960s.

O'Neill, William. *Coming Apart.* New York: Quadrangle, 1971. Informal history of the 1960s.

Videos

Crisis: Missiles in Cuba. Zenger Video, 1987. Social Studies School Service, 800-421-4246. Story of the Cuban missile crisis.

The Fabulous Sixties. MPI Home Video, 1970. 800-323-0442. Eleven-tape series.

Great Debates: John F. Kennedy and Richard M. Nixon. MPI Home Video, 1989.

Rachel Carson's Silent Spring. PBS Home Video, 1993. Documentary about the environmental activist.

Software

The Space Race. CD-ROM. First Educational Publishing,1995. 211 Congress Street, Boston, MA 02110.

Section 1 Overview

OBJECTIVES

1. To identify the factors that contributed to Kennedy's election in 1960.
2. To summarize the crises that developed over Cuba.
3. To show how Berlin symbolized the Cold War tensions of the early 1960s.

SKILLBUILDER

- Understanding geography: movement, human-environment interaction, p. 674

CRITICAL THINKING

- Making predictions, p. 671
- Finding main ideas, p. 672
- Analyzing motives, pp. 673, 676
- Recognizing effects, pp. 673, 675
- Summarizing, p. 676
- Evaluating decisions, p. 676
- Forming opinions, p. 676

FOCUS & MOTIVATE

5-MINUTE WARM-UP

Drawing Conclusions
To draw conclusions about the outcome of the Bay of Pigs invasion, have students read the *Life* magazine cover on page 673 and answer these questions.

1. Do you think the Bay of Pigs invasion was a success or a failure? What words on the magazine cover helped you draw that conclusion?
2. Whom do the writers seem to credit or blame for the outcome of the invasion?

 ***WARM-UP TRANSPARENCY 20***

▶ ***Starting with the Student***

- What do students think would happen in a nuclear war? Can anyone win such a war? Is there much chance of a nuclear war breaking out?
- Where are today's hot spots? Which countries or regions pose the greatest threat of nuclear war?

1 Kennedy and the Cold War

TERMS & NAMES
- John F. Kennedy
- flexible response
- Fidel Castro
- Berlin Wall
- hot line
- Limited Test Ban Treaty

LEARN ABOUT the election of 1960 and foreign affairs in the Kennedy administration
TO UNDERSTAND how Kennedy faced some of the most dangerous Soviet-American confrontations in the Cold War.

ONE AMERICAN'S STORY

John F. Kennedy became the 35th president of the United States on a crisp and sparkling day in January 1961. Appearing without a coat in freezing weather, he gave the impression of a man ready and determined to fight despite the elements. The words he spoke that day also issued a challenge. The world, the president said, was in "its hour of maximum danger," as Cold War tensions were running high. Rather than shrinking from the danger, the United States should actively confront the "iron tyranny" of communism throughout the world. He called upon all Americans to bear the necessary burden of this "long twilight struggle."

A PERSONAL VOICE

Let the word go forth from this time and place, to friend and foe alike, that the torch has been passed to a new generation of Americans, born in this century, tempered by war, disciplined by a hard and bitter peace, proud of our ancient heritage, and unwilling to witness or permit the slow undoing of those human rights to which this nation has always been committed. . . .

Let every nation know, whether it wishes us well or ill, that we shall pay any price, bear any burden, meet any hardship, support any friend, oppose any foe to assure the survival and the success of liberty.

JOHN F. KENNEDY, Inaugural Address, January 20, 1961

John F. Kennedy delivers his inaugural address.

Kennedy won praise for his well-crafted speech, but a question raised during the 1960 campaign was still on many minds. Did the young president have enough experience to back up the eloquent phrases with action? Several Cold War crises tested his leadership.

The Election of 1960

In 1960, as President Eisenhower's second term drew to a close, a mood of restlessness arose among voters. The economy was in a recession. The Soviet launch of *Sputnik 1* in 1957 and its development of long-range missiles had sparked lingering fears that the military power of the United States was falling behind that of the Soviet Union. Furthermore, several setbacks in 1960, including the U-2 incident and the alignment of Cuba with the Soviet Union, had Americans questioning whether the United States was losing the Cold War.

The Democratic nominee for president, Massachusetts senator John Kennedy, sounded the theme that the nation was "adrift." He promised active leadership "to get America moving again." His Republican opponent, Vice-President Richard M. Nixon, hoped to capitalize on President Eisenhower's enduring popularity. In fact, both candidates expressed very similar positions on policy issues.

LEADERSHIP for the 60's
KENNEDY ★ JOHNSON

The election in November 1960 was the closest since 1888. Kennedy won by fewer than 119,000 votes out of more than 68 million cast. Had a few thousand more people voted Republican in Illinois and Texas, the race would have gone to Nixon. Two factors helped put Kennedy over the top: television and the civil rights issue.

SECTION 1 RESOURCES

PRINT RESOURCES

IN-DEPTH RESOURCES: UNIT 6
Guided Reading, p. 1
Skillbuilder Practice: Making Predictions, p. 4
Geography Application: Divided Germany and the Berlin Wall, p. 5
Primary Sources: John F. Kennedy's Inaugural Address, p. 7; Political Cartoon, p. 9

READING STUDY GUIDE, p. 207

ACCESS FOR STUDENTS ACQUIRING ENGLISH
Guided Reading (Spanish), p. 225
Skillbuilder Practice: Making Predictions (Spanish), p. 228
Geography Application: Divided Germany and the Berlin Wall (Spanish), p. 229

SPANISH READING STUDY GUIDE, p. 207

FORMAL ASSESSMENT
Section Quiz, p. 248

ALTERNATIVE ASSESSMENT BOOK
See forms for supporting and scoring alternative activities.

TECHNOLOGY RESOURCES

CD-ROM *Our Times*
Grolier Multimedia Encyclopedia

VIDEO *American Portfolio: A Videodisc for U.S. History* user's guide, pp. 239–240, 243–244, 248

INTERNET http://www.mlushistory.com

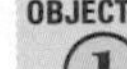

KENNEDY THE CANDIDATE Kennedy entered the race with a well-organized campaign, the backing of his large and wealthy family, and a handsome look and charisma that appealed to voters. Despite these assets, Kennedy also faced several obstacles. He was just 43 years old, which would make him the youngest president ever elected. Many people felt he was too inexperienced to lead the most powerful nation on earth.

There was also the question of his faith. Many Americans were concerned that having a Roman Catholic in the White House would lead either to influence of the Pope on American policies or to closer ties between church and state. However, Kennedy defused the religious issue by discussing it openly. "Whatever issue may come before me as President," he told a group of Protestant ministers in Houston, Texas, "I will make my decision . . . in the national interest, and without regard to outside religious pressure or dictates."

John F. Kennedy makes a point during a televised debate with Richard M. Nixon.

TELEVISED DEBATE A milestone of the campaign was the first televised debate ever between presidential candidates. Nixon, an expert on foreign policy, had agreed to the forum because he hoped to expose Kennedy's inexperience in world affairs. But the outcome of the debate hinged less on expertise than on image—how each candidate looked and spoke.

On September 26, 1960, 70 million TV viewers saw two candidates who both seemed articulate and knowledgeable on the issues. However, Nixon lost the image battle. Kennedy, who had been coached by television producers, played perfectly to the camera, and he scored many points with voters because he looked better than Nixon. *Time* magazine summed up the candidates' differences: "Kennedy was quick, aggressive, and cool. Nixon was strangely nervous, perspiring profusely, so badly made up . . . that under the baleful glare of floodlights he looked ill as well as ill at ease." Nixon's many years of experience had evaporated in one evening.

"That night, image replaced the printed word as the natural language of politics."

RUSSELL BAKER

THINK THROUGH HISTORY
A. Making Predictions *What effect do you think the televised debate would have on politics?*

A. Answer
Possible Answer: Voters would begin making decisions based on a candidate's perceived image rather than on his or her stand on the issues.

Kennedy's strong performance gave him a big boost in the polls, and he began to attract large and enthusiastic crowds on his campaign stops. His success in the debate also launched a new era in American politics: the television age. As journalist Russell Baker, who covered the Nixon campaign, said, "That night, image replaced the printed word as the natural language of politics."

KENNEDY AND KING A second major event of the campaign took place in October. Police in Atlanta, Georgia, arrested the Reverend Martin Luther King, Jr., and 52 other African-American demonstrators for sitting at a segregated lunch counter. Although the other demonstrators were released, King was sentenced to four months, hard labor—officially for a minor traffic violation. Despite the questionable sentence, the Eisenhower administration refused to intervene in the matter, and Nixon took no public position.

Hearing of the arrest and sentencing, Kennedy telephoned King's wife, Coretta, to express his sympathy. Meanwhile, Robert Kennedy, his brother and campaign manager, persuaded the judge who had sentenced King to release the civil rights leader on bail, pending appeal. News of the incident captured the immediate attention of the African-American community, whose votes helped carry key states for Kennedy in the Midwest and South.

KENNEDY TAKES COMMAND From the moment he took office, the Cold War occupied much of Kennedy's attention. During the campaign, Kennedy had criticized the Eisenhower administration for not being concerned enough about

OBJECTIVE
① INSTRUCT

The Election of 1960

Discussing Key Ideas
- Kennedy's skillful use of television and his stand on civil rights earn him a narrow victory in 1960.
- Kennedy develops a policy of flexible response, which enables the United States to fight limited wars while maintaining a nuclear balance of power with the Soviet Union.

IN-DEPTH RESOURCES: UNIT 6
Guided Reading, p. 1
Primary Source: JFK's Inaugural Address, p. 7

ACCESS FOR STUDENTS ACQUIRING ENGLISH
Guided Reading (Spanish), p. 225

MORE ABOUT . . .
The King Arrest

King's father, a Baptist minister who had supported Nixon, reversed his position after Kennedy contacted his son's wife. "Because this man," King, Sr., declared, "was willing to wipe the tears from my daughter[in-law]'s eyes, I've got a suitcase of votes, and I'm going to take them to Mr. Kennedy and dump them in his lap." Across the country, scores of other African-American Protestant ministers followed suit, urging their congregations to set aside the "religious question" in favor of the civil rights question.

TEACHING OPTION

Skillbuilder Mini-Lesson: Making Predictions

Explaining the Skill Historians often make predictions about what may happen in the future as the result of a decision or event. They think critically about the event and make realistic predictions about its possible outcomes and consequences.

Applying the Skill: Impact of Television on Politics
Many historians believe that John Kennedy's success in the televised debate with Richard Nixon brought about fundamental changes in the nature of politics. Ask students to explain the quote from Russell Baker on page 671: "That night, image replaced the printed word as the natural language of politics." *Superficial images replaced substance.*

Ask them what role television plays in politics and elections today. *Television reduces politics and elections to photo opportunities and soundbites.* Then have students make predictions about the future trends and consequences of television on politics. *Some students may say that television will become increasingly important as a means of creating candidates. Others may believe that there will be a backlash against television.*

IN-DEPTH RESOURCES: UNIT 6
Skillbuilder Practice: Making Predictions, p. 4

ANOTHER PERSPECTIVE

Eisenhower's Warning

Critical Thinking: Evaluating Ask students what Eisenhower feared might result from the development of a "military-industrial complex." *Possible Response: Industry and the military would become too powerful, eclipsing the government.* Why did Eisenhower believe that some military development was necessary? *Possible Response: Because he felt that the military had to be built up to counter the Soviet threat.*

OBJECTIVE
② INSTRUCT

Crises Over Cuba

▶ ***Starting with the Student*** Have students create a cluster diagram like the one below and list words and phrases associated with each topic. Students should list any facts, names, causes, effects, and quotes that help explain or describe the topic.

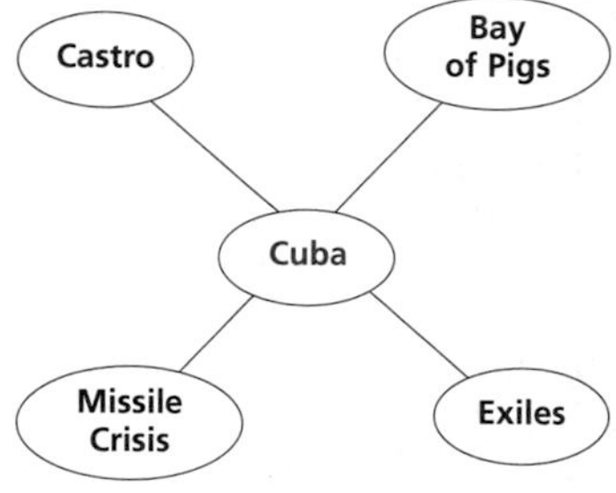

(continued on next page)

the Soviet threat. The Soviets, he said, were winning the race for allies in the so-called "third world," the economically less-developed countries of Asia, Africa, and Latin America. He had repeatedly blasted the Republicans for allowing communism to reach America's doorstep, in Cuba. As a defense against past criticisms that the Democrats were "soft" on communism, Kennedy took an especially hard line against the Soviets.

President Kennedy felt his most urgent task was to redefine the nation's nuclear strategy. The Eisenhower administration had relied on the policy of massive retaliation to deter Soviet aggression. However, the Soviets had built their stockpile of nuclear weapons and had developed the long-range missiles to deliver them. Threatening the use of nuclear arms over a minor conflict was not a risk Kennedy wished to take. Instead, Kennedy's advisers developed the policy of **flexible response.** In their view, the nation's conventional (nonnuclear) forces had been neglected during the buildup of nuclear arms and needed to be strengthened again. They believed a stronger military would give the president more options in international crises. Kennedy's defense secretary, Robert McNamara, explained the new policy.

EISENHOWER'S WARNING

The increase in defense spending during the Kennedy administration continued the trend in which corporations that supply the Defense Department were becoming more dominant in the American economy. Before leaving office, President Eisenhower warned against the dangers of what he called the "military-industrial complex." He included in his speech the following comments:

> This conjunction of an immense military establishment and a large arms industry is new in the American experience. The total influence—economic, political, even spiritual—is felt in every city, every statehouse, every office of the federal government. We recognize the imperative need for this development. Yet we must not fail to comprehend its grave implications. . . . The potential for the disastrous rise of misplaced power exists and will persist.

A PERSONAL VOICE

> The Kennedy administration worried that [the] reliance on nuclear weapons gave us no way to respond to large nonnuclear attacks without committing suicide. President Kennedy said we had put ourselves in the position of having to choose in a crisis between "inglorious retreat or unlimited retaliation." We decided to broaden the range of options by strengthening and modernizing the military's ability to fight a nonnuclear war.
>
> **ROBERT S. MCNAMARA,** *In Retrospect*

The policy of flexible response resulted in a large increase in defense spending. Kennedy boosted conventional military forces and created an elite branch of the army called the Special Forces—or Green Berets. He also tripled the overall nuclear capabilities of the United States. These changes enabled the United States to fight limited wars around the world, while also maintaining a nuclear balance of power with the Soviet Union. However, even as Kennedy hoped to reduce the risk of nuclear war, the world came perilously close to nuclear war under his command—over the island of Cuba.

THINK THROUGH HISTORY
B. *Finding Main Ideas* *What was the goal of the doctrine of flexible response?*

B. Answer To allow the U.S. to fight limited wars around the world while maintaining a nuclear balance of power with the Soviets.

Crises Over Cuba

The first test of Kennedy's foreign policy came just 90 miles off the coast of Florida. Only a few days before Kennedy took office, on January 3, 1961, Eisenhower had cut off diplomatic relations with Cuba, where a revolutionary leader named **Fidel Castro** had openly declared himself a Communist and welcomed aid from the Soviet Union.

THE CUBAN DILEMMA Castro rode to power on the promise of democracy. From 1956 to 1959, he led a guerrilla movement to topple dictator Fulgencio Batista. When Castro took control of the government in early 1959, he told reporters, "Revolutionaries are not born, they are made by poverty, inequality, and dictatorship." He then promised to eliminate these conditions from Cuba and "to revolutionize Cuba from the bottom up."

The United States was suspicious of Castro's intentions but nevertheless recognized the new government. Batista had been unpopular and corrupt, and many Americans perceived Castro as a freedom fighter. However, relations between the United States and Cuba soon worsened when Castro's government took control of three oil refineries owned by American and British firms. He

TEACHING OPTIONS

Exploring Themes

Science and Technology Discuss the fact that the United States and the Soviet Union had built up a stockpile of nuclear weapons by the early 1960s. Tell students that scientists who helped develop such weapons warned against their use. Then ask students why the U.S. government wanted to have nuclear weapons. *Possible Response: To keep pace with the Soviets in the arms race.* Do students think the weapons made Americans feel safer or more insecure? *Possible Response: Safer, because an enemy would be less likely to attack a country that possessed nuclear weapons.*

Teaching Less Proficient Readers

Chronological Order Help students understand the chronological order of events in Cuba. Remind students that chronological order is the order in which events take place. Then have them follow these steps as they read pages 672 to 675:

1. Draw a time line that spans the years from 1959, when Castro came to power, to 1973, when Castro cut down on exit permits.
2. Add events discussed in the text to the time line, including the Bay of Pigs invasion and the Cuban missile crisis.
3. Include any notes or details that help students remember what took place.

also broke up commercial farms into communes that would be worked by formerly landless peasants. American sugar companies, which controlled 75 percent of the crop land in Cuba, appealed to the U.S. government for help. Congress responded by erecting trade barriers against Cuban sugar.

To put his reforms into action, Castro relied increasingly on Soviet aid—and on political repression. Castro's charisma won many supporters among Cubans, as did his willingness to stand up to the United States, which had a long history of involvement in Cuban affairs. But many other Cubans felt betrayed. They saw Castro as a traitor to the revolution—a tyrant who had replaced one dictatorship with another. About 10 percent of Cuba's population went into exile, mostly to the United States. Within the large exile community of Miami, Florida, a counterrevolutionary movement took shape.

C. Answer Possible Answers: Kennedy had criticized Eisenhower for losing Cuba and was himself sensitive to appearing soft on communism; Castro took property of U.S. businesses; planners hoped that invasion would trigger mass uprising against Castro.

THINK THROUGH HISTORY C. *Analyzing Motives* *Why do you think Kennedy authorized the Bay of Pigs invasion?*

THE BAY OF PIGS In the summer of 1960, President Eisenhower gave the CIA permission to secretly train hundreds of Cuban exiles for an invasion of Cuba. The CIA and the exiles hoped that the invasion would trigger a mass uprising against Castro that would overthrow him.

Kennedy learned of the operation nine days after his election. He had his doubts about the plan, but he approved it anyway, even promising air support to the Cuban exiles. On the night of April 17, 1961, some 1,400 Cuban exiles landed on the island's southern coast at Bahia de Cochinos, the Bay of Pigs. Nothing went as planned. An air strike carried out two days before had failed to knock out the Cuban air force, although the CIA reported that it had. A small advance group sent to distract Castro's forces never reached shore. When the commando unit finally landed, it faced 20,000 Cuban troops, backed up by Soviet tanks and jet aircraft. The troops surrounded the exiles, killed some, and took others prisoner.

Castro turned the failed invasion into a public relations triumph. The Cuban media described in sensational detail the defeat of "North American mercenaries." In the United States, one commentator observed that Americans "look like fools to our friends, rascals to our enemies, and incompetents to the rest."

D. Answer Failure to oust Castro, loss of world prestige, embarrassment for JFK, ransom for captured commandos.

THINK THROUGH HISTORY D. *Recognizing Effects* *What were the consequences of the failed invasion for the United States?*

The disaster left Kennedy embarrassed. Privately, he asked, "How could that crowd at the CIA and the Pentagon be this wrong?" Publicly, he accepted blame for the fiasco. "I am the responsible officer of the government," said Kennedy.

Kennedy negotiated with Castro for the release of surviving commandos and ultimately paid a ransom of $53 million in food and medical supplies. In a speech in Miami, he promised exiles that they would one day return to a "free Havana." Although Kennedy warned that he would resist any further Communist expansion in the Western Hemisphere, Castro defiantly welcomed further Soviet aid.

THE CUBAN MISSILE CRISIS Castro had a powerful ally in Moscow—Soviet premier Nikita Khrushchev, who promised to defend Cuba with Soviet arms. During the summer of 1962, the flow of Soviet weapons to Cuba—including nuclear missiles—increased greatly. President Kennedy responded at first with a warning that the United States would not tolerate the presence of offensive nuclear weapons on Cuba. Then, on October 14, photographs taken by American U-2 planes provided the president with stark evidence that the Soviets were secretly building missile bases on Cuba—and that some contained

LIFE
RAW UNTOLD TRUTH BY MEN WHO FOUGHT Bay of Pigs
Heartbreaking Price They Paid for U.S. Miscalculations

top, **Fidel Castro celebrates after gaining power in Cuba;** ***above,*** **The Bay of Pigs fiasco enhanced the stature of Castro in Cuba and damaged U.S. prestige abroad.**

(continued from page 672)

▶ *Discussing Key Ideas*

- Fidel Castro rises to power in Cuba on the promise of democracy but declares himself a Communist after he takes control of the government.
- The failed Bay of Pigs invasion embarrasses the United States and enhances Castro's stature.
- The United States and Soviet Union come to the brink of nuclear war during the Cuban missile crisis.
- Many Cuban exiles blame Kennedy and the Democrats for "losing Cuba."

MORE ABOUT . . .
The Counter-Revolutionary Movement

Some Cuban exiles waged a psychological war using radio waves. Castro called it "an electronic war," the bombardment of Cuba with U.S.-sponsored radio messages. The war began in March 1960 when Eisenhower approved the creation of Radio Swan, a clandestine radio station set up on Swan Island in the Caribbean. Run by Cuban exiles, the station's mission was to prepare Cuba for a takeover at the Bay of Pigs. After Cuba had been blasted with messages, pro-Castro Radio Havana claimed, "Radio Swan is not a radio station but a cage of hysterical parrots." After the invasion failed, Cuban exiles moved the station to Miami, renamed it "Radio Americas," and continued broadcasting to Cuba.

TEACHING OPTION

Making Connections Across Cultures

Cubans in Miami Tell students that the part of Miami where Cuban exiles settled became known as Little Havana. Cubans called the area's main street Calle Ocho, or Eighth Street. In the 1960s, Calle Ocho developed into a center of Cuban-American culture, where restaurants served traditional island dishes such as fried bananas and cups of strong café Cubano—Cuban coffee. Today, Cubans make up about two-fifths of the population in Miami. Although overcrowding and a high rate of unemployment plague Little Havana, the Cubans in Miami have also made great progress. The city's strong Latin culture has attracted many banks and companies that deal with Latin-American trade. A Spanish-language newspaper is published daily. Most important, in 1985, Xavier Suarez became Miami's first Cuban-born mayor.

HISTORY FROM VISUALS

Cuban Missile Crisis, October 1962

Reading the Map Tell students that they can use the arcs on the map to calculate how long it would take a Cuban missile to reach an American city. Then ask them to estimate how long it would have taken for a missile to reach Los Angeles. *About 20 minutes.*

Extension Ask students why the U.S. range of quarantine extended through the northern part of Florida. *Possible Response: To prevent Soviet ships from entering American waters.*

IN-DEPTH RESOURCES: UNIT 6
Primary Source: Political Cartoon, p. 9

MORE ABOUT . . .

Kennedy's Speech to an Anxious Nation

On October 22, Kennedy urged Americans to support the blockade of Cuba with these words: "We have no wish to war with the Soviet Union, for we are a peaceful people who desire to live in peace with all other peoples . . . . The cost of freedom is always high, but Americans have always paid it. And one path we will never choose, and that is the path of surrender, or submission."

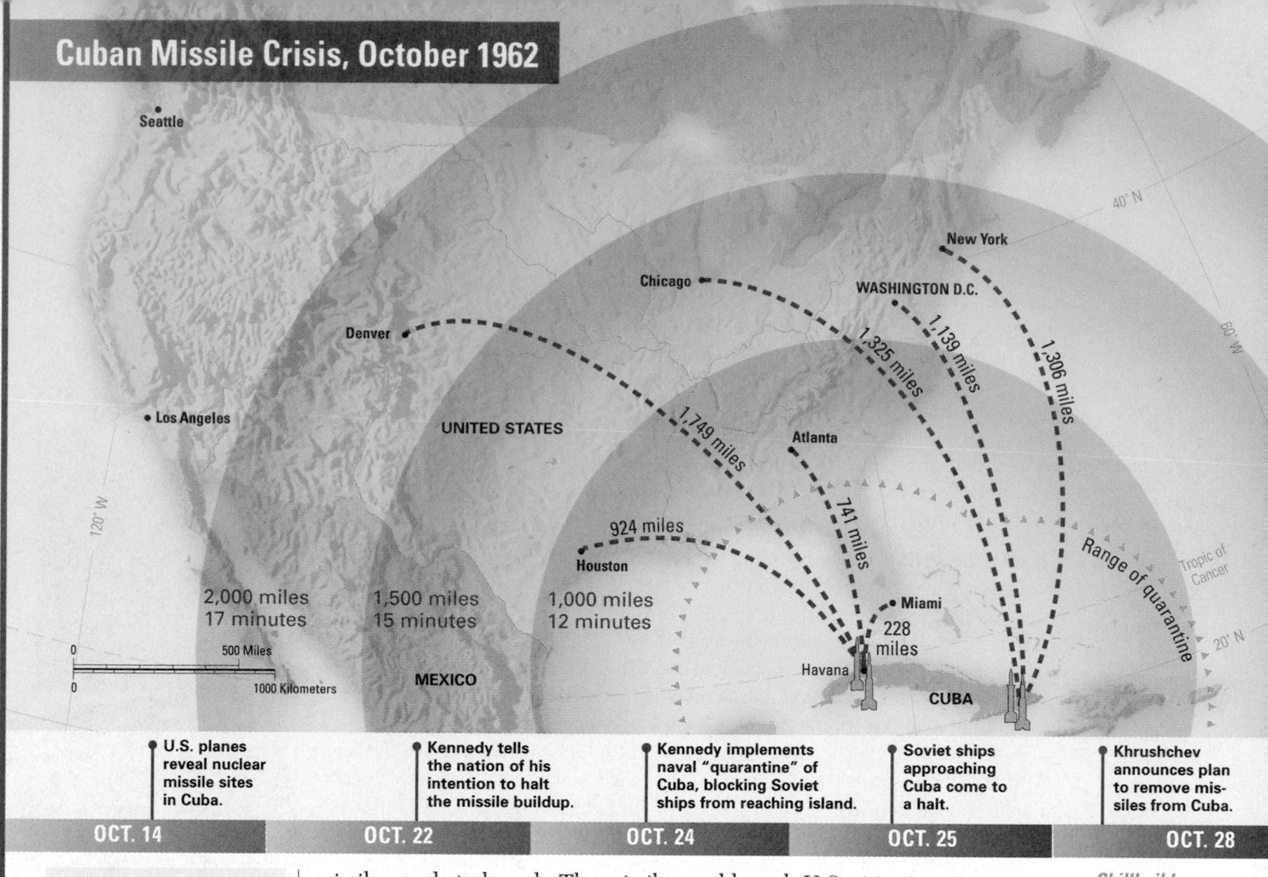

GEOGRAPHY SKILLBUILDER
MOVEMENT *About how long would it have taken for a missile launched from Cuba to reach New York?*
HUMAN-ENVIRONMENT INTERACTION *What was the range of the naval quarantine around Cuba?*

Skillbuilder Answer
Movement: Between 10 and 15 minutes. **Human-Environment Interaction:** 500 miles around the island.

missiles ready to launch. The missiles could reach U.S. cities in minutes.

On October 22, Kennedy delivered a speech to inform an anxious nation of the existence of Soviet missile sites in Cuba and his plans to remove them. He made it clear that any missile attack from Cuba would trigger an all-out attack on the Soviet Union.

For the next six days, the world faced the terrifying possibility of nuclear war. In the Atlantic, Soviet ships—presumably carrying more missiles—headed toward Cuba, while the U.S. Navy prepared to quarantine Cuba and prevent the ships from coming within 500 miles of the island. In Florida, nearly 200,000 men were being concentrated in the largest invasion force ever assembled in the United States.

C. Douglas Dillon, Kennedy's secretary of the treasury and a veteran of nuclear diplomacy, recalled those tension-filled days in October.

A PERSONAL VOICE

The only time I felt a fear of nuclear war or a use of nuclear weapons was on the very first day, when we'd decided that we had to do whatever was necessary to get the missiles out. There was always some background fear of what would eventually happen, and I think this is what was expressed when people said they feared they would never see another Saturday.

C. DOUGLAS DILLON, quoted in *On the Brink*

"We are eyeball to eyeball, and the other fellow just blinked."

DEAN RUSK

The first break in the crisis occurred when the Soviet ships suddenly halted to avoid a confrontation at sea. "We are eyeball to eyeball," commented Secretary of State Dean Rusk, "and the other fellow just blinked." A few days later, Khrushchev offered to remove the missiles in return for an American pledge not to invade Cuba. President Kennedy agreed and the crisis ended. Years later, Robert Kennedy, who served as attorney general in his brother's administration,

Block Schedule TEACHING OPTION **Time Needed: 30 Minutes**

Cooperative Activity: Keeping a Journal During the Cuban Missile Crisis

Task: Students will write journal entries about the Cuban missile crisis from the point of view of its key players.

Purpose: To help students understand the conflicts and tensions of the Cuban missile crisis.

Activity: Groups of four or five students should discuss the Cuban missile crisis by role-playing the key players. For example, students might role-play the behind-the-scenes preparations for Kennedy's speech to the nation. Or they might enact a phone call between the Americans and Khrushchev or Castro. Students should then collaborate on writing journal entries about the crisis from the point of view of the people they role-played.

Building a Portfolio: Students who believe that the journal entries are among their best work should include them in their portfolios.

ALTERNATIVE ASSESSMENT BOOK
Standards for Evaluating a Cooperative Activity

Standards for Evaluation
Journal entries should . . .
- succinctly describe the events that took place during the crisis
- express the point of view of the key players
- convey the doubts and fears felt by those who lived through the crisis

recalled the relief. "For a moment the world had stood still," he wrote, "and now it was going around again."

The crisis severely damaged Khrushchev's prestige in the Soviet Union and the world. Kennedy did not escape criticism either. The public hotly debated his actions. Some people criticized Kennedy for practicing brinkmanship, when private talks might have resolved the crisis without the threat of nuclear war. Others believed he had been too soft and had passed up an ideal chance to invade Cuba and oust Castro. (Soviet information that came to light in the 1990s suggests that, in fact, the CIA had underestimated the numbers of nuclear weapons and Soviet troops on the island, and that during the crisis, the Cubans had armed missiles in anticipation of an invasion by the United States.)

E. Answer Kennedy brought nation back from the brink of war; Khrushchev's prestige tarnished; Kennedy faced criticism from some for way he handled crisis; many Cuban exiles blamed Democrats for "losing Cuba" and switched allegiance to GOP; Castro limited exiles' access to Cuba.

THINK THROUGH HISTORY
E. *Recognizing Effects* *What were the results of the Cuban missile crisis?*

The effects of the crisis lasted long after the missiles had been removed. Many Cuban exiles blamed the Democrats for "losing Cuba" (a charge that Kennedy had earlier leveled at the Republicans) and switched their allegiance to the GOP. Meanwhile, Castro closed Cuba's doors to the exiles in November 1962 by banning all flights to and from Miami. When Cuba finally reopened its doors in 1965, hundreds of thousands of people took advantage of an agreement that allowed Cubans to join relatives in the United States. By the time Castro sharply cut down on exit permits in 1973, the Cuban population in Miami had increased to about 200,000.

KEY PLAYERS

JOHN F. KENNEDY
1917–1963

John F. "Jack" Kennedy grew up in a wealthy and politically powerful family. His father, Joseph P. Kennedy, had earned a fortune in business and was ambassador to Great Britain from 1937 to 1940. His mother, Rose, was the daughter of John F. Fitzgerald, a congressman and mayor of Boston.

The Kennedys instilled in Jack the drive to accomplish great things, and their wealth and influence helped him make the most of his abilities. He enlisted in the navy during World War II and was decorated for heroism. In 1946, Kennedy won his first seat in Congress from a Boston district where he had never lived. As a senator, he won a Pulitzer Prize for *Profiles in Courage.*

The energetic self-confidence that Jack Kennedy radiated also came, in part, from battles with his own physical frailties. Kennedy suffered many ailments, including severe back pain and Addison's disease—a debilitating condition that he treated with daily injections of cortisone. "At least one half of the days that he spent on this earth were days of intense physical pain," recalled his brother Robert.

NIKITA KHRUSHCHEV
1894–1971

"No matter how humble a man's beginnings," boasted Nikita Khrushchev, "he achieves the stature of the office to which he is elected." The son of a coal miner, Khrushchev became a Communist Party organizer in the 1920s. He advanced rapidly, becoming a member of the Central Committee in the 1930s and surviving dictator Joseph Stalin's brutal purges.

Khrushchev learned the lessons of dictatorship well. Within four years of Stalin's death in 1953, he had consolidated his power in the Soviet Union. He then denounced the Man of Steel and demoted most of Stalin's close associates.

During his regime, which ended in 1964, Khrushchev kept American nerves on edge with behavior that was alternately conciliatory and aggressive. For example, during a 1959 trip to the United States, he met for friendly talks with President Eisenhower and toured the country. The next year, in front of the UN General Assembly, he took off his shoe and angrily pounded it on a desk to protest the U-2 incident.

The Continuing Cold War

When Kennedy confronted Khrushchev in the Cuban missile crisis, he felt that more than Cuba was at stake. Kennedy believed that any sign of weakness might invite Khrushchev to test America's determination to contain communism elsewhere in the world. Ever present in Kennedy's mind was Berlin—a city where the Communist and non-Communist worlds directly confronted each other.

THE BERLIN CRISIS Soon after the Bay of Pigs fiasco, Kennedy was forced to turn his attention to a growing problem in West Berlin. By 1961, this city's prosperous economy made it a "showcase of democracy." In the 11 years since the Berlin Airlift, almost 3 million East Germans—20 percent of that country's population—had fled into West Berlin. This great stream of refugees vividly

KEY PLAYERS
Kennedy and Khrushchev

Critical Thinking: Compare and Contrast Have students compare Kennedy and Khrushchev. How are their backgrounds dissimilar? *Possible Responses: One was rich, the other poor; one was a war hero, the other escaped Stalin's purges.* What personality traits did they share? *Possible Responses: Both were driven, strong-willed, self-confident.* Then ask students what each man might have thought of the other.

OBJECTIVE
③ INSTRUCT

The Continuing Cold War

▶ ***Discussing Key Ideas***

- The Berlin Wall stems the flow of East German refugees but aggravates Cold War tensions.
- Kennedy and Khrushchev establish a telephone hot line and agree to a Limited Test Ban Treaty in an effort to ease tensions.

OUR TIMES
Bay of Pigs and the Berlin Wall

GROLIER MULTIMEDIA ENCYCLOPEDIA
President Kennedy's address on the Nuclear Test Ban

TEACHING OPTIONS

Making Connections Across Time

Relations with Cuba Today Tell students that relations still remain unfriendly between the United States and Castro's Cuba. Nonetheless, the United States still maintains a naval base in Cuba at Guantánamo Bay. Resentful of the American military presence, Castro shut off the base's fresh water supply in 1964. The United States answered by moving a plant to Guantánamo that converts ocean water into fresh water. In 1995, Castro attended a meeting with many other leaders at the United Nations. Although Castro received a warm welcome from the audience, many American leaders objected to his presence.

Making Connections Across the Curriculum

Literature Tell students that the Berlin Wall and the Cold War gave rise to a large body of espionage novels, filled with intricate plot lines and disillusioned, hardened spies. The novels of John le Carré, for example, depict a world filled with lies and betrayal. In such novels as le Carré's *The Spy Who Came in from the Cold,* secret agents track down the enemy but frequently compromise their principles in the process. Spy novels, such as those by le Carré, epitomize the distrust and paranoia of the Cold War era.

MORE ABOUT . . .
The Berlin Wall

At the stroke of midnight, on November 9, 1989, thousands of Germans took hammers and chisels and tore down the Berlin Wall. For the first time in almost 28 years, East and West Germans walked freely between the two zones, embracing each other, crying, and rejoicing.

IN-DEPTH RESOURCES: UNIT 6
Geography Application: Divided Germany and the Berlin Wall, p. 5

ASSESS & RETEACH

Section 1 Assessment

Have small groups of students get together to discuss and answer the questions.

Self-Assessment

To document what they've learned, have students create a time line listing the main events of Kennedy's presidency.

Section Quiz

FORMAL ASSESSMENT
Section Quiz, p. 248

Reteach

Use the map and accompanying time line on page 674 to review the Soviet-American confrontation during the Cuban missile crisis.

CLOSE

A series of Cold War crises occupied much of Kennedy's first term. Once these were behind him, the President planned to turn his attention to the nation's domestic issues. Unfortunately, Kennedy would never have the chance to achieve his domestic goals.

advertised the failure of East Germany's Communist government while also dangerously weakening that country's economy.

Khrushchev realized that this problem had to be solved quickly. At a summit meeting in Vienna, Austria, in June 1961, he threatened to sign a treaty with East Germany that would enable that country to close all the access roads to West Berlin. When Kennedy refused to give up U.S. access to West Berlin, Khrushchev furiously declared, "I want peace. But, if you want war, that is your problem."

After returning home, Kennedy told the nation in a televised address that Berlin was "the great testing place of Western courage and will." He pledged that "we cannot and will not permit the Communists to drive us out of Berlin."

Kennedy's determination and America's superior nuclear striking power prevented Khrushchev from closing the air and land routes between West Berlin and West Germany. Instead, the Soviet premier shocked the world with an unexpected decision. Just after midnight on August 13, 1961, East German troops began to unload concrete posts and rolls of barbed wire along the border between East and West Berlin. Within days, a concrete wall topped with barbed wire cut the city in two.

The Berlin Wall separated East Berlin and West Berlin.

The construction of the **Berlin Wall,** as this barrier was soon called, ended the Berlin crisis but further aggravated Cold War tensions. The wall—and its armed guards—successfully reduced the flow of East German refugees to a tiny trickle, thus solving Khrushchev's main problem. At the same time, however, the wall became an ugly symbol of Communist oppression.

THINK THROUGH HISTORY
F. Analyzing Motives *What led East Germany to erect the Berlin Wall? What were the effects of the wall?*

F. Answer **Motives:** Communists wanted to stem the flow of East German refugees into West Berlin and further isolate the thriving city. **Effects:** It ended the crisis but further aggravated Cold War tensions; it reduced the flow of refugees but became an ugly symbol of communism.

SEARCHING FOR WAYS TO EASE TENSIONS Showdowns between Kennedy and Khrushchev made both leaders aware of the gravity of split-second decisions that separated Cold War peace from nuclear disaster. Kennedy, in particular, searched for ways to tone down his hard-line stance. In April 1963, he announced that the two nations had established a **hot line** between the White House and the Kremlin. This hookup enabled leaders of the two countries to communicate at once should another crisis arise. Later that year, the United States and Soviet Union also agreed to a **Limited Test Ban Treaty** that barred nuclear testing in the atmosphere.

With the series of Cold War crises behind him, Kennedy turned more attention to the domestic issues facing the nation. In late November 1963, he prepared a speech to be given in Dallas, Texas, that declared that "a nation can be no stronger abroad than she is at home." Only an America, it went on, that "practices what it preaches" about equal rights, social justice, education, and economic prosperity will earn the world's respect. But Kennedy never had a chance to deliver this speech nor to achieve these domestic goals.

Section 1 Assessment

1. **TERMS & NAMES**
Identify:
- John F. Kennedy
- flexible response
- Fidel Castro
- Berlin Wall
- hot line
- Limited Test Ban Treaty

2. **SUMMARIZING** Using diagrams such as the one below, list two outcomes for each of these events: first Kennedy-Nixon debate, Bay of Pigs invasion, Cuban missile crisis, and construction of the Berlin Wall.

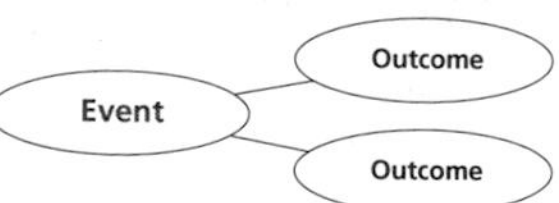

Which of these outcomes led directly to other events listed here or described in this section?

3. **EVALUATING DECISIONS** How well do you think President Kennedy handled the Cuban missile crisis? Justify your opinion with specific examples from the text.
THINK ABOUT
- Kennedy's decision to impose a naval "quarantine" of Cuba
- the nuclear showdown between the superpowers
- Kennedy's decision not to invade Cuba

4. **FORMING OPINIONS** Do you think Kennedy's actions justified his critics' accusations that he was too inexperienced in foreign affairs, or did his actions prove them wrong? Explain your response.
THINK ABOUT
- foreign policy changes in his administration
- his stance toward the Soviet Union
- his handling of foreign crises

ANSWERS

1. TERMS & NAMES

John F. Kennedy, p. 670
flexible response, p. 672
Fidel Castro, p. 672
Berlin Wall, p. 676
hot line, p. 676
Limited Test Ban Treaty, p. 676

2. SUMMARIZING

Possible Answers: Debate: Kennedy won support, TV became important in politics; Bay of Pigs: United States embarrassed, Cuba moved closer to Soviets; missile crisis: world at brink of nuclear war; Soviets backed down; Berlin Wall: increased Cold War tensions, symbolized Communist oppression.

3. EVALUATING DECISIONS

Possible Responses: Students giving the president high marks might say that the Cuban missiles were removed, nuclear war was averted, and there was no military engagement. Students giving him low marks might say that he risked nuclear war over the crisis.

4. FORMING OPINIONS

Possible Responses: Students may argue that Kennedy showed his inexperience by supporting the Bay of Pigs invasion and by being more aggressive than he needed to be in the Cuban missile crisis. Others may believe that he was generally successful in foreign policy and that he grew in the job.

❷ The New Frontier

TERMS & NAMES
- New Frontier
- mandate
- Peace Corps
- Alliance for Progress
- Warren Commission

LEARN ABOUT the goals of Kennedy's domestic program
TO UNDERSTAND why Kennedy had trouble securing congressional approval of his reform package.

ONE AMERICAN'S STORY

At 4 A.M. on May 5, 1961, American astronaut Alan Shepard climbed into *Freedom 7,* a tiny capsule sitting on top of a huge rocket booster. The capsule left the earth's atmosphere in a ball of fire and returned the same way—and inside it Shepard became the first American to travel into space. Years later, he recalled what his feelings had been when a naval crew fished him out of the Atlantic.

A PERSONAL VOICE

Until the moment I stepped out on the flight deck of the carrier festooned everywhere with red, white, and blue decorations, I hadn't realized the intensity of the emotions and feelings that so many people had for me, for the other astronauts, and for the whole manned space program. . . . I was very close to tears as I thought, it's no longer just our fight to get "out there." The struggle belongs to everyone in America. That was the best of all. From now on there was no turning back.

ALAN SHEPARD, *Moon Shot: The Inside Story of America's Race to the Moon*

The entire trip—from liftoff to splashdown—took only 15 minutes. But, like the Wright brothers' first brief flight, it reaffirmed the power of American ingenuity and inspired Americans with the belief that, with the right kind of effort, any achievement was possible. John F. Kennedy inspired many Americans with the same kind of belief. The nation's hopes were shaken, however, when his presidency was cut short by tragedy.

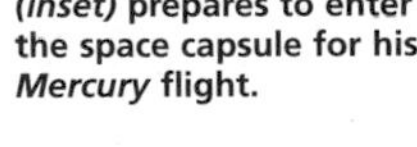

Astronaut Alan Shepard *(inset)* prepares to enter the space capsule for his *Mercury* flight.

The Camelot Years

President Kennedy's inauguration set the tone for a new era at the White House: one of grace, elegance, and wit. On the podium sat over one hundred writers, artists, and scientists that the Kennedys had invited. Robert Frost, the famous American poet, recited an inaugural poem. Opera singer Marian Anderson, who in 1939 had been barred from singing at Constitution Hall in the nation's capital because she was African American, sang the national anthem. Kennedy's inspiring speech called for hope, commitment, and sacrifice. "And so, my fellow Americans," he proclaimed, "ask not what your country can do for you—ask what you can do for your country."

During his term, Kennedy gave special recognition to American art and culture. The president and his beautiful young wife, Jacqueline, invited many artists, musicians, and celebrities to the White House to give performances or attend dinners and balls. The president appeared frequently on television, a medium that was well suited for conveying his charm and wit to the American people. These qualities also gained him wide admiration among the White House press corps, whose reports helped bolster Kennedy's public image.

"We stand today on the edge of a New Frontier."

JOHN F. KENNEDY

THE KENNEDY MYSTIQUE Critics of Kennedy's presidency argued that below the surface of Kennedy's smooth style, there was little substance. But the new

Section 2 Overview

OBJECTIVES

1. To explain the public's fascination with the Kennedys.
2. To summarize the domestic and foreign agenda of Kennedy's New Frontier.
3. To describe the tragic and controversial chain of events surrounding Kennedy's assassination.

SKILLBUILDER

- Interpreting graphs, p. 680

CRITICAL THINKING

- Developing historical perspective, p. 678
- Identifying problems, p. 679
- Analyzing issues, p. 679
- Theme: Science and Technology, p. 680
- Making inferences, p. 681
- Contrasting, p. 682
- Summarizing, p. 682
- Analyzing motives, p. 682
- Forming opinions, p. 682

FOCUS & MOTIVATE

5-MINUTE WARM-UP

Describing Mood
To understand the impact of Kennedy's death, have students look at the photo on page 681 and answer these questions.

1. What five adjectives would you use to describe the mood of the mourners in the photo?
2. How do you think the mourners reflected the mood of the nation?

WARM-UP TRANSPARENCY 20

▶ ***Starting with the Student***
- Do students believe that a lone assassin killed Kennedy?

SECTION 2 RESOURCES

PRINT RESOURCES

IN-DEPTH RESOURCES: UNIT 6
Guided Reading, p. 2
Literature: from *Paper Wings* by Marly Swick, p. 11
American Lives: Alan Shepard, p. 14

READING STUDY GUIDE, p. 209

ACCESS FOR STUDENTS ACQUIRING ENGLISH
Guided Reading (Spanish), p. 226

SPANISH READING STUDY GUIDE, p. 209

FORMAL ASSESSMENT
Section Quiz, p. 249

ALTERNATIVE ASSESSMENT BOOK
See forms for supporting and scoring alternative activities.

TECHNOLOGY RESOURCES

HUMANITIES TRANSPARENCIES
H43, The Nation Mourns

GEOGRAPHY TRANSPARENCIES
G28, Influence of Alliance for Progress

CD-ROM Electronic Library of Primary Sources

VIDEO *American Portfolio: A Videodisc for U.S. History* user's guide, pp. 244, 248

INTERNET http://www.mlushistory.com

OBJECTIVE

INSTRUCT

The Camelot Years

▶ ***Discussing Key Ideas***
- Kennedy gives special recognition to American art and culture.

(continued on next page)

(continued from page 677)

- The public is fascinated by the President and his family's glamour.
- Kennedy surrounds himself with young, bright advisers.

IN-DEPTH RESOURCES: UNIT 6
Guided Reading, p. 2

ACCESS FOR STUDENTS ACQUIRING ENGLISH
Guided Reading (Spanish), p. 226

OBJECTIVE
② INSTRUCT

The Promise of Progress

▶ ***Discussing Key Ideas***

- Kennedy outlines his New Frontier proposals but has difficulty fulfilling many of them because he lacks a popular mandate.
- Kennedy tries to stimulate economic growth by increasing government spending and lowering taxes.
- The President creates the Peace Corps to aid developing nations.
- The Soviet-manned launch in 1961 spurs the development of the U.S. space program.
- Kennedy turns his attention toward the issues of poverty and civil rights.

GEOGRAPHY TRANSPARENCIES
G28, Influence of Alliance for Progress

first family fascinated the public. After learning that JFK could read 1,600 words a minute, thousands of people enrolled in speed-reading courses. The first lady had an important influence on fashion and culture. Millions watched "Jackie's" televised tour of the White House and copied her latest hairstyle. The nation's newspapers and magazines filled their pages with pictures and stories about the president's young daughter Caroline and his infant son John.

President and Mrs. Kennedy enjoy time with their children, Caroline and John, Jr., while vacationing in Hyannis Port, Massachusetts.

The first family's youthful glamour seemed like a fairy tale come to life. The popular musical *Camelot,* which had opened on Broadway in 1960, portrayed the romance and adventure of King Arthur's court. Kennedy and his talented band of advisers reminded many of a modern-day Camelot. Years later, Jackie recalled her husband and the vision of Camelot.

THINK THROUGH HISTORY
A. Developing Historical Perspective *What factors help explain the public's fascination with the Kennedys as first family?*

A. Answer A young, attractive, energetic, and stylish couple; attention to arts and culture; young children; Kennedy's eloquence; television; admiring press.

A PERSONAL VOICE

> At night, before we'd go to sleep, Jack liked to play some records; and the song he loved most came at the very end of [the Camelot] record. The lines he loved to hear were: *Don't let it be forgot, that once there was a spot, for one brief shining moment that was known as Camelot.* There'll be great Presidents again . . . but there'll never be another Camelot again.
>
> JACQUELINE KENNEDY, quoted in *Life* magazine, John F. Kennedy Memorial Edition

THE BEST AND THE BRIGHTEST Kennedy surrounded himself with young intellectuals and businesspeople—a team of advisers that one journalist called "the best and the brightest." They included McGeorge Bundy, a Harvard University dean, as a national security adviser; Robert McNamara, president of Ford Motor Company, as secretary of defense; and Dean Rusk, president of the Rockefeller Foundation, as secretary of state. Of all the advisers who filled Kennedy's inner circle, he relied most heavily on his 35-year-old brother Robert, whom he appointed attorney general. "I see nothing wrong with giving Bobby some legal experience before he goes out to practice law," joked Kennedy when asked about his brother's youth.

The Promise of Progress

"We stand today on the edge of a New Frontier," Kennedy had announced upon accepting the nomination for president. He called on Americans to be "new pioneers" and explore "uncharted areas of science and space, . . . unconquered pockets of ignorance and prejudice, unanswered questions of poverty and surplus." Once elected, Kennedy set out to transform the broad vision of progress he had outlined in his campaign into a legislative agenda called the **New Frontier.**

For all the energetic idealism of his speeches, however, Kennedy had a difficult time turning his promise of a New Frontier into a reality. He offered Congress proposals to provide medical care for the aged, rebuild blighted urban areas, and aid education, but he simply lacked the votes he needed on Capitol Hill to pass the legislation. Kennedy faced the same conservative coalition of Republicans and Southern Democrats that had blocked Truman's Fair Deal, and he showed little skill in pushing his domestic reform measures through Congress.

Since Kennedy had been elected by the slimmest of margins, he lacked a popular **mandate**—a clear indication that the voters approved of his plans. As a result, Kennedy often felt it was in his best interest politically to play it safe.

TEACHING OPTIONS

Making Connections Across the Curriculum

Literature Tell students that the musical *Camelot* is based on the legend of King Arthur, a fictional ruler modeled on a real fifth- or sixth-century Celtic military leader. Many readers have been introduced to the Arthurian legends through Thomas Malory's *Le Morte d'Arthur,* which was first published in 1485. Malory's tales of King Arthur's court are populated by characters such as Sir Launcelot and Merlin the magician. Arthur rules a romantic world characterized by chivalry and magic. Ask students to discuss some of the similarities between Kennedy's presidency and King Arthur's court.

Making Connections Across Time

Clinton's Youthful Team Tell students that when President Bill Clinton assumed the presidency in 1992, he also surrounded himself with youthful advisers. Suggest that Clinton may have had Kennedy's example in mind, since JFK was one of Clinton's heroes. In fact, a meeting with the President first inspired young Bill Clinton to pursue a political career. Ask students to name some of the advantages and disadvantages of enlisting a group of young presidential advisers. *Possible Responses: Advantages—They're enthusiastic, energetic, creative, optimistic; Disadvantages—They're inexperienced, naive, unrealistic.*

THINK THROUGH HISTORY
B. *Identifying Problems* *Why did Kennedy have difficulty fulfilling many of his New Frontier proposals?*
B. Answer An uncooperative Congress and Kennedy's lack of a mandate.

There was no sense climbing out on a limb, he told his advisers, when he knew he would not be successful. Nevertheless, Kennedy did persuade Congress to enact measures to boost the economy, build the national defense, provide international aid, and fund a massive space program.

STIMULATING THE ECONOMY One domestic problem that the Kennedy team tackled head-on was the economy. By the late 1950s, the rate of growth in the economy had slowed considerably from its boom years after World War II, and by 1960 the country was stuck in a recession. Unemployment hovered around 6 percent, one of the highest levels since World War II. During the 1960 campaign, Kennedy had criticized the Eisenhower administration for not doing enough to stimulate growth and warned that the American economy was lagging behind that of the other Western democracies and also the Soviet Union. He promised that, if elected, he would "get America moving again."

To spur economic growth, Kennedy's advisers advocated the use of deficit spending, which had been the basis for Roosevelt's New Deal. They felt that stimulating economic growth depended on a combination of increased government spending and lower taxes for companies and individuals, even if it meant that the government spent more than it received as income. More public spending would pump money into the economy, and lower taxes would mean that people had more money left to invest and to spend.

Accordingly, the proposals Kennedy sent to Congress in 1961 called for increased spending. The biggest immediate beneficiary was the Department of Defense, which received a nearly 20 percent budget increase for new nuclear missiles, nuclear submarines, and an expansion of the armed services. Congress also approved a package that increased the minimum wage to $1.25 an hour, extended unemployment insurance, and provided assistance to cities with high unemployment. (See *deficit spending* on page 934 in the Economics Handbook.)

THINK THROUGH HISTORY
C. *Analyzing Issues* *Why do you think Kennedy chose to increase spending?*
C. Answer *Possible Answers:* He hoped that increased government spending would stimulate the economy; he wanted to strengthen the military.

"They are the best and best-liked unofficial ambassadors this nation has ever sent to lands overseas."

SARGENT SHRIVER, FIRST PEACE CORPS DIRECTOR

ADDRESSING POVERTY ABROAD One of the first campaign promises Kennedy fulfilled was the creation of the **Peace Corps,** a program of volunteer assistance to the developing nations of Asia, Africa, and Latin America. In March 1961, Congress funded the idea with a first-year budget of $30 million. Critics in the United States called the program a "boondoggle" and "Kennedy's Kiddie Korps," referring to the fact that many volunteers were young people just out of college. Some foreign observers questioned whether Americans could understand other cultures. "Here they come," said one woman in the Caribbean island of St. Lucia, "straight from school to people who manage very nicely earning nothing—to teach them about refrigeration and 'The Star-Spangled Banner.'"

A Peace Corps volunteer gives a piggy-back ride to a Nigerian girl.

Despite these reservations, the Peace Corps became a huge success. People of all ages and backgrounds signed up to work as agricultural advisers, teachers, health aides, or did whatever work the host country needed. By 1968, more than 35,000 volunteers had served in 60 nations around the world.

A second foreign aid program, the **Alliance for Progress,** offered economic and technical assistance to help Latin American countries improve their living standards. The program was intended, in part, to prevent Fidel Castro from exporting his revolutionary ideas to other Latin American countries. It earmarked money to build schools, houses, and sanitation facilities,

MORE ABOUT . . .
The Peace Corps

Kennedy voiced the need for a peace corps during his 1960 campaign. He declared: "There is not enough money in all America to relieve the misery of the underdeveloped world in a giant and endless soup kitchen. But there is enough know-how and knowledgeable people to help those nations help themselves." After his election, Kennedy appointed his brother-in-law, Sargent Shriver, director of the Peace Corps. Despite charges of nepotism—which were also leveled after the President named his brother attorney general—much of the early success of the Peace Corps was attributed to Shriver's leadership.

Block Schedule TEACHING OPTION **Time Needed: 30 Minutes**

Cooperative Activity: Writing an Advertisement for the Peace Corps

Task: Groups of four to five students will write an advertisement designed to persuade people to join the Peace Corps.

Purpose: To explore the purpose of the Peace Corps and the dedication of its volunteers.

Activity: Students should research the kind of work that Peace Corps volunteers carry out. Students might find information on the Peace Corps on the Internet or in other print or multimedia sources. Students should write an ad for a specific job in a specific country. They should include a list of an ideal applicant's qualifications, as well as an honest description of the work involved. If possible, students should also use photos or drawings of volunteers carrying out similar work.

Building a Portfolio: Students who add their advertisements to their portfolios should attach a note summarizing the qualities of a Peace Corps volunteer.

ALTERNATIVE ASSESSMENT BOOK
Standards for Evaluating a Cooperative Activity

Standards for Evaluation
Advertisements should . . .

- honestly describe the hard work involved
- summarize the qualities and experience required
- convey the idealism of the Peace Corps
- include pictures of volunteers at work

HISTORICAL SPOTLIGHT

Johnson and Mission Control

Critical Thinking: Analyzing

Ask students what Johnson's actions as chairman of the National Space Council reveal about the role he envisioned for himself as vice president. *Possible Response: He was ambitious and unwilling to be a passive vice president.*

IN-DEPTH RESOURCES: UNIT 6

American Lives: Alan Shepard, p. 14

ELECTRONIC LIBRARY OF PRIMARY SOURCES

On the Space Program by JFK and LBJ

HISTORY FROM VISUALS

U.S. Space Race Expenditures, 1957–1975

Reading the Graph Explain that the line graph shows the amount of money NASA spent per year, while the pie chart shows the total amount of money individual states received from NASA over a period of time. Ask students why the pie chart covers state contracts between 1961 and 1975. *Because the U.S. space program didn't really get under way until 1961.*

Extension Have students research the level of NASA spending between 1975 and 1995. Ask them to create a line graph showing the expenditures during this period. What caused spending to increase in the early 1980s? *The space shuttle program.*

HISTORICAL SPOTLIGHT

JOHNSON AND MISSION CONTROL

President Kennedy appointed Vice-President Johnson chairman of the National Space Council shortly after they assumed office in 1961. The chairman's duties were vague, but Johnson spelled them out: "He is to advise the president of what this nation's space policy ought to be." And Johnson's advice was to land a man on the moon.

Johnson soon picked out a new home for the moon program's Manned Spacecraft Center: Houston. Some NASA administrators wanted to consolidate the center and the launch site in Florida, However, when Johnson's friends at Humble Oil made a thousand acres of ranch land available for the new Mission Control, free of charge, the debate was over. Houston became the center of the new space program.

and also to encourage economic reforms such as breaking up large estates and giving farm workers land of their own. Between 1961 and 1969, the United States invested almost $12 billion in Latin America. While the money brought some development to the region, it failed to bring about fundamental reforms.

RACE TO THE MOON On April 12, 1961, radios all over the Soviet Union announced a new space triumph: "The world's first spaceship, *Vostok*, with a man on board, has been launched on . . . a round-the-world orbit." Soviet cosmonaut Yuri A. Gagarin had soared 188 miles into the sky and circled the earth in 108 minutes, becoming the first human in space.

The news stunned the United States. Kennedy viewed the Soviet success as a serious challenge that had to be met. At a special session of Congress, he announced that the United States "should commit itself to achieving the goal, before this decade is out, of landing a man on the moon and returning him safely to earth." Congress enthusiastically agreed. Within weeks, the National Aeronautics and Space Administration (NASA) began to construct new launch facilities at Cape Canaveral, Florida, and a mission control center in Houston, Texas. Meanwhile, Alan Shepard's brief flight in May 1961, while it did not orbit the earth, gave the program momentum.

It took less than a year for the United States to duplicate the Soviet feat. The payoff came on February 20, 1962, when Colonel John Glenn orbited the earth three times. Later that year, an experimental communications satellite called *Telstar* successfully relayed live television pictures across the Atlantic Ocean, from Maine to Europe. These achievements helped restore America's pride and prestige.

During the remainder of the decade, an excited nation watched as each new space flight brought the United States closer to its goal of sending humans to the moon. The goal was reached on July 20, 1969, when U.S. astronaut Neil Armstrong became the first person to set foot on the moon.

Skillbuilder Answer **Peak:** In 1966. **Benefit:** California.

The impact of the space program rippled through American society. The effort called for better education, and schools and colleges across the country expanded their science programs. The space program would never have been possible without numerous other scientific and technical developments, including computers and the miniaturized electronics made possible by transistors. By the same token, the huge federal funding for research and development gave rise to new industries and new developments, many of which had applications in business and industry—and also in new consumer goods. The spending also helped propel the rapid growth of Southern and Western states in particular, where many space- and defense-related industries sprang up.

THINK THROUGH HISTORY
D. THEME
Science and Technology
What effect did the space program have on other areas of American life?

D. Answer It improved education, particularly in science and math, and spurred many businesses and industries related to the program.

SKILLBUILDER
INTERPRETING GRAPHS
In which year did the federal government spend the most money on the space race? What state benefited the most?

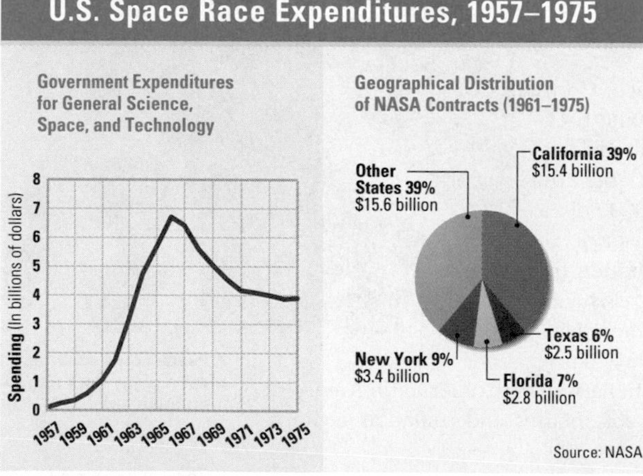

A NEW DOMESTIC AGENDA There were other places in America that received little benefit from the economic boom. In 1962, the problem of poverty in America came to national attention in Michael Harrington's book *The Other America.* Harrington used government statistics to profile the 42 million people in the United States who scraped by each year on less than $1,000 per person. The number of poor shocked many Americans.

TEACHING OPTIONS

Exploring Themes

Science and Technology Discuss the U.S. government's commitment to a lunar landing by the end of the decade. Ask students to summarize how the space program affected the American people. *Possible Response: It created new jobs in scientific research and development and caused greater emphasis to be placed on science education in schools.* Then ask students whether they think money should continue to be spent on the space program. Has the United States achieved all of its goals in space? Should space program funds be funneled into programs that are closer to home?

Making Connections Across the Curriculum

Science Tell students that, in the 1960s, the United States and the Soviet Union began developing simple space stations. A space station is a place where people can live and work for long periods of time. It orbits the earth while the crew carries out scientific research, such as analyzing the effects of microgravity and studying the stars and planets. In 1986, the Soviet space station Mir, which means "peace," was launched. Since then, Mir has rarely been unoccupied. The space station has even housed American astronauts and scientists involved in cooperative endeavors conducted by Russia and the United States.

While Harrington awakened the nation to the nightmare of poverty, the emergence of a mass movement against segregation delivered another wake-up call. Throughout the South, demonstrators raised their voices in the cry of "Freedom Now!" Kennedy had not pushed aggressively for legislation on the issues of poverty and civil rights, although he did step into some of the most controversial civil rights battles of the 1960s and effected changes by executive action. (See Chapter 21.) However, Kennedy now felt that it was time to live up to a campaign promise to be a president who "cares passionately about the fate of the people he leads."

E. Answer Towards taking more action on domestic problems, including poverty, civil rights, and the economy.

THINK THROUGH HISTORY
E. *Making Inferences* *In what directions did President Kennedy seem to be taking his administration in 1963?*

In 1963, Kennedy became, in many ways, a different leader than he had been in 1961 and 1962. During the year, he called for a "national assault on the causes of poverty." He also ordered Robert Kennedy's Justice Department to investigate racial injustices in the South. Finally, he presented Congress with a sweeping civil rights bill and a proposal to cut taxes by over $10 billion. Unfortunately, the test of his legislative leadership would never come.

Tragedy in Dallas

In the fall of 1963, Kennedy's performance as president seemed to have wide popular approval. In a national poll, almost 60 percent of the public gave him high marks. However, history often takes unexpected twists. No one could foresee that a terrible national tragedy lay just ahead.

"All the News That's Fit to Print" **The New York Times.** LATE CITY EDITION
NEW YORK, SATURDAY, NOVEMBER 23, 1963. TEN CENTS

KENNEDY IS KILLED BY SNIPER AS HE RIDES IN CAR IN DALLAS; JOHNSON SWORN IN ON PLANE

FOUR DAYS IN NOVEMBER On the sunny morning of November 22, 1963, *Air Force One,* the presidential aircraft, landed in Dallas, Texas. President and Mrs. Kennedy had come to Texas to mend political fences with members of the state's Democratic Party. Kennedy had expected a cool reception from the conservative state, but he basked instead in warm waves of applause from crowds that lined the streets of downtown Dallas.

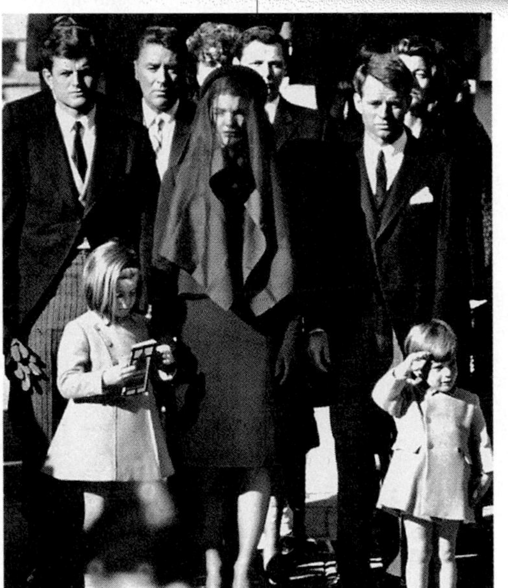

John Kennedy, Jr., salutes his father's casket as it is prepared for the trip to Arlington National Cemetery. His mother, his sister, and Attorney General Robert Kennedy look on.

Jacqueline sat next to her husband in the back seat of an open-air limousine. In front of them sat Texas Governor John Connally and his wife, Nellie. As the car approached a state building known as the Texas School Book Depository, Nellie Connally turned to Kennedy and said, "You can't say that Dallas isn't friendly to you today."

A few seconds later, rifle shots rang out, and Kennedy was shot in the head. He slumped over. His car raced to a nearby hospital, where doctors frantically tried to revive him, but it was too late. President Kennedy died less than an hour after he had been shot.

The tragic news flashed instantly across the nation and then around the world. As word of what happened spread through America's schools, offices, and homes, people reacted with disbelief. Questions were on everyone's lips: Who had killed the president, and why? What would happen next?

Millions of Americans turned on their television sets for answers. During the next four days, television became what one reporter called "the window of the world." A flood of dramatic pictures poured into the nation's living rooms. Viewers saw a somber Lyndon Baines Johnson take the oath of office aboard the

OBJECTIVE
③ INSTRUCT

Tragedy in Dallas

▶ *Starting with the Student*
Have students create a time line of events of the four days (22–25) in November.

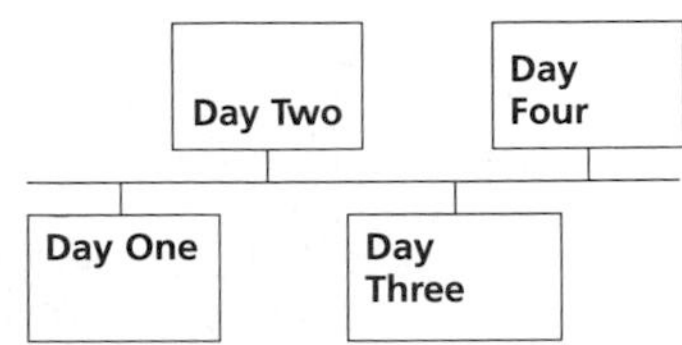

▶ *Discussing Key Ideas*
- People react with grief to Kennedy's assassination.
- The alleged assassin is shot on live television.
- The Warren Commission concludes that Oswald acted alone.

HUMANITIES TRANSPARENCIES
H43, The Nation Mourns

ELECTRONIC LIBRARY OF PRIMARY SOURCES
from "That Day in Dallas" by Tom Wicker

MORE ABOUT . . .
Kennedy's Assassination
Kennedy's death continued a strange and unhappy coincidence: Since 1840, every President elected in a year ending in zero had died while in office. These Presidents and the years of their election were Harrison (1840), Lincoln (1860), Garfield (1880), McKinley (1900), Harding (1920), Franklin Roosevelt (1940), and Kennedy (1960). Ronald Reagan, who was elected in 1980 but who—in spite of an assassination attempt—did not die in office, ended the chain.

TEACHING OPTIONS

Making Global Connections

The World Mourns the Fallen Leader Tell students that representatives and leaders from more than 90 countries attended Kennedy's funeral on November 25. Some of the world leaders were French President Charles de Gaulle and Ethiopian Emperor Haile Selassie. After President Kennedy's death, public buildings and other places throughout the world were named for him. In Great Britain, a one-acre area of land in the English meadow of Runnymede was set aside as part of a memorial to Kennedy.

Teaching Gifted and Talented Students

Debating Conspiracy Theories Encourage interested students to research the facts of Kennedy's assassination. Then have them get together to debate the following hypothesis: A lone gunman killed Kennedy. Students should:

- Get together in a group with students who hold a similar view.
- Discuss and prepare their case with group members.
- Use facts and logic during the debate to support their argument.
- Present charts and pictures to clarify points.
- Report to the rest of the class on the outcome of the debate.

NOW & THEN
Assassination Fascination
Critical Thinking: Analyzing Ask students why the Kennedy assassination continues to fascinate. Why are some people convinced that there was a conspiracy? *Possible Responses: Some facts haven't been adequately explained; people don't want to believe that someone like Oswald could alter the course of history; people distrust the government.*

ASSESS & RETEACH

Section 2 Assessment

Pair students with less proficient ones to answer the questions.

Self-Assessment

Ask students to make a list of the impressions they had of Kennedy and his presidency before reading Section 2. Then have them note whether their reading has confirmed or contradicted their preconceptions.

Section Quiz

FORMAL ASSESSMENT
Section Quiz, p. 249

Reteach

Use the Section Quiz to help students review the main concepts in Section 2.

CLOSE

Aided by his talented band of advisers, Kennedy worked to boost the economy, address poverty abroad, and develop the U.S. space program. After an assassin's bullet killed the President, the task of pushing through an ambitious domestic agenda fell to Lyndon Johnson.

NOW & THEN

ASSASSINATION FASCINATION

From the beginning, people have questioned the conclusions of the Warren Commission report. Even Chief Justice Warren admitted that "things will not be revealed in our lifetime." For decades, amateur investigators have delved into apparent inconsistencies in the official record. The questions raised by some of their findings have led to increasing public pressure on the government to tell all it knows about the assassination.

In response, Congress in 1992 passed the JFK Records Act, which created a panel to review all government and private files on the shooting and decide which should be made part of the public record.

Since the law was enacted, newly declassified information has added some weight to a body of evidence that JFK was shot from the front (the Warren Commission had concluded that a single bullet struck the president from behind) and that Oswald, thus, could not have acted alone. While such evidence challenges the Warren Commission's report, no information has yet surfaced that conclusively disproves its findings.

presidential airplane as the grief-stricken Jacqueline Kennedy stood at his side. They watched as Dallas police charged Lee Harvey Oswald with the murder of John F. Kennedy.

Strong evidence linked Oswald with the crime. Investigators found Oswald's palm print on the rifle used to kill the president. In addition, the 24-year-old former Marine had a suspicious past. After receiving a dishonorable discharge, Oswald briefly lived in the Soviet Union. He then returned to the United States and became an active supporter of Fidel Castro.

The capture of Lee Harvey Oswald did not end the nightmare. On Sunday, November 24, as millions of Americans watched live television coverage of Oswald being transferred from one jail to another, a Dallas nightclub owner named Jack Ruby suddenly stepped through a crowd of reporters. Then he shot the president's alleged assassin. Oswald died less than an hour later.

The next day, all work stopped as America mourned its fallen leader, whose body was laid to rest in Arlington National Cemetery. Kennedy's assassination and televised funeral, like the attack on Pearl Harbor, became a historic event that few could forget. To this day, most Americans who were alive at that time can recall exactly what they were doing when they first heard about the shooting of President Kennedy.

UNANSWERED QUESTIONS The entire chain of events was so bizarre that some people wondered if Oswald had acted as part of a conspiracy. In 1963, a commission presided over by Chief Justice Earl Warren began an extensive investigation that lasted ten months and yielded 26 volumes of testimony. The **Warren Commission** concluded that Kennedy had been shot by Oswald—"a sorry little loser"—acting on his own. In 1979, however, a congressional committee that reinvestigated the evidence concluded that Kennedy was probably shot by Oswald, but in a conspiracy with unknown people, and that it was possible that two persons had fired at the president. Besides these official inquiries, numerous other people have made their own investigations. Their explanations have ranged from a plot by anti-Castro Cubans, to a Communist-sponsored attack, to a conspiracy by the CIA.

THINK THROUGH HISTORY
F. Contrasting *How did the Warren Commission's findings differ from other theories?*
F. Answer It declared that Oswald acted alone, while others claimed a conspiracy.

What Americans did learn from the Kennedy assassination was that their system of government is remarkably sturdy. A crisis that would have crippled a dictatorship did not prevent a smooth transition to the presidency of Lyndon Johnson. In a moving speech to Congress, Johnson expressed his hope that "from the brutal loss of our leader we will derive not weakness but strength, that we can and will act and act now." Not long after this speech, Johnson drove through Congress the most ambitious domestic legislative package since the New Deal.

Section 2 Assessment

1. **TERMS & NAMES**
Identify:
- New Frontier
- mandate
- Peace Corps
- Alliance for Progress
- Warren Commission

2. **SUMMARIZING** Re-create the web below on a piece of paper and fill it in with programs of the New Frontier.

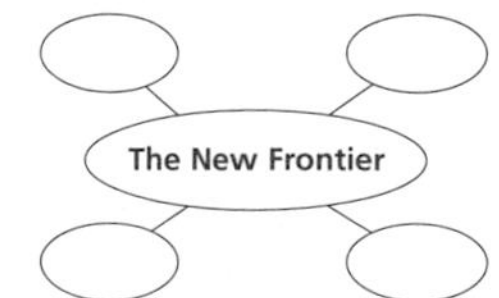

3. **ANALYZING MOTIVES** Why do you think Congress was so enthusiastic about allocating funds for the space program but rejected spending in education, social services, and other pressing needs?
THINK ABOUT
- the U.S.-Soviet space race
- Kennedy's commitment to the space program
- the costs and benefits of the space program

4. **FORMING OPINIONS** Do you think President Kennedy was a successful leader? Explain your viewpoint.
THINK ABOUT
- the reasons for his popularity
- the goals he expressed
- his legislative record
- his foreign policy

ANSWERS

1. TERMS & NAMES
New Frontier, p. 678
mandate, p. 678
Peace Corps, p. 679
Alliance for Progress, p. 679
Warren Commission, p. 682

2. SUMMARIZING
Possible Answer: Peace Corps, Alliance for Progress, moon program, tax cut, civil rights bill.

3. ANALYZING MOTIVES
Possible Response: It was largely a matter of national pride, since the Soviets had already sent a man into space.

4. FORMING OPINIONS
Possible Response: Students might argue that he was successful because he was popular and focused on projects that Congress would support. Others might argue that he was unsuccessful because he tended to react to events—such as to the Soviet threat, Harrington's *The Other America,* and the civil rights movement—rather than take the lead.

3 The Great Society

TERMS & NAMES
- Lyndon B. Johnson
- Economic Opportunity Act
- Great Society
- Medicare and Medicaid
- Immigration Act of 1965
- Warren Court
- reapportionment
- Miranda rights

LEARN ABOUT domestic events during Johnson's presidency
TO UNDERSTAND what Johnson's Great Society was.

ONE AMERICAN'S STORY

Larry Alfred served on the front lines of the war on poverty. In 1966, family finances forced Alfred to drop out of high school in Mobile, Alabama. He turned instead to the Job Corps, a federal program that provided training for young people from poor backgrounds. There he learned to operate heavy construction equipment, but his real dream was to help other people. So, on the advice of his Job Corps counselor, he read books on psychology and social work and decided to join VISTA—Volunteers in Service to America—often called the "domestic peace corps."

Both the Job Corps and VISTA sprang into being in 1964, when President Lyndon B. Johnson signed the Economic Opportunity Act. This sweeping law was the main offensive of Johnson's "war on poverty" and a cornerstone of the legislative agenda he called the Great Society.

VISTA assigned Alfred to work with a community of poor, mostly Latino farm laborers in Robstown, Texas, near the Mexican border. There he soon discovered that a number of children with mental and physical disabilities had no access to special assistance, education, or training. The main obstacle was in overcoming the stigma that parents often attached to children with disabilities, particularly mental retardation. So he established the Robstown Association for Retarded People, started an education program for the parents, sought state funds, and created a rehabilitation center.

At age 20, Larry Alfred was a high school dropout, Job Corps graduate, VISTA volunteer, and in Robstown, an authority on people with disabilities. Alfred embodied Johnson's ambitions for the Great Society in two ways. Its programs helped him turn his life around, and he went on to make a difference in other people's lives.

above, A VISTA volunteer in Chicago tutors children whose families had moved there from Appalachia; *left,* A VISTA volunteer in San Jon, New Mexico, works with Navajo laborers.

LBJ's Path to Power

"I don't quite know why it is," said one of **Lyndon B. Johnson's** friends in late 1963, "but whatever Lyndon *really* wants, he gets in the end." By the time LBJ, as Johnson was called, succeeded to the presidency, his ambition and drive had become legendary. In explaining his frenetic energy, Johnson once remarked, "That's the way I've been all my life. My daddy used to wake me up at dawn and shake my leg and say, 'Lyndon, every boy in town's got an hour's head start on you.'"

FROM THE TEXAS HILLS TO CAPITOL HILL A fourth-generation Texan, Lyndon Baines Johnson grew up in the dry Texas hill country of Blanco County, near Austin. His great-grandfather had been a pioneer, his grandfather a cowboy, and his father a businessman who served five terms in the Texas legislature. The Johnsons never knew great wealth, but they also never missed a meal—something that could not be said of many struggling farm families in the area.

LBJ entered politics in 1937 when he won a special election to fill a vacant seat in the U.S. House of Representatives. Johnson styled himself as a "New

SECTION 3 RESOURCES

PRINT RESOURCES

IN-DEPTH RESOURCES: UNIT 6
Guided Reading, p. 3
Primary Source: from *Unsafe at Any Speed,* p. 10
American Lives: Rachel Carson, p. 15

READING STUDY GUIDE, p. 211

ACCESS FOR STUDENTS ACQUIRING ENGLISH
Guided Reading (Spanish), p. 227

SPANISH READING STUDY GUIDE, p. 211

FORMAL ASSESSMENT
Section Quiz, p. 250

ALTERNATIVE ASSESSMENT BOOK
See forms for supporting and scoring alternative activities.

TECHNOLOGY RESOURCES

HUMANITIES TRANSPARENCIES
H44, Johnson Rag

CRITICAL THINKING TRANSPARENCIES
CT28, The Great Society
CT62, Federal Budget: 1952–1968

CD-ROM Electronic Library of Primary Sources

VIDEO *American Portfolio: A Videodisc for U.S. History* user's guide, pp. 240, 245

INTERNET http://www.mlushistory.com

Section 3 Overview

OBJECTIVES

1. To describe Johnson's path to the White House.
2. To explain Johnson's domestic agenda.
3. To summarize the goals of Johnson's Great Society.
4. To identify the reforms of the Warren Court.
5. To evaluate the impact of Great Society programs.

SKILLBUILDER

- Interpreting charts, p. 687

CRITICAL THINKING

- Analyzing motives, p. 684
- Theme: Economic Opportunity, p. 685
- Contrasting, p. 685
- Comparing, p. 686
- Theme: Immigration and Migration, p. 686
- Recognizing effects, pp. 689, 691
- Finding main ideas, p. 690
- Identifying problems, p. 691
- Summarizing, p. 691
- Synthesizing, p. 691

FOCUS & MOTIVATE

5-MINUTE WARM-UP

Recognizing Facts and Details
To explore the 1964 election, have students look at the button on page 685 and answer these questions.

1. What does the elephant symbolize?
2. What does the button suggest about voting trends among Republicans in 1964?

WARM-UP TRANSPARENCY 20

▶ ***Starting with the Student***
- Do students think that the government should try to right social wrongs?

OBJECTIVE
1 INSTRUCT

LBJ's Path to Power

▶ ***Discussing Key Ideas***
- Johnson imitates FDR's leadership style.

(continued on next page)

(continued from page 683)

- Johnson proves himself a master of party politics.
- Johnson's legislative skill and Southern Protestant background win him a slot on the Kennedy ticket.

IN-DEPTH RESOURCES: UNIT 6
Guided Reading, p. 3

ACCESS FOR STUDENTS ACQUIRING ENGLISH
Guided Reading (Spanish), p. 227

KEY PLAYER
Lyndon B. Johnson

Critical Thinking: Analyzing Ask students what Johnson's educational experience reveals about his character. *Possible Responses: Hard-working, self-reliant, caring.* Why did Johnson choose to sign the education act at his old schoolhouse? What does this action say about him as a politician? *Possible Response: He was shrewd. He knew that signing the act in that location would impress the public with the modesty of his background and the goodness of his heart.*

HUMANITIES TRANSPARENCIES
H44, Johnson Rag

OBJECTIVE
② INSTRUCT

Johnson's Domestic Agenda

▶ ***Discussing Key Ideas***

- Johnson pushes through Kennedy's civil rights and tax-cut bills.
- Johnson presses ahead with his own agenda—a war on poverty.

(continued on next page)

KEY PLAYER

LYNDON B. JOHNSON
1908–1973

LBJ received his degree in education from Southwest Texas State Teachers College in 1930. To finance his own education, Johnson took a year off from college to work at a Mexican-American school in Cotulla, Texas. He later taught English at the Sam Houston High School in Houston. At age 26, he became the state director of the National Youth Administration, a New Deal agency.

When he became president, Johnson pushed hard for the passage of the Elementary and Secondary Education Act. On April 11, 1965, he signed the act at the one-room schoolhouse near Stonewall, Texas, where his own education had begun. He asked his first teacher, Mrs. Kathryn Deadrich Loney ("Miss Kate") to sit at his side. Johnson also invited his former students to attend.

In recalling the experience, Johnson wrote, "My education had begun with what I learned in that schoolroom. Now what I had learned and experienced since that time had brought me back to fulfill a dream."

Dealer" and spokesperson for the small ranchers and struggling farmers of his district. His energetic politicking caught the eye of President Franklin Roosevelt, who took Johnson under his wing. Roosevelt helped the freshman representative secure key committee assignments in Congress and steer much-needed electrification and water projects to his Texas district. Johnson, in turn, idolized FDR and imitated his leadership style.

Once in the House, Johnson eagerly eyed a seat in the Senate. In 1948, after an exhausting, bitterly fought campaign, he won the Democratic primary election for the Senate by a margin of 87 votes out of over 900,000 cast. (In Texas at the time, the Democratic candidate was a shoo-in in the general election.) His opponent charged Johnson with illegal ballot-stuffing and fought the results all the way to the Supreme Court. The close result and allegations of fraud sent Johnson to his new position with the mocking nickname Landslide Lyndon—and the driving determination to win the approval of the voters and of his congressional colleagues.

Johnson proved himself a master of party politics and behind-the-scenes maneuvering, and he rose to the position of Senate majority leader in 1955. Standing six feet three, he dominated every room he entered. The tall Texan demonstrated great skill in the give-and-take needed to reach an agreement. People called his legendary ability to persuade senators to support his bills "the Johnson treatment." Referring to himself in the third person, Stewart Alsop, a writer for the *Saturday Evening Post,* explained what it was like to experience this treatment—which Johnson also used to win over reporters.

A PERSONAL VOICE

> The Majority Leader [Johnson] was, it seemed, in a relaxed, friendly, reminiscent mood. But by gradual stages this mood gave way to something rather like a human hurricane. Johnson was up, striding about his office, talking without pause, occasionally leaning over, his nose almost touching the reporter's, to shake the reporter's shoulder or grab his knee. . . . Appeals were made, to the Almighty, to the shades of the departed great, to the reporter's finer instincts and better nature, while the reporter, unable to get a word in edgewise, sat collapsed upon a leather sofa, eyes glazed, mouth half open.
>
> **STEWART ALSOP,** "The New President," *Saturday Evening Post,* December 14, 1963

It was through Johnson's deft handling of Congress that the nation passed the Civil Rights Act of 1957, a voting rights measure that was the first civil rights legislation since Reconstruction. Johnson's knack for achieving legislative results captured John F. Kennedy's attention, too. To Kennedy, Johnson's congressional connections and his Southern Protestant background compensated for his own drawbacks as a candidate, so he asked Johnson to be his running mate. Johnson's presence on the ticket helped Kennedy win key states in the South, especially Texas, which went Democratic by just a few thousand votes.

A. Answer Johnson brought balance to the presidential ticket because of his experience and influence in Congress and his Southern Protestant background.

THINK THROUGH HISTORY
A. Analyzing Motives *Why did Kennedy choose Johnson to be his running mate?*

Johnson's Domestic Agenda

The nation was still stunned by Kennedy's assassination as it watched and listened to President Johnson address a joint session of Congress on the fifth day of his administration. "All I have I would have given gladly not to be standing here today," he quietly began. He reminded his audience how Kennedy had inspired Americans to begin to solve national and world problems. "Let us continue," Johnson declared. In tribute to the nation's fallen leader, he urged Congress to move ahead on the civil rights and tax-cut bills Kennedy had sent to Capitol Hill.

TEACHING OPTION

Making Connections Across Time

Southern Democrats Today Draw students' attention to the fact that, as a Democrat, Johnson was a shoo-in in the Senate race in Texas. Tell students that the South had largely turned to the Democratic Party after Abraham Lincoln—a Republican—had led the Union to victory in the Civil War. Since then, the South had been a stronghold of white, male politicians who clung to Confederate beliefs. With politicians like Johnson, however, this tradition began to change. Over time, other socially liberal politicians came to power in the South. In addition, as Southern blacks gained more equal rights, many African Americans began to run for office—and win. Today, the South is governed by whites and blacks, men and women, and Democrats and Republicans—with few traditional Southern Democrats remaining. In fact, in 1976, 1992, and 1996, nontraditional Southern Democrats—first Jimmy Carter and then Bill Clinton—were elected to the White House.

Congress responded and in February 1964 passed a tax reduction of over $11 billion into law. As the Democrats had hoped, the tax cut spurred economic growth by stimulating consumer spending and business investment. More spending meant higher corporate profits, which actually increased tax revenues and lowered the federal budget deficit from $6 billion in 1964 to $4 billion in 1966.

It took Johnson several more months to push the civil rights bill through Congress, but he finally persuaded Southern senators to stop blocking its passage. In July, Johnson signed the Civil Rights Act of 1964, one of the most important achievements of the civil rights era. The act prohibited discrimination based on race, religion, national origin, and gender and granted the federal government new powers to enforce its provisions. (See Chapter 21 for more on this act.)

THE WAR ON POVERTY Following these successes, LBJ pressed ahead with his own ambitious agenda—to alleviate poverty. Like Kennedy before him, Johnson was appalled by the depth of poverty revealed in Michael Harrington's *The Other America,* and he believed that bold public action could change the lives of the millions of Americans who lived without hope of ever attaining the American dream. Early in 1964, he had declared "unconditional war on poverty in America" and proposed sweeping legislation designed to help Americans "on the outskirts of hope." (See *poverty* on page 937 in the Economics Handbook.)

THINK THROUGH HISTORY
B. THEME ***Economic Opportunity*** *What problems in American society did the Economic Opportunity Act seek to address?*

B. Answer The EOA sought to eliminate poverty.

In August 1964, Congress enacted the **Economic Opportunity Act** (EOA), approving nearly $1 billion for youth programs, antipoverty measures, small business loans, and job training. The EOA legislation created the Job Corps youth training program, the VISTA (Volunteers in Service to America) program, and Project Head Start, an education program for underprivileged preschoolers. It also established the Community Action Program, which encouraged poor people to participate in setting up public-works programs.

THE 1964 ELECTION Lyndon Johnson had brought the nation through a difficult time and had enjoyed legislative success. For the Republicans, ousting him from office in the election of 1964 would have been extremely difficult, even if they had nominated a candidate with wide appeal. As it was, they nominated a candidate with narrow appeal: conservative senator Barry Goldwater of Arizona. Goldwater believed the federal government had no business trying to right social and economic wrongs such as poverty, discrimination, and lack of opportunity. He attacked such long-established federal programs as Social Security, which he wanted to make voluntary, and the Tennessee Valley Authority, which he wanted to abolish.

In 1964, most American people were more in tune with Johnson's liberal goals. A majority of Americans believed that government could and should help solve the nation's social and economic problems. Moreover, in foreign affairs, Goldwater's hard-line rhetoric—including suggestions that he might use nuclear weapons on both Cuba and North Vietnam—frightened many people.

C. Answer LBJ won a landslide and mandate; he also had a liberal majority in Congress. JFK's slim victory had denied him a mandate.

THINK THROUGH HISTORY
C. *Contrasting* *How did the margin of victory of the 1964 election differ from that of 1960, and how might this difference have affected the two presidents' legislative records?*

Johnson capitalized heavily on these fears. His campaign produced a chilling television commercial in which a picture of a little girl counting the petals on a daisy dissolved into a picture of a mushroom cloud created by an atomic bomb. And where Goldwater advocated intervention in Vietnam, Johnson assured the American people that sending U.S. troops there "would offer no solution at all to the real problem of Vietnam."

LBJ won the election by a landslide. He received 61 percent of the popular vote—the highest percentage since 1936—and he received 90 percent of the electoral vote. The Democrats also increased their majority in Congress. For the first time since 1938, a Democratic president did not need the votes of conservative Southern Democrats in order to get laws passed. Now Johnson could launch his reform program in earnest.

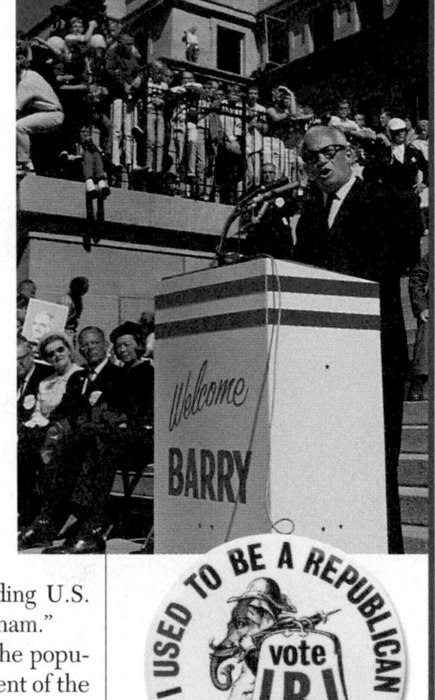

Senator Barry Goldwater delivers a speech while campaigning in Boise, Idaho, in 1964.

(continued from page 684)

- Capitalizing on the public's liberal bent, Johnson wins a landslide victory in 1964.

ELECTRONIC LIBRARY OF PRIMARY SOURCES

from *Citizens' Guide to the Civil Rights Act of 1964* by the National Lawyers Guild

from Civil Rights Act of 1964

MORE ABOUT . . .
Barry Goldwater

During the 1964 presidential election, Barry Goldwater knew his chances were slim at best. In his book of memoirs, he wrote: "Running for President was something like trying to stand up in a hammock. We knew from the polls a victory was not in our lane." Indeed, the polls continually showed Goldwater with 30 points to Johnson's 70. Still, Goldwater felt bitter after his crushing loss. "I think I could have accepted the defeat of the individual Barry Goldwater with humor and good grace. It was the apparent repudiation of all the beliefs and understandings I cherished—which had guided me in public life—that I found so hard to accept." Ironically, some of Goldwater's beliefs—reducing federal expenditures and balancing the budget—had been adopted by both Republicans and Democrats by the 1990s.

TEACHING OPTIONS

Exploring Themes

Economic Opportunity Discuss the programs under the Economic Opportunity Act. Ask students who the programs were meant to benefit. *Possible Responses: The poor, minorities.* Why did many of these people need assistance? *Possible Responses: Because of overcrowded urban conditions, unequal treatment, poor educational opportunities.* Are these programs better than welfare? Why or why not? *Possible Response: Better, because they help people help themselves.* Then ask students to identify government programs today that help people in economic need. How effective are these programs?

Making Connections Across Time

Campaign Commercials Tell students that, as television became an increasingly influential part of people's lives, politicians learned how to use it as a persuasive tool. In the 1988 presidential campaign, television dominated as never before. Playing on the public's concern with the rising crime rate, a Republican ad accused Democratic candidate Michael Dukakis of being soft on crime for furloughing Willie Horton, a black convict. Many people believe the ad contributed to Dukakis's overwhelming defeat. Ask students to discuss recent campaign ads that have attempted to capitalize on people's fears.

OBJECTIVE
③ INSTRUCT

Building the Great Society

▶ ***Starting with the Student*** Have students use a chart like the one below to organize what they learn about the Great Society programs. Students should list each program and describe its purpose.

Program	Purpose

▶ ***Discussing Key Ideas***
- Johnson presents his legislative program, which he calls the Great Society.
- Great Society programs bring about change in education, Social Security, housing, and immigration.
- The Great Society also seeks to protect the environment and consumers.

IN-DEPTH RESOURCES: UNIT 6
Primary Source: from *Unsafe at Any Speed,* p. 10
American Lives: Rachel Carson, p. 15

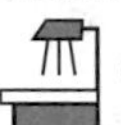
CRITICAL THINKING TRANSPARENCIES
CT28, The Great Society

NOW & THEN
Medicare on the Line
Critical Thinking: Evaluating Ask students whether they think cutbacks should be made in Medicare. Is Medicare an entitlement? Should other federal programs be cut to help balance the budget? Or is Medicare in its present state too expensive to maintain?

Building the Great Society

In May of 1964, Johnson had summed up his grand vision for America in a phrase: the **Great Society.** In a speech at the University of Michigan, the president declared that "the Great Society demands an end to poverty and racial injustice." But, he told the enthusiastic crowd, that was "just the beginning." Johnson envisioned a legislative program that would create not only a higher living standard and equal opportunity but also promote a richer quality of life.

NOW & THEN

MEDICARE ON THE LINE

When President Johnson signed the Medicare bill in 1965, only half of the nation's elderly had health insurance. Today, thanks largely to Medicare, most do. However, most experts agree that the country cannot afford to sustain Medicare in its present form for much longer, especially if the nation hopes to balance the federal budget.

Three trends are fueling these concerns: (1) people are living longer, (2) health care continues to become more advanced and more expensive, and (3) the large baby boomer generation is moving toward retirement age. Medicare costs are increasing 10 percent a year. In 1994, federal spending on Medicare was about $160 billion; in 2002, without changes in the program, it could top $345 billion.

Both Democrats and Republicans in Washington agree that cuts have to be made, but experience has shown that the issue is a political hot potato. Many people consider Medicare an "entitlement" that they expect to receive when they retire. Although most Americans want a balanced budget, a 1996 survey revealed that only 16 percent favored large cutbacks in Medicare to achieve it.

A PERSONAL VOICE

The Great Society is a place where every child can find knowledge to enrich his mind and to enlarge his talents. It is a place where leisure is a welcome chance to build and reflect, not a feared cause of boredom and restlessness. It is a place where the city of man serves not only the needs of the body and the demands of commerce but the desire for beauty and the hunger for community. It is a place where man can renew contact with nature. It is a place which honors creation for its own sake and for what it adds to the understanding of the race. It is a place where men are more concerned with the quality of their goals than the quantity of their goods.

LYNDON JOHNSON, "The Great Society," May 22, 1964

LBJ set lofty goals for his nation and for himself. Like his idol FDR, he wanted to change America. He also knew that he had to act quickly to capitalize on his new mandate. During the years 1965 and 1966, the Johnson administration introduced a flurry of bills to Congress. By the time Johnson left the White House in 1969, Congress had passed 206 of his measures. For most of them, the president personally led the battle to get them passed.

LANDMARK LEGISLATION Johnson considered education "the key which can unlock the door to the Great Society." The Elementary and Secondary Education Act of 1965 provided more than $1 billion in federal aid to help public and parochial schools purchase textbooks and new library materials. This was the first major federal aid package for education in the nation's history.

LBJ and Congress brought about the first major change in Social Security since its adoption in 1935 by establishing Medicare and Medicaid. **Medicare** provides hospital insurance and low-cost medical insurance for almost every American age 65 or older. **Medicaid** extended health insurance to welfare recipients.

D. Answer Both provide government-sponsored health insurance.

THINK THROUGH HISTORY
D. *Comparing* *How are Medicare and Medicaid similar?*

Congress also appropriated money to build some 240,000 units of low-rent public housing and help low- and moderate-income families pay for better private housing. It established a new federal department, the Department of Housing and Urban Development (HUD). As secretary of the new department, Johnson appointed Robert Weaver, the first African-American cabinet member in American history.

The Great Society also brought profound changes to the nation's immigration laws. The Immigration Act of 1924 and the National Origins Act of 1929 had established immigration quotas that discriminated strongly against people from outside Western Europe. The **Immigration Act of 1965** replaced the national origins system with an annual quota of 170,000 immigrants from the Eastern Hemisphere and 120,000 from the Western Hemisphere. Within this overall quota, no more than 20,000 persons from any one nation could enter the United States each year. Close relatives of American residents were exempt from the quotas. This act opened the door for many non-European immigrants to settle in the United States.

E. Answer It replaced the national origins system, which discriminated against people from outside Western Europe.

THINK THROUGH HISTORY
E. THEME ***Immigration and Migration*** *How did the Immigration Act of 1965 change the nation's immigration system?*

TEACHING OPTIONS

Exploring Themes

Immigration and Migration Discuss the Immigration Act of 1965. Ask students how the legislation affected immigration to the United States. *Possible Response: It allowed the influx of people from Asia, Latin America, and other non-European regions.* In what ways was the act consistent with the ideals and goals of the Great Society? *Possible Response: It offered the opportunity of a better life to people in need.* How does the act's provisions continue to affect the United States today? *Possible Response: People allowed into the country under the act have greatly influenced mainstream American culture and lifestyle.*

Making Connections Across the Curriculum

Government Discuss the creation of the Department of Housing and Urban Development. Ask students why the new federal department was created. *To address the problems of the nation's cities.* Why was the department considered necessary by the mid-1960s? *Possible Response: Explosive urban growth in the 1950s had resulted in many urban problems, including overcrowding and inadequate housing.* Then ask students to discuss any recently formed federal departments or programs, such as the war on drugs, created to address current problems.

Great Society Programs, 1964–1967

Category	Year	Program	Year	Program
Poverty	1964	**Tax Reduction Act** cut corporate and individual taxes to stimulate growth.	1965	**Medical Care Act** established Medicare and Medicaid programs.
	1964	**Economic Opportunity Act** created Job Corps, VISTA, Project Head Start, and other programs to fight "war on poverty."	1965	**Appalachian Regional Development Act** targeted aid for highways, health centers, and resource development in that economically depressed area.
Cities	1965	**Omnibus Housing Act** provided money for low-income housing.	1966	**Demonstration Cities and Metropolitan Area Redevelopment Act** funded slum rebuilding, mass transit, and other improvements for selected "model cities."
	1965	**Department of Housing and Urban Development** was formed to administer federal housing programs.		
Education	1965	**Elementary and Secondary Education Act** directed money to schools for textbooks, library materials, and special education.	1965	**National Foundation on the Arts and the Humanities** was created to financially assist painters, musicians, actors, and others in arts.
	1965	**Higher Education Act** funded scholarships and low-interest loans for college students.	1967	**Corporation for Public Broadcasting** was formed to fund educational TV and radio broadcasting.
Discrimination	1964	**Civil Rights Act** outlawed discrimination in public accommodations, housing, and jobs; increased federal power to prosecute civil rights abuses.	1965	**Voting Rights Act** ended the practice of requiring voters to pass literacy tests and permitted the federal government to monitor voter registration.
	1964	**Twenty-fourth Amendment** abolished the poll tax in federal elections.	1965	**Immigration Act** ended national-origins quotas established in 1924.
Environment	1965	**Wilderness Preservation Act** set aside over 9 million acres for national forest lands.	1965	**Clean Air Act Amendment** directed the federal government to establish emission standards for new motor vehicles.
	1965	**Water Quality Act** required states to clean up their rivers.	1967	**Air Quality Act** set federal air pollution guidelines and extended federal enforcement power.
Consumer Advocacy	1966	**Truth in Packaging Act** set standards for labeling consumer products.	1966	**Highway Safety Act** required states to set up highway safety programs.
	1966	**National Traffic and Motor Vehicle Safety Act** set federal safety standards for the auto and tire industries.	1966	**Department of Transportation** was created to deal with national air, rail, and highway transportation.

Skillbuilder Answer The programs were wide-ranging, which reflected an expanding role for the federal government in addressing certain areas of American society.

The Great Society addressed more than economic and social ills—it also embraced, among other things, protecting the environment and consumers. In 1962, *Silent Spring,* a book by Rachel Carson, had called attention to a hidden danger: the effects of pesticides on the environment. Carson's book and the following public outcry resulted in the Water Quality Act of 1965, which required states to clean up rivers. "Today we begin to be masters of our environment," declared Johnson as he signed the bill into law. He also ordered the federal government to search out the worst chemical polluters. "There is no excuse . . . for chemical companies and oil refineries using our major rivers as pipelines for toxic wastes." Such words and actions helped trigger the environmental movement in the United States. (See Chapter 24.)

Hand in hand with environmental protection arose a new concern for consumer protection. Consumer advocates convinced Congress to pass major safety laws, including a truth-in-packaging law that set standards for labeling consumer goods. Ralph Nader, a young lawyer, wrote a book, *Unsafe at Any Speed,* that sharply criticized the U.S. automobile industry for ignoring safety

SKILLBUILDER
INTERPRETING CHARTS
What did the Great Society programs indicate about the federal government's changing role?

Ralph Nader

Issues for the 21st Century

Curing the Health Care System

Connect medical programs in the 1960s to health care issues today by having students read pages 892–893. Then have them answer these questions.

1. Why did President Johnson want to establish Medicare and Medicaid? *To provide health care for the elderly and for the poor.*
2. Why are these medical programs in danger now? *Rising costs; running out of money; increasing numbers of seniors.*

HISTORY FROM VISUALS

Great Society Programs, 1964–1967

Reading the Chart Point out that the chart organizes the Great Society programs in distinct categories. Then ask students in which year the greatest number of programs were passed. *1965.* How is this fact connected to the results of the 1964 election? *Johnson hurried through a flurry of bills soon after the election to take advantage of his mandate.*

Extension Ask students what the scope of the Great Society programs suggests about the Johnson administration. *Possible Responses: The administration was ambitious, compassionate, liberal.* Why did the number of programs drop off after 1967? *Possible Response: Because Johnson began to focus his energies on the Vietnam War.*

Block Schedule TEACHING OPTION **Time Needed: 30 Minutes**

Cooperative Activity: Outlining Provisions for a Great Society Program

Task: Groups of four to five students will select a category and outline provisions for a Great Society-inspired program that addresses a problem today.

Purpose: To get a sense of the scope and purpose of the Great Society programs.

Activity: Students should get together in groups and discuss some of the major problems that face society today. Encourage students to use the categories and bills listed in the chart on page 687 to spark ideas. Students should then agree on a problem they would like to address and write an outline describing the problem and a proposed solution. The outline should detail the roles of the individuals and groups involved in the solution.

Building a Portfolio: Students who add their outlines to their portfolios should attach a note explaining the extent to which the government should involve itself in the issue.

ALTERNATIVE ASSESSMENT BOOK
Standards for Evaluating a Cooperative Activity

Standards for Evaluation
Outlines should . . .

- address an important problem in society
- describe the roles of the people involved in effecting a solution
- be consistent with the vision of the Great Society programs

OBJECTIVE

④ **INSTRUCT**

Reforms of the Warren Court

▶ ***Discussing Key Ideas***

- The Supreme Court reflects the wave of liberal reform that characterizes the Great Society.
- The Warren Court affects political representation in the United States by addressing the issue of reapportionment.
- The Warren Court expands the rights of people accused of crimes.

NOW & THEN

Creating Fair Legislative Districts

▶ ***Starting with the Student***

- Do students think that elected officials truly represent the people? Do students plan to vote when they reach voting age? Why or why not?
- Do students think that African Americans and other minorities are underrepresented in government? If so, what could be done to address this problem?

▶ ***Discussing Key Ideas***

- In 1982, Congress requires states to reapportion their congressional districts to increase minority candidates' chances of winning.
- Supporters of the act claim that boosting minority representation will help right past wrongs.
- Opponents charge that defining districts by race violates the right to equal protection.
- The Supreme Court declares the act unconstitutional and abolishes minority districts in several states.

concerns. His testimony helped persuade Congress to establish safety standards for automobiles and tires. Under prodding from Johnson and Betty Furness, the Special Assistant to the President for Consumer Affairs, Congress passed the Wholesome Meat Act of 1967. Because of consumer protection laws, said Johnson, "Americans can feel a little safer now in their homes, on the road, at the supermarket, and in the department store."

Reforms of the Warren Court

The wave of liberal reform that characterized the Great Society also swept through the Supreme Court of the 1960s. Beginning with the 1954 landmark decision *Brown* v. *Board of Education,* which ruled school segregation unconstitutional, the Court under Chief Justice Earl Warren had showed its willingness to take an activist stance on the leading issues of the day.

A series of major decisions in the 1960s made a lasting impact on American society. The **Warren Court** banned prayer in public schools and declared state-required loyalty oaths unconstitutional. It limited the power of communities to censor books and films and extended the meaning of free speech to include symbolic speech—such as the wearing of black armbands to school by antiwar students. Furthermore, the Court brought about significant change in the areas of congressional reapportionment and the rights of the accused.

CONGRESSIONAL REAPPORTIONMENT In a key series of decisions, the Warren Court addressed the issue of **reapportionment,** or the way in which states redraw election districts based on the changing number of people in them. By 1960, about 80 percent of Americans lived in cities and suburbs. However, many states failed to change their districts to reflect this development; instead, rural districts might have fewer than 200,000 people, while urban districts had

NOW & THEN

Creating Fair Legislative Districts

In the 1960s, the Supreme Court stepped into the debate about reapportionment by ordering states to redistrict according to the principle of "one person, one vote." In the 1990s, the Court visited the reapportionment issue again—this time over the question of how far redistricting can go to increase the political representation of minorities.

An act of Congress in 1982 required states to reapportion their congressional districts so as to increase minority candidates' chances of winning. Following the 1990 census, a wave of redistricting resulted in a record number of African Americans elected to the House. These included Cynthia McKinney of Georgia, who was one of 12 African Americans elected in 1992 to represent new black-majority districts in the South.

However, these "minority-majority" districts soon faced challenges in the courts. The challengers argued that creating these districts amounted to racial gerrymandering. Gerrymandering is the practice of drawing voting districts so as to unfairly benefit one group. Defining districts by race, opponents contended, violated the Fourteenth Amendment right to equal protection.

Supporters of the districts responded that in the past, gerrymandering had been used to intentionally dilute minority voting power. Therefore, the need to boost minority representation—to right past wrongs—demanded that special measures be taken.

The Supreme Court sided with the opponents. In a series of decisions from 1993 to 1996, the Court declared unconstitutional the use of race as a "predominant factor" in drawing congressional districts. It abolished minority districts in Texas, North Carolina, Louisiana, and Georgia—including Cynthia McKinney's home district. In one decision, Justice Anthony Kennedy wrote, "Just as the state may not . . . segregate citizens on the basis of race in its public parks . . . [it] may not separate its citizens into different voting districts based on race."

U.S. Representative Cynthia McKinney was left without a congressional district when the Supreme Court invalidated her Georgia district. In 1996, McKinney ran again in a reconfigured majority-white district and was easily reelected.

INTERACT WITH HISTORY

1. Forming Opinions

Possible Responses: *Students who agree with the arguments for creating race-based districts may assert that the districts will help right past wrongs and give minorities voting power proportional to their population in each state.*

Students who oppose creating race-based districts may say that such districts are unconstitutional, that it is wrong to use race or any other preferential factor to draw congressional districts. They may say that separating citizens into districts on the basis of race smacks of segregation.

2. Looking at an Election

Suggest that students do the following to research the November 1996 elections:

- use newspaper and other periodical sites on the Internet to pinpoint information
- research print and microfiche sources in a library
- write or speak to their representatives or other political experts
- study the weekly reports in the *Congressional Quarterly* and the *Guide to U.S. Elections*

more than 600,000. Thus the voters in rural areas had more representation—and also more power—than those in urban areas.

Baker v. *Carr* (1962) was the first of several decisions that established the principle of "one person, one vote" and made such patterns of representation illegal. In its decision, the Court asserted that the federal courts had the right to tell states to reapportion their districts for more equal representation. In subsequent decisions, including *Reynolds* v. *Sims* (1964), the Court ruled that congressional district boundaries should be redrawn so that they would be equal in population, and it extended the principle of "one person, one vote" to state legislative districts. These judicial decisions were extremely important, for they led to a significant shift of political power throughout the nation from rural areas to urban areas.

THINK THROUGH HISTORY
F. Recognizing Effects *How did the principle of "one person, one vote" affect political representation in the United States?*

F. Answer It equalized political representation among rural and urban areas by ending over-representation—and reducing power—of rural areas.

RIGHTS OF THE ACCUSED Other Warren Court decisions greatly expanded the rights of people accused of crimes. In *Mapp* v. *Ohio* (1961), the Court ruled that evidence seized illegally could not be used in state courts. This is called the exclusionary rule. In *Gideon* v. *Wainwright* (1963), the justices required criminal courts to provide free legal counsel to those who could not afford it. In *Escobedo* v. *Illinois* (1964), the justices ruled that an accused person has a right to have a lawyer present during questioning by police.

In 1966, the Court went one step further in *Miranda* v. *Arizona,* where it ruled that all suspects must be "read their rights" before questioning. These **Miranda rights** include (1) that suspects have a right to remain silent, (2) that anything they say may be used against them, and (3) that they have a right to a lawyer before and during interrogation.

These rulings greatly divided public opinion. Liberals praised the decisions, arguing that they placed necessary limits on police power and protected the right of all citizens to a fair trial. Conservatives, however, bitterly criticized the

Law enforcement officers often carry a card that contains the Miranda rights so they can read the rights to criminal suspects.

MORE ABOUT . . .
Ernesto Miranda

At Ernesto Miranda's trial in 1964 for the kidnap and rape of a young girl, the arresting officers admitted that no explanation of rights had been given to the suspect. The officers claimed that, because Miranda was an ex-convict, he knew his rights. Miranda was convicted and sentenced to twenty to thirty years in prison. He was released in 1966, however, following the Supreme Court's landmark decision. Ten years later, Miranda was stabbed to death in Phoenix in a fight over a card game. When a suspect in Miranda's murder was arrested, the police officer pulled out a card and read, "You have the right to remain silent. . . ."

Georgia's 11th District, 1992–1995

11th District
Atlanta
Augusta
Macon
Columbus
Savannah

African-American Population (percentage by county, per 1990 census)
- 0–24%
- 25–49%
- 50% and over

To comply with federal instructions, many states resorted to drawing oddly shaped districts to create a "minority majority." McKinney's 11th District, for example, was drawn after the 1990 census to ensure that a majority of the district's voters—64 percent—were African American. Stretching across 260 miles, the district was known as "Sherman's March," because—like the Union general—it swept from the outskirts of Atlanta to Savannah on the Atlantic Ocean.

INTERACT WITH HISTORY

1. **FORMING OPINIONS** The goal of the federal government was to increase the number of African Americans and other minority groups in Congress. The Supreme Court ruled that the manner in which the states tried to meet this goal—by creating race-based districts—was unconstitutional. Review the arguments for and against creating these districts. Which do you agree with more? Why?

   SEE SKILLBUILDER HANDBOOK, PAGE 919.

2. **LOOKING AT AN ELECTION** Conduct research to determine the results of the November 1996 congressional elections. How did African-American candidates fare at the polls? Did the abolition of minority and majority districts reduce their representation?

Visit http://www.mlushistory.com for more about gerrymandering.

Issues for the 21st Century

Crime and Public Safety

Connect the impact of the Warren Court decisions on crime to factors affecting crime today by having students read pages 884–887. Then have them answer these questions.

1. How did some of the Warren Court decisions contribute to an increased crime rate in the 1970s? *By expanding the rights of the accused, the decisions made convictions more difficult.*
2. What factors affect the crime rate today? What steps are being taken to curb crime? *Drug abuse, rising numbers of teens. Gun-control and three-strikes laws, new policing efforts.*

TEACHING OPTIONS

Making Connections Across Cultures

School Segregation Tell students that *Brown* v. *Board of Education* got its name from nine-year-old Linda Brown, whose parents wanted to remove her from the all-black school she attended. They contended—and had to prove—that separate schools were unequal by definition. After studying the case, the Supreme Court decided that racially separate schools could never be equal. Earl Warren stated: "To separate [black children] from others of similar age . . . solely because of their race generates a feeling of inferiority . . . that may affect their hearts and minds in a way unlikely ever to be undone."

Teaching Less Proficient Readers

Compare and Contrast Help students understand the conflicting opinions expressed in the Now & Then feature on pages 688 and 689. Have them follow these steps:

1. Create a two-column chart. Label one column Pro and label the other Con.
2. Read the feature once quickly and then slowly.
3. On the second reading, list the arguments people use to support minority-majority districts in the Pro column. List the arguments people use to oppose them in the Con column.
4. Look over the chart and form an opinion on the issue.

OBJECTIVE

5 INSTRUCT

Impact of the Great Society

▶ ***Discussing Key Ideas***

- Johnson extends the power of the federal government more than any president in the post-World War II era.
- The reforms made by the Great Society help create a new awareness of social problems.
- Debates over the effectiveness of the Great Society programs result in a conservative backlash.

CRITICAL THINKING TRANSPARENCIES

CT62, Federal Budget: 1952–1968

POINT/COUNTERPOINT

Debating the Great Society

Starting with the Student

▶ • Do students think that government programs encourage dependency? Or do such programs give people a boost and help them help themselves?

Discussing Key Ideas

▶ • Some advocates claim that the Great Society was a success because of the gains it made in civil rights.

- Defenders admit that the Great Society fell short of its goals but argue that it worked social and political wonders.
- Critics of the Great Society argue that it created oversized bureaucracies and rising budget deficits.
- Opponents assert that the Great Society created a culture of dependency.

Court. They claimed that *Gideon* and *Miranda* benefited criminal suspects and severely limited the power of the police to investigate crimes. During the late 1960s and 1970s, Republican candidates for office seized on the "crime issue," portraying liberals and Democrats as being soft on crime and citing the decisions of the Warren Court as major obstacles to fighting crime.

THINK THROUGH HISTORY
G. Finding Main Ideas *What were the differing reactions to the Warren Court decisions on the rights of the accused?*

G. Answer Liberals praised the decisions for protecting individual rights, while conservatives criticized the Court for protecting criminal suspects and limiting police power.

Impact of the Great Society

The Great Society and the Warren Court greatly changed the United States. People disagree on whether these changes left the nation better or worse off than before. However, most agree on one point: No president in the post–World War II era extended the power and reach of the federal government more than Lyndon Johnson.

The Johnson presidency oversaw an activist era in all three branches of government. The demand for reform helped create a new awareness of social problems, especially on matters of civil rights and the effects of poverty. The optimism spawned during the Kennedy era continued into the early years of the Johnson administration. The "war on poverty" did help reduce the suffering and want of

POINT

"The Great Society succeeded in prompting far-reaching social change."

Advocates of the Great Society contend that it bettered the lives of millions of Americans. Historian John Morton Blum notes, "The Great Society initiated policies that by 1985 had profound consequences: Blacks now voted at the same rate as whites, and nearly 6,000 blacks held public offices; almost every elderly citizen had medical insurance, and the aged were no poorer than Americans as a whole; a large majority of small children attended preschool programs."

Attorney Margaret Burnham argues that the civil rights gains alone justify the Great Society: "For tens of thousands of human beings . . . giving promise of a better life was significant. . . . What the Great Society affirmed was the responsibility of the federal government to take measures necessary to bring into the social and economic mainstream any segment of the people [who had been] historically excluded."

Many defenders of the Great Society acknowledge that it fell short of its goals but argue that this does not detract from its overall achievement. The historian Robert J. Lampman asserts that "even the successes [of the Great Society] have been called failures by reference to new and higher goals" and suggests that this "is evidence not of failure but of the problems of success." John Morton Blum agrees: "The Great Society had its failings. . . . But the Great Society also worked social and political wonders."

COUNTERPOINT

"Failures of the Great Society prove that government-sponsored programs do not work."

The major attack leveled at the Great Society is that it created "big government" and with it an oversized bureaucracy, too many regulations, waste and fraud, and rising budget deficits. As journalist David Alpern writes, big government resulted from the notion that government could solve all the nation's problems: "Oversold in the Johnsonian manner, the Great Society created unwieldy new mechanisms like the Office of Economic Opportunity and began 'throwing dollars at problems'. . . . Spawned in the process were vast new constituencies of government bureaucrats and beneficiaries whose political clout made it difficult to kill programs off."

Conservatives have criticized the Great Society's social welfare programs for creating a culture of dependency. Economist Paul Craig Roberts argues that increasing welfare negates the power of the free enterprise system: "The Great Society . . . reflected our lack of confidence in the institutions of a free society. We came to the view that it is government spending and not business innovation that creates jobs and that it is society's fault if anyone is poor." Speaker of the House Newt Gingrich contends that "the welfare state reduces the poor from citizens to clients." It "breaks up families, minimizes work incentives, blocks people from saving and acquiring property, and overshadows dreams of a promised future with a present despair born of poverty, violence, and hopelessness."

INTERACT WITH HISTORY

1. **FORMING OPINIONS** Do you think the Great Society was a success or a failure? Explain.

SEE SKILLBUILDER HANDBOOK, PAGE 919.

2. **ANALYZING SOCIAL PROBLEMS** Research the most pressing problems in your own neighborhood or precinct. Then propose a social program you think would address at least one of those problems while avoiding the pitfalls of the Great Society programs.

Visit http://www.mlushistory.com for more about the Great Society.

INTERACT WITH HISTORY

1. Forming Opinions

Possible Responses: *Success—Students may claim that the Great Society was a success because it resulted in great gains in civil rights, reduced the poverty level of many Americans, helped underprivileged children get a head start in school, and helped develop people's awareness of social problems.*

Failure—Students may claim that the Great Society was a failure because it fostered the creation of big government, negated the power of the free enterprise system, minimized work incentives, and mired dependents in a cycle of poverty and despair.

2. Analyzing Social Problems

After students identify a problem, suggest that they talk to the people involved to get ideas for addressing the issue. For example, students who think that their neighborhood should have a senior center might speak to elderly neighbors to determine their special needs. Social programs should:

- present a practical solution to a problem in students' neighborhoods
- propose a solution that takes people's needs into account but that also encourages independence
- not be too costly or involve excessive government interference

These preschoolers in a Head Start classroom are among the millions of Americans whose daily lives are still affected by Great Society programs.

THINK THROUGH HISTORY
H. *Identifying Problems* *What problems may have affected the success of the Great Society?*

H. Answer *Possible Answers:* Some programs were hastily conceived and proved difficult to accomplish; contributed to budget deficit problem; federal spending, deficits, and intervention sparked conservative backlash; Vietnam War drew away funds and attention of LBJ.

many people. The number of poor people fell from 25 percent of the population in 1962 to 11 percent in 1973. However, many of Johnson's proposals, though well intended, were hastily conceived and proved difficult to accomplish.

The massive tax cut won by Johnson spurred the economy. But the costs of funding the Great Society contributed to a growing budget deficit—a problem that has continued for more than three decades. Questions about government finances, as well as debates over the effectiveness of these programs and the role of the federal government, left a number of people disillusioned with the Great Society. A conservative backlash began to take shape as a new group of Republican leaders rose to power. In 1966, for example, a conservative Hollywood actor named Ronald Reagan swept to victory in the race for governor of California over the Democratic incumbent.

Thousands of miles away, the conflict in Vietnam also began to eat away at the Great Society, drawing away its funds as well as the attention of the president and of the people. The fear of communism was deeply rooted in the minds of Americans who came of age in the Cold War era. In Vietnam, Communist forces seemed to be gaining the upper hand. Four years after initiating the Great Society, Johnson, who ran as a peace candidate in 1964, would be labeled a "hawk"—a supporter of one of the most divisive wars in recent U.S. history.

Section  Assessment

1. TERMS & NAMES

Identify:
- Lyndon B. Johnson
- Economic Opportunity Act
- Great Society
- Medicare and Medicaid
- Immigration Act of 1965
- Warren Court
- reapportionment
- Miranda rights

2. SUMMARIZING In a two-column table, list four or more major Great Society programs and Warren Court rulings.

Great Society Programs	Warren Court Rulings
1.	1.
2.	2.
3.	3.
4.	4

Which item in each category do you consider the most significant? Why?

3. RECOGNIZING EFFECTS Explain how Lyndon Johnson's personal and political experiences might have influenced his actions as president.

THINK ABOUT
- his family background and education
- his relationship with Franklin Roosevelt
- his powers of persuasion

4. SYNTHESIZING In what ways were the 1960s an "activist" era in all three branches of the federal government? Support your answers with specific examples from the text.

THINK ABOUT
- Johnson's goals for his administration
- the major laws of the Great Society
- the changes brought about by the Warren Court

ANSWERS

1. TERMS & NAMES

Lyndon B. Johnson, p. 683
Economic Opportunity Act, p. 685
Great Society, p. 686
Medicare and Medicaid, p. 686
Immigration Act of 1965, p. 686
Warren Court, p. 688
reapportionment, p. 688
Miranda rights, p. 689

2. SUMMARIZING

Possible Answers: Great Society: Civil Rights Act of 1964, Economic Opportunity Act, Elementary and Secondary Education Act, Medicare, and Medicaid; Warren Court: *Brown* v. *Board of Education, Baker* v. *Carr, Escobedo* v. *Illinois, Miranda* v. *Arizona.*

3. RECOGNIZING EFFECTS

Possible Answers: Johnson's upbringing might have taught him about the hardships of those in need; as a New Dealer, he learned how the government could help people in need; in Congress, he learned the importance of political connections and clout, and the skills to negotiate political deals.

4. SYNTHESIZING

Possible Responses: People in all three branches brought about fundamental reforms that had lasting impact. It could also be called activist because the federal government expanded its role in an attempt to solve the country's social and economic problems.

MORE ABOUT . . .
Ronald Reagan

In the 1966 race for governor of California, the Democratic incumbent Pat Brown underestimated Ronald Reagan and scathingly referred to him as "an actor." This turned out to be a serious mistake in a state in which many people thought more highly of actors than of politicians. When Reagan was sworn in as governor at one minute after midnight on January 2, 1967, he turned to Senator George Murphy, a fellow former actor, and said, "Well, Murphy, here we are on 'The Late Late Show' again."

ASSESS & RETEACH

Section 3 Assessment

After students finish answering the questions, have them discuss their responses to item 2.

Self-Assessment

To explore what they've learned, have students jot down four or five words or phrases they associate with Johnson and the Great Society. Then have students compare and discuss their list with a partner.

Section Quiz

FORMAL ASSESSMENT
Section Quiz, p. 250

Reteach

Use the chart on page 687 to review the achievements of the Great Society.

CLOSE

After winning a landslide victory in the 1964 election, Johnson began pushing his ambitious Great Society programs through Congress. Johnson achieved real gains in civil rights, health care, and education. However, his grand vision for America would soon be distracted by the war in Vietnam.

CHAPTER 20

ASSESSMENT ANSWERS

REVIEWING THE CHAPTER

TERMS & NAMES

1. John F. Kennedy, p. 670
2. Fidel Castro, p. 672
3. Berlin Wall, p. 676
4. hot line, p. 676
5. New Frontier, p. 678
6. Peace Corps, p. 679
7. Warren Commission, p. 682
8. Great Society, p. 686
9. Medicare and Medicaid, p. 686
10. Miranda rights, p. 689

MAIN IDEAS

11. Kennedy looked better in the televised debates, and his brother helped get Martin Luther King, Jr., out of jail.
12. His prestige was boosted when Cubans repelled the U.S.-sponsored invasion, and he increased his ties to the Soviet Union.
13. The Soviets removed their missiles from Cuba, and nuclear war was avoided.
14. Kennedy's legislative agenda based on a broad vision of progress; he faced a conservative coalition in Congress of Republicans and Southern Democrats, and lacked a popular mandate.
15. The Peace Corps and Alliance for Progress.
16. The public deeply mourned the fallen leader.
17. To push through the civil rights and tax cut bills JFK had proposed and to create a "Great Society."
18. By providing job corps youth training programs, education programs, small business loans, medical care, and housing programs.
19. By establishing the principle of "one person, one vote," the Court made states reapportion their representative districts more fairly.
20. It forbade the use of illegally seized evidence, required that free legal counsel be provided to those who could not afford it, established that an accused person had the right to have a lawyer present during questioning, and required that suspects be read their rights at the time of arrest.

Chapter 20 Assessment

REVIEWING THE CHAPTER

TERMS & NAMES For each term below, write a sentence explaining its connection to the Kennedy and Johnson administrations. For each person below, explain his role during this time.

1. John F. Kennedy	**6. Peace Corps**
2. Fidel Castro	**7. Warren Commission**
3. Berlin Wall	**8. Great Society**
4. hot line	**9. Medicare and Medicaid**
5. New Frontier	**10. Miranda rights**

MAIN IDEAS

SECTION 1 *(pages 670–676)*

Kennedy and the Cold War

11. Explain the factors that led to Kennedy's victory over Nixon in the 1960 presidential campaign.
12. How did the Bay of Pigs invasion strengthen Castro's power in Cuba?
13. What were the most significant results of the Cuban missile crisis?

SECTION 2 *(pages 677–682)*

The New Frontier

14. What was Kennedy's New Frontier? Why did he have trouble getting his New Frontier legislation through Congress?
15. What two international aid programs were launched during the Kennedy administration?
16. How did Kennedy's assassination affect the public?

SECTION 3 *(pages 683–691)*

The Great Society

17. What were Johnson's goals as president?
18. Describe ways that Great Society programs addressed the problem of poverty.
19. How did the Supreme Court increase the political power of people in urban areas?
20. Explain how the Supreme Court expanded the protections provided to people accused of crimes.

THINKING CRITICALLY

1. **KENNEDY AND JOHNSON** Use a Venn diagram to show the major legislative programs of the New Frontier and the Great Society.

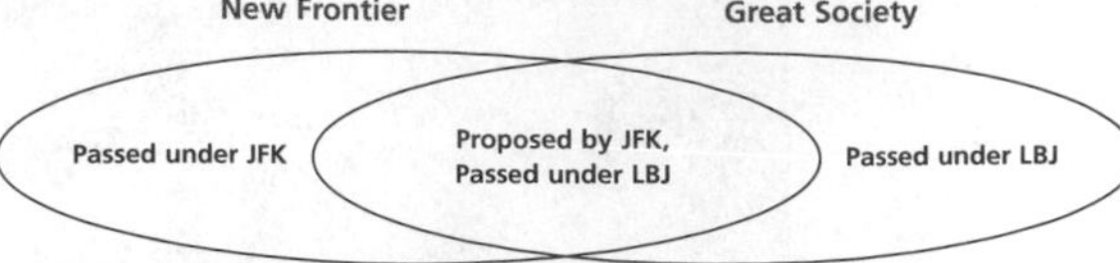

2. **EVALUATING LEADERSHIP** How important is the personality of a president in a democracy? Consider how Kennedy's mystique and Johnson's persuasive skills affected their success as presidents.
3. **SERVING ONE'S COUNTRY** Reread the quotation by John F. Kennedy on page 668. Do you agree with his view about the relationship between individuals and the country? Explain your opinion.
4. **GEOGRAPHY OF THE SUNBELT** The Kennedy and Johnson eras witnessed a transformation of the South—especially Florida. Summarize the events in this chapter that directly affected Florida. How are the changes they brought about felt today?
5. **TRACING THEMES** **ECONOMIC OPPORTUNITY** Do you think the Great Society helped people achieve their hopes of making life better for themselves and their children? Explain.
6. **ANALYZING PRIMARY SOURCES** Read the following excerpt from a speech by Arkansas Senator William Fulbright given less than two weeks after Kennedy was assassinated. Then answer the questions that follow.

> As we mourn the death of President Kennedy, it is fitting that we reflect on the character of our society and ask ourselves whether the assassination of the President was merely a tragic accident or a manifestation of some deeper failing in our lives and in our society.
>
> It may be that the tragedy was one which could have occurred anywhere at any time to any national leader. It may be that the cause lies wholly in the tormented brain of the assassin. It may be that the nation as a whole is healthy and strong and entirely without responsibility for the great misfortune which has befallen it. It would be comforting to think so.
>
> I for one do not think so. . . . Our national life, both past and present, has also been marked by a baleful [evil] and incongruous [inappropriate] strand of intolerance and violence.
>
> **J. WILLIAM FULBRIGHT,** speech delivered December 5, 1963

According to Fulbright, what does the death of Kennedy suggest about American society? Do you agree with him? Why or why not?

THINKING CRITICALLY

1. KENNEDY AND JOHNSON
Possible Answers:
Passed under JFK—Peace Corps, Alliance for Progress, space program.
Proposed by JFK, Passed under LBJ: tax cut, antipoverty legislation, civil rights bill.
Passed under LBJ—Elementary and Secondary Education Act, Medicare and Medicaid, HUD, Immigration Act of 1965, environmental and consumer laws.

2. EVALUATING LEADERSHIP
Students might argue that Kennedy's mystique and Johnson's persuasive skills made them effective leaders. Others might conclude that Kennedy accomplished little despite his charm and that Johnson's success depended more on the 1964 landslide than on his skills.

3. SERVING ONE'S COUNTRY
Students may agree that individuals should show their patriotism by serving their country. Others might disagree, arguing that the government of a nation should serve the citizens.

ALTERNATIVE ASSESSMENT

1. PROJECT FOR CITIZENSHIP
It is June 1963, and President Kennedy announces his intention to negotiate with the Soviets to limit or halt nuclear testing. What is your reaction to this plan—do you approve or disapprove? (See *Expressing Political Opinions* on page 113 in Projects for Citizenship.) Working with a partner, design and create a poster that supports or criticizes President Kennedy's proposal.

Research this question using the CD-ROM *Electronic Library of Primary Sources* and other resources.

- Consider key events such as the bombing of Hiroshima and Nagasaki, the Bay of Pigs invasion, the Cuban missile crisis, and the Berlin crisis.
- Review key sections of the Constitution of the United States to consider the responsibilities of the government to defend and protect the people of the United States.

2. DRAMATIZING KENNEDY'S LIFE
Cooperative Learning Working with a small group of classmates, prepare a short play based on John Kennedy's life.

- Discuss which traits of Kennedy you want to focus on in the play. Then select events from Kennedy's life that demonstrate that trait.
- Select the characters you will need for the play, and who will portray each one. Characters might include members of Kennedy's family, advisers, congressional leaders, foreign leaders, reporters, and others.
- Research your play. Look for details that provide insight into Kennedy's personality.

3. PORTFOLIO PROJECT

Use the Living History activity to expand your portfolio.

LIVING HISTORY

MAKING A CAMPAIGN COMMERCIAL
You have gathered ideas and written a script for a television political ad. Now revise and develop the script into a commercial you can present to the class. The final product could be in any of the following forms.

- Create a storyboard for the commercial. A storyboard is a series of sketches that depicts the sequence of images and text that will appear in the ad.
- Present the commercial live in the form of a skit.
- If you have access to video equipment, you may wish to tape the commercial.
- Present your commercial to the class. Add your work to your American history portfolio.

Bridge to Chapter 21

Review Chapter 20

THE KENNEDY ADMINISTRATION John F. Kennedy narrowly defeated Richard M. Nixon in the 1960 election. From President Kennedy's first days in office, the Cold War and foreign policy occupied much of his attention. In April 1961, the U.S. government backed Cuban exiles in a failed attempt to invade the island and overthrow Fidel Castro. In October 1962, the United States demanded that the Soviet Union remove missile sites it was building in Cuba. Rather than risk a nuclear confrontation, Soviet premier Nikita Khrushchev backed down. Between the two crises in Cuba, Kennedy also faced a crisis over West Berlin. After failing to pressure the United States to give up access to West Berlin, Khrushchev ordered the construction of a wall separating East and West Berlin.

In domestic areas, Kennedy presented several proposals to Congress, but most were blocked by conservatives there. He did gain approval for two programs, the Peace Corps and the Alliance for Progress, and for committing the nation to a moon landing before the end of the 1960s.

ASSASSINATION OF JFK On November 22, 1963, Kennedy was assassinated in Dallas, Texas. Lee Harvey Oswald was captured and charged with the murder. The nation mourned deeply for its fallen young leader. Lyndon B. Johnson, the new president, moved quickly to push through a tax cut and a civil rights bill that Kennedy had proposed.

THE JOHNSON YEARS In 1964, Johnson won a landslide victory and carried with him a solid Democratic majority into Congress. Johnson proposed and Congress approved a flurry of reform legislation known as the Great Society. Among these were federal aid to schools, Medicare, Medicaid, immigration reform, and pollution standards. The decisions of the Supreme Court under Chief Justice Earl Warren expanded the protection of individual liberties, caused more equitable reapportionment of legislative districts, and protected the rights of individuals accused of crimes.

Preview Chapter 21

The support by Kennedy and Johnson for civil rights legislation was part of a much larger drive for equality led by African Americans. In the 1950s and 1960s, African Americans successfully challenged segregation, won voting rights, and made other gains. You will learn about these and other significant developments in the next chapter.

ALTERNATIVE ASSESSMENT

1. PROJECT FOR CITIZENSHIP
Standards for Evaluation
A poster should meet the following criteria:

- Clearly presents a strong opinion on nuclear testing.
- Contains graphics—drawings, photographs, tables, and charts—that convey the opinion visually.
- Uses facts and visuals to appeal to the audience's emotions.
- Includes a catchy slogan or phrase that memorably summarizes the position.

2. DRAMATIZING KENNEDY'S LIFE
Standards for Evaluation
A play should meet the following criteria:

- Strongly conveys Kennedy's personality.
- Uses scenes from Kennedy's life to reveal his personality traits.
- Includes important people in the President's life.
- Sets an appropriate tone, which could be humorous, sad, joyous, or suspenseful.
- Engages the audience.

3. PORTFOLIO PROJECT
LIVING HISTORY
Standards for Evaluation
A commercial should meet the following criteria:

- Focuses on a relevant campaign theme.
- Conveys a clear message.
- Uses persuasive appeals targeted to a broad range of voters.

IN-DEPTH RESOURCES: UNIT 6
See the form for scoring this activity on page 17.

THINKING CRITICALLY

4. GEOGRAPHY OF THE SUNBELT
Possible Answers: The Cuban crisis triggered the growth of the Cuban community in Miami; when the space race began, new launch facilities were constructed at Cape Canaveral.

5. TRACING THEMES ECONOMIC OPPORTUNITY
Students might defend the Great Society for helping people out of poverty. Others might attack it for increasing government expenditures and causing individuals to rely on outside assistance.

6. ANALYZING PRIMARY SOURCES
Fulbright was concerned about violence and intolerance in the United States. Students might agree, pointing to the continuing presence of violent crime and racism. Others might disagree, arguing that an assassination is the work of one person or a small group and does not reflect on society as a whole.

CHAPTER 21

PLANNING GUIDE
Civil Rights

	Key Ideas	COPYMASTERS	ASSESSMENT
SECTION 1 Taking on Segregation *pp. 696–703*	*African Americans use strong organization and nonviolent tactics to confront the South's policies of segregation and racial inequality.*	***In-Depth Resources: Unit 6*** • Guided Reading, p. 18 • Skillbuilder Practice: Making Inferences, p. 21 • Geography Application: The *Brown* Decision, Ten Years Later, p. 22 • Primary Source: Crisis in Little Rock, p. 24 • American Lives: Rosa Parks, p. 31 ***Lesson Plans,*** pp. 171–172	PE ***Section 1 Assessment,*** p. 703 TE ***Self-Assessment,*** p. 703 ***Formal Assessment*** • Section Quiz, p. 259 ***Alternative Assessment Book*** • Standards for Evaluating a Cooperative Activity
SECTION 2 The Triumphs of a Crusade *pp. 704–710*	*Civil rights activists break down numerous racial barriers through continued social protest and the prompting of landmark legislation.*	***In-Depth Resources: Unit 6*** • Guided Reading, p. 19 • Primary Sources: Civil Rights Song, p. 25; *from* "I Have a Dream" by Martin Luther King, Jr., p. 26; Political Poster, p. 27 • Literature: from *And All Our Wounds Forgiven* by Julius Lester p. 28 • American Lives: A. Philip Randolph, p. 32 ***Lesson Plans,*** pp. 173–174	PE ***Section 2 Assessment,*** p. 710 TE ***Self-Assessment,*** p. 710 ***Formal Assessment*** • Section Quiz, p. 260 ***Alternative Assessment Book*** • Standards for Evaluating a Cooperative Activity
SECTION 3 Challenges and Changes in the Movement *pp. 711–717*	*The civil rights movement turns north, new leaders emerge, and the movement becomes more militant, thus leaving behind a mixed legacy.*	***In-Depth Resources: Unit 6*** • Guided Reading, p. 20 ***Lesson Plans,*** pp. 175–176	PE ***Section 2 Assessment,*** p. 717 TE ***Self-Assessment,*** p. 717 ***Formal Assessment*** • Section Quiz, p. 261 ***Alternative Assessment Book*** • Standards for Evaluating a Cooperative Activity
CHAPTER RESOURCES	**Chapter Overview** *After decades of discrimination, African Americans begin a struggle for equality. They make gains against unfair laws in the South, but as the movement reaches Northern cities, gains are fewer.*	***In-Depth Resources: Unit 6*** • Living History Project: Worksheet, p. 33; Standards, p. 34 ***Telescoping the Times*** • Chapter Summary, pp. 41–42 ***Planning for Block Schedules***	PE ***Chapter Assessment,*** pp. 720–721 PE ***Alternative Assessment,*** p. 721 ***Formal Assessment*** • Chapter Test, forms A and B, pp. 262–267 ***Test Generator*** ***Alternative Assessment Book*** See explanation and forms for different kinds of alternative assessments including portfolio assessment.

KEY
- PE Pupil's Edition
- TE Teacher's Edition
- **http://www.mlushistory.com**

TECHNOLOGY

 *Warm-Up Transparency* **21**
AMERICAN STORIES video series
- "Justice in Montgomery"

Electronic Library of Primary Sources
- Desegregation at Central High School by Craig Rains
- Desegregation at Central High School by Melba Pattillo Beals
- from *Stride Toward Freedom* by Martin Luther King, Jr.

 **INTERNET** *Brown* decision and NAACP

 *Warm-Up Transparency* **21**
Humanities Transparencies
- H27, March on Washington

Geography Transparencies
- G29, Before and After the Voting Rights Act of 1965

Grolier Multimedia Encyclopedia
- video of the Civil Rights March on Washington
- Pacifism and nonviolent movements

 **INTERNET** Civil Rights Museum and civil rights speeches

 *Warm-Up Transparency* **21**
Critical Thinking Transparencies
- CT29, Civil Rights Movement
- CT63, African-American Educational Attainment

 *Electronic Library of Primary Sources*
- *from* A Speech to Mississippi Youth by Malcolm X

 **INTERNET** Interact with History p. 719 (PE)

 *American Portfolio: A Videodisc for U.S. History,* user's guide, pp. 236, 237, 240, 246, 248

 *Chapter Summary Audiotapes*
- Unit 6, Chapter 21

 **INTERNET http://www. mlushistory.com**

Block Scheduling (90 MINUTES)

Day 1	Day 2	Day 3
Section 1, pp. 696–703  *AMERICAN STORIES* video series "Justice in Montgomery" *Section Assessment,* p. 703  COOPERATIVE ACTIVITIES • Researching Civil Rights Cases, p. 699 (TE) • Writing About Civil Rights Organizations, p. 702 (TE)	*Section 2,* pp. 704–710 *Section Assessment,* p. 710 COOPERATIVE ACTIVITY • Creating News Reports on the Birmingham Protest, p. 706 (TE)	*Section 3,* pp. 711–717 *Section Assessment,* p. 717 *Tracing Themes: Civil Rights,* pp. 718–719 *Chapter Assessment,* pp. 720–721  COOPERATIVE ACTIVITY • Creating a Historical Atlas, p. 715 (TE)

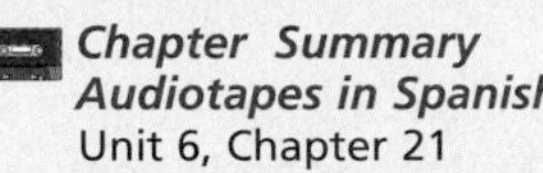

YEARLY PACING *Chapter 21 Total:* 3 days *Yearly Total:* 85 days

See *Planning for Block Schedules* for special activities and pacing strategies.

Customizing for Special Populations

Students Acquiring English

Access for Students Acquiring English: Spanish Translations
- Guided Reading for Sections 1–3, pp. 233–235
- Chapter Summary, pp. 231–232
- Skillbuilder Practice: Making Inferences, p. 236
- Geography Application: The *Brown* Decision, Ten Years Later, p. 237

Spanish Reading Study Guide, pp. 215–222

Translations of Chapter Summaries, Hmong, Cantonese, Vietnamese, and Cambodian

 *Chapter Summary Audiotapes in Spanish* Unit 6, Chapter 21

AMERICAN STORIES video series
- "Justice in Montgomery" (Spanish track)

INTERNET The Diverse Classroom

Gifted and Talented Students

In-Depth Resources: Unit 6
- Primary Sources: Crisis in Little Rock, p. 24; Civil Rights Song, p. 25; *from* "I Have a Dream" by Martin Luther King, Jr., p. 26; Political Poster, p. 27
- American Lives: Rosa Parks, p. 31; A. Philip Randolph, p. 32

Less Proficient Readers

In-Depth Resources: Unit 6
- Guided Reading for Sections 1–3, pp. 18–20
- Skillbuilder: Making Inferences, p. 21
- Geography Application: The *Brown* Decision, Ten Years Later, p. 22

Reading Study Guide
- pp. 215–222

Telescoping the Times
- Chapter Summary, pp. 41–42

Chapter Summary Audiotapes, Unit 6, Chapter 21

Connections to Literature READINGS FOR STUDENTS

In-Depth Resources: Unit 6
- **from *And All Our Wounds Forgiven* by Julius Lester,** p. 28

McDougal Littell *The Language of Literature*
American Literature
- **Martin Luther King, Jr., from *Stride Toward Freedom,*** p. 234
- **Malcolm X, "Necessary to Protect Ourselves,"** p. 239
- **Anne Moody, from *Coming of Age in Mississippi,*** p. 491
- **Robert Hayden, "Frederick Douglass,"** p. 497
- **Dudley Randall, "Ballad of Birmingham,"** p. 500
- **James Baldwin, "My Dungeon Shook,"** p. 791
- **Gwendolyn Brooks, "Life for My Child Is Simple,"** p. 799 **"Primer for Blacks,"** p. 799
- **Toni Morrison, "Thoughts on the African-American Novel,"** p. 805

McDougal Littell *Literature Connections*

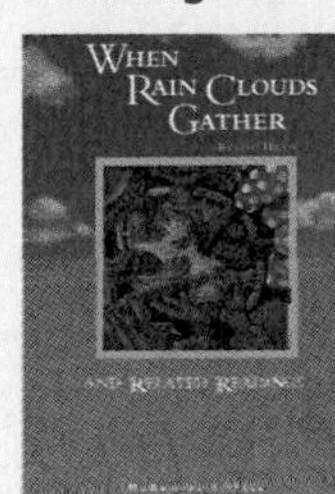

- **Bessie Head**
  When Rain Clouds Gather (with related readings) *Fleeing South Africa in the 1960s, Makhaya comes to a rural village in Botswana as that country approaches independence. The story resonates with the same issues of race, privilege, and identity that drove the civil rights movement in the United States.*
- **Mark Mathabane**
  Kaffir Boy *(with related readings) Born under the hopelessness of apartheid, Mark Mathabane raised himself up from squalor and desperation to win a scholarship to an American university. His extraordinary memoir of life under apartheid is a triumph of the human spirit over hatred.*

CHAPTER 21 OVERVIEW

Civil Rights

▶ *Accessing Prior Knowledge*

Ask students to give examples of people they know or have heard about who have fought against injustice. Have students describe the unfair treatment the people experienced and explain what they did to try to change it.

▶ *Predicting Outcomes*

Have students read the section heads and summaries on page 694. Then have them make predictions about the policies African Americans would confront in the South, the triumphs they would achieve, and the challenges and changes the civil rights movement would face when it turned north.

MORE ABOUT . . .
Medgar Evers

(1925–1963) In the spring of 1963, Medgar Evers went on television to expose the economic injustices faced by African Americans living in Jackson, Mississippi. Evers declared, "Tonight the Negro knows . . . about the new free nation[s] in Africa and knows that a Congo native can be a locomotive engineer, but in Jackson he cannot even drive a garbage truck." The bold speech made Evers a central target of racial hatred and on June 12, 1963, he was murdered in front of his house.

CHAPTER 21 Civil Rights

SECTION 1
Taking on Segregation
African Americans use strong organization and nonviolent tactics to confront the South's policies of segregation and racial inequality.

JUSTICE IN MONTGOMERY

SECTION 2
The Triumphs of a Crusade
Civil rights activists break down numerous racial barriers through continued social protest and the prompting of landmark legislation.

SECTION 3
Challenges and Changes in the Movement
The civil rights movement turns north, new leaders emerge, and the movement becomes more militant, thus leaving behind a mixed legacy.

"You can kill a man, but you can't kill an idea."
Medgar Evers

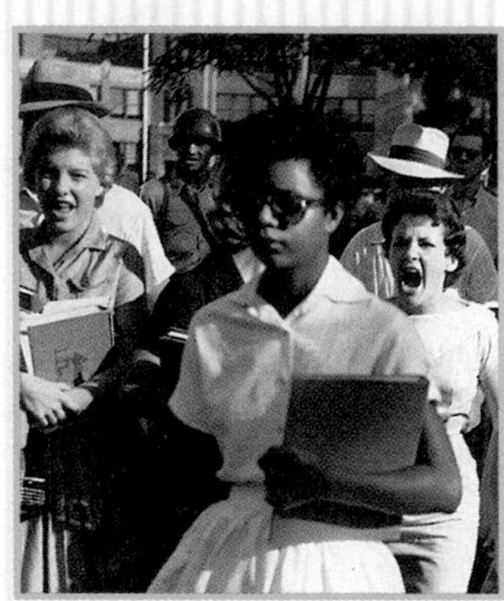

WE WANT TO SIT DOWN LIKE ANYONE ELSE

THE UNITED STATES

- **1954** *Brown v. Board of Education* decision orders the desegregation of public schools.
- **1955** Montgomery bus boycott begins.
- **1956** Dwight D. Eisenhower is reelected.
- **1957** School desegregation crisis occurs in Little Rock, Arkansas.
- **1957** Southern Christian Leadership Conference is formed.
- **1960** Students stage sit-ins across the South.
- **1960** John F. Kennedy is elected president.
- **1961** Attorney General Robert Kennedy steps up federal enforcement of civil rights laws.

THE WORLD

- **1956** Suez Canal crisis occurs in Egypt.
- **1957** African nation of Ghana wins independence.
- **1959** Fidel Castro assumes power in Cuba.
- **1960** South Africa leaves the British Commonwealth and outlaws the African National Congress (ANC).

THEMES IN CHAPTER 21

Constitutional Concerns

In the *Plessy* case in 1896, Justice John Marshall Harlan argued that segregation was wrong. This opinion was not validated by the Supreme Court until the *Brown* decision of 1954.

See Teacher's Edition note, p. 698.

Civil Rights

The civil rights movement exposed the ugly face of racial prejudice and pushed a reluctant federal government to take action on behalf of African Americans. Both Eisenhower and Kennedy had to use military force to enforce desegregation.

Although the Fifteenth Amendment guaranteed voting rights for all citizens regardless of "race, color, or previous condition of servitude," most Southern states restricted African Americans' access to the ballot. The civil rights movement changed that.

See Teacher's Edition notes, pp. 705, 708.

Democracy in America

There is no explicit right to work guaranteed by the Constitution, but some people feel that all Americans deserve to earn a decent living. Many African Americans feel that they have been denied economic equality through discrimination in the workplace.

See Teacher's Edition note, p. 712.

LIVING HISTORY

WRITING A BIOGRAPHICAL SKETCH

Civil rights activists began direct action during the 1950s and 1960s to win constitutional rights for African Americans. As you read the chapter, list important civil rights leaders. Then, choose a leader and write a biographical sketch about him or her. Use the text and other sources for information. Ask yourself the following questions as you begin writing:

- What event or situation caused the leader to become involved in the civil rights movement?
- What were the leader's major contributions to the movement?
- What were the effects of those contributions?
- How did the American people react to the leader's efforts?

PORTFOLIO PROJECT Save your biographical sketch in a folder for your American history portfolio. You will revise and share your writing at the end of the chapter.

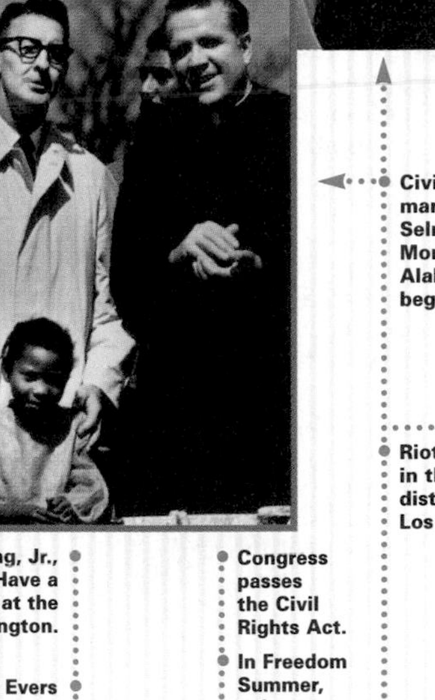

1962

- ANC leader Nelson Mandela is imprisoned.

1963

- Martin Luther King, Jr., delivers his "I Have a Dream" speech at the March on Washington.
- Medgar Evers is assassinated.
- Lyndon B. Johnson becomes president upon John F. Kennedy's assassination.

1964

- Congress passes the Civil Rights Act.
- In Freedom Summer, volunteers enroll African Americans to vote.
- Lyndon B. Johnson is elected president.

1965

- Civil rights march from Selma to Montgomery, Alabama, begins.
- Rioting erupts in the Watts district of Los Angeles.
- Congress passes the Voting Rights Act.
- Malcolm X is assassinated.

1966

- Cultural Revolution begins in China.

1967

- Race riots erupt in major U.S. cities.
- Civil war rages in Nigeria.

1968

- Martin Luther King, Jr., is assassinated.
- Richard M. Nixon is elected president.
- Tet offensive begins.

1969

- U.S. astronauts walk on the moon.

1970

- President Nasser of Egypt dies.

ALTERNATIVE ASSESSMENT

LIVING HISTORY

WRITING A BIOGRAPHICAL SKETCH

Discuss ways of writing a biographical sketch:

- Scan this chapter and outside sources for examples of people to write about.
- Choose a person and research that person's life.
- Decide which events, characteristics, and influences are most important about this person.
- Write the biographical sketch.

Project Planning Guide

Step 1	Choose the person to write about.
Step 2	Research that person's life.
Step 3	Make an outline of the important activities and events of that person's life.
Step 4	Write the biography.

IN-DEPTH RESOURCES: UNIT 6
See worksheet and standards for evaluation, pp. 33, 34.

RECOMMENDED RESOURCES

Books for the Teacher

Chafe, William H. *Civilities and Civil Rights: Greensboro, North Carolina, and the Black Struggle for Freedom.* New York: Oxford UP, 1980.

Morris, Aldon. D. *The Origins of the Civil Rights Movement.* New York: Free Press, 1984.

Ralph, James R. *Northern Protest: Martin Luther King, Jr., Chicago, and the Civil Rights Movement.* Cambridge: Harvard UP, 1993.

Books for the Student

Boyd, Herb. *Black Panthers for Beginners.* New York: Writers and Readers Publishing, Inc., 1995.

Goldfield, David. *Black, White, and Southern: Race Relations and Southern Culture, 1940 to the Present.* Baton Rouge: Louisiana State UP, 1990.

Kluger, Richard. *Simple Justice: The History of* Brown v. Board of Education *and Black America's Struggle for Equality.* New York: Knopf, 1975.

Videos

At the River I Stand. Dir. David Appleby. California Newsreel, 1993. Documentary of Martin Luther King's last civil rights campaign before his assassination.

Eyes on the Prize. PBS Home Video, 1986, 1989. 800-424-7963. 14-hour chronicle of the civil rights movement.

Simple Justice. PBS Home Video, 1993. Documentary about *Brown* v. *Board of Education.*

Software

Malcolm X: By Any Means Possible. Scholastic, 770 Broadway, New York, NY 10003.

Prejudice. Diskettes. Tom Snyder Productions, Inc., 1992. 800-342-0236.

Section 1 Overview

OBJECTIVES

1. To explain how *Plessy* v. *Ferguson* legalized segregation.
2. To describe NAACP's legal challenges to the *Plessy* decision.
3. To describe the divided reaction to the *Brown* decision.
4. To trace the development of the Montgomery bus boycott.
5. To explain the philosophy of Dr. Martin Luther King, Jr., and his role with the the SCLC.
6. To summarize the role young people played in the civil rights movement.

SKILLBUILDER

- Understanding geography: regions, p. 697

CRITICAL THINKING

- Theme: Constitutional Concerns, p. 697
- Developing historical perspective, p. 698
- Finding main ideas, pp. 698, 702
- Analyzing causes, p. 699
- Making inferences, p. 700
- Theme: Democracy in America, p. 701
- Contrasting, p. 703
- Summarizing, p. 703
- Analyzing motives, p. 703
- Drawing conclusions, p. 703

FOCUS & MOTIVATE

5-MINUTE WARM-UP

Making Judgments
To introduce the civil rights movement, have students study the photo on page 703 and answer these questions.

1. What characteristics did the demonstrators reveal by their actions?
2. What do you think motivated the white segregationists' actions?

WARM-UP TRANSPARENCY 21

▶ ***Starting with the Student*** Watch the video "Justice in Montgomery." Then use the *Teacher's Resource Book* as a guide to engage in extension activities using key primary sources.

(continued on next page)

1 Taking on Segregation

LEARN ABOUT school desegregation campaigns, the Montgomery bus boycott, and sit-ins
TO UNDERSTAND the beginnings of the civil rights movement.

TERMS & NAMES
- Thurgood Marshall
- *Brown* v. *Board of Education*
- Rosa Parks
- Dr. Martin Luther King, Jr.
- Southern Christian Leadership Conference
- Student Nonviolent Coordinating Committee
- sit-in

ONE AMERICAN'S STORY

Jo Ann Gibson Robinson drew back in self-defense as the white bus driver raised his hand as if to strike her. "Get up from there!" he shouted. The driver was furious because Robinson, laden with Christmas packages, had forgotten the rules and sat down in one of the front rows of the bus, which were reserved for whites. Robinson left the bus in tears. "I felt like a dog," she later said.

Humiliating incidents were not new to the African Americans who rode the segregated buses of Montgomery, Alabama, in the mid-1950s. The bus company required them to pay at the front and then exit and reboard at the rear. A few drivers considered it a joke to speed off before African American riders had a chance to get back on. In addition, if the seats in the white section were all taken, drivers could force black riders to yield their seats to whites.

Robinson, a professor at the all-black Alabama State College, was also president of the Women's Political Council, a group of professional African-American women determined to increase black political influence. The council petitioned city officials to ease the discrimination practiced on city buses. They also built a network of contacts in the African-American community so they would be able to coordinate citywide protests of injustice if necessary.

Jo Ann Gibson Robinson

A PERSONAL VOICE

> We had members in every elementary, junior high, and senior high school, and in federal, state, and local jobs. Wherever there were more than ten blacks employed, we had a member there. We were prepared to the point that we knew that in a matter of hours, we could corral the whole city.
>
> **JO ANN GIBSON ROBINSON,** quoted in *Voices of Freedom: An Oral History of the Civil Rights Movement*

On December 1, 1955, Robinson and other members of the council learned that the police had arrested an African-American woman for refusing to give up her seat on a bus. "Jo Ann, if you have ever planned to do anything with the council," a friend said, "now is your time." Robinson promptly sent out a call for all African Americans to boycott the city buses.

JUSTICE IN MONTGOMERY
Jo Ann Gibson Robinson and the Bus Boycott

The Segregation System

Segregated buses might never have rolled through the streets of Montgomery—or anywhere else in the United States—if the Civil Rights Act of 1875 had remained in force. This act outlawed segregation in public facilities by decreeing that "all persons . . . shall be entitled to the full and equal enjoyment of the accommodations . . . of inns, public conveyances on land or water, theaters, and other places of public amusement." In 1883, however, the Supreme Court declared the act unconstitutional.

WAITING ROOM
FOR COLORED ONLY
BY ORDER
POLICE DEPT.

Separate facilities, including bus and train station waiting rooms, were common throughout the South.

PLESSY V. FERGUSON During the 1890s, a number of other court decisions and state laws severely limited African-American rights. In 1890, Louisiana passed a law requiring railroads to provide "equal but separate accommodations for the white and colored races." In the *Plessy* v. *Ferguson* case in 1896, the Supreme Court

SECTION 1 RESOURCES

PRINT RESOURCES

IN-DEPTH RESOURCES: UNIT 6
Guided Reading, p. 18
Skillbuilder Practice: Making Inferences, p. 21
Geography Application: The *Brown* Decision, Ten Years Later, p. 22
Primary Source: Crisis in Little Rock, p. 24
American Lives: Rosa Parks, p. 31

READING STUDY GUIDE, p. 215

ACCESS FOR STUDENTS ACQUIRING ENGLISH
Guided Reading (Spanish), p. 233
Skillbuilder Practice: Making Inferences (Spanish), p. 236
Geography Application: The *Brown* Decision, Ten Years Later (Spanish), p. 237

SPANISH READING STUDY GUIDE, p. 215

FORMAL ASSESSMENT
Section Quiz, p. 259

ALTERNATIVE ASSESSMENT BOOK
See forms for supporting and scoring alternative activities.

TECHNOLOGY RESOURCES

CD-ROM Electronic Library of Primary Sources

VIDEO *American Stories* video series
American Portfolio: A Videodisc for U.S. History user's guide, pp. 236, 237, 240

INTERNET http://www.mlushistory.com

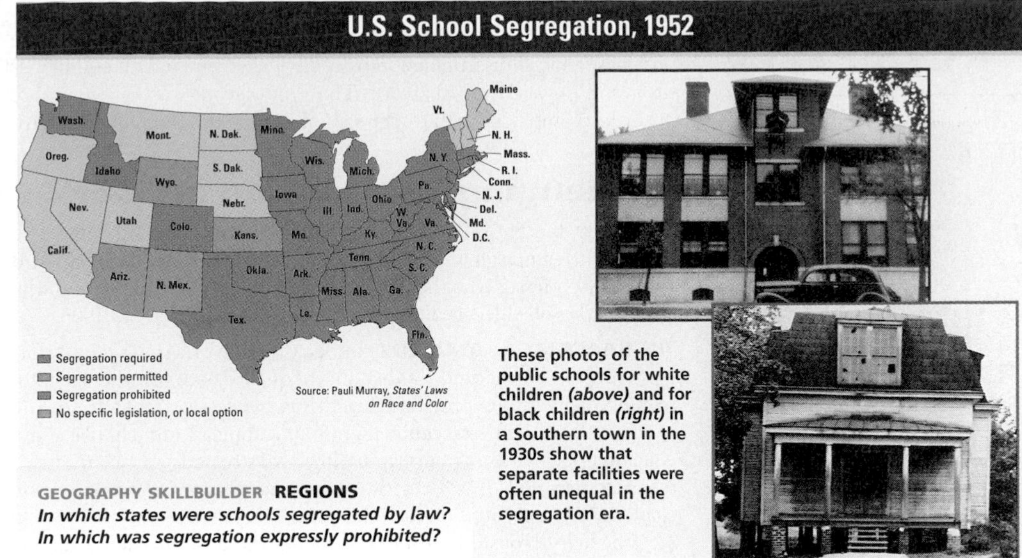

GEOGRAPHY SKILLBUILDER **REGIONS**
In which states were schools segregated by law? In which was segregation expressly prohibited?

These photos of the public schools for white children *(above)* and for black children *(right)* in a Southern town in the 1930s show that separate facilities were often unequal in the segregation era.

Skillbuilder Answer **Segregated by law:** All of the South. **Prohibited:** Much of the Northeast, upper Midwest, and Colorado, Idaho, and Washington.

ruled that this law did not violate the Fourteenth Amendment, which guarantees all Americans equal treatment under the law.

Armed with the *Plessy* decision, states throughout the nation, but especially in the South, passed what were known as Jim Crow laws, or laws aimed at separating the races. Laws forbade marriage between blacks and whites and established many other restrictions on social and religious contact between the races. There were separate schools, as well as separate streetcars, waiting rooms, railroad coaches, elevators, witness stands, and public restrooms. The facilities provided for blacks were always far inferior to those provided for whites. Nearly every day, African Americans faced humiliating signs that read, Colored Water; No Blacks Allowed; Whites Only.

THINK THROUGH HISTORY
A. THEME *Constitutional Concerns* *What were the effects of the Supreme Court decision* Plessy v. Ferguson?

A. Answer Since the Court ruled that segregation was not unconstitutional, many states, especially in the South, passed segregationist Jim Crow laws.

SEGREGATION CONTINUES INTO THE 20TH CENTURY In the late 1800s, some African Americans tried to escape Southern racism by moving north. This migration of Southern African Americans speeded up greatly during World War I, as many African-American sharecroppers abandoned the farms for the promise of industrial jobs in Northern cities. However, once African Americans reached the North, they discovered that racial prejudice and segregation patterns existed there as well. Most African Americans could find housing only in all-black neighborhoods. In addition, many white workers resented competition from blacks, resentment which sometimes led to violence.

In many ways, the events of World War II set the stage for the civil rights movement. First, the demand for soldiers in the early 1940s created a shortage of white male laborers, which opened up new job opportunities for African Americans, Latinos, and white women.

Second, about 700,000 African Americans served in the armed forces, which needed so many fighting men that they gradually had to end discriminatory policies that had kept African Americans from serving in fighting units. Many African-American soldiers returned from the war determined to fight for their own freedom now that they had helped defeat Fascist regimes overseas.

Third, during the war, civil rights organizations actively campaigned for African-American voting rights and challenged Jim Crow laws. In

ON THE WORLD STAGE

APARTHEID—SEGREGATION IN SOUTH AFRICA

In 1948, the white government of South Africa passed laws to ensure that the white minority would be able to retain control of the country. Those laws established a system known as apartheid, which means "separateness." Apartheid was a policy that divided South Africa's people into four rigidly segregated racial groups: whites, blacks, coloreds of mixed race, and Asians.

Apartheid laws restricted what jobs nonwhites could hold, where they could live, and what rights they could exercise. Because of apartheid, the black African majority suffered many inequalities—including being denied the right to vote.

In response to worldwide criticism, the South African government gradually repealed the apartheid laws, starting in the 1970s and concluding in 1991. In 1994, South Africans elected as president Nelson Mandela, a black anti-apartheid leader whom the white government had imprisoned for nearly 30 years.

(continued from page 696)

***AMERICAN STORIES* video series**
"Justice in Montgomery"
Videocassette: Volume 5

Videodisc: Disc 3, Side B, Chapter 2

OBJECTIVE

The Segregation System

Discussing Key Ideas
- *Plessy* v. *Ferguson* (1896) legalizes segregation.
- World War II inspires African Americans to fight for their rights.

IN-DEPTH RESOURCES: UNIT 6
Guided Reading, p. 18

ACCESS FOR STUDENTS ACQUIRING ENGLISH
Guided Reading (Spanish), p. 233

HISTORY FROM VISUALS

U.S. School Segregation, 1952

Reading the Map How many states permitted, but did not require, racial segregation? *Four.*

ON THE WORLD STAGE

Apartheid—Segregation in South Africa

Critical Thinking: Comparing Assign interested students to research the career of Nelson Mandela. Then, using the information on Martin Luther King, Jr., in this chapter, have them make a chart comparing the lives of the two men.

TEACHING OPTION

Making Connections Across the Curriculum

Language Arts Review the meaning of the term *metaphor* ("a figure of speech that makes a comparison between two things that are basically dissimilar"). Then read aloud this quote by a civil rights activist about life in the South.

> Black men and women lived behind a seemingly impenetrable wall of segregation. . . . There were Negro and white schools, Negro and white communities, Negro cemeteries, Negro jobs, Negro motels, Negro balconies. Sometimes there was no entrance at all, only a wall. . . . Beginning softly, then more and more insistently, men and women began to beat against the wall. Finally, in the mid-1950s, the wall began to crack.

Then ask these questions: What metaphor does the speaker use to describe segregation? *Segregation as a wall.* Is this an accurate metaphor? Why or why not? *Some students might say the metaphor is accurate because segregation separated people just like walls do. Others might say that people still had contact under segregation that would not be possible if real walls existed.* To guide reading for the rest of the section, direct students to look for the "tools" (another metaphor) that African Americans used to beat down the wall.

OBJECTIVE

② INSTRUCT

Challenging Segregation in Court

Discussing Key Ideas

- The NAACP exposes the unequal state of educational funding under segregation to challenge the Supreme Court precedent in *Plessy* v. *Ferguson.*
- The *Brown* decision overturns "separate but equal" and signals the end of legal segregation.

KEY PLAYER

Thurgood Marshall

Critical Thinking: Summarizing Have students use the *Readers' Guide to Periodical Literature* to find obituaries for Marshall published in national newsmagazines upon his death in 1993. Then ask them to summarize these obituaries.

IN-DEPTH RESOURCES: UNIT 6
Geography Application: The *Brown* Decision, Ten Years Later, p. 22

MORE ABOUT . . .

Charles Hamilton Houston

The grandson of runaway slaves, Charles Houston grew up in Washington, D.C., where he attended segregated schools. At age 15, he entered Amherst College and graduated with honors in 1915. In 1917, Houston entered World War I in a segregated unit. During his service, Houston endured such bitter racism that he vowed to fight segregation. In 1919, he entered Harvard Law School and went on to become the NAACP's first great lawyer.

KEY PLAYER

THURGOOD MARSHALL 1908–1993

Thurgood Marshall dedicated his life to fighting the indignities of a racist system he knew all too well. His father had labored as a steward at an all-white country club, his mother as a teacher at an all-black school. Marshall himself was denied admission to the University of Maryland Law School because of his race. One of the many lawsuits Marshall won for the NAACP forced that school to integrate.

In 1961, President John F. Kennedy nominated Marshall to the U.S. Court of Appeals. Lyndon Johnson picked Marshall for U.S. solicitor general in 1965 and two years later named him as the first African-American Supreme Court justice. In that role, he remained a strong advocate of civil rights until he retired in 1991.

After Marshall died in 1993, a copy of the *Brown* v. *Board of Education* decision was placed beside his casket. On it, an admirer wrote: "You shall always be remembered."

response to protests, President Roosevelt issued a presidential directive prohibiting racial discrimination by federal agencies and all companies that were engaged in war work. The groundwork was laid for more organized campaigns to end segregation throughout the United States.

THINK THROUGH HISTORY
B. Developing Historical Perspective *How did events during World War II lay the groundwork for African Americans to fight for civil rights?*
B. Answer Blacks had experienced better job opportunities; many veterans who had fought racist Germans wanted to resist racist Americans; civil rights groups had staged some successful protests.

Challenging Segregation in Court

Since 1909, the NAACP had fought to end segregation. One influential figure in this campaign was Charles Hamilton Houston, a brilliant Howard University professor who trained African-American law students and who also served as chief legal counsel for the NAACP from 1934 to 1938.

THE NAACP LEGAL STRATEGY In deciding the NAACP's legal strategy, Houston considered the blatant inequality between the separate schools many states provided for the two races. At that time, the nation spent ten times as much money educating a white child as it did educating an African-American child. It was to redress this injustice that Houston chose to focus the organization's limited resources on challenging segregated public education.

For help, Houston recruited some of his most able law students to prepare a battery of cases to take before the Supreme Court. In 1938, he placed the team under the direction of **Thurgood Marshall.** Over the next 23 years, Marshall and his NAACP lawyers would win 29 out of 32 cases argued before the Supreme Court.

Several of the cases that Marshall and his team of lawyers won became legal milestones, each one chipping away at the segregationist tenets of *Plessy* v. *Ferguson*. In the 1946 case *Morgan* v. *Virginia,* the Supreme Court declared unconstitutional those state laws mandating segregated seating on interstate buses. In 1950, the high court ruled in *Sweatt* v. *Painter* that state law schools must admit black applicants, even if separate black schools exist. In another 1950 case that Marshall and his team argued, the court ruled that blacks admitted to state graduate schools were entitled to the use of all the school's facilities.

BROWN V. BOARD OF EDUCATION Marshall's most stunning victory came on May 17, 1954, in the case known as ***Brown* v. *Board of Education*** of Topeka, Kansas. In this case, the court responded to a brilliant legal brief written by Marshall that addressed segregated education in four states—Kansas, South Carolina, Virginia, and Delaware. The court lumped the state cases together in a single ruling named for the case concerning nine-year-old Linda Brown. Her father, Oliver Brown, had charged the board of education of Topeka with violating Linda's rights by denying her admission to an all-white elementary school four blocks from her house. The state had directed Linda to cross a railroad yard and then take a bus to an all-black elementary school 21 blocks away.

THINK THROUGH HISTORY
C. Finding Main Ideas *What was the central issue raised in the* Brown v. Board of Education *ruling?*
C. Answer Segregation by race created a feeling of inferiority, so separate facilities made for inherently unequal experiences.

In a landmark verdict, the Supreme Court unanimously struck down segregation as unconstitutional. The Court's decision, written by Chief Justice Earl Warren, in part stated the following.

> To separate [African-American children] from others of similar age and qualifications solely because of their race generates a feeling of inferiority as to their status in the community that may affect their hearts and minds in a way unlikely ever to be undone. . . . We conclude that in the field of public education the doctrine of "separate but equal" has no place. Separate educational facilities are inherently unequal.
>
> CHIEF JUSTICE EARL WARREN, *Brown* v. *Board of Education*

TEACHING OPTIONS

Exploring Themes

Constitutional Concerns Explain the role of dissenting opinions as legal references in future cases. Then read this dissent in the *Plessy* case rendered by John Marshall Harlan: "Our Constitution is color-blind, and neither knows nor tolerates classes among citizens." Discuss how this opinion—the lone dissent in *Plessy*—was reflected in the majority opinion in the *Brown* case. Explore with students factors that may have influenced justices to rethink the 1896 majority opinion.

Making Connections Across Time

The* Brown *Case In 1979, the American Civil Liberties Union (ACLU) reopened the *Brown* case, arguing that 13 of Topeka's schools remained segregated because of de facto segregation in housing. In 1993, a federal court sided with the ACLU. Topeka responded by busing and by setting up magnet schools. "It's disheartening that we are still fighting," said Linda Brown Thompson, who was 11 when her parents joined the now famous class-action suit, "But we are dealing with human beings. As long as we are, there will always be those who feel the races should be separate."

Reaction to the *Brown* Decision

The ruling thrilled African Americans and many other Americans. "I was so happy, I was numb," declared Thurgood Marshall. The *Chicago Defender*, an African-American newspaper, pronounced, "[It's] a second emancipation proclamation."

The *Brown* decision immediately affected some 12 million schoolchildren in 21 states. Official reaction to the ruling was mixed. In Kansas and Oklahoma, state officials said they expected segregation to end with little trouble. In Texas the governor promised to comply but warned that plans might "take years" to work out. In Mississippi and Georgia, officials vowed total resistance. Governor Herman Talmadge of Georgia branded the decision "a flagrant abuse of judicial power" and pledged, "The people of Georgia . . . will map a program to insure . . . permanent segregation of the races."

RESISTANCE TO SCHOOL INTEGRATION Within a year of the *Brown* decision, more than 500 school districts in the nation had desegregated their classrooms. In the cities of Baltimore, St. Louis, and Washington, D.C., African-American and white students sat side by side for the first time in history. However, in areas where African Americans made up the majority of the population, whites often resisted desegregation because they feared losing control of the schools. In some places, the Ku Klux Klan reappeared and White Citizens Councils boycotted businesses that supported desegregation.

To hasten compliance, the Supreme Court handed down a second *Brown* ruling in 1955 that ordered district courts to implement school desegregation "with all deliberate speed." Neither Congress nor President Eisenhower moved to put teeth into the court order. In Congress, more than 90 Southern members issued the "Southern Manifesto," which denounced the *Brown* decision and called on the states to resist it "by all lawful means." Although the president accepted the Court's ruling as law, he also confided privately to an aide, "The fellow who tries to tell me that you can do these things by force is just plain nuts." Events in Little Rock, Arkansas, would soon force Eisenhower to act against this belief.

THINK THROUGH HISTORY
D. *Analyzing Causes* *Why weren't schools in all regions desegregated immediately after the* Brown *decision?*

D. Answer Some Southern whites and state officials resisted desegregation, and neither Eisenhower nor Congress forced them to act quickly.

As white students jeer her, Elizabeth Eckford tries to pass through lines of National Guardsmen and enter Little Rock Central High School in 1957.

CRISIS IN LITTLE ROCK In 1948, Arkansas had become the first Southern state to admit African Americans to the state universities without being required by a court order. By the 1950s, some scout troops and labor unions in Arkansas had quietly ended their Jim Crow practices. In Little Rock itself, citizens had elected two men to the school board who publicly backed desegregation—and the school superintendent, Virgil Blossom, had been working on a plan for gradual desegregation since 1953.

However, state politics created an explosive situation. Caught in a tight reelection race, Governor Orval Faubus jumped on the segregationist bandwagon. In September 1957, he ordered the National Guard to turn away the nine African-American students who had volunteered to integrate Little Rock's Central High School as the first step in Blossom's plan. That afternoon, a federal judge ordered Faubus to let the students into school the next day.

Eight members of the "Little Rock Nine" received phone calls from ministers who volunteered to escort the students to school for their safety. The family

OBJECTIVE
(3) INSTRUCT

Reaction to the *Brown* Decision

▶ ***Discussing Key Ideas***
- Some state and local governments balk at the *Brown* decision.
- In 1955, the Supreme Court orders district courts to enforce the *Brown* decision.
- Resistance to desegregation in Little Rock, Arkansas, leads President Eisenhower to send in the National Guard.

IN-DEPTH RESOURCES: UNIT 6
Primary Source: Crisis in Little Rock, p. 24

ELECTRONIC LIBRARY OF PRIMARY SOURCES
Desegregation at Central High School by Melba Pattillo Beals
Desegregation at Central High School by Craig Rains

Issues for the 21st Century

Exploring Education Today

Connect the *Brown* decision to education issues today by having students read pages 888-891. Then have them answer these questions.

1. What impact did *Brown v. Board of Education* have on schools and society? *It called for the desegregation of schools, which many people opposed.*
2. What are the major arguments in the debate over affirmative action in education today? *Pro: remedies past discrimination; Con: discriminates against nonminority students.*

Block Schedule TEACHING OPTION **Time Needed: 30 Minutes**

Cooperative Activity: Researching Civil Rights Cases

Task: Groups of students will research and explain Supreme Court decisions on civil rights cases.

Purpose: To track the Court's changing opinions on civil rights.

Activity: Divide the cases among the groups of students and have each group research their assigned case(s). They should learn the facts of the cases (date, plaintiffs, defendants, and legal issue) and the Supreme Court decisions (vote, majority opinion, and dissenting opinion). They should be prepared to explain their cases to the rest of the class.

1896 *Plessy* v. *Ferguson*
1938 *Missouri ex rel. Gaines* v. *Canada*
1944 *Smith* v. *Allwright*
1954 *Brown* v. *Board of Education of Topeka*
1971 *Swann* v. *Charlotte-Mecklenburg* [NC] *Board of Education*
1974 *Milliken* v. *Bradley*
1978 *Regents of the University of California* v. *Bakke*
1990 *Board of Education of Oklahoma City* v. *Dowell*
1995 *Adarand Constructors* v. *Peña*

OBJECTIVE

④ **INSTRUCT**

The Montgomery Bus Boycott

▶ ***Discussing Key Ideas***

- African Americans in Montgomery, Alabama, organize a boycott to protest discrimination on city buses.
- The boycott thrusts Martin Luther King, Jr., into the national spotlight.
- In a lawsuit filed by the boycotters, the Supreme Court outlaws segregated buses.

KEY PLAYER

Rosa Parks

Critical Thinking: Clarifying
Today a historic marker can be found at the bus stop where Rosa Parks began her famous ride. It begins, "At the bus stop on this site on December 1, 1955, . . ."

Assign pairs of students to complete the commemoration. Tell them to write no more than 50 words.

IN-DEPTH RESOURCES: UNIT 6
American Lives: Rosa Parks, p. 31

of the ninth student, Elizabeth Eckford, did not have a phone. The next morning, she put on the carefully ironed white-and-black dress she had made for her first day at an integrated school and set out alone.

On the sidewalk outside Central High, Eckford faced an abusive crowd of students and adults. Terrified, the 15-year-old Eckford searched the mob for a friendly face. "I looked into the face of an old woman, and it seemed a kind face," she later told one interviewer. "But when I looked at her again, she spat on me." Trailed by the mob, Eckford managed to make it to a bus stop, where two friendly whites stayed with her until the bus came.

The crisis in Little Rock forced Eisenhower to act. He placed the Arkansas National Guard under federal control and ordered a thousand paratroopers into Little Rock. Under the watchful eye of these soldiers, the nine African-American teenagers attended class. But even these soldiers could not protect the students from troublemakers who confronted them on stairways, in the halls, and in the cafeteria. Nor could the soldiers block interference by Faubus, who shut down Central High at the end of the school year rather than let integration continue.

The reports from Little Rock by network television news correspondents helped the nation to focus on the issue of desegregation. At the same time, on September 9, 1957, Congress passed the Civil Rights Act of 1957, the first civil rights law since Reconstruction. Sponsored by Senator Lyndon B. Johnson of Texas, the law gave the attorney general greater power over school desegregation. It also gave the federal government jurisdiction—or authority—over violations of African-American voting rights.

THINK THROUGH HISTORY
E. *Making Inferences* *Why do you think television coverage of the Little Rock incident helped the nation focus on desegregation?*

E. Answer
Possible Answer: Television allowed people to see the white separatists' cruel treatment of the African-American students.

KEY PLAYER

ROSA PARKS
1913–

Long before December 1955, Rosa Parks had protested segregation through everyday acts. She refused to use drinking fountains labeled "Colored Only." When possible, she shunned segregated elevators and climbed stairs instead.

Parks joined the Montgomery chapter of the NAACP in 1943 and became the organization's secretary. A turning point came for her in the summer of 1955, when she attended a workshop at the Highlander Folk School in Monteagle, Tennessee. Highlander's program was designed to promote integration by giving the students the experience of interracial living.

Returning to Montgomery, Parks was even more determined to fight segregation. As it happened, her act of protest against injustice on the buses inspired a whole community to join her cause.

The Montgomery Bus Boycott

The face-to-face confrontation at Central High School was not the only showdown over segregation in the mid-1950s. Impatient with the slow pace of change in the courts, African-American activists had begun taking direct action to win the rights promised to them by the Fourteenth and Fifteenth Amendments to the Constitution. Among those on the frontline of change was Jo Ann Robinson.

BOYCOTTING SEGREGATION Four days after the *Brown* decision in May 1954, Robinson wrote a letter to the mayor of Montgomery, Alabama, asking that bus drivers no longer be allowed to force riders in the "colored" section to yield their seats to whites. "More and more of our people are already arranging with neighbors and friends for rides to keep from being insulted and humiliated by bus drivers," Robinson warned. The mayor refused.

On December 1, 1955, **Rosa Parks,** a seamstress and an NAACP officer, took a seat in the front row of the "colored" section of a Montgomery bus. As the bus filled up, the driver ordered Parks and three other African-American passengers to empty the row they were occupying so that a white man could sit down without having to sit next to any African Americans. "It certainly was time for someone to stand up," recalled Parks wryly. "So I refused to move."

As Parks stared out the window, the bus driver said, "If you don't stand up, I'm going to call the police and have you arrested." The soft-spoken Parks replied, "You may do that."

News of Parks's arrest spread rapidly. Jo Ann Robinson and NAACP leader E. D. Nixon quickly organized a boycott of the buses. The leaders of the African-American community, including many ministers, formed the Montgomery Improvement Association to organize the

TEACHING OPTION

Skillbuilder Mini-Lesson: Making Inferences

Explaining the Skill Writers do not always explain every aspect of an event in detail. They rely on readers to make inferences, or draw conclusions, about the event by using clues in the text and by drawing on their own personal experience, historical knowledge, and common sense.

Applying the Skill: Crisis in Little Rock Have students answer the following questions to help them make inferences about the crisis in Little Rock.

What do clues in the text reveal about the outcome of the crisis? It helped focus attention on desegregation.

What do you know about the treatment of African Americans before 1957? They had endured discrimination and segregation for many years.

How do you think African Americans responded to the crisis in Little Rock? They were encouraged by the federal government's actions to enforce desegregation.

What inferences can you make about the crisis? It was a victory for African Americans.

IN-DEPTH RESOURCES: UNIT 6
Skillbuilder Practice: Making Inferences, p. 21

boycott. They elected the pastor of the Dexter Avenue Baptist Church, 26-year-old **Dr. Martin Luther King, Jr.,** to lead the group. "Well, I'm not sure I'm the best person for the position," King confided to Nixon. "But if no one else is going to serve, I'd be glad to try."

WALKING FOR JUSTICE On the night of December 5, 1955, an estimated crowd of 5,000 people gathered to hear the young pastor speak. With passion and eloquence, Dr. King made the following declaration.

> **A PERSONAL VOICE**
> There comes a time when people get tired of being trampled over by the iron feet of oppression. . . . I want it to be known—that we're going to work with grim and bold determination—to gain justice on buses in this city. And we are not wrong. . . . If we are wrong—the Supreme Court of this nation is wrong. If we are wrong—God Almighty is wrong. . . . If we are wrong—justice is a lie.
> DR. MARTIN LUTHER KING, JR., quoted in *Parting the Waters: America in the King Years, 1954–63*

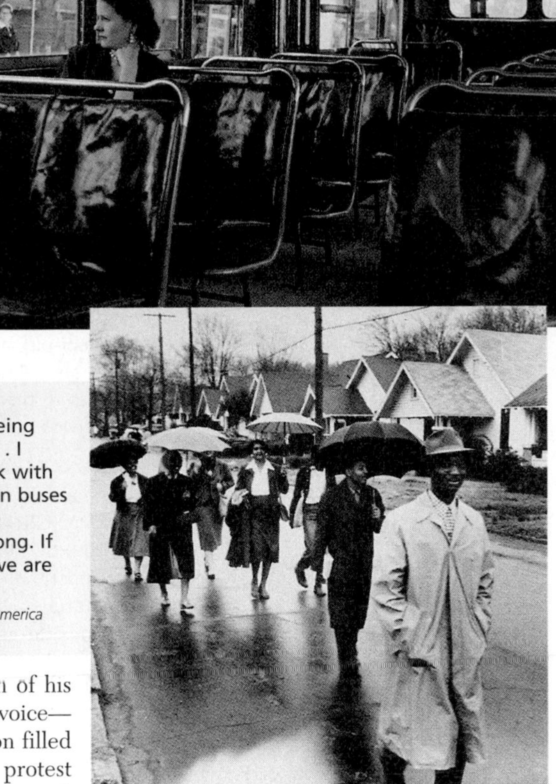

For over a year, Montgomery buses ran nearly empty while African Americans found other means to get where they wanted to go.

The impact of King's speech—the rhythm of his words, the power of his rising and falling voice—brought people to their feet. A sense of mission filled the audience as King proclaimed, "If you will protest courageously and yet with dignity, . . . historians will have to pause and say, 'There lived a great people—a black people—who injected a new meaning and dignity into the veins of civilization.'"

F. Answer They organized a peaceful boycott to protest segregation on the city's buses.

THINK THROUGH HISTORY
F. THEME Democracy in America *How did African Americans in Montgomery use the democratic process to protest segregation?*

For 381 days, African Americans refused to ride the buses in Montgomery. In most cases, they had to find other means of transportation by organizing car pools or walking long distances. The boycotters remained nonviolent even after a bomb ripped apart King's home. (Fortunately, no one was injured.) Finally, in late 1956, the Supreme Court outlawed bus segregation in response to a lawsuit filed by the boycotters. On December 21, King boarded a Montgomery bus and sat in the front. "It was a great ride," he declared.

ECONOMIC BACKGROUND

BOYCOTTS

A boycott's effectiveness lies in its ability to hit target companies where it hurts the most—in their pocketbooks. Aside from losing revenue, targeted companies often must devote resources to repairing their tarnished image. "They [boycotts] sap energy and time," said a spokesman for a recently targeted company. "And time is money."

Boycotts have become a popular form of protest in America today. There are even two newsletters, *Boycott Action News* and *Boycott Quarterly,* which track and report on various economic boycotts across the nation. (See *boycott* on page 933 in the Economics Handbook.)

Dr. King and the SCLC

The Montgomery bus boycott proved to the world that ordinary African Americans could unite and organize a successful protest movement. It also proved the power of nonviolent resistance, the peaceful refusal to obey unjust laws. Despite threats to his life and family, King urged his followers, "Let nobody pull you so low as to hate them."

CHANGING THE WORLD WITH SOUL FORCE King called his brand of nonviolent resistance "soul force." He based his ideas on the teachings of several people. From Jesus, he learned to love one's enemies. From writer Henry David Thoreau, he took the concept of civil disobedience—the refusal to obey an unjust law. From labor organizer A. Philip Randolph, he learned techniques for organizing massive demonstrations. From Mohandas Gandhi, the leader who helped

ECONOMIC BACKGROUND
Boycotts

Critical Thinking: Comparing Ask students to compare the reasons for the boycotts of the civil rights era with recent boycotts of companies, nations, or governments. Then have them create a list of companies, nations, or governments (if any) that they think should be boycotted.

OBJECTIVE
(5) INSTRUCT

Dr. King and the SCLC

▶ ***Discussing Key Ideas***
- Martin Luther King, Jr., seeks to promote civil rights through nonviolent resistance.
- King draws his ideas from the teachings of Thoreau, Gandhi, Jesus, and A. Philip Randolph.
- Young activists, impatient with the slow pace of change, organize the Student Nonviolent Coordinating Committee and vow to challenge the system.

ELECTRONIC LIBRARY OF PRIMARY SOURCES
from *Stride Toward Freedom* by Martin Luther King, Jr.

TEACHING OPTIONS

Teaching Less Proficient Readers

Activating Prior Knowledge Before less proficient readers read about the Montgomery bus boycott on pages 700–701, hold a discussion about boycotts. What are they? Have students ever experienced a boycott? What happened? Ask the following questions, recording responses on the board:

- What motivates a person to defy authority and risk jail?
- Why would a whole community organize a boycott?
- What can happen when enough people join a boycott?

Students should keep these questions in mind as they read about the Montgomery bus boycott and other protests.

Making Global Connections

Philosophies of Justice Read these quotations from Mohandas Gandhi. Then ask students to cite examples of how King's practice of soul force proved Gandhi's remarks.

- *Under a government which imprisons any unjustly, the only true place for a just man is in prison.*
- *It is possible for a single individual to defy the whole might of an unjust empire.*
- *When any group struggles properly and justly to achieve its own rights, it enlarges the rights of all.*

KEY PLAYER

Martin Luther King, Jr.

Critical Thinking: Evaluating Based on what students know about King's beliefs, have them write a speech that he might have delivered upon acceptance of an honorary degree. Speeches should be no more than two minutes long. Ask volunteers to do dramatic readings.

MORE ABOUT . . .

Ella Baker

Ella Baker wanted no credit for her work. Explained Baker:

> I have always felt it was a handicap for oppressed peoples to depend so largely upon a leader, because unfortunately in our culture, the charismatic leader usually becomes a leader because he has . . . been touted through the public media, which means that the media has made him, and the media may undo him.

Ask students to explain and comment on the validity of Baker's remark.

OBJECTIVE

(6) **INSTRUCT**

The Movement Spreads

▶ ***Discussing Key Ideas***

- Members of SNCC build on methods of protest used earlier by the Congress of Racial Equality (CORE).
- Sit-ins attract national media attention to the civil rights movement.

India throw off British rule, he learned that one could powerfully resist oppression without resorting to violence.

KEY PLAYER

MARTIN LUTHER KING, JR. 1929–1968

Born Michael Luther King, Jr., King had to adjust to a new name in 1934. In that year, his father—Rev. Michael Luther King, Sr.—returned home from a trip to Europe, where he had toured historic sites, including the site where Martin Luther had challenged the Roman Catholic Church and begun the Protestant Reformation. Upon his return home, the elder King changed his and his son's names to Martin.

Like Luther, the younger King became a reformer. He worked so diligently for civil rights that the Nobel Prize Committee gave him its coveted peace prize in 1964, making him the youngest person ever to receive the award.

Yet there was a side of King unknown to most people—his inner battle to overcome his hatred of the white bigots who lynched a neighbor, firebombed his own house, and spat at him. As a youth, he had once vowed "to hate all white people." As leader of the civil rights movement, King looked forward to a world in which people of all races respected each other. "Ultimately, we are trying to free all of America," he explained. "Negroes from the bonds of segregation and shame, whites from the bonds of bigotry and fear."

King summed up his philosophy by saying to white racists, "We will not hate you, but we cannot . . . obey your unjust laws. We will soon wear you down by our capacity to suffer. And in winning our freedom, we will so appeal to your heart and conscience that we will win you in the process."

Some African Americans questioned King's peaceful philosophy when, after the *Brown* decision, antiblack violence swept parts of the Deep South. The violence, aimed at keeping African Americans "in their place," included the highly publicized 1955 murder of Emmett Till—a 14-year-old who had allegedly flirted with a white woman. There were also shootings and beatings, some fatal, of civil rights workers. Despite these vicious attacks, King steadfastly preached the power of nonviolence.

THINK THROUGH HISTORY
G. *Finding Main Ideas* *What were the central points of Dr. King's philosophy?*

G. Answer "Soul force," or nonviolent resistance, which included acts of civil disobedience, demonstrations, and adherence to nonviolence.

FROM THE GRASSROOTS UP After the boycott ended, King joined with more than 100 ministers and civil rights leaders in 1957 to found the **Southern Christian Leadership Conference** (SCLC). The purpose of the SCLC, as stated by King, was "to carry on nonviolent crusades against the evils of second-class citizenship." Using African-American churches as a base, the SCLC planned to stage protests and demonstrations throughout the South.

Leaders of the SCLC hoped to build a movement from the grassroots up and to win the support of ordinary African Americans of all ages. King, president of the SCLC, used the power of his voice and ideas to fuel the movement's momentum. The nuts and bolts of organizing the SCLC fell to Ella Baker, a former NAACP activist and the granddaughter of a slave minister.

While with the NAACP, Baker had served as national field secretary, traveling over 16,000 miles throughout the South. From 1959 to 1961, Baker used her contacts to set up branches of the SCLC in 65 Southern cities. In April 1960, Baker helped students at Shaw University, an African-American university in Raleigh, North Carolina, to organize the **Student Nonviolent Coordinating Committee,** or SNCC, pronounced "snick" for short.

It had been six years since the *Brown* case, and many college students viewed the pace of change as too slow. Although these students risked a great deal—losing college scholarships, being expelled from college, being physically harmed—they were determined to challenge the system. SNCC, which hoped to harness the energy of these student protesters, would soon create one of the most important student activist movements in the nation's history.

The Movement Spreads

Although SNCC adopted King's ideas in part, its members had ideas of their own. Many wanted a more confrontational strategy and set out to reshape the civil rights movement.

DEMONSTRATING FOR FREEDOM The founders of SNCC had models to build on. In 1942, the Congress of Racial Equality (CORE) had staged the first **sit-ins,** in which African-American protesters sat down at segregated lunch counters in Chicago and refused to leave until they were served. In February 1960, African-American students from North Carolina's Agricultural and Technical College staged a sit-in at a whites-only lunch

Block Schedule TEACHING OPTION **Time Needed: 20 Minutes**

Cooperative Activity: Writing About Civil Rights Organizations

Task: Groups of students will research and write histories of civil rights organizations.

Purpose: To explain the development of civil rights organizations, movements, and activities.

Activity: Have groups choose one civil rights organization (such as the NAACP, CORE, SCLC, SNCC, the Urban League, the Montgomery Improvement Association, or the Greensboro Citizens Association) and research its origins, philosophy, leaders, and major activities. After writing a history of the organization, each group will share their findings with the class.

ALTERNATIVE ASSESSMENT BOOK
Standards for Evaluating a Cooperative Activity

Standards for Evaluation
Histories should . . .

- clearly describe the origins, leaders, and members of the organization
- list the major actions that the organization has taken
- explain how the organization has changed over time

Sit-in demonstrators, such as these at a Jackson, Mississippi, lunch counter, faced intimidation and humiliation from white segregationists.

counter at a Woolworth's store in Greensboro. This time, television crews brought coverage of the protest into homes throughout the United States.

Day after day, reporters captured the ugly face of racism—scenes of whites beating, jeering at, and pouring food over students who refused to strike back. The coverage sparked many other sit-ins across the South. Store managers called in the police, raised the price of food, and removed counter seats. But the movement continued and spread to the North. There students formed picket lines around national chain stores that maintained segregated lunch counters in the South.

THINK THROUGH HISTORY
H. *Contrasting* *How did the tactics of the student protesters from SNCC differ from those of the boycotters in Montgomery?*

H. Answer The students confronted businesses that had segregationist policies rather than boycotted them.

NO TURNING BACK By late 1960, students had descended on and desegregated Jim Crow lunch counters in some 48 cities in 11 states. They endured arrests, beatings, suspension from college, and tear gas and fire hoses, but the army of nonviolent students refused to back down. "My mother has always told me that I'm equal to other people," said Ezell Blair, Jr., one of the students who led the first sit-in in 1960. For the rest of the 1960s, many Americans persevered to prove Blair's mother correct.

Section 1 Assessment

1. TERMS & NAMES
Identify:
- Thurgood Marshall
- *Brown* v. *Board of Education*
- Rosa Parks
- Dr. Martin Luther King, Jr.
- Southern Christian Leadership Conference
- Student Nonviolent Coordinating Committee
- sit-in

2. SUMMARIZING Re-create the web diagram below on your paper. Then fill it in with examples of Supreme Court decisions, tactics, organizations, and leaders related to the early phases of the civil rights movement.

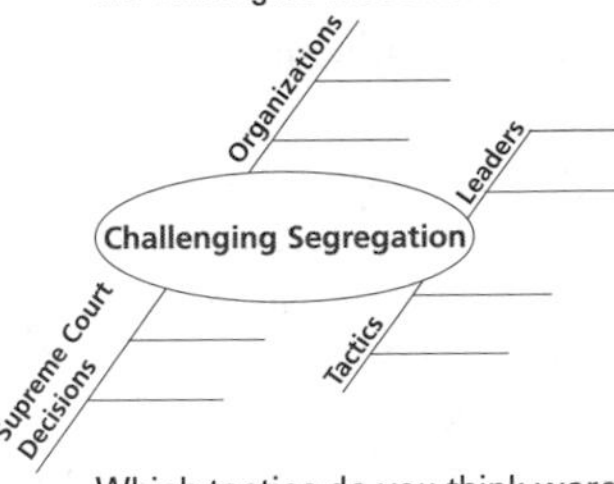

Which tactics do you think were most effective? Why?

3. ANALYZING MOTIVES Why did the civil rights movement use nonviolence? How successful was the tactic?

THINK ABOUT
- the Montgomery bus boycott
- television coverage of events
- sit-ins

4. DRAWING CONCLUSIONS After the *Brown* v. *Board of Education* ruling, what do you think was the most significant event of the civil rights movement prior to 1960? Why?

THINK ABOUT
- the role of civil rights leaders
- the results of confrontations and boycotts
- the role of grassroots organizations

ANSWERS

1. TERMS & NAMES

Thurgood Marshall, p. 698

Brown v. *Board of Education*, p. 698

Rosa Parks, p. 700

Dr. Martin Luther King, Jr., p. 701

Southern Christian Leadership Conference, p. 702

Student Nonviolent Coordinating Committee, p. 702

sit-in, p. 702

2. SUMMARIZING

Supreme Court Decisions—*Morgan* v. *Virginia; Sweatt* v. *Painter; Brown* v. *Board of Education.* **Tactics**—nonviolent resistance; legal action. **Organizations** —NAACP, SCLC, SNCC; CORE. **Leaders**—Thurgood Marshall; Dr. Martin Luther King, Jr.; Ella Baker; Jo Ann Robinson. ***Possible Responses:*** demonstrations, because they attracted media coverage; legal action, because it ended legal segregation.

3. ANALYZING MOTIVES

Reasons for nonviolence: Students might suggest that the tactic stemmed from the personal philosophy of Dr. King; that it had worked in other countries; or that nonviolent tactics would more effectively appeal to the nation's conscience. **Success:** Students might say the tactic was successful because it captured the sympathy of the nation; some might suggest that the toll could have been worse if violent tactics had been used. Other students might say that nonviolence did not go far enough to bring about immediate justice.

4. DRAWING CONCLUSIONS

Possible Responses: The crisis at Little Rock, because it forced the government to act; the Montgomery bus boycott, which brought Martin Luther King, Jr., into a leadership role.

MORE ABOUT . . .
The Greensboro Sit-Ins

The sit-ins in Greensboro, North Carolina, did not arise out of thin air—they happened because citizens organized. The four students who initiated the sit-ins at Greensboro were all members of the NAACP Youth Council, with links to civil rights activists who led sit-ins in Durham, North Carolina, and Nashville, Tennessee, in the late 1950s. The attention the media gave to the Greensboro sit-ins sparked more protests and led to the formation of SNCC.

ASSESS & RETEACH

Section 1 Assessment

Have students work in pairs to quiz each other on the questions.

Self-Assessment

Have students use the people in this section to create a game of Who Am I? After each speaker lists his or her accomplishments and then says the words "Who Am I?", the whole class should write down their answers on a sheet of paper. Students who guess incorrectly should write up their own "Who Am I?" description for the individual.

Section Quiz

FORMAL ASSESSMENT
Section Quiz, p. 259

Reteach

Use the list of Terms & Names to link each leader with the civil rights organizations and protest movements they were part of.

CLOSE

By the end of the 1950s, civil rights movements in the South had focused the nation's attention. Yet, when African Americans pressed for equality, they met massive resistance by many conservative whites.

Section 2 Overview

OBJECTIVES

1. To identify the goal of the freedom riders.
2. To explain how civil rights activism forced President Kennedy to act against segregation.
3. To state the motives behind the 1963 March on Washington.
4. To describe how civil rights organizers tried to secure passage of a voting rights act.

SKILLBUILDER

- Interpreting charts, p. 708

CRITICAL THINKING

- Analyzing motives, p. 705
- Theme: Civil Rights, p. 707
- Analyzing causes, pp. 708, 709
- Comparing, p. 710
- Summarizing, p.710
- Synthesizing, p. 710
- Recognizing effects, p. 710

FOCUS & MOTIVATE

5-MINUTE WARM-UP

Recognizing Point of View
To recognize the viewpoint of civil rights activists, have students read the Personal Voice on page 706 and answer these questions.

1. Why was King impatient to achieve integration?
2. Why did his son's question make King even more impatient for change?

WARM-UP TRANSPARENCY 21

▶ ***Starting with the Student***
Have students think about someone they know or know about who took a stand. Tell them to consider the issue involved, the action taken, and the price paid.

OBJECTIVE

① INSTRUCT

Riding for Freedom

▶ ***Discussing Key Ideas***

- Freedom riders expose Southern resistance to federal desegregation rulings.

(continued on next page)

2 The Triumphs of a Crusade

TERMS & NAMES

- freedom rider
- James Meredith
- Civil Rights Act of 1964
- Freedom Summer
- Robert Moses
- Fannie Lou Hamer
- Voting Rights Act of 1965

LEARN ABOUT the freedom rides, events in Birmingham and Selma, and Freedom Summer
TO UNDERSTAND how the civil rights movement pressured the federal government to end segregation and ensure voting

ONE AMERICAN'S STORY

James Peck, a white civil rights activist, was one of six whites and seven blacks who set out from Washington, D.C., in 1961 on a special bus ride through the South. The trip was part of CORE's attempt to test the Supreme Court decisions banning segregated seating on interstate bus routes and segregated facilities in bus terminals. The activists formed two interracial teams of freedom riders to travel through the South challenging segregation. They reasoned that if they provoked a violent reaction, the Kennedy administration would have to enforce the law.

Peck rode on Bus One. At the Alabama state line, a half dozen white racists got on the bus, carrying chains, brass knuckles, and pistols. They yanked the young African-American riders from their seats and shoved them into the aisle. Peck and a 60-year-old white freedom rider named Dr. Walter Bergman tried to intervene. The thugs knocked Peck unconscious and kicked Bergman repeatedly in the head until his brain hemorrhaged.

The ordeal for the freedom riders aboard Bus One didn't end there. On May 4, 1961—Mother's Day—they pulled into the Birmingham bus terminal. James Peck later recalled seeing the hostile mob that was waiting, some holding barely concealed iron bars.

Three days after he was beaten in Birmingham, freedom rider James Peck demonstrates in New York City to apply pressure on national bus companies to support desegregation in the South.

A PERSONAL VOICE

I looked at them and then I looked at Charles Person, who had been designated as my team mate to test the lunch counter. . . . When I looked at him, he responded by saying simply, "Let's go."

As we entered the white waiting room, . . . we were grabbed bodily and pushed toward the alleyway . . . and out of sight of onlookers in the waiting room, six of them started swinging at me with fists and pipes. Five others attacked Person a few feet ahead.

JAMES PECK, *Freedom Ride*

The mob beat Peck into unconsciousness. It took 53 stitches to sew up his badly battered head and face. The ride of Bus One had ended, but Bus Two continued southward on a journey that would shock the Kennedy administration into action.

Riding for Freedom

In Anniston, Alabama, about 200 angry whites attacked Bus Two, kicking its sides and slashing its tires. The driver managed to take the damaged bus six miles out of town before one of the slashed tires blew apart. The mob, which had driven after the bus, barricaded the door while someone smashed the rear window and tossed in a fire bomb. The **freedom riders** forced open the door and spilled out just before the bus exploded in a ball of flame.

NEW VOLUNTEERS CORE's freedom riders did not want to give up, but the bus companies refused to carry them any farther, so they ended their ride and nearly all of them boarded a flight to New Orleans. Then Diane Nash, a SNCC leader, called CORE director James Farmer to say that a group of Nashville students wanted to resume the freedom ride. "You know that may be suicide," warned Farmer. Nash answered, "We know that, but if we let them stop us with violence, the movement is dead! . . . Your troops have been badly battered. Let us pick up the baton and run with it."

SECTION 2 RESOURCES

PRINT RESOURCES

IN-DEPTH RESOURCES: UNIT 6
Guided Reading, p. 19
Primary Sources: Civil Rights Song, p. 25; *from* "I Have a Dream" by Martin Luther King, Jr., p. 26; Political Poster, p. 27
Literature: from *And All Our Wounds Forgiven* by Julius Lester, p. 28
American Lives: A. Philip Randolph, p. 32

READING STUDY GUIDE, p. 217

ACCESS FOR STUDENTS ACQUIRING ENGLISH
Guided Reading (Spanish), p. 234

SPANISH READING STUDY GUIDE, p. 217

FORMAL ASSESSMENT
Section Quiz, p. 260

ALTERNATIVE ASSESSMENT BOOK
See forms for supporting and scoring alternative activities.

TECHNOLOGY RESOURCES

HUMANITIES TRANSPARENCIES
H27, March on Washington

GEOGRAPHY TRANSPARENCIES
G29, Before and After the Voting Rights Act of 1965

CD-ROM *Grolier Multimedia Encyclopedia*

VIDEO *American Portfolio: A Videodisc for U.S. History* user's guide, pp. 245, 246, 248

INTERNET http://www.mlushistory.com

When the SNCC volunteers rode into Birmingham, Police Commissioner Eugene "Bull" Connor's men pulled them off the bus, beat them, and drove them into Tennessee. The determined young people returned to Birmingham and occupied the whites-only waiting room at the terminal, where they sat for 18 hours because the bus driver refused to risk his life transporting them. After receiving an angry phone call from U.S. Attorney General Robert Kennedy, bus company officials convinced the driver to proceed. The SNCC volunteers set out for Montgomery on May 20.

A. Answer To call attention to the South's refusal to abandon segregation and to force the federal government to enforce the Supreme Court's desegregation rulings.

In Alabama, a mob firebombed this bus of freedom riders and attacked passengers as they left.

ARRIVAL OF FEDERAL MARSHALS Although Alabama officials had promised Kennedy that the riders would be protected, no police were stationed near the Montgomery terminal when the bus arrived. Instead, a mob of whites—many carrying bats and lead pipes—fell upon the riders. John Doar, a Justice Department official on the scene, called the attorney general and reported what happened. "A bunch of men led by a guy with a bleeding face are beating [the passengers]. There are no cops. It's terrible. It's terrible. There's not a cop in sight. People are yelling, 'Get 'em, get 'em.' It's awful."

THINK THROUGH HISTORY
A. *Analyzing Motives* *What did the freedom riders hope to achieve?*

The violence provoked exactly the response the freedom riders had been hoping for. Newspapers throughout the nation and abroad denounced the beatings. Southern newspapers such as the *Atlanta Constitution,* which had criticized the freedom ride, expressed outrage that police had refused to protect the riders.

President John F. Kennedy decided to give the freedom riders more direct support. This time, the Justice Department sent 400 U.S. marshals to protect the riders on the last part of their journey to Jackson, Mississippi. In addition, the attorney general and the Interstate Commerce Commission issued an order banning segregation in all interstate travel facilities, including waiting rooms, restrooms, and lunch counters.

"We will continue our journey one way or another. . . . We are prepared to die."

JIM ZWERG,
FREEDOM RIDER

Standing Firm

As interstate travel facilities became more fully integrated, some civil rights workers turned their attention to integrating some Southern schools and pushing the movement into additional Southern towns. At each turn they encountered opposition from some whites.

"Violence is a fearful thing," recalled Avon Rollins of SNCC. "I remember when I had to take a stand, where the words wouldn't come out of my mouth, . . . because the fear was in me so strong."

INTEGRATING OLE MISS In September 1962, Air Force veteran **James Meredith** won a federal court case that allowed him to enroll in the all-white University of Mississippi, nicknamed Ole Miss. But when Meredith arrived on campus, he faced Governor Ross Barnett, who refused to let him register as a student.

Following the precedent set by Eisenhower in Little Rock, President Kennedy ordered federal marshals to escort Meredith to the registrar's office. Barnett responded with a heated radio appeal: "I call on every Mississippian to keep his faith and courage. We will never surrender." The broadcast turned out white demonstrators by the thousands.

On the night of September 30, riots broke out on campus that resulted in two deaths. It took more than 5,000 soldiers, 200 arrests, and 15 hours to stop the rioters. In the months that followed, federal officials accompanied Meredith

(continued from page 704)

- Violence against the freedom riders forces the Kennedy administration to intervene.

IN-DEPTH RESOURCES: UNIT 6
Guided Reading, p. 19

ACCESS FOR STUDENTS ACQUIRING ENGLISH
Guided Reading (Spanish), p. 234

MORE ABOUT . . .
Jim Zwerg

Zwerg, a white student, was among those brutally beaten in Montgomery. When a reporter asked a police commissioner to get an ambulance for Zwerg, the commissioner replied, "He hasn't asked for one." He was not allowed to go to the hospital with two black victims because of Alabama's segregation laws. Eventually, a black minister drove him to a Catholic hospital that agreed to treat him.

IN-DEPTH RESOURCES: UNIT 6
Primary Source: Civil Rights Song, p. 25

OBJECTIVE
② INSTRUCT

Standing Firm

▶ ***Discussing Key Ideas***
- Civil rights organizers turn their attention to integrating some Southern campuses and towns.
- Federal troops are needed to get James Meredith into the all-white University of Mississippi.
- Television coverage of the brutal treatment of marchers in Birmingham leads President Kennedy to call for passage of a new civil rights bill.

TEACHING OPTIONS

Exploring Themes

Civil Rights Efforts to desegregate the South exposed the unwillingness of federal and state governments to protect African Americans from racial discrimination and violence. Discuss with students why Kennedy (and Eisenhower before him) waited so long to defend the civil rights of African Americans. What precedents might have been set if Kennedy had not tried to protect freedom riders or marchers in Birmingham? Have them explain this remark by Kennedy: "The rights of every man are diminished when the rights of one man are threatened."

Teaching Gifted and Talented Students

Composing Civil Rights Songs Civil rights organizers shored up morale through song. Encourage musically talented students to create a song that freedom riders might have sung as they headed into the South. For models, refer students to *Everybody Says Freedom,* by Pete Seeger and Bob Reiser. Or share these opening lyrics from an impromptu song composed on one ride: *I'm taking a ride on the Greyhound bus line/I'm riding the front seat to Jackson this time/Hallelujah I'm a-traveling/Hallelujah ain't it fine/Hallelujah I'm a-traveling/Down freedom's main line.*

MORE ABOUT . . .
Fred Shuttlesworth

In June 1956, the white-controlled government in Alabama outlawed the NAACP. In response, Fred Shuttlesworth, a Birmingham minister and member of the outlawed NAACP, called a meeting to form a new organization to fight for civil rights in Birmingham—the Alabama Christian Movement for Human Rights (ACMHR). Shuttlesworth was determined to use direct action campaigns—like the Montgomery bus boycott—to desegregate Birmingham. For seven years before King came to Birmingham, ACMHR members protested segregation and endured arrests and violence in response.

MORE ABOUT . . .
"Letter from a Birmingham Jail"

King wrote his letter on scattered strips of paper that a friend smuggled out of jail. A complicated series of arrows and loops indicated how the strips should be connected. Another friend, Wyatt Walker, deciphered what he called King's "chicken-scratch" writing for a secretary. One sentence totaled more than 300 words. The typed version was smuggled back to King and resmuggled out. The process continued until a 20-page document emerged.

News photos and television coverage of police dogs attacking African Americans in Birmingham shocked the nation's conscience and spurred President Kennedy to present a major civil rights bill to Congress.

to class and protected his parents from nightriders who shot up their house.

HEADING INTO BIRMINGHAM By 1963, Reverend Fred Shuttlesworth, head of the Alabama Christian Movement for Human Rights, decided that something had to be done about Birmingham—a city known for its strict enforcement of total segregation in public life. The city also had a reputation for racial violence, including 18 bombings from 1957 to 1963.

Deciding that Birmingham would be the ideal place to test the power of nonviolence, Shuttlesworth invited Dr. Martin Luther King, Jr., and the SCLC to help desegregate the city. On April 3, 1963, King flew into Birmingham to hold planning meetings with members of the African-American community. "This is the most segregated city in America," he said. "We have to stick together if we ever want to change its ways."

After several days of demonstrations led by Shuttlesworth and others, King led a small band of marchers into the streets of Birmingham on Good Friday, April 12. Police Commissioner Bull Connor promptly arrested them. While sitting in his jail cell, Dr. King wrote an open letter to white religious leaders who felt he was pushing too hard, too fast.

A PERSONAL VOICE

I guess it is easy for those who have never felt the stinging darts of segregation to say, "Wait." But when you have seen vicious mobs lynch your mothers and fathers at whim; when you have seen hate-filled policemen curse, kick, brutalize and even kill your black brothers and sisters; . . . when you see the vast majority of your twenty million Negro brothers smothering in the air-tight cage of poverty; . . . when you have to concoct an answer for a five-year-old son asking: . . . "Daddy, why do white people treat colored people so mean?" . . . then you will understand why we find it difficult to wait.

DR. MARTIN LUTHER KING, JR., "Letter from a Birmingham Jail"

"I say, Segregation now! Segregation tomorrow! Segregation forever!"

GEORGE WALLACE,
ALABAMA GOVERNOR, 1963

On April 20, King posted bail and began to plan more demonstrations. On May 2, more than a thousand African-American children marched in Birmingham; Bull Connor arrested 959 of them. On May 3, a second "children's crusade" came face to face with Connor and his helmeted police force. As television cameras recorded the scene, the police swept the marchers off their feet with high-pressure fire hoses, set attack dogs on them, and clubbed those who fell. Millions of TV viewers heard the children screaming.

Continued protests, an economic boycott, and negative media coverage finally convinced Birmingham officials to meet King's demands for an end to segregation. Birmingham offered a stunning civil rights victory that inspired African Americans across the nation. In addition, it convinced President Kennedy that nothing short of a new civil rights act would end the disorder and satisfy the demands of African Americans—and many whites—for racial justice.

KENNEDY TAKES A STAND On June 11, 1963, President Kennedy used federal troops to force Governor George Wallace to honor a court order desegregating the University of Alabama. That evening, Kennedy addressed the nation and asked pointedly, "Are we to say to the world—and much more importantly, to each other—that this is the land of the free, except for the Negroes?" He referred directly to "repressive police action" and "demonstrations in the streets." Then, he demanded that Congress pass a sweeping civil rights bill.

Block Schedule TEACHING OPTION **Time Needed: 30 Minutes**

Cooperative Activity: Creating News Reports on the Birmingham Protest

Task: To create on-the-spot reports for a key event in each of these months in 1963: April, May, June, July, and August.

Purpose: To help students appreciate the impact of the media on the civil rights movement.

Activity: Divide the class into groups of five students and have them divide among themselves the months that are listed above. Direct students to use magazines from 1963, such as *Time, Newsweek,* or *U.S. News and World Report,* to locate accounts of dramatic incidents in the civil rights movement. Based on these accounts, instruct students to prepare a series of live "you-are-there" news reports for the rest of the class. Student reporters might deliver the report in person or reenact it on videotape.

ALTERNATIVE ASSESSMENT BOOK
Standards for Evaluating a Cooperative Activity

Standards for Evaluation
News reports should . . .
- demonstrate careful research of the incident
- accurately reflect the chronology of events
- clearly identify the people involved
- define terms and references

A tragic event just hours after Kennedy's speech highlighted the racial tension in much of the South. Shortly after midnight, a sniper shot and killed Medgar Evers—NAACP field secretary and World War II veteran—in the driveway of his home in Jackson, Mississippi. Police soon arrested white supremacist Byron de la Beckwith for the crime, but he was released after two trials resulted in hung juries. (De la Beckwith was finally convicted in 1994, after the case was reopened based on new evidence.) The release of de la Beckwith brought a new militancy to African Americans. With raised fists, many demanded, "Freedom now!"

You can kill a man but you can't kill an idea"
KEEP THE IDEA OF FREEDOM ALIVE
JOIN NAACP

This 1963 poster shows Myrlie Evers, who was the widow of NAACP activist Medgar Evers and who became head of the NAACP in 1995.

Marching to Washington

The civil rights bill that Kennedy sent to Congress guaranteed equal access to all public accommodations and gave the U.S. attorney general the power to file school desegregation suits. To persuade Congress to pass the bill, two veteran organizers—labor leader A. Philip Randolph and Bayard Rustin of the SCLC—summoned Americans to join in a massive march on Washington, D.C.

THE DREAM OF EQUALITY On August 28, 1963, more than 250,000 people—including about 75,000 whites—converged on the nation's capital. They assembled on the grassy slopes of the Washington Monument, and the movement's leaders, walking arm in arm, led the crowd to the sprawling plaza near the Lincoln Monument. There, for more than three hours, people listened to speakers demand the immediate passage of the civil rights bill.

THINK THROUGH HISTORY
B. THEME *Civil Rights* *Why did civil rights organizers ask their supporters to march on Washington?*

B. Answer To spur passage of the civil rights bill.

When Dr. Martin Luther King, Jr., appeared, the crowd exploded in applause. King eventually stopped reading from his prepared text and began an improvised speech in which he appealed for peace and racial harmony, punctuating his speech with the repeated refrain "I have a dream."

A PERSONAL VOICE

I have a dream that one day this nation will rise up and live out the true meaning of its creed: "We hold these truths to be self-evident; that all men are created equal." . . . I have a dream that my four little children will one day live in a nation where they will not be judged by the color of their skin but by the content of their character. . . . I have a dream that one day the state of Alabama . . . will be transformed into a situation where little black boys and black girls will be able to join hands with little white boys and white girls and walk together as sisters and brothers.

DR. MARTIN LUTHER KING, JR., "I Have a Dream"

Billed as a march for "jobs and freedom," the March on Washington was the largest such demonstration held in the United States up to that time.

OBJECTIVE

③ INSTRUCT

Marching to Washington

▶ ***Discussing Key Ideas***

- Civil rights activists organize a great protest march on Washington to pressure Congress into passing the civil rights bill.
- President Johnson pushes the Civil Rights Act of 1964 through Congress.

MORE ABOUT . . .

A. Philip Randolph

Randolph was founder of the nation's most powerful African-American labor union—the Brotherhood of Sleeping Car Porters. When African Americans were discriminated against in war-related industries, Randolph threatened to lead 100,000 demonstrators to Washington, D.C. FDR took the threat seriously and, in 1941, issued Executive Order 8802, prohibiting "discrimination in the employment of workers in defense industries or government because of race, creed, color, or national origin."

IN-DEPTH RESOURCES: UNIT 6

American Lives: A. Philip Randolph, p. 32

Primary Source: *from* "I Have a Dream" by Martin Luther King, Jr., p. 26

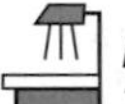
HUMANITIES TRANSPARENCIES

H27, March on Washington

GROLIER MULTIMEDIA ENCYCLOPEDIA

Pacifism and nonviolent movements video of the Civil Rights March on Washington

TEACHING OPTIONS

Making Connections Across Time

Myrlie Evers Today After her husband's assassination, Myrlie Evers-Williams endured two hung juries in the trial of Byron de la Beckwith, who was accused of the murder. In 1994, de la Beckwith was tried again and found guilty. The story is recounted in the 1996 movie *Ghosts of Mississippi.* In the 30 years since Medgar Evers's murder, Evers-Williams has never given up the fight for civil rights. She stayed active with grassroots organizations and lectured widely. In 1995, she became the chairperson of the NAACP Board of Directors.

Teaching Gifted and Talented Students

Identifying Political Differences Between SCLC and SNCC Many Americans have forgotten that a host of speakers addressed the crowd at the March on Washington in August 1963. Some of these speakers, such as John Lewis of SNCC and Martin Luther King, Jr., had different views on how to achieve equality most quickly and completely. Have students read King's "I Have a Dream" speech and the original (unaltered) version of Lewis's speech delivered at the March on Washington. Then have them list the points upon which the two men expressed divergent views and offer explanations about why they differed.

HISTORY FROM VISUALS

Civil Rights Acts of the 1950s and 1960s

Reading the Chart Point out that the chart details key points of four different civil rights acts.

Extension Ask students why Congress began passing so many pieces of civil rights legislation in the 1950s and 1960s. *Possible Responses: Because African Americans began calling for equal rights after fighting in World War II;* Brown v. Board of Education *and the crisis in Little Rock inspired African Americans and others to work for civil rights.*

OBJECTIVE

INSTRUCT

Fighting for Voting Rights

▶***Discussing Key Ideas***

- Violence and intimidation prevent millions of African Americans in the South from registering to vote.
- Civil rights workers try to win a voting rights act through two campaigns: Freedom Summer and a march from Selma, Alabama, to Montgomery.
- The Voting Rights Act of 1965 guarantees the right to vote for African Americans.

IN-DEPTH RESOURCES: UNIT 6
Primary Source: Political Poster, p. 27

Civil Rights Acts of the 1950s and 1960s

MAJOR CIVIL RIGHTS LEGISLATION
CIVIL RIGHTS ACT OF 1957 • Established federal Commission on Civil Rights and a Civil Rights Division in the Justice Department to enforce civil rights laws. • Enlarged federal power to protect voting rights.
CIVIL RIGHTS ACT OF 1964 • Banned discrimination in most employment and in public accommodations. • Enlarged federal power to protect voting rights and speed up school desegregation. • Established Equal Employment Opportunity Commission to ensure fair treatment in employment.
VOTING RIGHTS ACT OF 1965 • Eliminated voter literacy tests. • Enabled federal examiners to register voters.
CIVIL RIGHTS ACT OF 1968 • Prohibited discrimination in the sale or rental of most housing. • Strengthened antilynching laws.

SKILLBUILDER

INTERPRETING CHARTS

Which law do you think benefited the most people? Explain your choice.

Skillbuilder Answer
Possible Answer: The Civil Rights Act of 1964 because it banned discrimination in employment and public accommodations—areas that affect nearly everyone.

MORE VIOLENCE Two weeks after King's historic speech, a car sped past the Sixteenth Street Baptist Church in Birmingham, Alabama, and a rider in the car hurled a bomb through one of the church windows. The resulting explosion claimed the lives of four young girls. Two more African Americans died in the unrest that followed.

Two months later, on November 22, 1963, an assassin shot and killed John F. Kennedy. (See Chapter 20.) His successor, President Lyndon B. Johnson, pledged to carry on Kennedy's work by winning passage of the civil rights bill. "We have talked for 100 years or more," Johnson said. "It is time now to write the new chapter—and to write it in books of law." On July 2, 1964, President Johnson signed the **Civil Rights Act of 1964,** which prohibited discrimination because of race, religion, national origin, and gender. It gave all citizens the right to enter libraries, parks, washrooms, restaurants, theaters, and other public accommodations.

Fighting for Voting Rights

Meanwhile, civil rights workers in the South were planning a different campaign to influence the country's laws—by registering African-American voters who could elect legislators who supported civil rights. Because previous voter-registration drives had met with little success, CORE and SNCC planned a much larger effort for 1964. They hoped their campaign would receive national publicity that would in turn influence Congress to pass a voting rights act. SNCC concentrated its efforts in Mississippi, in a project that was popularly known as **Freedom Summer.**

FREEDOM SUMMER SNCC knew that challenging the system that kept more than 90 percent of African-American citizens from the polls would be a daunting task. Civil rights groups recruited white students from colleges across the country and then trained them in the techniques of nonviolent resistance. Some 1,000 volunteers—mostly white, about one-third female—went into Mississippi to help the mostly African-American SNCC staff members register voters.

Robert Moses, a former New York City schoolteacher who had quit his job and joined SNCC in 1961, led the voter project in Mississippi. By the summer of 1964, Moses had already been working for several years in Mississippi to register blacks to vote. "Mississippi has been called 'The Closed Society.' It is closed, locked," Moses said. "We think the key is in the vote."

THINK THROUGH HISTORY
C. ***Analyzing Causes*** *Why did civil rights groups organize Freedom Summer?*

C. Answer They hoped to call attention to the lack of voting rights in segregationist strongholds such as Mississippi, thereby winning passage of a federal voting rights act.

Immediately, the voter project encountered violent opposition. In June, while some of the volunteers were still receiving training back in Ohio, three

John Lewis, national chairman of SNCC, predicted that "1964 could really be the year for Mississippi." In that summer, college students from all over the country volunteered to go to Mississippi to help register that state's African-American voters.

TEACHING OPTIONS

Exploring Themes

Civil Rights The Fifteenth Amendment barred states from depriving citizens of the right to vote "on account of race, color, or previous condition of servitude." It also gave Congress the "power to enforce this article by appropriate legislation." Discuss with students how Southern states had violated this amendment. Then explore ways that civil rights workers tried to make the federal government honor its constitutional responsibility to African Americans.

Making Connections Across the Curriculum

Math Nearly two decades after Freedom Summer, math teacher Robert Moses started the Algebra Project—a system that uses real-life examples to teach mathematical concepts. For example: A central subway station might become the zero point, with routes to the east representing positive integers and routes to the west representing negative integers. The goal, said Moses in the early 1990s, "is to pump students into a broad mathematical pipeline."

civil rights workers, including one summer volunteer, disappeared in Mississippi. They were Michael Schwerner and Andrew Goodman, white activists from New York, and James Chaney, an African American from Mississippi. Investigators later learned that Klansmen, with the support of local police, had murdered the three and buried them in an earthen dam. By the end of the summer, the project had suffered 4 dead, 4 critically wounded, 80 beaten, and dozens of African-American churches and businesses bombed or burned. In spite of all the publicity the project received, Congress still did not pass a voting rights act.

A NEW POLITICAL PARTY To challenge Mississippi's white-controlled Democratic Party, SNCC organized the Mississippi Freedom Democratic Party (MFDP). Open to anyone, regardless of race, the MFDP hoped to unseat Mississippi's regular party delegates at the Democratic National Convention.

Fannie Lou Hamer, the daughter of Mississippi sharecroppers, won the honor of speaking for the MFDP at the convention. Hamer had registered to vote in 1962 at the cost of a crippling beating and her family's eviction from their farm. In June 1964, she spoke to the credentials committee at the Democratic convention in a prime-time televised address. Hamer described how she had been arrested for trying to register and taken to jail, where police forced other prisoners to beat her.

A PERSONAL VOICE

The first [prisoner] began to beat [me], and I was beat by the first until he was exhausted. . . . The second [prisoner] began to beat. . . . I began to scream and one white man got up and began to beat me in my head and tell me to "hush." . . . All of this on account we want to register, to become first-class citizens, and if the Freedom Democratic Party is not seated now, I question America.

FANNIE LOU HAMER, quoted in *The Civil Rights Movement: An Eyewitness History*

In response to Hamer's speech, telegrams and telephone calls poured in to the convention in support of seating the MFDP delegates. But President Johnson feared that such a move would cost him white votes throughout the South, so his administration pressured civil rights leaders to convince the MFDP to accept a compromise. The Democrats would give 2 of Mississippi's 68 seats to the MFDP, with a promise to ban discrimination at the 1968 convention.

When Hamer learned of the compromise, she exclaimed, "We didn't come all this way for no two seats when all of us is tired." The MFDP and many of their young supporters in SNCC felt that the leaders of other civil rights groups had betrayed them. This sense of betrayal was one of several factors that eventually led to conflict among various civil rights groups.

THINK THROUGH HISTORY
D. *Analyzing Causes* *Why did young people in SNCC and the MFDP feel betrayed by some civil rights leaders?*

D. Answer Because the leaders agreed to a compromise with the Johnson administration that kept most MFDP delegates from the Democratic convention.

THE SELMA CAMPAIGN At the start of 1965, the SCLC decided to conduct a major campaign in Selma, Alabama, where SNCC had been working for two years to register voters. African Americans accounted for more than half of Selma's population but for only about 3 percent of the total registered voters. Martin Luther King, Jr., and the SCLC hoped that a concentrated voter-registration drive in Selma would provoke a hostile white response—which would help convince the Johnson administration of the need to sponsor a federal voting-rights law.

By the end of January 1965, more than 2,000 African Americans had been arrested in demonstrations. Selma sheriff Jim Clark reacted as violently as Bull Connor in Birmingham, and his men brutally attacked civil rights demonstrators.

Dr. King and Coretta Scott King and others lead the Selma march in 1965.

HISTORICAL SPOTLIGHT

24TH AMENDMENT—BARRING POLL TAXES

On January 24, 1964, South Dakota became the 38th state to ratify the Twenty-fourth Amendment to the Constitution, thereby making it the law of the land. The key clause in the amendment read: "The right of citizens of the United States to vote in any primary or other election . . . shall not be denied or abridged by the United States or any State by reason of failure to pay any poll tax or other tax."

Poll taxes were often used to keep poor African Americans from voting. Although most states had already abolished their poll taxes by 1964, five Southern states—Alabama, Arkansas, Mississippi, Texas, and Virginia—still had such laws on the books. By making these laws unconstitutional, the Twenty-fourth Amendment gave the vote to millions who had been disqualified because of poverty.

HISTORICAL SPOTLIGHT

24th Amendment

Critical Thinking: Cause and Effect Have students analyze the causes and effects of the Twenty-fourth Amendment by using the graphic organizer below.

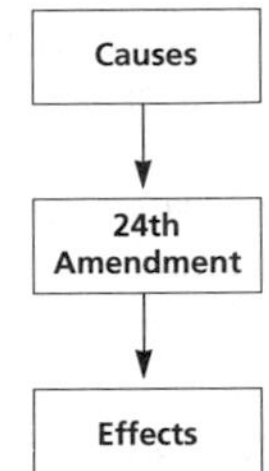

MORE ABOUT . . .

Fannie Lou Hamer

"We are sick and tired of being sick and tired." Fannie Lou Hamer used this phrase so many times in her speeches that it became her motto. Hamer also became known for another speech that sought to tear down economic and educational barriers that divided African Americans. "Whether you have a Ph.D., or no D, we're in this bag together," said Hamer. "And whether you're from Morehouse or Nohouse, we're still in this bag together."

TEACHING OPTIONS

Making Connections Across the Curriculum

U.S. Government The Voting Rights Act of 1965—and the later voting rights laws of 1970, 1975, and 1982—brought the federal government directly into the electoral process of the states. Have students find the provision in the Constitution that originally guaranteed states the right to manage federal elections. *Article I, Section 4, Clause 1.* Then have students research other federal laws, amendments (such as the Twenty-fourth), or court decisions that limited state conduct of elections.

Making Connections Across the Curriculum

Creative Writing The civil rights movement provided some of the most dramatic moments in American history, from the trial for the murder of Emmett Till and the March on Washington to the Montgomery bus boycott and the sit-ins in Greensboro. Ask students to write a poem or short story based on some aspect of the civil rights movement. The final products should be based on actual historical facts but should also express the emotion and drama of the era.

NOW & THEN

Integrating Government

Critical Thinking: Analyzing Assign interested students to find out more about changes in the number of African-American elected officials to Congress and the state legislatures since 1970. Have students show their findings in the form of a table or line graph. A possible source of information is the latest edition of *The American Almanac: Statistical Abstract of the United States.*

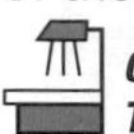 ***GEOGRAPHY TRANSPARENCIES***

G29, Before and After the Voting Rights Act of 1965

ASSESS & RETEACH

Section 2 Assessment

Have groups of four students each address one point from item 4 and then share the answers with each other.

Self-Assessment

Ask students to review the answers they gave for item 3. How might other factors have shaped opposition to the civil rights movement?

Section Quiz

FORMAL ASSESSMENT
Section Quiz, p. 260

Reteach

Use the Guided Reading Worksheet for Section 2 to help review the main ideas of the section.

IN-DEPTH RESOURCES: UNIT 6
Guided Reading, p. 19

CLOSE

Although civil rights activists across the South faced massive resistance in their efforts to achieve desegregation, they forced the federal government to pass monumental civil rights legislation.

African Americans in Mississippi line up to vote in primary elections in April 1966.

Then, in February, law officers shot and killed a demonstrator named Jimmie Lee Jackson. Dr. King responded by announcing a 50-mile protest march from Selma to the state capital, Montgomery. On Sunday, March 7, 1965, a group of about 600 protesters set out for Montgomery.

That night, news bulletins interrupted regular television programs to show what looked like a war. Clouds of tear gas swirled around fallen marchers, while police wearing gas masks and riding horses swung whips and clubs.

The scene sent shock waves across the country. Demonstrators from all over the United States poured into Selma to join the march. President Johnson responded by asking Congress for the swift passage of a new voting rights act. In his speech, Johnson openly embraced the rhetoric of the civil rights movement. Said the president, "Their cause must be our cause, too. It is not just Negroes, but all of us, who must overcome the crippling legacy of bigotry and injustice. And we *shall* overcome."

On Sunday, March 21, 3,000 marchers again set out for Montgomery, this time with federal protection. Two Nobel Peace Prize winners—Dr. Martin Luther King, Jr., and UN diplomat Ralph Bunche—led the procession. Under court order, only 250 marchers were supposed to enter the city limits, but nothing could stop the groundswell of support. An army of some 25,000 demonstrators joined the marchers as they walked into Montgomery.

NOW & THEN

INTEGRATING GOVERNMENT

During the 1996 Democratic National Convention, Rev. Jesse Jackson told a story that illustrates the political gains African Americans have made. Jackson's father, a World War II veteran, once pointed out a German-American citizen to his son. His father said, "We [Americans] fought to help free that [man's] country. Now he can go downtown and can vote and I can't."

In 1995, Jackson had the joy of seeing his son, Jesse Jackson, Jr., sworn in as a congressman from Illinois. The civil rights movement had so changed U.S. life that the man whose father couldn't vote because of race had a son in the U.S. House of Representatives.

THINK THROUGH HISTORY
E. *Comparing* *In what ways was the civil rights campaign in Selma similar to the one in Birmingham?*

E. Answer In both campaigns, civil rights workers encountered a violent response, and in both cases, TV coverage of that violence helped force the federal government to intervene.

VOTING RIGHTS ACT OF 1965 Ten weeks after the Selma-to-Montgomery march, Congress passed the **Voting Rights Act of 1965.** The act eliminated the literacy test that had disqualified so many voters. The act also stated that federal examiners could enroll voters denied suffrage by local officials. In Selma, the proportion of eligible African Americans who were registered to vote rose from 10 percent in 1964 to 60 percent in 1968. Overall the percentage of registered African-American voters in the South tripled.

Although the Voting Rights Act marked a major civil rights victory, some African Americans felt that the law did not go far enough. Centuries of segregation and discrimination had produced deep-rooted social and economic inequalities. In the mid-1960s, anger over these inequalities led to a series of violent disturbances in the cities of the North.

Section 2 Assessment

1. TERMS & NAMES *Identify:*
- freedom rider
- James Meredith
- Civil Rights Act of 1964
- Freedom Summer
- Robert Moses
- Fannie Lou Hamer
- Voting Rights Act of 1965

2. SUMMARIZING Write a newspaper headline that summarizes the historical significance of each date listed below.
- September 30, 1962
- April 12, 1963
- June 11, 1963
- June 12, 1963
- August 28, 1963
- November 22, 1963
- July 2, 1964

Choose a headline and write the first paragraph for the newspaper article.

3. SYNTHESIZING What assumptions and beliefs do you think guided the fierce opposition to the civil rights movement in the South? Support your answer with evidence from the text.

THINK ABOUT
- the social and political structure of the South
- Mississippi governor Ross Barnett's comment during his radio address
- the actions of police and some white Southerners

4. RECOGNIZING EFFECTS What was the outcome of each of the following events?
- freedom rides to Jackson, Mississippi
- demonstrations in Birmingham, Alabama
- formation of the Mississippi Freedom Democratic Party
- Selma-to-Montgomery march

ANSWERS

1. TERMS & NAMES

freedom rider, p. 704

James Meredith, p. 705

Civil Rights Act of 1964, p. 708

Freedom Summer, p. 708

Robert Moses, p. 708

Fannie Lou Hamer, p. 709

Voting Rights Act of 1965, p. 710

2. SUMMARIZING

Possible Responses: September 30, 1962: Backlash! Ole Miss Riot over Meredith's Enrollment; April 12, 1963: King Jailed in Birmingham After Leading Demonstration; June 11, 1963: Kennedy Orders Troops to Desegregate University of Alabama; June 12, 1963: Medgar Evers Murdered; August 28, 1963: March on Washington—King Declares "I Have a Dream"; November 22, 1963: Kennedy Killed by Sniper—Nation Mourns; July 2, 1964: Johnson Signs Civil Rights Act.

3. SYNTHESIZING

Possible Responses: Racism was deeply entrenched in the South; claiming racial superiority, some white Southerners feared that the civil rights movement would erode their power base and shake the foundations of the South's social and political structure, which was upheld by its system of segregation.

4. RECOGNIZING EFFECTS

Freedom rides: federal government issued an order banning segregation in all interstate travel facilities. **Birmingham:** city officials agreed to end segregation. **MFDP:** Fannie Lou Hamer addressed 1964 Democratic convention; as a compromise, the MFDP gained two seats at 1964 convention and the promise to ban discrimination at 1968 convention. **Selma:** President Johnson persuaded Congress to pass Voting Rights Act of 1965.

3 Challenges and Changes in the Movement

LEARN ABOUT disagreements among civil rights groups and the rise of black nationalism
TO UNDERSTAND why the civil rights movement had a mixed legacy.

TERMS & NAMES
- **de facto segregation**
- **de jure segregation**
- **Malcolm X**
- **Nation of Islam**
- **Stokely Carmichael**
- **Black Power**
- **Black Panthers**
- **Kerner Commission**
- **Civil Rights Act of 1968**
- **affirmative action**

ONE AMERICAN'S STORY

Alice Walker, the prize-winning novelist, became aware of the civil rights movement in 1960, when she was 16. Her mother had recently scraped together enough money to purchase a television.

A PERSONAL VOICE

Like a good omen for the future, the face of Dr. Martin Luther King, Jr., was the first black face I saw on our new television screen. And, as in a fairy tale, my soul was stirred by the meaning for me of his mission—at the time he was being rather ignominiously dumped into a police van for having led a protest march in Alabama—and I fell in love with the sober and determined face of the Movement.

ALICE WALKER, *In Search of Our Mothers' Gardens*

Alice Walker

The next year, Walker enrolled in Spelman College, an African-American college in Atlanta. While there, she demonstrated on weekends for an end to segregation. In 1963, Walker took part in King's March on Washington and then traveled to Africa to discover her spiritual roots. After returning to the United States in 1964, she married a civil rights attorney and, with him, moved to Mississippi, where she worked on voter registration, taught African-American history and writing, and wrote poetry and fiction.

Walker's interest in her African heritage was part of a trend among many African Americans in the mid-1960s who began to express pride in their African roots. In addition to emphasizing black identity, civil rights activists also began to call for changes to the social and economic structures that kept millions of African Americans in poverty. By 1964, more than one third of all African Americans lived in Northern cities, where they had trouble finding jobs or decent housing. Angry over these conditions and frustrated because the equality they hoped for was so slow in coming, some urban African Americans rioted in the years 1964 to 1968.

African Americans Seek Greater Equality

By 1965, the leading civil rights groups—while still sharing the goals of racial equality and greater opportunity—began to drift apart. New leaders emerged as the civil rights movement turned its attention to the North, where African Americans faced not legal racism but deeply entrenched and oppressive racial prejudice nonetheless.

NORTHERN SEGREGATION The problem in the North was **de facto segregation**—segregation that exists by practice and custom. De facto segregation can be harder to fight than **de jure segregation** (segregation by law), because eliminating it requires the transformation of racist attitudes rather than the repeal of Jim Crow laws. Activists in the mid-1960s would find it much more difficult to convince whites to share economic and social power with African Americans than to convince them to share lunch counters and bus seats.

De facto segregation intensified after African Americans migrated to Northern cities after World War II. This began a "white flight," in which great numbers of white city dwellers moved to the suburbs. By the mid-1960s, most

SECTION 3 RESOURCES

PRINT RESOURCES

IN-DEPTH RESOURCES: UNIT 6
Guided Reading, p. 20

READING STUDY GUIDE, p. 219

ACCESS FOR STUDENTS ACQUIRING ENGLISH
Guided Reading (Spanish), p. 235

SPANISH READING STUDY GUIDE, p. 219

FORMAL ASSESSMENT
Section Quiz, p. 261

ALTERNATIVE ASSESSMENT BOOK
See forms for supporting and scoring alternative activities.

TECHNOLOGY RESOURCES

CRITICAL THINKING TRANSPARENCIES
CT29, Civil Rights Movement
CT63, African-American Educational Attainment

CD-ROM Electronic Library of Primary Sources

VIDEO *American Portfolio: A Videodisc for U.S. History* user's guide, pp. 246, 248

INTERNET http://www.mlushistory.com

Section 3 Overview

OBJECTIVES

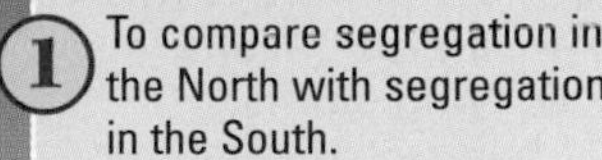
1. To compare segregation in the North with segregation in the South.

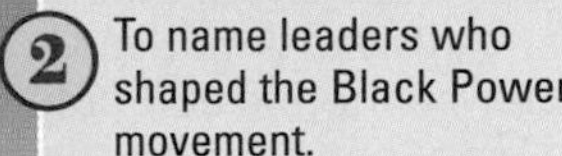
2. To name leaders who shaped the Black Power movement.

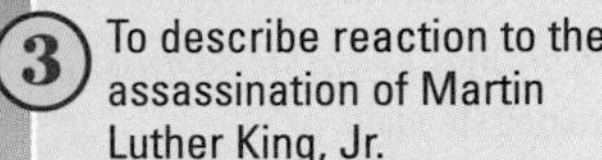
3. To describe reaction to the assassination of Martin Luther King, Jr.

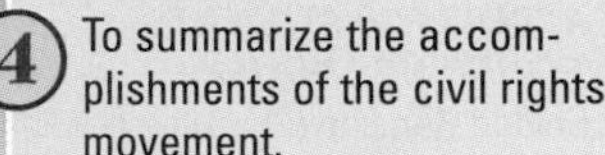
4. To summarize the accomplishments of the civil rights movement.

SKILLBUILDER
- Interpreting graphs, p. 717

CRITICAL THINKING
- Analyzing causes, p. 712
- Contrasting, p. 713
- Analyzing motives, p. 714
- Making inferences, pp. 715, 717
- Summarizing, pp. 716, 717
- Identifying problems, p. 717
- Comparing and contrasting, p. 717

FOCUS & MOTIVATE

5-MINUTE WARM-UP

Recognizing Fact and Detail
To explore riots in the 1960s, have students study the photos on page 712 and answer these questions.

1. How did the cities put down the riots?
2. What caused much of the property damage during the riots?

WARM-UP TRANSPARENCY 21

▶***Starting with the Student***
Ask students whether they think racial tensions are different in the North than in the South.

OBJECTIVE
① INSTRUCT

African Americans Seek Greater Equality

▶***Discussing Key Ideas***
- In the mid-1960s, differences over tactics create

(continued on next page)

(continued from page 711)

divisions in the civil rights movement.
- In the North, de facto segregation traps many African Americans in decaying slums.
- Urban riots reveal that many African Americans suffer economic and political inequality.

IN-DEPTH RESOURCES: UNIT 6
Guided Reading, p. 20

ACCESS FOR STUDENTS ACQUIRING ENGLISH
Guided Reading (Spanish), p. 235

MORE ABOUT . . .
The Harlem Riot

In assessing the Harlem riot of 1964, the poet Langston Hughes wrote:

> Old-timers . . . say, "White folks respect us more when they find out we mean business. When they only listen to our speeches or read our writing—if they ever do—they think we are just blowing off steam. But when rioters smash the plate glass windows of their stores, they know the steam has some force behind it."

Ask students to assess how this line of thinking also appealed to the new generation of civil rights leaders in the North.

MORE ABOUT . . .
The Watts Riot

National Guardsmen had to be called in to stem the rioting. In addition to the 34 people who were killed, almost 900 people were injured and over 3,500 people were arrested.

urban African Americans found themselves trapped in decaying slums, paying rent to landlords who often refused to comply with local housing and health ordinances. The schools provided for African-American children deteriorated along with their neighborhoods. Unemployment rates among African Americans were more than twice as high as those among whites.

The widely publicized gains in voting rights and desegregation of public accommodations made many urban African Americans impatient for discrimination in other areas to end. In addition, they were angry at the sometimes brutal treatment they received from the mostly white police force that patrolled their communities.

URBAN VIOLENCE ERUPTS In New York City in July 1964, a clash between white police and African-American teenagers ended in the death of a 15-year-old student. This incident sparked a race riot in central Harlem. Similar conflicts took place in other cities during that year. On August 11, 1965, only five days after President Johnson signed the Voting Rights Act into law, African Americans in Los Angeles exploded in anger against white authority. In Watts, the city's predominantly African-American neighborhood, police who were arresting a young man for drunk driving argued with the suspect's mother before onlookers. A riot broke out that lasted for six days. Thirty-four people were killed, and property valued at about $30 million was destroyed, making the Watts riot one of the worst race riots in the nation's history.

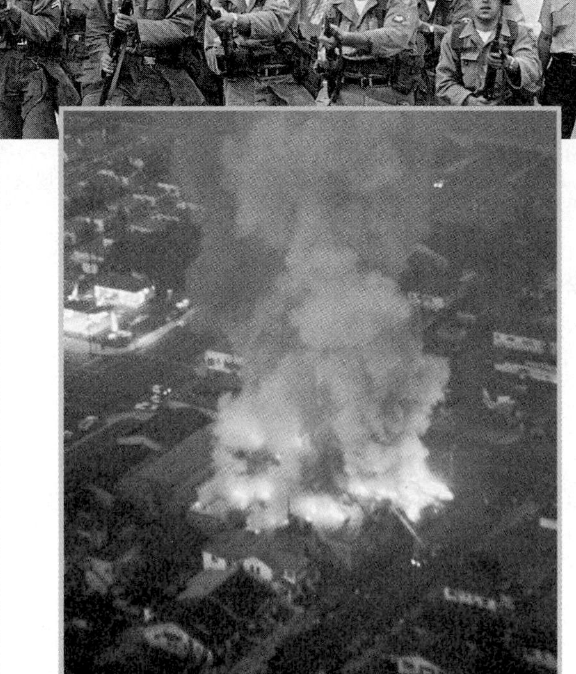

Between 1964 and 1968, more than 100 race riots erupted in major American cities. The worst included Watts in Los Angeles in 1965, *bottom*, and Detroit in 1967, *top*. In Detroit, 43 people were killed and property damage topped $40 million.

The next year, 1966, saw even more racial disturbances, and 1967 was the most violent year of all. In 1967 alone, riots and violent clashes took place in more than 100 cities—north and south, east and west.

The rage that African Americans were expressing baffled many whites, who could not understand why blacks would turn to violence just after winning so many important civil rights victories in the South. Some white leaders, however, realized that what African Americans wanted and needed was economic equality of opportunity in jobs, housing, and education.

THINK THROUGH HISTORY
A. *Analyzing Causes* *What were some of the causes of urban rioting in the 1960s?*

A. Answer
De facto segregation, police brutality, rundown communities and schools, and high unemployment.

As early as January 1964, even before the riots, President Johnson announced to Congress his War on Poverty, a program designed to help impoverished Americans of all races. But war in far-off Vietnam, a Southeast Asian country where the United States sent troops to fight Communists, soon siphoned off the money needed to fund what Johnson called the Great Society. In a fiery antiwar speech in 1967, Dr. Martin Luther King, Jr., declared, "The Great Society has been shot down on the battlefields of Vietnam."

TEACHING OPTIONS

Exploring Themes

Democracy in America Although not expressly written down in the Bill of Rights, Americans value the right to earn a decent living and freedom from economic want. Millions of African Americans in the 1960s felt that because of discrimination they had been denied economic rights as surely as they had been denied the right to vote. Challenge students to write an amendment guaranteeing Americans the right to work. As an extension, they might conduct a poll to see if voting-age members of their community would support such an amendment.

Teaching Less Proficient Readers

Interpreting Photographs Remind students that photographs serve as primary sources, or firsthand information, about the past. Working in pairs, have them write down all the things that these photographs tell them about the urban riots of 1965–1967. Suppose these two pictures were included in a photographic history of the civil rights movement. What caption would students write to summarize their content?

New Leaders Voice Discontent

The anger that sent rioters into the streets stemmed in part from African-American leaders who were reviving the belief that African Americans should take complete control of their communities, livelihoods, and culture. One such leader, **Malcolm X,** brought a Harlem audience to its feet in the early 1960s when he declared, "If you think we are here to tell you to love the white man, you have come to the wrong place."

AFRICAN-AMERICAN SOLIDARITY Malcolm X, born Malcolm Little, went to jail at age 20 for burglary. While in prison, he studied the teachings of Elijah Muhammad, the head of the **Nation of Islam,** or the Black Muslims. Malcolm changed his name to Malcolm X (dropping what he called his "slave name") and, after his release from prison in 1952, became a minister of the Islamic religion. Soon he was one of Elijah Muhammad's most famous disciples. A brilliant thinker and an engaging speaker, Malcolm X openly preached Elijah Muhammad's views that whites were the cause of the condition in which blacks found themselves and that blacks should separate from white society.

Malcolm's message appealed to many African Americans and their growing pride in their identity. At a New York press conference in March 1964, he also advocated armed self-defense.

A PERSONAL VOICE

Concerning nonviolence: it is criminal to teach a man not to defend himself when he is the constant victim of brutal attacks. It is legal and lawful to own a shotgun or a rifle. We believe in obeying the laws. . . . The time has come for the American Negro to fight back in self-defense whenever and wherever he is being unjustly and unlawfully attacked.

MALCOLM X, quoted in *EYEWITNESS: The Negro in American History*

The press gave a great deal of publicity to Malcolm X because his controversial statements made dramatic news stories. This publicity had two effects. First, his call for armed self-defense frightened most whites and many moderate African Americans. Second, reports of the attention Malcolm received awakened resentment in some other members of the Nation of Islam.

THINK THROUGH HISTORY
B. *Contrasting* *How did the ideas of Malcolm X differ from those of Martin Luther King, Jr.?*

B. Answer Malcolm X advocated self-defense, by violent means if necessary, and before 1964, rejected working with whites.

BALLOTS OR BULLETS? In March 1964, Malcolm broke with Elijah Muhammad over differences in strategy and doctrine and formed another Muslim organization. One month later, he embarked on a pilgrimage to Mecca, in Saudi Arabia, a trip required of followers of orthodox Islam. In Mecca, he learned that orthodox Islam preached the equality of all races, and he worshiped alongside people from many countries. Wrote Malcolm, "I have [prayed] . . . with fellow Muslims whose eyes were the bluest of blue, whose hair was the blondest of blond, and whose skin was the whitest of white."

The experience radically changed Malcolm's thinking. When he returned to the United States, he still burned with a hatred of racism and injustice, but his attitude toward whites had changed. When 1965 opened, he introduced a new slogan: "Ballots or bullets." In explaining the phrase, Malcolm told a follower, "Well, if you and I don't use the ballot, we're going to be forced to use the bullet. So let us try the ballot."

Malcolm believed that his life might be in danger because of his split with the Black Muslims. "No one can get out without trouble," he confided

KEY PLAYER

MALCOLM X
1925–1965

Malcolm X's early life left him alienated from white society. His father was allegedly killed by white racists, and his mother had an emotional collapse, leaving Malcolm and his siblings in the care of the state. At the end of eighth grade, Malcolm quit school and went first to Boston and then to New York, where he became a drug addict and a criminal. In 1946, a court sentenced him to ten years in prison.

While in prison, Malcolm joined the Nation of Islam, and after his release in 1952, he preached black superiority and separation from whites.

His 1964 pilgrimage to Mecca transformed his views. Instead of preaching separatism, he began to urge African Americans to identify with Africa and to work with world organizations and even progressive whites to attain equality. Although gunmen silenced his message, Malcolm X is a continuing inspiration for young African Americans.

OBJECTIVE
(2) INSTRUCT

New Leaders Voice Discontent

Discussing Key Ideas

- Malcolm X appeals to a growing sense of African-American pride.
- His later efforts to temper African-American separatism alienate many Black Muslims, three of whom assassinate him.
- Stokely Carmichael and the Black Panthers signal the growing radicalism of some segments of the African-American community.

KEY PLAYER
Malcolm X

Critical Thinking: Hypothesizing Assign teams of students to create a dialogue in which Malcolm X and Martin Luther King, Jr., discuss and debate their two philosophies for change. Have students reenact their dialogues, either in a live skit or in the form of a videotape.

ELECTRONIC LIBRARY OF PRIMARY SOURCES
from A Speech to Mississippi Youth by Malcolm X

TEACHING OPTIONS

Teaching Gifted and Talented Students

Writing a Book Review Assign your more able students to read *The Autobiography of Malcolm X, Where Do We Go from Here: Chaos or Community?* by Martin Luther King, Jr., or *Black Power* by Stokely Carmichael and Charles V. Hamilton. Tell them to write a review of the book from the perspective of the late 1960s. They might want to look at contemporary book reviews to get a sense of what people at the time thought about the book. In their review, students should critique the author's main arguments about race relations in the United States in the 1960s based on their knowledge of the time.

Making Global Connections

Creating Ties with Africa Before setting out on his *hajj,* or pilgrimage to Mecca, Malcolm X took the Muslim name of Malik El-Shabazz. After traveling through the Muslim world of the Middle East and Africa, Malcolm X (as he is still called) returned home to found the Organization of Afro-American Unity (OAAU)—a group set up to empower African Americans and to draw African nations into their struggle. Just before his death, Malcolm X tried to enlist African nations to petition the UN on behalf of African Americans in the United States.

MORE ABOUT . . .
Stokely Carmichael
Born in Port-of-Spain, Trinidad, Carmichael attended Howard University in Washington, D.C., in preference to the white universities that offered him scholarships. After his graduation in 1964, Carmichael plunged himself into the civil rights revolution. To this day, he often answers his phone with the words "Ready for the Revolution."

MORE ABOUT . . .
The Black Panthers
In 1974, the Panthers elected Elaine Brown as the group's first female leader. Among her community projects, Brown set up an award-winning learning center for poor children in Oakland, California. In 1977, Brown also organized a registration drive in which more than 100,000 African Americans signed up to vote. These new voters helped elect Lionel Wilson as Oakland's first-ever African-American mayor.

to a friend. On February 21, 1965, Malcolm X walked into Harlem's Audubon Ballroom to address a crowd of about 400 followers. No sooner had he begun speaking than three men rushed forward and shot him down. At age 39, Malcolm X was dead.

BLACK POWER In early June of 1966, tensions that had been building between SNCC and the other civil rights groups finally erupted in Mississippi. Here, James Meredith, the man who had integrated the University of Mississippi, set out on a 220-mile "march against fear." Meredith planned to walk all the way from the Tennessee border to Jackson. But on the second day of Meredith's march, a white man stopped him by firing a round of birdshot into his head, legs, and back. Meredith was too injured to continue.

Dr. Martin Luther King, Jr., of the SCLC, Floyd McKissick of CORE, and **Stokely Carmichael** of SNCC decided to lead their followers in a march to finish what Meredith had started. It soon became obvious that SNCC and CORE participants were quite militant, as they began to shout slogans similar to those of the black separatists who had followed Malcolm X. When King tried to rally the marchers with the familiar refrain of "We Shall Overcome," many SNCC workers—bitter over the violence they'd suffered during Freedom Summer—drowned out the song by singing, "We shall overrun."

On the night of June 17, police in Greenwood, Mississippi, arrested SNCC leader Stokely Carmichael for setting up a tent on the grounds of an all-black high school. That night marchers held a hastily organized rally to protest Carmichael's arrest. Near the end of the rally, he showed up on the platform, with his face swollen from a beating. The stunned crowd listened as Carmichael spoke.

Stokely Carmichael

> **A PERSONAL VOICE**
> This is the twenty-seventh time I have been arrested—and I ain't going to jail no more! . . . We been saying freedom for six years—and we ain't got nothin'. What we're gonna start saying now is BLACK POWER.
>
> STOKELY CARMICHAEL, quoted in *The Civil Rights Movement: An Eyewitness History*

The slogan **Black Power** electrified the night marchers. Some civil rights leaders, including King, urged Carmichael to stop using it because they believed it would provoke African-American violence and antagonize whites. Carmichael refused to heed their warnings. Black Power, he said, was a "call for black people to begin to define their own goals . . . [and] to lead their own organizations." He urged SNCC to stop recruiting whites and to focus on developing African-American pride.

THINK THROUGH HISTORY
C. *Analyzing Motives* *Why did some leaders of SNCC disagree with SCLC tactics?*

C. Answer Impatient for change and bitter over the violence of Freedom Summer, some SNCC leaders wanted African Americans to claim "Black Power" and to confront whites more directly.

BLACK PANTHERS Later that year, another development demonstrated the growing radicalism of some segments of the African-American community. In Oakland, California, in October 1966, Huey Newton and Bobby Seale founded a political party known as the **Black Panthers** to fight police brutality in the ghetto. The party also offered African Americans what it called "a program for the people," which advocated taking control of African-American communities, full employment, and decent housing. The program also supported an exemption of African Americans from military service—a reflection of the belief that the government drafted an unfair number of black youths to fight in Vietnam.

Most Panthers wore black berets, sunglasses, black leather jackets, black trousers, and shiny black shoes. To raise money for the organization, they sold copies of the writings of Mao Zedong, leader of the Chinese Communist revolution. The Panthers publicly preached armed revolt and adopted one of Mao's slogans: "Power flows out of the barrel of a gun."

Most white leaders feared and distrusted the Panthers and objected to their

TEACHING OPTIONS

Making Global Connections

Promoting Pan-Africanism In 1978, Stokely Carmichael changed his name to Kwame Ture, in honor of Kwame Nkrumah, the first president of independent Ghana and the so-called "Father of pan-Africanism," and Ahmed Sekou Toure, the first president of Guinea and an ardent supporter of Nkrumah. Carmichael became a citizen of Uganda in 1973 and is a staunch defender of pan-Africanism. He calls all people of the Black Diaspora "Africans," including African Americans. You might use Carmichael's story as a bridge to discussing the pan-Africanism of Marcus Garvey.

Making Connections Across Cultures

Kwanzaa Assign interested students to research Kwanzaa—a seven-day celebration of African-American culture that begins on December 26. Explain that Kwanzaa, which means "first fruits of harvest" in Swahili, was invented in 1966 by Maulana Karenga in reaction to the 1965 riots in Watts. Karenga, a black activist and educator in California, hoped the celebration would replace rage with pride. If possible, encourage a student familiar with the celebration to describe it to the class.

THINK THROUGH HISTORY
D. *Making Inferences* *Why was the public reaction to the Black Panthers mixed?*

revolutionary rhetoric. Several shootouts occurred between the Panthers and the police, and the FBI conducted investigations (sometimes using illegal tactics) of the organization. Even so, the Panthers' grassroots activities—the establishment of daycare centers, free breakfast programs, and other services—won support in the ghettos of America. The Panthers also drew recruits from SNCC, including Stokely Carmichael, who joined the party in June 1967.

1968—A Turning Point in Civil Rights

D. Answer Americans feared the Black Panthers' rhetoric and their involvement in violence; some poor African Americans benefited from their community programs.

Martin Luther King, Jr., objected to the Black Power movement that was taking root in the cities. King said, "I feel that . . . fiery, demagogic oratory in the black ghettos, urging Negroes to arm themselves, and prepare to engage in violence, . . . can reap nothing but grief." After Meredith's march against fear, King left the South to spread his message of nonviolence to Northern cities. He was planning to lead a Poor People's March on Washington, D.C., to press for government help for the nation's poor. This time, however, the people would have to march without King.

DR. KING'S DEATH Dr. King seemed to sense that death was near. On April 3, 1968, he addressed a crowd in Memphis, Tennessee, where he had gone to show his support for the city's striking garbage workers. "I may not get there with you," King said, "but I want you to know tonight that we as a people will get to the Promised Land." He then added, "And I'm happy tonight. I'm not fearing any man. Mine eyes have seen the glory of the coming of the Lord."

The next day, King stepped out onto the balcony of his hotel room. Across the street, James Earl Ray thrust a high-powered rifle out of a window and squeezed the trigger. King crumpled as a bullet crashed through his neck. An hour later, the man who dared to dream of racial peace lay dead from racial violence.

REACTIONS TO DR. KING'S DEATH The night King died, Robert F. Kennedy was campaigning for the Democratic presidential nomination. Fearful that King's death would spark riots, Kennedy's campaign advisers told him to cancel his appearance in an African-American neighborhood in Indianapolis. Kennedy rejected that advice, discarded his prepared speech, and made an impassioned plea for nonviolence.

Coretta Scott King mourns her husband at his funeral service.

A PERSONAL VOICE

For those of you who are black—considering the evidence . . . that there were white people who were responsible—you can be filled with bitterness, with hatred, and a desire for revenge. We can move in that direction as a country, in great polarization—black people amongst black, white people amongst white, filled with hatred toward one another.

Or we can make an effort, as Martin Luther King did, to understand and comprehend, and to replace that violence, that stain of bloodshed that has spread across our land, with an effort to understand with compassion and love.

ROBERT F. KENNEDY, "A Eulogy for Dr. Martin Luther King, Jr."

Robert F. Kennedy

HISTORICAL SPOTLIGHT

CONFRONTING THE NORTH

Martin Luther King, Jr.'s attempts to take his message to Northern cities also encountered many challenges. In 1966, for example, King spearheaded a campaign in Chicago to end de facto segregation there and create an "open city." On July 10, he led about 30,000 African Americans in a march on city hall.

In late July, when King led demonstrators through a neighborhood on Chicago's Southwest Side, angry whites threw rocks and bottles at the marchers. On August 5, hostile whites stoned King as he led 600 marchers. The next day, King left Chicago without accomplishing what he wanted, yet pledging to return.

Soon after, city officials signed an agreement to promote fair housing but later did little to carry out the agreement. At the time of King's death in 1968, Chicago was just as segregated as it had ever been.

HISTORICAL SPOTLIGHT
Confronting the North

Critical Thinking: Hypothesizing Ask students why they think the efforts of King, the SCLC, and other civil rights activists had such little success in Chicago. Have them consider the political clout of Mayor Richard J. Daley, the racial attitudes of white Chicagoans, and the size of the city.

OBJECTIVE
3 INSTRUCT

1968—A Turning Point in Civil Rights

Discussing Key Ideas
- Martin Luther King, Jr., tries to organize a Poor People's Campaign to counter the angry rhetoric of Black Power.
- King is assassinated in Memphis, where he was helping African-American trash collectors fight for fair treatment from the city.
- King's death sets off the worst wave of race riots in the nation's history.

Block Schedule TEACHING OPTION **Time Needed: 20 Minutes**

Cooperative Activity: Creating a Historical Atlas

Task: Groups of students will prepare a historical atlas on race relations in the United States.

Purpose: To help students understand that racial issues have touched many areas of the country during the 20th century.

Activity: Have pairs of students create an annotated map that shows important events or statistics about race relations in one state during one decade in the 20th century. They should choose states from different regions across the country to avoid several pairs working on the same place and time. For example, one pair might show the cities in California that experienced civil rights protests in the 1960s. A second pair might show the counties in Mississippi that lost the most African-American migrants during the 1940s. A third might show which districts in Michigan sent African-American representatives to the state legislature in the 1970s. When the maps are complete, students should collect them into one atlas book.

OBJECTIVE

④ **INSTRUCT**

Legacy of the Civil Rights Movement

▶ ***Discussing Key Ideas***

- The civil rights movement wipes de jure segregation from the law books of America.
- De facto segregation and unequal economic opportunity remain entrenched.
- The lingering effects of racism, as reported by the Kerner Commission, remain one of the greatest challenges facing the nation in the years ahead.

CRITICAL THINKING TRANSPARENCIES

CT29, Civil Rights Movement

CT63, African-American Educational Attainment

HISTORICAL SPOTLIGHT

Shirley Chisholm

Critical Thinking: Analyzing Discuss some of the problems Chisholm probably faced as a congresswoman. Then have students list some of the obstacles that an African American seeking the presidential nomination in 1964 would have encountered. *Possible Responses: Voting restrictions of African Americans; discrimination; more entrenched racism.*

Even though many leaders called for peace, rage over King's death led to the worst urban rioting in United States history. Some 125 cities exploded in flames. The hardest-hit cities included Baltimore, Chicago, Kansas City, and Washington, D.C. Not only racial but also political violence marred the year 1968. In June, Robert Kennedy himself was assassinated by a Jordanian immigrant who was angry over Kennedy's support of Israel.

Legacy of the Civil Rights Movement

On March 2, 1968, the **Kerner Commission,** which President Johnson had appointed to study the causes of urban violence, issued a 200,000-word report. In it, the panel named one main cause: white racism. Said the report, "This is our basic conclusion: Our nation is moving toward two societies, one black, one white—separate and unequal." The report called for the nation to create new jobs, construct new housing, and end de facto segregation in order to wipe out the destructive ghetto environment in which many African Americans lived. However, the Johnson administration chose to ignore many of the recommendations because of white opposition to such sweeping changes. So what had the civil rights movement accomplished?

CIVIL RIGHTS GAINS The civil rights movement brought about the end of de jure segregation. Constitutional and legal changes guaranteed the civil rights of all Americans under the laws. Congress passed the most important civil rights legislation since Reconstruction, including the **Civil Rights Act of 1968**—a law that banned discrimination in housing. Furthermore, in the decades following the integration of Little Rock Central High School and Ole Miss, the numbers of African Americans who finished high school and who went to college significantly increased.

HISTORICAL SPOTLIGHT

SHIRLEY CHISHOLM

African-American women such as Shirley Chisholm exemplified the advances won in the civil rights movement. In 1968, Chisholm became the first African-American woman elected to the United States House of Representatives. She held her Congressional seat until 1983.

In the mid-1960s, Chisholm served in the New York state assembly, representing a district that included the Bedford-Stuyvesant community in New York City. While there, she supported programs to establish public day-care centers and provide unemployment insurance to domestic workers.

In 1972, Chisholm gained national prominence by running for the Democratic presidential nomination. Despite the fact that she never won more than 7% of the vote in the primaries, she controlled 150 delegates at the Democratic convention in Miami and was invited by other candidates to help prevent George McGovern—the eventual nominee—from winning the nomination.

Another accomplishment of the civil rights movement was to give African Americans greater pride in their racial identity. Many African Americans adopted African-influenced styles—such as the Afro, a full, unstraightened hairstyle, and the dashiki, a loose, brightly colored tunic. College students demanded new Black Studies programs so they could study African-American history and literature. In the entertainment world, African Americans began to appear more frequently in movies and on television shows and commercials.

In addition, African Americans made substantial political gains. By 1970, an estimated two-thirds of eligible African Americans were registered to vote, and those voters brought about a significant increase in African-American elected officials. The number of African Americans holding elected office leaped from about 300 in 1965 to more than 7,000 in 1992. Many civil rights activists went on to become political leaders, among them Rev. Jesse Jackson, who ran for president in 1988; Vernon Jordan, who led voter-registration drives that enrolled about 2 million African Americans; and Andrew Young, who has been UN ambassador and Atlanta's mayor.

E. Answer End of legalized segregation; constitutional and legal protection of civil rights and voting rights; increased pride in racial identity; more African-American voters, elected officials, and high school and college graduates.

THINK THROUGH HISTORY
E. *Summarizing* *What were some accomplishments of the civil rights movement?*

UNFINISHED WORK The civil rights movement was remarkably successful in accomplishing the repeal of many discriminatory laws. Yet as the 1960s turned to the 1970s, the challenges for the movement changed. The issues it confronted—housing and job discrimination, educational inequality, poverty, and racism—involved the difficult task of changing people's attitudes and behavior. Some of the proposed solutions, such as more tax monies spent in the inner cities and the forced busing of schoolchildren, angered some whites, who resisted further changes. Public support for the civil rights movement also declined because some whites were frightened by the urban

TEACHING OPTIONS

Making Connections Across Cultures

African Americans in the Media Assign groups of students one of the major TV networks. For one week, have them keep logs on the appearance of African Americans in prime-time programming, starting with the evening news. Log entries might include these heads: Name of Program, Name of African American, Role Played, Length of Viewing Time (seconds/minutes on the screen).

Making Connections Across the Curriculum

U.S. Government In 1992, *Teaching Tolerance,* a biennial publication by the Southern Poverty Law Center, polled students on two questions: What causes most racial and ethnic conflicts between people? What do you think individuals can do to bring about greater understanding between different racial and ethnic groups? Have students use these questions to poll opinions in their own school and present results in the school newspaper.

riots and the rhetoric of the Black Panthers.

The trend of whites fleeing the cities for the suburbs increased the problem of de facto segregation. For example, by 1990 much of the progress toward school integration had been reversed. About 75 percent of African-American children in Northern cities and about 50 percent of African-American children in the South attended almost completely black schools. Lack of jobs also remained a serious problem for African Americans, who had a poverty rate three times greater than that for whites.

To help many African Americans—and other disadvantaged groups—gain education and jobs, the government in the 1960s began to promote **affirmative action.** Affirmative-action programs involve making special efforts to hire or enroll groups that have suffered from discrimination in the past. Many colleges and almost all companies that do business with the federal government adopted such programs.

In the late 1970s, some people began to criticize affirmative-action programs as "reverse discrimination" that set minority hiring or enrollment quotas and deprived whites of opportunities. In the 1980s, Republican administrations eased affirmative-action requirements for some government contractors. The fate of affirmative action—as of so much of the legacy of the civil rights movement—has still to be decided. In all the regions of the country today, African Americans and whites interact on a daily basis that could have only been imagined before the civil rights movement. In many respects, Dr. King's dream has been realized—yet much remains to be done.

Changes in Poverty and Education, 1959 and 1994

POVERTY STATUS

African-American Families: 1959 48.1%; 1994 31.3%

White Families: 1959 15.2%; 1994 9.4%

■ Families living in poverty ■ Families not living in poverty

COLLEGE EDUCATION

African Americans: 1959 3.3%; 1994 12.9%

Whites: 1959 8.6%; 1994 22.9%

■ Persons with four or more years of college ■ All other persons

Source: U.S. Bureau of the Census

SKILLBUILDER

INTERPRETING GRAPHS
Did the economic situation for African Americans get better or worse between 1959 and 1994 in terms of poverty status? How many times greater is the percentage of whites completing four or more years of college in 1994 than the percentage of African Americans?

Skillbuilder Answer **Poverty:** It improved because a smaller percentage was living in poverty. **College:** The percentage of whites is nearly two times greater.

F. Answer
Possible Answers: De facto segregation, joblessness and poverty among African Americans, fate of affirmative action.

THINK THROUGH HISTORY
F. Identifying Problems *What challenges still face the nation in the area of civil rights?*

Section 3 Assessment

1. TERMS & NAMES
Identify:
- de facto segregation
- de jure segregation
- Malcolm X
- Nation of Islam
- Stokely Carmichael
- Black Power
- Black Panthers
- Kerner Commission
- Civil Rights Act of 1968
- affirmative action

2. SUMMARIZING Create a time line of key events relating to the civil rights movement. Use the dates already plotted on the time line below as a guide.

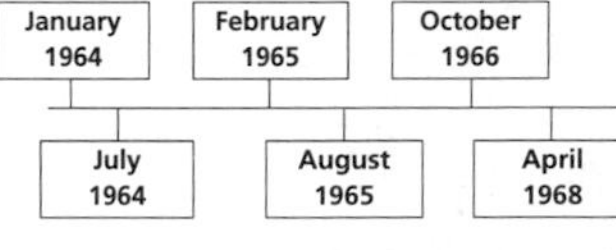

In your opinion, which event was most significant? Explain.

3. MAKING PREDICTIONS What if Dr. Martin Luther King, Jr., had not been assassinated? Speculate on how the civil rights movement might have been different. Support your answer with details from the text.

THINK ABOUT
- King's approach to civil rights issues
- King's status in the civil rights movement at the time of his death
- the immediate reaction to King's assassination

4. COMPARING AND CONTRASTING Compare and contrast the civil rights strategies of Malcolm X and Martin Luther King, Jr. Whose strategies do you think were more effective? Explain and support your response.

THINK ABOUT
- the goals and methods of each leader
- public reaction to each leader's methods
- the short-term and long-term effects of each leader's efforts

ANSWERS

1. TERMS & NAMES

de facto segregation, p. 711
de jure segregation, p. 711
Malcolm X, p. 713
Nation of Islam, p. 713
Stokely Carmichael, p. 714
Black Power, p. 714
Black Panthers, p. 714
Kerner Commission, p. 716
Civil Rights Act of 1968, p. 716
affirmative action, p. 717

2. SUMMARIZING

Possible Answers: January 1964—War on Poverty launched; July 1964—Harlem riot; February 1965—Malcolm X assassinated; August 1965—Watts riot; October 1966—Black Panthers founded; April 1968—King assassinated.

3. MAKING PREDICTIONS

Possible Responses: King was greatly admired and, had he lived, the movement might have been less splintered and not lost its momentum as quickly; the rage that fueled urban riots in about 125 cities after his assassination would not have been unleashed, and the white backlash to the civil rights movement might have been diminished.

4. COMPARING AND CONTRASTING

Possible Responses: Both wanted civil rights and greater opportunity for African Americans; King preached racial equality and used a nonviolent approach in demonstrations and marches; Malcolm X preached black separatism and urged African Americans to use armed self-defense. Some students may say King's strategies were more effective because his demonstrations caused civil rights legislation to be passed. Others may say Malcolm X was more effective because his strategies made people realize that African Americans needed to fight back.

HISTORY FROM VISUALS

Changes in Poverty and Education, 1959 and 1994

Comparing Graphs Point out that pie graphs make it easy to compare amounts or quantities of items. What two amounts are compared in the first set of graphs? *The poverty rates of African-American families and white families.* What two amounts are compared in the second set of graphs? *College attendance rates for African Americans and whites.*

Extension By comparing data in each set of graphs, what conclusions can students draw about the economic effect of the civil rights movement? *It helped improve the educational and economic situation for many African Americans but has not brought them to the same level as whites.*

ASSESS & RETEACH

Section 3 Assessment

Have students work in groups of four and compare their responses to question 3.

Self-Assessment

Direct students to write one question they think should have been included in the Section Assessment but was not.

Section Quiz

FORMAL ASSESSMENT
Section Quiz, p. 261

Reteach

Review the events in the time line in item 2 to reteach the major events in the section.

CLOSE

New leaders of the civil rights movement called for Black Power, and violence erupted in many American cities in the early 1960s. By 1968, the movement had brought about the end of de jure segregation, but economic and educational inequalities still remained.

Tracing Themes

OBJECTIVES

1. To recognize civil rights as a significant theme in America's history.
2. To trace the evolution of civil rights over time.

FOCUS & MOTIVATE

▶ ***Starting with the Student*** Have students think about the concept of civil rights.

- How do students define the term *civil rights?* What might they offer as an example of a civil right?
- Which documents, laws, organizations, and/or government institutions seem especially important in defining or guarding our civil rights? Explain.

MORE ABOUT . . .
Civil Rights

During the 19th century, American women also pressured for legal rights previously denied them. In the 1840s, many states passed laws granting married women the right to control their property and earnings, to participate in legal contracts, and to share in custody of their children. It took longer to win the right to vote. Although the 19th-century suffrage movement won some victories on a state-by-state basis, women could not vote nationwide until the Nineteenth Amendment to the U.S. Constitution was adopted in 1920.

TRACING THEMES
CIVIL RIGHTS

An Evolving Idea

Thomas Jefferson asserted in the Declaration of Independence that "all men are created equal" and are endowed with the "unalienable Rights" of "Life, Liberty and the Pursuit of Happiness." With these words, a new nation was founded on the principle that citizens have certain fundamental civil rights. These include the right to vote, the right to enjoy freedom of speech and religion, and others. For more than 200 years, the United States has stood as a worldwide example of a country committed to securing the rights of its people.

However, throughout the nation's history, some Americans have had to struggle to obtain even the most basic civil rights. Laws or customs prevented certain people from voting freely, from attending the school of their choice, and from eating in any restaurant they wish. Over time, many of these barriers have been torn down.

In recent years, the United States has tried to promote human rights in other countries through its foreign policy. Even as it does so, the United States continues to struggle to fulfill for all Americans the lofty ideals established by the nation's founders.

1791
BILL OF RIGHTS

During the Constitutional Convention, *below,* the question of a bill of rights arose, but none was included. After the Constitution was ratified, many people agreed that it needed to list the basic civil rights and liberties that the federal government could not take away from the people.

Accordingly, the nation ratified ten amendments to the Constitution—the Bill of Rights. It establishes such rights as freedom of speech, religion, and assembly, freedom of the press, and the right to a trial by jury. While these rights have been subject to interpretation over the nation's history, the Bill of Rights serves as the cornerstone of American democracy.

1868
THE FOURTEENTH AMENDMENT

In the engraving above, a crowd of black and white Americans celebrate the passage of the Civil Rights Act of 1866. This act recognized the citizenship of African Americans and granted the same civil rights to all people born in the United States except Native Americans.

The Fourteenth Amendment, ratified two years later, made these changes part of the Constitution. The Amendment declared that states cannot deny anyone "equal protection of the laws" and extended the right to vote to all 21-year-old males, including former slaves.

Despite these provisions, African Americans and other groups would struggle for the next 100 years to claim their full rights as U.S. citizens.

RECOMMENDED RESOURCES

Books

Belz, Herman. *Emancipation and Equal Rights: Politics and Constitutionalism in the Civil War Era.* New York: Norton, 1978.

Rutland, Robert. *The Birth of the Bill of Rights, 1776–1791.* Boston: Northeastern UP, 1991.

Totten, Samuel. *Human Rights.* Hillside, NJ: Enslow, 1989. Includes the UN's Universal Declaration of Human Rights.

Videos

Bill of Rights, Bill of Responsibilities. Cambridge Educational, 1995. A fast-paced commentary featuring comedian Bill Maher.

Fighting for Civil Rights. Coronet/MTI, 1993. Part 3 of the award-winning In the *Land of Jim Crow* series.

Software

African-American History—Slavery to Civil Rights. CD-ROM. Queue. From the slave trade to recent times; DOS version called *Black American History.*

Amnesty Interactive. CD-ROM. Voyager, 1994. Traces human rights from ancient to modern times.

1950s & 1960s

THE CIVIL RIGHTS MOVEMENT

Despite the Fourteenth Amendment and later the Fifteenth Amendment, which forbade states from denying anyone the right to vote on account of race, African Americans continued to live as second-class citizens, especially in the South. States passed laws aimed at separating the races and keeping blacks from the polls.

During the 1950s and 1960s, African Americans and other Americans led an organized and powerful movement to fight for racial equality. The movement often met with strong resistance, such as in Birmingham, Alabama, where police sprayed demonstrators with high-pressure fire hoses, *above.* Nevertheless, it succeeded in securing for African Americans the civil rights promised by the Declaration of Independence and Constitution. The civil rights movement has also been the basis for gaining equal rights by other groups, including other minorities, women, and people with disabilities.

1970s

HUMAN RIGHTS

President Jimmy Carter considered human rights an important foreign policy issue. Human rights are what Americans think of as their civil rights, including the right to vote and to receive a fair trial. The Carter administration tried to encourage greater freedom abroad by taking such steps as cutting off military aid to countries with poor human rights records.

While these efforts met with mixed results, the issue of human rights has continued to influence U.S. foreign policy. In the 1990s, for example, the U.S. government tried to push China for more democracy while keeping alive its trade ties with that country. As a private citizen, Jimmy Carter has also continued to champion human rights causes. In 1982, he and his wife, Rosalynn, founded the Carter Center, whose programs seek to end human rights abuses and promote democracy worldwide.

INTERACT WITH HISTORY

1. **ANALYZING ISSUES** The Fourteenth and Fifteenth Amendments both provided for the voting rights of African Americans. Based on what you have read on these two pages and in this chapter, how were these rights denied African Americans? How were they finally secured?

 SEE SKILLBUILDER HANDBOOK, PAGE 916.

2. **WRITING ABOUT RIGHTS** Have you or anyone you've known had their civil rights denied them in any way? How did you (or they) react? What did you (or they) do to improve the situation? Write an account of the incident and share it with your class.

Visit http://www.mlushistory.com for more about civil rights.

INSTRUCT

▶ *Starting with the Student*

- Have students make a civil rights time line with details from these pages and other major events in the history of civil rights.
- Encourage students to discuss current civil rights issues such as congressional districting, immigrants' rights, women's rights, and human rights around the globe. What factors limit the ability of people to exercise equal rights? *Possible Responses: economic inequality, racism.*

▶ *Discussing Key Ideas*

- The Declaration of Independence and Constitution, including the Bill of Rights, outline civil rights in the United States.
- Since America's founding, the concept of civil rights has evolved.

HISTORY FROM VISUALS

Reading the Images

Have students study the pictures and captions.

- Jot down adjectives to describe the different scenes. *Possible Responses: First formal; second jubilant; third oppressed; fourth dignified.*
- What ironies do you find in the captions' details or in the juxtaposition of any of these scenes? *Possible Responses: Violation of African-American civil rights juxtaposed with jubilation at passage of Fourteenth Amendment; a president from the South shows concern for human rights.*

INTERACT WITH HISTORY

1. Analyzing Issues

Possible Answers: *The rights were denied through poll taxes, unevenly applied literacy tests, other unfair voting qualifications (for example, you could not vote if your grandfather had not voted), intimidation of potential African-American voters, and gerrymandering to keep African Americans from office.*

They were secured through the civil rights movement, which helped change national opinion, and through resulting federal intervention and passage of federal laws like the Voting Rights Act of 1965.

2. Writing About Rights

Standards for Evaluation

Accounts should . . .

- identify the individuals involved and the setting (time and place) in which the incident occurred
- clarify the specific right or rights being violated
- indicate the reasons for the violation, if known
- capture the feelings of the victim
- describe the actions of the victim to improve the situation

Students might share their accounts in oral readings or group discussions.

CHAPTER 21
ASSESSMENT ANSWERS

REVIEWING THE CHAPTER

TERMS & NAMES

1. *Brown* v. *Board of Education,* p. 698
2. Rosa Parks, p. 700
3. Dr. Martin Luther King, Jr., p. 701
4. Student Nonviolent Coordinating Committee, p. 702
5. freedom rider, p. 704
6. Civil Rights Act of 1964, p. 708
7. Fannie Lou Hamer, p. 709
8. de facto segregation, p. 711
9. Malcolm X, p. 713
10. Black Power, p. 714

MAIN IDEAS

11. Jim Crow laws, passed in the South, were aimed at separating the races. Application of these laws included separate schools, streetcars, and public restrooms.
12. Rosa Parks was arrested for refusing to give up her bus seat to a white passenger.
13. Jesus' teachings to love one's enemies, Thoreau's concept of civil disobedience, Randolph's techniques for organizing massive demonstrations, Gandhi's use of nonviolent resistance.
14. Meredith won a federal court case allowing him to enroll in the University of Mississippi.
15. *Possible Responses:* Fannie Lou Hamer was beaten trying to register to vote; a bomb in a Birmingham church killed four African-American girls; in Mississippi, Klansmen, with the support of local police, murdered three civil rights activists.
16. King and the SCLC were invited there to help desegregate the city.
17. Black nationalism, self-determination, racial pride, self-respect, the use of self-defense.
18. Leaders felt that the slogan antagonized whites.
19. End of legalized segregation; increased pride in racial identity; more African-American voters, elected officials, and high school and college graduates.
20. De facto segregation, joblessness, and poverty among African Americans.

Chapter 21 Assessment

REVIEWING THE CHAPTER

TERMS & NAMES For each item below, write a sentence explaining its connection to the civil rights movement. For each person named below, explain his or her role in the movement.

1. ***Brown* v. *Board of Education***
2. **Rosa Parks**
3. **Dr. Martin Luther King, Jr.**
4. **Student Nonviolent Coordinating Committee**
5. **freedom rider**
6. **Civil Rights Act of 1964**
7. **Fannie Lou Hamer**
8. **de facto segregation**
9. **Malcolm X**
10. **Black Power**

MAIN IDEAS

SECTION 1 *(pages 696–703)*

Taking on Segregation

11. What were Jim Crow laws and how were they applied?
12. What incident sparked the Montgomery Bus Boycott?
13. What were the roots of Dr. Martin Luther King, Jr.'s beliefs in nonviolent resistance?

SECTION 2 *(pages 704–710)*

The Triumphs of a Crusade

14. What federal court case did James Meredith win in 1962?
15. Cite three examples of violence committed between 1962 and 1964 against African Americans and civil rights activists.
16. Why did Dr. Martin Luther King, Jr., go to Birmingham, Alabama, in 1963?

SECTION 3 *(pages 711–717)*

Challenges and Changes in the Movement

17. What were some of the key beliefs that Malcolm X advocated?
18. Why did some civil rights leaders urge Stokely Carmichael to stop using the slogan "black power"?
19. What were some accomplishments of the civil rights movement?
20. What challenges still face the nation in the area of civil rights?

THINKING CRITICALLY

1. **MEDIA INFLUENCE** On your own paper, draw a cluster diagram like the one shown below. Then, fill it in with four events from the civil rights movement that were broadcast on nationwide television and that you find the most compelling.

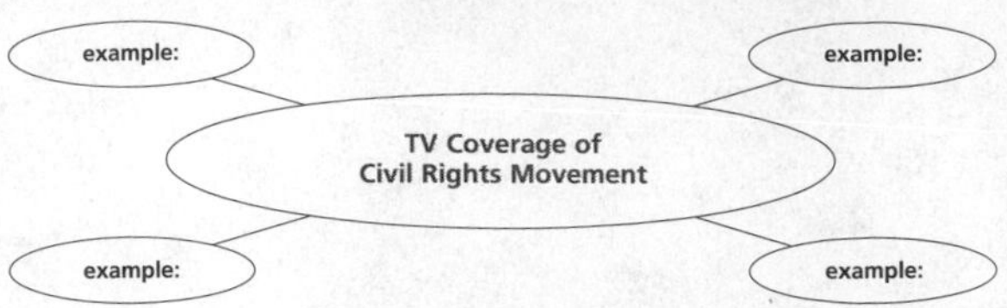

2. **THE CIVIL RIGHTS MOVEMENT** Overall, would you characterize the civil rights struggle as a unified or disunified movement? Explain.
3. **IMMORTAL IDEAS** Reread the quote by Medgar Evers on page 694. Do you agree with his statement? Cite examples from the text that support your answer.
4. **THE GEOGRAPHY OF SCHOOL SEGREGATION** Look carefully at the map of U.S. school segregation, on page 697. What regional differences do you think spurred civil rights activists to target the South before the North?
5. **TRACING THEMES** **CIVIL RIGHTS** African Americans and others have pressed for recognition of their civil rights since colonial times. Why do you think the civil rights movement finally achieved success in the 1950s and 1960s?
6. **ANALYZING PRIMARY SOURCES** Read the following excerpt from Malcolm X's speech "Prospects for Freedom in 1965," in which he denounces the police brutality that sparked the 1964 Harlem riot. Then answer the questions that follow.

> An illegal attack, an unjust attack, and an immoral attack can be made against you by any one. Just because a person has on a [police] uniform does not give him the right to come and shoot up your neighborhood. No, this is not right, and my suggestion would be that as long as the police department doesn't use those methods in white neighborhoods, they shouldn't come to Harlem and use them in our neighborhood. . . . It's not intelligent—and it [the Harlem riot] all started when a little boy was shot by a policeman.
>
> **MALCOLM X,** "Prospects for Freedom in 1965"

How does Malcolm X view violent police methods? What other instances might Malcolm X have cited to justify his condemnation of police brutality? Cite examples from the chapter.

THINKING CRITICALLY

1. MEDIA INFLUENCE

Possible Responses: The crisis at Central High School in Little Rock, Arkansas (1957); sit-ins at Greensboro, North Carolina (1960); the second "children's crusade" in Birmingham, Alabama (1963); Fannie Lou Hamer's speech to the Democratic National Convention (1964); the Selma march (1965).

2. THE CIVIL RIGHTS MOVEMENT

Possible Responses: Unified: all civil rights activists shared the same goals—freedom, justice, and equality; gender and age differences were surmounted; the March on Washington was a powerful display of unity. Disunified: violent versus nonviolent methods created divisiveness; Northern blacks and Southern blacks had different needs.

3. IMMORTAL IDEAS

Possible Responses: **Yes:** An idea can live on after a person dies because other people carry it on. **No:** Sometimes the person who believes in it most strongly must live to carry out the idea.

4. THE GEOGRAPHY OF SCHOOL DESEGREGATION

Possible Responses: As the map shows, primarily schools in Southern states were segregated by law. The legal racism—de

ALTERNATIVE ASSESSMENT

1. WRITING A RADIO OR TELEVISION EDITORIAL
The Supreme Court decision in *Brown* v. *Board of Education* set a new era of civil rights in motion. What did this decision mean in everyday terms? What impact did it have? Write a script for a radio or television editorial you might have filed in the aftermath of *Brown* v. *Board of Education*.

Use the CD-ROM *Electronic Library of Primary Sources* and other reference materials to review documents and issues related to the early civil rights movement.

- Your script should incorporate relevant historical background in addition to an analysis of one or more events. You might also include excerpts from news reports, interviews, and editorials of the day.

2. LEARNING FROM MEDIA
VIDEO View the McDougal Littell Video for Chapter 21, *Justice in Montgomery*. Discuss the following questions with a small group of classmates and then do the **Cooperative Learning** activity.

- According to the video, what role did Jo Ann Gibson Robinson and the African-American women of Montgomery play in the bus boycott?
- In your opinion, what responsibilities does an ordinary person have to stop injustice in his or her community?

Cooperative Learning You have just seen an account of the Montgomery bus boycott through the eyes of one person, Jo Ann Gibson Robinson, though there are many ways to learn about that event. With your group, decide how you would teach people about the boycott—from what perspective and with what materials. Then create a lesson plan or multimedia presentation to give to the class.

3. PORTFOLIO PROJECT
Use the Living History activity to expand your portfolio.

LIVING HISTORY

PRESENTING YOUR BIOGRAPHICAL SKETCH

You have written a biographical sketch of a civil rights leader. Now think about how you might revise it, considering the following suggestions:

- Did you provide vivid and precise details?
- Did you use quotations or anecdotes to add interest?
- Did you review your writing for errors and correct them?

Ask a classmate to read the biography and comment on content and organization.

After you have revised the biography, find a suitable photograph of the civil rights leader for your title page. Display the completed biography with those of your classmates. Add the biography to your American history portfolio.

Bridge to Chapter 22

Review Chapter 21

TAKING ON SEGREGATION Following World War II, the NAACP waged a successful campaign to challenge the legality of segregated public education. In 1954, the Supreme Court ruled in *Brown* v. *Board of Education* that school segregation was unconstitutional. In response, some white Southern officials vowed defiance. In 1957, President Eisenhower was forced to use federal power to integrate Central High School in Little Rock, Arkansas.

An earlier confrontation over segregation occurred in December 1955, when Rosa Parks was arrested in Montgomery, Alabama, for not yielding her bus seat to a white passenger. Under the leadership of Dr. Martin Luther King, Jr., African Americans held a year-long boycott of the city's buses. In late 1956, the Supreme Court outlawed segregation on public transportation.

CIVIL RIGHTS VICTORIES Across the South, activists used nonviolent means to break down racial barriers. Teams of young people staged sit-ins, held freedom rides, and registered black voters in the South. In 1963, thousands of people demonstrated in the March on Washington. Spurred by the mass movement, Congress passed the landmark Civil Rights Act of 1964 and Voting Rights Act of 1965.

CHANGES IN THE MOVEMENT In the North, new leaders emerged—Malcolm X, Stokely Carmichael, Huey Newton, and Bobby Seale—who advocated self-defense and militant tactics. Racial tensions persisted in northern cities, where African Americans faced the problems of deeply entrenched prejudice, police brutality, substandard housing and schools, and high unemployment. These conditions fueled the race riots that erupted in the mid-1960s.

Preview Chapter 22

While civil rights activists fought for equality at home, American soldiers were fighting on the battlefields in far-off Vietnam. Seeking to contain communism in Southeast Asia, the United States gradually increased its military involvement in Vietnam. You will learn about these and other significant developments in the next chapter.

ALTERNATIVE ASSESSMENT

1. WRITING AN EDITORIAL
Standards for Evaluation
An editorial should meet the following criteria:

- Takes a clear stand on the *Brown* decision.
- Incorporates relevant historical background from the civil rights movement.
- Accurately conveys contemporary arguments for and against the opinion.

2. LEARNING FROM MEDIA
Answer to the question:

- Robinson and the Women's Political Council called a one-day boycott on the day of Parks's trial. This started the year-long boycott. According to Robinson, if "people ask me about the boycott, I tell them, 'The black women did it.' And we did."

TEACHING THE MONTGOMERY BUS BOYCOTT
Standards for Evaluation

A lesson plan should meet the following criteria:

- Explains which materials should be used and why they were chosen.
- Mentions major aspects of the boycott including the history of segregation in Montgomery, the groups that organized the boycott, the groups that opposed it, and the leaders who emerged from the boycott.

A multimedia presentation should meet the following criteria:

- Uses a variety of media including photos, video, transcripts, and journals.
- Mentions all major aspects of the boycott.

3. PORTFOLIO PROJECT
LIVING HISTORY
Standards for Evaluation
Biographical sketches should meet the following criteria:

- Show the importance of the civil rights leader.
- Provide concrete details about the person's life.
- Show evidence of research from a variety of sources.

IN-DEPTH RESOURCES: UNIT 6
See the form for scoring this activity on page 34.

THINKING CRITICALLY

jure segregation—of the South was easier to tackle than the more subtle racism—de facto segregation—of the North.

5. TRACING THEMES CIVIL RIGHTS
Students might suggest some of the following factors: The impact of World War II on American society in raising African-American consciousness; actions by Franklin Roosevelt and later presidents in the area of civil rights; the *Brown* decision; effective organizing efforts of black churches; the successful leadership and tactics of Thurgood Marshall, Martin Luther King, Jr., and others; the influence of television and the national media; the emergence of youth activism among college students, both African American and white.

6. ANALYZING PRIMARY SOURCES
Possible Responses: As illegal, unjust, and immoral; as unjustifiably excessive; as a violation of the rights of citizens they are apprehending; as racially biased. Other examples of police brutality that Malcolm X might have cited include the tactics that Bull Connor's police force used against young demonstrators in Birmingham (May 1963); police support of Klansmen who murdered three civil rights activists (June 1964); police who forced prisoners to beat Fannie Lou Hamer after she was jailed for trying to register to vote (1962).

PLANNING GUIDE

CHAPTER 22

The Vietnam War Years

	Key Ideas	COPYMASTERS	ASSESSMENT
SECTION 1 **Moving Toward Conflict** *pp. 724–728*	*America slowly involves itself in the war in Vietnam as it seeks to halt the spread of communism.*	***In-Depth Resources: Unit 6*** • Guided Reading, p. 35 ***Lesson Plans,*** pp. 177–178	PE ***Section 1 Assessment,*** p. 728 TE ***Self-Assessment,*** p. 728 ***Formal Assessment*** • Section Quiz, p. 270 ***Alternative Assessment Book*** • Standards for Evaluating a Cooperative Activity
SECTION 2 **U.S. Involvement and Escalation** *pp. 729–734*	*The United States sends troops to fight in Vietnam, but the war quickly turns into a stalemate.*	***In-Depth Resources: Unit 6*** • Guided Reading, p. 36 • Skillbuilder Practice: Distinguishing Fact from Opinion, p. 40 • Primary Source: Letter from a Soldier in Vietnam, p. 45 • American Lives: Robert McNamara, p. 52 ***Lesson Plans,*** pp. 179–180	PE ***Section 2 Assessment,*** p. 734 TE ***Self-Assessment,*** p. 734 ***Formal Assessment*** • Section Quiz, p. 271 ***Alternative Assessment Book*** • Standards for Evaluating a Cooperative Activity
SECTION 3 **A Nation Divided** *pp. 735–740*	*An antiwar movement emerges in the United States, pitting those who oppose the government's war policy against those who support it.*	***In-Depth Resources: Unit 6*** • Guided Reading, p. 37 • Primary Sources: Protest Buttons, p. 46; The New Left, p. 47 ***Lesson Plans,*** pp. 181–182	PE ***Section 3 Assessment,*** p. 740 TE ***Self-Assessment,*** p. 740 ***Formal Assessment*** • Section Quiz, p. 272 ***Alternative Assessment Book*** • Standards for Evaluating a Cooperative Activity
SECTION 4 **1968: A Tumultuous Year** *pp. 741–746*	*A shocking enemy attack in Vietnam, two assassinations, and a chaotic political convention help make 1968 the most explosive year of the decade.*	***In-Depth Resources: Unit 6*** • Guided Reading, p. 38 • Geography Application: The Ho Chi Minh Trail, p. 41 • Primary Source: Lyndon B. Johnson on Vietnam and Reelection, p. 48 • American Lives: John Lewis, p. 53 ***Lesson Plans,*** pp. 183–184	PE ***Section 4 Assessment,*** p. 746 TE ***Self-Assessment,*** p. 746 ***Formal Assessment*** • Section Quiz, p. 273 ***Alternative Assessment Book*** • Standards for Evaluating a Cooperative Activity
SECTION 5 **The End of the War and Its Legacy** *pp. 747–753*	*The nation's longest war ends after nearly ten years and leaves a lasting impact on U.S. policy and American society.*	***In-Depth Resources: Unit 6*** • Guided Reading, p. 39 • Outline Map: The Vietnam War, p. 43 • Literature: from *In Country* by Bobbie Ann Mason, p. 49 ***Lesson Plans,*** pp. 185–186	PE ***Section 5 Assessment,*** p. 753 TE ***Self-Assessment,*** p. 753 ***Formal Assessment*** • Section Quiz, p. 274 ***Alternative Assessment Book*** • Standards for Evaluating a Cooperative Activity
CHAPTER RESOURCES	**Chapter Overview** *The United States enters a war in Vietnam, which results in the deaths of tens of thousands of American soldiers, the division of society into bitterly opposed camps, and a lasting impact on U.S. foreign policy.*	***In-Depth Resources: Unit 6*** • Living History Project: Worksheet, p. 54; Standards, p. 55 ***Telescoping the Times*** • Chapter Summary, pp. 43–44 ***Planning for Block Schedules***	PE ***Chapter Assessment,*** pp. 756–757 PE ***Alternative Assessment,*** p. 757 ***Formal Assessment*** • Chapter Test, forms A and B, pp. 275–280 ***Test Generator*** ***Alternative Assessment Book*** See explanation and forms for different kinds of alternative assessments including portfolio assessment.

KEY
- PE Pupil's Edition
- TE Teacher's Edition
- **http://www.mlushistory.com**

TECHNOLOGY

***Warm-Up Transparency* 22**

The War in Vietnam
- Geneva Accords
- Domino principle

Electronic Library of Primary Sources
- The Tonkin Gulf Resolution

INTERNET Vietnam War

***Warm-Up Transparency* 22**

The War in Vietnam
- Agent Orange
- Deforestation

Electronic Library of Primary Sources
- *from* "Peace Without Conquest" by Lyndon B. Johnson

INTERNET Land mines

***Warm-Up Transparency* 22**

***AMERICAN STORIES* video series**
- "Matters of Conscience"

INTERNET Women in Vietnam

***Warm-Up Transparency* 22**

Critical Thinking Transparencies
- CT64, Impact of Tet Offensive

The War in Vietnam
- Tet Offensive

Electronic Library of Primary Sources
- from *The Strategy of Confrontation*

INTERNET Tet offensive

***Warm-Up Transparency* 22**

Humanities Transparencies
- H28, Fall of Saigon
- H45, The Blind Leading the Blind

Geography Transparencies
- G30, Vietnam War: 1964–1975

Critical Thinking Transparencies
- CT30, The War in Vietnam

The War in Vietnam
- from the Pentagon Papers
- Supreme Court decision
- the boat people

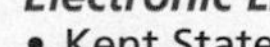

Electronic Library of Primary Sources
- Kent State

INTERNET Interact with History p. 755 (PE)

American Portfolio: A Videodisc for U.S. History, user's guide, pp.244–245, 251–253, 255

Chapter Summary Audiotapes
- Unit 6, Chapter 22

INTERNET http://www. mlushistory.com

Block Scheduling (90 MINUTES)

Day 1

Section 1, pp. 724–728

Section Assessment, p. 728

COOPERATIVE ACTIVITY
- Researching Buddhism, p. 726 (TE)

Day 2

Section 2, pp. 729–734

Section Assessment, p. 734

COOPERATIVE ACTIVITY
- Simulating a TV Interview, p. 733 (TE)

Day 3

Section 3, pp. 735–740

***AMERICAN STORIES* video series** "Matters of Conscience"

Section 4, pp. 741–746

Section Assessments, pp. 740, 746

COOPERATIVE ACTIVITIES
- Composing "Hawk" or "Dove" Song Lyrics, p. 739 (TE)
- Creating a 1968 Yearbook, p. 745 (TE)

Day 4

Section 5, pp. 747–753

American Literature: Literature of the Vietnam War, pp. 754–755

Chapter Assessment, pp. 756–757

COOPERATIVE ACTIVITY
- Writing Editorials, p. 749 (TE)

YEARLY PACING ***Chapter 22 Total:*** 4 days ***Yearly Total:*** 85 days

See *Planning for Block Schedules* for special activities and pacing strategies.

Customizing for Special Populations

Students Acquiring English

Access for Students Acquiring English: Spanish Translations
- Guided Reading for Sections 1–5, pp. 241–245
- Chapter Summary, pp. 239–240
- Skillbuilder Practice: Distinguishing Fact from Opinion, p. 246
- Geography Application: The Ho Chi Minh Trail, p. 247
- Outline Map: The Vietnam War, p. 249

Spanish Reading Study Guide, pp. 223–234

Translations of Chapter Summaries, Hmong, Cantonese, Vietnamese, and Cambodian

Chapter Summary Audiotapes in Spanish Unit 6, Chapter 22

***AMERICAN STORIES* video series**
- "Matters of Conscience" (Spanish track)

INTERNET The Diverse Classroom

Gifted and Talented Students

In-Depth Resources: Unit 6
- Primary Sources: Letter from a Soldier in Vietnam, p. 45; Protest Buttons, p. 46; The New Left, p. 47; Lyndon B. Johnson on Vietnam and Reelection, p. 48
- American Lives: Robert McNamara, p. 52; John Lewis, p. 53

Less Proficient Readers

In-Depth Resources: Unit 6
- Guided Reading for Sections 1–5, pp. 35–39
- Skillbuilder: Distinguishing Fact from Opinion, p. 40
- Geography Application: The Ho Chi Minh Trail, p. 41
- Outline Map: The Vietnam War, p. 43

Reading Study Guide
- pp. 223–234

Telescoping the Times
- Chapter Summary, pp. 43–44

Chapter Summary Audiotapes, Unit 6, Chapter 22

Connections to Literature READINGS FOR STUDENTS

In-Depth Resources: Unit 6
- **from *In Country* by Bobbie Ann Mason,** p. 49

McDougal Littell *The Language of Literature* American Literature
- **Estela Portillo Trambley, "Village,"** p. 937
- **George Olsen, from *Dear America: Letters Home from Vietnam,*** p. 945
- **Yusef Komunyakaa, "Camouflaging the Chimera,"** p.949
- **Wendy Wilder Larsen and Tran Thi Nga, "Deciding,"** p. 952
- **Tim O'Brien, "Ambush,"** p. 956
- **Lanford Wilson, *Wandering,*** p. 972
- **Denise Levertov, "At the Justice Department, November 15, 1969,"** p. 979

McDougal Littell *Literature Connections*

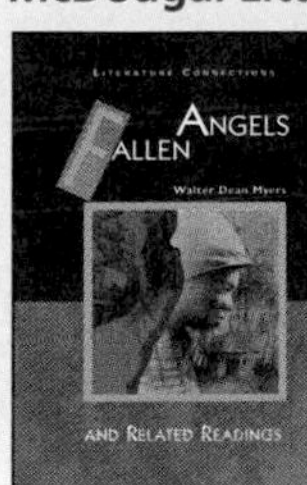

- **Walter Dean Myers** ***Fallen Angels*** *(with related readings) This novel presents the experiences of a small group of men who come of age in the Vietnam War. Richie Perry enlists in the army mainly to escape his problems at home and finds himself in the middle of a war that is more traumatic and confusing than the life he fled.*

OVERVIEW

The Vietnam War Years

▶ ***Accessing Prior Knowledge***

Ask students to discuss the images of the Vietnam War that they have seen in movies and on television. Which films represent the war realistically? Which films provide a distorted perspective of the war? What opinions have students formed about the Vietnam War?

▶ ***Predicting Outcomes***

Have students read the quotation from Henry Kissinger on this page. What price would the United States pay for its involvement in Vietnam during the 1960s and 1970s? What price would the country continue to pay?

MORE ABOUT . . .
Henry Kissinger

A Harvard professor of government and an authority on U.S. security policy, Kissinger joined the Nixon administration as national security advisor and later became Nixon's secretary of state. For his work as chief U.S. negotiator in the Vietnam peace talks, Kissinger was awarded the 1973 Nobel Peace Prize.

CHAPTER 22 The Vietnam War Years

SECTION 1
Moving Toward Conflict

America slowly involves itself in the war in Vietnam as it seeks to halt the spread of communism.

SECTION 2
U.S. Involvement and Escalation

The United States sends troops to fight in Vietnam, but the war quickly turns into a stalemate.

SECTION 3
A Nation Divided

An antiwar movement emerges in the United States, pitting those who oppose the government's war policy against those who support it.

MATTERS OF CONSCIENCE

SECTION 4
1968: A Tumultuous Year

A shocking enemy attack in Vietnam, two assassinations, and a chaotic political convention help make 1968 the most explosive year of the decade.

SECTION 5
The End of the War and Its Legacy

The nation's longest war ends after nearly ten years and leaves a lasting impact on U.S. policy and American society.

"Vietnam is still with us. . . . We paid an exorbitant price for the decisions that were made."

Henry Kissinger

THE UNITED STATES

- 1955: United States begins providing economic aid to South Vietnam.
- 1956: Dwight D. Eisenhower is reelected.
- 1957: President Eisenhower sends federal troops to enforce school desegregation in Little Rock.
- 1960: John F. Kennedy is elected president.
- 1963: Lyndon B. Johnson becomes president upon the assassination of John F. Kennedy.
- 1964: Congress passes the Tonkin Gulf Resolution in response to alleged North Vietnamese torpedo attacks.
- 1964: Lyndon B. Johnson is elected president.

THE WORLD

- 1954: Vietminh defeat the French at Dien Bien Phu.
- 1957: The National Liberation Front, or Vietcong, forms in South Vietnam.
- 1962: The African nation of Uganda becomes independent.
- 1964: Palestine Liberation Organization forms in the Middle East.

THEMES IN CHAPTER 22

America in the World

America's mission in Vietnam was to halt the spread of communism—a threat to democracy. Ironically, the South Vietnamese regimes that the U.S. supported were not very democratic themselves.

See Teacher's Edition note, p. 727.

Constitutional Concerns

Among the constitutional issues of the Vietnam War era were the president's powers as commander in chief and First Amendment rights. Both the Tonkin Gulf Resolution and the release of the Pentagon Papers sparked controversy.

See Teacher's Edition notes, pp. 727, 750.

Civil Rights

Initially, mainstream civil rights leaders were reluctant to criticize the Vietnam War, fearing they would jeopardize President Johnson's support for their cause. However, when the war threatened Great Society reforms, Dr. Martin Luther King, Jr., and other civil rights leaders voiced their opposition.

See Teacher's Edition note, p. 736.

Cultural Diversity

Many Vietnamese refugees seeking a homeland in the United States at the end of the war developed a cultural identity that was a blend of two traditions—Vietnamese and American.

See Teacher's Edition note, p. 752.

LIVING HISTORY

CREATING A VIETNAM WAR POSTER

In the 1960s and early 1970s, the American people viewed images of the Vietnam War and its effects in newspapers, magazines, and on television. Many of these images have remained forever in the minds of those who saw them. Create a poster that graphically depicts an aspect of the Vietnam War. Focus on a particular theme or time period of the war, using ideas presented in the chapter and images and scenes from outside sources. Consider the following suggestions as you develop your poster:

- Look for photographs of the war in newspapers, microfilm, magazines, and books.
- Look for appropriate quotations from veterans and government leaders.
- Use a computer to create captions.
- Experiment with arrangements of the visual images, quotations, and captions before affixing them to the poster.
- Add hand-drawn or painted designs or images.

PORTFOLIO PROJECT Save your poster in a folder for your American history portfolio. You will display and share your poster at the end of the chapter.

I WANT OUT

1965
- First U.S. ground troops arrive in Vietnam.
- U.S. troops quell an uprising in the Dominican Republic.

1966
- Mao Zedong begins the Cultural Revolution in China.

1967
- Antiwar protests intensify.

1968
- The Vietcong launch the Tet offensive.
- Martin Luther King, Jr., and Robert Kennedy are assassinated.
- Richard M. Nixon is elected president.
- Lyndon B. Johnson announces he will not seek reelection.

1968
- French students stage massive protests and strikes in Paris.

1969
- U.S. troops begin their withdrawal from Vietnam.

1970
- Ohio National Guardsmen shoot and kill four students at Kent State University.
- President Nixon orders an invasion of Cambodia.

1970
- Salvador Allende, a Marxist, is elected president of Chile.

1972
- Richard M. Nixon is reelected.

1972
- Ferdinand Marcos declares martial law in the Philippines.

1973
- United States signs a cease-fire with North Vietnam and Vietcong, ending American involvement in the Vietnam War.

1974
- Gerald R. Ford becomes president after Richard M. Nixon resigns.

1975
- Saigon falls; South Vietnam surrenders to the Communists.

ALTERNATIVE ASSESSMENT

LIVING HISTORY

CREATING A VIETNAM WAR POSTER

Offer students these suggestions for planning and creating their posters:

- Think about what you would like to communicate visually about the Vietnam War. Skim the photos and other illustrations in the chapter for ideas.
- Choose a theme or time period to help organize and guide your research.
- Investigate a variety of print sources for appropriate images.
- Create a thumbnail layout—a plan or design that shows the rough arrangement of the graphics and the words.
- Consider the reaction you want viewers to have when they see your poster.

Planning Guide

Step 1	Students choose a theme or time period.
Step 2	Students research several sources for images.
Step 3	Students create a rough layout.
Step 4	Students place their final posters in their portfolios.

IN-DEPTH RESOURCES: UNIT 6
See worksheet and standards for evaluation, pp. 54, 55.

RECOMMENDED RESOURCES

Books for the Teacher

Goldman, Eric F. *The Tragedy of Lyndon Johnson.* New York: Knopf, 1969. Johnson's presidency, including the impact of the Vietnam War.

Karnow, Stanley. *Vietnam.* New York: Viking, 1983. Thorough survey of the Vietnam War.

Wells, Tom. *The War Within.* New York: Holt, 1994. Polarization of American society over Vietnam.

Books for the Student

Caputo, Philip. *A Rumor of War.* New York: Ballantine, 1977. Compelling combat memoir.

McNamara, Robert. *In Retrospect.* New York: Vintage, 1995. Former secretary of defense's later thoughts on war.

Terry, Wallace. *Bloods.* New York: Ballantine, 1984. African-American veterans' oral histories of the Vietnam War.

Videos

Chicago 1968. PBS Home Video, 1995. Story of Democratic convention.

Fall of Saigon. Discovery Channel Home Video. Last days of South Vietnam.

No Time for Tears: Vietnam—The Women Who Served. West End Films, 1993. Documentary about women's experiences in Vietnam.

Vietnam: A Television History. PBS Video, 1983. Award-winning documentary in 13 parts.

Software

Passage to Vietnam. CD-ROM. Against All Odds/Interval Research, 1995.

The Wall. CD-ROM. Magnet Interactive, 1995.

The War in Vietnam: A Multimedia Chronicle. CD-ROM. Macmillan Digital, 212-654-8500.

Section 1 Overview

OBJECTIVES

1. To summarize Vietnam's history as a French colony and its struggle for independence.
2. To examine how the United States became involved in the Vietnam conflict.
3. To describe the expansion of U.S. military involvement under President Johnson.

SKILLBUILDER

- Understanding geography: movement, location, p. 726

CRITICAL THINKING

- Theme: America in the World, p. 725
- Analyzing causes, p. 726
- Forming generalizations, p. 727
- Theme: Constitutional Concerns, p. 728
- Summarizing, p. 728
- Analyzing effects, p. 728
- Forming opinions, p. 728

FOCUS & MOTIVATE

5-MINUTE WARM-UP

Recognizing Propaganda
To understand the Vietcong, have students look at the poster on page 726 and answer these questions.

1. How are the Vietcong portrayed? Use four adjectives to describe them.
2. How is the United States portrayed?

WARM-UP TRANSPARENCY 22

▶ ***Starting with the Student***
Ask students if they have ever tried to solve a problem that grew ever more complicated and more difficult to solve.

OBJECTIVE ① **INSTRUCT**

The Roots of American Involvement

▶ ***Discussing Key Ideas***
- France rules Indochina from the late 1800s until World War II.

(continued on next page)

1 Moving Toward Conflict

TERMS & NAMES
- Ho Chi Minh
- Vietminh
- domino theory
- Dien Bien Phu
- Geneva Accords
- Ngo Dinh Diem
- Vietcong
- Ho Chi Minh Trail
- Tonkin Gulf Resolution

LEARN ABOUT the early measures the United States took to stop the spread of communism in Vietnam
TO UNDERSTAND how America slowly became involved in a war in Vietnam.

ONE AMERICAN'S STORY

Lieutenant Colonel A. Peter Dewey

On the morning of September 26, 1945, Lieutenant Colonel A. Peter Dewey, the son of an Illinois congressman, was on his way to the Saigon airport in the Southeast Asian country of Vietnam. Only 28, Dewey served in the Office of Strategic Services, the chief intelligence-gathering body of the U.S. military and forerunner of the Central Intelligence Agency. Dewey had gone to Vietnam, which had recently been freed from Japanese rule during World War II, to assess what was becoming an explosive situation.

The Vietnamese, who had resisted Japanese occupation, now were preparing to fight the French. France, which until World War II had ruled Vietnam and its surrounding countries, sought—with British aid—to regain control of the region. Dewey saw nothing but disaster in this plan. "Cochinchina [southern Vietnam] is burning," he reported, "the French and British are finished here, and we [the United States] ought to clear out of Southeast Asia."

On his way to the airport, Dewey encountered a roadblock manned by several Vietnamese soldiers and made the fatal mistake of shouting at them in French. Presumably mistaking him for a French soldier, the Vietnamese guards shot him in the head. A. Peter Dewey, whose body was never recovered, was thus the first American to die in Vietnam.

Unfortunately, Dewey would not be the last. As Vietnam's independence effort came under Communist influence, the United States grew increasingly concerned about the small country's future. Eventually, America would fight a war to halt the spread of communism in Vietnam. The war would claim the lives of almost 60,000 Americans and more than 1.5 million Vietnamese. It also would divide the American nation as no other event since the Civil War.

The Roots of American Involvement

America's involvement in Vietnam began in 1950, during the French Indochina War, the name given to France's attempt to reestablish its rule in Vietnam after World War II. Seeking to strengthen its ties with France and help fight the spread of communism, the United States provided the French with massive amounts of economic and military support.

FRENCH RULE IN VIETNAM From the late 1800s until World War II—when the Japanese took over the area—France ruled Indochina, which consisted of Vietnam and neighboring Laos and Cambodia. French colonists took much of the land from the peasants and built large plantations, from which they extracted a large portion of the country's rice and rubber for their own profit. This situation sparked growing unrest among Vietnamese peasants, which in turn prompted a harsh French response. French rulers restricted freedom of speech and assembly and jailed many Vietnamese nationalists. These measures, however, failed to curb all dissent, as the Vietnamese staged several revolts and strikes during the 1930s.

The Indochinese Communist Party, founded in 1930, organized most of the uprisings. The party's leader was **Ho Chi Minh,** a thin, middle-aged man who sported a trademark goatee. Ho Chi Minh, whom the French had condemned to

SECTION 1 RESOURCES

PRINT RESOURCES

IN-DEPTH RESOURCES: UNIT 6
Guided Reading, p. 35

READING STUDY GUIDE, p. 223

ACCESS FOR STUDENTS ACQUIRING ENGLISH
Guided Reading (Spanish), p. 241

SPANISH READING STUDY GUIDE, p. 223

FORMAL ASSESSMENT
Section Quiz, p. 270

ALTERNATIVE ASSESSMENT BOOK
See forms for supporting and scoring alternative activities.

TECHNOLOGY RESOURCES

CD-ROM Electronic Library of Primary Sources
The War in Vietnam

VIDEO *American Portfolio: A Videodisc for U.S. History* user's guide, pp. 244–245

INTERNET http://www.mlushistory.com

death in 1930 for his rebellious activity, fled Vietnam that year. However, throughout the 1930s, Ho Chi Minh orchestrated Vietnam's growing independence movement from exile in the Soviet Union and later from China.

In 1941, a year after the Japanese took control of Vietnam, Ho Chi Minh returned home. That year, the Vietnamese Communists combined with other nationalist groups to form an organization called the **Vietminh.** The group sought Vietnam's independence from foreign rule. When the Allied defeat of Japan in August of 1945 forced the Japanese to leave Vietnam, that goal suddenly seemed a reality. On September 2, 1945, Ho Chi Minh stood in the middle of a huge crowd in the northern city of Hanoi and declared Vietnam an independent nation.

FRANCE BATTLES THE VIETMINH France, however, had no intention of relinquishing its former colony. French troops moved back into Vietnam in 1946, eventually driving the Vietminh out of the cities and regaining control of the country's southern half. Ho Chi Minh vowed to fight from the North to liberate the South from French control. "If ever the tiger pauses," Ho had said, referring to the Vietminh, "the elephant [France] will impale him on his mighty tusks. But the tiger will not pause, and the elephant will die of exhaustion and loss of blood."

In 1950, the United States entered the Vietnam struggle. That year, President Truman sent nearly $15 million in economic aid to France. Over the next four years the United States paid for much of France's war, pumping nearly $2.6 billion into the effort to defeat a man America had once supported. Ironically, during World War II, the United States had forged an alliance with Ho Chi Minh, supplying him with aid to resist the Japanese.

By 1950, however, Cold War fever had gripped much of the world. China and Eastern Europe had fallen to the Communists, and Korea appeared to be next. America saw a dual benefit in supporting France: maintaining an ally against the growing Soviet presence in Europe, and helping to stop another Asian country from turning Communist. While Ho Chi Minh promoted his cause as one of independence, the United States now saw their one-time ally as a Communist aggressor.

THINK THROUGH HISTORY
A. THEME *America in the World* *Why did the United States provide military aid to France?*

A. Answer To keep France as an ally against the Soviet Union in Europe and to keep communism from spreading to another Asian country.

KEY PLAYER

HO CHI MINH
1890–1969

Born Nguyen Tat Thanh to a poor family, Ho Chi Minh (which means "He Who Enlightens") found early work as a cook on a French steamship, which allowed him to visit such cities as Boston and New York.

Ho Chi Minh patterned the phrasing of the Vietnamese Declaration of Independence on the U.S. declaration. His admiration for the United States turned to disappointment, however, after the government chose to support France rather than his nationalist movement.

The Communist ruler's name lived on after his death in 1969. In 1975, the North Vietnamese Army conquered South Vietnam and changed the name of the South's capital from Saigon to Ho Chi Minh City.

THE VIETMINH DRIVE OUT THE FRENCH Upon entering the White House in 1953, President Eisenhower continued the policy of supplying aid to the French war effort. By this time, the United States had settled for a stalemate with the Communists in Korea, which only stiffened America's resolve to halt the spread of communism. During a news conference in 1954, Eisenhower explained the **domino theory,** in which he likened the countries on the brink of communism to a row of dominoes, waiting to fall one after the other. "You have a row of dominoes set up," the president said. "You knock over the first one, and what will happen to the last one is the certainty that it will go over very quickly."

Despite massive U.S. aid, however, the French could not retake Vietnam. The final blow came in May of 1954, when the Vietminh overran the French outpost at **Dien Bien Phu,** in northwestern Vietnam. Led by General Vo Nguyen Giap, the Vietminh surrounded the fort and pounded it with heavy artillery for nearly two months. Major Paul Grauwin of the French Army described the outpost's morgue on the first night of heavy bombardment.

A PERSONAL VOICE

The square hole was full [of dead]; outside, between the hole and the barbed wire, there were a hundred corpses, pell-mell, thrown on stretchers or onto the ground, stiffened in grotesque or tragic positions. Some were wrapped and tied in their tent cloth; others were dressed in their combat uniforms, motionless in the pose where death had surprised them.

MAJOR PAUL GRAUWIN, quoted in *Dien Bien Phu*

(continued from page 724)

- Ho Chi Minh declares Vietnam independent in 1945.
- Truman and Eisenhower support France's war against Vietnam.
- The Geneva Accords of 1954 temporarily divide Vietnam into North Vietnam and South Vietnam.

IN-DEPTH RESOURCES: UNIT 6
Guided Reading. p. 35

ACCESS FOR STUDENTS ACQUIRING ENGLISH
Guided Reading (Spanish), p. 241

THE WAR IN VIETNAM
Eisenhower introduces "falling domino" principle
Address on the Geneva Accords by John Foster Dulles

KEY PLAYER
Ho Chi Minh

Critical Thinking: Making Predictions Ask students what might have happened if the United States had supported Ho Chi Minh rather than France.

Issues for the 21st Century

Foreign Policy After the Cold War

Connect U.S. policy in Vietnam to foreign policy decisions today by having students read pages 878-879. Then have them answer these questions.

1. What foreign policy goals led to U.S. involvement in Vietnam? *Halting the spread of communism in Asia.*
2. What foreign policy decisions does the United States face today? *Whether the U.S. should actively promote democracy or trade with countries with poor human rights records.*

TEACHING OPTIONS

Making Connections Across Cultures

Chinese Influence in Vietnam Foreign domination of Vietnam did not begin with the French. After conquering Vietnam in 111 B.C., the Chinese ruled there for over a thousand years. They introduced their ideographic writing system, the Buddhist religion, and the cultivation of rice. This crop shaped the Vietnamese landscape—small villages set in rice fields surrounded by irrigation ditches, with jungles bordering the cultivated areas. Rebelling against Chinese rule, the Vietnamese won independence in A.D. 939. However, in subsequent centuries they often had to fight off further Chinese attempts at domination.

Making Global Connections

America and the Cold War The U.S. decision to assist France in its fight to retake Vietnam stemmed from American global concerns during the Cold War era. As the Iron Curtain descended in eastern Europe, the United States could not afford to antagonize France, an important European ally against Soviet encroachments in that region. In Asia, the fall of China to communism in the late 1940s intensified Western fears of the growing threat of Communist power worldwide, and the spread of communism to North Korea gave additional support to the domino theory.

HISTORY FROM VISUALS

Indochina, 1959

Reading the Map Explain that *parallel* refers to a line of latitude. On the map, the 17th parallel is labeled to indicate that the temporary division between North Vietnam and South Vietnam was at latitude 17 degrees north.

Extension Explain that many Vietnamese think that the shape of their country resembles two rice baskets dangling from a bamboo pole. Ask students to research the reasons for this comparison.

The United States Steps In

▶ ***Discussing Key Ideas***
- South Vietnamese president Ngo Dinh Diem cancels unifying elections because Ho Chi Minh is sure to win.
- Corruption and repressive policies pervade Diem's regime.
- In 1963, President Kennedy backs plans to overthrow Diem.

HISTORY FROM VISUALS

Vietcong Propaganda Poster

Reading the Poster Tell students that the slogan on the poster, "Better death than slavery," was echoed in the popular Cold War slogan, "Better dead than Red."

Extension Have students discuss why the poster might have drummed up support for the Vietcong.

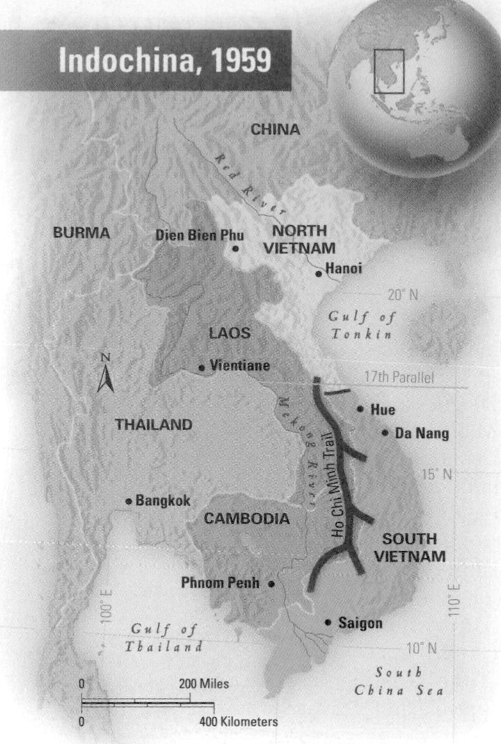

GEOGRAPHY SKILLBUILDER

MOVEMENT *Through which countries did the Ho Chi Minh Trail pass?* **LOCATION** *How might North Vietnam's location have enabled it to get aid from its ally, China?*

After the fall of Dien Bien Phu, the French surrendered and began to pull out of Vietnam. From May through July 1954, the countries of France, Great Britain, the Soviet Union, the United States, China, Laos, and Cambodia met in Geneva, Switzerland, with the Vietminh and with the South Vietnam's anti-Communist nationalists to hammer out a peace agreement. The **Geneva Accords** temporarily divided Vietnam along the 17th parallel. The Communists and their leader, Ho Chi Minh, controlled North Vietnam from the capital of Hanoi. The anti-Communist nationalists controlled South Vietnam from the port city of Saigon. An election to unify the country was called for in 1956.

The United States Steps In

In the wake of France's retreat, the United States took a more active role in halting the spread of communism in Vietnam. Wading deeper into the country's affairs, the administrations of President Eisenhower and then President John F. Kennedy provided economic and military aid to South Vietnam's non-Communist regime.

DIEM CANCELS ELECTIONS Although he directed a brutal and repressive regime, Ho Chi Minh won popular support in the North by breaking up large estates and redistributing land to peasants. Moreover, his years of fighting the Japanese and French had made him a national hero. Recognizing Ho Chi Minh's widespread popularity, South Vietnam's president, **Ngo Dinh Diem,** a strong anti-Communist, refused to take part in the countrywide election of 1956. The United States also sensed that a countrywide election might spell victory for Ho Chi Minh and therefore supported the cancellation of elections. The Eisenhower administration promised military aid and training to Diem in return for a stable reform government in the South.

The Vietcong saw the United States and South Vietnam as oppressors. This Vietcong propaganda poster reads, "Better death than slavery."

Diem, however, failed to hold up his end of the bargain. He ushered in a corrupt government that suppressed opposition of any kind and offered little or no land distribution to peasants. In addition, Diem, a devout Catholic, angered the country's large Buddhist population by restricting Buddhist practices.

By 1957, a Communist opposition group in the South, known as the **Vietcong,** had begun attacks on the Diem government, assassinating thousands of South Vietnamese government officials. While the group would later be called the National Liberation Front (NLF), the United States continued to refer to the fighters as the Vietcong.

Ho Chi Minh supported the group, which had strong Communist ties. In 1959, Ho Chi Minh began supplying arms to the Vietcong via a network of paths along the border of Vietnam, Laos, and Cambodia that became known as the **Ho Chi Minh Trail.** (See map above.) As the fighters stepped up their surprise attacks, or guerrilla tactics, South Vietnam grew more unstable. The Eisenhower administration took little action, however, deciding to "sink or swim with Ngo Dinh Diem."

KENNEDY AND VIETNAM The Kennedy administration, which entered the White House in 1961, also chose initially to "swim" with Diem. However, Kennedy was wary of accusations that Democrats were "soft" on

Skillbuilder Answers:
Movement: Laos and Cambodia.
Location: *Possible response:* China could easily deliver military and other supplies to North Vietnam.

THINK THROUGH HISTORY
B. *Analyzing Causes* *Why did the United States support the cancellation of Vietnam's unifying elections?*

B. Answer Because it appeared that Ho Chi Minh would win the election and possibly unify Vietnam under communism.

Block Schedule TEACHING OPTION **Time Needed: 20 Minutes**

Cooperative Activity: Researching Buddhism

Task: Pairs of students will research the beliefs and practices of Buddhists in Vietnam and their persecution under Diem's regime. Partners will then collaborate on compiling their findings in a short report.

Purpose: To explore world religions and reasons for religious intolerance.

Activity: Encourage students to use both library and Internet resources to gather information. Each report should include an explanation of the clash between Catholics and Buddhists under Diem's regime and the religious reasons for the Buddhists' political protests.

Building a Portfolio: Students should include their reports in their portfolios if they feel that this assignment represents their strongest work.

ALTERNATIVE ASSESSMENT BOOK
Standards for Evaluating a Cooperative Activity

Standards for Evaluation
Reports should . . .
- include information from a variety of sources
- contain accurate and relevant facts
- develop topic logically
- clarify relationships between different ideas

communism. Therefore, he increased financial aid to Diem's teetering regime and sent thousands of military advisers to help train South Vietnamese troops in their battle against the NLF. By the end of 1963, almost 16,000 U.S. military personnel were in South Vietnam.

A Buddhist monk sets himself on fire in a busy Saigon intersection in 1963 as a protest against the Diem regime.

Meanwhile, Diem's popularity plummeted because of ongoing corruption and lack of land reform. To combat the growing Vietcong presence in the South's countryside, the Diem administration initiated the strategic hamlet program, which meant moving all villagers to protected areas. Many Vietnamese deeply resented being moved from their home villages where they had lived for generations and where ancestors were buried.

THINK THROUGH HISTORY
C. Forming Generalizations *Why was the Diem regime so unpopular?*

C. Answer Corruption, repressive tactics, and persecution of Buddhists.

Diem also intensified his attack on Buddhism. Fed up with continuing Buddhist demonstrations, the South Vietnamese ruler imprisoned hundreds of Buddhist clerics and destroyed their temples. To protest, several Buddhist monks and nuns publicly burned themselves to death. Horrified, American officials urged Diem to stop the persecutions, but Diem refused.

It had become clear that for South Vietnam to remain stable, Diem would have to go. On November 1, 1963, a U.S.-supported military coup toppled Diem's regime. Against Kennedy's wishes, Diem was executed. A few weeks later, Kennedy too fell to an assassin's bullet. The presidency—along with the growing crisis in Vietnam—now belonged to Lyndon B. Johnson.

President Johnson Expands the Conflict

Shortly before his death, Kennedy had announced his intent to withdraw U.S. forces from South Vietnam. "In the final analysis, it's their war," he declared. Whether Kennedy would have in fact withdrawn from Vietnam remains a matter of debate. However, Lyndon Johnson escalated—or increased—the nation's role in Vietnam and eventually began what would become America's longest war.

THE SOUTH GROWS MORE UNSTABLE Diem's death brought more chaos to South Vietnam. A string of military leaders attempted to lead the country, but each regime was more unstable and inefficient than Diem's had been. Meanwhile, the Vietcong's influence in the countryside steadily grew.

To President Johnson, a Communist takeover of South Vietnam would be disastrous. As a Democratic president, Lyndon Johnson was particularly sensitive to being perceived as "soft" on communism. A Democrat, Harry Truman, had been president when China fell to the Communist Party in 1948, unleashing charges by some Republicans that the Democrats had "lost" China. In addition, many of Senator Joseph McCarthy's charges during the 1950s of Communist infiltrators in America had been directed against Democrats. For these political reasons, Johnson wanted to avoid being accused of "losing" Vietnam. "If I . . . let the Communists take over South Vietnam," Johnson said, "then . . . my nation would be seen as an appeaser, and we would find it impossible to accomplish anything . . . anywhere on the entire globe."

MORE ABOUT . . .
Ngo Dinh Diem

Ngo Dinh Diem was ill equipped to handle the changing times in his homeland. Along with his devout Catholicism, his Confucian training stressed obedience above all things. He had little understanding of either democracy or communism and, despite all the U.S. aid, little trust for anyone outside his family. In 1955, the British writer Graham Greene described Diem as "separated from the people by cardinals and police cars with wailing sirens and foreign advisers droning of global strategy."

OBJECTIVE
(3) INSTRUCT

President Johnson Expands the Conflict

▶ ***Starting with the Student***
Have students describe media images of politically unstable countries today.

- How do the situations in these countries compare with the growing unrest in Vietnam?

▶ ***Discussing Key Ideas***

- Diem's successors fail to curb the Vietcong's influence in South Vietnam.
- The Tonkin Gulf Resolution of 1964 grants President Johnson broad military powers in Vietnam.
- In February 1965, President Johnson escalates U.S. involvement in Vietnam.

ELECTRONIC LIBRARY OF PRIMARY SOURCES
The Tonkin Gulf Resolution

TEACHING OPTIONS

Exploring Themes

America in the World U.S. involvement in Vietnam was a mission to halt the spread of communism—perceived as a threat to democracy and free-market economies. Le Ly Hayslip (1949–), who grew up in central Vietnam, saw the struggle from a different perspective. In her autobiography *When Heaven and Earth Changed Places,* she wrote, "For you [American GIs], it was a simple thing: democracy against communism. For us, that was not our fight at all. How could it be? We knew little democracy and even less about communism. For most of us, it was a fight for independence—like the American Revolution."

Exploring Themes

Constitutional Concerns The Tonkin Gulf Resolution (see page 728), though short of a formal declaration of war, did grant the president broad war-making powers. During the debate over the resolution, Senator Wayne Morse of Oregon forecast, "I believe that history will record that we have made a great mistake in subverting and circumventing the Constitution of the United States, article 1, section 8 thereof [which gives Congress the power to declare war] by means of this resolution. . . ." Morse's words were prophetic. In 1973, Congress passed the War Powers Act to curb the president's war-making powers.

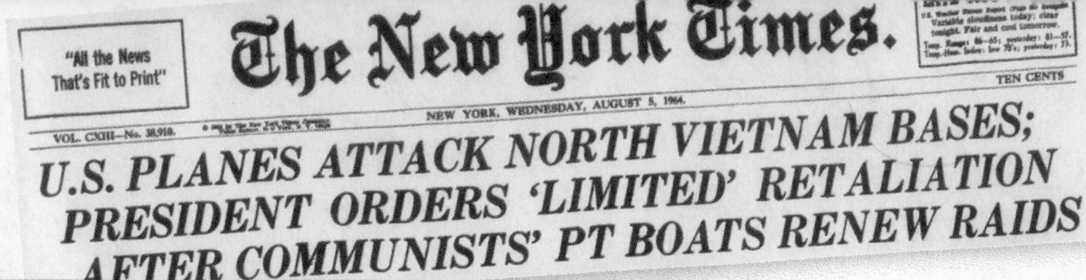
"All the News That's Fit to Print"

The New York Times.

VOL. CXIII—No. 38,918. NEW YORK, WEDNESDAY, AUGUST 5, 1964. TEN CENTS

U.S. PLANES ATTACK NORTH VIETNAM BASES; PRESIDENT ORDERS 'LIMITED' RETALIATION AFTER COMMUNISTS' PT BOATS RENEW RAIDS

A newspaper headline announces the U.S. military's reaction to the Gulf of Tonkin incident. During Operation Rolling Thunder, which followed, U.S. planes called Thunderchiefs dropped 750-pound bombs on Vietnamese targets.

THE TONKIN GULF RESOLUTION On August 2, 1964, a North Vietnamese patrol boat fired a torpedo at an American destroyer, the U.S.S. *Maddox,* which was patrolling in the Gulf of Tonkin off the North Vietnamese coast. The torpedo missed its target, but the *Maddox* inflicted heavy damage on the patrol boat.

Two days later, the *Maddox* and another destroyer were again off the North Vietnamese coast. In spite of bad weather, technicians reported enemy torpedoes. The American destroyers began firing. However, the crew of the *Maddox* later declared that they had neither seen nor heard hostile gunfire.

The alleged attack on the U.S. ships prompted Johnson to launch bombing strikes on North Vietnam. He also asked Congress for powers to take "all necessary measures to repel any armed attack against the forces of the United States and to prevent further aggression." Congress overwhelmingly approved Johnson's request, with only two senators voting against it. On August 7, Congress adopted the **Tonkin Gulf Resolution**. While not a declaration of war, it granted Johnson broad military powers in Vietnam.

Johnson did not tell Congress or the American people that the United States had been leading secret raids against North Vietnam. The *Maddox* had been in the Gulf of Tonkin to collect information for these raids. Furthermore, Johnson had prepared the resolution months beforehand and was only waiting for the chance to push it through Congress.

In February of 1965, President Johnson used his newly granted powers. In response to a Vietcong attack that killed eight Americans, Johnson unleashed Operation Rolling Thunder, the first sustained bombing of North Vietnam. In March of that year the first American combat troops began arriving in South Vietnam. By June, more than 50,000 U.S. soldiers were battling the Vietcong. The Vietnam War had become Americanized.

D. Answer It gave Johnson broad authority to widen America's role in the war.

THINK THROUGH HISTORY
D. THEME ***Constitutional Concerns*** *How did the expansion of presidential powers granted by the Tonkin Gulf Resolution lead to greater U.S. involvement in the Vietnam War?*

Section 1 Assessment

1. TERMS & NAMES

Identify:
- Ho Chi Minh
- Vietminh
- domino theory
- Dien Bien Phu
- Geneva Accords
- Ngo Dinh Diem
- Vietcong
- Ho Chi Minh Trail
- Tonkin Gulf Resolution

2. SUMMARIZING In a two-column chart like the one below, cite the Vietnam policy for each of the following presidents: Truman, Eisenhower, Kennedy, and Johnson.

President	Vietnam Policy

Choose one of the presidential policies and explain its purpose.

3. ANALYZING EFFECTS Why do you think the Geneva Accords of 1954 failed to bring a lasting peace in Vietnam? Support your answer with reasons.

THINK ABOUT
- the provisions of the Geneva Accords
- Ho Chi Minh's and Ngo Dinh Diem's goals
- the role of the U.S. in Vietnam

4. FORMING OPINIONS Do you think Congress was justified in passing the Tonkin Gulf Resolution? Use details from the text to support your response.

THINK ABOUT
- the questionable report of torpedo boat attacks on two U.S. destroyers
- the powers that the resolution would give the president
- the fact that the resolution was not a declaration of war

HISTORY FROM VISUALS
New York Times *Front-Page Headline*

Reading the Headline Point out that the headline is a capsule summary that answers questions beginning with the 5 *w's—who, what, when, where,* and *why.*

Extension Have students write a front-page headline for another important event discussed in this section.

ASSESS & RETEACH

Section 1 Assessment

Students might work in pairs to respond to the questions.

Self-Assessment

To assess what they have learned, students can write their own questions, exchange them with partners, and try to answer one another's questions.

Section Quiz

FORMAL ASSESSMENT
Section Quiz, p. 270

Reteach

Use the map and the other marginal features in Section 1 to help review the main ideas of this section.

CLOSE

After France's withdrawal from Vietnam, the country was temporarily divided into the Communist-controlled North and the nationalist-controlled South. U.S. military involvement escalated in 1965, when President Johnson unleashed the first sustained bombing of North Vietnam.

ANSWERS

1. TERMS & NAMES
- Ho Chi Minh, p. 724
- Vietminh, p. 725
- domino theory, p. 725
- Dien Bien Phu, p. 725
- Geneva Accords, p. 726
- Ngo Dinh Diem, p. 726
- Vietcong, p. 726
- Ho Chi Minh Trail, p. 726
- Tonkin Gulf Resolution, p. 728

2. SUMMARIZING

Possible Answers: Truman—economic aid to France; Eisenhower—economic and military aid to South Vietnam; Kennedy—economic and military aid to South Vietnam; Johnson—stepped-up U.S. military involvement. Possible explanations: Truman—containing communism; Eisenhower—domino theory; Kennedy—Democrats' hard-line anti-Communist stance; Johnson—maintaining America's anti-Communist reputation.

3. ANALYZING EFFECTS

Possible Responses: The geographical division of North and South Vietnam may have intensified the political division between Communist and anti-Communist nationalists; defying the Geneva Accords, the U.S. supported Diem's cancellation of the 1956 election.

4. FORMING OPINIONS

Possible Responses: Yes—Presidential authority should be broadened in response to emergency situations, such as bombing attacks. No—The circumstances surrounding the North Vietnamese attack were fuzzy and not adequately verified; Congress gave Johnson too much power over activities in Vietnam; Johnson deceived Congress about events in the Tonkin Gulf.

❷ U.S. Involvement and Escalation

TERMS & NAMES
- Robert McNamara
- Dean Rusk
- William Westmoreland
- napalm
- Agent Orange
- search-and-destroy mission
- credibility gap

LEARN ABOUT the reasons for U.S. escalation and the difficulty the United States encountered in fighting the Vietcong

TO UNDERSTAND why the war lasted longer than expected and began to lose support at home.

Section 2 Overview

OBJECTIVES

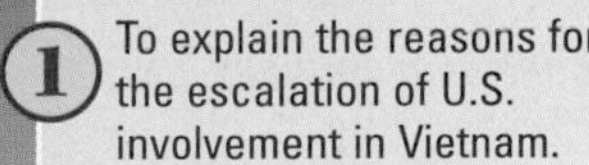

To explain the reasons for the escalation of U.S. involvement in Vietnam.

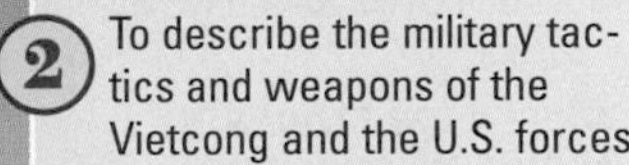

To describe the military tactics and weapons of the Vietcong and the U.S. forces.

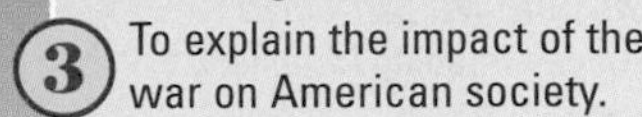

To explain the impact of the war on American society.

SKILLBUILDER
- Interpreting charts, p. 731

CRITICAL THINKING
- Contrasting, p. 730
- Identifying problems, p. 732
- Analyzing causes, p. 733
- Recognizing effects, p. 734
- Summarizing, p. 734
- Evaluating, p. 734
- Forming generalizations, p. 734

ONE AMERICAN'S STORY

Tim O'Brien, born in Austin, Minnesota, is a novelist who has written several books about his experience in Vietnam. O'Brien was drafted and sent to Vietnam in August of 1968, when he was 22. He spent the first seven months of his nearly two-year duty patrolling the fields outside of Chu Lai, a seacoast city in South Vietnam. O'Brien described one of the more nerve-racking experiences of the war: walking through the fields and jungles, many of which were filled with land mines and booby traps.

A PERSONAL VOICE

You do some thinking. You hallucinate. You look ahead a few paces and wonder what your legs will resemble if there is more to the earth in that spot than silicates and nitrogen. Will the pain be unbearable? Will you scream and fall silent? Will you be afraid to look at your own body, afraid of the sight of your own red flesh and white bone? . . .

It is not easy to fight this sort of self-defeating fear, but you try. You decide to be ultra-careful—the hard-nosed realistic approach. You try to second-guess the mine. Should you put your foot to that flat rock or the clump of weeds to its rear? Paddy dike or water? You wish you were Tarzan, able to swing on the vines. You trace the footprints of the men to your front. You give up when he curses you for following too closely; better one man dead than two.

TIM O'BRIEN, quoted in *A Life in a Year: The American Infantryman in Vietnam*

U.S. soldiers on patrol in Vietnam in November 1965.

Deadly traps were just some of the obstacles that U.S. troops faced in Vietnam as their attempt to defeat a resilient guerrilla army evolved into a bloody stalemate. As the influx of American ground troops into Vietnam failed to score a quick victory over the Communists, a mostly supportive U.S. population began to question its government's war policy.

The Decision to Escalate

Much of the nation supported Lyndon Johnson's determination to contain communism in Vietnam. Therefore, President Johnson began sending large numbers of American troops to fight alongside the South Vietnamese Army against the forces of the Vietcong and the North Vietnamese Army.

STRONG SUPPORT FOR CONTAINMENT In the 1964 presidential election, Lyndon Johnson soundly defeated his Republican opponent, Barry Goldwater. Johnson's victory was due in part to charges that Goldwater was an extreme anti-Communist who might push the United States into war with the Soviet Union. In contrast to Goldwater's heated, warlike language, Johnson's speeches were more moderate, yet he spoke determinedly about containing communism.

Even after Congress had approved the Tonkin Gulf Resolution, President Johnson voiced his opposition to sending U.S. ground troops to Vietnam. He

FOCUS & MOTIVATE

5-MINUTE WARM-UP

Interpreting Diagrams

To gain insight into the Vietcong's tactics, have students look at the diagram on page 731 and answer these questions.

1. How are firing posts in the tunnels an example of the Vietcong's guerrilla tactics?
2. What probably happened to enemy invaders who entered false tunnels?

 ***WARM-UP TRANSPARENCY 22***

▶ ***Starting with the Student***

Ask students how the expression "home-field advantage" might apply to U.S. troops waging a war on foreign soil.

SECTION 2 RESOURCES

PRINT RESOURCES

IN-DEPTH RESOURCES: UNIT 6
Guided Reading, p. 36
Skillbuilder Practice: Distinguishing Fact from Opinion, p. 40
Primary Source: Letter from a soldier in Vietnam, p. 45
American Lives: Robert McNamara, p. 52

READING STUDY GUIDE, p. 225

ACCESS FOR STUDENTS ACQUIRING ENGLISH
Guided Reading (Spanish), p. 242
Skillbuilder Practice: Distinguishing Fact from Opinion (Spanish), p. 246

SPANISH READING STUDY GUIDE, p. 225

FORMAL ASSESSMENT
Section Quiz, p. 271

ALTERNATIVE ASSESSMENT BOOK
See forms for supporting and scoring alternative activities.

TECHNOLOGY RESOURCES

CD-ROM Electronic Library of Primary Sources *The War in Vietnam*

VIDEO *American Portfolio: A Videodisc for U.S. History* user's guide, pp. 251–252, 255

INTERNET http://www.mlushistory.com

OBJECTIVE ① **INSTRUCT**

The Decision to Escalate

▶ ***Discussing Key Ideas***
- President Johnson dispatches the first American ground troops to Vietnam in March 1965.

(continued on next page)

(continued from page 729)

- Between 1965 and 1967, the number of U.S. troops in Vietnam more than doubles.

IN-DEPTH RESOURCES: UNIT 6
Guided Reading p. 36
American Lives: Robert McNamara, p. 52

ACCESS FOR STUDENTS ACQUIRING ENGLISH
Guided Reading (Spanish), p. 242

ELECTRONIC LIBRARY OF PRIMARY SOURCES
from "Peace Without Conquest" by Lyndon B. Johnson

HISTORICAL SPOTLIGHT

General William Westmoreland

Critical Thinking: Evaluating Ask students if providing deceptive information about enemy numbers and strength might have been justifiable during the Vietnam War. *Possible Responses: Yes—Such deceptions are sometimes necessary to boost the troops' and the public's morale. No—Such deceptions erode Americans' faith in government.*

OBJECTIVE

INSTRUCT

A War in the Jungle

▶ ***Starting with the Student***

- Ask students which they think is harder to face—an enemy whose strength and tactics are known or one whose strength and tactics are unknown. Why?

(continued on next page)

declared in 1964 that he was "not about to send American boys 9 or 10,000 miles away from home to do what Asian boys ought to be doing for themselves."

However, in March of 1965, that is precisely what the president did. Working closely with his foreign-policy advisers, particularly Secretary of Defense **Robert McNamara** and Secretary of State **Dean Rusk,** President Johnson began dispatching tens of thousands of U.S. soldiers to fight in Vietnam. While some Americans viewed Johnson's decision as contradictory to his position during the presidential campaign, most saw the president as following an established and popular policy of confronting communism anywhere in the world. That same year, for example, the Johnson administration also dispatched U.S. troops to the Dominican Republic, a small country in the Caribbean, to put down a rebellion the administration feared was Communist-inspired.

So, as American soldiers stepped onto the planes that would take them to fight in the thick jungles of Southeast Asia, Congress, as well as many Americans, strongly supported Johnson's strategy. A 1965 poll showed that 61 percent of Americans supported the U.S. policy in Vietnam, while only 24 percent opposed it.

To be sure, there were dissenters in the Johnson administration. In October of 1964, Undersecretary of State George Ball had argued against escalation, warning that "once on the tiger's back, we cannot be sure of picking the place to dismount." However, the president's closest advisers strongly urged escalation, believing the defeat of communism in Vietnam to be of vital importance to the future of America and the world. Dean Rusk stressed this view in a 1965 memo to President Johnson.

A PERSONAL VOICE

The integrity of the U.S. commitment is the principal pillar of peace throughout the world. If that commitment becomes unreliable, the communist world would draw conclusions that would lead to our ruin and almost certainly to a catastrophic war. So long as the South Vietnamese are prepared to fight for themselves, we cannot abandon them without disaster to peace and to our interests throughout the world.

DEAN RUSK, quoted in *In Retrospect*

HISTORICAL SPOTLIGHT

GENERAL WILLIAM WESTMORELAND

General Westmoreland retired from the military in 1972, but even in retirement, he could not escape the Vietnam War.

In 1982, almost seven years after the conflict had ended, CBS-TV aired a documentary entitled *The Uncounted Enemy: A Vietnam Deception.* The report, viewed by millions, asserted that General Westmoreland and the Pentagon had deceived the U.S. government about the enemy's size and strength during 1967 and 1968 to make it appear that U.S. forces were winning the war.

Westmoreland, claiming he was the victim of "distorted, false, and specious information . . . derived by sinister deception," filed a $120 million libel suit against CBS. The widely publicized suit was eventually settled, with both parties issuing statements pledging mutual respect. CBS, however, stood by its story.

THE TROOP BUILDUP ACCELERATES By the end of 1965, the U.S. government had sent more than 180,000 Americans to Vietnam. The American commander in South Vietnam, General **William Westmoreland,** continued to request more troops. Westmoreland, a tall and lean West Point graduate who served in World War II and Korea, was less than impressed with the fighting ability of the South Vietnamese Army, or the Army of the Republic of Vietnam (ARVN). The ARVN "cannot stand up to this pressure without substantial U.S. combat support on the ground," the general reported. "The only possible response is the aggressive deployment of U.S. troops." Throughout the early years of the war, the Johnson administration complied with Westmoreland's requests, and by 1967, the number of U.S. troops in Vietnam had climbed to about 500,000.

THINK THROUGH HISTORY
A. *Contrasting* *What differing opinions did Johnson's advisers have about Vietnam?*

A. Answer Some argued for U.S. escalation in Vietnam, claiming it was vital to stop the spread of communism, while George Ball argued against escalation, believing it would be easier to get into the Vietnam War than to get out.

A War in the Jungle

The United States entered the war in Vietnam believing that its superior weaponry would lead it to victory over the Vietcong. However, the jungle terrain and the enemy's guerrilla tactics soon turned the war into a frustrating stalemate.

AN ELUSIVE ENEMY Because the Vietcong lacked the high-powered weaponry of the American forces, they used hit-and-run and ambush tactics, as well as a keen knowledge of the jungle terrain, to their advantage. Moving

TEACHING OPTION

Skillbuilder Mini-Lesson: Distinguishing Fact from Opinion

Explaining the Skill Facts include events, dates, statistics, and statements that are generally known to be true. Opinions are personal judgments or beliefs. Typically, opinions are expressed as assertions, claims, predictions, and hypotheses. A person's opinion may turn out to be a fact.

Applying the Skill Have students work in small groups to make lists of the statements of fact and the statements of opinion included on this page of the text. Remind them that poll results are based on people's opinions. *Possible Responses: Facts—In March 1965, President Johnson sent tens of thousands of U.S. soldiers to fight in Vietnam; Johnson dispatched troops to the Dominican Republic to put down a rebellion. Opinions—Johnson's actions contradicted his position during the presidential campaign; defeating communism in Vietnam was vital to U.S. interests; the rebellion in the Dominican Republic was Communist-inspired.*

IN-DEPTH RESOURCES: UNIT 6
Skillbuilder Practice: Distinguishing Fact from Opinion, p. 40

secretly in and out of the general population, the Vietcong destroyed the notion of a frontline by attacking U.S. troops in both the cities and the countryside. Because some of the enemy lived amidst the civilian population, it became increasingly difficult for U.S. troops to discern friend from foe. A woman selling soft drinks to U.S. soldiers might be a Vietcong spy. A boy standing on the corner might be ready to throw a grenade.

In addition, the enemy laced the terrain with countless booby traps and land mines. American soldiers marching through South Vietnam's jungles and rice paddies dealt not only with sweltering heat and leeches but also with deadly traps. The enemy even turned U.S. weapons against the Americans. In a 1969 letter to his sister, Specialist Fourth Class Salvador Gonzalez described the tragic result from an unexploded U.S. bomb that the North Vietnamese Army had rigged.

A PERSONAL VOICE

Two days ago 4 guys got killed and about 15 wounded from the first platoon. Our platoon was 200 yards away on top of a hill. One guy was from Floral Park [in New York City]. He had five days left to go [before being sent home]. He was standing on a 250-lb. bomb that a plane had dropped and didn't explode. So the NVA [North Vietnamese Army] wired it up. Well, all they found was a piece of his wallet.

SALVADOR GONZALEZ, quoted in *Dear America: Letters Home from Vietnam*

Adding to the enemy's elusiveness was a network of elaborate tunnels that allowed the Vietcong to launch surprise attacks on American soldiers and then disappear quickly. The Vietnamese, who began building the tunnels during their war with the French, constructed even more in response to the massive U.S. bombings. The tunnels, which connected villages throughout the countryside, became home to many guerrilla fighters. Inside their underground world, the Vietcong ate and slept, stored munitions, built land mines, and treated their wounded. "The more the Americans tried to drive us

Skillbuilder Answer *Possible response:* They were able to make food, obtain water, and sleep down there, as well as tend to their wounded and store ammunition.

NOW & THEN

LAND MINES

The destructiveness of land mines still plagues much of the world today. As a result of past and present wars, roughly 110 million mines were still scattered throughout 64 countries in 1996. That year, nearly 2,000 victims lost either a limb or their life to a land mine each month. In Vietnam and Cambodia, more than 10 million mines remained in the ground.

Various relief, religious, and veterans organizations have urged the international community to ban the use of mines. The Vietnam Veterans of America Foundation, a group formed to examine the causes and consequences of the Vietnam War, has taken additional measures. Since 1991, it has supplied prosthetic limbs for Vietnamese and Cambodian mine victims.

SKILLBUILDER
INTERPRETING CHARTS
How were the Vietcong able to sustain themselves underground for such long periods of time?

Tunnels of the Vietcong

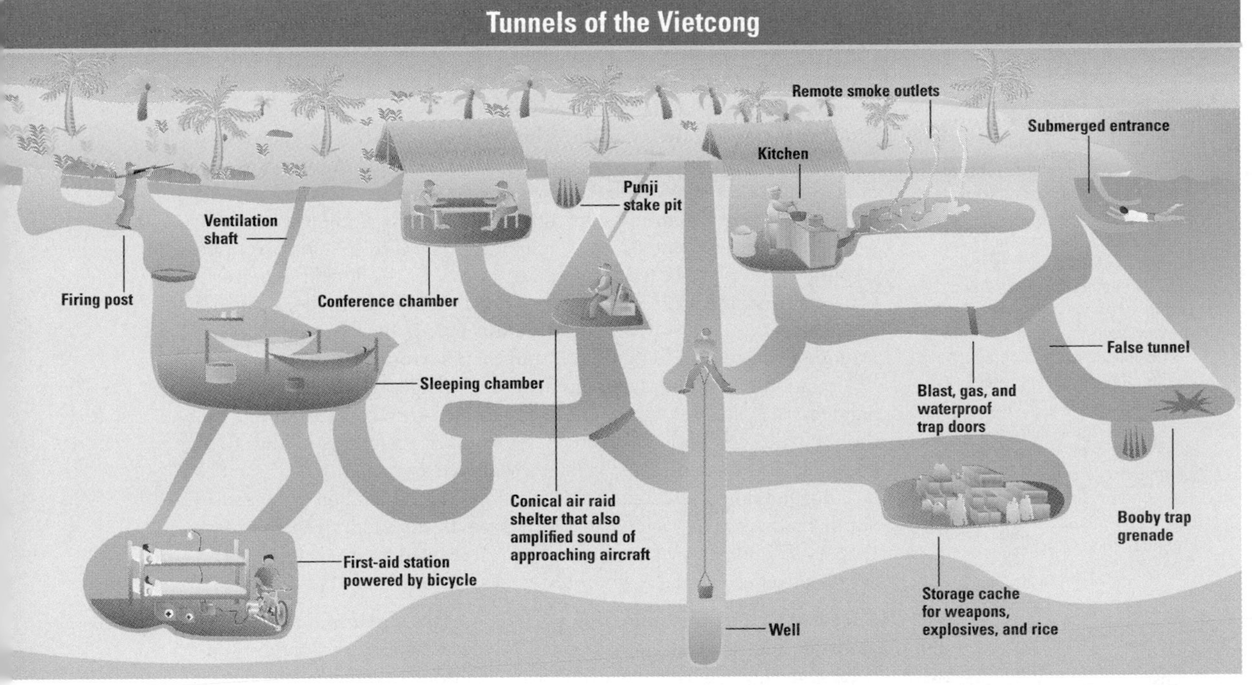

(continued from page 730)

▶ *Discussing Key Ideas*

- Vietcong military tactics stymie U.S. forces.
- U.S. chemical warfare harms the rural population and landscape.
- The frustrations of guerrilla combat, brutal jungle conditions, and the war's stalemate cause a decline in the morale of U.S. troops.

NOW & THEN
Land Mines

Critical Thinking: Recognizing Effects Ask students to explain the long-term consequences of the use of land mines. *Possible Responses: Unexploded mines remain a problem long after peace has been achieved; the mines may kill or mutilate friends as well as foes.*

HISTORY FROM VISUALS
Tunnels of the Vietcong

Reading the Chart As students read the labels identifying specific features and functions, remind them to visualize the tunnel system as the sum of its parts.

Extension Ask students to make two-column charts like the one below, in which they list the devices that protected tunnel users.

Protective Device	Function

TEACHING OPTIONS

Teaching Gifted and Talented Students

Oral Readings Salvador Gonzalez's letter quoted on this page is from *Dear America: Letters Home from Vietnam* (New York: Norton, 1985). Have students find this book or another collection of letters written during the Vietnam War. Ask them to present oral readings of letters to the class. Review the letters that students choose to ensure that their content and language are appropriate for a classroom presentation.

IN-DEPTH RESOURCES: UNIT 6
Primary Source: Letter from a soldier in Vietnam, p. 45

Making Connections Across the Curriculum

Geography Vietnam has a tropical climate, with heavy rainfall supporting lush jungles in many areas. In southern Vietnam, humidity is high for most of the year, with about 80 inches of annual rainfall in Ho Chi Minh City (formerly Saigon); temperatures rarely drop below the high 70s. In Hanoi to the north, average temperatures are somewhat lower, though rainfall is still plentiful. Monsoons, or seasonal winds, and typhoons affect Vietnam's climate. Summer monsoons bring the heaviest rainfall; typhoons often strike the coasts.

NOW & THEN
Agent Orange

Critical Thinking: Analyzing Motives Have a student clarify why the U.S. military dropped so much Agent Orange. *Possible Responses: To destroy the dense jungle foliage that concealed Vietcong guerrillas; to prevent the enemy from growing food.*

THE WAR IN VIETNAM CBS News video on Agent Orange; "Vietnam Deforestation Scars Expected to Last a Century"

MORE ABOUT . . .
Philip Caputo

After returning from Vietnam in 1967, Caputo worked briefly as a corporate publicist and then became a reporter with the *Chicago Tribune.* In 1973 he won a Pulitzer Prize for his reporting on primary-election fraud; four years later he won literary acclaim with his Vietnam memoir *A Rumor of War* (see page 755). Since then Caputo has published several novels, often set in war-torn lands, and *Means of Escape* (1991), a fictionalized memoir based on his experiences as a war correspondent.

away from our land, the more we burrowed into it," recalled Major Nguyen Quot of the Vietcong Army.

A FRUSTRATING WAR OF ATTRITION Not only may the United States have underestimated the Vietcong's ingenuity, but it also miscalculated the enemy's resolve. Westmoreland's strategy for defeating the Vietcong was to destroy their morale through a war of attrition, or the gradual wearing down of the enemy by continuous harassment. Introducing the concept of the body count, or the tracking of Vietcong killed in battle, the general believed that as the number of Vietcong dead rose, the enemy's surrender would become inevitable.

However, the Vietcong had no intention of quitting their fight. What Ho Chi Minh had told the French in the 1940s applied also to the Americans, "You can kill ten of my men for every one I kill of yours," he warned, "but even at those odds, you will lose and I will win." Despite absorbing significant casualties and the relentless pounding from U.S. bombers, the Vietcong—who received supplies from China and the Soviet Union—remained defiant. Defense Secretary McNamara confessed his early frustration over the Vietcong's resilience to a reporter in 1966. "I didn't think these people had the capacity to fight this way," he said. "If I had thought they would take this punishment and fight this well, . . . I would have thought differently at the start."

THINK THROUGH HISTORY
B. *Identifying Problems* *Why did the U.S. forces have difficulty fighting the Vietcong?*

B. Answer Because of the Vietcong's guerrilla tactics and their superior knowledge of the terrain.

General Westmoreland would say later that the United States never lost a battle in Vietnam. While the general's words may have been true, they underscored the degree to which America misunderstood the Vietcong. While the United States viewed the war strictly as a military struggle, the Vietcong saw it as a battle for their very existence, and they were ready to pay any price for victory. "The Communists were prepared to go on and on," explained Stanley Karnow, author of *Vietnam: A History*, "and they had factored their human costs into the equation."

NOW & THEN

AGENT ORANGE

The 13 million gallons of Agent Orange dumped on the jungles of Vietnam to destroy the foliage ended up harming some U.S. soldiers as well. After the war ended, researchers believed that toxins in the weed killer led to a wide range of health defects in humans, including skin diseases and cancer.

U.S. veterans eventually brought a class-action lawsuit against seven makers of Agent Orange. The suit was settled out of court with the establishment of a $180 million fund to compensate the roughly 250,000 veterans who claimed to be affected.

In addition, Congress in 1991 passed a bill providing disability benefits to veterans suffering from certain illnesses that were said to be related to exposure to Agent Orange.

THE BATTLE FOR "HEARTS AND MINDS" Another key part of the American strategy was to keep the Vietcong from winning the support of South Vietnam's rural population. Edward G. Lansdale, who helped found the special fighting unit known as the Green Berets, stressed the plan's importance. "Just remember this. Communist guerrillas hide among the people. If you win the people over to your side, the Communist guerrillas have no place to hide."

The campaign to win the "hearts and minds" of the South Vietnamese villagers proved more difficult than the Americans imagined. Some of the tactics the Americans used to battle the Vietcong also harmed much of the rural population. For instance, in their attempt to expose Vietcong tunnels and hideouts, the U.S. planes dropped **napalm,** a gasoline-based bomb that set fire to the jungle. American planes also sprayed **Agent Orange,** a leaf-killing toxic chemical that devastated the landscape. The saturation use of these weapons often wounded villagers and left villages and their surrounding area in ruins.

In addition, attempts to control the villages could turn heavy-handed. U.S. soldiers conducted **search-and-destroy missions,** uprooting villagers with suspected ties to the Vietcong, killing their livestock, and burning their villages. Many villagers fled into the cities or refugee camps, creating by 1967 more than 3 million refugees in South Vietnam. The irony of the strategy was summed up in February 1968 by a U.S. major whose forces had just leveled the town of Ben Tre: "We had to destroy the town in order to save it."

SINKING MORALE The frustrations of guerrilla warfare, the brutal jungle conditions, and the failure to make substantial headway against the enemy took their toll on the U.S. troops' morale. Philip Caputo, a marine lieutenant in

TEACHING OPTIONS

Making Connections Across Time

Agent Orange and Gulf War Syndrome Scientists took years to prove a link between exposure to Agent Orange and the diseases veterans claimed it caused. In 1993 the Veterans Administration expanded the list of illnesses for which Vietnam veterans exposed to Agent Orange could be compensated. Recently, many Persian Gulf War veterans have suffered from ailments possibly stemming from exposure to Iraqi chemical or biological weapons. An advisory committee appointed by President Clinton found no evidence of a "syndrome" but did recommend a more thorough investigation.

Making Connections Across Cultures

Vietnamese Family Names Vietnamese names, like Chinese and Japanese names, begin with family names, which are followed by given names. Thus, *Nguyen* was the family name of Nguyen Cao Ky, and *Diem* and *Nhu* were given names of the brothers Ngo Dinh Diem and Ngo Dinh Nhu. Because many Vietnamese share each family name (*Nguyen,* for example, is very common), Americans generally referred to Vietnam's leaders by given names.

Vietnam who later wrote several books about the war, summarized the soldiers' growing disillusionment, "When we marched into the rice paddies . . . we carried, along with our packs and rifles, the implicit convictions that the Vietcong could be quickly beaten. We kept the packs and rifles; the convictions, we lost."

As the war continued, American morale dropped steadily, as many soldiers turned to alcohol, marijuana, and other drugs. Low morale led a few soldiers even to murder their superior officers by "fragging" them, an action in which a soldier lobbed a fragmentation grenade (one that left no fingerprints) at an officer during battle. Morale would worsen during the later years of the war when soldiers realized they were fighting even as their government was negotiating for peace.

Another obstacle to successfully fighting the war was the continuing corruption and instability of the South Vietnamese government. Nguyen Cao Ky, a flamboyant air force general, led the government from 1965 to 1967. Ignoring U.S. pleas to step down, Ky refused to retire in favor of an elected civilian government. Mass demonstrations began, and by May of 1966, Buddhist monks were once again burning themselves in protest against the South Vietnamese government. South Vietnam was fighting a civil war within a civil war, leaving U.S. officials confused and angry.

C. Answer The frustrations of guerrilla warfare, the jungle conditions, and the continuing instability of the South Vietnamese government.

THINK THROUGH HISTORY
C. *Analyzing Causes* *What factors led to the low morale of U.S. troops?*

A soldier with the 61st Infantry Division wears symbols of both war and peace on his chest.

Despite the low morale among some U.S. troops, most soldiers firmly believed in their cause—to halt the spread of communism. They took patriotic pride in fulfilling their duty, just as their fathers had done in World War II.

Many American soldiers fought courageously. Particularly heroic were the thousands of soldiers who endured years of torture and confinement as prisoners of war. In 1966, Navy pilot Gerald Coffee's plane was shot down during a bombing mission over North Vietnam. Coffee spent the next seven years—until he was released in 1973 as part of a cease-fire agreement—struggling to stay alive in an enemy prison camp.

> **A PERSONAL VOICE**
> My clothes were filthy and ragged. . . . With no boots, my socks—which I'd been able to salvage—were barely recognizable. . . . Only a few threads around my toes kept them spread over my feet; some protection, at least, as I shivered through the cold nights curled up tightly on my morguelike slab. . . . My conditions and predicament were so foreign to me, so stifling, so overwhelming. I'd never been so hungry, so grimy, and in such pain.
>
> GERALD COFFEE, *Beyond Survival*

"We had to destroy the town in order to save it."

A U.S. MAJOR IN 1968

The Early War at Home

The Johnson administration thought the war would end quickly. When it dragged on, public support began to waver, and Johnson's domestic programs began to unravel.

THE GREAT SOCIETY SUFFERS As the number of U.S. troops in Vietnam continued to mount, the war grew more costly. As a result, the nation's economy began to suffer. The inflation rate, which had remained at 2 percent through most of the early 1960s, nearly tripled by 1969. President Johnson had been determined to pay for both the war and his Great Society programs.

MORE ABOUT . . .
Nguyen Cao Ky

Nguyen Cao Ky, a dashing pilot, along with his glamorous wife, liked to be seen in fashionable clothes. He was also rumored to be involved in the flourishing drug trade that preyed on U.S. troops during the Vietnam War. He was finally pressured from office in 1967, when the army general Nguyen Van Thieu was elected president of South Vietnam.

The Early War at Home

▶ ***Starting with the Student***
Ask students to describe combat scenes they have seen on the TV news.

- What do these broadcast images communicate about the grim reality of warfare?

▶ ***Discussing Key Ideas***

- War costs begin to drain the U.S. economy and undercut domestic reform programs.
- TV broadcasts of live combat cause public support for the war to wane.

Block Schedule TEACHING OPTION **Time Needed: 30 Minutes**

Cooperative Activity: Simulating a TV Interview

Task: Student pairs will role-play a war correspondent interviewing a U.S. soldier in Vietnam for a TV broadcast.

Purpose: To gain insight into journalists' and soldiers' perspectives on the Vietnam War around 1967.

Activity: Partners should decide which role each student will play. The student posing as the journalist should prepare a list of interview questions based on information in this section and other sources. The student portraying a soldier should research firsthand accounts of combat experiences during the war. The pair should then collaborate on writing a script of the interview, using a question-and-answer format. Allow time for partners to rehearse their interviews before performing them for the class. Students can present live interviews or create videotapes or audiotapes to play.

ALTERNATIVE ASSESSMENT BOOK
Standards for Evaluating a Cooperative Activity

MORE ABOUT . . .

J. William Fulbright

Best known for initiating the international scholarship program that bears his name, Fulbright served five terms as U.S. senator from Arkansas and was a mentor to the young Bill Clinton. Though he voted for the Tonkin Gulf Resolution in 1964, his opinion that the Johnson administration had deceived Congress prompted him to hold the 1966 hearings that lent respectability to the antiwar movement.

ASSESS & RETEACH

Section 2 Assessment

Have pairs of students evaluate each other's responses before finalizing them.

Self-Assessment

Have students make a time line of events, tracing U.S. involvement in Vietnam from the Truman administration to the Johnson administration. Have them identify events that they find difficult to understand.

Section Quiz

FORMAL ASSESSMENT
Section Quiz, p. 271

Reteach

Use the Guided Reading worksheet for Section 2 to help review the main ideas of the section.

IN-DEPTH RESOURCES: UNIT 6
Guided Reading, p. 36

CLOSE

Despite President Johnson's escalation of U.S. involvement in the war in Vietnam, the fighting did not move beyond a stalemate. Support for the war among U.S. citizens began to erode because of the war's toll on the U.S. economy and TV coverage of combat.

However, the cost of financing the Vietnam War became too great. In August of 1967, Johnson asked for a tax increase to help fund the war and to keep inflation in check. Congressional conservatives agreed, but only after demanding and receiving a $6 billion reduction in funding for Great Society programs. Vietnam was slowly claiming an early casualty: Johnson's grand vision of domestic reform.

Each night, Americans watched the images—which often were graphic and disturbing—of the Vietnam War.

THE LIVING-ROOM WAR By 1967, a majority of Americans still supported the war. However, cracks were beginning to show. The media, mainly television, helped heighten the nation's growing concern about the war. Vietnam was America's first "living-room war," in which footage of combat appeared nightly on the news in millions of homes. And what people saw on their television screens seemed to contradict the optimistic war scenario that the Johnson administration was painting.

Quoting body-count statistics that showed large numbers of Communists dying in battle, General Westmoreland continually reported that a Vietcong surrender was imminent. Victory "lies within our grasp—the enemy's hopes are bankrupt," he declared. Defense Secretary McNamara backed up the general's rosy analyses, saying that he could see "the light at the end of the tunnel."

However, the repeated television images of Americans in body bags told a different story. Communists may have been dying, but so too were Americans—nearly 16,000 between 1965 and 1967. Critics charged that a **credibility gap** was growing between what the Johnson administration reported and what was really happening.

One such critic was Senator J. William Fulbright, chairman of the powerful Senate Foreign Relations Committee. Fulbright, a former Johnson ally, charged the president with a "lack of candor" in portraying the war effort. In early 1966, the senator conducted a series of televised committee hearings in which he called forth members of the Johnson administration to defend their Vietnam policies. The Fulbright hearings delivered few major revelations, but they did contribute to the growing doubts about the war. One housewife appeared to capture the mood of Middle America when she told an interviewer, "I want to get out, but I don't want to give in."

By 1967, however, a small force outside of mainstream America, mainly from the ranks of the nation's youth, already had begun actively protesting the war. Their voices would grow louder and capture the attention of the entire nation.

D. Answer The continued reports of American casualties, television coverage, and the Johnson administration's growing credibility gap.

THINK THROUGH HISTORY
D. Recognizing Effects *What led to the growing concern in America about the Vietnam War?*

Section 2 Assessment

1. TERMS & NAMES
Identify:
- Robert McNamara
- Dean Rusk
- William Westmoreland
- napalm
- Agent Orange
- search-and-destroy mission
- credibility gap

2. SUMMARIZING Re-create the dual concept web below on your own paper. Then, show key military tactics and weapons of the Vietcong and Americans.

3. EVALUATING Evaluate the U.S. strategy for conducting the Vietnam War.

THINK ABOUT
- the war of attrition
- the battle for the "hearts and minds" of the South Vietnamese
- the support for South Vietnamese military leaders

4. FORMING GENERALIZATIONS What were the effects of the nightly TV coverage of the Vietnam War?

THINK ABOUT
- the image on the TV screen at the top of this page
- television images of Americans in body bags
- the Johnson administration's credibility gap

ANSWERS

1. TERMS & NAMES
- Robert McNamara, p. 730
- Dean Rusk, p. 730
- William Westmoreland, p. 730
- napalm, p. 732
- Agent Orange, p. 732
- search-and-destroy mission, p. 732
- credibility gap, p. 734

2. SUMMARIZING
Possible Responses: Vietcong: tactics—ambushes, hit-and-run attacks; weapons—booby traps, land mines. U.S.: tactics—large-scale bombing, search-and-destroy missions; weapons—napalm, Agent Orange, bombers.

3. EVALUATING
Possible Responses: The U.S. strategy seemed to fuel frustration. Military planners failed to take into account the Vietcong's unwillingness to surrender; the use of napalm, Agent Orange, and search-and-destroy missions undermined attempts to win the hearts and minds of the South Vietnamese; and continued support of a corrupt South Vietnamese government hindered the U.S. war effort.

4. FORMING GENERALIZATIONS
Possible Responses: Watching the graphic images of the Vietnam War each night caused many Americans to question the war; many Americans began to doubt the Johnson administration's reports that the enemy was near defeat, so that there was a growing credibility gap between what the administration reported about Vietnam and what seemed to be really happening.

3 A Nation Divided

TERMS & NAMES
- New Left
- Students for a Democratic Society
- Free Speech Movement
- dove
- hawk

LEARN ABOUT the growing antiwar movement in America
TO UNDERSTAND how the war sharply divided the American public.

ONE AMERICAN'S STORY

In 1969, Stephan Gubar was told to report to his local draft board. The young man was being called for possible military service in Vietnam. Gubar, 22, a veteran of the civil rights movement, had filed as a conscientious objector (CO), or someone who opposed war on the basis of religious or moral beliefs. Gubar was granted 1-A-O status, which meant that while he would not be forced to carry a weapon, he still qualified for noncombatant military duty. In 1969, he was drafted.

Gubar did his basic training at Fort Sam Houston, Texas. Along with other conscientious objectors, he received special training as a medic. Gubar described the memorable day when his training ended.

A PERSONAL VOICE

The thing that stands out most was . . . being really scared, being in formation and listening to the names and assignments being called. The majority of COs I knew had orders cut for Vietnam. And even though I could hear that happening, even though I could hear that every time a CO's name came up, the orders were cut for Vietnam, I still thought there was a possibility I might not go. Then, when they called my name and said "Vietnam," . . . I went to a phone and I called my wife. It was a tremendous shock.

STEPHAN GUBAR, quoted in *Days of Decision*

Stephan Gubar

Gubar was not alone in his anxiety. As American involvement in the Vietnam War escalated—and American casualties mounted—young men all over the country began to worry that they would be called on to fight and die in Vietnam. While many eligible young Americans proudly went off to war, some found ways to avoid serving, and still others simply refused to go. As the war progressed, it spurred a growing protest movement in America that sharply divided the country between supporters and opponents of the government's policy in Vietnam.

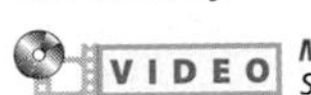
MATTERS OF CONSCIENCE
Stephan Gubar and the Vietnam War

A Working-Class War

The idea of fighting a war in a faraway place for what some believed was a questionable cause prompted a number of young Americans to avoid going to Vietnam. Because many middle-class and upper-class American youths were able—through college and other means—to avoid military service, most of the soldiers who fought in Vietnam were from the lower economic classes of American society.

A "MANIPULATABLE" DRAFT Most soldiers who fought in Vietnam were drafted into combat under the country's Selective Service System. Under this system, which had been established in the 1940s during World War II, all males had to register with their local draft boards when they turned 18. In the event of a war, the board called men between the ages of 18 and 26 into military service as they were needed. In a sign of America's growing doubts about the Vietnam War, many young men sought deferments from the draft.

Thousands of men attempted to find ways around the draft, which one man characterized as a "very manipulatable system." Because many medical excuses were honored, some men sought out sympathetic doctors to obtain medical

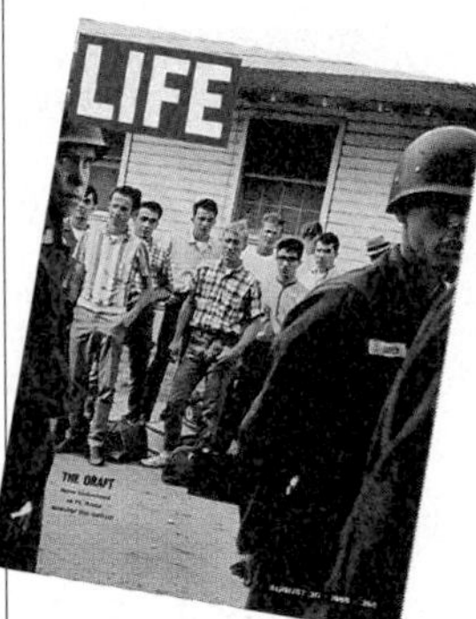

A *Life* magazine cover shows new draft inductees arriving for training at Fort Knox, Kentucky.

Section 3 Overview

OBJECTIVES

1. To explain the draft policies that made the Vietnam War a working-class war.
2. To trace the roots of opposition to the war.
3. To describe the antiwar movement.

SKILLBUILDER

- Interpreting graphs, p. 736

CRITICAL THINKING

- Theme: Civil Rights, p. 736
- Theme: Democracy in America, p. 737
- Finding main ideas, p. 738
- Contrasting, p. 739
- Identifying problems, p. 740
- Summarizing, p. 740
- Making decisions, p. 740
- Forming opinions, p. 740

FOCUS & MOTIVATE

5-MINUTE WARM-UP

Making Inferences
To understand the draft policies during the Vietnam War, have students read One American's Story on page 735 and answer these questions.

1. Why was Gubar shocked when he heard that he was being sent to Vietnam?
2. What did Gubar probably have to do when he got to Vietnam?

WARM-UP TRANSPARENCY 22

Starting with the Student
Watch the video "Matters of Conscience" to find out more about Stephan Gubar.

- Using the *Teacher's Resource Book* as a guide, have the class engage in extension activities involving primary sources.

***AMERICAN STORIES* video series**
"Matters of Conscience"
Videocassette: Volume 5

Videodisc: Disc 3, Side B, Chapter 3

SECTION 3 RESOURCES

PRINT RESOURCES

IN-DEPTH RESOURCES: UNIT 6
Guided Reading, p. 37
Primary Sources: Protest buttons, p. 46; The New Left, p. 47

READING STUDY GUIDE, p. 227

ACCESS FOR STUDENTS ACQUIRING ENGLISH
Guided Reading (Spanish), p. 243

SPANISH READING STUDY GUIDE, p. 227

FORMAL ASSESSMENT
Section Quiz, p. 272

ALTERNATIVE ASSESSMENT BOOK
See forms for supporting and scoring alternative activities.

TECHNOLOGY RESOURCES

VIDEO *American Stories* video series
American Portfolio: A Videodisc for U.S. History user's guide, pp. 246–247, 252–253, 255

INTERNET http://www.mlushistory.com

OBJECTIVE

① INSTRUCT

A Working-Class War

▶***Discussing Key Ideas***

- Draft policies favor young men from privileged backgrounds.
- Most American soldiers in Vietnam are minorities and lower-class whites.
- African Americans make up a disproportionately high percentage of U.S. ground combat troops.
- Most American women in Vietnam serve as military nurses or volunteers.

IN-DEPTH RESOURCES: UNIT 6
Guided Reading, p. 37

ACCESS FOR STUDENTS ACQUIRING ENGLISH
Guided Reading (Spanish), p. 243

HISTORY FROM VISUALS

U.S. Troop Strength in Vietnam

Reading the Graph Explain that line graphs show changes or trends over time. This line graph provides students with an instant overview of the steady increase (upward slope) in troops from 1963 to 1968, followed by the steady withdrawal of troops (downward slope).

Extension Have students convert the line graph into a bar graph.

deferments. Different draft boards had different qualifications, which prompted some men to change residences in order to stand before more lenient boards. Some Americans even joined the National Guard or Coast Guard, which often secured a deferment from service in Vietnam.

One of the most common ways to avoid the draft was to receive a college deferment, by which a young man enrolled in a university could put off his military service. Because most university students during the 1960s were white and some were financially well-off, many of the men who fought in Vietnam were lower-class whites or minorities who were less privileged economically. To be sure, a number of Americans who were drafted proudly went to Vietnam. Others volunteered to fight, their reasons ranging from a sense of duty to a feeling of patriotism. Nonetheless, with almost 80 percent of American soldiers coming from lower economic levels, Vietnam was a working-class war.

AFRICAN AMERICANS AND WOMEN IN VIETNAM African Americans served in disproportionate numbers in ground combat troops. During the first several years of the war, blacks accounted for more than 20 percent of American combat deaths despite representing only about 10 percent of the U.S. population. The Defense Department took steps to correct that imbalance by instituting a draft lottery system in 1969. Early in the war, though, the large number of black casualties angered African-American leaders, including Martin Luther King, Jr. King had refrained from speaking out against the war for fear that it would divert attention from the civil rights movement. However, he could no longer remain silent about the news he was hearing from Vietnam. In 1967 he lashed out against what he called the "cruel irony" of American blacks dying for a country that still regarded them as second-class citizens.

A. Answer American blacks were fighting and dying for a country that still discriminated against them.

THINK THROUGH HISTORY
A. THEME **Civil Rights** *Why did King call the disproportionate participation of African Americans in Vietnam a "cruel irony"?*

A PERSONAL VOICE

> We were taking the young black men who had been crippled by our society and sending them eight thousand miles away to guarantee liberties in Southeast Asia which they had not found in Southwest Georgia and East Harlem. . . . We have been repeatedly faced with the cruel irony of watching Negro and white boys on TV screens as they kill and die together for a nation that has been unable to seat them together in the same schools.
>
> **DR. MARTIN LUTHER KING, JR.,** quoted in *America's Vietnam War: A Narrative History*

Many African Americans experienced the same racism in Vietnam that they endured at home. Throughout the war, racial tensions between white and black soldiers ran high in many platoons. In some cases, the hostility led to violence. In 1967, a race riot erupted at the U.S. Army

Skillbuilder Answer
1965 through 1968.

SKILLBUILDER
INTERPRETING GRAPHS
What years signaled a rapid increase in the deployment of U.S. troops?

U.S. Troop Strength in Vietnam

536,000
600
500
400
300
200
100
0
Troops in Thousands
less than 25,000
1963 1964 1965 1966 1967 1968 1969 1970 1971 1972
Year-end figures

Source: *Statistical Abstract of the United States, 1976*

Despite racial tensions, black and white soldiers fought side by side in Vietnam.

TEACHING OPTION

Exploring Themes

Civil Rights By the late 1960s, Dr. Martin Luther King, Jr., and other prominent civil rights leaders were seeing the Vietnam War as a major setback in African Americans' struggle to achieve equality and justice. In a 1968 essay, King explained his opposition to the war: "The Great Society has become a victim of the war. I think there was a sincere desire in this country four or five years ago to move toward a genuinely great society, and I have little doubt that there would have been a gradual increase in Federal expenditures in this direction, rather than the gradual decline that has occurred, if the Vietnam War had been avoided.

"One of the incongruities of this situation is the fact that such a large number of the soldiers in the Armed Forces in Vietnam—especially the front-line soldiers who are actually doing the fighting—are Negroes. Negroes have always held the hope that if they really demonstrate they are great soldiers and if they really fight for America and help save American democracy, then when they come back home, America will treat them better. This has not been the case."

stockade at Long Binh, Vietnam. Two years later, black and white marines returning from war clashed at Camp Lejeune, North Carolina. The racism that gripped many military units was yet another factor that led to low troop morale in Vietnam.

While the U.S. military in the 1960s did not allow females to serve in combat, nearly 7,500 women served in Vietnam as army and navy nurses. Thousands more women volunteered their services in Vietnam to the American Red Cross and the United Services Organization (USO), which delivered hospitality and entertainment to the troops.

As the men who marched off to Vietnam fought against Communist guerrillas, some of the men who stayed home, as well as many women, waged a battle of their own. Shortly after U.S. troops began arriving in Vietnam, college campuses across the country erupted in protest as many of the nation's youths began to voice their opposition to the war.

Two U.S. nurses rest at Cam Ranh Bay, the major entry point for American supplies and troops in South Vietnam.

The Roots of Opposition

In the years prior to America's involvement in Vietnam, an atmosphere of protest already existed in many college campuses. In contrast to the general contentment that characterized the youths of the 1950s, students in the early 1960s had become more active socially and politically. Some had participated in the civil rights struggle, while others had answered President Kennedy's call to more actively pursue public service. By the mid-sixties, many youths believed the nation to be in need of fundamental change.

THE NEW LEFT The growing youth movement of the 1960s became known as the **New Left,** which encompassed many different activist groups and organizations. The movement was "new" in relation to the "old left" of the 1930s, which generally tried to move the nation toward socialism, and, in some cases, communism. While the New Left movement did not preach socialism, its followers demanded sweeping changes in American society.

Voicing these demands was one of the better-known New Left organizations, **Students for a Democratic Society** (SDS). Tom Hayden and Al Haber, two University of Michigan students, founded the group in 1959. Three years later, they convened a meeting in Port Huron, Michigan, to draft the group's declaration. Known as the Port Huron Statement, it began: "We are people of this generation, bred in at least modest comfort, housed now in universities, looking uncomfortably to the world we inherit." The statement, which charged that corporations and large government institutions had taken over America, called for a restoration of "participatory democracy" and greater individual freedom.

B. Answer Corporations and government institutions were growing too dominant and were inhibiting personal freedom.

THINK THROUGH HISTORY
B. THEME ***Democracy in America*** *What concerns did the New Left movement voice about American democratic society?*

In 1964, another New Left group gained prominence. At the University of California at Berkeley, the **Free Speech Movement** (FSM) grew out of a clash between students and administrators over free speech on campus. Led by Mario Savio, a philosophy major and a dynamic speaker, the FSM soon focused its criticism on what it called the American "machine," the nation's faceless and powerful business and government institutions.

CAMPUS ACTIVISM The strategies and tactics of the FSM and SDS soon spread to colleges throughout the country. There, students addressed mostly campus issues, such as dress codes, curfews, dormitory regulations, and mandatory Reserved Officer Training Corps (ROTC) programs. At Fairleigh Dickinson University in New Jersey, students marched merely as "an expression of general student discontent."

OBJECTIVE
② INSTRUCT

The Roots of Opposition

▶ ***Starting with the Student***
Ask students what changes they think are needed in contemporary society.

- How do these changes compare with those that young people advocated in the 1960s?

▶ ***Discussing Key Ideas***

- The New Left movement, including such activist groups as Students for a Democratic Society (SDS) and the Free Speech Movement (FSM), pushes for social and political change.
- SDS and FSM tactics spread to college campuses nationwide.
- College students begin joining together to protest the Vietnam War.

IN-DEPTH RESOURCES: UNIT 6
Primary Source: The New Left, p. 47

MORE ABOUT . . .
Tom Hayden

Hayden's antiwar activities included visits to North Vietnam in 1965 and 1967. Though some Americans condemned these trips, he did succeed in bringing back the first three released American POWs. He married the actress and activist Jane Fonda in 1973. During the couple's 16-year marriage, which ended in divorce, Hayden became a California state legislator and served for many years.

TEACHING OPTIONS

Teaching Less Proficient Readers

Questioning Techniques To help students build their comprehension skills, have student pairs follow these steps:

1. Read pages 737–740.
2. Change the headings and subheadings into questions beginning with the five *w's—who, what, where, when,* and *why.* Sample questions for this page follow:
   - What were the roots of opposition to the Vietnam War?
   - Who joined the New Left movement?
   - Why did campus activism spread in the mid-1960s?
3. Work together to answer the questions.

Making Connections Across Time

Women in the Military Women have had greater opportunities in the U.S. military since the Vietnam War era. In 1970, just over 40,000 women were in uniform; in 1990 there were more than 225,000. Women have advanced in all branches of the armed forces. For example, Carol Mutter, a U.S. Marine, became the first woman three-star general when she was promoted to that rank in 1996. The service academies have also opened their doors to women: West Point's first woman valedictorian graduated in June 1995. Students may wish to discuss problems still faced by women in the military—for example, resistance to women in combat duty.

OBJECTIVE

③ INSTRUCT

The Protest Movement Emerges

▶ ***Starting with the Student***

- What are some messages expressed in rock music today?
- What effects do social issues have on popular culture?

▶ ***Discussing Key Ideas***

- Campus protests mount as more college students become eligible for the draft.
- More young Americans resist the draft.
- The American public becomes deeply divided into opponents and supporters of the war.

IN-DEPTH RESOURCES: UNIT 6
Primary Source: Protest buttons, p. 46

HISTORICAL SPOTLIGHT

"The Ballad of the Green Berets"

Critical Thinking: Analyzing Tell students that the hit single "The Ballad of the Green Berets" was featured in the 1968 movie *The Green Berets,* starring John Wayne—an actor famous for his manly, tough-guy roles. Explain that some movie critics condemned the film as propaganda. Ask students if they think the song lyrics quoted on this page might also be considered propaganda. Why or why not?

With the onset of the Vietnam War, the students suddenly found a galvanizing issue. At campuses across the country, American youths joined together to protest the war.

The Protest Movement Emerges

Throughout the spring of 1965, a number of colleges began to host "teach-ins" to protest the war. At the University of Michigan, where only a year before, President Johnson had announced his sweeping Great Society program, teachers and students now assailed his war policy. "This is no longer a casual form of campus spring fever," journalist James Reston noted about the growing demonstrations. As the war continued, the protests grew and divided the country between those Americans who supported their government's policy in Vietnam and those who opposed it.

THE MOVEMENT GROWS In April of 1965, SDS helped organize a march on Washington, D.C., by some 20,000 protesters. By November of that year, a protest rally in Washington drew more than 30,000. Then, in January of 1966, the Johnson administration changed deferments for college students. Students now had to be in good academic standing to defer their military service. Campuses around the country erupted in protest. SDS called for civil disobedience at Selective Service Centers and openly counseled students to flee to Canada or Sweden. By the end of 1967, SDS had chapters on nearly 300 campuses.

The growing number of youths who opposed the war did so for different reasons. The most common reason for opposition was the belief that the conflict in Vietnam was basically a civil war and that the U.S. military had no business there. Others argued that the United States could not police the world and that the Vietnam War was draining American strength in important parts of the world such as Europe and the Middle East. Still others saw the war simply as morally unjust.

THINK THROUGH HISTORY
C. *Finding Main Ideas* *For what reasons did the protesters oppose the Vietnam War?*

C. Answer They felt that America had no business in Vietnam; the war was draining American strength from other parts of the world; the war was morally unjust.

HISTORICAL SPOTLIGHT

"THE BALLAD OF THE GREEN BERETS"

Not every Vietnam-era pop song about war was an antiwar song. At the top of the charts for five weeks in 1966 was "The Ballad of the Green Berets" by Staff Sergeant Barry Sadler of the U.S. Army Special Forces, known as the Green Berets:

Fighting soldiers from the sky,
Fearless men who jump and die,
Men who mean just what they say,
The brave men of the Green Beret.

The recording sold over a million copies in its first two weeks of release and was *Billboard* magazine's song of the year.

As the antiwar movement grew, it reached outside the college campuses and touched other groups in society. Small numbers of returning veterans also began to protest the war. Some antiwar veterans picketed the White House and tried to return their medals to President Johnson. In addition, many musicians took up the antiwar cause. Folk singers such as Peter, Paul and Mary and Joan Baez led the way as music became a popular protest vehicle. Soon protest songs even conquered the pop-music charts. Number one in September 1965 was "Eve of Destruction," in which singer Barry McGuire stressed the ironic fact that in the 1960s an American male could be drafted at 18 but had to be 21 to vote:

The Eastern world, it is exploding,
Violence flaring, bullets loading,
You're old enough to kill, but not for voting,
You don't believe in war, but what's that gun you're toting?

FROM PROTEST TO RESISTANCE From 1965 to 1967, the antiwar movement intensified. "We were having *no* effect on U.S. policy," recalled one protest leader. "So we thought we had to up the ante." In the spring of 1967, nearly half a million protesters of all ages gathered in New York's Central Park. Shouting "Burn cards, not people" and "Hell, no, we won't go!" hundreds tossed their draft cards into a bonfire. Many in the park were protesting for the first time. A housewife from New Jersey told a reporter, "So many of us are frustrated. We want to criticize this war because we think it's wrong, but we want to do it in the framework of loyalty."

TEACHING OPTIONS

Making Connections Across the Curriculum

Music Both Joan Baez and the folk-rock group Peter, Paul & Mary sang many songs composed by Bob Dylan. In fact, Peter, Paul & Mary's 1963 rendition of Dylan's protest song "Blowin' in the Wind" was the fastest-selling single in the history of Warner Brothers. Yet Dylan himself, the great folk-rock composer of the 1960s, soon moved away from the protest movement. "What Joan Baez is doing," he told the biographer Anthony Scaduto, "and all those people demonstrating, they're not gonna save the world. It's not true they can change men's hearts."

Making Connections Across the Curriculum

Literature Norman Mailer recorded his experiences during the October 21 march on the Pentagon—and his subsequent night in jail—in a 1968 book, *The Armies of the Night: History as a Novel, the Novel as History.* As the subtitle reveals, the book experiments with the boundaries between fiction and nonfiction. Winning both the Pulitzer Prize and the National Book Award, *The Armies of the Night* was praised by the critic Richard Gilman as a "rather wonderful achievement" in which "history and personality confront each other with a new sense of liberation."

Others were more radical in their view. David Harris, who would spend 20 months in jail for refusing to serve in Vietnam, explained his motives.

A PERSONAL VOICE

Theoretically, I can accept the notion that there are circumstances in which you have to kill people. I could not accept the notion that Vietnam was one of those circumstances. And to me that left the option of either sitting by and watching what was an enormous injustice . . . or [finding] some way to commit myself against it. And the position that I felt comfortable with in committing myself against it was total noncooperation—I was not going to be part of the machine.

DAVID HARRIS, quoted in *The War Within*

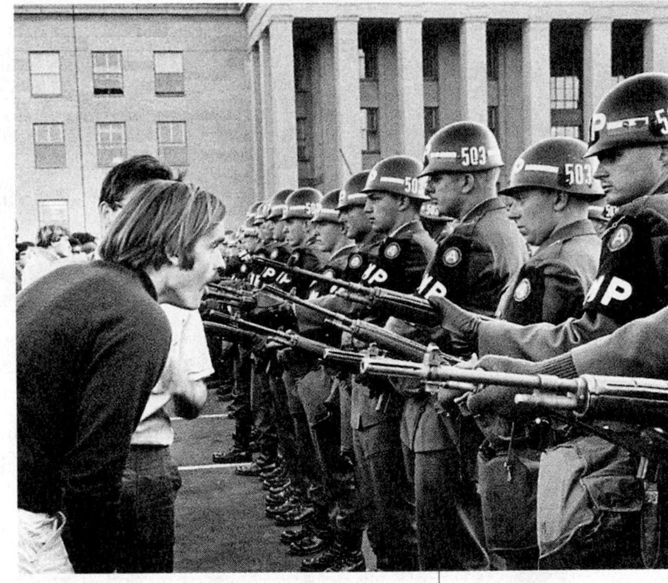

In a scene that grew more common as the Vietnam War dragged on, antiwar demonstrators in the United States confront military police.

Draft resistance continued from 1967 until President Nixon phased out the draft in the early 1970s. During these years, the U.S. government accused more than 200,000 men of draft offenses and imprisoned nearly 4,000 draft resisters. (Most won parole after 6 to 12 months behind bars, while some served four or five years.) Throughout these years, about 10,000 Americans fled to Canada rather than serve in the military.

In October of 1967, a demonstration at Washington's Lincoln Memorial drew about 75,000 protesters, including well-known figures like the poet Robert Lowell and the novelist Norman Mailer. When the speeches ended, about 30,000 demonstrators locked arms for a march on the Pentagon in order "to disrupt the center of the American war machine," as one organizer explained. As hundreds of protesters broke past the military police and mounted the Pentagon steps, they were met by tear gas and truncheons. About 1,500 demonstrators were injured and at least 700 arrested.

An American antiwar poster is a parody of the World War I Uncle Sam poster, "I Want You for the U.S. Army."

WAR DIVIDES THE NATION By 1967, Americans increasingly found themselves divided into two camps regarding the war. Those who strongly opposed the war and believed the United States should withdraw were known as **doves.** Feeling just as strongly that America should unleash a greater show of military force to end the war were the **hawks.**

THINK THROUGH HISTORY
D. Contrasting *How did the positions of the doves and the hawks differ?*

D. Answer The doves opposed America's involvement in the Vietnam War and called for U.S. troops to withdraw immediately. The hawks argued for a greater show of military force to end the war.

Despite the visibility of the antiwar protesters, a majority of American citizens in 1967 still remained committed to the war. In May of that year, a prowar march through the streets of Manhattan drew 20,000 people. During this time, a poll showed that two-thirds of Americans still felt that the war was justified. And while only 10 percent of Americans approved of the administration's present level of commitment in Vietnam, about 50 percent felt that "increased attacks" against North Vietnam would help win the war.

Others, while less certain about the U.S. role in Vietnam, were shocked to see protesters publicly criticize a war in which their fellow Americans were fighting and dying. A poll taken in December of 1967 showed that 70 percent of Americans believed the war protests were "acts of disloyalty." A firefighter

MORE ABOUT . . .
David Harris

During his antiwar activities Harris met and married the folksinger Joan Baez, who dedicated her 1969 recording *David's Album* to him. The couple divorced in 1973 but remained on amicable terms. Not long after the divorce, Harris began writing for *Rolling Stone* magazine. His first major article was an interview with Ron Kovic, the paraplegic ex-Marine who became one of the Vietnam War era's best-known antiwar veterans. Harris has also written full-length books, including *I Shoulda Been Home Yesterday* (1976), about his experiences in jail as a draft resister.

HISTORY FROM VISUALS
I Want Out

Reading the Poster To help students recognize the parody in this antiwar poster, have them examine James Montgomery Flagg's World War I "I Want You" poster, which appears on page 403 in this text. Have students draw comparisons between the two posters.

Extension Have students create a pro–Vietnam War poster based on the image and caption in the original "I Want You" recruiting poster.

Block Schedule TEACHING OPTION **Time Needed: 30 Minutes**

Cooperative Activity: Composing "Hawk" or "Dove" Song Lyrics

Task: Small groups of students will work together to compose and perform songs supporting or criticizing the Vietnam War.

Purpose: To discover how popular music can effectively convey political ideas.

Activity: Encourage musically talented students to compose an original music score to accompany the lyrics. Otherwise, students can write lyrics to a familiar tune. Performances of groups' songs may be live, videotaped, or recorded on audiocassette. Groups should distribute copies of the song lyrics so that classmates can follow along as they listen to the performances.

Building a Portfolio: Students who wish to add their lyrics to their portfolio should include a note explaining their role in creating the song.

ALTERNATIVE ASSESSMENT BOOK
Standards for Evaluating a Cooperative Activity

Standards for Evaluation
Song lyrics should . . .

- contain at least two verses and a chorus
- express a clear point of view about the war
- use humor or other emotional appeals to express a political message

MORE ABOUT . . .
Robert S. McNamara

In late 1967 McNamara quietly left his post as defense secretary, plagued by doubts about the Vietnam policy he had helped formulate. A controversial figure at the time, he provoked a new storm with his 1995 book *In Retrospect: The Tragedy and Lessons of Vietnam,* infuriating hawks and doves alike with his admission, "We were wrong, terribly wrong."

ASSESS & RETEACH

Section 3 Assessment

Have students work individually to answer the questions. Then have them share with the class their tree diagrams for item 2.

Self-Assessment

Have each student make a two-column chart with the headings "Hawks" and "Doves" and fill in each group's arguments about the war.

Section Quiz

FORMAL ASSESSMENT
Section Quiz, p. 272

Reteach

Repeat the video "Matters of Conscience," and discuss the issues that the video raises about the war.

AMERICAN STORIES
video series
"Matters of Conscience"

CLOSE

Controversy over the escalation of the Vietnam War divided the nation into supporters and opponents of the conflict. Despite nationwide campus protests, in 1967 most Americans remained committed to the war.

---

who lost his son in Vietnam articulated the bitter feelings a number of Americans felt toward the antiwar movement.

A PERSONAL VOICE

I'm bitter. . . . It's people like us who give up our sons for the country. . . . The college types, the professors, they go to Washington and tell the government what to do. . . . But their sons, they don't end up in the swamps over there, in Vietnam. No sir. They're deferred, because they're in school. Or they get sent to safe places. . . . What bothers me about the peace crowd is that you can tell from their attitude, the way they look and what they say, that they don't really love this country.

A FIREFIGHTER, quoted in *Working-Class War*

Responding to antiwar posters, Americans who supported the government's Vietnam policy developed their own slogans: "Support our men in Vietnam" and "America—love it or leave it."

This sign reflects the view of many Americans that the antiwar protests undermined the war effort in Vietnam.

JOHNSON REMAINS DETERMINED Throughout the turmoil and division that engulfed the country during the early years of the war, President Johnson remained firm. Attacked by doves for not withdrawing and by hawks for not increasing military power rapidly enough, Johnson continued his policy of slow escalation.

A PERSONAL VOICE

There has always been confusion, frustration, and difference of opinion in this country, when there is a war going on. . . . You know what President Roosevelt went through, and President Wilson in World War I. He had some senators from certain areas that gave him serious problems until victory was assured. . . . We are going to have these differences. No one likes war. All people love peace. But you can't have freedom without defending it.

LYNDON B. JOHNSON, quoted in *No Hail, No Farewell*

Johnson dismissed as "nervous nellies" members of Congress and other officials who questioned his war policies. As for the protesters who paraded outside his window, the president saw them as misguided and misinformed. They "wouldn't know a Communist if they tripped over one," he declared.

However, by the end of 1967, Johnson's policy—and the continuing stalemate—had begun to create turmoil within his own administration. In November, Defense Secretary McNamara, a key architect of U.S. escalation in Vietnam, quietly announced he was resigning to become head of the World Bank. "It didn't add up," McNamara recalled later. "What I was trying to find out was how . . . the war went on year after year when we stopped the infiltration [from North Vietnam] or shrunk it and when we had a very high body count and so on. It just didn't make sense."

As it happened, McNamara's resignation came on the threshold of the most tumultuous year of the sixties. In 1968 the war—and Johnson's presidency—would take a drastic turn for the worse.

E. Answer Doves attacked him for not pulling out, hawks attacked him for not escalating faster, and members of his own administration began doubting the policy.

THINK THROUGH HISTORY
E. *Identifying Problems* *What problems did Johnson face with his escalation policy?*

Section 3 Assessment

1. TERMS & NAMES

Identify:
- New Left
- Students for a Democratic Society
- Free Speech Movement
- dove
- hawk

2. SUMMARIZING Re-create the tree diagram below on your paper. Then fill it in with examples of student organizations, issues, and demonstrations of the New Left.

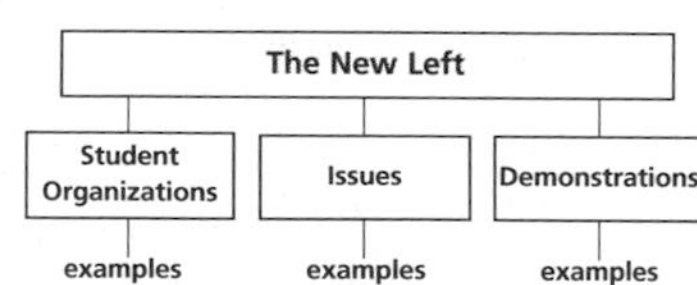

3. MAKING DECISIONS What choices did war draftees make during the Vietnam era?

THINK ABOUT
- university students
- antiwar demonstrators
- economically underprivileged whites and minorities

4. FORMING OPINIONS Do you agree, as many did, that antiwar protests were "acts of disloyalty"? Why or why not?

THINK ABOUT
- why protesters staged antiwar demonstrations
- comments that the protesters didn't "really love this country"
- the right to dissent in a democratic society

ANSWERS

1. TERMS & NAMES
- New Left, p. 737
- Students for a Democratic Society, p. 737
- Free Speech Movement, p. 737
- dove, p. 739
- hawk, p. 739

2. SUMMARIZING

Possible Answers: Student Organizations—Students for a Democratic Society; Free Speech Movement. Issues—opposition to Vietnam War; abolition of college deferments; campus issues. Demonstrations—march on Washington (April 1965); protest rally in Washington (November 1965); civil disobedience at Selective Service centers.

3. MAKING DECISIONS

Possible Responses: Many university students chose to defer their military service through the nation's college deferment plan; many antiwar demonstrators refused to serve in Vietnam, choosing to either leave the country, go to jail, or circumvent the authorities; many draftees also chose to serve proudly in Vietnam.

4. FORMING OPINIONS

Possible Responses: Agree—During wartime, Americans have the patriotic duty to support the soldiers who are risking their lives for their country and to show a unified front in the war effort; protests, especially burning draft cards, were flagrant displays of disloyalty that demoralized both U.S. soldiers in Vietnam and the American public. Disagree—There is a difference between patriotism and blind devotion; the people condemning the protesters were not closely examining the reasons for fighting the war; suppressing dissent is undemocratic.

❹ 1968: A Tumultuous Year

TERMS & NAMES
- Tet offensive
- Clark Clifford
- Robert Kennedy
- Eugene McCarthy
- Hubert Humphrey
- George Wallace

LEARN ABOUT the Tet offensive, the assassination of two national leaders, and the rioting at the Democratic National Convention
TO UNDERSTAND why 1968 stands out as the most explosive year of the 1960s.

ONE AMERICAN'S STORY

Early in the morning of June 5, 1968, John Lewis, the first chairman of the Student Nonviolent Coordinating Committee, fell to the floor and wept. Robert F. Kennedy, a leading Democratic candidate for president, had just been fatally shot. Lewis had strongly supported Kennedy, feeling that the candidate was "serious in his commitment to civil rights—you felt it was coming out of his gut, really." Two months earlier, when Dr. Martin Luther King, Jr., had fallen victim to an assassin's bullet, Lewis had told himself he still had Kennedy. And now they both were gone. Lewis, who later became a congressman from Georgia, recalled the lasting impact of these traumatic events from 1968.

A PERSONAL VOICE
There are people today who are afraid, In a sense, to hope or to have hope again, because of what happened in . . . 1968. Something was taken from us. The type of leadership that we had in a sense invested in, that we had helped to make and to nourish, was taken from us. . . . Something died in all of us with those assassinations.
JOHN LEWIS, quoted in *From Camelot to Kent State*

John Lewis

While the violent deaths of King and Kennedy left many Americans numb, the assassinations were but two of the traumatic events that rocked the nation in 1968. From a shocking setback in Vietnam to a chaotic Democratic National Convention in Chicago, the events of 1968 made it the most tumultuous year of a turbulent decade.

The Tet Offensive Turns the War

The year 1968 began with a daring surprise attack by the Vietcong on numerous cities in South Vietnam. The simultaneous strikes, while a military defeat for the Communist guerrillas, stunned the American public and caused many people with moderate views to begin turning against the war.

A SURPRISE ATTACK January 30 was the Vietnamese equivalent of New Year's Eve, the beginning of the lunar new year festivities known in Vietnam as Tet. Throughout that day in 1968, villagers—taking advantage of a week-long truce proclaimed for Tet—streamed into cities across South Vietnam to celebrate their New Year. At the time of the Tet celebration, many funerals were being held for victims of the war. Accompanying the funerals were the traditional firecrackers, flutes, and, of course, coffins.

As it turned out, the coffins contained weapons, and many of the villagers were Vietcong agents. That night the enemy launched an overwhelming attack on nearly 100 towns and cities in South Vietnam, as well as 12 U.S. air bases. The fighting was especially fierce in Saigon and in the former imperial capital of Hue. The Vietcong even attacked the U.S. embassy in Saigon, killing five Americans there. The **Tet offensive** continued for nearly a month before U.S. and South Vietnamese forces regained control of the cities.

Section 4 Overview

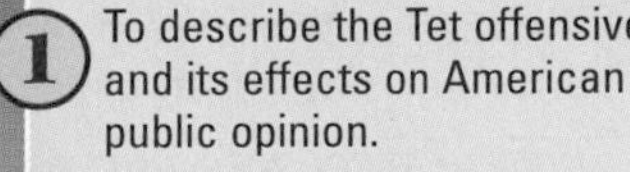

OBJECTIVES

1. To describe the Tet offensive and its effects on American public opinion.
2. To explain the domestic turbulence of 1968.
3. To describe the 1968 presidential election.

SKILLBUILDERS

- Interpreting tables, p. 746
- Understanding geography: location, p. 742

CRITICAL THINKING

- Analyzing issues, pp. 742, 744
- Analyzing motives, p. 743
- Analyzing causes, p. 746
- Summarizing, p. 746
- Analyzing, p. 746
- Comparing and contrasting, p. 746

FOCUS & MOTIVATE

5-MINUTE WARM-UP

Predicting Outcomes
To explore the impact of the 1968 Democratic convention, have students study the photo on page 745 and answer these questions.

1. What effect do you think the confrontation would have on those who opposed the war?
2. What effect do you think the confrontation would have on those who supported the war?

WARM-UP TRANSPARENCY 22

▶ ***Starting with the Student***
Ask students why a presidential adviser described the Vietnam War as a sinkhole.

SECTION 4 RESOURCES

PRINT RESOURCES

IN-DEPTH RESOURCES: UNIT 6
Guided Reading, p. 38
Geography Application: The Ho Chi Minh Trail, p. 41
Primary Source: Lyndon B. Johnson on Vietnam and Reelection, p. 48
American Lives: John Lewis, p. 53

READING STUDY GUIDE, p. 229

ACCESS FOR STUDENTS ACQUIRING ENGLISH
Guided Reading (Spanish), p. 244
Geography Application: The Ho Chi Minh Trail (Spanish), p. 247

SPANISH READING STUDY GUIDE, p. 229

FORMAL ASSESSMENT
Section Quiz, p. 273

ALTERNATIVE ASSESSMENT BOOK
See forms for supporting and scoring alternative activities.

TECHNOLOGY RESOURCES

CRITICAL THINKING TRANSPARENCIES
CT64, Impact of Tet Offensive

CD-ROM Electronic Library of Primary Sources
The War in Vietnam

VIDEO *American Portfolio: A Videodisc for U.S. History* user's guide, pp. 246–249, 255

INTERNET http://www.mlushistory.com

OBJECTIVE
① **INSTRUCT**

The Tet Offensive Turns the War

▶ ***Discussing Key Ideas***
- Early in 1968, North Vietnam and the Vietcong launch a surprise attack.

(continued on next page)

(continued from page 741)

- The Tet offensive sours the media's and the public's view of the war.
- By the end of February, President Johnson's popularity has plummeted.

IN-DEPTH RESOURCES: UNIT 6
Guided Reading p. 38
Primary Source: Lyndon B. Johnson on Vietnam and Reelection, p. 48

ACCESS FOR STUDENTS ACQUIRING ENGLISH
Guided Reading (Spanish), p. 244

HISTORY FROM VISUALS

Tet Offensive, Jan. 30–Feb. 24, 1968

Reading the Map Point out the numerous star-shaped symbols on the map, representing the major battle sites of the Tet offensive. Emphasize that the map shows the far-reaching geographic range of the surprise attacks.

Extension Ask students why the North Vietnamese and Vietcong forces may have decided to go through Laos and Cambodia to launch the Tet offensive. *Possible Responses: Because of bombing in Vietnam, the Ho Chi Minh Trail was the easiest means of entry; the North Vietnamese and Vietcong were less likely to surprise the South Vietnamese and American forces if they came through Vietnam.*

IN-DEPTH RESOURCES: UNIT 6
Geography Application: The Ho Chi Minh Trail, p. 41

CRITICAL THINKING TRANSPARENCIES
CT64, Impact of Tet Offensive

THE WAR IN VIETNAM
"Washington Feels Vietcong Offensive Failed to Gain Maximum Objectives"

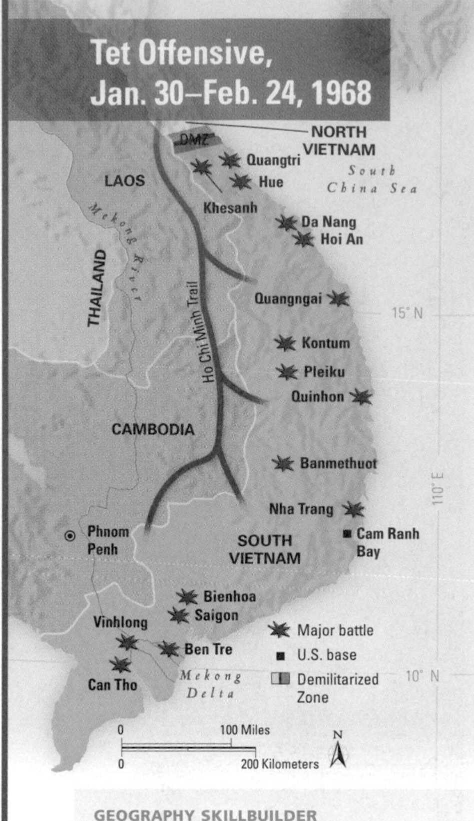

GEOGRAPHY SKILLBUILDER
LOCATION ***What were the geographical destinations of the Tet offensive attacks?***

Skillbuilder Answer
They were scattered all across South Vietnam.

General Westmoreland declared the attacks an overwhelming defeat for the Vietcong. The Communists' "well-laid plans went afoul," the general announced. He later added that "the enemy exposed himself by virtue of his strategy and he suffered heavy casualties." From a purely military standpoint, Westmoreland was right. The Vietcong lost about 32,000 soldiers during the month-long battle, while the American and ARVN forces lost little more than 3,000.

However, from a psychological—and political—standpoint, Westmoreland's claim could not have been more wrong. Despite its overall military failure, the Tet offensive greatly shook an American public that had come to believe that the enemy was close to defeat. The Johnson administration's credibility gap suddenly widened to a point from which it would never recover. Many Americans no longer believed the administration. The Pentagon's continued reports of favorable body counts, or massive Vietcong casualties, now rang hollow as Americans saw the shocking images of attacks on South Vietnam's major cities by an enemy that seemed to be everywhere.

TET CHANGES PUBLIC OPINION The aftershock from the Tet offensive reverberated throughout the United States, from its living rooms to its newsrooms to the White House. Despite the years of antiwar protest, a poll taken just before Tet showed that only 28 percent of Americans called themselves doves, while 56 percent claimed to be hawks. After Tet, both sides tallied 40 percent. The mainstream media, which had reported the war in a skeptical but generally balanced way, now openly criticized the war. One of the nation's most respected journalists, Walter Cronkite, told his viewers that it now seemed "more certain than ever that the bloody experience of Vietnam is to end in a stalemate." In a matter of weeks, the Tet offensive had changed millions of minds about the war.

THINK THROUGH HISTORY
A. *Analyzing Issues* *Why did American support for the war change after the Tet offensive?*

A. Answer
Because the enemy seemed much stronger and more numerous than Americans had thought.

Minds were also changing at the White House. To fill the defense secretary position left vacant by Robert McNamara's resignation, Johnson picked **Clark Clifford,** a trusted friend and strong supporter of the president's Vietnam policy. However, after settling in and studying the situation, Clifford concluded that the war was unwinnable. "We seem to have a sinkhole," Clifford said. "We put in more—they match it. I see more and more fighting with more and more casualties on the U.S. side and no end in sight to the action."

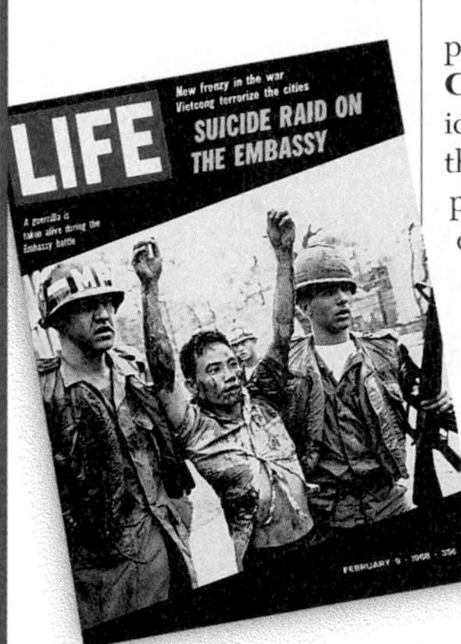

A *Life* magazine cover shows the capturing of a Vietcong guerrilla during the Tet offensive.

A NATION TURNS ON JOHNSON In the weeks following the Tet offensive, Johnson's popularity plummeted. In public opinion polls taken at the end of February 1968, nearly 60 percent of the American public disapproved of the president's handling of the war. Nearly half of the country now felt it had been a mistake to send American troops to Vietnam.

Even Dean Rusk, Johnson's secretary of state and another principal architect of the war, acknowledged that the mood of America had changed significantly after Tet. "It was clear to me in the spring of '68 that support for Vietnam at the grass-roots level had changed," Rusk recalled. "We had good support until that point, despite the campus demonstrations. War weariness eventually set in, and that was the watershed year." Johnson recognized the change, too. Upon learning of Cronkite's pessimistic analysis of the war, the president lamented, "If I've lost Walter, then it's over. I've lost Mr. Average Citizen."

TEACHING OPTIONS

Making Connections Across Cultures

Celebrating Tet Like the Chinese, the Vietnamese revere their dead ancestors, especially during Tet, the lunar new year celebration. As Tet draws near, the Vietnamese return to their native villages to reestablish bonds with relatives. Families visit graves and decorate them. On the 30th day of the final lunar month, families gather to prepare for the arrival of their ancestors' souls. At around 9 P.M., they set off firecrackers to ward off evil spirits. Women prepare soybean soup for the vigil, and the families recite prayers at their household ancestral altars. A seven-day festival follows.

Making Global Connections

Student Protests Abroad The student protests of the late 1960s were not confined to the United States. One of the most prominent student radicals abroad was Daniel Cohn-Bendit, whose left-wing politics earned him the nickname Danny the Red. The massive street protests that he organized in Paris crippled the French capital and even spread to cities as far away as Cairo, Egypt, and Karachi, Pakistan. Exiled from his native France, Cohn-Bendit settled in Frankfurt, Germany, where he continued his political activism.

Days of Loss and Rage

The growing division over Vietnam led to a shocking political development in the spring of 1968, a season in which Americans also endured two assassinations, a series of urban riots, and a surge in college campus protests.

JOHNSON WITHDRAWS Well before the Tet offensive, an antiwar coalition within the Democratic Party had taken steps to unseat President Johnson. The group sought a Democratic candidate to challenge Johnson in the 1968 presidential primary election. **Robert Kennedy,** a senator from New York, decided not to run, citing party loyalty. However, in December of 1967, Minnesota senator **Eugene McCarthy** answered the group's call. McCarthy, a strong critic of the war, declared he would run against Johnson on a platform to end the war in Vietnam. "In every other great war of the century," McCarthy declared, "we have had the support of what is generally accepted as the decent opinion of mankind. We do not have that today."

McCarthy's early campaign attracted little notice, but in the weeks following Tet, it picked up steam. In the New Hampshire Democratic primary in March 1968, the little-known senator shocked the nation by capturing 42 percent of the vote. While Johnson won the primary with 48 percent of the vote, the slim margin of victory was viewed as a defeat for the president. Influenced by Johnson's perceived weakness at the polls, Robert Kennedy declared his candidacy for president. The Democratic Party had become a house divided.

The Vietnam War and the divisiveness it caused within America took its toll on President Johnson.

On March 31, 1968, President Johnson responded to the growing division within his party and the country. In a televised address to the nation, Johnson announced a dramatic change in his Vietnam policy. The president declared that the United States would seek negotiations to end the war. In the meantime, the policy of U.S. escalation would end. The bombing of North Vietnam would eventually cease, and steps would be taken to ensure that the South Vietnamese played a larger role in the war.

The president paused and then ended his speech with a statement that shocked the nation. Declaring that he did not want the presidency to become "involved in the partisan divisions that are developing in this political year," Lyndon Johnson announced, "Accordingly, I shall not seek, and I will not accept, the nomination of my party for another term of president." The president was stepping down from national politics, his grand plan for domestic reform done in by a costly and divisive war. "That . . . war," Johnson later admitted, "killed the lady I really loved—the Great Society."

"If I've lost Walter [Cronkite], then it's over. I've lost Mr. Average Citizen."

LYNDON B. JOHNSON

THINK THROUGH HISTORY
B. *Analyzing Motives* *Why did President Johnson decide not to run again?*

B. Answer He believed that seeking a second term would cause further turmoil and divisiveness within the Democratic Party.

VIOLENCE AND PROTEST GRIP THE NATION The Democrats—as well as the nation—were in for more shock in 1968. Johnson's startling announcement had barely sunk in when America was rocked by the assassination of Dr. Martin Luther King, Jr., on April 4. In the wake of the civil rights leader's death, violence ripped through more than 100 U.S. cities as enraged followers of King burned buildings and destroyed neighborhoods.

Violence and rage engulfed the nation's capital for several days, as rioters set more than 700 fires. Federal army troops in full combat gear were called in to protect the Capitol and the White House. By the end of the week, 21,000 federal troops and 34,000 National Guardsmen had been called upon to subdue the rioting across the country. When it was all over, 46 persons were dead, more than 3,000 were injured and some 27,000 were arrested.

Just two months later, a bullet cut down yet another popular national figure. By June of 1968, Robert Kennedy had become a strong candidate in the

OBJECTIVE
② **INSTRUCT**

Days of Loss and Rage

▶ ***Starting with the Student***
Ask students to list the most compelling news stories that have been reported during their lifetimes.

- How do these stories compare with the shocking news stories of 1968?

▶ ***Discussing Key Ideas***

- The impressive showing of an antiwar candidate, Eugene McCarthy, in the New Hampshire Democratic primary prompts Robert Kennedy to join the presidential race.
- In March President Johnson announces a dramatic change in Vietnam policy and bows out of the presidential race.
- Martin Luther King, Jr., and Robert Kennedy are assassinated, and campus protests surge.

IN-DEPTH RESOURCES: UNIT 6
American Lives: John Lewis, p. 53

MORE ABOUT . . .
Robert Kennedy
Kennedy's candidacy attracted the support of African Americans and Latinos, whose causes he had championed in the past. Many antiwar Democrats also backed his bid for the White House. However, Kennedy's entering the race only after Johnson seemed vulnerable antagonized many McCarthy supporters, who mocked him as "Bobby-come-lately."

TEACHING OPTIONS

Making Global Connections

Soviet Union Invades Czechoslovakia The year 1968 was also a time of trauma in Eastern Europe. During the so-called Prague Spring, reformers in what was then the Communist nation of Czechoslovakia began initiating economic and political changes to make the country more democratic. Their hopes were crushed when Soviet, East German, Polish, and Hungarian troops invaded Czechoslovakia in August 1968. Though the Czechs' nonviolent resistance did not prevent the invaders from restoring hard-line Communists to authority, the Soviets again were cast as villains on the world stage.

Making Connections Across the Curriculum

Economics Johnson's TV speech also included his gloomy view of the war's economic toll: "Tonight we face the sharpest financial threat in the postwar era—a threat to the dollar's role as the keystone of international trade and finance in the world. . . . [In] 7 years of unparalleled prosperity . . . the real income of the average American, after taxes, rose by 30 percent—a gain as large as that of the preceding 19 years. So the steps that we must take to convince the world are exactly the steps we must take to sustain our own economic strength at home. In the past 8 months, prices and interest rates have risen because of our inaction."

MORE ABOUT . . .
Garry Wills

Wills began the 1960s as a conservative graduate student studying ancient Greek and ended the decade as a journalist who "had my suit jacket set on fire by a demonstrator, had a gun pulled on me by a man I was interviewing, and had gone to jail twice for blocking the entrances to the Senate and House chambers." Since then he has published several books, including the Pulitzer Prize–winning *Lincoln at Gettysburg.*

OBJECTIVE
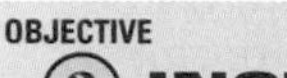
INSTRUCT

A Turbulent Race for President

▶ ***Discussing Key Ideas***
- Protests spark rioting in Chicago during the Democratic National Convention.
- Delegates at the Democratic convention bitterly debate the party's antiwar plank.
- Vice-President Hubert Humphrey wins the Democratic Party's presidential nomination.
- The Republican presidential candidate, Richard Nixon, wins the 1968 election.

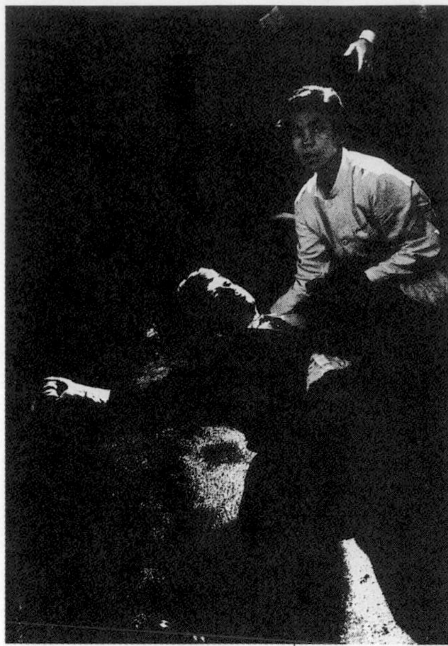

Hotel busboy Juan Romero was the first person to reach Robert Kennedy after he was shot. Kennedy had just won the California primary.

Democratic primary, drawing support heavily from minorities and urban Democratic voters. On June 4, Kennedy won the crucial California primary. Just after midnight, he gave a victory speech at a Los Angeles hotel. On his way out of the hotel, he passed through the hotel's kitchen. A young Palestinian immigrant, Sirhan Sirhan, was hiding in the kitchen with a gun. Sirhan, who later said he was angered by Kennedy's support of Israel, fatally shot the senator.

Jack Newfield, a speechwriter for Kennedy, described the anguish he and many Americans felt over the loss of two of the nation's leaders.

A PERSONAL VOICE

Things were not really getting better . . . we shall *not* overcome. . . . We had already glimpsed the most compassionate leaders our nation could produce, and they had all been assassinated. And from this time forward, things would get worse, Our best political leaders were part of memory now, not hope.

JACK NEWFIELD, quoted in *Nineteen Sixty-Eight*

Meanwhile, the nation's college campuses continued to erupt in protest. During the first six months of 1968, almost 40,000 students on more than 100 campuses took part in 221 major demonstrations. While many of the demonstrations continued to target U.S. involvement in the Vietnam War—which reached a peak of 536,000 American military personnel—students also clashed with university officials over campus and social issues. A massive student protest at Columbia University in New York City held the nation's attention for a week in April. There, students protesting the university's community policies took over several buildings. Police eventually restored order and arrested nearly 900 protesters.

Recalling the violence and turmoil that seemed to plague the nation in 1968, the journalist and historian Garry Wills wrote, "There was a sense everywhere . . . that things were giving way. That [people] had not only lost control of [their] history, but might never regain it."

THINK THROUGH HISTORY
C. *Analyzing Issues* *Why was 1968 characterized as a year of "lost control" in America?*

C. Answer The nation seemed to be losing control of everything from the Vietnam War to its college campuses. Even the future seemed uncertain with the assassination of two of the country's most promising leaders.

A Turbulent Race for President

The chaos and violence of 1968 climaxed in Chicago. Thousands of antiwar demonstrators converged on the city to protest at the Democratic National Convention in August of that year. The convention, which featured a bloody riot between protesters and police, fractured the Democratic Party and thus helped a nearly forgotten Republican win the White House.

TURMOIL IN CHICAGO With Lyndon Johnson stepping down and Robert Kennedy gone, the 1968 Democratic presidential primary race pitted Eugene McCarthy against Vice-President **Hubert Humphrey.** McCarthy, while still popular with the nation's antiwar segment, had little chance of defeating Humphrey, a loyal party man who had President Johnson's support. During the last week of August, the Democrats met at their convention in Chicago supposedly to choose a candidate. In reality, Humphrey's nomination had already been determined, a decision that upset many antiwar activists.

As the delegates arrived in Chicago, so too did nearly 10,000 protesters. Led by men such as SDS veteran Tom Hayden, many demonstrators sought to pressure the Democrats into adopting an antiwar platform. Others came to voice their displeasure with Humphrey's nomination. Still others, known as Yippies (members of the Youth International Party), had come hoping to provoke violence that might discredit the Democratic Party. Chicago's mayor, Richard J.

TEACHING OPTIONS

Teaching Less Proficient Readers

Tracking Presidential Candidates To help students better understand the 1968 presidential candidates, put the following "Who's Who" chart on the chalkboard, and have students fill in the missing information.

Presidential Candidate	Political Views
Hubert Humphrey (Democrat)	
Richard Nixon (Republican)	
George Wallace (American Independent)	

Teaching Gifted and Talented Students

Chicago Eight Have students research one of the following topics and present their findings in an oral report:

- the chaos at the 1968 Democratic National Convention
- the resulting Chicago Eight (later changed to Chicago Seven) trial
- one of the defendants in the trial—Tom Hayden, David Dellinger, Abbie Hoffman, Jerry Rubin, Rennie Davis, Lee Weiner, John Froines, or Bobby Seale

Encourage students to investigate primary sources and view videotapes of television news reports, if available.

Chicago police attempt to disperse antiwar demonstrators at the 1968 Democratic convention. Protesters shouted, "The whole world is watching!"

Daley, was determined to keep the protesters under control. With memories of the nationwide riots after King's death still fresh, Daley mobilized 12,000 Chicago police officers and 5,000 National Guardsmen. "As long as I am mayor," Daley vowed, "there will be law and order."

Order, however, soon collapsed. On August 28, as delegates cast votes for Humphrey, chaos engulfed the downtown park where the protesters had gathered to march on the convention. With television cameras focused on them, police moved into the crowd, sprayed the protesters with Mace and beat them with nightsticks. Many protesters tried to flee, while others retaliated, pelting the riot-helmeted police with rocks and bottles. "The whole world is watching!" protesters shouted, as police attacked demonstrators and bystanders alike.

The rioting soon spilled out of the park and into the downtown streets. One nearby hotel, observed a *New York Times* reporter, became a makeshift aid station.

A PERSONAL VOICE

Demonstrators, reporters, McCarthy workers, doctors, all began to stagger into the Hilton lobby, blood streaming from face and head wounds. The lobby smelled from tear gas, and stink bombs dropped by the Yippies. A few people began to direct the wounded to a makeshift hospital on the fifteenth floor, the McCarthy staff headquarters.

J. ANTHONY LUKAS, quoted in *Decade of Shocks*

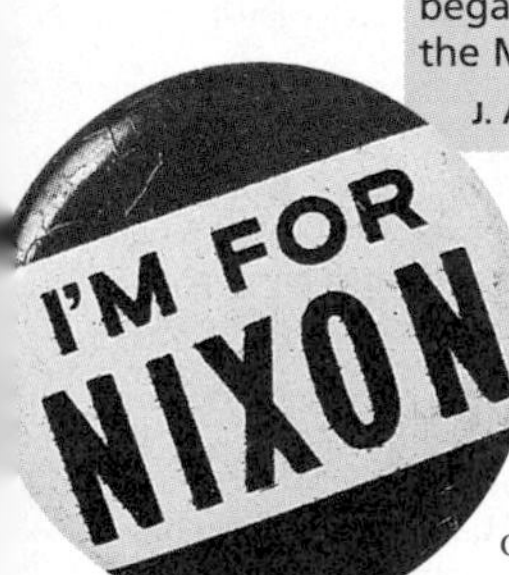

This button was made for Nixon's 1968 campaign.

Disorder of a different kind reigned inside the convention hall, where delegates bitterly debated an antiwar plank in the party platform. When word of the riot filtered into the hall, delegates angrily shouted at Daley, who returned their shouts with equal vigor. The whole world indeed was watching—on their televisions. The images of the Democrats—both inside and outside the convention hall—as a party of disorder became etched in the minds of millions of Americans.

NIXON TRIUMPHS A person who benefited from this turmoil was Republican presidential candidate Richard M. Nixon. By 1968, Nixon had achieved one of the greatest political comebacks in American politics. After his loss to Kennedy

MORE ABOUT . . .

Richard J. Daley

The last of the big-city political bosses, Daley had served in the Illinois legislature before being elected Chicago's mayor in 1955. A key supporter of John F. Kennedy's presidential bid in 1960, Daley's delivery of the Illinois vote helped give Kennedy his slim majority over Nixon. Daley maintained good relations with African Americans until the mid-1960s when violence erupted during civil rights marches–some led by Dr. Martin Luther King, Jr. Rioting also occurred after the assassination of King in 1968. It may have been in part because of those riots that Daley was so tough on protesters during the convention. In 1996 the Democrats returned to Chicago—now run by "Boss" Daley's son, Richard M. Daley—for a successful convention.

ELECTRONIC LIBRARY OF PRIMARY SOURCES

from *The Strategy of Confrontation*

Block Schedule TEACHING OPTION **Time Needed: 20 Minutes**

Cooperative Activity: Creating a 1968 Yearbook

Task: Groups of students will create 1968 yearbooks based on their research into key events in America and around the world.

Purpose: To chronicle the events of the most turbulent year of the decade.

Activity: Tell students to focus on only the major events of the year and to arrange information chronologically or geographically. Yearbooks might include captioned photos and magazine clippings (or photocopies of these), as well as original sketches, charts, and computer graphics. Each group member can perform a different task—for example, art research, drawing, creating computer graphics, paste-up, or caption writing.

ALTERNATIVE ASSESSMENT BOOK

Standards for Evaluating a Cooperative Activity

HISTORY FROM VISUALS

Election of 1968

Reading the Table Correlate the total numbers of electoral votes tallied in the third column of the table with the state-by-state results shown on the map. Point out that Wallace won states in the Deep South and that Humphrey triumphed in the Northeast.

Extension Have students use the information in the map to create a table with the headings "Candidate," "Party," and "States Won"

ASSESS & RETEACH

Section 4 Assessment

Have pairs of students work together to find evidence in the text to support their answers.

Self-Assessment

Have students create multiple-effects charts showing the short- and long-term consequences of the Tet offensive. Ask them to refer to their completed charts as they review their answers for item 3. Do they have new ideas to add?

Section Quiz

FORMAL ASSESSMENT
Section Quiz, p. 273

Reteach

Use the time lines students created for item 2 to review the turbulent events in the first half of 1968.

CLOSE

The Tet offensive changed public opinion about the war and contributed to Johnson's decision not to seek reelection. Two assassinations, urban riots, and campus protests rocked the nation. The chaotic Democratic convention helped pave the way for Republican Richard Nixon's win in November's presidential election.

Election of 1968

ELECTORAL AND POPULAR VOTES

Party	Candidate	Electoral votes	Popular votes
Republican	Richard M. Nixon	301	31,785,480
Democratic	Hubert H. Humphrey	191	31,275,166
American Independent	George C. Wallace	46	9,906,473

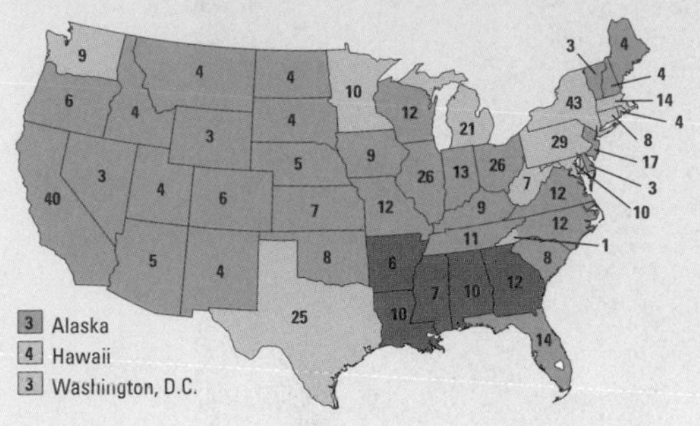

SKILLBUILDER
INTERPRETING TABLES ***By how many percentage points did Nixon defeat Humphrey in the popular vote? How large was Nixon's electoral vote victory?***

Skillbuilder Answers
Percent: Less than one percent (0.7). **Electoral:** 110 votes.

Richard M. Nixon flashes a victory signal on his way to winning the 1968 Republican nomination for president. Referring to recent years of turmoil, Nixon declared, "We have endured a long night. . . . Let us gather the light."

in the presidential race of 1960, Nixon tasted defeat again in 1962 when he ran for governor of California. His political career all but dead, Nixon joined a New York law firm. However, he never strayed far from politics. In 1966, Nixon campaigned for Republican candidates in congressional elections, helping Republicans win back 47 House seats and 3 Senate seats from Democrats. In 1968, Nixon announced his candidacy for president, and on the strength of his Republican alliances, as well as his voter appeal, he won the party's nomination.

During the presidential race, Nixon campaigned on a promise to restore law and order, which appealed to many middle-class Americans fed up with years of riots and protests. He also promised, in vague but appealing terms, to end the war in Vietnam. Nixon's candidacy was helped by the entry of former Alabama governor **George Wallace** into the race as a third-party candidate. Wallace, a Democrat running on the American Independent Party ticket, was a longtime champion of school segregation and states' rights. Labeled the "white backlash" candidate, Wallace captured five Southern states. In addition, he attracted a surprisingly high number of Northern white working-class voters disgusted with inner-city riots and antiwar protests.

In the end, Nixon defeated Humphrey by more than 100 electoral votes, despite capturing only 43 percent of the popular vote. By winning the presidency, Richard Nixon inherited the quagmire in Vietnam. He eventually would end America's involvement in Vietnam, but not before his war policies created even more protest and uproar within the country.

D. Answer The Democrats' disunity, Nixon's law-and-order stance, his vow to end the war, and the entry of George Wallace into the race.

THINK THROUGH HISTORY
D. *Analyzing Causes* *What factors led to Nixon's victory?*

Section 4 Assessment

1. TERMS & NAMES

Identify:
- Tet offensive
- Clark Clifford
- Robert Kennedy
- Eugene McCarthy
- Hubert Humphrey
- George Wallace

2. SUMMARIZING Create a time line of major events that occurred in 1968. Use the months already plotted on the time line below as a guide.

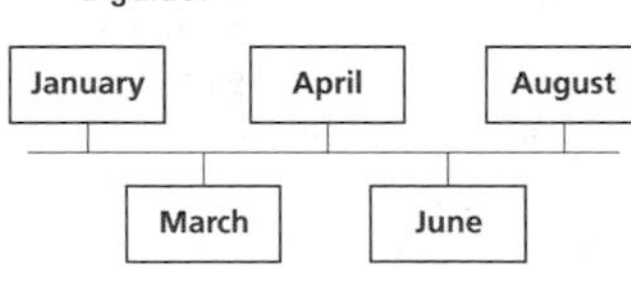

Which event do you think was most significant? Explain.

3. ANALYZING Why do you think the Tet offensive might be considered the turning point of the Vietnam War? Support your answer with reasons.

THINK ABOUT
- its effects on the Johnson administration's credibility
- its effects on public opinion
- Johnson's response to the split within the Democratic Party

4. COMPARING AND CONTRASTING Do you think there might have been a relationship between the violence of the Vietnam War and the growing climate of violence in the United States during 1968? Why or why not?

THINK ABOUT
- the heavy casualties during the month-long Tet offensive
- peak U.S. involvement in Vietnam in 1968
- Garry Wills's comment on page 744

ANSWERS

1. TERMS & NAMES
- Tet offensive, p. 741
- Clark Clifford, p. 742
- Robert Kennedy, p. 743
- Eugene McCarthy, p. 743
- Hubert Humphrey, p. 744
- George Wallace, p. 746

2. SUMMARIZING

Possible Responses: January—Tet offensive. March—Johnson's withdrawal from presidential race. April—King's assassination; urban riots. June—RFK's assassination. August—Clash between police and protesters at Democratic National Convention.

3. ANALYZING

Possible Responses: Widened the Johnson administration's credibility gap; prompted the mainstream media to criticize the war; caused Johnson's popularity to plummet; prompted Johnson's response to growing division within Democratic Party—the dramatic change in his Vietnam policy and withdrawal from the presidential race.

4. COMPARING AND CONTRASTING

Possible Responses: Yes—The war's atmosphere of violence spread to U.S. cities and college campuses. No—There was no cause-and-effect relationship between the two kinds of violence; neither King's nor Kennedy's assassination was related to the violence in Vietnam; the urban riots after King's assassination were related to the rage and anger over his death.

5 The End of the War and Its Legacy

TERMS & NAMES
- Vietnamization
- silent majority
- Pentagon Papers
- Henry Kissinger
- Khmer Rouge
- War Powers Act

LEARN ABOUT President Richard Nixon's Vietnamization policy and the end of the war
TO UNDERSTAND how the war had a lasting effect on America.

ONE AMERICAN'S STORY

Alfred S. Bradford served in Vietnam from September 1968 to August 1969. A member of the 25th Infantry Division, he was awarded several medals, including the Purple Heart, given to soldiers wounded in battle. Bradford went on to teach history at the universities of Missouri and Oklahoma. One day, Bradford's eight-year-old daughter, Elizabeth, inquired about his experience in Vietnam. "Daddy, why did you do it?" she asked. Bradford recalled what he had told himself.

A PERSONAL VOICE
Vietnam was my generation's adventure. I wanted to be part of that adventure and I believed that it was my duty as an American, both to serve my country and particularly not to stand by while someone else risked his life in my place. I do not regret my decision to go, but I learned in Vietnam not to confuse America with the politicians elected to administer America, even when they claim they are speaking for America, and I learned that I have a duty to myself and to my country to exercise my own judgment based upon my own conscience.

ALFRED S. BRADFORD, quoted in *Some Even Volunteered*

A U.S. soldier sits near Quang Tri, Vietnam, during a break in the fighting.

Bradford's mixed view of the war reflected the range of emotions many veterans felt about their service in Vietnam. The war left a deep and lasting impression on many Americans, from soldiers such as Bradford to citizens who did not serve. Richard Nixon had promised in 1968 to end the war, but it would take nearly five more years—and over 20,000 more American deaths—to end the nation's involvement in Vietnam. The legacy of the war was profound, as it dramatically affected the way Americans viewed their government and the world.

President Nixon and Vietnamization

In the summer of 1969, recently elected president Richard Nixon announced the first U.S. troop withdrawals from Vietnam. "We have to get rid of the nightmares we inherited," Nixon later told reporters. "One of the nightmares is war without end." However, as Nixon pulled out American troops, he continued the war against North Vietnam to achieve what he called "peace with honor"—a policy that some critics would charge prolonged the "war without end" for several more bloody years.

THE PULLOUT BEGINS As President Nixon settled into the White House in January of 1969, negotiations begun by the Johnson administration to end the war in Vietnam were going nowhere. During the peace talks in Paris, the warring factions argued over everything—including the shape of the negotiating table. The United States and South Vietnam insisted that all North Vietnamese forces withdraw from the South and that the government of Nguyen Van Thieu, then South Vietnam's ruler, remain in power. The North Vietnamese and Vietcong demanded that U.S. troops withdraw from South Vietnam and that the Thieu government step aside for a coalition government that would include the Vietcong.

SECTION 5 RESOURCES

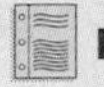
PRINT RESOURCES

IN-DEPTH RESOURCES: UNIT 6
Guided Reading, p. 39
Outline Map: The Vietnam War, p. 43
Literature: from *In Country* by Bobbie Ann Mason, p. 49

READING STUDY GUIDE, p. 231

ACCESS FOR STUDENTS ACQUIRING ENGLISH
Guided Reading (Spanish), p. 245
Outline Map: The Vietnam War (Spanish), p. 249

SPANISH READING STUDY GUIDE, p. 231

FORMAL ASSESSMENT
Section Quiz, p. 274

ALTERNATIVE ASSESSMENT BOOK
See forms for supporting and scoring alternative activities.

TECHNOLOGY RESOURCES

HUMANITIES TRANSPARENCIES
H28, Fall of Saigon; H45, The Blind Leading the Blind

GEOGRAPHY TRANSPARENCIES
G30, Vietnam War: 1964–1975

CRITICAL THINKING TRANSPARENCIES
CT30, The War in Vietnam

CD-ROM Electronic Library of Primary Sources
The War in Vietnam

VIDEO *American Portfolio: A Videodisc for U.S. History* user's guide, pp. 247, 252–253

INTERNET http://www.mlushistory.com

Section 5 Overview

OBJECTIVES

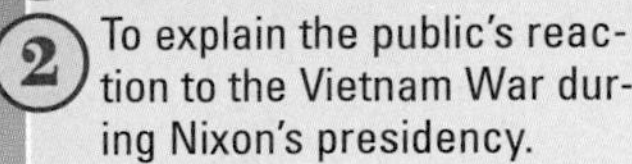
1. To describe Nixon's policy of Vietnamization.
2. To explain the public's reaction to the Vietnam War during Nixon's presidency.
3. To trace the end of U.S. involvement and the final outcome in Vietnam.
4. To examine the war's painful legacy in the United States and Southeast Asia.

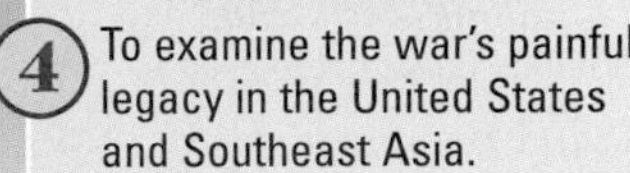

SKILLBUILDER
- Interpreting charts, p. 748

CRITICAL THINKING
- Summarizing, pp. 748, 753
- Analyzing issues, p. 749
- Making predictions, p. 750
- Evaluating decisions, p. 751
- Recognizing effects, p. 753
- Synthesizing, p. 753
- Making inferences, p. 753

FOCUS & MOTIVATE

5-MINUTE WARM-UP

Evaluating Judgments
To learn about Henry Kissinger, have students read the Key Player feature on page 750 and answer these questions.

1. What does Kissinger believe is interesting about most world leaders?
2. Why do you think Kissinger was drawn toward Nixon after the latter became president?

WARM-UP TRANSPARENCY 22

▶ ***Starting with the Student***
Ask students how the public reacts to politicians' unkept promises.

OBJECTIVE

1 INSTRUCT

President Nixon and Vietnamization

▶ ***Discussing Key Ideas***
- Negotiations to end the war reach a deadlock.

(continued on next page)

(continued from page 747)

- Nixon initiates a policy of Vietnamization—a gradual withdrawal of U.S. troops and replacement with South Vietnamese troops.
- A key goal of Vietnamization is to achieve "peace with honor."

IN-DEPTH RESOURCES: UNIT 6
Guided Reading p. 39

ACCESS FOR STUDENTS ACQUIRING ENGLISH
Guided Reading (Spanish), p. 245

HUMANITIES TRANSPARENCIES
H45, The Blind Leading the Blind

HISTORY FROM VISUALS

U.S. Aerial Bomb Tonnage

Reading the Chart Correlate the difference in bomb tonnage with the increased sophistication of military aircraft in the Vietnam War. Explain that the four bombers illustrated in the chart show the development of aircraft design over the years.

Extension Have students list other kinds of data that might be shown on charts about U.S. aerial bombing in wartime.

OBJECTIVE

② INSTRUCT

Trouble Continues on the Home Front

▶ ***Discussing Key Ideas***
- News accounts of the My Lai massacre horrify the American public.
- Nixon's invasion of Cambodia spurs nationwide campus protests.

(continued on next page)

In the midst of the stalled negotiations, Nixon announced his strategy to end America's involvement in Vietnam. Known as **Vietnamization,** the plan called for the gradual withdrawal of U.S. troops in order for the South Vietnamese to take on a more active combat role in the war. By August of 1969, the first 25,000 U.S. troops had returned home from Vietnam. Over the next three years, the number of American troops in Vietnam dropped from more than 500,000 to less than 25,000.

U.S. Aerial Bomb Tonnage

WORLD WAR I, WORLD WAR II, KOREAN WAR — 2.6 million tons

VIETNAM WAR — 6.2 million tons

Sources: *The U.S. Air Service in World War I, Vol. 1, 4; Vietnam War Almanac; Dictionary of the Vietnam War*

SKILLBUILDER
INTERPRETING CHARTS
What does the chart show about the type of war the U.S. fought in Vietnam?

Skillbuilder Answer
Possible response: The chart shows that the United States relied heavily on air power to defeat the Vietcong; the U.S. may have believed that a massive and unrelenting bombing campaign would greatly help in its strategy to demoralize the enemy.

"PEACE WITH HONOR" However, part of Nixon's Vietnamization policy was aimed at establishing what he called a "peace with honor." Nixon intended to maintain U.S. dignity in the face of its withdrawal from war. A further goal was the preservation of U.S. clout at the negotiation table, as President Nixon still demanded that the South Vietnamese government remain intact. With this objective—and even as the pullout had begun—Nixon secretly ordered a massive bombing campaign against supply routes and bases in North Vietnam. The president also ordered that bombs be dropped on the neighboring countries of Laos and Cambodia, which held a number of Vietcong sanctuaries. Nixon told aide H. R. Haldeman that he wanted the enemy to believe he was capable of anything.

A. Answer To withdraw U.S. troops while maintaining American might and dignity, as well as a strong negotiating position.

THINK THROUGH HISTORY
A. Summarizing *What was the goal of Nixon's "peace with honor" in Vietnam?*

A PERSONAL VOICE

I call it the madman theory, Bob. I want the North Vietnamese to believe I've reached the point where I might do *anything* to stop the war. We'll just slip the word to them that "for God's sake, you know Nixon is obsessed about Communists. We can't restrain him when he's angry—and he has his hand on the nuclear button . . ."—and Ho Chi Minh himself will be in Paris in two days begging for peace.

RICHARD M. NIXON, quoted in *The Price of Power*

Trouble Continues on the Home Front

Seeking to win support for his war policies, Richard Nixon appealed to what he called the **silent majority**—moderate, mainstream Americans who quietly supported the president's strategy. To be sure, many average Americans did support the president. However, the events of the war continued to divide the country.

THE MY LAI MASSACRE In November of 1969, Americans learned of a shocking event. That month, *New York Times* correspondent Seymour Hersh reported that on March 16, 1968, a U.S. platoon under the command of Lieutenant William Calley, Jr., entered the small village of My Lai in northern South Vietnam in search of Vietcong rebels. Finding no sign of the enemy, the troops rounded up the villagers and shot them. In all, the soldiers massacred more than 100 innocent Vietnamese—mostly women and children. "We huddled them up," recalled 22-year-old Private Paul Meadlo. "I poured about four clips into the group. . . . The mothers was hugging their children. . . . Well, we kept right on firing."

The troops insisted that they were following Lieutenant Calley's orders. When asked what his directive had been, one soldier answered, "Kill anything that breathed." Twenty-five army officers were charged with involve-

TEACHING OPTIONS

Teaching Less Proficient Readers

Clarifying Ideas As students read pages 748–753, have them follow the five steps of the SQ3R study method:

1. **Survey** the pages by skimming the paragraphs and the art, including the graphic on aerial bomb tonnage.
2. **Jot down** any **questions** about Vietnam or America.
3. **Reread** the pages, looking for answers to those questions.
4. **Record** any answers you find.
5. **Review** the information, checking for answers to any remaining questions.

Teaching Gifted and Talented Students

Discussing Political Strategy Have students research the tactics that Richard Nixon used, with the help of Vice-President Spiro Agnew, to enlist the support of the "silent majority." Students should then hold a panel discussion about the advantages and disadvantages of the strategy. Questions the panel might address include

- Who constituted the "silent majority" and the vocal minority?
- How did Nixon's and Agnew's criticism of the media play a role in polarizing these two groups?
- What other people did Nixon and Agnew criticize?

ment in the massacre and subsequent cover-up, but only Calley was convicted and imprisoned.

The My Lai massacre shook the nation. *Time* magazine called the incident "an American tragedy," and *Newsweek* appeared to capture the mood of the nation with its headline "A Single Incident in a Brutal War Shocks the American Conscience."

THE INVASION OF CAMBODIA Despite the shock over My Lai, however, the country's mood by 1970 seemed to be growing less explosive. American troops were on their way home, and it appeared that the war was finally winding down. Indeed, a *New York Times* survey of college campuses in 1969 had revealed that many students were shifting their attention from the antiwar movement to the environment.

Then on April 30, 1970, President Nixon announced that U.S. troops had invaded Cambodia. The "incursion" into Cambodia was launched, Nixon declared, to clear out North Vietnamese and Vietcong supply centers. Addressing potential critics, the president defended his action: "If when the chips are down, the world's most powerful nation . . . acts like a pitiful, helpless giant, the forces of totalitarianism and anarchy will threaten free nations . . . throughout the world."

Upon hearing of the invasion, college students across the country erupted in protest. In what became the first general student strike in the nation's history, more than 1.5 million students closed down some 1,200 campuses. The president of Columbia University called the month that followed the Cambodian invasion "the most disastrous month of May in the history of higher education."

KENT STATE Disaster struck hardest at Kent State University in Ohio, where a massive student protest led to the burning of the ROTC building. In response to the growing unrest, the local mayor called in the National Guard. On May 4, 1970, the guards fired into a crowd of campus protesters who were hurling rocks at them. The gunfire wounded nine people and killed four, including two who had not even participated in the rally.

Ten days later, similar violence rocked the mostly all-black college of Jackson State in Mississippi. National Guardsmen there confronted a group of antiwar demonstrators and fired on the crowd after several bottles were thrown. In the hail of bullets, 12 students were wounded and 2 were killed, both innocent bystanders.

Mary Ann Vecchio grieves over the body of Jeffrey Glenn Miller, a 20-year-old student shot by National Guard troops at Kent State.

B. Answer The shootings sparked heated debate as well as the resurgence of the "hardhats."

THINK THROUGH HISTORY
B. Analyzing Issues *How did the campus shootings demonstrate the continued divisions within the country?*

In a sign that America still remained sharply divided about the war, the country hotly debated the campus shootings. Polls indicated that many Americans supported the National Guard; respondents claimed that the students "got what they were asking for." The weeks following the campus turmoil brought new attention to a group known as "hardhats," construction workers and other blue-collar Americans who supported the U.S. government's war policies. In May of 1970, nearly 100,000 members of the Building and Construction Trades Council of New York held a rally outside city hall to support the government.

THE PENTAGON PAPERS Nixon's Cambodia policy, however, cost him significant political support. By first bombing and then invading Cambodia without

(continued from page 748)

- The slaying of student protesters and bystanders at Kent State and Jackson State rocks the nation.
- Publication of the top-secret Pentagon Papers further erodes support for the war.

MORE ABOUT . . .
Kent State

Over the years the ROTC had become a principal target of campus antiwar protests. Some students objected to being required to join the ROTC. Some wanted to ban the ROTC in order to create a manpower shortage in the U.S. military, since many officers were graduates of ROTC programs. Ironically, William Schroeder, one of the four students killed at Kent State, was an ROTC cadet, although he had begun to question the war effort. The killings at Kent State added fuel to a national student strike already scheduled in protest of the Cambodia invasion. In fact, it was at a protest connected with this strike that the Jackson State killings occurred.

ELECTRONIC LIBRARY OF PRIMARY SOURCES
On the Kent State Tragedy *from* the report by the Presidential Commission on Campus Unrest

Block Schedule TEACHING OPTION **Time Needed: 30 Minutes**

Cooperative Activity: Writing Editorials

Task: Groups of students will write newspaper editorials on issues related to the Vietnam War after 1968.

Purpose: To voice an opinion on a controversial issue.

Activity: Each group should choose an issue covered on pages 748–751. Examples include the My Lai massacre, the invasion of Cambodia, the student slayings at Kent State or Jackson State, or the release of the Pentagon Papers. Group members should review one another's rough drafts and suggest revisions.

Building a Portfolio: Remind students to choose their strongest work for their portfolio.

ALTERNATIVE ASSESSMENT BOOK
Standards for Evaluating a Cooperative Activity

Standards for Evaluation
Editorials should . . .

- express viewpoints supported with logical arguments
- reflect historical facts accurately
- persuade readers to consider the opinions presented

MORE ABOUT . . .
Daniel Ellsberg

Ellsberg had lost faith in the war by 1970. When he leaked the Pentagon Papers to the *New York Times,* Kissinger reportedly hit the roof. Ellsberg remained a lifelong antiwar activist; in 1991, he was arrested for protesting the Gulf War.

 ***THE WAR IN VIETNAM*** excerpts from the Pentagon Papers

OBJECTIVE
③ **INSTRUCT**

America's Longest War Ends

▶ ***Discussing Key Ideas***
- After Nixon's reelection, peace talks break off and U.S. bombings resume.
- In 1973, the United States and North Vietnam sign a cease-fire agreement, and the last U.S. combat troops withdraw from Vietnam.
- The cease-fire collapses, and in 1975 South Vietnam falls to North Vietnam.

 ***HUMANITIES TRANSPARENCIES*** H28, Fall of Saigon

KEY PLAYER
Henry Kissinger

Critical Thinking: Analyzing In the 1968 presidential campaign, Kissinger had backed Nelson Rockefeller. After Nixon won the election, he staffed his administration with some Rockefeller Republicans as a gesture of party unity. Discuss how the saying "Politics makes strange bedfellows" might be applied to Nixon and Kissinger.

even notifying Congress, the president stirred anger on Capitol Hill. On December 31, 1970, Congress repealed the Tonkin Gulf Resolution, which had given the president near independence in conducting policy in Vietnam.

Support for the war eroded even further when in June of 1971 former Defense Department worker Daniel Ellsberg leaked what became known as the **Pentagon Papers.** The 7,000-page document, written for Defense Secretary Robert McNamara, revealed among other things that the government drew up plans for entering the war even as President Lyndon Johnson promised that he would not send American troops to Vietnam. Furthermore, the papers showed that there was never any plan to end the war as long as the North Vietnamese persisted.

For many Americans, the Pentagon Papers confirmed their belief that the government had not been honest about its war intentions. The document, while not particularly damaging to the Nixon administration, supported what opponents of the war had been saying.

THINK THROUGH HISTORY
C. *Making Predictions* *How might the release of the Pentagon Papers have hurt the Nixon administration's war effort in Vietnam?*

C. Answer The release of the Pentagon Papers may have further eroded public support for the war and made Americans more distrustful of what the current administration was reporting about Vietnam.

HENRY KISSINGER
1923–

Henry Kissinger fled Germany with his family in 1938, to escape the Nazi persecution of the Jews. Kissinger, who helped negotiate America's withdrawal from Vietnam and who later would help forge historic new relations with China and the Soviet Union, held a deep interest in the concept of power. "You know," he once noted, "most of these world leaders, you wouldn't want to know socially. Mostly they are intellectual mediocrities. The thing that is interesting about them is . . . their power."

At first, Kissinger seemed an unlikely candidate to work for Richard Nixon. During the 1968 presidential campaign, Kissinger declared, "That man Nixon is not fit to be president." However, the two would become trusted colleagues. In August of 1974, two days before Nixon resigned as president amid the Watergate political scandal, he summoned Kissinger to the Lincoln Sitting Room upstairs in the White House. There, the two men reportedly knelt together, prayed, and then embraced.

America's Longest War Ends

In March of 1972, the North Vietnamese launched their largest attack on South Vietnam since the Tet offensive in 1968. President Nixon responded by ordering a massive bombing campaign against North Vietnamese cities, and the mining of Haiphong's harbor, into which Soviet and Chinese supply ships sailed. The Communists "have never been bombed like they are going to be bombed this time," Nixon vowed. The bombings halted the North Vietnamese attack, but the grueling stalemate continued. It was after this that the Nixon administration took steps to finally end America's involvement in Vietnam.

"PEACE IS AT HAND" By the middle of 1972, the country's growing social division and the looming presidential election prompted the Nixon administration to change its negotiating policy in Paris. Polls showed that more than 60 percent of Americans in 1971 felt that the United States should withdraw all troops from Vietnam by the end of the year.

Henry Kissinger, the president's adviser for national security affairs, served as Nixon's top negotiator in Vietnam. Kissinger, a German emigrant who had earned three degrees from Harvard, was an expert on international relations. Since 1969, Kissinger had been meeting privately with North Vietnam's chief negotiator, Le Duc Tho. Eventually, Kissinger dropped his insistence on the removal of all North Vietnamese troops from the South before the complete withdrawal of American troops. On October 26, 1972, one week before the presidential election, Kissinger announced, "Peace is at hand."

THE FINAL PUSH President Nixon won reelection, but the promised peace proved to be elusive. The Thieu regime, alarmed at the prospect of North Vietnamese troops stationed in South Vietnam, rejected Kissinger's plan. Talks broke off on December 16, and two days later, the president unleashed a ferocious bombing campaign against Hanoi and Haiphong, the two largest cities in North Vietnam. In what became known as the "Christmas bombings," U.S. planes dropped 100,000 bombs for 11 straight days, pausing only on Christmas Day.

At this point, calls to end the war resounded from the halls of Congress as well as from Beijing and Moscow. Everyone, it seemed, had finally grown weary of the war. The warring parties returned to the

TEACHING OPTIONS

Exploring Themes

Constitutional Concerns Though the Pentagon Papers controversy reflected the duplicity of Johnson's administration, Nixon felt that its content further undermined public faith in the war. His administration tried to stop its publication in a case that went all the way to the Supreme Court. While agreeing that the government could file criminal charges for theft or possession of classified documents, the court decided in the *New York Times*'s favor in the matter of publication.

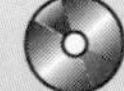 ***THE WAR IN VIETNAM*** texts of the Supreme Court decision in the Times-Post Case

Making Global Connections

Kissinger and Foreign Policy Nixon's visit to the People's Republic of China was one of the landmark foreign-policy achievements of his presidential administration. Kissinger was a chief behind-the-scenes negotiator for that historical visit. He also played a vital role in Mideast peace negotiations and developed the policy of better relations with the Soviet Union, called détente. He continued to be a major architect of U.S. foreign policy during President Ford's administration.

peace table, and on January 27, 1973, the United States signed an "agreement on ending the war and restoring peace in Vietnam." Under the agreement, North Vietnamese troops would remain in South Vietnam, which had Nixon's promise to respond "with full force" to any violation of the peace agreement. On March 29, 1973, the last U.S. combat troops left for home. For America, the Vietnam War had ended.

THE FALL OF SAIGON The war itself, however, raged on. Within months of the United States' departure, the cease-fire agreement between North and South Vietnam collapsed. In March of 1975, after several years of fighting, the North Vietnamese launched a full-scale invasion against the South. Thieu appealed to the United States for help. America provided economic aid but refused to send troops.

President Gerald Ford, who entered the White House after the Watergate political scandal forced Richard Nixon out, captured the nation's mood during a speech in New Orleans: "America can regain its sense of pride that existed before Vietnam. But it cannot be achieved by refighting a war that is finished as far as America is concerned." On April 30, 1975, North Vietnamese tanks rolled into Saigon and captured the city. Soon after, South Vietnam surrendered to North Vietnam.

D. Answer Because of the war's divisive effect on the country, as well as the desire to heal the country and move on.

THINK THROUGH HISTORY
D. *Evaluating Decisions* *Why might the United States have refused to reenter the war?*

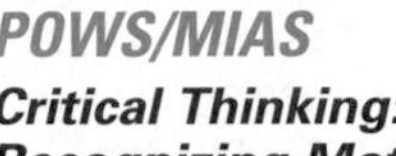

POWS/MIAS

An issue that remains alive for many Americans concerns the thousands of soldiers who did not return home from Vietnam. In 1995, the Pentagon reported that there were still 2,202 American soldiers missing in action (MIA) in Southeast Asia—1,618 in Vietnam.

While far more Americans are listed as missing from the Korean War (8,170) and World War II (78,750), locating missing soldiers in Vietnam has taken on a particular intensity. One reason is that despite the Vietnamese government's denial, a number of Americans believe that some U.S. soldiers may still be alive in Vietnam.

The United States has established an MIA office in Hanoi, whose staff members attempt to locate the remains of missing Americans and track down leads about the possibility of surviving soldiers.

The War's Painful Legacy

The Vietnam War exacted a terrible price from its participants. In all, 58,000 Americans were killed and some 365,000 were wounded. North and South Vietnamese deaths topped 1.5 million. In addition, the war left Southeast Asia highly unstable, which led to further war in Cambodia. In America, a nation attempted to come to grips with an unsuccessful war. In the end, the conflict in Vietnam left many Americans with a more cautious outlook on foreign affairs and a more cynical attitude toward their government.

AMERICAN VETERANS COPE BACK HOME While families welcomed home their sons and daughters, the nation as a whole extended a cold hand to its

Lieutenant Colonel Robert Stirm, a returning POW, receives a warm welcome from his family. The longest-held Vietnam POW was Lieutenant Everett Alvarez, Jr., of California. He was imprisoned for more than eight years.

NOW & THEN
POWS/MIAS

Critical Thinking: Recognizing Motives
Have students speculate on the reasons that the MIA issue remains alive for some Americans. *Possible Responses: Family members hold on to the hope that MIAs are still alive, since no final proof exists to the contrary; family members' sense of loss remains unresolved.*

OBJECTIVE
(4) INSTRUCT

The War's Painful Legacy

▶ ***Starting with the Student***
Have students discuss the homecomings that winning World Series and Super Bowl teams receive. Ask students to draw parallels between sports heroes and war heroes.

- Were the soldiers who served in Vietnam heroes? Why or why not?

▶ ***Discussing Key Ideas***
- Vietnam veterans receive a cold homecoming, and some face difficulties in readjusting to civilian life.
- The war's end ushers in a violent, chaotic period in Southeast Asia.
- The war still stirs up controversy and leads to major U.S. policy changes.

THE WAR IN VIETNAM video on the exodus of the boat people

TEACHING OPTION

Making Connections Across Cultures

Native American War Veterans Various tribal ceremonies helped many Native American veterans recover from the psychological trauma of Vietnam. For example, the "squaw dance," also called the Enemy Way, is a Navajo ritual for their returning warriors. As part of the four-day ceremony, a medicine man recounts the tale of the Hero Twins—slayers of the world's monsters. According to the story, "In the process of destroying the Monsters the Twins abused their special powers and weapons and disrupted the harmony in nature by killing some people. . . . [The Twins] thus needed a special ceremony to restore them to harmony. Thus was born the first 'Enemy Way.'"

A Kiowa veteran recalled the homecoming he received: "My people honored me as a warrior. We had a feast and my parents and grandparents thanked everyone who prayed for my safe return. We had a 'special' [a ritual ceremony] and I remembered as we circled the drum I got a feeling of pride. I felt good inside because that's the way the Kiowa people tell you that you've done well."

HISTORICAL SPOTLIGHT

Vietnam Veterans Memorial: The Wall

Maya Lin's vision of the memorial as a "journey, or passage" became a reality. Millions of people have made pilgrimages to the Wall, leaving notes and tokens of remembrance by the inscribed names of their loved ones. Have students research the objects that visitors have left at the Wall. Discuss why these objects might be considered historical artifacts or primary sources.

MORE ABOUT . . .

Vietnam Veterans Memorial

In addition to the Wall, the Vietnam Veterans Memorial site on the National Mall includes a sculpture of three soldiers, added in 1984, and the Vietnam's Women's Memorial, built in 1993.

MORE ABOUT . . .

Delayed Stress Syndrome

Among the legacies of the Vietnam War is a better understanding of delayed stress syndrome, also called posttraumatic stress disorder (PTSD). PTSD results from exposure to such life-threatening situations as warfare, terrorism, violent crime, and natural disasters. Since the 1970s the Veterans Administration has taken the lead in diagnosis and treatment of the disorder, which the American Psychiatric Association formally recognized in 1980.

America's Longest War, 1964–1973

- **1964** — Congress passes Tonkin Gulf Resolution, giving president broad military powers in Vietnam; President Johnson begins bombing North Vietnam.
- **1965** — First U.S. ground troops arrive in Vietnam to begin fighting the Vietcong and North Vietnamese Army.
- **1967** — Antiwar protests in the United States intensify.
- **1968** — Vietcong launch massive Tet offensive on numerous South Vietnamese cities.

returning Vietnam veterans. There were no brass bands, no victory parades, no cheering crowds. Instead, many veterans faced indifference or even hostility from an America still torn and bitter about the war. Lily Jean Lee Adams, who served as an army nurse in Vietnam, recalled arriving, while still in uniform, back at Oakland Army Base in 1970.

A PERSONAL VOICE

> In the bus terminal, people were staring at me and giving me dirty looks. I expected the people to smile, like, "Wow, she was in Vietnam, doing something for her country—wonderful." I felt like I had walked into another country, not my country. So I went into the ladies' room and changed.
>
> LILY JEAN LEE ADAMS, quoted in *A Piece of My Heart*

Many Vietnam veterans readjusted successfully to civilian life. However, about 15 percent of the 3.3 million soldiers who served developed delayed stress syndrome. These veterans had recurring nightmares about their war experience. Many suffered from severe headaches and memory lapses. Some veterans became highly apathetic, while others began abusing drugs or alcohol. Several thousand even committed suicide.

In 1982, the U.S. government, in an effort to honor the men and women who served in Vietnam, unveiled the Vietnam Veterans Memorial in Washington, D.C. The memorial consists of two black granite walls inscribed with the names of all the Americans who died in the war or who were then still listed as missing in action. Many Vietnam veterans, as well as their loved ones, have found visiting the memorial a deeply moving, even healing experience.

HISTORICAL SPOTLIGHT

VIETNAM VETERANS MEMORIAL: THE WALL

Shortly after 1980, a national competition was held to determine the Vietnam memorial's design. Maya Ying Lin, *above*, a 20-year-old architecture student of Chinese descent, submitted the winning design—a long, black granite wall on which are etched the names of the men and women who died or are missing in action, *below*.

"I didn't want a static object that people would just look at," Lin said, "but something they could relate to as on a journey, or passage, that would bring each to his own conclusions." Lin's design became known simply as the Wall.

FURTHER TURMOIL IN SOUTHEAST ASIA The end of the Vietnam War ushered in a new period of violence and chaos in Southeast Asia. In unifying Vietnam, the Communists initially held out a conciliatory hand to the South Vietnamese. "You have nothing to fear," declared Colonel Bui Tin of the North Vietnamese Army.

However, the Communists soon imprisoned more than 400,000 South Vietnamese in harsh "reeducation," or labor, camps. As the Communists imposed their rule throughout the land, nearly 1.5 million people fled Vietnam. They included citizens who had supported the U.S. war effort, as well as business owners, whom the Communists expelled when they began nationalizing the country's business sector.

Also fleeing the country was a large group of poor Vietnamese, known as boat people because they left on anything from freighters to barges to rowboats. Their efforts to reach safety across the South China Sea often met with tragedy, as nearly 50,000 perished on the high seas due to exposure, drowning, illness, or piracy.

The people of Cambodia also suffered greatly after the war. The U.S. invasion of Cambodia had unleashed a brutal civil war, in which a Communist group known as the **Khmer Rouge** seized power in 1975. In an effort to transform the country into a peasant society, the Khmer Rouge

TEACHING OPTIONS

Global Connections

Cambodia Led by Pol Pot, the Khmer Rouge created what is sometimes called Cambodia's "killing fields" and drove many Cambodians into neighboring Thailand. By 1977 Communist Vietnam was fighting the Khmer Rouge with the aid of Cambodian Communists. In 1979 Vietnam invaded Cambodia and toppled Pol Pot's regime. The new fighting, which resulted in more deaths and another wave of refugees to Thailand, continued sporadically until Vietnam withdrew its troops in 1989. Three years later a United Nations–brokered peace plan put Cambodia on the road to democracy.

Exploring Themes

Cultural Diversity Many of the Vietnamese refugees who fled to the United States after the war developed a new and unique cultural identity. As Hien Duc Do remarked, "Having left Vietnam at an early age [14], I have realized that I can never truly be a Vietnamese, and, at the same time, not having grown up in the United States, I can never fully be an American. In the final analysis, my life experience will not be that of a Vietnamese nor that of an American, but that of a Vietnamese-American. I need to merge the world of my parents with the opportunities, experiences, and hopes that America has to offer."

1969 — Paris peace talks begin in earnest; President Nixon announces Vietnamization of war—gradual withdrawal of U.S. troops.

1970 — President Nixon orders invasion of Cambodia to destroy enemy supply bases; American college campuses erupt in protest.

1972 — Nixon unleashes "Christmas bombings" on North Vietnamese cities after peace talks break off.

1973 — United States and North Vietnam sign a truce; the U.S. withdraws the last of its troops from Vietnam.

executed many government officials and academics. During its reign of terror, the Khmer Rouge is believed to have killed as many as 2 million Cambodians.

VIETNAM'S EFFECT ON AMERICA Even after it ended, the Vietnam War remained a subject of great controversy for Americans. Many hawks continued to insist that the war could have been won if the U.S. had employed more military power. They also blamed the antiwar movement at home for destroying American morale. Doves countered that the North Vietnamese had displayed incredible resiliency and that an increase in U.S. military force would have resulted only in a continuing stalemate. In addition, doves argued that an unrestrained war against North Vietnam might have prompted a military reaction from China or the Soviet Union.

The war resulted in several major U.S. policy changes. First, the government abolished the draft, which had stirred so much antiwar sentiment. The country also took steps to curb the president's war-making powers. In November 1973, Congress passed the **War Powers Act,** which stipulated that a president must inform Congress within 48 hours if U.S. forces are sent into a hostile area without a declaration of war. In addition, the troops may remain there no longer than 90 days unless Congress approves the president's actions or declares war.

E. Answer Many Americans viewed foreign affairs more cautiously and grew more cynical of their own government and political leaders.

In a broader sense, the Vietnam War significantly altered America's views on foreign policy. In what has been labeled the Vietnam syndrome, Americans now pause and consider possible risks to their own interests before deciding whether to intervene in the affairs of other nations.

Finally, the war contributed to an overall cynicism in Americans about their government and political leaders that persists today. Americans grew suspicious of a government that had provided so much misleading information—as the Johnson administration did—or concealed so many activities—as the Nixon administration did. Coupled with the Watergate scandal of the mid-1970s, the war diminished the optimism and faith in government that Americans felt during the Eisenhower and Kennedy years.

THINK THROUGH HISTORY
E. *Recognizing Effects* *In what way did the Vietnam War alter American attitudes?*

NOW & THEN

U.S. RECOGNITION OF VIETNAM

In July of 1995, more than 20 years after the Vietnam War ended, the United States extended full diplomatic relations to Vietnam. In announcing the resumption of ties with Vietnam, President Bill Clinton declared, "Let this moment . . . be a time to heal and a time to build." Demonstrating how the war still divides Americans, the president's decision drew both praise and criticism from members of Congress and veterans' groups.

In an ironic twist, Clinton nominated as ambassador to Vietnam a former prisoner of war from the Vietnam War, Douglas Peterson, a congress member from Florida. Peterson, a former air force pilot, was shot down over North Vietnam in 1966 and spent six and a half years in a Hanoi prison.

Section 5 Assessment

1. TERMS & NAMES
Identify:
- Vietnamization
- silent majority
- Pentagon Papers
- Henry Kissinger
- Khmer Rouge
- War Powers Act

2. SUMMARIZING Write a newspaper headline summarizing the historical significance of each date listed below.
- March 16, 1968
- April 30, 1970
- May 4, 1970
- May 14, 1970
- December 31, 1970
- January 27, 1973
- March 29, 1973

Choose a headline and write the first paragraph for the newspaper article.

3. SYNTHESIZING In your opinion, what was the effect of the U.S. government's deception about its policies and military conduct in Vietnam? Support your answer with evidence from the text.

THINK ABOUT
- the release of information surrounding the My Lai massacre
- the contents of the Pentagon Papers
- Nixon's secrecy in authorizing military maneuvers

4. MAKING INFERENCES How would you account for the cold homecoming American soldiers received when they returned from Vietnam? Support your answer with reasons.

THINK ABOUT
- how the Vietnam War ended
- America's divisiveness over its role in Vietnam
- the media coverage of the My Lai massacre

ANSWERS

1. TERMS & NAMES
- Vietnamization, p. 748
- silent majority, p. 748
- Pentagon Papers, p. 750
- Henry Kissinger, p. 750
- Khmer Rouge, p. 752
- War Powers Act, p. 753

2. SUMMARIZING
Possible Answers: March 16, 1968: Massacre at My Lai; April 30, 1970: Nixon Announces Invasion of Cambodia; May 4, 1970: Kent State Tragedy; May 14, 1970: Two Students Killed at Jackson State; December 31, 1970: Congress Repeals Tonkin Gulf Resolution; January 27, 1973: U.S. Signs Agreement to End Vietnam War; March 29, 1973: Last U.S. Combat Troops Leave Vietnam.

3. SYNTHESIZING
Possible Responses: Since Americans did not learn about the My Lai massacre until over 1½ years after it occurred, they distrusted government reports about Vietnam battles; the leaking of the Pentagon Papers in 1971 confirmed that the Johnson administration had not been entirely honest about its war intentions; Nixon's secretly ordering a massive bombing campaign in North Vietnam caused public mistrust.

4. MAKING INFERENCES
Possible Responses: The American public might have projected the war's failure onto the soldiers who fought it; though the war ended, many Americans' bitterness and cynicism persisted; the My Lai massacre might have tarnished the image of all U.S. soldiers.

NOW & THEN
U.S. Recognition of Vietnam

Critical Thinking: Forming an Opinion Have students debate whether the Clinton administration was justified in restoring diplomatic relations with Vietnam. Encourage students to consider economic and political factors, as well as deep-seated emotional factors, that may have led to this turnabout.

ASSESS & RETEACH

Section 5 Assessment
Have students work in small groups to discuss the questions and assess one another's responses.

Self-Assessment
Have students explore their understanding of the Vietnam War's legacy by listing in a chart the war's effects on each of the following: Vietnam veterans, Southeast Asia, U.S. policies, and U.S. attitudes.

Section Quiz
FORMAL ASSESSMENT
Section Quiz, p. 272

Reteach
Use the time line spanning the top of pages 752–753 to trace key events of the war, their causes, and their effects on America.

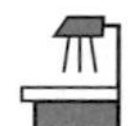
GEOGRAPHY TRANSPARENCIES
G30, Vietnam War: 1964–1975

CLOSE

After escalating bombings to achieve "peace with honor," the Nixon administration negotiated a cease-fire agreement and withdrew U.S. troops from Vietnam in 1973. The painful legacies of the controversial and divisive war still affect American life.

IN-DEPTH RESOURCES: UNIT 6
Outline Map: The Vietnam War, p. 43

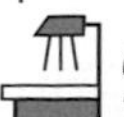
CRITICAL THINKING TRANSPARENCIES
CT30, The War in Vietnam

American Literature

OBJECTIVES

1. To explain the Vietnam War's influence on literature.
2. To identify the perceptions of the Vietnam War expressed in three literary excerpts.

FOCUS & MOTIVATE

▶ ***Starting with the Student*** Ask students what books they have read and what films they have seen about the Vietnam War.

- What general impressions did these works give of the Vietnam War and its warriors?
- How do the literary and film images compare with those in movies and novels set in other 20th-century wars?
- Why is literature about the Vietnam War so extensive and diverse?

MORE ABOUT . . .
Tim O'Brien

A gifted writer about the Vietnam War, Tim O'Brien was drafted just after graduating from Macalester College in 1968. A Minnesota native, he was deeply troubled by the war and even considered avoiding service. Instead, he fought valiantly in Vietnam and earned a Purple Heart. He completed his tour of duty in 1970 and won acclaim for his semifictional memoir *If I Die in a Combat Zone* in 1973. *Going After Cacciato* received the National Book Award.

AMERICAN LITERATURE

Literature of the Vietnam War

Throughout history, soldiers as well as citizens have written about the traumatic and moving experiences of war. The Vietnam War, which left a deep impression on America's soldiers and citizens alike, has produced its share of literature. From the surreal fantasy of *Going After Cacciato*, to the grim realism of *A Rumor of War*, much of this literature reflects the nation's lingering disillusionment with its involvement in the Vietnam War.

GOING AFTER CACCIATO

In *Going After Cacciato*, Vietnam veteran Tim O'Brien tells the story of Paul Berlin, a newcomer to Vietnam who fantasizes that his squad goes all the way to Paris, France, in pursuit of an AWOL soldier.

"How many days you been at the war?" asked Alpha's [Alpha Company's] mail clerk, and Paul Berlin answered that he'd been at the war seven days now.

The clerk laughed. "Wrong," he said. "Tomorrow, man, that's your first day at the war."

And in the morning PFC [Private First Class] Paul Berlin boarded a resupply chopper that took him fast over charred pocked mangled country, hopeless country, green skies and speed and tangled grasslands and paddies and places he might die, a million possibilities. He couldn't watch. He watched his hands. He made fists of them, opening and closing the fists. His hands, he thought, not quite believing. *His* hands.

Very quickly, the helicopter banked and turned and went down.

"How long you been at the war?" asked the first man he saw, a wiry soldier with ringworm in his hair.

PFC Paul Berlin smiled. "This is it," he said. "My first day."

Tim O'Brien, *Going After Cacciato* (1975)

RECOMMENDED RESOURCES

Books

Hayslip, Le Ly. *When Heaven and Earth Changed Places.* New York: Doubleday, 1989. A first-person account of a Vietnamese woman's experiences in the war.

O'Brien, Tim. *The Things They Carried.* Boston: Houghton, 1990. Interrelated stories capturing the Vietnam War era. Note: contains strong language.

Wyatt, David. *Out of the Sixties.* Cambridge UP, 1993. A study of storytelling and the Vietnam War generation.

Videos

A Rumor of War. Dir. Richard T. Heffron. USA Home Video, 1984. Acclaimed made-for-TV movie based on Caputo's book.

Vietnam: Chronicle of a War. CBS/Fox Video, 1981. Retrospective of the Vietnam War, based on CBS news broadcasts featuring Walter Cronkite and others.

Software

USA Wars: Vietnam. CD-ROM. Quanta Press. Brings the war to life with articles, images, facts, statistics, and the entire Vietnam Veterans Memorial database.

Vietnam: A Visual Investigation. CD-ROM. Medio, 1994.

754 Chapter 22

A RUMOR OF WAR

In *A Rumor of War,* considered to be among the best nonfiction accounts of the war, former marine Philip Caputo reflects on his years as a soldier in Vietnam.

At the age of twenty-four, I was more prepared for death than I was for life. . . . I knew how to face death and how to cause it, with everything on the evolutionary scale of weapons from the knife to the 3.5-inch rocket launcher. The simplest repairs on an automobile engine were beyond me, but I was able to field-strip and assemble an M-14 rifle blindfolded. I could call in artillery, set up an ambush, rig a booby trap, lead a night raid.

Simply by speaking a few words into a two-way radio, I had performed magical feats of destruction. Summoned by my voice, jet fighters appeared in the sky to loose their lethal droppings on villages and men. High-explosive bombs blasted houses to fragments, napalm sucked air from lungs and turned human flesh to ashes. All this just by saying a few words into a radio transmitter. Like magic.

PHILIP CAPUTO, *A Rumor of War* (1977)

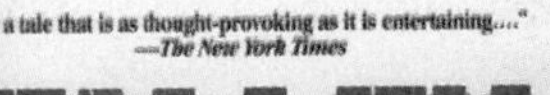

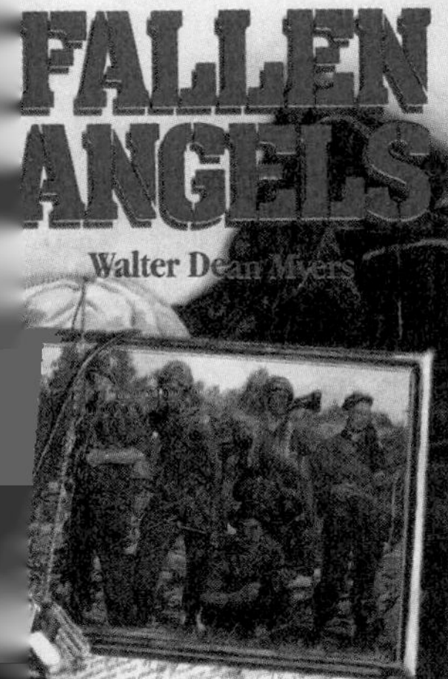

FALLEN ANGELS

Richie Perry, a 17-year-old Harlem youth, describes his harrowing tour of duty in Vietnam in Walter Dean Myers's novel *Fallen Angels.*

The war was about us killing people and about people killing us, and I couldn't see much more to it. Maybe there were times when it was right. I had thought that this war was right, but it was only right from a distance. Maybe when we all got back to the World and everybody thought we were heroes for winning it, then it would seem right from there. . . . But when the killing started, there was no right or wrong except in the way you did your job, except in the way that you were part of the killing.

What you thought about, what filled you up more than anything, was the being scared and hearing your heart thumping in your temples and all the noises, the terrible noises, the screeches and the booms and the guys crying for their mothers or for their wives.

WALTER DEAN MYERS, *Fallen Angels* (1988)

INTERACT WITH HISTORY

1. **COMPARING** What similar views about war do you think these three books convey?

SEE SKILLBUILDER HANDBOOK, PAGE 909.

2. **CHRONICLING A WAR** Choose a war in which the United States fought and research one aspect of the war (that is, a battle, or living conditions, or a march). Imagine you are a war correspondent in that war and write an article describing the event you have chosen.

INTERNET Visit http://www.mlushistory.com for more about American wars.

INSTRUCT

▶ *Discussing Key Ideas*

- American literature about the Vietnam War creatively expresses the multiple interpretations and enduring impact of that conflict.
- The portrayals of the war in the three literary works shown on these pages range from surrealistic to grimly realistic.

HISTORY FROM VISUALS

Reading the Images

Have students imagine that they are glancing at these jacket illustrations in a bookstore.

- Which cover is the most striking? Why?
- What words capture the overall effect of the images on each book jacket? *Possible Responses:* Going After Cacciato—*exultation, self-mastery;* A Rumor of War—*desolation, thoughtfulness;* Fallen Angels—*weariness, camaraderie.*
- Why might the publisher of *A Rumor of War* have selected a photograph, rather than a piece of fine art, for the jacket illustration? *Possible Response: The realism of a photograph underscores that the book is nonfiction—Caputo's memoir of his combat experiences.*

INTERACT WITH HISTORY

1. Comparing

Possible Answers: *These three books convey the grim reality of war instead of glorifying it; they paint portraits of disillusionment, horror, violence, fear, inhumanity, and senselessness.*

2. Chronicling a War

Standards for Evaluation
News articles should . . .

- focus on particular aspects or battles of the war
- begin with their most important points
- tell who, what, where, when, why, and how
- provide accurate facts and details
- be written with an objective, journalistic tone

CHAPTER 22
ASSESSMENT ANSWERS

REVIEWING THE CHAPTER

TERMS & NAMES

1. Ho Chi Minh, p. 724
2. Vietcong, p. 726
3. William Westmoreland, p. 730
4. Agent Orange, p. 732
5. dove, p. 739
6. hawk, p. 739
7. Tet offensive, p. 741
8. Robert Kennedy, p. 743
9. Vietnamization, p. 748
10. Pentagon Papers, p. 750

MAIN IDEAS

11. The resolution granted President Johnson broad war-making powers in Vietnam, which allowed him to escalate U.S. involvement in the war.
12. Countries on the brink of communism were like a row of dominoes. If South Vietnam fell to the Communists, the rest of Southeast Asia would follow in a kind of chain reaction.
13. The spread of communism jeopardized democracy.
14. The frustrations of guerrilla warfare; the brutal jungle conditions; the failure to overcome the enemy.
15. A highly disproportionate rate of combat deaths; racial tensions in many platoons.
16. Doves staged massive antiwar demonstrations; hawks urged a greater use of military force in Vietnam.
17. Johnson's high disapproval rating in public-opinion polls after the Tet offensive; the divisions within the Democratic Party.
18. The assassinations of Dr. Martin Luther King, Jr., and Robert Kennedy; the riots at the Democratic National Convention in Chicago.
19. The war itself raged on; the cease-fire agreement between North Vietnam and South Vietnam collapsed.
20. U.S. policy changes; American public's cynicism about the government.

Chapter 22 Assessment

REVIEWING THE CHAPTER

TERMS & NAMES For each item below, write a sentence explaining its connection to the Vietnam War. For each person or group of people named below, explain his or their role in the war's events.

1. Ho Chi Minh	**6. hawk**
2. Vietcong	**7. Tet offensive**
3. William Westmoreland	**8. Robert Kennedy**
4. Agent Orange	**9. Vietnamization**
5. dove	**10. Pentagon Papers**

MAIN IDEAS

SECTION 1 *(pages 724–728)*

Moving Toward Conflict

11. How did the Tonkin Gulf Resolution lead to greater U.S. involvement in Vietnam?
12. What was President Eisenhower's explanation of the domino theory?

SECTION 2 *(pages 729–734)*

U.S. Involvement and Escalation

13. Why did much of the American public and many in the Johnson administration support U.S. escalation in Vietnam?
14. Name three factors that contributed to the sinking morale among U.S. troops fighting in Vietnam.

SECTION 3 *(pages 735–740)*

A Nation Divided

15. What race-related problems existed for African-American soldiers who served in the Vietnam War?
16. What evidence was there that the country was sharply divided between hawks and doves?

SECTION 4 *(pages 741–746)*

1968: A Tumultuous Year

17. What circumstances set the stage for President Johnson's public announcement that he would not seek another term as president?
18. What acts of violence occurred in the United States during 1968 that dramatically altered the mood of the country?

SECTION 5 *(pages 747–753)*

The End of the War and Its Legacy

19. Briefly describe the military conflict in Vietnam soon after the last U.S. combat troops departed in 1973.
20. What were the immediate effects and more lasting legacies of the Vietnam War within America?

THINKING CRITICALLY

1. **PRESIDENTIAL POWER** Create a cause-and-effect web similar to the one shown for each of these congressional measures: (a) Tonkin Gulf Resolution (1964), (b) repeal of the Tonkin Gulf Resolution (1970), (c) War Powers Act (1973).

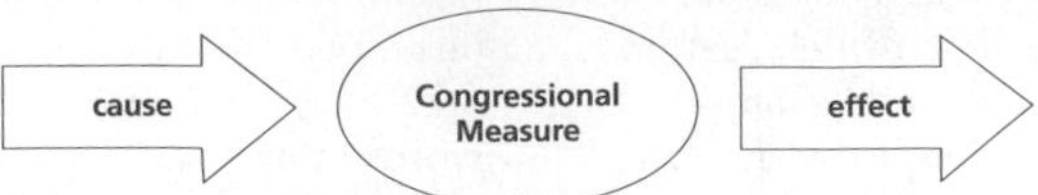

2. **TRACING THEMES DEMOCRACY IN AMERICA** Why do you think that many young Americans became so vocal in their condemnation of the Vietnam War?
3. **THE VIETNAM WAR'S LEGACY** Reread the quotation by Henry Kissinger on page 722. Explain what he meant. Do you agree or disagree? Explain your answer.
4. **GEOGRAPHY OF THE TET OFFENSIVE** Compare the maps on pages 726 and 742. How would you describe the geographic area involved in the Tet offensive?
5. **AMERICAN LITERATURE: LITERATURE OF THE VIETNAM WAR** In what ways do each of the literary excerpts on pages 754–755 broaden your understanding of the Vietnam War from a soldier's perspective? Based on these excerpts, what would you consider to be the gravest issues that young soldiers in Vietnam faced?
6. **ANALYZING PRIMARY SOURCES** Senator John Kerry was formerly a national coordinator of Vietnam Veterans Against the War after his service as a naval officer. Read the following excerpt from his speech delivered to the Senate Foreign Relations Committee in 1971. Then answer the questions that follow.

> We [veterans] are probably angriest about all we were told about Vietnam and about the mythical war against communism. We found that not only was it a civil war, an effort by a people who had for years been seeking their liberation from any colonial influence whatsoever, but also found that the Vietnamese whom we had enthusiastically molded after our own image were hard put to take up the fight against the threat we were supposedly saving them from.
>
> We found most people didn't even know the difference between communism and democracy. . . . They wanted everything to do with the war, particularly with this foreign presence of the United States of America, to leave them alone in peace, and they practiced the art of survival by siding with whichever military force was present at a particular time, be it Viet Cong, North Vietnamese, or American.
>
> **JOHN KERRY,** "Statement Before the Senate Foreign Relations Committee"

What does Kerry say about the false assumptions that guided U.S. foreign policy in Vietnam? Do you agree with his analysis? Why or why not?

THINKING CRITICALLY

1. PRESIDENTIAL POWER
Possible Responses: Tonkin Gulf Resolution: Causes—North Vietnamese torpedo boats allegedly attack two U.S. destroyers; Johnson asks Congress for powers to retaliate and prevent further aggression; effects—Johnson granted broad military powers; Johnson administration escalates U.S. military involvement in Vietnam. Repeal of Tonkin Gulf Resolution: Causes—Nixon's policy of bombing and invading Cambodia without notifying Congress; Congress's anger over Nixon's apparent abuse of power; effects—President's autonomy becomes limited in conducting Vietnam policies; Congress regains power in shaping Vietnam policies. War Powers Act: Causes—The outcome of the Vietnam War; fears that Nixon was setting a dangerous precedent of unchecked presidential power; effects—President's war-making powers curbed; balance of power between executive and legislative branches of government redefined.

2. TRACING THEMES DEMOCRACY IN AMERICA
Possible Responses: Since the draft board called men between the ages of 18 and 26 into military service, the Vietnam War directly affected young Americans; the war would take its greatest toll on this generation and would have a tremendous impact on shaping their adult lives; the tragedies at Kent State and Jackson State revealed that innocent students could, in a sense, also become casualties of the war.

3. THE VIETNAM WAR'S LEGACY
Possible Responses: In stating that "Vietnam is still with us," Kissinger meant that Vietnam not only continued to divide Americans but also still affected the way in which Americans viewed their government, as well as the world around them. Agree—The debate over the U.S. decision to restore full diplomatic relations with

ALTERNATIVE ASSESSMENT

1. MAKING DECISIONS

Imagine that the year is 1968, and you have been asked to write an editorial on the Vietnam War for your school newspaper. The month-long Tet offensive has just come to a close, and public support for the war has dropped dramatically. In light of this battle, decide where you stand on the war. Do you support further escalation, a change of strategy, gradual withdrawal, or immediate withdrawal?

Use the CD-ROM *Our Times*, your text, and other sources to research the Tet offensive and its impact on the American public.

- Talk to friends and family members who lived through the period and ask them how they felt about the war.
- Determine your stand on the war. Make a list of reasons that explains your position.
- Write an editorial that supports your decision.

2. LEARNING FROM MEDIA

VIDEO View the McDougal Littell Video for Chapter 22, *Matters of Conscience*. Discuss the following questions in small groups; then do the cooperative learning activity.

- What different views about the Vietnam War were expressed in the video?
- What were Stephan Gubar's choices when he was drafted?
- Why does Stephan say he feels guilt about having served in the war?
- **Cooperative Learning** Organize two teams for a debate. One team should argue for the side of the doves—those who believed that the United States should have quickly pulled out of Vietnam. The other team should argue on behalf of the hawks—those who promoted a greater show of military force in Vietnam. Research the arguments put forth by both sides and debate the issue before the class.

3. PORTFOLIO PROJECT

Use the Living History activity to expand your portfolio.

LIVING HISTORY

DISPLAYING A VIETNAM WAR POSTER

You have created a Vietnam War poster. Now consider the following questions as you review and assess your poster:

- Does it contain dynamic verbal and visual elements?
- Are the captions appropriate and interesting?
- Is the arrangement eye-catching?
- Are there any images or words you would like to add?

Make any final changes or additions and give your poster an appropriate title. With your classmates, create a classroom display of Vietnam War posters. Add your poster to your American history portfolio.

Bridge to Chapter 23

Review Chapter 22

BEGINNINGS OF THE VIETNAM WAR The Geneva Accords (1954) temporarily divided Vietnam into Communist-controlled North Vietnam and nationalist-controlled South Vietnam. Three years later, South Vietnamese Communists, called the Vietcong, began rebelling. To try to halt the spread of communism, Presidents Eisenhower and Kennedy both sent military advisers to Vietnam. In 1964, Congress passed the Tonkin Gulf Resolution, which granted President Johnson broad powers to escalate American military involvement. In 1965, Johnson authorized massive bombing of North Vietnam, and the first U.S combat troops arrived in Vietnam. Despite U.S. escalation, the war became bogged down in a stalemate.

THE HOME FRONT Back in the United States, the war spurred a growing antiwar movement that sharply divided the nation between supporters and opponents of the government's Vietnam policies. College campuses around the country erupted in protest. Many American youths staged demonstrations, while others displayed their resistance to the draft.

THE FINAL PHASES OF THE WAR AND ITS AFTERMATH The Tet offensive in 1968 stunned Americans and strengthened opposition to the war. Two months after Tet, President Johnson announced he would withdraw from the presidential race. Richard Nixon's victory in the 1968 presidential election paved the way for the end of U.S. involvement in Vietnam, but not before his war policies created even more nationwide protest. In 1973 the United States signed a peace agreement and withdrew its forces from Vietnam. The war left many Americans with a more cautious outlook on foreign affairs and a more cynical attitude toward the government.

Preview Chapter 23

Though the Vietnam War overshadowed Johnson's vision of the Great Society, Latinos, Native Americans, and women held fast to their dreams of gaining political power and improving their status. The Vietnam War also played a key role in fostering the emergence of a youth counterculture. You will learn about these and other significant developments in the next chapter.

ALTERNATIVE ASSESSMENT

1. MAKING DECISIONS

Standards for Evaluation
An essay should meet the following criteria:

- Explains what action student would have taken.
- Provides reasons to support the decision.
- Summarizes the probable consequences of the action.
- Includes authentic details, anecdotes, and facts from the period.

2. LEARNING FROM MEDIA

Answers to the questions:

- The war was wrong; the war was necessary to halt the spread of communism; eligible Americans' patriotic duty was to serve in the war.
- Gubar could have fled to Canada, gone to jail, or applied for a noncombatant role in Vietnam.
- Even though Gubar believed the war was wrong, he didn't stand up for that belief.

Standards for Evaluation
A debate should meet the following criteria:

- Opens with a clear statement of a viewpoint on the Vietnam War.
- Contains logical arguments based on research.
- Includes well-defended objections to the opposing side's viewpoint.

3. PORTFOLIO PROJECT

LIVING HISTORY

Standards for Evaluation
An effective Vietnam War poster should meet the following criteria:

- Grabs the attention of viewers.
- Presents a clear, coherent message.
- Uses a balanced layout of images.
- Leaves viewers with a personal insight into the Vietnam War.

IN-DEPTH RESOURCES: UNIT 6
See the form for scoring this activity on page 55.

THINKING CRITICALLY

Vietnam shows that the war still divides the country; in addition, Americans do indeed view their government more cynically and are less apt to approve of U.S. troops' intervening in another country's affairs. Disagree—The restoration of U.S. relations with Vietnam shows that the country is getting over the war; also, the United States remains the strongest nation in the world and continues to act confidently in its foreign relations.

4. GEOGRAPHY OF THE TET OFFENSIVE

Possible Response: The entire area of South Vietnam was under attack, but most battles took place along the coast, with some battles occurring in interior regions.

5. AMERICAN LITERATURE: LITERATURE OF THE VIETNAM WAR

Possible Response: The excerpts provide readers with a sense of immediacy and highly personal, brutally honest views of the Vietnam War. Among the gravest issues facing young soldiers were thoughts about their mortality, their powerlessness to control their destinies, the constant anticipation of death, and the overall unreal quality of war.

6. ANALYZING PRIMARY SOURCES

Possible Responses: False assumptions included that Vietnam was in the midst of a Communist revolution and that the Vietnamese would readily embrace democratic values. Agree—Above all else, the Vietnamese simply wanted to control their own destiny, and the real struggle of the Vietnamese was against foreign domination; the Americans were unwelcome intruders in a civil war. Disagree—Kerry is parroting the rhetoric of antiwar protesters; he is downplaying the threat of communism; he is subverting America's goal of preserving global freedom.

CHAPTER 23

PLANNING GUIDE

An Era of Social Change

	Key Ideas	COPYMASTERS	ASSESSMENT
SECTION 1 Latinos and Native Americans Seek Equality *pp. 760–765*	*The nation's Latinos and Native Americans demand greater equality.*	***In-Depth Resources: Unit 6*** • Guided Reading, p. 56 • Primary Sources: The Farm Worker Movement, p. 62; United Farm Workers Poster, p. 63 • American Lives: Cesar Chavez, p. 69 ***Lesson Plans,*** pp. 187–188	PE ***Section 1 Assessment,*** p. 765 TE ***Self-Assessment,*** p. 765 ***Formal Assessment*** • Section Quiz, p. 283 ***Alternative Assessment Book*** • Standards for Evaluating a Cooperative Activity
SECTION 2 Women Fight for Equality *pp. 768–772*	*A new feminist movement emerges during the 1960s, as women fight to improve their opportunities and status in society.*	***In-Depth Resources: Unit 6*** • Guided Reading, p. 57 • Geography Application: The Equal Rights Amendment, p. 60 • Primary Source: from *The Feminine Mystique*, p. 64 • American Lives: Betty Friedan, p. 70 ***Lesson Plans,*** pp. 189–190	PE ***Section 2 Assessment,*** p. 772 TE ***Self-Assessment,*** p. 772 ***Formal Assessment*** • Section Quiz, p. 284 ***Alternative Assessment Book*** • Standards for Evaluating a Cooperative Activity
SECTION 3 Culture and Counterculture *pp. 773–777*	*Groups of disillusioned youths shun the social activism of the times and choose instead to "drop out" of society and establish their own way of life.*	***In-Depth Resources: Unit 6*** • Guided Reading, p. 58 • Skillbuilder Practice: Comparing; Contrasting, p. 59 • Primary Source: Popular Song, p. 65 • Literature: from *Los Vendidos* by Luis Valdez, p. 66 ***Lesson Plans,*** pp. 191-192	PE ***Section 2 Assessment,*** p. 777 TE ***Self-Assessment,*** p. 777 ***Formal Assessment*** • Section Quiz, p. 285 ***Alternative Assessment Book*** • Standards for Evaluating a Cooperative Activity
CHAPTER RESOURCES	**Chapter Overview** *The civil rights movement inspires Latinos, Native Americans, and women to seek equality in American society. At the same time, the nation's young people adopt values that conflict with mainstream culture.*	***In-Depth Resources: Unit 6*** • Living History Project: Worksheet, p. 71; Standards, p. 72 ***Telescoping the Times*** • Chapter Summary, pp. 45–46 ***Planning for Block Schedules***	PE ***Chapter Assessment,*** pp. 780–781 PE ***Alternative Assessment,*** p. 781 ***Formal Assessment*** • Chapter Test, forms A and B, pp. 286–291 ***Test Generator*** ***Alternative Assessment Book*** See explanation and forms for different kinds of alternative assessments including portfolio assessment.

KEY
PE Pupil's Edition
TE Teacher's Edition
http://www.mlushistory.com

Block Scheduling (90 MINUTES)

Day 1

Section 1, pp. 760–765

Geography Spotlight: The Movement of Migrant Workers, pp. 766–767

Section Assessment, p. 765

 **COOPERATIVE ACTIVITY**
- Listing Native American Demands, p. 764 (TE)

Day 2

Section 2, pp. 768–772

Section Assessment, p. 772

 **COOPERATIVE ACTIVITY**
- Preparing Articles for *Ms.*, p. 770 (TE)

Day 3

Section 3, pp. 773–777

Daily Life: Signs of the Sixties, pp. 778–779

Section Assessment, p. 777

Chapter Assessment, pp. 780–781

COOPERATIVE ACTIVITY
- Producing a 1960s Music Video, p. 776 (TE)

YEARLY PACING *Chapter 23 Total:* 3 days *Yearly Total:* 85 days

See *Planning for Block Schedules* for special activities and pacing strategies.

TECHNOLOGY

 ***Warm-Up Transparency* 23**

Humanities Transparencies
- H29, Mural in Los Angeles

Geography Transparencies
- G31, Latino and Native American Population Centers, 1970

Grolier Multimedia Encyclopedia
- American Indian Movement

Electronic Library of Primary Sources
- The Birth of *La Causa* by Cesar Chavez

INTERNET Interact with History p. 767 (PE)

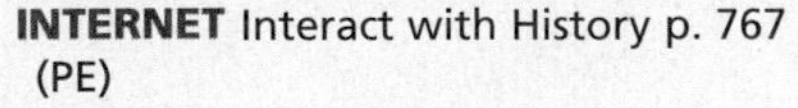

 ***Warm-Up Transparency* 23**

Critical Thinking Transparencies
- CT31, The Women's Movement
- CT65, Percentage of All Women Who Are Working, 1950–1995

Electronic Library of Primary Sources
- from *The Feminine Mystique* by Betty Friedan
- from NOW's Statement of Purpose

 **INTERNET** ERA, NOW, and Phyllis Schlafly

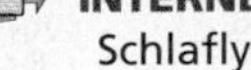

 ***Warm-Up Transparency* 23**

Our Times
- from *The Electric Kool-Aid Acid Test* by Tom Wolfe

 **INTERNET** Interact with History p. 779 (PE)

 ***American Portfolio: A Videodisc for U.S. History,*** user's guide, pp. 246–247, 249

 ***Chapter Summary Audiotapes***
- Unit 6, Chapter 23

 **INTERNET http://www.mlushistory.com**

Customizing for Special Populations

Students Acquiring English

Access for Students Acquiring English: Spanish Translations
- Guided Reading for Sections 1–3, pp. 253–255
- Chapter Summary, pp. 251–252
- Skillbuilder Practice: Comparing; Contrasting, p. 256
- Geography Application: The Equal Rights Amendment, p. 257

Spanish Reading Study Guide, pp. 235–242

Translations of Chapter Summaries, Hmong, Cantonese, Vietnamese, and Cambodian

Chapter Summary Audiotapes in Spanish Unit 6, Chapter 23

INTERNET The Diverse Classroom

Gifted and Talented Students

In-Depth Resources: Unit 6
- Primary Sources: The Farm Worker Movement, p. 62; United Farm Workers Poster, p. 63; from *The Feminine Mystique,* p. 64; Popular Song, p. 65
- American Lives: Cesar Chavez, p. 69; Betty Friedan, p. 70

Less Proficient Readers

In-Depth Resources: Unit 6
- Guided Reading for Sections 1–3, pp. 56–58
- Skillbuilder: Comparing; Contrasting, p. 59
- Geography Application: The Equal Rights Amendment, p. 60

Reading Study Guide
- pp. 235–242

Telescoping the Times
- Chapter Summary, pp. 45–46

Chapter Summary Audiotapes, Unit 6, Chapter 23

Connections to Literature READINGS FOR STUDENTS

In-Depth Resources: Unit 6
- **from *Los Vendidos* by Luis Valdez, p. 66**

McDougal Littell *The Language of Literature*
American Literature

- **Rodolfo Gonzales, from "I am Joaquin/Yo Soy Joaquin," p. 243**
- **Aurora Levins Morales and Rosario Morales, "Ending Poem," p. 328**
- **Luis J. Rodriquez, "Tía Chucha," p. 331**
- **Sylvia Plath, "Mirror," p. 882**
- **Anne Sexton, "Self in 1958," p. 885**
- **Lanford Wilson, *Wandering,* p. 972**
- **Denise Levertov, "At the Justice Department, November 15, 1969," p. 979**
- **Nikki Giovanni, "Revolutionary Dreams," p. 981**
- **Gloria Steinem, "Sisterhood," p. 984**
- **Anna Quindlen, from "Mother's Choice," p. 992**
- **Anne Tyler, "Teenage Wasteland," p. 996**
- **Nash Candelaria, "El Patrón," p. 1009**
- **Diane Burns, "Sure You Can Ask Me a Personal Question," p. 1020**
- **John Updike, "Separating," p. 1040**
- **Carlos Alberto Montaner, "Why Fear Spanish?" p. 1066**
- **Lorna Dee Cervantes, "Refugee Ship," p. 1068**
- **Gary Soto, "Mexicans Begin Jogging," p. 1113**
- **Pat Mora, "Legal Alien," p. 1116**

CHAPTER 23 OVERVIEW

An Era of Social Change

▸ ***Accessing Prior Knowledge***

Ask students what images, phrases, or symbols come to mind when they think about the 1960s. What people, songs, and films helped shape the era?

▸ ***Predicting Outcomes***

Ask students what Bob Dylan might have meant when he wrote, "The times they are a-changin'." Have them identify some of the ways in which American society and culture would change in the 1960s.

MORE ABOUT . . .
Bob Dylan

As a teenager Dylan, whose real name is Robert Zimmerman, listened to rock music and rhythm and blues. Because the local radio station in his small Minnesota hometown didn't play the type of music he liked, Dylan had to tune in to Southern radio stations, which he could get only late at night. He used to place his radio under the covers of his bed to keep from waking anyone.

CHAPTER 23 An Era of Social Change

SECTION 1
Latinos and Native Americans Seek Equality
The nation's Latinos and Native Americans demand greater equality.

SECTION 2
Women Fight for Equality
A new feminist movement emerges during the 1960s, as women fight to improve their opportunities and status in society.

SECTION 3
Culture and Counterculture
Groups of disillusioned youths shun the social activism of the times and choose instead to "drop out" of society and establish their own way of life.

"The times they are a-changin'."
Bob Dylan

THE UNITED STATES

- **1962** Cesar Chavez and Dolores Huerta found the National Farm Workers Association.
- **1963** Lyndon B. Johnson becomes president upon the assassination of John F. Kennedy.
- **1964** Lyndon B. Johnson is elected president.
- **1965** National Farm Workers Association joins Filipino farm workers in a strike against grape growers.
- **1966** National Organization for Women (NOW) is formed.
- **1966** National Farm Workers Association merges with another farm workers union to form the United Farm Workers Organizing Committee.
- **1967** The "summer of love" brings thousands of hippies to San Francisco.
- **1967** Twenty-fifth Amendment to the U.S. Constitution, providing guidelines for presidential and vice-presidential succession, takes effect.

1960

THE WORLD

- **1962** Chinese forces invade India.
- **1963** Civil war breaks out between Greeks and Turks on Cyprus.
- **1967** Six-Day War erupts between Israel and Arab nations.

THEMES IN CHAPTER 23

Immigration and Migration

During the 1960s, the Latino population in the United States grew from 3 million to more than 9 million. Most Latinos settled in large cities, where they often encountered discrimination.

See Teacher's Edition note, p. 761.

Civil Rights

The 1960s witnessed the struggle of Native Americans for greater equality. Impatience with the slow pace of reform, however, led to the formation of the American Indian Movement, which actively confronted the government.

See Teacher's Edition note, p. 763.

Women in America

For American women, the 1960s and 1970s were a time of consciousness-raising about "a woman's place." Many women struggled to find fulfillment beyond the bounds of home and family life.

See Teacher's Edition note, p. 769.

The American Dream

In the 1960s, members of the counterculture rejected the American dream and chose to drop out of mainstream society. Hippies sought to redefine the American dream by creating a society based on love.

See Teacher's Edition note, p. 775.

LIVING HISTORY

INVESTIGATING MUSIC OF THE 1960s

People strongly associate the 1960s with its popular music. The styles of music that were popular at the time included rhythm and blues, rock 'n' roll, protest songs, folk music, and others. Research a type of music from the 1960s that you find interesting. You will use the information you gather to create a documentary for radio.

- Be sure to investigate how the music you select influenced, or was influenced by, the events of the times. Also, find out how it influenced later musical styles.
- Research the people behind the music—the artists who wrote, performed, or produced it.
- Try to find selections of the music you are researching. Libraries are a good source.

PORTFOLIO PROJECT Save your research and any music selections in a folder for your American history portfolio. At the end of the chapter, you will prepare and present your music documentary.

BOYCOTT NON-UFW GRAPES

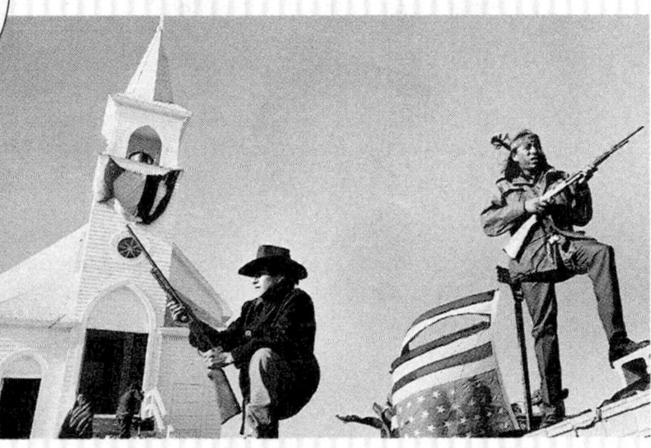

1968
- About 15,000 Mexican-American high school students in East Los Angeles boycott classes to protest poor conditions.
- Native American activists found the American Indian Movement (AIM).
- Richard M. Nixon is elected president.

1969
- Rock singer Janis Joplin is one of the many performers at the Woodstock music festival.
- President Charles de Gaulle of France resigns.

1970
- Grape boycott forces growers to sign contracts with the United Farm Workers Organizing Committee.
- Political party La Raza Unida is formed.
- Anwar el-Sadat becomes president of Egypt.

1971
- General Idi Amin Dada seizes power in Uganda.

1972
- Congress passes the Equal Rights Amendment.
- Gloria Steinem founds *Ms.* magazine.
- Richard M. Nixon is reelected.
- Earthquake kills 10,000 in Nicaragua.

1973
- Native Americans stage protest at Wounded Knee, South Dakota.

1974
- Gerald R. Ford becomes president after Richard M. Nixon resigns.

1975
- Congress passes the Indian Self-Determination and Education Assistance Act.

ALTERNATIVE ASSESSMENT

LIVING HISTORY

INVESTIGATING MUSIC OF THE 1960S

Help students carry out their investigation.

- Become familiar with a variety of songs from the 1960s—perhaps listening to records in a family member's or friend's collection, tuning in "oldies" radio stations, or checking out Web sites devoted to the music of the period.
- Narrow the documentary's focus. For example, a student exploring rock 'n' roll could concentrate on hard rock or on British invasion groups.
- Select the songs to be used in the documentary.
- Present a written script of the documentary, accompanied by a tape of the music to be used.

Have students create diagrams like the one below to organize their ideas for their documentary scripts.

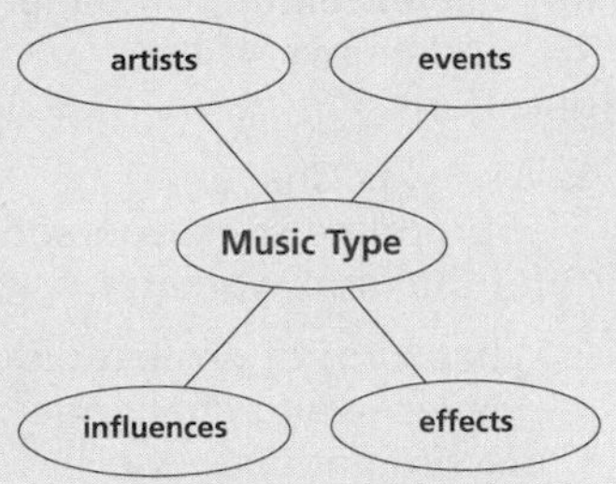

IN-DEPTH RESOURCES: UNIT 6
See worksheet and standards for evaluation, pp. 71, 72.

RECOMMENDED RESOURCES

Books for the Teacher

Matthiessen, Peter. *In the Spirit of Crazy Horse.* New York: Viking, 1983. FBI conflict with American Indian Movement.

Takaki, Ronald. *A Different Mirror.* Boston: Little, 1993. History of African Americans, Latinos, and Asian Americans in the United States.

Books for the Student

Friedan, Betty. *The Feminine Mystique.* Updated edition. New York: Dell, 1993. Includes thoughts 30 years after original publication.

Mankiller, Wilma, and Michael Wallis. *Mankiller.* New York: St. Martin's, 1993. Life of a Cherokee chief.

Shorris, Earl. *Latinos.* New York: Norton, 1992. Describes diverse Latino communities in the United States.

Videos

America: The Second Century: *The American Indian; Black Americans; Hispanic Americans; Women in America.* GPN, 402-472-2007.

American Indians, Yesterday and Today. Altschul Group, 847-328-6700.

Software

Her Heritage. CD-ROM. Pilgrim New Media, 800-997-5476.

The Native Americans. CD-ROM. Philips Media Software, 800-883-3767.

Section 1 Overview

OBJECTIVES

1. To describe the growth and diversity of the Latino population during the 1960s.
2. To summarize the efforts of Latinos to secure their civil rights.
3. To characterize the efforts of Native Americans to secure a number of reforms.

SKILLBUILDERS

- Interpreting graphs, p. 761
- Interpreting charts, p. 765

CRITICAL THINKING

- Theme: Immigration and Migration, p. 761
- Recognizing effects, p. 762
- Theme: Cultural Diversity, p. 763
- Theme: Civil Rights, p. 764
- Synthesizing, p. 765
- Summarizing, p. 765
- Contrasting, p. 765

FOCUS & MOTIVATE

5-MINUTE WARM-UP

Drawing Conclusions
To introduce Cesar Chavez, have students read the Key Player feature on page 762 and answer these questions.

1. Why was Chavez an appropriate spokesperson for the farm workers?
2. What form of protest did Chavez use to challenge discrimination in the theater?

WARM-UP TRANSPARENCY 23

▶ ***Starting with the Student***
- Do students think that violent methods are necessary to effect change?

OBJECTIVE
1 INSTRUCT

The Latino Presence Grows

▶ ***Discussing Key Ideas***
- During the 1960s, the Latino population in the United States triples.

(continued on next page)

1 Latinos and Native Americans Seek Equality

TERMS & NAMES
- **Cesar Chavez**
- **United Farm Workers Organizing Committee**
- **La Raza Unida**
- **American Indian Movement**

LEARN ABOUT the problems faced by Latinos and Native Americans ***TO UNDERSTAND*** their campaigns for civil rights and economic justice.

ONE AMERICAN'S STORY

Jessie Lopez de la Cruz's life changed one night in 1962, when Cesar Chavez came to her home. Chavez, a Mexican-American farm worker, was trying to organize a union for California's mostly Spanish-speaking farm workers. Although Jessie's husband had been attending union meetings, Jessie had always stayed home. So she was surprised when Chavez sat down at her kitchen table and said, "The women have to be involved. They're the ones working out in the fields with their husbands. If you can take the women out to the fields, you can certainly take them to meetings." Jessie sat up straight and said to herself, "*That's* what I want!" Before long she was out in the fields, talking to farm workers about the union.

A PERSONAL VOICE

Wherever I went to speak . . . I told them about . . . how we had no benefits, no minimum wage, nothing out in the fields—no restrooms, nothing. I'd ask people how they felt about these many years they had been working out in the fields . . . They would say, "I was working for so-and-so, and when I complained about something that happened there, I was fired." I said, "Well! Do you think we should be putting up with this in this modern age? . . . We can stand up! We can talk back! . . . This country is very rich, and we want a share of the money those growers make [off] our sweat and our work by exploiting us and our children!"

JESSIE LOPEZ DE LA CRUZ, quoted in *Moving the Mountain: Women Working for Social Change*

Mexican-American farm workers protest poor working conditions.

The efforts of Jessie Lopez de la Cruz were just one part of a larger Latino movement during the turbulent and revolutionary decade of the 1960s. As African Americans fought for their civil rights, Latinos and Native Americans also rose up to assert their rights, preserve their cultures, and improve their lives.

The Latino Presence Grows

Spanish-speaking Americans, or Latinos, have always been a large and diverse group. The country's Latino population includes people from several different areas: Mexico, Puerto Rico, Cuba, the Dominican Republic, other Caribbean islands, Central America, and South America. Because these groups all trace their roots back to Spanish-speaking countries of Latin America, people often group them together. However, each Latino group has its own history, its own pattern of settlement in the United States, and its own set of economic, social, cultural, and political concerns. During the 1960s, the Latino population in the United States grew from 3 million to more than 9 million.

During this time, the number of Mexicans settling in the United States rose. Mexican Americans, who have always made up the largest Latino group in the United States, once lived mostly in the Southwest and California. Some were the descendants of the nearly 100,000 Mexicans who had lived in territories ceded by Mexico to the United States after the war with Mexico in 1848. Others were the children and grandchildren of the million or so Mexicans who settled in the United States in the decade following Mexico's 1910 revolution. Still others came as *braceros*, or temporary laborers, during the 1940s and 1950s.

SECTION 1 RESOURCES

PRINT RESOURCES

IN-DEPTH RESOURCES: UNIT 6
Guided Reading, p. 56
Primary Sources: The Farm Worker Movement, p. 62; United Farm Workers Poster, p. 63
American Lives: Cesar Chavez, p. 69

READING STUDY GUIDE, p. 235

ACCESS FOR STUDENTS ACQUIRING ENGLISH
Guided Reading (Spanish), p. 253

SPANISH READING STUDY GUIDE, p. 235

FORMAL ASSESSMENT
Section Quiz, p. 283

ALTERNATIVE ASSESSMENT BOOK
See forms for supporting and scoring alternative activities.

TECHNOLOGY RESOURCES

HUMANITIES TRANSPARENCIES
H29, Mural in Los Angeles

GEOGRAPHY TRANSPARENCIES
G31, Latino and Native American Population Centers, 1970

CD-ROM *Grolier Multimedia Encyclopedia*
Electronic Library of Primary Sources

VIDEO *American Portfolio: A Videodisc for U.S. History* user's guide, pp. 246–247

INTERNET http://www.mlushistory.com

Latino Population in the United States and Selected Metropolitan Areas, 1970–1994

United States
1970 — 4%
1994 — 10%

Los Angeles
1970 — 18.3 %
1990 — 39.9%

Miami
1970 — 23.6 %
1990 — 62.5%

New York City
1970 — 7.3%
1990 — 24.4%

Chicago
1970 — 4.7%
1990 — 19.6%

Source: U.S. Bureau of the Census; U.S. Department of Commerce

Skillbuilder Answers
Largest: Miami.
Cities: Los Angeles and Miami.

SKILLBUILDER
INTERPRETING GRAPHS
Which city experienced the greatest percentage increase of Latinos between 1970 and 1990? In what two cities do Latinos represent more than one-third of the population?

About a million Puerto Ricans have lived in the United States since the 1960s. Most have settled in the Northeast, with about 600,000 in New York City alone. Lacking the needed skills and education, many Puerto Ricans had trouble finding work and getting ahead.

Hundreds of thousands of Cubans fled to the United States after the revolutionary leader Fidel Castro overthrew Cuba's dictator, Fulgencio Batista, in 1959. Most settled in or near Miami, turning that Florida city into a boom town. Large Cuban communities also formed in New York City and New Jersey. Many Cubans who fled to the United States were academics and professionals escaping Castro's Communist rule.

A. Answer Prejudice, job and housing discrimination, high unemployment, and poverty.

THINK THROUGH HISTORY
A. THEME
Immigration and Migration *What problems did different groups of Latino immigrants share?*

In addition, tens of thousands of Salvadorans, Guatemalans, Nicaraguans, and Colombians immigrated to the United States after the 1960s to escape civil war and chronic poverty.

Wherever they settled, during the 1960s many Latinos encountered ethnic prejudice and discrimination in jobs and housing. Most lived in segregated *barrios,* or neighborhoods. The Latino jobless rate was nearly 50 percent higher than that of whites, as was the percentage of families living in poverty.

HISTORICAL SPOTLIGHT

DESPERATE JOURNEYS

In the 1960s and 1970s, thousands of poor Mexicans illegally crossed the 2,000-mile border between the United States and Mexico each year. The journey these illegal aliens undertook was often made more difficult by "coyotes," dishonest guides who charged large amounts of money to help them cross the border.

Their problems didn't end when they entered the United States. Illegal immigrants were denied many social services, including unemployment insurance and food stamps. In addition, the Immigration and Naturalization Service urged businesses to refrain from hiring them. As a result, some owners stopped employing people with Latino names, including legal immigrants.

Latinos Fight for Change

As the presence of Latinos in the United States grew, so too did their cries for greater representation and better treatment. During the 1960s, Latinos demanded not only equal opportunity, but also a respect for their culture and heritage.

THE FARM WORKER MOVEMENT As Jessie Lopez de la Cruz stressed in her emotional speech, thousands of Mexican Americans working on California's fruit and vegetable farms found themselves subjected to long hours of backbreaking work for little pay and few benefits. **Cesar Chavez** believed that the only way to improve conditions for farm workers was to unionize them, so that they could bargain as a group for improved conditions and better treatment. In 1962, Chavez and Dolores Huerta established the National Farm Workers Association.

(continued from page 760)

- Many Latinos encounter ethnic prejudice.

IN-DEPTH RESOURCES, UNIT 6
Guided Reading, p. 56
Primary Source: United Farm Workers Poster, p. 63

ACCESS FOR STUDENTS ACQUIRING ENGLISH
Guided Reading (Spanish), p. 253

HISTORY FROM VISUALS
Latino Population in the United States and Selected Metropolitan Areas, 1970–1994

Reading the Graph Ask students why the increase in the percentage of Latinos was greatest in cities. *Employment opportunities drew Latinos to big cities.*

GEOGRAPHY TRANSPARENCIES
G31, Latino and Native American Population Centers, 1970

HISTORICAL SPOTLIGHT
Desperate Journeys

Critical Thinking: Identifying Problems Ask students what other problems confronted Mexican immigrants in the 1960s and 1970s. *Possible Responses: Crowded, unsafe housing, prejudice, limited access to health care and educational services.*

OBJECTIVE

INSTRUCT

Latinos Fight for Change

▶ ***Discussing Key Ideas***
- Led by Cesar Chavez, Mexican-American farm workers unionize.

(continued on next page)

TEACHING OPTIONS

Exploring Themes

Immigration and Migration Discuss how the growing Latino population affected American society. Ask students how the increased number of Latinos enriched society. *Possible Response: Latinos introduced elements of their culture, including language, literature, and cuisine.* Then ask what negative effects the influx of Latinos had on society. *Possible Responses: Overcrowding in cities; increased crime; higher unemployment.* Ask students what they think could be done to alleviate some of the problems. Should Latino immigration be limited? Does mainstream America need to change?

Teaching Less Proficient Readers

Clarifying Ideas Help students understand why the Latino population increased so much during the 1960s. Have students follow these steps:

1. Read pages 760–761 and study the graphs on page 761.
2. Create a cluster diagram, listing the Latin American countries and regions from which most of the immigrants came, including Mexico, Puerto Rico, Cuba, and Central America.
3. Jot down reasons why Latinos in each region decided to leave their homelands.
4. Add the city or cities where each group settled.

(continued from page 761)

- Latino "brown power" movements promote ethnic pride.
- Latinos begin organizing politically.

MORE ABOUT . . .
Cesar Chavez

Cesar Chavez attended at least 65 elementary schools—sometimes for only a day, a week, or a month. Like other migrant workers, Chavez's parents had to move from place to place looking for farm work. After witnessing the conditions of farm laborers firsthand, Chavez began working to help the Latino community. Although he was a quiet and rather self-effacing man, Chavez nonetheless captured the imagination and heart of people from all walks of life with his message of social justice. At least 17 million Americans joined his five-year boycott of California grapes.

IN-DEPTH RESOURCES: UNIT 6
Primary Source: The Farm Worker Movement, p. 62
American Lives: Cesar Chavez, p. 69

ELECTRONIC LIBRARY OF PRIMARY SOURCES
The Birth of *La Causa* by Cesar Chavez

KEY PLAYER
Cesar Chavez

Critical Thinking: Analyzing Ask students what Chavez's actions in the theater reveal about him. *He was proud, independent, and courageous.* How does his behavior as a teenager foreshadow his actions as a labor organizer when he was an adult? *Like his protest in the theater, the protests he organized as an adult were nonviolent.*

Four years later, Chavez merged this group with a Filipino agricultural union to form the **United Farm Workers Organizing Committee** (UFWOC).

Chavez and his fellow organizers insisted that California's large fruit and vegetable companies accept their union as the bargaining agent for the farm workers. In 1965, when California's grape growers refused to recognize the union, Chavez launched a nationwide boycott of the companies' grapes. Chavez, like Martin Luther King, Jr., believed in nonviolence to achieve his goals. His strategy was to win, through peaceful means, American public support for *La Causa,* or the cause of social and economic justice for farm workers.

The union sent farm workers across North America to convince supermarkets and shoppers not to buy California grapes. To call further attention to the workers' plight, Chavez, in 1968, went on a three-week fast in which he lost 35 pounds. He ended his fast by taking communion with Senator Robert F. Kennedy.

The efforts of the farm workers eventually paid off. In 1970, the grape growers finally signed contracts with the UFWOC. The new contracts guaranteed union workers higher wages and other benefits long denied them. "The boycott of grapes was the most near-perfect of nonviolent struggles," said Chavez afterward. (See *boycott* on page 933 in the Economics Handbook.)

CESAR CHAVEZ
1927–1993

Cesar Chavez spoke from experience when he said, "Many things in farm labor are terrible." As a teenager, Chavez moved with his family from farm to farm, picking such crops as grapes, apricots, and olives. "The worst crop was the olives," Chavez recalled, "the olives are so small you can never fill the bucket."

The seeds of protest grew early in Chavez, and one incident in particular seemed to signal his eventual climb to a life of activism. As a teenager, Chavez once went to see a movie, only to find that the theater was segregated—whites on one side of the aisle and Mexicans on the other side. "I really hadn't thought much about what I was going to do but I had to do something," Chavez recalled. The future union leader sat down in the whites-only section and stayed there until the police arrived and arrested him.

THINK THROUGH HISTORY
B. Recognizing Effects *What impact did the grape boycott have on grape growers?*
B. Answer It hurt their revenue as well as their public image and forced them to negotiate with the UFWOC.

CULTURAL PRIDE The activities of the California farm workers helped to inspire other Latino "brown power" movements across the country. In New York, Puerto Ricans began to demand that schools offer Spanish-speaking children classes taught in their own language as well as programs on their culture. In 1968, Congress enacted the Bilingual Education Act, which provided funds for schools to develop bilingual and cultural heritage programs for non-English-speaking children.

Young Mexican Americans started to call themselves Chicanos or Chicanas—a shortening of "Mexicanos" that expressed pride in their ethnic heritage. A Chicano community action group called the Brown Berets formed under the leadership of David Sanchez. In 1968, the Brown Berets organized school walkouts in East Los Angeles high schools. About 15,000 Chicano students walked out of class demanding smaller classes, more Chicano teachers and administrators, and programs designed to reduce the high Latino dropout rate. Militant Mexican-American students also won the establishment of Chicano studies programs at colleges and universities.

POLITICAL POWER Latinos also began organizing politically during the 1960s. Some worked within the two-party system to win support for Latino issues and candidates. For example, the Mexican American Political Association (MAPA), which sponsored candidates, registered and educated voters and lobbied for legislation that benefited the Latino community. In 1962, MAPA helped elect Los Angeles politician Edward Roybal to the House of Representatives. Roybal was the second Mexican American to serve in Congress. Henry Gonzalez, elected to the House of Representatives from Texas in 1961, was the first.

Others sought to create an independent Latino political movement. That was the dream of Texan José Angel Gutiérrez, who established **La Raza Unida** (the United People Party) in 1970. In the 1970s, La Raza Unida ran Latino candidates in five states and won positions on school boards and city councils, as well as several races for mayor.

Still other Latinos took on a more confrontational tone. Reies Tijerina, a one-time evangelical preacher, argued that the United States had stolen some

TEACHING OPTIONS

Making Connections Across Cultures

Latino Cultural Pride Tell students that many of the new Latino immigrants resisted assimilation into mainstream America. They preferred to retain their family-centered culture and their heritage. "We want to be here," explained Daniel Villanueva, who became a television executive, "but without losing our language and our culture." Ask students what aspects of American culture, if any, Latinos should be prepared—or required—to adopt.

HUMANITIES TRANSPARENCIES
H29, Mural in Los Angeles

Making Connections Across the Curriculum

Literature Tell students that since the 1950s, Latin American literature has received unprecedented international attention. The production during this period of many important novels by Latin American writers has been called the "boom." Many of the boom novelists write in a style that combines dreams and magic with everyday reality. The most famous of these authors is Gabriel García Márquez, who won the 1982 Nobel Prize in literature. His novel *One Hundred Years of Solitude* contains historical fact but also includes strange, fantastic events; startling characters; and unusual humor.

of the Latinos' land. In 1963, Tijerina founded the Alianza Federal de Mercedes (Federal Alliance of Land Grants) to help reclaim U.S. land taken from Mexican landholders in the 19th century.

Native Americans Struggle for Equality

Many people view Native Americans, like Latinos, as one group, despite the hundreds of distinct Native American tribes and nations in the United States. These diverse tribes and nations, however, have shared a mostly bleak existence in the United States. During the 1960s, many Native Americans joined together to demand improvements in their conditions.

NATIVE AMERICANS SEEK GREATER AUTONOMY Despite their cultural diversity, Native Americans have shared many of the same problems throughout the 20th century. As a group, Native Americans have been the poorest of Americans and have suffered from the highest unemployment rate. They have been more likely than any other group to suffer serious health problems, such as tuberculosis and alcoholism. Despite an increase in the Native American population during the 1960s, the death rate among Native American infants was nearly twice the national average, while the life expectancy of Native Americans was several years lower than for other Americans.

In an attempt to deal with these problems, the Eisenhower administration in 1953 enacted a termination policy designed to relocate Native Americans from isolated reservations into mainstream urban American life. The plan failed miserably. Most of the Native Americans who moved to the cities remained desperately poor.

In addition, many Native Americans refused to assimilate, or blend, into mainstream society. Native American nationalist Vine Deloria, Jr., expressed his opinion that young Native Americans viewed mainstream America as nothing more than "ice cream bars and heart trouble and neurosis and deodorants and getting up at six o'clock in the morning to mow your lawn in the suburbs." Deloria added that "when you get far enough from the reservation, you can see it's the urban man who has no identity."

THINK THROUGH HISTORY
C. THEME *Cultural Diversity*
Why did Native Americans resist assimilation?

C. Answer They viewed white culture as shallow and meaningless.

What Native Americans wanted was greater opportunity to control and govern their own lives. In 1961, representatives from 67 Native American groups met in Chicago and drafted the Declaration of Indian Purpose, which stressed the determination of Native Americans to "choose our own way of life." The declaration called for an end to the termination program in favor of new policies designed to create economic opportunities for Native Americans on their reservations. In 1965, President Lyndon Johnson responded to the Native Americans' call for more self-determination. As part of his Great Society program, Johnson established the National Council on Indian Opportunity to "ensure that programs reflect the needs and desires of the Indian people."

VOICES OF PROTEST Despite a change in the government's policies, many young Native Americans were dissatisfied with the slow pace of reform. Their discontent led in part to the growth of the **American Indian Movement** (AIM), an often militant Native American rights organization. AIM had begun in 1968 in Minneapolis as a self-defense group against police brutality. However, it soon turned its attention to the larger issue of Native American rights and branched out to northern and western states with large Native American populations.

NOW & THEN

BEN NIGHTHORSE CAMPBELL

Whereas many Native Americans, in seeking reforms, rejected assimilation with mainstream America, Ben Nighthorse Campbell has chosen to work within the system to improve the lives of Native Americans.

In 1992, Campbell was elected to the U.S. Senate from Colorado, marking the first time since 1929 that a Native American had been elected to the Senate. Campbell's father was North Cheyenne, and his great-grandfather, Black Horse, fought in the 1876 Battle of Little Bighorn—in which the Cheyenne and the Sioux defeated Lieutenant Colonel George Custer.

Campbell stated that while his new job called for him to address the problems of the entire nation, the needs of his fellow Native Americans remained a high priority. As a Native American, Campbell says, "you are measured by how much you've given to people, how much you help people."

OBJECTIVE
③ INSTRUCT

Native Americans Struggle for Equality

▶ ***Starting with the Student***
Have students use a chart similar to the one below to document the Native American struggle for equality during the 1960s. Ask them to list the actions taken by Native Americans and the results of those actions.

Action	Result

▶ ***Discussing Key Ideas***
- In the 1960s, Native Americans seek more control over their lives.
- The American Indian Movement brings a new spirit of militancy to the struggle for equality.
- AIM confronts the government—sometimes violently—to seek greater reforms for Native Americans.
- Native Americans win both legislative and legal battles.

NOW & THEN
Ben Nighthorse Campbell
Critical Thinking: Evaluating Ask students whether they think that Native Americans can achieve their goals by working within the system, as Campbell did, or that organizations such as AIM can accomplish more by agitating outside the system.

TEACHING OPTIONS

Exploring Themes

Civil Rights Discuss the Native American struggle for equal rights. Ask students what goals Native Americans sought to achieve in the 1960s. *Possible Responses: More control over their own lives; new economic opportunities; rights to lands taken by the government; improved living conditions on reservations; more say in children's education.* Then ask why these goals were important to Native Americans. *Possible Response: Many basic rights had been denied them for generations. Regaining the rights would be a major victory for the Native American people.*

Teaching Gifted and Talented Students

Researching AIM Encourage interested students to find out about the goals and accomplishments of AIM today. Have students
- search the Internet for information on the organization
- conduct a periodical search in the library for articles about AIM's activities
- create a poster that depicts the organization's activities
- present the poster to the class

GROLIER MULTIMEDIA ENCYCLOPEDIA
American Indian Movement

MORE ABOUT . . .
The Trail of Broken Treaties

When the Native Americans who took part in the Trail of Broken Treaties arrived in Washington, they did not plan to occupy the BIA building. The protesters first approached the BIA for help in finding a place to stay while they tried to make appointments with government officials. As Mary Crow Dog, who was one of the demonstrators, recalled, "Somebody suggested, 'Let's all go to the BIA.' It seemed a natural thing to do. . . . They would have to put us up. It was 'our' building after all."

The police, however, viewed the presence of a thousand Native Americans in the BIA offices as an occupation and surrounded the building. In response, the unarmed demonstrators blockaded doors and passageways with overturned desks and file cabinets. They also broke off a few table legs to defend themselves in case of attack. The AIM demonstrators left seven days later, when the Nixon administration promised to study their demands. The administration also agreed not to file criminal charges for the damage done to the BIA building. "Morally, it had been a great victory," wrote Mary Crow Dog. "We had faced White America collectively, not as individual tribes. We had stood up to the government and gone through our baptism of fire. We had not run."

AIM leader Dennis Banks speaks at the foot of Mount Rushmore, South Dakota, during a rally.

AIM's influence spread rapidly. For some, the new activism meant demanding the restoration of Native American lands, burial grounds, and fishing and timber rights. Others sought new respect for their cultures. Mary Crow Dog, a Lakota Sioux, described the impact of the movement on her reservation.

A PERSONAL VOICE

The American Indian Movement hit our reservation like a tornado. . . . Some people loved AIM, some hated it, but nobody ignored it. . . . My first encounter with AIM was at a pow-wow held in 1971. . . . One man, a Chippewa, stood up and made a speech. I had never heard anybody talk like that. He spoke about genocide and sovereignty, about tribal leaders selling out. . . . He had himself wrapped up in an upside-down American flag, telling us that every star in this flag represented a state stolen from the Indians. . . . Some people wept. An old man turned to me and said, "These are words I always wanted to speak, but had kept shut up within me."

MARY CROW DOG, quoted in *Lakota Women*

"If the government doesn't start living up to its obligations, armed resistance . . . will have to become a regular thing."

CHIPPEWA PROTESTER

CONFRONTING THE GOVERNMENT In its early years, AIM, as well as other groups, actively—and sometimes violently—confronted the government as it sought greater reforms for Native Americans. In November 1969, militants calling themselves the Indians of All Tribes seized Alcatraz Island, the site of a former federal prison in San Francisco Bay. While claiming the federally owned island as Native American territory "by right of discovery," they offered to pay for it with $24 in beads and cloth—the amount Dutch settlers paid native inhabitants for Manhattan Island in 1626. The group occupied the island for 18 months before federal officials finally removed them.

In 1972, AIM leader Russell Means organized a march known as the Trail of Broken Treaties in Washington, D.C., to protest the U.S. government's numerous treaty violations with Native Americans throughout history. Native Americans from across the country joined the marchers. The organizers called for the restoration of 110 million acres of land to Native American tribes. They also pushed for the abolition of the Bureau of Indian Affairs (BIA), an agency that many believed was inefficient and corrupt. The marchers temporarily occupied the BIA building, destroyed records, and caused $2 million in property damage.

The most violent demonstration occurred a year later, when AIM led nearly 200 Sioux to the tiny village of Wounded Knee, South Dakota—where the U.S. cavalry had massacred a Sioux village in 1890. To protest living conditions on their reservation, the Sioux seized the town and took eleven people hostage. After ten weeks of tense negotiations with the FBI, the situation erupted in a shootout that left one Native American dead and another one wounded. The confrontation ended with a government promise to reexamine Native American treaty rights.

D. Answer AIM used confrontational and sometimes violent tactics, such as occupying the Bureau of Indian Affairs, and taking hostages during a protest at Wounded Knee.

THINK THROUGH HISTORY
D. THEME ***Civil Rights*** *What tactics did AIM use in its attempts to gain reforms?*

NATIVE AMERICAN VICTORIES Although some of their actions led only to violence and stalemate, Native Americans did secure a number of reforms from both Congress and the federal courts. Congress passed the Indian Education Act in 1972 and the Indian Self-Determination and Education Assistance Act in 1975. These laws gave tribes much greater control over their own affairs and

Block Schedule TEACHING OPTION **Time Needed: 30 Minutes**

Cooperative Activity: Listing Native American Demands

Task: Representing the interests of the Sioux at the Wounded Knee demonstration, groups of four to five students will write lists of demands to present to the government.

Purpose: To explore in depth the Native American struggle for equality.

Activity: Students should research the 1973 demonstration and find out why the Sioux were protesting conditions on their reservation. Students should also research the Wounded Knee massacre of 1890 and some of the treaties made with the Sioux during that period. Have students write their lists on posters and decorate them with Native American symbols and artwork.

Building a Portfolio: Students who decide to add their list of demands to their portfolio should attach a note explaining why the Sioux staged the demonstration at Wounded Knee.

ALTERNATIVE ASSESSMENT BOOK
Standards for Evaluating a Cooperative Activity

Standards for Evaluation
Lists should . . .

- describe conditions on the Sioux reservation and detail changes that need to be made
- refer to any withheld treaty rights that should be restored
- be decorated with Native American symbols and artwork

Native American Legal Victories

1970
Taos of New Mexico regain possession of Blue Lake as well as surrounding forestland.

1971
Alaska Native Claims Settlement Act gives Aleut and Inuit tribes of Alaska 40 million acres and more than $962 million.

1979
Maine Implementing Act provides $81.5 million for Native tribes, including Penobscot and Passamaquoddy, to buy back land.

1980
U.S. awards Sioux $106 million for illegally taken land in South Dakota.

1988
U.S. awards Puyallup tribe $162 million for land claims in Washington.

especially over the education of their children. "This is the most wonderful revolution in Indian Country," commented a Native American educator, "the right to educate on our own terms."

Native Americans also regained rights to land through court action. Armed with copies of old land treaties that the U.S. government had broken, Native American groups took their cases to federal court, where they demanded portions of their land back. In 1970, the Taos of New Mexico regained possession of their sacred Blue Lake, as well as a portion of its surrounding forestland. Land claims by the Aleut and Inuit tribes of Alaska resulted in the Alaska Native Claims Settlement Act of 1971. This act gave more than 40 million acres to native peoples and paid out more than $962 million in cash. Throughout the 1970s and 1980s, Native Americans in Maine, Massachusetts, and South Carolina won settlements that provided legal recognition of their tribal lands as well as financial compensation.

E. Answer Education reform, land restitution, and financial compensation.

THINK THROUGH HISTORY
E. *Synthesizing* *What victories could the Native American movement claim?*

With Latinos and Native Americans rising up in the midst of African Americans' struggle for change, the 1960s and the early 1970s saw a wave of activism from the nation's minority groups. However, another group of Americans also pushed for changes during this era. Women, while not a minority group, felt in many ways like second-class citizens, and many joined together to demand equal treatment in society.

SKILLBUILDER
INTERPRETING CHARTS
What two things did Native Americans win throughout their years of legal victories?

Skillbuilder Answer
Land rights and monetary compensation.

Section  Assessment

1. TERMS & NAMES
Identify:
- Cesar Chavez
- United Farm Workers Organizing Committee
- La Raza Unida
- American Indian Movement

2. SUMMARIZING Create a Venn diagram like the one below to show the broad similarities between the issues faced by Latinos and Native Americans during the 1960s as well as their unique concerns.

Common Issues Faced by Latinos and Native Americans

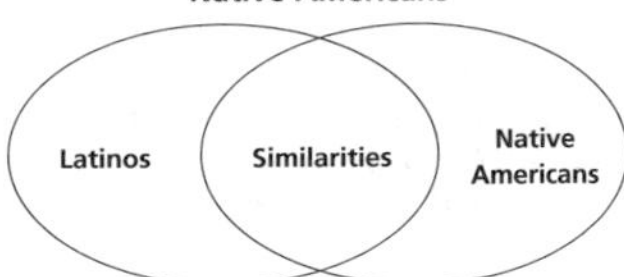

3. SYNTHESIZING What criteria would you establish for judging the effectiveness of an activist organization? Justify why your criteria are valid, based on the organizations discussed in this section.

THINK ABOUT
- UFWOC, MAPA, and La Raza Unida
- AIM and the Indians of All Tribes
- the leaders and activities of these organizations

4. CONTRASTING How did the Native American movement of the 1960s differ in general from the civil rights struggle of African Americans and Latinos?

THINK ABOUT
- Vine Deloria, Jr.'s, statement
- the Declaration of Indian Purpose
- the goals of AIM
- African Americans' and Latinos' desire for greater assimilation into mainstream society

ANSWERS

1. TERMS & NAMES
Cesar Chavez, p. 761
United Farm Workers Organizing Committee, p. 762
La Raza Unida, p. 762
American Indian Movement, p. 763

2. SUMMARIZING
Similarities: Great diversity within both groups; victims of prejudice, high unemployment, poverty, second-class citizenship; pride in their cultural heritage; concerns over their children's education; political activism; militant factions. Unique issues: Latinos—desire for greater assimilation into mainstream society; Native Americans—desire to remain outside mainstream society with greater autonomy.

3. SYNTHESIZING
Possible Responses: Strong leadership; clear-cut mission and goals; ability to enlist outside support; well-orchestrated demonstrations; unity among members; success in working for legislative measures and reforms.

4. CONTRASTING
Possible Response: Unlike African Americans and Latinos—most of whom sought assimilation into mainstream America—Native Americans attempted to better their lives while remaining removed from mainstream society.

HISTORY FROM VISUALS

Native American Legal Victories

Reading the Chart On a map, point out the sites of the legal victories. Ask students what these locations suggest about where Native Americans once lived. *Possible Response: They lived in vast, open spaces throughout the country.*

Extension Ask students why the restoration of lands is still important to Native Americans today. *Possible Response: Because the land represents their traditions and way of life.*

ASSESS & RETEACH

Section 1 Assessment

Have pairs of students take turns quizzing each other on the questions.

Self-Assessment

Draw on the board the Venn diagram in item 2 and have students discuss the issues they listed. Add students' ideas to the diagram on the board.

Section Quiz

FORMAL ASSESSMENT
Section Quiz, p. 283

Reteach

Use the Section Quiz to review key concepts in Section 1.

CLOSE

During the 1960s, Latinos and Native Americans fought for equal rights and economic justice. This era also witnessed a wave of activism by another oppressed group: women.

Geography Spotlight

OBJECTIVES

1. To trace the movements of migrant farm workers in the United States.
2. To recognize the role played by climate and growing seasons in the migrants' movements.

FOCUS & MOTIVATE

▶ ***Starting with the Student***
Ask students to think about jobs they've done that required manual labor.

- What did the jobs entail? Did they work indoors or outside?
- How did they feel physically after a full day's work?
- Did they feel a sense of satisfaction when the jobs were finished?

MORE ABOUT . . .
Migrant Farm Workers
The children of migrant farm workers often become migrant farm workers themselves. Because migrant families move so often, the children tend to fall behind in their education. In fact, only about a fifth of all migrant children attend school past the sixth grade. When these children grow up, they usually find that their education has prepared them for little other than farm work. As a result, generations of migrant families are caught in a cycle of poverty and despair.

GEOGRAPHY SPOTLIGHT

The Movement of Migrant Workers

WASHINGTON
MONTANA
OREGON
IDAHO
WYOMING
CALIFORNIA
NEVADA
UTAH
COLORADO
NEW MEXICO
ARIZONA

Pacific Coast paths
Midwest paths
Atlantic Coast paths
Year-round work
Migrant base areas

The nation's 3 million farm workers are responsible for harvesting much of the fruit and vegetables that families eat each day. There are two types of produce farm workers in the United States: workers who remain in one place most of the year; and migrant workers, who move with their entire family from one region to the next as the growing seasons change.

As the map shows, there were three major streams of migrant worker movements in the 1960s: the Pacific Coast, the Midwest, and the Atlantic Coast.

While these paths may have changed slightly since then, the movement of migrant workers into nearly every region of the nation continues today. The Pacific Coast region, with its year-round schedule and large harvests, offers laborers more steady work. Workers along the Midwest and East Coast streams, where crops are smaller, must keep moving in order to find work. Due to the winters, migrant workers in most of the Midwest and Atlantic regions can find work for only six months out of the year. During the winter months, many workers return to the nation's southernmost reaches, where they struggle to make a living, and wait until spring, when they once again head north.

THE PACIFIC COAST
Because California's moderate climate allows for year-round harvesting, most of the state's farm workers work on California's large fruit farms for most of the year. In addition, California produces large amounts of table grapes, a delicate fruit that requires specialized and constant care.

RECOMMENDED RESOURCES

Books

Altman, Linda Jacobs. *Cesar Chavez.* San Diego: Lucent, 1996. Biography of the charismatic labor leader who struggled to organize America's migrant farm workers.

Jiménez, Francisco. "The Circuit." *Cuentos Chicanos.* Ed. Rudolfo A. Anaya and Antonio Márquez. Rev. ed. Albuquerque: U of New Mexico P, 1984. Short story depicting the plight of migrant children.

Valle, Isabel. *Fields of Toil.* Pullman: Washington State UP, 1994. Traces the journey of a family of migrant farm laborers.

Videos

Cesar Chavez. Schlessinger Video Productions, 1995. Visual chronicle of Chavez's 30-year effort to organize migrant farm workers.

Harvest of Shame. FoxVideo, 1993. Renowned 1960 documentary on the exploitation of migrant farm workers in the United States.

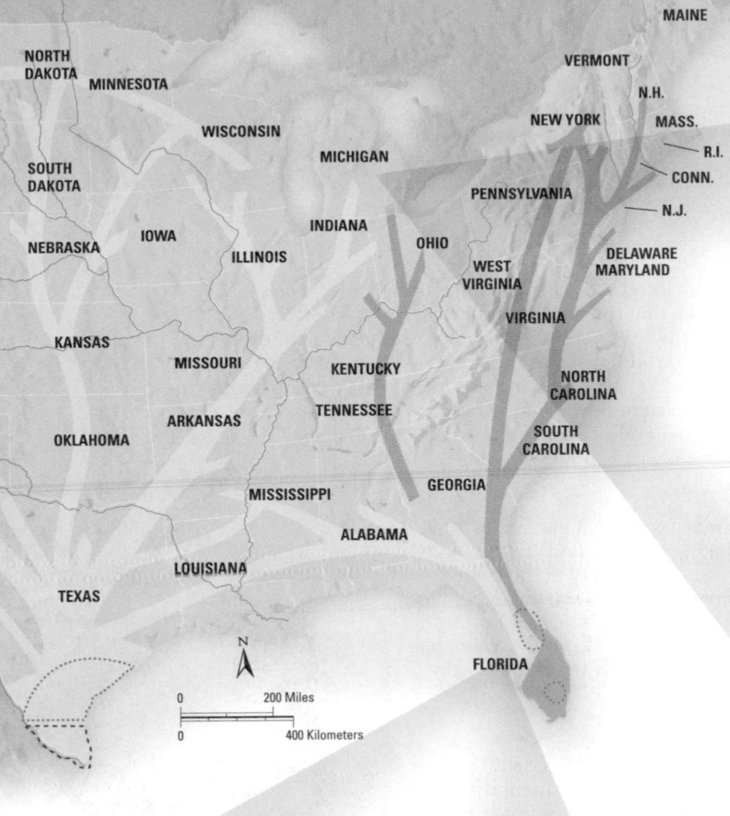

THE MIDWEST
These workers picking strawberries in Michigan will soon move on. For example, one family will travel to Ohio for the tomato harvest and then return to Michigan to pick apples before heading back to Texas for the winter months.

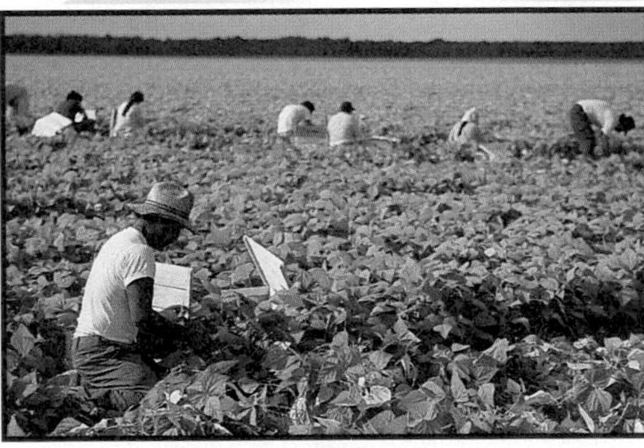

THE ATLANTIC COAST
While some workers along the Atlantic Coast stream remain in Florida, like the workers shown here picking beans, others travel as far north as New Hampshire and New York. There, they work from March through September, before returning to the South for the winter.

INTERACT WITH HISTORY

1. **FOLLOWING CHRONOLOGICAL ORDER** Retrace the 12-month activity of migrant workers along the Midwest and Atlantic Coast streams.
2. **CREATING A MAP** Use an outline map of the United States or of the world to trace work-related travel for some people in your community. Each student could track this information for a parent or a neighbor. The class could then place all of the results on a large map entitled "A Nation on the Move" and discuss certain aspects of the map.

SEE SKILLBUILDER HANDBOOK, PAGES 904 AND 932.

INTERNET Visit http://www.mlushistory.com for more about migrant workers.

INSTRUCT

Starting with the Student

- To help students understand the plight of migrant farm workers, you might show the class one of the videos listed under "Recommended Resources." Have students discuss their reactions to the video.
- Have students suggest ways to improve the situation of migrant farm workers.

Discussing Key Ideas

- In the 1960s, migrant farm workers follow three major streams of movement.
- Workers following the Midwest and Atlantic Coast paths must travel long distances to find seasonal work.

HISTORY FROM VISUALS

Reading the Images

Have students study the map and the photographs carefully.

- Which three states offer year-round work? *Florida, Texas, and California.* What conclusions can students draw about the climates of these states? *Possible Response: They have warm climates with year-round growing seasons.*
- Which group of paths shown on the map overlaps the other two groups? *The Midwest path.*
- On the basis of the photos, write four or five words that characterize migrant farm work. *Possible Responses: Backbreaking; monotonous; sweaty; dirty.*

INTERACT WITH HISTORY

1. Following Chronological Order

Possible Response: *During the winter months, migrant workers in the Midwest and Atlantic Coast streams seek employment in California, Florida, and Texas. They head north as the weather gets warmer and work in a number of Northern states during the summer and early fall. Once summer begins to fade into autumn, however, the workers once again move south.*

2. Creating a Map

Have students follow these steps:

- Ask parents or neighbors to discuss the travel involved in their jobs: business trips to meetings, conventions, and seminars or routes covered during work.
- Track the routes on a U.S. or world map.
- Work in groups of four or five to compile the information in group maps. Label the information and, if necessary, include legends indicating the meanings of any colors or symbols used.
- Share and discuss group maps in class.

Section 2 Overview

OBJECTIVES

1. To identify factors that led to the rise of the women's movement during the 1960s.
2. To describe some of the gains and losses of the women's movement in its early years.
3. To summarize the enduring legacy of the women's movement in employment, education, and politics.

SKILLBUILDER

- Interpreting graphs, p. 769

CRITICAL THINKING

- Recognizing effects, p. 769
- Analyzing causes, p. 770
- Analyzing motives, p. 772
- Theme: Women in America, p. 772
- Summarizing, p. 772
- Making predictions, p. 772
- Making inferences, p. 772

FOCUS & MOTIVATE

5-MINUTE WARM-UP

Recognizing Main Idea
To gain insight into the women's movement, have students read A Personal Voice on page 769 and answer these questions.

1. What point does Robin Morgan make about sexism?
2. Why is sexism so difficult to eliminate?

 ***WARM-UP TRANSPARENCY 23***

▶ ***Starting with the Student***
Ask students if they think women are discriminated against in American society. In what ways?

2 Women Fight for Equality

LEARN ABOUT the social and economic barriers that women faced in American society
TO UNDERSTAND the rise of a new and diverse women's movement during the 1960s.

TERMS & NAMES
- **feminism**
- **Betty Friedan**
- **National Organization for Women**
- **Gloria Steinem**
- **Equal Rights Amendment**
- **Phyllis Schlafly**
- **New Right**

ONE AMERICAN'S STORY

During the 1950s Betty Friedan seemed to be living the American dream. She had a loving husband, healthy children, and a house in the suburbs. According to the experts—doctors, psychologists, and women's magazines—that was all a woman needed to be happy and fulfilled. Why, then, wasn't she happy? What was wrong with her that this wasn't enough? When Friedan attended her fifteen-year college reunion in 1957, she found she was not alone in asking such questions. Many of her former classmates also were struggling with what Friedan would refer to as "the problem that has no name." Friedan eventually wrote a book, *The Feminine Mystique,* in which she addressed this seemingly indescribable problem.

A PERSONAL VOICE

The problem lay buried, unspoken, for many years in the minds of American women. It was a strange stirring, a sense of dissatisfaction, a yearning that women suffered in the middle of the twentieth century in the United States. Each suburban wife struggled with it alone. As she made the beds, shopped for groceries, matched slipcover material, ate peanut butter sandwiches with her children, chauffeured Cub Scouts and Brownies, lay beside her husband at night—she was afraid to even ask of herself the silent question—"Is this all?"

BETTY FRIEDAN, *The Feminine Mystique*

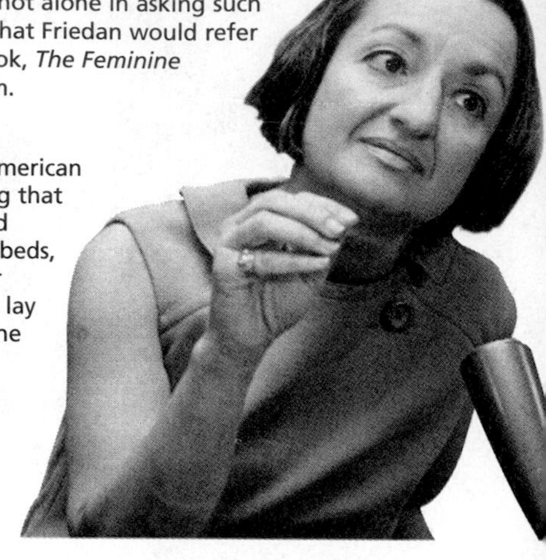
Betty Friedan

During the 1960s, more and more women answered Friedan's question with a resounding "no." As the nation's African Americans, Latinos, and Native Americans pushed for greater civil rights, many of the country's women also fought for equality in society.

A New Women's Movement Arises

The theory behind the women's movement of the 1960s was **feminism,** the belief that women should have economic, political, and social equality with men. Feminist beliefs gained momentum during the mid-1800s and led to woman suffrage, or women's right to vote, in 1920. The women's movement declined after this achievement. However, it reawakened during the 1960s, when many women began to recognize their social and economic inequality. This realization helped spark a new, powerful feminist movement.

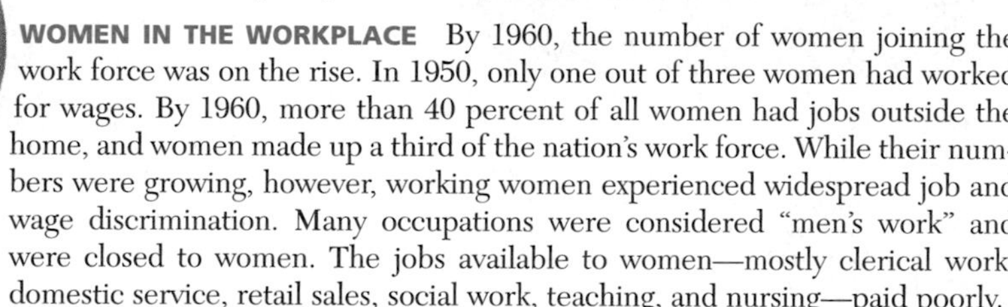

A button displays women's displeasure with their treatment in the workplace.

WOMEN IN THE WORKPLACE By 1960, the number of women joining the work force was on the rise. In 1950, only one out of three women had worked for wages. By 1960, more than 40 percent of all women had jobs outside the home, and women made up a third of the nation's work force. While their numbers were growing, however, working women experienced widespread job and wage discrimination. Many occupations were considered "men's work" and were closed to women. The jobs available to women—mostly clerical work, domestic service, retail sales, social work, teaching, and nursing—paid poorly.

The country largely ignored the discrimination women faced in the workplace, until President Kennedy appointed the Presidential Commission on the Status of Women in 1961. In 1963, the commission reported that women were

SECTION 2 RESOURCES

PRINT RESOURCES

IN-DEPTH RESOURCES: UNIT 6
Guided Reading, p. 57
Geography Application: The Equal Rights Amendment, p. 60
Primary Source: from *The Feminine Mystique*, p. 64
American Lives: Betty Friedan, p. 70

READING STUDY GUIDE, p. 237

ACCESS FOR STUDENTS ACQUIRING ENGLISH
Guided Reading (Spanish), p. 254
Geography Application: The Equal Rights Amendment (Spanish), p. 257

SPANISH READING STUDY GUIDE, p. 237

FORMAL ASSESSMENT
Section Quiz, p. 284

ALTERNATIVE ASSESSMENT BOOK
See forms for supporting and scoring alternative activities.

 **TECHNOLOGY RESOURCES**

CRITICAL THINKING TRANSPARENCIES
CT31, The Women's Movement
CT65, Percentage of All Women Who Are Working, 1950–1995

CD-ROM Electronic Library of Primary Sources

INTERNET http://www.mlushistory.com

Women in the Workplace, 1950–1993

WORKING WOMEN AND PERCENT OF LABOR FORCE

Year	Working women	Percent of labor force
1950	18 million	29%
1970	32 million	37%
1993	58 million	46%

MEDIAN INCOMES FOR WORKING WOMEN AND MEN

(symbol) = $2000

Year	Women	Men
1950	$953	$2,570
1970	$2,237	$6,670
1993	$22,469	$31,077

Sources: *Historical Statistics of the United States; Statistical Abstract of the United States 1978, 1995*

paid far less than men, even when doing the same jobs. Furthermore, women were seldom promoted to management positions, regardless of their education, experience, and ability. The discrimination that women faced in the workplace awakened many women to their unequal status in society.

SKILLBUILDER
INTERPRETING GRAPHS
For each year shown, what percentage of men's income did women make?

Skillbuilder Answers
1950: 37 percent; **1970:** 33 percent; **1993:** 72 percent.

SOCIAL ACTIVISM INSPIRES WOMEN Other sources of discontent for women stemmed from their involvement in the civil rights and antiwar movements. Although both movements inspired many women to take action on behalf of their beliefs, the discrimination they faced within the movements made them acutely aware of their inferior social status.

THINK THROUGH HISTORY
A. *Recognizing Effects* *What effects did the civil rights and the antiwar movements have on many women?*

A. Answer They spurred women to demonstrate for equality by both inspiring them to act and opening their eyes to their unequal treatment.

In these organizations, men led most of the activities, while women were assigned lesser roles. When women protested, the men usually brushed them aside. When activist Shulamith Firestone tried to raise the issue of women's rights with antiwar activists, one man told her, "Move on little girl; we have more important issues to talk about here than women's liberation."

Such experiences led some women to organize small groups to discuss their concerns. During these discussions, or "consciousness-raising" sessions, women shared their lives with each other and discovered that their experiences were not unique. Rather, they reflected a much larger pattern of sexism, or discrimination against women. Author Robin Morgan delineated this pattern.

A PERSONAL VOICE

It makes you very sensitive—raw, even, this consciousness. Everything, from the verbal assault on the street, to a "well-meant" sexist joke your husband tells, to the lower pay you get at work (for doing the same job a man would be paid more for), to television commercials, to rock-song lyrics, to the pink or blue blanket they put on your infant in the hospital nursery, to speeches by male "revolutionaries" that reek of male supremacy—everything seems to barrage your aching brain. . . . You begin to see how all-pervasive a thing is sexism.

ROBIN MORGAN, *Sisterhood is Powerful: An Anthology of Writings from the Women's Liberation Movement*

THE WOMEN'S MOVEMENT EMERGES In 1963, **Betty Friedan** published *The Feminine Mystique,* which captured the very discontent that many women were feeling. The book quickly became a bestseller. From across the country, women wrote to Friedan to thank her for exposing "the problem that has no name" and to tell her their own painful stories. "Thank God someone had the insight and courage to write it," an Iowa woman wrote.

Friedan's book helped galvanize a number of women throughout the nation. By the late 1960s, women across the country were coming together to work for change. "This is not a movement one 'joins,'" observed Robin Morgan. "The Women's Liberation movement exists where three or four friends or

OBJECTIVE ① **INSTRUCT**

A New Women's Movement Arises

▶ ***Discussing Key Ideas***

- Women encounter widespread job and wage discrimination.
- Women's experiences in the civil rights and antiwar movements increase their awareness of sexism in American society.
- Betty Friedan's *The Feminine Mystique* helps inspire a new women's movement.

IN-DEPTH RESOURCES, UNIT 6
Guided Reading, p. 57
American Lives: Betty Friedan, p. 70
Primary Source: from *The Feminine Mystique*, p. 64

ACCESS FOR STUDENTS ACQUIRING ENGLISH
Guided Reading (Spanish), p. 254

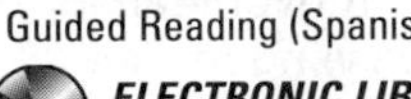

ELECTRONIC LIBRARY OF PRIMARY SOURCES
from *The Feminine Mystique* by Betty Friedan

HISTORY FROM VISUALS
Women in the Workplace,1950–1993

Reading the Graph Point out that the first graph shows the total number of working women and their percentage in the workforce in 1950, 1970, and 1993. The second graph shows the median incomes of men and women in those years.

Extension Ask students why the number of women in the work force and women's median income increased after 1970.

CRITICAL THINKING TRANSPARENCIES
CT65, Percentage of All Women Who Are Working, 1950–1995

TEACHING OPTIONS

Exploring Themes

Women in America Discuss some of the factors that sparked the women's movement in the 1960s. Ask students how the civil rights movement helped inspire the women's movement. *Possible Response: Working for the rights of others helped women become aware of inequalities in their own lives.* Point out that in the 1800s women's involvement in the antislavery movement and other causes helped to increase awareness of their own plight. Then ask students whether they think women's battle for equality is as important as the struggles of African Americans and other ethnic groups.

CRITICAL THINKING TRANSPARENCIES
CT31, The Women's Movement

Making Connections Across the Curriculum

Sociology Tell students that sociology deals with the attitudes, behaviors, and relationships in societies. The feminist movement of the 1960s and 1970s challenged and eventually influenced people's attitudes toward women. The movement also affected the relationship between men and women. Sociological studies have continued to study its effects and determine its influence on men, women, and children. Discuss the impact of the women's movement on society. Ask students whether they think the movement changed society for the better or for the worse.

OBJECTIVE

② INSTRUCT

The Movement Experiences Gains and Losses

▶ ***Starting with the Student***
Have students use a chart like the one below to record some of the gains and losses experienced by the women's movement.

Gains	Losses

▶ ***Discussing Key Ideas***

- The National Organization for Women is created to pursue women's goals.
- Radical and moderate factions form within the women's movement.
- With the ruling in *Roe* v. *Wade,* feminist groups win a battle in their fight for abortion rights.
- The New Right helps block ratification of the Equal Rights Amendment.

IN-DEPTH RESOURCES: UNIT 6
Geography Application: The Equal Rights Amendment, p. 60

ELECTRONIC LIBRARY OF PRIMARY SOURCES
from NOW's Statement of Purpose

KEY PLAYER
Gloria Steinem

Critical Thinking: Analyzing
Discuss the significance of the magazine's name. Tell students that *Ms.* was coined so that women would have a title that didn't reveal their marital status. Ask students why this was an important consideration in the women's movement.
Possible Response: Women were tired of being defined by their relationship to men.

neighbors decide to meet regularly . . . on the welfare lines, in the supermarket, the factory, the convent, the farm, the maternity ward. . . ."

The Movement Experiences Gains and Losses

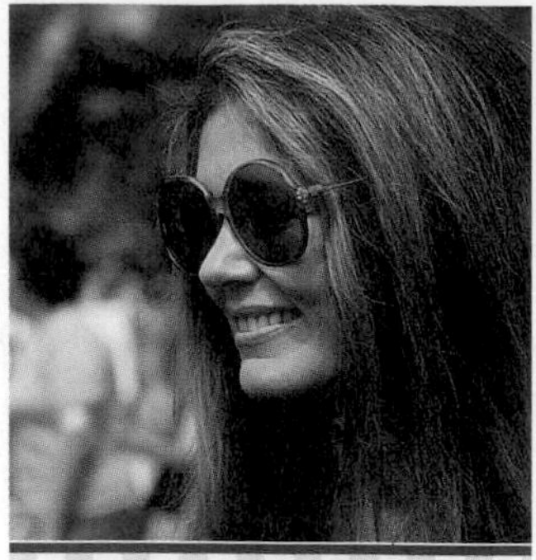

KEY PLAYER

GLORIA STEINEM
1934–

Gloria Steinem became one of the more prominent figures of the women's movement after she and several other women founded *Ms.* magazine in 1972. The magazine soon became a major voice of the women's movement.

Steinem said that she decided to start the feminist magazine after editors in the mainstream media continually rejected her stories about the women's movement: "Editors who had assumed I had some valuable biological insight into food, male movie stars, and textured stockings now questioned whether I or other women writers were biologically capable of writing objectively about feminism. That was the beginning."

Within a year of its first issue, *Ms.* had nearly 200,000 subscribers and kept many readers informed about events of the women's movement.

As the women's movement grew, it achieved remarkable political and social gains for women. Along the way, however, the movement also suffered setbacks, most notably in its attempt to ensure women's equality in the Constitution.

THE CREATION OF NOW Due in part to a backfired strategy by opponents of the Civil Rights Act of 1964, women had won the legal tools with which to fight discrimination. Opponents of the civil rights bill—which prohibited discrimination based on race, religion, and national origin—had added a provision outlawing discrimination based on gender, in an attempt to weaken support for the bill. Much to the dismay of its opponents, however, the bill passed with the gender provision included. One result of the provision was that the Equal Employment Opportunity Commission (EEOC)—an organization set up by the act to investigate discrimination claims by African Americans—also addressed women's job complaints.

By 1966, however, some women voiced dissatisfaction with the EEOC. They argued that the commission showed an overall lack of attention toward the flood of women's grievances. That year, several women, including Betty Friedan, created the **National Organization for Women** (NOW) to pursue more actively women's goals. "The time has come," the founders of NOW declared, "to confront with concrete action the conditions which now prevent women from enjoying the equality of opportunity . . . which is their right as individual Americans and as human beings."

THINK THROUGH HISTORY
B. ***Analyzing Causes***
What prompted women to establish NOW?

B. Answer Their dissatisfaction with the EEOC and the need for a more organized effort to combat sexism.

NOW moved into action quickly. Its members pushed for the creation of more child-care facilities and for improved educational opportunities for women. NOW also pressured the EEOC to enforce more vigorously the ban on gender discrimination in hiring. NOW's efforts prompted the EEOC to declare sex-segregated job ads illegal and issue guidelines to employers, stating that they could no longer refuse to hire women for traditionally male jobs.

A DIVERSE MOVEMENT In its first three years, NOW's ranks swelled from 300 to 175,000 members. Outside of NOW, a number of other women's groups sprang up around the country. In 1968 a militant group known as the New York Radical Women staged a well-publicized demonstration at the annual Miss America Pageant. To protest the concept of judging women's beauty, the women threw bras, girdles, wigs, and other "women's garbage" into a "Freedom Trash Can." They then crowned a sheep as "Miss America." In 1971, journalist **Gloria Steinem** helped found the National Women's Political Caucus, a moderate group that encouraged women to seek political office.

The radicals and moderates within the movement often quarreled over strategy. However, these diverse factions put aside their differences in August 1970 to join in the largest women's rights demonstration ever. To commemorate the 50th anniversary of woman suffrage, tens of thousands of women gathered from around the country and marched through New York City to promote women's equality.

By the early 1970s, the women's movement had scored several victories on the political and social fronts. In 1972, Congress passed a ban on gender discrimination in "any education program or activities receiving federal financial

Block Schedule TEACHING OPTION **Time Needed: 30 Minutes**

Cooperative Activity: Preparing Articles for Ms.

Task: Groups of five to six students will write, design, and produce articles for *Ms.*

Purpose: To explore the goals, interests, and accomplishments of the women's movement in the early 1970s.

Activity: Students should get together to discuss articles they would like to write for *Ms.* Some students might choose to research and write articles on the goals of the movement in the 1970s. Others might decide to "interview" important feminists of the time or to write human-interest features about women's experiences in the movement. Students should include photos and artwork with their articles.

Building a Portfolio: Students who add their article to their portfolio should attach a note explaining how the project affected their opinion of feminism.

ALTERNATIVE ASSESSMENT BOOK
Standards for Evaluating a Cooperative Activity

Standards for Evaluation
Articles should . . .

- deal with feminist issues and concerns of the 1970s
- include photos and artwork with feminist themes
- convey the authors' pride in the movement and optimism for the future

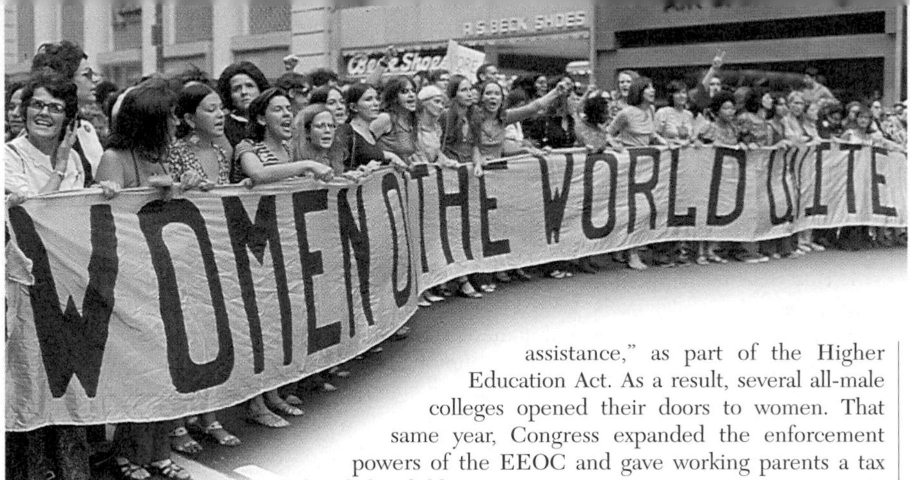

Thousands of women march through the streets of New York City during the summer of 1970 to promote women's equality.

assistance," as part of the Higher Education Act. As a result, several all-male colleges opened their doors to women. That same year, Congress expanded the enforcement powers of the EEOC and gave working parents a tax break for child-care expenses.

ROE V. WADE One of the more controversial issues that NOW and other feminist groups supported was a woman's right to have an abortion. In 1973, the Supreme Court ruled in the case *Roe* v. *Wade* that women had the right to choose an abortion during the first three months of pregnancy. In an editorial on the decision, the *New York Times* expressed hope that the ruling might "bring to end the emotional and divisive public argument . . ." However, this did not happen. Americans today remain divided over the abortion issue.

THE EQUAL RIGHTS AMENDMENT In what seemed at first to be another triumph for the women's movement, Congress passed the **Equal Rights Amendment** (ERA) in 1972. The amendment then needed ratification by 38 states—three-quarters of the 50 states—to become part of the Constitution. The ERA, which had first been introduced to Congress in 1923, would have guaranteed that "Equality of rights under the law shall not be denied or abridged by the United States or by any state on account of sex." The ERA's supporters argued that the amendment was needed to make sure that men and women could not be treated differently under the law solely because of their gender. It was, they said, a matter of "simple justice."

ANOTHER PERSPECTIVE

AFRICAN-AMERICAN WOMEN

The women's movement of the 1960s and 1970s was largely a white middle-class movement. By the 1960s, many African-American women expressed greater concern with racism and the attainment of civil rights than with sexism and inequality in the workplace. Ida Lewis, editor of the African-American magazine, *Essence*, advised, "The Women's Liberation Movement is basically a family quarrel between white women and white men. . . . And on general principles, it's not too good to get involved in family disputes."

CONSERVATIVES AND THE WOMEN'S MOVEMENT The amendment sparked fierce opposition from conservative religious groups, political organizations, and many women who opposed the feminist movement. These groups raised fears that the ERA would lead to "a parade of horribles," such as the drafting of women, the end of laws protecting homemakers, and same-sex marriages.

One prominent ERA opponent was **Phyllis Schlafly.** In 1972, Schlafly founded and became national chairman of the Stop-ERA campaign. Schlafly characterized the ERA as the work of radical feminists who "hate men, marriage, and children" and whose oppression existed "only in their distorted minds."

Phyllis Schlafly

A PERSONAL VOICE

The U.S. Constitution is not the place for symbols or slogans, it is not the proper device to alleviate psychological problems of personal inferiority. Symbols and slogans belong on bumper strips—not in the Constitution. It would be a tragic mistake for our nation to succumb to the tirades and demands of a few women who are seeking a constitutional cure for their personal problems.

PHYLLIS SCHLAFLY, quoted in *The Equal Rights Amendment: The History and the Movement*

The Stop-ERA campaign also attracted support from women who feared its impact on families. Many worried that the amendment would end a husband's responsibility to provide support to his wife and children.

ANOTHER PERSPECTIVE

African-American Women

Critical Thinking: Evaluating Ask students whether they agree with Ida Lewis's assessment that the women's movement was "basically a family quarrel between white women and white men."

MORE ABOUT . . .

Phyllis Schlafly

According to Schlafly, career success cannot compare with "the thrill, the satisfaction, and the fun of having and caring for babies, and watching them respond and grow under a mother's loving care. More babies multiply a woman's joy."

Issues for the 21st Century

Women and the Glass Ceiling

Connect the women's movement to issues affecting women today by having students read pages 894–895. Then have them answer these questions.

1. What did many women in the 1960s and 1970s hope to change in the workplace? *Unequal pay and opportunities; gender discrimination; more childcare facilities.*
2. Which of these goals had been achieved by the 1990s? Which goals remain to be fulfilled? *Better represented in nontraditional jobs, more equal pay; Women still earn less; unequal representation in top-level jobs.*

TEACHING OPTIONS

Making Connections Across Time

Jane Roe Today Tell students that the woman called Jane Roe in the 1973 Supreme Court case reversed her opinion on abortion in 1995. Claiming that abortion was "murderously wrong," the woman—Norma McCorvey—joined Operation Rescue, one of the most militant antiabortion groups in the country. The lawyer who won *Roe* v. *Wade* discounted her former client's reversal. "Jane Roe was a plaintiff," she said, "but the case was a class action on behalf of all women." McCorvey herself never had an abortion because her case was decided too late. She gave her baby daughter up for adoption in 1970.

Making Connections Across Cultures

Black Women in the Feminist Movement Tell students that many black women felt excluded from the feminist movement. They felt that the white leaders of the movement were not addressing black issues and concerns. They also believed that supporting the women's movement would undermine black men in their struggle against racism. However, not all black women shared this opinion. Shirley Chisholm, who in 1968 became the first black woman elected to the House of Representatives, was active in both the civil rights and women's movements. "I've suffered more discrimination as a woman," she said, "than as a black."

OBJECTIVE

③ INSTRUCT

The Movement's Legacy

▶ ***Discussing Key Ideas***

- The women's movement opens up new opportunities for women and changes their role in society.
- The movement changes the way women look at work and careers.

ASSESS & RETEACH

Section 2 Assessment

Have students work independently to answer the questions. Then have them meet in small groups to discuss their answers.

Self-Assessment

Have students make a list of the impressions they had about the women's movement before they read Section 2. Then have them note whether their reading has confirmed or contradicted their preconceptions.

Section Quiz

FORMAL ASSESSMENT
Section Quiz, p. 284

Reteach

Use the graphs on page 769 to review the progress women have made in the workplace since 1970.

CLOSE

In the 1960s, the women's movement began challenging traditional beliefs about a woman's place in society. The movement opened up new opportunities for women, particularly in the fields of education, employment, and politics. At the same time, many young people were rejecting mainstream American society and creating a counterculture.

During the 1970s, conservatives built on their opposition to ERA and the *Roe* v. *Wade* abortion decision by gaining support for what they called a new "pro-family" movement. Jo Anne Gasper, editor of a newsletter entitled *The Right Woman,* described this movement as a "broad-based coalition of social conservatives who recognize the value of the person, the importance of the family, the rights and responsibilities of parents, and the importance of restricting government so that there can be personal freedom."

This coalition of social conservatives—which focused on social, cultural, and moral issues—came to be known as the **New Right.** The New Right and the women's movement debated family-centered issues such as federally funded day care, which the New Right opposed. Throughout the 1970s, the New Right built grass-roots support for social conservatism; in fact, it would play a key role in the election of Ronald Reagan to the presidency in 1980.

THINK THROUGH HISTORY
C. *Analyzing Motives* *What concerns motivated those who opposed the ERA?*

C. Answer Fear of change and the perceived drastic effects the amendment might have had on traditional family life.

The Movement's Legacy

The New Right and the women's movement clashed most dramatically over ERA, however. By 1977, the ERA had won approval from 35 of the 38 states needed to ratify the amendment. At that point, however, the amendment stalled, as opposition to the ERA gained strength. By the end of 1982 (the deadline for ratification), no other states had approved the amendment. The ERA went down in defeat.

Women have made significant strides politically, as they have increased their presence in the U.S. Congress.

Despite ERA's defeat, the women's movement succeeded in opening up new opportunities for American women and dramatically altering their roles in society.

For instance, the movement left its mark on education. In 1970, 8 percent of all medical school graduates and 5 percent of all law school graduates were women. By 1992, those proportions had risen to 36 and 43 percent, respectively.

The women's movement also changed the way women looked at work and careers. In the 1950s, most women who took jobs had done so mainly to "help out." By the 1970s, many women were preparing themselves for lifetime careers. Still, many women ran into a "glass ceiling"—an invisible, but very real, resistance to promoting women into top positions.

The women's movement brought women into the political arena in growing numbers. Women held only 3.5 percent of elected state offices in 1969. By 1996, 25 percent of elected state officeholders were women. The number of women in Congress also has increased—from 19 in 1975 to 60 in 1997.

Most of all, the women's movement helped countless women open their lives to new possibilities. "We have lived the second American revolution," wrote Betty Friedan in 1976, "and our very anger said a 'new YES' to life."

D. Answer By opening up greater opportunities for women in the fields of education, employment, and politics.

THINK THROUGH HISTORY
D. THEME *Women in America* *In what ways did the women's movement help women progress in society?*

Section 2 Assessment

1. TERMS & NAMES
Identify:
- feminism
- Betty Friedan
- National Organization for Women
- Gloria Steinem
- Equal Rights Amendment
- Phyllis Schlafly
- New Right

2. SUMMARIZING Create a time line of key events relating to the women's movement. Use the dates already plotted on the time line below as a guide.

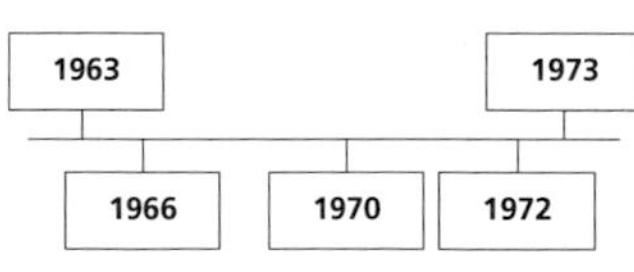

3. MAKING PREDICTIONS What if the Equal Rights Amendment had been ratified? Speculate on how women's lives might have been different. Use reasons to support your answer.

THINK ABOUT
- rights addressed by the amendment
- legal support that the amendment might have provided
- possible reactions from groups opposing the amendment

4. MAKING INFERENCES In 1976, Betty Friedan wrote, "We have lived the second American revolution." Do you think she is overstating the historical importance of the women's movement by comparing it to the American Revolution? Why or why not?

THINK ABOUT
- the movement's legacy
- what you already know about the American Revolution and its outcome

ANSWERS

1. TERMS & NAMES

feminism, p. 768
Betty Friedan, p. 769
National Organization for Women, p. 770
Gloria Steinem, p. 770
Equal Rights Amendment, p. 771
Phyllis Schlafly, p. 771
New Right, p. 772

2. SUMMARIZING

Possible Answers:
1963—Betty Friedan publishes *The Feminine Mystique.*
1966—National Organization for Women is formed.
1970—Demonstration commemorates 50th anniversary of woman suffrage.
1972—*Ms.* is founded; Congress passes Equal Rights Amendment and bans sex discrimination in federally assisted educational programs and activities.
1973—Supreme Court's ruling in *Roe* v. *Wade* legalizes abortion.

3. MAKING PREDICTIONS

Possible Answers: Women might have won more sex-discrimination lawsuits; the "glass ceiling" phenomenon might have been less of a problem for professional women; ratification might have spurred a powerful male backlash; Phyllis Schlafly and other opponents of ERA might have formed organizations to undermine the amendment.

4. MAKING INFERENCES

Possible Responses: Yes—Feminists were not like the American colonists who risked their lives fighting a war for independence and who formed a new nation. No—Feminists were nonviolent revolutionaries who were just as determined and committed to their cause as the early American revolutionaries.

③ Culture and Counterculture

TERMS & NAMES
- counterculture
- Haight-Ashbury
- The Beatles
- Woodstock

LEARN ABOUT the ideals and lifestyle of the counterculture movement of the 1960s ***TO UNDERSTAND*** its impact on young people in the 1960s and beyond.

ONE AMERICAN'S STORY

In 1966, Alex Forman packed up a guitar and little else and headed to San Francisco. Forman had decided to abandon his conventional life in mainstream America and live with thousands of others like himself in a more carefree setting. Forman recalled his early days in San Francisco's Haight-Ashbury district, which had attracted many young Americans seeking refuge from the violence and divisiveness of the sixties.

A PERSONAL VOICE

It was like paradise there. Everybody was in love with life and in love with their fellow human beings to the point where they were just sharing in incredible ways with everybody. Taking people in off the street and letting them stay in their homes. . . . You could walk down almost any street in Haight-Ashbury where I was living, and someone would smile at you and just go, "Hey, it's beautiful, isn't it?". . . It was a very special time.

ALEX FORMAN, quoted in *From Camelot to Kent State*

Members of the counterculture relax in a California park.

Forman was part of a movement known as the **counterculture.** Made up mostly of white middle-class youths, the counterculture—like other groups in society—had grown deeply disillusioned with America during the 1960s. However, unlike the other groups, which challenged the system, members of the counterculture chose to turn their backs on America and establish a new society based on peace and love. Although their efforts were short-lived, some aspects of the counterculture movement left an enduring mark on American society.

The Counterculture

In the late 1960s, the historian Theodore Roszak described the rise of these idealistic youths as the "counterculture." It was a culture, he said, so different from the mainstream "that it scarcely looks to many as a culture at all, but takes on the alarming appearance of a barbarian intrusion." The so-called alarming barbarians were mostly white middle-class college youths. And while they indeed did create a culture different from the mainstream, their lack of organization and direction—as well as the devastating effects of drug use—led to the counterculture's eventual collapse.

"TUNE IN, TURN ON, DROP OUT" Members of the counterculture, known as hippies, shared some of the beliefs of the New Left movement, namely that American society—and its materialism, technology, and war—had grown hollow. A number of hippies even participated in various New Left demonstrations, including its many protests against the Vietnam War. However, a majority of hippies chose to protest against society by leaving it.

Influenced heavily by the nonconformist beat movement of the 1950s, hippies eagerly embraced the credo voiced by Harvard psychology professor and counterculture philosopher Timothy Leary: "Tune in, turn on, drop out." Throughout the mid- and late 1960s, tens of thousands of idealistic

Throughout the late 1960s, thousands of hippies flocked to San Francisco's Haight-Ashbury district.

SECTION 3 RESOURCES

 **PRINT RESOURCES**

IN-DEPTH RESOURCES: UNIT 6
Guided Reading, p. 58
Skillbuilder Practice: Comparing; Contrasting, p. 59
Primary Source: Popular Song, p. 65
Literature: from *Los Vendidos* by Luis Valdez, p. 66

READING STUDY GUIDE, p. 239

ACCESS FOR STUDENTS ACQUIRING ENGLISH
Guided Reading (Spanish), p. 255
Skillbuilder Practice: Comparing; Contrasting (Spanish), p. 256

SPANISH READING STUDY GUIDE, p. 239

FORMAL ASSESSMENT
Section Quiz, p. 285

ALTERNATIVE ASSESSMENT BOOK
See forms for supporting and scoring alternative activities.

 **TECHNOLOGY RESOURCES**

CD-ROM *Our Times*

VIDEO *American Portfolio: A Videodisc for U.S. History* user's guide, pp. 247, 249

INTERNET http://www.mlushistory.com

Section 3 Overview

OBJECTIVES

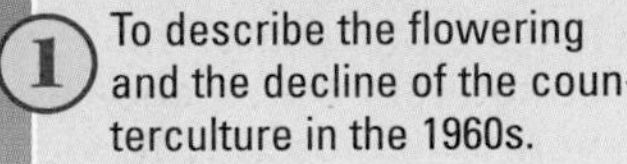

① To describe the flowering and the decline of the counterculture in the 1960s.

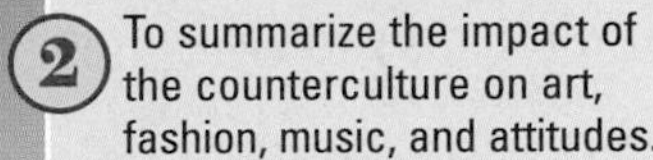

② To summarize the impact of the counterculture on art, fashion, music, and attitudes.

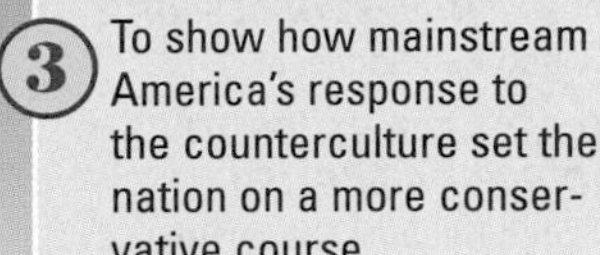

③ To show how mainstream America's response to the counterculture set the nation on a more conservative course.

CRITICAL THINKING

- Theme: The American Dream, p. 774
- Analyzing causes, p. 775
- Recognizing effects, p. 776
- Analyzing issues, p. 777
- Summarizing, p. 777
- Comparing and contrasting, p. 777
- Forming generalizations, p. 777

FOCUS & MOTIVATE

5-MINUTE WARM-UP

Recognizing Facts and Details

To explore the counterculture, have students look at the photos of young people on pages 773 and 776 and answer these questions.

1. What similarities of dress and appearance do the young people share?
2. What similar behavior is represented in both photos?

WARM-UP TRANSPARENCY 23

▶ ***Starting with the Student***

- What are some songs of the 1960s? How has the music of that period influenced the music students enjoy today?

OBJECTIVE ① **INSTRUCT**

The Counterculture

▶ ***Discussing Key Ideas***

- Members of the counterculture reject mainstream society and try to create an idyllic world of peace, love, and harmony.

(continued on next page)

(continued from page 773)

- Hippie life usually involves rock 'n' roll, outrageous clothing and appearance, and drugs.
- After a few years, the counterculture's peace and harmony give way to violence, drug abuse, and disillusionment.

IN-DEPTH RESOURCES: UNIT 6
Guided Reading, p. 58

ACCESS FOR STUDENTS ACQUIRING ENGLISH
Guided Reading (Spanish), p. 255

MORE ABOUT . . .
Communes

Many people who chose to live in communes sought to re-create the Garden of Eden by looking for beautiful, secluded spots in rural areas where they could live a spontaneous, hassle-free existence. Community relationships were valued above all else. This is how Rosabeth Moss Kanter described her communal experience: "The things that make up community are terribly subtle; it's the little things . . . making dinner with a crew once a week, remembering who's a vegetarian and needs a special meal. Expanded consciousness of others . . . nothing big and spectacular. The scenes that move me are the little things about our life together."

"How does it feel to be without a home . . . like a rolling stone?"

BOB DYLAN

young Americans left behind their established worlds of school, work, or home to live with one another in the streets, parks, and group homes. Their goal was to create, in the midst of what they viewed as a cold and cruel nation, an idyllic setting of peace, love, and harmony.

HIPPIE CULTURE The creation of this peace and love, which some called an Age of Aquarius, usually involved three things: rock 'n' roll music, colorful clothing and appearance, and the liberal use of drugs—both marijuana and a new hallucinogenic, or mind-altering, compound called LSD, or acid. Timothy Leary, an early experimenter with LSD, promoted the drug as a "liberating" and "mind-expanding" aid in the search for greater self-awareness and inner peace.

Aside from illegal drug use, hippies showed their rejection of the establishment by wearing what were then considered outrageous clothes. Many young men and women wore ragged jeans and tie-dyed T-shirts, as well as surplus military garments. In addition, many hippies enhanced their outfits with beads and Native American ornaments. Men grew long hair and beards. To many hippies, long hair symbolized the freedom to "do your own thing." To the older generation, long hair symbolized a lack of respect for social conventions. Signs went up across the country saying "Make America Beautiful—give a hippie a haircut."

THINK THROUGH HISTORY
A. THEME ***The American Dream*** *What was the counterculture movement's American dream?*

A. Answer To leave mainstream America and establish a new society of love and harmony.

Hippies also turned their backs on conventional home life. Many chose to live together in communes—group living arrangements in which the members renounced private property to live together in cooperation and harmony. For some, this meant establishing rural communes; for others, it meant crowding together in urban "crash pads." Scores of hippies flocked to Chicago's Old Town, Atlanta's Fourteenth Street, New York City's Greenwich Village, and especially San Francisco's **Haight-Ashbury** district. By the mid-sixties, Haight-Ashbury had become the hippie capital, mainly because of the availability of hallucinogenic drugs, which California did not outlaw until late 1966.

Many disillusioned youths also sought fulfillment through new and different religious experiences. Rejecting traditional forms of worship, scores of young men and women turned to the teachings of such Eastern religions as Zen Buddhism. According to the Zen philosophy, people attain enlightenment through meditation, self-contemplation, and intuition, rather than through the reading of scriptures.

Influenced by the preaching of spiritual gurus, such as Maharishi Mahesh Yogi of India, thousands of Americans began taking informal courses in mystical meditation and forming groups to practice what they learned. In 1968, the news media declared that more than 10,000 of the nation's youths had become "transcendental meditators." Later that year, *Life* magazine proclaimed 1968 to be the "Year of the Guru."

A prominent symbol of the counterculture movement was bright colors. Here, a woman and a Volkswagen bus sport such colors along a San Francisco street.

DECLINE OF THE MOVEMENT After only a few years, the counterculture's peace and harmony gave way to violence and disillusionment. The urban communes eventually turned seedy and dangerous, as they became havens for muggers, drug dealers, and runaways. "It got very ugly

TEACHING OPTION

Skillbuilder Mini-Lesson: Comparing; Contrasting

Explaining the Skill Finding similarities and differences between events, social or political groups, and movements can help historians understand the past more completely. For example, comparing the lifestyles and values of different groups can help historians identify trends or universal human needs.

Applying the Skill: Hippie Culture Make two columns on the chalkboard, labeled "Hippies" and "Establishment." Ask students to list as many differing characteristics of hippie culture and establishment, or mainstream culture, as they can find on this page. Point out that they may need to infer some characteristics of the establishment from the descriptions of the hippies. Also ask students if they find any similarities between the two groups. Here are some examples: hippies—long hair, rock 'n' roll music, hallucinogenic drugs, freedom to "do your own thing," outrageous clothes, communes, transcendental meditation; establishment—short hair, other kinds of music, objections to drug use, respect for social conventions, conventional clothing styles, traditional home life, regular jobs.

IN-DEPTH RESOURCES: UNIT 6
Skillbuilder Practice: Comparing; Contrasting, p. 59

very fast," Alex Forman recalled. "There were ripoffs, violence . . . people living on the street with no place to stay."

In 1969, two episodes of counterculture violence shocked America. In August, commune leader Charles Manson and his "family" murdered actress Sharon Tate. Four months later at the Altamont Raceway in California, the Hell's Angels motorcycle gang beat a man to death in front of the stage where the Rolling Stones, a British rock band, were playing.

B. Answer The Manson and Altamont murders, the dark side of the drug scene, and the hippies' inability to exist outside mainstream America.

By 1970, the widespread use of drugs had further eroded the counterculture movement. Many young people fell victim to the drugs they used, experiencing overdoses, drug dependence, and mental and physical breakdowns. The popular rock singer Janis Joplin and the legendary guitarist Jimi Hendrix both died of drug overdoses in 1970.

More than anything else, however, the hippies eventually discovered that they could not sustain themselves outside of mainstream America. Even though they tried to reject conventional society, many hippies found themselves ultimately dependent on it. Numerous hippies ended up panhandling on street corners and lined up at government offices, collecting welfare and food stamps to help them survive the trials of natural living. "We were together at the level of peace and freedom and love," said one disillusioned hippie. "We fell apart over who would cook and wash the dishes and pay the bills."

THINK THROUGH HISTORY
B. *Analyzing Causes* *What events hastened the decline of the counterculture movement?*

A Changing Culture

Although the counterculture movement was short-lived, some aspects of it—namely, its fashion, fine arts, and social attitudes—left a more lasting imprint on mainstream America and on the rest of the world.

ART AND FASHION The counterculture's rebellious style left its mark on the worlds of art and fashion. The 1960s saw the rise of popular, or pop, art. Pop artists, led by Andy Warhol, attempted to bring art into the mainstream. Warhol became famous for his bright silk-screen portraits of soup cans, Marilyn Monroe, and other icons of mass culture.

Andy Warhol created this image of movie actress and popular icon Marilyn Monroe.

To a larger extent, the counterculture's legacy lived on in the way many Americans dressed and groomed themselves. While most Americans did not adopt the outlandish look of hippies, many came out of the sixties wearing longer hair, more colorful clothing, and blue jeans, which became a staple in nearly every American's wardrobe.

ROCK MUSIC Perhaps the most lasting legacy of the counterculture movement was its music. During the 1960s, the hippie movement embraced rock 'n' roll—the offshoot of African-American rhythm and blues music that had captivated so many teenagers during the 1950s—as its loud and biting anthem of protest. However, as the years went on, rock music melded into the mainstream and is today one of the more recognizable characteristics of American youth.

The band that, perhaps more than any other, helped propel rock music into mainstream America was **the Beatles.** The British band, made up of four youths from working-class Liverpool, England, arrived in America in 1964 and immediately took the country by storm. By the time the Beatles broke up in 1971, the four "lads" from Liverpool had inspired a countless

MORE ABOUT . . . *The End of the Movement*

In 1969, the hippie activist Jerry Rubin published a book titled *Do It!,* in which he described his vision of the coming counterculture revolution. Rubin foresaw a "mass breakdown of authority, mass rebellion, total anarchy in every institution in the Western world. Tribes of long-hairs, blacks, armed women, workers, peasants and students will take over." Two years later, however, the revolution was dead.

OBJECTIVE
② INSTRUCT

A Changing Culture

Starting with the Student
Have students document details of the impact of the counterculture movement in a cluster diagram like this.

Discussing Key Ideas
- The rebelliousness of the counterculture influences styles of art and fashion.
- Hippies embrace rock music as their anthem of social protest and cultural change.
- The counterculture leaves a legacy of more relaxed attitudes toward sex, marriage, behavior, and relationships.

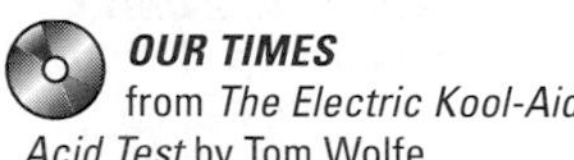
OUR TIMES from *The Electric Kool-Aid Acid Test* by Tom Wolfe

TEACHING OPTIONS

Exploring Themes

The American Dream Discuss the counterculture's rejection of mainstream society. Ask students to define the American dream. Which aspects of the traditional American dream did hippies renounce? *Possible Responses: Materialism; conventional home life; success in the workplace.* What did hippies value? What was their American dream? *Possible Responses: Peace; love; communal living.* Why did their dream sour? *Possible Response: Because they couldn't apply their ideals to practical, everyday life.* Then ask students whether the counterculture's American dream could be realized today.

Making Connections Across Time

Counterculture Fashion Returns Tell students that in the 1990s, bell-bottom jeans, tie-dyed shirts, and miniskirts made a comeback. These counterculture fashions and others became popular once again among nostalgic baby boomers and people of younger generations. Ask students why these items of clothing and other trappings of the counterculture have such an enduring hold on the imagination. Why do the 1960s continue to fascinate? *Possible Response: Because, even though they may have been illusory, the freedom and spirit of the period appeal to many people.*

MORE ABOUT . . .
The Beatles in America

In 1975, *Life* magazine published a list of "The 100 Events that Shaped America." The arrival of the Beatles on American soil in 1964 ranked number 96. Americans got their first look at the Fab Four on January 3 of that year, when television talk-show host Jack Paar aired a videotape of the group performing "She Loves You" to an audience of screaming, sobbing teenage girls. American critics were not impressed. One writer for the *New York Times* predicted that Beatlemania would never catch on in the United States: "On this side of the Atlantic, it is dated stuff." The journalist would soon eat his words. In 1996, 25 years after the Beatles broke up, the group once again reached the top of the charts with their *Anthology* albums.

MORE ABOUT . . .
Woodstock

The four young men who sponsored Woodstock set a $15,000 ceiling on payment for each musical act. However, Jimi Hendrix, the hottest musician in the country, wanted more. In the end, they compromised and paid Hendrix $32,000, but they had to lie to the other artists about the terms. "We told everyone that was because he was playing two sets at $16,000 each." As scheduled, Hendrix played his one and only set for the festival's finale.

IN-DEPTH RESOURCES: UNIT 6
Primary Source: Popular Song, p. 65

The Beatles, shown here on the cover of their album, *Sgt. Pepper's Lonely Hearts Club Band,* influenced fashion with their long hair and psychedelic clothing.

number of other bands and had won over millions of Americans to rock 'n' roll.

WOODSTOCK One dramatic example of rock 'n' roll's exploding popularity occurred in August 1969 on a farm in upstate New York. There, about 120,000 young people were expected to gather for a free music festival called "Woodstock Music and Art Fair, an Aquarian Exposition." More than 400,000 showed up. For three days, the most popular bands and musicians of the time performed, including Jimi Hendrix, Janis Joplin, Joe Cocker, Joan Baez, the Grateful Dead, and Jefferson Airplane.

Despite the huge crowd, the event, which became known simply as **Woodstock,** was remarkably peaceful and well-organized. However, not everyone remembered it as three days of bliss. Tom Mathews, a writer who attended the Woodstock festival, later recalled his experience there.

A PERSONAL VOICE

Woodstock, that three-day jamboree of peace, love and rock. Also rain. The last night of the concert I was standing in a narrow pit at the foot of the stage. I made the mistake of looking over the board fence separating the pit from Max Yasgur's hillside. When I peered up I saw 400,000 . . . people wrapped in wet, dirty ponchos, sleeping bags and assorted, tie-dyed mufti slowly slipping toward the stage. It looked like a human mudslide. . . . After that night, I couldn't get out of there fast enough.

TOM MATHEWS, "The Sixties Complex," *Newsweek,* September 5, 1988

A man and woman mak their own music at Woodstock. "If you wer part of this culture," no one Woodstock attend "you had to be there."

CHANGING ATTITUDES As the counterculture movement faded, its casual, "do your own thing" philosophy left an imprint on Americans' social attitudes. In particular, American attitudes toward sexual behavior became more permissive, leading to what became known as the sexual revolution. During the 1960s and 1970s, mass culture—which included books, magazines, and movies—began to more openly address subjects that had once been prohibited, particularly sexual behavior and explicit violence.

While some hailed the increasing permissiveness as a liberating force, others attacked it as a sign of moral decay. Millions of Americans opposed the country's increasingly permissive social behavior. While the counterculture movement eventually helped prompt many Americans to adopt more liberal attitudes about dress and appearance, music, and social behavior, the movement's immediate impact on the country produced the opposite effect.

C. Answer The counterculture influenced art, fashion, and music. It also led to the sexual revolution.

THINK THROUGH HISTORY
C. *Recognizing Effects* *What impact did the counterculture have on mainstream America?*

The Conservative Response

In the late 1960s, many mainstream Americans looked at the student rebellions, the increasing permissiveness, and the urban riots, and began to feel that the country was headed in the wrong direction. Many believed that the country was losing its moral compass—its sense of right and wrong. And increasingly, conservative voices began to express people's anger. For instance, at the Republican convention in Miami, a month after the tumultuous Democratic convention in Chicago, candidate Richard M. Nixon expressed that anger.

Block Schedule TEACHING OPTION **Time Needed: 30 Minutes**

Cooperative Activity: Producing a 1960s Music Video

Task: Groups of five to six students will select a song from the 1960s and create and record a music video based on it.

Purpose: To help students identify significant elements of the counterculture.

Activity: Group members should select a song from the 1960s. They should then brainstorm to create an appropriate video based on the song. The video should have a 1960s setting and be filled with the colors, clothes, and memorabilia of the time. One student in the group should direct the video, another should record it, and the rest should perform. Performers, who should be dressed as members of the counterculture, may lip-synch the song.

Building a Portfolio: Students who add their videos to their portfolio should attach a note to it, describing their role in the activity.

ALTERNATIVE ASSESSMENT BOOK
Standards for Evaluating a Cooperative Activity

Standards for Evaluation
Music videos should . . .

- celebrate and bring to life songs of the 1960s
- contain scenes filled with the colors, clothes, and trappings of the 1960s
- convey a sense of the freedom and abandon of the time

The Conservative Response

▶***Discussing Key Ideas***
- Conservative Americans voice their anger with student rebellions and the counterculture.
- The response of angry mainstream Americans helps propel Richard M. Nixon into the White House.

A PERSONAL VOICE

As we look at America we see cities enveloped in smoke and flame. We hear sirens in the night. We see Americans dying on distant battlefields abroad. We see Americans hating each other, fighting each other, killing each other at home. . . . Did we come all this way for this? . . . die in Normandy and Korea and Valley Forge for this? Listen to the . . . voice of the great majority of Americans, the forgotten Americans—the non-shouters; the non-demonstrators.

RICHARD M. NIXON, Republican Convention, August 8, 1968

In contrast to the Democratic convention in Chicago, the 1968 Republican convention was orderly and united—particularly in the delegates' opposition to the counterculture.

In 1968, conservative commentator William F. Buckley announced that his magazine, the *National Review,* was starting a newsletter to expose rebellious students, antiwar radicals, and Communist forces that he claimed were behind the New Left. FBI Director J. Edgar Hoover issued a warning to the nation's police officers that "revolutionary terrorism" was a threat to law and order on campuses and in cities. Other conservative critics warned the public that campus rebels posed a danger to traditional values and threatened to plunge American society into anarchy and lawlessness.

CONSERVATIVES ATTACK THE COUNTERCULTURE Conservatives also attacked the counterculture for what they saw as its decadent values: glorification of drug use, indulgent sexual behavior, and indifference toward work. In the view of psychiatrist Bruno Bettelheim, student rebels and members of the counterculture had been pampered in childhood; as young adults, they did not have the ability for delayed gratification.

D. Answer It resulted in a conservative backlash that helped propel Nixon to the White House.

THINK THROUGH HISTORY
D. Analyzing Issues *What role did the counterculture and antiwar movement play in helping Richard Nixon win the presidency?*

According to some conservative commentators, the counterculture had abandoned rational thought in favor of the senses and restraint for uninhibited self-expression. The counterculture, they believed, was undermining the capacity of young Americans to debate issues rationally.

The angry response of mainstream Americans to the disorders caused a profound change in the political landscape of the United States. By the end of the 1960s, conservatives were presenting their own solutions on such issues as lawlessness and crime, the size of the federal government, and welfare. This growing conservative movement would propel Richard M. Nixon into the White House—and set the nation on a more conservative course.

Section 3 Assessment

1. TERMS & NAMES
Identify:
- counterculture
- Haight-Ashbury
- The Beatles
- Woodstock

2. SUMMARIZING Re-create the organizational tree diagram below on your paper. Then fill in examples that illustrate the topics in the second row of boxes.

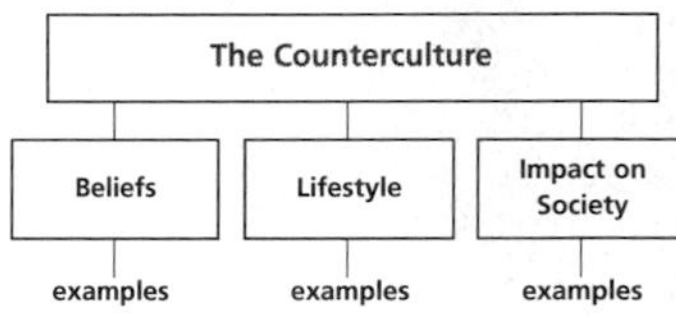

3. COMPARING AND CONTRASTING Compare the Woodstock rock concert in upstate New York with the Rolling Stones rock concert in California. What do you think each event came to symbolize?

THINK ABOUT
- the prevailing atmosphere at Woodstock
- the tragic result of the Rolling Stones concert
- the probable conclusions drawn about the events by proponents of the counterculture and by advocates of the conservative movement

4. FORMING GENERALIZATIONS A stereotype is a generalization made about a group. What stereotype do you think hippies might have formed about mainstream Americans? What stereotype do you think mainstream Americans might have formed about hippies? Why?

THINK ABOUT
- Alex Forman's comments in "A Personal Voice"
- hippies' values and lifestyle
- mainstream Americans' values and lifestyle

ANSWERS

1. TERMS & NAMES

counterculture, p. 773

Haight-Ashbury, p. 774

The Beatles, p. 775

Woodstock, p. 776

2. SUMMARIZING

Possible Answers:
Beliefs—Rejection of mainstream society's materialism and technology; opposition to war; vision of a society filled with peace, love, and harmony.
Lifestyle—Rock 'n' roll music; outrageous clothing; drug use; communal living.
Impact on Society—Pop art; men's and women's fashions, especially blue jeans; rock 'n' roll; conservative movement.

3. COMPARING AND CONTRASTING

Possible Response:
Woodstock probably came to symbolize the counterculture's ideals of peace and harmony. In the eyes of conservatives, the Rolling Stones concert probably symbolized the lawlessness and immorality of the counterculture.

4. FORMING GENERALIZATIONS

Possible Responses:
Stereotypes of mainstream Americans—Greedy and materialistic; old-fashioned and narrow-minded; insensitive and intolerant; prowar and ultraconservative.
Stereotypes of hippies—Flamboyant and shallow; lawless and immoral; self-absorbed and unrealistic; radical, violent, and disruptive.

ASSESS & RETEACH

Section 3 Assessment

Have students work in small groups to answer the questions.

Self-Assessment

Have students share the diagrams they created for item 2 in a class discussion of the counterculture movement.

Section Quiz

FORMAL ASSESSMENT
Section Quiz, p. 285

Reteach

Use the Guided Reading worksheet for Section 3 to review the section's main concepts.

CLOSE

Members of the 1960s counterculture movement rejected mainstream society's values and attempted to create a world of peace, love, and harmony. Though short-lived, the movement had a significant impact on art, fashion, music, and attitudes toward sex and human relationships. However, the counterculture and antiwar movements also sparked a conservative movement, which helped propel Richard Nixon into the White House.

OBJECTIVES

1. To identify some of the ways in which the wave of social change in the 1960s affected teenagers.
2. To summarize the types of music and movies popular in the 1960s.

FOCUS & MOTIVATE

▶ *Starting with the Student*

- Do students enjoy listening to music from the 1960s? What songs do they like?
- What kinds of music do students listen to today? How do these types of music compare with those popular in the 1960s?
- Which, if any, of the 1960s clothing styles and hairstyles do students admire?

MORE ABOUT . . .
Music of the 1960s

By the early 1960s, some of the energy of early rock 'n' roll had begun to dissipate. Elvis Presley had been drafted; Chuck Berry jailed (on charges that many deemed racially motivated); and Jerry Lee Lewis disgraced for marrying his 13-year-old cousin. Little Richard had left pop music to join the ministry, and plane and car crashes had claimed the lives of Buddy Holly, Ritchie Valens, the Big Bopper, and Eddie Cochran and injured two other early rockers, Carl Perkins and Gene Vincent. Then, in 1964, the British invasion began to breathe new life into rock 'n' roll.

DAILY LIFE 1960—1970

Signs of the Sixties

The wave of social change that swept across America during the 1960s affected the nation's teenagers as well. Abandoning the conservative and "clean-cut" look of the 1950s, many teens experimented with new and different appearances. In a declaration of their individuality and desire for more freedom, America's teens also reached out to a variety of new music and films during the 1960s.

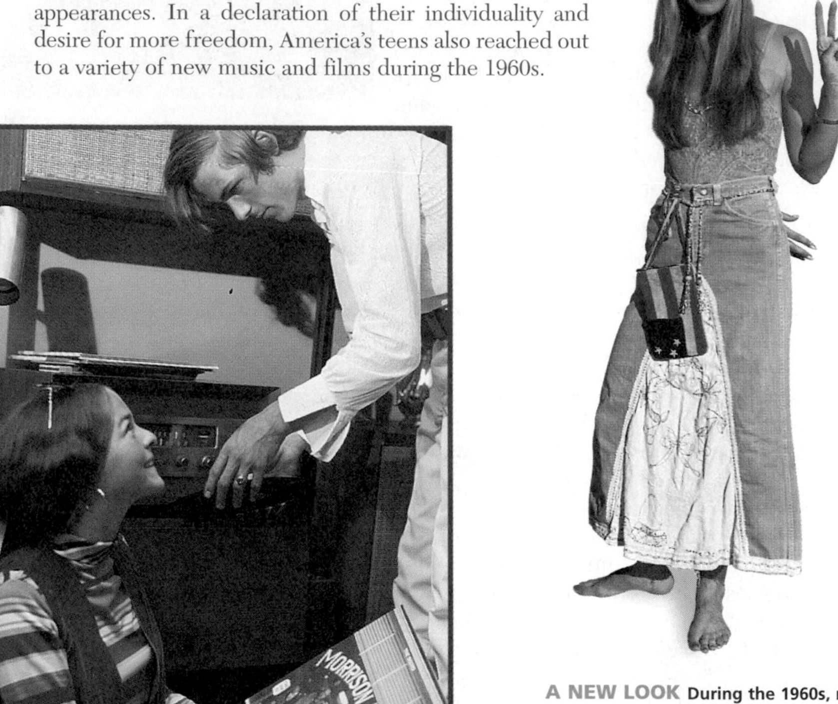

A NEW LOOK During the 1960s, many youths wore a wide range of unconventional clothing. Bright colors and psychedelic patterns became wildly popular. So, too, did the "natural" look of worn denim and hand-sewn or second-hand clothing. In addition, new grooming styles emerged, most notably evidenced in the way many young men and women grew their hair.

RECOMMENDED RESOURCES

Books

Howard, Gerald, ed. *The Sixties.* New York: Paragon, 1991. Art, politics, and the media in an explosive decade.

O'Neil, Doris C., ed. *Life—the '60s.* Boston: Little, 1989. A pictorial history.

Polsgrove, Carol. *It Wasn't Pretty, Folks, but Didn't We Have Fun?* New York: Norton, 1995. The 1960s as depicted in *Esquire* magazine.

Videos

Berkeley in the Sixties. Pacific Arts Video, 1993. The Free Speech Movement, antiwar protests, and counterculture at the California university.

Breaking Boundaries, Testing Limits. PBS Video, 1991. Focuses on the youth rebellion and the counterculture.

Flashing on the Sixties. Pacific Arts Video, 1993. Surveys some of the people, places, events, and ideals that helped shape the 1960s.

The History of Rock 'n' Roll. Time-Life, 1995. A ten-part series on rock music from rhythm and blues to rap.

GOING TO THE SHOW

As the nation's movie industry grew, more and more teenagers flocked to the cinema. Teens took in such diverse films as the counterculture classic *Easy Rider* and the science fiction classic *2001: A Space Odyssey (left),* which tells the story of HAL, a spaceship computer that develops a mind of its own.

THE RISE OF SOUL MUSIC

Rock 'n' roll's popularity continued to soar as teenagers listened to a wider variety of sounds in the 1960s. African-American soul artists, whose music had inspired the more popular white rock 'n' roll performers of the 1950s, grew widely popular themselves during the 1960s. During this decade, Detroit's Motown label produced the most popular and successful African-American artists, including Marvin Gaye, Stevie Wonder, and the Supremes *(right).*

A DIVERSE MUSIC SCENE

Scores of teenagers also tuned to surf music, a harmonic, light sound made popular by a California band, the Beach Boys. Other teens listened to the poetic and socially conscious lyrics of folk rock. Heavy, or psychedelic, rock, sung by bands such as the Doors (whose 1967 concert advertisement appears to the left), also found its way into many album collections.

DATA FILE

Popular songs

- "Blowin' in the Wind"
- "Surfin' USA"
- "Where Did Our Love Go?"
- "California Dreamin'"
- "Light My Fire"
- "Mrs. Robinson"
- "Aquarius/Let the Sunshine In"

Popular TV shows

- *The Dick Van Dyke Show*
- *The Beverly Hillbillies*
- *Green Acres*
- *The Addams Family*
- *The Man from U.N.C.L.E.*
- *Mission Impossible*
- *Laugh-In*
- *Bonanza*

Daily Life Data

1960: Alfred Hitchcock's *Psycho* terrified movie audiences across the nation.

1962: Wilt Chamberlain became the only professional basketball player to score 100 points in a game.

1963: The movie *Cleopatra,* which starred popular actress Elizabeth Taylor and cost $37 million, opened as the most expensive film to date.

1964: The Beatles arrived in America

1965: The miniskirt was introduced.

1966: The National Association of Broadcasters instructed disc jockeys to screen records for obscene or hidden meanings.

1967: The Green Bay Packers defeated the Kansas City Chiefs in the first Super Bowl.

1968: The government mandated that all new cars must be equipped with seat belts.

1969: Pantsuits became acceptable for everyday wear by women.

INTERACT WITH HISTORY

1. **DRAWING CONCLUSIONS** What conclusions can you draw about teenagers in the 1960s from the images and information in this feature?
2. **CREATING A GRAPH** Working with a small group, research the forms of entertainment that were popular during the 1960s. Then create a graph showing how much money was spent on each type of entertainment.

SEE SKILLBUILDER HANDBOOK, PAGES 920 AND 931.

Visit http://www.mlushistory.com for more about youth in the sixties.

INSTRUCT

▶ *Starting with the Student*

- Discuss the TV shows listed in the data file. Ask students to identify any of the shows' themes or characterizations that are typical of the 1960s.
- Ask students who made the popular recordings of the songs listed in the data file. *Peter, Paul & Mary; Beach Boys; Supremes; Mamas & Papas; Doors; Simon & Garfunkel; Fifth Dimension.* If possible, play some of these recordings, as well as hits by other 60s stars like Marvin Gaye, Stevie Wonder, and the Beatles.

▶ *Discussing Key Ideas*

- During the 1960s, many teenagers experiment with new looks in hair and clothing.
- Teenagers influence popular culture as they embrace a wide range of musical sounds and flock to the movies.

HISTORY FROM VISUALS

Reading the Images Have students study the illustrations and captions.

- What words would students use to characterize the "new look" of the 1960s? *Possible Responses: Natural; free; silly; colorful; dated.*
- How does the appearance of the Supremes compare with the look of a current music group?
- On the basis of the movie still, what current films do students think have been influenced by *2001?*

INTERACT WITH HISTORY

1. Drawing Conclusions

Possible Responses: *Teenagers were rebellious and wanted to express their individuality. They were also wild, self-confident, self-important, fun-loving, and innocent. Although teenagers thought they were being different, their appearance expressed little individuality as they conformed to an accepted "in" look. Teenage tastes dominated pop culture.*

2. Creating a Graph

You might suggest that each student in a group

- focus on one form of entertainment from the 1960s
- research that type of entertainment and report his or her findings to the group

Group members should then discuss how to organize the information and present it in a graph. After students have completed their graphs, ask them to compare the money spent on entertainment in the 1960s with the amount spent today.

CHAPTER 23
ASSESSMENT ANSWERS

REVIEWING THE CHAPTER

TERMS & NAMES

1. Cesar Chavez, p. 761
2. La Raza Unida, p. 762
3. American Indian Movement, p. 763
4. feminism, p. 768
5. Betty Friedan, p. 769
6. Equal Rights Amendment, p. 771
7. Phyllis Schlafly, p. 771
8. counterculture, p. 773
9. Haight-Ashbury, p. 774
10. Woodstock, p. 776

MAIN IDEAS

11. Mexicans; Cubans; Puerto Ricans; Salvadorans; Nicaraguans; Colombians.
12. Nonviolence; he launched a boycott to pressure California grape growers to recognize the United Farm Workers Organizing Committee.
13. Proclaiming Native Americans' goals and demanding greater autonomy; Johnson responded by establishing a National Council of Indian Opportunity.
14. The restoration of 110 million acres of land to Native American tribes and the abolition of the Bureau of Indian Affairs.
15. The creation of more child-care facilities, better educational opportunities for women, and EEOC enforcement of the ban on sex discrimination in hiring.
16. That women had the right to choose an abortion during the first three months of pregnancy.
17. Law, medicine, and politics.
18. A counterculture guru, Leary popularized the credo "Tune in, turn on, drop out" and promoted the use of LSD.
19. Chicago's Old Town; Atlanta's Fourteenth Street; New York City's Greenwich Village; San Francisco's Haight-Ashbury district.
20. It inspired a conservative backlash among mainstream Americans that led to a wave of Republican victories in elections.

Chapter 23 Assessment

REVIEWING THE CHAPTER

TERMS & NAMES For each item below, write a sentence explaining its connection to the 1960s. For each person or group of people named below, explain his or her role in events.

1. **Cesar Chavez**
2. **La Raza Unida**
3. **American Indian Movement**
4. **feminism**
5. **Betty Friedan**
6. **Equal Rights Amendment**
7. **Phyllis Schlafly**
8. **counterculture**
9. **Haight-Ashbury**
10. **Woodstock**

MAIN IDEAS

SECTION 1 *(pages 760–765)*

Latinos and Native Americans Seek Equality

11. Cite examples of groups that make up America's Latino population.
12. What strategy did both Cesar Chavez and Dr. Martin Luther King, Jr., use to achieve their goals? How did Chavez successfully apply this tactic?
13. What was the focus of the Declaration of Indian Purpose, drafted in 1961? How did President Johnson respond to the declaration in 1965?
14. What were the demands of the American Indian Movement organizers who staged "The Trail of Broken Treaties" march on Washington in 1972?

SECTION 2 *(pages 768–772)*

Women Fight for Equality

15. Name three changes that members of the National Organization of Women (NOW) advocated.
16. What was the Supreme Court's decision in the *Roe* v. *Wade* case?
17. What three traditionally male-dominated professions did women enter in much greater numbers as a result of the women's movement?

SECTION 3 *(pages 773–777)*

Culture and Counterculture

18. Briefly explain the role Timothy Leary played in the counterculture movement.
19. What urban areas became popular hangouts for hippies during the 1960s?
20. What unintended impact did the counterculture have on many mainstream Americans?

THINKING CRITICALLY

1. **PROMPTING REFORM** Re-create the diagram shown below. Then fill in the appropriate circles with key individual and shared achievements of Latinos, Native Americans, and feminists.

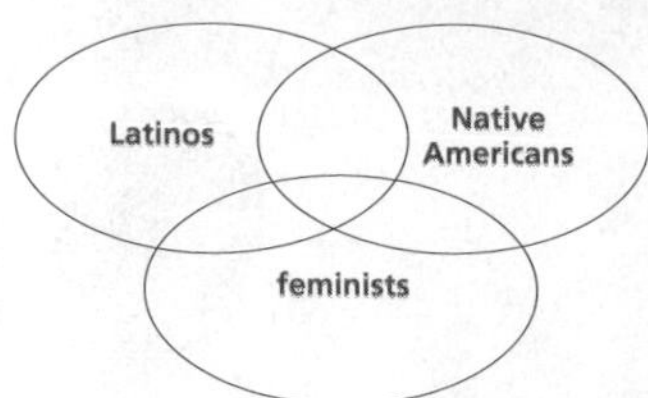

2. **TRACING THEMES WOMEN IN AMERICA** Imagine that the director of a history museum has asked you to submit a brief list of artifacts for exhibits featuring American women of the 1960s and early 1970s. What artifacts would you suggest? Use details from the text to help you develop your ideas.
3. **THE TURBULENT SIXTIES** Reread the line of song lyrics by Bob Dylan on page 758. Do you think the quotation captures the mood of the 1960s and early 1970s? Explain.
4. **VEHICLES FOR CHANGE** Consider the organizations that Latinos, Native Americans, and women formed during the 1960s. Which do you think was the most influential? Support your choice with reasons.
5. **GEOGRAPHY: THE MOVEMENT OF MIGRANT WORKERS** Refer to the map and information on pages 766–767. In light of their disruptive lifestyle, what social, economic, or medical problems do you think migrant workers and their families face?
6. **ANALYZING PRIMARY SOURCES** Read the following excerpt from *Always Running,* Luis J. Rodriguez's chronicle of growing up in Los Angeles during the late 1960s and early 1970s. Then answer the questions below.

> We [Mexican families] kept jumping hurdles, kept breaking from the constraints. . . . The [Los Angeles] River, for example, became a new barrier, keeping the Mexicans in their neighborhoods over on the vast east side of the city for years, except for forays downtown. School provided other restrictions: Don't speak Spanish; don't be Mexican—you don't belong. Railroad tracks divided us from communities where white people lived, such as South Gate and Lynwood across from Watts. We were invisible people in a city which thrived in glitter, big screens, and big names; but this glamour contained none of our names, none of our faces.
>
> The refrain "this is not your country" echoed for a long time.
>
> LUIS J. RODRIGUEZ, *Always Running*

According to Rodriguez, what were the gravest problems facing Mexican Americans during his youth? Why do you think some of these problems were eventually solved?

THINKING CRITICALLY

1. PROMPTING REFORM
Possible Answers: Individual achievements: Latinos—(1968) Bilingual Education Act; (1968) establishment of Chicano studies programs in colleges. Native Americans—(1972) Indian Education Act; (1975) Indian Self-Determination and Education Assistance Act. Feminists—(1972) Higher Education Act banning sex discrimination in federally funded education programs; increased numbers of women in law and medicine. Shared achievements: All groups—Education reform; greater political presence. Latinos and Native Americans—Stronger cultural identity. Latinos and feminists—Greater assimilation into mainstream society.

2. TRACING THEMES WOMEN IN AMERICA
Possible Answers: The transcript of a 1960s speech by Jessie Lopez de la Cruz; a photograph of Mary Crow Dog; a "Women Make Policy Not Coffee" button; a copy of Betty Friedan's *The Feminine Mystique;* a copy of *Ms.* magazine; a copy of *The Right Woman;* a woman's pair of ragged jeans and a tie-dyed T-shirt from the 1960s.

3. THE TURBULENT SIXTIES
Possible Responses: Yes—Those were turbulent times; Latinos, Native Americans, and women became a stronger presence and dramatically improved their social and political status; the rebelliousness of the youth counterculture jolted mainstream society. No—Mainstream America remained largely unchanged; many people still supported conventional family values, traditional roles of men and women, and mainstream lifestyles.

ALTERNATIVE ASSESSMENT

1. EXAMINING CULTURAL ARTIFACTS
How do the design trends of an era—seen in architecture, art, fashion, or industrial design—provide important clues to the past?

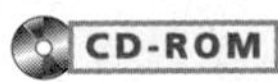

Use the CD-ROM *Our Times* and other reference materials to locate an image that depicts a popular style of the 1960s (for example, a building, a painting, clothing, a car, and so forth) and a contemporary version of the same object.

- Compare the two images you have selected. What is similar? What is different?
- Create a poster displaying the two images, and include a short essay that examines these objects as a product of their times.

2. SPEECHWRITING
Cooperative Learning Working in groups of four, have each member of the group imagine he or she is a speechwriter for one of the following people: Cesar Chavez, Russell Means, Betty Friedan, and Phyllis Schlafly. Each student should outline the person's main talking points based on his or her goals and philosophies. Focusing on these main points, the student should write a brief speech and read it before the group.

3. PORTFOLIO PROJECT
 Use the Living History activity to expand your portfolio.

LIVING HISTORY

PRESENTING A MUSIC DOCUMENTARY

You have researched a type of music from the 1960s that you find interesting. Now write a short radio documentary you can present to the class.

- Write a script for the narrative of the documentary.
- Try to use selections from songs, recordings of interviews, and other primary sources to explain by example.
- If you have access to audiotape equipment, you may wish to record your documentary.

 Present your taped or live documentary to the class. Add your written or recorded work to your American history portfolio.

Bridge to Chapter 24

Review Chapter 23

LATINOS AND NATIVE AMERICANS During the civil rights era, Latinos and Native Americans both struggled to gain greater equality, to preserve their cultures, and to improve their lives. Both formed organizations employing various strategies to achieve these aims. The United Farm Workers Organizing Committee's nationwide boycott of grapes, for example, forced California grape growers to meet the demands of union workers. The activism of organizations such as the American Indian Movement helped Native Americans secure educational reforms, greater control over governing their own affairs, and restoration of their land.

THE WOMEN'S MOVEMENT Taking their cue from the civil rights movement, women waged campaigns to surmount the social and economic barriers that impeded their progress in American society. The National Organization for Women pushed for more child-care facilities, better educational opportunities, fair hiring practices, and abortion rights—an issue that still sparks controversy today. Despite the defeat of the Equal Rights Amendment, the women's movement scored several victories, including vastly greater opportunities for women in education, employment, and politics.

THE COUNTERCULTURE Shunning the prevailing social activism of the 1960s, many disillusioned American youths opted to "drop out" of mainstream society. Hippies, the idealistic members of the counterculture, condemned materialism, technology, and war. However, publicized incidents of counterculture violence spelled the decline of this fleeting movement. Although the counterculture left its mark on music, fashion, and social attitudes, the movement also created a conservative backlash among many mainstream Americans.

Preview Chapter 24

Richard Nixon's victory in 1968 marked a turn toward conservatism. Later, his alleged involvement in the Watergate scandal led to his resignation. In the wake of this crisis, Nixon's successors, Gerald Ford and Jimmy Carter, both tried to restore a sense of trust in the presidency and to fix the ailing economy. You will learn about these and other significant developments in the next chapter.

ALTERNATIVE ASSESSMENT

1. EXAMINING CULTURAL ARTIFACTS
Standards for Evaluation
An essay should meet the following criteria:

- Compares an image of a popular item from the 1960s with a contemporary version of the same item.
- Discusses 1960s events that influenced the item's style.
- Contrasts the importance of the item in the 1960s with its significance today.
- Is accompanied by a poster that displays both images.

2. SPEECHWRITING
Standards for Evaluation
A speech should meet the following criteria:

- Accurately conveys the person's goals and philosophy.
- Develops two or three key points that clarify the person's position.
- Addresses the arguments or actions of opponents.
- Engages and stirs the audience.

3. PORTFOLIO PROJECT
LIVING HISTORY
Standards for Evaluation
A music documentary for radio should meet the following criteria:

- Uses selections from songs, interviews, or other primary sources.
- Includes an introduction that explains the scope of the documentary.
- Provides information on the factors that influenced the music.

IN-DEPTH RESOURCES: UNIT 6
See the form for scoring this activity on page 72.

THINKING CRITICALLY

4. VEHICLES FOR CHANGE
Organizations that students might cite include the United Farm Workers Organizing Committee, the American Indian Movement, and the National Organization for Women.

5. GEOGRAPHY: THE MOVEMENT OF MIGRANT WORKERS
Possible Response: Because migrant families must keep moving, they cannot settle down and live in a stable environment or develop close ties with other families; during the winter months, when there is no work, the families must struggle to earn money; because they don't stay at any one job for long, migrant families may be unable to obtain adequate health care.

6. ANALYZING PRIMARY SOURCES
Possible Answers: Among the problems Rodriguez cites are prejudice, suppression and rejection of Mexican culture, segregated living arrangements, and outsider status. Latino "brown power" movements, the reaffirmation of cultural pride, educational reforms, and the growing number of Latino political candidates helped solve some of these problems.

UNIT OVERVIEW

Passage to a New Century

HISTORY AND ART

The American Flag

Exhibit at Ellis Island Immigration Museum; design by MetaForm, Inc.; photograph by Norman McGrath; individual portraits on flag by Pablo Delano.

Art Note
Photographer Pablo Delano took hundreds of photographs that were assembled to create this image. It acts as both a symbol of America and a profound representation of the diversity of Americans.

▶ ***Previewing the Unit***
Unit 7 describes the turbulent presidency of Richard Nixon and the failure of his successors to fix the economic problems of the 1970s. A growing conservatism in the American public in the 1980s accompanies economic change and the end of the Cold War. In the 1990s, vast social changes reshape Americans' lives while the challenges and opportunities of a new century emerge.

UNIT 7

1968–1997

Passage to a New Century

"We should all be concerned about the future because we will have to spend the rest of our lives there."

CHARLES FRANKLIN KETTERING

782 UNIT 7

1 Ellis Island
More than 12 million immigrants passed through the reception facility on Ellis Island in New York Harbor from the time it opened in 1892. More than 40 percent of all Americans alive today have an ancestor who passed through the facility. Abandoned in 1954, Ellis Island became part of the Statue of Liberty National Monument in 1965. The statue was restored in 1986 on its hundredth anniversary. This step revived interest in Ellis Island, and it was reopened to the public in 1990 after being renovated.

2 Construction of the flag
The flag is composed of clear plastic prisms that are mounted on a metal frame. On the two outer faces of each prism is a photographic portrait of an American.

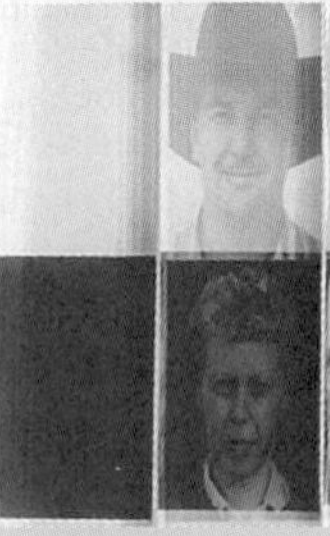

Discussing the Quotation

The actions of millions of immigrants—and of their millions of descendants—turned Kettering's abstract words into a vibrant reality. As one immigrant recalled in 1921:

> "I left my country because the jobs were scarce. I decided to take a chance and come to this new country."

FOR DISCUSSION:

- How did the immigrants who came to the United States view the future?
- How does understanding the past help us face the future?
- In facing the future, how will Americans deal with the social diversity revealed by the faces in this flag?

Discussing the Image

The flag made up of many faces offers a moving and varied portrait of the United States—a vision based not on the nation's land or resources or leaders but on the talent, determination, and diversity of its people.

FOR DISCUSSION:

- What other images have been used to represent the United States?
- Is this image a good way to symbolize the United States?
- What metaphors are also good ways to describe the United States?

3 Immigration museum
In 1990, the Ellis Island Immigration Museum opened. The museum includes photographs, passports, and belongings of immigrants; exhibits on how immigrants were processed at Ellis Island; and other films, images, and objects that reveal the immigrant experience.

4 The faces
Delano took 754 photographs of Americans representing all ages, both genders, all races, and all ethnic groups. Half were taken with a dark background and half with a light background to help create the red and white stripes of the flag.

5 "The Peopling of America"
The flag is one exhibit in a section of the museum called "The Peopling of America." This section includes displays that vividly provide data on immigration, including country-of-origin statistics.

CHAPTER 24

PLANNING GUIDE

An Age of Limits

	Key Ideas	COPYMASTERS	ASSESSMENT
SECTION 1 The Nixon Administration *pp. 786–792*	*President Richard M. Nixon attempts to move the country in a more conservative direction and ease Cold War tensions throughout the world.*	***In-Depth Resources: Unit 7*** • Guided Reading, p. 1 • Primary Source: Newspaper Front Page, p. 8 • American Lives: Henry Kissinger, p. 15 ***Lesson Plans,*** pp. 193–194	PE ***Section 1 Assessment,*** p. 792 TE ***Self-Assessment,*** p. 792 ***Formal Assessment*** • Section Quiz, p. 294 ***Alternative Assessment Book*** • Standards for Evaluating a Cooperative Activity
SECTION 2 Watergate: Nixon's Downfall *pp. 793–797*	*Richard Nixon's involvement in the cover-up of a campaign burglary forces him to resign from office—the only president to do so.*	***In-Depth Resources: Unit 7*** • Guided Reading, p. 2 • Primary source: from *All the President's Men* by Carl Bernstein and Bob Woodward, p. 9 • American Lives: Barbara Jordan, p. 16 ***Lesson Plans,*** pp. 195–196	PE ***Section 2 Assessment,*** p. 797 TE ***Self-Assessment,*** p. 797 ***Formal Assessment*** • Section Quiz, p. 295 ***Alternative Assessment Book*** • Standards for Evaluating a Cooperative Activity
SECTION 3 The Ford and Carter Years *pp. 800–807*	*In the wake of Watergate, Presidents Ford and Carter try to restore faith in America's leadership as they battle the worst economic crisis in decades.*	***In-Depth Resources: Unit 7*** • Guided Reading, p. 3 • Geography Application: Oil Consumption in the 1970s, p. 6 • Literature: from *Memories of the Ford Administration* by John Updike, p. 12 ***Lesson Plans,*** pp. 197–198	PE ***Section 3 Assessment,*** p. 807 TE ***Self-Assessment,*** p. 807 ***Formal Assessment*** • Section Quiz, p. 296 ***Alternative Assessment Book*** • Standards for Evaluating a Cooperative Activity
SECTION 4 Environmental Activism *pp. 808–813*	*Americans, struck by their sense of limitations, begin to address a growing number of environmental concerns.*	***In-Depth Resources: Unit 7*** • Guided Reading, p. 4 • Skillbuilder Practice: Analyzing Assumptions, p. 5 • Primary Sources: from *Love Canal: My Story* by Lois Gibbs, p. 10; from *Silent Spring* by Rachel Carson, p. 11 ***Lesson Plans,*** pp. 199–200	PE ***Section 4 Assessment,*** p. 813 TE ***Self-Assessment,*** p. 813 ***Formal Assessment*** • Section Quiz, p. 297 ***Alternative Assessment Book*** • Standards for Evaluating a Cooperative Activity
CHAPTER RESOURCES	**Chapter Overview** *Richard Nixon takes office as president, slowing down the growth of federal power and changing foreign policy. He resigns in disgrace during his second term, and his successors are unable to fix growing economic problems.*	***In-Depth Resources: Unit 7*** • Living History Project: Worksheet, p. 17; Standards, p. 18 ***Telescoping the Times*** • Chapter Summary, pp. 47–48 ***Planning for Block Schedules***	PE ***Chapter Assessment,*** pp. 814–815 PE ***Alternative Assessment,*** p. 815 ***Formal Assessment*** • Chapter Test, forms A and B, pp. 293–303 ***Test Generator*** ***Alternative Assessment Book*** See explanation and forms for different kinds of alternative assessments including portfolio assessment.

KEY
PE Pupil's Edition
TE Teacher's Edition
INTERNET http://www.mlushistory.com

TECHNOLOGY

 ***Warm-Up Transparency* 24**

 ***Grolier Multimedia Encyclopedia***
- Overview of Nixon's Political Career

 **INTERNET** Richard Nixon and world oil markets

---

 ***Warm-Up Transparency* 24**

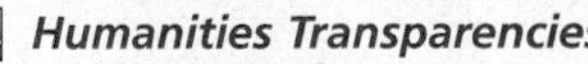 ***Humanities Transparencies***
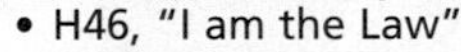
- H46, "I am the Law"

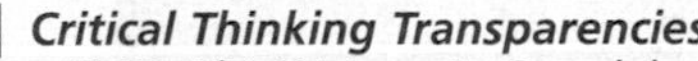 ***Critical Thinking Transparencies***
- CT32, The Watergate Scandal
- CT66, Shift in Presidential Politics

Our Times
- Richard Nixon and John Dean III

Electronic Library of Primary Sources
- Articles of Impeachment

 **INTERNET** Interact with History p. 799 (PE)

 ***Warm-Up Transparency* 24**

 ***Humanities Transparencies***
- H30, Bicentennial celebration

Geography Transparencies
- G32, OPEC

Grolier Multimedia Encyclopedia
- Overview of Ford's Political Career

Our Times
- Interview with Jimmy Carter

Electronic Library of Primary Sources
- Jimmy Carter, "On Energy"
- *from* "Victim-Victimizer: Why Excel?" by Rev. Jessie L. Jackson

 **INTERNET** Jimmy Carter

---

 ***Warm-Up Transparency* 24**

 ***AMERICAN STORIES* video series**
- "Poisoned Playground"

Our Times
- Essay on 1970s and Environmentalism

Grolier Multimedia Encyclopedia
- Video of Interview with Rachel Carson

Electronic Library of Primary Sources
- "Principles of Environmental Justice"

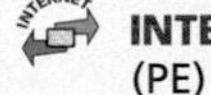 **INTERNET** Interact with History p. 811 (PE)

 ***American Portfolio: A Videodisc for U.S. History,*** user's guide, pp. 253–255

 ***Chapter Summary Audiotapes***
- Unit 7, Chapter 24

 **INTERNET http://www.mlushistory.com**

Block Scheduling (90 MINUTES)

Day 1
Section 1, pp. 786–792
Section 2, pp. 793–797
Section Assessments, pp. 792, 797
Daily Life: Television Reflects American Life, pp. 798–799

 **COOPERATIVE ACTIVITIES**
- Confirming a Supreme Court Judge, p. 789 (TE)
- Writing an Editorial about the Saturday Night Massacre, p. 796 (TE)

Day 2
Section 3, pp. 800–807
Section Assessment, p. 807

 **COOPERATIVE ACTIVITY**
- Writing a United Nations Speech for President Carter, p. 805 (TE)

Day 3
Section 4, pp. 808–813
Section Assessment, p. 813

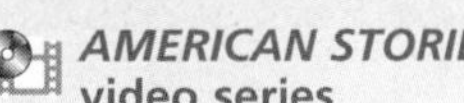 ***AMERICAN STORIES*** video series
- "Poisoned Playground"

Chapter Assessment, pp. 814–815

 **COOPERATIVE ACTIVITY**
- Debating the Use of Nuclear Energy, p. 812 (TE)

YEARLY PACING ***Chapter 24 Total:*** 3 days ***Yearly Total:*** 85 days

See *Planning for Block Schedules* for special activities and pacing strategies.

Customizing for Special Populations

Students Acquiring English
Access for Students Acquiring English: Spanish Translations
- Guided Reading for Sections 1–4 (Spanish), pp. 261–264
- Chapter Summary (Spanish), pp. 259–260
- Skillbuilder Practice: Analyzing Assumptions (Spanish), p. 265
- Geography Application: Oil Consumption in the 1970s (Spanish), p. 266

Spanish Reading Study Guide, pp. 243–252

Translations of Chapter Summaries, Hmong, Cantonese, Vietnamese, and Cambodian

Chapter Summary Audiotapes in Spanish
Unit 7, Chapter 24

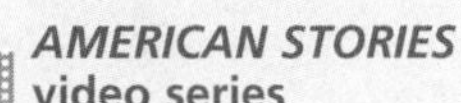 ***AMERICAN STORIES*** video series
- "Poisoned Playground" (Spanish track)

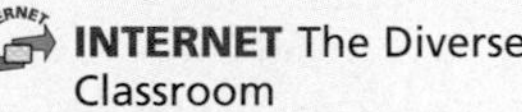 **INTERNET** The Diverse Classroom

Gifted and Talented Students
In-Depth Resources: Unit 7
- Primary Source: Newspaper Front Page, p. 8; from *All the President's Men* by Carl Bernstein and Bob Woodward, p. 9; from *Love Canal: My Story* by Lois Gibbs, p. 10; from *Silent Spring* by Rachel Carson, p. 11
- American Lives: Henry Kissinger, p. 15; Barbara Jordan, p. 16

Less Proficient Readers
In-Depth Resources: Unit 7
- Guided Reading for Sections 1–4, pp. 1–4
- Skillbuilder: Analyzing Assumptions, p. 5
- Geography Application: Oil Consumption in the 1970s, p. 6

Reading Study Guide
- pp. 243–252

Telescoping the Times
- Chapter Summary, pp. 47–48

Chapter Summary Audiotapes, Unit 7, Chapter 24

Connections to Literature READINGS FOR STUDENTS

In-Depth Resources: Unit 7
- **from *Memories of the Ford Administration* by John Updike,** p. 12

Enrichment Reading

- **Carl Bernstein and Bob Woodward**
  All the President's Men
  New York: Touchstone Books, 1994
  This book by two young reporters for The Washington Post *covers their investigation of the Watergate break-in. Their discoveries, and the story of their mysterious informant, make this fascinating reading as a coverup is linked to the White House and the president eventually resigns.*

- **Jeffrey Kluger and James A. Lovell**
  Lost Moon: The Perilous Voyage of Apollo 13
  Boston: Houghton, 1994
  A space capsule on the way to the moon is rocked by an explosion and loses the oxygen it needs for power and water. Can the three astronauts on board be brought back to Earth safely? The crisis brings out the best in hundreds of engineers and technicians on the ground and in the three astronauts who must remain calm and clear headed. They do make it, and this inspiring story is NOT fiction.

- **John Updike**
  Memories of the Ford Administration
  New York: Fawcett, 1993
  When a history professor is asked to record his impressions of the Ford administration, he uses that turbulent time—following the resignation of Richard Nixon—to recall a piece of turbulent personal history: his unfinished book on the 19th-century president James Buchanan.

OVERVIEW

An Age of Limits

▶ ***Accessing Prior Knowledge***

Ask students to give examples of things that can limit the power of a nation. What can a government do to overcome those limitations? What could citizens do to deal with those limitations.

▶ ***Predicting Outcomes***

Ask students what Jimmy Carter meant when he said, "We cannot afford everything, nor can we afford to lack boldness"? During the 1970s, what kinds of things will the United States not be able to afford? Why will boldness be necessary?

MORE ABOUT . . .
The First Moon Walk

Edwin "Buzz" Aldrin, Jr., was the second person to step on the moon. Aldrin's fellow astronaut, Neil Armstrong, stepped onto the moon's surface 19 minutes before him. The two astronauts spent about two hours on the moon, gathering rock samples and conducting tests.

CHAPTER 24

An Age of Limits

SECTION 1

The Nixon Administration

President Richard M. Nixon attempts to move the country in a more conservative direction and ease Cold War tensions throughout the world.

SECTION 2

Watergate: Nixon's Downfall

Richard Nixon's involvement in the cover-up of a campaign burglary forces him to resign from office—the only president to do so.

SECTION 3

The Ford and Carter Years

In the wake of Watergate, Presidents Ford and Carter try to restore faith in America's leadership as they battle the worst economic crisis in decades.

SECTION 4

Environmental Activism

Americans, struck by growing problems with pollution, begin to address environmental concerns.

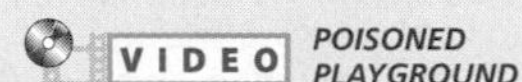

"We have learned . . . even our great nation has its recognized limits. . . . We cannot afford to do everything, nor can we afford to lack boldness as we meet the future."

Jimmy Carter, 1977

THE UNITED STATES

- **1968** Richard M. Nixon is elected president.
- **1969** Astronaut Edwin Aldrin, Jr., poses beside the American flag, as the U.S. becomes the first nation to put a person on the moon.
- **1970** America celebrates the first Earth Day.
- **1972** President Nixon is reelected.
- **1973** Senate begins its investigation into the Watergate break-in.
- **1973** Last U.S. troops leave Vietnam

THE WORLD

- **1969** Golda Meir becomes prime minister of Israel.
- **1970** Nigeria ends its 2½-year civil war.
- **1971** UN votes to admit China and expel Taiwan.
- **1973** Military junta, led by Augusto Pinochet Ugarte, seizes power in Chile.

THEMES IN CHAPTER 24

Economic Opportunity

Throughout the 1970s, many Americans grew anxious about their future, as the nation coped with its worst economic crisis in years. A decade of economic stagnation—which included bouts of increased unemployment and inflation—frustrated the successive administrations of Richard Nixon, Gerald Ford, and Jimmy Carter and left the country with a very real sense of its limitations.

See Teacher's Edition notes, pp. 790 and 802.

Constitutional Concerns

During the 1970s, Americans witnessed one of the most serious constitutional crises in U.S. history. The House of Representatives stood ready to impeach President Nixon for possible criminal wrongdoing. Before that could happen, Nixon resigned the presidency.

See Teacher's Edition note, p. 795.

Science and Technology

Adding to economic uncertainty were advancements in computer technology, which altered many of the nation's jobs and made some obsolete. Scientific advancements helped the United States battle another of its limitations: its finite natural resources.

See Teacher's Edition notes, pp. 804 and 809.

LIVING HISTORY

PREPARING AN EXHIBIT OF GLOBAL LINKS

Between 1968 and 1980, Americans became increasingly aware of economic and political links between their nation and other countries. With your classmates, prepare items for an exhibit that shows specific connections between the United States and other countries during these years.

Consider the following suggestions as you prepare individual items and displays for your exhibit:

- Use world maps or sections of world maps.
- Include three-dimensional objects—constructed or found—and audiovisual selections.
- Write comments that explain reasons for international links.

PORTFOLIO PROJECT Save your writing, maps, and other items in a folder for your American history portfolio. You will display and share your work at the end of the chapter.

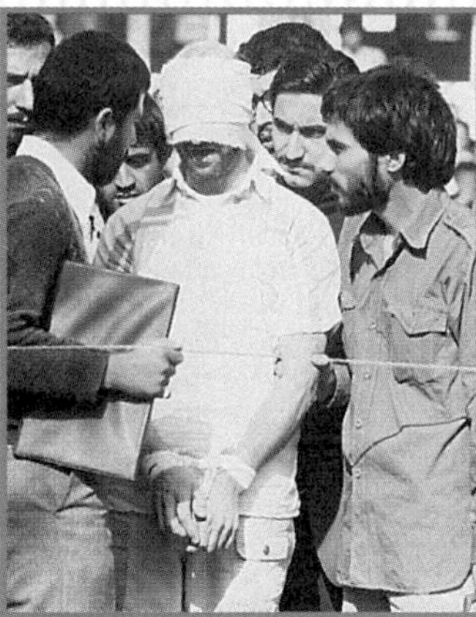

1974 — Vice-President Gerald R. Ford becomes president after Richard M. Nixon resigns.

1975 — South Vietnam surrenders to North Vietnam.

1976 — Jimmy Carter, shown with wife Rosalynn and daughter Amy, is elected president.

1977 — Andrew Young becomes the first African American to serve as U.S. ambassador to the United Nations.

1979 — In Iran, 52 Americans are taken hostage.

Israel and Egypt sign a peace treaty at the White House.

1979 — Soviet Union invades Afghanistan.

Ayatollah Khomeini seizes power in Iran.

1980 — Ronald Reagan is elected president.

ALTERNATIVE ASSESSMENT

LIVING HISTORY

PREPARING AN EXHIBIT OF GLOBAL LINKS

Discuss ways of preparing the exhibit:

- Look for maps of the Middle East in news magazines.
- Find political cartoons of the country's link to other nations, in particular cartoons satirizing the United States relationship with the OPEC nations (p. 790).
- Research further some of the chapter's global topics for items associated with the event. For example, a yellow ribbon came to symbolize the nation's support for the hostages.
- Look for dramatic photographs—such as long lines for gasoline and blindfolded hostages—in newspapers or newsmagazines.
- Find images of America's growing desire for foreign-made goods. Such images might include photographs of factories in China or Taiwan, or advertisements for Japanese automobiles.
- Look for tapes of news programs about the energy crunch or hostage situation. An example might be a tape of an early *Nightline* program, which began as a nightly program about the hostage crisis.

IN-DEPTH RESOURCES: UNIT 7
See worksheet and standards for evaluation, pp. 17, 18.

RECOMMENDED RESOURCES

Books for the Teacher

Bernstein, Carl, and Woodward, Bob. *The Final Days.* New York: Simon, 1976. A detailed look at the final days of the Nixon presidency.

Carter, Jimmy. *Keeping Faith: Memoirs of a President.* New York: Bantam, 1982.

Villaseñor, Victor. *Rain of Gold.* New York: Dell, 1991. A Mexican family's long history—similar to *Roots.*

Books for the Student

Lawson, Don. *America Held Hostage: The Iran Hostage Crisis and the Iran-Contra Affair.* New York: Watts, 1991.

Lazzari, Marie. *Environmental Viewpoints.* Detroit: Gale Research, Inc., Vol. 1 1992, Vol. 2 1993.

Videos

All the President's Men. Dir. Alan J. Pakula. Warner Home Video, 1976. Dramatic portrayal of Watergate investigation.

America Held Hostage. MPI Home Video, 1989. 800-323-0442. ABC News reports of hostage crisis.

Apollo 13. Dir. Ron Howard. MCA Universal Home Video, 1995, PG. Riveting story of a nearly disastrous moon mission.

1970s: A Crisis of Confidence. National Geographic Society, Educational Services, Washington, D.C., 20036, 800-368-2728.

Richard Nixon: Man and President. Library Video Company, 800-843-3620.

Software

Environment. Diskette. Tom Snyder Productions, Inc., 800-342-0236.

Foreign Policy: The Burdens of World Power. Diskette. Social Studies School Service, 10020 Jefferson Boulevard, Room 1311, P.O. Box 802, Culver City, CA, 90232-0802.

Section 1 Overview

OBJECTIVES

1. To summarize Richard Nixon's plans to lead the nation in a more conservative direction.
2. To describe how Nixon tried to win the support of Southern Democrats.
3. To list the steps Nixon took to battle stagflation.
4. To explain the importance of Nixon's visits to China and the Soviet Union.

CRITICAL THINKING

- Summarizing, pp. 786, 789, 791, 792
- Analyzing issues, p. 787
- Forming generalizations, p. 788
- Analyzing motives, p. 789
- Theme: Economic Opportunity, p. 790
- Drawing conclusions, p. 792
- Forming opinions, p. 792

FOCUS & MOTIVATE

5-MINUTE WARM-UP

Predicting Outcomes
To explore the effects of New Federalism, have students read "New Federalism" on pages 786–787 and answer these questions.

1. Define New Federalism.
2. What effect might New Federalism have on who controls government programs?

WARM-UP TRANSPARENCY 24

▶ ***Starting with the Student***

- Ask students how they would define a political conservative.
- Then read aloud the attributes ascribed to conservatives in William Safire's *New Political Dictionary: Defends the status quo, opposes rapid change, dislikes government regulation of the economy, favors state and local action over federal action.* Remind students to keep these traits in mind as they read about Nixon's administration.

1 The Nixon Administration

LEARN ABOUT President Nixon's domestic and foreign policy initiatives
TO UNDERSTAND how Nixon tried to lead the nation in a conservative direction and ease Cold War tensions.

TERMS & NAMES
- Richard M. Nixon
- New Federalism
- revenue sharing
- Family Assistance Plan
- Southern strategy
- stagflation
- OPEC
- realpolitik
- détente
- SALT I Treaty

ONE AMERICAN'S STORY

It was November of 1968 and Richard M. Nixon had just been elected president of the United States. President-elect Nixon asked Henry Kissinger to be his special adviser on foreign affairs. Kissinger did not particularly like Nixon, but he accepted, telling a surprised colleague, "I'm working for the presidency, not for Richard Nixon personally." However, in time the two men grew to be trusting colleagues. At the beginning of Nixon's second term in 1972, as the United States struggled to achieve an honorable peace in Vietnam, Kissinger reflected on his relationship with Nixon.

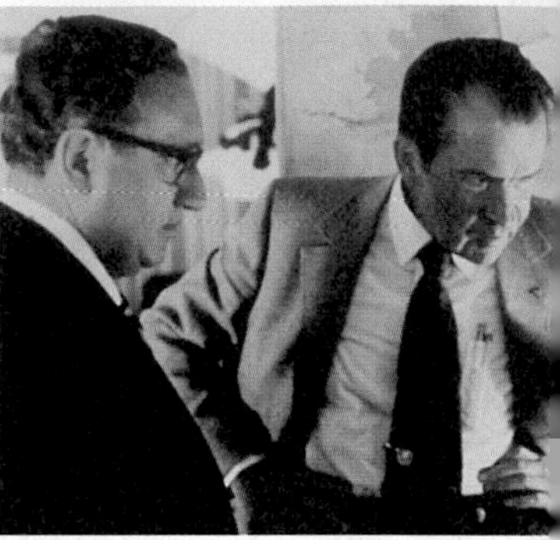

President Nixon confers with Henry Kissinger.

A PERSONAL VOICE

I . . . am not at all so sure I could have done what I've done with him with another president. Such a special relationship, I mean the relationship between the President and me, always depends on the style of both men. . . . I don't know many leaders who would entrust to their aide the task of negotiating with the North Vietnamese, informing only a tiny group of people of the initiative. Really, some things depend on the type of president.

HENRY KISSINGER, quoted in *The New Republic*, December 16, 1972

Nixon and Kissinger ended America's involvement in Vietnam. As the war wound down, the nation seemed to enter an era of limits. There were limits to U.S. power, as the nation's military had not been able to save South Vietnam from becoming Communist. Lyndon Johnson's Great Society programs seemed limited in their ability to eliminate poverty. And as the 1970s progressed, there seemed to be limits to the economic prosperity that the nation had experienced since World War II.

Into this era stepped a president who believed that there were also limits to what the federal government could accomplish. President Nixon would take action to reduce the power of the federal government and reverse the liberal policies of Lyndon Johnson. At the same time, he would seek to restore America's prestige and influence on the world stage—prestige that had been hit hard by the Vietnam experience.

Nixon's New Conservatism

President **Richard M. Nixon** entered office determined to turn America in a more conservative direction. Toward that end, he decreased the power of the federal government, dismantled a number of Great Society programs, and tried to instill a sense of order into a nation still divided over the continuing Vietnam War.

A. Answer To shrink the size and responsibility of the federal government by distributing some of its power to state and local governments.

THINK THROUGH HISTORY
A. ***Summarizing*** *What was the goal of Nixon's New Federalism?*

NEW FEDERALISM One of the main items on President Nixon's agenda was to decrease the size and influence of the federal government. Nixon believed that Lyndon Johnson's Great Society programs, by promoting greater federal involvement in dealing with social problems, had given the federal government too much responsibility. Nixon's plan, known as **New Federalism,** was to distribute a portion of federal power to state and local governments.

To implement this program, Nixon proposed a plan to give more financial freedom to local governments. Normally, the federal government told state and local governments how to spend their federal money. Under **revenue sharing,** state and local governments could spend their federal dollars however they saw fit within certain limitations. The revenue-sharing plan won support from financially strapped local governments, as well as

SECTION 1 RESOURCES

PRINT RESOURCES

IN-DEPTH RESOURCES: UNIT 7
Guided Reading, p. 1
Primary Source: Newspaper Front Page, p. 8
American Lives: Henry Kissinger, p. 15

READING STUDY GUIDE, p. 243

ACCESS FOR STUDENTS ACQUIRING ENGLISH
Guided Reading (Spanish), p. 261

SPANISH READING STUDY GUIDE, p. 243

FORMAL ASSESSMENT
Section Quiz, p. 294

ALTERNATIVE ASSESSMENT BOOK
See forms for supporting and scoring alternative activities.

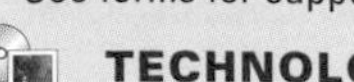

TECHNOLOGY RESOURCES

CD-ROM *Grolier Multimedia Encyclopedia*

VIDEO *American Portfolio: A Videodisc for U.S. History* user's guide, p. 253

INTERNET http://www.mlushistory.com

from conservatives who felt the national government had grown too large and unmanageable.

In 1972, the revenue-sharing bill became law. By the time the program ended in 1986, the federal government had dispensed more than $86 billion in unrestricted money to state and local governments, in one of the largest overhauls of federal spending since the New Deal.

WELFARE REFORM Nixon, however, was not so successful in his attempt to overhaul welfare. Unlike many conservatives, Nixon did not oppose welfare, but he did think it had grown cumbersome and inefficient. Nixon thought the welfare program would be more effective if the New Federalism approach were used. Consequently, in 1969 the president set out to restructure it. He advocated the so-called **Family Assistance Plan** (FAP), a set of reforms engineered by former Kennedy adviser Daniel Patrick Moynihan. Under the FAP, every family of four with no outside income would receive a basic federal payment of $1,600 a year, with a provision to earn up to $4,000 a year in supplemental income. Unemployed participants would have to take job training and accept any reasonable work offered them. (See *poverty* on page 937 in the Economics Handbook.)

Nixon presented the plan in conservative terms—as a program that would reduce the supervisory role of the federal government and make welfare recipients responsible for their own lives. The House approved the plan in 1970. However, when the bill reached the Senate, lawmakers from both sides of the aisle attacked it. Liberal legislators considered the minimum payments too low and the work requirement too stiff, while conservatives objected to the notion of guaranteed income. The bill went down in defeat.

NEW FEDERALISM'S TWO FACES In the end, Nixon's New Federalism enhanced several key federal programs as it dismantled others. Nixon had entered office as the first newly elected president to face a Congress controlled by the opposition party since Zachary Taylor in 1849. With the House and Senate in the hands of Democratic majorities, Nixon initially sought compromise on Capitol Hill as he attempted to move ahead with his New Federalism program. To win backing for his revenue-sharing plan, for example, Nixon supported a number of congressional measures to increase federal spending for some social programs. Without fanfare, the Nixon administration increased Social Security, Medicare, and Medicaid payments and made food stamps more accessible. Nixon also supported subsidized housing for low- and middle-income families, and he expanded the nation's Job Corps program.

However, the spirit of compromise between Congress and the White House soon deteriorated. Confronted by laws that he opposed, Nixon turned to a little-used presidential practice called impoundment. Nixon impounded, or withheld, necessary funds for programs, thus holding up their implementation. By 1973, Nixon had impounded almost $15 billion, affecting more than 100 federal programs, including those for health, housing, and education.

The federal courts eventually ordered the release of the impounded funds. They ruled that presidential impoundment was unconstitutional and that only Congress had the authority to decide how federal funds should be spent. However, in 1973 Nixon did use his presidential authority to abolish the Office of Economic Opportunity, a cornerstone of Johnson's antipoverty program.

B. Answer He increased several federal programs, including Social Security, Medicare, and Medicaid, while he dismantled other programs, most notably the Office of Economic Opportunity.

THINK THROUGH HISTORY
B. Analyzing Issues *In what ways did Nixon both strengthen and weaken federal programs?*

LAW-AND-ORDER POLITICS As President Nixon fought with Congress, he also battled the more liberal elements of society, including the antiwar movement. Nixon had been elected in 1968 on a dual promise to end the war in Vietnam

KEY PLAYER

RICHARD M. NIXON
1913–1994

The hurdles that Richard Nixon overcame to win the presidency in 1968 included his loss in the 1960 presidential race and a later defeat in the race for governor of California. But these were only two of the many obstacles he faced during his life.

While growing up, Nixon rose every day at 4 A.M. to help in his father's struggling grocery store. Nixon also worked as a janitor, a bean picker, and a barker at an amusement park. In the midst of its poverty, the Nixon family also endured episodes of tragedy. During his childhood, Nixon saw one brother die from meningitis and another from tuberculosis.

None of these traumatic experiences, however, dulled the future president's ambition. Nixon finished third in his law class at Duke University, and after serving in World War II, he launched his political career. After winning a seat in Congress in 1946, Nixon revealed the intense inner drive that would take him to the height of power—and also lead to his eventual downfall. "I had to win," he said. "That's the thing you don't understand. The important thing is to win."

OBJECTIVE
① INSTRUCT

Nixon's New Conservatism

Discussing Key Ideas
- Nixon works to decrease the size and influence of the federal government.
- Nixon practices law-and-order politics to curb dissent and appeal to mainstream Americans.

IN-DEPTH RESOURCES: UNIT 7
Guided Reading, p. 1

ACCESS FOR STUDENTS ACQUIRING ENGLISH
Guided Reading (Spanish), p. 261

KEY PLAYER
Richard M. Nixon

Critical Thinking: Analyzing Ask students what personality traits of Richard Nixon are revealed in the profile. *Possible Responses: Hard-working, determined, intelligent, driven.*

Issues for the 21st Century

Tough Choices on Entitlements

Connect entitlements in the 1970s to today by having students read pages 900–901. Then have them answer these questions.

1. Should Americans be entitled to a minimum income like that proposed in Nixon's FAP? *Answers will vary.*
2. In what ways is Social Security similar to and different from the FAP? *Similar: Both are entitlement programs. Different: Workers pay directly into the Social Security Fund. FAP was never enacted.*

TEACHING OPTIONS

Teaching Less Proficient Readers

Summarizing As students read pages 786–788, have them write a sentence summarizing the components of President Nixon's "New Conservatism." Use the list below as a guide.

1. Nixon's New Federalism program called for distributing more federal power back to state and local governments.
2. Under the revenue-sharing plan, local governments could . . .
3. Under the Family Assistance Plan, poor families would . . .
4. Federal programs which Nixon enhanced included . . .
5. The president dismantled federal programs related to . . .
6. To instill a sense of law and order, Nixon used . . .

Making Connections Across the Curriculum

U.S. Government Although Congress raises money and authorizes its use, the executive branch actually collects and spends funds. Congress oversees how money is spent and establishes guidelines, but normally the executive branch has flexibility in deciding exactly how programs will be implemented. When there is disagreement between the two branches over procedure and authority—as was the case when Nixon impounded funds—the courts must step in and interpret the powers granted by the Constitution.

HISTORICAL SPOTLIGHT

Americans Walk on the Moon

Critical Thinking: Analyzing Discuss with students the meaning of Neil Armstrong's quote. Then have students ask a parent or relative if they remember what they were doing the day the United States put a man on the moon.

IN-DEPTH RESOURCES: UNIT 7
Primary Source: Newspaper Front Page, p. 8

MORE ABOUT . . .

Spiro Agnew

While they were united in their attacks on liberals, Nixon and Agnew were hardly close. The president rarely consulted with Agnew on issues or policies. When asked if he had briefed Agnew about the decision to negotiate with China in 1971, Nixon answered, "Oh, of course not."

OBJECTIVE ② INSTRUCT

Nixon's Southern Strategy

▶ ***Discussing Key Ideas***

- Nixon hopes to win the support of conservative Southern Democrats by appealing to their unhappiness with federal desegregation and a liberal Supreme Court.
- To that end, the president attempts to slow several key civil rights initiatives and place more conservative judges on the Supreme Court.

and mend the divisiveness within America that the war had created. Throughout his first term, Nixon aggressively moved to fulfill both these pledges. The president de-escalated America's involvement in Vietnam and oversaw peace negotiations with North Vietnam. At the same time, he began the "law and order" policies that he had promised his "silent majority"—those middle-class Americans who wanted order restored to a country beset by urban riots and antiwar demonstrations.

To accomplish this goal, Nixon used the full resources of his office—sometimes illegally. The FBI illegally wiretapped numerous left-wing individuals and organizations. The FBI also infiltrated the ranks of the Students for a Democratic Society and radical African-American groups in an effort to spread conflict within the organizations.

In addition, the CIA investigated and compiled documents on thousands of American dissidents—people who objected to the government's policies. The administration even used the Internal Revenue Service to audit the tax returns of antiwar and civil rights activists. Viewing his opponents as personal assailants, Nixon began building an "enemies list" of prominent Americans whom the administration would harass. Remarked a top White House official, "anyone who opposes us, we'll destroy."

Nixon also enlisted the help of his combative vice-president, Spiro T. Agnew. In the fall of 1969, Nixon sent Agnew on a public speaking tour to attack the opposition. The vice-president repeatedly denounced the antiwar protesters and then turned his scorn on those who controlled the media, whom he viewed as liberal cheerleaders for the antiwar movement. Known for his colorful quotes, Agnew lashed out at the media and liberals as "an effete [weak] corps of impudent snobs," and "nattering nabobs of negativism."

HISTORICAL SPOTLIGHT

AMERICANS WALK ON THE MOON

Not all was political war during the Nixon administration. On July 20, 1969, one of America's long-held dreams became a reality. Nearly 10 years after John F. Kennedy challenged America to put a person on the moon, astronaut Neil Armstrong climbed down the ladder of his lunar module and stepped onto the surface of the moon. "That's one small step for a man," Armstrong said, "one giant leap for mankind."

Americans swelled with pride and accomplishment as they watched the historic moon landing on their televisions. Speaking to the astronauts from the White House, President Nixon said, "For every American, this has to be the proudest day of our lives."

Nixon's Southern Strategy

Even as President Nixon worked to steer the country along a more conservative course, he had his eyes on the 1972 presidential election. Nixon had won a slim majority in 1968—less than one percent of the popular vote. Shortly after entering the White House, he began working to forge a new conservative coalition to build on his support. In one approach, known as the **Southern strategy,** Nixon tried to attract Southern conservative Democrats by appealing to their unhappiness with federal desegregation policies and a liberal Supreme Court.

A NEW SOUTH Since Reconstruction, the South had been a Democratic stronghold. But by 1968 many white Southern Democrats had grown disillusioned with their party. In their eyes, the party—champion of the Great Society and civil rights—had grown too liberal.

This conservative backlash first surfaced in the 1968 election, when thousands of Southern Democrats helped former Alabama governor George Wallace, a conservative segregationist running as an independent, carry five Southern states and capture 13.5 percent of the popular vote.

Nixon wanted these voters. By winning over the Wallace voters and other discontented Democrats, the president and his fellow Republicans hoped not only to keep the White House but also to recapture a majority in Congress.

NIXON SLOWS INTEGRATION To attract white voters in the South, President Nixon decided on a policy of slowing the country's desegregation efforts. In September of 1969, shortly after being elected president, Nixon made clear his views on civil rights."There are those who want instant integration and those who want segregation forever. I believe we need to have a middle course between those two extremes," he said.

THINK THROUGH HISTORY
C. Forming Generalizations *Why had many Democratic voters in the South become potential Republican supporters by 1968?*

C. Answer They were unhappy with the Democratic leadership's desegregation policies, as well as the liberal leanings of the Supreme Court.

TEACHING OPTIONS

Making Connections Across Time

Life on Mars Having reached the moon, the United States may once again set its sights on Mars. In 1996, scientists reported that a meteorite that fell from Mars showed evidence of organic life on the large, red planet. Scientists added that the meteorite left Mars some 15 million years ago and had been orbiting the solar system ever since. The discovery of possible life on Mars "gives us a lot of reason to go back to Mars," said one scientist. The last major thrust of Mars exploration by the United States occurred in 1976, when the unmanned Viking 1 space probe landed on Mars.

Making Connections Across the Curriculum

Language Arts Review the meaning of the term *alliteration* with the class. *The repetition of consonant sounds at the beginnings of words or accented syllables.* Then point out Spiro Agnew's use of alliteration in his attacks on opponents. Have students translate the phrase "nattering nabobs of negativism" into more recognizable language. Discuss why Agnew's phrasing is effective. Then have students write their own alliterative phrase describing something with which they are familiar.

Throughout his first term, President Nixon worked to reverse several civil rights policies. In 1969, he ordered the Department of Health, Education, and Welfare (HEW) to delay desegregation plans for school districts in South Carolina and Mississippi. Nixon's actions violated the Supreme Court's second *Brown* v. *Board of Education* ruling—which called for the desegregation of schools "with all deliberate speed." In response to an NAACP suit, the high court ordered Nixon to abide by the second *Brown* ruling. The president did so reluctantly, and by 1972, nearly 90 percent of children in the South attended desegregated schools—up from about 20 percent in 1969.

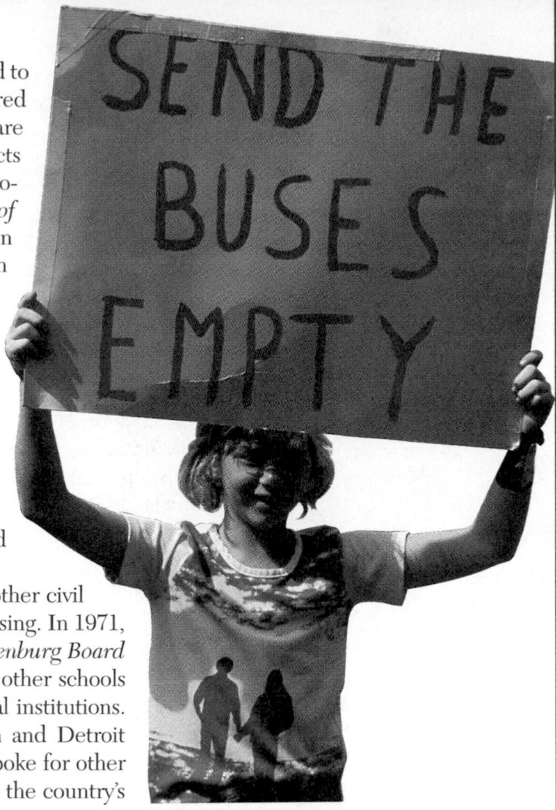

A demonstrator in Boston protests court-ordered school busing during the early 1970s.

In a further attempt to chip away at civil rights advances, Nixon opposed the extension of the Voting Rights Act of 1965. The act had added nearly one million African Americans to the voting rolls. Despite the president's opposition, Congress voted to extend the act.

THINK THROUGH HISTORY
D. ***Analyzing Motives*** *Why did President Nixon oppose the extension of the Voting Rights Act?*

D. Answer It was part of his "Southern strategy" to attract the support of white Southerners.

President Nixon then attempted to thwart yet another civil rights initiative—the integration of schools through busing. In 1971, the Supreme Court ruled in *Swann* v. *Charlotte-Mecklenburg Board of Education* that school districts may bus students to other schools to end the pattern of all-black or all-white educational institutions. White students and parents in cities such as Boston and Detroit angrily protested busing. One South Boston mother spoke for other white Northerners, many of whom still struggled with the country's racial integration process.

A PERSONAL VOICE

I'm not against any individual child. I am not a racist, no matter what those high-and-mighty suburban liberals with their picket signs say. I just won't have my children bused to some . . . slum school, and I don't want children from God knows where coming over here.

SOUTH BOSTON MOTHER, quoted in *The School Busing Controversy, 1970–75*

Nixon also opposed integration through busing and went on national television to urge Congress to halt the practice. While busing continued in some cities, Nixon had made his position clear to the country—and to the South.

A BATTLE OVER THE SUPREME COURT Civil rights was not the only issue over which President Nixon and the Supreme Court clashed. During the 1968 campaign, Nixon had criticized the Warren Court for being too liberal. Once in the White House, Nixon suddenly found himself with an opportunity to change the direction of the court. During Nixon's first term, four justices, including chief justice Earl Warren, left the bench through death, retirement, or resignation. President Nixon quickly moved to put a more conservative face on the Court. In 1969, he appointed U.S. Court of Appeals judge Warren Burger as chief justice. Burger's Senate confirmation went smoothly. However, Nixon's effort to fill a second vacancy could not have been rougher.

The Senate rejected Nixon's next two nominees—two conservative Southerners. The Senate claimed that one judge had engaged in questionable business dealings, while the other one was underqualified.

Eventually, Nixon placed on the bench three justices—Harry A. Blackmun, William H. Rehnquist, and Lewis Powell—who tilted the Court in a more conservative direction. However, the newly shaped

E. Answer It involved winning over disgruntled Southern Democrats by appealing to their unhappiness with integration and a liberal Supreme Court. To win these voters, Nixon slowed integration policies and attempted to appoint Supreme Court justices who were more conservative.

THINK THROUGH HISTORY
E. ***Summarizing*** *What was Nixon's Southern strategy and how did he implement it?*

HISTORICAL SPOTLIGHT

THE 26TH AMENDMENT

The 26th Amendment, ratified in 1971, extended voting rights to Americans 18 years old or older. The amendment was one example of the efforts in the 1960s and 1970s to expand opportunities to participate in government to more Americans.

At the time, liberals supported the amendment because they believed that young people were more likely to be liberal. Conservatives opposed the amendment because they didn't want to extend the vote to more liberals.

Opponents also argued that the amendment would be too expensive for states to administer and that 18 year olds were not mature enough to handle the responsibility. Many American youths, however, considered it unfair to be asked to fight and die for their country in Vietnam without being allowed to vote.

MORE ABOUT . . .
Busing

In addition to some whites, a few blacks also opposed busing. In the midst of the debate, black newspaper columnist William Raspberry wrote, "It has long seemed insane to me for black people to pursue whites from this neighborhood to that . . . because of some unspoken belief that black children could not get a proper education in the absence of white children."

MORE ABOUT . . .
Warren Burger

In nominating Burger for chief justice, Nixon said he was impressed by the "forcefulness and clarity" of Burger's opinions. The president also described Burger as "personally an impressive man." In one of the ironies of history, Burger himself would write the Supreme Court opinion that struck down Nixon's claim to executive privilege and ordered him to turn over the Watergate tapes. Nixon assailed the ruling as a blow to the power of the president. "I thought that the United States had lost," Nixon wrote about the decision. "I felt that the presidency itself was a casualty of this ruling."

HISTORICAL SPOTLIGHT
The 26th Amendment

Critical Thinking: Comparing Discuss with students some of the arguments for and against extending the vote to 18-year olds. How do these arguments compare to those made about woman suffrage or other voting rights movements?

Block Schedule TEACHING OPTION **Time Needed: 30 Minutes**

Cooperative Activity: Confirming a Supreme Court Judge

Task: Students will role-play U.S. senators and Supreme Court nominees and recreate a Supreme Court confirmation hearing.

Purpose: To help students understand some of the key issues related to the Supreme Court.

Activity: Divide students into groups of four. Three of the students will play U.S. senators, while the other student will act as a Supreme Court nominee. Have the entire group research a key issue which often faces the Supreme Court. Possible issues: First Amendment rights, the right to privacy, the right to bear arms. The student-senators will ask the nominee to explain his or her stance on the issue. Then each senator will explain why he or she agrees or disagrees with the nominee's stance. Have the groups hold their hearings simultaneously or one at a time before the class.

ALTERNATIVE ASSESSMENT BOOK
Standards for Evaluating a Cooperative Activity

OBJECTIVE

③ **INSTRUCT**

Nixon Confronts a Stagnant Economy

▶ ***Discussing Key Ideas***

- The United States enters a period of economic downswing brought on by numerous factors.
- Nixon's efforts to defeat stagflation meet with little success.

ON THE WORLD STAGE

The Yom Kippur War

Have students consult the world map on pages 942–943 to examine the geography of the Middle East, in particular the locations of Syria, Egypt, and Israel. Then have them research the history of Israel's fractious relationship with its Arab neighbors, including the Sinai invasion in 1956 and the Six-Day War in 1967. Have students create a chart like the one below detailing the cause and effect of each conflict.

	Cause	Effect
Sinai Invasion		
Six-Day War		

Court did not always take the conservative route—for example, it handed down the 1971 ruling in favor of racially integrating schools through busing.

Nixon Confronts a Stagnant Economy

One of the more pressing issues facing Richard Nixon was a troubled economy. Between 1967 and 1973, the nation's inflation rate doubled, from 3 percent to 6 percent. In addition, the unemployment rate, at nearly 4 percent when Nixon took office, climbed to almost 6 percent by 1971. Economists referred to the double hit of rising inflation and unemployment as **stagflation.** Nixon's attempts to fight stagflation mostly failed, and the nation's economic downswing would continue on throughout the 1970s, frustrating other administrations as well.

THE CAUSES OF STAGFLATION The economic problems of the late 1960s and early 1970s had several causes. One cause lay in Lyndon Johnson's attempt to pay for the Vietnam War and the Great Society through massive deficit spending, or spending more money than the government had collected in taxes. This influx of money into the economy had spurred the growth of inflation. Second, America had begun losing out in international trade markets to West Germany, Japan, and other rising industrial powers. Third, the nation could not absorb a flood of new workers—mainly baby boomers and women—into the labor market. Between 1965 and 1980, America's labor force grew by almost 30 million workers. The number of new jobs could not keep pace, leaving many unemployed.

Finally, the nation had begun to suffer for its heavy dependency on foreign oil. America received much of its petroleum from the oil-producing countries of the Middle East. Many of these countries belonged to a cartel called the Organization of Petroleum Exporting Countries, or **OPEC.** (A cartel is an organization that controls enough of the production of a commodity to set the price.) During the 1960s, OPEC gradually raised oil prices. Then in 1973, the Yom Kippur War broke out, with Israel against Egypt and Syria. When the United States sent massive military aid to Israel, its longtime ally, the Arab OPEC nations responded by cutting off all oil sales to the United States. (See *embargo* on page 934 in the Economics Handbook.)

ON THE WORLD STAGE

THE YOM KIPPUR WAR

On October 6, 1973, Syria and Egypt invaded Israel on Yom Kippur, the most sacred Jewish holiday. The war—the climax of years of intense border disputes—was short but brutal. Even though fighting lasted only three weeks, as many as 7,700 Egyptians, 7,700 Syrians, and 4,500 Israelis were killed or wounded.

Although the United States supplied massive amounts of military aid to Israel, U.S. officials also worked feverishly to broker a cease-fire between the warring nations. In what became known as "shuttle diplomacy," Secretary of State Henry Kissinger traveled back and forth between Middle Eastern countries in an attempt to forge a peace agreement. Kissinger's diplomatic efforts finally paid off. Israel signed an official peace accord with Egypt in January 1974 and one with Syria four months later.

From the fall of 1973 until March of 1974, when the oil embargo ended, American motorists faced long lines at gas stations. Across the nation, factories and schools closed. One New England mother of three lamented that her children were no better off at home. "We'll have heating problems at home, too," she said. "And I'm not sure I can keep them much warmer here." Moreover, when OPEC resumed selling its oil to the United States, the price had quadrupled. This sharp rise in oil prices only worsened the problem of inflation.

F. Answer Inflation prompted by Johnson's deficit spending, increased competition in international trade, too many new workers, and the OPEC oil embargo.

THINK THROUGH HISTORY
F. THEME ***Economic Opportunity*** *What factors brought on the country's economic problems in the late 1960s and early 1970s?*

NIXON BATTLES STAGFLATION President Nixon took several steps to combat stagflation, but none met with much success. To reverse deficit spending, Nixon attempted to raise taxes and cut the budget. Congress, however, refused to go along with this plan. In another effort to slow inflation, Nixon tried to reduce the amount of money in circulation by urging that interest rates be raised. This measure did little except drive the country into a mild recession, or an overall slowdown of the economy.

In August of 1971, the president turned to price and wage controls to stop inflation. He froze workers' wages as well as businesses' prices and fees for 90 days. Inflation eased for a short time, but the recession continued.

Gas pumps across the nation ran dry as a result of the OPEC oil embargo.

TEACHING OPTIONS

Exploring Themes

Economic Opportunity The economic downswing that gripped the nation during the Nixon administration would last for roughly a decade and frustrate other administrations as well. Throughout the 1970s, as inflation and unemployment rose and dipped, millions of Americans grew anxious about their economic opportunities. Playing a key role in the decade-long downturn was the rising cost of oil. Have students consider reasons for the high demand for oil in the United States. *It is a source of heating fuel for homes, gasoline for cars, and a key ingredient in materials such as plastic.*

Making Global Connections

Interdependence The onset of the economic crunch, in particular the oil embargo, awoke many Americans to the fact that the United States was part of—and sometimes dependent on—a larger world. In 1973, for example, the United States imported nearly 6.3 million barrels of crude oil a day, mainly from the Middle East. During the height of the 1973 oil embargo, U.S. Senator Dewey Bartlett of Oklahoma noted, "The sad, but true, fact is that in the near future we will have to spend more and more dollars abroad for crude oil and other petroleum products."

Nixon's Foreign Policy Triumphs

Richard Nixon admittedly preferred world affairs to domestic policy. "I've always thought this country could run itself domestically without a president," he had said in 1968. Throughout his presidency, Nixon's top priority was gaining an honorable peace in Vietnam. However, he also made significant advances in America's relationships with China and the Soviet Union.

KISSINGER AND REALPOLITIK The architect of Nixon's foreign policy was his adviser for national security affairs, Henry Kissinger. Kissinger, who would later become Nixon's secretary of state, promoted a philosophy known as **realpolitik,** from a German term meaning "realistic politics." In terms of foreign policy, realpolitik meant dealing with other nations in a practical and flexible manner, rather than by following a rigid policy. Kissinger believed in evaluating a nation's power, not its philosophy or beliefs. If a country was weak, Kissinger argued, it was often more practical to ignore that country, even if it was Communist.

On the other hand, Kissinger's philosophy called for the United States to fully confront the powerful nations of the globe. In the world of realpolitik, however, confrontation meant negotiation as well as military engagement. Realpolitik marked a departure from the policy of containment, which refused to recognize the world's major Communist countries. Kissinger urged the United States to recognize and deal directly with these nations. It was impractical, for example, to deny the existence of mainland China, which contained at least one-fifth of the world's population. It also was impractical not to ease relations with the Soviet Union, with its massive stockpile of nuclear weapons.

"I've always thought this country could run itself domestically without a president."

RICHARD M. NIXON

Nixon shared Kissinger's belief in realpolitik, and together the two men adopted a more flexible approach in dealing with Communist nations. They called their policy **détente**—a policy aimed at easing Cold War tensions. One of the most startling applications of détente came in early 1972 when President Nixon—who had risen in politics as a strong anti-Communist—visited Communist China.

THINK THROUGH HISTORY
G. ***Summarizing*** *What was the philosophy of realpolitik?*

G. Answer To deal with nations in a practical and flexible manner, rather than by following a rigid policy.

NIXON VISITS CHINA Since the takeover of mainland China by the Communists in 1949, the United States had not formally recognized the Chinese Communist government. In late 1971, Nixon reversed that policy. In a 90-second television speech, the president announced that he would visit China "to seek the normalization of relations between the two countries and to exchange views on questions of concern to both sides."

By going to China, Nixon was trying, in part, to take advantage of the decade-long rift between China and the Soviet Union. China had long criticized the Soviet Union as being too "soft" in its policies against the West. The two Communist superpowers officially broke ties in 1960. Nixon had thought about exploiting the fractured relationship for several years. "We want to have the Chinese with us when we sit down and negotiate with the Russians," he told a reporter in 1968.

President Nixon tours the Great Wall as part of his visit to China in 1972.

Nixon's visit to Beijing in February of 1972 scored high marks from the American public. U.S. television crews flooded American living rooms with news reports and film clips of Nixon at the Great Wall of China, at the Imperial Palace, and even toasting top Communist leaders at state dinners. Observers noted that

OBJECTIVE
④ INSTRUCT

Nixon's Foreign Policy Triumphs

▶ ***Discussing Key Ideas***
- Following the philosophy of realpolitik, Nixon and Kissinger work to relax Cold War tensions throughout the world.
- In the most visible sign of his attempt to ease Cold War animosities, Nixon visits China and the Soviet Union.

MORE ABOUT . . .
Nixon in China

The first-ever meeting between Nixon and Chinese leader Mao Zedong was marked by its light-heartedness. Mao joked that in his mind he had voted for Nixon. "I like rightists," the Chairman quipped. "I am comparatively happy when these people on the right come into power." Less friendly to Nixon was Mao's wife. "She obviously did not approve of the visit," Nixon wrote. "She said to me sharply, 'Why did you not come to China before now?'"

GROLIER MULTIMEDIA ENCYCLOPEDIA
Overview of Nixon's Political Career

TEACHING OPTIONS

Making Connections Across Time

U.S.-Sino Relations U.S.-Chinese relations today are strained, due mostly to arguments over human rights. Since the time of Nixon's visit, China has allowed more economic freedoms, including a growing amount of private enterprise. The world's most populous country, however, continues to crush attempts at social reform. The United States issued a report in 1997 claiming that China had jailed or exiled every active political dissident. The report called it an "accomplishment even post-Stalinist Russia could not achieve." A Chinese official called the report "an interference into China's internal affairs."

Teaching Gifted and Talented Students

Evaluating an Autobiographic Source After leaving government, Kissinger wrote two books about his White House experiences: *White House Years,* 1979, and *Years of Upheaval,* 1982. Assign students to read selections in these books that relate to the decision to open relations with China and the Soviet Union. Ask students what special insights Kissinger's account provides. Would students rely on such autobiographies as their main source of historical information? Why or why not?

MORE ABOUT . . .
Kissinger in Moscow

Before Nixon's arrival in Moscow, Kissinger met with Brezhnev to finalize the details of the visit. In preparing Brezhnev for the meeting, the Kremlin's top scholar on America advised the Soviet premier on one of Kissinger's most notable traits. "He has a huge ego and you can use it," the aide said. "Stroke him . . . deal with him as if he were an equal and not just a presidential assistant."

IN-DEPTH RESOURCES: UNIT 7
American Lives: Henry Kissinger, p. 15

ASSESS & RETEACH

Section 1 Assessment

Have students work in small groups to answer the questions. Draw the chart in question 2 on the board and complete it as a class.

Self-Assessment

Have students rate Nixon's performance as a president on a scale of 1 to 10 based on information in this section. Then have them share their ratings and reasons for them.

Section Quiz

FORMAL ASSESSMENT
Section Quiz, p. 294

Reteach

Use the Guided Reading Worksheet for Section 1 to help review the main ideas of the section.

IN-DEPTH RESOURCES: UNIT 7
Guided Reading, p. 1

CLOSE

President Richard Nixon attempted to steer the country in a more conservative direction by dismantling numerous federal programs and instilling a sense of law and order. On the world stage, Nixon worked to improve relations with Cold War adversaries China and the Soviet Union.

an important reason for the trip's popularity back home was Nixon's strong anti-Communist background. It seemed that Nixon, and no one else, could convince the American people that the time was right to negotiate with the Communists.

Besides the trip's enormous symbolic value, it also resulted in important agreements between the United States and China. The two nations agreed that neither would try to dominate the Pacific and that both would cooperate in settling disputes peacefully. The two nations also agreed to participate in scientific and cultural exchanges as well as to eventually reunite Taiwan with the mainland.

NIXON TRAVELS TO MOSCOW In May of 1972, three months after visiting Beijing, President Nixon headed to Moscow—the first U.S. president ever to visit the Soviet Union. By the time the president arrived for a summit meeting with Soviet premier Leonid Brezhnev, relations with the Soviet Union had already warmed. In 1971, the United States and the Soviet Union had crafted an agreement about Berlin. The Soviets promised to guarantee Western nations free access to West Berlin and to respect the city's independence. In return, the Western allies agreed to officially recognize East Germany.

Like his visit to China, Nixon's trip to the Soviet Union received wide acclaim. After a series of meetings called the Strategic Arms Limitation Talks (SALT), Nixon and Brezhnev signed the **SALT I Treaty.** This five-year agreement limited the number of intercontinental ballistic missiles (ICBMs) and submarine-launched missiles to 1972 levels.

The foreign policy triumphs with China and the Soviet Union, which came just months before the 1972 presidential election, helped Nixon win a second term in the White House. The administration's announcement, in October of 1972, that peace was imminent in Vietnam also played a significant role in Nixon's reelection.

However, peace in Vietnam proved elusive, and the Nixon administration grappled with the war for nearly six more months before finally ending America's involvement in Vietnam. By that time, another issue was about to dominate the Nixon administration—one that eventually led to the downfall of the president.

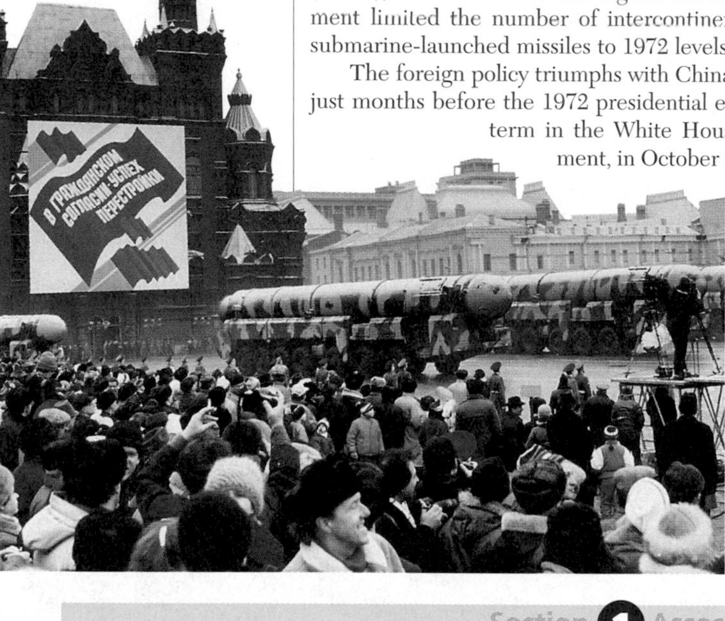

A 1973 military parade in Moscow displays the Soviet Union's arsenal, components of which were frozen at 1972 levels as a result of the SALT I Treaty.

H. Answer By coming just months before the 1972 presidential elections, these achievements helped Nixon win reelection.

THINK THROUGH HISTORY
H. Drawing Conclusions
Why was the timing of Nixon's foreign policy achievements particularly important?

Section 1 Assessment

1. TERMS & NAMES
Identify:
- Richard M. Nixon
- New Federalism
- revenue sharing
- Family Assistance Plan
- Southern strategy
- stagflation
- OPEC
- realpolitik
- détente
- SALT I Treaty

2. SUMMARIZING In a two-column chart similar to the one shown, list policies of Richard Nixon that promoted change and those that slowed it down.

Promoted Change	Slowed Change

In what ways do you think Nixon was most conservative? In which way was he least conservative? Explain.

3. DRAWING CONCLUSIONS Do you think Richard Nixon fulfilled his campaign promise to mend the divisiveness in the United States? Give examples to support your viewpoint.

THINK ABOUT
- his policy of law and order
- his views on busing and integration
- his Supreme Court appointments
- his economic reforms

4. FORMING OPINIONS In your opinion, did Nixon's policy of détente help solve the country's major foreign policy problems? Support your answer with evidence from the text.

THINK ABOUT
- the definition and origin of détente
- the effect of détente on U.S. dealings with Communist countries
- the effect of détente on the American public

ANSWERS

1. TERMS & NAMES
Richard M. Nixon, p. 786
New Federalism, p. 786
revenue sharing, p. 786
Family Assistance Plan, p. 787
Southern strategy, p. 788
stagflation, p. 790
OPEC, p. 790
realpolitik, p. 791
détente, p. 791
SALT I Treaty, p. 792

2. SUMMARIZING
Possible Answers: **Promoted Change:** Started revenue sharing program; supported Family Assistance Plan; visited China; visited Soviet Union; signed SALT I. **Slowed Change:** Impounded funds allocated by Congress; abolished Office of Economic Opportunity; slowed desegregation efforts; appointed conservative justices to the Supreme Court.

3. DRAWING CONCLUSIONS
Possible Responses: **Yes:** He tried to reduce protests, slow down integration, appoint Supreme Court justices who would resist change, and reduce economic suffering by wage and price controls. **No:** The creation of an "enemies list," his failure to support key civil rights legislation, his attempt to make the Supreme Court more conservative, and his inability to halt inflation all added to the country's divisiveness.

4. FORMING OPINIONS
Possible Responses: **Yes:** It brought improved relations with the Soviet Union and China. **No:** Although it improved foreign relations, enhanced Nixon's world image, and renewed the American public's confidence in Nixon, it did nothing to help the situation in Vietnam.

2 Watergate: Nixon's Downfall

LEARN ABOUT the events known as the Watergate scandal
TO UNDERSTAND why Watergate presented one of the most serious constitutional crises in U.S. history.

TERMS & NAMES
- Watergate
- H. R. Haldeman
- John Ehrlichman
- John Mitchell
- Committee to Reelect the President
- Judge John Sirica
- Saturday Night Massacre

ONE AMERICAN'S STORY

On July 25, 1974, Representative Barbara Jordan of Texas, a member of the House Judiciary Committee, sat before a packed hearing room and a television audience of millions. The Judiciary Committee faced a historic decision: should it recommend that President Richard M. Nixon be impeached? If the House voted for impeachment, the president would be tried in the Senate for crimes he had allegedly committed while in office. Addressing the room, Jordan cited the Constitution in urging her fellow committee members to investigate whether impeachment was appropriate.

U.S. representative Barbara Jordan

A PERSONAL VOICE

"We the people"—it is a very eloquent beginning. But when the Constitution of the United States was completed . . . I was not included in that "We the people." . . . But through the process of amendment, interpretation, and court decision, I have finally been included in "We the people." . . .

Today . . . [m]y faith in the Constitution is whole. It is complete. It is total. I am not going to sit here and be an idle spectator in the diminution, the subversion, the destruction of the Constitution. . . . Has the President committed offenses . . . which the Constitution will not tolerate? That is the question. We know that. We should now forthwith proceed to answer the question.

BARBARA JORDAN, quoted in *Notable Black American Women*

The committee eventually voted to recommend the impeachment of Richard Nixon for his role in the Watergate scandal. However, before Congress could take further action against him, the president resigned. Nixon's resignation, the first by a U.S. president, was the climax of a scandal that led to the imprisonment of 25 government officials and caused the most serious constitutional crisis in the United States since the impeachment of Andrew Johnson in 1868.

President Nixon and His White House

The **Watergate** scandal centered on the Nixon administration's attempt to cover up a burglary of the Democratic National Committee (DNC) headquarters at the Watergate apartment complex in Washington, D.C. However, the Watergate story began long before the actual burglary. Many historians believe that Watergate truly began with the personalities of Richard Nixon and his advisers, as well as with the changing role of the presidency.

AN IMPERIAL PRESIDENCY Over the course of the nation's history, the balance of power has shifted among the legislative, executive, and judicial branches of the federal government. By the time Richard Nixon took office, the executive branch—as a result of the Great Depression, World War II, and the Cold War—had become the most powerful branch. In his book *The Imperial Presidency*, the historian Arthur Schlesinger, Jr., argued that by the time of Richard Nixon, the executive branch had taken on an air of imperial, or supreme, authority.

Section 2 Overview

OBJECTIVES

1. To explain how Nixon and his advisers sought to increase the power of the presidency.
2. To summarize why the Watergate burglary occurred and why the Nixon administration covered it up.
3. To describe how the Watergate cover-up unraveled.
4. To explain why a House committee voted to impeach Nixon and what effect the Watergate scandal had on the country.

SKILLBUILDER

- Interpreting political cartoons, p. 796

CRITICAL THINKING

- Clarifying, p. 794
- Analyzing motives, p. 794
- Following chronological order, p. 795
- Drawing conclusions, p. 796
- Theme: Constitutional Concerns, p. 797
- Summarizing, p. 797
- Analyzing issues, p. 797
- Making predictions, p. 797

FOCUS & MOTIVATE

5-MINUTE WARM-UP

Making Inferences
To understand the Nixon presidency, have students read "An Imperial Presidency" on pages 793–794 and answer these questions.

1. What does Arthur Schlesinger mean by the term "imperial presidency"?
2. Does Schlesinger think the emergence of the "the imperial presidency" is a good thing?

WARM-UP TRANSPARENCY 24

▶***Starting with the Student***
Ask students how they react when they believe someone has lied to them. How would they react if they learned the president had lied to the country?

IN-DEPTH RESOURCES: UNIT 7
American Lives: Barbara Jordan, p. 16

SECTION 2 RESOURCES

PRINT RESOURCES

IN-DEPTH RESOURCES: UNIT 7
Guided Reading, p. 2
Primary Source: from *All the President's Men* by Carl Bernstein and Bob Woodward, p. 9
American Lives: Barbara Jordan, p. 16

READING STUDY GUIDE, p. 245

ACCESS FOR STUDENTS ACQUIRING ENGLISH
Guided Reading (Spanish), p. 262

SPANISH READING STUDY GUIDE, p. 245

FORMAL ASSESSMENT
Section Quiz, p. 295

ALTERNATIVE ASSESSMENT BOOK
See forms for supporting and scoring alternative activities.

TECHNOLOGY RESOURCES

HUMANITIES TRANSPARENCIES
H46, I Am the Law

CRITICAL THINKING TRANSPARENCIES
CT32, The Watergate Scandal
CT66, Shift in Presidential Politics, 1968–1972

CD-ROM *Our Times*
Grolier Multimedia Encyclopedia
Electronic Library of Primary Sources

VIDEO *American Portfolio: A Videodisc for U.S. History*
user's guide, pp. 253–255

INTERNET http://www.mlushistory.com

President Nixon and His White House

▶ ***Discussing Key Ideas***

- By the time Nixon arrives in the White House, the presidency has taken on an air of supreme, or imperial, authority.
- Nixon revels in this authority, as he distances himself from Congress and relies on a small group of close advisers.

IN-DEPTH RESOURCES: UNIT 7
Guided Reading, p. 2

ACCESS FOR STUDENTS ACQUIRING ENGLISH
Guided Reading (Spanish), p. 262

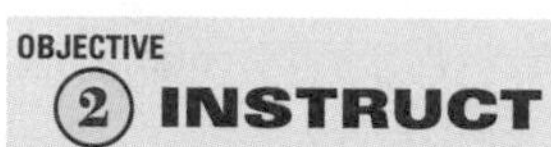

The Drive Toward Reelection

▶ ***Discussing Key Ideas***

- Seeking any and all advantages, officials with Nixon's reelection campaign burglarize the Democratic National Committee headquarters for information.
- Nixon agrees to a cover-up of the White House's involvement in the burglary.

CT66, Shift in Presidential Politics, 1968–1972

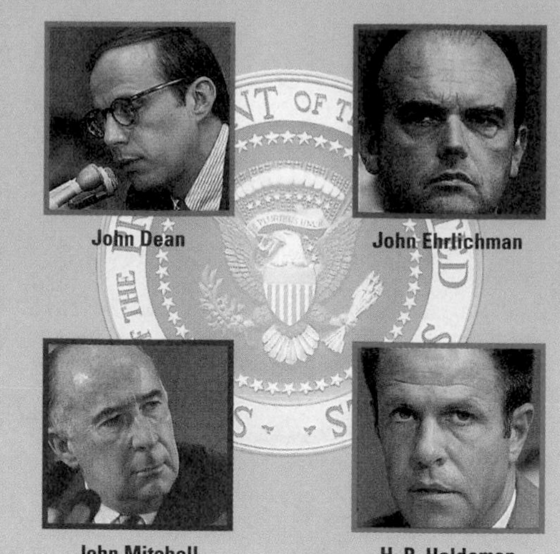

The "president's men," as they were called, formed a tight circle around Richard Nixon.

President Nixon settled into this imperial role with ease. Nixon believed, as he told a newspaper reporter in 1980, that "a president must not be one of the crowd. . . . People . . . don't want him to be down there saying, 'Look, I'm the same as you.'" Nixon expanded the power of the presidency and gave little thought to constitutional checks, as when he impounded funds for federal programs he opposed and ordered U.S. troops to invade Cambodia without congressional approval.

THINK THROUGH HISTORY
A. Clarifying *What is meant by "imperial presidency"?*

A. Answer The idea that the executive branch had become the most powerful of the three branches of government, acting as a supreme authority.

THE "PRESIDENT'S MEN" As he distanced himself from Congress, Nixon confided in a small and fiercely loyal group of advisers. They included **H. R. Haldeman,** chief of staff; **John Ehrlichman,** chief domestic adviser; and **John Mitchell,** the attorney general. These men had played key roles in Nixon's 1968 election victory and now helped the president direct White House policy.

These men also shared President Nixon's desire for secrecy and the consolidation of power. Through their personalities and their attitude toward the presidency, these men developed a sense that they were somehow above the law. This sense would, in turn, prompt President Nixon and his advisers to cover up their role in Watergate, and thus fuel the coming scandal.

The Drive Toward Reelection

Throughout his political career, Richard Nixon lived with the overwhelming fear of losing elections. In his 1972 reelection campaign, Nixon strived not only to defeat his opponent but to dominate him. "I vowed that I would never again enter an election at a disadvantage to . . . anyone on the level of political tactics," Nixon wrote. Toward this end, Nixon's campaign team sought advantages by any means possible, including an attempt to steal information from the DNC headquarters.

A BUNGLED BURGLARY At 2:30 A.M., June 17, 1972, a guard at the Watergate complex in Washington, D.C., caught five men breaking into the campaign headquarters of the DNC. The men were part of a team known as the plumbers, whose job it was to plug any government leaks to the media and to aid the Nixon administration in other—sometimes illegal—ways. The burglars had intended to photograph documents outlining Democratic Party strategy and to place wiretaps, or "bugs," on the office telephones. The press soon discovered that the group's leader, James McCord, was a former CIA agent. He was also an official of a group known as the **Committee to Reelect the President** (CRP). John Mitchell, who had resigned as attorney general to run Nixon's reelection campaign, was the CRP's director.

THINK THROUGH HISTORY
B. Analyzing Motives *Why would the Nixon campaign team take such a risky action as breaking into the opposition's headquarters?*

B. Answer Because of Nixon's overwhelming fear of losing and the team's belief that all means should be taken to defeat the opponent.

Just three days after the burglary, H.R. Haldeman noted in his diary Nixon's near obsession with how to respond to the break-in.

A PERSONAL VOICE

> We got back into the Democratic break-in again. . . . The more he [Nixon] thought about it, it obviously bothered him more, because he raised it in considerable detail today. . . . The P[resident] was concerned about what our counter-attack is. . . . He raised it again several times during the day, and it obviously is bothering him. . . . He called at home tonight, saying that he wanted to change the plan for his press conference and have it on Thursday instead of tomorrow, so that it won't look like he's reacting to the Democratic break-in thing.
>
> H. R. HALDEMAN, *The Haldeman Diaries*

TEACHING OPTIONS

Teaching Less Proficient Readers

Creating a Time Line Have less proficient readers create a Watergate time line to keep track of the scandal's many twists and turns. Starting with the Watergate burglary and ending with Nixon's resignation, students should list what they consider the major events of Watergate on a time line such as the one below. They may place as many events on their time line as they wish.

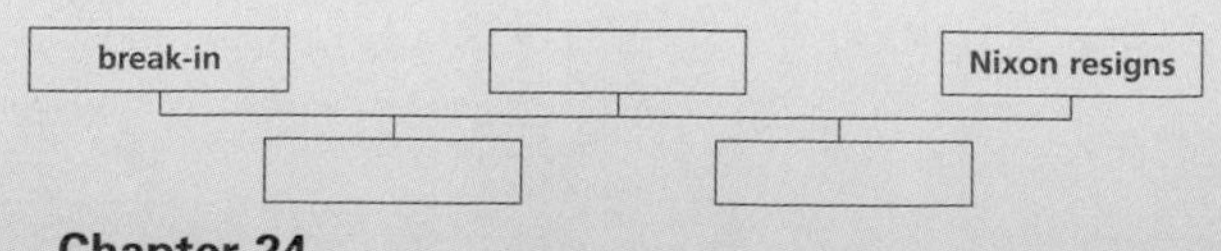

Teaching Gifted and Talented Students

Researching a Diary Have interested students read more of *The Haldeman Diaries,* particularly those excerpts that pertain to the Watergate scandal. Students should then write a brief paper answering the following questions: What new insight into the scandal did you learn? What more did you learn about the personality and behavior of Richard Nixon? Why might a diary be a useful source in researching historical persons or events?

At this point, the White House might have disowned the entire operation and demanded the resignation of everyone involved. But that would have meant getting rid of people upon whom Nixon heavily depended, such as Mitchell. The cover-up quickly began. Workers shredded all incriminating documents in Haldeman's office. The White House, with President Nixon's consent, asked the CIA to urge the FBI to stop its investigations into the burglary on the grounds of national security. In addition, the CRP passed out nearly $500,000 to the Watergate burglars to buy their silence after they were indicted in September of 1972.

THINK THROUGH HISTORY
C. *Following Chronological Order* *What steps did the White House take to cover up its involvement in the Watergate break-in?*

C. Answer Officials shredded documents, attempted to obstruct the investigation, and paid the Watergate burglars to remain silent.

Throughout the 1972 campaign, the Watergate burglary generated little interest among the American public and media. Only the *Washington Post* and two of its reporters, Bob Woodward and Carl Bernstein, kept on the story. In a series of articles, the reporters uncovered information that linked numerous members of the administration to the burglary. The White House denied each new *Post* allegation. Upon learning of an upcoming story that tied him to the burglars, Mitchell told Bernstein, "That's the most sickening thing I ever heard."

The White House reaction proved effective. Casting himself as a "global peacemaker"—in light of his China and Soviet Union summits and his promise of peace in Vietnam—Richard Nixon scored the largest victory of any Republican presidential candidate in history. The president captured nearly 61 percent of the popular vote on his way to soundly defeating George S. McGovern, a liberal senator from South Dakota. However, as Nixon savored his landslide victory, the storm clouds of Watergate were gathering on the horizon.

HISTORICAL SPOTLIGHT

WOODWARD AND BERNSTEIN

Bob Woodward and Carl Bernstein of the *Washington Post* seemed an unlikely team. Woodward, 29 (at right in the photo above), had graduated from Yale, while the 28-year-old Bernstein was a college dropout.

As the two men dug deeper into the Watergate scandal, a mysterious inside source known only as Deep Throat helped them along the way. There has been much debate over the identity of Deep Throat, which has been fueled by the reporters' continued refusal to identify their famous source.

While people lauded the two reporters for their dogged determination on the Watergate story, some Nixon officials remain bitter toward them. "I really believe [they] were on a personal crusade to bring down a president," said Gerald Warren, Nixon's deputy press secretary. Woodward denied that charge, saying, "We tried to do our job and, in fact, if you look at it, our coverage was pretty conservative."

The Cover-Up Unravels

In January of 1973, the trial of the Watergate burglars began. During the trial, all of the burglars except James McCord changed their pleas from innocent to guilty. McCord was found guilty by a jury. The trial's presiding judge, **Judge John Sirica,** made clear his belief that the Watergate burglars and their supervisors from the CRP, G. Gordon Liddy and E. Howard Hunt, had not acted alone. On March 20, a few days before the burglars were scheduled to be sentenced, McCord sent a letter to Sirica, in which he indicated that he had lied under oath. He also hinted that powerful members of the Nixon administration had been involved in the break-in.

THE SENATE INVESTIGATES WATERGATE McCord's revelation of possible White House involvement in the burglary rekindled public interest in Watergate. President Nixon moved quickly to stem the growing public concern. On April 30, 1973, Nixon dismissed White House counsel John Dean and announced the resignations of Haldeman and Ehrlichman. All three men had been involved in the Watergate affair. The president then went on television and denied any attempt at a cover-up. He announced that he was appointing a new attorney general, Elliot Richardson, and was authorizing him to appoint a special prosecutor to investigate Watergate. "There can be no whitewash at the White House," Nixon said.

The president's reassurances, however, came too late. In May 1973, the Senate began its own investigation of Watergate. A special committee, chaired by Senator Sam Ervin of North Carolina, began to call a parade of Nixon administration officials to give testimony. Throughout the summer and into the fall, millions of Americans sat glued to their televisions as the "president's men" testified one after another—and dropped several bombshells.

HISTORICAL SPOTLIGHT
Woodward and Bernstein

The mystery surrounding the identity of "Deep Throat" speaks to a controversial issue for journalists: the use of anonymous sources. Courts have sometimes ordered reporters to name an anonymous source who may be a witness to a crime or have knowledge vital to a case. Reporters have almost always refused, arguing that they promised to keep the source's name secret and that to reveal the name would undermine their ability to gather information from future sources. Ask students for their opinions on this issue.

IN-DEPTH RESOURCES: UNIT 7
Primary Source: from *All the President's Men* by Carl Bernstein and Bob Woodward, p. 9

OBJECTIVE
(3) INSTRUCT

The Cover-Up Unravels

Discussing Key Ideas

- The Senate begins investigating a possible White House connection to the Watergate break-in.
- During the Senate hearings several witnesses accuse numerous White House officials, including President Nixon, of orchestrating a cover-up.
- Nixon refuses to release White House tape recordings that could reveal his involvement in the cover-up.

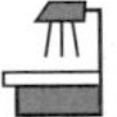

CRITICAL THINKING TRANSPARENCIES
CT32, The Watergate Scandal

TEACHING OPTIONS

Exploring Themes

Constitutional Concerns The Watergate scandal produced one of the most serious constitutional issues facing this country: the possibility of criminal activity by a sitting president. Make sure students understand the impeachment process as outlined in the Constitution. The House of Representatives has the sole power to bring impeachment charges against a president or any other civilian official of the U.S. government. A majority vote of the House is required for impeachment. The Senate then acts as a court to hear the charges brought against the impeached official. A two-thirds vote of the Senate is required for conviction.

Making Connections Across Cultures

Senator Edward Brooke In 1966, Edward Brooke of Massachusetts became the first African American to be elected to the U.S. Senate since 1876. He was also the first Republican senator to publicly call for President Nixon's resignation. Brooke, who was reelected in 1972, had served in World War II, where he rose to the rank of captain and received a Bronze Star for his work in intelligence. Although he was a Republican, he sparred with President Nixon over numerous issues, including civil rights.

MORE ABOUT . . .
Nixon and Dean

Nixon had been only too glad to involve Dean in the Watergate cover-up. "I am very impressed by him," Nixon wrote in his diary. "He has shown enormous strength." The president would soon change his opinion of Dean and deeply regret confiding in him.

OUR TIMES
transcript of White House conversation between Richard Nixon and John Dean III

HISTORY FROM VISUALS
Political Cartoons

Reading the Cartoon What building has been "transformed" into a giant tape recorder? *The White House.*

Extension The Watergate scandal, particularly Nixon's role in it, spawned numerous political cartoons. Have students work in pairs to create their own cartoon about the cover-up.

HUMANITIES TRANSPARENCIES
H46, I Am the Law

OBJECTIVE
④ INSTRUCT

The Fall of a President

▶ ***Discussing Key Ideas***
- The House Judiciary Committee adopts three articles of impeachment against President Nixon.
- Nixon releases the White House tapes, which reveal his involvement in the cover-up.
- Before the impeachment process can continue, President Nixon resigns from office.

"What did the president know and when did he know it?"

SENATOR HOWARD BAKER

"Divine right went out with the American Revolution and doesn't belong to White House aides."

SENATOR SAM ERVIN
IN RESPONSE TO THE WHITE HOUSE'S REQUEST THAT ITS AIDES TESTIFY IN PRIVATE

STARTLING TESTIMONY John Dean delivered the first bomb. In late June, during more than 30 hours of testimony, Dean provided a startling answer to Senator Howard Baker's repeated question, "What did the president know and when did he know it?" The former White House counsel answered that President Nixon had been deeply involved in the cover-up. The president quickly sent John Mitchell up to Capitol Hill to refute Dean's charges. Sitting before the Senate committee, Mitchell denied approving the break-in and wiretapping of the Democratic National Committee headquarters. He further stated that if there indeed was a cover-up, Nixon had no knowledge of it.

The hearings had suddenly reached an impasse as the committee attempted to sort out who was telling the truth. The answer came in July from an unlikely source: presidential aide Alexander Butterfield. Butterfield stunned the committee when he revealed that Nixon had taped virtually all of his presidential conversations. Butterfield later claimed that the taping system was installed "to help Nixon write his memoirs." However, for the Senate committee, the tapes were the key to revealing what Nixon knew and when he knew it.

THINK THROUGH HISTORY
D. ***Drawing Conclusions*** *What was significant about the revelation that Nixon taped his conversations?*

D. Answer The tapes of Nixon's private conversations would provide clear and convincing evidence as to what Nixon knew about Watergate and when he knew it.

THE SATURDAY NIGHT MASSACRE A year-long battle for the "Nixon tapes" followed. Archibald Cox, the special prosecutor whom Elliot Richardson had appointed to investigate the case, took the president to court in October 1973 to obtain the tapes. Nixon refused and ordered Attorney General Richardson to fire Cox. In what became known as the **Saturday Night Massacre,** Richardson refused the order and resigned. The deputy attorney general also refused the order, and he was fired. Solicitor General Robert Bork finally fired Cox. However, Cox's replacement, Leon Jaworski, proved equally determined to get the tapes. Shortly after the "massacre," the House Judiciary Committee began examining the possibility of an impeachment hearing.

The entire White House appeared to be under siege. Just days before the Saturday Night Massacre, Vice-President Spiro Agnew had resigned after it was revealed that he had accepted bribes from Maryland engineering firms before and during his term as vice-president. Acting under the Twenty-fifth Amendment, Nixon nominated the House minority leader, Gerald Ford, as his new vice-president. Congress quickly confirmed the nomination.

In light of Agnew's illegal activities, federal investigators began to study Nixon's own financial dealings. News reports revealed that Nixon had paid only $1,000 in taxes on a $200,000 income in 1971 and 1972. Nixon responded to the charges by uttering what the American people never imagined a president would have to say: "People have the right to know whether or not their president is a crook. Well, I am not a crook."

SKILLBUILDER
INTERPRETING POLITICAL CARTOONS
What does this cartoon imply about privacy in the Nixon White House?

Skillbuilder Answer *Possible Answer:* That there was very little privacy in the White House and that anyone's words might be taped.

The Fall of a President

In March 1974, a grand jury indicted Mitchell, Haldeman, Ehrlichman, and four other presidential aides on charges of conspiracy, obstruction of justice, and perjury. The investigation was closing in on the president of the United States.

NIXON RELEASES THE TAPES On April 30, 1974, President Nixon told a televised audience that he was releasing 1,254 pages of edited transcripts of White House conversations about Watergate. The president hoped that this would convince everyone of his truthfulness and leadership. If anything, the tapes only increased people's dismay. The president's vulgar language and lack of concern about fully addressing the growing Watergate scandal shocked many Americans. "We have seen the private man and we are appalled," declared the conservative *Chicago Tribune.*

Block Schedule TEACHING OPTION **Time Needed: 20 Minutes**

Cooperative Activity: Writing an Editorial about the Saturday Night Massacre

Task: Student groups will work together to write a newspaper editorial about Nixon's actions during the Saturday Night Massacre.

Purpose: To guide students in forming and relaying their opinion on the president's actions.

Activity: Divide students into groups of three or four. Have group members assign one another tasks in further researching the Saturday Night Massacre. One member might search for quotes from participants, another for public reaction, and another for several news editorials. Group members should combine their research and write an editorial about the event, addressing in particular the actions of President Nixon.

Building a Portfolio Students adding editorials to their portfolios should attach a note pointing out their contribution.

ALTERNATIVE ASSESSMENT BOOK
Standards for Evaluating a Cooperative Activity

Standards for Evaluation
Editorials should . . .
- summarize Nixon's actions
- state an opinion clearly and strongly
- support opinions with facts and examples
- suggest a course of action

Furthermore, Nixon's offering of edited tape transcripts failed to satisfy investigators. They demanded the unedited tapes. Nixon refused, and the case went before the Supreme Court. On July 24, 1974, the high court ruled unanimously that the president must surrender the tapes. The Court rejected Nixon's argument that doing so would violate national security. Evidence involving possible criminal activity could not be withheld, even by a president.

THE PRESIDENT RESIGNS Even without the original tapes, the House Judiciary Committee determined that there was enough evidence to impeach Richard Nixon. On July 27, the committee approved three articles of impeachment, charging the president with obstruction of justice, abuse of power, and contempt of Congress for refusing to obey a congressional subpoena to release the tapes.

E. Answer During the scandal, the president obstructed justice and abused power. The crisis revolved around the issue of whether a president could be held accountable for such misdeeds.

THINK THROUGH HISTORY
E. THEME ***Constitutional Concerns*** *How did the Watergate scandal create a constitutional crisis?*

On August 5, Nixon released the tapes. Despite a mysterious gap of 18 minutes, the tapes revealed the evidence for which investigators had been searching. A conversation with H. R. Haldeman on June 23, 1972—a week after the Watergate break-in—revealed that Nixon not only had known of his administration's role in the burglary but had agreed to the plan to obstruct the FBI's investigation.

The evidence now seemed overwhelming. On August 8, 1974, Richard M. Nixon announced his resignation from office. Defiant as always, Nixon admitted no guilt. He merely said that some of his judgments "were wrong." The next day, Nixon and his wife, Pat, climbed into the presidential helicopter that would take them to Andrews Air Force Base for their flight back home to California. Moments later, Gerald Ford was sworn in as the 38th president of the United States.

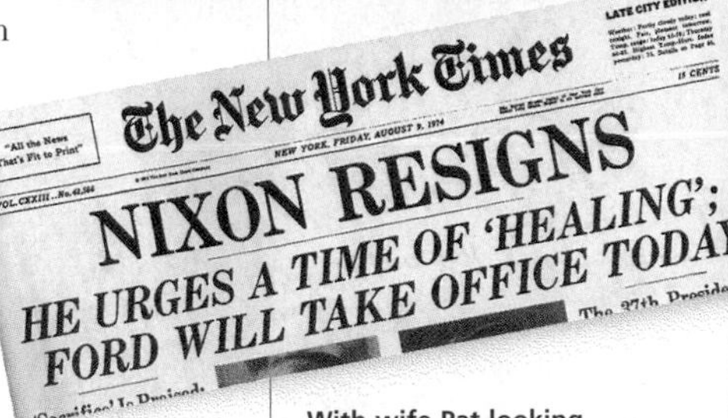
"All the News That's Fit to Print"
The New York Times
LATE CITY EDITION
NEW YORK, FRIDAY, AUGUST 9, 1974
NIXON RESIGNS
HE URGES A TIME OF 'HEALING';
FORD WILL TAKE OFFICE TODA

With wife Pat looking on, Richard Nixon bids farewell to his staff on his final day as president. "Always remember," he defiantly told them, "others may hate you, but those who hate you don't win unless you hate them, and then you destroy yourself."

THE EFFECTS OF WATERGATE The effects of Watergate have endured long after Nixon's resignation. Along with the divisive war in Vietnam, Watergate produced a deep disillusionment with the "imperial" presidency. A poll taken in 1974 showed that 43 percent of Americans had "hardly any" faith in the executive branch of government. In the years following Vietnam and Watergate, the American public developed a general cynicism about many public officials that still exists today.

During the rest of the 1970s, Gerald Ford and Jimmy Carter worked to restore the lost faith in the presidency. Unfortunately, each man would have to focus most of his attention on the country's worsening economic conditions.

Section 2 Assessment

1. TERMS & NAMES
Identify:
- Watergate
- H. R. Haldeman
- John Ehrlichman
- John Mitchell
- Committee to Reelect the President
- Judge John Sirica
- Saturday Night Massacre

2. SUMMARIZING In a diagram similar to the one below, list individuals or groups who helped uncover the Watergate scandal. Include people from the government and the media, as well as those on Nixon's staff who testified.

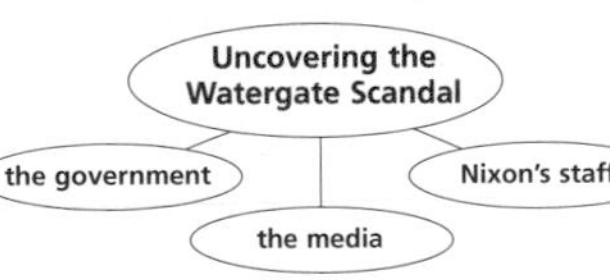

3. ANALYZING ISSUES Which events of the Watergate scandal do you think were most significant? Explain.

THINK ABOUT
- the intentions of the participants in each event
- the legal implications of each event
- the charges in the articles of impeachment

4. MAKING PREDICTIONS Imagine that Nixon had admitted to and apologized for the Watergate break-in immediately after it occurred. How might subsequent events have been different? Explain and support your answer.

THINK ABOUT
- the extent of the cover-up
- the impact of the cover-up on the nation
- the effect of the cover-up on Nixon's image

ANSWERS

1. TERMS & NAMES

Watergate, p. 793
H. R. Haldeman, p. 794
John Ehrlichman, p. 794
John Mitchell, p. 794
Committee to Reelect the President, p. 794
Judge John Sirica, p. 795
Saturday Night Massacre, p. 796

2. SUMMARIZING

Possible Responses: **The government:** Attorney General Elliot Richardson; special prosecutors Archibald Cox and Leon Jaworski; Senate committee headed by Sam Ervin; the House Judiciary Committee; Judge John Sirica; the Supreme Court. **The media:** *Washington Post* reporters Bob Woodward and Carl Bernstein. **Nixon's staff:** John Dean; presidential aide Alexander Butterfield.

3. ANALYZING ISSUES

Possible Responses: The initial burglary, because it was illegal, showed abuse of presidential power and led Nixon to cover up his actions; the subsequent cover-up, especially the destroying of evidence and bribing of the burglars, because these actions showed Nixon's contempt for law and Congress; Nixon's refusal to release the tapes, because it showed that he felt he was above the law and that Nixon, the "law and order" president, had something to hide.

4. MAKING PREDICTIONS

Possible Responses: Nixon's offenses would have been less significant and his public image would not have been as badly damaged; Americans might have respected his forthrightness and forgotten the matter after awhile; however, he probably would have lost some of the trust of the American people.

MORE ABOUT . . .
The Tapes

The White House attributed the mysterious gap in the tapes to a mistake by President Nixon's secretary, Rose Mary Woods. Woods said that while transcribing the tapes, she accidentally erased part of a June 20, 1972, conversation between Haldeman and Nixon. The explanation met with widespread skepticism.

ELECTRONIC LIBRARY OF PRIMARY SOURCES
Articles of Impeachment

GROLIER MULTIMEDIA ENCYCLOPEDIA
Nixon's Farewell Remarks

ASSESS & RETEACH

Section 2 Assessment
Ask students to answer the questions in small groups. Then have one member from each group read aloud the group's answer to question 3.

Self-Assessment
Have students explain in one or two paragraphs what they think President Nixon should have done differently regarding the Watergate affair.

Section Quiz
FORMAL ASSESSMENT
Section Quiz, p. 295

Reteach
Reexamine the key events of the Watergate affair using the bold, run-in headlines in the text.

CLOSE

President Nixon partook in an attempt to cover up the White House's involvement in a campaign burglary. However, the cover-up soon unraveled, forcing Nixon to become the first U.S. president to resign from office.

Daily Life

OBJECTIVES

1. To explain the growing realism of American TV in the 1970s.
2. To describe popular TV shows of the decade.

FOCUS & MOTIVATE

▶ ***Starting with the Student***
Ask students to think about popular TV shows today.

- Which seem the most realistic in their depiction of everyday life?
- What details make them realistic?

MORE ABOUT . . .
Alex Haley

Alex Haley, who served in the U.S. Coast Guard, admitted that he began writing to avoid boredom during long sea voyages. In 1965, Haley published *The Autobiography of Malcolm X,* which was based on interviews with Malcolm X. The book received wide critical praise. However, it was not until *Roots: The Saga of an American Family,* and the television adaptation that followed, that Haley became a household name. Haley said he began writing *Roots* after listening to his maternal grandmother talk about the family's history. He spent 12 years researching the book. *Roots* earned its author numerous accolades, including a special Pulitzer Prize. Haley died in 1992 at the age of 70.

Television Reflects American Life

Beginning in the late 1960s, television programming began to more closely reflect the realities of American life. Shows more often addressed relevant issues, more African-American characters appeared, and working women, as well as homemakers, were protrayed. By the 1970s, many of the most popular shows on television were multicultural and often controversial. Top-rated series presented the lives of African Americans (*Sanford and Son* and *Good Times*) and women living on their own (*One Day at a Time*). Another hit series, *M*A*S*H,* gave voice to antiwar sentiment. However, the 1970s were not all about relevance. Nostalgic comedies, such as *Happy Days,* and fantasy dramas, such as *Charlie's Angels,* were also big hits.

The 1970s also saw the rapid rise of quality children's programming on public broadcasting, which was created in 1967. Educational shows such as *Sesame Street* (whose Muppet character Cookie Monster appears on the *TV Guide* cover shown above) and *Zoom!* were deliberately fast-paced to appeal to the new generation of "television babies."

INDEPENDENT WOMEN ***The Mary Tyler Moore Show*** **depicted Mary Richards, a single woman living in Minneapolis and working as an assistant manager in a local TV news department. Mary symbolized the young career woman of the 1970s. She was professional and ambitious but also caring, optimistic, and funny. She dated but was not desperate for marriage—she enjoyed her independence.**

CULTURAL IDENTITY
The miniseries *Roots,* based on a book by Alex Haley, told the saga of four generations of an African-American family. The eight-part story began with Kunta Kinte, who was captured outside his West African village and taken to America as a slave. It ended with his great-grandson's setting off for a new life as a free man. The groundbreaking series, broadcast in January 1977, was one of the most-watched television events in history. The final episode reached an estimated 100 million viewers—71 percent of the TV audience—and was the highest-rated show up to that time.

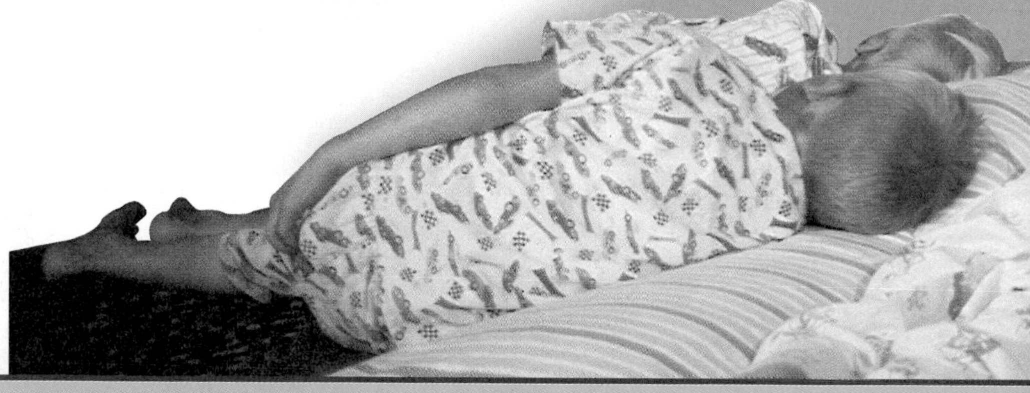

798

RECOMMENDED RESOURCES

Books

Alley, Robert S. *Love Is All Around.* New York: Delta, 1989. A book about the making of *The Mary Tyler Moore Show.*

Esslin, Martin. *The Age of Television.* San Francisco: Freeman, 1982. Written soon after the close of the 1970s, this study focuses on societal aspects of television.

Lesser, Gerald S. *Children and Television.* New York: Random, 1974. Lessons from Sesame Street detailed in a book published not very long after the show's creation.

Reiss, David S. *M*A*S*H.* Indianapolis: Bobbs-Merrill, 1980. An inside look at the popular TV show, with a foreword by star Alan Alda.

Videos

All in the Family 20th Anniversary Special. Columbia Pictures Home Video, 1991. A retrospective featuring the stars of the show and its creator, Norman Lear.

The Impact of Television. Encyclopædia Britannica, 1980. This look at TV features sequences from popular shows.

On Television. Films Inc., 1988. An exploration of TV as a social institution, hosted by Edwin Newman.

Roots, vol. 1. Dir. David Greene. Warner Home Video, 1977. The original six-part miniseries.

MULTICULTURALISM *Chico and the Man* was the first series set in a Mexican-American neighborhood, a barrio of East Los Angeles. It became an immediate hit after its debut in 1974. The program centered on the relationship between Ed Brown, a cranky Anglo garage owner, and Chico Rodriguez, an optimistic and energetic young Mexican-American he reluctantly hired. An attachment gradually grew between the two men from different backgrounds.

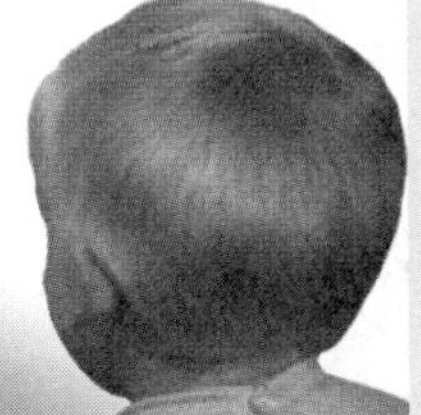

SOCIAL VALUES The most popular series of the 1970s was also the one that departed most radically from the idealized situation comedies of the 1950s and 1960s. *All in the Family* told the story of a working-class family in Queens, New York, headed by the bigoted Archie Bunker and his long-suffering wife, Edith. Through the barbs Bunker traded with his liberal son-in-law, "Meathead," and his African-American neighbor, George Jefferson, the show dealt openly with the divisions in American society. It also addressed controversial topics that had previously been taboo on TV, including politics, religious differences, and sexuality.

DATA FILE

TV facts of the 1970s

- American television sets were turned on an average of seven hours a day.
- The typical school-age child (6 to 18 years old) in America spent 25 percent more time watching TV than attending school.
- A congressional ban on TV cigarette commercials took effect in 1971.
- ABC negotiated an $8-million-a-year contract to televise *Monday Night Football*, first broadcast in September 1970.
- In 1972, President Nixon, accompanied by TV cameras and anchors from the major networks, made a surprise visit to China.
- From May until November 1973, the Senate Watergate hearings were the biggest daytime viewing event of the year.
- *Saturday Night Live*—a show that would launch the careers of Dan Aykroyd, Jane Curtin, Eddie Murphy, and many other comic actors—premiered in October 1975.
- WTCG-TV (later WTBS) in Atlanta, owned by Ted Turner, became the first "superstation" when it began satellite broadcasts to four cable systems in 1976.
- In November 1979, ABC began broadcasting late-night updates on the hostage crisis in Iran. These reports evolved into the program *Nightline.*

Other Popular Shows of the 1970s

Mod Squad
The Flip Wilson Show
Marcus Welby, M.D.
Hawaii Five-O
Adam-12
The Partridge Family
Maude
The Waltons
Little House on the Prairie
Laverne and Shirley
The Six Million Dollar Man
The Bionic Woman

INTERACT WITH HISTORY

1. **DEVELOPING HISTORICAL PERSPECTIVE** In what ways did television change to reflect American society in the 1970s? What factors might have influenced these changes?
2. **CREATING A GRAPH** Use the Internet or an almanac to find data on the number of televisions owned in the United States and the number of hours of TV watched every day. Make a graph that displays the data.

SEE SKILLBUILDER HANDBOOK, PAGES 913 AND 931.

INTERNET Visit http://www.mlushistory.com for more about television and mass culture.

INSTRUCT

▶ *Starting with the Student*
- Have students view and discuss 1970s TV shows on videocassette or in reruns.
- Encourage students to share opinions on the value of realistic TV. Should dramas and sitcoms be realistic? Why or why not?

▶ *Discussing Key Ideas*
- TV in the 1970s began increasingly to reflect everyday American life.
- Many of the shows dealt with racial division, multicultural heritage, independent working women, and other concerns and issues of the day.

HISTORY FROM VISUALS
Reading the Images
- Have students examine the photos on these pages.
- What does the central picture at the bottom of the page say about TV in the 1970s? *Possible Responses: Children spent much (or too much) time watching TV; it was viewed by children of all ages; it served as a baby sitter as more mothers worked; it dazed or dulled the minds of children; it brought families together; it drove families apart by cutting down on conversation and other interaction.*
- Ask students which spotlighted series or miniseries seems most interesting to them. Why?

INTERACT WITH HISTORY

1. Developing Historical Perspective

Possible Responses: *Television was more urban, more working class, more ethnic, more multicultural, and more independent. It showed working women and treated more social issues.*

Television became more reflective of its audience and the changing consumer market as African Americans and other groups grew more affluent; pressure came from women's and civil-rights groups to depict America with its rich diversity; loss of innocence with Vietnam War and Watergate made Americans more cynical, less accepting of unrealistic TV.

2. Creating a Graph

To help students complete this assignment, encourage them to take the following steps:

- Find data on the topics you are researching for your graph and think about how the numbers have changed over time.
- Organize your data by grouping information that comes from the same year and covers the same topics.
- Make a chart or graph with clear labels and an accurate scale that shows how the data has changed over time.

Section 3 Overview

OBJECTIVES

1. To describe Gerald Ford's attempts to combat the nation's economic problems.
2. To explain the reasons for Jimmy Carter's presidential election victory in 1976.
3. To identify the ways Carter tried to solve the nation's economic downswing.
4. To describe Jimmy Carter's foreign policy beliefs and their effect on U.S. foreign relations.
5. To summarize Carter's foreign policy triumphs and defeats in the Middle East.

SKILLBUILDERS

- Interpreting graphs, pp. 803, 804
- Understanding geography: location, p. 806

CRITICAL THINKING

- Contrasting, p. 801
- Analyzing causes, pp. 802, 804, 805
- Summarizing, p. 803
- Forming opinions, pp. 803, 807
- Identifying problems, p. 805
- Making inferences, p. 806
- Analyzing issues, p. 807
- Following chronological order, p. 807
- Comparing and contrasting, p. 807

FOCUS & MOTIVATE

5-MINUTE WARM-UP

Recognizing Facts and Details

To explore some of the issues of Gerald Ford's presidency, have students read the "One American's Story" on page 800 and answer these questions.

1. Whom did President Ford pardon?
2. What major problem beyond the Watergate scandal did the nation and President Ford face?

WARM-UP TRANSPARENCY 24

▶ ***Starting with the Student***
Ask students if they notice when prices increase on compact discs, gym shoes, or some of their other favorite items. What do they think causes this increase?

3 The Ford and Carter Years

TERMS & NAMES
- Gerald R. Ford
- Jimmy Carter
- National Energy Act
- human rights
- Camp David Accords
- Ayatollah Ruhollah Khomeini

LEARN ABOUT the domestic and foreign policies of the Ford and Carter administrations
TO UNDERSTAND how each man attempted to solve the country's worsening economic crisis and deal with an increasingly complex world.

ONE AMERICAN'S STORY

James D. Denney couldn't believe what he was hearing. Barely a month after Richard Nixon had resigned amid the Watergate scandal, President Gerald Ford had granted Nixon a full pardon. "Someone must write, 'The End,'" Ford had declared in a televised statement. "I have concluded that only I can do that." Denney sat down and wrote a letter to the editors of *Time* magazine, in which he voiced his anger at Ford's decision.

A PERSONAL VOICE

Justice may certainly be tempered by mercy, but there can be no such thing as mercy until justice has been accomplished by the courts. Since it circumvented justice, Mr. Ford's act was merely indulgent favoritism, a bland and unworthy substitute for mercy.

JAMES D. DENNEY, *Time*, September 23, 1974

James Denney's feelings were typical of the anger and the disillusionment with the presidency that many Americans felt in the aftermath of the Watergate scandal. During the 1970s, Presidents Gerald Ford and Jimmy Carter sought to restore America's faith in its leaders. However, both men had to focus much of their attention on battling the nation's worsening economic situation.

Two women protest President Ford's pardo of Richard Nixon.

Ford Travels a Rough Road

Upon taking office, **Gerald R. Ford** urged Americans to put the Watergate scandal behind them. "Our long national nightmare is over," he declared. However, the nation's nightmarish economy persisted, and Ford's policies offered little relief.

"A FORD, NOT A LINCOLN" Gerald Ford seemed to many to be a likable and honest man. Upon becoming vice-president after Spiro Agnew's resignation, Ford candidly admitted his limitations. "I'm a Ford, not a Lincoln," he remarked. Raised in Grand Rapids, Michigan, Ford was a product of the nation's heartland. Some people called him "square," but Ford saw nothing wrong with this. He once remarked, "It's . . . the straight, the square that accounts for the great stability of our nation. It's a quality to be proud of."

On September 8, 1974, President Ford pardoned Richard Nixon in an attempt to move the country beyond Watergate. The move cost Ford a good deal of public support. The president hoped to rebuild that support by scoring a victory on what many Americans considered to be the most pressing issue facing the nation: the troubled economy.

As this *Time* cover suggests, Americans looked to Gerald Ford to move the country beyond Watergate.

FORD TRIES TO "WHIP" INFLATION By the time Ford took office, America's economy had gone from bad to worse. Both inflation and unemployment continued to rise. After the massive OPEC oil-price increases in 1973, gasoline and heating oil costs had soared, pushing inflation from 6 percent to 11 percent by the end of 1974. In September 1974, the president invited the nation's top economic leaders to the White House to discuss economic

SECTION 3 RESOURCES

PRINT RESOURCES

IN-DEPTH RESOURCES: UNIT 7
Guided Reading, p. 3
Geography Application: Oil Consumption in the 1970s, p. 6
Literature: from *Memories of the Ford Administration* by John Updike, p. 12

READING STUDY GUIDE, p. 247

ACCESS FOR STUDENTS ACQUIRING ENGLISH
Guided Reading (Spanish), p. 263
Geography Application: Oil Consumption in the 1970s (Spanish), p. 266

SPANISH READING STUDY GUIDE, p. 247

FORMAL ASSESSMENT
Section Quiz, p. 296

ALTERNATIVE ASSESSMENT BOOK
See forms for supporting and scoring alternative activities.

TECHNOLOGY RESOURCES

HUMANITIES TRANSPARENCIES
H30, Bicentennial celebration

GEOGRAPHY TRANSPARENCIES
G32, OPEC (Organization of Petroleum Exporting Countries)

CD-ROM *Our Times*
Grolier Multimedia Encyclopedia
Electronic Library of Primary Sources

VIDEO *American Portfolio: A Videodisc for U.S. History* user's guide, pp. 254–255

INTERNET http://www.mlushistory.com

strategies. In the end, Ford promoted a program of massive citizen action, called "Whip Inflation Now" or WIN. The president called on Americans to cut back on their use of oil and gas and to take other energy-saving measures. (See *inflation* on page 936 in the Economics Handbook.)

In the absence of incentives, though, the plan fell flat. Ford then tried to curb inflation through a "tight money" policy. He cut government spending and encouraged the Federal Reserve Board to restrict credit through higher interest rates. These actions triggered the worst economic recession in 40 years.

FORD BATTLES THE CONGRESS As Ford implemented his economic programs, he continually battled a Democratic Congress intent on pushing its own economic agenda. The Democrats called for a federal jobs program to bring down unemployment, which had climbed to 8.5 percent in 1975. Ford rejected the plan, claiming that pumping more money into the economy would only increase inflation. Throughout his term, Ford vetoed bills to fund programs for health, education, and housing. During his two years as president, Ford vetoed more than 50 pieces of legislation.

THINK THROUGH HISTORY
A. *Contrasting* *How did Congress's economic agenda differ from Ford's?*
A. Answer Members of Congress wanted a federal jobs program to reduce unemployment, but Ford claimed that such a program would increase the flow of money into the economy, spurring inflation.

In the end, Ford's economic policies received mixed reviews. Inflation had dropped below 10 percent by 1975 and continued to decline slowly. Unemployment also retreated, but by 1976 it remained stuck at around 8 percent. Ford's policies, while holding stagflation steady, seemed to offer no lasting solutions.

FORD'S FOREIGN POLICY Ford fared slightly better in the international arena. With little experience in diplomacy, he relied heavily on Henry Kissinger, who continued to hold the key position of secretary of state. Following Kissinger's advice, Ford pushed ahead with Nixon's policy of negotiation with China and the Soviet Union. In November 1974, he met with Soviet premier Leonid Brezhnev to plan the next round of arms talks. Less than a year later, he traveled to Helsinki, Finland, to discuss the future of East-West relations. There, some 35 nations, including the Soviet Union, signed the so-called Helsinki Accords—a series of agreements that promised greater cooperation between the nations of Eastern and Western Europe.

However, like presidents before him, Ford encountered trouble in Southeast Asia. In 1975, the Communist government of Cambodia seized the U.S. merchant ship *Mayagüez* in the Gulf of Siam. Ford responded with a massive show of military force. He ordered two air strikes against Cambodia and sent a crack team of U.S. marines to rescue 39 crew members aboard the ship. The total operation cost the lives of 41 U.S. troops. Most Americans applauded the action as evidence of the country's strength. However, critics argued that the mission had cost more lives than it had saved and that the president had acted without consulting Congress.

Difficult Decisions IN HISTORY

PARDONING PRESIDENT NIXON

President Ford's pardon of Richard Nixon outraged many Americans. The *New York Times* called Ford's decision "a body blow to the president's own credibility and to the public's reviving confidence in the integrity of its government."

President Ford argued that the pardon of Richard Nixon was in the country's best interest. In the event of a Watergate trial, Ford argued, "ugly passions would again be aroused. . . . And the credibility of our free institutions . . . would again be challenged at home and abroad." Ford called the pardon decision "the most difficult of my life, by far."

1. How might the country have been affected if a former United States president had gone on trial for possible criminal wrongdoing?
2. If you had been in President Ford's position, would you have pardoned Richard Nixon? Why or why not?

Jimmy Carter Enters the White House

Gerald Ford won the Republican nomination for president in 1976. However, he had to fend off a powerful conservative challenge from former California governor Ronald Reagan. Because the Republicans seemed divided over Ford's leadership, and because Ford's economic policies had failed to provide substantial relief, the Democrats confidently eyed the White House. "We could run an aardvark this year and win," predicted one Democratic leader. The Democratic nominee was indeed a surprise: a nationally unknown peanut farmer and former governor of Georgia, **Jimmy Carter.**

OBJECTIVE
(1) INSTRUCT

Ford Travels a Rough Road

▶ ***Discussing Key Ideas***
- Ford's pardon of Nixon costs Ford public support.
- Ford battles the Congress as he attempts to improve the nation's economy.
- Ford signs the Helsinki Accords and encounters trouble in Cambodia.

IN-DEPTH RESOURCES: UNIT 7
Guided Reading, p. 3

ACCESS FOR STUDENTS ACQUIRING ENGLISH
Guided Reading (Spanish), p. 263

GROLIER MULTIMEDIA ENCYCLOPEDIA
Overview of Ford's Political Career

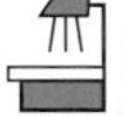
HUMANITIES TRANSPARENCIES
H30, Bicentennial celebration

DIFFICULT DECISIONS IN HISTORY
Pardoning President Nixon
Possible Responses:
1. *Some Americans might have felt vindicated, others might have felt ashamed.*
2. *Some might say that no one should be above the law; others might say that the pardon helped the nation get past the scandal.*

OBJECTIVE
(2) INSTRUCT

Jimmy Carter Enters the White House

▶ ***Discussing Key Ideas***
- Political outsider Jimmy Carter wins the 1976

(continued on next page)

TEACHING OPTIONS

Making Connections Across the Curriculum

U.S. Government Had Gerald Ford served longer, his combative relationship with Congress may have led him to veto even more bills. Remind students that the U.S. president has what is known as limited veto power. A two-thirds majority vote of both houses of Congress is required to override a presidential veto. Franklin Roosevelt, who served longer than any other president, vetoed the most bills, with a total of 635. Grover Cleveland, who served two terms, was second with 584. In third place was Harry Truman, who vetoed 250 bills sent to his desk.

Making Connections Across Time

Former President Carter As Jimmy Carter entered the White House, he probably had little idea he would be better known to some people for the life he has led since leaving the presidency. Considered one of the most active and influential former presidents in history, Carter continues to make his mark in this country and around the world. Through his organization, the Carter Center, he has launched a number of housing programs in Atlanta. Overseas, Carter has helped monitor elections in many Latin American and African countries. In 1994, he helped negotiate the removal of Haiti's military dictator.

(continued from page 801
presidential election, largely due to his personality and the nation's aversion to Washington politicians in the wake of Watergate.

KEY PLAYER
Jimmy Carter

While Jimmy Carter seemed to come from nowhere to win the 1976 presidential campaign, he in fact had had a substantial career in politics. Have students research Carter's political background and track his political ascendancy to the White House using a flow chart like the one below.

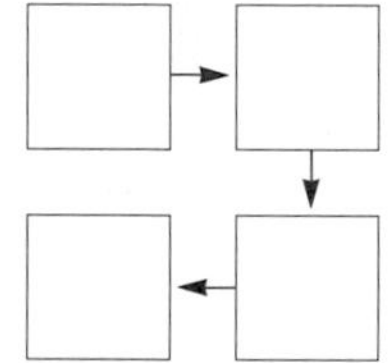

OUR TIMES
Interview with Jimmy Carter

OBJECTIVE
③ INSTRUCT

Carter's Domestic Agenda

▶ ***Discussing Key Ideas***
- Carter focuses much of his energy on improving the economy.
- Carter has limited success in battling the energy crisis, and the economy worsens as the president's measures fail to bring relief.
- Many of the nation's economic woes stem from high energy prices.

ELECTRONIC LIBRARY OF PRIMARY SOURCES
On Energy and National Goals by Jimmy Carter

KEY PLAYER

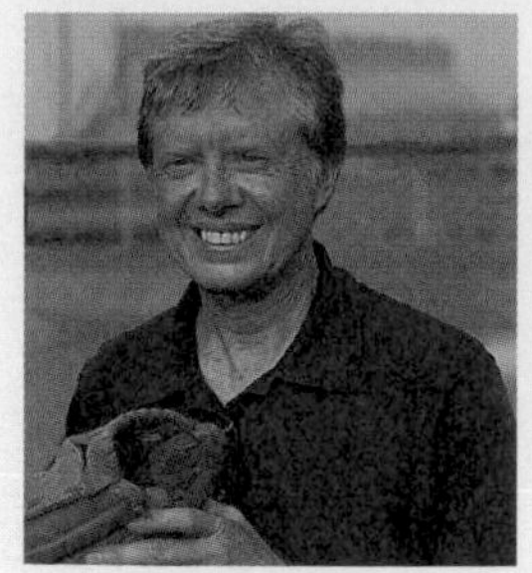

JIMMY CARTER
1924–

James Earl Carter, Jr., was born into relative prosperity. His father, Earl, owned a large farm and also ran a local store. However, Earl Carter, a disciplinarian who tried to instill a sense of hard work and responsibility in his son, refused to give Jimmy an allowance.

To earn money for himself, Carter and a friend undertook a variety of jobs. Throughout his childhood, Carter sold peanuts, ran a small hamburger and hot dog stand, collected newspapers and sold them to fish markets, and sold scrap iron.

Before entering politics, Carter joined the navy, where he excelled in electronics and naval tactics. In 1952, he joined a select group of officers who helped develop the world's first nuclear submarines. The group's commander was Captain Hyman G. Rickover. Carter later wrote that Rickover "had a profound effect on my life—perhaps more than anyone except my own parents. . . . He expected the maximum from us, but he always contributed more."

THE ELECTION OF 1976 During the post-Watergate era—in which cynicism toward the Washington establishment ran high—an outsider such as Jimmy Carter proved to be the right candidate for the time. The soft-spoken man from Plains, Georgia, promised to restore integrity to the nation's highest office. "I will never tell a lie to the American people," he said with a distinctive Southern drawl.

Throughout the presidential campaign, Carter and Ford squared off over the key issues of inflation, energy, and unemployment. However, Carter gained fewer points for his knowledge of economic issues than for his personality and sense of morality. He openly declared himself a born-again Christian, and he took pride in his pro–civil rights stance. In addition, Carter had a warm, direct campaign style. He would walk up to a stranger on the street, smile, and stick out his hand. "Hello, I'm Jimmy Carter and I'm running for president," he'd say. "I'd like your vote."

THINK THROUGH HISTORY
B. *Analyzing Causes* *What factors played a significant role in Carter's election?*

B. Answer Carter's personality and sense of morality, as well as his warm, direct campaign style.

Ford began the 1976 campaign well behind Carter in the polls. Although he narrowed the gap by election day, he could not close it. Jimmy Carter won a close election, claiming 40.8 million popular votes to Ford's 39.1 million.

GEORGIA COMES TO WASHINGTON From the very beginning, the new first family brought a down-to-earth style to Washington. Refusing the traditional limousine ride after his inauguration, Carter walked with his wife, Rosalynn, and daughter, Amy, down Pennsylvania Avenue to the White House. After settling into office, Carter stayed in touch with the people by holding Roosevelt-like "fireside chats" on radio and television. He also held "phone-ins" so that people could talk directly with their president.

However, Carter failed to reach out to Congress in a similar way. Because he had run as an outsider, Carter refused to play the "insider" game of compromise and deal making. Relying mainly on a team of advisers from Georgia, Carter even alienated himself from congressional members of his own party. Democrats on Capitol Hill often joined Republicans to sink the president's budget proposals, as well as his ambitious legislative agenda, which included major reforms of tax and welfare systems.

This campaign toy exaggerates Jimmy Carter's well-known smile and alludes to his occupation as a peanut farmer.

Carter's Domestic Agenda

Like Gerald Ford, President Carter focused much of his attention domestically on battling the country's energy and economic crises. While he met with some successes, Carter could not bring the United States out of its economic downswing.

CONFRONTING THE ENERGY CRISIS Carter considered the energy crisis to be the single most important issue facing the nation. A large part of the problem, the president believed, was America's overreliance on imported oil. On April 18, 1977, Carter sat before the nation and in a fireside chat urged his fellow Americans to cut their consumption of oil and gas.

A PERSONAL VOICE

The energy crisis has not yet overwhelmed us, but it will if we do not act quickly. It is a problem . . . likely to get progressively worse through the rest of this century. . . . Our decision about energy will test the character of the American people and the ability of the president and the Congress to govern this nation. This difficult effort will be the "moral equivalent of war," except that we will be uniting our efforts to build and not to destroy.

PRESIDENT CARTER, quoted in *Keeping Faith*

TEACHING OPTIONS

Exploring Themes

Economic Opportunity The economic anxiety that the nation began to feel under Presidents Nixon and Ford grew worse under Jimmy Carter. By 1978, the annual inflation rate had reached 7.6 percent and seemed poised to continue climbing. That year, Carter told the American people how rising inflation could adversely affect economic opportunity: "If inflation gets worse, . . . your purchasing power will continue to decline, . . . Our national productivity will suffer. The value of our dollar will continue to fall in world trade." The inflation rate did indeed get worse. By 1980, it had soared to 13.5 percent.

Teaching Less Proficient Readers

Clarifying As students read pages 802–804, help less proficient readers understand the concepts of inflation and foreign competition by providing them with everyday examples. Define inflation as an increase in prices due to an increase in the supply of money. Have students consider their experiences with inflation, such as the purchasing of gym shoes or compact discs. Next, have them consider closed stores or factories in their community. Tell them this may be an effect of foreign competition, in which some foreign-made goods outsold similar American-made items, driving U.S. companies out of business.

C. Answer The act placed a tax on gas-guzzling cars, encouraged the development of alternative energy sources, and removed price controls on oil and natural gas produced in the United States.

THINK THROUGH HISTORY
C. *Summarizing* *How did the National Energy Act help ease America's energy crisis?*

Carter asked Americans to turn down their thermostats to 65 degrees in the day and 55 degrees at night. He proposed a cabinet-level Department of Energy and presented Congress with more than 100 proposals on energy conservation and development. The battle over the president's energy policy started almost immediately. Representatives from oil- and gas-producing states fiercely resisted some of the proposals. Automobile manufacturers also lobbied against gas-rationing provisions. "It was impossible for me to imagine the bloody legislative battles we would have to win," Carter later wrote.

Out of the battle came the **National Energy Act.** The act placed a tax on gas-guzzling cars, removed price controls on oil and natural gas produced in the United States, and extended tax credits for the development of alternative energy supplies. By 1979, U.S. dependence on foreign oil had eased slightly. Private industry did its part by developing more gas-efficient automobiles and home heating systems. In addition, American citizens helped by lowering their thermostats and reinsulating their homes. A few also took advantage of a tax credit to install solar-heating panels.

THE ECONOMIC CRISIS WORSENS Unfortunately, these energy-saving measures could do little to combat a sudden new economic crisis. In the summer of 1979, renewed violence in the Middle East produced a second major fuel shortage in the United States. To make matters worse, OPEC announced another major price hike. In 1979 inflation soared from 7.6 percent to 11.3 percent. (See *inflation* on page 936 in the Economics Handbook.)

THINK THROUGH HISTORY
D. *Forming Opinions* *Do you think the government should use wage and price controls to discourage its citizens from spending money?*

D. Answer *Possible Answers:* Yes, if that is what is needed to help slow inflation. No, it goes too far in interfering with people's lives.

Faced with increasing pressure to act, Carter attempted an array of measures. He implemented voluntary wage and price freezes to slow inflation. He also tried to reduce the national debt through spending cuts. To stimulate business, Carter deregulated, or lifted government controls from, trucking, railroad, and shipping industries. To reduce the money supply, he convinced the Federal Reserve to raise interest rates.

None of these measures worked. Worse yet, Carter's scattershot approach convinced many people that he had no economic policy at all. Carter fueled this feeling of uncertainty by delivering his now-famous "malaise" speech, in which he complained of a "crisis of confidence" that had struck "at the very heart and soul of our national will." Carter's address made many Americans feel that their president had given up.

By 1980, inflation had climbed to nearly 14 percent, the highest rate since 1947. The standard of living in the United States slipped from first place to fifth place in the world. Carter's popularity slipped along with it. Polls put his approval rating at a dismal 26 percent, lower than Richard Nixon's lowest figures. The fact that this economic downswing—and Carter's inability to solve

ECONOMIC BACKGROUND

THE 1980S TEXAS OIL BOOM

The economic crisis that gripped the country in the late 1970s was largely caused by the increased cost of oil. The OPEC cartel raised the price of oil by agreeing to restrict oil production. The resulting decrease in the supply of oil in the market caused the price to go up.

Most Americans were hurt by the high energy prices. However, in areas that produced oil, such as Texas, the rise in prices led to a booming economy. Real-estate values—for land on which to drill for oil, as well as for office space in cities like Houston and Dallas—increased greatly. Young geologists right out of school collected large salaries from big oil companies. Meanwhile, the image of the hard-driving, independent Texas oil man was symbolized for much of the world by J. R. Ewing in the highly popular television show *Dallas*. (See *supply and demand* on page 939 in the Economics Handbook.)

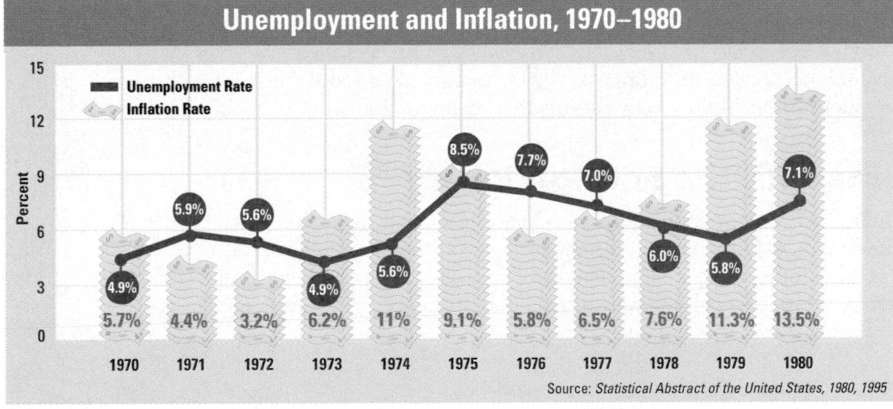

SKILLBUILDER
INTERPRETING GRAPHS
Which year saw the greatest degree of stagflation (inflation plus unemployment)?
Skillbuilder Answer 1980.

ECONOMIC BACKGROUND
The 1980s Texas Oil Boom

Critical Thinking: Hypothesizing Although the energy crisis of the 1970s was bad for the nation, the oil boom of the 1980s was good for Texas. Discuss with students other aspects of the economy that are good for part of the country, but harmful to other parts.

Extension What economic issues in the nation's past had similar regional characteristics? *Slavery and tariffs in the antebellum era.*

HISTORY FROM VISUALS
Unemployment and Inflation from 1970–1980

Reading the Graph Alert students to the two sets of data on the chart. The red line depicts the nation's unemployment rate each year between 1970 and 1980. The rows of dollar bills represent the rate of inflation during those same years.

Extension Using the latest *Statistical Abstract of the United States,* students should draw a chart like this one depicting the most recent five years of U.S. unemployment and inflation rates. Discuss with students any differences they notice between the two charts.

TEACHING OPTIONS

Making Connections Across the Curriculum

Economics Economists generally distinguish between two main types of inflation, which is defined as a sustained rise in the general price level, or a fall in the purchasing value of money. Demand-pull inflation occurs when total demand in the economy is rising faster than the production of goods and services. Because an increased demand in products normally raises their prices, the cost of many goods goes up. Cost-push inflation occurs when increases in the costs of production push prices up. This type of inflation resulted from the Middle East oil price hikes, which greatly increased the cost of producing oil-based goods.

Making Connections Across Time

The Economy and Politics Jimmy Carter would not be the only president to pay a political price for presiding over a stagnant economy. In 1992, the economy again played a key role in the defeat of an incumbent president. Throughout the election, Bill Clinton attacked President George Bush for his inability to revive the nation's stalled economy. Clinton's message resonated with the American public. According to a poll taken during the campaign, about 70 percent of the American people disapproved of Bush's handling of the economy. On election day, the nation's citizens voted Bush out of office.

HISTORY FROM VISUALS

Employment in Manufacturing and Service Industries, 1950–1994

Reading the Graph Tell students that the chart refers to the percentage of working Americans. In other words, in 1950, 60 percent of the nation's workers were employed in the service industry. By 1994, 79 percent of working Americans had jobs in the service sector.

Extension Have students consider their parents' jobs, as well as the jobs of some of their relatives and neighbors. Do they seem related to the service or manufacturing industries?

ELECTRONIC LIBRARY OF PRIMARY SOURCES
from "Victim-Victimizer: Why Excel?" by Reverend Jesse L. Jackson

A Human Rights Foreign Policy

▶ ***Discussing Key Ideas***

- Jimmy Carter rejects the philosophy of realpolitik in favor of a foreign policy based on human rights.
- Carter attempts to improve relations with Latin America by agreeing to relinquish U.S. control of the Panama Canal.
- Carter's policies lead to a breakdown in relations with the Soviet Union.

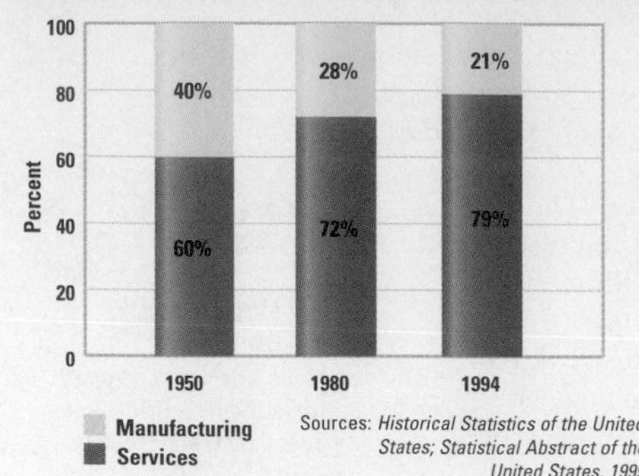

SKILLBUILDER
INTERPRETING GRAPHS
How much greater was the percentage of employment in service industries in 1994 than in 1950?
Skillbuilder Answer
19 percent.

it—visited the nation during an election year was one of the key factors in sending Ronald Reagan to the White House.

A CHANGING ECONOMY Many of the economic problems Jimmy Carter struggled with resulted from long-term trends in the economy. Since the 1950s, the rise of automation and foreign competition had reduced the number of manufacturing jobs. At the same time, the service sector of the economy expanded rapidly. This sector includes industries such as communications, transportation, and retail trade. During the 1970s, the shift toward a service-based economy accelerated, spurred on by the development of the tiny microchip that enabled computers to be cheaply mass-produced.

The rise of the service sector and the decline of manufacturing jobs meant big changes for some American workers. Workers left out of the shrinking pool of manufacturing jobs faced an increasingly complex job market. Many of the higher-paying service jobs required more education or specialized skills than did manufacturing jobs. The lower-skilled service jobs usually did not pay well.

Growing overseas competition during the 1970s caused further change in America's economy. The booming economies of West Germany and countries on the Pacific Rim (such as Japan, Taiwan, and Korea) cut into many U.S. markets. Many of the nation's primary industries—iron and steel, rubber, clothing, automobiles—had to cut back production, lay off workers, and even close plants.

Especially hard-hit were the automotive industries of the Northeast. There, high energy costs, foreign competition, and computerized production led companies to eliminate tens of thousands of jobs. As the 1970s drew to a close, a "Rustbelt" of deteriorating older industries stretched from Detroit to New York. To reduce costs, a number of corporations moved overseas or to Southern and Western states, where labor and energy costs were lower.

THINK THROUGH HISTORY
E. *Analyzing Causes* *What factors played a role in America's economic stagnation?*
E. Answer The technological revolution and growing overseas competition.

Allan Paul Bakke successfully sued the University of California at Davis, arguing that the medical school's affirmative-action policies were unconstitutional.

CARTER AND CIVIL RIGHTS Carter took special pride in his civil rights record. His administration included more African Americans and women than any before. In 1977, the president appointed civil rights leader Andrew Young as U.S. ambassador to the United Nations. Young was the first African American to hold that post. To the judicial branch alone, Carter appointed 28 African Americans, 29 women (including 6 African Americans), and 14 Latinos.

However, President Carter fell short of what many civil rights groups had expected in terms of legislation. Critics claimed that Carter—preoccupied with battles over energy and the economy—failed to give civil rights his full attention. Meanwhile, the courts began to turn against affirmative action. In 1978, the Supreme Court decided, in the case of *Regents of the University of California* v. *Bakke,* that the affirmative action policies of the university's medical school were unconstitutional. The decision made it more difficult for organizations to establish effective affirmative action programs.

A Human Rights Foreign Policy

Jimmy Carter gave a great deal of thought to human rights around the world. In fact, he based much of his foreign policy on human rights. Carter rejected the philosophy of realpolitik, the pragmatic policy of negotiating with powerful nations despite their behavior. Instead, the president strived for a foreign policy committed to human rights.

TEACHING OPTIONS

Connecting to Themes

Science and Technology The invention of the microchip, which is about the size of a fingernail, helped revolutionize American society. A microchip consists of tens of thousands of transistors on a single chip. Microchips, which can perform functions that in the past required the use of large computers, were introduced in 1971. Since then, the low cost and small size of microchips have led to their use in video games, digital watches, and microwave ovens. Microchips also have made possible the computerization of, among other things, gasoline pumps, store checkout lines, bank records, and medical instruments.

Making Connections Across Cultures

Desegregation Shortly after being elected president, Jimmy Carter became embroiled in a racial controversy surrounding the church in which he had worshiped nearly all of his life. The Plains Baptist Church did not allow African Americans, a fact that quickly came to light after Carter's presidential victory. Members of the church, including Carter, voted on the issue in an emergency meeting. The vote was 120 to 66 to admit African Americans. Carter, who voted to desegregate the church, stepped outside the old church and announced the decision to a throng of waiting reporters. "I was proud of my church," he declared.

ADVANCING HUMAN RIGHTS Jimmy Carter, like Woodrow Wilson, sought to use moral principles as a guide for U.S. foreign policy. He believed that the United States needed to commit itself to promoting **human rights**—such as the freedoms and liberties listed in the Declaration of Independence and the Bill of Rights—throughout the world.

Putting his principles into practice, President Carter cut off military aid to Argentina and Brazil, countries that had good relations with the United States but had imprisoned or tortured thousands of their own citizens. Carter followed up this action by establishing a Bureau of Human Rights in the State Department. "Human rights had become the central theme of our foreign policy in the minds of the press and public," Carter recalled. "It seemed that a spark had been ignited, and I had no inclination to douse the growing flames."

But as time went on, that flame cooled. Although many people favored Carter's idealism, supporters of the containment policy felt that the president's policy undercut allies such as Nicaragua, a dictatorial but anti-Communist country. Others argued that by supporting dictators in South Korea and the Philippines, Carter was acting inconsistently. In 1977, Carter's policies drew further criticism when his administration announced that it planned to give up ownership of the Panama Canal.

THINK THROUGH HISTORY
F. *Identifying Problems* *What problems did critics have with Carter's foreign-policy philosophy?*

F. Answer It undercut Cold War alliances, and was inconsistent in its treatment of dictators.

YIELDING THE PANAMA CANAL Since 1914, when the United States obtained full ownership of the Panama Canal, Panamanians had resented having their nation split in half by a foreign power. Shortly after 1964, President Lyndon Johnson began negotiations with the Panamanians to help ease tensions. Negotiations continued off and on into the Carter administration.

In 1977, the nations finally agreed to two treaties, one of which promised to turn over control of the Panama Canal to Panama on December 31, 1999. In 1978, the U.S. Senate, which had to ratify each treaty, approved both treaties by a vote of 68 to 32—one more vote than the required two-thirds. Public opinion also was divided. According to a Gallup poll, 45 percent of Americans favored the pacts, while 42 percent opposed them. Despite their cool reception by the American public, the treaties did bring about a warmer relationship between the United States and Latin America.

THE COLLAPSE OF DÉTENTE When Jimmy Carter took office, détente—the relaxation of tensions between the world's superpowers—had reached a high point. Beginning with President Nixon and continuing with President Ford, U.S. officials had worked to ease relations with the Communist superpowers of China and the Soviet Union.

However, Carter's firm insistence on human rights led to a breakdown in relations with the Soviet Union. President Carter's dismay over the Soviet Union's treatment of dissidents, or opponents of the government's policies, delayed a second round of SALT negotiations. President Carter and Soviet premier Leonid Brezhnev finally met in June of 1979 in Vienna, Austria, where they signed an agreement known as SALT II. Although the agreement did not reduce armaments, it did provide for limits on the number of strategic weapons and nuclear-missile launchers that each side could produce.

G. Answer Carter's concern over the Soviets' human rights violations and their invasion of Afghanistan.

THINK THROUGH HISTORY
G. *Analyzing Causes* *What led to the collapse of détente with the Soviet Union?*

The SALT II agreement, however, met sharp opposition in the Senate. Critics argued that it would put the United States at a military disadvantage. Then, in December 1979, the Soviets invaded the neighboring country of Afghanistan. When President Carter heard of the invasion, he activated the seldom-used White House–Kremlin hot line and protested to Brezhnev that the action was a "gross interference in

ON THE WORLD STAGE

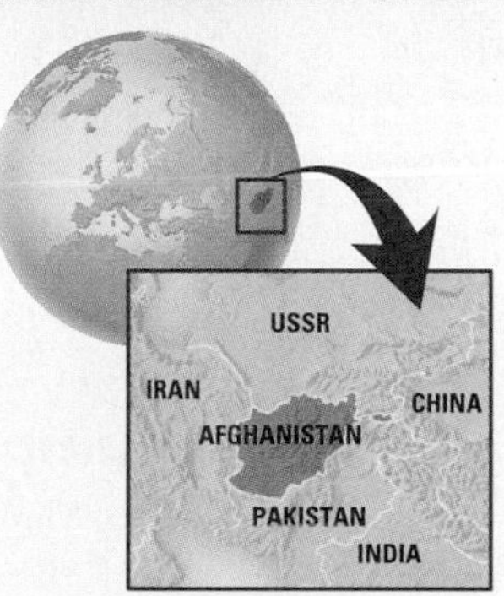
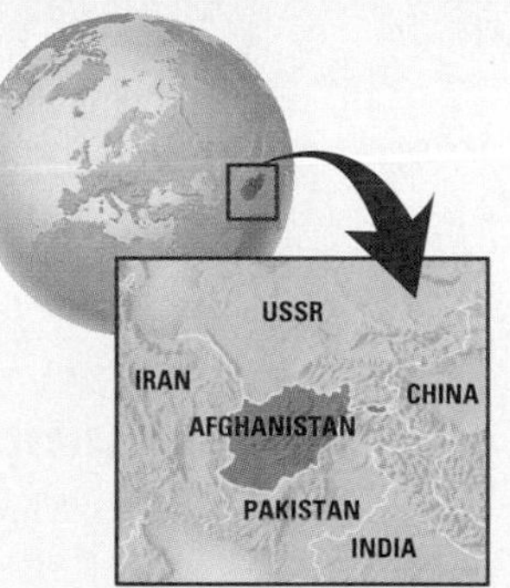

THE SOVIET–AFGHANISTAN WAR

Afghanistan, an Islamic country along the southern border of the Soviet Union, had had a pro-Soviet government for a number of years. However, a strong Muslim rebel group was intent on overthrowing the Afghan government.

Fearing that a rebel victory in Afghanistan might embolden the many Muslims living under Soviet rule, the Soviet Union sent troops to Afghanistan in late 1979 to try to crush the Muslim rebels.

While the Soviets had superior weaponry, the rebels fought the Soviets to a stalemate by using guerrilla tactics and a keen knowledge of the country's mountainous terrain.

In 1988, after suffering thousands of casualties, the Soviets began pulling out. Fighting within the country continued, and in 1992, the rebels overthrew the government. Some observers have considered Afghanistan to be "the Soviet Union's Vietnam."

ON THE WORLD STAGE
The Soviet-Afghanistan War

Critical Thinking: Summarizing After overthrowing the pro-Soviet government, the rebels began fighting among themselves for control of Afghanistan. Have students do outside research and write a brief report about the present situation in Afghanistan. Students should use the *Readers' Guide to Periodical Literature* for source information.

MORE ABOUT . . .
The Collapse of Détente

One of the more widely publicized events involving the breakdown of U.S.-Soviet relations was the correspondence between Carter and Soviet dissident Andrei Sakharov. Sakharov was a famous nuclear scientist who had been punished for his calls for political and social freedom. Sakharov wrote to Carter, asking him "to defend those who suffer because of their nonviolent struggle, for openness, . . ." Carter wrote back, "You may rest assured that the American people and our government will continue our firm commitment to promote respect for human rights not only in our own country but also abroad."

Block Schedule TEACHING OPTION **Time Needed: 20 Minutes**

Cooperative Activity: Writing a United Nations Speech for President Carter

Task: Students will act as speech writers for President Carter and write speeches for him to deliver before the United Nations regarding several foreign policy issues.

Purpose: To explore in depth Carter's responses to foreign policy issues he faced.

Activity: Divide students into groups of four or five. Have each group prepare a speech for President Carter on one of the following topics: the advancement of a human rights foreign policy; granting Panama control of the Panama Canal; or the collapse of détente with the Soviet Union. Have group members assign each other specific tasks. For example, several students will do further research on the topic; other students will write the speech; and another student will give the speech before the class.

Building a Portfolio: Students adding speeches to their portfolio should attach a note pointing out their contribution.

ALTERNATIVE ASSESSMENT BOOK
Standards for Evaluating a Cooperative Activity

Standards for Evaluation
Speeches should . . .

- show clear understanding of the topic
- express President Carter's point of view
- contain specific details and evidence to support the President's stance

HISTORY FROM VISUALS

Middle East, 1978–1982

Reading the Map Point out to students what the inset map depicts. *A close-up look at Israel and its neighboring countries.* Also, make sure students see where the inset area sits on the larger map.

Extension Ask students to look at the inset map and discuss why there might be so much tension between Israelis and the Palestinians living in the West Bank and Gaza Strip. *Possible Responses: The Israelis are basically living among the Palestinians whom they are controlling.*

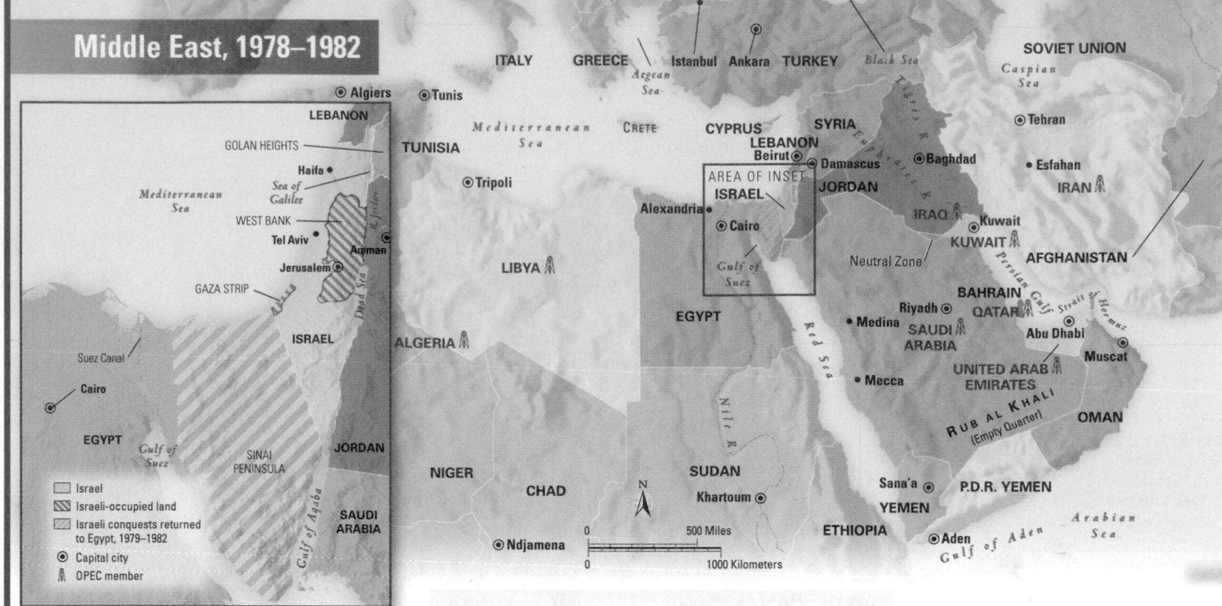

GEOGRAPHY SKILLBUILDER **LOCATION** *What OPEC countries are shown on the map?*

Skillbuilder Answer Iran, Iraq, Saudi Arabia, Algeria, Qatar, Kuwait, United Arab Emirates, and Libya.

the internal affairs of Afghanistan." As a result of the invasion, Carter refused to fight for the SALT II agreement, and the treaty died.

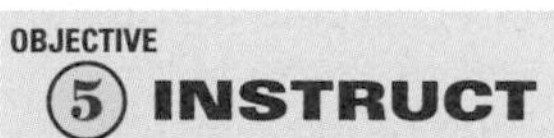

OBJECTIVE

(5) INSTRUCT

Triumph and Crisis in the Middle East

▶ ***Discussing Key Ideas***
- President Carter helps forge a peace between the rival nations of Israel and Egypt.
- Rebels in Iran overthrow their government and take 52 Americans hostage.
- The Carter administration spends more than a year negotiating for the hostages' release.

GEOGRAPHY TRANSPARENCIES
G32, OPEC (Organization of Petroleum Exporting Countries)

IN-DEPTH RESOURCES: UNIT 7
Geography Application: Oil Consumption in the 1970s, p. 6

Triumph and Crisis in the Middle East

Through long gasoline lines and high energy costs, Americans became all too aware of the troubles in the Middle East. In that area of ethnic, religious, and economic conflict, Jimmy Carter achieved one of his greatest diplomatic triumphs—and suffered his most tragic defeat.

A jubilant President Carter shakes hands with President Anwar el-Sadat of Egypt *(left)* and Prime Minister Menachem Begin of Israel *(right)* after the two Middle East leaders reached a peace agreement.

THE CAMP DAVID ACCORDS Jimmy Carter enjoyed a shining moment in a historic handshake between two long-time enemies—Egyptian president Anwar el-Sadat and Israeli prime minister Menachem Begin. Through negotiation and arm-twisting, Carter helped forge a peace between the two nations that marked the first major break in Middle Eastern hostilities since the creation of Israel in 1948.

In 1974, Henry Kissinger's shuttle diplomacy had helped end the Yom Kippur War between Egypt and Israel. At that time, Sadat and Begin had begun discussing an overall peace between the two nations. In the summer of 1978, Carter seized on the peace initiative. When the peace talks stalled, Carter invited Sadat and Begin to Camp David, the presidential retreat in Maryland.

THINK THROUGH HISTORY
H. *Making Inferences* *How might the Nixon administration's efforts have helped President Carter forge the Camp David Accords?*
H. Answer Kissinger's shuttle diplomacy initiated peace talks between Egypt and Israel.

After 13 days of intense negotiations, the three leaders reached two agreements known as the **Camp David Accords.** The first agreement provided for a five-year transition period during which Israel and Jordan would work out the issue of self-rule for the Palestinians, Arabs living on the West Bank and Gaza Strip—areas captured by Israel during earlier wars. The second agreement was aimed specifically at end-

TEACHING OPTIONS

Making Connections Across Time

Middle East Peace In 1993, peace in the Middle East took a giant step forward when Israel and the Palestinians signed a historic agreement giving the Palestinians self-rule in the Israeli-occupied lands where they live. As a result of the agreement, the Palestinians now govern Israel's West Bank and Gaza Strip. For years, Israel and the Palestine Liberation Organization had each claimed ownership of the lands and had waged bloody battles for their control. In 1997, the agreement was still being implemented, as the Israeli pullout from the West Bank region remained slow and painstaking.

Teaching Gifted and Talented Students

Exploring the Hostage Crisis Hamilton Jordan was an adviser to President Carter and later his Chief of Staff. His book, *Crisis, The Last Year of the Carter Presidency,* presents an inside look at the Carter administration's handling of events such as the Soviet invasion of Afghanistan and the hostage crisis in Iran. Have interested students read excerpts from the book that deal with the hostage crisis. Students then should write a brief report on what new insights they learned about the handling of the hostage crisis. In addition, have students evaluate Carter's handling of the hostage crisis using evidence to support their opinion. What, if anything, would they have done differently?

ing hostilities between Israel and Egypt. During a White House ceremony in March of 1979, Sadat and Begin signed a detailed peace treaty based on the accords. Under the treaty, Israel agreed to withdraw from the Sinai Peninsula, which it had seized from Egypt during the Six-Day War in 1967. In exchange, Egypt became the first Arab nation to recognize Israel's existence as a nation.

The treaty left many issues unresolved. For example, the document said little about the independence claims of Palestinians. Joking at the hard work ahead, Carter wrote playfully in his diary, "I resolved to do everything possible to get out of the negotiating business!" Little did the president know that his next Middle East negotiation would be his most painful.

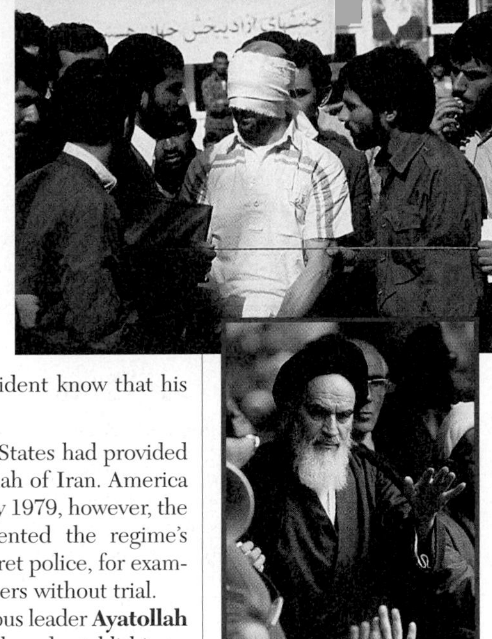

U.S. hostages were blindfolded and paraded through the streets of Tehran *(top)*. Iran's ruler, Ayatollah Ruhollah Khomeini *(above)*, supported the taking of the hostages.

THE IRAN HOSTAGE CRISIS Since the 1950s, the United States had provided political and military assistance to the government of the shah of Iran. America wanted an ally against communism and access to Iran's oil. By 1979, however, the shah's regime was in deep trouble. Many Iranians resented the regime's widespread corruption and dictatorial tactics. The shah's secret police, for example, tortured thousands of prisoners and executed many others without trial.

THINK THROUGH HISTORY
I. *Analyzing Issues* *How was Carter's treatment of the shah of Iran inconsistent with his foreign-policy philosophy?*

I. Answer Carter supported the shah, even though his regime was repressive and abusive toward its citizens.

In January 1979, revolution broke out. The Muslim religious leader **Ayatollah Ruhollah Khomeini** led the rebels in overthrowing the shah and establishing a religious state based on strict obedience to the Qur'an, the sacred book of Islam. Carter had supported the shah until the very end. In October of 1979, the president allowed the shah to enter the United States for cancer treatment.

The act infuriated the revolutionaries of Iran. On November 4, 1979, armed students seized the U.S. embassy in Tehran and took 52 Americans hostage. The militants demanded that the United States send the shah back to Iran in return for the release of the hostages.

Carter refused, and a painful year-long standoff followed. The president banned all trade with Iran and eventually severed diplomatic relations with the nation. Through it all, the United States continued quiet but intense efforts to free the hostages. Those efforts finally paid off in late 1980. However, because of last-minute delays and perhaps deliberate stalling by the Iranians, the hostages were not released until January 20, 1981, shortly after the new president, Ronald Reagan, took the oath of office.

Despite the hostages' release after 444 days in captivity, the crisis in Iran seemed to underscore the limits that Americans faced during the 1970s. Americans also realized during the 1970s that there were limits to the nation's environmental resources. This realization prompted both citizens and the government to actively address environmental concerns.

Section 3 Assessment

1. TERMS & NAMES
Identify:
- Gerald R. Ford
- Jimmy Carter
- National Energy Act
- human rights
- Camp David Accords
- Ayatollah Ruhollah Khomeini

2. FOLLOWING CHRONOLOGICAL ORDER Create a time line of the major events of the Ford and Carter administrations, using a form such as the one below.

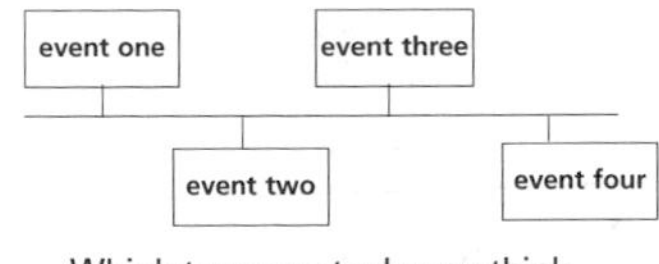

Which two events do you think were the most important? Why?

3. COMPARING AND CONTRASTING How were the actions taken by Presidents Ford and Carter to address the country's economic downturn similar? How did they differ?

THINK ABOUT
- Ford's "Whip Inflation Now" policy
- Carter's "moral equivalent of a war" speech
- Carter's legislative agenda

4. FORMING OPINIONS Do you agree with President Carter that human rights concerns should steer U.S. foreign policy? Why or why not?

THINK ABOUT
- the responsibility of promoting human rights
- the loss of good relations with certain countries
- the collapse of détente with the Soviet Union

ANSWERS

1. TERMS & NAMES
Gerald R. Ford, p. 800
Jimmy Carter, p. 801
National Energy Act, p. 803
human rights, p. 805
Camp David Accords, p. 806
Ayatollah Ruhollah Khomeini, p. 807

2. FOLLOWING CHRONOLOGICAL ORDER
Possible Answers:
Sept. 8, 1974: Ford pardons Nixon.
1975: Helsinki Accords signed.
1977: U.S. and Panama sign treaty.
March 1979: Sadat and Begin sign peace treaty.
Dec. 1979: Soviets invade Afghanistan.
Nov. 4, 1979: Iranians seize U.S. hostages.
1980: 14 percent inflation.

3. COMPARING AND CONTRASTING
Both emphasized the importance of energy conservation; both had trouble working with Congress; and both were largely unsuccessful. Ford put more emphasis on voluntary citizen action while Carter emphasized government action.

4. FORMING OPINIONS
Students may agree with President Carter and argue that the United States has a duty to stand up for human rights throughout the world. Others may disagree and contend that a strict foreign policy of any kind drives away allies and that the U.S. supported some countries with poor human rights records.

MORE ABOUT . . .
Anwar el-Sadat

Although Sadat won praise in the West for his peacemaking efforts, other Arab leaders and many of his fellow Egyptians assailed him for negotiating with Israel. Sadat's popularity in Egypt continued to plummet due to a worsening economic crisis and his suppression of growing dissent. On October 6, 1981, Muslim extremists opposed to his policies assassinated Sadat as he reviewed a military parade in Cairo.

ASSESS & RETEACH

Section 3 Assessment

Have students work in small groups to answer the questions. Ask the groups who agreed with President Carter in question 4 to hold an informal debate with the groups that disagreed with the president's policies.

Self-Assessment

Have students copy the title of this chapter on a sheet of paper: "An Age of Limits." Underneath, have them write what limits they believe Presidents Ford and Carter faced.

Section Quiz

FORMAL ASSESSMENT
Section Quiz, p. 296

Reteach

Have students work in pairs to summarize the main ideas of the text under each large red heading.

CLOSE

As Presidents Ford and Carter worked to move the country past the Watergate scandal, both men struggled in their attempts to fix the nation's worsening economy. On the world stage, President Carter guided a foreign policy based on human rights.

Section 4 Overview

OBJECTIVES

1. To summarize the origins of the environmental movement.
2. To identify key environmental issues in the 1970s.
3. To explain the goals of the continuing environmental movement.

CRITICAL THINKING

- Recognizing effects, pp. 809, 810
- Forming opinions, p. 811
- Theme: Science and Technology, p. 812
- Finding main ideas, p. 813
- Summarizing, p. 813
- Analyzing causes, p. 813

FOCUS & MOTIVATE

5-MINUTE WARM-UP

Distinguishing Fact from Nonfact

To understand the origins of the modern environmental movement, have students read the Key Player on page 809 and answer these questions.

1. Is it a fact or not a fact that Carson was born in Springdale, Pennsylvania?
2. Is it a fact or not a fact that poverty made Carson quiet and aloof?

WARM-UP TRANSPARENCY 24

▶ ***Starting with the Student***
Watch the video "Poisoned Playground" to see how one American fought for a safer environment in her town.

- Using the *Teacher's Resource Book* as a guide, hold a class discussion, explore the issues surrounding the crisis at Love Canal, and engage in extension activities using key primary sources.

***AMERICAN STORIES* video series**
"Poisoned Playground"
Videocassette: Volume 5

Videodisc: Disc 3, Side B, Chapter 4

IN-DEPTH RESOURCES: UNIT 9
Primary Source: from *Love Canal: My Story* by Lois Gibbs, p. 10

4 Environmental Activism

TERMS & NAMES
- Rachel Carson
- Earth Day
- environmentalist
- Environmental Protection Agency
- Three Mile Island

LEARN ABOUT America's efforts during the 1970s to address its environmental problems
TO UNDERSTAND how the nation attempted to strike a balance between environmental concerns and continued industrial growth.

ONE AMERICAN'S STORY

In 1973, Lois Gibbs and her family moved to Niagara Falls, New York, which Gibbs described as a "typical American small town." However, underneath this quiet town was a disaster in the making. In the 1890s, the Love Canal had been built to provide hydroelectric power for the Niagara Falls area. The canal ended up being used as a place for chemical companies to dump waste. In 1953, bulldozers filled in the canal. A school and rows of homes were built nearby.

From the day the school opened, parents complained of nauseous odors and black sludge near the grounds. In 1977, when Lois Gibbs's son fell sick, she decided to investigate the school's problems. Frustrated at nearly every turn, Gibbs refused to give up. She eventually uncovered the existence of the toxic waste site and mobilized the community to demand government action. In 1980, President Jimmy Carter authorized funds for many of Niagara Falls's families to move to safety. Years later, Lois Gibbs wrote a book detailing her efforts.

A PERSONAL VOICE

I want to tell you our story—my story—because I believe that ordinary citizens—using the tools of dignity, self-respect, common sense, and perseverance—can influence solutions to important problems in our society. . . . In solving any difficult problem, you have to be prepared to fight long and hard, sometimes at great personal cost; but it can be done. It must be done if we are to survive as a democratic society—indeed, if we are to survive at all.

LOIS GIBBS, *Love Canal: My Story*

Lois Gibbs

While her courage and determination were unique, Lois Gibbs's concerns about environmental hazards were shared by many Americans in the late 1970s. Through the Arab oil embargo and the OPEC price increases, Americans learned that their natural resources were not limitless. Many also realized that they also could no longer take the environment for granted. Throughout the 1970s, Americans—from grassroots organizations to the government—began a concerted effort to address the nation's environmental concerns.

POISONED PLAYGROUND
Lois Gibbs and the Crisis at Love Canal

The Roots of Environmentalism

Although many Americans began mobilizing in the 1970s to protect the environment, the realization that urban growth and industrial development were damaging the nation's natural resources had actually begun a decade earlier. In particular, a shocking book had awakened America's concerns about the environment and helped lay the groundwork for the activism of the 1970s.

This button was used to promote Earth Day.

RACHEL CARSON AND *SILENT SPRING* In 1962, **Rachel Carson,** a marine biologist, published a book entitled *Silent Spring.* In it, she attacked the growing use of pesticides—chemicals used to kill insects and rodents. Many owners of large farms sprayed a variety of pesticides on their crops to keep hungry insects from devouring their harvest. Carson argued that pesticides poisoned the very food they were intended to protect and as a result killed many birds and fish.

In her book, Carson warned that America faced a "silent spring," in which birds killed off by pesticides would no longer fill the air with song. "It was a

SECTION 4 RESOURCES

PRINT RESOURCES

IN-DEPTH RESOURCES: UNIT 7
Guided Reading, p. 4
Skillbuilder Practice: Analyzing Assumptions, p. 5
Primary Sources: from *Love Canal: My Story* by Lois Gibbs, p. 10; from *Silent Spring* by Rachel Carson, p. 11

READING STUDY GUIDE, p. 249

ACCESS FOR STUDENTS ACQUIRING ENGLISH
Guided Reading (Spanish), p. 264
Skillbuilder Practice: Analyzing Assumptions (Spanish), p. 265

SPANISH READING STUDY GUIDE, p. 249

FORMAL ASSESSMENT
Section Quiz, p. 297

ALTERNATIVE ASSESSMENT BOOK
See forms for supporting and scoring alternative activities.

TECHNOLOGY RESOURCES

CD-ROM *Our Times*
Grolier Multimedia Encyclopedia
Electronic Library of Primary Sources

VIDEO *American Stories* video series
American Portfolio: A Videodisc for U.S. History user's guide, p. 255

INTERNET http://www.mlushistory.com

spring without voices," she wrote. "On the mornings that had once throbbed with the dawn chorus of robins, catbirds, doves, jays, wrens and scores of other bird voices there was now no sound; only silence lay over the fields and woods and marsh." Carson argued that one pesticide in particular, DDT, was a threat even to humans. She contended that DDT, which is very slow to decay, made its way through the entire food chain—from plants to animals and ultimately to human beings.

Within six months of its publication, *Silent Spring* sold nearly half a million copies. It also prompted an immediate counterattack from many chemical companies, which attacked the book as inaccurate and threatened legal action against Carson. However, for a majority of Americans, Carson's book was an awakening to the danger that human activity posed to the natural environment. "There's no doubt about the impact of *Silent Spring;* it's a real shocker," declared a reviewer of the book. People throughout the country wrote to their representatives in Congress and to the president, demanding an investigation into the nation's pesticide use. Shortly after the book's publication, President Kennedy established an advisory committee to investigate the situation.

With Rachel Carson's prodding, the nation slowly began to focus more on environmental issues. In 1963, Congress passed the Clean Air Act, which regulated automotive and industrial emissions. Although Carson would not live to see the U.S. government outlaw DDT in 1972, her work helped many Americans realize that their everyday behavior, as well as the nation's industrial growth, had a damaging effect on the environment.

A. Answer It heightened Americans' awareness that many of their activities were potentially harmful to the environment.

THINK THROUGH HISTORY
A. *Recognizing Effects* *What effects did Rachel Carson's book have on the nation as a whole?*

KEY PLAYER

RACHEL CARSON
1907–1964

The marine biologist Rachel Carson was born far from the sea, in the small town of Springdale, Pennsylvania. She grew up with a brother and a sister in a two-story wooden house that had no plumbing, no furnace, and no electricity.

Carson was a sickly child who often had to remain at home, where her mother tutored her. Throughout her youth and into her college years, Carson was a studious, but quiet and aloof, person. "She just wasn't social," remembered a classmate. "Being poor had some bearing on that. She didn't have the clothes or the extra things a girl needed at college then."

Carson entered college intent on becoming a writer. During her sophomore year, she took a biology class to fulfill her science requirement. She quickly fell in love with the study of nature, and the next year she switched her major from English to science.

Environmental Concerns in the 1970s

Throughout the 1970s, the administrations of Richard Nixon and Jimmy Carter, along with numerous grassroots organizations, confronted such environmental issues as pollution, conservation, and the growth of nuclear energy.

Demonstrators gather in New York City's Central Park for the first Earth Day in 1970.

THE FIRST EARTH DAY The United States ushered in the 1970s—a decade in which it would actively address its environmental issues—fittingly enough with the first **Earth Day** celebration. In late 1969, Wisconsin's Senator Gaylord Nelson had suggested that Americans set aside April 22, 1970, as a day of serious discussion of environmental problems. On that day, nearly every community in the nation and more than 10,000 schools and 2,000 colleges hosted some type of environmental-awareness activity. The organizers of the first Earth Day, many of whom were antiwar and civil rights activists, spotlighted such problems as pollution, the growth of toxic waste, and the earth's dwindling resources.

The Earth Day celebration has endured. Each year on April 22, millions of people around the world gather to heighten public awareness of environmental problems.

THE GOVERNMENT TAKES ACTION President Nixon was not considered an **environmentalist,** or someone who takes an active role in advocating measures to protect the environment. However, Nixon recognized the nation's growing concern about the environment. In his 1970 State of the Union address he declared, "The great

OBJECTIVE
① INSTRUCT

The Roots of Environmentalism

▶ ***Discussing Key Ideas***
- Rachel Carson's *Silent Spring* prompts the nation to begin addressing environmental issues.

IN-DEPTH RESOURCES: UNIT 7
Guided Reading, p. 4

ACCESS FOR STUDENTS ACQUIRING ENGLISH
Guided Reading (Spanish), p. 264

KEY PLAYER
Rachel Carson

Critical Thinking: Comparing and Contrasting Some historians have compared *Silent Spring* to Harriet Beecher Stowe's *Uncle Tom's Cabin,* which awoke much of the nation to the horrors of slavery with its publication in 1852. Explore with students the effects of each book on society. Do students agree with the analogy? Why or why not?

IN-DEPTH RESOURCES: UNIT 7
Primary Source: from *Silent Spring* by Rachel Carson, p. 11

 ***GROLIER MULTIMEDIA ENCYCLOPEDIA***
Interview with Rachel Carson

OBJECTIVE
② INSTRUCT

Environmental Concerns in the 1970s

▶ ***Discussing Key Ideas***
- From the government to grass-roots groups, Americans in the 1970s

(continued on next page)

TEACHING OPTIONS

Exploring Themes

Science and Technology Technology, which some people consider a curse, has recently begun to play a key role in protecting the environment. America's scientific know-how—which spurred the creation of booming industries and the invention of the automobile—has also led to the development of such things as cleaner burning fuel and environmentally safe factory equipment. Science and technology now play the dual role of aiding the country's industrial and economic growth and helping in the fight to better protect our environment from the negative effects of such growth and progress.

Making Global Connections

Greenpeace Possibly the best known international environmental organization is Greenpeace. Founded in 1969 by a group of Canadian environmentalists, Greenpeace works to call attention to the world's environmental hazards. One reason the group is well known is its confrontational style. Greenpeace members often attempt to interfere with activities they consider to be harmful to the environment. The group's methods have sometimes drawn the wrath of governments. In 1985, France sunk a Greenpeace boat to prevent it from sailing into waters where the French were testing nuclear weapons.

(continued from page 809)

begin to more aggressively address environmental problems.
- The debate over nuclear energy intensifies after an accident at the Three Mile Island nuclear power plant.

NOW AND THEN

Air Pollution in California

▶ ***Starting with the Student***
- Ask students to consider places where they have endured air pollution. Was it alongside a passing bus? In an area of town with numerous factories?
- How did the pollution affect them? Did the odor offend them? Did the smoke make them cough?
- Ask students what they think eventually happens to air pollution.

▶ ***Discussing Key Ideas***
- There are two main types of waste matter that pollute the air. One type is particles of liquid or solid matter, such as lead. The other is gases, such as carbon monoxide.
- The biggest sources of air pollution are fuel combustion in cars, airplanes, homes, and factories.
- California—whose high population density and heavy traffic have created some of the most polluted air in the country—has led the way in passing laws to protect the environment.

ELECTRONIC LIBRARY OF PRIMARY SOURCES

"Principles of Environmental Justice" by People of Color Environmental Leadership

question of the seventies is: Shall we surrender to our surroundings or shall we make our peace with nature and begin to make reparations for the damage we have done to our air, to our land and to our water?"

President Nixon set out on a course that led to the passage of several landmark measures to protect the environment. In 1970, he consolidated 15 existing federal pollution programs into the **Environmental Protection Agency** (EPA). The new agency was given the power to set and enforce pollution standards, to conduct environmental research, and to assist state and local governments in pollution control. Today, the EPA remains the federal government's main instrument for dealing with environmental issues.

Nixon also signed a new Clean Air Act in 1970. The act gave the nation's industries five years to meet new pollution standards, including a mandate that automakers reduce the tailpipe emissions of their new cars by 90 percent. When automakers complained that they would be unable to meet this goal by 1975, the EPA extended the deadline to the 1980s. Automakers eventually complied by introducing the catalytic converter (which changes tailpipe pollutants into less harmful substances). The use of catalytic converters also forced consumers to use gasoline free of additives containing lead, a harmful pollutant.

Following the 1970 Clean Air Act, Congress passed laws that limited pesticide use, protected endangered species, and curbed strip mining—the practice

B. Answer Reducing automobile emissions by 90 percent by the 1980s.

THINK THROUGH HISTORY
B. Recognizing Effects *What was one eventual result of the Clean Air Act of 1970?*

NOW & THEN

Air Pollution in California

The term *air pollution* often makes people think of brown smog suffocating a city like a thick woolen blanket, but not all air pollution is so dramatically visible. Two types of waste matter pollute the air. One is particulates—particles of liquid or solid matter, such as lead. The other is gases, such as carbon monoxide, sulfur oxides, and nitrogen oxides. Nitrogen oxides react with other gases and sunlight to form ozone, a pollutant that causes respiratory problems.

The biggest sources of air pollution are fuel combustion in cars, airplanes, homes, factories, and power plants and the byproducts of industrial processes such as smelting ore and refining oil. Certain weather conditions can cause these pollutants to accumulate over cities in dangerous levels or to become visible as smog.

Southern California, because of its high population density and heavy traffic, has long had some of the most polluted air in the country. To counteract this, the state of California has been a pioneer in passing laws to protect the environment.

1974

Los Angeles has had serious problems with air pollution since the 1950s. The federal government's Clean Air Acts of 1965 and 1970 sought to help people in cities like Los Angeles by establishing stricter emission standards for automobiles and by requiring factories to reduce their sulfur oxide emissions. In addition, since 1970 California has had the strictest motor-vehicle emissions standards in the nation.

Environmental Progress in Los Angeles Region

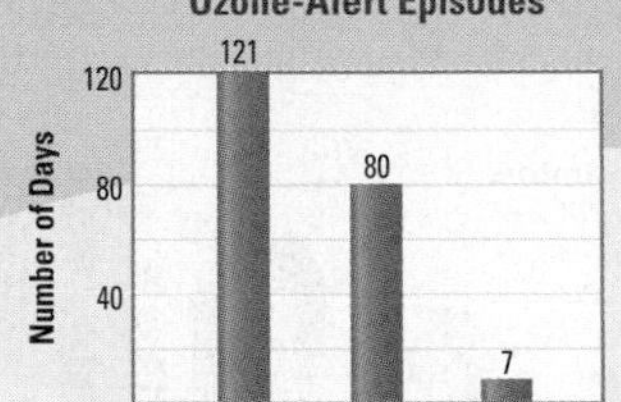

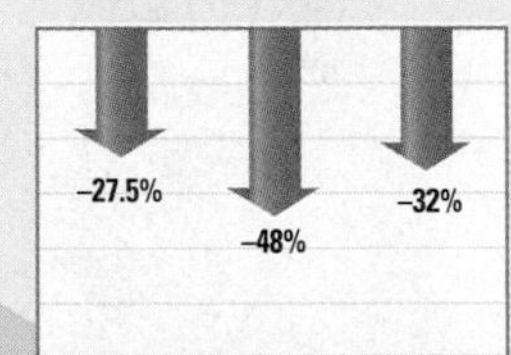

Source: California Air Resources Board

Southern California has experienced a steady improvement in air quality since 1976. Since that time, most U.S. cars have been equipped with catalytic converters, which greatly reduce the harmful emissions of individual automobiles.

TEACHING OPTION

Skillbuilder Mini-Lesson: Analyzing Assumptions

Explaining the Skill People and governments make decisions and take actions based on many things, including their assumptions, or beliefs that they take for granted. Examining the background and philosophy of a person or government can help historians understand the assumptions that lie behind historical actions.

Applying the Skill: Environmental Protection Refer students to the three paragraphs beginning on this page with "President Nixon set out . . .". Then ask them to analyze the assumptions behind the following actions:

1. Creation of the Environmental Protection Agency. *Government has a role in protecting the environment.*
2. Passage of the Clean Air Act of 1970. *Industries must take responsibility for addressing air pollution.*
3. Conservative complaints that new environmental laws burden business too much. *Good business is more important than a better environment.*
4. Liberal complaints that environmental laws do not go far enough. *Government should do whatever is necessary to ensure a clean environment.*

IN-DEPTH RESOURCES: UNIT 7
Skillbuilder Practice: Analyzing Assumptions, p. 5

of mining for ore and coal by digging gaping holes in the land. While it made significant advances in environmental protection, the Nixon administration failed to fully satisfy either the conservative or the liberal element of society. Conservatives complained that the new environmental laws placed too great a burden on business, and liberals contended that the new legislation did not go far enough.

BALANCING PROGRESS AND CONSERVATION IN ALASKA During the 1970s, the federal government took steps to ensure the continued well-being of the nation's largest, and one of its most ecologically sensitive, states. In 1968, the Atlantic Richfield Company announced the discovery of a gigantic oil field along Alaska's Arctic coast. In 1974, construction began on a pipeline to carry the oil 800 miles to the ice-free ports of the state's southern coast. The discovery of oil and the subsequent construction of a massive system to transport it created many new jobs and greatly increased state revenues.

However, the influx of new development also raised concerns about Alaska's wildlife environment, as well as the rights of its native peoples. In 1971, Nixon signed the Alaska Native Claims Settlement Act, which turned over millions of acres of land to the state's native tribes for conservation and tribal purposes. In 1978, President Carter enhanced this conservation effort by setting aside an additional 56 million acres in Alaska as national monuments. In 1980, Congress added another 104 million acres to the state's protected conservation areas.

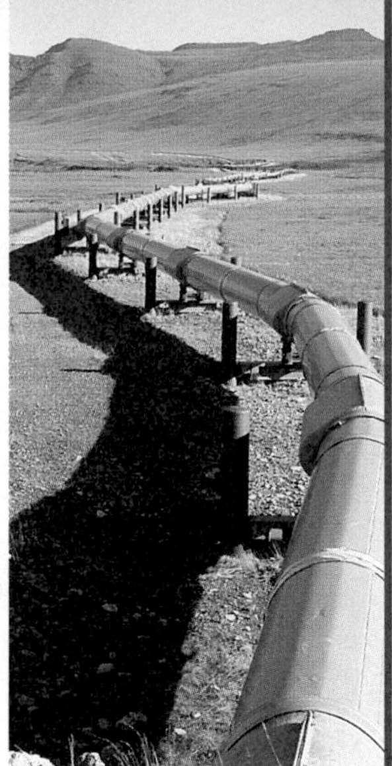

The Alaskan Pipeline stretches across hundreds of miles of tundra. Construction of the pipeline was completed in 1977 at a cost of $8 billion. In 1980, the high revenues from the oil allowed Alaska to abolish state income taxes for its residents.

1996

In 1996, California pioneered a new pollution-fighting measure by requiring the use of cleaner-burning gasoline in motor vehicles. Although more expensive, cleaner-burning gasoline immediately reduced pollution emissions. The California EPA estimated that ozone levels during the summer of 1996 were 18 percent lower than those in 1994 and 1995.

INTERACT WITH HISTORY

1. **FORMING OPINIONS** In your opinion, should all states adopt the California law requiring the use of cleaner-burning gasoline? Explain your answer by citing both the costs and benefits of adopting such legislation.

SEE SKILLBUILDER HANDBOOK, PAGE 919.

2. **RESEARCHING** Research another environmental problem, such as water pollution, indoor air pollution, toxic waste disposal, or global warming. Create a chart showing what measures have been taken to deal with the problem and whether the problem has improved or worsened. Present your chart to the class.

Visit http://www.mlushistory.com for more about environmentalism.

THE DEBATE OVER NUCLEAR ENERGY As the 1970s came to a close, Americans became acutely aware of the dangers that nuclear power plants posed to both humans and the environment. Since the 1950s, nuclear power advocates had argued that nuclear energy was the energy of the future. It was cheap, plentiful, and, they argued, environmentally safe. They pointed to years of safe operation at nuclear plants and called for larger and more powerful plants to meet the nation's growing energy needs. During the 1970s, as America realized the drawbacks to its heavy dependence on foreign oil for energy, nuclear power seemed an attractive alternative.

However, opponents of nuclear energy warned against the industry's growth. They contended that nuclear plants, and the wastes they produced, were potentially dangerous to humans and their environment. The construction of more nuclear power plants, they argued, increased the likelihood of accidents, which could lead to the accidental release of deadly radiation into the air.

THREE MILE ISLAND In the early hours of March 28, 1979, the concerns of nuclear energy opponents appeared to come true. That morning, one of the nuclear reactors at a plant on **Three Mile Island** near

MORE ABOUT . . .
Air Pollution

Some of the air pollution from cars and factories eventually returns to earth in the form of acid rain. Acid rain is a term for snow or rain that is polluted by certain chemical compounds in air pollution. Acid rain forms when water vapors in the clouds react with such acids as sulfuric acid and nitric acid. Acid rain harms lakes, rivers, and streams, killing fish and other aquatic life. Scientists believe it also damages forests and soil, as well as buildings and bridges.

OUR TIMES
Essay on 1970s and Environmentalism by Stephen Jay Gould

MORE ABOUT . . .
Nuclear Energy

One issue still concerns many people about nuclear energy: how to dispose of the radioactive waste created in producing nuclear energy. In 1995, the nation's 109 nuclear power plants were continuing to store their nuclear waste on site. However, observers believe that nearly one-third of the plants will run out of storage room before the end of the century. The government is searching for a permanent site to dump dangerous waste but does not expect to have a permanent burial site ready until 2010 at the earliest. One plan calls for burying the waste deep beneath the Yucca Mountains in southern Nevada about 100 miles northwest of Las Vegas.

INTERACT WITH HISTORY

1. Forming Opinions

Possible Responses:
Yes, it may cost a bit more at the gas pump, but cleaner air is worth it. Critics concerned about the cost should realize that increased air pollution could cause long-term health effects for many people, and that would be an even greater cost to society. No, most cars are already equipped with catalytic converters, which greatly reduce the harmful emissions from automobiles. Cleaner gasoline will not make that much difference, and besides, citizens should be able to buy the gasoline of their choice.

2. Researching

In researching an environmental problem, students might consult a number of possible sources, including:

1. Library resources, such as the *Readers' Guide to Periodical Literature,* newspaper indexes, and text indexes.
2. The web site of an individual state's Environmental Protection Agency or the U.S. Environmental Protection Agency.
3. The state or federal EPA office.

MORE ABOUT . . .
Nuclear Accidents

The world's worst nuclear reactor accident occurred on April 26, 1986, at the Chernobyl nuclear power plant in Ukraine, which was then part of the Soviet Union. "What happened was very simple," said a plant worker. "There was an explosion. . . . Fifteen seconds later there was a sudden shock, and a few seconds later a stronger shock." The blast released large amounts of radiation into the air. Soviet officials reported that 31 people died immediately and more than 200 others were hospitalized. However, the accident's legacy lives on in increased cancer rates and birth defects in the region. The Chernobyl plant continues to operate, but the surrounding city—which remains enveloped in low levels of radiation—has become a ghost town. The city, which once held 50,000 residents, now is home to only about 6,000 plant workers and safety technicians.

OBJECTIVE
③ INSTRUCT

A Continuing Movement

▶ ***Discussing Key Ideas***
- Americans continue to show great concern for the nation's environmental issues.
- As the 21st century dawns, the United States works to strike a balance between economic progress and conservation.

Harrisburg, Pennsylvania, malfunctioned. The reactor overheated after its cooling system failed, and fear quickly arose that radiation might escape and spread over the region. Two days later, low-level radiation actually did escape from the crippled reactor. Pennsylvania's governor ordered schools in the area closed. Officials evacuated some residents, while others fled on their own. One homemaker who lived near the plant recalled her desperate attempt to find safety.

A PERSONAL VOICE

On Friday, a very frightening thing occurred in our area. A state policeman went door-to-door telling residents to stay indoors, close all windows, and turn all air conditioners off. I was alone, as were many other homemakers, and my thoughts were focused on how long I would remain a prisoner in my own home. . . . Suddenly, I was scared, real scared. I decided to get out of there, while I could. I ran to the car not knowing if I should breathe the air or not, and I threw the suitcases in the trunk and was on my way within one hour. If anything dreadful happened, I thought that I'd at least be with my girls. Although it was very hot in the car, I didn't trust myself to turn the air conditioner on. It felt good as my tense muscles relaxed the farther I drove.

ANONYMOUS HOMEMAKER, quoted in *Accident at Three Mile Island: The Human Dimensions*

In all, more than 100,000 residents were evacuated from the surrounding area. On April 9, the Nuclear Regulatory Commission, the federal agency that monitors the nuclear power industry, announced that the immediate danger was over. President Carter inspected the site to help assure the public that the reactor was safe again. An investigation into the incident revealed that plant maintenance personnel had not been properly trained and that certain safety precautions at the plant were lax.

The events at Three Mile Island refueled the debate over nuclear power. Supporters of nuclear power pointed out that no one had been killed or seriously injured. Opponents countered by saying that chance alone had averted a tragedy. They demanded that the government call a halt to the construction of new power plants and gradually shut down existing nuclear facilities.

While the government did not do away with nuclear power, federal officials did recognize nuclear energy's potential danger to both humans and the environment. As a result of Three Mile Island, the Nuclear Regulatory Commission strengthened its safety standards and improved its inspection procedures. By 1988, at least 17 new nuclear power plants had opened in the United States, and none had suffered a breakdown.

C. Answer Opponents of nuclear power wanted the government to stop using nuclear plants. Instead, the Nuclear Regulatory Commission tightened its safety standards and improved its inspection procedures.

THINK THROUGH HISTORY
C. THEME ***Science and Technology*** *How did the Three Mile Island incident affect the use of nuclear power in America?*

In March 1979, a serious accident occurred at the nuclear energy plant at Three Mile Island, Pennsylvania (*bottom*).

Block Schedule TEACHING OPTION **Time Needed: 20 Minutes**

Cooperative Activity: Debating the Use of Nuclear Energy

Task: Student groups will debate the growing use of nuclear energy in the United States.

Purpose: To understand the arguments for and against the use of nuclear energy.

Activity: After choosing a position through a lottery, groups of three or four students will research the arguments either for or against the use of nuclear power. In researching their position, groups should consider such issues as the safety of nuclear power, the difference between nuclear power and other power sources, and public opinion about nuclear power. In researching its position, each group should also examine the state of nuclear energy in the United States today, including the current state of nuclear power in their county or state. Groups holding positions for and against the growth of nuclear energy will debate each other.

ALTERNATIVE ASSESSMENT BOOK
Standards for Evaluating a Cooperative Activity

A Continuing Movement

Although the environmental movement of the 1970s gained popular support, opponents of the movement also made their voices heard. In Tennessee, for example, where a federal dam project was halted because it threatened a certain species of fish, local developers took out ads asking residents to "tell the government that the size of your wallet is more important than some two-inch-long minnow." When confronted with environmental concerns, one unemployed steelworker spoke for others when he remarked, "Why worry about the long run, when you're out of work right now." The environmental movement that blossomed in the 1970s became in the 1980s and 1990s a struggle to balance environmental concerns with jobs and progress.

THINK THROUGH HISTORY
D. *Finding Main Ideas* *What was a major point of opposition to the environmental movement?*

D. Answer That the environmental initiatives sometimes cost people jobs.

As you will read in the next chapter, President Ronald Reagan's policy of deregulation, or reducing government restrictions on the way businesses may operate—created new challenges for the environmental movement during the 1980s. However, in the years since the first Earth Day, environmental issues have gained increasing attention and support. Environmentalists have continued to win battles on the local level, including the blocking of roads, airports, and other projects that they claimed would be ecologically dangerous.

In the 1990s, Americans began addressing new environmental problems. Scientists warned that industrial pollutants were depleting the earth's ozone layer, which protects the globe from the sun's most dangerous rays. In addition, some studies showed that the continued burning of fossil fuels (such as oil and coal) was contributing to a condition known as global warming, or a general rise in the earth's temperature.

One sociologist noted that the energy crisis and the environmental movement of the seventies "forced us all to accept a sense of our limits . . . to seek prosperity through conservation rather than growth." Today, America continues to seek prosperity, not by forsaking growth for conservation, but by trying to strike a workable balance between the two.

NOW & THEN

THE *EXXON VALDEZ* OIL SPILL

In 1994, a federal jury awarded almost $287 million in damages to thousands of Alaskans. The award was the climax of events that began in March 1989, when the giant oil tanker *Exxon Valdez* hit a reef in Prince William Sound, off the coast of Alaska, and dumped almost 11 million gallons of crude oil into the water. It was the largest oil spill in the country's history.

Within days, the black oil fouled more than 1,200 miles of coastline and beaches. At least 10 percent of the area's birds, sea otters, and other wildlife were killed, and commercial fishing in the area was seriously disrupted.

The jury also ordered the Exxon Corporation to pay $5 billion in punitive damages as a result of the spill. The size of these awards demonstrates that the nation has become serious about holding corporations responsible for damaging the environment.

A fisherman holds an oil-slicked bird after the *Exxon Valdez* oil spill.

Section  Assessment

1. TERMS & NAMES
Identify:
- Rachel Carson
- Earth Day
- environmentalist
- Environmental Protection Agency
- Three Mile Island

2. SUMMARIZING Re-create the web below on your paper and fill in events that illustrate the main idea in the center.

3. ANALYZING CAUSES Why do you think Rachel Carson's book *Silent Spring* had such impact when it appeared?

THINK ABOUT
- environmental awareness before the 1960s
- the message of *Silent Spring*
- the domestic agendas of the Kennedy, Johnson, and Nixon administrations

4. FORMING OPINIONS How much should the United States rely on nuclear power as a source of energy? Explain your view.

THINK ABOUT
- the safety of nuclear power
- the alternatives to nuclear power
- U.S. energy demands

ANSWERS

1. TERMS & NAMES

Rachel Carson, p. 808
Earth Day, p. 809
environmentalist, p. 809
Environmental Protection Agency, p. 810
Three Mile Island, p. 811

2. SUMMARIZING

Possible Answers:
Rachel Carson publishes *Silent Spring.*
In 1970, the first Earth Day is held.
Nixon organizes the EPA.
Three Mile Island raises concerns about nuclear power.
People struggle to balance environmental and economic concerns.

3. ANALYZING CAUSES

Possible Responses: Students might say that *Silent Spring* made people aware that chemical pesticides could harm even humans; it made people realize how human activity affects the environment. Others might point to the persuasive power of Carson's writing or the willingness of Kennedy, Johnson, and Nixon to act to protect the environment.

4. FORMING OPINIONS

Possible Responses: Supporters may argue that nuclear power should be widely used because it is cleaner than coal or oil, plentiful, and cheap, and its overall safety record is excellent. Opponents may argue that nuclear power is potentially very dangerous, that nuclear waste is difficult to dispose of, and that the high risks outweigh the benefits.

NOW AND THEN
The* Exxon Valdez *Oil Spill

Have students further research the aftermath of the *Exxon Valdez* oil spill, tracking the key events from the spill to the jury awards using a flow chart like the one below.

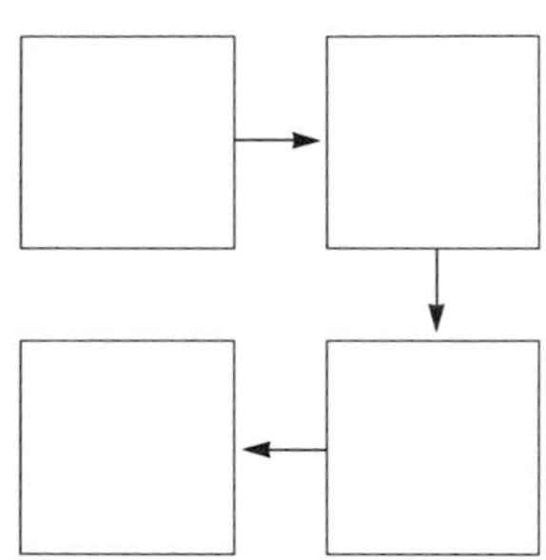

ASSESS & RETEACH

Section 4 Assessment

After answering the questions, have students pair up and check each other's answers. Students should note page references where missing information might be found.

Self-Assessment

Have each student write on an index card one action he or she might take each day to preserve and protect the earth. Collect these cards and post them on a bulletin board.

Section Quiz

FORMAL ASSESSMENT
Section Quiz, p. 297

Reteach

Replay the video, "Poisoned Playground," and discuss the environmental issues raised by the film.

***AMERICAN STORIES* video series**
"Poisoned Playground"

CLOSE

During the 1970s, as more Americans became aware of their economic and global limits, they also realized that their natural resources were not limitless. This realization moved the government, as well as average citizens, to more actively address the country's environmental concerns.

CHAPTER 24
ASSESSMENT ANSWERS

REVIEWING THE CHAPTER

TERMS & NAMES

1. Richard M. Nixon, p. 786
2. stagflation, p. 790
3. OPEC, p. 790
4. SALT I Treaty, p. 792
5. Watergate, p. 793
6. Saturday Night Massacre, p. 796
7. Camp David Accords, p. 806
8. Ayatollah Ruhollah Khomeini, p. 807
9. Rachel Carson, p. 808
10. Three Mile Island, p. 811

MAIN IDEAS

11. He tried to lessen the federal government's responsibilities through revenue sharing and welfare reform.
12. He tried to raise taxes, cut the budget, raise interest rates, and use wage and price controls.
13. His détente policy, based on the philosophy of realpolitik, sought to ease Cold War tensions. The result was a warmer relationship with China and the Soviet Union.
14. They shredded incriminating documents, paid off the Watergate burglars, lied while testifying, and tried to stop investigation of the burglary.
15. Nixon resigned as president, and many people lost faith in the government.
16. Under Ford, inflation and unemployment dropped somewhat and the United States joined with the Soviet Union and other countries in signing the Helsinki Accords.
17. Carter asked Americans to reduce energy consumption and pushed the National Energy Act through Congress.
18. Carter focused on human rights. Under him, the United States cut off military aid to Argentina and Brazil and criticized the Soviet Union's treatment of dissidents.
19. The publication of *Silent Spring;* Earth Day celebrations; the Three Mile Island accident.
20. It caused the government to strengthen its safety standards and improve its inspection procedures.

Chapter 24 Assessment

REVIEWING THE CHAPTER

TERMS & NAMES For each term below, write a sentence explaining its significance for the Nixon, Ford, and Carter administrations. For each person below, explain his or her role in the 1960s or 1970s.

1. **Richard M. Nixon**
2. **stagflation**
3. **OPEC**
4. **SALT I Treaty**
5. **Watergate**
6. **Saturday Night Massacre**
7. **Camp David Accords**
8. **Ayatollah Ruhollah Khomeini**
9. **Rachel Carson**
10. **Three Mile Island**

MAIN IDEAS

SECTION 1 *(pages 786–792)*

The Nixon Administration

11. In what ways did President Nixon attempt to reform the federal government?
12. How did Nixon try to combat stagflation?
13. Describe Nixon's foreign-policy philosophy and the results of that philosophy.

SECTION 2 *(pages 793–797)*

Watergate: Nixon's Downfall

14. In what ways did the participants in Watergate attempt to cover up the scandal?
15. What were the results of the Watergate scandal?

SECTION 3 *(pages 800–807)*

The Ford and Carter Years

16. What were Gerald Ford's greatest successes as president?
17. How did President Carter attempt to solve the energy crisis?
18. Describe Carter's foreign policy, using examples to show its impact.

SECTION 4 *(pages 808–813)*

Environmental Activism

19. What factors increased Americans' concerns about environmental issues during the 1960s and 1970s?
20. What was the impact of the Three Mile Island incident?

THINKING CRITICALLY

1. **ADVANCE OR RETREAT** Using a chart like the one below, identify one major development that occurred between 1968 and 1980 for each issue listed. Then indicate whether you think the impact of the development was positive (+) or negative (–) for the country as a whole.

Issue	Development	Impact
Economic conditions Racial harmony Democratic government Efficient energy use Environmental protection		

2. **PRESIDENTS AND THE ECONOMY** Review the economic policies of Presidents Nixon, Ford, and Carter. To what extent do you think each should be blamed or credited for changes in the economy during his administration?
3. **RECOGNIZING LIMITS** Reread the quotation from Jimmy Carter on page 784. How would you describe the feelings or tone that his statement conveys? Explain and support your opinion.
4. **GEOGRAPHY OF THE MIDDLE EAST** Look at the map on page 806. What U.S. interests do you think were served by helping to maintain peace in the Middle East?
5. **TRACING THEMES** **CONSTITUTIONAL CONCERNS** In your opinion, did the Watergate scandal primarily demonstrate flaws in the American system of government or show how well the system works? Explain.
6. **ANALYZING PRIMARY SOURCES** Read the following excerpt, from a 1973 interview with the environmental activist Barry Commoner, about the link between energy consumption and the environment. Then answer the questions that follow.

> **I've felt for a long time that the energy crisis is the cutting edge of the environmental crisis for [two reasons]. One is that it involves a counter-ecological step in that we're using nonrenewable resources, and that's a fundamental violation of a basic principle of ecology.**
>
> **The other reason is that in using fuel we inevitably pollute the environment with heat, with waste products and so on. So that for those reasons and also because energy—power—has become increasingly important in the design of new technology, which is the main source of the environmental crisis, the role of energy in industry and agriculture becomes a sort of red thread through the environmental crisis.**
>
> **BARRY COMMONER,** quoted in *Chicago Tribune,* November 19, 1973

According to Commoner, how was the energy crisis linked to the environmental crisis? Do you think Commoner's comments appropriately describe conditions that exist today? Explain.

THINKING CRITICALLY

1. ADVANCE OR RETREAT
Possible Answers: Economic conditions—High inflation and unemployment (–); Racial harmony—Nixon's retreat on integration and civil rights (–); Democratic government—Watergate scandal (–); Efficient energy use—Carter's energy conservation measure (+); Environmental protection—Clean Air Acts, banning of DDT (+).

2. PRESIDENTS AND THE ECONOMY
Possible Responses: Nixon could be blamed for allowing the recession to deepen by doing little to combat unemployment; Nixon could not, however, be blamed for OPEC price increases and the rise of foreign competition. Ford could be blamed for the failure of the WIN program but could be credited with moderate improvement in inflation and unemployment. Carter could be blamed for not establishing a consistent economic program and for allowing the inflation rate to reach nearly 14 percent; he could be credited for decreasing Americans' reliance on imported oil and gas.

3. RECOGNIZING LIMITS
Possible Responses: It conveys uncertainty—a holding back by saying we can't do everything, and a boldness in requiring us to move forward; it conveys pessimism by stressing limits and stating that we cannot do certain things; it conveys optimism by stressing boldness as we move into the future; it conveys realism—the nation cannot do or be everything; it expresses a sense of defeat in realization of limits.

ALTERNATIVE ASSESSMENT

1. PROJECT FOR CITIZENSHIP

What caused people to strike, protest, and demonstrate to express their beliefs during the 1960s and 1970s?

Write and deliver a three-minute speech that might have been given in a campus rally at a university somewhere in the world. See "Expressing Political Opinions" on page 113 in Projects for Citizenship.

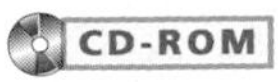

Use the *Our Times* CD-ROM, your text, and other sources to identify and research a social, political, or economic situation during this period.

- Your speech is an opportunity to express your thoughts and feelings about an issue that is of vital importance to you. Explain your position, and try to convince others to think the way you do or to take action.

2. LEARNING FROM MEDIA

VIDEO View the McDougal Littell video for Chapter 24, *Poisoned Playground*. Discuss the following questions in small groups and then do the cooperative learning activity:

- What obstacles did Lois Gibbs face in investigating conditions at Love Canal?
- How did Lois Gibbs's struggle affect her personal life?
- What finally prompted the government to evacuate the residents of Love Canal?

Cooperative Learning With a small group of classmates, discuss possible environmental problems in each group member's neighborhood, listing them on a sheet of paper. Compare lists with other groups to determine the most common problems. Discuss possible solutions to these problems.

3. PORTFOLIO PROJECT

Use the Living History activity to expand your portfolio.

LIVING HISTORY

SETTING UP AN EXHIBIT OF GLOBAL LINKS

You have prepared individual items that show international links. Now, with your classmates, set up an exhibit that displays these items. Consider the following suggestions as you organize your work:

- Divide your exhibit into sections, with each section representing a particular country.
- Prepare titles for sections of your exhibit.
- Arrange viewing and listening areas for videotapes and audiotapes.

After you have set up the exhibit, take notes and photographs as you view the displays. Explain in your notes which items you find most interesting and informative. Add your notes and photographs to your American history portfolio.

Bridge to Chapter 25

Review Chapter 24

NIXON'S PRESIDENCY Richard M. Nixon, elected president in 1968, attempted to move the nation in a more conservative direction. He took steps to reduce the size of the federal government, implement a policy of law and order, and slow down integration. In foreign policy, he sought to improve relations with China and the Soviet Union.

WATERGATE In June 1972, men employed by Nixon's reelection campaign broke into Democratic National Committee headquarters at the Watergate complex in Washington, D.C. When the burglars were caught, Nixon and his aides immediately tried to cover up the president's involvement. However, an investigation into the break-in revealed the cover-up and other scandals. To avoid impeachment, Nixon resigned in August 1974.

THE FORD AND CARTER YEARS The nation's economic downturn, which began under Nixon, continued under his two successors, Gerald Ford and Jimmy Carter. Each man tried to solve pressing energy and economic crises, with little success.

In foreign policy, Carter emphasized human rights and helped Israel and Egypt reach a historic peace agreement. However, in 1979, revolutionaries in Iran took 52 Americans hostage. They were not released until Carter left office in January 1981.

ENVIRONMENTAL ACTIVISM Awakened by the publication of Rachel Carson's *Silent Spring* and other events, Americans expressed concern for protecting the environment. The government responded with numerous environmental protection laws and the establishment of the Environmental Protection Agency in 1970. One issue of ongoing concern was the safety of nuclear energy. After the Three Mile Island incident in 1979, the federal government instituted tighter regulations on nuclear power plants.

Preview Chapter 25

The economic troubles of the 1970s caused discontent among voters. Capitalizing on this mood, a conservative, Ronald Reagan, won the presidency in 1980. He vowed to cut federal spending on domestic programs, cut regulations on business, cut taxes, and increase American military power. You will learn about these and other developments in the next chapter.

ALTERNATIVE ASSESSMENT

1. PROJECT FOR CITIZENSHIP

Standards for Evaluation

A speech should meet the following criteria:

- Focuses on one issue or event during the period.
- Expresses an opinion.
- Cites ample evidence from the text and other sources to support opinions.
- Uses forceful and moving language in order to convince others to change their view or to take action.

2. LEARNING FROM MEDIA

Answer to the questions:

- Lois Gibbs faced indifference from school officials and some town residents, as well as skepticism from state and federal officials.
- Her struggle forced her to spend time away from her family and caused tension in her marriage.
- Gibbs and her group held several EPA members hostage until their demands were met.

Standards for Evaluation

A discussion about local environmental problems should meet the following criteria:

- Addresses each group member's concerns.
- Involves all the groups in trying to determine solutions.

3. PORTFOLIO PROJECT

LIVING HISTORY

Standards for Evaluation

An exhibit should meet the following criteria:

- Uses items that clearly show economic or political links between the United States and other countries.
- Uses a balance of maps, pictures or drawings, three-dimensional objects, and audio-visual selections.
- Shows good organization.
- Contains labels and written comments that explain the events and global links of the exhibit.

IN-DEPTH RESOURCES: UNIT 7

See the form for scoring this activity on page 18.

THINKING CRITICALLY

4. GEOGRAPHY OF THE MIDDLE EAST

Possible Responses: Since the Middle East supplied the United States and other nations with much-needed oil, maintaining peace was important so as not to disrupt these trade links; maintaining peace helped limit the likelihood of increased influence from the neighboring Soviet Union over the region; maintaining peace helped keep a balance of power in the region between Israel, which was friendly to the United States, and other countries.

5. TRACING THEMES CONSTITUTIONAL CONCERNS

Possible Responses: Demonstrated flaws: It showed how a president can expand his power without giving any thought to constitutional checks; it showed how politicians and presidential advisers can become corrupt—desiring secrecy and power, and feeling that they are above the law. Showed how well government works: It showed how the system can provide for the investigation of presidential wrongdoing and create committees to investigate; it showed that a federal investigation can result in a grand jury indictment and that the House Judiciary Committee can impeach a president.

6. ANALYZING PRIMARY SOURCES

Possible Responses: Commoner argued that the use of energy is the main source of the environmental crisis. Yes: We are still using nonrenewable fuel resources that not only pollute the environment but will eventually be used up. No: Although we are still using fossil fuels, scientists are working to find alternative, renewable fuels.

CHAPTER 25

PLANNING GUIDE
The Conservative Tide

	Key Ideas	COPYMASTERS	ASSESSMENT
SECTION 1 A Conservative Movement Emerges *pp. 818–821*	*The new conservatism begins with the defeat of Barry Goldwater in 1964 and triumphs with the election of Ronald Reagan in 1980.*	***In-Depth Resources: Unit 7*** • Guided Reading, p. 19 • Skillbuilder Practice: Finding Main Ideas, p. 23 ***Lesson Plans,*** pp. 201–202	PE ***Section 1 Assessment,*** p. 821 TE ***Self-Assessment,*** p. 821 ***Formal Assessment*** • Section Quiz, p. 306 ***Alternative Assessment Book*** • Standards for Evaluating a Cooperative Activity
SECTION 2 Conservative Policies Under Reagan and Bush *pp. 822–826*	*President Reagan puts in place conservative policies concerning the nation's budget and the federal government.*	***In-Depth Resources: Unit 7*** • Guided Reading, p. 20 • Primary Sources: Political Cartoon, p. 28; *from* Ronald Reagan's Farewell Address, p. 29 • American Lives: Sandra Day O'Connor, p. 35 ***Lesson Plans,*** pp. 203–204	PE ***Section 2 Assessment,*** p. 826 TE ***Self-Assessment,*** p. 826 ***Formal Assessment*** • Section Quiz, p. 307 ***Alternative Assessment Book*** • Standards for Evaluating a Cooperative Activity
SECTION 3 American Society in a Conservative Age *pp. 827–833*	*Social issues of many kinds continue to concern the nation during the conservative backlash.*	***In-Depth Resources: Unit 7*** • Guided Reading, p. 21 • Geography Application: Latino Population in the 1980s, p. 24 • Primary Source: Civil Rights in the 1980s, p. 30 ***Lesson Plans,*** pp. 205–206	PE ***Section 3 Assessment,*** p. 833 TE ***Self-Assessment,*** p. 833 ***Formal Assessment*** • Section Quiz, p. 308 ***Alternative Assessment Book*** • Standards for Evaluating a Cooperative Activity
SECTION 4 Foreign Policy After the Cold War *pp. 836–841*	*Major changes throughout the world have a great impact on the direction of U.S. foreign policy.*	***In-Depth Resources: Unit 7*** • Guided Reading, p. 22 • Outline Map: U.S. Attention on the Middle East, p. 26 • Primary Source: The First Day of Desert Storm, p. 31 • American Lives: Daniel Inouye, p. 36 ***Lesson Plans,*** pp. 207–208	PE ***Section 4 Assessment,*** p. 841 TE ***Self-Assessment,*** p. 841 ***Formal Assessment*** • Section Quiz, p. 309 ***Alternative Assessment Book*** • Standards for Evaluating a Cooperative Activity
CHAPTER RESOURCES	**Chapter Overview** *A growing conservatism brings Ronald Reagan and George Bush to the presidency. Their policies change the American economy, while other forces transform American society and changes reshape the world.*	***In-Depth Resources: Unit 7*** • Living History Project: Worksheet, p. 37; Standards, p. 38 ***Telescoping the Times*** • Chapter Summary, pp. 49–50 ***Planning for Block Schedules***	PE ***Chapter Assessment,*** pp. 842–843 PE ***Alternative Assessment,*** p. 843 ***Formal Assessment*** • Chapter Test, forms A and B, pp. 310–315 ***Test Generator*** ***Alternative Assessment Book*** See explanation and forms for different kinds of alternative assessments including portfolio assessment.

KEY
PE Pupil's Edition
TE Teacher's Edition
http://www.mlushistory.com

TECHNOLOGY

***Warm-Up Transparency* 25**

Grolier Multimedia Encyclopedia
- Reagan's Political Career

INTERNET *National Review* and *The Nation*

***Warm-Up Transparency* 25**

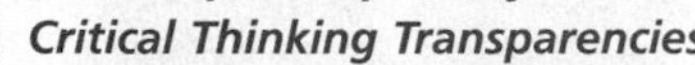
Critical Thinking Transparencies
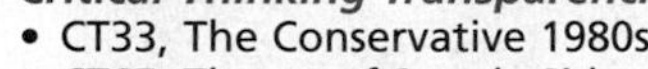
- CT33, The Conservative 1980s
- CT67, Theory of Supply-Side Economics

Electronic Library of Primary Sources
- On the Program for Economic Recovery by Ronald Reagan

INTERNET Ronald Reagan and George Bush

***Warm-Up Transparency* 25**

Grolier Multimedia Encyclopedia
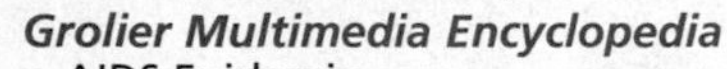
- AIDS Epidemic

INTERNET Interact with History, p. 835 (PE)

***Warm-Up Transparency* 25**

Humanities Transparencies
- H47, "Jobs That May Be Lost"

Geography Transparencies
- G33, The Cold War Ends, 1989–90

Grolier Multimedia Encyclopedia
- Iran-Contra Affair

Electronic Library of Primary Sources
- from *Setting Limits*

Our Times
- "Freedom Ascendant"

INTERNET Gorbachev and Tiananmen Square

American Portfolio: A Videodisc for U.S. History, user's guide, pp. 257–260

Chapter Summary Audiotapes
- Unit 7, Chapter 25

INTERNET http://www.mlushistory.com

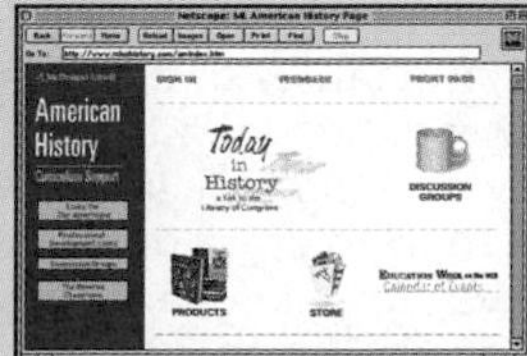

Block Scheduling (90 MINUTES)

Day 1
Section 1, pp. 818–821

Section Assessment, p. 821

COOPERATIVE ACTIVITY
- Diagramming the Shift to Conservatism, p. 820 (TE)

Day 2
Section 2, pp. 822–826

Section Assessment, p. 826

COOPERATIVE ACTIVITY
- Researching Supreme Court Decisions, p. 824 (TE)

Day 3
Section 3, pp. 827–833

Section Assessment, p. 833

COOPERATIVE ACTIVITY
- Developing a Plan for Better Schools, p. 829 (TE)

Day 4
Section 4, pp. 836–841

Section Assessment, p. 841

Geography Spotlight: Sunbelt, Rustbelt, Ecotopia, pp. 834–835

Chapter Assessment, pp. 842–843

COOPERATIVE ACTIVITY
- Creating a Foreign Affairs Time Line, p. 837 (TE)

YEARLY PACING ***Chapter 25 Total:*** 4 days ***Yearly Total:*** 85 days

See *Planning for Block Schedules* for special activities and pacing strategies.

Customizing for Special Populations

Students Acquiring English

Access for Students Acquiring English: Spanish Translations
- Guided Reading for Sections 1–4 (Spanish), pp. 270–273
- Chapter Summary (Spanish), pp. 268–269
- Skillbuilder Practice: Finding Main Ideas (Spanish), p. 274
- Geography Application: Latino Population in the 1980s (Spanish), p. 275
- Outline Map: U.S. Attention on the Middle East (Spanish), p. 277

Spanish Reading Study Guide, pp. 253–262

Translations of Chapter Summaries, Hmong, Cantonese, Vietnamese, and Cambodian

Chapter Summary Audiotapes in Spanish Unit 7, Chapter 25

INTERNET The Diverse Classroom

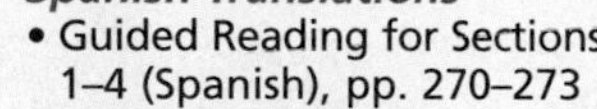

Gifted and Talented Students

In-Depth Resources: Unit 7
- Primary Sources: Political Cartoon, p. 28; *from* Ronald Reagan's Farewell Address, p. 29; Civil Rights in the 1980s, p. 30; The First Day of Desert Storm, p. 31
- American Lives: Sandra Day O'Connor, p. 35; Daniel Inouye, p. 36

Less Proficient Readers

In-Depth Resources: Unit 7
- Guided Reading for Sections 1–4, pp. 19–22
- Skillbuilder: Finding Main Ideas, p. 23
- Geography Application: Latino Population in the 1980s, p. 24
- Outline Map: U.S. Attention on the Middle East, p. 26

Reading Study Guide
- pp. 253–262

Telescoping the Times
- Chapter Summary, pp. 49–50

Chapter Summary Audiotapes, Unit 7, Chapter 25

Connections to Literature READINGS FOR STUDENTS

In-Depth Resources: Unit 7
- **from *The Bonfire of the Vanities* by Tom Wolfe,** p. 32

McDougal Littell *The Language of Literature* American Literature
- **Gregory Alan-Williams, from *A Gathering of Heroes,*** p. 1119
- **Peter Cameron, "Homework,"** p. 889

Enrichment Reading
- **Richard Russo**
  Nobody's Fool
  New York: Vintage, 1994
  In this quietly funny and moving novel, Russo follows the lives of quirky, flawed, yet likable characters in a deadbeat upstate New York town. Very much part of the economic disasters and hopes of the 1980s, these characters are real and vital.

- **Tom Wolfe**
  The Bonfire of the Vanities
  New York: Bantam, 1990
  Tom Wolfe wickedly assaults New York City politics and lifestyles of the 1980s in this wildly funny, bitter, and memorable novel. We see New York City from the perspective of Wall Street wizards, lawyers, mayors, civil rights leaders, journalists, and anyone who gets in between. Wolfe shows no favorites as he paints rich, poor, black, and white in absurd strokes.

OVERVIEW

The Conservative Tide

▶ ***Accessing Prior Knowledge***
Ask students what the phrase "conservative tide" suggests. Then, discuss the opening quotation.

▶ ***Predicting Outcomes***
Ask students what kinds of policies Ronald Reagan might offer when he becomes president if he truly believes that government is the problem. What might he try to do to the government that he will lead? How might he try to achieve his goals?

MORE ABOUT . . .
***Space Shuttle* Challenger**
The nation was stunned when on January 23, 1986, the space shuttle *Challenger* exploded in midair just 73 seconds after liftoff. The seven-member crew that died included Christa McAuliffe, a high school teacher from New Hampshire. She was the first civilian ever to have flown in a U.S. space mission.

CHAPTER 25 The Conservative Tide

SECTION 1
A Conservative Movement Emerges
The new conservatism begins with the defeat of Barry Goldwater in 1964 and triumphs with the election of Ronald Reagan in 1980.

SECTION 2
Conservative Policies Under Reagan and Bush
President Reagan implements conservative policies that affect the nation's economy and reduce the role of the federal government.

SECTION 3
American Society in a Conservative Age
Social issues of many kinds continue to concern the nation during the conservative backlash.

SECTION 4
Foreign Policy After the Cold War
Major changes throughout the world have a great impact on U.S. foreign policy.

"In this present crisis, government is not the solution to our problem; government is the problem."
Ronald Reagan, *first inaugural address, 1981*

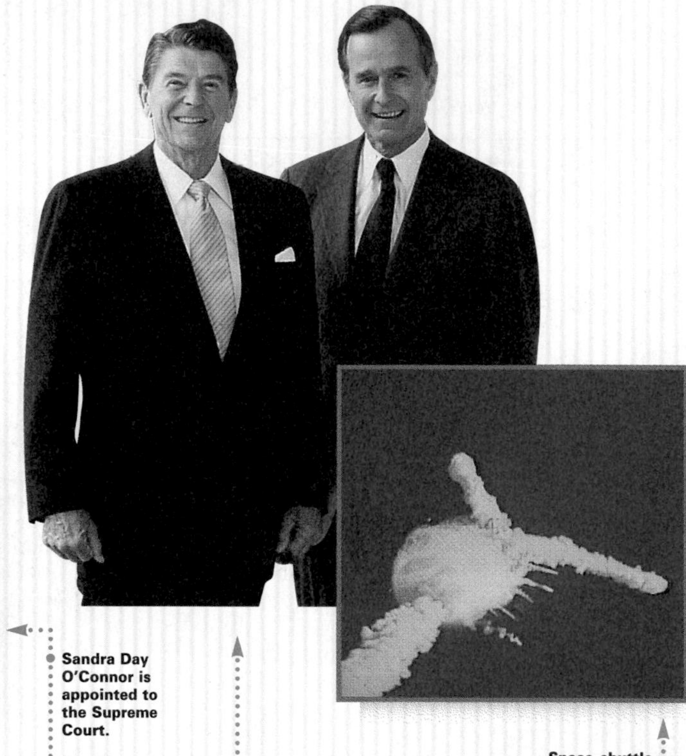

THE UNITED STATES

- 1980: Ronald Reagan is elected president.
- 1981: Sandra Day O'Connor is appointed to the Supreme Court. President Reagan is shot. Iran frees U.S. hostages.
- 1982: Equal Rights Amendment fails to win ratification.
- 1984: President Reagan is reelected.
- 1986: Space shuttle *Challenger* explodes. Iran arms deal is revealed.

THE WORLD

- 1980: Zimbabwe claims independence.
- 1982: Great Britain and Argentina go to war over the Falkland Islands.
- 1984: South African bishop Desmond Tutu receives the Nobel Peace Prize.
- 1986: Soviet Union suffers a disastrous accident at the Chernobyl nuclear power plant.

THEMES IN CHAPTER 25

Women in America
The Supreme Court was at the center of two events affecting women in the workplace: the appointment of the first woman justice to the Supreme Court and a hearing on charges of sexual harassment by a court nominee.
See Teacher's Edition, p. 825.

Civil Rights
A number of groups (including women, African Americans, Latinos, Native Americans, Asian Americans, and gays and lesbians) struggled to achieve equal rights in the 1980s under the administrations of Reagan and Bush.
See Teacher's Edition, p. 831.

Cultural Diversity
President Reagan set the upholding of traditional values as a major goal. But whose values are the traditional values? Some values indeed may be common to many of the diverse cultures found in this country. Other values vary by gender and ethnicity.
See Teacher's Edition, p. 832.

Constitutional Concerns
A major constitutional concern was raised by the Iran-Contra affair; it deals with the balance of powers between the presidency and the legislature. Can the nation tolerate one branch of government covertly working against another branch?
See Teacher's Edition, p. 839.

LIVING HISTORY

RESEARCHING POLITICAL POSITIONS

Watch a television news program, listen to a radio news program, or read a newsmagazine that features an interview with a conservative politician. Take notes on what the politician says about his or her positions. Consider the following questions:

- What does the politician say about social issues?
- What does the politician say about economic issues?
- What issues does the politician care most about?

PORTFOLIO PROJECT Save your notes about the interview in a folder for your American history portfolio. At the end of the chapter, you will compare that politician with Ronald Reagan or George Bush. Then you will present your comparison to the class.

1987
- President Reagan and Soviet leader Mikhail Gorbachev sign the Intermediate-Range Nuclear Forces Treaty.
- Stock market tumbles 500 points in one day.

1988
- George Bush is elected president.

1989
- *Exxon Valdez* spills oil along the coast of Alaska.
- Chinese troops kill student dissidents in Tiananmen Square in Beijing.
- Germans dismantle the Berlin Wall.

1990
- American troops defend Saudi Arabia from Iraq.
- Communist governments fall in Czechoslovakia, East Germany, and Hungary.
- Iraq invades Kuwait.

1991
- Persian Gulf War breaks out.
- Soviet Union breaks up.
- Yugoslavia dissolves in civil war.

1992
- Riots take place in Los Angeles after police officers are acquitted of brutality charges in the Rodney King case.
- Bill Clinton is elected president.

ALTERNATIVE ASSESSMENT

LIVING HISTORY

RESEARCHING POLITICAL POSITIONS

Discuss with students ways of researching political positions by taking notes on an interview.

- Be sure to note the source of the interview: radio talk show, television news, news magazine, or newspaper.
- Listen attentively or read carefully and take notes on the conservative politician's statements.
- Summarize notes about the politician's statements on social issues.
- Summarize notes about statements on economic issues.
- Think about ways in which the politician is like or different from Reagan and Bush.

Project Planning Guide

Step 1	Students choose a conservative politician.
Step 2	Students choose a medium (radio, television, newspaper, magazine).
Step 3	Students take careful notes of what the politician says.
Step 4	Students make comparisons and contrasts.

IN-DEPTH RESOURCES: UNIT 7
See worksheet and standards for evaluation, pp. 37, 38.

RECOMMENDED RESOURCES

Books for the Teacher

Ash, Timothy. *The Magic Lantern.* New York: Vintage, 1993. End of Cold War.

Cannon, Lou. *Ronald Reagan.* New York: Simon, 1990. Reagan's presidency.

Edelman, Marian Wright. *Families in Peril.* Cambridge: Harvard UP, 1987.

Faludi, Susan. *Backlash.* New York: Crown, 1991.

Smith, Hedrick. *The Power Game.* New York: Random House, 1988. Inner workings of Washington.

Books for the Student

Dionne, E. J., *Why Americans Hate Politics.* New York: Simon, 1991.

Johnson, Haynes. *Sleepwalking Through History: America in the Reagan Years.* New York: Norton, 1991.

Terkel, Studs. *The Great Divide.* New York: Pantheon, 1988. Oral history of the American dream as seen in 1980s.

Videos

America in Search of Itself. AIMS Media, 800-367-2467. Reagan wins presidency.

Colin Powell: An American Dream. Parade Video, 1995. Biography.

Colin Powell: A Soldier's Campaign. A&E Home Video, 1995. Biography.

One Thousand Days of the Reagan Presidency. MPI Home Video, 800-323-4442.

Software

Desert Storm: The War in the Gulf. CD-ROM. Time Warner Interactive, 800-482-3766.

Section 1 Overview

OBJECTIVES

1 To identify the reasons for the nation's swing toward conservatism.

2 To describe the emergence of Ronald Reagan as a conservative leader.

CRITICAL THINKING

- Forming generalizations, p. 819
- Clarifying, p. 819
- Finding main ideas, p. 820
- Summarizing, p. 821
- Analyzing causes, p. 821
- Analyzing motives, p. 821
- Synthesizing, p. 821

FOCUS & MOTIVATE

5-MINUTE WARM-UP

Recognizing Propaganda

To explore the appeal of the conservative message, have students read the One American's Story on page 818 and answer these questions.

1. Why does Noonan mention that all the young conservatives kept talking about freedom?
2. What does she suggest was the conservatives' notion of freedom?

WARM-UP TRANSPARENCY 25

▶Starting with the Student

- Ask students, What happens when things aren't going right or when they don't seem to be moving forward at all?
- Do students want to change something in their lives?
- Do students think an entire nation could feel that way?

1 A Conservative Movement Emerges

TERMS & NAMES
- Ronald Reagan
- entitlement program
- New Right
- reverse discrimination
- conservative coalition
- Moral Majority
- George Bush

LEARN ABOUT the conservative movement that swept the country
TO UNDERSTAND how conservatism changed American politics and led to the elections of Presidents Reagan and Bush.

ONE AMERICAN'S STORY

A daughter of hard-working Irish Catholic immigrant parents, Peggy Noonan grew up with a strong sense of social and political justice. As a child, she idolized the Kennedys; as a teenager, she devoured newspaper and magazine articles on social and political issues. After college, Noonan went to work for CBS, where she eventually gained a position as a news writer.

Over the years, Noonan came to realize that she was by nature a partisan—a supporter of a particular party or leader—rather than a journalist. Her political views became increasingly conservative. She won a job as a speechwriter for Ronald Reagan, whose commitment to his conservative values moved her deeply. Noonan recalled that her response to Reagan was not unusual.

A PERSONAL VOICE

The young people who came to Washington for the Reagan revolution came to make things better. . . . They looked at where freedom was and . . . where freedom wasn't and what that did, and they wanted to help the guerrilla fighters who were trying to overthrow the Communist regimes that had been imposed on them ten years ago while we were all watching "60 Minutes." The thing the young conservatives were always talking about, the constant subtext was freedom, freedom:
we'll free up more of your money,
we'll free up more of the world,
freedom freedom freedom—
It was the drumbeat that held a disparate group together, the rhythm that kept a fractious, not-made-in-heaven alliance in one piece.

PEGGY NOONAN, *What I Saw at the Revolution*

Peggy Noonan

Ever since Senator Barry Goldwater of Arizona had run for president in 1964, conservatives had argued that state governments, businesses, and individuals needed freedom from the heavy hand of Washington, D.C. During Ronald Reagan's campaign, that conviction gained a widespread following. It fueled a conservative sweep in the 1980 elections that brought Republican leadership to the presidency and the Senate.

The Conservative Movement Builds

By 1980, President Jimmy Carter was suffering from low ratings in public opinion polls. Economic troubles (including a high rate of inflation), the Iranian hostage crisis, and the nation's new conservatism eroded his popularity.

A TRADITION OF CHANGE Since early in its history, the United States has alternated between what historians call "public action and private interest." Sometimes voters have supported government action to solve social problems, whereas at other times they have become disillusioned with social experiments and preferred to concentrate on their individual economic well-being. Under the banner of progressivism, Presidents Theodore Roosevelt, William H. Taft, and Woodrow Wilson used the power of government to curb what they saw as the excesses of big business. During the 1920s, Presidents Warren Harding, Calvin Coolidge, and Herbert Hoover counteracted progressive policies with a conservative agenda that emphasized private interests over social reform.

SECTION 1 RESOURCES

PRINT RESOURCES

IN-DEPTH RESOURCES: UNIT 7
Guided Reading, p. 19
Skillbuilder Practice: Finding Main Ideas, p. 23

READING STUDY GUIDE, p. 253

ACCESS FOR STUDENTS ACQUIRING ENGLISH
Guided Reading (Spanish), p. 270
Skillbuilder Practice: Finding Main Ideas (Spanish), p. 274

SPANISH READING STUDY GUIDE, p. 253

FORMAL ASSESSMENT
Section Quiz, p. 306

ALTERNATIVE ASSESSMENT BOOK
See forms for supporting and scoring alternative activities.

TECHNOLOGY RESOURCES

CD-ROM *Grolier Multimedia Encyclopedia*

VIDEO *American Portfolio: A Videodisc for U.S. History* user's guide, pp. 258, 260

INTERNET http://www.mlushistory.com

When the Great Depression hit, the pendulum swung again. Franklin Roosevelt's New Deal and Harry Truman's Fair Deal focused on the use of government action to relieve social problems. Then Dwight Eisenhower brought a conservative perspective to the White House in the 1950s. John F. Kennedy's New Frontier and Lyndon Johnson's Great Society of the 1960s swung back to social reform. Conservatism returned during the Nixon and Ford administrations and reached a high point with the election of **Ronald Reagan.**

THE CONSERVATIVE BACKLASH By 1980, one out of every three households was receiving benefits from government programs. Yet many Americans resented the cost of maintaining these federal **entitlement programs**—programs that guaranteed and provided benefits to particular groups. Taxes were high, and inflation had reached nearly 15 percent. Many Americans feared they would not be able to provide for their children's college education or their own retirement.

In addition, some people had become frustrated with the government's civil rights policies. Congress had passed the Civil Rights Act of 1964 in an effort to eliminate racial discrimination. Over the years, however, judicial decisions and government regulations had broadened the reach of the act. A growing number of Americans viewed with skepticism what had begun as a movement toward equal opportunity. Although many people had rejected separate schools for blacks and whites as unfair and unequal, few wanted to bus their children long distances to achieve a fixed ratio of black and white students.

As the 1970s progressed, right-wing grassroots groups across the country emerged to support and promote single issues that reflected their key interests. Some members of this **New Right**—an alliance of conservative special-interest groups stressing cultural, social, and moral issues—fought any government regulation at all. Others fought specific government regulations in the form of busing, gun control, and antitrust laws. Many opposed legal abortion and the proposed Equal Rights Amendment (ERA). Some rejected laws promoting minority opportunities in employment or education—which they saw as **reverse discrimination** (discrimination against white people and specifically white men). Some called for a constitutional amendment to permit prayer in public schools. Others voted against anyone who favored increases in taxation. Of course, not all members of the New Right were single-issue voters. Many felt passionately about an overall philosophy of conservative government.

A. Answer A distrust of big government—including dislike of entitlement programs, taxes, and belief that civil rights policies had gone too far.

THINK THROUGH HISTORY
A. *Finding Main Ideas* *What main concern did conservatives have in common?*

THE CONSERVATIVE COALITION Between the mid-1960s and Reagan's victory in 1980, the conservative movement in the United States grew in strength. Eventually the groups on the right formed the **conservative coalition**—an alliance made up of some intellectuals, many business leaders, frustrated middle-class voters, disaffected Democrats, and fundamentalist Christian groups.

THINK THROUGH HISTORY
B. *Clarifying* *What was the conservative coalition?*

B. Answer An alliance made up of a variety of groups, including some intellectuals, many business leaders, frustrated middle-class voters, disaffected Democrats, and fundamentalist Christian groups.

There were a number of basic positions that were shared by most of the different groups that made up the conservative coalition. These included included opposition to big government, entitlements, and the use of busing and affirmative action to correct segregation, as well as a belief in a return to traditional moral standards.

Conservative intellectuals argued the cause of the conservative coalition in newspapers such as the *Wall Street Journal* and magazines such as the *National Review,* founded in 1955 by conservative intellectual William F. Buckley, Jr. Conservative "think tanks," such as the American Enterprise Institute and the Heritage Foundation, were founded to develop conservative policies and principles that would appeal to the majority of voters.

HISTORICAL SPOTLIGHT

WILLIAM F. BUCKLEY, JR.

Born in 1925 in New York City, William F. Buckley, Jr., is known for his conservative works. He first aired his conservative views in 1951, when he published *God and Man at Yale,* a book that attacked the liberal viewpoints he said were common at his alma mater.

He followed this publication with other political works, including *Up from Liberalism* (1959) and *The Unmaking of a Mayor* (1966), an account of his campaign for the mayorship of New York. When asked what he would do if he won the election, Buckley responded, "Demand a recount."

In 1955, Buckley founded the *National Review,* a magazine that continues to reflect and influence conservative political thought in America today.

OBJECTIVE
① INSTRUCT

The Conservative Movement Builds

▶ ***Starting with the Student*** Have students draw up a two-column chart. In one column they should list some of the actions taken by social reformers in the 1960s and 1970s. In a second column have them list the backlash that might have occurred.

Social Reform Actions	Backlashes
School busing	
Quotas	

▶ ***Discussing Key Ideas***
- In the 1980s, the country is ready for less government intervention.
- Conservatives form a coalition.

IN-DEPTH RESOURCES: UNIT 7
Guided Reading, p. 19

ACCESS FOR STUDENTS ACQUIRING ENGLISH
Guided Reading (Spanish), p. 270

HISTORICAL SPOTLIGHT
William F. Buckley, Jr.
Buckley has had greater influence as a writer and editor than he would have had as an elected official. Why might this be so? Have students list the attributes of Buckley that make him an influential journalist.

TEACHING OPTION

Skillbuilder Mini-Lesson: Finding Main Ideas

Explaining the Skill Finding the main idea means identifying one statement that an entire section or paragraph is about. Knowing how to find the main idea helps people understand the point a writer is trying to make—and how well the writer makes that point.

Applying the Skill To understand why the conservative movement gained strength in the 1960s and 1970s, it is important to find the main idea behind the movement. Ask students to list the causes of the conservative resurgence and then identify what they all have in common:

- Distrust of government regulation.
- Concern that entitlement programs were growing too quickly.
- Belief that taxes were too high.
- Belief that civil rights programs had gone too far.
- What these concerns have in common is that each expresses unease over the expansion of government power.

IN-DEPTH RESOURCES: UNIT 7
Skillbuilder Practice: Finding Main Ideas, p. 23

KEY PLAYER
Ronald Reagan
Critical Thinking: Synthesizing Have students synthesize Ronald Reagan's contributions to American life by designing a memorial to honor him. Students might work individually or in pairs. Suggested memorials include postage stamps, plaques, statues, poems, or pictures.

GROLIER MULTIMEDIA ENCYCLOPEDIA
Reagan's Political Career

OBJECTIVE
② **INSTRUCT**

Conservatives Win Political Power

▶ ***Starting with the Student*** Discuss with students what is required to turn beliefs into political action. Ask what the conservatives needed to become a political force. Some students might reply that the conservatives needed a leader who was also a charismatic political figure. Or they might respond that the conservatives needed political power.

▶ ***Discussing Key Ideas***
- Conservatives identify Ronald Reagan and George Bush as their political leaders.
- Reagan proves to have great appeal among the nation's voters.
- Reagan's election plus a Republican-controlled Senate provide conservatives with the opportunity to put their beliefs into action.

KEY PLAYER

RONALD REAGAN
1911–

Ronald Wilson Reagan was born in 1911 in Tampico, Illinois. He grew up in Dixon, Illinois, graduated from nearby Eureka College, and then worked as a sports announcer in Des Moines, Iowa. In 1937, Reagan moved to Hollywood and became a movie actor, eventually making 54 films. As president of the Screen Actors Guild, he worked actively to remove alleged Communist influences from the movie industry.

Reagan had the ability to express his ideas in simple and clear language that the average voter could understand. When he proposed a 10 percent cut in government spending on social programs, he stated, "We can lecture our children about extravagance until we run out of voice and breath. Or we can cut their extravagance by simply reducing their allowance."

A SUCCESS STRATEGY One of the most active segments of the conservative coalition was a confederation of various religious groups. These groups were encouraged and guided by Christian televangelists—evangelists, or preachers, who appear on religious telecasts—such as Jerry Falwell, Jim Bakker, Oral Roberts, Jimmy Swaggart, and Pat Robertson. Many of these religious conservatives came to call themselves the **Moral Majority.** The Moral Majority consisted mostly of evangelical and fundamentalist Christians who interpreted the Bible literally and believed in absolute standards of right and wrong. They condemned liberal attitudes and behaviors and argued for a restoration of traditional moral values. They worked toward their political goals by using direct-mail campaigns and raising money to support candidates.

As individual conservative groups formed networks, they created a movement dedicated to bringing back what they saw as traditional American values. They hoped their ideas would help to reduce the nation's high divorce rate, lower the number of out-of-wedlock births, encourage individual responsibility, and generally revive traditional values.

THINK THROUGH HISTORY
C. *Finding Main Ideas* *What were the main goals of the Moral Majority?*

C. Answer To restore traditional values and lifestyles and to reduce the divorce rate, reduce the number of children born to unmarried couples, and encourage individual responsibility in general.

A PERSONAL VOICE

Our nation's internal problems are the direct result of her spiritual condition. . . . Right living must be reestablished as an American way of life. . . . Now is the time to begin calling America back to God, back to the Bible, back to morality!

THE REVEREND JERRY FALWELL

Conservatives Win Political Power

By the mid-1970s, the strong conservative movement had four major goals:

- shrinking the federal government and lowering spending
- promoting traditional morality and values
- stimulating business by reducing government regulations and lowering taxes
- strengthening the national defense

But to achieve success politically, the conservative movement needed two things: a viable presidential candidate and an opportunity to present its case to the people. In the 1970s, conservatives found the candidate. In 1980, the conservative movement found its opportunity, and for the next 12 years Presidents Reagan and Bush were the primary spokespersons for and political leaders of both the Republican Party and the conservative movement in general.

REAGAN'S APPEAL In 1976, Ronald Reagan had lost the Republican nomination to the incumbent, Gerald Ford. But after a series of hard-fought primaries, Reagan won the 1980 nomination and chose **George Bush,** his leading competitor, as his running mate. Reagan and Bush ran against the incumbent president and vice-president, Jimmy Carter and Walter Mondale, who were nominated again by the Democrats despite their low standing in the opinion polls.

Originally a New Deal Democrat, Ronald Reagan had become a conservative Republican during the 1950s. He claimed that he had not left the Democratic Party but rather that the party had left him. As a spokesman for General Electric, he toured the country making speeches in favor of free enterprise and against big government. In 1964, he campaigned hard for Barry Goldwater, the Republican candidate for president. His speech nominating Goldwater at the 1964 Republican convention made Reagan a serious candidate for public office.

Block Schedule TEACHING OPTION **Time Needed: 20 Minutes**

Cooperative Activity: Diagramming the Shift to Conservatism

Task: Student groups will trace the fortunes of conservatism from the 1920s through the Reagan years of the 1980s.

Purpose: To understand the shifting political fortunes of conservatism in this century.

Activity: Groups of three or four students will each review a different decade (1920s, 1930s, and so forth), looking at federal spending, family values, business regulations, taxes, and national defense. They will present their findings as a chart that describes the time period covered, the various presidents during the decade, and their administrations' policies on the issues just mentioned.

Building a Portfolio: Students adding charts to their portfolios should attach a note pointing out their own contribution.

ALTERNATIVE ASSESSMENT BOOK
Standards for Evaluating a Cooperative Activity

Standards for Evaluation
Presentations should . . .
- show evidence of careful review and research using appropriate and various sources
- demonstrate an understanding of conservatism
- use specific details to back up groups' conclusions

In 1966 Reagan was elected governor of California, and in 1970 he was reelected.

THE 1980 PRESIDENTIAL ELECTION In 1980, changes in the voting population favored Reagan, as voters aged and moved in increasing numbers to the Sunbelt—the Southern and Southwestern regions of the country. In those regions, there was hostility to Washington and big government.

Reagan ran on a number of key issues. Supreme Court decisions on abortion, pornography, the teaching of evolution, and prayer in public schools all antagonized conservative voters in the country, and they rallied to Reagan. The Iranian hostage crisis and the weak economy under Carter, particularly the high rate of inflation, also helped Reagan. He also helped himself with a staunch anticommunism that led him to refer to the Soviet Union as the "evil empire."

Election of 1980

ELECTORAL AND POPULAR VOTES

Party	Candidate	Electoral votes	Popular vote
Republican	Ronald Reagan	489	43,904,153
Democratic	Jimmy Carter	49	35,483,883
Independent	John Anderson		5,720,060

3 Alaska
4 Hawaii
3 District of Columbia.

Thanks in part to his acting career and his long experience in the public eye, Reagan was an extremely effective candidate. In contrast to Carter, who often seemed stiff and nervous, Reagan was relaxed, charming, and affable. He loved making quips: "A recession is when your neighbor loses his job. A depression is when you lose yours. A recovery is when Jimmy Carter loses his." Reagan's long-standing skill at simplifying issues and presenting them clearly led his supporters to call him the Great Communicator. Also, his commitment to military and economic strength appealed to many Americans.

D. Answer Reagan's campaign benefited from high inflation, anxiety about the nation's future, and a burgeoning conservative mood.

THINK THROUGH HISTORY
D. Analyzing Causes *What factors led to Reagan's victory in 1980?*

Only 52.6 percent of American voters went to the polls in 1980. Reagan won the election by a narrow majority; he got 44 million votes, or 51 percent of the total. His support, however, was spread throughout the country, so that he carried 44 states and won 489 electoral votes. Republicans also gained control of the Senate for the first time since 1954. As Reagan assumed the presidency, many people were buoyed by his genial smile and his assertion that it was "morning again in America."

Now, at last, conservatives had elected one of their own—a true believer in less government, lower taxes, and traditional values. Once elected, Reagan worked aggressively to translate the conservative agenda into public policy.

Section 1 Assessment

1. TERMS & NAMES
Identify:
- Ronald Reagan
- entitlement program
- New Right
- reverse discrimination
- conservative coalition
- Moral Majority
- George Bush

2. SUMMARIZING Use a cluster diagram to record the issues that conservatives believed in strongly.

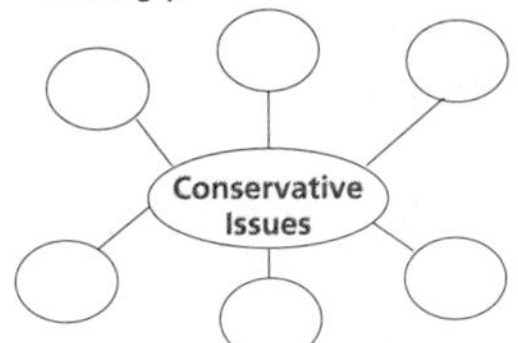

Choose one issue and explain in a paragraph the conservative position on that issue.

3. ANALYZING MOTIVES How did the leaders of the conservative movement of the 1980s want to change government?

THINK ABOUT
- the difference between the conservative view of government and the liberal view
- the groups that made up the conservative coalition
- conservatives' attitudes toward existing government programs

4. SYNTHESIZING Who were the main groups that made up the conservative coalition, and why did Ronald Reagan appeal to them?

THINK ABOUT
- their economic beliefs
- their political beliefs
- their religious beliefs

ANSWERS

1. TERMS & NAMES

Ronald Reagan, p. 819
entitlement program, p. 819
New Right, p. 819
reverse discrimination, p. 819
conservative coalition, p. 819
Moral Majority, p. 820
George Bush, p. 820

2. SUMMARIZING

Possible Answers:
reduce entitlement programs
end affirmative action
cut back government
end busing
stop regulating guns
outlaw abortion
defeat the ERA
allow school prayer
reduce taxes
strengthen national defense

3. ANALYZING MOTIVES

Possible Responses: The conservatives wanted to reduce government, lower taxes, and end liberal programs such as gun control, affirmative action, and busing. At the same time, they wanted government to increase national defense and to promote certain moral values.

4. SYNTHESIZING

Possible Responses: Reagan appealed to the Moral Majority because he opposed Supreme Court decisions on abortion, school prayer, and pornography. He appealed to people who favored free enterprise. He appealed to the struggling middle class because he promised to improve the economy. He appealed to many people because he seemed likable and was a good public speaker.

HISTORY FROM VISUALS

Election of 1980

Reading the Map Point out to students that the color green marks those states that voted for Ronald Reagan. The color vividly shows the extent of the Reagan landslide.

Extension Have students identify those states on the map that voted for Carter. *Hawaii, Minnesota, Georgia, Rhode Island, West Virginia, and Maryland, plus the District of Columbia.*

ASSESS & RETEACH

Section 1 Assessment

Have students individually answer the questions, then trade papers with a partner to compare the answers.

Self-Assessment

Ask students to reread the text and rewrite answers to any questions they found particularly perplexing.

Section Quiz

FORMAL ASSESSMENT
Section Quiz, p. 306

Reteach

Use the Guided Reading Worksheet for Section 1 to help review the main ideas of the section.

IN-DEPTH RESOURCES: UNIT 7
Guided Reading, p. 19

CLOSE

With the election of President Reagan, the conservatives had their national spokesperson and their political leader. This was their opportunity to effect national policy.

Section 2 Overview

OBJECTIVES

1. To summarize Reagan's economic programs.
2. To describe the changes that occurred in the makeup and decisions of the Supreme Court.
3. To identify results of federal deregulation of the savings and loan industry and of the Environmental Protection Agency.
4. To describe the presidential elections of 1984 and 1988.

SKILLBUILDER

- Interpreting political cartoons, p. 823

CRITICAL THINKING

- Clarifying, pp. 823, 825
- Making inferences, p. 825
- Analyzing causes, p. 826
- Summarizing, p. 826
- Analyzing motives, p. 826
- Forming opinions, p. 826

2 Conservative Policies Under Reagan and Bush

TERMS & NAMES
- Reaganomics
- supply-side economics
- Strategic Defense Initiative
- trade imbalance
- Sandra Day O'Connor
- William Rehnquist
- Geraldine Ferraro

LEARN ABOUT the programs of Presidents Reagan and Bush
TO UNDERSTAND how the conservative philosophy changed government policies and priorities.

ONE AMERICAN'S STORY

Throughout the 1980 presidential campaign and in the early days of his administration, President Reagan emphasized the perilous state of the economy during the Carter administration. In a speech to the nation on February 5, 1981—his first televised speech from the White House—Reagan announced his new economic program. He called for a reduction in income tax rates for individuals and a big reduction in government spending.

A PERSONAL VOICE

I'm speaking to you tonight to give you a report on the state of our Nation's economy. I regret to say that we're in the worst economic mess since the Great Depression. . . . It's time to recognize that we've come to a turning point. We're threatened with an economic calamity of tremendous proportions, and the old business-as-usual treatment can't save us. Together, we must chart a different course.

RONALD REAGAN, televised speech to the nation, February 5, 1981

President Reagan would deal with these problems by consistently stressing four conservative objectives: stimulate business by lowering taxes, promote traditional values, reduce the size and power of the federal government, and strengthen national defense.

President Ronald Reagan

"Reaganomics" Takes Over

As soon as Reagan took office, he worked to reduce the size and influence of the federal government, which, he thought, would encourage private investment. Since people were anxious about the economy in 1980, their concern opened the door for new approaches to taxes and the federal budget.

CUTTING GOVERNMENT PROGRAMS Reagan's strategy for downsizing the federal government included deep cuts in government spending on social programs. Yet his cuts did not affect all segments of the population equally. Entitlement programs that benefited the middle class, such as Social Security, Medicare, and veterans' pensions, remained intact. On the other hand, Congress slashed by 10 percent the budget for programs that benefited more limited groups: urban mass transit, food stamps, welfare benefits, job training, Medicaid, school lunches, and student loans. In 1981, Congress slashed domestic spending by over $40 billion—less than Reagan had asked for but still a huge sum.

REDUCING TAXES The second part of Reagan's policy called for lower taxes to accompany the reduced spending on social programs. This approach was the core of **Reaganomics**—a term used to refer to Reagan's economic policy, which involved large tax cuts to increase private investments, which in turn would, he thought, increase the nation's supply of goods and services. Reagan based his ideas on the work of economists such as George Gilder and Arthur Laffer.

FOCUS & MOTIVATE

5-MINUTE WARM-UP

Recognizing Point of View
To examine the effects of Reaganomics, have students read the Economic Background and Personal Voice on page 823 and answer these questions.

1. Are the points of view presented by Laffer and Stockman contradictory?
2. Who offers the more optimistic view of the 1981 tax cuts, Laffer or Stockman? Why?

WARM-UP TRANSPARENCY 25

Starting with the Student
- Have there been times when students felt others—teachers, parents—were running their lives?
- What were the issues? Control of money? Values?
- Could students' feelings have been shared by citizens who were weary of government control? What issues did those citizens want under their own control?

SECTION 2 RESOURCES

PRINT RESOURCES

IN-DEPTH RESOURCES: UNIT 7
Guided Reading, p. 20
Primary Sources: Political Cartoon, p. 28; *from* Ronald Reagan's Farewell Address, p. 29
Literature: from *The Bonfire of the Vanities* by Tom Wolfe, p. 32
American Lives: Sandra Day O'Connor, p. 35

READING STUDY GUIDE, p. 255

ACCESS FOR STUDENTS ACQUIRING ENGLISH
Guided Reading (Spanish), p. 271

SPANISH READING STUDY GUIDE, p. 255

FORMAL ASSESSMENT
Section Quiz, p. 307

ALTERNATIVE ASSESSMENT BOOK
See forms for supporting and scoring alternative activities.

TECHNOLOGY RESOURCES

CRITICAL THINKING TRANSPARENCIES
CT33, The Conservative 1980s
CT67, Theory of Supply Side Economics

CD-ROM Electronic Library of Primary Sources

VIDEO *American Portfolio: A Videodisc for U.S. History* user's guide, p. 257

INTERNET http://www.mlushistory.com

A PERSONAL VOICE

The most debilitating act a government can perpetrate on its citizens is to adopt policies that destroy the economy's production base, for it is the production base that generates any prosperity to be found in the society. U.S. tax policies over the last decade have had the effect of damaging this base by removing many of the incentives to economic advancement. It is necessary to restore those incentives if we are to cure our economic palsy.

ARTHUR LAFFER, *The Economics of the Tax Revolt: A Reader*

A. Answer That cutting taxes would lead to more investment, which in turn would lead to an increase in jobs and government revenue.

THINK THROUGH HISTORY
A. ***Clarifying*** *What were the main ideas of supply-side economics?*

Reaganomics rested heavily upon **supply-side economics,** which held that cutting tax rates—especially on investments—would give people incentives to work, save, and invest. According to this theory, increased business investment would create more jobs, as entrepreneurs and other suppliers developed new products and services. More workers would mean more taxpayers, which would cause government revenues to increase, even though tax rates were low. Using supply-side theory as his rationale, Reagan in 1981 signed into law a 25 percent cut in federal income taxes, spread out over three years.

INCREASING MILITARY SPENDING Meanwhile, Reagan authorized increases in military spending that more than offset cuts in social programs. Between 1981 and 1984, the Defense Department budget almost doubled. Indeed, the president revived two controversial weapons systems—the MX missile and the B-1 bomber. In 1983, Reagan asked the country's scientists to develop a defense system that would keep Americans safe from enemy missiles. Officially called the **Strategic Defense Initiative,** or SDI, the system quickly became known as Star Wars, after the title of a popular movie. The Defense Department estimated that the system would cost trillions of dollars.

ECONOMIC BACKGROUND

THE TRICKLE-DOWN THEORY

Ronald Reagan's budget director, David Stockman, used supply-side economics to draft the Economic Recovery Tax Act of 1981. His tax package cut income taxes and business taxes an average of 25 percent; the largest cuts went to those with the highest incomes. Administration officials defended the plan by claiming that prosperity would trickle down to the general population.

Later, after he left his position as director of the Office of Management and Budget, Stockman called the tax act a gift to the wealthy because it most benefited those with the greatest wealth. (See *supply-side economics* on page 939 in the Economics Handbook.)

A REVIVED AMERICAN ECONOMY As Reaganomics got under way, interest rates fell and the stock market soared, producing a long period of economic growth. The inflation rate dropped from a high of 14 percent in 1980 to 4 percent in 1988. Government revenues, however, did not increase as much as had been expected, resulting in large budget deficits.

The high interest rates that were necessary to curb inflation contributed to a severe recession during much of 1982. However, early in 1983 an economic upturn began as consumers went on a spending spree. Their confidence in the economy was bolstered by tax cuts, a decline in interest rates, and lower inflation. The stock market surged, unemployment declined, and the gross national product went up by almost 10 percent. The stock market boom lasted until 1987, when the market crashed, losing 508 points in one day. This fall was due in large part to automated and computerized buying and selling systems. However, the market recovered and then continued its upward trend.

Skillbuilder Answer **Wheel:** *Possible Answer:* The wheel is labeled "Deficits," so its flying off suggests that the federal deficit is spinning out of control. **Danger:** Inflation, because the stagecoach is named "Inflation Stage." **Opinion:** *Possible Answer:* The cartoonist is trying to indicate that President Reagan's efforts to control inflation have caused uncontrolled deficits despite Reagan's economic theories.

SKILLBUILDER
INTERPRETING POLITICAL CARTOONS
In this cartoon, President Reagan (with budget director David Stockman beside him) is trying to rein in the inflation stagecoach when a wheel suddenly flies off. What is the meaning of the wheel's flying off the coach? Besides deficits, what other economic danger is the artist pointing to? What opinion is the cartoonist trying to express?

THE NATIONAL DEBT CLIMBS During the Reagan and Bush years, the national debt soared from $900 billion in 1980 to almost $4 trillion in 1992, making the United States the world's leading debtor nation. Interest payments on this debt accounted for about 21 percent of the national budget—more than the budget for education, health, the environment, agriculture, transportation, space, science, and

OBJECTIVE
① INSTRUCT

"Reaganomics" Takes Over

▶ ***Discussing Key Ideas***
- Reagan believes small government is good.
- Many Americans are anxious about the economy.
- Reagan thinks tax cuts will help the economy.
- With less tax revenue, the federal deficit grows.
- Faced with a rising debt, Congress increases some taxes.

IN-DEPTH RESOURCES: UNIT 7
Guided Reading, p. 20
Primary Source: Political Cartoon, p. 28

ACCESS FOR STUDENTS ACQUIRING ENGLISH
Guided Reading (Spanish), p. 271

ELECTRONIC LIBRARY OF PRIMARY SOURCES
On the Program for Economic Recovery by Ronald Reagan

CRITICAL THINKING TRANSPARENCIES
CT33, The Conservative 1980s
CT67, Theory of Supply-Side Economics

ECONOMIC BACKGROUND
The Trickle-Down Theory

Have students visualize the trickle-down theory by drawing a cartoon or a graphic organizer. Ask students to label the different parts of their drawing.

HISTORY FROM VISUALS
Political Cartoon

Reading the Cartoon
Have students identify whom the passengers inside the stagecoach represent. *Possible Response:*

(continued on next page)

TEACHING OPTION

Teaching Less Proficient Readers

Charting Reaganomics Pair less proficient readers with more proficient ones to make a chart of the effects of Reaganomics. After students have read pages 822–823, have them draw up a chart that lists each of the subheads on the two pages. Then after each subhead list one example of Reagan's economic policy. The chart might look like this:

Economic Policy	Example
Cutting government programs	
Reducing taxes	
Increasing military spending	
A revived American economy	
The national debt climbs	

(continued from page 823)

Students might respond that they are the American people and that they are paying for the ride.

OBJECTIVE
② **INSTRUCT**

Judicial Power Shifts to the Right

▶ ***Discussing Key Ideas***

- Reagan and Bush appoint conservative justices to the Supreme Court.
- The new Court alters or overturns many past decisions made by more liberal Courts.

NOW & THEN
Clarence Thomas Versus Anita Hill

Have students write a paragraph defending or criticizing Anita Hill for bringing sexual harassment charges against Clarence Thomas. Ask them to be sure to give specific reasons to back up their argument.

MORE ABOUT . . .
Sandra Day O'Connor

Sandra Day O'Connor (b. 1930) was the first woman to be named to the Supreme Court. While judge of the Arizona State Court of Appeals, O'Connor had acquired a reputation for being "tough, but fair." She won easy approval to the Court.

IN-DEPTH RESOURCES: UNIT 7
American Lives: Sandra Day O'Connor, p. 35

technology combined. The interest payments on the national debt limited the amount of money available for investment in private enterprises. There was less money available to invest in technology and infrastructure (transportation systems, water and power lines, streets, and so forth). The country also faced a large foreign **trade imbalance**—that is, the nation was importing more goods than it was exporting. This imbalance meant that American dollars were going to other countries. On the other hand, the strong foreign competition spurred American companies to improve their products. (See *trade* on page 940 in the Economics Handbook.)

To reduce the budget deficit, Congress passed a sweeping new tax bill that provided for an increase in taxes other than those on income. In 1982, Reagan quietly signed it into law. Congress enacted another tax increase in 1984. In 1986 Reagan signed into law a new simplified tax system that lowered individual tax rates but raised business rates and eliminated hundreds of deductions.

Judicial Power Shifts to the Right

One of President Reagan's objectives was to promote traditional values and morality. Perhaps the most important way in which he accomplished this was through his appointments to the Supreme Court. Decisions of the Court affected many social issues, including crime, abortion, and First Amendment rights.

THE REAGAN–BUSH SUPREME COURT NOMINATIONS Reagan extended his conservative policies by naming conservative judges to the Supreme Court. He nominated **Sandra Day O'Connor,** Antonin Scalia, and Anthony M. Kennedy to fill the seats left by retiring judges. O'Connor was the first woman to be appointed to the Court. He also nominated Justice **William Rehnquist,** the most conservative justice on the court at the time, to the position of chief justice. By the end of his term in office, Reagan had appointed nearly half of all the federal district and appeals judges. These new appointees handed down conservative opinions on abortion rights and race discrimination.

President Bush later made the Court even less liberal when David H. Souter replaced the retiring justice William Brennan. He also nominated Clarence Thomas to take the place of Thurgood Marshall. However, controversy exploded when a law professor, Anita Hill, testified that Thomas had sexually harassed her when she worked for him in the 1980s at the Equal Employment Opportunity Commission (EEOC). The all-male Senate Judiciary Committee did not fully investigate the charges until after they became public knowledge. Thomas eventually won approval by a final vote of 52 to 48.

The Reagan and Bush appointments to the Supreme Court ended the liberal control over the Court that had begun under Franklin Roosevelt. These appointments became increasingly significant as the Court revisited constitutional issues related to such topics as discrimination, abortion, and affirmative action. In 1989, the Court, in a series of rulings, restricted a woman's right to an abortion. The Court also imposed new restrictions on civil rights laws that had been designed to protect the rights of women and minorities. In the 1990–1991 session, the Court narrowed the rights of arrested persons.

NOW & THEN

CLARENCE THOMAS VERSUS ANITA HILL

The effect of the televised Senate Judiciary Committee hearings on Clarence Thomas's nomination to the Supreme Court continues to this day. The hearings focused attention on sexual harassment and the lack of women in government. In the wake of the hearings, women's organizations stepped up campaigns against sexual harassment and in support of women candidates for political office. A record number of women were elected to Congress. Anita Hill continued to focus attention on the problem of sexual harassment in speeches she gave across the country.

While the hearings were going on, a gender gap developed—more women than men supported Hill, while men were more inclined to believe Thomas. The televised hearings dismayed many people, as senators on both sides of the nomination tried to discredit witnesses on the other side.

After the hearings had ended, most polls showed that more people believed Anita Hill than believed Clarence Thomas. Although there was not necessarily a direct causal relationship, the number of reported sexual harassment cases skyrocketed.

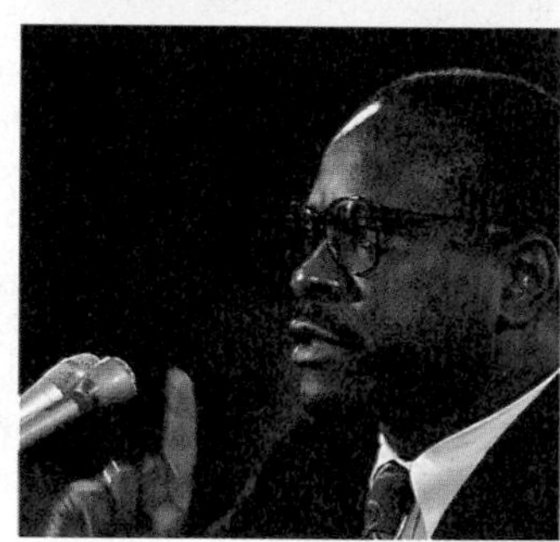

Anita Hill and Clarence Thomas testify before the Senate Judiciary Committee in October 1991.

Block Schedule TEACHING OPTION **Time Needed: 30 Minutes**

Cooperative Activity: Researching Supreme Court Decisions

Task: Student groups will research rulings by the Supreme Court during the Reagan and Bush years.

Purpose: To help students understand the changing attitudes of the Supreme Court.

Activity: Groups of three or four students will research one or two of the justices who served on the Court during the Reagan and Bush presidencies. They will make a tally of how the justices they research voted on topics such as abortion, discrimination, and affirmative action. Each group will also write a short report summarizing the records of the justices they researched. The groups will then meet together to combine their tallies and look at the Court as a whole.

Building a Portfolio: Students adding presentations to their portfolios should attach a note pointing out their own contribution.

ALTERNATIVE ASSESSMENT BOOK
Standards for Evaluating a Cooperative Activity

Standards for Evaluation
Reports should . . .

- demonstrate an understanding of the issues before the Court
- show the positions of the justices relative to the social and political values of the whole country
- be clear and well organized

Deregulating the Economy

Reagan achieved his third objective—reducing the size and power of the federal government—largely by deregulating, or cutting back on federal regulation of, industry. As part of his campaign for a smaller government, he removed price controls on oil and gas and eliminated federal health and safety inspections for nursing homes. He deregulated the airline industry (allowing airlines to abandon convenient but unprofitable air routes) and the savings and loan industry. One of the positive results of this deregulation was that it increased competition and often resulted in lower prices for the consumer.

THINK THROUGH HISTORY **B. *Making Inferences*** *What were some of the positive and negative effects of Reganomics?*

B. Answer Positive effects—encouraged growth, lowered inflation, decreased unemployment. Negative effects—created large budget deficit and contributed to trade imbalance.

In some cases Reagan's efforts at deregulation meant that government regulation simply stopped, since state or local governments were not able to pick up the burden of regulating airlines or controlling oil prices. In other cases, deregulation transferred financial burdens and a great deal of regulatory responsibility to state and local governments.

THE SAVINGS AND LOAN INDUSTRY Under the Reagan administration, the savings and loan industry was deregulated. Savings and loan institutions (sometimes called thrifts) were allowed to invest in commercial real estate, such as shopping malls, golf courses, and office buildings. Some S & Ls (as savings and loans are called) made risky loans on real estate. Even if they made risky investments, the government stood ready to pay individual investors up to $100,000 in savings insurance.

As the economy slowed down, many of the risky S & L investments lost large amounts of money. From 1988 to 1990, approximately 600 S & Ls failed, wiping out investors' savings. Charles Keating, president of Lincoln Savings and Loan in California, lost more than $2.6 billion of depositors' money. He made political contributions to several senators to keep his operation from being investigated. Keating and others like him were accused of having left the S & L industry in ruins. The federal government and the American taxpayer were left to clean up the mess.

THE ENVIRONMENT In a further effort at deregulation, President Reagan cut the budget of the Environmental Protection Agency (EPA), which had been established in 1970 to fight pollution and conserve natural resources. He ignored pleas from Canada to reduce acid rain and appointed administrators sympathetic to business to serve in environmentally sensitive offices. For example, James Watt, Reagan's secretary of the interior, sold millions of acres of public land to private developers—often at bargain prices. He opened the continental shelf to oil and gas drilling, which many people thought posed environmental risks. Watt also encouraged timber cutting in national forests and eased restrictions on coal mining.

C. Answer S & L failures and a drop in antipollution cases made apparent the negative aspects of deregulating the savings and loan industry and environmental protection.

THINK THROUGH HISTORY **C. *Clarifying*** *In what two areas were the negative aspects of deregulation particularly apparent during the Reagan and Bush years? Why?*

At the same time, EPA administrator Anne Gorsuch Burford and assistant administrator Rita Lavelle fired hundreds of inspectors at the Environmental Protection Agency. This caused a 75 percent drop in the number of antipollution cases referred to the Justice Department for prosecution. As a result of these actions, Watt came under fire from many quarters, and he resigned in 1983. Lavelle also resigned in 1983, and Burford was dismissed. The Reagan administration continued to oppose federal intervention to preserve the environment, though it did agree to support the 1980 Superfund bill, aimed at eliminating dangerous toxic waste sites.

HISTORICAL SPOTLIGHT

AN ASSASSINATION ATTEMPT

On March 30, 1981, President Reagan and other members of his staff were shot by a mentally unbalanced man named John Hinckley, Jr. While being wheeled into surgery to have a bullet removed, the president said to his wife, "Honey, I forgot to duck" (a line first used by boxer Jack Dempsey in the 1920s, after being knocked out in a bout). In the operating room, Reagan said to the team of surgeons, "I hope you fellas are Republicans." Reagan recovered speedily, and his popularity grew.

President Reagan is shot as he waves, and Secret Service agents shove him into the waiting presidential limousine.

OBJECTIVE **(3) INSTRUCT**

Deregulating the Economy

▶ ***Discussing Key Ideas***

- Reagan and conservatives want to reduce federal regulation of industry.
- Some regulatory responsibilities pass from the federal to state and local authorities; some regulations are discontinued altogether.
- Without regulation the savings and loan industry fares badly.
- Deregulation weakens the ability of the EPA to function well, and top officials resign or are dismissed.

HISTORICAL SPOTLIGHT

An Assassination Attempt

Discuss with students why President Reagan's comments and actions following the assassination attempt endeared him to the American people. Have students write a paragraph summarizing their views.

MORE ABOUT . . .

The S & L Crisis

In 1990 the head of the General Accounting Office told Congress that the total cost of bailing out the failed S & Ls would surpass the cost of the Marshall Plan, which rebuilt Europe after World War II. Other experts have reckoned the bailout cost as much as twice that of the Vietnam War, in comparable dollar value, and four times that of the Korean War.

TEACHING OPTIONS

Exploring Themes

Women in America Point out to students that during the Reagan and Bush presidencies the Supreme Court was a focus for discussion concerning the role of women in social, political, and business affairs. The first woman Supreme Court justice, Sandra Day O'Connor, was appointed. The testimony of Anita Hill, although it brought out many negative aspects of women's struggle for equality in the workplace, pushed the issue of sexual harassment to the forefront of the nation's consciousness.

Teaching Gifted and Talented Students

Government's Role in Business Some political commentators have labeled as an irony the government's stepping in and cleaning up problems created by deregulation. They point to the government's takeover of failed S & Ls and to the Federal Reserve Board's actions in preventing a breakdown of the stock market in 1987. Ask your gifted and talented students to research the government's actions in response to these economic crises. Have them write a paper pro or con on the thesis that Reagan's policies actually strengthened rather than weakened the role of government in business.

OBJECTIVE

④ INSTRUCT

Conservative Victories in 1984 and 1988

▶ *Starting with the Student*
Discuss with students conservative strengths and weaknesses going into the 1984 and 1988 campaigns.

▶ *Discussing Key Ideas*
- The conservative coalition remains intact going into the 1984 campaign.
- The support of the coalition, along with Reagan's popularity, sweeps him to victory in 1984.
- In 1988, much of the nation sees little reason for change, and Bush wins the election.

IN-DEPTH RESOURCES: UNIT 7
Primary Source: *from* Ronald Reagan's Farewell Address, p. 29

ASSESS & RETEACH

Section 2 Assessment
Have students answer the questions, note those that gave them trouble, and then note page references where answers can be found.

Self-Assessment
Have students identify those questions they were most unsure of and, with the help of a partner, locate the portion of the text that best helps them frame an answer.

Section Quiz

FORMAL ASSESSMENT
Section Quiz, p. 307

Reteach
Survey the students to find out what was difficult for them and then use the results of the survey to concentrate on that material.

CLOSE

During the Reagan and Bush presidencies conservative beliefs were transformed into political and economic policies.

Conservative Victories in 1984 and 1988

It was clear by 1984 that Reagan had forged a coalition of conservative voters who highly approved of his policies. These voters included

- businesspeople—who wanted to deregulate the economy
- Southerners—who welcomed the limits on federal power
- Westerners—who resented federal controls on mining and grazing
- "Reagan Democrats"—who agreed with Reagan on limiting federal government and thought that the Democratic Party had drifted too far to the left

Out of what conservatives saw as the major successes of his first term, Reagan had put together a strong conservative bloc of voters.

D. Answer
Reagan put together a winning coalition of business-people, Southern and Western voters, and disaffected Democrats. Bush built on Reagan's legacy and made effective use of negative ads.

THINK THROUGH HISTORY
D. *Analyzing Causes* *What factors contributed to Reagan's victory in 1984 and Bush's victory in 1988?*

THE 1984 PRESIDENTIAL ELECTION In 1984, Reagan and Bush won the Republican nominations for reelection without challenge. Walter Mondale, who had been vice-president under President Carter, won the Democratic Party's nomination and chose Representative **Geraldine Ferraro** of New York as his running mate. Ferraro became the first woman on a major party's presidential ticket.

Reagan and Bush maintained their popularity and won by a landslide, carrying every state but Mondale's Minnesota and the District of Columbia. As in 1980, Reagan received the bulk of his support from traditional Republicans, conservative Christians, and disaffected Democrats.

George Bush announces his presidential candidacy at a rally in 1987.

THE 1988 PRESIDENTIAL ELECTION Despite a deepening deficit, rising inflation, and foreign-policy scandals, a majority of Americans were economically comfortable, and they attributed their comfort to Reagan and Bush. When Michael Dukakis, the Democratic governor of Massachusetts, ran for the presidency in 1988 against George Bush, most voters saw little reason for change.

George Bush simply built on President Reagan's legacy by promising, "Read my lips: no new taxes" in his acceptance speech to the Republican convention. He stressed his commitment to the conservative ideas of the Moral Majority. Though Bush asserted that he wanted a "kinder, gentler" nation, his campaign sponsored a number of negative "attack ads." Some commentators believed that the ads contributed to the lowest voter turnout in 64 years. Only half of the eligible voters went to the polls in 1988. Fifty-three percent voted for George Bush, who won 426 electoral votes. Bush's electoral victory was viewed, as Reagan's had been, as a mandate for conservative social and political policies.

Section 2 Assessment

1. TERMS & NAMES
Identify:
- Reaganomics
- supply-side economics
- Strategic Defense Initiative
- trade imbalance
- Sandra Day O'Connor
- William Rehnquist
- Geraldine Ferraro

2. SUMMARIZING Use a diagram to explore the effects of Reaganomics.

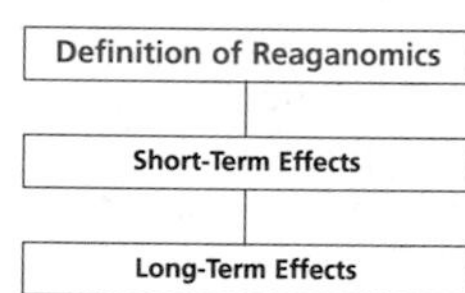

Explain in a paragraph whether you think Reaganomics was good or bad for the economy.

3. ANALYZING MOTIVES Why did Presidents Reagan and Bush think it was important to appoint more conservative justices to the Supreme Court?

THINK ABOUT
- the impact that the Supreme Court has on the nation's laws
- rulings that the Court made on social issues in the late 1980s and early 1990s

4. FORMING OPINIONS In your opinion, was deregulation generally good for the country, bad for the country, or a mixture of both? Explain.

THINK ABOUT
- the effect of deregulating the savings and loan industry
- the effect of cutting back on environmental regulations
- the effect of deregulation on the airline industry and other businesses

ANSWERS

1. TERMS & NAMES
Reaganomics, p. 822
supply-side economics, p. 823
Strategic Defense Initiative, p. 823
trade imbalance, p. 824
Sandra Day O'Connor, p. 824
William Rehnquist, p. 824
Geraldine Ferraro, p. 826

2. SUMMARIZING
Possible Answers:
Definition: Reagan's economic policies advocated large tax cuts to increase private investments, leading to an increase in the nation's supply of goods and services.
Short-Term Effects: Interest rates fell, stocks soared, inflation dropped, the economy grew.
Long-Term Effects: Increased national debt, budget deficit, trade imbalance, higher taxes.

3. ANALYZING MOTIVES
Possible Responses: The Supreme Court decides which laws are constitutional. Because Reagan and Bush supported the passage of more conservative laws, they wanted a conservative Court that would not strike down those laws. They hoped that a more conservative Court would strike down liberal laws and liberal judicial rulings, such as those allowing abortion.

4. FORMING OPINIONS
Possible Responses:
Deregulation was generally bad, because it led to many S & L failures and to exploitation of the environment. Deregulation was generally good, because it increased competition and often lowered prices. Deregulation was mixed, because it had both good and bad results.

3 American Society in a Conservative Age

LEARN ABOUT the social changes that occurred during the presidencies of Reagan and Bush
TO UNDERSTAND the effects of the new conservative movement in American politics.

TERMS & NAMES
- AIDS (acquired immune deficiency syndrome)
- pay equity
- L. Douglas Wilder
- Jesse Jackson
- affirmative action
- Selena Quintanilla-Perez

Section 3 Overview

OBJECTIVES

1. To identify national concerns about health issues, drug use, education, and the crisis of the cities.
2. To summarize political, economic, and social gains achieved by women.
3. To describe how conservative policies affected minority groups.

CRITICAL THINKING

- Summarizing, pp. 828, 829, 833
- Identifying problems, pp. 829, 830
- Theme: Women in America, p. 831
- Theme: Civil Rights, p. 832
- Theme: Cultural Diversity, p. 833
- Synthesizing, p. 833
- Making predictions, p. 833
- Comparing, p. 833

ONE AMERICAN'S STORY

Trevor Ferrell lived an ordinary life in Gladwyne, an affluent suburb 12 miles from downtown Philadelphia, Pennsylvania. Trevor had brothers and sisters, his own room, a favorite pillow, a fondness for video games, and a motorbike he loved to ride around the cul-de-sac where he lived. He did all right in school, though his parents and teachers thought he didn't work hard enough. In short, he seemed like a typical 11-year-old boy until he watched a television news report about homeless people in the City of Brotherly Love (as Philadelphia is sometimes called).

Trevor was astonished. "Do people really live like that?" he asked his parents. "I thought they lived like that in India, but not here, I mean in America." Trevor convinced his parents to drive downtown that night, where he gave a pillow and blanket to the first homeless man he saw. The next night, he returned with more blankets, and soon he and his family were taking food and clothing donated by neighbors to the homeless.

Trevor Ferrell listens to a homeless person on the corner of 12th and Chestnut streets in Philadelphia.

A PERSONAL VOICE

They have to live on the streets, and right after you see one of them, you see someone in a limousine pull up to a huge, empty mansion. It's such a difference. Some people can get anything they want, and these other people couldn't get a penny if they needed one.

TREVOR FERRELL, quoted in *Trevor's Place*

As Trevor saw, the restored American economy of the 1980s did not mean renewed prosperity for everyone in American society. As presidents Reagan and Bush pursued conservative domestic policies, people disagreed about the impact of these policies.

In these controversies, one truth emerged—American society during the 1980s was going through rapid changes. And Americans were at odds about how to deal with these changes.

Health, Education, and Cities in Crisis

In the 1980s, both in the cities (which supported large populations of poor people, minorities, and recent immigrants) and in rural and suburban areas, governments strove mightily to deal with crises in health, education, and safety. Americans directed their attention to issues such as AIDS, drug abuse, abortion, education, and the urban crisis.

HEALTH ISSUES One of the most troubling issues that Americans argued about in the 1980s was **AIDS (acquired immune deficiency syndrome).** Beginning in 1981, AIDS began spreading rapidly throughout the world. Caused by a virus that destroys the immune system, AIDS weakens the body so that it is prone to infections and normally rare cancers.

After years of intensive research, no cure had been found. AIDS is transmitted through bodily fluids, and most of the early victims of the disease were either homosexual men or intravenous drug users who shared needles. However, people also contracted AIDS through contaminated blood transfusions or by being born

FOCUS & MOTIVATE

5-MINUTE WARM-UP

Recognizing Facts and Details
To explore the problem of homelessness in the 1980s, have students read One American's Story on page 827 and answer these questions.

1. What did Trevor Ferrell think when he saw the news report on homelessness in Philadelphia?
2. What did he decide to do about the problem?

WARM-UP TRANSPARENCY 25

▶ ***Starting with the Student***
- What do students think are the greatest problems in their school community? Do they include the quality of their education? gangs? the treatment of women and minorities?

SECTION 3 RESOURCES

PRINT RESOURCES

IN-DEPTH RESOURCES: UNIT 7
Guided Reading, p. 21
Geography Application: Latino Population in the 1980s, p. 24
Primary Source: Civil Rights in the 1980s, p. 30

READING STUDY GUIDE, p. 257

ACCESS FOR STUDENTS ACQUIRING ENGLISH
Guided Reading (Spanish), p. 272
Geography Application: Latino Population in the 1980s (Spanish), p. 275

SPANISH READING STUDY GUIDE, p. 257

FORMAL ASSESSMENT
Section Quiz, p. 308

ALTERNATIVE ASSESSMENT BOOK
See forms for supporting and scoring alternative activities.

TECHNOLOGY RESOURCES

CD-ROM *Grolier Multimedia Encyclopedia*

VIDEO *American Portfolio: A Videodisc for U.S. History* user's guide, pp. 257, 259, 260

INTERNET http://www.mlushistory.com

OBJECTIVE
1 INSTRUCT

Health, Education, and Cities in Crisis

▶ ***Discussing Key Ideas***
- The rising incidence of AIDS troubles the nation.

(continued on next page)

(continued from page 827)

- Americans disagree about abortion.
- Reagan and Bush take a hard stand against drug dealers and users.
- Most Americans criticize the public schools.
- Cities face problems.

IN-DEPTH RESOURCES: UNIT 7
Guided Reading, p. 21

ACCESS FOR STUDENTS ACQUIRING ENGLISH
Guided Reading (Spanish), p. 272

ON THE WORLD STAGE
Worldwide AIDS
Ask students which of the 1996 statistics about AIDS most surprised them. Have students write several sentences summarizing what they learned.

GROLIER MULTIMEDIA ENCYCLOPEDIA
AIDS Epidemic

Issues for the 21st Century

Curing the Health Care System
Connect health-care issues in the 1980s with today by having students read pages 892–893 and answer these questions.

1. What effect did the spread of the AIDS virus have on public concerns over health care? *Possible Response: It raised concerns over the costs of treating AIDS sufferers.*
2. What obstacles might a person with a preexisting condition face in finding quality health care? *Health providers might deny coverage.*

ON THE WORLD STAGE

WORLDWIDE AIDS
In mid-1996, the World Health Organization estimated that 27.9 million children and adults worldwide had been infected with HIV (human immunodeficiency virus), which causes AIDS, and 21.8 million were living with HIV/AIDS. More than 7.7 million children and adults had developed full-blown AIDS, and at least 5.8 million people had already died. Over half of all AIDS cases occurred in people under 35 years old. Over 70 percent of all HIV infections throughout the world were the result of heterosexual activity.

to infected mothers. As the 1980s progressed, increasing numbers of heterosexuals began contracting AIDS as well. As the epidemic grew, so did concern over the rising cost of care for AIDS sufferers.

The AIDS quilt was displayed on the National Mall in Washington, D.C., in 1987. Each panel honors a person who died of AIDS.

ABORTION Many Americans were concerned about abortion in the 1980s. Abortion had been legal in the United States since 1973, when the Supreme Court ruled in *Roe* v. *Wade* that first-trimester abortions were protected by a woman's right to privacy. Opponents of legalized abortion quickly organized under the "pro-life" banner. They argued that human life began at conception and that no one had the right to terminate a human life by her individual decision. Proponents of legalized abortion described themselves as "pro-choice." They argued that reproductive choices were personal health-care matters and noted that many women had died from abortions performed by unskilled people in unsterile settings before the procedure was legalized.

In July of 1989, the Supreme Court ruled in *Webster* v. *Reproductive Health Care Services* that states had the right to impose new restrictions on abortion. As a result, abortion restrictions varied from state to state.

In May of 1991, the Court further limited abortion rights. It ruled in *Rust* v. *Sullivan* that the federal government could prevent doctors in government-sponsored health clinics from providing women with information about abortion—even if the women's health was at risk. Antiabortion activists applauded the new ruling, but abortion rights supporters argued that the ruling created one level of health care for the affluent and another for the poor. Many doctors felt that the decision violated professional ethics by telling them how to practice medicine. Congress passed a bill designed to overturn the Court's restrictions on abortion rights, but President Bush vetoed the bill. His veto was sustained by the Congress.

DRUG ABUSE Battles over abortion rights sometimes competed for public attention with concerns over rising drug abuse. Jobless youth in the cities and teenagers in the suburbs joined gangs to gain power and money by selling crack cocaine and other drugs. In 1980, only 10 cities reported serious problems, but by 1990, more than 125 cities had gang-related troubles. As crime and drug use rose, different factions promoted diverse approaches to the crisis. A few people argued that drugs should be legalized to reduce the power of gangs who made a living selling illegal drugs. Others called for more treatment facilities in order to treat addiction. The Reagan administration launched a war on drugs and supported moves to prosecute users as well as dealers.

A. Answer Launching a war on drugs, prosecuting users as well as dealers, random drug testing, cutting off college loans and public housing to drug users, educating people about drugs' effects, using the military to patrol the nation's borders to prevent drug smuggling.

"Just Say No!"
NANCY REAGAN, SLOGAN IN THE WAR ON DRUGS

The president called for random drug testing at government-related workplaces, and in 1988, Congress passed a law cutting off college loans and public housing for marijuana users. Congress also provided funds for antidrug education in the schools. Businesses and some institutions began random drug testing to identify drug users. The military used armed forces to patrol the nation's borders in an attempt to prevent drug smuggling. At the same time, First Lady Nancy Reagan toured the country with an antidrug campaign that admonished students to "Just Say No!" to drugs. These measures helped reduce drug use among middle-class Americans, but the availability of illegal drugs apparently remained the same.

THINK THROUGH HISTORY
A. Summarizing *What were some of the steps taken during the Reagan administration to combat drug use?*

President Bush followed in Reagan's footsteps and called for action against drugs, which he called "[our] gravest domestic threat." The president urged "a war on drugs"—by which he meant crack cocaine and similar substances.

TEACHING OPTIONS

Making Connections Across the Curriculum

Science For young American adults between the ages of 25 and 44, AIDS-related diseases had by 1994 become the second leading cause of death in men and the fifth leading cause in women. In major cities such as New York, Los Angeles, and San Francisco, AIDS had become the leading cause of death among young adult men. In New York City, AIDS was the leading cause of death among women aged 25 to 44. Major drug companies were working on developing new drugs (such as AZT) to fight the ravages of AIDS, but a cure still has not been found. Ask students to research the topic of an AIDS vaccine.

Making Connections Across the Curriculum

Writing Nancy Reagan's "Just Say No!" message was an emotional appeal to young people. In writing, emotional appeals make use of adjectives and adverbs that make an immediate, visceral appeal to the reader or listener. Pretend that you are writing slogans, ads, and bumper stickers for an antidrug campaign. What words and phrases would you use to appeal to your audience? Write an advertisement for a "Just Say No!" campaign.

Bush's program emphasized law enforcement: stopping drugs at the nation's borders, jailing drug-using Americans for long terms, and establishing a death penalty for drug dealers.

EDUCATION Education was another issue that stirred people's concerns about the future of their children. In 1983, a presidential commission issued a report on education, entitled *A Nation at Risk*. The report revealed that American students' test scores lagged behind those of students in most other industrialized nations. Further, the report showed that scores on standardized achievement tests had sunk below those in 1957, when the Soviets launched *Sputnik*. In addition, the report stated that 23 million Americans were unable to follow an instruction manual or fill out a job application form. It also noted that many 17-year-olds could not read a paragraph and draw an intelligent conclusion, or distinguish the state of Florida from Russia on an outline map.

The commission's findings and those of various scholars touched off a debate about education. The commission recommended more homework, longer school days, and an extended school year. It also promoted increased pay and merit raises for teachers, as well as a greater emphasis on basic subjects such as English, math, science, social studies, and computer science.

Some educators recommended more Head Start programs, smaller classes, tutorials, and an emphasis on critical thinking. Others advocated a system that would give parents who wanted to send their children to private schools the money that would have been spent on the children in public schools. Still others favored "magnet schools" and parental choice among public schools.

Whatever their ideas, most Americans agreed that the public schools were, at best, educating only half the students enrolled. Furthermore, students who dropped out of school stood little chance of earning a living in an economy that had become increasingly complex, in part because of the dawn of the computer age.

B. Answer Poor test scores, poor reading skills, poor math skills.

THINK THROUGH HISTORY
B. *Identifying Problems* *What problems of schools emerged during the 1980s?*

"Anyone who doubts that public education in the United States is in deep trouble has not been paying attention."

JOHN EGERTON, 1982

The tremendous growth in the use of personal computers during the 1980s made education even more important for students. The information age made it imperative that students learn to use the new technology, including the hardware of computers and keyboards as well as the software of different programs. Apple computers, IBM computers and their clones (similar machines), along with all the technology associated with them, became a growth industry in the 1980s and transformed the school and the workplace.

In April 1991, President Bush announced a bold new education initiative, "America 2000." He argued that choice was the salvation of American schools and recommended allowing parents to use public funds to send their children to schools of their choice—public, private, or religious. Bush also proposed the founding of 535 new schools that would serve as models of curriculum innovation. He also urged national achievement tests. First Lady Barbara Bush toured the country to promote reading and writing skills.

C. Answer More homework, longer school days, extended school year, increased pay for teachers, emphasis on basic subjects, Head Start programs, smaller classes, tutorials, parental choice, magnet schools, computers.

THINK THROUGH HISTORY
C. *Summarizing* *What were some of the proposals for improving schools?*

Barbara Bush visits with children at the Friendly Place, an East Harlem family center, in her effort to call attention to illiteracy.

THE URBAN CRISIS The crisis in education was closely connected to the crisis in the cities. Many undereducated students were in cities such as Baltimore, Chicago, Detroit, Philadelphia, and Washington, D.C.—municipalities whose populations had actually decreased during the 1980s. During the 1970s, the United States had become increasingly suburbanized as more and more white

MORE ABOUT . . .
Grading U.S. Education

The National Science Foundation and the United States Department of Education in 1989 issued a joint report comparing test scores of 24,000 thirteen-year-olds from around the world. They found that American students scored last in mathematics and near the bottom in science.

MORE ABOUT . . .
School Dropout Rates

By the late 1980s the dropout rate among high school freshmen was 26.7 percent. Among 18- and 19-year-olds, only 55 percent of Latino Americans completed high school. For African Americans, that rate was 65 percent, and for white Americans the number was 77 percent.

Block Schedule TEACHING OPTION **Time Needed: 20 Minutes**

Cooperative Activity: Developing a Plan for Better Schools

Task: Student groups will research topics related to school reform and develop a proposed plan of action for their local school or school district.

Purpose: To develop an awareness of the problems confronting public schools.

Activity: Students, working in groups of three or four, will research and report on one topic dealing with schools, such as national standards, national testing, traditional testing vs. alternative assessments and portfolios, rote knowledge vs. active learning, financing of public school education, or technology and education. Each group will frame one goal of a class proposal drafted for a potential audience of parents, teachers, administrators, and school board members.

Building a Portfolio: Students adding reports to their portfolios should attach a note pointing out their own contribution to the entry.

ALTERNATIVE ASSESSMENT BOOK
Standards for Evaluating a Cooperative Activity

Standards for Evaluation
Reports should . . .

- show evidence of thoughtful research using various sources
- present a plan of action
- support ideas with specific examples and evidence showing the need for reform

OBJECTIVE

(2) INSTRUCT

The Equal Rights Struggle

▶ ***Starting with the Student***
- Do students feel that male and female students should get the same grade for the same quality of work?
- Should they get the same pay for after-school work?
- Should the same principle apply to men and women in the work force?

▶ ***Discussing Key Ideas***
- Women's rights proponents feel disappointment at the failure of the ERA to gain ratification.
- Women are underrepresented in public affairs and organize to elect more women to public office.
- Women's groups call for pay equity and family work benefits.

MORE ABOUT . . .
Geraldine Ferraro

Geraldine Ferraro (b. 1935) became the first woman nominated to be vice-president by a major political party. Prior to her vice-presidential nomination Ferraro served three terms in Congress, representing a district in Queens, one of New York City's five boroughs. She built up a record of favoring benefits for women, the elderly, and labor and opposing restrictions on abortion. Following the defeat of the Mondale-Ferraro ticket, she ran unsuccessfully in 1992 for the Democratic nomination for senator from New York. She has also been talked about as a possible candidate for mayor of New York City.

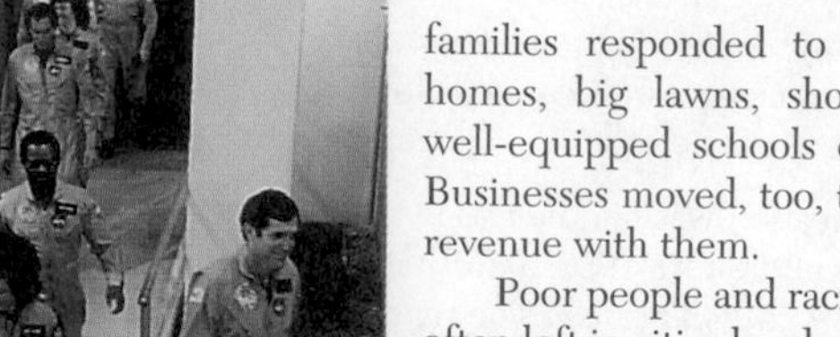

Difficult Decisions IN HISTORY

SENDING MONEY INTO SPACE

Under the Reagan administration, the government shifted the emphasis of the space program from scientific to military and commercial applications. Beginning in 1981, NASA directed a series of space shuttle flights. The agency hoped eventually to establish a manned space station, with the shuttle ferrying workers and materials to it. However the explosion of the space shuttle *Challenger* in 1986 caused a reexamination of ventures into space. Many people thought that the money spent on space ventures would be better spent on social, educational, and environmental needs.

1. Should the federal government spend money on space exploration when so many citizens require basic assistance?
2. If you were a legislator being asked to vote in favor of funding space exploration today, how would you vote? Why?

families responded to the lure of new homes, big lawns, shopping malls, and well-equipped schools outside the cities. Businesses moved, too, taking jobs and tax revenue with them.

Poor people and racial minorities were often left in cities burdened by high unemployment rates, crumbling infrastructure, inadequate funds for sanitation and health services, deteriorating schools, and growing social problems. To make matters worse, federal spending on cities dropped by more than 60 percent between 1981 and 1991. AFDC (Aid to Families with Dependent Children) benefits did not keep up with inflation. And despite inflation, federal funding for low-income housing fell from $32 billion in 1978 to less than $10 billion in 1990. By 1992, thousands of people were homeless, including many families with children. Cities were increasingly divided into wealthy neighborhoods and poverty-stricken areas.

One poverty-stricken area, south Central Los Angeles (which had erupted in violence in 1965 and 1968), erupted again in 1992. Four white police officers had been videotaped beating an African-American man named Rodney King, who had been fleeing the officers in a speeding car. A mostly white jury found the officers not guilty of brutality. This verdict resulted in riots that lasted five days and caused the deaths of 51 people. Approximately 2,400 people were injured and about $1 billion in property was damaged in the riots. Most of the damaged property belonged to merchants, who some rioters believed were exploiting their neighborhoods.

D. Answer Reaganomics led to deep cuts in aid for health, education, and social programs, which had been funded largely by the federal government.

THINK THROUGH HISTORY
D. ***Identifying Problems*** *What were some of the problems facing cities in the 1980s?*

The Equal Rights Struggle

Democratic vice-presidential candidate Geraldine Ferraro waves to the crowd during the 1984 campaign.

Within this environment of dwindling resources and social struggle, women worked to achieve economic and social gains.

POLITICAL LOSSES AND GAINS During the early 1980s, women's rights activists worked to obtain ratification of the Equal Rights Amendment (ERA). Although Congress had passed the amendment in 1972, it had not yet been ratified, or approved, by three-fourths of the states. Supporters of the amendment had until June 30, 1982, to gain ratification from 38 states. They obtained only 35 of the 38 ratifications they needed, and the ERA did not become law.

With the failure of the Equal Rights Amendment, women's organizations began to concentrate on electing women to public office. Elections in 1980 and 1982 revealed a gender gap, in which women followed different voting patterns than men. More women candidates began to run for office, and in 1984 the Democrats chose Geraldine Ferraro as their vice-presidential candidate. She had spoken of the necessity for women in all walks of life to continue working for equal opportunities in American society.

A PERSONAL VOICE

It is not just those of us who have reached the top who are fighting this daily battle. It is a fight in which all of us—rich and poor, career and home oriented, young and old—participate, simply because we are women.

GERALDINE FERRARO, quoted in *Vital Speeches of the Day*

TEACHING OPTIONS

Teaching Gifted and Talented Students

Looking at Your Own Community Ask your gifted and talented students to localize their study of urban crises in the 1980s by looking at their own city or the large city nearest their community. Ask them to interview local aldermen or city officials who served during the 1980s. Have them visit the city library for information about population growth, changing settlement patterns, and rising or falling tax revenues. Students can present their findings to the class, using visual aids such as graphs, maps, or flow charts when appropriate.

Teaching Less Proficient Readers

Finding Main Ideas and Supporting Details Pair less proficient readers with more proficient ones to identify the main ideas and supporting details in the section on the equal rights struggle. Have students follow these steps:

1. Read the text on the equal rights struggle on pages 830 and 831.
2. List the main idea for each paragraph.
3. Go back and list the details that support each of the main ideas.

During the 1980s, the number of women in Congress increased from 28 to 47, and the number of women senators tripled—from two to six. President Reagan also named two women to his cabinet: Elizabeth Dole became secretary of transportation, and Margaret Heckler became secretary of health and human services. Nevertheless, women remained underrepresented in political affairs and overrepresented among the ranks of the poor.

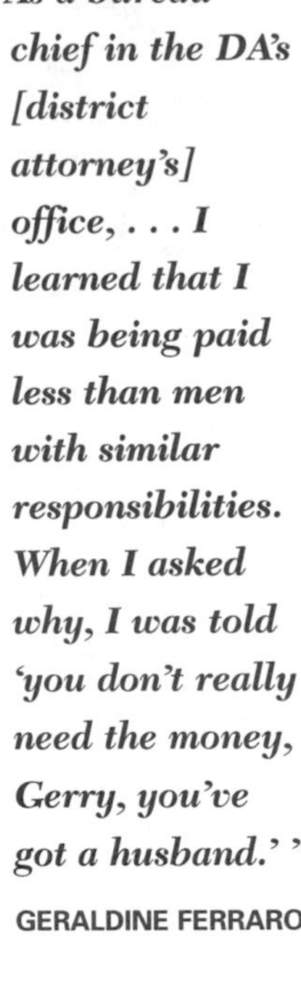

"As a bureau chief in the DA's [district attorney's] office, . . . I learned that I was being paid less than men with similar responsibilities. When I asked why, I was told 'you don't really need the money, Gerry, you've got a husband.'"

GERALDINE FERRARO

ECONOMIC AND SOCIAL GAINS Several factors contributed to what some called the feminization of poverty. By 1992, 57.8 percent of the nation's women were part of the work force, and a growing percentage of women worked as professionals and managers. However, in that year women earned only about 76 cents for every dollar men earned. Female college graduates earned only slightly more than male high-school graduates. Also, about 31 percent of female heads of household lived in poverty, and among African-American women the poverty rate was even higher. New trends in divorce settlements aggravated the situation. Under no-fault divorce, fewer women won alimony payments, and the courts rarely enforced the meager child support payments they awarded. As late as 1990, more than 25 percent of the spouses, mostly males, who owed child support still paid nothing at all.

To close the income gap that left so many women poor, women's organizations and unions proposed a system of **pay equity,** by which jobs would be rated on the basis of the amount of education they required, the amount of physical strength needed to perform them, and the number of people one supervised. Instead of relying on traditional pay scales, employers would establish pay rates that reflected each job's requirements. By 1989, 20 states had begun adjusting government jobs to offer pay equity for jobs of comparable worth. Many female employees received raises of up to 30 percent. Most private firms, however, resisted the idea because they believed it would be too expensive.

E. Answer Women were elected to public office in increasing numbers, and women employed on government jobs received raises through the implementation of pay equity.

Women also asked for other improvements in the workplace. Since many working women headed single-parent households or had children under the age of six, they pressed for family benefits. Government and corporate benefit packages began to include maternity leaves, flexible hours and workweeks, job sharing, and work-at-home arrangements. Some of these changes were launched by individual firms, while others required government intervention. Yet the Reagan administration sharply cut the federal budget for daycare, AFDC, and other similar programs. Congress passed a family-leave plan in 1991 that President Bush vetoed.

THINK THROUGH HISTORY
E. THEME ***Women in America*** *What gains did women make during the 1980s and early 1990s?*

The Fight for Rights Continues

Cuts in government programs and the backlash against civil rights initiatives, such as affirmative action, affected other groups as well.

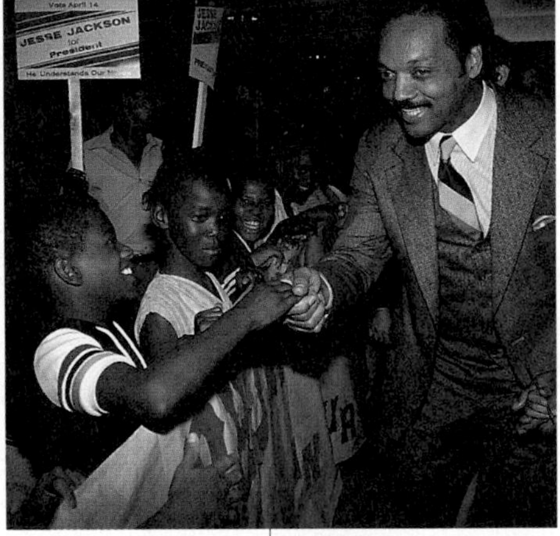

Jesse Jackson campaigns for the Democratic presidential nomination in 1984.

AFRICAN AMERICANS African Americans made striking political gains during the 1980s, even as their economic progress suffered. By the mid-1980s, African-American mayors governed dozens of cities, including Los Angeles, Detroit, Chicago, Atlanta, New Orleans, Philadelphia, and Washington, D.C. Hundreds of communities in both the North and the South had elected African Americans to serve as sheriffs, school board members, state legislators, and members of Congress. In 1990, **L. Douglas Wilder** of Virginia became the nation's first African-American governor. The Reverend **Jesse Jackson** ran for the Democratic presidential nomination in 1984 and 1988.

OBJECTIVE
(3) INSTRUCT

The Fight for Rights Continues

Discussing Key Ideas

- African Americans and Latino Americans see economic aid slashed by Reagan and Bush.
- Latino Americans and Asian Americans are the fastest-growing minorities during the 1980s.
- Some Latinos and non-Latinos differ in their views on bilingualism.
- Native Americans operate gambling casinos.
- Homosexual men and women become more politically active.

IN-DEPTH RESOURCES: UNIT 7
Geography Application: Latino Population in the 1980s, p. 24
Primary Source: Civil Rights in the 1980s, p. 30

MORE ABOUT . . .
Jesse Jackson's Campaign

In 1984, Jesse Jackson became the first African American to make a serious bid for the presidency. He tried again in 1988, when he was one of seven Democrats to enter the race for the Democratic nomination. Jackson claimed the second highest number of delegates (after Dukakis) in the New York State primary. Although Jackson lost the nomination to Dukakis, his good showing in the campaign helped him nail down some planks on minority rights in the party platform.

TEACHING OPTIONS

Making Connections Across Time

Women's Economic Status in the 1980s and Today In 1980, 51.5 percent of women worked outside the home. In 1994, 58.8 percent worked outside the home. Suggest to student groups that they interview working women to compare their experiences in the 1980s with women's current work experience. This should help students to become aware of issues faced by, and most important to, working women in the 1980s and 1990s.

Exploring Themes

Civil Rights Have students use a chart to summarize in a sentence one achievement by each group in pursuing equal rights.

Women	
African Americans	
Latinos	
Native Americans	
Asian Americans	
Gays and Lesbians	

NOW & THEN
Affirmative Action
Critical Thinking: Analyzing Results Discuss with students whether or not they see a trend developing in the 1980s and 1990s regarding affirmative action. How might they go about obtaining the information that would allow them to diagram the trend, if it exists? Have students outline the steps they might take to form an opinion.

MORE ABOUT . . .
Richmond v. J. A. Croson Company
In an attempt to redress past discrimination, Richmond, Virginia, like 190 other cities and 36 states, adopted a plan for affirmative action. In 1983, Richmond passed an ordinance that required at least 30 percent of all city construction work to be subcontracted to minority-owned companies. City records showed that although 50 percent of the population was black, only 0.67 percent of its prime construction contracts in recent years had been awarded to minority firms.

Similar affirmative action programs everywhere were thrown into turmoil when the Supreme Court in 1989 reversed its earlier support of affirmative action.

NOW & THEN

AFFIRMATIVE ACTION

In the 1996 presidential campaign, affirmative action became an issue. The Democratic candidate, President Clinton, favored current government policies supporting affirmative action, whereas the Republican candidate, Bob Dole, opposed affirmative action.

Presidents Reagan and Bush had actively opposed affirmative action and racial quotas throughout the 1980s.The Supreme Court's decision in *Richmond* v. *J. A. Croson Company* was one of a series of Supreme Court decisions that made it harder for minorities and women to sue in job-discrimination cases. In 1996, voters in California approved a referendum that did away with state affirmative action programs, but the referendum has been challenged on constitutional grounds in the courts.

However, the income gap between white Americans and African Americans was larger in 1988 than it had been in 1968. Middle-class African Americans sometimes moved into professional and managerial positions, but the poor faced a future of diminishing opportunities. In 1989, the newly conservative Supreme Court handed down a series of decisions that continued to change the nation's course on civil rights. In the case of *Richmond* v. *J. A. Croson Company,* for example, the Court further limited the scope of **affirmative-action,** policies that were designed to correct the effects of discrimination in the employment or education of minority groups or women. Other decisions by the Court outlawed contracts set aside for minority businesses. Sylvester Monroe, an African-American correspondent for *Newsweek* magazine, commented on the way many African Americans saw the backlash against affirmative action.

F. Answer It made it harder for minorities and women to win job-discrimination cases.

THINK THROUGH HISTORY
F. THEME
Civil Rights
How did the Croson decision affect affirmative action?

A PERSONAL VOICE

There's a finite pie and everybody wants his piece. Everybody is afraid of losing his piece of the pie. That's what the fight against affirmative action is all about. People feel threatened. As for blacks, they're passé. They're not in anymore. Nobody wants to talk about race.

SYLVESTER MONROE, quoted in *The Great Divide*

LATINOS Latinos became the fastest growing minority during the 1980s. By 1990, they constituted almost 9 percent of the population, and demographers estimated that Latinos would soon outnumber African Americans as the nation's largest minority group. About two out of three Latinos were Mexican Americans, who lived mostly in the Southwest. Puerto Ricans lived mainly in the Northeast, and Cubans lived primarily in Florida. Like African Americans, Latinos gained political power during the 1980s, when Toney Anaya became governor of New Mexico and Robert Martinez became governor of Florida. Several cities, including Denver, San Antonio, and Miami, elected mayors of Latino background. In August of 1988, President Reagan appointed Lauro Cavazos as secretary of education, and in 1990 President Bush named Dr. Antonia Coello Novello to the post of surgeon general.

Dr. Antonia Coello Novello served as surgeon general under President Bush.

Latino farm workers still suffered from low pay, unhealthy conditions, and high unemployment, but increasing numbers of Latinos held professional and technical positions. Latino salsa dancing and music gained widespread popularity, and by the early 1990s Tejano music had begun to gain mainstream attention. The murder of the young singer **Selena Quintanilla-Perez** in 1995 was even the subject of a commemorative edition of *People* magazine. Writers such as Sandra Cisneros and Oscar Hijuelos won literary awards for their books. Latino architecture and crafts—such as adobe houses, walled courtyards, and vivid woven rugs—became popular elements of American style. Such Latino foods as tapas, fajitas, tacos, jalapeño peppers, and jicama quickly found their way into mainstream American diets.

Many Latinos supported bilingual education. Some feared that abandoning Spanish would weaken their distinctive culture. In the words of Daniel Villanueva, a television executive, "We want to be here, but without losing our language and our culture. They are a richness, a treasure that we don't care to lose." The Bilingual Education Act of 1968 and the Voting Rights Act of 1975 enabled Spanish speakers to go to school and vote in their own language, but by the mid-1980s opposition to bilingualism was rising in some quarters. Critics argued that it slowed the rate at which Spanish-speaking people entered main-

TEACHING OPTIONS

Making Connections Across the Curriculum

Literature Ask students which of the authors mentioned on pages 832 (Sandra Cisnernos, Oscar Hijuelos) and 833 (Amy Tan, Maxine Hong Kingston) they are familiar with. Ask for suggestions of additional authors representing minority communities. If possible allow time for students to visit the school or community library and to meet with the librarian. Students may wish to prepare reports on a minority author of their choice and to include a brief excerpt from the author's work as part of their report.

Exploring Themes

Cultural Diversity Discuss with students the cultural diversity represented by the groups discussed on pages 831–833. Ask students which traditional values upheld by presidents Reagan and Bush are held in common by all the groups. *Some students may respond that broad values such as honesty, care for children, and a stable family life are accepted by all the groups. Students may also observe that some issues, such as civil rights, cut across minority lines, with some members in favor and some members in opposition.*

stream American life. They also feared that the nation would become split between English speakers and non–English speakers.

NATIVE AMERICANS During the 1980s, the Reagan administration slashed aid to Native Americans for health, education, and other services. Driven to find new sources of revenue, Native Americans began protesting federal and state regulations that restricted gambling on reservation lands. After the Supreme Court ruled in favor of Native Americans, many tribes opened Las Vegas–style casinos, which provided additional funding for the tribes that operated them. Nonetheless, the long-term problems faced by Native Americans have not been solved by gambling casinos, although the new wealth has helped to some extent.

G. Answer They defended their cultural identities by maintaining cultural traditions in language, literature, and architecture. They worked to see people from their backgrounds included in government.

THINK THROUGH HISTORY
G. THEME ***Cultural Diversity*** *How did racial and ethnic minorities defend their cultural identities in the 1980s?*

ASIAN AMERICANS Asian Americans were the second fastest-growing minority in the United States during the 1980s. By 1992, the U.S. population included about 8.3 million Asian Americans and Pacific Islanders. Asian Americans constituted 3.25 percent of the population.

Unlike African Americans and Latinos, Asian Americans made significant economic advances but few political strides, although Senator Daniel Inouye had long been an important Japanese-American politician who represented the state of Hawaii in the U.S. Senate. Many Asian Americans chose to attend college and pursued successful careers in business, science, or the arts. These included Amy Tan (author of *The Joy Luck Club*) and Maxine Hong Kingston (author of *The Woman Warrior*).

GAYS AND LESBIANS During the 1970s and 1980s, homosexual men and women emerged from political invisibility to work for legislation protecting their rights. By 1986, 26 states had reduced criminal penalties for homosexual relationships between consenting adults. During his term as president, George Bush increased funding for AIDS research and called for a study on hate crimes, including attacks on homosexuals. During the 1992 campaign, however, President Bush refused to support antidiscrimination legislation. Several speakers at the Republican National Convention in 1992 called gays immoral. However, by 1993, seven states and 110 communities had outlawed discrimination against homosexuals.

H. Answer Many minority groups made political rather than economic advances.

THINK THROUGH HISTORY
H. *Synthesizing* *How did minorities advance during the 1980s?*

Although various groups struggled for political power and economic success during the Reagan and Bush years, these competing groups tended to come together when the United States faced challenges abroad.

Gay and lesbian activists march in New York in 1983.

Section 3 Assessment

1. TERMS & NAMES
Identify:
- AIDS (acquired immune deficiency syndrome)
- pay equity
- L. Douglas Wilder
- Jesse Jackson
- affirmative action
- Selena Quintanilla-Perez

2. SUMMARIZING Use a chart to list some of the social problems of the Reagan and Bush years and how the government responded to them.

Social Problem	Government Response

Choose one issue and tell the class what other responses the government might have made.

3. MAKING PREDICTIONS How might improvements in the educational system help solve other social problems?

THINK ABOUT
- the impact education might have on health-related problems
- the impact that education might have on urban problems

4. COMPARING Compare the political gains and losses experienced by various groups during the Reagan and Bush administrations.

THINK ABOUT
- the experiences of women
- the experiences of African Americans
- the experiences of Latinos
- the experiences of other minorities

ANSWERS

1. TERMS & NAMES
AIDS (acquired immune deficiency syndrome), p. 827
pay equity, p. 831
L. Douglas Wilder, p. 831
Jesse Jackson, p. 831
affirmative action, p. 832
Selena Quintanilla-Perez, p. 832

2. SUMMARIZING
Possible Answers:
abortion—Supreme Court restricted access
drug abuse—"Just Say No!" campaign
low student test scores—"America 2000" education initiative
urban crisis—reduced federal spending on cities
equal rights for women—federal government cut budget for day care and cut AFDC; some states offered pay equity
equal rights for minorities—Supreme Court reversed affirmative action

3. MAKING PREDICTIONS
Possible Responses: Education might help discourage risky sexual behavior and drug use. Education makes workers more employable, so improved schools could help solve some urban problems, such as poverty and crime.

4. COMPARING
Possible Responses: More women and minorities were elected or appointed to office. Many Latinos encountered political opposition over their support for bilingual education. Some Native Americans gained more political autonomy as the Supreme Court struck down federal regulations restricting gambling on reservations. Asian Americans made economic advances but few political strides.

MORE ABOUT . . .
Native American Casinos
By 1996 Native Americans had opened more than 170 high-stakes bingo halls and casinos which grossed about $6 billion a year. The success of the casinos on Indian-owned land threatened other gambling interests, including state-operated lotteries. Many Native American communities used the gambling revenues to pay for badly needed improvements to schools, libraries, health care centers, homes, tribal industries, and other programs. "We've done everything we can to ensure that jobs are available to any of our people who want to work," said Marge Anderson, chief executive of the Mille Lacs Band of Ojibwe (in Minnesota).

ASSESS & RETEACH

Section 3 Assessment
Have students focus on question 4 which elicits a good overview of the section.

Self-Assessment
Have students return to the chart they made at the beginning of Section 3. Ask if they have learned what they had hoped to learn.

Section Quiz
FORMAL ASSESSMENT
Section Quiz, p. 308

Reteach
Review question 2 in the section assessment by drawing the graphic organizer on the chalkboard.

CLOSE

Men, women, and minorities vied for political power and economic gains in the 1980s. However, they agreed more than they differed when confronted with international challenges.

Geography Spotlight

OBJECTIVES

1. To describe regional population shifts in America in recent decades.
2. To identify the South and Southwest, or Sunbelt, as regions that have seen the greatest influx of people.

FOCUS & MOTIVATE

▶ ***Starting with the Student***
Ask students to consider the different parts or regions of America.

- If students could live in any part of the country, where would they live? Why?

MORE ABOUT . . .
Las Vegas, Nevada

Located in Nevada's southeastern corner, Las Vegas qualifies as one of the Sunbelt cities experiencing unprecedented growth in recent years. According to the U.S. Bureau of the Census, Las Vegas was one of the five fastest-growing American cities from 1990 to 1994. By the next year, according to a real-estate industry report, Las Vegas was the second largest new home market in the nation. A warm, sunny city surrounded by desert stretches, Las Vegas began growing after gambling was legalized in the state in 1931 and the nearby Hoover Dam was completed five years later.

GEOGRAPHY SPOTLIGHT

Sunbelt, Rustbelt, Ecotopia

Americans have always been on the move. Each year, hundreds of thousands of families move to new locations in search of better homes, jobs, and schools and for a host of other reasons. Sometimes people change addresses within the same locality. At other times they set off for different climates, crossing state lines and journeying thousands of miles to a different region.

As a geographical term, *region* is used to designate an area with common features or characteristics that set it apart from its surroundings. For example, the Mississippi Valley is a large physical region; Warren Woods is a small physical region. The term *region* is often used for groups of states that share an area and certain characteristics. New England, the Midwest, and the Pacific Coast are names given to some regions of this type.

As people move from place to place, from state to state, and from region to region, they gradually transform the balance of political and economic power in the nation. Each census in recent times has recorded how certain states have gained population and others have lost population. If the gains or losses are large enough, a state's representation in the U.S. House of Representatives will increase or decrease. In this way the movement of people translates directly into political power.

In the 1970s, people on the move created new names for regions. The South and Southwest were called the Sunbelt because their warm climate attracted many migrants. The West was sometimes called Ecotopia because of its varied scenery and ecological attractions. The North Central and Northeast regions were called the Rustbelt because many of their aging factories had been closed.

An aerial view of Miami, Florida

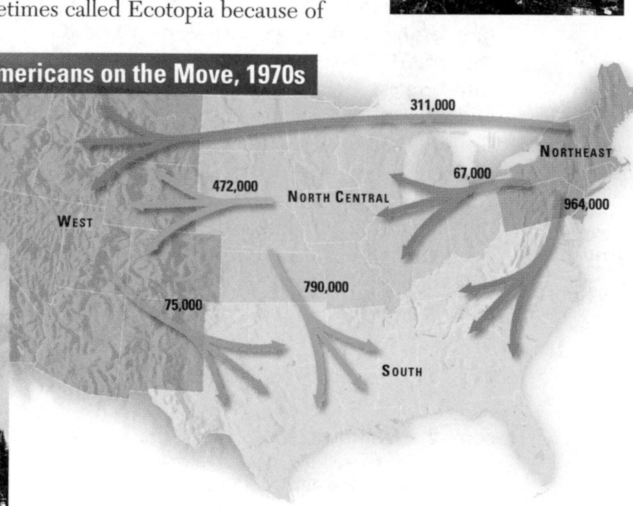

Source: Bernard L. Weinstein and Robert E. Firestine, *Regional Growth and Decline in the United States* (1978)

A posh hotel in downtown Los Angeles

REGIONAL EXCHANGES
As people moved from region to region between 1970 and 1975, the population center of the United States, which had generally moved westward for 17 decades, suddenly moved southward. The arrows show the net migration of Americans in the early 1970s. The West gained 311,000 from the Northeast plus 472,000 from the North Central region, for a total of 783,000 people. However, it also lost 75,000 people to the South, reducing its net gain to 708,000 people.

RECOMMENDED RESOURCES

Books and Pamphlets

Abbot, Carl. *The New Urban America.* Chapel Hill: U of North Carolina P, 1981. A study of Sunbelt cities and the political ramifications of their growth.

Bernard, Richard M., and Bradley R. Rice. *Sunbelt Cities.* Austin: U of Texas P, 1983. An examination of the growth and politics of Sunbelt cities since World War II.

Herbers, John. *The New Heartland.* New York: Times Books, 1986. A study of American migration beyond the suburbs and how it is changing the nation.

Population Trends in the 1980s. Washington, D.C.: Bureau of the Census, U.S. Department of Commerce, 1992. Pamphlet of statistics on national and state population trends and trends in internal migration.

Preston, Richard. *American Steel.* New York: Prentice, 1991. An account of efforts to resurrect America's Rustbelt by revitalizing the steel industry.

Videos

Top Ten Retirement Locations in the Sunbelt. Leisure Living, 1990. A tour of ten Sunbelt communities popular with retirees: Hot Springs, Arkansas; Phoenix and Tucson, Arizona; San Diego, California; Lakeland and Clearwater/St. Petersburg, Florida; Murray, Kentucky; Knoxville, Tennessee; and McAllen and San Antonio, Texas.

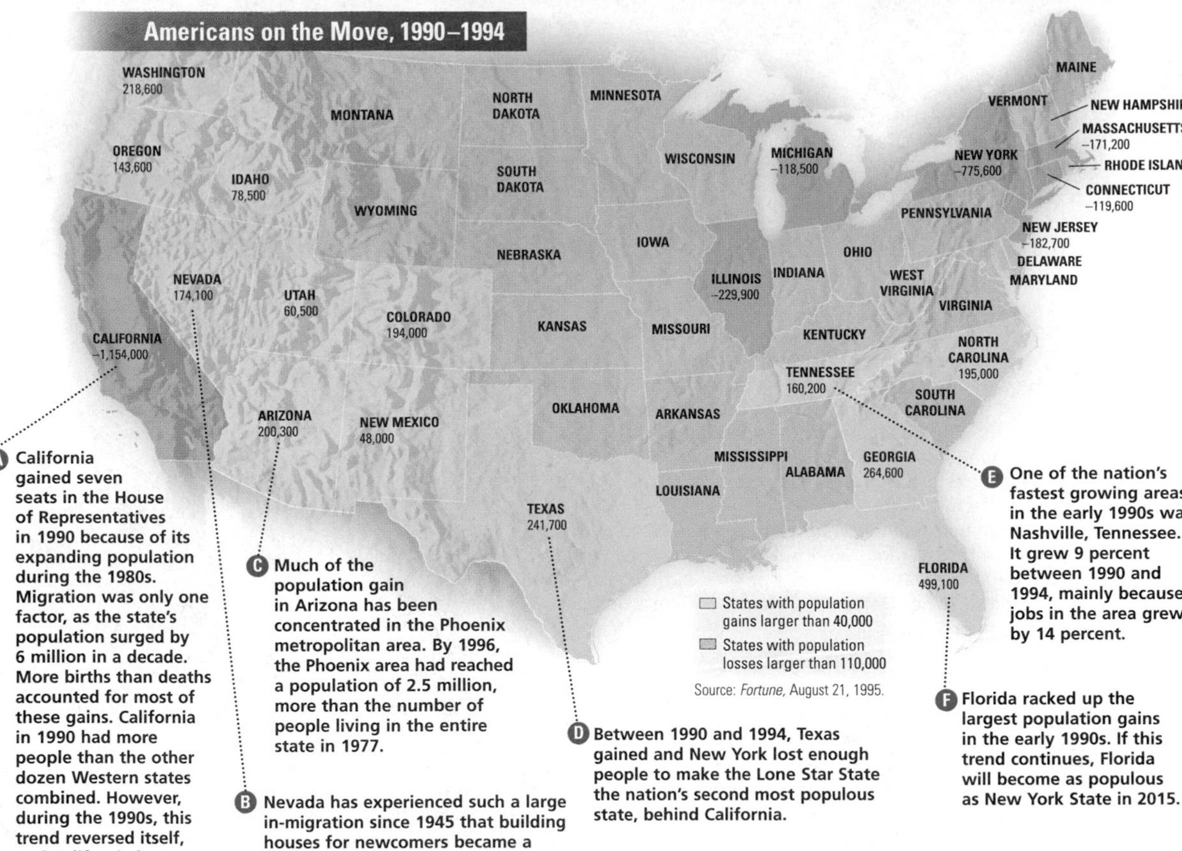

A California gained seven seats in the House of Representatives in 1990 because of its expanding population during the 1980s. Migration was only one factor, as the state's population surged by 6 million in a decade. More births than deaths accounted for most of these gains. California in 1990 had more people than the other dozen Western states combined. However, during the 1990s, this trend reversed itself, and California lost population during most of the decade.

B Nevada has experienced such a large in-migration since 1945 that building houses for newcomers became a major industry in the state. Only 3% of the existing residences were built before 1945.

C Much of the population gain in Arizona has been concentrated in the Phoenix metropolitan area. By 1996, the Phoenix area had reached a population of 2.5 million, more than the number of people living in the entire state in 1977.

D Between 1990 and 1994, Texas gained and New York lost enough people to make the Lone Star State the nation's second most populous state, behind California.

E One of the nation's fastest growing areas in the early 1990s was Nashville, Tennessee. It grew 9 percent between 1990 and 1994, mainly because jobs in the area grew by 14 percent.

F Florida racked up the largest population gains in the early 1990s. If this trend continues, Florida will become as populous as New York State in 2015.

CALIFORNIA'S POPULATION SHIFT In the 1980s, California steadily gained population as more people moved in than moved out. After 1988, however, the situation changed rapidly and the movement of people out of California exceeded in-migration.

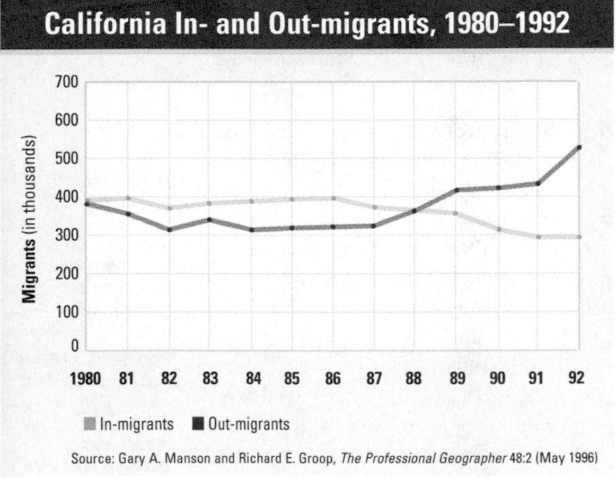

INTERACT WITH HISTORY

1. **COMPARING AND CONTRASTING** Which three states lost the most population between 1990 and 1994? Which three states gained the most population? Why do you think this happened?
2. **CREATING A MAP** Choose one of the most populous states and then make a demographic map of it. (*Demography* refers to human populations. Your map will show various aspects of the population of the state you have chosen, such as size, growth, density, distribution, and vital statistics.) Then display your map along with those of other students on a bulletin board in the classroom.

SEE SKILLBUILDER HANDBOOK, PAGES 909 AND 932.

Visit http://www.mlushistory.com for more about migration to the Sunbelt.

INSTRUCT

▶ *Starting with the Student*

- Have students speculate on reasons other than aging factories for Sunbelt growth in the 1970s. *Possible Responses: Cheaper housing; cheaper labor; lower taxes; air conditioning more widely available; crime and urban decay in the North.*
- Have students predict future regional population shifts and explain their predictions. *Some may predict a Sunbelt influx as Baby Boomers retire and seek the easier life of warmer climates. Some may feel global warming will make the Sunbelt less habitable. Others may base predictions on economic, social, or political factors.*

▶ *Discussing Key Ideas*

- Though the general trend of moving west continues, the 1970s see Americans also begin to move south.
- The influx to California ends in the late 1980s, but the influx to other parts of the so-called Sunbelt continues.

HISTORY FROM VISUALS

Reading the Images Have students study the maps.

- What was the northernmost state with a big population increase in the early 1990s? *Washington.*
- What generalizations can you make about the physical size of states that lost and gained population in the early 1990s? *Smaller lost population; larger, presumably less densely populated states gained.*

INTERACT WITH HISTORY

1. Comparing and Contrasting

Possible Responses: *California, New York, and Illinois lost the most people; Florida, Georgia, and Texas gained the most.*

Answers: *Among the factors students may cite are the recession at the start of the decade, which hit California harder than any other state; the natural disasters that California experienced in the first half of the decade; the passage of NAFTA, which prompted more companies to base themselves in Texas and Florida to be closer to trading partners in Latin America; the growth of Atlanta that came with an influx of new businesses, including CNN, and the buildup to the 1996 Olympics; and the high taxes and high cost of living in New York, Illinois, and California.*

2. Creating a Map

The most useful source for students to consult for demographic information is probably the *Statistical Abstract of the United States,* which is published annually by the U.S. Department of Commerce. Other sources might be recent encyclopedia articles about the various states.

Standards for Evaluation

Maps should be drawn to scale; provide accurate, up-to-date demographic information; and be clear and easy to read. Assign different states or regions to different students so that the final bulletin-board display covers the entire nation, including Alaska and Hawaii.

Section 4 Overview

OBJECTIVES

1. To identify changes in the Communist world that brought about an end to the Cold War.
2. To summarize U.S. actions taken to influence Central American and Caribbean affairs.
3. To trace the events leading to the Iran-Contra scandal and to analyze U.S. involvement in the Persian Gulf War.

SKILLBUILDERS

- Understanding geography: location, region, p. 839
- Understanding geography: region, movement, p. 841

CRITICAL THINKING

- Finding main ideas, p. 836
- Analyzing causes, p. 838
- Contrasting, p. 839
- Theme: Constitutional Concerns, p. 839
- Forming generalizations, pp. 840, 841
- Summarizing, p. 841
- Analyzing causes, p. 841

FOCUS & MOTIVATE

5-MINUTE WARM-UP

Recognizing Point of View
To explore differing views on American foreign policy after the Cold War, have students read the Point/Counterpoint on page 840 and answer these questions.

1. Why does General Schwarzkopf believe that the United States may need to intervene in regional conflicts?
2. Does Barbara Conry agree or disagree with Schwarzkopf's view?

WARM-UP TRANSPARENCY 25

▶ ***Starting with the Student***
- Ask students if they have ever been in an argument with someone when the cause of their disagreement suddenly seemed to disappear.
- Might the same thing happen in international affairs? Why or why not?

4 Foreign Policy After the Cold War

TERMS & NAMES
- Mikhail Gorbachev
- INF Treaty
- *glasnost*
- *perestroika*
- Commonwealth of Independent States
- Tiananmen Square
- Sandinista
- Contras
- Operation Desert Storm

LEARN ABOUT the end of the Cold War and the emergence of a global economy
TO UNDERSTAND America's search for a new role in the post-Cold War world.

ONE AMERICAN'S STORY

Colin Powell did not start out in life with any special privileges. He was born in Harlem and raised in the Bronx, where he enjoyed street games and tolerated school. Then, while attending the City College of New York, he joined the Reserve Officer Training Corps (ROTC). He got straight A's in ROTC, though his other grades were mediocre, and so he decided to make the army his career.

Powell served first in Vietnam, and then in Korea and West Germany. He rose in rank to become a general; then President Reagan made him national security adviser. In this post, Powell noted that the Soviet Union was a factor in all the administration's foreign policy decisions.

General Colin Powell

A PERSONAL VOICE

Our choosing sides in conflicts around the world was almost always decided on the basis of East-West competition. The new Soviet leader, Mikhail Gorbachev, however, was turning the old Cold War formulas on their head. . . . Ronald Reagan . . . had the vision and flexibility, lacking in many Cold Warriors [participants in the Cold War between the U.S. and the USSR], to recognize that Gorbachev was a new man in a new age offering new opportunities for peace.

COLIN POWELL, *My American Journey*

Though U.S. foreign policy in the early 1980s was marked by intense hostility toward the Soviet Union, drastic economic problems in the Soviet Union destroyed its ability to continue to vigorously wage the Cold War. Its new leaders began to look for a way out.

The Cold War Ends

In March of 1985, **Mikhail Gorbachev** became the general secretary of the Communist Party in the Soviet Union. He understood the economic weakness of the Soviet Union and initiated peace talks with the United States to lessen Cold War tensions.

GORBACHEV INITIATES REFORM Gorbachev represented a new generation of Soviet leaders. He recognized that better relations with the United States would allow the Soviets to reduce their military spending and reform their economy. An imaginative politician and skilled diplomat, Gorbachev initiated a series of arms-control meetings that led to the **INF Treaty** (Intermediate-Range Nuclear Forces Treaty). Reagan and Gorbachev signed this treaty on December 8, 1987, and the Senate ratified it in May 1988. The treaty eliminated two classes of weapons systems in Europe and allowed each nation to make on-site inspections of the other's military installations.

A. Answer He believed better relations would allow the Soviets to reduce military spending and reform their economy.

THINK THROUGH HISTORY
A. *Finding Main Ideas* *Why did Mikhail Gorbachev pursue better relations with the United States?*

Gorbachev advocated ***glasnost*** (openness in discussing social problems) and ***perestroika*** (economic and bureaucratic restructuring) in the Soviet Union. He restored private ownership of land and replaced central planning with local decision-making. He decreased censorship and held free elections.

SECTION 4 RESOURCES

PRINT RESOURCES

IN-DEPTH RESOURCES: UNIT 7
Guided Reading, p. 22
Primary Source: The First Day of Desert Storm, p. 31
Outline Map: U.S. Attention on the Middle East, p. 26
American Lives: Daniel Inouye, p. 36

READING STUDY GUIDE, p. 259

ACCESS FOR STUDENTS ACQUIRING ENGLISH
Guided Reading (Spanish), p. 273

SPANISH READING STUDY GUIDE, p. 259

FORMAL ASSESSMENT
Section Quiz, p. 309

ALTERNATIVE ASSESSMENT BOOK
See forms for supporting and scoring alternative activities.

TECHNOLOGY RESOURCES

HUMANITIES TRANSPARENCIES
H47, "Jobs That May Be Lost" by Walt Handelsman

GEOGRAPHY TRANSPARENCIES
G33, The Cold War Ends, 1989–1990

CD-ROM *Our Times*
Grolier Multimedia Encyclopedia
Electronic Library of Primary Sources

VIDEO *American Portfolio: A Videodisc for U.S. History* user's guide, pp. 258, 259

INTERNET http://www.mlushistory.com

SOVIET DISUNION The elections increased political tensions and led to a dramatic increase in nationalism on the part of the Soviet Union's non-Russian republics. By 1990, these republics had declared that local laws took priority over those of the central government.

Then, in the summer of 1991, a new Russian revolution took place. On August 19, Communist hardliners attempted a coup. They forced Gorbachev out of office and declared a state of emergency. Boris Yeltsin, president of the largest Soviet republic, Russia, climbed atop an armored truck and immediately called for a general strike in protest. Three days later, the coup was over and Gorbachev was back. On August 24, he resigned as head of the Communist Party and banned it from any further role in government.

The pressure for complete change, however, was overwhelming. In December of 1991, 14 non-Russian republics declared their independence and Gorbachev resigned as Soviet president. After 74 years, the Soviet Union dissolved. A loose federation known as the **Commonwealth of Independent States,** or CIS, took its place. In February of 1992, President George Bush and Russian president Boris Yeltsin issued a formal statement declaring an end to the Cold War and the beginning of a new era of "friendship and partnership." In January of 1993 they signed the START II pact, designed to cut both nations' nuclear arsenals by 75 percent.

ON THE WORLD STAGE

DEMOCRATIC ELECTIONS IN RUSSIA

This magazine cover showing the shattered image of Lenin, the first head of the USSR, symbolizes the breakup of the Soviet Union. After the Soviet Union dissolved in 1991, Boris Yeltsin continued as president of Russia. Yeltsin ended price controls and increased private ownership of business. The Russian parliament opposed Yeltsin's policies, even after a 1993 referendum showed that the majority of voters supported them.

In December of 1993, Russian voters installed a new parliament and approved a new constitution, parts of which resembled the U.S. Constitution. The election results heralded an era of increasing democracy in Russia. In 1996, Yeltsin won reelection as president of Russia, with his term not due to expire until 2000.

POLAND AND GERMANY Gorbachev's new policies led to massive changes in Eastern Europe as well as the Soviet Union. In 1988, when the Soviet Union was still intact, Gorbachev reduced the number of Soviet troops in Eastern Europe and allowed non-Communist parties to organize in satellite nations such as East Germany and Poland. He advised the satellite nations to move toward democracy.

That is exactly what they did. Poland moved immediately to establish a non-Communist government with a new constitution and a free-market economy. Embracing the once-outlawed Solidarity labor movement that had been growing throughout the 1980s, Polish voters supported an increasingly democratic government.

On November 9, 1989, East Germany opened the Berlin Wall, allowing free passage between the two parts of the city for the first time in 28 years. Berliners cheered and danced atop the wall, and rushed through what had once been heavily guarded checkpoints. East German border guards stood by and watched as Berliners pounded away with hammers and other tools at the despised wall. In early 1990, East Germany held its first free elections, and on October 3 of that year, the two German nations again became one.

Crowds welcome East Berliners into West Berlin as the Berlin Wall is being taken down in 1989.

EASTERN EUROPE Other European nations also adopted democratic reforms. Czechoslovakia withdrew from the Soviet bloc. The Baltic states of Latvia, Estonia, and Lithuania declared their independence from the Soviet Union. Hungary, Bulgaria, and Romania made successful transitions from communism.

Yugoslavia, however, collapsed. Four of its six republics seceded. Ethnic rivalries deteriorated into a brutal war among Muslims, Orthodox Serbs, and Roman Catholic Croats, who were dividing up Yugoslavia. Serbia backed Serb minorities that were stirring up civil unrest in Croatia and Bosnia.

OBJECTIVE
① **INSTRUCT**

The Cold War Ends

▶ ***Starting with the Student***
Discuss with students suitable metaphors for the collapse of the Soviet Union. *Students might suggest a stone wall that crumbles.*

▶ ***Discussing Key Ideas***
- Gorbachev begins reforms in the USSR.
- The breaking apart of the USSR brings an end to the Cold War.
- East and West Germany reunite.
- In China, communism continues.

IN-DEPTH RESOURCES: UNIT 7
Guided Reading, p. 22

ACCESS FOR STUDENTS ACQUIRING ENGLISH
Guided Reading (Spanish), p. 273

GEOGRAPHY TRANSPARENCIES
G33, The Cold War Ends, 1989–90

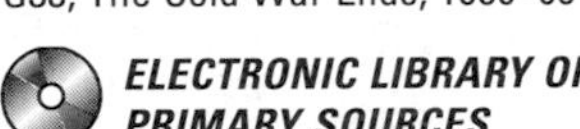

ELECTRONIC LIBRARY OF PRIMARY SOURCES
from *The United States and the World: Setting Limits* by Jeane J. Kirkpatrick

OUR TIMES
"Freedom Ascendant" by Taylor Branch

ON THE WORLD STAGE
Democratic Elections in Russia

Ask students why they think the Russian parliament continued to oppose Yeltsin's policies even after a majority of the people voted for them. *Possible answers include the reluctance of the old parliament to give up power and the persistence of strongly held beliefs.*

Block Schedule TEACHING OPTION **Time Needed: 20 Minutes**

Cooperative Activity: Creating a Foreign Affairs Time Line

Task: Student groups will construct a time line on foreign affairs that shows the Cold War.

Purpose: To understand the chronology of events relating to U.S. foreign affairs during the 1980s and to evaluate them for their negative or positive impact on the conservative agenda of the 1980s.

Activity: Students divide into three groups and each group researches foreign events in one part of the world in the 1980s: Europe and Asia, Central America and the Caribbean, and the Middle East. Each group will write out the most significant events in their area, to be organized into a class time line. Each event will be placed above the line if it positively affects the conservative agenda of the 1980s, and below the line if it negatively affects such an agenda. Three coordinators—one from each group—will need to meet together to design, coordinate, and produce the time line.

ALTERNATIVE ASSESSMENT BOOK
Standards for Evaluating a Cooperative Activity

Standards for Evaluation
Time line entries should . . .
- show evidence of careful research
- demonstrate an understanding of the significance of the events for the conservative agenda
- show a basic understanding of chronology

MORE ABOUT . . .
Tiananmen Square

Ironically, *Tiananmen* means the "Gate of Heavenly Peace." The gate itself overlooks the square, which has often been a place of national celebrations, with parades and fireworks. The students who began holding rallies in the square for a more democratic China were joined by tens of thousands. As the situation grew more and more out of control, the government called in military units from distant provinces. On June 3 the military moved in against the protesters, killing hundreds. Thousands more were arrested in the days that followed.

OBJECTIVE
② INSTRUCT

Central American and Caribbean Policy

▶ ***Discussing Key Ideas***
- Reagan and Bush think leftist governments in Central America and the Caribbean are a threat.
- The two administrations use both direct and indirect means to strengthen anti-Communist forces and weaken leftist governments.
- Reagan favors helping the Contras, who are anti-Communist Nicaraguan rebels, while Congress explicitly votes against such aid.
- In Grenada and again in Panama, the U.S. uses military force to suppress ties with Communist Cuba and to depose suspected drug trafficker Manuel Noriega.

The collapse of communism in the Soviet Union and Eastern Europe resulted in a formal end to the Cold War. The spread of democracy throughout the former Soviet empire suited American foreign policy, which looked to the spread of democracy to improve the prospects for peace and world trade.

THINK THROUGH HISTORY
B. Analyzing Causes *How did the end of the Cold War affect European politics and economics?*
B. Answer It brought democracy to Russia, reunited Germany, and brought freedom and a market economy to many of the countries of Eastern Europe. However, some ethnic rivalries intensified as a result of the changes sweeping Europe.

A Chinese protester defies the tanks in Tiananmen Square in 1989.

COMMUNISM CONTINUES IN CHINA Even before *perestroika* unfolded in the Soviet Union, economic reform began in China. Early in the 1980s, the Chinese Communist government loosened its grip on business and eliminated some price controls. Students in China began to demand freedom of speech and a greater voice in government.

In April 1989, university students in China held marches that quickly grew into large demonstrations in Beijing's **Tiananmen Square** and on the streets of other cities. In Tiananmen Square, Chinese students constructed a version of the Statue of Liberty to symbolize their struggle for democracy.

China's premier, Li Peng, ordered the military to crush the protesters. Soldiers killed hundreds of them; government officials ordered the arrest of others, and some of those were executed. The world's democratic countries watched these events on television with great dismay. By 1990 the Chinese government started more economic reforms. China's attempts at economic liberalization were encouraged by U.S. policymakers.

Central American and Caribbean Policy

Cold War considerations during the Reagan and Bush administrations continued to influence affairs in Central America and the Caribbean, where the United States opposed leftist governments in favor of governments friendly to it.

NICARAGUA The United States had had a presence in Nicaragua ever since 1912, when President Taft sent U.S. marines to protect American investments there. The marines left in 1933, but only after helping the dictator Anastasio Somoza come to power. When **Sandinista** rebels toppled the dictatorship of Somoza's son in 1979, President Carter recognized the new regime and sent it $83 million in economic aid. The Soviet Union and Cuba sent aid as well.

In 1981, however, President Reagan charged that Nicaragua was a Soviet outpost that was "exporting revolution" to other Central American countries. Reagan cut all aid to the Sandinista government and threw his support to guerrilla forces known as the **Contras** because they were against communism. By 1983, the Contra army had grown to nearly 10,000 men, and American officials from the CIA had moved in to direct operations—without congressional approval. In response, Congress passed the Boland Amendment, banning military aid to the Contras for two years, but Reagan's administration still managed to find ways to aid the Contras.

On February 25, 1990, Nicaraguan president Daniel Ortega held free elections, and Violeta de Chamorro was elected the nation's new president. Chamorro's supporters and the Sandinistas agreed to work together to rebuild Nicaragua.

GRENADA The Reagan administration had pursued indirect and covert means to influence politics in Central America, but on the tiny Caribbean island of Grenada, it used direct military force. After noting that the island was developing ties to Communist Cuba, President Reagan dispatched approximately 2,000 troops to the island in 1983. There they overthrew the pro-Cuban government, which was replaced by one friendlier to the United States. Eighteen American soldiers died in the attack, but Reagan declared that the invasion had been necessary to defend U.S. security.

PANAMA Six years later, in 1989, President Bush sent over 20,000 soldiers and marines into Panama to overthrow and arrest General Manuel Antonio Noriega on

TEACHING OPTIONS

Teaching Less Proficient Readers

Locating Place Names on a Map Less proficient readers may be confused by the number of different place names in this section of the text. They may find the text easier to understand if they can locate these places in relation to themselves. Have less proficient readers pair with more proficient readers. Make available to students a photocopy of a world map. As each new location is mentioned in the text, ask the paired readers to locate the site on their map, referring to atlases in their book and classroom if necessary.

Making Connections Across Cultures

Grenada Grenada, a country in the West Indies made up of the island of Grenada and the southern Grenadines, was settled first by the French, then became a British colony in 1783. Grenada achieved its independence in 1974. St. Georges is the capital and largest city. Most of the 110,000 people who make up the population are of African or mixed African and European ancestry. Tourists, who are essential to the economy of the country, rave about the balmy climate, sparkling beaches, and beautiful scenery.

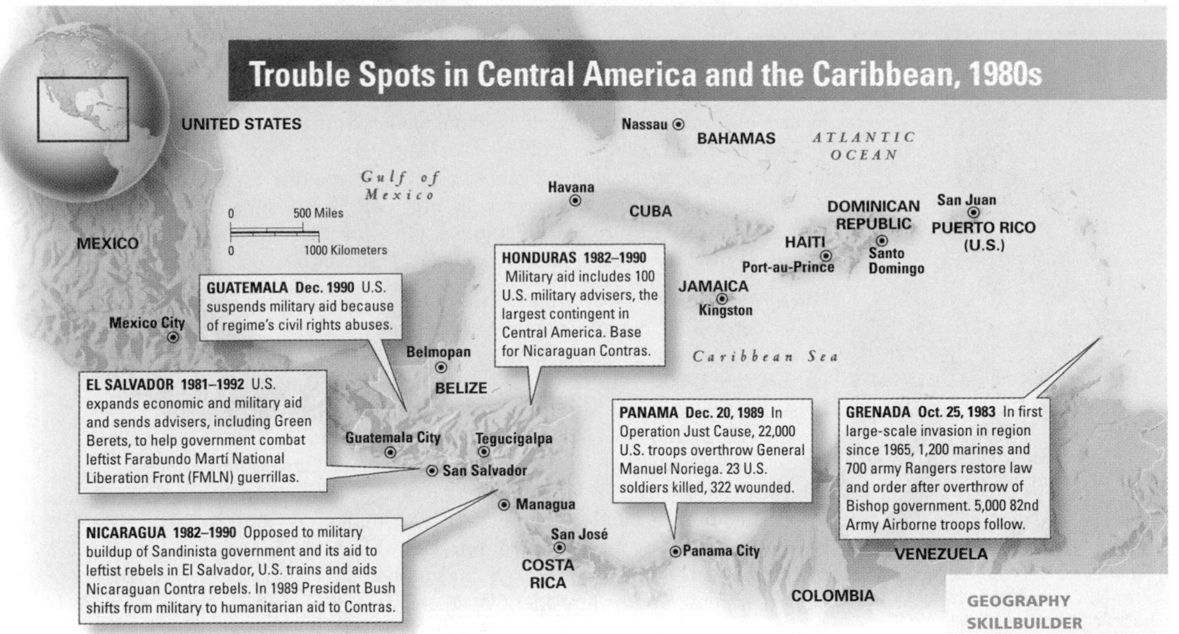
Trouble Spots in Central America and the Caribbean, 1980s
UNITED STATES
MEXICO
Gulf of Mexico
0 500 Miles
0 1000 Kilometers
Nassau
BAHAMAS
ATLANTIC OCEAN
Havana
CUBA
DOMINICAN REPUBLIC
San Juan
PUERTO RICO (U.S.)
HAITI
Port-au-Prince
Santo Domingo
JAMAICA
Kingston
Caribbean Sea
Mexico City
Belmopan
BELIZE
Guatemala City
Tegucigalpa
San Salvador
Managua
San José
COSTA RICA
Panama City
VENEZUELA
COLOMBIA
GUATEMALA Dec. 1990 U.S. suspends military aid because of regime's civil rights abuses.
HONDURAS 1982–1990 Military aid includes 100 U.S. military advisers, the largest contingent in Central America. Base for Nicaraguan Contras.
EL SALVADOR 1981–1992 U.S. expands economic and military aid and sends advisers, including Green Berets, to help government combat leftist Farabundo Martí National Liberation Front (FMLN) guerrillas.
PANAMA Dec. 20, 1989 In Operation Just Cause, 22,000 U.S. troops overthrow General Manuel Noriega. 23 U.S. soldiers killed, 322 wounded.
GRENADA Oct. 25, 1983 In first large-scale invasion in region since 1965, 1,200 marines and 700 army Rangers restore law and order after overthrow of Bishop government. 5,000 82nd Army Airborne troops follow.
NICARAGUA 1982–1990 Opposed to military buildup of Sandinista government and its aid to leftist rebels in El Salvador, U.S. trains and aids Nicaraguan Contra rebels. In 1989 President Bush shifts from military to humanitarian aid to Contras.

GEOGRAPHY SKILLBUILDER

LOCATION *Which Central American and Caribbean countries experienced an actual U.S. invasion of their territory in the 1980s?* **REGION** *Besides direct attack, what other techniques did the United States employ to influence countries in the Caribbean and Central American regions?*

Skillbuilder Answer **Location:** Grenada and Panama. **Region:** Providing economic and military aid, as well as dispatching military advisers, to nations it wished to influence.

charges of drug trafficking. Noriega had been receiving money since 1960 from the CIA, but he was also involved in the international drug trade. After he was indicted by a Miami grand jury, Noriega was taken by force by the American military and flown to Miami to stand trial. In April of 1992, Noriega was convicted and sentenced to 40 years in prison. Many Latin American governments deplored the "Yankee imperialism" of the action, but many Americans—and Panamanians—were pleased by the removal of a military dictator who supported drug smuggling.

THINK THROUGH HISTORY
C. Contrasting *Between 1980 and 1992, how did U.S. policies regarding Central America differ from those regarding Europe?*

C. Answer The government used direct intervention in Central America and diplomacy in Europe.

Middle East Trouble Spots

Results favorable to U.S. interests were more difficult to obtain in the Middle East. Negotiating conflicts between ever-shifting governments drew the United States into scandal and its first major war since Vietnam.

THE IRAN–CONTRA SCANDAL In 1983, terrorist groups loyal to Iran took a number of Americans hostage in Lebanon. Reagan denounced Iran and urged U.S. allies not to sell Iran arms for its war against Iraq. Three years later, in November of 1986, the American people learned that the Reagan administration had been violating its own public policy. Members of Reagan's staff had secretly sold Iran antitank and antiaircraft missiles in an attempt to free the hostages. What's more, they sent part of the profits from those illegal arms sales to the Contras in Nicaragua—in direct violation of the Boland Amendment. President Reagan held a press conference to explain what had happened.

THINK THROUGH HISTORY
D. THEME Constitutional Concerns *Do you think the Iran-Contra affair was a more serious constitutional crisis than Watergate?*

D. Answer Some students may say yes, because Iran-Contra involved a direct violation of law—the Boland Amendment. Others may say no, because Watergate threatened democracy at home and forced a president to resign.

A PERSONAL VOICE

I am deeply troubled that the implementation of a policy aimed at resolving a truly tragic situation in the Middle East has resulted in such controversy. As I've stated previously, I believe our policy goals toward Iran were well founded.

PRESIDENT REAGAN, presidential press conference, November 25, 1986

In the summer of 1987, special committees of both houses of Congress conducted a dramatic inquiry into the Iran-Contra affair in a month of joint televised hearings. Among those testifying was Lieutenant Colonel Oliver North, a member of the National Security Council staff who played a key role in providing aid to the Contras. North appeared in military uniform with a chestful of medals. In

HISTORY FROM VISUALS

Trouble Spots in Central America and the Caribbean, 1980s

Reading the Map Which operation involved the largest number of troops? *The invasion of Panama.*

Extension Have students list the operations in chronological order.

OBJECTIVE
3 INSTRUCT

Middle East Trouble Spots

▶ ***Starting with the Student*** Help students clarify the sequence of events in the Iran-Contra scandal by having them make charts that list dates given in the text along with what happened on each date.

Date	Event
1983	
1986	
1987	
1988	
1992	

▶ ***Discussing Key Ideas***

- An illicit trade of arms to Contras for Americans held hostage in Lebanon comes to light.
- Threatened by the loss of oil, the United States enters the Persian Gulf War in support of Saudi Arabia and Kuwait.

IN-DEPTH RESOURCES: UNIT 7
Primary Source: The First Day of Desert Storm, p.31
Outline Map: U.S. Attention on the Middle East, p. 26
American Lives: Daniel Inouye, p. 36

GROLIER MULTIMEDIA ENCYCLOPEDIA
Iran-Contra Affair

TEACHING OPTIONS

Exploring Themes

Constitutional Concerns Discuss with students the balance-of-powers issues raised by the Iran-Contra affair. The president is charged under the Constitution with making treaties with foreign governments with the advice and consent of the Senate. If members of Reagan's staff secretly sold arms to Iran and sent the moneys raised to Nicaraguan Contras without the president's knowledge, then they were acting beyond their areas of responsibility or accountability. If the president was aware of his staff's actions, then he was encouraging them to act in direct defiance of Congress, which had passed the Boland Amendment.

Making Connections Across Cultures

Nicaragua Nicaragua, the largest country in Central America, borders on both the Caribbean Sea and the Pacific Ocean. Its eastern coastline, on the Caribbean, was reached by Columbus in 1502; the first settlements were made by the Spanish in 1524. Managua is the largest city and the capital. Most Nicaraguans are people of mixed Spanish and Indian ancestry who practice the Roman Catholic religion and speak Spanish. Agriculture is the major economic activity, with coffee and cotton as the main crops. Many Nicaraguans are poor farmers, while others make their living by fishing, lumbering, or mining.

KEY PLAYER
H. Norman Schwarzkopf
Critical Thinking: Analyzing Primary Sources
Ask students to analyze Schwarzkopf's remarks about Saddam Hussein. Have them write a one- or two-sentence summary. Remind them that following the end of the war, Hussein retained control of Iraq. What qualities mentioned—or not mentioned—by Schwarzkopf allowed Hussein to do that?

POINT/COUNTERPOINT
Intervention Abroad

▶ ***Starting with the Student***
Ask students to name a recent story in the news about the possibility of U.S. military intervention abroad, perhaps as part of a multinational peacekeeping force.

- Do students have any friends or relatives in the military?
- Would they want a friend or relative of theirs to risk his or her life in a U.S. military action abroad?

▶ ***Discussing Key Ideas***

- Proponents of military intervention abroad believe that the U.S. must take the lead in defending and expanding democracy.
- Opponents of military intervention abroad believe that it is ineffective and that the U.S. should take care of its own problems at home and devote its resources to its own people.

KEY PLAYER

H. NORMAN SCHWARZKOPF
1934–

In 1988, Norman Schwarzkopf became commander in chief of forces in Asia and Africa. During the Persian Gulf War, more than 540,000 men and women served under the command of "Stormin' Norman." Schwarzkopf said of Saddam Hussein that he was "neither a strategist, nor is he schooled in the operational arts, nor is he a tactician, nor is he a general, nor is he a soldier. Other than that, he is a great military man."

defending his actions, North talked about patriotism and love of country. He asserted that he thought he was carrying out the president's wishes and that the end of helping the Contras justified almost any means. Viewers divided in their opinions about North, some viewing him as a hero and others as a villain.

After a congressional investigation, special prosecutor Lawrence E. Walsh early in 1988 indicted various members of the Reagan administration who were involved in the scandal. On Christmas Eve of 1992, President Bush pardoned a number of Reagan officials.

THE PERSIAN GULF WAR Regardless of the scandal surrounding the Iran-Contra affair, conflict with Iraq (Iran's long-standing enemy) and its leader, Saddam Hussein, soon eclipsed U.S. problems with Iran. During the 1980s, Iran and Iraq had fought a prolonged war, and Hussein found himself with enormous war debts to pay. In 1961 and again in 1973, Iraq had claimed that the oil-rich nation of Kuwait was part of Iraq. On August 2, 1990, Iraqi troops invaded a disputed area claimed by Kuwait. The Iraqi invaders looted Kuwait, then headed toward Saudi Arabia and its oil fields. If Iraq conquered Saudi Arabia as well as Kuwait, it would control one-half of the world's known oil reserves, which would threaten U.S. oil supplies.

THINK THROUGH HISTORY
E. *Forming Generalizations* *What issue led to conflict in the Middle East?*
E. Answer Control over the oil in the region

For several months, President Bush and Secretary of State James Baker organized an international coalition against Iraqi aggression. With the support of Congress and the UN, President Bush launched **Operation Desert Storm** to liberate Kuwait from Iraqi control. On January 16, 1991, the United States and its allies staged a massive air

POINT

"The United States must occasionally intervene militarily in regional conflicts."

Proponents of U.S. military intervention abroad agreed with General Norman Schwarzkopf that "as the only remaining superpower, we have an awesome responsibility to . . . the rest of the world."

"The United States must take the lead in promoting democracy," urged Morton H. Halperin, former director of the ACLU (American Civil Liberties Union). "To say 'Let the UN do it' is a cop-out," stated adviser Robert G. Neumann.

Political scientist Jane Sharp expressed a similar sentiment. "In weighing the cost of intervention, governments must also calculate the high costs of inaction." Offering a recent example, she asked, "Can any nation that has taken no action in Bosnia to stop the Serbian practice of ethnic cleansing continue to call itself civilized?"

COUNTERPOINT

"The United States should not intervene militarily in regional conflicts."

A foreign-policy analyst at the Cato Institute, Barbara Conry, stated that "intervention in regional wars is a distraction and a drain on resources." What's more, she argued, "it does not work." Recalling the presence of American troops in Lebanon, Conry argued that intervention not only jeopardized American soldiers, it often obstructed what it sought to achieve.

"The internal freedom of a political community can only be won by the members of that community," agreed Professor Stephen R. Shalom. He added that "using [military action] encourages quick fix solutions that ignore the underlying sources of conflict."

Author David Fromkin pointed out that "humanitarian goals tend to be broad . . . [while] armed interventions seem to be more successful when they are aimed at narrow, objective, tangible, and clearly defined goals."

INTERACT WITH HISTORY

1. **COMPARING AND CONTRASTING** What do you think are the strongest arguments for and against military intervention in regional conflicts?

SEE SKILLBUILDER HANDBOOK, PAGE 909.

2. **NEGOTIATING** With at least one partner, research the events leading up to U.S. involvement in one of these countries: Lebanon, Grenada, Panama, or Kuwait. Then negotiate to resolve the conflict.

INTERACT WITH HISTORY

1. Comparing and Contrasting

Possible Responses:

Arguments for military intervention:
- *U.S. must promote democracy*
- *U.S. must stop evil practices such as ethnic cleansing*

Arguments against military intervention:
- *may not work*
- *drain on resources*
- *distraction from domestic problems*

2. Negotiating

Following are the steps that students might follow in negotiating to resolve a conflict:

- Choose a country (e.g., Lebanon, Grenada, Panama, etc.).
- Do research in newspapers, magazines, and encyclopedias and on the Internet.
- Meet to pool the results of research.
- Come up with a sequence of events in U.S. involvement.
- Brainstorm solutions to resolve the conflict.

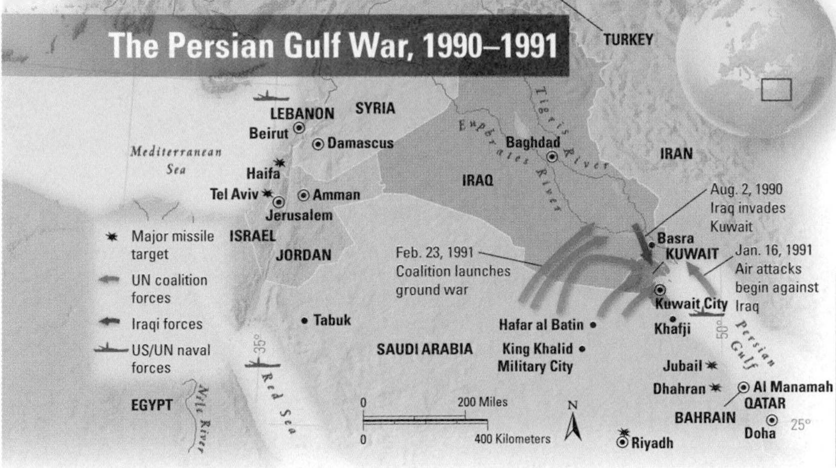

GEOGRAPHY SKILLBUILDER

REGION *What did UN coalition forces probably hope to achieve by moving forces into southern Iraq?* **MOVEMENT** *How did the movements of coalition ground forces show that the intention of the coalition in the Gulf War was primarily defensive, not offensive?*

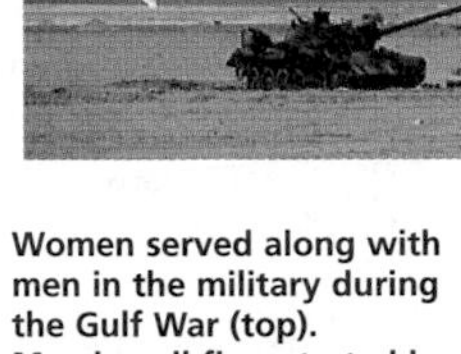

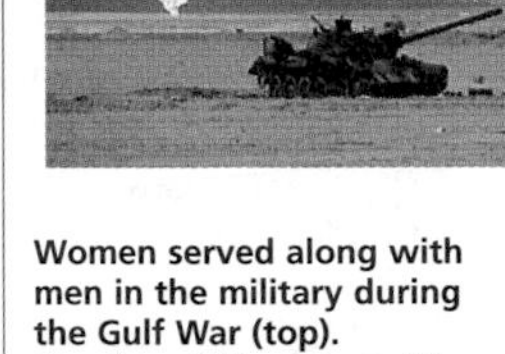

assault against Iraq. On February 23, they launched a successful ground offensive from Saudi Arabia. On February 28, President Bush announced a cease-fire. Operation Desert Storm was over. Kuwait was liberated.

A PERSONAL VOICE

We went halfway around the world to do what is moral and just and right. . . . We're coming home now proud, confident, heads held high. . . . We are Americans.

PRESIDENT GEORGE BUSH

Millions of Americans turned out for the victory parades that greeted returning soldiers. After the debacle in Vietnam, they were thrilled to win a war swiftly, with fewer than 400 casualties among UN coalition forces (although there were subsequently reports that Gulf veterans were suffering disabilities caused by chemicals used in the war). By contrast, Iraq had suffered 100,000 military and civilian deaths. Many of the dead were children under five, who died from outbreaks of cholera, typhoid, enteritis, and other diseases.

Despite his great achievement in the Persian Gulf War, President Bush was not as successful on the domestic front. He was hurt by rising deficits and a recession that began in 1990 and lasted through most of 1992. Bush was forced to raise taxes despite his campaign pledge, and his approval rating had dropped to 40 percent by 1992. The weak economy and the tax hike doomed Bush's reelection campaign, and 12 years of Republican leadership came to an end.

Women served along with men in the military during the Gulf War (top). Massive oil fires started by the Iraqis burned in Kuwait (bottom).

Skillbuilder Answer
Region: *Possible Answer:* By securing the area, coalition forces were probably hoping to cut Iraq off from further land access to Kuwait and also to isolate Iraqi forces already in Kuwait.
Movement: *Possible Answer:* Coalition forces did not strike deep into Iraq, only going far enough into the country to protect Kuwait.

Section  Assessment

1. TERMS & NAMES
Identify:
- Mikhail Gorbachev
- INF Treaty
- *glasnost*
- *perestroika*
- Commonwealth of Independent States
- Tiananmen Square
- Sandinista
- Contras
- Operation Desert Storm

2. SUMMARIZING Use a chart to explain U.S. foreign policy toward different world regions.

U.S. Foreign Policy
Europe
Central America and Caribbean
Middle East

Now write a paragraph in which you describe a trouble spot in one of these regions.

3. ANALYZING CAUSES What factors caused the end of the Cold War?

THINK ABOUT
- events in the Soviet Union
- events in Germany and Eastern Europe
- how U.S. leaders responded to those events

4. FORMING GENERALIZATIONS What factors do you think determined whether or not the United States intervened militarily in other nations?

THINK ABOUT
- economic factors
- geographic factors
- political factors

ANSWERS

1. TERMS & NAMES

Mikhail Gorbachev, p. 836
INF Treaty, p. 836
glasnost, p. 836
perestroika, p. 836
Commonwealth of Independent States, p. 837
Tiananmen Square, p. 838
Sandinista, p. 838
Contras, p. 838
Operation Desert Storm, p. 840

2. SUMMARIZING

Possible Answers:
Europe—INF Treaty, START II treaty, announce end of Cold War, encourage spread of democracy
Central America and Caribbean—cut aid to Sandinistas, send secret aid to the Contras, invade Grenada, seize Noriega
Middle East—secretly sell Iran weapons, Operation Desert Storm

3. ANALYZING CAUSES

Possible Responses: Gorbachev made reforms in the Soviet Union. Political tension and nationalism caused the Soviet Union to break apart and be replaced by the Commonwealth of Independent States. Poland established a non-Communist government. Germany reunited. U.S. leaders welcomed all these changes and vowed to work closely with the new democratic governments.

4. FORMING GENERALIZATIONS

Possible Responses: When the issue was democracy or the halt of communism, the United States often did not intervene militarily. When American lives, safety, and oil supplies were threatened, the United States did intervene.

HISTORY FROM VISUALS

The Persian Gulf War, 1990–1991

Reading the Map Where was the U.S. Navy deployed during the Persian Gulf conflict? *Mediterranean Sea, Red Sea, and Persian Gulf.*

Extension Based on information on the map and in the text, create a mini–time line for events of the Persian Gulf War.

ASSESS & RETEACH

Section 4 Assessment

Have students answer the questions and then compare answers with another student. Ask the student pairs to find text passages to support their answers.

Self-Assessment

Ask students to identify events covered in the chapter that they found hard to understand and to formulate one question they would like to ask the authors of the text.

Section Quiz

FORMAL ASSESSMENT
Section Quiz, p. 309

Reteach

Review the maps on pages 839 and 841, which carry much of the content of this section.

CLOSE

Bush continued to implement the conservative policies advocated by his predecessor, Ronald Reagan. But despite his campaign promise, Bush was obligated to raise taxes. After 12 years of conservative rule, the nation elected a Democratic president. Another swing of the pendulum was about to begin.

 ***HUMANITIES TRANSPARENCIES***
H47, "Jobs That May Be Lost" by Walt Handelsman

CHAPTER 25
ASSESSMENT ANSWERS

REVIEWING THE CHAPTER

TERMS & NAMES

1. Ronald Reagan, p. 819
2. entitlement program, p. 819
3. Moral Majority, p. 820
4. supply-side economics, p. 823
5. Geraldine Ferraro, p. 826
6. AIDS, p. 827
7. Mikhail Gorbachev, p. 836
8. Commonwealth of Independent States, p. 837
9. Contras, p. 838
10. Operation Desert Storm, p. 840

MAIN IDEAS

11. Public frustration over government's entitlement programs and civil rights policies.
12. Conservative voters in West, low voter turnout, frustration over hostage crisis, and high inflation.
13. Cutting social programs, lowering income taxes, increasing military spending.
14. They handed down conservative rulings on various issues.
15. Removal of government regulations on industries. Deregulation of airline industry resulted in increased competition and lower prices for consumer. Deregulation of savings and loan industry resulted in S & L failures.
16. African Americans made striking political gains, although economic progress lagged; Latinos became fastest-growing minority in 1980s, gaining both political and economic power; Native Americans faced long-term problems in health, employment, and education; Asian Americans made important economic advances but few political strides; gays and lesbians worked for legislation to protect their rights.
17. Ferraro's 1984 Democratic vice-presidential candidacy, increase in women in Congress, and push for pay equity.
18. Economic problems and nationalism in non-Russian republics.
19. The Reagan administration's selling weapons to Iran and using profits to aid Contras in Nicaragua; the executive branch deceived Congress.
20. Operation Desert Storm.

Chapter 25 Assessment

REVIEWING THE CHAPTER

TERMS & NAMES For each term below, write a sentence explaining its connection to the period from 1980 to 1992. For each person below, explain his or her role in the events of the period.

1. **Ronald Reagan**
2. **entitlement program**
3. **Moral Majority**
4. **Geraldine Ferraro**
5. **supply-side economics**
6. **AIDS**
7. **Mikhail Gorbachev**
8. **Commonwealth of Independent States**
9. **Contras**
10. **Operation Desert Storm**

MAIN IDEAS

SECTION 1 *(pages 818–821)*

A Conservative Movement Emerges

11. Briefly explain what brought about the conservative backlash of the 1980s.
12. What factors led to Ronald Reagan's victory in 1980?

SECTION 2 *(pages 822–826)*

Conservative Policies Under Reagan and Bush

13. What were the three economic tactics that formed the basis of Reaganomics?
14. How did Reagan's Supreme Court appointments affect the philosophy of the Court?
15. What is deregulation, and how did it affect certain industries in the 1980s?

SECTION 3 *(pages 827–833)*

American Society in a Conservative Age

16. What progress and obstacles did different minority groups experience in the 1980s?
17. What were some gains that women achieved as a result of the equal rights struggle of the 1980s?

SECTION 4 *(pages 836–841)*

Foreign Policy After the Cold War

18. What caused the downfall of the Soviet Union and the founding of the Commonwealth of Independent States?
19. What was the Iran-Contra scandal, and how did it pit presidential against congressional power?
20. Summarize the U.S. response to Iraq's invasion of Kuwait.

THINKING CRITICALLY

1. **FOLLOWING CHRONOLOGICAL ORDER** Choose two events from each of the sections of the chapter and place them in chronological order on a time line like the one below.

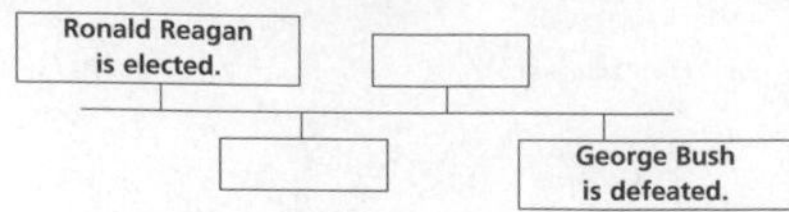

2. **CONSERVATIVE REFORM** Review the goals of the conservative movement and the actions the government took under Reagan and Bush. Evaluate how well the goals had been achieved by the end of George Bush's presidency. Use information from the chapter to support your answer.
3. **THE ROLE OF GOVERNMENT** Reread the quotation from President Reagan on page 816. Do you believe that big government is always a problem? Explain your answer.
4. **GEOGRAPHY OF CENTRAL AMERICA AND THE CARIBBEAN** Look at the map on page 839. Between 1982 and 1992, the United States intervened in this area many times for a variety of reasons. How might the presence of a Communist government on the island of Cuba have influenced U.S. actions in neighboring countries?
5. **TRACING THEMES IMMIGRATION AND MIGRATION** Movement of people affects the balance of political and economic power in the nation. Study the information in the Geography Spotlight on pages 824–825. If you were in charge of a national political party, how would these changes influence your plans for the next election?
6. **ANALYZING PRIMARY SOURCES** Read the following excerpt from a speech that Ronald Reagan gave at the 1992 Republican National Convention, when President Bush was running for reelection. Then answer the questions below.

> **We mustn't forget . . . the very different America that existed just 12 years ago; an America with 21 percent interest rates and back-to-back years of double-digit inflation; an America where mortgage payments doubled, paychecks plunged, and motorists sat in gas lines; an America whose leaders told us it was our own fault; that ours was a future of scarcity and sacrifice; and that what we really needed was another good dose of government control and higher taxes.**
>
> **It wasn't so long ago that the world was a far more dangerous place as well. It was a world where aggressive Soviet communism was on the rise and American strength was in decline. It was a world where our children came of age under the threat of nuclear holocaust.**
>
> **RONALD REAGAN,** speech at Republican National Convention, August 17, 1992

What picture did Reagan paint of the Democratic administration that preceded his own? What conclusions did he want people to draw about the choices in the 1992 election?

THINKING CRITICALLY

1. FOLLOWING CHRONOLOGICAL ORDER
Time lines may include the following information: 1982—ERA fails to pass; 1983—Reagan proposes Strategic Defense Initiative, invasion of Grenada; 1984—Geraldine Ferraro runs for vice-president, Jesse Jackson runs for president, Reagan and Bush win again; 1988—Jesse Jackson runs for president; 1989—Supreme Court rules on abortion; 1991—Operation Desert Storm, America 2000 education program, Anita Hill/Clarence Thomas hearings.

2. CONSERVATIVE REFORM
Possible Responses: Some goals were achieved, such as government deregulation of business, and cuts in taxes and social programs. Some failures were the rise of inflation and the national deficit, problems caused by the weakening of environmental and social agencies, and failure to win the drug war.

3. THE ROLE OF GOVERNMENT
Possible Responses: No, sometimes it is necessary to have a large base of operation to deal with national problems such as drug abuse or with military issues. Some would say that social and educational problems also need national attention, since they affect everyone. Students answering yes might cite the waste generated by national government or the ability of local agencies to better deal with the problems of their area.

ALTERNATIVE ASSESSMENT

1. **PRESENTING A CASE STUDY**
What causes natural resources to become depleted or endangered? What can be done in response?

Working with a small group, present a case study on an environmental problem that is significant to your future.

 Conduct research, using the CD-ROM *Our Times,* your textbook, and other sources.

- Your case study should consider why the problem is important and what recent events have had either a negative or a positive impact on it. For example, what role have industry, technology, urban development, and population growth played in the problem? What have environmental groups, industrial leaders, or politicians done in response? Use visuals, such as charts, maps, and photographs, to illustrate your presentation.
- Conclude with a look at the future. What actions might help to slow or reverse the situation? What could be done to prevent its happening again?

2. **DEBATING AN ISSUE**
Cooperative Learning With a small group of classmates, choose one issue that conservatives feel strongly about, and debate that issue before the class.

- Have one person present the conservative view and another present the liberal view.
- One member of your group should moderate the debate.
- Use your textbook and other resources to research the issue thoroughly. Present both sides of the issue as thoroughly and fairly as possible.
- Prepare a sheet that your classmates can use to judge the debate. You may want to suggest criteria such as "clear explanations," "adequate research," "use of supporting details," and "volume and pace of speaking."
- Conduct your debate in front of the class.

3. **PORTFOLIO PROJECT**
Use the Living History activity to expand your portfolio.

LIVING HISTORY

PRESENTING POLITICAL POSITIONS

After you read the chapter, use the notes you took to make a chart comparing the conservative politician today with Reagan or Bush. Then have a classmate review your chart and answer the following questions:

- Are the positions presented clearly? Do you understand what the politicians believe?
- Are the positions presented objectively, or can you tell what your classmate's opinion of them is?

When you have revised your chart on the basis of your classmate's comments, present it to the class. Then add it to your American history portfolio.

Bridge to Chapter 26

Review Chapter 25

CONSERVATIVE AGENDA The election of Ronald Reagan marked the peak of conservatism in late-20th-century politics. Encouraged by the strong support of the New Right and the Moral Majority, Reagan took steps to reduce the size of the federal government and to end entitlement programs to citizens. By his appointments to the Supreme Court, Reagan guaranteed conservative rulings on civil rights cases for years to come. Reaganomics was the conservative plan for energizing the flagging economy, but it had mixed results.

POLITICAL EMPOWERMENT Groups that had previously had limited representation in the political arena found political empowerment during the Reagan-Bush years. Women, minorities, and homosexuals gained more representation in American political life. However, divisive issues such as equal rights, abortion, education, and affirmative action combined to create a combative atmosphere in the halls of Congress and state and local legislatures.

CHANGES IN WORLD POLITICS The end of the Cold War occurred during Bush's presidency. The United States was faced with altering its foreign policy toward the once-powerful Communist bloc, which began to collapse in 1988. On other fronts, the United States continued to pursue an aggressive foreign policy of intervention, peaking with Operation Desert Storm in 1991.

Preview Chapter 26

Twelve years of conservative control were ended with the election of Bill Clinton in 1992. Clinton was the first "baby boomer" to be elected to the office of president. Finding an appropriate role for America in the increasingly globalized world, as well as dealing with thorny domestic issues, presented a great challenge to President Clinton. You will learn about these and other significant events in the next chapter.

ALTERNATIVE ASSESSMENT

1. PRESENTING A CASE STUDY
Standards for Evaluation
A case study should meet the following criteria:

- Addresses an environmental issue that is significant.
- Weighs both positive and negative impacts on the environment.
- Discusses the roles of industry, technology, urban development, and population growth in the crisis.
- Describes the contributions of various individuals and groups to solving the crisis.
- Uses visuals to illustrate the presentation.
- Speculates about the future.

2. DEBATING AN ISSUE
Standards for Evaluation
A debate should meet the following criteria:

- Provides clear explanations.
- Demonstrates adequate research.
- Makes use of supporting details.
- Gives each member of the group a clear function.

3. PORTFOLIO PROJECT
LIVING HISTORY
Standards for Evaluation:
A chart should meet the following criteria:

- Makes good use of accumulated notes.
- Compares Reagan or Bush with an important conservative politician of today, such as Newt Gingrich.
- Provides details about the two politicians being compared.
- Presents differences and similarities clearly.
- Shows good organization.
- Maintains a consistent focus.

IN-DEPTH RESOURCES: UNIT 7
See the form for scoring this activity on page 38.

THINKING CRITICALLY

4. GEOGRAPHY OF CENTRAL AMERICA AND THE CARIBBEAN
Possible Response: During this time period, the U.S. feared the spread of communism from Cuba to its nearby neighbors.

5. TRACING THEMES IMMIGRATION AND MIGRATION
Possible Responses: People are moving from the Rustbelt to the West, so there will be more voters in the Western states to be convinced of the importance of voting for your party. Issues in the Rustbelt might include the loss of jobs and the need for retraining and new industries. Issues in the West might include concerns about the environment, housing, and education. In the Sunbelt, the issues might relate to immigrants from other countries and concerns about water.

6. ANALYZING PRIMARY SOURCES
Possible Answers: Reagan wanted to make it seem as though the previous, Democratic administration had created a disaster. He wanted his listeners to think that if they voted for a Democrat in 1992, similarly terrible conditions would return. He was concerned that a Democratic president would undo some of the accomplishments of the conservative movement.

CHAPTER 26

PLANNING GUIDE

The United States in Today's World

	Key Ideas	COPYMASTERS	ASSESSMENT
SECTION 1 The Clinton Presidency *pp. 846–852*	*President Bill Clinton attempts to provide more economic security for all Americans. Republicans challenge some of his programs and win control of Congress.*	***In-Depth Resources: Unit 7*** • Guided Reading, p. 39 • Primary Sources: *from* Contract with America, p. 46; *from* "A Bridge to the Future" by Bill Clinton, p. 47 ***Lesson Plans,*** pp. 209–210	PE ***Section 1 Assessment,*** p. 852 TE ***Self-Assessment,*** p. 852 ***Formal Assessment*** • Section Quiz, p. 318 ***Alternative Assessment Book*** • Standards for Evaluating a Cooperative Activity
SECTION 2 The New Global Economy *pp. 853–857*	*Workers face new challenges to their economic security as the U.S. economy evolves.*	***In-Depth Resources: Unit 7*** • Guided Reading, p. 40 • Geography Application: The U.S. Trade in Goods, p. 44 • Primary Source: from *The Road Ahead* by Bill Gates, p. 48 • American Lives: Bill Gates, p. 52 • Literature: Selected Poems, p. 50 ***Lesson Plans,*** pp. 211–212	PE ***Section 2 Assessment,*** p. 857 TE ***Self-Assessment,*** p. 857 ***Formal Assessment*** • Section Quiz, p. 319 ***Alternative Assessment Book*** • Standards for Evaluating a Cooperative Activity
SECTION 3 Technology and Modern Life *pp. 860–865*	*New opportunities and challenges arise from technological developments in many industries, especially computers and communications.*	***In-Depth Resources: Unit 7*** • Guided Reading, p. 41 ***Lesson Plans,*** pp. 213–214	PE ***Section 3 Assessment,*** p. 865 TE ***Self-Assessment,*** p. 865 ***Formal Assessment*** • Section Quiz, p. 320 ***Alternative Assessment Book*** • Standards for Evaluating a Cooperative Activity
SECTION 4 The Changing Face of America *pp. 866–871*	*Demographic changes in the United States have significant implications for American society at the outset of the 21st century.*	***In-Depth Resources: Unit 7*** • Guided Reading, p. 42 • Skillbuilder Practice: Drawing Conclusions, p. 43 • Primary Source: Road Sign, p. 49 • American Lives: Wilma Mankiller, p. 53 ***Lesson Plans,*** pp. 215–216	PE ***Section 4 Assessment,*** p. 871 TE ***Self-Assessment,*** p. 871 ***Formal Assessment*** • Section Quiz, p. 321 ***Alternative Assessment Book*** • Standards for Evaluating a Cooperative Activity
CHAPTER RESOURCES	**Chapter Overview** *President Bill Clinton locks horns with a Republican Congress, reflecting the heated national debate over the country's direction. Americans face economic, technological, and demographic changes that are reshaping their lives and redefining the main issues that concern citizens.*	***In-Depth Resources: Unit 7*** • Living History Project: Worksheet, p. 54; Standards, p. 55 ***Telescoping the Times*** • Chapter Summary, pp. 51–52 ***Planning for Block Schedules***	PE ***Chapter Assessment,*** pp. 874–875 PE ***Alternative Assessment,*** p. 875 ***Formal Assessment*** • Chapter Test, forms A and B, pp. 322–327 ***Test Generator*** ***Alternative Assessment Book*** See explanation and forms for different kinds of alternative assessments including portfolio assessment.

KEY
PE Pupil's Edition
TE Teacher's Edition
http://www.mlushistory.com

TECHNOLOGY

 *Warm-Up Transparency* **26**

Geography Transparencies
- G34, Eligible Votes Cast, 1996

Critical Thinking Transparencies
- CT34, Federal Government Shutdown
- CT68, Federal Budget, 1945–1995

Electronic Library of Primary Sources
- Clinton's First Inaugural Address
- A Contract with America

INTERNET Newt Gingrich and the federal deficit

Warm-Up Transparency **26**

 **INTERNET** Welfare and GATT

 *Warm-Up Transparency* **26**

Grolier Multimedia Encyclopedia
- Computers and Privacy

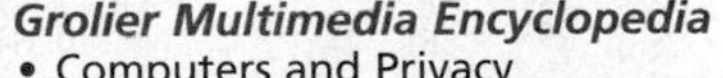

 *Electronic Library of Primary Sources*
- from *Being Digital* by Nicholas Negroponte

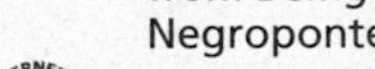

INTERNET Telecommunications Act

 *Warm-Up Transparency* **26**

Humanities Transparencies
- H48, Political Cartoon

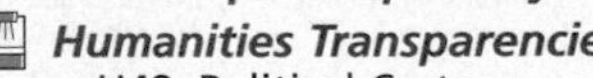

Electronic Library of Primary Sources
- from Mission Statement by the Organizing Committee of the Million Man March

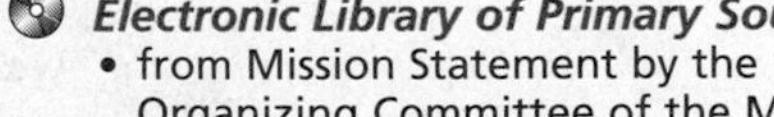

 **INTERNET** Interact with History p. 873 (PE)

 *American Portfolio: A Videodisc for U.S. History,* user's guide, pp. 192, 195–200

Chapter Summary Audiotapes
- Unit 7, Chapter 26

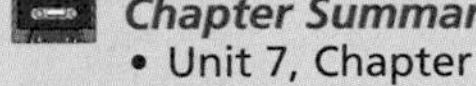

INTERNET **http://www.mlushistory.com**

Block Scheduling (90 MINUTES)

Day 1

Section 1, pp. 846–852

Section Assessment, p. 852

COOPERATIVE ACTIVITIES
- Graphing Election Results, p. 847 (TE)
- Researching Current Events, p. 851 (TE)

Day 2

Section 2, pp. 853–857

Section 3, pp. 860–865

Section Assessments, pp. 857, 865

American Literature: Women Writers Reflect American Diversity, pp. 858–859

COOPERATIVE ACTIVITIES
- Planning a Job Fair, p. 855 (TE)
- Researching International Trade, p. 856 (TE)
- Creating a Guide to the Internet, p. 863 (TE)

Day 3

Section 4, pp. 866–871

Section Assessment, p. 871

Tracing Themes: Cultural Diversity, pp. 872–873

Chapter Assessment, pp. 874–875

 **COOPERATIVE ACTIVITY**
- Predicting Local Demographics, p. 867 (TE)

YEARLY PACING *Chapter 26 Total:* 3 days *Yearly Total:* 85 days

See *Planning for Block Schedules* for special activities and pacing strategies.

Customizing for Special Populations

Students Acquiring English

Access for Students Acquiring English: Spanish Translations
- Guided Reading for Sections 1–4 (Spanish), pp. 281–284
- Chapter Summary (Spanish), pp. 279–280
- Skillbuilder Practice: Drawing Conclusions (Spanish), p. 285
- Geography Application: The U.S. Trade in Goods (Spanish), p. 286–287

Spanish Reading Study Guide, pp. 263–272

Translations of Chapter Summaries, Hmong, Cantonese, Vietnamese, and Cambodian

Chapter Summary Audiotapes in Spanish
Unit 7, Chapter 26

INTERNET The Diverse Classroom

Gifted and Talented Students

In-Depth Resources: Unit 7
- Primary Sources: *from* Contract with America, p. 46; *from* "A Bridge to the Future" by Bill Clinton, p. 47; from *The Road Ahead* by Bill Gates, p. 48; Road Sign, p. 49
- American Lives: Bill Gates, p. 52; Wilma Mankiller, p. 53

Less Proficient Readers

In-Depth Resources: Unit 7
- Guided Reading for Sections 1–4, pp. 39–42
- Skillbuilder: Drawing Conclusions, p. 43
- Geography Application: The U.S. Trade in Goods, p. 44

Reading Study Guide
- pp. 263–272

Telescoping the Times
- Chapter Summary, pp. 51–52

Chapter Summary Audiotapes, Unit 7, Chapter 26

Connections to Literature READINGS FOR STUDENTS

In-Depth Resources: Unit 7
- **Selected Poems,** p. 50–51

Enrichment Reading
- **Christopher Buckley**
  Thank You for Smoking
  New York: Harper, 1995
  Buckley skewers Washington politics, corporate power plays, media spin control, Hollywood pretensions and the human weakness for self-delusion and denial in this wickedly funny novel about the adventures of a spokesman for the tobacco lobby who will do anything to sell his product.

McDougal Littell *The Language of Literature*
American Literature

- **Lucy Honig, "English as a Second Language,"** p. 733
- **Wing Tek Lum, Jean Bethke Elshtain, Rodney King, Benjamin Spock, Achy Obejas, Baltasar Corrada, Colin Powell, "Voices from the Times,"** pp. 1037–1038
- **Carlos Alberto Montaner, "Why Fear Spanish?"** p. 1066
- **Gary Soto, "Mexicans Begin Jogging,"** p. 1113
- **Pat Mora, "Legal Alien,"** p. 1116

OVERVIEW

The United States in Today's World

▶ ***Accessing Prior Knowledge***

Ask students to discuss the most important things that are happening in the United States today. How do those things affect their daily lives?

▶ ***Predicting Outcomes***

Ask students what they think is the "common thread" that holds America together. What forces would weaken or strengthen that thread in the 1990s?

MORE ABOUT . . .
Madeleine Albright

As an emigrant fleeing the political turmoil of her native Czechoslovakia, Madeleine Albright came to understand what she called "the responsibilities of freedom." During President Clinton's first term, Albright served as the U.S. ambassador to the United Nations. When sworn in as secretary of state in 1997, Albright spoke of America's role in global affairs.

> "We must not shy from the mantle of leadership, nor hesitate to defend our interests, nor fail in our commitments, nor diverge from the principles that have defined, elevated and sustained our nation for more than 200 years."

CHAPTER 26

The United States in Today's World

SECTION 1
The Clinton Presidency
President Bill Clinton attempts to provide more economic security for all Americans. Republicans challenge some of his programs and win control of Congress.

SECTION 2
The New Global Economy
Workers face new challenges to their economic security as the U.S. economy evolves.

SECTION 3
Technology and Modern Life
New opportunities and challenges arise from technological developments in many industries, especially computers and communications.

SECTION 4
The Changing Face of America
Demographic changes in the United States have significant implications for American society at the outset of the 21st century.

"America is . . . like a quilt—many pieces, many colors, many sizes, all woven and held together by a common thread."
The Reverend Jesse Jackson

Janet Reno, the first female U.S. attorney general, testifies in Congress about the 1993 fire at the Branch Davidian compound in Waco, Texas.

THE UNITED STATES — 1992

Twenty-seventh Amendment to the Constitution, which deals with congressional pay raises, is ratified.

Bill Clinton (shown with Vice-President Al Gore) is elected president.

THE UNITED STATES — 1993

U.S. troops land in Somalia to provide humanitarian aid to the famine-stricken nation.

United States and Russia sign the START II pact to reduce nuclear weapons on both sides.

Terrorists bomb the World Trade Center in New York City.

THE WORLD — 1992

Boutros Boutros-Ghali becomes the secretary-general of the United Nations.

THE WORLD — 1993

South African government and the African National Congress agree to end white minority rule.

THEMES IN CHAPTER 26

America in the World
Commercial issues become the most important component of American foreign policy during President Clinton's tenure.
See Teacher's Edition note, p. 849.

Economic Opportunity
The government's pursuit of international trade agreements was fueled by the desire to expand foreign markets. At issue was the effect such agreements might have on the availability of jobs at home.
See Teacher's Edition, p. 854.

Science and Technology
Technological advances in the fields of medicine, communications, and entertainment affected many areas of American life and occasionally drew critical fire as well as praise.
See Teacher's Edition, p. 864.

Immigration and Migration
The changing ethnic makeup of the country and the high cost of providing services for legal and illegal immigrants brought immigration policies into focus once more.
See Teacher's Edition, p. 870.

LIVING HISTORY

PLANNING FOR THE 21ST CENTURY

During his 1992 presidential campaign, Bill Clinton posted in his campaign headquarters a sign listing three issues to focus on. Create a list of the three most important issues for 21st-century leaders to focus on. Use the following steps to create your list:

- Read news articles and interview friends and relatives to learn what issues people think will affect the future.
- Choose the three issues you think are the most crucial and rank them in order of importance.
- Find an editorial, an article, or a photograph that explains or illustrates a critical aspect of each issue.

PORTFOLIO PROJECT Save your list and the supporting articles and photographs in a folder for your American history portfolio. You will revise and share your work at the end of the chapter.

Astronauts on the space shuttle *Endeavour* repair the Hubble telescope in a dramatic space walk.

United States ends its relief efforts in Somalia.

In the 1994 elections, the Republican Party wins control of both houses of Congress for the first time since 1952.

Nation of Islam leader Louis Farrakhan leads the "Million Man March" in Washington, D.C.

Murrah Federal Building in Oklahoma City, Oklahoma, is bombed.

President Clinton is reelected.

Madelein Albright is the first woman to become secretary of state.

President Clinton signs bill to balance the budget by the year 2002.

1994 — 1995 — 1996 — 1997

1995

Peasants in the southern Mexican state of Chiapas rebel against the national government.

Russian armies invade the republic of Chechnya to try to squelch a separatist rebellion.

World Health Organization announces that more than 200 people have died in an outbreak of the Ebola virus in Zaire.

United Nations holds the Fourth World Conference on Women for 12 days in Beijing, China.

Israeli prime minister Yitzhak Rabin is assassinated.

ALTERNATIVE ASSESSMENT

LIVING HISTORY

PLANNING FOR THE 21ST CENTURY

Discuss ways of going about creating the list.

- Prepare questions to ask when interviewing friends and relatives.
- Use library resources or the Internet to locate a variety of articles from which to identify issues in the nation today.
- Develop criteria to use when ranking issues in order of importance.
- Create a checklist that includes all the steps in the process (research, selection, illustration).

Project Planning Guide

Step 1	**Students research possible issues by reading appropriate news articles.**
Step 2	**Students conduct interviews and compile the results.**
Step 3	**Students rank the issues in order of importance and select the top three.**
Step 4	**Students choose a photograph, editorial, or article to explain or illustrate each issue.**

IN-DEPTH RESOURCES: UNIT 7
See worksheet and standards for evaluation, pp. 54, 55.

RECOMMENDED RESOURCES

Books for the Teacher

Drew, Elizabeth. *Whatever It Takes: The Real Struggle for Political Power in America.* New York: Viking, 1997. A look at campaign fundraising in the 1996 election.

Woodward, Bob. *The Agenda.* New York: Pocket, 1994. First two years of Clinton White House.

Books for the Student

Costello, Cynthia, and Barbara Kivimac Krimgold. *The American Woman 1996–1997.* New York: Norton, 1996. Women at work.

Fischer, Daniel. *The Hubble: A New Window to the Universe.* New York: Copernicus, 1996.

Hodgson, Godfrey. *The World Turned Right Side Up.* Boston: Houghton, 1996.

Videos

The War Room. Dir. Chris Hegedus and D. A. Pennebaker. Vidmark Entertainment, 1994.

The Global Assembly Line. Dir. Lorraine Gray. New Day Films, 1986. Portrays people's lives in the "free trade zones" of developing countries and North America.

Software

Clinton: Portrait of a Victory. CD-ROM. Time Warner Interactive. Speeches, music, narration, and more than 300 photographs.

CNN Time Capsule 1994. CD-ROM. Vicarious Entertainment. More than 1,000 articles and photographs.

Section 1 Overview

OBJECTIVES

1. To summarize the issues of the 1992 presidential campaign.
2. To describe Clinton's stand on domestic and international issues.
3. To identify the effects of the Republican control of Congress.
4. To summarize the results of the 1996 election.
5. To list the issues that emerged during President Clinton's second term.

SKILLBUILDERS

- Interpreting political cartoons, p. 851
- Interpreting graphs, p. 852

CRITICAL THINKING

- Analyzing causes, pp. 847, 848
- Forming generalizations, p. 848
- Summarizing, pp. 849, 852
- Contrasting, p. 850
- Synthesizing, p. 852
- Recognizing effects, p. 852
- Analyzing issues, p. 852

FOCUS & MOTIVATE

5-MINUTE WARM-UP

Predicting Outcomes
To reflect on political leadership, have students read the Key Players on page 850 and answer these questions.

1. Why might Bill Clinton and Newt Gingrich become powerful political leaders in the 1990s?
2. Which of these two men might future generations more likely remember as a great leader?

WARM-UP TRANSPARENCY 26

▶ ***Starting with the Student***
Ask students whether they would select someone their age or someone older and more experienced if they were choosing a team captain or school president. Discuss these questions:

- What are the advantages and disadvantages of each choice?

(continued on next page)

❶ The Clinton Presidency

TERMS & NAMES
- Bill Clinton
- Twenty-seventh Amendment
- Hillary Rodham Clinton
- NAFTA
- Newt Gingrich
- Contract with America

LEARN ABOUT Bill Clinton's presidency
TO UNDERSTAND American politics during the 1990s.

ONE AMERICAN'S STORY

After Maya Angelou—poet, playwright, dancer, actress, singer, scholar, and activist—received the phone call from President-elect Bill Clinton in November 1992, she said, "I was bowled over." An admirer of Angelou's work, Clinton asked her to compose and deliver a poem at his inauguration. Robert Frost, in 1961, had been the first poet to deliver an inaugural poem. Angelou would be the first African American and the first woman to be so honored.

On inauguration day, 250,000 people gathered to watch in person, and millions more watched on television, as Angelou strode to the podium and delivered her poem, "On the Pulse of Morning." In the poem, Angelou expressed the optimism of the day, recalling the dream of Dr. Martin Luther King, Jr.

A PERSONAL VOICE

Lift up your faces, you have a piercing need
For this bright morning dawning for you.
History, despite its wrenching pain,
Cannot be unlived, but if faced
With courage, need not be lived again.

Lift up your eyes
Upon this day breaking for you.
Give birth again
To the dream.

MAYA ANGELOU, "On the Pulse of Morning"

Maya Angelou

Moments later, William Jefferson Clinton was inaugurated as the 42nd president of the United States. Clinton entered the presidency at a time when America was at a turning point. The breakup of the Soviet Union in 1991 had made the United States the undisputed winner of the Cold War. Yet a severe economic recession made many Americans uneasy about the future. They now looked to Clinton to restore a government that was more responsive to the people and to increase the economic security of all Americans.

Clinton Wins the Presidency

Governor **Bill Clinton** of Arkansas entered the presidential race with the energy of youth. The 46-year-old Clinton, who would be the first member of the baby-boom generation to win the presidency, campaigned as a "New Democrat." He took traditional liberal Democratic positions by proposing a shift in federal funds from defense to civilian programs, more public spending on the nation's infrastructure (roads, bridges, sewers, and power lines), and a national system for health care. However, Clinton also sought welfare reform and emphasized private business as the means to economic progress.

THE ELECTION OF 1992 After the U.S. victory in the Persian Gulf War, Republican president George Bush's popularity had soared to an 88 percent approval rating. In early 1992, however, his approval rating nose-dived to 40 percent as a worsening recession reduced U.S. incomes and boosted

SECTION 1 RESOURCES

PRINT RESOURCES

IN-DEPTH RESOURCES: UNIT 7
Guided Reading, p. 39
Primary Sources: *from* Contract with America, p. 46; *from* "A Bridge to the Future" by Bill Clinton, p. 47
Literature: Selected Poems, p. 50

READING STUDY GUIDE, p. 263

ACCESS FOR STUDENTS ACQUIRING ENGLISH
Guided Reading (Spanish), p. 281

SPANISH READING STUDY GUIDE, p. 263

FORMAL ASSESSMENT
Section Quiz, p. 318

ALTERNATIVE ASSESSMENT BOOK
See forms for supporting and scoring alternative activities.

TECHNOLOGY RESOURCES

GEOGRAPHY TRANSPARENCIES
G34, Percentage of Eligible Votes Cast, 1996 Presidential Election

CRITICAL THINKING TRANSPARENCIES
CT34, Shutdown of the Federal Government
CT68, Federal Budget, 1945–1995

CD-ROM Electronic Library of Primary Sources

INTERNET http://www.mlushistory.com

unemployment. In his run for reelection, President Bush tried to appeal to voters on the basis of his foreign-policy triumphs, but voters cared more about pocketbook issues. He could not convince the public that he had a clear strategy for ending the recession and creating jobs. Nor did he seem able to communicate a coherent vision of the country's future.

THINK THROUGH HISTORY
A. Analyzing Causes *What factors accounted for Bush's decline in popularity?*

A. Answer Voters cared more about domestic issues than they did about Bush's foreign-policy experience. The recession contributed to the decline.

Concern about the economy was so great that it created an opening for a third-party candidate—Texas billionaire H. Ross Perot. Perot drew strength from the surly mood of many voters. In fact, popular distrust of government contributed to the ratification of the **Twenty-seventh Amendment,** which prevents congressional pay raises from taking effect until after an election has occurred.

In his campaign, Bill Clinton also focused on the economy, making a number of proposals: (1) increasing government spending on the country's infrastructure to boost the economy, (2) cutting taxes for the middle class, (3) modifying the welfare system, and (4) balancing the budget by gradually reducing the size of government. Although Clinton would later back off on the middle-class tax cut, he convinced many Americans that he could ease their economic problems.

Clinton's biggest problem emerged from concerns about his character. When the public learned that he had managed to avoid military service during the Vietnam War, critics questioned his patriotism. In addition, Clinton's involvement in a failed 1979 real-estate investment in the Whitewater Development Company in Arkansas produced headlines questioning his ethics.

On the campaign trail, Clinton was able to overcome these concerns about his character, which to most voters seemed less important than the state of the economy. On election day, Clinton won 370 electoral votes to 168 for Bush. His 43 percent share of the popular vote, however, was the smallest winning percentage since that of Woodrow Wilson in the election of 1912. Bush received 38 percent of the popular vote, and Perot 19 percent.

HISTORICAL SPOTLIGHT

ROSS PEROT AND THIRD-PARTY CANDIDATES

Candidates of parties other than the Democrats or Republicans—third-party candidates—have usually had difficulty attracting voters in the United States. However, they have often provided an important way for Americans to express their discontent with politicians.

In the 1890s, the Populists offered many farmers a platform that they could not get from the Republicans or Democrats. Similarly, in 1968 former Alabama governor George Wallace ran for the presidency for the American Independent Party. He attracted the support of white Southern Democrats who opposed desegregation but would not vote for a Republican.

In 1992 Ross Perot tapped the discontent of people who felt that the Washington establishment had gotten too big and too far removed from common Americans. He ran as a candidate from outside the establishment and struck a nerve with people concerned about the deficit. He received a greater percentage of the popular vote than any third-party candidate since Teddy Roosevelt in 1912.

The Clinton Record

To improve government efficiency, Clinton attempted to streamline the federal bureaucracy and put his vice-president, Albert Gore, in charge of what he called "reinventing government." Clinton also tried to make government more inclusive by appointing more women and minorities to his cabinet. More important to Clinton, however, was his goal of strengthening American economic security, which included reform of the U.S. health-care system.

The candidates—Bill Clinton and Al Gore—and their wives celebrate victory in the 1992 presidential election.

(continued from page 846)

- Could the same approach be used to choose the nation's leader? Explain.

OBJECTIVE

① INSTRUCT

Clinton Wins the Presidency

▶ ***Discussing Key Ideas***
- The economy is the most important issue in the election of 1992.
- Ross Perot challenges the major political parties.
- Television remains an essential campaign tool.

IN-DEPTH RESOURCES: UNIT 7
Guided Reading, p. 39

ACCESS FOR STUDENTS ACQUIRING ENGLISH
Guided Reading (Spanish), p. 281

ELECTRONIC LIBRARY OF PRIMARY SOURCES
Clinton's First Inaugural Address

HISTORICAL SPOTLIGHT
Ross Perot and Third-Party Candidates

Critical Thinking: Synthesizing Have students review other third-party candidates such as Strom Thurmond, Eugene Debs, and the Republican Party in the 1850s. Why have no third-party candidates won the presidency in the 20th century?

OBJECTIVE

② INSTRUCT

The Clinton Record

▶ ***Discussing Key Ideas***
- Hillary Rodham Clinton leads an effort to reform health care.

(continued on next page)

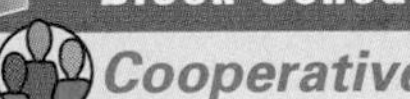
Block Schedule TEACHING OPTION **Time Needed: 20 Minutes**

Cooperative Activity: Graphing Election Results

Task: Student groups will research and graph results of the 1992 presidential election and will compare some of that data with similar data from a past election.

Purpose: To help students interpret election results by graphing in a variety of ways.

Activity: Students working in groups of three or four should use their textbook, library resources, and the Internet to gather data on the results of the 1992 presidential election. They should consider such variables as electoral votes, popular votes, voter turnout, and the breakdown of votes by state, gender, ethnic, or cultural group.

Each group member can work on graphing one set of results. Students should include one line graph, one pie or circle graph, and one bar graph. One student can create a graph comparing an aspect of the 1992 results with the same aspect in a past presidential election.

ALTERNATIVE ASSESSMENT BOOK
Standards for Evaluating a Cooperative Activity

Standards for Evaluation
Graphs should . . .
- show evidence of careful research
- demonstrate an understanding of different types of graphs
- demonstrate ability to correctly construct a variety of graphs

(continued from page 847)

- Bill Clinton inherits an enormous national debt.
- The NAFTA legislation causes controversy.
- Clinton argues for active U.S. participation in international affairs.

MORE ABOUT . . .
Hillary Rodham Clinton

Before coming to Washington, Hillary Rodham Clinton was a partner in the Rose Law Firm in Little Rock, Arkansas, and she was once named one of the nation's top 100 lawyers. Because of her active participation in social and legislative reform as First Lady, many commentators compared her to Eleanor Roosevelt.

MORE ABOUT . . .
The Economy in the 1990s

Most people agree that the economic news during Clinton's tenure has been positive, but some people think the traditional data hide weaknesses in the economy. One problem is that incomes are growing slowly despite low unemployment. Some argue that more people are working because families can't make ends meet on one income alone. Another problem is that gross domestic product and the productivity rate of individual workers are growing more slowly than in previous eras. All this means that average Americans are not getting richer like they used to.

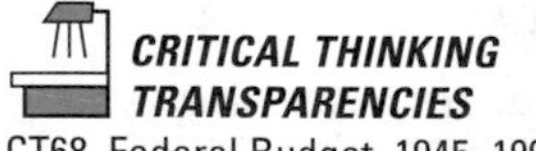
CRITICAL THINKING TRANSPARENCIES
CT68, Federal Budget, 1945–1995

HEALTH-CARE REFORM During the campaign, Clinton had pledged a sweeping reform to offer all Americans guaranteed, affordable health care. Indeed, as Clinton took office, an estimated 37 million Americans lacked medical insurance. Aware that Democratic senator Harris Wofford had used the issue of health-care reform to win a 1991 U.S. Senate race in Pennsylvania, Clinton decided to make "universal health care" the centerpiece of his administration.

Hillary Rodham Clinton explains the health-care reform plan to a Senate subcommittee.

The president appointed his wife, **Hillary Rodham Clinton,** an accomplished lawyer and child-welfare advocate, to head a task force on the issue. The first lady produced a reform plan in the form of a bill that ultimately ran to 1,342 pages. Clinton presented the bill to a joint session of Congress in September 1993 and labeled universal coverage "our most urgent priority." The plan would have extended coverage to every American, mandated that employers pay 80 percent of their workers' insurance costs, and provided for a national health board to monitor spiraling health-care costs.

Congress debated the Clinton health-care plan for a year. This lengthy debate allowed lobbyists for the bill's opponents—like small businesses and large insurance companies—plenty of time to mobilize against it. Although willing to compromise on minor points, President Clinton refused to negotiate on universal coverage. At first, about half of the American public supported the Clinton plan. However, intense lobbying and congressional debate, in which Republicans attacked the plan as "big government," sealed the plan's doom. The program never even came to the floor of Congress for a vote.

B. Answer Business and insurance interests lobbied against it; Clinton moved slowly and wouldn't compromise; the public viewed the plan as one that would increase the size of government.

THINK THROUGH HISTORY
B. *Analyzing Causes* *What factors led to the defeat of Clinton's health-care plan?*

CLINTON AND THE ECONOMY The most consistent characteristics of the American economy during the first five years of Clinton's presidency were steady growth with low interest rates, low inflation, falling unemployment, and a decreasing federal budget deficit. Meanwhile, the stock market soared to new heights, and economists began to view the ceaseless stream of economic good news in the mid-1990s as the natural order of things.

Nevertheless, the national debt continued to climb—to about $5.5 trillion by 1998. And although Clinton had promised tax cuts for the middle class and government expenditures for job training in his 1992 campaign, he bowed to political reality. To lower the deficit, he asked for higher taxes, primarily on the wealthy, and spending cuts, particularly on military appropriations.

The largest portion of federal expenditures, however, funded entitlement programs, whose costs had spiraled along with the deficit. These entitlement programs—including Social Security, Medicare, and Medicaid—guaranteed federal aid to all eligible American citizens. Most of the entitlement funds went to middle-class elderly and disabled persons and to poor children. These programs were popular, and most politicians, including President Clinton, hesitated to cut them. Even without cuts in entitlement programs, however, the Clinton plan, as modified by Congress, cut the federal budget deficit in half between 1992 and 1996.

C. Answer Politicians hesitate to cut these programs because most of the money from the programs goes to poor children or to powerful voting blocs of elderly and middle-class citizens.

THINK THROUGH HISTORY
C. *Forming Generalizations* *Why do politicians find it difficult to cut entitlement programs?*

TRADE AGREEMENT The North American Free Trade Agreement **(NAFTA)** was a central piece of legislation for both the Bush and Clinton administrations. The treaty, which the House passed in November 1993, lowered tariffs and brought Mexico into the free-trade zone that the United States and Canada had already established. Critics, including Ross Perot, had argued that NAFTA would weaken environmental regulations and result in the loss of American jobs

TEACHING OPTIONS

Teaching Less Proficient Readers

Clarifying Concepts Pair less proficient readers with more able readers and have them read "Clinton and the Economy." Ask each pair to create a graphic organizer showing ways in which Clinton might have reduced the national debt. The graphic organizer might be similar to the one below:

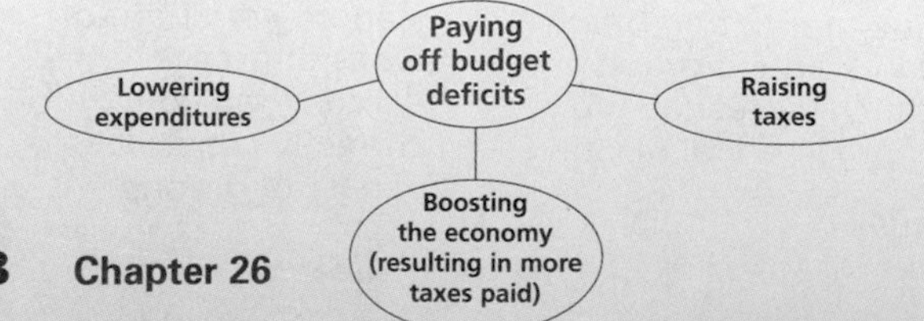

Making Connections Across the Curriculum

Economics Though President Clinton failed to gain approval of his plan for universal, affordable health care, substantial change occurred in the health care system over subsequent years, primarily due to competition. By the late 1990s, the growth in health maintenance organizations (HMOs), or prepaid health plans, and the increasing number of doctors abandoning their private practices to work for the HMOs has left more traditional medical establishments to consider mergers and other measures to ensure their survival.

to Mexico, where wages were lower than in the United States. Supporters, however, had argued that free trade and lower tariffs would strengthen all the participants' economies and that more U.S. jobs would be created as expanding Mexican markets bought U.S. goods. As advocates had predicted, trade with Mexico increased. But manufacturing plants moved to Mexico, costing many low-wage jobs and causing U.S. companies to keep wages low. (See *trade* on page 940 in the Economics Handbook.)

CLINTON'S FOREIGN POLICY The most important foreign policy challenge for the Clinton administration was to ease the instability that had followed the end of the Cold War. Following the collapse of the Soviet Union, American leaders supported Boris Yeltsin, the president of Russia, hoping that he could create a stable democracy in his country. The greatest concern was the Russian nuclear arsenal, which would pose a great risk if it were to fall into the hands of dictators. Aside from providing economic aid, the United States could only watch and wait and encourage the Russians to solve their problems in a peaceful, democratic manner.

The fall of Communist governments also revived ancient ethnic hatreds. When Yugoslavia disintegrated in 1991, Bosnian Serbs began a campaign called "ethnic cleansing," intended to remove Muslims and Croats from the parts of Bosnia that Serbs controlled. The United States, NATO, and the United Nations worked to restore peace in the region. In December, 1995, the presidents of Bosnia, Croatia, and Serbia signed the Dayton Peace Accords. Since then, the UN and NATO have tried to enforce the provisions of the agreement. By 1997, they had succeeded in holding elections but had little success in capturing people charged with war crimes—which threatened to undo the agreement.

Before assuming office in 1992, President Clinton had promised to force China to protect the human rights of its citizens. Once in office, however, Clinton backed away from that position in favor of protecting China's favorable trading status. Nevertheless, problems with China persisted. In 1996, the Chinese conducted naval exercises around Taiwan. Some feared that the exercises were a prelude to an invasion, but no invasion occurred. The United States responded by increasing diplomatic communication with China in order to reduce economic and human rights tensions there.

ON THE WORLD STAGE

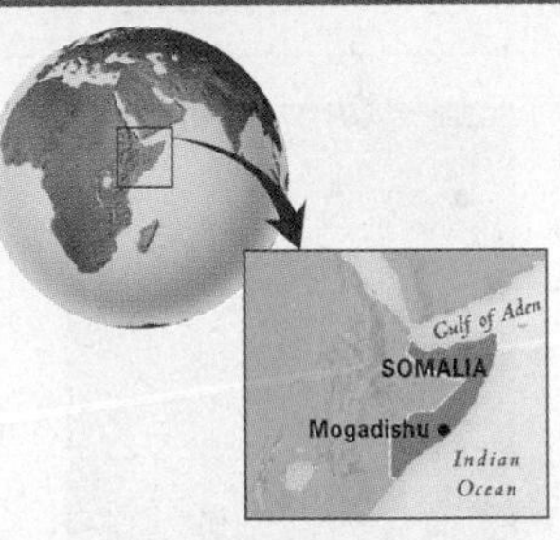

HUMANITARIAN RELIEF IN SOMALIA

In 1992, a deadly famine plagued Somalia, and an estimated 300,000 people died of starvation. Thirty thousand more Somalis were killed in fighting between warring ethnic groups, who stole relief supplies.

In December 1992, President Bush ordered U.S. marines to Somalia on a humanitarian mission named Operation Restore Hope. The marines tried to stop the theft of relief food in Somalia's capital, Mogadishu—an effort that saved an estimated 100,000 lives.

After 18 U.S. Army Rangers were killed in October 1993, however, President Clinton, responding to pressure, recalled the American troops and promised greater scrutiny of proposed humanitarian missions in the future.

The Republican Congress

In mid-1994, amid the failure of his health-care plan and recurring questions about Whitewater, Clinton saw his approval rating slump to 42 percent. Meanwhile, a Republican congressman from Georgia, **Newt Gingrich,** began to turn voters' dissatisfaction with Clinton into support for Republican candidates running in the midterm elections. His efforts led to a Republican victory and brought divided government back to Washington.

D. Answer The contract included tax cuts, harsher laws against crime, welfare reform, and a balanced-budget amendment.

THINK THROUGH HISTORY
D. *Summarizing* *List some of the provisions of the Contract with America.*

THE CONTRACT WITH AMERICA On September 27, 1994, on the steps of the Capitol, more than 300 Republican candidates signed Gingrich's **Contract with America.** The contract set forth ten items favored by an increasingly conservative electorate—among them, congressional term limits, a balanced-budget amendment, tax cuts, tougher crime laws, and welfare reform.

Republican congressional candidates hammered away at President Clinton and the

ON THE WORLD STAGE
Humanitarian Relief in Somalia

Critical Thinking: Analyzing Issues Ask students to tell why U.S. troops were unable to complete their mission in Somalia. *Possible Responses: Some students may respond that public opinion was against further aid after the deaths of U.S. servicemen. Others might attribute the cause to the fighting between ethnic groups within Somalia, which made safe distribution of relief goods impossible.*

OBJECTIVE
(3) INSTRUCT

The Republican Congress

▶ ***Starting with the Student*** Ask students to discuss the implications of having the Congress controlled by one party and the office of the president by another. Discuss these questions:

- What difficulties might this create?
- Under what circumstances might the country as a whole benefit from such an arrangement?

▶ ***Discussing Key Ideas***

- Republicans sign the Contract with America and take control of Congress.
- Conflict between Congress and the president leads to two shutdowns of federal government services.

(continued on next page)

TEACHING OPTIONS

Making Connections Across the Curriculum

Geography Have students locate each of the countries discussed on page 849 on a classroom map or globe. Some students may volunteer to bring to class specialized maps that give information about a particular region, such as a map that identifies areas of the Bosnian conflict or one that depicts Somalian refugee routes. Suggest to students that they look for such maps in past issues of magazines or on the Internet.

Exploring Themes

America in the World Expanding American commerce has always been a central tenet of U.S. foreign policy although it was less apparent during the Cold War. President Clinton vigorously strengthened the economic component of U.S. foreign policy. He created the National Economic Council, charged with coordinating domestic and foreign economic policies. Securing passage of NAFTA was one of the Clinton administration's major legislative successes in the areas of economic and foreign policy.

(continued from page 849)

- Clinton resists many conservative reforms, especially those related to entitlement programs.
- The president cooperates with the Republican Congress by signing into law a major overhaul of the welfare system.

ELECTRONIC LIBRARY OF PRIMARY SOURCES
A Contract with America by Newt Gingrich

IN-DEPTH RESOURCES: UNIT 7
from Contract with America p. 46

KEY PLAYERS
Clinton and Gingrich

Critical Thinking: Compare and Contrast Have students consider ways in which Clinton and Gingrich are similar and ways in which they differ. *Possible Responses: They are about the same age, both were reelected, both are tough on crime; they differ in their views on social issues such as changing Medicare.*

HISTORY FROM VISUALS
Political Cartoon

Reading the Cartoon Have students compare the effects of shutting down a family with the effects of shutting down the federal government. *Possible Response: Students may suggest that shutting down a family—and leaving children unfed or uncared for—would be impossible, and although it is possible to physically close government offices, the impact in lost wages and inefficient government functioning would hit millions of Americans.*

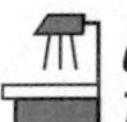

CRITICAL THINKING TRANSPARENCIES
CT34, Shutdown of the Federal Government

Democrats, using the contract as the hammer. In the elections of November 1994, the Republicans handed the Democrats a humiliating defeat. Voters turned control of both houses of Congress over to the Republicans for the first time since 1952 and placed 31 Republicans in the nation's governors' mansions. However, only 38 percent of eligible voters bothered to vote.

Chosen by acclamation as the new Speaker of the House, Newt Gingrich was jubilant.

A PERSONAL VOICE

I will never forget mounting the rostrum and looking over the House for the first time. It was an amazing experience. . . . The whole scene gave me a wonderful sense of the romance of America and the magic by which Americans share power and accept changes in government.

NEWT GINGRICH, *To Renew America*

KEY PLAYERS

BILL CLINTON
1946–

In 1992, Bill Clinton ran for president as a moderate, but in 1994 Republicans convinced voters that he had governed as a liberal during his first two years in office. As a result, the Republicans took control of Congress and controlled the national agenda throughout 1995.

Clinton reversed his fortunes, however, by opposing the Republicans' more unpopular positions, such as changing Medicare, and by taking control of their strongest issues, such as crime.

In 1996, Clinton forged compromises with Republicans on welfare and health-care reform. In the 1996 election, he became the first Democratic president to be reelected since FDR.

NEWT GINGRICH
1943–

In the summer of 1994, Newt Gingrich drafted his Contract with America. When Gingrich and the congressional Republicans took control of Congress in 1995, the House swiftly acted on the Contract with America, passing nine of the ten items within the first 100 days of the 104th Congress.

Gingrich eventually became highly unpopular, however, when Democrats attacked the Republican agenda as extreme. Nevertheless, as voters reelected Bill Clinton, they also retained Republican congressional majorities to pull Clinton and the Democrats to the center. Gingrich became the first Republican to be reelected speaker since the 1920s.

Gingrich and his fellow House Republicans spent their first days reforming Congress—cutting committees, staff, and special privileges. During the rest of their first 100 days in control of the House, they approved a constitutional amendment requiring a balanced federal budget by the year 2002, tried to increase defense spending, and promised tax cuts and welfare reform.

GOVERNMENT SHUTDOWNS Many Democrats and some Republicans in Congress, however, refused to go along with all of the conservative reforms. In the Senate, the balanced-budget amendment lost by one vote, and several other bills were either defeated or scaled back. Among these were efforts to repeal the ban on the sale of assault weapons and to cut federal environmental regulations.

Also, President Clinton began to fight back against the Republican Congress. In his first two years in office, Clinton had never issued a veto. In his second two years, he vetoed 15 bills.

Most notably, Clinton opposed Republican budgets that slowed the growth of entitlement programs. In late 1995, Clinton refused to compromise on the Republican budgets, and the congressional Republicans dug in their heels. The result was a shutdown of the federal government for a week in November, and again for several weeks in December 1995 and January 1996.

As a result of the shutdown, many government services were delayed, which inconvenienced citizens and federal employees alike. Although a third of the people polled blamed Clinton for the shutdown, even more people—44 percent—blamed Congress. Newt Gingrich's approval rating plunged to 22 percent. Fearing further voter disfavor, both sides agreed to a compromise in which Clinton

TEACHING OPTIONS

Teaching Gifted and Talented Students

Writing a Contract Have selected students write a "Contract with the Youth of America." Ask them to consider what, in their opinion, are the top ten issues affecting young people today. Suggest that they provide a legislative solution for each issue they identify. Students should write their contracts in a style that will make them suitable for oral presentation in a public setting, such as the steps of the U.S. Capitol.

Making Connections Across Time

Newt Gingrich's Reelection Ask students if they are aware of the circumstances that surrounded Newt Gingrich's 1997 reelection as Speaker of the House of Representatives. Some students may have followed media coverage of the House Ethics Committee's investigation of Gingrich. At issue was a complex case involving Gingrich's admitted misuse of tax-exempt nonpolitical resources—videos developed as part of a college course he was teaching—to achieve political goals for the Republican Party. Gingrich was reelected speaker prior to receiving a Congressional reprimand for his actions.

Skillbuilder Answer *Possible Answer:* The cartoonist took a dim view of the shutdowns. He sarcastically referred to the nation's leaders as "great statesmen" and indicated that shutting down the government is as impractical as shutting down family.

E. Answer As a presidential candidate, Clinton had promised to spend $10 billion to train welfare recipients to work. The bill he signed in 1996 contained no such provision for job training.

THINK THROUGH HISTORY
E. ***Contrasting*** *Contrast the welfare reform plan Clinton offered in 1992 with the one he signed in 1996.*

promised to balance the federal budget in seven years and Republicans promised to protect several of Clinton's favorite programs.

SKILLBUILDER
INTERPRETING POLITICAL CARTOONS
What point of view was the cartoonist expressing about federal government shutdowns?

WELFARE AND HEALTH REFORM Although the government shutdown dominated the headlines in late 1995 and early 1996, two bills signed into law in 1996 were more significant. Clinton had campaigned on the pledge to "end welfare as we know it." He had proposed to spend $10 billion to give welfare recipients training, education, and childcare so that they could seek higher-paying jobs. However, Congress had refused to approve this increased spending.

Instead, the Republican Congress crafted a bill that completely overhauled the welfare system. On July 31, 1996, President Clinton announced that he would sign the bill. It would cut $56 billion in welfare spending, limit the length of time people could receive benefits, and end the federal guarantee of welfare that had remained in place for 60 years. The new law would provide "block grants"—set amounts of federal funds—for the states to spend on welfare as they saw fit.

Liberal Democrats feared the consequences of eliminating the federal safety net for the poor, two-thirds of whom were children. New York senator Daniel Patrick Moynihan termed the legislation "an obscene act of political regression." Nevertheless, the bill passed. As Senator John Breaux of Louisiana argued, "It's not perfect. . . . But I think it's a major step in the right direction. It moves toward reform. It sets time limits."

In a less controversial action, the president signed into law a moderate health-care bill with bipartisan support. This bill made health insurance portable, so that workers could transfer their health insurance when they left their jobs, even if one of the people covered had a preexisting condition. However, the bill stopped short of establishing health care as a federal entitlement. The passage of these two laws removed welfare reform and health-care reform as issues in the 1996 election.

NOW & THEN

ENDING WELFARE ENTITLEMENTS

During Franklin D. Roosevelt's administration, the federal government for the first time assumed responsibility for the welfare of the nation's poor. Under the Social Security Act of 1935, Aid to Dependent Children, which later became Aid to Families with Dependent Children (AFDC), provided cash payments to a few hundred thousand families, most headed by widows.

Opponents of the program argued that people would become dependent on public assistance. By 1996, AFDC supported more than 4 million single mothers. Attacking a culture of dependency, politicians in both political parties pushed to end the federal government's guarantee of aid for America's needy. In 1996, Congress passed, and President Clinton signed, welfare reform legislation. It dissolved AFDC, but provided the states with federal funds to administer aid programs.

The Election of 1996

When Congress and Clinton began to compromise and pass legislation, their popularity rose among American voters. Early in the 1996 presidential campaign, President Clinton held large leads in public-opinion polls over Bob Dole, the Republican presidential nominee, and Ross Perot, the candidate of the newly established Reform Party.

THE 1996 CAMPAIGN After the nominating conventions in the summer, Clinton's lead in the polls was so large that some people thought the Democrats might regain control of Congress. Try as they might, Dole and Perot could not cut into Clinton's lead. Dole offered a 15 percent cut in the income tax and focused on scandals within the Clinton administration but did not gain any ground. Perot launched a television blitz attacking both major parties, but without success.

CLINTON REELECTED In the end, the strong economy and Clinton's improved working relationship with Congress convinced voters to back President Clinton. On election day, he won 49 percent of the popular vote, with Dole receiving 41 percent and Perot 8 percent. Despite Clinton's victory, there was no Democratic landslide, and the Republicans kept control of both houses of Congress.

Issues for the 21st Century

Tough Choices on Entitlements

Consider the state of entitlement reform by having students read pages 900–901. Then have them answer these questions.

1. How were federal entitlements affected by legislation in 1996? *Federal entitlements were ended.*
2. Was this legislation good for most Americans? Why? *Answers will vary.*

NOW & THEN
Ending Welfare Entitlements

Critical Thinking: Clarifying Ask students to cite the most important step the welfare reform bill took to limit recipients' dependence on public assistance. *Possible Response: Students should note limits on the length of time benefits can be received.* Then ask them what steps requested by Clinton were not taken. *Possible Responses: Clinton requested special training, education, and child care to prepare recipients for higher-paying jobs, but Congress refused.*

OBJECTIVE
(4) INSTRUCT

The Election of 1996

▶***Discussing Key Ideas***
- Voter apathy is high during the 1996 election.
- Clinton wins a second term, and the Republicans keep control of Congress.

IN-DEPTH RESOURCES: UNIT 7
from "A Bridge to the Future" by Bill Clinton, p. 47

Block Schedule TEACHING OPTION **Time Needed: 30 Minutes**

Cooperative Activity: Researching Current Events

Task: Small groups of students will research topics related to President Clinton's second term of office and a second Republican-dominated Congress.

Purpose: To learn how ongoing issues and new conflicts were handled in a second term of a Democratic president and a Republican Congress.

Activity: Each group will research one topic in the news that involves conflict or cooperation between President Clinton and Congress. Groups should present their information to the class in a format of their choosing, perhaps as a textbook page, as an oral presentation with visuals, or in a TV talk show. Students should incorporate quotations from key players involved in the issue.

Building a Portfolio: Students adding a presentation to their portfolio should attach a note explaining why they believe this is an example of their strongest work.

ALTERNATIVE ASSESSMENT BOOK
Standards for Evaluating a Cooperative Activity

Standards for Evaluation
Presentations should . . .
- show research using appropriate sources
- demonstrate an ability to identify significant information
- show creativity in the selection of accompanying quotations

OBJECTIVE

⑤ INSTRUCT

Clinton's Second Term

▶*Discussing Key Ideas*

- Popular calls for campaign finance reform lead to congressional investigations that discover illegalities in political fundraising practices.
- President Clinton and congressional Republicans set aside their partisan differences long enough to pass the first balanced budget since the 1960s.

ASSESS & RETEACH

Section 1 Assessment

Have students work individually to answer the questions and then trade papers with a partner to compare answers.

Self-Assessment

Ask students to identify passages in the text that helped them to answer each question.

Section Quiz

FORMAL ASSESSMENT
Section Quiz, p. 318

Reteach

Use the Geography Transparency for Section 1 to review voter turnout by state in 1996.

GEOGRAPHY TRANSPARENCIES
G34, Percentage of Eligible Votes Cast, 1996 Presidential Election

IN-DEPTH RESOURCES: UNIT 7
Guided Reading, p. 39

CLOSE

Although the split government of a Republican Congress and a Democratic president continued in Clinton's second term, the two parties had developed strategies for working together. Issues they confronted included the country's role in a changing world economy.

Voter Turnout, 1960–1996

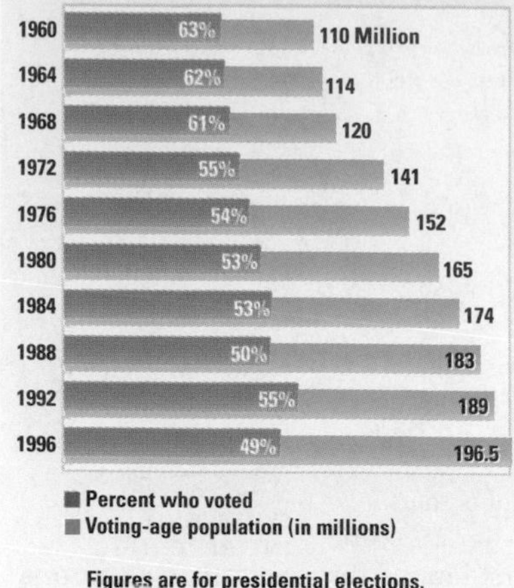

Figures are for presidential elections.
Source: Elections Research Center, Chevy Chase, Maryland.

SKILLBUILDER
INTERPRETING GRAPHS
What was the general trend in voter turnout between 1960 and 1996? In which election year did more than 100 million people cast ballots?

Skillbuilder Answer The rate of voter turnout generally declined. More than 100 million votes were cast in 1992 (55% of 189).

The biggest story of the election, however, was voter apathy. Exit polls showed that only 49 percent of eligible voters bothered to vote. Clinton's support came largely from women, especially single women. He also polled high numbers from blacks, Latinos, the elderly, and young voters. Dole's support came mainly from white, middle-class men.

THINK THROUGH HISTORY
F. *Synthesizing* *What factors contributed most to Clinton's reelection?*

F. Answer The strong economy; strong support among women and minorities; an improved working relationship with Congress.

Clinton's Second Term

In the immediate aftermath of the election, both President Clinton and Republican leaders pledged to set aside the bitter partisanship that had marked Clinton's first term. Nevertheless, Democrats and Republicans in Congress continued to attack each other as they looked ahead to future elections.

CAMPAIGN FINANCE REFORM The Republicans believed that they could most effectively damage the Democrats, including President Clinton, by exposing unethical and illegal fundraising efforts in the 1996 campaign. In the summer of 1997, congressional hearings into the fundraising tactics revealed a willingness by both major political parties to bend the rules. The Democrats had collected enormous sums of illegal money from foreigners and used the White House for fundraising. There was also evidence that the Republicans had raised campaign funds illegally, but to a lesser degree than the Democrats.

Meanwhile, some representatives and senators offered different plans to reform campaign financing. Some would have banned donations by political action committees in order to reduce the influence of special interests. Others would have lowered the upper limit on contributions or required full disclosure, the making public of the names of contributors. However, no bill gained enough support to pass.

BALANCING THE BUDGET Legislation to balance the budget, however, moved steadily ahead. In early August 1997, President Clinton and the Republican leadership agreed on a balanced-budget and tax-relief bill. It would reduce the deficit to zero by the year 2002 and provide tax relief to families with children, as well as a cut in the capital gains tax. Although some conservatives complained that tax cuts were too small and spending too high, and some liberals objected to cuts in social programs, the budget passed easily.

This bill would balance the budget for the first time since 1969. Many leaders hoped that it would lead to lower interest rates and increased economic growth. Most Americans also hoped that it would provide more security as they entered the new global economy of the 21st century.

Section 1 Assessment

1. TERMS & NAMES

Identify:

- Bill Clinton
- Twenty-seventh Amendment
- Hillary Rodham Clinton
- NAFTA
- Newt Gingrich
- Contract with America

2. SUMMARIZING Create a time line of Clinton's major actions during his first term as president, using a form such as the one below.

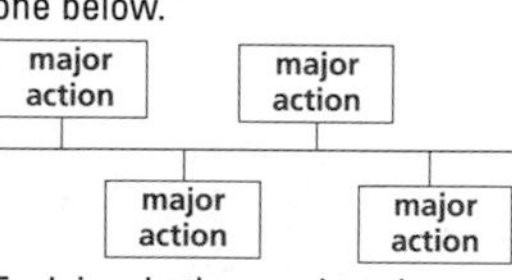

Explain whether each action was a success or a failure for Clinton.

3. RECOGNIZING EFFECTS How did voter dissatisfaction affect the 1992 presidential race?

THINK ABOUT

- what issues voters were upset about
- which candidates seemed to address those issues
- how voters responded at the polls

4. ANALYZING ISSUES On the basis of the events of Clinton's first term, would you characterize the United States in the 1990s as politically conservative, liberal, or somewhere in the middle? Explain your answer.

THINK ABOUT

- the response to Clinton's health-care reform plan
- the rise of Newt Gingrich and his loss of public approval
- the passage of welfare reform

ANSWERS

1. TERMS & NAMES

Bill Clinton, p. 846
27th Amendment, p. 847
Hillary Rodham Clinton, p. 848
NAFTA, p. 848
Newt Gingrich, p. 849
Contract with America, p. 849

2. SUMMARIZING

Students may include the following actions on their time lines. (Evaluations of success or failure may vary.)

September 1993—Presents health care bill to Congress
October 1993—Withdraws troops from Somalia
November 1993—Wins passage of NAFTA
November 1995 and January 1996—Argues with Congress over budget, leading to government shutdown
July 1996—Announces that he will sign welfare reform bill
August 1996—Announces that he will sign health care bill

3. RECOGNIZING EFFECTS

Possible Response: Students may note that dissatisfaction with the two major parties helped Ross Perot gain 19 percent of the vote. Also, dissatisfaction with the economy led voters to reject George Bush and elect Bill Clinton.

4. ANALYZING ISSUES

Possible Responses: Students who answer somewhere in the middle may point to the bipartisan bills that were passed during Clinton's first term and to the failure of either liberals or conservatives to dominate. Students who answer conservative may point to the failure of major health care reform, the rise of Newt Gingrich, and the passage of welfare reform. Those who answer liberal may point to the 1993 tax increase, Gingrich's loss of popularity, and Bob Dole's defeat.

2 The New Global Economy

TERMS & NAMES
- service sector
- downsize
- Bill Gates
- GATT

LEARN ABOUT America's role in a changing world economy
TO UNDERSTAND the economic challenges and opportunities facing Americans in the 21st century.

ONE AMERICAN'S STORY

The economy President Clinton inherited from President Bush was just beginning to pull out of a recession as Clinton took office. But some regions of the nation—particularly the Northeast—remained mired in stagnation. Near Kennebunkport, Maine, for example, the John Roberts clothing factory, which employed workers who did low-wage piecework, faced bankruptcy. Instead of letting the factory close, the workers, with the help of Mike Cavanaugh of the Clothing and Textile Workers Union, raised some money and turned the plant into an employee-owned company.

Ethel Beaudoin, who had worked in the factory for about 30 years, took a cut in pay for a chance at employee ownership. Although the pay cut was a hardship, she still had a positive outlook on the company's new direction.

A PERSONAL VOICE

It's a nice feeling to be part of the process . . . of deciding what this company buys for machinery and to know the customers more intimately. They're our customers, and it's a nicer feeling when the customers know that the coat that we put out is made by owners. It's almost like you're making it more personal.

ETHEL BEAUDOIN, quoted in *Divided We Fall*

Workers at the John Roberts clothing factory

Beaudoin's experience offered one example of the economic possibilities in America. A new global economy—brought about by new technologies, increased international competition, and the end of the Cold War—changed the nation's economic prospects. Still, despite all the positive economic news in the 1990s, some Americans still felt insecure.

The New Service and High-Tech Economy

In the mid-1990s, Americans heard a great deal of good news about the economy. The good news was that inflation had fallen to its lowest level since the 1960s. Ten million new jobs were created between 1993 and 1996. By 1997 the unemployment rate had fallen to 4.8 percent, the lowest it had been since 1973.

But there was some alarming news as well. For example, in many families both parents had to work, because it was harder to find jobs that paid well. Between 1989 and 1993, the median household income, adjusted for inflation, dropped from $33,585 to $31,241. In addition, the income gap between America's richest and poorest earners widened. In 1993, nearly 4 million working families earned too little to stay out of poverty.

There were varying explanations for this income stagnation. Liberal economists claimed that corporations were making unfair profits by manufacturing more of their goods in foreign countries that had lower labor costs. Conservative economists asserted that taxes were still too high, preventing companies from growing faster and creating more high-paying jobs. But no matter which side of the debate economists were on, they agreed that the American economy was going through significant changes.

Section 2 Overview

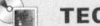

OBJECTIVES

1. To describe changes in the American workplace.
2. To explain increased competition for domestic and international markets.

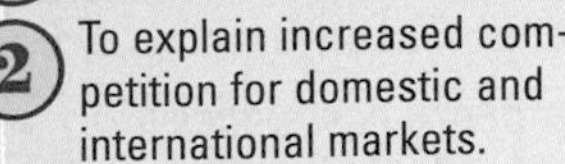

SKILLBUILDERS

- Interpreting graphs, p. 854
- Understanding geography: location, p. 856

CRITICAL THINKING

- Theme: The American Dream, p. 854
- Theme: Economic Opportunity, p. 855
- Recognizing effects, p. 857
- Summarizing. p. 857
- Drawing conclusions, p. 857

FOCUS & MOTIVATE

5-MINUTE WARM-UP

Drawing Conclusions
To discuss the impact of political leaders on the economy, have students read the Economic Background on page 854 and answer these questions.

1. Why is Alan Greenspan considered to be the most powerful man in the financial world?
2. Does he have too much power? Explain.

WARM-UP TRANSPARENCY 26

▶ ***Starting with the Student***
- Ask students where the manufactured objects they use every day—clothing, shoes, radio, TV, car—are made. Then ask them what impact they think a global economy might have on them and their families.

OBJECTIVE
(1) INSTRUCT

The New Service and High-Tech Economy

▶ ***Discussing Key Ideas***
- The income gap between wealthiest and poorest Americans widens.

(continued on next page)

SECTION 2 RESOURCES

PRINT RESOURCES

IN-DEPTH RESOURCES: UNIT 7
Guided Reading, p. 40
Geography Application: The U.S. Trade in Goods, p. 44
Primary Source: from *The Road Ahead* by Bill Gates, p. 48
American Lives: Bill Gates, p. 52

READING STUDY GUIDE, p. 265

ACCESS FOR STUDENTS ACQUIRING ENGLISH
Guided Reading (Spanish), p. 282
Geography Application: The U.S. Trade in Goods (Spanish), p. 286

SPANISH READING STUDY GUIDE, p. 265

FORMAL ASSESSMENT
Section Quiz, p. 319

ALTERNATIVE ASSESSMENT BOOK
See forms for supporting and scoring alternative activities.

TECHNOLOGY RESOURCES

INTERNET http://www.mlushistory.com

(continued from page 853)

- Temporary work and jobs expand in the service sector and in high technology.
- Young people suffer more unemployment and earn less than older workers.
- Union membership drops.

IN-DEPTH RESOURCES: UNIT 7
Guided Reading, p. 40

ACCESS FOR STUDENTS ACQUIRING ENGLISH
Guided Reading (Spanish), p. 282

ECONOMIC BACKGROUND
Greenspan and the Fed

Ask students to explain the analogy between a pacemaker and the Federal Reserve Board. Ask them if they think this is an apt comparison, and if so, why.

MORE ABOUT . . .
Downsizing Doublespeak

Apparently, some companies found it difficult to talk about laying off workers. Writer William Lutz collected ways businesses described the deed:

- career-change opportunity
- career-transition program
- involuntary severance
- rightsizing
- reshaping
- release of resources

In any case, the result was always the same—job loss.

HISTORY FROM VISUALS
Changes in Weekly Earnings, 1985–1995

Reading the Graphs
Remind students that the median figure is the earnings level above which half of all Americans fall and below which half of all Americans fall. Tell students that 1982 dollars were used

(continued on next page)

ECONOMIC BACKGROUND

GREENSPAN AND THE FED
Alan Greenspan has been chairman of the Federal Reserve Board (the Fed) since 1987, when he was appointed by President Ronald Reagan. The Fed has been described as the economic pacemaker of the United States because it helps determine how much money there will be in the American economy.

President Reagan chose Greenspan because he expected that Greenspan would promote policies to combat inflation. Greenspan has been successful in keeping inflation low, but at times critics have claimed that his efforts have helped keep the unemployment rate higher than necessary.

Greenspan is considered by many to be the most powerful man in the financial world. In December 1996, Greenspan asked whether "irrational exuberance has unduly escalated" stock prices. The next day, stock prices in Japan fell 3 percent, and U.S. stocks fell nearly 100 points. (See *interest rate* on page 936 in the Economics Handbook.)

THE EXPANDING SERVICE SECTOR In the 1990s, far-reaching changes in the U.S. workplace emerged. Chief among these changes were the loss of jobs in manufacturing and the explosive growth of jobs in the **service sector,** the part of the economy that provides services to consumers. By 1996, more than 60 percent of American workers held jobs in the service sector, which included store employees, medical professionals, lawyers, engineers, waitpeople, and teachers.

The largest growth in the service sector in the mid-1990s came in low-paying jobs, such as retail sales, fast-food vending, and janitorial work. In addition to the low pay these jobs offered, many were only part-time or temporary positions with limited benefits. For example, Manpower, Inc., a Milwaukee-based temporary services company, benefited from changes in the economy and became the largest U.S. employer. In 1993, fully 640,000 American workers cashed paychecks from the company, which generated earnings of almost $2 billion.

TEMPORARY WORKERS When Manpower, Inc., and other such companies first opened, they supplied temporary workers, often called temps, for emergencies or seasonal peak periods. Later, many corporations, instead of investing in salaries and benefits for a large full-time staff, began to **downsize**—reduce staff in order to streamline operations—and to hire temps, who were often less expensive. Many young workers who saw their parents work for one company until retirement found themselves working as "permalancers," long-term freelance workers. Experts projected that by the year 2000, 35 million workers—half of all workers and two-thirds of women workers—would be temps.

The increasing movement to temporary work had important consequences for the workers. Most temps had little job security and fewer benefits than permanent employees. Both of these factors in turn contributed to the general feeling of economic insecurity.

YOUNG WORKERS Another measure of economic insecurity in the 1990s was that three out of four young Americans expected to earn less money as adults than their parents did. In fact, younger workers continued to suffer higher rates of unemployment even when the jobless rate fell for older workers. In 1993, about one in seven workers between the ages of 16 and 25 lacked a job—double the national rate.

THINK THROUGH HISTORY
A. THEME ***The American Dream*** *How did the change from an industrial economy to a service economy affect Americans' economic security?*

A. Answer Unlike factory jobs, most jobs in the service sector paid low wages. Also, many service jobs provided only contract or part-time work.

SKILLBUILDER
INTERPRETING GRAPHS ***How did the change in men's earnings between 1985 and 1995 differ from the change in women's earnings? Which racial/ethnic group had the largest drop in earnings from 1990 to 1995?***

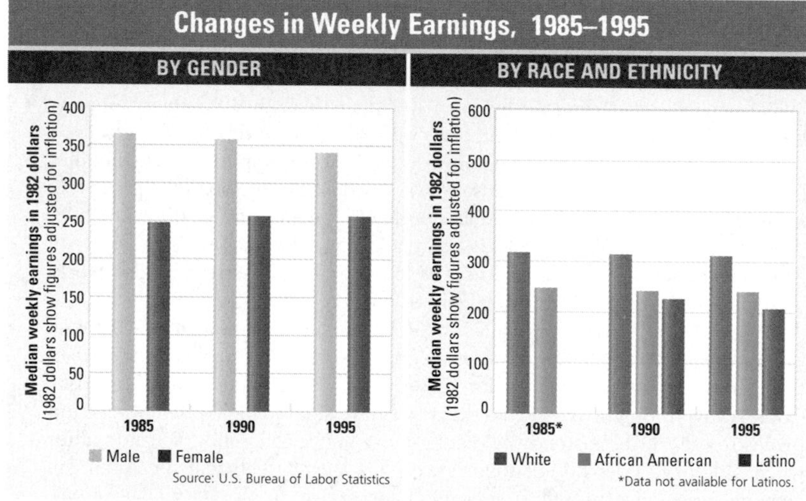

TEACHING OPTIONS

Making Connections Across the Curriculum

Economics Discuss with students the fluctuations of the stock market. Ask students to choose three stocks to follow in the newspaper for a month and to use a chart like this one to record changes.

Week	Stock	Increase	Decrease
Week 1			
Week 2			
Week 3			
Week 4			

Exploring Themes

Economic Opportunity Discuss with students the actions taken by the government during the 1990s that affected—or seemed to affect—workers' jobs. Point out that the federal government does not always make decisions based on the impact its actions might have on jobs in a particular city or company. In the pursuit of international trade agreements such as NAFTA, the federal government considered the economy of the nation as a whole. The assumption was that the expansion of U.S. markets abroad would benefit everyone—for example, by providing cheaper goods for American citizens.

High unemployment rates in the nation's cities hit young people harder than others. In 1994, for example, 18 percent of Detroit's workers, but almost 50 percent of its young people, were unemployed. The rise in joblessness among young people and the nation's shift to a service economy came at the expense of America's traditional workplaces, the farms and factories that had previously supported American families.

FARMS AND FACTORIES At the beginning of the 20th century, more Americans worked at farming than at any other single occupation. From the 1920s until the 1970s, though, industrial manufacturing was the nation's largest employment sector.

Starting in the 1970s, the United States experienced another wrenching change, as manufacturing jobs began to disappear. By 1996, only about 17 percent of America's workers worked in factories. Smokestack industries, such as automaking and steel production, declined in the 1970s, often because of international competition. In addition, by the 1980s and 1990s, automation had shifted many tasks from people to machines. In 1992, for example, a mere 140,000 steelworkers did the same work that 240,000 workers had accomplished ten years earlier. Larry Pugh, who managed a hospital in Waterloo, Iowa, talked about the downsizing of a farm equipment factory in his hometown.

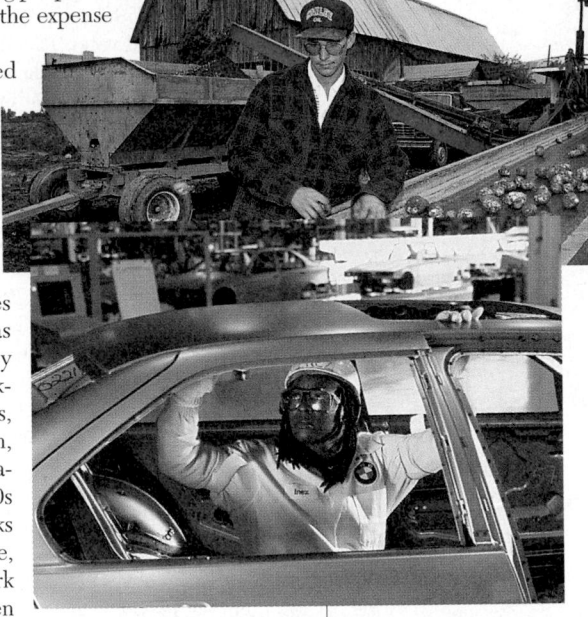

Despite steady growth in the economy, America's blue-collar workers on farms and in factories continued to feel economic insecurity in the 1990s.

A PERSONAL VOICE

There used to be seventeen thousand five hundred people working here. . . . Now there are six thousand. Those people spent their money. They bought the cars. They bought the houses. They were replaced by people that are at the minimum wage—seven or eight dollars an hour, not fifteen or twenty dollars an hour. These people can hardly eke out a living at today's wages.

LARRY PUGH, quoted in *Divided We Fall*

B. Answer Downsizing led to higher unemployment, particularly in cities. It also resulted in the hiring of more temporary workers in place of permanent employees.

THINK THROUGH HISTORY **B.** THEME *Economic Opportunity* *How did downsizing affect people?*

The decline in the number of industrial jobs caused by competition and automation contributed to a drop in union membership. In 1945, 35 percent of American workers belonged to unions; by 1995, only 15 percent of workers were union members. In the 1990s, unions had trouble organizing. Many high-tech and professional workers who already earned high wages felt no need for union membership, and low-wage service employees felt too vulnerable to risk their jobs in a strike. In this economy, some workers saw their incomes decline, while others—those with advanced training and specialized technical skills—saw their salaries rise and their economic security expand greatly.

HIGH-TECH INDUSTRIES In the mid-1990s, workers in high-tech fields made up about 20 percent of the work force. Management consultant Peter Drucker estimated that early in the 21st century, at least one in three workers would be a "knowledge worker." Unlike the factory work that had paid good wages even to semiskilled workers, the new high-tech jobs demanded that workers have specialized skills, creativity, and knowledge of computers. Most workers who landed high-tech jobs earned healthy salaries.

ECONOMIC BACKGROUND

HIGH-TECH LAYOFFS

Some experts have predicted that high-tech information jobs will employ one-third of the work force early in the 21st century. However, the companies that have been at the cutting edge of the technology revolution have been among the most aggressive in downsizing their work force. Between 1991 and 1995, for example, IBM laid off 85,000 workers, AT&T 83,000, and Xerox 10,000. While these layoffs were partially offset by hires in new companies that developed and used the new technology, the net result of the computer revolution in the 1990s has been a loss of jobs. (See *unemployment* on page 940 in the Economics Handbook.)

(continued from page 854)

to represent the earnings level for each year shown so that the graph would represent constant dollar values over time.

MORE ABOUT . . .
Job Shifts

An ironic result of the relatively dramatic shift in jobs from industrial to high-tech has been that some Americans in technical training schools are being trained for jobs that no longer exist. Technical school graduates experience growing difficulty in finding the jobs for which they entered school in the first place. The problem is likely to become worse with the increase in temporary or contract jobs. And the joblessness has not been limited to blue-collar workers. Stephen Roach of Morgan Stanley & Co. noted that during the early 1990s, little had been done to help "the new silent majority suffering from white-collar shock."

ECONOMIC BACKGROUND
High-Tech Layoffs

Critical Thinking: Forming Opinions Remind students that workers in high-tech jobs can usually count on good salaries—but increasingly must face possible job elimination at some point during their careers. Have students discuss whether they think layoffs by high-tech companies will deter young people from pursuing a career in high-tech industries.

IN-DEPTH RESOURCES: UNIT 7
Primary Source: from *The Road Ahead* by Bill Gates, p. 48
American Lives: Bill Gates, p. 52

Block Schedule TEACHING OPTION **Time Needed: 40 Minutes**

Cooperative Activity: Planning a Job Fair

Task: Student groups will organize a job fair focusing on new opportunities in the service sector and in high technology.

Purpose: To become aware of the changing job markets and of new job opportunities.

Activity: As a class, students will plan a job fair, brainstorming about what jobs should be included and what other classes or schools could be invited to their presentation.

Working in small groups, students will research one job or a group of related jobs and then prepare a presentation. They may also identify speakers who could be invited to talk about specific jobs. Groups should divide up other tasks such as publicizing the event and preparing a program.

Building a Portfolio: Students adding a presentation to their portfolio should attach a note pointing out their own contribution to the work.

ALTERNATIVE ASSESSMENT BOOK
Standards for Evaluating a Cooperative Activity

Standards for Evaluation
Presentations should . . .
- show efforts to identify current new jobs
- use details to describe the jobs
- be imaginative and effective

OBJECTIVE

② INSTRUCT

Change and the Global Economy

▶ ***Starting with the Student*** Ask students what trips to foreign countries they or their friends or family members have made during the past year. Then ask these questions:

- How many hours did it take to reach their destinations?
- What conclusions can they draw about the accessibility of international markets?

▶ ***Discussing Key Ideas***

- Clinton favors expanding U.S. trade abroad to meet international competition.
- Americans disagree over whether international trade agreements will result in the loss of jobs.

IN-DEPTH RESOURCES: UNIT 7
Geography Application: The U.S. Trade in Goods, p. 44

HISTORY FROM VISUALS

World Trading Blocs, 1996

Reading the Map Help students interpret the map by having them identify the members that make up some of the trading blocs. Begin by asking them what nations make up the Group of Seven. *U.S.A., Canada, Great Britain, France, Germany, Italy, Japan.*

Extension Have students use an almanac to find out to whom each country in the Group of Seven exported the most. *The U.S exported to Canada; Canada exported to the U.S.; Japan exported to the U.S.; Great Britain, France, Germany, and Italy, to the EU.*

By the 1990s, more than a few innovative entrepreneurs had turned cutting-edge ideas about computer technology into huge personal fortunes. **Bill Gates,** for example, was a sophomore at Harvard University in December 1974 when he saw a promising business opportunity. With his friend Paul Allen, Gates adapted the computer language BASIC for use in personal computers, which had recently come on to the market. Gates dropped out of college to found Microsoft, the computer software company that by 1997 had provided him with assets estimated at more than $39 billion, making him the wealthiest man in the world.

Change and the Global Economy

In 1900, airplanes hadn't yet flown and telephone service was barely 20 years old. U.S. trade with the rest of the world was worth about $2.2 billion (roughly 12 percent of the economy). Nearly a century later, New Yorkers could hop a supersonic jet and arrive in London within three hours, information traveled instantly by fax machine, and U.S. trade with other countries approached $2 trillion (more than 25 percent of the economy). As American companies competed for international and domestic markets, American workers competed with workers in other countries.

INTERNATIONAL TRADE The expansion of U.S. trade abroad was an important goal of President Clinton's foreign policy, as his support of NAFTA had shown. In 1994, in response to increasing international economic competition among trading blocs, the United States joined many other nations in adopting a new version of the General Agreement on Tariffs and Trade **(GATT).** The new treaty lowered trade barriers, such as tariffs, and established the World Trade Organization (WTO) to resolve trade disputes. Economists

World Trading Blocs, 1996

ORGANIZATIONS AND MEMBER COUNTRIES

- Organization of Petroleum Exporting Countries (OPEC)
- Asia Pacific Economic Cooperation (APEC) [countries with red borders]
- G-7 (Group of Seven)

Andean Group	
ASEAN	(Association of Southeast Asian Nations)
CACM/MCCA	(Central American Common Market)
CAEU	(Council of Arab Unity)
CARICOM	(Caribbean Community and Common Market)
CIS	(Commonwealth of Independent States)
EU	(European Union)
MERCOSUR	(Southern Cone Common Market)
NAFTA	(North American Free Trade Agreement)
SADC	(Southern African Development Community)
UDEAC	(Central African Customs and Economic Union)

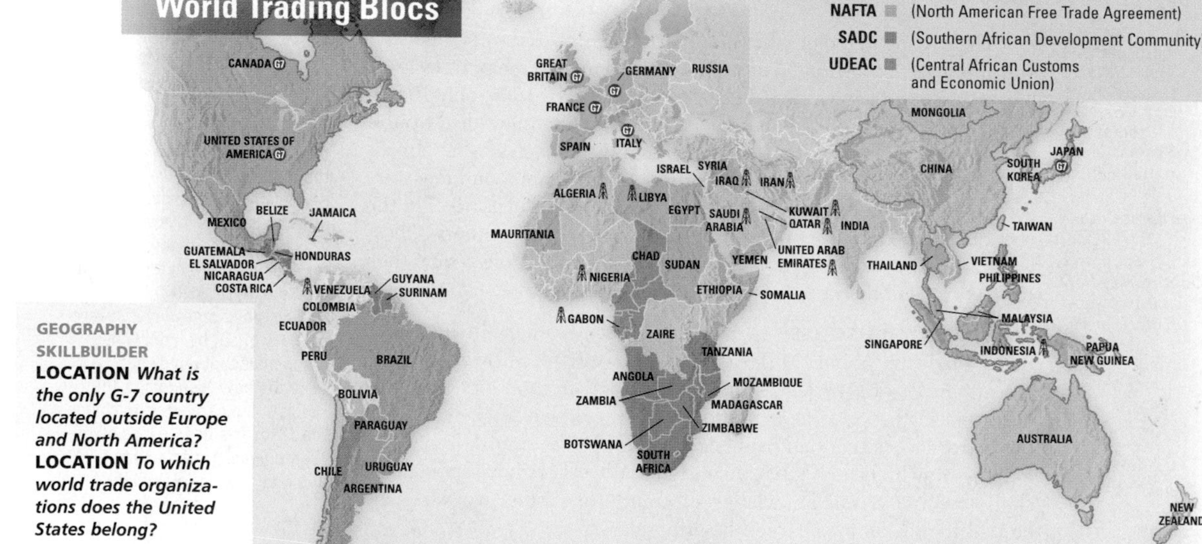

GEOGRAPHY SKILLBUILDER
LOCATION *What is the only G-7 country located outside Europe and North America?*
LOCATION *To which world trade organizations does the United States belong?*

Block Schedule TEACHING OPTION **Time Needed: 40 Minutes**

Cooperative Activity: Researching International Trade

Task: Student groups will research a world trading bloc and prepare a report on exports and imports of member countries.

Purpose: To recognize the importance of trading blocs in maintaining international trade.

Activity: Students will form pairs or small groups and choose a trading bloc represented by a color on the map. Each group will research the major exports and imports of countries in the bloc, the bloc's trading partners, and annual expenditures. Each group will then prepare a report and present it to the class, using graphs, charts, and product examples if they choose.

Building a Portfolio: Students adding a report to their portfolio should attach a note explaining their own contribution to the work.

ALTERNATIVE ASSESSMENT BOOK
Standards for Evaluating a Cooperative Activity

Standards for Evaluation
Reports should . . .

- use specific details to demonstrate knowledge of a country's exports and imports
- reflect accurate data from reliable sources
- be presented using effective oral presentation techniques

predicted that the treaty would have a positive overall effect on the U.S. economy. As President Clinton announced at a meeting of the Group of Seven (the world's seven leading economic powers) that year, "Trade as much as troops will increasingly define the ties that bind nations in the twenty-first century."

These international trade agreements, however, deepened American workers' fears of massive job flight to countries that produced the same goods as the United States but at a lower cost. Those fears had arisen in the 1970s, when less expensive but high-quality auto and steel imports from Japan and Germany had forced many U.S. factory workers out of high-paying jobs.

To remain competitive, many U.S. businesses felt the need to make their operations more global in order to produce goods as economically as possible. Indeed, the shipping label for a product of one American electronics company reads: "Made in one or more of the following countries: Korea, Hong Kong, Malaysia, Singapore, Taiwan, Mauritius, Thailand, Indonesia, Mexico, Philippines. The exact country of origin is unknown."

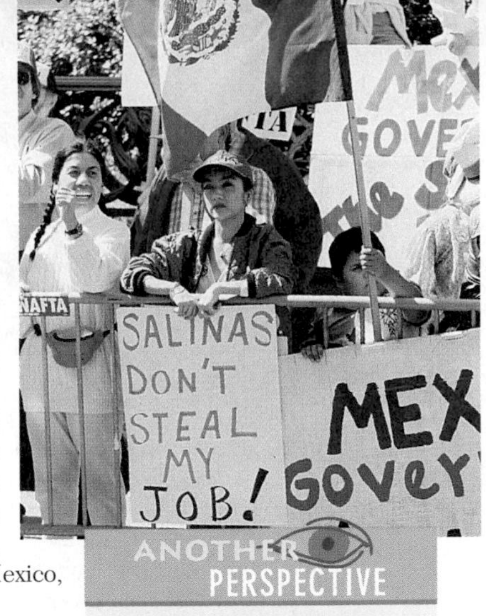

INTERNATIONAL COMPETITION During the 1990s, U.S. businesses felt pressure to cut costs wherever possible. To reduce labor costs, businesses frequently moved their operations to less economically advanced countries, such as Mexico, where wages were lower. Shortly after NAFTA took effect in 1994, 100,000 low-wage jobs were lost in U.S. manufacturing industries. However, exports to Canada and Mexico increased so much by 1997 that the Clinton administration estimated that NAFTA actually supported an increase of more than 300,000 more American jobs than existed in 1993.

Less economically advanced countries also offered some businesses an opportunity to evade the strict environmental regulations legislated in such developed nations as the United States. Just south of the U.S. border with Mexico, for example, foreign-owned *maquiladoras*, or assembly plants, often operated irresponsibly, dumping poisonous chemical wastes on Mexican soil. Critics of NAFTA feared that it would allow some U.S. companies to move to Mexico to avoid the strict environmental laws in the United States.

With the U.S. economy undergoing such extensive change at the end of the 20th century, feelings of insecurity were inevitable. Many Americans in all sectors of the economy feared being left behind by the rapid change. Other Americans, however, saw great opportunities for progress—especially from the endless stream of new technology.

C. Answer These trade agreements opened new markets but also made jobs more mobile. Companies exported work to countries with lower wages, costing Americans jobs.

THINK THROUGH HISTORY
C. *Recognizing Effects* *What were some of the effects of NAFTA and GATT?*

ANOTHER PERSPECTIVE

ECONOMICS AND IMMIGRATION

In 1996, the U.S.-Mexican border crossing between San Diego and Tijuana was one of the busiest in the world. Every day, some 40,000 people crossed the border there legally to work, shop, or visit. Many others crossed illegally elsewhere along the border. President Clinton tried to stem this tide by building a 14-mile wall along the border.

Some believed there was a better way to prevent illegal immigration to the United States—creating more jobs in Mexico. Carlos de Orduna, an executive at a Mexican assembly plant owned by a foreign company, said that few of his workers attempted to emigrate illegally. He argued, "If you have a job that allows you to live reasonably well, . . . why should you go to the United States?"

Section 2 Assessment

1. TERMS & NAMES
Identify:
- service sector
- downsize
- Bill Gates
- GATT

2. SUMMARIZING In a cluster diagram like the one below, record the major changes that occurred in the U.S. economy during the 1990s.

Which change has affected you the most? Explain.

3. RECOGNIZING EFFECTS Explain who was negatively affected by the changes in the economy and what negative effects they suffered.

THINK ABOUT
- who had the highest unemployment rates
- what types of jobs were eliminated
- what other negative effects there were

4. DRAWING CONCLUSIONS Considering the economic changes described in this section, how do you think workers can best prepare themselves for the future?

THINK ABOUT
- the trend of hiring more temporary employees
- the shift from agriculture and manufacturing to high-tech industries
- the skills that might prepare one for work in the global economy

ANSWERS

1. TERMS & NAMES

service sector, p. 854
downsize, p. 854
Bill Gates, p. 856
GATT, p. 856

2. SUMMARIZING

The cluster diagram might include the following words and phrases: expanding service sector, contract workers, "permalancers," downsizing, high unemployment, decline in industrial work, drop in union membership, "knowledge worker," high-tech industry, global economy, international trade, GATT.

3. RECOGNIZING EFFECTS

Possible Response: Students may say that young people, factory workers, and unskilled or uneducated workers lost jobs, that some workers employed by large corporations were replaced by temporary employees, and that even many workers who kept their jobs suffered small increases in wages and benefits because they were afraid to strike.

4. DRAWING CONCLUSIONS

Possible Response: Students may say that workers should prepare for self-employment, develop good job-hunting skills, get an education, learn about technology, learn foreign languages, be flexible, and be willing to constantly acquire new skills.

ANOTHER PERSPECTIVE
Economics and Immigration

Critical Thinking: Making Predictions Have students discuss the long-term impact of NAFTA. Among other questions, they could consider whether it might lead to environmental problems, spark economic growth in Mexico, or cause American industrial wages to stagnate.

ASSESS & RETEACH

Section 2 Assessment
Have students work in pairs to compare the cluster diagrams on changes in the economy that they created for item 2.

Self-Assessment
Ask students to review their responses to item 4. Have them expand their answers by adding any new or different ideas they might have for how workers can prepare for the future.

Section Quiz

FORMAL ASSESSMENT
Section Quiz, p. 319

Reteach
Have students work in small groups to merge their answers to item 2 on a single cluster diagram representing the whole group. Ask groups to put their diagrams on the board.

CLOSE

As the century came to a close, America's economic role at home and abroad was changing due in part to shifts in the workplace to high-technology industries.

American Literature

OBJECTIVES

1. To describe how contemporary women writers reflect diversity in America.
2. To explain how literature by female writers reflects women's experiences of American life.

FOCUS & MOTIVATE

▶ ***Starting with the Student*** Ask students to name American women writers whose work they have read.

- What issues and themes do these writers explore?
- Are these themes and issues different from those that male writers explore? If so, in what ways?

MORE ABOUT . . .

Nikki Giovanni

A product of the politically-charged 1960s, Nikki Giovanni began writing about African-American people and black power. She wrote about the issues of independence and self-determination before turning to family themes, including motherhood, children, and childhood memories. As Ida Lewis writes, Giovanni's "central core is always associated with her family: the family that produced her and the family she is producing."

AMERICAN LITERATURE

Women Writers Reflect American Diversity

The broadening of opportunities for American women that began in the late 1960s is as evident in literature as it is in other fields. Toni Morrison, Mary Oliver, Nikki Giovanni, Amy Tan, Anne Tyler, Alice Walker, Marge Piercy, Sandra Cisneros—these are just a few of the talented women novelists and poets who reflect the multicultural nature of American society. In the midst of such diversity, however, women's writing shares a common characteristic—that of conveying the American experience through the exploration of such issues as personal identity, nature, childhood, and family.

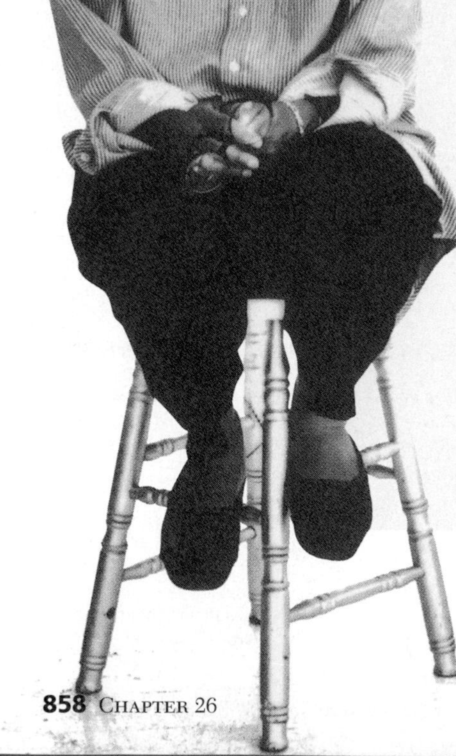

NIKKI GIOVANNI

In the late 1960s, Nikki Giovanni won instant attention as an African American poet writing about the Black Power movement. Since then her poetry has often focused on childhood, family ties, and other personal concerns. In the following poem, Giovanni deals with individual empowerment—even under less than ideal circumstances.

Choices

if i can't do
what i want to do
then my job is to not
do what i don't want
to do

it's not the same thing
but it's the best i can
do

if i can't have
what i want then
my job is to want
what i've got
and be satisfied
that at least there
is something more
to want

since i can't go
where i need
to go then i must go
where the signs point
though always understanding
parallel movement
isn't lateral

when i can't express
what i really feel
i practice feeling
what i can express
and none of it is equal
i know
but that's why mankind
alone among the mammals
learns to cry

NIKKI GIOVANNI, *Cotton Candy on a Rainy Day* (1978)

RECOMMENDED RESOURCES

Books

Alvarez, Julia. *¡Yo!* Chapel Hill: Algonquin, 1997. A novel of sisterhood, daughterhood, families, and friendships.

Erdrich, Louise. *The Beet Queen.* New York: Holt, 1986. A novel of families and friendships set in a small off-reservation town in North Dakota.

Giovanni, Nikki. *My House.* New York: Quill, 1983. Poetry that is mainly personal and autobiographical.

Growing Up Chicana/o: An Anthology. New York: William Morrow, 1993. Short stories by male and female Mexican American writers.

Morrison, Toni. *Beloved.* New York: New American Library, 1988. Fictional recreation of slavery and its effects.

Sound Recordings

Angelou, Maya. *I Know Why the Caged Bird Sings.* New York: Random, 1986. An abridgment of Angelou's award-winning autobiography, read by the author.

Cisneros, Sandra. *Woman Hollering Creek [and] House on Mango Street.* New York: Random House Audio Books. Taped abridgment of the novel and short stories.

Videos

Alice Walker. San Francisco: Contemporary Newsreel, 1992. A conversation with the contemporary novelist.

Breathing Lessons. Los Angeles: Republic Pictures, 1994. Film version of the novel by Anne Tyler.

The Joy Luck Club. Hollywood: Hollywood Pictures Home Video, 1993. The film based on the Amy Tan novel.

AMY TAN

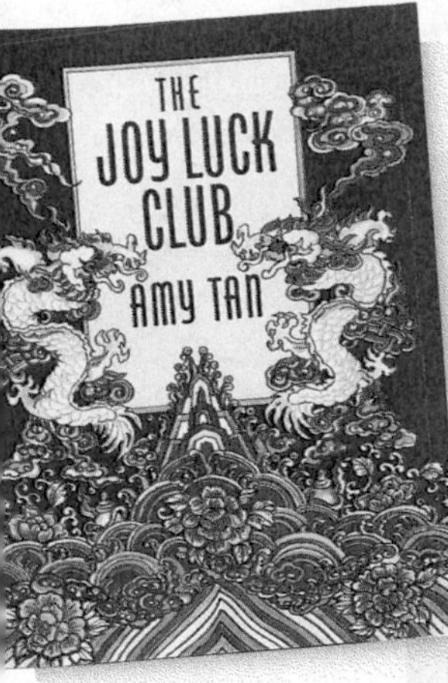

A native of San Francisco, Amy Tan draws on personal experiences in *The Joy Luck Club,* a series of interconnected stories about four Chinese-American daughters and their immigrant mothers. The title refers to the club that the four mothers establish for socializing and playing the game of mahjong.

My mother started the San Francisco version of the Joy Luck Club in 1949, two years before I was born. This was the year my mother and father left China with one stiff leather trunk filled only with fancy silk dresses. There was no time to pack anything else, my mother had explained to my father after they boarded the boat. Still his hands swam frantically between the slippery silks, looking for his cotton shirts and wool pants.

When they arrived in San Francisco, my father made her hide those shiny clothes. She wore the same brown-checked Chinese dress until the Refugee Welcome Society gave her two hand-me-down dresses, all too large in sizes for American women. The society was composed of a group of white-haired American missionary ladies from the First Chinese Baptist Church. And because of their gifts, my parents could not refuse their invitation to join the church. Nor could they ignore the old ladies' practical advice to improve their English through Bible study class on Wednesday nights and, later, through choir practice on Saturday mornings. This was how my parents met the Hsus, the Jongs, and the St. Clairs. My mother could sense that the women of these families also had unspeakable tragedies they had left behind in China and hopes they couldn't begin to express in their fragile English. Or at least, my mother recognized the numbness in these women's faces. And she saw how quickly their eyes moved when she told them her idea for the Joy Luck Club.

AMY TAN, *The Joy Luck Club* (1989)

SANDRA CISNEROS

Sandra Cisneros is one of many Chicana writers to win fame in recent years. In *The House on Mango Street,* she traces the experiences of a poor Hispanic girl named Esperanza (Spanish for hope) and her warm-hearted family. Nenny is her sister.

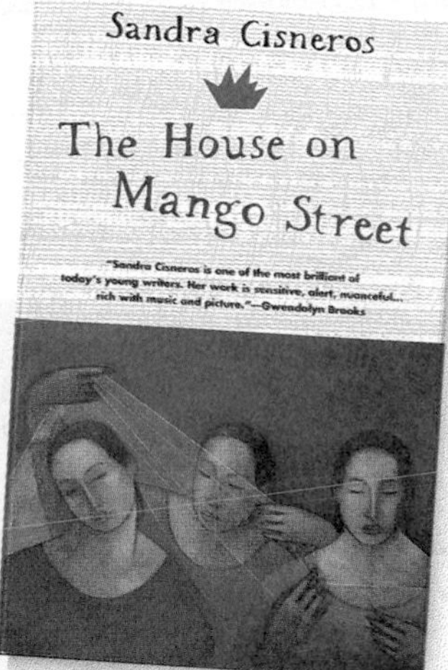

Four Skinny Trees

They are the only ones who understand me. I am the only one who understands them. Four skinny trees with skinny necks and pointy elbows like mine. Four who do not belong here but are here. Four raggedy excuses planted by the city. From our room we can hear them, but Nenny just sleeps and doesn't appreciate these things.

Their strength is secret. They send ferocious roots beneath the ground. They grow up and they grow down and grab the earth between their hairy toes and bite the sky with violent teeth and never quit their anger. This is how they keep.

Let one forget his reason for being, they'd all droop like tulips in a glass, each with their arms around the other. Keep, keep, keep, trees say when I sleep. They teach.

When I am too sad and too skinny to keep keeping, when I am a tiny thing against so many bricks, then it is I look at trees. When there is nothing left to look at on this street. Four who grew despite concrete. Four who reach and do not forget to reach. Four whose only reason is to be and be.

SANDRA CISNEROS, *The House on Mango Street* (1989)

INTERACT WITH HISTORY

1. **MAKING INFERENCES** From these selections, what can you infer about women's experiences in American life today? Cite passages to support your response.

SEE SKILLBUILDER HANDBOOK, PAGE 912.

2. **CREATING AN ANTHOLOGY** Working in a group, choose selections for an anthology of writing by contemporary American women. Write a "capsule biography" summarizing each writer's background and achievements.

Visit http://www.mlushistory.com for more about contemporary women writers.

INSTRUCT

▶ *Starting with the Student*

- Ask students who have read other works by these writers what they thought about the pieces they have read. Would they recommend that other students read these works? Explain.

▶ *Discussing Key Ideas*

- Much of the literature by women is domestic literature: it is set in the home or neighborhood and explores relationships between friends and family members.
- Women writers also commonly explore the theme of women's identity.
- As women writers bring their personal worlds into public view, they reflect America's diverse culture.

HISTORY FROM VISUALS

Book Covers

Reading the Images Have students look at the book cover for *The Joy Luck Club.* What do they make of the lively bands of curling color that suggest Chinese embroidery? What might this help them understand about the passage from the book?

Extension Ask students to write four or five words or phrases that describe the illustration on the cover of *The House on Mango Street. Possible Responses: Three women, serene, mysterious, perhaps sisters, related, Chicana, connected, interwoven. The woman in the middle appears to be controlling the other two like puppets.*

INTERACT WITH HISTORY

1. Making Inferences

Possible Responses: *"Choices":* A woman's choices are limited, but she must make the best out of the choices she has. *The Joy Luck Club:* Tan's mother was one of many who felt displaced and lonely in American society so she sought the company of women she sensed shared aspects of her background and plight. *The House on Mango Street:* In her city environment, the speaker, probably a "transplant," lacks the roots and secret strength the trees have, but she is inspired by them to keep going. Choice of passages for all three will vary.

2. Creating an Anthology

Standards for Evaluation
Anthologies should...

- include selections by several different contemporary American women writers
- provide short biographies that present the background and achievements of each author represented
- reflect American cultural diversity
- demonstrate characteristic themes of American women writers

Section 3 Overview

OBJECTIVES

1. To describe the explosive growth of communications technology and government regulations for the industry.
2. To identify specific uses of technological advances.
3. To summarize advances in technology that help to protect the environment.

SKILLBUILDER

- Interpreting graphs, p. 864

CRITICAL THINKING

- Theme: Science and Technology, p. 861
- Making predictions, pp. 862, 863
- Synthesizing, p. 862
- Contrasting, p. 865
- Summarizing, p. 865
- Making inferences, p. 865
- Forming opinions, p. 865

FOCUS & MOTIVATE

5-MINUTE WARM-UP

Predicting Outcomes
To predict some of the consequences of new technologies, have students read the headlines in this section and answer these questions.

1. What areas of life are most affected by new technologies?
2. Which types of new technologies are likely to have the greatest impact on the 21st century?

WARM-UP TRANSPARENCY 26

▶ ***Starting with the Student***
Discuss with students any new technologies they have used in the past few years. Ask them if they use a computer or CD-ROM at school or at home. Have them discuss the level of comfort they experience in working with new technologies as they appear on the market or in the classroom.

3 Technology and Modern Life

TERMS & NAMES
- information superhighway
- Internet
- e-mail
- Telecommunications Act
- magnetic resonance imaging
- genetic engineering

LEARN ABOUT developments in communications and other industries
TO UNDERSTAND the impact of technological advances in the late 20th century.

ONE AMERICAN'S STORY

In November 1995, Steven Jobs saw his net worth increase by more than a billion dollars in just one day. His company, Pixar, had just offered new stock in a booming stock market after producing the wildly successful computer-animated movie *Toy Story.*

Jobs first struck it rich in 1980, at age 25, when Apple Computer, the company he helped found, first sold its stock to the public. Five years later, however, Jobs broke ties with Apple. Eventually, he invested his considerable profits from Apple into a small firm specializing in computer animation. Jobs's goal was to make the first fully computer-animated feature film. His efforts resulted in *Toy Story,* which grossed more than $177 million in its first months at the box office. However, Jobs explained that it was not the promise of huge profits that motivated him.

Steven Jobs

A PERSONAL VOICE

The thing that drives me and my colleagues at both Apple and Pixar is that you see something very compelling to you, and you don't quite know how to get it, but you know, sometimes intuitively, it's within your grasp. And it's worth putting in years of your life to make it come into existence.

STEVEN JOBS, quoted in *Time,* February 19, 1996

Despite the success of *Toy Story,* the value of Pixar's stock rose and fell in the volatile technological market. Jobs returned to Apple in 1997. Nevertheless, exciting technological developments in many industries brought impressive fortunes to innovative people like Steven Jobs. These developments also enriched the lives of ordinary people.

Technology and Communications

In his State of the Union address in 1994, President Clinton urged Congress to pass legislation to "connect every classroom, every clinic, every library, every hospital in America into a national information superhighway by the year 2000." Clinton placed Vice-President Al Gore in charge of overseeing the government's participation in the developing electronic superhighway. According to Gore, the government's role would be to serve as "referee, facilitator, envisioner, definer." In other words, private industries would build the superhighway, but the government would keep the highway democratic, ensure affordable service for everyone, protect privacy and property rights, and develop incentives for investors.

THE INFORMATION SUPERHIGHWAY The **information superhighway**—a proposed computer communications network linking people and institutions across the nation and the world—promised to advance the communications revolution that had begun with the personal computer. Through an electronic connection, such as a cable-TV or phone line, participants could access remote computers that provided a mind-boggling array of media, from "video on demand" to computerized research libraries, from on-line shopping malls to

SECTION 3 RESOURCES

PRINT RESOURCES

IN-DEPTH RESOURCES: UNIT 7
Guided Reading, p. 41

READING STUDY GUIDE, p. 267

ACCESS FOR STUDENTS ACQUIRING ENGLISH
Guided Reading (Spanish), p. 283

SPANISH READING STUDY GUIDE, p. 267

FORMAL ASSESSMENT
Section Quiz, p. 320

ALTERNATIVE ASSESSMENT BOOK
See forms for supporting and scoring alternative activities.

TECHNOLOGY RESOURCES

CD-ROM *Grolier Multimedia Encyclopedia*
INTERNET http://www.mlushistory.com

personalized news broadcasts. Users weren't simply observers; they could interact with other users all over the world.

The information superhighway entered most people's consciousness through the explosive growth of the Internet during the 1990s. The **Internet** is a worldwide network that links computers and allows almost instant communication of texts, pictures, and sounds. Originally developed by the U.S. Department of Defense for research, the Internet enjoyed early popularity at universities.

In the 1990s, businesses and individuals began to log on—that is, to link their computer systems to the Internet. Experts estimated that by 1996, as many as 24 million North Americans were regularly using the Internet to send **e-mail** (electronic notes and messages), participate in discussion groups, or enjoy detailed graphics on the World Wide Web.

THINK THROUGH HISTORY
A. THEME ***Science and Technology*** *Explain the revolutionary nature of communicating via the Internet.*

A. Answer Communicating via the Internet provides nearly instantaneous transmission of texts, pictures, and sounds from a worldwide data network.

The modern communications revolution went far beyond the personal computer, cellular phones, and fax machines, however. For example, scientists at the Massachusetts Institute of Technology experimented with a "smart" office—a computerized desk that detects and monitors the workers who use it, responds to voice commands, and much more. These scientists also experimented with "bodycams," or minicomputers that are worn like earphones, like eyeglasses, or even in shoes and that provide on-the-spot links to the Internet.

TELECOMMUNICATIONS ACT OF 1996 The advances in computers and communications have had a real impact on American society. For example, because of fax machines, the Internet, and overnight shipping, people can more readily work out of their homes instead of going to an office every day. Technology has also given Americans more entertainment options. Cable service has multiplied the number of television channels available to many people. The Internet provides video games. CD-ROMs allow computer users to travel along the Oregon Trail or go on a voyage down the Nile River.

These changes have also brought rapid growth among the communications companies. To ensure that the industry provides consumers with the best service, the federal government took several steps in the mid-1990s. In February 1996, Congress passed the **Telecommunications Act,** which removed barriers that had previously prevented one type of communications company from starting up or buying another type of communications business. The law made it possible for local telephone companies and cable television companies to compete in providing telephone and cable service.

Experts predicted that this competition would result in increased choice for consumers. Industry observers expected that telecommunications companies would combine through mergers and acquisitions and create packages of services enabling consumers to obtain all the services they need from one company.

At first, the government was slow to recognize the implications of the new communications technology. In 1994, however, the Federal Communications Commission (FCC) began to auction the valuable rights to airwaves and in four auctions collected $9 billion. Then, in 1996, in the Communications Decency Act (part of the Telecommunications Act), the government barred the transmission of "indecent" materials over the Internet, though parts of the law were later struck down in court. In addition, Congress also called for a "V-chip" in television sets—a computer chip that would enable parents to block TV programs that they deemed inappropriate for their children.

The passage of the Telecommunications Act won applause from the communications industry but only mixed reviews from the public. Consumer activists worried that the law would concentrate ownership of communications media in too few hands and would fail to ensure equal access to new technologies for

ECONOMIC BACKGROUND

MEDIA MERGERS

The signing of the telecommunications bill in February 1996 put the final stamp of approval on a $19-billion merger between Capital Cities/ABC Inc. and the Walt Disney Company. The merger reflected the trend toward concentrating media influence in the hands of a few small but powerful conglomerates.

The FCC approved the merger only on the condition that Disney sell either its newspaper or its radio station in Fort Worth, Texas, and in Detroit, Michigan. The FCC also announced, however, that it planned to reconsider its regulations on cross-ownership. (See *monopoly* on page 937 in the Economics Handbook.)

Technology and Communications

▶ ***Starting with the Student*** Discuss the impact that technology has had on students' lives. Have them create a diagram on new technology similar to the one below:

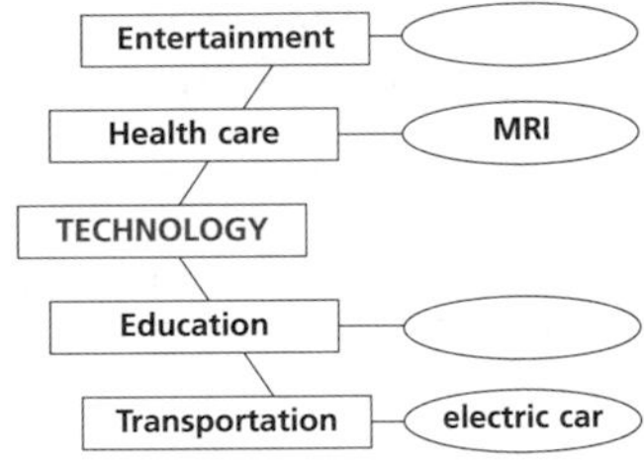

▶ ***Discussing Key Ideas***
- The Internet grows.
- Congress passes the Telecommunications Act of 1996.
- Controversy arises over efforts to regulate children's access to TV and the Internet.

IN-DEPTH RESOURCES: UNIT 7
Guided Reading, p. 41

ACCESS FOR STUDENTS ACQUIRING ENGLISH
Guided Reading (Spanish), p. 283

GROLIER MULTIMEDIA ENCYCLOPEDIA
Computers and Privacy

ELECTRONIC LIBRARY OF PRIMARY SOURCES
from *Being Digital* by Nicholas Negroponte

ECONOMIC BACKGROUND
Media Mergers
Critical Thinking: Analyzing Motives Ask students to discuss reasons for the FCC limits on cross-ownership of newspaper and radio and TV stations.

(continued on next page)

TEACHING OPTION

Teaching Less Proficient Readers

Outlining Help students understand the text on this page entitled "Telecommunications Act of 1996." Suggest that they use a standard outline form to organize the information in the passage. Write a sample outline on the board to which students can refer.

Student outlines might look like this:

I. Impact of computers and communication on society
  A. On home offices
  B. On entertainment
II. Growth of communications companies
  A. Federal regulations
  B. Benefits of competition
III. Implications of the new technology
  A. Federal response
    1. Auction of air waves
    2. The Communications Decency Act
  B. Public response
    1. For the government
    2. Against the government

Have volunteers write their outlines on the board.

(continued from page 861)

Possible Response: The government is reluctant to allow one individual or group to control the dissemination of information by owning all media outlets in a particular region.

OBJECTIVE

② **INSTRUCT**

Technology Enriches Lives

▶ ***Discussing Key Ideas***

- Technological advances in the 1990s affect all aspects of American life.
- Some technological advances meet with controversy.

MORE ABOUT . . .

Genetic Engineering

Worldwide, producers and consumers who favored genetic engineering and those who opposed it held equally strong opinions. The Plant Biotechnology Group at the University of Idaho, for example, saw its research as leading to the development of superior crops, which would be resistant to pests and diseases. In contrast, a group called the Pure Food Campaign protested the sale of the Flavr Savr® tomato and of a virus-resistant yellow crookneck squash called Freedom II® as well as the development of insect-resistant potatoes, corn, and cotton. The Pure Food Campaign based its opposition primarily on the not-yet-known but possible future risks and complications such altered plants might present.

rural residents and poor people. Civil rights advocates contended that the Communications Decency Act restricted free speech.

Technology Enriches Lives

The exciting advances in the telecommunications industry were matched by technological advances that revolutionized medicine, entertainment, education, transportation, and space exploration.

HEALTH CARE When Ken Mott, a physician on the staff of the World Health Organization in Geneva, Switzerland, was diagnosed with cancer in 1995, he turned to his computer. Mott used the Internet to find emotional support from other cancer patients and to examine new research data on the success of alternative treatments for the disease. Technological advances have led to better diagnoses, less painful treatments, and more effective medications and treatments for cancer and other illnesses.

People with AIDS (acquired immune deficiency syndrome) have increasingly benefited from advances in technology. By 1995, AIDS had killed more than 270,000 Americans, and it threatened about 1 million others who were infected with HIV, the virus that causes the disease. In the 1990s, improvements in tracking the spread of the virus through the body have made researchers better prepared to find a cure. In addition, new drugs that slow the multiplication of the virus in a person's system gave doctors and patients alike new hopes that a cure would soon be found. In addition, the U.S. Food and Drug Administration (FDA) responded to a call to speed up its lengthy process for approving new drugs and allowed doctors to offer terminally ill AIDS patients experimental drugs more quickly than before.

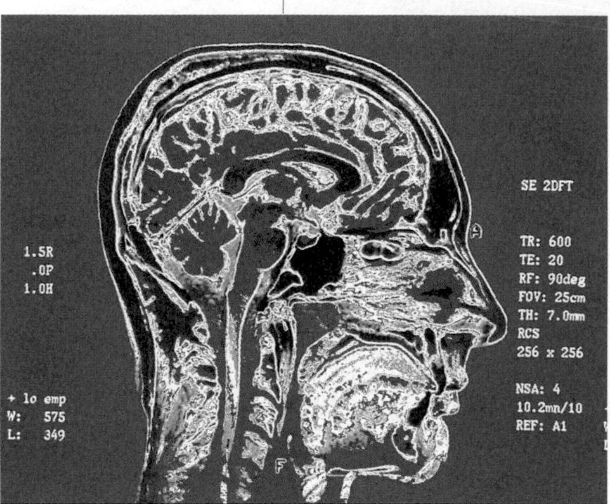

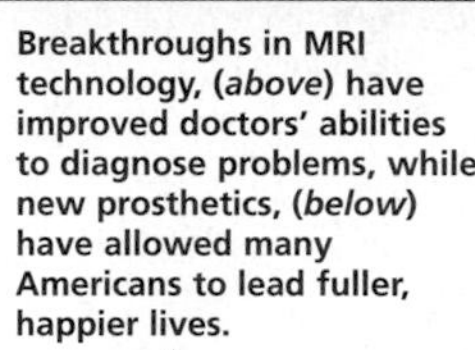

Breakthroughs in MRI technology, (*above*) have improved doctors' abilities to diagnose problems, while new prosthetics, (*below*) have allowed many Americans to lead fuller, happier lives.

Improved technology for making medical diagnoses offered new hope as well. **Magnetic resonance imaging** (MRI), for example, was used to produce cross-sectional images of any part of the body. Advances that will make the MRI procedure ten times faster will also make MRI more widely available and cheaper to use.

Technology also improved prosthetics—artificial limbs for amputees. Despite losing a leg to amputation, Leandro Stillitano continues to play soccer, and in 1988 Todd Schaffhauser ran 100 meters in 15.77 seconds. These remarkable athletes, along with many other amputees, have benefited from improvements in prosthetics, including lightweight titanium and carbon models that have given them a chance to resume their normal activities.

GENETIC ENGINEERING Not all technological advances have met with universal approval. The use of **genetic engineering**—the artificial changing of the molecular biology of organisms' cells—to alter food has aroused public concern. For example, the tomato that went on the market as the Flavr Savr® in 1994 looked ripe and red, just like a regular tomato, but had been genetically changed to remain ripe longer.

In 1996, international controversy arose over genetically altered soybeans and corn that were grown in the United States and shipped to Europe. In response to consumer pressure, the European Union moved to limit the

THINK THROUGH HISTORY
B. *Making Predictions* *How might the Telecommunications Act affect consumers?*

B. Answer *Possible Answer:* Consumers will probably enjoy increased choice and a greater variety of services.

THINK THROUGH HISTORY
C. *Synthesizing* *Describe how technology affected health care.*

C. Answer It improved diagnosis, medical research, and the field of prosthetics.

TEACHING OPTIONS

Making Connections Across the Curriculum

Science Suggest that students research areas discussed on pages 862–864 that have benefited from advances in technology. Some possible topics for research are these:

- new AIDS medications or drugs for other diseases
- magnetic resonance imaging
- prosthetics
- Hubble Space Telescope

Have students present their findings to the class in a panel discussion on new technologies.

Making Global Connections

International Health Care In addition to improvements in medical technology, advances in communications technology have had an impact on health care. Scientists throughout the world can have direct and instant communication in order to discuss experimental treatments, new drugs not yet approved for commercial distribution, rare organ transplants, or outbreaks of communicable diseases. Suggest that interested students explore the Internet pages maintained by agencies such as the Centers for Disease Control or the World Health Organization to observe medical applications of the communications technology at work.

importation of such products, allowing importation only if they were clearly labeled as having been genetically altered.

Critics of genetic engineering have raised questions about potential changes in the nutritional value of altered foods and the possibility that genetically altered foods might create unpredictable allergic reactions in the humans who eat them. However, the FDA holds that genetically engineered foods are safe and that they require no extra labeling.

ENTERTAINMENT AND MORE Like the Internet, multimedia devices of the 1990s—such as video games, virtual reality simulators, and CD-ROMs—often combined words, pictures, animation, narration, and music. They also engaged participants actively in receiving and communicating information. Among these devices, video games were used primarily for entertainment. However, virtual reality and CD-ROMs went beyond entertainment and provided applications in industry, medicine, and education.

Virtual reality began with the flight simulators used to train military and commercial pilots. Today, with a headset that holds tiny video screens and earphones, and with a data glove that translates hand movements to a computer screen, a participant can navigate a "virtual landscape." Beyond fun and games, however, builders and automobile engineers have used virtual reality to save money by creating visual, rather than physical, models of their buildings and cars. Doctors have used virtual reality to take a computerized tour of a patient's throat and lungs to check for medical problems.

THINK THROUGH HISTORY
D. *Making Predictions* *What new technological developments in entertainment do you expect to see in the next decade?*

D. Answer Some students might mention digital TV. Others might mention new developments on the Internet or in motion picture special effects.

The CD-ROM (Compact Disc Read-Only Memory) evolved from music CDs that contained code for sound waves. CD-ROMs also carry codes for pictures, text, and animation, and they play on a specially equipped computer. A single CD-ROM contains enough memory to hold all the text and pictures of two full-sized encyclopedias. By choosing items from an inviting list of CD-ROMs, people can access subjects ranging from art to zoology.

TECHNOLOGY AND EDUCATION Beyond the development of CD-ROM technology, improvements in communications began to open new opportunities for better education. During the 1990s, classrooms across the nation increasingly used computer networks to give students access to an almost unlimited range of information. Long-distance video and audio transmissions also opened new communications links for American students.

The most prominent additions to the classroom were computer networks. Some schools encouraged students to use the Internet both to gain access to and to share the wealth of information it contains. Other schools joined various networks, such as the Kids Network, which gave students the chance to share data with scientists. The scientists in turn produced reports based on the student-collected data.

Video transmissions also expanded educational opportunities, especially in rural areas. For example, the Alaskan Teleconferencing Network and the University of Alaska Computer Network provided video programming to Alaskan students in isolated communities. Other video programs became

HISTORICAL SPOTLIGHT

VIDEO GAMES

Video games first became popular in the early 1980s. In 1995, game players spent more than $6 billion on computer games. Today, about four out of ten households own video game systems.

Increasingly, game players are competing on-line with opponents on the Internet. In fact, experts estimate that annual expenditures on "multiplayer on-line gaming" will mushroom to $1 billion by the year 2000.

A 17-year-old player from Granbury, Texas, wakes up at 7 A.M. each morning to have an on-line chat with the friends he met while playing the game Subspace. He says, "It was a chance to blow them up. It's become a community."

MORE ABOUT . . .
Virtual Reality

One application of virtual reality, developed in England, enables viewers to assess their chances of escaping from a fire in a simulated structure. The program is called VEGAS, which stands for virtual egress analysis and simulation. Users can program the software so that the several dozen virtual occupants will respond as if they were children or elderly or handicapped persons. Programs can duplicate any existing structure. The results show possible structural flaws or places where bottlenecks will form during escape, the speed of smoke flow, and poor escape strategies of the occupants.

HISTORICAL SPOTLIGHT
Video Games

Critical Thinking Ask students to poll members of their classes to see how many hours per week, on average, students play video games. Students might also investigate which games are the most popular among their acquaintances and what percentage of class members have video game systems in their homes.

Block Schedule TEACHING OPTION **Time Needed: 20 Minutes**

Cooperative Activity: Cooperative Activity: Creating A Guide to the Internet

Task: Student groups will research the Internet and reviews of Internet pages and then compile a guide of home pages applicable to courses they are taking.

Purpose: To familiarize students with the educational uses of the Internet.

Activity: Students working in groups of three or four will compile an annotated list of Internet pages that provide information relevant to the subjects they are currently taking. Have students who have access to the Internet use the McDougal Littell website to explore Internet connections to *The Americans.* Students who do not have immediate access to the Internet can compile information from magazines, such as *Learning and Leading with Technology.*

ALTERNATIVE ASSESSMENT BOOK
Standards for Evaluating a Cooperative Activity

Standards for Evaluation
Guide entries should . . .

- evaluate the usefulness of Internet resources
- show a correlation between entries and students' curricula
- demonstrate the ability to maneuver on the Internet

OBJECTIVE
③ **INSTRUCT**

Progress on the Environment

▶ ***Starting with the Student***
Ask students what they currently do to protect the environment. Suggest that as they read, they complete a chart, such as the one below, showing ways in which Americans protect the environment and ways in which technology facilitates those actions.

Methods	How Technology Helps
Recycling	Extracting metal ores from recycled products
Using cleaner cars	
Using alternative energy sources	

▶ ***Discussing Key Ideas***
- Advances in technology create new methods of caring for the environment.
- Scientists design environmentally safer vehicles and develop alternatives to fossil fuels.

HISTORY FROM VISUALS

The Growth of Recycling, 1960–1993

Reading the Graph Ask students to identify the period in which the proportion of waste recycled increased the most. *1980–1993*

Extension Ask students how they would account for the rapid increase during that time period. *Possible Responses: more public awareness; more pressure by cities; more opportunities to recycle.*

Skillbuilder Answer
1970: About one-twelfth. **1993:** It had tripled, to nearly one-fourth.

SKILLBUILDER
INTERPRETING GRAPHS
Approximately what proportion of waste was recycled in 1970? By how much had the proportion increased by 1993?

The Growth of Recycling, 1960–1993

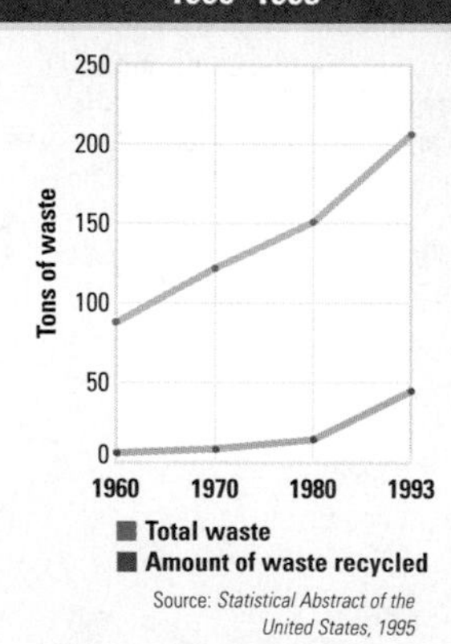

available not only on videotapes but also through broadcast transmissions and videodiscs. By using a digital scanner, a student can move through the lessons and other information provided on a videodisc.

TRANSPORTATION Advances in transportation in the United States involved making automobiles safer and making driving more convenient. In 1994, seat belts, which many states required drivers to wear, saved 9,200 lives. In the same year, air bags, a more recent safety device, saved nearly 400 lives. By 1996, all new car models boasted dual air bags. Experts predicted that the number of lives saved would multiply as air-bag installation increased. However, the public was increasingly concerned about design problems in air bags that had led to injury and even death of children and adults of small stature.

Technological advances also promised to make driving more convenient. Cars equipped with a navigation system linked to a satellite system called GPS (Global Positioning System) provided drivers with up-to-the-minute travel information. Drivers could tune in a channel on their radios to receive directions to restaurants or gas stations, as well as information on the best routes to use in order to avoid traffic jams or road construction projects.

SPACE EXPLORATION The United States continued to explore outer space, and the space program continued to provide technological advances for American society. Space shuttles regularly placed in orbit satellites that improved communications and research opportunities for earthbound scientists.

In 1993, American astronauts walked in space to repair the Hubble Space Telescope. Scientists had hoped that the telescope, launched in 1990, would provide spectacular views of the edges of the universe. Unfortunately, one of the telescope's mirrors was not properly set, hampering its vision. In a remarkably precise operation performed while orbiting the earth, the astronauts placed ten small mirrors in the telescope to correct the problems with the original mirror. Since the repair, astronomers have used the telescope to gather data about the formation of stars and galaxies.

Nearly as remarkable as the Hubble repair mission was the stay of American astronaut Shannon Lucid in the Russian space station *Mir.* The Russian space program had intended to relieve her from her duties aboard the space station in the summer of 1996. Because of budget restraints, however, the Russians were unable to make the mission, and Lucid had to wait until September 26, 1996, to return to the earth. Her 188-day stay on *Mir* was the longest stay in space of any American.

Dr. Shannon Lucid jokes with President Clinton after her record-breaking stay on the Russian space station *Mir.*

Progress on the Environment

Advanced technology led to a host of environmental developments in the 1990s. While many Americans took advantage of improved methods of recycling, scientists worked to create environmentally safer cars and new energy sources.

RECYCLING The most widespread method of protecting the environment was recycling. By the mid-1990s, more and more Americans were recycling. Cities such as Omaha, Houston, and Chicago were reforming old recycling plans or instituting new plans to become more efficient. In American offices, workers regularly recycled paper. At curbsides in towns and cities across the country, residents set out glass bottles and jars, plastic bottles, newspapers, phone books, paper bags, and aluminum cans for recycling. In fact, Americans recycled about two-thirds

TEACHING OPTIONS

Making Connections Across Time

Space Exploration Discuss with students current U.S. exploration in space and the advanced technologies that help ensure success. In 1996 and 1997, for example, the U.S. space program cooperated with Russian astronauts in experiments that focused on maintaining an orbiting space station that could house astronauts for weeks or months at a time. Point out that Dr. Shannon Lucid gained fame for her extended stay on the space station *Mir.*

Exploring Themes

Science and Technology For better or worse, changes in the field of science and technology have had a significant impact on American life during the 20th century. Discuss with students the positive and negative effects of technology on society. Most students may identify more positive than negative applications of technology—and most may persist in thinking of technology as "good" or "bad." Help students understand that technology itself is morally neutral. How a particular technology is used determines whether it has a positive or a negative impact.

of their cans. Industry experts claimed that producing the metal from ore would take about 95 percent more energy than it took to recycle the old metal.

DESIGNING A CLEANER CAR While Americans tried to reduce solid waste through recycling, they also worked to reduce the fossil fuel waste that produced air pollution. Designing a cleaner car was one effort. In California, for example, state regulations called for 10 percent of new vehicles to be "zero emission" (creating no air pollution), or battery-powered, by the year 2003.

Scientists had worked for decades to develop environmentally safer vehicles to meet the needs of mobile Americans. By 1996, one such vehicle—the electric car—had come into limited use. However, such cars, while clean, were expensive to operate. Nancy Hazard, associate director of the Northeast Sustainable Energy Association, worked to educate the public on the need for electric cars.

A PERSONAL VOICE

The present gasoline-based transportation system in the U.S. is leading the country to bankruptcy. One-third of the trade deficit is caused by imported oil and that percentage will grow unless we switch to electric vehicles—a move that can cut oil imports and . . . create well-paying domestic manufacturing jobs.

NANCY HAZARD, quoted in a news release of the Northeast Sustainable Energy Association

In addition to electric cars, people have proposed designing cars that run on relatively clean ethanol or methanol (manufactured from food byproducts) or solar-powered cars that would be affordable and convenient for consumers.

EXPLORING ALTERNATIVE ENERGY SOURCES Plans to develop electric cars were closely related to efforts to reduce American dependence on fossil fuels. Fossil fuels such as oil provided most of the energy in the United States in the 1990s but also contributed to urban air pollution, acid rain, and global warming.

E. Answer Solar power is abundant, ecologically neutral, and potentially cheap. Fossil fuels are finite and ecologically harmful.

In looking for an alternative to fossil fuels, scientists have experimented with energy sources such as nuclear, wind, and solar power. The latter two sources were environmentally safe, cheap, abundant, and renewable. Nuclear power, however, continued to raise the issue of long-term safety both in daily operations and in disposal.

THINK THROUGH HISTORY
E. *Contrasting* *Contrast the benefits and costs of solar energy and fossil fuels.*

The changes brought about by new technologies in the late 20th century, particularly in communications, came at a time when Americans were becoming acutely aware of the growing diversity of the nation's population. You will read about the changing face of America in Section 4.

Some experts hope to use windmills and wind turbines (*below*) and solar panels (*bottom*) to exploit the energy produced by the wind and the sun—which is equal to that in 1,000 trillion barrels of oil every year.

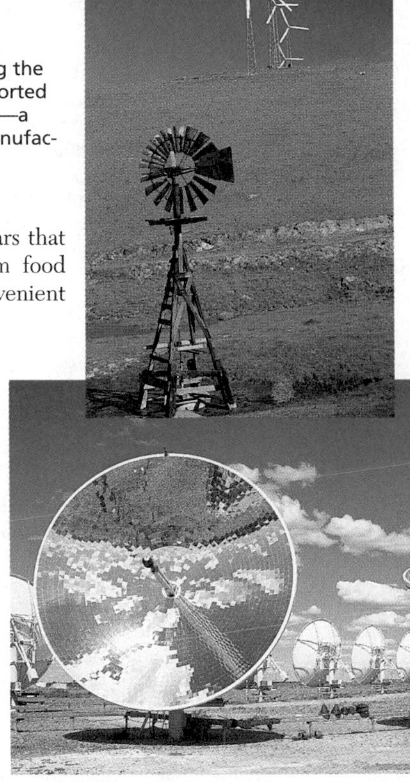

Section 3 Assessment

1. TERMS & NAMES
Identify:
- information superhighway
- Internet
- e-mail
- Telecommunications Act
- magnetic resonance imaging
- genetic engineering

2. SUMMARIZING On a chart such as the one shown, list four of the technological changes described in this section and explain how each change has affected your life.

Technological Change	Effect on My Life
1.	
2.	
3.	
4.	

Write a paragraph explaining how you expect one of these changes to affect your life.

3. MAKING INFERENCES Explain how government, business, and individuals are important to the existence of the information superhighway.

THINK ABOUT
- the costs of developing the superhighway
- the equipment and personnel needed to maintain it
- who uses the superhighway and why they use it

4. FORMING OPINIONS Which area of technological change described in this section do you think was the most important one for the country as a whole? Explain why.

THINK ABOUT
- changes in communications and transportation
- changes in health care
- changes in entertainment
- changes that benefit the environment

ANSWERS

1. TERMS & NAMES

information superhighway, p. 860

Internet, p. 861

e-mail, p. 861

Telecommunications Act, p. 861

magnetic resonance imaging, p. 862

genetic engineering, p. 862

2. SUMMARIZING

Student charts might include the following items: Internet, e-mail, V-chip, MRI, artificial limbs, virtual reality, CD-ROMs, air bags, Global Positioning System, electric cars, genetically engineered food

3. MAKING INFERENCES

Possible Response: Government helps regulate the superhighway and provides financial incentives for businesses that develop the networks, supercomputers, and so on, that make the superhighway work. Individuals also help finance the superhighway by paying businesses user fees. Information on the superhighway is provided by government, businesses, and individuals. These three groups all use the superhighway for research, communication, and advertising.

4. FORMING OPINIONS

Possible Response: Students may choose the communications revolution, because it will improve education; changes in transportation because they have improved safety and efficiency; health care changes, because they help save and improve lives; changes in entertainment, because they make life more fun; environmental changes, because of the need for clean air and water.

MORE ABOUT . . .
Electric Cars

Ask students, Which car do you think would win in a head-to-head contest—an electric car or a gasoline-powered one? A 1995 road rally created such a contest, sending electric, solar, hybrid electric, and gasoline-powered vehicles over a 300-mile course through the Northeast. The clear winner was an electric-powered car that achieved 65.2 miles per equivalent gallon; a gasoline-powered Geo Metro sedan, one of the best mileage cars produced in the United States, managed only 35.8 miles per equivalent gallon. The rally sponsors concluded that a gallon of crude oil converted into gasoline would take a car 35 miles down the road. The same amount of crude oil turned into electric power would enable a car to travel 70 miles.

ASSESS & RETEACH

Section 3 Assessment

Ask students to identify passages from the text that helped them answer the questions.

Self-Assessment

Have students review their answer to item 4. Ask them to evaluate how well they explained their answer, and to add to it or revise it if necessary.

Section Quiz

FORMAL ASSESSMENT
Section Quiz, p. 320

Reteach

Hold a debate on the pros and cons of technological change. Ask students to support their positions with details from the section.

CLOSE

Technological advances in communications, medicine, entertainment, and environmental protection changed Americans' lives.

Section 4 Overview

OBJECTIVES

1. To identify causes of the flight to the suburbs and the consequences of suburban growth.
2. To summarize reasons for, and the impact of, the rise in the elderly population.
3. To describe changing migration patterns and U.S. immigration policies.
4. To list challenges and opportunities for Americans as they move into the next century.

SKILLBUILDERS

- Interpreting graphs, p. 868
- Understanding geography: region, location, p. 869

CRITICAL THINKING

- Analyzing causes, p. 867
- Summarizing, pp. 868, 871
- Theme: Immigration and Migration, p. 869
- Comparing, p. 870
- Forming opinions, p. 871
- Hypothesizing, p. 871
- Making predictions, p. 861

FOCUS & MOTIVATE

5-MINUTE WARM-UP

Making Predictions
To predict the consequences of immigration for the United States in the 21st century, have students look at the map on page 869 and answer these questions.

1. Which states might have the greatest population growth in the 21st century?
2. How could population growth affect the politics in the states that grow most quickly?

WARM-UP TRANSPARENCY 26

▶ ***Starting with the Student***
Ask students questions like the following:

- Have you always lived in the same locality?
- Does your school draw students from the city, suburbs, or rural areas?
- Have neighbors and other families in your

(continued on next page)

4 The Changing Face of America

• telecommute

LEARN ABOUT social and cultural changes in the United States in the late 20th century
TO UNDERSTAND the challenges and opportunities of America's future.

ONE AMERICAN'S STORY

In the summer of 1996, at a summer camp in South Dakota, 40 Lakota Sioux teenagers practiced living as their ancestors had. The teens built tepees, tended to their horses, and dined on dried buffalo meat. Like 12 similar camps sponsored by a charitable foundation, the Wolakota Yukini Wicoti Camp on the Cheyenne River Indian Reservation taught young people traditional Native American ways of life. These camps represented one of the efforts of Native Americans to pass along to the younger generation an understanding of their traditions.

Many of the approximately 2 million Native Americans in the United States in the mid-1990s faced difficult problems. On the Cheyenne River Indian Reservation, for example, four out of five adults lacked jobs, and a high percentage of the population between the ages of 12 and 35 struggled with alcohol addiction. Gregg Bourland, chairman of the Cheyenne River Sioux, believed that by teaching Sioux values, the camp might accomplish the "rebirth of the Great Sioux Nation."

A PERSONAL VOICE

We call it seventh-generational thinking. Seven generations ago our ancestors loved us so much that we are still here as a people. We have to create a world not only for today, but for seven generations to come. The young people from this camp are going to be the messengers for the future.

GREGG BOURLAND, quoted in *Time*, August 26, 1996

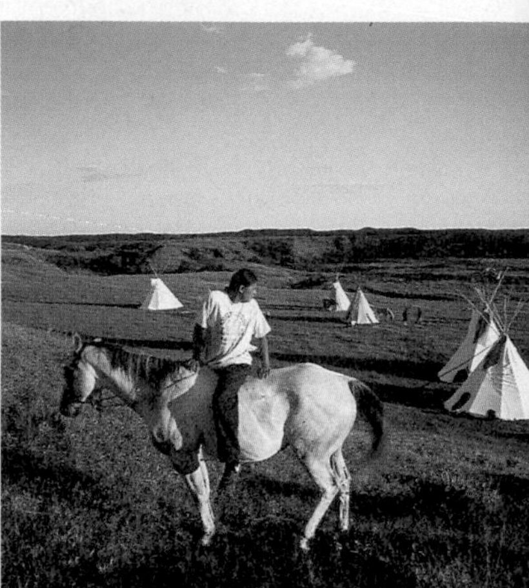

Wolakota Yukini Wicoti Camp, South Dakota

Bourland and other tribal leaders noted that Native Americans faced imposing problems but contended that they needed to seek their own solutions. Wilma Mankiller, leader of the Cherokee Nation from 1985 to 1994, acknowledged the crises Native Americans faced in health care, education, housing, and law enforcement. But she argued, "You can't dwell on problems if you want to bring change; you must be motivated by hope, by the feeling you can make a difference."

For five centuries, the ancestors of Gregg Bourland and Wilma Mankiller adapted to the millions of immigrants that came to North America. Native Americans and immigrants alike helped to reshape the land that Columbus first encountered in 1492. They built a great industrial nation where there once was none. At the outset of the 21st century, that nation continued to change. And Americans from all backgrounds, including new immigrants, contributed to these transformations.

The Suburban Nation

One of the most significant sociocultural changes in American history has been the movement of Americans from the cities to the suburbs. The years from 1950 to 1970 saw a widespread pattern of **urban flight,** the process in which Americans left the cities and moved to the suburbs. At mid-century, the population of cities exceeded that of suburbs. By 1970, the ratio became even. The 1990 census revealed that more than half of all Americans lived in suburbs. This transformation of the United States into a nation of suburbs has often intensified the problems of the cities.

CAUSES OF URBAN CHANGE Several factors contributed to the movement of Americans out of the cities. Because of the continued movement of job-seeking

SECTION 4 RESOURCES

PRINT RESOURCES

IN-DEPTH RESOURCES: UNIT 7
Guided Reading, p. 42
Skillbuilder Practice: Drawing Conclusions, p. 43
Primary Source: Road Sign, p. 49
American Lives: Wilma Mankiller, p. 53

READING STUDY GUIDE, p. 269

ACCESS FOR STUDENTS ACQUIRING ENGLISH
Guided Reading (Spanish), p. 284
Skillbuilder Practice: Drawing Conclusions (Spanish), p. 285

SPANISH READING STUDY GUIDE, p. 269

FORMAL ASSESSMENT
Section Quiz, p. 321

ALTERNATIVE ASSESSMENT BOOK
See forms for supporting and scoring alternative activities.

TECHNOLOGY RESOURCES

HUMANITIES TRANSPARENCIES
H48, Political cartoon

CD-ROM Electronic Library of Primary Sources

INTERNET http://www.mlushistory.com

Americans into urban areas in the 1950s and 1960s, many urban American neighborhoods became overcrowded. Overcrowding in turn contributed to such urban problems as increasing crime rates and decaying housing.

During the 1970s and 1980s, city dwellers who could afford to do so moved to the suburbs for more space, privacy, and security. Often, families left the cities because suburbs offered newer, less-crowded schools. As many middle-class Americans left cities for the suburbs, the economic base of many urban neighborhoods declined, and suburbs grew wealthy. Following the well-educated labor force, more industries relocated to suburban areas in the 1990s. High-tech industries established suburban "industrial parks," which reduced some of the job opportunities for urban residents who lacked transportation to commute to the new jobs. The economic base that provided tax money and supported city services in large cities such as New York, Detroit, and Philadelphia continued to shrink as people and jobs moved outward. In 1985, 14 out of the 21 counties with the highest per capita income in the nation were suburban.

The home office has become more popular as sophisticated communications technology has become more commonplace.

THINK THROUGH HISTORY
A. Analyzing Causes *List the factors that influenced middle-class residents to leave cities for suburbs.*

A. Answer Overcrowding; crime; better schools in the suburbs.

In addition, many downtown districts fell into disrepair as suburban shoppers abandoned city stores for suburban shopping malls. According to the 1990 census, the 31 most impoverished communities in the United States were in cities.

By the mid-1990s, however, as the property values in America's large cities declined, many people returned to live there. In a process called gentrification, they purchased and rehabilitated many stately homes dating from the cities' peak years. Old industrial sites and neighborhoods in locations convenient to downtown became popular, especially among young, single adults who preferred the excitement of city life and the uniqueness of urban neighborhoods to the often bland environment of the suburbs.

SUBURBAN LIVING While many suburbanites continued to commute to city jobs, during the 1990s, increasing numbers of workers began to **telecommute,** or use new communications technology, such as computers, modems, and fax machines, to work from their homes.

Another notable trend was the movement of minority populations to the suburbs. Nationwide, by the early 1990s, about 43 percent of the Latino population and more than half of the Asian-American population lived in suburbs.

Suburban growth led to intense competition between suburbs and cities, and among the suburbs themselves, for business and industry. Since low-rise suburban homes yielded low tax revenues, tax-hungry suburbs offered tax incentives for companies to locate within their borders. These incentives resulted in lower tax revenues for

Suburban space has drawn both citizens and businesses away from large cities.

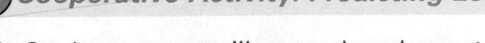

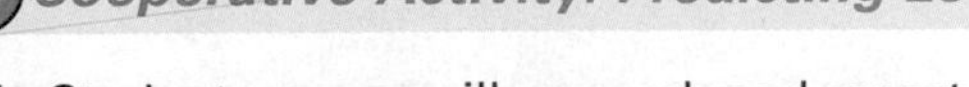

(continued from page 866)

community lived there for years, or is there a lot of moving out of the community?

- Do you think the change—or lack of change—in the area is indicative of the country as a whole? Explain.

OBJECTIVE
① INSTRUCT

The Suburban Nation

▶***Starting with the Student***
Discuss with students the movement of Americans to and from cities over the past 50 years. What kind of movement do they think will occur in the next decade?

Suggest to students that they might create a time line, similar to the one below, showing the movement of Americans over the past 50 years.

1950	Job seekers move into urban areas.
1960	
1970	Overcrowding sends many city dwellers into the suburbs.
1980	
1990	Industry and minorities relocate to the suburbs.
2000	

▶***Discussing Key Ideas***
- In the 1990s more than half of all Americans live in the suburbs.
- Suburban growth brings more minorities to the suburbs, increases competition for business and industry, and promotes suburban sprawl.

IN-DEPTH RESOURCES: UNIT 7
Guided Reading, p. 42

ACCESS FOR STUDENTS ACQUIRING ENGLISH
Guided Reading (Spanish), p. 284

Block Schedule TEACHING OPTION **Time Needed: 40 Minutes**

Cooperative Activity: Predicting Local Demographics

Task: Student groups will research and report on demographic changes in their own communities and predict future trends.

Purpose: To relate population studies to students' own lives.

Activity: Students working in small groups will examine their own cities or incorporated areas to determine demographic changes that have occurred over the past 20 years. Based on their reports, students will then form a hypothesis about future trends in their area, and explain the reasons for their opinions. If students live in a large city, they may wish to divide different wards of the city among the groups. They may also divide the work among groups by statistics about age, education, social or ethnic group, or types of employment.

Building a Portfolio: Students adding a report to their portfolio should indicate how they contributed to the project.

ALTERNATIVE ASSESSMENT BOOK
Standards for Evaluating a Cooperative Activity

Standards for Evaluation
Reports should . . .
- demonstrate an understanding of demographic changes
- show evidence of reliable research methods
- use specific details to support the hypothesis about future trends

OBJECTIVE

② INSTRUCT

The Graying of America

▶ ***Starting with the Student***

- Ask students to identify people they know who are baby boomers. Many of the students' parents, or their parents' older siblings, may be baby boomers.
- Have students estimate in what year the retirement of their parents will begin to peak, assuming that the age of retirement is 65.
- Ask them in what year most of them will retire.

▶ ***Discussing Key Ideas***

- The size of the elderly population swells to record highs in the 1990s.
- Programs aimed at taking care of the elderly's medical and financial needs are badly strained.

HUMANITIES TRANSPARENCIES

H48, Political Cartoon

HISTORY FROM VISUALS

Life Expectancy, 1970–2010

Reading the Graph Have students look at the graph and tell what the life expectancy is for females and males of their age. *Possible Responses: From around 70 to 73 years for men and around 78 to 79 for women.*

Extension Have students look for statistics that will enable them to compare their life expectancies with those of their parents and grandparents. Ask them how they account for the differences.

local governments—meaning that fewer funds were available for schools, libraries, and police departments. Consequently, taxes were often increased to fund these community services as well as to build the additional roads and other infrastructure necessary to support the new businesses.

Another consequence of suburban growth was suburban sprawl—the increasing spread of suburbs over land farther away from a central city—which contributed to environmental problems, such as flooding caused by inadequate drainage. In 1996, for example, heavy rains in the Midwest and the Northeast led to costly flooding of both suburban and urban areas.

The shift of populations from cities to suburbs was not the only significant change in American life in the 1990s. The American public was also growing older, and its aging raised complex issues for American policymakers.

The Graying of America

Born in 1946, Bill Clinton stood at the head of the huge baby-boom generation—the 60 million Americans who were born after World War II, between 1946 and 1961. As the baby boomers began to age, they would swell the ranks of the nation's already large elderly population.

As a result of falling birthrates and advances in medical care, the percentage of elderly people rose throughout most of the 20th century. In 1900, for example, the average life span was 46 years for men and 48 years for women. In 1993, a man could expect to live 72 years, and a woman 79 years. In 1950, only 1 in 12 Americans was over age 65. By 1990, 1 in 8 Americans was over 65. Because of the baby boomers, experts have predicted that by 2040, 1 in 5 Americans will be over 65. The older-than-85 population was expected to grow at an even faster rate.

Skillbuilder Answer
For men, almost 5 years higher; for women, about 4 years higher.

SKILLBUILDER
INTERPRETING GRAPHS ***How much higher was life expectancy for Americans born in 1990 than for Americans born in 1970?***

The graying of America placed new demands on the country's programs that provided care for the elderly. These programs, which had accounted for only 6 percent of the national budget in 1955, accounted for more than a third of the budget by the mid-1990s. It was projected that the programs would consume about 39 percent of the budget by 2005.

The major programs that provide care for the elderly are Medicare and Social Security. Medicare, which pays medical expenses for senior citizens, began in the mid-1960s, when most Americans had lower life expectancies. By 1995, the costs of this program had exceeded $150 billion.

Life Expectancy, 1970–2010

Life expectancy (in years)
100
95
90
85
80
75
70
65
60
1970
1980
1990
2000
2010
■ Female ■ Male

Source: *Statistical Abstract of the United States, 1995*

Social Security, which pays benefits to retired Americans, was designed to rely on continued funding from a vast number of younger workers who would contribute taxes to support a small number of retired workers. That system worked well when younger workers far outnumbered retirees and when most workers didn't live long after retirement.

In 1996, it took Social Security contributions from three workers to support every retiree. By 2030, however, with an increase in the number of elderly persons and an expected decline in the birthrate, there will be only two workers' contributions available to support each senior citizen. If Congress fails to restructure the system, Social Security will eventually pay out more money than it takes in. Some people have suggested that the system be reformed by raising deductions for current workers, taxing the benefits paid to wealthier Americans, and raising the age at which retirees can collect benefits.

B. Answer
Increased life expectancy; people living longer after retirement; the huge baby-boom generation; declining birthrate.

THINK THROUGH HISTORY
B. *Summarizing* *What are the factors that will force an eventual restructuring of Social Security?*

TEACHING OPTION

Skillbuilder Mini-Lesson: Drawing Conclusions

Explaining the Skill Drawing conclusions about the future involves analyzing statistics and other factual information and forming a prediction about the meaning and consequences of the information available to you. Sometimes conclusions are stated along with statistics, but reaching one's own conclusions about an issue can help foster a deeper understanding of that issue.

Applying the Skill: Social Security Ask students to examine the facts on this page about aging baby boomers and Social Security and to use those facts, their own experiences, and common sense to come up with a conclusion about the future of Social Security. Have them support their conclusions with evidence from the text. Most students will probably conclude that Social Security needs overhauling soon. Evidence includes the increasing numbers of retired citizens, the lengthening life expectancy of people after retirement, and the decline in the number of workers who will be paying into Social Security in the future.

IN-DEPTH RESOURCES: UNIT 7
Skillbuilder Practice: Drawing Conclusions, p. 43

Immigration in the 1990s

In addition to becoming increasingly suburban and elderly, the population of the United States has also been transformed by immigration. Between 1970 and 1995, the country's population swelled from 204 million to more than 260 million. Immigration accounted for much of that growth. As the nation's newest residents yearned for U.S. citizenship, however, other Americans debated the effects of immigration on American life.

A CHANGING IMMIGRANT POPULATION The most recent immigrants to the United States differed from immigrants of earlier years. The large numbers of immigrants who entered the country before and just after 1900 came from Europe. In contrast, about 45 percent of immigrants since the 1960s have come from the Western Hemisphere, primarily Mexico, and 30 percent from Asia.

THINK THROUGH HISTORY
C. THEME
Immigration and Migration
Contrast today's immigrants to the United States with the immigrants who came around 1900.

C. Answer In contrast to European immigrants who came around 1900, today's immigrants come largely from the Western hemisphere and Asia. As previous immigrants did, today's immigrants come for economic opportunities or to escape repressive governments.

Most immigrants left their homelands because of economic problems, though some fled oppressive governments or political turmoil. The chief lure of the United States was the opportunity it gave immigrants to earn a better living than they could in their home countries.

In Mexico, for example, between November 1994 and February 1995 millions of people fell into deeper poverty when the government decreased the value of the peso by 73 percent—making it harder to buy things because the peso was worth much less than before. As a result of this devaluation, almost a million Mexicans lost their jobs. The persistent lack of jobs motivated a portion of Mexico's young population—more than half its 100 million people were under age 25—to head north of the border in search of jobs.

Experts speculated that patterns of immigration in the early 21st century would result in changes in the ethnic and racial makeup of the United States. In 1996, 74 percent of the U.S. population consisted of non-Latino whites. The Census Bureau has predicted that by 2050 that figure will drop to 53 percent. The Latino population is expected to rise from 10 percent of the total population in 1996 to 25 percent in 2050, while the Asian population increases from 3 percent to 8 percent and the African-American population increases from 12 percent to 14 percent. Such predictions added to the continuing debate over U.S. immigration policies.

"We are at a period of historic change—the way we work; the way we live; the way we relate to each other; the way we relate to others beyond our borders."

BILL CLINTON

GEOGRAPHY SKILLBUILDER
REGION *Which four states received the greatest numbers of immigrants?*
LOCATION *Why do you think these states attracted so many immigrants?*

Skillbuilder Answer **Region:** California, New York, Texas, and Florida. **Location:** *Possible Answer:* They have the largest populations and therefore many job opportunities.

U.S. Immigration, 1995

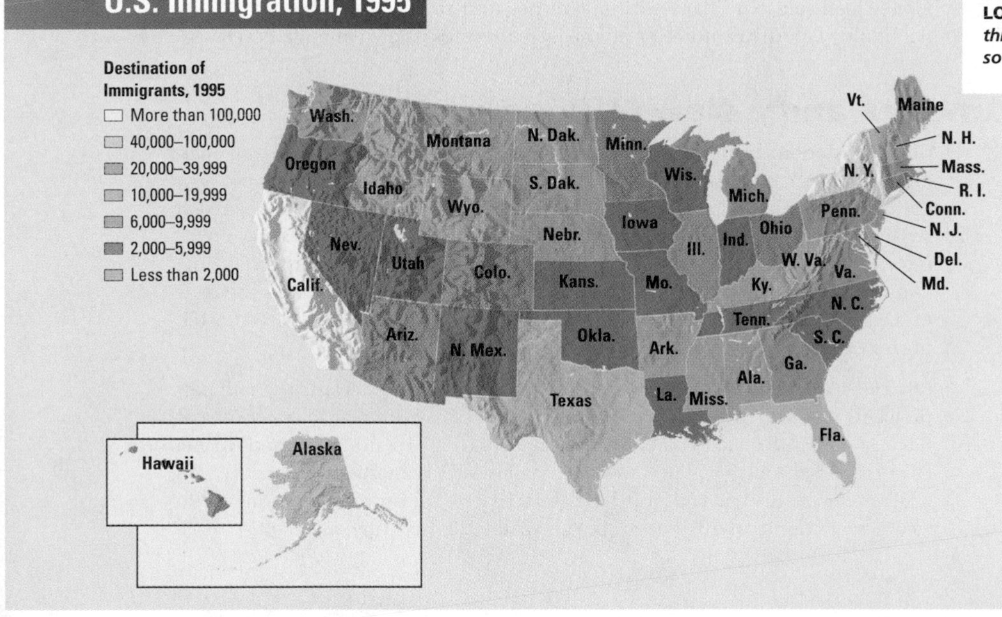

OBJECTIVE
③ INSTRUCT

Immigration in the 1990s

▶ *Starting with the Student*
- Ask students for their observations on the effects of immigration on American society. Ask them if they have noticed changes in the last four or five years.
- Have students consider how many different cultures are represented in the foods they eat, the music they listen to, and the books they read.
- Ask students if they are aware of any TV or radio shows for minority language or cultural groups in their area.

▶ *Discussing Key Ideas*
- The ethnic and racial makeup of the United States is changing as a result of new immigration patterns.
- The country debates future immigration policies.
- Hostility toward illegal immigrants increases.

HISTORY FROM VISUALS

U.S. Immigration, 1995

Reading the Map Ask students to indicate, according to the map, how many immigrants were located in their state in 1995.

Extension Have students look at state records or data on the Internet to determine the origins of major immigrant groups now located in their state.

TEACHING OPTIONS

Making Connections Across the Curriculum

Mathematics Have students graph the statistics about the U.S. racial and ethnic makeup cited on page 869. Help students understand that the 1996 figures total only 99 percent because they have been rounded to the nearest whole number. Put a completed graph on the board. Graphs might look like this:

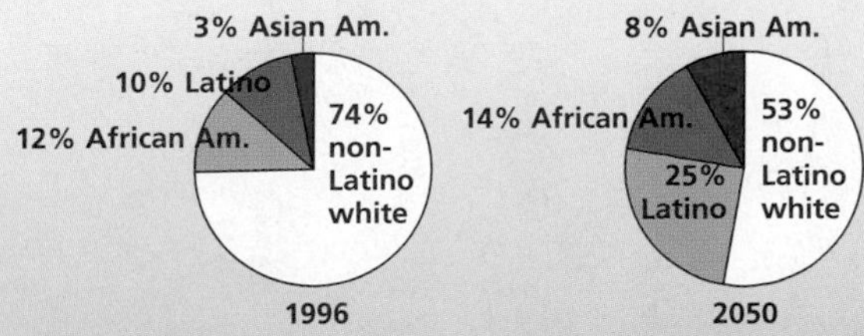

Making Connections Across Cultures

Cuban Immigrants Dating from the Bay of Pigs fiasco in 1961, Cubans fleeing Fidel Castro's Communist regime have landed by the thousands on the coasts of Florida. Relying on strong communal ties and sheer determination, Cuban workers parlayed small shops and family businesses into a multimillion-dollar economic presence in the state. With Castro's regime now heading into a decline, many Cuban Americans must decide whether to return to Cuba or stay in the United States—a decision made more difficult by the fact that the economic problems of cities like Miami threaten the economic base of the communities they have struggled so long to establish.

MORE ABOUT . . .
Illegal Immigrants

One 20th-century political commentator has called illegal immigrants to the United States the new "invisible Americans." Ignored by the middle- and upper-class people for whom they work, these immigrants nevertheless perform needed work that many Americans don't want to do. Moreover, these immigrants have every intention of staying for good.

OBJECTIVE
④ **INSTRUCT**

America and a New Millennium

▶ ***Starting with the Student*** Ask students to reflect on the feelings they've had each year on New Year's Eve. Help students recognize that many people think the coming of a new year means an opportunity to begin fresh. Discuss whether this feeling might be intensified at the turn of a century. Ask them how people might feel when one millennium—1,000 years—ends and another begins?

▶ ***Discussing Key Ideas***
- Americans face both old and new challenges as the century draws to a close.
- With the challenges come new opportunities presented by improvements in communication and technology.

ELECTRONIC LIBRARY OF PRIMARY SOURCES
from Mission Statement by the Organizing Committee of the Million Man March

DEBATES OVER IMMIGRATION POLICY Public opinion polls in 1994 revealed that only 6 percent of Americans believed that immigration should be increased, while almost two-thirds (63 percent) wanted to cut back immigration. Americans who opposed immigration argued that immigrants took jobs from other Americans or reduced wages because of competition, but many economists disagreed with that view.

Opponents of immigration found a strong spokesperson in Patrick Buchanan, a former speechwriter for President Nixon, who ran unsuccessfully for the Republican presidential nomination in 1992 and in 1996. Buchanan argued that the United States should erect a fence along the Mexican border to keep out illegal immigrants. In addition, he strongly opposed NAFTA, which he viewed as pitting working Americans against "Mexican folks who work for a buck an hour."

Candidates for U.S. citizenship are sworn in.

By the early 1990s, an estimated 3.2 million illegal immigrants had made their way to the United States. Most of these people had come from Mexico, but others had traveled north from El Salvador, Guatemala, and Haiti. Many illegal immigrants also arrived from Canada, Poland, China, and Ireland. Most of these illegal immigrants took jobs many Americans turned down, as sweatshop workers and domestic servants—often receiving the minimum wage or less and no benefits.

Hostility toward illegal immigration peaked in California and Florida, two states with high percentages of immigrants. In 1994, California passed Proposition 187, which cut off all education and nonemergency health benefits to illegal immigrants. That same year, California governor Pete Wilson demanded that the U.S. government reimburse the state for the $2.4 billion it was spending each year on undocumented aliens. In Florida, Governor Lawton Chiles filed suit in a Miami federal court against the U.S. government for "its continuing failure to enforce or rationally administer its own immigration laws."

D. Answer Americans fear job competition with immigrants who would work for low wages and the high social welfare expenses of immigrants.

THINK THROUGH HISTORY
D. *Comparing* *How are current arguments against immigration similar to those used in the past?*

America and a New Millennium

Since the nation's birth, the last decade of each century has been a time of challenge and change for Americans. In the last decade of the 18th century, the new nation was caught up in creating its national institutions and extending its reach to the West. As the 19th century came to a close, the United States was creating a new empire abroad, building new cities at home, rapidly industrializing, and becoming a world power. The end of the 20th century also marks the start of a new millennium, and it makes the sense of change and challenge on the horizon all the more dramatic.

CHALLENGES AHEAD As the century draws to a close, Americans face both new problems and old ones. Increasingly, terrorist acts pose a threat to Americans at home and abroad; recent bombings in Oklahoma City, New York City, and Atlanta have reminded Americans that world problems have domestic consequences. In addition, environmental concerns have become a global issue and have moved to center stage during the last few decades of the 20th century, as scientists have

TEACHING OPTIONS

Exploring Themes

Immigration and Migration Throughout the nation's history, U.S. immigration policies have fluctuated in reaction to the economic and political climate of the period. Years in which the country followed a restrictive immigration policy were usually followed by years of less restrictive policies, which in turn were succeeded by periods of greater restriction. Ask students how they would characterize the present period. *Possible Responses: Students may connect the changing U.S. ethnic and racial makeup to open immigration. Students may also cite the costs of providing services to illegal immigrants and newly arrived immigrants.*

warned of global warming, acid rain, and the loss of the earth's protective ozone layer. And poverty remains a problem for many Americans in the late 20th century, as the number of manufacturing jobs declines and government antipoverty programs are cut.

NEW OPPORTUNITIES For each challenge that Americans face, there are new opportunities ahead. As the century comes to a close, Americans look to a growing economy and hope to maintain the low unemployment and low inflation that marked the mid-1990s. General prosperity would help to reduce the problems of poverty that still persist in the nation.

To meet the challenges of the new millennium, Americans have invested in improved education and new technologies. Government data from 1995 revealed that 87 percent of both African-American and white young adults between the ages of 25 and 29 had completed high school. This figure is the highest percentage attained since the Census Bureau began collecting data on secondary school completion in 1947. Moreover, it suggests a narrowing of the educational gap that has so long separated blacks from whites.

E. Answer Possible responses: Optimistic students might point out America's strong economy, democratic traditions, and technological change. Pessimists might talk about persistent poverty and racism and, perhaps, declining moral values.

In addition to increasing the amount of time students spend in school, American educators are trying to enhance the quality of that time. Linking schools to the new communications networks will help students be more competitive in the global economy. Knowledge of advanced technology will help Americans find better jobs and make better products and thus improve the quality of life.

It is clear that the new century America faces will bring changes, but those changes need not deepen divisions among Americans. With effort and cooperation on the part of Americans, the changes could foster growth and tolerance. The 20th century has brought new ways of both destroying and enriching lives. What will the 21st bring? Much will depend on you—the dreamers, the decision makers, and the voters of the future.

THINK THROUGH HISTORY
E. *Forming Opinions* *Considering Americans' record at solving problems in the past, are you optimistic or pessimistic about America's future? Explain.*

HISTORICAL SPOTLIGHT

THE WORLD GAME INSTITUTE

Innovative programs around the country are preparing today's students to face tomorrow's challenges. For example, a nonprofit educational organization called the World Game Institute sponsors workshops in which student participants play a dynamic problem-solving game. Through cooperation and bartering, the students seek solutions to such problems as hunger, war, natural disaster, and disease. Private corporations, too, have begun to provide inner-city schools with computers, money for extra-curricular activities, and mentoring—the pairing of young people with adult advisers who provide them with advice and encouragement.

Section 4 Assessment

1. TERMS & NAMES

Identify:
- urban flight
- telecommute

2. SUMMARIZING Demography is the study of statistics about human populations. Use a table like the one below to summarize the demographic changes occurring in the United States.

Demographic Changes	
Urban distribution	
Age	
Ethnic and racial makeup	

3. HYPOTHESIZING As urban problems become more common in the suburbs, how might the residents of suburbs respond? Base your answer on existing behavior patterns.

THINK ABOUT
- the spread of suburbs farther and farther from the city
- the new ability to telecommute
- the tax problems that suburbs face

4. MAKING PREDICTIONS What do you think will be the biggest challenge facing the United States in the new millennium? Explain.

THINK ABOUT
- rundown cities and poverty
- the growing population of elderly persons
- the debate over immigration policy
- terrorism and crime

HISTORICAL SPOTLIGHT
The World Game Institute
Ask students to write a short paragraph proposing a problem they might like to tackle if they had a chance to attend the World Game Institute for a day.

ASSESS & RETEACH

Section 4 Assessment
Have students answer the questions individually and then compare answers with another student. Ask the student pairs to find text passages to support their answers.

Self-Assessment
Ask students to identify events from the chapter that they found hard to understand and to formulate one question they would like to ask the authors of the text.

Section Quiz
FORMAL ASSESSMENT
Section Quiz, p. 321

Reteach
Hold a group roundtable in which students can discuss their responses to item 4, "What will be the biggest challenge facing the United States in the new millennium?" Ask them to propose ways to handle that challenge.

CLOSE

The ending of one millennium and the beginning of a new 1,000 years left many Americans introspective about achievements made and promises yet unfulfilled.

ANSWERS

1. TERMS & NAMES

urban flight, p. 866
telecommute, p. 867

2. SUMMARIZING

Student charts may include the following possible responses:
Distribution: more suburban, less urban
Age: more senior citizens
Ethnic and racial makeup: more Asians and Hispanics, lower proportion of whites, about the same proportion of African Americans

3. HYPOTHESIZING

Possible Response: Students who say that people will move to new suburbs farther away from the city may cite the trend of suburban sprawl and the convenience of telecommuting. Students who say that people may start to move back to cities may cite the economic difficulties some suburbs are having.

4. MAKING PREDICTIONS

Possible Response: Some students may say poverty, because the gap between rich and poor is growing wider. Some may say the problem of funding Social Security, because if it goes bankrupt, the elderly will swell the ranks of the poor. Some may say health care, because many people still are without health insurance. Others may say crime and terrorism.

Cultural Diversity

OBJECTIVES

1. To trace America's historical experiences as a multicultural society.
2. To evaluate the benefits of America's multicultural heritage and of maintaining or abandoning one's ethnic heritage.

FOCUS & MOTIVATE

▶ ***Starting with the Student***
Ask students to think about ethnic heritage. Discuss the following questions:

- To what degree do you know and value your own ethnic heritage?
- What role do you think ethnic heritage should play in today's America?

MORE ABOUT . . .
Spanish Cowboys

The Mexican influence on American cowboys is evident in the language the cowboys used. Words such as *lasso, lariat, riata, chaps, mustang, pinto, palomino, stampede, rodeo, corral,* and even *ranch* all came to English from Spanish. It's also no accident that one old TV Western was called *Bonanza,* a Spanish word that became popular with miners hoping to strike it rich out West. Spanish cowboys were called *vaqueros,* a word still used by English speakers in parts of the Southwest.

TRACING THEMES
CULTURAL DIVERSITY

Sharing Cultures

Even before the first Europeans arrived in the Americas, a variety of cultural groups—coastal fishing societies, desert farmers, plains and woodland hunters—inhabited the North American continent. With the arrival of Europeans and Africans, the cultural mix grew even more diverse.

Although the diversity has often produced tension, it has also been beneficial for the United States. As different groups learned from one another about agriculture, technology, and social customs, American culture became a rich blend of cultures from around the world.

As these examples demonstrate, the United States has, throughout its history, been a place where cultures came together. As the nation moves into the 21st century, it will have to find ways to use its cultural diversity to help solve the problems of the future.

1610s to 1820s
SPANISH MISSION

The Spanish who established missions in the region that later became California, Texas, Arizona, and New Mexico had little interest in fostering cultural diversity. They tried to impose Spanish culture and Catholicism upon Native Americans. In spite of the missionaries' efforts, though, some Native Americans retained aspects of their original cultures even as they learned Spanish ways. For example, today many Pueblo Indians of New Mexico perform ancient dances, such as the Corn Dance, in addition to celebrating the feast days of Catholic saints.

1870s
COWBOYS

The American cowboy was a product of many cultures. The Spanish introduced cattle and horses to the Americas, and many of the techniques for raising cattle on large ranches developed in Mexico. When white Americans moved into Texas, they learned how to be cowboys from Mexicans. Cowboys were a diverse group; as the picture below shows, both whites and African Americans worked on ranches. However, as stories about the West spread into the popular culture, the truth became distorted, so that the roles of Mexicans and African Americans were largely ignored.

RECOMMENDED RESOURCES

Books

Buenker, John D., and Lorman A. Ratner. *Multiculturalism in the United States.* New York: Greenwood, 1992. A comparative guide to acculturation and ethnicity.

Daniels, Roger. *Coming to America.* New York: Harper, 1990. A history of immigration and ethnicity in American life.

Galens, Judy, et al., ed. *Gale Encyclopedia of Multicultural America.* Detroit: Gale Research, 1995. Reference.

Portes, Alejandro. *Immigrant America.* Berkeley: U of California P, 1990. A portrait of immigration.

Videos

Ethnic Diversity. PBS Video, 1993. Teens talk about prejudice.

Heritage of the Black West. National Geographic, 1995. African-American contributions to the history of the American West.

Old World, New World. Thames Television, 1977; dist. Media Guild. Late-19th-century European immigrants on their way to the United States.

Religion. National Geographic, 1993. The variety of religions in North America and the role of religion in our lives.

Software

Ellis Island—Immigrant Experience. Educational Activities, dist. ESI. Diskette. Students role-play the life of a different immigrant teenager each time they use the software.

1900s
THE "NEW" IMMIGRANTS

From 1890 to 1920, millions of southern and eastern European immigrants came to the United States. Many of them moved to cities and settled in neighborhoods populated by others from their country of origin, such as this neighborhood in New York City. This tended to foster cultural separation rather than cultural interaction—a situation that eased over time as the immigrants' children and grandchildren moved away from the old neighborhoods. Nevertheless, most large U.S. cities still have many neighborhoods that retain strong ethnic flavors.

1960s
CIVIL RIGHTS WORKERS

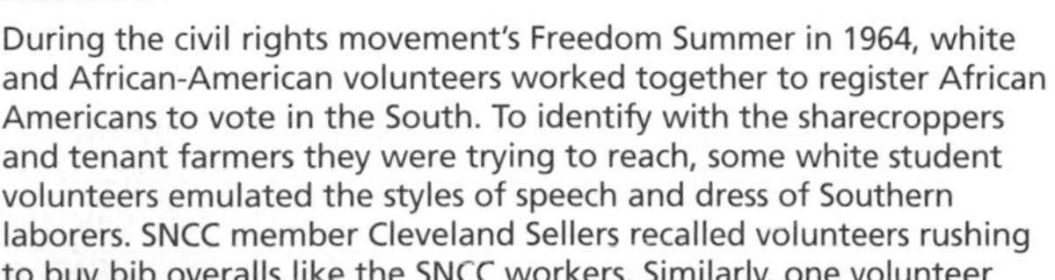

During the civil rights movement's Freedom Summer in 1964, white and African-American volunteers worked together to register African Americans to vote in the South. To identify with the sharecroppers and tenant farmers they were trying to reach, some white student volunteers emulated the styles of speech and dress of Southern laborers. SNCC member Cleveland Sellers recalled volunteers rushing to buy bib overalls like the SNCC workers. Similarly, one volunteer remembers that "everyone . . . got into talking like the SNCC staff . . . 'diggin' this and 'messin, with' that."

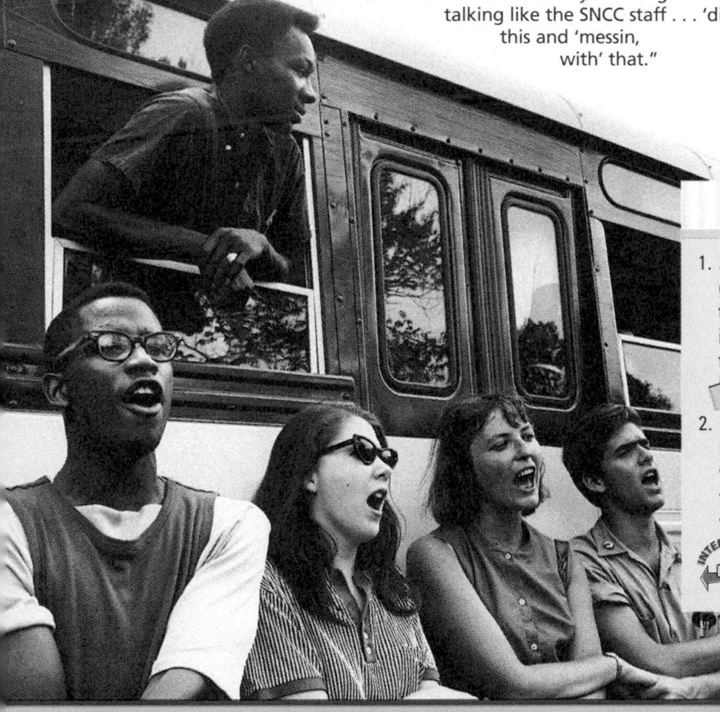

1990s
STUDENTS AND DIVERSITY

Many school districts across the United States provide a glimpse of the nation's future—in which diversity will increase to the point that there is no longer a majority group. The students pictured here are part of an advisory group helping their principal to address school problems in Los Angeles. As students such as these move into adulthood, the richness of their varied backgrounds and perspectives will help them make valuable contributions to America's economic and cultural life.

INTERACT WITH HISTORY

1. **ANALYZING MOTIVES** Why do you think some groups have tried to repress the culture of others over the course of history? Why have many groups persisted in retaining their cultural heritage? Write a brief explanation of your opinion and share it with the class.

SEE SKILLBUILDER HANDBOOK, PAGE 907.

2. **RESEARCHING YOUR PAST** What kinds of contributions to the cultural diversity of the United States have your own ancestors made? Research your own family history and write a brief explanation of your findings. Share it with the class.

INTERNET Visit http://www.mlushistory.com for more about cultural diversity.

INSTRUCT

▶ ***Starting with the Student***

- Have students work in groups to create maps with place names showing the many cultures that have shaped the United States.
- Encourage students to debate controversial issues related to the sharing of cultures, such as declaring English as America's legal language or using Ebonics in the classroom, as was recommended by the Oakland, California, school board in 1996.

▶ ***Discussing Key Ideas***

- America has always been a nation of diverse cultural heritages.
- Despite past conflicts, Americans' varied cultural heritages can make valuable contributions to American society as a whole.

HISTORY FROM VISUALS

Reading the Images Have students study the illustrations and accompanying details.

- Have students jot down adjectives describing their reactions to the different scenes depicted.
- Ask students why they think the truth about Mexican and African-American cowboys was largely ignored in the past. *Possible Responses: Racism and ethnocentrism; "winners" write history; Western dime novels, films, and TV shows of earlier decades were produced largely by whites and targeted to mainly white audiences.*

INTERACT WITH HISTORY

1. Analyzing Motives

Possible Answers: *Students may say that some groups have tried to repress the culture of others because of racism or because of long-standing ethnic conflicts. They may also point out that some groups might fear being overpowered or outnumbered by other groups. Many students may note that the groups that have persisted in retaining their cultural heritage are those that have formed relatively close communities in the United States.*

2. Researching Your Past

Standards for Evaluation
Explanations should . . .

- show evidence of a wide range of research sources, such as library references, personal interviews, family artifacts (for example, old photograph albums), church records, and contact with historical museums
- present the family historical information in an organized and coherent manner

CHAPTER 26
ASSESSMENT ANSWERS

REVIEWING THE CHAPTER

TERMS & NAMES
1. Bill Clinton, p. 846
2. NAFTA, p. 848
3. Contract with America, p. 849
4. service sector, p. 854
5. downsize, p. 854
6. GATT, p. 856
7. information superhighway, p. 860
8. Internet, p. 861
9. urban flight, p. 866
10. telecommute, p. 867

MAIN IDEAS

11. Possibilities include reducing the federal budget deficit, winning passage of NAFTA, signing the welfare reform bill, and signing a moderate health care reform bill.
12. The Republicans wanted to make large cuts in the budget; to block them, Democrats refused to pass spending bills; the resulting gridlock shut down government.
13. Clinton's foreign policy decisions consisted mainly of reactions to crises in other countries, such as Somalia and Bosnia.
14. Many workers lost jobs; others became temporary employees.
15. Service-sector and high-tech industries grew, while manufacturing and agriculture declined.
16. As the economy becomes more global, countries are bound as much by economic as by military alliances.
17. The Internet links people to government agencies, library databases, news media, and on-line catalogs.
18. Technology improved medicine, entertainment, education, automobile safety, and the environment.
19. Cities have grown poorer and more rundown; suburbs have sprawled farther from the city, grown more wealthy, and encountered problems with taxes and crime.
20. Possible Responses: Technology gives classrooms access to a wider range of information than was previously available. It also has expanded educational opportunities to students living in remote areas.

Chapter 26 Assessment

REVIEWING THE CHAPTER

TERMS & NAMES For each term below, write a sentence explaining its connection to the period from 1992 to the present. For each person below, explain his role in the events of the period.

1. **Bill Clinton**
2. **NAFTA**
3. **Contract with America**
4. **service sector**
5. **downsize**
6. **GATT**
7. **information superhighway**
8. **Internet**
9. **urban flight**
10. **telecommute**

MAIN IDEAS

SECTION 1 *(pages 846–852)*

The Clinton Presidency

11. Name three of President Clinton's most significant achievements during his first term.
12. How did both political parties contribute to the gridlock that shut down the government in 1995 and 1996?
13. How did world events shape Clinton's foreign policy?

SECTION 2 *(pages 853–857)*

The New Global Economy

14. How did downsizing affect U.S. workers?
15. Summarize which parts of the economy grew during the 1990s and which declined.
16. Explain what President Clinton meant when he said, "Trade as much as troops will increasingly define the ties that bind nations in the twenty-first century."

SECTION 3 *(pages 860–865)*

Technology and Modern Life

17. What resources of information, previously difficult to find, did the Internet make available?
18. How did changes in technology in the 1990s enrich American lives?

SECTION 4 *(pages 866–871)*

The Changing Face of America

19. How has urban flight changed both cities and suburbs?
20. In what ways has technology improved American education?

THINKING CRITICALLY

1. **CONFLICTING POLITICAL GOALS** Use a diagram similar to the one shown to list the political goals of President Clinton and Newt Gingrich. Indicate which goals were accomplished.

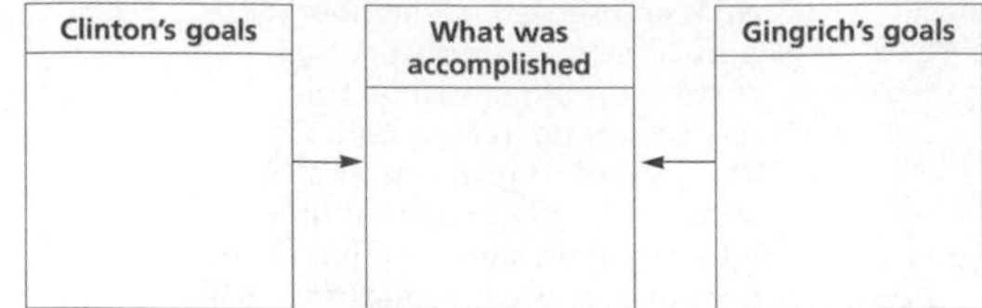

2. **NEW TECHNOLOGY** Compile a list of technological innovations of the late 20th century described in the chapter. Then predict what kinds of technological advancements might change American life during the 21st century.
3. **THE AMERICAN QUILT** Reread the quotation from Jesse Jackson on page 844. Do you agree with his description of American society? Why or why not?
4. **GEOGRAPHY OF IMMIGRATION** Look carefully at the map on page 869. What seems to have had a greater effect on the number of immigrants that a state received: how close it was to a border or how large a population it had? Explain why this might be.
5. **TRACING THEMES** **CULTURAL DIVERSITY** How important do you think it is for a nation to develop a single, unified culture? Support your opinion by using details from the chapter and the feature on pages 872–873.
6. **ANALYZING PRIMARY SOURCES** Read the following excerpt from an article published in *The Atlantic Monthly*. Then answer the questions below.

> In principle, we should admit immigrants whenever their economic contribution (to native well-being) will exceed the costs of providing social services to them. . . .
> Although we do not know how many immigrants to admit, simple economics and common sense suggest that the magic number should not be an immutable [unchangeable] constant regardless of economic conditions in the United States. A good case can be made for linking immigration to the business cycle: admit more immigrants when the economy is strong and the unemployment rate is low, and cut back on immigration when the economy is weak and the unemployment rate is high.
>
> **GEORGE J. BORJAS,** "The New Economics of Immigration," *The Atlantic Monthly,* November 1996

Do you agree with George Borjas that immigration policy should be designed to benefit the United States economically? What other factors besides potential economic impact should be used to decide what immigrants may enter the country?

THINKING CRITICALLY

1. CONFLICTING POLITICAL GOALS
Diagrams may include the following information:
Clinton's goals: cut middle-class taxes, reform health care, improve government efficiency, reduce the deficit.
What was accomplished: deficit reduced, bureaucracy reduced, welfare reform and limited health care reform passed.
Gingrich's goals: limit congressional terms, pass balanced-budget amendment, cut taxes, pass tougher crime laws and welfare reform.

2. NEW TECHNOLOGY
Possible Answers: Late-20th-century innovations: the Internet, CD-ROMs, fax machines, MRI, prosthetics, GPS, Hubble telescope. Possible advancements during the 21st century may include the more widespread use of electric cars and the integration of the television and the personal computer.

3. THE AMERICAN QUILT
Possible Responses: Some students may agree, saying that so many different groups have come together to make American society. Others may disagree, saying that they believe the groups do not share a common thread as Jackson suggests.

Review Chapter 26

ALTERNATIVE ASSESSMENT

1. **CREATING A PERSONAL TIME LINE**
   What impact have historical events during your lifetime had on you? Create an illustrated time line showing key historical events you believe have had an impact on your own life.

Conduct research using the CD-ROM *Our Times,* newspapers, interviews with relatives, and other resources.

- Identify both U.S. and global events.
- Construct a time line that identifies each event, including the year and place. Use magazine or newspaper pictures or headlines to illustrate the time line.
- Write a paragraph that explains which events had the most impact on you personally and why.

2. **MAKING DECISIONS**
   Review the information on American politics and economics in the first two sections of this chapter. The Cold War is over and the economy is growing. What should the government focus on now? Imagine that you are a member of Congress. What actions will you push the government to take? Use the following steps to help you make a decision:

- Identify the issues you feel are most important, and gather information about those issues.
- Decide what policies you want to pursue to address the issues you have identified.
- Predict the consequences of your actions. Will your constituents support you? Will you solve the problems you addressed?

3. **PORTFOLIO PROJECT**

Use the Living History activity to expand your portfolio.

LIVING HISTORY

SHARING 21ST-CENTURY GOALS

After you have compiled a list of the three main issues for the 21st century, have a friend read your list and answer these questions:

- Does the list clearly state the issues to be addressed?
- Do the supporting articles and photographs help you to understand the issue?
- Do any of the issues need to be explained further?

When you have revised the list on the basis of your friend's suggestions, write a letter to a newspaper or politician, explaining the list and your reason for sending it. Then add your list and your letter to your American history portfolio.

Review Chapter 26

POLITICAL SHIFTS Bill Clinton won the 1992 presidential election and had a mixed record as president. He failed to pass major health-care reform and drew criticism for raising taxes. He did succeed in lowering the budget deficit and gaining approval of NAFTA and welfare reform. In 1994, Republicans took control of Congress. Democrats blocked many Republican programs, leading to repeated government shutdowns that angered the public. Clinton's popularity rebounded, however, and he easily won reelection in 1996. In Clinton's second term, Congress investigated ways to reform campaign financing and passed a balanced budget.

ECONOMIC AND TECHNOLOGICAL CHANGE The American workplace continued to change as the service sector grew and manufacturing declined. International trade became more evident after the adoption of trade agreements such as GATT. Technology added to changes in the workplace as more businesses and individuals used the information superhighway. Technology also improved individual lives by making better products possible.

DEMOGRAPHIC CHANGES Because of overcrowding, crime, and other urban problems, many city dwellers fled to the suburbs. As baby boomers grew older, the average age in America rose—putting entitlement programs at risk. High immigration altered the ethnic and racial makeup of the U.S. population. Some experts predicted that by the year 2050, whites will no longer be in the majority. As the year 2000 approached, Americans looked for new ways to deal with the nation's problems.

LIVING HISTORY

COURSE-LONG PORTFOLIO PROJECT

After you have completed your theme portfolio, which you started as part of the thematic review on page 213, use the materials you have collected to create a museum exhibit on your theme. Present your museum exhibit to the class.

- Make a poster or diorama to display the visuals you have collected.
- Use any written sources you have collected to provide text for your visuals.

When you make your presentation, walk your audience through your exhibit. Be sure to answer clearly any questions they ask.

ALTERNATIVE ASSESSMENT

1. CREATING A PERSONAL TIME LINE
Standards for Evaluation
A time line should meet the following criteria:

- Identifies appropriate dates for U.S. and global events.
- Labels the place and year of the events clearly.
- Uses relevant pictures and headlines as illustrations.
- Includes a paragraph that cites reasons for the student's opinion.

2. MAKING DECISIONS
Standards for Evaluation
The student's decision-making process should meet the following criteria:

- Shows an awareness of the major political issues currently facing the nation.
- Demonstrates an understanding of the historical background of these issues.
- Offers logical solutions to the issues chosen as well as a thoughtful defense of the decisions made.

3. PORTFOLIO PROJECT
LIVING HISTORY
Standards for Evaluation
The letter and list of issues should meet the following criteria:

- Clearly explains the purpose of the letter and the list.
- Presents three crucial concerns of the 21st century.
- Explains each concern clearly.
- Includes well-chosen articles or illustrations.

IN-DEPTH RESOURCES: UNIT 7
See the form for scoring this activity on page 55.

COURSE-LONG PORTFOLIO PROJECT
LIVING HISTORY
Standards for Evaluation
The museum exhibit should meet the following criteria:

- Chooses appropriate topics that relate to the theme that is discussed.
- Uses accurate historical information about the topics used to exemplify the theme.
- Organizes visuals and text in a logical manner to communicate the historical development of the theme.

IN-DEPTH RESOURCES: UNIT 7
See the form for scoring this activity on page 57.

THINKING CRITICALLY

4. GEOGRAPHY OF IMMIGRATION
Possible Response: Students may note that states with large populations receive more immigrants than those with smaller populations and that this is a more consistent pattern than how close a state is to a border. Possible reasons for this include the tendency of immigrants to go to large cities to find work or to settle where relatives or people from their home country already reside.

5. TRACING THEMES CULTURAL DIVERSITY
Possible Responses: Students who think developing a unified culture is important may say that America can remain strong only if its people share a common vision. Students who disagree may say that America is a nation of many cultures and that forcing certain groups to abandon their culture and accept a common culture goes against the American tradition of individual liberty.

6. ANALYZING PRIMARY SOURCES
Possible Answer: Students who agree might contend that government officials should be more concerned with securing the economic well-being of native citizens than of immigrants. Those who disagree might say that reuniting families or helping people escape oppression are more important considerations than economics. Another factor that might be considered is that most Americans are themselves descendants of immigrants.

EPILOGUE

OVERVIEW

Issues for the 21st Century

▶ ***Accessing Prior Knowledge***

Ask students to review the topics listed on pages 876 and 877 and choose one that interests them.

- Are they themselves affected by this issue?
- Do they know anyone who is involved with the issue—either facing the problem or trying to find solutions?
- What impressions do they have about the issue through these acquaintances?
- What approaches can they think of that might be tried?

▶ ***Predicting Outcomes***

Ask students to read the brief descriptions of each topic. Which issues do they think will be most important in the 21st century? Which will be the most difficult to resolve?

EPILOGUE

Issues for the 21st Century

What are the toughest issues facing Americans now? Here are eight that grow out of themes and conflicts found throughout U.S. history. All eight will continue to be the subject of discussion and debate in the new century.

Soldiers help a wounded comrade during the 1991 Persian Gulf War.

Foreign Policy After the Cold War

page 878

How can the United States extend its democratic ideals—without stepping on other nations' toes?

The Debate over Immigration

page 880

Are too many immigrants entering the United States? Immigration policies continue to cause controversy.

Crime and Public Safety

page 884

Americans call for safer neighborhoods. Proposed solutions range from longer prison sentences to tighter gun control laws.

Exploring Education Today

page 888

Today, public schools in the United States—and those who run them—face difficult choices in terms of financing and reform. What direction should U.S. public education take?

Former Taiwan resident Candis Yen McCann joins 1,000 others in a swearing-in ceremony for new U.S. citizens, as her daughter waves the flag.

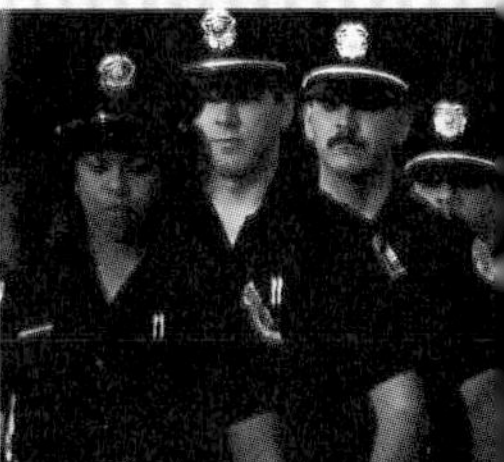

In the 1990s, women and minorities account for a larger percentage of new police recruits.

RECOMMENDED RESOURCES

Books for the Teacher

Anders, George. *Health Against Wealth: HMOs and the Breakdown of Medical Trust.* Boston: Houghton, 1996. How HMOs affect access to health care.

Bernstein, Richard and Ross H. Munro. *The Coming Conflict with China.* New York: Knopf, 1997. American relations with China.

Blair, Anita, et al. "Giving Women the Business," *Harper's,* December 1997. Discussion of the problems women face in the workplace.

Friedman, Lawrence. *Crime and Punishment in American History.* New York: Basic, 1993. Scholarly look at the history of criminal justice in the United States.

Glazer, Nathan. *We Are All Multiculturalists Now.* Cambridge, MA: Harvard UP, 1997. The consequences of multiculturalism for American society.

Hacker, Andrew. *Money: Who Has How Much and Why.* New York: Scribner, 1997. The distribution of wealth in the United States in the 1990s.

Books for the Student

"Affirmative Action: Redistribution or Equal Opportunity?" *Congressional Digest,* June-July 1996. Special issue devoted to the topic with several different points of view.

Costello, Cynthia, and Barbara Kivimac Krimgold. *The American Woman, 1996–1997.* New York: Norton, 1996. Essays and statistics on women in the workplace.

Madeleine Albright becomes U.S. secretary of state in 1997.

A family receives charitable assistance at a St. Vincent de Paul center in Phoenix, Arizona.

Curing the Health Care System

page 892

The health care system is failing millions of Americans—but should the goal be universal health care? U.S. policymakers look for a cure.

Women and the Glass Ceiling

page 894

Women continue to face obstacles in reaching top positions in their fields. Should the government play a role in promoting equal opportunity for women?

Breaking the Cycle of Poverty

page 896

A critical issue confronting the United States today is the millions of Americans who live in poverty. What proposed remedies are on the table?

Tough Choices About Entitlements

page 900

The aging of the American population has raised alarms about the future of Social Security. What must be done to fix Social Security and other government entitlement programs, such as Medicare?

Epilogue: Issues for the 21st Century

Below are page references to places in the Teacher's Edition that link historical topics to the articles in this Epilogue.

Foreign Policy After the Cold War
pp. 366, 609, 725

The Debate over Immigration
pp. 278, 439, 556

Crime and Public Safety
pp. 413, 454, 689

Exploring Education Today
pp. 233, 304, 699

Curing the Health Care System
pp. 645, 687, 828

Women and the Glass Ceiling
pp. 156, 339, 597, 771

Breaking the Cycle of Poverty
pp. 199, 263, 497, 661

Tough Choices About Entitlements
pp. 516, 787, 851

RECOMMENDED RESOURCES

Kennedy, David M. "Can We Still Afford to Be a Nation of Immigrants?" *Atlantic Monthly,* November 1996. Thoughtful essay on the past, present, and future of immigration.

Keve, Paul. *Crime Control and Justice in America.* Chicago: American Library Association, 1995. Fact-filled look at different aspects of crime and the criminal justice system.

Kozol, Jonathan. Savage *Inequalities: Children in America's Schools.* New York: Harper, 1992.

Videos

ABC News: Emergency! Health Care in America—A Town Meeting. 1993. MPI Home Video, 708-460-0555. Ordinary Americans and experts in panel discussion.

America in the 21st Century. 1990. PBS Home Video, 800-531-4727. Symposium that discusses economy, education, immigration among other topics.

America the Homeless. 1991. EcuFilm, 800-251-4091. 3-part series.

Careers in the 21st Century: Women in Non-Traditional Roles. 1992. Takeoff Multimedia, 800-462-5232. Advice from 22 women.

Software

Ethnic Newswatch. DOS, Windows CD-ROM. SoftLine Information, 800-524-7922.

Facts On File World News Digest: 1980–1996: Annual Cumulative Update. DOS, Mac, Windows CD-ROM. Facts On File News Services, 800-363-7976.

Foreign Policy After the Cold War

OBJECTIVES

1. To explain the foreign policy issues that have emerged since the end of the Cold War.
2. To describe the different goals that the United States can have for its foreign policy.

FOCUS & MOTIVATE

5-MINUTE WARM-UP

Interpreting Charts
To review American foreign policy during the Cold War, have students look at the chart on page 878 and answer these questions.

1. What actions in the chart did the United States take during the 1960s?
2. What was the purpose of most of the U.S. actions during the Cold War?

WARM-UP TRANSPARENCY EPILOGUE

▶ ***Starting with the Student***
Ask students in what ways they control their own lives. How do they feel when others make decisions for them? Then ask them what they think about the outer column quotation on page 879. How does the idea that "people like to vote" relate to U.S. foreign policy?

Foreign Policy After the Cold War

LEARN ABOUT foreign policy goals after the end of the Cold War
TO UNDERSTAND the evolving role of the United States in world affairs.

APPROACHING THE ISSUE "The United States stands at this time at the pinnacle of world power. It is a solemn moment for the American democracy. For with primacy in power is also joined an awe-inspiring accountability for the future." Winston Churchill's words, spoken in 1947, remain true as the 21st century begins.

Historical Perspective

The United States emerged from World War II ready to exert its influence in world affairs. For the next several decades, U.S. foreign policy had a clear goal: to prevent the spread of communism in the world. This aim prompted the key foreign policy decisions of the post-World War II era (see the chart below).

The Cold War ended when Russian leader Boris Yeltsin and President George Bush issued a statement promising future partnership in February 1992. The statement was the climax of several years of turmoil in the Communist bloc that had seen the end of the Soviet Union in 1991.

Since then, the United States has explored new goals and policies for its involvement in foreign affairs. What role should the nation play in the global arena?

Key Foreign Policy Actions During Cold War

U.S. ACTION	PURPOSE
• Establish Marshall Plan (1947)	• Halt Communist expansion by rebuilding Europe
• Form North Atlantic Treaty Organization (NATO) (1949)	• Counter Communist military threat in Europe
• Enter Korean War (1950s)	• Contain communism in Asia
• Force Soviets to remove nuclear missiles from Cuba (1962)	• Prevent Soviet establishment of base near U.S. mainland
• Enter Vietnam War (1960s)	• Contain communism in Asia
• Open ties with People's Republic of China (1970s)	• Weaken position of Soviet Union
• Improve relations with Arab nations (1970s)	• Weaken Soviet influence in Middle East
• Pursue nuclear arms reductions (1970s and 1980s)	• Limit threat of Communist-controlled nuclear arms
• Support Contra rebels in Nicaragua (1980s)	• Remove Communist regime in Western Hemisphere

Foreign Policy Goals

Americans debating the U.S. role in world affairs have focused on three issues: promoting democracy in the world, protecting human rights, and opening world markets to American goods.

PROMOTING DEMOCRACY Deputy Secretary of State Strobe Talbott states the position of those who urge an active American role in promoting democracy around the world.

A PERSONAL VOICE
[The more nations] that choose democratic forms of government, the safer and more prosperous Americans will be, since democracies are demonstrably more likely to maintain their international commitments, less likely to engage in terrorism or wreak environmental damage, and less likely to make war on each other.
STROBE TALBOTT, Deputy Secretary of State

Critics say that it is unrealistic to believe that democracy can be adopted everywhere. Former presidential candidate Pat Buchanan scoffs at the idea that American democracy "can be replicated [around the world] . . . if only we put enough men, money, and muscle into the great crusade."

History of Foreign Policy Since World War I

UNITED STATES

1917 United States abandons neutrality and enters World War I (pages 399–401).

1941 United States enters World War II (pages 563–565).

1945 United Nations created (page 607); Truman and Stalin clash at Potsdam (pages 607–608).

1946 United States adopts policy of containment against communism (page 609).

Block Schedule TEACHING OPTION **Time Needed: 20 Minutes**

Cooperative Activity: Debating Foreign Policy Goals

Task: Student groups will debate whether promoting democracy, protecting human rights, or opening world markets should be the central goal of American foreign policy.

Purpose: To help students understand the principles that shape American foreign policy decisions.

Activity: Divide the class into groups of eight or ten students, and then divide each group into two teams. Have both teams defend one goal for American foreign policy—promoting democracy, protecting human rights, or opening world markets. Within the groups, each student should prepare by researching current foreign policy issues confronting the United States. They should also discuss the effects that U.S. policies have had on other countries.

ALTERNATIVE ASSESSMENT BOOK
Standards for Evaluating a Cooperative Activity

Talbott disagrees. He points to the surge of democracy in many parts of the world in the 1990s. In places as diverse as Taiwan and Argentina, voters freely chose leaders. Although the shift to democracy can be "painful, suspenseful, and downright messy," democracy is attractive. "People," Talbott says, "like to vote."

PROTECTING HUMAN RIGHTS Since the 1970s, when President Jimmy Carter established a Bureau of Human Rights in the State Department, U.S. foreign policy has often emphasized basic human rights for people in other countries. But Aryeh Neier, former head of Human Rights Watch, argues that the United States has a dangerous double standard on human rights. While American leaders push smaller nations to fix human rights problems, they often ignore abuses by politically or economically important nations—nations like China, which is an important trading partner for the United States. Neier argues that this policy toward smaller nations will fail in the long run.

Jeffrey Garten, once a senior trade official in the Commerce Department, agrees that promoting human rights is important. However, to critics who argue that America should not trade with countries with poor records on human rights, Garten responds that increased trade improves the lives of people in both nations. By increasing wages abroad, Garten contends, U.S. companies raise the standard of living.

A Chinese demonstrator courageously stands in front of a column of tanks during the June 1989 demonstrations in Tiananmen Square in Beijing, China.

OPENING WORLD MARKETS The issue of protecting human rights is related to the U.S. goal of gaining its share of the emerging international markets—including those in China, Mexico, and Turkey. Some of these countries have had poor records on human rights, yet the United States has not imposed sanctions against them. As of 1997, China continued to receive "Most Favored Nation" (MFN) status, despite cases of human rights violations. Without this privileged trading status, duties on U.S. imports from China would rise from about 6 percent to 44 percent. However, China's MFN status must be renewed annually, and growing numbers in Congress say that they oppose this status unless China moves toward democracy.

Observers suggest that the best way to balance the need for gaining markets and protecting human rights is for several governments to pressure an offending nation to remedy human rights abuses. Many believe that the United States can play a leadership role in bringing about such cooperation.

"People like to vote."

STROBE TALBOTT, DEPUTY SECRETARY OF STATE

President Bill Clinton visited Mexico in 1997 to discuss trade policies. He is shown visiting Mexican schoolchildren with Hillary Rodham Clinton and President Ernesto Zedillo.

INTERACT WITH HISTORY

1. **FORMING OPINIONS** How actively do you think the United States should promote democracy? Why?

SEE SKILLBUILDER HANDBOOK, PAGE 919.

2. **MAKING DECISIONS** Suppose you were President of the United States. A country that trades with the United States has a poor human rights record. What would you do?

Visit http://www.mlushistory.com for more about U.S. foreign policy.

1961 Berlin Wall erected to divide Communist and noncommunist Berlin (pages 675–676).

1962 United States and Soviet Union confront each other in Cuban missile crisis (pages 673–675).

1965 First U.S. combat troops arrive in Vietnam (page 728).

1972 Nixon visits China and the Soviet Union (pages 791–792).

INSTRUCT

▶ *Discussing Key Ideas*
- The goals of U.S. foreign policy are changing now that the Cold War has ended.
- People disagree whether the main goal of U.S. foreign policy should be to promote democracy, protect human rights, or open world markets.

HISTORY FROM VISUALS

Chinese Protester

Reading the Photograph Have students look at the picture of the Chinese demonstrator standing in front of the tanks. Ask them how images from around the world like this one affect U.S. policies.

Possible Responses: Some might argue that such images inspire American citizens and leaders to support democratic movements while others might say that they tug at American heartstrings, but have no effect on policy.

Extension American policy toward China is a controversial issue. Many people feel that the Chinese government treats its people too harshly. Yet China offers a huge market that could benefit American business. Have students create a concept web that explores this issue. You could begin by listing these items on the board:

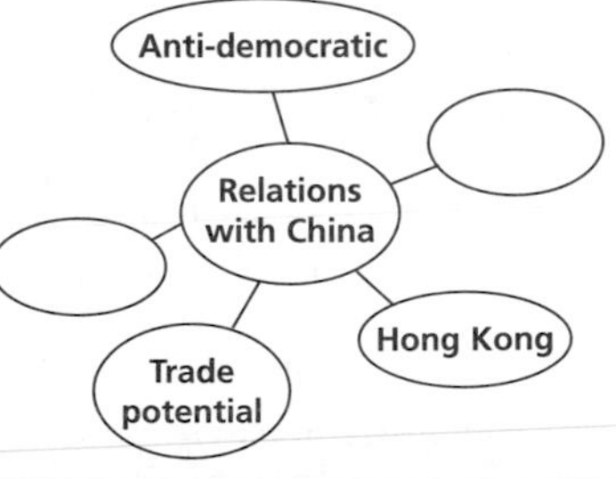

INTERACT WITH HISTORY

1. Forming Opinions

Possible Responses *Should not actively promote: The United States needs to respect the wishes of individual countries to choose their own form of government. Democracy might not be appropriate everywhere, and it would be costly—in lives and dollars—for the United States to try to impose it on every country.*

Should actively promote: The United States needs to take a strong stand to support democratic movements wherever they occur. Doing so will help people in other nations and help make Americans safer.

2. Making Decisions

Standards for Evaluation
Paragraphs should . . .

- explain clearly the course of action to be taken
- provide reasons for that action
- demonstrate an understanding of the limitations on what one country can do to influence another country

The Debate over Immigration

OBJECTIVES

1. To discuss the legal, economic, and moral aspects of immigration.
2. To describe the arguments for and against restricting immigration.

FOCUS & MOTIVATE

5-MINUTE WARM-UP

Interpreting Graphs

To analyze immigration patterns in the 1900s, have students look at the graph on page 881 and answer these questions.

1. During which years was immigration the lowest?
2. In which years was U.S. immigration greater than 1.2 million people?

WARM-UP TRANSPARENCY EPILOGUE

▶ ***Starting with the Student***

Ask students to review their own family's history of immigration.

- What led family members to immigrate to the United States?
- What experiences did they have when they arrived?
- How have their experiences affected how students view the issue of immigration?

OBJECTIVE

① INSTRUCT

▶ ***Discussing Key Ideas***

- More people immigrate to the United States between 1965 and 1997

(continued on next page)

The Debate over Immigration

LEARN ABOUT the political, economic, and social impact of legal and illegal immigration to the United States

TO UNDERSTAND why Americans disagree about what constitutes fair U.S. immigration policies.

APPROACHING THE ISSUE Briam Saiti left warring Bosnia and arrived in New York City, where he worked at a variety of jobs, saving money to send for his family. But his brother and parents may never be able to join him. Controversial new immigration laws may put tighter limits on who can come to live in the United States.

Historical Perspective

Thousands of years ago, Asians of unknown origin crossed the Bering land bridge to become the first immigrants to North America. Millions of people from Europe, Africa, Asia, and Latin America have come since.

These immigrant men and women helped build the country. Latino settlers formed cattle ranches and developed many of the tools and skills that American cowboys used. Chinese laborers dug tunnels out of mountains and laid the tracks to make the transcontinental railroad a reality. European farmers grew food and workers built cities and factories. African Americans—though not voluntary immigrants—helped to build the agriculture of the South and the industry of the North.

Chinese immigrants wait outside the hospital on Angel Island in San Francisco, 1910.

Americans have always felt pride in immigrants. In making Thanksgiving a national holiday in 1863, Abraham Lincoln announced with satisfaction that the number of free Americans had grown "by emancipation and by immigration."

But immigration has been argued hotly throughout American history as well. In the 1700s, Benjamin Franklin worried about the rising number of German immigrants to Pennsylvania. Anti-immigration sentiment spurred the nativist movement of the 1840s, led to the exclusion of Chinese immigrants in the 1880s, and produced a law strictly limiting immigration in the 1920s. Not until 1965 were those restrictions loosened. The result was an increase in immigration.

Shiu-Chen Chiang, age 84, recites the Pledge of Allegiance on June 19, 1996, in San Jose, California.

Recent Trends

In recent decades, economic troubles and rapid population growth hit Asia and Latin America. A hundred years before, these same factors drove millions of Europeans to move to the United States. These factors have the same effect now. Since 1965, when immigration law changed, 20 million people have come to the United States—more than during the peak years of 1890 to 1915. The number reached an all-time high of 1.8 million in 1990.

As that immigrant stream began, the U.S. economy was growing slowly. Losing their jobs and seeing their wages decline, many people blamed the high numbers of immigrants. The debate over immigration limits reopened.

History of Immigration

UNITED STATES

- **1751** Benjamin Franklin complains about German immigrants.
- **1854** Nativists form Know-Nothing Party to protest increase in immigration (page 169).
- **1882** Chinese Exclusion Act severely restricts immigration from China (page 279).
- **1896** President Cleveland vetoes bill requiring immigrants to pass literacy test (page 279).

Block Schedule — TEACHING OPTION — **Time Needed: 40 Minutes**

Cooperative Activity: Town Hall Discussion on Immigration

Task: Students play roles to discuss immigration policy in the United States.

Purpose: To understand the social and political aspects of immigration in the United States.

Activity: Have students assume the roles of U.S. leaders addressing the issue of immigration. One student should be president. Others should play the roles of congressional leaders and leaders of local areas that are affected by immigration—such as governors, mayors, journalists, or leaders of immigrants' rights groups. Choose one student to be a moderator who will lead the discussion on immigration issues. Have each of the students defend their views on immigration with statistics and information from the text and from other sources.

ALTERNATIVE ASSESSMENT BOOK
Standards for Evaluating a Cooperative Activity

SKILLBUILDER
INTERPRETING GRAPHS
The U.S. population was 76 million in 1900 and 249 million in 1990. In which year was the number of new immigrants a greater percentage of the population?

Immigrants become United States citizens in San Francisco, July 1996.

Illegal Immigration

Complicating the debate was the issue of illegal immigrants. By the early 1990s, 3.2 million people had entered the country illegally. Governor Pete Wilson of California echoed many Americans when he said, "There's a right way to come to America and a wrong way."

Legality was not the only issue—the influx of illegal immigrants hit the pocketbook. Though many of these immigrants worked, their jobs typically paid little and did not include health insurance. Many did seasonal work and found themselves unemployed part of the year. States faced increased costs for health care, education, welfare, and food stamps. Some citizens protested. In California in 1994, voters approved Proposition 187, which denied illegal immigrants access to public education and state-funded health care except in emergencies.

In 1996, Congress passed a spending bill that prevented illegal immigrants from receiving welfare, unemployment benefits, food stamps, and housing assistance. The law aimed at preventing illegal entry to the United States and made it easier to deport, or return, illegal immigrants, to their home countries.

Legal Immigration

Most Americans agree on the need to halt illegal immigration. But they divide sharply on whether to limit legal immigration. Some side with New York City mayor Rudolph Giuliani.

A PERSONAL VOICE

Immigrants are exactly what we need economically, and I think they're what we need morally. . . . [Immigrants] help us with the work they do, they challenge us with new ideas and new perspectives.

RUDOLPH GIULIANI, mayor, New York City

Others agree with Harold W. Ezell, formerly of the Immigration and Naturalization Service, which oversees immigration policy. Ezell says, "Immigration is good for America. But too much of a good thing can be harmful." The debate has four components: economic, political, cultural, and moral. →

Skillbuilder Answer
The percentage was greater in 1990 (.72%) than in 1900 (.66%).

1921 Emergency Quota Act begins era of limits on immigration (page 439).

1965 Immigration Act loosens restrictions in place since 1921 (page 686).

1994 California voters approve Proposition 187, excluding benefits to illegal immigrants (page 870).

1996 Congress passes laws that limit benefits to illegal immigrants.

(continued from page 880)

than did during the immigration boom of 1890 to 1915.
- Recent laws try to crack down on illegal immigration.
- Americans disagree on whether to limit legal immigration.

HISTORY FROM VISUALS

Immigrants Admitted to the U.S., 1900–1994

Reading the Graph What does the note at the bottom of the graph suggest about the 1990 data? *Possible Response: The large increase that year is an aberration caused by the one-time amnesty given illegal immigrants.*

MORE ABOUT . . .

The 1996 Law Affecting Illegal Immigration

The law Congress passed in 1996 originally placed limits on legal immigration as well as illegal immigraton. In its final version, the new law focused primarily on illegal immigration and took several steps:
- Authorized money to double the number of border patrol agents by the year 2000.
- Authorized money to lengthen the fence being built along a 14-mile stretch of the border south of San Diego, California.
- Ordered the Immigration and Naturalization Service to develop an identity card for immigrants that would feature an identifying device such as a retina scan.
- Reduced the procedures to deport aliens and required them to leave the country within 90 days of being so ordered.

TEACHING OPTIONS

Teaching Gifted and Talented Students

Researching Naturalization California governor Pete Wilson is quoted as saying, "There's a right way to come to America and a wrong way." Ask students to do research in the library or on the Internet to find the rules that immigrants are supposed to follow. Their research should include what immigrants must do to enter the country, how they apply for naturalization, and what they must do to become citizens. Have the students present their findings to the class.

Making Connections Across Time

Anti-Immigrant Sentiment in the Past The late 1800s was a period of strong anti-immigrant feeling, as shown by the passage of the Chinese Exclusion Act of 1882. Starting in 1895, Congress passed several bills requiring immigrants to pass a literacy test before they would be allowed to enter the country. In vetoing one of the bills, President Grover Cleveland said, "the time is quite within recent memory when . . . immigrants who, with their descendants, are now numbered among our best citizens [were called] undesirable." He called the bill "illiberal, narrow, and un-American."

OBJECTIVE
② INSTRUCT

▶ ***Starting with the Student***
Tell students to create a three-column chart to organize the information on immigrants' impact on the economy. They should give their paper the following headings:

Jobs	Wages	Government Benefits

They can list each fact provided in the article under the appropriate heading. They could mark each fact with a plus (+) if it shows immigration benefits the nation and a minus (-) if it shows that immigration is a drawback. Do the pluses outnumber the minuses?

▶ ***Discussing Key Ideas***
- Economists offer statistics showing that immigrants do not cost native-born Americans jobs.
- The rate at which immigrants are becoming citizens is increasing.
- Some people worry that rising numbers of immigrants will destroy the unity of American culture.
- Some people argue against laws that allow elderly immigrants to join their families already here.

"The U.S. has this terrible problem. . . . The smartest people in the world want to come here."

JENNIFER HUNT, ECONOMIST

Economic Arguments

The economic factors related to immigration can be complex.

JOBS One part of the argument has to do with jobs. Those who favor limits point out that 10 percent of all workers are now foreign born. They say that immigrants take jobs from American workers. Those against limits counter that these are jobs that native-born Americans do not want, including low-wage positions in the clothing, food processing, and restaurant industries. Other data suggest that the rise in immigration may not have harmed the economy. Unemployment fell from 7.1 percent in 1980 to under 5 percent in 1997, even though millions of immigrant workers joined the work force.

WAGES Another economic argument focuses on wages. Economists agree that immigrants have always worked for lower wages than native-born workers. Three Harvard University economists recently reported that one-third of the gap between low-paid and high-paid workers results from higher numbers of immigrant workers. But even those economists admit that other factors—the rise of foreign trade, the decline in union membership, and new technology—played a bigger role in lowering wages. Economist Jennifer Hunt of Yale University points out that immigrants' low wages benefit consumers by keeping prices low.

Opponents of limits on immigration suggest that immigrants also fill high-skilled, high-paying jobs. Current law allows 140,000 highly skilled immigrants to enter the country each year. When Congress debated lowering that limit, businesses lobbied hard—and successfully—to kill the bill. Economist Hunt saw the irony in the issue.

A PERSONAL VOICE
The U.S. has this terrible problem. . . . The smartest people in the world want to come here.
JENNIFER HUNT, economist, Yale University

GOVERNMENT SUPPORT Immigration increases government costs, supporters of limits say. Many immigrants are poor, and a high proportion are older than 65, a greater percentage than among the native-born population. These people require welfare, food stamps, Social Security, and Medicare and Medicaid.

Some economists say, however, that immigrants are not an economic drain but an economic gain. A calculation from the Cato Institute suggests that cutting immigration in half would cost the Social Security system $5.6 billion that immigrant workers pay in taxes each year. Jeffrey Passel of the Urban Institute estimates that in a recent year, immigrants paid $27 billion more in taxes than they used in services. Harvard economist George Borjas—an immigrant—disagrees, though. He thinks Passel's estimate ignores the fact that immigrants use local and state resources, such as education and public health care, far more than they pay in taxes to local and state governments.

"I hereby declare, on oath, that I absolutely and entirely renounce and abjure all allegiance and fidelity to any foreign prince, potentate, state or sovereignty, of whom or which I have heretofore been a subject or a citizen; that I will support and defend the Constitution and laws of the United States of America against all enemies, foreign and domestic; that I will bear true faith and allegiance to the same; that I will bear arms on behalf of the United States when required by the law; that I will perform noncombatant service in the armed forces of the United States when required by the law; that I will perform work of national importance under civilian direction when required by the law; and that I take this obligation freely without any mental reservation or purpose of evasion; so help me God."

Taking this oath of allegiance is part of the requirement for becoming a U.S. citizen.

TEACHING OPTIONS

Making Connections Across the Curriculum

Economics In discussing the Harvard study of wages, remind students that economists have to consider many factors when studying a phenomenon rather than assume that all effects result from one variable alone. To reinforce this idea, ask students to list things that can affect wages. The list should include: skills, cost-of-living, productivity, automation, danger of work, hours, and job competition. Point out that even if wages increase, some of these factors may act to limit that increase. For example, a skilled worker with no job competition may earn high wages, but if the cost-of-living is high due to a lack of cheap labor in other industries, part of the high wage is lost to high prices.

Making Connections Across the Curriculum

Civics Some students may have difficulty with the argument between Passel and Borjas in the section "Government Support." Help them by writing the following chart on the board and completing it with the participation of the whole class.

	Level of Government		
Program	Local	State	Federal

Elena Salas and her father, Miguel Salas (*center*), make their first Pledge of Allegiance at a citizenship ceremony for 11,000 people at Soldier Field in Chicago, 1996.

Political Arguments

The debate over immigration has had political overtones.

RESPONSIBILITIES OF CITIZENSHIP Some people want limits because, they say, many immigrants never become citizens. Immigrants should not enjoy the privileges of living in the United States without taking responsibility by voting, serving on juries, and so on, the argument goes. However, while the rate of immigrants' gaining citizenship was low for years, the trend has reversed. In 1996, 1.1 million immigrants took the oath of citizenship. Officials expect similar figures for the next few years.

VOTING TRENDS When immigrants do gain citizenship and vote, some say, they tend to vote in blocs, which reflects group thinking. Those who oppose limits say that earlier immigrant groups did the same thing. Just as these voting blocs broke up in the past, they say, voting patterns of today's immigrants will change.

Cultural Arguments

The diverse mix of people now living in the United States raises concerns that Americans will lose their common culture. Some say that at 8.7 percent of the population, foreigners are too numerous in America. Historian David Kennedy points out, however, that the percentage was much higher—14.7 percent—in 1910.

Those who favor limits say that new immigrants do not mix with other groups. They tend to live together in ethnic neighborhoods, dividing society. Others believe that ethnic neighborhoods do not weaken American culture, but enrich it by introducing new music, foods, and other cultural elements to the United States.

Moral Arguments

Some people feel the moral issues involved in immigration policies are often overlooked.

POLITICAL ASYLUM An area of moral debate is the question of asylum—providing a safe place for people trying to flee an oppressive foreign government. While immigration is allowed for political asylum, people fleeing economic oppression are turned away. Are such choices fair? In the words of social scientist Nathan Glazer, "Poorly paid officials must make decisions that would stump a professor of ethics."

FAMILY CONNECTIONS Some criticize rules that allow relatives of immigrants to enter the country. Representative Lamar Smith of Texas believes that these rules admit immigrants who "have no marketable skills, and end up on welfare." As Glazer notes, concern about the number of immigrants conflicts with sympathy for particular "neighbors and friends trying to bring in wives, children, parents, brothers, and sisters."

Alan Simpson, a former U.S. senator, believes that there are simply too many immigrants. Halt immigration for five years, he proposed, to gain "breathing space." Others believe that as a nation of immigrants, we have a moral obligation to allow immigration.

Americans remain divided. In one poll, 52 percent of those answering favored the Simpson idea. But in another poll, 60 percent of respondents agreed that "America should always welcome some immigrants." For a nation of immigrants, it is a tough question.

"Poorly paid officials must make decisions that would stump a professor of ethics."

NATHAN GLAZER, SOCIAL SCIENTIST

INTERACT WITH HISTORY

1. **INTERPRETING DATA** Using the graph of immigration and the time line, explain what particular events caused changes in immigration rates over time.
2. **FORMING OPINIONS** Should legal immigration be restricted? If so, what restrictions would you place? Support your answer with facts.

SEE SKILLBUILDER HANDBOOK, PAGE 919.

Visit http://www.mlushistory.com for more about immigration.

HISTORY FROM VISUALS

The Oath of Allegiance

Reading the Document Have students read the oath of allegiance on page 882. Ask them why the person must swear to "take this obligation freely without any mental reservation or purpose of evasion." *Possible Response: To be sure that the person swearing allegiance really means it.*

Extension Ask students the following questions:

- What do they think is the most important part of this oath?
- Is there anything they think should be added to this oath?
- Should all native-born citizens be required to take a similar oath?

INTERACT WITH HISTORY

1. Interpreting Data

Possible Responses *The graph shows a dramatic drop in immigration just after 1920, probably due to the Emergency Quota Act of 1921, which limited immigration. The Immigration Act of 1965 loosened restrictions and led to a boom in immigration that continued for three decades. Students may also note an increase in the late 1940s, which they could ascribe to the end of World War II.*

2. Forming Opinions

Standards for Evaluation
Paragraphs should . . .

- explain clearly the action they recommend
- use details from the text that support their positions
- recognize the arguments of the opposing point of view and offer counterarguments to refute them

Crime and Public Safety

OBJECTIVES

1. To identify trends in crime rates and crime-prevention techniques.
2. To describe different points of view on crime-prevention techniques.

FOCUS & MOTIVATE

5-MINUTE WARM-UP

Interpreting Graphs
To examine the relationship between unemployment and crime, have students look at the two graphs on page 884 and answer these questions.

1. In which year was the crime rate the highest?
2. Did the crime rate increase during the same years the unemployment rate increased?

WARM-UP TRANSPARENCY EPILOGUE

▶ ***Starting with the Student*** Ask the students what they think is the single biggest problem facing the nation today. Tabulate the results on the chalkboard. If crime ranks first, ask the class why this is the case. If crime is not ranked first, ask why not.

HISTORY FROM VISUALS
Crime and Unemployment, 1974–1994
Reading the Graphs Point out to students that crime rates are based on reported crimes. What does that

(continued on next page)

Crime and Public Safety

LEARN ABOUT factors that affect the U.S. crime rate and efforts to reduce crime in the United States
TO UNDERSTAND public perceptions of crime in America and ideas for creating a safer future.

APPROACHING THE ISSUE Each day, it seems, television news reports and newspaper headlines give grisly details about yet another violent crime. These reports have an impact. When asked by pollsters, 83 percent of Americans say that crime is a big problem in society today, according to the December 1996 issue of *U.S. News & World Report.* And in a 1996 poll reported in *American Demographics,* a third of all teens believed they would be shot or stabbed in their lifetime. How bad is crime in the United States—and what can be done about it?

Historical Perspective

In 1968, opinion polls reported that for the first time, Americans called crime the nation's single worst problem. Since then, crime has remained high on the list of national problems.

Crime rates generally increased during the 1970s, due in part to civil unrest, protests against the Vietnam War, and Supreme Court decisions that made convictions more difficult. But in the 1980s, the spread of crack cocaine abuse fueled a major jump in crime. From 1986 to the early 1990s, the rates of violent crimes and car thefts increased by more than 20 percent.

Beginning in 1993, however, these rates began to drop. In 1995, the FBI announced that violent crimes had fallen 3.2 percent from the previous year. The murder rate declined 7.4 percent in that period.

Recent Success Against Crime

Crime statistics from New York City were the most encouraging. Crime dropped in every single police precinct in the city in 1994, 1995, and 1996. Rates fell so much that New York alone accounted for one-third of the drop nationwide.

Experts have identified a few causes for falling crime rates.

- First, there simply are fewer males aged 15 to 29, the group most likely to commit crimes.

Skillbuilder Answer The unemployment rate rose and fell significantly. The crime rate was relatively steady.

SKILLBUILDER
INTERPRETING GRAPHS
How did the crime rate differ from the unemployment rate from 1974 to 1994?

Crime and Unemployment, 1974–1994

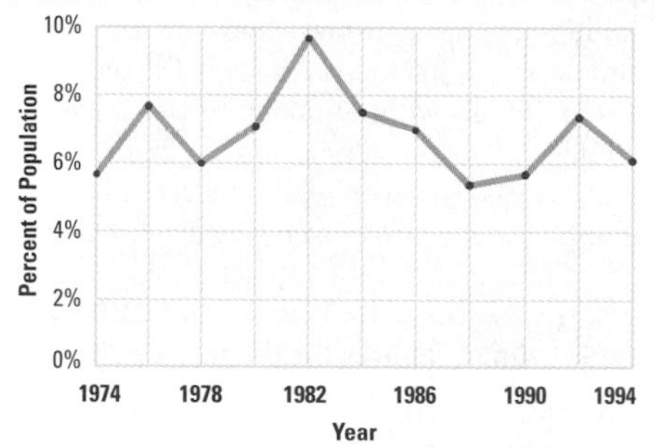

CRIME RATE

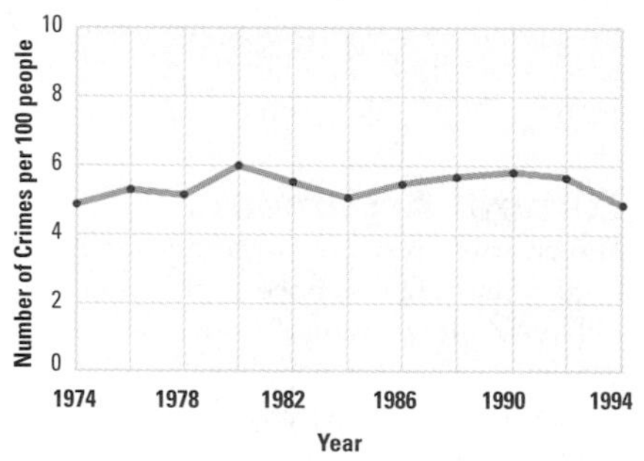

Sources: U.S. Bureau of Labor Statistics for unemployment rate; Federal Bureau of Investigation for crime rate.

History of Crime and Public Safety

UNITED STATES

- **1791** Second Amendment, protecting right to bear arms, is ratified as part of the Bill of Rights (page 74).
- **1844** New York City organizes first full-time, salaried police force (page 286).
- **1920s** Organized crime thrives because of Prohibition (page 455).
- **1968** Polls list crime as the most important domestic problem; President Nixon promises to restore law and order (page 746).

TEACHING OPTIONS

Teaching Less Proficient Readers

Using Graphic Organizers The article includes many statistics, some of which seem to contradict each other. To help less proficient students grasp them, have them construct a chart with headings like these:

Crime Going Up	Crime Going Down

Have them write each statistic under the appropriate heading as they read through the article.

Making Connections Across the Curriculum

Government Criminologists offer several explanations for the causes of crime. Have students write a letter to a member of the state or federal legislature that offers their own views and cites criminologists' explanations on how to reduce crime. For guidelines on how to write a persuasive letter, see Expressing a Political Opinion on page 113 in the Citizenship Handbook. Their letter should . . .

- describe the criminologists' views on the causes of crime
- explain why they think this is the case
- suggest laws or other actions that could solve the problem

Some communities have tested the effectiveness of police officers on bicycles, like these two in Alexandria, Virginia. Officials hope that officers on bicycles will encourage more community interaction with the police.

- Second, the trade in crack cocaine slowed.
- Third, the unemployment rate gradually decreased in the mid-1990s. Generally, when more people have jobs, crime rates fall.

NEW POLICING EFFORTS But the biggest factor seems to be new policing efforts. Police departments have taken officers out of patrol cars and put them back on the streets, walking a beat. They have taken a more active role in the neighborhood. In some communities, police emphasize a tough policy aimed at getting criminals off the street. In others, such as New Haven, Connecticut, they aim to *prevent* crime. Nicholas Pastore, chief of the New Haven police, sums up this view.

> A PERSONAL VOICE
> Arrest is a sign of failure. We try to identify those kids who are in greatest danger [of committing crimes] and throw everything the system has to offer at them.
> **NICHOLAS PASTORE,** chief, New Haven police

Such preventive crime methods usually include counseling and community outreach programs, an intense effort by those involved to intervene in young lives before a crime has occurred.

Public Alarm Remains

If crime has fallen so much, why do people still worry about it? Despite the decreases, rates are still very high. The murder rate in 1994 (9 victims for every 100,000 people in the population) far exceeds the 1965 rate (5.1 per 100,000). In addition, prison populations are soaring. Just over 200,000 people served time in prison in 1974. In 1995, the number topped 1 million—a five-fold increase.

Some observers also say that media coverage promotes widespread fear of crime. The Center for Media and Public Affairs studied national news broadcasts. Its researchers found that in 1995 the three networks ran 375 stories about murders—four times the number shown in 1990, when the murder rate was higher. A poll reinforced these findings. When asked *why* they called crime a problem, 76 percent of people polled named media reports.

"Arrest is a sign of failure."

NICHOLAS PASTORE, POLICE CHIEF

Continuing Efforts Against Crime

Crime, then, continues to command attention. Debate rages over whether crime rates will increase again. Also, experts split over two issues related to reducing crime further: gun control and tougher sentencing. →

Efforts to reduce juvenile crime include improved education for students like these at the California Youth Authority School.

1980s Increased drug abuse contributes to rising crime (page 828).

1993 Brady Act aims to reduce the spread of handguns.

1994 Republicans include tougher crime-prevention laws in their Contract with America (page 849).

1997 Supreme Court rules that certain provisions of the Brady Act are unconstitutional.

(continued from page 884)

suggest about the statistics? *Possible Response: The actual incidence of crime is probably somewhat higher since some crimes may go unreported.*

OBJECTIVE ① **INSTRUCT**

▶ ***Discussing Key Ideas***
- Crime rates fall dramatically in the early 1990s.
- Demographic and economic trends as well as new policing techniques contribute to the decrease in crime.
- People still see crime as a major problem, partly as a result of extensive crime coverage in the media.

HISTORY FROM VISUALS

Reading the Image Have students look at the photograph of the police officers. Ask them whether they think having police officers on bicycles or walking the streets instead of riding in patrol cars would have any impact on crime. What are their reasons for their beliefs?

Extension Have students devise their own suggestions for improving police efforts, both in terms of reducing crime and developing better relations with members of the community.

TEACHING OPTIONS

Making Connections Across the Curriculum

Civics Invite a police officer to the class to discuss issues related to crime in your community. Have students prepare questions beforehand. These questions might include: What are the crime trends in the community in recent years? Is the police department taking any steps toward community policing? If so, how? Have these approaches been effective in reducing crime? What should civilians do to help reduce crime? What problems—legal, economic, social, or political—make it most difficult for officers to effectively do their jobs?

Teaching Gifted and Talented Students

Conducting a Media Watch Ask students to evaluate local or national news broadcasts for one week to see how much media attention is given to crime news. They should compare the total time devoted to crime stories to the total time occupied by the news as a whole. They may also want to consider which kind of stories—on crime or other subjects—are used as the teaser before a commercial. Have them present their findings to the class.

OBJECTIVE

② INSTRUCT

▶ ***Starting with the Student***
Ask students what they think about the quotation by the Justice Department official on page 886.

- How do they see the incidence of violence among their peers?
- How easy is it for young people to get weapons?
- How likely are they to use weapons?

▶ ***Discussing Key Ideas***

- Some criminologists argue that a new crime wave will occur around 2005 when large numbers of children reach their teens.
- People debate whether the Second Amendment prevents the government from limiting Americans' access to guns and whether gun control is effective in fighting crime.
- Some analysts believe that the best way to fight crime is to give tougher sentences to convicted criminals.
- Several terrorist bombings in the mid-1990s raised fears of a surge in terrorist attacks.

Many police departments are working to hire more ethnic and racial minorities as well as women—as can be seen in this group of academy graduates in Miami, Florida.

"Instead of fists, youths today are settling their battles with bullets."

JUSTICE DEPARTMENT OFFICIAL

A NEW CRIME WAVE? Some social scientists agree with James Alan Fox, dean of Northeastern University's College of Criminal Justice, who predicts that a new crime wave is just over the horizon. They note that while the overall murder rate has declined since 1990, the rate among 14- to 17-year olds rose 22 percent in the same period. Indeed, from 1985 to 1994, the murder rate among that age group shot up 172 percent. Teens have been involved increasingly in other violent crimes as well. Combining these statistics with population trends produces, for some analysts, ominous results. There were about 39 million children under 10 in the late 1990s. By 2005, they will reach their teens. Criminologist Fox has sounded a warning.

A PERSONAL VOICE

So long as we fool ourselves into thinking that we're winning the war against crime, we may be blindsided by this bloodbath of teenage violence that is lurking in the future.

JAMES ALAN FOX, criminologist

Rising rates of drug abuse increase concerns over the future of this group. After falling for many years, drug-related arrests began to climb again in 1991. More significant, use of drugs by 12- to 17-year-olds doubled in the early 1990s.

However, some analysts dispute the dire predictions of rising crime rates. Franklin Zimring of the University of California, Berkeley, points out that the share of teens in the population in 2010—5.9 percent—will not be much higher than it was in 1994, 5.4 percent.

Zimring continues, "It's not the number of kids we have in the population, it's the lethal crime rate that is the problem." To reduce crime, gun-control advocates urge stricter controls on handguns.

GUN CONTROL In 1993, President Bill Clinton signed the Brady Act. The act was named for a former White House official, James Brady, seriously wounded in 1981 by a man who was shooting at President Reagan. The law called for states to place a five-day waiting period on the sale of handguns. During that period, police check the potential buyer's background. If they find a criminal record, a gun permit is denied. Many states and local communities have passed similar laws, aimed to slow the spread of handguns. Some observers credit these gun-control laws for subsequent drops in the crime rate. According to one report, police in four cities that have witnessed dropping homicide rates believe that local anti-gun laws have been a major cause.

The National Rifle Association (NRA), which is opposed to tougher gun-control laws, takes a different view. First, the NRA claims that the Brady Act itself has a minimal impact on reducing crime because it does not apply to states and municipalities that have their own gun laws. And it is these areas—including 28 states and Washington, D.C.—in which 75% of all violent crimes occur. At any rate, in June 1997, the Supreme Court ruled that the federal government could not force state or local officials to run background checks on potential buyers of handguns, thus weakening the law.

At the center of the gun-control issue lies a constitutional debate. The Second Amendment to the Constitution, ratified in 1791, states "A well-regulated militia being necessary to the security of a free state, the right of the people to keep and bear arms shall not be infringed." The NRA argues that gun-control laws violate this right. Others contend that the amendment was not intended to guarantee a right to personal weapons. Rather, its purpose is to protect "the state's right to maintain organized military units." This argument over the interpretation of the Second Amendment has stirred heated debate and is likely to continue.

Block Schedule TEACHING OPTION **Time Needed: 40 Minutes**

Cooperative Activity: Creating a Database on Crime

Task: Students will collect data on crime in their community.

Purpose: To help students understand the complexity of the issue of crime.

Activity: Have groups of four or five students conduct research to collect different types of data relating to crime in their community. One student might search the Internet for statistics on changes in the local crime rate, including changes in the types of crime that have been committed. Another student might search the library for judicial decisions on police practices. A third student might interview police officers and local community leaders to find how they try to address issues of crime.

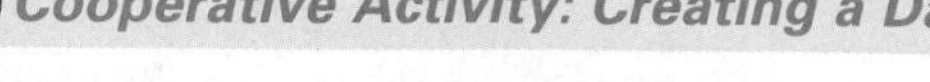

Building a Portfolio: Students should collect their findings into a well-organized database and place it in a folder in their portfolio.

ALTERNATIVE ASSESSMENT BOOK
Standards for Evaluating a Cooperative Activity

Standards for Evaluation
Databases should . . .

- organize data in a clear and comprehensible manner
- display statistical data in tables, charts, and graphs
- include textual data—such as interviews, speeches, articles—filed in an organized manner for future reference

GETTING TOUGH ON CRIME A headline in the conservative journal *National Review* sums up one position on crime: "Catch 'Em, Lock 'Em Up." William Bennett, former secretary of education and once head of the nation's antidrug effort, stated the position clearly.

A PERSONAL VOICE

Most prisoners are violent or repeat offenders. Prisons do cut crime.

WILLIAM BENNETT, former U.S. secretary of education

Social scientist James Q. Wilson points to Great Britain, where officials introduced a policy of more lenient prison sentences. Since then, burglary and auto theft rates have increased.

A 1982 article by Wilson and George L. Kelling offered what has been called the "broken windows" theory. By allowing minor crimes—vandalism, graffiti, public drinking—they said, police officials created an atmosphere that encouraged more serious crimes. By cracking down on these minor violations, police can raise the quality of life in an area and help reduce more serious crime.

To take a tough stand against crime, the federal government and many states have passed "three strikes" laws. Under these laws, any person found guilty of two earlier crimes receives a stiff sentence after conviction for a third. Chief Pastore dislikes these three-strikes laws. He charges that criminals fearful of getting caught a third time have become more likely to shoot police officers pursuing them.

Some experts charge that the get-tough policy suffers from another serious problem: racial bias. Although African Americans make up only 7 percent of California's population—and 20 percent of felony arrests—blacks account for 43 percent of those serving three-strikes sentences. Similar patterns are found nationwide. Blacks represent just 12 percent of the U.S. population and about 13 percent of those who reported using illegal drugs on a monthly basis. Yet three-quarters of all prison sentences for possession of drugs involve African Americans. Many analysts say that such differential treatment must end.

TERRORISM To complicate matters, a new form of violent crime is beginning to affect Americans—terrorism. In the mid-1990s, a series of terrorist bombings drew national attention, including the bombing of the World Trade Center in 1994, the 1995 Oklahoma City bombing, and the bombing at Centennial Park in Atlanta during the 1996 Olympics.

As a result, the federal government is beefing up efforts to prevent domestic terrorism. In April 1997, President Clinton signed a bill broadening the powers of the FBI to fight terrorism. But civil liberties groups and Republicans leery of handing more power to the federal government have fought some of the provisions of these bills such as expanded wiretapping authority.

While most people recognize the government's role in protecting public safety, few people agree on exactly how to achieve it. Americans will surely continue to struggle with these issues of criminal justice and civil liberties into the 21st century.

"Catch 'Em, Lock 'Em Up"

NATIONAL REVIEW HEADLINE

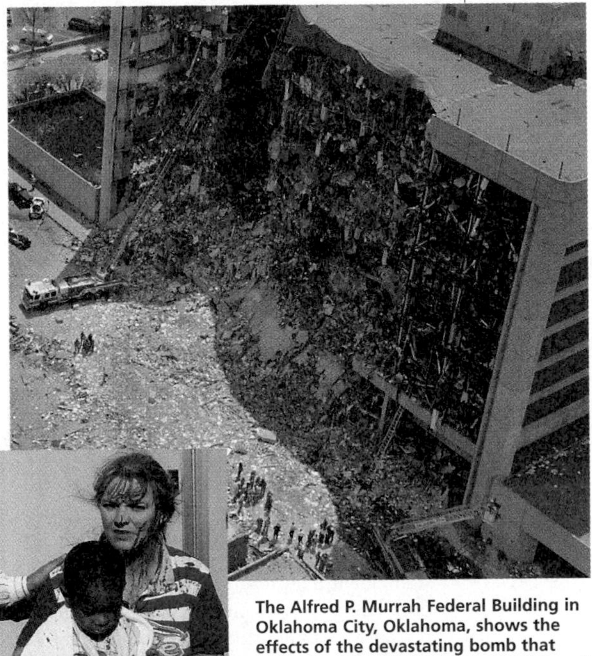

The Alfred P. Murrah Federal Building in Oklahoma City, Oklahoma, shows the effects of the devastating bomb that exploded there on April 19, 1995 (*above*). An injured woman holds a child who was also hurt in the blast (*below*).

INTERACT WITH HISTORY

1. **FINDING MAIN IDEAS** Recap the arguments for and against gun control, using references to the text.
2. **FORMING OPINIONS** Are tough prison sentences a good idea or not? Explain.

SEE SKILLBUILDER HANDBOOK, PAGES 911 AND 919.

Visit http://www.mlushistory.com for more about crime.

HISTORY FROM VISUALS

Reading the Photographs Have students look at the photographs of the Murrah Federal Building in Oklahoma City. Ask students if they think that media coverage of such events has any impact on terrorism. *Possible Responses: By giving prominence to the terrorists, it might encourage others to undertake similar attacks. Conversely, it might decrease the opportunity for terrorist acts by forcing authorities to increase security measures.*

Extension Ask students to discuss the issue of terrorism:

- How concerned are they about a possible terrorist attack?
- What powers are they willing to give authorities to seek out terrorists and prevent these attacks?

MORE ABOUT . . .
"Three Strikes" Laws

A report issued in 1996 found that while the federal government and 22 states have "three strikes" laws on the books, these laws are rarely applied. From 1994—when the federal law was passed—to 1996, the federal courts used these provisions only 9 times. Although California has applied the law extensively, no other state has. Officials in the criminal justice system say that the three-strike provisions are not needed because other existing laws punish criminals adequately.

INTERACT WITH HISTORY

1. Finding Main Ideas

Possible Responses *For gun control—The widespread availability of guns makes the streets more dangerous. The only way to reduce that danger is to limit access to guns.*

Against gun control—Americans have a constitutional right to bear arms. Gun control laws have little effect on criminals who can get weapons in other ways.

2. Forming Opinions

Possible Responses *Good idea—Tough sentences are a good idea because they send a message to criminals. Crime in England went up when sentences became more lenient.*

Bad idea—Tough sentences are not a good idea because they put people who committed minor crimes in prison with hardened criminals. The minor criminals then learn violent behavior and leave prison to commit even worse crimes.

Exploring Education Today

OBJECTIVES

1. To describe attempts to reform American public education.
2. To examine the issues of affirmative action and financing in education.

FOCUS & MOTIVATE

5-Minute Warm-Up

Interpreting Graphs To examine how the public views educational issues, have students look at the graph on page 889 and answer these questions.

1. Do you agree more with the views of the teachers or those of the public?
2. Which of the problems listed do you think is the most important?

WARM-UP TRANSPARENCY EPILOGUE

▶ ***Starting with the Student*** Have students give a grade—by secret ballot—to the education they received through the eighth grade. Did their schooling prepare them well for high school? What do they think could have been done better?

Exploring Education Today

LEARN ABOUT the problems that have arisen in many U.S. public school systems
TO UNDERSTAND the changes proposed to address those problems.

APPROACHING THE ISSUE The warning was clear. In 1983, the National Commission on Excellence in Education gave the nation's schools a failing grade. "The educational foundations of our society," its report said, "are presently being eroded by a rising tide of mediocrity that threatens our very future." The commission underscored the danger with the report's title: *A Nation at Risk.*

"The educational foundations of our society are . . . being eroded."

FROM *A NATION AT RISK*

Parents, political leaders, educators, and students all commented on the commission's report. In the years since the report, states and localities have tried many different approaches to improve American education. Yet a 1996 poll of parents and teachers (see the graph on the next page) identified continuing problems—and some new ones. What reform efforts have been tried? What are the advantages and disadvantages of these programs?

Historical Perspective

From the earliest days of the nation, American leaders stressed the importance of education. Thomas Jefferson wrote, "No other sure foundation can be devised for the preservation of freedom" than education. In the 19th century, reformers helped establish a system of government-supported public schools. By 1900, almost three-quarters of all eight- to fourteen-year-olds attended school. Even with these advances, some groups suffered. Public secondary education failed to reach most African Americans in the early 20th century, for instance. Not until 1954, with the Supreme Court decision in *Brown* v. *Board of Education of Topeka,* did federal court decisions call for an end to separate—usually inferior—schools for blacks.

In the 1960s, however, the nation's schools wrestled with severe problems. While more and more students attended college, overall achievement levels began to drop. Students in inner cities often entered decaying buildings and used dated materials. Meanwhile, many students in suburbs enjoyed new facilities and equipment. Violence and drugs in the schools raised issues of safety. Integrating white and minority students was easier to achieve on paper than in reality. By the time the National Commission on Excellence was formed, American education seemed to have reached a crisis.

The Key Issues

The debate on public education has focused on three key issues. First is the question of how to change schools to improve the quality of education. Second is the issue of school financing. Should different school systems in a state receive equal funding? The third issue has to do with affirmative action—programs intended to remedy past discrimination.

Improving Quality

People have offered many ideas on how to improve schools. Some critics say that lack of discipline is a major problem. A few of those critics have gone so far as to urge schools to require school uniforms to end fights that result from students wearing clothes with gang colors.

President Bill Clinton has backed the school uniform idea. He has also called for all schools in the country to be connected to the

History of Education
UNITED STATES

1821 Emma Willard opens Troy Female Seminary, an academic school for girls (page 156).

1837 Horace Mann begins push to spread public education.

1865 African Americans who had been slaves begin to create and attend schools (page 196).

1954 Supreme Court, in *Brown* v. *Board of Education,* rules segregated schools unconstitutional (page 698).

TEACHING OPTIONS

Making Connections Across the Curriculum

Civics Education is a matter of local jurisdiction. States have the power to establish school systems, and local communities have a great deal of authority in running their schools. The desire of parents and local leaders to maintain that control has kept federal involvement to a minimum. Of the $300 billion spent on K-12 public education, state and local governments contribute about 47 percent each. The remaining 6 percent—about $18 billion—comes from the federal government.

Teaching Less Proficient Readers

Making a Graphic Organizer Have students make a chart like the one below to help them organize information about the various ideas for improving education:

Proposal	Advantages	Disadvantages

As they read the text, they should fill in the appropriate information on each reform idea.

Long Beach, California, middle school students display their school uniforms.

Internet and its vast supply of information. Velma Walker, Director of the Office of Advanced Technology for the Detroit public schools, agrees.

A PERSONAL VOICE

If we elect to withhold telecommunications availability; worry about the fact that technology is changing so quickly; wait until prices go down . . . classrooms are renovated . . . we will inadvertently contribute to creating a class of "have-nots."

VELMA WALKER, educator

CHARTER SCHOOLS One reform receiving growing support is "charter schools." In this plan, certain schools receive a charter, or contract, from the state and offer innovations in education. In return for freedom to operate as they choose, charter schools promise to increase students' achievement levels. By the mid-1990s, about 450 such schools were in place in more than half the states.

A *Brookings Review* analysis of charter schools released in January 1996 describes their advantages. Charters may improve education because teachers, parents, and students are all committed to the educational philosophy of the school. And a 1995 study by the Education Commission of the States concludes that about half of the charter schools studied helped at-risk students, who needed help the most. This review also points out some drawbacks to charter schools. Noting that these schools are all relatively new, the report questions whether the staff can maintain its enthusiasm over time. Because many charter schools are operated as businesses, poor management can destroy them. Finally, most charter schools have small facilities and offer few extracurricular activities. →

Poll Results: What's Wrong with Schools?

Percentage (0–25)

	Teachers	Public
Lack of proper financial support	22%	13%
Lack of discipline	20%	15%
Pupils' lack of interest/ attitudes/truancy	16%	5%
Lack of family structure/ problems of home life	15%	4%
Use of drugs	7%	16%
Fighting/violence/gangs	7%	14%
Overcrowded schools	7%	8%

Source: Langdon, "Third Phi Delta Kappan Poll," *Phi Delta Kappan*, November 1996, pp. 245-46.

SKILLBUILDER

INTERPRETING GRAPHS

On what issue do teachers and the public disagree most? Why do you think this is so?

Skillbuilder Answer The public and teachers disagree most over pupil's lack of interest and lack of family structure. Students' opinions will vary.

1965	1983	1989	1996
Federal government begins providing aid to public schools (page 686).	Commission report *A Nation at Risk* severely criticizes public education (page 829).	Education summit issues Goals 2000 (page 829).	California voters ban affirmative action in education and other areas.

OBJECTIVE

1 INSTRUCT

Discussing Key Ideas

- A presidential commission states that the poor quality of education in America "threatens our very future."
- School uniforms, charter schools, and increased use of technology offer potential solutions to the problems that schools face.

HISTORY FROM VISUALS

Poll Results: What's Wrong with Schools?

Reading the Graph

On what problem do teachers and parents come closest to agreement? *Overcrowding.*

Extension Ask students to give their own rankings to these reasons given for problems in the schools:

- Lack of funding
- Outdated materials, equipment, and facilities
- Lack of discipline in the classroom
- Use of drugs
- Fighting, violence, or gang problems
- Overcrowding

Tabulate the results on the board and discuss them in class. What can students themselves do to help rectify these problems? What other problems do they believe hinder education?

TEACHING OPTION

Making Connections Across Cultures

International Performance on Math and Science Tests

One concern held by educators and the public at large is the performance of American students compared to students in other countries. The Third International Mathematics and Science Study compared the achievement scores of American eighth graders in math and science to those of comparable students around the world. The average score of U.S. students was 500 compared to an international average of 513. Twenty countries had a higher average score than the United States; seven had a lower score.

In science, the picture was somewhat better. The U.S. average score of 534 was higher than the international average of 516, although it still placed in the middle of the pack. Students from Singapore scored highest of all countries on both tests. Japanese students were third best on both tests. These scores resulted despite the fact that Japanese students have less homework than their American counterparts and watch just as much television. The difference, the study said, was in both content and methods. Japanese students are given a more rigorous course of study and taught to solve problems first and then discuss them.

OBJECTIVE

② INSTRUCT

▶ ***Starting with the Student***

- Ask students how—if at all—state and federal governments should fund and regulate local school districts.
- Ask students what role parents play in developing a school system that provides quality education.

▶ ***Discussing Key Ideas***

- Some people argue that school funding should be reformed through the use of vouchers.
- Some reformers want to equalize the amount of money spent in different school districts.
- Affirmative-action programs increase the number of women and minorities on college campuses, but recent court decisions have endangered those programs.

THE DEBATE OVER VOUCHERS Economist Milton Friedman first proposed a voucher system in a 1955 academic article. Since then, Friedman's proposal has received growing support on many fronts. In a voucher system, states issue a certificate worth several thousand dollars to parents, who then give it to a school of their choice. The school exchanges the voucher for payment from the government. Friedman believes that parents will seek schools that provide higher-quality education. Public schools will then be forced to compete with private and parochial schools, and with one another. The competition should increase the overall quality of education, supporters argue.

In 1990, Wisconsin adopted the nation's first voucher plan. Studies of the Milwaukee program showed parents very satisfied with the schools chosen. However, experts could not agree on whether the students involved actually improved in achievement.

Another debate rages over the question of who receives vouchers. William Miller, of the Institute for Justice, disagrees with Friedman's universal approach. He says that vouchers should only go to poorer families, whose children most acutely need school alternatives.

16A SUNDAY, SEPTEMBER 10, 1995 MILWAUKEE JOURNAL SENTINEL

Choice may redefine constitutional guarantee

U.S. Supreme court likely to rule on dispute over religious aspect

SCHMOKE ON Baltimore's bl

School Choice offers children hope for success

Under a voucher system, parents can choose to send their children to a private or parochial school as an alternative to their neighborhood public school.

GOALS 2000 Other reform proposals focus on what students should be learning. A 1989 education summit attended by the nation's governors and President George Bush produced a series of education goals to be achieved by the year 2000. The Goals 2000 plan established a panel to review progress toward these goals, many of which cannot be met, the group said, unless "states and local communities demand more from their students by setting rigorous standards for student achievement."

Financing Education

Some critics disagree with the emphasis on standards. Jonathan Kozol, a teacher and writer, blames the failures of American education on the fact that schools receive unequal resources.

> A PERSONAL VOICE
>
> Slogans, standards and exams do not teach reading. If all kids are to be judged by equal standards . . . then every one of them deserves an equal opportunity to meet them.
>
> **JONATHAN KOZOL,** educator

To Kozol, that means giving more money to poorer schools to equalize the expenditures for each pupil.

SCHOOLS AND TAXES In most states, school funding relies on property taxes—taxes paid on the value of real estate. Property taxes have the benefit of con-sistency over time, unlike sales taxes. Sales tax revenues can go up or down as the economy enjoys booms or bad times. Sales taxes are also regressive—they hit people with less income more heavily than they do people with more income, because poor people spend a larger proportion of their income on things subject to sales taxes.

Sales taxes are usually paid to the state, while property taxes go to local governments. When schools are funded primarily by property taxes, schools in poorer areas receive much less money than those in wealthier sections. According to the magazine *Washington Monthly*, one New Jersey town spends $13,394 per pupil on schooling. Another town just five miles away spends only $7,889. Court cases have raised legal challenges to unequal school funding in more than 20 states.

Meanwhile, in 1993, Michigan voters approved a plan that abandoned local property taxes as the basis of school funding. Now schools get their money from a smaller state-controlled property tax, an increased sales tax on consumer purchases, and increased taxes on purchases of such items as cigarettes and alcohol. Because the state sets property tax rates and monitors its school systems' budgets, it can even out inequalities.

Mike Casserly of the Council for Great City Schools likes the idea of taking funding away from communities and giving it to states to fix inequalities. He insists, however, that local school systems control how that money is spent.

TEACHING OPTIONS

Making Connections Across the Curriculum

Economics One economic question that arises from the issue of school financing is that of investment. Education is an important part of economic growth. When people are better educated and highly skilled, they are more productive and make themselves and everyone else wealthier. Nevertheless, people disagree on how to raise money for schools. Some people would like to see more money invested in education—to raise teachers' salaries, buy computers and textbooks, or construct better schools—in order to help students learn more and become more productive workers. Other people feel that taxes are already too high and argue that more money won't improve education.

Teaching Gifted and Talented Students

Making a Poster About Vouchers Have students make a poster that supports or opposes the idea of school vouchers. Students could use the library or Internet to research the issue further before deciding on their position regarding vouchers. Posters should . . .

- take a clear position on the issue
- give a convincing argument for their position
- use images and words in interesting ways

Affirmative Action

Starting with *Brown* v. *Board of Education* in 1954, federal courts ruled that school systems could not have separate schools for African Americans. Nevertheless, discrimination against blacks in education and employment continued. In response, President Lyndon Johnson issued Executive Order 11246 in September 1965. It required groups that did business with the federal government to take "affirmative action" to remedy the past discrimination against African Americans. Later, the policy came to include women and other minorities.

From the beginning, most Americans backed the idea of programs that gave women and minorities new opportunities. At the same time, a large majority disapproved of quotas, the setting aside of a certain number of jobs or college admissions for members of these groups.

This point became the focus of a court case challenging affirmative action. In the 1970s, Allan Bakke had twice been rejected by the medical school at the University of California, Davis, which instead admitted a number of minority students who had lower grades and test scores. Bakke argued that his rights had been denied. The Supreme Court, in *Regents of the University of California* v. *Bakke* (1978), ruled that the school had to admit Bakke—but also said that institutions could use race as one factor among others in determining admission.

Allan Paul Bakke successfully challenged the affirmative-action admission quotas of the medical school at the University of California at Davis.

Recently, however, a lower federal court issued a new ruling that challenged the *Bakke* decison. In *Hopwood* v. *Texas*, a federal judge ruled that a university could not legally have separate admissions tracks for white and minority candidates. The University of Texas Law School had used such a system to increase the number of minority students. But the court said that such a plan discriminates against nonminority students. The Supreme Court chose not to review the decision. Based on this new standard, colleges and universities across the country began reviewing their admissions policies.

In 1996, California was the site of a dispute over this issue. That year, voters passed an initiative that banned race or gender preferences in college admissions. According to *Science* magazine, "the percentage of black, Hispanic, and American Indian students in future freshman classes is expected to be halved."

George E. C. Hayes, Thurgood Marshall, and James Nabrit led the legal fight against segregation in *Brown* v. *Board of Education of Topeka* in 1954.

Opponents of affirmative action argue that it is not fair to use gender or race as the basis for decisions about jobs or college admissions. As former U.S. Representative Susan Molinari says, "Our country has long believed that people should be measured on their own merit." Jorge Amselle of the Center for Equal Opportunity argues, "We will never have a race-neutral society, as long as government continues to categorize people by race." But Frank Wu, a professor at Harvard Law School, dismisses this argument.

A PERSONAL VOICE

While no doubt "reverse discrimination" against whites occurs occasionally, regular discrimination against African Americans remains much more prevalent.

FRANK WU, professor, Harvard Law School

Sheila Jackson Lee, a U.S. representative from Texas, agrees with Wu, noting that "antidiscrimination laws are not sufficient to remedy the structural racial and gender discrimination that persists in our society today."

Clearly, the issue of how to reform American public education—and how to guarantee equal educational access for all—will continue to be the subject of debate for some time to come.

"Our country has long believed that people should be measured on their own merit."

SUSAN MOLINARI, FORMER MEMBER OF CONGRESS

INTERACT WITH HISTORY

1. **ANALYZING ISSUES** Discuss the advantages and disadvantages of the charter schools and vouchers. Do you agree that these plans can help improve public education? Explain why or why not.
2. **EVALUATING DECISIONS** In its *Bakke* decision, the Supreme Court struck down quotas for minorities but approved the use of race as one factor in deciding college admissions. Write an evaluation of that decision, explaining whether it was fair or unfair.

SEE SKILLBUILDER HANDBOOK, PAGES 916 AND 918.

INTERNET Visit http://www.mlushistory.com for more about education.

MORE ABOUT . . .
Affirmative Action

Dinesh D'Souza of the American Enterprise Institute, a conservative think tank, spoke in 1996 on the issue of affirmative action. He identified four basic alternative approaches that policy analysts offer to address the problem of discrimination in education:

- Use preferences in admissions and hiring decisions to achieve "proportional representation" of women and minorities in all areas of life.
- Abolish preferences except for African Americans, who require action to combat a long history of discrimination.
- End all preferences based on gender or race but allow programs that promote the participation of people who are economically disadvantaged.
- Allow steps to achieve proportional representation in government practices, but have no such programs in the private sector.

INTERACT WITH HISTORY

1. Analyzing Issues

Possible Responses *Charter schools: Advantages—can be suited to local needs, have committed participants, and give help to at-risk students. Disadvantages—loss of fervor over time, prospect of failure due to mismanagement, lack of facilities and extracurricular programs.*

Vouchers: Advantages—giving help to poorer families to find alternatives to public schools. Disadvantages—uncertainty over who should qualify for vouchers.

Agree or Disagree: Charter schools can be beneficial for those who attend but will not necessarily help all schools. Vouchers are an economic aid but may not improve quality.

2. Evaluating Decisions

Possible Response *The Bakke decision walked a fine line between upholding and overturning affirmative action. In striking down set-asides for minorities, though, the Court made it difficult for affirmative-action programs to work.*

Curing the Health Care System

OBJECTIVES

1. To explain the development of government-sponsored health programs.
2. To analyze the problem of people who do not have health insurance.

FOCUS & MOTIVATE

5-Minute Warm-Up

Recognizing Facts and Details
To explore the history of government-sponsored health programs in America, have students look at the time line on pages 892–893 and answer these questions.

1. Who was president when Medicare was established?
2. Which was established first—Medicaid or the Department of Health, Education, and Welfare?

WARM-UP TRANSPARENCY EPILOGUE

▶ **Starting with the Student** Have the class create a web diagram that presents the words and ideas they think of when they hear the term "health care." You can begin the diagram on the chalkboard in this way:

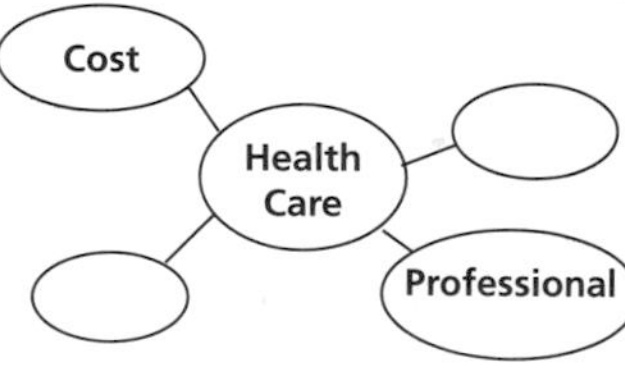

Curing the Health Care System

LEARN ABOUT the status of health care reform in the United States
TO UNDERSTAND the issues involved in providing health care to Americans.

APPROACHING THE ISSUE In his first term, President Bill Clinton declared that the health care system was in crisis. He urged Congress to pass a law guaranteeing health insurance for all Americans. Congress refused. By his second term, Clinton had abandoned that goal. But the question still remains whether a health care crisis exists in the United States. If so, what should be done about it?

Historical Perspective

In 1945, President Harry Truman first proposed universal health insurance, but Congress failed to enact it. It took the legislative skill of President Lyndon B. Johnson to enact Medicare in 1965. The program covered most of the cost of medical care for people over age 65.

Fast forward to the 1990s. Medicare and Medicaid (which covers the cost of medical care for the poor) take a greater share of federal spending. A sluggish economy in the early 1990s had Americans worried about soaring health care costs. The spread of the AIDS virus raised public alarm over how to meet the needs of the desperately ill. Hoping both to control costs and provide universal coverage, Clinton proposed a complex plan. However, lobbying by private insurers and the public's mistrust of big government programs killed the plan in Congress in 1994.

Many senior Americans, like these cyclists in Sun City, Arizona, have begun to get more exercise in order to stay healthy.

Health Care Reform Today

As the economy picked up, public anxiety over health care seemed to subside. Health care costs rose at a slower rate. And in 1996, a new law removed another concern. In the past, many Americans hesitated to change jobs because they were afraid of losing their health insurance. They could be denied coverage for *preexisting conditions*—medical conditions that are present when a person enters an insurance program. The Health Insurance Portability and Accountability Act of 1996 required insurers to provide coverage to new employees who had had health insurance before changing jobs.

Many Americans embraced this reform, but analysts pointed to growing problems with Medicare and Medicaid and with the number of uninsured Americans.

Medicare and Medicaid

The outlook on Medicare is simple. If nothing changes, Medicare Part A, which covers hospitalization, may run out of money early in the 21st century. Part B, which pays for doctors and medical tests, will take a growing share of the federal budget. The reasons are rising costs and population changes.

Americans are living longer now than they were in 1965—more than 5 years longer on average. As a result, seniors form a greater proportion of the population than before. More elderly people drive up the cost of Medicare. At the same time, the revenues targeted to pay

History of Health Care
UNITED STATES

1948 Congress rejects President Truman's plan for universal health insurance (page 641).

1953 Department of Health, Education, and Welfare is established.

1965 President Johnson and Congress enact Medicare and Medicaid into law (page 686).

1970s President Nixon increases funding for Medicare and Medicaid (page 787).

TEACHING OPTIONS

Making Connections Across Cultures

Health Care in Other Countries The governments of many nations run their countries' health care systems, which are financed by taxes. In Sweden, patients pay small fees for visits. This system costs about 10 percent of the nation's gross national product (GNP), and taxes are high. The British system pays for all coverage. Costs are only 8 percent of Britain's GNP, but facilities need improvements and patients have long waits for surgery. In Canada, the government acts as an insurer for all residents. The system costs less than that of the United States, but patients have long waits for elective procedures and sometimes have to travel long distances to see specialists.

Teaching Less Proficient Readers

Identifying Problems and Possible Solutions Students who are less proficient readers can benefit by charting the causes and possible solutions for the Medicaid problem. Have them create a chart similar to the one below and write the appropriate ideas on the blank lines.

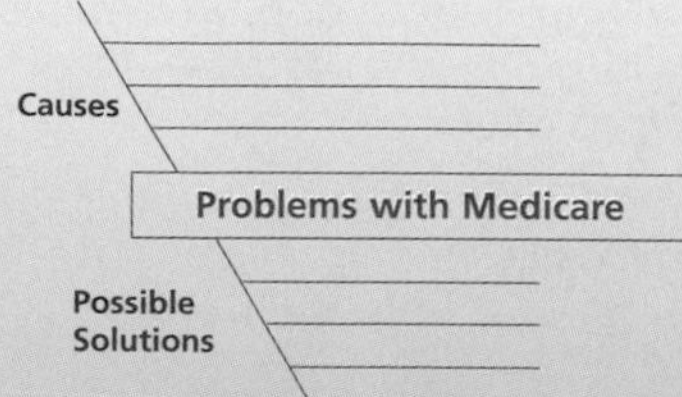

A Hispanic woman cuddles her daughter as they wait to see a pediatrician at Bellevue Hospital in New York City.

Medicare costs are expected to go down. As the population ages, fewer people will work and pay the taxes that fund Medicare. Today, five workers pay taxes for every person who receives Medicare. In 2030, only three workers will pay taxes per Medicare recipient. Workers' taxes will go up—especially if health costs continue to rise.

What is to be done? Medicare trustees say that Congress needs to boost the tax rate from 2.9 percent to 3.65 percent. The longer the delay, the greater the increase required. Another solution is to increase the share paid by the elderly. An older couple now pays more than $1,100 a year for Part B coverage. Increasing their premium can help fund the system. But some analysts point to the trade-offs.

A PERSONAL VOICE

Premiums already represent a significant burden for many elderly Americans. Any major hike risks pushing large numbers of the elderly into poverty.

DOUG BANDOW and MICHAEL TANNER, Cato Institute

Bandow and Tanner suggest raising the age of Medicare eligibility from 65 to 70.

MEDICAID Medicaid also faces an uncertain future. About 30 percent of annual Medicaid spending goes to the elderly poor. About half of all spending on elderly care in nursing homes comes from Medicaid. As the population ages, spending on Medicaid will increase. Also, recent changes in welfare laws may increase the number of poor people, which in turn will raise Medicaid costs.

The Uninsured Millions

The number of people without health insurance continues to rise (see the graph on this page). However, any thought of a government plan to guarantee coverage for those adults probably died with the Clinton plan in 1994.

It may be possible to lower the number of uninsured Americans, however. Some 10 million of the uninsured are children. Early in 1997, members of Congress from both parties joined to propose coverage for these "gap kids." They point out that health care for children is money well spent, and every dollar for preventive care saves $10 later. As Dr. Samuel Flint, head of the American Academy of Pediatrics, says, "If we have to make choices with limited resources, let's cover kids."

Uninsured Americans, 1980–1994

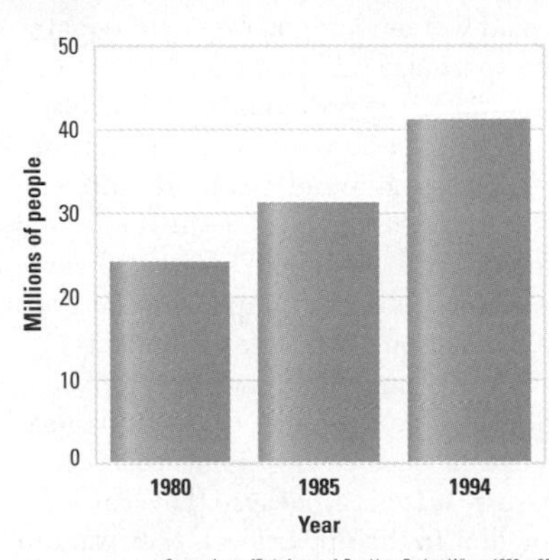

Source: Aaron, "End of an era," *Brookings Review*, Winter 1996, p.36

"Health care is too important for any modern society to permit many of its citizens to go without it."

HENRY J. AARON, DIRECTOR, BROOKINGS ECONOMIC STUDIES PROGRAM

SKILLBUILDER
INTERPRETING GRAPHS
What is the trend for the number of uninsured Americans? What factors do you think are contributing to this trend?

Skillbuilder Answer The numbers are rising. Students may mention higher health insurance costs and more part-time jobs.

INTERACT WITH HISTORY

1. **FINDING MAIN IDEAS** What factors are threatening the futures of Medicare and Medicaid?
2. **FORMING OPINIONS** Should the government provide coverage for the uninsured? If so, how should such a plan be funded?

SEE SKILLBUILDER HANDBOOK, PAGES 911 AND 919.

Visit http://www.mlushistory.com for more about health care.

1980 AIDS (Acquired Immune Deficiency Syndrome) is first identified, contributing to concerns over health care costs (pages 827–828).

1994 President Clinton's comprehensive health care bill fails to receive congressional approval (page 848).

1996 Congress passes Health Insurance Portability and Accountability Act (page 851).

INSTRUCT

▶ ***Discussing Key Ideas***
- President Bill Clinton's plan for health care reform fails.
- Analysts predict that Medicare and Medicaid will run short of money as fewer workers are available to support growing numbers of older people.
- Millions of people are without health insurance, but the government discusses measures to cover children.

HISTORY FROM VISUALS

Uninsured Americans, 1980–1994

Reading the Graph Ask students to find the rate of increase from 1980 (24 million people) to 1985 (31.3 million) and from 1985 to 1994 (41 million). Is the number of uninsured people rising more or less rapidly? *From 1980 to 1985, a period of 5 years, the number increased by 30 percent. From 1985 to 1994, a period of 9 years, the number increased by 31 percent. The number seems to be increasing at the slower rate—although the percentage increase is about the same, that increase took place over more years.*

Extension Have students do library or Internet research to find the number of uninsured people in the current year and calculate the percentage increase since 1994. Is the number growing more or less rapidly than before?

INTERACT WITH HISTORY

1. Finding Main Ideas

Possible Responses *The aging of the American population, with its higher health care costs; the expected decline in revenues targeted to pay for Medicare.*

2. Forming Opinions

Possible Responses *Responses will vary, but should show an understanding of the problems involved in providing health care coverage for all Americans.*

Women and the Glass Ceiling

OBJECTIVES

1. To describe obstacles to equality that women face in the workplace.
2. To examine the career gains women have made in the last few decades.

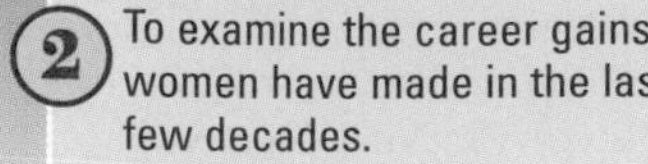

FOCUS & MOTIVATE

5-MINUTE WARM-UP

Recognizing Main Ideas
To consider the problems women face in the workplace, have students read Historical Perspective on page 894 and answer these questions.

1. What is the main idea of this passage?
2. What evidence supports this idea?

WARM-UP TRANSPARENCY EPILOGUE

▶ ***Starting with the Student*** Ask students what they think about the unequal representation of women in top-level corporate jobs.

- Should companies be required to provide more opportunities?
- Will women's positions gradually improve over time as the greater numbers of women now working inevitably rise in their careers?

Women and the Glass Ceiling

LEARN ABOUT women's representation at upper levels of the corporate ladder and their entry into new fields
TO UNDERSTAND issues of salary equity and upward mobility for women in the work force.

APPROACHING THE ISSUE In May 1996, *Working Woman* magazine passed on the following advice to women who want top business positions. It came from Catalyst, a nonprofit New York businesswomen's research and advocacy group: "Work harder than your male peers . . . and seek out difficult, high-visibility assignments. Oh—and your life outside the office? Kiss it goodbye."

"Work harder than your male peers."
CATALYST

Historical Perspective

In 1961, President John F. Kennedy named a commission to study the status of women in the workplace. Its report revealed that employers paid women less than men for equal work. The report also said that women were rarely promoted to top positions in their fields.

More than 30 years later, another presidential commission found that more women than ever before worked outside the home—46 percent. Yet women held only 10 percent of the most senior jobs in a sampling of the Fortune 500, the nation's 500 largest companies.

Some women who choose to pursue careers in business, government, or other organizations feel that a "glass ceiling" limits their career progress. It is glass because they can see through it to the upper levels they want to reach—but, like a ceiling, it stops them from rising higher.

Positive Trends

Women have made great strides in recent decades. For instance, they are entering new fields, including construction and such blue-collar jobs as equipment repair. In 1994, women held 9.3 percent of such jobs, up from 5.4 percent in 1974.

Women are also better represented in the academic world than ever before. M. R. C. Greenwood, a dean at the University of California at Davis, points out that in 1994, women received almost half of all the doctorate degrees issued by universities. According to Greenwood, more women are entering the sciences, a key to success in the high-tech industries of the future.

Nuala Beck, a consultant, sees better opportunities ahead for working women. She looks at trends among "knowledge workers"—managers, professionals, and those who use technology. In 1983, men in these jobs outnumbered women 3 to 2. In 1995, women had pulled almost even. The economy is moving toward industries that require these workers, and as a result, Beck says, the number of women in powerful positions will grow.

More and more women are developing careers in areas that used to be reserved for men—such as trading on the New York Stock Exchange (*below*).

History of Women at Work

UNITED STATES

1834	1850	1899	1900
Women working in Lowell, Massachusetts, textile mills strike (page 148).	One out of ten single white women works outside the home, earning half the pay of men to do the same job.	Average pay for women workers is $269 a year, compared with $498 for males (page 263).	One out of five women works outside the home (page 338).

Block Schedule TEACHING OPTION **Time Needed: 30 Minutes**

Cooperative Activity: Writing a Documentary Script

Task: To create a script for a documentary on the contemporary issues faced by working women.

Purpose: To understand the real life experiences of working women.

Activity: Divide the class into groups of 5 students. Have one student conduct research in the library or on the Internet to find statistical and narrative information about working women. Have the other students interview working women about their work experiences. When they have completed their interviews, have the students collaborate in writing a script that would provide the basis for a documentary on contemporary women and work.

Building a Portfolio: Have students save their scripts for their portfolio.

ALTERNATIVE ASSESSMENT BOOK
Standards for Evaluating a Cooperative Activity

Standards for Evaluation
Scripts should . . .

- Make connections between the experiences of the interviewees and the background research
- Use the evidence in the research and interviews to support a thesis on women and work

Money and Upward Mobility

Despite these positive signs, the key issues of unequal pay and unequal representation in top-level jobs remain.

SALARY DIFFERENCES In 1970, men earned an average of about three times what women earned. By the 1990s, the gap had narrowed. In 1993, the median income for women stood at $22,469, compared to $31,077 for men.

Kathleen Hall Jamieson, a university dean and author of *Beyond the Double Bind: Women and Leadership,* points out that even with unequal earnings, the story is not all bad.

> A PERSONAL VOICE
>
> Part-time work, time out of the labor force for childbearing and rearing, and a shorter work week account for some of the difference [in pay].
>
> **KATHLEEN HALL JAMIESON,** *Beyond the Double Bind: Women and Leadership*

Nevertheless, a survey by *Working Woman* found women's earnings trailing men's in career after career, as the chart at the right shows.

REACHING HIGHER As of 1997, women headed four major U.S. corporations. However, though women hold 10 percent of the senior jobs in Fortune 500 companies, only 2.4 percent held such elite positions as chief executive officer or president.

Why are women underrepresented in the top jobs? In one study, Catalyst asked male and female executives to comment on the issue of women heading companies. Almost 50 percent of male executives believed that the situation for women has greatly improved over five years ago. Only 23 percent of the women thought so.

Differences also arose over how to explain the situation. Male managers believed that women were held back because they lacked management experience and had not been in the work force long enough. However, most women executives blamed male stereotypes about women workers and the exclusion of women from what once was called the "old-boys' network" for impeding their progress.

Women's and Men's Average Earnings in Selected Careers

Career	Women	Men	Career	Women	Men
Accountant	$28,496	$38,844	Magazine art director	$40,546	$40,625
Advertising copywriter	53,000	58,000	Pediatrician	119,660	137,065
Computer operator	20,384	27,404	Personnel specialist	30,212	35,932
Cook	12,376	13,988	Pharmacist	53,650	52,200
Engineer	49,100	50,000	Real estate salesperson	26,832	33,800
Financial manager	33,020	48,984	Registered nurse	36,036	37,180
High school teacher	33,124	37,596	Retail sales worker	13,156	18,980
Insurance salesperson	23,556	40,404	Travel agent	23,600	28,200
Lawyer	49,816	60,892	University professor	57,790	65,080

Source: *"1997 salary report," Working Woman, January 1997, pp. 31–33, 69, 71, 73–76.*

SKILLBUILDER

INTERPRETING CHARTS ***Which career has the largest percentage gap between male and female earnings?***

One study revealed an overlooked trend in the management of corporations. In 1995, women—for the first time ever—held more than 10 percent of all seats on corporate boards of directors. Many companies accelerated their efforts to add women and minorities as directors. The reason was based on demographics. As the woman director of one company says, "To understand and serve our customer needs, we need to reflect our customer base."

Sandra Day O'Connor became the first woman to sit on the Supreme Court in 1981.

In 1997, Madeleine Albright became the first woman to hold the office of secretary of state.

INTERACT WITH HISTORY

1. **ANALYZING ISSUES** Which problem do you think is more important—unequal pay for equal work or limits on career advancement? Explain why.
2. **FORMING OPINIONS** Suppose another presidential commission studied women in the workplace in 2021. Would it find women's situation better, worse, or the same? Explain why.

SEE SKILLBUILDER HANDBOOK, PAGES 916 AND 919.

Visit http://www.mlushistory.com for more about women at work.

Skillbuilder Answer Pediatricians have the largest gap.

1920s Women enter new professions, such as secretarial work, but battle quotas and unequal wages (page 460).

1963 Presidential Commission on the Status of Women reports that women are paid less for equal work (pages 768-769).

1989 Twenty states begin adjusting pay scales to equalize pay for comparable work (page 831).

Six out of ten women work outside the home, but they only earn 76 cents for every dollar a man earns (page 831).

INSTRUCT

▶***Discussing Key Ideas***

- Women make professional progress, entering traditional male careers in larger numbers than ever before.
- Women are still paid less than men for the same work and are underrepresented in top-level management positions in most corporations.

HISTORY FROM VISUALS

Women's and Men's Average Earnings in Selected Careers

Reading the Table Ask students the following questions about the table: What is the gap in the traditional female career of registered nurse? *$1,144* What is the gap for retail sales worker, a career that is easy to enter? *$5,834* What are the gaps in the traditional male careers of financial manager and insurance salesperson? *$15,964; $16,848.*

Extension *Working Woman* magazine publishes its survey each year. Have students research the situation for the current year and compare it to the findings shown here. Where has the gap decreased? Where has it increased? *Answers will vary depending on the data for the current year.*

INTERACT WITH HISTORY

1. Analyzing Issues

Possible Responses *Unequal wages: Paying women unequally is more of a problem because it affects almost all women workers. Customs that keep women from advancing in their careers only affects a few.*

Limits on career advancement: Limits on career advancement are more of a problem because once women reach upper management levels, they can create policies to ensure that women throughout a company receive equal treatment.

2. Forming Opinions

Possible Response *A presidential commission in the future would find the situation somewhat better. As Jamieson points out, some of the difference in women's wages results from the fact that many women work part time or leave the workforce temporarily to raise children. As long as that trend continues, it is likely that women's wages will lag behind men's. Over the past 30 years, the distance has narrowed, however. This is partly because more and more women are entering higher-paying jobs. As long as that trend continues, the gap between men's and women's wages is likely to decrease.*

Breaking the Cycle of Poverty

OBJECTIVES

1. To describe the causes and extent of poverty in the United States.
2. To explore the impact of welfare reform on American society.

FOCUS & MOTIVATE

5-MINUTE WARM-UP

Making Judgments
To review the historical background of poverty in America, have students look at the time line on pages 896–897 and answer these questions.

1. Which event on the time line had the greatest impact on the history of poverty in America?
2. Which government program listed do you think did the most to combat poverty?

WARM-UP TRANSPARENCY EPILOGUE

▶ ***Starting with the Student***
Ask students if they know anyone who lives on an income below the poverty level. Discuss the following questions with them.

- What factors hinder these people from climbing out of poverty?
- What kinds of programs could the government use to help people escape poverty?

Breaking the Cycle of Poverty

LEARN ABOUT the causes of poverty in the United States and who constitutes the American poor
TO UNDERSTAND proposals for welfare reform and the impact of such reform on the American population.

APPROACHING THE ISSUE For people like "Gwenn," who grew up poor in the rural South, life is not easy. Gwenn is a single parent who takes classes and works full time. She intends to stay off welfare and get a better job. But Gwenn questions the fairness of a welfare system that allows her neighbors to be home with their children and collect welfare while she struggles with school and work.

In 1996, Congress and President Bill Clinton agreed on a new welfare system to remedy the kinds of inequities that Gwenn describes.

Historical Perspective

Some part of the American population has faced poverty since the "starving time" at Jamestown in 1607. In the 20th century, poverty was most widespread during the Great Depression of the 1930s. That economic disaster led to several new government programs such as the 1935 Social Security Act, which created a pension fund for retired people over age 65 and offered government aid to poor people for the first time.

Though the Depression ended with World War II, postwar prosperity did not last. In the 1960s, President Lyndon B. Johnson declared "unconditional war on poverty." The federal government launched programs to educate, train, and expand financial aid for the poor. The proportion of people living below the poverty level—the minimum income necessary to provide basic living standards—fell from 25 percent in 1962 to only 11 percent in 1973.

However, economic hard times reappeared in the late 1970s and the poverty rate began to rise. Facing rising prices and threatened job losses, many Americans became angry that tax dollars went to poor people who did not work. As a result, much of the public and a growing number of politicians called for changes in federal and state welfare programs. But to understand these calls for reform, it is important to look more closely at the people affected by poverty.

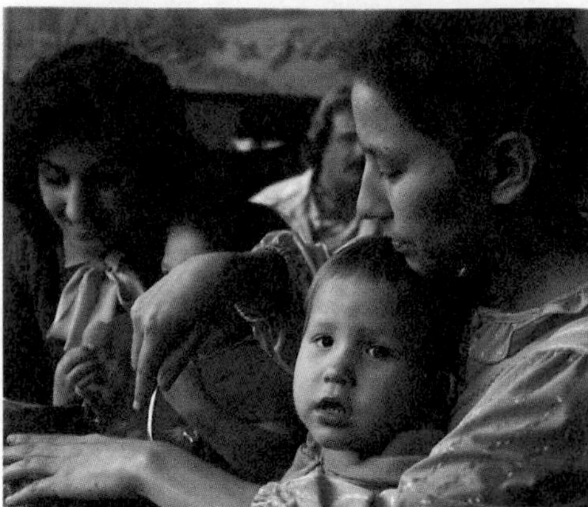
Some families, like this one in Phoenix, Arizona, rely on private charities to provide economic relief.

Americans in Poverty

The graph on U.S. poverty levels on the next page gives a partial statistical snapshot of poverty. But it does not give the complete picture.

THE WORKING POOR Not all poor people are without jobs. About 30 million people are part of the group called the working poor, who hold low-wage jobs with few benefits and almost never any health insurance. But as scholar Katherine Newman says, they are far from the stereotype that many Americans have of the poor.

History of Poverty
UNITED STATES

1894	1935	1962	1964
High unemployment in the wake of the Panic of 1893 leaves thousands homeless (page 237).	Social Security Act is passed; government gives aid to poor for first time (pages 515–516).	Michael Harrington's *The Other America* shocks the nation by revealing extent of poverty (680).	President Johnson announces War on Poverty (page 685).

TEACHING OPTIONS

Teaching Gifted and Talented Students

Minimum Wage One of the key issues regarding the working poor is the minimum wage. Have gifted and talented students research the debate over the minimum wage. They should answer such questions as: What is the current minimum wage? How has the value of the minimum wage changed over time relative to inflation? What workers are excluded from this minimum wage? What impact does a higher minimum wage have on workers? What impact does it have on employers? Ask them to report their findings to the class.

Teaching Less Proficient Readers

Creating a Concept Web Students who are less proficient readers can make a web that shows the causes of poverty outlined in the article. Have them reproduce the web below and fill in the five ovals with a description of the causes of poverty.

Poverty in the United States, 1978–1994

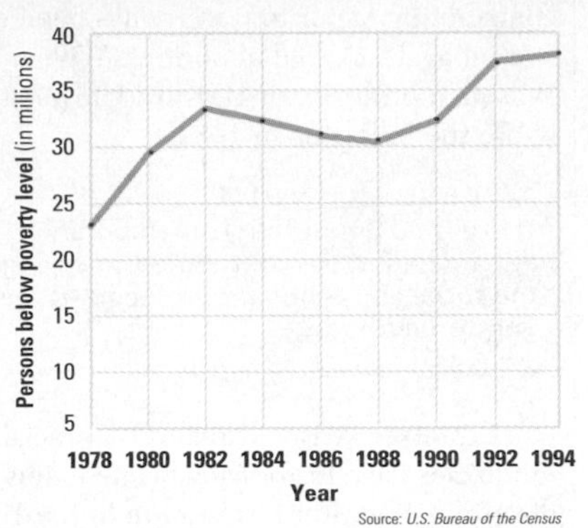

SKILLBUILDER
INTERPRETING GRAPHS
Which period showed the greatest increase in the number of people living below the poverty level? What factors do you think led to the increase?

CHILDREN Children account for a major share of the poor, and their numbers are growing rapidly for all ethnic groups. In 1969, 9.7 million children, or 14 percent of all children, were poor. By 1993, the number was 15.7 million, or almost 23 percent. The poverty rate among children in the United States is higher than in any other Western industrialized nation.

However, despite the statistical evidence, some analysts point out that concern over children's welfare doesn't translate into action.

> **A PERSONAL VOICE**
> Children are all the talk among policymakers and politicians. But we have only to look at the realities of their lives to see how little concern there is.
> **ROBERT ADAMS,** National Low Income Housing Coalition

THE HOMELESS Cuts in welfare and food stamp benefits in the 1980s brought the problem of homelessness to national attention. Today, the homeless account for a significant portion of the American poor. According to the National Alliance to End Homelessness (NAEH), about 750,000 Americans are without shelter on any given night. But sociology professor Christopher Jencks puts the number much lower, at about 325,000.

Many experts on the homeless believe that the lack of housing is simply a symptom of larger problems. These include unemployment, low-wage jobs, and high housing costs. They also may involve personal problems such as substance abuse. While many Americans seem to suffer from "compassion fatigue" and don't want to listen to warnings about homelessness, the problem, observers say, is not going to go away on its own.

THE UNEMPLOYED Across the nation, the poor often have failed to find the jobs they need. For example, when reform in Michigan cut the number of adults who could receive state aid, a University of Michigan study showed that only 20 percent of the people who used to receive welfare had found steady work. A *New York Times* report said that at the current rate of job growth for that state, it would take 21 years for all 470,000 adults who received welfare to get a job.

Some Causes of Poverty

Experts agree that some of the most important causes of poverty are lack of training, the economy, limited access to child care, poor education, and racial discrimination.

LACK OF TRAINING Lack of skills keeps many welfare recipients from finding, or keeping, jobs. They need more than job training. They also need training in work habits. According to a Kansas City welfare reform worker, employers are saying, "Send us people who get to work on time [and] can read and follow instructions." Programs in New York, Florida, and Missouri have had problems keeping former welfare recipients on the job. Many of these workers leave their jobs after a few months.

THE ECONOMY Other experts say that the biggest factor in finding jobs for the poor is the performance of the economy. Many critics argue that high welfare payments discourage work. But economist Paul Osterman found the local economic boom in Boston in the early 1980s dropped poverty rates even though welfare benefits rose. The reason, he said, was economic growth, which generated jobs. →

Skillbuilder Answer
1978–1982; Economic hard times led to the increase.

"The vast majority of poor people . . . work for a living."

KATHERINE NEWMAN
SCHOLAR

1970 President Nixon's welfare reform bill—the Family Assistance Plan—dies in the Senate (page 787).

1980s Welfare benefits and food stamps are cut under President Reagan (page 822).

1996 Congress passes the Personal Responsibility and Work Opportunity Act to completely overhaul the federal welfare system (page 851).

OBJECTIVE
① INSTRUCT

▶***Discussing Key Ideas***
- Almost 40 million people—many of them working poor and children—live below the poverty line.
- Estimates of the number of homeless people range from 325,000 to 750,000.
- Causes of poverty include lack of training for well-paying jobs, business cycles, lack of child care, poor education, and racial discrimination.

HISTORY FROM VISUALS

Poverty in the United States, 1978–1994

Reading the Graph The article states that about 30 million poor people are among the working poor. Ask students to find what percentage that represents of the approximately 38 million people below the poverty line. *Answer: 79 percent.*

Extension Have students compare this graph to the graph showing unemployment for a similar period on page 884. How do changes in unemployment parallel the changes shown on this graph? *Possible response: Unemployment rose sharply from 1979 to 1984, the same period that the number of poor people rose. Unemployment dipped from 1984 to 1989, when the number of poor people also declined. When unemployment began rising again in 1989, so did the number of poor people.*

TEACHING OPTIONS

Making Connections Across Cultures

Attitudes Toward Poverty The nations of Western Europe have extensive social welfare programs that provide aid to poor people and others in need. These programs are funded by taxes that are higher than in the United States, but also reflect a different attitude toward poverty. Social scientist Lester C. Thurow says that the approach in the United States—which sees poverty as a matter of personal responsibility—grows out of the national myth of rugged individualism. By contrast, historian Thomas Osborne says, Europeans "stress the role of economic systems and social injustices in producing poverty."

Making Connections Across the Curriculum

Art Have students take the role of a designer assigned to design a magazine cover for a special report on poverty. Each student should determine first what approach the magazine will take toward the issue—to simply report the status of the poor or to advocate particular solutions. Their design should . . .
- include a title for the in-depth report and an image that can be sketched
- have enough visual and verbal impact to lead people to buy the magazine
- be clearly and attractively presented

OBJECTIVE
② INSTRUCT

▶ *Discussing Key Ideas*

- Many states experiment with changes to the welfare system and see mixed results.
- The Personal Responsibility and Work Opportunity Act of 1996 makes radical changes in the nation's welfare system.
- States try to encourage private businesses to hire former welfare recipients as new workers.

MORE ABOUT . . .
Children in Poverty

A study by the Center for Children in Poverty looked at the number of children under age 6 who lived in poverty from 1970 to 1975 compared to those who lived in poverty from 1990 to 1994. It found the following growth rates between these times spans:

- Hispanic children: 42.8 percent
- white non-Hispanic children: 37.7 percent
- black non-Hispanic children: 19.1 percent
- children living in suburbs: 58.9 percent
- children living in rural areas: 45.4 percent
- children living in cities: 33.8 percent

CHILD CARE Another factor that holds back increased employment is limited access to child care. Economist David Gordon related the results of a study of mothers who received welfare. They could eke out a living, he found, by combining paid work and some outside support with welfare payments and food stamps. But, Gordon asked, suppose one of these mothers left welfare and took a full-time minimum wage job.

A PERSONAL VOICE

> If she is able to find free care for her kids, perhaps from a grandmother, then she can improve her standard of living by 20 percent. . . . [If] she cannot find free child care and has to pay the going rate, her standard of living . . . would decline by 20 percent.
>
> **DAVID GORDON,** economist

To help meet the need for child care, a 1996 federal welfare law included $3.5 billion in funding for day care.

POOR EDUCATION For millions of Americans, the U.S. public education system has failed to provide the tools necessary for climbing out of poverty. Anne Lewis, an education writer, thinks improved education is the key to breaking the cycle of poverty. She proposes four steps:

- Educate the parents of poor children, who will then encourage children to learn.
- Give welfare mothers effective job training.
- Push poor children toward college to give them a chance at a better future.
- Encourage literacy beginning at birth.

Lewis points out that "three-fourths of all welfare/food stamp recipients perform at the lowest levels of literacy." In turn, she notes, low levels of literacy generally lead to low employment rates and lower wages. By breaking that cycle, educators can play an important role in securing a better future for their students.

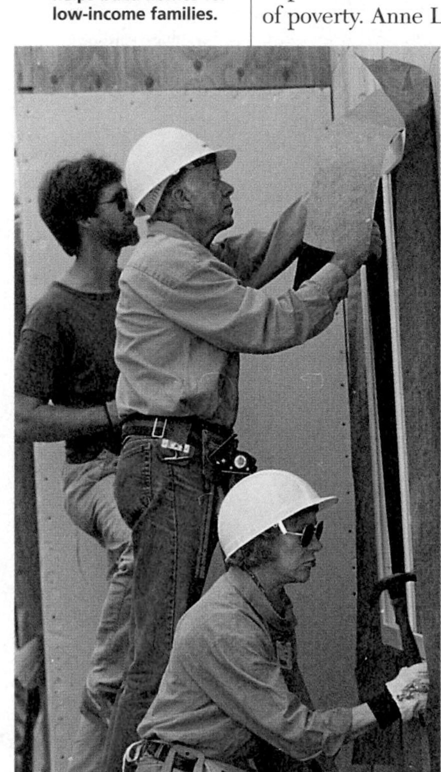

Former president Jimmy Carter and his wife, Rosalynn, donate their time and labor to Habitat for Humanity, an organization that helps build homes for low-income families.

DISCRIMINATION AND POVERTY Another contributing factor to poverty has been discrimination against racial minorities. William Julius Wilson, a professor at Harvard University, wrote the following in 1987.

A PERSONAL VOICE

> There is no doubt that contemporary discrimination has contributed to or aggravated the social and economic problems of the ghetto underclass.
>
> **WILLIAM JULIUS WILSON,** *The Truly Disadvantaged*

Professor Wilson explains that racial minorities have historically been victims of job discrimination. For instance, until the 1960s, most employers refused to employ African Americans for well-paying management positions.

The Civil Rights Act of 1964 forced companies to abandon obvious forms of discrimination, but subtle forms persist. For example, in the 1980s, Norman Drake, an African-American employee at a large defense contractor, complained when he was the only employee in his 75-person department not to receive a raise and a promotion. He was also the only minority in the department. Drake sued his employer for discrimination, and in 1992, a jury awarded him $925,000 in damages. Drake's and other cases show that discrimination still exists, blocking the economic progress of many minorities.

As the number of poor people has grown, calls to reform the U.S. welfare system have taken center stage. And reform efforts in some states—as early as 1987 in Wisconsin, for example—provided the motive for Congress to overhaul the federal system.

Welfare Reform by the States

Wisconsin, Virginia, and Maryland are just a few of the states that enacted their own welfare reforms. In Wisconsin, the number of welfare recipients dropped almost in half. Welfare numbers dipped in Maryland and Virginia as well.

All three states experienced this success partly because they enjoyed economic growth at the time. Paul Offner, a welfare policy analyst, notes that Wisconsin's success "shows what you can accomplish if you spend money." That state's program included heavy funding in the first years of reform to help former welfare recipients find jobs. Even there, success was

TEACHING OPTIONS

Making Connections Across the Curriculum

Economics One approach to welfare reform is called workfare. These programs sometimes hire former welfare recipients for public-service jobs. The problem is that these plans can hurt other workers. In New York, for instance, welfare recipients must work in state jobs until they get jobs in private business. The work they do in the state agencies, however, was often done in the past by unionized workers. Labor leaders protested the program, which they call "a union-busting tactic." In any event, well-paying union jobs in government departments were filled by low-wage non-union workers.

Making Connections Across the Curriculum

Language Arts Have students read the section on "Child Care." Then ask them to put themselves in the position of a speechwriter for a political leader. They have to write a brief speech about the usefulness of accessible child care in breaking the cycle of poverty. Speeches should . . .

- mention the high number of welfare families headed by single parents, especially single women
- offer practical solutions
- use clear and convincing language

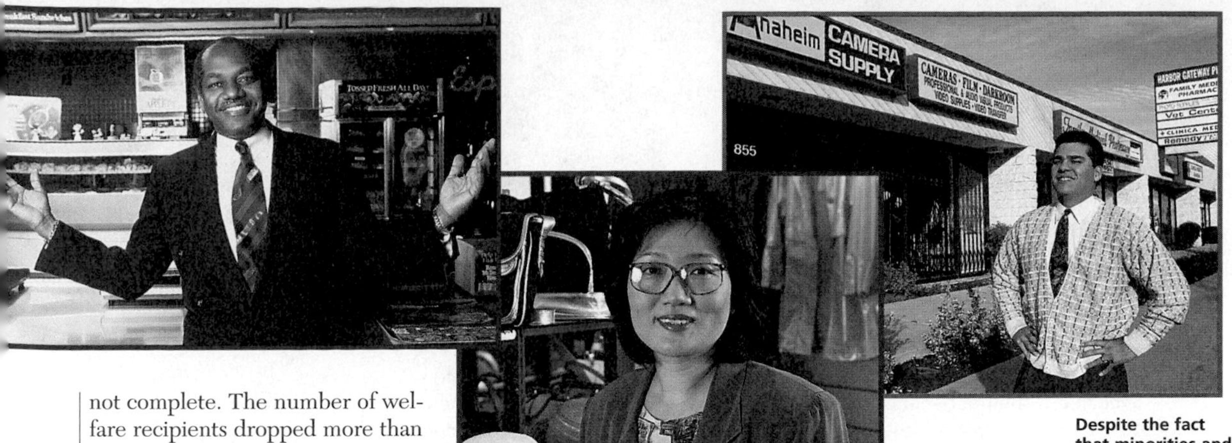

Despite the fact that minorities and women are more likely to live in poverty than white males are, many individuals from every background have established successful businesses and careers.

not complete. The number of welfare recipients dropped more than 70 percent in about half the state's counties. But in Milwaukee—with over half the state's welfare population—the decline was only 21 percent.

Nevertheless, state governments are working to encourage businesses to hire former welfare recipients. They grant employers tax credits and partial refunds of workers' wages.

In January of 1997, President Clinton urged businesses to make an effort to hire former welfare recipients. The next day, a Kansas City agency that helps connect welfare recipients with employers received 150 offers of jobs. TJX, a national retailer that operates T.J. Maxx, announced a plan in 1997 to hire up to 5,000 such workers by the year 2000.

Federal Welfare Reform

In 1996, the Republican Congress and President Clinton signed a bill—the Personal Responsibility and Work Opportunity Act—that cut more than $55 billion in welfare spending over six years and put a five-year limit on how long people could receive welfare payments. In addition, the bill cut benefits to recipients who had not found a job within two years.

Both proponents and critics of the law agreed on one thing: the law's success depended on putting welfare recipients to work. The federal government offered three incentives to encourage businesses to hire people from the welfare rolls: tax credits for employers who hire welfare recipients, wage subsidies, and establishment of enterprise zones, which provided tax breaks to companies that locate in economically depressed areas.

Despite waivers granted to various states that some claim weaken the law's effectiveness, most observers welcome the attempt to change the system from one that fosters dependence to one that encourages self-reliance.

Effects of Welfare Reform

Meanwhile, welfare analysts—from opposing sides of the debate—keep a wary eye on the impact of welfare reform. Liberal analysts, for example, fear the impact of the welfare reform law on children, while conservatives argue that the benefits of welfare reform outweigh the costs. And St. Louis mayor Freeman Bosley voices concern about the homeless. Seeing the massive changes the new welfare law will cause, he worries about increased homelessness among the American population.

A PERSONAL VOICE

These [welfare programs that existed before the 1996 welfare reform] are the programs and services that we know can help keep people out of soup kitchens and homeless shelters. Take them away—we know what will happen.

FREEMAN BOSLEY, mayor, St. Louis, Missouri

How U.S. policymakers will react to warnings like Bosley's remains to be seen. For now, most observers are watching carefully to see what the impact of welfare reform will be.

"It's time for American business to step up to the plate."

BERNARD CAMMARATA, PRESIDENT, TJX

INTERACT WITH HISTORY

1. **FORMING OPINIONS** Do you think the long-term benefits of welfare reform are likely to outweigh the short-range problems? Support your opinion.

SEE SKILLBUILDER HANDBOOK, PAGE 919.

2. **SOLVING PROBLEMS** What can be done to provide affordable child care to help the working poor?

Visit http://www.mlushistory.com for more about poverty.

MORE ABOUT . . .
Welfare to Work

Critics of welfare-to-work programs point out that politicians face a larger problem than they want to admit when it comes to placing welfare recipients into jobs. Aside from the fact that job training programs are expensive to run, there is also the possibility that there are not enough jobs for everyone on welfare. For example, an Urban League study on jobs in the Chicago area found that while there were 253,491 low-skilled, unemployed workers and welfare recipients in the Chicago area, there were only 47,102 entry-level job openings.

MORE ABOUT . . .
Bernard Cammarata

When Cammarata announced the planned hiring of 5,000 former welfare recipients at TJX, he underscored the importance of a strong economy in finding jobs for these people. He cited the combination of low-interest rates and low unemployment for creating the right climate for his actions. He also said that he hoped the results would prove to "be good for America and good for business."

INTERACT WITH HISTORY

1. Forming Opinions

Possible Responses *Benefits will outweigh problems: Students may suggest that reform that gets people off welfare and into jobs will result in greater financial prosperity for more people. They may predict that the shift from a system of dependence to one of self-reliance may have a positive impact on society as a whole.*

Benefits won't outweigh problems: Students may point out that some welfare recipients will not be able to find or hold jobs. They may suggest that homelessness will increase as well.

2. Solving Problems

Possible Response *Student responses will vary. Students might refer to government or corporate support of child-care programs.*

Tough Choices About Entitlements

OBJECTIVES

1. To examine the condition of the Social Security system and the impact of current demographic trends.
2. To analyze various suggestions for reforming Social Security.

Tough Choices About Entitlements

LEARN ABOUT projected problems of federal entitlement programs, especially Social Security, in the early 21st century
TO UNDERSTAND the variety of opinions about proposed changes to those programs.

FOCUS & MOTIVATE

5-MINUTE WARM-UP

Recognizing Facts and Details
To examine the history of entitlements in the United States, have students read Historical Perspective on page 900 and answer these questions.

1. What did Franklin Roosevelt say was the purpose of the Social Security Act?
2. In what year was Social Security extended?

WARM-UP TRANSPARENCY EPILOGUE

▶ ***Starting with the Student*** Check students' knowledge about Social Security with these questions:

- Does all the money in the system come from taxes paid by employees? *No, employers also contribute.*
- Are benefits paid only to retired and disabled workers? *No, for instance, spouses who did not work also receive benefits.*
- Are the taxes collected invested in stocks? *No, after paying benefits, any extra money is used to buy Treasury bills.*

APPROACHING THE ISSUE Economist Lester Thurow gives new meaning to the term *generation gap,* warning, "In the years ahead, class warfare [will] . . . mean not the poor against the rich but the young against the old." Economics may become a major issue dividing generations, as young workers shoulder the costs of Social Security, Medicare, and Medicaid—the three major federal entitlement programs funded by the federal government.

Historical Perspective

In the 1935 Social Security Act, the government promised to pay a pension to older Americans, funded by a tax on workers and employers. At that time, President Franklin D. Roosevelt said that Social Security was not intended to provide an individual's retirement income, but it was a base on which workers would build with private pension funds. In 1965, new laws extended Social Security support. In addition, the government assumed most health care costs for the elderly through the Medicare program and the poor through Medicaid.

These programs are called *entitlements* because their benefits are established by law rather than by appropriations by Congress.

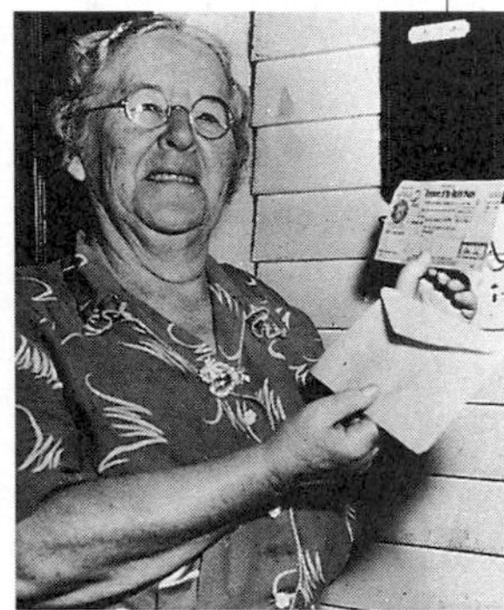

Miss Ida M. Fuller of Ludlow, Vermont, was one of the first Americans to receive Social Security benefits in 1940.

Social Security, Medicare, and Medicaid have received much attention because the U.S. population is aging. This aging population will put a severe financial strain on each program. Social Security is a good case study of the entitlements problem because this program benefits most Americans who reach retirement age.

Social Security: A Case Study

The threat to Social Security comes from a few important factors. First, when the baby boomers (those born between 1946 and 1964) retire, their huge numbers may overburden the entitlement programs. Second, Americans now live longer, so an individual's share of benefits from the program is greater than in the past. Third, slow growth in the rate of employment may limit tax receipts that fund the program.

Some experts predict disaster, and Americans have listened. In one poll, 61 percent said they doubted that Social Security would provide them with retirement income. Pete Peterson, a former U.S. secretary of commerce, has sounded the loudest alarms.

A PERSONAL VOICE
On our current path, entitlements will eventually consume all federal revenue, leaving nothing to pay for interest on the national debt, much less defense, education, and other discretionary expenditures.
PETER G. PETERSON, former U.S. secretary of commerce

Currently, Social Security collects more in taxes than it pays in benefits. The extra goes into a "trust fund" that is invested. Peterson warns that in the year 2029, payments will outweigh receipts and the system will have to dip into the trust fund until it is gone. Also, if no changes are made in the system, beginning in 2029, the fund will only be able to pay retirees 75 percent of the benefits due them.

Others, though, point to the conclusions of the Advisory Council on Social Security. That

History of Entitlements

UNITED STATES	1935	1950	1961	1965
	President Roosevelt signs Social Security Act, with Aid to Dependent Children (ADC) (pages 515–516).	ADC is renamed Aid to Families with Dependent Children (AFDC) and expanded (page 851).	Changes to Social Security allow full benefits at early retirement—age 62.	President Johnson signs Medicare and Medicaid into law (page 686).

TEACHING OPTIONS

Teaching Less Proficient Readers

Charting Problems and Possible Solutions Students who are less proficient readers can organize the information by using a grid to list the causes of and possible solutions to the problems of Social Security. Have them create a chart similar to the one below and write the appropriate ideas on the blank lines.

Causes	Possible Solutions

Making Connections Across the Curriculum

Civics The plan to have the government invest 40 percent of the Social Security fund draws criticism on one issue unrelated to Social Security itself. The concern is conflict of interest. Would the government—once it owned the stock of various companies—hesitate to enforce environmental, employment, or health and safety laws on those companies for fear of lowering the value of its investments? Ask students what they think could be done to prevent this potential conflict of interest in the 40 percent plan.

Social Security Recipients, 1950-2050

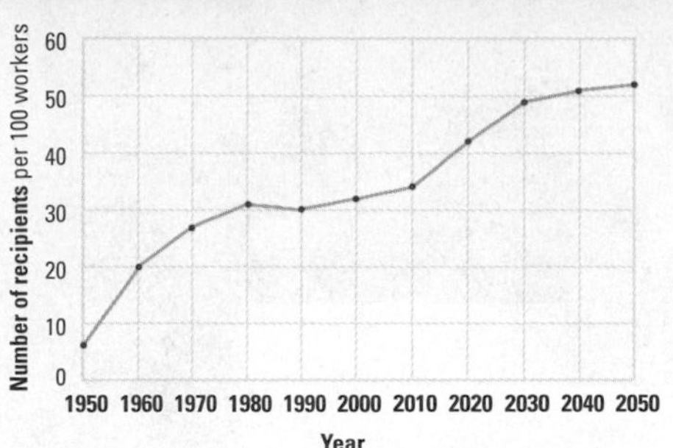

SKILLBUILDER
INTERPRETING GRAPHS
How does this graph support the analysis in the text of the problems facing Social Security?

panel found that the difference between the fund's tax receipts and its payments equals only 2.2 percent of total national payroll earnings over the next 70 years. In other words, with an immediate 2.2 percent payroll-tax contribution increase, the Social Security program would be completely funded until 2070. They agree with economist Laura D'Andrea Tyson.

> A PERSONAL VOICE
> Social Security doesn't face an impending crisis. It faces some understandable and predictable challenges that can be solved. . . . Creating a crisis atmosphere impedes the process of finding appropriate solutions.
>
> **LAURA D'ANDREA TYSON,** former chair of the President's Council of Economic Advisers

Options for Change

Panel members differed, however, on how to meet those challenges. Some wanted small tax hikes or benefit cuts. Others suggested raising the retirement age. All of their plans had a new feature: investing in stocks. The authors of this plan assume that such investments will increase the funds for Social Security.

- **The 40 Percent Plan.** Invest 40 percent of the Social Security fund in stocks, which the government would manage as a block.
- **The 1.6 Percent Plan.** Require workers to put 1.6 percent of their earnings—over and above their contributions to Social Security—into a retirement plan.
- **The 5 Percent Plan.** Provides a standard monthly benefit based on years of contribution and calls for 5 percent of a worker's Social Security tax to go to a retirement account controlled by the worker.

"Privatization"—channeling some income from payroll taxes into private-sector investments—is the core of the debate on Social Security. Supporters say that by investing in stocks, the Social Security fund could earn far more than it currently does. While stock prices can fall, the overall trend is for stock values to increase over time.

Critics of investing Social Security funds in the stock market warn, though, that stock prices *could* fall, leaving Social Security underfunded.

As of 1997, Congress had not taken any steps to reform Social Security. Most economists agree, however, that changes in the system must be made in the near future to avoid a crisis when large numbers of workers begin to retire early in the 21st century.

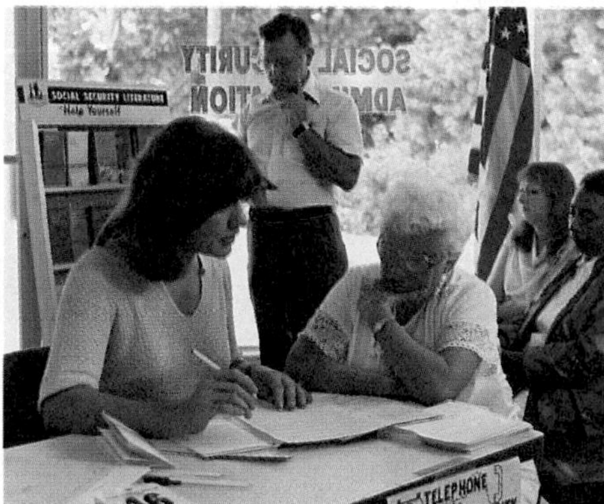

A Social Security employee in Florida helps a woman with her paperwork.

Skillbuilder Answer The graph shows the increase in the number of welfare recipients between 1950 and 1990, and projects expected increases to the year 2050.

"There's a legitimate question as to how much government should protect people from themselves."

SYLVESTER SCHIEBER,
ECONOMIST AND BENEFITS CONSULTANT

INTERACT WITH HISTORY

1. **SUMMARIZING** What factors contribute to the problems looming ahead for Social Security? Use details to support your answer.
2. **DRAWING CONCLUSIONS** How would the economy be both helped and hurt if Social Security benefits were cut? Explain your response.

SEE SKILLBUILDER HANDBOOK, PAGES 911 AND 919.

Visit http://www.mlushistory.com for more about entitlements.

INSTRUCT

▶***Discussing Key Ideas***
- Analysts foresee financial trouble for Social Security, Medicare, and Medicaid.
- When members of the baby boom generation retire, the government will have to pay out larger sums in benefits than it receives in contributions.
- Experts debate possible reforms such as increasing taxes, cutting benefits, or raising the retirement age.
- Another possible solution is to invest some Social Security funds in stocks.

HISTORY FROM VISUALS

Social Security Recipients, 1950–2050

Reading the Graph For every 100 workers paying taxes into the Social Security system, how many retirees were there in 1950? *About 8.* In 2000 (if trends continue)? *About 32.* In 2050? *About 52.*

Extension Have students find out what the current tax rate for Social Security is. They should find the rate for the contributions by employer and worker as well as the different rate for self-employed workers. What would be the effect of an increase in this tax?

1970s	1975	1983	1994
President Nixon increases Social Security payments (page 787).	Years of high inflation lead Congress to include cost-of-living adjustments for Social Security benefits.	Social Security is reformed to provide financial stability for many years.	President Clinton appoints Advisory Council on Social Security to report on system's financial health.

INTERACT WITH HISTORY

1. Summarizing

Possible Responses *The large number of people from the baby boom generation who are likely to retire at the same time; the fact that Americans live longer; slow growth in the rate of employment, which may limit tax revenues.*

2. Drawing Conclusions

Possible Responses *The economy would be helped because many people would be likely to continue working instead of retiring. The economy would be hurt because many of the oldest people would not be able to find jobs, but with smaller Social Security benefits they would not have the money to continue purchasing at the current rate.*

life

The
AMERICANS
REFERENCE SECTION

pursuit *of* happiness

liberty

Skillbuilder Handbook

Refer to the Skillbuilder Handbook when you need help in answering Think Through History questions, doing Interact with History activities, or answering questions in section assessments and chapter assessments. In addition, the handbook will help you create and interpret maps, charts, and graphs.

Section 1: Understanding Historical Readings

Section 2: Using Critical Thinking

Section 3: Print, Visual, and Technological Sources

Section 1: Understanding Historical Readings

1.1 Following Chronological Order

Chronological order is the order in which events happen in time. It is the framework for studying history. Without knowing the order in which things happened, historians could not get an accurate sense of the relationships among events.

UNDERSTANDING THE SKILL

Strategy: Finding clues in the text The following paragraph is about some events leading up to the Watergate scandal that brought down the Nixon administration. Notice how the time line below puts the events in chronological order.

THE PENTAGON PAPERS

The initial event that many historians believe led to Watergate took place on June 13, 1971, when the *New York Times* began publishing articles called the Pentagon Papers, which divulged government secrets about the U.S. involvement in Vietnam. The information had been leaked to the media by a former Defense Department official, Daniel Ellsberg. The Justice Department asked the courts to suppress publication of the articles, but on July 30, 1971, the Supreme Court ruled that the government could not censor the information being published. Two months later, in September, a group of special White House agents known as the plumbers burglarized the office of Ellsberg's psychiatrist in a vain attempt to find evidence against Ellsberg. President Nixon had authorized the creation of the plumbers in 1971, after the Pentagon Papers were published, to keep government secrets from leaking to the media and to help ensure his reelection in November 1972.

Look for clue words about time. These are words like *initial, first, next, then, before, after, finally,* and *by that time.*

Use specific dates provided in the text.

Watch for references to previous historical events that are included for background. Usually a change in the verb tense will indicate a previous event.

Strategy: Making a time line

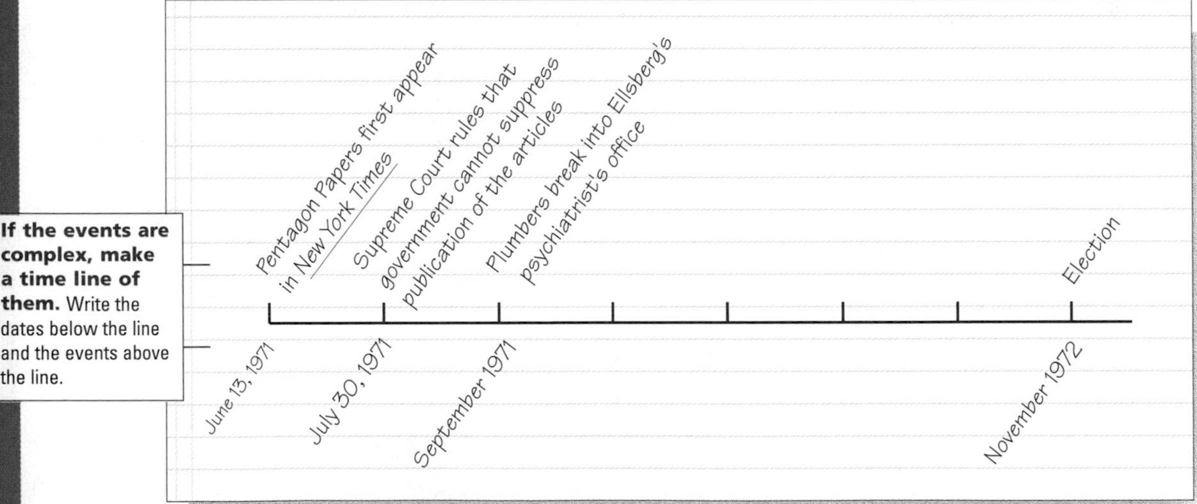

If the events are complex, make a time line of them. Write the dates below the line and the events above the line.

APPLYING THE SKILL

Make your own time line Skim Chapter 21, Section 2, "The Triumphs of a Crusade," to find out how the civil rights movement helped end segregation in the South. Make a list of the important dates you find, starting with the freedom ride in May 1961 and ending with the passage of the Voting Rights Act of 1965. Decide on a scale for a time line of the important dates. Use the model above to help you create your own time line, showing what happened on each date.

904 Skillbuilder Handbook

1.2 Clarifying; Summarizing

Clarifying means clearly understanding what you have read. One way to do this is by asking yourself questions about the material. In your answers, you restate in your own words what you have read.

When you **summarize,** you condense what you have read into fewer words, stating only the main ideas and the most important details. It is important to use your own words in a summary.

UNDERSTANDING THE SKILL

Strategy: Finding clues in the text The excerpt below describes a major oil spill. Following the excerpt is a summary that condenses the key information in the passage into a few sentences. The summary also clarifies.

Summarize: Look for topic sentences stating the main ideas. These are often at the beginning of a section or paragraph. In a summary, rewrite the main ideas in your own words.

THE *EXXON VALDEZ* OIL SPILL

In March 1989, the oil tanker *Exxon Valdez* ran aground in Prince William Sound along the coast of Alaska, dumping about 11 million gallons of crude oil into the sea. Within days, 1,800 miles of coastline were fouled with thick black oil that coated rocks and beaches. At least 10 percent of the area's birds, sea otters, and other animals were killed, and commercial fisheries estimated that they would lose at least 50 percent of the season's catch.

The captain of the *Exxon Valdez* was found guilty of negligence, and attempts were made to clean up the spill. Four years later, however, scientists found that pools of oil buried in coves were still poisoning shellfish, otters, and ducks, while several bird species failed to reproduce.

Between 1989 and 1994, Exxon spent about $2.1 billion in efforts to clean up Prince William Sound. In the meantime, some 34,000 commercial fishers and other Alaskans sued the company for damages, claiming that the oil spill had ruined their livelihoods.

In May of 1994, a federal grand jury decided that Exxon had been reckless in allowing a captain with a history of alcohol abuse to command the *Exxon Valdez*. The jury awarded almost $287 million in compensatory damages to the plaintiffs. They also ordered Exxon to pay $5 billion in punitive damages.

Clarify: Look up any words you do not recognize.

Summarize: Include the key facts and statistics. Pay attention to statements of fact, numbers, dates, quantities, percentages, and other data.

Strategy: Writing a summary

Clarify and summarize: Write a summary to clarify your understanding of the main ideas.

SUMMARY

In 1989, the oil freighter <u>Exxon Valdez</u> ran aground off the Alaskan coast, spilling 11 million gallons of crude oil. The water and coastline for hundreds of miles were badly polluted, and many animals died. Alaskans sued the oil company for lost income. Exxon paid for a cleanup effort that cost $2.1 billion and took many years. U.S. courts fined the company more than $5 billion and found it reckless for having allowed the ship's captain to continue in service despite a history of drinking problems.

APPLYING THE SKILL

Write your own summary Turn to Chapter 14, Section 1, and read the passage headed "Economic Troubles on the Horizon." Make notes of the main ideas. Look up any words you don't recognize. Then write a summary of the passage, using the model above as your guide.

1.3 Identifying Problems

Identifying problems means recognizing and understanding the difficulties faced by particular groups of people at particular times. Being able to focus on specific problems helps historians understand the course of historical events.

UNDERSTANDING THE SKILL

Strategy: Finding clues in the text The following passage tells about the experience of newcomers to Northern cities, like Boston and Philadelphia, in the late 1800s. Below the passage is a chart that organizes the information the passage contains about the problems those immigrants faced.

Look for the difficulties people faced. Ask yourself what problems a person or group had to overcome and how they searched for solutions.

Evaluate solutions to problems.

IMMIGRANT LIFE IN THE CITIES

The lure that drew people to the cities in many cases was the same one that had attracted settlers to the West and immigrants to America—opportunity. In these industrialized centers people saw a chance to escape poverty, find work, and carve out a better life.

Newcomers to the United States usually ended up in cities because they were the cheapest and most convenient places to live, not far from the ports where immigrants landed. Cities offered unskilled laborers steady jobs in mills and factories and provided the social support of neighborhoods of people with the same ethnic background. Living among people who shared their background enabled the newcomers to speak their own language while learning about their new home. Overcrowding soon became a problem, however—one that was intensified by the migration of people from America's rural areas.

Look for implied problems. Problems are sometimes stated indirectly. This sentence implies that immigrants were drawn to the cities because of limited opportunities elsewhere.

Sometimes the solution to one problem may be the cause of another problem. Overcrowding resulted when immigrants lived together in urban neighborhoods.

Strategy: Making a chart

Summarize the problems and solutions in a chart. Tell who had the problems, what the problems were, what steps the people took to solve the problems, and how those solutions affected them.

Problems	Solutions	Outcomes
poverty	coming to U.S. cities	jobs available
lack of opportunity	coming to U.S. cities	jobs, housing, communities
lack of transportation	living close to ports of entry	congenial living, but crowded
lack of work skills	factory and mill jobs not requiring a high level of training	enough jobs for the time being
unfamiliarity with country and language	living in ethnic communities	opportunity to learn with others, but overcrowding

APPLYING THE SKILL

Make your own chart Turn to Chapter 23, Section 2, "Women Fight for Equality." Read the section, noting the social and economic problems many women faced in the 1960s and 1970s. Then make a chart, like the one above, in which you summarize the information you found in the passage. Be sure to read to the end of the section so that you can evaluate the solutions and their outcomes.

906 Skillbuilder Handbook

1.4 Analyzing Motives

Analyzing motives means examining the reasons why a person, group, or government took a particular action. These reasons often go back to the needs, emotions, and prior experiences of the person or group, as well as their plans and objectives.

UNDERSTANDING THE SKILL

Strategy: Finding clues in the text The Mormon church was founded in 1830, in upstate New York, by Joseph Smith and several followers who believed that Smith had received a message directly from God. The following passage tells how the early Mormons were treated and why they moved west in the mid-1800s. The diagram below the passage summarizes the Mormons' motives for that journey.

The Mormon Migration

Some of the Mormons' beliefs alarmed and angered other Americans, who insulted the Mormons and sometimes became violent. Plagued by persecution and seeking to convert Native Americans, Smith and a growing band of followers determined to move west, settling in Commerce, Illinois, which he renamed Nauvoo in 1839. Within five years, the community had swelled to 20,000 members.

Serious conflict developed again when Smith allowed male members of the church to have more than one wife. This idea infuriated many of Smith's neighbors, and he was eventually murdered by a mob.

The Mormons rallied around a remarkable new leader, Brigham Young, who urged them to move farther west. There they found a desert area near a salt lake, just beyond the mountains of what was then part of Mexico. The salty water was useless for crops or animals. Dry and dusty winds blew. Because the land was not desirable to others, Young realized his people might be safe there. The Mormons began to build Salt Lake City.

Notice different kinds of motives. Some motives are negative, and others are positive. People usually have several motives for important actions.

Look for the influence of important individuals. Consider the role of leaders in motivating the behavior of people and groups.

Look for basic needs and human emotions. Needs include food, clothing, shelter, and safety. Emotions such as greed, ambition, compassion, and fear also motivate behavior.

Strategy: Making a diagram

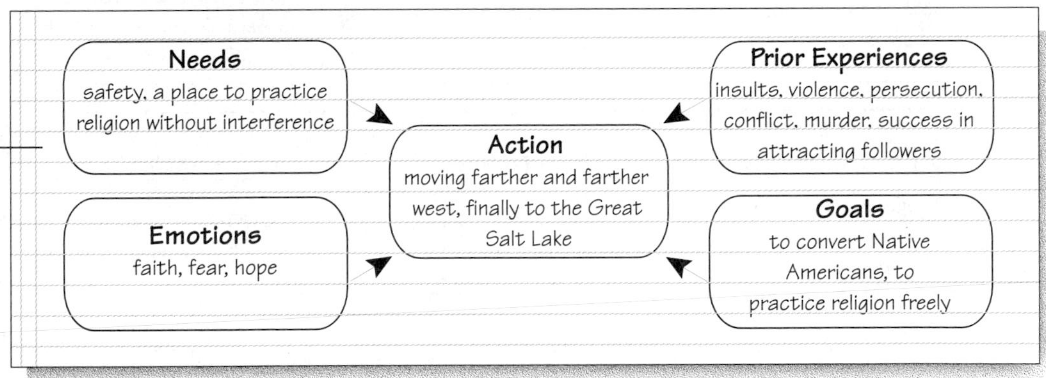

Make a diagram that summarizes motives and actions. List the important action in the middle of the diagram. Around it, list motives in different categories.

APPLYING THE SKILL

Make your own diagram Turn to Chapter 17, Section 3, and read the passage headed "The Atomic Bomb Ends the War." Take notes about President Truman's motives in dropping atomic bombs on Japanese cities. Using the model above as a guide, make a diagram in which you categorize Truman's motives under appropriate headings.

1.5 Analyzing Causes; Recognizing Effects

Historians not only want to know *what* happened in the past but also want to understand *why* things happened. Discovering **cause-and-effect relationships** helps historians see how events are related and why they took place.

UNDERSTANDING THE SKILL

Strategy: Finding clues in the text The following paragraphs describe the early events leading to the Battle of the Little Bighorn. The cause-and-effect diagram that follows the passage summarizes the chain of causes and effects.

Broken Treaties

The Treaty of 1868 had promised the Sioux that they could live forever in *Paha Sapa*, the Black Hills area of what is now South Dakota and Wyoming. The area was sacred to the Sioux. It was the center of their land, and the place where warriors went to await visions from their guardian spirits. The area also included the only good hunting ground remaining to them.

Unfortunately for the Sioux, the Black Hills contained large deposits of gold. As soon as white Americans learned that gold had been discovered, they poured into the Native Americans' territory and began staking claims.

Because the Sioux valued their land so highly, they appealed to the government to enforce the treaty terms and remove the miners. The government responded by sending out a commission to either lease mineral rights or buy *Paha Sapa* outright. The Sioux refused the commission's offer, whereupon the government sent in the Seventh Cavalry to remove not the miners but the Native Americans.

Cause: Look for reasons behind the events. Here the discovery of gold motivated the white Americans to move into Sioux territory.

Cause: Look for clue words indicating cause. These include *because, due to, since,* and *therefore.*

Effect: Look for clue words indicating consequences. These include *brought about, led to, as a result, thus, consequently,* and *responded.*

Notice that an effect may be the cause of another event, leading to a chain of causes and effects.

Strategy: Making a cause-and-effect diagram

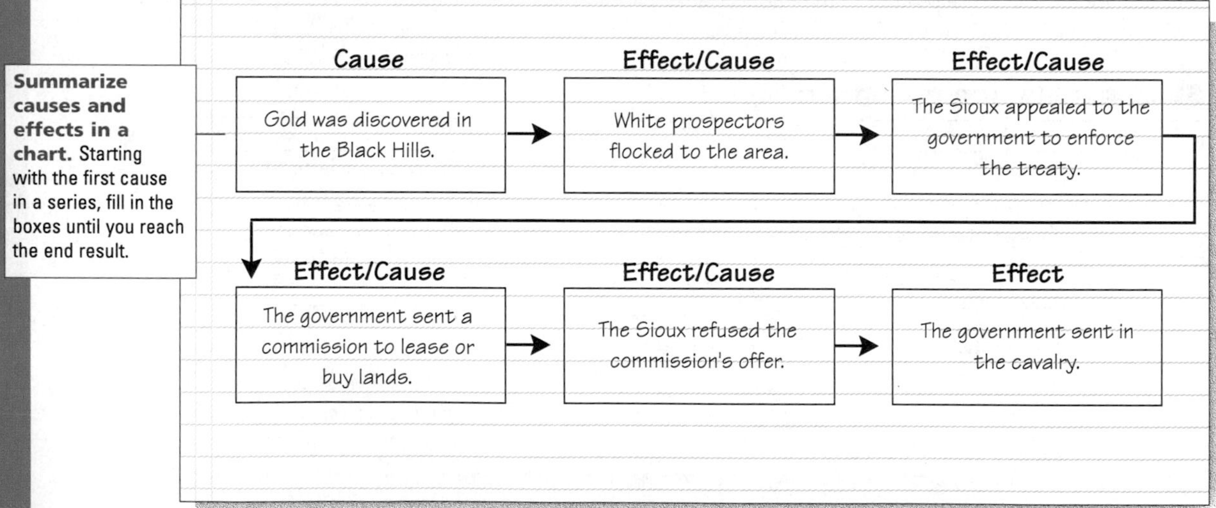

Cause
Gold was discovered in the Black Hills.
Effect/Cause
White prospectors flocked to the area.
Effect/Cause
The Sioux appealed to the government to enforce the treaty.
Effect/Cause
The government sent a commission to lease or buy lands.
Effect/Cause
The Sioux refused the commission's offer.
Effect
The government sent in the cavalry.

Summarize causes and effects in a chart. Starting with the first cause in a series, fill in the boxes until you reach the end result.

APPLYING THE SKILL

Make your own cause-and-effect diagram Turn to Chapter 11, Section 3, and read the passage headed "African Americans and the War." Take notes about the causes and effects of black migration. Make a diagram, like the one shown above, to summarize the information you find.

Section 1: Understanding Historical Readings

1.6 Comparing; Contrasting

Historians compare and contrast events, personalities, ideas, behaviors, beliefs, and institutions in order to understand them thoroughly. **Comparing** involves looking at the similarities and differences between two or more things. **Contrasting** means examining only the differences between them.

UNDERSTANDING THE SKILL

Strategy: Finding clues in the text The following passage describes life in colonial America during the last half of the 1600s. The Venn diagram below shows the similarities and differences between the Northern and Southern colonies.

Compare: Look for clue words indicating that two things are alike. Clue words include *both, all, like, as, likewise,* and *similarly.*

Compare: Look for features that two things have in common. Here you learn that both the Northern and the Southern colonies had slavery.

LIFE IN THE EARLY AMERICAN COLONIES

Not long after the English colonies were established, it became apparent that two very different ways of life were developing in the Northern and Southern colonies. In the South, both rich plantation owners and poorer frontier farmers sought land. Virginia and Maryland became known as the tobacco colonies. Large farms, but few towns, appeared there. Rivers served as the main roads.

Slavery existed in all the colonies, but it became a vital source of labor in the South. Most slaves in South Carolina remained unskilled, working mainly in the rice fields. By contrast, the New England and middle colonies did not rely on single staple crops, such as tobacco or rice. Most people were farmers, but they grew a wide variety of crops. A smaller number of workers made products like candles, iron bars, ropes, and sailing ships. The New England colonies traded actively with the islands of the West Indies. In addition to foods, they exported all kinds of other items, ranging from barrels to horses. In return, they imported sugar and molasses. All this trade resulted in the growth of small towns and larger port cities.

Contrast: Look for clue words that show how two things differ. Clue words include *different, differ, unlike, by contrast, however,* and *on the other hand.*

Contrast: Look for ways in which two things are different. Here you learn that unlike the South, the North did not rely on single crops.

Strategy: Making a Venn diagram

Compare and contrast: Summarize similarities and differences in a Venn diagram. Use one oval to describe one thing, the other oval to describe the thing you are comparing, and the overlapping area to show what the two things have in common.

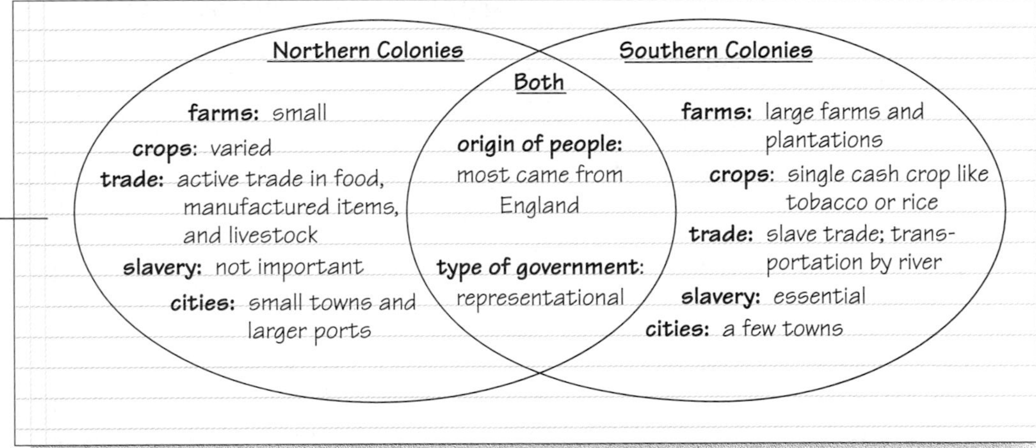

APPLYING THE SKILL

Make your own Venn diagram Turn to Chapter 5, Section 2, and read the passage headed "The Influence of Mexican Culture." Pay special attention to descriptions of the American cowboy and the Mexican vaquero. Make a Venn diagram showing what the two types of cowboy had in common and what made them different.

Section 1: Understanding Historical Readings

1.7 Distinguishing Fact from Opinion

Facts are dates, statistics, and accounts of events, or they are statements that are generally known to be true. Facts can be checked for accuracy. **Opinions** are the judgments, beliefs, and feelings of a writer or speaker.

UNDERSTANDING THE SKILL

Strategy: Finding clues in the text The following excerpt describes the 1886 Haymarket affair in Chicago. The chart summarizes the facts and opinions.

Facts: Look for specific events, dates, and statistics that can be verified. The factual account of the event continues through the first three paragraphs of the passage.

Opinion: Look for assertions, claims, hypotheses, and judgments. Here the speaker's opinion is expressed; the historian gives a factual account of the speech in which this opinion was expressed.

Opinion: Look for judgments the historian makes about events. In the last paragraph, the writer states the opinion that the event was a disaster and then backs up this opinion by explaining the negative consequences of the event.

THE HAYMARKET AFFAIR

At ten o'clock another speaker stepped forward, the main burden of his address being that there was no hope of improving the condition of workingmen through legislation; it must be through their own efforts. As he started to speak, a wind blew up, and it began to rain.

The speaker hurried to a conclusion, but at that point 180 police officers entered the square and headed for the speakers' platform. The captain in charge called on the meeting to disperse, "in the name of the people of the state of Illinois."

At that moment someone threw a bomb into the ranks of the policemen gathered about the speakers. After the initial shock and horror, the police opened fire on the 300 or 400 people who remained, and they in turn fled for their lives. One policeman had been killed by the bomb, and more than 60 injured. One member of the crowd was killed by police fire, and at least 12 were wounded. . . .

In almost every . . . way Haymarket was a disaster. It vastly augmented [increased] the already considerable paranoia of most Americans in regard to anarchists, socialists, communists, and radicals in general. It increased hostility toward "godless foreigners," a phrase that the prosecutor, Grinnell, had used frequently in referring to the defendants. It caused a serious impairment of freedom of speech in every part of the country.

Source: Page Smith, *The Rise of Industrial America* (New York: Penguin, 1990), pp. 244–256.

Strategy: Making a chart

Summarize facts and opinions in a chart. List the facts you learned in a passage as well as the opinions that were expressed.

FACTS	OPINIONS
Just after 10:00, as a speaker was finishing up and it was beginning to rain, someone threw a bomb into the ring of policemen surrounding the speakers. Numerous police were injured by the bomb, and civilians were injured when police fired into the crowd.	speaker: Workers must improve their own situations, since legislation can't do it for them. historian: Nothing good came of the Haymarket affair, and in fact it had many negative consequences. • increased paranoia about radicals • increased hostility toward foreigners • harmed freedom of speech

APPLYING THE SKILL

Make your own chart Read Chapter 7, Section 3, "The Emergence of the Political Machine." Make a chart in which you summarize the facts about political machines and the opinions on graft expressed by George Washington Plunkitt and James Pendergast.

910 Skillbuilder Handbook

1.8 Finding Main Ideas

Finding main ideas means identifying words that sum up what entire paragraphs or selections are about. To begin finding a main idea, identify the topic of a passage. Then think about each fact, example, or opinion you read and ask, What central idea do all these details explain or support? If the main idea is not directly stated, ask yourself, What central idea links all of these details?

UNDERSTANDING THE SKILL

Strategy: Finding clues in the text The following excerpt from President Richard M. Nixon's memoirs is about wiretapping, or bugging—the planting of a concealed microphone to get information. The diagram that follows identifies and organizes the information in the passage.

Nixon on Wiretapping

I had been in politics too long, and seen everything from dirty tricks to vote fraud. I could not muster much moral outrage over a political bugging.

Larry O'Brien [director of the Democratic National Committee] might affect astonishment and horror, but he knew as well as I did that political bugging had been around nearly since the invention of the wiretap. As recently as 1970 a former member of Adlai Stevenson's [Democratic candidate for president in 1952 and 1956] campaign staff had publicly stated that he had tapped the [John F.] Kennedy organization's phone lines at the 1960 Democratic convention. Lyndon Johnson felt that the Kennedys had had him tapped; Barry Goldwater said that his 1964 campaign had been bugged; and Edgar Hoover [director of the FBI, 1924–1972] told me that in 1968 Johnson had ordered my campaign plane bugged.

Source: Richard Nixon, *The Memoirs of Richard Nixon* (New York: Grosset & Dunlap, 1978), pp. 628–629.

Identify the topic by looking for repeated words or key words. This passage repeats the words *bugged, bugging, tapped,* and *wiretap.*

Ask whether any one sentence sums up the point of the whole passage. In this paragraph, the second sentence states Nixon's attitude toward bugging.

Decide what main idea the details or examples show. The many examples suggest that wiretapping was a common practice.

Look for clues that indicate examples. The dates indicate several different examples.

Strategy: Making a diagram

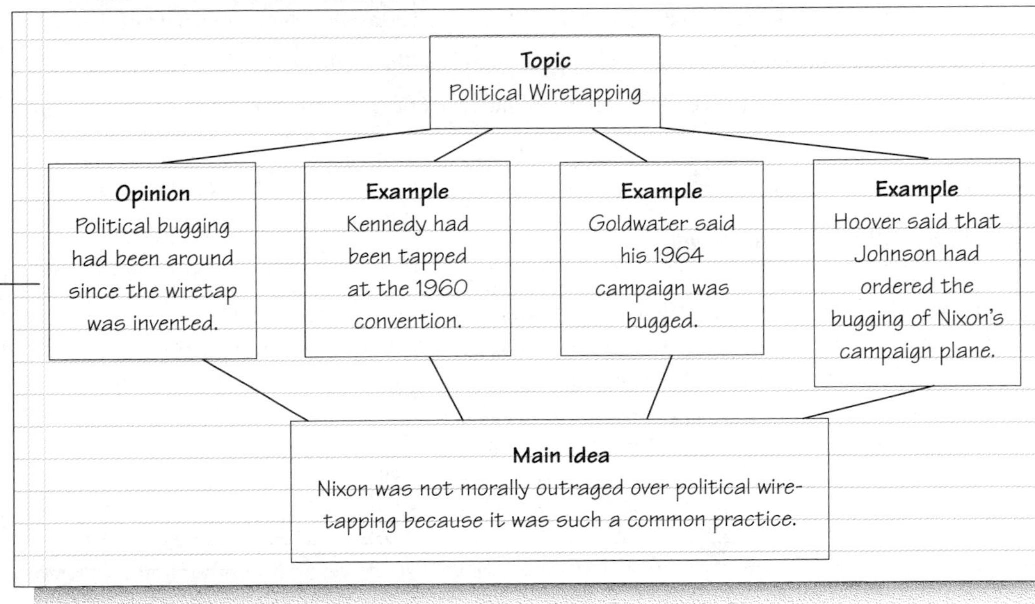

Topic
Political Wiretapping
Opinion
Political bugging had been around since the wiretap was invented.
Example
Kennedy had been tapped at the 1960 convention.
Example
Goldwater said his 1964 campaign was bugged.
Example
Hoover said that Johnson had ordered the bugging of Nixon's campaign plane.
Main Idea
Nixon was not morally outraged over political wiretapping because it was such a common practice.

State the topic and list the supporting details in a chart. Use the information you record to help you state the main idea.

APPLYING THE SKILL

Make your own diagram Turn to Chapter 26, Section 3, and read the passage headed "Space Exploration." Make a diagram, like the one above, to identify the topic, the most important details, and the main idea of the passage.

1.9 Making Inferences

Making inferences from a piece of historical writing means drawing conclusions based on facts, examples, and the author's use of language. For example, if you are reading about the Spanish-American-Cuban War, the writer may not come right out and explain why the United States fought that war. Therefore, you must make inferences about the reasons. To make inferences, use clues in the text and your own personal experience, historical knowledge, and common sense.

UNDERSTANDING THE SKILL

Strategy: Finding clues in the text The following passage is from a speech by President Ronald Reagan. In it, he describes the economic program that he presented to Congress in 1981. From Reagan's language and choice of facts, what can you infer about his opinions with regard to the economy? The chart below lists some inferences that can be drawn from the first paragraph.

On the Program for Economic Recovery

All of us are aware of the punishing inflation which has for the first time in 60 years held to double-digit figures for 2 years in a row. Interest rates have reached absurd levels of more than 20 percent and over 15 percent for those who would borrow to buy a home. All across this land one can see newly built homes standing vacant, unsold because of mortgage interest rates. Almost 8 million Americans are out of work. . . .

I am proposing a comprehensive four-point program . . . aimed at reducing the growth in government spending and taxing, reforming and eliminating regulations which are unnecessary and unproductive or counterproductive, and encouraging a consistent monetary policy aimed at maintaining the value of the currency.

Now, I know that exaggerated and inaccurate stories about these cuts have disturbed many people. . . . Some of you have heard from constituents, I know, afraid that social security checks, for example, were going to be taken away from them. . . . Those who, through no fault of their own, must depend on the rest of us—the poverty stricken, the disabled, the elderly, all those with true need—can rest assured that the social safety net of programs they depend on are exempt from any cuts.

From the facts in the text and historical knowledge, you can infer that Reagan is placing responsibility for the poor economy on the Democrats.

From Reagan's language, you can infer that he blames the poor economy on government spending and taxing.

From Reagan's language, you can infer that he is aware of criticism, although he finds it "exaggerated" and "inaccurate."

Strategy: Making a chart

Make your own inferences. Record clues in the text, as well as what you know about the topic on the basis of your own experience, knowledge, and common sense.

Clues in the Text: Facts, Examples, Language	Personal Experience, Historical Knowledge, Common Sense	Inference
• Inflation in double digits • Interest rates over 20% • 8 million unemployed • Inflation is "punishing" • Interest rates "absurd"	• Reagan defeated Democratic incumbent Jimmy Carter in the 1980 election.	Reagan blames the Democrats for the current economic problems.

APPLYING THE SKILL

Make your own chart Turn to Chapter 10, Section 3, and read the passage headed "The Impact of U.S. Territorial Gains." Create a chart like the one above, making inferences based on clues in the text and on your own personal experience, historical knowledge, and common sense.

2.1 Developing Historical Perspective

Historical perspective is an understanding of events and people in the context of their times. Using historical perspective can help you avoid judging the past solely in terms of present-day norms and values.

UNDERSTANDING THE SKILL

Strategy: Finding clues in the text The following passage is the opening portion of an address by President Theodore Roosevelt. Below it is a chart in which historical perspective is shown in a summary of the attitudes expressed in the passage.

Identify the historical figure, the occasion, and the date.

INAUGURAL ADDRESS, 1905
PRESIDENT THEODORE ROOSEVELT

My fellow-citizens, no people on earth have more cause to be thankful than ours, and this is said reverently, in no spirit of boastfulness in our own strength, but with gratitude to the Giver of Good who has blessed us with the conditions which have enabled us to achieve so large a measure of well-being and of happiness. To us as a people it has been granted to lay the foundations of our national life in a new continent. We are the heirs of the ages, and yet we have had to pay few of the penalties which in old countries are exacted by the dead hand of a bygone civilization. We have not been obliged to fight for our existence against any alien race; and yet our life has called for the vigor and effort without which the manlier and hardier virtues wither away. Under such conditions it would be our own fault if we failed; and the success which we have had in the past, the success which we confidently believe the future will bring, should cause in us no feeling of vainglory, but rather a deep and abiding realization of all which life has offered us; a full acknowledgment of the responsibility which is ours; and a fixed determination to show that under a free government a mighty people can thrive best, alike as regards the things of the body and the things of the soul.

Notice words, phrases, and settings that reflect the period. Here the language used by the president reflects the optimism of the progressive era.

Explain how people's actions and words reflected the attitudes, values, and passions of the era. Teddy Roosevelt's belief in what 19th-century Americans called "manly virtues" shines forth in the language that he employs to describe his nation and its destiny.

Look for clues to the attitudes, customs, and values of people living at the time. The language of the past, though occasionally high-flown and rhetorical, often reveals basic American attitudes toward other peoples and nations.

Strategy: Writing a summary

Use historical perspective to understand Roosevelt's attitudes. In a chart, list key words, phrases, and details from the passage, and then write a short paragraph synthesizing the basic values and attitudes it conveys.

Roosevelt's Inaugural Address	
• new continent • heirs of the ages • bygone civilization • vigor and effort • manlier and hardier virtues	Theodore Roosevelt seems to reveal a strong and resilient optimism about the American enterprise. His confidence is grounded in a deep religious faith in God (the "Giver of Good") and God's plan for the nation. Roosevelt clearly believes in the ability of the American people to solve whatever problems they face as they move into a bright future. Roosevelt's appeal to the manly virtues reflects typical attitudes and values of 19th- and early 20th-century Americans.

APPLYING THE SKILL

Write your own summary Turn to Chapter 8, Section 2, and read the One American's Story feature, which discusses ideas about educational reform in the late 19th century. Using historical perspective, summarize those ideas in a chart like the one above.

Section 2: Using Critical Thinking

2.2 Formulating Historical Questions

Formulating historical questions is important both as you read and as you do historical research. As you read, ask questions about the events—about what caused them, what made them important, and so forth. Then, when you are doing research, write questions that you want your research to answer. This step is critical—it will help you to guide and focus your research.

UNDERSTANDING THE SKILL

Strategy: Finding clues in the text At a women's rights convention in the mid-1800s, the delegates adopted a "Declaration of Sentiments" that set forth a number of grievances. The following passage is a description of that event. Below is a web diagram that organizes historical questions about the event.

Ask about the basic facts of the event. Who were the main people? What did they do? Where and when did the event take place?

Ask about the results produced by various causes. What were the results of the event?

SENECA FALLS, 1848

Elizabeth Cady Stanton and Lucretia Mott decided to act on their resolution to hold a women's rights convention. In 1848, it convened at Seneca Falls, New York, the small town that gave the convention its name. Stanton and Mott spent a day composing an agenda and a detailed statement of grievances. Stanton carefully modeled this "Declaration of Sentiments" on the Declaration of Independence. The second paragraph began, "We hold these truths to be self-evident: that all men and women are created equal. . . ." More than 300 women and men gathered at the convention. The participants approved all measures unanimously, except for one: women's right to vote. The franchise for women, though it passed, remained a controversial topic.

Ask about the cause of an event. Why did the event take place?

Ask about historical influences on a speaker or event. What other historical events was it similar to? How was it different?

Strategy: Making a web diagram

Investigate a topic in more depth by asking questions. Ask a large question, and then ask smaller questions to help you explore the larger question.

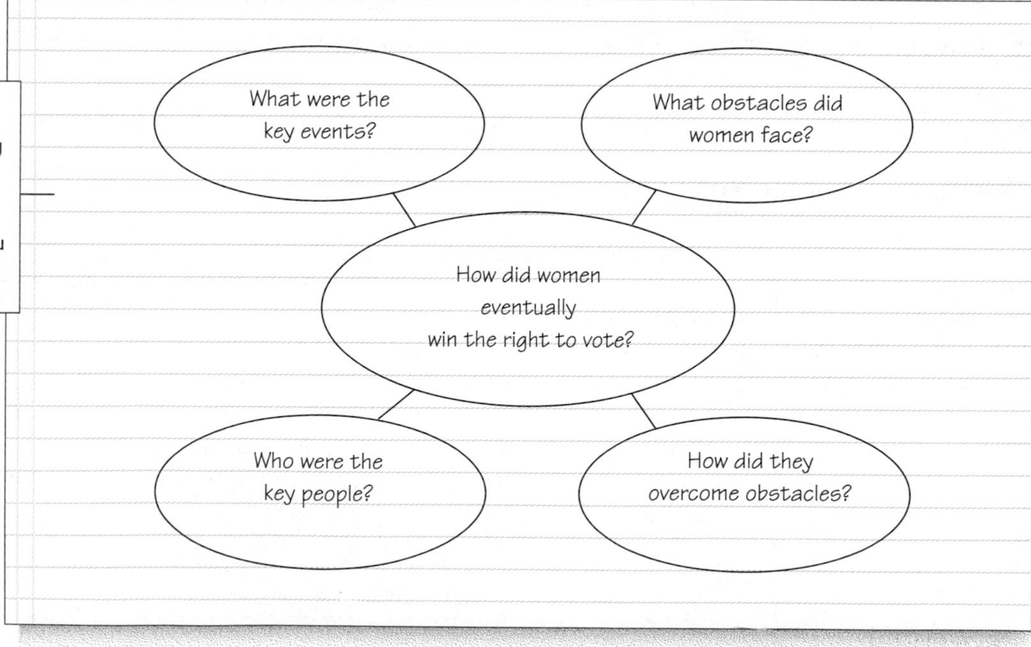

APPLYING THE SKILL

Make your own web diagram Turn to Chapter 22, Section 1, and read the passage headed "The Tonkin Gulf Resolution." Use a web diagram to write a historical question about the passage, along with smaller questions that could guide your research into the topic.

Section 2: Using Critical Thinking

2.3 Hypothesizing

Hypothesizing is the process of coming up with a possible theory or cause to explain historical events. This explanation can then be tested against the historical facts to see whether it is accurate. When you read history, hypothesizing is important because it helps you understand (1) why events occurred, (2) what the consequences of the events might be, and (3) what the significance of the events is.

UNDERSTANDING THE SKILL

As you read, form hypotheses about the important events. You could form the hypothesis that Gorbachev's new policies would deeply affect politics in the Soviet Union and Eastern Europe.

Read for facts that prove your hypothesis right or wrong. These facts support the hypothesis because they show that Gorbachev's policies affected politics in the Soviet Union.

Strategy: Finding clues in the text As the Cold War came to an end, people offered various hypotheses to explain why the Soviet Union broke up and to predict what would replace it. Read this passage and form your own hypothesis. Below the passage is a chart that presents a hypothesis and the facts used to support it.

THE COLD WAR ENDS

In March 1985, Mikhail Gorbachev became the general secretary of the Communist Party in the Soviet Union. He initiated a new policy of openness and reform within the USSR, putting an end to the collective ownership of resources, most government censorship, and controlled elections. A dramatic increase in nationalism on the part of the non-Russian republics followed the open elections, and in December 1991, all 14 republics declared independence. The USSR was replaced by a loose federation of republics called the Commonwealth of Independent States.

Gorbachev's new policies led to massive changes in Eastern Europe, as the satellite states, with his encouragement, moved toward democracy. On November 9, 1989, East Berlin opened the Berlin Wall, putting an end to the city's 28-year division. Berliners climbed atop the wall, cheering and dancing, and rushed through the previously well-armed checkpoints. East Germany soon held its first free elections, and the two Germanys were reunited. Hungary, Bulgaria, and Romania made successful transitions from communism, but Yugoslavia collapsed into warring factions.

This fact supports the hypothesis because it shows that Gorbachev's policies had a profound effect on politics in Eastern Europe.

Use a chart to summarize your hypothesis about events. Suppose that you are thinking about the effect of the end of the Cold War on American foreign and domestic policy. Use a chart to set out your hypothesis and the facts that support or contradict it.

Strategy: Making a chart

Hypothesis	Fact 1	Fact 2	Fact 3
Gorbachev's new policies would affect politics in Soviet Union and Eastern Europe	Fact: Increase in nationalism in non-Russian republics	Fact: USSR replaced by loose confederation	Fact: Massive change in Eastern Europe
	Whether it supports hypothesis: Yes	Whether it supports hypothesis: Yes	Whether it supports hypothesis: Yes

APPLYING THE SKILL

Make your own chart Turn to Chapter 24, Section 2, and read the passage headed "A Bungled Burglary." Make a chart in which you hypothesize about the consequences of the burglary at the Democratic National Committee headquarters. Then list facts and indicate whether they support the hypothesis.

Section 2: Using Critical Thinking

2.4 Analyzing Issues

An issue is a matter of public concern or debate. Issues in history are usually economic, social, political, or moral. Historical issues are often more complicated than they first appear. **Analyzing issues** means taking them apart to identify the different points of view in economic, social, political, or moral debates.

UNDERSTANDING THE SKILL

Strategy: Finding clues in the text The following passage describes working conditions in U.S. factories in the late 1800s and early 1900s. Notice how the cluster diagram below it helps you to analyze the issue of child labor.

CHILDREN AT WORK

Workers had little choice but to put up with deplorable conditions in aptly named sweatshops. Wages were so low that many families could not survive unless all their members, including children, worked. Between 1890 and 1910, 20 percent of boys and 10 percent of girls under age 15—some as young as five years old—held full-time jobs. A typical work week was 12 hours a day, six days a week. Many of these children worked from dawn to dusk, wasted by hunger and exhaustion that made them prone to crippling accidents for which there was no compensation. With little time or energy left for school, child laborers gave up their futures to help their families make ends meet.

Nonetheless, factory owners and some parents praised child labor for keeping children out of mischief. They believed idleness for children was bad and work provided healthy occupation.

The reformer Jacob Riis and others worked for decent conditions, better wages, and child-labor laws. The new labor unions joined the call for eight-hour days and better pay. Slowly public opinion turned against the use of child labor. Though it took many years and great effort, state legislatures finally passed laws banning or restricting child labor.

Look for a central problem with its causes and effects.

Look for facts and statistics. The numbers supplied by facts and statistics can help to flesh out the discussion of an issue.

Look for the other side to an issue. You need to look at all sides of an issue before deciding what you think.

Strategy: Making a cluster diagram

Issue: Should children under 15 have been allowed to work?

Facts:
- Children as young as 5 years old worked.
- Twenty percent of boys and 10 percent of girls under 15 held jobs.
- Workers typically put in 72 hours per week.
- Working conditions in many industries were strenuous, exhausting, and dangerous.

In favor of children working:
- **Who:** business owners, some parents
- **Reasons:** Idleness was bad, so working was good for children. Families needed income from children.

Against children working:
- **Who:** Jacob Riis and other reformers.
- **Reasons:** Working meant giving up school. Working conditions were inhumane.

If an issue is complex, make a diagram. A diagram can help you analyze an issue.

APPLYING THE SKILL

Make your own cluster diagram Read the passage headed "The Equal Rights Amendment" and "Conservatives and the Women's Movement" in Chapter 23, Section 2. Make a cluster diagram to analyze the issue and the positions of the people involved.

Section 2: Using Critical Thinking

2.5 Analyzing Assumptions and Biases

An **assumption** is a belief or an idea that is taken for granted. Sometimes people make assumptions based on evidence; sometimes they make unfounded assumptions. Whether assumptions are clearly stated or just implied, you can usually figure out what they are.

A bias is a prejudiced point of view. Historical accounts that are biased tend to be one-sided and reflect the personal prejudices of the historian.

UNDERSTANDING THE SKILL

Strategy: Finding clues in the text The following passage is from *The Americans at Home* by the Scottish minister David Macrae, who wrote the book after visiting the United States in the 1860s. Notice how the chart below the excerpt helps to summarize information about the writer's assumptions and biases.

Identify the author and information about him or her. Does the author belong to a special-interest group, religious organization, political party, or social movement that might promote a one-sided or slanted viewpoint on the subject?

THE AMERICANS AT HOME

BY DAVID MACRAE

[T]he American girls are very delightful. And in one point they fairly surpass the majority of English girls—they are all educated and well informed. . . . The admirable educational system . . . covering the whole area of society, has given them education whether they are rich or poor, has furnished them with a great deal of information, and has quickened their desire for more. An American girl will talk with you about anything, and . . . seem to feel interest in it. Their tendency is perhaps to talk too much, and . . . it seemed to me sometimes to make no perceptible difference whether they knew anything of the subject they talked about or not. But they usually know a little of everything; and their general intelligence and vivacity make them very delightful companions.

Examine the evidence. Is what the author relates consistent with other accounts? Is the behavior described consistent with human nature as you have observed it?

Search for clues. Are there words, phrases, statements, or images that might convey a positive or negative slant? What might these clues reveal about the author's bias?

Strategy: Making a chart

Make a chart of your analysis. For each of the heads listed on the left-hand side of the chart, summarize what information you can find in the passage.

David Macrae's impression of American Women	
speaker	David Macrae
date	1860s
occasion	book called The Americans at Home about Macrae's visit to the United States
tone	humorous or light-hearted
assumptions	American women are well-informed and stimulating companions, if inclined to talk too much about subjects of which they know little.
bias	Implicit in some of the author's comments seems to be a prejudice that women should defer to the superior knowledge of men.

APPLYING THE SKILL

Make your own chart Look at the opinions expressed by A. Mitchell Palmer in the feature A Personal Voice on page 431. Summarize his underlying assumptions and biases in a chart like the one shown.

Section 2: Using Critical Thinking

2.6 Evaluating Decisions and Courses of Action

Evaluating decisions means making judgments about the decisions that historical figures made. Historians evaluate decisions on the basis of their moral implications and their costs and benefits from different points of view.

Evaluating alternative courses of action means carefully judging the choices that historical figures were faced with, to better understand why they made the decisions they did.

UNDERSTANDING THE SKILL

Strategy: Finding clues in the text The following passage describes the decisions President John F. Kennedy had to make when he learned of Soviet missile bases in Cuba. As you read it, think about another decision he could have made at each turn of events. Below the passage is a chart in which one alternative response is analyzed.

The Cuban Missile Crisis

During the summer of 1962, the flow of Soviet weapons into Cuba—including nuclear missiles—greatly increased. President Kennedy responded cautiously at first, issuing a warning that the United States would not tolerate the presence of offensive nuclear weapons in Cuba. Then, on October 16, photographs taken by American U-2 planes showed the president that the Soviets were secretly building missile bases on Cuba. Some of the missiles, armed and ready to fire, could reach U.S. cities in minutes.

On the evening of October 22, the president made public the evidence of missiles and stated his ultimatum: any missile attack from Cuba would trigger an all-out attack on the Soviet Union. Soviet ships continued to head toward the island, while the U.S. navy prepared to stop them and U.S. invasion troops massed in Florida. To avoid confrontation, the Soviet ships suddenly halted. Then Soviet premier Khrushchev offered to remove the missiles from Cuba in exchange for a pledge not to invade the island. Kennedy agreed, and the crisis ended.

Some people criticized Kennedy for practicing brinkmanship when private talks might have resolved the crisis without the threat of nuclear war. Others believed he had been too soft and had passed up an ideal chance to invade Cuba and to oust its Communist leader, Castro.

Look at decisions made by individuals or by groups. Notice the decisions Kennedy made in response to Soviet actions.

Analyze a decision in terms of the alternatives that were possible. Both Kennedy and Khrushchev faced the alternative of either escalating or defusing the crisis.

Look at the outcome of the decisions.

Strategy: Making a chart

Make a chart of your analysis. The problem was that Soviet nuclear missiles were being shipped to Cuba. The decision to be made was how the United States should respond.

alternative	pros	cons	evaluation
Negotiate a settlement quietly, without threatening nuclear war.	1. Avoid the threat of nuclear war 2. Avoid frightening U.S. citizens	1. The U.S. would not have the public opportunity of looking like a strong world leader. 2. The government would lose favor with Cuban exiles living in the U.S.	your answer: Would this have been a good choice and why?

APPLYING THE SKILL

Make your own chart Turn to page 575 and read the discussion of the decision to intern Japanese Americans during World War II. Make a chart like the one shown to summarize the pros and cons of an alternative decision, and then write an evaluation of that decision.

2.7 Forming Opinions

Historians **form opinions** about the information they deal with. They support their opinions with references to facts, examples, and historical parallels. You might be asked, for instance, to decide in what circumstances violence in a political revolution is ever justified.

Decide what you think about a subject after reading all the information available to you. After reading this description, you might decide that no political cause justifies such violence against individuals. On the other hand, your opinion might be that, regrettable as such violence is, when a tyranny is overthrown, some servants of the old regime are bound to perish.

UNDERSTANDING THE SKILL

Strategy: Finding clues in the text The following passage includes comments on the French Revolution by Gouverneur Morris, one of the participants in the Constitutional Convention, and by Thomas Jefferson.

A Scene of Mob Violence

Gouverneur Morris was a visitor to Paris during the early days of the French Revolution. In the following journal entry he describes a scene of revolutionary mob violence: "The head and body of Mr. de Foulon are introduced in triumph. The head on a pike, the body dragged naked on the earth. Afterwards this horrible exhibition is carried through the different streets. His crime [was] to have accepted a place in the Ministry. This mutilated form of an old man of seventy five is shown to Bertier, his son in law, the intend't. [another official] of Paris, and afterwards he also is put to death and cut to pieces, the populace carrying the mangled fragments with a savage joy." Such violence was common during the French Revolution and shocked a good many Americans. However, Thomas Jefferson was a supporter of the Revolution, saying, "The liberty of the whole earth was depending on the issue of the contest, and . . . rather than it should have failed, I would have seen half the earth devastated."

Support your opinion with facts, quotations, and examples, including references to similar events in other historical eras. You might compare the violence on display in this episode of the French Revolution with the relative lack of mob violence in the American Revolution.

Look for the opinions of historians and other experts. Consider their opinions when forming your own.

Strategy: Making a chart

Summarize your opinion and supporting information in a chart. Write an opinion and then list facts, quotations, and examples that support your opinion.

Opinion: The French Revolution was especially violent and cruel.

facts:	quotations:	examples:
• Violence escalated. • Jacobins launched Reign of Terror. • Moderates were sent to guillotine. • Jacobins declared war on other countries.	"he also is put to death and cut to pieces"	Jacobins beheaded Louis XVI.

APPLYING THE SKILL

Make your own chart Read the Point/Counterpoint feature on page 530. Record your opinion and form your own opinion about the success or failure of the New Deal. Record your opinion in a chart like the one shown, providing supporting information to back it up.

2.8 Drawing Conclusions

Drawing conclusions involves analyzing the implications of what you have read and forming opinions about its meaning or consequences. To draw conclusions, you look closely at facts and then use your own experience and common sense to decide what those facts mean.

UNDERSTANDING THE SKILL

Strategy: Finding clues in the text The following passage tells about employment trends in the 1990s. The marginal boxes indicate some information from which conclusions can be drawn. In the diagram below, the information and conclusions are organized in a clear way.

Job Outlook in the Mid-1990s

Several trends have emerged in the workplace of the 1990s. Inflation is at its lowest level since the 1960s, and 10 million new jobs created between 1993 and 1996 have helped lower the unemployment rate to 5.1 percent. Median household income adjusted for inflation, however, has declined from $33,585 to $31,241, even though there are many households in which both parents work. And the gap between rich and poor continues to widen, with some executives receiving millions of dollars in compensation while 4 million families live below the poverty line.

Jobs in manufacturing have declined, while new jobs have appeared at a rapid rate in the service sector. In addition, many jobs once done by permanent employees of a company are done by temporary workers, who are paid only for the time they are needed and who typically do not receive benefits.

Three out of four young Americans think they will earn less in their lifetimes than their parents did. Unemployment in their age group continues at the same rate, while the unemployment rate for other adults has fallen. In 1993, about one in seven workers between the ages of 16 and 25 was out of work, double the national average.

Use the facts to draw a conclusion. Conclusion: In general, the economy is good in the mid-1990s.

Read carefully to understand all the facts. Conclusion: Income expectations are lower.

Ask questions of the material. What is the effect of these changes on job security? Conclusion: Job security is reduced.

Ask questions of the material. What might be the effect of these changes on young people? Conclusion: Jobs will be harder for young people to find.

Strategy: Making a diagram

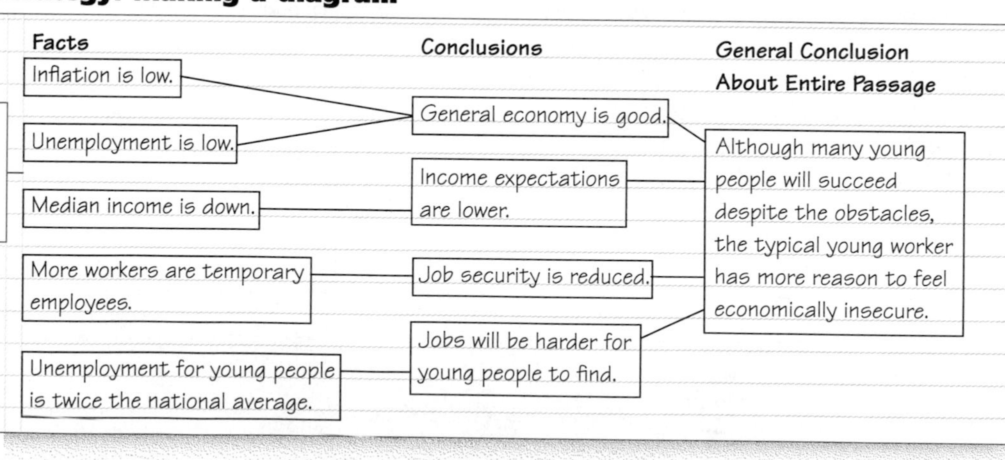

Summarize the data and your conclusion about it in a diagram.

APPLYING THE SKILL

Make your own diagram Turn to Chapter 26, Section 4, and read the passage headed "The Graying of America." Draw conclusions based on the facts in the passage. Using the model as a guide, create your own diagram, showing the facts and interim conclusions you have used to arrive at a general conclusion.

2.9 Synthesizing

Synthesizing is the skill historians use in developing interpretations of the past. Like detective work, synthesizing involves putting together clues, information, and ideas to form an overall picture of a historical event.

UNDERSTANDING THE SKILL

Strategy: Finding clues in the text The following passage describes the first settlers of the Americas. The marginal boxes indicate how some information leads toward a synthesis—an overall picture of Native American life.

Read carefully to understand the facts. Facts such as these enable you to base your interpretations on physical evidence.

Look for explanations that link the facts together. This assertion is based on the evidence provided by snares, nets, and bowls, which are mentioned in the next couple of sentences.

The First Americans

From the discovery of chiseled arrowheads and charred bones at ancient sites, it appears that the earliest Americans lived as big-game hunters. The woolly mammoth, their largest prey, provided them with food, clothing, and bones for constructing tools and shelters. People gradually shifted to hunting smaller game and gathering available plants. They fashioned baskets to collect nuts, wild rice, chokecherries, gooseberries, and currants. They invented snares, and later bows and arrows, to hunt small game, such as jackrabbits and deer. They wove nets to fish the streams and lakes.

Between 10,000 and 15,000 years ago, a revolution took place in what is now central Mexico. People began to raise plants as food. Maize may have been the first domesticated plant, with gourds, pumpkins, peppers, beans, and potatoes following. Agriculture spread to other regions.

The rise of agriculture brought tremendous changes to the Americas. Agriculture made it possible for people to remain in one place. It also enabled them to accumulate and store surplus food. As their surplus increased, people had the time to develop skills and more complex ideas about the world. From this agricultural base rose larger, more stable, and increasingly complex societies.

Consider what you already know that could apply. Your general knowledge will probably lead you to accept this statement as reasonable.

Bring together the information you have about a subject. This interpretation brings together different kinds of information to arrive at a new understanding of the subject.

Strategy: Making a cluster diagram

Summarize your synthesis in a diagram. Use a cluster diagram to organize the facts, opinions, examples, and interpretations that you have brought together to form a synthesis.

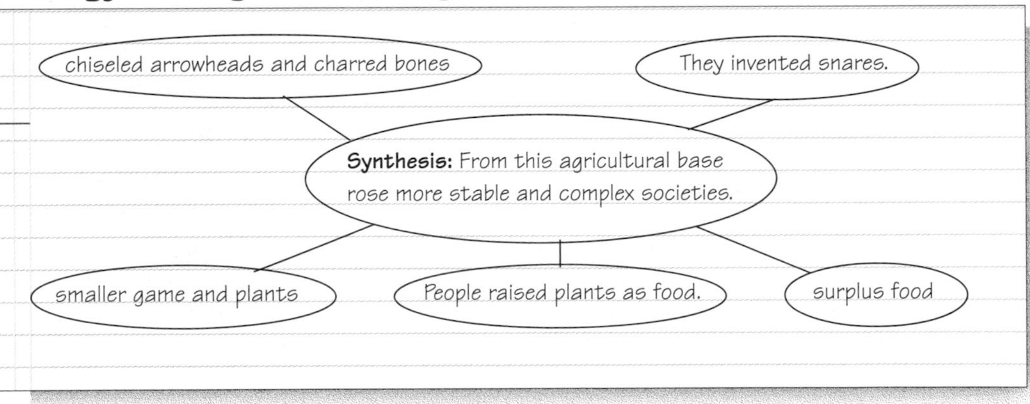

APPLYING THE SKILL

Make your own cluster diagram Turn to Chapter 13, Section 2, and read the passage headed "Women Shed Old Roles at Home and at Work." Look for information to support a synthesis about the fundamental changes in the family brought about by women's new opportunities.

Section 2: Using Critical Thinking

2.10 Making Predictions

Making predictions helps you think in greater depth about choices that historical figures faced. You can predict by evaluating the choices a leader or group faced and imagining what might have happened if a different course of action had been taken. You can also make predictions about what may happen in the future as the result of a decision.

UNDERSTANDING THE SKILL

Strategy: Finding clues in the text The following passage discusses the central weaknesses of the Treaty of Versailles, which ended World War I. Below the passage is a chart in which decisions taken by those who framed the treaty are listed, along with alternative decisions and predictions of their possible outcomes.

Identify the decisions.

Decide what other decisions might have been made.

Predict the outcomes of the alternative decisions.

WEAKNESSES OF THE TREATY OF VERSAILLES

First, the treaty humiliated Germany. The war-guilt clause caused Germans of all political viewpoints to detest the treaty. Furthermore, there was no way Germany could pay the huge financial reparations demanded by the Allies.

Second, the Bolshevik government in Russia was excluded from the peace conference. Russia, which had fought with the Allies and suffered higher casualties than any other nation, lost more territory than Germany did. The Union of Soviet Socialist Republics, as Russia was called after 1922, became determined to regain its former territory.

Third, the treaty ignored the claims of colonized people for self-determination. For example, the man who would later become known as Ho Chi Minh asked for a constitutional government that would give the Vietnamese people the same civil and political rights as the French. Instead of adopting Ho Chi Minh's proposal, however, President Wilson refused even to consider it.

Strategy: Making a Chart

Make a chart. Record decisions, alternatives, and possible outcomes.

Decision 1:	Decision 2:	Decision 3:
The treaty included a war-guilt clause.	Russia was excluded from the peace conference.	The treaty ignored the claims of colonized people.
Alternative decision:	**Alternative decision:**	**Alternative decision:**
The treaty had no war-guilt clause.	Russia was included in the peace negotiations.	The treaty respected the claims of colonized people.
Possible outcome:	**Possible outcome:**	**Possible outcome:**
Germany rebuilds. World War II does not occur.	Tension between the Soviet Union and the West decreases.	Tensions are reduced world-wide; Vietnam War is averted.

APPLYING THE SKILL

Make your own chart Turn to Chapter 20, Section 1, and read the passage headed "The Berlin Crisis." Make a chart, like the one above, in which you identify Kennedy's and Khrushchev's decisions, alternative decisions that these leaders might have made, and the outcomes that might have resulted.

922 Skillbuilder Handbook

2.11 Forming Generalizations

Forming generalizations means making broad judgments based on the information in texts. For instance, when reading about the Holocaust, you might form this generalization: "Most of Hitler's victims were Jews." When you form generalizations, you need to be sure they are valid. They must be based on sufficient evidence, and they must be consistent with the information given.

UNDERSTANDING THE SKILL

Strategy: Finding clues in the text The following three excerpts deal with Herbert Hoover and his relation to the Great Depression. Notice how the information in the web diagram below supports the generalization drawn.

Determine what information the sources have in common. All the sources suggest that people blamed Hoover for the Great Depression.

State your generalization in sentence form. A generalization often needs a qualifying word, such as *most, many,* or *some,* to make it valid.

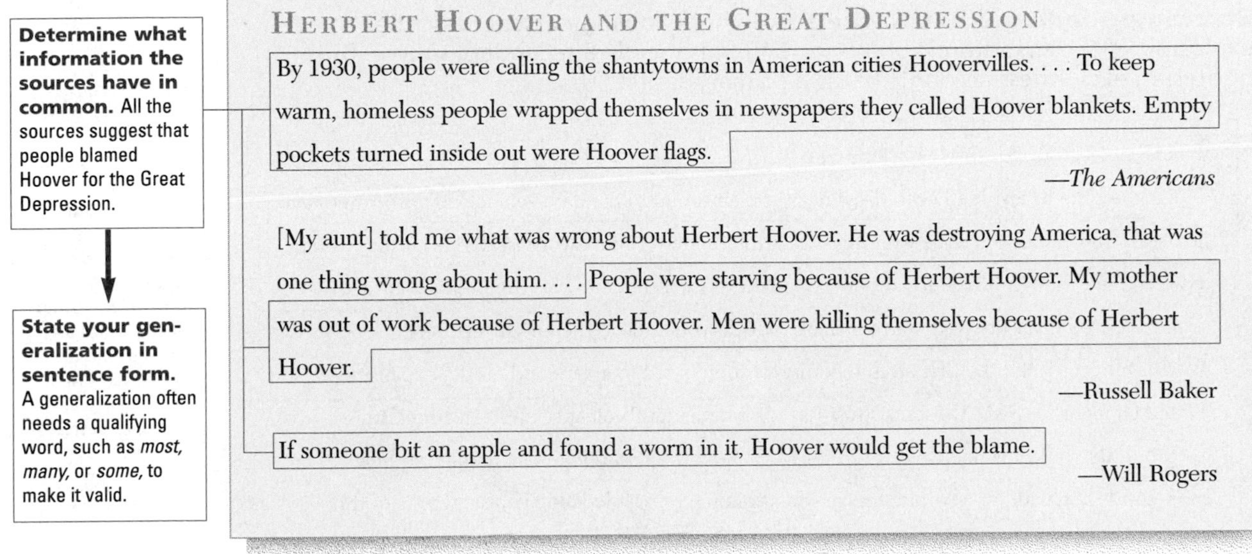

HERBERT HOOVER AND THE GREAT DEPRESSION

By 1930, people were calling the shantytowns in American cities Hoovervilles. . . . To keep warm, homeless people wrapped themselves in newspapers they called Hoover blankets. Empty pockets turned inside out were Hoover flags.

—*The Americans*

[My aunt] told me what was wrong about Herbert Hoover. He was destroying America, that was one thing wrong about him. . . . People were starving because of Herbert Hoover. My mother was out of work because of Herbert Hoover. Men were killing themselves because of Herbert Hoover.

—Russell Baker

If someone bit an apple and found a worm in it, Hoover would get the blame.

—Will Rogers

Strategy: Making a web diagram

Record the generalization in a diagram. Use a web diagram to record relevant information and make a valid generalization.

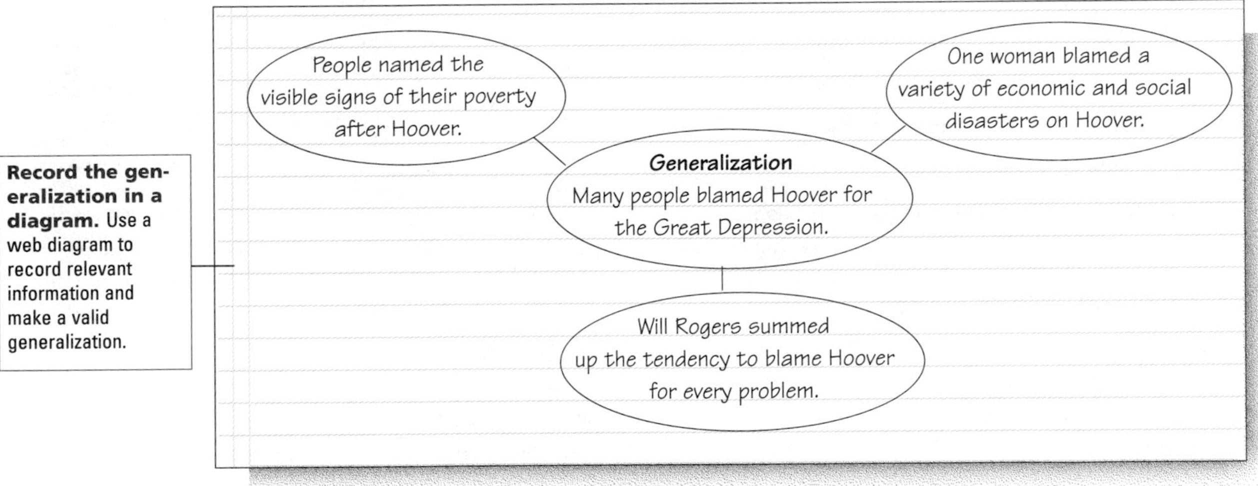
People named the visible signs of their poverty after Hoover.
One woman blamed a variety of economic and social disasters on Hoover.
Generalization
Many people blamed Hoover for the Great Depression.
Will Rogers summed up the tendency to blame Hoover for every problem.

APPLYING THE SKILL

Make your own diagram Study the Daily Life feature "Signs of the Sixties" on pages 778–779. Create a diagram like the one above, recording a generalization about teenagers during the sixties. Use information from the text, visuals, and data file to support your generalization.

3.1 Primary and Secondary Sources

Primary sources are written or created by people who were present at historical events, either as participants or as observers. Primary sources include letters, diaries, journals, speeches, newspaper articles, magazine articles, eyewitness accounts, and autobiographies.

Secondary sources are based on primary sources but are produced by people who were not present at the original events. They often combine information from a number of different accounts. Secondary sources include history books, historical essays, and biographies.

UNDERSTANDING THE SKILL

Strategy: Finding clues in the text The following passage describes the explosion of the first atomic bomb in 1945. It is mainly a secondary source, but it quotes an eyewitness account that is a primary source.

Secondary source: Look for information collected from several sources. Here the writer creates a composite picture of expectations before the explosion.

Primary source: Identify the author and evaluate his or her credentials. What qualifies the writer to report on the event? Here the writer actually worked on developing the bomb.

Primary source: Identify the title. Look for the name of the source and publication information, such as the date of a book or article.

Secondary source: Look for information collected after the event. A secondary source provides a perspective that is missing in a primary source.

THE FIRST ATOMIC BOMB

As the time to test the bomb drew near, the air around Los Alamos crackled with rumors and fears. At one end of the scale were fears that the bomb wouldn't work at all or, if it did, would not produce enough punch to amount to much. At the other end was the prediction that the explosion would set fire to the atmosphere, which would mean the end of the earth.

On July 16, 1945, the first atomic bomb was detonated in a dark and empty expanse of desert near Alamogordo, New Mexico. Otto Frisch, a Manhattan Project scientist, listened tensely to the countdown. In his book *What Little I Remember*, he described what happened next:

> And then without a sound, the sun was shining; or so it looked. The sand hills of the desert were shimmering in a very bright light, almost colorless and shapeless. . . . I turned round, but that object on the horizon which looked like a small sun was still too bright to look at. . . . After another ten seconds or so it had grown and . . . was slowly rising into the sky from the ground, with which it remained connected by a lengthening stem of swirling dust.

That blinding flash, which was visible 180 miles away, was followed by a deafening roar as a tremendous shock wave rolled across the trembling desert. The bomb not only worked, but it was more powerful than most had dared hope.

Strategy: Making a chart

Summarize information from primary and secondary sources in a chart.

Primary Source	Secondary Source
Author: Otto Frisch	Author: unknown
Qualifications: scientist working on Manhattan Project	Qualifications: had access to multiple accounts of the time leading up to and following the event
Information: detailed description, sensory observations, feeling of awe	Information: description of range of points of view and of information available only after the event

APPLYING THE SKILL

Make your own chart Turn to Chapter 25, Section 1, and read the One American's Story feature, which includes a quotation from Peggy Noonan. Make a chart, like the one above, in which you summarize information from the primary and secondary sources.

924 Skillbuilder Handbook

3.2 Visual, Audio, Multimedia Sources

In addition to written accounts, historians use many kinds of **visual sources,** including paintings, costume drawings, photographs, political cartoons, and advertisements. Visual sources are rich with historical details and sometimes convey the feelings and points of view of an era better than words do.

Spoken language has always been a primary means of passing on human history. **Audio sources**—such as recorded speeches, interviews, press conferences, and radio programs—continue the oral tradition today.

Movies, CD-ROMs, television, and computer software are the newest kind of historical sources, called **multimedia sources.** Often information found in other forms—such as writing, recordings, still photographs, and videotapes—is incorporated into a complex multimedia format with words, sounds, and pictures.

UNDERSTANDING THE SKILL

Strategy: Finding clues The following political cartoon shows President Calvin Coolidge playing the saxophone while big business dances. The chart below it summarizes historical information gained from interpreting the visual source.

Identify the subject. This cartoon deals with President Calvin Coolidge's relationship with big business.

Analyze the point of view. Is the subject shown in a positive or negative light? Big business is having a wonderful time, possibly at the public's expense. The president is small and relatively insignificant. The caption underscores the impression that big business is close to the president.

YES, SIR, HE'S MY BABY

Interpret the message. The cartoonist suggests a cozy relationship between the president and big business. Coolidge caters to big business, and business dances to his tune.

Identify important symbols and details. Big business is shown as a young, carefree, energetic flapper of the twenties. The president's saxophone is labeled "Praise," suggesting his positive attitude toward the oversized, fun-loving flapper.

Strategy: Making a chart

Summarize your interpretation of the cartoon in a simple chart.

Subject	Point of View	Symbols and Details	Message
President Coolidge's relationship with big business	Satirical of the Coolidge administration and of big business	Flapper: big business, carefree and overgrown President: playing a tune for business	Big business and the president are too close. Business is having too good a time—with the president's help.

APPLYING THE SKILL

Make your own chart Turn to the political cartoon on page 506, which presents an opinion about Franklin D. Roosevelt's New Deal programs. Use a chart like the one above to analyze and interpret the cartoon.

Section 3: Print, Visual, and Technological Sources

3.3 Interpreting Maps

Maps are representations of features on the earth's surface. Historians use maps to locate historical events, to demonstrate how geography has influenced history, and to illustrate human interaction with the environment.

Different kinds of maps are used for specific purposes.

Political maps show political units, from countries, states, and provinces to counties, districts, and towns. Each area is shaded a different color.

Physical maps show mountains, hills, plains, rivers, lakes, and oceans. They may include contour lines to indicate elevations of land and depths of water.

Historical maps illustrate such things as economic activity, political alliances, migrations, battles, population density, and changes over time.

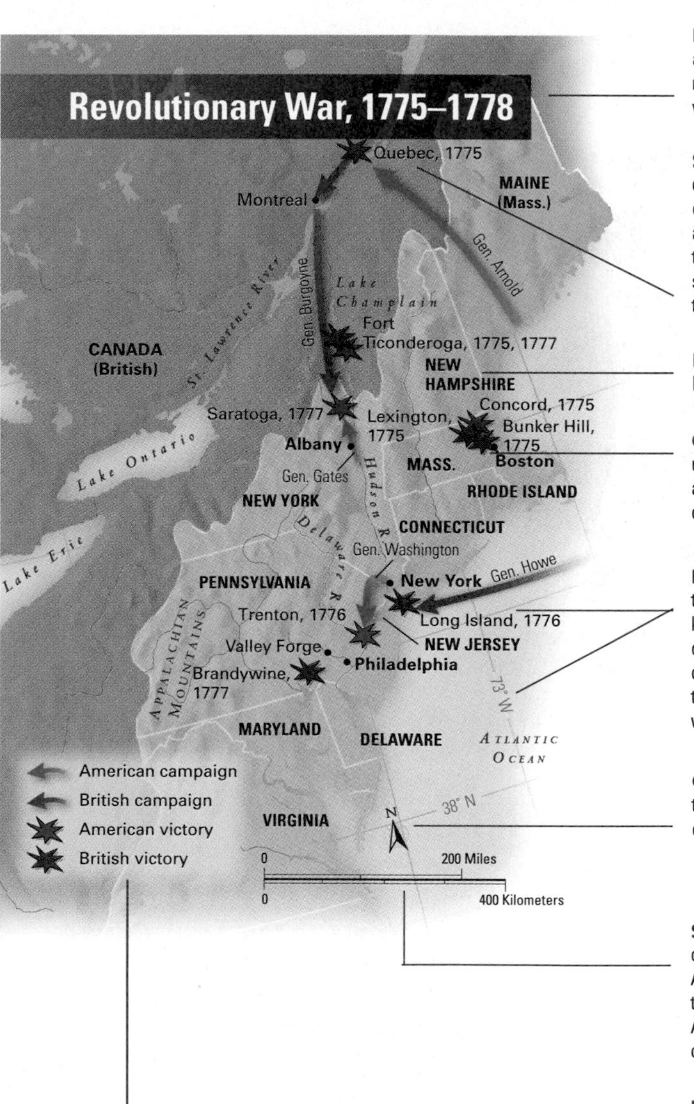

Lines Lines indicate boundaries between political areas, roads and highways, routes of exploration or migration, and rivers and other waterways. Lines may vary in width and color.

Symbols Cities, towns, and villages often appear as dots of different sizes, depending on their populations. A capital city is often shown as a star or a dot with a circle around it. An area's crops, products, resources, industries, and special features may be indicated by symbols, such as a cotton leaf for an area growing cotton and a tree silhouette for an area in which timber is important.

Labels The key places, such as cities, states, and bodies of water, are labeled.

Colors Different colors are used to indicate areas under different political or cultural influence. Colors are also used to show such variable features as population density and altitude.

Lines of longitude and latitude Lines of longitude and latitude appear on maps to indicate the absolute location of the area shown. Lines of latitude show distance north or south of the equator, measured in degrees along a meridian. Lines of longitude show distance in degrees east or west of the prime meridian, which runs through Greenwich, England.

Compass Rose A compass rose is a device indicating the map's orientation on the globe. It may show all four cardinal directions (N, S, E, W) or just one, north.

Scale A map's scale shows the ratio between a unit of length on the map and a unit of distance on the earth. A typical scale shows a one-inch segment and indicates the number of miles that length represents on the map. A map on which an inch represents 500 miles has a scale of 1:31,680,000

Legend or key A legend or key is a small table in which the symbols, types of lines, and special colors that appear in the map are listed and explained.

926 Skillbuilder Handbook

UNDERSTANDING THE SKILL

Strategy: Finding clues The historical maps below show European land claims in North America in 1754 and after 1763. Together they show changes over time.

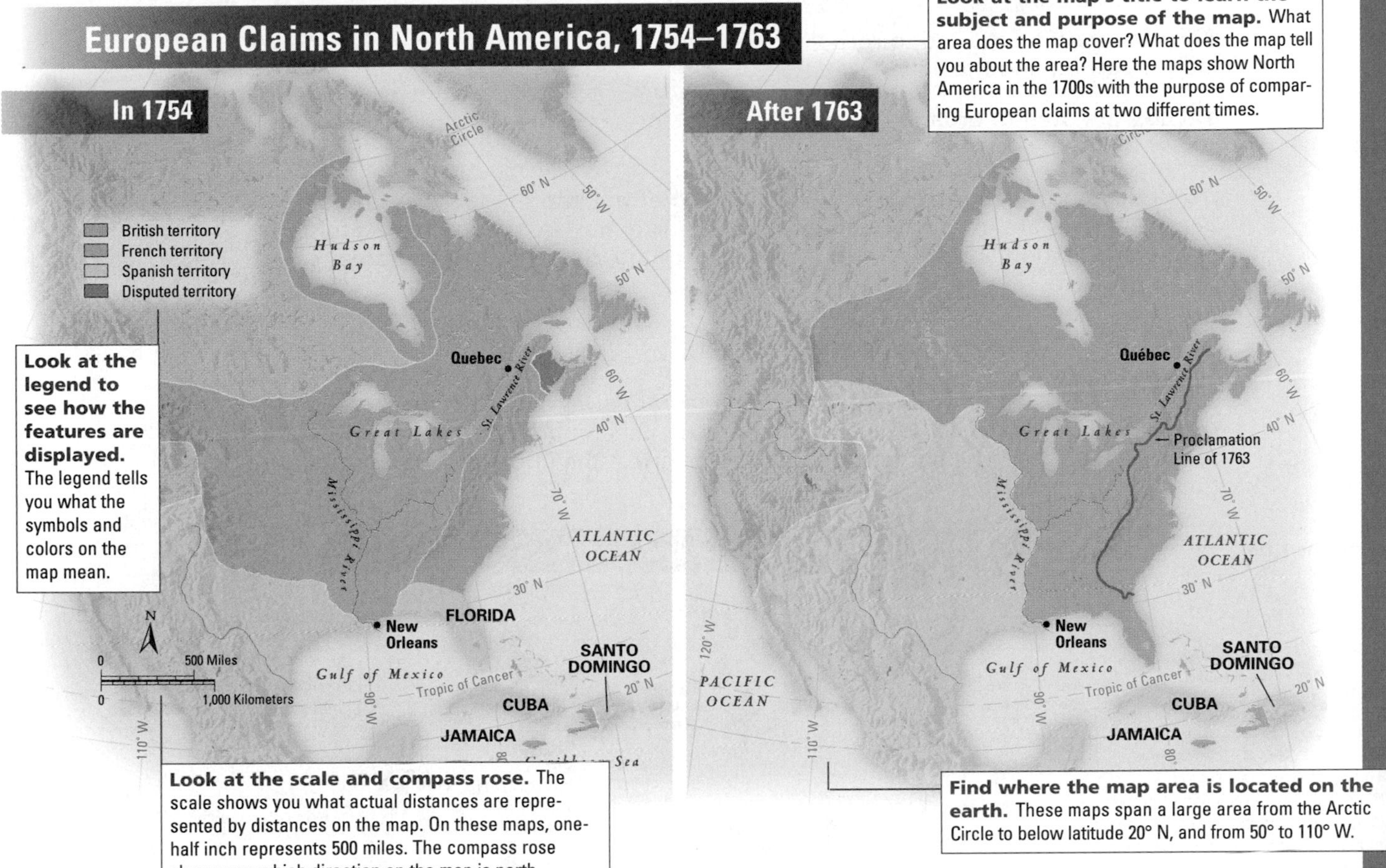
European Claims in North America, 1754–1763
In 1754
After 1763
British territory
French territory
Spanish territory
Disputed territory
Hudson Bay
Quebec
Québec
St. Lawrence River
Great Lakes
Mississippi River
Proclamation Line of 1763
ATLANTIC OCEAN
PACIFIC OCEAN
New Orleans
FLORIDA
Gulf of Mexico
Tropic of Cancer
SANTO DOMINGO
CUBA
JAMAICA
Arctic Circle
60° N
50° N
40° N
30° N
20° N
50° W
60° W
70° W
90° W
110° W
120° W
500 Miles
1,000 Kilometers
Look at the map's title to learn the subject and purpose of the map. What area does the map cover? What does the map tell you about the area? Here the maps show North America in the 1700s with the purpose of comparing European claims at two different times.
Look at the legend to see how the features are displayed. The legend tells you what the symbols and colors on the map mean.
Look at the scale and compass rose. The scale shows you what actual distances are represented by distances on the map. On these maps, one-half inch represents 500 miles. The compass rose shows you which direction on the map is north.
Find where the map area is located on the earth. These maps span a large area from the Arctic Circle to below latitude 20° N, and from 50° to 110° W.

Strategy: Making a chart

Relate the map to the five geographic themes by making a chart. The five themes are described on pages xxxiv–xxxv.

Location	Place	Region	Movement	Human-Environment Interaction
Large area from Arctic Circle to below 20° N, and from 50° to 110°W	North American continent	Western Hemisphere	Between 1754 and 1763, land claimed by France was largely taken over by the other two colonialist powers. Spain expanded its territories northward, while England consolidated and greatly expanded its holdings.	Europeans carved out political units in the continent, which already had inhabitants. The territories they claimed covered vast areas, with waterways and large mountain ranges to cross.

APPLYING THE SKILL

Make your own chart Study the map titled "Normandy Invasions, June 6, 1944" on pages 582–583. Make a chart, like the one shown above, in which you summarize what the map tells you in the five main subject areas.

Section 3: Print, Visual, and Technological Sources

3.4 Interpreting Charts

Charts are visual presentations of material. Historians use charts to organize, simplify, and summarize information in a way that makes it more meaningful or memorable. Several varieties of charts are commonly used.

Simple charts are used to consolidate information or to compare peoples, movements, parties, and the like.

Tables are used to organize numbers, percentages, or other information into columns and rows for easy reference.

Diagrams provide visual clues to the meaning of the information they contain. Venn diagrams are used for comparisons. Web diagrams are used to collect miscellaneous information around a central topic. Illustrated diagrams are sometimes called **infographics.**

UNDERSTANDING THE SKILL

Strategy: Finding clues The following diagram gives a visual representation of the cycle of poverty in which Southern sharecroppers found themselves trapped after the Civil War. The paragraph below summarizes the information contained in the diagram.

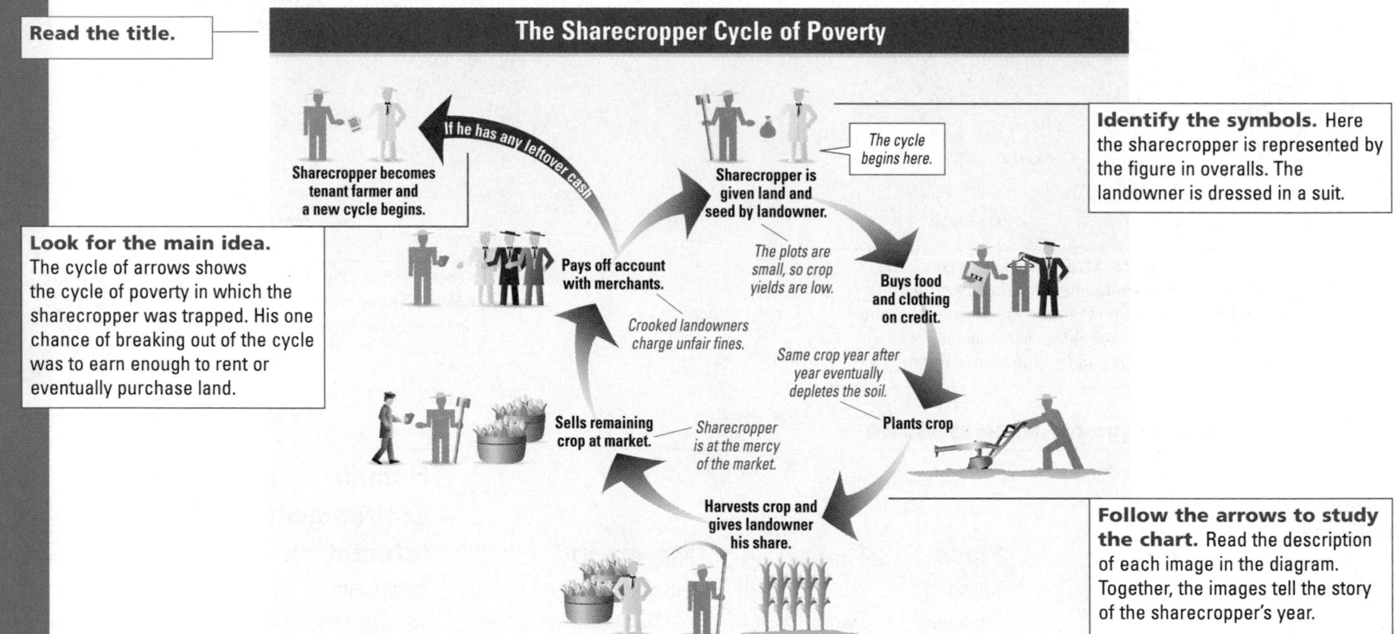
Read the title.
The Sharecropper Cycle of Poverty
Identify the symbols. Here the sharecropper is represented by the figure in overalls. The landowner is dressed in a suit.
The cycle begins here.
Sharecropper is given land and seed by landowner.
The plots are small, so crop yields are low.
Buys food and clothing on credit.
Same crop year after year eventually depletes the soil.
Plants crop
Harvests crop and gives landowner his share.
Sharecropper is at the mercy of the market.
Sells remaining crop at market.
Crooked landowners charge unfair fines.
Pays off account with merchants.
If he has any leftover cash
Sharecropper becomes tenant farmer and a new cycle begins.
Look for the main idea. The cycle of arrows shows the cycle of poverty in which the sharecropper was trapped. His one chance of breaking out of the cycle was to earn enough to rent or eventually purchase land.
Follow the arrows to study the chart. Read the description of each image in the diagram. Together, the images tell the story of the sharecropper's year.

Strategy: Writing a summary

Write a paragraph to summarize what you learned from the diagram.

Sharecroppers were given land and seed by a landowner. They were permitted to farm the land in exchange for a share of the crops they raised. The money they made from selling the rest of the crop often went to paying off their expenses. Usually, they had to renew the arrangement the next year, although some sharecroppers earned enough to break out of the cycle.

APPLYING THE SKILL

Write your own summary Turn to Chapter 5, Section 3, and study the diagram "Inventions That Tamed the Prairie." Write a paragraph in which you summarize what you learned from the diagram. Tell what impact the inventions had on Western agriculture.

928 Skillbuilder Handbook

3.5 Interpreting Graphs

Graphs show statistical information in a visual manner. Historians use graphs to visualize amounts, ratios, economic trends, and changes over time.

Line graphs typically show quantities on the vertical axis (up the left side) and time in years, months, or other units on the horizontal axis (across the bottom).

Pie graphs are useful for showing relative proportions. The circle represents the whole, such as an entire population, and the slices represent the parts belonging to various subgroups.

Bar graphs are commonly used to display information about quantities. Each small symbol stands for a given number or amount of something. It is easy to see at a glance how different quantities compare.

UNDERSTANDING THE SKILL

Strategy: Finding clues The graph below combines a bar graph with a line graph. The bars show the amount of wheat produced in each year from 1927 through 1934. The line shows the changing price of wheat over the same years.

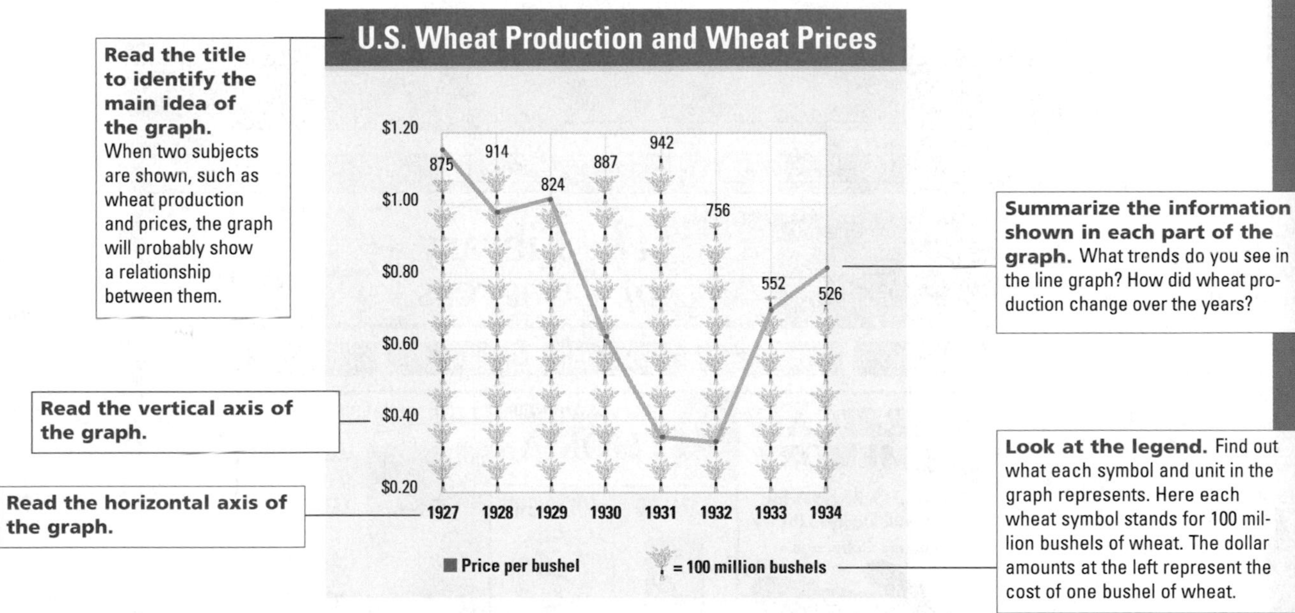

U.S. Wheat Production and Wheat Prices
Read the title to identify the main idea of the graph. When two subjects are shown, such as wheat production and prices, the graph will probably show a relationship between them.
$1.20
$1.00
$0.80
$0.60
$0.40
$0.20
875
914
824
887
942
756
552
526
1927
1928
1929
1930
1931
1932
1933
1934
Price per bushel
= 100 million bushels
Read the vertical axis of the graph.
Read the horizontal axis of the graph.
Summarize the information shown in each part of the graph. What trends do you see in the line graph? How did wheat production change over the years?
Look at the legend. Find out what each symbol and unit in the graph represents. Here each wheat symbol stands for 100 million bushels of wheat. The dollar amounts at the left represent the cost of one bushel of wheat.

Strategy: Writing a summary

Write a paragraph to summarize what you learned from the graph.

During the years from 1927 to 1931, U.S. farmers produced from 824,000 to 942,000 bushels of wheat per year. During the following three years, there was a steep decline in wheat production—from 756,000 bushels in 1932 to 526,000 bushels in 1934. Starting in 1929, wheat prices plunged, reaching a low of less than $0.40 per bushel in 1932. Only when wheat production dropped did prices begin to rise again. The graph suggests that wheat prices fluctuate depending on production, with wheat, like other commodities, bringing lower prices when it is abundant.

APPLYING THE SKILL

Write your own summary Turn to Chapter 19, Section 3, and look at the two graphs titled "Glued to the Set, 1950–1996." Study the graphs and write a paragraph in which you summarize what you learned from them. Tell how the two line graphs work together.

3.6 Using the Internet

The **Internet** is a network of computers associated with universities, libraries, news organizations, government agencies, businesses, and private individuals worldwide. Every page of information on the Internet has its own address, or **URL.**

With a computer connected to the Internet, you can reach pages provided by many organizations and services. You can find the call number of a library book, read an article in a periodical, view photographs, or receive moving pictures and sound.

The international collection of sites, known as the **World Wide Web** is a good source of up-to-the minute information about current events as well as in-depth research on historical subjects. This textbook contains many suggestions for navigating the Internet through the World Wide Web. You can begin by entering the address (URL) for McDougal Littell's site, which is

http://www.mlushistory.com

UNDERSTANDING THE SKILL

Strategy: Finding clues on the screen The computer screen below shows the Web page of the Library of Congress in Washington, D.C.

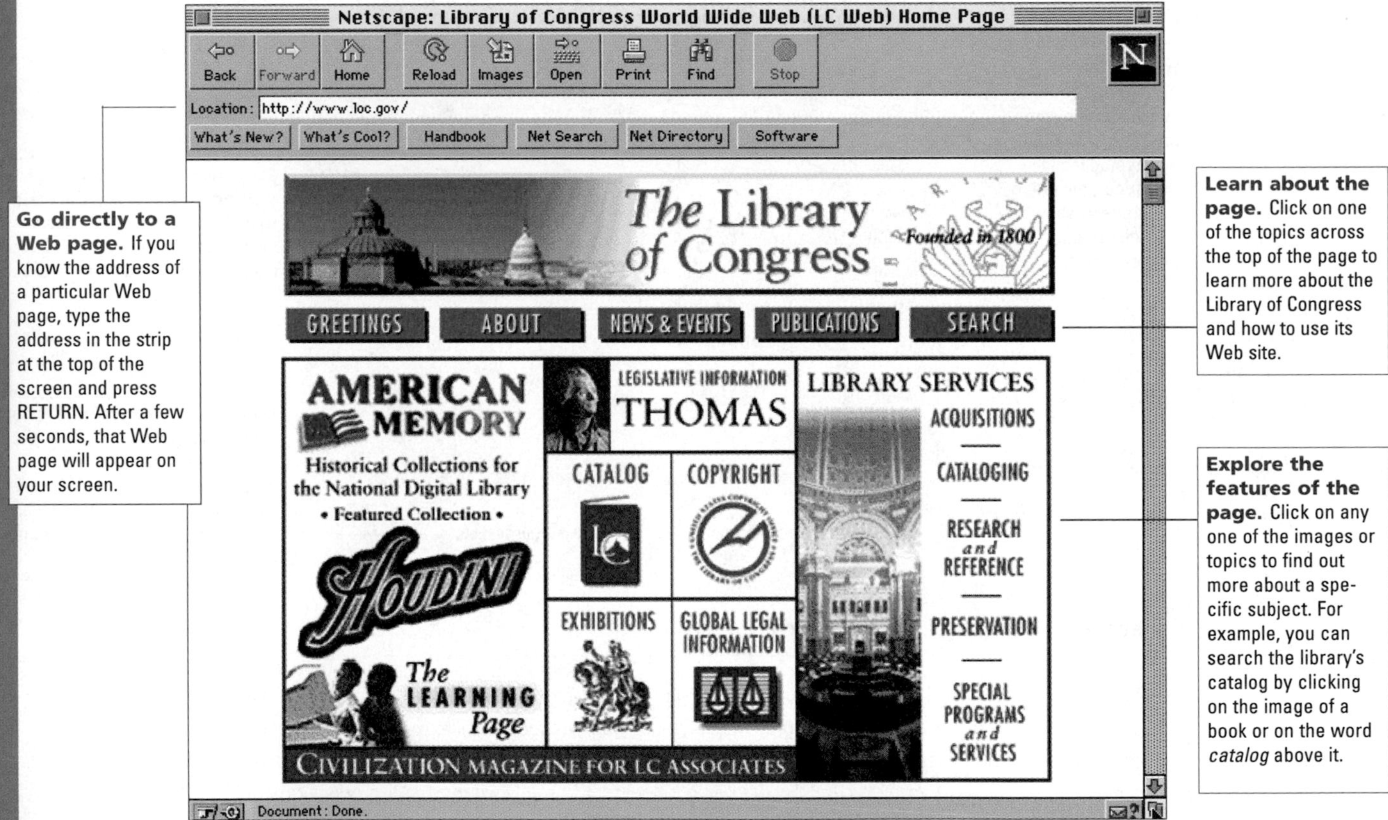

APPLYING THE SKILL

Do your own Internet research Turn to Chapter 21, Section 2, "The Triumphs of a Crusade." Read the section, making a list of topics you would like to research. If you have a computer with Internet access, go to the McDougal Littell site (http://www.mlushistory.com), where you will learn more about how to conduct a search.

3.7 Creating Graphs and Charts

Charts and **graphs** are visual representations of information. (See Sections 3.4 and 3.5 of this handbook for information on interpreting charts and graphs.) The three main types of graphs are bar graphs, line graphs, and pie graphs.

- Use a bar graph to display information about quantities and to compare related quantities.
- Use a line graph to show trends over time.
- Use a pie graph to show relative proportions.

UNDERSTANDING THE SKILL

Strategy: Finding clues in the text The following passage includes data about American commuting choices between 1960 and 1990. The bar graph below shows how the information in the passage might be represented.

Choose a title that sums up the information and includes a time span.

Note the dates. The years will appear along the horizontal axis of your graph.

Note the percentages. The percentages will appear along the vertical axis.

Organize the data. Group together numbers that provide information about the same year. Decide what symbols or colors you will use to represent each category of information.

American Commuting Choices, 1960–1990

In 1960, 64% of the population traveled to work by car, truck, or van; 12% took public transportation; 7% worked at home; and 17% either did not report the means of transportation or got to work by other means, such as by walking or bicycling. In 1970, 78% of the population went to work by car, truck, or van; 9% used public transportation; 4% worked at home; and 9% traveled by other means. By 1980, 84% of the population went to work by car, truck, or van while only, 6% took public transportation; a mere 2% worked at home, and 8% used other means. Trends held fairly steady in 1990, when 87% of the work force traveled to work by car, truck, or van; 5% took public transportation; 3% worked at home; and 5% went to work by other means.

Decide how best to represent the information. Data showing trends in more than one category are best represented in a bar graph.

Strategy: Creating a bar graph

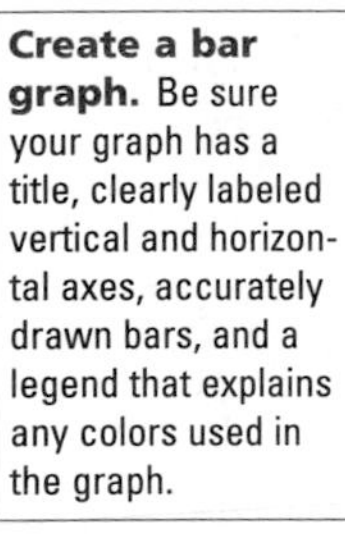

Create a bar graph. Be sure your graph has a title, clearly labeled vertical and horizontal axes, accurately drawn bars, and a legend that explains any colors used in the graph.

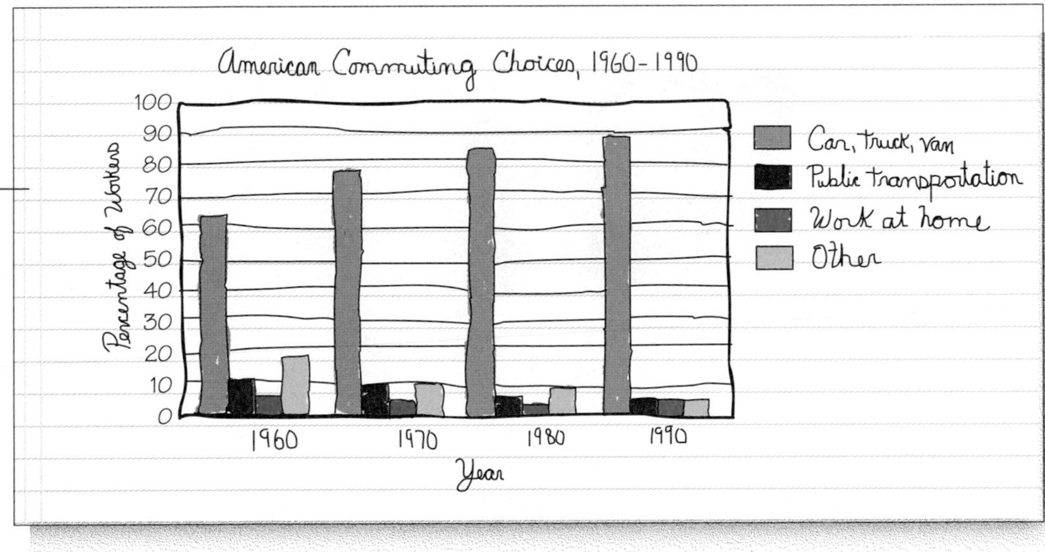

APPLYING THE SKILL

Create your own graph Turn to Chapter 26, Section 4, and read the passage headed "A Changing Immigration Population." Use a pie graph to display the information about the predicted ethnic distribution of the American population in 2050.

Section 3: Print, Visual, and Technological Sources

3.8 Creating Maps and Models

Maps and models are visual representations of information. **Maps** are scale representations, usually of land surfaces. (See Section 3.3 of this handbook for information on interpreting maps.) **Models** are three-dimensional representations. Historians make models of geographical areas, villages, cities, inventions, buildings, and other physical objects of historical importance. They sometimes use computers to create models.

Creating a map involves representing geographical data. When you draw a map, it is easiest to use an existing map as a guide. On the map you draw, you can show geographical information, as well as many other kinds of information, including data on climates, population trends, resources, or troop movements.

UNDERSTANDING THE SKILL

Strategy: Finding clues in the text The following chart shows the numbers of 1995 immigrants who planned to settle in the Southwestern states of the United States. Below it is a map that depicts the data given in the chart.

Determine what map you should use as a guide. Find a map of the Southwest that you can re-create. This will be your guide map.

IMMIGRANTS, BY SOUTHWESTERN STATE OF INTENDED RESIDENCE, 1995

Arizona	7,700	Nevada	4,306	Texas	49,963
California	166,482	New Mexico	2,758	Utah	2,831
Colorado	7,713				

Decide how best to show the data. These data can be grouped in three broad categories of numbers: more than 100,000; 10,000 to 100,000; and less than 10,000.

Strategy: Making a map

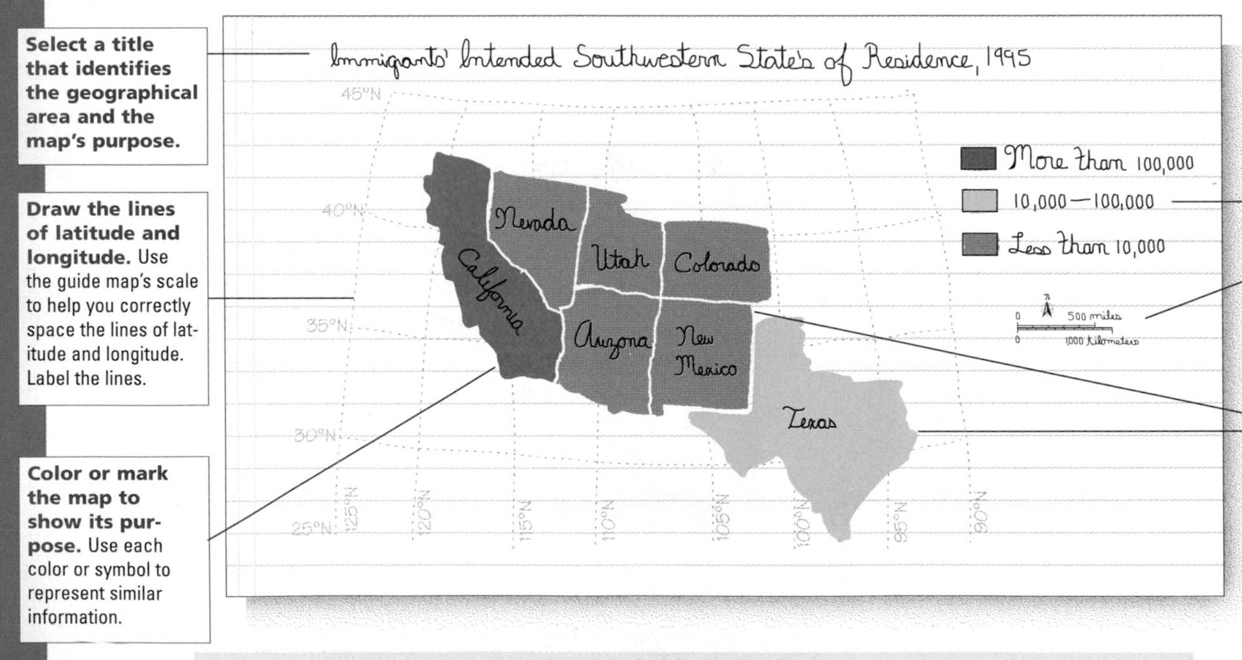

Select a title that identifies the geographical area and the map's purpose.

Draw the lines of latitude and longitude. Use the guide map's scale to help you correctly space the lines of latitude and longitude. Label the lines.

Color or mark the map to show its purpose. Use each color or symbol to represent similar information.

Provide user information. Include a key or legend explaining colors, symbols, or shading. Reproduce the scale and compass rose from the map you used as a guide.

Draw the borders. Plot the northernmost, southernmost, easternmost, and westernmost points of the map. Then draw the borders of the region, following your guide map carefully. Finally, sketch interior borders.

APPLYING THE SKILL

Make your own map Turn to page 610 and study the graph titled "The Marshall Plan." Use the process described above to draw a map that depicts the data. (You can use the map on page 609 as a guide.)

932 Skillbuilder Handbook

Note: Boldfaced words are terms that appear in this handbook.

boycott *A refusal to have economic dealings with a person, a business, an organization, or a country.* The purpose of a boycott is to show disapproval of particular actions or to force changes in those actions. A boycott often involves an economic act, such as refusing to buy a company's goods or services.

African Americans in Montgomery, Alabama (shown below), organized a bus boycott in December 1955 to fight bus segregation. The boycotters kept many buses nearly empty for 381 days before the Supreme Court outlawed bus segregation in December 1956.

American labor unions sometimes have used boycotts to win concessions for their members. Consumer groups, too, have organized boycotts to win changes in business practices. For an explanation of the effectiveness of boycotts, read the Economic Background on page 701.

business cycle *A pattern of increases and decreases in economic activity.* A business cycle generally consists of four distinct phases—expansion, peak, contraction, and trough, as shown in the graph in the next column.

An expansion is marked by increased business activity. The unemployment rate falls, businesses produce more, and consumers buy more goods and services. During a peak, business activity reaches a very high level. A contraction, or recession, occurs when business activity decreases. The unemployment rises, while both production and consumer spending fall. A deep and long-lasting contraction is called a **depression.** Business activity reaches its lowest point during a trough. After time, business activity starts to increase and a new business cycle begins. For more information on business cycles, read the Economic Background on page 237.

The Business Cycle

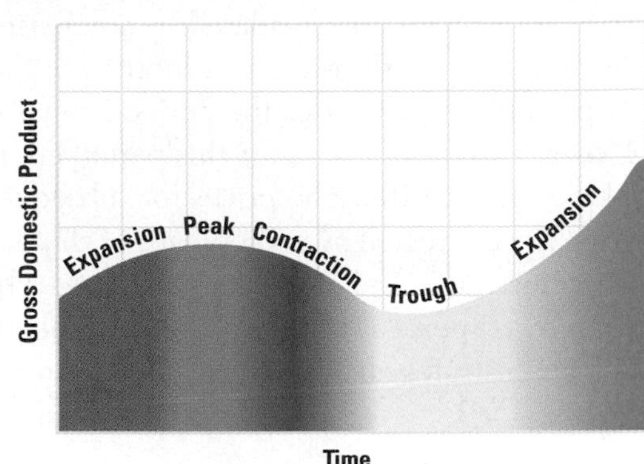

communism *An economic system based on one-party rule, government ownership of the means of production, and decision making by centralized authorities.* There is little or no private ownership of property and little or no political freedom. Under communism, government planners make economic decisions, such as which and how many goods and services should be produced. Individuals, therefore, have little say in a communist economy. Such a system, communists believed, would end inequality. For information on the ideas on which communism is based, read the Economic Background on page 431.

During the 20th century, most communist economies failed to achieve their goals. Economic decisions frequently were made to benefit only Communist Party officials. Also, government economic planning was inefficient, often creating shortages of goods. Those goods that were available were often of poor quality.

People became discontented with the lack of prosperity and political freedom and began to call for change. These demands led in the late 1980s and early 1990s to the collapse of Communist governments in the Soviet Union and Eastern Europe. Even those governments that clung to communism introduced elements of free enterprise. Some countries—such as China—have experienced significant economic growth but have not granted more political freedom to their citizens.

consumer price index (CPI) *A measure of the average prices of goods and services bought by consumers.* The CPI notes the prices of some 400 goods and services bought by average consumers on a regular basis. Items on which consumers spend a good deal of their income—such as food and housing—are given more weight in the CPI than items on which consumers spend less.

Price changes are calculated by comparing current prices with prices at a set time in the past. At present, the CPI uses the period from 1982 to 1984 as this base. Prices for this period are given a base value of 100. The prices for subsequent years are expressed as percentages of the base. Therefore, a CPI of 160 means that prices have risen by 60 percent since 1982–1984. The graph below illustrates changes in the CPI from 1980 to 1996.

Consumer Price Index, 1980–1996

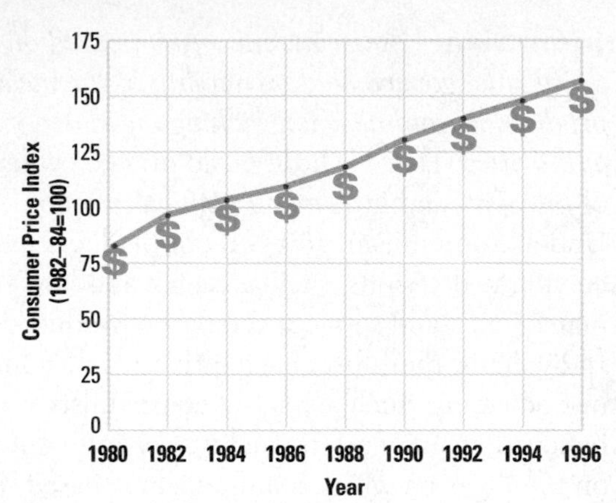

Source: *Economic Report of the President, 1997.*

deficit spending *A situation in which the government spends more money than it receives in revenues.* The government borrows or issues money to finance deficit spending.

For the most part, the government engages in deficit spending when the economy is in a contraction phase of the **business cycle.** In theory, the extra funds should stimulate business activity, pushing the economy into an expansion phase. As the economy recovers, revenues should increase, providing the government with a budget surplus. The government then can use the surplus to pay back the money it borrowed. For more information on deficit spending, read the Economic Background on page 531.

depression *A very severe and prolonged contraction in economic activity.* During a depression, consumer spending, production, levels, wages, prices, and profits fall sharply. Many businesses fail, and many workers lose their jobs.

The United States has experienced several economic depressions in its history. The worst was the Great Depression, which started in 1929 and lasted throughout the 1930s. Between 1929 and 1932, business activity in the United States decreased by an average of 10 percent each year. During the same period, some 40 percent of the country's banks failed, and prices for farm products dropped more than 50 percent. By 1933, the worst year of the Great Depression, 25 percent of American workers were unemployed—some, like the man shown below, reduced to selling apples on the street. For a personal account of life during the Great Depression, view the *American Stories* video "Broke but Not Broken: Ann Marie Low Remembers the Dust Bowl."

embargo *A government ban on trade with another nation.* In a civil embargo the nation imposing an embargo prevents exports to or imports from the country against which it has declared the embargo. A hostile embargo involves seizing the goods of another nation.

The major purpose of an embargo is to show disapproval of a nation's actions. For example, in 1979 the United States imposed a civil embargo on grain sales to the Soviet Union to protest the Soviet invasion of Afghanistan.

934 Economics Handbook

free enterprise *An economic system based on the private ownership of the means of production, free markets, and the right of individuals to make most economic decisions.* The free enterprise system is also called the free market system or capitalism. The United States has a free enterprise economic system.

In a free enterprise system, producers and consumers are motivated by self-interest. Producers want to make profits—the money left over after costs are subtracted from earnings. To maximize their profits, producers make the goods and services consumers want. Producers engage in competition—through lowering prices, advertising their products, and improving product quality—to encourage consumers to buy their goods. Consumers serve their self-interest by purchasing the best goods and services for the lowest price.

Government plays a limited, but important, role in most free-enterprise economies. It regulates economic activity to ensure there is fair competition. It also produces certain goods and services that private producers consider unprofitable.

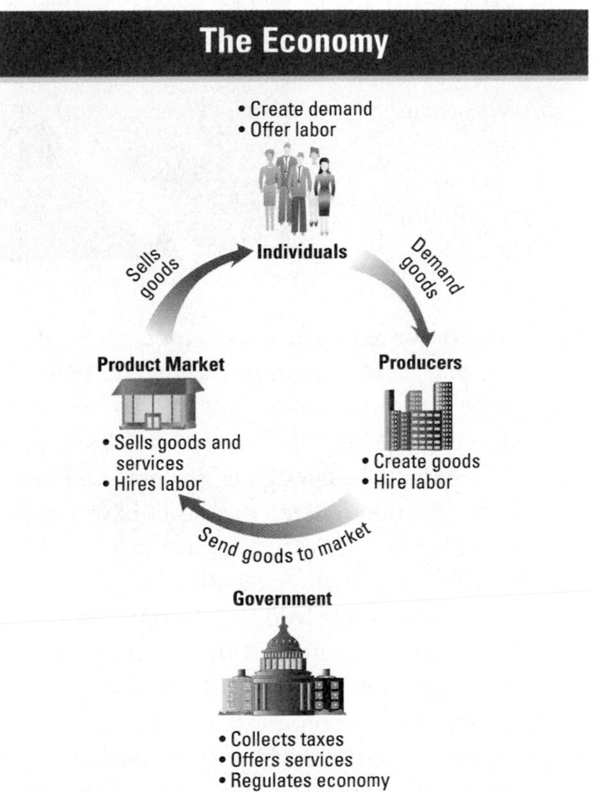

gold standard *A monetary system in which a country's basic unit of currency is valued at, and can be exchanged for, a fixed sum of gold.* This system has a number of advantages. To begin with, people have confidence in their currency, because they know it is backed by gold. Also, using the gold standard tends to curb **inflation,** since a government cannot put more currency into circulation than it can back with its gold supplies. This second advantage is also a weakness of the gold standard. During times of recession, a government may need the freedom to increase the amount of money in circulation to encourage economic growth. Many nations, including the United States, were on the gold standard from the 1870s to the early 1900s. Economic disruption during the Great Depression of the 1930s caused most nations to abandon the gold standard. The United States went off the gold standard in 1971.

gross domestic product (GDP) *The market value of all the goods and services produced in a nation within a specific time period, such as a quarter (three months) or a year.* It is the standard measure of how a nation's economy is performing.

GDP is calculated by adding four components: spending by individual consumers on goods and services; investment in such items as new factories, new factory machinery, and houses; government spending on goods and services; and net exports—the value of exports less the value of imports. GDP figures are presented in two ways. Nominal GDP is reported in current dollars. Real GDP is reported in constant dollars, or dollars adjusted for inflation.

Changes in the GDP indicate how well the economy is doing. If GDP is growing, the economy is probably in an expansion phase. If GDP is not increasing or is declining, the economy is probably in a contraction phase.

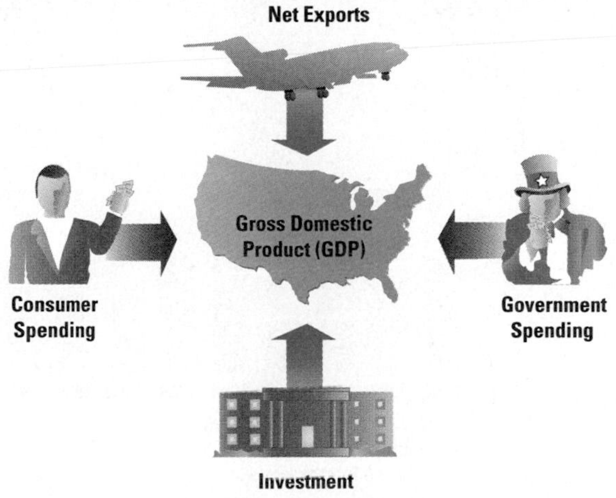

inflation *A sustained rise in the average level of prices.* Since more money is required to make purchases when prices rise, inflation is sometimes defined as a decrease in the purchasing value of money. Economists measure price changes with indexes. The most widely used index in the United States is the **consumer price index (CPI).**

Inflation may result if the demand for goods increases without an increase in the production of goods. Inflation may also take place if the cost of producing goods increases. Producers pass on such increased costs as higher wages and more expensive raw materials by charging consumers higher prices. For more information on the effects of inflation, read the Economic Background on page 62.

interest rate *The cost of borrowing money.* Interest is calculated as a yearly percentage, or rate, of the money borrowed. A 10 percent interest rate, therefore, would require a borrower to pay $10 per year for every $100 borrowed.

When interest rates are low, people will borrow more, because the cost of borrowing is lower. However, they will save and invest less, because the return on their savings or investment is lower. With high interest rates, people save and invest more but borrow less. Because interest rates affect the economy, the government takes steps to control them through the Federal Reserve System, the nation's central bank. The graph below shows the relationship between the rate of inflation and the interest rate over time.

Inflation and Interest Rates, 1980–1996

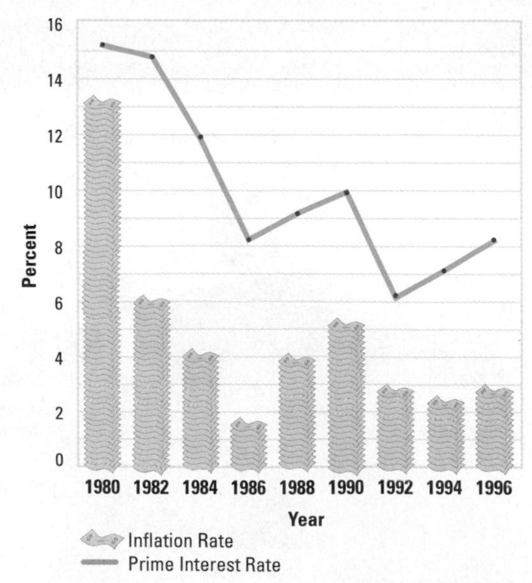

Source: *Economic Report of the President, 1997.*

Keynesian economics *The use of government spending to encourage economic activity by increasing the demand for goods.* This approach is based on the ideas of British economist John Maynard Keynes (shown below). In a 1936 study, Keynes pointed out that during economic downturns, more people are unemployed and have less income to spend. As a result, businesses cut production and lay off more workers.

Keynes's answer to this problem was for government to increase spending. This would stimulate demand for goods and services by replacing the decline in consumer demand. Government would want goods and services for its new programs. More people would be working and earning an income and, therefore, would want to buy more goods and services. Businesses would increase production to meet this new demand. As a result, the economy would soon recover.

Critics maintain, however, that Keynesian economics has led to the growth of government and to high taxes. For more information on Keynesian economics, read the Economic Background on page 531.

minimum wage *The minimum amount of money that employers must legally pay their employees for each hour of work.* The first federal minimum wage law, the Fair Labor Standards Act of 1938, set the base wage at 25 cents an hour. Since then, amendments to the act have raised this hourly rate to $5.15, effective in 1997. The Fair Labor Standards Act applies to workers in most businesses involved in interstate commerce.

The original intent of the minimum wage law was to ensure that all workers earned enough to survive. Some economists maintain that the law may have reduced the chances for unskilled workers to get jobs. They argue that the minimum wage increases labor costs for business. The graph on the next page shows changes in the minimum wage over a 10-year period.

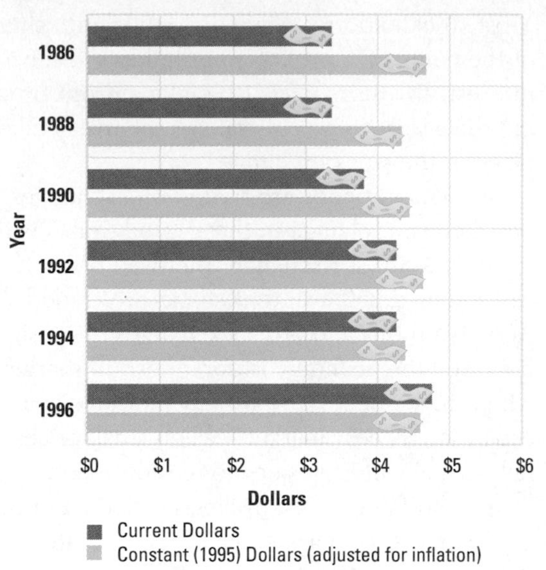

monopoly *A situation in which only one seller controls the production, supply, or pricing of a product for which there are no close substitutes.* In the United States, most basic public services, such as electrical power distributors, operate as local monopolies. This way of providing utilities is economically more efficient than having several competing companies running gas, electricity, or cable lines in the same area.

Monopolies, however, can be harmful to the economy. Since it has no competition, a monopoly does not need to respond to the wants of consumers by improving product quality or by charging fair prices. The government counters the threat of monopoly either by breaking up or regulating the monopoly.

national debt *The money owed by the federal government.* During wartime, during economic recession, or at other times, the federal government may employ **deficit spending.** However, the government may not pay back all the money it has borrowed to fund this policy. As a result, the government amasses a huge debt. By the late 1990s, the national debt of the United States stood in excess of $5 trillion, or about $20,000 for each citizen.

The rapid growth of the national debt since 1980 (see the graph at the top of the next column) has prompted many Americans to call for changes in government economic policies. Some suggest that the government raise taxes and cut spending to reduce the debt. Others recommend a constitutional amendment that would require the government to have a balanced budget—spending only as much as it takes in.

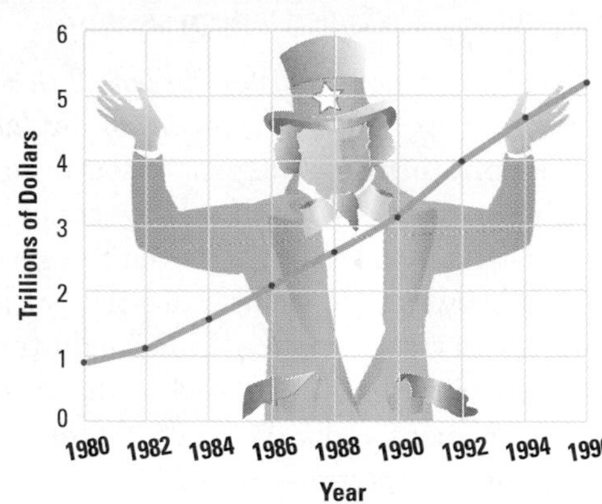

poverty *The lack of adequate income to maintain a minimum* ***standard of living.*** In the United States, this adequate income is referred to as the poverty line. For an explanation of how the poverty line is calculated, read the Economic Background on page 661. In the mid-1990s, more than 39 million Americans, or close to 14 percent of the country's population, lived in poverty.

While poverty rates have remained relatively steady over the last 25 to 30 years, inequality in the distribution of income has grown. Between 1967 and 1995, the share of income received by the wealthiest 20 percent of families increased by nearly 5 percent to 48.7 percent. In the same period, the poorest 20 percent of families' share of income fell from 4 percent to 3.7 percent.

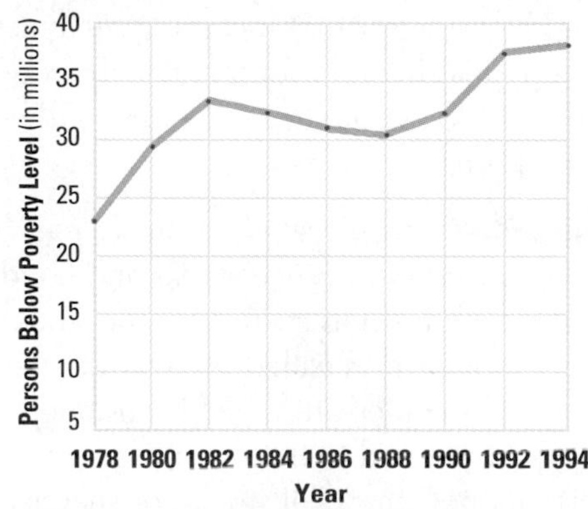

recession *A period of declining economic activity.* In economic terms, a recession takes place when **gross domestic product** falls for two quarters, or six months, in a row. The United States has experienced several of these business-cycle contractions in its history. On average, they have lasted about a year. If a recession persists and economic activity plunges, it is called a **depression.**

socialism *An economic system in which the government owns most of the means of production.* Like **communism,** the goal of socialism is to use the power of government to reduce inequality. Under socialism, however, the government usually owns only major industries, such as coal, steel, and transportation. Other industries are privately owned but regulated by the government. Government and individuals, therefore, share economic decision-making. Also, under socialism, the government may provide such services as reasonably priced health care.

Some countries, such as Sweden, are called democratic socialist countries. These nations have less government ownership of property than communist governments. They also have democratically elected governments.

Critics of socialism maintain that this system leads to less efficiency and higher taxes than does the **free enterprise system.**

standard of living *The overall economic situation in which people live.* Economists differ on how best to measure the standard of living. Some suggest average personal income, while others propose per capita **gross domestic product**—the GDP divided by the population. Another measure recommended by economists is the value of the goods and services bought by consumers during a year. In general terms, the nation's standard of living rises as these measures rise. Some people argue that the standard of living should not be measured in economic terms alone. They suggest that including such factors as pollution, health, and even political freedom would provide a more accurate view of the quality of life.

stock market *A place where stocks and bonds are bought and sold.* Since stocks and bonds together are known as securities, the stock market is sometimes called the securities market.

Large companies often need extra money to fund expansion and to help cover operating costs. To raise money, they sell stocks, or shares of ownership, in their companies or borrow by issuing bonds, or certificates of debt, promising to repay the money borrowed, plus interest.

Individuals invest in securities to make a profit. Most stockholders receive dividends, or a share of the company's profits. Bondholders receive interest. Investors may also make a profit by selling their securities. This sale of securities takes place in the stock exchange.

Stocks and bonds are traded on exchanges. The best known exchange in the United States is the New York Stock Exchange (pictured below). More than 2,250 different stocks are traded there. Activity on this and other exchanges often signals how well the economy is doing. A bull market—when stock prices rise—usually indicates economic expansion. A bear market—when stock prices fall—usually indicates economic contraction.

A rapid fall in stock prices is called a crash. The worst stock market crash in the United States came in October 1929. To help protect against another drastic stock market crash, the federal government set up the Securities and Exchange Commission (SEC), which regulates the trading of securities.

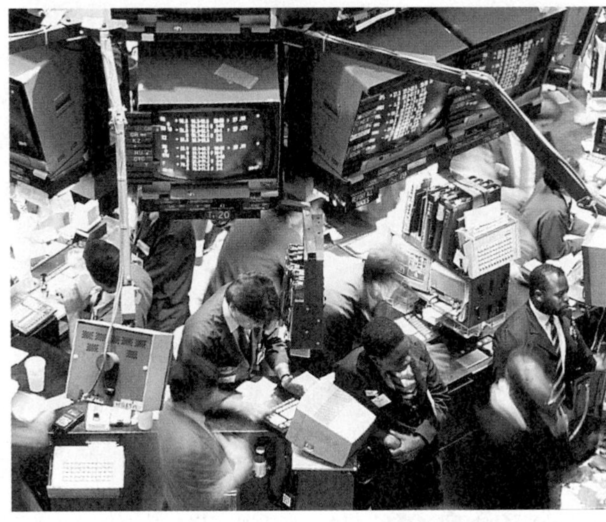

strike *A work stoppage by employees to gain higher wages and/or better working conditions.* The strike follows a failure in collective bargaining—the negotiation of contracts between labor unions and employers. Union members may decide to call a strike if they feel that negotiations with the employer are deadlocked. When strikes do occur, union representatives and employers try to negotiate a settlement. An outside party is sometimes asked to help work out an agreement. For a personal account of a strike, view the *American Stories* video, "A Child on Strike: The Testimony of Camella Teoli, Mill Girl."

supply and demand *The forces that determine prices of goods and services in a market economy.* Supply is the quantity of a good or service that producers are willing and able to produce at a set price. Demand is the quantity of a good or service consumers are willing and able to buy at a set price. Producers are willing to produce more of a good or service when prices are high. Conversely, consumers are willing to buy more of a good or service when prices are low. The price that satisfies both producers and consumers is the equilibrium, or market, price. It is the price at which the quantity produced and the quantity demanded are the same.

The table and graph below show supply and demand for a certain product. The line *S* shows the number of items producers are willing to make at various prices. The line *D* shows the number of items consumers are willing to buy at various prices. Point *E*, where the two lines intersect, is the equilibrium price. At prices above the equilibrium, consumers will demand less. Producers, therefore, will have to lower their prices to sell the surplus, or excess, products. At prices below the equilibrium, consumers will demand more. Producers will be able to raise their prices because the product is scarce, or in short supply.

Supply and Demand

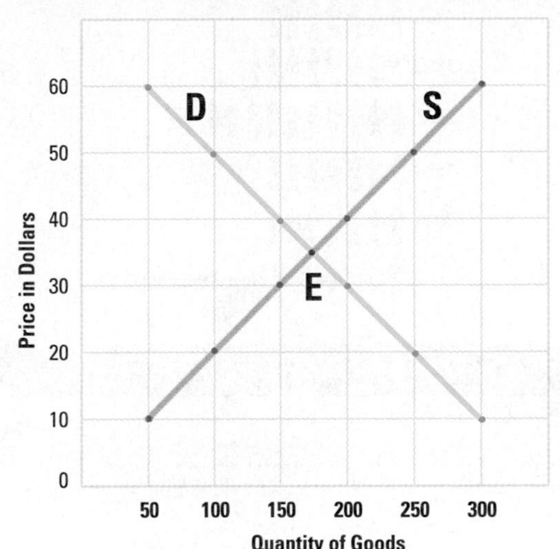

D — Demand
S — Supply
E ● Equilibrium Price

Supply and Demand Schedules

Demand	Price	Supply
50	$10	300
100	20	250
150	30	200
200	40	150
250	50	100
300	60	50

supply-side economics *Government policies designed to stimulate the production of goods and services, or the supply side of the economy.* Supply-side economists developed these policies in opposition to **Keynesian economics,** which they felt led to high tax rates, high inflation, a large national debt, and low economic growth.

Supply-side policies call for low tax rates. Lower taxes mean that people keep more of each dollar they earn. Therefore, supply-side economists argue, people will work harder in order to earn more. They will then use their extra income to save and invest. This investment will fund the development of new businesses and, as a result, create more jobs.

tariff *A fee charged for goods brought into a state or country from another state or country.* In the early 1800s, Congress created tariffs to raise revenue and to protect American products from foreign competition. Soon, however, special interests used tariffs to protect specific industries and increase profits.

Trade without tariffs is called free trade. In recent decades, a growing number of economists have favored free trade policies because they believe that such policies will help increase U.S. exports to other countries. In 1993, the North American Free Trade Agreement (NAFTA) established a free trade zone among the United States, Canada, and Mexico.

taxation *A method of raising revenues to finance government programs.* All levels of government—federal, state, and local—collect many kinds of taxes. Both corporations and individuals pay income tax, or taxes on earnings. Income taxes are the chief source of revenue for the federal government. Property taxes are the main source of funds for local governments. Property tax is calculated as a percentage of the assessed value of real estate, land, and improvements such as buildings. Sales taxes are an important source of income for state governments.

trade *The exchange of goods and services between countries.* Almost all nations produce goods that other countries need, and they sell (export) those goods to buyers in other countries. At the same time, they buy (import) goods from other countries as well. For example, Americans sell goods such as wheat to people in Japan and buy Japanese goods such as automobiles in return.

Nations that trade with one another often become dependent on one another's products. Sometimes this brings nations closer together, as it did the United States, Great Britain, and France before World War I. Other times it causes tension among nations, such as that between the United States and Arab oil-producing countries in the 1970s.

U.S. Foreign Trade, 1960–1995

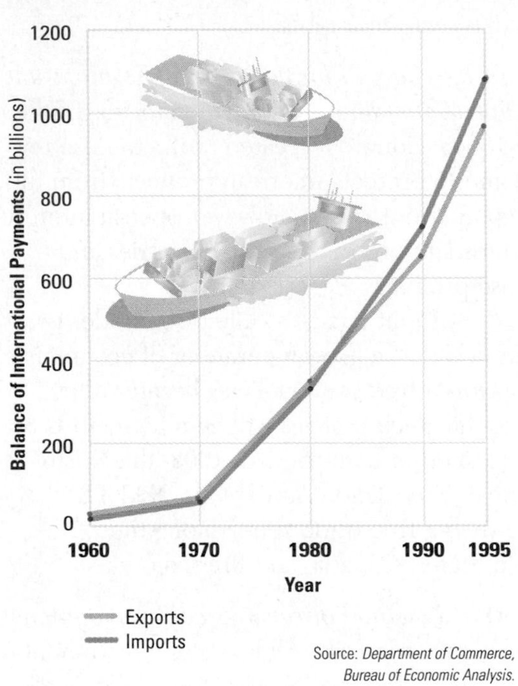

Source: *Department of Commerce, Bureau of Economic Analysis.*

trust *A form of business merger in which the major stockholders in several corporations turn over their stock to a group of trustees.* The trustees then run the separate corporations as one large company, or trust. In return for their stock, the stockholders of the separate corporations receive a share of the trust's profits.

American business leaders of the late 1800s used trusts to stifle competition and take control of particular industries. Trusts were outlawed by the Sherman Anti-Trust Act of 1890. However, business leaders eventually found other ways to merge corporations in an industry.

unemployment rate *The percentage of the labor force that is unemployed but actively looking for work.* The labor force consists of all civilians 16 years of age and older who are employed or unemployed but actively looking and available for work. The size of the labor force and the unemployment rate are determined by surveys conducted by the U.S. Bureau of the Census.

The unemployment rate provides an indicator of economic health. Rising unemployment rates signal a contraction in the economy, while falling rates indicate an economic expansion. The graph below shows two different methods of portraying unemployment in the United States.

Unemployment in the United States, 1980–1996

TOTAL UNEMPLOYED

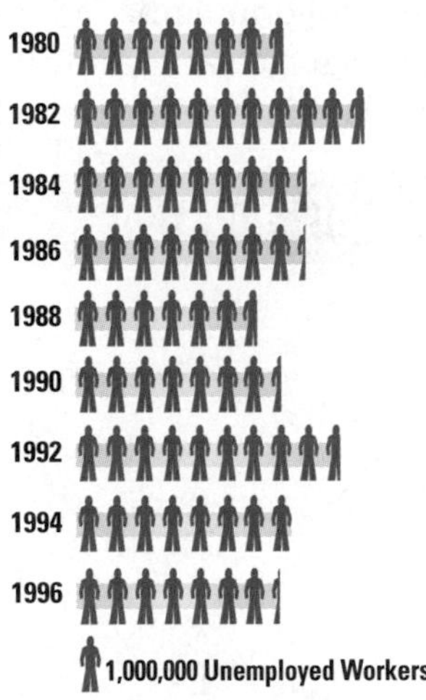

UNEMPLOYMENT RATE

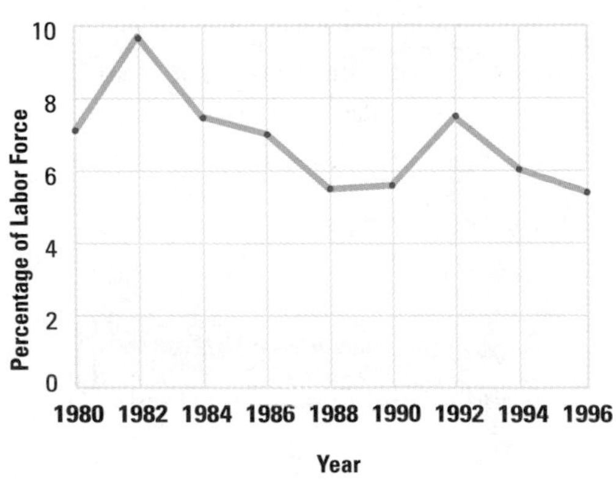

Source: *Economic Report of the President, 1997.*

ATLAS

The atlas contains a map of the world and several political, physical, and historical maps of the United States. It also contains a chart of important statistical trends in the history of the United States.

World: Political

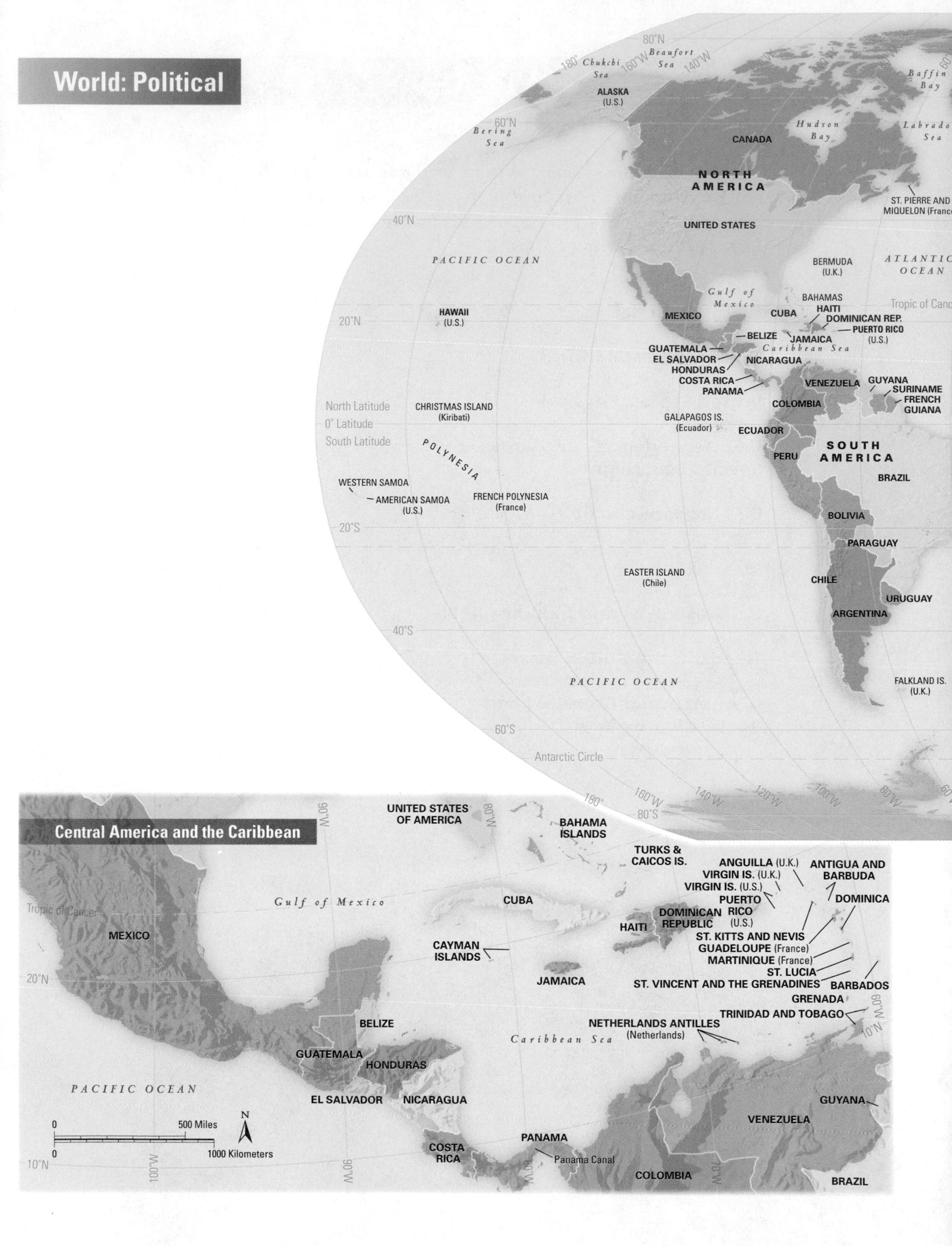

Chukchi Sea
Beaufort Sea
Baffin Bay
ALASKA (U.S.)
Bering Sea
Hudson Bay
Labrador Sea
CANADA
NORTH AMERICA
ST. PIERRE AND MIQUELON (France)
UNITED STATES
PACIFIC OCEAN
BERMUDA (U.K.)
ATLANTIC OCEAN
Gulf of Mexico
BAHAMAS
Tropic of Cancer
HAWAII (U.S.)
MEXICO
CUBA
HAITI
DOMINICAN REP.
PUERTO RICO (U.S.)
BELIZE
JAMAICA
GUATEMALA
EL SALVADOR
HONDURAS
COSTA RICA
PANAMA
Caribbean Sea
NICARAGUA
VENEZUELA
GUYANA
SURINAME
FRENCH GUIANA
COLOMBIA
North Latitude
0° Latitude
South Latitude
CHRISTMAS ISLAND (Kiribati)
GALAPAGOS IS. (Ecuador)
ECUADOR
POLYNESIA
PERU
SOUTH AMERICA
BRAZIL
WESTERN SAMOA
AMERICAN SAMOA (U.S.)
FRENCH POLYNESIA (France)
BOLIVIA
PARAGUAY
EASTER ISLAND (Chile)
CHILE
URUGUAY
ARGENTINA
PACIFIC OCEAN
FALKLAND IS. (U.K.)
Antarctic Circle
80°N
60°N
40°N
20°N
20°S
40°S
60°S
80°S
180°
160°W
140°W
120°W
100°W
80°W
60°W
Central America and the Caribbean
UNITED STATES OF AMERICA
BAHAMA ISLANDS
TURKS & CAICOS IS.
ANGUILLA (U.K.)
ANTIGUA AND BARBUDA
VIRGIN IS. (U.K.)
VIRGIN IS. (U.S.)
PUERTO RICO (U.S.)
DOMINICA
Gulf of Mexico
CUBA
DOMINICAN REPUBLIC
Tropic of Cancer
MEXICO
HAITI
ST. KITTS AND NEVIS
CAYMAN ISLANDS
GUADELOUPE (France)
MARTINIQUE (France)
ST. LUCIA
JAMAICA
ST. VINCENT AND THE GRENADINES
BARBADOS
GRENADA
TRINIDAD AND TOBAGO
BELIZE
NETHERLANDS ANTILLES (Netherlands)
Caribbean Sea
GUATEMALA
HONDURAS
PACIFIC OCEAN
EL SALVADOR
NICARAGUA
GUYANA
VENEZUELA
0
500 Miles
1000 Kilometers
N
PANAMA
COSTA RICA
Panama Canal
COLOMBIA
BRAZIL
20°N
10°N
100°W
90°W
80°W
70°W
60°W

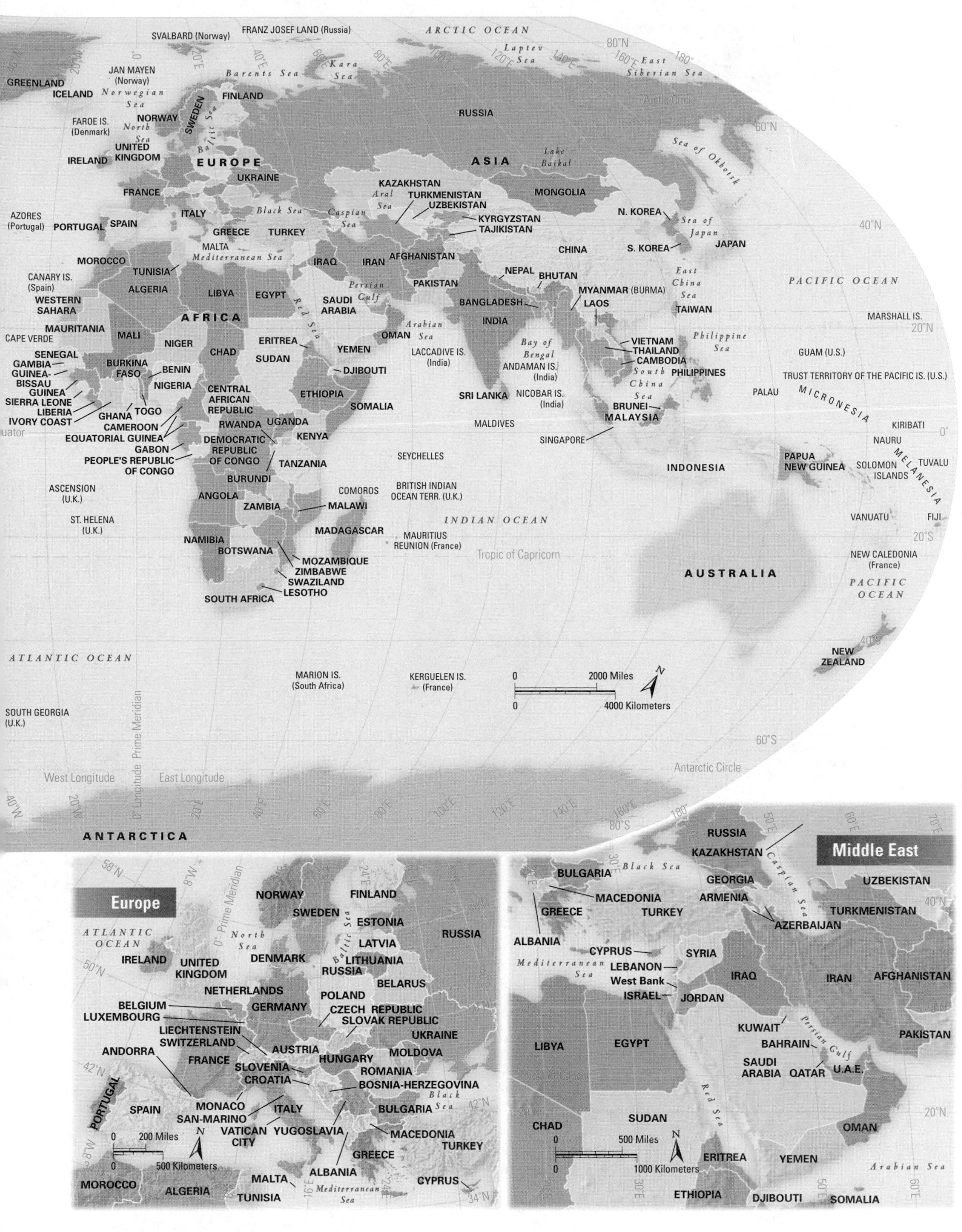

SVALBARD (Norway)
FRANZ JOSEF LAND (Russia)
ARCTIC OCEAN
Laptev Sea
East Siberian Sea
Kara Sea
Barents Sea
80°N
Arctic Circle
GREENLAND
JAN MAYEN (Norway)
ICELAND
Norwegian Sea
FINLAND
SWEDEN
NORWAY
FAROE IS. (Denmark)
North Sea
Baltic Sea
RUSSIA
60°N
Sea of Okhotsk
IRELAND
UNITED KINGDOM
EUROPE
ASIA
Lake Baikal
UKRAINE
KAZAKHSTAN
Aral Sea
TURKMENISTAN
UZBEKISTAN
MONGOLIA
FRANCE
AZORES (Portugal)
PORTUGAL
SPAIN
ITALY
Black Sea
Caspian Sea
KYRGYZSTAN
TAJIKISTAN
N. KOREA
Sea of Japan
40°N
GREECE
TURKEY
MALTA
Mediterranean Sea
CHINA
S. KOREA
JAPAN
MOROCCO
TUNISIA
IRAQ
IRAN
AFGHANISTAN
NEPAL
BHUTAN
East China Sea
CANARY IS. (Spain)
ALGERIA
LIBYA
EGYPT
Persian Gulf
PAKISTAN
MYANMAR (BURMA)
PACIFIC OCEAN
WESTERN SAHARA
Red Sea
SAUDI ARABIA
BANGLADESH
LAOS
TAIWAN
AFRICA
INDIA
MARSHALL IS.
MAURITANIA
Arabian Sea
20°N
CAPE VERDE
MALI
NIGER
ERITREA
OMAN
VIETNAM
Philippine Sea
CHAD
YEMEN
Bay of Bengal
THAILAND
SENEGAL
SUDAN
LACCADIVE IS. (India)
CAMBODIA
GUAM (U.S.)
GAMBIA
BURKINA FASO
BENIN
DJIBOUTI
ANDAMAN IS. (India)
South China Sea
PHILIPPINES
GUINEA-BISSAU
NIGERIA
TRUST TERRITORY OF THE PACIFIC IS. (U.S.)
GUINEA
CENTRAL AFRICAN REPUBLIC
ETHIOPIA
SRI LANKA
NICOBAR IS. (India)
PALAU
MICRONESIA
SIERRA LEONE
LIBERIA
GHANA
TOGO
SOMALIA
BRUNEI
IVORY COAST
CAMEROON
RWANDA
UGANDA
MALAYSIA
MALDIVES
KIRIBATI
EQUATORIAL GUINEA
DEMOCRATIC REPUBLIC OF CONGO
KENYA
SINGAPORE
NAURU
0°
GABON
PEOPLE'S REPUBLIC OF CONGO
SEYCHELLES
TANZANIA
PAPUA NEW GUINEA
SOLOMON ISLANDS
MELANESIA
TUVALU
BURUNDI
INDONESIA
ASCENSION (U.K.)
BRITISH INDIAN OCEAN TERR. (U.K.)
ANGOLA
COMOROS
ZAMBIA
MALAWI
ST. HELENA (U.K.)
INDIAN OCEAN
VANUATU
FIJI
MADAGASCAR
NAMIBIA
MAURITIUS
REUNION (France)
20°S
BOTSWANA
Tropic of Capricorn
MOZAMBIQUE
ZIMBABWE
NEW CALEDONIA (France)
SWAZILAND
AUSTRALIA
LESOTHO
PACIFIC OCEAN
SOUTH AFRICA
NEW ZEALAND
ATLANTIC OCEAN
MARION IS. (South Africa)
KERGUELEN IS. (France)
0
2000 Miles
0
4000 Kilometers
N
SOUTH GEORGIA (U.K.)
0° Longitude Prime Meridian
60°S
West Longitude
East Longitude
Antarctic Circle
ANTARCTICA
80°S
Europe
ATLANTIC OCEAN
NORWAY
FINLAND
SWEDEN
ESTONIA
North Sea
RUSSIA
LATVIA
IRELAND
UNITED KINGDOM
DENMARK
LITHUANIA
RUSSIA
BELARUS
NETHERLANDS
POLAND
BELGIUM
GERMANY
CZECH REPUBLIC
LUXEMBOURG
SLOVAK REPUBLIC
LIECHTENSTEIN
UKRAINE
SWITZERLAND
ANDORRA
AUSTRIA
MOLDOVA
FRANCE
HUNGARY
SLOVENIA
ROMANIA
CROATIA
BOSNIA-HERZEGOVINA
PORTUGAL
SPAIN
MONACO
ITALY
BULGARIA
Black Sea
SAN-MARINO
VATICAN CITY
YUGOSLAVIA
MACEDONIA
TURKEY
0
200 Miles
0
500 Kilometers
GREECE
MOROCCO
ALGERIA
MALTA
ALBANIA
TUNISIA
Mediterranean Sea
CYPRUS
Middle East
RUSSIA
KAZAKHSTAN
Caspian Sea
Black Sea
BULGARIA
GEORGIA
UZBEKISTAN
MACEDONIA
ARMENIA
GREECE
TURKEY
TURKMENISTAN
AZERBAIJAN
ALBANIA
CYPRUS
SYRIA
Mediterranean Sea
LEBANON
IRAQ
IRAN
AFGHANISTAN
West Bank
ISRAEL
JORDAN
KUWAIT
Persian Gulf
PAKISTAN
LIBYA
EGYPT
BAHRAIN
SAUDI ARABIA
QATAR
U.A.E.
Red Sea
SUDAN
CHAD
OMAN
0
500 Miles
0
1000 Kilometers
ERITREA
YEMEN
Arabian Sea
ETHIOPIA
DJIBOUTI
SOMALIA

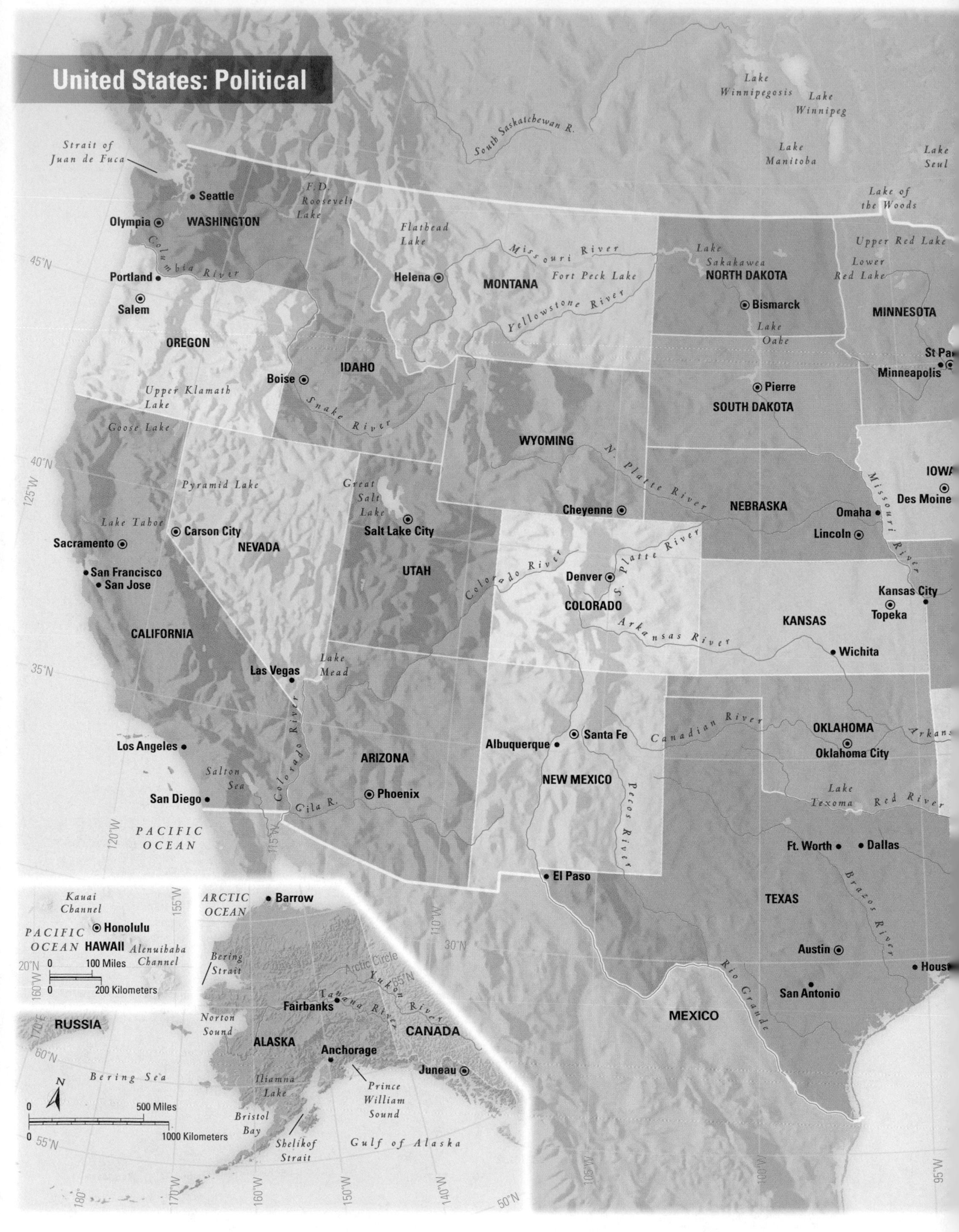
United States: Political
Strait of Juan de Fuca
Seattle
Olympia
WASHINGTON
F.D. Roosevelt Lake
Columbia River
Portland
Salem
OREGON
Upper Klamath Lake
Goose Lake
IDAHO
Boise
Snake River
Flathead Lake
Helena
MONTANA
Missouri River
Fort Peck Lake
Yellowstone River
NORTH DAKOTA
Lake Sakakawea
Bismarck
Lake Oahe
SOUTH DAKOTA
Pierre
MINNESOTA
Minneapolis
Upper Red Lake
Lower Red Lake
Lake of the Woods
Lake Winnipegosis
Lake Winnipeg
Lake Manitoba
South Saskatchewan R.
WYOMING
N. Platte River
Cheyenne
NEBRASKA
Omaha
Lincoln
Des Moine
Missouri River
Pyramid Lake
Great Salt Lake
Salt Lake City
Lake Tahoe
Carson City
NEVADA
Sacramento
San Francisco
San Jose
CALIFORNIA
UTAH
Colorado River
Denver
S. Platte River
COLORADO
Arkansas River
KANSAS
Kansas City
Topeka
Wichita
Las Vegas
Lake Mead
Colorado River
Los Angeles
Salton Sea
San Diego
ARIZONA
Phoenix
Gila R.
Albuquerque
Santa Fe
NEW MEXICO
Pecos River
Canadian River
OKLAHOMA
Oklahoma City
Lake Texoma
Red River
Ft. Worth
Dallas
El Paso
TEXAS
Brazos River
Austin
San Antonio
Rio Grande
MEXICO
PACIFIC OCEAN
Kauai Channel
PACIFIC OCEAN
Honolulu
HAWAII
Alenuihaha Channel
100 Miles
200 Kilometers
ARCTIC OCEAN
Barrow
Bering Strait
Arctic Circle
Yukon River
Tanana River
Fairbanks
Norton Sound
ALASKA
RUSSIA
CANADA
Anchorage
Juneau
Bering Sea
Iliamna Lake
Prince William Sound
Bristol Bay
Shelikof Strait
Gulf of Alaska
500 Miles
1000 Kilometers
45°N
40°N
35°N
30°N
125°W
120°W
115°W
110°W
105°W
100°W
95°W
20°N
160°W
155°W
170°E
60°N
55°N
50°N
180°
170°W
160°W
150°W
140°W

944 Atlas

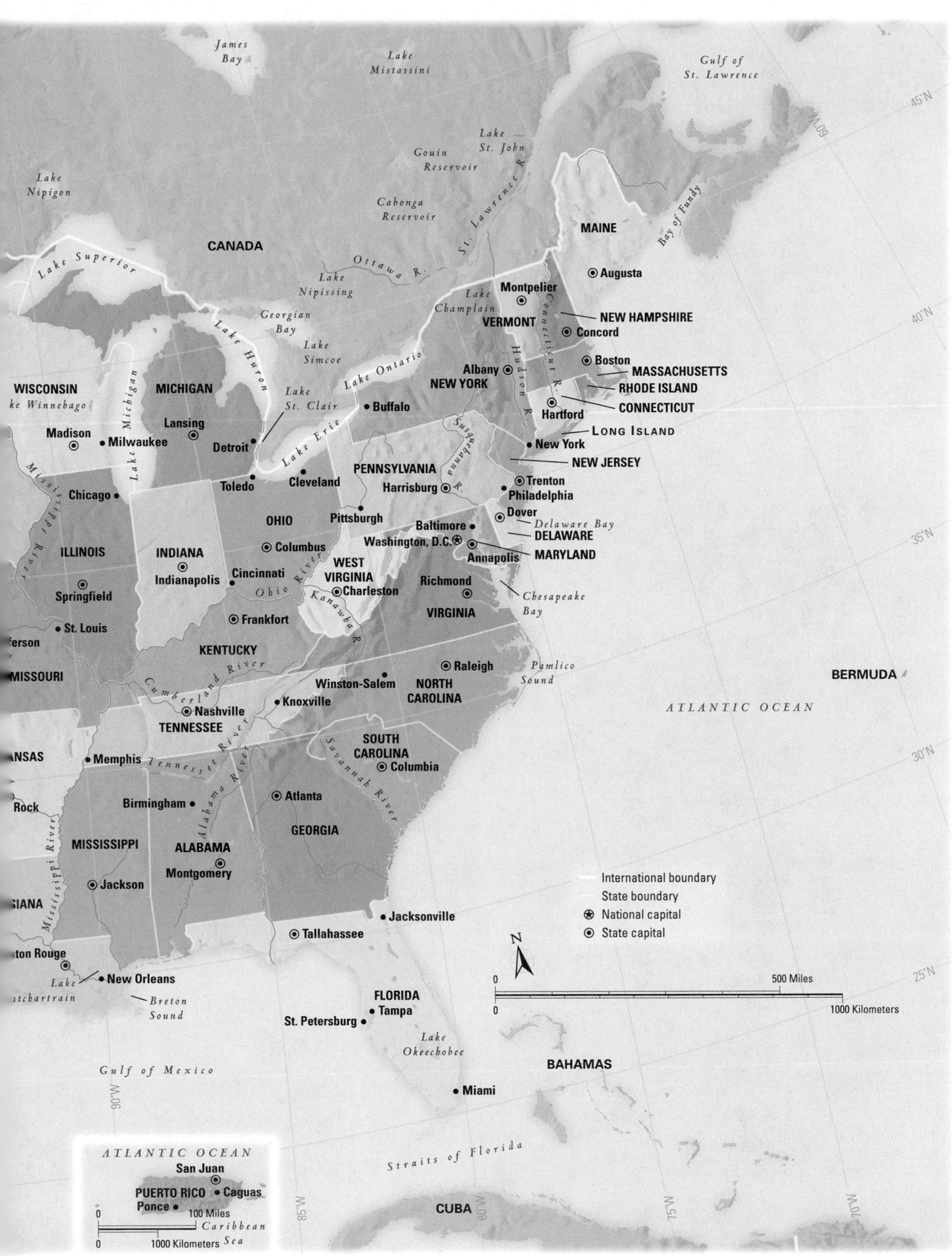

James Bay
Lake Mistassini
Gulf of St. Lawrence
Lake St. John
Gouin Reservoir
Lake Nipigon
Cabonga Reservoir
St. Lawrence R.
Bay of Fundy
MAINE
CANADA
Lake Superior
Ottawa R.
Augusta
Lake Nipissing
Lake Champlain
Montpelier
VERMONT
NEW HAMPSHIRE
Concord
Georgian Bay
Lake Huron
Lake Simcoe
Lake Ontario
Connecticut R.
Hudson R.
Albany
NEW YORK
Boston
MASSACHUSETTS
RHODE ISLAND
CONNECTICUT
Hartford
WISCONSIN
Lake Winnebago
Lake Michigan
MICHIGAN
Lake St. Clair
Buffalo
Lansing
Madison
Milwaukee
Detroit
Lake Erie
Susquehanna R.
Long Island
New York
NEW JERSEY
Mississippi River
Toledo
Cleveland
PENNSYLVANIA
Harrisburg
Trenton
Philadelphia
Chicago
OHIO
Pittsburgh
Dover
Delaware Bay
Baltimore
DELAWARE
Washington, D.C.
MARYLAND
Annapolis
ILLINOIS
INDIANA
Columbus
WEST VIRGINIA
Indianapolis
Cincinnati
Ohio River
Charleston
Richmond
Chesapeake Bay
Springfield
Kanawha R.
VIRGINIA
Frankfort
St. Louis
KENTUCKY
Raleigh
Pamlico Sound
Cumberland River
Winston-Salem
NORTH CAROLINA
BERMUDA
MISSOURI
Knoxville
Nashville
ATLANTIC OCEAN
TENNESSEE
SOUTH CAROLINA
Memphis
Tennessee River
Columbia
Savannah River
Birmingham
Alabama River
Atlanta
Rock
GEORGIA
MISSISSIPPI
ALABAMA
Montgomery
Jackson
International boundary
State boundary
National capital
State capital
Jacksonville
Tallahassee
N
0
500 Miles
0
1000 Kilometers
New Orleans
Lake
Breton Sound
FLORIDA
Tampa
St. Petersburg
Lake Okeechobee
BAHAMAS
Gulf of Mexico
Miami
ATLANTIC OCEAN
San Juan
PUERTO RICO
Caguas
Ponce
100 Miles
Caribbean Sea
1000 Kilometers
Straits of Florida
CUBA
45°N
40°N
35°N
30°N
25°N
60°W
90°W
85°W
80°W
75°W
70°W

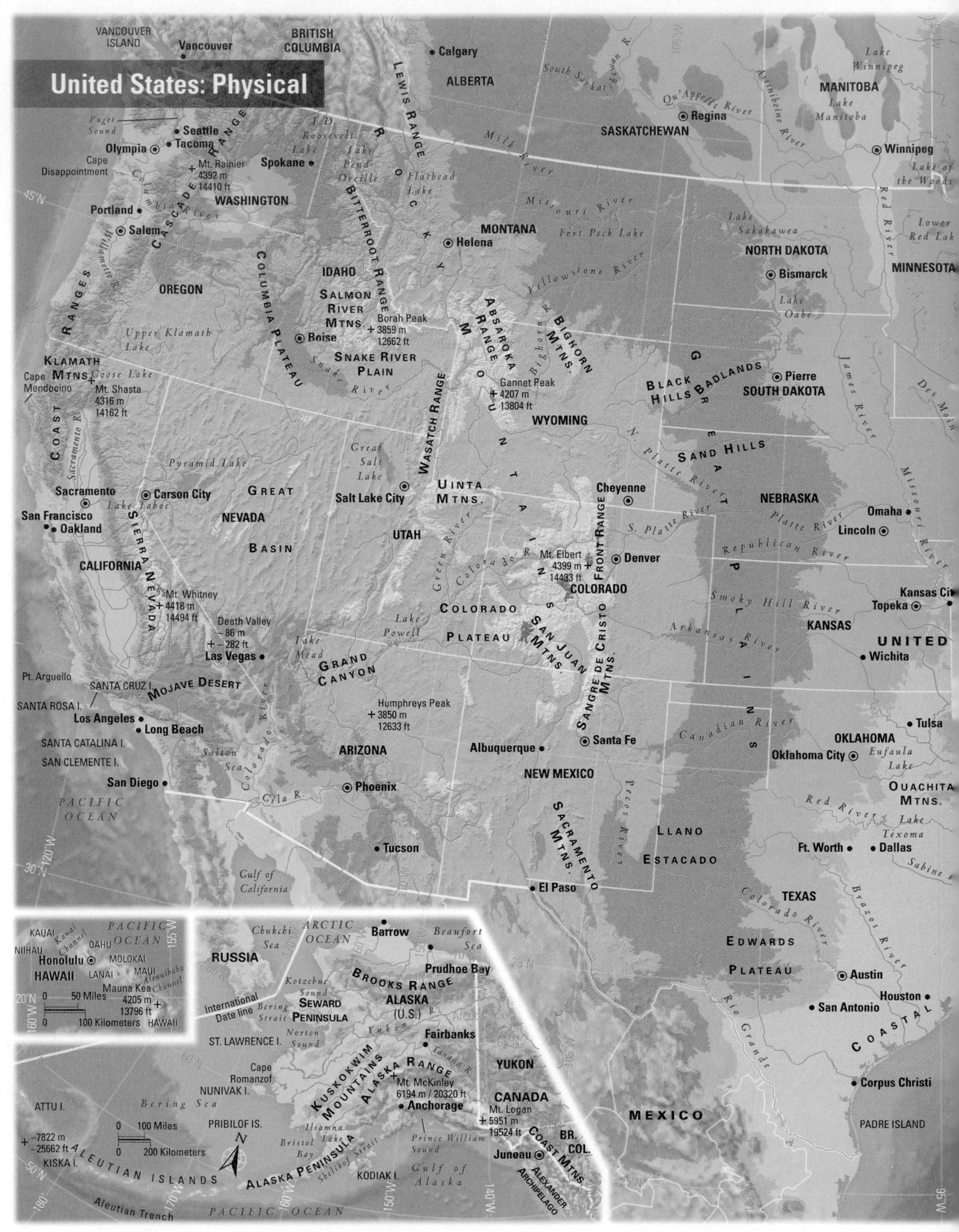
United States: Physical
VANCOUVER ISLAND
Vancouver
BRITISH COLUMBIA
Calgary
ALBERTA
SASKATCHEWAN
MANITOBA
Regina
Winnipeg
Lake Winnipeg
Lake Manitoba
Lake of the Woods
South Saskatchewan R.
Qu'Appelle River
Assiniboine River
Milk River
Puget Sound
Seattle
Tacoma
Olympia
Cape Disappointment
Mt. Rainier 4392 m 14410 ft
Spokane
WASHINGTON
Portland
Salem
Columbia River
Willamette R.
CASCADE RANGE
OREGON
LEWIS RANGE
ROCKY MOUNTAINS
F.D. Roosevelt Lake
Lake Pend Oreille
Flathead Lake
BITTERROOT RANGE
COLUMBIA PLATEAU
IDAHO
SALMON RIVER MTNS.
Borah Peak 3859 m 12662 ft
Boise
SNAKE RIVER PLAIN
Snake River
MONTANA
Helena
Missouri River
Fort Peck Lake
Yellowstone River
Lake Sakakawea
NORTH DAKOTA
Bismarck
MINNESOTA
Red River
Lower Red Lake
Lake Oahe
ABSAROKA RANGE
BIGHORN MTNS.
Bighorn R.
Gannet Peak 4207 m 13804 ft
WYOMING
BLACK HILLS
BADLANDS
Pierre
SOUTH DAKOTA
James River
Des Moines
COAST RANGES
Upper Klamath Lake
KLAMATH MTNS.
Cape Mendocino
Goose Lake
Mt. Shasta 4316 m 14162 ft
Sacramento R.
Pyramid Lake
Great Salt Lake
WASATCH RANGE
Salt Lake City
UINTA MTNS.
Sacramento
Carson City
Lake Tahoe
San Francisco
Oakland
GREAT BASIN
NEVADA
UTAH
SIERRA NEVADA
CALIFORNIA
Mt. Whitney 4418 m 14494 ft
Death Valley −86 m −282 ft
Las Vegas
Lake Mead
Lake Powell
Green River
Colorado R.
COLORADO PLATEAU
Cheyenne
FRONT RANGE
Denver
Mt. Elbert 4399 m 14433 ft
COLORADO
SAN JUAN MTNS.
SANGRE DE CRISTO MTNS.
N. Platte River
S. Platte River
SAND HILLS
GREAT PLAINS
NEBRASKA
Omaha
Platte River
Lincoln
Republican River
Smoky Hill River
Arkansas River
Kansas City
Topeka
KANSAS
UNITED
Wichita
Missouri River
GRAND CANYON
Pt. Arguello
SANTA CRUZ I.
SANTA ROSA I.
MOJAVE DESERT
Los Angeles
Long Beach
SANTA CATALINA I.
SAN CLEMENTE I.
Salton Sea
Colorado River
San Diego
PACIFIC OCEAN
Humphreys Peak 3850 m 12633 ft
ARIZONA
Phoenix
Gila R.
Tucson
Albuquerque
Santa Fe
NEW MEXICO
SACRAMENTO MTNS.
Pecos River
LLANO ESTACADO
El Paso
Canadian River
Tulsa
OKLAHOMA
Oklahoma City
Eufaula Lake
OUACHITA MTNS.
Red River
Lake Texoma
Ft. Worth
Dallas
Sabine
TEXAS
Colorado River
Brazos River
EDWARDS PLATEAU
Austin
Houston
San Antonio
COASTAL
Corpus Christi
PADRE ISLAND
Rio Grande
MEXICO
Gulf of California
KAUAI
Kauai Channel
NIIHAU
OAHU
PACIFIC OCEAN
Honolulu
MOLOKAI
HAWAII
LANAI
MAUI
Alenuihaha Channel
Mauna Kea 4205 m 13796 ft
0 50 Miles
0 100 Kilometers
HAWAII
ARCTIC OCEAN
Chukchi Sea
Barrow
Beaufort Sea
RUSSIA
Prudhoe Bay
BROOKS RANGE
Kotzebue Sound
International Date line
Bering Strait
SEWARD PENINSULA
ALASKA (U.S.)
Yukon R.
Norton Sound
ST. LAWRENCE I.
Fairbanks
Tanana R.
YUKON
Cape Romanzof
KUSKOKWIM MOUNTAINS
ALASKA RANGE
Mt. McKinley 6194 m / 20320 ft
NUNIVAK I.
Anchorage
CANADA
Mt. Logan 5951 m 19524 ft
ATTU I.
Bering Sea
PRIBILOF IS.
0 100 Miles
0 200 Kilometers
−7822 m −25662 ft
KISKA I.
ALEUTIAN ISLANDS
Bristol Bay
Iliamna Lake
ALASKA PENINSULA
Shelikof Strait
Prince William Sound
KODIAK I.
Gulf of Alaska
Juneau
COAST MTNS.
BR. COL.
ALEXANDER ARCHIPELAGO
Aleutian Trench
PACIFIC OCEAN
N

CANADA
ONTARIO
QUEBEC
HUDSON BAY LOWLANDS
LAURENTIAN HIGHLANDS
LAURENTIDE SCARP
NOTRE DAME MTNS.
LAURENTIAN SCARP
James Bay
Lake Mistassini
Harricana River
Lake Nipigon
Lake Abitibi
Gouin Reservoir
Cabonga Reservoir
Saguenay R.
Lake St. John
St. Maurice R.
St. Lawrence R.
Ottawa R.
Lake Nipissing
Gaspé PENINSULA
Cape Gaspé
NEWFOUNDLAND
Gulf of St. Lawrence
Cabot Strait
MAGDALEN IS.
PRINCE EDWARD ISLAND
Charlottetown
NEW BRUNSWICK
Fredericton
Halifax
NOVA SCOTIA
Bay of Fundy
Cape Sable
Quebec
Montreal
Ottawa
MAINE
Augusta
MESABI RANGE
ISLE ROYALE
Lake Superior
MANITOULIN I.
Lake Huron
Lake Simcoe
Lake Champlain
Montpelier
Mt. Washington 1917 m 6288 ft
VERMONT
NEW HAMPSHIRE
Concord
ADIRONDACK MTNS.
MASSACHUSETTS
Boston
Cape Cod
Worcester
Providence
Springfield
Hartford
NANTUCKET ISLAND
MARTHA'S VINEYARD
RHODE ISLAND
CONNECTICUT
New Haven
LONG ISLAND
New York
NEW JERSEY
Trenton
Philadelphia
Wilmington
Dover
Cape May
Delaware Bay
DELAWARE
MARYLAND
Annapolis
Baltimore
Washington, D.C.
Hudson River
Connecticut R.
WISCONSIN
Wisconsin R.
inneapolis
St. Paul
MICHIGAN
Lake Michigan
Madison
Milwaukee
Grand Rapids
Lansing
Flint
Lake St. Clair
Detroit
Windsor
Toronto
Lake Ontario
Hamilton
London
Syracuse
Albany
Rochester
Buffalo
NEW YORK
Lake Erie
Cleveland
Akron
Toledo
Chicago
IOWA
Des Moines
CENTRAL LOWLAND
PENNSYLVANIA
Harrisburg
Pittsburgh
Susquehanna R.
OHIO
Columbus
Dayton
Cincinnati
ILLINOIS
Springfield
INDIANA
Indianapolis
Ohio River
Wabash River
WEST VIRGINIA
Charleston
Kanawha R.
VIRGINIA
Richmond
James R.
Norfolk
Cape Charles
Chesapeake Bay
ATLANTIC OCEAN
BERMUDA
ISSOURI
Jefferson City
St. Louis
STATES
Louisville
Frankfort
KENTUCKY
Roanoke River
APPALACHIAN MOUNTAINS
CUMBERLAND PLATEAU
BLUE RIDGE MTNS.
HATTERAS ISLAND
Pamlico Sound
Cape Hatteras
Raleigh
NORTH CAROLINA
Cumberland River
Nashville
Knoxville
TENNESSEE
Mt. Mitchell 2037 m 6684 ft
Charlotte
SOUTH CAROLINA
Columbia
Pee Dee River
Savannah River
ZARK LATEAU
ARKANSAS
Arkansas River
Little Rock
Memphis
Tennessee River
Chattanooga
Atlanta
Birmingham
Charleston
COASTAL PLAIN
MISSISSIPPI
Mississippi River
Tombigbee R.
ALABAMA
Alabama R.
Montgomery
Chattahoochee R.
GEORGIA
Savannah
Jackson
LOUISIANA
Jacksonville
Mobile
Tallahassee
Baton Rouge
AIN
Lafayette
New Orleans
Lake Pontchartrain
Breton Sound
Cape San Blas
FLORIDA
Cape Canaveral
Gulf of Mexico
St. Petersburg
Tampa
Lake Okeechobee
Miami
Nassau
BAHAMAS
Cape Sable
FLORIDA KEYS
Straits of Florida
San Juan
PUERTO RICO
Caguas
Ponce
18°N
0
100 Miles
0
1000 Kilometers
68°W
Land Elevation
Higher than 13,000 ft
8,000 ft to 13,000 ft
4,000 ft to 8,000 ft
2,000 ft to 4,000 ft
1,000 ft to 2,000 ft
0 ft. to 1,000 ft.
Below sea level
Water Depth
0 ft. to 700 ft
700 ft to 9,800 ft
9,800 ft 19,700 ft
Deeper than 19,700 ft
International boundary
State boundary
National capital
State capital
Heights and depths
N
0
500 Miles
0
1,000 Kilometers
40°N
35°N
30°N
25°N
65°W
70°W
75°W
85°W
90°W

U.S. Dependencies and Areas of Special Sovereignty

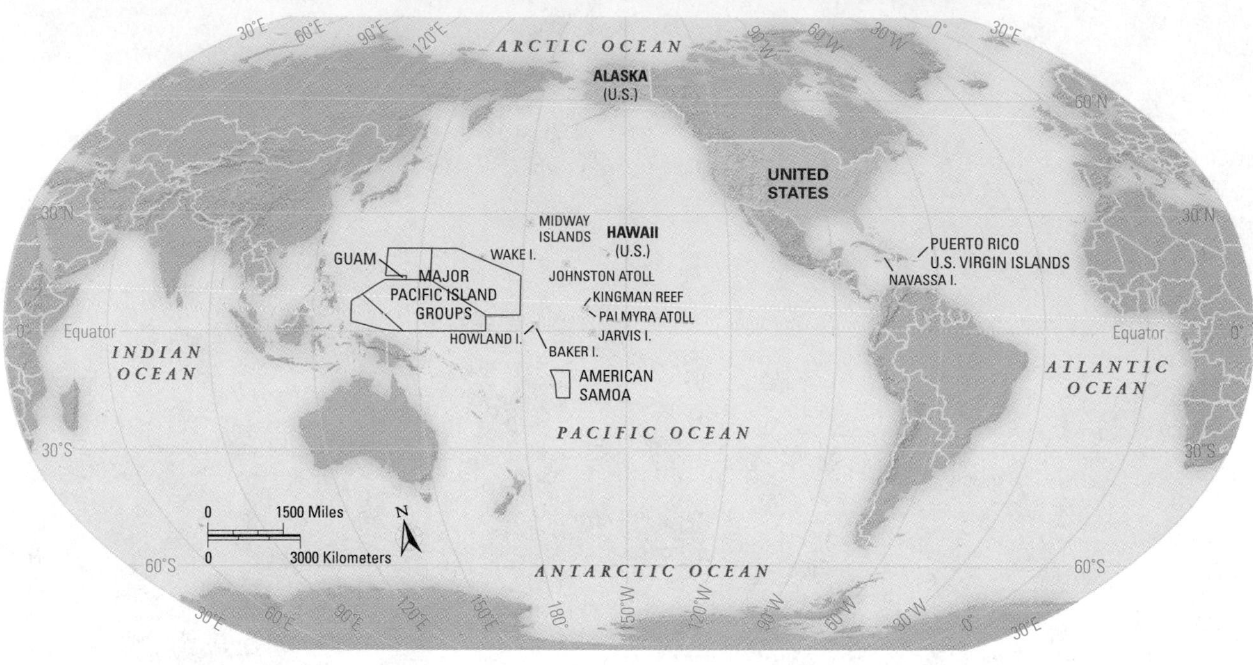

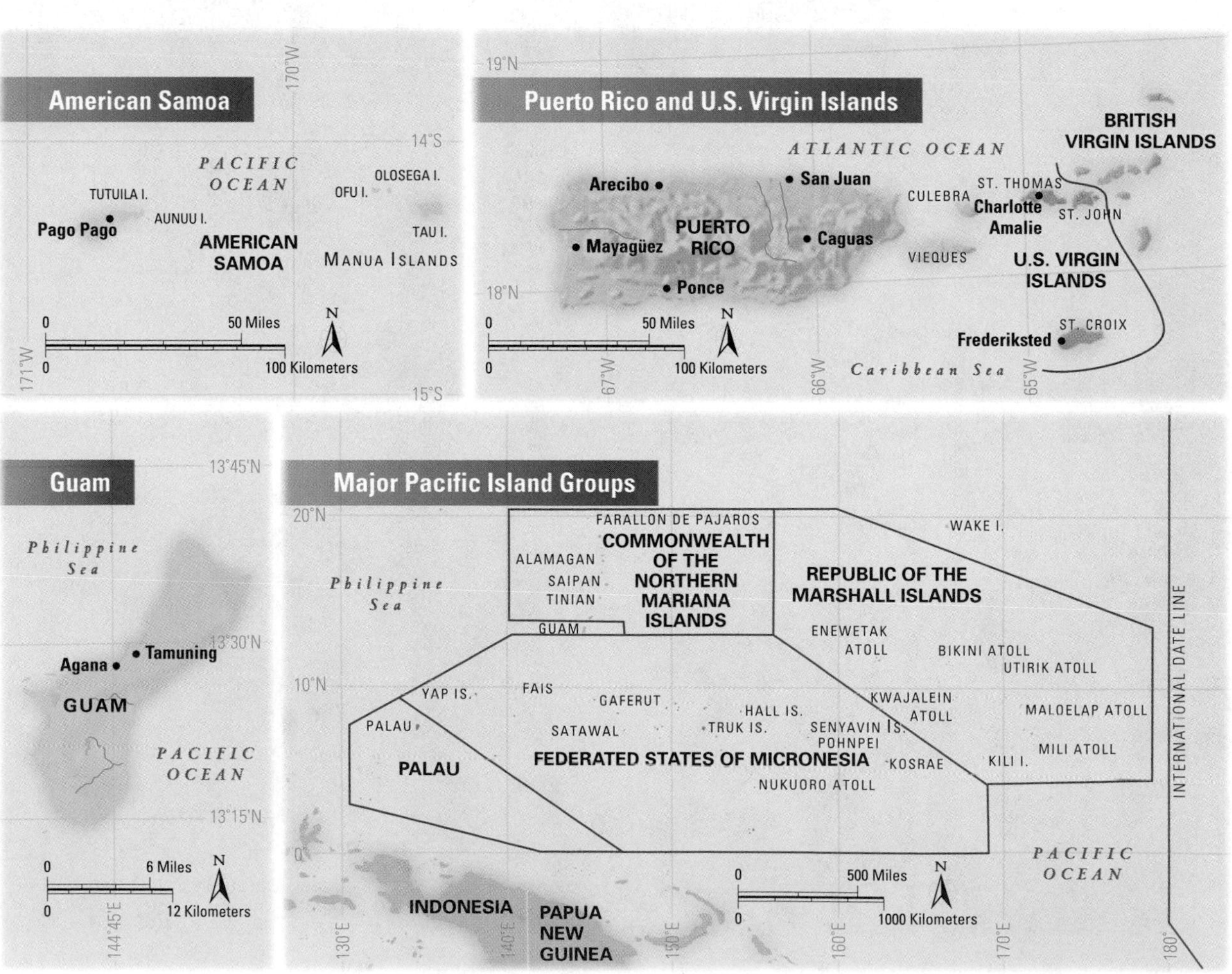

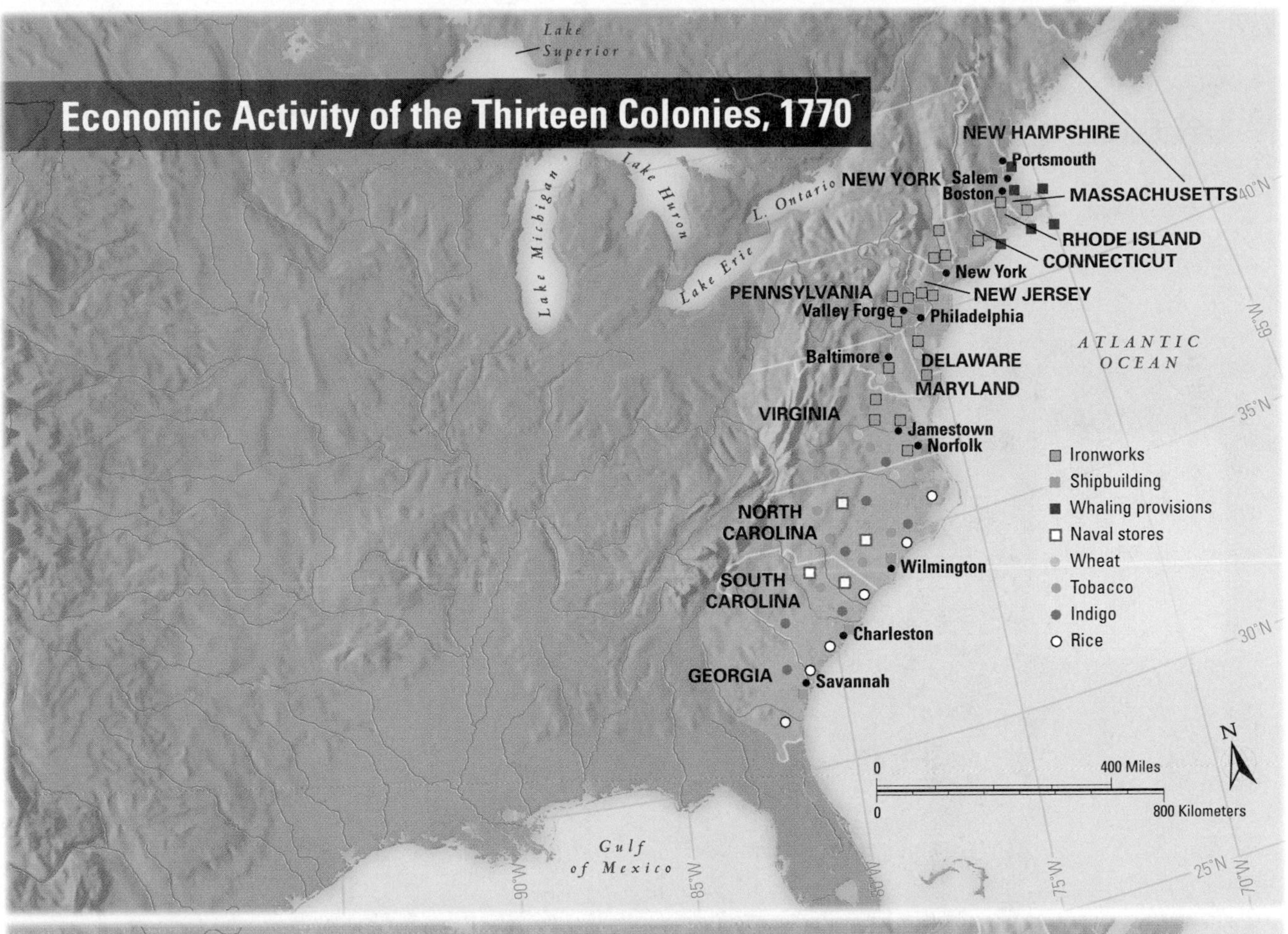
Economic Activity of the Thirteen Colonies, 1770
Lake Superior
Lake Michigan
Lake Huron
L. Ontario
Lake Erie
NEW HAMPSHIRE
Portsmouth
Salem
Boston
NEW YORK
MASSACHUSETTS
RHODE ISLAND
CONNECTICUT
New York
PENNSYLVANIA
NEW JERSEY
Valley Forge
Philadelphia
Baltimore
DELAWARE
MARYLAND
VIRGINIA
Jamestown
Norfolk
NORTH CAROLINA
Wilmington
SOUTH CAROLINA
Charleston
GEORGIA
Savannah
ATLANTIC OCEAN
Gulf of Mexico
Ironworks
Shipbuilding
Whaling provisions
Naval stores
Wheat
Tobacco
Indigo
Rice
0
400 Miles
0
800 Kilometers
N
40°N
35°N
30°N
25°N
90°W
85°W
80°W
75°W
70°W
65°W

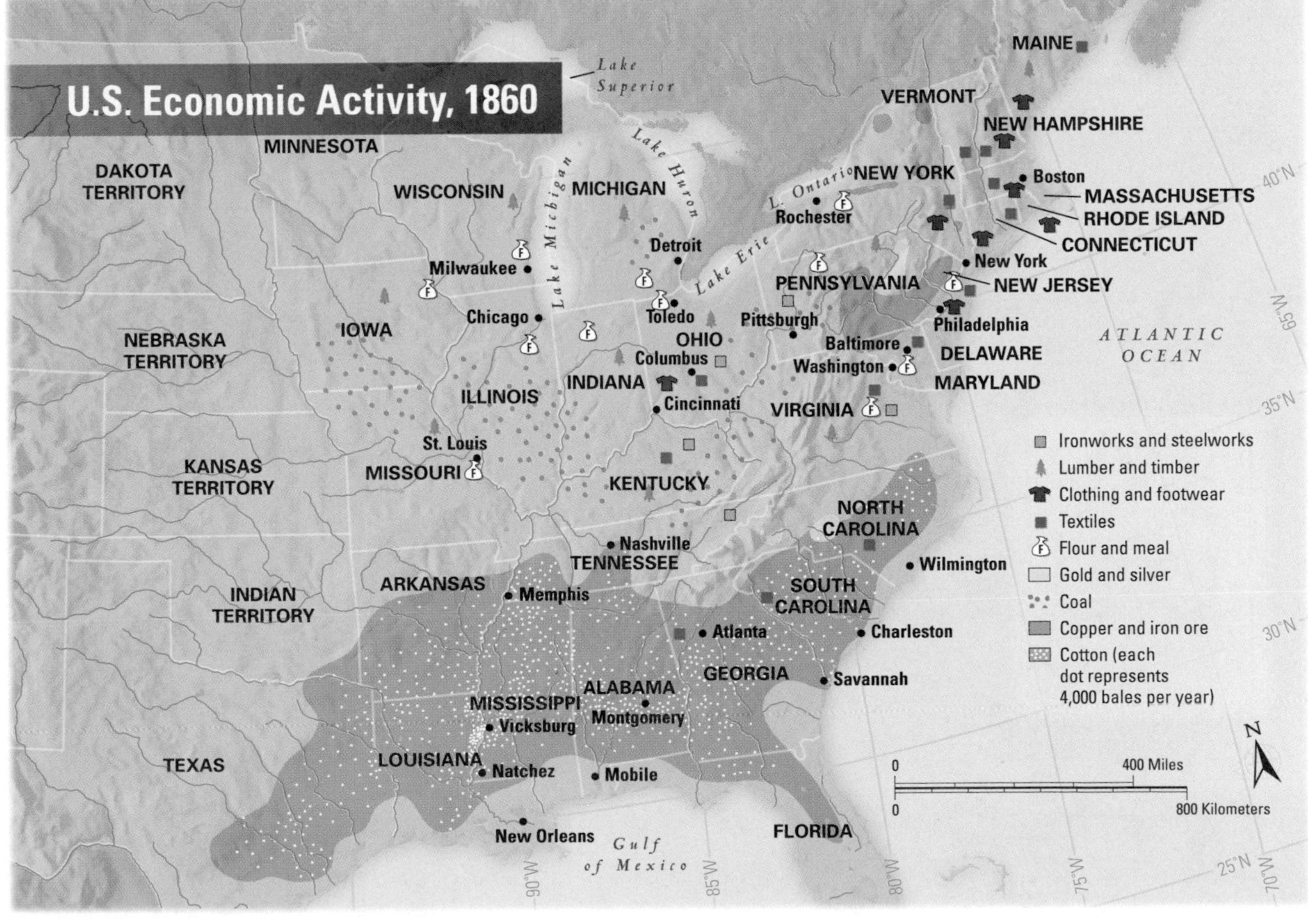
U.S. Economic Activity, 1860
Lake Superior
Lake Michigan
Lake Huron
L. Ontario
Lake Erie
MAINE
VERMONT
NEW HAMPSHIRE
NEW YORK
Boston
MASSACHUSETTS
RHODE ISLAND
CONNECTICUT
Rochester
New York
NEW JERSEY
PENNSYLVANIA
Philadelphia
DELAWARE
MARYLAND
Baltimore
Washington
VIRGINIA
MINNESOTA
DAKOTA TERRITORY
WISCONSIN
MICHIGAN
Detroit
Milwaukee
Chicago
Toledo
Pittsburgh
OHIO
Columbus
IOWA
NEBRASKA TERRITORY
ILLINOIS
INDIANA
Cincinnati
St. Louis
KANSAS TERRITORY
MISSOURI
KENTUCKY
NORTH CAROLINA
Nashville
TENNESSEE
Wilmington
ARKANSAS
Memphis
INDIAN TERRITORY
SOUTH CAROLINA
Atlanta
Charleston
GEORGIA
Savannah
ALABAMA
MISSISSIPPI
Vicksburg
Montgomery
TEXAS
LOUISIANA
Natchez
Mobile
New Orleans
FLORIDA
Gulf of Mexico
ATLANTIC OCEAN
Ironworks and steelworks
Lumber and timber
Clothing and footwear
Textiles
Flour and meal
Gold and silver
Coal
Copper and iron ore
Cotton (each dot represents 4,000 bales per year)
0
400 Miles
0
800 Kilometers
N
40°N
35°N
30°N
25°N
90°W
85°W
80°W
75°W
70°W
65°W

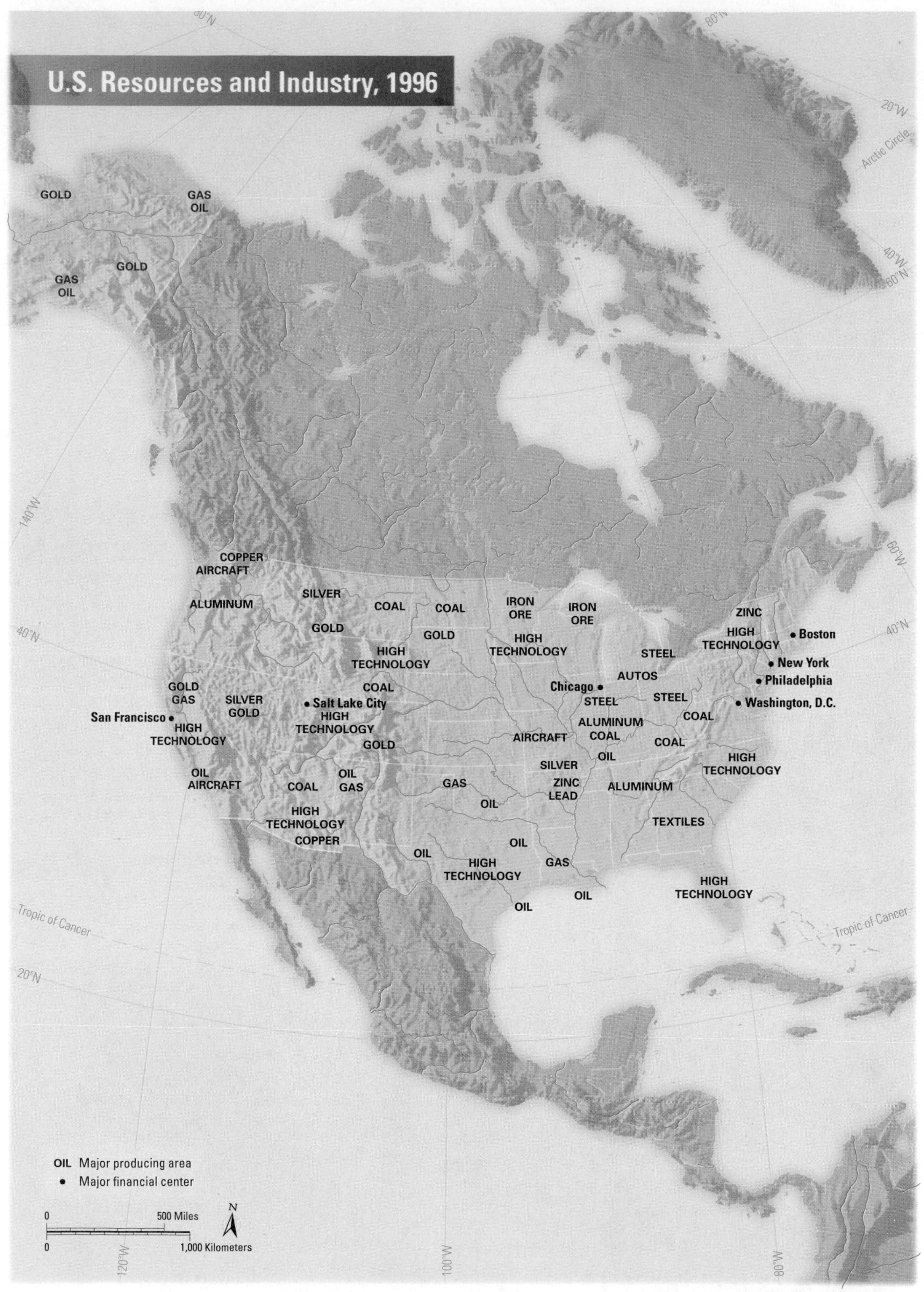
U.S. Resources and Industry, 1996
GOLD
GAS
OIL
GOLD
GAS
OIL
COPPER
AIRCRAFT
ALUMINUM
SILVER
COAL
COAL
IRON ORE
IRON ORE
ZINC
GOLD
GOLD
HIGH TECHNOLOGY
HIGH TECHNOLOGY
HIGH TECHNOLOGY
Boston
STEEL
New York
AUTOS
Philadelphia
Chicago
GOLD
GAS
COAL
SILVER
GOLD
Salt Lake City
HIGH TECHNOLOGY
STEEL
STEEL
Washington, D.C.
San Francisco
HIGH TECHNOLOGY
ALUMINUM
COAL
COAL
AIRCRAFT
COAL
GOLD
OIL
HIGH TECHNOLOGY
SILVER
OIL
AIRCRAFT
COAL
OIL
GAS
GAS
ZINC
LEAD
ALUMINUM
OIL
HIGH TECHNOLOGY
TEXTILES
COPPER
OIL
OIL
HIGH TECHNOLOGY
GAS
HIGH TECHNOLOGY
OIL
OIL
Tropic of Cancer
Tropic of Cancer
Arctic Circle
OIL Major producing area
• Major financial center
0
500 Miles
0
1,000 Kilometers
N
80°N
80°N
20°W
40°W
60°W
40°N
40°N
140°W
20°N
120°W
100°W
80°W

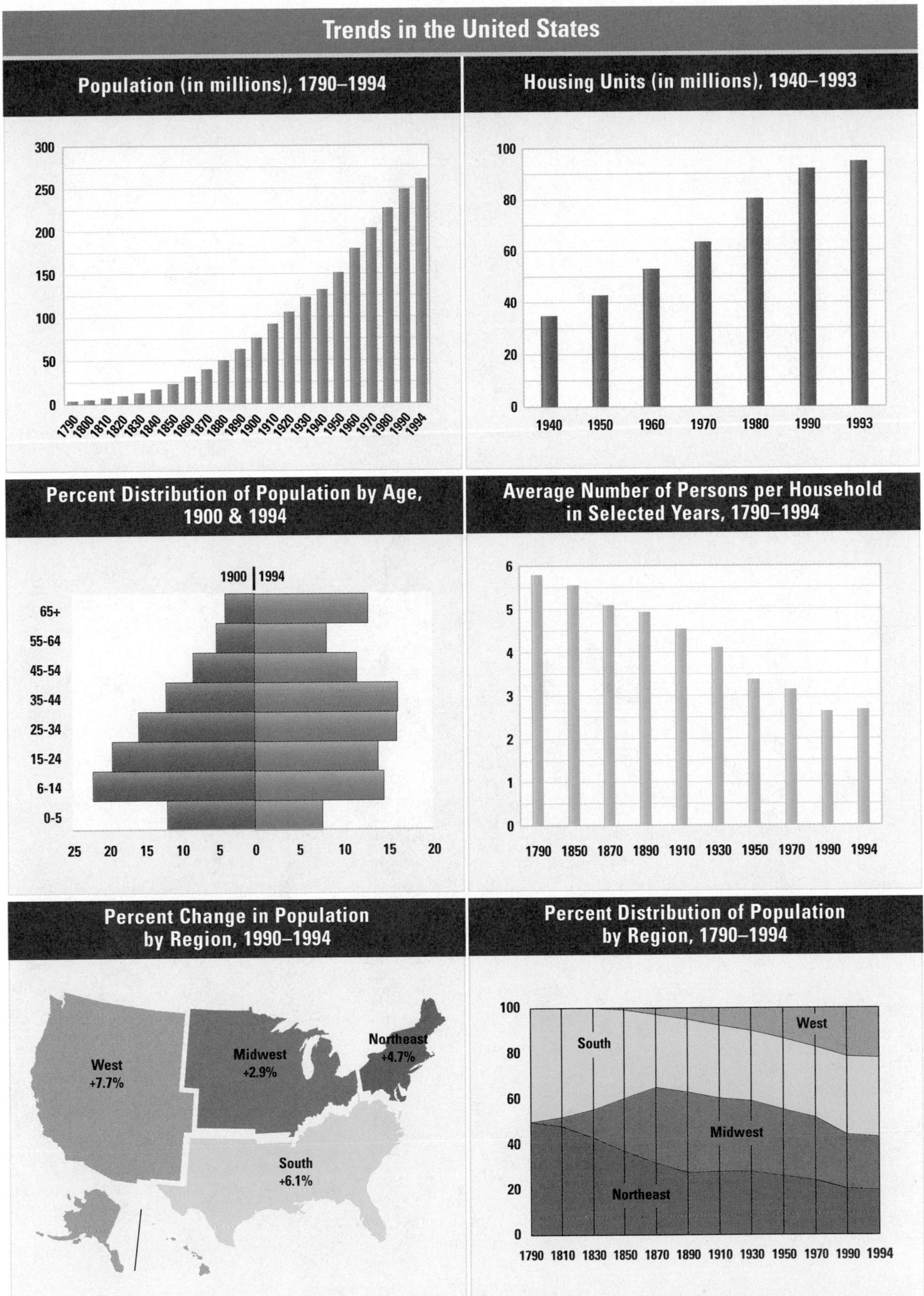

Sources: *Historical Statistics of the United States: Colonial Times to 1970; Statistical Abstract of the United States, 1995; American Housing Survey, 1993,* U.S. Census Bureau; George Thomas Kurian, *Datapedia of the United States: 1790–2000.*

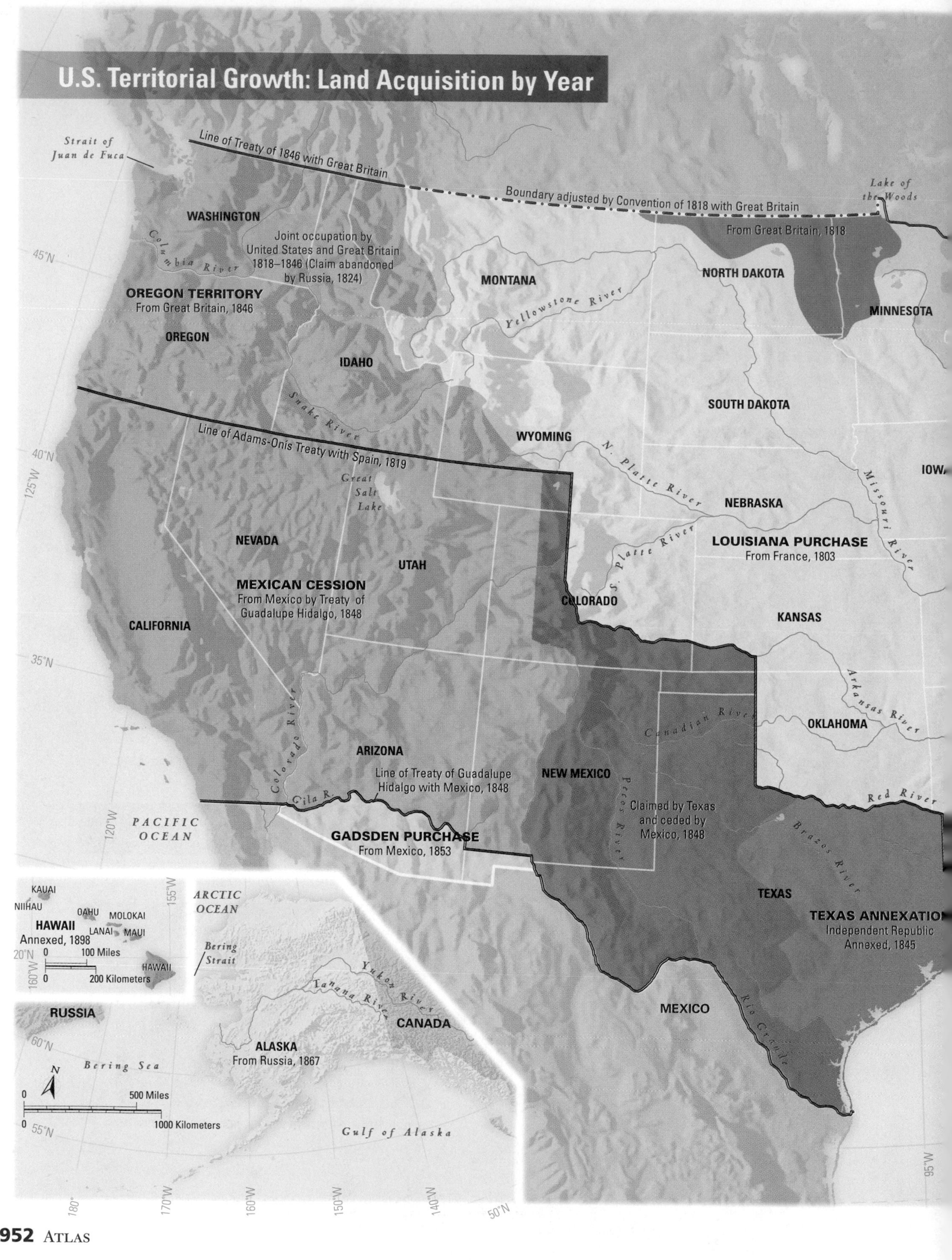

U.S. Territorial Growth: Land Acquisition by Year
Strait of Juan de Fuca
Line of Treaty of 1846 with Great Britain
Boundary adjusted by Convention of 1818 with Great Britain
Lake of the Woods
From Great Britain, 1818
WASHINGTON
Joint occupation by United States and Great Britain 1818–1846 (Claim abandoned by Russia, 1824)
Columbia River
OREGON TERRITORY
From Great Britain, 1846
OREGON
MONTANA
Yellowstone River
NORTH DAKOTA
MINNESOTA
IDAHO
SOUTH DAKOTA
Snake River
WYOMING
Line of Adams-Onis Treaty with Spain, 1819
N. Platte River
Great Salt Lake
NEBRASKA
Missouri River
IOWA
NEVADA
UTAH
LOUISIANA PURCHASE
From France, 1803
S. Platte River
MEXICAN CESSION
From Mexico by Treaty of Guadalupe Hidalgo, 1848
COLORADO
KANSAS
CALIFORNIA
Arkansas River
Canadian River
OKLAHOMA
Colorado River
ARIZONA
Line of Treaty of Guadalupe Hidalgo with Mexico, 1848
NEW MEXICO
Pecos River
Red River
Gila R.
Claimed by Texas and ceded by Mexico, 1848
Brazos River
PACIFIC OCEAN
GADSDEN PURCHASE
From Mexico, 1853
TEXAS
TEXAS ANNEXATION
Independent Republic Annexed, 1845
KAUAI
NIIHAU
OAHU
MOLOKAI
HAWAII
LANAI
MAUI
Annexed, 1898
100 Miles
200 Kilometers
ARCTIC OCEAN
Bering Strait
Yukon River
Tanana River
RUSSIA
CANADA
MEXICO
Rio Grande
ALASKA
From Russia, 1867
Bering Sea
500 Miles
1000 Kilometers
Gulf of Alaska

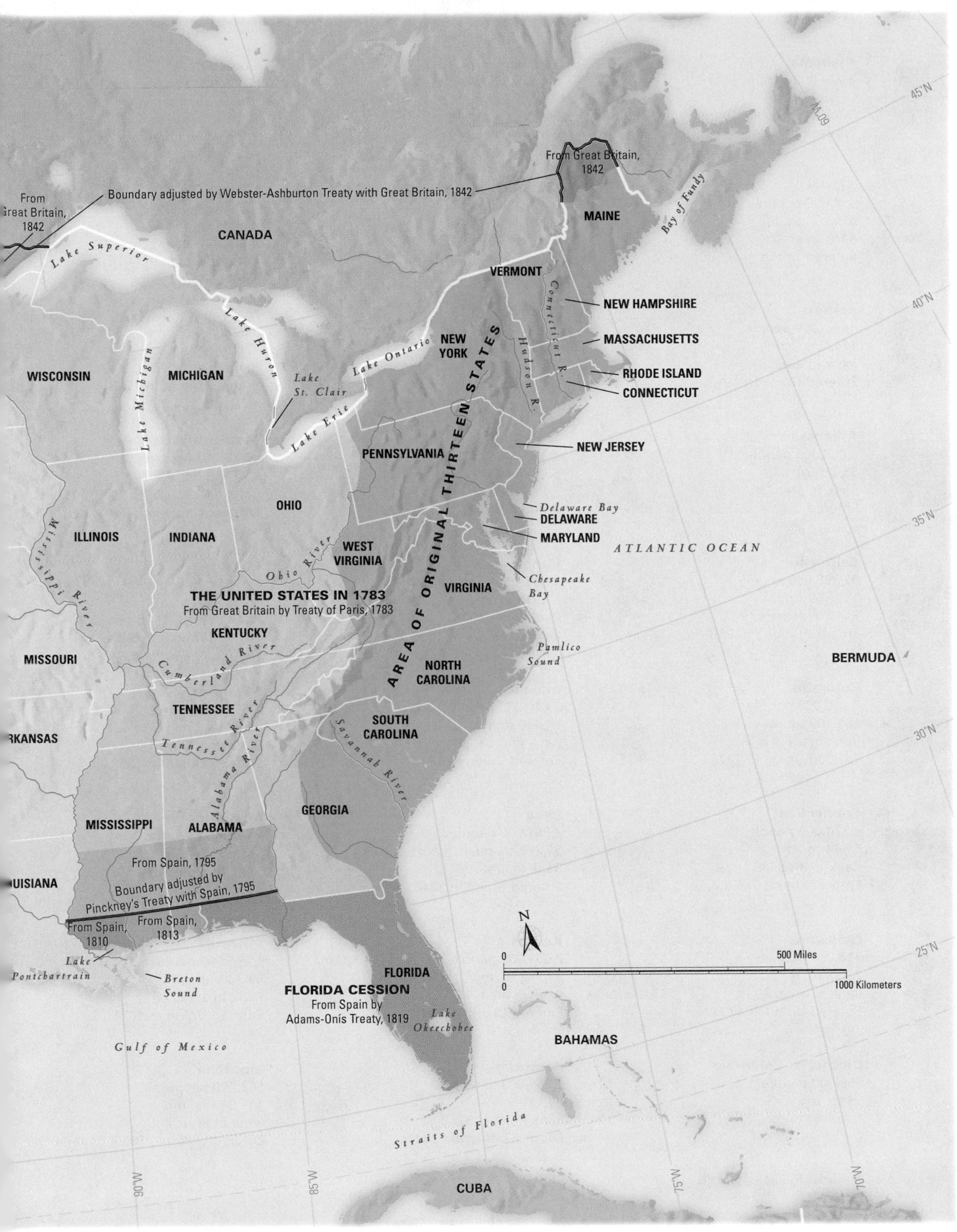

From Great Britain, 1842
Boundary adjusted by Webster-Ashburton Treaty with Great Britain, 1842
From Great Britain, 1842
CANADA
MAINE
Bay of Fundy
Lake Superior
VERMONT
NEW HAMPSHIRE
Connecticut R.
MASSACHUSETTS
Lake Huron
Lake Ontario
NEW YORK
Hudson R.
RHODE ISLAND
CONNECTICUT
WISCONSIN
MICHIGAN
Lake Michigan
Lake St. Clair
Lake Erie
AREA OF ORIGINAL THIRTEEN STATES
PENNSYLVANIA
NEW JERSEY
OHIO
Delaware Bay
DELAWARE
MARYLAND
ILLINOIS
INDIANA
WEST VIRGINIA
Ohio River
ATLANTIC OCEAN
Mississippi River
VIRGINIA
Chesapeake Bay
THE UNITED STATES IN 1783
From Great Britain by Treaty of Paris, 1783
KENTUCKY
Cumberland River
Pamlico Sound
MISSOURI
NORTH CAROLINA
BERMUDA
TENNESSEE
SOUTH CAROLINA
Tennessee River
Alabama River
Savannah River
GEORGIA
MISSISSIPPI
ALABAMA
From Spain, 1795
Boundary adjusted by Pinckney's Treaty with Spain, 1795
From Spain, 1810
From Spain, 1813
Lake Pontchartrain
Breton Sound
FLORIDA
FLORIDA CESSION
From Spain by Adams-Onís Treaty, 1819
Lake Okeechobee
Gulf of Mexico
BAHAMAS
Straits of Florida
CUBA
N
0
500 Miles
0
1000 Kilometers
45°N
40°N
35°N
30°N
25°N
90°W
85°W
75°W
70°W

Facts about the States

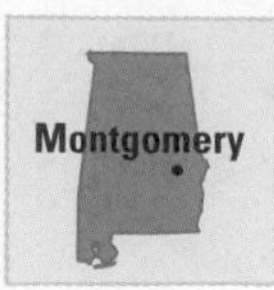

Alabama
4,724,000 people
52,237 sq. mi.
Rank in area: 30
Entered Union in 1819

Alaska
634,000 people
615,230 sq. mi.
Rank in area: 1
Entered Union in 1959

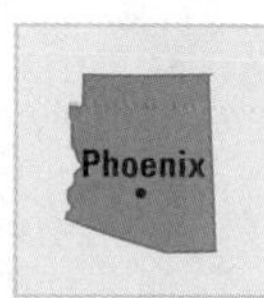

Arizona
4,072,000 people
114,006 sq. mi.
Rank in area: 6
Entered Union in 1912

Arkansas
2,468,000 people
53,182 sq. mi.
Rank in area: 28
Entered Union in 1836

California
32,398,000 people
158,869 sq. mi.
Rank in area: 3
Entered Union in 1850

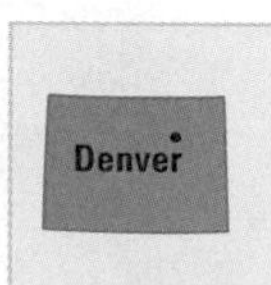

Colorado
3,710,000 people
104,100 sq. mi.
Rank in area: 8
Entered Union in 1876

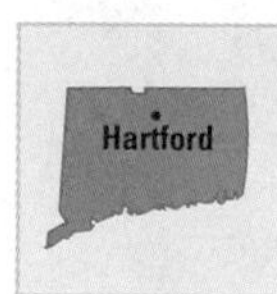

Connecticut
3,274,000 people
5,544 sq. mi.
Rank in area: 48
Entered Union in 1788

Delaware
718,000 people
2,397 sq. mi.
Rank in area: 49
Entered Union in 1787

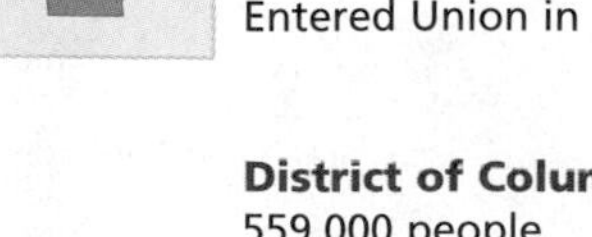

District of Columbia
559,000 people
68 sq. mi.

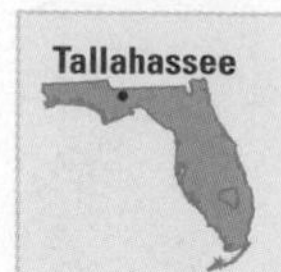

Florida
14,210,000 people
59,988 sq. mi.
Rank in area: 23
Entered Union in 1845

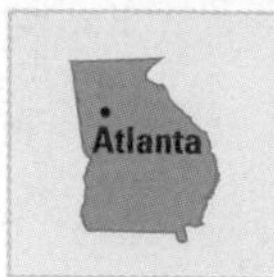

Georgia
7,102,000 people
58,977 sq. mi.
Rank in area: 24
Entered Union in 1788

Hawaii
1,221,000 people
6,459 sq. mi.
Rank in area: 47
Entered Union in 1959

Idaho
1,156,000 people
83,574 sq. mi.
Rank in area: 14
Entered Union in 1890

Illinois
11,853,000 people
57,918 sq. mi.
Rank in area: 25
Entered Union in 1818

Indiana
5,820,000 people
36,420 sq. mi.
Rank in area: 38
Entered Union in 1816

Iowa
2,861,000 people
56,276 sq. mi.
Rank in area: 26
Entered Union in 1846

Kansas
2,601,000 people
82,282 sq. mi.
Rank in area: 15
Entered Union in 1861

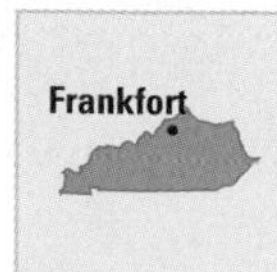

Kentucky
3,851,000 people
40,411 sq. mi.
Rank in area: 37
Entered Union in 1792

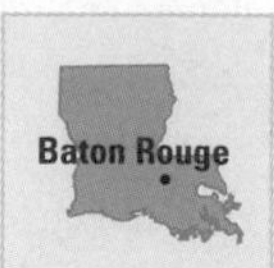

Louisiana
4,359,000 people
49,650 sq. mi.
Rank in area: 31
Entered Union in 1812

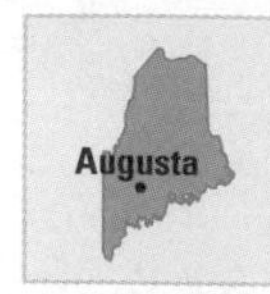

Maine
1,236,000 people
33,741 sq. mi.
Rank in area: 39
Entered Union in 1820

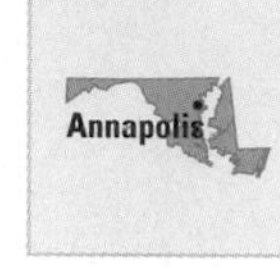

Maryland
5,078,000 people
12,297 sq. mi.
Rank in area: 42
Entered Union in 1788

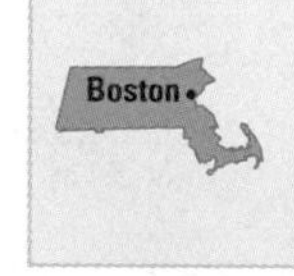

Massachusetts
5,976,000 people
9,241 sq. mi.
Rank in area: 45
Entered Union in 1788

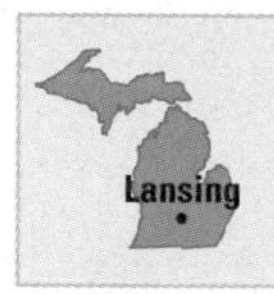

Michigan
9,575,000 people
96,705 sq. mi.
Rank in area: 11
Entered Union in 1837

Minnesota
4,619,000 people
86,943 sq. mi.
Rank in area: 12
Entered Union in 1858

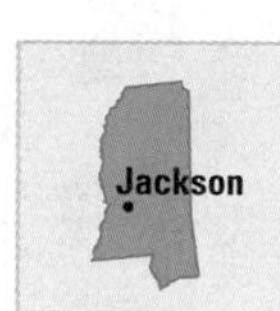

Mississippi
2,666,000 people
48,286 sq. mi.
Rank in area: 32
Entered Union in 1817

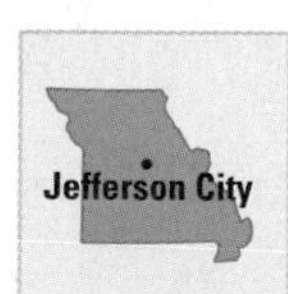

Missouri
5,286,000 people
69,709 sq. mi.
Rank in area: 21
Entered Union in 1821

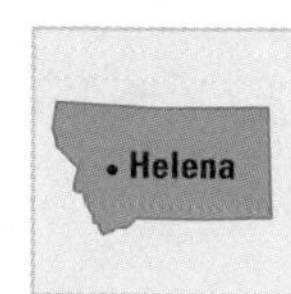

Montana
862,000 people
147,046 sq. mi.
Rank in area: 4
Entered Union in 1889

Population figures are for 1995.

954 **Facts About the States**

Nebraska
1,644,000 people
77,359 sq. mi.
Rank in area: 16
Entered Union in 1867

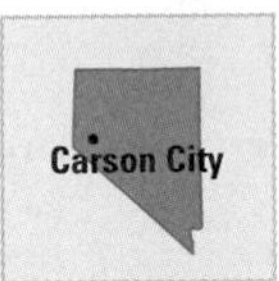

Nevada
1,477,000 people
110,567 sq. mi.
Rank in area: 7
Entered Union in 1864

New Hampshire
1,132,000 people
9,283 sq. mi.
Rank in area: 44
Entered Union in 1788

New Jersey
7,931,000 people
8,215 sq. mi.
Rank in area: 46
Entered Union in 1787

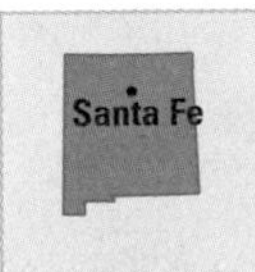

New Mexico
1,676,000 people
121,598 sq. mi.
Rank in area: 5
Entered Union in 1912

New York
18,178,000 people
53,989 sq. mi.
Rank in area: 27
Entered Union in 1788

North Carolina
7,150,000 people
52,672 sq. mi.
Rank in area: 29
Entered Union in 1789

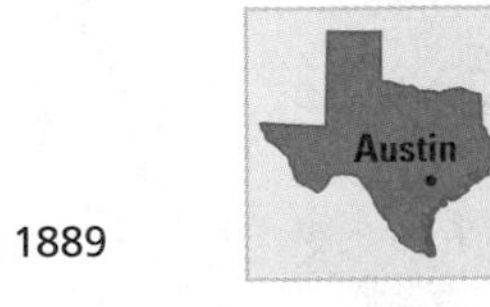

North Dakota
637,000 people
70,704 sq. mi.
Rank in area: 18
Entered Union in 1889

Ohio
11,203,000 people
44,828 sq. mi.
Rank in area: 34
Entered Union in 1803

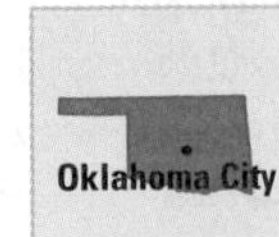

Oklahoma
3,271,000 people
69,903 sq. mi.
Rank in area: 20
Entered Union in 1907

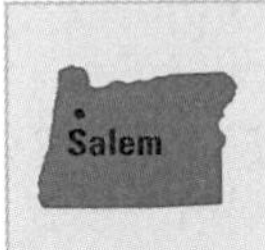

Oregon
3,141,000 people
97,093 sq. mi.
Rank in area: 10
Entered Union in 1859

Pennsylvania
12,134,000 people
45,759 sq. mi.
Rank in area: 33
Entered Union in 1787

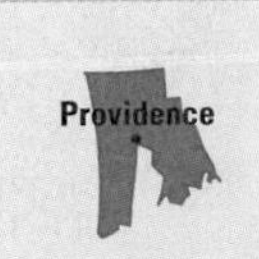

Rhode Island
1,001,000 people
1,231 sq. mi.
Rank in area: 50
Entered Union in 1790

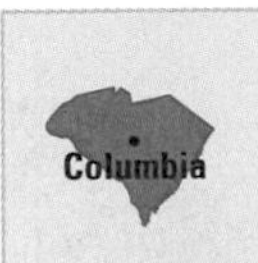

South Carolina
3,732,000 people
31,189 sq. mi.
Rank in area: 40
Entered Union in 1788

South Dakota
735,000 people
77,121 sq. mi.
Rank in area: 17
Entered Union in 1889

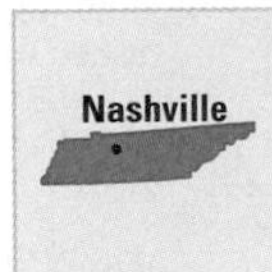
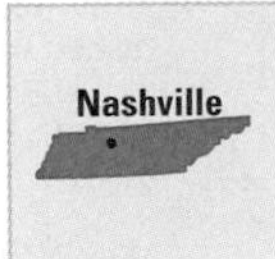

Tennessee
5,228,000 people
42,145 sq. mi.
Rank in area: 36
Entered Union in 1796

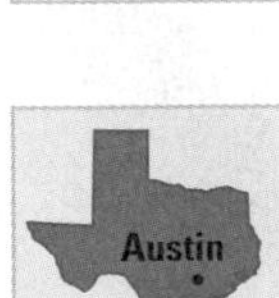
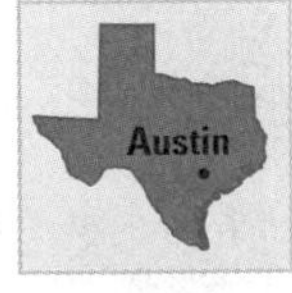

Texas
18,592,000 people
267,277 sq. mi.
Rank in area: 2
Entered Union in 1845

Utah
1,944,000 people
84,904 sq. mi.
Rank in area: 13
Entered Union in 1896

Vermont
579,000 people
9,615 sq. mi.
Rank in area: 43
Entered Union in 1791

Virginia
6,646,000 people
42,326 sq. mi.
Rank in area: 35
Entered Union in 1788

Washington
5,497,000 people
70,637 sq. mi.
Rank in area: 19
Entered Union in 1889

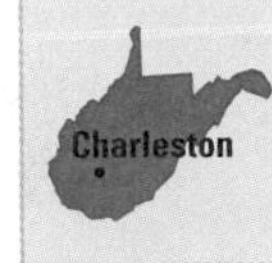

West Virginia
1,824,000 people
24,232 sq. mi.
Rank in area: 41
Entered Union in 1863

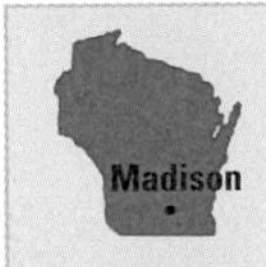

Wisconsin
5,159,000 people
65,500 sq. mi.
Rank in area: 22
Entered Union in 1848

Wyoming
487,000 people
97,819 sq. mi.
Rank in area: 9
Entered Union in 1890

United States: Major Dependencies (as of 1996)

American Samoa—57,000 people; 90 sq. mi.

Guam—153,000 people; 217 sq. mi.

Republic of the Marshall Islands—42,000 people; 70 sq. mi.

Federated States of Micronesia—102,000 people; 271 sq. mi.

Midway Island—500 people; 2 sq. mi.

Commonwealth of the Northern Mariana Islands—51,000 people; 189 sq. mi.

Commonwealth of Puerto Rico—3,813,000 people; 3,508 sq. mi.

Virgin Islands of the United States—97,000 people; 171 sq. mi.

Wake Island—302 people; 3 sq. mi.

Presidents of the United States

Here are some little-known facts about the Presidents of the United States:

- *Only former president to serve in Congress: John Quincy Adams*
- *First president born in the new United States: Martin Van Buren (8th president)*
- *Only president who was a bachelor: James Buchanan*
- *First left-handed president: James A. Garfield*
- *Largest president: William Howard Taft (6 feet, 2 inches; 326 pounds)*
- *Youngest president: Theodore Roosevelt (42 years old)*
- *Oldest president: Ronald Reagan (77 years old when he left office in 1989)*
- *First president born west of the Mississippi River: Herbert Hoover (born in West Branch, Iowa)*
- *First president born in the 20th century: John F. Kennedy (born May 29, 1917)*

1 **George Washington**
1789–1797
No Political Party
Birthplace: Virginia
Born: February 22, 1732
Died: December 14, 1799

2 **John Adams**
1797–1801
Federalist
Birthplace: Massachusetts
Born: October 30, 1735
Died: July 4, 1826

3 **Thomas Jefferson**
1801–1809
Republican
Birthplace: Virginia
Born: April 13, 1743
Died: July 4, 1826

4 **James Madison**
1809–1817
Republican
Birthplace: Virginia
Born: March 16, 1751
Died: June 28, 1836

5 **James Monroe**
1817–1825
Republican
Birthplace: Virginia
Born: April 28, 1758
Died: July 4, 1831

6 **John Quincy Adams**
1825–1829
Republican
Birthplace: Massachusetts
Born: July 11, 1767
Died: February 23, 1848

7 **Andrew Jackson**
1829–1837
Democratic Republican
Birthplace: South Carolina
Born: March 15, 1767
Died: June 8, 1845

8 **Martin Van Buren**
1837–1841
Democrat
Birthplace: New York
Born: December 5, 1782
Died: July 24, 1862

9 **William H. Harrison**
1841
Whig
Birthplace: Virginia
Born: February 9, 1773
Died: April 4, 1841

10 **John Tyler**
1841–1845
Whig
Birthplace: Virginia
Born: March 29, 1790
Died: January 18, 1862

11 **James K. Polk**
1845–1849
Democrat
Birthplace: North Carolina
Born: November 2, 1795
Died: June 15, 1849

12 **Zachary Taylor**
1849–1850
Whig
Birthplace: Virginia
Born: November 24, 1784
Died: July 9, 1850

13 **Millard Fillmore**
1850–1853
Whig
Birthplace: New York
Born: January 7, 1800
Died: March 8, 1874

14 **Franklin Pierce**
1853–1857
Democrat
Birthplace: New Hampshire
Born: November 23, 1804
Died: October 8, 1869

15 **James Buchanan**
1857–1861
Democrat
Birthplace: Pennsylvania
Born: April 23, 1791
Died: June 1, 1868

16 **Abraham Lincoln**
1861–1865
Republican
Birthplace: Kentucky
Born: February 12, 1809
Died: April 15, 1865

17 **Andrew Johnson**
1865–1869
Democrat
Birthplace: North Carolina
Born: December 29, 1808
Died: July 31, 1875

18 **Ulysses S. Grant**
1869–1877
Republican
Birthplace: Ohio
Born: April 27, 1822
Died: July 23, 1885

19 **Rutherford B. Hayes**
1877–1881
Republican
Birthplace: Ohio
Born: October 4, 1822
Died: January 17, 1893

20 **James A. Garfield**
1881
Republican
Birthplace: Ohio
Born: November 19, 1831
Died: September 19, 1881

21 **Chester A. Arthur**
1881–1885
Republican
Birthplace: Vermont
Born: October 5, 1829
Died: November 18, 1886

22 24 **Grover Cleveland**
1885–1889, 1893–1897
Democrat
Birthplace: New Jersey
Born: March 18, 1837
Died: June 24, 1908

23 **Benjamin Harrison**
1889–1893
Republican
Birthplace: Ohio
Born: August 20, 1833
Died: March 13, 1901

25 **William McKinley**
1897–1901
Republican
Birthplace: Ohio
Born: January 29, 1843
Died: September 14, 1901

26 **Theodore Roosevelt**
1901–1909
Republican
Birthplace: New York
Born: October 27, 1858
Died: January 16, 1919

27 **William H. Taft**
1909–1913
Republican
Birthplace: Ohio
Born: September 15, 1857
Died: March 8, 1930

28 **Woodrow Wilson**
1913–1921
Democrat
Birthplace: Virginia
Born: December 29, 1856
Died: February 3, 1924

29 **Warren G. Harding**
1921–1923
Republican
Birthplace: Ohio
Born: November 2, 1865
Died: August 2, 1923

30 Calvin Coolidge
1923–1929
Republican
Birthplace: Vermont
Born: July 4, 1872
Died: January 5, 1933

31 Herbert C. Hoover
1929–1933
Republican
Birthplace: Iowa
Born: August 10, 1874
Died: October 20, 1964

32 Franklin D. Roosevelt
1933–1945
Democrat
Birthplace: New York
Born: January 30, 1882
Died: April 12, 1945

33 Harry S. Truman
1945–1953
Democrat
Birthplace: Missouri
Born: May 8, 1884
Died: December 26, 1972

34 Dwight D. Eisenhower
1953–1961
Republican
Birthplace: Texas
Born: October 14, 1890
Died: March 28, 1969

35 John F. Kennedy
1961–1963
Democrat
Birthplace: Massachusetts
Born: May 29, 1917
Died: November 22, 1963

36 Lyndon B. Johnson
1963–1969
Democrat
Birthplace: Texas
Born: August 27, 1908
Died: January 22, 1973

37 Richard M. Nixon
1969–1974
Republican
Birthplace: California
Born: January 9, 1913
Died: April 22, 1994

38 Gerald R. Ford
1974–1977
Republican
Birthplace: Nebraska
Born: July, 14, 1913

39 James E. Carter, Jr.
1977–1981
Democrat
Birthplace: Georgia
Born: October 1, 1924

40 Ronald W. Reagan
1981–1989
Republican
Birthplace: Illinois
Born: February 6, 1911

41 George H. W. Bush
1989–1993
Republican
Birthplace: Massachusetts
Born: June 12, 1924

42 William J. Clinton
1993–
Democrat
Birthplace: Arkansas
Born: August 19, 1946

GLOSSARY

The Glossary is an alphabetical listing of many of the key terms from the chapters, along with their meanings. The definitions listed in the Glossary are the ones that apply to the way the words are used in this textbook. The Glossary gives the part of speech of each word. The following abbreviations are used:

adj. adjective *n.* noun *v.* verb

Pronunciation Key

Symbol	Examples	Symbol	Examples	Symbol	Examples
ă	**a**t, g**a**s	m	**m**an, see**m**	v	**v**an, sa**v**e
ā	**a**pe, d**ay**	n	**n**ight, mi**tt**en	w	**w**eb, t**w**ice
ä	f**a**ther, b**a**rn	ng	si**ng**, a**ng**er	y	**y**ard, law**y**er
âr	f**air**, d**are**	ŏ	**o**dd, n**o**t	z	**z**oo, rea**s**on
b	**b**ell, ta**b**le	ō	**o**pen, r**oa**d, gr**ow**	zh	trea**s**ure, gara**ge**
ch	**ch**in, lun**ch**	ô	**aw**ful, b**ough**t, h**o**rse	ə	**a**wake, ev**e**n, penc**i**l, pil**o**t, foc**u**s
d	**d**ig, bore**d**	oi	c**oi**n, b**oy**	ər	p**er**form, lett**er**
ĕ	**e**gg, t**e**n	o͝o	l**oo**k, f**u**ll		
ē	**e**vil, s**ee**, m**ea**l	o͞o	r**oo**t, gl**ue**, thr**ough**		
f	**f**all, lau**gh**, **ph**rase	ou	**ou**t, c**ow**	**Sounds in Foreign Words**	
g	**g**old, bi**g**	p	**p**ig, ca**p**	KH	*German* i**ch**, au**ch**; *Scottish* lo**ch**
h	**h**it, in**h**ale	r	**r**ose, sta**r**		
hw	**wh**ite, every**wh**ere	s	**s**it, fa**c**e	N	*French* e**n**tre, bo**n**, fi**n**
ĭ	**i**nch, f**i**t	sh	**sh**e, ma**sh**	œ	*French* f**eu**, c**oeu**r; *German* sch**ö**n
ī	**i**dle, m**y**, tr**ie**d	t	**t**ap, hoppe**d**		
îr	d**ear**, h**ere**	th	**th**ing, wi**th**	ü	*French* **u**tile, r**ue**; *German* gr**ü**n
j	**j**ar, **g**em, ba**dge**	*th*	**th**en, o**th**er		
k	**k**eep, **c**at, lu**ck**	ŭ	**u**p, n**u**t		
l	**l**oad, rat**tle**	ûr	f**ur**, **ear**n, b**ir**d, w**or**m		

Stress Marks

′ This mark indicates that the preceding syllable receives the primary stress. For example, in the word *lineage,* the first syllable is stressed: [lĭn′ē-ĭj].

′ This mark is used only in words in which more than one syllable is stressed. It indicates that the preceding syllable is stressed, but somewhat more weakly than the syllable receiving the primary stress. In the word *consumerism,* for example, the second syllable receives the primary stress, and the fourth syllable receives a weaker stress: [kən-so͞o′mə-rĭz′əm].

A

affirmative [ə-fûr′mə-tĭv] **action** *n.* a policy that seeks to correct the effects of past discrimination by favoring the groups who were previously disadvantaged. (p. 717)

Agent Orange *n.* a leaf-killing chemical sprayed by U.S. planes in Vietnam to expose Vietcong hideouts. (p. 732)

Agricultural Adjustment Act *n.* a law enacted in 1933 to raise crop prices by paying farmers to leave a certain amount of their land unplanted, thus lowering production. (p. 507)

AIDS [ādz] **(acquired immune deficiency syndrome)** *n.* a disease caused by a virus that weakens the immune system, making the body prone to infections and otherwise rare forms of cancer. (p. 827)

Alamo, the [ăl′ə-mō′] *n.* a mission in San Antonio, Texas, where Mexican forces massacred rebellious Texans in 1836. (p. 137)

Alien and Sedition [ā′lē-ən ənd sĭ-dĭsh′ən] **Acts** *n.* a series of four laws enacted in 1798 to reduce the political power of recent immigrants to the United States. (p. 83)

Alliance [ə-lī′əns] **for Progress** *n.* a U.S. foreign-aid program of the 1960s, providing economic and technical assistance to Latin American countries. (p. 679)

Allies [ə-līz′] *n.* **1.** in World War I, the group of nations—originally consisting of Great Britain, France, and Russia and later joined by the United States, Italy, and others—that opposed the Central Powers (p. 396). **2.** in World War II, the group of nations—including Great Britain, the Soviet Union, and the United States—that opposed the Axis powers. (p. 562)

American Federation of Labor (AFL) *n.* an alliance of trade and craft unions, formed in 1886. (p. 265)

American Indian Movement (AIM) *n.* a frequently militant organization that was formed in 1968 to work for Native American rights. (p. 763)

Americanization [ə-mĕr′ĭ-kə-nĭ-zā′shən] **movement** *n.* education program designed to help immigrants assimilate to American culture. (p. 283)

American System *n.* a pre-Civil War set of measures designed to unify the nation and strengthen its economy by means of protective tariffs, a national bank, and such internal improvements as the development of a transportation system. (p. 126)

anarchist [ăn′ər-kĭst] *n.* a person who opposes all forms of government. (p. 431)

Anasazi [ä′nə-sä′zē] *n.* a Native American group that lived on the mesa tops, cliff sides, and canyon bottoms of the Four Corners region (where the present-day states of Arizona, New Mexico, Colorado, and Utah meet) from about A.D. 100 to 1300. (p. 5)

Antifederalist [ăn′tē-fĕd′ər-ə-lĭst] *n.* an opponent of a strong central government. (p. 71)

appeasement [ə-pēz′mənt] *n.* the granting of concessions to a hostile power in order to keep the peace. (p. 549)

Articles of Confederation [kən-fĕd′ə-rā′shən] *n.* a document, adopted by the Continental Congress in 1777 and finally approved by the states in 1781, that outlined the form of government of the new United States. (p. 68)

assimilation [ə-sĭm′ə-lā′shən] *n.* a minority group's adoption of the beliefs and way of life of the dominant culture. (p. 219)

Atlantic Charter *n.* a 1941 declaration of principles in which the United States and Great Britain set forth their goals in opposing the Axis powers. (p. 562)

Axis [ăk′sĭs] **powers** *n.* the group of nations—including Germany, Italy, and Japan—that opposed the Allies in World War II. (p. 559)

Aztec [ăz′tĕk′] *n.* a Native American people that settled in the Valley of Mexico in the 1200s A.D. and later developed a powerful empire. (p. 5)

B

baby boom *n.* the sharp increase in the U.S. birthrate following World War II. (p. 645)

Battle of the Bulge *n.* a month-long battle of World War II, in which the Allies succeeded in turning back the last major German offensive of the war. (p. 584)

Battle of Wounded Knee [wo͞on′dĭd nē′] *n.* the massacre by U.S. soldiers of 300 unarmed Native Americans at Wounded Knee Creek, South Dakota, in 1890. (p. 221)

Bear Flag Republic *n.* the nation proclaimed by American settlers in California when they declared their independence from Mexico in 1846. (p. 140)

Beatles, the [bēt′lz] *n.* a British band that had an enormous influence on popular music in the 1960s. (p. 775)

beat movement *n.* a social and artistic movement of the 1950s, stressing unrestrained literary self-expression and nonconformity with the mainstream culture. (p. 655)

beatnik [bēt′nĭk] *n.* one of the unconventional, nonmaterialistic followers of the beat movement of the 1950s. (p. 655)

Benin [bə-nĭn′] *n.* a West African kingdom that flourished in the Niger Delta region (in what is now Nigeria) from the 14th to the 17th century. (p. 8)

Berlin airlift [bûr-lĭn′ âr′lĭft′] *n.* a 327-day operation in which U.S. and British planes flew food and supplies into West Berlin after the Soviets blockaded the city in 1948. (p. 611)

Berlin Wall *n.* a concrete wall that separated East Berlin and West Berlin from 1961 to 1989, built by the Communist East German government to prevent its citizens from fleeing to the West. (p. 676)

Bessemer [bĕs′ə-mər] **process** *n.* a cheap and efficient process for making steel, developed around 1850. (p. 247)

Bill of Rights *n.* the first ten amendments to the U.S. Constitution, added in 1791 and consisting of a formal list of citizens' rights and freedoms. (p. 72)

bimetallism [bī-mĕt′l-ĭz′əm] *n.* the use of both gold and silver as a basis for a national monetary system. (p. 238)

blacklist [blăk′lĭst′] *n.* a list of about 500 actors, writers, producers, and directors who were not allowed to work on Hollywood films because of their alleged Communist connections. (p. 621)

Black Panthers *n.* a militant African-American political organization formed in 1966 by Huey Newton and Bobby Seale to fight police brutality and to provide services in the ghetto. (p. 714)

Black Power *n.* a slogan—first used in the 1940s and revived by Stokely Carmichael in the 1960s—that encouraged African-American pride and political and social leadership. (p. 714)

Black Tuesday *n.* a name given to October 29, 1929, when stock prices fell sharply. (p. 485)

blitzkrieg [blĭts′krēg′] *n.* a sudden, massive attack with combined air and ground forces, intended to achieve a quick victory. (p. 551)

bonanza [bə-năn′zə] **farm** *n.* an enormous farm on which a single crop is grown. (p. 234)

Bonus [bō′nəs] **Army** *n.* a group of unemployed World War I veterans and their families who marched on Washington, D.C., in 1932 to demand the immediate payment of a bonus they had been promised for military service. (p. 498)

bootlegger [bo͞ot′lĕg′ər] *n.* a person who smuggled alcoholic beverages into the United States during Prohibition. (p. 455)

Boston Massacre [bô′stən măs′ə-kər] *n.* a clash between British soldiers and Boston colonists in 1770, in which five of the colonists were killed. (p. 50)

Boston Tea Party *n.* the dumping of 15,000 pounds of tea into Boston Harbor by colonists in 1773 to protest the Tea Act. (p. 51)

Boulder [bōl′dər] **Dam** *n.* a dam on the Colorado River—now called Hoover Dam—that was built during the Great Depression as part of a public-works program intended to stimulate business and provide jobs. (p. 497)

Boxer Rebellion *n.* a 1900 rebellion in which members of a Chinese secret society sought to free their country from Western influence. (p. 379)

bracero [brə-sâr′ō] *n.* a Mexican laborer allowed to enter the United States to work for a limited period of time. (p. 662)

bread line *n.* a line of people waiting for free food. (p. 491)

brinkmanship [brĭngk′mən-shĭp′] *n.* the practice of threatening an enemy with massive military retaliation for any aggression. (p. 626)

Brown* v. *Board of Education [broun′ vûr′səs bôrd′ əv ĕj′ə-kā′shən] *n.* a 1954 case in which the Supreme Court ruled that "separate but equal" education for black and white students was unconstitutional. (p. 698)

Bull Moose Party *n.* a name given to the Progressive Party, formed to support Theodore Roosevelt's candidacy for the presidency in 1912. (p. 352)

960 Glossary

buying on margin [mär′jĭn] *n.* the purchasing of stocks by paying only a small percentage of the price and borrowing the rest. (p. 485)

C

cabinet [kăb′ə-nĭt] *n.* the group of department heads who serve as the president's chief advisers. (p. 79)

Camp David Accords [ə-kôrdz′] *n.* two historic agreements between Israel and Egypt, reached in negotiations at Camp David in 1978. (p. 806)

carpetbagger [kär′pĭt-băg′ər] *n.* a Northerner who moved to the South after the Civil War. (p. 195)

Central Powers *n.* the group of nations—led by Germany, Austria-Hungary, and the Ottoman Empire—that opposed the Allies in World War I. (p. 396)

checks and balances *n.* the provisions in the U.S. Constitution that prevent any branch of the U.S. government from dominating the other two branches. (p. 71)

Chinese Exclusion Act *n.* a law, enacted in 1882, that prohibited all Chinese except students, teachers, merchants, tourists, and government officials from entering the United States. (p. 279)

CIA *n.* the Central Intelligence Agency—a U.S. agency created to gather secret information about foreign governments. (p. 626)

Civilian Conservation Corps [kôr] *n.* an agency, established as part of the New Deal, that put young unemployed men to work building roads, developing parks, planting trees, and helping in erosion-control and flood-control projects. (p. 507)

Civil Rights Act of 1964 *n.* a law that banned discrimination on the basis of race, sex, national origin, or religion in public places and most workplaces. (p. 708)

Civil Rights Act of 1968 *n.* a law that banned discrimination in housing. (p. 716)

civil service *n.* the nonmilitary branches of government administration. (p. 291)

Clayton Antitrust [klāt′n ăn′tē-trŭst′] **Act** *n.* a law, enacted in 1914, that made certain monopolistic business practices illegal and protected the rights of labor unions and farm organizations. (p. 355)

Cold War *n.* the state of hostility, without direct military conflict, that developed between the United States and the Soviet Union after World War II. (p. 610)

collective bargaining [kə-lĕk′tĭv bär′gə-nĭng] *n.* negotiations between the representatives of workers and employers to reach agreement on wages, benefits, hours, and working conditions. (p. 265)

Columbian Exchange [kə-lŭm′bē-ən ĭks-chānj′] *n.* the transfer—beginning with Columbus's first voyage—of plants, animals, and diseases between the Western Hemisphere and the Eastern Hemisphere. (p. 17)

Committee to Reelect the President *n.* an organization formed to run President Nixon's 1972 reelection campaign, which was linked to the break-in at the Democratic National Committee headquarters that set off the Watergate scandal. (p. 794)

Common Sense *n.* a pamphlet by Thomas Paine, published in 1776, that called for separation of the colonies from Britain. (p. 54)

Commonwealth [kŏm′ən-wĕlth′] **of Independent States** *n.* a loose confederation of former Soviet states, established after the dissolution of the Soviet Union in 1991. (p. 837)

Commonwealth* v. *Hunt [kŏm′ən-wĕlth′ vûr′səs hŭnt] *n.* an 1842 case in which the Supreme Court upheld workers' right to strike. (p. 149)

communism [kŏm′yə-nĭz′əm] *n.* an economic and political system based on one-party government and state ownership of property. (p. 430)

concentration [kŏn′sən-trā′shən] **camp** *n.* a prison camp operated by Nazi Germany in which Jews and other groups considered to be enemies of Adolf Hitler were starved while doing slave labor or were murdered. (p. 556)

conglomerate [kən-glŏm′ər-ĭt] *n.* a major corporation that owns a number of smaller companies in unrelated businesses. (p. 643)

Congress of Industrial Organizations *n.* a labor organization that broke away from the American Federation of Labor in 1938. (p. 521)

Congress of Racial Equality [rā′shəl ĭ-kwŏl′ĭ-tē] **(CORE)** *n.* an interracial group founded in 1942 by James Farmer to work against segregation in Northern cities. (p. 599)

conquistador [kŏng-kē′stə-dôr′] *n.* one of the Spaniards who traveled to the Americas as an explorer and conqueror in the 16th century. (p. 17)

conscientious objector [kŏn′shē-ĕn′shəs ŏb-jĕk′tər] *n.* a person who refuses, on moral grounds, to participate in warfare. (p. 405)

conscription [kən-skrĭp′shən] *n.* the drafting of citizens for military service. (p. 180)

conservation [kŏn′sûr-vā′shən] *n.* the planned management of natural resources, involving the protection of some wilderness areas and the development of others for the common good. (p. 346)

conservative coalition [kən-sûr′və-tĭv kō′ə-lĭsh′ən] *n.* a late-20th-century alliance of right-wing groups opposed to big government, entitlement programs, affirmative action, the busing of students to achieve integration, and the supposed moral decline of the U.S. people. (p. 819)

consumerism [kən-sōō′mə-rĭz′əm] *n.* a preoccupation with the purchasing of material goods. (p. 648)

containment [kən-tān′mənt] *n.* the blocking of another nation's attempts to spread its influence—especially the efforts of the United States to block the spread of Soviet influence during the late 1940s and early 1950s. (p. 609)

Contract [kŏn′trăkt′] **with America** *n.* a document that was drafted by Representative Newt Gingrich and signed by more than 300 Republican candidates in 1994, setting forth the Republicans' conservative legislative agenda. (p. 849)

Contras [kŏn′trəz] *n.* Nicaraguan rebels who received assistance from the Reagan administration in their efforts to overthrow the Sandinista government in the 1980s. (p. 838)

convoy [kŏn′voi′] **system** *n.* the protection of merchant ships from U-boat attacks by having the ships travel in large groups under the protection of warships. (p. 404)

counterculture [koun′tər-kŭl′chər] *n.* the culture of the young people who rejected mainstream American society in the 1960s, seeking to create an alternative society based on peace, love, and individual freedom. (p. 773)

credibility [krĕd′ə-bĭl′ĭ-tē] **gap** *n.* a public distrust of statements made by the government. (p. 734)

credit [krĕd′ĭt] *n.* an arrangement in which a buyer pays later for a purchase, often on an installment plan with interest charges. (p. 484)

Crédit Mobilier [krĕd′ĭt mō-bēl′yər] *n.* a construction company formed in 1868 by owners of the Union Pacific Railroad, who used it to fraudulently skim off railroad profits for themselves. (p. 255)

"Cross of Gold" speech *n.* an impassioned address by William Jennings Bryan at the 1896 Democratic Convention, in which he attacked the "gold bugs" who insisted that U.S. currency be backed only with gold. (p. 238)

culture shock *n.* the confusion and anxiety that result from living in an unfamiliar culture. (p. 278)

D

Dawes [dôz] **Act** *n.* a law, enacted in 1887, that was intended to "Americanize" Native Americans by distributing reservation land to individual owners. (p. 219)

D-Day *n.* a name given to June 6, 1944—the day on which the Allies launched an invasion of the European mainland during World War II. (p. 583)

debt peonage [dĕt′ pē′ə-nĭj] *n.* a system in which workers are bound in servitude until their debts are paid. (p. 313)

Declaration [dĕk′lə-rā′shən] **of Independence** *n.* the document, written by Thomas Jefferson in 1776, in which the delegates of the Continental Congress declared the colonies' independence from Britain. (p. 55)

de facto segregation [dĭ făk′tō sĕg′rĭ-gā′shən] *n.* racial separation established by practice and custom, not by law. (p. 711)

deficit [dĕf′ĭ-sĭt] **spending** *n.* a government's spending of more money than it receives in revenue. (p. 529)

de jure segregation [dē jŏŏr′ē sĕg′rĭ-gā′shən] *n.* racial separation established by law. (p. 711)

Democratic-Republican [dĕm′ə-krăt′ĭk rĭ-pŭb′lĭ-kən] *n.* a supporter of strong state governments. (p. 80)

department store *n.* a large retail store that offers a wide variety of goods and services. (p. 320)

détente [dā-tänt′] *n.* the flexible policy, involving a willingness to negotiate and an easing of tensions, that was adopted by President Richard Nixon and his adviser Henry Kissinger in their dealings with Communist nations. (p. 791)

direct relief [rĭ-lēf′] *n.* the giving of money or food by the government directly to needy people. (p. 493)

Dixiecrat [dĭk′sē-krăt′] *n.* one of the Southern delegates who, to protest President Truman's civil rights policy, walked out of the 1948 Democratic National Convention and formed the States' Rights Democratic Party. (p. 640)

dollar diplomacy [dĭ-plō′mə-sē] *n.* the U.S. policy of using the nation's economic power to exert influence over other countries. (p. 385)

domino theory [dŏm′ə-nō′ thē′ə-rē] *n.* the idea that if a nation falls under Communist control, nearby nations will also fall under Communist control. (p. 725)

double standard *n.* a set of principles granting greater sexual freedom to men than to women. (p. 459)

dove [dŭv] *n.* a person who opposed the Vietnam War and believed that the United States should withdraw from it. (p. 739)

Dow Jones [dou′ jōnz′] **Industrial Average** *n.* a measure based on the prices of the stocks of 30 large companies, widely used as a barometer of the stock market's health. (p. 487)

downsize [doun′sīz′] *v.* to dismiss numbers of permanent employees in an attempt to make operations more efficient and save money. (p. 854)

dumbbell tenement [dŭm′bĕl′ tĕn′ə-mənt] *n.* a long, narrow, five- or six-story building shaped like a barbell. (p. 284)

Dust Bowl *n.* the region, extending from Texas to North Dakota, that was made worthless for farming by drought and dust storms during the 1930s. (p. 490)

E

Earth Day *n.* a day set aside for environmental education, celebrated annually on April 22. (p. 809)

Economic Opportunity Act *n.* a law, enacted in 1964, that provided funds for youth programs, antipoverty measures, small-business loans, and job training. (p. 685)

egalitarianism [ĭ-găl′ĭ-târ′ē-ə-nĭz′əm] *n.* the belief that all people should have equal political, economic, social, and civil rights. (p. 65)

Eisenhower Doctrine [ī′zən-hou′ər dŏk′trĭn] *n.* a U.S. commitment to defend the Middle East against attack by any Communist country, announced by President Dwight D. Eisenhower in 1957. (p. 628)

e-mail [ē′māl′] *n.* the electronic messages that are sent and received over the Internet and other computer networks. (p. 861)

Emancipation Proclamation [prŏk′lə-mā′shən] *n.* an executive order issued by Abraham Lincoln on January 1, 1863, freeing the slaves in all regions in rebellion against the Union. (p. 179)

encomienda [ĕng-kô-myĕn′dä] *n.* a system in which Spanish authorities granted colonial landlords the service of Native Americans as forced laborers. (p. 18)

Enlightenment [ĕn-līt′n-mənt] *n.* an 18th-century intellectual movement that emphasized the use of reason and the scientific method as means of obtaining knowledge. (p. 37)

entitlement [ĕn-tīt′l-mənt] **program** *n.* a government program—such as Social Security, Medicare, or Medicaid—that guarantees and provides benefits to a specific group. (p. 819)

entrepreneur [ŏn′trə-prə-nûr′] *n.* a person who uses his or her own money to create a new business. (p. 144)

environmentalist [ĕn-vī′rən-mĕn′tl-ĭst] *n.* a person who works to protect the environment from destruction and pollution. (p. 809)

Environmental Protection Agency *n.* an agency established in 1970 to enforce pollution standards, to conduct environmental research, and to assist state and local governments in pollution control. (p. 810)

Equal Rights Amendment *n.* a proposed amendment to the U.S. Constitution that would prohibit any government discrimination on the basis of sex. (p. 771)

Espionage and Sedition [ĕs′pē-ə-näzh′ ənd sĭ-dĭsh′ən] **Acts** *n.* two laws, enacted in 1917 and 1918, that imposed harsh penalties on anyone interfering with or speaking against U.S. participation in World War I. (p. 413)

exoduster [ĕk′sə-dŭs′tər] *n.* an African American who migrated from the South to Kansas in the post-Reconstruction years. (p. 216)

F

Fair Deal *n.* President Harry S. Truman's economic program—an extension of Franklin Roosevelt's New Deal—which included measures to increase the minimum wage, to extend social security coverage, and to provide housing for low-income families. (p. 641)

Family Assistance Plan *n.* a welfare-reform proposal, approved by the House of Representatives in 1970 but defeated in the Senate, that would have guaranteed an income to welfare recipients who agreed to undergo job training and to accept work. (p. 787)

fascism [făsh′ĭz′əm] *n.* a political philosophy that advocates a strong, centralized, nationalistic government headed by a powerful dictator. (p. 544)

Federal Communications Commission (FCC) *n.* an agency that regulates U.S. communications industries, including radio and television stations. (p. 652)

Federal Deposit Insurance Corporation *n.* an agency created in 1933 to insure individuals' bank accounts, protecting people against losses due to bank failures. (p. 532)

Federal Home Loan Bank Act *n.* a law, enacted in 1931, that lowered home mortgage rates and allowed farmers to refinance their loans and avoid foreclosure. (p. 498)

Federalist [fĕd′ər-ə-lĭst] *n.* a supporter of the Constitution and of a strong national government. (p. 71)

Federal Reserve System *n.* a national banking system, established in 1913, that controls the U.S. money supply and the availability of credit in the country. (p. 356)

Federal Securities [sĭ-kyŏŏr′ĭ-tēz] **Act** *n.* a law, enacted in 1933, that required corporations to provide complete, accurate information on all stock offerings. (p. 506)

Federal Trade Commission *n.* a federal agency established in 1914 to investigate and stop unfair business practices. (p. 355)

feminism [fĕm′ə-nĭz′əm] *n.* the belief that women should have economic, political, and social equality with men. (p. 768)

Fifteenth Amendment *n.* an amendment to the U.S. Constitution, adopted in 1870, that prohibits the denial of voting rights to people because of their race or color or because they have previously been slaves. (p. 194)

flapper [flăp′ər] *n.* one of the free-thinking young women who embraced the new fashions and urban attitudes of the 1920s. (p. 458)

flexible response [flĕk′sə-bəl rĭ-spŏns′] *n.* a policy, developed during the Kennedy administration, that involved preparing for a variety of military responses to international crises rather than focusing on the use of nuclear weapons. (p. 672)

Fordney-McCumber Tariff [fôrd′nē mə-kŭm′bər tăr′ĭf] *n.* a set of regulations, enacted by Congress in 1922, that raised taxes on imports to record levels in order to protect American businesses against foreign competition. (p. 437)

Fourteen Points *n.* the principles making up President Woodrow Wilson's plan for world peace following World War I. (p. 417)

Fourteenth Amendment *n.* an amendment to the U.S. Constitution, adopted in 1868, that made all persons born or naturalized in the United States—including former slaves—citizens of the country. (p. 193)

franchise [frăn′chīz′] *n.* a business that has bought the right to use a parent company's name and methods, thus becoming one of a number of similar businesses in various locations. (p. 643)

freedom rider *n.* one of the civil rights activists who rode buses through the South in the early 1960s to challenge segregation. (p. 704)

Freedom Summer *n.* a 1964 project to register African-American voters in Mississippi. (p. 708)

free enterprise [ĕn′tər-prīz′] *n.* the economic system in which private businesses and individuals control the means of production. (p. 144)

Free Speech Movement *n.* an antiestablishment New Left organization that originated in a 1964 clash between students and administrators at the University of California at Berkeley. (p. 737)

French and Indian War *n.* a conflict in North America, lasting from 1754 to 1763, that was a part of a worldwide struggle between France and Britain and that ended with the defeat of France and the transfer of French Canada to Britain. (p. 39)

fundamentalism [fŭn′də-mĕn′tl-ĭz′əm] *n.* a Protestant religious movement grounded in the belief that all the stories and details in the Bible are literally true. (p. 456)

G

GATT [găt] *n.* the General Agreement on Tariffs and Trade—an international agreement first signed in 1947. In 1993, the agreement was amended to create the World Trade Organization, which seeks to lower trade barriers and establishes rules for resolving trade disputes. (p. 856)

genetic engineering [jə-nĕt′ĭk ĕn′jə-nîr′ĭng] *n.* the alteration of the molecular biology of organisms' cells in order to create new varieties of bacteria, plants, and animals. (p. 862)

Geneva Accords [jə-nē′və ə-kôrdz′] *n.* a 1954 peace agreement that divided Vietnam into Communist-controlled North Vietnam and non-Communist South Vietnam until unification elections could be held in 1956. (p. 726)

genocide [jĕn′ə-sīd′] *n.* the deliberate and systematic extermination of a particular racial, national, or religious group. (p. 555)

Gentlemen's Agreement *n.* a 1907–1908 agreement by the government of Japan to limit Japanese emigration to the United States. (p. 279)

Gettysburg Address [gĕt′ēz-bûrg′ ə-drĕs′] *n.* a famous speech delivered by Abraham Lincoln in November 1863, at the dedication of a national cemetery on the site of the Battle of Gettysburg. (p. 186)

Ghost Dance *n.* a Native American ritual intended to bring about the restoration of tribal life, popular among the Sioux prior to the Battle of Wounded Knee. (p. 221)

GI Bill of Rights *n.* a name given to the Servicemen's Readjustment Act, a 1944 law that provided financial and educational benefits for World War II veterans. (pp. 598, 636)

glasnost [gläs′nəst] *n.* the open discussion of social problems that was permitted in the Soviet Union in the 1980s. (p. 836)

Glass-Steagall [glăs′ stē′gəl] **Banking Act of 1933** *n.* the law that established the Federal Deposit Insurance Corporation to protect individuals' bank accounts. (p. 506)

Gone with the Wind *n.* a 1939 movie dealing with the life of Southern plantation owners during the Civil War—one of the most popular films of all time. (p. 524)

graft *n.* the illegal use of political influence for personal gain. (p. 288)

grandfather clause *n.* a provision that exempts certain people from a law on the basis of previously existing circumstances—especially a clause formerly in some Southern states' constitutions that exempted whites from the strict voting requirements used to keep African Americans from the polls. (p. 310)

Grange [grānj] *n.* the Patrons of Husbandry—a social and educational organization through which farmers attempted to combat the power of the railroads in the late 19th century. (p. 236)

Grapes of Wrath, The *n.* a novel by John Steinbeck, published in 1939, that deals with a family of Oklahomans who leave the Dust Bowl for California. (p. 527)

Great Awakening *n.* a revival of religious feeling in the American colonies during the 1730s and 1740s. (p. 38)

Great Depression *n.* a period, lasting from 1929 to 1941, in which the U.S. economy was in severe decline and millions of Americans were unemployed. (p. 486)

Great Migration [mī-grā′shən] *n.* the large-scale movement of African Americans from the South to Northern cities in the early 20th century. (p. 414)

Great Plains *n.* the vast grassland that extends through the west-central portion of the United States. (p. 214)

Great Potato Famine [făm′ĭn] n. in the mid-1800s, a blight on potatoes in Ireland that resulted in many deaths and increased immigration to America. (p. 149)

Great Society *n.* President Lyndon B. Johnson's program to reduce poverty and racial injustice and to promote a better quality of life in the United States. (p. 686)

H

Haight-Ashbury [hāt′ ăsh′bĕr-ē] *n.* a San Francisco district that became the "capital" of the hippie counterculture during the 1960s. (p. 774)

Harlem Renaissance [här′ləm rĕn′ĭ-säns′] *n.* a flowering of African-American artistic creativity during the 1920s, in the Harlem community of New York City. (p. 470)

hawk *n.* a person who supported U.S. involvement in the Vietnam War and believed that the United States should use increased military force to win it. (p. 739)

Hawley-Smoot Tariff [hô′lē smo͞ot′ tăr′ĭf] **Act** *n.* a law, enacted in 1930, that established the highest protective tariff in U.S. history, worsening the depression in America and abroad. (p. 489)

H-bomb *n.* the hydrogen bomb—a thermonuclear weapon much more powerful than the atomic bomb. (p. 625)

Ho Chi Minh [hō′ chē′ mĭn′] **Trail** *n.* a network of paths used by North Vietnam to transport supplies to the Vietcong in South Vietnam. (p. 726)

holding company *n.* a corporation formed to buy up the stock of other companies and thus create a monopoly. (p. 259)

Hollywood Ten *n.* ten witnesses from the film industry who refused to cooperate with the HUAC's investigation of Communist influence in Hollywood. (p. 621)

Holocaust [hŏl′ə-kôst′] *n.* the systematic murder of 11 million Jews and other people by the Nazis before and during World War II. (p. 554)

Homestead [hōm′stĕd′] **Act** *n.* a law, enacted in 1862, that provided 160 acres of free land in the West to anyone who would live on and cultivate it for five years. (p. 216)

homesteader [hōm′stĕd′ər] *n.* a settler on the free land made available by the Homestead Act. (p. 231)

horizontal consolidation [hôr′ĭ-zŏn′tl kən-sŏl′ĭ-dā′shən] *n.* the merging of companies that make similar products. (p. 258)

hot line *n.* a communication link established in 1963 to allow the leaders of the United States and the Soviet Union to contact each other in times of crisis. (p. 676)

HUAC [hyo͞o′ăk′] *n.* the House Committee on Un-American Activities—a congressional committee that investigated Communist influence inside and outside the U.S. government in the years following World War II. (p. 620)

human rights *n.* the rights and freedoms, such as those named in the Declaration of Independence and the Bill of Rights, to which all people are entitled. (p. 805)

I

immigration [ĭm′ĭ-grā′shən] n. coming and settling in a country of which one is not a native. (p. 149)

Immigration Act of 1965 *n.* a law that made it easier for non-European immigrants to settle in the United States. (p. 686)

imperialism [ĭm-pîr′ē-ə-lĭz′əm] *n.* the policy of extending a nation's authority over other countries by economic, political, or military means. (p. 364)

impressment [ĭm-prĕs′mənt] *n.* the forcible seizure of men for military service. (p. 121)

income tax *n.* a tax on individuals' earnings. (p. 182)

indentured [ĭn-dĕn′chərd] **servant** *n.* a person who has agreed to work for another for a limited period, often in return for travel expenses, shelter, and sustenance. (p. 23)

Industrial Workers of the World (IWW) *n.* a labor organization for unskilled workers, formed by a group of radical unionists and socialists in 1905. (p. 266)

inflation [ĭn-flā′shən] *n.* an increase in prices or decline in purchasing power caused by an increase in the supply of money. (p. 62)

information superhighway [sōō′pər-hī′wā] *n.* a proposed computer communications network that would link people and institutions throughout the world, providing individuals with services such as libraries, shopping, movies, and news. (p. 860)

INF Treaty *n.* the Intermediate-Range Nuclear Forces Treaty—a 1987 agreement between the United States and the Soviet Union that eliminated some weapons systems and allowed for on-site inspection of military installations. (p. 836)

initiative [ĭ-nĭsh′ə-tĭv] *n.* a procedure by which a legislative measure can be originated by the people rather than by lawmakers. (p. 336)

installment [ĭn-stôl′mənt] **plan** *n.* an arrangement in which a purchaser pays over an extended time, without having to put down much money at the time of purchase. (p. 445)

Internet [ĭn′tər-nĕt′] *n.* a worldwide network, originally developed by the U.S. Department of Defense, that links computers and allows almost immediate communication of texts, pictures, and sounds. (p. 861)

Interstate [ĭn′tər-stāt′] **Commerce Act** *n.* a law, enacted in 1887, that reestablished the federal government's right to supervise railroad activities and created a five-member Interstate Commerce Commission to do so. (p. 256)

Iroquois [ĭr′ə-kwoi′] *n.* a group of Native American peoples inhabiting the woodlands of the Northeast. (p. 6)

Islam [ĭs-läm′] *n.* a religion founded in Arabia in A.D. 622 by the prophet Muhammad; its believers are called Muslims. (p. 10)

isolationist [ī′sə-lā′shə-nĭst] *adj.* in opposition to political and economic entanglements with other countries. (p. 437)

J

Jacksonian democracy [jăk-sō′nē-an dĭ-mŏk′rə-sē] *n.* Jackson's political philosophy, based on his belief that common people were the source of American strength. (p. 127)

Japanese American Citizens League (JACL) *n.* an organization that pushed the U.S. government to compensate Japanese Americans for property they had lost when they were interned during World War II. (p. 601)

Jeffersonian republicanism [jĕf′ər-sō′nē-ən rĭ-pŭb′lĭ-kə-nĭz′əm] *n.* Jefferson's theory of government, which held that a simple government best suited the needs of the people. (p. 119)

Jim Crow laws *n.* laws enacted by Southern state and local governments to separate white and black people in public and private facilities. (p. 310)

joint-stock company *n.* a business in which investors pool their wealth for a common purpose. (p. 11)

judicial review *n.* the Supreme Court's power to declare an act of Congress unconstitutional. (p. 119)

Judiciary Act of 1789 *n.* a law that established the federal court system and the Supreme Court and that provided for the appeal of certain state court decisions to the federal courts. (p. 78)

Jungle, The *n.* a novel by Upton Sinclair, published in 1906, that portrayed the disgusting conditions prevalent in the meatpacking industry. (p. 341)

K

kamikaze [kä′mĭ-kä′zē] *adj.* involving or engaging in the deliberate crashing of a bomb-filled airplane into a military target. (p. 589)

Kellogg-Briand [kĕl′ôg′ brē-änd′] **Pact** *n.* a 1929 treaty in which 64 nations agreed to renounce war as a means of solving international disputes. (p. 437)

Kerner [kûr′nər] **Commission** *n.* a group that was appointed by President Johnson to study the causes of urban violence and that recommended the elimination of de facto segregation in American society. (p. 716)

Khmer Rouge [kmâr′ rōōzh′] *n.* a Communist group that seized power in Cambodia in 1975. (p. 752)

kickback [kĭk′băk′] *n.* the return of part of a payment, usually as a result of intimidation or a secret agreement. (p. 289)

King Philip's War *n.* a conflict, in the years 1675–1676, between New England colonists and Native American groups allied under the leadership of the Wampanoag chief Metacom. (p. 28)

Kongo [kŏng′gō] *n.* a group of small kingdoms along the Zaire River in Central Africa, united under a single leader in the late 1400s. (p. 9)

Korean [kə-rē′ən] **War** *n.* a conflict between North Korea and South Korea, lasting from 1950 to 1953, in which the United States, along with other UN countries, fought on the side of the South Koreans and China fought on the side of the North Koreans. (p. 615)

Kristallnacht [krĭ-stäl′näKHt′] *n.* a name given to the night of November 9, 1938, when gangs of Nazi storm troopers attacked Jewish homes, businesses, and synagogues in Germany. (p. 555)

Ku Klux Klan [kōō′ klŭks klăn′] *n.* a secret organization that used terrorist tactics in an attempt to restore white supremacy in Southern states after the Civil War. (p. 199)

L

La Raza Unida [lä rä′sä ōō-nē′dä] *n.* a Latino political organization founded in 1970 by José Angel Gutiérrez. (p. 762)

League of Nations *n.* an association of nations established in 1920 to promote international cooperation and peace. (p. 418)

Lend-Lease Act *n.* a law, enacted in 1941, that allowed the United States to ship arms and other supplies, without immediate payment, to nations fighting the Axis powers. (p. 561)

Limited Test Ban Treaty *n.* the 1963 treaty in which the United States and the Soviet Union agreed not to conduct nuclear-weapons tests in the atmosphere. (p. 676)

Linotype [lī′nə-tīp′] **machine** *n.* a keyboard-operated typesetting device that casts each line of type as a whole. (p. 302)

literacy [lĭt′ər-ə-sē] **test** *n.* a reading test formerly used in some Southern states to prevent African Americans from voting. (p. 310)

long drive *n.* the moving of cattle over trails to a shipping center. (p. 226)

longhorn [lông′hôrn′] *n.* a breed of sturdy long-horned cattle brought by the Spanish to Mexico and suited to the dry conditions of the Southwest. (p. 222)

Louisiana Purchase *n.* the 1803 purchase by the United States of France's Louisiana Territory—extending from the Mississippi River to the Rocky Mountains—for $15 million. (p. 119)

Lowell textile [lō′əl tĕks′tīl′] **mills** *n.* 19th century textile mills in Lowell, Massachusetts, that mainly employed young women. (p. 147)

Loyalist [loi′ə-lĭst] *n.* a colonist who supported the British government during the American Revolution. (p. 59)

Lusitania [lo͞o′sĭ-tā′nē-ə] *n.* a British passenger ship that was sunk by a German U-boat in 1915. (p. 399)

M

magnetic resonance imaging [măg-nĕt′ĭk rĕz′ə-nəns ĭm′ĭ-jĭng] *n.* a technology—often called MRI—used by physicians to produce cross-sectional images of any part of the human body. (p. 862)

mail-order catalog *n.* a book showing merchandise that can be ordered and delivered through the mail. (p. 321)

mandate [măn′dāt′] *n.* the authority to act that an elected official receives from the voters who elected him or her. (p. 678)

Manhattan Project [măn-hăt′n prŏj′ĕkt′] *n.* the U.S. program to develop an atomic bomb for use in World War II. (p. 590)

manifest destiny [măn′ə-fĕst′ dĕs′tə-nē] *n.* the 19th-century belief that the United States would inevitably expand westward to the Pacific Ocean and into Mexican territory. (p. 133)

Marbury* v. *Madison (mär′bar-ē vûr′səs măd′ĭ-sən) *n.* an 1803 case in which the Supreme Court ruled that it had the power to abolish legislative acts by declaring them unconstitutional; this power came to be known as judicial review. (p. 119)

market revolution *n.* the major change in the U.S. economy produced by people's beginning to buy and sell goods rather than make them for themselves. (p. 144)

Marshall [mär′shəl] **Plan** *n.* the program, proposed by Secretary of State George Marshall in 1947, under which the United States supplied economic aid to European nations to help them rebuild after World War II. (p. 610)

mass media [mē′dē-ə] *n.* the means of communication—such as television, newspapers, and radio—that reach large audiences. (p. 652)

McCarthyism [mə-kär′thē-ĭz′əm] *n.* the attacks, often unsubstantiated, by Senator Joseph McCarthy and others on people suspected of being Communists in the early 1950s. (p. 623)

Meat Inspection Act *n.* a law, enacted in 1906, that established strict cleanliness requirements for meatpackers and created a federal meat-inspection program. (p. 345)

mechanized [mĕk′ə-nīzd′] **warfare** *n.* military operations that depend on motorized vehicles, such as tanks and aircraft. (p. 406)

Medicaid [mĕd′ĭ-kād′] *n.* a program, established in 1965, that provides health insurance for people on welfare. (p. 686)

Medicare [mĕd′ĭ-kâr′] *n.* a federal program, established in 1965, that provides hospital insurance and low-cost medical insurance to Americans aged 65 and over. (p. 686)

melting pot *n.* a mixture of people from different cultures and races who blend together by abandoning their native languages and cultures. (p. 278)

mercantilism [mûr′kən-tē-lĭz′əm] *n.* an economic system in which nations seek to increase their wealth and power by obtaining large amounts of gold and silver and by establishing a favorable balance of trade. (p. 30)

mestizo [mĕs-tē′zō] *adj.* of mixed Spanish and Native American ancestry. (p. 18)

middle passage *n.* the transportation of slaves from Africa to the West Indies. (p. 34)

militarism [mĭl′ĭ-tə-rĭz′əm] *n.* the policy of building up armed forces in aggressive preparedness for war. (p. 395)

Miranda [mə-răn′də] **rights** *n.* the rights—including the right to remain silent and the right to consult an attorney—that every accused person must be informed of at the time of his or her arrest, according to the Supreme Court's 1966 decision in the case *Miranda* v. *Arizona.* (p. 689)

Missouri Compromise [kŏm′prə-mīz′] *n.* a series of laws enacted in 1820 to maintain the balance of power between slave states and free states. (p. 127)

monopoly [mə-nŏp′ə-lē] *n.* a complete control over an industry, achieved by buying up or driving out of business all competitors. (p. 259)

Monroe Doctrine [mən-rō′ dŏk′trĭn] *n.* a policy of U.S. opposition to any European interference in the affairs of the Western Hemisphere, announced by President Monroe in 1823. (p. 123)

Moral Majority [môr′əl mə-jôr′ĭ-tē] *n.* a political alliance of religious groups, consisting mainly of evangelical and fundamentalist Christians, that was active in the 1970s and 1980s, condemning liberal attitudes and behavior and raising money for conservative candidates. (p. 820)

Morrill [môr′əl] **Land Grant Acts** *n.* laws enacted in 1862 and 1890 to help create agricultural colleges by giving federal land to states. (p. 233)

muckraker [mŭk′rā′kər] *n.* one of the magazine journalists who exposed the corrupt side of business and public life in the early 1900s. (p. 332)

Munn* v. *Illinois [mŭn′ vûr′səs ĭl′ə-noi′] *n.* an 1877 case in which the Supreme Court upheld states' regulation of railroads for the benefit of farmers and consumers, thus establishing the right of government to regulate private industry to serve the public interest. (p. 256)

N

NAACP [ĕn′ dŭb′əl ā′ sē′ pē′] *n.* the National Association for the Advancement of Colored People—an organization founded in 1909 to promote full racial equality. (p. 347)

NACW *n.* the National Association of Colored Women—a social service organization founded in 1896. (p. 339)

NAFTA [năf′tə] *n.* the North American Free Trade Agreement—a 1993 treaty that lowered tariffs and brought Mexico into the free-trade zone established by the United States and Canada. (p. 848)

napalm [nā′päm′] *n.* a gasoline-based substance used in bombs that U.S. planes dropped in Vietnam in order to burn away jungle and expose Vietcong hideouts. (p. 732)

National Energy Act *n.* a law, enacted during the Carter administration, that established a tax on gas-guzzling automobiles, removed price controls on U.S. oil and natural gas, and provided tax credits for the development of alternative energy sources. (p. 803)

National Industrial Recovery Act *n.* a law enacted in 1933 to establish codes of fair practice for industries and to promote industrial growth. (p. 508)

National Labor Relations Board *n.* an agency created in 1935 to prevent unfair labor practices and to mediate disputes between workers and management. (p. 531)

National Organization for Women *n.* an organization founded in 1966 to pursue feminists' goals, such as better child-care facilities, improved educational opportunities, and an end to job discrimination. (p. 770)

National Trades' Union *n.* the first national association of trade unions, formed in 1834. (p. 149)

National Youth Administration *n.* an agency that provided young Americans with aid and employment during the Great Depression. (p. 513)

Nation of Islam [ĭs-läm′] *n.* a religious group, popularly known as the Black Muslims, founded by Elijah Muhammad to promote black separatism and the Islamic religion. (p. 713)

Navigation [năv′ĭ-gā′shən] **Acts** *n.* a series of laws enacted by Parliament, beginning in 1651, to tighten England's control of trade in its American colonies. (p. 31)

NAWSA *n.* the National American Woman Suffrage Association—an organization founded in 1890 to gain voting rights for women. (p. 339)

Nazism [nät′sĭz′əm] *n.* the political philosophy—based on extreme nationalism, racism, and militaristic expansionism—that Adolf Hitler put into practice in Germany from 1933 to 1945. (p. 544)

Neutrality Acts *n.* a series of laws enacted in 1935 and 1936 to prevent U.S. arms sales and loans to nations at war. (p. 546)

New Deal *n.* President Franklin Roosevelt's program to alleviate the problems of the Great Depression, focusing on relief for the needy, economic recovery, and financial reform. (p. 505)

New Deal Coalition [kō′ə-lĭsh′ən] *n.* an alliance of diverse groups—including Southern whites, African Americans, and unionized workers—who supported the policies of the Democratic Party in the 1930s and 1940s. (p. 520)

New Federalism [fĕd′ər-ə-lĭz′əm] *n.* President Richard Nixon's program to turn over part of the federal government's power to state and local governments. (p. 786)

New Frontier *n.* President John F. Kennedy's legislative program, which included proposals to provide medical care for the elderly, to rebuild blighted urban areas, to aid education, to bolster the national defense, to increase international aid, and to expand the space program. (p. 678)

New Left *n.* a youth-dominated political movement of the 1960s, embodied in such organizations as Students for a Democratic Society and the Free Speech Movement. (p. 737)

New Right *n.* a late-20th-century alliance of conservative special-interest groups concerned with cultural, social, and moral issues. (pp. 772, 819)

Nineteenth Amendment *n.* an amendment to the U.S. Constitution, adopted in 1920, that gave women the right to vote. (p. 358)

Nisei [nē-sā′] *n.* a U.S. citizen born of immigrant Japanese parents. (p. 575)

no man's land *n.* an unoccupied region between opposing armies. (p. 397)

nonaggression [nŏn′ə-grĕsh′ən] **pact** *n.* an agreement in which two nations promise not to go to war with each other. (p. 551)

North Atlantic Treaty Organization (NATO) *n.* a defensive military alliance formed in 1949 by ten Western European countries, the United States, and Canada. (p. 612)

Northwest Ordinance [ôr′dn-əns] **of 1787** *n.* a law that established a procedure for the admission of new states to the Union. (p. 69)

nullification [nŭl′ə-fĭ-kā′shən] *n.* a state's refusal to recognize an act of Congress that it considers unconstitutional. (p. 83)

Nuremberg [no͝or′əm-bûrg′] **trials** *n.* the court proceedings held in Nuremberg, Germany, after World War II, in which Nazi leaders were tried for war crimes. (p. 592)

O

Office of Price Administration (OPA) *n.* an agency established by Congress to control inflation during World War II. (p. 576)

Ohio gang *n.* a group of close friends and political supporters whom President Warren G. Harding appointed to his cabinet. (p. 439)

OPEC [ō′pĕk′] *n.* the Organization of Petroleum Exporting Countries—an economic association of oil-producing nations that is able to set oil prices. (p. 790)

Open Door notes *n.* messages sent by Secretary of State John Hay in 1899 to Germany, Russia, Great Britain, France, Italy, and Japan, asking the countries not to interfere with U.S. trading rights in China. (p. 379)

Operation Desert Storm [dĕz′ərt stôrm′] *n.* a 1991 military operation in which UN forces, led by the United States, drove Iraqi invaders from Kuwait. (p. 840)

Oregon Trail *n.* a route from Independence, Missouri, to Portland, Oregon, used by pioneers traveling to the Oregon Territory. (p. 134)

P

Panama Canal [păn′ə-mä′ kə-năl′] *n.* an artificial waterway cut through the Isthmus of Panama to provide a shortcut between the Atlantic and Pacific oceans, opened in 1914. (p. 384)

parity [păr′ĭ-tē] *n.* a government-supported level for the prices of agricultural products, intended to keep farmers' income steady. (p. 532)

Patriot [pā′trē-ət] *n.* a colonist who supported American independence from Britain. (p. 59)

patronage [pā′trə-nĭj] *n.* an officeholder's power to appoint people—usually those who have helped him or her get elected—to positions in government. (p. 291)

pay equity [ĕk′wĭ-tē] *n.* the basing of an employee's salary on the requirements of his or her job rather than on the traditional pay scales that have frequently provided women with smaller incomes than men. (p. 831)

Payne-Aldrich Tariff [pān' ôl'drĭch tăr'ĭf] *n.* a set of tax regulations, enacted by Congress in 1909, that failed to significantly reduce tariffs on manufactured goods. (p. 351)

Peace Corps *n.* an agency established in 1961 to provide volunteer assistance to developing nations in Asia, Africa, and Latin America. (p. 679)

Pendleton [pĕn'dl-tən] **Act** *n.* a law, enacted in 1883, that established a bipartisan civil service commission to make appointments to government jobs by means of the merit system. (p. 292)

Pentagon [pĕn'tə-gŏn'] **Papers** *n.* a 7,000-page document—leaked to the press in 1971 by the former Defense Department worker Daniel Ellsberg—revealing that the U.S. government had not been honest about its intentions in the Vietnam War. (p. 750)

perestroika [pĕr'ĭ-stroi'kə] *n.* the restructuring of the economy and the government instituted in the Soviet Union in the 1980s. (p. 836)

planned obsolescence [ŏb'sə-lĕs'əns] *n.* the designing of products to wear out or to become outdated quickly, so that people will feel a need to replace their possessions frequently. (p. 649)

Platt [plăt] **Amendment** *n.* a series of provisions that, in 1901, the United States insisted Cuba add to its new constitution, giving the United States the right to intervene in the country and the right to buy or lease Cuban land for naval and coaling stations. (p. 377)

Plessy* v. *Ferguson [plĕs'ē vûr'səs fûr'gə-sən] *n.* an 1896 case in which the Supreme Court ruled that separation of the races in public accommodations was legal, thus establishing the "separate but equal" doctrine. (p. 311)

political machine *n.* an organized group that controls a political party in a city and offers services to voters and businesses in exchange for political and financial support. (p. 288)

poll [pōl] **tax** *n.* an annual tax that formerly had to be paid in some Southern states by anyone wishing to vote. (p. 310)

Populism [pŏp'yə-lĭz'əm] *n.* a late-19th-century political movement seeking to advance the interests of farmers and laborers. (p. 236)

price support *n.* the maintenance of a price at a certain level through government intervention. (p. 483)

Proclamation [prŏk'lə-mā'shən] **of 1763** *n.* an order in which Britain prohibited its American colonists from settling west of the Appalachian Mountains. (p. 41)

progressive [prə-grĕs'ĭv] **movement** *n.* an early-20th-century reform movement seeking to return control of the government to the people, to restore economic opportunities, and to correct injustices in American life. (p. 330)

prohibition [prō'ə-bĭsh'ən] *n.* the banning of the manufacture, sale, and possession of alcoholic beverages. (p. 331)

protective tariff [prə-tĕk'tĭv tăr'ĭf] *n.* a tax on imported goods that is intended to protect a nation's businesses from foreign competition. (p. 80)

protectorate [prə-tĕk'tə-rĭt] *n.* a country whose affairs are partially controlled by a stronger power. (p. 377)

Pueblo [pwĕb'lō] *n.* a group of Native American peoples—descendants of the Anasazi—inhabiting the deserts of the Southwest. (p. 6)

Pure Food and Drug Act *n.* a law enacted in 1906 to halt the sale of contaminated foods and drugs and to assure truth in labeling. (p. 345)

Puritan [pyo͝or'ĭ-tn] *n.* a member of a group that wanted to eliminate all traces of Roman Catholic ritual and traditions in the Church of England. (p. 26)

Q

Quaker [kwā'kər] *n.* a member of the Society of Friends, a religious group persecuted for its beliefs in 17th-century England. (p. 29)

quota [kwō'tə] **system** *n.* a system that sets limits on how many immigrants from various countries a nation will admit each year. (p. 439)

R

ragtime [răg'tīm'] *n.* a form of music, originating in the 1880s, in which the styles of African-American spirituals and European music were blended. (p. 317)

ratification [răt'ə-fĭ-kā'shən] *n.* the official approval of the Constitution, or of an amendment, by the states. (p. 71)

rationing [răsh'ə-nĭng] *n.* a restriction of people's right to buy unlimited amounts of particular foods and other goods, often implemented during wartime to assure adequate supplies for the military. (p. 576)

Reaganomics [rā'gə-nŏm'ĭks] *n.* the economic policies of President Ronald Reagan, which were focused on the granting of large tax cuts in order to increase private investment. (p. 822)

realpolitik [rā-äl'pō'lĭ-tēk'] *n.* a political philosophy, advocated by Henry Kissinger in the Nixon administration, that involves dealing with other nations in a practical and flexible way rather than according to a rigid policy. (p. 791)

reapportionment [rē'ə-pôr'shən-mənt] *n.* the redrawing of election districts to reflect changes in population. (p. 688)

recall [rĭ-kôl'] *n.* a procedure for removing a public official from office by a vote of the people. (p. 336)

Reconstruction [rē'kən-strŭk'shən] *n.* the period of rebuilding that followed the Civil War, during which the defeated Confederate states were readmitted to the Union. (p. 192)

Reconstruction Finance [fə-năns'] **Corporation** *n.* an agency established in 1932 to provide emergency financing to banks, life-insurance companies, railroads, and other large businesses. (p. 498)

referendum [rĕf'ə-rĕn'dəm] *n.* a procedure by which a proposed legislative measure can be submitted to a vote of the people. (p. 336)

Reformation [rĕf'ər-mā'shən] *n.* a religious movement in 16th-century Europe, growing out of a desire for reform in the Roman Catholic Church and leading to the establishment of various Protestant churches. (p. 11)

reparations [rĕp'ə-rā'shənz] *n.* the compensation paid by a defeated nation for the damage or injury it inflicted during a war. (p. 418)

republic [rĭ-pŭb'lĭk] *n.* a government in which the citizens rule through elected representatives. (p. 68)

revenue [rĕv'ə-no͞o] **sharing** *n.* the distribution of federal money to state and local governments with few or no restrictions on how it is spent. (p. 786)

968 Glossary

reverse discrimination [dĭ-skrĭm′ə-nā′shən] *n.* an unfair treatment of members of a majority group—for example, white men—resulting from efforts to correct discrimination against members of other groups. (p. 819)

rock 'n' roll [rŏk′ən-rōl′] *n.* a form of popular music, characterized by heavy rhythms and simple melodies, that developed from rhythm and blues during the 1950s. (p. 656)

Roosevelt Corollary [rō′zə-vĕlt′ kôr′ə-lĕr-ē] *n.* an extension of the Monroe Doctrine, announced by President Theodore Roosevelt in 1904, under which the United States claimed the right to protect its economic interests by means of military intervention in the affairs of Western Hemisphere nations. (p. 384)

Rough Riders *n.* a volunteer cavalry regiment, commanded by Leonard Wood and Theodore Roosevelt, that served in the Spanish-American-Cuban War. (p. 373)

row [rō] **house** *n.* a single-family dwelling that shares side walls with other, similar houses. (p. 284)

rural free delivery *n.* the free government delivery of mail and packages to homes in rural areas, begun in 1896. (p. 321)

S

SALT I [sôlt′ wŭn′] **Treaty** *n.* a five-year agreement between the United States and the Soviet Union, signed in 1972, that limited the nations' numbers of intercontinental ballistic missiles and submarine-launched missiles. (p. 792)

Sand Creek Massacre [măs′ə-kər] *n.* an attack by U.S. soldiers on a Cheyenne encampment in the Colorado Territory in 1864, in which 200 Native American men, women, and children were killed. (p. 217)

Sandinista [săn′dĭ-nēs′tə] *adj.* belonging to a leftist group that overthrew the Nicaraguan government in 1979. (p. 838)

Santa Fe [săn′tə fā′] **Trail** *n.* a route from Independence, Missouri, to Santa Fe, New Mexico, used by traders in the early and mid 1800s. (p. 134)

satellite [săt′l-īt′] **nation** *n.* a country that is dominated politically and economically by another nation. (p. 609)

Saturday Night Massacre [măs′ə-kər] *n.* a name given to the resignation of the U.S. attorney general and the firing of his deputy in October 1973, after they refused to carry out President Nixon's order to fire the special prosecutor investigating the Watergate affair. (p. 796)

scab *n.* a person who works while others are on strike. (p. 267)

scalawag [skăl′ə-wăg′] *n.* a white Southerner who joined the Republican Party after the Civil War. (p. 195)

scientific management *n.* the application of scientific principles to increase efficiency in the workplace. (p. 332)

Scopes [skōps] **trial** *n.* a sensational 1925 court case in which the biology teacher John T. Scopes was tried for challenging a Tennessee law that outlawed the teaching of evolution. (p. 457)

search-and-destroy mission *n.* a U.S. military raid on a South Vietnamese village, intended to root out villagers with ties to the Vietcong but often resulting in the destruction of the village and the displacement of its inhabitants. (p. 732)

secession [sĭ-sĕsh′ən] *n.* the formal withdrawal of a state from the Union. (p. 165)

Second Great Awakening *n.* a 19th-century religious movement in which individual responsibility for seeking salvation was emphasized, along with the need for personal and social improvement. (p. 152)

Securities and Exchange [sĭ-kyŏŏr′ĭ-tēz ənd ĭks-chānj′] **Commission** *n.* an agency, created in 1934, that monitors the stock market and enforces laws regulating the sale of stocks and bonds. (p. 532)

segregation [sĕg′rĭ-gā′shən] *n.* the separation of people on the basis of race. (p. 310)

Selective [sĭ-lĕk′tĭv] **Service Act** *n.* a law, enacted in 1917, that required men to register for military service. (p. 402)

Seneca Falls [sĕn′ĭ-kə fôlz′] **Convention** *n.* a women's rights convention held in Seneca Falls, New York, in 1848. (p. 157)

service sector [sĕk′tər] *n.* the part of the economy that provides consumers with services rather than goods. (p. 854)

settlement house *n.* a community center providing assistance to residents—particularly immigrants—in a slum neighborhood. (p. 287)

Seventeenth Amendment *n.* an amendment to the U.S. Constitution, adopted in 1913, that provided for the election of U.S. senators by the people rather than by state legislatures. (p. 336)

shantytown [shăn′tē-toun′] *n.* a neighborhood in which people live in shacks. (p. 490)

sharecropping [shâr′krŏp′ĭng] *n.* a system in which landowners give farm workers land, seed, and tools in return for a part of the crops they raise. (p. 198)

Shays's [shā′zəz] **Rebellion** *n.* an uprising of debt-ridden Massachusetts farmers in 1787. (p. 70)

Sherman Antitrust [shûr′mən ăn′tē-trŭst′] **Act** *n.* a law, enacted in 1890, that was intended to prevent the creation of monopolies by making it illegal to establish trusts that interfered with free trade. (p. 260)

silent majority [mə-jôr′ĭ-tē] *n.* a name given by President Richard Nixon to the moderate, mainstream Americans who quietly supported his Vietnam War policies. (p. 748)

sit-in *n.* a form of demonstration used by African Americans to protest discrimination, in which the protesters sit down in a segregated business and refuse to leave until they are served. (p. 702)

Social Darwinism [sō′shəl där′wĭ-nĭz′əm] *n.* an economic and social philosophy—supposedly based on the biologist Charles Darwin's theory of evolution by natural selection—holding that a system of unrestrained competition will ensure the survival of the fittest. (p. 258)

Social Gospel [gŏs′pəl] **movement** *n.* a 19th-century reform movement based on the belief that Christians have a responsibility to help improve working conditions and alleviate poverty. (p. 287)

socialism [sō′shə-lĭz′əm] *n.* an economic and political system based on government ownership of business and property and on equal distribution of wealth. (p. 265)

Social Security Act *n.* a law enacted in 1935 to provide aid to retirees, the unemployed, people with disabilities, and dependent mothers and children. (p. 515)

soddy [sŏd′ē] *n.* a home built of blocks of turf. (p. 232)

Songhai [sông′hī′] *n.* an empire that, at the height of its power in the 1500s, controlled much of West Africa. (p. 8)

soup kitchen *n.* a place where free food is served to the needy. (p. 491)

Southern Christian Leadership Conference *n.* an organization formed in 1957 by Dr. Martin Luther King, Jr., and other leaders to work for civil rights through nonviolent means. (p. 702)

Southern strategy *n.* President Nixon's attempt to attract the support of Southern conservative Democrats who were unhappy with federal desegregation policies and the liberal Supreme Court. (p. 788)

speakeasy [spēk′ē′zē] *n.* a place where alcoholic drinks were sold and consumed illegally during Prohibition. (p. 454)

speculation [spĕk′yə-lā′shən] *n.* an involvement in risky business transactions in an effort to make a quick or large profit. (p. 485)

Square Deal *n.* President Theodore Roosevelt's program of progressive reforms designed to protect the common people against big business. (p. 342)

stagflation [stăg-flā′shən] *n.* an economic condition marked by both inflation and high unemployment. (p. 790)

Stalwart [stôl′wərt] *n.* a Republican who supported the New York political boss Roscoe Conkling and opposed civil service reform. (p. 292)

Stamp Act *n.* a 1765 law in which Parliament established the first direct taxation of goods and services within the British colonies in North America. (p. 49)

Strategic Defense Initiative [strə-tē′jĭk dĭ-fĕns′ ĭ-nĭsh′ə-tĭv] *n.* a proposed defense system—popularly known as Star Wars—intended to protect the United States against missile attacks. (p. 823)

strike *n.* a work stoppage intended to force an employer to respond to demands. (p. 148)

Student Nonviolent Coordinating [nŏn-vī′ə-lənt kō-ôr′dn-ā′tĭng] **Committee** *n.* an organization formed in 1960 to coordinate sit-ins and other protests and to give young blacks a larger role in the civil rights movement. (p. 702)

Students for a Democratic Society *n.* an antiestablishment New Left group, founded in 1960, that called for greater individual freedom and responsibility. (p. 737)

suburb [sŭb′ûrb′] *n.* a residential town or community near a city. (p. 636)

suffrage [sŭf′rĭj] *n.* the right to vote. (p. 339)

Sugar Act *n.* a trade law enacted by Parliament in 1764 in an attempt to reduce smuggling in the British colonies in North America. (p. 48)

supply-side economics *n.* the idea that a reduction of tax rates will lead to increases in jobs, savings, and investments, and therefore to an increase in government revenue. (p. 823)

T

Taino [tī′nō] *n.* a Native American people of the Caribbean islands—the first group encountered by Columbus and his men when they reached the Americas. (p. 14)

Tammany [tăm′ə-nē] **Hall** *n.* the Democratic political machine that dominated New York City in the late 19th century. (p. 290)

Teapot Dome scandal [skăn′dl] *n.* Secretary of the Interior Albert B. Fall's secret leasing of oil-rich public land to private companies in return for money and land. (p. 440)

Telecommunications [tĕl′ĭ-kə-myōō′nĭ-kā′shənz] **Act** *n.* a law enacted in 1996 to remove barriers that had previously prevented communications companies from engaging in more than one type of communications business. (p. 861)

telecommute [tĕl′ĭ-kə-myōōt′] *v.* to work at home for a company located elsewhere, by using such new communications technologies as computers, modems, and fax machines. (p. 867)

tenant [tĕn′ənt] **farming** *n.* a system in which farm workers supply their own tools and rent farmland for cash. (p. 199)

Tennessee Valley Authority *n.* a federal corporation established in 1933 to construct dams and power plants in the Tennessee Valley region. (p. 533)

termination [tûr′mə-nā′shən] **policy** *n.* the U.S. government's plan, announced in 1953, to give up responsibility for Native American tribes by eliminating federal economic support, discontinuing the reservation system, and redistributing tribal lands. (p. 663)

Tet offensive [tĕt′ ə-fĕn′sĭv] *n.* a massive surprise attack by the Vietcong on South Vietnamese towns and cities early in 1968. (p. 741)

Texas Revolution *n.* the 1836 rebellion in which Texas gained its independence from Mexico. (p. 137)

Thirteenth Amendment *n.* an amendment to the U.S. Constitution, adopted in 1865, that abolished slavery and involuntary servitude. (p. 190)

Tiananmen [tyän′än′mĕn′] **Square** *n.* the site of 1989 demonstrations in Beijing, China, in which Chinese students demanded freedom of speech and a greater voice in government. (p. 838)

Tonkin Gulf [tŏn′kĭn′ gŭlf′] **Resolution** *n.* a resolution adopted by Congress in 1964, giving the president broad powers to wage war in Vietnam. (p. 728)

totalitarian [tō-tăl′ĭ-târ′ē-ən] *adj.* characteristic of a political system in which the government exercises complete control over its citizens' lives. (p. 544)

trade imbalance [ĭm-băl′əns] *n.* a situation in which a country imports more goods than it exports. (p. 824)

Trail of Tears [tîrz] *n.* the routes along which the Cherokee people were forcibly removed from Georgia to the Indian Territory in 1838, with thousands of the Cherokee dying on the way. (p. 129)

transcendentalism [trăn′sĕn-dĕn′tl-ĭz′əm] *n.* a philosophical and literary movement of the 1800s that emphasized living a simple life and celebrated the truth found in nature and in personal emotion and imagination. (p. 153)

transcontinental [trăns′kŏn-tə-nĕn′tl] **railroad** *n.* a railroad line linking the Atlantic and Pacific coasts of the United States, completed in 1869. (p. 252)

Treaty of Guadalupe Hidalgo [gwäd′l-ōōp′ hĭ-däl′gō] *n.* the 1848 treaty ending the U.S. war with Mexico, in which Mexico ceded California and New Mexico to the United States. (p. 140)

970 Glossary

Treaty of Paris *n.* the 1783 treaty that ended the Revolutionary War, confirming the independence of the United States and setting the boundaries of the new nation. (p. 64)

Treaty of Tordesillas [tôr′də-sē′əs] *n.* the 1494 treaty in which Spain and Portugal agreed to divide the lands of the Western Hemisphere between them. (p. 16)

Treaty of Versailles [vər-sī′] *n.* the 1919 treaty that ended World War I. (p. 418)

trench warfare *n.* military operations in which the opposing forces attack and counterattack from systems of fortified ditches rather than on an open battlefield. (p. 397)

triangular [trī-ăng′gyə-lər] **trade** *n.* the transatlantic system of trade in which goods, including slaves, were exchanged between Africa, England, Europe, the West Indies, and the colonies in North America. (p. 34)

Truman Doctrine [trōō′mən dŏk′trĭn] *n.* a U.S. policy, announced by President Harry S. Truman in 1947, of providing economic and military aid to free nations threatened by internal or external opponents. (p. 610)

trust *n.* a method of consolidating competing companies, in which participants turn their stock over to a board of trustees, who run the companies as one large corporation. (p. 259)

Tweed Ring *n.* a group of corrupt New York politicians, led by William Marcy "Boss" Tweed, who took as much as $2 million from the city between 1869 and 1871. (p. 290)

Twenty-seventh Amendment *n.* amendment to the Constitution, adopted in 1992, that prevents Congressional pay raises from taking effect until after the next election has occurred. (p. 847)

two-party system *n.* a political system dominated by two major parties. (p. 80)

UV

Underground Railroad *n.* a system of routes along which runaway slaves were helped to escape to Canada or to safe areas in the free states. (p. 166)

Unitarian [yōō′nĭ-târ′ē-ən] *n.* member of a religious group that emphasizes reason and faith in the individual. (p. 153)

United Farm Workers Organizing Committee *n.* a labor union formed in 1966 to seek higher wages and better working conditions for Mexican-American farm workers in California. (p. 762)

United Nations (UN) *n.* an international peacekeeping organization to which most nations in the world belong, founded in 1945 to promote world peace, security, and economic development. (p. 592)

urban [ûr′bən] **flight** *n.* a migration of people from cities to the surrounding suburbs. (p. 866)

urbanization [ûr′bə-nĭ-zā′shən] *n.* the growth of cities. (p. 282)

urban renewal [rĭ-nōō′əl] *n.* the tearing down and replacing of buildings in rundown inner-city neighborhoods. (p. 661)

urban sprawl [sprôl′] *n.* the unplanned and uncontrolled spreading of cities into surrounding regions. (p. 442)

U.S.S. *Maine* *n.* a U.S. warship that mysteriously exploded and sank in the harbor of Havana, Cuba, on February 15, 1898. (p. 372)

U-2 incident *n.* the downing of a U.S. spy plane and capture of its pilot by the Soviet Union in 1960. (p. 629)

vaudeville [vôd′vĭl′] *n.* a form of stage entertainment that features a variety of short performances, including songs, dances, and comedy routines. (p. 317)

V-E Day *n.* a name given to May 8, 1945, on which General Eisenhower's acceptance of the unconditional surrender of Nazi Germany marked the end of World War II in Europe. (p. 585)

vertical integration [vûr′tĭ-kəl ĭn′tĭ-grā′shən] *n.* a company's taking over its suppliers and distributors to gain total control over the quality and cost of its product. (p. 258)

Vietcong [vē-ĕt′kŏng′] *n.* the South Vietnamese Communists who, with North Vietnamese support, fought against the government of South Vietnam in the Vietnam War. (p. 726)

Vietminh [vē-ĕt′mĭn′] *n.* an organization of Vietnamese Communists and other nationalist groups that between 1946 and 1954 fought for Vietnamese independence from the French. (p. 725)

Vietnamization [vē-ĕt′nə-mĭ-zā′shən] *n.* President Nixon's strategy for ending U.S. involvement in the Vietnam War, involving the gradual withdrawal of U.S. troops and their replacement with South Vietnamese forces. (p. 748)

Voting Rights Act of 1965 *n.* a law that made it easier for African Americans to register to vote by eliminating discriminatory literacy tests and authorizing federal examiners to enroll voters denied at the local level. (p. 710)

W

Wagner [wăg′nər] **Act** *n.* a law—also known as the National Labor Relations Act—enacted in 1935 to protect workers' rights after the Supreme Court declared the National Industrial Recovery Act unconstitutional. (p. 514)

war-guilt [wôr′ gĭlt′] **clause** *n.* a provision in the Treaty of Versailles by which Germany acknowledged that it alone was responsible for World War I. (p. 418)

war hawk *n.* one of the members of Congress who favored war with Britain in the early years of the 19th century. (p. 121)

War Industries Board *n.* an agency established during World War I to increase efficiency and discourage waste in war-related industries. (p. 410)

War Powers Act *n.* a law enacted in 1973, limiting a president's right to send troops into battle without consulting Congress. (p. 753)

War Production Board *n.* an agency established during World War II to coordinate the production of military supplies by U.S. industries. (p. 576)

Warren [wôr′ən] **Commission** *n.* a group, headed by Chief Justice Earl Warren, that investigated the assassination of President Kennedy and concluded that Lee Harvey Oswald was alone responsible for it. (p. 682)

Warren Court *n.* the Supreme Court during the period when Earl Warren was chief justice, noted for its activism in the areas of civil rights and free speech. (p. 688)

Warsaw [wôr′sô′] **Pact** *n.* a military alliance formed in 1955 by the Soviet Union and its Eastern European satellites. (p. 626)

Watergate [wô′tər-gāt′] *n.* a scandal arising from the Nixon administration's attempt to cover up its involvement in the 1972 break-in at the Democratic National Committee headquarters in the Watergate apartment complex. (p. 793)

web-perfecting [pər-fĕk′tĭng] **press** *n.* an electrically powered press that prints on both sides of a continuous roll of paper, then cuts, folds, and counts the pages. (p. 301)

Woodstock [wo͝od′stŏk′] *n.* a free music festival that attracted more than 400,000 young people to a farm in upstate New York in August 1969. (p. 776)

Works Progress Administration *n.* an agency, established as part of the New Deal, that provided the unemployed with jobs in construction, garment making, teaching, the arts, and other fields. (p. 513)

XYZ

XYZ Affair *n.* a 1797 incident in which French officials demanded a bribe from U.S. diplomats. (p. 83)

Yalta [yôl′tə] **Conference** *n.* a 1945 meeting at which the leaders of the United States, Great Britain, and the Soviet Union agreed on a set of measures to be implemented after the defeat of Germany. (p. 592)

yellow journalism [jûr′nə-lĭz′əm] *n.* the use of sensationalized and exaggerated reporting by newspapers or magazines to attract readers. (p. 371)

Zimmermann [zĭm′ər-mən] **note** *n.* a message sent in 1917 by the German foreign minister to the German ambassador in Mexico, proposing a German-Mexican alliance and promising to help Mexico regain Texas, New Mexico, and Arizona if the United States entered World War I. (p. 401)

972 Glossary

Spanish Glossary

A

affirmative action [acción afirmativa] *s.* medidas para corregir los efectos de la discriminación en los empleos y la educación; favorecen a grupos, como mujeres y minorías, que estaban en desventaja. (p. 717)

Agent Orange [Agente Naranja] *s.* químico tóxico exfoliante que fumigaron las tropas estadounidenses en Vietnam para poner al descubierto refugios del Vietcong. (p. 732)

Agricultural Adjustment Act [Ley de Ajustes Agrícolas] *s.* ley de 1933 que elevó el precio de las cosechas al pagarle a los granjeros para que no cultivaran cierta porción de sus tierras, reduciendo así la producción. (p. 507)

AIDS (acquired immune deficiency syndrome) [SIDA, síndrome de inmunodeficiencia adquirida] *s.* enfermedad causada por un virus que debilita el sistema inmunológico y hace que el cuerpo sea vulnerable a infecciones y formas poco comunes de cáncer. (p. 827)

Alamo, the [El Álamo] *s.* misión situada en San Antonio, Texas, en donde fuerzas mexicanas masacraron a rebeldes texanos en 1836. (p. 137)

Alien and Sedition Acts [Leyes de Extranjeros y de Sedición] *s.* serie de cuatro leyes aprobadas en 1798 para reducir el poder político de los nuevos inmigrantes. (p. 83)

Alliance for Progress [Alianza para el Progreso] *s.* propuesta del presidente Kennedy de ofrecer ayuda económica y técnica a los países latinoamericanos, en parte para contrarrestar la influencia de Fidel Castro. (p. 679)

Allies [Aliados] *s.* 1. en la I Guerra Mundial, naciones aliadas en un tratado contra Alemania y las otras Potencias Centrales; originalmente Gran Bretaña, Francia y Rusia; más adelante se unieron Estados Unidos, Japón, Italia y otros. (p. 396) 2. en la II Guerra Mundial, naciones asociadas contra el Eje, en particular Gran Bretaña, la Unión Soviética y Estados Unidos. (p. 562)

American Federation of Labor (AFL) [Federación Norteamericana del Trabajo] s. sindicato de trabajadores calificados creado en 1886 y dirigido por Samuel Gompers. (p. 265)

American Indian Movement (AIM) [Movimiento Indígena Americano] *s.* organización radical, a veces militante, creada en 1968 con el fin de luchar por los derechos de los amerindios. (p. 763)

Americanization movement [movimiento de americanización] *s.* programa educativo ideado para facilitar la asimilación de los inmigrantes a la cultura estadounidense. (p. 283)

American System [Sistema Americano] *s.* programa económico previo a la Guerra Civil diseñado para fortalecer y unificar a Estados Unidos por medio de aranceles proteccionistas, un banco nacional y un sistema de transporte eficiente. (p. 126)

anarchist [anarquista] *s.* persona que se opone a toda forma de gobierno. (p. 431)

Anasazi *s.* grupo amerindio que vivió cerca de la región de Four Corners —donde Arizona, New Mexico, Colorado y Utah se unen— de los años 100 a 1400 d.C., aproximadamente. (p. 5)

Antifederalist [antifederalista] *s.* oponente de la Constitución y de un gobierno central fuerte. (p. 71)

appeasement [apaciguamiento] *s.* política de ceder a las demandas de una potencia hostil con el fin de mantener la paz. (p. 549)

Articles of Confederation [Artículos de la Confederación] *s.* documento que sirvió como constitución para el nuevo gobierno de Estados Unidos, aprobado por los estados en 1781. (p. 68)

assimilation [asimilación] *s.* adopción, por parte de un grupo minoritario, de las creencias y estilo de vida de la cultura dominante. (p. 219)

Atlantic Charter [Carta del Atlántico] *s.* declaración de principios de 1941 en que Estados Unidos y Gran Bretaña establecieron sus objetivos contra las Potencias del Eje. (p. 562)

Axis powers [Potencias del Eje] *s.* países unidos contra los Aliados en la II Guerra Mundial; originalmente la Alemania nazi y la Italia fascista, y después Japón. (p. 559)

Aztec [azteca] *s.* pueblo también conocido como los mexica; se estableció en el valle de México en el siglo 13. (p. 5)

B

baby boom *s.* marcado aumento en el índice de natalidad en Estados Unidos después de la II Guerra Mundial, que originó la generación más numerosa en la historia del país, nacida entre 1947 y 1961. (p. 645)

Battle of the Bulge [Batalla del Bolsón] *s.* batalla de un mes de duración de la II Guerra Mundial, que se inició el 16 de diciembre de 1944, en la que fuerzas alemanas rompieron temporalmente las líneas de los Aliados pero al final sufrieron grandes pérdidas. (p. 584)

Battle of Wounded Knee [Batalla de Wounded Knee] *s.* masacre de 300 indígenas desarmados en Wounded Knee Creek, South Dakota, que puso fin en 1890 a las Guerras Indias. (p. 221)

Bear Flag Republic [República de la Bandera del Oso] *s.* territorio declarado como república por los colonos estadounidenses de California que se rebelaron contra México en 1846; también llamada República de California. (p. 140)

Beatles, the *s.* conjuntó inglés que tuvo gran influencia en la música popular en los años 60. (p. 775)

beat movement [movimiento beat] *s.* movimiento social y literario rebelde de los años 50. (p. 655)

beatnik *s.* uno de los jóvenes inconformistas, opuesto al materialismo, que seguía el movimiento beat de los años 50. (p. 655)

Benin *s.* reino de África occidental que existió en la actual Nigeria; floreció en los bosques del delta del Níger del siglo 14 al 17. (p. 8)

Berlin airlift [puente aéreo de Berlín] *s.* operación, de 327 días de duración, en la que aviones estadounidenses y británicos llevaron alimentos y provisiones a Berlín Occidental después de que la Unión Soviética bloqueó la ciudad en 1948. (p. 611)

Berlin Wall [Muro de Berlín] *s.* muro de concreto que separaba Berlín Oriental y Occidental, construido en 1961 bajo supervisión soviética por Alemania oriental para impedir que sus ciudadanos se escaparan; por mucho tiempo símbolo de la Guerra Fría, fue derribado en 1989. (p. 676)

Bessemer process [método Bessemer] *s.* técnica más eficiente de fabricar acero, desarrollada hacia 1850. (p. 247)

Bill of Rights [Carta de Derechos] *s.* primeras diez enmiendas a la Constitución que identifican los derechos de los ciudadanos; se adoptaron en 1791. (p. 72)

bimetallism [bimetalismo] *s.* sistema monetario nacional que utiliza el oro y la plata. (p. 238)

blacklist [lista negra] *s.* lista de unos 500 actores, escritores, productores y directores a quienes no se permitía trabajar en películas de Hollywood debido a sus supuestos vínculos comunistas. (p. 621)

Black Panthers [Panteras Negras] *s.* partido político afroamericano de carácter militante formado por Huey Newton y Bobby Seale en 1966 para luchar contra la violencia de la policía y suministrar servicios en el ghetto. (p. 714)

Black Power [Poder Negro] *s.* consigna de los años 40 revivida por Stokely Carmichael en los años 60, que pedía poder político y social para los afroamericanos. (p. 714)

Black Tuesday [Martes Negro] *s.* octubre 29 de 1929, día en que los precios de las acciones bajaron drásticamente al iniciarse la caída de la bolsa de valores. (p. 485)

blitzkrieg *s.* repentina ofensiva a gran escala, de fuerzas aéreas y terrestres, dirigida a obtener una victoria rápida. (p. 551)

bonanza farm [granja de bonanza] *s.* extensa granja dedicada a un solo cultivo, de 10,000 acres o más, muy común en las planicies de finales de la década de 1870 a mediados de la década de 1890. (p. 234)

Bonus Army *s.* 25,000 veteranos desempleados de la I Guerra Mundial que marcharon en Washington, D.C., en 1932 para exigir los bonos que les habían sido prometidos. (p. 498)

bootlegger *s.* persona que contrabandeaba bebidas alcohólicas durante la época de Prohibición. (p. 455)

Boston Massacre [Masacre de Boston] *s.* incidente que ocurrió en Boston en 1770, durante el cual tropas británicas mataron a cinco colonos. (p. 50)

Boston Tea Party [Motín del Té de Boston] *s.* protesta en 1773 contra el impuesto británico sobre el té, en la que los colonos arrojaron 15,000 libras de té a las aguas del puerto de Boston. (p. 51)

Boulder Dam [Presa de Boulder] *s.* presa del río Colorado construida durante la Depresión con fondos federales para estimular la economía; ahora llamada Presa Hoover. (p. 497)

Boxer Rebellion [Rebelión de los Boxer] *s.* rebelión encabezada en 1900 por los Boxer, sociedad secreta de China, para detener la difusión de la influencia occidental. (p. 379)

bracero *s.* trabajador mexicano que labora temporalmente en Estados Unidos, como los contratados durante la época de escasez de trabajadores agrícolas de 1942 a 1947. (p. 662)

bread line [cola para comer] *s.* fila de personas que esperan comida gratis, como ocurrió en la Depresión. (p. 491)

brinkmanship *s.* práctica de amenazar al enemigo con represalias militares extremas ante cualquier agresión, que caracterizó la carrera armamentista entre Estados Unidos y la Unión Soviética durante la Guerra Fría. (p. 626)

Brown v. Board of Education *s.* decisión de la Suprema Corte en 1954 que declaró que la segregación de estudiantes negros y blancos era inconstitucional. (p. 698)

Bull Moose Party [Partido Bull Moose] *s.* apodo del Partido Progresista, bajo el que Theodore Roosevelt aspiró, sin éxito, a la presidencia en 1912. (p. 352)

buying on margin [compra con margen] *s.* compra de acciones en la que se paga sólo una porción del valor de la acción al vendedor o corredor de bolsa, y se presta el resto. (p. 485)

C

cabinet [gabinete] *s.* asesores directos del presidente, por lo general jefes de departamentos, que coordinan y ponen en práctica la política gubernamental. (p. 79)

Camp David Accords [Acuerdos de Camp David] *s.* dos históricos acuerdos de paz entre Israel y Egipto, negociados en Camp David, Maryland, en 1978. (p. 806)

carpetbagger *s.* término despectivo para referirse a los norteños que se trasladaron al Sur después de la Guerra Civil y que apoyaban la Reconstrucción ordenada por el Congreso. (p. 195)

Central Powers [Potencias Centrales] *s.* en la I Guerra Mundial, el grupo de naciones —Alemania, Austro-Hungría y el imperio otomano— que se opuso a los Aliados. (p. 396)

checks and balances [control y compensación de poderes] *s.* sistema en el cual cada rama del gobierno controla o restringe a las demás ramas. (p. 71)

Chinese Exclusion Act [Ley de Exclusión de Chinos] *s.* ley de 1882 que prohibía la inmigración de ciudadanos chinos, con la excepción de estudiantes, maestros, comerciantes, turistas y funcionarios gubernamentales. (p. 279)

CIA *s.* Central Intelligence Agency (Agencia Central de Inteligencia), agencia gubernamental establecida en 1947 para espiar y realizar operaciones secretas en países extranjeros. (p. 626)

Civilian Conservation Corps [Cuerpo Civil de Conservación] *s.* agencia establecida como parte del New Deal con el fin de ocupar a jóvenes desempleados en trabajos como la construcción de carreteras y el cuidado de parques nacionales. (p. 507)

Civil Rights Act of 1964 [Ley de Derechos Civiles de 1964] *s.* ley que prohíbe la discriminación en lugares públicos, en la educación y en los empleos por cuestión de raza, color, sexo, nacionalidad o religión. (p. 708)

974 Spanish Glossary

Civil Rights Act of 1968 [Ley de Derechos Civiles de 1968] *s.* ley que prohíbe la discriminación en la vivienda. (p. 716)

civil service [servicio civil] *s.* cualquier servicio gubernamental en el que se obtiene un cargo mediante exámenes públicos. (p. 291)

Clayton Antitrust Act [Ley Antitrust Clayton] *s.* ley de 1914 que declaraba ilegales ciertas prácticas empresariales injustas y protegía el derecho de los sindicatos y organizaciones agrícolas a existir y a participar en actos de protesta. (p. 355)

Cold War [Guerra Fría] *s.* estado de hostilidad, sin llegar a conflictos armados, entre Estados Unidos y la Unión Soviética tras la II Guerra Mundial. (p. 610)

collective bargaining [negociación colectiva] *s.* negociaciones en grupo entre trabajadores y patronos para alcanzar acuerdos en cuanto a salarios, beneficios, horarios y condiciones de trabajo. (p. 265)

Columbian Exchange [Transferencia Colombina] *s.* transferencia —iniciada con el primer viaje de Colón a las Américas— de plantas, alimentos, animales y enfermedades entre el Hemisferio Occidental y el Hemisferio Oriental. (p. 17)

Committee to Reelect the President [Comité de Reelección del Presidente] *s.* grupo que dirigió la campaña para la reelección del presidente Nixon en 1972, cuya conexión con el allanamiento de la Sede Nacional del Partido Demócrata hizo estallar el escándalo Watergate. (p. 794)

Common Sense [Sentido común] *s.* folleto escrito en 1776 por Thomas Paine que exhortaba a la separación de las colonias británicas. (p. 54)

Commonwealth of Independent States [Comunidad de Estados Independientes] *s.* confederación amplia de Estados que quedó tras la disolución de la Unión Soviética en 1991. (p. 837)

Commonwealth* v. *Hunt *s.* caso judicial de 1842 en el cual la Suprema Corte ratificó el derecho de los obreros a la huelga. (p. 149)

communism [comunismo] *s.* sistema económico y político basado en un gobierno de un solo partido y en la propiedad estatal. (p. 430)

concentration camp [campo de concentración] *s.* campamento de presos operado por la Alemania nazi para judíos y otros grupos que consideraba enemigos de Adolfo Hitler; a los presos los mataban o los hacían morir de hambre y a causa de trabajos forzados. (p. 556)

conglomerate [conglomerado] *s.* corporación grande que posee compañías más pequeñas dedicadas a negocios no relacionados. (p. 643)

Congress of Industrial Organizations [Congreso de Organizaciones Industriales] *s.* organización sindical que se separó de la Federación Norteamericana del Trabajo en 1938. (p. 521)

Congress of Racial Equality (CORE) [Congreso de Igualdad Racial] *s.* grupo interracial, fundado por James Farmer en 1942, que luchaba contra la segregación en ciudades del Norte. (p. 599)

conquistador *s.* explorador y colonizador español de las Américas en el siglo 16. (p. 17)

conscientious objector [objetor de conciencia] *s.* persona que se opone a toda guerra por principio de conciencia. (p. 405)

conscription [conscripción] *s.* servicio militar obligatorio de ciertos miembros de la población. (p. 180)

conservation [conservación] *s.* práctica de preservar algunas zonas naturales y desarrollar otras por el bien común. (p. 346)

conservative coalition [coalición conservadora] *s.* alianza de fines del siglo 20 de grupos de ultraderecha opuestos a la ingerencia del gobierno, los programas de subvención, la acción afirmativa, la integración escolar por medio del transporte estudiantil y la presunta decadencia moral de la sociedad estadounidense. (p. 819)

consumerism [consumismo] *s.* gran interés en la compra de bienes materiales, como el que caracterizó a la clase media estadounidense a finales de los años 50. (p. 648)

containment [contención] *s.* política estadounidense de formar alianzas con países más pequeños y débiles con el fin de bloquear la expansión de la infuencia soviética tras la II Guerra Mundial. (p. 609)

Contract with America [Contrato con América] *s.* documento elaborado por el representante Newt Gingrich y firmado por 300 candidatos republicanos el 27 de septiembre de 1994, que presentaba sus planes legislativos conservadores. (p. 849)

Contras [la contra] *s.* fuerzas anticomunistas nicaragüenses que recibieron asistencia de la administración Reagan para derrocar al gobierno sandinista de Nicaragua. (p. 838)

convoy system [flotilla de escolta] *s.* medio de proteger los buques mercantes del ataque de submarinos al hacer que viajen con un grupo grande de destructores. (p. 404)

counterculture [contracultura] *s.* cultura de la juventud de los años 60 que rechazaba la sociedad tradicional y buscaba paz, amor y libertad individual. (p. 773)

credibility gap [falta de credibilidad] *s.* desconfianza del público en las declaraciones oficiales del gobierno, tales como las estadísticas de combate durante la Guerra de Vietnam. (p. 734)

credit [crédito] *s.* acuerdo en el que se compran artículos en el presente para ser cancelados en el futuro mediante un plan de cuotas con intereses. (p. 484)

Crédit Mobilier *s.* compañía constructora formada en 1868 por los dueños de la Union Pacific Railroad; se formó un escándalo al usarla ilegalmente para obtener ganancias y sobornar a funcionarios. (p. 255)

"Cross of Gold" speech [Discurso de la "Cruz de Oro"] *s.* exaltado discurso de William Jennings Bryan en la Convención Demócrata de 1896, en el que atacó a los que proponían un sistema monetario basado sólo en el oro. (p. 238)

culture shock [shock cultural] *s.* confusión y ansiedad generada por la inmersión en una cultura desconocida. (p. 278)

D

Dawes Act [Ley Dawes] *s.* ley aprobada por el Congreso en 1887 para "americanizar" a los indígenas distribuyendo a individuos la tierra de las reservaciones. (p. 219)

D-Day [Día D] *s.* junio 6 de 1944, día en que los Aliados emprendieron una invasión por tierra, mar y aire contra el Eje. (p. 583)

debt peonage [deuda por peonaje] *s.* sistema de servidumbre involuntaria en el que una persona es obligada a trabajar para pagar una deuda. (p. 313)

Declaration of Independence [Declaración de Independencia] *s.* documento escrito por Thomas Jefferson en 1776 que declaraba la independencia de las colonias de Gran Bretaña. (p. 55)

de facto segregation [segregación *de facto*] *s.* segregación racial impuesta por la práctica y la costumbre más que por las leyes, como era común en el Norte. (p. 711)

deficit spending [gasto deficitario] *s.* práctica por parte de un gobierno de gastar más de lo que recibe por concepto de rentas públicas. (p. 529)

de jure segregation [segregación *de jure*] *s.* segregación racial impuesta por la ley, como ocurría con las leyes Jim Crow en el Sur. (p. 711)

Democratic-Republican [demócrata-republicano] *s.* partidario de gobiernos estatales fuertes. (p. 80)

department store [tienda por departamentos] *s.* tienda grande al por menor, que ofrece una variedad de productos y servicios. (p. 320)

détente [distensión] *s.* política exterior estadounidense dirigida a disminuir las tensiones de la Guerra Fría; un ejemplo fue la visita del presidente Nixon a China en 1972. (p. 791)

direct relief [ayuda directa] *s.* alimentos o dinero que el gobierno da directamente a los necesitados. (p. 493)

Dixiecrat *s.* delegado sureño que se retiró de la convención del Partido Demócrata en 1948 para no apoyar la plataforma del partido sobre derechos civiles y formó un grupo denominado States' Rights Democratic Party. (p. 640)

dollar diplomacy [diplomacia del dólar] *s.* política de usar el poder económico o la influencia económica de Estados Unidos para proteger sus intereses empresariales del país o para alcanzar sus objetivos de política exterior en otros países. (p. 385)

domino theory [teoría del dominó] *s.* teoría basada en la analogía de piezas de dominó que caen: si una nación se vuelve comunista, las naciones vecinas inevitablemente se volverán comunistas también. (p. 725)

double standard [doble moral] *s.* conjunto de principios que permite mayor libertad sexual al hombre que a la mujer. (p. 459)

dove [paloma] *s.* persona que se oponía a la Guerra de Vietnam y creía que Estados Unidos debía retirarse. (p. 739)

Dow Jones Industrial Average [Promedio Industrial Dow Jones] *s.* medida que computa el valor de las acciones de un grupo selecto de compañías grandes; se usa como barómetro de los mercados bursátiles. (p. 487)

downsize [recortar] *v.* despedir trabajadores de una organización con el fin de hacer las operaciones más eficientes y ahorrar dinero. (p. 854)

dumbbell tenement [vecindad] *s.* edificio largo y estrecho, de cinco o seis pisos, con dos pabellones más anchos en los extremos. (p. 284)

Dust Bowl *s.* región entre Texas y North Dakota que quedó inservible para la agricultura debido a la sequía y a las tormentas de arena durante los años 30. (p. 490)

E

Earth Day [Día de la Tierra] *s.* día dedicado a la educación ambiental que desde 1970 se celebra el 22 de abril de cada año. (p. 809)

Economic Opportunity Act [Ley de Oportunidades Económicas] *s.* ley, promulgada en 1964, que adjudicó fondos a programas para la juventud, medidas para combatir la pobreza, préstamos para pequeños negocios y capacitación laboral. (p. 685)

egalitarianism [igualitarismo] *s.* creencia de que todas las personas deben tener igualdad de derechos políticos, económicos, sociales y civiles. (p. 65)

Eisenhower Doctrine [Doctrina Eisenhower] *s.* advertencia del presidente Eisenhower en 1957 de que Estados Unidos defendería el Oriente Medio contra el ataque de cualquier país comunista. (p. 628)

e-mail [correo electrónico] *s.* mensajes electrónicos enviados y recibidos por la Internet y otras redes de computadores. (p. 861)

Emancipation Proclamation [Proclama de Emancipación] *s.* orden ejecutiva de Abraham Lincoln el 1° de enero de 1863 que abolía la esclavitud en los estados "en rebelión". (p. 179)

encomienda *s.* institución colonial de España en las Américas que repartía indígenas a los conquistadores para hacer trabajos forzados. (p. 18)

Enlightenment [Ilustración] *s.* movimiento intelectual del siglo 18 que propugnaba la razón y los métodos científicos. (p. 37)

entitlement program [programa de subvención] *s.* programa gubernamental, tal como Social Security, Medicare y Medicaid, que brinda beneficios a grupos específicos. (p. 819)

entrepreneur [empresario] *s.* persona que usa su dinero para crear una empresa. (p. 144)

environmentalist [ambientalista] *s.* persona que procura proteger el medio ambiente de la destrucción y de la contaminación. (p. 809)

Environmental Protection Agency [Agencia de Protección Ambiental] *s.* agencia federal establecida en 1970 con el fin de supervisar los asuntos ambientales y controlar la contaminación. (p. 810)

Equal Rights Amendment [Enmienda de Igualdad de Derechos] *s.* enmienda constitucional propuesta que establece que "la igualdad de derechos bajo la ley no debe ser negada o restringida por el gobierno federal ni por ningún estado en razón del sexo". (p. 771)

Espionage and Sedition Acts [Leyes de Espionaje y Sedición] *s.* dos leyes aprobadas en 1917 y 1918, que castigaban fuertemente a quienes criticaran o bloquearan la participación de Estados Unidos en la II Guerra Mundial. (p. 413)

exoduster *s.* afroamericano que emigró del Sur a Kansas después de la Reconstrucción. (p. 216)

F

Fair Deal *s.* plan económico del presidente Truman que expandió el New Deal de Roosevelt; aumentó el salario mínimo, amplió el seguro social y le dio vivienda a familias de bajos recursos, entre otras medidas. (p. 641)

Family Assistance Plan [Plan de Asistencia Familiar] *s.* propuesta de reforma a los programas de beneficencia,

976 Spanish Glossary

aprobada por la Cámara de Representantes en 1970 pero rechazada por el Senado, que garantizaba un ingreso a los beneficiarios de ayuda pública que aceptaran capacitarse y emplearse en un oficio. (p. 787)

fascism [fascismo] *s.* filosofía política que propone un gobierno fuerte, centralizado, nacionalista, caracterizado por una rígida dictadura unipartidista. (p. 544)

Federal Communications Commission (FCC) [Comisión Federal de Comunicaciones] *s.* agencia del gobierno que regula y otorga licencias a la radio, la televisión, los teléfonos y otras industrias de comunicaciones. (p. 652)

Federal Deposit Insurance Corporation [Corporación Federal de Seguros de Depósitos] *s.* agencia creada en 1933 para garantizar depósitos bancarios individuales cuando un banco quiebra. (p. 532)

Federal Home Loan Bank Act [Ley Federal para Préstamos de Vivienda] *s.* ley aprobada en 1931 que redujo las cuotas hipotecarias y permitió a los agricultores refinanciar sus préstamos para prevenir juicios hipotecarios. (p. 498)

Federalist [federalista] *s.* partidario de la Constitución y de un gobierno nacional fuerte. (p. 71)

Federal Reserve System [Sistema de la Reserva Federal] *s.* sistema bancario nacional establecido por Woodrow Wilson en 1913 que controla el dinero circulante del país. (p. 356)

Federal Securities Act [Ley Federal de Valores] *s.* ley de 1933 que obliga a las corporaciones a suministrar información completa y fidedigna sobre sus ofertas de acciones. (p. 506)

Federal Trade Commission [Comisión Federal de Comercio] *s.* agencia federal establecida en 1914 para investigar y parar prácticas empresariales injustas. (p. 355)

feminism [feminismo] *s.* creencia, que inspiró el movimiento de la mujer de los años 60, de que la mujer debe tener igualdad económica, política y social con respecto al hombre. (p. 768)

Fifteenth Amendment [Enmienda 15] *s.* enmienda a la Constitución, adoptada en 1870, que establece que a nadie puede negársele el derecho al voto por motivos de raza, color o por haber sido esclavo. (p. 194)

flapper *s.* jovencita típica de los años 20 que actuaba y se vestía de manera atrevida y nada convencional. (p. 458)

flexible response [respuesta flexible] *s.* doctrina, desarrollada durante la administración Kennedy, de prepararse para una variedad de respuestas militares, en vez de concentrarse en las armas nuclerares. (p. 672)

Fordney-McCumber Tariff [Arancel Fordney-McCumber] *s.* serie de reglas, aprobada por el Congreso en 1922, que elevó a niveles sin precedentes los impuestos a las importaciones en 1922 para proteger las compañías estadounidenses de la competencia extranjera. (p. 437)

Fourteen Points [los catorce puntos] *s.* plan del presidente Wilson en pro de la paz mundial tras la I Guerra Mundial; estableció la Liga de las Naciones. (p. 417)

Fourteenth Amendment [Enmienda 14] *s.* enmienda a la Constitución, adoptada en 1868, que hace ciudadano a toda persona nacida o naturalizada en Estados Unidos. (p. 193)

franchise [franquicia] *s.* forma de negocio, común en la industria de la comida rápida, en la que individuos compran el derecho a usar el nombre y los métodos de una compañía matriz, con lo que la compañía se multiplica. (p. 643)

freedom rider *s.* activista de derechos civiles que enfrentó violentas reacciones al viajar en autobús a través del Sur a comienzos de los años 60 para poner a prueba la decisión de la Suprema Corte de prohibir la segregación en los autobuses de pasajeros. (p. 704)

Freedom Summer *s.* campaña de registro de votantes afroamericanos en el verano de 1964, organizada por el Congreso de Igualdad Racial y el SNCC (Comité Coordinador de Estudiantes no Violentos), que produjo violentas respuestas de los segregacionistas. (p. 708)

free enterprise [libre empresa] *s.* sistema económico en el que compañías privadas e individuos controlan los medios de producción. (p. 144)

Free Speech Movement [Movimiento de Libre Expresión] *s.* movimiento activista de los años 60 que surgió a raíz de un enfrentamiento entre los estudiantes y la administración de la Universidad de California en Berkeley en 1964; abordó muchos asuntos sociales y políticos. (p. 737)

French and Indian War [Guerra contra Franceses e Indígenas] *s.* guerra librada en Norteamérica (1757-1763) como parte de un conflicto mundial entre Francia y Gran Bretaña; finalizó con la derrota de Francia y el traspaso del Canadá francés a Gran Bretaña. (p. 39)

fundamentalism [fundamentalismo] *s.* movimiento religioso protestante basado en la interpretación textual, o palabra por palabra, de las escrituras. (p. 456)

G

GATT *s.* General Agreement on Tariffs and Trade (Acuerdo General de Aranceles y Comercio), acuerdo de comercio internacional, revisado en 1994 para crear la Organización Mundial de Comercio, que redujo las barreras arancelarias y estableció normas para resolver disputas comerciales. (p. 856)

genetic engineering [ingeniería genética] *s.* alteración de la biología molecular de las células de un organismo para crear nuevas variedades de bacterias, plantas o animales. (p. 862)

Geneva Accords [Acuerdos de Ginebra] *s.* plan de paz de Indochina en 1954 en el que Vietnam fue dividido temporalmente en Vietnam del Norte y Vietnam del Sur, mientras se celebraban las elecciones de 1956. (p. 726)

genocide [genocidio] *s.* exterminio deliberado y sistemático de un grupo de personas por su raza, nacionalidad o religión. (p. 555)

Gentlemen's Agreement [Acuerdo de Caballeros] *s.* acuerdo concertado durante 1907 y 1908, mediante el cual el gobierno de Japón limitó la emigración a Estados Unidos. (p. 279)

Gettysburg Address [Discurso de Gettysburg] *s.* famoso discurso de Abraham Lincoln durante la Guerra Civil al inaugurar un cementerio nacional en el campo de batalla de Gettysburg, Pennsylvania, el 19 de noviembre de 1863. (p. 186)

Ghost Dance *s.* ritual amerindio que evocaba la restauración de la vida tribal; popular entre los sioux antes de la Masacre de Wounded Knee en 1890. (p. 221)

GI Bill of Rights [Carta de Derechos de los Veteranos] *s.* nombre dado a la Ley de Reajuste de Militares de 1944, que ofrecía beneficios financieros y educativos a los veteranos de la II Guerra Mundial. (pp. 598, 636)

glasnost *s.* palabra rusa que se refiere a la discusión abierta de los problemas sociales que se dio en la Unión Soviética durante los años 80. (p. 836)

Glass-Steagall Banking Act of 1933 [Ley Bancaria Glass-Steagall] *s.* ley que aseguró los depósitos bancarios mediante la Corporación Federal de Seguros de Depósitos. (p. 506)

***Gone with the Wind** [Lo que el viento se llevó]* *s.* película de 1939 sobre la vida de los dueños de plantaciones del Sur durante la Guerra Civil. (p. 524)

graft [corrupción] *s.* acto de aprovecharse de un cargo político con el fin de ganar dinero, propiedades u otros bienes. (p. 288)

grandfather clause [cláusula del abuelo] *s.* estipulación que exime de cumplir una ley a ciertas personas por circunstancias previas; específicamente, cláusula de la constitución de algunos estados sureños que eximía a los blancos de los estrictos requisitos que impedían que los negros votaran. (p. 310)

Grange [la Granja] *s.* organización de granjeros que intentaron, a partir de la década de 1870, combatir el poder de los ferrocarriles. (p. 236)

***Grapes of Wrath, The** [Las uvas de la ira]* *s.* novela de John Steinbeck, publicada en 1939, sobre una familia de Oklahoma que se va de la región del Dust Bowl a California. (p. 527)

Great Awakening [Gran Despertar] *s.* serie de grandes asambleas religiosas en las décadas de 1730 y 1740 organizadas por predicadores viajeros como George Whitefield. (p. 38)

Great Depression [Gran Depresión] *s.* período de 1929 a 1941 en el que la economía estadounidense quebró y millones quedaron sin empleo. (p. 486)

Great Migration [Gran Migración] *s.* movimiento de cientos de miles de negros sureños a ciudades del Norte a principios de este siglo. (p. 414)

Great Plains [Grandes Llanuras] *s.* vasta pradera que cubre la porción centro-oeste de Estados Unidos. (p. 214)

Great Potato Famine [hambruna de la papa] *s.* hambre colectiva en Irlanda a mediados del siglo 19 a raíz de la pérdida de cosechas de papa por una plaga; causó muchas muertes y un aumento de la emigración a Estados Unidos. (p. 149)

Great Society [Gran Sociedad] *s.* ambicioso programa legislativo del presidente Lyndon B. Johnson para reducir la pobreza y la injusticia racial, y mejorar el nivel de vida. (p. 686)

H

Haight-Ashbury *s.* distrito de San Francisco, "capital" de la contracultura hippie durante los años 60. (p. 774)

Harlem Renaissance [Renacimiento de Harlem] *s.* período de sobresaliente creatividad afroamericana en el campo artístico durante los años 20 y 30, cuyo nombre viene de la zona de Harlem en New York City. (p. 470)

hawk [halcón] *s.* persona que respaldaba la Guerra de Vietnam y creía que Estados Unidos debía incrementar su fuerza militar para ganarla. (p. 739)

Hawley–Smoot Tariff Act [Ley de Aranceles Hawley-Smoot] *s.* ley de 1930 que estableció los más altos aranceles proteccionistas en la historia estadounidense, afectando negativamente el comercio internacional. (p. 489)

H-bomb [bomba de hidrógeno] *s.* bomba de hidrógeno, o termonuclear, mucho más poderosa que la bomba atómica, diseñada en la presidencia de Truman; detonó por primera vez en 1952. (p. 625)

Ho Chi Minh Trail [Sendero de Ho Chi Min] *s.* red de caminos por la que Vietnam del Norte abastecía al Vietcong en Vietnam del Sur. (p. 726)

holding company [compañía tenedora] *s.* compañía integrada para comprar acciones de otras compañías, y crear un monopolio. (p. 259)

Hollywood Ten [los Diez de Hollywood] *s.* diez testigos de la industria cinematográfica que se negaron a cooperar con la investigación de influencia comunista en Hollywood que realizó el Comité de la Cámara de Representantes sobre Actividades Antiamericanas. (p. 621)

Holocaust [Holocausto] *s.* asesinato sistemático de más de 11 millones de judíos y de otros grupos por los nazis antes y durante la II Guerra Mundial. (p. 554)

Homestead Act [Ley de la Heredad] *s.* ley aprobada por el Congreso en 1862 que ofrecía 160 acres de tierra gratis a quien viviera en ella y la cultivara por cinco años. (p. 216)

homesteader s. colono que vivía en tierras otorgadas por el gobierno a través de la Ley de la Heredad de 1862. (p. 231)

horizontal consolidation [consolidación horizontal] *s.* proceso mediante el cual compañías que fabrican productos similares se unen y reducen la competencia. (p. 258)

hot line [línea de emergencia] *s.* línea directa de comunicación entre la Casa Blanca y el Kremlin, establecida en 1963 para que los líderes de Estados Unidos y la Unión Soviética pudieran hablarse durante una crisis. (p. 676)

HUAC *s.* House Committee on Un-American Activities (Comité de la Cámara de Representantes sobre Actividades Antiamericanas), comité del Congreso creado en 1938 para investigar la influencia comunista dentro y fuera del gobierno. (p. 620)

human rights [derechos humanos] *s.* derechos y libertades considerados básicos, como los que establece la Declaración de Independencia y la Carta de Derechos. (p. 805)

I

immigration [inmigración] *s.* llegada a un país distinto al país natal para vivir en él. (p. 149)

Immigration Act of 1965 [Ley de Inmigración de 1965] *s.* ley que abrió las puertas a más inmigrantes de Asia y Latinoamérica al remplazar el sistema de inmigración por origen nacional. (p. 686)

978 Spanish Glossary

imperialism [imperialismo] *s.* política de controlar países por medios económicos, políticos o militares. (p. 364)

impressment [leva] *s.* práctica de reclutar hombres a la fuerza para prestar servicio militar. (p. 121)

income tax [impuesto sobre la renta] *s.* impuesto que retiene un porcentaje específico de los ingresos de un individuo. (p. 182)

indentured servant [sirviente por contrato] *s.* inmigrante que, a cambio de un pasaje para las Américas, se comprometía a trabajar de cuatro a siete años. (p. 23)

Industrial Workers of the World (IWW) *s.* también conocido como los Wobblies, sindicato de trabajadores de mano de obra no calificada creado en 1905. (p. 266)

inflation [inflación] *s.* fenómeno económico en el que hay un aumento constante en los precios por el incremento del dinero circulante; reduce el poder adquisitivo. (p. 62)

information superhighway [supercarretera de información] *s.* red de comunicación por computadoras propuesta para unir a personas e instituciones por todo el mundo y suministrar a individuos servicios de bibliotecas, compras, cines y noticias. (p. 860)

INF Treaty [Tratado sobre Fuerzas Nucleares Intermedias] *s.* tratado entre Estados Unidos y la Unión Soviética firmado en 1987, que eliminó algunas armas y permitió la inspección directa de emplazamientos de misiles. (p. 836)

initiative [iniciativa] *s.* reforma gubernamental que permite a los ciudadanos presentar proyectos de ley en el Congreso o en cuerpos legislativos estatales. (p. 336)

installment plan [pago a plazos] *s.* práctica de comprar a crédito mediante pagos regulares durante determinado período de tiempo. (p. 445)

Internet *s.* red mundial, originalmente diseñada por el Departamento de Defensa, que une computadors y permite una comunicación casi instantánea de textos, ilustraciones y sonidos. (p. 861)

Interstate Commerce Act [Ley de Comercio Interestatal] *s.* ley de 1887 que restablecía el derecho del gobierno federal a supervisar los ferrocarriles; creó una Comisión de Comercio Interestatal de cinco miembros. (p. 256)

Iroquois [iroqueses] *s.* grupo de pueblos amerindios que vivían en los bosques del Noreste. (p. 6)

Islam [islamismo] *s.* religión fundada en Arabia por el profeta Mahoma en el año 622; a sus seguidores se les llama musulmanes. (p. 10)

isolationist [aislacionista] *adj.* que se opone a participar en conflictos políticos y económicos con otros países. (p. 437)

J

Jacksonian democracy [democracia Jacksoniana] *s.* filosofía política de Jackson, basada en su creencia de que la gente común y corriente era la fuente de la fortaleza nacional. (p. 127)

Japanese Americans Citizens League (JACL) [Sociedad de Ciudadanos Americano-Japoneses] *s.* organización que presionó al gobierno a compensar a los estadounidenses de origen japonés por las propiedades que perdieron al ser internados durante la II Guerra Mundial. (p. 601)

Jeffersonian republicanism [republicanismo Jeffersoniano] *s.* teoría de gobierno de Jefferson; sostenía que un gobierno sencillo correspondía a las necesidades del pueblo. (p. 119)

Jim Crow laws [leyes Jim Crow] *s.* leyes impuestas por los gobiernos estatales y municipales del Sur con el fin de separar a blancos y negros en instalaciones públicas y privadas. (p. 310)

joint-stock company [sociedad de capitales] *s.* institución empresarial tipo corporación en la que inversionistas unen riquezas con un fin común; se usaron para financiar la exploración de las Américas. (p. 11)

judicial review [revisión judicial] *s.* poder de la Suprema Corte de declarar inconstitucional una ley del Congreso. (p. 119)

Judiciary Act of 1789 [Ley Judicial de 1789] *s.* ley que estableció el sistema de tribunales federales y la Suprema Corte. (p. 78)

Jungle, The *[La jungla]* *s.* novela publicada en 1906 por el periodista Upton Sinclair que denunciaba la insalubridad de la industria de carne; llevó a reformas nacionales. (p. 341)

K

kamikaze *adj.* que estrellaba deliberadamente un avión bombardero contra un buque estadounidense durante la II Guerra Mundial. (p. 589)

Kellogg-Briand Pact [Pacto Kellog-Briand] *s.* tratado de 1929 firmado por 64 naciones en el que acordaron renunciar a la guerra como medio para resolver disputas internacionales. (p. 437)

Kerner Commission [Comisión Kerner] *s.* grupo designado por el presidente Lyndon B. Johnson para estudiar las causas de la violencia urbana; recomendó eliminar la segregación *de facto* en la sociedad estadounidense. (p. 716)

Khmer Rouge *s.* grupo comunista que en 1975 tomó el poder en Camboya. (p. 752)

kickback [mordida] *s.* porción de los ingresos de un trabajador que se paga ilegalmente a un político o maquinaria política. (p. 289)

King Philip's War [Guerra del Rey Felipe] *s.* conflicto, en los años 1675 y 1676, entre los colonos de Nueva Inglaterra y grupos amerindios aliados bajo la dirección del cacique Metacom de los wampanoagas. (p. 28)

Kongo *s.* serie de pequeños reinos unidos bajo un líder a finales del siglo 15 en las selvas tropicales a lo largo del río Zaire (Congo) en África. (p. 9)

Korean War [Guerra de Corea] *s.* guerra de 1950 a 1953 entre Corea del Norte y Corea del Sur; China respaldó a Corea del Norte y las tropas de las Naciones Unidas, integradas en su mayoría por soldados estadounidenses, apoyaron a Corea del Sur. (p. 615)

Kristallnacht *s.* noviembre 9 de 1938, noche en que milicianos nazis atacaron viviendas, negocios y sinagogas judías en Alemania. (p. 555)

Ku Klux Klan *s.* sociedad secreta de hombres blancos en los estados sureños después de la Guerra Civil que desató terror para restaurar la supremacía blanca. (p. 199)

La Raza Unida *s.* organización política latina establecida en 1969 por José Ángel Gutiérrez. (p. 762)

League of Nations [Liga de las Naciones] *s.* organización internacional establecida en 1920 para promover la cooperación y la paz internacional. (p. 418)

Lend-Lease Act [Ley de Préstamo y Alquiler] *s.* ley, promulgada en 1941, que autorizó al gobierno a mandar armas y otros productos, sin pago inmediato, a las naciones que luchaban contra el Eje. (p. 561)

Limited Test Ban Treaty [Tratado de Limitación de Pruebas Nucleares] *s.* tratado de 1963 en que Estados Unidos y la Unión Soviética acordaron no realizar pruebas de armas nucleares en la atmósfera. (p. 676)

Linotype machine [linotipia] *s.* máquina de composición tipográfica que funde los caracteres por líneas completas, formando un solo bloque, no letra por letra. (p. 302)

literacy test [prueba de lectura] *s.* examen de lectura que se usaba en algunos estados sureños para impedir que los afroamericanos votaran. (p. 310)

long drive [arreo de ganado] *s.* proceso mediante el cual los vaqueros llevaban por tierra ganado hacia el mercado. (p. 226)

longhorn *s.* resistente raza de ganado vacuno de cuernos largos llevada por los españoles a México, muy apta para las condiciones de esa región. (p. 222)

Louisiana Purchase [Compra de Louisiana] *s.* compra de terrenos a Francia por 15 millones de dólares en 1803 de las tierras desde el río Mississippi hasta las montañas Rocosas. (p. 119)

Lowell textile mills [fábrica de textiles de Lowell] *s.* fábrica de textiles de Lowell, Massachusetts, del siglo 19; empleaba principalmente a trabajadoras jóvenes. (p. 147)

Loyalist [realista] *s.* colono que apoyaba al gobierno británico durante la Revolución Norteamericana. (p. 59)

Lusitania *s.* barco británico de pasajeros que se hundió cerca a costas irlandesas el 7 de mayo de 1915, tras ser atacado por un submarino alemán. (p. 399)

M

magnetic resonance imaging [imágenes por resonancia magnética] *s.* tecnología que utilizan los médicos para obtener imágenes de cortes transversales de cualquier parte del cuerpo humano. (p. 862)

mail-order catalog [catálogo por correo] *s.* folleto de mercancías que se pueden pedir y recibir por correo. (p. 321)

mandate [mandato] *s.* conquista de una porción suficientemente grande del voto, que indica que un líder elegido tiene apoyo popular para sus programas. (p. 678)

Manhattan Project [Proyecto Manhattan] *s.* programa estadounidense que se inició en 1942 con el fin de diseñar una bomba atómica para la II Guerra Mundial. La primera detonación atómica completa ocurrió en Alamogordo, New Mexico, el 16 de julio de 1945. (p. 590)

manifest destiny [destino manifiesto] *s.* término usado en la década de 1840 para describir la creencia de que Estados Unidos estaba inexorablemente destinado a adquirir más territorio, especialmente mediante su expansión hacia el oeste. (p. 133)

Marbury* v. *Madison *s.* caso de 1803 en que la Suprema Corte decidió que tenía el poder de abolir decretos legislativos declarándolos inconstitucionales; ese poder se conoce como revisión judicial. (p. 119)

market revolution [revolución mercantil] *s.* gran cambio económico que llevó a comprar y vender productos en lugar de hacerlos en el hogar. (p. 144)

Marshall Plan [Plan Marshall] *s.* plan formulado por el Secretario de Estado George Marshall en 1947, mediante el que se ofreció ayuda a países europeos con el fin de reparar los daños de la II Guerra Mundial. (p. 610)

mass media [medios informativos] *s.* medios de comunicación —tales como televisión, prensa y radio— que llegan a grandes audiencias. (p. 652)

McCarthyism [macartismo] *s.* ataques, a menudo sin respaldo, del senador Joseph McCarthy y otros contra presuntos comunistas en los años 50. (p. 623)

Meat Inspection Act [Ley de Inspección de la Carne] *s.* ley de 1906 que establecía estrictos requisitos sanitarios en las empacadoras de carne, así como un programa federal de inspección de carnes. (p. 345)

mechanized warfare [guerra mecanizada] *s.* guerra de máquinas con motores de gasolina y diesel. (p. 406)

Medicaid *s.* programa federal que se inició en 1965 para brindar atención médica a las personas que reciben ayuda pública. (p. 686)

Medicare *s.* programa federal que se inició en 1965 para brindar seguros médicos y de hospitalización a bajo costo a los mayores de 65 años. (p. 686)

melting pot [crisol de culturas] *s.* mezcla de personas de diferentes culturas y razas que se amalgaman y abandonan su idioma y cultura natal. (p. 278)

mercantilism [mercantilismo] *s.* sistema económico en que un país aumenta su riqueza y poder al incrementar su posesión de oro y plata, y al exportar más productos de los que importa. (p. 30)

mestizo *adj.* con mezcla de español e indígena. (p. 18)

middle passage [travesía intermedia] *s.* tramo de África a las Antillas; parte del triángulo comercial de esclavos. (p. 34)

militarism [militarismo] *s.* política de mantener una sólida organización militar como preparación agresiva para la guerra. (p. 395)

Miranda rights [derechos Miranda] *s.* derechos de un acusado, que estableció la decisión de la Suprema Corte *Miranda* v. *Arizona* de 1966; incluyen el derecho a guardar silencio hasta disponer de un abogado. (p. 689)

Missouri Compromise [Acuerdo de Missouri] *s.* serie de leyes de 1820 para mantener un equilibrio seccional entre los estados esclavistas y los estados libres. (p. 127)

monopoly [monopolio] *s.* control completo de una industria que se logra al comprar o arruinar a los competidores. (p. 259)

Monroe Doctrine [Doctrina Monroe] *s.* declaración del presidente Monroe en 1823 que establecía que Estados Unidos no permitiría la interferencia europea en los asuntos del Hemisferio Occidental. (p. 123)

Moral Majority [Mayoría Moral] *s.* coalición política de organizaciones religiosas conservadoras en los años 70 y 80 que recaudó dinero para respaldar agendas y

980 Spanish Glossary

candidatos conservadores, y condenó actitudes y comportamientos liberales. (p. 820)

Morrill Land Grant Acts [Leyes Morrill de Concesión de Tierras] *s.* leyes aprobadas en 1862 y 1890 que otorgaban tierras federales a los estados para financiar universidades agrícolas. (p. 233)

muckracker *s.* uno de los reporteros de revistas que desenmascaraban el lado corrupto de las empresas y de la vida pública a principios del siglo 20. (p. 332)

Munn v. Illinois *s.* caso de la Suprema Corte en 1877; estableció el derecho del gobierno federal a regular la industria privada en beneficio del interés público. (p. 256)

N

NAACP *s.* National Association for the Advancement of Colored People (Asociación Nacional para el Avance de la Gente de Color), organización fundada en 1909 y dedicada a la igualdad racial. (p. 347)

NACW *s.* National Association of Colored Women (Asociación Nacional de Mujeres de Color), organización de servicio social fundada en 1896. (p. 339)

NAFTA *s.* North American Free Trade Agreement (Tratado de Libre Comercio, TLC), tratado de 1993 que redujo aranceles e incorporó a México en la zona de libre comercio ya vigente entre Estados Unidos y Canadá. (p. 848)

napalm *s.* sustancia incendiaria de gasolina que lanzaban los aviones estadounidenses en Vietnam, con el fin de incendiar la selva y revelar los escondites del Vietcong. (p. 732)

National Energy Act [Ley Nacional de Energía] *s.* ley promulgada durante la administración Carter para aliviar la crisis energética; aplicó impuestos a los autos que usan gasolina de manera ineficiente y suspendió el control de precios del petróleo y el gas natural estadounidenses. (p. 803)

National Industrial Recovery Act [Ley Nacional de Recuperación Industrial] *s.* ley aprobada en 1933 que establecía agencias para supervisar industrias y suministrar empleos. (p. 508)

National Labor Relations Board [Junta Nacional de Relaciones Laborales] *s.* agencia creada en 1935 con el fin de prevenir prácticas laborales injustas y mediar en disputas laborales. (p. 531)

National Organization for Women [Organización Nacional de la Mujer] *s.* organización fundada en 1966 con el fin de impulsar metas feministas, tales como mejores guarderías, mayores oportunidades educativas y el fin de la discriminación laboral. (p. 770)

National Trades' Union [Unión Nacional de Sindicatos] *s.* primera asociación nacional de sindicatos, creada en 1834. (p. 149)

National Youth Administration [Administración Nacional de Recursos para la Juventud] *s.* programa que suministraba ayuda y empleos a jóvenes durante la Depresión. (p. 513)

Nation of Islam [Nación del Islam] *s.* grupo religioso, popularmente conocido como musulmanes negros, fundado por Elijah Muhammad para promover el separatismo negro y la religión islámica. (p. 713)

Navigation Acts [Leyes de Navegación] *s.* serie de leyes aprobadas a partir de 1651 que imponían un control más rígido del comercio en las colonias inglesas. (p. 31)

NAWSA *s.* National American Woman Suffrage Association (Asociación Nacional Americana del Sufragio Femenino), creada en 1890 para obtener derechos electorales para la mujer. (p. 339)

Nazism [nazismo] *s.* movimiento político basado en un extremo nacionalismo, racismo y expansionismo militar; instituido en Alemania como sistema de gobierno por Adolfo Hitler en 1933. (p. 544)

Neutrality Acts [Leyes de Neutralidad] *s.* serie de leyes aprobadas por el Congreso en 1935 y 1936 que prohibieron la venta y el alquiler de armas a naciones en guerra. (p. 546)

New Deal *s.* medidas económicas y políticas adoptadas por el presidente Franklin Roosevelt en los años 30 para promover recuperación económica, ayuda a los necesitados y reforma financiera. (p. 505)

New Deal Coalition [Coalición del New Deal] *s.* alianza temporal de distintos grupos, tales como blancos sureños, afroamericanos y sindicalistas, que apoyaban al Partido Demócrata en los años 30 y 40. (p. 520)

New Federalism [Nuevo Federalismo] *s.* programa del presidente Richard Nixon para distribuir una porción del poder del gobierno federal a gobiernos estatales y locales. (p. 786)

New Frontier [Nueva Frontera] *s.* agenda legislativa del presidente John F. Kennedy; tenía medidas de atención médica para ancianos, renovación urbana y apoyo a la educación, que fueron rechazadas por el Congreso, así como medidas que sí se aprobaron de defensa nacional, ayuda internacional y programas espaciales. (p. 678)

New Left [Nueva Izquierda] *s.* movimiento político juvenil de los años 60 con organizaciones como Students for a Democratic Society (Estudiantes por una Sociedad Democrática) y el Free Speech Movement (Movimiento de Libre Expresión). (p. 737)

New Right [Nueva Derecha] *s.* alianza política de grupos conservadores de fines del siglo 20, con énfasis en asuntos culturales, sociales y morales. (pp. 772, 819)

Nineteenth Amendment [Enmienda 19] *s.* enmienda a la Constitución adoptada en 1920 que le otorga a la mujer el derecho de votar. (p. 358)

Nisei *s.* ciudadano estadounidense de padres inmigrantes japoneses. (p. 575)

no man's land [tierra de nadie] *s.* en la I Guerra Mundial, extensión baldía de tierra entre trincheras de ejércitos enemigos. (p. 397)

nonaggression pact [pacto de no agresión] *s.* acuerdo entre dos naciones de no luchar entre sí. (p. 551)

North Atlantic Treaty Organization (NATO) [Organización del Tratado del Atlántico Norte] *s.* alianza militar defensiva formada en 1949 por diez países de Europa del oeste, Estados Unidos y Canadá. (p. 612)

Northwest Ordinance of 1787 [Ordenanza del Noroeste de 1787] *s.* procedimiento para la admisión de nuevos estados a la Unión. (p. 69)

nullification [anulación] *s.* rechazo de un estado a reconocer cualquier ley del Congreso que considere inconstitucional. (p. 83)

Nuremberg trials [juicios de Nuremberg] *s.* juicios llevados a cabo en Nuremberg, Alemania, inmediatamente después de la II Guerra Mundial, a líderes nazis por sus crímenes de guerra. (p. 592)

O

Office of Price Administration (OPA) [Oficina de Administración de Precios] *s.* agencia establecida por el Congreso durante la II Guerra Mundial con facultad para combatir la inflación al congelar los precios de la mayoría de los artículos. (p. 576)

Ohio gang [pandilla de Ohio] *s.* amigos y partidarios políticos del presidente Warren G. Harding, a quienes éste nombró a su gabinete. (p. 439)

OPEC *s.* Organization of Petroleum Exporting Countries (Organización de Países Exportadores de Petróleo, OPEP), alianza económica para ejercer influencia sobre los precios del petróleo. (p. 790)

Open Door notes [notas de Puertas Abiertas] *s.* notas que el Secretario de Estado John Hay envió a Gran Bretaña, Francia, Alemania, Italia, Japón y Rusia, instándolos a no interponerse en el comercio de Estados Unidos y China. (p. 379)

Operation Desert Storm [Operación Tormenta del Desierto] *s.* operación militar en la que fuerzas de las Naciones Unidas, encabezadas por Estados Unidos, liberaron a Kuwait y derrotaron al ejército iraquí. (p. 840)

Oregon Trail [Sendero de Oregon] *s.* camino que va de Independence, Missouri, a Portland, Oregon. (p. 134)

P

Panama Canal [canal de Panamá] *s.* canal artificial construido a través del istmo de Panamá para abrir paso entre los océanos Atlántico y Pacífico; se abrió en 1914. (p. 384)

parity [paridad] *s.* regulación de precios de ciertos productos agrícolas, apoyada por el gobierno, con el fin de mantener estables los ingresos agrícolas. (p. 532)

Patriot [patriota] *s.* colono que apoyaba la independencia norteamericana de Gran Bretaña. (p. 59)

patronage [clientelismo] *s.* sistema de otorgar empleos a personas que ayudan a la elección de un candidato. (p. 291)

pay equity [equidad salarial] *s.* sistema que basa el salario de un empleado en los requisitos del trabajo y no en escalas salariales tradicionales, que normalmente pagan menos a la mujer. (p. 831)

Payne-Aldrich Tariff [Arancel Payne-Aldrich] *s.* serie de reglamentos de impuestos, aprobados por el Congreso en 1909, que no logró reducir mucho los aranceles de productos manufacturados. (p. 351)

Peace Corps [Cuerpo de Paz] *s.* programa fundado en 1965 bajo iniciativa del presidente Kennedy, que envía voluntarios a las naciones en desarrollo de Asia, África y Latinoamérica para ayudar en escuelas, clínicas y otros proyectos. (p. 679)

Pendleton Act [Ley Pendleton] *s.* ley de 1883 que autorizaba nombrar empleados del servicio civil por mérito. (p. 292)

Pentagon Papers [Documentos del Pentágono] *s.* documento de 7,000 páginas que dejó filtrar a la prensa en 1971 el antiguo funcionario del Departamento de Defensa Daniel Ellsberg, donde se revela que el gobierno mintió sobre sus planes en la Guerra de Vietnam. (p. 750)

perestroika *s.* palabra rusa para designar la reestructuración económica y burocrática de la Unión Soviética que tuvo lugar en los años 80. (p. 836)

planned obsolescence [obsolencia planeada] *s.* diseño de artículos que se desgastan o pasan de moda muy pronto, para crear la necesidad de remplazarlos con frecuencia. (p. 649)

Platt Amendment [Enmienda Platt] *s.* serie de medidas que obligaba a Cuba a aceptar la intervención de Estados Unidos y el establecimiento de estaciones navales y carboníferas estadounidenses en sus puertos. (p. 377)

Plessy* v. *Ferguson *s.* caso de 1986 en que la Suprema Corte declaró legal la separación de razas en instalaciones públicas y estableció la doctrina de "separados aunque iguales". (p. 311)

political machine [maquinaria política] *s.* grupo organizado que controla un partido político en una ciudad y ofrece servicios a los votantes y negocios a cambio de apoyo político y financiero. (p. 288)

poll tax [impuesto para votar] *s.* impuesto anual que los ciudadanos debían pagar en algunos estados sureños para poder votar. (p. 310)

Populism [populismo] *s.* movimiento político de finales del siglo 19 que representaba los intereses de los granjeros y promovía una reforma del sistema monetario. (p. 236)

price support [apoyo de precios] *s.* apoyo de los precios de ciertos artículos al valor del mercado o por encima, algunas veces mediante la compra de excedentes por parte del gobierno. (p. 483)

Proclamation of 1763 [Proclama de 1763] *s.* decreto británico que prohibía que los colonos se instalaran al oeste de los montes Apalaches. (p. 41)

progressive movement [movimiento progresista] *s.* movimiento reformista de comienzos del siglo 20 cuyos objetivos eran mejorar el bienestar social, promover la moralidad, incrementar la justicia económica y devolver a la ciudadanía el control del gobierno. (p. 330)

prohibition [prohibición] *s.* prohibición de bebidas alcohólicas. (p. 331)

protective tariff [arancel proteccionista] *s.* impuesto aplicado a productos importados para proteger las empresas nacionales de la competencia extranjera. (p. 80)

protectorate [protectorado] *s.* nación cuyo gobierno y asuntos son controlados por una potencia más fuerte. (p. 377)

Pueblo *s.* amerindios descendientes de los anasazi; viven en los desiertos del Suroeste. (p. 6)

Pure Food and Drug Act [Ley de Pureza de Alimentos y Drogas] *s.* ley de 1906 que paró la venta de alimentos y drogas contaminadas y demandó etiquetas fidedignas. (p. 345)

Puritan [puritano] *s.* miembro de la Iglesia Anglicana que deseaba eliminar las tradiciones católicas y simplificar los servicios religiosos. (p. 26)

Q

Quaker [cuáquero] *s.* miembro de una secta religiosa considerada radical en el siglo 17, también conocida como Sociedad de Amigos. (p. 29)

quota system [sistema de cuotas] *s.* sistema que limita el número de inmigrantes de varios países que pueden ser admitidos a Estados Unidos cada año. (p. 439)

R

ragtime *s.* estilo de música que surgió en 1880 combinando la música espiritual negra y la música europea. (p. 317)

ratification [ratificación] *s.* aprobación oficial de la Constitución, o de una enmienda, por parte de los estados. (p. 71)

rationing [racionamiento] *s.* medida tomada durante tiempos de guerra para limitar la cantidad de ciertos alimentos y otros productos que cada persona puede comprar. (p. 576)

Reaganomics [reaganomía] *s.* nombre dado a la política económica del presidente Reagan, que abogaba por una gran reducción en los impuestos con el fin de incrementar la inversión privada y por consiguiente expandir el suministro de productos y servicios. (p. 822)

realpolitik *s.* enfoque de política exterior, identificado con Henry Kissinger y Richard Nixon, que propone hacer lo que resulte realista y práctico en lugar de seguir una política al pie de la letra. (p. 791)

reapportionment [nueva repartición] *s.* redistribución de distritos electorales cuando cambia el número de personas en un distrito. (p. 688)

recall [destitución] *s.* reforma gubernamental que permite a los votantes deponer a funcionarios públicos elegidos. (p. 336)

Reconstruction [Reconstrucción] *s.* período de reconstrucción después de la Guerra Civil y readmisión a la Unión de los estados de la Confederación que habían sido derrotados; de 1865 a 1877. (p. 192)

Reconstruction Finance Corporation [Corporación Financiera de la Reconstrucción] *s.* organización establecida en 1932 para dar financiación de emergencia a bancos, aseguradoras de vida, compañías ferroviarias y otras empresas grandes. (p. 498)

referendum [referendo] *s.* procedimiento que permite someter al voto popular propuestas legislativas. (p. 336)

Reformation [Reforma] *s.* movimiento religioso en la Europa de comienzos del siglo 16, encaminado a reformar la Iglesia Católica Romana; condujo a la formación del protestantismo. (p. 11)

reparations [reparación] *s.* compensación que paga una nación derrotada en una guerra por las pérdidas económicas del vencedor o por crímenes cometidos contra individuos. (p. 418)

republic [república] *s.* gobierno en el que los ciudadanos mandan por medio de sus representantes elegidos. (p. 68)

revenue sharing [distribución de rentas] *s.* plan puesto en práctica en 1972 que faculta a los gobiernos estatales y locales a invertir el dinero federal a su conveniencia. (p. 786)

reverse discrimination [discriminación a la inversa] *s.* tratamiento injusto de los miembros de un grupo mayoritario, típicamente hombres blancos, como resultado de los esfuerzos por remediar la discriminación contra otros grupos. (p. 819)

rock 'n' roll *s.* forma de música popular, caracterizada por ritmos fuertes y letras simples, que surgió de la música "rhythm and blues" y la música "country" durante los años 50. (p. 656)

Roosevelt Corollary [Corolario de Roosevelt] *s.* declaración de 1904 del presidente Theodore Roosevelt en que advertía que Estados Unidos intervendría militarmente en los asuntos de cualquier nación del Hemisferio Occidental para proteger sus intereses económicos si fuera necesario. (p. 384)

Rough Riders *s.* regimiento de caballería voluntario comandado por Leonard Wood y Theodore Roosevelt en la Guerra Española-Norteamericana-Cubana. (p. 373)

row house [casa de conjunto] *s.* vivienda familiar que comparte sus paredes laterales con otras casas similares. (p. 284)

rural free delivery [correo rural gratuito] *s.* entrega gubernamental gratis de correo y paquetes a zonas rurales; se inició en 1896. (p. 321)

S

SALT I Treaty [Tratado Salt I] *s.* acuerdo de cinco años entre Estados Unidos y la Unión Soviética que surgió de las Conversaciones sobre Limitación de Armas Estratégicas de 1972; limitó el número de misiles balísticos intercontinentales y de misiles de submarinos. (p. 792)

Sand Creek Massacre [Masacre de Sand Creek] *s.* ataque en 1864 a una aldea cheyenne en el Territorio de Colorado por parte de soldados del ejército federal, en el que murieron 200 hombres, mujeres y niños. (p. 217)

Sandinista *adj.* relativo a las fuerzas izquierdistas que derrocaron al gobierno nicaragüense en 1979; el presidente Reagan, quien respaldaba a la contra anticomunista, se les opuso. (p. 838)

Santa Fe Trail [Sendero de Santa Fe] *s.* camino que va de Independence, Missouri, a Santa Fe, New Mexico. (p. 134)

satellite nation [nación satélite] *s.* país dominado política y económicamente por otro. (p. 609)

Saturday Night Massacre [Masacre de Sábado en la Noche] *s.* nombre dado a la renuncia del procurador general y al despido de su comisionado el 20 de octubre de 1973, después de haberse negado a acatar la orden del presidente Nixon de despedir al fiscal especial en el caso Watergate. (p. 796)

scab [rompehuelgas] *s.* trabajador que no se une a una huelga o que trabaja en remplazo de un huelguista. (p. 267)

scalawag *s.* término despectivo para referirse a los sureños blancos que se unieron al Partido Republicano y apoyaron la Reconstrucción después de la Guerra Civil. (p. 195)

scientific management [administración científica] *s.* aplicación de principios científicos para simplificar y facilitar las tareas laborales. (p. 332)

Scopes trial [juicio de Scopes] *s.* sensacional juicio de 1925 en el que el maestro de biología John T. Scopes fue juzgado por desafiar una ley de Tennessee que prohibía la enseñanza de la evolución. (p. 457)

search-and-destroy mission [misión de búsqueda y destrucción] *s.* ataque militar estadounidense a aldeas de Vietnam del Sur con el fin de erradicar al Vietcong, que solía resultar en la destrucción de la aldea y el desplazamiento de sus habitantes. (p. 732)

secession [secesión] *s.* retiro formal de un estado de la Unión federal. (p. 165)

Second Great Awakening [Segundo Gran Despertar] *s.* movimiento religioso del siglo 19 que ponía énfasis en la responsabilidad individual para lograr la salvación y la superación personal y social. (p. 152)

Securities and Exchange Commission [Comisión de Valores y Cambios] *s.* agencia creada en 1934 para controlar el mercado bursátil y hacer cumplir las leyes que rigen la venta de acciones y bonos. (p. 532)

segregation [segregación] *s.* separación de la gente según su raza. (p. 310)

Selective Service Act [Ley de Servicio Selectivo] *s.* ley aprobada por el Congreso en mayo de 1917 que ordena que todos los hombres se inscriban para el servicio militar obligatorio. (p. 402)

Seneca Falls Convention [convención de Seneca Falls] *s.* convención de derechos femeninos celebrada en 1848 en Seneca Falls, New York. (p. 157)

service sector [sector de servicios] *s.* renglón de la economía que ofrece servicios en vez de productos. (p. 854)

settlement house [casa de beneficencia] *s.* centro comunitario en un barrio pobre que ayudaba a los residentes, particularmente a los inmigrantes. (p. 287)

Seventeenth Amendment [Enmienda 17] *s.* enmienda a la Constitución adoptada en 1913; dispone que los senadores federales sean elegidos por los votantes y no por cuerpos legislativos estatales. (p. 336)

shantytown [tugurio] *s.* vecindario muy pobre. (p. 490)

sharecropping [aparcería] *s.* sistema en el cual se da a los agricultores tierra, semillas, herramientas y alimentos para vivir, así como una parte de la cosecha, por cultivar la tierra. (p. 198)

Shays's Rebellion [Rebelión de Shays] *s.* sublevación de granjeros de Massachusetts en 1787 en protesta por los impuestos. (p. 70)

Sherman Antitrust Act [Ley Antitrust Sherman] *s.* ley contra los monopolios de 1890 que declaró ilegal la formación de consorcios que obstruyeran el libre comercio. (p. 260)

silent majority [mayoría silenciosa] *s.* nombre dado por el presidente Richard Nixon a los estadounidenses moderados que apoyaban silenciosamente su conducción de la Guerra de Vietnam. (p. 748)

sit-in *s.* forma de protesta —iniciada por el Congreso de Igualdad Racial en los años 40 y empleada con frecuencia en los años 60— en la que afroamericanos ingresaban a un lugar segregado, tal como el mostrador de un restaurante, y se negaban a salir hasta que se les sirviera. (p. 702)

Social Darwinism [darvinismo social] *s.* conjunto de creencias políticas y económicas basadas en la teoría del biólogo Charles Darwin sobre la selección natural o supervivencia del más apto; favorecía una competencia libre, no regulada, y creía que los individuos o grupos triunfaban porque eran genéticamente superiores. (p. 258)

Social Gospel movement [movimiento del Evangelio Social] *s.* movimiento de reforma del siglo 19 basado en la noción de que los cristianos tenían la responsabilidad social de mejorar las condiciones laborales y aliviar la pobreza urbana. (p. 287)

socialism [socialismo] *s.* sistema económico y político en el que los medios de producción son propiedad del gobierno; favorece una distribución igual de la riqueza. (p. 265)

Social Security Act [Ley de Seguro Social] *s.* ley aprobada por el Congreso en 1935 para crear un sistema federal de seguros para vejez, desempleo e incapacidad, financiado conjuntamente por empleados, patronos y gobierno. (p. 515)

soddy [choza de tepe] *s.* casa provisional hecha de césped, muy común en las llanuras, donde la madera era escasa. (p. 232)

Songhai *s.* imperio de África occidental en lo que hoy es Malí; su capital fue Tombuctú; alcanzó la cima de su poder hacia 1500. (p. 8)

soup kitchen [comedor de beneficencia] *s.* lugar donde se sirven alimentos gratis a los necesitados, muy común durante la Depresión. (p. 491)

Southern Christian Leadership Conference (SCLC) [Conferencia de Líderes Cristianos del Sur] *s.* organización formada en 1957 por el doctor Martin Luther King, Jr., y otros líderes para promover los derechos civiles sin violencia. (p. 702)

Southern strategy [estrategia sureña] *s.* estrategia del presidente Nixon de apelar a los demócratas conservadores sureños que estaban descontentos con la integración y con una Suprema Corte liberal. (p. 788)

speakeasy *s.* lugar donde se vendían bebidas alcohólicas ilegalmente, como ocurrió durante la Prohibición. (p. 454)

speculation [especulación] *s.* transacciones de alto riesgo con el fin de obtener ganancias rápidas o grandes. (p. 485)

Square Deal *s.* programa de reformas progresistas del presidente Theodore Roosevelt para proteger a la gente común y corriente de las grandes empresas. (p. 342)

stagflation [estanflación] *s.* situación económica en la que hay niveles altos de inflación y desempleo simultáneamente. (p. 790)

Stalwart *s.* republicano seguidor del "jefe" de New York City, Roscoe Conkling, quien favorecía el sistema de prebendas y se oponía a la reforma al servicio civil. (p. 292)

Stamp Act [Ley del Timbre] *s.* primer impuesto directo aplicado en 1765 por Gran Bretaña a una variedad de artículos y servicios, tales como documentos legales y periódicos. (p. 49)

Strateic Defense Initiative (SDI) [Iniciativa para la Defensa Estratégica] *s.* sistema de defensa propuesto en los años 80, popularmente conocido como la Guerra de las Galaxias, cuyo fin era proteger a Estados Unidos de ataques de misiles. (p. 823)

strike [huelga] *s.* interrupción del trabajo para presionar a un patrono a responder a ciertas demandas. (p. 148)

Student Nonviolent Coordinating Committee [Comité Coordinador de Estudiantes no Violentos] *s.* organización fundada en 1961, conocida como SNCC, para coordinar sit-ins y otras protestas, y para darles a los jóvenes negros mayor participación en el movimiento de derechos civiles. (p. 702)

Students for a Democratic Society [Estudiantes por una Sociedad Democrática] *s.* grupo activista de los años 60, conocido como SDS, que urgía una mayor libertad y responsabilidad individual. (p. 737)

suburb [suburbio] *s.* pueblo o comunidad residencial cerca de una ciudad. (p. 636)

suffrage [sufragio] *s.* derecho a votar. (p. 339)

Sugar Act [Ley del Azúcar] *s.* ley británica de 1764 que aplicó un impuesto comercial a la melaza, el azúcar y otras importaciones para reducir el contrabando en las colonias. (p. 48)

supply-side economics [economía de oferta] *s.* teoría económica, practicada por el presidente Ronald Reagan, que sostiene que recortar los impuestos de los ricos beneficia a todos pues aumenta empleos, ahorros e inversiones. (p. 823)

T

Taino *s.* pueblo amerindio que Colón y su tripulación vieron al arribar a la isla hoy conocida como San Salvador, el 12 de octubre de 1492. (p. 14)

Tammany Hall *s.* maquinaria política demócrata que dominaba a New York City a fines del siglo 19. (p. 290)

Teapot Dome scandal [escándalo de Teapot Dome] *s.* escándalo generado cuando Albert Fall, Secretario del Interior del presidente Warren G. Harding, concedió en secreto valiosas reservas de petróleo en Wyoming y California a compañías privadas a cambio de dinero y tierras. (p. 440)

Telecommunications Act [Ley de Telecomunicaciones] *s.* ley de 1996 que retiró las barreras que impedían que un tipo de compañía de comunicaciones ingresara a otro tipo de negocio en el mismo campo. (p. 861)

telecommute *v.* trabajar desde la casa para una compañía ubicada en otra parte, mediante la nueva tecnología de comunicaciones, como computadoras, modems y máquinas de fax. (p. 867)

tenant farming [agricultura de arrendatarios] *s.* sistema en el que los agricultores, llamados arrendatarios, ponen sus propias herramientas y animales, y pagan dinero por el arriendo de tierra para cultivar. (p. 199)

Tennessee Valley Authority [Autoridad del Valle de Tennessee] *s.* corporación federal creada en 1933 para construir presas y centrales eléctricas en la región del valle de Tennessee. (p. 533)

termination policy [política de terminación] *s.* programa del gobierno federal en 1953 de cesar su responsabilidad hacia las naciones amerindias y eliminar el apoyo económico federal, suspender el sistema de reservaciones y redistribuir las tierras tribales. (p. 663)

Tet offensive [ofensiva de Tet] *s.* sorpresivo ataque masivo del Vietcong a pueblos y ciudades de Vietnam del Sur a comienzos de 1968; la batalla, de un mes de duración, convenció a muchos estadounidenses de que no era posible ganar la guerra. (p. 741)

Texas Revolution [Revolución de Texas] *s.* rebelión de 1836 con la que Texas se independizó de México. (p. 137)

Thirteenth Amendment [Enmienda 13] *s.* enmienda a la Constitución, ratificada en 1865, que abolía la esclavitud y la servidumbre involuntaria. (p. 190)

Tiananmen Square [plaza Tianamen] *s.* lugar de protestas estudiantiles en 1989 en Beijing, China, por la falta de libertades democráticas, donde el gobierno atacó a los estudiantes. (p. 838)

Tonkin Gulf Resolution [Resolución del Golfo de Tonkin] *s.* resolución aprobada por el Congreso en 1964 que le otorgaba al presidente Johnson amplios poderes para la Guerra de Vietnam. (p. 728)

totalitarian [totalitario] *adj.* característico de un sistema político en que el gobierno ejerce completo control sobre la vida de los ciudadanos. (p. 544)

trade imbalance [déficit comercial] *s.* situación económica en la que un país importa más de lo que exporta. (p. 824)

Trail of Tears [Sendero de las Lágrimas] *s.* marcha obligada del pueblo cherokee desde Georgia hasta el Territorio Indio en 1838, durante la cual murieron miles. (p. 129)

transcendentalism [trascendentalismo] *s.* movimiento filosófico y literario que proponía llevar una vida sencilla y celebrar la verdad implícita de la naturaleza, la emoción personal y la imaginación. (p. 153)

transcontinental railroad [ferrocarril transcontinental] *s.* línea férrea finalizada en 1869 que unía la costa Atlántica y la costa Pacífica. (p. 252)

Treaty of Guadalupe Hidalgo [Tratado de Guadalupe Hidalgo] *s.* tratado de 1848 que puso fin a la guerra entre Estados Unidos y México, mediante el cual Estados Unidos obtuvo enormes tierras en el Oeste y el Suroeste. (p. 140)

Treaty of Paris [Tratado de París] *s.* tratado de 1783 que puso fin a la Guerra Revolucionaria Norteamericana y estableció las fronteras de la nueva nación. (p. 64)

Treaty of Tordesillas [Tratado de Tordesillas] *s.* tratado de 1494 que dividió las Américas entre España y Portugal mediante una línea vertical imaginaria en el Atlántico; cada país tenía poder sobre un lado de la línea. (p. 16)

Treaty of Versailles [Tratado de Versalles] *s.* tratado que puso fin a la I Guerra Mundial, firmado el 28 de junio de 1919. (p. 418)

trench warfare [guerra de trincheras] *s.* guerra en que los combatientes atacan desde un sistema de zanjas fortificadas y no en un campo abierto de batalla. (p. 397)

triangular trade [triángulo comercial de esclavos] *s.* red de rutas de África a las Antillas, las colonias norteamericanas, Inglaterra o Europa para traficar esclavos africanos y comerciar productos tales como ron y melaza. (p. 34)

Truman Doctrine [Doctrina Truman] *s.* declaración del presidente Truman en 1947, que establecía que Estados Unidos debía dar apoyo económico y militar para liberar a naciones amenazadas por fuerzas internas o externas. (p. 610)

trust *s.* método de unir compañías competidoras, en que los participantes entregan sus acciones a una junta única que maneja las distintas compañías como una sola corporación. (p. 259)

Tweed Ring *s.* grupo de políticos corruptos de New York encabezados por William Marcy "Boss" Tweed; le robaron a la ciudad cerca de $200 millones entre 1869 y 1871. (p. 290)

Twenty-seventh Amendment [Enmienda 27] *s.* enmienda a la Constitución, adoptada en 1992, que pospone los aumentos salariales que se aprueba el Congreso hasta después de las siguientes elecciones. (p. 847)

two-party system [bipartidismo] *s.* sistema político dominado por dos partidos. (p. 80)

UV

Underground Railroad [Ferrocarril Subterráneo] *s.* red secreta de personas que ayudaban a los esclavos fugitivos a escapar a lo largo de diversas rutas hacia Canadá o hacia zonas seguras en los estados libres. (p. 166)

Unitarian [unitario] *s.* miembro de un grupo religioso que destaca la razón y la fe en el individuo. (p. 153)

United Farm Workers Organizing Committee [Comité Organizador de Trabajadores Agrícolas Unidos] *s.* sindicato establecido en 1966 por César Chávez para mejorar los salarios y las condiciones laborales de los trabajadores agrícolas. (p. 762)

United Nations (UN) [Naciones Unidas] *s.* organización internacional promotora de la paz a la que pertenecen la mayoría de naciones, fundada en 1945 para fomentar la paz, la seguridad y el desarrollo económico del mundo. (p. 592)

urban flight [huida urbana] *s.* migración de las ciudades a los suburbios aledaños. (p. 866)

urbanization [urbanización] *s.* movimiento de personas a una ciudad. (p. 282)

urban renewal [renovación urbana] *s.* práctica que se inició con la Ley Nacional de Vivienda de 1949, de remplazar vecindarios urbanos derruidos por viviendas nuevas para gente de bajos recursos. (p. 661)

urban sprawl [explosión urbana] *s.* expansión desordenada y desmedida de las ciudades a las áreas aledañas. (p. 442)

U.S.S. *Maine* *s.* buque de guerra estadounidense que explotó y naufragó misteriosamente el 15 de febrero de 1898 en el puerto de La Habana, Cuba. (p. 372)

U-2 incident [incidente del U-2] *s.* derribo en 1960 de un avión espía estadounidense U-2 en suelo soviético; complicó las conversaciones de paz entre Estados Unidos y la Unión Soviética. (p. 629)

vaudeville [teatro de variedades] *s.* espectáculo popular de tablas con una variedad de canciones, bailes y comedias. (p. 317)

V-E Day [Día V-E] *s.* mayo 8 de 1945, día de la victoria europea, cuando el general Eisenhower aceptó la rendición incondicional de Alemania; puso fin a la II Guerra Mundial en Europa. (p. 585)

vertical integration [integración vertical] *s.* proceso mediante el cual una compañía se adueña de sus proveedores y distribuidores, con lo que obtiene control total sobre la calidad y el costo de su producción. (p. 258)

Vietcong *s.* rebeldes comunistas de Vietnam del Sur apoyados por Vietnam del Norte a partir de 1959. (p. 726)

Vietminh [Vietmin] *s.* organización de comunistas vietmanitas y otros grupos nacionalistas que luchó contra los franceses por la independencia de Vietnam de 1946 a 1954. (p. 725)

Vietnamization [vietnamización] *s.* plan del presidente Nixon de retiro gradual de las tropas estadounidenses de Vietnam y su remplazo por el ejército vietnamita. (p. 748)

Voting Rights Act of 1965 [Ley de Derechos Electorales de 1965] *s.* ley para facilitarles a los afroamericanos inscribirse para votar; eliminó las pruebas discriminatorias de lectura y escritura, y autorizó a los examinadores federales inscribir votantes rechazados a nivel local. (p. 710)

W

Wagner Act [Ley Wagner] *s.* ley—también conocida como Ley Nacional de Relaciones Laborales—promulgada en 1935 para proteger los derechos de los trabajadores después de que la Corte Suprema consideró la Ley Nacional de Recuperación Industrial (NIRA) era inconstitucional. (p. 514)

war-guilt clause [cláusula de culpabilidad] *s.* cláusula del Tratado de Versalles que obligaba a Alemania a reconocer que había sido única responsable de la I Guerra Mundial. (p. 418)

war hawk [halcón] *s.* congresista de principios del siglo 19 a favor de la guerra con Gran Bretaña. (p. 121)

War Industries Board [Junta de Industrias Bélicas] *s.* junta establecida en 1917 que animaba a las compañías a usar técnicas de producción en masa para mejorar la eficiencia durante la I Guerra Mundial. (p. 410)

War Powers Act [Ley de Poderes de Guerra] *s.* ley aprobada en 1973 tras la Guerra de Vietnam que limitaba el derecho de un presidente a enviar tropas a combatir sin consultar con el Congreso. (p. 753)

War Production Board [Junta de Producción Bélica] *s.* agencia establecida durante la II Guerra Mundial para coordinar la producción de suministros militares por la industria nacional. (p. 576)

Warren Commission [Comisión Warren] *s.* grupo encabezado por Earl Warren, presidente de la Suprema Corte, que realizó la investigación oficial del asesinato del presidente Kennedy y concluyó que Lee Harvey Oswald había actuado por su cuenta. (p. 682)

Warren Court [la Corte Warren] *s.* la Suprema Corte de la que fue presidente Earl Warren, que se destacó por sus actividades en torno a los derechos civiles y la libre expresión. (p. 688)

Warsaw Pact [Pacto de Varsovia] *s.* alianza militar formada en 1955 por la Unión Soviética y las naciones satélite de Europa del este. (p. 626)

Watergate *s.* serie de escándalos en que el presidente Nixon trató de encubrir la participación de su comité de relección en el allanamiento de la sede del Partido Demócrata, en los apartamentos Watergate, en 1972. (p. 793)

web-perfecting press [prensa de bobina] *s.* prensa eléctrica que imprime a ambos lados de un rollo de papel y luego corta, dobla y cuenta las páginas. (p. 301)

Woodstock *s.* festival gratuito de música que atrajo a más de 400,000 jóvenes a una granja del estado de New York en agosto de 1969. (p. 776)

Works Progress Administration [Administración para el Progreso de Obras] *s.* agencia gubernamental del New Deal que empleó a personal desocupado en construcción de escuelas y hospitales, reparación de carreteras, enseñanza, escritura y artes. (p. 513)

XYZ

XYZ Affair [Asunto XYZ] *s.* incidente diplomático de 1797 en el que funcionarios franceses trataron de sobornar a funcionarios estadounidenses para entrevistarse con un alto ministro francés. (p. 83)

Yalta Conference [Conferencia de Yalta] *s.* reunión en 1945 de representantes de Estados Unidos, Gran Bretaña y la Unión Soviética, durante la cual se decidió la división de Alemania en cuatro zonas ocupadas, la celebración de elecciones libres en Europa del este y que la Unión Soviética le declarara la guerra a Japón. (p. 592)

yellow journalism [prensa amarillista] *s.* uso de métodos sensacionalistas en periódicos o revistas para atraer o influenciar lectores. (p. 371)

Zimmermann note [nota Zimmermann] *s.* mensaje enviado por el canciller alemán en 1917 al canciller mexicano en el que prometía a México los estados de Texas, New Mexico y Arizona si se aliaba a Alemania en contra de Estados Unidos en la I Guerra Mundial. (p. 401)

Index

An *i* preceding a page number in italics refers to an illustration on the page. An *m* or a *c* preceding a page number in italics refers to a map or a chart on the page.

B

D

F

H

K

L

M

N

S

T

U

XYZ

Skills Index

Boldface page numbers refer to Skillbuilder Handbook sections in which the corresponding skills are discussed.

Critical Thinking Skills

Reading Skills

Using Visuals and Technology

Research, Writing, and Presentation Skills

Portfolio and Citizenship Projects

Acknowledgments

Text Acknowledgments

Chapter 5, page 241: Excerpt from "El Corrido de Gregorio Cortez," from *With His Pistol in His Hands: A Border Ballad and Its Hero* by Américo Paredes. Copyright © 1958, renewed 1986. By permission of the University of Texas Press. By permission of the author and the University of Texas Press.

Chapter 7, page 277: Excerpt from "The Reminiscences of Edward Ferro," Columbia University, Oral History Research Office, 1968. Used with permission.

Chapter 13, page 477: "First Fig" by Edna St. Vincent Millay, from *Collected Poems,* published by HarperCollins. Copyright 1922, 1950 by Edna St. Vincent Millay. Reprinted by permission of Elizabeth Barnett, literary executor.

"Dream Variations," from *Collected Poems* by Langston Hughes. Copyright © 1994 by the Estate of Langston Hughes. Reprinted by permission of Alfred A. Knopf, Inc.

Chapter 14, page 499: Excerpt from "A. Everette McIntyre," from *Hard Times* by Studs Terkel. Copyright © 1970 by Studs Terkel. By permission of Random House, Inc.

Chapter 16, page 554: Excerpt from Gerda Weissmann Klein's interview in the film *One Survivor Remembers,* a production of Home Box Office and the United States Holocaust Museum. By permission of Gary Greenberg for Gerda Weissmann Klein.

Chapter 17, page 570: Excerpts from "Wife's Recorded Message Made Many Long for Home" by Charles Swanson, from *We Pulled Together . . . and Won!* (Reminisce Books). By permission of Charles Swanson.

Chapter 22, page 731: Excerpt from *Dear America: Letters Home from Vietnam,* edited by Bernard Edelman for the New York Vietnam Veterans Memorial Commission. Published originally by W. W. Norton & Company, 1985.

page 738: Excerpt from "Eve of Destruction," words and music by P. F. Sloan. Copyright © 1965 by Duchess Music Corporation. Sole selling agent MCA Music Publishing, a division of MCA Inc. International copyright secured. All rights reserved.

Excerpt from "The Ballad of the Green Berets" by Barry Sadler: Eastaboga Music.

page 747: Excerpt from the epilogue of *Some Even Volunteered* by Alfred S. Bradford. Copyright © 1994 by Alfred S. Bradford. By permission of Greenwood Publishing Group, Inc., Westport, Conn.

Chapter 25, page 834, map: "Migration Patterns: Where Americans Are Going," from *Regional Growth and Decline in the United States* (1978) by Bernard L. Weinstein and Robert E. Firestine. Used by permission of Bernard L. Weinstein, University of North Texas, Denton, Texas.

page 835, graph: "California In- and Outmigrants, 1980–1981 to 1992–1993," from *The Professional Geographer.* Reproduced courtesy of Blackwell Publishers, Inc., Malden, Mass.

page 835, map: "Where Americans Are Moving" by Joseph Spiers, from *Fortune*, August 21, 1995. Copyright © 1995 Time, Inc. All rights reserved.

Chapter 26, page 846: Excerpt from "On the Pulse of Morning" by Maya Angelou. Copyright © 1993 by Maya Angelou. Reprinted by permission of Random House, Inc.

page 858: "Choices" from *Cotton Candy on a Rainy Day* by Nikki Giovanni. Copyright © 1978 by Nikki Giovanni. By permission of William Morrow & Company, Inc.

page 859: Excerpt from *The Joy Luck Club* by Amy Tan. Reprinted by permission of G. P. Putnam's Sons, a division of The Putnam Publishing Group, from *The Joy Luck Club* by Amy Tan. Copyright © 1989 by Amy Tan.

"Four Skinny Trees," from *The House on Mango Street* by Sandra Cisneros. Copyright © 1984 by Sandra Cisneros. Published by Vintage Books, a division of Random House, Inc., and in hardcover by Alfred A. Knopf. Reprinted by permission of Susan Bergholz Literary Services, New York. All rights reserved.

Art Credits

COVER AND FRONTISPIECE

Ben Nighthorse Campbell: AP/Wide World Photos.

Elizabeth Dole: Copyright © 1989 Rick Reinhard/Impact Visuals/PNI.

Barbara Jordan: AP/Wide World Photos.

John F. Kennedy: *John F. Kennedy* (1970), Aaron Shikler. Courtesy of the White House Historical Association.

Dr. Martin Luther King, Jr.: Photo by Howard Sochurek/*Life* Magazine. Copyright © Time, Inc.

Gerda Weissmann Klein: Courtesy of HBO.

Liliuokalani: Culver Pictures.

Maya Lin: Copyright © Richard Howard/Black Star/PNI.

Sandra Day O'Connor: Copyright © 1993 Ron Sachs/Archive Photos/PNI.

Ronald Reagan: Ronald Reagan Presidential Library.

Franklin Delano Roosevelt: Archive Photos.

General Norman Schwarzkopf: Copyright © 1991 David Turnley, Detroit Free Press/Black Star/PNI.

Beverly Scott: Courtesy of Beverly Scott.

ART CREDITS

viii *center* Copyright © National Maritime Museum Picture Library, London; *second from bottom* The Granger Collection, New York; *bottom* AP/Wide World Photos; **ix** *top* Tray depicting Reverend Lemuel Haynes in the pulpit (early 19th century), probably English. Papier maché, 25¹¹⁄₁₆″ × 20¹⁵⁄₁₆″. Museum of Art, Rhode Island School of Design, gift of Miss Lucy T. Aldrich; *second from top, second from bottom, bottom* The Granger Collection, New York; **x** *top, Portrait of a Sioux Man and Woman* (date unknown), Gertrude Käsebier. Copyright © Smithsonian Institution; *second from top* National Museum of American History/Smithsonian Institution; *second from bottom* National Park Service/Statue of Liberty National Monument; *bottom* Culver Pictures; **xi** *top* Corbis-Bettmann; *center, bottom* The Granger Collection, New York; **xii** *top* Copyright © Henry Ford Museum and Greenfield Village, Dearborn, Michigan; *second from top* Fisk University, Nashville, Tennessee; *second from bottom* Conservative Research Department, Conservative Party, London; *bottom, Franklin D. Roosevelt at Hill Top Cottage, with Ruthie Bie and Fala* (1941), Margaret Suckley. Photograph. Franklin D. Roosevelt Library; **xiii** *top* Courtesy of the Spertus Museum, Chicago; *second from bottom* AP/Wide World Photos; *bottom* Courtesy of *TV Guide*; **xiv** *top* Archive Photos; Blank Archives; *second from top* AP/Wide World Photos; *second from bottom* Photo by Sharon Hoogstraten; *bottom* Copyright © John Paul Filo; **xv** *top* Copyright © 1973 Dennis Brack/Black Star; *center* Courtesy of the Ronald Reagan Library; *bottom* Copyright © Uniphoto, Inc.; **xvii** *top left* Reproduced from *Prospectus: The True History of the Beaumont Oil Fields* by Pattillo Higgins. Copyright © 1902 Pattillo Higgins. Courtesy of the estate of Pattillo Higgins; *bottom left* Courtesy of Tony Kahn; *top right* Courtesy of Brigham Young University; *center right* Beinecke Rare Book and Manuscript Library, Yale University; *bottom right* UPI/Corbis-Bettmann; **xviii** *top left, top right* Corbis-Bettmann; *bottom left* National Archives; *bottom right* Courtesy of Bantam Doubleday Books; **xxi** *left* University of Illinois at Chicago Library, Jane Addams Memorial Collection; *center* Culver Pictures; *right, Life* Magazine. Copyright © Time, Inc.; **xxii** *top, Abraham Lincoln* (about 1858), Fetter's Picture Gallery photograph. National Portrait Gallery, Smithsonian Institution/Art Resource, New York; *bottom* The Granger Collection, New York; **xxiii** *left* Corbis-Bettmann; *right* Reproduced from *Dust Bowl Diary* by Ann Marie Low, by permission of the University of Nebraska Press. Copyright © 1984 by the University of Nebraska Press; **xxiv** *left* Magnum Photos; **xxv** *left* AP/Wide World Photos; *right* Copyright © 1985 Steve Leonard/Black Star; **xxvi** *left, center* UPI/Corbis-Bettmann; *right* Corbis-Bettmann; **xxxii** *left* UPI/Corbis-Bettmann; *right* NASA (National Aeronautics and Space Administration); **xxxiii** *left* The Granger Collection, New York; *top right* H. Armstrong Roberts; *bottom right* Photo by Howard Sochurek/*Life* Magazine. Copyright © Time, Inc.; **xxxiv–xxxv** Copyright © 1991 Woodward Payne; **xxxv** Copyright © Hazel Hankin/Stock Boston/PNI.

Chapter 1

xxxvi–1 *Washington Addressing the Constitutional Convention* (1856), Junius Brutus Stearns. Oil on canvas, 37½″ × 54″. Virginia Museum of Fine Arts, Richmond, Virginia, gift of Edgar William and Bernice Chrysler Garbisch. Photo by Ron Jennings, Copyright © Virginia Museum of Fine Arts; **2** *left* Copyright © T. Linck/SuperStock; *right, Portrait of a Man, called Christopher Columbus* (1519), Sebastiano del Piombo. Oil on canvas, 42″ × 34¾″. The Metropolitan Museum of Art, gift of J. Pierpont Morgan, 1900. Copyright © 1979 The Metropolitan Museum of Art; **3** *top left, Benjamin Franklin*, Charles Willson Peale. Historical Society of Pennsylvania; *bottom left* Courtesy of the Department of Library Services, American Museum of Natural History; *right* The Granger Collection, New York; **4** *left* Courtesy Arizona State Museum, University of Arizona, Tucson, Arizona. Copyright © Jerry Jacka, 1996; *right* Phoebe Hearst Museum of Anthropology, University of California at Berkeley; **5** Reconstruction of the Valley of Mexico, Lake Texcoco, and Great Tenochtitlan. Museum of Mexico City. Copyright © C. Lenars/Explorer; **6** Courtesy of the National Museum of the American Indian/Smithsonian Institution #17/6228; **7** The Philbrook Museum of Art, Tulsa, Oklahoma; **8** Copyright © Aldona Sabalis/Photo Researchers, Inc.; **9** *Portrait of a King* (11th–12th century), unknown Yoruba artist. Bronze, height 12³⁄₁₆″. National Commission for Museums and Monuments, Nigeria; **10** Photos by Sharon Hoogstraten; **11** The Granger Collection, New York; **12** The Granger Collection, New York; **13** Copyright © National Maritime Museum Picture Library, London; **14** The Granger Collection, New York; **16** The Granger Collection, New York; **18** The Granger Collection, New York; **19** *Nuestra Señora* (1938), Polly Duncan. Watercolor, colored pencil, graphite, and heightening on paper, 22⅟₁₆″ × 14¹⁵⁄₁₆″. Copyright © Board of Trustees, National Gallery of Art, Washington, D.C.; **20** *left* Copyright © Jim Corwin/Photo Researchers, Inc.; *top center* Copyright © 1994 Bob Schatz/Liaison International; *bottom center* Copyright © United States Postal Service; *top right* Copyright © Paul S. Howell/Liaison International; *bottom right* Copyright © Sylvain Grandadam/Photo Researchers, Inc.; **22** *left* The Granger Collection, New York; *right, Nova Britannia* (1609), Robert Johnson, London, title page (*KC 1609). Rare Books Division, The New York Public Library, Astor, Lenox and Tilden Foundations; **23** The Granger Collection, New York; **24** Kenneth D. Lyons; **25** The Granger Collection, New York; **26** *left* Copyright © Kindra Clineff/The Picture Cube, Inc.; *right* Pilgrim Society, Plymouth, Massachusetts; **27** The Granger Collection, New York; **28** Culver Pictures; **30** *top left*, Silver gorget (about 1757), Joseph Richardson. Historical Society of Pennsylvania; *bottom left, William Penn's Treaty with the Indians* (about 1840), Edward Hicks. Giraudon/Art Resource, New York; *top right* Copyright © 1995 William S. Nawrocki/Nawrocki Stock Photo, Inc; *bottom right* Copyright © 1995 Larry Stevens/Nawrocki Stock Photo, Inc.; **31** Overmantle (mid-18th century), unknown artist. Oil on wood panel from the Moses Marcy House, Old Sturbridge Village, Southbridge, Massachusetts. Photo by Henry E. Peach; **33** Copyright © Taylor Lewis. Courtesy Catherine Fallin, Kerhonkson, New York; **34** *left, Slaves Below Deck of Albanez* (date unknown), Francis Meynell. Copyright © National Maritime Museum Picture Library, London; *right* The Newberry Library, Chicago; **35** The Granger Collection, New York; **36** *SE Prospect of the City of Philadelphia* (1720), Peter Cooper. Library Company of Philadelphia; **37** The Granger Collection, New York; **38** *left, Benjamin Franklin* (about 1785), Joseph Siffred Duplessis. Oil on canvas, 28½″ × 23½″. National Portrait Gallery, Smithsonian Institution, gift of the Morris and Gwendolyn Cafritz Foundation/Art Resource, New York; *right* The Granger Collection, New York; **40** The Granger Collection, New York; **42** *left, Celebrating Couple: General Jackson and His Lady* (date unknown), Reverend H. Young. Pen and watercolor, 10¼″ × 7⅝″. Courtesy, Museum of Fine Arts, Boston (Massachusetts), gift of Maxim Karolik; **42–43** Abby Aldrich Rockefeller Folk Art Center, Williamsburg, Virginia; **43** *top* Abby Aldrich Rockefeller Folk Art Center, Williamsburg, Virginia; *bottom* Library of Congress.

Chapter 2

46 *left* The Granger Collection, New York; *right* National Archives. Photo by Sharon Hoogstraten; **47** *left, right* The Granger Collection, New York; **48** Stock Montage; **49** Rare Books and Manuscripts Division, The New York Public Library, Astor, Lenox and Tilden Foundations; **50** *The Boston Massacre (The Bloody Massacre)* (1770), Paul Revere. Hand-colored engraving, 10¼″ × 9⅛″. The Metropolitan Museum of Art, gift of Mrs. Russell Sage, 1909. Copyright © 1979 The Metropolitan Museum of Art; **51** *left* Courtesy, American Antiquarian Society; *right, A View of the Town of Concord* (about 1775), artist unknown. Oil on canvas. Photograph courtesy of the Concord Museum, Concord, Massachusetts; **53** *Attack on Bunker's Hill, with the Burning of Charles Town* (about 1783), unknown artist. Oil on canvas, 23⅞″ × 30½″ × 1½″ framed. Copyright © 1996 Board of Trustees, National Gallery of Art, Washington, D.C., gift of Edgar William and Bernice Chrysler Garbisch; **54** *top* Library of Congress; *center* The Granger Collection, New York; *bottom* From *The National Archives of the United States* by Herman J. Viola. Photo by Jonathan Wallen. Published by Harry N. Abrams, Inc., New York; **56** *top* The Granger Collection, New York; *bottom* National Archives; **57** Courtesy of the Massachusetts Historical Society; **58** *top* Library of Congress; *bottom* National Archives. Photo by Sharon Hoogstraten; **59** Collection of Mrs. Jackson C. Boswell, Arlington, Virginia. Courtesy of the Frick Art Reference Library; **61** The Granger Collection, New York; **62** *Molly Pitcher at the Battle of Monmouth* (1854), Dennis Malone Carter. Oil on canvas, 42″ × 56″. Courtesy of Fraunces Tavern Museum, New York City, gift of Herbert P. Whitlock, 1913; **64** Photo by Sharon Hoogstraten; **66** *top, Governor and Mrs. Mifflin*, J. S. Copley. The Historical

Society of Pennsylvania; *bottom* Courtesy of the Seneca Falls (New York) Historical Society; **66–67** The Granger Collection, New York; **67** *top* Photo by Sharon Hoogstraten; *bottom* AP/Wide World Photos; **68** Detail of *John Jay, Statesman* (1783–1808), begun by Gilbert Stuart and completed by John Trumbull. National Portrait Gallery, Smithsonian Institution/Art Resource, New York; **70** *top* Stock Montage; *bottom* The Granger Collection, New York; **72** AP/Wide World Photos; **73** Copyright © Sasa Karlj. AP/Wide World Photos; **74** The Granger Collection, New York; **75** Copyright © Susan Walsh. AP/Wide World Photos; **76** Copyright © Tony Stone Images; **77** Clements Library, University of Michigan; **78** The Granger Collection, New York; **79** *left, Alexander Hamilton* (about 1796), James Sharples, the elder. Pastel on paper. National Portrait Gallery, Smithsonian Institution/Art Resource, New York; *right* Corbis-Bettmann; **80** *left* Museum of the City of New York; *right* The Granger Collection, New York; **81** *Taking of the Bastille, 14 July 1789* (late 1700s), unknown artist. Chateau, Versailles, France. Giraudon/Art Resource, New York; **82** *top* Chicago Historical Society; *bottom* Corbis-Bettmann.

The Living Constitution
87 Corbis-Bettmann; **88** The Granger Collection, New York; **91** Copyright © Herblock, from *The Herblock Gallery*, Simon & Schuster, 1968; **96** *top* The Granger Collection, New York; *bottom* AP/Wide World Photos; **99** "The Federal Edifice: On the Erection of the Eleventh Pillar," cartoon from the *Massachusetts Centinel*, August 2, 1788. Courtesy of the New-York Historical Society, New York City; **101** AP/Wide World Photos; **103** AP/Wide World Photos; **104** Corbis-Bettmann; **105** AP/Wide World Photos; **107** *top* AP/Wide World Photos; *bottom* Copyright © Robert E. Daemmrich/ Tony Stone Images; **108** *left* Detail of *Daniel Boardman* (1789), Ralph Earl. Oil on canvas, 81⅝″ × 55¼″. Copyright © 1996 Board of Trustees, National Gallery of Art, Washington, D.C., gift of Mrs. W. Murry Crane; **108–109** Corbis-Bettmann; **109** *top* Copyright © Robert E. Daemmrich/Tony Stone Images; *bottom* FPG International; **111** Vaughn Shoemaker, reprinted with permission, *The Chicago Sun-Times,* Copyright © 1996; **112** Photo by Sharon Hoogstraten; **113** Copyright © David Young-Wolff/ PhotoEdit; **114** Copyright © Michelle Bridwell/PhotoEdit; **115** Copyright © PhotoEdit.

Chapter 3
116 *left* The Granger Collection, New York; *right, Andrew Jackson* (1845), Thomas Sully. Oil on canvas, 20⅜″ × 17¼″. Copyright © 1996 Board of Trustees, National Gallery of Art, Washington, D.C. Andrew W. Mellon Collection; **117** *top left* Detail of *Trail of Tears* (date unknown), Robert Lindneux. Woolaroc Museum, Bartlesville, Oklahoma; *bottom left* Corbis-Bettmann; *right* Courtesy of the Smithsonian Institution, Washington, D.C.; **118** Courtesy of Mrs. V. James Taranik; **119** Detail of *John Marshall, Chief Justice of the United States* (about 1832), William James Hubard. National Portrait Gallery, Smithsonian Institution/Art Resource, New York; **120** *top left* Stock Montage; *bottom left* American Philosophical Society Library; *top right, Mandan Village* (date unknown), Karl Bodmer, from *Travels in the Interior of North America* by Maximilian Prince zu Wied. Yale Collection of Western Americana, Beinecke Rare Book and Manuscript Library, Yale University; *bottom right* National Museum of American History, Smithsonian Institution [75-2348]; **121** The Granger Collection, New York; **124** The Granger Collection, New York; **125** *top, Slater's Mill,* unknown date and artist. Oil on canvas. Smithsonian Institution, Washington, D.C.; *bottom* National Museum of American History, Smithsonian Institution [73-11287]; **128** The Granger Collection, New York; **130** *left, John Caldwell Calhoun* (about 1820), attributed to Charles Bird King. National Portrait Gallery, Smithsonian Institution/Art Resource, New York; *right, Daniel Webster (1782–1852), Statesman* (about 1828), Chester Harding. National Portrait Gallery, Smithsonian Institution/Art Resource, New York; **131** Library of Congress; **133** The Granger Collection, New York; **134** Courtesy, Colorado Historical Society; **137** *Dawn at the Alamo* (1876–1883), Henry Arthur McArdle. Oil on canvas, 7′ × 12′. Texas State Capitol, Austin. Photo courtesy of the State Preservation Board, Austin, Texas; **138** *left* The Granger Collection, New York; *right* Corbis-Bettmann; **141** *left, View of San Francisco (Formerly Yerba Buena)* (1847), Victor Prevost. Oil on canvas, 25″ × 30″. California Historical Society, gift of the Ohio Historical Society; *right* The Bancroft Library, University of California, Berkeley; **142** Copyright © Smithsonian Institution, Washington, D.C.; **142–143** National Archives; **143** *top* Idaho State Historical Society. Photo number 1254-D-1; *bottom* Copyright © Ric Ergenbright Photography; **144** The Granger Collection, New York; **145** The Granger Collection, New York; **146** *left* Courtesy of the Smithsonian Institution, Washington, D.C.; *right* H. Armstrong Roberts; **147** *top* The Granger Collection, New York; *bottom* Photo by Sharon Hoogstraten; **149** *The Bay and Harbor of New York* (about 1855), Samuel Waugh. Oil on canvas, 99⅛″ × 198″. Museum of the City of New York, gift of Mrs. Robert M. Littlejohn; **150** *left* Courtesy George Eastman House, Rochester, New York; *right* American Textile History Museum, Lowell, Massachusetts; **150–151** Library of Congress; **151** *Haymaking* (1864), Winslow Homer. Oil on canvas, 16″ x 11″. Columbus Museum of Art, Ohio, museum purchase, Howald Fund; **152** Historical Society of Pennsylvania, Leon Gardiner Collection; **153** Tray depicting Reverend Lemuel Haynes in the pulpit (early 19th century), probably English. Papier maché, 25¹¹⁄₁₆″ × 20¹⁵⁄₁₆″. Museum of Art, Rhode Island School of Design, gift of Miss Lucy T. Aldrich; **154** The Granger Collection, New York; **155** *left* Massachusetts Commandery, Military Order of the Loyal Legion and the United States Military History Institute, Carlisle, Pennsylvania; *right* Collection of the New-York Historical Society, neg. 48169; **156** The Granger Collection, New York; **157** The Granger Collection, New York; **158** The Granger Collection, New York; **159** *top, Harriet Tubman Series No. 10* (1939–1940), Jacob Lawrence. Casein tempera on gessoed hard board, 17⅞″ × 12″. Courtesy of the Hampton University Museum, Hampton, Virginia; *bottom* Jacket from *Narrative of the Life of Frederick Douglass*. Used by permission of Dell Books, a division of Bantam Doubleday Dell Publishing Group, Inc. Cover art from the National Portrait Gallery, Smithsonian Institution/Art Resource, New York.

Chapter 4
162 *right* The Granger Collection, New York; **163** *left, center* The Granger Collection, New York; **164** The Granger Collection, New York; **167** The Granger Collection, New York; **169** *top, bottom* The Granger Collection, New York; **170** *top* Ontario County (New York) Historical Society; *bottom* The Granger Collection, New York; **171** *left, Stephen Douglas* (about 1860), Mathew Brady. Photograph, albumen silver print, 3⅜″ × 2⅛″. National Portrait Gallery, Smithsonian Institution/Art Resource, New York; *right* The Granger Collection, New York; **174** *left* The Granger Collection, New York; *right* The Library Company of Philadelphia; **174–175** Corbis-Bettmann; **175** Copyright © 1957, Burt Glinn/Magnum Photos; **176** Beverley R. Robinson Collection, United States Naval Academy Museum, Annapolis, Maryland. Accession number 51.7.667; **178** *top, bottom* The Granger Collection, New York; **179** *left, Abraham Lincoln, Sixteenth President of the United States* (1864), William Willard. National Portrait Gallery, Smithsonian Institution/Art Resource, New York; *right* Corbis-Bettmann; **180** Corbis-Bettmann; **181** Chicago Historical Society; **182** The Granger Collection, New York; **183** The Granger Collection, New York; **184** *Mary Boykin Chesnut* (1856), Samuel Osgood. On loan from Serena Williams Miles Van Rensselaer. National Portrait Gallery, Smithsonian Institution/Art Resource, New York; **187** *left, right* Library of Congress; **188** Chicago Historical Society; **189** The Granger Collection, New York; **190** Corbis-Bettmann; **191** *left* Illinois State Historical Library; *right* The Granger Collection, New York; **192** Copyright © 1956, 1978 by Pauli Murray. Reprinted by permission of Frances Collin, literary agent; **193** Culver Pictures; **194** The Granger Collection, New York; **195** *top* Corbis-Bettmann; *bottom* The Granger Collection, New York; **196** *left* Copyright © 1995 Smithsonian Institution; *right* The Granger Collection, New York; **197** *left* Copyright © Tom McCarthy/PhotoEdit; *right* Copyright © 1993 Dennis Brack/Black Star; **199** Culver Pictures; **201** Library of Congress; **204** *The Bay and Harbor of New York* (about 1855), Samuel Waugh. Oil on canvas, 99⅛″ × 198″. Museum of the City of New York, gift of Mrs. Robert M. Littlejohn; **205** *left* Copyright © Sylvain Grandadam/Photo Researchers, Inc.; *right, Taking of the Bastille, 14 July 1789* (late 1700s), unknown artist. Chateau, Versailles, France. Giraudon/Art Resource, New York; **206** *top* The Granger Collection, New York; *bottom* Corbis-Bettmann; **207** *top* Museum of American Political Life, University of Hartford, West Hartford, Connecticut; *bottom, Molly Pitcher at the Battle of Monmouth* (1854), Dennis Malone Carter. Oil on canvas, 42″ × 56″. Courtesy of Fraunces Tavern Museum, New York City, gift of Herbert P. Whitlock, 1913; **208** *top, Slater's Mill,* unknown date and artist. Oil on canvas. Smithsonian Institution,

Art Credits (Cont.)

Washington, D.C.; *bottom* Courtesy of the Smithsonian Institution, Washington, D.C.; **209** The Granger Collection, New York.

Chapter 5

210–211 The Granger Collection, New York; **212** *left, right* The Granger Collection, New York; **213** *top left* Courtesy of the National Museum of the American Indian/Smithsonian Institution #s2336; *bottom left* The Granger Collection, New York; *right* Archive Photos; **214** *left* Copyright © The Detroit Institute of Arts, Founders Society Purchase with funds from Flint Ink Corporation; *right* Courtesy of Brigham Young University; **215** *top* The Granger Collection, New York; *inset, Portrait of a Sioux Man and Woman* (date unknown), Gertrude Käsebier. Photographic History Collection, National Museum of American History, Smithsonian Institution; **216** Kansas State Historical Society, Topeka; **218** *left* The Granger Collection, New York; *right* American Museum of Natural History, New York. Photo by Lee Boltin; **219** *top* Buffalo Bill Historical Center, Cody, Wyoming. Gift of Olin Corporation, Winchester Arms Collection; *bottom* Corbis-Bettmann; **220** T. Ulrich/H. Armstrong Roberts; **222** Montana Historical Society, Helena; **223** *And So, Unemotionally, There Began One of the Wildest and Strangest Journeys Ever Made in Any Land* (date unknown), William Henry David Koerner. Oil on canvas, 22¼″ × 72¼″. Buffalo Bill Historical Center, Cody, Wyoming; **224** Montana Historical Society, Helena; **225** The Granger Collection, New York; **228** *bottom left* Photo by E. A. Hegg. Special Collections Division, University of Washington Libraries, Seattle. Negative number 1312; **228–229** Photo by J. G. Wison. Denver Public Library, Western History Department Collection; **229** *top left, Miners Underground* (1897), unknown photographer. Glass plate negative. Amon Carter Museum, Fort Worth, Texas, Mazzulla Collection; *top right, bottom* Photos by Chuck Lawliss; **230** *Pioneer Woman* (date unknown), Harvey Dunn. Hazel L. Meyer Memorial Library, De Smet, South Dakota; **231** *left* Library of Congress; *right* Kansas State Historical Society, Topeka; **232** The Granger Collection, New York; **234** State Historical Society of North Dakota; **235** Kansas State Historical Society, Topeka; **236** Culver Pictures; **238** Courtesy of the Chicago Tribune/Chicago American Photo File. Copyright © KMTV; **239** The Granger Collection, New York; **240** The Granger Collection, New York; **241** *left* Detail of *Vaquero* (modeled 1980/cast 1990), Luis Jiménez. Cast fiberglass and epoxy. Courtesy of the National Museum of American Art, Smithsonian Institution, Washington, D.C./Art Resource, New York. Gift of Judith and Wilbur L. Ross, Jr.; *right* Photograph by William Stinson Soule, Archives & Manuscripts Division of the Oklahoma Historical Society. Courtesy of the Oklahoma Historical Society (neg. no. 3969).

Chapter 6

244 *top left* Archives of Labor and Urban Affairs, Wayne State University, Detroit, Michigan; *top right* Library of Congress; *bottom center* The Granger Collection, New York; **245** *left* Library of Congress; *right* The Granger Collection, New York; **246** Reproduced from *Prospectus: The True History of the Beaumont Oil Fields* by Pattillo Higgins. Copyright © 1902 Pattillo Higgins. Courtesy of the estate of Pattillo Higgins; **248** *left* National Museum of American History/Smithsonian Institution; *center, right* The Granger Collection, New York; **250** *top left* From the *Atlas of Cuyahoga County, Ohio*, Titus, Simmons and Titus; *bottom left* Western Reserve Historical Society, Cleveland, Ohio; **250–251** From the *Atlas of Cuyahoga County, Ohio*, Titus, Simmons and Titus; **251** *top right* Western Reserve Historical Society, Cleveland, Ohio; *bottom right* Cleveland Public Library/Corbis-Bettmann; **252** *left* Union Pacific Railroad, San Francisco, California; *right* Historic Pullman Foundation Archives, Chicago; **253** *On the Kansas Pacific Railway: Number 8, Roundhouse at Armstrong, Kansas* (date unknown), Robert Benecke. Courtesy, DeGolyer Library, Southern Methodist University, Dallas; **255** The Granger Collection, New York; **256** The Granger Collection, New York; **257** The Granger Collection, New York; **258** *top* Harry Ransom Humanities Research Center, The University of Texas at Austin; *bottom* The Granger Collection, New York; **259** Library of Congress; **260** Library of Congress; **262** The Granger Collection, New York; **263** *top* George Eastman House Collection; *bottom* Photographs and Prints Division, Shomburg Center for Research in Black Culture, The New York Public Library, Astor, Lenox and Tilden Foundations; **264** *left* Courtesy of George Eastman House; *top right* H. Armstrong Roberts; *bottom right* Corbis-Bettmann; **265** *left* Copyright © Lawrence Migdale/Stock Boston; *right* Corbis-Bettmann; **267** The Granger Collection, New York; **268** *top left* Eugene Debs Collection/Tamiment Institute Library, New York University; *top right, bottom* The Granger Collection, New York.

Chapter 7

272 *left* The Granger Collection, New York; *right* Corbis-Bettmann; **273** *left* National Park Service/Statue of Liberty National Monument; *center, right* The Granger Collection, New York; **274** Courtesy of the Fong See family; **276** National Park Service/Statue of Liberty National Monument; **277** *top left* Culver Pictures; *top right* New York Academy of Medicine Library; *bottom right* California Department of Parks and Recreation Photographic Archives; **278** Underwood Photo Archives, San Francisco, California; **280** *inset left, inset bottom right* The Granger Collection, New York; *inset top right* Underwood Photo Archives, San Francisco, California; **280–281** *background* W. Metzen/H. Armstrong Roberts; *foreground* The Granger Collection, New York; **281** *inset top left* H. Armstrong Roberts; *inset bottom left, The Medicine Robe* (1915), Maynard Dixon. Oil on canvas, 40″ × 30″. Buffalo Bill Historical Center, Cody, Wyoming, gift of Mr. and Mrs. Godwin Pelissero; *inset right* Copyright © Bob Daemmrich/Stock Boston/PNI; **282** The Granger Collection, New York; **285** *top right* Library of Congress; *bottom left* The Granger Collection, New York; *bottom right* Corbis-Bettmann; **286** *background* The Granger Collection, New York; *foreground* University of Illinois at Chicago Library, the Jane Addams Memorial Collection; **287** University of Illinois at Chicago Library, the Jane Addams Memorial Collection; **288** Corbis-Bettmann; **290** *top, bottom* The Granger Collection, New York; **291** The Granger Collection, New York; **292** *top, center, bottom* The Granger Collection, New York.

Chapter 8

296 *left* Corbis-Bettmann; *right* The Granger Collection, New York; **297** *top left* Copyright © Smithsonian Institution; *bottom left* The Brooklyn Historical Society; **298** Library of Congress; **299** Library of Congress; **300** *left* "Plan of the Center of the City, Showing the Present Street and Boulevard System," plate 111 from *Plan of Chicago* (1909), Daniel H. Burnham and Edward H. Bennett, Chicago, partnership 1903–1912. Ink and watercolor on paper, 131.1 cm × 102.4 cm. On permanent loan to the Art Institute of Chicago from the City of Chicago, 19.148.1966. Photograph copyright © The Art Institute of Chicago. All rights reserved; *bottom center* The Granger Collection, New York; **301** Copyright © Smithsonian Institution; **302** *left* Corbis-Bettmann; *right* Copyright © Eastman Kodak Company; **303** Culver Pictures; **304** Library of Congress; **306** Moorland-Spingarn Research Center, Howard University Archives; **307** *The Champion Single Sculls (Max Schmitt in a Single Scull)* (1871), Thomas Eakins. Oil on canvas, 32¼″ × 46¼″. The Metropolitan Museum of Art, purchase, The Alfred N. Punnett Endowment Fund and George D. Pratt Gift, 1934 (34.92); **308** *top, bottom* The Granger Collection, New York; **309** The Granger Collection, New York; **310** *left, right* The Granger Collection, New York; **313** Corbis-Bettmann; **314** Culver Pictures; **316** *top* Boston Public Library; *bottom* Culver Pictures; **317** The Granger Collection, New York; **318** *left, right* The Granger Collection, New York; **319** *left* From *Passing Parade: A History of Popular Culture in the Twentieth Century* by Richard Malthy, Oxford University Press, Copyright © 1988; **320** The Granger Collection, New York; **321** Courtesy of Sears Roebuck and Company; **322** *The Picnic Grounds* (1906–1907), John Sloan. Oil on canvas, 30¼″ × 42¼″ × 2″. Copyright © 1996 Whitney Museum of American Art, New York; **322–323** The Granger Collection, New York; **323** *top* Collection of the New-York Historical Society; *bottom* Library of Congress.

Chapter 9

326–327 Corbis-Bettmann; **328** *left, right* Corbis-Bettmann; **329** *left, right* The Granger Collection, New York; *center* UPI/Corbis-Bettmann; **330** Corbis-Bettmann; **331** *top* UPI/Corbis-Bettmann; *bottom* Archive Photos; **333** Corbis-Bettmann; **334** Cleveland Public Library; **335** *left* Corbis-Bettmann; *right* Archives & Information Services Division, Texas State Library, Austin; **337** The Granger Collection, New York; **338** Corbis-Bettmann; **339** Corbis-Bettmann; **340** *left* The Granger Collection, New York; *right* Culver

1016 Acknowledgments

Pictures; **341** *left* Corbis-Bettmann; *right* Doubleday, Page and Company, New York, 1906, second issue; **342** Corbis-Bettmann; **343** Corbis-Bettmann; **344** UPI/Corbis-Bettmann; **346** *top, bottom* The Granger Collection, New York; **347** Corbis-Bettmann; **348** The Granger Collection, New York; **349** *top* The Granger Collection, New York; *bottom* Jacket from *The Jungle*. Used by permission of University of Illinois Press. Cover art from the Chicago Historical Society; **350** The Granger Collection, New York; **351** Corbis-Bettmann; **352** *left* The Granger Collection, New York; *right* Corbis-Bettmann; **354** Corbis-Bettmann; **355** UPI/Corbis-Bettmann; **357** Archive Photos; **358** Archive Photos.

Chapter 10
362 Culver Pictures; **363** *top left* Archive Photos; *bottom left* The Granger Collection, New York; *right* Panama Canal Company; **364** Corbis-Bettmann; **365** The Granger Collection, New York; **367** Hawaiian Historical Society; **368** *left, right* The Granger Collection, New York; **369** *top* Copyright © 1968 Philip Jones Griffiths/Magnum Photos; *inset* Reuters/Corbis-Bettmann; *bottom* Photo by George Rodger/*Life* Magazine. Copyright © 1944 Time, Inc.; **370** Corbis-Bettmann; **371** *top* The Granger Collection, New York; *bottom* Culver Pictures; **373** The Granger Collection, New York; **375** From *Puerto Rico: A Political and Cultural History*, Arturo Morales Carrion; **377** The Granger Collection, New York; **378** Keystone-Mast Collection (24039), UCR/California Museum of Photography, University of California, Riverside; **379** The Granger Collection, New York; **382** UPI/Corbis-Bettmann; **383** *top* The Granger Collection, New York; *bottom* Corbis-Bettmann; **384** *left* Theodore Roosevelt Collection, Harvard College Library; *right* Archive Photos; **385** *left* Reuters/Corrine Dufka/Archive Photos; *right* Copyright © Hires/Merillon/Gamma-Liasion; **387** The Granger Collection, New York; **388** Panama Canal Company; **389** *top* Copyright © 1979 New York News Inc; *bottom* Copyright © Will and Deni McIntyre/Tony Stone Images.

Chapter 11
392 The Granger Collection, New York; **393** *left* Culver Pictures/PNI; *center, right* The Granger Collection, New York; **394** Culver Pictures; **397** Corbis-Bettmann; **400** Corbis-Bettmann; **402** Corbis-Bettmann; **403** *top* The Granger Collection, New York; *bottom* UPI/Corbis-Bettmann; **406** *left* Corbis-Bettmann; *center* RIA-Novosti/Sovfoto/PNI; *right* Archive Photos; **407** *left, right* The Granger Collection, New York; **409** *Oliver Wendell Holmes* (1935), Clara E. Sipprell. National Portrait Gallery, Smithsonian Institution/Art Resource, New York; **410** Corbis-Bettmann; **411** The Granger Collection, New York; **412** The Granger Collection, New York; **413** Corbis-Bettmann; **414** Panel no. 1: "During the World War There Was a Great Migration North by Southern Negroes" from *The Migration of the Negro* mural series (1940–1941), Jacob Lawrence. Tempera on masonite, 12″ × 18″. Acquired though Downtown Gallery, 1942. The Phillips Collection, Washington, D.C.; **416** *left* UPI/Corbis-Bettmann; *right* Corbis-Bettmann; **417** *Edith Bolling Galt Wilson, First Lady* (1924), Emile Alexay. National Portrait Gallery, Smithsonian Institution/Art Resource, New York; **418** Corbis-Bettmann; **420** The Granger Collection, New York; **421** Corbis-Bettmann; **422** *left* Corbis-Bettmann; *right* UPI/Corbis-Bettmann; **423** *left* Corbis-Bettmann; *right* UPI/Corbis-Bettmann.

Chapter 12
426–427 *Drouth Stricken Area* (1934), Alexandre Hogue. Oil on canvas, 30″ × 42¼″. Dallas Museum of Art, Dallas Art Association Purchase; **428** *left* The Granger Collection, New York; *right* UPI/Corbis-Bettmann; **429** *top left* Stock Montage; *center left* UPI/Corbis-Bettmann; *bottom* Copyright © Henry Ford Museum and Greenfield Village, Dearborn, Michigan; *right* Corbis-Bettmann; **430** From *The Jewish Americans*, Copyright © 1982 by Milton Meltzer. Thomas Y. Crowell Junior Books/Harper Collins Children's Books; **432** *top* Detail of *Sacco and Vanzetti* (1932), Ben Shahn. Tempera, 21″ × 48″. Private collection. Copyright © 1997 Estate of Ben Shahn/Licensed by VAGA, New York, NY; *bottom* UPI/Corbis-Bettmann; **433** Library of Congress; **435** UPI/Corbis-Bettmann; **436** Copyright © Underwood Photo Archives, San Francisco, California; **437** Detail of *Warren Gamaliel Harding* (about 1923), Margaret Lindsay William. National Portrait Gallery, Smithsonian Institution/Art Resource, New York; **439** UPI/Corbis-Bettmann; **440** Stock Montage; **441** H. Armstrong Roberts; **442** *inset top* Minnesota Historical Society; *insets bottom left and right* Brown Brothers; **443** Courtesy of United Airlines; **444** *left* Culver Pictures; *right* Copyright © 1931 (renewed 1959) by the Condé Nast Publications, Inc.; **446** *center left* Chicago Historical Society; *bottom left* Montgomery Ward and Company, Chicago; **446–447** Joseph J. Pennell Collection, Kansas Collection, University of Kansas Libraries; **447** *top* Copyright © J. McDermott/Tony Stone Images; *bottom* Copyright © Camerique Stock Photos.

Chapter 13
450 *left* Library of Congress; *center* Illustration by William Cotten, *Vanity Fair*, January 1931. Copyright © 1931 (renewed 1959) by the Condé Nast Publications, Inc.; *right* Archive Photos/Frank Driggs Collection; **451** *left, center* UPI/Corbis-Bettmann; *right* Copyright © United States Postal Service; **452** Corbis-Bettmann; **453** *New York Street Scene* (1920), Joaquin Torres-García. Oil on paper mounted on cradled wood panel, 18 3/8″ × 25 7/8″. Hirshhorn Museum and Sculpture Garden, Smithsonian Institution, gift of Joseph H. Hirshhorn, 1972; **454** *left, right* Underwood and Underwood/Corbis-Bettmann; **455** Detail of *Al Capone* (1929), Jun Fujita. Photograph. Chicago Historical Society; **456** UPI/Corbis-Bettmann; **457** UPI/Corbis-Bettmann; **458** UPI/Corbis-Bettmann; **459** *top, bottom* Culver Pictures; **460** Courtesy George Eastman House; **462** *left* Brown Brothers; *center* Culver Pictures; *right* Corbis-Bettmann; **463** *top* Archive Photos/Frank Driggs Collection; *center left* Photo by Sharon Hoogstraten; *center right* Library of Congress; *bottom* Corbis-Bettmann; **464** UPI/Corbis-Bettmann; **465** *left* Rare Books and Manuscripts Division, New York Public Library, Astor, Lenox and Tilden Foundations; *center* Culver Pictures; *right* National Museum of American History, Smithsonian Institution; **466** Brown Brothers; **467** *top left, top center* UPI/Corbis-Bettmann; *top right* Corbis-Bettmann; *bottom right* Photofest; **468** *left, Radiator Building—Night, New York* (1927), Georgia O'Keeffe. Oil on canvas. The Alfred Stieglitz Collection, Fisk University Art Galleries, Nashville, Tennessee; *right* Photofest/Copyright © The Walt Disney Corporation; **469** Corbis-Bettmann; **470** Beinecke Rare Book and Manuscript Library, Yale University; **471** Fisk University, Nashville, Tennessee; **472** UPI/Corbis-Bettmann; **473** *Black Belt* (1934), Archibald J. Motley, Jr. Oil on canvas, 31⅞″ × 39⅜″. Hampton University Museum, Hampton, Virginia; **474** Archive Photos/Frank Driggs Collection; **475** Archive Photos/Frank Driggs Collection; **476** Book cover from first edition, *The Great Gatsby* by F. Scott Fitzgerald (New York: Charles Scribner's Sons, 1925). Used by permission of Scribner, a division of Simon and Schuster; **477** *left, Langston Hughes* (about 1920), Winold Reiss. National Portrait Gallery, Smithsonian Institution/Art Resource, New York; *right, Edna St. Vincent Millay* (1930), unknown photographer. National Portrait Gallery, Smithsonian Institution/Art Resource, New York.

Chapter 14
480 *left* Archive Photos; *right* Cover copyright © 1933 (renewed 1961) by the Condé Nast Publications, Inc. Courtesy of *Vanity Fair*; **481** *left* Copyright © M. Howell/Camerique/H. Armstrong Roberts, Inc.; *center* Photo by Dorothea Lange, Collection of the Oakland Museum; *right* Courtesy of the Chicago Historical Society; **482** AP/Wide World Photos; **485** *Dies Irae (October 29, 1929)*, James Naumburg Rosenberg. National Museum of American Art, Washington, D.C./Art Resource, New York; **486** *left* Courtesy Dow Jones Archive; *right* C. Ursillo/H. Armstrong Roberts; **486–487** H. Armstrong Roberts; **488** Conservative Research Department, Conservative Party, London; **490** Franklin D. Roosevelt Library and UPI/Corbis-Bettmann; *right* Reproduced from *Dust Bowl Diary* by Ann Marie Low, by permission of the University of Nebraska Press. Copyright © 1984 by the University of Nebraska Press; **491** Courtesy of the Chicago Historical Society; **493** UPI/Corbis-Bettmann; **494** Farm Security Administration; **495** Library of Congress; **496** Detail of *Herbert Clark Hoover* (1931), Douglas Chandor. Oil on canvas. National Portrait Gallery, Smithsonian Institution/Art Resource, New York; **497** *top* Reprinted from the *Albany Evening News*, June 7, 1931, with permission of the *Times Union*, Albany, New York; *bottom, Construction of a Dam* (1937), William Gropper. Mural study done for Department of the Interior, Washington, D.C. National Museum of American Art, Washington, D.C./Art Resource, New York; **498** UPI/Corbis-Bettmann.

Chapter 15
502 *left* UPI/Corbis-Bettmann; *top right, Waiting Outside Relief Station, Urbana, Ohio, 1938*, Ben Shahn. Photograph courtesy of

Art Credits (Cont.)

the Library of Congress; *bottom right* Corbis-Bettmann; **503** *left* Copyright © 1934 (renewed 1962) by the Condé Nast Publications, Inc.; *center* Library of Congress; *right* UPI/Corbis-Bettmann; **504** Copyright © 1984 John Gutmann; **505** *left*, *Franklin Delano Roosevelt* (1935), Henry Salem Hubbell. National Portrait Gallery, Smithsonian Institution/Art Resource, New York; *right* Detail of *Anna Eleanor Roosevelt* (1949), Douglas Chandor. Oil on canvas, 49½″ × 38¼″. Gift of the White House Historical Association; **506** Stock Montage; **507** Library of Congress; **508** *Franklin D. Roosevelt at Hill Top Cottage, with Ruthie Bie and Fala* (1941), Margaret Suckley. Photograph. Franklin D. Roosevelt Library; **509** Stock Montage, Copyright © 1937 by the Des Moines Register and Tribune Company. Reprinted with permission; **510** Corbis-Bettmann; **511** *Migrant Mother, Nipomo, California* (1936), Dorothea Lange, 9⅝″ × 7½″. Courtesy of the Library of Congress; **512** Photofest; **513** Library of Congress; **514** UPI/Corbis-Bettmann; **515** *top* The Granger Collection, New York; *center* Corbis-Bettmann; *bottom* Library of Congress; **516** Library of Congress; **517** *left* UPI/Corbis-Bettmann; **518** *left* Detail of *Mary McLeod Bethune* (1943–1944), Betsy Graves Reyneau. National Portrait Gallery, Smithsonian Institution/Art Resource, New York; *inset* UPI/Corbis-Bettmann; **519** UPI/Corbis-Bettmann; **520** UPI/Corbis-Bettmann; **521** *left* AP/Wide World Photos; *center* UPI/Corbis-Bettmann; *right* The Granger Collection, New York; **522** NYT Pictures; **523** Library of Congress; **524** *top* Photofest; *bottom* The Granger Collection, New York; **525** *left*, *right* Photofest; **526** *left* Library of Congress; *right*, *Industries of California* (1934), Ralph Stackpole. Photo courtesy of the San Francisco (California) Art Commission. Photo by Malcolm Kimberlin; **527** *American Gothic* (1930), Grant Wood. Oil on beaver board, 74.3 cm × 62.4 cm. All rights reserved. The Art Institute of Chicago, Friends of American Art Collection, 1930.934/VAGA, New York, NY; **528** *top* Library of Congress; *bottom* Houghton Mifflin Company, Boston; **529** Franklin D. Roosevelt Library and AP/Wide World Photos; **532** Library of Congress; **533** *Norris Dam* (1935), Paul Sample. From the collection of the New Britain (Connecticut) Museum of American Art, John Butler Talcott Fund. Photograph by E. Irving Blomstrann; **534** *Suspended Power* (1939), Charles Sheeler. Oil on canvas, 33″ × 26″. Dallas Museum of Art, gift of Edmund J. Kahn; **535** *top* Courtesy of the Tennessee Valley Authority; *bottom* Copyright © Roderick Beebe/Gamma-Liasion.

Chapter 16

538–539 National Archives/PhotoAssist, Inc./Woodfin Camp; **540** *left* UPI/Bettmann; *right*, *Albert Einstein Among Other Immigrants* (date unknown), Ben Shahn. Scala/Art Resource, New York/VAGA, New York; **541** *top left* AP/Wide World Photos; *bottom left* Corbis-Bettmann; *right background* American Stock Photo/Archive; *right foreground* Black Star; **542** *left* UPI/Corbis-Bettmann; *right* Copyright © The Hulton Getty Picture Collection Limited; **544** Copyright © SuperStock; **545** *left* UPI/Corbis-Bettmann; *center* Archive Photos/G. D. Hackett; *right* Corbis-Bettmann; **547** Copyright © The Washington Post. Reprinted with permission; **548** Corbis-Bettmann; **549** *top* Archive Photos/G. D. Hackett; *bottom* Photo by Hugh Jaeger/*Life* Magazine. Copyright © 1970 Time, Inc.; **551** *top* March of Time/*Life* Magazine. Copyright © Time, Inc.; **553** *left* Copyright © John Topham/Black Star; *right* Woodfin Camp; **554** *right* Photo courtesy of Gerda Weissmann Klein/Hill and Wang Publishers; **555** Courtesy of the Spertus Museum, Chicago; **556–557** U.S. Army Military History Institute; **557** *inset top*, *bottom* UPI/Corbis-Bettmann; **558** Magnum Photos; **559** *Washington Times-Herald*/Franklin D. Roosevelt Library; **560** National Archives; **562** UPI/Corbis-Bettmann; **563** AP/Wide World Photos; **565** *left* United States Navy; *right* Archive Photos/Thornton.

Chapter 17

568 *top left* Corbis-Bettmann; *top right*, *bottom* UPI/Corbis-Bettmann; **569** *left*, *right* National Archives; *center* United States Marine Corps/National Archives; **570** Courtesy of Charles Swanson; **571** UPI/Corbis-Bettmann; **572** UPI/Corbis-Bettmann; **573** *top* Photo courtesy of the Franklin D. Roosevelt Library; *bottom* AP/Wide World Photos; **574** Corbis-Bettmann; **576** *center* UPI/Corbis-Bettmann; *right* AP/Wide World Photos; **577** *top left* Culver Pictures; *bottom left* Archive Photos; *right* Photo by Eric Schaal/*Life* Magazine. Copyright © Time, Inc.; **578** Courtesy of Adrienne McGrath; **580** UPI/Corbis-Bettmann; **581** AP/Wide World Photos; **583** *top* Imperial War Museum, London; *center* National Archives; *bottom* Copyright © 1944 Robert Capa/Magnum Photos; **584** UPI/Corbis-Bettmann; **585** *New York Daily News* photo; **586** UPI/Corbis-Bettmann; **587** National Archives/PhotoAssist, Inc./Woodfin Camp; **589** Courtesy of the U.S. Navy/PhotoAssist, Inc./Woodfin Camp; **590** *top* Corbis-Bettmann; *bottom* UPI/Corbis-Bettmann; **591** *top* Courtesy of the Air Force Administration/Photo Assist, Inc./Woodfin Camp; *bottom* Copyright © 1945 Yosuke Yamahata/Magnum Photos; **593** National Archives; **594** *center left* Copyright © Dan McCoy/Rainbow; *bottom* Copyright © George Hall/Check Six/PNI; *top right background* AP/Wide World Photos; **594–595** Copyright © Hank Morgan/Rainbow; **595** *top right* Sovfoto/Eastfoto; *bottom right* Copyright © 1993 Larry Mulvehill/Rainbow/PNI; **596** *Twice a Patriot* (1943), unknown artist. Lithograph. Amistad Foundation Collection at the Wadsworth Atheneum, Hartford, Connecticut; **597** Brown Brothers; **598** *left* Corbis-Bettmann; *inset* Alan B. Taylor Collection; **599** AP/Wide World Photos; **601** Photo by Eliot Elisofon/*Life* Magazine. Copyright © 1942 Time, Inc.

Chapter 18

604 *center* AP/Wide World Photos; *bottom right* Photo by Carl Mydans/*Life* Magazine. Copyright © Time, Inc.; **605** *top left* Photofest; *bottom left* Photo by Hank Walker/*Life* Magazine. Copyright © Time, Inc.; *right* Sovfoto/Eastfoto; **606** *top* UPI/Corbis-Bettmann; *bottom* Copyright © United States Postal Service; **607** *left* Archive Photos; *right* AP/Wide World Photos; **610** *left* UPI/Corbis-Bettmann; *right* AP/Wide World Photos; **611** AP/Wide World Photos; **613** Archive Photos; **614** *left*, *right* AP/Wide World Photos; **617** *top* Courtesy of Beverly Scott; *bottom* Photo by Carl Mydans/*Life* Magazine. Copyright © Time, Inc.; **619** Courtesy of Tony Kahn; **620** *top*, *Paul Bustill Robeson as Othello* (1943–1944), Betsy Graves Reyneau. National Portrait Gallery, Smithsonian Institution/Art Resource, New York; *bottom* Photofest; **621** Photofest; **622** *left* UPI/Corbis-Bettmann; *top right*, *bottom right* Corbis-Bettmann; **623** *left* AP/Wide World Photos; *right* From *Herblock Special Report* (W. W. Norton and Company, 1974); **624** *top center* Photofest; *left* From *Herblock's Here and Now* (Simon and Schuster, 1955); **625** AP/Wide World Photos; **626** AP/Wide World Photos; **629** *top* Photri, Inc.; *bottom left* AP/Wide World Photos; *bottom right* ITAR-TASS/Sovfoto; **630** Courtesy of Bantam Doubleday Books; **631** *left* Courtesy of Bantam Books; *right* Courtesy of Republic Entertainment, Inc.

Chapter 19

634 *GI Homecoming* (1945), Norman Rockwell. Oil on canvas. Copyright © 1945 The Norman Rockwell Family Trust. Photo courtesy of the Norman Rockwell Museum at Stockbridge, New York; **634–635** Copyright © SuperStock; **635** *left* Archive Photos/Blank Archives. Photo by Sharon Hoogstraten; *center*, *The Problem We All Live With* (1964), Norman Rockwell. Oil on canvas. Copyright © 1964 The Norman Rockwell Family Trust. Photo courtesy of the Norman Rockwell Museum at Stockbridge, New York; *right* Hake's Americana and Collectibles, York, Pennsylvania. Photograph by Stephen Mays, New York; **636** Archive Photos/Harold M. Lambert; **637** Photo by J. R. Eyerman/*Life* Magazine. Copyright © 1953 Time, Inc.; **639** *left* Baseball Hall of Fame Library, Cooperstown, New York; *right* Culver Pictures; **640** *top*, *Wipe Out Discrimination* (1949), Milton Ackoff. Offset lithograph, printed in color, 43⅞″ × 32¾″. The Museum of Modern Art, New York, gift of the Congress of Industrial Organizations. Photography Copyright © 1998 The Museum of Modern Art, New York; *bottom* UPI/Corbis-Bettmann; **641** Cousley Historical Collections. Photo by Stephen Mays, New York; **642** Photo by Carl Iwasaki/*Life* Magazine. Copyright © 1953 Time, Inc.; **643** Copyright © SuperStock; **644** Archive/Lambert; **645** *top* Popper Foto/Archive; *bottom* Corbis-Bettmann; **646** *top* National Bowling Hall of Fame and Museum, St. Louis; *bottom* UPI/Corbis-Bettmann; **647** *top left*, *bottom left* H. Armstrong Roberts; *top center* Copyright © SuperStock; *top right* Photo by Alan Grant/*Life* Magazine. Copyright © Time, Inc.; *bottom right* R. Walker/H. Armstrong Roberts; **648** Copyright © The Curtis Publishing Company; **649** Archive Photos/Michael Barson Collection; **650** *left*, *right*, *bottom* Park Forest Public Library, Park Forest, Illinois; **651** *top left*, *top center*, *center right* Park Forest Public Library, Park Forest, Illinois; *top right* Copyright © Dab Weiner, courtesy Sandra Weiner; *bottom* Courtesy of the Lincoln

1018 Acknowledgments

Mall, Matteson, Illinois; **652** Michael Ochs Archives; **653** Courtesy of *TV Guide*; **654** Photofest; **655** Globe Photos, Inc.; **656** *background* Copyright © Stephen G. St. John/National Geographic Society; *background* Photo by Paul Schutzer/*Life* Magazine. Copyright © 1958 Time, Inc.; **657** Archive Photos/Frank Driggs; **658** *left* Photofest; *right* Equinox Archives; **659** *top* R. Walker/H. Armstrong Roberts; *center* UPI/Corbis-Bettmann; *bottom* Copyright © 1987 Dennis Brack/Black Star/PNI; **660** The Granger Collection, New York; **662** UPI/Corbis-Bettmann; **663** *Milwaukee* (Wisconsin) *Journal/Milwaukee Sentinel*.

Chapter 20
666–667 Copyright © Ivan Massar/Black Star; **668** *top left* Courtesy of the John F. Kennedy Library; *bottom left* Courtesy Life Pictures. Copyright © 1963 Time, Inc.; *right* AP/Wide World Photos; **669** *left* NASA (National Aeronautics and Space Administration); *right* UPI/Corbis-Bettmann; **670** *left* Archive Photos/Blank Archives; *right* Copyright © 1961 Black Star; **671** AP/Wide World Photos; **673** *top* Copyright © Burt Glinn/Magnum Photos; *bottom* Courtesy Life Pictures. Copyright © 1963 Time, Inc.; **675** *left* UPI/Corbis-Bettmann; *right* AP/Wide World Photos; **676** AP/Wide World Photos; **677** *top*, *inset* NASA (National Aeronautics and Space Administration); **678** Courtesy of the John F. Kennedy Library; **679** *top* Photo by Sharon Hoogstraten; *bottom* UPI/Corbis-Bettmann; **681** *top* Copyright © 1963, 1964 by The New York Times Company. Reprinted by permission; *bottom* *New York Daily News* photo; **683** *top*, *bottom* Courtesy of VISTA; **684** UPI/Corbis-Bettmann; **685** *top* AP/Wide World Photos; *bottom* Museum of American Political Life, University of Hartford, West Hartford, Connecticut. Photo by Sally Andersen-Bruce; **687** Archive Photos; **688** AP/Wide World Photos; **689** Photo by Sharon Hoogstraten; **691** Copyright © Paul Conklin/PhotoEdit.

Chapter 21
694 *left*, *right* UPI/Corbis-Bettmann; *center* Photo by Don Uhrbroch/*Life* Magazine. Copyright © Time, Inc.; **695** *top left* Copyright © 1996 Bob Adelman/Magnum Photos; *bottom left* Copyright © Flip Schulke/Black Star; *right* Photo by Frank Dandridge/*Life* Magazine. Copyright © Time, Inc.; **696** *left* Archive Photos/Express Newspapers; *right* Courtesy Arthur L. Freeman; **697** *top*, *bottom* Library of Congress; **698** Archive Photos/Consolidated News; **699** UPI/Corbis-Bettmann; **700** AP/Wide World Photos; **701** *top* Dan Weiner, courtesy of Sandra Weiner; *bottom* Photo by Grey Villet/*Life* Magazine. Copyright © 1956 Time, Inc.; **702** AP/Wide World Photos; **703** AP/Wide World Photos; **704** UPI/Corbis-Bettmann; **705** UPI/Corbis-Bettmann; **706** AP/Wide World Photos; **707** *top* AP/Wide World Photos; *bottom* Copyright © Flip Schulke/Black Star; **708** Copyright © 1964 Steve Schapiro/Black Star; **709** Copyright © Ivan Massar/Black Star; **710** Copyright © Flip Schulke/Black Star; **711** UPI/Corbis-Bettmann; **712** *top* UPI/Corbis-Bettmann; *bottom* Photo by J. R. Eyerman/*Life* Magazine. Copyright © Time, Inc.; **713** Copyright © 1964 John Launois/Black Star; **714** *top* Ken Regan/Camera 5; *bottom* Photo by Sharon Hoogstraten; **715** *left* Black Star; *right* Corbis-Bettmann; **716** AP/Wide World Photos; **718** *left*, *right* The Granger Collection, New York; **719** *left* Copyright © 1963 Charles Moore/Black Star; *right* UPI/Corbis-Bettmann.

Chapter 22
722 Democratic Republic of Vietnam; **723** *top* UPI/Corbis-Bettmann; *center left* Copyright © 1967 James Pickerell/Black Star; *bottom left* Peter Newark's American Pictures; *right* Copyright © John Paul Filo; **725** AP/Wide World Photos; **727** AP/Wide World Photos; **728** *top* Copyright © 1963, 1964 by The New York Times Company. Reprinted by permission; *bottom* U.S. Armed Forces; **729** Copyright © Co Rentmeester; **730** Defense Audio Visual Agency, Washington, D.C.; **732** U.S. Armed Forces; **733** The Granger Collection, New York; **734** UPI/Corbis-Bettmann; **735** *top* Courtesy of Stephan Gubar; *bottom* Photo by Mark Kauffman/*Life* Magazine. Copyright © 1965 Time, Inc.; **736** Copyright © 1967 James Pickerell/Black Star; **737** *top* AP/Wide World Photos; *bottom* Photo by Sharon Hoogstraten; **739** *top* UPI/Corbis-Bettmann; *bottom* Peter Newark's American Pictures; **740** Copyright © 1995 Burt Glinn/Magnum Photos; **741** Copyright © 1996 Danny Lyon/Magnum Photos; **742** *Life* Magazine. Copyright © Time, Inc.; **743** Courtesy of Jack Kightlinger; **744** Photo by Bill Eppridge/*Life* Magazine. Copyright © Time, Inc.; **745** *top* Copyright © Jeffrey Blankfort/Jeroboam; *bottom* Photo by Sharon Hoogstraten; **746** Photo by V. Merritt. Copyright © Time, Inc.; **747** Copyright © Donald J. Weber; **749** Copyright © John Paul Filo; **750** UPI/Corbis-Bettmann; **751** *bottom* AP/Wide World Photos; *center right* Photo by Sharon Hoogstraten; **752** *top* Copyright © 1993 Richard Howard/Black Star/PNI; *bottom* Copyright © Seny Norasingh/Light Sensitive; **754** From *Going After Cacciato* (jacket cover) by Tim O'Brien. Used by permission of Delacorte Press/Seymour Lawrence, a division of Bantam Doubleday Dell Publishing Group, Inc.; **754–755** *background* UPI/Corbis-Bettmann; **755** *left* Cover illustration by Jim Dietz from *Fallen Angels* by Walter Dean Myers. Illustration Copyright © 1988 by Jim Dietz. Reprinted with permission of Scholastic, Inc.; *right* Courtesy of Random House.

Chapter 23
758 *left* UPI/Corbis-Bettmann; *right* Copyright © 1980 Arnold Zann/Black Star; **758–759** *bottom background* Photo by Ron Rutkowski; **759** *left* Photofest; *center* Photo by Sharon Hoogstraten; *right* UPI/Corbis-Bettmann; **760** Copyright © 1995 Paul Fusco/Magnum Photos; **761** *background* Copyright © 1991 Naoki Okamoto/Black Star; **762** *top* Photo by Arthur Schatz/*Life* Magazine. Copyright © Time, Inc.; *bottom* Archive Photos/Jon Hammer; **763** AP/Wide World Photos; **764** Copyright © Rick Smolan; **765** *left* Copyright © Art Wolfe/Tony Stone Images; *center* Copyright © Sara Gray/Tony Stone Images; *right* Copyright © Tim Davis/Allstock; **766** Copyright © T Resource/Tony Stone Images; **767** *left* Copyright © Richard Elliot/Tony Stone Images; *right* Copyright © Bruce Forster/Tony Stone Images; **768** *right* UPI/Corbis-Bettmann; **770** *top* Copyright © Mark Klamkin/ Black Star; *bottom* Permission to reprint granted for one time by *Ms.* magazine. Copyright © 1972; **771** *top* Copyright © Werner Wolff/Black Star; *bottom* Copyright © Lynda Gordon/Gamma-Liasion; **772** Library of Congress; **773** *top* Copyright © Bob Fitch/Black Star; *bottom* UPI/Corbis-Bettmann; **774** *top left* Copyright © 1995 Elliot Landy/Magnum Photos; *bottom left* Corbis-Bettmann; *right* Photo by Sharon Hoogstraten; **775** *Marilyn Monroe* (1967), Andy Warhol. Screenprint on white paper, 36″ × 36″. The Andy Warhol Foundation, Inc./Art Resource, New York; **776** *left* Courtesy of Apple Records/EMI Records Ltd.; *right* Photo by Bill Eppridge/*Life* Magazine. Copyright © Time, Inc.; **777** UPI/Corbis-Bettmann; **778** *left* Copyright © Archive Photos; *right* Copyright © Coni Kaufman/Southern Stock/PNI; *bottom center* UPI/Corbis-Bettmann; **778–779** Photofest; **779** *center* Photofest; *center background* Photo by Sharon Hoogstraten; *bottom left*, *Poster #75*, Bonnie MacLean. Copyright © 1967 Bill Graham.

Chapter 24
782–783 National Park Service/Statue of Liberty National Monument. Photo Copyright © Norman McGrath; **784** *left* NASA (National Aeronautics and Space Administration); *right* Copyright © Dennis Brack/Black Star; **785** *top left* AP/Wide World Photos; *bottom left* Copyright © 1974 Time, Inc. Reprinted by permission; *bottom center* Copyright © 1977 Alex Webb/Magnum Photos; *right* Copyright © Ledru/Sygma; **786** UPI/Corbis-Bettmann; **787** Copyright © 1968 Dennis Brack/Black Star; **788** NASA (National Aeronautics and Space Administration); **789** Copyright © Ira Wyman/Sygma; **790** Copyright © 1974 Dennis Brack/Black Star; **791** Corbis-Bettmann; **792** AP/Wide World Photos; **793** AP/Wide World Photos; **794** *background* H. Armstrong Roberts; *top left*, *bottom left* AP/Wide World Photos; *top right*, *bottom right* Copyright © J. P. Laffront/Sygma; **795** Copyright © 1973 Dennis Brack/Black Star; **796** *top left*, *bottom left* AP/Wide World Photos; *right* Reprinted by permission of Tribune Media Services; **797** *top* Copyright © 1974 Harry Benson; *bottom* Copyright © 1974 by The New York Times Company. Reprinted by permission; **798** *top left* Courtesy of *TV Guide; top right*, *center* Photofest; **798–799** Copyright © 1976 Maurice Rosen/Magnum Photos; **799** *top left*, *top right* Photofest; **800** *left* Copyright © 1974 Time, Inc. Reprinted by permission; *right* Copyright © Bill Pierce/*Time* Magazine; **802** *left* Copyright © Owen Franken/Sygma; *right* Museum of American Political Life, University of Hartford, West Hartford, Connecticut. Photo by Sally Andersen-Bruce; **804** AP/Wide World Photos; **806** Courtesy of the Jimmy Carter Library; **807** *top* Copyright © Alain Mingam/Gamma-Liaison; *bottom* Copyright © Alain Dejean/Sygma; **808** *left* Photo by Sharon Hoogstraten; *right* UPI/Corbis-Bettmann; **809** *left* Copyright © Covello-Launois/Black Star; *right* Copyright © 1962 Eric Hartmann/Magnum Photos; **810** Copyright © 1974 Paul Fusco/Magnum Photos; **811** *left* Copyright © Bill Ross/Westlight;

Art Credits (Cont.)

right Copyright © Leonard Lee Rue III/Stock Boston; **812** Copyright © 1994 John McGrail; **813** UPI/Corbis-Bettmann.

Chapter 25
816 *left* Reuters/Corbis-Bettmann; *center* Courtesy of the Ronald Reagan Library; *right* UPI/Corbis-Bettmann; **817** *left* Copyright © Brad Markel/Gamma-Liasion; *right* Copyright © 1990 Christopher Morris/Black Star; **818** Copyright © 1988 Dennis Brack/Black Star; **819** Copyright © 1971 John Messina/Black Star; **820** Detail of *Ronald Wilson Reagan* (1989), Henry C. Casselli. National Portrait Gallery, Smithsonian Institution/Art Resource, New York; **822** Copyright © 1991 Dennis Brack/Black Star; **823** Cartoon by Pat Oliphant. Copyright © Universal Press Syndicate; **824** *top, bottom* Copyright © 1991 Dennis Brack/Black Star; **825** AP/Wide World Photos; **826** Copyright © 1987 Dennis Brack/Black Star; **827** From *Trevor's Place: The Story of the Boy Who Brings Hope to the Homeless*. Copyright © 1985 by Frank and Janet Ferrell; **828** Copyright © Brad Markel/Gamma-Liasion; **829** AP/Wide World Photos; **830** *top* NASA (National Aeronautics and Space Administration); *bottom* Copyright © 1985 Steve Leonard/Black Star; **831** Copyright © 1994 P. F. Bentley/Black Star; **832** Copyright © 1991 Dennis Brack/Black Star; **833** Copyright © 1983 Christopher Morris/Black Star; **834** *left* Copyright © Daniel Barbier/Image Bank; *right* Copyright © Andrea Pistolesi/Image Bank; **836** United States Government; **837** *left* AP/Wide World Photos; *right* Copyright © 1989 by National Review, Inc., 150 East 35th Street, New York, NY 10016. Reprinted by permission; **838** Copyright © 1989 Stuart Franklin/Magnum Photos; **840** AP/Wide World Photos; **841** *top* Copyright © 1991 David Turnley, Detroit Free Press/Black Star; *bottom* Copyright © Giles Bassignac/Gamma-Liaison.

Chapter 26
844 *left* Reuters/Corbis-Bettmann; *right* Reuters/Win McNamee/Archive Photos; **845** *left* AP/Wide World/NASA TV; *center* Copyright © Rod Rolle/Gamma-Liaison; *right* Copyright © 1993 Dennis Brack/Black Star; **846** Copyright © 1993 Jim Stratford/Black Star; **847** Reuters/Corbis-Bettmann; **848** John Duricka/AP/Wide World Photos; **849** AP/Wide World Photos; **850** *left* Reuters/Corbis-Bettmann; *right* AP/Wide World Photos; **851** Copyright © 1996 Peter Hannan; **853** Courtesy of Mike Cavanaugh/UNITE; **854** UPI/Corbis-Bettmann; **855** *top* Copyright © Tom Cheek/Stock Boston/PNI; *bottom* Copyright © 1994 Thomas Hoepker/Magnum Photos; **857** Reuters/Corbis-Bettmann; **858** Copyright © Barron Claiborne/Outline; **859** *left* Jacket from *The Joy Luck Club*. Used by permission of G. P. Putnam's Sons. Cover illustration copyright © Gretchen Schields; *right* Jacket from *The House on Mango Street*. Used by permission of Vintage Books, a division of Random House, Inc., New York. Cover design by Lorraine Louie, illustration by Nivia Gonzalez; **860** Copyright © Rick Browne/Stock Boston/PNI; **862** *top, bottom* Copyright © Dan McCoy/Rainbow/PNI; **863** Copyright © 1993 Seth Resnic/Stock Boston/PNI; **864** AP/Wide World Photos; **865** *top* Copyright © Joe Sohm/Chromsohm/Stock Boston/PNI; *bottom* Copyright © Dave Jacobs/Tony Stone Images; **866** Photo by William F. Campbell/*Life* Magazine. Copyright © Time, Inc.; **867** *top* Copyright © 1995 C/B/Productions/The Stock Market; *bottom left* Copyright © 1991 Kenneth Jarecke/Contact Press Images; *bottom right* Copyright © Tom Carroll/Phototake, NYC/PNI; **870** Copyright © 1996 Erich Hartmann/Magnum Photos; **871** Copyright © David Young-Wolff/Tony Stone Images; **872** *left, Mission Francisco Solano de Sonoma* (date unknown), Oriana Day. Fine Arts Museums of San Francisco (California), gift of Eleanor Martin, 37573; *top right* FPG International; *bottom right* Courtesy of the Colorado Historical Society; **873** *top* Copyright © 1990 Alon Reininger/Contact Press Images/PNI; *bottom* Copyright © 1964 Steve Shapiro/Black Star.

Epilogue
876 *top* Copyright © 1991 David Turnley/PNI; *bottom left* Copyright © Bizuayehu Tesfaye/AP/Wide World Photos; *bottom right* Copyright © 1995 Peter Marlow/Magnum Photos; **877** *left* Copyright © 1996 Jaffe/Gamma-Liaison; *right* Copyright © 1985 Paul Fusco/Magnum Photos; **879** *top* Copyright © 1989 Jeff Widener/AP/Wide World Photos; *bottom* Copyright © 1997 Gregory Bull/AP/Wide World Photos; **880** *left* The Granger Collection, New York; *right* Copyright © Paul Sakuma/AP/Wide World Photos; **881** Copyright © AP/Wide World Photos; **882–883** Copyright © 1996 Chicago Tribune, Carl Wagner/AP/Wide World Photos; **885** *top* Copyright © 1992 Tom Horan/AP/Wide World Photos; *bottom* Copyright © A. Ramey/PhotoEdit; **886** Copyright © 1995 Peter Marlow/Magnum Photos; **887** AP/Wide World Photos; *inset* Copyright © 1995 David Longstreath/AP/Wide World Photos; **889** Copyright © Mingasson/Gamma-Liaison; **890** Reprinted with the permission of the *Milwaukee Journal Sentinel;* **891** *left, right* AP/Wide World Photos; **892** Copyright © 1980 David Hurn/Magnum Photos; **893** Copyright © 1992 Richard Falco/PNI; **894** Copyright © 1996 Wally Santana/AP/Wide World Photos; **895** *top* Copyright © Westenberger/Gamma-Liaison; *bottom* Copyright © 1996 Jaffe/Gamma-Liaison; **896** Copyright © 1985 Paul Fusco/Magnum Photos; **898** AP/Wide World Photos; **899** *left, center* Copyright © Michael Newman/PhotoEdit; *right* Copyright © Tony Freeman/PhotoEdit; **900** AP/Wide World Photos; **901** Copyright © 1982 Randy Taylor/Sygma.

Handbooks
925 Culver Pictures; **933** *Life* Magazine. Copyright © 1956 Time, Inc.; **934** UPI/Corbis-Bettmann; **936** AP/Wide World Photos; **938** Copyright © 1996 Wally Santana/AP/Wide World Photos.

McDougal Littell Inc. has made every effort to locate the copyright holders for the images used in this book and to make full acknowledgement for their use. Omissions brought to our attention will be corrected in subsequent editions.

1020 Acknowledgments